C000173905

The Bible

Contemporary English Version

HarperCollins*Publishers*

HarperCollins*Publishers*
77–85 Fulham Palace Road, London W6 8JB
www.fireandwater.com

Contemporary English Version Bible

For permission to use excerpts of the CEV please contact Permissions, The British
and Foreign Bible Society, Stonehill Green, Westlea, Swindon, Wiltshire, SN5 7DG

Title	ISBN
CEV Compact Blue Hardback	0 00 220222 0
CEV Compact Paperback	0 00 220220 4

BFBS/10M/2000/1.4

Text design by Martin Richards.
Typeset in Stone Serif 8/9pt reduced 32% using Corel Ventura 8 by The British and
Foreign Bible Society.
Production arranged by The British and Foreign Bible Society.
www.biblesociety.org.uk
Cover design by HarperCollins*Publishers*
Printed in Great Britain by The Bath Press, Bath.

Contents

Books of the Bible in alphabetical order

How to read the Bible

The Bible is a collection of sixty-six separate books, written by many different authors and in several quite different styles. The CEV translators have tried very hard to make the original meaning clear, but it can still be difficult to understand how any single passage is supposed to make a difference here and now.

We need to know when, why, and how the Bible was put together, before we can apply it in our lives today. The books of the Bible were written over a long period, during which the cultures in which the writers lived changed, as did the way God dealt with his people. God began by speaking through individual prophets, but Jesus promised that we could all have our own relationship with him. So while some things are still clear today, others have to be understood in their own cultural and historical context before we can benefit from them.

Story — *Genesis, Exodus, the Gospels and Historical Books (see Contents)*
These books can contain political comment, and will always illustrate spiritual truths, but their main purpose is to tell about a specific period in the life of God's people.

Prophecy — *Major Prophets, Minor Prophets, Revelation (see Contents)*
These books comment on the current situation and foretell what will happen in the future. Often God's people have disobeyed him, and he promises to give them good things if they will follow him again, but to destroy them if they carry on disobeying.

Poetry — *see Contents*
Some of these books began life as hymns or songs which were used in worship. Others describe particular aspects of human experience, and some do comment on recent or past history. Some prophecy is in poetic form, eg. Isaiah 40—66.

Letters — *see Contents*
Most of the letters in the New Testament were written by one person to a group of Christians, either one church or several. They were probably read out in church, and they deal with issues of belief or behaviour, particularly problems in the local church.

Law — *for example Leviticus, Deuteronomy*
These books were intended to show the new nation of Israel, called to be God's people, how to live in the right way. The Law places worship at the centre of life for God's people, but also gives rules intended to ensure every part of life reflects God's justice and love.

Wisdom — *for example Proverbs, Job in the poetic books*
Books in this form often express our human experiences. They seek to give insights on trusting God, on times of joy and sadness, as well as on human nature, which aren't necessarily limited to any historical period.

Note: in the Bible text, * indicates a footnote (see bottom of page), ' an endnote (see end of each book).

A Time-Line of the Bible

Creation
earliest times Humans created in God's image

Disobedience
earliest times Humans fall into sin (Adam and Eve),
Cain and Abel, Noah and the flood, Tower of
Babel

God's People — Israel
c. 2000 BC	Abraham is called and travels into Canaan	
c. 1650 BC	The sons of Jacob move to Egypt	
c. 1250 BC	Moses leads the Israelites out of Egypt, and God calls them to be the nation who will serve him	
probably late 13th century BC	Conquering and settling in Canaan	
12th and 11th centuries BC	Israel led by military liberators called "judges"	
c. 1030–1010 BC	Israel ruled by King Saul	
c. 1010–970 BC	Israel ruled by King David	
c. 970–931 BC	Israel ruled by King Solomon	
931 BC	Israel splits into two (Israel and Judah)	*about a thousand years*
722/721 BC	The people of the north (Israel) go into exile in Assyria	
587/586 BC	The people of the south (Judah) go into exile in Babylon	
539 BC	The return from exile begins	
	The time between the Old and the New Testaments	
probably 6 BC	The coming of the king — Jesus' birth	

When the Christian calendar was worked out in the
sixth century, a mistake in working back to the date of
Jesus' birth meant that it was a few years out.

probably 30 AD The death and resurrection of Jesus
c. 41–65 AD The travels and ministry of Paul

**Jesus recognized as
king over everything**
the future Jesus returns to set up the new heavens and
earth

About the Contemporary English Version

The *Contemporary English Version* is distinctive among Bible translations because it takes seriously the words of the apostle Paul that "faith comes by hearing".

Traditional translations of the Bible count on the reader's ability to decipher a written text. The CEV differs by considering the needs of both the reader **and** the hearer, who may not be familiar with traditional biblical jargon.

The CEV is an audio translation in print form, crafted to be read aloud without stumbling, heard without misunderstanding, and listened to with appreciation.

Like all other serious translations of the Bible, the CEV is concerned primarily with **faithfulness** to the **meaning** of the biblical text. In order to ensure the accuracy of the CEV, the Old Testament was translated directly from the Hebrew and Aramaic texts published by the United Bible Societies (*Biblia Hebraica Stuttgartensia*, 4th edition corrected). The New Testament was translated directly from the Greek text published by the United Bible Societies (3rd edition corrected and compared with the 4th revised edition).

Over a period of ten years, more than a hundred people contributed towards the creating and crafting of the CEV. Key people within this group are Translation Consultants of the United Bible Societies, which is the most experienced Bible translation organisation in the world. These consultants are from a wide variety of denominations and nationalities, including Africa, the Americas, Asia, and Europe. And for these consultants, translating the Word of God is much more than an academic pursuit — it is something that grows out of their faith commitment to Jesus Christ.

Each biblical book went through a series of thorough reviews before final approval was given by the American Bible Society Board of Trustees. It is this process of constant review — with prayers for the guidance of the Holy Spirit — that ensures the reliability of the CEV.

Three features of the Contemporary English Version

1. Reliable

The CEV is reliable, because the translation team has done its homework. A clear example is found in Jeremiah 23.23-24. The **meaning** of these two verses is that the Lord is not some local, tribal deity, who cannot be everywhere at the same time and see everything that happens on earth. In the CEV the context clearly identifies the speaker as the Lord, and the passage appears as follows in a traditional translation and in the CEV:

Traditional	CEV
"Am I only a God nearby,"	*The Lord said:* . . .
declares the LORD,	I am everywhere —
"and not a God far away?	both near and far,
Can anyone hide in secret places	in heaven and on earth.
so that I cannot see him?"	There are no secret places
declares the LORD.	where you can hide from me.
"Do not I fill heaven and earth?"	
declares the LORD.	

Each of the above translations is a reliable rendering of the Hebrew text. The difference is that the CEV uses economy of words and exactness of language to faithfully communicate the meaning to persons who must depend upon **hearing** the text read to them.

There is a need for emphasis to be placed on **hearing** the Bible:

• more people hear the Bible than read it for themselves
• many people do not read for pleasure
• for new readers the sounds of words are important
• experienced readers often read poetry and lyrical prose aloud
• hearing reinforces understanding
• hearing assists memorisation
• an ear-oriented text can serve as the basis for printed material, but the reverse is not necessarily true.

Genesis 1.1,2 demonstrates how the CEV faithfully communicates meaning in a creative style and format:

Traditional	CEV
In the beginning God created	In the beginning God
the heavens and the earth.	created the heavens
Now the earth was formless and empty,	and the earth.
darkness was over the	The earth was barren,
surface of the deep, and the	with no form of life;
Spirit of God was hovering over	it was under a roaring ocean
the waters.	covered with darkness.
	But the Spirit of God
	was moving over the water.

Several important observations may be made about the way these verses are translated in the CEV.

• First, the initial sentence ("In the beginning God created the heavens and the earth") represents a somewhat literal rendering of the Hebrew text. Such renderings are rare in the CEV. However, in this particular instance, after a number of options were considered, it was concluded that this was the most poetic and effective of them all. One translation has "the universe" in place of the more descriptive "the heavens and the earth". The CEV, on the other hand, retains the figurative expression and supplements it with a note: " 'The heavens and the earth' stood for the universe."
• Second, in keeping with contemporary biblical scholarship, the CEV provides a note indicating an alternative rendering of the opening words; "Or 'When God began to create the heavens and the earth, the earth was barren with no form of life.' "

- Third, the Hebrew phrase translated "Spirit of God" may also mean "a mighty wind", which is indicated by a note as well.
- Fourth, the Hebrew conjunction traditionally rendered "And" ("**And** the Spirit . . .") is legitimately translated "**But**", which more effectively draws the reader's attention to the events to follow.
- Fifth, the parallel phrases traditionally rendered "the surface of the deep" and "the waters" are confusing to many readers. So confusing in fact, that at a translation seminar in Thailand a prospective translator said, "Draw me a picture, and I can translate this passage." In the CEV the picture is drawn by "telescoping" the two phrases into one: "over the water", which clearly refers back to "the ocean".
- Finally, but of major importance, is the observation that the poetic format allows the text to make an opening statement of supreme significance:

In the beginning **God**
created the heavens and the earth.

The opening verse of the Gospel of John is another example of a passage where clarity of meaning in the CEV is the result of careful research. In the English-speaking world, a "word" is something either spoken or written, and so a literal rendering of the Greek text ("In the beginning was the Word") is problematic for persons unfamiliar with the theological background of the author and original readers of this Gospel. For this reason, the CEV translates the entire verse as: "In the beginning was the one who is called the Word. The Word was with God and was truly God."

2. Readable

Recently there has been much discussion about the readability levels of different Bible translations. Most readability formulae focus on sentence length and choice of vocabulary, with others including such factors as sentence structure. Unfortunately, these measurements tend to be mechanical and do not take into consideration the **interest** level:

- Is the text appealing to the eyes?
- Is it easy to read aloud?
- Does it make for easy listening?
- Are the words and sentence patterns familiar?
- Does it capture and hold the reader's interest?
- Are the thoughts easy to follow and understand?

Compare the **interest** level of another translation of Psalm 29.3,4 with the CEV. The first translation has a series of five consecutive choppy clauses, each beginning with the word "*the*", while the CEV combines pleasing rhythmic patterns with powerful imagery and an appealing sequence of sounds:

Traditional	CEV

The voice of the LORD is over the waters;
  the God of glory thunders,
  the LORD thunders over the mighty
        waters.
The voice of the LORD is powerful;
  the voice of the LORD is majestic.
	The voice of the LORD
	  echoes over the oceans.
	The glorious LORD God
	thunders above the roar
	  of the raging sea,
	and his voice is mighty
	  and marvellous.

In the CEV every attempt has been made to avoid a series of unaccented syllables, as well as potential tongue twisters and "jingly" expressions. For example, "Your teeth will be **too few to do** their work, and **you** will be blind, **too**" (Ecclesiastes 12.3) is difficult to read aloud. In the CEV this verse is translated, "Your teeth will decay, and your eyesight fail", which is both clear and concise as well as easy to memorise. On the other hand, "The Word became flesh and **blood** and moved into the neighbour**hood**" (John 1.14) sounds like something from a rap session. "The Word became a human being and lived here with us" is how the verse appears in the CEV.

The readability level of a translation is significantly lessened when pronoun references are ambiguous. For example, in the following translation of John 19.29,30, "It is finished" must grammatically refer to the sour wine, though that is not the intention of the Greek text: "A jar of sour wine was sitting there, so they soaked a sponge in it, put it on a hyssop branch, and held it up to his lips. When Jesus had tasted it, he said, 'It is finished!'" The CEV makes every attempt to avoid such confusion of pronoun references.

The question and answer in Psalm 119.9 ("How may a young person live a pure life? By obeying your word.") could be read and **heard** as a question without an answer ("How may a young person live a pure life by obeying your word?"). In the CEV the problem is resolved by shifting to a statement: "Young people can live a clean life by obeying your word." A similar problem occurs in Psalm 89.47 ("Why did you create us? For nothing?"), which may be heard as "Why did you create us for nothing?" The CEV has "Why did you empty our lives of all meaning?".

3. Relevant

In the CEV traditional theological terms have been faithfully translated from the original languages into concepts that are relevant for today's readers.

Many theological terms used in traditional translations were borrowed from the Latin Vulgate by John Wycliffe in 1384 and are not translated from the original Greek. For example, "justify" is a word of Latin origin and is used today to mean making an excuse for questionable behaviour. But the apostle Paul uses the Greek word to describe God's activity in accepting us and making us acceptable even though we are undeserving of his kindness. As one theologian expressed it: "God says, 'You are guilty, but I **accept** you as though you had never sinned!' That's what we mean by 'justification'."

In many contexts, the word "grace" is **not** a translation of the Greek word "charis" but a "sounding out" of the Latin word "gratia". In Romans 3.24 of the CEV, "charis" is translated "God treats us much better than we deserve", while in Hebrews 4.16 "throne of grace" is translated "throne of our merciful God" and "find grace" as "be treated with undeserved kindness".

Compare the contemporary **relevance** of the two following translations of Romans 3.24–26, where the CEV focuses upon the communication of the **meaning** of the Greek words. As Martin Luther said, "Words must obey and follow the meaning and not the meaning the words."

Traditional

(All) are **justified** freely by his **grace** through the **redemption** that came by Christ Jesus. God presented him as a **sacrifice of atonement**, through faith in his blood. He did this to demonstrate his justice, because in his **forbearance** he had left the sins committed beforehand unpunished — he did it to demonstrate his justice at the present time, so as to be just and the one who **justifies** those who have faith in Jesus.

CEV

God treats us much better than we deserve, and because of Christ Jesus, he freely accepts us and sets us free from our sins. God sent Christ to be our sacrifice. Christ offered his life's blood, so that by faith in him we could come to God. And God did this to show that in the past he was right to be patient and forgive sinners. This also shows that God is right when he accepts people who have faith in Jesus.

The *Contemporary English Version* invites you to read, to hear, to understand, and to share the Word of God now as never before!

The Old Testament

Genesis

A quick look at this book

The name "Genesis" comes from a Greek word meaning "beginning". And this is a book of beginnings, because it talks about the beginning of the universe, the beginning of the human race, and the beginning of the people of Israel.

The first part of Genesis (1—11) tells about creation and the human race up to the time of Abraham. Everything God created was good, but the first two human beings, Adam and Eve, disobeyed him and brought evil into the world. People became so sinful that God decided to send a flood to kill everyone except a man named Noah and his family. They worshipped God, and so God told them to build a large boat to save themselves and a few of each kind of animals and birds. After the flood people again spread out over the earth, and most of them stopped worshipping God.

The rest of the book of Genesis (12—50) contains the story of Abram and his family. God chose them to be the beginning of his own special people. God also changed Abram's name to Abraham, and the name of Abram's wife Sarai to Sarah. Abraham and his wife Sarah had no children, but God promised that they would have a child and that their descendants would some day have their own land and be a blessing for all nations.

Abraham and Sarah moved to Canaan, the land that God had promised to give their descendants. Abraham and Sarah had a son, Isaac, when they were very old. Isaac later had two sons, Jacob and Esau. As the book concludes, Jacob's twelve sons and their families are living in Egypt. One of these brothers, Joseph, had become the governor of

Egypt. But Joseph knew that God would some day keep his promise to his people:

> Before Joseph died, he told his brothers, "I won't live much longer. But God will take care of you and lead you out of Egypt to the land he promised Abraham, Isaac, and Jacob."
>
> (50.24)

The story of creation

CHAPTER 1

¹ In the beginning God
   created the heavens
   and the earth.*
² The earth was barren,
   with no form of life;*
   it was under a roaring ocean
   covered with darkness.
   But the Spirit of God*
   was moving over the water.

The first day

³ God said, "I command light to shine!" And light started shining. ⁴ God looked at the light and saw that it was good. He separated light from darkness ⁵ and named the light "Day" and the darkness "Night". Evening came and then morning — that was the first day.*

The second day

⁶ God said, "I command a dome to separate the water above it from the water below it." ⁷ And that's what happened. God made the dome ⁸ and named it "Sky". Evening came and then morning — that was the second day.

The third day

⁹ God said, "I command the water under the sky to come together in one place, so there will be dry ground." And that's what happened. ¹⁰ God named the dry ground "Land", and he named the water "Sea". God looked at what he had done and saw that it was good.

¹¹ God said, "I command the earth to produce all kinds of plants, including fruit trees and grain." And that's what happened.

¹² The earth produced all kinds of vegetation. God looked at what he had done, and it was good. ¹³ Evening came and then morning — that was the third day.

The fourth day

¹⁴ God said, "I command lights to appear in the sky and to separate day from night and to show the time for seasons, special days, and years. ¹⁵ I command them to shine on the earth." And that's what happened. ¹⁶ God made two powerful lights, the brighter one to rule the day and the other* to rule the night. He also made the stars. ¹⁷ Then God put these lights in the sky to shine on the earth, ¹⁸ to rule day and night, and to separate light from darkness. God looked at what he had done, and it was good. ¹⁹ Evening came and then morning — that was the fourth day.

The fifth day

²⁰ God said, "I command the sea to be full of living creatures, and I command birds to fly above the earth." ²¹ So God made the giant sea monsters and all the living creatures that swim in the sea. He also made every kind of bird. God looked at what he had done, and it was good. ²² Then he gave the living creatures his blessing — he told the sea creatures to live everywhere in the sea and the birds to live everywhere on earth. ²³ Evening came and then morning — that was the fifth day.

The sixth day

²⁴ God said, "I command the earth to give life to all kinds of tame animals, wild animals, and reptiles." And that's what happened. ²⁵ God made every one of them. Then he looked at what he had done, and it was good.

²⁶ God said, "Now we will make humans, and they will be like us. We will let them rule the fish, the birds, and all other living creatures."

²⁷ So God created humans to be like himself; he made men and women. ²⁸ God gave them his blessing and said:

> Have a lot of children! Fill the earth with people and bring it under your control.

---

*1.1 the heavens and the earth: "The heavens and the earth" stood for the universe.
*1.5 the first day: A day was measured from evening to evening.
See also: 1.3: 2 Cor 4.6.   1.6–8: 2 Pet 3.5.

*1.16 the brighter . . . the other: The sun and the moon. But they are not called by their names, because in Old Testament times some people worshipped the sun and the moon as though they were gods.
See also: 1.26: 1 Cor 11.7.   1.27,28: Gen 5.1,2.
1.27: Matt 19.4; Mark 10.6.

Rule over the fish in the sea, the birds in the sky, and every animal on the ground.

²⁹ I have provided all kinds of fruit and grain for you to eat. ³⁰ And I have given the green plants as food for everything else that breathes. These will be food for animals, both wild and tame, and for birds.

³¹ God looked at what he had done. All of it was very good! Evening came and then morning — that was the sixth day.

CHAPTER 2

¹ So the heavens and the earth and everything else were created.

The seventh day

² By the seventh day God had finished his work, and so he rested. ³ God blessed the seventh day and made it special because on that day he rested from his work.

⁴ That's how God created the heavens and the earth.

The Garden of Eden

When the LORD God made the heavens and the earth, ⁵ no grass or plants were growing anywhere. God had not yet sent any rain, and there was no one to work the land. ⁶ But streams' came up from the ground and watered the earth.

⁷ The LORD God took a handful of soil and made a man.* God breathed life into the man, and the man started breathing. ⁸ The LORD made a garden in a place called Eden, which was in the east, and he put the man there.

⁹ The LORD God placed all kinds of beautiful trees and fruit trees in the garden. Two other trees were in the middle of the garden. One of the trees gave life — the other gave the power to know the difference between right and wrong.

¹⁰ From Eden a river flowed out to water the garden, then it divided into four rivers. ¹¹ The first one is the River Pishon that flows through the land of Havilah, ¹² where pure gold, rare perfumes, and precious stones are found. ¹³ The second is the River Gihon that winds through Ethiopia.* ¹⁴ The River Tigris

that flows east of Assyria is the third, and the fourth is the River Euphrates.

¹⁵ The LORD God put the man in the Garden of Eden to take care of it and to look after it. ¹⁶ But the LORD told him, "You may eat fruit from any tree in the garden, ¹⁷ except the one that has the power to let you know the difference between right and wrong. If you eat any fruit from that tree, you will die before the day is over!"

¹⁸ The LORD God said, "It isn't good for the man to live alone. I need to make a suitable partner for him." ¹⁹⁻²⁰ So the LORD took some soil and made animals and birds. He brought them to the man to see what names he would give each of them. Then the man named the tame animals and the birds and the wild animals. That's how they got their names.

None of these was the right kind of partner for the man. ²¹ So the LORD God made him fall into a deep sleep, and he took out one of the man's ribs. Then after closing the man's side, ²² the LORD made a woman out of the rib.

The LORD God brought her to the man, ²³ and the man exclaimed,

"Here is someone like me!
She is part of my body,
   my own flesh and bones.
She came from me, a man.
   So I will name her Woman!"*

²⁴ That's why a man will leave his own father and mother. He marries a woman, and the two of them become like one person. ²⁵ Although the man and his wife were both naked, they were not ashamed.

The first sin and the first murder

CHAPTER 3

The first sin

¹ The snake was more cunning than any of the other wild animals that the LORD God had made. One day it came to the woman and asked, "Did God tell you not to eat fruit from any tree in the garden?"

² The woman answered, "God said we could eat fruit from any tree in the garden,

---

*2.7 man: In Hebrew "man" comes from the same word as "soil".
*2.13 Ethiopia: The Hebrew text has "Cush", which was a region south of Egypt that included parts of the present countries of Ethiopia and Sudan.
See also: 2.2,3: Exod 20.11. 2.2: Heb 4.4,10. 2.7: 1 Cor 15.45. 2.9: Rev 2.7; 22.2,14.

*2.23 a man . . . Woman: In Hebrew the words "man" and "woman" are similar.
See also: 2.24: Matt 19.5; Mark 10.7,8; 1 Cor 6.16; Eph 5.31. 3.1: Matt 12.9; 20.2.

³ except the one in the middle. He told us not to eat fruit from that tree or even to touch it. If we do, we will die."

⁴ "No, you won't!" the snake replied.

⁵ "God understands what will happen on the day you eat fruit from that tree. You will see what you have done, and you will know the difference between right and wrong, just as God does."

⁶ The woman stared at the fruit. It looked beautiful and tasty. She wanted the wisdom that it would give her, and she ate some of the fruit. Her husband was there with her, so she gave some to him, and he ate it too.

⁷ Straight away they saw what they had done, and they realized they were naked. Then they sewed fig leaves together to make something to cover themselves.

⁸ Late in the afternoon a breeze began to blow, and the man and woman heard the LORD God walking in the garden. They were frightened and hid behind some trees.

The trouble with sin

⁹ The LORD called out to the man and asked, "Where are you?"

¹⁰ The man answered, "I was naked, and when I heard you walking through the garden, I was frightened and hid!"

¹¹ "How did you know you were naked?" God asked. "Did you eat any fruit from that tree in the middle of the garden?"

¹² "It was the woman you put here with me," the man said. "She gave me some of the fruit, and I ate it."

¹³ The LORD God then asked the woman, "What have you done?"

"The snake tricked me," she answered. "And I ate some of that fruit."

¹⁴ So the LORD God said to the snake:

"Because of what you have done,
you will be the only animal
    to suffer this curse —
for as long as you live,
you will crawl on your stomach
    and eat dust.
¹⁵ You and this woman
    will hate each other;
your descendants and hers
    will always be enemies.
One of hers will strike you
    on the head,
and you will strike him
    on the heel."

¹⁶ Then the LORD said to the woman:

"You will suffer terribly
    when you give birth.
But you will still desire
your husband,
    and he will rule over you."

¹⁷ The LORD said to the man:

"You listened to your wife
    and ate fruit from that tree.
And so, the ground
will be under a curse
    because of what you did.
As long as you live,
you will have to struggle
    to grow enough food.
¹⁸ Your food will be plants,
but the ground will produce
    thorns and thistles.
¹⁹ You will have to sweat
    to earn a living;
you were made out of soil,
and you will once again
    turn into soil."

²⁰ The man Adam* named his wife Eve* because she would become the mother of all who live.

²¹ Then the LORD God made clothes out of animal skins for the man and his wife.

²² The LORD said, "These people now know the difference between right and wrong, just as we do. But they must not be allowed to eat fruit from the tree that lets them live for ever." ²³ So the LORD God sent them out of the Garden of Eden, where they would have to work the ground from which the man had been made. ²⁴ Then God put winged creatures at the entrance to the garden and a flaming, flashing sword to guard the way to the life-giving tree.

CHAPTER 4

Cain murders Abel

¹ Adam* and Eve had a son. Then Eve said, "I'll name him Cain because I got* him with the help of the LORD." ² Later she had another son and named him Abel.

---

*3.20 The man Adam: In Hebrew "man" and "Adam" are the same.
*3.20 Eve: In Hebrew "Eve" sounds like "living".
*4.1 Adam: See the note at 3.20.
*4.1 Cain . . . got: In Hebrew "Cain" sounds like "got".

See also: 3.17,18: Heb 6.8.   3.22: Rev 22.14.

was the ancestor of Seba, Havilah, Sabtah, Raamah, and Sabteca.

Raamah was the ancestor of Sheba and Dedan.

Cush was also the ancestor of Nimrod, a mighty warrior whose strength came from the LORD. Nimrod is the reason for the saying, "You hunt like Nimrod with the strength of the LORD!" Nimrod first ruled in Babylon, Erech, and Accad, all of[•] which were in Babylonia.[•] From there Nimrod went to Assyria and built the great city of Nineveh. He also built Rehoboth-Ir and Calah, as well as Resen, which is between Nineveh and Calah.

Egypt was the ancestor of Ludim, Anamim, Lehabim, Naphtuhim, Pathrusim, Casluhim, and Caphtorim, the ancestor of the Philistines.[•]

Canaan's sons were Sidon and Heth. He was also the ancestor of the Jebusites, the Amorites, the Girgashites, the Hivites, the Arkites, the Sinites, the Arvadites, the Zemarites, and the Hamathites.

Later the Canaanites spread from the territory of Sidon and went as far as Gaza in the direction of Gerar. They also went as far as Lasha in the direction of Sodom, Gomorrah, Admah, and Zeboiim.

The descendants of Shem

21-31 Shem's descendants had their own languages, tribes, and land. He was the elder brother of Japheth and the ancestor of the tribes of Eber.

Shem was the ancestor of Elam, Asshur, Arpachshad, Lud, and Aram.

Aram was the ancestor of Uz, Hul, Gether, and Mash.

Arpachshad was the father of Shelah and the grandfather of Eber, whose first son was named Peleg,* because it was during his time that tribes divided up the earth. Eber's second son was Joktan.

Joktan was the ancestor of Almodad, Sheleph, Hazarmaveth, Jerah, Hadoram, Uzal, Diklah, Obal, Abimael, Sheba, Ophir, Havilah, and Jobab. Their land reached from Mesha in the direction of Sephar, the hill country in the east.

32 This completes the list of Noah's descendants. After the flood their descendants became nations and spread all over the world.

CHAPTER 11

The tower of Babel

1 At first everyone spoke the same language, 2 but after some of them moved from the east[•] and settled in Babylonia,[•] 3-4 they said:

Let's build a city with a tower that reaches to the sky! We'll use hard bricks and tar instead of stone and mortar. We'll become famous, and we won't be scattered all over the world.

5 But when the LORD came down to look at the city and the tower, 6 he said:

These people are working together because they all speak the same language. This is just the beginning. Soon they will be able to do anything they want. 7 Come on! Let's go down and confuse them by making them speak different languages — then they won't be able to understand each other.

8-9 So the people had to stop building the city, because the LORD confused their language and scattered them all over the earth. That's how the city of Babel* got its name.

The descendants of Shem

10-11 Two years after the flood, when Shem was one hundred, he had a son named Arpachshad. He had more children and died at the age of six hundred. This is a list of his descendants:

12 When Arpachshad was thirty-five, he had a son named Shelah. 13 Arpachshad had more children and died at the age of four hundred and thirty-eight.

14 When Shelah was thirty, he had a son named Eber. 15 Shelah had more children and died at the age of four hundred and thirty-three.

16 When Eber was thirty-four, he had a son named Peleg. 17 Eber had more children and died at the age of four hundred and sixty-four.

18 When Peleg was thirty, he had a son named Reu. 19 Peleg had more children and died at the age of two hundred and thirty-nine.

20 When Reu was thirty-two he had a son named Serug. 21 Reu had more children and died at the age of two hundred and thirty-nine.

---

*10.21–31 Peleg: In Hebrew "Peleg" means "divided".

*11.8,9 Babel: In Hebrew "Babel" sounds like "confused".

²² When Serug was thirty, he had a son named Nahor. ²³ Serug had more children and died at the age of two hundred and thirty.

²⁴ When Nahor was twenty-nine, he had a son named Terah. ²⁵ Nahor had more children and died at the age of one hundred and forty-eight.

The descendants of Terah

²⁶⁻²⁸ After Terah was seventy years old, he had three sons: Abram, Nahor, and Haran, who became the father of Lot. Terah's sons were born in the city of Ur in Chaldea,* and Haran died there before the death of his father. The following is the story of Terah's descendants.

²⁹⁻³⁰ Abram married Sarai, but she was not able to have any children. And Nahor married Milcah, who was the daughter of Haran and the sister of Iscah.

³¹ Terah decided to move from Ur to the land of Canaan. He took along Abram and Sarai and his grandson Lot, the son of Haran. But when they came to the city of Haran,* they decided to settle there instead. ³² Terah lived to be two hundred and five years old and died in Haran.

The Lord chooses Abram

CHAPTER 12

¹ The LORD said to Abram:

Leave your country, your family, and your relatives and go to the land that I will show you. ² I will bless you and make your descendants into a great nation. You will become famous and be a blessing to others. ³ I will bless anyone who blesses you, but I will put a curse on anyone who puts a curse on you. Everyone on earth will be blessed because of you.'

⁴⁻⁵ Abram was seventy-five years old when the LORD told him to leave the land of Haran. He obeyed and left with his wife Sarai, his nephew Lot, and all the possessions and slaves they had got while in Haran.

When they came to the land of Canaan, ⁶ Abram went as far as the sacred tree of Moreh in a place called Shechem. The Canaanites were still living in the land at that time, ⁷ but the LORD appeared to Abram and promised, "I will give this land to your family for ever." Abram then built an altar there for the LORD.

⁸ Abram travelled to the hill country east of Bethel and camped between Bethel and Ai, where he built another altar and worshipped the LORD. ⁹ Later, Abram started out towards the Southern Desert.

Abram in Egypt

¹⁰⁻¹¹ The crops failed, and there was no food anywhere in the land. So Abram and his wife Sarai went to live in Egypt for a while. But just before they got there, he said, "Sarai, you are really beautiful! ¹² When the Egyptians see how lovely you are, they will murder me because I am your husband. But they won't kill you. ¹³ Please save my life by saying that you are my sister."

¹⁴ As soon as Abram and Sarai arrived in Egypt, the Egyptians noticed how beautiful she was. ¹⁵ The king's officials told him about her, and she was taken to his house. ¹⁶ The king was good to Abram because of Sarai, and Abram was given sheep, cattle, donkeys, slaves, and camels.

¹⁷ Because of Sarai, the LORD struck the king and everyone in his palace with terrible diseases. ¹⁸ Finally, the king sent for Abram and said to him, "What have you done to me? Why didn't you tell me Sarai was your wife? ¹⁹ Why did you make me believe she was your sister? Now I've married her. Take her and go! She's your wife."

²⁰ So the king told his men to let Abram and Sarai take their possessions and leave.

Abram and Lot

CHAPTER 13

Abram and Lot separate

¹ Abram and Sarai took everything they owned and went to the Southern Desert. Lot went with them.

² Abram was very rich. He owned many cattle, sheep, and goats, and had a lot of silver and gold. ³ Abram moved from place to place in the Southern Desert. And finally, he went north and set up his tents between Bethel and

---

*11.26–28 Ur in Chaldea: Chaldea was a region at the head of the Persian Gulf. Ur was on the main trade routes from Mesopotamia to the Mediterranean Sea.
*11.31 Haran: About 885 kilometres north-west of Ur.
See also: 12.1: Acts 7.2,3; Heb 11.8.   12.3: Gal 3.8.

See also: 12.7: Acts 7.5; Gal 3.16.   12.13: Gen 20.2; 26.7.

Ai, [4] where he had earlier camped and built an altar. There he worshipped the LORD.

[5] Lot, who was travelling with him, also had sheep, goats, and cattle, as well as his own family and slaves. [6-7] At this time the Canaanites and the Perizzites were living in the same area, and so there wasn't enough pasture land left for Abram and Lot with all their animals. Besides this, the men who took care of Abram's animals and the ones who took care of Lot's animals started quarrelling.

[8] Abram said to Lot, "We are close relatives. We shouldn't argue, and our men shouldn't be fighting one another. [9] There is plenty of land for you to choose from. Let's separate. If you go north, I'll go south; if you go south, I'll go north."

[10] This happened before the LORD had destroyed the cities of Sodom and Gomorrah. And when Lot looked around, he saw there was plenty of water in the Jordan Valley. All the way to Zoar the valley was as green as the garden of the LORD or the land of Egypt. [11] So Lot chose the whole Jordan Valley for himself, and as he started towards the east, he and Abram separated. [12] Abram stayed in the land of Canaan. But Lot settled near the cities of the valley and put up his tents not far from Sodom, [13] where the people were evil and sinned terribly against the LORD.

Abram moves to Hebron

[14] After Abram and Lot had gone their separate ways, the LORD said to Abram:

Look around to the north, south, east, and west. [15] I will give you and your family all the land you can see. It will be theirs for ever! [16] I will give you more descendants than there are specks of dust on the earth, and some day it will be easier to count the specks of dust than to count your descendants. [17] Now walk back and forth across the land, because I am giving it to you.

[18] Abram took down his tents and went to live near the sacred trees of Mamre at Hebron, where he built an altar in honour of the LORD.

CHAPTER 14

Abram rescues Lot

[1] About this time, King Amraphel of Babylonia,* King Arioch of Ellasar, King Chedorlaomer of Elam, and King Tidal of Goiim [2] attacked King Bera of Sodom, King Birsha of Gomorrah, King Shinab of Admah, King Shemeber of Zeboiim, and the king of Bela, also known as the city of Zoar.

[3-4] King Chedorlaomer and his allies had ruled these last five kings for twelve years, but in the thirteenth year the kings rebelled and came together in Siddim Valley, which is now covered by the southern part of the Dead Sea.

[5] A year later King Chedorlaomer and his allies attacked and defeated the Rephaites in Ashteroth-Karnaim, the Zuzites in Ham, and the Emites in Shaveh-Kiriathaim. [6] They also defeated the Horites in the hill country of Edom,* as far as El-Paran, near the desert.

[7] They went back to the city of Enmishpat, better known as Kadesh. Then they captured all the land that belonged to the Amalekites, and they defeated the Amorites who were living in Hazazon-Tamar.

[8-9] At Siddim Valley, the armies of the kings of Sodom, Gomorrah, Admah, Zeboiim, and Bela fought the armies of King Chedorlaomer of Elam, King Tidal of Goiim, King Amraphel of Babylonia, and King Arioch of Ellasar. The valley [10] was full of tar pits, and when the troops from Sodom and Gomorrah started running away, some of them fell into the pits. Others escaped to the hill country. [11] Their enemies took everything of value from Sodom and Gomorrah, including their food supplies. [12] They also captured Abram's nephew Lot, who lived in Sodom. They took him and his possessions and then left.

[13] At this time Abram the Hebrew was living near the oaks that belonged to Mamre the Amorite. Mamre and his brothers Eshcol and Aner were Abram's friends. Someone who had escaped from the battle told Abram [14] that his nephew Lot had been taken away. Three hundred and eighteen of Abram's servants were fighting men, so he took them and followed the enemy as far north as the city of Dan.

[15] That night, Abram divided up his troops, attacked from all sides, and won a great victory. But some of the enemy escaped to the town of Hobah north of Damascus, [16] and Abram went after them. He brought back his nephew Lot, together with Lot's possessions and the women and everyone else who had been captured.

See also: 13.10: Gen 2.10. 13.15: Acts 7.5.

Abram is blessed by Melchizedek

17 Abram returned after he had defeated King Chedorlaomer and the other kings. Then the king of Sodom went to meet Abram in Shaveh Valley, which is also known as King's Valley.

18 King Melchizedek of Salem was a priest of God Most High. He brought out some bread and wine 19 and said to Abram:

> "I bless you in the name
>   of God Most High,
>   Creator of heaven and earth.
> 20 All praise belongs
>   to God Most High
>   for helping you defeat
>   your enemies."

Then Abram gave Melchizedek a tenth of everything.

21 The king of Sodom said to Abram, "All I want are my people. You can keep everything else."

22 Abram answered:

> The LORD God Most High made the heavens and the earth. And I have promised him 23 that I won't keep anything of yours, not even a sandal strap or a piece of thread. Then you can never say that you are the one who made me rich. 24 Let my share be the food that my men have eaten. But Aner, Eshcol, and Mamre went with me, so give them their share of what we brought back.

The Lord's promises to Abram

CHAPTER 15

1 Later the LORD spoke to Abram in a vision, "Abram, don't be afraid! I will protect you and reward you greatly."

2 But Abram answered, "LORD All-Powerful, you have given me everything I could ask for, except children. And when I die, Eliezer of Damascus will get all I own.∗ 3 You have not given me any children, and this servant of mine will inherit everything."

4 The LORD replied, "No, he won't! You will have a son of your own, and everything you have will be his." 5 Then the LORD took Abram outside and said, "Look at the sky and see if you can count the stars. That's how many descendants you will have."

6 Abram believed the LORD, and the LORD was pleased with him.

The LORD makes another promise to Abram

7 The LORD said to Abram, "I brought you here from Ur in Chaldea, and I gave you this land."

8 Abram asked, "LORD God, how can I know the land will be mine?"

9 Then the LORD told him, "Bring me a three-year-old cow, a three-year-old female goat, a three-year-old ram, a dove, and a young pigeon."

10 Abram obeyed the LORD. Then he cut∗ the animals in half and laid the two halves of each animal opposite each other on the ground. But he did not cut the doves and pigeons in half. 11 And when birds came down to eat the animals, Abram chased them away.

12 As the sun was setting, Abram fell into a deep sleep, and everything became dark and frightening. 13-15 Then the LORD said:

> Abram, you will live to an old age and die in peace.
>   But I solemnly promise that your descendants will live as foreigners in a land that doesn't belong to them. They will be forced into slavery and abused for four hundred years. But I will terribly punish the nation that enslaves them, and they will leave with many possessions.
> 16 Four generations later,∗ your descendants will return here and take this land, because only then will the people who live here∗ be so sinful that they deserve to be punished.

17 Some time after sunset, when it was very dark, a smoking cooking pot∗ and a flaming fire went between the two halves of each animal. 18 At that time the LORD made an agreement with Abram and told him:

> I will give your descendants the land east of the River Shihor∗ on the border of Egypt as far as the River Euphrates. 19 They will

---

∗15.16 Four generations later: This may refer to the "four hundred years" of verses 13–15.
∗15.17 smoking cooking pot: One possible meaning for the difficult Hebrew text. The smoke and fire represent the presence of the LORD.
∗15.18 River Shihor: See Joshua 13.2–7.

See also: 15.6: Rom 4.3; Gal 3.6; Jam 2.23.
15.12: Job 4.13,14.   15.13: Exod 1.1–14; Acts 7.6.
15.14: Exod 12.40,41; Acts 7.7.   15.18: Acts 7.5.

possess the land of the Kenites, the
Kenizzites, the Kadmonites, [20] the Hittites,
the Perizzites, the Rephaites, [21] the
Amorites, the Canaanites, the Girgashites,
and the Jebusites.

Abram, Hagar, and Ishmael

CHAPTER 16

[1] Abram's wife Sarai had not been able to have
any children. But she owned a young Egyptian
slave woman named Hagar, [2] and Sarai said to
Abram, "The LORD has not given me any
children. Sleep with my slave, and if she has a
child, it will be mine."* Abram agreed, [3] and
Sarai gave him Hagar to be his wife. This
happened after Abram had lived in the land of
Canaan for ten years. [4] Later, when Hagar
knew she was going to have a baby, she
became proud and was hateful to Sarai.

[5] Then Sarai said to Abram, "It's all your
fault!* I gave you my slave woman, but she
has been hateful to me ever since she found
out she was pregnant. You have done me
wrong, and you will have to answer to the
LORD for this."

[6] Abram said, "All right! She's your slave,
and you can do whatever you want with her."
But Sarai began treating Hagar so harshly that
she finally ran away.

[7] Hagar stopped to rest at a spring in the
desert on the road to Shur. While she was
there, the angel of the LORD came to her
[8] and asked, "Hagar, where have you come
from, and where are you going?"

She answered, "I'm running away from
Sarai, my owner."

[9] The angel said, "Go back to Sarai and be
her slave. [10-11] I will give you a son, who will
be called Ishmael,* because I have heard your
cry for help. And later I will give you so many
descendants that no one will be able to count
them all. [12] But your son will live far from his
relatives; he will be like a wild donkey,
fighting everyone, and everyone fighting
him."

[13] Hagar thought, "Have I really seen God
and lived to tell about it?"* So from then on
she called him, "The God who Sees Me".*
[14] That's why people call the well between

Kadesh and Bered, "The Well of the Living
One who Sees Me".*
[15-16] Abram was eighty-six years old when
Hagar gave birth to their son, and he named
him Ishmael.

God changes Abram's name to Abraham and promises him a son

CHAPTER 17

[1] Abram was ninety-nine years old when the
LORD appeared to him again and said, "I am
God All-Powerful. If you obey me and always
do right, [2] I will keep my solemn promise to
you and give you more descendants than can
be counted." [3] Abram bowed with his face to
the ground, and God said:

[4-5] I promise that you will be the father of
many nations. That's why I now change
your name from Abram to Abraham.*
[6] I will give you a lot of descendants, and in
the future they will become great nations.
Some of them will even be kings.
[7] I will always keep the promise I have
made to you and your descendants,
because I am your God and their God.
[8] I will give you and them the land in
which you are now a foreigner. I will give
the whole land of Canaan to your family
for ever, and I will be their God.
[9] Abraham, you and all future members
of your family must promise to obey me.
[10-11] As the sign that you are keeping this
promise, you must circumcise every man
and boy in your family. [12-13] From now on,
your family must circumcise every baby
boy when he is eight days old. You must
even circumcise any man or boy you have
as a slave, both those born in your homes
and those you buy from foreigners. This
will be a sign that my promise to you will
last for ever. [14] Any man who isn't
circumcised hasn't kept his promise to me
and cannot be one of my people.
[15] Abraham, your wife's name will now
be Sarai instead of Saraí. [16] I will bless her,
and you will have a son by her. She will
become the mother of nations, and some
of her descendants will even be kings.

*16.2 Sleep . . . mine: It was the custom for a wife
who could not have children to let her husband sleep
with one of her slave women. The children of the
slave would belong to the wife.
*16.10,11 Ishmael: In Hebrew "Ishmael" sounds like
"God hears".

*17.4,5 Abraham: In Hebrew "Abraham" sounds like
"father of many nations".
See also: 16.15: Gal 4.22. 17.5: Rom 4.17.
17.7: Luke 1.55. 17.8: Acts 7.5. 17.10: Acts 7.8; Rom 4.11.

13

17 Abraham bowed with his face to the ground and thought, "I am almost a hundred years old. How can I become a father? And Sarah is ninety. How can she have a child?" So he started laughing. 18 Then he asked God, "Why not let Ishmael* inherit what you have promised me?"

19 But God answered:

No! You and Sarah will have a son. His name will be Isaac,* and I will make an everlasting promise to him and his descendants.

20 I have heard what you asked me to do for Ishmael, and so I will also bless him with many descendants. He will be the father of twelve princes, and I will make his family a great nation. 21 But your son Isaac will be born about this time next year, and the promise I am making to you and your family will be for him and his descendants for ever.

22 God finished speaking to Abraham and then left.

23-27 On that same day Abraham obeyed God by circumcising Ishmael. Abraham was also circumcised, and so were all other men and boys in his household, including his servants and slaves. He was ninety-nine years old at the time, and his son Ishmael was thirteen.

CHAPTER 18

The LORD promises Abraham a son

1 One hot summer afternoon Abraham was sitting by the entrance to his tent near the sacred trees of Mamre, when the LORD appeared to him. 2 Abraham looked up and saw three men standing nearby. He quickly ran to meet them, bowed with his face to the ground, 3 and said, "Please come to my home where I can serve you. 4 I'll have some water brought, so you can wash your feet, then you can rest under the tree. 5 Let me get you some food to give you strength before you leave. I would be honoured to serve you."

"Thank you very much," they answered. "We accept your offer."

6 Abraham quickly went to his tent and said to Sarah, "Hurry! Get a large sack of flour and make some bread." 7 After saying this, he rushed off to his herd of cattle and

picked out one of the best calves, which his servant quickly prepared. 8 He then served his guests some yoghurt and milk together with the meat.

While they were eating, he stood near them under the trees, 9 and they asked, "Where is your wife Sarah?"

"She is there in the tent," Abraham answered.

10 One of the guests was the LORD, and he said, "I'll come back about this time next year, and when I do, Sarah will already have a son."

Sarah was behind Abraham, listening at the entrance to the tent. 11 Abraham and Sarah were very old, and Sarah was well past the age for having children. 12 So she laughed and said to herself, "Now that I am worn out and my husband is old, will I really know such happiness?"*

13 The LORD asked Abraham, "Why did Sarah laugh? Does she doubt that she can have a child in her old age? 14 I am the LORD! There is nothing too difficult for me. I'll come back next year at the time I promised, and Sarah will already have a son."

15 Sarah was so frightened that she lied and said, "I didn't laugh."

"Yes, you did!" he answered.

Abraham, Lot, Sodom, and Gomorrah

Abraham prays for Sodom

16 When the three men got ready to leave, they looked down towards Sodom, and Abraham walked part of the way with them.

17 The LORD said to himself, "I should tell Abraham what I am going to do, 18 since his family will become a great and powerful nation that will be a blessing to all other nations on earth.▸ 19 I have chosen him to teach his family to obey me for ever and to do what is right and fair. Then I will give Abraham many descendants, just as I promised."

20 The LORD said, "Abraham, I have heard that the people of Sodom and Gomorrah are doing all kinds of evil things. 21 Now I am going down to see for myself if those people really are that bad. If they aren't, I want to know about it."

---

*17.18 Ishmael: Ishmael was the son of Sarah's slave Hagar (see 16.1–16).
*17.19 Isaac: In Hebrew "Isaac" sounds like "laugh."
See also: 18.2a: Heb 13.2.

*18.12 know such happiness: Either the joy of making love or the joy of having children.
See also: 18.10: Rom 9.9. 18.12: 1 Pet 3.6.
18.14: Luke 1.37.

22 The men turned and started towards Sodom. But the LORD stayed with Abraham, 23 who asked, "LORD, when you destroy the evil people, are you also going to destroy those who are good? 24 Wouldn't you spare the city if there are only fifty good people in it? 25 You surely wouldn't let them be killed when you destroy the evil ones. You are the judge of all the earth, and you do what is right."

26 The LORD replied, "If I find fifty good people in Sodom, I will save the city to keep them from being killed."

27 Abraham answered, "I am nothing more than the dust of the earth. Please forgive me, LORD, for daring to speak to you like this. 28 But suppose there are only forty-five good people in Sodom. Would you still wipe out the whole city?"

"If I find forty-five good people," the LORD replied, "I won't destroy the city."

29 "Suppose there are just forty good people?" Abraham asked.

"Even for them," the LORD replied, "I won't destroy the city."

30 Abraham said, "Please don't be angry, LORD, if I ask you what you will do if there are only thirty good people in the city."

"If I find thirty," the LORD replied, "I still won't destroy the city."

31 Then Abraham said, "I don't have any right to ask you, LORD, but what would you do if you find only twenty?"

"Because of them, I won't destroy the city," was the LORD's answer.

32 Finally, Abraham said, "Please don't get angry, LORD, if I speak just once more. Suppose you find only ten good people there."

"For the sake of ten good people," the LORD told him, "I still won't destroy the city."

33 After speaking with Abraham, the LORD left, and Abraham went back home.

CHAPTER 19

The evil city of Sodom

1 That evening the two angels* arrived in Sodom, while Lot was sitting near the city gate.* When Lot saw them, he got up, bowed down low, 2 and said, "Gentlemen, I am your servant. Please come to my home. You can wash your feet, spend the night, and be on your way in the morning."

They told him, "No, we'll spend the night in the city square." 3 But Lot kept insisting, until they finally agreed and went home with him. He baked some bread,* cooked a meal, and they ate.

4 Before Lot and his guests could go to bed, every man in Sodom, young and old, came and stood outside his house 5 and started shouting, "Where are your visitors? Send them out, so we can have sex with them!"

6 Lot went outside and shut the door behind him. 7 Then he said, "Friends, please don't do such a terrible thing! 8 I have two daughters who have never been married. I'll bring them out, and you can do what you want with them. But don't harm these men. They are guests in my home."

9 "Don't get in our way," the crowd answered. "You're an outsider. What right do you have to order us around? We'll do worse things to you than we're going to do to them."

The crowd kept arguing with Lot. Finally, they rushed towards the door to break it down. 10 But the two angels in the house reached out and pulled Lot safely inside. 11 Then they struck everyone in the crowd blind, and none of them could even find the door.

12-13 The two angels said to Lot, "The LORD has heard many terrible things about the people of Sodom, and he has sent us here to destroy the city. Take your family and leave. Take every relative you have in the city, as well as the men your daughters are going to marry."

14 Lot went to the men who were engaged to his daughters and said, "Hurry and get out of here! The LORD is going to destroy this city." But they thought he was joking, and they laughed at him.

15 Early the next morning the two angels tried to make Lot hurry and leave. They said, "Take your wife and your two daughters and get out of here as fast as you can! If you don't, every one of you will be killed when the LORD destroys the city." 16 At first, Lot just stood there. But the LORD wanted to save him. So the angels took Lot, his wife, and his two daughters by the hand and led them out of the city. 17 When they were outside, one of the angels said, "Run for your lives! Don't

---

*19.1 two angels:** The two men of 18.22.
*19.1 near the city gate:** In a large area where the people would gather for community business and for meeting with friends.

*19.3 bread:** The Hebrew text has "bread without yeast", which could be prepared quickly when guests came without warning.

See also: 19.5–8: Judg 19.22–24. 19.11: 2 King 6.18.
19.16: 2 Pet 2.7.

15

even look back. And don't stop in the valley. Run to the hills, where you will be safe."

18-19 Lot answered, "You have done us a great favour, sir. You have saved our lives, but please don't make us go to the hills. That's too far away. The city will be destroyed before we can get there, and we will be killed when it happens. 20 There's a town near here. It's only a small place, but my family and I will be safe, if you let us go there."

21 "All right, go there," he answered. "I won't destroy that town. 22 Hurry! Run! I can't do anything until you are safely there."

The town was later called Zoar* because Lot had said it was small.

Sodom and Gomorrah are destroyed

23 The sun was coming up as Lot reached the town of Zoar, 24 and the LORD sent burning sulphur down like rain on Sodom and Gomorrah. 25 He destroyed those cities and everyone who lived in them, as well as their land and the trees and grass that grew there.

26 On the way, Lot's wife looked back and was turned into a block of salt.

27 That same morning Abraham got up and went to the place where he had stood and spoken with the LORD. 28 He looked down towards Sodom and Gomorrah and saw smoke rising from all over the land — it was like a flaming furnace.

29 When God destroyed the cities of the valley where Lot lived, he remembered his promise to Abraham and saved Lot from the terrible destruction.

Moab and Ammon

30 Lot was afraid to stay on in Zoar. So he took his two daughters and moved to a cave in the hill country. 31 One day his elder daughter said to her sister, "Our father is old, and there are no men anywhere for us to marry. 32 Let's get our father drunk! Then we can sleep with him and have children." 33 That night they got their father drunk, and the elder daughter got in bed with him, but he was too drunk even to know she was there.

34 The next day the elder daughter said to her sister, "I slept with my father last night. We'll get him drunk again tonight, so you can go to bed with him, and we can each have a child." 35 That night they got their father drunk, and this time the younger sister slept with him. But once again he was too drunk even to know she was there.

36 That's how Lot's two daughters had their children. 37 The elder daughter named her son Moab,* and he is the ancestor of the Moabites. 38 The younger daughter named her son Benammi,* and he is the ancestor of the Ammonites.

Abraham, Sarah, and Isaac

CHAPTER 20

Abraham and Sarah at Gerar

1 Abraham moved to the Southern Desert, where he settled between Kadesh and Shur. Later he went to Gerar, and while there 2 he told everyone that his wife Sarah was his sister. So King Abimelech of Gerar had Sarah brought to him. 3 But God came to Abimelech in a dream and said, "You have taken a married woman, and for this you will die!"

4-5 Abimelech said to the Lord, "Don't kill me! I haven't slept with Sarah. Didn't they say they were brother and sister? I am completely innocent."

6 God spoke to Abimelech in another dream and said:

I know you are innocent. That's why I kept you from sleeping with Sarah and doing anything wrong. 7 Her husband is a prophet. Let him go back to him, and his prayers will save you from death. But if you don't return her, you and all your people will die.

8 Early the next morning Abimelech sent for his officials, and when he told them what had happened, they were frightened. 9 Abimelech then called in Abraham and said:

Look what you've done to us! What have I ever done to you? Why did you make me and my nation guilty of such a terrible sin? 10 What were you thinking when you did this?

11 Abraham answered:

I did it because I didn't think any of you respected God, and I was sure that someone would kill me to get my wife. 12 Besides, she is my half sister. We have the same father, but different mothers.

---

*19.22 Zoar: In Hebrew "Zoar" sounds like "small".

See also: 19.24,25: Matt 10.15; 11.23,24; Luke 10.12; 17.29; 2 Pet 2.6. 19.26: Luke 17.32.

*19.37 Moab: In Hebrew "Moab" sounds like "from (my) father".

*19.38 Benammi: In Hebrew "Benammi" means "son of my relative".

See also: 20.2: Gen 12.13; 26.7.

¹³ When God made us leave my father's home and start wandering, I told her, "If you really love me, you will tell everyone that I am your brother."

¹⁴ Abimelech gave Abraham some sheep, cattle, and slaves. He sent Sarah back ¹⁵ and told Abraham that he could settle anywhere in his country. ¹⁶ Then he said to Sarah, "I have given your brother a thousand pieces of silver as proof to everyone that you have done nothing wrong."*

¹⁷⁻¹⁸ Meanwhile, God had kept Abimelech's wife and slaves from having children. But Abraham prayed, and God let them start having children again.

CHAPTER 21

Sarah has a son

¹ The LORD was good to Sarah and kept his promise. ² Although Abraham was very old, Sarah had a son exactly at the time God had said. ³ Abraham named his son Isaac, ⁴ and when the boy was eight days old, Abraham circumcised him, just as the LORD had commanded.

⁵ Abraham was a hundred years old when Isaac was born, ⁶ and Sarah said, "God has made me laugh.* Now everyone will laugh with me. ⁷ Who would have dared to tell Abraham that some day I would have a child? But in his old age, I have given him a son."

⁸ The time came when Sarah no longer had to nurse Isaac,* and on that day Abraham gave a big feast.

Hagar and Ishmael are sent away

⁹⁻¹⁰ One day, Sarah noticed Hagar's son Ishmael* playing,* and she said to Abraham, "Get rid of that Egyptian slave woman and her son! I don't want him to inherit anything. It should all go to my son."*

---

*21.6 God has made me laugh: In Hebrew "Isaac" sounds like "laugh."
*21.8 no longer had to nurse Isaac: In ancient Israel mothers nursed their children until they were about three years old. Then there was a family celebration.
*21.9,10 Ishmael: The son of Abraham and Hagar, who was Sarah's slave woman (see 16.1–16).
*21.9,10 Get rid . . . son: When Abraham accepted Ishmael as his son, it gave Ishmael the right to inherit part of what Abraham owned. But slaves who were given their freedom lost the right to inherit such property.

See also: 21.2: Heb 11.11. 21.4: Gen 17.12; Acts 7.8. 21.10: Gal 4.29,30.

¹¹ Abraham was worried about Ishmael. ¹² But God said, "Abraham, don't worry about your slave woman and the boy. Just do what Sarah tells you. Isaac will inherit your family name, ¹³ but the son of the slave woman is also your son, and I will make his descendants into a great nation."

¹⁴ Early the next morning Abraham gave Hagar an animal skin full of water and some bread. Then he put the boy on her shoulder and sent them away.

They wandered around in the desert near Beersheba, ¹⁵ and after they had run out of water, Hagar put her son under a bush. ¹⁶ Then she sat down a long way off, because she could not bear to watch him die. And she cried bitterly.

¹⁷ When God heard the boy crying, the angel of God called out to Hagar from heaven and said, "Hagar, why are you worried? Don't be afraid. I have heard your son crying. ¹⁸ Help him up and hold his hand, because I will make him the father of a great nation." ¹⁹ Then God let her see a well. So she went to the well and filled the skin with water, then gave some to her son.

²⁰⁻²¹ God blessed Ishmael, and as the boy grew older, he became an expert with his bow and arrows. He lived in the Paran Desert, and his mother chose an Egyptian woman for him to marry.

A peace treaty

²² About this time Abimelech and his army commander Phicol said to Abraham, "God blesses everything you do! ²³ Now I want you to promise in the name of God that you will always be loyal to me and my descendants, just as I have always been loyal to you in this land where you have lived as a foreigner." ²⁴ And so, Abraham promised.

²⁵ One day, Abraham told Abimelech, "Some of your servants have taken over one of my wells."

²⁶ "This is the first I've heard about it," Abimelech replied. "Why haven't you said something before? I don't have any idea who did it." ²⁷ Abraham gave Abimelech some sheep and cattle, and then the two men made a peace treaty.

²⁸ Abraham separated seven female lambs from his flock of sheep, ²⁹ and Abimelech asked, "Why have you done this?"

³⁰ Abraham told him, "I want you to accept these seven lambs as proof that I dug this

See also: 21.12: Rom 9.7; Heb 11.18. 21.22: Gen 26.26.

well." ³¹ So they called the place Beersheba,* because they made a treaty there.

³² When the treaty was completed, Abimelech and his army commander Phicol went back to the land of the Philistines. ³³ Abraham planted a tamarisk tree* in Beersheba and worshipped the eternal LORD God. ³⁴ Then Abraham lived a long time as a foreigner in the land of the Philistines.

CHAPTER 22

The LORD tells Abraham to offer Isaac as a sacrifice

¹ Some years later God decided to test Abraham, so he spoke to him.

Abraham answered, "Here I am, LORD."

² The LORD said, "Go and get Isaac, your only son, the one you dearly love! Take him to the land of Moriah, and I will show you a mountain where you must sacrifice him to me on the fires of an altar." ³ So Abraham got up early the next morning and chopped wood for the fire. He put a saddle on his donkey and left with Isaac and two servants for the place where God had told him to go.

⁴ Three days later Abraham looked into the distance and saw the place. ⁵ He told his servants, "Stay here with the donkey, while my son and I go over there to worship. We will come back."

⁶ Abraham put the wood on Isaac's shoulder, but he carried the hot coals and the knife. As the two of them walked along, ⁷⁻⁸ Isaac said, "Father, we have the coals and the wood, but where is the lamb for the sacrifice?"

"My son," Abraham answered, "God will provide the lamb."

The two of them walked on, and ⁹ when they reached the place that God had told him about, Abraham built an altar and placed the wood on it. Next, he tied up his son and put him on the wood. ¹⁰ He then took the knife and got ready to kill his son. ¹¹ But the LORD's angel shouted from heaven, "Abraham! Abraham!"

"Here I am!" he answered.

¹² "Don't hurt the boy or harm him in any way!" the angel said. "Now I know that you

truly obey God, because you were willing to offer him your only son."

¹³ Abraham looked up and saw a ram caught by its horns in the bushes. So he took the ram and sacrificed it in place of his son.

¹⁴ Abraham named that place "The LORD will Provide". And even now people say, "On the mountain of the LORD it will be provided."*

¹⁵ The LORD's angel called out from heaven a second time:

¹⁶ You were willing to offer the LORD your only son, and so he makes you this solemn promise, ¹⁷ "I will bless you and give you such a large family, that some day your descendants will be more numerous than the stars in the sky or the grains of sand along the beach. They will defeat their enemies and take over the cities where their enemies live. ¹⁸ You have obeyed me, and so you and your descendants will be a blessing to all nations on earth."

¹⁹ Abraham and Isaac went back to the servants who had come with him, and they returned to Abraham's home in Beersheba.

The children of Nahor

²⁰⁻²³ Abraham's brother Nahor had married Milcah, and Abraham was later told that they had eight sons. Uz was their firstborn; Buz was next, and then there was Kemuel who became the father of Aram; their other five sons were: Chesed, Hazo, Pildash, Jidlaph, and Bethuel, who became the father of Rebekah. ²⁴ Nahor also had another wife.* Her name was Reumah, and she had four sons: Tebah, Gaham, Tahash, and Maacah.

CHAPTER 23

Sarah's death and burial

¹⁻² When Sarah was one hundred and twenty-seven years old, she died in Kiriath-Arba, better known as Hebron, in the land of Canaan. After Abraham had mourned for her, ³ he went to the Hittites and said, ⁴ "I live as a foreigner in your land, and I don't own any property where I can bury my wife. Please let me buy a piece of land."

---

*21.31 Beersheba: Meaning "Well of Good Fortune" or "Peace Treaty Well".
*21.33 tamarisk tree: A tall shade tree that has deep roots and needs little water.
See also: 22.1-13: Heb 11.17-19. 22.2: 2 Chron 3.1.
22.9: Jam 2.21.

*22.24 another wife: This translates a Hebrew word for a woman who was legally bound to a man, but without the full privileges of a wife.
See also: 22.16,17: Heb 6.13,14. 22.17: Heb 11.12.
22.18: Acts 3.25. 23.4: Heb 11.9,13; Acts 7.16.

5-6 "Sir," they answered, "you are an important man. Choose the best place to bury your wife. None of us would refuse you a resting place for your dead."

7 Abraham bowed down 8 and replied, "If you are willing to let me bury my wife here, please ask Zohar's son Ephron 9 to sell me Machpelah Cave at the end of his field. I'll pay what it's worth, and all of you can be witnesses."

10 Ephron was sitting there near the city gate, when Abraham made this request, and he answered, 11 "Sir, the whole field, including the cave, is yours. With my own people as witnesses, I freely give it to you as a burial place for your dead."

12 Once again, Abraham bowed down 13 and said to Ephron, "In front of these witnesses, I offer you the full price, so I can bury my wife. Please accept my offer."

14-15 "But sir," the man replied, "the property is worth only four hundred pieces of silver. Why should we haggle over such a small amount? Take the land. It's yours."

16-18 Abraham accepted Ephron's offer and paid him the four hundred pieces of silver in front of everyone at the city gate. That's how Abraham got Ephron's property east of Hebron,* which included the field with all its trees, as well as Machpelah Cave at the end of the field. 19 So Abraham buried his wife Sarah in Machpelah Cave that was in the field 20 he had bought from the Hittites.

Rebekah, a wife for Isaac

CHAPTER 24

1 Abraham was now a very old man. The LORD had made him rich, and he was successful in everything he did. 2 One day, Abraham called in his most trusted servant and said to him, "Solemnly promise me 3 in the name of the LORD, who rules heaven and earth, that you won't choose a wife for my son Isaac from the people here in the land of Canaan. 4 Instead, go back to the land where I was born and find a wife for him from among my relatives."

5 But the servant asked, "What if the young woman I choose refuses to leave home and come here with me? Should I send Isaac there to look for a wife?"

6 "No!" Abraham answered. "Don't ever do that, no matter what. 7 The LORD who rules heaven brought me here from the land where I was born and promised that he would give this land to my descendants for ever. When you go back there, the LORD will send his angel ahead of you to help you find a wife for my son. 8 If the woman refuses to come along, you don't have to keep this promise. But don't ever take my son back there." 9 So the servant gave Abraham his word that he would do everything he had been told to do.

10 Soon after that, the servant loaded ten of Abraham's camels with valuable gifts. Then he set out for the city in northern Syria,* where Abraham's brother Nahor lived.
11 When he got there, he let the camels rest near the well outside the city. It was late afternoon, the time when the women came out for water. 12 The servant prayed:

You, LORD, are the God my master Abraham worships. Please keep your promise to him and let me find a wife for Isaac today. 13 The young women of the city will soon come to this well for water, 14 and I'll ask one of them for a drink. If she gives me a drink and then offers to get some water for my camels, I'll know she is the one you have chosen and that you have kept your promise to my master.

15-16 While he was still praying, a beautiful unmarried young woman came by with a water jar on her shoulder. She was Rebekah, the daughter of Bethuel, the son of Abraham's brother Nahor and his wife Milcah. Rebekah walked past Abraham's servant, then went over to the well, and filled her water jar. When she started back, 17 Abraham's servant ran to her and said, "Please let me have a drink of water."

18 "I'll be glad to," she answered. Then she quickly took the jar from her shoulder and held it while he drank. 19-20 After he had finished, she said, "Now I'll give your camels all the water they want." She quickly poured out water for them, and she kept going back for more, until his camels had drunk all they wanted. 21 Abraham's servant did not say a word, but he watched everything Rebekah did, because he wanted to know for certain if this was the woman the LORD had chosen.

22 The servant had brought along an expensive gold ring and two large gold bracelets. When Rebekah had finished bringing the water, he gave her the ring for her nose* and the bracelets for her arms.
23 Then he said, "Please tell me who your

---

*24.22 ring for her nose: Nose-rings were popular jewellery items, as were earrings.

father is. Does he have room in his house for me and my men to spend the night?"

²⁴ She answered, "My father is Bethuel, the son of Nahor and Milcah. ²⁵ We have a place where you and your men can stay, and we also have enough straw and feed for your camels."

²⁶ Then the servant bowed his head and prayed, ²⁷ "I thank you, LORD God of my master Abraham! You have led me to his relatives and kept your promise to him."

²⁸ Rebekah ran straight home and told her family everything. ²⁹⁻³⁰ Her brother Laban heard her tell what the servant had said, and he saw the ring and the bracelets she was wearing. So Laban ran out to Abraham's servant, who was standing by his camels at the well. ³¹ Then Laban said, "The LORD has brought you safely here. Come home with me. There's no need for you to keep on standing outside. I have a room ready for you in our house, and there's also a place for your camels."

³² Abraham's servant went home with Laban, where Laban's servants unloaded his camels and gave them straw and feed. Then they brought water into the house, so Abraham's servant and his men could wash their feet. ³³ After that, they brought in food. But the servant said, "Before I eat, I must tell you why I have come."

"Go ahead and tell us," Laban answered.
³⁴ The servant explained:

I am Abraham's servant. ³⁵ The LORD has been good to my master and has made him very rich. He has given him many sheep, goats, cattle, camels, and donkeys, as well as a lot of silver and gold, and many slaves. ³⁶ Sarah, my master's wife, didn't have any children until she was very old. Then she had a son, and my master has given him everything. ³⁷ I solemnly promised my master that I would do what he said. And he told me, "Don't choose a wife for my son from the women in this land of Canaan. ³⁸ Instead, go back to the land where I was born and find a wife for my son from among my relatives."

³⁹ I asked my master, "What if the young woman refuses to come with me?"

⁴⁰ My master answered, "I have always obeyed the LORD, and he will send his angel to help you find my son a wife from among my own relatives. ⁴¹ But if they refuse to let her come back with you, then you are freed from your promise."

⁴² When I came to the well today, I silently prayed, "You, LORD, are the God my master Abraham worships, so please lead me to a wife for his son ⁴³ while I am here at the well. When a young woman comes out to get water, I'll ask her to give me a drink. ⁴⁴ If she gives me a drink and offers to get some water for my camels, I'll know she is the one you have chosen."

⁴⁵ Even before I had finished praying, Rebekah came by with a water jar on her shoulder. When she had filled the jar, I asked her for a drink. ⁴⁶ She quickly lowered the jar from her shoulder and said, "Have a drink. Then I'll get water for your camels." So I drank, and after that she got some water for my camels. ⁴⁷ I asked her who her father was, and she answered, "My father is Bethuel the son of Nahor and Milcah." Straight away I put the ring in her nose and the bracelets on her arms. ⁴⁸ Then I bowed my head and gave thanks to the God my master Abraham worships. The LORD had led me straight to my master's relatives, and I had found a wife for his son.

⁴⁹ Now please tell me if you are willing to do the right thing for my master. Will you treat him fairly, or do I have to look for another young woman?

⁵⁰ Laban and Bethuel answered, "The LORD has done this. We have no choice in the matter. ⁵¹ Take Rebekah with you; she can marry your master's son, just as the LORD has said." ⁵² Abraham's servant bowed down and thanked the LORD. ⁵³ Then he gave clothing, as well as silver and gold jewellery, to Rebekah. He also gave expensive gifts to her brother and her mother.

⁵⁴ Abraham's servant and the men with him ate and drank, then spent the night there. The next morning they got up, and the servant told Rebekah's mother and brother, "I would like to go back to my master now."

⁵⁵ "Let Rebekah stay with us for a week or ten days," they answered. "Then she may go."

⁵⁶ But he said, "Don't make me stay any longer. The LORD has already helped me find a wife for my master's son. Now let us return."

⁵⁷ They answered, "Let's ask Rebekah what she wants to do." ⁵⁸ They called her and asked, "Are you willing to leave with this man at once?"

"Yes," she answered.

⁵⁹ So they agreed to let Rebekah and an old family servant woman* leave immediately with Abraham's servant and his men. ⁶⁰ They gave Rebekah their blessing and said, "We pray that God will give you many children and grandchildren and that he will help them defeat their enemies." ⁶¹ Afterwards, Rebekah and the young women who were to travel with her prepared to leave. Then they got on camels and left with Abraham's servant and his men.

⁶² At that time Isaac was living in the southern part of Canaan near a place called "The Well of the Living One who Sees Me".*

⁶³⁻⁶⁵ One evening he was walking out in the fields, when suddenly he saw a group of people approaching on camels. So he started towards them. Rebekah saw him coming; she got down from her camel, and asked, "Who is that man?"

"He is my master Isaac," the servant answered. Then Rebekah covered her face with her veil.*

⁶⁶ The servant told Isaac everything that had happened.

⁶⁷ Isaac took Rebekah into the tent* where his mother had lived before she died, and Rebekah became his wife. He loved her and was comforted over the loss of his mother.

The death of Abraham

CHAPTER 25

Abraham marries Keturah

¹ Abraham married Keturah, ² and they had six sons: Zimran, Jokshan, Medan, Midian, Ishbak, and Shuah. ³ Later, Jokshan became the father of Sheba and Dedan, and when Dedan grew up, he had three sons: Asshurim, Letushim, and Leummim. ⁴ Midian also had five sons: Ephah, Epher, Hanoch, Abida, and Eldaah.

⁵⁻⁶ While Abraham was still alive, he gave gifts to the sons of Hagar and Keturah. He also sent his sons to live in the east far from

his son Isaac, and when Abraham died, he left everything to Isaac.

The death of Abraham

⁷⁻⁸ Abraham died at the ripe old age of one hundred and seventy-five. ⁹⁻¹⁰ His sons Isaac and Ishmael buried him east of Hebron* in Machpelah Cave that was part of the field Abraham had bought from Ephron son of Zohar the Hittite. Abraham was buried there beside his wife Sarah. ¹¹ God blessed Isaac after this, and Isaac moved to a place called "The Well of the Living One who Sees Me".*

Ishmael's descendants

¹² Ishmael was the son of Abraham and Hagar, the slave woman of Sarah. ¹³ Ishmael had twelve sons, in this order: Nebaioth, Kedar, Adbeel, Mibsam, ¹⁴ Mishma, Dumah, Massa, ¹⁵ Hadad, Tema, Jetur, Naphish, and Kedemah. ¹⁶ Each of Ishmael's sons was a tribal chief, and a village was named after each of them.

¹⁷⁻¹⁸ Ishmael had settled in the land east of his brothers, and his sons* settled everywhere from Havilah to Shur, east of Egypt on the way to Asshur.* Ishmael was one hundred and thirty-seven when he died.

Isaac and his family

The birth of Esau and Jacob

¹⁹ Isaac was the son of Abraham, ²⁰ and he was forty years old when he married Rebekah, the daughter of Bethuel. She was also the sister of Laban, the Aramean from northern Syria.*

Almost twenty years later, ²¹ Rebekah still had no children. So Isaac asked the LORD to let her have a child, and the LORD answered his prayer.

²² Before Rebekah gave birth, she knew she was going to have twins, because she could feel them inside her, fighting each other. She thought, "Why is this happening to me?" Finally, she asked the LORD why her twins were fighting, ²³ and he told her:

> "Your two sons will become
>   two separate nations.
> The younger of the two
>   will be stronger,
> and the elder son
>   will be his servant."

---

*24.59 old family servant woman: Probably Deborah, who had taken care of Rebekah from the time she was born (see 35.8).
*24.63-65 covered . . . veil: Since the veiling of a bride was part of the wedding ceremony, this probably means that she was willing to become the wife of Isaac.
*24.67 took . . . tent: This shows that Rebekah is now the wife of Isaac and the successor of Sarah as the leading woman in the tribe.

*25.17,18 Havilah to Shur . . . Asshur: The exact location of these places is not known.
See also: 25.10: Gen 23.3–16. 25.23: Rom 9.12.

24 When Rebekah gave birth, 25 the first baby was covered with red hair, so he was named Esau.* 26 The second baby grabbed his brother's heel, so they named him Jacob.* Isaac was sixty years old when they were born.

Esau sells his rights as the firstborn son

27 As Jacob and Esau grew older, Esau liked the outdoors and became a good hunter, while Jacob settled down and became a shepherd. 28 Esau would take the meat of wild animals to his father Isaac, and so Isaac loved him more, but Jacob was his mother's favourite son.

29 One day, Jacob was cooking some stew, when Esau came home hungry 30 and said, "I'm starving to death! Give me some of that red stew at once!" That's how Esau got the name "Edom".*

31 Jacob replied, "Sell me your rights as the firstborn son."*

32 "I'm about to die," Esau answered. "What good will those rights do me?"

33 But Jacob said, "Promise me your birthrights, here and now!" And that's what Esau did. 34 Jacob then gave Esau some bread and some of the bean stew, and when Esau had finished eating and drinking, he just got up and left, showing how little he thought of his rights as the firstborn.

CHAPTER 26

Isaac and Abimelech

1 Once during Abraham's lifetime, the fields had not produced enough grain, and now the same thing happened. So Isaac went to King Abimelech of the Philistines in the land of Gerar, 2 because the LORD had appeared to Isaac and said:

Isaac, stay away from Egypt! I will show you where I want you to go. 3 You will live there as a foreigner, but I will be with you and bless you. I will keep my promise to your father Abraham by giving this land to you and your descendants.

4 I will give you as many descendants as there are stars in the sky, and I will give your descendants all this land. They will be a blessing to every nation on earth,* 5 because Abraham did everything I told him to do.

6 Isaac moved to Gerar 7 with his beautiful wife Rebekah. He was afraid that someone might kill him to get her, and so he told everyone that Rebekah was his sister. 8 After Isaac had been there a long time, King Abimelech looked out of a window and saw Isaac hugging and kissing Rebekah.

9 Abimelech called him in and said, "Rebekah must be your wife! Why did you say she is your sister?"

"Because I thought someone would kill me," Isaac answered.

10 "Don't you know what you've done?" Abimelech exclaimed. "If someone had slept with her, you would have made our whole nation guilty!" 11 Then Abimelech warned his people that anyone who even touched Isaac or Rebekah would be put to death.

12 Isaac planted grain and had a good harvest that same year. The LORD blessed him, 13 and Isaac was so successful that he became very rich. 14 In fact, the Philistines were jealous of the large number of sheep, goats, and slaves that Isaac owned, 15 and they stopped up the wells that Abraham's servants had dug before his death. 16 Finally, Abimelech said, "Isaac, I want you to leave our country. You have become too powerful to stay here."

17 Isaac left and settled in Gerar Valley, 18 where he cleaned out those wells that the Philistines had stopped up. Isaac also gave each of the wells the same name* that Abraham had given to them. 19 While his servants were digging in the valley, they found a spring-fed well. 20 But the shepherds of Gerar Valley quarrelled with Isaac's shepherds and claimed the water belonged to them. So the well was named "Quarrel", because they had quarrelled with Isaac.

21 Isaac's servants dug another well, and the shepherds also quarrelled about it. So that well was named "Jealous". 22 Finally, they dug one more well. There was no quarrelling this time, and the well was named "Lots of Room", because the LORD had given them room and would make them very successful.

23 Isaac went on to Beersheba, 24 where the LORD appeared to him that night and told him, "Don't be afraid! I am the God who was

---

*25.25 Esau: In Hebrew "Esau" sounds like "hairy".
*25.26 Jacob: In Hebrew "Jacob" sounds like "heel".
*25.30 Edom: In Hebrew "Edom" sounds like "red".
*25.31 rights . . . son: The firstborn son inherited the largest amount of property, as well as the leadership of the family.
See also: 25.33: Heb 12.16.   26.3,4: Gen 22.16–18.

*26.18 gave . . . same name: By doing this Isaac claimed ownership of the wells.
See also: 26.7: Gen 12.13; 20.2.

worshipped by your father Abraham, my servant. I will be with you and bless you, and because of Abraham I will give you many descendants." 25 Isaac built an altar there and worshipped the LORD. Then he set up camp, and his servants started digging a well.

26 Meanwhile, Abimelech had left Gerar and was taking his adviser Ahuzzath and his army commander Phicol to see Isaac. 27 When they arrived, Isaac asked, "Why are you here? Didn't you send me away because you hated me?"

28 They answered, "We now know for certain that the LORD is with you, and we have decided there needs to be a peace treaty between you and us. So let's make a solemn agreement 29 not to harm each other. Remember, we have never hurt you, and when we sent you away, we let you go in peace. The LORD has truly blessed you."

30 Isaac gave a big feast for them, and everyone ate and drank. 31 Early the next morning Isaac and the others made a solemn agreement, then he let them go in peace.

32 Later that same day Isaac's servants came and said, "We've struck water!" 33 So Isaac named the well Shibah,* and the town is still called Beersheba.*

Esau's foreign wives

34 When Esau was forty, he married Judith the daughter of Beeri the Hittite and Basemath the daughter of Elon the Hittite. 35 But these two women brought a lot of grief to his parents Isaac and Rebekah.

CHAPTER 27

Isaac blesses Jacob

1 After Isaac had become old and almost blind, he called in his firstborn son Esau, who asked him, "Father, what can I do for you?"

2 Isaac replied, "I am old and might die at any time. 3 So take your bow and arrows, then go out in the fields, and kill a wild animal. 4 Cook some of that tasty food that I love so much and bring it to me. I want to eat it once more and give you my blessing before I die."

5 Rebekah had been listening, and as soon as Esau left to go hunting, 6 she said to Jacob, "I heard your father tell Esau 7 to kill a wild animal and cook some tasty food for your

father before he dies. Your father said this because he wants to bless your brother with the LORD as his witness. 8 Now, my son, listen carefully to what I want you to do. 9 Go and kill two of your best young goats and bring them to me. I'll cook the tasty food that your father loves so much. 10 Then you can take it to him, so he can eat it and give you his blessing before he dies."

11 "My brother Esau is a hairy man," Jacob reminded her. "And I am not. 12 If my father touches me and realizes I am trying to trick him, he will put a curse on me instead of giving me a blessing."

13 Rebekah insisted, "Let his curse fall on me! Just do what I say and bring me the meat." 14 So Jacob brought the meat to his mother, and she cooked the tasty food that his father liked. 15 Then she took Esau's best clothes and put them on Jacob. 16 She also covered the smooth part of his hands and neck with goatskins 17 and gave him some bread and the tasty food she had cooked.

18 Jacob went to his father and said, "Father, here I am."

"Which one of my sons are you?" his father asked.

19 Jacob replied, "I am Esau, your firstborn, and I have done what you told me. Please sit up and eat the meat I have brought. Then you can give me your blessing."

20 Isaac asked, "My son, how did you find an animal so quickly?"

"The LORD your God was kind to me," Jacob answered.

21 "My son," Isaac said, "come closer, where I can touch you and find out if you really are Esau." 22 Jacob went closer. His father touched him and said, "You sound like Jacob, but your hands feel hairy like Esau's." 23 And so Isaac blessed Jacob, thinking he was Esau.

24 Isaac asked, "Are you really my son Esau?"

"Yes, I am," Jacob answered.

25 So Isaac told him, "Serve me the wild meat, and I can give you my blessing."

Jacob gave him some meat, and he ate it. He also gave him some wine, and he drank it. 26 Then Isaac said, "Son, come over here and kiss me." 27 While Jacob was kissing him, Isaac caught the smell of his clothes and said:

> "The smell of my son
> is like a field
>   the LORD has blessed.

---

*26.33 Shibah: In Hebrew "Shibah" sounds something like "good luck" and "promise".
*26.33 Beersheba: See the note at 21.31.
See also: 26.26: Gen 21.22.

See also: 27.27-29: Heb 11.20.

28 God will bless you, my son,
    with dew from heaven
and with fertile fields,
    rich with grain and grapes.
29 Nations will be your servants
    and bow down to you.
You will rule over your brothers,
    and they will kneel
    at your feet.
Anyone who curses you
    will be cursed;
anyone who blesses you
    will be blessed."

30 Straight after Isaac had given Jacob his blessing and Jacob had gone, Esau came back from hunting. 31 He cooked the tasty food, brought it to his father, and said, "Father, please sit up and eat the meat I have brought you, so you can give me your blessing."

32 "Who are you?" Isaac asked.

"I am Esau, your firstborn son."

33 Isaac started trembling and said, "Then who brought me some wild meat just before you came in? I ate it and gave him a blessing that cannot be taken back."

34 Esau cried loudly and begged, "Father, give me a blessing too!"

35 Isaac answered, "Your brother tricked me and stole your blessing."

36 Esau replied, "My brother deserves the name Jacob,* because he has already cheated me twice. The first time he cheated me out of my rights as the firstborn son, and now he has cheated me out of my blessing." Then Esau asked his father, "Don't you still have any blessing left for me?"

37 "My son," Isaac answered, "I have made Jacob the ruler over you and your brothers, and all of you will be his servants. I have also promised him all the grain and grapes that he needs. There's nothing left that I can do for you."

38 "Father," Esau asked, "don't you have more than one blessing? You can surely give me a blessing too!" Then Esau started crying again.

39 So his father said:

"Your home will be far
    from that fertile land,
where dew comes down
    from the heavens.

40 You will live by the power
    of your sword
    and be your brother's slave.
But when you decide to be free,
    you will break loose."

41 Esau hated his brother Jacob because he had stolen the blessing that was supposed to be his. So he said to himself, "Just as soon as my father dies, I'll kill Jacob."

42 When Rebekah found out what Esau planned to do, she sent for Jacob and told him, "Son, your brother Esau is just waiting for the time when he can kill you. 43 Now listen carefully and do what I say. Go to the home of my brother Laban in Haran 44 and stay with him for a while. When Esau stops being angry 45 and forgets what you have done to him, I'll send for you to come home. Why should I lose both of my sons on the same day?"*

46 Rebekah later told Isaac, "Those Hittite wives of Esau are making my life miserable! If Jacob marries a Hittite woman, I'd be better off dead."

CHAPTER 28

Isaac's instructions to Jacob

1 Isaac called in Jacob, then gave him a blessing, and said:

Don't marry any of those Canaanite women. 2 Go at once to your mother's father Bethuel in northern Syria* and choose a wife from one of the daughters of Laban, your mother's brother. 3 I pray that God All-Powerful will bless you with many descendants and let you become a great nation. 4 May he bless you with the land he gave Abraham, so that you will take over this land where we now live as foreigners.

5 Isaac then sent Jacob to stay with Rebekah's brother Laban, the son of Bethuel the Aramean.

Esau marries the daughter of Ishmael

6 Esau found out that his father Isaac had blessed Jacob and had warned him not to marry any of the Canaanite women. He also learnt that Jacob had been sent to find a wife in northern Syria* 7 and that he had obeyed

---

*27.36 Jacob: In Hebrew "Jacob" sounds like "cheat".
See also: 27.29: Gen 12.3. 27.36: Gen 25.29–34.
27.38: Heb 12.17. 27.39,40: Heb 11.20.

*27.45 lose . . . day: Esau would be hunted down as a murderer if he killed Jacob, and so Rebekah would lose both of her sons.
See also: 27.40: Gen 36.8; 2 King 8.20. 28.4: Gen 17.4–8.

his father and mother. [8] Esau already had several wives, but he realized at last how much his father hated the Canaanite women. [9] So he married Ishmael's daughter Mahalath, who was the sister of Nebaioth* and the granddaughter of Abraham.

Jacob and his family

Jacob's dream at Bethel

[10] Jacob left the town of Beersheba and started out for Haran. [11] At sunset he stopped for the night and went to sleep, resting his head on a large rock. [12] In a dream he saw a ladder* that reached from earth to heaven, and God's angels were going up and down on it.

[13] The LORD was standing beside the ladder* and said:

I am the LORD God who was worshipped by Abraham and Isaac. I will give to you and your family the land on which you are now sleeping. [14] Your descendants will spread over the earth in all directions and will become as numerous as the specks of dust. Your family will be a blessing to all people.* [15] Wherever you go, I will watch over you, then later I will bring you back to this land. I won't leave you — I will do all I have promised.

[16] Jacob woke up suddenly and thought, "The LORD is in this place, and I didn't even know it." [17] Then Jacob became frightened and said, "This is a fearsome place! It must be the house of God and the ladder* to heaven."

[18] When Jacob got up early the next morning, he took the rock that he had used for a pillow and stood it up for a place of worship. Then he poured olive oil on the rock to dedicate it to God, [19] and he named the place Bethel.* Before that it had been named Luz.

[20] Jacob solemnly promised God, "If you go with me and watch over me as I travel, and if you give me food and clothes [21] and bring me safely home again, you will be my God. [22] This rock will be your house, and I will give back to you a tenth of everything you give me."

CHAPTER 29

Jacob arrives at Laban's home

[1] As Jacob continued on his way to the east, [2] he looked out in a field and saw a well where shepherds took their sheep for water. Three flocks of sheep were lying around the well, which was covered with a large rock. [3] Shepherds would roll the rock away when all their sheep had gathered there. Then after the sheep had been watered, the shepherds would roll the rock back over the mouth of the well.

[4] Jacob asked the shepherds, "Where are you from?"

"We're from Haran," they answered.

[5] Then he asked, "Do you know Nahor's grandson Laban?"

"Yes we do," they replied.

[6] "How is he?" Jacob asked.

"He's fine," they answered. "And here comes his daughter Rachel with the sheep."

[7] Jacob told them, "Look, the sun is still high up in the sky, and it's too early to bring in the rest of the flocks. Water your sheep and take them back to the pasture."

[8] But they replied, "We can't do that until they all get here, and the rock has been rolled away from the well."

[9] While Jacob was still talking with the men, his cousin Rachel came up with her father's sheep. [10] When Jacob saw her and his uncle's sheep, he rolled the rock away and watered the sheep. [11] He then kissed Rachel and started crying because he was so happy. [12] He told her that he was the son of her aunt Rebekah, and she ran and told her father about him.

[13] As soon as Laban heard the news, he ran out to meet Jacob. He hugged and kissed him and brought him to his home, where Jacob told him everything that had happened. [14] Laban said, "You are my nephew, and you are like one of my own family."

Jacob marries Leah and Rachel

After Jacob had been there for a month, [15] Laban said to him, "You shouldn't have to work without pay, just because you are a relative of mine. What do you want me to give you?"

[16-17] Laban had two daughters. Leah was older than Rachel, but her eyes didn't sparkle,* while Rachel was beautiful and had a good figure. [18] Since Jacob was in love with Rachel, he answered, "If you will let me marry Rachel, I'll work seven years for you."

[19] Laban replied, "It's better for me to let you marry Rachel than for someone else to

---

*28.9 Nebaioth: Ishmael's eldest son (see 25.13).
*28.19 Bethel: In Hebrew "Bethel" means "House of God".
See also: 28.12: John 1.51. 28.13: Gen 13.14,15.
28.14: Gen 12.3; 22.18.

have her. So stay and work for me." 20 Jacob worked seven years for Laban, but the time seemed like only a few days, because he loved Rachel so much.

21 Jacob said to Laban, "The time is up, and I want to marry Rachel now!" 22 So Laban gave a big feast and invited all their neighbours. 23 But that evening he brought Leah to Jacob, who married her and spent the night with her. 24 Laban also gave Zilpah to Leah as her servant woman.

25 The next morning Jacob found out that he had married Leah, and he asked Laban, "Why did you do this to me? Didn't I work to get Rachel? Why did you trick me?"

26 Laban replied, "In our country the elder daughter must get married first. 27 After you spend this week* with Leah, you may also marry Rachel. But you will have to work for me another seven years."

28-30 At the end of the week of celebration, Laban let Jacob marry Rachel, and he gave her his servant woman Bilhah. Jacob loved Rachel more than he did Leah, but he had to work another seven years for Laban.

31 The LORD knew that Jacob loved Rachel more than he did Leah, and so he gave children to Leah, but not to Rachel. 32 Leah gave birth to a son and named him Reuben,* because she said, "The LORD has taken away my sorrow. Now my husband will love me more than he does Rachel." 33 She had a second son and named him Simeon,* because she said, "The LORD has heard that my husband doesn't love me." 34 When Leah's third son was born, she said, "Now my husband will hold me close. So this son was named Levi.* 35 She had one more son and named him Judah,* because she said, "I'll praise the LORD!"

CHAPTER 30

Problems between Rachel and Leah

1 Rachel was very jealous of Leah for having children, and she said to Jacob, "I'll die if you don't give me some children!"

2 But Jacob became upset with Rachel and answered, "Don't blame me! I'm not God."

3 "Here, take my servant Bilhah," Rachel told him. "Have children by her, and I'll let them be born on my knees to show that they are mine."

4 Then Rachel let Jacob marry Bilhah, 5 and they had a son. 6 Rachel named him Dan,* because she said, "God has answered my prayers. He has judged me and given me a son." 7 When Bilhah and Jacob had a second son, 8 Rachel said, "I've struggled hard with my sister, and I've won!" So she named the boy Naphtali.*

9 When Leah realized she could not have any more children, she let Jacob marry her servant Zilpah, 10 and they had a son. 11 "I'm really lucky," Leah said, and she named the boy Gad.* 12 When they had another son, 13 Leah exclaimed, "I'm happy now, and all the women will say how happy I am." So she named him Asher.*

Love flowers

14 During the time of the wheat harvest, Reuben found some love flowers* and took them to his mother Leah. Rachel asked Leah for some of them, 15 but Leah said, "It's bad enough that you stole my husband! Now you want my son's love flowers too."

"All right," Rachel answered. "Let me have the flowers, and you can sleep with Jacob tonight."

16 That evening when Jacob came in from the fields, Leah told him, "You're sleeping with me tonight. I hired you with my son's love flowers."

They slept together that night, 17 and God answered Leah's prayers by giving her a fifth son. 18 Leah shouted, "God has rewarded me for letting Jacob marry my servant," and she named the boy Issachar.*

19 When Leah had another son, 20 she exclaimed, "God has given me a wonderful

---

*29.27 this week: The wedding feast lasted for seven days (see Judges 14.12,17).
*29.32 Reuben: In Hebrew "Reuben" means "Look, a son!"
*29.33 Simeon: In Hebrew "Simeon" sounds like "someone who hears".
*29.34 hold me close . . . Levi: In Hebrew "Levi" sounds like "hold (someone) close".
*29.35 Judah: In Hebrew "Judah" sounds like "praise".

*30.6 Dan: In Hebrew "Dan" means "judge".
*30.8 Naphtali: In Hebrew "Naphtali" means "struggle" or "contest".
*30.11 Gad: In Hebrew "Gad" means "lucky".
*30.13 Asher: In Hebrew "Asher" means "happy".
*30.14 love flowers: Also called "mandrakes", a flowering plant that was thought to give sexual powers.
*30.18 Issachar: In Hebrew "Issachar" sounds like "reward".

gift, and my husband will praise me for giving him six sons." So she named the boy Zebulun.* ²¹ Later, Leah had a daughter and named her Dinah.

²²⁻²³ Finally, God remembered Rachel — he answered her prayer by giving her a son. "God has taken away my disgrace," she said. ²⁴ "I'll name the boy Joseph,* and I'll pray that the LORD will give me another son."

Jacob and Laban

²⁵ After Joseph was born, Jacob said to Laban, "Release me from our agreement* and let me return to my own country. ²⁶ You know how hard I've worked for you, so let me take my wives and children and leave."

²⁷⁻²⁸ But Laban told him, "If you really are my friend, stay on, and I'll pay whatever you ask. I'm sure* the LORD has blessed me because of you."

²⁹ Jacob answered:

You've seen how hard I've worked for you, and you know how your flocks and herds have grown under my care. ³⁰ You didn't have much before I came, but the LORD has blessed everything I have ever done for you. Now it's time for me to start looking after my own family.

³¹ "How much do you want me to pay you?" Laban asked.

Then Jacob told him:

I don't want you to pay me anything. Just do one thing, and I'll take care of your sheep and goats. ³² Let me go through your flocks and herds and take the sheep and goats that are either spotted or speckled* and the black lambs. That's all you need to give me. ³³ In the future you can easily find out if I've been honest. Just look and see if my animals are either spotted or speckled, or if the lambs are black. If they aren't, they've been stolen from you.

³⁴ "I agree to that," was Laban's response. ³⁵ Before the end of the day, Laban had separated his spotted and speckled animals and the black lambs from the others and had put his sons in charge of them. ³⁶ Then Laban made Jacob keep the rest of the sheep and goats at a distance of three days' journey.

³⁷ Jacob cut branches from some poplar trees and from some almond and evergreen trees. He peeled off part of the bark and made the branches look spotted and speckled. ³⁸ Then he put the branches where the sheep and goats would see them* while they were drinking from the water trough. The goats mated there ³⁹ in front of the branches, and their young were spotted and speckled.

⁴⁰ Some of the sheep that Jacob was keeping for Laban were already spotted. And when the others were ready to mate, he made sure that they faced in the direction of the spotted and black ones. In this way, Jacob built up a flock of sheep for himself and did not put them with the other sheep. ⁴¹ When the stronger sheep were mating near the drinking place, Jacob made sure that the spotted branches were there. ⁴² But he would not put out the branches when the weaker animals were mating. So Jacob got all the healthy animals, and Laban got what was left. ⁴³ Jacob soon became rich and successful. He owned many sheep, goats, camels, and donkeys, as well as a lot of slaves.

CHAPTER 31

Jacob runs from Laban

¹ Jacob heard that Laban's sons were complaining, "Jacob is now a rich man, and he got everything he owns from our father." ² Jacob also noticed that Laban was not as friendly as he had been before. ³ One day the LORD said, "Jacob, go back to your relatives in the land of your ancestors, and I will bless you."

⁴ Jacob sent for Rachel and Leah to meet him in the field where he kept his sheep, ⁵ and he told them:

Your father isn't as friendly with me as he used to be, but the God my ancestors worshipped has been on my side. ⁶ You

---

*30.20 Zebulun: In Hebrew "Zebulun" sounds like "give" and "praise".
*30.24 Joseph: In Hebrew "Joseph" sounds like "take away" and "add".
*30.25 Release . . . agreement: Jacob had agreed to work seven years for each of Laban's two daughters (see 29.18).
*30.32 spotted or speckled: In ancient times sheep were usually white, and goats were usually black or dark brown; only a few sheep would have black spots, and only a few goats would have white spots.

*30.38 would see them: It was believed by some that what sheep and goats saw at the time of breeding would determine the colour of their young.

know that I have worked hard for your father [7] and that he keeps cheating me by changing my wages time after time. But God has protected me. [8] When your father said the speckled sheep would be my wages, all of them were speckled. And when he said the spotted ones would be mine, all of them were spotted. [9] That's how God has taken sheep and goats from your father and given them to me.

[10] Once, when the flocks were mating, I dreamed that all the rams were either spotted or speckled. [11] Then God's angel called me by name. I answered, [12] and he said, "Notice that all the rams are either spotted or speckled. I know everything Laban is doing to you, [13] and I am the God you worshipped at Bethel,* when you poured olive oil on a rock and made a promise to me. Leave here straight away and return to the land where you were born."

[14] Rachel and Leah said to Jacob:

There's nothing left for us to inherit from our father. [15] He treats us like foreigners and has even cheated us out of the bride price* that should have been ours. [16] Now do whatever God tells you to do. Even the property God took from our father and gave to you really belongs to us and our children.

[17] Then Jacob, his wives, and his children got on camels and left [18] for the home of his father Isaac in Canaan. Jacob took all the flocks, herds, and other property that he had got in northern Syria.*

[19] Before Rachel left, she stole the household idols* while Laban was out shearing his sheep.

[20] Jacob tricked Laban the Aramean* by not saying that he intended to leave. [21] When Jacob crossed the River Euphrates and headed for the hill country of Gilead, he took with him everything he owned.

Laban catches up with Jacob

[22] Three days later Laban found out that Jacob had gone. [23] So he took some of his relatives along and chased after Jacob for seven days, before catching up with him in the hill country of Gilead. [24] But God appeared to Laban in a dream that night and warned, "Don't say a word to Jacob. Don't make a threat or a promise."

[25] Jacob had set up camp in the hill country of Gilead, when Laban and his relatives came and set up camp in another part of the hill country. Laban went to Jacob [26] and said:

Look what you've done! You've tricked me and run off with my daughters like a kidnapper. [27] Why did you sneak away without telling me? I would have given you a going-away party with singing and with music on tambourines and harps. [28] You didn't even give me a chance to kiss my own grandchildren and daughters goodbye. That was really foolish. [29] I could easily hurt you, but the God your father worshipped has warned me not to make any threats or promises.

[30] I can understand why you were eager to return to your father, but why did you have to steal my idols?

[31] Jacob answered, "I left secretly because I was afraid you would take your daughters from me by force. [32] If you find that any one of us has taken your idols, I'll have that person killed. Let your relatives be witnesses. Show me what belongs to you, and you can take it back." Jacob did not realize that Rachel had stolen the household idols.

[33] Laban searched the tents of Jacob, Leah, and the two servant women,* but did not find the idols. Then he started for Rachel's tent. [34] She had already hidden them in the cushion she used as a saddle and was sitting on it. Laban searched everywhere and did not find them. [35] Rachel said, "Father, please don't be angry with me for not getting up; I am having my period." Laban kept on searching, but still did not find the idols.

[36] Jacob became very angry and said to Laban:

What have I done wrong? Have I committed some crime? Is that why you hunted me down? [37] After searching through everything I have, did you find anything of yours? If so, put it here, where

---

*31.15 bride price: Usually the husband-to-be paid a bride price to the father of the bride. But Jacob didn't pay Laban a bride price for either Rachel or Leah. Instead he was tricked into working fourteen years to get the bride he loved. So there was no money for either of Laban's daughters.

*31.19 household idols: These were thought to protect the household from danger. It is also possible that the person who had them would inherit the family property.

See also: 31.13: Gen 28.18-22.

*31.33 two servant women: Bilhah and Zilpah (see 30.4,9).

your relatives and mine can see it. Then we can decide what to do.

³⁸ In all the twenty years that I've worked for you, not one of your sheep or goats has had a miscarriage, and I've never eaten even one of your rams. ³⁹ If a wild animal killed one of your sheep or goats, I paid for it myself. In fact, you demanded the full price, whether the animal was killed during the day or at night.* ⁴⁰ I sweated every day, and I couldn't sleep at night because of the cold.

⁴¹ I had to work fourteen of these twenty long years to earn your two daughters and another six years to buy your sheep and goats. During that time you kept changing my wages. ⁴² If the fearsome God* worshipped by Abraham and my father Isaac had not been on my side, you would have sent me away without a thing. But God saw my hard work, and he knew the trouble I was in, so he helped me. Then last night he told you how wrong you were.

Jacob and Laban make an agreement

⁴³ Laban said to Jacob, "Leah and Rachel are my daughters, and their children belong to me. All these sheep you are taking are really mine too. In fact, everything you have belongs to me. But there is nothing I can do to keep my daughters and their children. ⁴⁴ So I am ready to make an agreement with you, and we will pile up some large rocks here to remind us of the agreement."

⁴⁵ After Jacob had set up a large rock, ⁴⁶ he told his men to get some more rocks and pile them up next to it. Then Jacob and Laban ate a meal together beside the rocks. ⁴⁷ Laban named the pile of rocks Jegar Sahadutha.* But Jacob named it Galeed.* ⁴⁸ Laban said to Jacob, "This pile of rocks will remind us of our agreement." That's why the place was named Galeed. ⁴⁹ Laban also said, "This pile of rocks means that the LORD will watch us both while we are apart from each other." So the place was also named Mizpah.*

⁵⁰ Then Laban said:

If you ill-treat my daughters or marry other women, I may not know about it, but remember, God is watching us! ⁵¹⁻⁵² Both this pile of rocks and this large rock have been set up between us as a reminder. I must never go beyond them to attack you, and you must never go beyond them to attack me. ⁵³ My father Nahor, your grandfather Abraham, and their ancestors all worshipped the same God, and he will make sure that we each keep the agreement.

Then Jacob made a promise in the name of the fearsome God* his father Isaac had worshipped. ⁵⁴ Jacob killed an animal and offered it as a sacrifice there on the mountain, and he invited his men to eat with him. After the meal they spent the night on the mountain. ⁵⁵ Early the next morning, Laban kissed his daughters and his grandchildren goodbye, then he left to go back home.

CHAPTER 32

Jacob gets ready to meet Esau

¹ As Jacob was on his way back home, some of God's angels came and met him. ² When Jacob saw them, he said, "This is God's camp." So he named the place Mahanaim.*

³ Jacob sent messengers on ahead to Esau, who lived in the land of Seir, also known as Edom. ⁴ Jacob told them to say to Esau, "Master, I am your servant! I have lived with Laban all this time, ⁵ and now I own cattle, donkeys, and sheep, as well as many slaves. Master, I am sending these messengers in the hope that you will be kind to me."

⁶ When the messengers returned, they told Jacob, "We went to your brother Esau, and now he is heading this way with four hundred men."

⁷ Jacob was so frightened that he divided his people, sheep, cattle, and camels into two groups. ⁸ He thought, "If Esau attacks one group, perhaps the other can escape."

⁹ Then Jacob prayed:

You, LORD, are the God who was worshipped by my grandfather Abraham and by my father Isaac. You told me to return home to my family, and you promised to be with me and make me successful. ¹⁰ I don't deserve all the good things you have done for me, your servant.

---

*31.39 you demanded . . . night: A shepherd was not responsible for sheep and goats killed by wild animals, if the shepherd could supply proof of how they were killed.

*31.47 Jegar Sahadutha: In Aramaic "Jegar Sahadutha" means "a pile of rocks to remind us".

*31.47 Galeed: In Hebrew "Galeed" means "a pile of rocks to remind us".

*31.49 Mizpah: In Hebrew "Mizpah" sounds like "a place from which to watch".

*32.2 Mahanaim: In Hebrew "Mahanaim" means "two camps".

When I first crossed the Jordan, I had only my walking stick, but now I have two large groups of people and animals. ¹¹ Please rescue me from my brother. I am afraid he will come and attack not only me, but my wives and children as well. ¹² But you have promised that I would be a success and that some day it will be as hard to count my descendants as it is to count the stars in the sky.

¹³ After Jacob had spent the night there, he chose some animals as gifts for Esau: ¹⁴⁻¹⁵ two hundred female goats and twenty males, two hundred female sheep and twenty males, thirty female camels with their young, forty cows and ten bulls, and twenty female donkeys and ten males.

¹⁶ Jacob put servants in charge of each herd and told them, "Go ahead of me and keep a space between each herd." ¹⁷ Then he said to the servant in charge of the first herd, "When Esau meets you, he will ask whose servant you are. He will want to know where you are going and who owns those animals in front of you. ¹⁸ So tell him, 'They belong to your servant Jacob, who is coming this way. He is sending them as a gift to his master Esau.'"

¹⁹ Jacob also told the men in charge of the second and third herds and those who followed to say the same thing when they met Esau. ²⁰ And Jacob told them to be sure to say that he was just behind them. Jacob hoped the gifts would make Esau friendly, so Esau would be glad to see him when they met. ²¹ Jacob's men took the gifts on ahead of him, but he spent the night in camp.

Jacob's name is changed to Israel

²²⁻²³ Jacob got up in the middle of the night and took his wives, his eleven children, and everything he owned across to the other side of the River Jabbok for safety. ²⁴ Afterwards, Jacob went back and spent the rest of the night alone.

A man came and fought with Jacob until just before daybreak. ²⁵ When the man saw that he could not win, he struck Jacob on the hip and threw it out of joint. ²⁶ They kept on wrestling until the man said, "Let go of me! It's almost daylight."

"You can't go until you bless me," Jacob replied.

²⁷ Then the man asked, "What is your name?"

"Jacob," he answered.

²⁸ The man said, "Your name will no longer be Jacob. You have wrestled with God and with men, and you have won. That's why your name will be Israel."*

²⁹ Jacob said, "Now tell me your name."

"Don't you know who I am?" he asked. And he blessed Jacob.

³⁰ Jacob said, "I have seen God face to face, and I am still alive." So he named the place Peniel.* ³¹ The sun was coming up as Jacob was leaving Peniel. He was limping because he had been struck on the hip, ³² and the muscle on his hip joint had been injured. That's why even today the people of Israel don't eat the hip muscle of any animal.

CHAPTER 33

Jacob meets Esau

¹ Later that day Jacob met Esau coming with his four hundred men. So Jacob made his children walk with him. ² The two servant women, Zilpah and Bilhah, together with their children went first, followed by Leah and her children, then by Rachel and Joseph. ³ Jacob himself walked in front of them all, bowing to the ground seven times as he came near his brother.

⁴ But Esau ran towards Jacob and hugged and kissed him. Then the two brothers started crying.

⁵ When Esau noticed the women and children he asked, "Whose children are these?"

Jacob answered, "These are the ones the LORD has been kind enough to give to me, your servant."

⁶ Then the two servant women and their children came and bowed down to Esau. ⁷ Next, Leah and her children came and bowed down; finally, Joseph and Rachel also came and bowed down.

⁸ Esau asked Jacob, "What did you mean by these herds I met along the road?"

"Master," Jacob answered, "I sent them so that you would be friendly to me."

⁹ "But, brother, I already have plenty," Esau replied. "Keep them for yourself."

¹⁰ "No!" Jacob said. "Please accept these gifts as a sign of your friendship for me. When you welcomed me and I saw your face, it was like seeing the face of God. ¹¹ Please

---

*32.28 Israel: In Hebrew one meaning of "Israel" is "a man who wrestles with God."
*32.30 Peniel: In Hebrew "Peniel" means "face of God."

See also: 32.12: Gen 22.17. 32.24-26: Hos 12.3,4.

See also: 32.28: Gen 35.10. 32.29: Judg 13.17,18.

accept these gifts I brought to you. God has been good to me, and I have everything I need." Jacob kept insisting until Esau accepted the gifts.

¹² "Let's get ready to travel," Esau said. "I'll go along with you."

¹³ But Jacob answered, "Master, you know travelling is hard on children, and I have to look after the sheep and goats that are nursing their young. If my animals travel too much in one day, they will all die. ¹⁴ Why don't you go on ahead and let me travel along slowly with the children, the herds, and the flocks. We can meet again in the country of Edom."

¹⁵ Esau replied, "Let me leave some of my men with you."

"You don't have to do that," Jacob answered. "I am happy, simply knowing that you are friendly to me."

¹⁶ So Esau left for Edom. ¹⁷ But Jacob went to Succoth,* where he built a house for himself and set up shelters for his animals. That's why the place is called Succoth.

Jacob arrives at Shechem

¹⁸ After leaving northern Syria,* Jacob arrived safely at Shechem in Canaan and set up camp outside the city. ¹⁹ The land where he camped was owned by the descendants of Hamor, the father of Shechem. So Jacob paid them one hundred pieces of silver* for the property, ²⁰ then he set up his tents and built an altar there to honour the God of Israel.

CHAPTER 34

Dinah is raped

¹ Dinah, the daughter of Jacob and Leah, went to visit some of the women who lived there. ² She was seen by Hamor's son Shechem, the leader of the Hivites, and he grabbed her and raped her. ³ But Shechem was attracted to Dinah, so he told her how much he loved her. ⁴ He even asked his father to get her for his wife.

⁵ Meanwhile, Jacob heard what had happened. But his sons were out in the fields with the cattle, so he did not do anything at the time. ⁶ Hamor arrived at Jacob's home ⁷ just as Jacob's sons were coming in from work. When they learnt that their sister had been raped, they became furiously angry.

Nothing is more disgraceful than rape, and it should not be tolerated in Israel.

⁸ Hamor said to Jacob and his sons:

My son Shechem really loves Dinah. Please let him marry her. ⁹ Why don't you start letting your families marry into our families and ours marry into yours? ¹⁰ You can share this land with us. Move freely about until you find the property you want; then buy it and settle down here.

¹¹ Shechem added, "Do this favour for me, and I'll give whatever you want. ¹² Ask anything, no matter how expensive. I'll do anything, just let me marry Dinah."

¹³ Jacob's sons wanted to get even with Shechem and his father because of what had happened to their sister. ¹⁴ So they tricked them by saying:

You're not circumcised!* It would be a disgrace for us to let you marry Dinah now. ¹⁵ But we will let you marry her, if you and the other men in your tribe get circumcised. ¹⁶ Then your families can marry into ours, and ours can marry into yours, and we can live together like one nation. ¹⁷ But if you don't agree to get circumcised, we'll take Dinah and leave this place.

¹⁸ Hamor and Shechem liked what was said. ¹⁹ Shechem was the most respected person in his family, and he was so in love with Dinah that he hurried off to get everything done. ²⁰ The two men met with the other leaders of their city and told them:

²¹ These people really are friendly. Why not let them move freely about until they find the property they want? There's enough land here for them and for us. Then our families can marry into theirs, and theirs can marry into ours.

²² We have to do only one thing before they will agree to stay here and become one nation with us. Our men will have to be circumcised like their men. ²³ Just think! We'll get their property, as well as their flocks and herds. All we have to do is to agree, and they will live here with us.

²⁴ Every grown man followed this advice and got circumcised.

---

*33.17 Succoth: In Hebrew "Succoth" means "shelters".

See also: 33.19: Josh 24.32; John 4.5.

*34.14 You're not circumcised: Israelite boys were circumcised when they were eight days old, and no uncircumcised man could be part of the people of Israel.

Dinah's brothers take revenge

²⁵ Three days later the men who had been circumcised were still weak from pain. So Simeon and Levi,* two of Dinah's brothers, attacked with their swords and killed every man in town, ²⁶ including Hamor and Shechem. Then they took Dinah and left. ²⁷ Jacob's other sons came and took everything they wanted. All this was done because of the horrible thing that had happened to their sister. ²⁸ They took sheep, goats, donkeys, and everything else that was in the town or the fields. ²⁹ After taking everything of value from the houses, they dragged away the wives and children of their victims.

³⁰ Jacob said to Simeon and Levi, "Look what you've done! Now I'm in real trouble with the Canaanites and Perizzites who live around here. There aren't many of us, and if they attack, they'll kill everyone in my household."

³¹ They answered, "Was it right to let our own sister be treated that way?"

CHAPTER 35

Jacob returns to Bethel

¹ God told Jacob, "Return to Bethel, where I appeared to you when you were running from your brother Esau. Make your home there and build an altar for me."

² Jacob said to his family and to everyone else who was travelling with him:

Get rid of your foreign gods! Then make yourselves acceptable to worship God and put on clean clothes. ³ Afterwards, we'll go to Bethel. I will build an altar there for God, who answered my prayers when I was in trouble and who has always been at my side.

⁴ So everyone gave Jacob their idols and their earrings,* and he buried them under the oak tree near Shechem.

⁵ While Jacob and his family were travelling through Canaan, God terrified the people in the towns so much that no one dared bother them. ⁶ Finally, they reached Bethel, also known as Luz. ⁷ Jacob built an altar there and called it "God of Bethel", because that was the place where God had appeared to him when

he was running from Esau. ⁸ While they were there, Rebekah's personal servant Deborah* died. They buried her under an oak tree and called it "Weeping Oak".

God blesses Jacob at Bethel

⁹⁻¹¹ After Jacob came back to the land of Canaan, God appeared to him again. This time he gave Jacob a new name and blessed him by saying:

I am God All-Powerful, and from now on your name will be Israel* instead of Jacob. You will have many children. Your descendants will become nations, and some of the men in your family will even be kings. ¹² I will give you the land that I promised Abraham and Isaac, and it will belong to your family for ever.

¹³ After God had gone, ¹⁴ Jacob set up a large rock, so that he would remember what had happened there. Then he poured wine and olive oil on the rock to show that it was dedicated to God, ¹⁵ and he named the place Bethel.*

Benjamin is born

¹⁶ Jacob and his family had left Bethel and were still a long way from Ephrath, when the time came for Rachel's baby to be born. ¹⁷ She was having a rough time, but the woman who was helping her said, "Don't worry! It's a boy." ¹⁸ Rachel was at the point of death, and just before dying, she said, "I'll name him Benoni."* But Jacob called him Benjamin.*

¹⁹ Rachel was buried beside the road to Ephrath, which is also called Bethlehem. ²⁰ Jacob set up a tombstone over her grave, and it is still there. ²¹ Jacob, also known as Israel, travelled to the south of Eder Tower, where he set up camp.

²² During their time there, Jacob's eldest son Reuben slept with Bilhah, who was one of Jacob's other wives.* And Jacob found out about it.

---

*34.25 Simeon and Levi: Dinah's full brothers.
*35.4 earrings: These would have had symbols of foreign gods on them.
See also: 35.1: Gen 28.11–17.

*35.8 Deborah: See 24.59 and the note there.
*35.9–11 Israel: See the note at 32.28.
*35.15 Bethel: See the note at 28.19.
*35.18 Benoni: In Hebrew "Benoni" means "Son of my Sorrow".
*35.18 Benjamin: In Hebrew "Benjamin" can mean "Son at my Right Side" (the place of power).
*35.22 other wives: See the note at 22.24. Bilhah had been Rachel's servant woman (see 29.28–30).
See also: 35.9–11: Gen 32.28.   35.11,12: Gen 17.4–8.
35.14,15: Gen 28.18,19.   35.22: Gen 49.4.

Jacob's twelve sons

23-26 Jacob had twelve sons while living in northern Syria.* His firstborn Reuben was the son of Leah, who later gave birth to Simeon, Levi, Judah, Issachar, and Zebulun. Leah's servant Zilpah had two sons: Gad and Asher.

Jacob and his wife Rachel had Joseph and Benjamin. Rachel's servant woman Bilhah had two more sons: Dan and Naphtali.

Isaac dies

27 Jacob went to his father Isaac at Hebron, also called Mamre or Kiriath-Arba, where Isaac's father Abraham had lived as a foreigner. 28-29 Isaac died at the ripe old age of one hundred and eighty, then his sons Esau and Jacob buried him.

Esau and his family

CHAPTER 36

1 Esau, also known as Edom, had many descendants. 2 He married three Canaanite women: the first was Adah, the daughter of Elon the Hittite; the second was Oholibamah, the daughter of Anah and the granddaughter of Zibeon the Hivite; 3 the third was Basemath, who was Ishmael's daughter and Nebaioth's sister.

4-5 Esau and his three wives had five sons while in Canaan. Adah's son was Eliphaz; Basemath's son was Reuel; Oholibamah's three sons were Jeush, Jalam, and Korah.

6 Esau took his children and wives, his relatives and servants, his animals and possessions he had got while in Canaan, and moved far from Jacob. 7 He did this because the land was too crowded and could not support him and his brother with their flocks and herds. 8 That's why Esau made his home in the hill country of Seir.

9-14 Esau lived in the hill country of Seir and was the ancestor of the Edomites. Esau had three wives: Adah, Basemath, and Oholibamah. Here is a list of his descendants: Esau and Adah had a son named Eliphaz, whose sons were Teman, Omar, Zepho, Gatam, and Kenaz. Timna was the other wife* of Esau's son Eliphaz, and she had a son named Amalek.

Esau and Basemath had a son named Reuel, whose sons were Nahath, Zerah, Shammah, and Mizzah.

Esau and Oholibamah had three sons: Jeush, Jalam, and Korah.

Chiefs and leaders in Edom

15 Esau and Adah's eldest son was Eliphaz, and the clans that descended from him were Teman, Omar, Zepho, Kenaz, 16 Korah, Gatam, and Amalek. These and Esau's other descendants lived in the land of Edom.

17 The clans that descended from Esau and Basemath's son Reuel were Nahath, Zerah, Shammah, and Mizzah.

18 The clans that descended from Esau and Oholibamah the daughter of Anah were Jeush, Jalam, and Korah. 19 All of these clans descended from Esau, who was also known as Edom.

20 Seir was from the Horite tribe that had lived in Edom before the time of Esau. The clans that had descended from him were Lotan, Shobal, Zibeon, Anah, 21 Dishon, Ezer, and Dishan.

22 Lotan's sons were Hori and Heman; his sister was Timna.

23 Shobal's sons were Alvan, Manahath, Ebal, Shepho, and Onam.

24 Zibeon's sons were Aiah and Anah — the same Anah who found an oasis* in the desert while taking the donkeys of his father out to pasture.

25 Anah's children were Dishon and Oholibamah.

26 Dishon's sons were Hemdan, Eshban, Ithran, and Cheran.

27 Ezer's sons were Bilhan, Zaavan, and Akan.

28 Dishan's sons were Uz and Aran.

29 The clans of the Horites were Lotan, Shobal, Zibeon, Anah, 30 Dishon, Ezer, and Dishan, and they lived in the land of Seir.

31-39 Before there were kings in Israel, the following kings ruled Edom one after another:

> Bela son of Beor from Dinhabah;
> Jobab son of Zerah from Bozrah;
> Husham from the land of Teman;
> Hadad son of Bedad from Avith (Bedad had defeated the Midianites in Moab);
> Samlah from Masrekah;
> Shaul from the city of Rehoboth on the River Euphrates;
> Baalhanan son of Achbor;
> Hadar from the city of Pau (his wife Mehetabel was the daughter of Matred and the granddaughter of Mezahab).

---

*36.9–14 other wife: See the note at 22.24.
See also: 35.27: Gen 13.18. 36.2: Gen 26.34.
36.3: Gen 28.9.

[40] The clans that descended from Esau took their names from their families and the places where they lived. They are Timna, Alvah, Jetheth, [41] Oholibamah, Elah, Pinon, [42] Kenaz, Teman, Mibzar, [43] Magdiel, and Iram. These clans descended from Esau, who was known as Edom, the father of the Edomites. They took their names from the places where they settled.

Joseph is sold by his brothers as a slave

CHAPTER 37

Joseph and his brothers

[1] Jacob lived in the land of Canaan, where his father Isaac had lived, [2] and this is the story of his family.

When Jacob's son Joseph was seventeen years old, he took care of the sheep with his brothers, the sons of Bilhah and Zilpah.* But he was always telling his father all sorts of bad things about his brothers.

[3] Jacob loved Joseph more than he did any of his other sons, because Joseph was born after Jacob was very old. Jacob had given Joseph a fine coat* [4] to show that he was his favourite son, and so Joseph's brothers hated him and would not be friendly to him.

[5] One day, Joseph told his brothers what he had dreamed, and they hated him even more. [6] Joseph said, "Let me tell you about my dream. [7] We were out in the field, tying up bundles of wheat. Suddenly my bundle stood up, and your bundles gathered around and bowed down to it."

[8] His brothers asked, "Do you really think you are going to be king and rule over us?" Now they hated Joseph more than ever because of what he had said about his dream.

[9] Joseph later had another dream, and he told his brothers, "Listen to what else I dreamed. The sun, the moon, and eleven stars bowed down to me."

[10] When he told his father about this dream, his father became angry and said, "What's that supposed to mean? Are your mother and I and your brothers all going to come and bow down in front of you?"

[11] Joseph's brothers were jealous of him, but his father kept wondering about the dream.

Joseph is sold and taken to Egypt

[12] One day when Joseph's brothers had taken the sheep to a pasture near Shechem, [13] his father Jacob said to him, "I want you to go to your brothers. They are with the sheep near Shechem."

"Yes, sir," Joseph answered.

[14] His father said, "Go and find out how your brothers and the sheep are doing. Then come back and let me know." So he sent him from Hebron Valley.

Joseph was near Shechem [15] and wandering through the fields, when a man asked, "What are you looking for?"

[16] Joseph answered, "I'm looking for my brothers who are watching the sheep. Can you tell me where they are?"

[17] "They're not here any more," the man replied. "I overheard them say they were going to Dothan."

Joseph left and found his brothers in Dothan. [18] But before he got there, they saw him coming and made plans to kill him. [19] They said to one another, "Look, here comes the hero of those dreams! [20] Let's kill him and throw him into a pit and say that some wild animal ate him. Then we'll see what happens to those dreams."

[21] Reuben heard this and tried to protect Joseph from them. "Let's not kill him," he said. [22] "Don't murder him or even harm him. Just throw him into a dry well out here in the desert." Reuben planned to rescue Joseph later and take him back to his father.

[23] When Joseph came to his brothers, they pulled off his fine coat* [24] and threw him into a dry well.

[25] As Joseph's brothers sat down to eat, they looked up and saw a caravan of Ishmaelites coming from Gilead. Their camels were loaded with all kinds of spices that they were taking to Egypt. [26] So Judah said, "What will we gain if we kill our brother and hide his body? [27] Let's sell him to the Ishmaelites and not harm him. After all, he is our brother." And the others agreed.

[28] When the Midianite merchants came by, Joseph's brothers took him out of the well, and for twenty pieces of silver they sold him to the Ishmaelites* who took him to Egypt.

[29] When Reuben returned to the well and did not find Joseph there, he tore his clothes in sorrow. [30] Then he went back to his brothers and said, "The boy is gone! What am I going to do?"

---

*37.2 Bilhah and Zilpah: See 30.1–13.

See also: 37.11: Acts 7.9.   37.28: Acts 7.9.

[31] Joseph's brothers killed a goat and dipped Joseph's fine coat in its blood. [32] After this, they took the coat to their father and said, "We found this! Look at it carefully and see if it belongs to your son."

[33] Jacob knew it was Joseph's coat and said, "It's my son's coat! Joseph has been torn to pieces and eaten by some wild animal."

[34] Jacob mourned for Joseph a long time, and to show his sorrow he tore his clothes and wore sackcloth.* [35] All Jacob's children came to comfort him, but he refused to be comforted. "No," he said, "I will go to my grave, mourning for my son." So Jacob kept on grieving.

[36] Meanwhile, the Midianites had sold Joseph in Egypt to a man named Potiphar, who was the king's' official in charge of the palace guard.

Judah and Tamar

CHAPTER 38

[1] About that time Judah left his brothers in the hill country and went to live near his friend Hirah in the town of Adullam. [2] While there he met the daughter of Shua, a Canaanite man. Judah married her, [3] and they had three sons. He named the first one Er, [4] she named the next one Onan. [5] The third one was born when Judah was in Chezib, and she named him Shelah.

[6] Later, Judah chose Tamar as a wife for Er, his eldest son. [7] But Er was very evil, and the LORD took his life. [8] So Judah told Onan, "It's your duty to marry Tamar and have a child for your brother."*

[9] Onan knew the child would not be his,* and when he had sex with Tamar, he made sure that she would not get pregnant. [10] The LORD wasn't pleased with Onan and took his life too.

[11] Judah did not want the same thing to happen to his son Shelah, and he told Tamar, "Go home to your father and live there as a widow until my son Shelah is grown up." So Tamar went to live with her father.

[12] Some years later Judah's wife died, and he mourned for her. He then went with his friend Hirah to the town of Timnah, where his sheep were being sheared. [13] Tamar found out that her father-in-law Judah was going to Timnah to shear his sheep. [14] She also realized that Shelah was now a grown man, but she had not been allowed to marry him. So she decided to dress in something other than her widow's clothes and to cover her face with a veil. After this, she sat outside the town of Enaim on the road to Timnah.

[15] When Judah came along, he did not recognize her because of the veil. He thought she was a prostitute [16] and asked her to sleep with him. She asked, "What will you give me if I do?"

[17] "One of my young goats," he answered.

"What will you give me to keep until you send the goat?" she asked.

[18] "What do you want?" he asked in return.

"The ring on that cord around your neck," was her reply. "I also want the special walking stick* you have with you." He gave them to her, they slept together, and she became pregnant.

[19] After returning home, Tamar took off the veil and dressed in her widow's clothes again.

[20] Judah sent his friend Hirah to take a goat to the woman, so he could get back the ring and walking stick, but she wasn't there. [21] Hirah asked the people of Enaim, "Where is the prostitute who sat along the road outside your town?"

"There's never been one here," they answered.

[22] Hirah went back and told Judah, "I couldn't find the woman, and the people of Enaim said no prostitute had ever been there."

[23] "If you couldn't find her, we'll just let her keep the things I gave her," Judah answered. "And we'd better forget about the goat, or else we'll look like fools."

---

*37.34 sackcloth: A rough dark-coloured cloth made from goat or camel hair and used to make grain sacks. It was worn in times of trouble or sorrow.
*38.8 It's your duty . . . child . . . brother: If a man died without having children, his brother was to marry the dead man's wife and have a child, who was to be considered the child of the dead brother (see Deuteronomy 25.5–6).
*38.9 the child . . . not be his: When Judah died, Onan would get his dead brother's share of the inheritance, but if his dead brother had a son, the inheritance would go to him instead.

*38.18 ring . . . walking stick: The ring was shaped like a cylinder and could be rolled over soft clay as a way of sealing special documents. The walking stick was probably a symbol of power and the sign of leadership in the tribe, though it may have been a shepherd's rod.

²⁴ About three months later someone told Judah, "Your daughter-in-law Tamar has behaved like a prostitute, and now she's pregnant!"

"Drag her out of town and burn her to death!" Judah shouted.

²⁵ As Tamar was being dragged off, she sent someone to tell her father-in-law, "The man who gave me this ring, this cord, and this walking stick is the one who got me pregnant."

²⁶ "Those are mine!" Judah admitted. "She's a better person than I am, because I broke my promise to let her marry my son Shelah." After this, Judah never slept with her again.

²⁷⁻²⁸ Tamar later gave birth to twins. But before either of them was born, one of them stuck a hand out of her womb. The woman who was helping tied a red thread around the baby's hand and explained, "This one came out first."

²⁹ Straight away his hand went back in, and the other child was born first. The woman then said, "What an opening you've made for yourself!" So they named the baby Perez.* ³⁰ When the brother with the red thread came out, they named him Zerah.*

Joseph in Egypt

CHAPTER 39

Joseph and Potiphar's wife

¹ The Ishmaelites took Joseph to Egypt and sold him to Potiphar, the king's* official in charge of the palace guard. ²⁻³ So Joseph lived in the home of Potiphar, his Egyptian owner.

Soon Potiphar realized that the LORD was helping Joseph to be successful in whatever he did. ⁴ Potiphar liked Joseph and made him his personal assistant, putting him in charge of his house and all his property. ⁵ Because of Joseph, the LORD began to bless Potiphar's family and fields. ⁶ Potiphar left everything up to Joseph, and with Joseph there, the only decision he had to make was what he wanted to eat.

Joseph was well-built and handsome, ⁷ and Potiphar's wife soon noticed him. She asked him to make love to her, ⁸ but he refused and

said, "My master isn't worried about anything in his house, because he has placed me in charge of everything he owns. ⁹ No one in my master's house is more important than I am. The only thing he hasn't given me is you, and that's because you are his wife. I won't sin against God by doing such a terrible thing as this." ¹⁰ She kept begging Joseph day after day, but he refused to do what she wanted or even to go near her.

¹¹ One day, Joseph went to Potiphar's house to do his work, and none of the other servants were there. ¹² Potiphar's wife grabbed hold of his coat and said, "Make love to me!" Joseph ran out of the house, leaving her hanging on to his coat.

¹³ When this happened, ¹⁴ she called in her servants and said, "Look! This Hebrew has come just to make fools of us. He tried to rape me, but I screamed for help. ¹⁵ And when he heard me scream, he ran out of the house, leaving his coat with me."

¹⁶ Potiphar's wife kept Joseph's coat until her husband came home. ¹⁷ Then she said, "That Hebrew slave of yours tried to rape me! ¹⁸ But when I screamed for help, he left his coat and ran out of the house."

¹⁹ Potiphar became very angry ²⁰ and threw Joseph in the same prison where the king's prisoners were kept.

While Joseph was in prison, ²¹ the LORD helped him and was good to him. He even made the jailer like Joseph so much that ²² he put him in charge of the other prisoners and of everything that was done in the jail. ²³ The jailer did not worry about anything, because the LORD was with Joseph and made him successful in all that he did.

CHAPTER 40

Joseph tells the meaning of the prisoners' dreams

¹⁻³ While Joseph was in prison, both the king's* personal servant* and his chief cook made the king angry. So he had them thrown into the same prison with Joseph. ⁴ They spent a long time in prison, and Potiphar, the official in charge of the palace guard, made Joseph their servant.

⁵ One night each of the two men had a dream, but their dreams had different

---

*38.29 Perez: In Hebrew "Perez" sounds like "opening".
*38.30 Zerah: In Hebrew "Zerah" means "bright", probably referring to the red thread.
See also: 39.2; Acts 7.9.

*40.1–3 personal servant: The Hebrew text has "cup bearer", an important and trusted official in the royal court, who personally served wine to the king.
See also: 39.21; Acts 7.9.

meanings. [6] The next morning, when Joseph went to see the men, he could tell they were upset, [7] and he asked, "Why are you so worried today?"

[8] "We each had a dream last night," they answered, "and there is no one to tell us what they mean."

Joseph replied, "Doesn't God know the meaning of dreams? Now tell me what you dreamed."

[9] The king's personal servant told Joseph, "In my dream I saw a vine [10] with three branches. As soon as it budded, it blossomed, and its grapes became ripe. [11] I held the king's cup and squeezed the grapes into it, then I gave the cup to the king."

[12] Joseph said:

This is the meaning of your dream. The three branches stand for three days, [13] and in three days the king will pardon you. He will make you his personal servant again, and you will serve him his wine, just as you used to do. [14] But when these good things happen, please don't forget to tell the king about me, so I can get out of this place. [15] I was kidnapped from the land of the Hebrews, and here in Egypt I haven't done anything to deserve being thrown in jail.

[16] When the chief cook saw that Joseph had given a good meaning to the dream, he told Joseph, "I also had a dream. In it I was carrying three breadbaskets stacked on top of my head. [17] The top basket was full of all kinds of baked things for the king, but birds were eating them."

[18] Joseph said:

This is the meaning of your dream. The three baskets are three days, [19] and in three days the king will cut off your head. He will hang your body on a pole, and birds will come and peck at it.

[20] Three days later, while the king was celebrating his birthday with a dinner for his officials, he sent for his personal servant and the chief cook. [21] He put the personal servant back in his old job [22] and had the cook put to death.

Everything happened just as Joseph had said it would, [23] but the king's personal servant completely forgot about Joseph.

CHAPTER 41

Joseph interprets the king's dreams

[1] Two years later the king* of Egypt dreamed he was standing beside the River Nile. [2] Suddenly, seven fat, healthy cows came up from the river and started eating grass along the bank. [3] Then seven ugly, skinny cows came up out of the river and [4] ate the fat, healthy cows. When this happened, the king woke up.

[5] The king went back to sleep and had another dream. This time seven full heads of grain were growing on a single stalk. [6] Later, seven other heads of grain appeared, but they were thin and scorched by the east wind. [7] The thin heads of grain swallowed the seven full heads. Again the king woke up, and it had only been a dream.

[8] The next morning the king was upset. So he called in his magicians and wise men and told them what he had dreamed. None of them could tell him what the dreams meant.

[9] The king's personal servant said:

Now I remember what I was supposed to do. [10] When you were angry with me and your chief cook, you threw us both in jail in the house of the captain of the guard. [11] One night we both had dreams, and each dream had a different meaning. [12] A young Hebrew, who was a servant of the captain of the guard, was there with us at the time. When we told him our dreams, he explained what each of them meant, [13] and everything happened just as he said it would. I got my job back, and the cook was put to death.

[14] The king sent for Joseph, who was quickly brought out of jail. He shaved, changed his clothes, and went to the king.

[15] The king said to him, "I had a dream, yet no one can explain what it means. I am told that you can interpret dreams."

[16] "Your Majesty," Joseph answered, "I can't do it myself, but God can give a good meaning to your dreams."

[17] The king told Joseph:

I dreamed I was standing on the bank of the River Nile. [18] I saw seven fat, healthy cows come up out of the river, and they began feeding on the grass. [19] Next, seven skinny, bony cows came up out of the river. I have never seen such terrible looking cows anywhere in Egypt. [20] The

---

See also: 41.8: Dan 2.2.

skinny cows ate the fat ones. [21] But you couldn't tell it, because these skinny cows were just as skinny as they were before. Straight away, I woke up.

[22] I also dreamed that I saw seven heads of grain growing on one stalk. The heads were full and ripe. [23] Then seven other heads of grain came up. They were thin and scorched by a wind from the desert. [24] These heads of grain swallowed the full ones. I told my dreams to the magicians, but none of them could tell me the meaning of the dreams.

[25] Joseph replied:

Your Majesty, both of your dreams mean the same thing, and in them God has shown what is going to do. [26] The seven good cows stand for seven years, and so do the seven good heads of grain. [27] The seven skinny, ugly cows that came up later also stand for seven years, as do the seven bad heads of grain that were scorched by the east wind. The dreams mean there will be seven years when there won't be enough grain.

[28] It is just as I said — God has shown what he intends to do. [29] For seven years Egypt will have more than enough grain, [30] but that will be followed by seven years when there won't be enough. The good years of plenty will be forgotten, and everywhere in Egypt people will be starving. [31] The famine will be so bad that no one will remember that once there had been plenty. [32] God has given you two dreams to let you know that he has definitely decided to do this and that he will do it soon.

[33] Your Majesty, you should find someone who is wise and will know what to do, so that you can put him in charge of all Egypt. [34] Then appoint some other officials to collect one-fifth of every crop harvested in Egypt during the seven years when there is plenty. [35] Give them the power to collect the grain during those good years and to store it in your cities. [36] It can be stored until it is needed during the seven years when there won't be enough grain in Egypt. This will keep the country from being destroyed because of the lack of food.

Joseph is made governor over Egypt

[37] The king[*] and his officials liked this plan. [38] So the king said to them, "No one could possibly handle this better than Joseph, since the Spirit of God is with him."

[39] The king told Joseph, "God is the one who has shown you these things. No one else is as wise as you are or knows as much as you do. [40] I'm putting you in charge of my palace, and everybody will have to obey you. No one will be over you except me. [41] You are now governor of all Egypt!"

[42] Then the king took off his royal ring and put it on Joseph's finger. He gave him fine clothes to wear and placed a gold chain around his neck. [43] He also let him ride in the chariot next to his own, and people shouted, "Make way for Joseph!" So Joseph was governor of Egypt.

[44] The king told Joseph, "Although I'm king, no one in Egypt is to do anything without your permission." [45] He gave Joseph the Egyptian name Zaphenath Paneah. And he let him marry Asenath, the daughter of Potiphera, a priest in the city of Heliopolis.[*] Joseph travelled all over Egypt.

[46] Joseph was thirty when the king made him governor, and he went everywhere for the king. [47] For seven years there were big harvests of grain. [48] Joseph collected and stored up the extra grain in the cities of Egypt near the fields where it was harvested. [49] In fact, there was so much grain that they stopped keeping record, because it was like counting the grains of sand along the beach.

[50] Joseph and his wife had two sons before the famine began. [51] Their first son was named Manasseh, which means, "God has let me forget all my troubles and my family back home." [52] His second son was named Ephraim, which means "God has made me a success[*] in the land where I suffered."[*]

[53] Egypt's seven years of plenty came to an end, [54] and the seven years of famine began, just as Joseph had said. There was not enough food in other countries, but all over Egypt there was plenty. [55] When the famine finally struck Egypt, the people asked the king for food, but he said, "Go to Joseph and do what he tells you to do."

[56] The famine became bad everywhere in Egypt, so Joseph opened the storehouses and sold the grain to the Egyptians. [57] People from all over the world came to Egypt, because the famine was severe in their countries.

See also: 41.40: Acts 7.10.   41.42: Dan 5.29.
41.54: Acts 7.11.   41.55: John 2.5.

Joseph and his brothers

CHAPTER 42

Joseph's brothers go to Egypt to buy grain

1 When Jacob found out there was grain in Egypt, he said to his sons, "Why are you just sitting here, staring at one another? 2 I have heard there is grain in Egypt. Now go down and buy some, so we won't starve to death."

3 Ten of Joseph's brothers went to Egypt to buy grain. 4 But Jacob did not send Joseph's younger brother Benjamin with them; he was afraid that something might happen to him. 5 So Jacob's sons joined others from Canaan who were going to Egypt because of the terrible famine.

6 Since Joseph was governor of Egypt and in charge of selling grain, his brothers came to him and bowed with their faces to the ground. 7-8 They did not recognize Joseph, but straight away he knew who they were, though he pretended not to know. Instead, he spoke harshly and asked, "Where do you come from?"

"From the land of Canaan," they answered. "We've come here to buy grain."

9 Joseph remembered what he had dreamed about them and said, "You're spies! You've come here to find out where our country is weak."

10 "No sir," they replied. "We're your servants, and we have only come to buy grain. 11 We're honest men, and we come from the same family — we're not spies."

12 "That isn't so!" Joseph insisted. "You've come here to find out where our country is weak."

13 But they explained, "Sir, we come from a family of twelve brothers. The youngest is still with our father in Canaan, and one of our brothers is dead."

14 Joseph replied:

It's just like I said. You're spies, 15 and I'm going to find out who you really are. I swear by the life of the king that you won't leave this place until your youngest brother comes here. 16 Choose one of you to go after your brother, while the rest of you stay here in jail. That will show whether you are telling the truth. But if you are lying, I swear by the life of the king that you are spies!

17 Joseph kept them all under guard for three days, 18 before saying to them:

Since I respect God, I'll give you a chance to save your lives. 19 If you are honest men, one of you must stay here in jail, and the rest of you can take the grain back to your starving families. 20 But you must bring your youngest brother to me. Then I'll know that you are telling the truth, and you won't be put to death.

Joseph's brothers agreed 21 and said to one another, "We're being punished because of Joseph. We saw the trouble he was in, but we refused to help him when he begged us. That's why these terrible things are happening."

22 Reuben spoke up, "Didn't I tell you not to harm the boy? But you wouldn't listen, and now we have to pay the price for killing him."

23 They did not know that Joseph could understand them, since he was speaking through an interpreter. 24 Joseph turned away from them and cried, but soon he turned back and spoke to them again. Then he had Simeon tied up and taken away while they watched.

Joseph's brothers return to Canaan

25 Joseph gave orders for his brothers' grain sacks to be filled with grain and for their money* to be put in their sacks. He also gave orders for them to be given food for their journey home. After this was done, 26 they each loaded the grain on their donkeys and left.

27 When they stopped for the night, one of them opened his sack to get some grain for his donkey, and straight away he saw his money bag. 28 "Here's my money!" he told his brothers. "Right here in my sack."

They were trembling with fear as they stared at one another and asked themselves, "What has God done to us?"

29 When they returned to the land of Canaan, they told their father Jacob everything that had happened to them:

30 The governor of Egypt was rude and treated us like spies. 31 But we told him, "We're honest men, not spies. 32 We come

*42.25 money: Probably in the form of small pieces of silver and/or other precious or semi-precious metals; there were no coins or paper money at this time.

See also: **42.2:** Acts 7.12. **42.9:** Gen 37.5–10.

See also: **42.22:** Gen 37.21,22.

from a family of twelve brothers. The youngest is still with our father in Canaan, and the other is dead."

³³ Then the governor of Egypt told us, "I'll find out if you really are honest. Leave one of your brothers here with me, while you take the grain to your starving families. ³⁴ But bring your youngest brother to me, so I can be certain that you are honest men and not spies. After that, I'll let your other brother go free, and you can stay here and trade."

³⁵ When the brothers started emptying their sacks of grain, they found their money bags in them. They were frightened, and so was their father Jacob, ³⁶ who said, "You have already taken my sons Joseph and Simeon from me. And now you want to take away Benjamin! Everything is against me."

³⁷ Reuben spoke up, "Father, if I don't bring Benjamin back, you can kill both of my sons. Trust me with him, and I will bring him back."

³⁸ But Jacob said, "I won't let my son Benjamin go down to Egypt with the rest of you. His brother is already dead, and he is the only son I have left.* I am an old man, and if anything happens to him on the way, I'll die from sorrow, and all of you will be to blame."

CHAPTER 43

Joseph's brothers return to Egypt with Benjamin

¹ The famine in Canaan got worse, ² until finally, Jacob's family had eaten all the grain they had bought in Egypt. So Jacob said to his sons, "Go back and buy some more grain."

³⁻⁵ Judah replied, "The governor strictly warned us that we would not be allowed to see him unless we brought our youngest brother with us. If you let us take Benjamin along, we will go and buy grain. But we won't go without him!"

⁶ Jacob asked, "Why did you cause me so much trouble by telling the governor you had another brother?"

⁷ They answered, "He asked a lot of questions about us and our family. He wanted to know if you were still alive and if we had any more brothers. All we could do was answer his questions. How could we know he would tell us to bring along our brother?"

⁸ Then Judah said to his father, "Let Benjamin go with me, and we will leave straight away, so that none of us will starve to death. ⁹ I promise to bring him back safely, and if I don't, you can blame me as long as I live. ¹⁰ If we had not wasted all this time, we could already have been there and back twice."

¹¹ Their father said:

If Benjamin must go with you, take the governor a gift of some of the best things from our own country, such as perfume, honey, spices, pistachio nuts, and almonds.* ¹² Also take along twice the amount of money for the grain, because there must have been some mistake when the money was put back in your sacks. ¹³ Take Benjamin with you and leave right away.

¹⁴ When you go in to see the governor, I pray that God All-Powerful will be good to you and that the governor will let your other brother and Benjamin come back home with you. If I must lose my children, I suppose I must.

¹⁵ The brothers took the gifts, twice the amount of money, and Benjamin. Then they hurried off to Egypt. When they stood in front of Joseph, ¹⁶ he saw Benjamin and told the servant in charge of his house, "Take these men to my house. Slaughter an animal and cook it, so they can eat with me at midday."

¹⁷ The servant did as he was told and took the brothers to Joseph's house. ¹⁸ But on the way they got worried and started thinking, "We are being taken there because of the money that was put back in our sacks last time. He will arrest us, make us his slaves, and take our donkeys."

¹⁹ So when they arrived at Joseph's house, they said to the servant in charge, ²⁰ "Sir, we came to Egypt once before to buy grain. ²¹ But when we stopped for the night, we each found in our grain sacks the exact amount we had paid. We have brought that money back, ²² together with enough money to buy more grain. We don't know who put the money in our sacks."

²³ "It's all right," the servant replied. "Don't worry. The God you and your father worship must have put the money there,

---

*42.38 only son I have left: Jacob had only two sons by Rachel, his favourite wife.

*43.11 honey, spices, pistachio nuts, and almonds: Some of these foods were still available in Canaan, but the main food was bread, and there was no grain to make bread.

because I received your payment in full." Then he brought Simeon out to them.

²⁴ The servant took them into Joseph's house and gave them water to wash their feet. He also tended their donkeys. ²⁵ The brothers got their gifts ready to give to Joseph at midday, since they had heard they were going to eat there.

²⁶ When Joseph came home, they gave him the gifts they had brought, and they bowed down to him. ²⁷ After Joseph had asked how they were, he said, "What about your elderly father? Is he still alive?"

²⁸ They answered, "Your servant our father is still alive and well." And again they bowed down to Joseph.

²⁹ When Joseph looked around and saw his brother Benjamin, he said, "This must be your youngest brother, the one you told me about. God bless you, my son."

³⁰ Straight away he rushed off to his room and cried because of his love for Benjamin. ³¹ After washing his face and returning, he was able to control himself and said, "Serve the meal!"

³² Joseph was served at a table by himself, and his brothers were served at another. The Egyptians sat at yet another table, because Egyptians felt it was disgusting to eat with Hebrews. ³³ To the surprise of Joseph's brothers, they were seated in front of him according to their ages, from the eldest to the youngest. ³⁴ They were served food from Joseph's table, and Benjamin was given five times as much as each of the others. So Joseph's brothers drank with him and had a good time.

CHAPTER 44

The missing cup

¹⁻² Later, Joseph told the servant in charge of his house, "Fill the men's grain sacks with as much as they can hold and put their money in the sacks. Also put my silver cup in the sack of the youngest brother." The servant did as he was told.

³ Early the next morning, the men were sent on their way with their donkeys. ⁴ But they had not gone far from the city when Joseph told the servant, "Go after those men! When you catch them, say, 'My master has been good to you. So why have you stolen his silver cup? ⁵ Not only does he drink from his cup, but he also uses it to learn about the future. You have done a terrible thing.'"

⁶ When the servant caught up with them, he said exactly what Joseph had told him to say. ⁷ But they replied, "Sir, why do you say such things? We would never do anything like that! ⁸ We even returned the money we found in our grain sacks when we got back to Canaan. So why would we want to steal any silver or gold from your master's house? ⁹ If you find that one of us has the cup, then kill him, and the rest of us will become your slaves."

¹⁰ "Good!" the man replied, "I'll do what you have said. But only the one who has the cup will become my slave. The rest of you can go free."

¹¹ Each of the brothers quickly put his sack on the ground and opened it. ¹² Joseph's servant started searching the sacks, beginning with the one that belonged to the eldest brother. When he came to Benjamin's sack, he found the cup. ¹³ This upset the brothers so much that they began tearing their clothes in sorrow. Then they loaded their donkeys and returned to the city.

¹⁴ When Judah and his brothers got there, Joseph was still at home. So they bowed down to Joseph, ¹⁵ who asked them, "What have you done? Didn't you know I could find out?"

¹⁶ "Sir, what can we say?" Judah replied. "How can we prove we are innocent? God has shown that we are guilty. And now all of us are your slaves, especially the one who had the cup."

¹⁷ Joseph told them, "I would never punish all of you. Only the one who was caught with the cup will become my slave. The rest of you are free to go home to your father."

Judah pleads for Benjamin

¹⁸ Judah went over to Joseph and said:

Sir, you have as much power as the king* himself, and I am only your slave. Please don't get angry if I speak. ¹⁹ You asked us if our father was still alive and if we had any more brothers. ²⁰ So we told you, "Our father is a very old man. In fact, he was already old when Benjamin was born. Benjamin's brother is dead. Now Benjamin is the only one of the two brothers who is still alive, and our father loves him very much."

²¹ You ordered us to bring him here, so you could see him for yourself. ²² We told you that our father would die if Benjamin left him. ²³ But you warned us that we could never see you again, unless our

youngest brother came with us. ²⁴ So we returned to our father and reported what you had said.

²⁵ Later our father told us to come back here and buy more grain. ²⁶ But we answered, "We can't go back to Egypt without our youngest brother. We will never be let in to see the governor, unless he is with us."

²⁷ Sir, our father then reminded us that his favourite wife had given birth to two sons. ²⁸ One of them was already missing and had not been seen for a long time. My father thinks the boy was torn to pieces by some wild animal, ²⁹ and he said, "I am an old man. If you take Benjamin from me, and something happens to him, I will die of a broken heart."

³⁰ That's why Benjamin must be with us when I go back to my father. He loves him so much ³¹ that he will die if Benjamin doesn't come back with me. ³² I promised my father that I would bring him safely home. If I don't, I told my father he could blame me the rest of my life.

³³ Sir, I am your slave. Please let me stay here in place of Benjamin and let him return home with his brothers. ³⁴ How can I face my father if Benjamin isn't with me? I couldn't bear to see my father in such sorrow.

CHAPTER 45

Joseph tells his brothers who he is

¹ Since Joseph could no longer control his feelings in front of his servants, he sent them out of the room. When he was alone with his brothers, he told them, "I am Joseph." ² Then he cried so loudly that the Egyptians heard him and told about it in the king's palace.

³ Joseph asked his brothers if his father was still alive, but they were too frightened to answer. ⁴ Joseph told them to come closer to him, and when they did, he said:

Yes, I am your brother Joseph, the one you sold into Egypt. ⁵ Don't worry or blame yourselves for what you did. God is the one who sent me ahead of you to save lives.

⁶ There has already been a famine for two years, and for five more years no one will plough fields or harvest grain. ⁷ But God sent me on ahead of you to keep your families alive and to save you in this wonderful way. ⁸ After all, you weren't

really the ones who sent me here — it was God. He made me the highest official in the king's court and placed me over all Egypt.

⁹ Now hurry back and tell my father that his son Joseph says, "God has made me ruler of Egypt. Come here as quickly as you can. ¹⁰ You will live near me in the region of Goshen with your children and grandchildren, as well as with your sheep, goats, cattle, and everything else you own. ¹¹ I will take care of you there during the next five years of famine. But if you don't come, you and your family and your animals will starve to death."

¹² All of you, including my brother Benjamin, can tell by what I have said that I really am Joseph. ¹³ Tell my father about my great power here in Egypt and about everything you have seen. Hurry and bring him here.

¹⁴ Joseph and Benjamin hugged each other and started crying. ¹⁵ Joseph was still crying as he kissed each of his other brothers. After this, they started talking with Joseph.

¹⁶ When it was told in the palace that Joseph's brothers had come, the king and his officials were happy. ¹⁷ So the king said to Joseph:

Tell your brothers to load their donkeys and return to Canaan. ¹⁸ They must bring their father and their families here. I will give them the best land in Egypt, and they can eat and enjoy everything that grows on it. ¹⁹ Also tell your brothers to take some wagons from Egypt for their wives and children to ride in. And they must be sure to bring their father. ²⁰ They can leave their possessions behind, because they will be given the best of everything in Egypt.

²¹ Jacob's sons agreed to do what the king had said. And Joseph gave them wagons and food for their trip home, just as the king had ordered. ²² Joseph gave some new clothes to each of his brothers, but to Benjamin he gave five new outfits and three hundred pieces of silver. ²³ To his father he sent ten donkeys loaded with the best things in Egypt, and ten other donkeys loaded with grain and bread and other food for the return trip. ²⁴ Then he sent his brothers off and told them, "Don't argue on the way home!"

²⁵ Joseph's brothers left Egypt, and when they arrived in Canaan, ²⁶ they told their

See also: 45.1: Acts 7.13.

See also: 45.9–11: Acts 7.14.

father that Joseph was still alive and was the ruler of Egypt. But their father was so surprised that he could not believe them. [27] Then they told him everything Joseph had said. When he saw the wagons Joseph had sent, he felt much better [28] and said, "Now I can believe you! My son Joseph must really be alive, and I will get to see him before I die."

Jacob and his family go to Egypt

CHAPTER 46

[1] Jacob packed up everything he owned and left for Egypt. On the way he stopped near the town of Beersheba and offered sacrifices to the God his father Isaac had worshipped. [2] That night, God spoke to him and said, "Jacob! Jacob!"

"Here I am," Jacob answered.

[3] God said, "I am God, the same God your father worshipped. Don't be afraid to go to Egypt. I will give you so many descendants that one day they will become a nation. [4] I will go with you to Egypt, and later I will bring your descendants back here. Your son Joseph will be at your side when you die."

[5-7] Jacob and his family set out from Beersheba and headed for Egypt. His sons put him in the wagon that the king* had sent for him, and they put their small children and their wives in the other wagons. Jacob's whole family went to Egypt, including his sons, his grandsons, his daughters, and his granddaughters. They took along their animals and everything else they owned.

[8-15] When Jacob went to Egypt, his children who were born in northern Syria* also went along with their families.

Jacob and his wife Leah had a total of thirty-three children, grandchildren, and great-grandchildren, but two of their grandchildren had died in Canaan.

Their eldest son Reuben took his sons Hanoch, Pallu, Hezron, and Carmi.

Their son Simeon took his sons Jemuel, Jamin, Ohad, Jachin, Zohar, and Shaul, whose mother was a Canaanite.

Their son Levi took his sons Gershon, Kohath, and Merari.

Their son Judah took his sons Shelah, Perez, and Zerah. Judah's sons Er and Onan

had died in Canaan. Judah's son Perez took his sons Hezron and Hamul.

Their son Issachar took his sons Tola, Puvah, Jashub,* and Shimron.

Their son Zebulun took his sons Sered, Elon, and Jahleel.

Their daughter Dinah also went.

[16-18] Jacob and Zilpah, the servant woman Laban had given his daughter Leah, had a total of sixteen children, grandchildren, and great-grandchildren.

Their son Gad took his sons Ziphion, Haggi, Shuni, Ezbon, Eri, Arodi, and Areli.

Their son Asher took his sons Imnah, Ishvah, Ishvi, and Beriah, who took his sons Heber and Malchiel.

Serah, the daughter of Asher, also went.

[19-22] Jacob and Rachel had fourteen children and grandchildren.

Their son Joseph was already in Egypt, where he had married Asenath, daughter of Potiphera, the priest of Heliopolis.* Joseph and Asenath had two sons Manasseh and Ephraim.

Jacob and Rachel's son Benjamin took his sons Bela, Becher, Ashbel, Gera, Naaman, Ehi, Rosh, Muppim, Huppim, and Ard.

[23-25] Jacob and Bilhah, the servant woman Laban had given his daughter Rachel, had seven children and grandchildren.

Their son Dan took his son Hushim.

Their son Naphtali took his sons Jahzeel, Guni, Jezer, and Shillem.

[26] Sixty-six members of Jacob's family went to Egypt with him, not counting his daughters-in-law. [27] Jacob's two grandsons who were born there made it a total of seventy members of Jacob's family in Egypt.

[28] Jacob had sent his son Judah ahead of him to ask Joseph to meet them in Goshen. [29] So Joseph got in his chariot and went to meet his father. When they met, Joseph hugged him father around the neck and cried for a long time. [30] Jacob said to Joseph, "Now that I have seen you and know you are still alive, I am ready to die."

[31] Then Joseph said to his brothers and to everyone who had come with them:

I must go and tell the king* that you have arrived from Canaan. [32] I will tell him that you are shepherds and that you have

See also: 46.6: Acts 7.15.   See also: 46.20: Gen 41.50–52. 46.27: Acts 7.14.

43

brought your sheep, goats, cattle, and everything else you own. 33 The king will call you in and ask what you do for a living. 34 When he does, be sure to say, "We are shepherds. Our families have always raised sheep." If you tell him this, he will let you settle in the region of Goshen.

Joseph wanted them to say this to the king, because the Egyptians did not like to have anything to do with people who raised sheep.

CHAPTER 47

1-2 Joseph took five of his brothers to the king and told him, "My father and my brothers have come from Canaan. They have brought their sheep, goats, cattle, and everything else they own to the region of Goshen."

Then he introduced his brothers to the king, 3 who asked them, "What do you do for a living?"

"Sir, we are shepherds," was their answer. "Our families have always raised sheep. 4 But in our country all the pastures are dried up, and our sheep have no grass to eat. So we, your servants, have come here. Please let us live in the region of Goshen."

5 The king said to Joseph, "It's good that your father and brothers have arrived. 6 I will let them live anywhere they choose in the land of Egypt, but I suggest that they settle in Goshen, the best part of our land. I would also like your finest shepherds to look after my own sheep and goats."

7 Then Joseph brought his father Jacob and introduced him to the king. Jacob gave the king his blessing, 8 and the king asked him, "How old are you?"

9 Jacob answered, "I have lived only a hundred and thirty years, and I have had to move from place to place. My parents and my grandparents also had to move from place to place. But they lived much longer, and their life was not as hard as mine." 10 Then Jacob gave the king his blessing once again and left. 11 Joseph obeyed the king's orders and gave his father and brothers some of the best land in Egypt near the city of Rameses. 12 Joseph also provided food for their families.

A famine in Egypt

13 The famine was bad everywhere in Egypt and Canaan, and the people were suffering terribly. 14 So Joseph sold them the grain that had been stored up, and he put the money*

in the king's' treasury. 15 But when everyone had run out of money, the Egyptians came to Joseph and demanded, "Give us more grain! If you don't, we'll soon be dead, because our money's all gone."

16 "If you don't have any money," Joseph answered, "give me your animals, and I'll let you have some grain." 17 From then on, they brought him their horses and donkeys and their sheep and goats in exchange for grain. Within a year Joseph had collected every animal in Egypt. 18 Then the people came to him and said:

Sir, there's no way we can hide the truth from you. We are broke, and we don't have any more animals. We have nothing left except ourselves and our land. 19 Don't let us starve and our land be ruined. If you'll give us grain to eat and seed to plant, we'll sell ourselves and our land to the king. We'll become his slaves.

20 The famine became so severe that Joseph finally bought every piece of land in Egypt for the king 21 and made everyone the king's slaves, 22 except the priests. The king gave the priests a regular food allowance, so they did not have to sell their land. 23 Then Joseph said to the people, "You and your land now belong to the king. I'm giving you seed to plant, 24 but one-fifth of your crops must go to the king. You can keep the rest as seed or as food for your families."

25 "Sir, you have saved our lives!" they answered. "We are glad to be slaves of the king." 26 Then Joseph made a law that one-fifth of the harvest would always belong to the king. Only the priests did not lose their land.

Jacob becomes an old man

27 The people of Israel made their home in the land of Goshen, where they became prosperous and had large families. 28 Jacob himself lived there for seventeen years, before dying at the age of one hundred and forty-seven. 29 When Jacob knew he did not have long to live, he called in Joseph and said, "If you really love me, you must make a solemn promise not to bury me in Egypt. 30 Instead, bury me in the place where my ancestors are buried."

"I will do what you have asked," Joseph answered.

---

*47.14 money: See the note at 42.25.

See also: 47.29,30: Gen 49.29–32; 50.6.

31 "Will you give me your word?" Jacob asked.

"Yes, I will," Joseph promised. After this, Jacob bowed down and prayed at the head of his bed.

Jacob blesses his family and dies

CHAPTER 48

Jacob blesses Joseph's two sons

1 Joseph was told that his father Jacob had become very sick. So Joseph went to see him and took along his two sons, Manasseh and Ephraim. 2 When Joseph arrived, someone told Jacob, "Your son Joseph has come to see you." Jacob sat up in bed, but it took almost all his strength.

3 Jacob told Joseph:

God All-Powerful appeared to me at Luz in the land of Canaan, where he gave me his blessing 4 and promised, "I will give you a large family with many descendants that will grow into a nation. And I am giving you this land that will belong to you and your family for ever."

5 Then Jacob went on to say:

Joseph, your two sons Ephraim and Manasseh were born in Egypt, but I accept them as my own, just as Reuben and Simeon are mine. 6 Any children you have later will be considered yours, but their inheritance will come from Ephraim and Manasseh. 7 Unfortunately, your mother Rachel died in Canaan after we had left northern Syria' and before we reached Bethlehem.' And I had to bury her along the way.

8-10 Jacob was very old and almost blind. He did not recognize the two boys, and so he asked Joseph, "Who are these boys?"

Joseph answered, "They are my sons. God has given them to me here in Egypt."

"Bring them to me," Jacob said. "I want to give them my blessing." Joseph brought the boys to him, and he hugged and kissed them.

11 Jacob turned to Joseph and told him, "For many years I thought you were dead and that I would never see you again. But now God has even let me live to see your children." 12 Then Joseph made his sons

move away from Jacob's knees,* and Joseph bowed down in front of him with his face to the ground.

13 After Joseph got up, he brought his two sons over to Jacob again. He led his younger son Ephraim to the left side of Jacob and his elder son Manasseh to the right. 14 But before Jacob gave them his blessing, he crossed his arms, putting his right hand on the head of Ephraim and his left hand on the head of Manasseh. 15 Then he gave Joseph his blessing and said:

My grandfather Abraham and my father Isaac worshipped the LORD God. He has been with me all my life, 16 and his angel has kept me safe. Now I pray that he will bless these boys and that my name and the names of Abraham and Isaac will live on because of them. I ask God to give them many children and many descendants as well.

17 Joseph did not like it when he saw his father place his right hand on the head of the younger son. So he tried to move his father's right hand from Ephraim's head and place it on Manasseh. 18 Joseph said, "Father, you have made a mistake. This is the elder boy. Put your right hand on him."

19 But his father said, "Son, I know what I am doing. It's true that Manasseh's family will some day become a great nation. But Ephraim will be even greater than Manasseh, because his descendants will become many great nations."

20 Jacob told him that in the future the people of Israel would ask God's blessings on one another by saying, "I pray for God to bless you as much as he blessed Ephraim and Manasseh." Jacob put Ephraim's name first to show that he would be greater than Manasseh. 21 After that, Jacob said, "Joseph, you can see that I won't live much longer. But God will be with you and will lead you back to the land he promised our family long ago. 22 Meanwhile, I'm giving you the hillside' I captured from the Amorites."

---

*48.12 move . . . Jacob's knees: The two boys were placed either on or between Jacob's knees, as a sign that he had accepted them as his sons.

See also: 48.3,4: Gen 28.13,14. 48.7: Gen 35.16–19.   See also: 48.20: Heb 11.21.

CHAPTER 49

Jacob blesses his sons

1-2 Jacob called his sons together and said:

My sons, I am Jacob,
   your father Israel.
Come, gather around,
   as I tell your future.

3 Reuben, you are my eldest,
   born at the peak of my powers;
   you were an honoured leader.
4 Uncontrollable as a flood,
   you slept with my wife
   and disgraced my bed.
And so you no longer deserve
   the place of honour.

5 Simeon and Levi, you are brothers,
   each a gruesome sword.
6 I never want to take part
   in your plans or deeds.
You slaughtered people
   in your anger,
   and you crippled cattle
   for no reason.
7 Now I place a curse on you
   because of your fierce anger.
Your descendants
   will be scattered
   among the tribes of Israel.

8 Judah, you will be praised
   by your brothers;
they will bow down to you,
   as you defeat your enemies.
9 My son, you are a lion
   ready to eat your victim!
You are terribly fierce;
   no one will bother you.
10 You will have power and rule
   until nations obey you⟩
   and come bringing gifts.
11 You will tie your donkey
   to a choice grapevine
and wash your clothes
   in wine from those grapes.
12 Your eyes are darker than wine,
   your teeth whiter than milk.

13 Zebulun, you will settle
   along the seashore
and provide safe harbours
   as far north as Sidon.

14 Issachar, you are a strong donkey
   resting in the meadows.⟩

15 You found them so pleasant
   that you worked too hard
   and became a slave.

16 Dan,* you are the tribe
   that will bring justice
   to Israel.
17 You are a snake that bites
   the heel of a horse,
   making its rider fall.

18 Our LORD, I am waiting
   for you to save us.

19 Gad,* you will be attacked,
   then attack your attackers.

20 Asher, you will eat food
   fine enough for a king.

21 Naphtali, you are a wild deer
   with lovely fawns.⟩

22 Joseph, you are a fruitful vine
   growing near a stream
   and climbing a wall.⟩
23 Enemies attacked with arrows,
   refusing to show mercy.
24 But you stood your ground,
   swiftly shooting back
with the help of Jacob's God,
   the All-Powerful One —
his name is the Shepherd,
   Israel's mighty rock.*
25 Your help came from the God
   your father worshipped,
   from God All-Powerful.
God will bless you with rain
   and streams from the earth;
   he will bless you
   with many descendants.
26 My son, the blessings I give
   are better than the promise
   of ancient mountains
   or eternal hills.⟩
Joseph, I pray these blessings
   will come to you,
because you are the leader
   of your brothers.

27 Benjamin, you are a fierce wolf,
   destroying your enemies
   morning and evening.

---

*49.16 Dan: In Hebrew "Dan" means "justice" or "judgment".
*49.19 Gad: In Hebrew "Gad" sounds like "attack".
*49.24 mighty rock: The Hebrew text has "rock", which is sometimes used in poetry to compare the LORD to a mountain where his people can run for protection from their enemies.

See also: 49.9: Num 24.9; Rev 5.5.

28 These are the twelve tribes of Israel, and this is how Jacob gave each of them their proper blessings.

Jacob's death

29-31 Jacob told his sons:

Soon I will die, and I want you to bury me in Machpelah Cave. Abraham bought this cave as a burial place from Ephron the Hittite, and it is near the town of Mamre in Canaan. Abraham and Sarah are buried there, and so are Isaac and Rebekah. I buried Leah there too. 32 Both the cave and the land that goes with it were bought from the Hittites.

33 When Jacob had finished giving these instructions to his sons, he lay down on his bed and died.

CHAPTER 50

1 Joseph started crying, then leaned over to hug and kiss his father.

2 Joseph gave orders for Jacob's body to be embalmed, 3 and it took the usual forty days. The Egyptians mourned seventy days for Jacob. 4 After the time of mourning was over, Joseph said to the Egyptian leaders, "If you consider me your friend, please speak to the king' for me. 5 Just before my father died, he made me promise to bury him in his burial cave in Canaan. If the king will give me permission to go, I will come back here."

6 The king answered, "Go to Canaan and keep your promise to your father."

7-9 When Joseph left Goshen with his brothers, his relatives, and his father's relatives to bury Jacob, many of the king's highest officials and even his military chariots and cavalry went along. The Israelites left behind only their children, their cattle, and their sheep and goats.

10 After crossing the River Jordan and reaching Atad's threshing place, Joseph made everyone mourn and weep seven days for his father. 11 The Canaanites saw this and said, "The Egyptians are in great sorrow." Then they named the place "Egypt in Sorrow".'

12 So Jacob's sons did just as their father had instructed. 13 They took him to Canaan and buried him in Machpelah Cave, the burial place Abraham had bought from Ephron the Hittite.

14 After the funeral, Joseph, his brothers, and everyone else returned to Egypt.

Joseph dies

Joseph's promise to his brothers

15 After Jacob died, Joseph's brothers said to each other, "What if Joseph still hates us and wants to get even with us for all the cruel things we did to him?"

16 So they sent this message to Joseph:

Before our father died, 17 he told us, "You did some cruel and terrible things to Joseph, but you must ask him to forgive you."

Now we ask you to forgive the terrible things we did. After all, we serve the same God that your father worshipped.

When Joseph heard this, he started crying. 18 At once, Joseph's brothers came and bowed down to the ground in front of him and said, "We are your slaves."

19 But Joseph told them, "Don't be afraid! I have no right to change what God has decided. 20 You tried to harm me, but God made it turn out for the best, so that he could save all these people, as he is now doing. 21 Don't be afraid! I will take care of you and your children." After Joseph said this, his brothers felt much better.

Joseph's death

22 Joseph lived in Egypt with his brothers until he died at the age of one hundred and ten. 23 Joseph lived long enough to see Ephraim's children and grandchildren. He also lived to see the children of Manasseh's son Machir, and he welcomed them into his family. 24 Before Joseph died, he told his brothers, "I won't live much longer. But God will take care of you and lead you out of Egypt to the land he promised Abraham, Isaac, and Jacob. 25 Now promise me that you will take my body with you when God leads you to that land." 26 So Joseph died in Egypt at the age of one hundred and ten; his body was embalmed and put in a coffin.

See also: 49.30: Gen 23.3–20. 49.31: a Gen 25.9,10; b Gen 35.29. 49.33: Acts 7.15. 50.5: Gen 47.29–31. 50.13: Acts 7.16.

See also: 50.25: Exod 13.19; Josh 24.32; Heb 11.22.

Additional Notes

'1.1,2 In . . . life: Or "When God began to create the heavens and the earth, the earth was barren with no form of life."

'1.2 the Spirit of God: Or "a mighty wind".

'2.6 streams: Or "mist".

'4.7 you would be smiling: Or "I would have accepted your offering."

'4.8 Cain said to his brother Abel, "Let's . . . walk": Most ancient translations; Hebrew "Cain spoke to his brother Abel."

'4.15 No: Three ancient translations; Hebrew "Very well!"

'4.16 Wandering: The Hebrew text has "Nod", which means "wandering".

'4.26 worshipping the LORD: Or "worshipping in the name of the LORD."

'6.1,2 supernatural beings: Or "angels".

'6.3 I won't . . . for ever: One possible meaning for the difficult Hebrew text.

'6.3 No one . . . years: Or "In fact, they will all be destroyed in about one hundred years" (that is, at the time of the flood).

'6.16 roof: Or "window".

'6.16 leave . . . sides: One possible meaning for the difficult Hebrew text.

'6.18 boat: One possible meaning for the difficult Hebrew text of verse 18.

'8.13 made . . . boat: One possible meaning for the difficult Hebrew text.

'10.2–5 Dodanim: Most Hebrew manuscripts; some Hebrew manuscripts and one ancient translation have "Rodanim".

'10.6–20 and Accad, all of: Or "Accad, and Calneh".

'10.6–20 Babylonia: The Hebrew text has "Shinar", another name for Babylonia.

'10.6–20 Casluhim, and Caphtorim, the ancestor of the Philistines: Hebrew "Caphtorim, and Casluhim, the ancestor of the Philistines". The Philistines were from Caphtor (see Jeremiah 47.4; Amos 9.7), better known as Crete.

'11.2 from the east: Or "to the east".

'11.2 Babylonia: See the note at 10.6–20.

'12.3 Everyone . . . you: Or "Everyone on earth will ask me to bless them as I have blessed you."

'12.15 the king's: The Hebrew text has "Pharaoh's", a Hebrew word sometimes used for the king of Egypt.

'14.1 Babylonia: See the note at 10.6–20.

'14.6 Edom: The Hebrew text has "Seir", another name for Edom.

'15.2 And . . . own: One possible meaning for the difficult Hebrew text.

'15.10 cut: In Hebrew "cut" sounds something like "agreement". What follows shows that the LORD is making an agreement with Abram.

'15.16 people who live here: The Hebrew text has "Amorites", a name sometimes used of the people who lived in Palestine before the Israelites.

'16.5 It's . . . fault: Or "I hope you'll be punished for what you did to me!"

'16.13 Have . . . it: One possible meaning for the difficult Hebrew text.

'16.13 The God who Sees Me: Or "The God I have Seen".

'16.14 The Well . . . Me: Or "Beer-Lahai-Roi" (see 25.11).

'18.18 that will be . . . on earth: Or "and all other nations on earth will ask me to bless them as I have blessed his family."

'20.16 as proof . . . wrong: One possible meaning for the difficult Hebrew text.

'21.9,10 playing: Hebrew; one ancient translation "playing with her son Isaac".

'22.14 The LORD will Provide . . . it will be provided: Or "The LORD will be Seen . . . the LORD will be seen" or "It (a ram) will be Seen . . . it (a ram) will be seen".

'23.16–18 Hebron: The Hebrew text has "Mamre", a place just north of Hebron.

'24.10 northern Syria: The Hebrew text has "Aram-Naharaim", probably referring to the land around the city of Haran (see also "Paddan-Aram" in 25.20; 28.2,6; 31.18,20; 33.18; 35.23–26; 46.8–15; and "Paddan" in 48.7).

'24.62 who Sees Me: Or "I Have Seen".

'25.9,10 Hebron: See the note at 23.16–18.

'25.11 The Well . . . Sees Me: Or "Beer-Lahai-Roi" (see 16.14).

'25.17,18 sons: Or "descendants".

'25.20 northern Syria: See the note at 24.10.

'25.23 two separate nations: Or "two nations always in conflict".

'26.4 They . . . on earth: Or "All nations on earth will ask me to bless them."

'28.2 northern Syria: See the note at 24.10.

'28.6 northern Syria: See the note at 24.10.

'28.12 ladder: Or "stairway".

'28.13 the ladder: Or "Jacob" or "the stairway" (see the note at 28.12).

'28.14 Your family . . . people: Or "All people will ask me to bless them as I have blessed your family."

'28.17 ladder: See the note at 28.12.

'29.16,17 but her eyes didn't sparkle: Or "and her eyes sparkled".

'30.27,28 I'm sure: The Hebrew text means to find out by some kind of magic, such as fortune-telling.

'31.13 you . . . Bethel: Or "who appeared to you at Bethel".

'31.18 northern Syria: See the note at 24.10.

'31.20 the Aramean: Meaning someone from northern Syria (see the note at 24.10).

'31.42 fearsome God: One possible meaning for the difficult Hebrew text.

'31.53 fearsome God: See the note at 31.42.

'33.18 northern Syria: See the note at 24.10.

'33.19 pieces of silver: Or "lambs" or "cattle".

'35.23–26 northern Syria: See the note at 24.10.

'36.24 an oasis: One possible meaning for the difficult Hebrew text.

'37.3 fine coat: Or "a coat of many colours" or "a coat with long sleeves".

'37.23 fine coat: See the note at 37.3.

˒37.28 Midianite . . . Ishmaelites: According to 25.1,2,12 both the Midianites and the Ishmaelites were descendants of Abraham, and in Judges 8.22–24 the two names are used of the same people. It is possible that in this passage "Ishmaelite" has the meaning "nomadic traders", while "Midianite" refers to their ethnic origin.
˒37.36 the king's: See the note at 12.15.
˒39.1 the king's: See the note at 12.15.
˒40.1–3 the king's: See the note at 12.15.
˒41.1 the king: See the note at 12.15.
˒41.37 The king: See the note at 12.15.
˒41.45 Heliopolis: The Hebrew text has "On", which is better known by its Greek name "Heliopolis".
˒41.52 God has made me a success: Or "God has given me children".
˒41.52 Ephraim . . . suffered: In Hebrew "Ephraim" actually means either "fertile land" or "pasture land".
˒44.18 the king: See the note at 12.15.
˒45.2 the king's: See the note at 12.15.
˒46.5–7 the king: See the note at 12.15.
˒46.8–15 northern Syria: See the note at 24.10.
˒46.8–15 Jashub: The Samaritan Hebrew Text and one ancient translation; the Standard Hebrew Text "Iob".
˒46.19–22 Heliopolis: See the note at 41.45.
˒46.31 the king: See the note at 12.15.
˒47.14 the king: See the note at 12.15.
˒47.21 made . . . slaves: One ancient translation and the Samaritan Hebrew Text; the Standard Hebrew Text "made everyone move to the cities".
˒48.7 northern Syria: See the note at 24.10.
˒48.7 Bethlehem: The Hebrew text has "Ephrath, that is, Bethlehem".
˒48.22 the hillside: Or "a larger share than your brothers, the land".
˒49.10 until . . . you: One possible meaning for the difficult Hebrew text.
˒49.14 resting . . . meadows: One possible meaning for the difficult Hebrew text.
˒49.21 with lovely fawns: Or "speaking lovely words".
˒49.22 wall: One possible meaning for the difficult Hebrew text.
˒49.26 eternal hills: One possible meaning for the difficult Hebrew text.
˒50.4 the king: See the note at 12.15.
˒50.11 Egypt in Sorrow: Or "Abel-Mizraim".

Exodus

A quick look at this book

The title "Exodus" comes from a Greek word meaning "going out", and this book tells how the Lord set his people Israel free from slavery and brought them out of Egypt.

The book of Exodus teaches that the Lord is the one true God and the ruler of all creation. And when the Lord decides to do something, no one can stop him.

Exodus can be divided into three parts. Most of the events in the first part (1—13) take place in Egypt, where the people of Israel had been made slaves by the king. The Lord heard their cries for help and chose Moses to set them free. Moses was an Israelite who had been adopted by an Egyptian princess.

When Moses demanded that the Israelites be set free, the king refused. And so the Lord told Moses to bring ten disasters on Egypt. These disasters have often been called "the ten plagues". Finally, the king let the Israelites leave Egypt.

The second part of the book (14—18) includes events that happened while the people of Israel were on their way to Mount Sinai, God's holy mountain. The king of Egypt quickly changed his mind about setting them free, and he ordered his army to capture them. But the Lord protected Israel and destroyed the Egyptian army. Then, as the Israelites travelled through the desert, the Lord provided food and water for them.

The final part of Exodus (19—40) takes place at Mount Sinai, where the Lord appeared to Moses. The Lord gave him the Ten Commandments, as well as laws for worship, sacrifice, and everyday life, and instructions on making the sacred tent and its furnishings, the altars, and the priestly clothes. But this part also tells how the people made an idol and disobeyed the first of the Ten Commandments:

I am the LORD your God, the one who brought you out of Egypt where you were slaves. Do not worship any god except me.

(20.2,3)

The people of Israel become slaves

CHAPTER 1

The people of Israel suffer

¹⁻⁵ When Jacob went to Egypt, his son Joseph was already there. So Jacob took his eleven other sons and their families. They were: Reuben, Simeon, Levi, Judah, Issachar, Zebulun, Benjamin, Dan, Naphtali, Gad, and Asher. Altogether, Jacob had seventy children, grandchildren, and great-grandchildren* who went with him.

⁶ After Joseph, his brothers, and everyone else in that generation had died, ⁷ the people of Israel became so numerous that the whole region of Goshen was full of them.

⁸ Many years later a new king came to power. He did not know what Joseph had done for Egypt, ⁹ and he told the Egyptians:

There are too many of those Israelites in our country, and they are becoming more powerful than we are. ¹⁰ If we don't outsmart them, their families will keep growing larger. And if our country goes to war, they could easily fight on the side of our enemies and escape from Egypt.

¹¹ The Egyptians put slave bosses in charge of the people of Israel and tried to wear them down with hard work. Those bosses forced them to build the cities of Pithom and Rameses,* where the king* could store his supplies. ¹² But even though the Israelites were ill-treated, their families grew larger, and they took over more land. Because of this, the Egyptians hated them more than before ¹³ and made them work so hard ¹⁴ that

their lives were miserable. The Egyptians were cruel to the people of Israel and forced them to make bricks and to mix mortar and to work in the fields.

¹⁵ Finally, the king called in Shiphrah and Puah, the two women who helped the Hebrew* mothers when they gave birth. ¹⁶ He told them, "If a Hebrew woman gives birth to a girl, let the child live. If the baby is a boy, kill him!"

¹⁷ But the two women were faithful to God and did not kill the boys, even though the king had told them to. ¹⁸ The king called them in again and asked, "Why are you letting those baby boys live?"

¹⁹ They answered, "Hebrew women have their babies much quicker than Egyptian women. By the time we arrive, their babies are already born." ²⁰⁻²¹ God was good to the two women because they truly respected him, and he blessed them with children of their own.

The Hebrews kept increasing ²² until finally, the king gave a command to everyone in the nation, "As soon as a Hebrew boy is born, throw him into the River Nile! But you can let the girls live."

Moses is born and grows up

CHAPTER 2

¹ A man from the Levi tribe married a woman from the same tribe, ² and she later had a baby boy. He was a beautiful child, and she kept him inside for three months. ³ But when she could no longer keep him hidden, she made a basket out of reeds and covered it with tar. She put him in the basket and placed it in the tall grass along the edge of the River Nile. ⁴ The baby's elder sister* stood at a distance to see what would happen to him.

⁵ About that time one of the king's* daughters came down to take a bath in the river, while her servant women walked along the river bank. She saw the basket in the tall grass and sent one of the young women to pull it out of the water. ⁶ When the king's daughter opened the basket, she saw the baby and felt sorry for him because he was crying. She said, "This must be one of the Hebrew babies."

---

*1.1–5 seventy children . . . great-grandchildren: See Genesis 46.8–27.
*1.11 Pithom and Rameses: This is the only mention of Pithom in the Bible; its exact location is unknown, though it was probably in the northern Delta of Egypt. Rameses is the famous Delta city that was the home of Rameses II; its exact location is also unknown.

See also: 1.1–4: Gen 46.8–27. **1.7:** Acts 7.17.
1.8: Acts 7.18. **1.10:** Acts 7.19.

---

*1.15 Hebrew: An earlier term for "Israelite".
*2.4 elder sister: Miriam, the sister of Moses and Aaron.
See also: 1.22: Acts 7.19. **2.2:** Acts 7.20; Heb 11.23.

7 At once the baby's elder sister came up and asked, "Do you want me to get a Hebrew woman to take care of the baby for you?"

8 "Yes," the king's daughter answered.

So the girl brought the baby's mother, 9 and the king's daughter told her, "Take care of this child, and I will pay you."

The baby's mother carried him home and took care of him. 10 And when he was old enough, she took him to the king's daughter, who adopted him. She named him Moses* because she said, "I pulled him out of the water."

Moses escapes from Egypt

11 After Moses had grown up, he went out to where his own people were hard at work, and he saw an Egyptian beating one of them. 12 Moses looked around to see if anyone was watching, then he killed the Egyptian and hid his body in the sand.

13 When Moses went out the next day, he saw two Hebrews fighting. So he went to the man who had started the fight and asked, "Why are you beating up one of your own people?"

14 The man answered, "Who put you in charge of us and made you our judge? Are you planning to kill me, just as you killed that Egyptian?"

This frightened Moses because he was sure that people must have found out what had happened. 15 When the king* heard what Moses had done, the king wanted to kill him. But Moses escaped and went to the land of Midian.

One day, Moses was sitting there by a well, 16 when the seven daughters of Jethro, the priest of Midian,* came up to water their father's sheep and goats. 17 Some shepherds tried to chase them away, but Moses came to their rescue and watered their animals.

18 When Jethro's daughters returned home, their father asked, "Why have you come back so early today?"

19 They answered, "An Egyptian rescued us from the shepherds, and he even watered our sheep and goats."

20 "Where is he?" Jethro asked. "Why did you leave him out there? Invite him to eat with us."

21 Moses agreed to stay on with Jethro, who later let his daughter Zipporah marry Moses. 22 And when she had a son, Moses said, "I will name him Gershom,* since I am a foreigner in this country."

23 After the death of the king of Egypt, the Israelites still complained because they were forced to be slaves. They cried out for help, 24 and God heard their loud cries. He did not forget the promise he had made to Abraham, Isaac, and Jacob, 25 and because he knew what was happening to his people, he felt sorry for them.

God sends Moses to speak to the king of Egypt

CHAPTER 3

God speaks to Moses

1 One day, Moses was taking care of the sheep and goats of his father-in-law Jethro, the priest of Midian, and Moses decided to lead them across the desert to Sinai,* the holy mountain. 2 There an angel of the LORD appeared to him from a burning bush. Moses saw that the bush was on fire, but it was not burning up. 3 "This is strange!" he said to himself. "I'll go over and see why the bush isn't burning up."

4 When the LORD saw Moses coming near the bush, he called him by name, and Moses answered, "Here I am."

5 God replied, "Don't come any closer. Take off your sandals — the ground where you are standing is holy. 6 I am the God who was worshipped by your ancestors Abraham, Isaac, and Jacob."

Moses was afraid to look at God, and so he hid his face.

7 The LORD said:

I have seen how my people are suffering as slaves in Egypt, and I have heard them beg for my help because of the way they are being ill-treated. I feel sorry for them, 8 and I have come down to rescue them from the Egyptians.

I will bring my people out of Egypt into a country where there is good land, rich with milk and honey. I will give them the land where the Canaanites, Hittites, Amorites, Perizzites, Hivites, and Jebusites now live.

---

*2.10 Moses: In Hebrew "Moses" sounds like "pull out".

See also: 2.10: Acts 7.21. 2.11–14: Acts 7.23–28. 2.11: Heb 11.24. 2.15: Acts 7.29; Heb 11.27.

*2.22 Gershom: In Hebrew "Gershom" sounds like "foreigner".

See also: 2.24: Gen 15.13,14. 3.2–10: Acts 7.30–34.

⁹ My people have begged for my help, and I have seen how cruel the Egyptians are to them. ¹⁰ Now go to the king! I am sending you to lead my people out of his country."

¹¹ But Moses said, "Who am I to go to the king and lead your people out of Egypt?"

¹² God replied, "I will be with you. And you will know that I am the one who sent you, when you worship me on this mountain after you have led my people out of Egypt."

¹³ Moses answered, "I will tell the people of Israel that the God their ancestors worshipped has sent me to them. But what should I say, if they ask me your name?"

¹⁴⁻¹⁵ God said to Moses:

I am the eternal God. So tell them that the LORD,* whose name is "I Am," has sent you. This is my name for ever, and it is the name that people must use from now on.

¹⁶ Call together the leaders of Israel and tell them that the God who was worshipped by Abraham, Isaac, and Jacob has appeared to you. Tell them I have seen how terribly they are being treated in Egypt, ¹⁷ and I promise to lead them out of their troubles. I will give them a land rich with milk and honey, where the Canaanites, Hittites, Amorites, Perizzites, Hivites, and Jebusites now live.

¹⁸ The leaders of Israel will listen to you. Then you must take them to the king of Egypt and say, "The LORD God of the Hebrews has appeared to us. Let us walk three days into the desert, where we can offer a sacrifice to him." ¹⁹ But I know that the king of Egypt won't let you go unless something forces him to. ²⁰ So I will use my mighty power to perform all kinds of miracles and strike down the Egyptians. Then the king will send you away.

²¹ After I punish the Egyptians, they will be so afraid of you that they will give you anything you want. You are my people, and I will let you make many things with you when you leave the land of Egypt. ²² Every Israelite woman will go to her Egyptian neighbours or to any Egyptian woman living in her house. She will ask them for gold and silver jewellery and for their finest

clothes. The Egyptians will give them to you, and you will put these fine things on your sons and daughters. You will carry all this away when you leave Egypt.

CHAPTER 4

The LORD gives great power to Moses

¹ Moses asked the LORD, "Suppose everyone refuses to listen to my message, and no one believes that you really appeared to me?"

² The LORD answered, "What's that in your hand?"

"A walking stick," Moses replied.

³ "Throw it down!" the LORD commanded. So Moses threw the stick on the ground. It immediately turned into a snake, and Moses jumped back.

⁴ "Pick it up by the tail!" the LORD told him. And when Moses did this, the snake turned back into a walking stick.

⁵ "Do this," the LORD said, "and the Israelites will believe that you have seen me, the God who was worshipped by their ancestors Abraham, Isaac, and Jacob."

⁶ Next, the LORD commanded Moses, "Put your hand inside your shirt." Moses obeyed, and when he took it out, his hand had turned white as snow — like someone with leprosy.*

⁷ "Put your hand back inside your shirt," the LORD told him. Moses did so, and when he took it out again, it was as healthy as the rest of his body.

⁸⁻⁹ Then the LORD said, "If no one believes either of these miracles, take some water from the River Nile and pour it on the ground. The water will immediately turn into blood."

¹⁰ Moses replied, "I have never been a good speaker. I wasn't one before you spoke to me, and I'm not one now. I am slow at speaking, and I can never think of what to say."

¹¹ But the LORD answered, "Who makes people able to speak or makes them deaf or unable to speak? Who gives them sight or makes them blind? Don't you know that I am the one who does these things? ¹² Now go! When you speak, I will be with you and give you the words to say."

¹³ Moses begged, "LORD, please send someone else to do it."

¹⁴ The LORD became irritated with Moses and said:

---

*3.14,15 LORD: The Hebrew text has "Yahweh," which is usually translated "LORD" in the CEV. Since it seems related to the word translated "I am", it may mean "I am the one who is" or "I will be what I will be" or "I am the one who brings into being".

See also: 3.13: Exod 6.2,3. 3.14: Rev 1.4,8. 3.21,22: Exod 12.35,36.

*4.6 leprosy: The word translated "leprosy" was used for many different kinds of skin diseases.

What about your brother Aaron, the Levite? I know he is a good speaker. He is already on his way here to visit you, and he will be happy to see you again. 15-16 Aaron will speak to the people for you, and you will be like me, telling Aaron what to say. I will be with both of you as you speak, and I will tell each of you what to do. 17 Now take this walking stick and use it to perform miracles.

Moses returns to Egypt

18 Moses went to his father-in-law Jethro and asked, "Please let me return to Egypt to see if any of my people are still alive."

"All right," Jethro replied. "I hope all goes well."

19 But even before this, the LORD had told Moses, "Leave the land of Midian and return to Egypt. Everyone who turned to kill you is dead." 20 So Moses put his wife and sons on donkeys and headed for Egypt, holding the walking stick that had the power of God.

21 On the way the LORD said to Moses:

When you get to Egypt, go to the king and work the miracles I have shown you. But I will make him so stubborn that he will refuse to let my people go. 22 Then tell him that I have said, "Israel is my firstborn son, 23 and I commanded you to release him, so he could worship me. But you refused, and now I will kill your firstborn son."

Zipporah's son is circumcised

24 One night while Moses was in camp, the LORD was about to kill him. 25 But Zipporah* circumcised her son with a flint knife. She touched his* legs with the skin she had cut off and said, "My dear son, this blood will protect you."* 26 So the LORD did not harm Moses. Then Zipporah said, "Yes, my dear, you are safe because of this circumcision."*

Aaron is sent to meet Moses

27 The LORD sent Aaron to meet Moses in the desert. So Aaron met Moses at Mount Sinai* and greeted him with a kiss. 28 Moses told Aaron what God had sent him to say; he also told him about the miracles God had given him the power to perform.

29 Later they brought together the leaders of Israel, 30 and Aaron told them what the

LORD had sent Moses to say. Then Moses worked the miracles for the people, 31 and everyone believed. They bowed down and worshipped the LORD because they knew that he had seen their suffering and was going to help them.

CHAPTER 5

Moses and Aaron go to the king of Egypt

1 Moses and Aaron went to the king* of Egypt and told him, "The LORD God says, 'Let my people go into the desert, so they can honour me with a celebration there.'"

2 "Who is this LORD and why should I obey him?" the king replied. "I refuse to let you and your people go!"

3 They answered, "The LORD God of the Hebrews has appeared to us. Please let us walk three days into the desert where we can offer sacrifices to him. If you don't, he may strike us down with terrible troubles or with war."

4-5 The king said, "Moses and Aaron, why are you keeping these people from working? Look how many you are keeping from doing their work. Now everyone get back to work!"

6 That same day the king gave orders to his slave bosses and to the men directly in charge of the Israelite slaves. He told them:

7 Don't give the slaves any more straw* to put in their bricks. Force them to find their own straw wherever they can, 8 but they must make the same number of bricks as before. They are lazy, or else they would not beg me to let them go and sacrifice to their God. 9 Make them work so hard that they won't have time to listen to these lies.

10 The slave bosses and the men in charge of the slaves went out and told them, "The king says he will not give you any more straw. 11 Go and find your own straw wherever you can, but you must still make as many bricks as before."

12 The slaves went all over Egypt, looking for straw. 13 But the slave bosses were hard on them and kept saying, "Each day you have to make as many bricks as you did when you were given straw." 14 The bosses beat the men in charge of the slaves and said, "Why didn't

---

*4.25 Zipporah: The wife of Moses (see 2.16–21).
*4.25 his: Either Moses or the boy.
See also: 4.23: Exod 12.29.

*5.7 straw: The straw made the mud bricks stronger and kept them from shrinking, cracking, or losing their shape.

you force the slaves to make as many bricks yesterday and today as they did before?"

¹⁵ Finally, the men in charge of the slaves went to the king and said, "Why are you treating us like this? ¹⁶ No one brings us any straw, but we are still ordered to make the same number of bricks. We are beaten with whips, and your own people are to blame."

¹⁷ The king replied, "You are lazy— nothing but lazy! That's why you keep asking me to let you go and sacrifice to your LORD. ¹⁸ Get back to work! You won't be given straw, but you must still make the same number of bricks."

¹⁹ The men knew they were in deep trouble when they were ordered to make the same number of bricks each day. ²⁰ After they left the king, they went to see Moses and Aaron, who had been waiting for them. ²¹ Then the men said, "We hope the LORD will punish both of you for making the king and his officials hate us. Now they even have an excuse to kill us."

The LORD's promise to Moses

²² Moses left then and prayed, "Our LORD, why have you brought so much trouble on your people? Is that why you sent me here? ²³ Ever since you told me to speak to the king,ᵏ he has caused nothing but trouble for these people. And you haven't done a thing to help."

CHAPTER 6

¹ The LORD God told Moses:

Soon you will see what I will do to the king. Because of my mighty power, he will let my people go, and he will even chase them out of his country.

² My name is the LORD.* ³ But when I appeared to Abraham, Isaac, and Jacob, I came as God All-Powerful and did not use my name. ⁴ I made an agreement and promised them the land of Canaan, where they were living as foreigners. ⁵ Now I have seen how the people of Israel are suffering because of the Egyptians, and I will keep my promise.

⁶ Here is my message for Israel: "I am the LORD! And with my mighty power I will punish the Egyptians and free you from slavery. ⁷ I will accept you as my people, and I will be your God. Then you will

know that I was the one who rescued you from the Egyptians. ⁸ I will bring you into the land that I solemnly promised Abraham, Isaac, and Jacob, and it will be yours. I am the LORD!"

⁹ When Moses told this to the Israelites, they were too discouraged and ill-treated to believe him.

¹⁰ Then the LORD told Moses ¹¹ to demand that the king of Egypt let the Israelites leave. ¹² But Moses replied, "I'm not a powerful speaker. If the Israelites won't listen to me, why should the king of Egypt?" ¹³ But the LORD sent Aaron and Moses with a message for the Israelites and for the king; he also ordered Aaron and Moses to free the people from Egypt.

Family record of Aaron and Moses

¹⁴ The following men were the heads of their ancestral clans:

The sons of Reuben, Jacob'sˡ eldest son, were Hanoch, Pallu, Hezron, and Carmi.

¹⁵ The sons of Simeon were Jemuel, Jamin, Ohad, Jachin, Zohar, and Shaul, the son of a Canaanite woman.

¹⁶ Levi lived to be one hundred and thirty-seven; his sons were Gershon, Kohath, and Merari.

¹⁷ Gershon's sons were Libni and Shimei.

¹⁸ Kohath lived to be one hundred and thirty-three; his sons were Amram, Izhar, Hebron, and Uzziel.

¹⁹ Merari's sons were Mahli and Mushi. All of the above were from the Levi tribe.

²⁰ Amram lived to be one hundred and thirty-seven. He married his father's sister Jochebed, and they had two sons, Aaron and Moses.

²¹ Izhar's sons were Korah, Nepheg, and Zichri.

²² Uzziel's sons were Mishael, Elzaphan, and Sithri.

²³ Aaron married Elisheba. She was the daughter of Amminadab and the sister of Nahshon; they had four sons, Nadab, Abihu, Eleazar, and Ithamar.

²⁴ Korah's sons were Assir, Elkanah, and Abiasaph.

²⁵ Aaron's son Eleazar married one of Putiel's daughters, and their son was Phinehas. This ends the list of those who were the heads of clans in the Levi tribe.

---

*6.2 My name is the LORD: See the note at 3.14,15.
See also: 6.2,3: Gen 17.1; 28.3; 35.11; Exod 3.13-15.

See also: 6.16-19: Num 3.17-20; 26.57,58; 1 Chron 6.16-19.

26 The LORD had commanded Aaron and Moses to lead every family and tribe of Israel out of Egypt, 27 and so they ordered the king of Egypt to set the people of Israel free.

The LORD commands Moses and Aaron to speak to the king

28 When the LORD spoke to Moses in the land of Egypt, 29 he said, "I am the LORD. Tell the king' of Egypt everything I say to you."

30 But Moses answered, "You know I am a very poor speaker, and the king will never listen to me."

The first nine disasters

CHAPTER 7

1 The LORD said:

I am going to let your brother Aaron speak for you. He will tell your message to the king, just as a prophet speaks my message to the people. 2 Tell Aaron everything I say to you, and he will order the king to let my people leave his country. 3-4 But I will make the king so stubborn that he won't listen to you. He won't listen even when I do many terrible things to him and his nation. Then I will bring a final punishment on Egypt, and the king will let Israel's families and tribes go. 5 When this happens, the Egyptians will know that I am the LORD.

6 Moses and Aaron obeyed the LORD 7 and spoke to the king. At the time, Moses was eighty years old, and Aaron was eighty-three.

A stick turns into a snake

8-9 The LORD said, "Moses, when the king' asks you and Aaron to perform a miracle, command Aaron to throw his walking stick down in front of the king, and it will turn into a snake."

10 Moses and Aaron went to the king and his officials and did exactly as the LORD had commanded — Aaron threw the stick down, and it turned into a snake. 11 Then the king called in the wise men and the magicians, who used their secret powers to do the same thing — 12 they threw down sticks that turned into snakes. But Aaron's snake swallowed theirs. 13 The king behaved just as the LORD had said and stubbornly refused to listen.

The River Nile turns into blood

14 The LORD said to Moses:

The Egyptian king' stubbornly refuses to change his mind and let the people go. 15 Tomorrow morning take the stick that turned into a snake, then wait beside the River Nile for the king. 16 Tell him, "The LORD God of the Hebrews sent me to order you to release his people, so they can worship him in the desert. But until now, you have paid no attention.

17 "The LORD is going to do something to show you that he really is the LORD. I will strike the Nile, and the water will turn into blood. 18 The fish will die, the river will stink, and none of you Egyptians will be able to drink the water."

19 Moses, then command Aaron to hold his stick over the water. And when he does, every drop of water in Egypt will turn into blood, including rivers, canals, ponds, and even the water in buckets and jars.

20 Moses and Aaron obeyed the LORD. Aaron held out his stick, then struck the Nile, as the king and his officials watched. The river turned into blood, 21 the fish died, and the water smelt so bad that none of the Egyptians could drink it. Blood was everywhere in Egypt.

22 But the Egyptian magicians used their secret powers to do the same thing. The king did just as the LORD had said — he stubbornly refused to listen. 23 Then he went back to his palace and never gave it a second thought. 24 The Egyptians had to dig holes along the banks of the Nile for drinking water, because water from the river was unfit to drink.

Frogs

25 Seven days after the LORD had struck the Nile,

CHAPTER 8

1 he said to Moses:

Go to the palace and tell the king' of Egypt that I order him to let my people go, so they can worship me. 2 If he refuses, I will cover his entire country with frogs. 3 Warn the king that the Nile will be full of frogs, and from there they will spread into the royal palace, including the king's bedroom and even his bed. Frogs will enter the homes of his officials and will find their

See also: 7.3: Acts 7.36.

See also: 7.17: Rev 16.4.

way into ovens and into the bowls of bread dough. 4 Frogs will be crawling on everyone — the king, his officials, and every citizen of Egypt.

5 Moses, now command Aaron to hold his stick over the water. Then frogs will come from all rivers, canals, and ponds in Egypt, and they will cover the land.

6 Aaron obeyed, and suddenly frogs were everywhere in Egypt. 7 But the magicians used their secret powers to do the same thing.

8 The king sent for Moses and Aaron and told them, "If you ask the LORD to take these frogs away from me and my people, I will let your people go and offer sacrifices to him."

9 "All right," Moses answered. "You choose the time when I am to pray for the frogs to stop bothering you, your officials, and your people, and for them to leave your houses and be found only in the river."

10 "Do it tomorrow!" the king replied.

"As you wish," Moses agreed. "Then everyone will discover that there is no god like the LORD, 11 and frogs will no longer be found anywhere, except in the Nile."

12 After Moses and Aaron left the palace, Moses begged the LORD to do something about the frogs he had sent as punishment for the king. 13 The LORD listened to Moses, and frogs died everywhere — in houses, yards, and fields. 14 The dead frogs were placed in piles, and the whole country began to stink. 15 But when the king saw that things were now better, he again did just as the LORD had said and stubbornly refused to listen to Moses and Aaron.

Gnats

16 The LORD said to Moses, "Command Aaron to strike the ground with his walking stick, and everywhere in Egypt the dust will turn into gnats." 17 They obeyed, and when Aaron struck the ground with the stick, gnats started swarming on people and animals. In fact, every speck of dust in Egypt turned into a gnat. 18 When the magicians tried to use their secret powers to do this,' they failed, and gnats stayed on people and animals.

19 The magicians told the king,' "God has done this."

But, as the LORD had said, the king was too stubborn to listen.

Flies

20 The LORD said to Moses:

Early tomorrow morning, while the king' is on his way to the river, go and say to him, "The LORD commands you to let his people go, so they can worship him. 21 If you don't, he will send swarms of flies to attack you, your officials, and every citizen of your country. Houses will be full of flies, and the ground will crawl with them.

22-23 "The LORD's people in Goshen won't be bothered by flies, but your people in the rest of the country will be tormented by them. That's how you will know that the LORD is here in Egypt. This miracle will happen tomorrow."

24 The LORD kept his promise — the palace and the homes of the royal officials swarmed with flies, and the rest of the country was infested with them as well. 25 Then the king sent for Moses and Aaron and told them, "Go and sacrifice to your God, but stay here in Egypt."

26 "That's impossible!" Moses replied. "Any sacrifices we offer to the LORD our God would disgust the Egyptians, and they would stone us to death. 27 No indeed! The LORD has ordered us to walk three days into the desert before offering sacrifices to him, and that's what we have to do."

28 Then the king told him, "I'll let you go into the desert to offer sacrifices, if you don't go very far. But in the meantime, pray for me."

29 "Your Majesty," Moses replied, "I'll pray for you as soon as I leave, and by tomorrow the flies will stop bothering you, your officials, and the citizens of your country. Only make sure that you're telling the truth this time and that you really intend to let our people offer sacrifices to the LORD."

30 After leaving the palace, Moses prayed, 31 and the LORD answered his prayer. Not a fly was left to pester the king, his officials, or anyone else in Egypt. 32 But the king turned stubborn again and would not let the people go.

CHAPTER 9

Dead animals

1 The LORD sent Moses with this message for the king' of Egypt:

The LORD God of the Hebrews commands you to let his people go, so they can worship him. 2 If you keep refusing, 3 he will bring a terrible disease on your horses and donkeys, your camels and cattle, and your sheep and goats. ⁴ But the LORD will protect the animals that belong to the people of Israel, and none of theirs will die. ⁵ Tomorrow is the day the LORD has set to do this.

⁶ It happened the next day — all the animals belonging to the Egyptians died, but the Israelites did not lose even one. ⁷ When the king found out, he was still too stubborn to let the people go.

Sores

⁸ The LORD said to Moses and Aaron:

Take a few handfuls of ashes from a stove and let Moses throw them into the air. Be sure the king is watching. ⁹ The ashes will blow across the land of Egypt, causing sores to break out on people and animals.

¹⁰ So they took a few handfuls of ashes and went to the king.' Moses threw them into the air, and sores immediately broke out on the Egyptians and their animals. ¹¹ The magicians were suffering so much from the sores, that they could not even come to Moses. ¹² Everything happened just as the LORD had told Moses — he made the king too stubborn to listen to Moses and Aaron.

Hailstones

¹³ The LORD told Moses to get up early the next morning and say to the king:'

The LORD God of the Hebrews commands you to let his people go, so they can worship him! ¹⁴ If you don't, he will send his worst plagues to strike you, your officials, and everyone else in your country. Then you will find out that no one can oppose the LORD. ¹⁵ In fact, he could already have sent a terrible disease and wiped you from the face of the earth. ¹⁶ But he has kept you alive, just to show you his power and to bring honour to himself everywhere in the world.

¹⁷ You are still determined not to let the LORD's people go. ¹⁸ All right. At this time tomorrow, he will bring on Egypt the worst hailstorm in its history. ¹⁹ You had better give orders for every person and every animal in Egypt to take shelter. If they don't, they will die.

²⁰ Some of the king's officials were frightened by what the LORD had said, and they hurried off to make sure their slaves and animals were safe. ²¹ But others paid no attention to his threats and left their slaves and animals out in the open.

²² Then the LORD told Moses, "Stretch your arm towards the sky, so that hailstones will fall on people, animals, and crops in the land of Egypt." ²³⁻²⁴ Moses pointed his walking stick towards the sky, and hailstones started falling everywhere. Thunder roared, and lightning flashed back and forth, striking the ground. This was the worst storm in the history of Egypt. ²⁵ People, animals, and crops were pounded by the hailstones, and bark was stripped from trees. ²⁶ Only Goshen, where the Israelites lived, was safe from the storm.

²⁷ The king sent for Moses and Aaron and told them, "Now I have really sinned! My people and I are guilty, and the LORD is right. ²⁸ We can't stand any more of this thunder and hail. Please ask the LORD to make it stop. Your people can go — you don't have to stay in Egypt any longer."

²⁹ Moses answered, "As soon as I leave the city, I will lift my arms in prayer. When the thunder and hail stop, you will know that the earth belongs to the LORD. ³⁰ But I am certain that neither you nor your officials really fear the LORD God."

³¹ Meanwhile, the flax and barley crops had been destroyed by the storm because they were ready to ripen. ³² But the wheat crops' ripen later, and they were not damaged.

³³ After Moses left the royal palace and the city, he lifted his arms in prayer to the LORD, and the thunder, hail, and drenching rain stopped. ³⁴ When the king realized that the storm was over, he disobeyed once more. He and his officials were so stubborn ³⁵ that he refused to let the Israelites go. This was exactly what the LORD had said would happen.

CHAPTER 10

Locusts

¹ The LORD said to Moses:

Go back to the king.' I have made him and his officials stubborn, so that I could work these miracles. ² I did this because I want you to tell your children and your grandchildren about my miracles and about my harsh treatment of the Egyptians. Then all of you will know that I am the LORD.

3 Moses and Aaron went to the king and told him that the LORD God of the Hebrews had said:

> How long will you stubbornly refuse to obey? Release my people so they can worship me. 4 Do this by tomorrow, or I will cover your country with so many locusts* 5 that you won't be able to see the ground. Most of your crops were ruined by the hailstones, but these locusts will destroy what little is left, including the trees. 6 Your palace, the homes of your officials, and all other houses in Egypt will overflow with more locusts than have ever been seen in this country.

After Moses left the palace, 7 the king's officials asked, "Your Majesty, how much longer is this man going to be a trouble-maker? Why don't you let the people leave, so they can worship the LORD their God? Don't you know that Egypt is a disaster?"

8 The king had Moses and Aaron brought back, and he said, "All right, you may go and worship the LORD your God. But first tell me who will be going."

9 "Everyone, young and old," Moses answered. "We will even take our sheep, goats, and cattle, because we want to hold a celebration in honour of the LORD."

10 The king replied, "The LORD had better watch over you on the day I let you leave with your families! You're up to no good. 11 Do you want to worship the LORD? All right, take only the men and go." Then Moses and Aaron were chased out of the palace.

12 The LORD told Moses, "Stretch your arm towards Egypt. Swarms of locusts will come and eat everything left by the hail."

13 Moses held out his walking stick, and the LORD sent an east wind that blew across Egypt the rest of the day and all that night. By morning, locusts 14 were swarming everywhere. Never before had there been so many locusts in Egypt, and never again will there be so many. 15 The ground was black with locusts, and they ate everything left on the trees and in the fields. Nothing green remained in Egypt — not a tree or a plant.

16 At once the king sent for Moses and Aaron. He told them, "I have sinned against the LORD your God and against you. 17 Forgive me one more time and ask the LORD to stop these insects from killing every living plant."

18 Moses left the palace and prayed. 19 Then the LORD sent a strong west wind* that swept the locusts into the Red Sea.* Not one locust was left anywhere in Egypt, 20 but the LORD made the king so stubborn that he still refused to let the Israelites go.

Darkness

21 The LORD said to Moses, "Stretch your arm towards the sky, and everything will be covered with darkness thick enough to touch." 22 Moses stretched his arm towards the sky, and Egypt was covered with darkness for three days. 23 During that time, the Egyptians could not see each other or leave their homes, but there was light where the Israelites lived.

24 The king' sent for Moses and told him, "Go and worship the LORD! And take your families with you. Just leave your sheep, goats, and cattle."

25 "No!" Moses replied. "You must let us offer sacrifices to the LORD our God, 26 and we won't know which animals we will need until we get there. That's why we can't leave even one of them here."

27 This time the LORD made the king so stubborn 28 that he said to Moses, "Get out and stay out! If you ever come back, you're dead!"

29 "Have it your way," Moses answered. "You won't see me again."

The last disaster and the first Passover

CHAPTER 11

Moses warns the Egyptians that the LORD will kill their firstborn sons

1 The LORD said to Moses:

> I am going to punish the king' of Egypt and his people one more time. Then the

---

*10.4 locusts: A type of grasshopper that comes in swarms and causes great damage to crops.
See also: 10.14,15: Rev 9.2,3.

*10.19 Red Sea: Hebrew *yam suph*, here referring to the Gulf of Suez, since the term is extended to include the north-western arm of the Red Sea (see also the note at 13.18).
See also: 10.22: Psa 105.28; Rev 16.10.

king will gladly let you leave his land, so that I will stop punishing the Egyptians. He will even chase you out. ² Now go and tell my people to ask their Egyptian neighbours for gold and silver jewellery.

³ So the LORD made the Egyptians greatly respect the Israelites, and everyone, including the king and his officials, considered Moses an important leader.

⁴ Moses went to the king and said:

I have come to let you know what the LORD is going to do. About midnight he will go through the land of Egypt, ⁵ and wherever he goes, the firstborn son in every family will die. Your own son will die, and so will the son of the lowest slave woman. Even the firstborn males of cattle will die. ⁶ Everywhere in Egypt there will be loud crying. Nothing like this has ever happened before or will ever happen again.

⁷ But there won't be any need for the Israelites to cry. Things will be so quiet that not even a dog will be heard barking. Then you Egyptians will know that the LORD is good to the Israelites, even while he punishes you. ⁸ Your leaders will come and bow down, begging me to take my people and leave your country. Then we will leave.

Moses was very angry; he turned and left the king.

⁹ What the LORD had earlier said to Moses came true. He had said, "The king of Egypt won't listen. Then I will perform even more miracles." ¹⁰ So the king of Egypt saw Moses and Aaron work miracles, but the LORD made him stubbornly refuse to let the Israelites leave his country.

CHAPTER 12

The Passover

¹ Some time later the LORD said to Moses and Aaron:

² This month* is to be the first month of the year for you. ³ Tell the people of Israel that on the tenth day of this month the head of each family must choose a lamb or a young goat for his family to eat. ⁴⁻⁵ If any family is too small to eat the whole animal, they must share it with their next-door

neighbours. Choose either a sheep or a goat, but it must be a one-year-old male that has nothing wrong with it. And it must be large enough for everyone to have some of the meat.

⁶ Each family must take care of its animal until the evening of the fourteenth day of the month, when the animals are to be killed. ⁷ Some of the blood must be put on the two doorposts and above the door of each house where the animals are to be eaten. ⁸ That night the animals are to be roasted and eaten, together with bitter herbs and thin bread made without yeast. ⁹ Don't eat the meat raw or boiled. The entire animal, including its head, legs, and insides, must be roasted. ¹⁰ Eat what you want that night, and the next morning burn whatever is left. ¹¹ When you eat the meal, be dressed and ready to travel. Have your sandals on, carry your walking stick in your hand, and eat quickly. This is the Passover Festival in honour of me, your LORD.

¹² That same night I will pass through Egypt and kill the firstborn son in every family and the firstborn male of all animals. I am the LORD, and I will punish the gods of Egypt. ¹³ The blood on the houses will show me where you live, and when I see the blood, I will pass over you. Then you won't be bothered by the terrible disasters I will bring on Egypt.

¹⁴ Remember this day and celebrate it each year as a festival in my honour. ¹⁵ For seven days you must eat bread made without yeast. And on the first of these seven days, you must remove all yeast from your homes. If you eat anything made with yeast during this festival, you will no longer be part of Israel. ¹⁶ Meet together for worship on the first and seventh days of the festival. The only work you are allowed to do on either of these two days is that of preparing the bread.

¹⁷ Celebrate this Festival of Thin Bread as a way of remembering the day that I brought your families and tribes out of Egypt. And do this each year. ¹⁸ Begin on the evening of the fourteenth day of the first month by eating bread made without yeast. Then continue this celebration until the evening of the twenty-first day.

¹⁹ During these seven days no yeast is allowed in anyone's home, whether they

*12.2 This month: Abib (also called Nisan), the first month of the Hebrew calendar, from about mid-March to mid-April.

See also: 12.1–13: Lev 23.5; Num 9.1–5; 28.16; Deut 16.1,2.

See also: 12.14–20: Exod 23.15; 34.18; Lev 23.6–8; Num 28.17–25; Deut 16.3–8.

are native Israelites or not. If you are caught eating anything made with yeast, you will no longer be part of Israel. 20 Stay away from yeast, no matter where you live. No one is allowed to eat anything made with yeast!

21 Moses called the leaders of Israel together and said:

Each family is to pick out a sheep and kill it for Passover. 22 Make a brush from a few small branches of a hyssop plant and dip the brush in the bowl that has the blood of the animal in it. Then brush some of the blood above the door and on the posts at each side of the door of your house. After this, everyone is to stay inside. 23 During that night the LORD will go through the country of Egypt and kill the firstborn son in every Egyptian family. He will see where you have put the blood, and he will not come into your house. His angel that brings death will pass over and not kill your firstborn sons.

24-25 After you have entered the country promised to you by the LORD, you and your children must continue to celebrate Passover each year. 26 Your children will ask you, "What are we celebrating?" 27 And you will answer, "The Passover animal is killed to honour the LORD. We do these things because on that night long ago the LORD passed over the homes of our people in Egypt. He killed the firstborn sons of the Egyptians, but he saved our children from death."

After Moses finished speaking, the people of Israel knelt down and worshipped the LORD. 28 Then they left and did what Moses and Aaron had told them to do.

Death for the firstborn sons

29 At midnight the LORD killed the firstborn son of every Egyptian family, from the son of the king* to the son of every prisoner in jail. He also killed the firstborn male of every animal that belonged to the Egyptians.

30 That night the king, his officials, and everyone else in Egypt got up and started crying bitterly. In every Egyptian home, someone was dead.

The people of Israel escape from Egypt

31 During the night the king* sent for Moses and Aaron and told them, "Get your people out of my country and leave us alone! Go and worship the LORD, as you have asked. 32 Take your sheep, goats, and cattle, and get out. But ask your God to be kind to me."

33 The Egyptians did everything they could to get the Israelites to leave their country fast. They said, "Please hurry and leave. If you don't, we will all be dead." 34 So the Israelites quickly made some bread dough and put it in pans. But they did not mix any yeast in the dough to make it rise. They wrapped cloth around the pans and carried them on their shoulders.

35 The Israelites had already done what Moses had told them to do. They had gone to their Egyptian neighbours and asked for gold and silver and for clothes. 36 The LORD had made the Egyptians friendly towards the people of Israel, and they gave them whatever they asked for. In this way they carried away the wealth of the Egyptians when they left Egypt.

37 The Israelites walked from the city of Rameses to the city of Succoth. There were about six hundred thousand of them, not counting women and children. 38 Many other people went with them as well, and there were also a lot of sheep, goats, and cattle. 39 They left Egypt in such a hurry that they did not have time to prepare any food except the bread dough made without yeast. So they baked it and made thin bread.

40-41 The LORD's people left Egypt exactly four hundred and thirty years after they had arrived. 42 On that night the LORD kept watch for them, and on this same night each year Israel will always keep watch in honour of the LORD.

Instructions for Passover

43 The LORD gave Moses and Aaron the following instructions for celebrating Passover:

No one except Israelites may eat the Passover meal.

44 Your slaves may eat the meal if they have been circumcised, 45 but no foreigners who work for you are allowed to have any.

See also: 12.23: Heb 11.28. 12.29: Exod 4.22–32.

See also: 12.35,36: Exod 3.21,22. 12.40: Gen 15.13; Gal 3.17.

61

⁴⁶ The entire meal must be eaten inside, and no one may leave the house during the celebration.

No bones of the Passover lamb may be broken. ⁴⁷ And all Israelites must take part in the meal.

⁴⁸ If anyone who isn't an Israelite wants to celebrate Passover with you, every man and boy in that family must first be circumcised. Then they may join in the meal, just like native Israelites. No uncircumcised man or boy may eat the Passover meal! ⁴⁹ This law applies both to native Israelites and to those foreigners who live among you.

⁵⁰ The Israelites obeyed everything the LORD had commanded Moses and Aaron to tell them. ⁵¹ And on that same day the LORD brought Israel's families and tribes out of Egypt.

CHAPTER 13

Dedication of the firstborn

¹ The LORD said to Moses, ² "Dedicate to me the firstborn son of every family and the firstborn males of your flocks and herds. These belong to me."

The Festival of Thin Bread

³⁻⁴ Moses said to the people:

Remember this day in the month of Abib.* It is the day when the LORD's mighty power rescued you from Egypt, where you were slaves. Do not eat anything made with yeast. ⁵ The LORD promised your ancestors that he would bring you into the land of the Canaanites, Hittites, Amorites, Hivites, and Jebusites. It is a land rich with milk and honey.

Each year during the month of Abib, celebrate these events in the following way: ⁶ for seven days you are to eat bread made without yeast, and on the seventh day you are to celebrate a festival in honour of the LORD. ⁷ During those seven days, you must not eat anything made with yeast or even have yeast anywhere near your homes. ⁸ Then on the seventh day you must explain to your children that you do this because the LORD brought you out of Egypt.

⁹ This celebration will be like wearing a sign on your hand or on your forehead, because then you will pass on to others the teaching of the LORD, whose mighty power brought you out of Egypt. ¹⁰ Celebrate this festival each year at the same time.

¹¹ The LORD will give you the land of the Canaanites, just as he promised you and your ancestors. ¹² From then on, you must give him every firstborn son from your families and every firstborn male from your animals, because these belong to him. ¹³ You can save the life of a firstborn donkey* by sacrificing a lamb; if you don't, you must break the donkey's neck. You must save every firstborn son.

¹⁴ In the future your children will ask what this ceremony means. Explain it to them by saying, "The LORD used his mighty power to rescue us from slavery in Egypt. ¹⁵ The king* stubbornly refused to set us free, so the LORD killed the firstborn male of every animal and the firstborn son of every Egyptian family. This is why we sacrifice to the LORD every firstborn male of every animal and save every firstborn son."

¹⁶ This ceremony will serve the same purpose as a sign on your hand or on your forehead to tell how the LORD's mighty power rescued us from Egypt.

The LORD leads his people

¹⁷ After the king* had finally let the people go, the LORD did not lead them through Philistine territory,* though that was the shortest way. God had said, "If they are attacked, they may decide to return to Egypt." ¹⁸ So he led them around through the desert and towards the Red Sea.*

The Israelites left Egypt, prepared for battle.

---

*13.13 donkey: This was the only "unclean" animal that had to be saved; the firstborn of all "clean" animals (sheep, goats, cattle) had to be sacrificed. Donkeys were important because they were the basic means of transport.

*13.17 Philistine territory: The shortest land route from the Nile Delta to Canaan; it was the southern section of the major road that led to Megiddo and then on to Mesopotamia by way of Asia Minor.

*13.18 Red Sea: Hebrew *yam suph* "Sea of Reeds", one of the marshes or fresh water lakes, near the eastern part of the Nile Delta. This identification is based on Exodus 13.17—14.9, which lists the towns on the route of the Israelites before crossing the sea. In the Greek translation of the Scriptures made about 200 BC, the "Sea of Reeds" was named "Red Sea".

See also: 13.12: Exod 34.19,20; Luke 2.23.

---

*13.3,4 Abib: Or Nisan, the first month of the Hebrew calendar, from about mid-March to mid-April.

See also: 12.46: Num 9.12; John 19.36.   13.2: Num 3.13; Luke 2.23.

¹⁹ Moses made them take along the bones of Joseph, whose dying words had been, "God will come to your rescue, and when he does, be sure to take along my bones."

²⁰ The people of Israel left Succoth and camped at Etham at the border of Egypt near the desert. ²¹⁻²² During the day the LORD went ahead of his people in a thick cloud, and during the night he went ahead of them in a flaming fire. That way the LORD could lead them at all times, whether day or night.

The people cross the Red Sea

CHAPTER 14

¹ At Etham the LORD said to Moses:

² Tell the people of Israel to turn back and camp across from Pi-Hahiroth near Baal-Zephon, between Migdol and the Red Sea. ³ The king* will think they were afraid to cross the desert and that they are wandering around, trying to find another way to leave the country. ⁴ I will make the king stubborn again, and he will try to catch you. Then I will destroy him and his army. People everywhere will praise me for my victory, and the Egyptians will know that I really am the LORD.

The Israelites obeyed the LORD and camped where he told them.

⁵ When the king of Egypt heard that the Israelites had finally left, he and his officials changed their minds and said, "Look what we have done! We let them get away, and they will no longer be our slaves."

⁶ The king got his war chariot and army ready. ⁷ He commanded his officers in charge of his six hundred best chariots and all his other chariots to start after the Israelites. ⁸ The LORD made the king so stubborn that he went after them, even though the Israelites proudly* went on their way. ⁹ But the king's horses and chariots and soldiers caught up with them while they were camping near the Red Sea near Pi-Hahiroth and Baal-Zephon.

¹⁰ When the Israelites saw the king coming with his army, they were frightened and begged the LORD for help. ¹¹ They also complained to Moses, "Wasn't there enough room in Egypt to bury us? Is that why you brought us out here to die in the desert? Why did you bring us out of Egypt anyway?

¹² While we were there, didn't we tell you to leave us alone? We would rather be slaves in Egypt than die in this desert!"

¹³ But Moses answered, "Don't be afraid! Be brave, and you will see the LORD save you today. These Egyptians will never bother you again. ¹⁴ The LORD will fight for you, and you won't have to do a thing."

¹⁵ The LORD said to Moses, "Why do you keep calling out to me for help? Tell the Israelites to move forward. ¹⁶ Then hold your walking stick over the sea. The water will open up and make a road where they can walk through on dry ground. ¹⁷ I will make the Egyptians so stubborn that they will go after you. Then I will be praised because of what happens to the king and his chariots and cavalry. ¹⁸ The Egyptians will know for sure that I am the LORD."

¹⁹ All this time God's angel had gone ahead of Israel's army, but now he moved behind them. A large cloud had also gone ahead of them, ²⁰ but now it had moved between the Egyptians and the Israelites. The cloud gave light to the Israelites, but made it dark for the Egyptians, and during the night they could not come any closer.

²¹ Moses stretched his arm over the sea, and the LORD sent a strong east wind that blew all night until there was dry land where the water had been. The sea opened up, ²² and the Israelites walked through on dry land with a wall of water on each side.

²³ The Egyptian chariots and cavalry went after them. ²⁴ But before daylight the LORD looked down at the Egyptian army from the fiery cloud and made them panic. ²⁵ Their chariot wheels got stuck,* and it was hard for them to move. So the Egyptians said to one another, "Let's leave these people alone! The LORD is on their side and is fighting against us."

²⁶ The LORD told Moses, "Stretch your arm towards the sea — the water will cover the Egyptians and their cavalry and chariots." ²⁷ Moses stretched out his arm, and at daybreak the water rushed towards the Egyptians. They tried to run away, but the LORD drowned them in the sea. ²⁸ The water came and covered the chariots, the cavalry, and the whole Egyptian army that had followed the Israelites into the sea. Not one of them was left alive. ²⁹ But the sea had made a wall of water on each side of the Israelites; so they walked through on dry land.

See also: 13.19: Gen 50.25; Josh 24.32.   See also: 14.22: 1 Cor 10.1,2; Heb 11.29.

³⁰ On that day, when the Israelites saw the bodies of the Egyptians washed up on the shore, they knew that the LORD had saved them. ³¹ Because of the mighty power he had used against the Egyptians, the Israelites worshipped him and trusted him and his servant Moses.

CHAPTER 15

The song of Moses

¹ Moses and the Israelites sang this song in praise of the LORD:

I sing praises to the LORD
for his great victory!
He has thrown the horses
and their riders into the sea.
² The LORD is my strength,
the reason for my song,
because he has saved me.
I praise and honour the LORD —
he is my God and the God
of my ancestors.
³ The LORD is his name,
and he is a warrior!
⁴ He threw the chariots and army
of Egypt's king'
into the Red Sea,*
and he drowned the best
of the king's officers.
⁵ They sank to the bottom
just like stones.

⁶ With the tremendous force
of your right arm, our LORD,
you crushed your enemies.
⁷ What a great victory was yours,
as you defeated everyone
who opposed you.
Your fiery anger wiped them out,
as though they were straw.
⁸ You were so furious
that the sea piled up like a wall,
and the ocean depths
curdled like cheese.

⁹ Your enemies boasted
that they would
pursue and capture us,
divide up our possessions,
treat us as they wished,
then take out their swords
and kill us there.
¹⁰ But when you got furious,

they sank like lead,
swallowed by ocean waves.

¹¹ Our LORD, no other gods
compare with you —
Majestic and holy!
Fearsome and glorious!
Miracle worker!
¹² When you signalled
with your right hand,
your enemies were swallowed
deep into the earth.

¹³ The people you rescued
were led by your powerful love
to your holy place.
¹⁴ Nations learnt of this and trembled —
Philistines shook with horror.
¹⁵ The leaders of Edom and of Moab
were terrified.
Everyone in Canaan fainted,
¹⁶ struck down by fear.
Our LORD, your powerful arm
kept them still as a rock
until the people you rescued
for your very own had marched by.

¹⁷ You will let your people settle
on your chosen mountain,
where you built your home
and your temple.
¹⁸ Our LORD, you will rule for ever!

The song of Miriam

¹⁹ The LORD covered the royal Egyptian cavalry and chariots with the sea, after the Israelites had walked safely through on dry ground. ²⁰ Miriam the sister of Aaron was a prophet. So she took her tambourine and led the other women out to play their tambourines and to dance. ²¹ Then she sang to them:

"Sing praises to the LORD
for his great victory!
He has thrown the horses
and their riders into the sea."

Moses leads the people to Mount Sinai

Bitter water at Marah

²² After the Israelites left the Red Sea,* Moses led them through the Shur Desert for three days, before finding water. ²³ They did find water at Marah, but it was bitter, which is

---

*15.4 Red Sea: See the note at 13.18.
See also: 15.1: Rev 15.3. 15.2: Psa 118.14; Isa 12.2.

*15.22 Red Sea: See the note at 13.18.

how that place got its name.* ²⁴ The people complaining about, not us — we are complained and said, "Moses, what are we going to drink?"

²⁵ Moses asked the LORD for help, and the LORD told him to throw a piece of wood into the water. Moses did so, and the water became fit to drink.

At Marah the LORD tested his people and also gave them some laws and teachings. ²⁶ Then he said, "I am the LORD your God, and I cure your diseases. If you obey me by doing right and by following my laws and teachings, I won't punish you with the diseases I sent on the Egyptians."

²⁷ Later the Israelites came to Elim, where there were twelve springs and seventy palm trees. So they camped there.

CHAPTER 16

The LORD sends food from heaven

¹ On the fifteenth day of the second month after the Israelites had escaped from Egypt, they left Elim and started through the western edge of the Sinai Desert* in the direction of Mount Sinai. ² There in the desert they started complaining to Moses and Aaron, ³ "We wish the LORD had killed us in Egypt. When we lived there, we could at least sit down and eat all the bread and meat we wanted. But you have brought us out here into this desert, where we are going to starve."

⁴ The LORD said to Moses, "I will send bread* down from heaven like rain. Each day the people can go out and gather only enough for that day. That's how I will see if they obey me. ⁵ But on the sixth day of each week they must gather and cook twice as much."

⁶ Moses and Aaron told the people, "This evening you will know that the LORD was the one who rescued you from Egypt. ⁷ And in the morning you will see his glorious power, because he has heard your complaints against him. Why should you grumble to us? Who are we?"

⁸ Then Moses continued, "You will know it is the LORD when he gives you meat each evening and more than enough bread each morning. He is really the one you are

complaining about, not us — we are nobodies — but the LORD has heard your complaints."

⁹ Moses turned to Aaron and said, "Bring the people together, because the LORD has heard their complaints."

¹⁰ Aaron was speaking to them, when everyone looked out towards the desert and saw the bright glory of the LORD in a cloud. ¹¹ The LORD said to Moses, ¹² "I have heard my people complain. Now tell them that each evening they will have meat and each morning they will have more than enough bread. Then they will know that I am the LORD their God."

¹³ That evening a lot of quails came and landed everywhere in the camp, and the next morning dew covered the ground. ¹⁴ After the dew had gone, the desert was covered with thin flakes that looked like frost. ¹⁵ The people had never seen anything like this, and they started asking each other, "What is it?"*

Moses answered, "This is the bread that the LORD has given you to eat. ¹⁶ And he orders you to gather about two litres for each person in your family — that should be more than enough."

¹⁷ They did as they were told. Some gathered more and some gathered less, ¹⁸ according to their needs, and none was left over.

¹⁹ Moses told them not to keep any overnight. ²⁰ Some of them disobeyed, but the next morning what they kept was stinking and full of worms, and Moses was angry.

²¹ Each morning everyone gathered as much as they needed, and in the heat of the day the rest melted. ²² However, on the sixth day of the week, everyone gathered enough to have four litres, instead of two. When the leaders reported this to Moses, ²³ he told them that the LORD had said, "Tomorrow is the Sabbath, a sacred day of rest in honour of me. So gather all you want to bake or boil, and make sure you save enough for tomorrow."

²⁴ The people obeyed, and the next morning the food smelt fine and had no worms. ²⁵ "You may eat the food," Moses said. "Today is the Sabbath in honour of the LORD, and there won't be any of this food on the ground today. ²⁶ You will find it there for the first six days of the week, but not on the Sabbath."

---

*15.23 Marah . . . name: In Hebrew "Marah" means "bitter".

*16.4 bread: This was something like a thin wafer, and it was called "manna", which in Hebrew means, "What is it?"

See also: 16.4: John 6.31.

*16.15 What is it: See the note at 16.4.

See also: 16.15: 1 Cor 10.3. 16.18: 2 Cor 8.15.
16.23: Exod 20.8-11.

²⁷ A few of the Israelites did go out to look for some, but there was none. ²⁸ Then the LORD said, "Moses, how long will you people keep disobeying my laws and teachings? ²⁹ Remember that I was the one who gave you the Sabbath. That's why on the sixth day I provide enough bread for two days. Everyone is to stay at home and rest on the Sabbath." ³⁰ And so they rested on the Sabbath.

³¹ The Israelites called the bread manna.* It was white like coriander seed and delicious as wafers made with honey. ³² Moses told the people that the LORD had said, "Store up two litres of this manna, because I want future generations to see the food I gave you during the time you were in the desert after I rescued you from Egypt."

³³ Then Moses told Aaron, "Put some manna in a jar and store it in the place of worship for future generations to see."

³⁴ Aaron followed the LORD's instructions and put the manna in front of the sacred chest for safekeeping. ³⁵⁻³⁶ The Israelites ate manna for forty years, before they came to the border of Canaan that was a settled land.ˀ

CHAPTER 17

The LORD gives water from a rock

This is also told in Numbers 20.1–13

¹ The Israelites left the desert and moved from one place to another each time the LORD ordered them to. Once they camped at Rephidim,* but there was no water for them to drink.

² The people started complaining to Moses, "Give us some water!"

Moses replied, "Why are you complaining to me and trying to put the LORD to the test?"

³ But the people were thirsty and kept on complaining, "Moses, did you bring us out of Egypt just to let us and our families and our animals die of thirst?"

⁴ Then Moses prayed to the LORD, "What am I going to do with these people? They are about to stone me to death!"

⁵ The LORD answered, "Take some of the leaders with you and go ahead of the rest of the people. Also take along the walking stick you used to strike the River Nile, ⁶ and when

you get to the rock at Mount Sinai,ˀ I will be there with you. Strike the rock with the stick, and water will pour out for the people to drink." Moses did this while the leaders watched.

⁷ The people had complained and tested the LORD by asking, "Is the LORD really with us?" So Moses named that place Massah, which means "testing" and Meribah, which means "complaining".

Israel defeats the Amalekites

⁸ When the Israelites were at Rephidim, they were attacked by the Amalekites. ⁹ So Moses told Joshua, "Have some men ready to attack the Amalekites tomorrow. I will stand on a hilltop, holding this walking stick that has the power of God."

¹⁰ Joshua led the attack as Moses had commanded, while Moses, Aaron, and Hur stood on the hilltop. ¹¹ The Israelites out-fought the Amalekites as long as Moses held up his arms, but they started losing whenever he had to lower them. ¹² Finally, Moses was so tired that Aaron and Hur got a rock for him to sit on. Then they stood beside him and supported his arms in the same position until sunset. ¹³ That's how Joshua defeated the Amalekites.

¹⁴ Afterwards, the LORD said to Moses, "Write an account of this victory and read it to Joshua. I want the Amalekites to be forgotten for ever."

¹⁵ Moses built an altar and named it "The LORD Gives me Victory". ¹⁶ Then Moses explained, "This is because I depended on the LORD.ˀ But in future generations, the LORD will have to fight the Amalekites again."

CHAPTER 18

Jethro visits Moses

¹ Jethro was the priest of Midian and the father-in-law of Moses. And he heard what the LORD God had done for Moses and his people, after rescuing them from Egypt.

²⁻⁴ In the meantime, Moses had sent his wife Zipporah and her two sons to stay with Jethro, and he had welcomed them. Moses was still a foreigner in Midian when his first son was born, and so Moses said, "I'll name him Gershom."*

---

*16.31 manna: See the note at 16.4.
*17.1 Rephidim: The last stopping place for the Israelites between the Red Sea and Mount Sinai; the exact location is not known.

See also: 16.31: Num 11.7,8. 16.33: Heb 9.4.
16.35: Josh 5.12. 17.1–7: Num 20.2–13.

*18.2–4 Gershom: See the note at 2.22.
See also: 17.14: Deut 25.17–19; 1 Sam 15.2–9.
18.2,3: Exod 2.21,22. 18.3: Acts 7.29.

When his second son was born, Moses said, "I'll name him Eliezer,* because the God my father worshipped has saved me from the king of Egypt."*

5-6 While Israel was camped in the desert near Mount Sinai,♦ Jethro sent Moses this message: "I am coming to visit you, and I am bringing your wife and two sons."

7 When they arrived, Moses went out and bowed down in front of Jethro, then kissed him. After they had greeted each other, they went into the tent, 8 where Moses told him everything the LORD had done to protect Israel against the Egyptians and their king. He also told him how the LORD had helped them in all their troubles.

9 Jethro was so pleased to hear this good news about what the LORD had done, 10 that he shouted, "Praise the LORD! He rescued you and the Israelites from the Egyptians and their king. 11 Now I know that the LORD is the greatest God, because he has rescued Israel from their arrogant enemies." 12 Jethro offered sacrifices to God. Then Aaron and Israel's leaders came to eat with Jethro there at the place of worship.

Judges are appointed

This is also told in Deuteronomy 1.9-18

13 The next morning Moses sat down at the place where he decided legal cases for the people, and everyone crowded around him until evening. 14 Jethro saw how much Moses had to do for the people, and he asked, "Why are you the only judge? Why do you let these people crowd around you from morning till evening?"

15 Moses answered, "Because they come here to find out what God wants them to do. 16 They bring their complaints to me, and I make decisions on the basis of God's laws."

17 Jethro replied:

That isn't the best way to do it. 18 You and the people who come to you will soon be worn out. The job is too much for one person; you can't do it alone. 19 God will help you if you follow my advice. You should be the one to speak to God for the people, 20 and you should teach them God's laws and show them what they must do to live right.

21 You will need to appoint some competent leaders who respect God and are trustworthy and honest. Then put them over groups of ten, fifty, a hundred, and a thousand. 22 These judges can handle the ordinary cases and bring the more difficult ones to you. Having them to share the load will make your work easier. 23 This is the way God wants it done. You won't be under nearly as much stress, and everyone else will return home feeling satisfied.

24 Moses followed Jethro's advice. 25 He chose some competent leaders from every tribe in Israel and put them over groups of ten, fifty, a hundred, and a thousand. 26 They served as judges, deciding the easy cases themselves, but bringing the more difficult ones to Moses.

27 After Moses and his father-in-law Jethro had said goodbye to each other, Jethro returned home.

The Ten Commandments and other laws

CHAPTER 19

At Mount Sinai

1-2 The Israelites left Rephidim.* Then two months after leaving Egypt, they arrived at the desert near Mount Sinai, where they set up camp at the foot of the mountain.

3 Moses went up the mountain to meet with the LORD God, who told him to say to the people:

4 You saw what I did in Egypt, and you know how I brought you here to me, just as a mighty eagle carries its young. 5 Now if you will faithfully obey me, you will be my very own people. The whole world is mine, 6 but you will be my holy nation and serve me as priests.

Moses, that is what you must tell the Israelites.

7 After Moses went back, he reported to the leaders what the LORD had said, 8 and they promised, "We will do everything the LORD has commanded." So Moses told the LORD about this.

9 The LORD said to Moses, "I will come to you in a thick cloud and let the people hear me speak to you. Then they will always trust

---

*18.2-4 Eliezer: In Hebrew "Eliezer" means "God has helped me".

*18.2-4 saved . . . Egypt: See 2.1-15.

*19.1,2 Rephidim: See the note at 17.1.

See also: 19.5,6: 1 Pet 2.9. 19.5: Deut 4.20; 7.6; 14.2; 26.18; Titus 2.14. 19.6: Rev 1.6; 5.10.

you." Again Moses reported to the people what the LORD had told him.

¹⁰ Once more the LORD spoke to Moses:

Go back and tell the people that today and tomorrow they must get themselves ready to meet me. They must wash their clothes ¹¹ and be ready by the day after tomorrow, when I will come down to Mount Sinai, where all of them can see me.

¹² Warn the people that they are forbidden to touch any part of the mountain. Anyone who does will be put to death, ¹³ either with stones or arrows, and no one must touch the body of a person killed in this way. Even an animal that touches this mountain must be put to death. You may go up the mountain only after a signal is given on the trumpet.

¹⁴ After Moses went down the mountain, he gave orders for the people to wash their clothes and make themselves acceptable to worship God. ¹⁵ He told them to be ready in three days and not to have sex in the meantime.

The LORD comes to Mount Sinai

¹⁶ On the morning of the third day there was thunder and lightning. A thick cloud covered the mountain, a loud trumpet blast was heard, and everyone in camp trembled with fear. ¹⁷ Moses led them out of the camp to meet God, and they stood at the foot of the mountain.

¹⁸ Mount Sinai was covered with smoke because the LORD had come down in a flaming fire. Smoke poured out of the mountain just like a furnace, and the whole mountain shook. ¹⁹ The trumpet blew louder and louder. Moses spoke, and God answered him with thunder.

²⁰ The LORD came down to the top of Mount Sinai and told Moses to meet him there. ²¹ Then he said, "Moses, go and warn the people not to cross the boundary that you set at the foot of the mountain. They must not cross it to come and look at me, because if they do, many of them will die. ²² Only the priests may come near me, and they must obey strict rules before I let them. If they don't, they will be punished."

²³ Moses replied, "The people cannot come up the mountain. You warned us to stay away because it is holy."

²⁴ Then the LORD told Moses, "Go down and bring Aaron back here with you. But the priests and people must not try to push their way through, or I will rush at them like a flood!"

²⁵ After Moses had gone back down, he told the people what the LORD had said.

CHAPTER 20

The Ten Commandments

This is also told in Deuteronomy 5.1–21

¹ God said to the people of Israel:

² I am the LORD your God, the one who brought you out of Egypt where you were slaves.

³ Do not worship any god except me.

⁴ Do not make idols that look like anything in the sky or on earth or in the sea under the earth. ⁵ Don't bow down and worship idols. I am the LORD your God, and I demand all your love. If you reject me, I will punish your families for three or four generations. ⁶ But if you love me and obey my laws, I will be kind to your families for thousands of generations.

⁷ Do not misuse my name.* I am the LORD your God, and I will punish anyone who misuses my name.

⁸ Remember that the Sabbath Day belongs to me. ⁹ You have six days when you can do your work, ¹⁰ but the seventh day of each week belongs to me, your God. No one is to work on that day — not you, your children, your slaves, your animals, or the foreigners who live in your towns. ¹¹ In six days I made the sky, the earth, the seas, and everything in them, but on the seventh day I rested. That's why I made the Sabbath a special day that belongs to me.

¹² Respect your father and your mother, and you will live a long time in the land I am giving you.

¹³ Do not murder.

*20.7 misuse my name: Probably includes breaking promises, telling lies after swearing to tell the truth, using the LORD's name as a curse word or a magic formula, and trying to control the LORD by using his name.

See also: 20.4,5: Exod 34.17; Lev 19.4; 26.1; Deut 4.15–18; 27.15. 20.5,6: Exod 34.6,7; Num 14.18; Deut 7.9,10. 20.7: Lev 19.12. 20.8: Exod 16.23–30; 31.12–14. 20.9,10: Exod 23.12; 31.15; 34.21; 35.2; Lev 23.3. 20.11: Gen 2.1–3; Exod 31.17. 20.12: a Deut 27.16; Matt 15.4; 19.19; Mark 7.10; 10.19; Luke 18.20; Eph 6.2; b Eph 6.3. 20.13: Gen 9.6; Lev 24.17; Matt 5.21; 19.18; Mark 10.19; Luke 18.20; Rom 13.9; Jam 2.11.

See also: 19.12,13: Heb 12.18–20. 19.16: Rev 4.5. 19.16–18: Deut 4.11,12.

¹⁴ Be faithful in marriage.
¹⁵ Do not steal.
¹⁶ Do not tell lies about others.
¹⁷ Do not want to take anything that belongs to someone else. Don't want to take anyone's house, wife or husband, slaves, oxen, donkeys or anything else.

The people are afraid

This is also told in Deuteronomy 5.23–33

¹⁸ The people trembled with fear when they heard the thunder and the trumpet and saw the lightning and the smoke coming from the mountain. They stood a long way off ¹⁹ and said to Moses, "If you speak to us, we will listen. But don't let God speak to us, or we will die!"

²⁰ "Don't be afraid!" Moses replied. "God has come only to test you, so that by obeying him you won't sin." ²¹ But when Moses went near the thick cloud where God was, the people stayed a long way off.

Idols and altars

²² The Lᴏʀᴅ told Moses to say to the people of Israel:

With your own eyes, you saw me speak to you from heaven. ²³ So you must never make idols of silver or gold to worship in place of me.♦

²⁴ Build an altar out of earth, and offer on it your sacrifices* of sheep, goats, and cattle. Wherever I choose to be worshipped, I will come down to bless you. ²⁵ If you ever build an altar for me out of stones, do not use any tools to chisel the stones, because that would make the altar unfit. ²⁶ And don't build an altar that requires steps; you might expose yourself when you climb up.

CHAPTER 21

Hebrew slaves

This is also told in Deuteronomy 15.12–18

¹ The Lᴏʀᴅ gave Moses the following laws for his people:

² If you buy a Hebrew slave, he must remain your slave for six years. But in the seventh year you must set him free, without cost to him. ³ If he was single at the time you bought him, he alone must be set free. But if he was married at the time, both he and his wife must be given their freedom. ⁴ If you give him a wife, and they have children, only the man himself must be set free; his wife and children remain the property of his owner.

⁵ But suppose the slave loves his wife and children so much that he won't leave without them. ⁶ Then he must stand beside either the door or the doorpost at the place of worship,♦ while his owner punches a small hole through one of his ears with a sharp metal rod. This makes him a slave for life.

⁷ A young woman who was sold by her father doesn't gain her freedom in the same way that a man does. ⁸ If she doesn't please the man who bought her to be his wife, he must let her be bought back.* He cannot sell her to foreigners; this would break the contract he made with her. ⁹ If he selects her as a wife for his son, he must treat her as his own daughter.

¹⁰ If the man later marries another woman, he must continue to provide food and clothing for the one he bought and to treat her as a wife. ¹¹ If he fails to do any of these things, she must be given her freedom without cost.

Murder and other violent crimes

The Lᴏʀᴅ said:

¹² Death is the punishment for murder.
¹³ But if you did not intend to kill someone, and I, the Lᴏʀᴅ, let it happen anyway, you may run for safety to a place that I have set aside. ¹⁴ If you plan in advance to murder someone, there's no escape, not even by holding on to my altar.* You will be dragged off and killed.

---

*20.24 sacrifices: The Hebrew text mentions two types of sacrifices: sacrifices to please the Lᴏʀᴅ (traditionally called "whole burnt offerings") and sacrifices to ask the Lᴏʀᴅ's blessing (traditionally called "peace offerings").

See also: 20.14: Lev 20.10; Matt 5.27; 19.18; Mark 10.19; Luke 18.20; Rom 13.9; Jam 2.11.   20.15: Lev 19.11; Matt 19.18; Mark 10.19; Luke 18.20; Rom 13.9. 20.16: Exod 23.1; Matt 19.18; Mark 10.19; Luke 18.20. 20.17: Rom 7.7; 13.9.   20.18,19: Heb 12.18,19. 20.25: Deut 27.5–7; Josh 8.31.

*21.8 bought back: Either by her family or by another Israelite who wanted to marry her.
*21.14 altar: As a rule, anyone who ran to the altar was safe from the death penalty, until proved guilty.
See also: 21.2–6: Lev 25.39–46.   21.12: Lev 24.17. 21.13: Num 35.10–34; Deut 19.1–13; Josh 20.1–9.

¹⁵ Death is the punishment for attacking your father or mother.

¹⁶ Death is the punishment for kidnapping. If you sell the person you kidnapped, or if you are caught with that person, the penalty is death.

¹⁷ Death is the punishment for cursing your father or mother.

¹⁸ Suppose two of you are arguing, and you hit the other with either a rock or your fist, without causing a fatal injury. If the victim has to stay in bed, ¹⁹ and later has to use a stick when walking outside, you must pay for the loss of time and do what you can to help until the injury is completely healed. That's your only responsibility.

²⁰ Death is the punishment for beating to death any of your slaves. ²¹ However, if the slave lives a few days after the beating, you are not to be punished. After all, you have already lost the services of that slave who was your property.

²² Suppose a pregnant woman suffers a miscarriage* as the result of an injury caused by someone who is fighting. If she isn't badly hurt, the one who injured her must pay whatever fine her husband demands and the judges approve. ²³ But if she is seriously injured, the payment will be life for life, ²⁴ eye for eye, tooth for tooth, hand for hand, foot for foot, ²⁵ burn for burn, cut for cut, and bruise for bruise.

²⁶ If you hit one of your slaves and cause the loss of an eye, the slave must be set free. ²⁷ The same law applies if you knock out a slave's tooth — the slave goes free.

²⁸ A bull that kills someone with its horns must be killed and its meat destroyed, but the owner of the bull isn't responsible for the death.

²⁹ Suppose you own a bull that has been in the habit of attacking people, but you have refused to keep it fenced in. If that bull kills someone, both you and the bull must be put to death by stoning. ³⁰ However, you may save your own life by paying whatever fine is demanded. ³¹ This same law applies if the bull gores someone's son or daughter. ³² If the bull kills a slave, you must pay the slave owner thirty pieces of silver for the loss of the slave, and the bull must be killed by stoning.

³³ Suppose someone's ox or donkey is killed by falling into an open pit that you dug or left uncovered on your property.

³⁴ You must pay for the dead animal, and it becomes yours.

³⁵ If your bull kills someone else's, yours must be sold. Then the money from your bull and the meat from the dead bull must be divided equally between you and the other owner.

³⁶ If you refuse to fence in a bull that is known to attack others, you must pay for any animal it kills, but the dead animal will belong to you.

CHAPTER 22

Property laws

The LORD said:

¹ If you steal an ox and slaughter or sell it, you must replace it with five oxen; if you steal a sheep and slaughter it or sell it, you must replace it with four sheep. ²⁻⁴ But if you cannot afford to replace the animals, you must be sold as a slave to pay for what you have stolen. If you steal an ox, donkey, or sheep, and are caught with it still alive, you must pay the owner double.

If you happen to kill a burglar who breaks into your home after dark, you are not guilty. But if you kill someone who breaks in during the day, you are guilty of murder.

⁵ If you allow any of your animals to stray from your property and graze* in someone else's field or vineyard, you must repay the damage from the best part of your own harvest of grapes and grain.

⁶ If you carelessly let a fire spread from your property to someone else's, you must pay the owner for any crops or fields destroyed by the fire.

⁷ Suppose a neighbour asks you to keep some silver or other valuables, and they are stolen from your house. If the thief is caught, the thief must repay double. ⁸ But if the thief isn't caught, some judges* will decide if you are the guilty one.

⁹ Suppose two people claim to own the same ox or donkey or sheep or piece of clothing. Then the judges* must decide the case, and the guilty person will pay the owner double.

¹⁰ Suppose a neighbour who is going to be away asks you to keep a donkey or an ox or a sheep or some other animal, and it dies or gets injured or is stolen while no one is looking. ¹¹ If you swear with me as your witness that you did not harm the animal, you do not have to replace it. Your word is enough. ¹² But if the animal was stolen

---

See also: 21.16: Deut 24.7. 21.17: Lev 20.9; Matt 15.4; Mark 7.10. 21.24: Lev 24.19,20; Deut 19.21; Matt 5.38.

70

while in your care, you must replace it. ¹³ If the animal was attacked and killed by a wild animal, and you can show the remains of the dead animal to its owner, you do not have to replace it.

¹⁴ Suppose you borrow an animal from a neighbour, and it gets injured or dies while the neighbour isn't around. Then you must replace it. ¹⁵ But if something happens to the animal while the owner is present, you do not have to replace it. If you had leased the animal, the money you paid the owner will cover any harm done to it.

Laws for everyday life

The LORD said:

¹⁶ Suppose a young woman has never been married and isn't engaged. If a man talks her into having sex, he must pay the bride price* and marry her. ¹⁷ But if her father refuses to let her marry the man, the bride price must still be paid.

¹⁸ Death is the punishment for witchcraft.

¹⁹ Death is the punishment for having sex with an animal.

²⁰ Death is the punishment for offering sacrifices to any god except me.

²¹ Do not ill-treat or abuse foreigners who live among you. Remember, you were foreigners in Egypt.

²² Do not ill-treat widows or orphans. ²³ If you do, they will beg for my help, and I will come to their rescue. ²⁴ In fact, I will get so angry that I will kill your men and make widows of their wives and orphans of their children.

²⁵ Don't charge interest when you lend money to any of my people who are in need. ²⁶ Before sunset you must return any coat taken as security for a loan, ²⁷ because that is the only cover the poor have when they sleep at night. I am a merciful God, and when they call out to me, I will come to help them.

²⁸ Don't speak evil of me* or of the ruler of your people.

²⁹ Don't fail to give me the offerings of grain and wine that belong to me.*

Dedicate to me your firstborn sons ³⁰ and the firstborn of your cattle and sheep. Let the animals stay with their mothers for seven days, then on the eighth day give them to me, your God.

³¹ You are my chosen people, so don't eat the meat of any of your livestock that was killed by a wild animal. Instead, feed the meat to dogs.

CHAPTER 23

Equal justice for all

The LORD said:

¹ Don't spread harmful rumours or help a criminal by giving false evidence.

² Always tell the truth in court, even if everyone else is* dishonest and stands in the way of justice. ³ And don't favour the poor, simply because they are poor.

⁴ If you find an ox or a donkey that has wandered off, take it back where it belongs, even if the owner is your enemy.

⁵ If a donkey is overloaded and falls down, you must do what you can to help, even if it belongs to someone who doesn't like you.*

⁶ Make sure that the poor are given equal justice in court. ⁷ Don't bring false charges against anyone or sentence an innocent person to death. I won't forgive you if you do.

⁸ Don't accept bribes. Judges are blinded and justice is twisted by bribes.

⁹ Don't ill-treat foreigners. You were foreigners in Egypt, and you know what it is like.

Laws for the Sabbath

The LORD said:

¹⁰ Plant and harvest your crops for six years, ¹¹ but let the land rest during the seventh year. The poor are to eat what they want from your fields, vineyards, and olive trees during that year, and when they have all they want from your fields, leave the rest for wild animals.

¹² Work the first six days of the week, but rest and relax on the seventh day. This law is not only for you, but for your oxen,

---

*22.16 **bride price:** It was the custom for a man to pay his wife's family a bride price before the actual wedding ceremony took place.

See also: 22.16,17: Deut 22.28,29. **22.18:** Deut 18.10,11. **22.19:** Lev 18.23; 20.15,16; Deut 27.21. **22.20:** Deut 17.2–7. **22.21,22:** Exod 23.9; Lev 19.33,34; Deut 24.17,18; 27.19. **22.25:** Lev 25.35–38; Deut 15.7–11; 23.19,20. **22.26,27:** Deut 24.10–13. **22.28:** Acts 23.5.

See also: 22.31: Lev 17.15. **23.1:** Exod 20.16; Lev 19.11,12; Deut 5.20. **23.3:** Lev 19.15. **23.4,5:** Deut 22.1–4. **23.6–8:** Lev 19.15; Deut 16.19. **23.9:** Exod 22.21; Lev 19.33,34; Deut 24.17,18; 27.19. **23.10,11:** Lev 25.1–7. **23.12:** Exod 20.9–11; 31.15; 34.21; 35.2; Lev 23.3; Deut 5.13,14.

donkeys, and slaves, as well as for any foreigners among you.

¹³ Make certain that you obey everything I have said. Don't pray to other gods or even mention their names.

Three annual festivals

This is also told in Exodus 34.18–26; Deuteronomy 16.1–17

The LORD said:

¹⁴ Celebrate three festivals each year in my honour.

¹⁵ Celebrate the Festival of Thin Bread by eating bread made without yeast, just as I have commanded.* Do this at the proper time during the month of Abib,* because it is the month when you left Egypt. And make certain that everyone brings the proper offerings.

¹⁶ Celebrate the Harvest Festival* each spring when you start harvesting your wheat, and celebrate the Festival of Shelters* each autumn when you pick your fruit.

¹⁷ Your men must come to these three festivals each year to worship me.

¹⁸ Do not offer bread made with yeast when you sacrifice an animal to me. And make sure that the fat of the animal is burnt that same day.

¹⁹ Each year bring the best part of your first harvest to the place of worship.

Don't boil a young goat in its mother's milk.

A promise and a warning

The LORD said:

²⁰ I am sending an angel to protect you and to lead you into the land I have ready for you. ²¹ Carefully obey everything the angel says, because I am giving him complete authority, and he won't tolerate rebellion.

²² If you faithfully obey him, I will be a fierce enemy of your enemies. ²³ My angel will lead you into the land of the Amorites, Hittites, Perizzites, Canaanites, Hivites, and Jebusites, and I will wipe them out. ²⁴ Don't worship their gods or follow their customs. Instead, destroy their idols and shatter their stone images.

²⁵ Worship only me, the LORD your God! I will bless you with plenty of food and water and keep you strong. ²⁶ Your women will give birth to healthy children, and everyone will live a long life.

²⁷ I will terrify those nations and make your enemies so confused that they will run from you. ²⁸ I will make the Hivites, Canaanites, and Hittites panic as you approach. ²⁹ But I won't do all this in the first year, because the land would become poor, and wild animals would be everywhere. ³⁰ Instead, I will force out your enemies little by little and give your nation time to grow strong enough to take over the land.

³¹ I will see that your borders reach from the Red Sea* to the River Euphrates and from the Mediterranean Sea to the desert. I will let you defeat the people who live there, and you will force them out of the land. ³² But you must not make any agreements with them or with their gods. ³³ Don't let them stay in your land. They will trap you into sinning against me and worshipping their gods.

CHAPTER 24

The people agree to obey God

¹ The LORD said to Moses, "Come up to me on this mountain. Bring along Aaron, as well as his two sons Nadab and Abihu, and seventy of Israel's leaders. They must worship me at a distance, ² but you are to come near. Don't let anyone else come up."

³ Moses gave the LORD's instructions to the people, and they promised, "We will do everything the LORD has commanded!" ⁴ Then Moses wrote down what the LORD had said.

The next morning Moses got up early. He built an altar at the foot of the mountain and set up a large stone for each of the twelve tribes of Israel. ⁵ He also sent some young

---

*23.15 as I have commanded:** See 12.14–20.
*23.15 Abib:** See the note at 13.3,4.
*23.16 Harvest Festival:** Traditionally called the "Festival of Weeks" and known in New Testament times as "Pentecost".
*23.16 Festival of Shelters:** The Hebrew text has "Festival of Ingathering" (so also in 34.22), which was the final harvesting of crops and fruits before the autumn rains began. But the usual name was "Festival of Shelters".
See also: 23.15: Exod 12.14–20; Lev 23.6–8; Num 28.17–25. 23.16: a Lev 23.15–21; Num 28.26–31; b Lev 23.39–43. 23.19: Deut 26.2; Exod 34.26; Deut 14.21.

*23.31 Red Sea:** Hebrew *yam suph*, here referring to the Gulf of Aqaba, since the term is extended to include the north-eastern arm of the Red Sea (see also the note at 13.18).

men to burn offerings and to sacrifice bulls as special offerings* to the LORD. ⁶ Moses put half of the blood from the animals into bowls and sprinkled the rest on the altar. ⁷ Then he read aloud the LORD's commands and promises, and the people shouted, "We will obey the LORD and do everything he has commanded!"

⁸ Moses took the blood from the bowls and sprinkled it on the people. Next, he told them, "With this blood the LORD makes his agreement with you."

⁹ Moses and Aaron, together with Nadab and Abihu and the seventy leaders, went up the mountain ¹⁰ and saw the God of Israel. Under his feet was something that looked like a pavement made out of sapphire,* and it was as bright as the sky.

¹¹ Even though these leaders of Israel saw God, he did not punish them. So they ate and drank.

Moses on Mount Sinai

¹² The LORD said to Moses, "Come up on the mountain and stay here for a while. I will give you the two flat stones on which I have written the laws that my people must obey." ¹³ Moses and Joshua his assistant got ready, then Moses started up the mountain to meet with God.

¹⁴ Moses had told the leaders, "Wait here until we come back. Aaron and Hur will be with you, and they can settle any arguments while we are away."

¹⁵ When Moses went up on Mount Sinai, a cloud covered it, ¹⁶ and the bright glory of the LORD came down and stayed there. The cloud covered the mountain for six days, and on the seventh day the LORD told Moses to come into the cloud. ¹⁷⁻¹⁸ Moses did so and stayed there forty days and nights. To the people, the LORD's glory looked like a blazing fire on top of the mountain.

Instructions for the sacred tent, its furnishings, and the sacred chest

CHAPTER 25

The sacred tent
This is also told in Exodus 35.4–9

¹ The LORD said to Moses:

² Tell everyone in Israel who wants to give gifts that they must bring them to you. ³ Here is a list of what you are to collect: gold, silver, and bronze; ⁴ blue, purple, and red wool; fine linen; goat hair; ⁵ tanned ram skins; fine leather; acacia wood; ⁶ olive oil for the lamp; sweet-smelling spices to mix with the oil for dedicating the tent and ordaining the priests; ⁷ and onyx* stones for the sacred apron and the breastpiece. ⁸ I also want them to build a special place where I can live among my people. ⁹ Make it and its furnishings exactly like the pattern I will show you.

The sacred chest
This is also told in Exodus 37.1–9

The LORD said to Moses:

¹⁰ Tell the people to build a chest of acacia wood one hundred and ten centimetres long, sixty-six centimetres wide, and sixty-six centimetres high. ¹¹ Cover it inside and out with pure gold and put a gold edging around the lid. ¹² Make four gold rings and fasten one of them to each of the four legs of the chest. ¹³ Make two poles of acacia wood. Cover them with gold ¹⁴ and put them through the rings, so the chest can be carried by the poles. ¹⁵ Don't ever remove the poles from the rings. ¹⁶ When I give you the Ten Commandments written on two flat stones, put them inside the chest.

¹⁷ Cover the lid of the chest with pure gold. ¹⁸⁻¹⁹ Then hammer out two winged creatures of pure gold and fasten them to the lid at the ends of the chest. ²⁰ The creatures must face each other with their wings spread over the chest. ²¹ Inside it place the two flat stones with the Ten Commandments and put the gold lid on

*24.5 special offerings: Often translated "peace offerings", which were to make peace between God and his people, who ate certain parts of the sacrificed animal.
*24.10 sapphire: A precious stone, blue in colour.
See also: 24.8: a Matt 26.28; Mark 14.24; Luke 22.20; 1 Cor 11.25; Heb 10.29; b Heb 9.19,20. 24.18: Deut 9.9.

*25.7 onyx: A precious stone with bands of different colours.
See also: 25.17: Heb 9.5.

top of the chest. 22 I will meet you there*
between the two creatures and tell you what
my people must do and what they must not
do.

The table for the sacred bread

This is also told in Exodus 37.10–16

The LORD said:

23 Make a table of acacia wood eighty-eight
centimetres long, forty-four centimetres
wide, and sixty-six centimetres high.
24-25 Cover it with pure gold and put a gold
edging around it with a border seventy-five
millimetres wide.* 26 Make four gold rings
and attach one to each of the legs 27-28 near
the edging. The poles for carrying the table
are to be placed through these rings and
are to be made of acacia wood covered with
gold. 29-30 The table is to be kept in the holy
place, and the sacred loaves of bread must
always be put on it. All bowls, plates, jars,
and cups for wine offerings are to be made
of pure gold and set on this table.

The lampstand

This is also told in Exodus 37.17–24

The LORD said:

31 Make a lampstand of pure gold. The
whole lampstand, including its decorative
flowers, must be made from a single piece
of hammered gold 32 with three branches
on each of its two sides. 33 There are to be
three decorative almond blossoms on each
branch 34 and four on the stem. 35 There
must also be a blossom where each pair of
branches comes out from the stem. 36 The
lampstand, including its branches and
decorative flowers, must be made from a
single piece of hammered gold. 37 The
lamp on the top and those at the end of
each of its six branches must be made so as
to shine towards the front of the
lampstand. 38 The tongs and trays for
taking care of the lamps are to be made of
pure gold. 39 The lampstand and its
equipment will require thirty-five
kilogrammes of pure gold, 40 and they must
be made according to the pattern I showed
you on the mountain.

CHAPTER 26

Curtains and coverings for the sacred tent

This is also told in Exodus 36.8–19

The LORD said to Moses:

1 Furnish the sacred tent with curtains
made from ten pieces of the finest linen.
They must be woven with blue, purple,
and red wool and embroidered with figures
of winged creatures. 2 Make each piece
twelve metres long and two metres wide
3 and sew them together into two curtains
with five sections each. 4-6 Put fifty loops of
blue cloth along one of the wider sides of
each curtain, then fasten the two curtains
at the loops with fifty gold hooks.

7-8 As the material for the tent, use goat
hair to weave eleven sections thirteen
metres by two metres each. 9 Sew five of
the sections together to make one panel.
Then sew the other six together to make a
second panel, and fold the sixth section
double over the front of the tent. 10 Put
fifty loops along one of the wider sides of
each panel 11 and fasten the two panels at
the loops with fifty bronze hooks. 12-13 The
panel of goat hair will be a metre longer
than the tent itself, so fold fifty centimetres
of the material behind the tent and on
each side as a protective covering. 14 Make
two more coverings — one with ram skins
dyed red and the other with fine leather.

The framework for the sacred tent

This is also told in Exodus 36.20–34

The LORD said:

15 Build a framework of acacia wood for the
walls of the sacred tent. 16 Each frame is to
be four metres high and sixty-six
centimetres wide 17 with two wooden pegs
near the bottom. 18-21 Place two silver
stands under each frame with sockets for
the pegs, so the frames can be joined
together. Twenty of these frames are to be
used along the south side and twenty more
along the north. 22 For the back wall along
the west side use six frames 23-24 with two
more at the south-west and north-west
corners. Make certain that these corner
frames are joined from top to bottom.
25 Altogether, this back wall will have eight
frames with two silver stands under each
one.

---

*25.22 I will meet you there: It was believed that God
had his earthly throne on the lid of the sacred chest.
See also: 25.30: Lev 24.5–8. 25.40: Acts 7.44; Heb 8.5.

26-27 Make five crossbars for each of the wooden frames, 28 with the centre crossbar running the full length of the wall. 29 Cover the frames and the crossbars with gold and attach gold rings to let the crossbars through. 30 Then set up the tent in the way I showed you on the mountain.

The curtain inside the sacred tent
This is also told in Exodus 36.35–38

The LORD said:

31-33 Make a curtain to separate the holy place from the most holy place. Use fine linen woven with blue, purple, and red wool, and embroidered with figures of winged creatures. Cover four acacia wood posts with gold and set them each on a silver stand. Then fasten gold hooks to the posts and hang the curtain there.

34 Inside the most holy place, you must put the sacred chest that has the place of mercy on its lid.* 35 Outside the curtain put the table for the sacred bread on the right side and the gold lampstand on the left.

36 For the entrance to the tent, use a piece of fine linen woven with blue, purple, and red wool and embroidered with fine needlework. 37 Cover five acacia wood posts with gold and set them each on a bronze stand. Then put gold hooks on the posts and hang the curtain there.

CHAPTER 27
The altar for offering sacrifices
This is also told in Exodus 38.1–7

The LORD said to Moses:

1 Use acacia wood to build an altar two and a quarter metres square and one and a third metres high, 2 and make each of the four top corners stick up like the horn of a bull. Then cover the whole altar with bronze, including the four horns. 3 All the equipment for the altar must also be made of bronze — the pans for the hot ashes, the shovels, the sprinkling bowls, the meat forks, and the fire pans. 4-5 Half-way up the altar build a ledge around it, and cover the

bottom half of the altar with a decorative bronze grating. Then attach a bronze ring beneath the ledge at the four corners of the altar. 6-7 Cover two acacia wood poles with bronze and put them through the rings for carrying the altar. 8 Construct the altar in the shape of an open box, just as you were shown on the mountain.

The courtyard around the sacred tent
This is also told in Exodus 38.9–20

The LORD said:

9-15 Surround the sacred tent with a courtyard forty-four metres long on the south and north and twenty-two metres wide on the east and west. Use twenty bronze posts on bronze stands for the south and north and ten for the west. Then hang a curtain of fine linen on the posts along each of these three sides by using silver hooks and rods.

Place three bronze posts on each side of the entrance at the east and hang a curtain six and two thirds metres wide on each set of posts. 16 Use four more of these posts for the entrance way, then hang on them an embroidered curtain of fine linen nine metres long and woven with blue, purple, and red wool. 17-18 The curtains that surround the courtyard must be two and a quarter metres high and are to be hung from the bronze posts with silver hooks and rods. 19 The rest of the equipment for the sacred tent must be made of bronze, including the pegs for the tent and for the curtain surrounding the courtyard.

The oil for the lamp in the holy place
This is also told in Leviticus 24.1–4

The LORD said to Moses:

20 Command the people of Israel to supply you with the purest olive oil. Do this so the lamp will keep burning 21 in front of the curtain that separates the holy place from the most holy place, where the sacred chest is kept. Aaron and his sons are responsible for keeping the lamp burning every night in the sacred tent. The Israelites must always obey this command.

---

*26.34 place of mercy on its lid: It was believed that God had his earthly throne on the lid of the sacred chest, and from this place he showed mercy to his people.
See also: 26.33: Heb 6.19; 9.3–5.

Instructions for priests, sacrifices, and the Sabbath

CHAPTER 28

The clothes for the high priest

This is also told in Exodus 39.1–7

The LORD said to Moses:

¹ Send for your brother Aaron and his sons Nadab, Abihu, Eleazar, and Ithamar. They are the ones I have chosen from Israel to serve as my priests. ² Make Aaron some beautiful clothes that are worthy of a high priest. ³ Aaron is to be dedicated as my high priest, and his clothes must be made only by persons who possess skills that I have given them. ⁴ Here are the items that need to be made: a breastpiece, a priestly apron, a robe, an embroidered shirt, a turban, and a sash. These sacred clothes are to be made for your brother Aaron and his sons who will be my priests. ⁵ Only gold and fine linen, woven with blue, purple, and red wool, are to be used for making these clothes.

The apron for the high priest

This is also told in Exodus 39.2–7

The LORD said:

⁶⁻⁸ The entire priestly apron must be made of fine linen skilfully woven with blue, purple, and red wool, and decorated with gold. It is to have two shoulder straps to support it and a sash that fastens around the waist.

⁹⁻¹² Put two onyx* stones in gold settings, then attach one to each of the shoulder straps. On one of these stones engrave the names of Israel's first six sons in the order of their birth. And do the same with his remaining six sons on the other stone. In this way Aaron will always carry the names of the tribes of Israel when he enters the holy place, and I will never forget my people.

¹³⁻¹⁴ Attach two gold settings to the shoulder straps and fasten them with two braided chains of pure gold.

The breastpiece for the high priest

This is also told in Exodus 39.8–21

The LORD said:

¹⁵ From the same costly material make a breastpiece for the high priest to use in

learning what I want my people to do. ¹⁶ It is to be twenty-two centimetres square and folded double ¹⁷ with four rows of three precious stones: in the first row put a carnelian, a chrysolite, and an emerald; ¹⁸ in the second row a turquoise, a sapphire, and a diamond; ¹⁹ in the third row a jacinth, an agate, and an amethyst; ²⁰ and in the fourth row a beryl, an onyx, and a jasper.* Mount the stones in delicate gold settings ²¹ and engrave on each of them the name of one of the twelve tribes of Israel.

²²⁻²⁵ Attach two gold rings to the upper front corners of the breastpiece and fasten them with two braided gold chains to gold settings on the shoulder straps. ²⁶ Attach two other gold rings to the lower inside corners next to the apron ²⁷ and two more near the bottom of the shoulder straps just above the sash. ²⁸ Then take a blue cord and tie the two lower rings on the breastpiece to those on the apron. This will keep the breastpiece in place.

²⁹ In this way Aaron will have the names of the twelve tribes of Israel written on his heart each time he enters the holy place, and I will never forget my people. ³⁰ He must also wear on his breastpiece the two small objects* that he uses to receive answers from me.

The other high-priestly clothes

This is also told in Exodus 39.22–26,30,31

The LORD said:

³¹ Under his apron Aaron must wear a robe of blue wool ³² with an opening in the centre for his head. Be sure to bind the material around the collar to keep it from fraying. ³³⁻³⁴ Along the hem of the robe weave pomegranates* of blue, purple, and red wool with a gold bell between each of

---

*28.20 jasper: The stones mentioned in verses 17–20 are of different colours: *carnelian* is deep red or reddish white; *chrysolite* is olive green; *emerald* is green; *turquoise* is blue or blue green; *sapphire* is blue; *diamond* is colourless or white; *jacinth* is reddish orange; *agate* has circles of brown and white; *amethyst* is deep purple; *beryl* is green or bluish green; *onyx* has bands of different colours; and *jasper* is usually green or clear.

*28.30 two small objects: The Hebrew text has "urim and thummim", which may have been made of wood, stone, or metal, and were used in some way to receive answers from God.

*28.33,34 pomegranates: A bright red fruit that looks like an apple.

See also: 28.30: Num 27.21; Deut 33.8; Ezra 2.63; Neh 7.65.

*28.9–12 onyx: See the note at 25.7.

them. 35 If Aaron wears these clothes when he enters the holy place as my high priest, the sound of the bells will be heard, and his life will not be in danger.

36 On a narrow strip of pure gold engrave the words: "Dedicated to the LORD".
37 Fasten it to the front of Aaron's turban with a blue cord, 38 so he can wear it on his forehead. This will show that he will take on himself the guilt for any sins the people of Israel commit in offering their gifts to me, and I will forgive them.

39 Make Aaron's robe and turban of fine linen and decorate his sash with fine needlework.

The clothes for the other priests

This is also told in Exodus 39.27–29

The LORD said:

40 Since Aaron's sons are priests, they should also look dignified. So make robes, sashes, and special caps for them. 41 Then dress Aaron and his sons in these clothes, pour olive oil on their heads, and ordain them as my priests.

42 Make linen shorts for them that reach from the waist down to the thigh, so they won't expose themselves. 43 Whenever they enter the sacred tent or serve at the altar or enter the holy place, they must wear these shorts, or else they will be guilty and die. This same rule applies to any of their descendants who serve as priests.

CHAPTER 29

Instructions for ordaining priests

This is also told in Leviticus 8.1–36

The LORD said to Moses:

1 When you ordain one of Aaron's sons as my priest, choose a young bull and two rams that have nothing wrong with them.
2 Then from your finest flour make three batches of dough without yeast. Shape some of it into larger loaves, some into smaller loaves mixed with olive oil, and the rest into thin wafers brushed with oil. 3 Put all this bread in a basket and bring it when you come to sacrifice the three animals to me.
4 Bring Aaron and his sons to the entrance of the sacred tent and make them wash themselves. 5 Dress Aaron in the priestly shirt, the robe that goes under the sacred apron, the apron itself, the breastpiece, and the sash. 6 Put on his

turban with its narrow strip of engraved gold 7 and then ordain him by pouring olive oil on his head.

8 Next, dress Aaron's sons in their special shirts 9 and caps and their sashes,* then ordain them, because they and their descendants will always be priests.

10 Lead the bull to the entrance of the sacred tent, where Aaron and his sons will lay their hands on its head. 11 Kill the bull near my altar in front of the tent. 12 Use a finger to smear some of its blood on each of the four corners of the altar and pour out the rest of the blood on the ground next to the altar. 13 Then take the fat from the animal's insides, as well as the lower part of the liver and the two kidneys with their fat, and send them up in smoke on the altar.
14 But the meat, the skin, and the food still in the bull's stomach must be burnt outside the camp as an offering to ask forgiveness for the sins of the priests.*

15 Bring one of the rams to Aaron and his sons and make them lay their hands on its head. 16 Kill the ram and splatter its blood against all four sides of the altar. 17 Cut up the ram, wash its insides and legs, and lay all its parts on the altar, including the head. 18 Then make sure that the whole animal goes up in smoke with a smell that pleases me.

19 Bring the other ram to Aaron and his sons and make them lay their hands on its head. 20 Kill the ram and place some of its blood on Aaron's right ear lobe, his right thumb, and the big toe of his right foot. Do the same for each of his sons and splatter the rest of the blood against the four sides of the altar. 21 Then take some of the blood from the altar, mix it with the oil used for ordination, and sprinkle it on Aaron and his clothes, and also on his sons and their clothes. This will show that they and their clothes have been dedicated to me.

22 This ram is part of the ordination service. So remove its right hind leg,* its fat tail, the fat on its insides, as well as the lower part of the liver and the two kidneys with their fat. 23 Take one loaf of each kind of bread* from the basket, 24 and put this

---

29.14 for the sins of the priests: When a sacrifice for the forgiveness of sins was made for someone other than priests, the part that was not burnt on the altar could be eaten by the priests (see Leviticus 5.13; 6.26).
29.22 right hind leg: This was usually given to the officiating priest (see Leviticus 7.33).
29.23 each kind of bread: See verses 2,3.
See also: 29.18: Eph 5.2; Phil 4.18.

bread, together with the meat, into the hands of Aaron and his sons. Then they will lift it all up' to show that it is dedicated to me. ²⁵ After this, the meat and bread are to be placed on the altar and sent up in smoke with a smell that pleases me.

²⁶ You may eat the choice ribs from this second ram, but you must first lift them up' to show that this meat is dedicated to me.

²⁷⁻²⁸ In the future, when anyone from Israel offers the ribs and a hind leg of a ram either to ordain a priest or to ask for my blessing, the meat belongs to me, but it may be eaten by the priests. This law will never change.

²⁹⁻³⁰ After Aaron's death, his priestly clothes are to be handed down to each descendant who succeeds him as high priest, and these clothes must be worn during the seven-day ceremony of ordination.

³¹ Boil the meat of the ordination ram in a sacred place, ³² then Aaron and his sons are to eat it together with the three kinds of bread* at the entrance to the sacred tent. ³³ At their ordination, a ceremony of forgiveness was performed for them with this sacred food, and only they have the right to eat it. ³⁴ If any of the sacred food is left until morning, it must be burnt up.

³⁵ Repeat this ordination ceremony for Aaron and his sons seven days in a row, just as I have instructed you. ³⁶ Each day you must offer a bull as a sacrifice for sin and as a way of purifying the altar. In addition, you must smear the altar with olive oil to make it completely holy. ³⁷ Do this for seven days, and the altar will become so holy that anyone who touches it will become holy.

Daily sacrifices

This is also told in Leviticus 6.8–13; Numbers 28.1–8

The LORD said:

³⁸ Each day you must sacrifice two lambs a year old, ³⁹ one in the morning and one in the evening. ⁴⁰⁻⁴¹ With each lamb offer one kilogramme of your finest flour mixed with a litre of your finest olive oil, and also pour out a litre of wine as an offering. The smell of this sacrifice on the fires of the altar will be pleasing to me. ⁴²⁻⁴³ You and your descendants must always offer this sacrifice on the altar at the entrance to the sacred tent.

People of Israel, I will meet and speak with you there, and my shining glory will

make the place holy. ⁴⁴ Because of who I am, the tent will become sacred, and Aaron and his sons will become worthy to serve as my priests. ⁴⁵ I will live among you as your God, ⁴⁶ and you will know that I am the LORD your God, the one who rescued you from Egypt, so that I could live among you.

CHAPTER 30

The altar for burning incense

This is also told in Exodus 37.25–28

The LORD said to Moses:

¹ Build an altar of acacia wood where you can burn incense. ² Make it forty-five centimetres square and ninety centimetres high, and make each of its four corners stick up like the horn of a bull. ³ Cover it with pure gold and put a gold edging around it. ⁴ Then below the edging on opposite sides attach two gold rings through which you can put the poles for carrying the altar. ⁵ These poles are also to be made of acacia wood covered with gold.

⁶ Put the altar in front of the inside curtain of the sacred tent. The chest with the place of mercy* is kept behind that curtain, and I will talk with you there. ⁷⁻⁸ From now on, when Aaron tends the lamp each morning and evening, he must burn sweet-smelling incense to me on the altar. ⁹ Burn only the proper incense on the altar and never use it for grain sacrifices or animal sacrifices or drink offerings. ¹⁰ Once a year Aaron must purify the altar by smearing on its four corners* the blood of an animal sacrificed for sin, and this practice must always be followed. The altar is sacred because it is dedicated to me.

The money for the sacred tent

¹¹ The LORD said to Moses:

¹² Find out how many grown men there are in Israel and require each of them to pay me to keep him safe from danger while you are counting them. ¹³⁻¹⁵ Each man over nineteen, whether rich or poor, must pay me the same amount of money, weighed according to the official standards. ¹⁶ This money is to be used for the upkeep of the sacred tent, and because of it, I will never forget my people.

---

*30.6 place of mercy: See the note at 26.34.
*30.10 four corners: See 27.2; 30.2.
See also: 30.13: Exod 38.25,26; Matt 17.24.

The large bronze bowl

This is also told in Exodus 38.8

17 The LORD said to Moses:

18-21 Make a large bronze bowl and a bronze stand for it. Then put them between the altar for sacrifice and the sacred tent, so the priests can wash their hands and feet before entering the tent or offering a sacrifice on the altar. Each priest in every generation must wash himself in this way, or else he will die there.

The oil for dedication and ordination

This is also told in Exodus 37.29

22 The LORD said to Moses:

23-25 Mix four litres of olive oil with the following costly spices: six kilogrammes of myrrh, three kilogrammes of cinnamon, three kilogrammes of cane, and six kilogrammes of cassia. Measure these according to the official standards. Then use this sacred mixture 26 for dedicating the tent and chest, 27 the table with its equipment, the lampstand with its equipment, the incense altar with all its utensils, 28 the altar for sacrifices, and the large bowl with its stand. 29 By dedicating them in this way, you will make them so holy that anyone who even touches them will become holy.

30 When you ordain Aaron and his sons as my priests, sprinkle them with some of this oil, 31 and say to the people of Israel: "This oil must always be used in the ordination service of a priest. It is holy because it is dedicated to the LORD. 32 So treat it as holy! Don't ever use it for everyday purposes or mix any for yourselves. 33 If you do, you will no longer belong to the LORD's people."

The sweet-smelling incense

The LORD said:

34-35 Mix equal amounts of the costly spices stacte, onycha, galbanum, and pure frankincense, then add salt to make the mixture pure and holy. 36 Pound some of it into powder and sprinkle it in front of the sacred chest, where I meet with you. Be sure to treat this incense as something very holy. 37 It is truly holy because it is dedicated to me, so don't ever make any for yourselves. 38 If you ever make any of it to use as

perfume, you will no longer belong to my people.

CHAPTER 31

The LORD chooses Bezalel and Oholiab

This is also told in Exodus 35.30—36.1

1 The LORD said to Moses:

2 I have chosen Bezalel[*] from the Judah tribe to make the sacred tent and its furnishings. 3-5 Not only have I filled him with my Spirit, but I have given him wisdom and made him a skilled craftsman who can create objects of art with gold, silver, bronze, stone, and wood. 6 I have appointed Oholiab[*] from the tribe of Dan to work with him, and I have also given skills to those who will help them make everything exactly as I have commanded you: 7-11 the sacred tent with its furnishings, the sacred chest with its place of mercy, the table with all that is on it, the lamp with its equipment, the incense altar, the altar for sacrifices with its equipment, the bronze bowl with its stand, the beautiful priestly clothes for Aaron and his sons, the oil for dedication and ordination services, and the sweet-smelling incense for the holy place.

Laws for the Sabbath

12-13 Moses told the Israelites that the LORD had said:

The Sabbath belongs to me. Now I command you and your descendants always to obey the laws of the Sabbath. By doing this, you will know that I have chosen you as my own. 14-15 Keep the Sabbath holy. You have six days to do your work, but the Sabbath is mine, and it must remain a day of rest. If you work on the Sabbath, you will no longer be part of my people, and you will be put to death.

16 Every generation of Israelites must respect the Sabbath. 17 This day will always serve as a reminder, both to me and to the Israelites, that I made the heavens and the earth in six days, then on the seventh day I rested and relaxed.

18 When God had finished speaking to Moses on Mount Sinai, he gave him the two flat stones on which he had written all his laws with his own hand.

See also: 30.18: Exod 38.8. 30.22-38: Exod 37.29.

See also: 31.15: Exod 20.8-11; 23.12; 34.21; 35.2; Lev 23.3; Deut 5.12-14. 31.17: Exod 20.11.

The people make an idol

CHAPTER 32

This is also told in Deuteronomy 9.6-29

[1] After the people saw that Moses had been on the mountain for a long time, they went to Aaron and said, "Make us an image of a god who will lead and protect us. Moses brought us out of Egypt, but nobody knows what has happened to him."

[2] Aaron told them, "Bring me the gold earrings that your wives and sons and daughters are wearing." [3] Everybody took off their earrings and brought them to Aaron, [4] then he melted them and made an idol in the shape of a young bull.

All the people said to one another, "This is the god who brought us out of Egypt!"

[5] When Aaron saw what was happening, he built an altar in front of the idol and said, "Tomorrow we will celebrate in honour of the LORD." [6] The people got up early the next morning and killed some animals to be used for sacrifices and others to be eaten. Then everyone ate and drank so much that they began to carry on like wild people.

[7] The LORD said to Moses:

Hurry back down! Those people you led out of Egypt are acting like fools. [8] They have already stopped obeying me and have made themselves an idol in the shape of a young bull. They have bowed down to it, offered sacrifices, and said that it is the god who brought them out of Egypt. [9] Moses, I have seen how stubborn these people are, [10] and I'm angry enough to destroy them, so don't try to stop me. But I will make your descendants into a great nation.

[11] Moses tried to get the LORD God to change his mind:

Our LORD, you used your mighty power to bring these people out of Egypt. Now don't become angry and destroy them. [12] If you do, the Egyptians will say that you brought your people out here into the mountains just to get rid of them. Please don't be angry with your people. Don't destroy them!

[13] Remember the solemn promise you made to Abraham, Isaac, and Jacob. You promised that some day they would have as many descendants as there are stars in the sky and that you would give them land.

[14] So even though the LORD had threatened to destroy the people, he changed his mind and let them live.

[15-16] Moses went back down the mountain with the two flat stones on which God had written all his laws with his own hand, and he had used both sides of the stones.

[17] When Joshua heard the noisy shouts of the people, he said to Moses, "A battle must be going on down in the camp."

[18] But Moses replied, "It doesn't sound like they are shouting because they have won or lost a battle. They are singing wildly!"

[19] As Moses got closer to the camp, he saw the idol, and he also saw the people dancing around. This made him so angry that he threw down the stones and broke them to pieces at the foot of the mountain. [20] He melted the idol the people had made, and he ground it into powder. He scattered it in their water and made them drink it. [21] Moses asked Aaron, "What did these people do to harm you? Why did you make them sin in this terrible way?"

[22] Aaron answered:

Don't be angry with me. You know as well as I do that they are determined to do evil. [23] They even told me, "That man Moses led us out of Egypt, but now we don't know what has happened to him. Make us a god to lead us." [24] Then I asked them to bring me their gold earrings. They took them off and gave them to me. I threw the gold into a fire, and out came this bull.

[25] Moses knew that the people were out of control and that it was Aaron's fault. And now they had made fools of themselves in front of their enemies. [26] So Moses stood at the gate of the camp and shouted, "Everyone who is on the LORD's side come over here!"

Then the men of the Levi tribe gathered around Moses, [27] and he said to them, "The LORD God of Israel commands you to strap on your swords and go through the camp, killing your relatives, your friends, and your neighbours."

[28] The men of the Levi tribe followed his orders, and that day they killed about three thousand men. [29] Moses said to them, "You obeyed the LORD and did what was right, and so you will serve as his priests for the people of Israel. It was hard for you to kill your own sons and brothers, but the LORD has blessed you and made you his priests today."

See also: 32.1: Acts 7.40. 32.4: 1 King 12.28; Acts 7.41.
32.6: 1 Cor 10.7. 32.11-14: Num 14.13-19.
32.13: Gen 22.16,17; Gen 17.8.

30 The next day Moses told the people, "This is a terrible thing you have done. But I will go back to the LORD to see if I can do something to keep this sin from being held against you."

31 Moses returned to the LORD and said, "The people have committed a terrible sin. They have made a gold idol to be their god. 32 But I beg you to forgive them. If you don't, please wipe my name out of your book."*

33 The LORD replied, "I will wipe out of my book the name of everyone who has sinned against me. 34 Now take my people to the place I told you about, and my angel will lead you. But when the time comes, I will punish them for this sin."

35 So the LORD punished the people of Israel with a terrible disease for talking Aaron into making the gold idol.

The Lord makes promises, renews his agreement, and gives more laws to Israel

CHAPTER 33

The LORD tells Israel to leave Mount Sinai

1 The LORD said to Moses:

You led the people of Israel out of Egypt. Now get ready to lead them to the land I promised their ancestors Abraham, Isaac, and Jacob. 2-3 It is a land rich with milk and honey, and I will send an angel to force out those people who live there — the Canaanites, the Amorites, the Hittites, the Perizzites, the Hivites, and the Jebusites. I would go with my people, but they are so rebellious that I would destroy them before they get there.

4-5 Even before the LORD said these harsh things, he had told Moses, "These people really are rebellious, and I would kill them at once, if I went with them. But tell them to take off their jewellery, then I'll decide what to do with them." So the people started mourning, 6 and after leaving Mount Sinai,ᵇ they stopped wearing jewellery.

The LORD is with his people

7 Moses decided to set up a tent far from camp. He called it the "meeting tent", and whoever needed some message from the LORD would go there. 8 Each time Moses went out to the tent, everyone would stand at the entrance to their own tents and watch him enter.

9-11 Then they would bow down because a thick cloud would come down in front of the tent, and the LORD would speak to Moses face to face, just like a friend. Afterwards, Moses would return to camp, but his young assistant Joshuaᵃ would stay at the tent.

The LORD promises to be with his people

12 Moses said to the LORD, "I know that you have told me to lead these people to the land you promised them. But you have not told me who my assistant will be. You have said that you are my friend and that you are pleased with me. 13 If this is true, let me know what your plans are, then I can obey and continue to please you. And don't forget that you have chosen this nation to be your own."

14 The LORD said, "I will go with you and give you peace."

15 Then Moses replied, "If you aren't going with us, please don't make us leave this place. 16 But if you do go with us, everyone will know that you are pleased with your people and with me. That way, we will be different from the rest of the people on earth."

17 So the LORD told him, "I will do what you have asked, because I am your friend and I am pleased with you."

18 Then Moses said, "I pray that you will let me see you in all your glory."

19 The LORD answered:

All right. I am the LORD, and I show mercy and kindness to anyone I choose. I will let you see my glory and hear my holy name, 20 but I won't let you see my face, because anyone who sees my face will die. 21 There is a rock not far from me. Stand beside it, 22 and before I pass by in all my shining glory, I will put you in a large crack in the rock. I will cover your eyes with my hand until I have passed by. 23 Then I will take my hand away, and you will see my back. You will not see my face.

*32.32 your book: The people of Israel believed that the LORD kept a record of the names of his people, and anyone whose name was removed from that book no longer belonged to the LORD.

See also: 32.32: Psa 69.28; Rev 3.5. 33.1: a Gen 12.7; b Gen 26.3; c Gen 28.13.

See also: 33.19: Rom 9.15.

CHAPTER 34

The second set of commandments

This is also told in Deuteronomy 10.1–5

¹ One day the LORD said to Moses, "Cut two flat stones like the first ones I made, and I will write on them the same commandments that were on the two you broke. ² Be ready tomorrow morning to come up Mount Sinai and meet me at the top. ³ No one is to come with you or to be on the mountain at all. Don't even let the sheep and cattle graze at the foot of the mountain." ⁴ So Moses cut two flat stones like the first ones, and early the next morning he carried them to the top of Mount Sinai, just as the LORD had commanded.

⁵ The LORD God came down in a cloud and stood beside Moses there on the mountain. God spoke his holy name, "the LORD".*

⁶ Then he passed in front of Moses and called out, "I am the LORD God. I am merciful and very patient with my people. I show great love, and I can be trusted. ⁷ I keep my promises to my people for ever, but I also punish them and their children, and also their grandchildren and great-grandchildren."

⁸ Moses quickly bowed down to the ground and worshipped the LORD. ⁹ He prayed, "LORD, if you really are pleased with me, I pray that you will go with us. It is true that these people are sinful and rebellious, but forgive our sin and let us be your people."

A promise and its demands

This is also told in Exodus 23.14–19;
Deuteronomy 7.1–5; 16.1–17

¹⁰ The LORD said:

I promise to perform miracles for you that have never been seen anywhere on earth. Neighbouring nations will stand in fear and know that I was the one who did these marvellous things. ¹¹ I will force out the Amorites, the Canaanites, the Hittites, the Perizzites, the Hivites, and the Jebusites, but you must do what I command you today. ¹² Don't make treaties with any of those people. If you do, it will be like falling into a trap. ¹³ Instead, you must destroy their altars and tear down the sacred poles* they

use in the worship of the goddess Asherah. ¹⁴ I demand your complete loyalty — you must not worship any other god! ¹⁵ Don't make treaties with the people there, or you will soon find yourselves worshipping their gods and taking part in their sacrificial meals. ¹⁶ Your men will even marry their women and be influenced to worship their gods.

¹⁷ Don't make metal images of gods.

¹⁸ Don't fail to observe the Festival of Thin Bread in the month of Abib.* Obey me and eat bread without yeast for seven days during Abib, because that is the month you left Egypt.

¹⁹ The firstborn males of your families and of your flocks and herds belong to me. ²⁰ You can save the life of a firstborn donkey* by sacrificing a lamb; if you don't, you must break the donkey's neck. You must save every firstborn son.

Bring an offering every time you come to worship.

²¹ Do your work in six days and rest on the seventh day, even during the seasons for ploughing and harvesting. ²² Celebrate the Harvest Festival* each spring when you start harvesting your wheat, and celebrate the Festival of Shelters* each autumn when you pick your fruit.

²³ Your men must come to worship me three times a year, because I am the LORD God of Israel. ²⁴ I will force the nations out of your land and enlarge your borders. Then no one will try to take your property when you come to worship me these three times each year.

²⁵ When you sacrifice an animal on the altar, don't offer bread made with yeast. And don't save any part of the Passover meal for the next day.

²⁶ I am the LORD your God, and you must bring the first part of your harvest to the place of worship.

Don't boil a young goat in its mother's milk.

---

*34.5 the LORD: See the note at 3.14,15.
*34.13 sacred poles: Or "trees", used as symbols of Asherah, the goddess of fertility.

*34.18 Abib: See the note at 13.3,4.
*34.20 donkey: See the note at 13.13.
*34.22 Harvest Festival: See the note at 23.16.
*34.22 Festival of Shelters: See the note at 23.16.

See also: 34.6,7: Exod 20.5,6; Num 14.18; Deut 5.9,10; 7.9,10. 34.13: Deut 16.21.

See also: 34.17: Exod 20.4; Lev 19.4; Deut 5.8; 27.15.
34.18: Exod 12.14–20; Lev 23.6–8; Num 28.16–25.
34.19: Exod 13.2. 34.20: Exod 13.13. 34.21: Exod 20.9,10; 23.12; 31.15; 35.2; Lev 23.3; Deut 5.13,14.
34.22: a Lev 23.15–21; Num 28.26–31; b Lev 23.39–43.
34.25: Exod 12.10. 34.26: a Deut 26.2; b Deut 14.21.

27 The LORD told Moses to put these laws in writing, as part of his agreement with Israel. 28 Moses stayed on the mountain with the LORD for forty days and nights, without eating or drinking. And he wrote down the Ten Commandments, the most important part of God's agreement with his people.

Moses comes down from Mount Sinai

29 Moses came down from Mount Sinai, carrying the Ten Commandments. His face was shining brightly because the LORD had been speaking to him. But Moses did not know at first that his face was shining. 30 When Aaron and the others looked at Moses, they saw that his face was shining, and they were afraid to go near him. 31 Moses called out for Aaron and the leaders to come to him, and he spoke with them. 32 Then the rest of the people of Israel gathered around Moses, and he gave them the laws that the LORD had given him on Mount Sinai.

33 The face of Moses kept shining, and after he had spoken with the people, he covered his face with a veil. 34 Moses would always remove the veil when he went into the sacred tent to speak with the LORD. And when he came out, he would tell the people everything the LORD had told him to say. 35 They could see that his face was still shining. So after he had spoken with them, he would put the veil back on and leave it on until the next time he went to speak with the LORD.

CHAPTER 35

Laws for the Sabbath

1 Moses called together the people of Israel and told them that the LORD had said:

2 You have six days in which to do your work. But the seventh day must be dedicated to me, your LORD, as a day of rest. Whoever works on the Sabbath will be put to death. 3 Don't even build a cooking fire at home on the Sabbath.

Offerings and gifts for the sacred tent and the priestly clothes

Offerings for the sacred tent

This is also told in Exodus 25.1–9; 35.10–19

4 Moses told the people of Israel that the LORD had said:

5 I would welcome an offering from anyone who wants to give something. You may bring gold, silver, or bronze; 6 blue, purple, or red wool; fine linen; goat hair; 7 tanned ram skin or fine leather; acacia wood; 8 olive oil for the lamp; sweet-smelling spices for the oil of dedication and for the incense; or 9 onyx* stones or other gems for the sacred apron and breastpiece.

10 If you have any skills, you should use them to help make what I have commanded: 11 the sacred tent with its covering and hooks, its framework and crossbars, and its post and stands; 12 the sacred chest with its carrying poles, its place of mercy, and the curtain in front of it; 13 the table with all that goes on it, including the sacred bread; 14 the lamp with its equipment and oil; 15 the incense altar with its carrying poles and sweet-smelling incense; the ordination oil; the curtain for the entrance to the sacred tent; 16 the altar for sacrifices with its bronze grating, its carrying poles, and its equipment; the large bronze bowl with its stand; 17 the curtains with the posts and stands that go around the courtyard; 18 the pegs and ropes for the tent and the courtyard; 19 and the finely woven priestly clothes for Aaron and his sons.

Gifts for the LORD

20 Moses finished speaking, and everyone left. 21 Then those who wanted to bring gifts to the LORD, brought them to be used for the sacred tent, the worship services, and the priestly clothes. 22 Men and women came willingly and gave all kinds of gold jewellery such as pins, earrings, rings, and necklaces. 23 Everyone brought their blue, purple, and red wool, their fine linen, and their cloth made of goat hair, as well as their ram skins dyed red and their fine leather. 24 Anyone

---

See also: **34.29–35:** 2 Cor 3.7–16. **35.2:** Exod 20.8–11; 23.12; 31.15; 34.21; Lev 23.3; Deut 5.12–14.

*35.9 onyx: See the note at 25.7.

who had silver or bronze or acacia wood brought it as a gift to the LORD. ²⁵ The women who were good at weaving cloth brought the blue, purple, and red wool and the fine linen they had made. ²⁶ And the women who knew how to make cloth from goat hair were glad to do so.

²⁷ The leaders brought different kinds of jewels to be sewn on the special clothes and the breastpiece for the high priest. ²⁸ They also brought sweet-smelling spices to be mixed with the incense and olive oil that were for the lamps and for ordaining the priests. ²⁹ Moses had told the people what the LORD wanted them to do, and many of them decided to bring their gifts.

Bezalel and Oholiab

This is also told in Exodus 31.1–11

³⁰ Moses said to the people of Israel:

The LORD has chosen Bezalel* of the Judah tribe. ^{31–33} Not only has the LORD filled him with his Spirit, but he has given him wisdom and made him a skilled craftsman who can create objects of art with gold, silver, bronze, stone, and wood. ³⁴ The LORD is urging him and Oholiab* from the tribe of Dan to teach others. ³⁵ And he has given them all kinds of artistic skills, including the ability to design and embroider with blue, purple, and red wool and to weave fine linen.

CHAPTER 36

Moses said:

¹ The LORD has given to Bezalel, Oholiab, and others the skills needed for building a place of worship, and they will follow the LORD's instructions.

² Then Moses brought together these workers who were eager to work, ³ and he gave them the money that the people of Israel had donated for building the place of worship. In fact, so much money was being given each morning, ⁴ that finally everyone stopped working ⁵ and said, "Moses, there is already more money than we need for what the LORD has assigned us to do." ⁶ So Moses sent word for the people to stop giving, and they did. ⁷ But there was already more than enough to do what needed to be done.

Skilled workers make the sacred tent and its furnishings

The curtains and coverings for the sacred tent

This is also told in Exodus 26.1–14

^{8–9} The skilled workers got together to make the sacred tent and its linen curtains woven with blue, purple, and red wool and embroidered with figures of winged creatures. Each of the ten panels was twelve metres long and two metres wide, ¹⁰ and they were sewn together to make two curtains with five panels each. ^{11–13} Then fifty loops of blue cloth were put along one of the wider sides of each curtain, and the two curtains were fastened together at the loops with fifty gold hooks.

^{14–15} As the material for the tent, goat hair was used to weave eleven sections thirteen metres by two metres each. ¹⁶ These eleven sections were joined to make two panels, one with five and the other with six sections. ¹⁷ Fifty loops were put along one of the wider sides of each panel, ¹⁸ and the two panels were fastened at the loops with fifty bronze hooks. ¹⁹ Two other coverings were made — one with fine leather and the other with ram skins dyed red.

The framework for the sacred tent

This is also told in Exodus 26.15–30

²⁰ Acacia wood was used to build the framework for the walls of the sacred tent. ²¹ Each frame was four metres high and sixty-six centimetres wide ^{22–26} with two wooden pegs near the bottom. Then two silver stands were placed under each frame with sockets for the pegs, so they could be joined together. Twenty of these frames were used along the south side and twenty more along the north. ²⁷ Six frames were used for the back wall along the west side ^{28–29} with two more at the south-west and north-west corners. These corner frames were joined from top to bottom. Altogether, along the back wall there were eight frames with two silver stands under each of them.

^{31–33} Five crossbars were made for each of the wooden frames, with the centre crossbar running the full length of the wall. ³⁴ The frames and crossbars were covered with gold, and gold rings were attached to the frames to run the crossbars through.

The inside curtain for the sacred tent

This is also told in Exodus 26.31–37

35 They made the inside curtain* of fine linen woven with blue, purple, and red wool, and embroidered with figures of winged creatures. 36 They also made four acacia wood posts and covered them with gold. Then gold rings were fastened to the posts, which were set on silver stands.

37 For the entrance to the tent, they used a curtain of fine linen woven with blue, purple, and red wool and embroidered with fancy needlework. 38 They made five posts, covered them completely with gold, and set them each on a gold-covered bronze stand. Finally, they attached hooks for the curtain.

CHAPTER 37

The sacred chest

This is also told in Exodus 25.10–22

1 Bezalel built a chest of acacia wood one hundred and ten centimetres long, sixty-six centimetres wide, and sixty-six centimetres high. 2 He covered it inside and out with pure gold and put a gold edging around the top. 3 He made four gold rings and fastened one of them to each of the four legs of the chest. 4 Then he made two poles of acacia wood, covered them with gold, 5 and put them through the rings, so the chest could be carried by the poles.

6 The entire lid of the chest, which was also covered with pure gold, was the place of mercy.* 7–9 On each of the two ends of the chest he made a winged creature of hammered gold. They faced each other, and their wings covered the place of mercy.

The table for the sacred bread

This is also told in Exodus 25.23–30

10 Bezalel built a table of acacia wood eighty-eight centimetres long, forty-four centimetres wide, and sixty-six centimetres high. 11–12 He covered it with pure gold and put a gold edging around it with a border seventy-five millimetres wide.• 13 He made four gold rings and attached one to each of the legs 14 near the edging. The poles for carrying the table were placed through these rings 15 and were made of acacia wood

covered with gold. 16 Everything that was to be set on the table was made of pure gold — the bowls, plates, jars, and cups for wine offerings.

The lampstand

This is also told in Exodus 25.31–40

17 Bezalel made a lampstand of pure gold. The whole lampstand, including its decorative flowers, was made from a single piece of hammered gold, 18 with three branches on each of its two sides. 19 There were three decorative almond blossoms on each branch 20 and four on the stem. 21 There was also a blossom where each pair of branches came out from the stem. 22 The lampstand, including its branches and decorative flowers, was made from a single piece of hammered pure gold. 23–24 The lamp and its equipment, including the tongs and trays, were made of about thirty-five kilogrammes of pure gold.

The altar for burning incense

This is also told in Exodus 30.1–5

25 For burning incense, Bezalel made an altar of acacia wood. It was forty-five centimetres square and ninety centimetres high with each of its four corners sticking up like the horn of a bull. 26 He covered it with pure gold and put a gold edging around it. 27 Then below the edging on opposite sides he attached two gold rings through which he put the poles for carrying the altar. 28 These poles were also made of acacia wood and covered with gold.

The oil for dedication and the incense

This is also told in Exodus 30.22–38

29 Bezalel mixed the oil for dedication and the sweet-smelling spices for the incense.

CHAPTER 38

The altar for offering sacrifices

This is also told in Exodus 27.1–8

1 Bezalel built an altar of acacia wood for offering sacrifices. It was two and a quarter metres square and one and a third metres high 2 with each of its four corners sticking up like the horn of a bull, and it was completely covered with bronze. 3 The equipment for the altar was also made of bronze — the pans for the hot ashes, the

*36.35 inside curtain: Separating the holy place from the most holy place.

*37.6 place of mercy: See the note at 26.34.

See also: 37.29: Exod 30.22–38.

shovels, the meat forks, and the fire pans.
⁴ Half-way up the altar he built a ledge
around it and covered the bottom half of the
altar with a decorative bronze grating. ⁵ Then
he attached a bronze ring beneath the ledge
at the four corners to put the poles through.
⁶ He covered two acacia wood poles with
bronze and ⁷ put them through the rings for
carrying the altar, which was shaped like an
open box.

The large bronze bowl

This is also told in Exodus 30.18–21

⁸ Bezalel made a large bowl and a stand out of
bronze from the mirrors of the women who
helped at the entrance to the sacred tent.

The courtyard around the sacred tent

This is also told in Exodus 27.9–19

⁹⁻¹⁷ Around the sacred tent Bezalel built a
courtyard forty-four metres long on the south
and north and twenty-two metres wide on
the east and west. He used twenty bronze
posts on bronze stands for the south and
north and ten for the west. Then he hung a
curtain of fine linen on the posts along each
of these three sides by using silver hooks and
rods. He placed three bronze posts on each
side of the entrance at the east and hung a
curtain six and two thirds metres wide on
each set of posts.

¹⁸⁻¹⁹ For the entrance to the courtyard,
Bezalel made a curtain nine metres long,
which he hung on four bronze posts that
were set on bronze stands. This curtain was
the same height as the one for the rest of the
courtyard and was made of fine linen
embroidered with blue, purple, and red wool.
He hung the curtain on the four posts, using
silver hooks and rods. ²⁰ The
pegs for the tent and for the curtain around
the tent were made of bronze.

The sacred tent

²¹⁻²³ Bezalel had worked closely with
Oholiab,* who was an expert at designing and
engraving, and at embroidering blue, purple,
and red wool. The two of them completed
the work that the LORD had commanded.

Moses made Aaron's son Ithamar
responsible for keeping record of the metals
used for the sacred tent. ²⁴ According to the
official weights, the amount of gold given
was a thousand kilogrammes, ²⁵ and the

silver that was collected when the people
were counted* came to three thousand four
hundred and thirty kilogrammes. ²⁶ Everyone
who was counted paid the required amount,
and there was a total of 603,550 men who
were twenty years old or older.

²⁷ Thirty-four kilogrammes of the silver
were used to make each of the one hundred
stands for the sacred tent and the curtain.
²⁸ The remaining thirty kilogrammes of silver
were used for the hooks and rods and for
covering the tops of the posts.

²⁹ Two thousand four hundred and
twenty-five kilogrammes of bronze were
given. ³⁰ And it was used to make the stands
for the entrance to the tent, the altar and its
grating, the equipment for the altar, ³¹ the
stands for the posts that surrounded the
courtyard, including those at the entrance to
the courtyard, and the pegs for the tent and
the courtyard.

The priestly clothes are made

CHAPTER 39

Making the priestly clothes

This is also told in Exodus 28.1–14

¹ Beautiful priestly clothes were made of blue,
purple, and red wool for Aaron to wear when
he performed his duties in the holy place.
This was done exactly as the LORD had
commanded Moses.

²⁻³ The entire priestly apron was made of
fine linen, woven with blue, purple, and red
wool. Thin sheets of gold were hammered
out and cut into threads that were skilfully
woven into the apron. ⁴⁻⁵ It had two shoulder
straps to support it and a sash that fastened
around the waist. ⁶ Onyx* stones were placed
in gold settings, and each one was engraved
with the name of one of Israel's sons. ⁷ Then
these were attached to the shoulder straps of
the apron, so the LORD would never forget
his people. Everything was done exactly as
the LORD had commanded Moses.

---

*38.25 counted: See 30.11–16; Numbers 1.
*39.6 Onyx: See the note at 25.7.
See also: 38.26: Matt 17.24.

See also: 38.8: Exod 30.18. 38.25,26: Exod 30.11–16.

The breastpiece

This is also told in Exodus 28.15–30

[8] The breastpiece was made with the same materials and designs as the priestly apron. [9] It was twenty-two centimetres square and folded double [10] with four rows of three precious stones: a carnelian, a chrysolite, and an emerald were in the first row; [11] a turquoise, a sapphire, and a diamond were in the second row; [12] a jacinth, an agate, and an amethyst were in the third row; [13] a beryl, an onyx, and a jasper* were in the fourth row. They were mounted in a delicate gold setting, [14] and on each of them was engraved the name of one of the twelve tribes of Israel.

[15-18] Two gold rings were attached to the upper front corners of the breastpiece and fastened with two braided gold chains to gold settings on the shoulder straps. [19] Two other gold rings were attached to the lower inside corners next to the apron, [20] and two more near the bottom of the shoulder straps just above the sash. [21] To keep the breastpiece in place, a blue cord was used to tie the two lower rings on the breastpiece to those on the apron. These things were done exactly as the LORD had commanded Moses.

The clothes for the priests

This is also told in Exodus 28.31–43

[22] The priestly robe was made of blue wool [23] with an opening in the centre for the head. The material around the collar was bound so as to keep it from fraying. [24-26] Along the hem of the robe were woven pomegranates* of blue, purple, and red wool with a bell of pure gold between each of them. This robe was to be worn by Aaron when he performed his duties.

[27-29] Everything that Aaron and his sons wore was made of fine linen woven with blue, purple, and red wool, including their robes and turbans, their fine caps and underwear, and even their sashes that were embroidered with needlework.

[30] "Dedicated to the LORD" was engraved on a narrow strip of pure gold, [31] which was fastened to Aaron's turban. These things were done exactly as the LORD had commanded Moses.

The work is completed

This is also told in Exodus 35.10–19

[32] So the people of Israel finished making everything the LORD had told Moses to make. [33] Then they brought it all to Moses: the sacred tent and its equipment, including the hooks, the framework and crossbars, and its posts and stands; [34] the covering of tanned ram skins and fine leather; the inside curtain; [35] the sacred chest with its carrying poles and the place of mercy; [36] the table with all that goes on it, including the sacred bread; [37] the lampstand of pure gold, together with its equipment and oil; [38] the gold-covered incense altar; the ordination oil and the sweet-smelling incense; the curtain for the entrance to the tent; [39] the bronze altar for sacrifices with its bronze grating, its carrying poles, and its equipment; the large bronze bowl with its stand; [40] the curtain with its posts and cords, and its pegs and stands that go around the courtyard; everything needed for the sacred tent; [41] and the finely woven priestly clothes for Aaron and his sons.

[42-43] When Moses saw that the people had done everything exactly as the LORD had commanded, he gave them his blessing.

The sacred tent is set up

CHAPTER 40

[1] The LORD said to Moses:

[2] Set up my tent on the first day of the year* [3] and put the chest with the Ten Commandments behind the inside curtain* of the tent. [4] Bring in the table and set on it those things that are needed for it. Also bring in the lampstand and attach the lamps to it. [5] Then place the gold altar of incense in front of the sacred chest and hang a curtain at the entrance to the tent. [6] Set the altar for burning sacrifices in front of the entrance to my tent. [7] Put the large bronze bowl between the tent and the altar and fill the bowl with water. [8] Surround the tent and the altar with the wall of curtains and hang the curtain that was made for the entrance.

[9] Use the sacred olive oil to dedicate the tent and everything in it to me. [10] Do the same thing with the altar for offering sacrifices and its equipment [11] and with the

---

*39.13 jasper: For the stones mentioned in verses 10–13, see the note at 28.20.
*39.24–26 pomegranates: See the note at 28.33,34.

*40.2 first day of the year: See the note at 12.2.
*40.3 inside curtain: See the note at 36.35.

bowl and its stand. ¹² Bring Aaron and his sons to the entrance of the tent and make them wash themselves. ¹³ Dress Aaron in the priestly clothes, then use the sacred olive oil to ordain him and dedicate him to me as my priest. ¹⁴ Put the priestly robes on Aaron's sons ¹⁵ and ordain them in the same way, so they and their descendants will always be my priests.

¹⁶ Moses followed the LORD's instructions. ¹⁷ And on the first day of the first month* of the second year, the sacred tent was set up. ¹⁸ The posts, stands, and framework were put in place, ¹⁹ then the two layers of coverings were hung over them. ²⁰ The stones with the Ten Commandments written on them were stored in the sacred chest, the place of mercy* was put on top of it, and the carrying poles were attached. ²¹ The chest was brought into the tent and set behind the curtain in the most holy place. These things were done exactly as the LORD had commanded Moses.

²² The table for the sacred bread was put along the north wall of the holy place, ²³ after which the bread was set on the table. ²⁴ The lampstand was put along the south wall, ²⁵ then the lamps were attached to it there in the presence of the LORD. ²⁶ The gold incense altar was set up in front of the curtain, ²⁷ and sweet-smelling incense was burnt on it. These things were done exactly as the LORD had commanded Moses.

²⁸ The curtain was hung at the entrance to the sacred tent. ²⁹ Then the altar for offering sacrifices was put in front of the tent, and animal sacrifices and gifts of grain were offered there. ³⁰ The large bronze bowl was placed between the altar and the entrance to the tent. It was filled with water, ³¹ then Moses and Aaron, together with Aaron's sons, washed their hands and feet. ³² In fact, they washed each time before entering the tent or offering sacrifices at the altar. These things were done exactly as the LORD had commanded Moses.

³³ Finally, Moses had the curtain hung around the courtyard.

The glory of the LORD

³⁴ Suddenly the sacred tent was covered by a thick cloud and filled with the glory of the LORD. ³⁵ And so, Moses could not enter the tent. ³⁶ Whenever the cloud moved from the tent, the people would break camp and follow; ³⁷ then they would set up camp and stay there, until it moved again. ³⁸ No matter where the people travelled, the LORD was with them. Each day his cloud was over the tent, and each night a fire could be seen in the cloud.

Additional notes

*1.11 the king: The Hebrew text has "Pharaoh", a Hebrew word sometimes used for the title of the king of Egypt.

*2.5 the king's: See the note at 1.11.

*2.15 the king: See the note at 1.11.

*2.16 Jethro, the priest of Midian: Hebrew "the priest of Midian". But see 3.1; 4.18; 18.1,2–4 where his name is given. In the Hebrew of verse 18 he is spoken of as "Reuel", which may have been the name of the tribe to which Jethro belonged.

*3.1 Sinai: The Hebrew text has "Horeb", another name for Sinai.

*3.12 I will be with you . . . out of Egypt: Or "I will be with you. This bush is a sign that I am the one sending you, and it is a promise that you will worship me on this mountain after you have led my people out of Egypt."

*4.25 My dear son . . . you: Or "My dear husband, you are a man of blood" (meaning Moses).

*4.26 you are . . . circumcision: Or "you are a man of blood".

*4.27 Mount Sinai: Hebrew "the mountain of God".

*5.1 the king: See the note at 1.11.

*5.23 the king: See the note at 1.11.

*6.14 Jacob: The Hebrew text has "Israel", Jacob's name after God renamed him.

*6.29 the king: See the note at 1.11.

*7.8,9 the king: See the note at 1.11.

*7.14 The Egyptian king: See the note at 1.11.

*8.1 the king: See the note at 1.11.

*8.18 to do this: Or "to get rid of the gnats".

*8.19 the king: See the note at 1.11.

*8.20 the king: See the note at 1.11.

*9.1 the king: See the note at 1.11.

*9.10 the king: See the note at 1.11.

*9.13 the king: See the note at 1.11.

*9.32 wheat crops: The Hebrew text mentions two kinds of wheat.

*10.1 the king: See the note at 1.11.

*10.19 west wind: The Hebrew text has "wind from the sea", referring to the Mediterranean Sea (see verse 13).

*10.24 The king: See the note at 1.11.

*11.1 the king: See the note at 1.11.

*12.29 the king: See the note at 1.11.

*12.31 the king: See the note at 1.11.

*13.15 The king: See the note at 1.11.

*13.17 the king: See the note at 1.11.

---

*40.17 first month: See the note at 12.2.

*40.20 place of mercy: See the note at 26.34.

See also: 40.34: 1 King 8.10,11; Isa 6.4; Ezek 43.4,5; Rev 15.8.

’**14.2 Red Sea:** Hebrew *hayyam* "the Sea", understood as *yam suph*, "Sea of Reeds" (see also the note at 13.18).

’**14.3 The king:** See the note at 1.11.

’**14.8 proudly:** Or "victoriously".

’**14.25 stuck:** The Samaritan Hebrew text and two ancient translations; Hebrew "came off".

’**15.4 Egypt's king:** See the note at 1.11.

’**16.1 the western edge of the Sinai Desert:** Hebrew "the Sin Desert".

’**16.35,36 land:** The Hebrew text adds, "An omer is one tenth of an ephah." In the CEV "omer" is usually translated "two litres".

’**17.6 Sinai:** See the note at 3.1.

’**17.16 This . . . Lord:** One possible meaning for the difficult Hebrew text.

’**18.5,6 Mount Sinai:** See the note at 4.27.

’**20.23 in place of me:** Or "together with me".

’**21.6 at the place of worship:** The Hebrew text has "in the presence of God", which probably refers to the place where God was worshipped.

’**21.22 suffers a miscarriage:** Or "gives birth before her time".

’**22.5 graze:** Or "eat everything".

’**22.8 some judges:** Or "I".

’**22.9 the judges:** Or "I".

’**22.28 me:** Or "your judges".

’**22.29 Don't fail . . . me:** One possible meaning for the difficult Hebrew text.

’**23.2 everyone else is:** Or "the authorities are".

’**23.5 you:** One possible meaning for the difficult Hebrew text of verse 5.

’**25.24,25 a gold edging . . . wide:** Or "a gold edging around it seventy-five millimetres wide".

’**29.9 their sashes:** One ancient translation; Hebrew "the sashes of Aaron and his sons".

’**29.24 lift it all up:** Or "wave it all".

’**29.26 lift them up:** Or "wave them".

’**31.2 Bezalel:** Hebrew "Bezalel, son of Uri and grandson of Hur".

’**31.6 Oholiab:** Hebrew "Oholiab son of Ahisamach".

’**33.6 Mount Sinai:** See the notes at 3.1 and 4.27.

’**33.9–11 Joshua:** Hebrew "Joshua son of Nun".

’**35.30 Bezalel:** See the note at 31.2.

’**35.34 Oholiab:** See the note at 31.6.

’**37.11,12 a gold edging . . . wide:** See the note at 25.24,25.

’**38.21–23 Bezalel . . . Oholiab:** Hebrew "Bezalel son of Uri and grandson of Hur of the Judah tribe had worked closely with Oholiab son of Ahisamach from the tribe of Dan."

Leviticus

A quick look at this book

Leviticus tells how the Lord continued to give laws and instructions to Moses. The book's name is related to the word "Levite", a term referring to a person who belonged to the tribe of Levi. Levites were to be special servants of the Lord at the sacred tent, and the priests came from one of the Levite families. Much of the book deals with the responsibilities of the priests and other Levites, for example, sacrifices, gifts to the Lord, and religious festivals. But this book also contains laws about what animals could be used for food, what materials could be used for clothing, and how to care for the poor.

Most of the book is made up of laws, but it has a few stories telling what happened when the people or priests obeyed or disobeyed God's instructions. God was quick to punish those who rebelled, but he also made this promise to those who would obey him:

I will walk with you — I will be your God, and you will be my people. I am the LORD your God, and I rescued you from Egypt, so that you would never again be slaves. I have set you free; now walk with your heads held high.

(26.12,13)

Laws about sacrifices

CHAPTER 1

1-3 The LORD spoke to Moses from the sacred tent and gave him instructions for the community of Israel to follow when they offered sacrifices.

Sacrifices to please the LORD

The LORD said:

Sacrifices to please me* must be completely burnt on the bronze altar.*

Bulls or rams or goats* are the animals to be used for these sacrifices. If the animal is a bull, it must not have anything wrong with it. Lead it to the entrance of the sacred tent, and I will let you know if it is* acceptable to me. ⁴ Lay your hand on its head, and I will accept the animal as a sacrifice for taking away your sins.

⁵ After the bull is killed in my presence, some priests from Aaron's family will offer

---

*1.1-3 Sacrifices to please me: These sacrifices have traditionally been called "whole burnt offerings" because the whole animal was burnt on the altar. A main purpose of such sacrifices was to please the LORD with the smell of the sacrifice, and so in the CEV they are often called "sacrifices to please the LORD".
*1.1-3 bronze altar: This altar for offering sacrifices was in front of the entrance to the sacred tent; it was made of acacia wood covered with bronze. A smaller altar for offering incense was inside the tent; it was made of acacia wood covered with gold.

its blood to me by splattering it against the four sides of the altar.

⁶ Skin the bull and cut it up, ⁷ while the priests pile wood on the altar fire to make it start blazing. ⁸⁻⁹ Wash the bull's insides and hind legs, so the priests can lay them on the altar with the head, the fat, and the rest of the animal. A priest will then send all of it up in smoke with a smell that pleases me.

¹⁰ If you sacrifice a ram or a goat, it must not have anything wrong with it. ¹¹ Lead the animal to the north side of the altar, where it is to be killed in my presence. Then some of the priests will splatter its blood against the four sides of the altar.

¹²⁻¹³ Cut up the animal and wash its insides and hind legs. A priest will put these parts on the altar with the head, the fat, and the rest of the animal. Then he will send all of it up in smoke with a smell that pleases me.

¹⁴ If you offer a bird for this kind of sacrifice, it must be a dove or a pigeon. ¹⁵ A priest will take the bird to the bronze altar, where he will wring its neck and pull its head on the fire. Then he will drain out its blood on one side of the altar, ¹⁶ remove the bird's craw with what is in it,ᵛ and throw them on the ash heap at the east side of the altar.* ¹⁷ Finally, he will take the bird by its wings, tear it partially open,ᵛ and send it up in smoke with a smell that pleases me.

CHAPTER 2

Sacrifices to give thanks to the Lord

The Lord said:

¹ When you offer sacrifices to give thanks to me,* you must use only your finest flour. Put it in a dish, sprinkle olive oil and incense on the flour, ² and take it to the priests from Aaron's family. One of them will scoop up the incense together with a handful of the flour and oil. Then, to show that the whole offering belongs to me, the priest will lay this part on the bronze altar and send it up in smoke with a smell that pleases me. ³ The

rest of this sacrifice is for the priests; it is very holy because it was offered to me.

⁴ If you bake bread in an oven for this sacrifice, use only your finest flour, but without any yeast. You may make the flour into a loaf mixed with olive oil, or you may make it into thin wafers and brush them with oil.

⁵ If you cook bread in a shallow pan for this sacrifice, use only your finest flour. Mix it with olive oil, but do not use any yeast. ⁶ Then break the bread into small pieces and sprinkle them with oil. ⁷ If you cook your bread in a pan with a lid on it, you must also use the finest flour mixed with oil.

⁸ You may prepare sacrifices to give thanks in any of these three ways. Bring your sacrifice to a priest, and he will take it to the bronze altar*. ⁹ Then, to show that the whole offering belongs to me, the priest will lay part of it on the altar and send it up in smoke with a smell that pleases me. ¹⁰ The rest of this sacrifice is for the priests; it is very holy because it was offered to me.

¹¹ Yeast and honey must never be burnt on the altar, so don't ever mix either of these in a grain sacrifice. ¹² You may offer either of them separately,ᵛ when you present the first part of your harvest to me, but they must never be burnt on the altar.

¹³ Salt is offered when you make an agreement with me, so sprinkle salt on these sacrifices.

¹⁴ Freshly cut grain, either roasted or coarsely ground,ᵛ must be used when you offer the first part of your grain harvest. ¹⁵ You must mix in some olive oil and put incense on top, because this is a grain sacrifice. ¹⁶ A priest will sprinkle all the incense and some of the grain and oil on the altar and send them up in smoke to show that the whole offering belongs to me.

CHAPTER 3

Sacrifices to ask the Lord's blessing

The Lord said:

¹ When you offer sacrifices to ask my blessing,* you may offer either a bull or a

---

*1.16 ash heap at the east side of the altar: Ashes were piled here, then once a day they were taken to the ash heap outside the camp (see 4.11,12; 6.10,11).
*2.1 sacrifices to give thanks to me: These sacrifices have traditionally been called "grain offerings". A main purpose of such sacrifices was to thank the Lord with a gift of grain, and so in the CEV they are sometimes called "sacrifices to give thanks to the Lord".

*2.8 bronze altar: See the note at 1.1–3.
*3.1 sacrifices to ask my blessing: These sacrifices have traditionally been called "peace offerings" or "offerings of well-being". A main purpose was to ask for the Lord's blessing, and so in the CEV they are sometimes called "sacrifices to ask the Lord's blessing".

cow, but there must be nothing wrong with the animal. [2] Lead it to the entrance of the sacred tent, lay your hand on its head, and have it killed there. A priest from Aaron's family will splatter its blood against the four sides of the altar.

[3] Offer all the fat on the animal's insides, [4] as well as the lower part of the liver and the two kidneys with their fat. [5] Some of the priests will lay these pieces on the altar and send them up in smoke with a sacrifice that is offered to please me.*

[6] Instead of a bull or a cow, you may offer any sheep or goat that has nothing wrong with it. [7] If you offer a sheep, you must present it to me at the entrance to the sacred tent. [8] Lay your hand on its head and have it killed there. A priest will then splatter its blood against the four sides of the altar.

[9] Offer the fat on the tail, the tailbone, and the insides, [10] as well as the lower part of the liver and the two kidneys with their fat. [11] One of the priests will lay these pieces on the altar and send them up in smoke as a food offering for me.

[12] If you offer a goat, you must also present it to me [13] at the entrance to the sacred tent. Lay your hand on its head and have it killed there. A priest will then splatter its blood against the four sides of the altar.

[14] Offer all the fat on the animal's insides, [15] as well as the lower part of the liver and the two kidneys with their fat. [16] One of the priests will put these pieces on the altar and send them up in smoke as a food offering with a smell that pleases me.

All fat belongs to me. [17] So you and your descendants must never eat any fat or any blood, not even in the privacy of your own homes.' This law will never change.

CHAPTER 4

Sacrifices for sin

This is also told in Leviticus 6.24–30

[1] The LORD told Moses [2] to say to the community of Israel:

Offer a sacrifice to ask forgiveness when you sin by accidentally doing something I have told you not to do.

When the high priest sins

The LORD said:

[3] When the high priest sins, he makes everyone else guilty too. And so, he must sacrifice a young bull that has nothing wrong with it. [4] The priest will lead the bull to the entrance of the sacred tent, lay his hand on its head, and kill it there. [5] He will take a bowl of the blood inside the tent, [6] dip a finger in the blood, and sprinkle some of it seven times towards the sacred chest behind the curtain. [7] Then, in my presence, he will smear some of the blood on each of the four corners of the incense altar, before pouring out the rest at the foot of the bronze altar* near the entrance to the tent.

[8-10] The priest will remove the fat from the bull, just as he does when he sacrifices a bull to ask my blessing.* This includes the fat on the insides, as well as the lower part of the liver and the two kidneys with their fat. He will then send it all up in smoke.

[11-12] The skin and flesh of the bull, together with its legs, insides, and the food still in its stomach, are to be taken outside the camp and burnt on a wood fire near the ash heap.*

When the whole nation sins

The LORD said:

[13] When the nation of Israel disobeys me without meaning to, the whole nation is still guilty. [14] Once you realize what has happened, you must sacrifice a young bull to ask my forgiveness. Lead the bull to the entrance of the sacred tent, [15] where your tribal leaders will lay their hands on its head, before having it killed in my presence.

[16] The priest will take a bowl of the animal's blood inside the sacred tent, [17] dip a finger in the blood, and sprinkle some of it seven times towards the sacred chest behind the curtain. [18] Then, in my presence, he must smear some of the blood on each of the four corners of the incense altar, before pouring out the rest at the foot of the bronze altar* near the entrance to the tent. [19-21] After this, the priest will remove the fat from the bull and send it

---

*3.5 sacrifice . . . to please me: See the note at 1.1–3.

*4.7,18 incense altar . . . bronze altar: See the note at 1.1–3.
*4.8–10 to ask my blessing: See the note at 3.1.
*4.11,12 ash heap: See the note at 1.16.

up in smoke on the altar. Finally, he will burn its remains outside the camp, just as he did with the other bull. By this sacrifice the sin of the whole nation will be forgiven.

When a tribal leader sins

The LORD God said:

²² Any tribal leader who disobeys me without meaning to is still guilty. ²³ As soon as the leader realizes what has happened, he must sacrifice a goat* that has nothing wrong with it. ²⁴ This is a sacrifice for sin. So he will lay his hand on the animal's head, before having it killed in my presence at the north side of the bronze altar. ²⁵ The priest will dip a finger in the blood, smear some of it on each of the four corners of the altar, and pour out the rest at the foot of the altar. ²⁶ Then he must send all the fat up in smoke, just as he does when a sacrifice is offered to ask my blessing.* By this sacrifice the leader's sin will be forgiven.

When ordinary people sin

The LORD said:

²⁷ When any of you ordinary people disobey me without meaning to, you are still guilty. ²⁸ As soon as you realize what you have done, you must sacrifice a female goat that has nothing wrong with it. ²⁹ Lead the goat to the north side of the bronze altar and lay your hand on its head, before having it killed. ³⁰ Then a priest will dip a finger in the blood; he will smear some of it on each of the four corners of the altar and pour out the rest at the foot of the altar. ³¹ After this, the priest will remove all the fat, just as he does when an animal is sacrificed to ask my blessing.* The priest will then send the fat up in smoke with a smell that pleases me. This animal is sacrificed so that I will forgive you ordinary people when you sin.

³² If you offer a lamb instead of a goat as a sacrifice for sin, it must be a female that has nothing wrong with it. ³³ Lead the lamb to the altar and lay your hand on its head, before having it killed. ³⁴ The priest will dip a finger in the blood, smear some of it on each of the four corners of the

altar, and pour out the rest at the foot of the altar. ³⁵ After this, all the fat must be removed, just as when an animal is sacrificed to ask my blessing. Then the priest will send it up in smoke to me, together with a food offering, and your sin will be forgiven.

CHAPTER 5

The LORD said:

¹ If you refuse to testify in court about something you saw or know has happened, you have sinned and can be punished.

² You are guilty and unfit to worship me, if you accidentally touch the dead body of any kind of unclean animal.

³ You are guilty if you find out that you have accidentally touched any waste that comes from a human body.

⁴ You are guilty the moment you realize that you have made a hasty promise to do something good or bad.

⁵ As soon as you discover that you have committed any of these sins, you must confess what you have done. ⁶ Then you must bring a female sheep or goat to me as the price for your sin. A priest will sacrifice the animal, and you will be forgiven.

⁷ If you are poor and cannot afford to bring an animal, you may bring two doves or two pigeons. One of these will be a sacrifice to ask my forgiveness, and the other will be a sacrifice to please me.

⁸ Give both birds to the priest, who will offer one as a sacrifice to ask my forgiveness. He will wring its neck without tearing off its head, ⁹ splatter some of its blood on one side of the bronze altar, and drain out the rest at the foot of the altar. ¹⁰ Then he will follow the proper rules for offering the other bird as a sacrifice to please me.

You will be forgiven when the priest offers these sacrifices as the price for your sin.

¹¹ If you are so poor that you cannot afford doves or pigeons, you may bring one kilogramme of your finest flour. This is a sacrifice to ask my forgiveness, so don't sprinkle olive oil or sweet-smelling incense on it. ¹² Give the flour to a priest, who will scoop up a handful and send it up in smoke together with the other offerings. This is a reminder that all the flour belongs to me. ¹³ By offering this sacrifice, the

*4.26,31 sacrifice . . . blessing: See the note at 3.1.
See also: 4.27–31: Num 15.27,28.

priest pays the price for any of these sins you may have committed. The priest gets the rest of the flour, just as he does with grain sacrifices.

Sacrifices to make things right

This is also told in Leviticus 7.1-10

14-15 The LORD told Moses what the people must do to make things right when they find out they have cheated the LORD without meaning to:

If this happens, you must either sacrifice a ram that has nothing wrong with it or else pay the price of a ram with the official money used by the priests. In addition, you must pay what you owe plus a fine of twenty per cent. Then the priest will offer the ram as a sacrifice to make things right, and you will be forgiven.

17-19 If you break any of my commands without meaning to, you are still guilty, and you can be punished. When you realize what you have done, you must either bring to the priest a ram that has nothing wrong with it or else pay him for one. The priest will then offer it as a sacrifice to make things right, and you will be forgiven.

CHAPTER 6

Other sins that need sacrifices or payments

This is also told in Numbers 5.5-10

1-3 The LORD told Moses what the people must do when they commit other sins against the LORD:

You have sinned if you rob or cheat someone, if you keep back money or valuables left in your care, or if you find something and claim not to have it.

4 When this happens, you must return what doesn't belong to you 5 and pay the owner a fine of twenty per cent. 6-7 In addition, you must either bring to the priest a ram that has nothing wrong with it or else pay him for one. The priest will then offer it as a sacrifice to make things right, and you will be forgiven for what you did wrong.

Daily sacrifices

This is also told in Exodus 29.38-43; Numbers 28.1-8

8-9 The LORD told Moses to tell Aaron and his sons how to offer the daily sacrifices that are sent up in smoke to please the LORD:*

You must put the animal for the sacrifice on the altar in the evening and let it stay there all night. But make sure the fire keeps burning. 10 The next morning you will dress in your priestly clothes, including your linen underwear. Then clean away the ashes left by the sacrifices and pile them beside the altar. 11 Change into your everyday clothes, take the ashes outside the camp, and pile them in the special place.*

12 The fire must never go out, so put wood on it each morning. After this, you are to lay an animal on the altar next to the fat that you sacrifice to ask my blessing.* Then send it all up in smoke to me.

13 The altar fire must always be kept burning — it must never go out.

Sacrifices to give thanks to the LORD

The LORD said:

14 When someone offers a sacrifice to give thanks to me,* the priests from Aaron's family must bring it to the front of the bronze altar, 15 where one of them will scoop up a handful of the flour and oil, together with all the incense on it. Then, to show that the whole offering belongs to me, he will lay all of this on the altar and send it up in smoke with a smell that pleases me. 16-17 The rest of it is to be baked without yeast and eaten by the priests in the sacred courtyard of the sacred tent. This bread is very holy, just like the sacrifices for sin or for making things right, and I have given this part to the priests from what is offered to me on the altar.

18 Only the men in Aaron's family are allowed to eat this bread, and they must go through a ceremony to be made holy before touching it.* This law will never change.

---

*6.8,9 to please the LORD: See the note at 1.1-3.
*6.11 ashes . . . in the special place: See the note at 1.16.
*6.12 sacrifice to ask my blessing: See the note at 3.1.
*6.14 a sacrifice to give thanks to me: See the note at 2.1.

See also: 6.1-7: Num 5.5-8.

When priests are ordained

¹⁹ The LORD spoke to Moses ²⁰ and told him what sacrifices the priests must offer on the morning and evening of the day they are ordained:

It is the same as the regular morning and evening sacrifices — half a kilogramme of flour ²¹ mixed with olive oil and cooked in a shallow pan. The bread must then be crumbled into small pieces¹ and sent up in smoke with a smell that pleases me. ²²⁻²³ Each of Aaron's descendants who is ordained as a priest must perform this ceremony and make sure that the bread is completely burnt on the altar. None of it may be eaten!

Sacrifices for sin

This is also told in Leviticus 4.1,2

²⁴ The LORD told Moses ²⁵ how the priests from Aaron's family were to offer the sacrifice for sin:

This sacrifice is very sacred, and the animal must be killed in my presence at the north side of the bronze altar. ²⁶ The priest who offers this sacrifice must eat it in the sacred courtyard of the sacred tent, ²⁷ and anyone or anything that touches the meat will be holy.* If any of the animal's blood is splattered on the clothes of the priest, they must be washed in a holy place. ²⁸ If the meat was cooked in a clay pot, the pot must be destroyed,* but if it was cooked in a bronze pot, the pot must be scrubbed and rinsed with water.

²⁹ This sacrifice is very holy, and only the priests may have any part of it. ³⁰ None of the meat may be eaten from the sacrifices for sin that require blood to be brought into the sacred tent.* These sacrifices must be completely burnt.

CHAPTER 7

Sacrifices to make things right

This is also told in Leviticus 5.14–19

The LORD said:

¹ The sacrifice to make things right is very sacred. ² The animal must be killed in the same place where the sacrifice to please

me* is killed, and the animal's blood must be splattered against the four sides of the bronze altar. ³ Offer all the animal's fat, including the fat on its tail and on its insides, ⁴ as well as the lower part of the liver and the two kidneys with their fat. ⁵ One of the priests will lay these pieces on the altar and send them up in smoke to me. ⁶ This sacrifice for making things right is very holy. Only the priests may eat it, and they must eat it in a holy place.*

⁷ The ceremony for this sacrifice and the one for sin are alike, and the meat may be eaten only by the priest who performs this ceremony of forgiveness.

⁸ In fact, the priest who offers a sacrifice to please me* may keep the skin of the animal, ⁹ just as he may eat the bread from a sacrifice to give thanks to me.* ¹⁰ All other grain sacrifices — with or without olive oil in them — are to be divided equally among the priests of Aaron's family.

Sacrifices to ask the LORD's blessing

The LORD said:

¹¹ Here are the instructions for offering a sacrifice to ask my blessing:* ¹² If you offer it to give thanks, you must offer some bread together with it. Use the finest flour to make three kinds of bread without yeast — two in the form of loaves mixed with olive oil and one in the form of thin wafers brushed with oil. ¹³ You must also make some bread with yeast. ¹⁴ Give me one loaf or wafer from each of these four kinds of bread, after which they will belong to the priest who splattered the blood against the bronze altar.

¹⁵ When you offer an animal to ask a blessing from me or to thank me, the meat belongs to you, but it must be eaten the same day. ¹⁶ It is different with the sacrifices you offer when you make me a promise or voluntarily give me something. The meat from those sacrifices may be kept and eaten the next day, ¹⁷⁻¹⁸ but any that is left must be destroyed. If you eat any after the second day, your sacrifice will be useless and unacceptable, and you will be both disgusting and guilty.

6.28 clay pot . . . destroyed: Juice from the meat cannot be completely cleaned from a clay pot.
6.30 that require blood . . . tent: See 4.1–21.

7.2,8 sacrifice to please me: See the note at 1.1–3.
7.6 holy place: The courtyard of the sacred tent (see 6.16,17).
7.9 sacrifice to give thanks to me: See the note at 2.1.
7.11 sacrifice to ask my blessing: See the note at 3.1.

¹⁹ Don't eat any of the meat that touches something unclean. Instead, burn it. The rest of the meat may be eaten by anyone who is clean and acceptable to me. ²⁰⁻²¹ But don't eat any of this meat if you have become unclean by touching something unclean from a human or an animal or from any other creature. If you do, you will no longer belong to the community of Israel.

²² The LORD told Moses ²³ to say to the people:

Don't eat the fat of cattle, sheep, or goats. ²⁴ If one of your animals dies or is killed by some wild animal, you may do anything with its fat except eat it. ²⁵ If you eat the fat of an animal that can be used as a sacrifice to me, you will no longer belong to the community of Israel. ²⁶ And no matter where you live, you must not eat the blood of any bird or animal, ²⁷ or you will no longer belong to the community of Israel.

²⁸ The LORD also told Moses ²⁹⁻³⁰ to say to the people of Israel:

If you want to offer a sacrifice to ask my blessing, you must bring the part to be burnt and lay it on the bronze altar. But you must first lift up⁺ the choice ribs with their fat to show that the offering is dedicated to me. ³¹ A priest from Aaron's family will then send the fat up in smoke, but the ribs belong to the priests. ³²⁻³³ The upper joint of the right hind leg is for the priest who offers the blood and the fat of the animal. ³⁴ I have decided that the people of Israel must always give the choice ribs and the upper joint of the right hind leg to Aaron's descendants ³⁵ who have been ordained as priests to serve me. ³⁶ This law will never change. I am the LORD!

³⁷ These are the ceremonies for sacrifices to please the LORD, to give him thanks, and to ask his blessing or his forgiveness, as well as the ceremonies for those sacrifices that demand a payment and for the sacrifices that are offered when priests are ordained. ³⁸ While Moses and the people of Israel were in the desert at Mount Sinai, the LORD commanded them to start offering these sacrifices.

Ordaining the priests

CHAPTER 8

The ceremony for ordaining priests
This is also told in Exodus 29.1–37

¹ The LORD said to Moses:

² Send for Aaron and his sons, as well as their priestly clothes, the oil for ordination, the bull for the sin offering, the two rams, and a basket of bread made without yeast. ³ Then bring the whole community of Israel together at the entrance to the sacred tent.

⁴ Moses obeyed the LORD, and when everyone had come together, he said, "We are here to follow the LORD's instructions."

⁶ After Moses told Aaron and his sons to step forward, he made them wash themselves. ⁷ He put the priestly shirt and robe on Aaron and wrapped the sash around his waist. Then he put the sacred apron on Aaron and fastened it with the finely woven belt. ⁸ Next, he put on Aaron the sacred breastpiece that was used in learning what the LORD wanted his people to do. ⁹ He placed the turban on Aaron's head, and on the front of the turban was the narrow strip of thin gold as a sign of his dedication to the LORD.

¹⁰ Moses then dedicated the sacred tent and everything in it to the LORD by sprinkling them with some of the oil for ordination. ¹¹ He sprinkled the bronze altar seven times, and he sprinkled its equipment, as well as the large bronze bowl and its base. ¹² He also poured some of the oil on Aaron's head to dedicate him to the LORD. ¹³ At last, Moses dressed Aaron's sons in their shirts, then tied sashes around them and put special caps on them, just as the LORD had commanded.

¹⁴ Moses led out the bull that was to be sacrificed for sin, and Aaron and his sons laid their hands on its head. ¹⁵ After it was killed, Moses dipped a finger in the blood and smeared some of it on each of the four corners of the bronze altar, before pouring out the rest at the foot of the altar. This purified the altar and made it a fit place for offering the sacrifice for sin. ¹⁶ Moses then took the fat on the bull's insides, as well as the lower part of the liver and the two kidneys with their fat, and sent them up in smoke on the altar fire. ¹⁷ Finally, he took the skin and the flesh of the bull, together with the food

See also: 7.26,27; Gen 9.4; Lev 17.10–14; 19.26; Deut 12.16,23; 15.23.

96

still in its stomach, and burnt them outside the camp, just as the LORD had commanded.

18 Moses led out the ram for the sacrifice to please the LORD.* After Aaron and his sons had laid their hands on its head, 19 Moses killed the ram and splattered its blood against the four sides of the altar. 20-21 Moses had the animal cut up, and he washed its insides and hind legs. Then he laid the head, the fat, and the rest of the ram on the altar and sent them up in smoke with a smell that pleased the LORD. All this was done just as the LORD had commanded.

22 Moses led out the ram for the ceremony of ordination. Aaron and his sons laid their hands on its head, 23 and it was killed. Moses smeared some of its blood on Aaron's right ear lobe, some on his right thumb, and some on the big toe of his right foot. 24 Moses did the same thing for Aaron's sons, before splattering the rest of the blood against the four sides of the altar. 25 He took the animal's fat tail, the fat on its insides, and the lower part of the liver and the two kidneys with their fat, and the right hind leg. 26 Then he took from a basket some of each of the three kinds of bread* that had been made without yeast and had been dedicated to the LORD.

27 Moses placed the bread on top of the meat and gave it all to Aaron and his sons, who lifted it up⸵ to show that it was dedicated to the LORD. 28 After this, Moses placed it on the fires of the altar and sent it up in smoke with a smell that pleased the LORD. This was part of the ordination ceremony. 29 Moses lifted up⸵ the choice ribs of the ram to show that they were dedicated to the LORD. This was the part that the LORD had said Moses could have.

30 Finally, Moses sprinkled the priestly clothes of Aaron and his sons with some of the oil for ordination and with some of the blood from the altar. So Aaron and his sons, together with their priestly clothes, were dedicated to the LORD.

31 Moses said to Aaron and his sons:

The LORD told me that you must boil this meat at the entrance to the sacred tent and eat it there with the bread. 32 Burn what is left over 33 and stay near the entrance to the sacred tent until the ordination ceremony ends seven days from now. 34 We have obeyed the LORD in everything that has been done today, so that your sins may be forgiven.⸵ 35 The LORD has told me that you must stay near the entrance to the tent for seven days and nights, or else you will die.

36 Aaron and his sons obeyed everything that the LORD had told Moses they must do.

Aaron's first sacrifices

CHAPTER 9

1 Eight days later Moses called together Aaron, his sons, and Israel's leaders. 2 Then he said to Aaron:

Find a young bull and a ram that have nothing wrong with them. Offer the bull to the LORD as a sacrifice for sin and the ram as a sacrifice to please him.*

3 Tell the people of Israel that they must offer sacrifices as well. They must offer a goat* as a sacrifice for sin, and a bull and a ram as a sacrifice to please the LORD. The bull and the ram must be a year old and have nothing wrong with them. 4 Then the people must offer a bull and a ram as a sacrifice to ask the LORD's blessing* and also a grain sacrifice* mixed with oil. Do this, because the LORD will appear to you today.

5 After the animals and the grain had been brought to the front of the sacred tent, and the people were standing there in the presence of the LORD, 6 Moses said:

The LORD has ordered you to do this, so that he may appear to you in all his glory. 7 Aaron, step up to the altar and offer the sacrifice to please the LORD, then offer the sacrifices for the forgiveness of your sins and for the sins of the people, just as the LORD has commanded.

8 Aaron stepped up to the altar and killed the bull that was to be the sacrifice for his sins. 9 His sons brought him the blood. He dipped a finger in it, smeared some on the four corners of the bronze altar, and poured out the rest at its foot. 10 But he sent up in smoke the fat, the kidneys, and the lower part of the

---

*8.18 sacrifice to please the LORD: See the note at 1.1-3.
*8.26 three kinds of bread: Made from the finest wheat flour; olive oil was mixed into part of the dough, and some of it was made into thin wafers brushed with oil (see Exodus 29.2,3).

*9.2 sacrifice to please him: See the note at 1.1-3.
*9.4 to ask the LORD's blessing: See the note at 3.1.
*9.4 grain sacrifice: To give thanks to the LORD (see the note at 2.1).
See also: 9.7: Heb 7.27.

liver, just as the LORD had commanded
Moses. ¹¹ Then Aaron burnt the skin and the
flesh outside the camp.

¹² After Aaron had killed the ram that was
sacrificed to please the LORD, Aaron's sons
brought him the blood, and he splattered it
against all four sides of the altar. ¹³ They
brought him each piece of the animal,
including the head, and he burnt them all on
the altar. ¹⁴ He washed the insides and the
hind legs and also sent them up in smoke.

¹⁵ Next, Aaron sacrificed the goat for the
sins of the people, as he had done with the
sacrifice for his own sins. ¹⁶ And so, he burnt
this sacrifice on the altar in the proper way.
¹⁷ He also presented the grain sacrifice and
burnt a handful of the flour on the altar as
part of the morning sacrifice.

¹⁸ At last, he killed the bull and the ram as a
sacrifice to ask the LORD's blessing on the
people. Aaron's sons brought him the blood,
and he splattered it against the four sides of
the altar. ¹⁹ His sons placed all the fat, as well
as the kidneys and the lower part of the liver
²⁰ on top of the choice ribs. ²¹ Then Aaron
burnt the fat on the altar and lifted up* these
ribs and the right hind leg to show that these
were dedicated to the LORD. This was done
just as the LORD had instructed Moses.

²² Aaron held out his hand and gave the
people his blessing, before coming down
from the bronze altar where he had offered
the sacrifices. ²³ He and Moses went into the
sacred tent, and when they came out, they
gave the people their blessing. Then the LORD
appeared to the people in all his glory. ²⁴ The
LORD sent fiery flames that burnt up
everything on the altar, and when everyone
saw this, they shouted and fell to their knees
to worship the LORD.

Two priests are killed

CHAPTER 10

Nadab and Abihu

¹ Nadab and Abihu were two of Aaron's sons,
but they disobeyed the LORD by burning
incense to him on a fire pan, when they were
not supposed to.* ² Suddenly the LORD sent
fiery flames and burnt them to death. ³ Then
Moses told Aaron that this was exactly what
the LORD had meant when he said:

"I demand respect
 from my priests,

and I will be praised
 by everyone!"

Aaron was speechless.

⁴ Moses sent for Mishael and Elzaphan, the
two sons of Aaron's uncle Uzziel. Then he
told them, "Take these two dead relatives of
yours outside the camp far from the entrance
to the sacred tent." ⁵ So they dragged the
dead men away by their clothes.

⁶ Then Moses told Aaron and his other two
sons, Eleazar and Ithamar:

Don't show your sorrow by leaving your
hair uncombed and tearing your priestly
clothes, or the LORD will get angry. He will
kill the three of you and punish everyone
else. It's all right for your relatives, the
people of Israel, to mourn for those he
destroyed by fire. ⁷ But you are the LORD's
chosen priests, and you must not leave the
sacred tent, or you will die.

Aaron and his two sons obeyed Moses.

⁸ The LORD said to Aaron:

⁹ When you or your sons enter the sacred
tent, you must never drink beer or wine. If
you do, you will die there! This law will
never change. ¹⁰ You must learn the
difference between what is holy and what
isn't holy and between the clean and the
unclean. ¹¹ You must also teach the people
of Israel everything that I commanded
Moses to say to them.

¹² Moses told Aaron and his two sons, Eleazar
and Ithamar:

The grain sacrifice that was offered to give
thanks to the LORD* is very holy. So make
bread without yeast from the part that
wasn't sent up in smoke and eat it beside
the altar. ¹³ The LORD has said that this
belongs to you and your sons, and that it
must be eaten in a holy place. ¹⁴⁻¹⁵ But the
choice ribs and the hind leg that were lifted
up* may be eaten by your entire family, as
long as you do so in an acceptable place.*
These parts are yours from the sacrifices
that the people offer to ask the LORD's
blessing.* This is what the LORD has
commanded, and it will never change.

*10.12 grain sacrifice . . . to give thanks to the
LORD: See the note at 2.1.
*10.14,15 acceptable place: See 6.24–30.
*10.14,15 to ask the LORD's blessing: See the note
at 3.1.

See also: 9.18: Lev 3.1–11. 9.22: Num 6.22–26.

See also: 10.12,13: Lev 6.14–18. 10.14,15: Lev 7.30–34.

16 When Moses asked around and learnt that the ram for the sin sacrifice had already been burnt on the altar, he became angry with Eleazar and Ithamar and said, 17 "Why didn't you eat the meat from this sacrifice in an acceptable place? It is very holy, and the LORD has given you this sacrifice to remove Israel's sin and guilt. 18 Whenever an animal's blood isn't brought into the sacred tent, I commanded you to eat its meat in an acceptable place, but you burnt it instead."

19 Their father Aaron replied, "Today two of my sons offered the sacrifice for sin and the sacrifice to please the LORD, and look what has happened to me! Would the LORD have approved if I had eaten the sacrifice for sin?"

20 Moses was satisfied with Aaron's reply.

Laws about what is clean and unclean

CHAPTER 11

Clean and unclean animals

This is also told in Deuteronomy 14.3–21

1 The LORD told Moses and Aaron 2 to say to the community of Israel:

You may eat 3 any animal that has divided hoofs and chews the cud.* 4-8 But you must not eat animals such as camels, rock badgers, and rabbits that chew the cud but don't have divided hoofs. And you must not eat pigs — they have divided hoofs, but don't chew the cud. All these animals are unclean,* and you are forbidden even to touch their dead bodies.

9-12 You may eat anything that lives in water and has fins and scales. But it would be disgusting for you to eat anything else that lives in water, and you must not even touch their dead bodies.

13-19 Eagles, vultures, buzzards, crows, ostriches, hawks, seagulls, owls, pelicans, storks, herons, hoopoes,• and bats are also disgusting, and you are forbidden to eat any of them.

20-23 The only winged insects you may eat are locusts, grasshoppers, and crickets. All other winged insects that crawl are too disgusting for you to eat.

24-28 Don't even touch the dead bodies of animals that have divided hoofs but don't chew the cud. And don't touch the dead bodies of animals that have paws. If you do, you must wash your clothes, but you are still unclean until evening.

29-30 Moles, rats, mice, and all kinds of lizards are unclean. 31 Anyone who touches their dead bodies or anything touched by their dead bodies becomes unclean until evening. 32 If something made of wood, cloth, or leather touches one of their dead bodies, it must be washed, but it is still unclean until evening. 33 If any of these animals is found dead in a clay pot, the pot must be broken to pieces, and everything in it becomes unclean. 34 If you pour water from this pot on any food, that food becomes unclean, and anything drinkable in the pot becomes unclean.

35 If the dead body of one of these animals touches anything else, including ovens and stoves, that thing becomes unclean and must be destroyed. 36 A spring or a cistern where one of these dead animals is found is still clean, but anyone who touches the animal becomes unclean. 37 If the dead body of one of these animals is found lying on seeds that have been set aside for planting, the seeds remain clean. 38 But seeds that are soaking in water become unclean, if the dead animal is found in the water.

39 If an animal that may be eaten happens to die, and you touch it, you become unclean until evening. 40 If you eat any of its meat or carry its body away, you must wash your clothes, but you are still unclean until evening.

41-42 Don't eat any of those disgusting little creatures that crawl or walk close to the ground. 43 If you eat any of them, you will become just as disgusting and unclean as they are. 44 I am the LORD your God, and you must dedicate yourselves to me and be holy, just as I am holy. Don't become disgusting by eating any of these unclean

---

*11.3 chews the cud: Some animals that eat grass and leaves have more than one stomach and chew their food a second time after it has been partly digested in the first stomach. This partly digested food is called the "cud."

*11.4–8 unclean: In the Old Testament "clean" and "unclean" refer to whatever makes a person, animal, or object acceptable or unacceptable to God. For example, a person became unclean by eating certain foods, touching certain objects, and having certain kinds of diseases or bodily discharges.

See also: 10.17; Lev 6.24–26.

See also: 11.44: Lev 19.2; 1 Pet 1.16.

creatures. 45 I brought you out of Egypt so that I could be your God. Now you must become holy, because I am holy!

46-47 I have given these laws so that you will know what animals, birds, and fish are clean and may be eaten, and which ones are unclean and may not be eaten.

CHAPTER 12

What women must do after giving birth

1 The LORD told Moses 2 to say to the community of Israel:

If a woman gives birth to a son, she is unclean for seven days, just as she is during her monthly period. 3 Her son must be circumcised on the eighth day, 4 but her loss of blood keeps her from being completely clean for another thirty-three days. During this time she must not touch anything holy or go to the place of worship. 5 Any woman who gives birth to a daughter is unclean for two weeks, just as she is during her period. And she won't be completely clean for another sixty-six days.

6 When the mother has completed her time of cleansing, she must come to the front of the sacred tent and bring to the priest a year-old lamb as a sacrifice to please me* and a dove or a pigeon as a sacrifice for sin. 7 After the priest offers the sacrifices to me, the mother will become completely clean from her loss of blood, whether her child is a boy or a girl. 8 If she cannot afford a lamb, she can offer two doves or two pigeons, one as a sacrifice to please me and the other as a sacrifice for sin.

CHAPTER 13

Skin diseases

1 The LORD told Moses and Aaron to say to the people:

2 If sores or boils or a skin rash should break out and start spreading on your body, you must be brought to Aaron or to one of the other priests. 3 If the priest discovers that the hair in the infected area has turned white and that the infection

seems more than skin deep, he will say, "This is leprosy* — you are unclean."

4 But if the infected area is white and only skin deep, and if the hair in it hasn't turned white, the priest will order you to stay away from everyone else for seven days. 5 If the disease hasn't spread by that time, he will order you to stay away from everyone else for another seven days. 6 Then if the disease hasn't got any worse or spread, the priest will say, "You are clean. It was only a sore. After you wash your clothes, you may go home."

7 However, if the disease comes back, you must return to the priest. 8 If it is discovered that the disease has started spreading, he will say, "This is leprosy — you are unclean."

9 Any of you with a skin disease must be brought to a priest. 10 If he discovers that the sore spot is white with pus and that the hair around it has also turned white, 11 he will say, "This is leprosy. You are unclean and must stay away from everyone else."

12-13 But if the disease has run its course and only the scars remain, he will say, "You are clean." 14-15 If the sores come back and turn white with pus, he will say, "This is leprosy — you are unclean."

16-17 However, if the sores heal and only white spots remain, the priest will say, "You are now clean."

18-19 If you have a sore that either swells or turns reddish-white after it has healed, then you must show it to a priest. 20 If he discovers that the hair in the infected area has turned white and that the infection seems more than skin deep, he will say, "This is leprosy — you are unclean." 21 But if the white area is only on the surface of the skin and hasn't got any worse, and if the hair in it hasn't turned white, he will make you stay away from everyone else for seven days.

22 If the sore begins spreading during this time, the priest will say, "You are unclean because you have a disease." 23 But if it doesn't spread, and only a scar remains, he will say, "You are now clean."

24 If you have a burn that gets infected and turns red or reddish-white, 25 a priest must examine it. Then if he discovers that the hair in the infected area has turned white and that the infection seems more than skin deep, he will say, "The burn has turned into leprosy, and you are unclean."

---

*12.6 sacrifice to please me: See the note at 1.1–3.
See also: 12.3: Gen 17.12; Luke 2.21. 12.8: Luke 2.24.

*13.3 leprosy: The word translated "leprosy" was used for many different kinds of skin diseases.

26 But if the priest finds that the hair in the infected area hasn't turned white and that the sore is only skin deep and it is healing, he will make you stay away from everyone else for seven days. 27 On the seventh day the priest will examine you again, and if the infection is spreading, he will say, "This is leprosy — you are unclean." 28 However, if the infection hasn't spread and has begun to heal, and if only a scar remains from the burn, and you are clean."

29 If you have a sore on your head or chin, 30 it must be examined by a priest. If the infection seems more than skin deep, and the hair in it has thinned out and lost its colour, he will say, "This is leprosy — you are unclean." 31 On the other hand, if he discovers that the itchy spot is only skin deep, but that the hair still isn't healthy, he will order you to stay away from everyone else for seven days. 32 By that time, if the itch hasn't spread, if the hairs seem healthy, and if the itch is only skin deep, 33 you must shave off the hairs around the infection, but not those on it. Then the priest will tell you to stay away from everyone else for another seven days. 34 By that time, if the itch hasn't spread and seems no more than skin deep, he will say, "You are clean; now you must wash your clothes."

35-36 Later, if the itch starts spreading, even though the hair is still healthy, the priest will say, "You are unclean." 37 But if he thinks you are completely well, he will say, "You are clean."

38 If white spots break out on your skin, 39 but the priest discovers that it is only a rash, he will say, "You are clean."

40-41 If you become bald on any part of your head, you are still clean. 42-43 But if a priest discovers that a reddish-white sore has broken out on the bald spot and looks like leprosy, he will say, 44 "This is leprosy — you are unclean."

45 If you ever have leprosy, you must tear your clothes, leave your hair uncombed, cover the lower part of your face, and go around shouting, "I'm unclean! I'm unclean!" 46 As long as you have the disease, you are unclean and must live alone outside the camp.

47-50 If a greenish or reddish spot* appears anywhere on any of your clothing or on anything made of leather, you must let the priest examine the clothing or the leather. He will put it aside for seven days, 51 and if the mildew has spread in that time, he will say, "This is unclean 52 because the mildew has spread." Then he will burn the clothing or the piece of leather.

53 If the priest discovers that the mildew hasn't spread, 54 he will tell you to wash the clothing or leather and put it aside for another seven days, 55 after which he will examine it again. If the spot hasn't spread, but is still greenish or reddish, the clothing or leather is unclean and must be burnt. 56 But if the spot has faded after being washed, he will tear away the spot. 57 Later, if the spot reappears elsewhere on the clothing or the leather, you must burn it. 58 Even if the spot completely disappears after being washed, it must be washed again before it is clean.

59 These are the rules for deciding if clothing is clean or unclean after a spot appears on it.

CHAPTER 14

The ceremony for people healed of leprosy

1 The LORD told Moses to say to the people:

2-3 After you think you are healed of leprosy,* you must ask for a priest to come outside the camp and examine you. And if you are well, 4 he will order someone to bring out two live birds that are acceptable for sacrifice, together with a stick of cedar wood, a piece of red yarn, and a branch from a hyssop plant. 5 The priest will order someone to kill one of the birds over a clay pot of spring water. 6 Then he will dip the other bird, the cedar, the red yarn, and the hyssop in the blood of the dead bird. 7 Next, he will sprinkle you seven times with the blood and say, "You are now clean." Finally, he will release the bird and let it fly away.

8 After this you must wash your clothes, shave your entire body, and take a bath before you are completely clean. You may move back into camp, but you must not enter your tent for seven days. 9 Then you must once again shave your head, face, and eyebrows, as well as the hair on the rest of your body. Finally, wash your

---

*13.47-50 spot: The Hebrew word translated "spot" and "mildew" in verses 47-59 is the same one translated "leprosy" earlier in the chapter.

*14.2,3 leprosy: See the note at 13.3.

See also: 14.2: Matt 8.4; Mark 1.44; Luke 5.14; 17.14.

clothes and take a bath, and you will be completely clean.

¹⁰ On the eighth day you must bring to the priest two rams and a year-old female lamb that have nothing wrong with them; also bring a third of a litre of olive oil and three kilogrammes of your finest flour mixed with oil. ¹¹ Then the priest will present you and your offerings to me at the entrance to my sacred tent. ¹² There he will offer one of the rams, together with the one third of a litre of oil, as a sacrifice to make things right.* He will also lift them up* to show that they are dedicated to me. ¹³ This sacrifice is very holy. It belongs to the priest and must be killed in the same place where animals are killed as sacrifices for sins and as sacrifices to please me.*

¹⁴ The priest will smear some of the blood from this sacrifice on your right ear lobe, some on your right thumb, and some on the big toe of your right foot. ¹⁵ He will then pour some of the olive oil into the palm of his left hand, ¹⁶ dip a finger of his right hand into the oil, and sprinkle some of it seven times towards the sacred tent. ¹⁷ Next, he will smear some of the oil on your right ear lobe, some on your right thumb, and some on the big toe of your right foot, ¹⁸⁻²⁰ and pour the rest of the oil from his palm on your head. Then he will offer the other two animals — one as a sacrifice for sin and the other as a sacrifice to please me, together with a grain sacrifice. After this you will be completely clean.

²¹ If you are poor and cannot afford to offer this much, you may offer a ram as a sacrifice to make things right, together with a third of a litre of olive oil and one kilogramme of flour mixed with oil as a grain sacrifice. The priest will then lift these up* to dedicate them to me. ²² Depending on what you can afford, you must also offer either two doves or two pigeons, one as a sacrifice for sin and the other as a sacrifice to please me. ²³ The priest will offer these to me in front of the sacred tent on the eighth day.

²⁴⁻²⁵ The priest will kill this ram for the sacrifice to make things right, and he will lift it up* with the olive oil in dedication to me. Then he will smear some of the blood on your right ear lobe, some on your right thumb, and some on the big toe of your right foot.

²⁶ The priest will pour some of the olive oil into the palm of his left hand, ²⁷ then dip a finger of his right hand in the oil and sprinkle some of it seven times towards the sacred tent. ²⁸ He will smear some of the oil on your right ear lobe, some on your right thumb, and some on the big toe of your right foot, just as he did with the blood of the sacrifice to make things right. ²⁹⁻³¹ And he will pour the rest of the oil from his palm on your head.

Then, depending on what you can afford, he will offer either the doves or the pigeons together with the grain sacrifice. One of the birds is the sacrifice for sin, and the other is the sacrifice to please me. After this you will be completely clean.

³² These are the things you must do if you have leprosy and cannot afford the usual sacrifices to make you clean.

When mildew is in a house

³³ The LORD told Moses and Aaron to say to the people:

³⁴ After I have given you the land of Canaan as your permanent possession, here is what you must do, if I ever put mildew* on the walls of any of your homes. ³⁵ First, you must say to a priest, "I think mildew is on the wall of my house."

³⁶ The priest will reply, "Empty the house before I inspect it, or else everything in it will be unclean."

³⁷ If the priest discovers greenish or reddish spots that go deeper than the surface of the walls, ³⁸ he will have the house closed for seven days. ³⁹ Then he will return and check to see if the mildew has spread. ⁴⁰⁻⁴¹ If so, he will order someone to scrape the plaster from the walls, remove the filthy stones, then haul everything off and dump it in an unclean place outside the town. ⁴² Afterwards the wall must be repaired with new stones and fresh plaster.

⁴³ If the mildew appears a second time, ⁴⁴ the priest will come and say, "This house is unclean. It's covered with mildew that can't be removed." ⁴⁵ Then he will have the house torn down and every bit of wood, stone, and plaster hauled off to an unclean place outside the town. ⁴⁶ Meanwhile, if any of you entered the house while it was closed, you will be unclean until evening.

---

*14.12 sacrifice to make things right: See 7.1–10.
*14.13 sacrifices to please me: See the note at 1.1–3.

*14.34 mildew: The Hebrew word translated "mildew" is the same one translated "leprosy" and "spot" in chapter 13.

⁴⁷ And if you either slept or ate in the house, you must wash your clothes.

⁴⁸ On the other hand, if the priest discovers that mildew hasn't reappeared after the house was newly plastered, he will say, "This house is clean — the mildew has gone." ⁴⁹ Then, to show that the house is now clean, he will get two birds, a stick of cedar wood, a piece of red yarn, and a branch from a hyssop plant and bring them to the house. ⁵⁰ He will kill one of the birds over a clay pot of spring water ⁵¹⁻⁵² and let its blood drain into the pot. Then he will dip the cedar, the hyssop, the yarn, and the other bird into the mixture of blood and water. Next, he will sprinkle the house seven times with the mixture, then the house will be completely clean. ⁵³ Finally, he will release the bird and let it fly away, ending the ceremony for purifying the house.

⁵⁴⁻⁵⁷ These are the things you must do if you discover that you are unclean because of an itch or a sore, or that your clothing or house is unclean because of mildew.

CHAPTER 15

Sexual uncleanness

¹ The LORD told Moses and Aaron ² to say to the community of Israel:

Any man with an infected penis is unclean, ³ whether it is stopped up or keeps dripping. ⁴ Anything that he rests on or sits on is also unclean, ⁵⁻⁷ and if you touch either these or him, you must wash your clothes and take a bath, but you still remain unclean until evening.

⁸ If you are spat on by the man, you must wash your clothes and take a bath, but you still remain unclean until evening. ⁹⁻¹⁰ Any saddle or seat on which the man sits is unclean. And if you touch or carry either of these, you must wash your clothes and take a bath, but you still remain unclean until evening. ¹¹ If the man touches you without first washing his hands, you must wash your clothes and take a bath, but you still remain unclean until evening. ¹² Any clay pot that he touches must be destroyed, and any wooden bowl that he touches must be washed.

¹³ Seven days after the man gets well, he will be considered clean, if he washes his clothes and takes a bath in spring water. ¹⁴ On the eighth day he must bring either two doves or two pigeons to the front of

my sacred tent and give them to a priest. ¹⁵ The priest will offer one of the birds as a sacrifice for sin and the other as a sacrifice to please me,* then I will consider the man completely clean.

¹⁶ Any man who has a flow of semen must take a bath, but he still remains unclean until evening. ¹⁷ If the semen touches anything made of cloth or leather, these must be washed, but they still remain unclean until evening. ¹⁸ After having sex, both the man and the woman must take a bath, but they still remain unclean until evening.

¹⁹ When a woman has her monthly period, she remains unclean for seven days, and if you touch her, you must take a bath, but you remain unclean until evening. ²⁰⁻²³ Anything that she rests on or sits on is also unclean, and if you touch either of these, you must wash your clothes and take a bath, but you still remain unclean until evening. ²⁴ Any man who has sex with her during this time becomes unclean for seven days, and anything he rests on is also unclean.

²⁵ Any woman who has a flow of blood outside her regular monthly period is unclean until it stops, just as she is during her monthly period. ²⁶ Anything that she rests on or sits on during this time is also unclean, just as it would be during her period. ²⁷ If you touch either of these, you must wash your clothes and take a bath, but you still remain unclean until evening.

²⁸ Seven days after the woman gets well, she will be considered clean. ²⁹ On the eighth day, she must bring either two doves or two pigeons to the front of my sacred tent and give them to a priest. ³⁰ He will offer one of the birds as a sacrifice for sin and the other as a sacrifice to please me; then I will consider the woman completely clean.

³¹ When any of you are unclean, you must stay away from the rest of the community of Israel. Otherwise, my sacred tent will become unclean, and the whole nation will die.

³²⁻³³ These are the things you men must do if you become unclean because of an infected penis or if you have a flow of semen. And these are the things you women must do when you become unclean either because of your monthly period or an unusual flow of blood. This is

*15.15 sacrifice to please me: See the note at 1.1–3.

also what you men must do if you have sex with a woman who is unclean.

Laws about the Great Day of Forgiveness

CHAPTER 16

¹⁻² Two of Aaron's sons had already lost their lives for disobeying the LORD,* so the LORD told Moses to say to Aaron:

I, the LORD, appear in a cloud over the place of mercy on the sacred chest, which is behind the inside curtain* of the sacred tent. And I warn you not to go there except at the proper time. Otherwise, you will die!

³ Before entering this most holy place, you must offer a bull as a sacrifice for your sins* and a ram as a sacrifice to please me.* ⁴ You will take a bath and put on the sacred linen clothes, including the underwear, the robe, the sash, and the turban. ⁵ Then the community of Israel will bring you a ram and two goats, both of them males. The goats are to be used as sacrifices for sin, and the ram is to be used as a sacrifice to please me.

⁶ Aaron, you must offer the bull as a sacrifice of forgiveness for your own sins and for the sins of your family. ⁷ Then you will lead the two goats into my presence at the front of the sacred tent, ⁸ where I will show you* which goat will be sacrificed to me and which one will be sent into the desert to the demon Azazel.* ⁹ After you offer the first goat as a sacrifice for sin, ¹⁰ the other one must be presented to me alive, before you send it into the desert to take away the sins of the people.

¹¹ You must offer the bull as a sacrifice to ask forgiveness for your own sins and for the sins of your family. ¹² Then you will take a fire pan of live coals from the bronze altar, together with two handfuls of finely ground incense, into the most holy place. ¹³ There you will present them to me by placing the incense on the coals, so that the place of mercy will be covered with a cloud of smoke. Do this, or you will die there! ¹⁴ Next, use a finger to sprinkle some of the blood on the place of mercy, which is on the lid of the sacred chest; then sprinkle blood seven times in front of the chest.

¹⁵ Aaron, you must next sacrifice the goat for the sins of the people, and you must sprinkle its blood inside the most holy place, just as you did with the blood of the bull. ¹⁶ By doing this, you will take away the sins that make both the most holy place and the people of Israel unclean. Do the same for the sacred tent, which is here among the people. ¹⁷ Only you are allowed in the sacred tent from the time you enter until the time you come out. ¹⁸ After leaving the tent, you will purify the bronze altar by smearing each of its four corners with some of the blood from the bull and from the goat. ¹⁹ Use a finger to sprinkle the altar seven times with the blood, and it will be completely clean from the sins of the people.

²⁰ After you have purified the most holy place, the sacred tent, and the bronze altar, you must bring the live goat to the front of the tent. ²¹ There you will lay your hands on its head, while confessing every sin the people have committed, and you will appoint someone to lead the goat into the desert, so that it can take away their sins. ²² Finally, this goat that carries the heavy burden of Israel's sins must be released deep in the desert.

²³⁻²⁴ Aaron, after this you must go inside the sacred tent, take a bath, put on your ordinary priestly clothes, and leave there the clothes you put on before entering the most holy place. Then you will come out and offer sacrifices to please me and sacrifices for your sins and for the sins of the people. ²⁵ The fat from these sacrifices for sin must be sent up in smoke on the bronze altar.

²⁶ The one who led the goat into the desert and sent it off to the demon Azazel must take a bath and wash his clothes before coming back into camp. ²⁷ The remains of the bull and the goat whose blood was taken into the most holy place must be taken outside the camp and burnt.

---

*16.1,2 lost . . . disobeying the LORD: See 10.1,2.
*16.1,2 inside curtain: That separated the holy place from the most holy place.
*16.3 for your sins: See 4.3–12.
*16.3 sacrifice to please me: See the note at 1.1–3.
*16.8 I will show you: The Hebrew text has "you must cast lots to find out". Pieces of wood or stone (called "lots") were used to find out what God wanted his people to do.
*16.8 Azazel: It was believed that a demon named Azazel lived in the desert.

See also: 16.2: Heb 6.19. 16.3: Heb 9.7.

See also: 16.15: Heb 9.12. 16.23: Ezek 44.19.
16.27: Heb 13.11.

²⁸ And whoever does this must take a bath and change clothes before coming back into camp.

The LORD told Moses to say to the people:

²⁹ On the tenth day of the seventh month* of each year, you must go without eating to show sorrow for your sins, and no one, including foreigners who live among you, is allowed to work. ³⁰ This is the day on which the sacrifice for the forgiveness of your sins will be made in my presence, ³¹ and from now on, it must be celebrated each year. Go without eating and make this a day of complete rest just like the Sabbath. ³² The high priest must offer the sacrifices for cleansing from sin, while wearing the sacred linen clothes. ³³ He will offer these sacrifices for the most holy place, the sacred tent, the bronze altar, all the priests, and for the whole community. ³⁴ You must celebrate this day each year — it is the Great Day of Forgiveness* for all the sins of the people of Israel.

Moses did exactly as the LORD had commanded.

Laws on various subjects

CHAPTER 17

Where to offer sacrifices

¹ The LORD told Moses ² to tell Aaron, his sons, and everyone else in Israel:

³⁻⁴ Whenever you kill any of your cattle, sheep, or goats as sacrifices to me, you must do it at the entrance to the sacred tent. If you don't, you will be guilty of pouring out blood, and you will no longer belong to the community of Israel. ⁵ And so, when you sacrifice an animal to ask my blessing,* it must not be done out in a field, ⁶ but in front of the sacred tent. Then a priest can splatter its blood against the bronze altar and send its fat up in smoke with a smell that pleases me. ⁷ Don't ever

turn from me again and offer sacrifices to goat-demons. This law will never change.

⁸ Remember! No one in Israel, including foreigners, is to offer a sacrifice anywhere ⁹ except at the entrance to the sacred tent. If you do, you will no longer belong to my people.

Do not eat blood

The LORD said:

¹⁰ I will turn against any of my people who eat blood. This also includes any foreigners living among you. ¹¹ Life is in the blood, and I have given you the blood of animals to sacrifice in place of your own. That's also why I have forbidden you to eat blood. ¹³ Even if you should hunt and kill a bird or an animal, you must drain out the blood and cover it with soil.

¹⁴ The life of every living creature is in its blood. That's why I have forbidden you to eat blood and why I have warned you that anyone who does will no longer belong to my people.

¹⁵ If you happen to find a dead animal and eat it, you must take a bath and wash your clothes, but you are still unclean until evening. ¹⁶ If you don't take a bath, you will suffer for what you did wrong.

CHAPTER 18

Forbidden sex

¹ The LORD told Moses ² to tell the people of Israel:

I am the LORD your God! ³ So don't follow the customs of Egypt where you used to live or those of Canaan where I am bringing you. ⁴ I am the LORD your God, and you must obey my teachings. ⁵ Obey them and you will live. I am the LORD.

⁶ Don't have sex with any of your close relatives, ⁷ especially your own mother. This would disgrace your father. ⁸ And don't disgrace him by having sex with any of his other wives. ⁹ Don't have sex with your sister or stepsister, whether you grew up together or not. ¹⁰ Don't disgrace yourself by having sex with your granddaughter ¹¹ or half sister ¹²⁻¹³ or a sister of your father or mother. ¹⁴ Don't

---

*16.29 seventh month: Tishri (also called Ethanim), the seventh month of the Hebrew calendar, from about mid-September to mid-October.
*16.34 Great Day of Forgiveness: Traditionally known as the Day of Atonement.
*17.5 sacrifice . . . to ask my blessing: See the note at 3.1.
See also: 16.29-34: Lev 23.26-32; Num 29.7-11.

See also: 17.10: Gen 9.4; Lev 7.26,27; 19.26; Deut 12.16,23; 15.23.   17.11: Heb 9.22.   18.5: Neh 9.29; Ezek 18.9; 20.11-13; Luke 10.28; Rom 10.5; Gal 3.12.   18.8: Lev 20.11; Deut 22.30; 27.20.   18.9: Lev 20.17; Deut 27.22.
18.12-14: Lev 20.19,20.

disgrace your uncle by having sex with his wife. ¹⁵ Don't have sex with your daughter-in-law ¹⁶ or sister-in-law. ¹⁷ And don't have sex with the daughter or granddaughter of any woman that you have earlier had sex with. You may be having sex with a relative, and that would make you unclean. ¹⁸ As long as your wife is alive, don't cause trouble for her by taking one of her sisters as a second wife.

¹⁹ When a woman is having her monthly period, she is unclean, so don't have sex with her.

²⁰ Don't have sex with another man's wife — that would make you unclean.

²¹ Don't sacrifice your children on the altar fires to the god Molech. I am the LORD your God, and that would disgrace me.

²² It is disgusting for a man to have sex with another man.

²³ Anyone who has sex with an animal is unclean.

²⁴ Don't make yourselves unclean by any of these disgusting practices of those nations that I am forcing out of the land for you. They made themselves ²⁵ and the land so unclean, that I punished the land because of their sins, and I made it vomit them up. ²⁶⁻²⁷ Now don't do these sickening things that make the land filthy. Instead, obey my laws and teachings. ²⁸ Then the land won't become sick of you and vomit you up, just as it did them. ²⁹⁻³⁰ If any of you do these vulgar, disgusting things, you will be unclean and no longer belong to my people. I am the LORD your God, and I forbid you to follow their sickening way of life.

CHAPTER 19

Moral and religious laws

¹ The LORD told Moses ² to say to the community of Israel:

I am the LORD your God. I am holy, and you must be holy too! ³⁻⁴ Respect your father and your mother, honour the Sabbath, and don't make idols or images. I am the LORD your God.

⁵ When you offer a sacrifice to ask my blessing,* be sure to follow my instructions. ⁶ You may eat the meat either on the day of the sacrifice or on the next day, but you must burn anything left until the third day. ⁷ If you eat any of it on the third day, the sacrifice will be disgusting to me, and I will reject it. ⁸ In fact, you will be punished for not respecting what I say is holy, and you will no longer belong to the community of Israel.

⁹ When you harvest your grain, always leave some of it standing along the edges of your fields and don't pick up what falls on the ground. ¹⁰ Don't strip your grapevines clean or gather the grapes that fall off the vines. Leave them for the poor and for those foreigners who live among you. I am the LORD your God.

¹¹ Do not steal or tell lies or cheat others.

¹² Do not misuse my name by making promises you don't intend to keep. I am the LORD your God.

¹³ Do not steal anything or cheat anyone, and don't fail to pay your workers at the end of each day.*

¹⁴ I am the LORD your God, and I command you not to make fun of the deaf or to cause a blind person to stumble.

¹⁵ Be fair, no matter who is on trial — don't favour either the poor or the rich.

¹⁶ Don't be a gossip, but never hesitate to speak up in court, especially if your testimony can save someone's life.*

¹⁷ Don't hold grudges. On the other hand, it's wrong not to correct someone who needs correcting. ¹⁸ Stop being angry and don't try to take revenge. I am the LORD, and I command you to love others as much as you love yourself.

¹⁹ Breed your livestock animals only with animals of the same kind, and don't plant two kinds of seed in the same field or wear clothes made of different kinds of material.

²⁰ If a man has sex with a slave woman who is promised in marriage to someone else, he must pay a fine, but they are not to

---

19.5 to ask my blessing: See the note at 3.1.
19.13 to pay . . . end of each day: Day labourers needed their wages to buy food for their evening meal, which was the main meal of the day.

See also: 18.15: Lev 20.12. 18.16: Lev 20.21. 18.17: Lev 20.14; Deut 27.23. 18.19: Lev 20.18. 18.20: Lev 20.10. 18.21: Lev 20.1–5. 18.22: Lev 20.13. 18.23: Exod 22.19; Lev 20.15,16; Deut 27.21. 19.2: Lev 11.44,45; 1 Pet 1.16. 19.3: a Exod 20.12; Deut 5.16; b Exod 20.8; Deut 5.12. 19.4: a Lev 26.1; b Exod 20.23; 34.17; Deut 17.25.

See also: 19.9,10: Lev 27.15; Deut 24.19–22. 19.11: a Exod 20.15; Deut 5.19; b Exod 20.16; Deut 5.20. 19.12: Exod 20.7; Deut 5.11; Matt 5.33. 19.13: Deut 24.14,15. 19.14: Deut 27.18. 19.15: Exod 23.6–8; Deut 16.19. 19.17: Matt 18.15. 19.18: Matt 5.43; 19.19; 22.39; Mark 12.31; Luke 10.27; Rom 13.9; Gal 5.14; Jam 2.8. 19.19: Deut 22.9–11.

be put to death. After all, she was still a slave at the time. ²¹⁻²² The man must bring a ram to the entrance of the sacred tent and give it to a priest, who will then offer it as a sacrifice to me, so the man's sins will be forgiven.

²³ After you enter the land, you will plant fruit trees, but you are not to eat any of their fruit for the first three years. ²⁴ In the fourth year the fruit must be set apart, as an expression of thanks ²⁵ to me, the LORD God. Do this, and in the fifth year, those trees will produce an abundant harvest of fruit for you to eat.

²⁶ Don't eat the blood of any animal. Don't practise any kind of witchcraft. ²⁷⁻²⁸ I forbid you to shave any part of your head or beard or to cut and tattoo yourself as a way of worshipping the dead.

²⁹ Don't let your daughters serve as temple prostitutes — this would bring disgrace both to them and the land.

³⁰ I command you to respect the Sabbath and the place where I am worshipped.

³¹ Don't make yourselves disgusting to me by going to people who claim they can talk to the dead.

³² I command you to show respect for older people and to obey me with fear and trembling.

³³ Don't ill-treat any foreigners who live in your land. ³⁴ Instead, treat them as well as you treat citizens and love them as much as you love yourself. Remember, you were once foreigners in the land of Egypt. I am the LORD your God.

³⁵⁻³⁶ Use honest scales and don't cheat when you weigh or measure anyone.

I am the LORD your God. I rescued you from Egypt, ³⁷ and I command you to obey my laws.

CHAPTER 20

Penalties for disobeying God's laws

¹ The LORD told Moses ² to say to the community of Israel:

Death by stoning is the penalty for any citizens or foreigners in the country who

sacrifice their children to the god Molech. ³ They have disgraced both the place where I am worshipped and my holy name, and so I will turn against them and no longer let them belong to my people. ⁴ Some of you may let them get away with human sacrifice, ⁵ but not me. If any of you worship Molech, I will turn against you and your entire family, and I will no longer let you belong to my people.

⁶ I will be your enemy if you go to someone who claims to speak with the dead, and I will destroy you from among my people. ⁷ Dedicate yourselves to me and be holy because I am the LORD your God. ⁸ I have chosen you as my people, and I expect you to obey my laws.

⁹ If you curse your father or mother, you will be put to death, and it will be your own fault.

¹⁰ If any of you men have sex with another man's wife, both you and the woman will be put to death.

¹¹ Having sex with one of your father's wives disgraces him. So both you and the woman will be put to death, just as you deserve. ¹² It isn't natural to have sex with your daughter-in-law, and both of you will be put to death, just as you deserve. ¹³ It's disgusting for men to have sex with one another, and those who do will be put to death, just as they deserve. ¹⁴ It isn't natural for a man to marry both a mother and her daughter, and so all three of them will be burnt to death. ¹⁵⁻¹⁶ If any of you have sex with an animal, both you and the animal will be put to death, just as you deserve.

¹⁷ If you marry one of your sisters, you will be punished, and the two of you will be disgraced by being openly forced out of the community. ¹⁸ If you have sex with a woman during her monthly period, both you and the woman will be cut off from the people of Israel. ¹⁹ The sisters of your father and mother are your own relatives, and you will be punished for having sex with any of them. ²⁰ If you have sex with your uncle's wife, neither you nor she will ever have any children. ²¹ And if you marry

See also: **19.26:** a Gen 9.4; Lev 7.26,27; 17.10–14; Deut 12.16,23; 15.23; b Deut 18.10.   **19.27,28:** Lev 21.5; Deut 14.1.   **19.29:** Deut 23.17.   **19.30:** Lev 26.2.
19.31: Deut 18.11; 1 Sam 28.3; 2 King 23.4; Isa 8.19.
19.33,34: Exod 22.21; Deut 24.17,18; 27.19.
19.35,36: Deut 25.13–16; Prov 20.10; Ezek 45.10.

20.9: Exod 21.17; Matt 15.4; Mark 7.10.
20.10: Exod 20.14; Lev 18.20; Deut 5.18.   **20.11:** Lev 18.8; Deut 22.30; 27.20.   **20.12:** Lev 18.15.   **20.13:** Lev 18.22.
20.14: Lev 18.17; Deut 27.23.   **20.15,16:** Exod 22.19; Lev 18.23; Deut 27.21.   **20.17:** Lev 18.9; Deut 27.22.
20.18: Lev 18.19.   **20.19,20:** Lev 18.12–14.
20.21: Lev 18.16.

your sister-in-law, neither of you will ever have any children.* ²² Obey my laws and teachings. Or else the land I am giving you will become sick of you and throw you out. ²³ The nations I am chasing out did these disgusting things, and I hated them for it, so don't follow their example. ²⁴ I am the LORD your God, and I have promised you their land that is rich with milk and honey. I have chosen you to be different from other people. ²⁵ That's why you must make a difference between animals and birds that I have said are clean and unclean* — this will keep you from becoming unclean. ²⁶ I am the LORD, the holy God. You have been chosen to be my people, and so you must be holy too.

²⁷ If you claim to receive messages from the dead, you will be put to death by stoning, just as you deserve.

Rules for priests to follow

CHAPTER 21

¹ The LORD gave Moses these instructions for Aaron's sons, the priests:

Touching a dead body will make you unclean. So don't go near a dead relative, ² except your mother, father, son, daughter, brother, ³ or an unmarried sister, who has no husband to take care of her. ⁴ Don't make yourself unclean by attending the funeral of someone related to you by marriage.* ⁵ Don't shave any part of your head or trim your beard or cut yourself to show that you are mourning. ⁶ I am the LORD your God, and I have chosen you alone to offer sacrifices of food to me on the altar. That's why you must keep yourselves holy. ⁷ Don't marry a divorced woman or a woman who has served as a temple prostitute. You are holy, ⁸ because I am holy. And so, you must be treated with proper respect, since you offer food sacrifices to me, the God of holiness.

⁹ If any of you priests has a daughter who disgraces you by serving as a temple prostitute, she must be burnt to death.

¹⁰ If you are the high priest, you must not leave your hair uncombed or tear your clothes in order to mourn for the dead. ¹¹ Don't make yourself unclean by going near a dead body, not even that of your own father or mother. ¹² If you leave the sacred place to attend a funeral, both you and the sacred place become unclean, because you are the high priest.

¹³ If you are the high priest, you must marry only a virgin ¹⁴ from your own tribe. Don't marry a divorced woman or any other woman who has already had sex, including a temple prostitute. ¹⁵ In this way, your descendants will be qualified to serve me. Remember — I am the LORD, and I have chosen you.

¹⁶ The LORD told Moses ¹⁷⁻¹⁸ to say to Aaron:

No descendant of yours can ever serve as my priest if he is blind or lame, if his face is disfigured, if one leg is shorter than the other, ¹⁹ if either a foot or a hand is crippled, ²⁰ if he is a hunchback or a dwarf, if an eye or his skin is diseased, or if his testicles have been damaged. ²¹ These men may not serve as my priests and burn sacrifices to me. ²² They may eat the food offerings presented to me, ²³ but they may not enter the sacred place or serve me at the altar. Remember — I am the LORD, the one who makes a priest holy.

²⁴ Moses told all this to Aaron, his sons, and the people of Israel.

CHAPTER 22

The offerings are holy

¹ The LORD told Moses ² to say to Aaron and his sons:

I am the LORD God, and I demand that you honour my holy name by showing proper respect for the offerings brought to me by the people of Israel. ³ If any of you are unclean when you accept an offering for me, I will no longer let you serve as a priest. ⁴ None of you may take part in the sacred meals while you have a skin disease or an infected penis, or after you have been near a dead body or have had a flow of semen, ⁵ or if you have touched an unclean creature of any sort, including an unclean person. ⁶⁻⁷ Once you are unclean, you must

---

*20.21 And . . . children: According to Deuteronomy 25.5,6 a man was supposed to marry his brother's widow if his brother had died without having children. Otherwise, such marriages were forbidden (see also Matthew 22.23–33; Mark 12.18–27; Luke 20.27–40).

*20.25 clean and unclean: See the note at 11.4–8.

See also: 21.5: Lev 19.27,28; Deut 14.1.

take a bath, but you still cannot eat any of the sacred food until evening. 8 I command you not to eat anything that is killed by a wild animal or dies a natural death. This would make you unclean. 9 Obey me, or you will die on duty for disgracing the place of worship. Remember — I am the LORD, the one who makes a priest holy.

10 Only you priests and your families may eat the food offerings; these are too sacred for any of your servants. 11 However, any slave that you own, including those born into your household, may eat this food. 12 If your daughter marries someone who isn't a priest, she can no longer have any of this food. 13 But if she returns to your home, either widowed or divorced, and has no children, she may join in the meal. Only members of a priestly family can eat this food, 14 and anyone else who accidentally does so, must pay for the food plus a fine of twenty per cent.

15 I warn you not to treat lightly the offerings that are brought by the people of Israel. 16 Don't let them become guilty of eating this sacred food. Remember — I am the LORD, the one who makes these offerings holy.

Acceptable sacrifices

17 The LORD told Moses 18 to tell Aaron and his sons and everyone else the rules for offering sacrifices. He said:

The animals that are to be completely burnt on the altar 19-20 must have nothing wrong with them, or else I won't accept them. Bulls or rams or goats' are the animals to be used for these sacrifices.

21 When you offer a sacrifice to ask my blessing,* there must be nothing wrong with the animal. This is true, whether the sacrifice is part of a promise or something you do voluntarily. 22 Don't offer an animal that is blind or injured or that has an infection or a skin disease. 23 If one of your cattle or lambs has a leg that is longer or shorter than the others, you may offer it voluntarily, but not as part of a promise. 24 As long as you live in this land, don't offer an animal with injured testicles. 25 And don't bring me animals you bought from a foreigner. I won't accept them,

because they are no better than one that has something wrong with it.

26 The LORD told Moses to say:

27 Newborn cattle, sheep, or goats must remain with their mothers for seven days, but on the eighth day, you may send them up in smoke to me, and I will accept the offering. 28 Don't sacrifice a newborn animal and its mother on the same day.

29 When you offer a sacrifice to give thanks* to me, you must do it in a way that is acceptable. 30 Eat all the meat that same day and don't save any for the next day. I am the LORD your God!

31 Obey my laws and teachings — I am the LORD. 32-33 I demand respect from the people of Israel, so don't disgrace my holy name. Remember — I am the one who chose you to be priests and rescued all of you from Egypt, so that I would be your LORD.

Instructions for religious festivals

CHAPTER 23

1 The LORD told Moses 2 to say to the community of Israel:

I have chosen certain times for you to come together and worship me.

3 You have six days when you can do your work, but the seventh day of each week is holy because it belongs to me. No matter where you live, you must rest on the Sabbath and come together for worship. This law will never change.

Passover and the Festival of Thin Bread

This is also told in Numbers 28.16–25

The LORD said:

4-5 Passover is another time when you must come together to worship me, and it must be celebrated on the evening of the fourteenth day of the first month* of each year.

6 The Festival of Thin Bread begins on the fifteenth day of that same month; it lasts

---

*22.29 sacrifice to give thanks:** See 7.12.
*23.4,5 first month:** Abib (also called Nisan), the first month of the Hebrew calendar, from about mid-March to mid-April.

See also: 23.3: Exod 20.8–10; 23.12; 31.15; 34.21; 35.2; Deut 5.12–14. **23.5:** Exod 12.1–13; Deut 16.1,2.
23.6–8: Exod 12.14–20; 23.15; 34.18; Deut 16.3–8.

---

*22.21 sacrifice to ask my blessing:** See the note at 3.1.
See also: 22.20: Deut 17.1.

seven days, and during this time you must honour me by eating bread made without yeast. [7] On the first day of this festival you must rest from your work and come together for worship. [8] Each day of this festival you must offer sacrifices. Then on the final day you must once again rest from your work and come together for worship.

Offering the first part of the harvest

[9] The LORD told Moses [10] to say to the community of Israel:

After you enter the land I am giving you, the first bundle of wheat from each crop must be given to me. So bring it to a priest [11] on the day after the Sabbath. He will lift it up* in dedication to me, and I will accept you. [12] You must also offer a sacrifice to please me.* So bring the priest a one-year-old lamb that has nothing wrong with it [13] and two kilogrammes of your finest flour mixed with olive oil. Then he will place these on the bronze altar and send them up in smoke with a smell that pleases me. Together with these, you must bring a litre of wine as a drink offering. [14] I am your God, and I forbid you to eat any new grain or anything made from it until you have brought these offerings. This law will never change.

The Harvest Festival

This is also told in Numbers 28.26–31

The LORD said:

[15] Seven weeks after you offer this bundle of grain, each family must bring another offering of new grain. [16] Do this exactly fifty days later, which is the day following the seventh Sabbath. [17] Bring two loaves of bread to be lifted up* in dedication to me. Each loaf is to be made with yeast and with two kilogrammes of the finest flour from the first part of your harvest.

[18] At this same time, the entire community of Israel must bring seven lambs that are a year old, a young bull, and two rams. These animals must have nothing wrong with them, and they must be offered as a sacrifice to please me.* You must also offer the proper grain and wine sacrifices with each animal.* [19] Offer a goat* as a sacrifice for sin, and two rams a year old as a sacrifice to ask my blessing.* [20] The priest will lift up* the rams together with the bread in dedication to me. These offerings are holy and are my gift to the priest. [21] This is a day of celebration and worship, a time of rest from your work. You and your descendants must obey this law.

[22] When you harvest your grain, always leave some of it standing around the edges of your fields and don't pick up what falls on the ground. Leave it for the poor and for those foreigners who live among you. I am the LORD your God!

The Festival of Trumpets

This is also told in Numbers 29.1–6

[23] The LORD told Moses [24-25] to say to the people of Israel:

The first day of the seventh month* must be a day of complete rest. Then at the sound of the trumpets, you will come together to worship and to offer sacrifices on the altar.

The Great Day of Forgiveness

This is also told in Numbers 29.7–11

[26] The LORD God said to Moses:

[27] The tenth day of the seventh month* is the Great Day of Forgiveness.* It is a solemn day of worship; everyone must go without eating to show sorrow for their sins, and sacrifices must be burnt. [28] No one is to work on that day — it is the Great Day of Forgiveness, when sacrifices will be offered to me, so that I will forgive your sins. [29] I will destroy anyone who refuses to go without eating. [30-31] None of my people are ever to do any work on that day — not now or in the future. And I will wipe out those who do! [32] This is a time of complete rest just like the Sabbath, and everyone must go without eating from the evening of the ninth to the evening of the tenth.

---

*23.12,18 sacrifice to please me: See the note at 1.1–3.
*23.18 proper grain . . . animal: See Numbers 15.1–16.
See also: 23.15-21: Exod 23.16; 34.22; Deut 16.9–12.

*23.19 sacrifice to ask my blessing: See the note at 3.1.
*23.24,25,27 seventh month: See the note at 16.29.
*23.27 Great Day of Forgiveness: See the note at 16.34.
See also: 23.22: Lev 19.9,10; Deut 24.19–22.
23.26–32: Lev 16.29–34.

The Festival of Shelters

This is also told in Numbers 29.12–40

33 The LORD told Moses 34 to say to the community of Israel:

Beginning on the fifteenth day of the seventh month,* and continuing for seven days, everyone must celebrate the Festival of Shelters in honour of me. 35 No one is to do any work on the first day of the festival — it is a time when everyone must come together for worship. For seven days, sacrifices must be offered on the altar. The eighth day is also to be a day of complete rest, as well as a day of offering sacrifices on the altar and of coming together for worship.

37 I have chosen these festivals as times when my people must come together for worship and when animals, grain, and wine are to be offered on the proper days. 38 These festivals must be celebrated in addition to the Sabbaths and the times when you offer special gifts or sacrifices to keep a promise or as a voluntary offering.

39 Remember to begin the Festival of Shelters on the fifteenth day of the seventh month after you have harvested your crops. Celebrate this festival for seven days in honour of me and don't do any work on the first day or on the day following the festival. 40 Pick the best fruit from your trees* and cut leafy branches to use during the time of this joyous celebration in my honour. 41 I command you and all your descendants to celebrate this festival during the seventh month of each year. 42 For seven days every Israelite must live in a shelter, 43 so future generations will know that I made their ancestors live in shelters when I brought them out of Egypt. I am the LORD your God.

44 This is how Moses instructed the people of Israel to celebrate the LORD's festivals.

CHAPTER 24

Caring for the lamps

This is also told in Exodus 27.20,21

1 The LORD told Moses 2 to say to the community of Israel:

You must supply the purest olive oil for the lamps in the sacred tent, so they will keep burning. 3–4 Aaron will set up the gold lampstand in the holy place of the sacred tent. Then he will light the seven lamps that must be kept burning there in my presence, every night from now on. This law will never change.

The sacred bread

The LORD said:

5 Use your finest flour to bake twelve loaves of bread about two kilogrammes each, 6 then take them into the sacred tent and lay them on the gold table in two rows of six loaves. 7 Beside each row put some pure incense that will be set up by fire in place of the bread as an offering to me. 8 Aaron must lay fresh loaves on the table each Sabbath, and priests in all generations must continue this practice as part of Israel's agreement with me. 9 This bread will always belong to Aaron and his family; it is very holy because it was offered to me, and it must be eaten in a holy place.*

Punishment for cursing the LORD

10–11 Shelomith, the daughter of Dibri from the tribe of Dan, had married an Egyptian, and they had a son. One day their son got into a fight with an Israelite man in camp and cursed the name of the LORD. So the young man was dragged off to Moses, 12 who had him guarded while everyone waited for the LORD to tell them what to do.

13 Finally, the LORD said to Moses:

14 This man has cursed me! Take him outside the camp and make the witnesses lay their hands on his head. Then command the whole community of Israel to stone him to death. 15–16 And warn the others that everyone who curses me will die in the same way, whether they are Israelites by birth or foreigners living among you.

17 Death is also the penalty for murder, 18 but the killing of an animal that belongs to someone else requires only that the animal be replaced. 19 Personal injuries to others must be dealt with in keeping with the crime — 20 a broken bone for a broken bone, an eye for an eye, or a tooth for a

---

*23.34 seventh month: See the note at 16.29.
See also: 23.33–36: Deut 16.13–15.

*24.9 holy place: See the note at 7.6.
See also: 24.5,6: Exod 25.30. 24.9: Matt 12.4; Mark 2.26; Luke 6.4. 24.17: Exod 21.12. 24.20: Exod 21.23–25; Deut 19.21; Matt 5.38.

tooth. ²¹ It's possible to pay the owner for an animal that has been killed, but death is the penalty for murder. ²² I am the LORD your God, and I demand equal justice both for you Israelites and for those foreigners who live among you.

²³ When Moses finished speaking, the people did what the LORD had told Moses, and they stoned to death the man who had cursed the LORD.

CHAPTER 25
The seventh year
This is also told in Deuteronomy 15.1–11

¹ When Moses was on Mount Sinai, the LORD told him ² to say to the community of Israel:

After you enter the land that I am giving you, it must be allowed to rest one year out of every seven. ³ You may raise grain and grapes for six years, ⁴ but the seventh year you must let your fields and vineyards rest in honour of me, your LORD. ⁵ This is to be a time of complete rest for your fields and vineyards, so don't harvest anything they produce.

⁶⁻⁷ However, you and your slaves and your hired workers, as well as any domestic or wild animals, may eat whatever grows on its own.

The Year of Celebration
The LORD said to his people:

⁸ Once every forty-nine years ⁹ on the tenth day of the seventh month,* which is also the Great Day of Forgiveness,* trumpets are to be blown everywhere in the land. ¹⁰ This fiftieth year* is sacred – it is a time of freedom and of celebration when everyone will receive back their original property, and slaves will return home to their families. ¹¹ This is a year of complete celebration, so don't plant any seed or harvest what your fields or vineyards produce. ¹² In this time of sacred celebration you may eat only what grows on its own.

¹³ During this year, all property must go back to its original owner. ¹⁴⁻¹⁵ So when

you buy or sell farmland, the price is to be determined by the number of crops it can produce before the next Year of Celebration. Don't try to cheat. ¹⁶ If it is a long time before the next Year of Celebration, the price will be higher, because what is really being sold are the crops that the land can produce. ¹⁷ I am the LORD your God, so obey me and don't cheat anyone.

¹⁸⁻¹⁹ If you obey my laws and teachings, you will live safely in the land and enjoy its abundant crops. ²⁰ Don't ever worry about what you will eat during the seventh year when you are forbidden to plant or harvest. ²¹ I will see to it that you harvest enough in the sixth year to last for three years. ²² In the eighth year you will live on what you harvested in the sixth year, but in the ninth year you will eat what you plant and harvest in the eighth year.

²³ No land may be permanently bought or sold. It all belongs to me – it isn't your land, and you only live there for a little while.

²⁴ When property is being sold, the original owner must be given the first chance to buy it.

²⁵ If any of you Israelites become so poor that you are forced to sell your property, your closest relative must buy it back, ²⁶ if that relative has the money. Later, if you can afford to buy it, ²⁷ you must pay enough to make up for what the present owner will lose on it before the next Year of Celebration, when the property would become yours again. ²⁸ But if you don't have the money to pay the present owner a fair price, you will have to wait until the Year of Celebration, when the property will once again become yours.

²⁹ If you sell a house in a walled city, you have only one year in which to buy it back. ³⁰ If you don't buy it back before that year is up, it becomes the permanent property of the one who bought it, and it will not be returned to you in the Year of Celebration. ³¹ But a house out in a village may be bought back at any time just like a field. And it must be returned to its original owner in the Year of Celebration. ³² If any Levites own houses inside a walled city, they will always have the right to buy them back. ³³ And any houses that they do not buy back will be returned to them in the Year of Celebration, because these homes

*25.9 seventh month: See the note at 16.29.
*25.9 Great Day of Forgiveness: See the note at 16.34.
*25.10 fiftieth year: The year following seven periods of seven years.
See also: 24.22; Num 15.16. 25.1–7: Exod 23.10,11.

are their permanent property among the people of Israel. [34] No pasture land owned by the Levi tribe can ever be sold; it is their permanent possession.

Help for the poor

The LORD said:

[35] If any of your people become poor and unable to support themselves, you must help them, just as you are supposed to help foreigners who live among you. [36-37] Don't take advantage of them by charging any kind of interest or selling them food for profit. Instead, honour me by letting them stay where they now live. [38] Remember — I am the LORD your God! I rescued you from Egypt and gave you the land of Canaan, so that I would be your God.

[39] Suppose some of your people become so poor that they have to sell themselves and become your slaves. [40] Then you must treat them as servants, rather than as slaves. And in the Year of Celebration they are to be set free, [41] so they and their children may return home to their families and property. [42] I brought them out of Egypt to be my servants, not to be sold as slaves. [43] So obey me, and don't be cruel to the poor.

[44] If you want slaves, buy them from other nations [45] or from the foreigners who live in your own country, and make them your property. [46] You can own them, and even leave them to your children when you die, but do not make slaves of your own people or be cruel to them.

[47] Even if some of you Israelites become so much in debt that you must sell yourselves to foreigners in your country, [48] you still have the right to be set free by a relative, such as a brother [49] or uncle or cousin, or some other family member. In fact, if you ever get enough money, you may buy your own freedom [50] by paying your owner for the number of years you would still be a slave before the next Year of Celebration. [51-52] The longer the time until then, the more you will have to pay. [53] And even while you are the slaves of foreigners in your own country, your people must make sure that the slaves are not ill-treated. [54] If you cannot gain your freedom in any of these ways, both you and your children will still be set free in

the Year of Celebration. [55] People of Israel, I am the LORD your God, and I brought you out of Egypt to be my own servants.

Blessings and punishments

CHAPTER 26

Blessings for obeying the LORD

The LORD said:

[1] I am the LORD your God! So don't make or worship any sort of idols or images. [2] Respect the Sabbath and honour the place where I am worshipped, because I am the LORD.

[3] Faithfully obey my laws, [4] and I will send rain to make your crops grow and your trees produce fruit. [5] Your harvest of grain and grapes will be so abundant, that you won't know what to do with it all. You will eat and be satisfied, and you will live in safety. [6] I will bless your country with peace, and you will rest without fear. I will wipe out the dangerous animals and protect you from enemy attacks. [7] You will chase and destroy your enemies, [8] even if there are only five of you and a hundred of them, or only a hundred of you and ten thousand of them. [9] I will treat you with such kindness that your nation will grow strong, and I will also keep my promises to you. [10] Your barns will overflow with grain each year. [11] I will live among you and never again look on you with disgust. [12] I will walk with you — I will be your God, and you will be my people. [13] I am the LORD your God, and I rescued you from Egypt, so that you would never again be slaves. I have set you free; now walk with your heads held high.

Punishment for disobeying the LORD

The LORD said:

[14-15] If you disobey me and my laws, and if you break our agreement, [16] I will punish you terribly, and you will be ruined. You will be struck with incurable diseases and with fever that leads to blindness and depression. Your enemies will eat the crops you plant, [17] and I will turn from you and let you be destroyed by your attackers. You will even run at the very rumour of attack.

See also: 25.35: Deut 15.7,8. 25.37: Exod 22.25; Deut 23.19,20. 25.39-46: Exod 21.2-6; Deut 15.12-18.

See also: 26.1: a Lev 19.4; b Exod 20.4; Deut 5.8; 16.21,22; 27.1. 26.3-5: Deut 11.13-15; 28.1-14. 26.12: 2 Cor 6.16. 26.14-33: Deut 28.15-68.

[18] Then, if you still refuse to obey me, I will punish you seven times for each of your sins, [19] until your pride is completely crushed. I will hold back the rain, so the sky above you will be like iron, and the ground beneath your feet will be like copper. [20] All your hard work will be for nothing — and there will be no harvest of grain or fruit.

[21] If you keep rebelling against me, I'll punish you seven times worse, just as your sins deserve! [22] I'll send wild animals to attack you, and they will gobble up your children and livestock. So few of you will be left that your roads will be deserted.

[23] If you remain my enemies after this, [24] I'll remain your enemy and punish you even worse. [25] War will break out because you broke our agreement, and if you escape to your walled cities, I'll punish you with horrible diseases, and you will be captured by your enemies. [26] You will have such a shortage of bread, that ten women will be able to bake their bread in the same oven. Each of you will get only a few crumbs, and you will go hungry.

[27] Then if you don't stop rebelling, [28] I'll really get furious and punish you terribly for your sins! [29] In fact, you will be so desperate for food that you will eat your own children. [30] I'll destroy your shrines and tear down your incense altars, leaving your dead bodies piled on top of your idols. And you will be disgusting to me. [31] I'll wipe out your towns and your places of worship and will no longer be pleased with the smell of your sacrifices. [32] Your land will become so desolate that even your enemies who settle there will be shocked when they see it. [33] After I destroy your towns and ruin your land with war, I'll scatter you among the nations.

[34-35] While you are prisoners in foreign lands, your own land will enjoy years of rest and refreshment, as it should have done each seventh year when you lived there. [36-37] In the land of your enemies, you will tremble at the rustle of a leaf, as though it were a sword. And you will become so weak that you will stumble and fall over each other, even when no one is chasing you. [38] Many of you will die in foreign lands, [39] and others of you will waste away in sorrow as the result of your sins and the sins of your ancestors.

[40-41] Then suppose you realize that I turned against you and brought you to the land of your enemies because both you and your ancestors had stubbornly sinned against me. If you humbly confess what you have done and start living right, [42] I'll keep the promise I made to your ancestors Abraham, Isaac, and Jacob. I will bless your land [43] and let it rest during the time that you are in a foreign country, paying for your rebellion against me and my laws.

[44] No matter what you have done, I am still the LORD your God, and I will never completely reject you or become absolutely disgusted with you there in the land of your enemies. [45] While nations watched, I rescued your ancestors from Egypt so that I would be their God. Yes, I am your LORD, and I will never forget our agreement.

[46] Moses was on Mount Sinai when the LORD gave him these laws and teachings for the people of Israel.

Laws about promises and offerings to the Lord

CHAPTER 27

Making promises to the LORD

[1] The LORD told Moses [2] to say to the community of Israel:

If you ever want to free someone who has been promised to me, you may do so by paying the following amounts, weighed according to the official standards:

fifty pieces of silver for men aged twenty to sixty, and thirty pieces for women; twenty pieces of silver for young men aged five to twenty, and ten pieces for young women; fifteen pieces of silver for men aged sixty and above and ten pieces for women; five pieces of silver for boys aged one month to five years, and three pieces for girls.

[8] If you have promised to give someone to me and can't afford to pay the full amount for that person's release, you will be taken

See also: 26.42: a Gen 28.13,14; b Gen 26.3,4; c Gen 17.7,8.

114

to a priest, and he will decide how much you can afford.

⁹ If you promise to sacrifice an animal to me, it becomes holy, and there is no way you can set it free. ¹⁰ If you try to substitute any other animal, no matter how good, for the one you promised, they will both become holy and must be sacrificed. ¹¹ Donkeys are unfit for sacrifice, so if you promise me a donkey,* you must bring it to the priest, ¹² and let him determine its value. ¹³ But if you want to buy it back, you must pay an additional twenty per cent.

¹⁴ If you promise a house to me, a priest will set the price, whatever the condition of the house. ¹⁵ But if you decide to buy it back, you must pay an additional twenty per cent.

¹⁶ If you promise part of your family's land to me, its value must be determined by the amount of seed needed to plant the land, and the rate will be ten pieces of silver for every twenty kilograms of seed. ¹⁷ If this promise is made in the Year of Celebration,* the land will be valued at the full price. ¹⁸ But any time after that, the price will be worked out according to the number of years before the next Year of Celebration. ¹⁹ If you decide to buy back the land, you must pay the price plus an additional twenty per cent, ²⁰ but you cannot buy it back once someone else has bought it. ²¹ When the Year of Celebration comes, the land becomes holy because it belongs to me, and it will be given to the priests.

²² If you promise me a field that you have bought, ²³ its value will be decided by a priest, according to the number of years before the next Year of Celebration, and the money you pay will be mine. ²⁴ However, on the next Year of Celebration, the land will go back to the family of its original owner. ²⁵ Every price will be set by the official standards.

Various offerings

The LORD said:

²⁶ All firstborn animals of your flocks and herds are already mine, and so you cannot promise any of them to me. ²⁷ If you

promise me a donkey,* you may buy it back by adding an additional twenty per cent to its value. If you don't buy it back, it can be sold to someone else for whatever a priest has said it is worth.

²⁸ Anything that you completely dedicate to me must be completely destroyed.* It cannot be bought back or sold. Every person, animal, and piece of property that you dedicate completely is only for me. ²⁹ In fact, any humans who have been promised to me in this way must be put to death.

³⁰ Ten per cent of everything you harvest is holy and belongs to me, whether it grows in your fields or on your fruit trees. ³¹ If you want to buy back this part of your harvest, you may do so by paying what it is worth plus an additional twenty per cent.

³² When you count your flocks and herds, one out of ten of every newborn animal* is holy and belongs to me, ³³ no matter how good or bad it is. If you substitute one animal for another, both of them become holy, and neither can be bought back.

³⁴ Moses was on Mount Sinai when the LORD gave him these laws for the people of Israel.

---

*27.27 donkey: See the note at verse 11.
*27.28 completely dedicate . . . completely destroyed: In order to show that something belonged completely to the LORD and could not be used by anyone else, it was destroyed. This law most often applied to towns and people captured in war (see Joshua 6.16,17).
See also: 27.28: Num 18.14. 27.30–33: Num 18.21; Deut 14.22–29.

Additional notes

*1.1–3 goats: Hebrew "male goats".
*1.1–3 if it is: Or "if you are".
*1.16 with what is in it: One possible meaning for the difficult Hebrew text.
*1.17 tear it partially open: Or "tear it open without pulling off the wings".
*2.12 You . . . separately: One possible meaning for the difficult Hebrew text.
*2.14 either . . . ground: Or "roasted and coarsely ground".
*3.17 not even . . . homes: Or "no matter where you live".
*4.23 goat: See the note at 1.1–3.
*6.18 and they . . . touching it: One possible meaning for the difficult Hebrew text.
*6.21 crumbled . . . pieces: One possible meaning for the difficult Hebrew text.

---

*27.11 Donkeys . . . donkey: The Hebrew text has "If you promise me an unclean animal", which probably refers to a donkey (see Exodus 13.13; 34.20).
*27.17 Year of Celebration: See 25.8–34.

'**6.27 that touches . . . holy:** One possible meaning for the difficult Hebrew text.
'**7.29,30 lift up:** Or "wave".
'**8.27 lifted it up:** See the note at 7.29,30.
'**8.29 lifted up:** See the note at 7.29,30.
'**8.34 forgiven:** One possible meaning for the difficult Hebrew text of verse 34.
'**9.3 goat:** See the note at 1.1–3.
'**9.21 lifted up:** See the note at 7.29,30.
'**10.1 when they . . . to:** One possible meaning for the difficult Hebrew text.
'**10.14,15 lifted up:** See the note at 7.29,30.
'**11.13–19 Eagles . . . hoopoes:** Some of the birds in this list are difficult to identify.
'**14.12 lift them up:** See the note at 7.29,30.
'**14.21 lift these up:** See the note at 7.29,30.
'**14.24,25 lift it up:** See the note at 7.29,30.
'**19.16 but never . . . someone's life:** One possible meaning for the difficult Hebrew text.
'**19.20 time:** One possible meaning for the difficult Hebrew text of verse 20.
'**21.4 marriage:** One possible meaning for the difficult Hebrew text of verse 4.
'**22.19,20 goats:** See the note at 1.1–3.
'**23.11 lift it up:** See the note at 7.29,30.
'**23.17 lifted up:** See the note at 7.29,30.
'**23.19 goat:** See the note at 1.1–3.
'**23.20 lift up:** See the note at 7.29,30.
'**23.40 best fruit from your trees:** One possible meaning for the difficult Hebrew text.
'**27.32 one out of ten of every newborn animal:** Or "one out of every ten animals".

Numbers

A quick look at this book

The book of Numbers continues the history of the people of Israel after they escaped from Egypt, and it tells what happened during the forty years when the Israelites lived in the desert on their journey from Mount Sinai to Canaan. This book is named "Numbers" because it begins with Moses counting the Israelites to find out the number of people in each of Israel's twelve tribes.

Numbers can be divided into three parts. In the first part (1.1—10.10) the Lord tells Moses to count the people, and then he gives Moses instructions for setting up Israel's camp and for assigning the Levites their duties. This part ends with everyone celebrating Passover and offering sacrifices to the Lord.

The second part (10.11—21.20) includes events that happened while the Israelites were on their way to Moab, a nation living east of the River Jordan. This was a very difficult journey through the desert, and the people often complained and even rebelled against Moses and against God. The Israelites refused to enter Canaan after hearing about the nations that lived there, and so the Lord punished the Israelites by making them remain in the desert for forty years. This part of Numbers ends with the people camped in Moab near Mount Pisgah.

The third part of the book (21.21—36.13) begins with the Israelites conquering the land just east of the River Jordan, from the border with Moab in the south to Lake Galilee in the north. Then the king of Moab hired the foreign prophet Balaam to curse the people of Israel. But the Lord told Balaam to bless the Israelites, and Balaam obeyed.

The Israelites prepared to cross the River Jordan and conquer the land of Canaan, although some of the people decided to settle east of the Jordan. The Israelites were counted a second time, then the Lord appointed Joshua to be Israel's next leader and chose other leaders to help Joshua divide the land among the tribes. The book concludes with the Lord giving the Israelites more laws.

Numbers is about people who were rebellious and discouraged and who refused to believe that the Lord would take care of them. But the book also shows how the Lord protected them in war and gave them food and water in the barren desert. The Lord wanted the Israelites to realize that he did not want them to be destroyed; he wanted to bless them, just as Aaron prayed:

"I pray that the LORD
will bless and protect you,
and that he will show you mercy
and kindness.
May the LORD be good to you
and give you peace."

(6.24–26)

The people of Israel are counted

CHAPTER 1

¹ The people of Israel had left Egypt and were living in the Sinai Desert. Then on the first day of the second month* of the second year, Moses was in the sacred tent when the LORD said:

²⁻³ I want you and Aaron to find out how many people are in each of Israel's clans and families. And make a list of all the men twenty years and older who are able to fight in battle. ⁴⁻¹⁵ The following twelve family leaders, one from each tribe, will help you:

Elizur son of Shedeur from Reuben,
Shelumiel son of Zurishaddai
    from Simeon,
Nahshon son of Amminadab
    from Judah,

Nethanel son of Zuar from Issachar,
Eliab son of Helon from Zebulun,
Elishama son of Ammihud
    from Ephraim,
Gamaliel son of Pedahzur
    from Manasseh,
Abidan son of Gideoni from Benjamin,
Ahiezer son of Ammishaddai from Dan,
Pagiel son of Ochran from Asher,
Eliasaph son of Deuel from Gad,
and Ahira son of Enan from Naphtali.

¹⁶⁻¹⁷ Moses and Aaron, together with these twelve tribal leaders, ¹⁸ called together the people that same day. They were counted according to their clans and families. Then Moses and the others listed the names of the men twenty years and older, ¹⁹ just as the LORD had commanded. ²⁰⁻⁴⁶ The number of men from each tribe who were at least twenty years old and strong enough to fight in Israel's army was as follows:

46,500 from Reuben,
    the eldest son of Jacob,ʼ
59,300 from Simeon,
45,650 from Gad,
74,600 from Judah,
54,400 from Issachar,
57,400 from Zebulun,
40,500 from Ephraim,
32,200 from Manasseh,
35,400 from Benjamin,
62,700 from Dan,
41,500 from Asher,
53,400 from Naphtali.

The total number of men registered by Moses, Aaron, and the twelve leaders was 603,550.

⁴⁷ But those from the Levi tribe were not included ⁴⁸ because the LORD had said to Moses:

⁴⁹ When you count the Israelites, do not include those from the Levi tribe. ⁵⁰⁻⁵¹ Instead, give them the job of caring for the sacred tent, its furnishings, and the objects used for worship. They will camp around the tent, and whenever you move, they will take it down, carry it to the new camp, and set it up again. Anyone else who tries to go near it must be put to death.

⁵² The rest of the Israelites will camp in their own groups and under their own banners. ⁵³ But the Levites will camp around the sacred tent to make sure that no one goes near it and makes me furious with the Israelites.

*1.1 second month: Ziv, the second month of the Hebrew calendar, from about mid-April to mid-May.
See also: 1.1–46: Num 26.1–51.

118

[54] The people of Israel did everything the LORD had commanded.

CHAPTER 2

Instructions for setting up Israel's camp

[1] The LORD told Moses and Aaron [2] how the Israelites should arrange their camp:

Each tribe must set up camp under its own banner and under the flags of its ancestral families. These camps will be arranged around the sacred tent, but not close to it.

[3-4] Judah and the tribes that march with it must set up camp on the east side of the sacred tent, under their own banner. The 74,600 troops of the tribe of Judah will be arranged by divisions and led by Nahshon son of Amminadab. [5-6] On one side of Judah will be the tribe of Issachar, with Nethanel son of Zuar as the leader of its 54,400 troops. [7-8] On the other side will be the tribe of Zebulun, with Eliab son of Helon as the leader of its 57,400 troops. [9] These 186,400 troops will march into battle first.

[10-11] Reuben and the tribes that march with it must set up camp on the south side of the sacred tent, under their own banner. The 46,500 troops of the tribe of Reuben will be arranged by divisions and led by Elizur son of Shedeur. [12-13] On one side of Reuben will be the tribe of Simeon, with Shelumiel son of Zurishaddai as the leader of its 59,300 troops. [14-15] On the other side will be the tribe of Gad, with Eliasaph son of Deuel as the leader of its 45,650 troops. [16] These 151,450 troops will march into battle second.

[17] Marching behind Reuben will be the Levites, arranged in groups, just as they are camped. They will carry the sacred tent and their own banners.

[18-19] Ephraim and the tribes that march with it must set up camp on the west side of the sacred tent, under their own banner. The 40,500 troops of the tribe of Ephraim will be arranged by divisions and led by Elishama son of Ammihud. [20-21] On one side of Ephraim will be the tribe of Manasseh, with Gamaliel son of Pedahzur as the leader of its 32,200 troops. [22-23] On the other side will be the tribe of Benjamin, with Abidan son of Gideoni as the leader of its 35,400 troops. [24] These 108,100 troops will march into battle third.

[25-26] Dan and the tribes that march with it must set up camp on the north side of the sacred tent, under their own banner. The 62,700 troops of the tribe of Dan will be arranged by divisions and led by Ahiezer son of Ammishaddai. [27-28] On one side of Dan will be the tribe of Asher, with Pagiel son of Ochran as the leader of its 41,500 troops. [29-30] On the other side will be the tribe of Naphtali with Ahira son of Enan as the leader of its 53,400 troops. [31] These 157,600 troops will march into battle last.

[32] So all the Israelites in the camp were counted according to their ancestral families. The troops were arranged by divisions and totalled 603,550. [33] The only Israelites not included were the Levites, just as the LORD had commanded Moses.

[34] Israel did everything the LORD had told Moses. They arranged their camp according to clans and families, with each tribe under its own banner. And that was the order by which they marched into battle.

CHAPTER 3

The sons of Aaron

[1] When the LORD talked with Moses on Mount Sinai, [2] Aaron's four sons, Nadab, Abihu, Eleazar, and Ithamar, [3] were the ones to be ordained as priests. [4] But the LORD killed Nadab and Abihu in the Sinai Desert when they used fire that was unacceptable[*] in their offering to the LORD.[*] And because Nadab and Abihu had no sons, only Eleazar and Ithamar served as priests with their father Aaron.

The duties of the Levites

[5] The LORD said to Moses:

[6] Assign the Levi tribe to Aaron the priest. They will be his assistants [7] and will work at the sacred tent for him and for all the Israelites. [8] The Levites will serve the community by being responsible for the furnishings of the tent. [9] They are assigned to help Aaron and his sons, [10] who have been appointed to be priests. Anyone else who tries to perform the duties of a priest must be put to death.

[11-13] Moses, I have chosen these Levites from all Israel, and they will belong to me in a special way. When I killed the

---

*3.4 the LORD killed Nadab and Abihu . . . to the LORD: See Leviticus 10.1,2.
See also: 3.2: Num 26.60.   3.4: Lev 10.1,2; Num 26.61.
3.13: Exod 13.2.

firstborn sons of the Egyptians, I decided that the firstborn sons in every Israelite family and the firstborn males of their flocks and herds would be mine.* But now I accept these Levites in place of the firstborn sons of the Israelites.

The Levites are counted

14 In the Sinai Desert the LORD said to Moses, 15 "Now I want you to count the men and boys in the Levi tribe by families and by clans. Include every one at least a month old." 16 So Moses obeyed and counted them.

17 Levi's three sons, Gershon, Kohath, and Merari, had become the heads of their own clans. 18 Gershon's sons were Libni and Shimei. 19 Kohath's sons were Amram, Izhar, Hebron, and Uzziel. 20 And Merari's sons were Mahli and Mushi. These were the sons and grandsons of Levi, and they had become the leaders of the Levite clans.

21 The two Gershon clans were the Libnites and Shimeites, 22 and they had seven thousand five hundred men and boys at least one month old. 23 The Gershonites were to camp on the west side of the sacred tent, 24 under the leadership of Eliasaph son of Lael. 25 Their duties at the tent included taking care of the tent itself, along with its outer covering, the curtain for the entrance, 26 the curtains hanging inside the courtyard around the tent, as well as the curtain and ropes for the entrance to the courtyard and its altar. The Gershonites were responsible for setting these things up and taking them down.

27 The four Kohath clans were the Amramites, Izharites, Hebronites, and the Uzzielites, 28 and they had eight thousand six hundred* men and boys at least one month old. 29 The Kohathites were to camp on the south side of the sacred tent, 30 under the leadership of Elizaphan son of Uzziel. 31 Their duties at the tent included taking care of the sacred chest, the table for the sacred bread, the lampstand, the altars, the objects used for worship, and the curtain in front of the most holy place. The Kohathites were responsible for setting these things up and taking them down.

32 Eleazar son of Aaron was the head of the Levite leaders, and he made sure that the work at the sacred tent was done.

33 The two Merari clans were the Mahlites and the Mushites, 34 and they had six thousand two hundred men and boys at least one month old. 35 The Merarites were to camp on the north side of the sacred tent, under the leadership of Zuriel son of Abihail. 36-37 Their duties included taking care of the tent frames and the pieces that held the tent up: the bars, the posts, the stands, and its other equipment. They were also in charge of the posts that supported the courtyard, as well as their stands, tent pegs, and ropes. The Merari clans were responsible for setting these things up and taking them down.

38 Moses, Aaron, and his sons were to camp in front of the sacred tent, on the east side, and to make sure that the Israelites worshipped in the proper way. Anyone else who tried to do the work of Moses and Aaron was to be put to death.

39 So Moses and Aaron obeyed the LORD and counted the Levites by their clans. The total number of Levites at least one month old was twenty-two thousand.

The Levites are accepted as substitutes for the firstborn sons

40 The LORD said to Moses, "Make a list and count the firstborn sons at least one month old in each of the Israelite families. 41 They belong to me, but I will accept the Levites as substitutes for them, and I will accept the Levites' livestock as substitutes for the Israelites' firstborn livestock."

42 Moses obeyed the LORD and counted the firstborn sons; 43 there were 22,273 of them.

44 Then the LORD said, 45 "The Levites will belong to me and will take the place of the firstborn sons; their livestock will take the place of the Israelites' firstborn livestock. 46 But since there are more firstborn sons than Levites, the extra two hundred and seventy-three men and boys must be bought back from me. 47 For each one, you are to collect five pieces of silver, weighed according to the official standards. 48 This money must then be given to Aaron and his sons."

49 Moses collected the silver from the extra two hundred and seventy-three firstborn men and boys, 50 and it amounted to one thousand three hundred and sixty-five pieces of silver, weighed according to the official standards. 51 Then he gave it to Aaron and his sons, just as the LORD had commanded.

---

*3.11-13 When I killed . . . mine: See Exodus 13.1,2,11-16.

CHAPTER 4

The duties of the Kohathite clans

¹ The LORD told Moses and Aaron:

²⁻³ Find out how many men between the ages of thirty and fifty are in the four Levite clans of Kohath. Count only those who are able to work at the sacred tent.

⁴ The Kohathites will be responsible for carrying the sacred objects used in worship at the sacred tent. ⁵ When the Israelites are ready to move their camp, Aaron and his sons will enter the tent and take down the curtain that separates the sacred chest from the rest of the tent. They will cover the chest with this curtain, ⁶ and then with a piece of fine leather, and cover it all with a solid blue cloth. After this they will put the carrying poles in place.

⁷ Next, Aaron and his sons will use another blue cloth to cover the table for the sacred bread.* On the cloth they will place the dishes, the bowls for incense, the cups, the jugs for wine, as well as the bread itself. ⁸ They are to cover all of this with a bright red cloth, and then with a piece of fine leather, before putting the carrying poles in place.

⁹ With another blue cloth they will cover the lampstand, along with the lamps, the lamp snuffers, the fire pans, and the jars of oil for the lamps. ¹⁰ All of this will then be covered with a piece of fine leather and placed on a carrying frame.

¹¹ The gold incense altar* is to be covered with a blue cloth, and then with a piece of fine leather, before its carrying poles are put in place.

¹² Next, Aaron and his sons will take blue cloth and wrap all the objects used in worship at the sacred tent. These will need to be covered with a piece of fine leather, then placed on a carrying frame.

¹³ They are to remove the ashes from the bronze altar and cover it with a purple cloth. ¹⁴ On that cloth will be placed the

utensils used at the altar, including the fire pans, the meat forks, the shovels, and the sprinkling bowls. All of this will then be covered with a piece of fine leather, before the carrying poles are put in place.

¹⁵ When the camp is ready to be moved, the Kohathites will be responsible for carrying the sacred objects and the furnishings of the sacred tent. But Aaron and his sons must have already covered those things so the Kohathites won't touch them and die.

¹⁶ Eleazar son of Aaron the priest will be in charge of the oil for the lamps, the sweet-smelling incense, the grain for the sacrifices, and the olive oil used for dedications and ordinations. Eleazar is responsible for seeing that the sacred tent, its furnishings, and the sacred objects are taken care of.

¹⁷⁻²⁰ The Kohathites must not go near or even look at the sacred objects until Aaron and his sons have covered those objects. If they do, their entire clan will be wiped out. So make sure that Aaron and his sons go into the tent with them and tell them what to carry.

The duties of the Gershonite clans

²¹ The LORD said to Moses:

²²⁻²³ Find out how many men between the ages of thirty and fifty are in the two Levite clans of Gershon. Count only those who are able to work at the sacred tent.

²⁴ The Gershonites will be responsible ²⁵ for carrying the curtains of the sacred tent, its two outer coverings,* the curtain for the entrance to the tent, ²⁶ the curtains hanging around the courtyard of the tent, and the curtain and ropes for the entrance to the courtyard. The Gershonites are to do whatever needs to be done to take care of these things, ²⁷ and they will carry them wherever Aaron and his sons tell them to. ²⁸ These are the duties of the Gershonites at the sacred tent, and Ithamar son of Aaron will make sure they do their work.

The duties of the Merarite clans

²⁹⁻³⁰ The LORD said:

Moses, find out how many men between thirty and fifty are in the two Levite clans of Merari, but count only those who are able to work at the sacred tent.

*4.7 sacred bread: This bread was offered to the LORD and was a symbol of his presence in the sacred tent. It was put out on a special table and was replaced with fresh bread each Sabbath (Leviticus 24.5–9).

*4.11 gold incense altar: This altar for offering incense was inside the sacred tent; it was made of acacia wood covered with gold. A large altar for offering sacrifices was in front of the entrance to the tent; it was made of acacia wood covered with bronze (see verse 13).

*4.25 two outer coverings: See Exodus 26.14.

31 The Merarites will be responsible for carrying the frames of the tent and its other pieces, including the bars, the posts, the stands, 32 as well as the posts that support the courtyard, together with their stands, tent pegs, and ropes. The Merarites are to be told exactly what objects they are to carry, 33 and Ithamar son of Aaron will make sure they do their work.

The Levites are counted again

34-49 Moses, Aaron, and the other Israelite leaders obeyed the LORD and counted the Levi tribe by families and clans, to find out how many men there were between the ages of thirty and fifty who could work at the sacred tent. There were two thousand seven hundred and fifty Kohathites, two thousand six hundred and thirty Gershonites, and three thousand two hundred Merarites, making a total of eight thousand five hundred and eighty. Then they were all assigned their duties.

Various laws and the dedication of the Levites

CHAPTER 5

People are sent outside the camp

1 The LORD told Moses 2-3 to say to the people of Israel, "Put out of the camp everyone who has leprosy* or a bodily discharge or who has touched a dead body. Now that I live among my people, their camp must be kept clean."

4 The Israelites obeyed the LORD's instructions.

The penalty for committing a crime

This is also told in Leviticus 6.1-7

5 The LORD told Moses 6 to say to the community of Israel:

If any of you commit a crime against someone, you have sinned against me. 7 You must confess your guilt and pay the victim in full for whatever damage has been done, plus a fine of twenty per cent. 8 If the victim has no relative who can accept this money, it belongs to me and must be paid to the priest. In addition to that payment, you

must take a ram for the priest to sacrifice so your sin will be forgiven.

9-10 When you make a donation to the sacred tent, that money belongs only to the priest, and each priest will keep what is given to him.

A suspicious husband

11 The LORD told Moses 12-14 to say to the people of Israel:

Suppose a man becomes jealous and suspects that his wife is unfaithful, but he has no proof. 15 He must take his wife to the priest, together with one kilogramme of ground barley as an offering to find out if she is guilty. No olive oil or incense is to be put on that offering.

16 The priest is to make the woman stand at my altar, 17 where he will pour sacred water into a clay jar and stir in some dust from the floor of the sacred tent. 18-22 Next, he will remove her veil, then hand her the barley offering, and say, "If you have been faithful to your husband, this water won't harm you. But if you have been unfaithful, it will bring down the LORD's curse — you will never be able to give birth to a child, and everyone will curse your name."

Then the woman will answer, "If I am guilty, let it happen just as you say."

23 The priest will write these curses on special paper and wash them off into the bitter water, 24 so that when the woman drinks this water, the curses will enter her body. 25 He will take the barley offering from her and lift it up' in dedication to me, the LORD. Then he will place it on my altar 26 and burn part of it as a sacrifice. After that, the woman must drink the bitter water.

27 If the woman has been unfaithful, the water will immediately make her unable to have children, and she will be a curse among her people. 28 But if she is innocent, her body will not be harmed, and she will still be able to have children.

29-30 This is the ceremony that must take place at my altar when a husband suspects that his wife has been unfaithful. The priest must make the woman stand in my presence and carefully follow these instructions. 31 If the husband is wrong, he will not be punished; but if his wife is guilty, she will be punished.

---

*5.2,3 leprosy: The word translated "leprosy" was used for many different kinds of skin diseases.
See also: 5.5-8: Lev 6.1-7.

122

CHAPTER 6

Rules for Nazirites

¹ The LORD told Moses ² to say to the people of Israel:

If any of you want to dedicate yourself to me by vowing to become a Nazirite, ³ you must no longer drink any wine or beer or use any kind of vinegar. Don't drink grape juice or eat grapes or raisins — ⁴ not even the seeds or skins.

⁵ Even the hair of a Nazirite is sacred to me, and as long as you are a Nazirite, you must never cut your hair.

⁶ During the time that you are a Nazirite, you must never go close to a dead body, ⁷⁻⁸ not even that of your father, mother, brother, or sister. That would make you unclean. Your hair is the sign that you are dedicated to me, so remain holy.

⁹ If someone suddenly dies near you, your hair is no longer sacred, and you must shave it seven days later during the ceremony to make you clean. ¹⁰ Then on the next day, bring two doves or two pigeons to the priest at the sacred tent. ¹¹ He will offer one of the birds as a sacrifice for sin and the other as a sacrifice to please me.* You will then be forgiven for being too near a dead body, and your hair will again become sacred. ¹² But the dead body made you unacceptable, so you must make another vow to become a Nazirite and be dedicated once more. Finally, a year-old ram must be offered as the sacrifice to make things right.

¹³ When you have completed your promised time of being a Nazirite, go to the sacred tent ¹⁴ and offer three animals that have nothing wrong with them: a year-old ram as a sacrifice to please me, a year-old female lamb as a sacrifice for sin, and a full-grown ram as a sacrifice to ask my blessing.* ¹⁵ Wine offerings and grain sacrifices must also be brought with these animals. Finally, you are to bring a basket of bread made with your finest flour and olive oil, but without yeast. Also bring some thin wafers brushed with oil.

¹⁶ The priest will take these gifts to my altar and offer them, so that I will be pleased and will forgive you. ¹⁷ Then he will sacrifice the ram and offer the wine, grain, and bread.

¹⁸ After that, you will stand at the entrance to the sacred tent, shave your head, and put the hair in the fire where the priest has offered the sacrifice to ask my blessing.

¹⁹ Once the meat from the ram's shoulder has been boiled, the priest will take it, along with one loaf of bread and one wafer brushed with oil, and give them to you. ²⁰ You will hand them back to the priest, who will lift them up* in dedication to me. Then he can eat the meat from the ram's shoulder, its choice ribs, and its hind leg, because this is his share of the sacrifice. After this, you will no longer be a Nazirite and will be free to drink wine.

²¹ These are the requirements for Nazirites. However, if you can afford to offer more, you must do so.

The blessing for the people

²² The LORD told Moses, ²³ "When Aaron and his sons bless the people of Israel, they must say:

²⁴ I pray that the LORD
    will bless and protect you,
²⁵ and that he will show you mercy
    and kindness.
²⁶ May the LORD be good to you
    and give you peace."

²⁷ Then the LORD said, "If Aaron and his sons ask me to bless the Israelites, I will give them my blessing."

CHAPTER 7

The leaders bring gifts to the sacred tent

¹ When Moses had finished setting up the sacred tent, he dedicated it to the LORD, together with its furnishings, the altar, and its equipment. ² Then the twelve tribal leaders of Israel, the same men who had been in charge of counting the people,* came to the tent ³ with gifts for the LORD. They

---

*6.11 sacrifice to please me: This sacrifice has traditionally been called a "whole burnt offering", because the whole animal was burnt on the altar. A main purpose of such a sacrifice was to please the LORD with the smell of the sacrifice, and so in the CEV it is often called "a sacrifice to please the LORD".
*6.14 sacrifice to ask my blessing: This sacrifice has traditionally been called a "peace offering" or an "offering of well-being". A main purpose of such a sacrifice was to ask the LORD's blessing, and so in the CEV it is often called a "sacrifice to ask the LORD's blessing".

See also: 6.3: Luke 1.15. 6.13-21: Acts 21.23,24.

*7.2 the same men . . . the people: See 1.1–19.

brought six strong carts and twelve oxen — one ox from each leader and a cart from every two.

⁴ The LORD said to Moses, ⁵ "Accept these gifts, so the Levites can use them here at the sacred tent for carrying the sacred things."

⁶ Then Moses took the carts and oxen and gave them to the Levites, ⁷⁻⁸ who were under the leadership of Ithamar son of Aaron. Moses gave two carts and four oxen to the Gershonites for their work, and four carts and eight oxen to the Merarites for their work. ⁹ But Moses did not give any to the Kohathites, because they were in charge of the sacred objects that had to be carried on their shoulders.

¹⁰ On the day the altar was dedicated, the twelve leaders brought offerings for its dedication. ¹¹ The LORD said to Moses, "Each day one leader is to give his offering for the dedication."

¹²⁻⁸³ So each leader brought the following gifts:

a silver bowl that weighed one and a half kilogrammes and a silver sprinkling bowl weighing almost a kilogramme, both of them filled with flour and olive oil as grain sacrifices and weighed according to the official standards;

a small gold dish filled with incense;

a young bull, a full-grown ram, and a year-old ram as sacrifices to please the LORD;*

a goat* as a sacrifice for sin;

and two bulls, five full-grown rams, five goats, and five rams a year old as sacrifices to ask the LORD's blessing.*

The tribal leaders brought their gifts and offerings in the following order:

> On the first day Nahshon from Judah,
> on the second day Nethanel
>   from Issachar,
> on the third day Eliab from Zebulun,
> on the fourth day Elizur from Reuben,
> on the fifth day Shelumiel from Simeon,
> on the sixth day Eliasaph from Gad,
> on the seventh day Elishama
>   from Ephraim,
> on the eighth day Gamaliel
>   from Manasseh,
> on the ninth day Abidan from Benjamin,
> on the tenth day Ahiezer from Dan,

> on the eleventh day Pagiel from Asher,
> on the twelfth day Ahira from Naphtali.

⁸⁴⁻⁸⁸ And so when the altar was dedicated to the LORD, these twelve leaders brought the following gifts:

twelve silver bowls and twelve silver sprinkling bowls, weighing a total of almost twenty-eight kilogrammes, according to the official standards;

twelve gold dishes filled with incense and weighing over a kilogramme;

twelve bulls, twelve full-grown rams, and twelve rams a year old as sacrifices to please the LORD, along with the proper grain sacrifices;

twelve goats as sacrifices for sin;

and twenty-four bulls, sixty full-grown rams, sixty goats, and sixty rams a year old as sacrifices to ask the LORD's blessing.

⁸⁹ Whenever Moses needed to talk with the LORD, he went into the sacred tent, where he heard the LORD's voice coming from between the two winged creatures above the lid of the sacred chest.

CHAPTER 8

Aaron puts the gold lamps in place

¹ The LORD said to Moses, ² "Tell Aaron to put the seven lamps on the lampstand so they shine towards the front."

³ Aaron obeyed and placed the lamps as he was told. ⁴ The lampstand was made of hammered gold from its base to the decorative flowers on top, exactly like the pattern the LORD had described to Moses.

Instructions for ordaining the Levites

⁵ The LORD said to Moses:

⁶ The Levites must be acceptable to me before they begin working at the sacred tent. So separate them from the rest of the Israelites ⁷ and sprinkle them with the water that washes away their sins. Then tell them to shave their entire bodies and wash their clothes.

⁸ They are to bring a bull and its proper grain sacrifice of flour mixed with olive oil. And they must bring a second bull as a sacrifice for sin.

⁹ Then you, Moses, will call together all the people of Israel and make the Levites go to my sacred tent, ¹⁰ where the people will place their hands on them. ¹¹ Aaron

---

*7.12-83 sacrifices to please the LORD: See the note at 6.11.

*7.12-83 sacrifices to ask the LORD's blessing: See the note at 6.14.

See also: 8.1-4: Exod 25.31-40; 37.17-24.

will present the Levites to me as a gift from the people, so that the Levites will do my work.

¹² After this, the Levites are to place their hands on the heads of the bulls. Then one of the bulls will be sacrificed for the forgiveness of sin, and the other to make sure that I am pleased. ¹³ The Levites will stand at my altar in front of Aaron and his sons, who will then dedicate the Levites to me.

¹⁴ This ceremony will show that the Levites are different from the other Israelites and belong to me in a special way. ¹⁵ After they have been made acceptable and have been dedicated, they will be allowed to work at my sacred tent. ¹⁶ They are mine and will take the place of the firstborn Israelite sons. ¹⁷ When I killed the eldest sons of the Egyptians, I decided that the firstborn sons in each Israelite family would be mine, as well as every firstborn male from their flocks and herds. ¹⁸ But now I have chosen these Levites as substitutes for the firstborn sons, ¹⁹ and I have given them as gifts to Aaron and his sons to serve at the sacred tent. I will hold them responsible for what happens to anyone who gets too close to the sacred tent.*

The Levites are dedicated to the LORD

²⁰ Moses, Aaron, and the other Israelites made sure that the Levites did everything the LORD had commanded. ²¹ The Levites sprinkled themselves with the water of forgiveness and washed their clothes. Then Aaron brought them to the altar and offered sacrifices to forgive their sins and make them acceptable to the LORD. ²² After this, the Levites worked at the sacred tent as assistants to Aaron and his sons, just as the LORD had commanded.

²³ The LORD also told Moses, ²⁴⁻²⁵ "Levites who are between the ages of twenty-five and fifty can work at my sacred tent. But once they turn fifty, they must retire. ²⁶ They may help the other Levites in their duties, but they must no longer be responsible for any work themselves. Remember this when you assign their duties."

Passover is celebrated and a cloud covers the sacred tent

CHAPTER 9

Regulations for celebrating Passover

¹ During the first month of Israel's second year in the Sinai Desert,* the LORD had told Moses ² to say to the people, "Celebrate Passover ³ in the evening of the fourteenth day of this month* and do it by following all the regulations." ⁴⁻⁵ Moses told the people what the LORD had said, and they celebrated Passover there in the desert in the evening of the fourteenth day of the first month.

⁶ Some people in Israel's camp had touched a dead body and had become unfit to worship the LORD, and they could not celebrate Passover. But they asked Moses and Aaron, ⁷ "Even though we have touched a dead body, why can't we celebrate Passover and offer sacrifices to the LORD at the same time as everyone else?"

⁸ Moses said, "Wait here while I go into the sacred tent and find out what the LORD says about this."

⁹ The LORD then told Moses ¹⁰ to say to the community of Israel:

If any of you or your descendants touch a dead body and become unfit to worship me, or if you are away on a long journey, you may still celebrate Passover. ¹¹ But it must be done in the second month,* in the evening of the fourteenth day. Eat the Passover lamb with thin bread and bitter herbs, ¹² and don't leave any of it until morning or break any of the animal's bones. Be sure to follow these regulations.

¹³ But if any of you refuse to celebrate Passover when you are not away on a journey, you will no longer belong to my people. You will be punished because you did not offer sacrifices to me at the proper time.

*9.1 first month . . . Sinai Desert: The book of Numbers begins in the second month of the second year (see 1.1), so 9.1–5 refers to a Passover celebration that had already taken place.
*9.3 this month: Abib (also called Nisan), the first month of the Hebrew calendar, from about mid-March to mid-April.
*9.11 second month: See the note at 1.1.
See also: 9.1–5: Exod 12.1–13.   9.12: Exod 12.46; John 19.36.

¹⁴ Anyone, including foreigners who live among you, can celebrate Passover, if they follow all the regulations.

The cloud over the sacred tent

This is also told in Exodus 40.34–38

¹⁵⁻¹⁶ As soon as the sacred tent was set up,* a thick cloud appeared and covered it. The cloud was there each day, and during the night, a fire could be seen in it. ¹⁷⁻¹⁹ The LORD used this cloud to tell the Israelites when to move their camp and where to set it up again. As long as the cloud covered the tent, the Israelites did not break camp. But when the cloud moved, they followed it, and wherever it stopped, they camped and stayed there, ²⁰⁻²² whether it was only one night, a few days, a month, or even a year. As long as the cloud remained over the tent, the Israelites stayed where they were. But when the cloud moved, so did the Israelites. ²³ They obeyed the LORD's commands and went wherever he directed Moses.

The people begin their journey

CHAPTER 10

The silver trumpets

¹ The LORD told Moses:

² Have two trumpets made out of hammered silver. These will be used to call the people together and to give the signal for moving your camp. ³ If both trumpets are blown, everyone is to meet with you at the entrance to the sacred tent. ⁴ But if just one is blown, only the twelve tribal leaders need to come together.

⁵⁻⁶ Give a signal on a trumpet when it is time to break camp. The first blast will be the signal for the tribes camped on the east side, and the second blast will be the signal for those on the south. ⁷ But when you want everyone to come together, sound a different signal on the trumpet. ⁸ The priests of Aaron's family will be the ones to blow the trumpets, and this law will never change.

⁹ Whenever you go into battle against an enemy attacking your land, give a warning signal on the trumpets. Then I, the LORD, will hear it and rescue you. ¹⁰ During the celebration of the New Moon Festival and other religious festivals, sound the trumpets while you offer sacrifices. This will be a reminder that I am the LORD your God.

The Israelites begin their journey

¹¹ On the twentieth day of the second month* of that same year, the cloud over the sacred tent moved on. ¹² So the Israelites broke camp and left the Sinai Desert. And some time later, the cloud stopped in the Paran Desert.* ¹³ This was the first time the LORD had told Moses to command the people of Israel to move on.

¹⁴ Judah and the tribes that camped beside it marched out first, carrying their banner. Nahshon son of Amminadab was the leader of the Judah tribe, ¹⁵ Nethanel son of Zuar was the leader of the Issachar tribe, ¹⁶ and Eliab son of Helon was the leader of the Zebulun tribe.

¹⁷ The sacred tent had been taken down, and the Gershonites and the Merarites carried it, marching behind the Judah camp.

¹⁸ Reuben and the tribes that camped beside it marched out second, carrying their banner. Elizur son of Shedeur was the leader of the Reuben tribe, ¹⁹ Shelumiel son of Zurishaddai was the leader of the Simeon tribe, ²⁰ and Eliasaph son of Deuel was the leader of the Gad tribe.

²¹ Next were the Kohathites, carrying the objects for the sacred tent, which was to be set up before they arrived at the new camp.

²² Ephraim and the tribes that camped beside it marched next, carrying their banner. Elishama son of Ammihud was the leader of the Ephraim tribe, ²³ Gamaliel son of Pedahzur was the leader of the Manasseh tribe, ²⁴ and Abidan son of Gideoni was the leader of the Benjamin tribe.

²⁵ Dan and the tribes that camped beside it were to protect the Israelites against an attack from behind, and so they marched last, carrying their banner. Ahiezer son of Ammishaddai was the leader of the tribe of Dan, ²⁶ Pagiel son of Ochran was the leader of the Asher tribe, ²⁷ and Ahira son of Enan was the leader of the Naphtali tribe.

---

*9.15,16 As soon as the sacred tent was set up: According to Exodus 40.17, this took place "on the first day of the first month of the second year" of the Israelites' stay in the desert.

*10.11 second month: See the note at 1.1.
*10.12 the Paran Desert: Probably a general name for the northernmost part of the Sinai Desert.

28 This was the order in which the Israelites marched each time they moved their camp.

29 Hobab* the Midianite, the father-in-law of Moses, was there. And Moses said to him, "We're leaving for the place the LORD has promised us. He has said that all will go well for us. So come along, and we will make sure that all goes well for you."

30 "No, I won't go," Hobab answered. "I'm returning home to be with my own people."

31 "Please go with us!" Moses said. "You can be our guide because you know the places to camp in the desert. 32 Besides that, if you go, we will give you a share of the good things the LORD gives us."

33 The people of Israel began their journey from Mount Sinai.* They travelled three days, and the Levites who carried the sacred chest led the way, so the LORD could show them where to camp. 34 And the cloud always stayed with them.

35 Each day as the Israelites began their journey, Moses would pray, "Our LORD, defeat your enemies and make them run!" 36 And when they stopped to set up camp, he would pray, "Our LORD, stay close to Israel's thousands and thousands of people."

The people complain

CHAPTER 11

1 One day the Israelites started complaining about their troubles. The LORD heard them and became so angry that he destroyed the outer edges of their camp with fire.

2 When the people begged Moses to help, he prayed, and the fire went out. 3 They named the place "Burning",* because in his anger the LORD had set their camp on fire.

The people grumble about being hungry

4 One day some worthless foreigners among the Israelites became greedy for food, and even the Israelites themselves began moaning, "We don't have any meat! 5 In Egypt we could eat all the fish we wanted, and there were cucumbers, melons, onions, and garlic. 6 But we're starving out here, and the only food we have is this manna."

7 The manna was like small whitish seeds 8-9 and tasted like something baked with sweet olive oil. It appeared at night with the dew. In the morning the people would collect the manna, grind or crush it into flour, then boil it and make it into thin wafers.

10 The Israelites stood around their tents complaining. Moses heard them and was upset that they had made the LORD angry. 11 He prayed:

I am your servant, LORD, so why are you doing this to me? What have I done to deserve this? You've made me responsible for all these people, 12 but they're not my children. You told me to nurse them along and to carry them to the land you promised their ancestors. 13 They keep whining for meat, but where can I get meat for them? 14 This job is too much for me. How can I take care of all these people by myself? 15 If this is the way you're going to treat me, just kill me now and end my miserable life!

Seventy leaders are chosen to help Moses

16 The LORD said to Moses:

Choose seventy of Israel's respected leaders and go with them to the sacred tent. 17 While I am talking with you there, I will give them some of your authority, so they can share responsibility for my people. You will no longer have to care for them by yourself.

18 As for the Israelites, I have heard them complaining about not having meat and about being better off in Egypt. So tell them to make themselves acceptable to me, because tomorrow they will have meat. 19-20 In fact, they will have meat day after day for a whole month — not just a few days, or even ten or twenty. They turned against me and wanted to return to Egypt. Now they will eat meat until they get sick of it.

21 Moses replied, "At least six hundred thousand grown men are here with me. How can you say there will be enough meat to feed them and their families for a whole month? 22 Even if we butchered all our sheep and cattle, or caught every fish in the sea, we wouldn't have enough to feed them."

23 The LORD answered, "I can do anything! Watch and you'll see my words come true."

24 Moses told the people what the LORD had said. Then he chose seventy respected leaders and went with them to the sacred tent. While the leaders stood in a circle around the tent,

See also: **10.35:** Psa 68.1. **11.7,8:** Exod 16.31. **11.9:** Exod 16.13–15.

Moses went inside, 25 and the LORD spoke with him. Then the LORD took some authority* from Moses and gave it to the seventy leaders. And when the LORD's Spirit took control of them, they started shouting like prophets. But they did it only this one time.

26 Eldad and Medad were two leaders who had not gone to the tent. But when the Spirit took control of them, they began shouting like prophets in camp. 27 A boy ran to Moses and told him about Eldad and Medad. 28 Joshua* was there helping Moses, as he had done since he was young. And he said to Moses, "Sir, you must stop them!"

29 But Moses replied, "Are you concerned what this might do to me? I wish the LORD would give his Spirit to all his people so everyone could be a prophet." 30 Then Moses and the seventy leaders went back to camp.

The LORD sends quails

31 Some time later the LORD sent a strong wind that blew quails in from the sea until Israel's camp was completely surrounded with birds, piled up about a metre high for miles in every direction. 32 The people picked up quails for two days — each person collected at least a thousand kilogrammes. Then they spread them out to dry. 33 But before the meat could be eaten, the LORD became angry and sent a disease through the camp.

34 After they had buried the people who had been so greedy for meat, they called the place "Graves for the Greedy".*

35 Israel then broke camp and travelled to Hazeroth.

Miriam and Aaron are jealous of Moses

CHAPTER 12

1-3 Although Moses was the most humble person in all the world, Miriam and Aaron started complaining, "Moses had no right to marry that woman from Ethiopia!* Who does he think he is? The LORD has spoken to us, not just to him."

The LORD heard their complaint 4 and told Moses, Aaron, and Miriam to come to the entrance of the sacred tent. 5 There the LORD appeared in a cloud and told Aaron and Miriam to come closer. 6 Then after commanding them to listen carefully, he said:

"I, the LORD, speak to prophets
  in visions and dreams.
7 But my servant Moses
  is the leader of my people.
8 He sees me face to face,
  and everything I say to him
  is perfectly clear.
You have no right to criticize
  my servant Moses."

9 The LORD became angry with Aaron and Miriam. And after the LORD left 10 and the cloud disappeared from over the sacred tent, Miriam's skin turned white with leprosy.* When Aaron saw what had happened to her, 11 he said to Moses, "Sir, please don't punish us for doing such a foolish thing. 12 Don't let Miriam's flesh rot away like a child born dead!"

13 Moses prayed, "LORD God, please heal her."

14 But the LORD replied, "Miriam would be disgraced for seven days if her father had punished her by spitting in her face. So make her stay outside the camp for seven days, before coming back."

15 The people of Israel did not move their camp until Miriam returned seven days later. 16 Then they left Hazeroth and set up camp in the Paran Desert.

Twelve men are sent into Canaan

CHAPTER 13

Twelve men are sent into Canaan
This is also told in Deuteronomy 1.19–33

1 The LORD said to Moses, 2 "Choose a leader from each tribe and send them into Canaan to explore the land I am giving you."

3 So Moses sent twelve tribal leaders from Israel's camp in the Paran Desert 4-16 with orders to explore the land of Canaan. And here are their names:

Shammua son of Zaccur from Reuben,
Shaphat son of Hori from Simeon,
Caleb son of Jephunneh from Judah,
Igal son of Joseph from Issachar,

---

*12.1–3 Ethiopia: The Hebrew text has "Cush", which was a region south of Egypt that included parts of the present countries of Ethiopia and Sudan.

*12.10 leprosy: See the note at 5.2,3.
See also: 12.7: Heb 3.2. 12.14: Num 5.2,3.

Joshua son of Nun from Ephraim,*
Palti son of Raphu from Benjamin,
Gaddiel son of Sodi from Zebulun,
Gaddi son of Susi from Manasseh,
Ammiel son of Gemalli from Dan,
Sethur son of Michael from Asher,
Nahbi son of Vophsi from Naphtali,
and Geuel son of Machi from Gad.

17 Before Moses sent them into Canaan, he said:

After you go through the Southern Desert of Canaan, continue north into the hill country 18 and find out what those regions are like. Be sure to remember how many people live there, how strong they are, 19–20 and if they live in open towns or walled cities. See if the land is good for growing crops and find out what kinds of trees grow there. It's time for grapes to ripen, so try to bring back some of the fruit that grows there.

21 The twelve men left to explore Canaan from the Zin Desert in the south all the way to the town of Rehob near Lebo-Hamath in the north. 22 As they went through the Southern Desert, they came to the town of Hebron, which was seven years older than the Egyptian town of Zoan. In Hebron, they saw the three Anakim* clans of Ahiman, Sheshai, and Talmai. 23–24 When they got to Bunch Valley,* they cut off a branch with such a huge bunch of grapes, that it took two men to carry it on a pole. That's why the place was called Bunch Valley. Along with the grapes, they also took back pomegranates* and figs.

The men report back to the people

25 After exploring the land of Canaan for forty days, 26 the twelve men returned to Kadesh in the Paran Desert and told Moses, Aaron, and the people what they had seen. They showed them the fruit 27 and said:

Look at this fruit! The land we explored is rich with milk and honey. 28 But the people who live there are strong, and their cities are large and walled. We even saw the three Anakim* clans. 29 Besides that, the Amalekites live in the Southern Desert; the Hittites, Jebusites, and Amorites are in the

hill country; and the Canaanites* live along the Mediterranean Sea and the River Jordan.

30 Caleb calmed down the crowd and said, "Let's go and take the land. I know we can do it!"

31 But the other men replied, "Those people are much too strong for us." 32 Then they started spreading rumours and saying, "We won't be able to grow anything in that soil. And the people are like giants. 33 In fact, we saw the Nephilim who are the ancestors of the Anakim. They were so big that we felt as small as grasshoppers."

The people rebel and are punished

CHAPTER 14

The Israelites rebel against Moses

1 After the Israelites heard the report from the twelve men who had explored Canaan, the people cried all night 2 and complained to Moses and Aaron, "We wish we had died in Egypt or somewhere out here in the desert! 3 Is the LORD leading us into Canaan, just to have us killed and our women and children captured? We'd be better off in Egypt." 4 Then they said to one another, "Let's choose our own leader and go back."

5 Moses and Aaron bowed down to pray in front of the crowd. 6 Joshua and Caleb tore their clothes in sorrow 7 and said:

We saw the land ourselves, and it's very good. 8 If we obey the LORD, he will surely give us that land rich with milk and honey. 9 So don't rebel. We have no reason to be afraid of the people who live there. The LORD is on our side, and they won't stand a chance against us!

10 The crowd threatened to stone Moses and Aaron to death. But just then, the LORD appeared in a cloud at the sacred tent.

Moses prays for the people

11 The LORD said to Moses, "I have done great things for these people, and they still reject me by refusing to believe in my power. 12 So they will no longer be my people. I will

---

*13.22,28 Anakim: Perhaps a group of people of great stature (see Deuteronomy 2.10,11,20,21).
*13.23,24 pomegranates: A bright red fruit that looks like an apple.

*13.29 Amalekites . . . Hittites . . . Jebusites . . .
Amorites . . . Canaanites: These people lived in Canaan before the Israelites.
See also: 13.33: Gen 6.4. 14.9: Heb 3.16.

destroy them, but I will make you the ancestor of a nation even stronger than theirs."

13-16 Moses replied:

With your mighty power you rescued your people from Egypt, so please don't destroy us here in the desert. If you do, the Egyptians will hear about it and tell the people of Canaan. Those Canaanites already know that we are your people, and that we see you face to face. And they have heard how you lead us with a thick cloud during the day and flaming fire at night. But if you kill us, they will claim it was because you weren't powerful enough to lead us into Canaan as you promised.

17 Show us your great power, LORD. You promised 18 that you love to show mercy and kindness. And you said that you are very patient, but that you will punish everyone guilty of doing wrong — not only them but their children and grandchildren as well.

19 You are merciful, and you treat people better than they deserve. So please forgive these people, just as you have forgiven them ever since they left Egypt.

20 Then the LORD said to Moses:

In answer to your prayer, I do forgive them. 21 But as surely as I live and my power has no limit, 22-23 I swear that not one of these Israelites will enter the land I promised to give to their ancestors. These people have seen my power in Egypt and in the desert, but they will never see Canaan. They have disobeyed and tested me too many times.

24 My servant Caleb isn't like the others. So because he has faith in me, I will allow him to cross into Canaan, and his descendants will settle there.

25 Now listen, Moses! The Amalekites and the Canaanites live in the valleys of Canaan.* And tomorrow morning, you'll need to turn round and head back into the desert towards the Red Sea.*

The Israelites are punished for complaining

26 The LORD told Moses and Aaron 27-28 to give this message to the people of Israel:

You sinful people have complained against me too many times! Now I swear by my own life that I will give you exactly what you wanted.* 29 You will die here in the desert, and your dead bodies will cover the ground. You have insulted me, and none of you men who are over twenty years old 30 will enter the land I promised to give you as your own — only Caleb and Joshua will.

31 You were worried that your own children would be captured. But I, the LORD, will let them enter the land you have rejected. 32 You will die here in the desert! 33 Your children will wander around in this desert forty years, suffering because of your sins, until all of you are dead. 34 I will cruelly punish you every day for the next forty years — one year for each day that the land was explored. 35 You sinful people who ganged up against me will die here in the desert.

36 Ten of the men sent to explore the land had brought back bad news and had made the people complain against the LORD. 37 So he sent a deadly disease that killed those men, 38 but he let Joshua and Caleb live.

The Israelites fail to enter Canaan

This is also told in Deuteronomy 1.41–45

39 The people of Israel were very sad after Moses gave them the LORD's message. 40 So they got up early the next morning and got ready to head towards the hill country of Canaan. They said, "We were wrong to complain about the LORD. Let's go into the land that he promised us."

41 But Moses replied, "You're disobeying the LORD! Your plan won't work, 42-43 so don't even try it. The LORD refuses to help you, because you turned your backs on him. The Amalekites and the Canaanites are your enemies, and they will attack and defeat you."

44 But the Israelites ignored Moses' and marched towards the hill country, even though the sacred chest and Moses did not go with them. 45 The Amalekites and the

---

*14.25 The Amalekites and the Canaanites . . . valleys of Canaan: That is, all possible ways into Canaan were blocked.
*14.25 Red Sea: Hebrew *yam suph*, here referring to the Gulf of Aqaba, since the term is extended to include the north-eastern arm of the Red Sea (see also the note at Exodus 13.18).

See also: 14.13–19: Exod 32.11–14. 14.18: Exod 20.5,6; 34.6,7; Deut 5.9,10; 7.9,10. 14.21–23: Heb 3.18. 14.24: Josh 14.9–12.

*14.27,28 wanted: See verse 2.
See also: 14.29: Heb 3.17. 14.33: Acts 7.36.

Canaanites came down from the hill country, defeated the Israelites, and chased them as far as the town of Hormah.

Laws and punishments

CHAPTER 15

Laws about sacrifices

¹ The LORD told Moses ² to give the Israelites the following laws about offering sacrifices:

³ Bulls or rams or goats' are the animals that you may burn on the altar as sacrifices to please me.* You may also offer sacrifices voluntarily or because you made a promise, or because they are part of your regular religious ceremonies. The smell of the smoke from these sacrifices is pleasing to me.

⁴⁻⁵ If you sacrifice a young ram or goat, you must also offer a kilogramme of your finest flour mixed with a litre of olive oil as a grain sacrifice. A litre of wine must also be poured on the altar.

⁶⁻⁷ And if the animal is a full-grown ram, you must offer two kilogrammes of flour mixed with one and a half litres of olive oil. One and a half litres of wine must also be poured on the altar. The smell of this smoke is pleasing to me.

⁸ If a bull is offered as a sacrifice to please me or to ask my blessing,* ⁹ you must offer three kilogrammes of flour mixed with two litres of olive oil. ¹⁰ Two litres of wine must also be poured on the altar. The smell of this smoke is pleasing to me.

¹¹⁻¹³ If you are a native Israelite, you must obey these rules each time you offer a bull, a ram, or a goat as a sacrifice. ¹⁴ And the foreigners who live among you must also follow these rules. ¹⁵⁻¹⁶ This law will never change. I am the LORD, and I consider all people the same, whether they are Israelites or foreigners living among you.

¹⁷⁻¹⁹ When you eat food in the land that I am giving you, remember to set aside some of it as an offering to me. ²⁰ From the first batch of bread dough that you make after each new grain harvest, make a loaf of bread and offer it to me, just as you offer grain. ²¹ All your descendants must follow this law and offer part of the first batch of bread dough.

²²⁻²³ The LORD also told Moses to tell the people what must be done if they ever disobey his laws:

²⁴ If all of you disobey one of my laws without meaning to, you must offer a bull as a sacrifice to please me, together with a grain sacrifice, a wine offering, and a goat as a sacrifice for sin. ²⁵ Then the priest will pray and ask me to forgive you. And since you did not mean to do wrong, and you offered sacrifices, ²⁶ the sin of everyone — both Israelites and foreigners among you — will be forgiven.

²⁷ But if one of you does wrong without meaning to, you must sacrifice a year-old female goat as a sacrifice for sin. ²⁸ The priest will then ask me to forgive you, and your sin will be forgiven.

²⁹ The law will be the same for anyone who does wrong without meaning to, whether an Israelite or a foreigner living among you.

³⁰⁻³¹ But if one of you does wrong on purpose, whether Israelite or foreigner, you have sinned against me by disobeying my laws. You will be sent away and will no longer live among the people of Israel.

A man put to death for gathering firewood on the Sabbath

³² Once, while the Israelites were travelling through the desert, a man was caught gathering firewood on the Sabbath.* ³³ He was taken to Moses, Aaron, and the rest of the community. ³⁴ But no one knew what to do with him, so he was not allowed to leave.

³⁵ Then the LORD said to Moses, "Tell the people to take that man outside the camp and stone him to death!" ³⁶ So he was killed, just as the LORD had commanded Moses.

The tassels on the people's clothes

³⁷ The LORD told Moses ³⁸ to say to the people of Israel, "Sew tassels on to the bottom edge of your clothes and tie a purple string to each tassel. ³⁹⁻⁴⁰ These will remind you that you must obey my laws and teachings. And when you do, you will be dedicated to me and won't follow your own sinful desires. ⁴¹ I am the LORD your God who led you out of Egypt."

---

*15.3 sacrifices to please me: See the note at 6.11.
*15.8 to ask my blessing: See the note at 6.14.
See also: 15.16: Lev 24.22.

*15.32 a man . . . Sabbath: No work was to be done on the Sabbath (see Exodus 31.12–17).
See also: 15.27,28: Lev 4.27–31. 15.38: Deut 22.12.

The people rebel

CHAPTER 16

Korah, Dathan, and Abiram lead a rebellion

¹⁻² Korah son of Izhar was a Levite from the Kohathite clan. One day he called together Dathan, Abiram, and On* from the Reuben tribe, and the four of them decided to rebel against Moses. So they asked two hundred and fifty respected Israelite leaders for their support, and together they went to Moses ³ and Aaron and said, "Why do you think you're so much better than anyone else? We're part of the LORD's holy people, and he's with all of us. What makes you think you're the only ones in charge?"

⁴ When Moses heard this, he knelt down to pray.* ⁵ Then he said to Korah and his followers:

Tomorrow morning the LORD will show us the person he has chosen to be his priest, and that man will faithfully serve him.

⁶⁻⁷ Korah, now here is what you and your followers must do: get some fire pans, fill them with coals and incense, and place them near the sacred tent. And the man the LORD chooses will be his priest.* Korah, this time you Levites have gone too far!

⁸⁻⁹ You know that the God of Israel has chosen you Levites from all Israel to serve him by being in charge of the sacred tent and by helping the community to worship in the proper way. What more do you want? ¹⁰ The LORD has given you a special responsibility, and now, Korah, you think you should also be his priest. ¹¹ You and your followers have rebelled against the LORD, not against Aaron.

¹² Then Moses sent for Dathan and Abiram, but they sent back this message: "We won't come! ¹³ It's bad enough that you took us from our rich farmland in Egypt to let us die here in the desert. Now you also want to boss us around! ¹⁴ You keep promising us rich farmlands with fertile fields and vineyards — but where are they? Stop trying to trick these people. No, we won't come to see you."

¹⁵ Moses was very angry and said to the LORD, "Don't listen to these men! I haven't done anything wrong to them. I haven't taken as much as a donkey."

¹⁶ Then he said to Korah, "Tomorrow you and your followers must go with Aaron to the LORD's sacred tent. ¹⁷ Each of you take along your fire pan with incense in it and offer the incense to the LORD."

¹⁸ The next day the men placed incense and coals in their fire pans and stood with Moses and Aaron at the entrance to the sacred tent. ¹⁹ Meanwhile, Korah had convinced the rest of the Israelites to rebel against their two leaders.

When that happened, the LORD appeared in all his glory ²⁰ and said to Moses and Aaron, ²¹ "Get away from the rest of the Israelites so I can kill them at once!"

²² But the two men bowed down and prayed, "Our God, you gave these people life. Why would you punish everyone here when only one man has sinned?"

²³ The LORD answered Moses, ²⁴ "Tell the people to stay away from the tents of Korah, Dathan, and Abiram."

²⁵ Moses walked over to Dathan and Abiram, and the other leaders of Israel followed. ²⁶ Then Moses warned the people, "Get away from the tents of these sinful men! Don't touch anything that belongs to them or you'll be wiped out." ²⁷ So everyone moved away from those tents, except Korah, Dathan, Abiram, and their families.

²⁸ Moses said to the crowd, "The LORD has chosen me and told me to do these things — it wasn't my idea. And here's how you will know: ²⁹ if these men die a natural death, it means the LORD hasn't chosen me. ³⁰ But suppose the LORD does something that has never been done before. For example, what if a huge crack appears in the ground, and these men and their families fall into it and are buried alive, together with everything they own? Then you will know they have turned their backs on the LORD!"

³¹ As soon as Moses said this, the ground under the men opened up ³²⁻³³ and swallowed them alive, together with their families and everything they owned. Then the ground closed back up, and they were gone.

³⁴ The rest of the Israelites heard their screams, so they ran off, shouting, "We don't want that to happen to us!"

---

*16.6,7 get some fire pans . . . his priest: Only priests could offer incense at the sacred altar; anyone else who tried would be killed. In this case, the man who lived would be the one the LORD had chosen.

See also: 16.1: Jude 11.

35 Suddenly the LORD sent a fire that burnt up the two hundred and fifty men who had offered incense to him.

36 Then the LORD said to Moses, 37 "Tell Aaron's son Eleazar to take the fire pans from the smouldering fire and scatter the coals. The pans are now sacred, 38 because they were used for offering incense to me. Have them hammered into a thin layer of bronze as a covering for the altar. Those men died because of their sin, and now their fire pans will become a warning for the rest of the community."

39 Eleazar collected the pans and had them hammered into a thin layer of bronze as a covering for the altar, 40 just as the LORD had told Moses. The pans were a warning to the Israelites that only Aaron's descendants would be allowed to offer incense to the LORD. Anyone else who tried would be punished like Korah and his followers.

The Israelites rebel and are punished

41 The next day the people of Israel again complained against Moses and Aaron, "The two of you killed some of the LORD's people!"

42 As the people crowded around them, Moses and Aaron turned towards the sacred tent, and the LORD appeared in his glory in the cloud covering the tent. 43 So Moses and Aaron walked to the front of the tent, 44 where the LORD said to them, 45 "Stand back! I am going to wipe out these Israelites once and for all."

They immediately bowed down and prayed. 46 Then Moses told Aaron, "Grab your fire pan and fill it with hot coals from the altar. Put incense in it, then quickly take it to where the people are and offer it to the LORD, so they can be forgiven. The LORD is very angry, and people have already started dying!"

47-48 Aaron did exactly what he had been told. He ran over to the crowd of people and stood between the dead bodies and the people who were still alive. He placed the incense on the pan, then offered it to the LORD and asked him to forgive the people's sin. The disease immediately stopped spreading, and no one else died from it. 49 But fourteen thousand seven hundred Israelites were dead, not counting those who had died with Korah and his followers. 50 Aaron walked back and stood with Moses at the sacred tent.

CHAPTER 17

Aaron's walking stick blooms and produces almonds

1 The LORD told Moses:

2-3 Call together the twelve tribes of Israel and tell the leader of each tribe to write his name on the walking stick he carries as a symbol of his authority. Make sure Aaron's name is written on the one from the Levi tribe, then collect all the sticks.

4 Place these sticks in the tent in front of the sacred chest where I appear to you. 5 I will then choose a man to be my priest, and his stick will sprout. After that happens, I won't have to listen to any more complaints about you.

6 Moses told the people what the LORD had commanded, and they gave him the walking sticks from the twelve tribal leaders, including Aaron's from the Levi tribe. 7 Moses took them and placed them in the LORD's sacred tent.

8 The next day when Moses went into the tent, flowers and almonds were already growing on Aaron's stick. 9 Moses brought the twelve sticks out of the tent and showed them to the people. Each of the leaders found his own and took it.

10 But the LORD told Moses, "Put Aaron's stick back! Let it stay near the sacred chest as a warning to anyone who might think about rebelling. If these people don't stop their grumbling about me, I will wipe them out." 11 Moses did what he was told.

12 The Israelites cried out to Moses, "We're done for 13 and doomed if we even get near the sacred tent!"

Priests and Levites

CHAPTER 18

The duties of the priests and Levites

1 The LORD said to Aaron:

You, your sons, and the other Levites of the Kohath clan, are responsible for what happens at the sacred tent.* And you and your sons will be responsible for what the priests do. 2 The Levites are your relatives and are here to help you in your service at the tent. 3 You must see that they perform their duties. But if they go near any of the

See also: 17.8-10: Heb 9.4.

sacred objects or the altar, all of you will die. ⁴ No one else is allowed to take care of the sacred tent or to do anything connected with it. ⁵ Follow these instructions, so I won't become angry and punish the Israelites ever again.

⁶ I alone chose the Levites from all the other tribes to belong to me, and I have given them to you as your helpers. ⁷ But only you and your sons can serve as priests at the altar and in the most holy place. Your work as priests is a gift from me, and anyone else who tries to do that work must be put to death.

The priests' share of offerings given to the LORD

This is also told in Deuteronomy 18.1–8

⁸⁻⁹ The LORD said to Aaron:

I have put you in charge of the sacred gifts and sacrifices that the Israelites bring to me. And from now on, you, your sons, and your descendants will receive part of the sacrifices for sin, as well as part of the grain sacrifices, and the sacrifices to make things right. Your share of these sacrifices will be the parts not burnt on the altar. ¹⁰ Since these things are sacred, they must be eaten near the sacred tent, but only men are allowed to eat them.

¹¹ You will also receive part of the special gifts and offerings that the Israelites bring to me. Any member of your family who is clean and acceptable for worship can eat these things. ¹² For example, when the Israelites bring me the first batches of oil, wine, and grain, you can have the best parts of those gifts. ¹³ And the first part of the crops from their fields and vineyards also belongs to you. The people will offer this to me, then anyone in your family who is clean may have some of it.

¹⁴ Everything in Israel that has been completely dedicated to me* will now belong to you.

¹⁵ The firstborn son in every Israelite family, as well as the firstborn males of their flocks and herds, belong to me. But a firstborn son and every firstborn

donkey* must be bought back from me. ¹⁶ The price for a firstborn son must be at least one month old will be five pieces of silver, weighed according to the official standards. ¹⁷ However, all firstborn cattle, sheep, and goats belong to me and cannot be bought back. Splatter their blood on the altar and send their fat up in smoke, so I can smell it and be pleased. ¹⁸ You are allowed to eat the meat of those animals, just as you can eat the choice ribs and the right hind leg of the special sacrifices.

¹⁹ From now on, the sacred offerings that the Israelites give to me will belong to you, your sons, and your daughters. This is my promise to you and your descendants, and it will never change.

²⁰ You will not receive any land in Israel as your own. I am the LORD, and I will give you whatever you need.

What the Levites receive

The LORD said to Aaron:

²¹ Ten per cent of the Israelites' crops and one out of every ten of their newborn animals belong to me. But I am giving all this to the Levites as their pay for the work they do at the sacred tent. ²²⁻²³ They are the only ones allowed to work at the tent, and they must not let anyone else come near it. Those who do must be put to death, and the Levites will also be punished. This law will never change.

Since the Levites won't be given any land in Israel as their own, ²⁴ they will be given the crops and newborn animals that the Israelites offer to me.

What the Levites must give

²⁵ The LORD told Moses ²⁶ to say to the Levites:

When you receive from the people of Israel ten per cent of their crops and newborn animals, you must offer a tenth of that to me. ²⁷ Just as the Israelites give me part of their grain and wine, you must set aside part of what you receive ²⁸ as an offering to me. That amount must then be given to Aaron, ²⁹ so the best of what you receive will be mine.

---

*18.14 that has been completely dedicated to me: This translates a Hebrew word that describes property and things that were taken away from humans and given to God for ever. Sometimes such things had to be completely destroyed (see Joshua 6.15–19).
See also: 18.14: Lev 27.28.

*18.15 donkey: The Hebrew text has "unclean animal", which probably refers to a donkey (see Exodus 13.13; 34.20).
See also: 18.21: Lev 27.30–33; Deut 14.22–29.

30 After you have dedicated the best parts to me, you can eat the rest, just as the Israelites eat part of their grain and wine after offering them to me.' 31 Your share may be eaten anywhere by anyone in your family, because it is your pay for working at the sacred tent. 32 You won't be punished for eating it, as long as you have already offered the best parts to me.

The gifts and sacrifices brought by the people must remain sacred, and if you eat any part of them before they are offered to me, you will be put to death.

Becoming clean

CHAPTER 19

The ceremony to wash away sin

1-2 The LORD gave Moses and Aaron the following law:

The people of Israel must bring Moses a reddish-brown cow that has nothing wrong with it and that has never been used for ploughing. 3 Moses will give it to Eleazar the priest, then it will be led outside the camp and killed while Eleazar watches. 4 He will dip his finger into the blood and sprinkle it seven times in the direction of the sacred tent. 5 Then the whole cow, including its skin, meat, blood, and insides must be burnt. 6 A priest* is to throw a stick of cedar wood, a hyssop* branch, and a piece of red yarn into the fire.

7 After the ceremony, the priest is to take a bath and wash his clothes. Only then can he go back into the camp, but he remains unclean and unfit for worship until evening. 8 The man who burnt the cow must also wash his clothes and take a bath, but he is also unclean until evening.

9 A man who isn't unclean must collect the ashes of the burnt cow and store them outside the camp in a clean place. The people of Israel can mix these ashes with the water used in the ceremony to wash away sin. 10 The man who collects the ashes must wash his clothes, but will remain unclean until evening. This law must always be obeyed by the people of Israel and the foreigners living among them.

What must be done after touching a dead body

The LORD said:

11 If you touch a dead body, you will be unclean for seven days. 12 But if you wash with the water mixed with the cow's ashes on the third day and again on the seventh day, you will be clean and acceptable for worship. You must wash yourself on those days; if you don't, you will remain unclean. 13 Suppose you touch a dead body, but refuse to be made clean by washing with the water mixed with ashes. You will be guilty of making my sacred tent unclean and will no longer belong to the people of Israel.

14 If someone dies in a tent while you are there, you will be unclean for seven days. And anyone who later enters the tent will also be unclean. 15 Any open jar in the tent is unclean.

16 If you touch the body of someone who was killed or who died of old age, or if you touch a human bone or a grave, you will be unclean for seven days.

17-18 Before you can be made clean, someone who is clean must take some of the ashes from the burnt cow and stir them into a pot of spring water. That same person must dip a hyssop branch in the water and ashes, then sprinkle it on the tent and everything in it, including everyone who was inside. If you have touched a human bone, a grave, or a dead body, you must be sprinkled with that water. 19 If this is done on the third day and on the seventh day, you will be clean. Then after you take a bath and wash your clothes, you can worship that evening.

20 If you are unclean and refuse to be made clean by washing with the water mixed with ashes, you will be guilty of making my sacred tent unclean, and you will no longer belong to the people of Israel. 21 These laws will never change.

The man who sprinkled the water and the ashes on you when you were unclean must also wash his clothes. And whoever touches this water is unclean until evening. 22 When you are unclean, everything you touch becomes unclean, and anyone who touches you will be unclean until evening.

---

*19.6 hyssop: A plant with small clusters of blue flowers and sweet-smelling leaves.
See also: 19.9: Heb 9.13.

On the way to Moab

CHAPTER 20

Water from a rock

This is also told in Exodus 17.1–7

¹ The people of Israel arrived at the Zin Desert during the first month* and set up camp near the town of Kadesh. It was there that Miriam died and was buried.

² The Israelites had no water, so they went to Moses and Aaron ³ and complained, "Moses, we'd be better off if we had died along with the others in front of the LORD's sacred tent.* ⁴ You brought us into this desert, and now we and our livestock are going to die! ⁵ Egypt was better than this horrible place. At least there we had grain and figs and grapevines and pomegranates.* But now we don't even have any water."

⁶ Moses and Aaron went to the entrance of the sacred tent, where they bowed down. The LORD appeared to them in all his glory ⁷⁻⁸ and said, "Moses, get your walking stick.* Then you and Aaron call the people together and command that rock to give you water. That's how you will provide water for the people of Israel and their livestock."

⁹ Moses obeyed and took his stick from the sacred tent. ¹⁰ After he and Aaron had gathered the people around the rock, he said, "Look, you rebellious people, and you will see water flow from this rock!" ¹¹ He raised his stick in the air and struck the rock two times. At once, water gushed from the rock, and the people and their livestock had water to drink.

¹² But the LORD said to Moses and Aaron, "Because you refused to believe in my power, these people did not respect me. And so, you will not be the ones to lead them into the land I have promised."

¹³ The Israelites had complained against the LORD, and he had shown them his holy power by giving them water to drink. So they named the place Meribah, which means "Complaining."

Israel isn't allowed to go through Edom

¹⁴ Moses sent messengers from Israel's camp near Kadesh with this message for the king of Edom:

We are Israelites, your own relatives, and we're sure you have heard the terrible things that have happened to us. ¹⁵ Our ancestors settled in Egypt and lived there a long time. But later the Egyptians were cruel to us, ¹⁶ and when we begged our LORD for help, he answered our prayer and brought us out of that land.

Now we are camped at the border of your territory, near the town of Kadesh. ¹⁷ Please let us go through your country. We won't go near your fields and vineyards, and we won't drink any water from your wells. We will stay on the main road* until we leave your territory.

¹⁸ But the Edomite king answered, "No, I won't let you go through our country! And if you try, we will attack you."

¹⁹ Moses sent back this message: "We promise to stay on the main road, and if any of us or our livestock drink your water, we will pay for it. We just want to pass through."

²⁰ But the Edomite king insisted, "You can't go through our land!"

Then Edom sent out its strongest troops ²¹ to keep Israel from passing through its territory. So the Israelites had to go in another direction.

Aaron dies

²² After the Israelites had left Kadesh and had gone as far as Mount Hor ²³ on the Edomite border, the LORD said, ²⁴ "Aaron, this is where you will die. You and Moses disobeyed me at Meribah, and so you will not enter the land I promised the Israelites. ²⁵ Moses, go with Aaron and his son Eleazar to the top of the mountain. ²⁶ Then take Aaron's priestly robe from him and place it on Eleazar. Aaron will die there."

²⁷ Moses obeyed, and everyone watched as he and Aaron and Eleazar walked to the top of Mount Hor. ²⁸ Moses then took the priestly

---

*20.1 first month: See the note at 9.3.
*20.3 if we had died . . . sacred tent: See 16.41–49.
*20.5 pomegranates: See the note at 13.23,24.
*20.7,8 walking stick: A symbol of his authority.
See also: 20.2–13; Exod 17.1–7.

*20.17 the main road: The Hebrew text has "the King's Highway," which was an important trade route through what is today the country of Jordan. It connected the city of Damascus in Syria with the Gulf of Aqaba in southern Jordan.
See also: 20.28: Exod 29.29; Num 33.38; Deut 10.6.

robe from Aaron and placed it on Eleazar. Aaron died there.

When Moses and Eleazar came down, ²⁹ the people knew that Aaron had died, and they mourned his death for thirty days.

CHAPTER 21

Israel defeats the Canaanites at Hormah

¹ The Canaanite king of Arad lived in the Southern Desert of Canaan, and when he heard that the Israelites were on their way to the village of Atharim, he attacked and took some of them hostage.

² The Israelites prayed, "Our LORD, if you will help us defeat these Canaanites, we will completely destroy their towns and everything in them, to show that they belong to you."*

³ The LORD answered their prayer and helped them wipe out the Canaanite army and completely destroy their towns. That's why one of the towns is named Hormah, which means "Destroyed Place".

Moses makes a bronze snake

⁴ The Israelites had to go around the territory of Edom, so when they left Mount Hor, they headed south towards the Red Sea.* But along the way, the people became so impatient ⁵ that they complained against God and said to Moses, "Did you bring us out of Egypt, just to let us die in the desert? There's no water out here, and we can't stand this awful food!"

⁶ The LORD then sent poisonous snakes that bit and killed many of them.

⁷ Some of the people went to Moses and admitted, "It was wrong of us to insult you and the LORD. Now please ask him to make these snakes go away."

Moses prayed, ⁸ and the LORD answered, "Make a snake out of bronze and place it on top of a pole. Anyone who gets bitten can look at the snake and won't die."

⁹ Moses obeyed the LORD. And all of those who looked at the bronze snake lived, even

though they had been bitten by the poisonous snakes.

Israel's journey to Moab

¹⁰ As the Israelites continued their journey to Canaan, they camped at Oboth, ¹¹ then at Iye-Abarim in the desert east of Moab, ¹² and then in the Zered Gorge. ¹³ After that, they crossed the gorge of the River Arnon and camped in the Moabite desert bordering Amorite territory. The Arnon was the border between the Moabites and the Amorites. ¹⁴ A song in *The Book of the LORD's Battles** mentions the town of Waheb with its creeks in the territory of Suphah. It also mentions the River Arnon, ¹⁵ with its valleys that lie beside the Moabite border and extend to the town of Ar.

¹⁶ From the Arnon, the Israelites went to the well near the town of Beer, where the LORD had said to Moses, "Call the people together, and I will give them water to drink."

¹⁷ That's also the same well the Israelites sang about in this song:

Let's celebrate!
    The well has given us water.
¹⁸ With their royal sceptres,
    our leaders pointed out
    where to dig the well.

The Israelites left the desert and camped near the town of Mattanah, ¹⁹ then at Nahaliel, and then at Bamoth. ²⁰ Finally, they reached Moabite territory, where they camped near Mount Pisgah* in a valley overlooking the desert north of the Dead Sea.

Israel defeats King Sihon the Amorite

This is also told in Deuteronomy 2.26–37

²¹ The Israelites sent this message to King Sihon of the Amorites:

²² Please let us pass through your territory. We promise to stay away from your fields and vineyards, and we won't drink any water from your wells. As long as we're in your land, we won't get off the main road.*

*21.2 completely destroy . . . belong to you: The complete destruction of a town and everything in it, including its people and animals, showed that the town belonged to the LORD and could no longer be used by humans.
*21.4 Red Sea: See the note at 14.25.
See also: 21.1: Num 33.40. 21.4: Deut 2.1.
21.5,6: 1 Cor 10.9. 21.9: 2 Kings 18.4; John 3.14.

*21.14 The Book of the LORD's Battles: This may have been a collection of ancient war songs.
*21.20 Mount Pisgah: This probably refers to the highest peak in the Abarim Mountains in Moab.
*21.22 the main road: See the note at 20.17.

23 But Sihon refused to let Israel travel through his land. Instead, he called together his entire army and marched into the desert to attack Israel near the town of Jahaz. 24 Israel defeated them and took over the Amorite territory from the gorge of the River Arnon in the south to the gorge of the River Jabbok in the north. Beyond the Jabbok was the territory of the Ammonites, who were much stronger than Israel.

25 The Israelites settled in the Amorite towns, including the capital city of Heshbon with its surrounding villages. 26 King Sihon had ruled from Heshbon, after defeating the Moabites and taking over their land north of the Arnon gorge. 27 That's why the Amorites had written this poem about Heshbon:

> Come and rebuild Heshbon,
>   King Sihon's capital city!
> 28 His armies marched out
>   like fiery flames,
> burning down the town of Ar
> and destroying* the hills
>   along the River Arnon.
> 29 You Moabites are done for!
>   Your god Chemosh
>   deserted your people;
> they were captured, taken away
>   by King Sihon the Amorite.
> 30 We completely defeated Moab.
>   The towns of Heshbon and Dibon,
>   of Nophah and Medeba
>   are ruined and gone.*

31 After the Israelites had settled in the Amorite territory, 32 Moses sent some men to explore the town of Jazer. Later, the Israelites captured the villages surrounding it and forced out the Amorites who lived there.

Israel defeats King Og of Bashan

This is also told in Deuteronomy 3.1–11

33 The Israelites headed towards the region of Bashan, where King Og ruled, and he led his entire army to Edrei to meet Israel in battle. 34 The LORD said to Moses, "Don't be afraid of Og. I will help you defeat him and his army, just as you did King Sihon who ruled in Heshbon. Og's territory will be yours." 35 So the Israelites wiped out Og, his family, and his entire army — there were no survivors. Then Israel took over the land of Bashan.

See also: 21.28,29: Jer 48.45,46.

The messages of Balaam

CHAPTER 22

1 Israel moved from there to the hills of Moab, where they camped across the River Jordan from the town of Jericho.

King Balak of Moab hires Balaam to curse Israel

2-3 When King Balak* of Moab and his people heard how many Israelites there were and what they had done to the Amorites, he and the Moabites were terrified and panicked. 4 They said to the Midianite leaders, "Those Israelites will wipe out everything in sight, like a bull eating grass in a field."

So King Balak 5 sent a message to Balaam son of Beor who lived among his relatives in the town of Pethor near the River Euphrates. It said:

> I need your help. A huge group of people has come here from Egypt and settled near my territory. 6 They are too powerful for us to defeat, so would you come and place a curse on them? Perhaps then we can drive them out. I know that anyone we bless will be successful, but anyone you curse will fail.

7 The leaders of Moab and Midian left and took along money to pay Balaam for his work. When they got to his house, they gave him Balak's message.

8 "Spend the night here," Balaam replied, "and tomorrow I will tell you the LORD's answer." So the officials stayed at his house.

9 During the night, God asked Balaam, "Who are these people at your house?"

10 "They are messengers from King Balak of Moab," Balaam answered. "He sent them 11 to ask me to go to Moab and place a curse on the people who have come there from Egypt. They have settled everywhere around him, and he wants to drive them out."

12 But God replied, "Don't go with Balak's messengers. I have blessed those people who have come from Egypt, so don't curse them."

13 The next morning, Balaam said to Balak's officials, "Go back home. The LORD says I cannot go with you."

14 The officials left and told Balak that Balaam refused to come.

*22.2,3 Balak: Hebrew "Balak son of Zippor".
See also: 22.5: Num 31.8; 2 Pet 2.15,16.

44-47 There were 53,400 men from the tribe of Asher; they were from the clans of Imnah, Ishvi, and Beriah, and from the two clans of Heber and Malchiel, the sons of Beriah. Asher's daughter was Serah.

48-50 There were 45,400 men from the tribe of Naphtali; they were from the clans of Jahzeel, Guni, Jezer, and Shillem.

51 The total number of Israelite men listed was 601,730.

52 The LORD said to Moses, 53 "Divide the land of Canaan among these tribes, according to the number of people in each one, 54 so the larger tribes have more land than the smaller ones. 55-56 I will show you* what land to give each tribe, and they will receive as much land as they need, according to the number of people in it."

57 The tribe of Levi included the clans of the Gershonites, Kohathites, Merarites, 58 as well as the clans of Libni, Hebron, Mahli, Mushi, and Korah. Kohath the Levite was the father of Amram, 59 the husband of Levi's daughter Jochebed, who was born in Egypt. Amram and Jochebed's three children were Aaron, Moses, and Miriam. 60 Aaron was the father of Nadab, Abihu, Eleazar, and Ithamar. 61 But Nadab and Abihu had died when they offered fire that was unacceptable to the LORD.*

62 In the tribe of Levi there were 23,000 men and boys at least a month old. They were not listed with the other tribes, because they would not receive any land in Canaan.

63 Moses and Eleazar counted the Israelites while they were camped in the hills of Moab across the River Jordan from Jericho. 64 None of the people that Moses and Aaron had counted in the Sinai Desert were still alive, 65 except Caleb son of Jephunneh and Joshua son of Nun. The LORD had said that everyone else would die there in the desert.*

---

*26.55,56 I will show you: The Hebrew text has "Cast lots to find out". Pieces of wood or stone (called "lots") were used to find out what the LORD wanted his people to do.
*26.61 Nadab and Abihu . . . the LORD: See 3.1-4 and Leviticus 10.1,2.
*26.64,65 None of the people . . . the desert: See 14.26-30.

See also: 26.52-56: Num 34.13; Josh 14.1,2.
26.60: Num 3.2. 26.61: Lev 10.1,2; Num 3.4.
26.65: Num 14.26-35.

The daughters of Zelophehad are given land

CHAPTER 27

1 Zelophehad* was from the Manasseh tribe, and he had five daughters, whose names were Mahlah, Noah, Hoglah, Milcah, and Tirzah.

2 One day his daughters went to the sacred tent, where they met with Moses, Eleazar, and some other leaders of Israel, as well as a large crowd of Israelites. The young women said:

3 You know that our father died in the desert. But it was for something he did wrong, not for joining with Korah in rebelling against the LORD.

Our father left no sons 4 to carry on his family name. But why should his name die out for that reason? Give us some land like the rest of his relatives in our clan, so our father's name can live on.

5 Moses asked the LORD what should be done, 6 and the LORD answered:

7 Zelophehad's daughters are right. They should each be given part of the land their father would have received.

8 Tell the Israelites that when a man dies without a son, his daughter will inherit his land. 9 If he has no daughter, his brothers will inherit the land. 10 But if he has no brothers, his father's brothers will inherit the land. 11 And if his father has no brothers, the land must be given to his nearest relative in the clan. This is my law, and the Israelites must obey it.

Joshua is appointed Israel's leader

This is also told in Deuteronomy 31.1-8

12 The LORD said to Moses, "One day you will go up into the Abarim Mountains, and from there you will see the land I am giving the Israelites. 13 After you have seen it, you will die,* just like your brother Aaron, 14 because both of you disobeyed me at

---

*27.12,13 One day . . . you will die: The story of Moses' death is in Deuteronomy 34.1-8.
See also: 27.7: Num 36.2. 27.12-14: Deut 3.23-27; 32.48-52.

Meribah near the town of Kadesh in the Zin Desert. When the Israelites insulted me there, you didn't believe in my holy power."*

¹⁵ Moses replied, ¹⁶ "You are the LORD God, and you know what is in everyone's heart. So I ask you to appoint a leader for Israel. ¹⁷ Your people need someone to lead them into battle, or else they will be like sheep wandering around without a shepherd."

¹⁸ The LORD answered, "Joshua son of Nun can do the job. Place your hands on him to show that he is the one to take your place. ¹⁹ Then go with him and make him stand in front of Eleazar the priest and the Israelites. Appoint Joshua as their new leader ²⁰ and tell them they must now obey him, just as they obey you. ²¹ But Joshua must depend on Eleazar to find out from me' what I want him to do as he leads Israel into battle."

²² Moses followed the LORD's instructions and took Joshua to Eleazar and the people, ²³ then he placed his hands on Joshua and appointed him Israel's leader.

Various laws and sacrifices for Israel's festivals

CHAPTER 28

Regular daily sacrifices

This is also told in Exodus 29.38–43; Leviticus 6.8–13

¹ The LORD told Moses ² to say to the people of Israel:

Offer sacrifices to me at the appointed times of worship, so that I will smell the smoke and be pleased.

³ Each day offer two rams a year old as sacrifices to please me.* The animals must have nothing wrong with them; ⁴ one will be sacrificed in the morning, and the other in the evening. ⁵ Along with each of them, one kilogramme of your finest flour mixed with a litre of olive oil must be offered as a grain sacrifice. ⁶ This sacrifice to please me was first offered on Mount Sinai. ⁷ Finally, along with each of these two sacrifices, a litre of wine must be poured on the altar as a drink offering. ⁸ The second ram will be

sacrificed that evening, along with the other offerings, just like the one sacrificed that morning. The smell of the smoke from these sacrifices will please me.

The sacrifice on the Sabbath

The LORD said:

⁹⁻¹⁰ On the Sabbath, in addition to the regular daily sacrifices,* you must sacrifice two rams a year old to please me.* These rams must have nothing wrong with them, and they will be sacrificed with a drink offering and two kilogrammes of your finest flour mixed with olive oil.

The sacrifices on the first day of the month

The LORD said:

¹¹ On the first day of each month, bring to the altar two bulls, one full-grown ram, and seven rams a year old that have nothing wrong with them. Then offer these as sacrifices to please me.* ¹² Three kilogrammes of your finest flour mixed with olive oil must be offered with each bull as a grain sacrifice. Two kilogrammes of flour mixed with oil must be offered with the ram, ¹³ and one kilogramme of flour mixed with oil must be offered with each of the young rams. The smell of the smoke from these sacrifices will please me.

¹⁴⁻¹⁵ Offer two litres of wine as a drink offering with each bull, one and a half litres with the ram, and one litre with each of the young rams.

Finally, you must offer a goat* as a sacrifice for sin.

These sacrifices are to be offered on the first day of each month, in addition to the regular daily sacrifices.*

The sacrifices during Passover and the Festival of Thin Bread

This is also told in Leviticus 23.4–8

The LORD said:

¹⁶ Celebrate Passover in honour of me on the fourteenth day of the first month* of each year. ¹⁷ The following day will begin

---

27.14 both of you . . . my holy power: See 20.1–13.
28.3 sacrifices to please me: See the note at 6.11.
See also: 27.17: 1 King 22.17; Ezek 34.5; Matt 9.36; Mark 6.34. 27.18: Exod 24.13. 27.21: Exod 28.30; 1 Sam 14.41; 28.6. 27.23: Deut 31.23.

28.9,10,14,15 regular daily sacrifices: See 28.1–8.
28.9,10,11 sacrifice(s) . . . to please me: See the note at 6.11.
28.16 first month: See the note at 9.3.
See also: 28.16: Exod 12.1–13; Deut 16.1,2.
28.17–25: Exod 12.14–20; 23.15; 34.18; Deut 16.3–8.

the Festival of Thin Bread, which will last for a week. During this time you must honour me by eating bread made without yeast.

18 On the first day of this festival, you must rest from your work and come together for worship. 19 Bring to the altar two bulls, one full-grown ram, and seven rams a year old that have nothing wrong with them. And then offer these as sacrifices to please me.* 20 Three kilogrammes of your finest flour mixed with olive oil must be offered with each bull as a grain sacrifice. Two kilogrammes of flour mixed with oil must be offered with the ram, 21 and one kilogramme of flour mixed with oil must be offered with each of the young rams. 22 Also offer a goat* as a sacrifice for the sins of the people. 23-24 All of these are to be offered in addition to the regular daily sacrifices,* and the smoke from them will please me. 25 Then on the last day of the festival, you must once again rest from work and come together for worship.

The sacrifices during the Harvest Festival

This is also told in Leviticus 23.15-22

The LORD said:

26 On the first day of the Harvest Festival, you must rest from your work, come together for worship, and bring a sacrifice of new grain. 27 Offer two young bulls, one full-grown ram, and seven rams a year old as sacrifices to please me.* 28 Three kilogrammes of your finest flour mixed with olive oil must be offered with each bull as a grain sacrifice. Two kilogrammes of flour mixed with oil must be offered with the ram, 29 and one kilogramme of flour mixed with oil must be offered with each of the young rams. 30 Also offer a goat* as a sacrifice for sin. 31 The animals must have nothing wrong with them and are to be sacrificed along with the regular daily sacrifices.*

CHAPTER 29

The sacrifices at the Festival of Trumpets

This is also told in Leviticus 23.23-25

The LORD said:

1 On the first day of the seventh month,* you must rest from your work and come together to celebrate at the sound of the trumpets. 2 Bring to the altar one bull, one full-grown ram, and seven rams a year old that have nothing wrong with them. And then offer these as sacrifices to please me.* 3 Three kilogrammes of your finest flour mixed with olive oil must be offered with the bull as a grain sacrifice. Two kilogrammes of flour mixed with oil must be offered with the ram, 4 and one kilogramme of flour mixed with oil must be offered with each of the young rams. 5 You must also offer a goat* as a sacrifice for sin. 6 These sacrifices are to be made in addition to the regular daily sacrifices* and the sacrifices for the first day of the month.* The smoke from these sacrifices will please me.

The sacrifices on the Great Day of Forgiveness

This is also told in Leviticus 23.26-32

The LORD said:

7 The tenth day of the seventh month* is the Great Day of Forgiveness.* On that day you must rest from all work and come together for worship. Show sorrow for your sins by going without food, 8 and bring to the altar one young bull, one full-grown ram, and seven rams a year old that have nothing wrong with them. Then offer these as sacrifices to please me.* 9 Three kilogrammes of your finest flour mixed with olive oil must be offered with the bull as a grain sacrifice. Two kilogrammes of flour mixed with oil must be offered with the ram, 10 and one kilogramme of flour mixed with oil must be offered with each of

---

*28.19,27 sacrifices to please me: See the note at 6.11.
*28.23,24,31 regular daily sacrifices: See 28.1-8.
See also: 28.26-31: Exod 23.16; 34.22; Deut 16.9-12.

*29.1,7 seventh month: Tishri (also called Ethanim), the seventh month of the Hebrew calendar, from about mid-September to mid-October.
*29.2,8 sacrifices to please me: See the note at 6.11.
*29.6 regular daily sacrifices: See 28.1-8.
*29.6 sacrifices . . . month: See 28.11-15.
*29.7 Great Day of Forgiveness: Traditionally known as the Day of Atonement.
See also: 29.7-11: Lev 16.29-34.

the young rams. ¹¹ A goat* must also be sacrificed for the sins of the people. You will offer these sacrifices in addition to the sacrifice to ask forgiveness and the regular daily sacrifices.*

The sacrifices during the Festival of Shelters

This is also told in Leviticus 23.33–44

The LORD said:

¹² Beginning on the fifteenth day of the seventh month* and continuing for seven days, everyone must celebrate the Festival of Shelters in honour of me.

¹³ On the first day, you must rest from your work and come together for worship. Bring to the altar thirteen bulls, two full-grown rams, and fourteen rams a year old that have nothing wrong with them. Then offer these as sacrifices to please me.* ¹⁴ Three kilogrammes of your finest flour mixed with olive oil must be offered with each bull as a grain sacrifice. Two kilogrammes of flour mixed with oil must be offered with each of the rams, ¹⁵ and one kilogramme of flour mixed with oil must be offered with each of the young rams. ¹⁶ You must also offer a goat* as a sacrifice for sin. These are to be offered in addition to the regular daily sacrifices.*

¹⁷⁻³⁴ For the next six days of the festival, you will sacrifice one less bull than the day before, so that on the seventh day, seven bulls will be sacrificed. The other sacrifices and offerings must remain the same for each of these days.

³⁵ On the eighth day, you must once again rest from your work and come together for worship. ³⁶ Bring to the altar one bull, one full-grown ram, and seven rams a year old that have nothing wrong with them. Then offer these as sacrifices to please me. ³⁷ You must also offer the proper grain sacrifices and drink offerings of wine with each animal. ³⁸ And offer a goat* as the sacrifice to ask forgiveness for the people. These sacrifices are made in addition to the regular daily sacrifices.*

³⁹ You must offer all these sacrifices to me at the appointed times of worship, together with any offerings that are voluntarily given or given because of a promise.

⁴⁰ Moses told the people of Israel everything the LORD had told him about the sacrifices.

CHAPTER 30

Making promises to the LORD

¹ The LORD told Moses to say to Israel's tribal leaders:

² When one of you men makes a promise to the LORD,* you must keep your word.

³ Suppose a young woman who is still living with her parents makes a promise to the LORD. ⁴ If her father hears about it and says nothing, she must keep her promise. ⁵ But if he hears about it and objects, then she no longer has to keep her promise. The LORD will forgive her, because her father did not agree with the promise.

⁶⁻⁷ Suppose a woman makes a promise to the LORD and then gets married. If her husband later hears about the promise but says nothing, she must do what she said, whether she meant it or not. ⁸ But if her husband hears about the promise and objects, she no longer has to keep it, and the LORD will forgive her.

⁹ Widows and divorced women must keep every promise they make to the LORD.

¹⁰ Suppose a married woman makes a promise to the LORD. ¹¹ If her husband hears about the promise and says nothing, she must do what she said. ¹² But if he hears about the promise and does object, she no longer has to keep it. The LORD will forgive her, because her husband would not allow her to keep the promise. ¹³ Her husband has the final say about any promises she makes to the LORD. ¹⁴ If her husband hears about a promise and says nothing about it for a whole day, she must do what she said — since he did not object, the promise must be kept. ¹⁵ But if he waits until the next day to stop her from keeping her promise, he is the one who must be punished.

¹⁶ These are the laws that the LORD gave Moses about husbands and wives, and about young daughters who still live at home.

---

*29.11,16,38 regular daily sacrifices: See 28.1–8.
*29.12 seventh month: See the note at 29.1.
*29.13 sacrifices to please me: See the note at 6.11.
See also: 29.12–38: Lev 23.34; Deut 16.13–15.

*30.2 a promise to the LORD: Either the promise of a gift or the promise to do something.
See also: 30.2: Deut 23.21–23; Matt 5.33.

Israel defeats Midian and prepares to cross the River Jordan

CHAPTER 31

Israel's war against Midian

[1] The LORD said to Moses, [2] "Before you die, make sure that the Midianites are punished for what they did to Israel."*

[3] Then Moses told the people, "The LORD wants to punish the Midianites. So tell our men to prepare for battle. [4] Each tribe will send a thousand men to fight."

[5] Twelve thousand men were picked from the tribes of Israel, and after they were prepared for battle, [6] Moses sent them off to war. Phinehas the son of Eleazar went with them and took along some things from the sacred tent* and the trumpets for sounding the battle signal.

[7] The Israelites fought against the Midianites, just as the LORD had commanded Moses. They killed all the men, [8] including Balaam son of Beor and the five Midianite kings, Evi, Rekem, Zur, Hur, and Reba. [9] The Israelites captured every woman and child, then led away the Midianites' cattle and sheep, and took everything else that belonged to them. [10] They also burnt down the Midianite towns and villages.

[11] Israel's soldiers gathered together everything they had taken from the Midianites, including the captives and the animals. [12-13] Then they returned to their own camp in the hills of Moab across the River Jordan from Jericho, where Moses, Eleazar, and the other Israelite leaders met the troops outside camp.

[14] Moses became angry with the army commanders [15] and said, "I can't believe you let the women live! [16] They are the ones who followed Balaam's advice and invited our people to worship the god Baal-Peor. That's why the LORD punished us by killing so many of our people. [17] You must put to death every boy and all the women who have ever had sex. [18] But do not kill the young women who have never had sex. You may keep them for yourselves."

[19] Then Moses said to the soldiers, "If you killed anyone or touched a dead body, you are unclean and have to stay outside the camp for seven days. On the third and seventh days, you must go through a ceremony to make yourselves and your captives clean. [20] Then wash your clothes and anything made from animal skin, goat's hair, or wood."

[21-23] Eleazar then explained, "If you need to purify something that won't burn, such as gold, silver, bronze, iron, tin, or lead, you must first place it in a hot fire. After you take it out, sprinkle it with the water that purifies. Everything else should only be sprinkled with the water. Do all of this, just as the LORD commanded Moses. [24] Wash your clothes on the seventh day, and after that, you will be clean and may return to the camp."

Everything taken from the Midianites is divided

[25] The LORD told Moses:

[26-27] Make a list of everything taken from the Midianites, including the captives and the animals. Then divide them between the soldiers and the rest of the people. Eleazar the priest and the family leaders will help you.

[28-29] From the half that belongs to the soldiers, set aside for the LORD one out of every five hundred people or animals and give these to Eleazar.

[30] From the half that belongs to the people, set aside one out of every fifty and give these to the Levites in charge of the sacred tent.

[31] Moses and Eleazar followed the LORD's instructions [32-35] and listed everything that had been taken from the Midianites. The list included 675,000 sheep and goats, 72,000 cattle, 61,000 donkeys, and 32,000 young women who had never had sex.

[36-47] Each half included 337,500 sheep and goats, 36,000 cattle, 30,500 donkeys, and 16,000 young women. From the half that belonged to the soldiers, Moses counted out 675 sheep and goats, 72 cattle, 61 donkeys, and 32 women and gave them to Eleazar to be dedicated to the LORD. Then from the half that belonged to the people, Moses set aside one out of every fifty animals and women, as the LORD had said, and gave them to the Levites.

[48] The army commanders went to Moses [49] and said, "Sir, we have counted our troops,

---

*31.2 Midianites . . . to Israel: See 25.1–18.
*31.6 Phinehas . . . sacred tent: Phinehas would serve as the priest during the battle, so he took along the things needed to ask God what he wanted done.
See also: 31.16: Num 25.1–9.

and not one soldier is missing. ⁵⁰ So we want to give the LORD all the gold jewellery we took from the Midianites. It's our gift to him for watching over us and our troops."

⁵¹ Moses and Eleazar accepted the jewellery from the commanders, ⁵² and its total weight was nearly two hundred kilogrammes. ⁵³ This did not include the things that the soldiers had kept for themselves. ⁵⁴ So Moses and Eleazar placed the gold in the LORD's sacred tent to remind Israel of what had happened.*

CHAPTER 32

Land east of the River Jordan is settled

This is also told in Deuteronomy 3.12–22

¹ The tribes of Reuben and Gad owned a lot of cattle and sheep, and they saw that the regions of Jazer and Gilead had good pasture land. ² So they went to Moses, Eleazar, and the other leaders of Israel and said, ³⁻⁴ "The LORD has helped us capture the land around the towns of Ataroth, Dibon, Jazer, Nimrah, Heshbon, Elealeh, Sebam, Nebo, and Beon. That's good pasture land, and since we own cattle and sheep, ⁵ would you let us stay here east of the River Jordan and have this land as our own?"

⁶ Moses answered:

You mean you'd stay here while the rest of the Israelites go into battle? ⁷ If you did that, it would discourage the others from crossing over into the land the LORD promised them. ⁸ This is exactly what happened when I sent your ancestors from Kadesh-Barnea to explore the land. ⁹ They went as far as Eshcol Valley, then returned and told the people that we should not enter it. ¹⁰ The LORD became very angry. ¹¹ And he said that no one who was twenty years or older when they left Egypt would enter the land he had promised to Abraham, Isaac, and Jacob. Not one of those people believed in the LORD's power, ¹² except Caleb and Joshua.* They remained faithful to the LORD, ¹³ but he was so angry with the others that he forced them to wander around in the desert forty years. By that time everyone who had sinned against him had died.

¹⁴ Now you people of Reuben and Gad are doing the same thing and making the LORD even angrier. ¹⁵ If you reject the LORD, he will once again abandon his people and

leave them here in the desert. And you will be to blame!

¹⁶ The men from Reuben and Gad replied:

Let us build places to keep our sheep and goats, and towns for our wives and children, ¹⁷ where they can stay and be safe. Then we'll prepare to fight and lead the other tribes into battle. ¹⁸ We will stay with them until they have settled in their own tribal lands. ¹⁹ The land on this side of the River Jordan will be ours, so we won't expect to receive any on the other side.

²⁰ Moses said:

You promised that you would be ready to fight for the LORD. ²¹ You also agreed to cross the Jordan and stay with the rest of the Israelites, until the LORD forces our enemies out of the land. If you do these things, ²² then after the LORD helps Israel capture the land, you can return to your own land. You will no longer have to stay with the others. ²³ But if you don't keep your promise, you will sin against the LORD and be punished.

²⁴ Go ahead and build towns for your wives and children, and places for your sheep and goats. Just be sure to do what you have promised.

²⁵ The men from Reuben and Gad answered:

Sir, we will do just what you have said. ²⁶ Our wives and children and sheep and cattle will stay here in the towns in Gilead. ²⁷ But those of us who are prepared for battle will cross the Jordan and fight for the LORD.

²⁸ Then Moses said to Eleazar, Joshua, and the family leaders, ²⁹ "Make sure that the tribes of Gad and Reuben prepare for battle and cross the River Jordan with you. If they do, then after the land is in your control, give them the region of Gilead as their tribal land. ³⁰ But if they break their promise, they will receive land on the other side of the Jordan, like the rest of the tribes."

³¹ The tribes of Gad and Reuben replied, "We are your servants and will do whatever the LORD has commanded. ³² We will cross the River Jordan, ready to fight for the LORD in Canaan. But the land we will inherit as our own will be on this side of the river."

³³ So Moses gave the tribes of Gad, Reuben, and half of Manasseh* the territory and towns that King Sihon the Amorite had ruled, as

See also: 32.8,9: Num 13.17–33; 32.10–13: Num 14.26–35.   See also: 32.28–32: Josh 1.12–15.

well as the territory and towns that King Og of Bashan had ruled.*

³⁴ The tribe of Gad rebuilt the towns of Dibon, Ataroth, Aroer, ³⁵ Atroth-Shophan, Jazer, Jogbehah, ³⁶ Beth-Nimrah, and Beth-Haran. They built walls around them and also built places to keep their sheep and goats.

³⁷ The tribe of Reuben rebuilt Heshbon, Elealeh, Kiriathaim, ³⁸ Sibmah, as well as the towns that used to be known as Nebo and Baal-Meon. They renamed all those places.

³⁹ The clan of Machir from the tribe of East Manasseh went to the region of Gilead, captured its towns, and forced out the Amorites. ⁴⁰ So Moses gave the Machirites the region of Gilead, and they settled there.

⁴¹ Jair from the Manasseh tribe captured villages and renamed them "Villages of Jair."*

⁴² Nobah captured the town of Kenath with its villages and renamed it Nobah.

CHAPTER 33

Israel's journey from Egypt to Moab

¹ As Israel travelled from Egypt under the command of Moses and Aaron, ² Moses kept a list of the places where they camped, just as the LORD had instructed. Here is the record of their journey:

³⁻⁴ Israel left the Egyptian city of Rameses on the fifteenth day of the first month.* This was the day after the LORD had punished Egypt's gods by killing the firstborn sons in every Egyptian family. So while the Egyptians were burying the bodies, they watched the Israelites proudly* leave their country.

⁵ After the Israelites left Rameses, they camped at Succoth, ⁶ from there, they moved their camp to Etham on the edge of the desert. ⁷ Then they turned back towards Pi-Hahiroth, east of Baal-Zephon, and camped near Migdol. ⁸ They left Pi-Hahiroth,* crossed the Red Sea,* walked three days into the Etham Desert and camped at Marah. ⁹ Next, they camped at Elim, where there were twelve springs of water and seventy palm trees. ¹⁰ They left Elim and camped near the Red Sea,* ¹¹ then turned east and camped

along the western edge of the Sinai Desert.*

¹²⁻¹⁴ From there they went to Dophkah, Alush, and Rephidim, where they had no water.* ¹⁵ They left Rephidim and finally reached the Sinai Desert.

¹⁶⁻³⁶ As Israel travelled from the Sinai Desert to Kadesh in the Zin Desert, they camped at Kibroth-Hattaavah, Hazeroth, Rithmah, Rimmon-Perez, Libnah, Rissah, Kehelathah, Mount Shepher, Haradah, Makheloth, Tahath, Terah, Mithkah, Hashmonah, Moseroth, Bene-Jaakan, Hor-Haggidgad, Jotbathah, Abronah, Ezion-Geber, and finally Kadesh. ³⁷ When they left Kadesh, they came to Mount Hor, on the border of Edom.

³⁸ That's where the LORD commanded Aaron the priest to go to the top of the mountain. Aaron died there on the first day of the fifth month,* forty years after the Israelites left Egypt. ³⁹ He was one hundred and twenty-three years old at the time.

⁴⁰ It was then that the Canaanite king of Arad, who lived in the Southern Desert of Canaan, heard that Israel was headed that way.

⁴¹⁻⁴⁷ The Israelites left Mount Hor and headed towards Moab. Along the way, they camped at Zalmonah, Punon, Oboth, Iye-Abarim in the territory of Moab, Dibon-Gad, Almon-Diblathaim, at a place near Mount Nebo in the Abarim Mountains, ⁴⁸ and finally in the lowlands of Moab across the River Jordan from Jericho. ⁴⁹ Their camp stretched from Beth-Jeshimoth to Acacia.

The LORD's command to conquer Canaan

⁵⁰ While Israel was camped in the lowlands of Moab across the River Jordan from Jericho, the LORD told Moses ⁵¹ to give the people of Israel this message:

When you cross the River Jordan and enter Canaan, ⁵² you must force out the people living there. Destroy their idols and tear down their altars. ⁵³ Then settle in the land — I have given it to you as your own.

⁵⁴ I will show you* how to divide the land among the tribes, according to the

---

*33.3,4 **first month:** See the note at 9.3.

*33.8 **Red Sea:** Hebrew *hayyam* "the Sea", understood as *yam suph*, "Sea of Reeds" (see also note at Exodus 13.18).

*33.10 **Red Sea:** Hebrew *yam suph*, here referring to the Gulf of Suez, since the term is extended to include the north-western arm of the Red Sea (see also the note at Exodus 13.18).

*33.12–14 **Rephidim . . . no water:** See Exodus 17.1–7.

*33.38 **fifth month:** Ab, the fifth month of the Hebrew calendar, from about mid-July to mid-August.

*33.54 **I will show you:** See the note at 26.55,56.

See also: 33.38: Num 20.22–28; Deut 10.6; 32.50.
33.40: Num 21.1.   33.54: Num 26.54–56.

number of clans in each one, so that the larger tribes will have more land than the smaller ones.

⁵⁵ If you don't force out all the people there, they will be like pointed sticks in your eyes and thorns in your back. They will always be trouble for you, ⁵⁶ and I will treat you as cruelly as I planned to treat them.

CHAPTER 34

Israel's borders

¹ The LORD told Moses ² to tell the people of Israel that their land in Canaan would have the following borders:

³ The southern border will be the Zin Desert and the north-west part of Edom. This border will begin at the south end of the Dead Sea. ⁴ It will go west from there, but will turn southward to include Scorpion Pass, the village of Zin, and the town of Kadesh-Barnea. From there, the border will continue to Hazar-Addar and on to Azmon. ⁵ It will run along the Egyptian Gorge and end at the Mediterranean Sea.

⁶ The western border will be the Mediterranean Sea.

⁷ The northern border will begin at the Mediterranean, then continue eastward to Mount Hor.* ⁸ After that, it will run to Lebo-Hamath and across to Zedad, which is the northern edge of your land. ⁹ From Zedad, the border will continue east to Ziphron and end at Hazar-Enan.

¹⁰ The eastern border will begin at Hazar-Enan in the north, then run south to Shepham, ¹¹ and on down to Riblah on the east side of Ain. From there, it will go south to the eastern hills of Lake Galilee,* ¹² then follow the River Jordan down to the north end of the Dead Sea.

The land within those four borders will belong to you.

¹³ Then Moses told the people, "You will receive the land inside these borders. It will be yours, but the LORD has commanded you to divide it among the nine and a half tribes. ¹⁴ The tribes of Reuben, Gad, and East Manasseh have already been given their land ¹⁵ across from Jericho, east of the River Jordan."

The leaders who will divide the land

¹⁶ The LORD said to Moses, ¹⁷ "Eleazar the priest and Joshua son of Nun will divide the land for the Israelites. ¹⁸ One leader from each tribe will help them, ¹⁹⁻²⁸ and here is the list of their names:

Caleb son of Jephunneh from Judah,
Shemuel son of Ammihud from Simeon,
Elidad son of Chislon from Benjamin,
Bukki son of Jogli from Dan,
Hanniel son of Ephod from Manasseh,
Kemuel son of Shiphtan from Ephraim,
Elizaphan son of Parnach from Zebulun,
Paltiel son of Azzan from Issachar,
Ahihud son of Shelomi from Asher,
and Pedahel son of Ammihud
    from Naphtali."

²⁹ These are the men the LORD commanded to help Eleazar and Joshua divide the land for the Israelites.

CHAPTER 35

The towns for the Levites

¹ While the people of Israel were still camped in the lowlands of Moab across the River Jordan from Jericho, the LORD told Moses ² to say to them:

When you receive your tribal lands, you must give towns and pastures to the Levi tribe. ³ That way, the Levites will have towns to live in and pastures for their animals. ⁴⁻⁵ The pasture around each of these towns must be in the shape of a square, with the town itself in the centre. The pasture is to measure nine hundred metres on each side, with four hundred and fifty metres of land outside each of the town walls. This will be the Levites' pasture land.

⁶ Six of the towns you give them will be Safe Towns where a person who has accidentally killed someone can run for protection. But you will also give the Levites forty-two other towns, ⁷ so they will have a total of forty-eight towns with their surrounding pastures.

⁸ Since the towns for the Levites must come from Israel's own tribal lands, the larger tribes will give more towns than the smaller ones.

---

*34.7 Mount Hor: Not the same as in 33.37.
See also: 34.13: Num 26.52-56. 34.13-15: Josh 14.1-5.

See also: 35.1-8: Josh 21.1-42.

The Safe Towns

This is also told in Deuteronomy 19.1–13; Joshua 20.1–9

⁹ The LORD then told Moses ¹⁰ to tell the people of Israel:

After you have crossed the River Jordan and are settled in Canaan, ¹¹ choose Safe Towns, where a person who has accidentally killed someone can run for protection. ¹² If the victim's relatives think it was murder, they might try to take revenge.* Anyone accused of murder can run to one of these Safe Towns for protection and not be killed before a trial is held.

¹³ There are to be six of these Safe Towns, ¹⁴ three on each side of the River Jordan. ¹⁵ They will be places of protection for anyone who lives in Israel and accidentally kills someone.

Laws about murder and accidental killing

The LORD said:

¹⁶⁻¹⁸ Suppose you hit someone with a piece of iron or a large stone or a dangerous wooden tool. If that person dies, then you are a murderer and must be put to death ¹⁹ by one of the victim's relatives.* He will take revenge for his relative's death as soon as he finds him.

²⁰⁻²¹ Or suppose you get angry and kill someone by pushing or hitting or by throwing something. You are a murderer and must be put to death by one of the victim's relatives.

²²⁻²⁴ But if you are not angry and accidentally kill someone in any of these ways, the townspeople must hold a trial and decide if you are guilty. ²⁵ If they decide that you are innocent, you will be protected from the victim's relative and sent to stay in one of the Safe Towns until the high priest dies. ²⁶ But if you ever leave the Safe Town ²⁷ and are killed by the victim's relative, he cannot be punished for killing you. ²⁸ You must stay inside the town until the high priest dies; only then can you go back home.

²⁹ The community of Israel must always obey these laws.

³⁰ Death is the penalty for murder. But no one accused of murder can be put to death unless there are at least two witnesses to the crime. ³¹ You cannot give someone money to escape the death penalty; you must pay with your own life! ³² And if you have been proved innocent of murder and are living in a Safe Town, you cannot pay to go back home; you must stay there until the high priest dies.

³³⁻³⁴ I, the LORD, live among you people of Israel, so your land must be kept pure. But when a murder takes place, blood pollutes the land, and it becomes unclean. If that happens, the murderer must be put to death, so the land will be clean again. Keep murder out of Israel!

CHAPTER 36

The laws about married women and land

¹ One day the family leaders from the Gilead clan of the Manasseh tribe went to Moses and the other family leaders of Israel ² and said, "Sir, the LORD has said that he will show* what land each tribe will receive as their own. And the LORD has commanded you to give the daughters of our relative Zelophehad the land that he would have received. ³ But if they marry men from other tribes of Israel, the land they receive will become part of that tribe's inheritance and will no longer belong to us. ⁴ Even when land is returned to its original owner in the Year of Celebration,* we will not get back Zelophehad's land — it will belong to the tribe into which his daughters married."

⁵ So Moses told the people that the LORD had said:

These men from the Manasseh tribe are right. ⁶ I will allow Zelophehad's daughters to marry anyone, as long as those men belong to one of the clans of the Manasseh tribe.

⁷ Tribal land must not be given to another tribe — it will remain the property

*35.12 the victim's relatives . . . revenge: At this time in Israel's history, the clan would appoint the closest male relative to find and kill a person who had killed a member of their clan.
*35.19 one of the victim's relatives: See the note at 35.12.
See also: 35.9–28: Deut 19.2–4; Josh 20.1–9.

*36.2 that he will show: See the note at 26.55,56.
*36.4 Year of Celebration: This was a sacred year for Israel, traditionally called the "Year of Jubilee". During this year, all property had to go back to its original owner. But here, the property was not sold; it became part of the other tribe's land when the daughter who owned it married into that tribe. So the property could not be returned even during this year.
See also: 35.30: Deut 17.6; 19.15. 36.2: Num 27.7.

of the tribe that received it. [8-9] In the future, any daughter who inherits land must marry someone from her own tribe. Israel's tribal land is never to be passed from one tribe to another.

[10-11] Mahlah, Tirzah, Hoglah, Milcah, and Noah the daughters of Zelophehad obeyed the LORD and married their uncles' sons [12] and remained part of the Manasseh tribe. So their land stayed in their father's clan.

[13] These are the laws that the LORD gave to Moses and the Israelites while they were camped in the lowlands of Moab across the River Jordan from Jericho.

Additional notes

[1.20-46] Jacob: The Hebrew text has "Israel", Jacob's name after God renamed him.

[3.4] fire that was unacceptable: One possible meaning for the difficult Hebrew text.

[3.28] eight thousand six hundred: Hebrew; some manuscripts of one ancient translation "eight thousand three hundred".

[5.25] lift it up: Or "wave it".

[6.20] lift them up: See the note at 5.25.

[7.12-83] goat: Hebrew "male goat".

[8.19] I will hold . . . sacred tent: One possible meaning for the difficult Hebrew text.

[10.29] Hobab: Hebrew "Hobab son of Reuel".

[10.33] Mount Sinai: Hebrew "the LORD's mountain".

[11.3] Burning: Or "Taberah".

[11.25] some authority: Or "some of the Spirit's power".

[11.28] Joshua: Hebrew "Joshua son of Nun".

[11.34] Graves for the Greedy: Or "Kibroth-Hattaavah".

[13.4-16] Joshua . . . Ephraim: Hebrew "Hoshea son of Nun from Ephraim; Moses renamed him Joshua."

[13.23,24] Bunch Valley: Or "Eshcol Valley".

[14.30] Caleb and Joshua: Hebrew "Caleb son of Jephunneh and Joshua son of Nun".

[14.44] ignored Moses: One possible meaning for the difficult Hebrew text.

[15.3] goats: See the note at 7.12-83.

[16.1,2] Dathan, Abiram, and On: Hebrew "Dathan and Abiram the sons of Eliab, and On son of Peleth".

[16.4] he knelt down to pray: Or "he fell to his knees in sorrow".

[18.1] are responsible . . . sacred tent: Or "are to make sure that no one gets near the sacred tent."

[18.30] just as the Israelites . . . to me: One possible meaning for the difficult Hebrew text.

[19.6] A priest: Or "Eleazar".

[21.28] destroying: One ancient translation; Hebrew "the rulers of".

[21.30] gone: One possible meaning for the difficult Hebrew text of verse 30.

[22.32] I don't think you should go to Moab: One possible meaning for the difficult Hebrew text.

[23.14] a field . . . where lookouts were stationed: Or "Zophim Field on the top of Mount Pisgah."

[24.3] my words are true: One possible meaning for the difficult Hebrew text.

[24.6] grove of palm trees: Or "green valley".

[24.8] shooting them with arrows: One possible meaning for the difficult Hebrew text.

[24.15] my words are true: See the note at 24.3.

[24.17] you Moabites: Or "the territories of Moab".

[24.17] destroy: The Standard Hebrew Text; the Samaritan Hebrew Text "the skulls of".

[24.17] those tribes . . . desert: The Hebrew text has "the descendants of Sheth", which probably refers to the people who lived in the desert areas of Canaan before the Israelites.

[24.19] every town there: Or "Ir in Moab".

[24.20] but . . . for ever: One possible meaning for the difficult Hebrew text.

[24.22] them: One possible meaning for the difficult Hebrew text of verse 22.

[24.23] destruction: One possible meaning for the difficult Hebrew text of verse 23.

[25.7 Phinehas . . . Aaron: Hebrew "Phinehas, son of Eleazar and grandson of Aaron".

[26.4] just as . . . Egypt: One possible meaning for the difficult Hebrew text.

[26.5-7] Jacob: See the note at 1.20-46.

[27.1] Zelophehad: Hebrew "Zelophehad son of Hepher son of Gilead son of Machir son of Manasseh son of Joseph".

[27.21] from me: The Hebrew text has "by the urim", something used by the priests to get answers from the LORD.

[28.14,15] goat: See the note at 7.12-83.

[28.22] goat: See the note at 7.12-83.

[28.30] goat: See the note at 7.12-83.

[29.5] goat: See the note at 7.12-83.

[29.11] goat: See the note at 7.12-83.

[29.16] goat: See the note at 7.12-83.

[29.38] goat: See the note at 7.12-83.

[31.54] to remind . . . happened: Or "so the LORD would continue to help Israel."

[32.12] Caleb and Joshua: Hebrew "Caleb son of Jephunneh the Kenizzite and Joshua son of Nun".

[32.33] half of Manasseh: Or "East Manasseh".

[32.33] ruled: One possible meaning for the difficult Hebrew text of verse 33.

[32.41] Villages of Jair: Or "Havvoth-Jair".

[33.3,4] proudly: Or "bravely".

[33.8] Pi-Hahiroth: Two ancient translations and the Samaritan Hebrew Text; the Standard Hebrew Text "a place near Hahiroth".

[33.11] the western edge of the Sinai Desert: Hebrew "the Sin Desert".

[34.11] Lake Galilee: The Hebrew text has "Lake Chinnereth", an earlier name for Lake Galilee.

Deuteronomy

A quick look at this book

It was almost time for the people of Israel to
cross the River Jordan and conquer Canaan.
But God refused to let Moses lead them into
the land. Instead, Moses had been told that he
was going to die on the eastern side of the
Jordan. So Moses gave several farewell
speeches to the people of Israel in which he
repeated many of God's laws.

Because Moses was giving these laws to Israel
for a second time, the book is now called
"Deuteronomy", which comes from a Greek
phrase meaning "second law".

Moses also reminded the Israelites about the
past forty years. God had rescued them from
Egypt and taken care of them in the desert, but
they had not always been faithful or obedient
to him.

Moses told the Israelites that if they kept their
agreement to worship and obey the Lord, they
would be a successful and powerful nation.
But if they broke their agreement and
worshipped idols, the Lord promised to put
terrible curses on the people. They would be
defeated by their enemies and lose their land
and their lives.

Much later, when Jesus was asked which one
of God's commands was the most important,
he answered by quoting one of the commands
from Deuteronomy:

> Listen, Israel! The LORD our God is the only true
> God! So love the LORD your God with all your
> heart, soul, and strength.
>
> (6.4,5)

CHAPTER 1

The final speeches of Moses

1-5 This book contains the speeches that Moses
made while Israel was in the land of Moab,
camped near the town of Suph in the desert
east of the River Jordan. The town of Paran
was in one direction from their camp, and the
towns of Tophel, Laban, Hazeroth, and
Dizahab* were in the opposite direction.
 Earlier, Moses had defeated the Amorite
King Sihon of Heshbon. Moses had also
defeated King Og of Bashan, who used to live
in Ashtaroth for part of the year and in Edrei
for the rest of the year.

---

*1.1-5 Suph . . . Paran . . . Tophel, Laban, Hazeroth,
and Dizahab: The exact location of these towns is not
known.
See also: 1.4: Num 21.21-35.

Although it takes only eleven days to walk from Mount Sinai* to Kadesh-Barnea by way of the Mount Seir road, these speeches were not made until forty years after Israel left Egypt.*

THE FIRST SPEECH: MOSES REVIEWS THE PAST

The LORD's command at Mount Sinai

The LORD had given Moses his laws for the people of Israel. And on the first day of the eleventh month,* Moses began explaining those laws by saying:

⁶ People of Israel, when we were in our camp at Mount Sinai,* the LORD our God told us:

You have stayed here long enough. ⁷ Leave this place and go into the land that belongs to the Amorites and the land of their neighbours the Canaanites. This land includes the valley of the River Jordan, the hill country, the western foothills, the Southern Desert, the Mediterranean coast, the Lebanon Mountains, and all the territory as far as the River Euphrates. ⁸ I give you this land, just as I promised your ancestors Abraham, Isaac, and Jacob. Now you must go and take the land.

Leaders were appointed

This is also told in Exodus 18.13–27

Moses said:

⁹ Straight after the LORD commanded us to leave Mount Sinai,* I told you:

Israel, being your leader is too big a job for one person. ¹⁰ The LORD our God has blessed us, and so now there are as many of us as there are stars in the sky. ¹¹ God has even promised to bless us a thousand times more, and I pray that he will. ¹² But I cannot take care of all your problems and settle all your arguments alone. ¹³ Each tribe must choose some experienced men who are known for their wisdom and understanding, and I will make those men the official leaders of their tribes.

¹⁴ You answered, "That's a good idea!" ¹⁵ Then I took these men, who were already wise and respected leaders, and I appointed them as your official leaders. Some of them became military officers in charge of groups of a thousand, or a hundred, or fifty, or ten, ¹⁶ and others became judges. I gave these judges the following instructions:

When you settle legal cases, your decisions must be fair. It doesn't matter if the case is between two Israelites, or between an Israelite and a foreigner living in your community. ¹⁷ And it doesn't matter if one is helpless and the other is powerful. Don't be afraid of anyone! No matter who comes to your court, God will help you make a fair decision.

If any case is too hard for you, bring the people to me, and I will make the decision.

¹⁸ After I gave these instructions to the judges, I taught you the LORD's commands.

Men were sent to explore the hill country

This is also told in Numbers 13.1–33

Moses said to Israel:

¹⁹ The LORD had commanded us to leave Mount Sinai* and go to the hill country that belonged to the Amorites, so we started out into the huge desert. You remember how frightening it was, but soon we were at Kadesh-Barnea, ²⁰-²¹ and I told you, "We have reached the hill country. It belongs to the Amorites now, but the LORD our God is giving it to us. He is the same God our ancestors worshipped, and he has told us to go in and take this land, so don't hesitate and be afraid."

²² Then all of you came to me and said, "Before we go into the land, let's send some men to explore it. When they come back, they can tell us about the towns we will find and what roads we should take to get there."

²³ It seemed like a good idea, so I chose twelve men, one from each tribe. ²⁴ They explored the hill country as far as Bunch Valley* ²⁵ and even brought back some of the fruit. They said, "The LORD our God is giving us good land."

---

*1.1–5 Egypt: The Israelites would soon enter Canaan, but they would have entered the land of Canaan from Kadesh-Barnea forty years earlier if they had not rebelled against God (see verses 6–40).
*1.1–5 eleventh month: Shebat, the eleventh month of the Hebrew calendar, from about mid-January to mid-February.

*1.24 Bunch Valley: Or "Eshcol Valley," famous for its large bunches of grapes.

Israel refused to obey the LORD

This is also told in Numbers 14.1–45

Moses said to Israel:

²⁶ You did not want to go into the land, and you refused to obey the LORD your God. ²⁷ You stayed in your tents and grumbled, "The LORD must hate us — he brought us out of Egypt, just so he could hand us over to the Amorites and get rid of us. ²⁸ We are afraid, because the men who explored the land told us that the cities are large, with walls that reach to the sky. The people who live there are taller and stronger than we are,' and some of them are Anakim.* We have nowhere to go."

²⁹ Then I said, "Don't worry! ³⁰ The LORD our God will lead the way. He will fight on our side, just as he did when we saw him do all those things to the Egyptians. ³¹ And you know that the LORD has taken care of us the whole time we've been in the desert, just as you might carry one of your children."

³² But you still would not trust the LORD, ³³ even though he had always been with us in the desert. During the daytime, the LORD was in the cloud, leading us in the right direction and showing us where to camp. And at night, he was there in the fire.*

³⁴ You had made the LORD angry, and he said:

³⁵ You people of this generation are evil, and I refuse to let you go into the good land that I promised your ancestors. ³⁶ Caleb son of Jephunneh is the only one of your generation that I will allow to go in. He obeyed me completely, so I will give him and his descendants the land he explored.

³⁷ The LORD was even angry with me because of you people, and he said, "Moses, I won't let you go into the land either. ³⁸ Instead, I will let Joshua' your assistant lead Israel to conquer the land. So encourage him."

³⁹ Then the LORD spoke to you again:

People of Israel, you said that your innocent young children would be taken prisoner in the battle for the land. But some day I will let them go into the land, and with my help they will conquer it and live there.

⁴⁰ Now, turn round and go back into the desert by way of Red Sea* Road.

⁴¹ Then you told me, "We disobeyed the LORD our God, but now we want to obey him. We will go into the hill country and fight, just as he told us to do." So you picked up your weapons, thinking it would be easy to take over the hill country.

⁴² But the LORD said, "Moses, warn them not to go into the hill country. I won't help them fight, and their enemies will defeat them."

⁴³ I told you what the LORD had said, but you paid no attention. You disobeyed him and went into the hill country anyway. You thought you were so great! ⁴⁴ But when the Amorites in the hill country attacked from their towns, you ran from them as you would run from a swarm of bees. The Amorites chased your troops into Seir* as far as Hormah, killing them as they went. ⁴⁵ Then you came back to the place of worship at Kadesh-Barnea and wept, but the LORD would not listen to your prayers.

Israel spent years in the desert

Moses said to Israel:

⁴⁶ After we had been in Kadesh for a few months, we obeyed the LORD and headed back into the desert by way of Red Sea* Road.

CHAPTER 2

¹ We spent many years wandering around outside the hill country of Seir,* ² until the LORD said:

Moses, ³ Israel has wandered in these hills long enough. Turn and go north. ⁴ And give the people these orders: "Be very careful, because you will soon go through the land that belongs to your relatives, the

---

*1.28 Anakim: Perhaps a group of people of great stature that lived in or near Palestine before the Israelites. See also 2.10,11,20,21; Numbers 13.33.
*1.33 The cloud . . . the fire: See Exodus 40.34–38; Numbers 9.15–23.
See also: 1.26: Deut 9.23; Heb 3.16. 1.31: Acts 13.18. 1.32: Heb 3.19. 1.34,35: Heb 3.18.

---

*1.40 Red Sea: Hebrew *yam suph*, here referring to the Gulf of Aqaba, since the term is extended to include the north-eastern arm of the Red Sea (see also the note at 11.4).
*1.44 Seir: An area of hills and mountains that was part of the territory of Edom.
*1.46 Red Sea: See the notes at 1.40; 11.4.
*2.1 hill country of Seir: See the note at 1.44.
See also: 2.1: Num 21.4. 2.4: Gen 36.8.

descendants of Esau.* They are afraid of you, ⁵ but don't start a war with them. I have given them the hill country of Seir, so I won't give any of it to you, not even enough to set a foot on. ⁶ And as you go through their land, you will have to buy food and water from them."

⁷ The LORD has helped us and taken care of us during the past forty years that we have been in this huge desert. We've had everything we needed, and the LORD has blessed us and made us successful in whatever we have done.

⁸ We went past the territory that belonged to our relatives, the descendants of Esau.* We followed Arabah Road that starts in the south at Elath and Ezion-Geber, then we turned on to the desert road that leads to Moab.

⁹ The LORD told me, "Don't try to start a war with Moab. Leave them alone, because I gave the land of Ar* to them,* and I will not let you have any of it."

Tribes that lived near Canaan

¹⁰ Before the LORD gave the Moabites their land, a large and powerful tribe lived there. They were the Emim, and they were as tall as the Anakim. ¹¹ The Moabites called them Emim, though others sometimes used the name Rephaim* for both the Anakim and the Emim.

¹² The Horites used to live in Seir, but the Edomites* took over that region. They killed many of the Horites and forced the rest of

them to leave, just as Israel did to the people in the land that the LORD gave them.

Israel crossed the Zered Gorge

Moses said to Israel:

¹³ When we came to the Zered Gorge along the southern border of Moab, the LORD told us to cross the gorge into Moab, and we did. ¹⁴ This was thirty-eight years after we left Kadesh-Barnea, and by that time all the men who had been in the army at Kadesh-Barnea had died, just as the LORD had said they would. ¹⁵⁻¹⁶ The LORD kept getting rid of* them until finally none of them were left.

¹⁷ Then the LORD told me, ¹⁸ "Moses, now go past the town of Ar and cross Moab's northern border ¹⁹ into Ammon. But don't start a war with the Ammonites. Leave them* their land, and I won't give any of it to Israel."

More nations that lived near Canaan

²⁰ Before the Ammonites conquered the land that the LORD had given them, some of the Rephaim used to live there, although the Ammonites called them Zamzummim. ²¹ The Zamzummim were a large and powerful tribe and were as tall as the Anakim.* But the LORD helped the Ammonites, and they killed many of the Zamzummim and forced the rest to leave. Then the Ammonites settled there. ²² The LORD helped them as he had helped the Edomites,* who killed many of the Horites in Seir and forced the rest to leave before settling there themselves.

²³ A group called the Avvim used to live in villages as far south as Gaza, but the Philistines* killed them and settled on their land.

Israel crossed the Arnon Gorge

Moses said:

²⁴ After we went through Ammon, the LORD told us:

---

*2.4 your relatives, the descendants of Esau: Esau was the brother of Jacob, the ancestor of the nation of Israel. Esau's descendants were also known as the nation of Edom.
*2.8 We went past . . . Esau: According to Numbers 20.14–21, the king of Edom did not let the Israelites go through his land.
*2.9 Ar: One of the main cities of Moab (see Numbers 21.28); sometimes it may have stood for the whole territory of Moab.
*2.9 them: The Hebrew text has "the descendants of Lot"; the nation of Moab descended from Moab, who was the son of Lot, the nephew of Abraham.
*2.10,11 Emim . . . Anakim . . . Rephaim: These may refer to a group or groups of people of great stature that lived in or near Palestine before the Israelites (see also Numbers 13.33).
*2.12 Edomites: The Hebrew text has "the descendants of Esau", who became the nation of Edom.
See also: 2.9: Gen 19.37.

*2.19 them: The Hebrew text has "descendants of Lot"; the nation of Ammon descended from Benammi, who was the son of Lot, the nephew of Abraham.
*2.21 Anakim: See the notes at 1.28; 2.10,11.
*2.22 Edomites: See the note at 2.12.
*2.23 Philistines: The Hebrew text has "the Caphtorim from Caphtor", probably referring to the Philistines who originally came from Crete.
See also: 2.14: Num 14.28–35. 2.19: Gen 19.38.

Israel, pack up your possessions, take down your tents, and cross the gorge of the River Arnon.* The territory of the Amorite King Sihon of Heshbon lies on the other side of the river, but I now give you his land. So attack and take it! 25 Today I will start making all other nations afraid of you. They will tremble with fear when anyone mentions you, and they will be terrified when you appear.

The defeat of King Sihon of Heshbon

This is also told in Numbers 21.21–30

Moses said to Israel:

26 After we had crossed the Arnon and had set up camp in the Kedemoth Desert, I sent messengers to King Sihon of Heshbon, telling him that his nation and ours could be at peace. I said:

27 Please let Israel go across your country. We will walk straight through, without turning off the road. 28-29 You can even sell us food and water, and we will pay with silver. We need to reach the River Jordan and cross it, because the LORD our God is giving us the land on the west side. The Edomites and Moabites′ have already let us cross their land. Please let us cross your land as well.

30-31 But Sihon refused to let us go across his country, because the LORD made him stubborn and eager to fight us. The LORD told me, "I am going to help you defeat Sihon and take his land, so attack him!"

32 We met Sihon and his army in battle at Jahaz, 33 and the LORD our God helped us defeat them. We killed Sihon, his sons, and everyone else in his army. 34 Then we captured and destroyed every town in Sihon's kingdom, killing everyone, 35 but keeping the livestock and everything else of value. 36 The LORD helped us capture every town from the gorge of the River Arnon north to the boundary of Gilead, including the town of Aroer on the edge of the gorge and the town in the middle of the gorge. 37 However, we stayed away from all the Ammonite towns, both in the hill country and near the River Jabbok, just as the LORD had commanded.

CHAPTER 3

The defeat of King Og of Bashan

This is also told in Numbers 21.31–35

Moses said to Israel:

1 When we turned on to the road that leads to Bashan, King Og of Bashan led out his whole army to fight us at Edrei. 2 But the LORD told me, "Moses, don't be afraid of King Og. I am going to help you defeat him and his army and take over his land. Destroy him and his people, just as you did with the Amorite King Sihon of Heshbon."

3-6 The LORD our God helped us destroy Og and his army and conquer his entire kingdom of Bashan, including the Argob region. His kingdom had lots of villages and sixty towns with high walls and gates that locked with bars. We completely destroyed* them all, killing everyone, 7 but keeping the livestock and everything else of value.

8 Sihon and Og had ruled Amorite kingdoms east of the River Jordan. Their land stretched from the gorge of the River Arnon in the south to Mount Hermon in the north, and we captured it all. 9 Mount Hermon is called Mount Sirion by the people of Sidon, and it is called Mount Senir by the Amorites. 10 We captured all the towns in the highlands, all of Gilead, and all of Bashan as far as Salecah and Edrei, two of the towns that Og had ruled.

Og's coffin

11 King Og was the last of the Rephaim,* and his coffin′ is in the town of Rabbah in Ammon. It is made of hard black rock* and is four metres long and almost two metres wide.

The land east of the River Jordan is divided

This is also told in Numbers 32.1–42

Moses said to Israel:

12-17 I gave some of the land and towns we captured to the tribes of Reuben and Gad. Their share started at the gorge of the River

---

*3.3–6 completely destroyed: The Hebrew word means that the town was given completely to the LORD, and since it could not be used for normal purposes any more, it had to be destroyed. Every person was killed and sometimes all the animals as well.
*3.11 Rephaim: See the note at 2.10,11.
*3.11 hard black rock: The Hebrew text has "iron", which probably refers to basalt, a hard black rock.

---

*2.24 gorge of the River Arnon: The northern boundary of Moab's territory and the southern boundary of Sihon's kingdom.

Arnon in the south, took in the town of Aroer on the edge of the gorge, and went far enough north to include the southern half of the Gilead region. The northern part of their land went as far east as the upper gorge of the River Jabbok, which formed their border with the Ammonites.* I also gave them the eastern side of the valley of the River Jordan, from Lake Galilee' south to the Dead Sea' below the slopes of Mount Pisgah.

I gave the northern half of Gilead and all of the Bashan region to half the tribe of Manasseh.' Bashan had belonged to King Og, and the Argob region in Bashan used to be called the Land of the Rephaim. Jair from the Manasseh tribe conquered the Argob region as far west as the kingdoms of Geshur and Maacah. The Israelites even started calling Bashan by the name "Villages of Jair,"* and that is still its name. I gave the northern half of Gilead to the Machir clan.'

18-19 At that time I told the men of Reuben, Gad, and East Manasseh:

The LORD our God told me to give you this land with its towns, and that's what I have done. Now your wives and children can stay here with your large flocks of sheep and goats and your large herds of cattle. But all of you men who can serve in our army must cross the River Jordan and help the other tribes, because they are your relatives. 20 The LORD will let them defeat the enemy nations on the west side of the Jordan and take their land. Afterwards, you can come back here to the land I gave you.

21-22 Then I told Joshua, "You saw how the LORD our God helped us destroy King Sihon and King Og. So don't be afraid! Wherever you go, the LORD will fight on your side and help you destroy your enemies."

God refused to let Moses enter Canaan

Moses said to Israel:

23 At that time I prayed and begged, 24 "Our LORD, it seems that you have just begun to show me your great power. No other god in

the sky or on earth is able to do the mighty things that you do. 25 The land west of the Jordan is such good land. Please let me cross the Jordan and see the hills and the Lebanon Mountains."

26 But the LORD was angry with me because of you people,* and he refused to listen. "That's enough!" he said. "I don't want to hear any more. 27 Climb to the top of Mount Pisgah and look north, south, east, and west. Take a good look, but you are not going to cross the River Jordan. 28 Joshua will lead Israel across the Jordan to take the land, so help him be strong and brave and tell him what he must do."

29 After this we stayed in the valley at Beth-Peor.

CHAPTER 4

Israel must obey God

Moses said:

1 Israel, listen to these laws and teachings! If you obey them, you will live, and you will go in and take the land that the LORD is giving you. He is the God your ancestors worshipped, 2 and now he is your God. I am telling you everything he has commanded, so don't add anything or take anything away.

3 You saw how he killed everyone who worshipped the god Baal-Peor.* 4 But all of you who were faithful to the LORD your God are still alive today.

5-8 No other nation has laws that are as fair as the ones the Lord my God told me to give you. If you faithfully obey them when you enter the land, you will show other nations how wise you are. In fact, everyone who hears about your laws will say, "That great nation certainly is wise!" And what makes us greater than other nations? We have a God who is close to us and answers our prayers.

9 You must be very careful not to forget the things you have seen God do on your own. Keep reminding yourselves, and tell your children and grandchildren as well. 10 Do you remember the day you stood in the LORD's presence at Mount Sinai? The LORD said, "Moses, bring the people of Israel here. I want to speak to them so they will

---

*3.12–17 The northern part . . . border with the Ammonites: The River Jabbok flowed from south to north, then it turned west and formed the northern border of the land belonging to the Reuben and Gad tribes.

See also: 3.18–20: Josh 1.12–15. 3.23–27: Num 27.12–14; Deut 32.48–52.

*3.26 But the LORD . . . people: See 1.37.
*4.3 Baal-Peor: See Numbers 25.1–9.
See also: 4.2: Rev 22.18,19. 4.3: Num 25.1–9.

obey me as long as they live, and so they will teach their children to obey me too."

¹¹ Mount Sinai' was surrounded by deep dark clouds, and fire went up to the sky. You came to the foot of the mountain, ¹² and the LORD spoke to you from the fire. You could hear him and understand what he was saying, but you couldn't see him. ¹³ The LORD said he was making an agreement with you, and he told you that your part of the agreement is to obey the Ten Commandments. Then the LORD wrote these Commandments on two flat stones.

¹⁴ That's when the LORD commanded me to give you the laws and teachings you must obey in the land that you will conquer west of the River Jordan.

Don't worship idols

Moses said to Israel:

¹⁵ When God spoke to you from the fire, he was invisible. So be careful ¹⁶ not to commit the sin of worshipping idols. Don't make idols to be worshipped, whether they are shaped like men, women, ¹⁷ animals, birds, ¹⁸ reptiles, or fish. ¹⁹ And when you see the sun or moon or stars, don't be tempted to bow down and worship them. The LORD put them there for all the other nations to worship. ²⁰ But you are the LORD's people, because he led you through fiery trials and rescued you from Egypt.

²¹ The LORD was angry with me because of what you said,' and he told me that he would not let me cross the River Jordan into the good land that he is giving you.* ²² So I must stay here and die on this side of the Jordan, but you will cross the river and take the land.

²³ Always remember the agreement that the LORD your God made with you, and don't make an idol in any shape or form. ²⁴ The LORD will be angry if you worship other gods, and he can be like a fire destroying everything in its path.

²⁵⁻²⁶ Soon you will cross the River Jordan and settle down in the land. Then in the years to come, you will have children, and they will give you grandchildren. After

many years, you might lose your sense of right and wrong and make idols, even though the LORD your God hates them. So I am giving you fair warning today, and I call the earth and the sky as witnesses. If you ever make idols, the LORD will be angry, and you won't have long to live, because the LORD will let you be wiped out. ²⁷ Only a few of you will survive, and the LORD will force you to leave the land and will scatter you among the nations. ²⁸ There you will have to worship gods made of wood and stone, and these are nothing but idols that can't see or hear or eat or smell.

²⁹⁻³⁰ In all your troubles, you may finally decide that you want to worship only the LORD. And if you turn back to him and obey him completely, he will again be your God. ³¹ The LORD your God will have mercy — he won't destroy you or desert you. The LORD will remember his promise, and he will keep the agreement he made with your ancestors.

³²⁻³⁴ When the LORD your God brought you out of Egypt, you saw how he fought for you and showed you his great power by performing terrifying miracles. You became his people, and at Mount Sinai you heard him talking to you out of fiery flames. And yet you are still alive! Has anything like this ever happened since the time God created humans? No matter where you go or who you ask, you will get the same answer. No one has ever heard of another god even trying to do such things as the LORD your God has done for you.

³⁵⁻³⁶ The LORD wants you to know he is the only true God, and he wants you to obey him. That's why he let you see his mighty miracles and his fierce fire on earth, and why you heard his voice from that fire and from the sky.

³⁷ The LORD loved your ancestors and decided that you would be his people. So the LORD used his great power to bring you out of Egypt. ³⁸ Now you face other nations more powerful than you are, but the LORD has already started forcing them out of their land and giving it to you.

³⁹ So remember that the LORD is the only true God, whether in the sky above or on the earth below. ⁴⁰ Today I am explaining his laws and teachings. And if you always obey them, you and your descendants will live long and be successful in the land the LORD is giving you.

4.21 The LORD was angry . . . giving you: See 1.37; 3.26.

See also: **4.11,12:** Exod 19.16–18; Heb 12.18,19. **4.13:** Exod 31.18; 34.28; Deut 9.10. **4.14:** Exod 21.1. **4.16:** Exod 20.4; Lev 26.1; Deut 5.8; 27.15. **4.17,18a:** Rom 1.23. **4.20:** Exod 19.5; Deut 7.6; 14.2; 26.18; Titus 2.14; 1 Pet 2.9. **4.21:** Num 20.12. **4.24:** Heb 12.29.

See also: **4.27,28:** Deut 28.36. **4.29:** Jer 29.13. **4.35:** Mark 12.32.

Safe Towns

41-43 Moses said, "People of Israel, you must set aside the following three towns east of the River Jordan as Safe Towns: Bezer in the desert highlands belonging to the Reuben tribe; Ramoth in Gilead, belonging to the Gad tribe; and Golan in Bashan, belonging to the Manasseh tribe. If you kill a neighbour without meaning to, and if you had not been angry with that person, you can run to one of these towns and find safety."*

THE SECOND SPEECH: MOSES TELLS WHAT THE LORD DEMANDS

Israel at Beth-Peor

44-46 The Israelites had come from Egypt and were camped east of the River Jordan near Beth-Peor, when Moses gave these laws and teachings. The land around their camp had once belonged to King Sihon of Heshbon. But Moses and the Israelites defeated him 47 and King Og of Bashan, and took their lands. These two Amorite kings had ruled the territory east of the River Jordan 48 from the town of Aroer on the edge of the gorge of the River Arnon, north to Mount Hermon.* 49 Their land included the eastern side of the Jordan valley, as far south as the Dead Sea* below the slopes of Mount Pisgah.

CHAPTER 5

The Ten Commandments

This is also told in Exodus 20.1–17

1 Moses called together the people of Israel and said:

Today I am telling you the laws and teachings that you must follow, so listen carefully. 2 The LORD our God made an agreement with our nation at Mount Sinai.* 3 That agreement wasn't only with* our ancestors but with us, who are here today. 4 The LORD himself spoke to you out of the fire, 5 but you were afraid of the fire and refused to go up the mountain. So I spoke with the LORD for you, then I told you that he had said:

6 I am the LORD your God, the one who brought you out of Egypt where you were slaves.

7 Do not worship any god except me.

8 Do not make idols that look like anything in the sky or on earth or in the ocean under the earth. 9 Don't bow down and worship idols. I am the LORD your God, and I demand all your love. If you reject me and worship idols, I will punish your families for three or four generations. 10 But if you love me and obey my laws, I will be kind to your families for thousands of generations.

11 Do not misuse my name.* I am the LORD your God, and I will punish anyone who misuses my name.

12 Show respect for the Sabbath Day — it belongs to me. 13 You have six days when you can do your work, 14 but the seventh day of the week belongs to me, your God. No one is to work on that day — not you, your children, your oxen or donkeys or any other animal, not even those foreigners who live in your towns. And don't make your slaves do any work. 15 This special day of rest will remind you that I reached out my mighty arm and rescued you from slavery in Egypt.

16 Respect your father and mother, and you will live a long and successful life in the land I am giving you.

17 Do not murder.

18 Be faithful in marriage.

19 Do not steal.

20 Do not tell lies about others.

21 Do not want to take anything that belongs to someone else. Don't want to take anyone's wife or husband, house, land, slaves, oxen, donkeys, or anything else.

22 When we were gathered on the mountain, the LORD spoke to us in a loud voice from the dark fiery cloud. The LORD gave us these

---

*4.41–43 find safety: From the victim's clan, who might appoint one of their men to track down and put to death the killer (see also 19.1–13).

See also: 4.41–43: Josh 20.8,9.

*5.11 misuse my name: Probably includes breaking promises, telling lies after swearing to tell the truth, using the LORD's name as a curse word or a magic formula, and trying to control the LORD by using his name.

See also: 5.8,9: Lev 26.1; Deut 4.15–18; 27.15.
5.9,10: Exod 34.6,7; Num 14.18; Deut 7.9,10.
5.11: Lev 19.12. 5.12: Exod 16.23–30; 31.12–14.
5.13,14: Exod 23.12; 31.15; 34.21; 35.2; Lev 23.3.
5.16: a Deut 27.16; Matt 15.4; 19.19; Mark 7.10; 10.19;
Luke 18.20; Eph 6.2; b Eph 6.3. 5.17: Gen 9.6; Lev 24.17;
Matt 5.21; 19.18; Mark 10.19; Luke 18.20. 5.18: Matt 5.27; 19.18; Mark 10.19;
Luke 18.20; Rom 13.9; Jam 2.11. 5.19: Lev 19.11; Matt 19.18;
Mark 10.19; Luke 18.20; Rom 13.9. 5.20: Exod 23.1;
Matt 19.18; Mark 10.19; Luke 18.20. 5.21: Rom 7.7; 13.9.
5.22–27: Heb 12.18,19.

commands, and only these. Then he wrote
them on two flat stones and gave them to me.

The people were afraid

This is also told in Exodus 20.18–21

Moses said to Israel:

²³ When fire blazed from the mountain,
and you heard the voice coming from the
darkness, your tribal leaders came to me
²⁴ and said:

Today the LORD our God has shown us how
powerful and glorious he is. He spoke to us
from the fire, and we learnt that people can
live, even though God speaks to them.
²⁵ But we don't want to take a chance on
being killed by that terrible fire, and if we
keep on hearing the LORD's voice, we will
die. ²⁶ Has anyone else ever heard the only
true God speaking from fire, as we have?
And even if they have, would they live to
tell about it? ²⁷ Moses, go up close and
listen to the LORD. Then come back and tell
us, and we will do everything he says.

²⁸ The LORD heard you and said:

Moses, I heard what the people said to you,
and I approve. ²⁹ I wish they would always
worship me with fear and trembling and be
this willing to obey me! Then they and
their children would always enjoy a
successful life. ³⁰ Now, tell them to return to their tents,
³¹ but you come back here to me. After I tell
you my laws and teachings, you will repeat
them to the people, so they can obey these
laws in the land I am giving them.

Moses said to Israel:

³² Israel, you must carefully obey the
LORD's commands. ³³ Follow them, because
they make a path that will lead to a long
successful life in the land the LORD your
God is giving you.

CHAPTER 6

The most important commandment

Moses said to Israel:

¹ The LORD told me to give you these laws
and teachings,' so you can obey them in
the land he is giving you. Soon you will
cross the River Jordan and take that land.
² And if you and your descendants want to
live a long time, you must always worship
the LORD and obey his laws. ³ Pay attention,

Israel! Our ancestors worshipped the LORD,
and he promised to give us this land that is
rich with milk and honey. Be careful to
obey him, and you will become a successful
and powerful nation.

⁴ Listen, Israel! The LORD our God is the
only true God!' ⁵ So love the LORD your
God with all your heart, soul, and strength.
⁶ Memorize his laws ⁷ and tell them to your
children over and over again. Talk about
them all the time, whether you're at home
or walking along the road or going to bed at
night, or getting up in the morning. ⁸ Write
down copies and tie them to your wrists
and foreheads to help you obey them.
⁹ Write these laws on the door frames of
your homes and on your town gates.

Worship only the LORD

Moses said to Israel:

¹⁰ The LORD promised your ancestors
Abraham, Isaac, and Jacob that he would
give you this land. Now he will take you
there and give you large towns, with good
buildings that you didn't build, ¹¹ and
houses full of good things that you didn't
put there. The LORD will give you wells*
that you didn't have to dig, and vineyards
and olive orchards that you didn't have to
plant. But when you have eaten so much
that you can't eat any more, ¹² don't forget
it was the LORD who set you free from
slavery and brought you out of Egypt.
¹³ Worship and obey the LORD your God
with fear and trembling, and promise that
you will be loyal to him.

¹⁴ Don't have anything to do with gods
that are worshipped by the nations around
you. ¹⁵ If you worship other gods, the LORD
will be furious and wipe you off the face of
the earth. The LORD your God is with you,
¹⁶ so don't try to make him prove that he
can help you, as you did at Massah.*
¹⁷ Always obey the laws that the LORD has
given you ¹⁸⁻¹⁹ and live in a way that pleases
him. Then you will be able to go in and
take this good land from your enemies, just
as he promised your ancestors.

*6.11 wells: Cisterns cut into the rock to collect
rainwater.
*6.16 Massah: See Exodus 17.1–7; Numbers 20.2–13.
See also: 6.4: Matt 12.29. 6.5: Matt 22.37; Mark 12.30;
Luke 10.27. 6.6–9: Deut 11.18–20. 6.10: a Gen 12.7;
b Gen 26.3; c Gen 28.13. 6.13: Matt 4.10; Luke 4.8.
6.16: a Matt 4.7; Luke 4.12; b Exod 17.1–7.

²⁰ Some day your children will ask, "Why did the LORD give us these laws and teachings?"

²¹ Then you will answer:

We were slaves of the king of Egypt, but the LORD used his great power and set us free. ²² We saw him perform miracles and make horrible things happen to the king, his officials, and everyone else. ²³ The LORD rescued us from Egypt, so he could bring us into this land, as he had promised our ancestors. ²⁴⁻²⁵ That's why the LORD our God demands that we obey his laws and worship him with fear and trembling. And if we do, he will protect us and help us be successful.

CHAPTER 7

Force the other nations out of the land

This is also told in Exodus 34.11–16

Moses said:

¹ People of Israel, the LORD your God will help you take the land of the Hittites, the Girgashites, the Amorites, the Canaanites, the Perizzites, the Hivites, and the Jebusites. These seven nations have more people and are stronger than Israel, but when you attack them, ² the LORD will force them out of the land. Then you must destroy them without mercy. Don't make any peace treaties with them, ³ and don't let your sons and daughters marry any of them. ⁴ If you do, those people will lead your descendants to worship other gods and to turn their backs on the LORD. That will make him very angry, and he will quickly destroy Israel.

⁵ So when you conquer these nations, tear down the altars where they worship their gods. Break up their sacred stones, cut down the poles* that they use in worshipping the goddess Asherah, and throw their idols in the fire.

The LORD's chosen people

Moses said:

⁶ Israel, you are the chosen people of the LORD your God. There are many nations on this earth, but he chose only Israel to be his very own. ⁷ You were the weakest of all nations, ⁸ but the LORD chose you because

he loves you and because he had made a promise to your ancestors. Then with his mighty arm, he rescued you from the king of Egypt, who had made you his slaves.

⁹ You know that the LORD your God is the only true God. So love him and obey his commands, and he will faithfully keep his agreement with you and your descendants for a thousand generations. ¹⁰ But if you turn against the LORD, he will quickly destroy you. ¹¹ So be sure to obey his laws and teachings I am giving you today.

The LORD will bless you if you obey

This is also told in Deuteronomy 28.1–14; Leviticus 26.3–13

Moses said to Israel:

¹² If you completely obey these laws, the LORD your God will be loyal and keep the agreement he made with you, just as he promised our ancestors. ¹³ The LORD will love you and bless you by giving you many children and plenty of food, wine, and olive oil. Your herds of cattle will have many calves, and your flocks of sheep will have many lambs. ¹⁴ God will bless you more than any other nation — your families will grow and your livestock increase. ¹⁵ You will no longer suffer with the same horrible diseases that you sometimes had in Egypt. You will be healthy, but the LORD will make your enemies suffer from those diseases.

Destroy the nations and their gods

Moses said to Israel:

¹⁶ When the LORD helps you defeat your enemies, you must destroy them without pity! And don't get trapped into worshipping their gods.

¹⁷ You may be thinking, "How can we destroy these nations? They are more powerful than we are." ¹⁸ But stop worrying! Just remember what the LORD your God did to Egypt and its king. ¹⁹ You saw how the LORD used his tremendous power to work great miracles and bring you out of Egypt. And he will work miracles for you when you face these enemies you fear so much. ²⁰ Some of them may try to survive by hiding from you, but the LORD will make them panic, and soon they will be dead. ²¹ So don't be frightened

---

*7.5 poles: Or "trees," used as symbols of Asherah, the goddess of fertility.

See also: 7.1: Acts 13.19.   7.5: Deut 12.3.   7.6: Exod 19.5; 4.20; 14.2; 26.18; Titus 2.14; 1 Pet 2.9.

See also: 7.9,10: Exod 20.5,6; 34.6,7; Num 14.18; Deut 5.9,10.   7.12–16: Deut 11.13–17.

when you meet them in battle. The LORD your God is great and fearsome, and he will fight at your side.

²² As you attack these nations, the LORD will force them out little by little. He won't let you get rid of them all at once — if he did, there wouldn't be enough people living in the land to keep down the number of wild animals. ²³⁻²⁴ But when you attack your enemies, the LORD will make them panic, and you will easily destroy them. You will defeat them one after another until they are gone, and no one will remember they ever lived.

²⁵ After you conquer a nation, burn their idols. Don't get trapped into wanting the silver or gold on an idol. Even the metal on an idol is disgusting to the LORD, ²⁶ so destroy it. If you bring it home with you, both you and your house will be destroyed. Stay away from those disgusting idols!

CHAPTER 8

The LORD takes care of you

Moses said:

¹ Israel, do you want to go into the land the LORD promised your ancestors? Do you want to capture it, live there, and become a powerful nation? Then be sure to obey every command I am giving you.

² Don't forget how the LORD your God has led you through the desert for the past forty years. He wanted to find out if you were truly willing to obey him and depend on him, ³ so he made you go hungry. Then he gave you manna,* a kind of food that you and your ancestors had never even heard about. The LORD was teaching you that people need more than food to live — they need every word that the LORD has spoken.

⁴ Over the past forty years, your clothing hasn't worn out, and your feet haven't swollen. ⁵ So keep in mind that the LORD has been correcting you, just as parents correct their children. ⁶ Obey the commands the LORD your God has given you and worship him with fear and trembling.

⁷ The LORD your God is bringing you into a good land with streams that flow from springs in the valleys and hills. ⁸⁻⁹ You can dig for copper in those hills, and the stones are made of iron ore. And you won't go hungry. Wheat and barley fields are everywhere, and so are vineyards and orchards full of fig, pomegranate,* and olive trees, and there is plenty of honey.

Don't forget the LORD

Moses said to Israel:

¹⁰ After you eat and are full, give praise to the LORD your God for the good land he gave you. ¹¹ Make sure that you never forget the LORD or disobey his laws and teachings that I am giving you today. If you always obey them, ¹² you will have plenty to eat, and you will build good houses to live in. ¹³ You will get more and more cattle, sheep, silver, gold, and other possessions.

¹⁴ But when all this happens, don't be proud! Don't forget that you were once slaves in Egypt and that it was the LORD who set you free. ¹⁵ Remember how he led you in that huge and frightening desert where poisonous snakes and scorpions live. There was no water, but the LORD split open a rock, and water poured out so you could drink. ¹⁶ He also gave you manna,* a kind of food your ancestors had never even heard about. The LORD was testing you to make you trust him, so that later on he could be good to you.

¹⁷ When you become successful, don't say, "I'm rich, and I've earned it all myself." ¹⁸ Instead, remember that the LORD your God gives you the strength to make a living. That's how he keeps the promise he made to your ancestors.

¹⁹⁻²⁰ But I'm warning you — if you forget the LORD your God and worship other gods, the LORD will destroy you, just as he destroyed the nations you fought.

CHAPTER 9

Why the LORD will help Israel

Moses said:

¹ Israel, listen to me! You will soon cross the River Jordan and go into the land to force out the nations that live there. They are more powerful than you are, and the walls around their cities reach to the sky. ² Some of these nations are descendants of

---

*8.3 manna: See Exodus 16.1–36.
See also: 8.3: Matt 4.4; Luke 4.4.

*8.8,9 pomegranate: A bright red fruit that looks like an apple.
*8.16 manna: See the note at 8.3.
See also: 8.11–16: Hos 13.5,6.

the Anakim.* You know how tall and strong they are, and you've heard that no one can defeat them in battle. ³ But the LORD your God has promised to go ahead of you, like a raging fire burning everything in its path. So when you attack your enemies, it will be easy for you to destroy them and take their land.

⁴⁻⁶ After the LORD helps you wipe out these nations and conquer their land, don't think he did it because you are such good people. You aren't good — you are stubborn! No, the LORD is going to help you, because the nations that live there are evil, and because he wants to keep the promise he made to your ancestors Abraham, Isaac, and Jacob.

When Israel made an idol

This is also told in Exodus 32

Moses said to Israel:

⁷ Don't ever forget how you kept rebelling and making the LORD angry the whole time you were in the desert. You rebelled from the day you left Egypt until the day you arrived here.

⁸ At Mount Sinai* you made the LORD so angry that he was going to destroy you. ⁹⁻¹¹ It happened during those forty days and nights that I was on the mountain, without anything to eat or drink. He had told me to come up there so he could give me the agreement he made with us. And this agreement was actually the same Ten Commandments* he had announced to you when he spoke from the mountain. The LORD had written them on two flat stones with his own hand. But after giving me the two stones, ¹² he said:

Moses, hurry down the mountain to those people you led out of Egypt. They have already disobeyed me and committed the terrible sin of making an idol.

¹³ I've been watching the Israelites, and I've seen how stubborn and rebellious they are. ¹⁴ So don't try to stop me! I am going to wipe them out, and no one on earth will remember they ever lived. Then I will let your descendants become an even bigger and more powerful nation than Israel.

Moses said:

¹⁵ Fire was raging on the mountaintop as I went back down, carrying the two stones

with the commandments on them. ¹⁶ I saw how quickly you had sinned and disobeyed the LORD your God. There you were, worshipping the metal idol you had made in the shape of a calf. ¹⁷ So I threw down the two stones and smashed them before your very eyes.

¹⁸⁻²⁰ I bowed down at the place of worship and prayed to the LORD, without eating or drinking for forty days and nights. You had committed a terrible sin by making that idol, and the LORD hated what you had done. He was angry enough to destroy all of you and Aaron as well. So I prayed for you and Aaron as I had done before, and this time the LORD answered my prayers.*

²¹ It was a sin for you to make that idol, so I threw it into the fire to melt it down. Then I took the lump of gold, ground it into powder, and threw the powder into the stream flowing down the mountain.

²² You also made the LORD angry when you were staying at Taberah,* at Massah,* and at Kibroth-Hattaavah.* ²³ Then at Kadesh-Barnea the LORD said, "I am giving you the land, so go ahead and take it!" But since you didn't trust the LORD, you rebelled and disobeyed his command.*

²⁴ In fact, you've rebelled against the LORD for as long as he' known you.

²⁵ After you had made the idol in the shape of a calf, the LORD said he was going to destroy you. So I bowed down in front of the sacred tent for forty days and nights, ²⁶ and I prayed:

Our LORD, please don't wipe out your people. You used your great power to rescue them from Egypt and to make them your very own. ²⁷ Israel's ancestors Abraham, Isaac, and Jacob obeyed you faithfully. Think about them, and not about Israel's stubbornness, evil, and sin. ²⁸ If you destroy your people, the Egyptians will say, "The LORD promised to give Israel land, but he wasn't powerful enough to keep his promise. In fact, he hated them so

---

*9.2 Anakim: See the notes at 1.28; 2.10,11.

See also: 9.9: Exod 24.18.

*9.18–20 as I had done before . . . prayers: This may refer to Moses' praying for Israel before he came down from the mountain (see Exodus 32.11–14).
*9.22 Taberah: See Numbers 11.1–3.
*9.22 Massah: See the note at 6.16.
*9.22 Kibroth-Hattaavah: See Numbers 11.31–34.
*9.23 Kadesh-Barnea . . . you rebelled and disobeyed his command: See Numbers 13,14.

See also: 9.19: Heb 12.21. 9.22: a Num 11.3; b Exod 17.7; c Num 11.34. 9.23: a Num 13.17; b Deut 1.21; c Num 13.31; Deut 1.26; Heb 3.16.

much that he took them into the desert and killed them." [29] But you, our LORD, chose the people of Israel to be your own, and with your mighty power you rescued them from Egypt.

CHAPTER 10

The second set of commandments

This is also told in Exodus 34.1–10

Moses said to the people:

[1] The LORD to'd me to chisel out two flat stones, just like the ones he had given me earlier. He also commanded me to make a wooden chest, then come up the mountain and meet with him. [2] He told me that he would write the same words on the new stones that he had written on the ones I broke, and that I could put these stones in this sacred chest.

[3] So I made a chest out of acacia wood, and I chiselled two flat stones like the ones I broke. Then I carried the stones up the mountain, [4] where the LORD wrote the Ten Commandments on them, just as he had done the first time. The commandments were exactly what he had announced from the fire, when you were gathered at the mountain.

After the LORD returned the stones to me, [5] I took them down the mountainside and put them in the chest, just as he had commanded. And they are still there.

Aaron died

This is also told in Numbers 20.22–29

Moses said to Israel:

[6] Later we set up camp at the wells belonging to the descendants of Jaakan.' Then we moved on and camped at Moserah, where Aaron died and was buried, and his son Eleazar became the priest. [7] Next, we camped at Gudgodah and then at Jotbathah, where there are flowing streams.

The Levites were appointed to carry the chest

Moses said to Israel:

[8] After I put the two stones in the sacred chest,' the LORD chose the tribe of Levi, not only to carry the chest, but also to serve as his priests at the place of worship and to bless the other tribes in his name. And they

still do these things. [9] The LORD promised that he would always provide for the tribe of Levi, and that's why he won't give them any land, when he divides it among the other tribes.

The LORD answered the prayers of Moses

This is also told in Exodus 34.9,10,27–29

Moses said to Israel:

[10] When I had taken the second set of stones up the mountain, I spent forty days and nights there, just as I had done before. Once again, the LORD answered my prayer and did not destroy you. [11] Instead, he told me, "Moses, get ready to lead the people into the land that I promised their ancestors."*

What the LORD wants

Moses said:

[12] People of Israel, what does the LORD your God want from you? The LORD wants you to respect and follow him, to love and serve him with all your heart and soul, [13] and to obey his laws and teachings that I am giving you today. Do this, and all will go well for you.

[14] Everything belongs to the LORD your God, not only the earth and everything on it, but also the sky and the highest heavens. [15] Yet the LORD loved your ancestors and wanted them to belong to him. So he chose them and their descendants rather than any other nation, and today you are still his people.

[16] Remember your agreement with the LORD and stop being so stubborn. [17] The LORD your God is more powerful than all other gods and lords, and his tremendous power is to be feared. His decisions are always fair, and you cannot bribe him to change his mind. [18] The LORD defends the rights of orphans and widows. He cares for foreigners and gives them food and clothing. [19] And you should also care for them, because you were foreigners in Egypt. [20] Respect the LORD your God, serve only him, and make promises in his name alone. [21] Offer your praises to him, because you

10.11 lead … ancestors: The LORD would later tell Moses that he would not be allowed to enter the land (see 1.37; 3.23–28; Numbers 20.10–12).

See also: 10.6: Num 20.28; 33.38. 10.8: Num 3.5–8.

See also: 10.10: Exod 34.28. 10.17: 1 Tim 6.15; Rev 17.14; 19.16; Acts 10.34; Rom 2.11; Gal 2.6; Eph 6.9.

have seen him work such terrifying miracles for you.

²² When your ancestors went to live in Egypt, there were only seventy of them. But the LORD has blessed you, and now there are more of you than there are stars in the sky.

CHAPTER 11

If you are loyal to the LORD, he will bless you

Moses said to Israel:

¹ The LORD is your God, so you must always love him and obey his laws and teachings. ² Remember, he corrected you and not your children. You are the ones who saw the LORD use his mighty power ³ when he worked miracles in Egypt, making terrible things happen to the king and all his people. ⁴ And when the Egyptian army chased you in their chariots, you saw the LORD drown them and their horses in the Red Sea.* Egypt still suffers from that defeat!

⁵ You saw what the LORD did for you while you were in the desert, right up to the time you arrived here. ⁶ And you saw how the LORD made the ground open up in the middle of our camp underneath the tents of Dathan and Abiram,* who were swallowed up along with their families, their animals, and their tents.

⁷ With your own eyes, you saw the LORD's mighty power do all these things.

⁸ Soon you will cross the River Jordan, and if you obey the laws and teachings I'm giving you today, you will be strong enough to conquer the land ⁹ that the LORD promised your ancestors and their descendants. It's rich with milk and honey, and you will live there and enjoy it for a long time. ¹⁰ It's better land than you had in Egypt, where you had to struggle just to water your crops.* ¹¹ But the hills and valleys in the promised land are

watered by rain from heaven,* ¹² because the LORD your God keeps his eye on this land and takes care of it all year long.

¹³ The LORD your God commands you to love him and to serve him with all your heart and soul. If you obey him, ¹⁴⁻¹⁵ he will send rain at the right seasons,* so you will have more than enough food, wine, and olive oil, and there will be plenty of grass for your cattle.

¹⁶ But watch out! You will be tempted to turn your backs on the LORD. And if you worship other gods, ¹⁷ the LORD will become angry and keep the rain from falling. Nothing will grow in your fields, and you will die and disappear from the good land that the LORD is giving you.

¹⁸ Memorize these laws and think about them. Write down copies and tie them to your wrists and your foreheads to help you obey them. ¹⁹ Teach them to your children. Talk about them all the time — whether you're at home or walking along the road or going to bed at night, or getting up in the morning. ²⁰ Write them on the door frames of your homes and on your town gates. ²¹ Then you and your descendants will live a long time in the land that the LORD promised your ancestors. Your families will live there as long as the sky is above the earth.

²² Love the LORD your God and obey all the laws and teachings that I'm giving you today. If you live the way the LORD wants, ²³ he will help you take the land. And even though the nations there are more powerful than you, the LORD will force them to leave when you attack. ²⁴ You will capture the land everywhere you go, from the Southern Desert to the Lebanon Mountains, and from the River Euphrates west to the Mediterranean Sea. ²⁵ No one will be able to stand up to you. The LORD will make everyone terrified of you, just as he promised.

²⁶ You have a choice — do you want the LORD to bless you, or do you want him to put a curse on you? ²⁷ Today I am giving you his laws, and if you obey him, he will

---

*11.4 Red Sea: Hebrew *yam suph* "Sea of Reeds", one of the marshes or fresh water lakes near the eastern part of the Nile Delta. This identification is based on Exodus 13.7–14.9, which lists towns on the route of the Israelites before crossing the sea. In the Greek translation of the Scriptures made about 200 BC, the "Sea of Reeds" was named "Red Sea".

See also: 10.22: a Gen 46.27; b Gen 15.5; 22.17.
11.3: Exod 7.8–12.13.   11.4: Exod 14.28.
11.6: Num 16.31,32.

*11.10,11 to water your crops . . . rain from heaven: Egypt was flat and had very little rain. All water for crops had to come from the River Nile.
*11.14,15 rain . . . seasons: In Palestine, almost all the rain for the year comes during the months from October to April.

See also: 11.13–17: Lev 26.3–5; Deut 7.12–16; 28.1–14.
11.18–20: Deut 6.6–9.   11.24,25: Josh 1.3–5.

bless you. 28 But if you disobey him and worship those gods that have never done anything for you, the LORD will put a curse on you.

29 After the LORD your God helps you take the land, you must have a ceremony where you announce his blessings from Mount Gerizim and his curses from Mount Ebal. 30 You know that these two mountains are west of the River Jordan in land now controlled by the Canaanites living in the Jordan valley. The mountains are west of the road near the sacred trees of Moreh on the other side of Gilgal.

31 Soon you will cross the River Jordan to conquer the land that the LORD your God is giving you. And when you have settled there, 32 be careful to obey his laws and teachings that I am giving you today.

CHAPTER 12

Only one place to worship the LORD

Moses said to Israel:

1 Now I'll tell you the laws and teachings that you have to obey as long as you live. Your ancestors worshipped the LORD, and he is giving you this land. 2 But the nations that live there worship other gods. So after you capture the land, you must completely destroy their places of worship — on mountains and hills or in the shade of large trees. 3 Wherever these nations worship their gods, you must tear down their altars, break their sacred stones, burn the sacred poles* used in worshipping the goddess Asherah, and smash their idols to pieces. Destroy these places of worship so completely that no one will remember they were ever there. 4 Don't worship the LORD your God in the way these nations worship their gods.

5–19 Soon you will cross the Jordan, and the LORD will help you conquer your enemies and let you live in peace, there in the land he has given you. But after you are settled, life will be different. You must not offer sacrifices anywhere you want. Instead, the LORD will choose a place somewhere in Israel where you must go to worship him. All your sacrifices and offerings must be taken there, including

sacrifices to please the LORD* and any gift you promise or voluntarily give him. That's where you must also take one tenth of your grain, wine, and olive oil,* as well as the firstborn of your cattle, sheep, and goats.* You and your family and servants will eat your gifts and sacrifices* and celebrate there at the place of worship, because the LORD your God has made you successful in everything you have done. And since Levites will not have any land of their own, you must ask some of them to come along and celebrate with you.

Sometimes you may want to kill an animal for food and not as a sacrifice. If the LORD has blessed you and given you enough cows or sheep or goats, then you can butcher one of them where you live. You can eat it just like the meat from a deer or gazelle that you kill when you go hunting. And even those people who are unclean and unfit for worship can have some of the meat. But you must not eat the blood of any animal — let the blood drain out on the ground.

20–21 The LORD has promised that later on he will give Israel more land, and some of you may not be able to travel all the way from your homes to the place of worship each time you are hungry for meat.* But the LORD will give you cattle, sheep, and goats, and you can butcher any of those animals at home and eat as much as you want. 22 It is the same as eating the meat from a deer or a gazelle that you kill when you go hunting. And in this way, anyone

---

*12.3 sacred poles: See the note at 7.5.

See also: 11.29: Deut 27.11–14; Josh 8.33–35.
12.3: Deut 7.5. 12.16: Gen 9.4; Lev 7.26,27; 17.10–14; 19.26; Deut 15.23.

---

*12.5–19 sacrifices to please the LORD: These sacrifices have traditionally been called "whole burnt offerings" because the whole animal was burnt on the altar. A main purpose of such sacrifices was to please the LORD with the smell of the sacrifice, and so in the CEV they are often called "sacrifices to please the LORD".
*12.5–19 one tenth of your grain, wine, and olive oil: The Israelites had to give one tenth of their harvest of these products to the LORD each year (see 14.22–29; 26.12,13; Leviticus 27.30–33).
*12.5–19 the firstborn of your cattle, sheep, and goats: The Israelites had to sacrifice these to the LORD (see 15.19–22).
*12.5–19 sacrifices: Some sacrifices were completely burnt on the altar; in other sacrifices, part of the animal was burnt and part was given to the priests, but most of the meat was eaten by the worshippers as a sacred meal.
*12.20,21 meat: Usually eaten only on special occasions, such as during a sacred meal when sacrifices were offered to the LORD.

who is unclean and unfit for worship can have some of the meat.*

23-24 But don't eat the blood. It is the life of the animal, so let it drain out on the ground before you eat the meat. 25 Do you want the LORD to make you successful? Do you want your children to be successful even after you are gone? Then do what pleases the LORD and don't eat blood.

26-27 All sacrifices and offerings to the LORD must be taken to the place where he chooses to be worshipped. If you offer a sacrifice to please the LORD, all of its meat must be burnt on the altar. You can eat the meat from certain kinds of sacrifices, but you must always pour out the animal's blood on the altar.

28 If you obey these laws, you will be doing what the LORD your God says is right and good. Then he will help you and your descendants be successful.

Worship the LORD in the right way

Moses said:

29 Israel, as you go into the land and attack the nations that are there, the LORD will get rid of them, and you can have their land.

30 But that's when you must be especially careful not to ask, "How did those nations worship their gods? Shouldn't we worship the LORD in the same way?" 31 No, you should not! The LORD hates the disgusting way those nations worship their gods, because they even burn their sons and daughters as sacrifices.

32 Obey all the laws and teachings I am giving you. Don't add any, and don't take any away.

CHAPTER 13

Don't worship other gods

Moses said to Israel:

1-2 Some day a prophet' may come along who is able to perform miracles or tell what will happen in the future. Then the prophet may say, "Let's start worshipping some new gods — some gods that we know nothing about." 3 If the prophet says this, don't listen! The LORD your God will be watching to find out whether or not you love him

with all your heart and soul. 4 You must be completely faithful to the LORD. Worship and obey only the LORD and do this with fear and trembling, 5 because he rescued you from slavery in Egypt.

If a prophet tells you to disobey the LORD your God and to stop worshipping him, then that prophet is evil and must be put to death.

6-10 Someone else may say to you, "Let's worship other gods." That person may be your best friend, your brother or sister, your son or daughter, or your own dear wife or husband. But you must not listen to people who say such things. Instead, you must stone them to death. You must be the first to throw the stones, then others from the community will finish the job. Don't show any pity.

The gods worshipped by other nations have never done anything for you or your ancestors. People who ask you to worship other gods are trying to get you to stop worshipping the LORD, who rescued you from slavery in Egypt. So put to death anyone who asks you to worship another god. 11 And when the rest of Israel hears about it, they will be afraid, and no one else will ever do such an evil thing again.

12 After the LORD your God gives you towns to live in, you may hear a rumour about one of the towns. 13 You may hear that some worthless people have talked everyone there into worshipping other gods, even though these gods had never done anything for them. 14 You must carefully find out if the rumour is true. Then if the people of that town have actually done such a disgusting thing in your own country, 15 you must take your swords and kill every one of them, and their livestock too. 16-17 Gather all the possessions of the people who lived there, and pile them up in the market place, without keeping anything for yourself. Set the pile and the whole town on fire, and don't ever rebuild the town. The whole town will be a sacrifice to the LORD your God. Then he won't be angry any more, and he will have mercy on you and make you successful, just as he promised your ancestors. 18 That's why you must do what the LORD your God says is right. I am giving you his laws and teachings today, and you must obey them.

---

*12.22 anyone . . . the meat: Only those who were properly prepared for worship, or "clean", could eat a sacred meal, but anyone could eat this kind of meat.

See also: 12.23,24: Lev 17.10–14. 12.32: Deut 4.2; Rev 22.18,19.

CHAPTER 14

Don't mourn like other nations

Moses said:

[1] People of Israel, you are the LORD's children, so when you mourn for the dead, you must not cut yourselves or shave your forehead.* [2] Out of all the nations on this earth, the LORD your God chose you to be his own. You belong to the LORD, so don't behave like those who worship other gods.

Animals that can be eaten

This is also told in Leviticus 11.1–47

Moses said:

[3] Don't eat any disgusting animals. [4-5] You may eat the meat of cattle, sheep, and goats; wild sheep and goats; and gazelles, antelopes, and all kinds of deer. [6] It is all right to eat meat from any animals that have divided hoofs and also chew the cud.*

[7] But don't eat camels, rabbits, and rock badgers. These animals chew the cud but do not have divided hoofs. You must treat them as unclean. [8] And don't eat pork, since pigs have divided hoofs, but they do not chew their cud. Don't even touch a dead pig!

[9] You can eat any fish that has fins and scales. But there are other creatures that live in the water, [10] and if they do not have fins and scales, you must not eat them. Treat them as unclean.

[11] You can eat any clean bird. [12-18] But don't eat the meat of any of the following birds: eagles, vultures, falcons, kites, ravens, ostriches, owls, seagulls, hawks, pelicans, ospreys, cormorants, storks, herons, and hoopoes.* [19] Swarming insects are unclean, so don't eat them. [20] However, you are allowed to eat certain kinds of winged insects.*

[21] You belong to the LORD your God, so if you happen to find a dead animal, don't eat

its meat. You may give it to foreigners who live in your town or sell it to foreigners who are visiting your town.

Don't boil a young goat in its mother's milk.

Give the LORD ten per cent of your harvest

Moses said:

[22] People of Israel, every year you must set aside ten per cent of your grain harvest. [23] Also set aside ten per cent of your wine and olive oil, and the firstborn of every cow, sheep, and goat. Take these to the place where the LORD chooses to be worshipped, and eat them there. This will teach you to always respect the LORD your God.

[24] But suppose you can't carry that ten per cent of your harvest to the place where the LORD chooses to be worshipped. If you live too far away, or if the LORD gives you a big harvest, [25] then sell this part and take the money there instead. [26] When you and your family arrive, spend the money on food for a big celebration. Buy cattle, sheep, goats, wine, beer, and if there are any other kinds of food that you want, buy those too. [27] And since people of the Levi tribe won't own any land for growing crops, remember to ask the Levites to celebrate with you.

[28] Every third year, instead of using the ten per cent of your harvest for a big celebration, bring it into town and put it in a community storehouse. [29] The Levites have no land of their own, so you must give them food from the storehouse. You must also give food to the poor who live in your town, including orphans, widows, and foreigners. If they have enough to eat, then the LORD your God will be pleased and make you successful in everything you do.

CHAPTER 15

Loans

This is also told in Leviticus 25.1–7

Moses said:

[1-2] Every seven years you must announce, "The LORD says loans do not need to be paid back." Then if you have loaned money to another Israelite, you can no longer ask

---

*14.6 chew the cud: Some animals that eat grass and leaves have more than one stomach, and they chew their food a second time, after it has been partly digested in the first stomach. This partly digested food is called "cud."

*14.20 certain kinds of winged insects: These were locusts, crickets, and grasshoppers; see Leviticus 11.21,22.

See also: 14.1: Lev 19.28; 21.5. 14.2: Exod 19.5,6; Deut 4.20; 7.6; 26.18; Titus 2.14; 1 Pet 2.9. 14.21: Exod 23.19; 34.26.

See also: 14.22-29: Lev 27.30–33; Num 18.21.

for payment.* ³ This law applies only to loans you have made to other Israelites. Foreigners will still have to pay back what you have loaned them.

⁴⁻⁶ No one in Israel should ever be poor. The LORD your God is giving you this land, and he has promised to make you very successful, if you obey his laws and teachings that I'm giving you today. You will lend money to many nations, but you won't have to borrow. You will rule many nations, but they won't rule you.

⁷ After the LORD your God gives land to each of you, there may be poor Israelites in the town where you live. If there are, then don't be mean and selfish with your money. ⁸ Instead, be kind and lend them what they need. ⁹ Be careful! Don't say to yourself, "Soon it will be the seventh year, and then I won't be able to get my money back." It would be horrible for you to think that way and to be so selfish that you refuse to help the poor. They are your relatives, and if you don't help them, they may ask the LORD to decide whether you have done wrong. And he will say that you are guilty. ¹⁰ You should be happy to give the poor what they need, because then the LORD will make you successful in everything you do.

¹¹ There will always be some Israelites who are poor and needy. That's why I am commanding you to be generous with them.

Setting slaves free

This is also told in Exodus 21.1–11

Moses said to Israel:

¹² If any of you buy Israelites as slaves, you must set them free after six years. ¹³ And don't just tell them they are free to leave — ¹⁴ give them sheep and goats and a good supply of grain and wine. The more the LORD has given you, the more you should give them. ¹⁵ I am commanding you to obey the LORD as a reminder that you were slaves in Egypt before he set you free. ¹⁶ But one of your slaves may say, "I love you and your family, and I would be better off staying with you, so please don't make me

leave." ¹⁷ Take the slave to the door of your house and push a sharp metal rod through one ear lobe and into the door. Such slaves will belong to you for life, whether they are men or women.

¹⁸ Don't complain when you have to set a slave free. After all, you got six years of service at half the cost of hiring someone to do the work.*

Firstborn animals

This is also told in Leviticus 27.26,27; Numbers 18.15–18

Moses said to Israel:

¹⁹ If the firstborn animal of a cow or sheep or goat is a male, it must be given to the LORD. Don't put firstborn cattle to work or cut wool from firstborn sheep. ²⁰ Instead, each year you must take the firstborn of these animals to the place where the LORD your God chooses to be worshipped. You and your family will sacrifice them to the LORD and then eat them as part of a sacred meal.

²¹ But if the animal is lame or blind or has something else wrong with it, you must not sacrifice it to the LORD your God. ²² You can butcher it where you live, and eat it just like the meat of a deer or gazelle that you kill while hunting. Even those people who are unclean and unfit for worship can have some. ²³ But you must never eat the blood of an animal — let it drain out on the ground.

CHAPTER 16

Passover

This is also told in Exodus 12.1–20; Leviticus 23.4–8

Moses said:

¹ People of Israel, you must celebrate Passover in the month of Abib,* because one night in that month years ago, the LORD your God rescued you from Egypt. ² The Passover sacrifice must be a cow, a sheep, or a goat, and you must offer it at the place where the LORD chooses to be worshipped. ³⁻⁴ Eat all the meat of the Passover sacrifice that same night. But don't

---

15.1,2 The LORD says . . . no longer ask for payment: Or " 'The LORD says loans do not need to be paid back this year.' Then if you have loaned money to another Israelite, you cannot ask for payment until the next year."

See also: 15.7,8: Lev 25.35.   15.11: Matt 26.11; Mark 14.7; John 12.8.   15.12–18: Lev 25.39–46.

16.1 in the month of Abib: Abib (also called Nisan), the first month of the Hebrew calendar, from about mid-March to mid-April. Passover was celebrated on the evening of the fourteenth of Abib (see Exodus 12.6; Leviticus 23.4,5).

See also: 15.19: Exod 13.12.   15.23: Gen 9.4; Lev 7.26,27; 17.10–14; 19.26; Deut 12.16,23.   16.1–8: Exod 12.1–20; Lev 23.5–8; Num 28.16–25.

serve bread made with yeast at the Passover meal. Serve the same kind of thin bread that you ate when you were slaves suffering in Egypt* and when you had to leave Egypt quickly. As long as you live, this thin bread will remind you of the day you left Egypt.

For seven days following Passover,* don't make any bread with yeast. In fact, there should be no yeast anywhere in Israel.

5 Don't offer the Passover sacrifice in any town where you happen to live. 6 It must be offered at the place where the LORD chooses to be worshipped. Kill the sacrifice at sunset, the time of day when you left Egypt.* 7 Then cook it and eat it there at the place of worship, returning to your tents the next morning.

8 Eat thin bread for the next six days. Then on the seventh day, don't do any work. Instead, come together and worship the LORD.

The Harvest Festival

This is also told in Exodus 34.22; Leviticus 23.15–21

Moses said to Israel:

9 Seven weeks after you start your grain harvest, 10–11 go to the place where the LORD chooses to be worshipped and celebrate the Harvest Festival* in honour of the LORD your God. Bring him an offering as large as you can afford, depending on how big a harvest he has given you. Be sure to take along your sons and daughters and all your servants. Also invite the poor, including Levites, foreigners, orphans, and widows. 12 Remember that you used to be slaves in Egypt, so obey these laws.

The Festival of Shelters

This is also told in Leviticus 23.33–43; Numbers 29.12–38

Moses said to Israel:

13–15 After you have finished the grain harvest and the grape harvest,* take your sons and daughters and all your servants to the place where the LORD chooses to be worshipped. Celebrate the Festival of Shelters for seven days. Also invite the poor, including Levites, foreigners, orphans, and widows.

The LORD will give you big harvests and make you successful in everything you do. You will be completely happy, so celebrate this festival in honour of the LORD your God.

Three festivals at the place of worship

This is also told in Exodus 23.14–17

Moses said:

16 Each year there are three festivals when all Israelite men must go to the place where the LORD chooses to be worshipped. These are the Festival of Thin Bread, the Harvest Festival,* and the Festival of Shelters. And don't forget to take along a gift for the LORD. 17 The bigger the harvest the LORD gives you, the bigger your gift should be.

Treat everyone with justice

Moses said to Israel:

18–19 After you are settled in the towns that you will receive from the LORD your God, the people in each town must appoint judges and other officers. Those of you who become judges must be completely fair when you make legal decisions, even if someone important is involved. Don't take bribes to give unfair decisions. Bribes keep people who are wise from seeing the truth and turn honest people into liars.*

20 People of Israel, if you want to enjoy a long and successful life, make sure that everyone is treated with justice in the land the LORD is giving you.

Don't set up sacred poles or stones

Moses said to Israel:

21 When you build the altar for offering sacrifices to the LORD your God, don't set up a sacred pole* for the worship of the goddess Asherah. 22 And don't set up a sacred stone! The LORD hates these things.

---

*16.3,4 seven days following Passover:** This period was called the Festival of Thin Bread (see also verse 16).
*16.10,11 Harvest Festival:** Traditionally called the "Festival of Weeks", and known in New Testament times as "Pentecost".
*16.13–15 After you . . . harvest:** Leviticus 23.34 gives the exact date as the fifteenth day of the seventh month of the Hebrew calendar, which would be early in October.
See also: 16.9–12: Lev 23.15–21; Num 28.26–31. 16.13–15: Lev 23.33–36,39–43; Num 29.12–38.

*16.16 Harvest Festival:** See the note at 16.10,11.
*16.21 sacred pole:** See the note at 7.5.
See also: 16.19: Exod 23.6–8; Lev 19.15. 16.21: Exod 34.13. 16.22: Lev 26.1.

CHAPTER 17

Sacrifices that have something wrong with them

Moses said to Israel:

¹ If an ox or a sheep has something wrong with it, don't offer it as a sacrifice to the LORD your God — he will be disgusted!

Put to death people who worship idols

Moses said to Israel:

²⁻³ The LORD your God is giving you towns to live in. But later, a man or a woman in your town may start worshipping other gods, or even the sun, moon, or stars.* I have warned you not to worship other gods, because whoever worships them is disobeying the LORD and breaking the agreement he made with you. ⁴ So when you hear that someone in your town is committing this disgusting sin, you must carefully find out if that person really is guilty. ⁵⁻⁷ But you will need two or three witnesses — one witness isn't enough to prove a person guilty.

Get rid of those who are guilty of such evil. Take them outside your town gates and let everyone stone them to death. But the witnesses must be the first to throw stones.

Difficult cases

Moses said to Israel:

⁸⁻¹² It may be difficult to find out the truth in some legal cases in your town. You may not be able to decide if someone was killed accidentally or murdered. Or you may not be able to tell whether an injury or some property damage was done by accident or on purpose. If the case is too difficult, take it to the court at the place where the LORD your God chooses to be worshipped.

This court will be made up of one judge and several priests* who serve at the LORD's altar. They will explain the law to you and give you their decision about the case. Do exactly what they tell you, or you will be put to death. ¹³ When other Israelites hear about it, they will be afraid and obey the decisions of the court.

The king

Moses said:

¹⁴ People of Israel, after you capture the land the LORD your God is giving you, and after you settle on it, you will say, "We want a king, just like the nations around us."

¹⁵ Go ahead and appoint a king, but make sure that he is an Israelite and that he is the one the LORD has chosen.

¹⁶ The king should not have many horses, especially those from Egypt. The LORD has said his people are never to go back there again. ¹⁷ And the king must not have a lot of wives — they might tempt him to be unfaithful to the LORD.* Finally, the king must not try to get huge amounts of silver and gold.

¹⁸ The official copy of God's laws' will be kept by the priests of the Levi tribe. So, as soon as anyone becomes king, he must go to the priests and write out a copy of these laws while they watch. ¹⁹ Each day the king must read and obey these laws, so that he will learn to worship the LORD with fear and trembling ²⁰ and not think that he's better than everyone else.

If the king completely obeys the LORD's commands, he and his descendants will rule Israel for many years.

CHAPTER 18

Special privileges for priests and Levites

This is also told in Numbers 18.8–32

Moses said to Israel:

¹ The people of the Levi tribe, including the priests, will not receive any land. Instead, they will receive part of the sacrifices that are offered to the LORD, ² because he has promised to provide for them in this way.

³ When you sacrifice a bull or sheep, the priests will be given the shoulder, the jaws, and the stomach.* ⁴ In addition, they will

---

*17.2,3 sun, moon, or stars: Some people thought these were gods and worshipped them.

*17.8–12 several priests: The Hebrew text has "the priests, the Levites"; priests belonged to the Levi tribe.

See also: 17.3: Exod 22.20. 17.6: Num 35.30; Deut 19.15; Matt 18.16; 2 Cor 13.1; 1 Tim 5.19; Heb 10.28.
17.7: 1 Cor 5.13.

*17.17 a lot of wives . . . unfaithful to the LORD: A king would often marry the daughter of another king whom he was making a treaty with. These foreign women would naturally want to worship their own gods, and would want their husband the king to do so as well.

*18.3 stomach: Certain portions of the stomach were considered a delicacy.

See also: 17.14: 1 Sam 8.5. 17.16: 1 Kings 10.28; 2 Chron 1.16; 9.28. 17.17: a 1 King 11.1–8; b 1 King 10.14–22,27; 2 Chron 1.15; 9.27. 18.2: Num 18.20.

receive the first part of your grain harvest and part of your first batches of wine and olive oil.* You must also give them the first wool that is cut from your sheep each year. 5 Give these gifts to the priests, because the LORD has chosen them and their descendants out of all the tribes of Israel to be his special servants at the place of worship.

6 Any Levite can leave his home town, and go to the place where the LORD chooses to be worshipped, 7 and then be a special servant of the LORD* there, just like all the other Levites. 8 Some Levites may have money from selling family possessions, and others may not. But all Levites serving at the place of worship will receive the same amount of food from the sacrifices and gifts brought by the people.

Don't do disgusting things

Moses said to Israel:

9 Soon you will go into the land that the LORD your God is giving you. The nations that live there do things that are disgusting to the LORD, and you must not follow their example. 10–11 Don't sacrifice your son or daughter. And don't try to use any kind of magic or witchcraft to tell fortunes* or to cast spells or to talk with spirits of the dead.

12 The LORD is disgusted with anyone who does these things, and that's why he will help you destroy the nations that are in the land. 13 Never be guilty of doing any of these disgusting things!

A prophet like Moses

Moses said to Israel:

14 You will go in and take the land from nations that practise magic and witchcraft. But the LORD your God won't allow you to do those things. 15 Instead, he will choose one of your own people to be a prophet just like me, and you must do what that prophet says. 16 You were asking for a prophet the day you were gathered at

Mount Sinai* and said to the LORD, "Please don't let us hear your voice or see this terrible fire again — if we do, we will die!"

17 Then the LORD told me:

Moses, they have said the right thing. 18 So when I want to speak to them, I will choose one of them to be a prophet like you. I will give my message to that prophet, who will tell the people exactly what I have said. 19 Since the message comes from me, anyone who doesn't obey the message will have to answer to me.

20 But if I haven't spoken, and a prophet claims to have a message from me, you must kill that prophet, and you must also kill any prophet who claims to have a message from another god.

Moses said to Israel:

21 You may be asking yourselves, "How can we tell if a prophet's message really comes from the LORD?" 22 You will know, because if the LORD says something will happen, it will happen. And if it doesn't, you will know that the prophet was falsely claiming to speak for the LORD. Don't be afraid of any prophet whose message doesn't come from the LORD.

CHAPTER 19

Safe Towns

This is also told in Numbers 35.9–28; Joshua 20.1–9

Moses said to Israel:

1 Soon you will go into the land and attack the nations. The LORD your God will destroy them and give you their lands, towns, and homes. Then after you are settled, 2–4 you must choose three of your towns to be Safe Towns. Divide the land into three regions with one Safe Town near the middle of each, so that a Safe Town can be easily reached from anywhere in your land.

Then, if one of you accidentally kills someone, you can run to a Safe Town and find protection from being put to death. But you must not have been angry with the person you killed.

5 For example, suppose you and a friend go into the forest to cut wood. You are chopping down a tree with an axe, when the axe head slips off the handle, hits your friend, and kills him. You can run to one of

---

*18.4 grain . . . olive oil: An Israelite was supposed to offer the first part of the harvest as a gift to the LORD (see Leviticus 23.10,11).
*18.10,11 tell fortunes: Fortune-tellers thought they could learn secrets or learn about the future by watching the flight of birds or looking at the livers of animals or in many other ways.
See also: 18.10: a Lev 19.26; b Exod 22.18.
18.11: Lev 19.31. 18.13: Matt 5.48. 18.15: Acts 3.22; 7.37.

See also: 18.19: Acts 3.23. 19.1–13: Josh 20.1–9.

the Safe Towns and save your life. 6 You don't deserve to die, since you did not mean to harm your friend. But he did get killed, and his relatives might be very angry. They might even choose one of the men from their family to track you down and kill you. If it is too far to one of the Safe Towns, the victim's relative might be able to catch you and kill you. 7 That's why I said there must be three Safe Towns.

8-9 Israel, the LORD your God has promised that if you obey his laws and teachings I'm giving you, and if you always love him, then he will give you the land he promised your ancestors. When that happens, you must name three more Safe Towns in the new territory. 10 You will need them, so innocent people won't be killed on your land while they are trying to reach a Safe Town that is too far away. You will be guilty of murder, if innocent people lose their lives because you didn't name enough Safe Towns in the land the LORD your God will give you.

11 But what if you really do commit murder? Suppose one of you hates a neighbour. So you wait in a deserted place, kill the neighbour, and run to a Safe Town. 12 If that happens, the leaders of your town must send messengers to bring you back from the Safe Town. They will hand you over to one of the victim's relatives, who will put you to death.

13 Israel, for the good of the whole country, you must kill anyone who murders an innocent person. Never show mercy to a murderer!

Boundary marks

Moses said to Israel:

14 In the land the LORD is giving you, there are already stones set up to mark the boundaries between fields. So don't move those stones.

Witnesses must tell the truth

Moses said to Israel:

15 Before you are convicted of a crime, at least two witnesses must be able to testify that you did it.

16 If you accuse someone of a crime, but seem to be lying, 17-18 then both you and the accused must be taken to the court at

the place where the LORD is worshipped. There the priests and judges will find out if you are lying or telling the truth.

If you are lying and the accused is innocent, 19-21 then you will be punished without mercy. You will receive the same punishment the accused would have received if found guilty, whether it means losing an eye, a tooth, a hand, a foot, or even your life.

Israel, the crime of telling lies in court must be punished. And when people hear what happens to witnesses that lie, everyone else who testifies in court will tell the truth.

CHAPTER 20

Laws for going to war

Moses said to Israel:

1 If you have to go to war, you may find yourselves facing an enemy army that is bigger than yours and that has horses and chariots. But don't be afraid! The LORD your God rescued you from Egypt, and he will help you fight. 2 Before you march into battle, a priest will go to the front of the army 3 and say, "Soldiers of Israel, listen to me! Today when you go into battle, don't be afraid of the enemy, and when you see them, don't panic. 4 The LORD your God will fight beside you and help you win the battle."

5 Then the tribal officials will say to the troops:

If any of you have built a new house, but haven't yet moved in, you may go home. It isn't right for you to die in battle and for somebody else to live in your new house.

6 If any of you have planted a vineyard but haven't had your first grape harvest, you may go home. It isn't right for you to die in battle and for somebody else to enjoy your grapes.

7 If any of you are engaged to be married, you may go back home and get married. It isn't right for you to die in battle and for somebody else to marry the woman you are engaged to.

8 Finally, if any of you are afraid, you may go home. We don't want you to discourage the other soldiers.

9 When the officials have finished giving these orders, they will appoint officers to be in command of the army.

See also: **19.14:** Deut 27.17. **19.15:** Num 35.30; Deut 17.6; Matt 18.16; John 8.17; 2 Cor 13.1; 1 Tim 5.19; Heb 10.28.

See also: **19.21:** Exod 21.23–25; Lev 24.19,20; Matt 5.38.

10-15 Before you attack a town that is far from your land, offer peace to the people who live there. If they surrender and open their town gates, they will become your slaves. But if they reject your offer of peace and try to fight, surround their town and attack. Then, after the LORD helps you capture it, kill all the men. Take the women and children as slaves and keep the livestock and everything else of value.

16 Whenever you capture towns in the land the LORD your God is giving you, be sure to kill all the people and animals. 17 He has commanded you to completely wipe out the Hittites, the Amorites, the Canaanites, the Perizzites, the Hivites, and the Jebusites. 18 If you allow them to live, they will persuade you to worship their disgusting gods, and you will be unfaithful to the LORD.

19 When you are attacking a town, don't chop down its fruit trees, not even if you have had the town surrounded for a long time. Fruit trees aren't your enemies, and they produce food that you can eat, so don't cut them down. 20 You may need wood to make ladders and towers to help you get over the walls and capture the town. But use only trees that you know are not fruit trees.

CHAPTER 21

Unsolved murder

Moses said to Israel:

1 Suppose the body of a murder victim is found in a field in the land the LORD your God is giving you, and no one knows who the murderer is. 2 The judges and other leaders from the towns around there must find out what town is the closest to where the body was found. 3 The leaders from that town will go to their cattle herds and choose a young cow that has never been put to work.* 4-5 They and some of the priests will take this cow to a nearby valley where there is a stream, but no crops. Once they reach the valley, the leaders will break the cow's neck.

The priests must be there, because the LORD your God has chosen them to be his special servants at the place of worship. The LORD has chosen them to bless the people in his name and to be judges in all legal cases, whether property or injury is involved.

6 The town leaders will wash their hands over the body of the dead cow 7 and say, "We had no part in this murder, and we don't know who did it. 8-9 But since an innocent person may be a beautiful woman, you, our LORD, to accept this sacrifice and forgive Israel. We beg you, our LORD, to accept this sacrifice and forgive Israel. We beg you, our people, and you rescued us. Please don't hold this crime against us."

If you obey the LORD and do these things, he will forgive Israel.

Marrying a woman taken prisoner in war

Moses said to Israel:

10 From time to time, you men will serve as soldiers and go off to war. The LORD your God will help you defeat your enemies, and you will take many prisoners. 11-13 One of these prisoners may be a beautiful woman, and you may want to marry her. But first you must bring her into your home, and she must shave her head, cut her nails, get rid of her foreign clothes, and start wearing Israelite clothes. She will mourn a month for her father and mother, then you can marry her.

14 Later on, if you are not happy with the woman, you can divorce her, and she can go free. But you have slept with her as your wife, so you cannot sell her as a slave or make her into your own slave.

Rights of a firstborn son

Moses said to Israel:

15-17 Suppose a man has two wives and loves one more than the other. The first son of either wife is the man's firstborn son, even if the boy's mother is the wife the man doesn't love. Later, when the man is near death and is dividing up his property, he must give a double share to his firstborn son, simply because he was the first to be born.

A son who rebels

Moses said to Israel:

18 A father and a mother may have a stubborn and rebellious son who refuses to obey them even after he has been punished. 19 If a son is like that, his parents must drag him to the town gate, where the leaders of the town hold their meetings.

21.3 young cow . . . work: Cows and oxen pulled ploughs and wagons.

20 The parents will tell the leaders, "This son of ours is stubborn and never obeys. He spends all his time drinking and feasting."

21 The men of the town will stone that son to death, because they must get rid of the evil he brought into the community. Everyone in Israel will be afraid when they hear how he was punished.

The body of a criminal

Moses said to Israel:

22 If a criminal is put to death, and you hang the dead body on a tree, 23 you must not let it hang there overnight. Bury it the same day, because the dead body of a criminal will bring God's curse on the land. The LORD your God is giving this land to you, so don't make it unclean by leaving the bodies of executed criminals on display.

CHAPTER 22

Helping others

Moses said to Israel:

1 If you see a cow or sheep wandering around lost, take the animal back to its owner. 2 If the owner lives too far away, or if you don't know who the owner is, take the animal home with you and take care of it. The owner will come looking for the animal, and then you can give it back. 3 That's what you should do if you find anything that belongs to someone else. Do whatever you can to help, whether you find a cow or sheep or donkey or some clothing. 4 Oxen and donkeys that carry heavy loads can stumble and fall, and be unable to get up by themselves. So as you walk along the road, help anyone who is trying to get an ox or donkey back on its feet.

Don't pretend to be the opposite sex

Moses said to Israel:

5 Women must not pretend to be men, and men must not pretend to be women.◆ The LORD your God is disgusted with people who do that.

Don't take a mother bird

Moses said to Israel:

6-7 As you walk along the road, you might see a bird's nest in a tree or on the ground. If the mother bird is in the nest with either her eggs or her baby birds, you are allowed to take the baby birds or the eggs, but not the mother bird. Let her go free, and the LORD will bless you with a long and successful life.

Put a wall around your flat roof

Moses said to Israel:

8 If you build a house, make sure to put a low wall around the edge of the flat roof.◆ Then if someone falls off the roof and is killed, it won't be your fault.

Laws against mixing different things

Moses said to Israel:

9 If you plant a vineyard, don't plant any other fruit tree or crop in it. If you do plant something else there, you must bring to the place of worship everything you harvest from the vineyard.

10 Don't hitch an ox and a donkey to your plough at the same time.

11 When you weave cloth for clothing, you can use thread made of flax◆ or wool, but not both together. 12 And when you make a coat, sew a tassel on each of the four corners.

When a husband accuses his wife

Moses said to Israel:

13 Suppose a man starts hating his wife soon after they are married. 14 He might tell ugly lies about her, and say, "I married this woman, but when we slept together, I found out she wasn't a virgin."

15 If this happens, the bride's father and mother must go to the town gate to show the town leaders the proof that the woman was a virgin. 16 Her father will say, "I let my daughter marry this man, but he started hating her 17 and accusing her of not being a virgin. But he is wrong, because here is proof that she was a virgin!" Then the bride's parents will show them the bed sheet from the woman's wedding night.

---

*22.8 **flat roof:** Houses usually had flat roofs. In hot dry weather, it was cooler on the roof than in the house, and so roofs were used for sleeping and living quarters, and for entertaining guests.*

*22.11 **flax:** The stalks of flax plants were harvested, soaked in water, and dried, then their fibres were separated and spun into thread, which was woven into linen cloth.*

See also: 21.23: Gal 3.13. 22.1–4: Exod 23.4,5.

See also: 22.9–11: Lev 19.19. 22.12: Num 15.37–41.

¹⁸ The town leaders will beat the man with a whip ¹⁹ because he accused his bride of not being a virgin. He will have to pay her father one hundred pieces of silver and will never be allowed to divorce her.

²⁰ But if the man was right and there is no proof that his bride was a virgin, ²¹ the men of the town will take the woman to the door of her father's house and stone her to death.

This woman brought evil into your community by sleeping with someone before she got married, and you must get rid of that evil by killing her.

Laws about illegal sex

Moses said:

²² People of Israel, if a man is caught having sex with someone else's wife, you must put them both to death. That way, you will get rid of the evil they have done in Israel.

²³⁻²⁴ If a man is caught in town having sex with an engaged woman who isn't screaming for help, they both must be put to death. The man is guilty of having sex with a married woman.* And the woman is guilty because she didn't call for help, even though she was inside a town and people were nearby. Take them both to the town gate and stone them to death. You must get rid of the evil they brought into your community.

²⁵ If an engaged woman is raped out in the country, only the man will be put to death. ²⁶ Do not punish the woman at all; she has done nothing wrong, and certainly nothing deserving death. This crime is like murder, ²⁷ because the woman was alone out in the country when the man attacked her. She screamed, but there was no one to help her.

²⁸ Suppose a woman isn't engaged to be married, and a man talks her into sleeping with him. If they are caught, ²⁹ they will be forced to get married. He must give her father fifty pieces of silver as a bride price and* can never divorce her.

³⁰ A man must not marry a woman who was married to his father. This would be a disgrace to his father.

CHAPTER 23

Who cannot become one of the Lord's people

Moses said to Israel:

¹ If a man's private parts have been crushed or cut off,* he cannot fully belong to the Lord's people.

² No one born outside a legal marriage, or any of their descendants for ten generations, can fully belong to the Lord's people.

³ No Ammonites or Moabites, or any of their descendants for ten generations, can become part of Israel, the Lord's people. ⁴ This is because when you came out of Egypt, they refused to provide you with food and water. And besides, they hired Balaam* to put a curse on you. ⁵ But the Lord your God loves you, so he refused to listen to Balaam and turned Balaam's curse into a blessing. ⁶ Don't even think of signing a peace treaty with Moab or Ammon.

⁷ But Edomites are your relatives, and you lived as foreigners in the country of Egypt. Now you must be kind to Edomites and Egyptians ⁸ and let their great-grandchildren become part of Israel, the Lord's people.

Keep the army camp acceptable

Moses said to Israel:

⁹ When you men go off to fight your enemies, make sure your camp is acceptable to the Lord.

¹⁰ For example, if something happens at night that makes a man unclean and unfit for worship, he* must go outside the camp and stay there ¹¹ until late afternoon. Then he must take a bath, and at sunset he can go back into camp.

¹² Set up a place outside the camp to be used as a toilet area. ¹³ And make sure that you have a small shovel in your equipment. When you go out to the toilet area, use the shovel to dig a hole. Then, after you relieve yourself, bury the waste in the hole. ¹⁴ You must keep your camp clean of filthy and disgusting things. The Lord is always

---

*22.23,24 engaged woman . . . married woman: An engaged woman was legally married, but had not yet slept with her husband or started living with him.
See also: 22.28,29: Exod 22.16,17. **22.30:** Lev 18.8; 20.11; Deut 27.20.

*23.1 a man's private parts have been crushed or cut off: This was sometimes done to show devotion to pagan gods.
See also: 23.3–5: Neh 13.1,2. **23.4:** Num 22.1–6. **23.5:** Num 23.7—24.9.

present in your camp, ready to rescue you and give you victory over your enemies. But if he sees something disgusting in your camp, he may turn around and leave.

Runaway slaves from other countries

Moses said:

¹⁵ When runaway slaves from other countries come to Israel and ask for protection, you must not hand them back to their owners. ¹⁶ Instead, you must let them choose which one of your towns they want to live in. Don't be cruel to runaway slaves.

Temple prostitutes

Moses said:

¹⁷ People of Israel, don't any of you ever be temple prostitutes.* ¹⁸ The LORD your God is disgusted with men and women who are prostitutes of any kind, and he will not accept a gift from them, even if it had been promised to him.

Interest on loans

Moses said:

¹⁹ When you lend money, food, or anything else to another Israelite, you are not allowed to charge interest. ²⁰ You can charge a foreigner interest. But if you charge other Israelites interest, the LORD your God will not let you be successful in the land you are about to take.

Sacred promises to the LORD

Moses said:

²¹ People of Israel, if you make a sacred promise to give a gift to the LORD, then do it as soon as you can. If the LORD has to come looking for the gift you promised, you will be guilty of breaking that promise. ²² On the other hand, if you never make a sacred promise, you can't be guilty of breaking it. ²³ You must keep whatever promises you make to the LORD. After all, you are the one who chose to make the promises.

Eating someone else's produce

Moses said:

²⁴ If you go into a vineyard that belongs to someone else, you are allowed to eat as many grapes as you want while you are there. But don't take any with you when you leave. ²⁵ In the same way, if you are in a grain field that belongs to someone else, you can pick heads of grain and eat the kernels. But don't cut down the stalks of grain and take them with you.

CHAPTER 24

A law about divorce

Moses said to Israel:

¹ Suppose a woman was divorced by her first husband because he found something disgraceful about her.ᵇ He wrote out divorce papers, gave them to her, and sent her away. ² Later she married another man, ³ who then either divorced her in the same way or died. ⁴ Since she has slept with her second husband, she cannot marry her first husband again. Their marriage would pollute the land that the LORD your God is giving you, and he would be disgusted.

Newlyweds

Moses said to Israel:

⁵ If a man and a woman have been married less than one year, he must not be sent off to war or sent away to do forced labour. He must be allowed to stay home for a year and be happy with his wife.

Loans

Moses said to Israel:

⁶ When you lend money to people, you are allowed to keep something of theirs as a guarantee that they will pay back the loan. But don't take one or both of their millstones, or else they may starve. They need these stones for grinding grain into flour to make bread.

Kidnapping

Moses said to Israel:

⁷ If you are guilty of kidnapping Israelites and forcing them into slavery, you will be

---

*23.17 temple prostitutes: Some Canaanites worshipped by going to their temples and having sex with prostitutes who represented their gods.
See also: 23.17: Lev 19.29. **23.19,20:** Exod 22.25; Lev 25.36,37; Deut 15.7–11. **23.21:** Num 30.1–16; Matt 5.33.

See also: 24.1: Matt 5.31; 19.7; Mark 10.4. **24.7:** Exod 21.16.

put to death to remove this evil from the community.

Skin diseases

Moses said to Israel:

⁸ I have told the priests* what to do if any of you have leprosy,* so do exactly what they say. ⁹ And remember what the Lord your God did to Miriam* after you left Egypt.

Loans

Moses said to Israel:

¹⁰ When you lend money to people, you are allowed to keep something of theirs as a guarantee that the money will be paid back. But you must not go into their house to get it. ¹¹ Wait outside, and they will bring out the item you have agreed on.

¹² Suppose someone is so poor that a coat is the only thing that can be offered as a guarantee on a loan. Don't keep the coat overnight. ¹³ Instead, give it back before sunset, so the owner can keep warm and sleep and ask the Lord to bless you. Then the Lord your God will notice that you have done the right thing.

Poor people's wages

Moses said:

¹⁴ If you hire poor people to work for you, don't hold back their pay,* whether they are Israelites or foreigners who live in your town. ¹⁵ Pay them their wages at the end of each day, because they live in poverty and need the money to survive. If you don't pay them on time, they will complain about you to the Lord, and he will punish you.

The death penalty

Moses said to Israel:

¹⁶ Parents must not be put to death for crimes committed by their children, and children must not be put to death for crimes committed by their parents. Don't put anyone to death for someone else's crime.

Don't ill-treat the powerless

Moses said to Israel:

¹⁷ Make sure that orphans and foreigners are treated fairly. And if you lend money to a widow and want to keep something of hers to guarantee that she will pay you back, don't take any of her clothes. ¹⁸ You were slaves in Egypt until the Lord your God rescued you. That's why I am giving you these laws.

Leave some of your harvest for the poor

Moses said to Israel:

¹⁹ If you forget to bring in a stack of harvested grain, don't go back in the field to get it. Leave it for the poor, including foreigners, orphans, and widows, and the Lord will make you successful in everything you do.

²⁰ When you harvest your olives, don't try to get them all for yourself, but leave some for the poor. ²¹ And when you pick your grapes, go over the vines only once, then let the poor have what is left. ²² You lived in poverty as slaves in Egypt until the Lord your God rescued you. That's why I am giving you these laws.

CHAPTER 25

Whipping as punishment for a crime

Moses said to Israel:

¹⁻² Suppose you and someone else each accuse the other of doing something wrong, and you go to court, where the judges decide you are guilty. If your punishment is to be beaten with a whip,* one of the judges will order you to lie down, and you will receive the number of lashes you deserve. ³ Forty lashes is the most that you can be given, because more than that might make other Israelites think you are worthless.

Don't muzzle an ox

Moses said to Israel:

⁴ Don't muzzle an ox while it is threshing grain.*

---

*24.8 the priests: See the note at 17.8–12.
*24.8 leprosy: The word "leprosy" was used for many different kinds of skin diseases.
*24.9 what the Lord your God did to Miriam: See Numbers 12.1–16.

See also: 24.8: Lev 13.1—14.54. 24.9: Num 12.10. 24.10–13: Exod 22.26,27. 24.14,15: Lev 19.13. 24.16: 2 King 14.6; 2 Chron 25.4; Ezek 18.20.

*25.4 threshing grain: Oxen were used at the threshing place to walk on heads of grain, or pull heavy slabs of wood over it, to separate the kernels from the husks.

See also: 24.17,18: Exod 23.9; Lev 19.33,34; Deut 27.19. 24.19–21: Lev 19.9,10; 23.22. 25.3: 2 Cor 11.24. 25.4: 1 Cor 9.9; 1 Tim 5.18.

A son for a dead brother

Moses said to Israel:

5-6 Suppose two brothers are living on the same property, when one of them dies without having a son to carry on his name. If this happens, his widow must not marry anyone outside the family. Instead, she must marry her late husband's brother, and their first son will be the legal son of the dead man.

7 But suppose the brother refuses to marry the widow. She must go to a meeting of the town leaders at the town gate and say, "My husband died without having a son to carry on his name. And my husband's brother refuses to marry me so I can have a son."

8 The leaders will call the living brother to the town gate and try to persuade him to marry the widow. But if he doesn't change his mind and marry her, 9 she must go over to him while the town leaders watch. She will pull off one of his sandals and spit in his face, while saying, "That's what happens to a man who won't help provide descendants for his dead brother." 10 From then on, that man's family will be known as "the family of the man whose sandal was pulled off".

When two men fight

Moses said to Israel:

11 If two men are fighting, and the wife of one man tries to rescue her husband by grabbing the other man's private parts, 12 you must cut off her hand. Don't have any mercy.

Be honest in business

Moses said to Israel:

13-14 Don't try to cheat people by having two sets of weights or measures, one to get more when you are buying, and the other to give less when you are selling. 15 If you weigh and measure things honestly, the LORD your God will let you enjoy a long life in the land he is giving you. 16 But the LORD is disgusted with anyone who cheats or is dishonest.

Wipe out Amalek

Moses said:

17 People of Israel, do you remember what the Amalekites did to you after you came out of Egypt? 18 You were tired, and they followed along behind, attacking those who could not keep up with the others. This showed that the Amalekites have no respect for God.

19 The LORD your God will help you capture the land, and he will give you peace. But when that day comes, you must wipe out Amalek so completely that no one will remember they ever lived.

CHAPTER 26

Give the LORD the first part of your harvest

Moses said to Israel:

1 The LORD is giving you the land, and soon you will conquer it, settle down, 2 and plant crops. And when you begin harvesting each of your crops, the very first things you pick must be put in a basket. Take them to the place where the LORD your God chooses to be worshipped, 3 and tell the priest, "Long ago the LORD our God promised our ancestors that he would give us this land. And today, I thank him for keeping his promise and giving me a share of the land."

4 The priest will take the basket and set it in front of the LORD's altar. 5 Then, standing there in front of the place of worship, you must pray:

My ancestor was homeless,
an Aramean who went to live in Egypt.
There were only a few
in his family then,
but they became great and powerful,
a nation of many people.

6 The Egyptians were cruel
and had no pity on us.
They ill-treated our people
and forced us into slavery.
7 We called out for help
to you, the LORD God of our ancestors.
You heard our cries;
you knew we were in trouble
and abused.

See also: 25.5,6: Matt 22.24; Mark 12.19; Luke 20.28.
25.7-10: Ruth 4.7,8. 25.13-16: Lev 19.35,36.

See also: 25.17-19: Exod 17.8-14; 1 Sam 15.2-9.
26.2: Exod 23.19.

8 Then you terrified the Egyptians
with your mighty miracles
and rescued us from Egypt.
9 You brought us here
and gave us this land
rich with milk and honey.
10 Now, LORD, I bring to you
the best of the crops
that you have given me.

After you say these things, place the basket in front of the LORD's altar and bow down to worship him.
11 Then you and your family must celebrate by eating a meal at the place of worship to thank the LORD your God for giving you such a good harvest. And remember to invite the Levites and the foreigners who live in your town.

Ten per cent of the harvest

Moses said to Israel:

12 Every year you are to give ten per cent of your harvest to the LORD.* But every third year,* this ten per cent must be given to the poor who live in your town, including Levites, foreigners, orphans, and widows. That way, they will have enough to eat.
13 Then you must pray:

Our LORD and our God, you have said that ten per cent of my harvest is sacred. I have obeyed your command and given this to the poor, including the Levites, foreigners, orphans, and widows.
14 I have not eaten any of this sacred food while I was in mourning; in fact, I never touched it when I was unclean.* And none of it has been offered as a sacrifice to the spirits of the dead. I have done everything exactly as you commanded.
15 Our LORD, look down from your temple in heaven and bless your people Israel. You promised our ancestors that you would give us this land rich with milk and honey, and you have kept your promise.

The LORD is your God, and you are his people

Moses said to Israel:

16 Today the LORD your God has commanded you to obey these laws and teachings with all your heart and soul.
17 In response, you have agreed that the LORD will be your God, that you will obey all his laws and teachings, and that you will listen when he speaks to you.
18 Since you have agreed to obey the LORD, he has agreed that you will be his people and that you will belong to him, just as he promised. 19 The LORD created all nations, but he will make you more famous than any of them, and you will receive more praise and honour. You will belong only to the LORD your God, just as he promised.

CHAPTER 27

Build an altar on Mount Ebal

1 Moses stood together with the leaders and told the people of Israel:

Obey all the laws and teachings that I am giving you today. 2-4 Soon you will enter the land that the LORD your God is giving to you. He is the God that your ancestors worshipped, and he has promised that this land is rich with milk and honey.
After you cross the River Jordan, go to Mount Ebal. Set up large slabs of stone, then cover them with white plaster and write on them a copy of these laws.
5 At this same place, build an altar for offering sacrifices to the LORD your God. But don't use stones that have been cut with iron tools. 6 Look for stones that can be used without being cut. Then offer sacrifices to please the LORD,* burning them completely on the altar. 7 Next, offer sacrifices to ask the LORD's blessing,* and serve the meat at a sacred meal where you will celebrate in honour of the LORD.

---

*26.12 Every year . . . LORD: See 14.22–29.
*26.12 every third year: Probably the third and sixth years of the seven-year cycle described in 15.1–11 and Leviticus 25.1–7.
*26.14 in mourning . . . unclean: Touching a dead body made a person unclean and unfit to worship God. Ten per cent of the harvest belonged to God, and was not to be touched by an unclean person.
See also: 26.12: Deut 14.28,29.

*27.6 sacrifices to please the LORD: See the note at 12.5–19.
*27.7 sacrifices to ask the LORD's blessing: These sacrifices have traditionally been called "peace offerings" or "offerings of well-being". A main purpose was to ask for the LORD's blessing, and so in the CEV they are sometimes called "sacrifices to ask the LORD's blessing".
See also: 26.18: Exod 19.5; Deut 4.20; 7.6; 14.2; Titus 2.14; 1 Pet 2.9. 27.2–8: Josh 8.30–32. 27.5,6: Exod 20.25.

⁸ Don't forget to write out a copy of these laws on the stone slabs that you are going to set up. Make sure that the writing is easy to read.

Curses on those who disobey

⁹ Moses stood together with the priests* and said, "Israel, be quiet and listen to me! Today you have become the people of the LORD your God.* ¹⁰ So you must obey his laws and teachings that I am giving you."

¹¹ That same day, Moses gave them the following instructions:

¹²⁻¹³ After you cross the River Jordan, you will go to Mount Gerizim and Mount Ebal.* The tribes of Simeon, Levi, Judah, Issachar, Ephraim, Manasseh,* and Benjamin will go up on Mount Gerizim, where they will bless the people of Israel. The tribes of Reuben, Gad, Asher, Zebulun, Dan, and Naphtali will go up on Mount Ebal where they will agree to the curses.

¹⁴⁻²⁶ The people of the Levi tribe will speak each curse in a loud voice, then the rest of the people* will agree to that curse by saying, "Amen!" Here are the curses:

We ask the LORD to put a curse on anyone who makes an idol or worships idols, even secretly. The LORD is disgusted with idols.

We ask the LORD to put a curse on all who do not show respect for their father and mother.

We ask the LORD to put a curse on anyone who moves the rocks that mark boundaries.

We ask the LORD to put a curse on anyone who tells blind people to go the wrong way.

We ask the LORD to put a curse on anyone who keeps the poor from getting justice, whether these poor are foreigners, widows, or orphans.

We ask the LORD to put a curse on any man who sleeps with his father's wife; that man has shown no respect for his father's marriage.

We ask the LORD to put a curse on anyone who has sex with an animal.

We ask the LORD to put a curse on any man who sleeps with his sister or his half-sister or his mother-in-law.

We ask the LORD to put a curse on anyone who commits murder, even when there are no witnesses to the crime.

We ask the LORD to put a curse on anyone who accepts money to murder an innocent victim.

We ask the LORD to put a curse on anyone who refuses to obey his laws.

And so, to each of these curses, the people will answer, "Amen!"

CHAPTER 28

The LORD will bless you if you obey

Moses said to Israel:

¹⁻² Today I am giving you the laws and teachings of the LORD your God. Always obey them, and the LORD will make Israel the most famous and important nation on earth, and he will bless you in many ways.

³ The LORD will make your businesses and your farms successful.

⁴ You will have many children. You will harvest large crops, and your herds of cattle and flocks of sheep and goats will produce many young.

⁵ You will have plenty of bread* to eat.

⁶ The LORD will make you successful in your daily work.

⁷ The LORD will help you defeat your enemies and make them scatter in all directions.

⁸ The LORD your God is giving you the land, and he will make sure you are successful in everything you do. Your harvests will be so large that your storehouses will be full.

⁹ If you follow and obey the LORD, he will make you his own special people, just as he promised. ¹⁰ Then everyone on earth will know that you belong to the LORD, and they will be afraid of you.

¹¹ The LORD will give you a lot of children and make sure that your animals give birth to many young. The LORD promised your

---

*27.9 priests: See the note at 17.8–12.
*27.9 Today you have become the people of the LORD your God: As a result of the agreement that the LORD had made with them, recorded in 26.16–19.
*27.12,13 Mount Gerizim and Mount Ebal: These mountains were separated by a valley.
*27.12,13 Ephraim, Manasseh: The Hebrew text has "Joseph"; the descendants of Joseph formed the two tribes of Ephraim and Manasseh.

See also: 27.12: Deut 11.29; Josh 8.33–35.
27.15: Exod 20.4; 34.17; Lev 19.4; 26.1; Deut 4.15–18; 5.8.
27.16: Exod 20.12; Deut 5.16. 27.17: Deut 19.14.
27.18: Lev 19.14. 27.19: Exod 22.21; 23.9; Lev 19.33,34;
Deut 24.17,18. 27.20: Lev 18.8; 20.11; Deut 22.30.
27.21: Exod 22.19; Lev 18.23; 20.15. 27.22: Lev 18.9; 20.17.
27.23: Lev 18.17; 20.14. 27.26: Gal 3.10.

*28.5 bread: The main food of the Israelites.
See also: 28.1–14: Deut 11.13–17.

ancestors that this land would be yours, and he will make it produce large crops for you.

¹² The LORD will open the storehouses of the skies where he keeps the rain, and he will send rain on your land at just the right times. He will make you successful in everything you do. You will have plenty of money to lend to other nations, but you won't need to borrow any yourself.

¹³ Obey the laws and teachings that I'm giving you today, and the LORD your God will make Israel a leader among the nations, and not a follower. Israel will be wealthy and powerful, not poor and weak. ¹⁴ But you must not reject any of his laws and teachings or worship other gods.

The LORD will put curses on you if you disobey

This is also told in Leviticus 26.14–46

Moses said:

¹⁵ Israel, today I am giving you the laws and teachings of the LORD your God. And if you don't obey them all, he will put many curses on you.

¹⁶ Your businesses and farms will fail.

¹⁷ You won't have enough bread* to eat.

¹⁸ You'll have only a few children, your crops will be small, and your herds of cattle and flocks of sheep and goats won't produce many young.

¹⁹ The LORD will make you fail in everything you do.

²⁰ No matter what you try to accomplish, the LORD will confuse you, and you will feel his anger. You won't last long, and you may even meet with disaster, all because you rejected the LORD.

²¹⁻²³ The LORD will send terrible diseases to attack you, and you will never be well again. You will suffer with burning fever and swelling and pain until you die somewhere in the land that you captured.

The LORD will make the sky overhead seem like a bronze roof that keeps out the rain, and the ground under your feet will become as hard as iron. Your crops will be scorched by the hot east wind or ruined by mildew. ²⁴ He will send dust and sandstorms instead of rain, and you will be wiped out.

²⁵ The LORD will let you be defeated by your enemies, and you will scatter in all directions. You will be a horrible sight for the other nations to see, ²⁶ and no one will disturb the birds and wild animals while they eat your dead bodies.

²⁷ The LORD will make you suffer with diseases that will cause oozing sores or crusty itchy patches on your skin or boils like the ones that are common in Egypt. And there will be no cure for you! ²⁸ You will become insane and go blind. The LORD will make you so confused, ²⁹ that even in bright sunshine you will have to feel your way around like a blind person, who cannot tell day from night. For the rest of your life, people will beat and rob you, and no one will be able to stop them.

³⁰ A man will be engaged to a woman, but before they can get married, she will be raped by enemy soldiers. Some of you will build houses, but never get to live in them. If you plant a vineyard, you won't be around long enough to enjoy the first harvest. ³¹ Your cattle will be killed while you watch, but you won't get to eat any of the meat. Your donkeys and sheep will be stolen from you, and no one will be around to force your enemies to give them back. ³² Your sons and daughters will be dragged off to a foreign country, while you stand there helpless. And even if you watch for them until you go blind, you will never see them again.

³³ You will work hard on your farms, but everything you harvest will be eaten by foreigners, who will ill-treat you and abuse you for the rest of your life.

³⁴ What you see will be so horrible that you will go insane, ³⁵ and the LORD will punish you from head to toe with boils that never heal.

³⁶ The LORD will let you and your king be taken captive to a country that you and your ancestors have never even heard of, and there you will have to worship idols* made of wood and stone. ³⁷ People of nearby countries will shudder when they see your terrible troubles, but they will still make fun of you.

³⁸ You will plant a lot of seed, but gather a small harvest, because locusts* will eat your crops. ³⁹ You will plant vineyards and work hard at taking care of them, but you

---

*28.17 bread: See the note at 28.5.

*28.36 have to worship idols: It was sometimes thought that only the gods of a country could be worshipped within the borders of that country.
*28.38 locusts: A type of grasshopper that comes in swarms and causes great damage to plant life.

won't gather any grapes, much less get any wine, and the vines themselves will be eaten by worms. 40 Even if your olive trees grow everywhere in your country, the olives will fall off before they are ready, and there won't be enough olive oil for combing your hair.*

41 Even your infant sons and daughters will be taken as prisoners of war.

42 Locusts* will eat your crops and strip your trees of leaves and fruit.

43 Foreigners in your towns will become wealthy and powerful, while you become poor and powerless. 44 You will be so short of money that you will have to borrow from those foreigners. They will be the leaders in the community, and you will be the followers.

More curses for disobedience

Moses said:

45 Israel, if you don't obey the laws and teachings that the LORD your God is giving you, he will send these curses to chase, attack, and destroy you. 46 Then everyone will look at you and your descendants and realize that the LORD has placed you under a curse.

47 If the LORD makes you wealthy, but you don't joyfully worship and honour him, 48 he will send enemies to attack you and make you their slaves. Then you will live in poverty with nothing to eat, drink, or wear, and your owners will work you to death.

49 Foreigners who speak a strange language will be sent to attack you without warning, just like an eagle swooping down. 50 They won't show any mercy, and they will have no respect for old people or pity for children. 51 They will take your cattle, sheep, goats, grain, wine, and olive oil, then leave you to starve.

52 All over the land that the LORD your God gave you, the enemy army will surround your towns. You may feel safe inside your town walls, but the enemy will tear them down, 53 while you wait in horror. Finally, you will get so hungry that you will eat the sons and daughters that the LORD gave you. 54-55 Because of hunger, a man who had been gentle and kind will eat his own children and refuse to share the meal with his brother or wife or with his

other children. 56-57 A woman may have grown up in such luxury that she never had to put a foot on the ground. But times will be so bad that she will secretly eat both her newborn baby and the afterbirth, without sharing any with her husband or her other children.

Disobedience brings destruction

Moses said to Israel:

58 You must obey everything in *The Book of God's Law*. Because if you don't respect the LORD, 59 he will punish you and your descendants with incurable diseases, 60 like those you were so afraid of in Egypt.

61 Remember! If the LORD decides to destroy your nation, he can use any disease or disaster, not just the ones written in *The Book of God's Law*.

62 There are as many of you now as the stars in the sky, but if you disobey the LORD your God, only a few of you will be left. 63 The LORD is happy to make you successful and to help your nation grow while you conquer the land. But if you disobey him, he will be just as happy to pull you up by your roots.

64 Those of you who survive will be scattered to every nation on earth, and you will have to worship stone and wood idols* that never helped you or your ancestors. 65 You will be restless — always longing for home, but never able to return. 66 You will live in constant fear of death. 67 Each morning you will wake up to such terrible sights that you will say, "I wish it were night!" But at night you will be terrified and say, "I wish it were day!"

68 I told you never to go back to Egypt. But now the LORD himself will load you on ships and send you back. Then you will even try to sell yourselves as slaves, but no one will be interested.

CHAPTER 29

The agreement in Moab

1 So Moses finished telling the Israelites what they had to do in order to keep the agreement the LORD was making with them in Moab, which was in addition to the one the LORD had made with them at Mount Sinai.*

---

*28.40 olive oil . . . hair: Olive oil was used for combing the hair.
*28.42 Locusts: See the note at 28.38.

*28.64 have to worship . . . idols: See the note at 28.36.
See also: 28.57: 2 King 6.28,29; Lam 4.10.

THE THIRD SPEECH: ISRAEL MUST KEEP ITS AGREEMENT WITH THE LORD

The LORD is your God

²⁻³ Moses called the nation of Israel together and told them:

> When you were in Egypt, you saw the LORD perform great miracles that caused trouble for the king, his officials, and everyone else in the country. ⁴⁻⁶ He has even told you, "For forty years I, the LORD, led you through the desert, but your clothes and your sandals didn't wear out, and I gave you special food.' I did these things so you would realize that I am your God."
>
> But the LORD must give you a change of heart before you truly understand what you have seen and heard.
>
> ⁷ When we first camped here, King Sihon of Heshbon and King Og of Bashan attacked, but we defeated them. ⁸ Then we captured their land and divided it among the tribes of Reuben, Gad, and East Manasseh.

Keep the agreement

Moses said:

> ⁹ Israel, the LORD has made an agreement with you, and if you keep your part, you will be successful in everything you do.
>
> ¹⁰⁻¹² Today everyone in our nation is standing here in the LORD's presence, including leaders and officials, parents and children, and even those foreigners who cut wood and carry water for us. We are at this place of worship to promise that we will keep our part of the agreement with the LORD our God.
>
> ¹³⁻¹⁵ In this agreement, the LORD promised that you would be his people and that he would be your God. He first made this promise to your ancestors Abraham, Isaac, and Jacob, and today the LORD is making this same promise to you. But it isn't just for you; it is also for your descendants.
>
> ¹⁶⁻¹⁷ When we lived in Egypt, you saw the Egyptians worship disgusting idols of wood, stone, silver, and gold. Then as we travelled through other nations, you saw those people worship other disgusting idols. ¹⁸ So make sure that everyone in your tribe remains faithful to the LORD and never starts worshipping gods of other nations.

If even one of you worships idols, you will be like the root of a plant that produces bitter, poisonous fruit. ¹⁹ You may be an Israelite and know all about the LORD's agreement with us, but you won't bless you if you rebel against him. You may think you can get away with it, but you will cause the rest of Israel to be punished along with you.' ²⁰⁻²¹ The LORD will be furious, and instead of forgiving you, he will separate you from the other tribes. Then he will destroy you, by piling on you all the curses in *The Book of God's Law,* and you will be forgotten for ever.

²² The LORD will strike your country with diseases and disasters. Your descendants and foreigners from distant countries will see that your land ²³ has become a scorching desert of salt and sulphur, where nothing is planted, nothing sprouts, and nothing grows. It will be as lifeless as the land around the cities of Sodom, Gomorrah, Admah, and Zeboiim, after the LORD became angry and destroyed them.*

²⁴ People from other nations will ask, "Why did the LORD destroy this country? Why was he so furious?"

²⁵ And they will be given this answer:

> Our ancestors worshipped the LORD, but after he brought them out of Egypt and made an agreement with them, they rejected the agreement ²⁶ and decided to worship gods that had never helped them. The LORD had forbidden Israel to worship these gods, ²⁷⁻²⁸ and so he became furious and punished the land with all the curses in *The Book of God's Law.* Then he pulled up Israel by the roots and tossed them into a foreign country, where they still are today.

²⁹ The LORD our God hasn't explained the present or the future, but he has commanded us to obey the laws he gave to us and our descendants.

CHAPTER 30

The LORD will bring you back

Moses said to Israel:

> ¹ I have told you everything the LORD your God will do for you, and I've also told you the curses he will put on you if you reject

---

29.23 Sodom . . . destroyed them: See Genesis 18.16–28.
See also: 29.23: Gen 19.24,25.

See also: **29.7:** a Num 21.21–30; b Num 21.31–35. **29.8:** Num 32.33. **29.18:** Heb 12.15.

185

him. He will scatter you in faraway countries, but when you realize that he is punishing you, ² return to him with all your heart and soul and start obeying the commands I have given to you today. ³⁻⁴ Then he will stop punishing you and treat you with kindness. He may have scattered you to the furthest countries on earth, but he will bring you back ⁵ to the land that had belonged to your ancestors and make you even more successful and powerful than they ever were.

⁶ You and your descendants are stubborn, but the LORD will make you willing to obey him and love him with all your heart and soul, and you will enjoy a long life.

⁷ The LORD your God will remove the curses from you and put them on those enemies who hate and attack you.

⁸ You will again obey the laws and teachings of the LORD, ⁹ and he will bless you with many children, large herds and flocks, and abundant crops. The LORD will be happy to do good things for you, just as he did for your ancestors. ¹⁰ But you must decide once and for all to worship him with all your heart and soul and to obey everything in *The Book of God's Law.*

Choose life, not death

Moses said to Israel:

¹¹ You know God's laws, and it isn't impossible to obey them. ¹² His commands aren't in heaven, so you can't excuse yourselves by saying, "How can we obey the LORD's commands? They are in heaven, and no one can go up to get them, then bring them down and explain them to us." ¹³ And you can't say, "How can we obey the LORD's commands? They are across the sea, and someone must go across, then bring them back and explain them to us." ¹⁴ No, these commands are nearby and you know them by heart. All you have to do is obey!

¹⁵ Today I am giving you a choice. You can choose life and success or death and disaster. ¹⁶⁻¹⁸ I am commanding you to be loyal to the LORD, to live the way he has told you, and to obey his laws and teachings. You are about to cross the River Jordan and take the land that he is giving you. If you obey him, you will live and become successful and powerful.

On the other hand, you might choose to disobey the LORD and reject him. So I'm

warning you that if you bow down and worship other gods, you won't have long to live.

¹⁹ Now I call the sky and the earth to be witnesses that I am offering you this choice. Will you choose for the LORD to make you prosperous and give you a long life? Or will he put you under a curse and kill you? Choose life! ²⁰ Be completely faithful to the LORD your God, love him, and do whatever he tells you. The LORD is the only one who can give life, and he will let you live a long time in the land that he promised to your ancestors Abraham, Isaac, and Jacob.

CHAPTER 31

FINAL SPEECHES AND THE DEATH OF MOSES

Joshua is appointed the leader of Israel

¹ Moses again spoke to the whole nation of Israel:

² I am a hundred and twenty years old, and I am no longer able to be your leader. And besides that, the LORD your God has told me that he won't let me cross the River Jordan. ³⁻⁵ But he has promised that he and Joshua will lead you across the Jordan to attack the nations that live on the other side. The LORD will destroy those nations just as he destroyed Sihon and Og, those two Amorite kings. Just remember — whenever you capture a place, kill everyone who lives there.

⁶ Be brave and strong! Don't be afraid of the nations on the other side of the Jordan. The LORD your God will always be at your side, and he will never abandon you.

⁷ Then Moses called Joshua up in front of the crowd and said:

Joshua, be brave and strong as you lead these people into their land. The LORD made a promise long ago to Israel's ancestors that this land would some day belong to Israel. That time has now come, and you must divide up the land among the people. ⁸ The LORD will lead you into the land. He will always be with you and help you, so don't ever be afraid of your enemies.

See also: **30.20:** a Gen 12.7; b Gen 26.3; c Gen 28.13.
31.2: Num 20.12. **31.4:** Num 21.21–35. **31.8:** Josh 1.5; Heb 13.5.

Read these laws

9 Moses wrote down all these laws and teachings and gave them to the priests and the leaders of Israel. The priests were from the Levi tribe, and they carried the sacred chest that belonged to the LORD. 10-11 Moses told these priests and leaders:

Each year the Israelites must come together to celebrate the Festival of Shelters at the place where the LORD chooses to be worshipped. You must read these laws and teachings to the people at the festival every seventh year, the year when loans do not need to be repaid.* 12-13 Everyone must come — men, women, children, and even the foreigners who live in your towns. And each new generation will listen and learn to worship the LORD their God with fear and trembling and to do exactly what is said in God's Law.

Israel will reject the Lord

14 The LORD told Moses, "You will soon die, so bring Joshua to the sacred tent, and I will appoint him the leader of Israel."

Moses and Joshua went to the sacred tent, 15 and the LORD appeared in a thick cloud right over the entrance to the tent. 16 The LORD said:

Moses, you will soon die. But Israel is going into a land where other gods are worshipped, and Israel will reject me and start worshipping these gods. The people will break the agreement I made with them, 17 and I will be so furious that I will abandon them and ignore their prayers. I will send disasters and suffering that will nearly wipe them out. Finally, they will realize that the disasters happened because I abandoned them. 18 They will pray to me, but I will ignore them because they were evil and started worshipping other gods.

19 Moses and Joshua, I am going to give you the words to a new song. Write them down and teach the song to the Israelites. If they learn it, they will know what I want them to do, and so they will have no excuse for not obeying me. 20 For I am bringing them into the land that I promised their ancestors. It is a land rich with milk and honey, and the Israelites will have more

than enough food to eat. But they will get fat and turn their backs on me and start worshipping other gods. The Israelites will reject me and break the agreement that I made with them.

21 When I punish the Israelites and their descendants with suffering and disasters, I will remind them that they know the words to this song, so they have no excuse for not obeying me.

I will give them the land that I promised, but I know the way they are going to live later on.

22 Moses wrote down the words to the song* straight away, and he taught it to the Israelites.

23 The LORD told Joshua, "Be brave and strong! I will help you lead the people of Israel into the land that I have promised them."

24 Moses wrote down all these laws and teachings in a book, 25 then he went to the Levites who carried the sacred chest and said:

26 This is *The Book of God's Law.* Keep it beside the sacred chest that holds the agreement the LORD your God made with Israel. This book is proof that you know what the LORD wants you to do. 27 I know how stubborn and rebellious you and the rest of the Israelites are. You have rebelled against the LORD while I have been alive, and it will only get worse after I am gone. 28 So call together the leaders and officials of the tribes of Israel. I will bring this book and read every word of it to you, and I will call the sky and the earth as witnesses that all of you know what you are supposed to do.

29 I am going to die soon, and I know that in the future you will stop caring about what is right and what is wrong, and so you will disobey the LORD and stop living the way I told you to live. The LORD will be angry, and terrible things will happen to you.

The song of Moses

30 Moses called a meeting of all the people of Israel, so he could teach them the words to the song that the LORD had given him. And here are the words:

---

*31.10,11 every seventh year . . . repaid: See 15.1,2 and the note there.

See also: 31.10: a Deut 15.12; b Deut 16.13-15.

*31.22 the words to the song: See 32.1-43.

See also: 31.23: Num 27.23; Josh 1.6.

CHAPTER 32

¹ Earth and Sky, listen to what I say!
² Israel, I will teach you.
My words will be like gentle rain
on tender young plants,
or like dew on the grass.

³ Join with me in praising
the wonderful name
of the LORD our God.
⁴ The LORD is a mighty rock,*
and he never does wrong.
God can always be trusted
to bring justice.
⁵ But you lie and cheat
and are unfaithful to him.
You have disgraced yourselves
and are no longer worthy
to be his children.*
⁶ Israel, the LORD is your Father,
the one who created you,
but you repaid him
by being foolish.
⁷ Think about past generations.
Ask your parents
or any of your elders.
They will tell you
⁸ that God Most High
gave land to every nation.
He assigned a guardian angel
to each of them,*
⁹ but the LORD himself
takes care of Israel.*

¹⁰ Israel, the LORD discovered you
in a barren desert
filled with howling winds.
God became your fortress,
protecting you as though
you were his own eyes.
¹¹ The LORD was like an eagle
teaching its young to fly,
always ready to swoop down
and catch them on its back.
¹² Israel, the LORD led you,
and without the aid
of a foreign god,
¹³ he helped you capture the land.
Your fields were rich with grain.
Olive trees grew in your stony soil,

and honey was found
among the rocks.
¹⁴ Your flocks and herds
produced milk and yoghurt,
and you got choice meat
from your sheep and goats
that grazed in Bashan.
Your wheat was the finest,
and you drank the best wine.

¹⁵ Israel,* you grew fat and rebelled
against God, your Creator;
you rejected the Mighty Rock,*
your only place of safety.
¹⁶ You made God jealous and angry
by worshipping disgusting idols
and foreign gods.
¹⁷ You offered sacrifices
to demons, those useless gods*
that never helped you,
new gods that your ancestors
never worshipped.
¹⁸ You turned away
from God, your Creator;
you forgot the Mighty Rock,*
the source of your life.
¹⁹ You were the LORD's children,
but you made him angry.
Then he rejected you ²⁰ and said,
"You are unfaithful
and can't be trusted.
So I won't answer your prayers;
I'll just watch and see
what happens to you.
²¹ You worshipped worthless idols,
and made me jealous and angry!
Now I will send a cruel*
and worthless nation
to make you jealous and angry.

²² "My people, I will breathe out fire
that sends you down
to the world of the dead.
It will scorch your farmlands
and burn deep down
under the mountains.
²³ I'll send disaster after disaster
to strike you like arrows.
²⁴ You'll be struck by starvation
and deadly diseases,
by the fangs of wild animals
and poisonous snakes.

---

*32.4 mighty rock: The Hebrew text has "rock",
which is sometimes used in poetry to compare the
LORD to a mountain where his people can run for
protection from their enemies.
See also: 32.8: Acts 17.26.

*32.15,18 Mighty Rock: See the note at 32.4.
*32.16,17 disgusting idols . . . foreign
gods . . . demons . . . those useless gods: Different
ways of referring to gods of other nations.
See also: 32.17: 1 Cor 10.20. 32.21: a 1 Cor 10.22;
b Rom 10.19.

²⁵ Young and old alike
    will be killed in the streets
    and terrified at home.
²⁶ "I wanted to scatter you,
    so no one would remember
    that you had ever lived.
²⁷ But I dreaded the sound
    of your enemies saying,
    'We defeated Israel with no help
    from the LORD.' "

²⁸ People of Israel, that's what the LORD
    has said to you.
    But you don't have good sense,
    and you never listen to advice.
²⁹ If you did, you could see
    where you are headed.
³⁰ How could one enemy soldier
    chase a thousand of Israel's troops?
    Or how could two of theirs
    pursue ten thousand of ours?
    It can only happen if the LORD
    stops protecting Israel
    and lets the enemy win.
³¹ Even our enemies know
    that only our God is a Mighty Rock.*

³² Our enemies are grapevines
    rooted in the fields
    of Sodom and Gomorrah.*
    The grapes they produce
    are full of bitter poison;
³³ their wine is more deadly
    than cobra venom.
³⁴ But the LORD has written
    a list of their sins
    and locked it in his vault.
³⁵ Soon our enemies will get
    what they deserve* —
    suddenly they will slip,
    and total disaster will quickly follow.

³⁶ When only a few
    of the LORD's people remain,
    when their strength is gone,
    and some of them are slaves,
    the LORD will feel sorry for them
    and give them justice.

³⁷ But first the LORD will say,
    "You ran for safety to other gods —
    couldn't they help you?

³⁸ You offered them wine
    and your best sacrifices.
    Can't those gods help you now
    or give you protection?
³⁹ Don't you understand?
    I am the only God;
    there are no others.
    I am the one who takes life
    and gives it again.
    I punished you with suffering.
    But now I will heal you,
    and nothing can stop me!

⁴⁰ "I make this solemn promise:
    just as I live for ever,
⁴¹ I will take revenge
    on my hateful enemies.
    I will sharpen my sword
    and let it flash like lightning.
⁴² My arrows will get drunk
    on enemy blood;
    my sword will taste the flesh
    and the blood of the enemy.
    It will kill prisoners,
    and cut off the heads
    of their leaders.'"

⁴³ Tell the heavens to celebrate
    and all gods to bow down
    to the LORD,'
    because he will take revenge
    on those hateful enemies
    who killed his people.
    He will forgive the sins of Israel
    and purify their land.'

⁴⁴⁻⁴⁵ Moses spoke the words of the song so that all the Israelites could hear, and Joshua' helped him. When Moses had finished, ⁴⁶ he said, "Always remember this song I have taught you today. And let it be a warning that you must teach your children to obey everything written in *The Book of God's Law.* ⁴⁷ The Law isn't empty words. It can give you a long life in the land that you are going to take."

Moses sees the land and blesses the tribes of Israel

Moses will see the land

⁴⁸ Later that day the LORD said to Moses:

⁴⁹ Go up into the Abarim Mountain range here in Moab across the Jordan valley from Jericho. And when you reach the top of

*32.31 Mighty Rock: See the note at 32.4.
*32.32 Sodom and Gomorrah: Two cities that the LORD destroyed because their people were so evil (see Genesis 18.16—19.28).

See also: 32.35: Rom 2.19; Heb 10.30. 32.36a: Psa 135.14.

See also: 32.43: Rom 5.10; Rev 19.2.
32.48-52: Num 27.12-14; Deut 3.23-27.

Mount Nebo, you will be able to see the land of Canaan, which I am giving to Israel. [50] Then you will die and be buried on the mountaintop, just as your brother Aaron died and was buried on Mount Hor. [51] Both of you were unfaithful to me at Meribah Spring near Kadesh in the Zin Desert.* I am God, but there in front of the Israelites, you did not treat me with the honour and respect I deserve. [52] So I will give the land to the people of Israel, but you will only get to see it from a distance.

CHAPTER 33

Moses blesses the tribes of Israel

[1] Moses was a prophet, and before he died, he blessed the tribes of Israel by saying:

> [2] The LORD came from Mount Sinai.
> From Edom, he gave light
>   to his people,
> and his glory was shining
>   from Mount Paran.
> Thousands of his warriors
>   were with him, and fire
>   was at his right hand.[b]
> [3] The LORD loves the tribes of Israel,[c]
>   and he protects his people.
> They listen to his words
>   and worship at his feet.
> [4-5] I called a meeting
>   of the tribes of Israel[d]
>   and gave you God's Law.
> Then you and your leaders
>   made the LORD your king.
>
> [6] Tribe of Reuben, you will live,
>   even though your tribe
>   will always be small.[e]
>
> [7] The LORD will listen to you,
>   tribe of Judah, as you beg
>   to come safely home.
> You fought your enemies alone;[f]
>   now the LORD will help you.
>
> [8] At Massah and Meribah Spring,*
>   the LORD tested you, tribe of Levi.
> You were faithful,[g]
>   and so the priesthood[h] belongs
>   to the Levi tribe.

> [9] Protecting Israel's agreement
>   with the LORD
> was more important to you
>   than the life of your father or mother,
>   or brothers or sisters,
>   or your own children.*
>
> [10] You teach God's laws to Israel,[i]
>   and at the place of worship
>   you offer sacrifices and burn incense.
> [11] I pray that the LORD will bless
>   everything you do,
> and make you strong enough
>   to crush your enemies.
>
> [12] The LORD Most High[j] loves you,
>   tribe of Benjamin.
> He will live among your hills
>   and protect you.
>
> [13] Descendants of Joseph,
>   the LORD will bless you
> with precious water
>   from deep wells
> and with dew from the sky.
> [14] Month by month, your fruit
>   will ripen in the sunshine.
> [15] You will have a rich harvest
>   from the slopes of the ancient hills.
> [16] The LORD who appeared
>   in the burning bush
> wants to give you the best
>   the land can produce,
> and it will be a princely crown
>   on Joseph's head.
>
> [17] The armies of Ephraim and Manasseh
>   are majestic and fierce
> like a bull or a wild ox.
> They will run their spears
>   through faraway nations.
>
> [18] Be happy, Zebulun,
>   as your boats set sail;
> be happy, Issachar, in your tents.
> [19] The sea will make you wealthy,
>   and from the sandy beach
>   you will get treasure.*
> So invite the other tribes[k]
>   to celebrate with you
>   and offer sacrifices to God.
>
> [20] Tribe of Gad,
>   the LORD will bless you
>   with more land.

---

*32.51 Both of you were unfaithful . . . the Zin Desert: See Numbers 20.1-13.
*33.8 Massah and Meribah Spring: See Exodus 17.1-7; Numbers 20.1-13.
See also: 33.8: a Exod 28.30; b Exod 17.7; c Exod 17.7; Num 20.13.

*33.9 Protecting Israel's agreement . . . your own children: See Exodus 32.25-29.
*33.19 sandy beach . . . treasure: Possibly a reference to glass made from sand; glass was rare and very valuable.

So shout his praises!
Your tribe is like a lion
   ripping up its victim.
21 Your leaders met together
   and chose the best land
      for your tribe,
   but you obeyed the LORD
      and helped the other tribes.*

22 Tribe of Dan, you are like a lion cub,
   startled by a snake.♪

23 The LORD is pleased with you,
   people of Naphtali.
He will bless you
   and give you the land
      to the west and the south.♪

24 The LORD's greatest blessing
   is for you, tribe of Asher.
You will be the favourite
   of all the other tribes.
You will be rich with olive oil
25 and have strong town gates
   with bronze and iron bolts.
Your people will be powerful
   for as long as they live.

26 Israel,♪ no other god is like ours —
   the clouds are his chariot
as he rides across the skies
   to come and help us.
27 The eternal God
   is our hiding place;
   he carries us in his arms.
When God tells you
   to destroy your enemies,
   he will make them run.
28 Israel, you will live in safety;
   your enemies will be gone.♪
The dew will fall from the sky,
   and you will have plenty
      of grain and wine.
29 The LORD has rescued you
   and given you more blessings
      than any other nation.
He protects you like a shield
   and is your majestic sword.
Your enemies will bow in fear,
   and you will trample on their backs.

The death of Moses

CHAPTER 34

1 Some time later, Moses left the lowlands of
Moab. He went up Mount Pisgah to the peak
of Mount Nebo,* which is across the River
Jordan from Jericho. The LORD showed him all
the land as far north as Gilead and the town of
Dan. 2 He let Moses see the territories that
would soon belong to the tribes of Naphtali,
Ephraim, Manasseh, and Judah, as far west as
the Mediterranean Sea. 3 The LORD also
showed him the land in the south, from the
valley near the town of Jericho, known as The
City of Palm Trees, down to the town of Zoar.

4 The LORD said, "Moses, this is the land I
was talking about when I solemnly promised
Abraham, Isaac, and Jacob that I would give
land to their descendants. I have let you see it,
but you will not cross the Jordan and go in."

5 And so, Moses the LORD's servant died
there in Moab, just as the LORD had said. 6 The
LORD buried him in a valley near the town of
Beth-Peor, but even today no one knows
exactly where. 7 Moses was a hundred and
twenty years old when he died, yet his
eyesight was still good, and his body was
strong.

8 The people of Israel stayed in the
lowlands of Moab, where they mourned and
grieved thirty days for Moses, as was their
custom.

Joshua becomes the leader of Israel

9 Before Moses died, he had placed his hands
on Joshua, and the LORD had given Joshua
wisdom. The Israelites paid attention to what
Joshua said and obeyed the commands that
the LORD had given Moses.

Moses was a great prophet

10 There has never again been a prophet in
Israel like Moses. The LORD spoke face to face
with him 11 and sent him to perform
powerful miracles in the presence of the king
of Egypt and his entire nation. 12 No one else
has ever had the power to do such great
things as Moses did for everyone to see.

---

*33.21 tribes: One possible meaning for the difficult
Hebrew text of verse 21. The Gad tribe asked for
some of the land east of the River Jordan, but
promised that their warriors would cross the Jordan
and help the other tribes take over the land west of
the Jordan (see Numbers 32.1–33; Joshua 4.10–13).

*34.1 Mount Pisgah . . . Mount Nebo: Mount Nebo
was probably one peak of the ridge known as Mount
Pisgah.

See also: 34.4: a Gen 12.7; b Gen 26.3; c Gen 28.13.
34.10: Exod 33.11.

Additional notes

'1.1–5 Mount Sinai: The Hebrew text has "Horeb", another name for Mount Sinai.
'1.6 Mount Sinai: See the note at 1.1–5.
'1.9 Mount Sinai: See the note at 1.1–5.
'1.19 Mount Sinai: See the note at 1.1–5.
'1.28 The people . . . we are: Most Hebrew manuscripts; a few Hebrew manuscripts and one ancient translation "The people who live there are stronger than we are, and there are more of them than there are of us."
'1.38 Joshua: Hebrew "Joshua son of Nun".
'2.15,16 getting rid of: Or "sending diseases on".
'2.28,29 Edomites and Moabites: Hebrew "descendants of Esau, who live in Seir and Moabites who live in Ar".
'3.11 coffin: Or "bed".
'3.12–17 Lake Galilee: The Hebrew text has "Lake Chinnereth", an earlier name.
'3.12–17 the Dead Sea: Hebrew "the Sea of the Arabah, the Salt Sea".
'3.12–17 half the tribe of Manasseh: Or "East Manasseh".
'3.12–17 Villages of Jair: Or "Havvoth-Jair".
'3.12–17 Machir clan: One of the clans of the Manasseh tribe.
'4.10 Mount Sinai: See the note at 1.1–5.
'4.11 Mount Sinai: See the note at 1.1–5.
'4.21 what you said: Or "you people".
'4.48 Hermon: The Hebrew text also includes the name "Sion", probably another form of "Sirion", the name used by the Sidonians.
'4.49 the Dead Sea: Hebrew "the Sea of the Arabah".
'5.2 Mount Sinai: See the note at 1.1–5.
'5.3 wasn't only with: Hebrew "wasn't with".
'6.1 these laws and teachings: Or "the following commandment with its laws and teachings" (see 6.4,5).
'6.4 The LORD . . . true God: Or "Only the LORD is our God."
'7.20 make them . . . dead: Or "send hornets to kill them".
'9.8 Mount Sinai: See the note at 1.1–5.
'9.9–11 Ten Commandments: Hebrew "commandments".
'9.24 he has: The Samaritan Hebrew Text and one ancient translation; the Standard Hebrew Text "I have".
'10.6 the wells . . . Jaakan: Or "Beeroth Bene-Jaakan".
'10.8 After . . . chest: Or "After Israel reached Jotbathah".
'11.6 Dathan and Abiram: Hebrew "Dathan and Abiram, the sons of Eliab from the Reuben tribe".
'11.10 where . . . crops: One possible meaning for the difficult Hebrew text.
'13.1,2 a prophet: Hebrew adds "or a dreamer of dreams", another name for a prophet.
'14.1 when you mourn . . . forehead: Or "you must not worship Baal, cutting yourselves and shaving your forehead."

'14.12–18 eagles . . . hoopoes: Some of the birds in this list are difficult to identify.
'15.18 six years . . . work: Or "six years of service, and it cost you no more than if you had hired someone to do the work"; or "six years of service, for what you would have had to pay a worker for two years."
'16.3,4 the same kind . . . in Egypt: One possible meaning for the difficult Hebrew text.
'16.6 sunset, the time of day when you left Egypt: Or "sunset on the same date as when you left Egypt".
'16.18,19 turn . . . liars: Or "keep innocent people from getting justice".
'17.18 God's laws: Or "God's laws for the king".
'18.7 a special servant of the LORD: Or "one of the LORD's priests".
'18.16 Mount Sinai: See the note at 1.1–5.
'22.5 pretend to be men . . . pretend to be women: Or "wear men's clothing . . . wear women's clothing".
'22.28,29 talks him into sleeping with him . . . bride price and: Or "forces her to have sex. 29 Then if they are caught, he will have to marry her. He must give her father fifty pieces of silver as a bride price and".
'23.4 Balaam: Hebrew "Balaam son of Beor from Pethor".
'23.10 if something . . . worship, he: Or "if a man has a flow of semen at night, he is unclean and unfit for worship, and he".
'24.1 something disgraceful about her: One possible meaning for the difficult Hebrew text.
'24.14 don't hold back their pay: The Dead Sea Scrolls; the Standard Hebrew Text "treat them right".
'25.1,2 whip: Or "rod".
'27.14–26 the rest of the people: Or "all the people who are standing on Mount Ebal".
'29.1 Mount Sinai: See the note at 1.1–5.
'29.4–6 I gave . . . food: Hebrew "you didn't eat bread or drink any wine or beer."
'29.19 you will cause the rest of Israel to be punished along with you: Hebrew "The mud will be swept away as well as the dust."
'32.5 and are unfaithful . . . children: One possible meaning for the difficult Hebrew text.
'32.8 He assigned . . . them: The Dead Sea Scrolls and one ancient translation; the Standard Hebrew Text "So there were as many nations as Israel (that is, Jacob) had children".
'32.9 Israel: The Hebrew text has "Jacob", another name for Israel's ancestor.
'32.15 Israel: The Standard Hebrew Text has "Jeshurun", a rare name for Israel related to a word meaning "honest". The Samaritan Hebrew Text and one ancient translation also use "Jacob", another name for the ancestor of the nation of Israel.
'32.21 cruel: One possible meaning for the difficult Hebrew text.
'32.35 our enemies . . . deserve: The Samaritan Hebrew Text and one ancient translation; the Standard Hebrew Text "I will pay them back".

up the chest by its carrying poles and went on ahead.

7 The LORD told Joshua, "Beginning today I will show the people that you are their leader, and they will know that I am helping you as I helped Moses. 8 Now, tell the priests who are carrying the chest to go a little way into the river and stand there."

9 Joshua spoke to the people:

Come here and listen to what the LORD our God said he will do! 10 The Canaanites, the Hittites, the Hivites, the Perizzites, the Girgashites, the Amorites, and the Jebusites control the land on the other side of the river. But the living God will be with you and will force them out of the land when you attack. And now, God is going to prove that he's powerful enough to force them out. 11-13 Just watch the sacred chest that belongs to the LORD, the ruler of the whole earth. As soon as the priests carrying the chest step into the Jordan, the water will stop flowing and pile up as if someone had built a dam across the river.

The LORD has also said that each of the twelve tribes should choose one man to represent it.

14 The Israelites packed up and left camp. The priests carrying the chest walked in front, 15 until they came to the River Jordan. The water in the river had risen over its banks, as it often does in springtime.* But as soon as the feet of the priests touched the water, 16-17 the river stopped flowing, and the water started piling up at the town of Adam near Zarethan. No water flowed towards the Dead Sea, and the priests stood in the middle of the dry river bed near Jericho while everyone else crossed over.

CHAPTER 4

The people set up a monument

1 After Israel had crossed the Jordan, the LORD said to Joshua:

2-3 Tell* one man from each of the twelve tribes to pick up a large rock from where the priests are standing. Then tell the men to set up those rocks as a monument at the place where you camp tonight.

4 Joshua chose twelve men; he called them together, 5 and told them:

Go to the middle of the river bed where the sacred chest is, and pick up a large rock. Carry it on your shoulder to our camp. There are twelve of you, so there will be one rock for each tribe. 6-7 Some day your children will ask, "Why are these rocks here?" Then you can tell them how the water stopped flowing when the chest was being carried across the river. These rocks will always remind our people of what happened here today.

8 The men followed the instructions that the LORD had given Joshua. They picked up twelve rocks, one for each tribe, and carried them to the camp, where they put them down.

9 Joshua told some other men to set up a monument next to the place where the priests were standing. This monument was also made of twelve large rocks, and it is still there in the middle of the river.

The people of Israel set up camp at Gilgal

10-13 The army got ready for battle and crossed the Jordan. They marched quickly past the sacred chest* and into the desert near Jericho. Forty thousand soldiers from the tribes of Reuben, Gad, and East Manasseh* led the way, as Moses had ordered.*

The priests stayed where they were until the army had followed the orders that the LORD had given Moses and Joshua. Then the army watched as the priests carried the chest the rest of the way across.

14-18 "Joshua," the LORD said, "tell the priests to come up from the Jordan and bring the chest with them." So Joshua went over to the priests and told them what the LORD had said. And as soon as the priests carried the chest past the highest place that the flood waters of the Jordan had reached, the river flooded its banks again.

That's how the LORD showed the Israelites that Joshua was their leader.* For the rest of Joshua's life, they respected him as they had respected Moses.

---

*3.15 springtime: Or "harvest time"; the grain harvest was in late spring.

*4.10–13 the sacred chest: The Hebrew text has "the LORD". The army was marching past the sacred chest, which was a symbol of God's throne on earth (see 1 Samuel 4.4 and Exodus 25.10–22; 37.1–9).
*4.10–13 Moses . . . ordered: See Numbers 32.16–32; Joshua 1.12–16.
*4.14–18 leader: See 3.7.

¹⁹ It was the tenth day of the first month* of the year when Israel crossed the River Jordan. They set up camp at Gilgal, which was east of the land controlled by Jericho. ²⁰ The men who had carried the twelve rocks from the Jordan brought them to Joshua, and they made them into a monument. ²¹ Then Joshua told the people:

Years from now your children will ask you why these rocks are here. ²²⁻²³ Tell them, "The LORD our God dried up the River Jordan so we could walk across. He did the same thing here for us that he did for our people at the Red Sea,* ²⁴ because he wants everyone on earth to know how powerful he is. And he wants us to worship only him."

CHAPTER 5

¹ The Amorite kings west of the River Jordan and the Canaanite kings along the Mediterranean Sea lost their courage and their will to fight, when they heard how the LORD had dried up the River Jordan to let Israel go across.

Israel gets ready to celebrate Passover

² While Israel was camped at Gilgal, the LORD said, "Joshua, make some flint knives* and circumcise the rest of the Israelite men and boys."*

³ Joshua made the knives, then circumcised those men and boys at Haaraloth Hill.* ⁴⁻⁷ This had to be done, because none of Israel's baby boys had been circumcised during the forty years that Israel had wandered through the desert after leaving Egypt.

And why had they wandered for forty years? It was because straight after they left Egypt, the men in the army had disobeyed the LORD. And the LORD had said, "None of you men will ever live to see the land that I promised Israel. It is a land rich with milk and honey, and some day your children will live there, but not before you do here in the desert."

⁸ Everyone who had been circumcised needed time to heal, and they stayed in camp.

⁹ The LORD told Joshua, "It was a disgrace for my people to be slaves in Egypt, but now I have taken away that disgrace." So the Israelites named the place Gilgal,* and it still has that name.

¹⁰ Israel continued to camp at Gilgal in the desert near Jericho, and on the fourteenth day of the same month,* they celebrated Passover.

¹¹⁻¹² The next day, God stopped sending the Israelites manna* to eat each morning, and they started eating food grown in the land of Canaan. They ate roasted grain* and thin bread* made of the barley they had gathered from nearby fields.

Israel captures Jericho

¹³ One day, Joshua was near Jericho when he saw a man standing some distance in front of him. The man was holding a sword, so Joshua walked up to him and asked, "Are you on our side or on our enemies' side?"

¹⁴ "Neither," he answered. "I am here because I am the commander of the LORD's army."

Joshua fell to his knees and bowed down to the ground. "I am your servant," he said. "Tell me what to do."

¹⁵ "Take off your sandals," the commander answered. "This is a holy place."

So Joshua took off his sandals.

CHAPTER 6

¹ Meanwhile, the people of Jericho had been locking the gates in their town wall because

---

*4.19 first month: Abib (also called Nisan), the first month of the Hebrew calendar, from about mid-March to mid-April.

*4.22,23 Red Sea: See the note at 2.10.

*5.2 flint knives: Flint is a stone that can be chipped until it forms a very sharp edge.

*5.2 circumcise . . . men and boys: They could not celebrate Passover unless they were circumcised (see Exodus 12.43–49).

See also: 5.6: Num 14.28–35.

*5.9 Gilgal: In Hebrew "Gilgal" sounds like "take away."

*5.10 the same month: See the note at 4.19.

*5.11,12 manna: The special food that God provided for the Israelites while they were in the desert for forty years. It was about the size of a small seed, and it appeared on the ground during the night, except on the Sabbath. It was gathered early in the morning, ground up, and then baked or boiled (see Exodus 16.13–35; Numbers 11.4–9).

*5.11,12 roasted grain: Roasted grain was made by cooking the grain in a dry pan or on a flat rock, or by holding a bunch of grain stalks over a fire.

*5.11,12 thin bread: Bread made without yeast. Israelites were not supposed to eat bread made with yeast for the week following Passover. That week is called the Festival of Thin Bread (see Exodus 12.14–20; 13.3–7).

See also: 5.10: Exod 12.1–13. 5.12: Exod 16.35.

they were afraid of the Israelites. No one could go out or come in.

²-³ The LORD said to Joshua:

With my help, you and your army will defeat the king of Jericho and his army, and you will capture the town. Here is how to do it: march slowly around Jericho once a day for six days. ⁴ Take along the sacred chest and have seven priests walk in front of it, carrying trumpets.*

But on the seventh day, march slowly around the town seven times while the priests blow their trumpets. ⁵ Then the priests will blast on their trumpets, and everyone else will shout. The wall will fall down, and your soldiers can go straight in from every side.

⁶ Joshua called the priests together and said, "Take the chest and make seven priests carry trumpets and march ahead of it."

⁷-¹⁰ Next, he gave the army their orders: "March slowly around Jericho. A few of you will go ahead of the chest to guard it, but most of you will follow it. Don't shout the battle cry or yell or even talk until the day I tell you to. Then let out a shout!"

As soon as Joshua finished giving the orders, the army started marching. One group of soldiers led the way, with seven priests marching behind them and blowing trumpets. Then came the priests carrying the chest, followed by the rest of the soldiers. ¹¹ They obeyed Joshua's orders and carried the chest once around the town before returning to camp for the night.

¹²-¹⁴ Early the next morning, Joshua and everyone else started marching around Jericho in the same order as the day before. One group of soldiers was in front, followed by the seven priests with trumpets and the priests who carried the chest. The rest of the army came next. The seven priests blew their trumpets while everyone marched slowly around Jericho and back to camp. They did this once a day for six days.

¹⁵ On the seventh day, the army got up at daybreak. They marched slowly around Jericho as they had done for the past six days, except on this day they went around seven times. ¹⁶ Then the priests blew the trumpets, and Joshua yelled:

Get ready to shout! The LORD will let you capture this town. ¹⁷ But you must destroy

it and everything in it, to show that it now belongs to the LORD.* The woman Rahab helped the spies we sent,* so protect her and the others who are inside her house. But kill everyone else in the town. ¹⁸-¹⁹ The silver and gold and everything made of bronze and iron belong to the LORD and must be put in his treasury. Be careful to follow these instructions, because if you see something you want and take it, the LORD will destroy Israel. And it will be all your fault.*

²⁰ The priests blew their trumpets again, and the soldiers shouted as loud as they could. The walls of Jericho fell flat. Then the soldiers rushed up the hill, went straight into the town, and captured it. ²¹-²⁵ They killed everyone, men and women, young and old, everyone except Rahab and the others in her house. They even killed every cow, sheep, and donkey.

Joshua said to the two men who had been spies, "Rahab kept you safe when I sent you to Jericho. We promised to protect her and her family, and we will keep that promise. Now go into her house and bring them out."

The two men went into Rahab's house and brought her out, along with her father and mother, her brothers, and her other relatives. Rahab and her family had to stay in a place just outside the Israelite army camp.* But later they were allowed to live among the Israelites, and her descendants still do.

The Israelites took the silver and gold and the things made of bronze and iron and put them with the rest of the treasure that was kept at the LORD's house.* Finally, they set fire to Jericho and everything in it.

²⁶ After Jericho was destroyed, Joshua warned the people, "Some day a man will rebuild Jericho, but the LORD will put a curse on him, and the man's eldest son will die

---

*6.17 destroy . . . now belongs to the LORD: Destroying a city and everything in it, including its people and animals, showed that it belonged to the LORD and could no longer be used by humans.
*6.17 sent: See 2.1,21.
*6.21-25 camp: Rahab and her family were Canaanites and were considered unclean. If they stayed in the Israelite army camp, the Lord would not help the Israelite army in battle (see Deuteronomy 23.9–14). However, Rahab and her family later became part of Israel.
*6.21-25 the LORD's house: A name for the place of worship, which at that time was the sacred tent.
See also: 6.20: Heb 11.30. 6.25: Heb 11.31.
6.26: 1 King 16.34.

---

*6.4 trumpets: These were hollowed-out ram's horns.

when he starts to build the town wall. And by the time he finishes the wall and puts gates in it, all his children will be dead."*

27 The LORD helped Joshua in everything he did, and Joshua was famous everywhere in Canaan.

Achan disobeys the Lord

CHAPTER 7

1 The LORD had said that everything in Jericho belonged to him.* But Achan* from the Judah tribe took some of the things from Jericho for himself. And so the LORD was angry with the Israelites, because one of them had disobeyed him.*

2 While Israel was still camped near Jericho, Joshua sent some spies with these instructions: "Go to the town of Ai and find out whatever you can about the region around the town."

The spies left and went to Ai, which is east of Bethel and near Beth-Aven. 3 They went back to Joshua and reported, "You don't need to send the whole army to attack Ai — two or three thousand troops will be enough. Why bother the whole army for a town that small?"

4-5 Joshua sent about three thousand soldiers to attack Ai. But the men of Ai fought back and chased the Israelite soldiers away from the town gate and down the hill to the stone quarries.* Thirty-six Israelite soldiers were killed, and the Israelite army felt discouraged.

6 Joshua and the leaders of Israel tore their clothes and put dust on their heads to show their sorrow. They lay face down on the ground in front of the sacred chest until sunset. 7 Then Joshua said:

Our LORD, did you bring us across the River Jordan just so the Amorites could destroy us? This wouldn't have happened if we had agreed to stay on the other side of the Jordan. 8 I don't even know what to say to you, since Israel's army has turned and run from the enemy. 9 Everyone will think you weren't strong enough to protect your people. Now the Canaanites and everyone else who lives in the land will surround us and wipe us out.

10 The LORD answered:

Stop lying there on the ground! Get up! 11 I said everything in Jericho belonged to me and had to be destroyed. But the Israelites have kept some of the things for themselves. They stole from me and hid what they took. Then they lied about it. 12 What they stole was supposed to be destroyed, and now Israel itself must be destroyed. I cannot help you any more until you do exactly what I have said. That's why Israel turns and runs from its enemies instead of standing up to them.

13 Tell the people of Israel, "Tomorrow you will meet with the LORD your God, so make yourselves acceptable to worship him. The LORD says that you have taken things that should have been destroyed. You won't be able to stand up to your enemies until you get rid of those things.

14 "Tomorrow morning everyone must gather near the place of worship. You will come forward tribe by tribe, and the LORD will show which tribe is guilty. Next, the clans in that tribe must come forward, and the LORD will show which clan is guilty. The families in that clan must come, and the LORD will point out the guilty family. Finally, the men in that family must come, 15 and the LORD will show who stole what should have been destroyed. That man must be put to death, his body burnt, and his possessions thrown into the fire. He has done a terrible thing by breaking the sacred agreement that the LORD made with Israel."

16 Joshua got up early the next morning and brought each tribe to the place of worship, where the LORD showed that the Judah tribe was guilty. 17 Then Joshua brought the clans of Judah to the LORD, and the LORD showed that the Zerah clan was guilty. One by one he brought the leader of each family in the Zerah clan to the LORD, and the LORD showed that Zabdi's family was guilty. 18 Finally, Joshua brought each man in Zabdi's family to the LORD, and the LORD showed that Achan was the guilty one.

19 "Achan," Joshua said, "the LORD God of Israel has decided that you are guilty. Is this true? Tell me what you did, and don't try to hide anything."

20 "It's true," Achan answered. "I sinned and disobeyed the LORD God of Israel. 21-22 While we were in Jericho, I saw a beautiful Babylonian robe, two hundred pieces of silver, and a gold bar that weighed

*7.1 belonged to him: See the note at 6.17.
*7.1 the LORD was angry . . . disobeyed him: Even though only one person had disobeyed, it meant that the LORD's instructions to the people of Israel had not been followed, and the whole nation was held responsible.

the same as fifty pieces of gold. I wanted them for myself, so I took them. I dug a hole under my tent and hid the silver, the gold, and the robe."

Joshua told some people to run to Achan's tent, where they found the silver, the gold, and the robe. ²³ They brought them back and put them in front of the sacred chest, so Joshua and the rest of the Israelites could see them. ²⁴ Then everyone took Achan and the things he had stolen to Trouble Valley.* They also took along his sons and daughters, his cattle, donkeys, and sheep, his tent, and everything else that belonged to him.

²⁵ Joshua said, "Achan, you caused us a lot of trouble. Now the LORD is paying you back with the same kind of trouble."

The people of Israel then stoned to death Achan and his family. They made a fire and burnt the bodies, together with what Achan had stolen, and all his possessions. ²⁶ They covered the remains with a big pile of rocks, which is still there. Then the LORD stopped being angry with Israel.

That's how the place came to be called Trouble Valley.

The battle at Ai

CHAPTER 8

Israel destroys the town of Ai

¹⁻² The LORD told Joshua:

Don't be afraid, and don't be discouraged by what happened at the town of Ai. Take the army and attack again. But first, make part of the army set up an ambush on the other side of the town. I will help you defeat the king of Ai and his army, and you will capture the town and the land around it. Destroy Ai and kill its king as you did at Jericho. But you may keep the livestock and everything else you want.

³⁻⁴ Joshua quickly got the army ready to attack Ai. He chose thirty thousand of his best soldiers and gave them these orders:

Tonight, while it is dark, march to Ai and take up a position behind the town. Get as close to the town as you can without being seen, but be ready to attack.

⁵⁻⁶ The rest of the army will come with me and attack near the gate. When the people of Ai come out to fight, we'll run away and let them chase us. They will think we are running from them just like

the first time. But when we've let them chase us far enough away, ⁷ you come out of hiding. The LORD our God will help you capture the town. ⁸ Then set it on fire, as the LORD has told us to do. Those are your orders, ⁹ now go!

The thirty thousand soldiers went to a place on the west side of Ai, between Ai and Bethel, where they could hide and wait to attack.

That night, Joshua stayed in camp with the rest of the army. ¹⁰ Early the next morning he got his troops ready to move out, and he and the other leaders of Israel led them to Ai. ¹¹ They set up camp in full view of the town, across the valley to the north. ¹² Joshua had already sent five thousand soldiers to the west side of the town to hide and wait to attack. ¹³ Now all his troops were in place. Part of the army was in the camp to the north of Ai, and the others were hiding to the west, ready to make a surprise attack. That night, Joshua went into the valley.*

¹⁴⁻¹⁵ The king of Ai saw Joshua's army, so the king and his troops hurried out early the next morning to fight them. Joshua and his army pretended to be beaten, and they let the men of Ai chase them towards the desert. The king and his army were facing the Jordan Valley as Joshua had planned.

The king did not realize that some Israelite soldiers were hiding behind the town. ¹⁶⁻¹⁷ So he called out every man in Ai to go after Joshua's troops. They all rushed out to chase the Israelite army, and they left the town gates wide open. Not one man was left in Ai or in Bethel.*

Joshua let the men of Ai chase him and his army further and further away from Ai. ¹⁸ Finally, the LORD told Joshua, "Point your sword* at the town of Ai, because now I am going to help you defeat it!"

As soon as Joshua pointed his sword at the town, ¹⁹ the soldiers who had been hiding got up and ran into the town. They captured it and set it on fire.

²⁰⁻²¹ When Joshua and his troops saw smoke rising from the town, they knew that the other part of their army had captured it. So they turned and attacked.

The men of Ai looked back and saw smoke rising from their town. But they could not escape, because the soldiers they had been chasing had suddenly turned and started fighting. ²²⁻²⁴ Meanwhile, the other Israelite

---

*8.13 valley: This may refer either to the Jordan Valley or to the valley between the Israelite camp and Ai.

soldiers had come from the town and attacked the men of Ai from the rear. The Israelites captured the king of Ai and brought him to Joshua. They also chased the rest of the men of Ai into the desert and killed them.*

The Israelite army went back to Ai and killed everyone there. 25-26 Joshua kept his sword pointed at the town of Ai until every last one of Ai's twelve thousand people was dead. 27 But the Israelites took the animals and the other possessions of the people of Ai, because this was what the LORD had told Joshua to do.

28-29 Joshua made sure every building in Ai was burnt to the ground. He told his men to kill the king of Ai and hang his body on a tree. Then at sunset he told the Israelites to take down the body,* throw it in the gateway of the town, and cover it with a big pile of rocks. Those rocks are still there, and the town itself has never been rebuilt.

Joshua reads the blessings and curses
This is also told in Deuteronomy 27.1-26

30-32 One day, Joshua led the people of Israel to Mount Ebal, where he told some of his men, "Build an altar for offering sacrifices to the LORD. And use stones that have never been cut with iron tools,* because that is what Moses taught in *The Book of the Law*."*

Joshua offered sacrifices to please the LORD* and to ask his blessing.* Then with the Israelites still watching, he copied parts of *The Book of the Law* of Moses on to stones.

33-35 Moses had said that everyone in Israel was to go to the valley between Mount Ebal and Mount Gerizim, where they were to be blessed. So everyone went there, including the foreigners, the leaders, officials, and judges. Half of the people stood on one side of the valley, and half on the other side, with

the priests from the Levi tribe standing in the middle with the sacred chest. Then in a loud voice, Joshua read the blessings and curses from *The Book of the Law* of Moses.*

The people of Gibeon trick the leaders of Israel

CHAPTER 9

1-2 The kings west of the River Jordan heard about Joshua's victories, and so they got together and decided to attack Joshua and Israel. These kings were from the hill country and from the foothills to the west, as well as from the Mediterranean coast as far north as the Lebanon Mountains. Some of them were Hittites, others were Amorites or Canaanites, and still others were Perizzites, Hivites, or Jebusites.

3 The people of Gibeon had also heard what Joshua had done to Jericho and Ai. 4 So they decided that some of their men should pretend to be messengers from a faraway country.* The men put worn-out bags on their donkeys and found some old wineskins that had cracked and had been sewn back together. 5 Their sandals were old and patched, and their clothes were worn out. They even took along some dry and crumbly bread. 6 Then they went to the Israelite camp at Gilgal, where they said to Joshua and the men of Israel, "We have come from a country that is far from here. Please make a peace treaty with us."

7-8 The Israelites replied, "But perhaps you really live near us. We can't make a peace treaty with you if you live nearby."*

The Gibeonites* said, "If you make a peace treaty with us, we will be your servants."

"Who are you?" Joshua asked. "Where do you come from?"

They answered:

9 We are your servants, and we live far from here. We came because the LORD our God is so famous. We heard what the LORD did in Egypt 10 and what he did to those two Amorite kings on the other side of the Jordan: King Og of Bashan, who lived in Ashtaroth, and King Sihon of Heshbon.

11 Our leaders and everyone who lives in our country told us to meet with you and

---

*8.28,29 take down the body: See Deuteronomy 21.22,23.
*8.30-32 use stones . . . iron tools: See Exodus 20.25.
*8.30-32 sacrifices to please the LORD: These sacrifices have been traditionally called "whole burnt offerings" because the whole animal was burnt on the altar. A main purpose of such sacrifices was to please the LORD with the smell of the sacrifice, and so in the CEV they are often called "sacrifices to please the LORD".
*8.30-32 to ask his blessing: These sacrifices have traditionally been called "peace offerings", or "offerings of well-being". A main purpose was to ask for the LORD's blessing, and so in the CEV they are often called "sacrifices to ask the LORD's blessing".
See also: 8.30-32: Deut 27.2-8. 8.31: Exod 20.25. 8.33-35: Deut 11.29; 27.11-14.

*9.7,8 nearby: See Deuteronomy 20.10-18.
See also: 9.7: Exod 23.32; 34.12; Deut 7.2. 9.10: Num 21.21-35.

tell you that all of us are your servants. They said to ask you to make a peace treaty with our people. They told us to be sure and take along enough food for our journey. [12] See this dry, crumbly bread of ours? It was hot out of the oven when we packed the food on the day we left our homes. [13] These cracked wineskins were new when we filled them, and our clothes and sandals are worn out because we have travelled so far.

[14] The Israelites tried some of the food,* but they did not ask the LORD if he wanted them to make a treaty. [15] So Joshua made a peace treaty with the messengers and promised that Israel would not kill their people. Israel's leaders swore that Israel would keep this promise.

[16-17] A couple of days later,* the Israelites found out that these people actually lived in the nearby towns of Gibeon, Chephirah, Beeroth, and Kiriath-Jearim.* So the Israelites left the place where they had camped and arrived at the four towns two days later.* [18] But they did not attack the towns, because the Israelite leaders had sworn in the name of the LORD that they would let these people live.

The Israelites complained about their leaders' decision not to attack, [19-21] but the leaders reminded them, "We promised these people in the name of the LORD God of Israel that we would let them live, so we must not harm them. If we break our promise, God will punish us. We'll let them live, but we'll make them cut wood and carry water for our people."

[22] Joshua told some of his soldiers, "I want to meet with the Gibeonite leaders. Bring them here."

When the Gibeonites came, Joshua said, "You live close to us. Why did you lie by claiming you lived far away? [23] Now you are under a curse, and your people will have to send workers to cut wood and carry water for the place of worship."*

[24] The Gibeonites answered, "The LORD your God told his servant Moses that you were to kill everyone who lives here and take their land for yourselves. We were afraid you would kill us, and so we tricked you into making a peace treaty. But we agreed to be

your servants, [25] and you are strong enough to do anything to us that you want. We just ask you to do what seems right."

[26] Joshua did not let the Israelites kill the Gibeonites, [27] but he did tell the Gibeonites that they would have to be servants of the nation of Israel. They would have to cut firewood and bring it for the priests to use for burning sacrifices on the LORD's altar, wherever the LORD decided the altar would be. The Gibeonites would also have to carry water for the priests. And that is still the work of the Gibeonites.

Joshua commands the sun to stand still

CHAPTER 10

[1] King Adonizedek of Jerusalem* heard that Joshua had captured and destroyed the town of Ai, and then killed its king as he had done at Jericho. He also learnt that the Gibeonites had signed a peace treaty with Israel. [2] This frightened Adonizedek and his people. They knew that Gibeon was a large town, as big as the towns that had kings, and even bigger than the town of Ai had been. And all the men of Gibeon were warriors. [3] So Adonizedek sent messages to the kings of four other towns: King Hoham of Hebron, King Piram of Jarmuth, King Japhia of Lachish, and King Debir of Eglon. The messages said, [4] "The Gibeonites have signed a peace treaty with Joshua and the Israelites. Come and help me attack Gibeon!"

[5] When these five Amorite kings called their armies together and attacked Gibeon, [6] the Gibeonites sent a message to the Israelite camp at Gilgal: "Joshua, please come and rescue us! The Amorite kings from the hill country have joined together and are attacking us. We are your servants, so don't let us down. Please hurry!"

[7] Joshua and his army, including his best warriors, left Gilgal. [8] "Joshua," the LORD said, "don't be afraid of the Amorites. They will run away when you attack, and I will help you defeat them."

[9] Joshua marched all night from Gilgal to Gibeon and made a surprise attack on the Amorite camp. [10] The LORD made the enemy panic, and the Israelites started killing them right and left. They* chased the Amorite

---

*9.14 tried . . . food: Probably to see if it really was old or to show that they wanted peace.
*9.16,17 Gibeon, Chephirah, Beeroth, and Kiriath-Jearim: These towns were thirty to fifty kilometres west of the Israelite camp at Gilgal.

*10.1 Jerusalem: Jerusalem was not an Israelite city at this time.

troops up the road to Beth-Horon and kept on killing them, until they reached the towns of Azekah and Makkedah.* [11] And while these troops were going down through Beth-Horon Pass,* the LORD made huge hailstones fall on them all the way to Azekah. More of the enemy soldiers died from the hail than from the Israelite weapons.

[12-13] The LORD was helping the Israelites defeat the Amorites that day. So about midday, Joshua prayed to the LORD loud enough for the Israelites to hear:

> "Our LORD, make the sun stop
>   in the sky over Gibeon,
> and the moon stand still
>   over Aijalon Valley."*
> So the sun and the moon
>   stopped and stood still
> until Israel defeated its enemies.

This poem can be found in *The Book of Jashar*.* The sun stood still and didn't go down for about a whole day. [14] Never before and never since has the LORD done anything like that for someone who prayed. The LORD was really fighting for Israel.

[15] After the battle, Joshua and the Israelites went back to their camp at Gilgal.

Israel takes over much of the land of Canaan

Joshua kills the five enemy kings

[16] While the enemy soldiers were running from the Israelites, the five enemy kings ran away and hid in a cave near Makkedah. [17] Joshua's soldiers told him, "The five kings have been found in a cave near Makkedah."

[18] Joshua answered, "Roll some big stones over the mouth of the cave and leave a few soldiers to guard it. [19] But you and everyone else must keep following the enemy troops, because they will be safe if they reach their walled towns. Don't let them get away! The LORD our God is helping us get rid of them."

[20] So Joshua and the Israelites almost wiped

out the enemy soldiers. Only a few safely reached their walled towns.

[21] The Israelite army returned to their camp at Makkedah, where Joshua was waiting for them. No one around there dared say anything bad about the Israelites. [22] Joshua told his soldiers, "Now, move the rocks from the entrance to the cave and bring those five kings to me."

[23] The soldiers opened the entrance to the cave and brought out the kings of Jerusalem, Hebron, Jarmuth, Lachish, and Eglon. [24] After Joshua had called the army together, he forced the five kings to lie down on the ground. Then he called his officers forward and told them, "You fought these kings along with me, so put your feet on their necks." The officers did, [25] and Joshua continued, "Don't ever be afraid or discouraged. Be brave and strong. This is what the LORD will do to all your enemies."

[26] Joshua killed the five kings and told his men to hang each body on a tree. Then at sunset [27] he told some of his troops, "Take the bodies down and throw them into the cave where the kings were found. Cover the entrance to the cave with big rocks."

Joshua's troops obeyed his orders, and those rocks are still there.

Joshua continues the fighting

[28] Later that day, Joshua captured Makkedah and killed its king and everyone else in the town, just as he had done at Jericho.

[29] Joshua and his army left Makkedah and attacked the town of Libnah. [30] The LORD let them capture the town and its king, and they killed the king and everyone else, just as they had done at Jericho.

[31] Joshua then led his army to Lachish, and they set up camp around the town. They attacked, [32] and the next day the LORD let them capture the town. They killed everyone, as they had done at Libnah. [33] King Horam of Gezer arrived to help Lachish, but Joshua and his troops attacked and destroyed him and his army.

[34] From Lachish, Joshua took his troops to Eglon, where they set up camp surrounding the town. They attacked, [35] captured it that same day, then killed everyone, as they had done at Lachish.

[36] Joshua and his army left Eglon and attacked Hebron. [37] They captured the town and the nearby villages, then killed everyone, including the king. They destroyed Hebron in the same way they had destroyed Eglon.

---

*10.10 Makkedah: A total distance of about forty kilometres.
*10.11 Beth-Horon Pass: A three-kilometre long, steeply-sloping valley between the towns of Upper Beth-Horon and Lower Beth-Horon.
*10.12,13 Aijalon Valley: A valley south-west of Beth-Horon Pass.
*10.12,13 Book of Jashar: This book may have been a collection of ancient war songs.
See also: 10.13: 2 Sam 1.18.

³⁸ Joshua and the Israelite army turned and attacked Debir. ³⁹ They captured the town, and its nearby villages. Then they destroyed Debir and killed its king, together with everyone else, just as they had done with Hebron and Libnah.

⁴⁰ Joshua captured towns everywhere in the land: in the central hill country and the foothills to the west, in the Southern Desert and the region that slopes down towards the Dead Sea. Whenever he captured a town, he would kill the king and everyone else, as the LORD God of Israel had commanded.

⁴¹ Joshua wiped out towns from Kadesh-Barnea to Gaza, everywhere in the region of Goshen,* and as far north as Gibeon.

⁴²⁻⁴³ The LORD fought on Israel's side, so Joshua and the Israelite army were able to capture these kings and take their land. They fought one battle after another, then they went back to their camp at Gilgal after capturing all that land.

CHAPTER 11

Joshua captures towns in the north

¹ King Jabin of Hazor heard about Joshua's victories, so he sent messages to many nearby kings and asked them to join him in fighting Israel. He sent these messages to King Jobab of Madon, and the kings of Shimron and Achshaph, ² the kings in the northern hill country and in the valley of the River Jordan south of Lake Galilee,* and the kings in the foothills and in Naphtath-Dor to the west.

³ He sent messages to the Canaanite kings in the east and the west, to the Amorite, Hittite, Perizzite, and Jebusite kings in the hill country, and to the Hivite kings in the region of Mizpah, near the foot of Mount Hermon.*

⁴⁻⁵ The kings and their armies went to Merom Pond,* where they set up camp, and got ready to fight Israel. It seemed as though there were more soldiers and horses and chariots than there are grains of sand on a beach.

⁶ The LORD told Joshua:

Don't let them frighten you! I'll help you defeat them, and by this time tomorrow they will be dead.

When you attack, the first thing you have to do is to cripple their horses. Then after the battle is over,* burn their chariots.

⁷ Joshua and his army made a surprise attack against the enemy camp at Merom Pond. ⁸⁻⁹ and crippled the enemies' horses.* Joshua followed the LORD's instructions, and the LORD helped Israel defeat the enemy. The Israelite army then chased enemy soldiers as far as Misrephoth-Maim to the north-west,* the city of Sidon to the north, and Mizpeh Valley to the north-east.* None of the enemy soldiers escaped alive. The Israelites came back after the battle and burnt the enemy's chariots.

¹⁰ Up to this time, the king of Hazor had controlled the kingdoms that had joined together to attack Israel, so Joshua led his army back and captured Hazor. They killed its king ¹¹ and everyone else, then they set the town on fire.

¹²⁻¹⁵ Joshua captured all the towns where the enemy kings had ruled. These towns were built on small hills,* and Joshua did not set fire to any of these towns, except Hazor. The Israelites kept the animals and everything of value from these towns, but they killed everyone who lived in them, including their kings. That's what the LORD had told his servant Moses to do, that's what Moses had told Joshua to do, and that's exactly what Joshua did.

¹⁶ Joshua and his army took control of the northern and southern hill country, the foothills to the west, the Southern Desert, the whole region of Goshen,* and the Jordan valley. ¹⁷⁻¹⁸ They took control of the land from Mount Halak near the country of Edom in the south to Baal-Gad in Lebanon Valley at the foot of Mount Hermon in the north. Joshua and his army were at war with the kings in this region for a long time, but finally they captured and put to death the last king.

¹⁹⁻²⁰ The LORD had told Moses that he wanted the towns in this region destroyed and their people killed without mercy. That's

---

*10.41 Goshen: A region between the hill country of Judah and the desert further south. Not the same Goshen as in Genesis 47.4–6.
*11.3 Mizpah, near the foot of Mount Hermon: Probably the same region as Mizpeh Valley in verses 8,9, but different from the two other places named Mizpeh in 15.37–41; 18.25–28, and also different from the Mizpah mentioned in Genesis 31.49 and Judges 10.17.

*11.8,9 north-east: These three areas were thirty to fifty-five kilometres north of Merom.
*11.12–15 small hills: Towns were often built on top of the ruins of a previous town that had been destroyed. When this happened many times at one place, a hill was formed.
*11.16 Goshen: See the note at 10.41.
See also: 11.20: Deut 7.16.

why the LORD made the people in the towns stubborn and determined to fight Israel. The only town that signed a peace treaty with Israel was the Hivite town of Gibeon. The Israelite army captured the rest of the towns in battle.

²¹ During this same time, Joshua and his army killed the Anakim* from the northern and southern hill country. They also destroyed the towns where the Anakim had lived, including Hebron, Debir, and Anab. ²² There were not any Anakim left in the regions where the Israelites lived, although there were still some in Gaza, Gath, and Ashdod.*

²³ That's how Joshua captured the land, just as the LORD had commanded Moses, and Joshua divided it up among the tribes.

Finally, there was peace in the land.

CHAPTER 12

The kings defeated by the Israelites

¹ Before Moses died, he and the people of Israel had defeated two kings east of the River Jordan. These kings had ruled the region from the gorge of the River Arnon in the south to Mount Hermon in the north, including the eastern side of the Jordan valley.

² The first king whom Moses and the Israelites defeated was an Amorite, King Sihon of Heshbon.* The southern border of his kingdom ran down the middle of the Arnon gorge, taking in the town of Aroer on the northern edge of the gorge. The River Jabbok separated Sihon's kingdom from the Ammonites on the east. Then the Jabbok turned north and became his northern border, so his kingdom included the southern half of the region of Gilead. ³ Sihon also controlled the eastern side of the Jordan valley from Lake Galilee⁰ south to Beth-Jeshimoth and the Dead Sea. In addition to these regions, he ruled the town called Slopes of Mount Pisgah⁰ and the land south of there at the foot of the hill.

⁴ Next, Moses and the Israelites defeated King Og of Bashan,* who lived in the town of

Ashtaroth part of each year and in Edrei the rest of the year. Og was one of the last of the Rephaim.* ⁵ His kingdom stretched north to Mount Hermon, east to the town of Salecah, and included the land of Bashan as far west as the borders of the kingdoms of Geshur and Maacah. He also ruled the northern half of Gilead.

⁶ Moses, the LORD's servant, had led the people of Israel in defeating Sihon and Og. Then Moses gave their land to the tribes of Reuben, Gad, and East Manasseh.

⁷⁻⁸ Later, Joshua and the Israelites defeated many kings west of the River Jordan, from Baal-Gad in Lebanon Valley in the north to Mount Halak near the country of Edom in the south. This region included the hill country and the foothills, the Jordan valley and its western slopes, and the Southern Desert. Joshua and the Israelites took this land from the Hittites, the Amorites, the Canaanites, the Perizzites, the Hivites, and the Jebusites. Joshua divided up the land among the tribes of Israel.

The Israelites defeated the kings of the following towns west of the River Jordan:

⁹⁻²⁴ Jericho, Ai near Bethel, Jerusalem, Hebron, Jarmuth, Lachish, Eglon, Gezer, Debir, Geder, Hormah, Arad, Libnah, Adullam, Makkedah, Bethel, Tappuah, Hepher, Aphek, Lasharon,⁰ Madon, Hazor, Shimron-Meron, Achshaph, Taanach, Megiddo, Kedesh, Jokneam on Mount Carmel, Dor in Naphath-Dor, Goiim in Galilee,⁰ and Tirzah.⁰

There were thirty-one of these kings in all.

Land that Israel did not take over

CHAPTER 13

¹ Many years later, the LORD told Joshua:

Now you are very old, but there is still a lot of land that Israel has not yet taken. ²⁻⁷ First, there is the Canaanite territory that starts at the River Shihor just east of Egypt and goes north to Ekron. The southern part of this region belongs to the

---

*11.21 Anakim: Perhaps a group of people of great stature that lived in Palestine before the Israelites (see Numbers 13.33 and Deuteronomy 2.10,11,20,21).
*11.22 Gaza, Gath, and Ashdod: Towns in Philistia.
*12.2 King Sihon of Heshbon: See Numbers 21.21–31.
*12.4 King Og of Bashan: See Numbers 21.33–35.
See also: 12.1–5: Num 21.21–35; Deut 2.26–3.11.

*12.4 Rephaim: Perhaps a group of people of great stature that lived in Palestine before the Israelites (see Deuteronomy 2.10,11,20,21).
See also: 12.6: Num 32.33; Deut 3.12.   13.6: Num 33.54.

Avvites and the Geshurites,* and the land around Gaza, Ashdod, Ashkelon, Gath, and Ekron belongs to the five Philistine rulers.

The other Canaanite territory is in the north. Its northern border starts at the town of Arah, which belongs to the Sidonians. From there, it goes to Aphek,* then along the Amorite border* to Hamath Pass.* The eastern border starts at Hamath Pass and goes south to Baal-Gad at the foot of Mount Hermon, and its southern boundary runs west from there to Misrephoth-Maim.* This northern region includes the Lebanon Mountains and the land that belongs to the Gebalites* and the Sidonians who live in the hill country from the Lebanon Mountains to Misrephoth-Maim.

With my help, Israel will capture these Canaanite territories and force out the people who live there. But you must divide up the land from the River Jordan to the Mediterranean Sea* among the nine tribes and the half of Manasseh that don't have any land yet. Then each tribe will have its own land.

Tribal lands that Moses had assigned east of the Jordan

8 Moses had already given land east of the River Jordan to the tribes of Reuben, Gad, and half of Manasseh. 9 This region stretched north from the town in the middle of the valley of the River Arnon, and included the town of Aroer on the northern edge of the valley. It covered the flat lands of Medeba north of Dibon, 10 and took in the towns that had belonged to Sihon, the Amorite king of Heshbon. Some of these towns were as far east as the Ammonite border.

11-12 Geshur and Maacah were part of this region, and so was the whole territory that King Og had ruled, that is, Gilead, Mount Hermon, and all of Bashan as far east as Salecah. Og had lived in Ashtaroth and Edrei part of each year, and he had lived in Edrei the rest of the year. Og had been one of the last of the Rephaim,* but Moses had defeated Sihon

and Og and their people* and had forced them to leave their land. 13 However, the Israelites did not force the people of Geshur and Maacah to leave, and they still live there among the Israelites.

Moses did not give land to the Levi tribe

14 Moses did not give any land to the Levi tribe, because the LORD God of Israel had told them, "Instead of land, you will receive the sacrifices offered at my altar."

Moses gave land to the Reuben tribe

15 Moses gave land to each of the clans in the Reuben tribe. 16 Their land started in the south at the town in the middle of the valley of the River Arnon, took in the town of Aroer on the northern edge of the valley, and went as far north as the flat lands around Medeba. 17-21 The Amorite King Sihon had lived in Heshbon and had ruled the towns in the flat lands. Now Heshbon belonged to Reuben, and so did the following towns in the flat lands: Dibon, Bamoth-Baal, Beth-Baal-Meon, Jahaz, Kedemoth, Mephaath, Kiriathaim, Sibmah, Zereth-Shahar on the hill in the valley, Beth-Peor, Slopes of Mount Pisgah, and Beth-Jeshimoth.

Moses defeated Sihon and killed him and the Midianite chiefs who ruled parts of his kingdom for him. Their names were Evi, Rekem, Zur, Hur, and Reba. 22 The Israelites also killed Balaam the son of Beor, who had been a fortune-teller.

23 This region with its towns and villages was the land for the Reuben tribe, and the River Jordan was its western border.

Moses gave land to the Gad tribe

24 Moses also gave land to each of the clans in the Gad tribe. 25 It included the town of Jazer, and in the Gilead region their territory took in the land and towns as far east as the town of Aroer* just west of Rabbah.* This was about half of the land that had once belonged to the Ammonites. 26 The land given to Gad stretched from Heshbon in the south to Ramath-Mizpeh and Betonim in the north, and even further north to Mahanaim and Lidebor.* 27 Gad also received the eastern

---

*13.2-7 Geshurites: Not the same Geshur as in 12.5 and 13.11. One ancient translation has "Gezerites". Gezer was a town north of Ekron that the Israelites did not capture (see Judges 1.29).
*13.2-7 Aphek: Not the same Aphek as in 12.9–24.
*13.11,12 Rephaim: See the note at 12.4.
See also: 13.8: Num 32.33; Deut 3.12.

*13.25 Aroer: Not the same town as the Aroer in verse 16.
*13.25 Rabbah: The capital city of Ammon.
See also: 13.14: Deut 18.1.

half of the Jordan valley, which had been ruled by King Sihon of Heshbon. This territory stretched as far north as Lake Galilee,* and included the towns of Beth-Haram, Beth-Nimrah, Succoth, and Zaphon. 28 These regions with their towns and villages were given to the Gad tribe.

Moses gave land to half of the Manasseh tribe

29 Moses gave land east of the River Jordan to half of the clans from the Manasseh tribe.
30-31 Their land started at Mahanaim and took in the region that King Og of Bashan had ruled, including Ashtaroth and Edrei, the two towns where he had lived. The villages where the Jair clan settled were part of Manasseh's land, and so was the northern half of the region of Gilead. The clans of this half of Manasseh had sixty towns in all.

The Manasseh tribe is sometimes called the Machir tribe, after Manasseh's son Machir.

32 That was how Moses divided up the Moab Plains to the east of Jericho on the other side of the River Jordan, so these two and a half tribes would have land of their own. 33 But Moses did not give any land to the Levi tribe, because the LORD had promised that he would always provide for them.

Tribal lands west of the Jordan

CHAPTER 14

1-5 Nine and a half tribes still did not have any land, although two and a half tribes had already received land east of the River Jordan. Moses had divided that land among them, and he had also said that the Levi tribe would not receive a large region like the other tribes. Instead, the people of Levi would receive towns and the nearby pastures for their sheep, goats, and cattle. And since the descendants of Joseph had become the two tribes of Ephraim and Manasseh, there were still nine and a half tribes that needed land. The LORD had told Moses that he would show those tribes* how to divide up the land of Canaan.

When the priest Eleazar, Joshua, and the leaders of the families and tribes of Israel met to divide up the land of Canaan, the LORD showed them how to do it.

Joshua gives Hebron to Caleb

6 One day while the Israelites were still camped at Gilgal, Caleb the son of Jephunneh went to talk with Joshua. Caleb belonged to the Kenaz clan, and many other people from the Judah tribe went with Caleb. He told Joshua:

You know that back in Kadesh-Barnea the LORD talked to his prophet Moses about you and me. 7 I was forty years old at the time Moses sent me from Kadesh-Barnea into Canaan as a spy. When I came back and told him about the land, everything I said was true. 8 The other spies said things that made our people afraid, but I completely trusted the LORD God. 9 The same day I came back, Moses told me, "Since you were faithful to the LORD God, I promise that the places where you went as a spy will belong to you and your descendants for ever."

10 Joshua, it was forty-five years ago that the LORD told Moses to make that promise, and now I am eighty-five. Even though Israel has moved from place to place in the desert, the LORD has kept me alive all this time as he said he would. 11 I'm just as strong today as I was then, and I can still fight as well in battle.

12 So I'm asking you for the hill country that the LORD promised me that day. You were there. You heard the other spies talk about that part of the hill country and the large, walled towns where the Anakim* live. But perhaps the LORD will help me take their land, just as he promised.

13 Joshua prayed that God would help Caleb, then he gave Hebron to Caleb and his descendants. 14 And Hebron still belongs to Caleb's descendants, because he was faithful to the LORD God of Israel.

15 Hebron used to be called Arba's Town,* because Arba had been one of the greatest* of the Anakim.

There was peace in the land.

---

*14.1-5 he would show those tribes: The Hebrew text has "those tribes must cast lots to find out". Pieces of wood or stone (called "lots") were used to find out what God wanted his people to do.

See also: 13.33: Num 18.20; Deut 18.2.
14.2: Num 26.52-56; 34.13. 14.3.4: Num 32.33; 34.14,15; Deut 3.12-17.

*14.12 Anakim: See the note at 11.21.
See also: 14.6: Num 14.30. 14.7: Num 13.1-30.
14.9: Num 14.24.

CHAPTER 15

Judah's land

¹ The clans of the Judah tribe were given land that went south along the border of Edom, and at its furthest point south it even reached the Zin Desert. ² Judah's southern border started at the south end of the Dead Sea. ³ As it went west from there, it ran south of Scorpion Pass* to Zin, and then came up from the south to Kadesh-Barnea. It continued past Hezron up to Addar, turned towards Karka, ⁴ and ran along to Azmon. After that, it followed the Egyptian Gorge and ended at the Mediterranean Sea. This was also Israel's southern border.

⁵ Judah's eastern border ran the full length of the Dead Sea.

The northern border started at the northern end of the Dead Sea. ⁶ From there it went up to Beth-Hoglah, continued north of Beth-Arabah, and went up to the Monument of Bohan,* who belonged to the Reuben tribe. ⁷ From there, it went to Trouble Valley* and Debir,* then turned north and went to Gilgal,* which is on the north side of the valley across from Adummim Pass. It continued on to Enshemesh, Enrogel, ⁸ and up through Hinnom Valley on the land sloping south from Jerusalem. The city of Jerusalem itself belonged to the Jebusites.

Next, the border went up to the top of the mountain on the west side of Hinnom Valley and at the north end of Rephaim Valley. ⁹ At the top of the mountain it turned and went to Nephtoah Spring and then to the ruins* on Mount Ephron. From there, it went to Baalah, which is now called Kiriath-Jearim.

¹⁰ From Baalah the northern border curved west to Mount Seir and then ran along the northern ridge of Mount Jearim, where Chesalon is. Then it went down to Beth-Shemesh* and over to Timnah.

¹¹ It continued along the hillside north of Ekron, curved around to Shikkeron, and then went to Mount Baalah. After going to Jabneel, the border finally ended at the Mediterranean Sea, ¹² which was Judah's western border.

The clans of Judah lived within these borders.

Caleb's land

This is also told in Judges 1.12–15

¹³ Joshua gave Caleb some land among the people of Judah, as God had told him to do. Caleb's share was Hebron, which at that time was known as Arba's Town,* because Arba was the famous ancestor of the Anakim.*

¹⁴ Caleb attacked Hebron and forced the three Anakim clans of* Sheshai, Ahiman, and Talmai to leave. ¹⁵ Next, Caleb started a war with the town of Debir, which at that time was called Kiriath-Sepher. ¹⁶ He told his men, "The man who captures Kiriath-Sepher can marry my daughter Achsah."

¹⁷ Caleb's nephew Othniel* captured Kiriath-Sepher, and Caleb let him marry Achsah. ¹⁸ Straight after the wedding, Achsah started telling Othniel that he* ought to ask her father for a field. She went to see her father, and while she was getting down from* her donkey, Caleb asked her, "What's bothering you?"

¹⁹ She answered, "I need your help. The land you gave me is in the Southern Desert, so I really need some spring-fed ponds* for a water supply."

Caleb gave her a couple of small ponds, named Higher Pond and Lower Pond.*

Towns in Judah's land

²⁰ The following is a list of the towns in each region given to the Judah clans:

²¹⁻³² The first region was in the Southern Desert along the border with Edom, and it had the following twenty-nine towns with their surrounding villages:

Kabzeel, Eder, Jagur, Kinah, Dimonah, Aradah,* Kedesh, Hazor of Ithnan,* Ziph, Telem, Bealoth, Hazor-Hadattah, Kerioth-Hezron, which is also called Hazor, Amam, Shema, Moladah, Hazar-Gaddah, Heshmon, Beth-Pelet, Hazar-Shual, Beersheba and its surrounding villages,* Baalah, Iim, Ezem, Eltolad, Chesil, Hormah, Ziklag, Madmannah, Sansannah, Lebaoth, Shilhim, and Enrimmon.*

³³⁻³⁶ The second region was in the northern part of the lower foothills, and it had the following fourteen towns with their surrounding villages:

Eshtaol, Zorah, Ashnah, Zanoah, En-Gannim, Tappuah, Enam, Jarmuth,

---

*15.7 Debir: Not the same town as in 10.38,39.
*15.7 Gilgal: Not the same Gilgal as in 4.19.

*15.13 Anakim: See the note at 11.21.
See also: 15.13,14: Judg 1.20.

Adullam, Socoh, Azekah, Shaaraim, Adithaim, Gederah, and Gederothaim.

37-41 The third region was in the southern part of the lower foothills, and it had the following sixteen towns with their surrounding villages:

Zenan, Hadashah, Migdalgad, Dilan, Mizpeh, Joktheel, Lachish, Bozkath, Eglon, Cabbon, Lahmas,* Chitlish, Gederoth, Beth-Dagon, Naamah, and Makkedah.

42-44 The fourth region was in the central part of the lower foothills, and it had the following nine towns with their surrounding villages:

Libnah, Ether, Ashan, Iphtah, Ashnah, Nezib, Keilah, Achzib, and Mareshah.

45-47 The fifth region was along the Mediterranean coast, and it had the following towns with their surrounding settlements and villages:

Ekron and the towns between there and the coast, Ashdod and the larger towns nearby, Gaza, the towns from Gaza to the Egyptian Gorge, and the towns along the coast of the Mediterranean Sea.

48-51 The sixth region was in the south-western part of the hill country, and it had the following eleven towns with their surrounding villages:

Shamir, Jattir, Socoh, Dannah, Kiriath-Sannah, which is now called Debir, Anab, Eshtemoh,* Anim, Goshen, Holon, and Giloh.

52-54 The seventh region was in the south-central part of Judah's hill country, and it had the following nine towns with their surrounding villages:

Arab, Dumah,* Eshan, Janim, Beth-Tappuah, Aphekah, Humtah, Kiriath-Arba, which is now called Hebron, and Zior.

55-57 The eighth region was in the south-eastern part of the hill country, and it had the following ten towns with their surrounding villages:

Maon, Carmel, Ziph, Juttah, Jezreel,* Jokdeam,* Zanoah, Kain, Gibeah,* and Timnah.

58-59 The ninth region was in the central part of Judah's hill country, and it had the following six towns with their surrounding villages:

Halhul, Beth-Zur, Gedor, Maarath, Beth-Anoth, and Eltekon.

The tenth region was in the north-central part of Judah's hill country, and it had the following eleven towns with their surrounding villages:

Tekoa, Ephrath, which is also called Bethlehem, Peor, Etam, Culon, Tatam, Shoresh, Kerem, Gallim, Bether, and Manahath.*

60 The eleventh region was in the northern part of Judah's hill country, and it had the following two towns with their surrounding villages:

Rabbah, and Kiriath-Baal, which is also called Kiriath-Jearim.

61-62 The twelfth region was in the desert along the Dead Sea, and it had the following six towns with their surrounding villages:

Beth-Arabah, Middin, Secacah, Nibshan, Salt Town, and En-Gedi.

The Jebusites

63 The Jebusites lived in Jerusalem, and the people of the Judah tribe could not capture the city and get rid of them. That's why Jebusites still live in Jerusalem along with the people of Judah.*

CHAPTER 16

Ephraim's land

1-4 Ephraim and Manasseh are the two tribes descended from Joseph, and the following is a description of the land they received. The southern border of their land started at the River Jordan east of the spring at Jericho. From there it went west through the desert up to the hill country around Bethel. From Bethel it went to Luz and then* to the border of the Archites in Ataroth.* It continued west down to the land that belonged to the Japhlet

---

*15.55–57 Jezreel: Not the same Jezreel as in 19.17–23.
*15.55–57 Gibeah: Not the same Gibeah as in 18.25–28.

*15.63 Jebusites . . . Judah: Israel captured Jerusalem in King David's time, but even then the Jebusites were not forced to leave.
*16.1–4 Ataroth: This is the same Ataroth as Ataroth-Addar in verse 5, but a different Ataroth from the one in verses 6–8.
See also: 15.63: Judg 1.21; 2 Sam 5.6; 1 Chron 11.4.

clan, then went on to Lower Beth-Horon, Gezer, and the Mediterranean Sea.

⁵ The following is a description of the land that was divided among the clans of the Ephraim tribe. Their southern border started at Ataroth-Addar and went west to Upper Beth-Horon ⁶⁻⁸ and the Mediterranean Sea. Their northern border started on the east at Janoah, curved a little to the north, then came back south to Michmethath and Tappuah, where it followed the Kanah Gorge west to the Mediterranean Sea.

The eastern border started on the north near Janoah and went between Janoah on the south-west and Taanath-Shiloh on the north-east. Then it went south to Ataroth, Naarah, and on as far as the edge of the land that belonged to Jericho. At that point it turned east and went to the River Jordan. The clans of Ephraim received this region as their tribal land. ⁹ Ephraim also had some towns and villages that were inside Manasseh's tribal land.

¹⁰ Ephraim could not force the Canaanites out of Gezer, so there are still some Canaanites who live there among the Israelites. But now these Canaanites have to work as slaves for the Israelites.

CHAPTER 17

Manasseh's land west of the River Jordan

¹⁻⁶ Manasseh was Joseph's eldest son, and Machir was Manasseh's eldest son. Machir had a son named Gilead, and some of his descendants had already received the regions of Gilead and Bashan because they were good warriors. The other clans of the Manasseh tribe descended from Gilead's sons Abiezer, Helek, Asriel, Shechem, Hepher, and Shemida. The following is a description of the land they received.

Hepher's son Zelophehad did not have any sons, but he did have five daughters: Mahlah, Noah, Hoglah, Milcah, and Tirzah. One day the clans that were descendants of Zelophehad's five daughters went to the priest Eleazar, Joshua, and the leaders of Israel. The people of these clans said, "The LORD told Moses to give us land just as he gave land to our relatives."⁎

Joshua followed the LORD's instructions and gave land to these five clans, as he had given

land to the five clans that had descended from Hepher's brothers.⁎ So Manasseh's land west of the River Jordan was divided into ten parts.

⁷ The land of the Manasseh tribe went from its northern border with the Asher tribe south to Michmethath, which is to the east of Shechem. The southern border started there, but curved even further south to include the people who lived around Tappuah Spring.⁎ ⁸ The town of Tappuah was on Manasseh's border with Ephraim. Although the land around Tappuah belonged to Manasseh, the town itself belonged to Ephraim.

⁹⁻¹⁰ Then the border went west to the Kanah Gorge and ran along the northern edge of the gorge to the Mediterranean Sea. The land south of the gorge belonged to Ephraim. And even though there were a few towns that belonged to Ephraim north of the gorge, the land north of the gorge belonged to Manasseh.

The western border of Manasseh was the Mediterranean Sea, and the tribe shared a border with the Asher tribe on the north-west and with the Issachar tribe on the north-east.

¹¹ Manasseh was supposed to have the following towns with their surrounding villages inside the borders of Issachar's and Asher's tribal lands:

Beth-Shan, Ibleam, Endor, Taanach, Megiddo, and Dor, which is also called Naphath.⁎

¹² But the people of Manasseh could not capture these towns, so the Canaanites kept on living in them. ¹³ When the Israelites grew stronger, they made the Canaanites in these towns work as their slaves, though they never did force them to leave.

Joseph's descendants ask for more land

¹⁴ One day the Joseph tribes⁎ came to Joshua and asked, "Why didn't you give us more land? The LORD has always been kind to us, and we have too many people for this small region."

¹⁵ Joshua replied, "If you have so many people that you don't have enough room in the hill country of Ephraim, then go into the forest that belonged to the Perizzites and the Rephaim.⁎ Clear out the trees and make more room for yourselves there."

⁎**17.1-6 The LORD told Moses . . . relatives:** See Numbers 27.1-11; 36.1-12.
See also: 16.10: Judg 1.29. **17.4:** Num 27.1-7.

⁎**17.14 Joseph tribes:** Ephraim and the half of Manasseh that lived west of the River Jordan.
⁎**17.15 Rephaim:** See the note at 12.4.
See also: 17.12,13: Judg 1.27,28.

16 "Even if we do that," they answered, "there still won't be enough land for us in the hill country. And we can't move down into Jezreel Valley, because the Canaanites who live in Beth-Shan and in other parts of the valley have iron chariots."

17 "Your tribes do have a lot of people," Joshua admitted. "I'll give you more land. Your tribes are powerful, 18 so you can have the rest of the hill country, but it's a forest, and you'll have to cut down the trees and clear the land. You can also have Jezreel Valley. Even though the Canaanites there are strong and have iron chariots, you can force them to leave the valley."

CHAPTER 18

Joshua gives out the rest of the land

1 After Israel had captured the land, they met at Shiloh and set up the sacred tent.* 2 There were still seven tribes without any land, 3-7 so Joshua told the people:

The Judah tribe has already settled in its land in the south, and the Joseph tribes* have settled in their land in the north. The tribes of Gad, Reuben, and East Manasseh already have the land that the LORD's servant Moses gave them east of the River Jordan. And the people of Levi won't get a single large region of the land like the other tribes. Instead, they will serve the LORD as priests.

But the rest of you haven't done a thing to take over any land. The LORD God who was worshipped by your ancestors has given you the land, and now it's time to go ahead and settle there.

Seven tribes still don't have any land. Each of these tribes should choose three men, and I'll send them to explore the remaining land. They will divide it into seven regions, write a description of each region, and bring these descriptions back to me. I will find out* from the LORD our God what region each tribe should get.

8 Just before the men left camp, Joshua repeated their orders: "Explore the land and write a description of it. Then come back to Shiloh, and I will find out from the LORD how to divide the land."

9 The men left and went across the land, dividing it into seven regions. They wrote

down a description of each region, town by town, and returned to Joshua at the camp at Shiloh. 10 Joshua found out from the LORD how to divide the land, and he told the tribes what the LORD had decided.

Benjamin's land

11 Benjamin was the first tribe chosen to receive land. The region for its clans lay between the Judah tribe on the south and the Joseph tribes* on the north. 12 Benjamin's northern border started at the River Jordan and went up the ridge north of Jericho, then on west into the hill country as far as the Beth-Aven Desert. 13-14 From there it went to Luz, which is now called Bethel. The border ran along the ridge south of Luz, then went to Ataroth-Orech* and on as far as the mountain south of Lower Beth-Horon. At that point it turned south and became the western border. It went as far as south as Kiriath-Baal, a town in Judah now called Kiriath-Jearim.

15 Benjamin's southern border started at the edge of Kiriath-Jearim and went east to the ruins* and on to Nephtoah Spring. 16 From there it went to the bottom of the hill at the northern end of Rephaim Valley. The other side of this hill faces Hinnom Valley, which is on the land that slopes south from Jerusalem.* The border went down through Hinnom Valley until it reached Enrogel. 17 At Enrogel the border curved north and went to Enshemesh and on east to Geliloth,* which is across the valley from Adummim Pass. Then it went down to the Monument of Bohan,* who belonged to the Reuben tribe. 18 The border ran along the hillside north of Beth-Arabah,* then down into the Jordan Valley. 19 Inside the valley it went south as far as the northern hillside of Beth-Hoglah. The last section of the border went from there to the northern end of the Dead Sea,* at the mouth of the River Jordan. 20 The River Jordan itself was Benjamin's eastern border.

These were the borders of Benjamin's tribal land, where the clans of Benjamin lived.

21-24 One region of Benjamin's tribal land had twelve towns with their surrounding villages. Those towns were Jericho, Beth-Hoglah, Emek-Keziz, Beth-Arabah, Zemaraim, Bethel, Avvim, Parah, Ophrah, Chephar-Ammoni, Ophni, and Geba.

25-28 In the other region there were the following fourteen towns with their

---

*18.3-7 Joseph tribes: See the note at 17.14.
*18.3-7 find out: Hebrew "cast lots to find out" (see the note at 14.1–5).

*18.11 Joseph tribes: See the note at 17.14.

surrounding villages: Gibeon, Ramah,
Beeroth, Mizpeh, Chephirah, Mozah, Rekem,
Irpeel, Taralah, Zelah, Haeleph, Gibeah,
Kiriath-Jearim,* and Jerusalem, which is also
called Jebusite Town.

These regions are the tribal lands of
Benjamin.

CHAPTER 19

Simeon's land

¹ Simeon was the second tribe chosen to
receive land, and the region for its clans was
inside Judah's borders. ²⁻⁶ In one region of
Simeon's tribal land there were the following
thirteen towns with their surrounding
villages:

Beersheba, Shema,* Moladah, Hazar-Shual,
Balah, Ezem, Eltolad, Bethul, Hormah,
Ziklag, Beth-Marcaboth, Hazar-Susah,
Beth-Lebaoth, and Sharuhen.

⁷ In another region, Simeon had the
following four towns with their surrounding
villages:

Enrimmon,* Tachan,* Ether, and Ashan.

⁸ Simeon's land also included all the other
towns and villages as far south as
Baalath-Beer, which is also called Ramah of
the South.

⁹ Simeon's tribal land was actually inside
Judah's territory. Judah had received too
much land for the number of people in its
tribe, so part of Judah's land was given to
Simeon.

Zebulun's land

¹⁰⁻¹² Zebulun was the third tribe chosen to
receive land. The southern border for its
clans started in the west at the edge of
the gorge near Jokneam. It went east to the edge
of the land that belongs to the town of
Dabbesheth, and continued on to Maralah
and Sarid. It took in the land that belongs to
Chislothtabor, then ended at Daberath.

The eastern border went up to Japhia ¹³ and
continued north to Gath-Hepher, Ethkazin,
and Rimmonah,* where it curved* towards
Neah ¹⁴ and became the northern border.
Then it curved south around Hannathon and
went as far west as Iphtahel Valley.

¹⁵ Zebulun had twelve towns with their
surrounding villages. Some of these were

Kattath, Nahalal, Shimron, Jiralah,* and
Bethlehem.*

¹⁶ This is the tribal land, and these are the
towns and villages of the Zebulun clans.

Issachar's land

¹⁷⁻²³ Issachar was the fourth tribe chosen to
receive land. The northern border for its
clans went from Mount Tabor east to the
River Jordan. Their land included the
following sixteen towns with their
surrounding villages:

Jezreel, Chesulloth, Shunem, Hapharaim,
Shion, Anaharath, Debirath,* Kishion,
Ebez, Remeth, En-Gannim, Enhaddah,
Beth-Pazzez, Tabor,* Shahazumah and
Beth-Shemesh.*

Asher's land

²⁴⁻²⁶ Asher was the fifth tribe chosen to
receive land, and the region for its clans
included the following towns:

Helkath, Hali, Beten, Achshaph,
Allammelech, Amad, and Mishal.

Asher's southern border ran from the
Mediterranean Sea south-east along the River
Shihor-Libnath at the foot of Mount Carmel,
²⁷ then east to Beth-Dagon. On the
south-east, Asher shared a border with
Zebulun along the Iphtahel Valley. On the
eastern side their border ran north to
Beth-Emek, went east of Cabul, and then on
to Neiel, ²⁸ Abdon,* Rehob, Hammon, Kanah,
and as far north as the city of Sidon.
²⁹⁻³¹ Then it turned west to become the
northern border and went to Ramah* and the
fortress-city of Tyre.* Near Tyre it turned
towards Hosah and ended at the
Mediterranean Sea.

Asher had a total of twenty-two towns with
their surrounding villages, including
Mahalab,* Achzib, Acco,* Aphek, and Rehob.

Naphtali's land

¹²⁻³⁴ Naphtali was the sixth tribe chosen to
receive land. The southern border for its

---

*19.15 Bethlehem: This town is different from the
Bethlehem in 15.58,59.
*19.17–23 Beth-Shemesh: Not the same
Beth-Shemesh as in 15.10 or 19.35–39.
*19.29–31 Ramah: Not the same Ramah as in
18.25–28 or 19.35–39.
*19.29–31 fortress-city of Tyre: Tyre was a walled
city built on an island about a kilometre from shore.

See also: 19.2–8: 1 Chron 4.28–33.

clans started in the west, where the tribal lands of Asher and Zebulun meet near Hukkok. From that point it ran east and south-east along the border with Zebulun as far as Aznoth-Tabor. From there the border went east to Heleph, Adami-Nekeb, Jabneel,* then to the town called Oak in Zaanannim,* and Lakkum. The southern border ended at the River Jordan, at the edge of the town named Jehudah.* Naphtali shared a border with Asher on the west.

35-39 The Naphtali clans received this region as their tribal land, and it included nineteen towns with their surrounding villages. The following towns had walls around them:

Ziddim, Zer, Hammath, Rakkath, Chinnereth, Adamah, Ramah,* Hazor, Kedesh, Edrei,* Enhazor, Iron, Migdalel, Horem, Beth-Anath, and Beth-Shemesh.*

Dan's land

40-46 Dan was the seventh tribe chosen to receive land, and the region for its clans included the following towns:

Zorah, Eshtaol, Ir-Shemesh,* Shaalabbin, Aijalon, Ithlah, Elon, Timnah, Ekron, Eltekeh, Gibbethon, Baalath, Jehud, Azor,* Beneberak, Gath-Rimmon, Mejarkon, and Rakkon.

Dan's tribal land* went almost as far as Joppa. 47-48 Its clans received this land and these towns with their surrounding villages.

Later, when enemies* forced them to leave their tribal land, they went to the town of Leshem. They attacked the town, captured it, and killed the people who lived there. Then they settled there themselves and renamed the town Dan after their ancestor.

Joshua's land

49-51 The Israelites were still gathered in Shiloh in front of the sacred tent,* when Eleazar the priest, Joshua, and the family leaders of Israel finished giving out the land to the tribes. The LORD had told the people to give Joshua whatever town he wanted. So Joshua chose Timnath-Serah in the hill country of Ephraim, and the people gave it to him. Joshua went to Timnath-Serah, rebuilt it, and lived there.

Towns for protecting people accused of murder

CHAPTER 20

The Safe Towns
This is also told in Numbers 35.9-15; Deuteronomy 19.1-13

1 One day the LORD told Joshua:

2 When Moses was still alive, I told him to tell the Israelites about the Safe Towns. Now you tell them that it is time to set up these towns. 3-4 If a person accidentally kills someone and the victim's relatives say it was murder, they might try to take revenge.* Anyone accused of murder can run to one of the Safe Towns and be safe from the victim's relatives. The one needing protection will stand at the entrance to the town gate and explain to the town leaders what happened. Then the leaders will bring that person in and provide a place to live in their town.

5 One of the victim's relatives might come to the town, looking for revenge. But the town leaders must not simply hand over the person accused of murder. After all, the accused and the victim had been neighbours, not enemies. 6 The citizens of that Safe Town must come together and hold a trial. They may decide that the victim was killed accidentally and that the accused is not guilty of murder.

Everyone found not guilty* must still live in the Safe Town until the high priest dies. Then they can go back to their own towns and their homes that they had to leave behind.

*19.32-34 Jabneel: This town is not the same Jabneel as in 15.11.
*19.35-39 Ramah: See the note at 19.29-31.
*19.35-39 Edrei: Not the same Edrei as the town in Bashan east of the River Jordan where King Og had lived (see 12.4; 13.11,12,30,31).
*19.35-39 Beth-Shemesh: Not the same Beth-Shemesh as in 15.10 or 19.17-23.
*19.40-46 Ir-Shemesh: Possibly the same town as the Beth-Shemesh of 15.10.
*19.47,48 enemies: Probably the Philistines.
See also: 19.47: Judg 18.27-29.

*20.3,4 revenge: At this time in Israel's history, the clan could appoint a close male relative to find and kill a person who had killed a member of their clan.
*20.6 not guilty: If the person was found to be guilty of murder, the citizens of the Safe Town were to let the victim's relatives kill the murderer (see Deuteronomy 19.11-13).
See also: 20.1-9: Num 35.9-34; Deut 4.41-43; 19.1-13.

7 The Israelites decided that the following three towns west of the River Jordan would be Safe Towns:

> Kedesh in Galilee in Naphtali's hill country, Shechem in Ephraim's hill country, and Kiriath-Arba in Judah's hill country. Kiriath-Arba is now called Hebron.

8 The Israelites had already decided on the following three towns east of the River Jordan:

> Bezer in the desert flat lands of Reuben, Ramoth in Gilead, which was a town that belonged to Gad, and Golan in Bashan, which belonged to Manasseh.

9 These Safe Towns were set up, so that if Israelites or even foreigners who lived in Israel accidentally killed someone, they could run to one of these towns. There they would be safe until a trial could be held, even if one of the victim's relatives came looking for revenge.

Towns for the Levi tribe

CHAPTER 21

1-2 While the Israelites were still camped at Shiloh in the land of Canaan, the family leaders of the Levi tribe went to speak to the priest Eleazar, Joshua, and the family leaders of the other Israelite tribes. The leaders of Levi said, "The LORD told Moses that you have to give us towns and provide pastures for our animals."*

3 Since the LORD had said this, the leaders of the other Israelite tribes agreed to give some of the towns and pastures from their tribal lands to Levi. 4 The leaders asked the LORD to show them* in what order the clans of Levi would be given towns, and which towns each clan would receive.

The Kohath clans were first. The descendants of Aaron, Israel's first priest,* were given thirteen towns from the tribes of Judah, Simeon, and Benjamin. 5 The other members of the Kohath clans received nine towns from the tribes of Ephraim, Dan, and West Manasseh. 6 The clans that were descendants of Gershon were given thirteen towns from the tribes of Issachar, Asher, Naphtali, and East Manasseh. 7 The clans that

were descendants of Merari* received twelve towns from the tribes of Reuben, Gad, and Zebulun.

8 The LORD had told Moses that he would show the Israelites which towns and pastures to give to the clans of Levi, and he did.

Towns from Judah, Simeon, Benjamin

9-19 The descendants of Aaron from the Kohath clans of Levi were priests, and they were chosen to receive towns first. They were given thirteen towns and the pasture land around them. Nine of these towns were from the tribes of Judah and Simeon and four from Benjamin.

Hebron, Libnah, Jattir, Eshtemoa, Holon, Debir, Ashan,* Juttah, and Beth-Shemesh were from Judah and Simeon. Hebron, in the hill country of Judah, was earlier called Arba's Town.* It had been named after Arba, the ancestor of the Anakim.* Hebron's pasture lands went along with the town, but its farmlands and the villages around it had been given to Caleb.* Hebron was also one of the Safe Towns for people who had accidentally killed someone.

Gibeon, Geba, Anathoth, and Almon were from Benjamin.

Towns from Ephraim, Dan, West Manasseh

20-26 The rest of the Kohath clans of the Levi tribe received ten towns and the pasture land around them. Four of these towns were from the tribe of Ephraim, four from Dan, and two from West Manasseh.

Shechem, Gezer, Kibzaim, and Beth-Horon were from Ephraim. Shechem in the hill country, and it was also one of the Safe Towns for people who had accidentally killed someone.

Elteke, Gibbethon, Aijalon, and Gath-Rimmon were from Dan.

Taanach and Jibleam* were from West Manasseh.

Towns from East Manasseh, Issachar, Asher, Naphtali

27-33 The clans of Levi that were descendants of Gershon received thirteen towns and the pasture land around them. Two of these towns were from the tribe of East Manasseh, four from Issachar, four from Asher, and three from Naphtali.

---

*21.1,2 The LORD told Moses . . . animals: See Numbers 35.1–8.
*21.4 asked the LORD to show them: Hebrew "cast lots to find out". See the note at 14.1–5.
See also: 21.2: Num 35.1–8.

*21.4–7 Kohath . . . Gershon . . . Merari: Sons of Levi, the ancestor of the tribe of Levi.
*21.9–19 Anakim: See the note at 11.21.
*21.9–19 Caleb: See 14.6–14.

Golan in Bashan and Beeshterah were from East Manasseh.

Kishion, Daberath, Jarmuth, and En-Gannim were from Issachar.

Mishal, Abdon, Helkath, and Rehob were from Asher.

Kedesh in Galilee, Hammothdor, and Kartan were from Naphtali. Golan in Bashan and Kedesh in Galilee were also Safe Towns for people who had accidentally killed someone.

Towns from Zebulun, Reuben, Gad

34-40 The rest of the Levi clans were descendants of Merari, and they received twelve towns with the pasture land around them. Four towns were from the tribe of Zebulun, four from Reuben, and four from Gad.

Jokneam, Kartah, Rimmonah,* and Nahalal were from Zebulun.

Bezer, Jazah, Kedemoth, and Mephaath were from Reuben. Bezer was in the desert flat lands east of the River Jordan across from Jericho.*

Ramoth in Gilead, Mahanaim, Heshbon, and Jazer were from Gad.

Bezer and Ramoth in Gilead were Safe Towns* for people who had accidentally killed someone.

41-42 The people of the Levi tribe had a total of forty-eight towns within Israel, and they had pastures around each one of their towns.

Israel settles in the land

43 The LORD gave the Israelites the land he had promised their ancestors, and they captured it and settled in it. 44 There still were enemies around Israel, but the LORD kept his promise to let his people live in peace. And whenever the Israelites did have to go to war, no enemy could defeat them. The LORD always helped Israel win. 45 The LORD promised to do many good things for Israel, and he kept his promise every time.

The eastern tribes return home

CHAPTER 22

The two and a half tribes return home

1 Joshua called the men of the tribes of Reuben, Gad, and East Manasseh to a meeting, and he told them:

2-3 You have obeyed every command of the LORD your God and of his servant Moses.

And you have done everything I've told you to do. It's taken a long time, but you have stayed and helped your relatives. 4 The LORD promised to give peace to your relatives, and that's what he has done. Now it's time for you to go back to your own homes in the land that Moses gave you east of the River Jordan.

5 Moses taught you to love the LORD your God, to be faithful to him, and to worship and obey him with your whole heart and with all your strength. So be very careful to do everything Moses commanded.

6-9 You've become rich from what you've taken from your enemies. You have big herds of cattle, lots of silver, gold, bronze, and iron, and plenty of clothes. Take everything home with you and share it with the people of your tribe.

I pray that God will be kind to you. You are now free to go home.

The tribes of Reuben and Gad started back to Gilead, their own land. Moses had given the land of Bashan to the East Manasseh tribe, so they started back along with Reuben and Gad. God had told Moses that these two and a half tribes should conquer Gilead and Bashan, and they had done so.

Joshua had given land west of the River Jordan to the other half of the Manasseh tribe, so they stayed at Shiloh in the land of Canaan with the rest of the Israelites.

10-11 The tribes of Reuben, Gad, and East Manasseh reached the western side of the Jordan Valley* and built a huge altar there beside the river.

When the rest of the Israelites heard what these tribes had done,* 12 the Israelite men met at Shiloh to get ready to attack the two and a half tribes. 13 But first they sent a priest, Phinehas the son of Eleazar, to talk with the two and a half tribes. 14 Each of the tribes at Shiloh sent the leader of one of its families along with Phinehas.

15 Phinehas and these leaders went to Gilead and met with the tribes of Reuben, Gad, and East Manasseh. They said:

16 All the LORD's people have gathered together and have sent us to find out why you are unfaithful to our God. You have

---

*22.10,11 built a huge altar . . . tribes had done: According to Deuteronomy 12.5–14, the LORD wanted the Israelites to have only one altar for offering sacrifices. To build another altar would be to disobey the LORD.

See also: 22.16: Deut 12.13,14.

See also: 22.2: Num 32.20–32; Jam 1.12–15.

turned your backs on the LORD by building that altar. Why are you rebelling against him? 17 Wasn't our people's sin at Peor* terrible enough for you? The LORD punished us by sending a horrible sickness that killed many of us, and we still suffer because of that sin.' 18 Now you are turning your backs on the LORD again.

If you don't stop rebelling against the LORD at once, he will be angry with the whole nation. 19 If you don't think your land is a fit place to serve God, then move across the Jordan and live with us in the LORD's own land, where his sacred tent is. But don't rebel against the LORD our God or against us by building another altar besides the LORD's own altar.' 20 Don't you remember what happened when Achan was unfaithful* and took some of the things that belonged to God? This made God angry with the entire nation. Achan died because he sinned, but he also caused the death of many others.

21 The tribes of Reuben, Gad, and East Manasseh answered:

22 The LORD is the greatest God! We ask him to be our witness, because he knows whether or not we were rebellious or unfaithful when we built that altar. If we were unfaithful, then we pray that God won't rescue us today. Let us tell you why we built that altar, 23 and we ask the LORD to punish us if we are lying. We didn't build it so we could turn our backs on the LORD. We didn't even build it so we could offer animal or grain sacrifices to please the LORD or ask his blessing.

24-25 We built that altar because we were worried. Some day your descendants might tell our descendants, "The LORD made the River Jordan the boundary between us Israelites and you people of Reuben and Gad. The LORD is Israel's God, but you're not part of Israel, so you can't take part in worshipping the LORD."

Your descendants might say that and try to make our descendants stop worshipping and obeying the LORD. 26 That's why we decided to build the altar. It isn't for offering sacrifices, not even sacrifices to please the LORD.* 27-29 To build another altar for offering sacrifices would be the same as

turning our backs on the LORD and rebelling against him. We could never do that! No, we built the altar to remind us and you and the generations to come that we will worship the LORD. And so we will keep bringing our sacrifices to the LORD's altar, there in front of his sacred tent. Now your descendants will never be able to say to our descendants, "You can't worship the LORD."

But if they do say this, our descendants can answer back, "Look at this altar our ancestors built! It's like the LORD's altar, but it isn't for offering sacrifices. It's here to remind us and you that we belong to the LORD, just as much as you do."

30-31 Phinehas and the clan leaders were pleased when they heard the tribes of Reuben, Gad, and East Manasseh explain why they had built the altar. Then Phinehas told them, "Today we know that the LORD is helping us. You have not been unfaithful to him, and this means that the LORD will not be angry with us."

32 Phinehas and the clan leaders left Gilead and went back to Canaan to tell the Israelites about their meeting with the Reuben and Gad tribes. 33 The Israelites were happy and praised God. There was no more talk about going to war and wiping out the tribes of Reuben and Gad.

34 The people of Reuben and Gad named the altar "A Reminder to us all that the LORD is our God."'

Joshua's farewell speeches and death

CHAPTER 23

1 The LORD let Israel live in peace with its neighbours for a long time, and Joshua lived to a ripe old age. 2 One day he called a meeting of the leaders of the tribes of Israel, including the old men, the judges, and the officials. Then he told them:

I am now very old. 3 You have seen how the LORD your God fought for you and helped you defeat the nations who lived in this land. 4-5 There are still some nations left, but the LORD has promised you their land. So when you attack them, he will make them run away. I have already divided their land among your tribes, as I did with the land of the nations I defeated between the River Jordan and the Mediterranean Sea.

*22.17 our people's sin at Peor: See Numbers 25.
*22.20 Achan was unfaithful: See 7.1-26.
*22.26 sacrifices to please the LORD: See the note at 8.30-32.
See also: 22.17: Num 25.1-9. 22.20: Josh 7.1-26.

⁶ Be sure that you carefully obey everything written in *The Book of the Law* of Moses and do exactly what it says.

⁷ Don't have anything to do with the nations that live around you. Don't worship their gods or pray to their idols or make promises in the names of their gods. ⁸ Be as faithful to the LORD as you have always been.

⁹ When you attacked powerful nations, the LORD made them run away, and no one has ever been able to stand up to you. ¹⁰ Any one of you can defeat a thousand enemy soldiers, because the LORD God fights for you, just as he promised. ¹¹ Be sure to love the LORD your God always.

¹²⁻¹³ Don't ever turn your backs on him by marrying people from the nations that are left in the land. Don't even make friends with them. I tell you that if you are friendly with those nations, the LORD won't chase them away when you attack. Instead, they'll be like a trap for your feet, a whip on your back, and thorns in your eyes. And finally, none of you will be left in this good land that the LORD has given you.

¹⁴ I will soon die, as everyone must. But deep in your hearts you know that the LORD has kept every promise he made to you. Not one of them has been broken.

¹⁵⁻¹⁶ Yes, when the LORD makes a promise, he does what he has promised. But when he makes a threat, he will also do what he has threatened. The LORD is our God. He gave us this wonderful land and made an agreement with us that we would worship only him. But if you worship other gods, it will make the LORD furious. He will start getting rid of you, and soon not one of you will be left in this good land that he has given you.

CHAPTER 24

We will worship and obey the LORD

¹ Joshua called the tribes of Israel together for a meeting at Shechem. He made the leaders, including the old men, the judges, and the officials, come up and stand near the sacred tent. ² Then Joshua told everyone to listen to this message from the LORD, the God of Israel:

Long ago your ancestors lived on the other side of the River Euphrates, and they worshipped other gods. This continued until the time of your ancestor Terah and his two sons, Abraham and Nahor. ³ But I brought Abraham across the River Euphrates and led him through the land of Canaan. I blessed him by giving him Isaac, the first in a line of many descendants. ⁴ Then I gave Isaac two sons, Jacob and Esau. I let Esau live in the hill country of Mount Seir, but your ancestor Jacob and his children went to live in Egypt.

⁵⁻⁶ Later I sent Moses and his brother Aaron to help your people, and I made all those horrible things happen to the Egyptians. I brought your ancestors out of Egypt, but the Egyptians got in their chariots and on their horses and chased your ancestors, catching up with them at the Red Sea.* ⁷ Your people cried to me for help, so I put a dark cloud between them and the Egyptians. Then I opened up the sea and let your people walk across on dry ground. But when the Egyptians tried to follow, I commanded the sea to swallow them, and they drowned while you watched.

You lived in the desert for a long time, ⁸ then I brought you into the land east of the River Jordan. The Amorites were living there, and they fought you. But with my help, you defeated them, wiped them out, and took their land. ⁹ King Balak decided that his nation Moab would go to war against you, so he asked Balaam* to come and put a curse on you. ¹⁰ But I wouldn't listen to Balaam, and I rescued you by making him bless you instead of curse you.

¹¹ You crossed the River Jordan and came to Jericho. The rulers of Jericho fought you, and so did the Amorites, the Perizzites, the Canaanites, the Hittites, the Girgashites, the Hivites, and the Jebusites. I helped you defeat them all. ¹² Your enemies ran from you, but not because you had swords and bows and arrows. I made your enemies panic and run away, as I had done with the two Amorite kings east of the River Jordan.

¹³ You didn't have to work for this land — I gave it to you. Now you live in towns you didn't build, and you eat grapes

---

*24.5,6 Red Sea: See the note at 2.10.

See also: 24.3: a Gen 12.1–9; b Gen 21.1–3. 24.4: a Gen 25.24–26; b Gen 36.8; Deut 2.5; c Gen 46.1–7. 24.5: Exod 3.1–12.42. 24.6,7: Exod 14.1–31. 24.8: Num 21.21–35. 24.9,10: Num 22.1–24.25. 24.11: a Josh 3.14–17; b Josh 6.1–21. 24.12: Exod 23.28; Deut 7.20. 24.13: Deut 6.10,11.

See also: 23.10: a Deut 32.30; b Deut 3.22. 24.2: Gen 11.27.

218

and olives from vineyards and trees you
didn't plant.

¹⁴ Then Joshua told the people:

Worship the LORD, obey him, and always
be faithful. Get rid of the idols your
ancestors worshipped when they lived on
the other side of the River Euphrates and in
Egypt. ¹⁵ But if you don't want to worship
the LORD, then choose now! Will you
worship the same idols your ancestors did?
Or since you're living on land that once
belonged to the Amorites, perhaps you'll
worship their gods. I won't. My family and
I are going to worship and obey the LORD!

¹⁶ The people answered:

We could never worship other gods or stop
worshipping the LORD. ¹⁷ The LORD is our
God. We were slaves in Egypt as our
ancestors had been, but we saw the LORD
work miracles to set our people free and to
bring us out of Egypt. Even though other
nations were all around us, the LORD
protected us wherever we went. ¹⁸ And
when we fought the Amorites and the
other nations that lived in this land, the
LORD made them run away. Yes, we will
worship and obey the LORD, because the
LORD is our God.

¹⁹ Joshua said:

The LORD is fearsome; he is the one true
God, and I don't think you are able to
worship and obey him in the ways he
demands. You would have to be
completely faithful, and if you sin or rebel,
he won't let you get away with it. ²⁰ If you
turn your backs on the LORD and worship
the gods of other nations, the LORD will
turn against you. He will make terrible
things happen to you and wipe you out,
even though he had been good to you
before.

²¹ But the people shouted, "We won't worship
any other gods. We will worship and obey
only the LORD!"

²² Joshua said, "You have heard yourselves
say that you will worship and obey the LORD.
Isn't that true?"

"Yes, it's true," they answered.

²³ Joshua said, "But you still have some
idols, like those the other nations worship.
Get rid of your idols! You must decide once
and for all that you really want to obey the
LORD God of Israel."

²⁴ The people said, "The LORD is our God,
and we will worship and obey only him."

²⁵ Joshua helped Israel make an agreement
with the LORD that day at Shechem. Joshua
made laws for Israel ²⁶ and wrote them down
in *The Book of the Law*ʼ of God. Then he set up
a large stone under the oak tree at the place
of worship in Shechem ²⁷ and told the
people, "Look at this stone. It has heard
everything that the LORD has said to us. Our
God can call this stone as a witness if we ever
reject him."

²⁸ Joshua sent everyone back to their
homes.

Joshua, Joseph, and Eleazar are buried

²⁹ Not long afterwards, the LORD's servant
Joshua died at the age of one hundred and
ten. ³⁰ The Israelites buried him in his own
land at Timnath-Serah, north of Mount Gaash
in the hill country of Ephraim.

³¹ As long as Joshua lived, Israel worshipped
and obeyed the LORD. There were other
leaders old enough to remember everything
that the LORD had done for Israel. And for as
long as these men lived, Israel continued to
worship and obey the LORD.

³² When the people of Israel left Egypt, they
brought the bones of Joseph along with them.
They took the bones to the town of Shechem
and buried them in the field that Jacob had
bought for one hundred pieces of silverʼ from
Hamor, the founder of Shechem. The town
and the field bothʼ became part of the land
belonging to the descendants of Joseph.

³³ When Eleazar the priestʼ died, he was
buried in the hill country of Ephraim on a hill
that belonged to his son Phinehas.

See also: 24.30: Josh 19.49,50. 24.32: Gen 33.19; 50.24,25;
Exod 13.19; John 4.5; Acts 7.16.

Additional notes

ʼ1.6-8 the Law: Or "Teachings".
ʼ2.14 We pray . . . promise: Or "If you save our lives,
we will save yours!"
ʼ3.2 Two days later: The Hebrew text has "At the end
of three days", two days after they had set up camp.
ʼ3.3,4 the priests: The Hebrew text has "the priests,
the Levites"; priests belonged to the tribe of Levi.
ʼ4.1-3 Joshua . . . Tell: Or "Joshua, you and the other
leaders must tell".
ʼ4.10-13 Forty thousand soldiers from the tribes of
Reuben, Gad, and East Manasseh: Or "There were
forty thousand soldiers altogether, and those from the
tribes of Reuben, Gad, and East Manasseh".

⟩5.3 Haaraloth Hill: Or "Foreskin Hill".

⟩6.18,19 Be careful . . . fault: One ancient translation; Hebrew "Don't keep any of it for yourself. If you do, the LORD will destroy both you and Israel."

⟩6.26 by the time . . . dead: Or "when he puts gates into the town wall, his youngest son will die."

⟩7.1 Achan: The Hebrew text has "Achan, son of Carmi, grandson of Abdi, and great-grandson of Zerah".

⟩7.2 of Ai: Or "called The Ruins".

⟩7.4,5 stone quarries: Or "Shebarim".

⟩7.24 Trouble Valley: Or "Achor Valley".

⟩8.16,17 Ai or in Bethel: Hebrew; one ancient translation "Ai".

⟩8.18 sword: Or "spear".

⟩8.22–24 Joshua. They also chased . . . them: Or "Joshua. The men of Ai had chased the Israelites into the desert, but the Israelites killed them there."

⟩8.30–32 taught . . . Law: Or "commanded . . . Teachings".

⟩8.30–32 Law: See the note at 1.6–8.

⟩8.33–35 the blessings . . . Moses: Or "all of *The Book of the Law* of Moses, including the blessings and the curses."

⟩9.4 So . . . country: One possible meaning for the difficult Hebrew text.

⟩9.7,8 Gibeonites: Hebrew "Hivites".

⟩9.16,17 A couple . . . later: The Hebrew text has "At the end of three days", meaning two days after the day the treaty was made.

⟩9.16,17 A couple of days . . . later: Or "A couple of days later, the Israelites moved their camp to the area near the towns of Gibeon, Chephirah, Beeroth, and Kiriath-Jearim. When they arrived, they realized that they had made a peace treaty with the people of these nearby towns!"

⟩9.23 the place of worship: The Hebrew text has "God's house", which at that time was the sacred tent.

⟩10.10 They: Or "The LORD".

⟩11.2 Lake Galilee: The Hebrew text has "Lake Chinnereth", an earlier name.

⟩11.4,5 Pond: Or "Gorge".

⟩11.6 When . . . over: Or "After the battle is over, cripple their horses and burn their chariots."

⟩11.8,9 and crippled the enemies' horses: It is also possible that the Israelites crippled the enemies' horses after the battle at the same time they burnt the enemies' chariots; see the note at 11.6.

⟩11.8,9 Misreroth-Maim . . . north-west: Or "the town of Misrephoth to the north-west" or "the River Misrephoth".

⟩12.3 Lake Galilee: See the note at 11.2.

⟩12.3 the town called Slopes of Mount Pisgah: Or "the slopes of Mount Pisgah".

⟩12.9–24 Aphek, Lasharon: Or "Aphek in the Sharon Plain".

⟩12.9–24 Galilee: One ancient translation; Hebrew "Gilgal".

⟩12.9–24 Jericho . . . Tirzah: There are some differences in this list between the Hebrew and several ancient translations.

⟩13.2–7 Amorite border: What had been the southern border of the old Amorite kingdom of Amurru.

⟩13.2–7 Hamath Pass: Or "Lebo-Hamath".

⟩13.2–7 Misrephoth-Maim: Or "Misrephoth" or "the River Misrephoth".

⟩13.2–7 Gebalites: Gebal was another name for Byblos.

⟩13.2–7 from . . . Sea: One ancient translation; the Hebrew text does not have these words.

⟩13.11,12 Sihon . . . people: Or "the Rephaim".

⟩13.26 Lidebor: This may be another name for Lodebar, a town a few kilometres east of the River Jordan and about sixteen kilometres south of Lake Galilee.

⟩13.27 Lake Galilee: See the note at 11.2.

⟩14.15 Arba's Town: Or "Kiriath-Arba".

⟩14.15 Arba's Town, because . . . greatest: Hebrew; one ancient translation "Arba's Town. It was one of the main towns."

⟩15.3 Scorpion Pass: Or "Akrabbim Pass".

⟩15.5 at . . . Dead Sea: One possible meaning for the difficult Hebrew text.

⟩15.6 Monument of Bohan: Or "Bohan Rock", possibly a natural rock formation.

⟩15.7 Trouble Valley: See the note at 7.24.

⟩15.9 ruins: Hebrew; one ancient translation "towns".

⟩15.10 Beth-Shemesh: Probably the same town as the Ir-Shemesh of 19.41–46. Two other towns were also named Beth-Shemesh (see 19.17–23 and 19.35–39).

⟩15.13 Arba's Town: See the note at 14.15.

⟩15.14 clans of: Or "warriors".

⟩15.17 Caleb's nephew Othniel: Hebrew "Othniel the son of Caleb's brother Kenaz".

⟩15.18 Achsah . . . Othniel . . . he: Hebrew; one manuscript of one ancient translation and two ancient translations of the parallel in Judges 1.14 "Othniel . . . Achsah . . . she".

⟩15.18 getting down from: One possible meaning for the difficult Hebrew text.

⟩15.19 spring-fed ponds: Or "wells".

⟩15.19 small ponds . . . Pond . . . Pond: Or "wells . . . Well . . . Well".

⟩15.21–32 Aradah: One possible meaning for the difficult Hebrew text.

⟩15.21–32 Hazor of Ithnan: One ancient translation; Hebrew "Hazor and Ithnan".

⟩15.21–32 its . . . villages: One ancient translation; Hebrew "Biziothiah".

⟩15.21–32 Enrimmon: One ancient translation; Hebrew "Ain and Rimmon".

⟩15.37–41 Lahmas: Most Hebrew manuscripts; many other Hebrew manuscripts and one manuscript of one ancient translation "Lahmam".

⟩15.48–51 Eshtemoh: Another spelling for the name Eshtemoa (see 21.9–19).

⟩15.52–54 Dumah: Most Hebrew manuscripts; some Hebrew manuscripts and one ancient translation "Rumah".

⟩15.55–57 Jokdeam: Hebrew; one ancient translation "Jorkeam".

'**15.58,59 The tenth region . . . Manahath:** One ancient translation; the Hebrew text does not have these words.

'**16.1–4 it . . . then:** Or "which is also called Luz, it went".

'**17.1–6 the clans that were descendants of Zelophehad's five daughters . . . Hepher's brothers:** Or "Zelophehad's five daughters went to the priest Eleazar, Joshua, and the leaders of Israel. The five sisters said, 'The LORD told Moses to give us land just as he gave land to our relatives.' Joshua followed the LORD's instructions and gave land to these five sisters, as he had given land to Hepher's brothers."

'**17.7 to include . . . Tappuah Spring:** Hebrew; one ancient translation "to Jassiben-Tappuah" or "and turns towards Tappuah Spring".

'**17.11 Dor . . . Naphath:** One possible meaning for the difficult Hebrew text.

'**18.1 sacred tent:** Or "meeting tent".

'**18.13,14 Ataroth-Orech:** One ancient translation; Hebrew "Ataroth-Addar".

'**18.15 the ruins:** One possible meaning for the difficult Hebrew text.

'**18.16 Jerusalem:** Hebrew "the Jebusite town."

'**18.17 Gelioth:** Probably another name for Gilgal.

'**18.17 Monument of Bohan:** See the note at 15.6.

'**18.18 hillside north of Beth-Arabah:** One ancient translation (see also the border description in 15.6); Hebrew "the northern hillside overlooking the Jordan Valley".

'**18.19 northern . . . Dead Sea:** One possible meaning for the difficult Hebrew text.

'**18.25–28 Kiriath-Jearim:** One ancient translation; Hebrew "Kiriath".

'**19.2–6 Shema:** One ancient translation and some manuscripts of another ancient translation (see also the list at 15.21–32); Hebrew and some manuscripts of one ancient translation "Sheba". The list in 1 Chronicles 4.28 does not have either "Shema" or "Sheba".

'**19.7 Enrimmon:** Some Hebrew manuscripts and one ancient translation; most Hebrew manuscripts "Ain, Rimmon".

'**19.7 Tachan:** Some manuscripts of one ancient translation; the Hebrew text does not have this word.

'**19.13 Rimmonah:** Or "Rimmon".

'**19.13 Rimmonah . . . curved:** One possible meaning for the difficult Hebrew text.

'**19.15 Jiralah:** Some Hebrew manuscripts and two ancient translations; most Hebrew manuscripts "Idalah".

'**19.17–23 Debirath:** One ancient translation; Hebrew "Rabbith". Debirath is probably the same place as Daberath in verse 12.

'**19.17–23 Mount Tabor . . . Tabor:** In Hebrew the name "Tabor" is used only once. It was probably intended as the name of a town at the foot of Mount Tabor and which formed one point on the northern border of Issachar.

'**19.28 Abdon:** A few Hebrew manuscripts and one ancient translation; most Hebrew manuscripts "Ebron".

'**19.29–31 Mahalab:** One possible meaning for the difficult Hebrew text.

'**19.29–31 Acco:** One ancient translation; Hebrew "Ummah".

'**19.32–34 the town . . . Zaanannim:** Or "the oak tree in the town of Zaananim".

'**19.32–34 at . . . Jehudah:** One possible meaning for the difficult Hebrew text.

'**19.40–46 Azor:** Some manuscripts of one ancient translation; the Hebrew text does not have this word.

'**19.40–46 Gath-Rimmon, Mejarkon, and Rakkon. Dan's tribal land:** Or "Gath-Rimmon, and Rakkon. Dan's tribal land also included the River Yarkon and".

'**19.49–51 sacred tent:** See the note at 18.1.

'**21.4 The descendants . . . priest:** between three ancient translations "The priests, the descendants of Aaron". The male descendants of Aaron would also be priests.

'**21.9–19 Ashan:** One ancient translation and the parallel in 1 Chronicles 6.59; Hebrew "Ain".

'**21.9–19 Arba's Town:** See the note at 14.15.

'**21.20–26 Jibleam:** One ancient translation and the parallel in 1 Chronicles 6.70; Hebrew "Gath-Rimmon".

'**21.34–40 Rimmonah:** One possible meaning for the difficult Hebrew text.

'**21.34–40 Bezer . . . Jericho:** One possible meaning for the difficult Hebrew text.

'**21.34–40 Bezer and Ramoth in Gilead were Safe Towns:** One ancient translation; Hebrew "Ramoth in Gilead was a Safe Town."

'**22.10,11 western . . . valley:** Or "the town of Geliloth, which is in the land of Canaan near the River Jordan".

'**22.17 we still . . . sin:** Or "There are still people in Israel who want to worship other gods."

'**22.19 or against . . . altar:** Or "by building another altar besides the LORD's own altar. That would even make us into rebels along with you."

'**22.34 named . . . God:** Or "gave a name to the altar. They explained, 'This altar is here to remind us all that the LORD is our God' "; most Hebrew manuscripts. A few Hebrew manuscripts and one ancient translation "named the altar 'Reminder'. They explained, 'This altar is here to remind us all that the LORD is our God.' "

'**23.6 Law:** See the note at 1.6–8.

'**24.1 near . . . tent:** Or "in front of the sacred chest"; Hebrew "in the presence of God".

'**24.9 King Balak . . . Balaam:** The Hebrew text has "King Balak the son of Zippor . . . Balaam the son of Beor."

'**24.26 Law:** See the note at 1.6–8.

'**24.32 pieces of silver:** One possible meaning for the difficult Hebrew word.

'**24.32 town . . . both:** One possible meaning for the difficult Hebrew text.

'**24.33 Eleazar the priest:** Hebrew "Eleazar the son of Aaron".

Judges

A quick look at this book

The book of Judges tells how the Israelites kept rejecting the Lord and worshipping idols. Each time they did this, the Lord punished them by letting other nations attack and defeat them. As a result, the Israelites turned back to the Lord and asked for his help, and he sent a special leader called a "judge", who helped them defeat their enemies. A time of peace followed, and the Israelites were faithful to the Lord for as long as the judge lived. But then they again rejected the Lord. All these things happened time after time.

Some judges may have led the entire nation, but usually a judge led a few tribes at the most. Israel at this time was a loosely-bound group of tribes, and the Israelites did not think of themselves as being a single, united country. They did not yet have a king, and so

during this time "everyone did what they thought was right" (21.25). But the people had to learn that they were to worship only the Lord, and when they were unfaithful, the Lord punished them.

Israel captures only part of the land

CHAPTER 1

The tribes of Judah and Simeon fight the Canaanites

¹ After the death of Joshua, the Israelites asked the LORD, "Which of our tribes should attack the Canaanites first?"

² "Judah!" the LORD answered. "I'll help them take the land."

³ The people of Judah went to their relatives, the Simeon tribe, and said, "Canaanites live in the land God gave us. Help us fight them, and we will help you."

Troops from Simeon came to help Judah. ⁴⁻⁵ Together they attacked an army of ten thousand Canaanites and Perizzites at Bezek, and the LORD helped Judah defeat them. During the battle, Judah's army found out where the king of Bezek' was, and they attacked there. ⁶ Bezek tried to escape, but soldiers from Judah caught him. They cut off his thumbs and big toes, ⁷ and he said, "I've cut off the thumbs and big toes of seventy kings and made those kings crawl around under my table for scraps of food. Now God is paying me back."

The army of Judah took the king of Bezek along with them to Jerusalem, where he died.

8 They attacked Jerusalem,* captured it, killed everyone who lived there, and then burnt it to the ground.

9 Judah's army fought the Canaanites who lived in the hill country, the Southern Desert, and the foothills to the west. 10 After that, they attacked the Canaanites who lived at Hebron, defeating the three clans called* Sheshai, Ahiman, and Talmai. At that time, Hebron was called Kiriath-Arba.

11 From Hebron, Judah's army went to attack Debir, which at that time was called Kiriath-Sepher. 12 Caleb* told his troops, "The man who captures Kiriath-Sepher can marry my daughter Achsah."

13 Caleb's nephew Othniel captured Kiriath-Sepher, so Caleb let him marry Achsah. Othniel was the son of Caleb's younger brother Kenaz.* 14 Straight after the wedding, Achsah started telling Othniel that he' ought to ask her father for a field. She went to see her father, and while she was getting down from' her donkey, Caleb asked, "What's bothering you?"

15 She answered, "I need your help. The land you gave me is in the Southern Desert, so please give me some spring-fed ponds for a water supply."

Caleb gave her a couple of small ponds named Higher Pond and Lower Pond.'

16 The people who belonged to the Kenite clan were the descendants of the father-in-law of Moses. They left Jericho' with the people of Judah and settled near Arad in the Southern Desert of Judah not far from the Amalekites.'

17 Judah's army helped Simeon's army attack the Canaanites who lived at Zephath. They completely destroyed* the town and renamed it Hormah.*

18-19 The LORD helped the army of Judah capture Gaza, Ashkelon, Ekron, and the land near those towns. They also took the hill country. But the people who lived in the valleys had iron chariots, so Judah was not able to make them leave or to take their land.

20 The tribe of Judah gave the town of Hebron to Caleb, as Moses had told them to do. Caleb defeated the three Anakim* clans' and took over the town.

The Benjamin tribe does not capture Jerusalem

21 The Jebusites were living in Jerusalem, and the Benjamin tribe did not defeat them or capture the town. That's why Jebusites still live in Jerusalem along with the people of Benjamin.

The Ephraim and Manasseh tribes capture Bethel

22-23 The Ephraim and Manasseh tribes* were getting ready to attack Bethel, which at that time was called Luz. And the LORD helped them when they sent spies to find out as much as they could about Bethel. 24 While the spies were watching the town, a man came out, and they told him, "If you show us how our army can get into the town,* we will make sure that you aren't harmed." 25 The man showed them, and the two Israelite tribes attacked Bethel, killing everyone except the man and his family. The two tribes made the man and his family leave, 26 so they went to the land of the Hittites,* where he built a town. He named the town Luz, and that is still its name.

Israel does not get rid of all the Canaanites

27-28 Canaanites lived in the towns of Beth-Shan, Taanach, Dor, Ibleam, Megiddo, and all the villages nearby. The Canaanites were determined to stay, and the Manasseh

---

*1.8 Jerusalem: This probably refers to towns and villages belonging to Jerusalem but lying in Judah's territory south of the city wall. Jerusalem itself was just inside Benjamin's territory, but was not captured by Israel at this time (see verse 21; Joshua 15.5–9; 18.15–18).
*1.12 Caleb: One of the leaders of Judah; see Joshua 14.6–14 and Numbers 13.6,30; 14.6,10,20–24. For verses 12–15, see Joshua 15.13–19.
*1.17 completely destroyed: The Hebrew word means that the town was given completely to the LORD, and since it could not be used for normal purposes any more, it had to be destroyed.
*1.17 Hormah: In Hebrew "Hormah" sounds like "completely destroyed".

*1.20 Anakim: Perhaps a group of people of great stature that lived in Palestine before the Israelites (see Numbers 13.33 and Deuteronomy 2.10,11,20,21).
*1.22,23 The Ephraim and Manasseh tribes: The Hebrew text has "The Joseph family", which was divided into these two tribes after Joseph's sons.
*1.24 If you . . . town: Sometimes there were small doors in the town wall that could be opened from the inside even when the main town gates were shut and locked.
*1.26 land of the Hittites: The Hittites had an empire centred in what is now Turkey. At one time their empire reached south into Syria, north of Israel.
See also: 1.20: Josh 15.13,14. 1.21: Josh 15.63; 2 Sam 5.6; 1 Chron 11.4. 1.27,28: Josh 17.11–13.

tribe never did get rid of them. But later on, when the Israelites grew more powerful, they made slaves of the Canaanites.

²⁹ The Ephraim tribe did not get rid of the Canaanites who lived in Gezer, so the Canaanites lived there with Israelites all around them.

³⁰ The Zebulun tribe did not get rid of the Canaanites who lived in Kitron and Nahalol, and the Canaanites stayed there with Israelites around them. But the people of Zebulun did force the Canaanites into slave labour.

³¹⁻³² The Asher tribe did not get rid of the Canaanites who lived in Acco, Sidon, Ahlab, Achzib, Helbah, Aphik, and Rehob, and the Asher tribe lived with Canaanites all around them.

³³ The Naphtali tribe did not get rid of the Canaanites who lived in Beth-Shemesh and Beth-Anath, but they did force the Canaanites into slave labour. The Naphtali tribe lived with Canaanites around them.

³⁴ The Amorites* were strong enough to keep the tribe of Dan from settling in the valleys, so Dan had to stay in the hill country.

³⁵ The Amorites on Mount Heres and in Aijalon and Shaalbim were also determined to stay. Later on, as Ephraim and Manasseh grew more powerful, they forced those Amorites into slave labour.

The Amorite-Edomite border

³⁶ The old Amorite-Edomite border used to go from Sela through Scorpion Pass* into the hill country.*

The Lord chooses judges for Israel

CHAPTER 2

The Lord's angel speaks to Israel

¹ The Lord's angel went from Gilgal to Bochim* and gave the Israelites this message from the Lord:

> I promised your ancestors that I would give this land to their families, and I brought your people here from Egypt. We made an agreement that I promised never to break, ² and you promised not to make any peace

treaties with the other nations that live in the land. Besides that, you agreed to tear down the altars where they sacrifice to their idols. But you didn't keep your promise.

³ And so, I'll stop helping you defeat your enemies. Instead, they will be there to trap* you into worshipping their gods.

⁴ The Israelites started crying loudly, ⁵ and they offered sacrifices to the Lord. From then on, they called that place "Crying".*

Israel stops worshipping the Lord

⁶⁻⁹ Joshua had been faithful to the Lord. And after Joshua sent the Israelites to take the land they had been promised, they remained faithful to the Lord until Joshua died at the age of one hundred and ten. He was buried on his land in Timnath-Heres, in the hill country of Ephraim north of Mount Gaash. Even though Joshua was gone, the Israelites were faithful to the Lord during the lifetime of those men who had been leaders with Joshua and who had seen the wonderful things the Lord had done for Israel.

¹⁰ After a while the people of Joshua's generation died, and the next generation did not know the Lord or any of the things he had done for Israel. ¹¹⁻¹³ The Lord had brought their ancestors out of Egypt, and they had worshipped him. But now the Israelites stopped worshipping the Lord and worshipped the idols of Baal and Astarte, as well as the idols of other gods from nearby nations.

The Lord was so angry ¹⁴⁻¹⁵ with the Israelites that he let other nations raid Israel and steal their crops and other possessions. Enemies were everywhere, and the Lord always let them defeat Israel in battle. The Lord had warned Israel he would do this, and now the Israelites were miserable.

The Lord chooses leaders for Israel

¹⁶ From time to time, the Lord would choose special leaders known as judges.* These judges would lead the Israelites into battle and defeat the enemies that made raids on them. ¹⁷ In years gone by, the Israelites had been faithful to the Lord, but now they were quick to be unfaithful or to refuse even to

---

*1.34 Amorites: Used in the general sense of nations that lived in Canaan before the Israelites.
*2.1 Bochim: In Hebrew "Bochim" means "crying" (see verse 5).
See also: 1.29: Josh 16.10. 2.2: Exod 34.12,13; Deut 7.2–5.

*2.5 Crying: Or "Bochim".
*2.16 special leaders known as judges: The Hebrew text has "judges". In addition to leading Israelites in battle, these special leaders also decided legal cases and sometimes performed religious duties.
See also: 2.9: Josh 19.49,50.

listen to these judges. The Israelites would disobey the LORD, and instead of worshipping him, they would worship other gods.

[18] When enemies made life miserable for the Israelites, the LORD would feel sorry for them. He would appoint a judge and help that judge rescue Israel from its enemies. The LORD would be kind to Israel as long as that judge lived. [19] But afterwards, the Israelites would become even more sinful than their ancestors had been. The Israelites were stubborn — they simply would not stop worshipping other gods or following the teachings of other religions.

The LORD lets enemies test Israel

[20] The LORD was angry with Israel and said:

The Israelites have broken the agreement I made with their ancestors. They won't obey me, [21] so I'll stop helping them defeat their enemies. Israel still had a lot of enemies when Joshua died, [22] and I'm going to let those enemies stay. I'll use them to test Israel, because then I can find out if Israel will worship and obey me as their ancestors did.

[23] That's why the LORD had not let Joshua get rid of all those enemy nations straight away.

CHAPTER 3

[1-2] And the LORD had another reason for letting these enemies stay. The Israelites needed to learn how to fight in war, just as their ancestors had done. Each new generation would have to learn by fighting [3] the Philistines and their five rulers, as well as the Canaanites, the Sidonians, and the Hivites who lived in the Lebanon Mountains from Mount Baal-Hermon to Hamath Pass.'

[4] Moses had told the Israelites what the LORD had commanded them to do, and now the LORD was using these nations to find out if Israel would obey. [5-6] But they refused. And it was because of the Canaanites, Hittites, Amorites, Perizzites, Hivites, and Jebusites who lived all around them. Some of the Israelites married the people of these nations, and that's how they started worshipping foreign gods.

Othniel, Ehud, and Shamgar

Othniel

[7] The Israelites sinned against the LORD by forgetting him and worshipping idols of Baal

and Astarte. [8] This made the LORD angry, so he let Israel be defeated by King Cushan Rishathaim of northern Syria,' who ruled Israel eight years and made everyone pay taxes. [9] The Israelites begged the LORD for help, and he chose Othniel to rescue them. Othniel was the son of Caleb's younger brother Kenaz.' [10] The Spirit of the LORD took control of Othniel, and he led Israel in a war against Cushan Rishathaim. The LORD gave Othniel victory, [11] and Israel was at peace until Othniel died about forty years later.

Ehud

[12] Once more the Israelites started disobeying the LORD. So he let them be defeated by King Eglon of Moab, [13] who had joined forces with the Ammonites and the Amalekites to attack Israel. Eglon and his army captured Jericho.' [14] Then he ruled Israel for eighteen years and forced the Israelites to pay heavy taxes.

[15-16] The Israelites begged the LORD for help, and the LORD chose Ehud' from the Benjamin tribe to rescue them. They put Ehud in charge of taking the taxes to King Eglon, but before Ehud went, he made a double-edged dagger. Ehud was left-handed, so he strapped the dagger to his right thigh, where it would be hidden under his robes.

[17-18] Ehud and some other Israelites took the taxes to Eglon, who was a very fat man. As soon as they gave the taxes to Eglon, Ehud said it was time to go home.

[19-20] Ehud went with the other Israelites as far as the statues* at Gilgal.* Then he turned back and went upstairs to the cool room* where Eglon had his throne. Ehud said, "Your Majesty, I need to talk with you in private."

Eglon replied, "Don't say anything yet!" His officials left the room, and Eglon stood up as Ehud came closer.

"Yes," Ehud said, "I have a message for you from God!" [21] Ehud pulled out the dagger with his left hand and shoved it so far into Eglon's stomach [22-23] that even the handle was buried in his fat. Ehud left the dagger there. Then after closing and locking the doors to the room, he climbed through a window on to the porch' [24] and left.

---

*3.19,20 statues: Or "stone idols" or "stone monuments".

*3.19,20 Gilgal: About two and a half kilometres from Jericho, where Eglon probably was (see verse 13).

*3.19,20 upstairs . . . cool room: Houses usually had flat roofs, and sometimes a room was built on one corner of the roof where it could best catch the breeze and be kept cooler than the rest of the house.

When the king's officials came back and saw that the doors were locked, they said, "The king is probably inside relieving himself." 25 They stood there waiting until they felt foolish, but Eglon never opened the doors. Finally, they unlocked the doors and found King Eglon lying dead on the floor. 26 But by that time, Ehud had already escaped past the statues.*

Ehud went to the town of Seirah 27-28 in the hill country of Ephraim and started blowing a signal on a trumpet. The Israelites came together, and he shouted, "Follow me! The LORD will help us defeat the Moabites."

The Israelites followed Ehud down to the Jordan Valley, and they captured the places where people cross the river on the way to Moab. They would not let anyone go across, 29 and before the fighting was over, they killed about ten thousand Moabite warriors — not one escaped alive.

30 Moab was so badly defeated that it was a long time before they were strong enough to attack Israel again. And Israel was at peace for eighty years.

Shamgar

31 Shamgar the son of Anath was the next to rescue Israel. In one battle, he used a sharp wooden pole* to kill six hundred Philistines.

Deborah, Barak, and Jael

CHAPTER 4

Deborah and Barak

1 After the death of Ehud, the Israelites again started disobeying the LORD. 2 So the LORD let the Canaanite King Jabin of Hazor conquer Israel. Sisera, the commander of Jabin's army, lived in Harosheth-Ha-Goiim. 3 Jabin's army had nine hundred iron chariots, and for twenty years he made life miserable for the Israelites, until finally they begged the LORD for help.

4 Deborah the wife of Lappidoth was a prophet and a leader* of Israel during those days. 5 She would sit under Deborah's Palm Tree between Ramah and Bethel in the hill country of Ephraim, where Israelites would come and ask her to settle their legal cases.

6 One day, Barak the son of Abinoam was in Kedesh in Naphtali, and Deborah sent word for him to come and talk with her. When he arrived, she said:

I have a message for you from the LORD God of Israel! You are to get together an army of ten thousand men from the Naphtali and Zebulun tribes and lead them to Mount Tabor. 7 The LORD will trick Sisera into coming out to fight you at the River Kishon. Sisera will be leading King Jabin's army as usual, and they will have their chariots, but the LORD has promised to help you defeat them.

8 "I'm not going unless you go!" Barak told her.

9 "All right, I'll go!" she replied. "But I'm warning you that the LORD is going to let a woman defeat Sisera, and no one will honour you for winning the battle."

Deborah and Barak left for Kedesh, 10 where Barak called together the troops from Zebulun and Naphtali. Ten thousand soldiers gathered there, and Barak led them out from Kedesh. Deborah went too.

11 At this time, Heber of the Kenite clan was living near the village of Oak in Zaanannim,* not far from Kedesh. The Kenites were descendants of Hobab, the father-in-law of Moses, but Heber had moved and had set up his tents away from the rest of the clan.

12 When Sisera learnt that Barak had led an army to Mount Tabor, 13 he called his troops together and got all nine hundred iron chariots ready. Then he led his army away from Harosheth-Ha-Goiim to the River Kishon.

14 Deborah shouted, "Barak, it's time to attack Sisera! Because today the LORD is going to help you defeat him. In fact, the LORD has already gone on ahead to fight for you."

Barak led his ten thousand troops down from Mount Tabor. 15 And during the battle, the LORD confused Sisera, his chariot drivers, and his whole army. Everyone was so afraid of Barak and his army, that even Sisera jumped down from his chariot and tried to escape. 16 Barak's forces went after Sisera's chariots and army as far as Harosheth-Ha-Goiim.

Sisera's entire army was wiped out. 17 Only Sisera escaped. He ran to Heber's camp, because Heber and his family had a peace treaty with the king of Hazor. Sisera went to the tent that belonged to Jael, Heber's wife. 18 She came out to greet him and said, "Come in, sir! Please come on in. Don't be afraid."

---

*3.26 statues: See the note at 3.19,20.
*3.31 sharp wooden pole: The Hebrew text has "cattle-prod", a pole with a sharpened tip or metal point at one end.
*4.4 leader: See 2.16 and the note there.

After they had gone inside, Sisera lay down, and Jael covered him with a blanket.

¹⁹ "Could I have a little water?" he asked. "I'm thirsty."

Jael opened a leather bottle and poured him some milk, then she covered him up again.

²⁰ "Stand at the entrance to the tent," Sisera told her. "If someone comes by and asks if anyone is inside, tell them 'No.' "

²¹ Sisera was exhausted and soon fell fast asleep. Jael took a hammer and drove a tent-peg through his head into the ground, and he died.

²² Meanwhile, Barak had been following Sisera, and Jael went out to meet him. "The man you're looking for is inside," she said. "Come in and I'll show him to you."

They went inside, and there was Sisera — dead and stretched out with a tent-peg through his skull.

²³ That same day the Israelites defeated the Canaanite King Jabin, and his army was no longer powerful enough to attack the Israelites. ²⁴ Jabin grew weaker while the Israelites kept growing stronger, and at last the Israelites destroyed him.

CHAPTER 5

Deborah and Barak sing for the LORD

¹ After the battle was over that day, Deborah and Barak sang this song:

² We praise you, LORD!
   Our soldiers volunteered,
      ready to follow you.
³ Listen, kings and rulers,
   while I sing for the LORD,
      the God of Israel.

⁴⁻⁵ Our LORD, God of Israel,
   when you came from Seir,
      where the Edomites live,
   rain poured from the sky,
      the earth trembled,
      and mountains shook.

⁶ In the time of Shamgar son of Anath,
   and now again in Jael's time,
   roads were too dangerous
      for caravans.
   Travellers had to take the back roads,
⁷ and villagers couldn't work
      in their fields.◆
   Then Deborah◆ took command,
      protecting Israel as a mother
      protects her children.

⁸ The Israelites worshipped other gods,
   and the gates of their towns
      were then attacked.
   But they had no shields
      or spears to fight with.
⁹ I praise you, LORD,
   and I am grateful
   for those leaders and soldiers
      who volunteered.
¹⁰ Listen, everyone!
   Whether you ride a donkey
      with a padded saddle
      or have to walk.
¹¹ Even those who carry water◆
   to the animals will tell you,
   "The LORD has won victories,
      and so has Israel."

   Then the LORD's people marched
      down to the town gates
¹² and said, "Deborah, let's go!
   Let's sing as we march.
   Barak, capture your enemies."

¹³ The LORD's people who were left
   joined with their leaders
      and fought at my side.◆
¹⁴ Troops came from Ephraim,
   where Amalekites once lived.
   Others came from Benjamin;
   officers and leaders came
      from Machir and Zebulun.
¹⁵ The rulers of Issachar
      came along with Deborah,
   and Issachar followed Barak
      into the valley.

   But the tribe of Reuben
      was no help at all!◆
¹⁶ Reuben, why did you stay
      among your sheep pens?◆
   Was it to listen to shepherds
      whistling for their sheep?
   No one could understand
      why Reuben wouldn't come.◆
¹⁷ The people of Gilead stayed
      across the Jordan.
   Why did the tribe of Dan
      remain on their ships
   and the tribe of Asher
      stay along the coast
      near the harbours?
¹⁸ But soldiers of Zebulun and Naphtali
   risked their lives
      to attack the enemy.◆
¹⁹ Canaanite kings fought us
   at Taanach by the stream
      near Megiddo◆ —

See also: 5.4–5: Exod 19.18.

but they couldn't rob us of our silver.*
²⁰ From their pathways in the sky
the stars* fought Sisera,
²¹ and his soldiers were swept away
by the ancient River Kishon.

I will march on and be brave.

²² Sisera's horses galloped off,
their hoofs thundering in retreat.

²³ The LORD's angel said,
"Put a curse on Meroz Town!
Its people refused
to help the LORD fight
his powerful enemies."

²⁴ But honour Jael, the wife of Heber
from the Kenite clan.
Give more honour to her
than to any other woman
who lives in tents.
Yes, give more honour to her
than to any other woman.

²⁵ Sisera asked for water,
but Jael gave him milk —
cream in a fine cup.
²⁶ She reached for a tent-peg
and held a hammer
in her right hand.
And with a blow to the head,
she crushed his skull.
²⁷ Sisera sank to his knees
and fell dead at her feet.

²⁸ Sisera's mother looked out
through her window.
"Why is he taking so long?"
she asked.
"Why haven't we heard
his chariots coming?"
²⁹ She and her wisest women
gave the same answer:
³⁰ "Sisera and his troops
are finding treasures to bring back —
a woman, or perhaps two,
for each man,
and beautiful dresses
for those women to wear."◆

³¹ Our LORD, we pray
that all your enemies
will die like Sisera.
But let everyone who loves you
shine brightly like the sun at dawn.

---

*5.19 rob us of our silver: The army that won a
battle would take everything of value from the dead
enemy soldiers.
*5.20 stars: In ancient times, the stars were
sometimes regarded as supernatural beings.

Gideon

CHAPTER 6

Midian steals everything from Israel

There was peace in Israel for about forty years.
¹ Then once again the Israelites started
disobeying the LORD, so he let the nation of
Midian control Israel for seven years. ² The
Midianites were so cruel that many Israelites
ran to the mountains and hid in caves.

³ Every time the Israelites would plant crops,
the Midianites invaded Israel together with
the Amalekites and other eastern nations.
⁴⁻⁵ They rode in on their camels, set up their
tents, and then let their livestock eat the crops
as far as the town of Gaza. The Midianites stole
food, sheep, cattle, and donkeys. Like a swarm
of locusts,* they could not be counted, and
they ruined the land wherever they went.
⁶⁻⁷ The Midianites took almost everything
that belonged to the Israelites, and the
Israelites begged the LORD for help. ⁸⁻⁹ Then
the LORD sent a prophet to them with this
message:

I am the LORD God of Israel, so listen to
what I say. You were slaves in Egypt, but I
set you free and led you out of Egypt into
this land. And when nations here made life
miserable for you, I rescued you and
helped you get rid of them and take their
land. ¹⁰ I am your God, and I told you not
to worship Amorite gods, even though you
are living in the land of the Amorites. But
you refused to listen.

The LORD chooses Gideon

¹¹ One day an angel from the LORD went to
the town of Ophrah and sat down under the
big tree that belonged to Joash, a member of
the Abiezer clan. Joash's son Gideon was
nearby, threshing grain in a shallow pit,
where he could not be seen by the Midianites.
¹² The angel appeared and spoke to Gideon,
"The LORD is helping you, and you are a
strong warrior."
¹³ Gideon answered, "Please don't take this
wrong, but if the LORD is helping us, then why
have all these awful things happened? We've
heard how the LORD performed miracles and
rescued our ancestors from Egypt. But those
things happened long ago. Now the LORD has
abandoned us to the Midianites."

---

*6.4,5 locusts: Insects like grasshoppers that travel in
swarms and cause great damage to crops.

¹⁴ Then the LORD himself said, "Gideon, you will be strong, because I am giving you the power to rescue Israel from the Midianites."

¹⁵ Gideon replied, "But how can I rescue Israel? My clan is the weakest one in Manasseh, and everyone else in my family is more important than I am."

¹⁶ "Gideon," the LORD answered, "you can rescue Israel because I am going to help you! Defeating the Midianites will be as easy as beating up one man."

¹⁷ Gideon said, "It's hard to believe that I'm actually talking to the LORD. Please do something so I'll know that you really are the LORD. ¹⁸ And wait here until I bring you an offering."

"All right, I'll wait," the LORD answered.

¹⁹ Gideon went home and killed a young goat, then started boiling the meat. Next, he opened a big sack of flour and made it into thin bread.* When the meat was done, he put it in a basket and poured the broth into a clay cooking pot. He took the meat, the broth, and the bread and placed them under the big tree.

²⁰ God's angel said, "Gideon, put the meat and the bread on this rock, and pour the broth over them." Gideon did as he was told. ²¹ The angel was holding a walking stick, and he touched the meat and the bread with the end of the stick. Flames jumped from the rock and burnt up the meat and the bread.

When Gideon looked, the angel was gone. ²² Gideon realized that he had seen one of the LORD's angels. "Oh!" he moaned. "Now I'm going to die."*

²³ "Calm down!" the LORD told Gideon. "There's nothing to be afraid of. You're not going to die."

²⁴ Gideon built an altar for worshipping the LORD and called it "The LORD Calms our Fears". It still stands there in Ophrah, a town in the territory of the Abiezer clan.

Gideon tears down Baal's altar

²⁵ That night the LORD spoke to Gideon again:

Get your father's second-best bull, the one that's seven years old. Use it to pull down the altar where your father worships Baal

and cut down the sacred pole* next to the altar. ²⁶ Then build an altar for worshipping me on the highest part of the hill where your town is built. Use layers of stones for my altar, not just a pile of rocks. Cut up the wood from the pole, make a fire, kill the bull, and burn it as a sacrifice to me.

²⁷ Gideon chose ten of his servants to help him, and they did everything God had said. But since Gideon was afraid of his family and the other people in town, he did it all at night.

²⁸ When the people of the town got up the next morning, they saw that Baal's altar had been knocked over, and the sacred pole next to it had been cut down. Then they noticed the new altar covered with the remains of the sacrificed bull.

²⁹ "Who could have done such a thing?" they asked. And they kept on asking, until finally someone told them, "Gideon the son of Joash did it."

³⁰ The men of the town went to Joash and said, "Your son Gideon knocked over Baal's altar and cut down the sacred pole next to it. Hand him over, so we can kill him!"

³¹ The crowd pushed closer and closer, but Joash replied, "Are you trying to take revenge for Baal? Are you trying to rescue Baal? If you are, you will be the ones who are put to death, and it will happen before another day dawns. If Baal really is a god, let him take his own revenge on someone who tears down his altar."

³² That same day, Joash changed Gideon's name to Jerubbaal, explaining, "He tore down Baal's altar, so let Baal take revenge himself."*

Gideon defeats the Midianites

³³ All the Midianites, Amalekites, and other eastern nations got together and crossed the River Jordan. Then they invaded the land of Israel and set up camp in Jezreel Valley.

³⁴ The LORD's Spirit took control of Gideon, and Gideon blew a signal on a trumpet to tell the men in the Abiezer clan to follow him. ³⁵ He also sent messengers to the tribes of Manasseh, Asher, Zebulun, and Naphtali, telling the men of these tribes to come and join his army. Then they set out towards the enemy camp.

³⁶⁻³⁷ Gideon prayed to God, "I know that you promised to help me rescue Israel, but I need proof. Tonight I'll put some wool on the

---

*6.19 thin bread: Bread made without yeast, since there was no time for the dough to rise.

*6.22 Now I'm going to die: The Hebrew text has "I have seen an angel of the LORD face to face." Some people believed that if they saw one of the LORD's angels, they would die (see 13.22).

*6.25 sacred pole: Or "sacred tree", used as a symbol of Asherah, the Canaanite goddess of fertility.

*6.32 Jerubbaal . . . take revenge himself: In Hebrew, "Jerubbaal" means "Let Baal take revenge".

stone floor of that threshing-place over there. If you really will help me rescue Israel, then tomorrow morning let there be dew on the wool, but let the stone floor be dry."

[38] And that's just what happened. Early the next morning, Gideon got up and checked the wool. He squeezed out enough water to fill a bowl. [39] But Gideon prayed to God again. "Don't be angry with me," Gideon said. "Let me try this just one more time, so I'll really be sure you'll help me. Only this time, let the wool be dry and the stone floor be wet with dew."

[40] That night, God made the stone floor wet with dew, but he kept the wool dry.

CHAPTER 7

[1] Early the next morning, Gideon and his army got up and moved their camp to Fear Spring.* The Midianite camp was to the north, in the valley at the foot of Moreh Hill.*

[2] "Gideon," the LORD said, "your army is too big. I can't let you win with this many soldiers. The Israelites would think that they had won the battle all by themselves and that I didn't have anything to do with it. [3] So call your troops together and tell them that anyone who is really afraid can leave Mount Gilead* and go home."

Twenty-two thousand men returned home, leaving Gideon with only ten thousand soldiers.

[4] "Gideon," the LORD said, "you still have too many soldiers. Take them down to the spring and I'll test them. I'll tell you which ones can go along with you and which ones must go back home."

[5] When Gideon led his army down to the spring, the LORD told him, "Watch how each man gets a drink of water. Then divide them into two groups — those who lap the water like a dog and those who kneel down to drink."

[6] Three hundred men scooped up water in their hands and lapped it, and the rest knelt to get a drink. [7] The LORD said, "Gideon, your army will be made up of everyone who lapped the water from their hands. Send the others home. I'm going to rescue Israel by helping you and your army of three hundred defeat the Midianites."

[8] Then Gideon gave these orders, "You three hundred men stay here. The rest of you may go home, but leave your food and trumpets with us."

Gideon's army camp was on top of a hill overlooking the Midianite camp in the valley.

[9] That night, the LORD said to Gideon. "Get up! Attack the Midianite camp. I am going to let you defeat them, [10] but if you're still afraid, you and your servant Purah should sneak down to their camp. [11] When you hear what the Midianites are saying, you'll be brave enough to attack."

Gideon and Purah worked their way to the edge of the enemy camp, where soldiers were on guard duty. [12] The camp was huge. The Midianites, Amalekites, and other eastern nations covered the valley like a swarm of locusts.* And it would be easier to count the grains of sand on a beach than to count their camels. [13] Gideon overheard one enemy guard telling another, "I had a dream about a flat* loaf of barley bread that came tumbling into our camp. It hit the headquarters tent,* and the tent tipped over and fell down."

[14] The other soldier answered, "Your dream must have been about Gideon, the Israelite commander. It means God will let him and his army defeat the Midianite army and everyone else in our camp."

[15] As soon as Gideon heard about the dream and what it meant, he bowed down to praise God. Then he went back to the Israelite camp and shouted, "Let's go! The LORD is going to let us defeat the Midianite army."

[16] Gideon divided his little army into three groups of one hundred men, and he gave each soldier a trumpet and a large clay jar with a burning torch inside. [17-18] Gideon said, "When we get to the enemy camp, spread out and surround it. Then wait for me to blow a signal on my trumpet. As soon as you hear it, blow your trumpets and shout, 'Fight for the LORD! Fight for Gideon!' "

[19] Gideon and his group reached the edge of the enemy camp a few hours after dark, just after the new guards had come on duty.* Gideon and his soldiers blew their trumpets

---

*7.12 locusts: See the note at 6.4,5.
*7.19 a few hours after dark, just . . . duty: The Hebrew text has "at the beginning of the second watch, just . . . duty." The night was divided into three periods called "watches", each about four hours long, and different guards would come on duty at the beginning of each watch. The first watch began at sunset, so the beginning of the second watch would have been shortly after 10:00 PM.

---

*7.1 Moreh Hill: About 8 kilometres north of Fear Spring.
*7.3 Mount Gilead: Usually "Gilead" refers to an area east of the River Jordan, but in this verse it refers to a place near Jezreel Valley west of the Jordan.
See also: 7.3: Deut 20.8.

and smashed the clay jars that were hiding the torches. [20] The rest of Gideon's soldiers blew the trumpets they were holding in their right hands. Then they smashed the jars and held the burning torches in their left hands. Everyone shouted, "Fight with your swords for the LORD and for Gideon!"

[21] The enemy soldiers started yelling and tried to run away. Gideon's troops stayed in their positions surrounding the camp [22] and blew their trumpets again. As they did, the LORD made the enemy soldiers pull out their swords and start fighting each other.

The enemy army tried to escape from the camp. They ran to Acacia Tree Town, towards Zeredah,* and as far as the edge of the land that belonged to the town of Abel-Meholah near Tabbath.*

[23] Gideon sent word for more Israelite soldiers to come from the tribes of Naphtali, Asher, and both halves of Manasseh* to help fight the Midianites. [24] He also sent messengers to tell all the men who lived in the hill country of Ephraim, "Come and help us fight the Midianites! Put guards at every spring, stream, and well, as far as Beth-Barah before the Midianites can get to them. And guard the River Jordan."

Troops from Ephraim did exactly what Gideon had asked, [25] and they even helped chase the Midianites on the east side of the River Jordan. These troops captured Raven and Wolf,* the two Midianite leaders. They killed Raven at a large rock that has come to be known as Raven Rock, and they killed Wolf near a wine-pit that has come to be called Wolf Wine-pit.*

The men of Ephraim brought the heads of the two Midianite leaders to Gideon.

CHAPTER 8

[1] But the men were really upset with Gideon and complained, "When you went to war with Midian, you didn't ask us to help! Why did you treat us like that?"

[2] Gideon answered:

Don't be upset! Even though you came later, you were able to do much more than I did. It's just like the grape harvest: the grapes your tribe doesn't even bother to

pick are better than the best grapes my family can grow. [3] Besides, God chose you to capture Raven and Wolf. I didn't do a thing compared to you.

By the time Gideon had finished talking, the men of Ephraim had calmed down and were no longer angry with him.

Gideon finishes destroying the Midianite army

[4] After Gideon and his three hundred troops had chased the Midianites as far as the River Jordan, they were exhausted. The town of Succoth was nearby, so he went there and asked, "Please give my troops some food. They are worn out, but we have to keep chasing Zebah and Zalmunna, the two Midianite kings."

[6] The town leaders of Succoth answered, "Why should we feed your army? We don't know if you really will defeat Zebah and Zalmunna."

[7] "Just wait!" Gideon said. "After the LORD helps me defeat them, I'm coming back here. I'll make a whip out of thorns and rip the flesh from your bones."

[8] After leaving Succoth, Gideon went to Penuel and asked the leaders there for some food. But he got the same answer as he had got at Succoth. [9] "I'll come back safe and sound," Gideon said, "but when I do, I'm going to tear down your tower!"*

[10] Zebah and Zalmunna were in Karkor* with an army of fifteen thousand troops. They were all that was left of the army of the eastern nations, because one hundred and twenty thousand of their warriors had been killed in the battle.

[11] Gideon reached the enemy camp by going east along Nomad* Road past Nobah and Jogbehah. He made a surprise attack, [12] and the enemy panicked. Zebah and Zalmunna tried to escape, but Gideon chased and captured them.

[13] After the battle, Gideon set out for home. As he was going through Heres Pass, [14] he caught a young man who lived in Succoth. Gideon asked him who the town officials of Succoth were, and the young man wrote down seventy-seven names.

---

*7.22 Acacia Tree Town . . . Zeredah . . . Abel-Meholah near Tabbath: These were places east of the River Jordan.
*7.23 both halves of Manasseh: Half of Manasseh lived east of the River Jordan, and the other half lived on the west.

*8.9 tower: Towers were often part of a town wall.
*8.10 Karkor: About 160 kilometres east of the Dead Sea.
*8.11 Nomad: A person who lives in a tent and moves from place to place.
See also: 8.3–5: Psa 83.11.

¹⁵ Gideon went to the town officials and said, "Here are Zebah and Zalmunna. Remember how you made fun of me? You said, 'We don't know if you really will defeat those two Midianite kings. So why should we feed your worn-out army?' "

¹⁶ Gideon made a whip from thorn plants and used it to beat the town officials.
¹⁷ Afterwards he went to Penuel, where he tore down the tower and killed all the town officials' there.

¹⁸ Then Gideon said, "Zebah and Zalmunna, tell me about the men you killed at Tabor."

"They were a lot like you," the two kings answered. "They were dignified, almost like royalty."

¹⁹ "They were my very own brothers!" Gideon said. "I swear by the living LORD that if you had let them live, I would let you live."

²⁰ Gideon turned to Jether, his eldest son. "Kill them!" Gideon said.

But Jether was young,* and he was too afraid even to pull out his sword.

²¹ "What's the matter, Gideon?" Zebah and Zalmunna asked. "Do it yourself, if you're not too much of a coward!"

Gideon jumped up and killed them both. Then he took the fine gold ornaments from the necks of their camels.

The Israelites ask Gideon to be their king

²² After the battle with the Midianites, the Israelites said, "Gideon, you rescued us! Now we want you to be our king. Then after your death, your son and then your grandson will rule."

²³ "No," Gideon replied, "I won't be your king, and my son won't be king either. Only the LORD is your ruler. ²⁴ But I will ask you to do one thing: give me all the earrings you took from the enemy."

The enemy soldiers had been Ishmaelites,* and they wore gold earrings.

²⁵ The Israelite soldiers replied, "Of course we will give you the earrings." Then they spread out a robe on the ground and tossed

the earrings on it. ²⁶ The total weight of this gold was nearly twenty kilograms. In addition, there was the gold from the camels' ornaments and from the beautiful jewellery worn by the Midianite kings. Gideon also took their purple robes.

²⁷⁻²⁹ Gideon returned to his home in Ophrah and had the gold made into a statue, which the Israelites soon started worshipping. They became unfaithful to God, and even Gideon and his family were trapped into worshipping the statue.'

The Midianites had been defeated so badly that they were no longer strong enough to attack Israel. And so Israel was at peace for the remaining forty years of Gideon's life.

Gideon dies

³⁰ Gideon had many wives and seventy sons. ³¹ He even had a wife* who lived at Shechem.* They had a son, and Gideon named him Abimelech.

³² Gideon lived to be an old man. And when he died, he was buried in the family tomb in his home town of Ophrah, which belonged to the Abiezer clan.

³³ Soon after Gideon's death, the Israelites turned their backs on God again. They set up idols of Baal and worshipped Baal Berith' as their god. ³⁴ The Israelites forgot that the LORD was their God, and that he had rescued them from the enemies who lived around them. ³⁵ Besides all that, the Israelites were unkind to Gideon's family, even though Gideon had done so much for Israel.

Abimelech

CHAPTER 9

Abimelech tries to be king

¹ Abimelech the son of Gideon' went to Shechem. While there, he met with his mother's relatives ² and told them to say to the leaders of Shechem, "Do you think it would be good to have all seventy of Gideon's sons ruling us? Wouldn't you rather have just one man as king? Abimelech would make a good king, and he's related to us."

---

*8.20 young: Gideon wanted to insult the kings by having them killed by a young boy.
*8.24 Ishmaelites: According to Genesis 25.1,2,12, both Ishmaelites and Midianites were descendants of Abraham. It is possible that in this passage "Ishmaelites" has the meaning "nomadic traders", while "Midianites" (verses 22,26–29) refers to their ethnic origin.

*8.31 wife: This translates a Hebrew word for a woman who was legally bound to a man, but without the full privileges of a wife.
*8.31 who lived at Shechem: Sometimes marriages were arranged so that the wife lived with her parents, and the husband visited her from time to time.

³ Abimelech's uncles talked it over with the leaders of Shechem who agreed, "Yes, it would be better for one of our relatives to be king." ⁴ Then they gave Abimelech seventy pieces* of silver from the temple of their god Baal Berith.⁑

Abimelech used the silver to hire a gang of rough soldiers who would do anything for money. ⁵ Abimelech and his soldiers went to his father's home in Ophrah and brought out Gideon's other sons to a large rock, where they murdered all seventy. Gideon's youngest son Jotham hid from the soldiers, but he was the only one who escaped.

⁶ The leaders of Shechem, including the priests and the military officers,⁑ met at the tree next to the sacred rock⁑ in Shechem to crown Abimelech king. ⁷ Jotham heard what they were doing. So he climbed to the top of Mount Gerizim and shouted down to the people who were there at the meeting:

Leaders of Shechem,
   listen to me,
and perhaps God
   will listen to you.

⁸ Once the trees searched
   for someone to be king;
they asked the olive tree,
   "Will you be our king?"
⁹ But the olive tree replied,
   "My oil brings honour
      to people and gods.
I won't stop making oil,
   just so my branches can wave
      above the other trees."

¹⁰ Then they asked the fig tree,
   "Will you be our king?"
¹¹ But the fig tree replied,
   "I won't stop growing
      my delicious fruit,
just so my branches can wave
   above the other trees."

¹² Next they asked the grape vine,
   "Will you be our king?"
¹³ But the grape vine replied,
   "My wine brings cheer
      to people and gods.
I won't stop making wine,
   just so my branches can wave
      above the other trees."

¹⁴ Finally, they went
   to the thorn bush and asked,
   "Will you be our king?"

¹⁵ The thorn bush replied,
   "If you really want me
      to be your king,
then come into my shade
   and I will protect you.
But if you're deceiving me,
   I'll start a fire
that will spread out and destroy
   the cedars of Lebanon."*

After Jotham had finished telling this story, he said:

¹⁶⁻¹⁸ My father Gideon risked his life for you when he fought to rescue you from the Midianites. Did you reward Gideon by being kind to his family? No, you did not! You attacked his family and killed all seventy of his sons on that rock.

And was it right to make Abimelech your king? He's merely the son of my father's slave girl.* But just because he's your relative, you made him king of Shechem.

¹⁹ So, you leaders of Shechem, if you treated Gideon and his family the way you should have, then I hope you and Abimelech will make each other very happy. ²⁰ But if it was wrong to treat Gideon and his family the way you did, then I pray that Abimelech will destroy you with fire, and I pray that you will do the same to him.

²¹ Jotham ran off and went to live in the town of Beer, where he could be safe from his brother Abimelech.

Abimelech destroys Shechem

²² Abimelech had been a military commander of Israel for three years, ²³⁻²⁴ when God decided to punish him and the leaders of Shechem for killing Gideon's seventy sons.

So God turned the leaders of Shechem against Abimelech. ²⁵ Then they sent some men to hide on the hilltops and watch for Abimelech and his troops, while they sent others to rob everyone who went by on the road. But Abimelech found out what they were doing.

²⁶ One day, Gaal son of Ebed went to live in Shechem. His brothers moved there too, and soon the leaders of Shechem started trusting him.

²⁷ The time came for the grape harvest, and the people of Shechem went into their

---

*9.4 seventy pieces: Nearly 800 grammes.

*9.15 cedars of Lebanon: The cedars that grew in the Lebanon mountains were some of the largest trees in that part of the world.

*9.16–18 son of . . . slave girl: See 8.31.

vineyards and picked the grapes. They put the grapes in their wine-pits and walked on them to squeeze out the juice in order to make wine. Then they went into the temple of their god and threw a big party. There was a lot of eating and drinking, and before long they were cursing Abimelech.

[28] Gaal said:

Hamor was the founder of Shechem, and one of his descendants should be our ruler. But Abimelech's father was Gideon, so Abimelech isn't really one of us. He shouldn't be our king, and we shouldn't have to obey him or Zebul, who rules Shechem for him. [29] If I were the ruler of Shechem, I'd get rid of that Abimelech. I'd tell him, "Get yourself an even bigger army, and we will still defeat you."

[30] Zebul was angry when he found out what Gaal had said. [31] And so he sent some messengers to Abimelech. But they had to pretend to be doing something else, or they would not have been allowed to leave Shechem.' Zebul told the messengers to say:

Gaal the son of Ebed has come to Shechem along with his brothers, and they have persuaded the people to let Gaal rule Shechem instead of you. [32] This is what I think you should do. Lead your army here during the night and hide in the fields. [33] Get up the next morning at sunrise and rush out of your hiding places to attack the town. Gaal and his followers will come out to fight you, but you will easily defeat them.

[34] So one night, Abimelech led his soldiers to Shechem. He divided them into four groups, and they all hid near the town.

[35] The next morning, Gaal went out and stood in the opening of the town gate. Abimelech and his soldiers left their hiding places, [36] and Gaal saw them. Zebul was standing there with Gaal, and Gaal remarked, "Zebul, that looks like a crowd of people coming down from the mountaintops."

"No," Zebul answered, "it's just the shadows of the mountains. It only looks like people moving."

[37] "But Zebul, look over there," Gaal said. "There's a crowd coming down from the sacred mountain,' and another group is coming along the road from the tree where people talk with the spirits of the dead."

[38] Then Zebul replied, "What good is all your boasting now? You were the one who said Abimelech shouldn't be the ruler of Shechem. Out there is the army that you made fun of. So go out and fight them!"

[39] Gaal and the leaders of Shechem went out and fought Abimelech. [40] Soon the people of Shechem turned and ran back into the town. However, Abimelech and his troops were close behind and killed many of them along the way.

[41] Abimelech stayed at Arumah,* and Zebul forced Gaal and his brothers out of Shechem.

[42] The next morning, the people of Shechem were getting ready to work in their fields as usual, but someone told Abimelech about it. [43] Abimelech divided his army into three groups and set up an ambush in the fields near Shechem. When the people came out of the town, he and his army rushed out from their hiding places and attacked.

[44] Abimelech and the troops with him ran to the town gate and took control of it, while two other groups attacked and killed the people who were in the fields. [45] He and his troops fought in Shechem all day, until they had killed everyone in town. Then he and his men tore down the houses and buildings and scattered salt* everywhere.

[46] Earlier that day, the leaders of the temple of El Berith' at Shechem had heard about the attack. So they went into the temple fortress, [47] but Abimelech found out where they were. [48] He led his troops to Mount Zalmon, where he took an axe and chopped off a tree branch. He lifted the branch on to his shoulder and shouted, "Hurry! Cut off a branch just as I did."

[49] When they all had branches, they followed Abimelech back to Shechem. They piled the branches against the fortress and set them on fire, burning down the fortress and killing about one thousand men and women.

[50] After destroying Shechem, Abimelech went to Thebez. He surrounded the town and captured it. [51] But there was a tall fortress in the middle of the town, and the town leaders and everyone else went inside. Then they barred the gates and went up to the flat roof. [52] Abimelech and his army rushed to the fortress and tried to force their way inside. Abimelech himself was about to set the heavy wooden doors on fire, [53] when a woman on the roof dropped a large rock* on his head

---

*9.41 Arumah: About eight kilometres from Shechem.
*9.45 scattered salt: This may have been part of a ceremony to place a curse on the town.
*9.53 large rock: One that was used in the grinding of grain.

See also: 9.53: 2 Sam 11.21.

and cracked his skull. ⁵⁴ The soldier who carried his weapons was nearby, and Abimelech told him, "Take out your sword and kill me. I don't want people to say that I was killed by a woman!"

So the soldier ran his sword through Abimelech. ⁵⁵ And when the Israelite soldiers saw that their leader was dead, they went back home.

⁵⁶ That's how God punished Abimelech for killing his brothers and bringing shame on his father's family. ⁵⁷ God also punished the people of Shechem for helping Abimelech.ᵇ Everything happened just as Jotham's curse said it would.

Tola, Jair, and Jephthah

CHAPTER 10

Tola

¹ Tola was the next person to rescue Israel. He belonged to the Issachar tribe, but he lived in Shamir, a town in the hill country of Ephraim. His father was Puah, and his grandfather was Dodo. ² Tola was a leader* of Israel for twenty-three years, then he died and was buried in Shamir.

Jair

³ The next leader* of Israel was Jair, who lived in Gilead. He was a leader for twenty-two years. ⁴ He had thirty sons, and each son had his own mule* and was in charge of one town in Gilead. Those thirty towns are still called The Settlements of Jair.ᵇ ⁵ When he died, he was buried in the town of Kamon.

Israel is unfaithful again

⁶ Before long, the Israelites began disobeying the Lord by worshipping Baal, Astarte, and gods from Syria, Sidon, Moab, Ammon, and Philistia.

⁷ The Lord was angry with Israel and decided to let Philistia and Ammon conquer them. ⁸ So the same year that Jair died, Israel's army was crushed by these two nations. For eighteen years, Ammon was cruel to the Israelites who lived in Gilead, the region east of the River Jordan that had once belonged to the Amorites. ⁹ Then the Ammonites began crossing the Jordan and

attacking the tribes of Judah, Benjamin, and Ephraim. Life was miserable for the Israelites. ¹⁰ They begged the Lord for help and confessed, "We were unfaithful to you, our Lord. We stopped worshipping you and started worshipping idols of Baal."

¹¹⁻¹² The Lord answered:

In the past when you came crying to me for help, I rescued you. At one time or another I've rescued you from the Egyptians, the Amorites, the Ammonites, the Philistines, the Sidonians, the Amalekites, and the Maonites.ᵇ ¹³⁻¹⁴ But I'm not going to rescue you any more! You've left me and gone off to worship other gods. If you're in such big trouble, go and cry to them for help!

¹⁵ "We have been unfaithful," the Israelites admitted. "If we must be punished, do it yourself, but please rescue us from the Ammonites."

¹⁶ Then the Israelites got rid of the idols of the foreign gods, and they began worshipping only the Lord. Finally, there came a time when the Lord could no longer stand to see them suffer.

The Ammonites invade Gilead

¹⁷ The rulers of Ammon called their soldiers together and led them to Gilead, where they set up camp.

The Israelites gathered at Mizpah* and set up camp there. ¹⁸ The leaders of Gilead asked each other, "Who can lead an attack on the Ammonites?" Then they agreed, "If we can find someone who can lead the attack, we'll make him the ruler of Gilead."

CHAPTER 11

Jephthah

¹⁻⁵ The leaders of the Gilead clan decided to ask a brave warrior named Jephthah son of Gilead to lead the attack against the Ammonites.

Even though Jephthah belonged to the Gilead clan, he had earlier been forced to leave the region where they had lived. Jephthah was the son of a prostitute, but his half-brothers were the sons of his father's wife.

---

*10.2,3 leader: See 2.16 and the note there.
*10.4 each son had his own mule: A sign that the family was wealthy.

*10.17 Mizpah: In chapters 10–12, Mizpah is the name of a town in Gilead (see 11.29), not the same town as the Mizpah of chapters 20,21.

One day his half-brothers told him, "You don't really belong to our family, so you can't have any of the family property." Then they forced Jephthah to leave home.

Jephthah went to the country of Tob, where he was joined by a number of men who would do anything for money.

So the leaders of Gilead went to Jephthah and said, ⁶ "Please come back to Gilead! If you lead our army, we will be able to fight off the Ammonites."

⁷ "Didn't you hate me?" Jephthah replied. "Weren't you the ones who forced me to leave my family? You're coming to me now, just because you're in trouble."

⁸ "But we do want you to come back," the leaders said. "And if you lead us in battle against the Ammonites, we will make you the ruler of Gilead."

⁹ "All right," Jephthah said. "If I go back with you and the LORD lets me defeat the Ammonites, will you really make me your ruler?"

¹⁰ "You have our word," the leaders answered. "And the LORD is a witness to what we have said."

¹¹ So Jephthah went back to Mizpah* with the leaders of Gilead. The people of Gilead gathered at the place of worship and made Jephthah their ruler. Jephthah also made promises to them.

¹² After the ceremony, Jephthah sent messengers to say to the king of Ammon, "Are you trying to start a war? You have invaded my country, and I want to know why!"

¹³ The king of Ammon replied, "Tell Jephthah that the land really belongs to me, all the way from the River Arnon in the south, to the River Jabbok in the north, and west to the River Jordan. When the Israelites came out of Egypt, they stole it. Tell Jephthah to return it to me, and there won't be any war."

¹⁴ Jephthah sent the messengers back to the king of Ammon, ¹⁵ and they told him that Jephthah had said:

Israel hasn't taken any territory from Moab or Ammon. ¹⁶ When the Israelites came from Egypt, they travelled in the desert to the Red Sea* and then to Kadesh. ¹⁷ They sent messengers to the king of Edom and

said, "Please, let us go through your country." But the king of Edom refused. They also sent messengers to the king of Moab, but he wouldn't let them cross his country either. And so the Israelites stayed at Kadesh.

¹⁸ A little later, the Israelites set out into the desert, going east of Edom and Moab, and camping on the eastern side of the gorge of the River Arnon. The Arnon is the eastern border of Moab, and since the Israelites didn't cross it, they didn't even set foot in Moab.

¹⁹ The Israelites sent messengers to the Amorite King Sihon of Heshbon. "Please," they said, "let our people go through your country to get to our own land."

²⁰ Sihon didn't think the Israelites could be trusted, so he called his army together. They set up camp at Jahaz, then they attacked the Israelite camp. ²¹ But the LORD God helped Israel defeat Sihon and his army. Israel took over all of the Amorite land where Sihon's people had lived, ²² from the River Arnon in the south to the River Jabbok in the north, and from the desert in the east to the River Jordan in the west.

²³ The messengers also told the king of Ammon that Jephthah had said:

The LORD God of Israel helped his nation get rid of the Amorites and take their land. Now do you think you're going to take over that same territory? ²⁴ If Chemosh your god* takes over a country and gives it to you, don't you have a right to it? And if the LORD takes over a country and gives it to us, the land is ours!

²⁵ Are you better than Balak the son of Zippor? He was the king of Moab, but he didn't quarrel with Israel or start a war with us.

²⁶ For three hundred years, Israelites have been living in Heshbon and Aroer and the nearby villages, and in the towns along the Arnon gorge. If the land really belonged to you Ammonites, you wouldn't have waited until now to try to get it back.

---

*11.11 Mizpah: See the note at 10.17.
*11.16 Red Sea: Hebrew *yam suph*, here referring to the Gulf of Aqaba, since the term is extended to include the north-eastern arm of the Red Sea (see also the note at Exodus 13.18).
See also: 11.17: Num 20.14–21.

*11.24 Chemosh your god: Chemosh was actually the national god of Moab, not Ammon. The land that Ammon was trying to take over had belonged to the Moabites before belonging to the Amorites (see Numbers 21.26). So the Ammonites may have thought that Chemosh controlled it.
See also: 11.18: Num 21.4. 11.19–22: Num 21.21–24. 11.25: Num 22.1–6.

²⁷ I haven't done anything to you, but it's certainly wrong of you to start a war. I pray that the LORD will show whether Israel or Ammon is in the right.

²⁸ But the king of Ammon paid no attention to Jephthah's message.

²⁹ Then the LORD's Spirit took control of Jephthah, and Jephthah went through Gilead and Manasseh, raising an army. Finally, he arrived at Mizpah in Gilead, where ³⁰ he promised the LORD, "If you will let me defeat the Ammonites ³¹ and come home safely, I will sacrifice to you whoever comes out to meet me first."

³² From Mizpah, Jephthah attacked the Ammonites, and the LORD helped him defeat them.

³³ Jephthah and his army destroyed the twenty towns between Aroer and Minnith, and others as far as Abel-Keramim. After that, the Ammonites could not invade Israel any more.

Jephthah's daughter

³⁴ When Jephthah returned to his home in Mizpah, the first one to meet him was his daughter. She was playing a tambourine and dancing to celebrate his victory, and she was his only child.

³⁵ "Oh!" Jephthah cried. Then he tore his clothes in sorrow and said to his daughter, "I made a sacred promise to the LORD, and I must keep it. Your coming out to meet me has broken my heart."

³⁶ "Father," she said, "you made a sacred promise to the LORD, and he let you defeat the Ammonites. Now, you must do what you promised, even if it means I must die. ³⁷ But first, please let me spend two months, wandering in the hill country with my friends. We will cry together, because I can never get married and have children."

³⁸ "Yes, you may have two months," Jephthah said.

She and some other girls left, and for two months they wandered in the hill country, crying because she could never get married and have children. ³⁹ Then she went back to her father. He did what he had promised, and she never got married.

That's why ⁴⁰ every year, Israelite girls walk around for four days, weeping for* Jephthah's daughter.

CHAPTER 12

The Ephraim tribe fights Jephthah's army

¹ The men of the Ephraim tribe got together an army and went across the River Jordan to Zaphon to meet with Jephthah. They said, "Why did you go to war with the Ammonites without asking us to help? Just for that, we're going to burn down your house with you inside!"

² "But I did ask for your help," Jephthah answered. "That was back when the people of Gilead and I were having trouble with the Ammonites, and you wouldn't do a thing to help us. ³ So when you weren't coming, we risked our lives and attacked the Ammonites. And the LORD let us defeat them. There's no reason for you to come here today to attack me."

⁴ But the men from Ephraim said, "You people of Gilead are nothing more than refugees from Ephraim. You even live on land that belongs to the tribes of Ephraim and Manasseh."*

So Jephthah called together the army of Gilead, then they attacked and defeated the army from Ephraim. ⁵ The army of Gilead also posted guards at all the places where the soldiers from Ephraim could cross the River Jordan to return to their own land.

Whenever one of the men from Ephraim would try to cross the river, the guards would say, "Are you from Ephraim?"

"No," the man would answer, "I'm not from Ephraim."

⁶ The guards would then tell them to say "Shibboleth", because they knew that people of Ephraim could say "Sibboleth", but not "Shibboleth".

If the man said "Sibboleth", the guards would grab him and kill him there. Altogether, forty-two thousand men from Ephraim were killed in the battle and at the Jordan.

⁷ Jephthah was a leader* of Israel for six years, before he died and was buried in his home town Mizpah† in Gilead.

Ibzan, Elon, and Abdon

Ibzan

⁸ Ibzan, the next leader* of Israel, came from Bethlehem. ⁹ He had thirty daughters and

---

See also: 11.35: Num 30.2.

*12.7,8 leader: See at 2.16 and the note there.

thirty sons, and he let them all marry outside his clan.

Ibzan was a leader for seven years, [10] before he died and was buried in Bethlehem.

Elon

[11] Elon from the Zebulun tribe was the next leader* of Israel. He was a leader for ten years, [12] before he died and was buried in Aijalon that belonged to the Zebulun tribe.

Abdon

[13-15] Abdon the son of Hillel was the next leader* of Israel. He had forty sons and thirty grandsons, and each one of them had his own donkey.* Abdon was a leader for eight years, before he died and was buried in his home town of Pirathon, which is in the part of the hill country of Ephraim where Amalekites used to live.

Samson

CHAPTER 13

Samson is born

[1] Once again the Israelites started disobeying the LORD. So he let the Philistines take control of Israel for forty years.

[2] Manoah from the tribe of Dan lived in the town of Zorah. His wife was not able to have children, [3-5] but one day an angel from the LORD appeared to her and said:

> You have never been able to have any children, but very soon you will be pregnant and have a son. He will belong to God* from the day he is born, so his hair must never be cut. And even before he is born, you must not drink any wine or beer or eat any food forbidden by God's laws.
>
> Your son will begin to set Israel free from the Philistines.

[6] She went to Manoah and said, "A prophet who looked like an angel of God came and talked to me. I was so frightened, that I didn't

even ask where he was from. He didn't tell me his name, [7] but he did say that I'm going to have a baby boy. I'm not supposed to drink any wine or beer or eat any food forbidden by God's laws. Our son will belong to God for as long as he lives."

[8] Then Manoah prayed, "Our LORD, please send that prophet again and let him tell us what to do for the son we are going to have."

[9] God answered Manoah's prayer, and the angel went back to Manoah's wife while she was resting in the fields. Manoah wasn't there at the time, [10] so she found him and said, "That same man is here again! He's the one I saw the other day."

[11] Manoah went with his wife and asked the man, "Are you the one who spoke to my wife?"

"Yes, I am," he answered.

[12] Manoah then asked, "When your promise comes true, what rules must he obey and what will be his work?"

[13] "Your wife must be careful to do everything I told her," the LORD's angel answered. [14] "She must not eat or drink anything made from grapes. She must not drink wine or beer or eat anything forbidden by God's laws. I told her exactly what to do."

[15] "Please," Manoah said, "stay here with us for just a little while, and we'll prepare a young goat for you to eat." [16] Manoah didn't realize that he was really talking to one of the LORD's angels.

The angel answered, "I can stay for a little while, although I won't eat any of your food. But if you would like to offer the goat as a sacrifice to the LORD, that would be fine."

[17] Manoah said, "Tell us your name, so we can honour you after our son is born."

[18] "No," the angel replied. "You don't need to know my name. And if you did, you couldn't understand it."

[19] So Manoah took a young goat over to a large rock he had chosen for an altar, and he built a fire on the rock. Then he killed the goat, and offered it with some grain as a sacrifice to the LORD. But then an amazing thing happened. [20] The fire blazed up towards the sky, and the LORD's angel went up towards heaven in the fire. Manoah and his wife bowed down low when they saw what happened.

[21] The angel was gone, but Manoah and his wife realized that he was one of the LORD's

---

*12.11,13–15 leader: See 2.16 and the note there.

*12.13–15 each . . . donkey: A sign that the family was wealthy.

*13.3–5 belong to God: The Hebrew text has "be a Nazirite of God". Nazirites were dedicated to God and had to follow special rules to stay that way (see Numbers 6.1,21).

See also: 13.5: Num 6.1–5.

angels. [22] Manoah said, "We have seen an angel." Now we're going to die."*

[23] "The LORD isn't going to kill us," Manoah's wife responded. "The LORD accepted our sacrifice and grain offering, and he let us see something amazing. Besides, he told us that we're going to have a son."

[24] Later, Manoah's wife did give birth to a son, and she named him Samson. As the boy grew, the LORD blessed him. [25] Then, while Samson was staying at Dan's Camp* between the towns of Zorah and Eshtaol, the Spirit of the LORD took control of him.

CHAPTER 14

Samson gets married

[1] One day, Samson went to Timnah, where he saw a Philistine woman. [2] When he got back home, he told his parents, "I saw a Philistine woman in Timnah, and I want to marry her. Get her for me!"*

[3] His parents answered, "There are a lot of women in our clan and even more in the rest of Israel. Those Philistines are pagans. Why would you want to marry one of their women?"

"She looks good to me," Samson answered. "Get her for me!"

[4] At that time, the Philistines were in control of Israel, and the LORD wanted to stir up trouble for them. That's why he made Samson desire that woman.

[5] As Samson and his parents reached the vineyards near Timnah, a fierce young lion suddenly roared and attacked Samson. [6] But the LORD's Spirit took control of Samson, and with his bare hands he tore the lion apart, as though it had been a young goat. His parents didn't know what he had done, and he didn't tell them.

[7] When they got to Timnah, Samson talked to the woman, and he was sure that she was the one for him.

[8] Later,* Samson returned to Timnah for the wedding. And when he came near the place where the lion had attacked, he left the road to see what was left of the lion. He was surprised to see that bees were living in the lion's skeleton, and that they had made some honey. [9] He scooped up the honey in his hands and ate some of it as he walked along.

When he got back to his parents, he gave them some of the honey, and they ate it too. But he didn't tell them he had found the honey in the skeleton of a lion.*

[10] While Samson's father went to make the final arrangements with the bride and her family, Samson threw a big party,* as grooms* usually did. [11] When the Philistines saw what Samson was like, they told thirty of their young men to stay with him at the party.

[12] Samson told the thirty young men, "This party will last for seven days. Let's make a bet: I'll tell you a riddle, and if you can tell me the right answer before the party is over, I'll give each one of you a shirt and a full change of clothing. [13] But if you can't tell me the answer, then each of you will have to give me a shirt and a full change of clothing."

"It's a bet!" the Philistines said. "Tell us the riddle."

[14] Samson said:

> Once so strong and mighty —
> now so sweet and tasty!

Three days went by, and the Philistine young men had not come up with the right answer. [15] Finally, on the seventh* day of the party they went to Samson's bride and said, "You had better trick your husband into telling you the answer to his riddle. Have you invited us here just to rob us? If you don't find out the answer, we will burn you and your family to death."

[16] Samson's bride went to him and started crying in his arms. "You must really hate me," she sobbed. "If you loved me at all, you would have told me the answer to your riddle."

"But I haven't even told my parents the answer!" Samson replied. "Why should I tell you?"

[17] For the entire seven days of the party, she had been whining and trying to get the answer from him. But that seventh day she put so much pressure on Samson that he finally gave in and told her the answer. She went straight to the young men and told them.

[18] Before sunset that day, the men of the town went to Samson with this answer:

---

*13.22 We have seen an angel. Now we're going to die: Some people believed that if they saw the LORD or one of the LORD's angels, they would die.

*14.2 Get her for me: At that time, parents arranged marriages for their children.

*14.9 But he didn't tell them . . . skeleton of a lion: To eat honey that had touched a skeleton was against God's laws (see Leviticus 11.27–40).

*14.10 party: The Hebrew term means a party that involved a lot of drinking.

A lion is the strongest —
    honey is the sweetest!

Samson replied,

This answer you have given me
    doubtless came
    from my bride-to-be.

¹⁹ Then the LORD's Spirit took control of Samson. He went to Ashkelon,* where he killed thirty men and took their clothing. Samson then gave it to the thirty young men at Timnah and stormed back home to his own family.

²⁰ The father of the bride made Samson's wife marry one of the thirty young men who had been at Samson's party.▸

CHAPTER 15

¹ Later, during the wheat harvest, Samson went to visit the young woman he thought was still his wife.* He brought along a young goat as a gift and said to her father, "I want to go into my wife's bedroom."

"You can't do that," he replied. ² "When you left the way you did, I thought you were divorcing* her. So I arranged for her to marry one of the young men who were at your party. But my younger daughter is even prettier, and you can have her as your wife."

³ "This time," Samson answered, "I have a good reason for really hurting some Philistines."

Samson takes revenge

⁴ Samson went out and caught three hundred foxes and tied them together in pairs with oil-soaked rags around their tails. ⁵ Then Samson took the foxes into the Philistine wheat fields that were ready to be harvested. He set the rags on fire and let the foxes go. The wheat fields went up in flames, and so did the stacks of wheat that had already been cut. Even the Philistine vineyards and olive orchards burnt.

⁶ Some of the Philistines started asking around, "Who could have done such a thing?"

"It was Samson," someone told them. "He married the daughter of that man in Timnah, but then the man gave Samson's wife to one of the men at the wedding."

The Philistine leaders went to Timnah and burnt to death Samson's wife and her father.▸

⁷ When Samson found out what they had done, he went to them and said, "You killed them! And I won't rest until I get even with you." ⁸ Then Samson started hacking them to pieces with his sword.

Samson left Philistia and went to live in the cave at Etam Rock. ⁹ But it wasn't long before the Philistines invaded Judah* and set up a huge army camp at Jawbone.▸

¹⁰ The people of Judah asked, "Why have you invaded our land?"

The Philistines answered, "We've come to get Samson. We're going to do the same things to him that he did to our people."

¹¹ Three thousand men from Judah went to the cave at Etam Rock and said to Samson, "Don't you know that the Philistines rule us, and they will punish us for what you did?"

"I was only getting even with them," Samson replied. "They did the same things to me first."

¹² "We came here to tie you up and turn you over to them," said the men of Judah.

"I won't put up a fight," Samson answered, "but you have to promise not to hurt me yourselves."

¹³⁻¹⁴ "We promise," the men said. "We will only tie you up and turn you over to the Philistines. We won't kill you." Then they tied up his hands and arms with two brand-new ropes and led him away from Etam Rock.

When the Philistines saw that Samson was being brought to their camp at Jawbone, they started shouting and ran towards him. But the LORD's Spirit took control of Samson, and Samson broke the ropes, as though they were pieces of burnt cloth. ¹⁵ Samson glanced around and spotted the jawbone of a donkey. The jawbone had not yet dried out, so it was still hard and heavy. Samson grabbed it and started hitting Philistines — he killed a thousand of them! ¹⁶ After the fighting was over, he made up this poem about what he had done to the Philistines:

I used a donkey's jawbone
    to kill a thousand men;
I beat them with this jawbone
    over and over again.▸

---

*14.19 Ashkelon: Another Philistine town.
*15.1 Samson went to visit . . . his wife: See the note at 8.31.
*15.2 divorcing: It was often very easy for a husband to divorce his wife.

*15.9 Judah: Samson belonged to the Dan tribe, but his hide-out in the cave at Etam Rock was in Judah, a few kilometres south-west of Bethlehem.

17 Samson tossed the jawbone on the ground and decided to call the place Jawbone Hill.* It is still called that today.

18 Samson was so thirsty that he prayed, "Our LORD, you helped me win a battle against a whole army. Please don't let me die of thirst now. Those heathen Philistines will carry off my dead body."

19 Samson was tired and weary, but God sent water gushing from a rock.* Samson drank some and felt strong again.

Samson named the place Caller Spring,* because he had called out to God for help. The spring is still there at Jawbone.

20 Samson was a leader* of Israel for twenty years, but the Philistines were still the rulers of Israel.

CHAPTER 16

Samson carries off the gates of Gaza

1 One day while Samson was in Gaza, he saw a prostitute and went to her house to spend the night. 2 The people who lived in Gaza found out he was there, and they decided to kill him at dawn. So they went to the city gate and waited all night in the guardrooms on each side of the gate.*

3 But Samson got up in the middle of the night and went to the town gate. He pulled the gate doors and doorposts out of the wall and put them on his shoulders. Then he carried them all the way to the top of the hill that overlooks Hebron,* where he set the doors down, still closed and locked.

Delilah tricks Samson

4 Some time later, Samson fell in love with a woman named Delilah, who lived in Sorek Valley. 5 The Philistine rulers* went to Delilah and said, "Trick Samson into telling you what makes him so strong and what can make him weak. Then we can tie him up so he can't get away. If you find out his secret, we will each give you eleven hundred pieces of silver."*

6 The next time Samson was at Delilah's house, she asked, "Samson, what makes you

so strong? How can I tie you up so you can't get away? Come on, you can tell me."

7 Samson answered, "If someone ties me up with seven new bowstrings that have never been dried,* it will make me just as weak as anyone else."

8-9 The Philistine rulers gave seven new bowstrings to Delilah. They also told some of their soldiers to go to Delilah's house and hide in the room where Samson and Delilah were. If the bowstrings made Samson weak, they would be able to capture him.

Delilah tied up Samson with the bowstrings and shouted, "Samson, the Philistines are attacking!"

Samson snapped the bowstrings, as though they were pieces of scorched string. The Philistines had not found out why Samson was so strong.

10 "You lied and made me look like a fool," Delilah said. "Now tell me. How can I really tie you up?"

11 Samson answered, "Use some new ropes. If I'm tied up with ropes that have never been used, I'll be just as weak as anyone else."

12 Delilah got new ropes and again some Philistines hid in the room. Then she tied up Samson's arms and shouted, "Samson, the Philistines are attacking!"

Samson snapped the ropes as if they were threads.

13 "You're still lying and making a fool of me," Delilah said. "Tell me how I can tie you up!"

"My hair is in seven braids," Samson replied. "If you weave my braids into the threads on a loom* and nail the loom to a wall, then I will be as weak as anyone else."

14 While Samson was asleep, Delilah wove his braids into the threads on a loom and nailed the loom to a wall.* Then she shouted, "Samson, the Philistines are attacking!"

Samson woke up and pulled the loom free from its posts in the ground and from the nails in the wall. Then he pulled his hair free from the woven cloth.

15 "Samson," Delilah said, "you claim to love me, but you don't mean it! You've made me look like a fool three times now, and you still haven't told me why you are so strong."

---

*16.20 leader: See 2.16 and the note there.
*16.2 guardrooms . . . gate: The gate was often in a part of the town wall that was thicker and taller than the rest of the wall, and that had rooms where guards stayed when they were on duty.
*16.3 Hebron: About sixty-five kilometres from Gaza.
*16.5 Philistine rulers: There were five rulers, each one controlling part of Philistia.
*16.5 silver: About 60 kilogrammes of silver altogether.

*16.7 new bowstrings . . . dried: The string for a bow was often made from sinews or internal organs of animals. These strings were made while the animal tissues were still moist, and they became much stronger, once they were dry.
*16.13 loom: A large wooden frame on which cloth is woven.

¹⁶ Delilah started nagging and pestering him day after day, until he couldn't stand it any longer.

¹⁷ Finally, Samson told her the truth. "I have belonged to God* ever since I was born, so my hair has never been cut. If it were ever cut off, my strength would leave me, and I would be as weak as anyone else."

¹⁸ Delilah realized that he was telling the truth. So she sent someone to tell the Philistine rulers, "Come to my house one more time. Samson has finally told me the truth."

The Philistine rulers went to Delilah's house, and they brought along the silver they had promised her. ¹⁹ Delilah had lulled Samson to sleep with his head resting in her lap. She signalled to one of the Philistine men as she began cutting off Samson's seven braids. And by the time she had finished, Samson's strength was gone. Delilah tied him up ²⁰ and shouted, "Samson, the Philistines are attacking!"

Samson woke up and thought, "I'll break loose and escape, just as I always do." He did not realize that the LORD had stopped helping him.

²¹ The Philistines grabbed Samson and put out his eyes. They took him to the prison in Gaza and chained him up. Then they put him to work, turning a millstone to grind grain. ²² But they didn't cut his hair any more, so it started growing back.

²³ The Philistine rulers threw a big party and sacrificed a lot of animals to their god Dagon. The rulers said:

Samson was our enemy,
but our god Dagon
helped us capture him!

²⁴⁻²⁵ Everyone there was having a good time, and they shouted, "Bring out Samson — he's still good for a few more laughs!"

The rulers had Samson brought from the prison, and when the people saw him, this is how they praised their god:

Samson ruined our crops
and killed our people.
He was our enemy,
but our god helped us
capture him.

They made fun of Samson for a while, then they told him to stand near the columns that supported the roof. ²⁶ A young man was leading Samson by the hand, and Samson

said to him, "I need to lean against something. Take me over to the columns that hold up the roof."

²⁷ The Philistine rulers were celebrating in a temple packed with people and with three thousand* more on the flat roof. They had all been watching Samson and making fun of him.*

²⁸ Samson prayed, "Please remember me, LORD God. The Philistines put out my eyes, but make me strong one last time, so I can take revenge for at least one of my eyes!"*

²⁹ Samson was standing between the two middle columns that held up the roof. He felt around and found one column with his right hand, and the other with his left hand. ³⁰ Then he shouted, "Let me die with the Philistines!" He pushed against the columns as hard as he could, and the temple collapsed with the Philistine rulers and everyone else still inside. Samson killed more Philistines when he died than he had killed during his entire life.

³¹ His brothers and the rest of his family went to Gaza and took his body back home. They buried him in his father's tomb,* which was between Zorah and Eshtaol.

Samson was a leader* of Israel for twenty years.

The tribe of Dan and their place of worship

CHAPTER 17

Micah makes idols and hires a priest

¹ Micah* belonged to the Ephraim tribe and lived in the hill country. ² One day he told his mother, "Do you remember those eleven hundred pieces of silver* that were stolen from you? I was there when you put a curse on whoever stole them. Well, I'm the one who did it."

His mother answered, "I pray that the LORD will bless* you, my son."

³⁻⁴ Micah returned the silver to his mother, and she said, "I give this silver to the LORD, so my son can use it to make an idol--

---

*16.17 belonged to God: See the note at 13.3-5.

*16.27 They . . . him: Samson may have been in a courtyard visible from the roof.
*16.31 buried him in his father's tomb: Several family members were often buried in one tomb.
*16.31 leader: See 2.16 and the note there.
*17.2 eleven hundred . . . silver: About 13 kilogrammes.
*17.2 curse . . . bless: A curse could not be taken back, but it could be made powerless by a blessing.

Turning to her son, she said, "Micah, now the silver belongs to you."

But Micah handed it back to his mother. She took two hundred pieces* of the silver and gave them to a silver worker, who made them into an idol.* They kept the idol in Micah's house. 5 He had a shrine for worshipping God there at his home, and he had made some idols and a sacred priestly apron. Micah chose one of his own sons to be the priest for his shrine.

6 This was before kings ruled Israel, so all the Israelites did whatever they thought was right.

7-8 One day a young Levite came to Micah's house in the hill country of Ephraim. He had been staying with one of the clans of Judah in Bethlehem, but he had left Bethlehem to find a new place to live* where he could be a priest.♦

9 "Where are you from?" Micah asked.

"I am a Levite from Bethlehem in Judah," the man answered, "and I'm on my way to find a new place to live."

10 Micah said, "Why don't you stay here with me? You can be my priest and tell me what God wants me to do. Every year I'll give you ten pieces of silver and one complete set of clothes, and I'll provide all your food."

The young man went for a walk, 11-12 then he agreed to stay with Micah and be his priest. He lived in Micah's house, and Micah treated him like one of his own sons.

13 Micah said, "I have a Levite as my own priest. Now I know that the LORD will be kind to me."

CHAPTER 18

1 These things happened before kings ruled Israel.

The tribe of Dan takes Micah's priest and idols

About this time, the tribe of Dan was looking for a place to live. The other tribes had land, but the people of Dan did not really have any to call their own. 2 The tribe chose five warriors to represent its clans and told them, "Go and find some land where we can live."

The warriors left the area of Zorah and Eshtaol and went into the hill country of Ephraim. One night they stayed at Micah's house, 3 because they heard the young Levite talking, and they knew from his accent that he was from the south. They asked him, "What are you doing here? Who brought you here?"

4 The Levite replied, "Micah hired me as his priest." Then he told them how well Micah had treated him.

5 "Please talk to God for us," the men said. "Ask God if we will be successful in what we are trying to do."

6 "Don't worry," answered the priest. "The LORD is pleased with what you are doing."

7 The five men left and went to the town of Laish, whose people were from Sidon,♦ but Sidon was too far away to protect them. Even though their town had no walls, the people thought they were safe from attack. So they had not asked anyone else♦ for protection, which meant that the tribe of Dan could easily take over Laish.♦

8 The five men went back to Zorah and Eshtaol, where their relatives asked, "Did you find any land?"

9-10 "Let's go!" the five men said. "We saw some very good land with enough room for all of us, and it has everything we will ever need. What are you waiting for? Let's attack and take it. You'll find that the people think they're safe, but God is giving the land to us."

11 Six hundred men from the tribe of Dan strapped on their weapons and left Zorah and Eshtaol with their families.♦ 12 One night they camped near Kiriath-Jearim in the territory of Judah, and that's why the place just west of Kiriath-Jearim is still known as Dan's Camp.♦ 13 Then they went into the hill country of Ephraim.

When they came close to Micah's house, 14 the five men who had been spies asked the other warriors, "Did you know that someone in this village has several idols and a sacred priestly apron? What do you think we should do about it?"

15-18 The six hundred warriors left the road and went to the house on Micah's property where the young Levite priest lived. They stood at the gate and greeted the priest. Meanwhile, the five men who had been there before went into Micah's house and took the sacred priestly apron and the idols.

"Hey!" the priest shouted. "What do you think you're doing?"

---

*17.3,4 two hundred pieces: About 2 kilogrammes.
*17.3,4 idol: Probably carved from wood and covered with the silver.
*17.7,8 place to live: The people of the Levi tribe did not have a large area of land like the other tribes.
See also: 17.6: Judg 21.25.

¹⁹ "Quiet!" the men said. "Keep your mouth shut and listen. Why don't you come with us and be our priest, so you can tell us what God wants us to do? You could stay here and be a priest for one man's family, but wouldn't you rather be the priest for a clan or even a whole tribe of Israel?"

²⁰ The priest really liked that idea. So he took the apron and the idols and joined the others ²¹ from the tribe of Dan. Then they turned and left, after putting their children, their cattle, and the rest of their other possessions in front.

²² They had travelled for some time, before Micah asked his neighbours to help him get his things back. He and his men caught up with the people of Dan ²³ and shouted for them to stop.

They turned to face him and asked, "What's wrong? Why did you bring all these men?"

²⁴ Micah answered, "You know what's wrong. You stole the gods' I made, and you took my priest. I don't have anything left."

²⁵ "We don't want to hear any more about it," the people of Dan said. "And if you make us angry, you'll only get yourself and your family killed." ²⁶ After saying this, they turned and left.

Micah realized there was no way he could win a fight with them, and so he went back home.

The tribe of Dan captures Laish

²⁷⁻²⁸ The tribe of Dan took Micah's priest and the things Micah had made, and headed for Laish, which was in a valley controlled by the town of Beth-Rehob. Laish was defenceless, because it had no walls and was too far from Sidon for the Sidonians to help defend it. The leaders of Laish had not even asked nearby towns to help them in case of an attack.

The warriors from Dan made a surprise attack on Laish, killing everyone and burning it down. Then they rebuilt the town and settled there themselves. ²⁹ But they named it Dan, after one of Israel's* sons, who was the ancestor of their tribe.

³⁰⁻³¹ Even though the place of worship* was in Shiloh, the people of Dan set up the idol Micah had made. They worshipped the idol, and the Levite was their priest. His name was Jonathan, and he was a descendant of Gershom the son of Moses.' His descendants served as priests for the tribe of Dan, until the people of Israel were taken away as prisoners by their enemies.

Civil war against the tribe of Benjamin

CHAPTER 19

A woman is murdered

¹ Before kings ruled Israel, a Levite* was living deep in the hill country of the Ephraim tribe. He married* a woman from Bethlehem in Judah, ² but she was unfaithful and went back to live with her family in Bethlehem.

Four months later ³ her husband decided to try and talk her into coming back. So he went to Bethlehem, taking along a servant and two donkeys. He talked with his wife, and she invited him into her family's home. Her father was glad to see him ⁴ and did not want him to leave. So the man stayed three days, eating and drinking with his father-in-law.

⁵ When everyone got up on the fourth day, the Levite started getting ready to go home. But his father-in-law said, "Don't leave until you have a bite to eat. You'll need strength for your journey."

⁶ The two men sat down together and ate a big meal. "Come on," the man's father-in-law said. "Stay tonight and have a good time."

⁷ The Levite tried to leave, but his father-in-law insisted, and he spent one more night. ⁸ On the fifth day, the man got up early to leave, but his wife's father said, "You need to keep up your strength! Why don't you leave straight after lunch?" So the two of them started eating.

⁹ Finally, the Levite got up from the meal, so he and his wife and servant could leave. "Look," his father-in-law said, "it's already late afternoon, and if you leave now, you won't get very far before dark. Stay with us one more night and enjoy yourself. Then you can get up early tomorrow morning and start home."

¹⁰ But the Levite decided not to spend the night there again. He had the saddles put on his two donkeys, then he and his wife and servant travelled as far as Jebus, which is now

---

*18.29 Israel's: Israel was another name for Jacob, the father of the twelve ancestors of the tribes of Israel.
*18.30,31 place of worship: The Hebrew text has "house of God," which at this time was probably the sacred tent.

*19.1 a Levite: Someone from the Levi tribe, which had no tribal lands of its own.
*19.1 married: See the note at 8.31.

called Jerusalem. ¹¹ It was beginning to get dark, and the man's servant said, "Let's stop and spend the night in this town where the Jebusites live."

¹² "No," the Levite answered. "They aren't Israelites, and I refuse to spend the night there. We'll stop for the night at Gibeah, ¹³ because we can make it to Gibeah or perhaps even to Ramah* before dark."

¹⁴ They walked on and reached Gibeah in the territory of Benjamin just after sunset. ¹⁵ They left the road and went into Gibeah. But the Levite couldn't find a house where anyone would let them spend the night, and they sat down in the open area just inside the town gates.

¹⁶ Soon an old man came in through the gates on his way home from working in the fields. Most of the people who lived in Gibeah belonged to the tribe of Benjamin, but this man was originally from the hill country of Ephraim. ¹⁷ He noticed that the Levite was just in town to spend the night. "Where are you going?" the old man asked. "Where did you come from?"

¹⁸ "We've come from Bethlehem in Judah," the Levite answered. "We went there on a visit. Now we're going to the place where the LORD is worshipped, and later we will return to our home in the hill country of Ephraim. But no one here will let us spend the night* in their home. ¹⁹ We brought food for our donkeys and bread and wine for ourselves, so we don't need anything except a place to sleep."

²⁰ The old man said, "You are welcome to spend the night in my home and to be my guest, but don't stay out here!"

²¹ The old man brought them into his house and fed their donkeys. Then he and his guests washed their feet* and began eating and drinking. ²² They were having a good time, when some worthless men of that town surrounded the house and started banging on the door and shouting, "A man came to your house tonight. Send him out, so we can have sex with him!"

²³ The old man went outside and said, "My friends, please don't commit such a horrible crime against a man who is a guest in my house. ²⁴ Let me send out my daughter instead. She's a virgin. And I'll even send out the man's wife.* You can rape them or do whatever else you want, but please don't do such a horrible thing to this man."

²⁵ The men refused to listen, so the Levite grabbed his wife and shoved her outside. The men raped her and abused her all night long. Finally, they let her go just before sunrise, ²⁶ and it was almost daybreak when she went back to the house where her husband* was staying. She collapsed at the door and lay there until sunrise.

²⁷ About that time, her husband woke up and got ready to leave. He opened the door and went outside, where he found his wife lying at the door with her hands on the doorstep. ²⁸ "Get up!" he said. "It's time to leave."

But his wife didn't move.♦

He lifted her body on to his donkey and left. ²⁹ When he got home, he took a butcher's knife and cut her body into twelve pieces. Then he told some messengers, "Take one piece to each tribe of Israel ³⁰ and ask everyone if anything like this has ever happened since Israel left Egypt. Tell them to think about it, talk it over, and tell us what should be done."

Everyone who saw a piece of the body said, "This is horrible! Nothing like this has ever happened since the day Israel left Egypt."

CHAPTER 20

Israel gets ready for war

¹⁻³ The Israelites called a meeting of the nation. And since they were God's people, the meeting was held at the place of worship in Mizpah. Men who could serve as soldiers came from everywhere in Israel — from Dan in the north, Beersheba in the south, and Gilead east of the River Jordan. Four hundred thousand of them came to Mizpah, and they each felt the same about what those men from the tribe of Benjamin had done.

News about the meeting at Mizpah reached the tribe of Benjamin.

---

*19.13 Gibeah . . . Ramah: It was about five kilometres from Jerusalem to Gibeah, and another five kilometres to Ramah.
*19.18 spend the night: People usually considered it a duty to ask travellers to spend the night in their homes, since there were often no other places to stay.
*19.21 washed their feet: This was a custom, since people wore open sandals and their feet would be dirty after walking on the earth roads or working in the fields.
See also: 19.22–24: Gen 19.5–8.

*19.24 wife: See the note at 8.31.
*19.26 husband: Or "owner"; the Hebrew word may mean that she was his slave and had no legal rights.
See also: 19.29: 1 Sam 11.7.

As soon as the leaders of the tribes of Israel took their places, the Israelites said, "How could such a horrible thing happen?"

⁴ The husband of the murdered woman answered:

My wife* and I went into the town of Gibeah in Benjamin to spend the night. ⁵ Later that night, the men of Gibeah surrounded the house. They wanted to kill me, but instead they raped and killed my wife. ⁶ It was a terrible thing for Israelites to do! So I cut up her body and sent pieces everywhere in Israel.

⁷ You are the people of Israel, and you must decide today what to do about the men of Gibeah.

⁸ The whole army was in agreement, and they said, "None of us will go home. ⁹⁻¹⁰ We'll send one tenth of the men from each tribe to get food for the army. And we'll ask God* who should attack Gibeah, because those men* deserve to be punished for committing such a horrible crime in Israel."

¹¹ Everyone agreed that Gibeah had to be punished.

¹² The tribes of Israel sent messengers to every town and village in Benjamin. And wherever the messengers went, they said, "How could those worthless men in Gibeah do such a disgusting thing? ¹³ We can't allow such a terrible crime to go unpunished in Israel! Hand the men over to us, and we will put them to death."

But the people of Benjamin refused to listen to the other Israelites. ¹⁴ Men from towns all over Benjamin's territory went to Gibeah and got ready to fight Israel. ¹⁵ The Benjamin tribe had twenty-six thousand soldiers, not counting the seven hundred who were Gibeah's best warriors. ¹⁶ In this army there were seven hundred left-handed experts who could sling a stone* at a target the size of a hair and hit it every time.

¹⁷ The other Israelite tribes organized their army and found they had four hundred thousand experienced soldiers. ¹⁸ So they went to the place of worship at Bethel* and asked God, "Which tribe should be the first to attack the people of Benjamin?"

"Judah," the LORD answered.

¹⁹ The next morning the Israelite army moved its camp to a place near Gibeah. ²⁰ Then they left their camp and got into position to attack the army of Benjamin.

The war between Israel and Benjamin

²¹ Benjamin's soldiers came out of Gibeah and attacked, and when the day was over, twenty-two thousand Israelite soldiers lay dead on the ground.

²²⁻²⁴ The people of Israel went to the place of worship and cried until sunset. Then they asked the LORD, "Should we attack the people of Benjamin again, even though they are our relatives?"

"Yes," the LORD replied, "attack them again!"

The Israelite soldiers encouraged each other to be brave and to fight hard. Then the next day they went back to Gibeah and took up the same positions as they had before.

²⁵ That same day, Benjamin's soldiers came out of Gibeah and attacked, leaving another eighteen thousand Israelite soldiers dead on the battlefield.

²⁶⁻²⁸ The people of Israel went to the place of worship at Bethel,* where the sacred chest was being kept. They sat on the ground, crying and not eating for the rest of the day. Then about sunset, they offered sacrifices to please the LORD and to ask his blessing.* Phinehas* the priest then prayed, "Our LORD, the people of Benjamin are our relatives. Should we stop fighting or attack them again?"

"Attack!" the LORD answered. "Tomorrow I will let you defeat them."

²⁹ The Israelites surrounded Gibeah, but stayed where they could not be seen. ³⁰ Then the next day, they took the same positions as twice before, ³¹⁻⁴¹ but this time they had a different plan. They said, "When the men of Benjamin attack, we will run off and let them chase us away from the town and into the country roads."

The soldiers of Benjamin attacked the Israelite army and started pushing it back from the town. They killed about thirty Israelites in the fields and along the road between Gibeah and Bethel. The men of Benjamin were thinking, "We're mowing them down like we did before."

The Israelites were running away, but they headed for Baal-Tamar, where they regrouped. They had set an ambush, and they were sure it

---

*20.4 wife: See the note at 8.31.

*20.9,10 ask God: The Hebrew text has "use lots to decide"; small pieces of wood or stone called "lots" were used to find out what God wanted his people to do.

*20.16 sling a stone: Using a sling made from a leather strap.

*20.26–28 sacrifices . . . blessing: See Leviticus 1–3.

would work. Ten thousand of Israel's best soldiers had been hiding west of Gibeah,* and as soon as the men of Benjamin chased the Israelites into the countryside, these ten thousand soldiers made a surprise attack on the town gates. They dashed in and captured Gibeah, killing everyone there. Then they set the town on fire, because the smoke would be the signal for the other Israelite soldiers to turn and attack the soldiers of Benjamin.

The fighting had been so heavy around the soldiers of Benjamin, that they did not know the trouble they were in. But then they looked back and saw clouds of smoke rising from the town. They looked in front and saw the soldiers of Israel turning to attack. This terrified them, because they realized that something horrible was happening. And it was horrible — over twenty-five thousand* soldiers of Benjamin died that day, and those who were left alive knew that the LORD had given Israel the victory.

42 The men of Benjamin headed down the road towards the desert, trying to escape from the Israelites. But the Israelites stayed just behind them, keeping up their attack. Men even came out of the nearby towns to help kill the men of Benjamin, 43 who were having to fight on all sides. The Israelite soldiers never let up their attack.* They chased and killed the warriors of Benjamin as far as a place directly east of Gibeah,* 44 until eighteen thousand of these warriors lay dead.

45 Some other warriors of Benjamin turned and ran down the road towards Rimmon Rock in the desert. The Israelites killed five thousand of them on the road, then chased the rest until they had killed* two thousand more.

46 Twenty-five thousand soldiers of Benjamin died that day, all of them experienced warriors. 47 Only six hundred of them finally made it into the desert to Rimmon Rock, where they stayed for four months.

48 The Israelites turned back and went to every town in Benjamin's territory, killing all the people and animals, and setting the towns on fire.

CHAPTER 21

Wives for the men of Benjamin

1 When the Israelites had met at Mizpah before the war with Benjamin,* they had made this sacred promise: "None of us will ever let our daughters marry any man from Benjamin."

2 After the war with Benjamin, the Israelites went to the place of worship at Bethel and sat there until sunset. They cried loudly and bitterly 3 and prayed, "Our LORD, you are the God of Israel. Why did you let this happen? Now one of our tribes is almost gone."

4 Early the next morning, the Israelites built an altar and offered sacrifices to please the LORD and to ask his blessing.* 5 Then they asked each other, "Did any of the tribes of Israel fail to come to the place of worship? We made a sacred promise that anyone who didn't come to the meeting at Mizpah would be put to death."

6 The Israelites were sad about what had happened to the Benjamin tribe, and they said, "One of our tribes was almost wiped out. 7 Only a few men of Benjamin weren't killed in the war. We need to get wives for them, so the tribe won't completely disappear. But how can we do that, after promising in the LORD's name that we wouldn't let them marry any of our daughters?"

8-9 Again the Israelites asked, "Did any of the tribes stay away from the meeting at Mizpah?"

After asking around, they discovered that no one had come from Jabesh in Gilead.

10-11 So they sent twelve thousand warriors with these orders: "Attack Jabesh in Gilead and kill everyone, except the women who have never been married."

12 The warriors attacked Jabesh in Gilead, and returned to their camp in Canaan* with four hundred young women.

13 The Israelites met and sent messengers to the men of Benjamin at Rimmon Rock, telling them that the Israelites were willing to make peace with them. 14 So the men of Benjamin came back from Rimmon Rock, and the Israelites let them marry the young women from Jabesh. But there weren't enough women.

15 The Israelites were very sad, because the LORD had almost wiped out one of their tribes. 16 Then their national leaders said:

All the women of the Benjamin tribe were killed. How can we get wives for the men of Benjamin who are left? 17 If they don't have children, one of the Israelite tribes will die out. 18 But we can't let the men of Benjamin marry any of our daughters. We made a

*21.4 sacrifices . . . blessing: See the note at 20.26–28.
*21.12 in Canaan: Jabesh was in Gilead, across the River Jordan from the land of Canaan.

*21.1 the Israelites . . . Benjamin: See 20.1–3.

247

sacred promise not to do that, and if we break our promise, we will be under our own curse.

¹⁹ Then someone suggested, "What about the LORD's Festival that takes place each year in Shiloh? It's held north of Bethel, south of Lebonah, and just east of the road that goes from Bethel to Shechem."

²⁰ The leaders told the men of Benjamin who still did not have wives:

Go to Shiloh and hide in the vineyards near the festival. ²¹ Wait there for the young women of Shiloh to come out and perform their dances. Then rush out and grab one of the young women, then take her home as your wife. ²² If the fathers or brothers of these young women complain about this, we'll say, "Be kind enough to let those men keep your daughter. After all, we couldn't get enough wives for all the men of Benjamin in the battle at Jabesh. And because you didn't give them permission to marry your daughters, you won't be under the curse we earlier agreed on."

²³ The men of Benjamin went to Shiloh and hid in the vineyards. The young women soon started dancing, and each man grabbed one of them and carried her off. Then the men of Benjamin went back to their own land and rebuilt their towns and started living in them again.

²⁴ Afterwards, the rest of the Israelites returned to their homes and families.

Israel was not ruled by a king

²⁵ In those days Israel wasn't ruled by a king, and everyone did what they thought was right.

See also: 21.25: Judg 17.6.

Additional notes

¹1.4,5 king of Bezek: Or "Adoni-Bezek".
¹1.10 clans called: Or "warriors".
¹1.13 Othniel was the son of . . . Kenaz: Or "Othniel and Caleb both belonged to the Kenaz clan, but Othniel was younger than Caleb."
¹1.14 Achsah . . . Othniel . . . he: Hebrew; two ancient translations "Othniel . . . Achsah . . . she".
¹1.14 getting down from: One possible meaning for the difficult Hebrew text.
¹1.15 spring-fed ponds . . . small ponds . . . Higher Pond and Lower Pond: Or "wells . . . wells . . . Higher Well and Lower Well."
¹1.16 Jericho: The Hebrew text has "Town of Palm Trees", another name for Jericho.

¹1.16 not far . . . Amalekites: One possible meaning for the difficult Hebrew text.
¹1.20 clans: See the note at 1.10.
¹1.36 Scorpion Pass: Or "Akrabbim Pass".
¹1.36 country: One possible meaning for the difficult Hebrew text of verse 36.
²2.3 trap: One possible meaning for the difficult Hebrew text.
³3.3 Hamath Pass: Or "Lebo-Hamath".
³3.8 northern Syria: The Hebrew text has "Aram-Naharaim", probably referring to the land around the city of Haran (see Genesis 24.10; 25.20; 28.2,6; 31.18,20; 33.18; 35.23–26; 46.8–15; 48.7).
³3.9 Othniel was the son of . . . Kenaz: See the note at 1.13.
³3.13 Jericho: See the note at 1.16.
³3.15,16 Ehud: Hebrew "Ehud the son of Gera".
³3.22,23 he climbed . . . porch: One possible meaning for the difficult Hebrew text.
⁴4.11 the village . . . Zaanannim: Or "the oak tree in the town of Zaanannim".
⁵5.7 villagers . . . fields: One possible meaning for the difficult Hebrew text.
⁵5.7 Deborah: Or "I, Deborah".
⁵5.8 The Israelites . . . attacked: One possible meaning for the difficult Hebrew text.
⁵5.11 Even . . . water: One possible meaning for the difficult Hebrew text.
⁵5.13 side: One possible meaning for the difficult Hebrew text of verse 13.
⁵5.15 But . . . at all: Or "But the people of Reuben couldn't make up their minds."
⁵5.16 sheep pens: Or "campfires".
⁵5.16 No . . . come: See the note at 5.15.
⁵5.18 to attack the enemy: One possible meaning for the difficult Hebrew text.
⁵5.19 stream near Megiddo: Probably refers to one of the streams that flow into the River Kishon.
⁵5.30 and beautiful . . . wear: One possible meaning for the difficult Hebrew text.
⁷7.1 Fear Spring: Or "Harod Spring".
⁷7.13 flat: Or "mouldy".
⁷7.13 the headquarters tent: Or "a tent".
⁷7.22 Zeredah: Some Hebrew manuscripts; most Hebrew manuscripts "Zererah"; these may be different names for the town of Zarethan in the Jordan Valley.
⁷7.25 Raven and Wolf: Or "Oreb and Zeeb".
⁷7.25 Raven Rock . . . Wolf Wine-pit: Or "Oreb Rock . . . Zeeb Wine-pit".
⁸8.17 all . . . officials: Or "every man in town".
⁸8.27–29 statue . . . statue: Or "sacred priestly apron . . . apron".
⁸8.33 Baal Berith: Or "Baal of the Agreement" or "the Lord of the Agreement".
⁹9.1 Gideon: The Hebrew text has "Jerubbaal", another name for Gideon (see 6.32).
⁹9.4 Baal Berith: See the note at 8.33.
⁹9.6 including the priests and the military officers: The Hebrew text has "and the Millo house", another

Ruth and Boaz get married

CHAPTER 4

[1] Meanwhile, Boaz had gone to the meeting place at the town gate and was sitting there when the other close relative came by. So Boaz invited him to come over and sit down, and he did. [2] Then Boaz got ten of the town leaders and also asked them to sit down. After they had sat down, [3] he said to the man:

Naomi has come back from Moab and is selling the land that belonged to her husband Elimelech. [4] I am telling you about this, since you are his closest relative and have the right to buy the property. If you want it, you can buy it now. These ten men and the others standing here can be witnesses. But if you don't want the property, let me know, because I am next in line.

The man replied, "I will buy it!"

[5] "If you do buy it from Naomi," Boaz told him, "you must also marry Ruth. Then if you have a son by her, the property will stay in the family of Ruth's first husband."

[6] The man answered, "If that's the case, I don't want to buy it! That would make problems with the property I already own.* You may buy it yourself, because I cannot."

[7] To make a sale legal in those days, one person would take off a sandal and give it to the other. [8] So after the man had agreed to let Boaz buy the property, he took off one of his sandals and handed it to Boaz.

[9] Boaz told the town leaders and everyone else:

All of you are witnesses that today I have bought from Naomi the property that belonged to Elimelech and his two sons, Chilion and Mahlon. [10] You are also witnesses that I have agreed to marry Mahlon's widow Ruth, the Moabite woman. This will keep the property in his family's name, and he will be remembered in this town.

[11] The town leaders and the others standing there said:

We are witnesses to this. And we pray that the LORD will give your wife many children, just as he did Leah and Rachel, the wives of Jacob. May you be a rich man in the tribe of Ephrath and an important man in Bethlehem. [12] May the children you have by this young woman make your family as famous as the family of Perez,* the son of Tamar and Judah.

[13] Boaz married Ruth, and the LORD blessed her with a son. [14] After his birth, the women said to Naomi:

Praise the LORD! Today he has given you a grandson to take care of you. We pray that the boy will grow up to be famous everywhere in Israel. [15] He will* make you happy and take care of you in your old age, because he is the son of your daughter-in-law. And she loves you more than seven sons of your own would love you.

[16] Naomi loved the boy and took good care of him. [17] The neighbourhood women named him Obed, but they called him "Naomi's Boy".

When Obed grew up he had a son named Jesse, who later became the father of King David. [18-22] Here is a list of the ancestors of David: Jesse, Obed, Boaz, Salmon, Nahshon, Amminadab, Ram, Hezron, and Perez.

---

*4.12 Perez: One of the sons of Judah; he was an ancestor of Boaz and of many others who lived in Bethlehem.
See also: 4.12: Gen 38.27–30.

Additional notes

*1.13 Life . . . me: Or "I'm sorry that the LORD has turned against me and made life so hard for you."

*1.17 even by death: Or "by anything but death".

*2.7 she has . . . rest: One possible meaning for the difficult Hebrew text.

*2.20 He: Or "The LORD".

*3.15,16 When . . . her: Some Hebrew manuscripts and two ancient translations; most Hebrew manuscripts "Boaz went back to town. [16] Naomi asked Ruth".

*4.14,15 We pray that . . . famous . . . [15] He will: Or "We pray that the LORD will be praised everywhere in Israel. [15] Your grandson will".

---

*4.6 property . . . own: This property would then have to be shared with Ruth and her children as well as with his own family.
See also: 4.7,8: Deut 25.9. 4.10: Deut 25.5,6.
4.11: Gen 29.31.

1 Samuel

A quick look at this book

The First Book of Samuel is actually the first
half of a single book that was divided into two
parts, 1 and 2 Samuel, because together they

were too long to fit on one scroll. The books
are named after one of the main characters,
who was a prophet and also the last judge to
lead Israel.

The first part of 1 Samuel (1—7) tells about the
life of Samuel and how he helped Israel's army
fight against enemies that were making raids
in Israel. But when he grew old, the people
decided to ask the Lord for a king who could
lead the army.

In the second part of this book (8.1—15.35) the
Lord told Samuel to appoint Saul son of Kish to
be the first king of Israel. Saul and his eldest
son Jonathan won several battles against the
Ammonites and Philistines, but Saul did not
completely obey the Lord.

In the third part of the book (15.36—31.13),
the Lord told Samuel to secretly appoint a
young man named David to be the next king.
The book tells how David soon became a
national hero after he killed the giant Philistine
warrior, Goliath from Gath. But as David
continued to become more popular, Saul
became suspicious of David. Saul tried to have
him killed, even though David was married to
Saul's daughter Michal and was best friends
with Saul's son Jonathan. The rest of 1 Samuel
tells how David escaped and became the
leader of his own small army in the desert. Saul
continued to hunt for David, and so David
finally had to lead his followers to Philistia to
be safe from Saul.

The book concludes with the death of Saul and
his sons in a battle with the Philistine army.
The Lord was keeping his promise to make
David the king of Israel:

[17] Eli's sons did not show any respect for the sacrifices that the people offered. This was a terrible sin, and it made the LORD very angry.

Hannah visits Samuel

[18] The boy Samuel served the LORD and wore a special linen garment* [19] and the clothes* his mother made for him. She would bring new clothes every year, when she and her husband came to offer sacrifices at Shiloh.

[20] Eli would always bless Elkanah and his wife and say, "Samuel was born in answer to your prayers. Now you have given him to the LORD. I pray that the LORD will bless you with more children to take his place." After Eli had blessed them, Elkanah and Hannah would return home.

[21] The LORD was kind to Hannah, and she had three more sons and two daughters. But Samuel grew up at the LORD's house in Shiloh.

Eli warns his sons

[22] Eli was now very old, and he heard what his sons were doing to the people of Israel.*

[23-24] "Why are you doing these awful things?" he asked them. "I've been hearing nothing but complaints about you from all the LORD's people. [25] If you harm another person, God can help make things right between the two of you. But if you commit a crime against the LORD, no one can help you!"

But the LORD had already decided to kill them. So he kept them from listening to their father.

A prophet speaks to Eli

[26] Each day the LORD and his people liked Samuel more and more.

[27] One day a prophet came to Eli and gave him this message from the LORD:

When your ancestors were slaves of the king of Egypt, I came and showed them who I am. [28-29] Out of all the tribes of Israel, I chose your family to be my priests. I wanted them to offer sacrifices and burn

incense to me and to find out from me what I want my people to do. I commanded everyone to bring their sacrifices here where I live, and I allowed you and your family to keep those that were not offered to me on the altar.

But you honour your sons instead of me! You don't respect* the sacrifices and offerings that are brought to me, and you've all got fat from eating the best parts.

[30] I am the LORD, the God of Israel. I promised to let your family serve me as priests for ever, but now I tell you that I cannot do this any longer! I honour anyone who honours me, but I put a curse on anyone who hates me. [31] The time will come when I will kill you and everyone else in your family. Not one of you will live to an old age.

[32] Your family* will have a lot of trouble. I will be kind to Israel,* but everyone in your family will die young. [33] If I let anyone from your family be a priest, his* life will be full of sadness and sorrow. But most of the men in your family will die a violent death!* [34] To prove to you that I will do these things, your two sons, Hophni and Phinehas, will die on the same day.

[35] I have chosen someone else to be my priest, someone who will be faithful and obey me. I will always let his family serve as priests and help my chosen king. [36] But if anyone is left from your family, he will come to my priest and beg for money or a little bread. He may even say to my priest, "Please let me be a priest, so I will at least have something to eat."

CHAPTER 3

The LORD speaks to Samuel

[1-2] Samuel served the LORD by helping Eli the priest, who was by that time almost blind. In those days, the LORD hardly ever spoke directly to people, and he did not appear to them in dreams very often. But one night, Eli was asleep in his room, [3] and Samuel was sleeping on a mat near the sacred chest in the LORD's house. They had not been awake very long* [4] when the LORD called out Samuel's name.

"Here I am!" Samuel answered. [5] Then he ran to Eli and said, "Here I am. What do you want?"

---

*2.18 a special linen garment: Either a loin cloth or a jacket or an apron worn only by priests.
*2.19 clothes: The Hebrew word means a sleeveless coat or robe that was worn by priests. Samuel was a small child, but his mother made him clothes just like those worn by priests.
See also: 2.26: Luke 2.52. 2.28: a Exod 28.1–4; b Lev 7.35,36.

*3.3 They . . . long: The Hebrew text has "The lamp was still burning". An olive oil lamp would go out after a few hours if the wick was not adjusted.
See also: 2.34: 1 Sam 4.11.

"I didn't call you," Eli answered. "Go back to bed."

Samuel went back.

⁶ Again the LORD called out Samuel's name. Samuel got up and went to Eli. "Here I am," he said. "What do you want?"

Eli told him, "Son, I didn't call you. Go back to sleep."

⁷ The LORD had not spoken to Samuel before, and Samuel did not recognize the voice. ⁸ When the LORD called out his name for the third time, Samuel went to Eli again and said, "Here I am. What do you want?"

Eli finally realized that it was the LORD who was speaking to Samuel. ⁹ So he said, "Go back and lie down! If someone speaks to you again, answer, 'I'm listening, LORD. What do you want me to do?'"

Once again Samuel went back and lay down.

¹⁰ The LORD then stood beside Samuel and called out as he had done before, "Samuel! Samuel!"

"I'm listening," Samuel answered. "What do you want me to do?"

¹¹ The LORD said:

Samuel, I am going to do something in Israel that will shock everyone who hears about it! ¹² I will punish Eli and his family, just as I promised. ¹³ He knew that his sons refused to respect me,* and he let them get away with it, even though I said I would punish his family for ever. ¹⁴ I warned Eli that sacrifices or offerings could never make things right! His family has done too many disgusting things.

¹⁵ The next morning, Samuel got up and opened the doors to the LORD's house. He was afraid to tell Eli what the LORD had said. ¹⁶ But Eli told him, "Samuel, my boy, come here!"

"Here I am," Samuel answered.

¹⁷ Eli said, "What did God say to you? Tell me everything. I pray that God will punish you terribly if you don't tell me every word he said!"

¹⁸ Samuel told Eli everything. Then Eli said, "He is the LORD, and he will do what's right."

The LORD helps Samuel

¹⁹ As Samuel grew up, the LORD helped him and made everything Samuel said come true. ²⁰ From the town of Dan in the north to the town of Beersheba in the south, everyone in the country knew that Samuel was truly the LORD's prophet. ²¹ The LORD often appeared to Samuel at Shiloh and told him what to say.

CHAPTER 4

¹ Then Samuel would speak to the whole nation of Israel.

The sacred chest is captured and returned

The Philistines capture the sacred chest

One day the Israelites went out to fight the Philistines. They set up camp near Ebenezer, and the Philistines camped at Aphek. ² The Philistines made a fierce attack. They defeated the Israelites and killed about four thousand of them.

³ The Israelite army returned to their camp, and the leaders said, "Why did the LORD let us lose to the Philistines today? Let's get the sacred chest where the LORD's agreement with Israel is kept. Then the LORD* will help us and rescue us from our enemies."

⁴ The army sent some soldiers to bring back the sacred chest from Shiloh, because the LORD All-Powerful has his throne on the winged creatures on top of the chest.

As Eli's two sons, Hophni and Phinehas, ⁵ brought the chest into camp, the army cheered so loudly that the ground shook. ⁶ The Philistines heard the noise and said, "What are those Hebrews shouting about?"

When the Philistines learnt that the sacred chest had been brought into the camp, ⁷ they were scared to death and said:

The gods have come into their camp. Now we're in real trouble! Nothing like this has ever happened to us before. ⁸ We're in big trouble! Who can save us from these powerful gods? They're the same gods who made all those horrible things happen to the Egyptians in the desert.

⁹ Philistines, be brave and fight hard! If you don't, those Hebrews will rule us, just as we've been ruling them. Fight and don't be afraid.

¹⁰ The Philistines did fight. They killed thirty thousand Israelite soldiers, and all the rest ran off to their homes. ¹¹ Hophni and Phinehas were killed, and the sacred chest was captured.

Eli dies

¹² That same day a soldier from the tribe of Benjamin ran from the battlefront to Shiloh. He had torn his clothes and put earth on his

See also: 4.4: Exod 25.22.

head to show his sorrow. ¹³ He went into town and told the news about the battle, and everyone started crying.

Eli was afraid that something might happen to the sacred chest. So he was sitting on his chair beside the road, just waiting. ¹⁴⁻¹⁵ He was ninety-eight years old and blind, but he could hear everyone crying, and he asked, "What's all that noise?"

The soldier hurried over and told Eli, ¹⁶ "I escaped from the fighting today and ran here."

"Young man, what happened?" Eli asked.

¹⁷ "Israel ran away from the Philistines," the soldier answered. "Many of our people were killed, including your two sons, Hophni and Phinehas. But worst of all, the sacred chest was captured."

¹⁸ Eli was still sitting on a chair beside the wall of the town gate. And when the man said that the Philistines had taken the sacred chest, Eli fell backwards. He was a very heavy old man, and the fall broke his neck and killed him. He had been a leader* of Israel for forty years.

¹⁹ The wife of Phinehas was about to give birth. And soon after she heard that the sacred chest had been captured and that her husband and his father had died, her baby came. The birth was very hard, ²⁰ and she was dying. But the women taking care of her said, "Don't be afraid — it's a boy!"

She didn't pay any attention to them. ²¹⁻²² Instead she kept thinking about losing her husband and her father-in-law. So she said, "My son will be named Ichabod,* because the glory of Israel left our country when the sacred chest was captured."

CHAPTER 5

God causes trouble for the Philistines

¹ The Philistines took the sacred chest from near Ebenezer to the town of Ashdod. ² They brought it into the temple of their god Dagon and put it next to the statue of Dagon, which they worshipped.

³ When the people of Ashdod got up early the next morning, they found the statue lying face down on the floor in front of the sacred chest. They put the statue back where it belonged. ⁴ But early the next morning, it had fallen over again and was lying face

down on the floor in front of the chest. The body of the statue was still in one piece, but its head and both hands had broken off and were lying on the stone floor in the doorway. ⁵ This is the reason the priests and everyone else step over that part of the doorway when they enter the temple of Dagon in Ashdod.

⁶ The LORD caused a lot of trouble for the people of Ashdod and their neighbours. He made sores break out all over their bodies,' and everyone was in a panic.' ⁷ Finally, they said, "The God of Israel did this. He is the one who caused all this trouble for us and our god Dagon. We've got to get rid of this chest."

⁸ The people of Ashdod called all the Philistine rulers to Ashdod, and they asked them, "What can we do with the sacred chest that belongs to the God of Israel?"

"Send it to Gath," the rulers answered. But after they took it there, ⁹ the LORD made sores break out on everyone in town. The people of Gath were frightened, ¹⁰ so they sent the sacred chest to Ekron. But before they could take it through the town gates, the people of Ekron started screaming, "They've brought the sacred chest that belongs to the God of Israel! It will kill us and our families too!"

The Philistines send back the sacred chest

¹¹ The people of Ekron called for another meeting of the Philistine rulers and told them, "Send this chest back where it belongs. Then it won't kill us."

Everyone was in a panic, because God was causing a lot of people to die, ¹² and those who had survived were suffering from the sores. They all cried to their gods for help.

CHAPTER 6

¹ After the sacred chest had been in Philistia for seven months,' ² the Philistines called in their priests and fortune-tellers, and asked, "What should we do with this sacred chest? Tell us how to send it back where it belongs!"

³ "Don't send it back without a gift," the priests and fortune-tellers answered. "Send along something to Israel's God to make up for taking the chest in the first place. Then you will be healed, and you will find out why the LORD was causing you so much trouble."

⁴ "What should we send?" the Philistines asked.

The priests and fortune-tellers answered:

---

*4.18 leader: The Hebrew word means that Eli may have been an army commander, a judge, and a priest.
*4.21,22 Ichabod: Ichabod means "where is the glory?" or "there is no glory".

There are five Philistine rulers, and they all have the same disease that you have. ⁵ So make four gold models of the sores and five gold models of the rats that are wiping out your crops. If you honour the God of Israel with this gift, perhaps he will stop causing trouble for you and your gods and your crops. ⁶ Don't be like the Egyptians and their king. They were stubborn, but when Israel's God had finished with them, they had to let Israel go.

⁷ Get a new cart and two cows that have young calves and that have never pulled a cart. Hitch the cows to the cart, but take the calves back to their barn. ⁸ Then put the chest on the cart. Put the gold rats and sores in a bag and put it on the cart next to the chest. Then send it on its way.

⁹ Watch to see if the chest goes on up the road to the Israelite town of Beth-Shemesh. If it goes back to its own country, you will know that it was the LORD who made us suffer so badly. But if the chest doesn't go back to its own country, then the LORD had nothing to do with the disease that hit us — it was simply bad luck.

¹⁰ The Philistines followed their advice. They hitched up the two cows to the cart, but they kept their calves in a barn. ¹¹ Then they put the chest on the cart, along with the bag that had the gold rats and sores in it.

¹² The cows went straight up the road towards Beth-Shemesh, mooing as they went. The Philistine rulers followed them until they got close to Beth-Shemesh.

¹³ The people of Beth-Shemesh were harvesting their wheat* in the valley. When they looked up and saw the chest, they were so happy that they stopped working and started celebrating.

¹⁴⁻¹⁵ The cows left the road and pulled the cart into a field that belonged to Joshua from Beth-Shemesh, and they stopped beside a huge rock. Some men from the tribe of Levi were there. So they took the chest off the cart and placed it on the rock, and then they did the same thing with the bag of gold rats and sores. A few other people chopped up the cart and made a fire. They killed the cows and burnt them as sacrifices to the LORD. After that, they offered more sacrifices.

¹⁶ When the five rulers of the Philistines saw what had happened, they went back to Ekron that same day.

¹⁷ That is how the Philistines sent gifts to the LORD to make up for taking the sacred chest. They sent five gold sores, one each for their towns of Ashdod, Gaza, Ashkelon, Gath, and Ekron. ¹⁸ They also sent one gold rat for each walled town and for every village that the five Philistine rulers controlled. The huge stone* where the Levites set the chest is still there in Joshua's field as a reminder of what happened.

The sacred chest is sent to Kiriath-Jearim

¹⁹ Some of the men of Beth-Shemesh looked inside the sacred chest, and the LORD God killed seventy* of them. This made the people of Beth-Shemesh very sad, ²⁰ and they started saying, "No other God is like the LORD! Who can go near him and still live? We'll have to send the chest away from here. But where can we send it?"

²¹ They sent messengers to tell the people of Kiriath-Jearim, "The Philistines have sent back the sacred chest. Why don't you take it and keep it there with you?"

CHAPTER 7

¹ The people of Kiriath-Jearim got the chest and took it to Abinadab's house, which was on a hill in their town. They chose his son Eleazar to take care of it, ² and it stayed there for twenty years.

During this time everyone in Israel was very sad and begged the LORD for help.*

Samuel as the leader of Israel

The people of Israel turn back to the LORD

³ One day, Samuel told all the people of Israel, "If you really want to turn back to the LORD, then prove it. Get rid of your foreign idols, including the ones of the goddess Astarte. Turn to the LORD with all your heart and worship only him. Then he will rescue you from the Philistines."

⁴ The people got rid of their idols of Baal and Astarte and began worshipping only the LORD.

⁵ Then Samuel said, "Tell everyone in Israel to meet together at Mizpah, and I will pray to the LORD for you."

---

*6.13 wheat: The wheat harvest took place in May and June.

See also: 7.1: 2 Sam 6.2–4; 1 Chron 13.5–7.

6 The Israelites met together at Mizpah with Samuel as their leader. They drew water from the well and poured it out as an offering to the LORD. On that same day they went without eating to show their sorrow, and they confessed they had been unfaithful to the LORD.

The Philistines attack Israel

7 When the Philistine rulers found out about the meeting at Mizpah, they sent an army there to attack the people of Israel.

The Israelites were afraid when they heard that the Philistines were coming. 8 "Don't stop praying!" they told Samuel. "Ask the LORD our God to rescue us."

9-10 Samuel begged the LORD to rescue Israel, then he sacrificed a young lamb to the LORD. Samuel had not even finished offering the sacrifice when the Philistines started to attack. But the LORD answered his prayer and made thunder crash all around them. The Philistines panicked and ran away. 11 The men of Israel left Mizpah and went after them as far as the hillside below Beth-Car, killing every enemy soldier they caught.

12-13 The Philistines were so badly beaten that it was quite a while before they attacked Israel again. After the battle, Samuel set up a monument between Mizpah and the rocky cliffs. He named it "Help Monument"* to remind Israel how much the LORD had helped them.

For as long as Samuel lived, the LORD helped Israel fight the Philistines. 14 The Israelites were even able to recapture their towns and territory between Ekron and Gath.

Israel was also at peace with the Amorites.*

Samuel is a leader in Israel

15 Samuel was a leader* in Israel all his life. 16 Every year he would go around to the towns of Bethel, Gilgal, and Mizpah where he served as judge for the people. 17 Then he would go back to his home in Ramah and do the same thing there. He also had an altar built for the LORD at Ramah.

Saul, the first king of Israel

CHAPTER 8

The people of Israel want a king

1-2 Samuel had two sons. The elder one was Joel, and the younger one was Abijah. When Samuel was getting old, he let them be leaders* at Beersheba. 3 But they were not like their father. They were dishonest and accepted bribes to give unfair decisions.

4 One day the nation's leaders came to Samuel at Ramah 5 and said, "You are an old man. You set a good example for your sons, but they haven't followed it. Now we want a king to be our leader,* just like all the other nations. Choose one for us!"

6 Samuel was upset to hear the leaders say they wanted a king, so he prayed about it. 7 The LORD answered:

Samuel, do everything they want you to do. I am really the one they have rejected as their king. 8 Ever since the day I rescued my people from Egypt, they have turned from me to worship idols. Now they are turning away from you. 9 Do everything they ask, but warn them and tell them how a king will treat them.

10 Samuel told the people who were asking for a king what the LORD had said:

11 If you have a king, this is how he will treat you. He will force your sons to join his army. Some of them will ride in his chariots, some will serve in the cavalry, and others will run ahead of his own chariot.* 12 Some of them will be officers in charge of a thousand soldiers, and others will be in charge of fifty. Still others will have to farm the king's land and harvest his crops, or make weapons and parts for his chariots. 13 Your daughters will have to make perfume or do his cooking and baking.

14 The king will take your best fields, as well as your vineyards and olive orchards, and give them to his own officials. 15 He will also take a tenth of your grain and grapes and give it to his officers and officials.

16 The king will take your slaves and your best young men and your donkeys and

*7.14 Amorites: In this verse, the non-Israelite peoples of Canaan.
*7.15 leader: The Hebrew word could mean an army commander, a judge, and a religious leader.

*8.1,2 leaders: See the note at 7.15.
*8.5 leader: See the note at 7.15.
*8.11 others . . . chariot: These men were probably his bodyguards.
See also: 8.5: Deut 17.14.

make them do his work. ¹⁷ He will also take a tenth of your sheep and goats. You will become the king's slaves, ¹⁸ and you will finally cry out for the LORD to save you from the king you wanted. But the LORD won't answer your prayers.

¹⁹⁻²⁰ The people would not listen to Samuel. "No!" they said. "We want to be like other nations. We want a king to rule us and lead us in battle."

²¹ Samuel listened to them and then told the LORD exactly what they had said. ²² "Do what they want," the LORD answered. "Give them a king."

Samuel told the people to go back to their homes.

CHAPTER 9

Saul meets Samuel

¹ Kish was a wealthy man who belonged to the tribe of Benjamin. His father was Abiel, his grandfather was Zeror, his great-grandfather was Becorath, and his great-great-grandfather was Aphiah. ² Kish had a son named Saul, who was better looking and more than a head taller than anyone else in all Israel.

³ Kish owned some donkeys, but they had run off. So he told Saul, "Take one of the servants and go and look for the donkeys."

⁴ Saul and the servant went through the hill country of Ephraim and the territory of Shalishah, but they could not find the donkeys. Then they went through the territories of Shaalim and Benjamin, but still there was no sign of the donkeys. ⁵ Finally they came to the territory where the clan of Zuph* lived. "Let's go back home," Saul told his servant. "If we don't go back soon, my father will stop worrying about the donkeys and start worrying about us!"

⁶ "Wait!" the servant answered. "There's a man of God who lives in a town near here. He's amazing! Everything he says comes true. Let's talk to him. Perhaps he can tell us where to look."

⁷ Saul said, "How can we talk to the prophet when I don't have anything to give him? We don't even have any bread left in our sacks. What can we give him?"

⁸ "I have a small piece of silver," the servant answered. "We can give him that, and then he will tell us where to look for the donkeys."

⁹⁻¹⁰ "Great!" Saul replied. "Let's go to the man who can see visions!" He said this because in those days God would answer questions by giving visions to prophets.

Saul and his servant went to the town where the prophet lived. ¹¹ As they were going up the hill to the town, they met some young women coming out to get water,* and the two men said to them, "We're looking for the man who can see visions. Is he in town?"

¹² "Yes, he is," they replied. "He's in town today because there's going to be a sacrifice and a sacred meal at the place of worship. In fact, he's just ahead of you. Hurry ¹³ and you should find him just inside the town gate. He's on his way out to the place of worship to eat with the invited guests. They can't start eating until he blesses the sacrifice. If you go now, you should find him."

¹⁴ They went to the town, and just as they were going through the gate, Samuel was coming out on his way to the place of worship.

¹⁵ The day before Saul came, the LORD had told Samuel, ¹⁶ "I've seen how my people are suffering, and I've heard their call for help. About this time tomorrow I'll send you a man from the tribe of Benjamin, who will rescue my people from the Philistines. I want you to pour olive oil* on his head to show that he will be their leader."

¹⁷ Samuel looked at Saul, and the LORD told Samuel, "This is the man I told you about. He's the one who will rule Israel."

¹⁸ Saul went over to Samuel in the gateway and said, "A man who can see visions lives here in town. Could you tell me the way to his house?"

¹⁹ "I am the one who sees visions!" Samuel answered. "Go on up to the place of worship. You will eat with me today, and in the morning I'll answer your questions. ²⁰ Don't worry about your donkeys that ran off three days ago. They've already been found. Everything of value in Israel now belongs to you and your family."

²¹ "Why are you telling me this?" Saul asked. "I'm from Benjamin, the smallest tribe in Israel, and my clan is the least important in the tribe."

*9.5 Zuph: Samuel's father Elkanah was from the Zuph clan.

*9.11 water: Towns were often built on a hill near a source of water, which would often be down in the valley outside the town. It was usually the job of women to get water for their family.
*9.16 olive oil: Olive oil was poured on the head of someone who was chosen to be a priest, a prophet, or a king.

Saul eats with Samuel and stays at his house

²² Samuel took Saul and his servant into the dining room at the place of worship. About thirty people were there for the dinner, but Samuel gave Saul and his servant the places of honour. ²³⁻²⁴ Then Samuel told the cook, "I gave you the best piece of meat and told you to set it aside. Bring it here now."

The cook brought the meat over and set it down in front of Saul. "This is for you," Samuel told him. "Go ahead and eat it. I had this piece saved especially for you, and I invited these guests to eat with us."

After Saul and Samuel had finished eating, ²⁵ they went down from the place of worship and back into town. A bed was set up for Saul on the flat roof* of Samuel's house, ²⁶ and Saul slept there.

About sunrise the next morning,' Samuel called up to Saul on the roof, "Time to get up! I'll help you get started on your way."

Saul got up. He and Samuel left together ²⁷ and had almost reached the edge of town when Samuel stopped and said, "Tell your servant to go on. Stay here with me for a few minutes, and I'll tell you what God has told me."

Samuel tells Saul he will be king

After the servant had gone,

CHAPTER 10

¹ Samuel took a small jar of olive oil and poured it on Saul's head. Then he kissed* Saul and told him:

The Lord has chosen you to be the leader and ruler of his people.' ² When you leave me today, you'll meet two men near Rachel's tomb at Zelzah in the territory of Benjamin. They'll tell you, "The donkeys you've been looking for have been found. Your father has forgotten about them, and now he's worrying about you! He's wondering how he can find you."

³ Go on from there until you reach the big oak tree at Tabor, where you'll meet three men on their way to worship God at Bethel. One of them will be leading three young goats, another will be carrying three round loaves of bread, and the last one will be carrying a clay jar of wine. ⁴ After they greet you, they'll give you two loaves of bread.

⁵ Next, go to Gibeah,' where the Philistines have an army camp. As you're going into the town, you'll meet a group of prophets coming down from the place of worship. They'll be going along prophesying while others are walking in front of them, playing small harps, small drums, and flutes.

⁶ The Spirit of the Lord will suddenly take control of you.' You'll become a different person and start prophesying along with them. ⁷ After these things happen, do whatever you think is right! God will help you.

⁸ Then you should go to Gilgal. I'll come a little later, so wait for me. It may even take a week for me to get there, but when I come, I'll offer sacrifices and offerings to the Lord. I'll also tell you what to do next.

Saul goes back home

⁹ As Saul turned around to leave Samuel, God made Saul feel like a different person. That same day, everything happened just as Samuel had said. ¹⁰ When Saul arrived at Gibeah, a group of prophets met him. The Spirit of God suddenly took control of him,' and there in the middle of the group he began prophesying.

¹¹ Some people who had known Saul for a long time saw that he was speaking and behaving like a prophet. They said to each other, "What's happened? How can Saul be a prophet?"

¹² "Why not?" one of them answered. "Saul has as much right to be a prophet as anyone else!" That's why everyone started saying, "How can Saul be a prophet?"

¹³ After Saul stopped prophesying, he went to the place of worship.

¹⁴ Later, Saul's uncle asked him, "Where have you been?"

Saul answered, "Looking for the donkeys. We couldn't find them, so we went to talk with Samuel."

¹⁵ "And what did he tell you?" Saul's uncle asked.

¹⁶ Saul answered, "He told us the donkeys had been found." But Saul didn't mention that Samuel had chosen him to be king.

---

*9.25 roof: Guests often slept on the flat roof of their host's house, where it was cool and breezy.
*10.1 kissed: Relatives or close friends often greeted one another with a kiss. But this may have been a ceremonial kiss after Samuel poured oil on Saul's head to show that he was to be the king.

See also: **10.12:** 1 Sam 19.23,24.

**The LORD shows Israel
that Saul will be king**

[17] Samuel sent messengers to tell the Israelites to come to Mizpah and meet with the LORD. [18] When everyone had arrived, Samuel said:

The LORD God of Israel told me to remind you that he had rescued you from the Egyptians and from the other nations that abused you.

[19] God has rescued you from your troubles and hard times. But you have rejected your God and have asked for a king. Now each tribe and clan must come near the place of worship so the LORD can choose a king.

[20] Samuel brought each tribe, one after the other, to the altar, and the LORD chose the Benjamin tribe. [21] Next, Samuel brought each clan of Benjamin there, and the LORD chose the Matri clan. Finally, Saul the son of Kish was chosen. But when they looked for him, he was nowhere to be found.

[22] The people prayed, "Our LORD, is Saul here?"

"Yes," the LORD answered, "he is hiding behind the baggage."

[23] The people ran and got Saul and brought him into the middle of the crowd. He was more than a head taller than anyone else. [24] "Look closely at the man the LORD has chosen!" Samuel told the crowd. "There is no one like him!"

The crowd shouted, "Long live the king!"

[25] Samuel explained the rights and duties of a king and wrote them all in a book. He put the book in a temple building at one of the places where the LORD was worshipped. Then Samuel sent everyone home.

[26] God had encouraged some young men to become followers of Saul, and when he returned to his home town of Gibeah, they went with him. [27] But some worthless fools said, "How can someone like Saul rescue us from our enemies?" They did not want Saul to be their king, and so they didn't bring him any gifts. But Saul kept calm.

CHAPTER 11

**Saul rescues the town
of Jabesh in Gilead**

[1] About this time,[•] King Nahash of Ammon came with his army and surrounded the town of Jabesh in Gilead. The people who lived there told Nahash, "If you will sign a peace treaty with us, you can be our ruler, and we will pay taxes to you."

[2] Nahash answered, "Certainly, I'll sign a treaty! But not before I insult Israel by putting out the right eye of every man who lives in Jabesh."

[3] The town leaders said, "Give us seven days so we can send messengers everywhere in Israel to ask for help. If no one comes here to save us, we will surrender to you."

[4] Some of the messengers went to Gibeah, Saul's home town. They told what was happening at Jabesh, and everyone in Gibeah started crying. [5] Just then, Saul came in from the fields, walking behind his oxen.

"Why is everyone crying?" Saul asked.

They told him what the men from Jabesh had said. [6] Then the Spirit of God suddenly took control of Saul and made him furious. [7] Saul killed two of his oxen, cut them up in pieces, and gave the pieces to the[•] messengers. He told them to show the pieces to everyone in Israel and say, "Saul and Samuel are getting an army together. Come and join them. If you don't, this is what will happen to your oxen!"

The LORD made the people of Israel terribly afraid. So all the men came together [8] at Bezek. Saul had them organized and counted. There were three hundred thousand from Israel and thirty thousand[•] from Judah.

[9] Saul and his officers sent the messengers back to Jabesh with this promise: "We will rescue you tomorrow afternoon." The messengers went back to the people at Jabesh and told them that they were going to be rescued.

Everyone was encouraged! [10] So they told the Ammonites, "We will surrender to you tomorrow, and then you can do whatever you want to."

[11] The next day, Saul divided his army into three groups and attacked before daylight. They started killing Ammonites and kept it up until afternoon. A few Ammonites managed to escape, but they were scattered far from each other.

[12] The Israelite soldiers went to Samuel and demanded, "Where are the men who said they didn't want Saul to be king? Bring them to us, and we will put them to death!"

[13] "No you won't!" Saul told them. "The LORD rescued Israel today, and no one will be put to death."

Saul is accepted as king

[14] "Come on!" Samuel said. "Let's go to Gilgal and make an agreement that Saul will continue to be our king."

¹⁵ Everyone went to the place of worship at Gilgal, where they agreed that Saul would be their king. Saul and the people sacrificed animals to ask for the LORD's blessing,* and they had a big celebration.

Samuel's farewell speech

CHAPTER 12

¹ Samuel told the Israelites:

I have given you a king, just as you asked. ² You have seen how I have led you ever since I was a young man. I'm already old. My hair is grey, and my own sons are grown up. Now you must see how well your king will lead you.

³ Let me ask this. Have I ever taken anyone's ox or donkey or forced you to give me anything? Have I ever hurt anyone or taken a bribe to give an unfair decision? Answer me so the LORD and his chosen king can hear you. And if I have done any of these things, I will give it all back.

⁴ "No," the Israelites answered. "You've never cheated us in any way!"

⁵ Samuel said, "The LORD and his chosen king are witnesses to what you have said."

"That's true," they replied.

⁶ Then Samuel told them:

The LORD brought your ancestors out of Egypt and chose Moses and Aaron to be your leaders. ⁷ Now the LORD will be your judge. So stand here and listen, while I remind you that the LORD has saved you and your ancestors from your enemies.

⁸ After Jacob went to Egypt, your ancestors cried out to the LORD for help, and he sent Moses and Aaron. They led your ancestors out of Egypt and settled them in this land. ⁹ But your ancestors forgot the LORD, so he let them be defeated by the Philistines, the king of Moab, and Sisera, the commander of Hazor's army.

¹⁰ Again your ancestors cried out to the LORD for help. They said, "We have sinned! We stopped worshipping you, our LORD, and started worshipping Baal and Astarte. But now, if you rescue us from our enemies, we will worship you."

¹¹ The LORD sent Gideon,ᵇ Bedan, Jephthah, and Samuel to rescue you from your enemies, and you didn't have to worry about being attacked. ¹² Then you saw that King Nahash of Ammon was going to attack you. And even though the LORD your God is your king, you told me, "This time it's different. We want a king to rule us!"

¹³ You asked for a king, and you chose one. Now he stands here where all of you can see him. But it was really the LORD who made him your king. ¹⁴ If you and your king want to be followers of the LORD, you must worship himᶜ and do what he says. Don't be stubborn! ¹⁵ If you're stubborn and refuse to obey the LORD, he will turn against you and your king.ᵈ

¹⁶ Just stand here and watch the LORD show his mighty power. ¹⁷ Isn't this the dry season?* I'm going to ask the LORD to send a thunderstorm. When you see it, you will realize how wrong you were to ask for a king.

¹⁸ Samuel prayed, and that same day the LORD sent a thunderstorm. Everyone was afraid of the LORD and of Samuel. ¹⁹ They told Samuel, "Please, pray to the LORD your God for us! We don't want to die. We have sinned many times in the past, and we were very wrong to ask for a king."

²⁰ Samuel answered:

Even though what you did was wrong, you don't need to be afraid. But you must always follow the LORD and worship him with all your heart. ²¹ Don't worship idols! They don't have any power, and they can't help you or save you when you're in trouble. ²² But the LORD has chosen you to be his own people. He will always take care of you so that everyone will know how great he is.

²³ I would be disobeying the LORD if I stopped praying for you! I will always teach you how to live right. ²⁴ You also must obey the LORD — you must worship him with all your heart and remember the great things he has done for you. ²⁵ But if you and your king do evil, the LORD will wipe you out.

---

*11.15 sacrificed . . . blessing: This kind of sacrifice is described in Leviticus 3; 7.11–36; 19.5–8. People who offered these sacrifices were allowed to eat most of the meat, and they could invite others to share it with them.

See also: 12.6: Exod 6.26. 12.8: Exod 2.23.
12.9: a Judg 4.2; b Judg 13.1; c Judg 3.12.
12.10: Judg 10.10–15.

*12.17 the dry season: The Hebrew text has "time for wheat harvest", which was usually in the spring, the beginning of the dry season.

See also: 12.11: a Judg 7.1; b Judg 4.6; c Judg 11.29;
d 1 Sam 3.20. 12.12: 1 Sam 8.19.

265

Saul disobeys the Lord, and the Lord rejects him as king

CHAPTER 13

¹ Saul was a young man* when he became king, and he ruled Israel for two years.
² Then* he chose three thousand men from Israel to be full-time soldiers and sent everyone else* home. Two thousand of these troops stayed with him in the hills around Michmash and Bethel. The other thousand were stationed with Jonathan* at Gibeah* in the territory of Benjamin.

³ Jonathan led an attack on the Philistine army camp at Geba.* The Philistine camp was destroyed, but* the other Philistines heard what had happened. Then Saul told his messengers, "Go to every village in the country. Give a signal with the trumpet, and when the people come together, tell them what has happened."

⁴ The messengers then said to the people of Israel, "Saul has destroyed the Philistine army camp at Geba." Now the Philistines really hate Israel, so every town and village must send men to join Saul's army at Gilgal."

⁵ The Philistines called their army together to fight Israel. They had three thousand* chariots, six thousand cavalry, and as many foot soldiers as there are grains of sand on the beach. They went to Michmash and set up camp there east of Beth-Aven.*

⁶ The Israelite army realized that they were outnumbered and were going to lose the battle. Some of the Israelite men hid in caves or in clumps of bushes,* and some ran to places where they could hide among large rocks. Others hid in tombs* or in deep

dry pits. ⁷ Still others* went to Gad and Gilead on the other side of the River Jordan.

Saul stayed at Gilgal. His soldiers were shaking with fear, ⁸ and they were starting to run off and leave him. Saul waited there seven days, just as Samuel had ordered him to do,* but Samuel did not come. ⁹ Finally, Saul commanded, "Bring me some animals, so we can offer sacrifices to please the LORD and ask for his help."

Saul killed one of the animals, ¹⁰ and just as he was placing it on the altar, Samuel arrived. Saul went out to welcome him.

¹¹ "What have you done?" Samuel asked.

Saul answered, "My soldiers were leaving in all directions, and you didn't come when you were supposed to. The Philistines were gathering at Michmash, ¹² and I was worried that they would attack me here at Gilgal. I hadn't offered a sacrifice to ask for the LORD's help, so I forced myself to offer a sacrifice on the altar fire."

¹³ "That was stupid!" Samuel said. "You didn't obey the LORD your God. If you had obeyed him, someone from your family would always have been king of Israel. ¹⁴ But no, you disobeyed, and so the LORD won't choose anyone else from your family to be king. In fact, he has already chosen the one he wants to be the next leader of his people." ¹⁵ Then Samuel left Gilgal.

Part of Saul's army had not deserted him, and he led them to Gibeah in Benjamin to join his other troops. Then he counted them* and found that he still had six hundred men. ¹⁶ Saul, Jonathan, and their army set up camp at Geba in Benjamin.

Jonathan attacks the Philistines

The Philistine army was camped at Michmash. ¹⁷ Each day they sent out patrols to attack and rob villages and then destroy them. One patrol would go north along the road to Ophrah in the region of Shual. ¹⁸ Another patrol would go west along the road to Beth-Horon. A third patrol would go east towards the desert on the road to the ridge that overlooks Zeboim Valley.

¹⁹ The Philistines would not allow any Israelites to learn how to make iron tools. "If

*13.2 everyone else: People who were not full-time soldiers, but fought together with the army when the nation was in danger.
*13.2 Jonathan: Saul's son (see verse 16).
*13.2 Michmash . . . Bethel . . . Gibeah: These three towns form a triangle, with Bethel to the north.
*13.3 Geba: Geba was between Gibeah and Michmash.
*13.5 Beth-Aven: This Beth-Aven was probably about one and a half kilometres south-west of Michmash, between Michmash and Geba.
*13.6 tombs: The Hebrew word may mean a room cut into solid rock and used as a burial place, or it may mean a cellar.

13.7 Still others: This translates a Hebrew word which may be used of wandering groups of people who sometimes became outlaws or hired soldiers (see also 14.21).
*13.8 Samuel . . . to do: See 10.8.
See also: 13.8: 1 Sam 10.8. 13.14: Acts 13.22.

we allowed that," they said, "those worthless Israelites would make swords and spears."

20-21 Whenever the Israelites wanted to get an iron point put on a cattle prod,* they had to go to the Philistines. Even if they wanted to sharpen plough-blades, picks, axes, sickles,* and pitchforks* they still had to go to them. And the Philistines charged high prices. 22 So, whenever the Israelite soldiers had to go into battle, none of them had a sword or a spear except Saul and his son Jonathan. 23 The Philistines moved their camp to the pass at Michmash,

CHAPTER 14

1-3 and Saul was in Geba* with his six hundred men. Saul's own tent was set up under a fruit tree* by the threshing place* at the edge of town. Ahijah was serving as priest, and part of his jobs was to get answers from the LORD for Saul. Ahijah's father was Ahitub, and his father's brother was Ichabod. Ahijah's grandfather was Phinehas, and his great-grandfather Eli had been the LORD's priest at Shiloh.

One day, Jonathan told the soldier who carried his weapons that he wanted to attack the Philistine camp on the other side of the valley. So they slipped out of the Israelite camp without anyone knowing it. Jonathan didn't even tell his father he was leaving.

4-5 Jonathan decided to get to the Philistine camp by going through the pass that led between Shiny Cliff and Michmash to the north and Thorn Bush Cliff* and Geba to the south.

6 Jonathan and the soldier who carried his weapons talked as they went towards the Philistine camp. "It's just the two of us against all those godless men," Jonathan said. "But the LORD can help a few soldiers win a battle just as easily as he can help a whole army. Perhaps the LORD will help us win this battle."

7 "Do whatever you want," the soldier answered. "I'll be with you."

8 "This is what we will do," Jonathan said. "We will go across and let them see us. 9 If they agree to come down the hill and fight where we are, then we won't climb up to their camp. 10 But we will go if they tell us to

come up the hill and fight. That will mean the LORD is going to help us win."

11-12 Jonathan and the soldier stood at the bottom of the hill where the Philistines could see them. "Look! Those worthless Israelites have crawled out of the holes where they've been hiding." Then they yelled down to Jonathan and the soldier, "Come up here, and we will teach you a thing or two!"

Jonathan turned to the soldier and said, "Follow me! The LORD is going to let us win."

13 Jonathan crawled up the hillside with the soldier following him. When they got to the top, Jonathan killed the Philistines who attacked from the front, and the soldier killed those who attacked from behind.* 14 Before they had gone thirty metres,* they had killed about twenty Philistines.

15 The whole Philistine army panicked — those in camp, those on guard duty, those in the fields, and those on raiding patrols. All of them were afraid and confused. Then God sent an earthquake, and the ground began to tremble.*

Israel defeats the Philistines

16 Saul's lookouts at Geba* saw that the Philistine army was running in every direction, like melted wax. 17 Saul told his officers, "Call the roll and find out who left our camp." When they had finished, they found out that Jonathan and the soldier who carried his weapons were missing.

18 At that time, Ahijah was serving as priest for the army of Israel, and Saul told him, "Come over here! Let's ask God what we should do."* 19 Just as Saul finished saying this, he could see that the Philistine army camp was getting more and more confused, and he said, "Ahijah, never mind!"

20 Saul quickly called his army together, then led them to the Philistine camp. By this time the Philistines were so confused that they were killing each other.

21 There were also some hired soldiers* in the Philistine camp, who now switched to Israel's side and fought for Saul and Jonathan.

22 Many Israelites had been hiding in the hill country of Ephraim. And when they heard that the Philistines were running away, they came out of hiding and joined in chasing the Philistines.

---

*13.20,21 cattle prod: A pole used to poke cattle and make them move.
*14.1–3 fruit tree: Hebrew "pomegranate tree". A pomegranate is a bright red fruit that looks like an apple.

*14.21 hired soldiers: See the note at 13.7.

²³⁻²⁴ So the LORD helped Israel win the battle that day.

Saul's curse on anyone who eats

Saul had earlier told his soldiers, "I want to get even with those Philistines by sunset. If any of you eat before then, you will be under a curse!" So he made them swear not to eat.

By the time the fighting moved past Beth-Aven,* the Israelite troops were weak from hunger. ²⁵⁻²⁶ The army and the people who lived nearby had gone into a forest, and they came to a place where honey was dripping on the ground.' But no one ate any of it, because they were afraid of being put under the curse.

²⁷ Jonathan did not know about Saul's warning to the soldiers. So he dipped the end of his walking stick in the honey and ate some with his fingers. He felt stronger and more alert. ²⁸ Then a soldier told him, "Your father swore that anyone who ate food today would be put under a curse, and we agreed not to eat. That's why we're so weak."

²⁹ Jonathan said, "My father has caused you a lot of trouble. Look at me! I had only a little of this honey, but already I feel strong and alert. ³⁰ I wish you had eaten some of the food the Philistines left behind. We would have been able to kill a lot more of them."

³¹ By evening the Israelite army was exhausted killing Philistines all the way from Michmash to Aijalon.* ³² They grabbed the food they had captured from the Philistines and started eating. They even killed sheep and cows and calves right on the ground and ate the meat without draining the blood.* ³³ Someone told Saul, "Look! The army is disobeying the LORD by eating meat before the blood drains out."

"You're right," Saul answered. "They are being unfaithful to the LORD! Hurry! Roll a big rock over here." ³⁴ Then tell everyone in camp to bring their cattle and lambs to me. They can kill the animals on this rock,* then eat the meat. That way no one will disobey the LORD by eating meat with blood still in it."

That night the soldiers brought their cattle over to the big rock and killed them there. ³⁵ It was the first altar Saul had built for offering sacrifices to the LORD.*

The army rescues Jonathan

³⁶ Saul said, "Let's attack the Philistines again while it's still dark. We can fight them all night. Let's kill them and take everything they own!"

The people answered, "We will do whatever you want."

"Wait!" Ahijah the priest said. "Let's ask God what we should do."

³⁷ Saul asked God, "Should I attack the Philistines? Will you help us win?"

This time God did not answer. ³⁸ Saul called his army officers together and said, "We have to find out what sin has kept God from answering. ³⁹ I swear by the living LORD that whoever sinned must die, even if it turns out to be my own son Jonathan."

No one said a word.

⁴⁰ Saul told his army, "You stand on that side of the priest, and Jonathan and I will stand on the other side."

Everyone agreed.

⁴¹ Saul prayed, "Our LORD, God of Israel, why haven't you answered me today? Please show us who sinned. Was it my son Jonathan and I, or was it your people Israel?"'

The answer came back that Jonathan or Saul had sinned, not the army. ⁴² Saul told Ahijah, "Now ask the LORD to decide between Jonathan and me."

The answer came back that Jonathan had sinned. ⁴³ "Jonathan," Saul exclaimed, "tell me what you did!"

"I dipped the end of my walking stick in some honey and ate a little. Now you say I have to die!"

⁴⁴ "Yes, Jonathan. I swear to God that you must die."

⁴⁵ "No!" the soldiers shouted. "God helped Jonathan win the battle for us. We won't let you kill him. We swear to the LORD that we won't let you kill him or even lay a hand on him!" So the army kept Saul from killing Jonathan.

---

*14.23,24 Beth-Aven: See the note at 13.5.
*14.31 Aijalon: About 30 kilometres west of Michmash.
*14.32 blood: The Israelites are supposed to drain the blood from a butchered animal before the meat was cooked and eaten (see Genesis 9.4; Leviticus 17.11; Deuteronomy 12.23).
*14.34 kill . . . rock: That is, up off the ground so the blood could drain out.
See also: 14.33: Gen 9.4; Lev 7.26,27; 17.10–14; 19.26; Deut 12.16,23; 15.23.

*14.35 offering sacrifices to the LORD: Even when animals were killed for food, it was often done as a sacrifice to the LORD.
See also: 14.41: Num 27.21; 1 Sam 28.6.

⁴⁶ Saul stopped hunting down the Philistines, and they went home.

Saul fights his enemies

⁴⁷⁻⁴⁸ When Saul became king, the Moabites, the Ammonites, the Edomites, the kings of Zobah, the Philistines, and the Amalekites had all been robbing the Israelites. Saul fought back against these enemies and stopped them from robbing Israel. He was a brave commander and always won his battles.*

Saul's family

⁴⁹⁻⁵¹ Saul's wife was Ahinoam, the daughter of Ahimaaz. They had three sons: Jonathan, Ishvi,* and Malchishua. They also had two daughters: the elder one was Merab, and the younger one was Michal.

Abner, Saul's cousin, was the commander of the army. Saul's father Kish and Abner's father Ner were sons of Abiel.

War with the Philistines

⁵² Saul was at war with the Philistines for as long as he lived. Whenever he found a good warrior or a brave man, Saul made him join his army.

CHAPTER 15

Saul disobeys the LORD

¹ One day, Samuel told Saul:

The LORD made me choose you to be king of his people, Israel. Now listen to this message from the LORD: ² "When the Israelites were on their way out of Egypt, the nation of Amalek attacked them. I am the LORD All-Powerful, and now I'm going to make Amalek pay!

³ "Go and attack the Amalekites! Destroy them and all their possessions. Don't have any pity. Kill their men, women, children, and even their babies. Slaughter their cattle, sheep, camels, and donkeys."

⁴ Saul sent messengers who told every town and village to send men to join the army at Telaim. There were two hundred and ten thousand troops in all, and fifty thousand of these were from Judah. Saul organized them,

⁵ then led them to a valley near one of the towns in* Amalek, where they got ready to make a surprise attack. ⁶ Some Kenites lived nearby, and Saul told them, "Your people were kind to our nation when we left Egypt, and I don't want you to get killed when I wipe out the Amalekites. Leave here and stay away from them."

The Kenites left, ⁷ and Saul attacked the Amalekites from Havilah* to Shur, which is just east of Egypt. ⁸ Every Amalekite was killed except King Agag. ⁹ Saul and his army let Agag live, and they also spared the best sheep and cattle. They didn't want to destroy anything of value, so they only killed the animals that were worthless or weak.*

The LORD rejects Saul

¹⁰ The LORD told Samuel, ¹¹ "Saul has stopped obeying me, and I'm sorry that I made him king."

Samuel was angry, and he cried out in prayer to the LORD all night. ¹² Early the next morning he went to talk with Saul. Someone told him, "Saul went to Carmel, where he had a monument built so everyone would remember his victory. Then he left for Gilgal."

¹³ Samuel finally caught up with Saul,* and Saul told him, "I hope the LORD will bless you! I have done what the LORD told me."

¹⁴ "Then why," Samuel asked, "do I hear sheep and cattle?"

¹⁵ "The army took them from the Amalekites," Saul explained. "They kept the best sheep and cattle, so they could sacrifice them to the LORD your God. But we destroyed everything else."

¹⁶ "Stop!" Samuel said. "Let me tell you what the LORD told me last night."

"All right," Saul answered.

¹⁷ Samuel continued, "You may not think you're very important, but the LORD chose you to be king, and you are in charge of the tribes of Israel. ¹⁸ When the LORD sent you on this mission, he told you to wipe out those worthless Amalekites. ¹⁹ Why didn't you listen to the LORD? Why did you keep the animals and make him angry?"

²⁰ "But I did listen to the LORD!" Saul answered. "He sent me on a mission, and I went. I captured King Agag and destroyed his nation. ²¹ All the animals are going to be destroyed* anyway. That's why the army

---

*14.49-51 Ishvi: Also known as Eshbaal (see 1 Chronicles 8.33; 9.39) and Ishbosheth (see 2 Samuel 2.8-13; 3.8-15; 4.5-12).

See also: 15.1: 1 Sam 10.1. 15.2: Exod 17.8-14; Deut 25.17-19.

*15.21 animals . . . destroyed: The Hebrew means things that were set aside for God. They could not be used for anything else, so they had to be destroyed.

brought the best sheep and cattle to Gilgal as sacrifices to the LORD your God."

22 "Tell me," Samuel said. "Does the LORD really want sacrifices and offerings? No! He doesn't want your sacrifices. He wants you to obey him. 23 Rebelling against God or disobeying him because you are proud is just as bad as worshipping idols or asking them for advice. You refused to do what God told you, so God has decided that you can't be king."

24 "I have sinned," Saul admitted. "I disobeyed both you and the LORD. I was afraid of the army, and I listened to them instead. 25 Please forgive me and come back with me so I can worship the LORD."

26 "No!" Samuel replied, "You disobeyed the LORD, and I won't go back with you. Now the LORD has said that you can't be king of Israel any longer."

27 As Samuel turned to go, Saul grabbed the edge of Samuel's robe. It tore! 28 Samuel said, "The LORD has torn the kingdom of Israel away from you today, and he will give it to someone who is better than you. 29 Besides, the eternalᵇ God of Israel isn't a human being. He doesn't tell lies or change his mind."

30 Saul said, "I did sin, but please honour me in front of the leaders of the army and the people of Israel. Come back with me, so I can worship the LORD your God."

31 Samuel followed Saul back, and Saul worshipped the LORD. 32 Then Samuel shouted, "Bring me King Agag of Amalek!"

Agag came in chains,ᶜ and he was saying to himself, "Surely they won't kill me now."ᵈ

33 But Samuel said, "Agag, you have snatched children from their mothers' arms and killed them. Now your mother will be without children." Then Samuel chopped Agag to pieces at the place of worship in Gilgal.

34 Samuel went home to Ramah, and Saul returned to his home in Gibeah. 35 Even though Samuel felt sad about Saul, Samuel never saw him again.

The Lord chooses David to be the next king

The LORD was sorry he had made Saul the king of Israel.

CHAPTER 16

1 One day he said, "Samuel, I've rejected Saul, and I refuse to let him be king any

longer. Stop feeling sad about him. Put some olive oil* in a small container* and go and visit a man named Jesse, who lives in Bethlehem. I've chosen one of his sons to be my king."

2 Samuel answered, "If I do that, Saul will find out and have me killed."

"Take a calf with you," the LORD replied. "Tell everyone that you've come to offer it as a sacrifice to me, 3 then invite Jesse to the sacrifice.* When I show you which one of his sons I have chosen, pour the olive oil on his head."

4 Samuel did what the LORD told him and went to Bethlehem. The town leaders went to meet him, but they were terribly afraid and asked, "Is this a friendly visit?"

5 "Yes, it is!" Samuel answered. "I've come to offer a sacrifice to the LORD. Get yourselves ready* to take part in the sacrifice and come with me." Samuel also invited Jesse and his sons to come to the sacrifice, and he got them ready to take part.

6 When Jesse and his sons arrived, Samuel noticed Jesse's eldest son, Eliab. "He must be the one the LORD has chosen," Samuel said to himself.

7 But the LORD told him, "Samuel, don't think Eliab is the one just because he's tall and handsome. He isn't the one I've chosen. People judge others by what they look like, but I judge people by what is in their hearts."

8 Jesse told his son Abinadab to go over to Samuel, but Samuel said, "No, the LORD hasn't chosen him."

9 Next, Jesse sent his son Shammah to him, and Samuel said, "The LORD hasn't chosen him either."

10 Jesse sent all seven of his sons over to Samuel. Finally, Samuel said, "Jesse, the LORD hasn't chosen any of these young men. 11 Do you have any more sons?"

"Yes," Jesse answered. "My youngest son David is out taking care of the sheep."

"Send for him!" Samuel said. "We won't start the ceremony until he gets here."

12 Jesse sent for David. He was a healthy, good-looking boy with a sparkle in his eyes.

---

*16.1 olive oil: See the note at 9.16.
*16.1 small container: Hebrew "horn"; animal horns were sometimes hollowed out and used as containers.
*16.3 sacrifice: A sacrifice often involved a dinner where the meat from the sacrificed animal would be served.
*16.5 Get yourselves ready: The people of Israel sometimes had to perform certain ceremonies to make themselves acceptable to God.

See also: **15.27,28:** 1 Sam 28.17; 1 King 11.30,31.

As soon as David came, the LORD told Samuel, "He's the one! Get up and pour the olive oil on his head."*

[13] Samuel poured the oil on David's head while his brothers watched. At that moment, the Spirit of the LORD took control of David and stayed with him from then on.

Samuel returned home to Ramah.

David plays the harp for Saul

[14] The Spirit of the LORD had left Saul, and an evil spirit from the LORD was terrifying him. [15] "It's an evil spirit from God that's frightening you," Saul's officials told him. [16] "Your Majesty, let us go and look for someone who is good at playing the harp. He can play for you whenever the evil spirit from God bothers you, and you'll feel better."

[17] "All right," Saul answered. "Find me someone who is good at playing the harp and bring him here."

[18] "A man named Jesse who lives in Bethlehem has a son who can play the harp," one official said. "He's a brave warrior, he's good-looking, he can speak well, and the LORD is with him."

[19] Saul sent a message to Jesse: "Tell your son David to leave your sheep and come here to me."

[20] Jesse loaded a donkey with bread and a goatskin full of wine,* then he told David to take the donkey and a young goat to Saul. [21] David went to Saul and started working for him. Saul liked him so much that he put David in charge of carrying his weapons. [22] Not long after this, Saul sent another message to Jesse: "I really like David. Please let him stay with me."

[23] Whenever the evil spirit from God bothered Saul, David would play his harp. Saul would relax and feel better, and the evil spirit would go away.

David kills Goliath

CHAPTER 17

Goliath challenges Israel's army

[1] The Philistines got ready for war and brought their troops together to attack the town of Socoh in Judah. They set up camp at Ephes-Dammim, between Socoh and Azekah.* [2-3] King Saul and the Israelite army set up camp on a hill overlooking Elah Valley, and they got ready to fight the Philistine army that was on a hill on the other side of the valley.

[4] The Philistine army had a hero named Goliath who was from the town of Gath and was about three metres* tall. [5-6] He wore a bronze helmet and had bronze armour to protect his chest and legs. The chest armour alone weighed about fifty-seven kilogrammes. He carried a bronze sword strapped on his back, [7] and his spear was so big that the iron spearhead alone weighed about seven kilogrammes. A soldier always walked in front of Goliath to carry his shield.

[8] Goliath went out and shouted to the army of Israel:

> Why are you lining up for battle? I'm the best soldier in our army, and all of you are in Saul's army. Choose your best soldier to come out and fight me! [9] If he can kill me, our people will be your slaves. But if I kill him, your people will be our slaves. [10] Here and now I challenge Israel's whole army! Choose someone to fight me!

[11] Saul and his men heard what Goliath said, but they were so frightened of Goliath that they couldn't do a thing.

David meets King Saul

[12] David's father Jesse was an old man, who belonged to the Ephrath clan and lived in Bethlehem in Judah. Jesse had eight sons: [13-14] the eldest was Eliab, the next was Abinadab, and Shammah was the third. The three of them had gone off to fight in Saul's army.

David was Jesse's youngest son. [15] He took care of his father's sheep, and he went back and forth between Bethlehem and Saul's camp.

[16] Goliath came out and gave his challenge every morning and every evening for forty days.

[17] One day, Jesse told David, "Hurry and take this sack of roasted grain and these ten loaves of bread to your brothers at the army camp. [18] And here are ten large chunks of cheese to take to their commanding officer. Find out how your brothers are doing and

---

*16.12 olive oil on his head: See the note at 9.16.
*16.20 wine: Wine was sometimes kept in bottles made of goatskin sewn up with the fur on the outside.

*17.1 Socoh and Azekah: Socoh was controlled by the Israelites, while Azekah was in Philistine hands.

bring back something that shows that they're all right. ¹⁹ They're with Saul's army, fighting the Philistines in Elah Valley."

²⁰ David obeyed his father. He got up early the next morning and left someone else in charge of the sheep; then he loaded the supplies and started off. He reached the army camp just as the soldiers were taking their places and shouting the battle cry. ²¹ The army of Israel and the Philistine army stood there facing each other.

²² David left his things with the man in charge of supplies and ran up to the battle line to ask his brothers if they were well. ²³ While David was talking with them, Goliath came out from the line of Philistines and started boasting as usual. David heard him.

²⁴ When the Israelite soldiers saw Goliath, they were scared and ran off. ²⁵ They said to each other, "Look how he keeps coming out to insult us. The king is offering a big reward to the man who kills Goliath. That man will even get to marry the king's daughter, and no one in his family will have to pay taxes again."

²⁶ David asked some soldiers standing nearby, "What will a man get for killing this Philistine and stopping him from insulting our people? Who does that worthless Philistine think he is? He's making fun of the army of the living God!"

²⁷ The soldiers told David what the king would give the man who killed Goliath.

²⁸ David's eldest brother Eliab heard him talking with the soldiers. Eliab was angry with him and said, "What are you doing here, anyway? Who's taking care of that little flock of sheep out in the desert? You spoilt brat! You came here just to watch the fighting, didn't you?"

²⁹ "Now what have I done?" David answered. "Can't I even ask a question?" ³⁰ Then he turned and asked another soldier the same thing he had asked the others, and he got the same answer.

³¹ Some soldiers overheard David talking, so they told Saul what David had said. Saul sent for David, and David came. ³² "Your Majesty," he said, "this Philistine shouldn't turn us into cowards. I'll go out and fight him myself!"

³³ "You don't have a chance against him," Saul replied. "You're only a boy, and he's been a soldier all his life."

³⁴ But David told him:

Your Majesty, I take care of my father's sheep. And when one of them is dragged off by a lion or a bear, ³⁵ I go after it and

beat the wild animal until it lets the sheep go. If the wild animal turns and attacks me, I grab it by the throat and kill it.

³⁶ Sir, I have killed lions and bears that way, and I can kill this worthless Philistine. He shouldn't have made fun of the army of the living God! ³⁷ The LORD has rescued me from the claws of lions and bears, and he will keep me safe from the hands of this Philistine.

"All right," Saul answered, "go ahead and fight him. And I hope the LORD will help you."

³⁸ Saul had his own military clothes and armour put on David, and he gave David a bronze helmet to wear. ³⁹ David strapped on a sword and tried to walk around, but he was not used to wearing those things.

"I can't move with all this stuff on," David said. "I'm just not used to it."

David took off the armour ⁴⁰ and picked up his shepherd's stick. He went out to a stream and picked up five smooth stones and put them in his leather bag. Then with his sling in his hand, he went straight towards Goliath.

David kills Goliath

⁴¹ Goliath came towards David, walking behind the soldier who was carrying his shield. ⁴² When Goliath saw that David was just a healthy, good-looking boy, he made fun of him. ⁴³ "Do you think I'm a dog?" Goliath asked. "Is that why you've come after me with a stick?" He cursed David in the name of the Philistine gods ⁴⁴ and shouted, "Come on! When I'm finished with you, I'll feed you to the birds and wild animals!"

⁴⁵ David answered:

You've come out to fight me with a sword and a spear and a dagger. But I've come out to fight you in the name of the LORD All-Powerful. He is the God of Israel's army, and you have insulted him too!

⁴⁶ Today the LORD will help me defeat you. I'll knock you down and cut off your head, and I'll feed the bodies of the other Philistine soldiers to the birds and wild animals. Then the whole world will know that Israel has a real God. ⁴⁷ Everybody here will see that the LORD doesn't need swords or spears to save his people. The LORD always wins his battles, and he will help us defeat you.

⁴⁸ When Goliath started forward, David ran towards him. ⁴⁹ He put a stone in his sling and swung the sling around by its straps. When he

let go of one strap, the stone flew out and hit Goliath on the forehead. It cracked his skull, and he fell face down on the ground. ⁵⁰ David defeated Goliath with a sling and a stone. He killed him without even using a sword.

⁵¹ David ran over and pulled out Goliath's sword. Then he used it to cut off Goliath's head.

When the Philistines saw what had happened to their hero, they started running away. ⁵² But the soldiers of Israel and Judah let out a battle cry and went after them as far as Gath* and Ekron. The bodies of the Philistines were scattered all along the road from Shaaraim to Gath and Ekron.

⁵³ When the Israelite army returned from chasing the Philistines, they took what they wanted from the enemy camp. ⁵⁴ David took Goliath's head to Jerusalem, but he kept Goliath's weapons in his own tent.

David becomes one of Saul's officers

⁵⁵ After King Saul had watched David go out to fight Goliath, Saul turned to the commander of his army and said, "Abner, who is that young man?"

"Your Majesty," Abner answered, "I swear by your life that I don't know."

⁵⁶ "Then find out!" Saul told him.

⁵⁷ When David came back from fighting Goliath, he was still carrying Goliath's head.

Abner took David to Saul, ⁵⁸ and Saul asked, "Who are you?"

"I am David the son of Jesse, a loyal Israelite from Bethlehem."

CHAPTER 18

¹ David and Saul finished talking, and soon David and Jonathan* became best friends. Jonathan thought as much of David as he did of himself. ² From that time on, Saul kept David in his service and would not let David go back to his own family.

³ Jonathan liked David so much that they promised they would always be loyal friends. ⁴ Jonathan took off the robe that he was wearing and gave it to David. He also gave him his military clothes,* his sword, his bow and arrows, and his belt.

⁵ David was a success in everything that Saul sent him to do, and Saul made him a high officer in his army. That pleased everyone, including Saul's other officers.

---

*18.1 Jonathan: See the note at 13.2.
*18.4 military clothes: Or "armour".

See also: 17.50: 2 Sam 21.19. 17.51: 2 Sam 21.29.

Saul tries to kill David

Saul becomes David's enemy

⁶ David had killed Goliath, the battle was over, and the Israelite army set out for home. As the army went along, women came out of each Israelite town to welcome King Saul. They were singing happy songs and dancing to the music of tambourines and harps. ⁷ They sang:

> Saul has killed
>   a thousand enemies;
> David has killed
>   ten thousand enemies!

⁸ This song made Saul very angry, and he thought, "They are saying that David has killed ten times more enemies than I ever did. Next they will want to make him king." ⁹ Saul never again trusted David.

¹⁰ The next day the LORD let an evil spirit take control of Saul, and he began acting like a mad man inside his house. David began to play the harp for Saul as usual, but this time Saul had a spear in his hand. ¹¹ Saul thought, "I'll pin David to the wall." He threw the spear at David twice, but David dodged and got away both times.

¹² Saul was afraid of David, because the LORD was helping David and was no longer helping him. ¹³ Saul put David in charge of a thousand soldiers and sent him out to fight. ¹⁴ The LORD helped David, and he and his soldiers always won their battles. ¹⁵ This made Saul even more afraid of David. ¹⁶ But everyone else in Judah and Israel was loyal to* David, because he led the army in battle.

¹⁷ One day, Saul told David, "If you'll be brave and fight the LORD's battles for me, I'll let you marry my eldest daughter Merab." But Saul was really thinking, "I don't want to kill David myself, so I'll let the Philistines do it for me."

¹⁸ David answered, "How could I possibly marry your daughter? I'm not very important, and neither is my family."

¹⁹ But when the time came for David to marry Saul's daughter Merab, Saul told her to marry Adriel from the town of Meholah.

²⁰ Saul had another daughter. Her name was Michal, and Saul found out that she was in love with David. This made Saul happy, ²¹ and he thought, "I'll tell David he can marry Michal, but I'll set it up so that the Philistines will kill him." He told David, "I'm

---

See also: 18.7: 1 Sam 21.11; 29.5.

going to give you a second chance to marry one of my daughters."

22-23 Saul ordered his officials to speak to David in private, so they went to David and said, "Look, the king likes you, and all his officials are loyal to you. Why not ask the king if you can marry his daughter Michal?"

"I'm not rich* or famous enough to marry Princess Michal!" David answered.

24 The officials went back to Saul and told him exactly what David had said. 25 Saul was hoping that the Philistines would kill David, and he told his officials to tell David, "The king doesn't want any silver or gold. He only wants to get even with his enemies. All you have to do is to bring back proof that you have killed a hundred Philistines!"* 26 The officials told David, and David wanted to marry the princess.

King Saul had set a time limit, and before it ran out, 27 David and his men left and killed two hundred Philistines. He brought back the proof and showed it to Saul, so he could marry Michal. Saul agreed to let David marry Michal. 28 Saul knew that she loved David,' and he also realized that the LORD was helping David. 29 But knowing those things made Saul even more afraid of David, and he was David's enemy for the rest of his life.

30 The Philistine rulers kept coming to fight Israel, but whenever David fought them, he won. He was famous because he won more battles against the Philistines than any of Saul's other officers.

Jonathan, Michal, Samuel, and Ahimelech help David

CHAPTER 19

Saul tries to have David killed

1 One day, Saul told his son Jonathan and his officers to kill David. But Jonathan liked David a lot, 2-3 and he warned David, "My father is trying to have you killed, so be very careful. Hide in a field tomorrow morning, and I'll bring them there. Then I'll talk to him

about you, and if I find out anything, I'll let you know."

4-5 The next morning, Jonathan reminded Saul about the many good things David had done for him. Then he said, "Why do you want to kill David? He hasn't done anything to you. He has served in your army and has always done what's best for you. He even risked his life to kill Goliath. The LORD helped Israel win a great victory that day, and it made you happy."

6 Saul agreed and promised, "I swear by the living LORD that I won't have David killed!"

7 Jonathan called to David and told him what Saul had said. Then he brought David to Saul, and David served in Saul's army just as he had done before.

8 The next time there was a war with the Philistines, David fought hard and forced them to retreat.

Michal helps David escape

9-10 One night, David was in Saul's home, playing the harp for him. Saul was sitting there, holding a spear, when an evil spirit from the LORD took control of him. Saul tried to pin David to the wall with the spear, but David dodged, and it stuck in the wall. David ran out of the house and escaped.

11 Saul sent guards to watch David's house all night and then to kill him in the morning.

Michal, David's wife, told him, "If you don't escape tonight, they'll kill you tomorrow!" 12 She helped David go through a window and climb down to the ground.* As David ran off, 13 Michal put a statue in his bed. She put goat hair on its head and dressed it in some of David's clothes.

14 The next morning, Saul sent guards to arrest David. But Michal told them, "David is sick."

15 Saul sent the guards back and told them, "Get David out of his bed and bring him to me, so I can have him killed."

16 When the guards went in, all they found in the bed was the statue with the goat hair on its head.

17 "Why have you tricked me this way?" Saul asked Michal. "You helped my enemy get away!"

She answered, "He said he would kill me if I didn't help him escape!"

---

*18.22,23 not rich: It was the custom for a man to give the bride's father some silver or gold in order to marry his daughter, and it would take a large amount to marry the daughter of the king.

*18.25 proof . . . Philistines: Hebrew "one hundred Philistine foreskins." In ancient times soldiers sometimes cut off body parts of their dead enemies to prove how many they had killed.

*19.12 ground: The house was probably built into the town wall, allowing David to come down outside the wall.

See also: 19.11: Psa 59 Title.

Samuel helps David escape

¹⁸ Meanwhile, David went to Samuel at Ramah and told him what Saul had done. Then Samuel and David went to Prophets Village* and stayed there.

¹⁹ Someone told Saul, "David is at Prophets Village in Ramah."

²⁰ Saul sent a few soldiers to bring David back. They went to Ramah and found Samuel in charge of a group of prophets who were all prophesying. Then the Spirit of God took control of the soldiers and they started prophesying too.

²¹ When Saul heard what had happened, he sent another group of soldiers, but they prophesied the same way. He sent a third group of soldiers, but the same thing happened to them. ²² Finally, Saul left for Ramah himself. He went as far as the deep pit* at the town of Secu, and he asked, "Where are Samuel and David?"

"At Prophets Village in Ramah," the people answered.

²³ Saul left for Ramah. But as he walked along, the Spirit of God took control of him, and he started prophesying. Then, when he reached Prophets Village, ²⁴ he stripped off his clothes and prophesied in front of Samuel. He dropped to the ground and lay there naked all day and night. That's how the saying started, "Is Saul now a prophet?"

CHAPTER 20

Jonathan helps David escape

¹ David escaped from Prophets Village. Then he ran to see Jonathan and asked, "Why does your father Saul want to kill me? What have I done wrong?"

² "My father can't be trying to kill you! He never does anything without telling me about it. Why would he hide this from me? It can't be true!"

³ "Jonathan, I swear it's true! But your father knows how much you like me, and he didn't want to break your heart. That's why he didn't tell you. I swear by the living LORD and by your own life that I'm only one step ahead of death."

⁴ Then Jonathan said, "Tell me what to do, and I'll do it."

⁵ David answered:

Tomorrow is the New Moon Festival,* and I'm supposed to have dinner with your father. But instead, I'll hide in a field until the evening of the next day. ⁶ If Saul wonders where I am, tell him, "David asked me to let him go to his home town of Bethlehem, so he could take part in a sacrifice his family makes there every year."

⁷ If your father says it's all right, then I'm safe. But if he gets angry, you'll know he wants to harm me. ⁸ Be kind to me. After all, it was your idea to promise the LORD that we would always be loyal friends. If I've done anything wrong, kill me yourself, but don't hand me over to your father.

⁹ "Don't worry," Jonathan said. "If I find out that my father wants to kill you, I'll certainly let you know."

¹⁰ "How will you do that?" David asked.

¹¹ "Let's go out to this field, and I'll tell you," Jonathan answered.

When they got there, ¹² Jonathan said:

I swear by the LORD God of Israel, that two days from now I'll know what my father is planning. Of course I'll let you know if he's friendly towards you. ¹³ But if he wants to harm you, I promise to tell you and help you escape. And I ask the LORD to punish me severely if I don't keep my promise.

I pray that the LORD will bless you, just as he used to bless my father. ¹⁴⁻¹⁵ Some day the LORD will wipe out all your enemies. Then if I'm still alive, please be as kind to me as the LORD has been. But if I'm dead, be kind to my family.

¹⁶ Jonathan and David made an agreement that even David's descendants would have to keep.* Then Jonathan said, "I pray that the LORD will take revenge on our descendants if they break our promise."*

¹⁷ Jonathan thought as much of David as he did of himself, so he asked David to promise once more that he would be a loyal friend. ¹⁸ After this Jonathan said:

Tomorrow is the New Moon Festival, and people will wonder where you are, because your place will be empty. ¹⁹ By the day after tomorrow, everyone will think you've been gone a long time.* Then go to the place where you hid before and stay beside

---

*19.22 pit: A cistern, a large pit dug down into the rock and used for storing rainwater.
See also: 19.24: 1 Sam 10.11,12. 20.5: Num 28.11.

*20.5 New Moon Festival: The first day of the month, when Israelites offered special sacrifices to the LORD and had special sacred meals.
See also: 20.15: 2 Sam 9.1.

Going-Away Rock.' ²⁰ I'll shoot three arrows at a target off to the side of the rock, ²¹ and send my servant to find the arrows.

You'll know if it's safe to come out by what I tell him. If it is safe, I swear by the living LORD that I'll say, "The arrows are on this side of you! Pick them up!" ²² But if it isn't safe, I'll say to the boy, "The arrows are further away!" This will mean that the LORD wants you to leave, and you must go. ²³ But he will always watch us to make sure that we keep the promise we made to each other.

²⁴ So David hid there in the field.

During the New Moon Festival, Saul sat down to eat ²⁵ by the wall, just as he always did. Jonathan sat across from him,' and Abner sat next to him. But David's place was empty. ²⁶ Saul didn't say anything that day, because he was thinking, "Something must have happened to make David unfit to be at the Festival.* Yes, something must have happened."

²⁷ The day after the New Moon Festival, when David's place was still empty, Saul asked Jonathan, "Why hasn't that son of Jesse come to eat with us? He wasn't here yesterday, and he still isn't here today!"

²⁸⁻²⁹ Jonathan answered, "The reason David hasn't come to eat with you is that he begged me to let him go to Bethlehem. He said, 'Please let me go. My family is offering a sacrifice, and my brother told me I have to be there. Do me this favour and let me slip away to see my brothers.' "

³⁰ Saul was furious with Jonathan and yelled, "You're no son of mine, you traitor! I know you've chosen to be loyal to that son of Jesse. You should be ashamed of yourself! And your own mother should be ashamed that you were ever born. ³¹ You'll never be safe, and your kingdom will be in danger as long as that son of Jesse is alive. Turn him over to me now! He deserves to die!"

³² "Why do you want to kill David?" Jonathan asked. "What has he done?"

³³ Saul threw his spear at Jonathan and tried to kill him. Then Jonathan was sure that his father really did want to kill David.

³⁴ Jonathan was angry that his father had insulted David' so terribly. He got up, left the table, and didn't eat anything all that day.

³⁵ In the morning, Jonathan went out to the field to meet David. He took a servant boy along ³⁶ and told him, "When I shoot the arrows, you run and find them for me."

The boy started running, and Jonathan shot an arrow so that it would go beyond him. ³⁷ When the boy got near the place where the arrow had landed, Jonathan shouted, "Isn't the arrow on past you?" ³⁸ Jonathan shouted to him again, "Hurry up! Don't stop!"

The boy picked up the arrows and brought them back to Jonathan, ³⁹ but he had no idea about what was going on. Only Jonathan and David knew. ⁴⁰ Jonathan gave his weapons to the boy and told him, "Take these back into town."

⁴¹ After the boy had gone, David got up from beside the mound' and bowed very low three times. Then he and Jonathan kissed* each other and cried, but David cried louder. ⁴² Jonathan said, "Take care of yourself. And remember, we have each asked the LORD to watch and make sure that we and our descendants keep our promise for ever."

David left and Jonathan went back to town.

CHAPTER 21

Ahimelech helps David

¹ David went to see Ahimelech, a priest who lived in the town of Nob. Ahimelech was trembling with fear as he came out to meet David. "Why are you alone?" Ahimelech asked. "Why isn't anyone else with you?"

² "I'm on a mission for King Saul," David answered. "He ordered me not to tell anyone what the mission is all about, so I told my soldiers to stay somewhere else. ³ Do you have any food you can give me? Could you spare five loaves of bread?"

⁴ "The only bread I have is the sacred bread," the priest told David. "You can have it if your soldiers didn't sleep with women last night."*

⁵ "Of course we didn't sleep with women," David answered. "I never let my men do that when we're on a mission. They have to be acceptable to worship God even when we're

---

*20.26 unfit . . . Festival: During the New Moon Festival a sacred meal was served that could only be eaten by people who were properly prepared. Some of the things that could make a person unfit are listed in Leviticus 7.20,21; 15.2,31; 22.4–8; Deuteronomy 23.10,11.

*20.41 kissed: A common way of greeting or saying goodbye in biblical times (see Mark 14.44).

*21.4 night: Having sex was one of the things that would make someone temporarily unfit to take part in worship or a sacred meal (see Exodus 19.15; Leviticus 15.18).

See also: 21.1–6: Matt 12.3,4; Mark 2.25,26; Luke 6.3.

on an ordinary mission, and today we're on a special mission."

⁶ The only bread the priest had was the sacred bread that he had taken from the place of worship after putting out the fresh loaves. So he gave it to David.

⁷ It so happened that one of Saul's officers was there, worshipping the LORD that day. His name was Doeg the Edomite,* and he was the strongest of* Saul's shepherds.

⁸ David asked Ahimelech, "Do you have a spear or a sword? I had to leave so quickly on this mission for the king that I didn't bring along my sword or any other weapons."

⁹ The priest answered, "The only sword here is the one that belonged to Goliath the Philistine. You were the one who killed him in Elah Valley, and so you can take his sword if you want to. It's wrapped in a cloth behind the statue."

"It's the best sword there is," David said. "I'll take it!"

David runs from Saul

David tries to find safety in Gath

¹⁰ David kept on running from Saul that day until he came to Gath,* where he met with King Achish. ¹¹ The officers of King Achish were also there, and they asked Achish, "Isn't David a king back in his own country? Don't the Israelites dance and sing,

"Saul has killed
a thousand enemies;
David has killed
ten thousand enemies?"

¹² David thought about what they were saying, and it made him afraid of Achish. ¹³ So in front of everyone, he pretended to be insane. He acted confused and scratched on the doors of the town gate, while drooling in his beard.

¹⁴ "Look at him!" Achish said to his officers. "You can see he's mad. Why did you bring him to me? ¹⁵ I have enough mad people without your bringing another one here. Keep him away from my palace!"

CHAPTER 22

People join David

¹ When David escaped from the town of Gath, he went to Adullam Cave. His brothers and the rest of his family found out where he was, and they followed him there. ² A lot of other people joined him too. Some were in trouble, others were angry or in debt, and David was soon the leader of four hundred men.

³ David left Adullam Cave and went to the town of Mizpeh in Moab, where he talked with the king of Moab. "Please," David said, "let my father and mother stay with you until I find out what God will do with me." ⁴ So he brought his parents to the king of Moab, and they stayed with him while David was in hiding.

⁵ One day the prophet Gad told David, "Don't stay here! Go back to Judah." David then left and went to Hereth Forest.

Saul kills the priests of the Lord

⁶ Saul was sitting under a small tree on top of the hill at Gibeah when he heard that David and his men had been seen. Saul was holding his spear, and his officers were standing in front of him. ⁷ He told them:

Listen to me! You belong to the Benjamin tribe,* so if that son of Jesse ever becomes king, he won't give you fields or vineyards. He won't make you officers in charge of thousands or hundreds as I have done. ⁸ But you're all plotting against me! Not one of you told me that my own son Jonathan had made an agreement with him. Not one of you cared enough to tell me that Jonathan had helped one of my officers* rebel. Now that son of Jesse is trying to ambush me.

⁹ Doeg the Edomite was standing with the other officers and spoke up, "When I was in the town of Nob, I saw that son of Jesse. He was visiting the priest Ahimelech the son of Ahitub. ¹⁰ Ahimelech talked to the LORD for

---

*21.7 Edomite: A person from the country of Edom, to the south of Israel.
*21.10 Gath: One of the five main Philistine towns.
See also: 21.6: Lev 24.5–9. 21.9: 1 Sam 17.51.
21.11: 1 Sam 18.7; 29.5. 21.12: Psa 56 Title.
21.13: Psa 34 Title.

*22.7 You . . . Benjamin tribe: David was from the Judah tribe and would have given special privileges to the people of his own tribe rather than to those of Benjamin.
*22.7,8 son of Jesse . . . officers: That is, David. Saul avoids even saying David's name.
See also: 22.1: Psa 57 Title; Psa 142 Title.
22.9,10: 1 Sam 21.7–9; Psa 52 Title.

him, then gave him food and the sword that had belonged to Goliath the Philistine."

¹¹ Saul sent a message to Ahimelech and his whole family of priests at Nob, ordering them to come to him. When they came, ¹² Saul told them, "Listen to me, you son of Ahitub."

"Certainly, Your Majesty," Ahimelech answered.

¹³ Saul demanded, "Why did you plot against me with that son of Jesse? You helped him rebel against me by giving him food and a sword, and by talking with God for him. Now he's trying to ambush me!"

¹⁴ "Your Majesty, none of your officers is more loyal than David!" Ahimelech replied. "He's your son-in-law and the captain of your bodyguard. Everyone in your family respects him. ¹⁵ This isn't the first time I've talked with God for David, and it's never made you angry before! Please don't accuse me or my family like this. I have no idea what's going on!"

¹⁶ "Ahimelech," Saul said, "you and your whole family are going to die."

¹⁷ Saul shouted to his bodyguards, "These priests of the LORD helped David! They knew he was running away, but they didn't tell me. Kill them!"

But the king's officers would not attack the priests of the LORD.

¹⁸ Saul turned to Doeg, who was from Edom, and said, "Kill the priests!"

On that same day, Doeg killed eighty-five priests. ¹⁹ Then he attacked the town of Nob, where the priests had lived, and he killed everyone there — men, women, children, and babies. He even killed their cattle, donkeys, and sheep.

Only Abiathar escapes from Nob

²⁰ Ahimelech's son Abiathar was the only one who escaped. He ran to David ²¹ and told him, "Saul has murdered the priests at Nob!"

²² David answered, "That day when I saw Doeg, I knew he would tell Saul! Your family died because of me. ²³ Stay here. Isn't the same person trying to kill both of us? Don't worry! You'll be safe here with me."

David refuses to kill Saul

CHAPTER 23

David rescues the town of Keilah

¹ One day some people told David, "The Philistines keep attacking the town of Keilah and stealing grain from the threshing place."

² David asked the LORD, "Should I attack these Philistines?"

"Yes," the LORD answered. "Attack them and rescue Keilah."

³ But David's men said, "Look, even here in Judah we're afraid of the Philistines. We will be terrified if we try to fight them at Keilah!"*

⁴ David asked the LORD about it again. "Leave at once," the LORD answered. "I will give you victory over the Philistines at Keilah."

⁵ David and his men went there and fiercely attacked the Philistines. They killed many of them, then led away their cattle, and rescued the people of Keilah.

⁶⁻⁸ Meanwhile, Saul heard that David was in Keilah. "God has let me catch David," Saul said. "David is trapped inside a walled town where the gates can be locked." Saul decided to go there and surround the town, in order to trap David and his men. He sent messengers who told the towns and villages, "Send men to serve in Saul's army!"

By this time, Abiathar had joined David in Keilah and had brought along everything he needed to get answers from God.

⁹ David heard about Saul's plan to capture him, and he told Abiathar, "Let's ask God what we should do."

¹⁰ David prayed, "LORD God of Israel, I was told that Saul is planning to come here. What should I do? Suppose he threatens to destroy the town because of me. ¹¹ Would the leaders of Keilah turn me over to Saul? Or is he really coming? Please tell me, LORD."

"Yes, he will come," the LORD answered.

¹² David asked, "Would the leaders of Keilah hand me and my soldiers over to Saul?"

"Yes, they would," the LORD answered.

¹³ David and his six hundred men got out of there fast and started moving from place to place. Saul heard that David had left Keilah, and he decided not to go after him.

Jonathan says David will be king

¹⁴ David stayed in hide-outs in the hill country of Ziph Desert. Saul kept searching, but God never let Saul catch him.

¹⁵ One time, David was at Horesh in Ziph Desert. He was afraid because* Saul had come to the area to kill him. ¹⁶ But Jonathan went

---

*23.3 Keilah: Keilah was probably not controlled by Israelites at this time.

to see David, and God helped him encourage David. [17] "Don't be afraid," Jonathan said. "My father Saul will never get his hands on you. In fact, you're going to be the next king of Israel, and I'll be your highest official. Even my father knows it's true."

[18] They both promised the LORD that they would always be loyal to each other. Then Jonathan went home, but David stayed at Horesh.

David escapes from Saul

[19] Some people from the town of Ziph went to Saul at Gibeah and said, "Your Majesty, David has a hide-out not far from us! It's near Horesh, somewhere on Mount Hachilah south of Jeshimon.* [20] If you come, we will help you catch him."

[21] Saul told them:

You've done me a big favour, and I pray that the LORD will bless you. [22] Now please do just a little more for me. Find out exactly where David is, as well as where he goes, and who has seen him there. I've been told that he's very cunning. [23] Find out where all his hiding places are and come back when you're sure. Then I'll go with you. If he is still in the area, or anywhere among the clans of Judah, I'll find him.

[24] The people from Ziph went back ahead of Saul, and they found out that David and his men were still south of Jeshimon in the Maon Desert. [25] Saul and his army set out to find David. But David heard that Saul was coming, and he went to a place called The Rock, one of his hide-outs in Maon Desert.

Saul found out where David was and started closing in on him. [26] Saul was going around a hill on one side, and David and his men were on the other side, trying to get away. Saul and his soldiers were just about to capture David and his men, [27] when a messenger came to Saul and said, "Come quickly! The Philistines are attacking Israel and taking everything."

[28] Saul stopped going after David and went back to fight the Philistines. That's why the place is called "Escape Rock".

[29] David left and went to live in the hide-outs at En-Gedi.

CHAPTER 24

David lets Saul live

[1] When Saul got back from fighting off the Philistines, he heard that David was in the desert around En-Gedi. [2] Saul led three thousand of Israel's best soldiers out to look for David and his men near Wild Goat Rocks at En-Gedi. [3] There were some sheep pens along the side of the road, and one of them was built around the entrance to a cave. Saul went into the cave to relieve himself.

David and his men were hiding at the back of the cave. [4] They whispered to David, "The LORD told you he was going to let you defeat your enemies and do whatever you want with them. This must be the day the LORD was talking about."

David sneaked over and cut off a small piece* of Saul's robe, but Saul didn't notice a thing. [5] Afterwards, David was sorry that he had even done that, [6-7] and he told his men, "Stop talking foolishly. We're not going to attack Saul. He's my king, and I pray that the LORD will keep me from doing anything to harm his chosen king."

Saul left the cave and started down the road. [8] Soon, David also got up and left the cave. "Your Majesty!" he shouted from a distance.

Saul turned around to look. David bowed down very low [9] and said:

Your Majesty, why do you listen to people who say that I'm trying to harm you? [10] You can see for yourself that the LORD gave me the chance to catch you in the cave today. Some of my men wanted to kill you, but I wouldn't let them do it. I told them, "I will not harm the LORD's chosen king!" [11] Your Majesty, look at what I'm holding. You can see that it's a piece of your robe. If I could cut off a piece of your robe, I could have killed you. But I let you live, and that should prove I'm not trying to harm you or to rebel. I haven't done anything to you, and yet you keep trying to ambush and kill me.

[12] I'll let the LORD decide which one of us has done right. I pray that the LORD will punish you for what you're doing to me, but I won't do anything to you. [13] An old proverb says, "Only evil people do evil things," and so I won't harm you.

---

*23.19 **Jeshimon**: A place in the desert near the southern border of Judah.
See also: 23.18: 1 Sam 18.3.   23.19: Psa 54 Title.

See also: 24.3: Psa 57 Title; Psa 142 Title.
24.6: 1 Sam 26.11.

¹⁴ Why should the king of Israel be out chasing me, anyway? I'm as worthless as a dead dog or a flea. ¹⁵ I pray that the LORD will help me escape and show that I am in the right.

¹⁶ "David, my son — is that you?" Saul asked. Then he started crying ¹⁷ and said:

David, you're a better person than I am. You treated me with kindness, even though I've been cruel to you. ¹⁸ You've told me how you were kind enough not to kill me when the LORD gave you the chance. ¹⁹ If you really were my enemy, you wouldn't have let me leave here alive. I pray that the LORD will give you a big reward for what you did today.

²⁰ I realize now that you will be the next king, and a powerful king at that. ²¹ Promise me with the LORD as your witness, that you won't wipe out my descendants. Let them live to keep my family name alive.

²² So David promised, and Saul went home. David and his men returned to their hide-out.

CHAPTER 25

Samuel dies

¹ Samuel died, and people from all over Israel gathered to mourn for him when he was buried at his home* in Ramah. Meanwhile, David moved his camp to Paran Desert.᾽

Abigail keeps David from killing innocent people

²⁻³ Nabal was a very rich man who lived in Maon. He owned three thousand sheep and a thousand goats, which he kept at Carmel.* His wife Abigail was sensible and beautiful, but he was from the Caleb clan᾽ and was rough and mean.

⁴ One day, Nabal was in Carmel, while his servants cut the wool from his sheep. David was in the desert when he heard about it. ⁵⁻⁶ So he sent ten men to Carmel with this message for Nabal:

I hope that you and your family are healthy and that all is going well for you. ⁷ I've heard that you are cutting the wool from your sheep.

When your shepherds were with us in Carmel, we didn't harm them, and nothing was ever stolen from them. ⁸ Ask your shepherds, and they'll tell you the same thing.

My servants are your servants, and you are like a father to me. This is a day for celebrating,* so please be kind and share some of your food with us.

⁹ David's men went to Nabal and gave him David's message, then they waited for Nabal's answer.

¹⁰ This is what he said:

Who does this David think he is? That son of Jesse is just one more slave on the run from his master, and there are too many of them these days. ¹¹ What makes you think I would take my bread, my water, and the meat that I've had cooked for my own servants* and give it to you? Besides, I'm not sure that David sent you!᾽

¹² The men returned to their camp and told David everything Nabal had said.

¹³ "Everybody get your swords!" David ordered.

They all strapped on their swords. Two hundred men stayed behind to guard the camp, but the other four hundred followed David.

¹⁴⁻¹⁶ Meanwhile, one of Nabal's servants told Abigail:

David's men were often nearby while we were taking care of the sheep in the fields. They were very good to us, they never hurt us, and nothing was ever stolen from us while they were nearby. With them around day or night, we were as safe as we would have been inside a walled city.

David sent some messengers from the desert to wish our master well, but he shouted insults at them. ¹⁷ He's a bully who won't listen to anyone.

Isn't there something you can do? Please think of something! Or else our master and his family and everyone who works for him are all doomed.

---

*25.1 at his home: Hebrew "in his house". Family tombs were sometimes underneath the house or in the courtyard of the house.
*25.2,3 Carmel: About one and a half kilometres north of Maon in the Southern Desert of Judah.
See also: 24.14: 1 Sam 26.20.

*25.8 celebrating: Cutting the wool from the sheep was a time for celebrating as well as for work.
*25.11 servants: Hebrew "shearers", the servants who cut the wool from the sheep.

18 Abigail quickly got together two hundred loaves of bread, two large clay jars of wine, the meat from five sheep, a large sack of roasted grain, a hundred handfuls of raisins, and two hundred handfuls of dried figs. She loaded all the food on donkeys 19 and told her servants, "Take this on ahead, and I'll catch up with you." She didn't tell her husband Nabal what she was doing.

20 Abigail was riding her donkey on the path that led around the hillside, when suddenly she met David and his men heading straight at her.

21 David had just been saying, "I wasted my time guarding Nabal's things in the desert and keeping them from being stolen! I was good to him, and now he pays me back with insults. 22 I swear that by morning, there won't be a man or boy left from his family or his servants' families. I pray that God will punish me* if I don't do it!"

23 Abigail quickly got off her donkey and bowed down in front of David. 24 Then she said:

Sir, please let me explain! 25 Don't pay any attention to that good-for-nothing Nabal. His name means "fool", and it really fits him!

I didn't see the men you sent, 26–27 but please take this gift of food that I've brought and share it with your followers. The LORD has kept you from taking revenge and from killing innocent people. But I hope your enemies and anyone else who wants to harm you will end up like Nabal. I swear this by the living LORD and by your life.

28 Please forgive me if I say a little more. The LORD will always protect you and your family, because you fight for him. I pray that you won't ever do anything evil as long as you live. 29 The LORD your God will keep you safe when your enemies try to kill you. But he will snatch away their lives quicker than you can throw a stone from a sling.

30 The LORD has promised to do many good things for you, even to make you the ruler of Israel. The LORD will keep his promises to you, 31 and now your conscience will be clear, because you won't be guilty of taking revenge and killing innocent people.

When the LORD does all those good things for you, please remember me.

32 David told her:

I praise the LORD God of Israel! He must have sent you to meet me today. 33 And you

should also be praised. Your good sense kept me from taking revenge and killing innocent people. 34 If you hadn't come to meet me so quickly, every man and boy in Nabal's family and in his servants' families would have been killed by morning. I swear by the living LORD God of Israel who protected you that this is the truth.

35 David accepted the food Abigail had brought. "Don't worry," he said. "You can go home now. I'll do what you asked."

36 Abigail went back home and found Nabal throwing a party fit for a king. He was very drunk and feeling good, so she didn't tell him anything that night. 37 But when he sobered up the next morning, Abigail told him everything that had happened. Nabal had a heart attack, and he lay in bed as still as a stone. 38 Ten days later, the LORD took his life.

39–40 David heard that Nabal had died. "I praise the LORD!" David said. "He has judged Nabal guilty for insulting me. The LORD kept me from doing anything wrong, and he made sure that Nabal hurt only himself with his own evil."

David and Abigail are married

Abigail was still at Carmel. So David sent messengers to ask her if she would marry him.

41 She bowed down and said, "I would willingly be David's slave and wash his servants' feet."

42 Abigail quickly got ready and went back with David's messengers. She rode on her donkey, while five of her servant women walked beside her. She and David were married as soon as she arrived.

43 David had earlier married Ahinoam from the town of Jezreel, so both she and Abigail were now David's wives.* 44 Meanwhile, Saul had arranged for Michal* to marry Palti the son of Laish, who came from the town of Gallim.

CHAPTER 26

David again lets Saul live

1 Once again,* some people from Ziph went to Gibeah to talk with Saul. "David has a hide-out on Mount Hachilah near Jeshimon out in the desert," they told him.

---

*25.43 wives: See the note at 1.2.
*25.44 Michal: David's first wife (see 18.20—19.17).
*26.1 again: See 23.19.
See also: 25.44: 2 Sam 3.14-16. 26.1: Psa 54 Title.

² Saul took three thousand of Israel's best soldiers and went to look for David there in Ziph Desert. ³ Saul set up camp on Mount Hachilah, which is across the road from Jeshimon. But David was hiding out in the desert.

When David heard that Saul was following him, ⁴ he sent some spies to find out if it was true. ⁵ Then he sneaked up to Saul's camp. He noticed that Saul and his army commander Abner the son of Ner were sleeping in the middle of the camp, with soldiers sleeping all around them. ⁶ David asked Ahimelech the Hittite and Joab's brother Abishai,* "Which one of you will go with me into Saul's camp?"

"I will!" Abishai answered.

⁷ That same night, David and Abishai crept into the camp. Saul was sleeping, and his spear was stuck in the ground not far from his head. Abner and the soldiers were sound asleep all around him.

⁸ Abishai whispered, "This time God has let you get your hands on your enemy! I'll pin him to the ground with one thrust of his own spear."

⁹ "Don't kill him!" David whispered back. "The LORD will punish anyone who kills his chosen king. ¹⁰ As surely as the LORD lives, the LORD will kill Saul, or Saul will die a natural death or be killed in battle. ¹¹ But I pray that the LORD will keep me from harming his chosen king. Let's grab his spear and his water jar and get out of here!"

¹² David took the spear and the water jar, then left the camp. None of Saul's soldiers knew what had happened or even woke up — the LORD had made all of them fall sound asleep. ¹³ David and Abishai crossed the valley and went to the top of the next hill, where they were at a safe distance. ¹⁴ "Abner!" David shouted towards Saul's army. "Can you hear me?"

Abner shouted back. "Who dares disturb the king?"

¹⁵ "Abner, what kind of a man are you?" David replied. "Aren't you supposed to be the best soldier in Israel? Then why didn't you protect your king? Anyone who went into your camp could have killed him tonight.* ¹⁶ You're a complete failure! I swear by the living LORD that you and your men deserve to die for not protecting the LORD's chosen king.

Look and see if you can find the king's spear and the water jar that were near his head."

¹⁷ Saul could tell it was David's voice, and he called out, "David, my son! Is that you?"

"Yes it is, Your Majesty. ¹⁸ Why are you after me? Have I done something wrong, or have I committed a crime? ¹⁹ Please listen to what I have to say. If the LORD has turned you against me, perhaps a sacrifice will make him change his mind. But if some people have turned you against me, I hope the LORD will punish them! They have forced me to leave the land that belongs to the LORD and have told me to worship foreign gods.* ²⁰ Don't let me die in a land far away from the LORD. I'm no more important than a flea! Why should the king of Israel hunt me down as if I were a bird in the mountains?"

²¹ "David, you had the chance to kill me today. But you didn't. I was very wrong about you. It was a terrible mistake for me to try to kill you. I've acted like a fool, but I'll never try to harm you again. You're like a son to me, so please come back."

²² "Your Majesty, here's your spear! Let one of your soldiers come and get it. ²³ The LORD put you in my power today, but you are his chosen king and I wouldn't harm you. The LORD rewards people who are faithful and live right. ²⁴ I saved your life today, and I pray that the LORD will protect me and keep me safe."

²⁵ "David, my son, I pray that the Lord will bless you and make you successful!"

David in Philistia

CHAPTER 27

Saul went back home. David also left, ¹ but he thought to himself, "One of these days, Saul is going to kill me. The only way to escape from him is to go to Philistia. Then I'll be outside Israel, and Saul will give up trying to catch me."

²⁻³ David and his six hundred men went across the border to stay in Gath with King Achish the son of Maoch. His men brought their families with them. David brought his wife Ahinoam whose home town was Jezreel, and he also brought his wife Abigail who had been married to Nabal from Carmel. ⁴ When Saul found out that David had run off to Gath, he stopped trying to catch him.

---

*26.6 Abishai: Hebrew "Abishai the son of Zeruiah". Zeruiah was David's elder sister, so Abishai and Joab were David's nephews (see 1 Chronicles 2.12–17; 2 Samuel 17.25 and the note there).
See also: 26.11: 1 Sam 24.26.

*26.19 gods: In ancient times it was often believed that gods (even the God of Israel) could only be properly worshipped in their own countries, and only a country's gods should be worshipped in that country.

⁵ One day, David was talking with Achish and said, "If you are happy with me, then let me live in one of the towns in the countryside. I'm not important enough to live here with you in the royal city."

⁶ Achish gave David the town of Ziklag that same day, and Ziklag has belonged to the kings of Judah ever since.

⁷ David was in Philistia for a year and four months. ⁸ The Geshurites, the Girzites, and the Amalekites lived in the area from Telam to Shur* and on as far as Egypt, and David often attacked their towns. ⁹ Whenever David and his men attacked a town, they took the sheep, cattle, donkeys, camels, and the clothing, and killed everyone who lived there.

After he returned from a raid, David always went to see Achish, ¹⁰ who would ask, "Where did you attack today?"*

David would answer, "Oh, we attacked some desert town that belonged to the Judah tribe." Sometimes David would say, "Oh, we attacked a town in the desert where the Jerahmeel clan lives" or "We attacked a town in the desert where the Kenites* live."

¹¹ That's why David killed everyone in the towns he attacked. He thought, "If I let any of them live, they might come to Gath and tell what I've really been doing."

David made these raids all the time he was in Philistia. ¹² But Achish trusted David and thought, "David's people must be furious with him. From now on he will have to take orders from me."

Saul talks with Samuel's ghost

CHAPTER 28

¹⁻³ Samuel had died some time earlier,* and people from all over Israel had attended his funeral in his home town of Ramah.

Meanwhile, Saul had been trying to get rid of everyone who spoke with the spirits of the dead.* But one day the Philistines brought their soldiers together to attack Israel.

Achish told David, "Of course, you know that you and your men must fight as part of our Philistine army."

David answered, "That will give you a chance to see for yourself just how well we can fight!"

"In that case," Achish said, "you and your men will always be my bodyguards."

⁴ The Philistines went to Shunem and set up camp. Saul called the army of Israel together, and they set up their camp in Gilboa. ⁵ Saul took one look at the Philistine army and started shaking with fear. ⁶ So he asked the LORD what to do. But the LORD would not answer, either in a dream or by a priest or a prophet. ⁷ Then Saul told his officers, "Find me a woman who can talk to the spirits of the dead. I'll go to her and find out what's going to happen."

His servants told him, "There's a woman at Endor who can talk to spirits of the dead."

⁸ That night, Saul put on different clothing so nobody would recognize him. Then he and two of his men went to the woman, and asked, "Will you bring up the ghost of someone for us?"

⁹ The woman said, "Why are you trying to trick me and get me killed? You know King Saul has got rid of everyone who talks to the spirits of the dead!"

¹⁰ Saul replied, "I swear by the living LORD that nothing will happen to you because of this."

¹¹ "Who do you want me to bring up?" she asked.

"Bring up the ghost of Samuel," he answered.

¹² When the woman saw Samuel, she screamed. Then she turned to Saul and said, "You've tricked me! You're the king!"

¹³ "Don't be afraid," Saul replied. "Just tell me what you see."

She answered, "I see a spirit rising up out of the ground."

¹⁴ "What does it look like?"

"It looks like an old man wearing a robe."

Saul knew it was Samuel, so he bowed down low.

¹⁵ "Why are you bothering me by bringing me up like this?" Samuel asked.

"I'm terribly worried," Saul answered. "The Philistines are about to attack me. God has turned his back on me and won't answer any more by prophets or by dreams. What should I do?"

---

*27.10 Jerahmeel . . . Kenites: These were clans of the Judah tribe.
*28.1–3 earlier: See 25.1.
*28.1–3 dead: Many people believed that it was possible to talk to spirits of the dead, and that these spirits could tell the future.
See also: 28.1: 1 Sam 25.1.

See also: 28.6: Num 27.21. 28.7: Lev 20.27; Deut 18.10,11.

16 Samuel said:

If the LORD has turned away from you and is now your enemy, don't ask me what to do. 17 I've already told you: the LORD has sworn to take the kingdom from you and give it to David. And that's just what he's doing! 18 When the LORD was angry with the Amalekites, he told you to destroy them, but you didn't do it. That's why the LORD is doing this to you. 19 Tomorrow the LORD will let the Philistines defeat Israel's army, then you and your sons will join me down here in the world of the dead.

20 At once, Saul collapsed and lay stretched out on the floor, terrified at what Samuel had said. He was weak because he had not eaten anything since the day before.

21 The woman came over to Saul, and when she saw that he was completely terrified, she said, "Your Majesty, I listened to you and risked my life to do what you asked. 22 Now please listen to me. Let me get you a little something to eat. It will give you strength for your walk back to camp."

23 "No, I won't eat!"

But his officers and the woman kept on urging Saul, until he finally agreed. He got up off the floor and sat on the bed. 24 Straight away the woman killed a calf that she had been fattening up. She cooked part of the meat and baked some thin bread.* 25 Then she served the food to Saul and his officers, who ate and left before daylight.

David rescues the families of his troops

CHAPTER 29

The Philistines send David back

1 The Philistines had brought their whole army to Aphek,* while Israel's army was camping near Jezreel Spring. 2-3 The Philistine rulers and their troops were marching past the Philistine army commanders in groups of a hundred and a thousand. When David and his men marched by at the end with Achish, the commanders said, "What are these worthless Israelites doing here?"

"They are David's men," Achish answered. "David used to be one of Saul's officers, but he left Saul and joined my army a long time ago. I've never had even one complaint about him."

4 The Philistine army commanders were angry and shouted:

Send David back to the town you gave him. We won't have him going into the battle with us. He could turn and fight against us! Saul would take David back as an officer if David brought him the heads of our soldiers. 5 The Israelites even dance and sing,

"Saul has killed
   a thousand enemies;
David has killed
   ten thousand enemies!"

6 Achish called David over and said:

I swear by the living LORD that you've been honest with me, and I want you to fight by my side. I don't think you've done anything wrong from the day you joined me until this very moment. But the other Philistine rulers don't want you to come along. 7 Go back home and try not to upset them.

8 "But what have I done?" David asked. "Do you know of anything I've ever done that would keep me from fighting the enemies of my king?"*

9 Achish said:

I believe that you're as good as an angel of God, but our army commanders have decided that you can't fight in this battle. 10 You and your troops will have to go back to the town I gave you.ʼ Get up and leave tomorrow morning as soon as it's light. I am pleased with you, so don't let any of this bother you.ʼ

11 David and his men got up early in the morning and headed back towards Philistia, while the Philistines left for Jezreel.

CHAPTER 30

David rescues his soldiers' families

1 It took David and his men three days to reach Ziklag. But while they had been away, the Amalekites had been raiding in the desert

---

*28.24 thin bread: Bread made without yeast; since there was no time for the bread to rise.
*29.1 Aphek: The events of chapter 29 probably took place as the Philistine army was on its way to Shunem, which they reached in 28.4.
See also: 28.17: 1 Sam 15.28. 28.18: 1 Sam 15.3–9.

*29.8 my king: David may be referring to either Saul or Achish.
See also: 29.5: 1 Sam 18.7; 21.11.

around there. They had attacked Ziklag, burnt it to the ground, ² and had taken away the women and children. ³ When David and his men came to Ziklag, they saw the burnt-out ruins and learnt that their families had been taken captive. ⁴ They started crying and kept it up until they were too weak to cry any more. ⁵ David's two wives, Ahinoam and Abigail, had been taken captive with everyone else.

⁶ David was desperate. His soldiers were so upset over what had happened to their sons and daughters that they were thinking about stoning David to death. But he felt the LORD God giving him strength, ⁷ and he said to the priest, "Abiathar, let's ask God what to do."

Abiathar brought everything he needed to get answers from God, and he went over to David. ⁸ Then David asked the LORD, "Should I go after the people who raided our town? Can I catch up with them?"

"Go after them," the LORD answered. "You will catch up with them, and you will rescue your families."

⁹⁻¹⁰ David led his six hundred men to Besor Gorge, but two hundred of them were too tired to go across. So they stayed behind, while David and the other four hundred men crossed the gorge.

¹¹ Some of David's men found an Egyptian out in a field and took him to David. They gave the Egyptian some bread, and he ate it. Then they gave him a drink of water, ¹² some dried figs, and two handfuls of raisins. This was the first time in three days he had tasted food or water. Now he felt much better.

¹³ "Who is your master?" David asked. "And where do you come from?"

"I'm from Egypt," the young man answered. "I'm the servant of an Amalekite, but he left me here three days ago because I was sick. ¹⁴ We had attacked some towns in the desert where the Cherethites live, in the area that belongs to Judah, and in the desert where the Caleb clan lives. And we burnt down Ziklag."

¹⁵ "Will you take me to those Amalekites?" David asked.

"Yes, I will, if you promise with God as a witness that you won't kill me or hand me over to my master."

¹⁶ He led David to the Amalekites. They were eating and drinking everywhere, celebrating because of what they had taken from Philistia and Judah. ¹⁷ David attacked just before sunrise the next day and fought

until sunset.' Four hundred Amalekites rode away on camels, but they were the only ones who escaped.

¹⁸ David rescued his two wives and everyone else the Amalekites had taken from Ziklag. ¹⁹ No one was missing — young or old, sons or daughters. David brought back everything that had been stolen, ²⁰ including their livestock.

David also took the sheep and cattle that the Amalekites had with them, but he kept these separate from the others. Everyone agreed that these would be David's reward.

²¹ On the way back, David went to the two hundred men he had left at Besor Gorge, because they had been too tired to keep up with him. They came towards David and the people who were with him. When David was close enough, he greeted the two hundred men and asked how they were doing.

²² Some of David's men were good-for-nothings, and they said, "Those men didn't go with us to the battle, so they don't get any of the things we took back from the Amalekites. Let them take their wives and children and go!"

²³ But David said:

My friends, don't be so greedy with what the LORD has given us! The LORD protected us and gave us victory over the people who attacked us. ²⁴ Who would pay attention to you, anyway? Soldiers who stay behind to guard the camp get as much as those who go into battle.

²⁵ David made this a law for Israel, and it has been the same ever since.

²⁶ David went back to Ziklag with everything that he had taken from the Amalekites. He sent some of these things as gifts to his friends who were leaders of Judah, and he told them, "We took these things from the LORD's enemies. Please accept them as a gift."

²⁷⁻³¹ This is a list of the towns where David sent gifts: Bethel,* Ramoth in the Southern Desert, Jattir, Aroer, Siphmoth, Eshtemoa, Racal, the towns belonging to the Jerahmeelites and the Kenites, Hormah, Bor-Ashan, Athach, and Hebron. He also sent gifts to the other towns where he and his men had travelled.

See also: 30.5: 1 Sam 25.42,43. 30.7: 1 Sam 22.20-23.

*30.27-31 Bethel: Or "Bethuel" (see Joshua 19.4).

Saul and his sons die in battle against the Philistines

CHAPTER 31

¹ Meanwhile, the Philistines were fighting Israel at Mount Gilboa. Israel's soldiers ran from the Philistines, and many of them were killed. ² The Philistines closed in on Saul and his sons, and they killed his sons Jonathan, Abinadab, and Malchishua. ³ The fighting was fierce around Saul, and he was badly wounded by enemy arrows.

⁴ Saul told the soldier who carried his weapons, "Kill me with your sword! I don't want those worthless Philistines to torture me and make fun of me." But the soldier was afraid to kill him.

Saul then took out his own sword; he stuck the blade into his stomach, and fell on it. ⁵ When the soldier knew that Saul was dead, he killed himself in the same way.

⁶ Saul was dead, his three sons were dead, and the soldier who carried his weapons was dead. They and all his soldiers died on that same day. ⁷ The Israelites on the other side of Jezreel Valley* and the other side of the Jordan learnt that Saul and his sons were dead. They saw that the Israelite army had run away too. So they ran away too, and the Philistines moved into the towns the Israelites had left behind.

⁸ The day after the battle, when the Philistines returned to the battlefield to take the weapons of the dead Israelite soldiers, they found Saul and his three sons lying dead on Mount Gilboa. ⁹ The Philistines cut off Saul's head and pulled off his armour. Then they put his armour in the temple of the goddess Astarte, and they nailed his body to the city wall of Beth-Shan. They also sent messengers everywhere in Philistia to spread the good news in the temples of their idols and among their people.

¹¹ The people who lived in Jabesh in Gilead heard what the Philistines had done to Saul's body. ¹² So one night, some brave men from Jabesh went to Beth-Shan. They took down the bodies of Saul and his sons, then brought them back to Jabesh and burnt them. ¹³ They buried the bones under a small tree in Jabesh, and for seven days, they went without eating to show their sorrow.

*31.7 Jezreel Valley: Hebrew "valley". Shunem (see 28.4) and Gilboa (see verse 1) were across the Jezreel Valley from each other.

Additional notes

1.1 Ramah: The Hebrew has "Ramathaim," a longer form of "Ramah" (see verse 19).

1.3 Eli . . . priests: One ancient translation; Hebrew "Hophni and Phinehas, the two sons of Eli, served the LORD as priests."

1.23 the LORD . . . promised: The Dead Sea Scrolls and two ancient translations; the Standard Hebrew Text "the LORD will do what he said."

1.24,25 When it was the time of year to go to Shiloh again, Hannah and Elkanah: The Dead Sea Scrolls and one ancient translation; the Standard Hebrew Text "she."

1.24,25 a three-year-old bull: The Dead Sea Scrolls and two ancient translations; the Standard Hebrew Text "three bulls."

1.28 Elkanah: Or "They" or "Samuel."

2.2 god: The Hebrew text has "holy one", a term for supernatural beings or gods.

2.2 mountain: One possible meaning for the difficult Hebrew text of verse 2.

2.22 Israel: The Dead Sea Scrolls and one ancient translation; the Standard Hebrew Text adds "He heard that his sons were even sleeping with the women who worked at the entrance to the sacred tent."

2.28,29 don't respect: The Standard Hebrew Text; the Dead Sea Scrolls and one ancient translation "are greedy for."

2.32 Your family: Or "My house of worship".

2.31,32 No one . . . to Israel: The Standard Hebrew Text; the Dead Sea Scrolls and one ancient translation do not have these words.

2.33 his: The Dead Sea Scrolls and one ancient translation; the Standard Hebrew Text "your."

2.33 die a violent death: The Dead Sea Scrolls and one ancient translation; the Standard Hebrew Text "die."

3.13 refused . . . me: Or "were insulting everyone."

4.3 LORD: Or "chest".

5.6 sores . . . bodies: Or "He struck them with bubonic plague".

5.6 panic: Two ancient translations add "Rats came from their ships, and people were dying night and left."

6.1 months: One ancient translation adds "and rats were everywhere" or "and rats ate the crops".

6.18 stone: A few Hebrew manuscripts; most Hebrew manuscripts "meadow" or "stream".

6.19 seventy: A few Hebrew manuscripts; most Hebrew manuscripts "seventy men, fifty thousand men".

7.2 Israel . . . help: Or "Israel turned to the Lord and begged him for help."

7.12,13 Help Monument: Or "Ebenezer".

9.20 Everything . . . family: Or "You and your family are all Israel wants."

9.25,26 was set . . . morning: One ancient translation; Hebrew "Samuel spoke with Saul on the flat roof of his house. They got up early the next morning, about sunrise, and . . . ".

10.1 people: One ancient translation adds "You will rule the Lord's people and save them from their enemies who are all around them. These things will prove that what I say is true."

10.5 Gibeah: The Hebrew text has "Gibeah of God", which may or may not have been the same Gibeah as Saul's home town.

10.6 take . . . you: Or "will take control of you in a powerful way."

10.10 suddenly . . . him: Or "came over him in a powerful way."

10.12 Why not . . . anyone else: Or "He certainly is! He's probably the leader of the prophets!" or "How can he be? Those prophets are nobodies!"

10.27—11.1 But Saul . . . time: The Standard Hebrew Text; the Dead Sea Scrolls add "King Nahash of Ammon was making the people of Gad and Reuben miserable. He was putting out everyone's right eye, and no one in Israel could stop him. He had put out the right eye of every Israelite man who lived east of the River Jordan. Only seven thousand men had escaped from the Ammonites, and they had gone into the town of Jabesh in Gilead. About a month later . . . ".

11.7 the: Or "some other".

11.8 three hundred thousand . . . thirty thousand: The Dead Sea Scrolls and some ancient translations have different numbers.

12.11 Gideon: The Hebrew text has "Jerubbaal", another name for "Gideon".

12.14 If . . . him: Or "If you and your king want things to go well for you, then you must worship the LORD."

12.15 and your king: One ancient translation; Hebrew "and your ancestors" or "as he was against your ancestors".

13.1 a young man: One possible meaning for the difficult Hebrew text; several manuscripts of one ancient translation have "thirty years old".

13.1,2 for . . . Then: One possible meaning for the difficult Hebrew text.

13.3 led an attack . . . destroyed, but: Or "killed the Philistine military governor who lived at Geba, and . . . ".

13.4 destroyed . . . Geba: Or "killed the Philistine military governor who lived at Geba."

13.5 three thousand: Some ancient translations; Hebrew "thirty thousand".

13.6 in . . . bushes: Or "in cracks in the rocks".

13.15 Then Samuel . . . counted them: Two ancient translations; Hebrew "Then Samuel left Gilgal and went to Gibeah in Benjamin. Saul counted his army".

13.20,21 sickles: One ancient translation; Hebrew "plough-blades".

13.20,21 pitchforks: One possible meaning for the difficult Hebrew text.

14.1–3 Geba: Or "Gibeah". In 13.16 and 14.5 the name "Geba" is used, while 14.2,16 have "Gibeah". In ancient Hebrew writing there is only one letter different between the two words.

14.1–3 threshing place: Or "in Migron".

14.4,5 Shiny Cliff . . . Thorn Bush Cliff: Or "Bozez Cliff . . . Seneh Cliff".

14.13 Jonathan killed . . . from behind: Or "Jonathan attacked the Philistines with his sword, and the soldier killed those who fell to the ground wounded."

14.14 thirty metres: One possible meaning for the difficult Hebrew text.

14.15 Then . . . tremble: Or "Then the ground began to tremble, and everyone was in a terrible panic." Or "Then the ground began to tremble, and God made them all panic."

14.16 Geba: See the note at 14.1–3.

14.18 At that time . . . should do: One ancient translation; Hebrew "Saul told Ahijah, 'Bring the sacred chest,' because at that time it was with the army of Israel."

14.25,26 The army . . . ground: One possible meaning for the difficult Hebrew text.

14.33 over here: One ancient translation; Hebrew "today".

14.41 why . . . Israel: One ancient translation; Hebrew "give me an answer."

14.47,48 won his battles: One ancient translation; Hebrew "hurt them".

15.5 one . . . in: Or "the town of".

15.7 from Havilah: One ancient translation; Hebrew "from the valley" (see 15.5).

15.9 animals . . . weak: One possible meaning for the difficult Hebrew text.

15.13 Saul: One ancient translation adds "Saul had sacrificed to the LORD the best animals they had taken from Amalek, when Samuel came up to him . . . ".

15.29 eternal: Or "glorious".

15.32 in chains: One possible meaning for the difficult Hebrew text.

15.32 Surely . . . now: Or Hebrew; one ancient translation "It would have been better to die in battle!"

17.4 about three metres: The Standard Hebrew Text; the Dead Sea Scrolls and some manuscripts of one ancient translation have "about two metres".

17.52 Gath: One ancient translation; Hebrew "a valley".

18.16 was loyal to: Or "loved".

18.28 she . . . David: Hebrew; one ancient translation "all Israel was loyal to David".

19.18 Prophets Village: Or "Naioth".

20.16 Jonathan . . . keep: Or, continuing Jonathan's statement to David, "You and your descendants must not kill off my descendants."

20.16 I pray . . . promise: Or "I pray that the LORD take revenge on you if you break our promise!"

20.19 By . . . time: One possible meaning for the difficult Hebrew text.

20.19 Going-Away Rock: Or "Ezel Rock"; one ancient translation "that mound" (see 20.41).

20.25 sat . . . him: One ancient translation; Hebrew "stood up".

20.34 insulted David: Or "insulted him" (that is, Jonathan).

20.41 the mound: One ancient translation; Hebrew "from the south side".

21.7 the strongest of: Or "in charge of".

23.15 He . . . because: Or "He saw that".

24.4 small piece: Hebrew "corner" or "lower hem".

'25.1 Paran Desert: Hebrew; some manuscripts of one ancient translation "Maon Desert".

'25.2,3 from the Caleb clan: Or "behaved like a dog".

'25.11 I'm not sure . . . sent you: Or "I don't know where you come from."

'25.22 me: One ancient translation; Hebrew "my enemies".

'26.15 Anyone . . . tonight: Or "Someone went into your camp to kill him tonight."

'27.8 lived . . . Shur: One ancient translation; Hebrew "had lived for a long time in Shur".

'27.10 Where . . . today: A few Hebrew manuscripts, the Dead Sea Scrolls, and three ancient translations; most Hebrew manuscripts "Didn't you make a raid today?"

'29.10 go . . . you: One ancient translation; these words are not in the Hebrew text.

'29.10 I am . . . bother you: One ancient translation; these words are not in the Hebrew text.

'30.17 just . . . sunset: Or "at dusk, and fought until sunset on the next day."

2 Samuel

A quick look at this book

The Second Book of Samuel is actually the second half of a single book that was divided into two parts, 1 and 2 Samuel, because together they were too long to fit on one scroll. Most of 2 Samuel is a history of the rule of King David.

After the death of King Saul, the people of the Judah tribe chose David to be their king. And for the next seven years David was at war with Saul's son, King Ishbosheth of Israel. Then David became king of the entire nation.

David captured Jerusalem from the Jebusites, made it his new capital, and brought the sacred chest there. He wanted to build a temple to honour the Lord and as a place to

keep the sacred chest, but the Lord refused to let him do so. Instead, the Lord promised that David would be a powerful ruler and that one of his descendants would always be king.

David conquered the enemies of Israel and became the ruler of a small empire. But he also had an affair with Bathsheba, the wife of an army officer who was away at war. As a result, the Lord allowed David to have serious troubles later on, and many of those troubles came from within his own family. For example, one of David's sons, Amnon, raped David's daughter Tamar. Amnon was then killed by David's son Absalom, who later led a rebellion against David.

David wasn't perfect, but he was loyal to the Lord and worshipped only him. And for as long as Judah continued as a nation, the Lord kept the promise he made to David:

> Now I promise that you and your descendants
> will be kings. I'll choose one of your sons to be
> king when you reach the end of your life and
> are buried in the tomb of your ancestors. I'll
> make him a strong ruler, and no one will be
> able to take his kingdom away from him . . .
> I will be his father, and he will be my son.
>
> (7.11–14)

David mourns for Saul

CHAPTER 1

David finds out about Saul's death

¹ Saul was dead.

Meanwhile, David had defeated the Amalekites and returned to Ziklag. ² Three days later, a soldier came from Saul's army. His clothes were torn, and earth was on his head.* He went to David and knelt down in front of him.

³ David asked, "Where did you come from?"

The man answered, "From Israel's army. I barely escaped with my life."

⁴ "Who won the battle?" David asked.

The man said, "Our army turned and ran, but many were wounded and died. Even King Saul and his son Jonathan are dead."

⁵ David asked, "How do you know Saul and Jonathan are dead?"

⁶ The young man replied:

I was on Mount Gilboa and saw King Saul leaning on his spear. The enemy's war chariots and cavalry were closing in on him. ⁷ When he turned round and saw me, he called me over. I went and asked what he wanted.

⁸ Saul asked me, "Who are you?"

"An Amalekite," I answered.

⁹ Then he said, "Kill me! I'm dying, and I'm in terrible pain."*

¹⁰ So I killed him. I knew he was too badly wounded to live much longer. Then I took his crown and his arm-band, and I brought them to you, Your Majesty. Here they are.

¹¹ Straight away, David and his soldiers tore their clothes in sorrow. ¹² They cried all day long and would not eat anything. Everyone was sad because Saul, his son Jonathan, and many of the LORD's people had been killed in the battle.

¹³ David asked the young man, "Where is your home?"

The man replied, "My father is an Amalekite, but we live in Israel."

¹⁴⁻¹⁶ David said to him, "Why weren't you afraid to kill the LORD's chosen king? And you even told what you did. It's your own fault that you're going to die!"

Then David told one of his soldiers, "Come here and kill this man!"

David sings in memory of Saul

¹⁷ David sang a song in memory of Saul and Jonathan, ¹⁸ and he ordered his men to teach the song to everyone in Judah. He called it "The Song of the Bow", and it can be found in *The Book of Jashar*.* This is the song:

¹⁹ Israel, your famous hero
    lies dead on the hills,
and your mighty warriors
    have fallen!

²⁰ Don't tell it in Gath
    or spread the news
    in the streets of Ashkelon.
The godless Philistine women
    will be happy
    and jump for joy.

²¹ Don't let dew or rain fall
    on the hills of Gilboa.
Don't let its fields
    grow offerings for God.
There the warriors' shields
    were smeared with mud,
and Saul's own shield
    was left unpolished.*

²² The arrows of Jonathan struck,
    and warriors died.
The sword of Saul cut
    the enemy apart.

²³ It was easy to love Saul
    and Jonathan.
Together in life,
    together in death,
they were faster than eagles
    and stronger than lions.

²⁴ Women of Israel, cry for Saul.
He brought you fine red cloth
    and jewellery made of gold.

²⁵ Our warriors have fallen
    in the heat of battle,
and Jonathan lies dead
    on the hills of Gilboa.

²⁶ Jonathan, I miss you most!
    I loved you like a brother.
You were truly loyal to me,
    more faithful than a wife
    to her husband.*

²⁷ Our warriors have fallen,
    and their weapons*
    are destroyed.

---

*1.2 His clothes . . . his head: People tore their clothes and put earth on their heads to show they were sad because someone had died.

See also: 1.6-10; 1 Sam 31.1-6; 1 Chron 10.1-6.
1.18: Josh 10.13.

290

*1.18 The Book of Jashar: This book may have been a collection of ancient war songs.
*1.21 unpolished: Some shields were made of leather and were polished with olive oil.
*1.27 weapons: This may refer to Saul and Jonathan.

David, king of Judah

CHAPTER 2

[1] Later, David asked the LORD, "Should I go back to one of the towns of Judah?"

The LORD answered, "Yes."

David asked, "Which town should I go to?"

"Go to Hebron," the LORD replied.

[2] David went to Hebron with his two wives, Ahinoam and Abigail. Ahinoam was from Jezreel, and Abigail was the widow of Nabal from Carmel. [3] David also took his men and their families to live in the villages near Hebron.

[4] The people of Judah met with David at Hebron and poured olive oil on his head to show that he was their new king. Then they told David, "The people from Jabesh in Gilead buried Saul."

[5] David sent messengers to tell them:

The LORD bless you! You were kind enough to bury Saul your ruler, [6] and I pray that the LORD will be kind and faithful to you. I will be your friend because of what you have done. [7] Saul is dead, but the tribe of Judah has made him their king. So be strong and have courage.

Ishbosheth becomes king of Israel

[8] Abner the son of Ner* had been the general of Saul's army. He took Saul's son Ishbosheth* across the River Jordan to Mahanaim [9] and made him king of Israel,* including the areas of Gilead, Asher,* Jezreel, Ephraim, and Benjamin. [10] Ishbosheth was forty years old at the time, and he ruled for two years. But the tribe of Judah made David

their king, [11] and he ruled from Hebron for seven and a half years.

The war between David and Ishbosheth

[12] One day, Abner and the soldiers of Ishbosheth* left Mahanaim and went to Gibeon. [13] Meanwhile, Joab the son of Zeruiah* was leading David's soldiers, and the two groups met at the pool in Gibeon.* Abner and his men sat down on one side of the pool, while Joab and his men sat on the other side. [14] Abner yelled to Joab, "Let's get some of our best soldiers to stand up and fight each other!"

Joab agreed, [15] and twelve of Ishbosheth's men from the tribe of Benjamin got up to fight twelve of David's men. [16] They grabbed each other by the hair and stabbed each other in the side with their daggers. They all died there! That's why the place in Gibeon is called "Field of Daggers".* [17] Then everyone started fighting. Both sides fought very hard, but David's soldiers defeated Abner and the soldiers of Israel.

[18] Zeruiah's three sons were there: Joab, Abishai, and Asahel. Asahel could run as fast as a deer in an open field, [19] and he ran straight after Abner, without looking to the right or to the left.

[20] When Abner turned and saw him, he said, "Is that you, Asahel?"

Asahel answered, "Yes it is."

[21] Abner said, "There are soldiers all around. Stop chasing me and fight one of them! Kill him and take his clothes and weapons for yourself."

But Asahel refused to stop.

[22] Abner said, "If you don't turn back, I'll have to kill you! Then I could never face your brother Joab again."

[23] But Asahel would not turn back, so Abner struck him in the stomach with the back end of his spear. The spear went all the way through and came out of his back. Asahel fell down and died. Everyone who saw Asahel lying dead just stopped and stood still. [24] But Joab and Abishai went after Abner.

---

*2.8 son of Ner: Abner was Saul's cousin (see 1 Samuel 14.50).

*2.8 Ishbosheth: One ancient translation has "Ishbaal" (see also 1 Chronicles 8.33). In Hebrew "baal" means "lord" and was used as the name of a Canaanite god. The people of Israel often changed "baal" to "bosheth" (which means "shame") in personal names. Ishbosheth was probably called Ishvi or Ishyo in 1 Samuel 14.49.

*2.9 Israel: Sometimes "Israel" means the northern tribes and does not include the tribes of Judah and Simeon. That is how it is used in this verse.

*2.9 Asher: The Hebrew text has "Ashur", which is the Hebrew name for the Assyrians. It may be another spelling for Asher (one of the tribes of Israel) or it may refer to Geshur (a small area between Gilead and Jezreel, east of Lake Galilee).

See also: 2.2: 1 Sam 25.42,43. 2.4: 1 Sam 31.11–13.

---

*2.12 Ishbosheth: See the note at 2.8.

*2.13 the son of Zeruiah: Zeruiah was David's elder sister, who was David's nephew (see 1 Chronicles 2.12–17 and the note at 2 Samuel 17.25).

*2.13 pool in Gibeon: This pool was just inside the city wall and was used for storing water. It was in the shape of a circle and was about 11 metres wide and about 11 metres deep.

Finally, about sunset, they came to the hill of Ammah, not far from Giah on the road to Gibeon Desert. 25 Abner brought the men of Benjamin together in one group on top of a hill, and they got ready to fight.

26 Abner shouted to Joab, "Aren't we ever going to stop killing each other? Don't you know that the longer we keep on doing this, the worse it's going to be when it's all over? When are you going to order your men to stop chasing their own relatives?"

27 Joab shouted back, "I swear by the living God, if you hadn't spoken, my men would have chased their relatives all night!" 28 Joab took his trumpet and blew the signal for his soldiers to stop chasing the soldiers of Israel. Straight away, the fighting stopped.

29 Abner and his troops marched through the Jordan Valley all that night. Then they crossed the river and marched all morning* until they arrived back at Mahanaim.

30 As soon as Joab stopped chasing Abner, he got David's troops together and counted them. There were nineteen missing besides Asahel. 31 But David's soldiers had killed 360 of Abner's men from the tribe of Benjamin. 32 Joab and his troops carried Asahel's body to Bethlehem and buried him in the family burial place. Then they marched all night and reached Hebron before sunrise.

CHAPTER 3

1 This battle was the beginning of a long war between the followers of Saul and the followers of David. Saul's power grew weaker, but David's grew stronger.

David's sons born in Hebron

This is also told in 1 Chronicles 3.1–4

2-5 Several of David's sons were born while he was living in Hebron. His eldest son was Amnon, whose mother was Ahinoam from Jezreel. David's second son was Chileab, whose mother was Abigail, who had been married to Nabal from Carmel. Absalom was the third. His mother was Maacah, the daughter of King Talmai of Geshur. The fourth was Adonijah, whose mother was Haggith. The fifth was Shephatiah, whose mother was Abital. The sixth was Ithream, whose mother was Eglah, another one of David's wives.

Abner decides to help David

6 As the war went on between the families of David and Saul, Abner was gaining more

power than ever in Saul's family. 7 He had even slept with a wife* of Saul by the name of Rizpah the daughter of Aiah. But Saul's son Ishbosheth* told Abner, "You shouldn't have slept with one of my father's wives!"

8 Abner was very angry at what Ishbosheth had said, and he told Ishbosheth:

Am I some kind of worthless dog from Judah? I've always been loyal to your father's family and to his relatives and friends. I haven't turned you over to David. And yet you talk to me as if I've committed a crime with this woman.

9 I ask God to punish me if I don't help David get what the LORD promised him! 10 God said that he wouldn't let anyone in Saul's family ever be king again and that David would be king instead. He also said that David would rule both Israel and Judah, all the way from Dan in the north to Beersheba in the south.*

11 Ishbosheth was so afraid of Abner that he could not even answer.

12 Abner sent some of his men to David with this message: "You should be the ruler of the whole nation. If you make an agreement with me, I will persuade everyone in Israel to make you their king."

13 David sent this message back: "Good! I'll make an agreement with you. But before I will even talk with you about it, you must get Saul's daughter Michal back for me."

14 David sent a few of his officials to Ishbosheth to give him this message: "Give me back my wife Michal! I killed a hundred Philistines so I could marry her."*

15 Ishbosheth sent some of his men to take Michal away from her new husband, Paltiel the son of Laish. 16 Paltiel followed Michal and the men all the way to Bahurim, crying as he walked. But he went back home after Abner ordered him to leave.

17 Abner talked with the leaders of the tribes of Israel and told them, "You've wanted to make David your king for a long time now. 18 So do it! After all, God said he

---

*3.7 wife: This translates a Hebrew word for a woman who was legally bound to a man, but without the full privileges of a wife.

*3.7 Ishbosheth: See the note at 2.8.

*3.10 from . . . south: Hebrew "from Dan to Beersheba." This was one way of describing all of the Israelite land, from north to south.

*3.14 I killed . . . marry her: See 1 Samuel 18.20–27.

See also: 3.10: 1 Sam 15.28. 3.14: 1 Sam 18.27.

would use his servant David to rescue his people Israel from their enemies, especially from the Philistines."

¹⁹ Finally, Abner talked with the tribe of Benjamin. Then he left for Hebron to tell David everything that the tribe of Benjamin and the rest of the people of Israel wanted to do. ²⁰ Abner took twenty soldiers with him, and when they got to Hebron, David gave a big feast for them.

²¹ After the feast, Abner said, "Your Majesty, let me leave now and bring Israel here to make an agreement with you. You'll be king of the whole nation, just as you've been wanting."

David told Abner he could leave, and he left without causing any trouble.

Joab kills Abner

²² Soon after Abner had left Hebron, Joab and some of David's soldiers came back, bringing a lot of things they had taken from an enemy village. ²³ Just after they arrived, someone told Joab, "Abner visited the king, and the king let him go. Abner even left without causing any trouble."

²⁴ Joab went to David and said, "What have you done? Abner came to you, and you let him go. Now he's long gone! ²⁵ You know Abner — he wants to trick you. He wants to find out how strong your army is and to know everything you're doing."

²⁶ Joab left David, then he sent some messengers to catch up with Abner. They brought him back from the well at Sirah,ᵇ but David did not know anything about it. ²⁷ When Abner returned to Hebron, Joab pretended he wanted to talk privately with him. So he took Abner into one of the small rooms that were part of the town gate and stabbed him in the stomach. Joab killed him because Abner had killed Joab's brother Asahel.

Abner's funeral

²⁸ David heard how Joab had killed Abner, and he said, "I swear to the LORD that I am completely innocent of Abner's death! ²⁹ Joab and his family are the guilty ones. I pray that Joab's family will always be sick with sores and other skin diseases. May they all be cowards,ᵇ and may they die in war or starve to death."

³⁰ Joab and his brother Abishai killed Abner because he had killed their brother Asahel in the battle at Gibeon.

³¹ David told Joab and everyone with him, "Show your sorrow by tearing your clothes and wearing sackcloth!ᵃ Walk in front of Abner's body and cry!"

David walked behind the stretcher on which Abner's body was being carried. ³² Abner was buried in Hebron, while David and everyone else stood at the tomb and cried loudly. ³³ Then the king sang a funeral song about Abner:

> Abner, why should you
>   have died like an outlaw?ᵇ
> ³⁴ No one tied your hands
>   or chained your feet,
>   yet you died as a victim
>   of murderers.

Everyone started crying again. ³⁵ Then they brought some food to David and told him he would feel better if he had something to eat. It was still daytime, and David said, "I swear to God that I'll not take a bite of bread or anything else until sunset!"

³⁶ Everyone noticed what David did, and they liked it, just as they always liked what he did. ³⁷ Now the people of Judah and Israel were certain that David had nothing to do with killing Abner.

³⁸ David said to his officials, "Don't you realize that today one of Israel's great leaders has died? ³⁹ I am the chosen king, but Joab and Abishai have more power than I do. So God will have to pay them backᵇ for the evil thing they did."

CHAPTER 4

Ishbosheth is killed

¹ Ishboshethᵇ felt like giving up after he heard that Abner had died in Hebron. Everyone in Israel was terrified.

² Ishbosheth had put the two brothers Baanah and Rechab in charge of the soldiers who raided enemy villages. Rimmon was their father, and they were from the town of Beeroth, which belonged to the tribe of Benjamin. ³ The people who used to live in Beeroth had run away to Gittaim, and they still live* there.

*3.31 sackcloth: Sackcloth was a rough, dark-coloured cloth made from goat or camel hair and was used to make grain sacks. People wore sackcloth or tore their clothes in times of trouble or sorrow.
*4.3 live: The Hebrew word means that they did not have the full legal rights of citizens.

293

⁴ Saul's son Jonathan had a son named Mephibosheth,* who had not been able to walk since he was five years old. It happened when someone from Jezreel told his nurse that Saul and Jonathan had died.* She hurried off with the boy in her arms, but she fell and injured his legs.

⁵ One day about midday, Rechab and Baanah went to Ishbosheth's house. It was a hot day, and he was resting ⁶⁻⁷ in his bedroom. The two brothers went into the house, pretending to get some flour. But once they were inside, they stabbed Ishbosheth in the stomach and killed him. Then they cut off his head and took it with them.

Rechab and Baanah walked through the Jordan valley all night long. ⁸ Finally they turned west and went to Hebron. They went in to see David and told him, "Your Majesty, here is the head of Ishbosheth, the son of your enemy Saul who tried to kill you! The LORD has let you get even with Saul and his family."

⁹ David answered:

I swear that only the LORD rescues me when I'm in trouble! ¹⁰ When a man came to Ziklag and told me that Saul was dead, he thought he deserved a reward for bringing good news. But I grabbed him and killed him.

¹¹ You evil men have done something much worse than he did. You've killed an innocent man in his own house and on his own bed. I'll make you pay for that. I'll wipe you from the face of the earth!

¹² Then David said to his troops, "Kill these two brothers! Cut off their hands and feet and hang their bodies by the pool in Hebron. But bury Ishbosheth's head in Abner's tomb near Hebron." And they did.

David, king of all Israel

CHAPTER 5

David becomes king of Israel

This is also told in 1 Chronicles 11.1–3

¹ Israel's leaders met with David at Hebron and said, "We are your relatives. ² Even when Saul was king, you led our nation in battle. And the LORD promised that some day you would rule Israel and take care of us like a shepherd."

³ During the meeting, David made an agreement with the leaders and asked the LORD to be their witness. Then the leaders poured olive oil on David's head to show that he was now the king of Israel.

⁴ David was thirty years old when he became king, and he ruled for forty years. ⁵ He lived in Hebron for the first seven and a half years and ruled only Judah. Then he moved to Jerusalem, where he ruled both Israel and Judah for thirty-three years.

How David captured Jerusalem

This is also told in 1 Chronicles 11.4–9; 14.1–2

⁶ The Jebusites lived in Jerusalem, and David led his army there to attack them. The Jebusites did not think he could get in, so they told him, "You can't get in here! We could drive you away, even if we couldn't see or walk!"

⁷⁻⁹ David told his troops, "You will have to go up through the water tunnel to get those Jebusites. I hate people like them who can't walk or see!"

That's why there is still a rule that says, "Only people who can walk and see are allowed in the temple."*

David captured the fortress on Mount Zion, then he moved there and named it David's City. He had the city rebuilt, starting with the landfill to the east. ¹⁰ David became a great and strong ruler, because the LORD All-Powerful was on his side.

¹¹ King Hiram of Tyre sent some officials to David. Carpenters and stone workers came with them, and they brought cedar logs so they could build David a palace.

¹² David knew that the LORD had made him king of Israel and that he had made him a powerful ruler for the good of his people.

David's sons born in Jerusalem

This is also told in 1 Chronicles 14.3–7

¹³ After David left Hebron and moved to Jerusalem, he married many women* from Jerusalem,* and he had a lot of children. ¹⁴ His sons who were born there were

---

*4.4 Mephibosheth: Some manuscripts of one ancient translation have "Mephibaal." In 1 Chronicles 8.34 and 9.40 he is called "Meribbaal". See the note on "baal" and "bosheth" at 2.8.
*4.4 Saul . . . died: See 1 Samuel 31.1–6.
See also: 4.4: 2 Sam 9.3. 4.10: 2 Sam 1.1–16.

*5.13 married many women: Some of these women were second-class wives (see the note at 3.7).
See also: 5.4,5: 1 King 2.11; 1 Chron 3.4; 29.27.
5.6: Josh 15.63; Judg 1.21.

Shammua, Shobab, Nathan, Solomon, [15] Ibhar, Elishua, Nepheg, Japhia, [16] Elishama, Eliada,* and Eliphelet.

David fights the Philistines

This is also told in 1 Chronicles 14.8-17

[17] The Philistines heard that David was now king of Israel, and they came into the hill country to try and capture him. But David found out and went into his fortress.* [18] So the Philistines camped in Rephaim Valley.*

[19] David asked the LORD, "Should I attack the Philistines? Will you let me win?"

The LORD told David, "Attack! I will let you win."

[20] David attacked the Philistines and defeated them. Then he said, "I watched the LORD break through my enemies like a mighty flood." So he named the place "The Lord Broke Through".' [21] David and his troops also carried away the idols that the Philistines had left behind.

[22] Some time later, the Philistines came back into the hill country and camped in Rephaim Valley. [23] David asked the LORD what he should do, and the LORD answered:

Don't attack them from the front. Circle around behind and attack them among the balsam' trees. [24] Wait until you hear a sound like troops marching through the tops of the trees. That sound will mean I have marched out ahead of you to fight the Philistine army.

[25] David obeyed the LORD and defeated the Philistines. He even chased them all the way from Geba to the entrance to Gezer.

CHAPTER 6

David brings the sacred chest back to Jerusalem

This is also told in 1 Chronicles 13.1-14; 15.1-16.3,43

[1] David brought together thirty thousand of Israel's best soldiers and [2] led them to Baalah in Judah, which was also called

Kiriath-Jearim. They were going there' to get the sacred chest and bring it back to Jerusalem. The throne of the LORD All-Powerful is above the winged creatures* on top of this chest, and he is worshipped there.'

[3] They put the sacred chest on a new ox cart and started bringing it down the hill from Abinadab's house. Abinadab's sons Uzzah and Ahio were guiding the ox cart, [4] with Ahio' walking in front of it. [5] Some of the people of Israel were playing music on small harps and other stringed instruments, and on tambourines, castanets, and cymbals. David and the others were happy, and they danced for the LORD with all their might.

[6] But when they came to Nacon's threshing-floor, the oxen stumbled, so Uzzah reached out and took hold of the sacred chest. [7] The LORD God was very angry with Uzzah for doing this, and he killed Uzzah there beside the chest.

[8] David got angry with God for killing Uzzah. He named that place "Bursting Out Against Uzzah",' and that's what it's still called.

[9] David was afraid of the LORD and thought, "Should I take the sacred chest to my city?" [10] He decided not to take it there. Instead, he turned off the road and took it to the home of Obed-Edom, who was from Gath.'

[11-12] The chest stayed there for three months, and the LORD greatly blessed Obed-Edom, his family, and everything he owned. Then someone told King David, "The LORD has done this because the sacred chest is in Obed-Edom's house."

Straight away, David went to Obed-Edom's house to get the chest and bring it to David's City. Everyone was celebrating. [13] The people carrying the chest walked six steps, then David sacrificed an ox and a choice cow. [14] He was dancing for the LORD with all his might, but he wore only a linen cloth.* [15] He and everyone else were celebrating by shouting and blowing horns while the chest was being carried along.

---

*5.16 Eliada: See 1 Chronicles 3.8. 1 Chronicles 14.7 has "Baalyada".

*5.17 fortress: Probably the fortress of Adullam, which was David's former hide-out (see 1 Samuel 22.1,4; 24.22). Or it could refer to the older walled city of Jerusalem, called the "fortress on Mount Zion" in verses 7-9.

*5.18 Rephaim Valley: A few kilometres south-west of Jerusalem.

See also: 6.2: Exod 25.22.

*6.2 winged creatures: Two golden statues of winged creatures were on top of the sacred chest and were symbols of the LORD's throne on earth (see Exodus 25.18).

*6.14 only a linen cloth: The Hebrew word is "ephod", which can mean either a piece of clothing like a skirt that went from the waist to the knee or a garment like an apron or a jacket that only the priests wore.

See also: 6.3: 1 Sam 7.1,2. 6.11: 1 Chron 26.4,5.

¹⁶ Saul's daughter Michal looked out of her window and watched the chest being brought into David's City. But when she saw David jumping and dancing for the LORD, she was disgusted.

¹⁷ They put the chest inside a tent that David had set up for it. David worshipped the LORD by sacrificing animals and burning them on an altar,* ¹⁸ then he blessed the people in the name of LORD All-Powerful.
¹⁹ He gave all the men and women in the crowd a small loaf of bread, some meat, and a handful of raisins, and everyone went home.

Michal talks to David

²⁰ David went home so he could ask the LORD to bless his family. But Saul's daughter Michal went out and started yelling at him. "You were really great today!" she said. "You acted like a dirty old man, dancing around half-naked in front of your servants' slave-girls."

²¹ David told her, "The LORD didn't choose your father or anyone else in your family to be the leader of his people. The LORD chose me, and I was celebrating in honour of him.
²² I'll show you just how great I can be! I'll even be disgusting to myself. But those slave-girls you talked about will still honour me!"

²³ Michal never had any children.

The Lord's promise to David

CHAPTER 7

The LORD's message to David

This is also told in 1 Chronicles 17.1–15

¹ King David moved into his new palace, and the LORD let his kingdom be at peace. ² Then one day, as David was talking with Nathan the prophet, David said, "Look around! I live in a palace made of cedar, but the sacred chest has to stay in a tent."

³ Nathan replied, "The LORD is with you, so do what you want!"

⁴ That night, the LORD told Nathan ⁵ to go to David and give him this message:

David, you are my servant, so listen to what I say. Why should you build a temple for me? ⁶ I didn't live in a temple when I

brought my people out of Egypt, and I don't live in one now. A tent has always been my home wherever I have gone with them. ⁷ I chose leaders and told them to be like shepherds for my people Israel. But did I ever say anything to even one of them about building a cedar temple for me?

⁸ David, this is what I, the LORD All-Powerful, say to you. I brought you in from the fields where you took care of sheep, and I made you the leader of my people. ⁹ Wherever you went, I helped you and destroyed your enemies right in front of your eyes. I have made you one of the most famous people in the world.

¹⁰ I have given my people Israel a land of their own where they can live in peace, and they won't have to tremble with fear any more. Evil nations won't bother them, as they did ¹¹ when I let judges rule my people. And I have kept your enemies from attacking you.

Now I promise that you and your descendants will be kings. ¹² I'll choose one of your sons to be king when you reach the end of your life and are buried in the tomb of your ancestors. I'll make him a strong ruler, ¹³ and no one will be able to take his kingdom away from him. He will be the one to build a temple for me. ¹⁴ I will be his father, and he will be my son.

When he does wrong, I'll see that he is corrected, just as children are corrected by their parents. ¹⁵ But I will never put an end to my agreement with him, as I put an end to my agreement with Saul, who was king before you. ¹⁶ I will make sure that one of your descendants will always be king.

¹⁷ Nathan told David exactly what he had heard in the vision.

David gives thanks to the LORD

This is also told in 1 Chronicles 17.16–27

¹⁸ David went into the tent he had set up for the sacred chest. Then he sat there and prayed:

LORD All-Powerful, my family and I don't deserve what you have already done for us, ¹⁹ and yet you have promised to do even more. Is this the way you usually treat people?* ²⁰ I am your servant, and you know my thoughts, so there is nothing more that I need to say. ²¹ You have done

---

*6.17 sacrificing . . . altar: The Hebrew mentions two kinds of sacrifices. In one kind of sacrifice, the whole animal was burnt on the altar. In the other kind, only part was burnt, and the worshippers ate the rest, as in verse 19 (see Leviticus 1.2–17; 3.1–17).

See also: **6.19,20:** 1 Chron 16.43.

See also: **7.12:** Psa 89.3,4; 132.11; John 7.42; Acts 2.30.
7.14: Psa 89.26,27; 2 Cor 6.18; Heb 1.5. **7.16:** Psa 89.36,37.

this wonderful thing, and you have let me know about it, because you wanted to keep your promise.

²² LORD All-Powerful, you are greater than all others. No one is like you, and you alone are God. Everything we have heard about you is true. ²³ And there is no other nation on earth like Israel, the nation you rescued from slavery in Egypt to be your own. You became famous by using great and wonderful miracles to force other nations and their gods out of your land, so your people could live here.' ²⁴ You have chosen Israel to be your people for ever, and you have become their God.

²⁵ And now, LORD God, please do what you have promised me and my descendants. ²⁶ Then you will be famous for ever, and everyone will say, "The LORD God All-Powerful rules Israel, and David's descendants are his chosen kings." ²⁷ After all, you really are Israel's God, the LORD All-Powerful. You've told me that you will let my descendants be kings. That's why I have the courage to pray to you like this, even though I am only your servant.

²⁸ LORD All-Powerful, you are God. You have promised me some very good things, and you can be trusted to do what you promise. ²⁹ Please bless my descendants and let them always be your chosen kings. You have already promised, and I'm sure that you will bless my family for ever.

The wars of King David

CHAPTER 8

A list of David's victories in war

This is also told in 1 Chronicles 18.1–13

¹ Later, David attacked and badly defeated the Philistines. Israel was now free from their control.'

² David also defeated the Moabites. Then he made their soldiers lie down on the ground, and he measured them off with a rope. He would measure off two lengths of the rope and have those men killed, then he would measure off one length and let those men live. The people of Moab had to accept David as their ruler and pay taxes to him.

³ David set out for the River Euphrates to build a monument* there. On his way,' he

---

defeated the king of Zobah, whose name was Hadadezer the son of Rehob. ⁴ In the battle, David captured seventeen hundred cavalry' and twenty thousand foot soldiers. He also captured war chariots, but he destroyed all but one hundred of them.' ⁵ When troops from the Aramean kingdom of Damascus came to help Hadadezer, David killed twenty thousand of them. ⁶ He left some of his soldiers in Damascus, and the Arameans had to accept David as their ruler and pay taxes to him.

Everywhere David went, the LORD helped him win battles.

⁷ Hadadezer's officers had carried their arrows in gold cases hung over their shoulders, but David took these cases' and brought them to Jerusalem. ⁸ He also took a lot of bronze from the cities of Betah and Berothai, which had belonged to Hadadezer.

⁹⁻¹⁰ King Toi of Hamath and King Hadadezer had been enemies. So when Toi heard that David had attacked and defeated' Hadadezer's whole army, he sent his son Joram to praise and congratulate David. Joram also brought him gifts made of silver, gold, and bronze. ¹¹ David gave these to the LORD, just as he had done with the silver and gold that he had captured from ¹² Edom,' Moab, Ammon, Philistia, and from King Hadadezer of Zobah.

¹³ David fought the Edomite' army in Salt Valley and killed eighteen thousand of their soldiers. When he returned, he built a monument.' ¹⁴ David left soldiers all through Edom, and the people of Edom had to accept him as their ruler.

Wherever David went, the LORD helped him.

A list of David's officials

This is also told in 1 Chronicles 18.14–17

¹⁵ David ruled all Israel with fairness and justice.

¹⁶ Joab the son of Zeruiah was the commander in chief of the army.

Jehoshaphat the son of Ahilud kept the government records.

¹⁷ Zadok the son of Ahitub, and Abiathar the son of Ahimelech,' were the priests.

Seraiah was the secretary.

¹⁸ Benaiah the son of Jehoiada was the commander of' David's bodyguard.'

David's sons were priests.

---

*8.3 monument: Kings sometimes set up monuments in lands they had conquered.

See also: 7.23: Deut 4.34.

See also: 8.13: Psa 60 Title.

CHAPTER 9

David is kind to Mephibosheth

¹ One day, David thought, "I wonder if any of Saul's family are still alive. If they are, I will be kind to them, because I made a promise to Jonathan." ² David called in Ziba, one of the servants of Saul's family. David said, "So you are Ziba."

"Yes, Your Majesty, I am."

³ David asked, "Are any of Saul's family still alive? If there are, I want to be kind to them."

Ziba answered, "One of Jonathan's sons is still alive, but he can't walk."

⁴ "Where is he?" David asked.

Ziba replied, "He lives in Lo-Debar with Machir the son of Ammiel."

⁵⁻⁶ David sent some servants to bring Jonathan's son from Lo-Debar. His name was Mephibosheth,* and he was the grandson of Saul. He came to David and knelt down.

David asked, "Are you Mephibosheth?"

"Yes, I am, Your Majesty."

⁷ David said, "Don't be afraid. I'll be kind to you because Jonathan was your father. I'm going to give you back the land that belonged to your grandfather Saul. Besides that, you will always eat with me at my table."

⁸ Mephibosheth knelt down again and said, "Why should you care about me? I'm worth no more than a dead dog."

⁹ David called in Ziba, Saul's chief servant, and told him, "Since Mephibosheth is Saul's grandson, I've given him back everything that belonged to your master Saul and his family. ¹⁰ You and your fifteen sons and twenty servants will work for Mephibosheth. You will farm his land and bring in his crops, so that Saul's family and servants* will have food. But Mephibosheth will always eat with me at my table."

¹¹⁻¹³ Ziba replied, "Your Majesty, I will do exactly what you tell me to do." So Ziba's family and servants worked for Mephibosheth.

Mephibosheth was lame, but he lived in Jerusalem and ate at David's* table, just like one of David's own sons. And he had a young son of his own, named Mica.

CHAPTER 10

Israel fights Ammon

This is also told in 1 Chronicles 19.1–19

¹ Some time later, King Nahash of Ammon died, and his son Hanun became king. ² David said, "Nahash was kind to me, and I will be kind to his son." So he sent some officials to the country of Ammon to tell Hanun how sorry he was that his father had died.

³ But Hanun's officials told him, "Do you really believe David is honouring your father by sending these people to comfort you? He probably sent them to spy on our city, so he can destroy it." ⁴ Hanun arrested David's officials and had their beards shaved off on one side of their faces. He had their robes cut off just below the waist, and then he sent them away. ⁵ They were terribly ashamed.

When David found out what had happened to his officials, he sent a message and told them, "Stay in Jericho until your beards grow back. Then you can come home."

⁶ The Ammonites realized that they had made David very angry, so they hired more foreign soldiers. Twenty thousand of them were foot soldiers from the Aramean cities of Beth-Rehob and Zobah, one thousand were from the king of Maacah, and twelve thousand were from the region of Tob. ⁷ David heard what they had done, and he sent out Joab with all his well-trained soldiers.

⁸ The Ammonite troops came out and got ready to fight in front of the gate to their city. The Arameans from Zobah and Rehob and the soldiers from Tob and Maacah formed a separate group in the nearby fields.

⁹ Joab saw that he had to fight in front and behind at the same time, and he picked some of the best Israelite soldiers to fight the Arameans. ¹⁰ He put his brother Abishai in command of the rest of the army and made them fight the Ammonites. ¹¹ Joab told his brother, "If the Arameans are too much for me to handle, you can come and help me. If the Ammonites are too strong for you, I'll come and help you. ¹² Be brave and fight hard to protect our people and the cities of our God. I pray that the LORD will do whatever pleases him."

¹³ Joab and his soldiers attacked the Arameans, and the Arameans ran from them. ¹⁴ When the Ammonite soldiers saw that the Arameans had run away, they ran from Abishai's soldiers and went back into their own city. Joab stopped fighting the Ammonites and returned to Jerusalem.

---

*9.5,6 Mephibosheth: Or "Mephibaal" (see the note at 4.4).
See also: 9.1: 1 Sam 20.15–17. 9.3: 2 Sam 4.4.

¹⁵ The Arameans realized they had lost the battle, so they brought all their troops together again. ¹⁶ Hadadezer sent messengers to call in the Arameans who were on the other side of the River Euphrates. Then Shobach, the commander of Hadadezer's army, led them to the town of Helam.

¹⁷ David found out what the Arameans were doing, and he brought Israel's whole army together. They crossed the River Jordan and went to Helam, where the Arameans were ready to meet them. ¹⁸ The Arameans attacked, but then they ran from Israel. David killed seven hundred chariot drivers and forty thousand cavalry.* He also killed Shobach, their commander.

¹⁹ When the kings who had been under Hadadezer's rule saw that Israel had beaten them, they made peace with Israel and accepted David as their ruler. The Arameans were afraid to help Ammon any more.

David's affair with Bathsheba

CHAPTER 11

David and Bathsheba

This is also told in 1 Chronicles 20.1a

¹ It was now spring, the time when kings go to war.* David sent out the whole Israelite army under the command of Joab and his officers. They destroyed the Ammonite army and surrounded the capital city of Rabbah, but David stayed in Jerusalem.

²⁻⁴ Late one afternoon, David got up from a nap and was walking around on the flat roof of his palace. A beautiful young woman was down below in her courtyard, bathing as her religion required.* David happened to see her, and he sent one of his servants to find out who she was.

The servant came back and told David, "Her name is Bathsheba. She is the daughter of Eliam, and she is the wife of Uriah the Hittite."

David sent some messengers to bring her to his palace. She came to him, and he slept with her. Then she returned home. ⁵ But later, when she found out that she was going to have a baby, she sent someone to David with this message: "I'm pregnant!"

⁶ David sent a message to Joab: "Send Uriah the Hittite to me."

Joab sent Uriah ⁷ to David's palace, and David asked him, "Is Joab well? How is the army doing? And how about the war?" ⁸ Then David told Uriah, "Go home and clean up."* Uriah left the king's palace, and David had dinner sent to Uriah's house. ⁹ But Uriah didn't go home. Instead, he slept outside the entrance to the royal palace, where the king's guards slept.

¹⁰ Someone told David that Uriah had not gone home. So the next morning David asked him, "Why didn't you go home? Haven't you been away for a long time?"

¹¹ Uriah answered, "The sacred chest and the armies of Israel and Judah are camping out somewhere in the fields* with our commander Joab and his officers and troops. Do you really think I would go home to eat and drink and sleep with my wife? I swear by your life that I would not!"

¹² Then David said, "Stay here in Jerusalem today, and I will send you back tomorrow."

Uriah stayed in Jerusalem that day. Then the next day, ¹³ David invited him for dinner. Uriah ate with David and drank so much that he got drunk, but he still did not go home. He went out and slept on his mat near the palace guards. ¹⁴ Early the next morning, David wrote a letter and told Uriah to deliver it to Joab. ¹⁵ The letter said: "Put Uriah on the front line where the fighting is the worst. Then pull the troops back from him, so that he will be wounded and die."

¹⁶ Joab had been carefully watching the city of Rabbah, and he put Uriah in a place where he knew there were some of the enemy's best soldiers. ¹⁷ When the men of the city came out, they fought and killed some of David's soldiers — Uriah the Hittite was one of them.

¹⁸ Joab sent a messenger to tell David everything that was happening in the war. ¹⁹ He gave the messenger these orders:

When you finish telling the king everything that has happened, ²⁰ he may get angry and ask, "Why did you go so near the city to fight? Didn't you know they would shoot arrows from the wall? ²¹ Don't you know how Abimelech the son of Gideon* was killed at Thebez? Didn't a woman kill him by dropping a large rock from the top of the city wall? Why did you go so close to the city walls?"

---

*11.2–4 as . . . required: This bathing was often a requirement for worshipping God.
See also: 11.1: 1 Chron 20.1.

*11.8 and clean up: Or "and sleep with your wife".
See also: 11.21: Judg 9.53.

Then you tell him, "One of your soldiers who was killed was Uriah the Hittite."

²² The messenger went to David and reported everything Joab had told him. ²³ He added, "The enemy chased us from the wall and out into the open fields. But we pushed them back as far as the city gate. ²⁴ Then they shot arrows at us from the top of the wall. Some of your soldiers were killed, and one of them was Uriah the Hittite."

²⁵ David replied, "Tell Joab to cheer up and not to be upset about what happened. You never know who will be killed in a war. Tell him to strengthen his attack against the city and break through its walls."ᵇ

²⁶ When Bathsheba heard that her husband was dead, she mourned for him. ²⁷ Then after the time for mourning was over, David sent someone to bring her to the palace. She became David's wife, and they had a son.

CHAPTER 12

The Lᴏʀᴅ's message for David

The Lᴏʀᴅ was angry at what David had done, ¹ and he sent Nathan the prophet to tell this story to David:

A rich man and a poor man lived in the same town. ² The rich man owned a lot of sheep and cattle, ³ but the poor man had only one little lamb that he had bought and raised. The lamb became a pet for him and his children. He even let it eat from his plate and drink from his cup and sleep on his lap. The lamb was like one of his own children.

⁴ One day someone came to visit the rich man, but the rich man didn't want to kill any of his own sheep or cattle and serve it to the visitor. So he stole the poor man's little lamb and served it instead.

⁵ David was furious with the rich man and said to Nathan, "I swear by the living Lᴏʀᴅ that the man who did this deserves to die! ⁶ And because he didn't have any pity on the poor man, he will have to pay four times what the lamb was worth."

⁷ Then Nathan told David:

You are that rich man! Now listen to what the Lᴏʀᴅ God of Israel says to you: "I chose you to be the king of Israel. I kept you safe from Saul ⁸ and even gave you his house and his wives. I let you rule Israel and Judah, and if that had not been enough, I would have given you much more. ⁹ Why

did you disobey me and do such a horrible thing? You murdered Uriah the Hittite by letting the Ammonites kill him, so you could take his wife.

¹⁰ Because you wouldn't obey me and took Uriah's wife for yourself, your family will never live in peace. ¹¹ Someone from your own family will cause you a lot of trouble, and I will take your wives and give them to another man before your very eyes. He will go to bed with them while everyone looks on. ¹² What you did was in secret, but I will do this in the open for everyone in Israel to see.

¹³⁻¹⁴ David said, "I have disobeyed the Lᴏʀᴅ."

"Yes, you have!" Nathan answered. "You showed you didn't care what the Lᴏʀᴅ wanted.ᵇ He has forgiven you, and you won't die. But your newborn son will." ¹⁵ Then Nathan went back home.

David's young son dies

The Lᴏʀᴅ made David's young son very sick. ¹⁶ So David went without eating to show his sorrow, and he begged God to make the boy well. David would not sleep on his bed, but spent each night lying on the floor. ¹⁷ His officials stood beside him and tried to talk him into getting up. But he would not get up or eat with them.

¹⁸ After the child had been sick for seven days, he died, but the officials were afraid to tell David. They said to each other, "Even when the boy was alive, David wouldn't listen to us. How can we tell him his son is dead? He might do something terrible!"

¹⁹ David noticed his servants whispering, and he knew the boy was dead. "Has my son died?" he asked his servants.

"Yes, he has," they answered.

²⁰ David got up off the floor; he took a bath, combed his hair, and dressed. He went into the Lᴏʀᴅ's tent and worshipped, then he went back home. David asked for something to eat, and when his servants brought him some food, he ate it.

²¹ His officials said, "What are you doing? You went without eating and cried for your son while he was alive! But now that he's dead, you're up and eating."

²² David answered:

While he was still alive, I went without food and cried because there was still hope.

See also: 12.1: Psa 51 Title.

See also: 12.11,12: 2 Sam 16.22.

me and said, "Hand over your son! We're going to put him to death for killing his brother." But what they really want is to get rid of him, so they can take over our land.

Please don't let them put out my only flame of hope! There won't be anyone left on this earth to carry on my husband's name.

8 "Go home," David told her. "I'll take care of this matter for you."

9 The woman said, "I hope your decision doesn't cause any problems for you. But if it does, you can blame me."

10 He said, "If anyone gives you any trouble, bring them to me, and it won't happen again!"

11 "Please," she replied, "swear by the LORD your God that no one will be allowed to kill my son!"

He said, "I swear by the living LORD that no one will touch even a hair on his head!"

12 Then she asked, "Your Majesty, may I say something?"

"Yes," he answered.

13 The woman said:

Haven't you been hurting God's people? Your own son had to leave the country. And when you judged in my favour, it was the same as admitting that you should have let him come back. 14 We each must die and disappear like water poured out on the ground. But God doesn't take our lives.' Instead, he finds ways of bringing us back when we run away.

15 Your Majesty, I came here to tell you about my problem, because I was afraid of what someone might do to me. I decided to come to you, because I thought you could help. 16 In fact, I knew that you would listen and save my son and me from those who want to take the land that God gave us.'

17 I can rest easy now that you have given your decision. You know the difference between right and wrong just like an angel of God, and I pray that the LORD your God will be with you.

18 Then David said to the woman, "Now I'm going to ask you a question, and don't try to hide the truth!"

The woman replied, "Please go ahead, Your Majesty."

19 David asked, "Did Joab put you up to this?"

The woman answered, "Your Majesty, I swear by your life that no one can hide the truth from you. Yes, Joab did tell me what to say, 20 but only to show you the other side of this problem. You must be as wise as the angel of God to know everything that goes on in this country."

21 David turned to Joab and said, "It seems that I have already given my decision. Go and bring Absalom back."

22 Joab bowed very low and said, "Your Majesty, I thank you for giving your permission. It shows that you approve of me."

23 Joab went to Geshur to get Absalom. But when they came back to Jerusalem, 24 David told Joab, "I don't want to see my son Absalom. Tell him to stay away from me." So Absalom went to his own house without seeing his father.

Absalom was handsome

25 No one in all Israel was as handsome and well-built as Absalom. 26 He got his hair cut once a year, and when the hair was weighed, it came to over two kilograms.

27 Absalom had three sons. He also had a daughter named Tamar, who grew up to be very beautiful.

Absalom finally sees David

28 Absalom lived in Jerusalem for two years without seeing his father. 29 He wanted Joab to talk to David for him. So one day he sent a message asking Joab to come over, but Joab refused. Absalom sent another message, but Joab still refused. 30 Finally, Absalom told his servants, "Joab's barley field is next to mine. Go and set it on fire!" And they did.

31 Joab went to Absalom's house and demanded, "Why did your servants set my field on fire?"

32 Absalom answered, "You didn't pay any attention when I sent for you. I want you to ask my father why he told me to come back from Geshur. I was better off there. I want to see my father now! If I'm guilty, let him kill me."

33 Joab went to David and told him what Absalom had said. David sent for Absalom, and Absalom came. He bowed very low, and David leaned over and kissed him.

See also: 14.17: 2 Sam 19.27.

Absalom leads a rebellion

CHAPTER 15

¹ Some time later, Absalom got himself a chariot with horses to pull it, and he had fifty men to run in front. ² He would get up early each morning and wait by the side of the road that led to the city gate.* Anyone who had a complaint to bring to King David would have to go that way, and Absalom would ask each of them, "Where are you from?"

If they said, "I'm from a tribe in the north," ³ Absalom would say, "You deserve to win your case. But the king doesn't have anyone to hear complaints like yours. ⁴ I wish someone would make me the judge around here! I would be fair to everyone."

⁵ Whenever anyone would come to Absalom and start bowing down, he would reach out and hug and kiss them. ⁶ That's how he treated everyone from Israel who brought a complaint to the king. Soon everyone in Israel liked Absalom better than they liked David.

⁷ Four years* later, Absalom said to David, "Please, let me go to Hebron. I have to keep a promise that I made to the LORD, ⁸ when I was living with the Arameans in Geshur. I promised that if the LORD would bring me back to live in Jerusalem, I would worship him in Hebron."*

⁹ David gave his permission, and Absalom went to Hebron. ¹⁰⁻¹² He took two hundred men from Jerusalem with him, but they had no idea what he was going to do. Absalom offered sacrifices in Hebron and sent someone to Gilo to tell David's adviser Ahithophel to come.

More and more people were joining Absalom and supporting his plot. Meanwhile, Absalom had secretly sent some messengers to the northern tribes of Israel. The messengers told everyone, "When you hear the sound of the trumpets, you must shout, 'Absalom now rules as king in Hebron!'"

David has to leave Jerusalem

¹³ A messenger came and told David, "Everyone in Israel is on Absalom's side!"

¹⁴ David's officials were in Jerusalem with him, and he told them, "Let's get out of here! We'll have to leave soon, or none of us will escape from Absalom. Hurry! If he moves fast, he could catch us while we're still here. Then he will kill us and everyone else in the city."

¹⁵ The officials said, "Your Majesty, we'll do whatever you say."

¹⁶⁻¹⁷ David left behind ten of his wives* to take care of the palace, but the rest of his family and his officials and soldiers went with him.

They stopped at the last house at the edge of the city. ¹⁸ Then David stood there and watched while his regular troops and his bodyguards* marched past. The last group was the six hundred soldiers who had followed him from Gath.* Their commander was Ittai.

¹⁹ David spoke to Ittai and said, "You're a foreigner from the town of Gath. You don't have to leave with us. Go back and join the new king! ²⁰ You haven't been with me very long, so why should you have to follow me, when I don't even know where I'm going? Take your soldiers and go back. I pray that the Lord will be* kind and faithful to you."

²¹ Ittai answered, "Your Majesty, just as surely as you and the LORD live, I will go where you go, no matter if it costs me my life."

²² "Then come on!" David said.

So Ittai and all his men and their families walked on past David.

David sends the sacred chest back to Jerusalem

²³ The people of Jerusalem were crying and moaning as David and everyone with him passed by. He led them across Kidron Valley* and along the road towards the desert.

²⁴ Zadok and Abiathar the priests were there along with several men from the tribe of Levi who were carrying the sacred chest. They set the chest down, and left it there until David and his followers had gone out of the city.

²⁵ Then David said:

Zadok, take the sacred chest back to Jerusalem. If the LORD is pleased with me, he will bring me back and let me see it and his tent again. ²⁶ But if he says he isn't pleased with me, then let him do what he knows is best.

²⁷ Zadok, you are a good judge of things,* so return to the city and don't cause any trouble. Take your son Ahimaaz with you. Abiathar and his son Jonathan will also go back. ²⁸ I'll wait at the river crossing in the desert until I hear from you.

²⁹ Zadok and Abiathar took the sacred chest back into Jerusalem and stayed there.

---

*15.16,17 wives: See the note at 3.7.
*15.18 the six . . . Gath: These were Philistine soldiers who were loyal to David.
*15.23 Kidron Valley: This was considered the eastern boundary of Jerusalem.

30 David went on up the slope of the Mount of Olives. He was barefoot and crying, and he covered his head to show his sorrow. Everyone with him was crying, and they covered their heads too.

31 Someone told David, "Ahithophel is helping Absalom plot against you!"

David said, "Please, LORD, keep Ahithophel's plans from working!"

David sends Hushai back as a spy

32 When David reached the top of the Mount of Olives, he met Hushai the Archite* at a place of worship. Hushai's robe was torn, and dust was on his head.* 33 David told him:

If you come with me, you might slow us down.* 34 Go back into the city and tell Absalom, "Your Majesty, I am your servant. I will serve you now, just as I served your father in the past."

Hushai, if you do that, you can help me ruin Ahithophel's plans. 35 Zadok and Abiathar the priests will be there with you, and you can tell them everything you hear in the palace. 36 Then they can send their sons Ahimaaz and Jonathan to tell me what you've heard.

37 David's adviser Hushai slipped back into Jerusalem, just about the same time that Absalom was coming in.

CHAPTER 16

Ziba gives food to David

1 David had started down the other side of the Mount of Olives, when he was met by Ziba, the chief servant of Mephibosheth.* Ziba had two donkeys that were carrying two hundred loaves of bread, a hundred handfuls of raisins, a hundred figs,* and some wine.

2 "What's all this?" David asked.

Ziba said, "The donkeys are for your family to ride. The bread and fruit are for the people to eat, and the wine is for them to drink in the desert when they are tired out."

3 "And where is Mephibosheth?" David asked.

Ziba answered, "He stayed in Jerusalem, because he thinks the people of Israel want him to rule the kingdom of his grandfather Saul."

4 David then told him, "Everything that used to belong to Mephibosheth is now yours."

Ziba said, "Your Majesty, I am your humble servant, and I hope you will be pleased with me."

Shimei curses David

5 David was near the town of Bahurim when a man came out and started cursing him. The man was Shimei the son of Gera, and he was one of Saul's distant relatives. 6 He threw stones at David, at his soldiers, and at everyone else, including the bodyguards who walked on each side of David.

7 Shimei was yelling at David, "Get out of here, you murderer! You good-for-nothing, 8 the LORD is paying you back for killing so many in Saul's family. You stole his kingdom, but now the LORD has given it to your son Absalom. You're a murderer, and that's why you're in such big trouble!"

9 Abishai said, "Your Majesty, this man is as useless as a dead dog! He shouldn't be allowed to curse you. Let me go over and chop off his head."

10 David replied, "What will I ever do with you and your brother Joab? If Shimei is cursing me because the LORD has told him to, then who are you to tell him to stop?"

11 Then David said to Abishai and all his soldiers:

My own son is trying to kill me! Why shouldn't this man from the tribe of Benjamin want me dead even more? Let him curse all he wants. Perhaps the LORD did tell him to curse me. 12 But if the LORD hears these curses and sees the trouble I'm in, perhaps he will have pity on me instead.

13 David and the others went on down the road. Shimei went along the hillside by the road, cursing and throwing stones and earth at them. 14 When David and those with him came to the River Jordan, they were tired out. But after they rested, they* felt much better.

Hushai meets Absalom

15 By this time, Absalom, Ahithophel, and the others had reached Jerusalem. 16 David's friend Hushai came to Absalom and said, "Long live the king! Long live the king!"

---

*15.32 Archite: The Archites were part of the tribe of Benjamin (see Joshua 16.2).

*15.32 Hushai's . . . head: See the note at 1.2.

*15.33 you might slow us down: Hushai was probably very old.

*16.1 chief servant of Mephibosheth: See 9.1–13.

See also: 16.1: 2 Sam 9.9,10. 16.3: 2 Sam 19.25–27.

¹⁷ But Absalom asked Hushai, "Is this how you show loyalty to your friend David? Why didn't you go with him?"

¹⁸ Hushai answered, "The LORD and the people of Israel have chosen you to be king. I can't leave. I have to stay and serve the one they've chosen. ¹⁹ Besides, it seems right for me to serve you, just as I served your father."

Ahithophel's advice

²⁰ Absalom turned to Ahithophel and said, "Give us your advice! What should we do?"

²¹ Ahithophel answered, "Some of your father's wives* were left here to take care of the palace. You should have sex with them. Then everyone will find out that you have publicly disgraced your father. This will make you and your followers even more powerful."

²² Absalom had a tent set up on the flat roof of the palace, and everyone watched as he went into the tent with his father's wives.

²³ Ahithophel gave such good advice in those days that both Absalom and David thought it came straight from God.

CHAPTER 17

¹ Ahithophel said to Absalom:

Let me choose twelve thousand men and attack David tonight, ² while he is tired and discouraged. He will panic, and everyone with him will run away. I won't kill anyone except David, ³ since he's the one you want to get rid of. Then I'll bring the whole nation back to you like a bride coming home to her husband.' This way there won't be a civil war.

Hushai fools Absalom

⁴ Hushai and all the leaders of the tribes of Israel agreed that Ahithophel had a good plan. ⁵ Then Absalom said, "Bring in Hushai the Archite. Let's hear what he has to say."

⁶ Hushai came in, and Absalom told him what Ahithophel had planned. Then Absalom said, "Should we do what he says? And if we shouldn't, can you come up with anything better?"

⁷ Hushai said:

This time Ahithophel's advice isn't so good. ⁸ You know that your father and his followers are real warriors. Now they are as fierce as a mother bear whose cubs have

just been killed. Besides, your father has a lot of experience in fighting wars, and he won't be spending the night with the others. ⁹ He has probably already found a hiding place in a cave or somewhere else.

As soon as anyone hears that some of your soldiers have been killed, everyone will think your whole army has been destroyed. ¹⁰ Then even those who are as brave as a lion will lose their courage. All Israel knows what a great warrior your father is and what brave soldiers he has.

¹¹ My advice is to gather all the fighting men of Israel from the town of Dan in the north down to the town of Beersheba in the south. You will have more soldiers than there are grains of sand on the seashore. Absalom, you should lead them yourself, ¹² and we will all go to fight David wherever he is. We will fall on him just as dew falls and covers the ground. He and all his soldiers will die! ¹³ If they go into a walled town, we will put ropes around that town and drag it into the river. We won't leave even one small piece of a stone.

¹⁴ Absalom and the others liked Hushai's plan better than Ahithophel's plan. This was because the LORD had decided to keep Ahithophel's plan from working and to cause trouble for Absalom.

Jonathan and Ahimaaz tell David the news

¹⁵ Straight away, Hushai went to Zadok and Abiathar. He told them what advice Ahithophel had given to Absalom and to the leaders of Israel. He also told them about the advice he had given. ¹⁶ Then he said, "Hurry! Send someone to warn David not to spend the night on this side of the river. He must get across the river, so he and the others won't be wiped out!"

¹⁷ Jonathan and Ahimaaz* had been waiting at Rogel Spring* because they did not want to be seen in Jerusalem. A servant girl went to the spring and gave them the message for David. ¹⁸ But a young man saw them and went to tell Absalom. So Jonathan and Ahimaaz left and hurried to the house of a man who lived in Bahurim. Then they climbed down into a well in the courtyard. ¹⁹ The man's wife put the cover on the well

---

*16.21 wives: See the note at 3.7.
See also: 16.22: 2 Sam 12.11,12.

*17.17 Jonathan and Ahimaaz: See 15.27.
*17.17 Rogel Spring: South of Jerusalem in Kidron Valley.

and poured grain on top of it, so the well could not be seen.*

20 Absalom's soldiers came to the woman and demanded, "Where are Ahimaaz and Jonathan?"

The woman answered, "They went across the stream."

The soldiers went off to look for the two men. But when they did not find the men, they went back to Jerusalem.

21 After the soldiers had gone, Jonathan and Ahimaaz climbed out of the well. They went to David and said, "Hurry! Get ready to cross the river!" Then they told him about Ahithophel's plan.

22 David and the others got ready and started crossing the River Jordan. By sunrise all of them were on the other side.

Ahithophel kills himself

23 When Ahithophel saw that Absalom and the leaders of Israel were not going to follow his advice, he saddled his donkey and rode back to his home in Gilo. He told his family and servants what to do. Then he hanged himself, and they buried him in his family's burial place.

Absalom puts Amasa in charge of the army

24 David went to the town of Mahanaim, and Absalom crossed the River Jordan with the army of Israel. 25 Absalom put Amasa in Joab's place as commander of the army. Amasa's father was Ithra* from the family of Ishmael,* and his mother was Abigal,* the daughter of Nahash and the sister of Joab's mother Zeruiah. 26 The Israelites under Absalom's command set up camp in the region of Gilead.

Friends bring supplies to David

27 After David came to the town of Mahanaim, Shobi the son of Nahash came from Rabbah in Ammon,* Machir the son of

Ammiel came from Lo-Debar, and Barzillai the Gileadite came from Rogelim.

28-29 Here is a list of what they brought: sleeping mats, blankets, bowls, pottery jars, wheat, barley, flour, roasted grain, beans, lentils, honey, yoghurt, sheep, and cheese.

They brought the food for David and the others because they knew that everyone would be hungry, tired, and thirsty from being out in the desert.

CHAPTER 18

David gets ready for battle

1 David divided his soldiers into groups of a hundred and groups of a thousand. Then he chose officers to be in command of each group. 2 He sent out one-third of his army under the command of Joab, another third under the command of Abishai the son of Zeruiah, and the rest under the command of Ittai from Gath. He told the soldiers, "I'm going into battle with you."

3 But the soldiers said, "No, don't go into battle with us! It won't matter to our enemies if they make us all run away, or even if they kill half of us. But you are worth ten thousand of us. It would be better for you to stay in town and send help if we need it."

4-6 David said, "All right, if you think I should."

Then in a voice loud enough for everyone to hear, he said, "Joab! Abishai! Ittai! For my sake, be sure that Absalom comes back unharmed."

David stood beside the town gate as his army marched past in groups of a hundred and in groups of a thousand.

Joab kills Absalom

The war with Israel took place in Ephraim Forest. 7-8 Battles were being fought all over the forest, and David's soldiers were winning. Twenty thousand soldiers were killed* that day, and more of them died from the dangers of the forest than from the fighting itself.

9 Absalom was riding his mule under a huge tree when his head* caught in the branches. The mule ran off and left Absalom hanging in mid-air. Some of David's soldiers happened to pass by, 10 and one of them went and told Joab, "I saw Absalom hanging in a tree!"

11 Joab said, "You saw Absalom? Why didn't you kill him? I would have given you ten pieces of silver and a special belt."

---

*17.19 The man's wife . . . seen: Everyone would have thought that the woman was drying grain on a mat that she had spread on the ground.
*17.25 Amasa . . . Abigal: Abigal and Zeruiah (Joab's mother) were full sisters, and David was evidently their half-brother with the same mother, but a different father. This made Amasa one of David's nephews (see 1 Chronicles 2.12–17).
*17.27 Shobi . . . Ammon: Shobi was probably the new king of the Ammonites whom David had appointed after he captured Rabbah (see 2 Samuel 10.1–3; 12.26–31).

[12] The man answered, "Even if you paid me a thousand pieces of silver here and now, I still wouldn't touch the king's son. We all heard King David tell you and Abishai and Ittai not to harm Absalom. [13] He always finds out what's going on. I would have been risking my life to kill Absalom, because you would have let me take the blame."

[14] Joab said, "I'm not going to waste any more time on you!"

Absalom was still alive, so Joab took three spears and stuck them through Absalom's chest. [15] Ten of Joab's bodyguards came over and finished him off. [16] Then Joab blew a trumpet to signal his troops to stop chasing Israel's soldiers. [17] They threw Absalom's body into a deep pit in the forest and put a big pile of rocks over it.

Meanwhile, the people of Israel had all run back to their own homes.

[18] When Absalom was alive, he had set up a stone monument for himself in King's Valley. He explained, "I don't have any sons* to keep my name alive." He called it Absalom's Monument, and that is the name it still has today.*

Ahimaaz wants to tell David

[19] Ahimaaz the son of Zadok said, "Joab, let me run and tell King David that the LORD has rescued him from his enemies."

[20] Joab answered, "You're not the one to tell the king that his son is dead. You can take him a message some other time, but not today."

[21] Someone from Ethiopia* was standing there, and Joab told him, "Go and tell the king what you have seen." The man knelt down in front of Joab and then got up and started running.

[22] Ahimaaz spoke to Joab again, "No matter what happens, I still want to run. And besides, the Ethiopian has already left."

Joab said, "Why should you run? You won't get a reward for the news you have!"

[23] "I'll run no matter what!" Ahimaaz insisted.

"All right then, run!" Joab said.

Ahimaaz took the road through the Jordan Valley and outran the Ethiopian.

[24] Meanwhile, David was sitting between the inner and outer gates* in the city wall. One of his soldiers was watching from the roof of the gate-tower. He saw a man running towards the town [25] and shouted down to tell David.

David answered, "If he's alone, he must have some news."

The runner was getting closer, [26] when the soldier saw someone else running. He shouted down to the gate, "Look! There's another runner!"

David said, "He must have some news too."

[27] The soldier on the roof shouted, "The first one runs just like Ahimaaz the son of Zadok."

This time David said, "He's a good man. He must have some good news."

[28] Ahimaaz called out, "We won! We won!" Then he bowed low to David and said, "Your Majesty, praise the LORD your God! He has given you victory over your enemies."

[29] "Is my son Absalom all right?" David asked.

Ahimaaz said, "When Joab sent your personal servant and me, I saw a noisy crowd. But I don't know what it was all about."

[30] David told him, "Stand over there and wait."

Ahimaaz went over and stood there. [31] The Ethiopian came and said, "Your Majesty, today I have good news! The LORD has rescued you from all your enemies!"

[32] "Is my son Absalom all right?" David asked.

The Ethiopian replied, "I wish that all Your Majesty's enemies and everyone who tries to harm you would end up like him!"

David cries for Absalom

[33] David started trembling. Then he went up to the room above the city gate to cry. As he went, he kept saying, "My son Absalom! My son, my son Absalom! I wish I could have died instead of you! Absalom, my son, my son, my son!"

CHAPTER 19

[1] Someone told Joab, "The king is crying because Absalom is dead."

---

*18.18 I don't have any sons: According to 14.27, Absalom had three sons. But they could have died young or been put to death for Absalom's murder of Amnon.

*18.18 today: That is, at the time of writing. This monument is not the same as the structure now known as "Absalom's Tomb", which was built at least 600 years later.

*18.21 Ethiopia: The Hebrew text has "Cush", which was a region south of Egypt that included parts of the present countries of Ethiopia and Sudan.

*18.24 between . . . gates: The city gate was often like a tower in the city wall, with one gate on the outside of the wall and another gate on the inside of the wall.

² David's army found out he was crying because his son had died, and their day of victory suddenly turned into a day of sadness. ³ The troops were sneaking into Mahanaim, just as if they had run away from a battle and were ashamed.

⁴ David held his hands over his face and kept on crying loudly, "My son, Absalom! Absalom, my son, my son!"

⁵ Joab went to the house where David was staying and told him:

You've made your soldiers ashamed! Not only did they save your life, they saved your sons and daughters and wives as well. ⁶ You're more loyal to your enemies than to your friends. What you've done today has shown your officers and soldiers that they don't mean a thing to you. You would be happy if Absalom was still alive, even if the rest of us were dead.

⁷ Now get up! Go out there and thank them for what they did. If you don't, I swear by the LORD that you won't even have one man left on your side tomorrow morning. You may have had a lot of troubles in the past, but this will be the worst thing that has ever happened to you!

⁸ David got up and went to the town gate and sat down. When the people heard that he was sitting there, they came to see him.

Israel and Judah want David back

After Israel's soldiers had all returned home, ⁹⁻¹⁰ everyone in Israel started arguing. They were saying to each other, "King David rescued us from the Philistines and from our other enemies. But then we chose Absalom to be our new leader, and David had to leave the country to get away. Absalom died in battle, so why hasn't something been done to bring David back?"

¹¹ When David found out what they were saying, he sent a message to Zadok and Abiathar the priests. It said:

Say to the leaders of Judah, "Why are you the last tribe to think about bringing King David back home? ¹² He is your brother, your own relative! Why haven't you done anything to bring him back?" ¹³ And tell Amasa, "You're my nephew, and with God as a witness, I swear I'll make you commander of my army instead of Joab."

¹⁴ Soon the tribe of Judah again became followers of David, and they sent him this

message: "Come back, and bring your soldiers with you."

David starts back for Jerusalem

¹⁵ David started back and had gone as far as the River Jordan when he met the people of Judah. They had gathered at Gilgal and had come to help him cross the river.

¹⁶ Shimei* the son of Gera was there with them. He had hurried from Bahurim to meet David. Shimei was from the tribe of Benjamin, and ¹⁷ a thousand others from Benjamin had come with him.

Ziba, the chief servant of Saul's family, also came to the River Jordan. He and his fifteen sons and twenty servants waded across* to meet David. ¹⁸ Then they brought David's family and servants back across the river, and they did everything he wanted them to do.

Shimei meets with David

Shimei crossed the River Jordan and bowed down in front of David. ¹⁹ He said, "Your Majesty, I beg you not to punish me! Please, forget what I did when you were leaving Jerusalem. Don't even think about it. ²⁰ I know I was wrong. That's why I wanted to be the first one from the northern tribes to meet you."

²¹ But Abishai shouted, "You should be killed for cursing the LORD's chosen king!"

²² David said, "Abishai, whatever will I do with you and your brother Joab? Is it your job to tell me who has done wrong? I've been made king of all Israel today, and no one will be put to death!" ²³ Then David promised Shimei that he would not be killed.

Mephibosheth meets with David

²⁴ Mephibosheth, the grandson of Saul, also came to meet David. He had missed David so much that he had not taken a bath or trimmed his beard or washed his clothes the whole time David was gone.

²⁵ After they had gone back to Jerusalem, Mephibosheth came to see David, who asked him, "Why didn't you go with me?"

²⁶ He answered, "Your Majesty, you know I can't walk. I told my servant to saddle a donkey for me* so I could go with you. But my servant left without me, and ²⁷ then he lied about me. You're as wise as an angel of

*19.16 Shimei: See 16.5-13.

See also: 19.16: 2 Sam 16.5-13. 19.24: 2 Sam 9.1-13; 16.1-4.

God, so do what you think is right. [28] After all, you could have killed my whole family and me. But instead, you let me eat at your own table. Your Majesty, what more could I ask?"

[29] David answered, "You've said enough! I've decided to divide the property* between you and David."

[30] Mephibosheth replied, "He can have it all! I'm just glad you've come home safely."

Barzillai returns home

[31] Barzillai came from Rogelim in Gilead to meet David at the River Jordan and go across with him. [32] Barzillai was eighty years old. He was very rich and had sent food to David in Mahanaim.

[33] David said to him, "Cross the river and go to Jerusalem with me. I will take care of you."

[34] Barzillai answered:

Your Majesty, why should I go to Jerusalem? I don't have much longer to live. [35] I'm already eighty years old, and my body is almost numb. I can't taste my food or hear the sound of singing, and I would be nothing but a burden. [36] I'll cross the river with you, but I'll only go a little way on the other side. You don't have to be so kind to me. [37] Just let me return to my home town, where I can some day be buried near my father and mother. My servant Chimham* can go with you, and you can treat him as your own.

[38] David said, "I'll take Chimham with me, and whatever you ask me to do for him, I'll do. And if there's anything else you want, I'll also do that."

[39] David's soldiers went on across the river, while he stayed behind to say goodbye to Barzillai and to wish him well. Barzillai returned home, but [40] Chimham crossed the river with David.

Israel and Judah argue

All of Judah's army and half of Israel's army were there to help David cross the river.
[41] The soldiers from Israel came to him and said, "Why did our relatives from Judah sneak you and your family and your soldiers across the Jordan?"

[42] The people of Judah answered, "Why are you so angry? We are the king's relatives. He

didn't give us any food, and we didn't take anything for ourselves!"

[43] Those from Israel said, "King David belongs to us ten times more than he belongs to you.* Why didn't you think we were good enough to help us? After all, we were the first ones to think of bringing him back!"

The people of Judah spoke more harshly than the people of Israel.

CHAPTER 20

Sheba rebels against David

[1] A troublemaker from the tribe of Benjamin was there. His name was Sheba the son of Bichri, and he blew a trumpet to get everyone's attention. Then he said, "People of Israel, David the son of Jesse doesn't belong to us! Let's go home."

[2] So they stopped following David and went off with Sheba. But the people of Judah stayed close to David all the way from the Jordan to Jerusalem.

David's ten wives

[3] David had left ten of his wives in Jerusalem to take care of his palace. But when he came back, he had them taken to another house, and he placed soldiers there to guard them. He gave them whatever they needed, but he never slept with any of them again.* They had to live there for the rest of their lives as if they were widows.

The army goes after Sheba

[4] David said to Amasa, "Three days from now I want you and all of Judah's army to be here!"

[5] Amasa started bringing the army together, but it was taking him more than three days. [6] So David said to Abishai, "Sheba will hurt us more than Absalom ever did. Take my best soldiers and go after him. We don't want him to take over any walled cities and get away from us.'"

Joab kills Amasa

[7] Abishai left Jerusalem to try and capture Sheba. He took along Joab and his soldiers, as

---

*19.43 King David . . . you: In this verse "Israel" stands for the ten northern tribes and does not include the tribe of Judah in the south.

*20.3 he . . . again: Because of what Absalom had done (see 16.21,22).

See also: 20.1: 1 King 12.16; 2 Chron 10.16.
20.3: 2 Sam 16.22.

---

*19.29 the property: The property that had belonged to Saul (see 9.7; 16.4).

See also: 19.31: 2 Sam 17.27–29.

well as David's bodyguard[c] and best troops.
[8] They had gone as far as the big rock at Gibeon when Amasa caught up with them. Joab had a dagger strapped around his waist over his military uniform, but it fell out as he started towards Amasa.

[9] Joab said, "Amasa, my cousin, how are you?" Then Joab took hold of Amasa's beard with his right hand, so that he could greet him with a kiss. [10] Amasa did not see the dagger in Joab's other hand. Joab stuck it in Amasa's stomach, and his insides spilt out on the ground. Joab only struck him once, but Amasa was dying.

Joab and his brother Abishai went off to chase Sheba. [11] One of Joab's soldiers stood by Amasa and shouted, "If any of you like Joab, and if you are for David, then follow Joab!"

[12] Amasa was still rolling in his own blood in the middle of the road. The soldier who had shouted noticed that everyone who passed by would stop, so he dragged Amasa off the road and covered him with a blanket. [13] After this, no one else stopped. They all walked straight past him on their way to help Joab capture Sheba.

Sheba hides out in the town of Abel

[14] Sheba had gone through all the tribes of Israel when he came to the town of Abel Beth-Maacah. All his best soldiers[c] met him there and followed him into the town.

[15] Joab and his troops came and surrounded Abel, so that no one could go in or come out. They made an earth ramp up to the town wall and then started to use a battering ram to knock the wall down.

A wise woman saves the town

[16] A wise woman shouted from the top of the wall,[c] "Listen to me! Listen to me! I have to talk to Joab! Tell him to come here!" [17] When he came, the woman said, "Are you Joab?"

"Yes, I am," he answered.

She said, "Please, listen to what I have to say."

"All right," he said. "I'll listen."

[18] She said, "Long ago people used to say, 'If you want good advice, go to the town of Abel to get it.' The answers they got here were all that was needed to settle any problem. [19] We are Israelites, and we want peace! You can trust us. Why are you trying to destroy a town that's like a mother in Israel? Why do you want to wipe out the LORD's people?"

[20] Joab answered, "No, no! I'm not trying to wipe you out or destroy your town! [21] That's not it at all. There's a man in your town from the hill country of Ephraim. His name is Sheba, and he is the leader of a rebellion against King David. Turn him over to me, and we will leave your town alone."

The woman told Joab, "We will throw his head over the wall."

[22] She went to the people of the town and talked them into doing it. They cut off Sheba's head and threw it to Joab.

Joab blew a signal on his trumpet, and the soldiers returned to their homes. Joab went back to David in Jerusalem.

Another list of David's officials*

[23] Joab was the commander of Israel's entire army.

Benaiah the son of Jehoiada was in command of David's bodyguard.[c]

[24] Adoram[c] was in charge of the slave-labour force.

Jehoshaphat the son of Ahilud kept government records.

[25] Sheva was the secretary.

Zadok and Abiathar were the priests.

[26] Ira from Jair was David's priest.

Other events from David's rule

CHAPTER 21

The Gibeonites hang Saul's descendants

[1] While David was king, there were three years in a row when the nation of Israel could not grow enough food. So David asked the LORD for help, and the LORD answered, "Saul and his family are guilty of murder, because he had the Gibeonites killed."

[2] The Gibeonites were not Israelites; they were descendants of the Amorites. The people of Israel had promised not to kill them,* but Saul had tried to kill them because he wanted Israel and Judah to control all the land.

David called the Gibeonites to him, and he talked with them. [3] He said, "What can I do to

---

*20.23 Another list of David's officials: See also the list in 8.16,17.
*21.2 promised . . . them: See Joshua 9.3–27.
See also: 21.2: Josh 9.3–15.

make up for what Saul did, so that you'll ask the LORD to be kind to his people again?"*

4 The Gibeonites answered, "Silver and gold from Saul and his family are not enough. On the other hand, we don't have the right to put any Israelite to death."

David said, "I'll do whatever you ask."*

5 They replied, "Saul tried to kill all our people so that none of us would be left in the land of Israel. 6 Give us seven of his descendants. We will hang* these men near the place where the LORD is worshipped in Gibeah, the home town of Saul, the LORD's chosen king."

"I'll give them to you," David said.

7 David had made a promise to Jonathan with the LORD as his witness, to spare Jonathan's son Mephibosheth, the grandson of Saul. 8 But Saul and Rizpah the daughter of Aiah had two sons named Armoni and Mephibosheth. Saul's daughter Merab* had five sons whose father was Adriel the son of Barzillai from Meholah.* David took Rizpah's two sons and Merab's five sons and 9 turned them over to the Gibeonites, who hanged* all seven of them on the mountain near the place where the LORD was worshipped. This happened right at the beginning of the barley harvest.*

Rizpah takes care of the bodies

10 Rizpah spread out some sackcloth* on a nearby rock. She wouldn't let the birds land on the bodies during the day, and she kept the wild animals away at night. She stayed there from the beginning of the harvest until it started to rain.*

The burial of Saul and his descendants

11-12 Earlier the Philistines had killed Saul and Jonathan on Mount Gilboa and had hung their bodies in the town square at Beth-Shan. The people of Jabesh in Gilead had secretly taken the bodies away, but David found out what Saul's wife* Rizpah had done, and he went to the leaders of Jabesh to get the bodies of Saul and his son Jonathan. 13-14 David had their bones taken to the land of Benjamin and buried in a side room in Saul's family burial place. Then he gave orders for the bones of the men who had been hanged* to be buried there. It was done, and God answered prayers to bless the land.

The descendants of the Rephaim

This is also told in 1 Chronicles 20.4–8

15 One time David got very tired when he and his soldiers were fighting the Philistines. 16 One of the Philistine warriors was Ishbibenob, who was a descendant of the Rephaim,* and he tried to kill David. Ishbibenob was armed with a new sword,* and his bronze spearhead* alone weighed about three and a half kilogrammes. 17 But Abishai* came to the rescue and killed the Philistine.

David's soldiers told him, "We can't let you risk your life in battle any more! You give light to our nation, and we want that flame to keep burning."

18 There was another battle with the Philistines at Gob, where Sibbecai from Hushah killed a descendant of the Rephaim named Saph.

19 There was still another battle with the Philistines at Gob. A soldier named Elhanan killed Goliath* from Gath, whose spear shaft was like a weaver's beam.* Elhanan's father was Jair* from Bethlehem.

20 There was another war, this time in Gath. One of the enemy soldiers was a

---

*21.3 ask . . . again: Saul's guilt had become a curse on Israel that had resulted in famine. For the effects of this curse to be removed, the Gibeonites would have to ask the LORD to be kind to Israel.
*21.8 Merab: Some Hebrew manuscripts and some manuscripts of one ancient translation. Most other manuscripts have "Michal," Saul's daughter who was one of David's wives, but she never had any children (see 2 Samuel 6.23). According to 1 Samuel 18.19, Merab was Saul's daughter, and she married Adriel from Meholah.
*21.9 This . . . harvest: This would have been late in April.
*21.10 sackcloth: See the note at 3.31.
*21.10 started to rain: This may have been the beginning of the rainy season in September or October. It usually didn't rain from May to September. Or, it may have been a sign that now there would be enough rain again.

See also: 21.7: 1 Sam 20.15–17; 2 Sam 9.1–7.
21.8: 1 Sam 18.19.

*21.11,12 wife: See the note at 3.7.
*21.16 Rephaim: This may refer to a group of people of great stature that lived in Palestine before the Israelites.
*21.17 Abishai: David's nephew, the brother of Joab.
*21.19 Goliath: According to 1 Chronicles 20.5, Elhanan killed the brother of Goliath.
*21.19 weaver's beam: When a weaver made cloth, one set of threads was tied on to a large wooden rod that was known as a weaver's beam.

See also: 21.12: 1 Sam 31.8–13. 21.17: 1 King 11.36; Psa 132.17.

descendant of the Rephaim. He was as big as a giant and had six fingers on each hand and six toes on each foot. 21 But when he made fun of Israel, David's nephew Jonathan killed him. Jonathan was the son of David's brother Shimei.

22 David and his soldiers killed these four men who were descendants of the Rephaim from Gath.

Two poems by David

CHAPTER 22

David sings to the Lord

This is also told in Psalm 18.1–50

1 David sang a song to the LORD after the LORD had rescued him from his enemies, especially Saul. These are the words to David's song:

2 Our LORD and our God,
   you are my mighty rock,*
   my fortress, my protector.
3 You are the rock where I am safe.
   You are my shield,
   my powerful weapon,'
   and my place of shelter.

   You rescue me and keep me
   from being hurt.
4 I praise you, our LORD!
   I prayed to you,
   and you rescued me
   from my enemies.
5 Death, like ocean waves,
   surrounded me,
   and I was almost swallowed
   by its flooding waters.

6 Ropes from the world
   of the dead had coiled around me,
   and death had set a trap in my path.
7 I was in terrible trouble
   when I called out to you,
   but from your temple you heard me
   and answered my prayer.
8 Earth shook and shivered!
   The columns supporting the sky*
   rocked back and forth.

   You were angry
9 and breathed out smoke.
   Scorching heat and fiery flames
   spewed from your mouth.

10 You opened the heavens
    like curtains,
    and you came down
    with storm clouds under your feet.
11 You rode on the backs
    of flying creatures.*
    You appeared' with the wind as wings.
12 Darkness was your tent!
    Thunderclouds filled the sky,
    hiding you from sight.
13 Fiery coals lit up the sky
    in front of you.

14 LORD Most High, your voice
    thundered from the heavens.
15 You scattered your enemies
    with arrows of lightning.
16 You roared at the sea,
    and its deepest channels could be seen.
    You snorted,
    and the earth shook
    to its foundations.

17 You reached down from heaven,
    and you lifted me
    from deep in the ocean.
18 You rescued me from enemies
    who were hateful
    and too powerful for me.
19 On the day disaster struck,
    they came and attacked,
    but you defended me.
20 When I was fenced in,
    you freed and rescued me
    because you love me.
21 You are good to me, LORD,
    because I do right,
    and you reward me
    because I am innocent.
22 I do what you want
    and never turn to do evil.
23 I keep your laws in mind
    and never turn away
    from your teachings.
24 I obey you completely
    and guard against sin.
25 You have been good to me
    because I do right;
    you have rewarded me
    for being innocent
    by your standards.

*22.2 mighty rock: The Hebrew text has "rock," which is sometimes used in poetry to compare the LORD to a mountain where his people can run for protection from their enemies.
*22.8 columns . . . sky: The sky was sometimes described as a dome that was held up by a foundation or pillars.

*22.11 flying creatures: These were supernatural beings (see the note at 6.2).

313

26 You are always loyal
   to your loyal people,
and you are faithful to the faithful.
27 With all who are sincere
   you are sincere,
but you treat the unfaithful
   as their deeds deserve.
28 You rescue the humble,
   but you look for ways
to put down the proud.

29 Our LORD and God,
   you are my lamp.
You turn darkness to light.
30 You help me defeat armies
   and capture cities.

31 Your way is perfect, LORD,
   and your word is correct.
You are a shield for those
   who run to you for help.
32 You alone are God!
   Only you are a mighty rock.*
33 You are my strong fortress,
   and you set me free.
34 You make my feet run as fast
   as those of a deer,
and you help me stand
   on the mountains.

35 You teach my hands to fight
   and my arms to use
   a bow of bronze.
36 You alone are my shield,
   and by coming to help me,
   you have made me famous.
37 You clear the way for me,
   and now I won't stumble.

38 I kept chasing my enemies
   until I caught them
   and destroyed them.
39 I destroyed them!
   I stuck my sword
through my enemies,
   and they were crushed
   under my feet.
40 You helped me win victories
   and forced my attackers
   to fall victim to me.
41 You made my enemies run,
   and I killed them.
42 They cried out for help,
   but no one saved them;
they called out to you,
   but there was no answer.

43 I ground them to dust,
   and I squashed them
   like mud in the streets.

44 You rescued me
   from my stubborn people
and made me the leader
   of foreign nations,
who are now my slaves.
45 They obey and come crawling.
46 They have lost all courage
   and from their fortresses
   they come trembling.

47 You are the living LORD!
   I will praise you!
You are a mighty rock.*
   I will honour you
   for keeping me safe.
48 You took revenge for me,
   and you put nations in my power.
49 You protected me
   from violent enemies,
and you made me much greater
   than all of them.

50 I will praise you, LORD,
   and I will honour you
   among the nations.
51 You give glorious victories
   to your chosen king.
Your faithful love for David
and for his descendants will never end.

CHAPTER 23

David's last words

1 These are the last words
   of David the son of Jesse.
The God of Jacob chose David
   and made him a great king.
The Mighty God of Israel loved him.*
When God told him to speak,
   David said:
2 The Spirit of the LORD
   has told me what to say.
3 Our Mighty Rock,*
   the God of Jacob, told me,
"A ruler who obeys God
   and does right
4 is like the sunrise
   on a cloudless day,
or like rain that sparkles
   on the grass."*

---

*22.32 mighty rock: See the note at 22.2.
See also: 22.34: Hab 3.19.

*22.47; 23.3 mighty rock: See the note at 22.2.
See also: 22.50: Rom 15.9.

5 I have ruled this way,
    and God will never break
        his promise to me.
God's promise is complete
    and unchanging;
he will always help me
    and give me what I hope for.
6 But evil people are pulled up
    like thorn bushes.
They are not dug up by hand,
7 but with a sharp spear
    and are burnt on the spot.

David's warriors

The Three Warriors

This is also told in 1 Chronicles 11.10–19

8 These are the names of David's warriors: Ishbosheth* the son of Hachmon* was the leader of the Three Warriors.* In one battle, he killed eight hundred men with his spear.*

9 The next one of the Three Warriors was Eleazar the son of Dodo the Ahohite. One time when the Philistines were at war with Israel, he and David dared the Philistines to fight them. Every one of the Israelite soldiers turned and ran, 10 except Eleazar. He killed Philistines until his hand was cramped, and he couldn't let go of his sword. When Eleazar finished, all the Israelite troops had to do was come back and take the enemies' weapons and armour. The LORD gave Israel a great victory that day.

11 Next was Shammah the son of Agee the Hararite. One time the Philistines brought their army together to destroy a crop of peas growing in a field near Lehi. The rest of Israel's soldiers ran away from the Philistines, 12 but Shammah stood in the middle of the field and killed the Philistines. The crops were saved, and the LORD gave Israel a great victory.

13 One year at harvest time, the Three Warriors* went to meet David at Adullam Cave.* The Philistine army had set up camp in Rephaim Valley 14 and had taken over

Bethlehem. David was in his fortress, 15 and he was very thirsty. He said, "I wish I had a drink from the well by the gate at Bethlehem."

16 The Three Warriors* sneaked into the Philistine camp and got some water from the well near Bethlehem's gate. But after they brought the water back to David, he refused to drink it. Instead, he poured it out as a sacrifice 17 and said to the LORD, "I can't drink this water! It's like the blood of these men who risked their lives to get it for me."

The Three Warriors did these brave deeds.

The Thirty Warriors

This is also told in 1 Chronicles 11.20–47

18 Joab's brother Abishai was the leader of the Thirty Warriors,* and in one battle he killed three hundred men with his spear. He was as famous as the Three Warriors 19 and certainly just as famous as the rest of the Thirty Warriors. He was the commander of the Thirty Warriors, but he still did not become one of the Three Warriors.

20 Benaiah the son of Jehoiada was a brave man from Kabzeel who did some amazing things. He killed two of Moab's best fighters,* and on a snowy day he went down into a pit and killed a lion. 21 Another time, he killed an Egyptian, as big as a giant.* The Egyptian was armed with a spear, but Benaiah only had a club. Benaiah grabbed the spear from the Egyptian and killed him with it. 22-23 Benaiah did these things. He never became one of the Three Warriors, but he was just as famous as they were and certainly just as famous as the rest of the Thirty Warriors. David made him the leader of his bodyguard.

24-39 Some of the Thirty Warriors were:

Asahel the brother of Joab
Elhanan the son of Dodo from Bethlehem
Shammah from Harod
Elika from Harod
Helez the Paltite
Ira the son of Ikkesh from Tekoa
Abiezer from Anathoth
Mebunnai* the Hushathite
Zalmon the Ahohite
Maharai from Netophah
Heleb the son of Baanah from Netophah
Ittai the son of Ribai from Gibeah of the
    tribe of Benjamin
Benaiah from Pirathon

---

*23.8 Ishbosheth: Hebrew "Josheb Bashebeth", which seems to be another spelling of Ishbosheth. See the note at 2.8, although this is a different Ishbosheth.
*23.8 the Three Warriors: The most honoured group of warriors. They may have been part of the Thirty Warriors. "Three" and "thirty" are spelt almost the same in Hebrew, so there is some confusion in the manuscripts as to which group is being talked about in some places in the following lists.
*23.13 Adullam Cave: This may have happened during the time that David was an outlaw (see 1 Samuel 22.1–6).

*23.18 the Thirty Warriors: The second most honoured group of warriors. They may have also been officers in the army (see the note at 23.8).

315

Hiddai from the streams on Mount Gaash
Abialbon from Beth-Arabah
Azmaveth from Bahurim'
Eliahba from Shaalbon
Jashen'
Jonathan the son of Shammah the
    Hararite'
Ahiam the son of Sharar the Hararite
Eliphelet the son of Ahasbai from Maacah
Eliam the son of Ahithophel from Gilo
Hezro from Carmel
Paarai the Arbite
Igal the son of Nathan from Zobah
Bani the Gadite
Zelek from Ammon
Naharai from Beeroth, who carried the
    weapons of Joab the son of Zeruiah
Ira the Ithrite
Gareb the Ithrite
Uriah the Hittite

There were thirty-seven in all.

David counts the people of Israel, and Israel is punished

CHAPTER 24

David counts the people

This is also told in 1 Chronicles 21.1-6

[1] The LORD was angry with Israel again, and he made David think it would be a good idea to count the people in Israel and Judah. [2] So David told Joab and the army officers,' "Go to every tribe in Israel, from the town of Dan in the north all the way south to Beersheba, and count everyone who can serve in the army. I want to know how many there are."

[3] Joab answered, "I hope the LORD your God will give you a hundred times more soldiers than you already have. I hope you will live to see that day! But why do you want to do a thing like this?"

[4] But when David refused to change his mind, Joab and the army officers went out and started counting the people. [5] They crossed the River Jordan and began with' Aroer and the town in the middle of the river valley. From there they went towards Gad and on as far as Jazer. [6] They went to Gilead and to Kadesh in Syria.' Then they went to Dan, Ijon,' and on towards Sidon. [7] They came to the fortress of Tyre, then went through every town of the Hivites and the Canaanites. Finally, they went to Beersheba in the Southern Desert of Judah. [8] After they

had gone through the whole land, they went back to Jerusalem. It had taken them nine months and twenty days.

[9] Joab came and told David, "In Israel there are eight hundred thousand who can serve in the army, and in Judah there are five hundred thousand."

The LORD punishes David

This is also told in 1 Chronicles 21.7-17

[10] After David had everyone counted, he felt guilty and told the LORD, "What I did was stupid and terribly wrong. LORD, please forgive me."

[11] Before David even got up the next morning, the LORD had told David's prophet Gad [12-13] to take a message to David. Gad went to David and told him:

You must choose one of three ways for the LORD to punish you: will there be seven' years when the land won't grow enough food for your people? Or will your enemies chase you and make you run from them for three months? Or will there be three days of horrible disease in your land? Think about it and decide, because I have to give your answer to God, who sent me.

[14] David was really frightened and said, "It's a terrible choice to make! But the LORD is kind, and I'd rather be punished by him than by anyone else."

[15-16] So that morning, the LORD sent an angel to spread a horrible disease everywhere in Israel, from Dan to Beersheba. And before it was over, seventy thousand people had died.

When the angel was about to destroy Jerusalem, the LORD felt sorry for all the suffering he had caused and told the angel, "That's enough! Don't touch them." This happened at the threshing place that belonged to Araunah the Jebusite.

[17] David saw the angel killing everyone and told the LORD, "These people are like sheep with me as their shepherd.' I have sinned terribly, but they have done nothing wrong. Please, punish me and my family instead of them!"

David buys Araunah's threshing place

This is also told in 1 Chronicles 21.18—22.1

[18-19] That same day the prophet Gad came and told David, "Go to the threshing place that belongs to Araunah and build an altar there for the LORD."

So David went.

²⁰ Araunah looked and saw David and his soldiers coming up towards him. He went over to David, bowed down low, ²¹ and said, "Your Majesty! Why have you come to see me?"

David answered, "I've come to buy your threshing place. I have to build the LORD an altar here, so this disease will stop killing the people."

²² Araunah said, "Take whatever you want and offer your sacrifice. Here are some oxen for the sacrifice. You can use the threshing-boards* and the wooden yokes for the fire. ²³ Take them — they're yours! I hope the LORD your God will be pleased with you."

²⁴ But David answered, "No! I have to pay you what they're worth. I can't offer the LORD my God a sacrifice that I got for nothing." So David bought the threshing place and the oxen for fifty pieces of silver. ²⁵ Then he built an altar for the LORD. He sacrificed animals and burnt them on the altar.

The LORD answered the prayers of the people, and no else died from the terrible disease.

---

*24.22 threshing-boards: Heavy boards with bits of rock or metal on the bottom. They were dragged across the grain to separate the husks from the kernels.

Additional notes

›1.9 in terrible pain: Or "very weak".

›1.26 You . . . husband: Or "You loved me more than a wife could possibly love her husband."

›2.16 Field of Daggers: Or "Field of Opponents" or "Battlefield".

›2.29 all morning: One possible meaning for the difficult Hebrew text.

›3.12 You . . . nation: Or "I like you."

›3.26 well at Sirah: Or "oasis of Sirah" or "cistern at Sirah".

›3.29 cowards: One possible meaning for the difficult Hebrew text.

›3.33 outlaw: Or "fool".

›3.39 God . . . back: Or "I pray that God will pay them back".

›4.1 Ishbosheth: Hebrew "The son of Saul."

›5.7–9 You will . . . or see: One possible meaning for the difficult Hebrew text.

›5.7–9 capital: Or "palace".

›5.13 from Jerusalem: Or "in Jerusalem".

›5.20 The Lord Broke Through: Or "Baal-Perazim".

›5.23 balsam: One possible meaning for the difficult Hebrew text.

›6.2 to Baalah . . . there: The Dead Sea Scrolls and 1 Chronicles 13.6; the Standard Hebrew Text "from Baalah in Judah. They had gone there".

›6.2 he is worshipped there: Or "the chest belongs to him."

›6.3,4 Ahio . . . Ahio: Or "his brother . . . his brother".

›6.8 Bursting . . . Uzzah: Or "Perez-Uzzah".

›6.10 Gath: Or perhaps "Gittaim".

›7.19 Is this . . . people: One possible meaning for the difficult Hebrew text.

›7.23 You . . . here: One possible meaning for the difficult Hebrew text.

›8.1 Israel . . . control: Or "David also took the town of Metheg-Ammah away from them."

›8.3 David . . . way: One possible meaning for the difficult Hebrew text. It may have been Hadadezer who was going to the River Euphrates. And he may have gone there either to build a monument or to put down a rebellion.

›8.4 seventeen hundred cavalry: Hebrew; one ancient translation and 1 Chronicles 18.4 "a thousand chariots and seven thousand cavalry".

›8.4 He also captured . . . them: Or "He crippled all but one hundred of the horses".

›8.7 Hadadezer's . . . cases: Or "Hadadezer's soldiers carried gold shields, but David took these shields".

›8.9,10 defeated: Or "killed".

›8.12 Edom: Some Hebrew manuscripts and two ancient translations (see also 1 Chronicles 18.11); most Hebrew manuscripts "Aram". In Hebrew the words for "Edom" and "Aram" look almost alike.

›8.13 Edomite: Some Hebrew manuscripts and two ancient translations (see also 1 Chronicles 18.12); most Hebrew manuscripts "Aramean". In Hebrew the words for "Edomite" and "Aramean" look almost alike.

›8.13 built a monument: Or "was famous".

›8.17 Abiathar the son of Ahimelech: One ancient translation and 1 Samuel 22.11–23; Hebrew "Ahimelech the son of Abiathar".

›8.18 was the commander of: Not in the Hebrew text of this verse, but see 1 Chronicles 18.17.

›8.18 David's bodyguard: The Hebrew text has "the Cherethites and the Pelethites", who were foreign soldiers hired by David to be his bodyguard.

›9.10 Saul's family and servants: Some manuscripts of one ancient translation; Hebrew "the son of your master".

›9.11–13 David's: Hebrew "my".

›10.18 cavalry: The Hebrew manuscripts and ancient translations differ as to how many and what kind of soldiers were killed.

›11.1 when . . . war: Or "when the messengers had gone to Ammon" (see 10.2) or "the time when the kings had gone to war" (see 10.6–8).

›11.11 somewhere in the fields: Or "at Succoth".

›11.21 Gideon: The Hebrew text has Jerubbesheth, which stands for "Jerubbaal", another name for Gideon. See Judges 6.32 and the note on "bosheth" at 2.8 ("besheth" means the same as "bosheth").

›11.25 break . . . walls: Or "destroy it."

›12.13,14 what . . . wanted: One manuscript of one ancient translation; one Hebrew manuscript "what the LORD had said"; most Hebrew manuscripts "what the enemies of the Lord would think".

ᵃ**12.30 the statue of their god Milcom:** Or "their king."

ᵃ**12.30 David . . . crown:** Or "and David wore the crown."

ᵃ**12.31 tear . . . walls:** One possible meaning for the difficult Hebrew text.

ᵃ**13.6 special bread:** Or "heart-shaped bread" or "dumplings."

ᵃ**13.18 long . . . sleeves:** One possible meaning for the difficult Hebrew text.

ᵃ**13.21 But Amnon . . . unhappy:** The Dead Sea Scrolls and one ancient translation; these words are not in the Standard Hebrew Text.

ᵃ**13.27 Absalom prepared . . . king:** One ancient translation; these words are not in the Hebrew text.

ᵃ**13.32 David's nephew:** The Hebrew text has "the son of David's brother Shimeah."

ᵃ**13.34 the road to Horonaim:** Or "the road behind him" or "the road to the west".

ᵃ**13.34 He . . . Road:** One ancient translation; these words are not in the Hebrew text.

ᵃ**13.39 David . . . Absalom:** Or "David was comforted over the loss of Amnon, and he no longer wanted to take his army there to capture Absalom."

ᵃ**14.9 I hope . . . me:** Or "May I speak some more?"

ᵃ**14.14 take our lives:** Or "make any exceptions".

ᵃ**14.16 take . . . us:** Or "make sure we have no part in God's people."

ᵃ**15.2 the city gate:** Or "the entrance to the king's palace."

ᵃ**15.7 Four years:** The Hebrew text has "forty years".

ᵃ**15.8 in Hebron:** Some manuscripts of one ancient translation; these words are not in the Hebrew text.

ᵃ**15.18 bodyguards:** See the note at 8.18.

ᵃ**15.20 I pray . . . be:** One ancient translation; these words are not in the Hebrew text.

ᵃ**15.27 you . . . things:** Or "You are a prophet" or "You are not a prophet".

ᵃ**16.1 figs:** Or "pomegranates", a bright red fruit that looks like an apple.

ᵃ**16.14 they:** Hebrew "he".

ᵃ**17.3 back to you . . . husband:** One ancient translation; Hebrew "back to you. The man you are chasing is like bringing back the whole nation."

ᵃ**17.25 Ithra:** Or "Jether".

ᵃ**17.25 the family of Ishmael:** Some manuscripts of one ancient translation; other manuscripts of the same translation "the town of Jezreel"; Hebrew "the people of Israel".

ᵃ**18.7,8 Twenty . . . killed:** This may refer to the total number or to the number of Absalom's soldiers who were killed.

ᵃ**18.9 head:** Or "hair".

ᵃ**18.33 son:** In Hebrew, this verse is 19.1.

ᵃ**19.17 waded across:** Or "rushed".

ᵃ**19.26 I told . . . me:** Two ancient translations; Hebrew, "I said, 'I will saddle a donkey for myself.' "

ᵃ**19.37 My servant Chimham:** Or "My son Chimham".

ᵃ**20.6 get . . . us:** One possible meaning for the difficult Hebrew text.

ᵃ**20.7 bodyguard:** See the note at 8.18.

ᵃ**20.14 best soldiers:** One ancient translation; the

difficult Hebrew text may mean either "Berites" or "Bichrites", Sheba's relatives.

ᵃ**20.16 the top of the wall:** Or "the town".

ᵃ**20.23 David's bodyguard:** See the note at 8.18.

ᵃ**20.24 Adoram:** One ancient translation "Adoniram" (see 1 Kings 4.6; 5.14).

ᵃ**21.4 I'll . . . ask:** Or "What are you asking me to do for you?"

ᵃ**21.6 hang:** One possible meaning for the difficult Hebrew text.

ᵃ**21.8 Meholah:** Also known as Abel-Meholah.

ᵃ**21.9 hanged:** One possible meaning for the difficult Hebrew text.

ᵃ**21.13,14 hanged:** See the note at 21.9.

ᵃ**21.16 new sword:** One possible meaning for the difficult Hebrew text.

ᵃ**21.16 spearhead:** Or "helmet".

ᵃ**21.19 Jari:** Or "Jaare".

ᵃ**22.3 powerful weapon:** The Hebrew text has "the horn", which refers to the horn of a bull, one of the most powerful animals in ancient Palestine.

ᵃ**22.11 appeared:** Most Hebrew manuscripts; some Hebrew manuscripts "swooped down" (see Psalm 18.10).

ᵃ**23.1 The Mighty . . . him:** Or "He wrote Israel's favourite songs."

ᵃ**23.4 sparkles . . . grass:** Or "makes the grass grow."

ᵃ**23.8 the son of Hachmon:** Or "the Tahchemonite" (see 1 Chronicles 11.11).

ᵃ**23.8 with . . . spear:** One possible meaning for the difficult Hebrew text (see 1 Chronicles 11.11).

ᵃ**23.13 the Three Warriors:** Or "three warriors"; Hebrew "three of the thirty most important".

ᵃ**23.16 the Three Warriors:** Or "three warriors".

ᵃ**23.20 Moab's best fighters:** Or "big lions in Moab"; one ancient translation "sons of Ariel from Moab".

ᵃ**23.21 Egyptian . . . giant:** 1 Chronicles 11.23; in this verse the Hebrew text has "good-looking Egyptian."

ᵃ**23.24–39 Mebunnai:** Or "Sibbecai" (see 1 Chronicles 11.26–47).

ᵃ**23.24–39 Bahurim:** Or "Barhum".

ᵃ**23.24–39 Jashen:** Hebrew "sons of Jashen".

ᵃ**23.24–39 Jonathan . . . Hararite:** Some manuscripts of one ancient translation (see 1 Chronicles 26–47). In the Hebrew text Jonathan and Shammah are separate members of the list.

ᵃ**24.2 Joab . . . officers:** Some manuscripts of one ancient translation (see 24.4); 1 Chronicles 21.2; Hebrew "Joab, the officer of the army".

ᵃ**24.5 began with:** Some manuscripts of one ancient translation; Hebrew "set up camp in".

ᵃ**24.6 Kadesh in Syria:** Or "the lower slopes of Mount Hermon."

ᵃ**24.6 Dan, Ijon:** Or "Danjaan", an unknown place.

ᵃ**24.12,13 seven:** Hebrew; some manuscripts of one ancient translation "three" (see 1 Chronicles 21.12).

ᵃ**24.17 as their shepherd:** The Dead Sea Scrolls, and some manuscripts of two ancient translations (see 1 Chronicles 21.17); these words are not in the Standard Hebrew Text of this verse.

1 Kings

A quick look at this book

The First Book of Kings is the first half of a
single book that was divided into two parts,
1 and 2 Kings, because together they were too
long to fit on one scroll. These books continue
the history of Israel.

The book of 1 Kings has three parts. The first
part (1—2) tells about the last years of

King David's life and how his son Solomon
became the king of Israel. The second part
(3—11) includes events from Solomon's rule
and tells how famous and rich he was. Much
of this second part tells how Solomon built and
dedicated the temple in Jerusalem. The last
part of the book (12—22) reports what
happened after Solomon's death — the
northern tribes rebelled against Rehoboam his
son, and the nation of Israel was divided into
two separate kingdoms: Judah in the south
and Israel in the north. This part of 1 Kings
includes stories about the kings of these two
kingdoms. The book concludes with the rule of
King Jehoshaphat of Judah and King Ahaziah
of Israel.

Each king in the book is judged according to
his faithfulness to the Lord. If the king was
faithful and obeyed God's Law, he was praised
as being good; but if he disobeyed and did
wrong, he was condemned as being evil. All
the kings of Israel were judged to be evil,
because they rejected the Lord and
worshipped idols. However, most of the kings
of Judah were judged to be good, because
they followed the example of their ancestor
King David and worshipped the Lord.

The First Book of Kings also includes the
familiar stories about Elijah the prophet, who
opposed the evil King Ahab and Queen Jezebel
of the northern kingdom. Elijah warned the
people of Israel to obey the Lord and not to
worship other gods. Elijah wanted to prove
that the Lord was the one true God, and so he
arranged a contest between the Lord and the
pagan god Baal. Elijah and the prophets of

Baal would offer a sacrifice to their own God, but the fire on the altars would not be lit. Elijah explained to the people:

> How much longer will you try to have things both ways? If the LORD is God, worship him! But if Baal is God, worship him! . . . The prophets of Baal will pray to their god, and I will pray to the LORD. The one who answers by starting the fire is God.

(18.21,24)

Solomon becomes king

CHAPTER 1

David in his old age

¹ King David was now an old man, and he always felt cold, even under a lot of blankets. ² His officials said, "Your Majesty, we will look for a young woman to take care of you. She can lie down beside you and keep you warm." ³⁻⁴ They looked everywhere in Israel until they found a very beautiful young woman named Abishag, who lived in the town of Shunem.* They brought her to David, and she took care of him. But David did not have sex with her.

Adonijah tries to become king

⁵⁻⁶ Adonijah was the son of David and Haggith. He was Absalom's younger brother* and was very handsome. One day, Adonijah started boasting, "I'm going to make myself king!" So he got some chariots and horses, and he hired fifty men as bodyguards. David did not want to hurt his feelings, so he never asked Adonijah why he was doing these things.

⁷ Adonijah met with Joab the son of Zeruiah and Abiathar the priest and asked them if they would help him become king. Both of them agreed to help. ⁸ But Zadok the priest, Benaiah the son of Jehoiada, Nathan the prophet, Shimei, Rei,* and David's bodyguards all refused.

⁹ Adonijah invited his brothers and David's officials from Judah to go with him to Crawling Rock* near Rogel Spring, where he sacrificed some sheep, cattle, and fat calves.* ¹⁰ But he did not invite Nathan, Benaiah, David's bodyguards, or his own brother Solomon.

¹¹ When Nathan heard what had happened, he asked Bathsheba, Solomon's mother:

> Have you heard that Adonijah the son of Haggith has made himself king? But David doesn't know a thing about it. ¹² You and your son Solomon will be killed, unless you do what I tell you. ¹³ Go and say to David, "You promised me that Solomon would be the next king. So why is Adonijah now king?"
>
> ¹⁴ While you are still talking to David, I'll come in and tell him that everything you said is true.

¹⁵ Meanwhile, David was in his bedroom where Abishag was taking care of him because he was so old. Bathsheba went in ¹⁶ and bowed down.

"What can I do for you?" David asked. ¹⁷ Bathsheba answered:

> Your Majesty, you promised me in the name of the LORD your God that my son Solomon would be the next king. ¹⁸ But Adonijah has already been made king, and you didn't know anything about it. ¹⁹ He sacrificed a lot of cattle, calves, and sheep. And he invited Abiathar the priest, Joab your army commander, and all your sons to be there, except Solomon, your loyal servant.
>
> ²⁰ Your Majesty, everyone in Israel is waiting for you to announce who will be the next king. ²¹ If you don't, they will say that Solomon and I have rebelled. They will treat us like criminals and kill us as soon as you die.

²² Just then, Nathan the prophet arrived. ²³ Someone told David that he was there, and Nathan came in. He bowed with his face to the ground ²⁴ and said:

> Your Majesty, did you say that Adonijah would be king? ²⁵ Earlier today, he sacrificed a lot of cattle, calves, and sheep. He invited the army commanders, Abiathar, and all your sons to be there. Now they are eating and drinking and shouting,

---

*1.3,4 Shunem: A town in northern Israel, just north of Jezreel Valley.
*1.5,6 brother: Since Absalom was dead, Adonijah was now David's eldest living son and would be next in line to be king.
See also: 1.5: 2 Sam 3.4.

*1.9 sacrificed . . . calves: This was part of a ceremony where Adonijah was made the new king.
See also: 1.11: 2 Sam 12.24.

"Long live King Adonijah!" 26 But he didn't invite me or Zadok the priest or Benaiah or Solomon. 27 Did you say they could do this without telling the rest of us who would be the next king?

Solomon becomes king

28 David said, "Tell Bathsheba to come here." She came and stood in front of him.

29-30 Then he said, "The living LORD God of Israel has kept me safe. And so today, I will keep the promise I made to you in his name: Solomon will be the next king!"

31 Bathsheba bowed with her face to the ground and said, "Your Majesty, I pray that you will live a long time!"

32 Then David said, "Tell Zadok, Nathan, and Benaiah to come here."

When they arrived, 33 he told them:

Take along some of my officials and let Solomon ride my own mule to Gihon Spring. 34 When you get there, Zadok and Nathan will make Solomon the new king of Israel. Then after the ceremony* is over, make someone blow a trumpet and tell everyone to shout, "Long live King Solomon!" 35 Bring him back here, and he will take my place as king. He is the one I have chosen to rule Israel and Judah.

36 Benaiah answered, "We will do it, Your Majesty. I pray that the LORD your God will let it happen. 37 The LORD has always watched over you, and I pray that he will now watch over Solomon. May the LORD help Solomon to be an even greater king than you."

38 Zadok, Nathan, and Benaiah left and took along the two groups of David's special bodyguards.* Solomon rode on David's mule as they led him to Gihon Spring. 39 Zadok the priest brought some olive oil from the sacred tent and poured it on Solomon's head to show that he was now king. A trumpet was blown and everyone shouted, "Long live King Solomon!" 40 Then they played flutes and celebrated as they followed Solomon back to Jerusalem. They made so much noise that the ground shook.

41 Adonijah and his guests had almost finished eating when they heard the noise. Joab also heard the trumpet and asked, "What's all that noise about in the city?"

42 Just then, Jonathan son of Abiathar came running up. "Come in," Adonijah said. "An important man like you must have some good news."

43 Jonathan answered:

No, I haven't! David has just announced that Solomon will be king. 44-45 Solomon rode David's own mule to Gihon Spring, and Zadok, Nathan, Benaiah, and David's special bodyguards* went with him. When they got there, Zadok and Nathan made Solomon king. Then everyone celebrated all the way back to Jerusalem. That's the noise you hear in the city. 46 Solomon is now king.

47 And listen to this! David's officials told him, "We pray that your God will help Solomon to be an even greater king!"

David was in his bed at the time, but he bowed 48 and prayed, "I praise you, LORD God of Israel. You have made my son Solomon king and have let me live to see it."

49 Adonijah's guests shook with fear when they heard this news, and they left as fast as they could. 50 Adonijah himself was afraid of what Solomon might do to him, so he ran to the sacred tent and grabbed hold of the corners of the altar for protection.*

51 Someone told Solomon, "Adonijah is afraid of you and is holding on to the corners of the altar. He wants you to promise that you won't kill him."

52 Solomon answered, "If Adonijah doesn't cause any trouble, I won't hurt him. But if he does, I'll have him killed." 53 Then he sent someone to the altar to get Adonijah.

After Adonijah came and bowed down, Solomon said, "Adonijah, go home."

David's final words and his death

CHAPTER 2

David's instructions to Solomon

1 Not long before David died, he told Solomon:

2 My son, I will soon die, as everyone must. But I want you to be strong and brave. 3 Do what the LORD your God commands and

---

*1.34 the ceremony: Part of this ceremony was pouring olive oil on Solomon's head to show that he was now king.

*1.50 the corners . . . for protection: The four corners of some ancient altars looked like animal horns. Since the entire altar was sacred, anyone holding on to its corners was supposed to be safe from being killed.

follow his teachings. Obey everything written in the Law of Moses. Then you will be a success, no matter what you do or where you go. 4 You and your descendants must always faithfully obey the LORD. If you do, he will keep the solemn promise he made to me that someone from our family will always be king of Israel.

5 Solomon, don't forget what Joab did to me by killing Abner son of Ner and Amasa son of Jether, the two commanders of Israel's army. He killed them as if they were his enemies in a war, but he did it when there was no war.* He is guilty, and now it's up to you to punish him 6 in the way you think best. Whatever you do, don't let him die peacefully in his old age.

7 The sons of Barzillai from Gilead helped me when I was running from your brother Absalom.* Be kind to them and let them eat at your table.

8 Be sure to do something about Shimei son of Gera from Bahurim in the territory of Benjamin. He cursed and insulted me the day I went to Mahanaim. But later, when he came to meet me at the River Jordan, I promised that I wouldn't kill him.* 9 Now you must punish him. He's an old man, but you're wise enough to know that you must have him killed.

David dies

10-11 David was king of Israel forty years. He ruled seven years from Hebron and thirty-three years from Jerusalem. Then he died and was buried in Jerusalem. 12 His son Solomon became king and took control of David's kingdom.

Solomon takes control of the kingdom

Adonijah is killed

13 One day, Adonijah went to see Bathsheba, Solomon's mother, and she asked, "Is this a friendly visit?"

"Yes. 14 I just want to talk with you."

"All right," she told him, "go ahead."

15 "You know that I was king for a little while," Adonijah replied. "And everyone in Israel accepted me as their ruler. But the LORD wanted my brother to be king, so now things have changed. 16 Would you do me a favour?"

"What do you want?" Bathsheba asked.

17 "Please ask Solomon to let me marry Abishag. He won't say no to you."

18 "All right," she said. "I'll ask him."

19 When Bathsheba went to see Solomon, he stood up to meet her, then bowed low. He sat back down and had another throne brought in, so his mother could sit at his right side.* 20 Bathsheba sat down and then asked, "Would you do me a small favour?"

Solomon replied, "Mother, just tell me what you want, and I will do it."

21 "Allow your brother Adonijah to marry Abishag," she answered.

22 Solomon said:

What? Let my elder brother marry Abishag? You may as well ask me to let him rule the kingdom! And why don't you ask such favours for Abiathar and Joab?

23 I swear in the name of the LORD that Adonijah will die because he asked for this! If he doesn't, I pray that God will severely punish me. 24 The LORD made me king in my father's place and promised that the kings of Israel would come from my family. Yes, I swear by the living LORD that Adonijah will die today.

25 "Benaiah," Solomon shouted, "go and kill Adonijah." So Adonijah died.

Abiathar is sent back home

26 Solomon sent for Abiathar the priest and said:

Abiathar, go back home to Anathoth! You ought to be killed too, but I won't do it now. When my father David was king, you were in charge of the sacred chest, and you went through a lot of hard times with my father. 27 But I won't let you be a priest of the LORD any more.

And so the promise that the LORD had made at Shiloh about the family of Eli came true.*

---

*2.5 war: See 2 Samuel 3.22–27 and 20.7–10.
*2.7 Absalom: See 2 Samuel 17.27–29.
*2.8 him: See 2 Samuel 16.5–14 and 19.16–23.

See also: 2.5: a 2 Sam 3.27; b 2 Sam 20.10.
2.7: 2 Sam 17.27–29.   2.8: 2 Sam 16.5–13; 19.16–23.
2.11: 2 Sam 5.4,5; 1 Chron 3.4.   2.12: 1 Chron 29.23.

*2.19 at his right side: The place of honour.
*2.27 the promise . . . came true: See
1 Samuel 2.27–34.

See also: 2.17: 1 King 1.3,4.   2.26: a 2 Sam 15.24;
b 1 Sam 22.20–23.   2.27: 1 Sam 2.27–36.

Joab is killed

28 Joab had not helped Absalom try to become king, but he had helped Adonijah. So when Joab learnt that Adonijah had been killed, he ran to the sacred tent and grabbed hold of the corners of the altar for protection.* 29 When Solomon heard about this, he sent someone to ask Joab, "Why did you run to the altar?"

Joab sent back his answer, "I was afraid of you, and I ran to the LORD for protection."

Then Solomon shouted, "Benaiah, go and kill Joab!"

30 Benaiah went to the sacred tent and yelled, "Joab, the king orders you to come out!"

"No!" Joab answered. "Kill me right here."

Benaiah went back and told Solomon what Joab had said.

31-32 Solomon replied:

Do what Joab said. Kill him and bury him! Then my family and I won't be responsible for what he did to Abner the commander of Israel's army and to Amasa the commander of Judah's army. He killed those innocent men without my father knowing about it. Both of them were better men than Joab. Now the LORD will make him pay for those murders. 33 Joab's family will always suffer because of what he did, but the LORD will always bless David's family and his kingdom with peace.

34 Benaiah went back and killed Joab. His body was taken away and buried near his home in the desert.

35 Solomon put Benaiah in Joab's place as army commander, and he put Zadok in Abiathar's place as priest.

Shimei is killed

36 Solomon sent for Shimei and said, "Build a house here in Jerusalem and live in it. But whatever you do, don't leave the city! 37 If you ever cross Kidron Valley and leave Jerusalem, you will be killed. And it will be your own fault."

38 "That's fair, Your Majesty," Shimei answered. "I'll do that." So Shimei lived in Jerusalem from then on.

39 About three years later, two of Shimei's servants ran off to King Achish in Gath. When Shimei found out where they were, 40 he saddled his donkey and went after them. He found them and brought them back to Jerusalem.

41 Someone told Solomon that Shimei had gone to Gath and was back. 42 Solomon sent for him and said:

Shimei, you promised in the name of the LORD that you would never leave Jerusalem. I warned you that you would die if you did. You agreed that this was fair, didn't you? 43 You have disobeyed me and have broken the promise you made to the LORD.

44 I know you remember all the cruel things you did to my father David. Now the LORD is going to punish you for what you did. 45 But the LORD will bless me and make my father's kingdom strong for ever.

46 "Benaiah," Solomon shouted, "kill Shimei." So Shimei died.

Solomon was now in complete control of his kingdom.

Solomon's wisdom and his officials

CHAPTER 3

The LORD makes Solomon wise

This is also told in 2 Chronicles 1.1–13

1 Solomon signed a treaty with the king of Egypt and married his daughter. She lived in the older part of Jerusalem† until the palace, the LORD's temple, and the wall around Jerusalem were completed.

2 At that time, there was no temple for worshipping the LORD, and everyone offered sacrifices at the local shrines. 3 Solomon loved the LORD and followed his father David's instructions, but Solomon also offered sacrifices and burnt incense at the shrines.

4 The most important shrine was in Gibeon, and Solomon had offered more than a thousand sacrifices on that altar. 5 One night while Solomon was in Gibeon, the LORD God appeared to him in a dream and said, "Solomon, ask for anything you want, and I will give it to you."

6 Solomon answered:

My father David, your servant, was honest and did what you commanded. You were always loyal to him, and you gave him a son who is now king. 7 LORD God, I'm your servant, and you've made me king in my father's place. But I'm very young and know so little about being a leader. 8 And now I must rule your chosen people, even though there are too many of them to count.

*2.28 the corners . . . for protection: See the note at 1.50.

9 Please make me wise and teach me the difference between right and wrong. Then I will know how to rule my people. If you don't, there is no way I could rule this great nation of yours.

10-11 God said:

Solomon, I'm pleased that you asked for this. You could have asked to live a long time or to be rich. Or you could have asked for your enemies to be destroyed. Instead, you asked for wisdom to make right decisions. 12 So I'll make you wiser than anyone who has ever lived or ever will live. 13 I'll also give you what you didn't ask for. You'll be rich and respected as long as you live, and you'll be greater than any other king. 14 If you obey me and follow my commands, as your father David did, I'll let you live a long time.

15 Solomon woke up and realized that God had spoken to him in the dream. He went back to Jerusalem and stood in front of the sacred chest, where he offered sacrifices to please the Lord* and sacrifices to ask his blessing.* Then Solomon gave a feast for his officials.

Solomon makes a difficult decision

16 One day two women* came to King Solomon, 17 and one of them said:

Your Majesty, this woman and I live in the same house. Not long ago my baby was born at home, 18 and three days later her baby was born. Nobody else was there with us.

19 One night while we were all asleep, she rolled over on her baby, and she died. 20 Then while I was still asleep, she got up and took my son out of my bed. She put him in her bed, then she put her dead baby next to me.

21 In the morning when I got up to feed my son, I saw that he was dead. But when I looked at him in the light, I knew he wasn't my son.

22 "No!" the other woman shouted. "He was your son. My baby is alive!"

"The dead baby is yours," the first woman yelled. "Mine is alive!"

They argued back and forth in front of Solomon, 23 until finally he said, "Both of you say this live baby is yours. 24 Someone bring me a sword."

A sword was brought, and Solomon ordered, 25 "Cut the baby in half! That way each of you can have part of him."

26 "Please don't kill my son," the baby's mother screamed. "Your Majesty, I love him very much, but give him to her. Just don't kill him."

The other woman shouted, "Go ahead and cut him in half. Then neither of us will have the baby."

27 Solomon said, "Don't kill the baby." Then he pointed to the first woman, "She is his real mother. Give the baby to her."

28 Everyone in Israel was amazed when they heard how Solomon had made his decision. They realized that God had given him wisdom to judge fairly.

CHAPTER 4

Solomon's officials

1-6 Here is a list of Solomon's highest officials while he was king of Israel:

Azariah son of Zadok was the priest;
Elihoreph and Ahijah sons of Shisha were the secretaries;
Jehoshaphat son of Ahilud kept the government records;
Benaiah son of Jehoiada was the army commander;
Zadok and Abiathar were priests;
Azariah son of Nathan was in charge of the regional officers;
Zabud son of Nathan was a priest and the king's adviser;
Ahishar was the prime minister;
Adoniram son of Abda was in charge of the forced labour.

7 Solomon chose twelve regional officers, who took turns bringing food for him and his household. Each officer provided food from his region for one month of the year. 8 These were the twelve officers:

The son of Hur was in charge of the hill country of Ephraim.

9 The son of Deker was in charge of the towns of Makaz, Shaalbim, Beth-Shemesh, and Elon-Beth-Hanan.

10 The son of Hesed was in charge of the towns of Arubboth and Socoh, and the region of Hepher.

---

*3.15 sacrifices to please the Lord: See Leviticus 1.1–17.
*3.15 sacrifices to ask his blessing: See Leviticus 3.1–17.

[11] The son of Abinadab was in charge of Naphath-Dor and was married to Solomon's daughter Taphath.

[12] Baana son of Ahilud was in charge of the towns of Taanach and Megiddo. He was also in charge of the whole region of Beth-Shan near the town of Zarethan, south of Jezreel from Beth-Shan to Abel-Meholah to the other side of Jokmeam.

[13] The son of Geber was in charge of the town of Ramoth in Gilead and the villages in Gilead belonging to the family of Jair, a descendant of Manasseh. He was also in charge of the region of Argob in Bashan, which had sixty walled towns with bronze bars on their gates.

[14] Ahinadab son of Iddo was in charge of the territory of Mahanaim.

[15] Ahimaaz was in charge of the territory of Naphtali and was married to Solomon's daughter Basemath.

[16] Baana son of Hushai was in charge of the territory of Asher and the town of Bealoth.

[17] Jehoshaphat son of Paruah was in charge of the territory of Issachar.

[18] Shimei son of Ela was in charge of the territory of Benjamin.

[19] Geber son of Uri was in charge of Gilead, where King Sihon of the Amorites and King Og of Bashan had lived.

And one officer was in charge of the territory of Judah.'

The size of Solomon's kingdom

[20] There were so many people living in Judah and Israel while Solomon was king that they seemed like grains of sand on a beach. Everyone had enough to eat and drink, and they were happy.

[21] Solomon ruled every kingdom between the River Euphrates and the land of the Philistines down to Egypt. These kingdoms paid him taxes as long as he lived.

[22] Every day, Solomon needed five thousand litres of fine flour, ten thousand litres of coarsely-ground flour, [23] ten grain-fed cattle, twenty pasture-fed cattle, one hundred sheep, as well as deer, gazelles, and geese.

[24] Solomon ruled the whole region west of the River Euphrates, from Tiphsah to Gaza, and he was at peace with all the countries around him. [25] Everyone living in Israel, from the town of Dan in the north to Beersheba in the south, was safe as long as Solomon lived.

Each family sat undisturbed beneath its own grape vines and fig trees.

[26] Solomon had forty thousand stalls of chariot horses and twelve thousand chariot soldiers.

[27] Each of the twelve regional officers brought food to Solomon and his household for one month of the year. They provided everything he needed, [28] as well as barley and straw for the horses.

Solomon's wisdom

[29] Solomon was brilliant. God had blessed him with insight and understanding. [30-31] He was wiser than anyone else in the world, including the wisest people of the east and of Egypt. He was even wiser than Ethan the Ezrahite, and Mahol's three sons, Heman, Calcol, and Darda. Solomon became famous in every country around Judah and Israel. [32] Solomon wrote three thousand wise sayings and composed more than a thousand songs. [33] He could talk about all kinds of plants, from large trees to small bushes, and he taught about animals, birds, reptiles, and fish. [34] Kings all over the world heard about Solomon's wisdom and sent people to listen to him teach.

Building and dedication of the Jerusalem temple

CHAPTER 5

Solomon asks Hiram to help build the temple

This is also told in 2 Chronicles 2.1–16

[1] King Hiram of Tyre* had always been friends with Solomon's father David. When Hiram learnt that Solomon was king, he sent some of his officials to meet with Solomon.

[2] Solomon sent a message back to Hiram:

[3] Remember how my father David wanted to build a temple where the LORD his God could be worshipped? But enemies kept attacking my father's kingdom, and he never had the chance. [4] Now, thanks to the LORD God, there is peace in my kingdom and no trouble or threat of war anywhere.

---

*5.1 Tyre: The most important city in Phoenicia. It was on the coast of the Mediterranean Sea north of Israel, in what is today southern Lebanon.

See also: 4.26: 1 King 10.26; 2 Chron 1.14; 9.25.
4.31: Psa 89 Title. 4.32: Prov 1.1; 10.1; 25.1; Song 1.1.

⁵ The LORD God promised my father that when his son became king, he would build a temple for worshipping the LORD. So I've decided to do that.

⁶ I'd like you to send your workers to cut down cedar trees in Lebanon for me. I will pay them whatever you say and will even make my workers help them. We both know that your workers are more experienced than anyone else at cutting timber.

⁷ Hiram was so happy when he heard Solomon's request that he said, "I am grateful that the LORD gave David such a wise son to be king of that great nation!" ⁸ Then he sent back his answer:

I received your message and will give you all the cedar and pine logs you need. ⁹ My workers will carry them down from Lebanon to the Mediterranean Sea. They will tie the logs together and float them along the coast to wherever you want them. Then they will untie the logs, and your workers can take them from there.

To pay for the logs, you can provide the grain I need for my household.

¹⁰ Hiram gave Solomon all the cedar and pine logs he needed. ¹¹ In return, Solomon gave Hiram two thousand tonnes of wheat and four hundred thousand litres of pure olive oil each year.

¹² The LORD kept his promise and made Solomon wise. Hiram and Solomon signed a treaty and never went to war against each other.

Solomon's workers

¹³ Solomon ordered thirty thousand people from all over Israel to cut logs for the temple, ¹⁴ and he put Adoniram in charge of these workers. Solomon divided them into three groups of ten thousand. Each group worked one month in Lebanon and had two months off at home.

¹⁵ He also had eighty thousand workers to cut stone in the hill country of Israel, seventy thousand workers to carry the stones, ¹⁶ and over three thousand assistants to keep track of the work and to supervise the workers.

¹⁷ He ordered the workers to cut and shape large blocks of good stone for the foundation of the temple.

¹⁸ Solomon's and Hiram's men worked with men from the city of Gebal,* and together they got the stones and logs ready for the temple.

CHAPTER 6

The outside of the temple is completed

¹ Solomon's workers started building the temple during Ziv,* the second month of the year. It had been four years since Solomon became king of Israel, and four hundred and eighty years since the people of Israel left Egypt.

² The inside of the LORD's temple was twenty-seven metres long, nine metres wide, and thirteen and a half metres high.

³ A four-and-a-half-metre porch went all the way across the front of the temple. ⁴ The windows were narrow on the outside but wide on the inside.

⁵⁻⁶ Along the sides and back of the temple, there were three levels of storage rooms. The rooms on the bottom level were just over two metres wide, the rooms on the middle level were over two and a half metres wide, and those on the top level were just over three metres wide. There were ledges on the outside of the temple that supported the beams of the storage rooms, so that nothing was built into the temple walls.

⁷ Solomon did not want the noise of hammers and axes to be heard at the place where the temple was being built. So he made the workers shape the blocks of stone at the quarry.

⁸ The entrance to the bottom storage rooms was on the south side of the building, and stairs to the other rooms were also there. ⁹ The roof of the temple was made out of beams and cedar boards.

The workers finished building the outside of the temple. ¹⁰ Storage rooms just over two metres high were all around the temple, and they were attached to the temple by cedar beams.

¹¹ The LORD told Solomon:

¹²⁻¹³ If you obey my commands and do what I say, I will keep the promise I made to your father David. I will live among my people Israel in this temple you are building, and I will not desert them.

¹⁴ So Solomon's workers finished building the temple.

See also: 5.5: 2 Sam 7.12,13; 1 Chron 17.11,12.
5.14: 1 King 12.18.

*5.18 Gebal: Later known as Byblos.
*6.1 Ziv: The second month of the Hebrew calendar, from about mid-April to mid-May.

The inside of the temple is furnished

This is also told in 2 Chronicles 3.8–14

15 The floor of the temple was made out of pine, and the walls were lined with cedar from floor to ceiling.'

16 The most holy place was in the back of the temple, and it was nine metres square. Cedar boards standing from floor to ceiling' separated it from the rest of the temple.

17 The temple's main room was eighteen metres long, and it was in front of the most holy place.

18 The inside walls were lined with cedar to hide the stones, and the cedar was decorated with carvings of gourds and flowers.

19 The sacred chest was kept in the most holy place. 20–22 This room was nine metres long, nine metres wide, and nine metres high, and it was lined with pure gold. There were also gold chains across the front of the most holy place. The inside of the temple, as well as the cedar altar in the most holy place, was covered with gold.

23 Solomon had two statues of winged creatures* made from olive wood to put in the most holy place. Each creature was four and a half metres tall 24–26 and four and a half metres across. They had two wings, and the wings were just over two metres long.

27 Solomon put them next to each other in the most holy place. Their wings were spread out and reached across the room. 28 The creatures were also covered with gold.

29 The walls of the two rooms were decorated with carvings of palm trees, flowers, and winged creatures. 30 Even the floor was covered with gold.

31–32 The two doors to the most holy place were made out of olive wood and were decorated with carvings of palm trees, flowers, and winged creatures. The doors and the carvings were covered with gold. The door frame came to a point at the top.

33–34 The two doors to the main room of the temple were made out of pine, and each one had two sections' so they could fold open. The door frame was shaped like a rectangle and was made out of olive wood. 35 The doors were covered with gold and were decorated with carvings of palm trees, flowers, and winged creatures.

36 The inner courtyard of the temple had walls made out of three layers of cut stones with one layer of cedar beams.

37 Work began on the temple during Ziv,* the second month of the year, four years after Solomon became king of Israel. 38 Seven years later the workers finished building it during Bul,* the eighth month of the year. It was built exactly as it had been planned.

CHAPTER 7

Solomon's palace is built

1 Solomon's palace took thirteen years to build.

2–3 Forest Hall was the largest room in the palace. It was forty-four metres long, twenty-two metres wide, and thirteen and a half metres high, and was lined with cedar from Lebanon. It had four rows of cedar pillars, fifteen in a row, and they held up forty-five cedar beams. The ceiling was covered with cedar. 4 Three rows of windows on each side faced each other, 5 and there were three doors on each side near the front of the hall.

6 Pillar Hall was twenty-two metres long and thirteen and a half metres wide. A covered porch supported by pillars went all the way across the front of the hall.

7 Solomon's throne was in Justice Hall, where he judged cases. This hall was completely lined with cedar.

8 The section of the palace where Solomon lived was behind Justice Hall and looked exactly like it. He had a similar place built for his wife, the daughter of the king of Egypt.

9 From the foundation all the way to the top, these buildings and the courtyard were made out of the best stones' carefully cut to size, then smoothed on every side with saws. 10 The foundation stones were huge, good stones — some of them four and a half metres long and others three and a half metres long. 11 The cedar beams and other stones that had been cut to size were on top of these foundation stones. The walls around the palace courtyard were made out of three layers of cut stones with one layer of cedar beams, just like the front porch and the inner courtyard of the temple.

---

*6.23 statues of winged creatures: These were symbols of the LORD's throne on earth (see Exodus 25.18–22).

See also: 6.16: Exod 26.33,34. **6.22:** Exod 30.1–3. **6.23–28:** Exod 25.18–20.

*6.37 Ziv: See the note at 6.1.
*6.38 Bul: The eighth month of the Hebrew calendar, from about mid-October to mid-November.

See also: 7.8: 1 King 3.1.

Hiram makes the bronze furnishings

This is also told in 2 Chronicles 3.15–17; 4.1–10

13-14 Hiram was a skilled bronze worker from the city of Tyre.* His father was now dead, but he also had been a bronze worker from Tyre, and his mother was from the tribe of Naphtali.

King Solomon asked Hiram to come to Jerusalem and make the bronze furnishings to use for worship in the LORD's temple, and he agreed to do it.

15 Hiram made two bronze columns eight metres tall and almost two metres across. 16 For the top of each column, he also made a bronze cap just over two metres high. 17 The caps were decorated with seven rows of designs that looked like chains,* 18 with two rows of designs that looked like pomegranates.*

19 The caps for the columns of the porch were almost two metres high and were shaped like lilies.* 20 The chain designs on the caps were just above the rounded tops of the two columns, and there were two hundred pomegranates in rows around each cap. 21 Hiram placed the two columns on each side of the main door of the temple. The column on the south side was called Jachin,* and the one on the north was called Boaz.*

22 The lily-shaped caps were on top of the columns.

This completed the work on the columns.

23 Hiram also made a large bowl called the Sea. It was just over two metres deep, about four and a half metres across, and thirteen and a half metres around. 24 Two rows of bronze gourds were around the outer edge of the bowl, ten gourds to about every forty-five centimetres. 25 The bowl itself sat on top of twelve bronze bulls with three bulls facing outwards in each of four directions. 26 The sides of the bowl were seventy-five millimetres thick, and its rim was like a cup that curved outwards like flower petals. The bowl held about forty thousand litres.

27 Hiram made ten moveable bronze stands, each one over a metre high, almost two metres long, and almost two metres wide. 28-29 The sides were made with panels attached to frames decorated with flower designs. The panels themselves were decorated with figures of lions, bulls, and winged creatures. 30-31 Each stand had four bronze wheels and axles and a round frame sixty-eight centimetres across, held up by four supports forty-five centimetres high. A small bowl rested in the frame. The supports were decorated with flower designs, and the frame with carvings.

The side panels of the stands were square, 32 and the wheels and axles were underneath them. The wheels were about sixty-eight centimetres high 33 and looked like chariot wheels. The axles, rims, spokes, and hubs were made out of bronze.

34-35 Around the top of each stand was a twenty-two-centimetre strip, and there were four braces* attached to the corners of each stand. The panels and the supports were attached to the stands, 36 and the stands were decorated with flower designs and figures of lions, palm trees, and winged creatures. 37 Hiram made the ten bronze stands from the same mould, so they were exactly the same size and shape.

38 Hiram also made ten small bronze bowls, one for each stand. The bowls were almost two metres across and could hold about eight hundred litres.

39 He put five stands on the south side of the temple, five stands on the north side, and the large bowl at the south-east corner of the temple.

40 Hiram made pans for hot ashes, and also shovels and sprinkling bowls.

A list of everything inside the temple

This is also told in 2 Chronicles 4.11–5.1

This is a list of the bronze items that Hiram made for the LORD's temple: 41 two columns; two bowl-shaped caps for the tops of the columns; two chain designs on the caps; 42 four hundred pomegranates* for the chain designs; 43 ten moveable stands; ten small bowls for the stands; 44 a large bowl; twelve bulls that held up the bowl; 45 pans for hot ashes, and also shovels and sprinkling bowls.

Hiram made these bronze things for Solomon 46 near the River Jordan between

---

*7.13,14 Hiram . . . city of Tyre: This is not the same person as "King Hiram of Tyre" (see 5.1).
*7.18 pomegranates: One possible meaning for the difficult Hebrew text of verse 18. A pomegranate is a bright red fruit that looks like an apple. In ancient times, it was a symbol of life.
*7.21 Jachin: Or "He makes secure".
*7.21 Boaz: Or "He is strong."

*7.34,35 braces: Or "handles".
*7.42 pomegranates: See the note at 7.18.
See also: 7.38: Exod 30.17–21.

Succoth and Zarethan by pouring melted bronze into clay moulds.

⁴⁷ There were so many bronze things that Solomon never bothered to weigh them, and no one ever knew how much bronze was used.

⁴⁸ Solomon gave orders to make the following temple furnishings out of gold: the altar; the table that held the sacred loaves of bread;* ⁴⁹ ten lampstands that went in front of the most holy place; flower designs; lamps and tongs; ⁵⁰ cups, lamp snuffers, and small sprinkling bowls; dishes for incense; fire pans; and the hinges for the doors to the most holy place and the main room of the temple.

⁵¹ After the LORD's temple was finished, Solomon put into its storage rooms everything that his father David had dedicated to the LORD, including the gold and the silver.

CHAPTER 8

Solomon brings the sacred chest to the temple

This is also told in 2 Chronicles 5.2—6.2

¹⁻² The sacred chest had been kept on Mount Zion, also known as the city of David. But Solomon decided to have the chest moved to the temple while everyone was in Jerusalem, celebrating the Festival of Shelters during Ethanim,* the seventh month of the year.

Solomon called together the important leaders of Israel. ³⁻⁴ Then the priests and the Levites carried to the temple the sacred chest, the sacred tent, and the objects used for worship. ⁵ Solomon and a crowd of people walked in front of the chest, and along the way they sacrificed more sheep and cattle than could be counted.

⁶ The priests carried the chest into the most holy place and put it under the winged creatures, ⁷ whose wings covered the chest and the poles used for carrying it. ⁸ The poles were so long that they could be seen from just outside the most holy place, but not from anywhere else. And they stayed there from then on.

⁹ The only things kept in the chest were the two flat stones Moses had put there when the LORD made his agreement with the people of Israel at Mount Sinai,* after bringing them out of Egypt.

¹⁰ Suddenly a cloud filled the temple as the priests were leaving the most holy place. ¹¹ The LORD's glory was in the cloud, and the light from it was so bright that the priests could not stay inside to do their work. ¹² Then Solomon prayed:

"Our LORD, you said that you
    would live in a dark cloud.
¹³ Now I have built a glorious temple
    where you can live for ever."

Solomon speaks to the people

This is also told in 2 Chronicles 6.3–11

¹⁴ Solomon turned towards the people standing there. Then he blessed them ¹⁵⁻¹⁶ and said:

Praise the LORD God of Israel! Long ago he brought his people out of Egypt. He later kept his promise to make my father David the king of Israel. The LORD also said that he had not chosen the city where his temple would be built.

¹⁷ So when David wanted to build a temple for the LORD God of Israel, ¹⁸ the LORD said, "It's good that you want to build a temple where I can be worshipped. ¹⁹ But you're not the one to do it. Your son will build a temple to honour me."

²⁰ The LORD has done what he promised. I am the king of Israel like my father, and I've built a temple for the LORD our God. ²¹ I've also made a place in the temple for the sacred chest. And in that chest are the two flat stones on which is written the solemn agreement the LORD made with our ancestors when he led them out of Egypt.

Solomon prays at the temple

This is also told in 2 Chronicles 6.12–42

²² Solomon stood facing the altar with everyone standing behind him. Then he lifted his arms towards heaven ²³ and prayed:

LORD God of Israel, no other god in heaven or on earth is like you!

---

*7.48 sacred loaves of bread: This bread was offered to the LORD and was a symbol of the LORD's presence in the temple. It was put out on a special table, and was replaced with fresh bread each week (see Leviticus 24.5–9).

*8.1,2 Ethanim: The seventh month of the Hebrew calendar, from about mid-September to mid-October.

See also: 7.48: a Exod 30.1–3; b Exod 25.23–30.
7.49: Exod 25.31–40. 7.51: 2 Sam 8.11; 1 Chron 18.11.
8.1: 2 Sam 6.12–16; 1 Chron 15.25–29. 8.2: Lev 23.34.

See also: 8.9: Deut 10.5. 8.10,11: Exod 40.34,35.
8.12: Psa 18.11; 97.2. 8.16: 2 Sam 7.4–11; 1 Chron 17.3–10.
8.17,18: 2 Sam 7.1–3; 1 Chron 17.1,2. 8.19: 2 Sam 7.12,13;
1 Chron 17.11,12.

You never forget the agreement you made with your people, and you are loyal to anyone who faithfully obeys your teachings. 24 My father David was your servant, and today you have kept every promise you made to him.

25 LORD God of Israel, you promised my father that someone from his family would always be king of Israel, if they do their best to obey you, just as he did. 26 Please keep this promise you made to your servant David.

27 There's not enough room in all of heaven for you, LORD God. How could you possibly live on earth in this temple I have built? 28 But I ask you to answer my prayer. 29 This is the temple where you have chosen to be worshipped. Please watch over it day and night and listen when I turn towards it and pray. 30 I am your servant, and the people of Israel belong to you. So whenever any of us look towards this temple and pray, answer from your home in heaven and forgive our sins.

31 Suppose someone accuses a person of a crime, and the accused has to stand in front of the altar in your temple and say, "I swear I am innocent!" 32 Listen from heaven and decide who is right. Then punish the guilty person and let the innocent one go free.

33 Suppose your people Israel sin against you, and then an enemy defeats them. If they come to this temple and beg for forgiveness, 34 listen from your home in heaven. Forgive them and bring them back to the land you gave their ancestors.

35 Suppose your people sin against you, and you punish them by holding back the rain. If they turn towards this temple and pray in your name and stop sinning, 36 listen from your home in heaven and forgive them. The people of Israel are your servants, so teach them to live right. And please send rain on the land you promised them for ever.

37 Sometimes the crops may dry up or rot or be eaten by locusts* or grasshoppers, and your people will be starving. Sometimes enemies may surround their towns, or your people will become sick with deadly diseases. 38 Listen when anyone in Israel truly feels sorry and sincerely prays with arms lifted towards your temple. 39 You know what is in everyone's heart. So from your home in heaven answer their prayers, according to the way they live and what is in their hearts. 40 Then your people will worship and obey you for as long as they live in the land you gave their ancestors.

41-42 Foreigners will hear about you and your mighty power, and some of them will come to live among your people Israel. If any of them pray towards this temple, 43 listen from your home in heaven and answer their prayers. Then everyone on earth will worship you, just like your people Israel, and they will know that I have built this temple to honour you.

44 Our LORD, sometimes you will order your people to attack their enemies. Then your people will turn towards this temple I have built for you in your chosen city, and they will pray to you. 45 Answer their prayers from heaven and give them victory.

46 Everyone sins. But when your people sin against you, suppose you get angry enough to let their enemies drag them away to foreign countries. 47-49 Later, they may feel sorry for what they did and ask your forgiveness. Answer them when they pray towards this temple I have built for you in your chosen city, here in this land you gave their ancestors. From your home in heaven, listen to their sincere prayers and do what they ask. 50 Forgive your people no matter how much they have sinned against you. Make the enemies who defeated them be kind to them. 51 Remember, they are the people you chose and rescued from Egypt that was like a blazing fire to them.

52 I am your servant, and the people of Israel belong to you. So listen when any of us pray and cry out for your help. 53 When you brought our ancestors out of Egypt, you told your servant Moses to say to them, "From all people on earth, the LORD God has chosen you to be his very own."

Solomon blesses the people

54 When Solomon finished his prayer at the altar, he was kneeling with his arms lifted towards heaven. He stood up, 55 turned towards the people, blessed them, and said loudly:

56 Praise the LORD! He has kept his promise and given us peace. Every good thing he promised to his servant Moses has happened.

---

*8.37 locusts: A type of grasshopper that comes in swarms and causes great damage to plant life.

See also: 8.25: 1 King 2.4. 8.27: 2 Chron 6.
8.29: Deut 12.11.

See also: 8.56: Deut 12.10; Josh 21.44,45.

⁵⁷ The LORD our God was with our ancestors to help them, and I pray that he will be with us and never abandon us. ⁵⁸ May the LORD help us obey him and follow all the laws and teachings he gave our ancestors.

⁵⁹ I pray that the LORD our God will remember my prayer day and night. May he help everyone in Israel each day, in whatever way we need it. ⁶⁰ Then every nation will know that the LORD is the only true God.

⁶¹ Obey the LORD our God and follow his commands with all your heart, just as you are doing today.

Solomon dedicates the temple

This is also told in 2 Chronicles 7.4–10

⁶²⁻⁶³ Solomon and the people dedicated the temple to the LORD by offering twenty-two thousand cattle and one hundred and twenty thousand sheep as sacrifices to ask the LORD's blessing.* ⁶⁴ On that day, Solomon dedicated the courtyard in front of the temple and made it acceptable for worship. He offered the sacrifices there because the bronze altar in front of the temple was too small.

⁶⁵ Solomon and the huge crowd celebrated the Festival of Shelters at the temple for seven days.* There were people from as far away as the Egyptian Gorge in the south and Lebo-Hamath in the north. ⁶⁶ Then on the eighth day, he sent everyone home. They said goodbye and left, very happy because of all the good things the LORD had done for his servant David and his people Israel.

Other events during Solomon's rule

CHAPTER 9

The LORD appears to Solomon again

This is also told in 2 Chronicles 7.11–22

¹ The LORD's temple and Solomon's palace were now finished, and Solomon had built everything he wanted. ² Some time later the LORD appeared to him again in a dream, just as he had done at Gibeon. ³ The LORD said:

I heard your prayer and what you asked me to do. This temple you have built is where I

will be worshipped for ever. It belongs to me, and I will never stop watching over it.

⁴ You must obey me, as your father David did, and be honest and fair. Obey my laws and teachings, ⁵ and I will keep my promise to David that someone from your family will always be king of Israel.

⁶ But if you or any of your descendants disobey my commands or start worshipping foreign gods, ⁷ I will no longer let my people Israel live in this land I gave them. I will desert this temple where I said I would be worshipped. Then people everywhere will think this nation is only a joke and will make fun of it. ⁸ This temple will become a pile of rocks!* Everyone who walks by will be shocked, and they will ask, "Why did the LORD do such a terrible thing to his people and to this temple?" ⁹ Then they will answer, "We know why the LORD did this. The people of Israel rejected the LORD their God, who rescued their ancestors from Egypt, and they started worshipping other gods."

Other things Solomon did

This is also told in 2 Chronicles 8.1–18

¹⁰ It took twenty years for the LORD's temple and Solomon's palace to be built. ¹¹ Later, Solomon gave King Hiram of Tyre twenty towns in the region of Galilee to repay him for the cedar, pine, and gold he had given Solomon.

¹² When Hiram went to see the towns, he did not like them. ¹³ He said, "Solomon, my friend, are these the kind of towns you want to give me?" So Hiram called the region Cabul because he thought it was worthless.* ¹⁴ He sent Solomon only five thousand kilogrammes of gold.

¹⁵ After Solomon's workers had finished the temple and the palace, he ordered them to fill in the land on the east side of Jerusalem,* to build a wall around the city, and to rebuild the towns of Hazor, Megiddo, and Gezer.

¹⁶ Earlier, the king of Egypt had captured the town of Gezer; he burnt it to the ground and killed the Canaanite people living there. Then he gave it to his daughter as a wedding

---

*8.62,63 sacrifices to ask the LORD's blessing: See Leviticus 3.1–17.

See also: 9.2: 1 King 3.5; 2 Chron 1.7.

*9.13 Cabul . . . worthless: Cabul sounds like the Hebrew word for "worthless".

*9.15 fill . . . Jerusalem: The Hebrew text has "build the Millo", which probably refers to a landfill to strengthen and extend the hill where the city was built.

See also: 9.5: 1 King 2.4. 9.8: 2 King 25.9; 2 Chron 36.19.

present when she married Solomon. 17 So
Solomon had the town rebuilt.

Solomon made his workers rebuild Lower
Beth-Horon, 18 Baalath, and Tamar in the
desert of Judah. 19 They also built towns
where he could keep his supplies and his
chariots and horses. Solomon made them
build whatever he wanted in Jerusalem,
Lebanon, and anywhere in his kingdom.

20-22 Solomon did not force the Israelites to
do his work. They were his soldiers, officials,
leaders, commanders, chariot captains, and
chariot drivers. But he did make slaves of the
Amorites, Hittites, Perizzites, Hivites, and
Jebusites who were living in Israel. These
were the descendants of those foreigners the
Israelites could not destroy, who
remained Israel's slaves.

23 Solomon appointed five hundred and
fifty officers to be in charge of his workers
and to watch over his building projects.

24 Solomon's wife, the daughter of the king
of Egypt, moved from the older part of
Jerusalem* to her new palace. Then Solomon
had the land on the east side of Jerusalem
filled in.*

25 Three times a year, Solomon burnt
incense and offered sacrifices to the LORD on
the altar he had built.

Solomon had now finished building the
LORD's temple.

26 He also had a lot of ships at Ezion-Geber,
a town in Edom near Eloth on the Red Sea.*
27-28 King Hiram let some of his experienced
sailors go to the country of Ophir* with
Solomon's own sailors, and they brought
back about fourteen thousand kilogrammes
of gold for Solomon.

CHAPTER 10

The Queen of Sheba visits Solomon
This is also told in 2 Chronicles 9.1–12

1 The Queen of Sheba heard how famous
Solomon was, so she went to Jerusalem to
test him with difficult questions. 2 She took
along several of her officials, and she loaded
her camels with gifts of spices, jewels, and

gold. When she arrived, she and Solomon
talked about everything she could think of.
3 He answered every question, no matter how
difficult it was.

4-5 The Queen was amazed at Solomon's
wisdom. She was breathless when she saw his
palace, the food on his table, his officials, his
servants in their uniforms, the people who
served his food, and the sacrifices he offered
at the LORD's temple. 6 She said:

Solomon, in my own country I had heard
about your wisdom and all you've done.
7 But I didn't believe it until I saw it with
my own eyes! And there's so much I didn't
hear about. You are wiser and richer than I
was told. 8 Your wives* and officials are
lucky to be here where they can listen to
the wise things you say.

9 I praise the LORD your God. He is
pleased with you and has made you king of
Israel. The LORD loves Israel, so he has
given them a king who will rule fairly and
honestly.

10 The Queen of Sheba gave Solomon more
than four thousand kilogrammes of gold,
many jewels, and more spices than anyone
had ever brought into Israel.

11-13 In return, Solomon gave her the gifts
he would have given any other ruler, but he
also gave her everything else she wanted.
Then she and her officials went back to their
own country.

Solomon's wealth
This is also told in 2 Chronicles 9.13–28

King Hiram's ships brought gold, juniper
wood, and jewels from the country of Ophir.
Solomon used the wood to make steps* for
the temple and palace, and harps and other
stringed instruments for the musicians. It was
the best juniper wood anyone in Israel had
ever seen.

14 Solomon received almost twenty-three
thousand kilogrammes of gold a year. 15 The
merchants and traders, as well as the kings of
Arabia and rulers from Israel, also gave him
gold.

16 Solomon made two hundred gold shields
and used almost seven kilogrammes of gold
for each one. 17 He also made three hundred
smaller gold shields, using almost two
kilogrammes of gold for each one, and he put the
shields in his palace in Forest Hall.

18 His throne was made of ivory and
covered with pure gold. 19-20 The back of the
throne was rounded at the top, and it had

---

*9.24 the land . . . filled in: See the note at 9.15.
*9.26 Red Sea: Hebrew *yam suph*, here referring to
the Gulf of Aqaba, since the term is extended to
include the north-eastern arm of the Red Sea (see also
the note at Exodus 13.11).
*9.27,28 Ophir: The location of this place is not
known.
See also: 9.25: Exod 23.17; 34.23; Deut 16.16.
10.1–10: Matt 12.42; Luke 11.31.

arm rests on each side. There was a statue of a lion on both sides of the throne, and there was a statue of a lion at both ends of each of the six steps leading up to the throne. No other throne in the world was like Solomon's.

²¹ Since silver was almost worthless in those days, everything was made of gold, even the cups and dishes used in Forest Hall.

²² Solomon had a lot of seagoing ships.* Every three years he sent them out with Hiram's ships to bring back gold, silver, and ivory, as well as monkeys and peacocks.'

²³ He was the richest and wisest king in the world. ²⁴ People from every nation wanted to hear the wisdom God had given him. ²⁵ Year after year people came and brought gifts of silver and gold, as well as clothes, weapons, spices, horses, or mules.

²⁶ Solomon had one thousand four hundred chariots and twelve thousand horses that he kept in Jerusalem and other towns.

²⁷ While he was king, there was silver everywhere in Jerusalem, and cedar was as common as ordinary sycamore trees in the foothills.

²⁸⁻²⁹ Solomon's merchants bought his horses and chariots in the regions of Musri and Kue.* They paid about six hundred pieces of silver for a chariot and a hundred and fifty pieces of silver for a horse. They also sold horses and chariots to the Hittite and Syrian kings.

Solomon's unfaithfulness, enemies, and death

CHAPTER 11

Solomon disobeys the LORD

¹⁻² The LORD did not want the Israelites to worship foreign gods, so he had warned them not to marry anyone who was not from Israel.

Solomon loved his wife, the daughter of the king of Egypt. But he also loved some women from Moab, Ammon, and Edom, and others from Sidon and the land of the Hittites. ³⁻⁴ Seven hundred of his wives were daughters of kings, but he also married three hundred other women.*

As Solomon got older, some of his wives led him to worship their gods. He wasn't like his father David, who had worshipped only the LORD God. ⁵ Solomon also worshipped Astarte the goddess of Sidon, and Milcom the disgusting god of Ammon. ⁶ Solomon's father had obeyed the LORD with all his heart, but Solomon disobeyed and did what the LORD hated.

⁷ Solomon built shrines on a hill east of Jerusalem to worship Chemosh the disgusting god of Moab, and Molech the disgusting god of Ammon. ⁸ In fact, he built a shrine for each of his foreign wives, so all of them could burn incense and offer sacrifices to their own gods.

⁹⁻¹⁰ The LORD God of Israel had appeared to Solomon twice and warned him not to worship foreign gods. But Solomon disobeyed and did it anyway. This made the LORD very angry, ¹¹ and he said to Solomon:

You did what you wanted and not what I told you to do. Now I'm going to take your kingdom from you and give it to one of your officials. ¹² But because David was your father, you will remain king as long as you live. I will wait until your son becomes king, then I will take the kingdom from him. ¹³ When I do, I will still let him rule one tribe, because I have not forgotten that David was my servant and Jerusalem is my city.

Hadad becomes an enemy of Solomon

¹⁴ Hadad was from the royal family of Edom, and here is how the LORD made him Solomon's enemy:

¹⁵⁻¹⁶ Some time earlier, when David conquered the nation of Edom,* Joab his army commander went there to bury those who had died in battle. Joab and his soldiers stayed in Edom six months, and during that time they killed every man and boy who lived there.

¹⁷⁻¹⁹ Hadad was a boy at the time, but he escaped to Midian with some of his father's officials. At Paran some other men joined

---

*10.22 seagoing ships: The Hebrew text has "ships of Tarshish", which may have been a Phoenician city in Spain. "Ships of Tarshish" probably means large, seagoing ships.
*10.28,29 Musri and Kue: Hebrew "Egypt and Kue". Musri and Kue were regions in what is today south-east Turkey.

See also: 10.26: 1 King 4.26. 10.27: Deut 17.17.
10.28: Deut 17.16. 11.1: Deut 17.17. 11.2: Exod 34.16; Deut 7.3,4.

*11.3,4 other women: This translates a Hebrew word for a woman who was legally bound to a man, but without the full privileges of a wife.
*11.15,16 Edom: See 2 Samuel 8.13,14.

them, and they went to the king of Egypt. The king liked Hadad and gave him food, some land, and a house, and even let him marry the sister of Queen Tahpenes. [20] Hadad and his wife had a son named Genubath, and the queen let the boy grow up in the palace with her own children.

[21] When Hadad heard that David and Joab were dead, he said to the king, "Your Majesty, please let me go back to my own country."

[22] "Why?" asked the king. "Do you want something I haven't given you?"

"No, I just want to go home."

Rezon becomes an enemy of Solomon

[23] Here is how God made Rezon son of Eliada an enemy of Solomon:

Rezon had run away from his master, King Hadadezer of Zobah. [24-25] He formed his own small army and became its leader after David had defeated Hadadezer's troops.* Then Rezon and his army went to Damascus, where he became the ruler of Syria and an enemy of Israel.

Both Hadad and Rezon were enemies of Israel while Solomon was king, and they caused him a lot of trouble.

The LORD makes a promise to Jeroboam

[26] Jeroboam was from the town of Zeredah in Ephraim. His father Nebat had died, but his mother Zeruah was still alive. Jeroboam was one of Solomon's officials, but even he rebelled against Solomon. [27] Here is how it happened:

While Solomon's workers were filling in the land on the east side of Jerusalem* and repairing the city walls, [28] Solomon noticed that Jeroboam was a hard worker. So he put Jeroboam in charge of the work force from Manasseh and Ephraim.

[29-30] One day when Jeroboam was leaving Jerusalem, he met Ahijah, a prophet from Shiloh. No one else was anywhere around. Suddenly, Ahijah took off his new coat and ripped it into twelve pieces. [31] Then he said:

Jeroboam, take ten pieces of this coat and listen to what the LORD God of Israel says to you. "Jeroboam, I am the LORD God, and I am about to take Solomon's

kingdom from him and give you ten tribes to rule. [32] But Solomon will still rule one tribe,* since he is the son of David my servant, and Jerusalem is my chosen city.

[33] "Solomon and the Israelites are not like their ancestor David. They will not listen to me, obey me, or do what is right. They have turned from me to worship Astarte the goddess of Sidon, Chemosh the god of Moab, and Milcom the god of Ammon.

[34] "Solomon is David's son, and David was my chosen leader, who did what I commanded. So I will let Solomon be king until he dies. [35] Then I will give you ten tribes to rule, [36] but Solomon's son will still rule one tribe. This way, my servant David will always have a descendant ruling in Jerusalem, the city where I have chosen to be worshipped.

[37] "You will be king of Israel and will rule every nation you want. [38] I'll help you if you obey me. And if you do what I say, as my servant David did, I will always let someone from your family rule in Israel, just as someone from David's family will always rule in Judah. The nation of Israel will be yours.

[39] "I will punish the descendants of David, but not for ever."

[40] When Solomon learnt what the LORD had told Jeroboam, Solomon tried to kill Jeroboam. But he escaped to King Shishak of Egypt and stayed there until Solomon died.

Solomon dies

This is also told in 2 Chronicles 9.29–31

[41] Everything else Solomon did while he was king is written in the book about him and his wisdom. [42] After he had ruled forty years from Jerusalem, [43] he died and was buried there in the city of his father David. His son Rehoboam then became king.

---

*11.24,25 troops: See 2 Samuel 8.3–6.
*11.27 filling . . . Jerusalem: See the note at 9.15.

*11.31,32 ten tribes . . . one tribe: By this time the tribe of Simeon had become part of the tribe of Judah. "One tribe" refers to Judah. Instead of "one tribe", one ancient translation has "two tribes".

The northern tribes of Israel rebel against King Rehoboam

CHAPTER 12

Some of the people rebel against Rehoboam

This is also told in 2 Chronicles 10.1–19

¹ Rehoboam went to Shechem where everyone was waiting to crown him king.

² Jeroboam son of Nebat heard what was happening, and he stayed in Egypt,' where he had gone to hide from Solomon. ³ But the people from the northern tribes of Israel sent for him. Then together they went to Rehoboam and said, ⁴ "Your father Solomon forced us to work very hard. But if you make our work easier, we will serve you and do whatever you ask."

⁵ "Give me three days to think about it," Rehoboam replied, "then come back for my answer." So the people left.

⁶ Rehoboam went to some leaders who had been his father's senior officials, and he asked them, "What should I tell these people?"

⁷ They answered, "If you want them to serve and obey you, then you should do what they ask today. Tell them you will make their work easier."

⁸ But Rehoboam refused their advice and went to the younger men who had grown up with him and were now his officials. He asked, "What do you think I should say to these people who asked me to make their work easier?"

¹⁰ His younger advisers said:

Here's what we think you should say to them: "Compared to me, my father was weak.' ¹¹ He made you work hard, but I'll make you work even harder. He punished you with whips, but I'll use whips with pieces of sharp metal!"

¹² Three days later, Jeroboam and the others came back. ¹³ Rehoboam ignored the advice of the older advisers. ¹⁴ He spoke bluntly and told them exactly what his own advisers had suggested: "My father made you work hard, but I'll make you work even harder. He punished you with whips, but I'll use whips with pieces of sharp metal!"

¹⁵⁻¹⁹ When the people realized that Rehoboam would not listen to them, they shouted: "We don't have to be loyal to David's family. We can do what we want. Come on, people of Israel, let's go home! Rehoboam can rule his own people."

Adoniram' was in charge of the forced labour, and Rehoboam sent him to talk to the people. But they stoned him to death. Then Rehoboam ran to his chariot and hurried back to Jerusalem.

So the people from the northern tribes of Israel went home, leaving Rehoboam to rule only the people from the towns in Judah. Ever since that day, the people of Israel have opposed David's family in Judah. All this happened just as the LORD's prophet Ahijah had told Jeroboam.

²⁰ When the Israelites heard that Jeroboam was back, they called everyone together. Then they sent for Jeroboam and made him king of Israel. Only the people from the tribe of Judah* remained loyal to David's family.

Shemaiah warns Rehoboam

This is also told in 2 Chronicles 11.1–4

²¹ After Rehoboam returned to Jerusalem, he decided to attack Israel and take control of the whole country. So he called together one hundred and eighty thousand soldiers from the tribes of Judah and Benjamin.

²² Meanwhile, God told Shemaiah the prophet ²³ to give Rehoboam and everyone from Judah and Benjamin this warning: ²⁴ "Don't go to war against the people from Israel — they are your relatives. Go home! I am the LORD, and I made these things happen."

Rehoboam and his army obeyed the LORD and went home.

King Jeroboam of Israel makes two gold statues of calves

²⁵ Jeroboam rebuilt Shechem in Ephraim and made it a stronger town, then he moved there. He also fortified the town of Penuel.

²⁶⁻²⁷ One day, Jeroboam started thinking, "Everyone in Israel still goes to the temple in

---

*12.20 Israelites . . . Israel . . . Judah: From this time on, "Israel" usually refers to the northern kingdom, and "Israelites" refers to the people who lived there. The southern kingdom is called "Judah".

See also: 12.16: 2 Sam 20.1.

Jerusalem to offer sacrifices to the LORD. What if they become loyal to David's family again? They will kill me and accept Rehoboam as their king."

²⁸ Jeroboam asked for advice and then made two gold statues of calves. He showed them to the people and said, "Listen everyone! You won't have to go to Jerusalem to worship any more. Here are your gods* who rescued you from Egypt." ²⁹⁻³⁰ Then he put one of the gold calves in the town of Bethel. He put the other one in the town of Dan, and the crowd walked out in front as the calf was taken there.* What Jeroboam did was a terrible sin.

³¹ Jeroboam built small places of worship at the shrines* and appointed men who were not from the tribe of Levi to serve as priests. ³²⁻³³ He also decided to start a new festival for the Israelites on the fifteenth day of the eighth month, just like the one in Judah.* On that day, Jeroboam went to Bethel and offered sacrifices on the altar to the gold calf he had put there. Then he assigned the priests their duties.

Prophets condemn Jeroboam

CHAPTER 13

A prophet condemns the altar at Bethel

¹⁻² One day, Jeroboam was standing at the altar in Bethel, ready to make an offering. Suddenly one of God's prophets* arrived from Judah and shouted:

> The LORD sent me with a message about this altar. A child named Josiah will be born into David's family. He will sacrifice on this altar the priests who make offerings here, and human bones will be burnt on it.

³ You will know that the LORD has said these things when the altar splits in half, and the ashes on it fall to the ground.

⁴ Jeroboam pointed at the prophet and shouted, "Grab him!" But straight away, Jeroboam's hand became stiff, and he could not move it. ⁵ The altar split in half, and the ashes fell to the ground, just as the prophet had warned.

⁶ "Please pray to the LORD your God and ask him to heal my hand," Jeroboam begged.

The prophet prayed, and Jeroboam's hand was healed.

⁷ "Come home with me and eat something," Jeroboam said. "I want to give you a gift for what you have done."

⁸ "No, I wouldn't go with you, even if you offered me half of your kingdom. I won't eat or drink here either. ⁹ The LORD said I can't eat or drink anything and that I can't go home the same way I came." ¹⁰ Then he started home down a different road.

An old prophet from Bethel

¹¹ At that time an old prophet lived in Bethel, and one of his sons told him what the prophet from Judah had said and done.

¹² "Show me which way he went," the old prophet said, and his sons pointed out the road. ¹³ "Put a saddle on my donkey," he told them. After they did, he got on the donkey ¹⁴ and rode off to look for the prophet from Judah.

The old prophet found him sitting under an oak tree and asked, "Are you the prophet from Judah?"

"Yes, I am."

¹⁵ "Come home with me," the old prophet said, "and have something to eat."

¹⁶ "I can't go back with you," the prophet replied, "and I can't eat or drink anything with you. ¹⁷ The LORD warned me not to eat or drink or to go home the same way I came."

¹⁸ The old prophet said, "I'm a prophet too. One of the LORD's angels told me to take you to my house and give you something to eat and drink."

The prophet from Judah did not know that the old prophet was lying, ¹⁹ so he went home with him and ate and drank.

²⁰ During the meal the LORD gave the old prophet ²¹ a message for the prophet from Judah:

> Listen to the LORD's message. You have disobeyed the LORD your God. ²² He told you not to eat or drink anything here, but you came home and ate with me. And so, when you die, your body won't be buried in your family tomb.

²³ After the meal the old prophet got a donkey ready, ²⁴ and the prophet from Judah left. Along the way, a lion attacked and killed him, and the donkey and the lion stood there beside his dead body.

---

*12.32,33 the one in Judah: This probably refers to the Festival of Shelters.

See also: 12.28: Exod 32.4. 12.32,33: Lev 23.33,34.
13.2: 2 King 23.15,16.

25 Some people walked by and saw the body with the lion standing there. They ran into Bethel, telling everyone what they had seen.

26 When the old prophet heard the news, he said, "That must be the prophet from Judah. The LORD warned him, but he disobeyed. So the LORD sent a lion to kill him."

27 The old prophet told his sons to saddle his donkey, and when it was ready, 28 he left. He found the body lying on the road, with the donkey and lion standing there. The lion had not eaten the body or attacked the donkey. 29 The old prophet picked up the body, put it on his own donkey, and took it back to Bethel, so he could bury it and mourn for the prophet from Judah.

30 He buried the body in his own family tomb and cried for the prophet. 31 He said to his sons, "When I die, bury my body next to this prophet. 32 I'm sure that everything he said about the altar in Bethel and the shrines in Samaria will happen."

33 But Jeroboam kept on doing evil things. He appointed men to be priests at the local shrines, even if they were not Levites. In fact, anyone who wanted to be a priest could be one. 34 This sinful thing led to the downfall of his kingdom.

CHAPTER 14

Jeroboam's son dies

1 About the same time, Abijah son of Jeroboam got sick. 2-3 Jeroboam told his wife:

Disguise yourself so no one will know you're my wife, then go to Shiloh, where the prophet Ahijah lives. Take him ten loaves of bread, some small cakes, and honey, and ask him what will happen to our son. He can tell you, because he's the one who told me I would become king.

4 She got ready and left for Ahijah's house in Shiloh.

Ahijah was now old and blind, 5 but the LORD told him, "Jeroboam's wife is coming to ask about her son. I will tell you what to say to her."

Jeroboam's wife came to Ahijah's house, pretending to be someone else. 6 But when Ahijah heard her walking up to the door, he said:

Come in! I know you're Jeroboam's wife — why are you pretending to be someone else? I have some bad news for you. 7 Give your husband this message

from the LORD God of Israel: "Jeroboam, you know that I, the LORD, chose you over anyone else to be the leader of my people Israel. 8 I even took David's kingdom away from his family and gave it to you. But you are not like my servant David. He always obeyed me and did what was right.

9 "You have made me very angry by rejecting me and making idols out of gold. Jeroboam, you have done more evil things than any king before you.

10 "Because of this, I will destroy your family by killing every man and boy in it, whether slave or free. I will wipe out your family, just as fire burns up rubbish. 11 Dogs will eat the bodies of your relatives who die in town, and vultures will eat the bodies of those who die in the country. I, the LORD, have spoken and will not change my mind!"

12 That's the LORD's message to your husband. As for you, go back home, and straight after you get there, your son will die. 13 Everyone in Israel will mourn at his funeral. But he will be the last one from Jeroboam's family to receive a proper burial, because he's the only one the LORD God of Israel is pleased with.

14 The LORD will soon choose a new king of Israel, who will destroy Jeroboam's family. And I mean very soon.* 15 The people of Israel have made the LORD angry by setting up sacred poles* for worshipping the goddess Asherah. So the LORD will punish them until they shake like grass in a stream. He will take them out of the land he gave to their ancestors, then scatter them as far away as the River Euphrates. 16 Jeroboam sinned and caused the Israelites to sin. Now the LORD will desert Israel.

17 Jeroboam's wife left and went back home to the town of Tirzah. As soon as she set foot in her house, her son died. 18 Everyone in Israel came and mourned at his funeral, just as the LORD's servant Ahijah had said.

Jeroboam dies

19 Everything else Jeroboam did while he was king, including the battles he won, is written in *The History of the Kings of Israel*. 20 He was king of Israel for twenty-two years, then he died, and his son Nadab became king.

---

*14.15 sacred poles: Or "trees", used as symbols of Asherah, the goddess of fertility.
See also: 14.10: 1 King 15.29.

Kings of Judah and Israel

King Rehoboam of Judah

This is also told in 2 Chronicles 11.5–12.16

²¹ Rehoboam son of Solomon was forty-one years old when he became king of Judah, and he ruled seventeen years from Jerusalem, the city where the LORD had chosen to be worshipped. His mother Naamah was from Ammon.

²² The people of Judah disobeyed the LORD and made him even angrier than their ancestors had. ²³ They also built their own local shrines and stone images of foreign gods, and they set up sacred poles* for worshipping the goddess Asherah on every hill and in the shade of large trees. ²⁴ Even worse, they allowed prostitutes* at the shrines, and followed the disgusting customs of the foreign nations that the LORD had forced out of Canaan.

²⁵ After Rehoboam had been king for four years, King Shishak of Egypt attacked Jerusalem. ²⁶ He took everything of value from the temple and the palace, including Solomon's gold shields.

²⁷ Rehoboam had bronze shields made to replace the gold ones, and he ordered the guards at the city gates to keep them safe. ²⁸ Whenever Rehoboam went to the LORD's temple, the guards carried the shields. But they always took them back to the guardroom as soon as he had finished.

²⁹ Everything else Rehoboam did while he was king is written in *The History of the Kings of Judah*. ³⁰ He and Jeroboam were constantly at war. ³¹ Rehoboam's mother Naamah was from Ammon, but when Rehoboam died, he was buried beside his ancestors in Jerusalem.* His son Abijam then became king.

CHAPTER 15

King Abijam of Judah

This is also told in 2 Chronicles 13.1–22

¹ Abijam became king of Judah in Jeroboam's eighteenth year as king of Israel, ² and he

ruled from Jerusalem for three years. His mother was Maacah the daughter of Abishalom.

³ Abijam did not truly obey the LORD his God as his ancestor David had done. Instead, he was sinful just like his father Rehoboam. ⁴⁻⁵ David had always obeyed the LORD's commands by doing right, except in the case of Uriah.* And since Abijam was David's great-grandson, the LORD kept Jerusalem safe and let Abijam have a son who would be the next king.

⁶⁻⁷ The war that had broken out between Rehoboam and Jeroboam continued during the time that Abijam was king.

Everything else Abijam did while he was king is written in *The History of the Kings of Judah*. ⁸ Abijam died and was buried in Jerusalem,* and his son Asa became king.

King Asa of Judah

This is also told in 2 Chronicles 15.16–16.6,11–13

⁹ Asa became king of Judah in the twentieth year of Jeroboam's rule in Israel, ¹⁰ and he ruled forty-one years from Jerusalem. His grandmother was Maacah the daughter of Abishalom.

¹¹ Asa obeyed the LORD, as David had done. ¹² He forced the prostitutes* at the shrines to leave the country, and he got rid of the idols his ancestors had made. ¹³ His own grandmother Maacah had made an idol of Asherah, and Asa took it and burnt it in Kidron Valley. Then he removed Maacah from her position as queen mother.*

¹⁴ As long as Asa lived, he was completely faithful to the LORD, even though he did not destroy the local shrines. ¹⁵ He placed in the temple all the silver and gold objects that he and his father had dedicated to the LORD.

¹⁶ Asa was always at war with King Baasha of Israel. ¹⁷ One time, Baasha invaded Judah and captured the town of Ramah. He started making the town stronger, so he could put troops there to stop people from going in and out of Judah.

¹⁸ When Asa heard about this, he took the silver and gold from his palace and from the

---

14.23 sacred poles: See the note at 14.15.

14.24 prostitutes: Men and women sometimes served at the shrines as prostitutes in the worship of Canaanite gods, but the LORD had forbidden the people of Israel to worship in this way (see Deuteronomy 23.17,18).

See also: **14.23:** 2 King 17.9,10. **14.24:** Deut 23.17. **14.25:** 2 Chron 12.2–8. **14.26:** 1 King 10.16,17; 2 Chron 9.15,16.

15.4,5 Uriah: A Hittite who served in David's army; David had him killed so he could marry his wife Bathsheba (see 2 Samuel 11.1–27).

15.12 prostitutes: See the note at 14.24.

15.13 queen mother: Or "the mother of the king", an important position in biblical times (see 2.19).

See also: **15.4:** 1 King 11.36. **15.5:** 2 Sam 11.1–27. **15.6:** 2 Chron 13.3–21. **15.12:** 2 Chron 15.8–15.

LORD's temple. He gave it to some of his officials and sent them to Damascus with this message for King Benhadad* of Syria: ¹⁹ "Our fathers signed a peace treaty. Why don't we do the same thing? This silver and gold is a present for you. So, would you please break your treaty with Baasha and force him to leave my country?"

²⁰ Benhadad did what Asa asked and sent the Syrian army into Israel. They captured the towns of Ijon, Dan, and Abel-Bethmaacah, and the territories of Chinneroth and Naphtali. ²¹ When Baasha heard about it, he left Ramah and went back to Tirzah.

²² Asa ordered everyone in Judah to carry away the stones and wood Baasha had used to strengthen the town of Ramah. Then he used these same stones and wood to fortify the town of Geba in the territory of Benjamin and the town of Mizpah.

²³ Everything else Asa did while he was king, including his victories and the towns he rebuilt, is written in *The History of the Kings of Judah*. When he got older, he had a foot disease. ²⁴ Asa died and was buried in the tomb of his ancestors in Jerusalem.* His son Jehoshaphat then became king.

King Nadab of Israel

²⁵ Nadab son of Jeroboam became king of Israel in Asa's second year as king of Judah, and he ruled two years. ²⁶ Nadab disobeyed the LORD by following the evil example of his father, who had caused the Israelites to sin.

²⁷⁻²⁸ Baasha son of Ahijah was from the tribe of Issachar, and he made plans to kill Nadab. When Nadab and his army went to attack the town of Gibbethon in Philistia, Baasha killed Nadab there. So in the third year of Asa's rule, Baasha became king of Israel.

²⁹ The LORD's prophet Ahijah had earlier said, "Not one man or boy in Jeroboam's family will be left alive." And, as soon as Baasha became king, he killed everyone in Jeroboam's family, ³⁰ because Jeroboam had made the LORD God of Israel angry by sinning and causing the Israelites to sin.

³¹ Everything else Nadab did while he was king is written in *The History of the Kings of Israel*.

³² King Asa of Judah and King Baasha of Israel were always at war.

King Baasha of Israel

³³ Baasha son of Ahijah became king of Israel in Asa's third year as king of Judah, and he ruled twenty-four years from Tirzah. ³⁴ Baasha also disobeyed the LORD by acting like Jeroboam, who had caused the Israelites to sin.

CHAPTER 16

¹ The LORD sent Jehu son of Hanani to say to Baasha:

² Nobody knew who you were until I, the LORD, chose you* to be the leader of my people Israel. And now you're acting exactly like Jeroboam by causing the Israelites to sin. What you've done has made me so angry ³ that I will destroy you and your family, just as I did the family of Jeroboam. ⁴ Dogs will eat the bodies of your relatives who die in town, and vultures will eat the bodies of those who die in the country.

⁵⁻⁷ Baasha made the LORD very angry, and that's why the LORD gave Jehu this message for Baasha and his family. Baasha constantly disobeyed the LORD by following Jeroboam's sinful example — but even worse, he killed everyone in Jeroboam's family!

Everything else Baasha did while he was king, including his brave deeds, is written in *The History of the Kings of Israel*. Baasha died and was buried in Tirzah, and his son Elah became king.

King Elah of Israel

⁸ Elah son of Baasha became king of Israel after Asa had been king of Judah for twenty-five years, and he ruled from Tirzah for two years.

⁹ Zimri commanded half of Elah's chariots, and he made plans to kill Elah.

One day, Elah was in Tirzah, getting drunk at the home of Arza, his prime minister, ¹⁰ when Zimri went there and killed Elah. So Zimri became king in the twenty-seventh year of Asa's rule in Judah.

¹¹ As soon as Zimri became king, he killed everyone in Baasha's family. Not one man or boy in his family was left alive — even his close friends were killed. ¹² Baasha's family was completely wiped out, just as the LORD's prophet Jehu had warned. ¹³ Baasha and Elah sinned and caused the Israelites to sin, and they made the LORD angry by worshipping idols.

¹⁴ Everything else Elah did while he was king is written in *The History of the Kings of Israel.*

King Zimri of Israel

¹⁵⁻¹⁶ Zimri became king of Israel in Asa's twenty-seventh year as king of Judah, but he ruled only seven days from Tirzah.

Israel's army was camped near Gibbethon in Philistia under the command of Omri. The soldiers heard that Zimri had killed Elah, and they made Omri their king that same day. ¹⁷ At once, Omri and his army marched to Tirzah and attacked. ¹⁸ When Zimri saw that the town was captured, he ran into the strongest part of the palace and killed himself by setting it on fire. ¹⁹ Zimri had disobeyed the LORD by following the evil example of Jeroboam, who had caused the Israelites to sin.

²⁰ Everything else Zimri did while he was king, including his rebellion against Elah, is written in *The History of the Kings of Israel.*

King Omri of Israel

²¹ After Zimri died, some of the Israelites wanted Tibni son of Ginath to be king, but others wanted Omri. ²² Omri's followers were stronger than Tibni's, so Tibni was killed, and Omri became king of Israel ²³ in the thirty-first year of Asa's rule in Judah.

Omri ruled Israel for twelve years. The first six years he ruled from Tirzah, ²⁴ then he bought the hill of Samaria from Shemer for six thousand pieces of silver. He built a town there and named it Samaria, after Shemer who had owned the hill.

²⁵ Omri did more evil things than any king before him. ²⁶ He acted just like Jeroboam and made the LORD God of Israel angry by causing the Israelites to sin and to worship idols.

²⁷ Everything else Omri did while he was king, including his brave deeds, is written in *The History of the Kings of Israel.* ²⁸ Omri died and was buried in Samaria, and his son Ahab became king.

King Ahab of Israel

²⁹ Ahab son of Omri became king of Israel in the thirty-eighth year of Asa's rule in Judah, and he ruled twenty-two years from Samaria.

³⁰ Ahab did more things to displease the LORD than any king before him. ³¹ He acted just like Jeroboam. Even worse, he married Jezebel the daughter of King Ethbaal of

Sidon* and started worshipping Baal. ³² Ahab built an altar and temple for Baal in Samaria ³³ and set up a sacred pole* for worshipping the goddess Asherah. Ahab did more to make the LORD God of Israel angry than any king of Israel before him.

³⁴ While Ahab was king, a man from Bethel named Hiel rebuilt the town of Jericho. But while Hiel was laying the foundation for the town wall, his eldest son Abiram died. And while he was finishing the gates, his youngest son Segub died. This happened just as the LORD had told Joshua to say many years ago.*

Elijah the prophet

CHAPTER 17

Elijah stops the rain

¹ Elijah was a prophet from Tishbe in Gilead.* One day he went to King Ahab and said, "I'm a servant of the living LORD, the God of Israel. And I swear in his name that it won't rain until I say so. There won't even be any dew on the ground."

² Later, the LORD said to Elijah, ³ "Leave and go across the River Jordan so you can hide near Cherith Brook. ⁴ You can drink water from the brook, and eat the food I've told the ravens to bring you."

⁵ Elijah obeyed the LORD and went to live near Cherith Brook. ⁶ Ravens brought him bread and meat twice a day, and he drank water from the brook. ⁷ But after a while, it dried up because there was no rain.

Elijah helps a widow in Zarephath

⁸ The LORD told Elijah, ⁹ "Go to the town of Zarephath in Sidon and live there. I've told a widow in that town to give you food."

¹⁰ When Elijah came near the town gate of Zarephath, he saw a widow gathering sticks for a fire. "Would you please bring me a cup of water?" he asked. ¹¹ As she left to get it, he asked, "Would you also please bring me a piece of bread?"

---

*16.31 Sidon: One of the most important cities in Phoenicia. It was on the coast of the Mediterranean Sea, north of Israel, in what is today southern Lebanon.
*16.33 sacred pole: See the note at 14.15.
*16.34 a man from Bethel . . . ago: See Joshua 6.26.
See also: 16.34: Josh 6.26. 17.1: Jam 5.17.
17.9: Luke 4.25,26.

¹² The widow answered, "In the name of the living LORD your God, I swear that I don't have any bread. All I have is a handful of flour and a little olive oil. I'm on my way home now with these few sticks to cook what I have for my son and me. After that, we will starve to death."

¹³ Elijah said, "Everything will be fine. Do what you said. Go home and prepare something for yourself and your son. But first, please make a small piece of bread and bring it to me. ¹⁴ The LORD God of Israel has promised that your jar of flour won't run out and your bottle of oil won't dry up before he sends rain for the crops."

¹⁵ The widow went home and did exactly what Elijah had told her. She and Elijah and her family had enough food for a long time. ¹⁶ The LORD kept the promise that his prophet Elijah had made, and she did not run out of flour or oil.

Elijah brings a boy back to life

¹⁷ Several days later, the son of the woman who owned the house* got sick, and he kept getting worse, until finally he died.

¹⁸ The woman shouted at Elijah, "What have I done to you? I thought you were God's prophet. Did you come here to cause the death of my son as a reminder that I've sinned against God?"*

¹⁹ "Bring me your son," Elijah said. Then he took the boy from her arms and carried him upstairs to the room where he was staying. Elijah laid the boy on his bed ²⁰ and prayed, "LORD God, why did you do such a terrible thing to this woman? She's letting me stay here, and now you've let her son die." ²¹ Elijah stretched himself out over the boy three times, while praying, "LORD God, bring this boy back to life!"

²² The LORD answered Elijah's prayer, and the boy started breathing again. ²³ Elijah picked him up and carried him downstairs. He gave the boy to his mother and said, "Look, your son is alive."

²⁴ "You are God's prophet!" the woman replied. "Now I know that you really do speak for the LORD."

---

*17.17 the woman who owned the house: This may or may not be the same woman as the widow in verses 8–16.

*17.18 Did you . . . God: In ancient times people sometimes thought that if they sinned, something terrible would happen to them.

See also: 17.21: 2 King 4.34,35.

CHAPTER 18

Elijah proves he is the LORD's prophet

¹⁻² For three years no rain fell in Samaria, and there was almost nothing to eat anywhere. The LORD said to Elijah, "Go and meet with King Ahab. I will soon make it rain." So Elijah went to see Ahab.

³⁻⁴ At that time Obadiah was in charge of Ahab's palace, but he faithfully worshipped the LORD. In fact, when Jezebel was trying to kill the LORD's prophets, Obadiah hid a hundred of them in two caves and gave them food and water.

Ahab sent for Obadiah ⁵ and said, "We have to find something for our horses and mules to eat. If we don't, we will have to kill them. Let's look around every brook and spring in the country for some grass. ⁶ You go one way, and I'll go the other." Then they left in separate directions.

⁷ As Obadiah was walking along, he met Elijah. Obadiah recognized him, bowed down, and asked, "Elijah, is it really you?"

⁸ "Yes. Go and tell Ahab I'm here."

⁹ Obadiah replied:

King Ahab would kill me if I told him that. And I haven't even done anything wrong. ¹⁰ I swear to you in the name of the living LORD your God that the king has looked everywhere for you. He sent people to look in every country, and when they couldn't find you, he made the leader of each country swear that you were not in that country. ¹¹ Do you really want me to tell him you're here?

¹² What if the LORD's Spirit takes you away as soon as I leave? When Ahab comes to get you, he won't find you. Then he will surely kill me.

I have worshipped the LORD since I was a boy. ¹³ I even hid a hundred of the LORD's prophets in caves when Jezebel was trying to kill them. I also gave them food and water. Do you really want me to tell Ahab you're here? He will kill me!

¹⁵ Elijah said, "I'm a servant of the living LORD All-Powerful, and I swear in his name that I will meet with Ahab today."

¹⁶ Obadiah left and told Ahab where to find Elijah.

Ahab went to meet Elijah, ¹⁷ and when he saw him, Ahab shouted, "There you are, the biggest troublemaker in Israel!"

¹⁸ Elijah answered:

You're the troublemaker — not me! You and your family have disobeyed the LORD's commands by worshipping Baal.

19 Call together everyone from Israel to meet me on Mount Carmel. Be sure to bring along the four hundred and fifty prophets of Baal and the four hundred prophets of Asherah who eat at Jezebel's table.'

20 Ahab got everyone together, then they went to meet Elijah on Mount Carmel. 21 Elijah stood in front of them and said, "How much longer will you try to have things both ways? If the LORD is God, worship him! But if Baal is God, worship him!"

The people did not say a word.

22 Then Elijah continued:

I am the LORD's only prophet, but Baal has four hundred and fifty prophets.

23 Bring us two bulls. Baal's prophets can take one of them, kill it, and cut it in pieces. Then they can put the meat on the wood without lighting the fire. I will do the same thing with the other bull, and I won't light a fire under it either.

24 The prophets of Baal will pray to their god, and I will pray to the LORD. The one who answers by starting the fire is God.

"That's a good idea," everyone agreed.

25 Elijah said to Baal's prophets, "There are more of you, so you go first. Pick out a bull and get it ready, but don't light the fire. Then pray to your god."

26 They chose their bull, then they got it ready and prayed to Baal all morning, asking him to start the fire. They danced around the altar and shouted, "Answer us, Baal!" But there was no answer.

27 At midday, Elijah began making fun of them. "Pray louder!" he said. "Baal must be a god. Perhaps he's daydreaming or using the toilet or travelling somewhere. Or perhaps he's asleep, and you have to wake him up."

28 The prophets kept shouting louder and louder, and they cut themselves with swords and knives until they were bleeding. This was the way they worshipped, 29 and they kept it up all afternoon. But there was no answer of any kind.

30 Elijah told everyone to gather around him while he repaired the LORD's altar. 31-32 Then he used twelve stones to build an altar in honour of the LORD. Each stone stood for one of the tribes of Israel, which was the name the LORD had given to their ancestor Jacob. Elijah

dug a ditch around the altar, large enough to hold almost fourteen litres. 33 He placed the wood on the altar, then they cut the bull into pieces and laid the meat on the wood.

He told the people, "Fill four large jars with water and pour it over the meat and the wood." After they did this, 34 he told them to do it two times. They did exactly as he said 35 until finally, the water ran down the altar and filled the ditch.

36 When it was time for the evening sacrifice, Elijah prayed:

Our LORD, you are the God of Abraham, Isaac, and Israel. Now, prove that you are the God of this nation, and that I, your servant, have done this at your command. 37 Please answer me, so these people will know that you are the LORD God, and that you will turn their hearts back to you.'

38 The LORD immediately sent fire, and it burnt up the sacrifice, the wood, and the stones. It scorched the ground everywhere around the altar and dried up every drop of water in the ditch. 39 When the crowd saw what had happened, they all bowed down and shouted, "The LORD is God! The LORD is God!"

40 Just then, Elijah said, "Grab the prophets of Baal! Don't let any of them get away."

So the people captured the prophets and took them to the River Kishon, where Elijah killed every one of them.

It starts to rain

41 Elijah told Ahab, "Get something to eat and drink. I hear a heavy rain coming."

42 Ahab left, but Elijah climbed back to the top of Mount Carmel. Then he stooped down with his face almost to the ground 43 and said to his servant, "Look towards the sea."

The servant left. And when he came back, he said, "I looked, but I didn't see anything." Elijah told him to look seven more times.

44 After the seventh time the servant replied, "I see a small cloud coming this way. But it's no bigger than a fist."

Elijah told him, "Tell Ahab to get his chariot ready and start home now. Otherwise, the rain will stop him."

45-46 A few minutes later, it got very cloudy and windy, and rain started pouring down. So Elijah wrapped his coat around himself, and the LORD gave him strength to run all the way to Jezreel. Ahab followed him.

See also: 18.31: Gen 32.28; 35.10.

See also: 18.42-45: Jam 5.18.

CHAPTER 19

Elijah runs away
from Ahab and Jezebel

¹ Ahab told his wife Jezebel what Elijah had done and that he had killed the prophets. ² She sent a message to Elijah: "You killed my prophets. Now I'm going to kill you! I pray that the gods will punish me even more severely if I don't do it by this time tomorrow."

³ Elijah was afraid when he got her message, and he ran to the town of Beersheba in Judah. He left his servant there, ⁴ then walked another whole day into the desert. Finally, he came to a large bush and sat down in its shade. He begged the LORD, "I've had enough. Just let me die! I'm no better off than my ancestors." ⁵ Then he lay down in the shade and fell asleep.

Suddenly an angel woke him up and said, "Get up and eat." ⁶ Elijah looked around, and by his head was a jar of water and some baked bread. He sat up, ate and drank, then lay down and went back to sleep.

⁷ Soon the LORD's angel woke him again and said, "Get up and eat, or else you'll get too tired to travel." ⁸ So Elijah sat up and ate and drank.

The food and water made him strong enough to walk forty more days. At last, he reached Mount Sinai,' the mountain of God, ⁹ and he spent the night there in a cave.

The LORD appears to Elijah

While Elijah was on Mount Sinai, the LORD asked, "Elijah, why are you here?"

¹⁰ He answered, "LORD God All-Powerful, I've always done my best to obey you. But your people have broken their solemn promise to you. They have torn down your altars and killed all your prophets, except me. And now they are even trying to kill me!"

¹¹ "Go out and stand on the mountain," the LORD replied. "I want you to see me when I pass by."

All at once, a strong wind shook the mountain and shattered the rocks. But the LORD was not in the wind. Next, there was an earthquake, but the LORD was not in the earthquake. ¹² Then there was a fire, but the LORD was not in the fire.

Finally, there was a gentle breeze,' ¹³ and when Elijah heard it, he covered his face with his coat. He went out and stood at the entrance to the cave.

The LORD' asked, "Elijah, why are you here?"

¹⁴ Elijah answered, "LORD God All-Powerful, I've always done my best to obey you. But your people have broken their solemn promise to you. They have torn down your altars and killed all your prophets, except me. And now they are even trying to kill me!"

¹⁵ The LORD said:

Elijah, you can go back to the desert near Damascus. And when you get there, appoint* Hazael to be king of Syria. ¹⁶ Then appoint Jehu son of Nimshi to be king of Israel, and Elisha son of Shaphat' to take your place as my prophet.

¹⁷ Hazael will start killing the people who worship Baal. Jehu will kill those who escape from Hazael, and Elisha will kill those who escape from Jehu.

¹⁸ But seven thousand Israelites have refused to worship Baal, and they will live.

Elisha becomes Elijah's assistant

¹⁹ Elijah left and found Elisha ploughing a field with a pair of oxen. There were eleven other men in front of him, and each one was also ploughing with a pair of oxen. Elijah went over and put his own coat on Elisha.*

²⁰ Elisha stopped ploughing and ran after him. "Let me kiss my parents goodbye, then I'll go with you," he said.

"You can go," Elijah said. "But remember what I've done for you."

²¹ Elisha left and took his oxen with him. He killed them and boiled them over a fire he had made with the wood from his plough. He gave the meat to the people who were with him, and they ate it. Then he left with Elijah and became his assistant.

---

*19.15 appoint: This would have included a ceremony in which olive oil would be poured on his head to show that he was now king.
*19.19 put . . . Elisha: This was a sign that Elijah wanted Elisha to follow him and become a prophet.

See also: 19.14: Rom 11.3. 19.15: 2 King 8.7-13. 19.16: 2 King 9.1-6. 19.18: Rom 11.4.

See also: 19.4: Jon 4.3. 19.10: Rom 11.3.

King Ahab and Queen Jezebel

CHAPTER 20

Syria attacks Israel

¹ King Benhadad of Syria* called his army together. He was joined by thirty-two other kings with their horses and chariots, and together they marched to Samaria and attacked. ² Benhadad sent a messenger to tell King Ahab of Israel, ³ "Ahab, give me your silver and gold, your wives,* and your strongest sons!"

⁴ "Your Majesty," Ahab replied, "everything I have is yours, including me."

⁵ Later, Benhadad sent another messenger to say to Ahab, "I have already told you to give me your silver and gold, your wives, and your children. ⁶ But tomorrow at this time, I will send my officials into your city to search my palace and the houses of your officials. They will take everything else that you' own."

⁷ Ahab called a meeting with the leaders of Israel and said, "Benhadad is causing real trouble. He told me to give him my wives and children, as well as my silver and gold. And I agreed."

⁸ "Don't listen to him!" they answered. "You don't have to do what he says."

⁹ So Ahab sent someone to tell Benhadad, "Your Majesty, I'll give you my silver and gold, and even my wives and children. But I won't let you have anything else."

When Benhadad got his answer, ¹⁰ he replied, "I'll completely destroy Samaria! There won't even be enough of it left for my soldiers to carry back in their hands. If I don't do it, I pray that the gods will punish me terribly."

¹¹ Ahab then answered, "Benhadad, don't boast before the fighting even begins. Wait and see if you live through it."

¹² Meanwhile, Benhadad and the other kings had been drinking in their tents. But when Ahab's reply came, he ordered his soldiers to prepare to attack Samaria, and they all got ready.

¹³ At that very moment, a prophet ran up to Ahab and said, "You can see that Benhadad's army is very strong. But the LORD has

promised to help you defeat them today. Then you will know that the LORD is in control."

¹⁴ "Who will fight the battle?" Ahab asked.

The prophet answered, "The young bodyguards who serve the district officials."

"But who will lead them into battle?" Ahab asked.

"You will!" the prophet replied.

¹⁵ So Ahab called together the two hundred and thirty-two bodyguards and the seven thousand troops in Israel's army, and he got them ready to fight the Syrians.

Israel defeats the Syrians

¹⁶⁻¹⁷ At midday, King Ahab and his Israelite army marched out of Samaria, with the young soldiers in front.

King Benhadad of Syria and the thirty-two kings with him were drunk when the scouts he had sent out ran up to his tent, shouting, "We just now saw soldiers marching out of Samaria!"

¹⁸ "Take them alive!" Benhadad ordered. "I don't care if they have come out to fight or to surrender."

¹⁹ The young soldiers led Israel's troops into battle, ²⁰ and each of them attacked and killed an enemy soldier. The rest of the Syrian army turned and ran, and the Israelites went after them. Benhadad and some others escaped on horses, ²¹ but Ahab and his soldiers followed them and captured' their horses and chariots.

Ahab and Israel's army crushed the Syrians. ²² Later, the prophet* went back and warned Ahab, "Benhadad will attack you again next spring. Build up your troops and make sure you have some good plans."

Syria attacks Israel again

²³ Meanwhile, Benhadad's officials went to him and explained:

Israel's gods are mountain gods. We fought Israel's army in the hills, and that's why they defeated us. But if we fight them on flat land, there's no way we can lose.

²⁴ Here's what you should do. First, get rid of those thirty-two kings and put army commanders in their places. ²⁵ Then get more soldiers, horses, and chariots, so your army will be as strong as it was before. We'll fight Israel's army on flat land and wipe them out.

Benhadad agreed and did what they suggested.

---

*20.1 King Benhadad of Syria: This is probably not the same Benhadad mentioned in 15.18–21.
*20.3 wives: Having more than one wife was allowed in those times.

*20.22 the prophet: See verse 13.

26 In the spring, Benhadad got his army together, and they marched to the town of Aphek to attack Israel. 27 The Israelites also prepared to fight. They marched out to meet the Syrians, and the two armies camped facing each other. The Syrians covered the whole area, but the Israelites looked like two little flocks of goats.

28 The prophet went to Ahab and said, "The Syrians think the LORD is a god of the hills and not of the valleys. So he has promised to help you defeat their powerful army. Then you will know that the LORD is in control."

29 For seven days the two armies stayed in their camps, facing each other. Then on the seventh day the fighting broke out, and before sunset the Israelites had killed one hundred thousand Syrian troops. 30 The rest of the Syrian army ran back to Aphek, but the town wall fell and crushed twenty-seven thousand of them.

Benhadad also escaped to Aphek and hid in the back room of a house. 31 His officials said, "Your Majesty, we've heard that Israel's kings keep their agreements. We will wrap sackcloth around our waists, put ropes around our heads, and ask Ahab to let us live."

32 They dressed in sackcloth and put ropes on their heads, then they went to Ahab and said, "Your servant Benhadad asks you to let him live."

"Is he still alive?" Ahab asked. "Benhadad is like a brother to me."

33 Benhadad's officials were trying to understand what Ahab was thinking, and when he said "brother," they quickly replied, "You're right! You and Benhadad are like brothers."

"Go and get him," Ahab said.

When Benhadad came out, Ahab asked him to climb up into his chariot.

34 Benhadad said, "I'll give back the towns my father took from your father. And you can have shops in Damascus, just as my father had in Samaria."

Ahab replied, "If you do these things, I'll let you go free." Then they signed a peace treaty, and Ahab let Benhadad go.

A prophet condemns Ahab

35 About this time the LORD commanded a prophet to say to a friend, "Hit me!" But the friend refused, 36 and the prophet told him, "You disobeyed the LORD, and as soon as you walk away, a lion will kill you." The friend left, and suddenly a lion killed him.

37 The prophet found someone else and said, "Hit me!" So this man beat him up.

38 The prophet left and put a bandage over his face to disguise himself. Then he went and stood beside the road, waiting for Ahab to pass by.

39 When Ahab went by, the prophet shouted, "Your Majesty, right in the heat of battle, someone brought me a prisoner to me and told me to guard him. He said if the prisoner got away, I would either be killed or forced to pay three thousand pieces of silver. 40 But I got busy doing other things, and the prisoner escaped."

Ahab answered, "You will be punished just as you have said."

41 The man quickly tore the bandage off his face, and Ahab saw that he was one of the prophets. 42 The prophet said, "The LORD told you to kill Benhadad, but you let him go. Now you will die in his place, and your people will die in place of his people."

43 Ahab went back to Samaria, angry and depressed.

CHAPTER 21

Jezebel has Naboth killed

1 Naboth owned a vineyard in Jezreel near King Ahab's palace.

2 One day, Ahab said, "Naboth, your vineyard is near my palace. Give it to me so I can turn it into a vegetable garden. I'll give you a better vineyard or pay whatever you want for yours."

3 Naboth answered, "This vineyard has always been in my family. I won't let you have it."

4 So Ahab went home, angry and depressed because of what Naboth had told him. He lay on his bed, just staring at the wall and refusing to eat a thing.

5 Jezebel his wife came in and asked, "What's wrong? Why won't you eat?"

6 "I asked Naboth to sell me his vineyard or to let me give him a better one," Ahab replied. "And he told me I couldn't have it."

7 "Aren't you the king of Israel?" Jezebel asked. "Get out of bed and eat something! Don't worry, I'll get Naboth's vineyard for you."

8-10 Jezebel wrote a letter to each of the leaders of the town where Naboth lived. In the letters she said:

Call everyone together and tell them to go without eating* today. When they come together, give Naboth a seat at the front. Get two liars to sit facing him and swear that Naboth has cursed God and the king. Then take Naboth outside and stone him to death!

She signed Ahab's name to the letters and sealed them with his seal. Then she sent them to the town leaders.

¹¹ After receiving her letters, they did exactly what she had asked. ¹² They told the people that it was a day to go without eating, and when they all came together, they seated Naboth at the front. ¹³ The two liars came in and sat facing Naboth. Then they accused him of cursing God and the king, so the people dragged Naboth outside and stoned him to death.

¹⁴ The leaders of Jezreel sent a message back to Jezebel that said, "Naboth is dead."

¹⁵ As soon as Jezebel got their message, she told Ahab, "Now you can have the vineyard Naboth refused to sell. He's dead." ¹⁶ Ahab got up and went to take over the vineyard.

Elijah condemns Ahab

¹⁷ The LORD said to Elijah the prophet, ¹⁸ "King Ahab of Israel is in Naboth's vineyard right now, taking it over. ¹⁹ Go and tell him that I say, 'Ahab, you murdered Naboth and took his property. And so, in the very spot where dogs licked up Naboth's blood, they will lick up your blood.' "

When Elijah found him, ²⁰ Ahab said, "So, my enemy, you've found me at last."

Elijah answered:

Yes, I have! Ahab, you have managed to do everything the LORD hates. ²¹ Now you will be punished. You and every man and boy in your family will die, whether slave or free. ²² Your whole family will be wiped out, just like the families of King Jeroboam and King Baasha. You've made the LORD very angry by sinning and causing the Israelites to sin.

²³ And as for Jezebel, dogs will eat her body there in Jezreel. ²⁴ Dogs will also eat the bodies of your relatives who die in town, and vultures will eat the bodies of those who die in the country.

²⁵⁻²⁹ When Ahab heard this, he tore his clothes and wore sackcloth day and night. He was depressed and refused to eat.

Some time later, the LORD said, "Elijah, do you see how sorry Ahab is for what he did? I won't punish his family while he is still alive. I'll wait until his son is king."

No one was more determined than Ahab to disobey the LORD. And Jezebel encouraged him. Worst of all, he had worshipped idols, just as the Amorites* had done before the LORD forced them out of the land and gave it to Israel.

CHAPTER 22

Micaiah warns Ahab about disaster

This is also told in 2 Chronicles 18.2–27

¹ For the next three years there was peace between Israel and Syria. ² During the third year King Jehoshaphat of Judah went to visit King Ahab of Israel.

³ Ahab asked his officials, "Why haven't we tried to get Ramoth in Gilead back from the Syrians? It belongs to us." ⁴ Then he asked Jehoshaphat, "Would you go to Ramoth with me and attack the Syrians?"

"Just tell me what to do," Jehoshaphat answered. "My army and horses are at your command. ⁵ But first, let's ask the LORD."

⁶ Ahab sent for about four hundred prophets and asked, "Should I attack the Syrians at Ramoth?"

"Yes!" the prophets answered. "The Lord will help you defeat them."

⁷ But Jehoshaphat said, "Just to make sure, is there another of the LORD's prophets we can ask?"

⁸ "We could ask Micaiah son of Imlah," Ahab said. "But I hate Micaiah. He always has bad news for me."

"Don't say that!" Jehoshaphat replied. ⁹ Then Ahab sent someone to bring Micaiah as soon as possible.

¹⁰ All this time, Ahab and Jehoshaphat were dressed in their royal robes and were seated on their thrones at the threshing place near the gate of Samaria. They were listening to the prophets tell them what the LORD had said.

¹¹ Zedekiah son of Chenaanah was one of the prophets. He had made some horns out of iron and shouted, "Ahab, the LORD says

---

*21.8–10 to go without eating: People sometimes came together to worship and went without eating to show that they were sorry for their sins.
See also: 21.23: 2 King 9.36.

*21.25–29 Amorites: A name sometimes used of the people who lived in Palestine before the Israelites.

you will attack the Syrians like a bull with iron horns and wipe them out!"

¹² All the prophets agreed that Ahab should attack the Syrians at Ramoth, and they promised that the LORD would help him defeat them.

¹³ Meanwhile, the messenger who went to get Micaiah whispered, "Micaiah, all the prophets have good news for Ahab. Now go and say the same thing."

¹⁴ "I'll say whatever the living LORD tells me to say," Micaiah replied.

¹⁵ Then Micaiah went to Ahab, and Ahab asked, "Micaiah, should I attack the Syrians at Ramoth?"

"Yes!" Micaiah answered. "The LORD will help you defeat them."

¹⁶ "Micaiah, I've told you over and over again to tell me the truth!" Ahab shouted. "What does the LORD really say?"

¹⁷ He answered, "In a vision* I saw Israelite soldiers walking around in the hills like sheep without a shepherd to guide them. The LORD said, 'This army has no leader. They should go home and not fight.' "

¹⁸ Ahab turned to Jehoshaphat and said, "I told you he would bring bad news!"

¹⁹ Micaiah replied:

Listen to this! I also saw the LORD seated on his throne with every creature in heaven gathered around him. ²⁰ The LORD asked, "Who can trick Ahab and make him go to Ramoth where he will be killed?"

They talked about it for a while, ²¹ then finally a spirit came forward and said to the LORD, "I can trick Ahab."

"How?" the LORD asked.

²² "I'll make Ahab's prophets lie to him."

"Good!" the LORD replied. "Now go and do it."

²³ This is exactly what has happened, Ahab. The LORD made all your prophets lie to you, and he knows you will soon be destroyed.

²⁴ Zedekiah walked up to Micaiah and slapped him on the face. Then he asked, "Do you really think the LORD would speak to you and not to me?"

²⁵ Micaiah answered, "You'll find out on the day you have to hide in the back room of some house."

²⁶ Ahab shouted, "Arrest Micaiah! Take him to Prince Joash and Governor Amon of Samaria. ²⁷ Tell them to put him in prison and to give him nothing but bread and water until I come back safely."

²⁸ Micaiah said, "If you do come back, I was wrong about what the LORD wanted me to say." Then he told the crowd, "Don't forget what I said!"

Ahab dies at Ramoth

This is also told in 2 Chronicles 18.28–34

²⁹ Ahab and Jehoshaphat led their armies to Ramoth in Gilead. ³⁰ Before they went into battle, Ahab said, "Jehoshaphat, I'll disguise myself, but you wear your royal robe." Then Ahab disguised himself and went into battle.

³¹ The king of Syria had ordered his thirty-two chariot commanders to attack only Ahab. ³² So when they saw Jehoshaphat in his robe, they thought he was Ahab and started to attack him. But when Jehoshaphat shouted out to them, ³³ they realized he wasn't Ahab, and they left him alone.

³⁴ However, during the fighting a soldier shot an arrow without even aiming, and it hit Ahab where two pieces of his armour joined. He shouted to his chariot driver, "I've been hit! Get me out of here!"

³⁵ The fighting lasted all day, with Ahab propped up in his chariot so he could see the Syrian troops. He bled so much that the bottom of the chariot was covered with blood, and by evening he was dead.

³⁶ As the sun was going down, someone in Israel's army shouted to the others, "Retreat! Go back home!"

³⁷ Ahab's body was taken to Samaria and buried there. ³⁸ Some workers washed his chariot near a spring in Samaria, and prostitutes washed themselves in his blood.* Dogs licked Ahab's blood off the ground, just as the LORD had warned.

³⁹ Everything else Ahab did while he was king, including the towns he strengthened and the palace he built and furnished with ivory, is written in *The History of the Kings of Israel*. ⁴⁰ Ahab died, and his son Ahaziah became king.

---

*22.17 vision: In ancient times, prophets often told about future events from what they had seen in visions or dreams.

See also: **22.17:** Num 27.17; Matt 9.36; Mark 6.34.
22.19: Job 1.6; Isa 6.1.

King Jehoshaphat of Judah and King Ahaziah of Israel

King Jehoshaphat of Judah

This is also told in 2 Chronicles 20.31–21.1

⁴¹ Jehoshaphat son of Asa became king of Judah in Ahab's fourth year as king of Israel. ⁴² Jehoshaphat was thirty-five years old when he became king, and he ruled from Jerusalem for twenty-five years. His mother was Azubah daughter of Shilhi.

⁴³⁻⁴⁶ Jehoshaphat obeyed the LORD, just as his father Asa had done, and during his rule he was at peace with the king of Israel.

He got rid of the rest of the prostitutes* from the local shrines, but he did not destroy the shrines, and they were still used as places for offering sacrifices.

Everything else Jehoshaphat did while he was king, including his brave deeds and military victories, is written in *The History of the Kings of Judah*.

⁴⁷ The country of Edom had no king at the time, so a lower official ruled the land.

⁴⁸ Jehoshaphat had seagoing ships* built to sail to Ophir for gold. But they were wrecked at Ezion-Geber and never sailed. ⁴⁹ Ahaziah son of Ahab offered to let his sailors go with Jehoshaphat's sailors, but Jehoshaphat refused.

⁵⁰ Jehoshaphat died and was buried beside his ancestors in Jerusalem,' and his son Jehoram became king.

King Ahaziah of Israel

⁵¹ Ahaziah son of Ahab became king of Israel in the seventeenth year of Jehoshaphat's rule in Judah, and he ruled two years from Samaria.

⁵² Ahaziah disobeyed the LORD, just as his father, his mother, and Jeroboam had done. They all led Israel to sin. ⁵³ Ahaziah worshipped Baal and made the LORD God of Israel very angry, just as his father had done.

*22.43–46 prostitutes: See the note at 14.24.
*22.48 seagoing ships: See the note at 10.22.

Additional notes

'1.8 Shimei, Rei: Or "Shimei his adviser".
'1.9 Crawling Rock: Or "Zoheleth Rock".
'1.38 the two . . . bodyguards: The Hebrew text has "the Cherethites and the Pelethites", who were foreign soldiers hired by David to be part of his bodyguard.

'1.44,45 David's special bodyguards: See the note at 1.38.
'2.10,11 Jerusalem: Hebrew "the city of David".
'2.22 And why . . . Joab: One possible meaning for the difficult Hebrew text.
'2.29 he sent someone . . . for protection: One ancient translation; these words are not in the Hebrew text.
'3.1 the older . . . Jerusalem: Hebrew "the city of David".
'3.2 local shrines: The Hebrew text has "high places", which were local places to worship God or foreign gods.
'3.16 women: Hebrew "prostitutes".
'4.19 of Judah: One ancient translation; these words are not in the Hebrew text.
'6.15 from floor to ceiling: One possible meaning for the difficult Hebrew text.
'6.16 standing . . . ceiling: One possible meaning for the difficult Hebrew text.
'6.33,34 two sections: One possible meaning for the difficult Hebrew text.
'7.9 From . . . best stones: One possible meaning for the difficult Hebrew text.
'7.17 seven rows . . . chains: One possible meaning for the difficult Hebrew text.
'7.19 lilies: One possible meaning for the difficult Hebrew text of verse 19.
'8.9 Sinai: Hebrew "Horeb".
'8.65 seven days: One ancient translation; Hebrew "seven days and seven more days, fourteen days in all."
'9.8 a pile of rocks: Some ancient translations; Hebrew "high".
'9.24 the older . . . Jerusalem: See the note at 3.1.
'10.8 wives: Two ancient translations; Hebrew "men".
'10.11–13 steps: Or "stools" or "railings".
'10.22 peacocks: Or "baboons".
'12.2 he stayed in Egypt: Hebrew; two ancient translations "he returned from Egypt" (see also 2 Chronicles 10.2).
'12.10 Compared . . . weak: Hebrew "My little finger is bigger than my father's waist."
'12.15–19 Adoniram: Two ancient translations (see also 4.6 and 5.14); Hebrew "Adoram".
'12.28 Here are your gods: Or "Here is your God".
'12.29,30 the crowd . . . taken there: One possible meaning for the difficult Hebrew text.
'12.31 shrines: See the note at 3.2.
'13.1,2 one of God's prophets: Hebrew "a man of God".
'14.14 And I mean very soon: One possible meaning for the difficult Hebrew text.
'14.23 local shrines: See the note at 3.2.
'14.31 Jerusalem: See the note at 2.10,11.
'15.8 Jerusalem: See the note at 2.10,11.
'15.18 Benhadad: Hebrew "Benhadad son of Tabrimmon son of Hezion".
'15.24 Jerusalem: See the note at 2.10,11.

ᵗ**16.2 Nobody . . . you:** Hebrew "I pulled you up out of the dust".

ᵗ**17.1 from Tishbe in Gilead:** Or "from the settlers in Gilead".

ᵗ**18.36 this nation:** Hebrew "Israel".

ᵗ**18.37 will turn . . . to you:** One possible meaning for the difficult Hebrew text.

ᵗ**19.8 Sinai:** See the note at 8.9.

ᵗ**19.12 a gentle breeze:** Or "a soft whisper" or "hardly a sound".

ᵗ**19.13 The LORD:** Hebrew "A voice".

ᵗ**19.16 Shaphat:** Hebrew "Shaphat from Abel-Meholah".

ᵗ**20.6 you:** Hebrew; three ancient translations "they".

ᵗ**20.21 captured:** One ancient translation; Hebrew "attacked".

ᵗ**22.38 prostitutes . . . blood:** Or "they cleaned his weapons".

ᵗ**22.50 Jerusalem:** See the note at 2.10,11.

2 Kings

A quick look at this book

The Second Book of Kings is the second half of
a single book that was divided into two parts,
1 and 2 Kings, because together they were too
long to fit on one scroll. The book of 2 Kings
continues the history of the two separate
kingdoms of Judah and Israel.

The book of 2 Kings has two main parts. The
first part (1—17) is the history of the two
kingdoms until 722 BC, when the northern
kingdom was conquered by the Assyrians.
Samaria, the capital city of Israel, was
destroyed, and the people of that kingdom

were taken as prisoners to Assyria. Only Judah,
the southern kingdom, was left.

The second part of the book (18—25) is the
history of Judah until 586 BC, when it was
conquered by King Nebuchadnezzar of
Babylonia. Jerusalem, the capital city, was
completely destroyed, and many of the people
of Judah and Jerusalem were led away as
prisoners to Babylonia. King Nebuchadnezzar
then made Gedaliah ruler of those left in
Judah. The book concludes with some hope for
Judah's future: King Jehoiachin is released
from prison in Babylon and is invited to eat
with the Babylonian king every day.

According to the book of 2 Kings, Israel and
Judah were destroyed because the people
refused to be faithful to the Lord. He had sent
prophets over and over again to warn the
people and their kings to stop worshipping
other gods and to turn back to him. Finally, the
people were punished. The two kingdoms
were destroyed, and the people were forced to
live in foreign nations, far from their own land.
The fall of Jerusalem is one of the most
important events in Israel's history. The book
itself explains why this disaster took place:

> *The people of Judah and Jerusalem had made*
> *the LORD so angry that he finally turned his*
> *back on them. That's why these horrible things*
> *were happening.*

(24.20b)

Elijah the prophet condemns King Ahaziah of Israel

CHAPTER 1

1-2 Soon after King Ahab of Israel died, the country of Moab rebelled against his son King Ahaziah.*

One day, Ahaziah fell through the wooden slats around the porch on the flat roof of his palace in Samaria, and he was badly injured. So he sent some messengers to the town of Ekron* with orders to ask the god Baalzebub if he would get well.

3 About the same time, an angel from the LORD sent Elijah the prophet from Tishbe to say to the king's messengers, "Ahaziah has rejected Israel's own God by sending you to ask Baalzebub about his injury. 4 Tell him that because he has done this, he's on his deathbed!" And Elijah did what he was told.

5 When the messengers returned to Ahaziah, he asked, "Why are you back so soon?"

6 "A man met us along the road with a message for you from the LORD," they answered. "The LORD wants to know why you sent us to ask Baalzebub about your injury and why you don't believe there's a God in Israel. The man also told us that the LORD says you're going to die."

7 "What did the man look like?" Ahaziah asked.

8 "He was hairy* and had a leather belt around his waist," they answered.

"It must be Elijah!" replied Ahaziah. 9 So at once he sent an army officer and fifty soldiers to meet Elijah.

Elijah was sitting on top of a hill* at the time. The officer went up to him and said, "Man of God, the king orders you to come down and talk with him."

10 "If I am a man of God," Elijah answered, "God will send down fire on you and your fifty soldiers." Fire immediately came down from heaven and burnt up the officer and his men.

11 Ahaziah sent another officer and fifty more soldiers to Elijah. The officer said, "Man of God, the king orders you to come and see him at once."

12 "If I am a man of God," Elijah answered, "fire will destroy you and your fifty soldiers." And God sent down fire* from heaven on the officer and his men.

13 Ahaziah sent a third army officer and fifty more soldiers. This officer went up to Elijah, then he got down on his knees and begged, "Man of God, please be kind to me and these fifty servants of yours. Let us live! 14 Fire has already wiped out the other officers and their soldiers. Please don't let it happen to me."

15 The angel from the LORD said to Elijah, "Go with him and don't be afraid." So Elijah got up and went with the officer.

16 When Elijah arrived, he told Ahaziah, "The LORD wants to know why you sent messengers to Ekron to ask Baalzebub about your injury. Don't you believe there's a God in Israel? Ahaziah, because you did that, the LORD says you will die."

17 Ahaziah died, just as the LORD had said. But since Ahaziah had no sons, Joram* his brother* then became king. This happened in the second year that Jehoram son of Jehoshaphat was king of Judah.* 18 Everything else Ahaziah did while he was king is written in *The History of the Kings of Israel.*

Elisha the prophet

CHAPTER 2

The LORD takes Elijah away

1 Not long before the LORD took Elijah up into heaven in a strong wind, Elijah and Elisha* were leaving Gilgal. 2 Elijah said to Elisha, "The LORD wants me to go to Bethel, but you must stay here."

Elisha replied, "I swear by the living LORD and by your own life that I will stay with you no matter what!" And he went with Elijah to Bethel.

3 A group of prophets who lived there asked Elisha, "Do you know that today the LORD is going to take away your master?"

---

*1.1,2 the country . . . King Ahaziah: The story of Moab's rebellion is in 3.4-27.
*1.1,2 Ekron: An important Philistine town about sixty-five kilometres south-west of Samaria.
*1.9 a hill: Probably Mount Carmel.
*1.9 Man of God: Another name for a prophet of the LORD.
See also: 1.8: Matt 3.4; Mark 1.6. 1.10: Luke 9.54.

*1.17 This happened . . . Judah: According to 3.1, this was also the eighteenth year of Jehoshaphat's rule in Judah. In biblical times, a father and son would sometimes rule as kings at the same time. This way, when the father died, the son would already have control of the kingdom (see also 8.16).
See also: 1.12: Luke 9.54.

"Yes, I do," Elisha answered. "But don't remind me of it."

[4] Elijah then said, "Elisha, now the LORD wants me to go to Jericho, but you must stay here."

Elisha replied, "I swear by the living LORD and by your own life, that I will stay with you no matter what!" And he went with Elijah to Jericho.

[5] A group of prophets who lived there asked Elisha, "Do you know that today the LORD is going to take away your master?"

"Yes, I do," Elisha answered. "But don't remind me of it."

[6] Elijah then said to Elisha, "Now the LORD wants me to go to the River Jordan, but you must stay here."

Elisha replied, "I swear by the living LORD and by your own life that I will never leave you!" So the two of them walked on together.

[7] Fifty prophets followed Elijah and Elisha from Jericho, then stood at a distance and watched as the two men walked towards the river. [8] When they got there, Elijah took off his coat, then he rolled it up and struck the water with it. At once a path opened up through the river, and the two of them walked across on dry ground.

[9] After they had reached the other side, Elijah said, "Elisha, the LORD will soon take me away. What can I do for you before that happens?"

Elisha answered, "Please give me twice as much of your power as you give the other prophets, so I can be the one who takes your place as their leader."

[10] "It won't be easy," Elijah answered. "It can happen only if you see me as I am being taken away."

[11] Elijah and Elisha were walking along and talking, when suddenly there appeared between them a flaming chariot pulled by fiery horses. Straight away, a strong wind took Elijah up into heaven. [12] Elisha saw this and shouted, "Israel's cavalry and chariots have taken my master away!" After Elijah had gone, Elisha tore his clothes in sorrow.

[13] Elijah's coat had fallen off, so Elisha picked it up and walked back to the River Jordan. [14] He struck the water with the coat and wondered, "Will the LORD perform miracles for me as he did for Elijah?" As soon as Elisha did this, a dry path opened up through the water, and he walked across.

[15] When the prophets from Jericho saw what happened, they said to each other, "Elisha now has Elijah's power."

They walked over to him, bowed down, [16] and said, "There are fifty strong men here with us. Please let them go and look for your master. Perhaps the Spirit of the LORD carried him off to some mountain or valley."

"No," Elisha replied, "they won't find him."

[17] They kept begging until he was embarrassed to say no. He finally agreed, and the prophets sent the men out. They looked three days for Elijah but never found him. [18] They returned to Jericho, and Elisha said, "I told you that you wouldn't find him."

Elisha makes the water pure at Jericho

[19] One day the people of Jericho said, "Elisha, you can see that our city is in a good spot. But the water from our spring is so bad that it even keeps our crops from growing."

[20] He replied, "Put some salt in a new bowl and bring it to me."

They brought him the bowl of salt, [21] and he carried it to the spring. He threw the salt into the water and said, "The LORD has made this water pure again. From now on you'll be able to grow crops, and no one will starve."

[22] The water has been fine ever since, just as Elisha said.

Some boys make fun of Elisha

[23] Elisha left and headed towards Bethel. Along the way some boys started making fun of him by shouting, "Go away, baldy! Get out of here!"

[24] Elisha turned round and stared at the boys. Then he cursed them in the name of the LORD. Straight away two bears ran out of the woods and ripped to pieces forty-two of the boys.

[25] Elisha went up to Mount Carmel, then returned to Samaria.

CHAPTER 3

King Joram of Israel

[1] Joram* son of Ahab became king of Israel in Jehoshaphat's eighteenth year as king of Judah.* Joram ruled twelve years from Samaria [2] and disobeyed the LORD by doing wrong. He tore down the stone image his

---

*3.1 Joram: See the note at 1.17 and additional note 1.12.

*3.1 Joram . . . Judah: See 1.17 and 8.16 and the notes there.

father had made to honour Baal, and so he wasn't as sinful as his parents. ³ But he kept doing the sinful things that Jeroboam son of Nebat had led Israel to do.*

The country of Moab rebels against Israel

⁴ For many years the country of Moab had been controlled by Israel and was forced to pay taxes to the kings of Israel. King Mesha of Moab raised sheep, so he paid the king of Israel one hundred thousand lambs and the wool from one hundred thousand rams. ⁵ But soon after the death of Ahab, Mesha rebelled against Israel.

⁶ One day, Joram left Samaria and called together Israel's army. ⁷ He sent this message to King Jehoshaphat of Judah, "The king of Moab has rebelled. Will you go with me to attack him?"

"Yes, I will," Jehoshaphat answered. "I'm on your side, and my soldiers and horses are at your command. ⁸ But which way should we go?"

"We will march through Edom Desert," Joram replied.

⁹ So Joram, Jehoshaphat, and the king of Edom led their troops out. But seven days later, there was no drinking water left for them or their animals. ¹⁰ Joram cried out, "This is terrible! The LORD must have led us out here to be captured by Moab's army."

¹¹ Jehoshaphat said, "Which of the LORD's prophets are with us? We can find out from him what the LORD wants us to do."

One of Joram's officers answered, "Elisha son of Shaphat is here. He was one of Elijah's closest followers."

¹² Jehoshaphat replied, "He can give us the LORD's message."

The three kings went over to Elisha, ¹³ and he asked Joram, "Why did you come to me? Go and talk to the prophets of the foreign gods your parents worshipped."*

"No," Joram answered. "It was the LORD who led us out here, so that Moab's army could capture us."

¹⁴ Elisha said to him, "I serve the LORD All-Powerful, and as surely as he lives, I swear I wouldn't even look at you if I didn't respect King Jehoshaphat." ¹⁵ Then Elisha said, "Send for someone who can play the harp."

The harpist began playing, and the LORD gave Elisha this message for Joram:

¹⁶ The LORD says that this dry river bed will be filled with water.* ¹⁷ You won't feel any wind or see any rain, but there will be plenty of water for you and your animals.

¹⁸ That simple thing isn't all the LORD is going to do. He will also help you defeat Moab's army. ¹⁹ You will capture all their walled cities and important towns. You will chop down every good tree and stop up every spring of water, then ruin their fertile fields by covering them with rocks.

²⁰ The next morning, while the sacrifice was being offered, water suddenly started flowing from the direction of Edom, and it flooded the land.

²¹ Meanwhile, the people of Moab had heard that the three kings were coming to attack them. They had called together all their fighting men, from the youngest to the oldest, and these troops were now standing at their border, ready for battle. ²² When they got up that morning, the sun was shining across the water, making it look red. The Moabite troops took one look ²³ and shouted, "Look at that blood! The armies of those kings must have fought and killed each other. Come on, let's go and take what's left in their camp."

²⁴ But when they arrived at Israel's camp, the Israelite soldiers came out and attacked them, until they turned and ran away. Israel's army chased them all the way back to Moab, and even there they kept up the attack.* ²⁵ The Israelites destroyed the Moabite towns. They chopped down the good trees and stopped up the springs of water, then covered the fertile fields with rocks.

Finally, the only city left standing was Kir-Hareseth, but soldiers armed with slings surrounded and attacked it. ²⁶ King Mesha of Moab saw that he was about to be defeated. So he took along seven hundred soldiers with swords and tried to break through the front line where the Edomite troops were positioned. But he failed. ²⁷ He then grabbed his eldest son who was to be the next king and sacrificed him as an offering on the city wall. The Israelite troops were so horrified that* they left the city and went back home.

---

*3.3 the sinful things . . . to do: When Jeroboam became king of Israel, he made two gold statues of calves and put them in the towns of Bethel and Dan, so the people of Israel could worship them (see 1 Kings 12.26–30).

*3.13 the prophets . . . worshipped: These were prophets of the Canaanite god Baal and the goddess Asherah (see 1 Kings 16.30–33; 18.19).

CHAPTER 4

Elisha helps a poor widow

¹ One day the widow of one of the LORD's prophets said to Elisha, "You know that before my husband died, he was a follower of yours and a worshipper of the LORD. But he owed a man some money, and now that man is on his way to take my two sons as his slaves."

² "Perhaps there's something I can do to help," Elisha said. "What do you have in your house?"

"Sir, I have nothing but a small bottle of olive oil."

³ Elisha told her, "Ask your neighbours for their empty jars. And after you've borrowed as many as you can, ⁴ go home and shut the door behind you and your sons. Then begin filling the jars with oil and set each one aside as you fill it." ⁵ The woman left.

Later, when she and her sons were back inside their house, the two sons brought her the jars, and she began filling them.

⁶ At last, she said to one of her sons, "Bring me another jar."

"We don't have any more," he answered, and the oil stopped flowing from the small bottle.

⁷ After she told Elisha what had happened, he said, "Sell the oil and use part of the money to pay what you owe the man. You and your sons can live on what is left."

Elisha brings a rich woman's son back to life

⁸ Once, while Elisha was in the town of Shunem,* he met a rich woman who invited him to her home for dinner. After that, whenever he was in Shunem, he would have a meal there with her and her husband.

⁹ Some time later the woman said to her husband, "I'm sure the man who comes here so often is a prophet of God. ¹⁰ Why don't we build him a small room on the flat roof of our house? We can put a bed, a table and chair, and an oil lamp in it. Then whenever he comes, he can stay with us."

¹¹ The next time Elisha was in Shunem, he stopped at their house and went up to his room to rest. ¹²⁻¹³ He said to his servant Gehazi, "This woman has been very helpful. Ask her to come up here to the roof for a moment." She came, and Elisha told Gehazi to say to her, "You've gone to a lot of trouble

for us, and we want to help you. Is there something we can request the king or army commander to do?"*

The woman answered, "With my relatives nearby, I have everything I need."

¹⁴ "Then what can we do for her?" Elisha asked Gehazi.

Gehazi replied, "I do know that her husband is old, and that she doesn't have a son."

¹⁵ "Ask her to come here again," Elisha told his servant. He called for her, and she came and stood in the doorway of Elisha's room.

¹⁶ Elisha said to her, "Next year at this time, you'll be holding your own baby son in your arms."

"You're a man of God," the woman replied. "Please don't lie to me."

¹⁷ But a few months later, the woman got pregnant. She gave birth to a son, just as Elisha had promised.

¹⁸ One day while the boy was still young, he was out in the fields with his father, where the workers were harvesting the crops. ¹⁹ Suddenly he shouted, "My head hurts. It hurts a lot!"

"Carry him back to his mother," the father said to his servant. ²⁰ The servant picked up the boy and carried him to his mother. The boy lay on her lap all morning, and by midday he was dead. ²¹ She carried him upstairs to Elisha's room and laid him across the bed. Then she walked out and shut the door behind her.

²² The woman called to her husband, "I need to see the prophet. Let me use one of the donkeys. Send a servant along with me, and let me leave now, so I can get back quickly."

²³ "Why do you need to see him today?" her husband asked. "It's not the Sabbath or time for the New Moon Festival."

"That's all right," she answered. ²⁴ She saddled the donkey and said to her servant, "Let's go. And don't slow down unless I tell you to." ²⁵ She left at once for Mount Carmel* to talk with Elisha.

When Elisha saw her coming, he said, "Gehazi, look! It's the woman from Shunem. ²⁶ Run and meet her. And ask her if everything is all right with her and her family."

---

*4.8 Shunem: A town in Israel, about forty kilometres north of Samaria.

*4.12,13 request the king . . . do: Elisha may have meant that he could ask these leaders to lower her taxes.

*4.25 Mount Carmel: About forty kilometres from Shunem.

See also: 4.16: Gen 18.4.

"Everything is fine," she answered Gehazi. 27 But as soon as she got to the top of the mountain, she went over and grabbed Elisha by the feet.

Gehazi started towards her to push her away, when Elisha said, "Leave her alone! Don't you see how sad she is? But the LORD hasn't told me why."

28 The woman said, "Sir, I begged you not to get my hopes up, and I didn't even ask you for a son."

29 "Gehazi, get ready and go to her house," Elisha said. "Take along my walking stick, and when you get there, lay it on the boy's face. Don't stop to talk to anyone, even if they try to talk to you."

30 But the boy's mother said to Elisha, "I swear by the living LORD and by your own life that I won't leave without you." So Elisha got up and went with them.

31 Gehazi ran on ahead and laid Elisha's walking stick on the boy's face, but the boy didn't move or make a sound. Gehazi ran back to Elisha and said, "The boy didn't wake up."

32 Elisha arrived at the woman's house and went straight to his room, where he saw the boy's body on his bed. 33 He walked in, shut the door, and prayed to the LORD. 34 Then he got on the bed and stretched out over the dead body, with his mouth on the boy's mouth, his eyes on his eyes, and his hand on his hands. As he lay there, the boy's body became warm. 35 Elisha got up and walked back and forth in the room, then he went back and leaned over the boy's body. The boy sneezed seven times and opened his eyes.

36 Elisha called out to Gehazi, "Ask the boy's mother to come here." Gehazi did, and when she was at the door, Elisha said, "You can take your son."

37 She came in and bowed down at Elisha's feet. Then she picked up her son and left.

Elisha makes some stew taste better

38 Later, Elisha went back to Gilgal, where there was almost nothing to eat, because the crops had failed.

One day while the prophets who lived there were meeting with Elisha, he said to his servant, "Prepare a big pot of stew for these prophets."

39 One of them went out into the woods to gather some herbs. He found a wild vine and picked as much of its fruit as he could carry,

but he didn't know that the fruit was very sour. When he got back, he cut up the fruit and put it in the stew.

40 The stew was served, and when the prophets started eating it, they shouted, "Elisha, this stew tastes terrible! We can't eat it."

41 "Bring me some flour," Elisha said. He sprinkled the flour in the stew and said, "Now serve it to them." And the stew tasted fine.

Elisha feeds a hundred people

42 A man from the town of Baal-Shalishah* brought Elisha some freshly cut grain and twenty loaves of bread made from the first barley that was harvested. Elisha said, "Give it to the people so they can eat."

43 "There's not enough here for a hundred people," his servant said.

"Just give it to them," Elisha replied. "The LORD has promised there will be more than enough."

44 So the servant served the bread and grain to the people. They ate and still had some left over, just as the LORD had promised.

CHAPTER 5

Elisha heals Naaman

1 Naaman was the commander of the Syrian army. The LORD had helped him and his troops defeat their enemies, so the king of Syria respected Naaman very much. Naaman was a brave soldier, but he had leprosy.*

2 One day while the Syrian troops were raiding Israel, they captured a girl, and she became a servant of Naaman's wife. 3 Some time later the girl said, "If your husband Naaman would go to the prophet in Samaria, he would be cured of his leprosy."

4 When Naaman told the king what the girl had said, 5 the king replied, "Go ahead! I will give you a letter to take to the king of Israel."

Naaman left and took along thirty thousand pieces of silver, six thousand pieces of gold, and ten new outfits. 6 He also carried the letter to the king of Israel. It said, "I am sending my servant Naaman to you. Would you cure him of his leprosy?"

---

*4.42 Baal-Shalishah: The exact location of this town is not known, but it was probably somewhere near Shechem.
*5.1 leprosy: The word translated "leprosy" was used for many different kinds of skin diseases.

See also: 4.34,35: 1 King 17.21.
See also: 5.1–14: Luke 4.27.

7 When the king of Israel read the letter, he tore his clothes in fear and shouted, "That Syrian king believes I can cure this man of leprosy! Does he think I'm God with power over life and death? He must be trying to pick a fight with me."

8 As soon as Elisha the prophet* heard what had happened, he sent the Israelite king this message: "Why are you so afraid? Send the man to me, so that he will know there is a prophet in Israel."

9 Naaman left with his horses and chariots and stopped at the door of Elisha's house. 10 Elisha sent someone outside to say to him, "Go and wash seven times in the River Jordan. Then you'll be completely cured."

11 But Naaman stormed off, grumbling, "Why couldn't he come out and talk to me? I thought he would be sure to stand in front of me and pray to the LORD his God, then wave his hand over my skin and cure me. 12 What about the River Abana* or the River Pharpar? Those rivers in Damascus are just as good as any river in Israel. I could have washed in them and been cured."

13 His servants went over to him and said, "Sir, if the prophet had told you to do something difficult, you would have done it. So why don't you do what he said? Go and wash and be cured."

14 Naaman walked down to the Jordan; he waded out into the water and stooped down in it seven times, just as Elisha had told him. Straight away, he was cured, and his skin became as smooth as a child's.

15 Naaman and his officials went back to Elisha. Naaman stood in front of him and announced, "Now I know that the God of Israel is the only God in the whole world. Sir, would you please accept a gift from me?"

16 "I am a servant of the living LORD," Elisha answered, "and I swear that I will not take anything from you."

Naaman kept begging, but Elisha kept refusing. 17 Finally Naaman said, "If you won't accept a gift, then please let me take home as much soil as two mules can pull in a wagon. Sir, from now on I will offer sacrifices only to the LORD.* 18 But I pray that the LORD will forgive me when I go into the temple of the god Rimmon and bow down there with the king of Syria."

19 "Go home, and don't worry about that," Elisha replied. Then Naaman left.

---

*5.17 let me take . . . the LORD: It was believed that the LORD had to be worshipped in Israel or on soil taken from Israel.

356

Elisha places a curse on Gehazi

After Naaman had gone only a short distance, 20 Gehazi said to himself, "Elisha let that Syrian off too easily. He should have taken Naaman's gift. I swear by the living LORD that I will talk to Naaman myself and get something from him." 21 So he hurried after Naaman.

When Naaman saw Gehazi running after him, he got out of his chariot to meet him. Naaman asked, "Is everything all right?"

22 "Yes," Gehazi answered. "But my master has sent me to tell you about two young prophets from the hills of Ephraim. They came asking for help, and now Elisha wants to know if you would give them three thousand pieces of silver and some new clothes?"

23 "Certainly," Naaman replied. "But why don't you take twice that amount of silver?" He convinced Gehazi to take it all, then put the silver in two bags. He handed the bags and the clothes to his two servants, and they carried them for Gehazi.

24 When they reached the hill where Gehazi lived, he took the bags from the servants and placed them in his house, then sent the men away. After they had gone, 25 Gehazi went in and stood in front of Elisha, who asked, "Gehazi, where have you been?"

"Nowhere, sir," Gehazi answered.

26 Elisha asked, "Don't you know that my spirit was there when Naaman got out of his chariot to talk with you? Gehazi, you have no right to accept money or clothes, olive orchards or vineyards, sheep or cattle, or servants. 27 Because of what you've done, Naaman's leprosy* will now be on you and your descendants for ever!"

Suddenly, Gehazi's skin became white with leprosy, and he left.

CHAPTER 6

Elisha makes an axe head float

1 One day the prophets said to Elisha, "The place where we meet with you is too small. 2 Why don't we build a new meeting place near the River Jordan? Each of us could get some wood, then we could build it."

"That's a good idea," Elisha replied, "get started."

3 "Aren't you going with us?" one of the prophets asked.

"Yes, I'll go," Elisha answered, 4 and he left with them.

---

*5.27 leprosy: See the note at 5.1.

They went to the River Jordan and began chopping down trees. ⁵ While one of the prophets was working, his axe head fell off and dropped into the water. "Oh!" he shouted. "Sir, I borrowed this axe."

⁶ "Where did it fall in?" Elisha asked. The prophet pointed to the place, and Elisha cut a stick and threw it into the water at that spot. The axe head floated to the top of the water.

⁷ "Now get it," Elisha told him. And the prophet reached in and grabbed it.

Elisha stops an invasion of the Syrian army

⁸ Time after time, when the king of Syria was at war against the Israelites, he met with his officers and announced, "I've decided where we will set up camp."

⁹ Each time, Elisha would send this warning to the king of Israel: "Don't go near there. That's where the Syrian troops have set up camp."* ¹⁰ So the king would warn the Israelite troops in that place to be on guard.

¹¹ The king of Syria was furious when he found out what was happening. He called in his officers and asked, "Which one of you has been telling the king of Israel our plans?"

¹² "None of us, Your Majesty," one of them answered. "It's an Israelite named Elisha. He's a prophet, so he can tell his king everything — even what you say in your own room."

¹³ "Find out where he is!" the king ordered. "I'll send soldiers to bring him here."

They learnt that Elisha was in the town of Dothan* and reported it to the king. ¹⁴ He ordered his best troops to go there with horses and chariots. They marched out during the night and surrounded the town.

¹⁵ When Elisha's servant got up the next morning, he saw that Syrian troops had the town surrounded. "Sir, what are we going to do?" he asked.

¹⁶ "Don't be afraid," Elisha answered. "There are more troops on our side than on theirs." ¹⁷ Then he prayed, "LORD, please help him to see." And the LORD let the servant see that the hill* was covered with fiery horses and flaming chariots all around Elisha.

¹⁸ As the Syrian army came closer, Elisha prayed, "LORD, make those soldiers blind!" And the LORD blinded them with a bright light.

¹⁹ Elisha told the enemy troops, "You've taken the wrong road and are in the wrong town. Follow me. I'll lead you to the man you're looking for." Elisha led them straight to the capital city of Samaria.

²⁰ When all the soldiers were inside the city, Elisha prayed, "LORD, now let them see again." The LORD let them see that they were standing in the middle of Samaria.

²¹ The king of Israel saw them and asked Elisha, "Should I kill them, sir?"

²² "No!" Elisha answered. "You didn't capture these troops in battle, so you have no right to kill them. Instead, give them something to eat and drink and let them return to their leader."

²³ The king ordered a huge meal to be prepared for Syria's army, and when they finished eating, he let them go.

For a while, the Syrian troops stopped invading Israel's territory.

King Benhadad of Syria attacks Samaria

²⁴ Some time later, King Benhadad of Syria* called his entire army together, then they marched to Samaria and attacked. ²⁵ They kept up the attack until there was nothing to eat in the city. In fact, a donkey's head cost about eighty pieces of silver, and a small bowl of pigeon droppings* cost five pieces of silver.

²⁶ One day as the king of Israel* was walking along the top of the city wall, a woman shouted to him, "Please, Your Majesty, help me!"

²⁷ "Let the LORD help you!" the king said. "Do you think I have grain or wine to give you?" ²⁸ Then he asked, "What's the matter anyway?"

The woman answered, "Another woman and I were so hungry that we agreed to eat our sons. She said if we ate my son one day, we could eat hers the next day. ²⁹ So yesterday we cooked my son and ate him. But today when I went to her house to eat her son, she had hidden him."

---

*6.13 Dothan: About fifteen kilometres north of Samaria.

*6.17 the hill: The hill on which the town was built.

*6.24 King Benhadad of Syria: This may or may not be the same Benhadad mentioned in 1 Kings 20.1. Several of the Syrian kings were named Benhadad.

*6.25 pigeon droppings: This may have been used for food or to burn for fuel. It also may have been a popular name for roasted beans or the shells of certain seeds.

*6.26 the king of Israel: Probably either Jehoahaz or Jehoash, but possibly even Joram.

See also: 6.29: Deut 28.57; Lam 4.10.

357

30 The king tore off his clothes in sorrow, and since he was on top of the city wall, the people saw that he was wearing sackcloth underneath. 31 He said, "I pray that God will punish me terribly, if Elisha's head is still on his shoulders by this time tomorrow."
32 Then he sent a messenger to Elisha.

Elisha was at home at the time, and the important leaders of Israel were meeting with him. Even before the king's messenger arrived, Elisha told the leaders, "That murderer* is sending someone to cut off my head. When you see him coming, shut the door and don't let him in. I'm sure the king himself will be just behind him."

33 Before Elisha finished talking, the messenger* came up and said, "The LORD has made all these terrible things happen to us. Why should I think he will help us now?"

CHAPTER 7

1 Elisha answered, "I have a message for you. The LORD promises that tomorrow here in Samaria, you will be able to buy a large sack of flour or two large sacks of barley for almost nothing."

2 The chief officer there with the king replied, "I don't believe it! Even if the LORD sent a rainstorm, it couldn't produce that much grain by tomorrow."

"You will see it happen, but you won't eat any of the food," Elisha warned him.

The Syrian army stops its attack

3 About the same time, four men with leprosy* were just outside the gate of Samaria. They said to each other, "Why should we sit here, waiting to die? 4 There's nothing to eat in the city, so we would starve if we went inside. But if we stay out here, we will die for certain. Let's sneak over to the Syrian army camp and surrender. They might kill us, but they might not." 5-6 That evening the four men got up and left for the Syrian camp.

As they walked towards the camp, the Lord caused the Syrian troops to hear what sounded like the roar of a huge force of cavalry. The soldiers said to each other, "Listen! The king of Israel must have hired Hittite and Egyptian troops to attack us. Let's get out of here!" So they ran out of their camp that night, leaving their tents and horses and donkeys.

When the four men with leprosy reached the edge of the Syrian camp, no one was there. They walked into one of the tents, where they ate and drank, before carrying off clothes, as well as silver and gold. They hid all this, then walked into another tent; they took what they wanted and hid it too.

9 They said to each other, "This isn't right. Today is a day to celebrate, and we haven't told anyone else what has happened. If we wait until morning, we will be punished. Let's go to the king's palace straight away and tell the good news."

10 They went back to Samaria and shouted up to the guards at the gate, "We've just come from the Syrian army camp, and all the soldiers are gone! The tents are empty, and the horses and donkeys are still tied up. We didn't see or hear anybody."

11 The guards reported the news to the king's palace. 12 The king got out of bed and said to his officers, "I know what those Syrians are doing. They know we're starving, so they're hiding in the fields, hoping we will go out to look for food. When we do, they can capture us and take over our city."

13 One of his officers replied, "We have a few horses left — why don't we let some men take five of them and go to the Syrian camp and see what's happening? We're going to die anyway like those who have already died."* 14 They found two chariots, and the king commanded the men to find out what had happened to the Syrian troops.

15 The men rode as far as the River Jordan. All the way they saw clothes and equipment that the Syrians had thrown away as they escaped. Then they went back to the king and told him what they had seen.

16 At once the people went to the Syrian camp and carried off what was left. They took so much that a large sack of flour and two large sacks of barley sold for almost nothing, just as the LORD had promised.

17 The king of Israel had put his chief officer in charge of the gate, but he died when the people trampled him as they rushed out of the city. 18 Earlier, when the king was at Elisha's house, Elisha had told him that flour or barley would sell for almost nothing. 19 But the officer refused to believe that even the LORD could do that. So Elisha warned him that he would see it happen, but would not eat any of the food. 20 And that's exactly what happened — the officer was trampled to death.

---

*6.33 messenger: Or "king" (see 7.2,18); the two Hebrew words are very similar.
*7.3 leprosy: See the note at 5.1.

CHAPTER 8

The woman from Shunem is given back her land

¹ Elisha told the woman whose son he had brought back to life,* "The LORD has warned that there will be no food here for seven years. Take your family and go and live somewhere else for a while." ² The woman did exactly what Elisha had said and went to live in Philistine territory.

She and her family lived there seven years. ³ Then she returned to Israel and immediately begged the king to give back her house and property.

⁴ Meanwhile, the king was asking Gehazi the servant of Elisha about the amazing things Elisha had been doing. ⁵ While Gehazi was telling him that Elisha had brought a dead boy back to life, the woman and her son arrived.

"Here's the boy, Your Majesty," Gehazi said. "And this is his mother."

⁶ The king asked the woman to tell her story, and she told him everything that had happened. He then said to one of his officials, "I want you to make sure that this woman gets back everything that belonged to her, including the money her crops have made since the day she left Israel."

Hazael kills Benhadad

⁷ Some time later Elisha went to the capital city of Damascus to visit King Benhadad of Syria, who was sick. And when Benhadad was told he was there, ⁸ he said to Hazael,* "Go and see Elisha the man of God and get him to ask the LORD if I will get well. And take along a gift for him."

⁹ Hazael left with forty camel loads of the best things made in Damascus as a gift for Elisha. He found the prophet and said, "Your servant, King Benhadad, wants to know if he will get well."

¹⁰ "Tell him he will," Elisha said to Hazael. "But the LORD has already told me that Benhadad will definitely die." ¹¹ Elisha stared at him until Hazael was embarrassed, then Elisha began crying.*

¹² "Sir, why are you crying?" Hazael asked.

Elisha answered, "Because I know the terrible things you will do to the people of Israel. You will burn down their walled cities and slaughter their young men. You will even crush the heads of their babies and rip open their pregnant women."

¹³ "How could I ever do anything like that?" Hazael replied. "I'm only a servant and don't have that kind of power."

"Hazael, the LORD has told me that you will be the next king of Syria."

¹⁴ Hazael went back to Benhadad and told him, "Elisha said that you will get well." ¹⁵ But the very next day, Hazael got a thick blanket; he soaked it in water and held it over Benhadad's face until he died. Hazael then became king.

Kings of Judah and Israel

King Jehoram of Judah

This is also told in 2 Chronicles 21.2-20

¹⁶ Jehoram son of Jehoshaphat became king of Judah in Joram's fifth year as king of Israel, while Jehoshaphat was still king of Judah.* ¹⁷ Jehoram was thirty-two years old when he became king, and he ruled eight years from Jerusalem.

¹⁸ Jehoram disobeyed the LORD by doing wrong. He married Ahab's daughter and was as sinful as Ahab's family and the kings of Israel. ¹⁹ But the LORD refused to destroy Judah, because he had promised his servant David that someone from his family would always rule in Judah.

²⁰ While Jehoram was king, the people of Edom rebelled and chose their own king. ²¹ So Jehoram* and his cavalry marched to Zair, where the Edomite army surrounded him and his commanders. During the night he attacked the Edomites, but he was defeated, and his troops escaped to their homes.* ²² Judah was never able to regain control of Edom. Even the town of Libnah* rebelled at that time.

²³ Everything else Jehoram did while he was king is written in *The History of the Kings of Judah.* ²⁴ Jehoram died and was buried beside his ancestors in Jerusalem.* His son Ahaziah then became king.

---

*8.16 while Jehoshaphat . . . Judah: In biblical times, a father and son would sometimes rule as kings at the same time. That way, when the father died, his son would already have control of the kingdom.
*8.22 Even the town of Libnah: This was a town on the border between Philistia and Judah, which means that Jehoram was facing rebellion on two sides of his kingdom.
See also: 8.13: 1 King 19.15. 8.19: 1 King 11.36. 8.20: Gen 27.40.

*8.1 Elisha . . . life: See 4.8–37.
*8.8 Hazael: Probably one of Benhadad's officials.
See also: 8.1: 2 King 4.8–37.

King Ahaziah of Judah

This is also told in 2 Chronicles 22.1–6

25 Ahaziah son of Jehoram became king of Judah in the twelfth year of Joram's rule in Israel. 26 Ahaziah was twenty-two years old when he became king, and he ruled from Jerusalem for only one year. His mother was Athaliah, a granddaughter of King Omri of Israel. 27 Since Ahaziah was related to Ahab's family,* he acted just like them and disobeyed the LORD by doing wrong.

28 Ahaziah went with King Joram of Israel to attack King Hazael and the Syrian troops at Ramoth in Gilead. Joram was wounded in that battle, 29 so he went to the town of Jezreel to recover. Ahaziah went there to visit him.

CHAPTER 9

Jehu becomes king of Israel

1 One day, Elisha called for one of the other prophets and said:

Take this bottle of olive oil and get ready to go to the town of Ramoth in Gilead. 2 When you get there, find Jehu son of Jehoshaphat and grandson of Nimshi. Take him to a place where the two of you can be alone, 3 then pour olive oil on his head to show that he is the new king. Say to him, "The LORD has chosen you to be king of Israel." Then leave quickly — don't wait for anything!

4 The young prophet left for Ramoth. 5 When he arrived, the army officers were meeting together. "Sir, I have a message for you," he said.

"For which one of us?" Jehu asked.

"You, sir," the prophet answered. 6 So Jehu got up and went inside.* The prophet poured olive oil on Jehu's head and told him:

The LORD God of Israel has this message for you: "I am the LORD, and I have chosen you to be king of my people Israel. 7 I want you to wipe out the family of Ahab, so Jezebel will be punished for killing the prophets and my other servants. 8 Every man and boy in Ahab's family must die, whether slave or free. 9 His whole family

must be destroyed, just like the families of Jeroboam son of Nebat and Baasha son of Ahijah. 10 As for Jezebel, her body will be eaten by dogs in the town of Jezreel. There won't be enough left of her to bury."

Then the young prophet opened the door and ran out.

11 Jehu went back to his officers, and one of them asked, "What did that mad prophet want? Is everything all right?"

"You know him and how he talks," Jehu answered.

12 "No, we don't. What did he say?" they asked.

"He had a message from the LORD," Jehu replied. "He said that the LORD has chosen me to be the next king of Israel."

13 They quickly grabbed their coats and spread them out on the steps where Jehu was standing. Someone blew a trumpet, and everyone shouted, "Jehu is king!"

Jehu kills Joram and Ahaziah

14-16 King Joram* of Israel had been badly wounded in the battle at Ramoth, trying to defend it against King Hazael and the Syrian army. Joram was now recovering in Jezreel, and King Ahaziah of Judah was there, visiting him.

Meanwhile, Jehu was in Ramoth, making plans to kill Joram. He said to his officers, "If you want me to be king, then don't let anyone leave this town. They might go to Jezreel and tell Joram." Then Jehu got in his chariot and rode to Jezreel.

17 When the guard in the watchtower at Jezreel saw Jehu and his men riding up, he shouted to the king, "I see some men coming this way."

Joram ordered, "Send someone out to ask them if this is a friendly visit."

18 One of the soldiers rode out and said to Jehu, "King Joram wants to know if this is a friendly visit."

"What's it to you?" Jehu asked. "Just stay behind me with the rest of my troops!"

About the same time the guard in the watchtower said, "Your Majesty, the rider got there, but he isn't coming back."

19 So Joram sent out another rider, who rode up to Jehu and said, "The king wants to know if this is a friendly visit."

"What's it to you?" Jehu asked. "Just get behind me with the rest of my troops!"

---

*8.27 Since . . . family: Ahaziah's mother was Ahab's daughter (see verse 18).
*9.6 went inside: The officers were probably meeting outside in an open courtyard of some building.
See also: 9.6: 1 King 19.16.

See also: 9.10: 1 King 21.23.

20 The guard in the watchtower said, "Your Majesty, the rider got there, but he isn't coming back either. Wait a minute! One man is a reckless chariot driver — it must be Jehu!"

21 Joram commanded, "Get my chariot ready." Then he and Ahaziah got in their chariots and rode out to meet Jehu. They all met on the land that had belonged to Naboth.*
22 Joram asked, "Jehu, is this a peaceful visit?"

"How can there be peace?" Jehu asked. "Your mother Jezebel has caused everyone to worship idols and practise witchcraft."

23 "Ahaziah, let's get out of here!" Joram yelled. "It's a trap!" As Joram tried to escape, 24 Jehu shot an arrow. It hit Joram between his shoulders, then it went through his heart and came out of his chest. He fell over dead in his chariot.

25-26 Jehu commanded his assistant Bidkar, "Get Joram's body and throw it in the field that Naboth once owned. Do you remember when you and I used to ride side by side behind Joram's father Ahab? It was then that the LORD swore to Ahab that he would be punished in the same field where he had killed Naboth and his sons. So throw Joram's body there, just as the LORD said."

27 Ahaziah saw all this happen and tried to escape to the town of Beth-Haggan, but Jehu caught up with him and shouted, "Kill him too!" So his troops shot Ahaziah with an arrow while he was on the road to Gur near Ibleam. He went as far as Megiddo, where he died. 28 Ahaziah's officers put his body in a chariot and took it back to Jerusalem, where they buried him beside his ancestors.

29 Ahaziah had become king of Judah in the eleventh year of the rule of Ahab's son Joram.

Jehu kills Jezebel

30 Jehu headed towards Jezreel, and when Jezebel heard he was coming, she put on eye shadow and brushed her hair. Then she stood at the window, waiting for him to arrive. 31 As he walked through the city gate, she shouted down to him, "Why did you come here, you murderer? To kill the king? You're no better than Zimri!"*

32 He looked up towards the window and asked, "Is anyone up there on my side?"

A few palace workers stuck their heads out of a window, 33 and Jehu shouted, "Throw her out of the window!" They threw her down, and her blood splattered on the walls and on the horses that trampled her body.*

34 Jehu left to get something to eat and drink. Then he told some workers, "Even though she was evil, she was a king's daughter,* so make sure she has a proper burial."

35 But when they went out to bury her body, they found only her skull, her hands, and her feet. 36 They reported this to Jehu, and he said, "The LORD told Elijah the prophet that Jezebel's body would be eaten by dogs here in Jezreel. 37 And he warned that her bones would be spread all over the ground like manure, so that no one could tell who it was."

CHAPTER 10

Jehu kills all of Ahab's descendants

1 Ahab still had seventy descendants living in Samaria. So Jehu wrote a letter to each of the important leaders and officials of the town,* and to those who supported Ahab. In the letters he wrote:

2 Your town is strong, and you're protected by chariots and an armed cavalry. And I know that King Ahab's descendants live there with you. So as soon as you read this letter, 3 choose the best person for the job and make him the next king. Then be prepared to defend Ahab's family.

4 The officials and leaders read the letters and were very frightened. They said to each other, "Jehu has already killed King Joram and King Ahaziah! We have to do what he says." 5 The prime minister, the mayor of the city, as well as the other leaders and Ahab's supporters, sent this answer to Jehu, "We are your servants, Your Majesty, and we will do whatever you tell us. But it's not our place to choose someone to be king. You do what you think is best."

6 Jehu then wrote another letter which said, "If you are on my side and will obey me, then prove it. Bring me the heads of the descendants of Ahab! And be here in Jezreel by this time tomorrow."

The seventy descendants of King Ahab were living with some of the most important people of the city. 7 And when these people

---

*9.21 the land . . . Naboth: See 1 Kings 21.
*9.31 Zimri: An Israelite king who killed King Elah and his family so he could become king, but who ruled only seven days (see 1 Kings 16.8–20).
See also: 9.26: 1 King 21.19.

*9.34 She . . . daughter: Her father was King Ethbaal of Sidon (see 1 Kings 16.31).
See also: 9.36: 1 King 21.23.

read Jehu's second letter, they called together all seventy of Ahab's descendants. They killed them, put their heads in baskets, and sent them to Jezreel.

⁸ When Jehu was told what had happened, he said, "Put the heads in two piles at the city gate, and leave them there until morning."

⁹ The next morning, Jehu went out and stood where everyone could hear him, and he said, "You people are not guilty of anything. I'm the one who plotted against Joram and had him killed. But who killed all these men? ¹⁰ Listen to the words of the LORD's servant Elijah promised about Ahab's family will come true."*

¹¹ Then Jehu killed the rest of Ahab's relatives living in Jezreel, as well as his royal officials, his priests, and his closest friends. No one in Ahab's family was left alive in Jezreel.

¹²⁻¹³ Jehu left for Samaria, and along the way, he met some relatives of King Ahaziah of Judah at a place where shepherds meet.* He asked, "Who are you?"

"We are relatives of Ahaziah," they answered. "We're going to visit his family."

¹⁴ "Take them alive!" Jehu said to his officers. So they grabbed them and led them to the well near the shepherds' meeting place, where they killed all forty-two of them.

¹⁵ As Jehu went on, he saw Jehonadab son of Rechab* coming to meet him. Jehu greeted him, then said, "Jehonadab, I'm on your side. Are you on mine?"

"Yes, I am."

"Then give me your hand," Jehu answered. He helped Jehonadab into his chariot ¹⁶ and said, "Come with me and see how faithful I am to the LORD."

They rode together in Jehu's chariot ¹⁷ to Samaria. Jehu killed everyone there who belonged to Ahab's family, as well as all his officials. Everyone in his family was now dead, just as the LORD had promised Elijah.

Jehu kills all the worshippers of Baal

¹⁸ Jehu called together the people in Samaria and said:

King Ahab sometimes worshipped Baal, but I will be completely faithful to Baal. ¹⁹ I'm going to offer a huge sacrifice to him. So invite his prophets and priests, and be sure everyone who worships him is there. Anyone who doesn't come will be killed.

But this was a trick — Jehu was really planning to kill the worshippers of Baal. ²⁰ He said, "Announce a day of worship for Baal!" After the day had been announced, ²¹ Jehu sent an invitation to everyone in Israel. All the worshippers of Baal came, and the temple was filled from one end to the other. ²² Jehu told the official in charge of the sacred robes to make sure that everyone had a robe to wear.

²³ Jehu and Jehonadab went into the temple, and Jehu said to the crowd, "Look around and make sure that only the worshippers of Baal are here. No one who worships the LORD is allowed in." ²⁴ Then they began to offer sacrifices to Baal.

Earlier, Jehu had ordered eighty soldiers to wait outside the temple. He had warned them, "I will get all these worshippers here, and if any of you let even one of them escape, you will be killed instead!"

²⁵ As soon as Jehu finished offering the sacrifice, he told the guards and soldiers, "Come in and kill them! Don't let anyone escape." They slaughtered everyone in the crowd and threw the bodies outside. Then they went back into the temple ²⁶ and carried out the image of Baal. They burnt it ²⁷ and broke it into pieces, then they completely destroyed Baal's temple. And since that time, it's been nothing but a public toilet.*

²⁸ That's how Jehu stopped the worship of Baal in Israel. ²⁹ But he did not stop the worship of the gold statues of calves at Dan and Bethel that Jeroboam had made for the people to worship.*

³⁰ Later the LORD said, "Jehu, you have done right by destroying Ahab's entire family, just as I had planned. So I will make sure that the next four kings of Israel will come from your own family."

³¹ But Jehu did not completely obey the commands of the LORD God of Israel. Instead, he kept doing the sinful things that Jeroboam had caused the Israelites to do.

Jehu dies

³² In those days the LORD began to reduce the size of Israel's territory. King Hazael of Syria defeated the Israelites and took control ³³ of the regions of Gilead and Bashan east of the River Jordan and north of the town of Aroer near the River Arnon. This was the land

---

*10.10 Everything . . . come true: See
1 Kings 21.17–24.

See also: 10.11: Hos 1.4.

*10.29 gold statues . . . to worship: See
1 Kings 12.26–30.

See also: 10.29: 1 King 12.28–30.

where the tribes of Gad, Reuben, and Manasseh had once lived. 34 Everything else Jehu did while he was king, including his brave deeds, is written in *The History of the Kings of Israel*. 35 Jehu died and was buried in Samaria, and his son Jehoahaz became king. 36 Jehu had ruled Israel twenty-eight years from Samaria.

CHAPTER 11

Queen Athaliah of Judah

This is also told in 2 Chronicles 22.10–12

1 As soon as Athaliah heard that her son King Ahaziah was dead, she decided to kill any relative who could possibly become king. She would have done that, 2 but Jehosheba rescued Joash son of Ahaziah just as he was about to be murdered. Jehosheba, who was Jehoram's' daughter and Ahaziah's half-sister, hid her nephew Joash and his personal servant in a bedroom in the LORD's temple where he was safe from Athaliah. 3 Joash hid in the temple with Jehosheba* for six years while Athaliah ruled as queen of Judah.

Jehoiada makes Joash king of Judah

This is also told in 2 Chronicles 23.1–21

4 Joash son of Ahaziah had hidden in the LORD's temple six years. Then in the seventh year, Jehoiada the priest sent for the commanders of the king's special bodyguards' and the commanders of the palace guards. They met him at the temple, and he asked them to make a promise in the name of the LORD. Then he brought out Joash 5 and said to them:

Here's what I want you to do. Three of your guard units will be on duty on the Sabbath. I want one unit to guard the palace. 6 Another unit will guard Sur Gate, and the third unit will guard the palace gate and relieve the palace guards.
7 The other two guard units are supposed to be off duty on the Sabbath. But I want both of them to stay here at the temple and protect King Joash. 8 Make sure they follow him wherever he goes, and tell them to keep their swords ready to kill anyone who tries to get near him.

9 The commanders followed Jehoiada's orders. Each one called together his guards – those coming on duty and those going off duty. 10 Jehoiada brought out the swords and shields that had belonged to King David and gave them to the commanders. 11 Then they gave the weapons to their guards, who took their positions around the temple and the altar to protect Joash on every side.

12 Jehoiada brought Joash outside, where he placed the crown on his head and gave him a copy of instructions for ruling the nation. Olive oil was poured on his head to show that he was now king, while the crowd clapped and shouted, "Long live the king!"
13 Queen Athaliah heard the crowd and went to the temple. 14 There she saw Joash standing by one of the columns, which was the usual place for the king. The singers' and the trumpet players were standing next to him, and the people were celebrating and blowing trumpets. Athaliah tore her clothes in anger and shouted, "You betrayed me, you traitors!"
15 Straight away, Jehoiada said to the army commanders, "Kill her! But don't do it anywhere near the LORD's temple. Take her out in front of the troops and kill anyone who is with her!" 16 So the commanders dragged her to the gate where horses are led into the palace, and they killed her there.

17 Jehoiada the priest asked King Joash and the people to promise that they would be faithful to each other and to the LORD. 18 Then the crowd went to the temple built to honour Baal and tore it down. They smashed the altars and idols and killed Mattan the priest of Baal in front of the altars.

After Jehoiada had placed guards around the LORD's temple, 19 he called together all the commanders, the king's special bodyguards,' the palace guards, and the people. They led Joash from the temple, through the Guards' Gate, and into the palace. He took his place on the throne and became king of Judah. 20 Everyone celebrated because Athaliah had been killed and Jerusalem was peaceful again. 21 Joash was only seven years old when this happened.

---

*11.3 Jehosheba: Jehosheba was the wife of Jehoiada the priest (see 2 Chronicles 22.11), which is why she could hide Joash in one of the private bedrooms used only by the priests.

See also: 11.14: 2 King 23.3.

CHAPTER 12

King Joash of Judah

This is also told in 2 Chronicles 24.1–16

[1] Joash* became king of Judah in Jehu's seventh year as king of Israel, and he ruled forty years from Jerusalem. His mother Zibiah was from the town of Beersheba.

[2] Jehoiada the priest taught Joash what was right, and so for the rest of his life Joash obeyed the LORD. [3] But even Joash did not destroy the local shrines,* and they were still used as places for offering sacrifices.

[4] One day, Joash said to the priests, "Collect all the money that has been given to the LORD's temple, whether from taxes or gifts, [5] and use it to repair the temple. You priests can contribute your own money too."*

[6] But the priests never started repairing the temple. So in the twenty-third year of his rule, [7] Joash called for Jehoiada and the other priests and said, "Why aren't you using the money to repair the temple? Don't take any more money for yourselves. It is only to be used to pay for the repairs." [8] The priests agreed that they would not collect any more money or be in charge of the temple repairs.

[9] Jehoiada found a wooden box; he cut a hole in the top of it and set it on the right side of the altar where people went into the temple. Whenever someone gave money to the temple, the priests guarding the entrance would put it into this box. [10] When the box was full of money, the king's secretary and the chief priest would count the money and put it in bags. [11] Then they would give it to the men supervising the repairs to the temple. Some of the money was used to pay the builders, the woodworkers, [12] the stonecutters, and the men who built the walls. And some was used to buy wood and stone and to pay any other costs for repairing the temple.

[13] While the repairs were being made, the money that was given to the temple was not used to make silver bowls, lamp snuffers, small sprinkling bowls, trumpets, or anything gold or silver for the temple. [14] It went only to pay for repairs. [15] The men in charge were honest, so no one had to keep track of the money.

[16] The fines that had to be paid along with the sacrifices to make things right and the sacrifices for sin did not go to the temple. This money belonged only to the priests.

[17] About the same time, King Hazael of Syria attacked the town of Gath and captured it. Next, he decided to attack Jerusalem. [18] So Joash collected everything he and his ancestors Jehoshaphat, Jehoram, and Ahaziah had dedicated to the LORD, as well as the gold in the storage rooms in the temple and palace. He sent it all to Hazael as a gift, and when Hazael received it, he ordered his troops to leave Jerusalem.

[19] Everything else Joash did while he was king is written in *The History of the Kings of Judah*. [20-21] At the end of his rule, some of his officers rebelled against him. Jozabad* son of Shimeath and Jehozabad son of Shomer murdered him in a building where the land was filled in on the east side of Jerusalem,* near the road to Silla. Joash was buried beside his ancestors in Jerusalem,* and his son Amaziah became king.

CHAPTER 13

King Jehoahaz of Israel

[1] Jehoahaz son of Jehu became king of Israel in the twenty-third year of Joash's rule in Judah. Jehoahaz ruled seventeen years from Samaria [2] and disobeyed the LORD by doing wrong. He never stopped following the example of Jeroboam, who had caused the Israelites to sin.

[3] The LORD was angry with the Israelites, so he let King Hazael of Syria and his son Benhadad rule over them for a long time. [4] Jehoahaz prayed to the LORD for help, and the LORD saw how terribly Hazael was treating the Israelites. He answered Jehoahaz [5] by sending Israel a leader who rescued them from the Syrians,* and the Israelites lived in peace as they had before. [6-7] But Hazael had defeated Israel's army so badly that Jehoahaz had only ten chariots, fifty cavalry troops, and ten thousand regular soldiers left in his army.

The Israelites kept sinning and following the example of Jeroboam's family. They did not tear down the sacred poles* that had been set up in Samaria for the worship of the goddess Asherah.

---

*12.20,21 where . . . Jerusalem: The Hebrew text has "on the Millo," which probably refers to a landfill to strengthen and extend the hill where the city was built.
*13.5 by sending . . . the Syrians: The name of this leader is not given, but it may refer to Elisha the prophet, King Jehoash of Israel, or his son King Jeroboam.
*13.6,7 sacred poles: Or "trees," used as symbols of Asherah, the goddess of fertility.

[8] Everything else Jehoahaz did while he was king, including his brave deeds, is written in *The History of the Kings of Israel.* [9] Jehoahaz died and was buried in Samaria, and his son Jehoash became king.

King Jehoash of Israel

[10] Jehoash became king of Israel in the thirty-seventh year of Joash's rule in Judah, and he ruled sixteen years from Samaria. [11] He disobeyed the LORD by doing just like Jeroboam, who had caused the Israelites to sin.

[12] Everything else Jehoash did while he was king, including his war against King Amaziah of Judah, is written in *The History of the Kings of Israel.* [13] Jehoash died and was buried in Samaria beside the other Israelite kings. His son Jeroboam then became king.

Elisha the prophet dies

[14] Some time before the death of King Jehoash, Elisha the prophet was very sick and about to die. Jehoash went in and stood beside him, crying. He said, "Master, what will Israel's chariots and cavalry be able to do without you?"

[15-16] "Grab a bow and some arrows," Elisha told him, "and hold them in your hand." Jehoash grabbed the bow and arrows and held them. Elisha placed his hand on the king's hand [17] and said, "Open the window facing east." When it was open, Elisha shouted, "Now shoot!" Jehoash shot an arrow and Elisha said, "That arrow is a sign that the LORD will help you completely defeat the Syrian army at Aphek."

[18] Elisha said, "Pick up the arrows and hit the ground with them." Jehoash grabbed the arrows and hit the ground three times, then stopped. [19] Elisha became angry with the king and exclaimed, "If you had struck it five or six times, you would completely wipe out the Syrians. Now you will defeat them only three times."

[20] Elisha died and was buried.

Every year in the spring, Moab's leaders sent raiding parties into Israel. [21] Once, while some Israelites were burying a man's body, they saw a group of Moabites. The Israelites quickly threw the body into Elisha's tomb and ran away. As soon as the man's body touched the bones of Elisha, the man came back to life and stood up.

Israel defeats Syria

[22] Israel was under the power of King Hazael of Syria during the entire rule of Jehoahaz. [23] But the LORD was kind to the Israelites and showed them mercy because of his solemn agreement with their ancestors Abraham, Isaac, and Jacob. In fact, he has never turned his back on them or let them be completely destroyed.

[24] Hazael died, and his son Benhadad then became king of Syria. [25] King Jehoash of Israel attacked and defeated the Syrian army three times. He took back from Benhadad all the towns Hazael had captured in battle from his father Jehoahaz.

CHAPTER 14

King Amaziah of Judah

This is also told in 2 Chronicles 25.1–24

[1] Amaziah son of Joash became king of Judah in the second year of Jehoash's rule in Israel. [2] Amaziah was twenty-five years old when he became king, and he ruled twenty-nine years from Jerusalem, which was also the home town of his mother Jehoaddin.

[3] Amaziah followed the example of his father Joash by obeying the LORD and doing right. But he was not as faithful as his ancestor David. [4] Amaziah did not destroy the local shrines*, and they were still used as places for offering sacrifices.

[5] As soon as Amaziah had control of Israel, he arrested and killed the officers who had murdered his father. [6] But the children of those officers were not killed. The LORD had commanded in the Law of Moses that only the people who sinned were to be punished, not their parents or children.*

[7] While Amaziah was king, he killed ten thousand Edomite soldiers in Salt Valley. He captured the town of Sela and renamed it Joktheel, which is still its name.

[8] One day, Amaziah sent a message to King Jehoash of Israel: "Come out and face me in battle!"

[9] Jehoash sent back this reply:

Once upon a time, a small thorn bush in Lebanon announced that his son was going to marry the daughter of a large cedar tree. But a wild animal came along and trampled the small bush.

*14.6 The LORD had commanded . . . children: See Deuteronomy 24.16.

See also: 13.14: 2 King 2.12.

See also: 14.6: Deut 24.16.

[10] Amaziah, you think you're so powerful because you defeated Edom. Go ahead and celebrate — but stay at home. If you cause any trouble, both you and your kingdom of Judah will be destroyed.

[11] But Amaziah refused to listen. So Jehoash and his troops marched to the town of Beth-Shemesh in Judah to attack Amaziah and his troops. [12] During the battle, Judah's army was crushed. Every soldier from Judah ran back home, [13] and Jehoash captured Amaziah.

Jehoash then marched to Jerusalem and broke down the city wall from Ephraim Gate to Corner Gate, a section nearly two hundred metres long. [14] He took the gold and silver, as well as everything of value from the LORD's temple and the king's treasury. He took hostages, then returned to Samaria.

[15] Everything else Jehoash did while he was king, including his brave deeds and how he defeated King Amaziah of Judah, is written in *The History of the Kings of Israel.* [16] Jehoash died and was buried in Samaria beside the other Israelite kings. His son Jeroboam then became king.

[17] Fifteen years after Jehoash died, [18-20] some people in Jerusalem plotted against Amaziah. He was able to escape to the town of Lachish, but another group of people caught him and killed him there. His body was taken back to Jerusalem on horseback and buried beside his ancestors.

Everything else Amaziah did while he was king is written in *The History of the Kings of Judah.* [21] After his death the people of Judah made his son Azariah king, even though he was only sixteen at the time. [22] Azariah was the one who later recaptured and rebuilt the town of Elath.

King Jeroboam the Second of Israel

[23] Jeroboam son of Jehoash became king of Israel in the fifteenth year of Amaziah's rule in Judah. Jeroboam ruled forty-one years from Samaria. [24] He disobeyed the LORD by following the evil example of Jeroboam son of Nebat, who had caused the Israelites to sin.

[25] Jeroboam extended the boundaries of Israel from Lebo-Hamath in the north to the Dead Sea in the south, just as the LORD had promised his servant Jonah son of Amittai, who was a prophet from Gath-Hepher. [26] The LORD helped Jeroboam do this because he had seen how terribly the Israelites were

suffering, whether slave or free, and no one was left to help them. [27] And since the LORD had promised he would not let Israel be completely destroyed, he helped Jeroboam rescue them.

[28] Everything else Jeroboam did while he was king, including his brave deeds and how he recaptured the towns of Damascus and Hamath,* is written in *The History of the Kings of Israel.* [29] Jeroboam died and was buried, and his son Zechariah became king.

CHAPTER 15

King Azariah of Judah
This is also told in 2 Chronicles 26.1–23

[1] Azariah son of Amaziah became king of Judah in Jeroboam's twenty-seventh year as king of Israel. [2] He was only sixteen years old when he became king, and he ruled fifty-two years from Jerusalem, which was also the home town of his mother Jecoliah.

[3] Azariah obeyed the LORD by doing right, as his father Amaziah had done. [4] But Azariah did not destroy the local shrines,* and they were still used as places for offering sacrifices.

[5] The LORD punished Azariah with leprosy* for the rest of his life. He wasn't allowed to live in the royal palace, so his son Jotham lived there and ruled in his place.

[6] Everything else Azariah did while he was king is written in *The History of the Kings of Judah.* [7] Azariah died and was buried beside his ancestors in Jerusalem. His son Jotham then became king.

King Zechariah of Israel

[8] Zechariah son of Jeroboam became king of Israel in the thirty-eighth year of Azariah's rule in Judah, but he ruled only six months from Samaria. [9] Like his ancestors, Zechariah disobeyed the LORD by following the evil ways of Jeroboam son of Nebat, who had caused the Israelites to sin.

[10] Shallum son of Jabesh plotted against Zechariah and killed him in public.* Shallum then became king. [11-12] So the LORD had kept his promise to Jehu that the next four kings of Israel would come from his family.*

Everything else Zechariah did while he was king is written in *The History of the Kings of Israel.*

14.28 Damascus and Hamath: See the note at 5.1.
15.5 leprosy: See the note at 5.1.
15.11,12 So the LORD . . . family: See 10.28–31.
See also: 15.7: Isa 6.1. 15.12: 2 King 10.30.

King Shallum of Israel

13 Shallum became king of Israel in the thirty-ninth year of Azariah's* rule in Judah. But only one month after Shallum became king, 14-16 Menahem son of Gadi came to Samaria from Tirzah and killed him. Menahem then became king. The town of Tiphsah would not surrender to him, so he destroyed it and all the surrounding towns as far as Tirzah. He killed everyone living in Tiphsah, and with his sword he even ripped open pregnant women.

Everything else Shallum did while he was king, including his plot against Zechariah, is written in *The History of the Kings of Israel*.

King Menahem of Israel

17 Menahem became king of Israel in Azariah's thirty-ninth year as king of Judah, and he ruled Israel ten years from Samaria. 18 He constantly disobeyed the LORD by following the example of Jeroboam son of Nebat, who had caused the Israelites to sin.

19 During Menahem's rule, King Tiglath Pileser* of Assyria invaded Israel. He agreed to help Menahem keep control of his kingdom, if Menahem would pay him thirty-four thousand kilogrammes of silver. 20 So Menahem ordered every rich person in Israel to give him fifty pieces of silver, and he gave it all to Tiglath Pileser, who stopped his attack and left Israel.

21 Everything else Menahem did while he was king is written in *The History of the Kings of Israel*. 22 Menahem died, and his son Pekahiah became king.

King Pekahiah of Israel

23 Pekahiah became king of Israel in the fiftieth year of Azariah's rule in Judah, and he ruled two years from Samaria. 24 He disobeyed the LORD and caused the Israelites to sin, just as Jeroboam son of Nebat had done.

25 Pekah son of Remaliah was Pekahiah's chief officer, but he made plans to kill the king. So he and fifty men from Gilead broke into the strongest part of the palace in Samaria and murdered Pekahiah, together with Argob and Arieh.* Pekah then became king.

26 Everything else Pekahiah did while he was king is written in *The History of the Kings of Israel*.

King Pekah of Israel

27 Pekah son of Remaliah became king of Israel in Azariah's fifty-second year as king of Judah, and he ruled twenty years from Samaria. 28 He disobeyed the LORD and followed the evil example of Jeroboam son of Nebat, who had caused the Israelites to sin.

29 During Pekah's rule, King Tiglath Pileser of Assyria marched into Israel. He captured the territories of Gilead and Galilee, including the towns of Ijon, Abel-Bethmaacah, Janoah, Kedesh, and Hazor, as well as the entire territory of Naphtali. Then he took Israelites from those regions to Assyria as prisoners.*

30 In the twentieth year of Jotham's rule in Judah, Hoshea son of Elah plotted against Pekah and murdered him. Hoshea then became king of Israel.

31 Everything else Pekah did while he was king is written in *The History of the Kings of Israel*.

King Jotham of Judah

This is also told in 2 Chronicles 27.1-9

32 Jotham son of Azariah* became king of Judah in the second year of Pekah's rule in Israel. 33 Jotham was twenty-five years old when he became king, and he ruled sixteen years from Jerusalem. His mother Jerusha was the daughter of Zadok.

34 Jotham followed the example of his father by obeying the LORD and doing right. 35 It was Jotham who rebuilt the Upper Gate that led into the court around the LORD's temple. But the local shrines* were not destroyed, and they were still used as places for offering sacrifices.

36 Everything else Jotham did while he was king is written in *The History of the Kings of Judah*. 37 During his rule, the LORD let King Rezin of Syria and King Pekah of Israel start attacking Judah. 38 Jotham died and was buried beside his ancestors in Jerusalem, and his son Ahaz became king.

CHAPTER 16

King Ahaz of Judah

This is also told in 2 Chronicles 28.1-27

1 Ahaz son of Jotham became king of Judah in the seventeenth year of Pekah's rule in Israel.

*15.19 Tiglath Pileser: The Hebrew text has "Pul", another name for Tiglath Pileser, who ruled Assyria from 745 to 727 BC.

*15.29 prisoners: The events in this verse probably took place around 733 BC.

² He was twenty years old at the time, and he ruled from Jerusalem for sixteen years.

Ahaz wasn't like his ancestor David. Instead, he disobeyed the LORD ³ and was even more sinful than the kings of Israel. He sacrificed his own son, which was a disgusting custom of the nations that the LORD had forced out of Israel. ⁴ Ahaz offered sacrifices at the local shrines', as well as on every hill and in the shade of large trees.

⁵⁻⁶ While Ahaz was ruling Judah, the king of Edom recaptured the town of Elath from Judah and forced out the people of Judah. Edomites' then moved into Elath, and they still live there.

About the same time, King Rezin of Syria and King Pekah of Israel marched to Jerusalem and attacked, but they could not capture it.

⁷ Ahaz sent a message to King Tiglath Pileser of Assyria that said, "Your Majesty, King Rezin and King Pekah are attacking me, your loyal servant. Please come and rescue me." ⁸ Along with the message, Ahaz sent silver and gold from the LORD's temple and from the palace treasury as a gift for the Assyrian king.

⁹ As soon as Tiglath Pileser received the message, he and his troops marched to Syria. He captured the capital city of Damascus, then he took the people living there to the town of Kir as prisoners and killed King Rezin.*

¹⁰ Later, Ahaz went to Damascus to meet Tiglath Pileser. And while Ahaz was there, he saw an altar and sent a model of it back to Uriah the priest, along with the plans for building one. ¹¹ Uriah followed the plans and built an altar exactly like the one in Damascus, finishing it just before Ahaz came back.

¹² When Ahaz returned, he went to see the altar and to offer sacrifices on it. He walked up to the altar ¹³ and poured wine over it. Then he offered sacrifices to please the LORD, to give him thanks, and to ask for his blessings.* ¹⁴ After that, he had the bronze altar moved aside,' so his new altar would be right in front of the LORD's temple. ¹⁵ He told Uriah the priest:

From now on, the morning and evening sacrifices as well as all gifts of grain and wine are to be offered on this altar. The sacrifices for the people and for the king must also be offered here. Sprinkle the blood from all the sacrifices on it, but leave the bronze altar for me to use for prayer and finding out what God wants me to do.

¹⁶ Uriah did everything Ahaz told him.

¹⁷ Ahaz also had the side panels and the small bowls taken off the moveable stands in the LORD's temple. He had the large bronze bowl, called the Sea, removed from the bronze bulls on which it rested and had it placed on a stand made of stone. ¹⁸ He took down the special tent that was used for worship on the Sabbath' and closed up the private entrance that the kings of Judah used for going into the temple. He did all these things to please Tiglath Pileser.

¹⁹ Everything else Ahaz did while he was king is written in *The History of the Kings of Judah.* ²⁰ Ahaz died and was buried beside his ancestors in Jerusalem,' and his son Hezekiah became king.

King Hoshea of Israel and the defeat of the northern kingdom

CHAPTER 17

¹ Hoshea son of Elah became king of Israel in the twelfth year of Ahaz's rule in Judah, and he ruled nine years from Samaria. ² Hoshea disobeyed the LORD and sinned, but not as much as the earlier Israelite kings had done.

³ During Hoshea's rule, King Shalmaneser of Assyria* invaded Israel; he took control of the country and made Hoshea pay taxes. ⁴ But later, Hoshea refused to pay the taxes and asked King So of Egypt to help him rebel. When Shalmaneser found out, he arrested Hoshea and put him in prison.

Samaria is destroyed and the Israelites are taken to Assyria

⁵ Shalmaneser invaded Israel and attacked the city of Samaria for three years, ⁶ before capturing it in the ninth year of Hoshea's

---

*16.9 King Rezin: This probably took place around 734 BC, before the events in 15.29.
*16.13 offered . . . blessings: In traditional translations, these sacrifices are usually called "whole burnt offerings", "grain offerings", and "peace offerings". These are described in Leviticus 1—3.

See also: 16.3: Deut 12.31. 16.5: Isa 7.1.
16.14: Exod 27.1,2; 2 Chron 4.1.

*17.3 King Shalmaneser of Assyria: The son of Tiglath Pileser, who ruled Assyria from 727 to 722 BC.
See also: 16.17: 1 King 7.23–39; 2 Chron 4.2–6.
16.20: Isa 14.28.

rule. The Assyrian king* took the Israelites away to Assyria as prisoners. He forced some of them to live in the town of Halah, others to live near the River Habor in the territory of Gozan, and still others to live in towns where the Median people lived.

⁷ All of this happened because the people of Israel had sinned against the LORD their God, who had rescued them from Egypt, where they had been slaves. They worshipped foreign gods, ⁸ followed the customs of the nations that the LORD had forced out of Israel, and were just as sinful as the Israelite kings. ⁹ Even worse, the Israelites tried to hide their sins from the LORD their God. They built their own local shrines everywhere in Israel — from small towns to large, walled cities. ¹⁰ They also built stone images of foreign gods and set up sacred poles* for the worship of Asherah on every hill and under every shady tree. ¹¹ They offered sacrifices at the shrines,* just as the foreign nations had done before the LORD forced them out of Israel. They did sinful things that made the LORD very angry.

¹² Even though the LORD had commanded the Israelites not to worship idols,* they did it anyway. ¹³ So the LORD made sure that every prophet warned Israel and Judah with these words: "I, the LORD, command you to stop doing sinful things and start obeying my laws and teachings! I gave them to your ancestors, and I told my servants the prophets to repeat them to you."

¹⁴ But the Israelites would not listen; they were as stubborn as their ancestors who had refused to worship the LORD their God. ¹⁵ They ignored the LORD's warnings and commands, and they rejected the solemn agreement he had made with their ancestors. They worshipped worthless idols and became worthless themselves. The LORD had told the Israelites not to do the things that the foreign nations around them were doing, but Israel became just like them.

¹⁶ The people of Israel disobeyed all the commands of the LORD their God. They made two gold statues of calves and set up a sacred pole for Asherah; they also worshipped the

stars and the god Baal. ¹⁷ They used magic and witchcraft and even sacrificed their own children. The Israelites were determined to do whatever the LORD hated. ¹⁸ The LORD became so furious with the people of Israel that he allowed them to be carried away as prisoners.

Only the people living in Judah were left, ¹⁹ but they also disobeyed the LORD's commands and acted like the Israelites. ²⁰ So the LORD turned his back on everyone in Israel and Judah* and let them be punished and defeated until no one was left.

²¹ Earlier, when the LORD took the northern tribes away from David's family,* the people living in northern Israel chose Jeroboam son of Nebat as their king. Jeroboam caused the Israelites to sin and to stop worshipping the LORD. ²² The people kept on sinning like Jeroboam, ²³ until the LORD got rid of them, just as he had warned his servants the prophets.

That's why the people of Israel were taken away as prisoners to Assyria, and that's where they remained.

Foreigners are resettled in Israel

²⁴ The king of Assyria took people who were living in the cities of Babylon, Cuthah, Avva, Hamath, and Sepharvaim, and forced them to move to Israel. They took over the towns where the Israelites had lived, including the capital city of Samaria.

²⁵ At first these people did not worship the LORD, so he sent lions to attack them, and the lions killed some of them. ²⁶ A messenger told the king of Assyria, "The people you moved to Israel don't know how to worship the god of that country. So he sent lions that have attacked and killed some of them."

²⁷ The king replied, "Get one of the Israelite priests we brought here and send him back to Israel. He can live there and teach them about the god of that country." ²⁸ One of the Israelite priests was chosen to go back to Israel. He lived in Bethel and taught the people how to worship the LORD.

²⁹ But in towns all over Israel, the different groups of people made statues of their own gods, then they placed these idols in local Israelite' shrines. ³⁰ The people from Babylonia made the god Succoth-Benoth; those from Cuthah made the god Nergal;

---

*17.6 The Assyrian king: Probably Sargon, Shalmaneser's successor. Shalmaneser died after the city of Samaria was captured (722 BC) but before the people were taken away as prisoners (720 BC). Sargon ruled Assyria from 721 to 705 BC.
*17.10 sacred poles: See the note at 13.6,7.
*17.12 the LORD . . . idols: See Exodus 20.4,5.
See also: 17.10: 1 King 14.23. **17.16:** 1 King 12.28.

*17.21 when the LORD . . . family: See
1 Kings 11.29–39.
See also: 17.17: Deut 18.10.

those from Hamath made Ashima; [31] those from Avva made Nibhaz and Tartak; and the people from Sepharvaim sacrificed their children to their own gods Adrammelech and Anammelech. [32-33] They worshipped their own gods, just as they had before they were taken away to Israel. They also worshipped the LORD, but they chose their own people to be priests at the shrines. [34] Everyone followed their old customs. None of them worshipped only the LORD, and they refused to obey the laws and commands that the LORD had given to the descendants of Jacob, the man he named Israel. [35] At the time when the LORD had made his solemn agreement with the people of Israel, he told them:

Do not worship any other gods! Do not bow down to them or offer them a sacrifice. [36] Worship only me! I am the one who rescued you from Egypt with my mighty power. Bow down to me and offer sacrifices. [37] Never worship any other god, always obey my laws and teachings, [38] and remember the solemn agreement between us.

I will say it again: do not worship any god [39] except me. I am the LORD your God, and I will rescue you from all your enemies.

[40] But the people living in Israel ignored this command and kept on following their old customs. [41] They did worship the LORD, but they also worshipped their own idols. Their descendants did the same thing.

King Hezekiah of Judah and the Assyrian invasion

CHAPTER 18

King Hezekiah of Judah

This is also told in 2 Chronicles 29.1,2; 31.1

[1] Hezekiah son of Ahaz became king of Judah in the third year of Hoshea's rule in Israel. [2] Hezekiah was twenty-five years old when he became king, and he ruled twenty-nine years from Jerusalem. His mother Abi was the daughter of Zechariah.

[3] Hezekiah obeyed the LORD, just as his ancestor David had done. [4] He destroyed the local shrines*, then tore down the images of foreign gods and cut down the sacred pole*

for worshipping the goddess Asherah. He also smashed the bronze snake Moses had made. The people had named it Nehushtan* and had been offering sacrifices to it.

[5] Hezekiah trusted the LORD God of Israel. No other king of Judah was like Hezekiah, either before or after him. [6] He was completely faithful to the LORD and obeyed the laws the LORD had given to Moses for the people. [7] The LORD helped Hezekiah, so he was successful in everything he did. He even rebelled against the king of Assyria, refusing to be his servant. [8] Hezekiah defeated the Philistine towns as far away as Gaza — from the smallest towns to the large, walled towns.

[9] During the fourth year of Hezekiah's rule, which was the seventh year of Hoshea's rule in Israel, King Shalmaneser of Assyria led his troops to Samaria, the capital city of Israel. They attacked [10] and captured it three years later,* in the sixth year of Hezekiah's rule and the ninth year of Hoshea's rule. [11] The king of Assyria* took the Israelites away as prisoners; he forced some of them to live in the town of Halah, others to live near the River Habor in the territory of Gozan, and still others to live in towns where the Median people lived. [12] All of that happened because the people of Israel had not obeyed the LORD their God. They rejected the solemn agreement he had made with them, and they ignored everything that the LORD's servant Moses had told them.

King Sennacherib of Assyria invades Judah

This is also told in 2 Chronicles 32.1–19; Isaiah 36.1–22

[13] In the fourteenth year of Hezekiah's rule in Judah, King Sennacherib of Assyria invaded the country and captured every walled city,* except Jerusalem. [14] Hezekiah sent this message to Sennacherib, who was in the town of Lachish: "I know I am guilty of rebellion. But I will pay you whatever you want, if you stop your attack."

---

*18.4 sacred pole: See the note at 13.6,7.

See also: 17.34: Gen 32.28; 35.10. 17.35: Exod 20.5; Deut 5.9. 17.36: Deut 6.13. 18.4: Num 21.9.

*18.4 the bronze snake . . . Nehushtan: See Numbers 21.8,9. "Nehushtan" is a nickname that sounds like the Hebrew words for "snake" and "bronze".
*18.10 three years later: When the Israelites measured time, part of a year could be counted as a whole year.
*18.11 The king of Assyria: Probably Sargon, Shalmaneser's successor (see the note at 17.6).
*18.13 King Sennacherib . . . walled city: Sennacherib ruled Assyria 705–681 BC, and this event probably took place in 701 BC.

Sennacherib told Hezekiah to pay ten thousand kilogrammes of silver and a thousand kilogrammes of gold. 15 So Hezekiah collected all the silver from the LORD's temple and the royal treasury. 16 He even stripped the gold that he had used to cover the doors and doorposts* in the temple. He gave it all to Sennacherib.

17 The king of Assyria ordered his three highest military officers to leave Lachish and take a large army to Jerusalem. When they arrived, the officers stood on the road near the cloth makers' shops along the canal from the upper pool. 18 They called out to Hezekiah, and three of his highest officials came out to meet them. One of them was Hilkiah's son Eliakim, who was the prime minister. The other two were Shebna, assistant to the prime minister, and Joah son of Asaph, keeper of the government records.

19 One of the Assyrian commanders told them:

I have a message for Hezekiah from the great king of Assyria. Ask Hezekiah why he feels so sure of himself. 20 Does he think he can plan and win a war with nothing but words? Who is going to help him, now that he has turned against the king of Assyria? 21 Is he depending on Egypt and its king? That's the same as leaning on a broken stick, and it will go right through his hand. 22 Is Hezekiah now depending on the LORD your God? Didn't Hezekiah tear down all except one of the LORD's altars and places of worship?* Didn't he tell the people of Jerusalem and Judah to worship at that one place?

23 The king of Assyria wants to make a bet with you people. He will give you two thousand horses, if you have enough troops to ride them. 24 How could you even defeat our lowest ranking officer, when you have to depend on Egypt for chariots and cavalry? 25 Don't forget that it was the LORD who sent me here with orders to destroy your nation!

26 Eliakim, Shebna, and Joah said, "Sir, we don't want the people listening from the city wall to understand what you are saying. So please speak to us in Aramaic instead of Hebrew."

*18.22 worship: Hezekiah actually had torn down the places where idols were worshipped, and he had told the people to worship the LORD at the one place of worship in Jerusalem. But the Assyrian leader was confused and thought these were also places where the LORD was supposed to be worshipped.

27 The Assyrian army commander answered, "My king sent me to speak to everyone, not just to you leaders. These people will soon have to eat their own body waste and drink their own urine! And so will the three of you."

28 Then, in a voice loud enough for everyone to hear, he shouted in Hebrew:

Listen to what the great king of Assyria says! 29 Don't be fooled by Hezekiah. He can't save you. 30 Don't trust him when he tells you that the LORD will protect you from the king of Assyria. 31 Stop listening to Hezekiah! Pay attention to my king. Surrender to him. He will let you keep your own vineyards, fig trees, and cisterns 32 for a while. Then he will come and take you away to a country just like yours, where you can plant vineyards, raise your own grain, and have plenty of olive oil and honey. Believe me, you won't starve there.

Hezekiah claims the LORD will save you. But don't be fooled by him. 33 Were any other gods able to defend their land against the king of Assyria? 34 What happened to the gods of Hamath and Arpad? What about the gods of Sepharvaim, Hena, and Ivvah? Were the gods of Samaria able to protect their land against the Assyrian forces? 35 None of these gods kept their people safe from the king of Assyria. Do you think the LORD your God can do any better?

36-37 Eliakim, Shebna, and Joah had been warned by King Hezekiah not to answer the Assyrian commander. So they tore their clothes in sorrow and reported to Hezekiah everything the commander had said.

CHAPTER 19

Hezekiah asks Isaiah the prophet for advice

This is also told in Isaiah 37.1–13

1 As soon as Hezekiah heard the news, he tore off his clothes in sorrow and put on sackcloth. Then he went into the temple of the LORD. 2 He told Prime Minister Eliakim, Assistant Prime Minister Shebna, and the senior priests to dress in sackcloth and tell the prophet Isaiah:

3 These are difficult and disgraceful times. Our nation is like a woman too weak to give birth, when it's time for her baby to be born. 4 Please pray for those of us who are

left alive. The king of Assyria sent his army commander to insult the living God. Perhaps the LORD heard what he said and will do something, if you will pray.

5 When these leaders went to Isaiah, 6 he told them that the LORD had this message for Hezekiah:

I am the LORD. Don't worry about the insulting things that have been said about me by these messengers from the king of Assyria. 7 I will upset him with rumours about what's happening in his own country. He will go back, and there I will make him die a violent death.

8 Meanwhile, the commander of the Assyrian forces heard that the king had left the town of Lachish and was now attacking Libnah. So he went there.

9 About this same time the king of Assyria learnt that King Tirhakah of Ethiopia* was on his way to attack him. Then the king of Assyria sent some messengers with this note for Hezekiah:

10 Don't trust your God or be fooled by his promise to defend Jerusalem against me. 11 You have heard how we Assyrian kings have completely wiped out other nations. What makes you feel so safe? 12 The Assyrian kings before me destroyed the towns of Gozan, Haran, Rezeph, and everyone from Eden who lived in Telassar. What good did their gods do them? 13 The kings of Hamath, Arpad, Sepharvaim, Hena, and Ivvah have all disappeared.

Hezekiah prays

This is also told in Isaiah 37.14–20

14 After Hezekiah had read the note from the king of Assyria, he took it to the temple and spread it out for the LORD to see. 15 He prayed:

LORD God of Israel, your throne is above the winged creatures.* You created the heavens and the earth, and you alone rule the kingdoms of this world. 16 But just look how Sennacherib has insulted you, the living God.

17 It is true, our LORD, that Assyrian kings have turned nations into deserts. 18 They destroyed the idols of wood and stone that the people of those nations had made and worshipped. 19 But you are our LORD and our God! We ask you to keep us safe from the Assyrian king. Then everyone in every kingdom on earth will know that you are the only God.

The LORD's answer to Hezekiah

This is also told in Isaiah 37.21–35

20 Isaiah went to Hezekiah and told him that the LORD God of Israel had said:

Hezekiah, I heard your prayer about King Sennacherib of Assyria. 21 Now this is what I say to that king:

The people of Jerusalem
hate and make fun of you;
they laugh behind your back.

22 Sennacherib, you cursed,
shouted, and sneered at me,
the holy God of Israel.
23 You let your officials
insult me, the Lord.
And here is what you
have said about yourself,
"I led my chariots
to the highest heights
of Lebanon's mountains.
I went deep into its forest,
cutting down the best cedar
and cypress trees.
24 I dried up every stream
in the land of Egypt,
and I drank water from wells I had dug."

25 Sennacherib, now listen
to me, the Lord.
I planned all this long ago.
And you don't even realize
that I alone am the one
who decided that you
would do these things.
I let you make ruins of fortified cities.
26 Their people became weak,
terribly confused.
They were like wild flowers
or tender young grass
growing on a flat roof,
scorched before it matures.*

*19.9 Ethiopia: The Hebrew text has "Cush", which was a region south of Egypt that included parts of the present countries of Ethiopia and Sudan.
*19.15 winged creatures: Two winged creatures made of gold were on the top of the sacred chest and were symbols of the LORD's throne on earth (see Exodus 25.18; 2 Samuel 6.2).
See also: 19.15: Exod 25.22.

*19.26 tender young grass . . . matures: Many of the houses had roofs made of packed earth. Grass would sometimes grow out of the roof, but would die quickly because of the sun and hot winds.

27 I know all about you,
   even how fiercely angry
     you are with me.
28 I have seen your pride
   and the tremendous hatred
     you have for me.
   Now I will put a hook in your nose,
     a bit in your mouth,*
   then I will send you back
     to where you came from.

29 Hezekiah, I will tell you what's going to
happen. This year you will eat crops that
grow on their own, and the next year you
will eat whatever springs up where those
crops grew. But the third year you will
plant grain and vineyards, and you will eat
what you harvest. 30 Those who survive in
Judah will be like a vine that puts down
deep roots and bears fruit. 31 I, the LORD
All-Powerful, will see to it that some who
live in Jerusalem will survive.

32 I promise that the king of Assyria won't
get into Jerusalem, or shoot an arrow into
the city, or even surround it and prepare to
attack. 33 As surely as I am the LORD, he will
return by the way he came and will never
enter Jerusalem. 34 I will protect it for
myself and for my servant David.

The death of King Sennacherib
This is also told in Isaiah 37.36-38

35 That same night the LORD sent an angel to
the camp of the Assyrians, and he killed one
hundred and eighty-five thousand of them.
And so the next morning, the camp was full
of dead bodies. 36 After this King Sennacherib
went back to Assyria and lived in the city of
Nineveh. 37 One day he was worshipping in
the temple of his god Nisroch, when his sons,
Adrammelech and Sharezer, killed him with
their swords. They escaped to the land of
Ararat, and his son Esarhaddon became king.*

CHAPTER 20

Hezekiah gets sick and almost dies
This is also told in 2 Chronicles 32.24-26;
Isaiah 38.1-8,21,22

1 About this time, Hezekiah got sick and was
almost dead. Isaiah the prophet went in and

told him, "The LORD says you won't ever get
well. You are going to die, so you had better
start doing what needs to be done."

2 Hezekiah turned towards the wall and
prayed, 3 "Don't forget that I have been
faithful to you, LORD. I have obeyed you with
all my heart, and I do whatever you say is
right." After this, he cried hard.

4 Before Isaiah got to the middle court of
the palace, 5 the LORD sent him back to
Hezekiah with this message:

Hezekiah, you are the ruler of my people,
and I am the LORD God, who was
worshipped by your ancestor David.
I heard you pray, and I saw you cry. I will
heal you, so that three days from now you
will be able to worship in my temple.
6 I will let you live fifteen years more, while
I protect you and your city from the king
of Assyria. I will defend this city as an
honour to me and to my servant David.

7 Then Isaiah said to the king's servants,
"Bring some mashed figs and place them on
the king's open sore. He will then get well."

8 Hezekiah asked Isaiah, "Can you prove
that the LORD will heal me, so that I can
worship in his temple in three days?"

9 Isaiah replied, "The LORD will prove to
you that he will keep his promise. Will the
shadow made by the setting sun on the
stairway go forward ten steps or back ten
steps?"*

10 "It's normal for the sun to go forward,"
Hezekiah answered. "But how can it go
back?"

11 Isaiah prayed, and the LORD made the
shadow go back ten steps on the stairway
built for King Ahaz.*

The LORD is still with Hezekiah
This is also told in Isaiah 39.1-8

12 Merodach* Baladan, the son of Baladan,
was now king of Babylonia.* And when he
learnt that Hezekiah had been sick, he sent
messengers with letters and a gift for him.
13 Hezekiah welcomed* the messengers and
showed them all the silver, the gold, the
spices, and the fine oils that were in his
storehouse. He even showed them where he
kept his weapons. Nothing in his palace or in
his entire kingdom was kept hidden from
them.

---

*19.28 I will put . . . your mouth: This is how the
Assyrians treated their prisoners, and now the LORD
will treat Sennacherib the same way.
*19.37 Esarhaddon became king: Ruled Assyria
681–669 BC.

*20.12 Merodach Baladan . . . Babylonia: Ruled
Babylonia 722–710 and 704–703 BC.

373

¹⁴ Isaiah asked Hezekiah, "Where did these men come from? What did they want?"

"They came all the way from Babylonia," Hezekiah answered.

¹⁵ "What did you show them?" Isaiah asked.

Hezekiah answered, "I showed them everything in my kingdom."

¹⁶ Then Isaiah told Hezekiah:

I have a message for you from the LORD. ¹⁷ One day everything you and your ancestors have stored up will be taken to Babylonia. The LORD has promised that nothing will be left. ¹⁸ Some of your own sons will be taken to Babylonia, where they will be disgraced and made to serve in the king's palace.

¹⁹ Hezekiah thought, "At least our nation will be at peace for a while." So he told Isaiah, "The message you brought me from the LORD is good."

Hezekiah dies

This is also told in 2 Chronicles 32.32,33

²⁰ Everything else Hezekiah did while he was king, including how he made the upper pool and tunnel to bring water into Jerusalem, is written in *The History of the Kings of Judah.* ²¹ Hezekiah died, and his son Manasseh became king.

Two evil kings of Judah: Manasseh and Amon

CHAPTER 21

King Manasseh of Judah

This is also told in 2 Chronicles 33.1–20

¹ Manasseh was twelve years old when he became king of Judah, and he ruled fifty-five years from Jerusalem. His mother was Hephzibah. ² Manasseh disobeyed the LORD by following the disgusting customs of the nations that the LORD had forced out of Israel. ³ He rebuilt the local shrines* that his father Hezekiah had torn down. He built altars for the god Baal and set up a sacred pole* for worshipping the goddess Asherah, just as King Ahab of Israel had done. And he faithfully worshipped the stars in heaven.

⁴ In the temple, where only the LORD was supposed to be worshipped, Manasseh built altars for pagan gods ⁵ and for the stars. He placed these altars in both courts of the temple, ⁶⁻⁷ and even set up the pole for Asherah there. Manasseh practised magic and witchcraft; he asked fortune-tellers for advice and sacrificed his own son. He did many sinful things and made the LORD very angry.

Years ago the LORD had told David and his son Solomon:

Jerusalem is the place I prefer above all others in Israel. It belongs to me, and there I will be worshipped for ever. ⁸ If my people will faithfully obey all the commands in the Law of my servant Moses, I will never make them leave the land I gave to their ancestors.

⁹ But the people of Judah disobeyed the LORD. They listened to Manasseh and did even more sinful things than the nations the LORD had wiped out.

¹⁰ One day the LORD said to some of his prophets:

¹¹ King Manasseh has done more disgusting things than the Amorites,* and he has led my people to sin by forcing them to worship his idols. ¹² Now I, the LORD God of Israel, will destroy both Jerusalem and Judah! People will hear about it but won't believe it. ¹³ Jerusalem is as sinful as Ahab and the people of Samaria were. So I will wipe out Jerusalem and be done with it, just as someone wipes water off a plate and turns it over to dry.

¹⁴ I will even get rid of my people who survive. They will be defeated and robbed by their enemies. ¹⁵ My people have done what I hate and have not stopped making me angry since their ancestors left Egypt.

¹⁶ Manasseh was guilty of causing the people of Judah to sin and disobey the LORD. He also refused to protect innocent people — he even let so many of them be killed* that their blood filled the streets of Jerusalem.

¹⁷ Everything else Manasseh did while he was king, including his terrible sins, is written in *The History of the Kings of Judah.* ¹⁸ He died and was buried in Uzza Garden near his palace, and his son Amon became king.

---

*21.3 sacred pole: See the note at 13.6,7.
See also: 20.17: 2 King 24.13; 2 Chron 36.10.
20.18: 2 King 24.14,15; Dan 1.1–7.   21.2: Jer 15.4.

*21.11 Amorites: Here used in the general sense of nations that lived in Canaan before the Israelites.
See also: 21.4: 2 Sam 7.13.   21.7,8: 1 King 9.3–5; 2 Chron 7.12–18.

King Amon of Judah

This is also told in 2 Chronicles 33.21–25

19 Amon was twenty-two years old when he became king of Judah, and he ruled from Jerusalem for two years. His mother Meshullemeth was the daughter of Haruz from Jotbah. 20 Amon disobeyed the LORD, just as his father Manasseh had done. 21 Amon worshipped the idols Manasseh had made and 22 refused to be faithful to the LORD, the God his ancestors had worshipped.

23 Some of Amon's officials plotted against him and killed him in his palace. 24–26 He was buried in Uzza Garden. Soon after that, the people of Judah killed the murderers of Amon, then they made his son Josiah king.

Everything else Amon did while he was king is written in *The History of the Kings of Judah.*

The rule of King Josiah and "The Book of God's Law"

CHAPTER 22

King Josiah of Judah

This is also told in 2 Chronicles 34.1,2

1 Josiah was eight years old when he became king of Judah, and he ruled thirty-one years from Jerusalem. His mother Jedidah was the daughter of Adaiah from Bozkath. 2 Josiah always obeyed the LORD, just as his ancestor David had done.

Hilkiah finds *The Book of God's Law*

This is also told in 2 Chronicles 34.8–28

3 After Josiah had been king for eighteen years, he told Shaphan,• one of his highest officials:

Go to the LORD's temple 4 and ask Hilkiah the high priest to collect from the guards all the money that the people have donated. 5 Tell Hilkiah to give it to the men supervising the repairs to the temple. They can use some of the money to pay 6 the workers, and with the rest of it they can buy wood and stone for the repair work. 7 They are honest, so we won't ask them to keep track of the money.

8 While Shaphan was at the temple, Hilkiah handed him a book and said, "Look what I found here in the temple — *The Book of God's Law.*"

Shaphan read it, 9 then went back to Josiah and reported, "Your officials collected the money in the temple and gave it to the men supervising the repairs. 10 But there's something else, Your Majesty. The priest Hilkiah gave me this book." Then Shaphan read it out loud.

11 When Josiah heard what was in *The Book of God's Law,* he tore his clothes in sorrow. 12 At once he called together Hilkiah, Shaphan, Ahikam son of Shaphan, Achbor son of Micaiah, and his own servant Asaiah. He said, 13 "The LORD must be furious with me and everyone else in Judah, because our ancestors did not obey the laws written in this book. Go and find out what the LORD wants us to do."

14 The five men left straight away and went to talk with Huldah the prophet. Her husband was Shallum,• who was in charge of the king's clothes. Huldah lived in the northern part of Jerusalem, and when they met in her home, 15 she said:

You were sent here by King Josiah, and this is what the LORD God of Israel says to him: 16 "Josiah, I am the LORD! And I will see to it that this country and everyone living in it will be destroyed. It will happen just as this book says." 17 The people of Judah have rejected me. They have offered sacrifices to foreign gods and have worshipped their own idols. I cannot stand it any longer. I am furious.

18 "Josiah, listen to what I am going to do. 19 I noticed how sad you were when you read that this country and its people would be completely wiped out. You even tore your clothes in sorrow, and I heard you cry. 20 So I will let you die in peace, before I destroy this place."

The men left and took Huldah's answer back to Josiah.

CHAPTER 23

Josiah reads *The Book of God's Law*

This is also told in 2 Chronicles 34.29–33

1 King Josiah called together the older leaders of Judah and Jerusalem. 2 Then he went to the LORD's temple, together with the people of Judah and Jerusalem, the priests, and the prophets. Finally, when everybody was there,

he read aloud *The Book of God's Law** that had been found in the temple.

[3] After Josiah had finished reading, he stood by one of the columns. He asked the people to promise in the LORD's name to obey the LORD faithfully and to follow his commands. The people agreed to do everything written in the book.

Josiah follows the teachings of God's Law

This is also told in 2 Chronicles 34.3–7

[4] Josiah told Hilkiah the priest, the assistant priests, and the guards at the temple door to go into the temple and bring out the things used to worship Baal, Asherah, and the stars. Josiah had these things burnt in Kidron Valley just outside Jerusalem, and he had the ashes carried away to the town of Bethel.

[5] Josiah also got rid of the pagan priests at the local shrines in Judah and around Jerusalem. These were the men whom the kings of Judah had appointed to offer sacrifices to Baal and to the sun, moon, and stars. [6] Josiah had the sacred pole* for Asherah brought out of the temple and taken to Kidron Valley, where it was burnt. He then had its ashes ground into dust and scattered over the public cemetery there. [7] He had the buildings torn down where the male prostitutes* lived next to the temple, and where the women wove sacred robes* for the idol of Asherah.

[8] In almost every town in Judah, priests had been offering sacrifices to the LORD at local shrines.* Josiah brought these priests to Jerusalem and had their shrines made unfit for worship — every shrine from Geba just north of Jerusalem to Beersheba in the south. He even tore down the shrine at Beersheba that was just to the left of Joshua Gate, which was named after the highest official of the city. [9] Those local priests could not serve at the LORD's altar in Jerusalem, but they were allowed to eat sacred bread,* just like the priests from Jerusalem.

[10] Josiah sent some men to Hinnom Valley just outside Jerusalem with orders to make the altar there unfit for worship. That way, people could no longer use it for sacrificing their children to the god Molech. [11] He also got rid of the horses that the kings of Judah used in their ceremonies to worship the sun, and he destroyed the chariots along with them. The horses had been kept near the entrance to the LORD's temple, in a courtyard* close to where an official named Nathan-Melech lived.

[12] Some of the kings of Judah, especially Manasseh, had built altars in the two courts of the temple and in the room that Ahaz had built on the palace roof. Josiah had these altars torn down and smashed to pieces, and he had the pieces thrown into Kidron Valley, just outside Jerusalem. [13] After that, he closed down the shrines that Solomon had built east of Jerusalem and south of Spoil Hill to honour Astarte the disgusting goddess of Sidon, Chemosh the disgusting god of Moab, and Milcom the disgusting god of Ammon.* [14] He tore down the stone images of foreign gods and cut down the sacred pole used in the worship of Asherah. Then he had the whole area covered with human bones.*

[15] But Josiah had not finished yet. At Bethel he destroyed the shrine and the altar that Jeroboam son of Nebat had built and that had caused the Israelites to sin. Josiah had the shrine and the Asherah pole burnt and ground into dust. [16] As he looked around, he saw graves on the hillside. He had the bones in them dug up and burnt on the altar, so that it could no longer be used. This happened just as God's prophet had said when Jeroboam was standing at the altar, celebrating a festival.*

---

*23.2 *The Book of God's Law*: The Hebrew text has "The Book of God's Agreement", which is the same as "The Book of God's Law" in 22.8,11. In traditional translations this is called "The Book of the Covenant".
*23.6 sacred pole: See the note at 13.6,7.
*23.7 male prostitutes: Young men or boys sometimes served as prostitutes in the worship of Canaanite gods, but the LORD had forbidden the people of Israel and Judah to worship in this way (see Deuteronomy 23.17,18).
*23.7 sacred robes: Or "coverings".
See also: 23.4–6: 2 King 21.3; 2 Chron 33.3.

*23.9 sacred bread: The Hebrew text has "thin bread", which may be either the pieces of thin bread made without yeast to be eaten during the Passover Festival (see verses 21–23) or the baked flour used in sacrifices to give thanks to the LORD (see Leviticus 2.4,5).
*23.13 the shrines . . . Ammon: See 1 Kings 11.5–7.
*23.14 Then he . . . human bones: This made the whole area unfit for the worship of any god.
*23.16 just . . . festival: See 1 Kings 13.1,2.
See also: 23.10: a Jer 7.31; 19.1–6; 32.35; b Lev 18.21.
23.12: 2 King 21.5; 2 Chron 33.5.   23.13: 1 King 11.7.
23.15: 1 King 12.33.   23.16: 1 King 13.2.

Then Josiah saw the grave of the prophet who had said this would happen [17] and he asked,‣ "Whose grave is that?"

Some people who lived nearby answered, "It belongs to the prophet from Judah who told what would happen to this altar."

[18] Josiah replied, "Then leave it alone. Don't dig up his bones." So they did not disturb his bones or the bones of the old prophet from Israel who had also been buried there.*

[19] Some of the Israelite kings had made the LORD angry by building pagan shrines all over Israel. So Josiah sent troops to destroy these shrines just as he had done to the one in Bethel. [20] He killed the priests who served at them and burnt their bones on the altars.

After all that, Josiah went back to Jerusalem.

Josiah and the people of Judah celebrate Passover

This is also told in 2 Chronicles 35.1–19

[21] Josiah told the people of Judah, "Celebrate Passover in honour of the LORD your God, just as it says in *The Book of God's Law*."*

[22] This festival had not been celebrated in this way since kings ruled Israel and Judah. [23] But in Josiah's eighteenth year as king of Judah, everyone came to Jerusalem to celebrate Passover.

The LORD is still angry with the people of Judah

[24] Josiah got rid of every disgusting person and thing in Judah and Jerusalem — including magicians, fortune-tellers, and idols. He did his best to obey every law written in the book that the priest Hilkiah found in the LORD's temple. [25] No other king before or after Josiah tried as hard as he did to obey the Law of Moses.

[26] But the LORD was still furious with the people of Judah because Manasseh had done so many things to make him angry. [27] The LORD said, "I will desert the people of Judah, just as I deserted the people of Israel. I will reject Jerusalem, even though I chose it to be mine. And I will abandon this temple built to honour me."

Josiah dies in battle

This is also told in 2 Chronicles 35.20—36.1

[28] Everything else Josiah did while he was king is written in *The History of the Kings of Judah*. [29] During Josiah's rule, King Neco of Egypt led his army north to the River Euphrates to help the king of Assyria. Josiah led his troops north to fight Neco, but when they met in battle at Megiddo, Josiah was killed.* [30] A few of Josiah's servants put his body in a chariot and took it back to Jerusalem, where they buried it in his own tomb. Then the people of Judah found his son Jehoahaz and poured olive oil on his head to show that he was their new king.

The last kings of Judah

King Jehoahaz of Judah

This is also told in 2 Chronicles 36.2–4

[31] Jehoahaz was twenty-three years old when he became king of Judah, and he ruled from Jerusalem only three months. His mother Hamutal was the daughter of Jeremiah from Libnah. [32] Jehoahaz disobeyed the LORD, just as some of his ancestors had done.

[33] King Neco of Egypt had Jehoahaz arrested and put in prison at Riblah* near Hamath. Then he forced the people of Judah to pay him three thousand four hundred kilogrammes of silver and thirty-four kilogrammes of gold as taxes. [34] Neco appointed Josiah's son Eliakim king of Judah, and changed his name to Jehoiakim. He took Jehoahaz as a prisoner to Egypt, where he died.

[35] Jehoiakim forced the people of Judah to pay higher taxes, so he could give Neco the silver and gold he demanded.

King Jehoiakim of Judah

This is also told in 2 Chronicles 36.5–8

[36] Jehoiakim was twenty-five years old when he was appointed king, and he ruled

---

*23.18 old prophet . . . there: See 1 Kings 13.11–32.
*23.21 *The Book of God's Law*: See the note at verse 2.
See also: 23.17: 1 King 13.30–32.

*23.29 killed: At this time, King Neco of Egypt (609–595 BC) was fighting on the side of the Assyrians. He marched north to fight the Babylonian army and help Assyria keep control of its land. Since Josiah considered Assyria an enemy, he set out to stop Neco and the Egyptian troops.
*23.33 Riblah: An important town in Syria on the River Orontes.
See also: 23.34: Jer 22.11,12. 23.36: Jer 22.18,19; 26.1–6; 35.1–19.

eleven years from Jerusalem. His mother Zebidah was the daughter of Pedaiah from Rumah. [37] Jehoiakim disobeyed the LORD by following the example of his ancestors.

CHAPTER 24

[1] During Jehoiakim's rule, King Nebuchadnezzar of Babylonia* invaded and took control of Judah. Jehoiakim obeyed Nebuchadnezzar for three years, but then he rebelled.

[2] At that time, the LORD started sending troops to rob and destroy towns in Judah. Some of these troops were from Babylonia, and others were from Syria, Moab, and Ammon. The LORD had sent his servants the prophets to warn Judah about this, [3] and now he was making it happen. The country of Judah was going to be wiped out, because Manasseh had sinned [4] and caused many innocent people to die. The LORD would not forgive this.

[5] Everything else Jehoiakim did while he was king is written in *The History of the Kings of Judah.* [6] Jehoiakim died, and his son Jehoiachin became king.

[7] King Nebuchadnezzar defeated King Neco of Egypt and took control of his land from the Egyptian Gorge all the way north to the River Euphrates. So Neco never invaded Judah again.*

King Jehoiachin of Judah is taken to Babylon

This is also told in 2 Chronicles 36.9,10

[8] Jehoiachin was eighteen years old when he became king of Judah, and he ruled only three months from Jerusalem. His mother Nehushta was the daughter of Elnathan from Jerusalem. [9] Jehoiachin disobeyed the LORD, just as his father Jehoiakim had done.

[10] King Nebuchadnezzar of Babylonia sent troops to attack Jerusalem soon after Jehoiachin became king. [11] During the attack, Nebuchadnezzar himself arrived at the city. [12] Jehoiachin immediately

surrendered, together with his mother and his servants, as well as his army officers and officials. Then Nebuchadnezzar had Jehoiachin arrested. These things took place in the eighth year of Nebuchadnezzar's rule in Babylonia.*

[13] The LORD had warned* that some day the treasures would be taken from the royal palace and from the temple, including the gold objects that Solomon had made for the temple. And that's exactly what Nebuchadnezzar ordered his soldiers to do. [14] He also led away as prisoners the Jerusalem officials, the military leaders, and the skilled workers — ten thousand in all. Only the very poorest people were left in Judah.

[15] Nebuchadnezzar took Jehoiachin to Babylon, along with his mother, his wives, his officials, and the most important leaders of Judah. [16] He also led away seven thousand soldiers, one thousand skilled workers, and anyone who would be useful in battle.

[17] Then Nebuchadnezzar appointed Jehoiachin's uncle Mattaniah king of Judah and changed his name to Zedekiah.

King Zedekiah of Judah

This is also told in 2 Chronicles 36.11–16; Jeremiah 52.1–3

[18] Zedekiah was twenty-one years old when he was appointed king of Judah, and he ruled from Jerusalem for eleven years. His mother Hamutal was the daughter of Jeremiah from Libnah. [19] Zedekiah disobeyed the LORD, just as Jehoiakim had done. [20] It was Zedekiah who finally rebelled against Nebuchadnezzar.

The people of Judah and Jerusalem had made the LORD so angry that he finally turned his back on them. That's why these horrible things were happening.

---

*24.1 King Nebuchadnezzar of Babylonia: Ruled Babylonia 605–562 BC.
*24.7 again: Nebuchadnezzar defeated the Egyptian army in 605 BC at the town of Carchemish. But a few years later, he was forced to retreat all the way back to Babylonia, which allowed Jehoiakim to rebel (see verse 1).

See also: 24.1: Jer 25.1–38; Dan 1.1,2. 24.12: Jer 22.24–30; 24.1–10; 29.1,2.

*24.12 Babylonia: These events took place in 597 BC.
*24.13 warned: See 20.16–18.

See also: 24.15: Ezek 17.12. 24.17: Jer 37.1; Ezek 17.13. 24.18: Jer 27.1–22; 28.1–17. 24.20: Ezek 17.15.

Jerusalem is destroyed and the people are taken to Babylonia

CHAPTER 25

Jerusalem is captured and destroyed

This is also told in 2 Chronicles 36.17–21; Jeremiah 52.3–30

¹ In Zedekiah's ninth year as king, on the tenth day of the tenth month,* King Nebuchadnezzar of Babylonia led his entire army to attack Jerusalem. The troops set up camp outside the city and built ramps up to the city walls. ²⁻³ After a year and a half, all the food in Jerusalem was gone. Then on the ninth day of the fourth* month, ⁴ the Babylonian troops broke through the city wall.* That same night, Zedekiah and his soldiers tried to escape through the gate near the royal garden, even though they knew the enemy had the city surrounded. They headed towards the desert, ⁵ but the Babylonian troops caught up with them near Jericho. They arrested Zedekiah, but his soldiers scattered in every direction.

⁶ Zedekiah was taken to Riblah, where Nebuchadnezzar put him on trial and found him guilty. ⁷ Zedekiah's sons were killed right in front of him. His eyes were then put out, and he was put in chains and dragged off to Babylon.

⁸ About a month later,* in Nebuchadnezzar's nineteenth year as king, Nebuzaradan, who was his official in charge of the guards, arrived in Jerusalem. ⁹ Nebuzaradan burnt down the LORD's temple, the king's palace, and every important building in the city, as well as all the houses. ¹⁰ Then he ordered the Babylonian soldiers to break down the walls around Jerusalem. ¹¹ He led away as prisoners the people left in the city, including those who had become loyal to Nebuchadnezzar. ¹² Only some of the poorest people were left behind to work the vineyards and the fields.

¹³ The Babylonian soldiers took the two bronze columns that stood in front of the temple, the ten moveable bronze stands, and the large bronze bowl called the Sea. They broke them into pieces so they could take the bronze to Babylonia. ¹⁴ They carried off the bronze things used for worship at the temple, including the pans for hot ashes, and the shovels, snuffers, and also the dishes for incense, ¹⁵ as well as the fire pans and the sprinkling bowls. Nebuzaradan ordered his soldiers to take everything made of gold or silver.

¹⁶ The pile of bronze from the columns, the stands, and the large bowl that Solomon had made for the temple was too large to be weighed. ¹⁷ Each column had been eight metres tall with a bronze cap over one metre high. These caps were decorated with bronze designs — some of them like chains and others like pomegranates.*

¹⁸ Next, Nebuzaradan arrested Seraiah the chief priest, Zephaniah his assistant, and three temple officials. ¹⁹ Then he arrested one of the army commanders, the king's five personal advisers, and the officer in charge of gathering the troops for battle. He also found sixty more soldiers who were still in Jerusalem. ²⁰ Nebuzaradan led them all to Riblah ²¹ near Hamath, where Nebuchadnezzar had them killed.

The people of Judah no longer lived in their own country.

Gedaliah is made ruler and King Jehoiachin is released from prison

Gedaliah is made ruler of the people left in Judah

This is also told in Jeremiah 40.7–9; 41.1–3

²² King Nebuchadnezzar appointed Gedaliah son of Ahikam* to rule the few people still living in Judah. ²³ When the army officers and troops heard that Gedaliah was their ruler, the officers met with him at Mizpah. These men were Ishmael son of Nethaniah, Johanan son of Kareah, Seraiah son of Tanhumeth from Netophah, and Jaazaniah from Maacah.

---

*25.1 tenth month: Tebeth, the tenth month of the Hebrew calendar, from about mid-December to mid-January.
*25.4 wall: Jerusalem was destroyed in 586 BC.
See also: 25.1: Jer 21.1–10; 34.1–5; Ezek 24.2.
25.4: Ezek 33.21. 25.7: Ezek 12.13. 25.9: 1 King 9.8.

*25.17 pomegranates: A bright red fruit that looks like an apple.
See also: 25.13: a 1 King 7.15–26; 2 Chron 3.15–17;
b 1 King 7.23–26; 2 Chron 4.2–5. 25.14: 1 King 7.45;
2 Chron 4.16. 25.22–24: Jer 40.7–9.

24 Gedaliah said to them, "Everything will be fine, I promise. We don't need to be afraid of the Babylonian rulers, if we live here peacefully and do what Nebuchadnezzar says."

25 Ishmael* was from the royal family. And about two months after Gedaliah began his rule,* Ishmael and ten other men went to Mizpah. They killed Gedaliah and his officials, including those from Judah and those from Babylonia. 26 After that, the army officers and all the people in Mizpah, whether important or not, were afraid of what the Babylonians might do. So they left Judah and went to Egypt.

Jehoiachin is set free

This is also told in Jeremiah 52.31–34

27 Jehoiachin was a prisoner in Babylon for thirty-seven years. Then Evil-Merodach became king of Babylonia,* and in the first year of his rule, on the twenty-seventh day of the twelfth month,* he let Jehoiachin out of prison. 28 Evil-Merodach was kind to Jehoiachin and honoured him more than any of the other kings held prisoner there. 29 Jehoiachin was even allowed to wear his own clothes, and he ate at the king's table every day. 30 As long as Jehoiachin lived, he was paid a daily allowance to buy whatever he needed.

*25.27 Evil-Merodach . . . Babylonia: The son of Nebuchadnezzar, who ruled Babylonia from 562 to 560 BC.

*25.27 twelfth month: Adar, the twelfth month of the Hebrew calendar, from about mid-February to mid-March.

See also: 25.25: Jer 41.1–3. 25.26: Jer 43.5–7.

Additional notes

'1.8 hairy: Or "wearing a furry coat".

'1.12 God sent down fire: Or "A mighty fire came down".

'1.17 Joram: The Hebrew text has "Jehoram", another spelling of the name.

'1.17 his brother: Some ancient translations (see also 3.1); these words are not in the Hebrew text.

'2.1 Elisha: Hebrew "the man of God".

'2.12 Israel's . . . away: Or "Master, you were like cavalry and chariots for the people of Israel!"

'3.16 that . . . water: Or "you must dig holes everywhere in this river bed."

'3.24 chased . . . attack: One possible meaning for the difficult Hebrew text.

'3.27 The Israelite . . . that: One possible meaning for the difficult Hebrew text.

'5.8 the prophet: Hebrew "the man of God".

'5.12 River Abana: Most Hebrew manuscripts; some Hebrew manuscripts and two ancient translations "River Amana".

'6.9 have set up camp: Or "are going".

'6.32 That murderer: Hebrew "That murderer's son".

'7.13 We're going . . . died: One possible meaning for the difficult Hebrew text.

'8.11 Elisha stared . . . crying: Or "Hazael stared at him until Elisha was embarrassed and began to cry."

'8.21 Jehoram: The Hebrew text has "Joram", another spelling of the name.

'8.21 he attacked . . . homes: One possible meaning for the difficult Hebrew text.

'8.24 Jerusalem: Hebrew "the city of David".

'9.14–16 Joram: See the note at 1.17.

'9.33 horses . . . her body: Two ancient translations; Hebrew "horses. Then Jehu trampled her body."

'10.1 the town: Two ancient translations; Hebrew "Jezreel".

'10.12,13 at a place where shepherds meet: Or "at Betheked of the Shepherds".

'10.15 Jehonadab son of Rechab: Or "Jehonadab the chariot driver".

'10.27 public toilet: Or "rubbish dump".

'11.2 Jehoram's: The Hebrew text has "Joram's", another spelling of the name.

'11.4 the king's special bodyguards: The Hebrew text has "the Carites", who were probably foreign soldiers hired to serve as royal bodyguards.

'11.14 singers: Two ancient translations; Hebrew "commanders".

'11.19 the king's special bodyguards: See the note at 11.4.

'12.1 Joash: The Hebrew text has "Jehoash", another spelling of the name.

'12.3 local shrines: The Hebrew text has "high places", which were local places to worship God or foreign gods.

'12.5 You priests . . . money too: One possible meaning for the difficult Hebrew text.

'12.20,21 Jozabad: Some manuscripts of the Hebrew text; other manuscripts "Jozacar".

'12.20,21 Jerusalem: See the note at 8.24.

'13.14 Master . . . without you: Or "Master, you were like chariots and cavalry for Israel!"

'14.4 local shrines: See the note at 12.3.

'14.28 how he recaptured . . . Hamath: One possible meaning for the difficult Hebrew text.

'15.4 local shrines: See the note at 12.3.

'15.10 in public: Hebrew; some manuscripts of one ancient translation "in Ibleam".

'15.13 Azariah's: The Hebrew text has "Uzziah's", another spelling of the name.

'15.25 together with Argob and Arieh: One possible meaning for the difficult Hebrew text.

'15.32 Azariah: See the note at 15.13.

'15.35 local shrines: See the note at 12.3.

'16.4 local shrines: See the note at 12.3.

'**16.5,6 the king of Edom . . . Edomites:** The Hebrew text has "King Rezin of Syria . . . Syrians"; in Hebrew, there is only one letter difference between "Edom" and "Aram", which is the usual Hebrew name for Syria in the Bible (see also 2 Chronicles 28.17).

'**16.14 aside:** Hebrew "to the north".

'**16.18 the special tent . . . Sabbath:** One possible meaning for the difficult Hebrew text.

'**16.20 Jerusalem:** See the note at 8.24.

'**17.11 shrines:** See the note at 12.3.

'**17.20 Israel and Judah:** Or "Israel", that is, the northern kingdom only.

'**17.29 Israelite:** The Hebrew text has "Samaritan", which is a later word to describe the people who lived in northern Israel at this time.

'**18.4 local shrines:** See the note at 12.3.

'**18.16 doorposts:** One possible meaning for the difficult Hebrew text.

'**20.9 Will . . . steps:** One possible meaning for the difficult Hebrew text.

'**20.11 the shadow . . . Ahaz:** One possible meaning for the difficult Hebrew text.

'**20.12 Merodach:** The Hebrew text has "Berodach", another spelling of the name.

'**20.13 welcomed:** Or "listened to".

'**21.3 local shrines:** See the note at 12.3.

'**21.16 He also refused . . . killed:** Or "He killed so many innocent people".

'**22.3 Shaphan:** Hebrew "Shaphan son of Azaliah son of Meshullam".

'**22.14 Shallum:** Hebrew "Shallum son of Tikvah son of Harhas".

'**23.5 local shrines:** See the note at 12.3.

'**23.8 local shrines:** See the note at 12.3.

'**23.11 in a courtyard:** One possible meaning for the difficult Hebrew text.

'**23.16,17 said when Jeroboam . . . asked:** One ancient translation; Hebrew "said. ¹⁷ Then Josiah asked".

'**25.2,3 fourth:** This word is not in the Hebrew text here, but see the parallel in Jeremiah 52.5,6.

'**25.8 About a month later:** Hebrew "On the seventh day of the fifth month".

'**25.22 Ahikam:** Hebrew "Ahikam son of Shaphan".

'**25.25 Ishmael:** Hebrew "Ishmael son of Nethaniah son of Elishama".

'**25.25 about two months . . . his rule:** Hebrew "in the seventh month".

1 Chronicles

A quick look at this book

The First Book of Chronicles is the first half of a
single book that was divided into two parts,
1 and 2 Chronicles, because together they
were too long to fit on one scroll. These two
books retell the history of Israel from a slightly
different viewpoint than that of Samuel and
Kings, although many of the same stories are
repeated.

King David is the most important person in the
book of 1 Chronicles. He is the one who made
Jerusalem the centre for the worship of the
Lord God, and who made sure the Lord was
worshipped in the proper way. David is also

honoured as the founder of the temple, even
though it was his son Solomon who actually
built it.

Much of 1 Chronicles is made up of lists that
trace the descendants of Adam to the time of
King Saul (1–9). After reporting how Saul died
(10), the rest of the book (11–29) focuses on
King David, and these chapters can be divided
into four parts. The first part (11–12) tells how
David became king and made Jerusalem his
capital city. This part also includes information
about David's warriors and military officers.
The second part (13–16) describes how David
moved the sacred chest to its new home in
Jerusalem. The third part (17–20) includes
events during his rule, and the final part
(21–29) describes his preparations for
building the Lord's temple and his instructions
to his son Solomon about the proper worship
of the Lord.

In 1 Chronicles, David is used as an example of
someone who faithfully worships and obeys
the Lord. At the end of David's rule, he praises
the Lord in front of everyone in Israel and says:

*I praise you for ever, LORD! You are the God
our ancestor Jacob worshipped. Your power is
great, and your glory is seen everywhere in
heaven and on earth. You are king of the entire
world, and you rule with strength and power.*

(29.10b–12a)

Descendants of Adam until the time of King Saul

CHAPTER 1

The descendants of Adam

This is also told in Genesis 5.1–32; 10.1–32; 11.10–32

[1-4] Adam was the father of Seth, and his descendants were Enosh, Kenan, Mahalalel, Jared, Enoch, Methuselah, Lamech, and Noah, who had three sons: Shem, Ham, and Japheth.

[5] Japheth was the father of Gomer, Magog, Madai, Javan, Tubal, Meshech, and Tiras, and they were the ancestors of the kingdoms named after them. [6] Gomer was the ancestor of Ashkenaz, Riphath,' and Togarmah. [7] Javan was the ancestor of Elishah, Tarshish, Kittim, and Dodanim.'

[8] Ham was the father of Ethiopia,* Egypt, Put, and Canaan, and they were the ancestors of the kingdoms named after them. [9] Ethiopia was the ancestor of Seba, Havilah, Sabta, Raamah, and Sabteca. Raamah was the ancestor of Sheba and Dedan. [10] Ethiopia was also the father of Nimrod, the world's first mighty warrior. [11] Egypt was the ancestor of Ludim, Anamim, Lehabim, Naphtuhim, [12] Pathrusim, Casluhim, and Caphtorim, the ancestor of the Philistines.' [13] Canaan's eldest son was Sidon; his other son was Heth. [14-16] Canaan was also the ancestor of the Jebusites, the Amorites, the Girgashites, the Hivites, the Arkites, the Sinites, the Arvadites, the Zemarites, and the Hamathites.

[17] Shem was the father of Elam, Asshur, Arpachshad, Lud, Aram, Uz, Hul, Gether, and Meshech;' they were the ancestors of the kingdoms named after them. [18] Arpachshad was Shelah's father and Eber's grandfather. [19] Eber named his first son Peleg,* because in his time the earth was divided into tribal regions. Eber's second son was Joktan, [20-23] the ancestor of Almodad, Sheleph, Hazarmaveth, Jerah, Hadoram, Uzal, Diklah, Ebal, Abimael, Sheba, Ophir, Havilah, and Jobab. [24-27] Shem's descendants included Arpachshad, Shelah, Eber, Peleg, Reu, Serug, Nahor, Terah, and Abram, later renamed Abraham.

Abraham's family

This is also told in Genesis 25.1–4,12–16

[28] Abraham was the father of Isaac and Ishmael.

[29-31] Ishmael had twelve sons, who were born in the following order: Nebaioth, Kedar, Adbeel, Mibsam, Mishma, Dumah, Massa, Hadad, Tema, Jetur, Naphish, and Kedemah. [32] Abraham and his slave woman Keturah had six sons: Zimran, Jokshan, Medan, Midian, Ishbak, and Shuah. Jokshan was the father of Sheba and Dedan. [33] Midian was the father of Ephah, Epher, Hanoch, Abida, and Eldaah.

Esau's family

This is also told in Genesis 36.1–14

[34] Abraham's son Isaac was the father of Esau and Jacob.' [35] Esau was the father of Eliphaz, Reuel, Jeush, Jalam, and Korah. [36] Eliphaz was the father of Teman, Omar, Zephi, Gatam, Kenaz, Timna, and Amalek. [37] Reuel was the father of Nahath, Zerah, Shammah, and Mizzah.

The first Edomites and their kings

This is also told in Genesis 36.20–43

[38] Seir was the father of Lotan, Shobal, Zibeon, Anah, Dishon, Ezer, and Dishan. [39] Lotan was the father of Hori and Homam; Lotan's sister was Timna. [40] Shobal was the father of Alvan,' Manahath, Ebal, Shephi, and Onam. Zibeon was the father of Aiah and Anah.

[41] Anah was the father of Dishon and the grandfather of Hemdan,' Eshban, Ithran, and Cheran. [42] Ezer was the father of Bilhan, Zaavan, and Jaakan.' Dishan' was the father of Uz and Aran.

[43] Before kings ruled in Israel, Bela son of Beor ruled the country of Edom from its capital of Dinhabah. [44] After Bela's death, Jobab son of Zerah from Bozrah became king. [45] After Jobab's death, Husham from the land of Teman became king. [46] After Husham's death, Hadad son of Bedad became king and ruled from Avith. Earlier, Bedad had defeated the Midianites in the territory of Moab. [47] After Hadad's death, Samlah from Masrekah became king; [48] after Samlah's death, Shaul from the town of Rehoboth on the River Euphrates became king; [49] and after Shaul's death, Baal Hanan son of Achbor became king. [50] After Baal Hanan's death, Hadad ruled from Pai. His wife was Mehetabel, the daughter of Matred and granddaughter of Mezahab.

---

*1.8 Ethiopia: The Hebrew text has "Cush", which was a region south of Egypt that included parts of the present countries of Ethiopia and Sudan.
*1.19 Peleg: In Hebrew "Peleg" means "divided".

383

[51] The Edomite clans' were Timna, Alvah,' Jetheth, [52] Oholibamah, Elah, Pinon, [53] Kenaz, Teman, Mibzar, [54] Magdiel, and Iram.

CHAPTER 2

The descendants of Judah

[1-2] Jacob' was the father of twelve sons: Reuben, Simeon, Levi, Judah, Issachar, Zebulun, Dan, Joseph, Benjamin, Naphtali, Gad, and Asher.

[3] Judah and his Canaanite wife Bathshua had three sons: Er, Onan, and Shelah. But the LORD had Er put to death, because he disobeyed and did what the LORD hated. [4] Judah and his daughter-in-law Tamar also had two sons: Perez and Zerah.

[5] Perez was the father of Hezron and Hamul. [6] Zerah was the father of Zimri, Ethan, Heman, Calcol, and Darda.' [7] Achan,' who was a descendant of Zerah and the son of Carmi, caused trouble for Israel, because he kept for himself things that belonged only to the LORD.* [8] Ethan's son was Azariah.

The ancestors of King David

[9] Hezron was the father of Jerahmeel, Ram, and Caleb.' [10] Ram was the father of Amminadab and the grandfather of Nahshon, a tribal leader of Judah. [11] Nahshon's descendants included Salma, Boaz, [12] Obed, and Jesse. [13-15] Jesse had seven sons, who were born in the following order: Eliab, Abinadab, Shimea, Nethanel, Raddai, Ozem, and David. [16] Jesse also had two daughters: Zeruiah and Abigail. Zeruiah was the mother of Abishai, Joab, and Asahel. [17] Abigail's husband was Jether, who was a descendant of Ishmael, and their son was Amasa.

The descendants of Hezron

[18] Hezron's son Caleb married Azubah, and their daughter was Jerioth,' the mother of Jesher, Shobab, and Ardon. [19] After the death of Azubah, Caleb married Ephrath. Their son Hur [20] was the father of Uri and the grandfather of Bezalel.

[21] When Hezron was sixty years old, he married the daughter of Machir, who settled the region of Gilead. Their son Segub [22] was the father of Jair, who ruled twenty-three villages in the region of Gilead. [23] Some time later the

nations of Geshur and Aram captured sixty towns in that region, including the villages that belonged to Jair, as well as the town of Kenath and the nearby villages. Everyone from the region of Gilead was a descendant of Machir.

[24] After the death of Hezron, Caleb married Ephrath, his father's wife. Their son was Asshur,' who later settled the town of Tekoa.

The descendants of Jerahmeel

[25] Jerahmeel, Hezron's eldest son, was the father of Ram, Bunah, Oren, and Ahijah. [26] Jerahmeel had a second wife, Atarah, who gave birth to Onam. [27] Ram was the father of Maaz, Jamin, and Eker. [28] Onam was the father of Shammai and Jada.

Shammai was the father of Nadab and Abishur. [29] Abishur married Abihail, and their two sons were Ahban and Molid. [30] Nadab was the father of Seled and Appaim. Seled had no children; [31] Appaim's son was Ishi, the father of Sheshan and the grandfather of Ahlai. [32] Jada was the father of Jether and Jonathan. Jether had no children, [33] but Jonathan had two sons: Peleth and Zaza.

[34-35] Sheshan had no sons, and so he let one of his daughters marry Jarha, his Egyptian slave. Their son was Attai, [36] the father of Nathan and the grandfather of Zabad. [37-41] Zabad's descendants included Ephlal, Obed, Jehu, Azariah, Helez, Eleasah, Sismai, Shallum, Jekamiah, and Elishama.

The descendants of Caleb

[42] Caleb, Jerahmeel's brother, had the following descendants: Mesha,' Ziph, Mareshah,' Hebron,' and Hebron's four sons, Korah, Tappuah, Rekem, and Shema. [43] Shema was the father of Raham and the grandfather of Jorkeam. Rekem was the father of Shammai, [45] the grandfather of Maon, and the great-grandfather of Bethzur.

[46] Ephah was one of Caleb's wives,* and their sons were Haran, Moza, and Gazez. Haran named his son after his brother Gazez. [47] Ephah was the daughter of Jahdai, who was also the father of Regem, Jotham, Geshan, Pelet, and Shaaph.'

[48] Maacah was another of Caleb's wives,* and their sons were Sheber and Tirhanah. [49] Later, they had two more sons: Shaaph the father of Madmannah, and Sheva the father of Machbenah and Gibea. Caleb's daughter was Achsah. [50-51] All of these were Caleb's descendants.

---

*2.7 Achan: The Hebrew text has "Achar", which means "trouble".
*2.7 Achan . . . the LORD: See Joshua 7.1–26.
See also: 2.7: Josh 7.1.

*2.46,48 wives: See the note at 3.9.

Hur, the eldest son of Caleb and Ephrath, had three sons: Shobal, Salma, and Hareph, who settled the town of Beth-Gader. [52] Shobal, who settled the town of Kiriath-Jearim, was the ancestor of Haroeh, half of the Menuhoth clan, [53] and the clans that lived near Kiriath-Jearim; they were the Ithrites, the Puthites, the Shumathites, and the Mishraites. The Zorathites and the Eshtaolites were descendants of the Mishraites.

[54] Salma settled the town of Bethlehem and was the ancestor of the Netophathites, the people of Atroth-Bethjoab, half of the Manahathite clan, and the Zorites. [55] Salma was also the ancestor of the clans in Jabez that kept the court and government records; they were the Tirathites, the Shimeathites, and the Sucathites. These clans were the descendants of Hammath the Kenite, who was also the ancestor of the Rechabites.

CHAPTER 3

The descendants of King David

[1-4] King David ruled from Hebron for seven years and six months, and during that time he had six sons, who were born in the following order: Amnon, Daniel, Absalom, Adonijah, Shephatiah, and Ithream. Ahinoam from Jezreel was the mother of Amnon; Abigail from Carmel was the mother of Daniel; Maacah daughter of King Talmai of Geshur was the mother of Absalom; Haggith was the mother of Adonijah; Abital was the mother of Shephatiah; and Eglah was the mother of Ithream.

David then ruled from Jerusalem for thirty-three years, [5] and during that time, he had thirteen more sons. His wife Bathsheba* daughter of Ammiel gave birth to Shimea, Shobab, Nathan, and Solomon. [6-8] David's other sons included Ibhar, Elishua,* Eliphelet, Nogah, Nepheg, Japhia, Elishama, Eliada, and Eliphelet. [9] David's other wives* also gave birth to sons. Tamar was his daughter.

The descendants of King Solomon

[10-15] Solomon's descendants included the following kings: Rehoboam, Abijah, Asa, Jehoshaphat, Jehoram,* Ahaziah, Joash, Amaziah, Azariah, Jotham, Ahaz, Hezekiah, Manasseh, Amon, and Josiah and his four

sons, Johanan, Jehoiakim, Zedekiah, and Jehoahaz.* [16] Jehoiakim was the father of Jehoiachin and Zedekiah.

[17] Jehoiachin, who was taken to Babylon as a prisoner, had seven sons: Shealtiel, [18] Malchiram, Pedaiah, Shenazzar, Jekamiah, Hoshama, and Nedabiah. [19] Pedaiah had two sons: Zerubbabel and Shimei. Zerubbabel was the father of Meshullam, Hananiah, and Shelomith their sister. [20] He also had five other sons: Hashubah, Ohel, Berechiah, Hasadiah, and Jushabhesed. [21] Hananiah's descendants were Pelatiah, Jeshaiah, Rephaiah, Arnan, Obadiah, and Shecaniah,* [22] the father of Shemaiah and the grandfather of Hattush, Igal, Bariah, Neariah, and Shaphat. [23] Neariah was the father of Elioenai, Hizkiah, and Azrikam. [24] Elioenai was the father of Hodaviah, Eliashib, Pelaiah, Akkub, Johanan, Delaiah, and Anani.

CHAPTER 4

The descendants of Judah

[1] Judah was the father of five sons: Perez, Hezron, Carmi, Hur, and Shobal. [2] Shobal was the father of Reaiah, the grandfather of Jahath, and the great-grandfather of Ahumai and Lahad. These men all belonged to the Zorathite clan.

[3-4] Hur was the eldest son of Caleb and Ephrath. Some of his descendants settled the town of Bethlehem. Hur's other descendants included Etam, Penuel, and Ezer. Etam's sons* were Jezreel, Ishma, and Idbash, and his daughter was Hazzelelponi. Penuel settled the town of Gedor, and Ezer settled the town of Hushah.

[5] Ashhur, who settled the town of Tekoa, had two wives: Helah and Naarah. [6] Ashhur and Naarah were the parents of Ahuzzam, Hepher, Temeni, and Haahashtari. [7] Ashhur and Helah were the parents of Zereth, Izhar, and Ethnan.

[8] Koz, the father of Anub and Zobebah, was also the ancestor of the clans of Aharhel, the son of Harum.

[9] Jabez was a man who got his name because of the pain he caused his mother during birth.* But he was still the most respected son in his family. [10] One day he prayed to Israel's God, "Please bless me and give me a lot of land. Be with me so I will be safe from harm."* And God did just what Jabez had asked.

---

*3.9 other wives: This translates a Hebrew word for women who were legally bound to a man, but without the full privileges of a wife.

See also: 3.4: 2 Sam 5.4,5; 1 King 2.11; 1 Chron 29.27.
3.5: 2 Sam 11.3.

*4.9 Jabez . . . pain . . . birth: In Hebrew "Jabez" sounds like "pain".

[11] Chelub was the brother of Shuhah and the father of Mehir. Later, Mehir had a son, Eshton, [12] whose three sons were Bethrapha, Paseah, and Tehinnah. It was Tehinnah who settled the town of Nahash.* These men and their families lived in the town of Recah.

[13] Kenaz was the father of Othniel and Seraiah. Othniel had two sons: Hathath and Meonothai,* [14] who was the father of Ophrah. Seraiah was the father of Joab, who settled a place called "Valley of Crafts" because the people who lived there were experts in making things.

[15] Caleb son of Jephunneh had three sons: Iru, Elah, and Naam. Elah was the father of Kenaz.

[16] Jehallelel was the father of Ziph, Ziphah, Tiria, and Asarel.

[17-18] Ezrah was the father of Jether, Mered, Epher, and Jalon. Mered was married to Bithiah the daughter of the king of Egypt. They had a daughter named Miriam and two sons: Shammai and Ishbah. It was Ishbah who settled the town of Eshtemoa. Mered was also married to a woman from the tribe of Judah, and their sons were Jered, Heber, and Jekuthiel. Jered settled the town of Gedor; Heber settled the town of Soco; and Jekuthiel settled the town of Zanoah.

[19] A man named Hodiah was married to the sister of Naham. Hodiah's descendants included Keilah the Garmite clan and Eshtemoa of the Maacathite clan.

[20] Shimon was the father of Amnon, Rinnah, Benhanan, and Tilon.

Ishi was the father of Zoheth and Benzoheth.

[21-22] Judah also had a son named Shelah, whose descendants included Jokim and the people of the town of Cozeba, as well as Er who settled the town of Lecah and Laadah who settled the town of Mareshah. The people who lived in Beth-Ashbea were also descendants of Shelah, and they were experts in weaving cloth. Shelah was the ancestor of Joash and Saraph, two men who married Moabite women and then settled near Bethlehem* — but these family records are very old. [23] The members of these clans were the potters who lived in the towns of Netaim and Gederah and worked for the king.

The descendants of Simeon

[24] Simeon had five sons: Nemuel, Jamin, Jarib, Zerah, and Shaul. [25] The descendants of Shaul included his son Shallum, his grandson Mibsam, and his great-grandson Mishma. [26] The descendants of Mishma included his son Hammuel, his grandson Zaccur, and his great-grandson Shimei. [27] Shimei had sixteen sons and six daughters. But his brothers did not have as many children, so the Simeon tribe was smaller than the Judah tribe.

[28-31] Before David became king, the people of the Simeon tribe lived in the following towns: Beersheba, Moladah, Hazar-Shual, Bilhah, Ezem, Tolad, Bethuel, Hormah, Ziklag, Beth-Marcaboth, Hazarsusim, Bethbiri, and Shaaraim. [32] They also lived in the five villages of Etam, Ain, Rimmon, Tochen, and Ashan, [33] as well as in the nearby villages as far as the town of Baal. These are the places where Simeon's descendants had settled, according to their own family records.

[34-38] As their families and clans became larger, the people of Simeon had the following leaders: Meshobab, Jamlech, Joshah son of Amaziah, Joel, Jehu,* Elioenai, Jaakobah, Jeshohaiah, Asaiah, Adiel, Jesimiel, Benaiah, and Ziza.* [39] When the people needed more pasture land for their flocks and herds, they looked as far as the eastern side of the valley where the town of Gerar* is, [40] and they found a lot of good pasture land that was quiet and undisturbed. This had once belonged to the Hamites, [41] but when Hezekiah was king of Judah, the descendants of Simeon attacked and forced the Hamites and Meunites off the land, then settled there.

[42] Some time later, five hundred men from the Simeon tribe went into Edom* under the command of Pelatiah, Neariah, Rephaiah, and Uzziel the sons of Ishi. [43] They killed the last of the Amalekites and lived there from then on.

CHAPTER 5

The descendants of Reuben

[1] Reuben was the eldest son of Jacob,* but he lost his rights as the firstborn son* because he slept with one of his father's wives.* The honour of the firstborn son was then given to Joseph, [2] even though it was the Judah tribe that became the most powerful and produced a leader.

---

*5.1 rights as the firstborn son: The firstborn son inherited the largest amount of property, as well as the leadership of the family.
*5.1 wives: See Genesis 35.22; 49.3,4.

See also: 4.28-33: Josh 19.2-8. 5.1: Gen 35.22; 49.3,4. 5.2: Gen 49.8-10.

3 Reuben had four sons: Hanoch, Pallu, Hezron, and Carmi.

4-6 The descendants of Joel included Shemaiah, Gog, Shimei, Micah, Reaiah, Baal, and Beerah, a leader of the Reuben tribe. Later, King Tiglath Pileser of Assyria took Beerah away as prisoner.

7-8 The family records also include Jeiel, who was a clan leader, Zechariah, and Bela son of Azaz and grandson of Shema of the Joel clan. They lived in the territory around the town of Aroer, as far north as Nebo and Baal-Meon, 9 and as far east as the desert just west of the River Euphrates. They needed this much land because they owned too many cattle to keep them all in Gilead.

10 When Saul was king, the Reuben tribe attacked and defeated the Hagrites, then took over their land east of Gilead.

The descendants of Gad

11 The tribe of Gad lived in the region of Bashan, north of the Reuben tribe. Gad's territory extended all the way to the town of Salecah. 12 Some of the clan leaders were Joel, Shapham, Janai, and Shaphat. 13 Their relatives included Michael, Meshullam, Sheba, Jorai, Jacan, Zia, and Eber.

14 They were all descendants of Abihail, whose family line went back through Huri, Jaroah, Gilead, Michael, Jeshishai, Jahdo, and Buz. 15 Ahi, the son of Abdiel and the grandson of Guni, was the leader of their clan.

16 The people of Gad lived in the towns in the regions of Bashan and Gilead, as well as in the pasture land of Sharon. 17 Their family records were written when Jotham was king of Judah and Jeroboam was king of Israel.

18 The tribes of Reuben, Gad, and East Manasseh had 44,760 soldiers trained to fight in battle with shields, swords, bows, and arrows. 19 They fought against the Hagrites and the tribes of Jetur, Naphish, and Nodab. 20 Whenever these soldiers went to war against their enemies, they prayed to God and trusted him to help. That's why the tribes of Reuben, Gad, and East Manasseh defeated the Hagrites and their allies.

21 These Israelite tribes captured fifty thousand camels, two hundred and fifty thousand sheep, two thousand donkeys, and one hundred thousand people. 22 Many of the Hagrites died in battle, because God was fighting this battle against them. The tribes

of Reuben, Gad, and East Manasseh lived in that territory until they were taken as prisoners to Assyria.*

The tribe of East Manasseh

23 East Manasseh was a large tribe, so its people settled in the northern region of Bashan, as far north as Baal-Hermon,* Senir, and Mount Hermon. 24 Epher, Ishi, Eliel, Azriel, Jeremiah, Hodaviah, and Jahdiel were their clan leaders; they were well-known leaders and brave soldiers.

The tribes of Reuben, Gad, and East Manasseh are defeated

25 The people of the tribes of Reuben, Gad, and East Manasseh were unfaithful to the God their ancestors had worshipped, and they started worshipping the gods of the nations that God had forced out of Canaan. 26 So God sent King Tiglath Pileser* of Assyria to attack these Israelite tribes. The king led them away as prisoners to Assyria, and from then on, he forced them to live in Halah, Habor, Hara, and near the River Gozan.

CHAPTER 6

The descendants of Levi

1 Levi was the father of Gershon, Kohath, and Merari.

2 Kohath was the father of Amram, Izhar, Hebron, and Uzziel. 3 Amram was the father of Aaron, Moses, and Miriam.

Aaron had four sons: Nadab, Abihu, Eleazar, and Ithamar.

4-14 Eleazar's descendants included Phinehas, Abishua, Bukki, Uzzi, Zerahiah, Meraioth, Amariah, Ahitub, Zadok, Ahimaaz, Azariah, Johanan, Azariah the priest who served in the temple built by King Solomon, Amariah, Ahitub, Zadok, Shallum, Hilkiah, Azariah, Seraiah, and Jehozadak. 15 King Nebuchadnezzar of Babylonia took Jehozadak to Babylon as prisoner when the LORD let the people of Judah and Jerusalem be dragged from their land.*

---

*5.22 they were taken as prisoners to Assyria: See 2 Kings 15.29; 17.5–23.

*5.23 Baal-Hermon: The location of this place is unknown.

*6.15 King Nebuchadnezzar . . . dragged from their land: See 2 Kings 24.8–17; 25.1–21.

See also: 5.26: a 2 Kings 15.19; b 2 King 15.29; c 2 Kings 17.6.

16 Levi's three sons had sons of their own. 17 Gershon was the father of Libni and Shimei. 18 Kohath was the father of Amram, Izhar, Hebron, and Uzziel. 19 Merari was the father of Mahli and Mushi. These descendants of Levi each became leaders of their own clans.

20-21 Gershon's descendants included Libni, Jahath, Zimmah, Joah, Iddo, Zerah, and Jeatherai.

22-24 Kohath's descendants included Amminadab, Korah, Assir, Elkanah, Ebiasaph, Assir, Tahath, Uriel, Uzziah, and Shaul.

25 Elkanah was the father of Amasai and Ahimoth. 26-27 Ahimoth's descendants included Elkanah, Zophai, Nahath, Eliab, Jeroham, and Elkanah.

28 Samuel was the father of Joel* and Abijah, born in that order.

29-30 Merari's descendants included Mahli, Libni, Shimei, Uzzah, Shimea, Haggiah, and Asaiah.

The temple musicians

31 After King David had the sacred chest moved to Jerusalem, he appointed musicians from the Levi tribe to be in charge of the music at the place of worship. 32 These musicians served at the sacred tent and later at the LORD's temple that King Solomon built.

33-38 Here is a list of these musicians and their family lines:

Heman from the Kohathite clan was the director. His ancestors went all the way back to Jacob and included Joel, Samuel, Elkanah, Jeroham, Eliel, Toah, Zuph, Elkanah, Mahath, Amasai, Elkanah, Joel, Azariah, Zephaniah, Tahath, Assir, Ebiasaph, Korah, Izhar, Kohath, and Levi.

39-43 Asaph was Heman's relative and served as his assistant. Asaph's ancestors included Berechiah, Shimea, Michael, Baaseiah, Malchijah, Ethni, Zerah, Adaiah, Ethan, Zimmah, Shimei, Jahath, Gershon, and Levi.

44-47 Ethan was also Heman's relative and served as his assistant. Ethan belonged to the Merari clan, and his ancestors included Kishi, Abdi, Malluch, Hashabiah, Amaziah, Hilkiah, Amzi, Bani, Shemer, Mahli, Mushi, Merari, and Levi.

48 The rest of the Levites were appointed to work at the sacred tent.

The descendants of Aaron

49 Only Aaron and his descendants were allowed to offer sacrifices and incense on the

two altars at the sacred tent.* They were in charge of the most holy place and the ceremonies to forgive sins, just as God's servant Moses had commanded.

50-53 Aaron's descendants included his son Eleazar, Phinehas, Abishua, Bukki, Uzzi, Zerahiah, Meraioth, Amariah, Ahitub, Zadok, and Ahimaaz.

The towns for the Levites

This is also told in Joshua 21.1–42

54 Aaron's descendants belonged to the Levite clan of Kohath, and they were the first group chosen to receive towns to live in. 55 They received the town of Hebron in the territory of Judah and the pasture land around it. 56 But the farmland and villages around Hebron were given to Caleb son of Jephunneh. 57-59 So Aaron's descendants received the following Safe Towns* and the pasture land around them: Hebron, Libnah, Jattir, Eshtemoa, Hilen, Debir, Ashan, and Beth-Shemesh. 60 From the Benjamin tribe they were given the towns of Geba, Alemeth, and Anathoth and the pasture land around them. Thirteen towns were given to Aaron's descendants.

61 The rest of the Levite clan of Kohath received ten towns from West Manasseh.

62 The Levite clan of Gershon received thirteen towns from the tribes of Issachar, Asher, Naphtali, and East Manasseh in Bashan.

63 The Levite clan of Merari received twelve towns from the tribes of Reuben, Gad, and Zebulun.

64 So the people of Israel gave the Levites towns to live in and the pasture land around them. 65 All the towns were chosen with the LORD's help,* including those towns from the tribes of Judah, Simeon, and Benjamin.

66 Some of the families of the Kohath clan received their towns from the tribe of Ephraim. 67-69 These families received the following Safe Towns and the pasture land around them: Shechem in the hill country, Gezer, Jokmeam, Beth-Horon, Aijalon, and Gath-Rimmon. 70 And from West Manasseh

---

*6.57-59 Safe Towns: These were special towns set aside where a person who had accidentally killed someone could run for protection from the victim's relatives (see Numbers 35.9–15; Deuteronomy 19.1–13; Joshua 20.1–9).

*6.65 with the LORD's help: The Hebrew text has "by lot." Pieces of wood or stone (called "lots") were used to find out what God wanted his people to do.

they received Aner and Bileam, together with their pasture land.

⁷¹ The Gershonite clan received two towns from the tribe of East Manasseh: Golan in Bashan and Ashtaroth, including the pasture land around them. ⁷²⁻⁷³ The Gershonites also received four towns from the tribe of Issachar: Kedesh, Daberath, Ramoth, and Anem, including the pasture land around them. ⁷⁴⁻⁷⁵ The Gershonites received four towns from the tribe of Asher: Mashal, Abdon, Hukok, and Rehob, including the pasture land around them. ⁷⁶ Finally, the Gershonites received three towns from the tribe of Naphtali: Kedesh in Galilee, Hammon, and Kiriathaim, including the pasture land around them.

⁷⁷ The rest of the Merari clan received the towns of Rimmono and Tabor and their pasture land from the tribe of Zebulun. ⁷⁸⁻⁷⁹ They also received four towns east of the River Jordan from the tribe of Reuben: Bezer in the flat lands, Jahzah, Kedemoth, and Mephaath, including the pastures around them. ⁸⁰⁻⁸¹ And from the tribe of Gad the Merarites received the towns of Ramoth in Gilead, Mahanaim, Heshbon, and Jazer, including the pasture land around them.

CHAPTER 7

The descendants of Issachar

¹ Issachar was the father of four sons: Tola, Puah, Jashub, and Shimron.

² Tola was the father of Uzzi, Rephaiah, Jeriel, Jahmai, Ibsam, and Shemuel, who were all brave soldiers and family leaders in their clan. There were 22,600 people in Tola's family by the time David became king.

³ Uzzi was the father of Izrahiah and the grandfather of Michael, Obadiah, Joel, and Isshiah, who were also family leaders. ⁴ Their families were so large that they had 36,000 soldiers in their clans. ⁵ In fact, according to family records, the tribe of Issachar had a total of 87,000 warriors.

The descendants of Benjamin and Dan

⁶ Benjamin was the father of three sons: Bela, Becher, and Jediael.

⁷ Bela was the father of Ezbon, Uzzi, Uzziel, Jerimoth, and Iri. They were all brave soldiers and family leaders in their father's clan. The number of soldiers in their clan was 22,034.

⁸ Becher was the father of Zemirah, Joash, Eliezer, Elioenai, Omri, Jeremoth, Abijah, Anathoth, and Alemeth. ⁹ The official family

records listed 20,200 soldiers in the families of this clan, as well as their family leaders.

¹⁰ Jediael was the father of Bilhan and the grandfather of Jeush, Benjamin, Ehud, Chenaanah, Zethan, Tarshish, and Ahishahar. ¹¹ They were family leaders in their clan, which had 17,200 soldiers prepared to fight in battle. ¹² Ir was the father of Shuppim and Huppim, who also belonged to this clan.

Dan* was the father of Hushim.

The descendants of Naphtali

¹³ Naphtali's mother was Bilhah,* and he was the father of Jahziel, Guni, Jezer, and Shallum.

The descendants of Manasseh

¹⁴ Manasseh and his Syrian wife* were the parents of Asriel and Machir the father of Gilead. ¹⁵ Machir found a wife for Huppim and one for Shuppim. Machir had a sister named Maacah.

Zelophehad was also a descendant of Manasseh, and he had five daughters.*

¹⁶ Machir and his wife Maacah were the parents of Peresh and Sheresh. Peresh was the father of Ulam and Rekem. ¹⁷ Ulam was the father of Bedan. These were all descendants of Gilead, the son of Machir and the grandson of Manasseh.

¹⁸ Gilead's sister Hammolecheth was the mother of Ishhod, Abiezer, and Mahlah.

¹⁹ Shemida, another descendant of Manasseh, was the father of Ahian, Shechem, Likhi, and Aniam.

The descendants of Ephraim

²⁰ Ephraim was the father of Shuthelah and the ancestor of Bered, Tahath, Eleadah, Tahath, ²¹ Zabad, and Shuthelah.

Ephraim had two other sons, Ezer and Elead. But they were killed when they tried to steal livestock from the people who lived in the territory of Gath. ²² Ephraim mourned for his sons a long time, and his relatives came to comfort him. ²³ Some time later his wife gave birth to another son, and Ephraim named him Beriah, because he was born during a time of misery.*

²⁴ Ephraim's daughter was Sheerah. She built the towns of Lower Beth-Horon, Upper Beth-Horon, and Uzzen-Sheerah.

---

*7.13 Bilhah: One of Jacob's wives and the mother of Dan and Naphtali (see Genesis 46.23–25).
*7.14 wife: See the note at 3.9.
*7.23 Beriah . . . misery: In Hebrew "Beriah" sounds like "in misery".

²⁵ Ephraim also had a son named Rephah, and his descendants included Resheph, Telah, Tahan, ²⁶ Ladan, Ammihud, Elishama, ²⁷ Nun, and Joshua.

²⁸ The descendants of Ephraim took over the territory as far south as Bethel, as far east as Naaran, and as far west as Gezer. Their territory included all the villages around these towns, as well as Shechem, Ayyah, and the nearby villages.

²⁹ The descendants of Manasseh settled in the territory that included Beth-Shan, Taanach, Megiddo, Dor, and the nearby villages.

The descendants of Joseph* lived in these towns and villages.

The descendants of Asher

³⁰ Asher had four sons, Imnah, Ishvah, Ishvi, and Beriah, and one daughter, Serah.

³¹ Beriah was the father of Heber and Malchiel the father of Birzaith. ³² Heber was the father of three sons, Japhlet, Shomer, and Hotham, and one daughter, Shua. ³³ Japhlet was the father of Pasach, Bimhal, and Ashvath. ³⁴ Shomer was the father of Ahi, Rohgah, Hubbah, and Aram. ³⁵ And Japhlet's brother Hotham* was the father of Zophah, Imna, Shelesh, and Amal. ³⁶ Zophah was the father of Suah, Harnepher, Shual, Beri, Imrah, ³⁷ Bezer, Hod, Shamma, Shilshah, Ithran, and Beera. ³⁸ Jether was the father of Jephunneh, Pispa, and Ara.

³⁹ Ulla was the father of Arah, Hanniel, and Rizia.

⁴⁰ These were the descendants of Asher, and they were all respected family leaders and brave soldiers. The tribe of Asher had a total of 26,000 soldiers.

CHAPTER 8

More descendants of Benjamin

¹ Benjamin had five sons, who were born in the following order: Bela, Ashbel, Aharah, ² Nohah, and Rapha. ³ Bela was the father of Addar, Gera, Abihud, ⁴ Abishua, Naaman, Ahoah, ⁵ Gera, Shephuphan, and Huram.

⁶⁻⁷ Ehud was the father of Naaman, Ahijah, and Gera. They were clan leaders in the town of Geba, but were later forced to move to the town of Manahath, and Gera led the way. He had two sons: Uzza and Ahihud.

⁸⁻¹¹ Shaharaim and his wife Hushim had two sons: Abitub and Elpaal. But Shaharaim later divorced her and his other wife, Baara. Then he moved to the country of Moab and married Hodesh, and they had seven sons:

Jobab, Zibia, Mesha, Malcam, Jeuz, Sachia, and Mirmah. They were all family leaders in his clan. ¹² Elpaal was the father of Eber, Misham, and Shemed, who settled the towns of Ono and Lod, as well as the nearby villages.

¹³ Beriah and Shema were family leaders in the clan that lived in the town of Aijalon and that forced out the people of Gath.

¹⁴⁻¹⁶ Beriah's descendants included Ahio, Shashak, Jeremoth, Zebadiah, Arad, Eder, Michael, Ishpah, and Joha. ¹⁷⁻¹⁸ Elpaal's descendants included Zebadiah, Meshullam, Hizki, Heber, Ishmerai, Izliah, and Jobab. ¹⁹⁻²¹ Shimei's descendants included Jakim, Zichri, Zabdi, Elienai, Zillethai, Eliel, Adaiah, Beraiah, and Shimrath. ²²⁻²⁵ Shashak's descendants included Ishpan, Eber, Eliel, Abdon, Zichri, Hanan, Hananiah, Elam, Anthothijah, Iphdeiah, and Penuel. ²⁶⁻²⁷ Jeroham's descendants included Shamsherai, Shehariah, Athaliah, Jaareshiah, Elijah, and Zichri. ²⁸ These were the family leaders in their ancestor's clan, and they and their descendants lived in Jerusalem.

²⁹ Jeiel* settled the town of Gibeon. He and his wife Maacah lived there ³⁰ along with their sons, who were born in the following order: Abdon, Zur, Kish, Baal, Ner,* Nadab, ³¹ Gedor, Ahio, Zecher, ³² and Mikloth the father of Shimeah. Some of them went to live in Jerusalem near their relatives.

The descendants of King Saul

³³ Ner was the father of Kish and the grandfather of King Saul.

Saul had four sons: Jonathan, Malchishua, Abinadab, and Eshbaal.* ³⁴ Jonathan was the father of Meribbaal,* the grandfather of Micah, ³⁵ and the great-grandfather of Pithon, Melech, Tarea, and Ahaz. ³⁶ Saul's other descendants were Jehoaddah, Alemeth, Azmaveth, Zimri, Moza, ³⁷ Binea, Raphah, Eleasah, Azel, ³⁸ as well as Azel's six sons: Azrikam, Bocheru, Ishmael, Sheariah, Obadiah, and Hanan. ³⁹ Azel's brother Eshek was the father of Ulam, Jeush, and Eliphelet. ⁴⁰ Ulam's sons were brave soldiers who were experts at using a bow and arrows. They had a total of one hundred and fifty children and grandchildren.

All of these belonged to the tribe of Benjamin.

---

*8.33 Eshbaal: Also called "Ishbosheth" (see 2 Samuel 2.8 and the note there).
*8.34 Meribbaal: Also called "Mephibosheth" (see 2 Samuel 4.4 and the note there).

CHAPTER 9

The people who returned from Babylonia and settled in Jerusalem

¹ Everyone in Israel was listed in the official family records that were included in the history of Israel's kings.

The people of Judah were taken to Babylonia as prisoners because they sinned against the LORD. ² And the first people to return to their towns included priests, Levites, temple workers, and other Israelites. ³ People from the tribes of Judah, Benjamin, Ephraim, and Manasseh settled in Jerusalem.

⁴⁻⁶ There were six hundred and ninety people from the Judah tribe who settled in Jerusalem. They were all descendants of Judah's three sons: Perez, Shelah, and Zerah. Their leaders were Uthai, Asaiah, and Jeuel. Uthai was the son of Ammihud and a descendant of Omri, Imri, Bani, and Perez. Asaiah was a descendant of Shelah; Jeuel was a descendant of Zerah.

⁷⁻⁹ There were also nine hundred and fifty-six family leaders from the Benjamin tribe who settled in Jerusalem. They included: Sallu son of Meshullam, grandson of Hodaviah, and great-grandson of Hassenuah; Ibneiah son of Jeroham; Elah son of Uzzi and grandson of Michri; Meshullam son of Shephatiah, grandson of Reuel, and great-grandson of Ibnijah.

The priests who settled in Jerusalem

¹⁰⁻¹² Here is a list of priests who settled in Jerusalem: Jedaiah; Jehoiarib; Jachin; Azariah, who was a temple official, and whose ancestors included Hilkiah, Meshullam, Zadok, Meraioth, and Ahitub; Adaiah son of Jeroham, whose ancestors included Pashhur and Malchijah; Maasai son of Adiel, whose ancestors included Jahzerah, Meshullam, Meshillemith, and Immer.

¹³ There was a total of 1,760 priests, all of them family leaders in their clan and trained in the work at the temple.

The Levites who settled in Jerusalem

¹⁴⁻¹⁶ Here is a list of Levites who settled in Jerusalem: Shemaiah from the Merari clan, whose ancestors included Hasshub, Azrikam, and Hashabiah; Bakbakkar; Heresh; Galal; Mattaniah son of Mica, whose ancestors included Zichri and Asaph; Obadiah son of Shemaiah, whose ancestors included Galal and Jeduthun; Berechiah son of Asa and

grandson of Elkanah, who had lived in the villages near the town of Netophah.

The temple guards who settled in Jerusalem

¹⁷ Shallum, Akkub, Talmon, Ahiman, and their relatives were the guards at the temple gates. Shallum was the leader of this clan, ¹⁸ and for a long time they had been the guards at the King's Gate on the east side of the city. Before that, their ancestors guarded the entrance to the Levite camp.

¹⁹ Shallum son of Kore,* as well as the other men in the Korahite clan, guarded the entrance to the temple, just as their ancestors had guarded the entrance to the sacred tent. ²⁰ Phinehas son of Eleazar had supervised their work because the LORD was with him.

²¹ Zechariah son of Meshelemiah was also one of the guards at the temple.

²² There was a total of two hundred and twelve guards, all of them listed in the family records in their towns. Their ancestors had been chosen by King David and by Samuel the prophet to be responsible for this work, ²³ and now they guarded the temple gates.

²⁴ There was one full-time guard appointed to each of the four sides of the temple. ²⁵ Their assistants lived in the villages outside the city, and every seven days a group of them would come into the city and take their turn at guard duty. ²⁶ The four full-time guards were Levites, and they supervised the other guards and were responsible for the rooms in the temple and the supplies kept there. ²⁷ They guarded the temple day and night and opened its doors every morning.

The duties of the Levites

²⁸ Some of the Levites were responsible for the equipment used in worship at the temple, and they had to count everything before and after it was used. ²⁹ Others were responsible for the temple furnishings and its sacred objects, as well as the flour, wine, olive oil, incense, and spices. ³⁰ But only the priests could mix the spices. ³¹ Mattithiah, Shallum's eldest son, was a member of the Levite clan of Korah, and he was in charge of baking the bread used for offerings.* ³² The Levites from the Kohath clan were in charge of baking the sacred loaves of bread for each Sabbath.*

*9.31 the bread used for offerings: See Leviticus 2.4–7.
*9.32 the sacred loaves of bread for each Sabbath: See Leviticus 24.5–9.

See also: 9.2,3: Ezra 2.27; Neh 7.73.

^{33} The Levite family leaders who were the musicians also lived at the temple. They had no other responsibilities, because they were on duty day and night.

^{34} All these men were family leaders in the Levi tribe and were listed that way in their family records. They lived in Jerusalem.

King Saul's family

This is also told in 1 Chronicles 8.29–38

^{35} Jeiel had settled the town of Gibeon, where he and his wife Maacah lived. ^{36} They had ten sons, who were born in the following order: Abdon, Zur, Kish, Baal, Ner, Nadab, ^{37} Gedor, Ahio, Zechariah, and Mikloth ^{38} the father of Shimeam. Some of them went to live in Jerusalem near their relatives.

^{39} Ner was the father of Kish and the grandfather of King Saul.

Saul had four sons: Jonathan, Malchishua, Abinadab, and Eshbaal.* $^{40-41}$ Jonathan was the father of Meribbaal,* the grandfather of Micah, and the great-grandfather of Pithon, Melech, Tahrea, and Ahaz.* $^{42-44}$ The descendants of Ahaz included Jarah, Alemeth, Azmaveth, Zimri, Moza, Binea, Rephaiah, Eleasah, and Azel and his six sons: Azrikam, Bocheru, Ishmael, Sheariah, Obadiah, and Hanan.

The death of Saul and his sons

CHAPTER 10

This is also told in 1 Samuel 31.1–13

^{1} The Philistines fought against Israel in a battle at Mount Gilboa. Israel's soldiers ran from the Philistines, and many of them were killed. ^{2} The Philistines closed in on Saul and his sons and killed three of them: Jonathan, Abinadab, and Malchishua. ^{3} The fighting was fierce around Saul, and he was badly wounded by enemy arrows.

^{4} Saul told the soldier who carried his weapons, "Kill me with your sword! I don't want those godless Philistines to torture and make fun of me."

But the soldier was afraid to kill him. Then Saul stuck himself in the stomach with his own sword and fell on the blade. ^{5} When the soldier realized that Saul was dead, he killed himself in the same way.

^{6} Saul, three of his sons, and all his male relatives were dead. ^{7} The Israelites who lived in Jezreel Valley* learnt that their army had run away and that Saul and his sons were dead. They ran away too, and the Philistines moved into the towns the Israelites left behind.

^{8} The next day the Philistines came back to the battlefield to carry away the weapons of the dead Israelite soldiers. When they found the bodies of Saul and his sons on Mount Gilboa, ^{9} they took Saul's weapons, pulled off his armour, and cut off his head. Then they sent messengers everywhere in Philistia to spread the news among their people and to thank the idols of their gods. ^{10} They put Saul's armour in the temple of their gods and hung his head in the temple of their god Dagon.

^{11} When the people who lived in Jabesh in Gilead heard what the Philistines had done to Saul, ^{12} some brave men went to get his body and the bodies of his three sons. The men brought the bodies back to Jabesh, where they buried them under an oak tree. Then for seven days, they went without eating to show their sorrow.

^{13} Saul died because he was unfaithful and disobeyed the LORD. He even asked advice from a woman who talked to spirits of the dead, ^{14} instead of asking the LORD. So the LORD had Saul killed and gave his kingdom to David, the son of Jesse.

David becomes king of Israel and captures Jerusalem

CHAPTER 11

David becomes king of Israel

This is also told in 2 Samuel 5.1–3

^{1} Israel's leaders met with David at Hebron and said, "We are your relatives, ^{2} and we know that you have led our army into battle, even when Saul was still our king. The LORD God has promised that you would rule our country and take care of us like a shepherd. ^{3} So we have come to crown you king of Israel!"

David made an agreement with the leaders and asked the LORD to be their witness. Then the leaders poured olive oil on David's head

---

*9.39 Eshbaal: See the note at 8.33.
*9.40 Meribbaal: See the note at 8.34.

See also: 10.13: a 1 Sam 13.8–14; 15.1–24; b Lev 19.31; 20.6; 1 Sam 28.7,8.

to show that he was now king of Israel. This happened just as the LORD's prophet Samuel had said.

David captures Jerusalem

This is also told in 2 Samuel 5.6–10

⁴ Jerusalem was called Jebus at the time, and David led Israel's army to attack the town. ⁵ The Jebusites said, "You won't be able to get in here!" But David captured the fortress of Mount Zion, which is now called the City of David.

⁶ David had told his troops, "The first soldier to kill a Jebusite will become my army commander." And since Joab son of Zeruiah attacked first, he became commander. ⁷ Later, David moved to the fortress — that's why it's called the City of David. ⁸ He had the city rebuilt, starting at the landfill on the east side.* Meanwhile, Joab supervised the repairs to the rest of the city.

⁹ David became a great and strong ruler, because the LORD All-Powerful was on his side.

David's warriors

The Three Warriors

This is also told in 2 Samuel 23.8–17

¹⁰ The LORD had promised that David would become king, and so everyone in Israel gave David their support. Certain warriors also helped keep his kingdom strong.

¹¹ The first of these warriors was Jashobeam the son of Hachmoni, the leader of the Three Warriors.* In one battle he killed three hundred men with his spear.

¹² Another one of the Three Warriors was Eleazar son of Dodo the Ahohite. ¹³ During a battle against the Philistines at Pas-Dammim, all the Israelite soldiers ran away, ¹⁴ except Eleazar, who stayed with David. They took

their positions in a nearby barley field and defeated the Philistines! The LORD gave Israel a great victory that day.

¹⁵ One time the Three Warriors* went to meet David among the rocks at Adullam Cave. The Philistine army had set up camp in Rephaim Valley ¹⁶ and had taken over Bethlehem. David was in a fortress, ¹⁷ and he said, "I'm very thirsty. I wish I had a drink of water from the well by the gate to Bethlehem."

¹⁸ The Three Warriors sneaked through the Philistine camp and got some water from the well near Bethlehem's gate. They took it back to David, but he refused to drink it. Instead, he poured out the water as a sacrifice to the LORD ¹⁹ and said, "Drinking this water would be like drinking the blood of these men who risked their lives to get it for me."

The Three Warriors did these brave deeds.

The Thirty Warriors

This is also told in 2 Samuel 23.18–39

²⁰ Joab's brother Abishai was the leader of the Thirty Warriors,* and in one battle he killed three hundred men with his spear. He was just as famous as the Three Warriors ²¹ and was more famous than the rest of the Thirty Warriors. He was their commander, but he never became one of the Three Warriors.

²² Benaiah the son of Jehoiada was a brave man from Kabzeel who did some amazing things. One time he killed two of Moab's best fighters, and one snowy day he went into a pit and killed a lion. ²³ Another time he killed an Egyptian who was over two metres tall and was armed with a spear. Benaiah only had a club, so he grabbed the spear from the Egyptian and killed him with it. ²⁴ Benaiah did things like that; he was just as brave as the Three Warriors, ²⁵ even though he never became one of the Three Warriors. And he was certainly as famous as the rest of the Thirty Warriors. So David made him the leader of his own bodyguard.

²⁶⁻⁴⁷ Here is a list of the other famous warriors:

Asahel the brother of Joab; Elhanan the son of Dodo from Bethlehem; Shammoth from Haror; Helez from Pelon; Ira the son of

---

*11.8 the landfill on the east side: The Hebrew text has "the Millo", which probably refers to a landfill to strengthen and extend the hill where the city was built.
*11.11 Three Warriors: One ancient translation and 2 Samuel 23.8; Hebrew "Thirty Warriors". The "Three Warriors" was the most honoured group of warriors and may have also been officers in the army and part of the Thirty Warriors. "Three" and "thirty" are spelt almost the same in Hebrew, so there is some confusion in the manuscripts as to which group is being talked about in some places in the following lists.
See also: 11.4: Josh 15.63; Judg 1.21.

*11.20 Thirty Warriors: One ancient translation; Hebrew "Three Warriors". The "Thirty Warriors" was the second most honoured group of warriors and they may have also been officers in the army.

Ikkesh from Tekoa; Abiezer from Anathoth; Sibbecai the Hushathite; Ilai* the Ahohite; Maharai from Netophah; Heled the son of Baanah from Netophah; Ithai the son of Ribai from Gibeah in Benjamin; Benaiah from Pirathon; Hurai* from near the streams on Mount Gaash; Abiel from Arbah; Azmaveth from Baharum; Eliahba from Shaalbon; Hashem* the Gizonite; Jonathan the son of Shagee from Harar; Ahiam the son of Sachar the Hararite; Eliphal the son of Ur; Hepher from Mecherah; Ahijah from Pelon; Hezro from Carmel; Naarai the son of Ezbai; Joel the brother of Nathan; Mibhar the son of Hagri; Zelek from Ammon; Naharai from Beeroth who carried Joab's weapons; Ira the Ithrite; Gareb the Ithrite; Uriah the Hittite; Zabad the son of Ahlai; Adina the son of Shiza, a leader in the Reuben tribe, and thirty of his soldiers; Hanan the son of Maacah; Joshaphat from Mithan; Uzzia from Ashterah; Shama and Jeiel the sons of Hotham from Aroer; Jediael and Joha the sons of Shimri from Tiz; Eliel from Mahavah; Jeribai and Joshaviah the sons of Elnaam; Ithmah from Moab; Eliel, Obed, and Jaasiel from Mezobah.

CHAPTER 12

David's men at Ziklag

1 Some time earlier, David had gone to live in the town of Ziklag to escape from King Saul. While David was there, several brave warriors joined him to help fight his battles.*

Warriors from the Benjamin tribe

2 Several of these warriors were from King Saul's own tribe of Benjamin. They were experts at using a bow and arrows, and they could shoot an arrow or sling a stone with either hand. 3–7 Their leaders were Ahiezer and Joash, the sons of Shemaah from Gibeah. Here is a list of those men from Benjamin: Jeziel and Pelet the sons of Azmaveth; Beracah and Jehu from Anathoth; Ishmaiah from Gibeon, who was the leader of the Thirty Warriors; Jeremiah, Jahaziel, Johanan, and Jozabad from Gederah; Eluzai, Jerimoth, Bealiah, Shemariah, and Shephatiah from

Haruph; Elkanah, Isshiah, Azarel, Joezer, and Jashobeam from the Korah clan; Joelah and Zebadiah the sons of Jeroham from Gedor.

Warriors from the Gad tribe

8 Men from the tribe of Gad also joined David at his fortress in the desert and served as his warriors. They were also brave soldiers — fierce as lions and quick as gazelles. They were always prepared to fight with shields and spears. 9–13 There were eleven of them, ranked in the following order: Ezer the leader, then Obadiah, Eliab, Mishmannah, Jeremiah, Attai, Eliel, Johanan, Elzabad, Jeremiah, and Machbannai.

14 All these men were army officers; some were high-ranking officers over a thousand troops, and others were officers over a hundred troops. 15 Earlier, they had crossed the River Jordan when it flooded, and they chased out the people who lived in the valleys on each side of the river.

Warriors from the Benjamin and Judah tribes

16 One time a group of men from the tribes of Benjamin and Judah went to the fortress where David was staying. 17 David met them outside and said, "If you are coming as friends to fight on my side, then stay and join us. But if you try to turn me over to my enemies, the God our ancestors worshipped will punish you, because I have done nothing wrong."

18 Amasai, who later became the leader of the Thirty Warriors, was one of these men who went to David. God's Spirit took control of him, and he said, "We will join you, David son of Jesse! You and your followers will always be successful, because God fights on your side."

So David agreed to let them stay, and he even put them in charge of his soldiers who raided enemy villages.

Warriors from the Manasseh tribe

19 Some of the warriors who joined David were from the tribe of Manasseh. They had earlier gone with David when he agreed to fight on the side of the Philistines against King Saul. But as soon as the Philistine rulers realized that David might turn against them and rejoin Saul, they sent David away to the town of Ziklag. 20 That's when the following men from Manasseh joined him: Adnah, Jozabad, Jediael, Michael, Jozabad, Elihu, and Zillethai. They had all been

---

*12.1 David had gone . . . battles: Ziklag was the Philistine town that King Achish of Gath gave David in return for his loyalty (see 1 Samuel 27.6). This happened during the time when David was living as an outlaw, so the events in this chapter actually took place before chapter 11 when David became king of Israel.

commanders in Saul's army [21] and brave soldiers, and so David made them officers in his army. They fought on his side when enemy troops attacked.

[22] Day after day, new men came to join David, and soon he had a large, powerful army.

David's men at Hebron

[23-37] The kingdom of Israel had been taken away from Saul, and it now belonged to David. He was ruling from Hebron, and thousands of well-trained soldiers from each tribe went there to crown David king of all Israel, just as the LORD had promised. These soldiers, who were always prepared for battle, included: 6,800 from Judah, who were armed with shields and spears; 7,100 from Simeon; 4,600 from Levi, including Jehoiada, who was a leader from Aaron's descendants, and his 3,700 men, as well as Zadok, who was a brave soldier, and 22 of his relatives, who were also officers; 3,000 from Benjamin, because this was Saul's own tribe and most of the men had remained loyal to him; 20,800 from Ephraim, who were not only brave, but also famous in their clans; 18,000 from West Manasseh, who had been chosen to help make David king; 200 leaders from Issachar, along with troops under their command — these leaders knew the right time to do what needed to be done; 50,000 from Zebulun, who were not only loyal, but also trained to use any weapon; 1,000 officers from Naphtali and 37,000 soldiers armed with shields and spears; 28,600 from Dan; 40,000 from Asher; and 120,000 from the tribes of Reuben, Gad, and East Manasseh, who were armed with all kinds of weapons.

[38] All these soldiers voluntarily came to Hebron because they wanted David to become king of Israel. In fact, everyone in Israel wanted the same thing. [39] The soldiers stayed in Hebron three days, eating and drinking what their relatives had prepared for them. [40] Other Israelites from as far away as the territories of Issachar, Zebulun, and Naphtali brought cattle and sheep to slaughter for food. They also brought donkeys, camels, mules, and oxen that were loaded down with flour, dried figs, wine, and olive oil.

Everyone in Israel was very happy.

The sacred chest is moved to Jerusalem

CHAPTER 13

David moves the sacred chest to Jerusalem
This is also told in 2 Samuel 6.1–12a

[1] Some time later, David talked with his army commanders, [2-3] and then announced to the people of Israel:

> While Saul was king, the sacred chest was ignored. But now it's time to bring the chest to Jerusalem. We will invite everyone in Israel to come here, including the priests and the Levites in the towns surrounded by pasture land. But we will do these things only if you agree, and if the LORD our God wants us to.

[4] The people agreed this was the right thing to do.

[5] David gathered everyone from the River Shihor in Egypt to Lebo-Hamath in the north. [6] Then he led them to Baalah in Judah, which was also called Kiriath-Jearim. They went there to get the sacred chest and bring it to Jerusalem, because it belonged to the LORD God, whose throne is above the winged creatures* on the lid of the chest.

[7] The sacred chest was still at Abinadab's house,* and when David and the crowd arrived there, they brought the chest outside and placed it on a new ox cart. Abinadab's sons' Uzzah and Ahio guided the cart, [8] while David and the crowd danced and sang praises to the LORD with all their might. They played music on small harps and other stringed instruments, and on tambourines, cymbals, and trumpets.

[9] But when they came to Chidon's threshing place, the oxen stumbled, and Uzzah reached out and took hold of the chest to stop it from falling. [10] The LORD God was very angry at Uzzah for doing this, and he killed Uzzah there beside the chest.

[11] David then got angry with God for killing Uzzah. So he named that place

---

*13.6 winged creatures: Two golden statues of winged creatures were on top of the sacred chest and were symbols of the LORD's throne on earth (see Exodus 25.18).

*13.7 The sacred chest . . . Abinadab's house: See 1 Samuel 6.19—7.2.

See also: 13.5: 1 Sam 7.1,2. 13.6: Exod 25.22.

"Attack on Uzzah",' and it's been called that ever since.

¹² David was afraid of what the LORD might do to him, and he asked himself, "Should I really be the one to take care of the sacred chest?" ¹³ So instead of taking it to Jerusalem, David decided to take it to the home of Obed-Edom, who lived in the town of Gath.

¹⁴ The chest stayed there for three months, and the LORD blessed Obed-Edom, his family, and everything he owned.

CHAPTER 14

David's palace in Jerusalem
This is also told in 2 Samuel 5.11–16

¹ King Hiram of Tyre sent some officials to David. They brought along carpenters and stone workers, and enough cedar logs to build David a palace. ² David now knew that the LORD had made him a powerful king of Israel for the good of his people.

³ After David moved to Jerusalem, he married more women and had more sons and daughters. ⁴⁻⁷ His children born there were Shammua, Shobab, Nathan, Solomon, Ibhar, Elishua, Elpelet, Nogah, Nepheg, Japhia, Elishama, Beeliada,' and Eliphelet.

David defeats the Philistines
This is also told in 2 Samuel 5.17–25

⁸ When the Philistines heard that David had become king of Israel, they came to capture him. But David heard about their plan and marched out to meet them in battle. ⁹ The Philistines had already camped in Rephaim Valley and were raiding the nearby villages.

¹⁰ David asked God, "Should I attack the Philistines? Will you help me win?"

The LORD told David, "Yes, attack them! I will give you victory."

¹¹ David and his army marched to Baal-Perazim, where they attacked and defeated the Philistines. He said, "I defeated my enemies because God used me to break through them like a mighty flood." So he named the place "The Lord Broke Through."' ¹² Then David ordered his troops to burn the idols that the Philistines had left behind.

¹³ Some time later, the Philistines came back into the hill country and camped in Rephaim Valley. ¹⁴ David asked God what he should do, and God answered, "Don't attack them from the front. Circle around behind them where the balsam' trees are. ¹⁵ Wait there until you hear the treetops making the sound of marching troops. That sound will mean I have marched out ahead of you to fight the Philistine army. So you must then attack quickly!"

¹⁶ David obeyed God and he defeated the Philistines. He even chased them all the way from Gibeon to the entrance to Gezer.

¹⁷ From then on, David became even more famous, and the LORD made all the nations afraid of him.

CHAPTER 15

David gets ready to bring the sacred chest to Jerusalem

¹ David had several buildings built in Jerusalem, and he had a tent set up where the sacred chest would be kept. ² He said, "Only Levites will be allowed to carry the chest, because the LORD has chosen them to do that work and to serve him for ever."

³ Next, David invited everyone to come to Jerusalem and watch the sacred chest being carried to the place he had set up for it. ⁴ He also sent for Aaron's descendants and for the Levites. The Levites who came were: ⁵ Uriel, the leader of the Kohath clan, and one hundred and twenty of his relatives; ⁶ Asaiah, the leader of the Merari clan, and two hundred and twenty of his relatives; ⁷ Joel, the leader of the Gershon clan, and one hundred and thirty of his relatives; ⁸ Shemaiah, the leader of the Elizaphan clan, and two hundred of his relatives; ⁹ Eliel, the leader of the Hebron clan, and eighty of his relatives; and ¹⁰ Amminadab, the leader of the Uzziel clan, with one hundred and twelve of his relatives.

¹¹ David called together these six Levites and the two priests, Zadok and Abiathar. ¹² He said to them, "You are the leaders of the clans in the Levi tribe. You and your relatives must first go through the ceremony to make yourselves clean and acceptable to the LORD. Then you may carry the sacred chest that belongs to the LORD God of Israel and bring it to the place I have prepared for it. ¹³ The first time we tried to bring the chest to Jerusalem, we didn't ask the LORD what he wanted us to do. He was angry with us, because you Levites weren't there to carry the chest."

¹⁴ The priests and the Levites made themselves clean. They were now ready to carry the sacred chest ¹⁵ on poles that rested

See also: 13.14: 1 Chron 26.4,5.   See also: 15.2: Deut 10.8.   15.15: Exod 25.14.

396

on their shoulders, just as the LORD had told Moses to do.

¹⁶ David then told the leaders to choose some Levites to sing and play music on small harps, other stringed instruments, and cymbals. ¹⁷⁻²¹ The men chosen to play the cymbals were Heman the son of Joel, his relative Asaph the son of Berechiah, and Ethan the son of Kushaiah from the Merari clan. Some of their assistants played the smaller harps: they were Zechariah, Aziel, Shemiramoth, Jehiel, Unni, Eliab, Maaseiah, and Benaiah. Others played the larger harps: they were Mattithiah, Eliphelehu, Mikneiah, Azaziah, and two of the temple guards, Obed-Edom and Jeiel.

²² Chenaniah was chosen to be the music director, because he was a skilled musician.

²³⁻²⁴ Four Levites were then appointed to guard the sacred chest. They were Berechiah, Elkanah, Obed-Edom, and Jehiah.

Finally, David chose priests to walk in front of the sacred chest and blow trumpets. They were Shebaniah, Joshaphat, Nethanel, Amasai, Zechariah, Benaiah, and Eliezer.

The sacred chest is brought to Jerusalem
This is also told in 2 Samuel 6.12–22

²⁵ David, the leaders of Israel, and the army commanders were very happy as they went to Obed-Edom's house to get the sacred chest. ²⁶ God gave the Levites the strength they needed to carry the chest, and so they sacrificed seven bulls and seven rams. ²⁷ David, the Levites, Chenaniah the music director, and all the musicians were wearing linen robes, and David was also wearing a linen cloth.* ²⁸ While the sacred chest was being carried into Jerusalem, everyone was celebrating by shouting and playing music on horns, trumpets, cymbals, harps, and other stringed instruments.

²⁹ Saul's daughter Michal* looked out of her window and watched the chest being brought into David's City. But when she saw David jumping and dancing in honour of the LORD, she was disgusted.

*15.27 a linen cloth: The Hebrew word is "ephod", which can mean either a piece of clothing like a skirt that went from the waist to the knee or a garment like an apron or jacket that only the priests wore.
*15.29 Michal: One of David's wives.

CHAPTER 16

¹ They put the sacred chest inside the tent that David had set up for it, then they offered sacrifices to please the LORD* and sacrifices to ask his blessing.* ² After David had finished, he blessed the people in the name of the LORD ³ and gave every person in the crowd a small loaf of bread, some meat, and a handful of raisins.

⁴ David appointed some of the Levites to serve at the sacred chest; they were to play music and sing praises to the LORD God of Israel. ⁵ Asaph was their leader, and Zechariah was his assistant. Jeiel, Shemiramoth, Jehiel, Mattithiah, Eliab, Benaiah, Obed-Edom, and another man named Jeiel were appointed to play small harps and stringed instruments. Asaph himself played the cymbals, ⁶ and the two priests Benaiah and Jahaziel were to blow trumpets every day in front of the sacred chest.

David's song of praise
This is also found in Psalms 105.1–15; 96.1–13; 106.1,47,48

⁷ That same day, David instructed Asaph and his relatives for the first time to sing these praises to the LORD:

⁸ Praise the LORD
  and pray in his name!
 Tell everyone what he has done.
⁹ Sing praises to the LORD!
  Tell about his miracles.
¹⁰ Celebrate and worship
  his holy name with all your heart.

¹¹ Trust the LORD
  and his mighty power.
 Worship him always.
¹² Remember his miracles
  and all his wonders
  and his fair decisions.
¹³ You belong to the family
  of Israel, his servant;

*16.1 sacrifices to please the LORD: These sacrifices have traditionally been called "whole burnt offerings" because the whole animal was burnt on the altar. A main purpose of such sacrifices was to please the LORD with the smell of the sacrifice, and so in the CEV they are often called "sacrifices to please the LORD".
*16.1 sacrifices to ask his blessing: These sacrifices have traditionally been called "peace offerings" or "offerings of well-being". A main purpose was to ask for the LORD's blessing, and so in the CEV they are sometimes called "sacrifices to ask the LORD's blessing".

397

you are his chosen ones,
  the descendants of Jacob.

¹⁴ The LORD is our God,
  bringing justice everywhere on earth.
¹⁵ We must never forget
  his agreement and his promises,
  not in thousands of years.
¹⁶⁻¹⁷God made an eternal promise
  to Abraham, Isaac, and Jacob
¹⁸ when he said, "I'll give you
  the land of Canaan."

¹⁹ At the time there were
  only a few of us,
  and we were homeless.
²⁰ We wandered from nation to nation,
  from one country to another.
²¹ God did not let anyone
  ill-treat our people.
  Instead he protected us
  by punishing rulers
²² and telling them,
  "Don't touch my chosen leaders
  or harm my prophets!"

²³ Everyone on this earth,
  sing praises to the LORD.
  Day after day announce,
  "The LORD has saved us!"
²⁴ Tell every nation on earth,
  "The LORD is wonderful
  and does marvellous things!
²⁵ The LORD is great and deserves
  our greatest praise!
  He is the only God
  worthy of our worship.
²⁶ Other nations worship idols,
  but the LORD created the heavens.
²⁷ Give honour and praise to the LORD,
  whose power and beauty
  fill his holy temple."

²⁸ Tell everyone of every nation,
  "Praise the glorious power of the LORD.
²⁹ He is wonderful! Praise him
  and bring an offering
  into his temple.
  Worship the LORD,
  majestic and holy.
³⁰ Everyone on earth, now tremble!"

  The world stands firm,
  never to be shaken.
³¹ Tell the heavens and the earth
  to be glad and celebrate!

And announce to the nations,
  "The LORD is King!"
³² Command the ocean to roar
  with all its creatures
  and the fields to rejoice
  with all their crops.
³³ Then every tree in the forest
  will sing joyful songs to the LORD.
  He is coming to judge
  all people on earth.

³⁴ Praise the LORD
  because he is good to us,
  and his love never fails.
³⁵ Say to him, "Save us, LORD God!
  Bring us back from among the nations.
  Let us celebrate and shout
  in praise of your holy name.
³⁶ LORD God of Israel,
  you deserve to be praised
  for ever and ever."

After David finished, the people shouted,
"Amen! Praise the LORD!"

David appoints worship leaders at Jerusalem and Gibeon

³⁷ David chose Asaph and the Levites in his clan to be in charge of the daily worship at the place where the sacred chest was kept. ³⁸ Obed-Edom and sixty-eight of his relatives were their assistants, and Hosah and Obed-Edom the son of Jeduthun were the guards.

³⁹ David also chose Zadok the priest and his relatives who were priests to serve at the LORD's sacred tent at Gibeon. ⁴⁰ They were to offer sacrifices on the altar every morning and evening, just as the LORD had commanded in the Law he gave Israel. ⁴¹ Heman and Jeduthun were their assistants, as well as the other men who had been chosen to praise the LORD for his never-ending love. ⁴² Heman and Jeduthun were also responsible for blowing the trumpets, and for playing the cymbals and other instruments during worship at the tent. The Levites in Jeduthun's clan were the guards at Gibeon.

⁴³ After that, everyone went home, and David went home to his family.

See also: 16.16: a Gen 12.7; b Gen 26.3.
16.17,18: Gen 28.13. 16.21,22: Gen 20.3–7.

See also: 16.34: 2 Chron 5.13; 7.3; Ezra 3.11; Psa 100.5; 106.1; 107.1; 118.1; 136.1; Jer 33.11. 16.43: 2 Sam 6.19,20.

Solomon will build the Lord's temple

CHAPTER 17

The LORD's message to David

This is also told in 2 Samuel 7.1-17

¹ Soon after David moved into his new palace, he said to Nathan the prophet, "Look around! I live in a palace made of cedar, but the sacred chest is kept in a tent."

² Nathan replied, "The LORD is with you — do what you want."

³ That night, the LORD told Nathan ⁴ to go to David and tell him:

David, you are my servant, so listen carefully: you are not the one to build a temple for me. ⁵ I didn't live in a temple when I brought my people out of Egypt, and I don't live in one now. A tent has always been my home wherever I have gone with them. ⁶ I chose special leaders and told them to be like shepherds for my people Israel. But did I ever say anything to even one of them about building a cedar temple for me?

⁷ David, this is what I, the LORD All-Powerful, say to you. I brought you in from the fields where you took care of sheep, and I made you the leader of my people. ⁸ Wherever you went, I helped you and destroyed your enemies right in front of your eyes. I have made you one of the most famous people in the world.

⁹ I have given my people Israel a land of their own where they can live in peace. They will no longer have to tremble with fear — evil nations won't bother them, as they did ¹⁰ when I let judges rule my people, and I will keep your enemies from attacking you.

Now I promise that like you, your descendants will be kings. ¹¹ I'll choose one of your sons to be king when you reach the end of your life and are buried beside your ancestors. I'll make him a strong ruler, ¹² and no one will be able to take his kingdom away from him. He will be the one to build a temple for me. ¹³ I will be like a father to him, and he will be like a son to me. I will never put an end to my agreement with him, as I put an end to my agreement with Saul, who was king before you. ¹⁴ I will make sure that your son and

his descendants will rule my people and my kingdom for ever.

¹⁵ Nathan told David exactly what the LORD had said.

David gives thanks to the LORD

This is also told in 2 Samuel 7.18-29

¹⁶ David went into the tent he had set up for the sacred chest. He sat there and prayed:

LORD God, my family and I don't deserve what you have already done for us, ¹⁷ and yet you have promised to do even more for my descendants. You are treating me as if I am a very important person.* ¹⁸ I am your servant, and you know my thoughts. What else can I say, except that you have honoured me? ¹⁹ It was your choice to do these wonderful things for me and to make these promises.

²⁰ No other god is like you, LORD — you alone are God. Everything we have heard about you is true. ²¹ And there is no other nation on earth like Israel, the nation you rescued from slavery in Egypt to be your own. You became famous by using great and wonderful miracles to force other nations and their gods out of your land, so that your people could live here. ²² You have chosen Israel to be your people for ever, and you have become their God.

²³ LORD God, please do what you promised me and my descendants. ²⁴ Then you will be famous for ever, and everyone will say, "The LORD All-Powerful rules Israel and is their God."

My kingdom will be strong, ²⁵ because you are my God, and you have promised that my descendants will be kings. That's why I have the courage to pray to you like this, even though I am only your servant.

²⁶ You are the LORD God, and you have made this good promise to me. ²⁷ Now please bless my descendants for ever, and let them always be your chosen kings. You have already blessed my family, and I know you will bless us for ever.

David's military victories

CHAPTER 18

A list of David's victories in war

This is also told in 2 Samuel 8.1-14

¹ Later, David attacked and defeated the Philistines. He captured their town of Gath and the nearby villages.

See also: **17.13:** 2 Cor 6.18; Heb 1.5.

² David also defeated the Moabites, and so they had to accept him as their ruler and pay taxes to him.

³ While King Hadadezer of Zobah was trying to gain control of the territory near the River Euphrates, David met him in battle at Hamath and defeated him. ⁴ David captured one thousand chariots, seven thousand chariot drivers, and twenty thousand soldiers. And he crippled all but one hundred of the horses.

⁵ When troops from the Syrian kingdom of Damascus came to help Hadadezer, David killed twenty-two thousand of them. ⁶ Then David stationed some of his troops in Damascus, and the people there had to accept David as their ruler and pay taxes to him.

Everywhere David went, the LORD helped him win battles.

⁷ Hadadezer's officers had carried gold shields, but David took these shields and brought them back to Jerusalem. ⁸ He also took a lot of bronze from the cities of Tibhath and Cun, which had belonged to Hadadezer. Later, Solomon used this bronze to make the large bowl called the Sea, and to make the pillars and other furnishings for the temple.

⁹⁻¹⁰ King Tou of Hamath and King Hadadezer had been enemies. So when Tou heard that David had defeated Hadadezer's whole army, he sent his son Hadoram to congratulate David on his victory. Hadoram also brought him gifts made of gold, silver, and bronze. ¹¹ David gave these gifts to the LORD, just as he had done with the silver and gold he had captured from Edom, Moab, Ammon, Philistia, and Amalek.

¹² Abishai the son of Zeruiah defeated the Edomite army in Salt Valley and killed eighteen thousand of their troops. ¹³ Then he stationed troops in Edom, and the people there had to accept David as their ruler.

Everywhere David went, the LORD gave him victory in war.

A list of David's officials

This is also told in 2 Samuel 8.15–18

¹⁴ David ruled all Israel with fairness and justice.

¹⁵ Joab the son of Zeruiah was the commander in chief of the army.

Jehoshaphat the son of Ahilud kept the government records.

¹⁶ Zadok the son of Ahitub and Ahimelech the son of Abiathar were the priests.

Shavsha was the secretary.

¹⁷ Benaiah the son of Jehoiada was the commander of David's bodyguard.⁺

David's sons were his highest-ranking officials.

CHAPTER 19

Israel fights Ammon and Syria

This is also told in 2 Samuel 10.1–19

¹ Some time later, King Nahash of Ammon died, and his son Hanun became king. ² David said, "Nahash was kind to me, so I will be kind to his son." He sent some officials to Ammon to tell Hanun how sorry he was that his father had died.

But when David's officials arrived at Ammon, ³ the Ammonite leaders said to Hanun, "Do you really believe King David is honouring your father by sending these men to comfort you? He probably sent them to spy on our country, so he can come and destroy it."

⁴ Hanun arrested David's officials and had their beards shaved off and their robes cut off just below the waist, and then he sent them away. ⁵ They were terribly ashamed.

When David found out what had happened to his officials, he sent a message that told them, "Stay in Jericho until your beards grow back. Then you can come home."

⁶ The Ammonites realized they had made David furious. So they paid thirty-four thousand kilograms of silver to hire chariot troops from Mesopotamia and from the Syrian kingdoms of Maacah and Zobah. ⁷ Thirty-two thousand troops, as well as the king of Maacah and his army, came and camped near Medeba. The Ammonite troops also left their towns and came to prepare for battle.

⁸ David heard what was happening, and he sent out Joab with his army. ⁹ The Ammonite troops marched to the entrance of the city* and prepared for battle, while the Syrian troops took their positions in the open fields.

¹⁰ Joab saw that the enemy troops were lined up on both sides of him. So he picked some of the best Israelite soldiers to fight the Syrians. ¹¹ Then he put his brother Abishai in command of the rest of the army and told

---

See also: **18.8:** 1 King 7.40–47; 2 Chron 4.11–18.
18.12: Psa 60 Title.

400

---

*19.9 the city: Probably Rabbah, the capital city of Ammon.

them to fight against the Ammonites. ¹² Joab told his brother, "If the Syrians are too much for me to handle, come and help me. And if the Ammonites are too strong for you, I'll come and help you. ¹³ Be brave and fight hard to protect our people and the towns of our LORD God. I pray he will do whatever pleases him."

¹⁴ Joab and his soldiers attacked the Syrians, and the Syrians ran from them. ¹⁵ When the Ammonite troops saw that the Syrians had run away, they ran from Abishai's soldiers and went back into their own city. Joab then returned to Jerusalem.

¹⁶ As soon as the Syrians realized they had been defeated, they sent for their troops that were stationed on the other side of the River Euphrates. Shophach, the commander of Hadadezer's army, led these troops to Ammon.

¹⁷ David found out what the Syrians were doing, and he brought Israel's entire army together. They crossed the River Jordan, and he commanded them to take their positions facing the Syrian troops.

Soon after the fighting began, ¹⁸ the Syrians ran from Israel. David killed seven thousand chariot troops and forty thousand regular soldiers. He also killed Shophach, their commander.

¹⁹ When the kings who had been under Hadadezer's rule saw that Israel had defeated them, they made peace with David and accepted him as their new ruler. The Syrians never helped the Ammonites again.

CHAPTER 20

The end of the war with Ammon

This is also told in 2 Samuel 11.1; 12.26-31

¹ The next spring, the time when kings go to war, Joab marched out in command of the Israelite army and destroyed towns all over the country of Ammon. He attacked the capital city of Rabbah and left it in ruins. But David stayed in Jerusalem.

² Later, David himself went to Rabbah, where he took the crown from the statue of their god Milcom.♦ The crown was made of about thirty-four kilogrammes of gold, and there was a valuable jewel on it. David put the jewel on his crown,♦ then carried off everything else of value. ³ He forced the people of Rabbah to work with saws, iron picks, and axes. He also did the same

thing with the people in all the other Ammonite towns.

David then led Israel's army back to Jerusalem.

The descendants of the Rephaim

This is also told in 2 Samuel 21.15-22

⁴ Some time later, Israel fought a battle against the Philistines at Gezer. During this battle, Sibbecai from Hushah killed Sippai, a descendant of the Rephaim,* and the Philistines were defeated.

⁵ In another battle against the Philistines, Elhanan the son of Jair killed Lahmi the brother of Goliath from Gath, whose spear shaft was like a weaver's beam.*

⁶ Another one of the Philistine soldiers who was a descendant of the Rephaim was as big as a giant and had six fingers on each hand and six toes on each foot. During a battle at Gath, ⁷ he made fun of Israel, so David's nephew Jonathan♦ killed him.

⁸ David and his soldiers killed these three men from Gath who were descendants of the Rephaim.

David's preparations for building the temple

CHAPTER 21

David counts the people

This is also told in 2 Samuel 24.1-9

¹ Satan decided to cause trouble for Israel by making David think it was a good idea to find out how many people there were in Israel and Judah. ² David told Joab and the army commanders, "Count everyone in Israel, from the town of Beersheba in the south all the way north to Dan. Then I will know how many people can serve in my army."

³ Joab answered, "Your Majesty, even if the LORD made your kingdom a hundred times larger, you would still rule everyone in it. Why do you need to know how many soldiers there are? Don't you think that would make the whole nation angry?"

---

*20.4 Rephaim: This may refer to a group of people of great stature that lived in Palestine before the Israelites.
*20.5 weaver's beam: When a weaver made cloth, one set of threads was tied on to a large wooden rod that was known as a weaver's beam.

See also: 20.5: 1 Sam 17.4-7.

See also: 20.1: 2 Sam 11.1.

4 But David would not change his mind. And so Joab went everywhere in Israel and Judah and counted the people. He returned to Jerusalem 5 and told David that the total number of men who could serve in the army was one million one hundred thousand in Israel and four hundred and seventy thousand in Judah. 6 Joab refused to include anyone from the tribes of Levi and Benjamin, because he still disagreed with David's orders.

God punishes Israel

This is also told in 2 Samuel 24.10–17

7 David's order to count the people made God angry, and he punished Israel. 8 David prayed, "I am your servant. But what I did was stupid and terribly wrong. Please forgive me."

9 The LORD said to Gad, one of David's prophets, 10 "Tell David that I will punish him in one of three ways. But he will have to choose which one it will be."

11 Gad went to David and told him:

You must choose how the LORD will punish you: 12 Will there be three years when the land won't grow enough food for its people? Or will your enemies constantly defeat you for three months? Or will the LORD send a horrible disease to strike your land for three days? Think about it and decide, because I have to give your answer to God who sent me.

13 David was miserable and said, "It's a terrible choice to make! But the LORD is kind, and I'd rather be punished by him than by anyone else."

14 So the LORD sent a horrible disease on Israel, and seventy thousand Israelites died. 15 Then he sent an angel to destroy the city of Jerusalem. But just as the angel was about to do that, the LORD felt sorry for all the suffering he had caused the people, and he told the angel, "Stop! They have suffered enough." This happened at the threshing place that belonged to Araunah* the Jebusite.

16 David saw the LORD's angel in the air, holding a sword over Jerusalem. He and the leaders of Israel, who were all wearing sackcloth,* bowed with their faces to the ground, 17 and David prayed, "It's my fault! I sinned by ordering the people to be

counted. They have done nothing wrong — they are innocent sheep. LORD God, please punish me and my family. Don't let the disease wipe out your people."

David buys Araunah's threshing place

This is also told in 2 Samuel 24.18–25

18 The LORD's angel told the prophet Gad to tell David that he must go to Araunah's threshing place and build an altar in honour of the LORD. 19 David followed the LORD's instructions.

20 Araunah and his four sons were threshing wheat at the time, and when they saw the angel, the four sons ran to hide. 21 Just then, David arrived, and when Araunah saw him, he stopped his work and bowed down.

22 David said, "Would you sell me your threshing place, so I can build an altar on it to the LORD? Then this disease will stop killing the people. I'm willing to pay whatever you say it's worth."

23 Araunah answered, "Take it, Your Majesty, and do whatever you want with it. I'll even give you the oxen for the sacrifice and the wheat for the grain sacrifice. And you can use the threshing-boards* for the fire. It's all yours!"

24 But David replied, "No! I want to pay you what they're worth. I can't just take something from you and then offer the LORD a sacrifice that cost me nothing."

25 So David paid Araunah six hundred gold coins for his threshing place. 26 David built an altar and offered sacrifices to please the LORD* and sacrifices to ask his blessing.* David prayed, and the LORD answered him by sending fire down on the altar. 27 Then the LORD commanded the angel to put the sword away.*

28 When David saw that the LORD had answered his prayer, he offered more sacrifices there at the threshing place, 29–30 because he was afraid of the angel's sword and did not want to go all the way to

---

*21.23 threshing-boards: Heavy boards with bits of rock or metal on the bottom. They were dragged across the grain to separate the husks from the kernels.
*21.26 sacrifices to please the LORD: See the note at 16.1.
*21.26 sacrifices to ask his blessing: See the note at 16.1.
*21.27 the LORD commanded the angel to put the sword away: See verse 16.

*21.16 sackcloth: A rough, dark-coloured cloth made from goat or camel hair and used to make grain sacks. It was worn in times of trouble or sorrow.

Gibeon. That's where the sacred tent that Moses had made in the desert was kept, as well as the altar where sacrifices were offered to the LORD.

CHAPTER 22

[1] David said, "The temple of the LORD God must be built here at this threshing place. And the altar for offering sacrifices will also be here."

David prepares to build the temple

[2] David ordered the foreigners living in Israel to come to Jerusalem. Then he assigned some to cut blocks of stone for building the temple. [3] He got a large supply of iron to make into nails and hinges for the doors, and he provided so much bronze that it could not be weighed. [4] He also had cedar logs brought in from the cities of Sidon and Tyre.

[5] He said, "The temple for the LORD must be great, so that everyone in the world will know about it. But since my son Solomon is young and has no experience, I will make sure that everything is ready for the temple to be built."

That's why David did all these things before he died.

David instructs Solomon to build the temple

[6] David sent for his son Solomon and told him to build a temple for the LORD God of Israel. [7] He said:

My son, I wanted to build a temple where the LORD my God would be worshipped. [8] But some time ago, he told me, "David, you have killed too many people and have fought too many battles. That's why you are not the one to build my temple. [9] But when your son becomes king, I will give him peace throughout his kingdom. His name will be Solomon, because during his rule I will keep Israel safe and peaceful.* [10] Solomon will build my temple. He will be like a son to me, and I will be like a father to him. In fact, one of his descendants will always rule in Israel."

[11] Solomon, my son, I now pray that the LORD your God will be with you and keep his promise to help you build a temple for

him. [12] May he give you wisdom and knowledge, so that you can rule Israel according to his Law. [13] If you obey the laws and teachings that the LORD gave Moses, you will be successful. Be strong and brave and don't get discouraged or be afraid of anything.

[14] I have all the supplies you'll need to build the temple: you have more than three thousand tonnes of gold and over thirty-four thousand tonnes of silver. There's also plenty of wood, stone, and more bronze and iron than you could weigh. Ask for anything else you need. [15] I have also assigned men who will cut and lay the stone. And there are carpenters and people who are experts in working with [16] gold, silver, bronze, and iron. You have plenty of workers to do the job. Now get started, and I pray that the LORD will be with you in your work.

[17] David then gave orders for the leaders of Israel to help Solomon. [18] David said:

The LORD our God has helped me defeat all the people who lived here before us, and he has given you peace from all your enemies. Now this land belongs to the LORD and his people. [19] Obey the LORD your God with your heart and soul. Begin work on the temple to honour him, so that the sacred chest and the things used for worship can be kept there.

CHAPTER 23

David assigns the Levites their duties

[1] David was old when he chose his son Solomon to be king of Israel. [2] Some time later, David called together all of Israel's leaders, priests, and Levites. [3] He then counted the Levite men who were at least thirty years old, and the total was thirty-eight thousand. [4] He said, "Twenty-four thousand of the Levites will be in charge of the temple, six thousand will be temple officials and judges, [5] four thousand will be guards at the temple, and four thousand will praise the LORD by playing the musical instruments I have given them."

[6] David then divided the Levites into three groups according to the clans of Levi's sons, Gershon, Kohath, and Merari. [7] Gershon had two sons: Ladan and Shimei. [8] Ladan was the father of Jehiel, Zetham, and Joel. [9] They were all family leaders among

---

*22.9 Solomon . . . safe and peaceful: In Hebrew "Solomon" sounds like "peace".

See also: 22.7–10: 2 Sam 7.1–16; 1 Chron 17.1–14.

See also: 22.13: Josh 1.6–9. 23.1: 1 King 1.1–40.

their father's descendants. Shimei was the father of Shelomoth, Haziel, and Haran.
¹⁰⁻¹¹ Later, Shimei had four more sons, in the following order: Jahath, Zina, Jeush, and Beriah. But Jeush and Beriah didn't have many children, so their descendants were counted as one family.

¹² Kohath had four sons: Amram, Izhar, Hebron, and Uzziel. ¹³ Amram was the father of Aaron and Moses. Aaron and his descendants were chosen to be in charge of all the sacred things. They served the LORD by offering sacrifices to him and by blessing the people in his name. ¹⁴⁻¹⁵ Moses, the man of God, was the father of Gershom and Eliezer, and their descendants were considered Levites. ¹⁶ Gershom's eldest son was Shebuel. ¹⁷ Rehabiah, who was Eliezer's only son, had many children. ¹⁸ The second son born to Kohath was Izhar, and his eldest son was Shelomith. ¹⁹ Hebron, the third son of Kohath, was the father of Jeriah, Amariah, Jahaziel, and Jekameam. ²⁰ Kohath's youngest son, Uzziel, was the father of Micah and Isshiah.

²¹ Merari had two sons: Mahli and Mushi. Mahli was the father of Eleazar and Kish.
²² Eleazar had no sons, only daughters, and they married their uncle's sons. ²³ Mushi, the second son of Merari, was the father of Mahli, Eder, and Jeremoth.

²⁴ These were the clans and families of the tribe of Levi. Those who were twenty years and older were assigned to work at the LORD's temple.

²⁵ David said:

The LORD God of Israel has given his people peace, and he will live in Jerusalem for ever. ²⁶ And so, the Levites won't need to move the sacred tent and the things used for worship from place to place.
²⁷ From now on, all Levites at least twenty years old ²⁸ will serve the LORD by helping Aaron's descendants do their work at the temple, by keeping the courtyards and rooms of the temple clean, and by making sure that everything used in worship stays pure. ²⁹ They will also be in charge of the sacred loaves of bread, the flour for the grain sacrifices, the thin wafers, and any offerings to be baked, and the flour mixed with olive oil. These Levites will weigh and measure these offerings.

³⁰ Every morning and evening, the Levites are to give thanks to the LORD and sing praises to him. ³¹ They must also give thanks and sing praises when sacrifices are offered on each Sabbath, as well as during New Moon Festivals and other religious feasts. There must always be enough Levites on duty at the temple to do everything that needs to be done. ³² They were once in charge of taking care of the sacred tent; now they are responsible for the temple and for helping Aaron's descendants.

CHAPTER 24

David assigns the priests their duties

¹ Aaron's descendants were then divided into work groups. Aaron had four sons: Nadab, Abihu, Eleazar, and Ithamar. ² But Nadab and Abihu died long before their father, without having any sons. That's why Eleazar and Ithamar served as priests.

³ David divided Aaron's descendants into groups, according to their assigned work. Zadok, one of Eleazar's descendants, and Ahimelech, one of Ithamar's descendants, helped David.

⁴ Eleazar's descendants were divided into sixteen groups, and Ithamar's were divided into eight groups, because Eleazar's family included more family leaders. ⁵ However, both families included temple officials and priests, and so to make sure the work was divided fairly, David asked God what to do.*

⁶ As each group was assigned their duties, Shemaiah the son of Nethanel the Levite wrote down the name of the family leader in charge of that group. The witnesses were David and his officials, as well as Zadok the priest, Ahimelech the son of Abiathar, and the family leaders from the clans of the priests and the Levites.

⁷⁻¹⁸ Each group of priests went by the name of its family leader, and they were assigned their duties in the following order: Jehoiarib, Jedaiah, Harim, Seorim, Malchijah, Mijamin, Hakkoz, Abijah, Jeshua, Shecaniah, Eliashib, Jakim, Huppah, Jeshebeab, Bilgah, Immer, Hezir, Happizzez, Pethahiah, Jehezkel, Jachin, Gamul, Delaiah, Maaziah.
¹⁹ These men were assigned their duties at the temple, just as the LORD God of Israel had commanded their ancestor Aaron.

See also: 23.13: Exod 28.1. 23.26: Deut 10.8.
23.28–32: Num 3.5–9.

*24.5 asked God what to do: The Hebrew text has "cast lots" (see the note at 6.65).
See also: 24.2: Lev 10.1,2.

The rest of the Levites are assigned their duties

20 Here is a list of the other descendants of Levi:

> Amram was the ancestor of Shubael and Jehdeiah.

21 Rehabiah was the ancestor of Isshiah, the eldest son in his family.

22 Izhar was the father of Shelomoth and the grandfather of Jahath.

23 Hebron had four sons, in the following order: Jeriah, Amariah, Jahaziel, and Jekameam.

24 Uzziel was the father of Micah and the grandfather of Shamir.

25 Isshiah, Micah's brother, was the father of Zechariah.

26 Merari was the father of Mahli, Mushi, and Jaaziah.

27 Jaaziah had three sons: Shoham, Zaccur, and Ibri. 28-29 Mahli was the father of Eleazar and Kish. Eleazar had no sons, but Kish was the father of Jerahmeel. 30 Mushi had three sons: Mahli, Eder, and Jerimoth.

These were the descendants of Levi, according to their clans. 31 Each one was assigned his duties in the same way that their relatives the priests had been assigned their duties. David, Zadok, Ahimelech, and the family leaders of the priests and Levites were the witnesses.

CHAPTER 25

David assigns the temple musicians their duties

1 David and the temple officials chose the descendants of Asaph, Heman, and Jeduthun to be in charge of music. They were to praise the LORD by playing cymbals, harps, and other stringed instruments. Here is a list of the musicians and their duties:

2 Asaph's four sons, Zaccur, Joseph, Nethaniah, and Asarelah, were under the direction of their father and played music whenever the king told them to.

3 Jeduthun's six sons, Gedaliah, Zeri, Jeshaiah, Shimei,♭ Hashabiah, and Mattithiah, were under the direction of their father and played harps and sang praises to the LORD.

4 Heman had fourteen sons: Bukkiah, Mattaniah, Uzziel, Shebuel, Jerimoth, Hananiah, Hanani, Eliathah, Giddalti, Romamtiezer, Joshbekashah, Mallothi, Hothir, Mahazioth. 5 Heman was one of the king's prophets, and God honoured Heman by giving him fourteen sons and three daughters. 6 His sons were under his direction and played cymbals, harps, and other stringed instruments during times of worship at the temple.

Asaph, Jeduthun, and Heman took their orders directly from the king.

7 There were two hundred and eighty-eight of these men, and all of them were skilled musicians. 8 David assigned them their duties by asking the LORD what he wanted.* Everyone was responsible for something, whether young or old, teacher or student.

9-31 The musicians were divided into twenty-four groups of twelve, and each group went by the name of their family leader. They were assigned their duties in the following order: Joseph, Gedaliah, Zaccur, Zeri, Nethaniah, Bukkiah, Asarelah, Jeshaiah, Mattaniah, Shimei, Uzziel, Hashabiah, Shebuel, Mattithiah, Jerimoth, Hananiah, Joshbekashah, Hanani, Mallothi, Eliathah, Hothir, Giddalti, Mahazioth, and Romamtiezer.

CHAPTER 26

The temple guards are assigned their duties

1 The temple guards were also divided into groups according to clans.

Meshelemiah son of Kore was from the Korah clan and was a descendant of Asaph. 2 He had seven sons, who were born in the following order: Zechariah, Jediael, Zebadiah, Jathniel, 3 Elam, Jehohanan, and Eliehoenai.

4-5 Obed-Edom had been blessed with eight sons: Shemaiah, Jehozabad, Joah, Sachar, Nethanel, Ammiel, Issachar, and Peullethai.

6-7 Shemaiah was the father of Othni, Rephael, Obed, Elzabad, Elihu, and Semachiah. They were all respected leaders in their clan. 8 There were sixty-two descendants of Obed-Edom who were strong enough to be guards at the temple.

9 Eighteen descendants of Meshelemiah were chosen for this work.

10-11 Hosah, from the Merari clan, was the father of Shimri, Hilkiah, Tebaliah, and Zechariah. Hosah had made Shimri the family leader, even though he was not the eldest son. Thirteen men from Hosah's family were chosen to be temple guards.

---

*25.8 asking the LORD what he wanted: The Hebrew text has "casting lots" (see the note at 6.65).
See also: 26.4,5; 2 Sam 6.11; 1 Chron 13.14.

¹² The guards were divided into groups, according to their family leaders, and they were assigned duties at the temple, just like the other Levites. ¹³ Each group, no matter how large or small, was assigned a gate to guard, and they let the LORD show them what he wanted done.*

¹⁴ Shelemiah* was chosen to guard the East Gate. Zechariah his son was a wise man and was chosen to guard the North Gate.

¹⁵ Obed-Edom was then chosen to guard the South Gate, and his sons were chosen to guard the storerooms. ¹⁶ Shuppim and Hosah were chosen to guard the West Gate and the Shallecheth Gate on the upper road.

The guards were assigned the following work schedule: ¹⁷ each day six guards were on duty on the east side of the temple, four were on duty on the north side, and four were on duty on the south side. Two guards were stationed at each of the two storerooms, ¹⁸ four were stationed along the road leading to the west courtyard,* and two guards stayed in the court itself.

¹⁹ These were the guard duties assigned to the men from the clans of Korah and Merari.

Guards are assigned to the treasury

²⁰ The Levites who were relatives of the Korahites and the Merarites were* in charge of guarding the temple treasury and the gifts that had been dedicated to God.

²¹ Ladan was from the Gershon clan and was the father of Jehieli. Many of his other descendants were family leaders in the clan.*

²² Jehieli was the father of Zetham and Joel, and they were responsible for guarding the treasury.

²³ Other guards at the treasury were from the Kohathite clans of Amram, Izhar, Hebron, and Uzziel.

²⁴ Shebuel was a descendant of Gershom the son of Moses. He was the chief official in charge of the temple treasury. ²⁵ The descendants of Gershom's brother Eliezer included Rehabiah, Jeshaiah, Joram, Zichri, and Shelomoth.

²⁶ Shelomoth and his relatives were in charge of all the gifts that were dedicated to the LORD. These included the gifts that King David had dedicated, as well as those dedicated by the family leaders, army officers, and army commanders. ²⁷ And whenever valuable things were captured in battle, these men brought some of them to the temple. ²⁸ Shelomoth and his relatives were responsible for any gifts that had been given to the temple, including those from Samuel the prophet, King Saul the son of Kish, Abner the son of Ner,* and Joab the son of Zeruiah.

Other officers are assigned their duties

²⁹ Chenaniah from the Izhar clan and his sons were government officials and judges. They did not work at the temple.

³⁰ Hashabiah from the Hebron clan and one thousand seven hundred of his skilled relatives were the officials in charge of all religious and government business in the Israelite territories west of the River Jordan.

³¹⁻³² Jerijah was the leader of the Hebron clan. David assigned him and two thousand seven hundred of his relatives, who were all respected family leaders, to be the officials in charge of all religious and government business in the tribes of Reuben, Gad, and East Manasseh. David found out about these men during the fortieth year of his rule, when he had a list made of all the families in the Hebron clan. They were from the town of Jazer in the territory of Gilead.

CHAPTER 27

David assigns army commanders

¹ Each month a group of twenty-four thousand men served as soldiers in Israel's army. These men, who included the family leaders, army commanders, and officials of the king, were under the command of the following men, arranged by the month of their service:

² In the first month, Jashobeam the son of Zabdiel, ³ a descendant of Perez;

⁴ in the second month, Dodai the Ahohite, whose assistant was Mikloth;*

⁵ in the third month, Benaiah the son of Jehoiada the priest, ⁶ who was the leader of the Thirty Warriors,* and whose son Ammizabad was also an army commander;*

⁷ in the fourth month, Asahel the brother of Joab, whose son Zebadiah took over command after him;

⁸ in the fifth month, Shamhuth from the Izrah clan;

---

*26.13 they let the LORD show them what he wanted done: The Hebrew text has "they cast lots to find out what the LORD wanted done" (see the note at 6.65).

*26.28 Abner the son of Ner: Abner was King Saul's uncle (see 9.39).

*27.6 Thirty Warriors: See the note at 11.20.

⁹ in the sixth month, Ira the son of Ikkesh from Tekoa;

¹⁰ in the seventh month, Helez from Pelon in the territory of Ephraim;

¹¹ in the eighth month, Sibbecai from Hushah of the Zerah clan;

¹² in the ninth month, Abiezer from Anathoth in the territory of Benjamin;

¹³ in the tenth month, Maharai from Netophah of the Zerah clan;

¹⁴ in the eleventh month, Benaiah from Pirathon in the territory of Ephraim;

¹⁵ in the twelfth month, Heldai from Netophah, who was a descendant of Othniel.

David assigns tribal leaders

¹⁶⁻²² Here is a list of the leaders of each tribe in Israel:

Eliezer son of Zichri was over Reuben; Shephatiah son of Maacah was over Simeon; Hashabiah son of Kemuel was over the Levites, and Zadok the priest was over the descendants of Aaron; Elihu the brother of David was over Judah; Omri son of Michael was over Issachar; Ishmaiah son of Obadiah was over Zebulun; Jerimoth son of Azriel was over Naphtali; Hoshea son of Azaziah was over Ephraim; Joel son of Pedaiah was over West Manasseh; Iddo son of Zechariah was over East Manasseh; Jaasiel son of Abner was over Benjamin; Azarel son of Jeroham was over Dan.

²³ When David decided to count the people of Israel, he gave orders not to count anyone under twenty years of age, because the LORD had promised long ago that Israel would have as many people as there are stars in the sky. ²⁴ Joab the son of Zeruiah had begun to count the people, but he stopped when the LORD began punishing Israel. So the total number was never included in David's official records.

Officials in charge of the king's property

²⁵ Azmaveth the son of Adiel was in charge of the king's personal storage rooms. Jonathan the son of Uzziah was in charge of the king's other storerooms that were in the towns, the villages, and the defence towers in Israel. ²⁶ Ezri the son of Chelub was in charge of the workers who farmed the king's land. ²⁷ Shimei from Ramah was in charge of the vineyards, and Zabdi from Shepham was in charge of storing the wine.

²⁸ Baal Hanan from Geder was in charge of the olive and sycamore trees in the western foothills, and Joash was in charge of storing the olive oil.

²⁹ Shitrai from Sharon was responsible for the cattle that were kept in Sharon Plain, and Shaphat son of Adlai was responsible for those kept in the valleys.

³⁰ Obil the Ishmaelite was in charge of the camels, Jehdeiah from Meronoth was in charge of the donkeys, and Jaziz the Hagrite was in charge of the sheep and goats.

³¹ These were the men in charge of David's royal property.

David's personal advisers

³² David's uncle Jonathan was a wise and intelligent adviser. He and Jehiel the son of Hachmoni taught David's sons.

³³ Ahithophel and Hushai the Archite were two of David's advisers. ³⁴ Jehoiada the son of Benaiah was the king's adviser after Ahithophel, and later, Abiathar was his adviser.

Joab was commander of Israel's army.

CHAPTER 28

David gives Solomon the plans for the temple

¹ David called a meeting in Jerusalem for all Israel's leaders, including the tribal leaders, the government officials, the army commanders, the officials in charge of the royal property and livestock, the palace officials, and the brave warriors.

² After everyone was there, David stood up and said:

Listen to me, my people. I wanted to build a place where the sacred chest would be kept, so we could go there and worship the LORD our God. I have prepared all the supplies for building a temple, ³ but the LORD has refused to let me build it, because he said I have killed too many people in battle.

⁴ The LORD God chose Judah to be the leading tribe in Israel. Then from Judah, he chose my father's family, and from that family, he chose me to be the king of Israel, and he promised that my descendants will also rule as kings. ⁵ The LORD has blessed me with many sons, but he chose my son Solomon to be the next king of Israel. ⁶ The LORD said to me, "Your son Solomon will

See also: 27.23: Gen 15.5; 22.17; 26.4. 27.24: 2 Sam 24.15; 1 Chron 21.1–14.

See also: 28.2–7: 2 Sam 7.1–16; 1 Chron 17.1–14.

build my temple, and it will honour me. Solomon will be like a son to me, and I will be like a father to him. [7] If he continues to obey my laws and commands, his kingdom will never end."

[8] My friends, you are the LORD's people. And now, with God as your witness, I want you to promise that you will do your best to obey everything the LORD God has commanded us. Then this land will always belong to you and your descendants.

[9] Solomon, my son, worship God and obey him with all your heart and mind, just as I have done. He knows all your thoughts and your reasons for doing things, and so if you turn to him, he will hear your prayers. But if you ignore him, he will reject you for ever. [10] The LORD has chosen you to build a temple for worshipping him. Be confident and do the work you have been assigned.

[11] After David finished speaking, he gave Solomon the plans for building the main rooms of the temple, including the porch, the storerooms, the rooms upstairs and downstairs, as well as the most holy place. [12] He gave Solomon his plans for the courtyards and the open areas around the temple, and for the rooms to store the temple treasures and gifts that had been dedicated to God.

[13] David also gave Solomon his plans for dividing the priests and the Levites into groups, as well as for the work that needed to be done at the temple and for taking care of the objects used for worship. [14] He told Solomon how much gold and silver was to be used in making the sacred objects, [15] including the lampstands and lamps, [16] the gold table which held the sacred loaves of bread, the tables made of silver, [17] the meat forks, the bowls and cups, [18] the gold incense altar, and the gold statue of a chariot for the winged creatures* which were on the lid of the sacred chest.

[19] David then said to Solomon:

The LORD showed me how his temple is to be built. [20] But you must see that everything is done according to these plans. Be confident, and never be afraid of anything or get discouraged. The LORD my God will help you do everything needed to finish the temple, so it can be used for worshipping him. [21] The priests and Levites have been assigned their duties, and all the skilled workers are prepared to do their work. The people and their leaders will do anything you tell them.

The people bring gifts for building the temple

CHAPTER 29

[1] David told the crowd:

God chose my son Solomon to build the temple, but Solomon is young and has no experience. This is not just any building — this is the temple for the LORD God! [2] That's why I have done my best to get everything Solomon will need to build it — gold, silver, bronze, iron, wood, turquoise, coloured gems, all kinds of precious stones, and marble.

[3] Besides doing all that, I have promised to give part of my own gold and silver as a way of showing my love for God's temple. [4] More than a hundred tonnes of my finest gold and almost two hundred and forty tonnes of my silver will be used to decorate its walls [5] and to make the gold and silver objects. Now, who else will show their dedication to the LORD by giving gifts for building his temple?

[6] After David finished speaking, the family leaders, the tribal leaders, the army commanders, and the government officials voluntarily gave gifts [7] for the temple. These gifts included more than a hundred and seventy tonnes of gold, over three hundred and forty tonnes of silver, six hundred and twenty tonnes of bronze, and more than three thousand four hundred tonnes of iron. [8] Everyone who owned precious stones also donated them to the temple treasury, where Jehiel from the Levite clan of Gershon guarded them.

[9] David and the people were very happy that so much had been given to the LORD, and they all celebrated.

David praises the LORD

[10] Then, in front of everyone, David sang praises to the LORD:

I praise you for ever, LORD! You are the God our ancestor Jacob* worshipped. [11] Your power is great, and your glory is seen everywhere in heaven and on earth. You are king of the entire world, [12] and you rule with strength and power. You make people rich and powerful and famous. [13] We thank you, our God, and praise you.

---

*28.18 winged creatures: See the note at 13.6.

See also: 29.1,2: 1 Chron 22.5. 29.11: Matt 6.13.

¹⁴ But why should we be happy that we have given you these gifts? They belong to you, and we have only given back what is already yours. ¹⁵ We are only foreigners living here on earth for a while, just as our ancestors were. And we will soon be gone, like a shadow that suddenly disappears. ¹⁶ Our LORD God, we have brought all these things for building a temple to honour you. They belong to you, and you gave them to us. ¹⁷ But we are happy, because everyone has voluntarily given you these things. You know what is in everyone's heart, and you are pleased when people are honest. ¹⁸ Always make us eager to give, and help us be faithful to you, just as our ancestors Abraham, Isaac, and Jacob faithfully worshipped you. ¹⁹ And give Solomon the desire to obey your laws and teachings completely, and the desire to build the temple for which I have provided these gifts.

²⁰ David then said to the people, "Now it's your turn to praise the LORD, the God your ancestors worshipped!" So everyone praised the LORD, and they bowed down to honour him and David their king.

Solomon is crowned king

²¹ The next day, the Israelites slaughtered a thousand bulls, a thousand rams, and a thousand lambs, and they offered them as sacrifices to please the LORD,* along with offerings of wine. ²² The people were very happy, and they ate and drank there at the LORD's altar.

That same day, Solomon was crowned king. The people celebrated and poured olive oil on Solomon's head to show that he would be their next king. They also poured oil on Zadok's head to show that he was their priest.

²³ So Solomon became king after David his father. Solomon was successful, and everyone in Israel obeyed him. ²⁴ Every official and every soldier, as well as all David's other sons, were loyal to him. ²⁵ The LORD made Solomon a great king, and the whole nation was amazed at how famous he was. In fact, no other king of Israel was as great as Solomon.

*29.21 sacrifices to please the LORD: See the note at 16.1.
See also: 29.23: 1 King 2.12.

The death of David

²⁶ David the son of Jesse was king of Israel ²⁷ for forty years. He ruled from Hebron for seven years and from Jerusalem for thirty-three years. ²⁸ David was rich and respected and lived to be an old man. Then he died, and his son Solomon became king.

²⁹ Everything David did while he was king is included in the history written by the prophets Samuel, Nathan, and Gad. ³⁰ They wrote about his powerful rule and about the things that happened not only to him, but also to Israel and the other nations.

See also: 29.27: 2 Sam 5.4,5; 1 Chron 3.4.

Additional notes

*1.6 Riphath: Most Hebrew manuscripts and two ancient translations (see also Genesis 10.2–5); some Hebrew manuscripts "Diphath". In Hebrew the letters "d" and "r" look almost exactly the same.
*1.7 Dodanim: Most Hebrew manuscripts and one ancient translation (see also Genesis 10.2–5); some Hebrew manuscripts "Rodanim". In Hebrew the letters "d" and "r" look almost exactly the same.
*1.12 Casluhim, and Caphtorim, the ancestor of the Philistines: The Hebrew text has "Casluhim, the ancestor of the Philistines, and Caphtorim"; but see Jeremiah 47.4 and Amos 9.7.
*1.17 Meshech: Most Hebrew manuscripts; a few Hebrew manuscripts and some manuscripts of one ancient translation "Mash" (see also Genesis 10.21–31).
*1.34 Jacob: The Hebrew text has "Israel", which was Jacob's name after God renamed him.
*1.40 Alvan: Or "Alian".
*1.41 Hemdan: Most Hebrew manuscripts and one manuscripts of one ancient translation (see also Genesis 36.26); other Hebrew manuscripts "Hamran".
*1.42 Jaakan: Or "Akan" (see Genesis 36.27).
*1.42 Dishan: The Hebrew text has "Dishon", another spelling of the name (see Genesis 36.28).
*1.51 The Edomite clans: Or "The leaders of the Edomite clans".
*1.51 Alvah: Or "Aliah".
*2.1,2 Jacob: See the note at 1.34.
*2.6 Darda: Most Hebrew manuscripts and two ancient translations (see also 1 Kings 4.30,31); some Hebrew manuscripts "Dara".
*2.9 Caleb: The Hebrew text has "Chelubai", another form of the name.
*2.18 married Azubah . . . Jerioth: One possible meaning for the difficult Hebrew text.
*2.24 After the death of Hezron . . . Ashhur: Two ancient translations; Hebrew "After Hezron died in Caleb-Ephrath, Abijah his wife gave birth to Ashhur."

²2.42 Mesha: Hebrew; one ancient translation "Mareshah".

²2.42 following descendants . . . Mareshah: One possible meaning for the difficult Hebrew text.

²2.47 Shaaph: One possible meaning for the difficult Hebrew text of verse 47.

³3.5 Bathsheba: Two ancient translations (see also 2 Samuel 11); Hebrew "Bathshua".

³3.6-8 Elishua: Some Hebrew manuscripts and some manuscripts of one ancient translation (see also 2 Samuel 5.14,15); most Hebrew manuscripts "Elishama".

³3.10-15 Jehoram: The Hebrew text has "Joram", another spelling of the name.

³3.10-15 Jehoahaz: The Hebrew text has "Shallum", probably another name for Jehoahaz (see also 2 Kings 23.30).

³3.21 Shecaniah: One possible meaning for the difficult Hebrew text of verse 21.

⁴4.3 Etam's sons: Some manuscripts of one ancient translation; Hebrew "Etam's ancestors".

⁴4.10 I . . . harm: Or "keep me from harm, so I won't cause any pain."

⁴4.12 who settled the town of Nahash: Or "who was the father of Irnahash."

⁴4.13 and Meonothai: Two ancient translations; these words are not in the Hebrew text.

⁴4.14 Valley of Crafts: Hebrew "Geharashim".

⁴4.21,22 who married Moabite women and then settled near Bethlehem: Or "who ruled in Moab and Jashubi-Lahem" or "who ruled in Moab but then returned to Lahem".

⁴4.34-38 Jehu: Hebrew "Jehu son of Joshibiah son of Seraiah son of Asiel".

⁴4.34-38 Ziza: Hebrew "Ziza son of Shiphi son of Allon son of Jedaiah son of Shimri son of Shemaiah".

⁴4.39 Gerar: One ancient translation; Hebrew "Gedor".

⁴4.42 Edom: The Hebrew text has "Mount Seir", a common name for the nation of Edom.

⁵5.1 Jacob: See the note at 1.34.

⁵5.26 King Tiglath Pileser: The Hebrew text also includes "King Pul", another name by which he was known.

⁶6.28 Joel: Two ancient translations (see also verse 33 and 1 Samuel 8.1,2); this name is not in the Hebrew text.

⁶6.49 the two altars at the sacred tent: The Hebrew text mentions two different altars: a large altar for offering sacrifices, and a smaller altar for offering incense.

⁷7.12 Dan: The Hebrew text has "Aher", which can mean "someone else" (see Genesis 46.23-25).

⁷7.15 Zelophehad . . . daughters: One possible meaning for the difficult Hebrew text (see also Numbers 26.28-33).

⁷7.29 Joseph: Hebrew "Joseph son of Israel".

⁷7.35 Hotham: The Hebrew text has "Helem", another spelling of the name.

⁸8.29 Jeiel: One ancient translation and 9.35; the Hebrew text does not have this name.

⁸8.30 Ner: One ancient translation and 9.36; the Hebrew text does not have this name.

⁹9.19 Shallum son of Kore: Hebrew "Shallum son of Kore, grandson of Ebiasaph, and great-grandson of Korah".

⁹9.41 and Ahaz: Most ancient translations and 8.35; the Hebrew text does not have this name.

¹⁰10.7 Jezreel Valley: Hebrew "the valley".

¹¹11.15 the Three Warriors: Hebrew "three of the thirty most important warriors".

¹¹11.20,21 Warriors: One possible meaning for the difficult Hebrew text of these verses.

¹¹11.26-47 Ilai: Or "Zalmon" (see 2 Samuel 23.24-39).

¹¹11.26-47 Hurai: Or "Hiddai" (see 2 Samuel 23.24-39).

¹¹11.26-47 Hashem: One ancient translation; Hebrew "the sons of Hashem".

¹³13.7 Abinadab's sons: These words are not in the Hebrew text, but see 2 Samuel 6.3.

¹³13.11 Attack on Uzzah: Or "Perez-Uzzah".

¹⁴14.4-7 Beeliada: Or "Eliada" (see 3.6-8).

¹⁴14.11 The Lord Broke Through: Or "Baal-Perazim".

¹⁴14.14 balsam: One possible meaning for the difficult Hebrew text.

¹⁷17.17 You are treating me . . . person: One possible meaning for the difficult Hebrew text.

¹⁸18.17 David's bodyguard: The Hebrew text has "the Cherethites and the Pelethites", who were foreign soldiers hired by David to be his bodyguard.

²⁰20.2 the statue of their god Milcom: Or "their king."

²⁰20.2 David put the jewel on his crown: Or "David put the crown on his head".

²⁰20.7 David's nephew Jonathan: Hebrew "Jonathan son of Shimea, David's brother".

²¹21.15 Araunah: The Hebrew text has "Ornan", another spelling of Araunah (see 2 Samuel 24.16).

²⁴24.26,27 Ibri: One possible meaning for the difficult Hebrew text of verses 26,27.

²⁵25.3 Shimei: One Hebrew manuscript and two ancient translations; other Hebrew manuscripts do not have this name.

²⁶26.14 Shelemiah: Another spelling for Meshelemiah.

²⁶26.18 courtyard: One possible meaning for the difficult Hebrew text.

²⁶26.20 The Levites . . . were: One ancient translation; Hebrew "Ahijah the Levite was".

²⁶26.21 Many of his other . . . clan: One possible meaning for the difficult Hebrew text.

²⁷27.4 whose . . . Mikloth: One possible meaning for the difficult Hebrew text.

²⁷27.6 whose son Ammizabad . . . army commander: One possible meaning for the difficult Hebrew text.

²⁹29.10 Jacob: See the note at 1.34.

2 Chronicles

A quick look at this book

The Second Book of Chronicles continues the history of Israel that was begun in 1 Chronicles. This book repeats information and many stories that are in 1 and 2 Kings, but from a slightly different viewpoint.

The book of 2 Chronicles begins with the rule of King Solomon, then tells the history of the two separate kingdoms of Judah and Israel down to the fall of Jerusalem in 586 BC.

King Solomon is honoured as the ideal king of Israel. The first part of 2 Chronicles (1—9) includes events from his rule, especially the building and dedication of the temple in Jerusalem and the beginning of worship there.

The second part of the book (10—36) begins with the rebellion of the northern tribes of Israel and the division of the country into two separate kingdoms, Judah in the south and Israel in the north. This part of 2 Chronicles is the history of Judah down to the time of Jerusalem's fall and destruction. Unlike 2 Kings, the book of 2 Chronicles includes very little information about the northern kingdom. According to 2 Chronicles, the people of Israel were sinful and turned their backs on the Lord, and so their history did not deserve to be told.

The Second Book of Chronicles, like 1 Chronicles, is very concerned that the Lord be worshipped in the proper way. Hezekiah and Josiah are two of the most respected kings of Judah, because they were always faithful to the Lord and did many things to see that he was properly worshipped and that his Law was obeyed.

This book tells how Jerusalem was destroyed and the people of Judah were led away as prisoners to Babylonia. But the book concludes with hope for the Jews. King Cyrus of Persia lets them return to Judah, and he promises:

> The LORD God will watch over any of his people who want to go back to Judah.

(36.23b)

Solomon's wisdom and wealth

CHAPTER 1

The LORD makes Solomon wise

This is also told in 1 Kings 3.1–15

¹ King Solomon, the son of David, was now in complete control of his kingdom, because the LORD God had blessed him and made him a powerful king. ²⁻³ At that time, the sacred tent that Moses the servant of the LORD had made in the desert was still kept at Gibeon, and in front of the tent was the bronze altar that Bezalel* had made.

One day, Solomon told the people of Israel, the army commanders, the officials, and the family leaders, to go with him to the place of worship at Gibeon, even though his father King David had already moved the sacred chest from Kiriath-Jearim to the tent that he had set up for it in Jerusalem. Solomon and the others went to Gibeon to worship the LORD, ⁶ and there at the bronze altar, Solomon offered a thousand animals as sacrifices to please the LORD.*

⁷ God appeared to Solomon that night in a dream and said, "Solomon, ask for anything you want, and I will give it to you."

⁸ Solomon answered:

LORD God, you have always loyal to my father David, and now you have made me king of Israel. ⁹ I am supposed to rule these people, but there are as many of them as there are specks of dust on the ground. So keep the promise you made to my father ¹⁰ and make me wise. Give me the knowledge I'll need to be the king of this great nation of yours.

¹¹ God replied:

Solomon, you could have asked me to make you rich or famous or to let you live a long time. Or you could have asked for your enemies to be destroyed. Instead, you asked for wisdom and knowledge to rule

my people. ¹² So I will make you wise and intelligent. But I will also make you richer and more famous than any king before or after you.

¹³ Solomon then left Gibeon and returned to Jerusalem, the capital city of Israel.

Solomon's wealth

This is also told in 1 Kings 10.26–29

¹⁴ Solomon had a force of one thousand four hundred chariots and twelve thousand horses that he kept in Jerusalem and other towns. ¹⁵ While Solomon was king of Israel, there was silver and gold everywhere in Jerusalem, and cedar was as common as ordinary sycamore trees in the foothills.

¹⁶⁻¹⁷ Solomon's merchants bought his horses and chariots in the regions of Musri and Kue.* They paid six hundred pieces of silver for a chariot and a hundred and fifty pieces of silver for a horse. They also sold horses and chariots to the Hittite and Syrian kings.

Building and dedication of the Jerusalem temple

CHAPTER 2

Solomon asks Hiram to help build the temple

This is also told in 1 Kings 5.1–12

¹ Solomon decided to build a temple where the LORD would be worshipped, and also to build a palace for himself. ² He assigned seventy thousand men to carry building supplies and eighty thousand to cut stone from the hills. And he chose three thousand six hundred men to supervise these workers.

³ Solomon sent the following message to King Hiram of Tyre:

Years ago, when my father David was building his palace, you supplied him with cedar logs. Now will you send me supplies? ⁴ I am building a temple where the LORD my God will be worshipped. Sweet-smelling incense will be burnt there, and sacred bread will be offered to him. Worshippers will offer sacrifices to the LORD every

---

*1.6 sacrifices to please the LORD: These sacrifices have traditionally been called "whole burnt offerings", because the whole animal was burnt on the altar. A main purpose of such sacrifices was to please the LORD with the smell of the sacrifice, and so in the CEV they are often called "sacrifices to please the LORD".
See also: 1.4: 2 Sam 6.1–17; 1 Chron 13.5–14; 15.25—16.1.
1.5: Exod 38.1–7.   1.9: Gen 13.16; 28.14.

*1.16,17 Musri and Kue: Hebrew "Egypt and Kue". Musri and Kue were regions in what is today south-east Turkey.
See also: 1.14: 1 King 4.26.   1.16: Deut 17.16.

morning and evening, every Sabbath, and on the first day of each month, as well as during all our religious festivals. These things will be done for all time, just as the LORD has commanded.

⁵ This will be a great temple, because our God is greater than all other gods. ⁶ No one can ever build a temple large enough for God — even the heavens are too small a place for him to live in! All I can do is build a place where we can offer sacrifices to him.

⁷ Send me a worker who can not only carve, but who can work with gold, silver, bronze, and iron, as well as make brightly-coloured cloth. The person you send will work here in Judah and Jerusalem with the skilled workers that my father has already hired.

⁸ I know that you have workers who are experts at cutting timber in Lebanon. So would you please send me some cedar, pine, and juniper logs? My workers will be there to help them, ⁹ because I'll need a lot of timber to build such a large and glorious temple. ¹⁰ I will pay your woodcutters two thousand tonnes of wheat, the same amount of barley, four hundred thousand litres of wine, and that same amount of olive oil.

¹¹ Hiram sent his answer back to Solomon:

I know that the LORD must love his people, because he has chosen you to be their king. ¹² Praise the LORD God of Israel who made heaven and earth! He has given David a son who is not only wise and clever, but who has the knowledge to build a temple for the LORD and a palace for himself.

¹³ I am sending Huram Abi to you. He is very bright. ¹⁴ His mother was from the Israelite tribe of Dan, and his father was from Tyre. Not only is Huram an expert at working with gold, silver, bronze, iron, stone, and wood, but he can also make coloured cloth and fine linen. And he can carve anything if you give him a pattern to follow. He can help your workers and those hired by your father King David.

¹⁵ Go ahead and send the wheat, barley, olive oil, and wine you promised to pay my workers. ¹⁶ I will tell them to start cutting down trees in Lebanon. They will cut as many as you need, then tie them together into rafts, and float them down along the

coast to Joppa. Your workers can take them to Jerusalem from there.

Solomon's work force

¹⁷ Solomon counted all the foreigners who were living in Israel, just as his father David had done when he was king, and the total was 153,600. ¹⁸ He assigned 70,000 of them to carry building supplies and 80,000 of them to cut stone from the hills. He chose 3,600 others to supervise the workers and to make sure the work was completed.

CHAPTER 3

The temple is built

This is also told in 1 Kings 6.1-38

¹⁻² Solomon's workers began building the temple in Jerusalem on the second day of the second month,* four years after Solomon had become king of Israel. It was built on Mount Moriah where the LORD had appeared to David at the threshing place that had belonged to Araunah* from Jebus.

³ The inside of the temple was twenty-seven metres long and nine metres wide, according to the older standards.* ⁴ Across the front of the temple was a porch nine metres wide and nine metres* high. The inside walls of the porch were covered with pure gold.

⁵ Solomon had the inside walls of the temple's main room panelled first with pine and then with a layer of gold, and he had them decorated with carvings of palm trees and designs that looked like chains. ⁶ He used precious stones to decorate the temple, and he used gold imported from Parvaim* ⁷ to decorate the ceiling beams, the doors, the door frames, and the walls. Solomon also made the workers carve designs of winged creatures into the walls.

⁸ The most holy place was nine metres square, and its walls were covered with over twenty tonnes of fine gold. ⁹ Five hundred and seventy grammes of gold was used to cover the heads of the nails. The walls of the small storage rooms were also covered with gold.*

---

* **3.1,2 second month:** Ziv, the second month of the Hebrew calendar, from about mid-April to mid-May.
* **3.3 according to the older standards:** There were possibly two different standards of measurement during Israel's history.
* **3.6 Parvaim:** An unknown place.

See also: 2.6: 1 King 8.27; 2 Chron 6.18.   **See also:** 3.1: Gen 22.22. 3.8: Exod 26.33,34.

¹⁰ Solomon had two statues of winged creatures* made to put in the most holy place, and he covered them with gold. ¹¹⁻¹³ Each creature had two wings and was four and a half metres from the tip of one wing to the tip of the other wing. Solomon set them next to each other in the most holy place, facing the doorway. Their wings were spread out and reached all the way across the nine-metre wall.

¹⁴ A curtain* was made of fine linen woven with blue, purple, and red wool, and embroidered with designs of winged creatures.

The two columns

This is also told in 1 Kings 7.15–22

¹⁵ Two columns were made for the entrance to the temple. Each one was five and a half metres tall and had a cap on top that was over two metres high. ¹⁶ The top of each column was decorated with designs that looked like chains* and with a hundred carvings of pomegranates.* ¹⁷ Solomon had one of the columns placed on the south side of the temple's entrance; it was called Jachin.* The other one was placed on the north side of the entrance; it was called Boaz.*

CHAPTER 4

The furnishings for the temple

This is also told in 1 Kings 7.23–51

¹ Solomon had a bronze altar made that was nine metres square and four and a half metres high. ² He also gave orders to make a large metal bowl called the Sea. It was four and a half metres across, just over two metres deep, and thirteen and a half metres around. ³ Its outer edge was decorated with two rows of carvings of bulls, ten bulls to about every forty-five centimetres, all made from the same piece of metal as the bowl. ⁴ The bowl itself sat on top of twelve bronze bulls, with

three bulls facing outwards in each of four directions. ⁵ The sides of the bowl were seventy-five millimetres thick, and its rim was in the shape of a cup that curved outwards like flower petals. The bowl held about sixty thousand litres.

⁶ He also made ten small bowls and put five on each side of the large bowl. The small bowls were used to wash the animals that were burnt on the altar as sacrifices, and priests used the water in the large bowl to wash their hands.

⁷ Ten gold lampstands were also made according to the plans. Solomon placed these lampstands inside the temple, five on each side of the main room. ⁸ He also made ten tables and placed them in the main room, five on each side. And he made a hundred small gold sprinkling bowls.

⁹ Solomon gave orders to build two courtyards: a smaller one that only priests could use and a larger one. The doors to these courtyards were covered with bronze. ¹⁰ The large bowl called the Sea was placed near the south-east corner of the temple.

¹¹ Huram made shovels, sprinkling bowls, and pans for hot ashes. Here is a list of the other furnishings he made for God's temple: ¹² two columns, two bowl-shaped caps for the tops of these columns, two chain designs on the caps, ¹³ four hundred pomegranates* for the chain designs, ¹⁴ the stands and the small bowls, ¹⁵ the large bowl and the twelve bulls that held it up, ¹⁶ pans for hot ashes, as well as shovels and meat forks.

Huram made all these things out of polished bronze ¹⁷ by pouring melted bronze into the clay moulds he had set up near the River Jordan, between Succoth and Zeredah. ¹⁸ There were so many bronze furnishings that no one ever knew how much bronze it took to make them.

¹⁹ Solomon also gave orders to make the following temple furnishings out of gold: the altar, the tables that held the sacred loaves of bread,* ²⁰ the lampstands and the lamps that burnt in front of the most holy place, ²¹ flower designs, lamps and tongs, ²² lamp snuffers, small sprinkling bowls, ladles, fire

---

*3.10 statues of winged creatures: These were symbols of the LORD's throne on earth (see Exodus 25.18–22).

*3.14 A curtain: To separate the most holy place from the main room of the temple.

*3.16 pomegranates: A pomegranate is a small red fruit that looks like an apple. In ancient times, it was a symbol of life.

*3.17 Jachin: Or "He (God) makes secure."

*3.17 Boaz: Or "He (God) is strong."

See also: 3.10–13: Exod 25.18–20. 3.14: Exod 26.31.
4.1: Exod 27.1,2.

*4.13 pomegranates: See the note at 3.16.

*4.19 sacred loaves of bread: This bread was offered to the LORD and was a symbol of the LORD's presence in the temple. It was put out on special tables, and was replaced with fresh bread every week (see Leviticus 24.5–9).

See also: 4.6: Exod 30.17–21. 4.7: Exod 25.31–40.
4.8: Exod 25.23–30.

pans, and the doors to the most holy place and the main room of the temple.

CHAPTER 5

¹ After the LORD's temple was finished, Solomon put in its storage rooms everything that his father David had dedicated to the LORD, including the gold and silver, and the objects used in worship.

Solomon brings the sacred chest to the temple
This is also told in 1 Kings 8.1–13

²⁻³ The sacred chest had been kept on Mount Zion, also known as the City of David. But Solomon decided to have the chest moved to the temple while everyone was in Jerusalem to celebrate the Festival of Shelters during the seventh month.*
    Solomon called together all the important leaders of Israel. ⁴⁻⁵ Then the priests and the Levites picked up the sacred chest, the sacred tent, and the objects used for worship, and they carried them to the temple. ⁶ Solomon and a crowd of people walked in front of the chest, and along the way they sacrificed more sheep and cattle than could be counted.
    ⁷ The priests carried the chest into the most holy place and put it under the winged creatures,* ⁸ whose wings covered the chest and the poles used for carrying it. ⁹ The poles were so long that they could be seen from just outside the most holy place, but not from anywhere else. And they stayed there from then on.
    ¹⁰ The only things kept in the chest were the two flat stones Moses had put there when the LORD made his agreement with the people of Israel at Mount Sinai,* after bringing them out of Egypt.
    ¹¹⁻¹³ The priests of every group had gone through the ceremony to make themselves clean and acceptable to the LORD. The Levite musicians, including Asaph, Heman, Jeduthun, and their sons and relatives, were wearing robes of fine linen. They were standing on the east side of the altar, playing cymbals, small harps, and other stringed

instruments. One hundred and twenty priests were with these musicians, and they were blowing trumpets.
    They were praising the LORD by playing music and singing:

> "The LORD is good,
>   and his love never ends."

Suddenly a cloud filled the temple as the priests were leaving the holy place. ¹⁴ The LORD's glory was in that cloud, and the light from it was so bright that the priests could not stay inside to do their work.

CHAPTER 6

¹ Solomon prayed:

> "Our LORD, you said that you
>   would live in a dark cloud.
> ² Now I've built a glorious temple
>   where you can live for ever."

Solomon speaks to the people
This is also told in 1 Kings 8.14–21

³ Solomon turned towards the people standing there. Then he blessed them ⁴⁻⁶ and said:

Praise the LORD God of Israel! He brought his people out of Egypt long ago and later kept his promise to make my father David the king of Israel. The LORD also promised him that Jerusalem would be the city where his temple will be built, and now that promise has come true.
    ⁷ When my father wanted to build a temple for the LORD God of Israel, ⁸ the LORD said, "It's good that you want to build a temple where I can be worshipped. ⁹ But you're not the one to do it. Your son will build the temple to honour me."
    ¹⁰ The LORD has done what he promised. I am now the king of Israel, and I've built a temple for the LORD our God. ¹¹ I've also put the sacred chest in the temple. And in that chest are the two flat stones on which is written the solemn agreement the LORD made with our ancestors when he rescued them from Egypt.

Solomon prays at the temple
This is also told in 1 Kings 8.22–53

¹²⁻¹³ Earlier, Solomon had a bronze platform made that was about two metres square and

---

*5.2,3 seventh month: Tishri (also called Ethanim), the seventh month of the Hebrew calendar, from about mid-September to mid-October.
*5.7 winged creatures: See the note at 3.10.

See also: 5.1: 2 Sam 8.11; 1 Chron 18.11.
5.2: 2 Sam 6.12–15; 1 Chron 15.25–28. 5.10: Deut 10.5.
5.13: 1 Chron 16.34; 2 Chron 7.3; Ezra 3.11; Psa 100.5; 106.1; 107.1; 118.1; 136.1; Jer 33.11. 5.13,14: Exod 40.34,35.

See also: 6.4–9: 2 Sam 7.1–13; 1 Chron 17.1–12.

over a metre high, and he put it in the centre of the outer courtyard near the altar. Solomon stood on the platform facing the altar with everyone standing behind him. Then he lifted his arms towards heaven; he knelt down ¹⁴ and prayed:

LORD God of Israel, no other god in heaven or on earth is like you!

You never forget the agreement you made with your people, and you are loyal to anyone who faithfully obeys your teachings. ¹⁵ My father David was your servant, and today you have kept every promise you made to him.

¹⁶ You promised that someone from his family would always be king of Israel, if they do their best to obey you, just as he did. ¹⁷ Please keep this promise you made to your servant David. ¹⁸ There's not enough room in all of heaven for you, LORD God. How could you possibly live on earth in this temple I have built? ¹⁹ But I ask you to answer my prayer. ²⁰ This is the temple where you have chosen to be worshipped. Please watch over it day and night and listen when I turn towards it and pray. ²¹ I am your servant, and the people of Israel belong to you, and so whenever any of us look towards this temple and pray, answer from your home in heaven and forgive our sins.

²² Suppose someone accuses a person of a crime, and the accused has to stand in front of the altar in your temple and say, "I swear I am innocent!" ²³ Listen from heaven and decide who is right. Then punish the guilty person and let the innocent one go free.

²⁴ Suppose your people Israel sin against you, and then an enemy defeats them. If they come to this temple and beg for forgiveness, ²⁵ listen from your home in heaven. Forgive them and bring them back to the land you gave their ancestors.

²⁶ Suppose your people sin against you, and you punish them by holding back the rain. If they stop sinning and turn towards this temple to pray in your name, ²⁷ listen from your home in heaven and forgive them. The people of Israel are your servants, so teach them to live right. And send rain on the land you promised them for ever.

²⁸ Sometimes the crops may dry up or rot or be eaten by locusts* or grasshoppers, and your people will be starving. Sometimes enemies may surround their towns, or your people will become sick with deadly diseases. ²⁹ Please listen when anyone in Israel truly feels sorry and sincerely prays with arms lifted towards your temple. ³⁰ You know what is in everyone's heart. So from your home in heaven answer their prayers, according to what they do and what is in their hearts. ³¹ Then your people will worship you and obey you for as long as they live in the land you gave their ancestors.

³² Foreigners will hear about you and your mighty power, and some of them will come to live among your people Israel. If any of them pray towards this temple, ³³ listen from your home in heaven and answer their prayers. Then everyone on earth will worship you, just as your own people Israel do, and they will know that I have built this temple in your honour.

³⁴ Sometimes you will order your people to attack their enemies. Then your people will turn towards this temple I have built for you in your chosen city, and they will pray to you. ³⁵ Answer their prayers from heaven and give them victory.

³⁶ Everyone sins. But when your people sin against you, suppose you get angry enough to let their enemies drag them away to foreign countries. ³⁷⁻³⁹ Later, they may feel sorry for what they did and ask your forgiveness. Answer them when they pray towards this temple I have built for you in your chosen city, here in this land you gave their ancestors. From your home in heaven, listen to their sincere prayers and forgive your people who have sinned against you.

⁴⁰ LORD God, hear us when we pray in this temple. ⁴¹ Come to your new home, where we have already placed the sacred chest, which is the symbol of your strength. I pray that when the priests announce your power to save people, those who are faithful to you will celebrate what you've done for them. ⁴² Always remember the love you had for your servant David,ᵇ so that you will not reject your chosen kings.

See also: 6.16: 1 King 2.4. 6.18: 2 Chron 2.6. 6.20: Deut 12.11.

*6.28 locusts: A type of grasshopper that comes in swarms and causes great damage to crops.
See also: 6.41-42: Psa 132.8-10.

416

CHAPTER 7

Solomon dedicates the temple

This is also told in 1 Kings 8.62–66

¹ As soon as Solomon finished praying, fire came down from heaven and burnt up the offerings. The LORD's dazzling glory then filled the temple, ² and the priests could not go in.

³ When the crowd of people saw the fire and the LORD's glory, they knelt down and worshipped the LORD. They prayed:

> "The LORD is good,
> and his love never ends."

⁴⁻⁵ Solomon and the people dedicated the temple to the LORD by sacrificing twenty-two thousand cattle and one hundred and twenty thousand sheep. ⁶ Everybody stood up during the ceremony. The priests were in their assigned places, blowing their trumpets. And the Levites faced them, playing the musical instruments that David had made for them to use when they praised the LORD for his never-ending love.

⁷ On that same day, Solomon dedicated the courtyard in front of the temple and got it ready to be used for worship. The bronze altar he had made was too small, so he used the courtyard to offer sacrifices to please the LORD* and grain sacrifices, and also to send up in smoke the fat from the other offerings.

⁸ For seven days, Solomon and the crowd celebrated the Festival of Shelters, and people came from as far away as the Egyptian Gorge in the south and Lebo-Hamath in the north. ⁹ On the next day, everyone came together for worship. They had celebrated a total of fourteen days; seven days for the dedication of the altar and seven more days for the festival. ¹⁰ Then on the twenty-third day of the seventh month,* Solomon sent everyone home. They left very happy because of all the good things the LORD had done for David and Solomon, and for his people Israel.

The LORD appears to Solomon again

This is also told in 1 Kings 9.1–9

¹¹ The LORD's temple and Solomon's palace were now finished. In fact, everything Solomon had planned to do was completed.

¹² Some time later, the LORD appeared to Solomon in a dream and said:

I heard your prayer, and I have chosen this temple as the place where sacrifices will be offered to me.

¹³ Suppose I hold back the rain or send locusts* to eat the crops or make my people suffer with deadly diseases. ¹⁴ If my own people will humbly pray and turn back to me and stop sinning, then I will answer them from heaven. I will forgive them and make their land fertile once again. ¹⁵ I will hear the prayers made in this temple, ¹⁶ because it belongs to me, and this is where I will be worshipped for ever. I will never stop watching over it.

¹⁷ Your father David obeyed me, and now, Solomon, you must do the same. Obey my laws and teachings, ¹⁸ and I will keep my solemn promise to him that someone from your family will always be king of Israel.

¹⁹ But if you or any of the people of Israel disobey my laws or start worshipping foreign gods, ²⁰ I will pull you out of this land I gave you. I will desert this temple where I said I would be worshipped, so that people everywhere will think it is only a joke and will make fun of it. ²¹ This temple is now magnificent. But when these things happen, everyone who walks by it will be shocked and will ask, "Why did the LORD do such a terrible thing to his people and to this temple?" ²² Then they will answer, "It was because the people of Israel rejected the LORD their God, who rescued their ancestors from Egypt, and they started worshipping other gods."

Other events during Solomon's rule

CHAPTER 8

Other things Solomon did

This is also told in 1 Kings 9.10–28

¹ It took twenty years for the LORD's temple and Solomon's palace to be built. ² After that, Solomon's workers rebuilt the towns that Hiram had given him. Then Solomon sent Israelites to live in those towns.

³ Solomon attacked and captured the town of Hamath-Zobah. ⁴ He made his workers

---

*7.7 sacrifices to please the LORD: See the note at 1.6.
*7.10 seventh month: See the note at 5.2,3.

See also: 7.1: Lev 9.23-24. 7.3: 1 Chron 16.34; 2 Chron 5.13;
Ezra 3.11; Psa 100.5; 106.1; 107.1; 118.1; 136.1; Jer 33.11.

*7.13 locusts: See the note at 6.28.

See also: 7.18: 1 King 2.4.

build the town of Tadmor in the desert and some towns in Hamath where he could keep his supplies. 5 He strengthened Upper Beth-Horon and Lower Beth-Horon by adding walls and gates that could be locked. 6 He did the same thing to the town of Baalath and to the cities where he kept supplies, chariots, and horses. Solomon made his workers build whatever he wanted in Jerusalem, Lebanon, and anywhere else in his kingdom.

7-9 Solomon did not force the Israelites to do his work. Instead, they were his soldiers, officers, army commanders, and cavalry troops. But he did make slaves of the Hittites, Amorites, Perizzites, Hivites, and Jebusites who were living in Israel. These were the descendants of those foreigners the Israelites did not destroy, and they remained Israel's slaves.

10 Solomon appointed two hundred and fifty officers to be in charge of his workers.

11 Solomon's wife, the daughter of the king of Egypt, moved from the part of Jerusalem called David's City to her new palace that Solomon had built. The sacred chest had been kept in David's City, which made his palace sacred, and so Solomon's wife could no longer live there.

12 Solomon offered sacrifices to the LORD on the altar he had built in front of the temple. 13 He followed the requirements that Moses had given for sacrifices offered on the Sabbath, on the first day of each month, the Festival of Thin Bread, the Harvest Festival, and the Festival of Shelters.

14 Solomon then assigned the priests and the Levites their duties at the temple, and he followed the instructions that his father David had given him. Some of the Levites were to lead music and help the priests in their duties, and others were to guard the temple gates 15 and the storage rooms. The priests and Levites followed these instructions exactly.

16 Everything Solomon had planned to do was now finished — from the laying of the temple's foundation to its completion.

17 Solomon went to Ezion-Geber and Eloth, two Edomite towns on the Red Sea.* 18 Hiram sent his ships and some of his experienced sailors. They went with Solomon's own sailors to the country of Ophir* and brought

back more than fifteen thousand kilogrammes of gold for Solomon.

CHAPTER 9

The Queen of Sheba visits Solomon

This is also told in 1 Kings 10.1–13

1 The Queen of Sheba heard how famous Solomon was, so she went to Jerusalem to test him with difficult questions. She took along several of her officials, and she loaded her camels with gifts of spices, jewels, and gold. When she arrived, she and Solomon talked about everything she could think of. 2 She answered every question, no matter how difficult it was.

3-4 The Queen was amazed at Solomon's wisdom. She was breathless when she saw his palace,* the food on his table, his officials, all his servants in their uniforms, and the sacrifices he offered at the LORD's temple. 5 She said:

Solomon, in my own country I had heard about your wisdom and all you've done. 6 But I didn't believe it until I saw it with my own eyes! And there's so much I didn't hear about. You are greater than I was told. 7 Your people and officials are lucky to be here where they can listen to the wise things you say.

8 I praise the LORD your God. He is pleased with you and has made you king of Israel. God loves the people of this country and will never desert them, so he has given them a king who will rule fairly and honestly.

9 The Queen of Sheba gave Solomon more than four thousand kilogrammes of gold, a large amount of jewels, and the best spices anyone had ever seen.

10-12 In return, Solomon gave her everything she wanted — even more than she had given him. Then she and her officials went back to their own country.

Solomon's wealth

This is also told in 1 Kings 10.14–29

Hiram's and Solomon's sailors brought gold, juniper wood, and jewels from the country of Ophir. Solomon used the wood to make steps* for the temple and palace, and harps and other stringed instruments for the musicians. Nothing like these had ever been made in Judah.

*8.17 Red Sea: Hebrew *yam suph*, here referring to the Gulf of Aqaba, since the term is extended to include the north-eastern arm of the Red Sea (see also the note at Exodus 13.18).
*8.18 Ophir: The location of this place is not known.

See also: 8.13: a Num 28.9,10; b Num 28.11–15; c Exod 23.14–17; 34.22,23; Num 28.16–29.39; Deut 16.16.

See also: 9.1–9: Matt 12.42; Luke 11.31.

¹³ Solomon received almost twenty-three thousand kilogrammes of gold each year, ¹⁴ not counting what the merchants and traders brought him. The kings of Arabia and the leaders of Israel also gave him gold and silver.

¹⁵ Solomon made two hundred gold shields that weighed over three kilogrammes each. ¹⁶ He also made three hundred smaller gold shields that weighed almost two kilogrammes, and he put these shields in his palace in Forest Hall.

¹⁷ His throne was made of ivory and covered with pure gold. ¹⁸ It had a gold footstool attached to it and arm rests on each side. There was a statue of a lion on each side of the throne, ¹⁹ and there were two lion statues on each of the six steps leading up to the throne. No other throne in the world was like Solomon's.

²⁰ Solomon's cups and dishes in Forest Hall were made of pure gold, because silver was almost worthless in those days.

²¹ Solomon had a lot of seagoing ships.* Every three years he sent them out with Hiram's ships to bring back gold, silver, and ivory, as well as monkeys and peacocks.*

²² Solomon was the richest and wisest king in the world. ²³⁻²⁴ Year after year, other kings came to hear the wisdom God had given him. And they brought gifts of silver and gold, as well as clothes, weapons, spices, horses, and mules.

²⁵ Solomon had four thousand stalls for his horses and chariots, and he owned twelve thousand horses that he kept in Jerusalem and other towns.

²⁶ He ruled all the nations from the River Euphrates in the north to the land of Philistia in the south, as far as the border of Egypt.

²⁷ While Solomon was king, there was silver everywhere in Jerusalem, and cedar was as common as the sycamore trees in the western foothills. ²⁸ Solomon's horses were brought in from other countries, including Musri.*

The death of Solomon

This is also told in 1 Kings 11.41-43

²⁹ Everything else Solomon did while he was king is written in the records of Nathan the prophet, Ahijah the prophet from Shiloh, and Iddo the prophet who wrote about Jeroboam son of Nebat. ³⁰ After Solomon had ruled forty years from Jerusalem, ³¹ he died and was buried in the city of his father David. His son Rehoboam then became king.

The northern tribes of Israel rebel against King Rehoboam

CHAPTER 10

This is also told in 1 Kings 12.1-20

¹ Rehoboam went to Shechem where everyone was waiting to crown him king.

² Jeroboam son of Nebat heard what was happening, and he returned from Egypt, where he had gone to hide from Solomon. ³ The people from the northern tribes of Israel sent for him. Then together they went to Rehoboam and said, ⁴ "Your father Solomon forced us to work very hard. But if you make our work easier, we will serve you and do whatever you ask."

⁵ Rehoboam replied, "Come back in three days for my answer." So the people left.

⁶ Rehoboam went to some leaders who had been his father's senior officials, and he asked them, "What should I tell these people?"

⁷ They answered, "If you want them to serve and obey you, then you should be kind and promise to make their work easier."

⁸ But Rehoboam refused their advice and went to the younger men who had grown up with him and were now his officials. ⁹ He asked, "What do you think I should say to these people who asked me to make their work easier?"

¹⁰ His younger advisers said:

Here's what we think you should say to them: "Compared to me, my father was weak.* ¹¹ He made you work hard, but I'll make you work even harder. He punished you with whips, but I'll use whips with pieces of sharp metal!"

---

*9.21 seagoing ships: The Hebrew text has "ships of Tarshish", which may have been a Phoenician city in Spain. "Ships of Tarshish" probably means large, seagoing ships.
*9.28 Musri: See the note at 1.16,17.
See also: 9.25: 1 King 4.26. 9.26: Gen 15.18; 1 King 4.21. 9.28: Deut 17.16.

12 Three days later, Jeroboam and the others came back. 13 Rehoboam ignored the advice of the older advisers. He spoke bluntly 14 and told them exactly what his own advisers had suggested. He said: "My father made you work hard, but I'll make you work even harder. He punished you with whips, but I'll use whips with pieces of sharp metal!"

15-19 When the people realized that Rehoboam would not listen to them, they shouted: "We don't have to be loyal to David's family. We can do what we want. Come on, people of Israel, let's go home! Rehoboam can rule his own people."

Adoniram* was in charge of the work force, and Rehoboam sent him to talk to the people. But they stoned him to death. Then Rehoboam ran to his chariot and hurried back to Jerusalem.

Everyone from Israel's northern tribes went home, leaving Rehoboam to rule only the people from Judah. And since that day, the people of Israel have been opposed to David's descendants in Judah.* All this happened just as Ahijah the LORD's prophet from Shiloh had told Jeroboam.

Kings of Judah

CHAPTER 11

Shemaiah the prophet warns Rehoboam

This is also told in 1 Kings 12.21-24

1 After Rehoboam returned to Jerusalem, he decided to attack Israel and regain control of the whole country. So he called together one hundred and eighty thousand soldiers from the tribes of Judah and Benjamin.

2 Meanwhile, the LORD told Shemaiah the prophet 3 to tell Rehoboam and everyone from Judah and Benjamin, 4 "The LORD warns you not to go to war against the people from the northern tribes — they are your relatives. Go home! The LORD is the one who made these things happen."

Rehoboam and his army obeyed the LORD's message and did not attack Jeroboam and his troops.

Rehoboam fortifies cities in Judah

5 Rehoboam ruled from Jerusalem, and he had several cities in Judah turned into fortresses so he could use them to defend his country. These cities included 6 Bethlehem, Etam, Tekoa, 7 Beth-Zur, Soco, Adullam, 8 Gath, Mareshah, Ziph, 9 Adoraim, Lachish, Azekah, 10 Zorah, Aijalon, and Hebron. After he had fortified these cities in the territories of Judah and Benjamin, 11 he assigned an army commander to each of them and stocked them with supplies of food, olive oil, and wine, 12 as well as with shields and spears. He used these fortified cities to keep control of Judah and Benjamin.

The priests and the Levites support Rehoboam

13 The priests and Levites from the northern tribes of Israel gave their support to King Rehoboam. 14 And since Jeroboam and the kings of Israel who followed him would not allow any Levites to serve as priests, most Levites left their towns and pasture lands in Israel and moved to Jerusalem and other towns in Judah. 15 Jeroboam chose his own priests to serve at the local shrines* in Israel and at the places of worship where he had set up statues of goat-demons and of calves.

16 But some of the people from Israel wanted to worship the LORD God, just as their ancestors had done. So they followed the priests and Levites to Jerusalem, where they could offer sacrifices to the LORD. 17 For the next three years, they lived in Judah and were loyal to Rehoboam and his kingdom, just as they had been loyal to David and Solomon.

Rehoboam's family

18 Rehoboam married Mahalath, whose father was Jerimoth son of David, and whose mother was Abihail the daughter of Eliab and granddaughter of Jesse. 19 Rehoboam and Mahalath had three sons: Jeush, Shemariah, and Zaham. 20 Then Rehoboam married Maacah the daughter of Absalom. Their sons were Abijah, Attai, Ziza, and Shelomith.

21 Rehoboam had eighteen wives, but he also married sixty other women,* and he was the father of twenty-eight sons and sixty

---

*10.15-19 the people of Israel have been opposed . . . Judah: From this time on, "Israel" usually refers only to the northern kingdom. The southern kingdom is called "Judah".

See also: 10.16: 2 Sam 20.1.

*11.21 other women: This translates a Hebrew word for women who were legally bound to a man, but without the full privileges of a wife.

See also: 11.15: 1 King 12.31.

daughters. Rehoboam loved his wife Maacah the most, [22] so he chose their eldest son Abijah to be the next king. [23] Rehoboam was wise enough to put one of his sons in charge of each fortified city in his kingdom. He gave them all the supplies they needed and found wives for every one of them.

CHAPTER 12

King Shishak of Egypt invades Judah

This is also told in 1 Kings 14.25–28

[1] Soon after Rehoboam had control of his kingdom, he and everyone in Judah stopped obeying the LORD. [2] So in the fifth year of Rehoboam's rule, the LORD punished them for their unfaithfulness and allowed King Shishak of Egypt to invade Judah. [3] Shishak attacked with his army of one thousand two hundred chariots and sixty thousand cavalry troops, as well as Egyptian soldiers from Libya, Sukkoth, and Ethiopia.* [4] He captured every one of the fortified cities in Judah and then marched to Jerusalem.

[5] Rehoboam and the leaders of Judah had gone to Jerusalem to escape Shishak's invasion. And while they were there, Shemaiah the prophet told them, "The LORD says that because you have disobeyed him, he has now abandoned you. The LORD will not help you against Shishak!"

[6] Rehoboam and the leaders were sorry for what they had done and admitted, "The LORD is right. We have deserted him."

[7] When the LORD heard this, he told Shemaiah:

The people of Judah are truly sorry for their sins, and so I won't let Shishak completely destroy them. But because I am still angry, [8] he will conquer and rule them.

Then my people will know what it's like to serve a foreign king instead of serving me.

[9] Shishak attacked Jerusalem and took all the valuable things from the temple and from the palace, including Solomon's gold shields. [10] Rehoboam had bronze shields made to replace the gold ones, and he ordered the guards at the city gates to keep them safe. [11] Whenever Rehoboam went to the LORD's temple, the guards carried the shields. But they always took them back to the guardroom as soon as he had finished worshipping.

[12] Rehoboam turned back to the LORD, and so the LORD did not let Judah be completely destroyed, and Judah was prosperous again.

Rehoboam's rule in Judah

This is also told in 1 Kings 14.21,29–31

[13] Rehoboam was forty-one years old when he became king, and he ruled seventeen years from Jerusalem, the city where the LORD had chosen to be worshipped. His mother Naamah was from Ammon. Rehoboam was a powerful king, [14] but he still did wrong and refused to obey the LORD.

[15] Everything else Rehoboam did while he was king, including a history of his family, is written in the records of the two prophets, Shemaiah and Iddo. During Rehoboam's rule, he and King Jeroboam of Israel were constantly at war. [16] When Rehoboam died, he was buried beside his ancestors in Jerusalem, and his son Abijah became king.

CHAPTER 13

King Abijah of Judah

This is also told in 1 Kings 15.1–8

[1] Abijah* became king of Judah in Jeroboam's eighteenth year as king of Israel, [2] and he ruled from Jerusalem for three years. His mother was Micaiah the daughter of Uriel from Gibeah.

Some time later, Abijah and King Jeroboam of Israel went to war against each other. [3] Abijah's army had four hundred thousand troops, and Jeroboam met him in battle with eight hundred thousand troops.

[4] Abijah went to the top of Mount Zemaraim* in the hills of Ephraim and shouted:

Listen, Jeroboam and all you Israelites! [5] The LORD God of Israel has made a solemn promise that every king of Israel will be from David's family. [6] But Jeroboam, you were King Solomon's official, and you rebelled. [7] Then straight after Rehoboam became king, you and your bunch of worthless followers challenged Rehoboam, who was too young to know how to stop you.

---

*12.3 Ethiopia: The Hebrew text has "Cush," which was a region south of Egypt that included parts of the present countries of Ethiopia and Sudan.

See also: 12.9: 1 King 10.16,17; 2 Chron 9.15,16.

*13.4 Mount Zemaraim: Probably on the northern border of the territory of Benjamin.

8 Now you and your powerful army think you can stand up to the kingdom that the LORD has given to David's descendants. The only gods you have are those gold statues of calves that Jeroboam made for you. 9 You don't even have descendants of Aaron on your side, because you forced out the LORD's priests and Levites. In their place, you appoint ordinary people to be priests, just as the foreign nations do. In fact, anyone with a bull and seven rams to the altar can become a priest of your so-called gods.

10 But we have not turned our backs on the LORD God! Aaron's own descendants serve as our priests, and the Levites are their assistants. 11 Twice every day they offer sacrifices and burn incense to the LORD. They set out the sacred loaves of bread on a table that has been purified, and they light the lamps in the gold lampstand every day at sunset. We follow the commands of the LORD our God — you have rejected him! 12 That's why God is on our side and will lead us into battle when the priests sound the signal on the trumpets. It's no use, Israelites. You might as well give up. There's no way you can defeat the LORD, the God your ancestors worshipped.

13 But while Abijah was talking, Jeroboam had sent some of his troops to attack Judah's army from behind, while the rest attacked from the front. 14 Judah's army realized they were trapped, and so they prayed to the LORD. The priests blew the signal on the trumpet, 15 and the troops let out a battle cry. Then with Abijah leading them into battle, God defeated Jeroboam and Israel's army. 16 The Israelites ran away, and God helped Judah's soldiers slaughter 17 five hundred thousand enemy troops. 18 Judah's army won because they had trusted the LORD God of their ancestors.

19 Abijah kept up his attack on Jeroboam's army and captured the Israelite towns of Bethel, Jeshanah, and Ephron, as well as the villages around them.

20 Jeroboam never regained his power during the rest of Abijah's rule. The LORD punished Jeroboam, and he died, but Abijah became more powerful.

21 Abijah had a total of fourteen wives, twenty-two sons, and sixteen daughters. 22 Everything Abijah said and did while he was king is written in the records of Iddo the prophet.

CHAPTER 14

King Asa of Judah

1 Abijah died and was buried in Jerusalem. Then his son Asa became king, and Judah had ten years of peace.

2 Asa obeyed the LORD his God and did right. 3 He destroyed the local shrines* and the altars to foreign gods. He smashed the stone images of gods and cut down the sacred poles* used in worshipping the goddess Asherah. 4 Then he told everyone in Judah to worship the LORD God, just as their ancestors had done, and to obey his laws and teachings. 5 He destroyed every local shrine and incense altar in Judah.

6 The LORD blessed Judah with peace while Asa was king, and so during that time, Asa fortified many of the towns. 7 He said to the people, "Let's build walls and defence towers for these towns, and put in gates that can be locked with bars. This land still belongs to us, because we have obeyed the LORD our God. He has given us peace from all our enemies." The people did everything Asa had suggested.

8 Asa had a large army of brave soldiers: three hundred thousand of them were from the tribe of Judah and were armed with shields and spears; two hundred and eighty thousand were from Benjamin and were armed with bows and arrows.

Judah defeats Ethiopia's army

9 Zerah from Ethiopia* led an army of a million soldiers and three hundred chariots to the town of Mareshah* in Judah. 10 Asa met him there, and the two armies prepared for battle in Zephathah Valley.

11 Asa prayed:

LORD God, only you can help a powerless army defeat a stronger one. So we depend on you to help us. We will fight against this powerful army to honour your name, and we know that you won't be defeated. You are the LORD our God.

12 The LORD helped Asa and his army defeat the Ethiopians. The enemy soldiers ran away, 13 but Asa and his troops chased them as far as Gerar. It was a total defeat — the Ethiopians could not even fight back!*

---

*14.3 sacred poles: Or "trees", used as symbols of Asherah, the goddess of fertility.
*14.9 Ethiopia: See the note at 12.3.
*14.9 Mareshah: About forty kilometres south-west of Jerusalem.

The soldiers from Judah took everything that had belonged to the Ethiopians. 14 The people who lived in the villages around Gerar learnt what had happened and were afraid of the LORD. So Judah's army easily defeated them and carried off everything of value that they wanted from these towns. 15 They also attacked the camps where the shepherds lived and took a lot of sheep, goats, and camels. Then they went back to Jerusalem.

CHAPTER 15

Asa destroys the idols in Judah

1 Some time later, God spoke to Azariah son of Oded. 2 At once, Azariah went to Asa and said:

Listen to me, King Asa and you people of Judah and Benjamin. The LORD will be with you and help you, as long as you obey and worship him. But if you disobey him, he will desert you.

3 For a long time, the people of Israel did not worship the true God or listen to priests who could teach them about God. They refused to obey God's Law. 4 But whenever trouble came, Israel turned back to the LORD their God and worshipped him.

5 There was so much confusion in those days that it wasn't safe to go anywhere in Israel. 6 Nations were destroying each other, and cities were wiping out other cities, because God was causing trouble and unrest everywhere.

7 So you must be brave. Don't give up! God will honour you for obeying him.

8 As soon as Asa heard what Azariah the prophet said, he gave orders for all the idols in Judah and Benjamin to be destroyed, including those in the towns he had captured in the territory of Ephraim. He also repaired the LORD's altar that was in front of the temple porch.

9 Asa called together the people from Judah and Benjamin, as well as the people from the territories of Ephraim, West Manasseh, and Simeon who were living in Judah. Many of these people were now loyal to Asa, because they had seen that the LORD was with him.

10 In the third month of the fifteenth year of Asa's rule, they all met in Jerusalem. 11 That same day, they took seven hundred bulls and seven thousand sheep and goats from what they had brought back from Gerar and sacrificed them as offerings to the LORD.

12 They made a solemn promise to faithfully worship the LORD God their ancestors had worshipped, 13 and to put to death anyone who refused to obey him. 14 The crowd solemnly agreed to keep their promise to the LORD, then they celebrated by shouting and blowing trumpets and horns. 15 Everyone was happy because they had made this solemn promise, and in return, the LORD blessed them with peace from all their enemies.

16 Asa's grandmother Maacah had made a disgusting idol of the goddess Asherah, so he cut it down, crushed it, and burnt it in Kidron Valley. Then he removed Maacah from her position as queen mother.* 17 As long as Asa lived, he was faithful to the LORD, even though he did not destroy the local shrines† in Israel. 18 He placed in the temple all the silver and gold objects that he and his father had dedicated to God.

19 There was peace in Judah until the thirty-fifth year of Asa's rule.

CHAPTER 16

King Baasha of Israel invades Judah

This is also told in 1 Kings 15.16–22

1 In the thirty-sixth year of Asa's rule, King Baasha of Israel invaded Judah and captured the town of Ramah. He started making the town stronger, and he put troops there to stop people from going in and out of Judah.

2 When Asa heard about this, he took the silver and gold from his palace and from the LORD's temple. Then he sent it to Damascus with this message for King Benhadad of Syria: 3 "I think we should sign a peace treaty, just as our fathers did. This silver and gold is a present for you. Would you please break your treaty with King Baasha of Israel and force him to leave my country?"

4 Benhadad did what Asa asked and sent the Syrian army into Israel. They captured the towns of Ijon, Dan, Abel-Maim,† and all the towns in Naphtali where supplies were kept. 5 When Baasha heard about it, he stopped his work on the town of Ramah.

6 Asa ordered everyone in Judah to carry away the stones and wood Baasha had used to fortify Ramah. Then he fortified the towns of Geba and Mizpah with these same stones and wood.

---

*15.16 queen mother: Or "the mother of the king", which was an important position in biblical times (see 1 Kings 2.19).

Hanani the prophet condemns Asa

[7] Soon after that happened, Hanani the prophet went to Asa and said:

You depended on the king of Syria instead of depending on the LORD your God. And so, you will never defeat the Syrian army. [8] Remember how powerful the Ethiopian* and Libyan army was, with all their chariots and cavalry troops! You trusted the LORD to help you then, and you defeated them. [9] The LORD is constantly watching everyone, and he gives strength to those who faithfully obey him. But you have done a foolish thing, and your kingdom will never be at peace again.

[10] When Asa heard this, he was so angry that he put Hanani in prison. Asa was also cruel to some of his people.'

Asa dies

This is also told in 1 Kings 15.23,24

[11] Everything Asa did while he was king is written in *The History of the Kings of Judah and Israel.* [12] In the thirty-ninth year of his rule, he got a very bad foot disease, but he relied on doctors and refused to ask the LORD for help. [13] He died two years later.

[14] Earlier, Asa had his own tomb cut out of a rock hill in Jerusalem. So he was buried there, and the tomb was filled with spices and sweet-smelling oils. Then the people built a bonfire in his honour.

CHAPTER 17

King Jehoshaphat of Judah

[1] Jehoshaphat son of Asa became king and strengthened his defences against Israel. [2] He assigned troops to the fortified cities in Judah, as well as to other towns in Judah and to those towns in Ephraim that his father Asa had captured.

[3-4] When Jehoshaphat's father had first become king of Judah, he was faithful to the LORD and refused to worship the god Baal as the kings of Israel did. Jehoshaphat followed his father's example and obeyed and worshipped the LORD. And so the LORD blessed Jehoshaphat [5] and helped him keep firm control of his kingdom. The people of Judah brought gifts to Jehoshaphat, but even after he became very rich and respected, [6] he remained completely faithful to the LORD. He destroyed all the local shrines* in Judah, including the places where the goddess Asherah was worshipped.

[7] In the third year of Jehoshaphat's rule, he chose five officials and gave them orders to teach the LORD's Law in every city and town in Judah. They were Benhail, Obadiah, Zechariah, Nethanel, and Micaiah. [8] Their assistants were the following nine Levites: Shemaiah, Nethaniah, Zebadiah, Asahel, Shemiramoth, Jehonathan, Adonijah, Tobijah, and Tob-Adonijah. Two priests, Elishama and Jehoram, also went along. [9] They carried with them a copy of the LORD's Law wherever they went and taught the people from it.

[10] The nations around Judah were afraid of the LORD's power, so none of them attacked Jehoshaphat. [11] Philistines brought him silver and other gifts to keep peace. Some of the Arab people brought him seventy-seven hundred rams and the same number of goats.

[12] As Jehoshaphat became more powerful, he built fortresses and cities [13] where he stored supplies. He also kept in Jerusalem some experienced soldiers [14] from the Judah and Benjamin tribes. These soldiers were grouped according to their clans.

Adnah was the commander of the troops from Judah, and he had three hundred thousand soldiers under his command. [15] Jehohanan was second in command, with two hundred and eighty thousand soldiers under him. [16] Amasiah son of Zichri, who had volunteered to serve the LORD, was third in command, with two hundred thousand soldiers under him.

[17] Eliada was a brave warrior who commanded the troops from Benjamin. He had two hundred thousand soldiers under his command, all of them armed with bows and shields. [18] Jehozabad was second in command, with one hundred and eighty thousand soldiers under him. [19] These were the troops who protected the king in Jerusalem, not counting those he had assigned to the fortified cities throughout the country.

CHAPTER 18

Micaiah warns King Ahab of Israel

This is also told in 1 Kings 22.1–28

[1] Jehoshaphat was now very rich and famous. He signed a treaty with King Ahab of Israel by arranging the marriage of his son and Ahab's daughter.

---

*16.8 Ethiopian: See the note at 12.3.

2 One day, Jehoshaphat went to visit Ahab in his capital city of Samaria. Ahab slaughtered sheep and cattle and prepared a big feast to honour Jehoshaphat and the officials with him. Ahab talked about attacking the city of Ramoth in Gilead,* 3 and finally asked, "Jehoshaphat, would you go with me to attack Ramoth?"

"Yes," Jehoshaphat answered. "My army is at your command. 4 But first let's ask the LORD what to do."

5 Ahab sent for four hundred prophets and asked, "Should I attack the city of Ramoth?"

"Yes!" the prophets answered. "God will help you capture the city."

6 But Jehoshaphat said, "Just to make sure, is there another of the LORD's prophets we can ask?"

7 "We could ask Micaiah son of Imlah," Ahab said. "But I hate Micaiah. He always has bad news for me."

"Don't say that!" Jehoshaphat replied.

8 Then Ahab sent someone to bring Micaiah as soon as possible.

9 All this time, Ahab and Jehoshaphat were dressed in their royal robes and were seated on their thrones at the threshing place near the gate of Samaria, listening to the prophets tell them what the LORD had said.

10 Zedekiah son of Chenaanah was one of the prophets. He had made some horns out of iron and shouted, "Ahab, the LORD says you will attack the Syrians like a bull with iron horns and wipe them out!"

11 All the prophets agreed that Ahab should attack the Syrians at Ramoth and promised that the LORD would help him defeat them.

12 Meanwhile, the messenger who went to get Micaiah whispered, "Micaiah, all the prophets have good news for Ahab. Now go and say the same thing."

13 "I'll say whatever the living LORD my God tells me to say," Micaiah replied.

14 Then Micaiah went up to Ahab, who asked, "Micaiah, should we attack Ramoth?"

"Yes!" Micaiah answered. "The LORD will help you capture the city."

15 Ahab shouted, "Micaiah, I've told you over and over again to tell me the truth! What does the LORD really say?"

16 Micaiah answered, "In a vision* I saw Israelite soldiers wandering around, lost in the hills like sheep without a shepherd. The LORD said, 'These troops have no leader. They should go home and not fight.'"

17 Ahab turned to Jehoshaphat and said, "I told you he would bring me bad news!"

18 Micaiah replied:

I then saw the LORD seated on his throne with every creature in heaven gathered around him. 19 The LORD asked, "Who can trick Ahab and make him go to Ramoth where he will be killed?"

They talked about it for a while, 20 then finally came forward and said to the LORD, "I can trick Ahab."

"How?" the LORD asked.

21 "I'll make Ahab's prophets lie to him."

"Good!" the LORD replied. "Now go and do it. You will be successful."

22 Ahab, this is exactly what has happened. The LORD made all your prophets lie to you, and he knows you will soon be destroyed.

23 Zedekiah walked over and slapped Micaiah on the face. Then he asked, "Do you really think the LORD would speak to you and not to me?"

24 Micaiah answered, "You'll find out on the day you have to hide in the back room of some house."

25 Ahab shouted, "Arrest Micaiah! Take him to Prince Joash and Governor Amon of Samaria. 26 Tell them to put him in prison and to give him nothing but bread and water until I come back safely."

27 Micaiah said, "If you do come back, I was wrong about what the LORD wanted me to say." Then he told the crowd, "Don't forget what I said!"

Ahab dies at Ramoth

This is also told in 1 Kings 22.29-35

28 Ahab and Jehoshaphat led their armies to Ramoth in Gilead. 29 Before they went into battle, Ahab said, "Jehoshaphat, I'll disguise myself, but you wear your royal robe." Ahab disguised himself and went into battle.

30 The king of Syria had ordered his chariot commanders to attack only Ahab. 31 So when

---

*18.2 attacking the city of Ramoth in Gilead: The Syrians had taken control of Ramoth (see 1 Kings 22.3,4).

*18.16 vision: In ancient times, prophets often told about future events from what they had seen in visions or dreams.

See also: 18.16: Num 27.17; Ezek 34.5; Matt 9.36; Mark 6.34.

they saw Jehoshaphat in his robe, they thought he was Ahab and started to attack him. But Jehoshaphat prayed, and the LORD made the Syrian soldiers stop. ³² And when they realized he wasn't Ahab, they left him alone.

³³ However, during the fighting a soldier shot an arrow without even aiming, and it hit Ahab between two pieces of his armour. He shouted to his chariot driver, "I've been hit! Get me out of here!"

³⁴ The fighting lasted all day, with Ahab propped up in his chariot so he could see the Syrian troops. He stayed there until evening, and by sundown he was dead.

CHAPTER 19

¹ Jehoshaphat returned safely to his palace in Jerusalem. ² But the prophet Jehu son of Hanani met him and said:

By helping with wicked Ahab, you have made friends with someone who hates the LORD. Now the LORD God is angry with you! ³ But not everything about you is bad. You destroyed the sacred poles* used in worshipping the goddess Asherah — that shows you have tried to obey the LORD.

Jehoshaphat appoints judges to settle cases

⁴ Jehoshaphat lived in Jerusalem, but he often travelled through his kingdom, from Beersheba in the south to the edge of the hill country of Ephraim in the north. He talked with the people and convinced them to turn back to the LORD God and worship him, just as their ancestors had done.

⁵ He assigned judges to each of the fortified cities in Judah ⁶ and told them:

Be careful when you make your decisions in court, because these are the LORD's people, and he will know what you decide. ⁷ So do your work in honour of him and know that he won't allow you to be unfair to anyone or to take bribes.

⁸ Jehoshaphat also chose some Levites, some priests, and some of the family leaders, and he appointed them to serve as judges in Jerusalem. ⁹ He told them:

Faithfully serve the LORD! ¹⁰ The people of Judah will bring you legal cases that involve every type of crime, including murder. You must settle these cases and

warn the people to stop sinning against the LORD, so that he won't get angry and punish Judah. Remember, if you follow these instructions, you won't be held responsible for anything that happens.

¹¹ Amariah the high priest will have the final say in any religious case. And Zebadiah the leader⁺ of the Judah tribe, will have the final say in all other cases. The rest of the Levites will serve as your assistants. Be brave, and I pray that the LORD will help you do right.

CHAPTER 20

Moab and Ammon are defeated

¹ Some time later, the armies of Moab and Ammon, together with the Meunites,⁺ went to war against Jehoshaphat. ² Messengers told Jehoshaphat, "A large army from Edom⁺ east of the Dead Sea has invaded our country. They have already reached En-Gedi."*

³ Jehoshaphat was afraid, so he asked the LORD what to do. He then told the people of Judah to go without eating to show their sorrow. ⁴ They immediately left for Jerusalem to ask for the LORD's help.

⁵ After everyone from Judah and Jerusalem had come together at the LORD's temple, Jehoshaphat stood in front of the new courtyard ⁶ and prayed:

You, LORD, are the God our ancestors worshipped, and from heaven you rule every nation in the world. You are so powerful that no one can defeat you. ⁷ Our God, you forced out the nations who lived in this land before your people Israel came here, and you gave it to the descendants of your friend Abraham for ever. ⁸ Our ancestors lived in this land and built a temple to honour you. ⁹ They believed that whenever this land is struck by war or disease or famine, your people can pray to you at the temple, and you will hear their prayer and save them.

¹⁰ You can see that the armies of Ammon, Moab, and Edom are attacking us! Those are the nations you would not let our ancestors invade on their way from Egypt, so these nations were not destroyed. ¹¹ Now they are coming to take back the

---

*20.2 En-Gedi: The Hebrew text has "Hazazon-Tamar, also known as En-Gedi", a city on the west shore of the Dead Sea, about forty kilometres south-east of Jerusalem.

See also: 20.7: Isa 41.8; Jam 2.23. 20.10: Deut 2.4-19.

*19.3 sacred poles: See the note at 14.3.

land you gave us. 12 Aren't you going to punish them? We won't stand a chance when this army attacks. We don't know what to do — we are begging for your help.

13 While every man, woman, and child of Judah was standing there at the temple, 14 the LORD's Spirit suddenly spoke to Jahaziel, a Levite from the Asaph clan.◦ 15 Then Jahaziel said:

Your Majesty and everyone from Judah and Jerusalem, the LORD says that you don't need to be afraid or let this powerful army discourage you. God will fight on your side! 16 So here's what you must do. Tomorrow the enemy armies will march through the desert around the town of Jeruel. March down and meet them at the town of Ziz as they come up the valley. 17 You won't even have to fight. Just take your positions and watch the LORD rescue you from your enemy. Don't be afraid. Just do as you're told. And as you march out tomorrow, the LORD will be there with you.

18 Jehoshaphat bowed low to the ground and everyone worshipped the LORD. 19 Then some Levites from the Kohath and Korah clans stood up and shouted praises to the LORD God of Israel.

20 Early the next morning, as everyone got ready to leave for the desert near Tekoa, Jehoshaphat stood up and said, "Listen my friends, if we trust the LORD God and believe what these prophets have told us, the LORD will help us, and we will be successful." 21 Then he explained his plan and appointed men to march in front of the army and praise the LORD for his holy power by singing:◦

"Praise the LORD!
    His love never ends."

22 As soon as they began singing, the LORD confused the enemy camp, 23 so that the Ammonite and Moabite troops attacked and completely destroyed those from Edom. Then they turned against each other and fought until the entire camp was wiped out! 24 When Judah's army reached the tower that overlooked the desert, they saw that every soldier in the enemy's army was lying dead on the ground. 25 So Jehoshaphat and his troops went into the camp to carry away everything of value. They found a large herd of livestock,◦ a lot of equipment, clothes,◦ and other valuable things. It took them three days to carry it all away, and there was still some left over.

26 Then on the fourth day, everyone came together in Beracah Valley and sang praises to the LORD. That's why that place was called Praise Valley.◦

27-28 Jehoshaphat led the crowd back to Jerusalem. And as they marched, they played harps and blew trumpets. They were very happy because the LORD had given them victory over their enemies, so when they reached the city, they went straight to the temple.

29 When the other nations heard how the LORD had fought against Judah's enemies, they were too afraid 30 to invade Judah. The LORD let Jehoshaphat's kingdom be at peace.

Jehoshaphat dies
This is also told in 1 Kings 22.41-50

31 Jehoshaphat was thirty-five years old when he became king of Judah, and he ruled from Jerusalem for twenty-five years. His mother was Azubah daughter of Shilhi. 32 Jehoshaphat obeyed the LORD, just as his father Asa had done, 33 but he did not destroy the local shrines.◦ So the people still worshipped foreign gods, instead of faithfully serving the God their ancestors had worshipped.

34 Everything else Jehoshaphat did while he was king is written in the records of Jehu son of Hanani that are included in *The History of the Kings of Israel*.

35 While Jehoshaphat was king, he signed a peace treaty with Ahaziah the wicked king of Israel. 36 They agreed to build several seagoing ships◦ at Ezion-Geber. 37 But the prophet Eliezer◦ warned Jehoshaphat, "The LORD will destroy these ships because you have supported Ahaziah." The ships were wrecked and never sailed.

CHAPTER 21

1 Jehoshaphat died and was buried beside his ancestors in Jerusalem, and his son Jehoram became king.

King Jehoram of Judah
This is also told in 2 Kings 8.16-24

2 King Jehoshaphat had seven sons: Jehoram, Azariah, Jehiel, Zechariah, Azariah, Michael, and Shephatiah. 3 Jehoshaphat gave each of them silver and gold, as well as other

---

*20.26 Beracah Valley . . . sang praises . . . Praise Valley: In Hebrew the name "Beracah" means "praise".
*20.36 seagoing ships: See the note at 9.21.

See also: 20.15-17: Deut 20.1-4. 20.17: Exod 14.13,14.

valuable gifts. He also put them in charge of the fortified cities in Judah, but he had chosen his eldest son Jehoram to succeed him as king.

⁴ After Jehoram had taken control of Judah, he had his brothers killed, as well as some of the nation's leaders. ⁵ He was thirty-two years old when he became king, and he ruled eight years from Jerusalem.

⁶ Jehoram married Ahab's daughter and followed the sinful example of Ahab's family and the other kings of Israel. He disobeyed the LORD by doing wrong, ⁷ but because the LORD had made a solemn promise to King David that someone from his family would always rule in Judah, he refused to wipe out David's descendants.

⁸ While Jehoram was king, the people of Edom rebelled and chose their own king. ⁹ Jehoram, his officers, and his cavalry marched to Edom, where the Edomite army surrounded them. He escaped during the night, ¹⁰ but Judah was never able to regain control of Edom. Even the town of Libnah* rebelled at that time.

Those things happened because Jehoram had turned away from the LORD, the God his ancestors had worshipped. ¹¹ Jehoram even built local shrines* in the hills of Judah and let the people sin against the LORD by worshipping foreign gods.

¹² One day, Jehoram received a letter from Elijah the prophet that said:

I have a message for you from the LORD God your ancestor David worshipped. He knows that you have not followed the example of Jehoshaphat your father or Asa your grandfather. ¹³ Instead you have acted like those sinful kings of Israel and have encouraged the people of Judah to stop worshipping the LORD, just as Ahab and his descendants did. You even murdered your own brothers, who were better men than you.

¹⁴ Because you have done these terrible things, the LORD will severely punish the people in your kingdom, including your own family, and he will destroy everything you own. ¹⁵ You will be struck with a painful stomach disease and suffer until you die.

¹⁶ The LORD later caused the Philistines and the Arabs who lived near the Ethiopians* to become angry with Jehoram. ¹⁷ They invaded Judah and stole the royal property from the palace, and they led Jehoram's wives and sons away as prisoners. The only one left behind was Ahaziah,' his youngest son.

¹⁸ After this happened, the LORD struck Jehoram with an incurable stomach disease. ¹⁹ About two years later, Jehoram died in terrible pain. No bonfire was built to honour him, even though the people had done this for his ancestors.

²⁰ Jehoram was thirty-two years old when he became king, and he ruled eight years from Jerusalem. He died, and no one even felt sad. He was buried in Jerusalem, but not in the royal tombs.

CHAPTER 22

King Ahaziah of Judah

This is also told in 2 Kings 8.25–29; 9.21,27,28

¹ Earlier, when the Arabs led a raid against Judah, they killed all of Jehoram's sons, except Ahaziah, the youngest one. So the people of Jerusalem crowned him their king. ² He was twenty-two* years old at the time, and he ruled only one year from Jerusalem.

Ahaziah's mother was Athaliah, a granddaughter of King Omri of Israel, ³ and she encouraged her son to sin against the LORD. He followed the evil example of King Ahab and his descendants. ⁴ In fact, after his father's death, Ahaziah sinned against the LORD by appointing some of Ahab's relatives to be his advisers.

Their advice led to his downfall. ⁵ He listened to them and went with King Joram of Israel to attack King Hazael and the Syrian troops at Ramoth in Gilead. Joram was wounded in that battle, ⁶ and he went to the town of Jezreel to recover. And Ahaziah later went there to visit him. ⁷ It was during that visit that God had Ahaziah put to death.

When Ahaziah arrived at Jezreel, he and Joram went to meet with Jehu, grandson of Nimshi. The LORD had already told Jehu to kill every male in Ahab's family, ⁸ and while Jehu was doing that, he saw some of Judah's leaders and Ahaziah's nephews who had come with Ahaziah. Jehu killed them on the spot, ⁹ then gave orders to find Ahaziah. Jehu's officers found him hiding in Samaria. They brought Ahaziah to Jehu, who

---

*21.10 Even the town of Libnah: This was a town on the border between Philistia and Judah, which means that Jehoram was facing rebellion on both sides of his kingdom.

See also: 21.7: 1 King 11.36. 21.8: Gen 27.40.

*21.16 Ethiopians: See the note at 12.3.

immediately put him to death. They buried Ahaziah only because they respected Jehoshaphat his grandfather, who had done his best to obey the LORD.

There was no one from Ahaziah's family left to become king of Judah.

Queen Athaliah of Judah

This is also told in 2 Kings 11.1-3

¹⁰ As soon as Athaliah heard that her son King Ahaziah was dead, she decided to kill any relative who could possibly become king. She would have done just that, ¹¹ but Jehosheba' rescued Joash son of Ahaziah just as the others were about to be murdered. Jehosheba, who was Jehoram's daughter and Ahaziah's half-sister, was married to Jehoiada the priest. So she was able to hide her nephew Joash and his personal servant in a bedroom in the LORD's temple where he was safe from Athaliah. ¹² Joash hid in the temple with them for six years while Athaliah ruled as queen of Judah.

CHAPTER 23

Jehoiada makes Joash king of Judah

This is also told in 2 Kings 11.4-21

¹ After Ahaziah's son Joash had hidden in the temple for six years, Jehoiada the priest knew that something had to be done. So he made sure he had the support of several army officers. They were Azariah son of Jeroham, Ishmael son of Jehohanan, Azariah son of Obed, Maaseiah son of Adaiah, and Elishaphat son of Zichri. ² These five men went to the towns in Judah and called together the Levites and the clan leaders. They all came to Jerusalem ³ and gathered at the temple, where they agreed to help Joash. Jehoiada said to them:

Joash will be our next king, because long ago the LORD promised that one of David's descendants would always be king. ⁴ Here is what we will do. Three groups of priests and Levites will be on guard duty on the Sabbath — one group will guard the gates of the temple, ⁵ one will guard the palace, and the other will guard Foundation Gate. The rest of you will stand guard in the temple courtyards. ⁶ Only the priests and Levites who are on duty will be able to enter the temple, because they will be the only ones who have gone through the

ceremony to make themselves clean and acceptable. The others must stay outside in the courtyards, just as the LORD has commanded. ⁷ You Levites must protect King Joash. Don't let him out of your sight! And keep your swords ready to kill anyone who comes into the temple.

⁸ The Levites and the people of Judah followed Jehoiada's orders. The guards going off duty were not allowed to go home, and so each commander had all his guards available — those going off duty as well as those coming on duty. ⁹ Jehoiada went into the temple and brought out the swords and shields that had belonged to King David, and he gave them to the commanders. ¹⁰ They gave the weapons to the guards, and Jehoiada then made sure that the guards took their positions around the temple and the altar to protect the king on every side.

¹¹ Jehoiada and his sons brought Joash outside, where they placed the crown on his head and gave him a copy of the instructions for ruling the nation. Olive oil was poured on his head to show that he was now king, and the crowd cheered and shouted, "Long live the king!"

¹² As soon as Queen Athaliah heard the crowd cheering for Joash, she went to the temple. ¹³ There she saw Joash standing by one of the columns near the entrance, which was the usual place for the king. The commanders and the trumpet players were standing next to him, and the musicians were playing instruments and leading the people as they celebrated and blew trumpets. Athaliah tore her clothes in anger and shouted, "You betrayed me, you traitors!"

¹⁴ Straight away, Jehoiada said to the army commanders, "Don't kill her near the LORD's temple. Take her out in front of the troops, and be sure to kill all her followers!" ¹⁵ She tried to escape, but the commanders caught and killed her near the gate where horses are led into the palace.

¹⁶ Jehoiada asked King Joash and the people to join with him in being faithful to the LORD. They agreed, ¹⁷ then rushed to the temple of the god Baal and tore it down. They smashed the altars and the idols and killed Mattan the priest of Baal in front of the altars.

¹⁸ Jehoiada assigned the priests and Levites their duties at the temple, just as David had done. They were in charge of offering sacrifices to the LORD according to the Law of Moses, and they were responsible for leading the celebrations with singing. ¹⁹ Jehoiada

ordered the guards at the temple gates to keep out anyone who was unclean.

²⁰ Finally, Jehoiada called together the army commanders, the most important citizens of Judah, and the government officials. The crowd of people followed them as they led Joash from the temple, through the Upper Gate, and into the palace, where he took his place as king of Judah.

²¹ Everyone celebrated because Athaliah had been killed and Jerusalem was peaceful again.

CHAPTER 24

King Joash of Judah

This is also told in 2 Kings 12.1–16

¹ Joash was only seven years old when he became king of Judah, and he ruled forty years from Jerusalem. His mother Zibiah was from the town of Beersheba.

² While Jehoiada the priest was alive, Joash obeyed the LORD by doing right. ³ Jehoiada even chose two women for Joash to marry so he could have a family.

⁴ Some time later, Joash decided it was time to repair the temple. ⁵ He called together the priests and Levites and said, "Go everywhere in Judah and collect the annual tax from the people. I want this done straight away — we need that money to repair the temple."

But the Levites were in no hurry to follow the king's orders. ⁶ So he sent for Jehoiada the high priest and asked, "Why didn't you send the Levites to collect the taxes? The LORD's servant Moses and the people agreed long ago that this tax would be collected and used to pay for the upkeep of the sacred tent. ⁷ And now we need it to repair the temple because the sons of that evil woman Athaliah came in and wrecked it. They even used some of the sacred objects to worship the god Baal."

⁸ Joash gave orders for a wooden box to be made and had it placed outside, near the gate of the temple. ⁹ He then sent letters everywhere in Judah and Jerusalem, asking everyone to bring their taxes to the temple, just as Moses had required their ancestors to do.

¹⁰ The people and their leaders agreed, and they brought their money to Jerusalem and placed it in the box. ¹¹ Each day, after the Levites took the box into the temple, the king's secretary and the high priest's assistant would take out the money and count it. Then the empty box would be taken back outside.

This happened day after day, and soon a large amount of money was collected. ¹² Joash and Jehoiada turned the money over to the men who were supervising the repairs to the temple. They used the money to hire stonecutters, carpenters, and experts in working with iron and bronze.

¹³ These workers went straight to work repairing the temple, and when they had finished, it looked as good as new. ¹⁴ They did not use all the tax money for the repairs, so the rest of it was handed over to Joash and Jehoiada, who then used it to make dishes and other gold and silver objects for the temple.

Sacrifices to please the LORD* were offered regularly in the temple for as long as Jehoiada lived. ¹⁵ He died at the ripe old age of one hundred and thirty years, ¹⁶ and he was buried in the royal tombs in Jerusalem, because he had done so much good for the people of Israel, for God, and for the temple.

Joash turns away from the LORD

¹⁷ After the death of Jehoiada the priest, the leaders of Judah went to Joash and talked him into doing what they wanted. ¹⁸ Straight away, the people of Judah stopped worshipping in the temple of the LORD God, and they started worshipping idols and the symbols of the goddess Asherah. These sinful things made the LORD God angry with the people of Judah and Jerusalem, ¹⁹ but he still sent prophets who warned them to turn back to him. The people refused to listen.

²⁰ God's Spirit spoke to Zechariah son of Jehoiada the priest, and Zechariah told everyone that God was saying: "Why are you disobeying me and my laws? This will only bring punishment! You have deserted me, so now I will desert you."

²¹⁻²² King Joash forgot that Zechariah's father had always been a loyal friend. So when the people of Judah plotted to kill Zechariah, Joash joined them and gave orders for them to stone him to death in the courtyard of the temple. As Zechariah was dying, he said, "I pray that the LORD will see this and punish all of you."

Joash is killed

²³ In the spring of the following year, the Syrian army invaded Judah and Jerusalem,

---

*24.14 Sacrifices to please the LORD: See the note at 1.6.

See also: 24.6: Exod 30.11–16.

See also: 24.20,21: Matt 23.35; Luke 11.51.

killing all the nation's leaders. They collected everything of value that belonged to the people and took it back to their king in Damascus. 24 The Syrian army was very small, but the LORD let them defeat Judah's large army, because he was punishing Joash and the people of Judah for turning away from him.

25-26 Joash was severely wounded during the battle, and as soon as the Syrians left Judah, two of his officials, Zabad and Jehozabad,* decided to avenge the death of Zechariah. They plotted and killed Joash while he was in bed, recovering from his wounds. Joash was buried in Jerusalem, but not in the royal tombs. 27 *The History of the Kings* also tells more about the sons of Joash, what the prophets said about him, and how he repaired the temple. Amaziah son of Joash became king after his father's death.

CHAPTER 25

King Amaziah of Judah

This is also told in 2 Kings 14.1–6

1 Amaziah was twenty-five years old when he became king, and he ruled twenty-nine years from Jerusalem, the home town of his mother Jehoaddin.*

2 Even though Amaziah obeyed the LORD by doing right, he refused to be completely faithful. 3 For example, as soon as he had control of Judah, he arrested and killed the officers who had murdered his father. 4 But the children of those officers were not killed; the LORD had commanded in the Law of Moses that only the people who sinned were to be punished.*

Edom is defeated

This is also told in 2 Kings 14.7

5 Amaziah sent a message to the tribes of Judah and Benjamin and called together all the men who were twenty years and older. Three hundred thousand men went to Jerusalem, all of them ready for battle and able to fight with spears and shields. Amaziah grouped these soldiers according to their clans and put them under the command of his army officers. 6 Amaziah also paid about three thousand four hundred kilograms of silver to hire one hundred thousand soldiers from Israel.

7 One of God's prophets said, "Your Majesty, don't let these Israelite soldiers march into battle with you. The LORD has refused to help anyone from the northern kingdom of Israel, 8 and so he will let your enemies defeat you, even if you fight hard. He is the one who brings both victory and defeat."

9 Amaziah replied, "What am I supposed to do about all the silver I paid those troops?"

"The LORD will give you back even more than you paid," the prophet answered.

10 Amaziah ordered the troops from Israel to go home, but when they left, they were furious with the people of Judah.

11 After Amaziah got his courage back, he led his troops to Salt Valley, where he killed ten thousand Edomite soldiers in battle. 12 He captured ten thousand more soldiers and dragged them to the top of a high cliff. Then he pushed them over the side, and they were all killed on the rocks below.

13 Meanwhile, the Israelite troops that Amaziah had sent home raided the towns in Judah between Samaria and Beth-Horon. They killed three thousand people and carried off their possessions.

14 After Amaziah had defeated the Edomite army, he returned to Jerusalem. He took with him the idols of the Edomite gods and set them up. Then he bowed down and offered them sacrifices. 15 This made the LORD very angry, and he sent a prophet to ask Amaziah, "Why would you worship these foreign gods that couldn't even save their own people from your attack?"

16 But before the prophet finished speaking, Amaziah interrupted and said, "You're not one of my advisers! Don't say another word, or I'll have you killed."

The prophet stopped. But then he added, "First you sinned and now you've ignored my warning. It's clear that God has decided to punish you!"

Israel defeats Judah

This is also told in 2 Kings 14.8–14

17 King Amaziah of Judah talked with his officials, then sent a message to King Jehoash* of Israel: "Come out and face me in battle!"

18 Jehoash sent back a reply that said:

Once upon a time, a small thorn bush in Lebanon arranged the marriage between his son and the daughter of a large cedar tree. But a wild animal came along and trampled the small bush.

---

*25.4 the LORD had commanded . . . punished: See Deuteronomy 24.16.

See also: 25.4: Deut 24.16.

[19] Amaziah, you think you're so powerful because you defeated Edom. But stay at home and do your celebrating. If you cause any trouble, both you and your kingdom of Judah will be destroyed.

[20] God made Amaziah stubborn because he was planning to punish him for worshipping the Edomite gods. Amaziah refused to listen to Jehoash's warning, [21] so Jehoash led his army to the town of Beth-Shemesh in Judah to attack Amaziah and his troops. [22] During the battle, Judah's army was crushed. Every soldier from Judah ran back home, [23] and Jehoash captured Amaziah.

Jehoash took Amaziah with him when he went to attack Jerusalem. Jehoash broke down the city wall from Ephraim Gate to Corner Gate, a section nearly two hundred metres long. [24] He carried away the gold, the silver, and all the valuable furnishings from God's temple where the descendants of Obed-Edom stood guard. He robbed the king's treasury, took hostages, then returned to Samaria.

Amaziah is killed

This is also told in 2 Kings 14.15–20

[25] Amaziah lived fifteen years after Jehoash died. [26] Everything else Amaziah did while he was king is written in *The History of the Kings of Judah and Israel.*

[27] As soon as Amaziah started disobeying the LORD, some people in Jerusalem plotted against Amaziah. He was able to escape to the town of Lachish, but another group of people caught him and killed him there. [28] His body was taken to Jerusalem on horseback and buried beside his ancestors.

CHAPTER 26

King Uzziah of Judah

This is also told in 2 Kings 14.21,22; 15.1–7

[1-3] After the death of King Amaziah, the people of Judah crowned his son Uzziah' king, even though he was only sixteen at the time. Uzziah ruled fifty-two years from Jerusalem, the home town of his mother Jecoliah. During his rule, he recaptured and rebuilt the town of Elath.

[4] He obeyed the LORD by doing right, as his father Amaziah had done. [5] Zechariah was Uzziah's adviser and taught him to obey God. And so, as long as Zechariah was alive, Uzziah was faithful to God, and God made him successful.

[6] While Uzziah was king, he started a war against the Philistines. He smashed the walls of the cities of Gath, Jabneh, and Ashdod, then rebuilt towns around Ashdod and in other parts of Philistia. [7] God helped him defeat the Philistines, the Arabs living in Gur-Baal, and the Meunites. [8] Even the Ammonites paid taxes to Uzziah. He became very powerful, and people who lived as far away as Egypt heard about him.

[9] In Jerusalem, Uzziah built fortified towers at the Corner Gate, the Valley Gate, and the place where the city wall turned inward.' [10] He also built defence towers out in the desert.

He owned such a large herd of livestock in the western foothills and in the flat lands, that he had cisterns dug there to catch the rainwater. He loved farming, so he had crops and vineyards planted in the hill country wherever there was fertile soil, and he hired farmers to take care of them.

[11] Uzziah's army was always ready for battle. Jeiel and Maaseiah were the officers who kept track of the number of soldiers, and these two men were under the command of Hananiah, one of Uzziah's officials. [12-13] There were 307,500 trained soldiers, all under the command of 2,600 clan leaders. These powerful troops protected the king against any enemy. [14] Uzziah supplied his army with shields, spears, helmets, armour, bows, and stones used for slinging. [15] Some of his skilled workers invented machines that could shoot arrows and sling large stones. Uzziah set these up in Jerusalem at his defence towers and at the corners of the city wall.

God helped Uzziah become more and more powerful, and he was famous all over the world.

Uzziah becomes too proud

[16] Uzziah became proud of his power, and this led to his downfall.

One day, Uzziah disobeyed the LORD his God by going into the temple and burning incense as an offering to him.* [17] Azariah the priest and eighty other brave priests followed Uzziah into the temple [18] and said, "Your Majesty, this isn't right! You are not allowed to burn incense to the LORD. That must be

---

* 26.16 going into the temple and burning incense as an offering to him: This was to be done only by priests (see Exodus 30.1–10; Numbers 16.39,40).
See also: 26.18: Exod 30.7,8; Num 3.10.

done only by priests who are descendants of Aaron. You will have to leave! You have sinned against the LORD, and so he will no longer bless you."

[19] Uzziah, who was standing next to the incense altar at the time, was holding the incense burner, ready to offer incense to the LORD. He became very angry when he heard Azariah's warning, and leprosy* suddenly appeared on his forehead! [20] Azariah and the other priests saw it and immediately told him to leave the temple. Uzziah realized that the LORD had punished him, so he hurried to get outside.

[21] Uzziah had leprosy for the rest of his life. He was no longer allowed in the temple or in his own palace. That's why his son Jotham lived there and ruled in his place.

[22] Everything else Uzziah did while he was king is in the records written by the prophet Isaiah son of Amoz. [23] Since Uzziah had leprosy, he could not be buried in the royal tombs. Instead, he was buried in a nearby cemetery that the kings owned. His son Jotham then became king.

CHAPTER 27

King Jotham of Judah

This is also told in 2 Kings 15.32-38

[1] Jotham was twenty-five years old when he became king of Judah, and he ruled from Jerusalem for sixteen years. Jerushah his mother was the daughter of Zadok.

[2] Jotham obeyed the LORD and did right. He followed the example of his father Uzziah, except he never burnt incense in the temple as his father had done. But the people of Judah kept sinning against the LORD.

[3] Jotham rebuilt the Upper Gate of the temple and did a lot of work to repair the wall near Mount Ophel. [4] He built towns in the mountains of Judah and built fortresses and defence towers in the forests.

[5] During his rule he attacked and defeated the Ammonites. Then every year for the next three years, he forced them to pay three thousand four hundred kilogrammes of silver, one thousand tonnes of wheat, and one thousand tonnes of barley.

[6] Jotham remained faithful to the LORD his God and became a very powerful king.

[7] Everything else Jotham did while he was king, including the wars he fought, is written in *The History of the Kings of Israel and Judah*. [8] After he had ruled Judah sixteen years, he died at the age of forty-one. [9] He was buried in Jerusalem, and his son Ahaz became king.

CHAPTER 28

King Ahaz of Judah

This is also told in 2 Kings 16.1-4

[1] Ahaz was twenty years old when he became king of Judah, and he ruled from Jerusalem for sixteen years.

Ahaz was nothing like his ancestor David. Ahaz disobeyed the LORD [2] and was as sinful as the kings of Israel. He made idols of the god Baal, [3] and he offered sacrifices in Hinnom Valley. Worst of all, Ahaz sacrificed his own sons, which was a disgusting custom of the nations that the LORD had forced out of Israel. [4] Ahaz offered sacrifices at the local shrines,* as well as on every hill and in the shade of large trees.

Syria and Israel attack Judah

This is also told in 2 Kings 16.5,6

[5-6] Ahaz and the people of Judah sinned and turned away from the LORD, the God their ancestors had worshipped. So the LORD punished them by letting their enemies defeat them.

The king of Syria attacked Judah and took many of its people to Damascus as prisoners. King Pekah* of Israel later defeated Judah and killed one hundred and twenty thousand of its bravest soldiers in one day. [7] During that battle, an Israelite soldier named Zichri killed three men from Judah: Maaseiah the king's son; Azrikam, the official in charge of the palace; and Elkanah, the king's second in command. [8] The Israelite troops captured two hundred thousand women and children and took them back to their capital city of Samaria, along with a large amount of their possessions. They did these things even though the people of Judah were their own relatives.

Oded the prophet condemns Israel

[9] Oded lived in Samaria and was one of the LORD's prophets. He met Israel's army on their way back from Judah and said to them:

---

*26.19 leprosy: The word translated "leprosy" was used for many different kinds of skin diseases.
See also: 26.23: Isa 6.1.

See also: 28.5,6: 2 King 16.5; Isa 7.1.

The LORD God of your ancestors let you defeat Judah's army only because he was angry with them. But you should not have been so cruel! 10 If you make slaves of the people of Judah and Jerusalem, you will be as guilty as if sinning against the LORD.

11 Send these prisoners back home — they are your own relatives. If you don't, the LORD will punish you in his anger.

12 About the same time, four of Israel's leaders arrived. They were Azariah son of Johanan, Berechiah son of Meshillemoth, Jehizkiah son of Shallum, and Amasa son of Hadlai. They agreed with Oded that the Israelite troops were wrong, 13 and they said:

If you bring these prisoners into Samaria, that will be one more thing we've done to sin against the LORD. And he is already angry enough with us.

14 So in front of the leaders and the crowd, the troops handed over their prisoners and the property they had taken from Judah. 15 The four leaders took some of the stolen clothes and gave them to the prisoners who needed something to wear. They later gave them all a new change of clothes and shoes, then provided something for them to eat and drink, and cleaned their wounds with olive oil. They gave donkeys to those who were too weak to walk, and led all of them back to Jericho, the city known for its palm trees. The leaders then returned to Samaria.

Ahaz asks the king of Assyria for help

This is also told in 2 Kings 16.7–9

16-18 Some time later, the Edomites attacked the eastern part of Judah again and carried away prisoners. And at the same time, the Philistines raided towns in the western foothills and in the Southern Desert. They conquered the towns of Beth-Shemesh, Aijalon, Gederoth, Soco, Timnah, and Gimzo, including the villages around them. Then some of the Philistines went to live in these places.

Ahaz sent a message to King Tiglath Pileser of Assyria and begged him for help. 19 But God was punishing Judah with these disasters, because Ahaz had disobeyed him and refused to stop Judah from sinning. 20 So Tiglath Pileser came to Judah, but instead of helping, he made things worse. 21 Ahaz gave him gifts from the LORD's temple and the king's palace, as well as from the homes of

Israel's other leaders. The Assyrian king still refused to help Ahaz.

The final sin of Ahaz and his death

22 Even after all these terrible things happened to Ahaz, he sinned against the LORD even worse than before. 23 He said to himself, "The Syrian gods must have helped their kings defeat me. Perhaps if I offer sacrifices to those gods, they will help me." That was the sin that finally led to the downfall of Ahaz, as well as to the destruction of Judah.

24 Ahaz collected all the furnishings of the temple and smashed them to pieces. Then he locked the doors to the temple and set up altars to foreign gods on every street corner in Jerusalem. 25 In every city and town in Judah he built local shrines* to worship foreign gods. All this made the LORD God of his ancestors very angry.

26 Everything else Ahaz did while he was king is written in *The History of the Kings of Judah and Israel.* 27 Ahaz died and was buried in Jerusalem, but not in the royal tombs. His son Hezekiah then became king.

King Hezekiah and the Assyrian invasion

CHAPTER 29

King Hezekiah of Judah

This is also told in 2 Kings 18.1–3

1 Hezekiah was twenty-five years old when he became king of Judah, and he ruled twenty-nine years from Jerusalem. His mother was Abijah daughter of Zechariah. 2 Hezekiah obeyed the LORD by doing right, just as his ancestor David had done.

The temple is purified

3 In the first month* of the first year of Hezekiah's rule, he unlocked the doors to the LORD's temple and had them repaired.* 4 Then he called the priests and Levites to the east courtyard of the temple 5 and said:

---

*29.3 first month: Abib (also called Nisan), the first month of the Hebrew calendar, from about mid-March to mid-April.
*29.3 he unlocked the doors . . . repaired: King Ahaz had locked the doors and stopped everyone from worshiping the LORD (see 28.24,25).
See also: 28.27: Isa 14.28.

It's time to purify the temple of the LORD God of our ancestors. You Levites must first go through the ceremony to make yourselves clean, then go into the temple and bring out everything that is unclean and unacceptable to the LORD. ⁶ Some of our ancestors were unfaithful and disobeyed the LORD our God. Not only did they turn their backs on the LORD, but they also completely ignored his temple. ⁷ They locked the doors, then let the lamps go out and stopped burning incense and offering sacrifices to him. ⁸ The LORD became terribly angry with the people of Judah and Jerusalem, and everyone was shocked and horrified at what he did to punish them. Not only were ⁹ our ancestors killed in battle, but our own children and wives were taken captive.

¹⁰ So I have decided to renew our agreement with the LORD God of Israel. Perhaps then he will stop being so angry with us. ¹¹ Let's not waste any time, my friends. You are the ones who have been chosen to be the LORD's priests and to offer him sacrifices.

¹²⁻¹⁴ When Hezekiah finished talking, the following Levite leaders went to work:

Mahath son of Amasai and Joel son of Azariah from the Kohath clan; Kish son of Abdi and Azariah son of Jehallelel from the Merari clan; Joah son of Zimmah and Eden son of Joah from the Gershon clan; Shimri and Jeuel from the Elizaphan clan; Zechariah and Mattaniah from the Asaph clan; Jehuel and Shimei from the Heman clan; Shemaiah and Uzziel from the Jeduthun clan.

¹⁵ These leaders gathered together the rest of the Levites, and they all went through the ceremony to make themselves clean. Then they began to purify the temple according to the Law of the LORD, just as Hezekiah had commanded.

¹⁶ The priests went into the temple and carried out everything that was unclean. They put these things in the courtyard, and from there, the Levites carried them outside the city to Kidron Valley.

¹⁷ The priests and Levites began their work on the first day of the first month.* It took them one week to purify the courtyards of the temple and another week to purify the temple. On the sixteenth day of that same month ¹⁸ they went back to Hezekiah and said:

Your Majesty, we have finished our work. The entire temple is now pure again, and so

is the altar and its utensils, as well as the table for the sacred loaves of bread and its utensils. ¹⁹ And we have brought back all the things that King Ahaz took from the temple during the time he was unfaithful to God. We purified them and put them back in front of the altar.

Worship in the temple

²⁰ Straight away, Hezekiah called together the officials of Jerusalem, and they went to the temple. ²¹ They brought with them seven bulls, seven rams, seven lambs, and seven goats' as sacrifices to take away the sins of Hezekiah's family and of the people of Judah, as well as to purify the temple. Hezekiah told the priests, who were descendants of Aaron, to sacrifice these animals on the altar.

²² The priests killed the bulls, the rams, and the lambs, then splattered the blood on the altar. ²³ They took the goats to Hezekiah and the worshippers, and they laid their hands on the animals. ²⁴ The priests then killed the goats and splattered the blood on the altar as a sacrifice to take away the sins of everyone in Israel, because Hezekiah had commanded that these sacrifices be made for all the people of Israel.

²⁵ Next, Hezekiah assigned the Levites to their places in the temple. He gave them cymbals, harps, and other stringed instruments, according to the instructions that the LORD had given King David and the two prophets, Gad and Nathan. ²⁶ The Levites were ready to play the instruments that had belonged to David; the priests were ready to blow the trumpets.

²⁷ As soon as Hezekiah gave the signal for the sacrifices to be burnt on the altar, the musicians began singing praises to the LORD and playing their instruments, ²⁸ and everyone worshipped the LORD. This continued until the last animal was sacrificed.

²⁹ After that, Hezekiah and the crowd of worshippers knelt down and worshipped the LORD. ³⁰ Then Hezekiah and his officials ordered the Levites to sing the songs of praise that David and Asaph the prophet had written. And so they bowed down and joyfully sang praises to the LORD.

³¹ Hezekiah said to the crowd, "Now that you are once again acceptable to the LORD, bring sacrifices and offerings to give him thanks."

The people did this, and some of them voluntarily brought animals to be offered as sacrifices. ³² Seventy bulls, one hundred

---

*29.17 first month: See the note at 29.3.

rams, and two hundred lambs were brought as sacrifices to please the LORD;* ³³ six hundred bulls and three thousand sheep were brought as sacrifices to ask the LORD's blessing.* ³⁴ There were not enough priests to skin all these animals, because many of the priests had not taken the time to go through the ceremony to make themselves clean. However, since all the Levites had made themselves clean, they helped the priests until the last animal was skinned. ³⁵ Besides all the sacrifices that were burnt on the altar, the fat from the other animal sacrifices was burnt, and the offerings of wine were poured over the altar.

So the temple was once again used for worshipping the LORD. ³⁶ Hezekiah and the people of Judah celebrated, because God had helped them make this happen so quickly.

CHAPTER 30

Hezekiah prepares to celebrate Passover

¹⁻⁴ Passover wasn't celebrated in the first month,* which was the usual time, because many of the priests were still unclean and unacceptable to serve, and because not everyone in Judah had come to Jerusalem for the festival. So Hezekiah, his officials, and the people agreed to celebrate Passover in the second month.*

Hezekiah sent a message to everyone in Israel and Judah, including those in the territories of Ephraim and West Manasseh, inviting them to the temple in Jerusalem for the celebration of Passover in honour of the LORD God of Israel. ⁵ Everyone from Beersheba in the south to Dan in the north was invited. This was the largest crowd of people that had ever celebrated Passover, according to the official records.

⁶ Hezekiah's messengers went everywhere in Israel and Judah with the following letter:

People of Israel, now that you have survived the invasion of the Assyrian kings,* it's time for you to turn back to the LORD God our ancestors Abraham, Isaac and Jacob worshipped. If you do this, he will stop being angry. ⁷ Don't follow the example of your ancestors and your Israelite relatives in the north. They were unfaithful to the LORD, and he punished them horribly. ⁸ Don't be stubborn like your ancestors. Decide now to obey the LORD our God! Come to Jerusalem and worship him in the temple that will belong to him for ever. Then he will stop being angry, ⁹ and the enemies who have captured your families will show pity and send them back home. The LORD God is kind and merciful, and if you turn back to him, he will no longer turn his back on you.

¹⁰ The messengers went to every town in Ephraim and West Manasseh as far north as the territory of Zebulun, but everyone laughed and insulted them. ¹¹ Only a few people from the tribes of Asher, West Manasseh, and Zebulun were humble and went to Jerusalem. ¹² God also made everyone in Judah eager to do what Hezekiah and his officials had commanded.

Passover is celebrated

¹³ In the second month,* a large crowd of people gathered in Jerusalem to celebrate the Festival of Thin Bread.* ¹⁴ They took all the foreign altars and incense altars in Jerusalem and threw them into Kidron Valley.

¹⁵⁻¹⁷ Then, on the fourteenth day of that same month, the Levites began killing the lambs for Passover, because many of the worshippers were unclean and were not allowed to kill their own lambs. Meanwhile, some of the priests and Levites felt ashamed because they had not gone through the ceremony to make themselves clean. They immediately went through that ceremony and went to the temple, where they offered sacrifices to please the LORD.* Then the priests and Levites took their positions, according to the Law of Moses, the servant of God.

---

*29.32 sacrifices to please the LORD: See the note at 1.6.
*29.33 sacrifices to ask the LORD's blessing: These sacrifices have traditionally been called "peace offerings" or "offerings of well-being". A main purpose was to ask for the LORD's blessing, and so in the CEV they are sometimes called "sacrifices to ask the LORD's blessing".
*30.1–4 first month: See the note at 29.3.
*30.1–4 second month: See the note at 3.1,2.
See also: 30.2,3; Num 9.9–11.

*30.6 the invasion of the Assyrian kings: See 2 Kings 17.1–22.
*30.13 second month: See the note at 3.1,2.
*30.13 the Festival of Thin Bread: The celebration of this Festival began one day after Passover. And so these two festivals were often referred to as one.
*30.15–17 sacrifices to please the LORD: See the note at 1.6.

As the Levites killed the lambs, they handed some of the blood to the priests, who splattered it on the altar.

18-19 Most of the people who came from Ephraim, West Manasseh, Issachar, and Zebulun had not made themselves clean, but they ignored God's Law and ate the Passover lambs anyway. Hezekiah found out what they had done and prayed, "LORD God, these people are unclean according to the laws of holiness. But they are worshipping you, just as their ancestors did. So, please be kind and forgive them." 20 The LORD answered Hezekiah's prayer and did not punish them.

21 The worshippers in Jerusalem were very happy and celebrated the Festival for seven days. The Levites and priests sang praises to the LORD every day and played their instruments. 22 Hezekiah thanked the Levites for doing such a good job, leading the celebration.

The worshippers celebrated for seven days by offering sacrifices, by eating the sacred meals, and by praising the LORD God of their ancestors. 23 Everyone was so excited that they agreed to celebrate seven more days.

24 So Hezekiah gave the people one thousand bulls and seven thousand sheep to be offered as sacrifices and to be used as food for the sacred meals. His officials gave one thousand bulls and ten thousand sheep, and many more priests agreed to go through the ceremony to make themselves clean.

25 Everyone was very happy, including those from Judah and Israel, the priests and Levites, and the foreigners living in Judah and Israel. 26 It was the biggest celebration in Jerusalem since the days of King Solomon, the son of David. 27 The priests and Levites asked God to bless the people, and from his home in heaven, he did.

CHAPTER 31

The people destroy the local shrines

This is also told in 2 Kings 18.4

1 After the Festival, the people went to every town in Judah and smashed the stone images of foreign gods and cut down the sacred poles* for worshipping the goddess Asherah. They destroyed all the local shrines* and foreign altars in Judah, as well as those in the territories of Benjamin, Ephraim, and West Manasseh. Then everyone went home.

Offerings for the priests and Levites

2 Hezekiah divided the priests and Levites into groups, according to their duties. Then he assigned them the responsibilities of offering sacrifices to please the LORD* and sacrifices to ask his blessing.* He also appointed people to serve at the temple and to sing praises at the temple gates. 3 Hezekiah provided animals from his own herds and flocks to use for the morning and evening sacrifices, as well as for the sacrifices during the Sabbath celebrations, the New Moon Festivals, and the other religious feasts required by the Law of the LORD.

4 He told the people of Jerusalem to bring the offerings that were to be given to the priests and Levites, so that they would have time to serve the LORD with their work. 5 As soon as the people heard what the king wanted, they brought a tenth of everything they owned, including their best grain, wine, olive oil, honey, and other crops. 6 The people from the other towns of Judah brought a tenth of their herds and flocks, as well as a tenth of anything they had dedicated to the LORD. 7 The people started bringing their offerings to Jerusalem in the third month,* and the last ones arrived four months later. 8 When Hezekiah and his officials saw these offerings, they thanked the LORD and the people.

9 Hezekiah asked the priests and Levites about the large amount of offerings. 10 The high priest at the time was Azariah, a descendant of Zadok, and he replied, "Ever since the people have been bringing us their offerings, we have had more than enough food and supplies. The LORD has certainly blessed his people. Look at how much is left over!"

11 So the king gave orders for storerooms to be built in the temple, and when they were completed, 12-13 all the extra offerings were taken there. Hezekiah and Azariah then appointed Conaniah the Levite to be in charge of these storerooms. His brother Shimei was his assistant, and the following Levites worked with them: Jehiel, Azaziah, Nahath, Asahel, Jerimoth, Jozabad, Eliel, Ismachiah, Mahath, and Benaiah. 14 Kore son of Imnah was assigned to guard the East Gate, and he was put in charge of receiving the offerings voluntarily

---

*31.1 sacred poles: See the note at 14.3.

*31.2 sacrifices to please the LORD: See the note at 1.6.
*31.2 sacrifices to ask his blessing: See the note at 29.33.
*31.7 third month: Sivan, the third month of the Hebrew calendar, from about mid-May to mid-June.
See also: 31.3: Num 28.1—29.39. 31.4,5: Num 18.12,13,21.

given to God and of dividing them among the priests and Levites. 15-16 He had six assistants who were responsible for seeing to it that all the priests in the other towns of Judah also got their share of these offerings. They were Eden, Miniamin, Jeshua, Shemaiah, Amariah, and Shecaniah.

Every priest and every Levite over thirty* years old who worked daily in the temple received part of these offerings, according to their duties. 17 The priests were listed in the official records by clans, and the Levites twenty years old and older were listed by their duties. 18 The official records also included their wives and children, because they had also been faithful in keeping themselves clean and acceptable to serve the LORD.

19 Hezekiah also appointed other men to take food and supplies to the priests and Levites whose homes were in the pasture land around the towns of Judah. But the priests had to be descendants of Aaron, and the Levites had to be listed in the official records.

20-21 Everything Hezekiah did while he was king of Judah, including what he did for the temple in Jerusalem, was right and good. He was a successful king, because he obeyed the LORD God with all his heart.

CHAPTER 32

King Sennacherib of Assyria invades Judah

This is also told in 2 Kings 18.13–37; Isaiah 36.1–22

1 After King Hezekiah had faithfully obeyed the LORD's instructions by doing these things, King Sennacherib of Assyria invaded Judah. He attacked the fortified cities and thought he would capture every one of them.

2 As soon as Hezekiah learnt that Sennacherib was planning to attack Jerusalem, 3-4 he and his officials worked out a plan to cut off the supply of water outside the city, so that the Assyrians would have no water when they came to attack. The officials got together a large work force that stopped up the springs and streams near Jerusalem.

5 Hezekiah's workers also repaired the broken sections of the city wall. Then they built defence towers and an outer wall to help protect the one already there. The landfill on the east side* of David's City was also strengthened.

He gave orders to make a large supply of weapons and shields, 6 and he appointed army commanders over the troops. Then he gathered the troops together in the open area in front of the city gate and said to them:

7 Be brave and confident! There's no reason to be afraid of King Sennacherib and his powerful army. We are much more powerful, 8 because the LORD our God fights on our side. The Assyrians must rely on human power alone.

These words encouraged the army of Judah.

9 When Sennacherib and his troops were camped at the town of Lachish, he sent a message to Hezekiah and the people in Jerusalem. It said:

10 I am King Sennacherib of Assyria, and I have Jerusalem surrounded. Do you think you can survive my attack? 11 Hezekiah your king is telling you that the LORD your God will save you from me. But he is lying, and you'll die of hunger and thirst. 12 Didn't Hezekiah tear down all except one of the LORD's altars and places of worship?* And didn't he tell you people of Jerusalem and Judah to worship at that one place?

13 You've heard what my ancestors and I have done to other nations. Were the gods of those nations able to defend their land against us? 14 None of those gods kept their people safe from the kings of Assyria. Do you really think your God can do any better? 15 Don't be fooled by Hezekiah! No god of any nation has ever been able to stand up to Assyria. Believe me, your God cannot keep you safe!

16 The Assyrian officials said terrible things about the LORD God and his servant Hezekiah. 17 Sennacherib's letter even made fun of the LORD. It said, "The gods of other nations could not save their people from Assyria's army, and neither will the God that Hezekiah worships." 18 The officials said all these things in Hebrew, so that everyone listening from the city wall would understand and be terrified and surrender. 19 The officials talked about the LORD God as if he were nothing but an ordinary god or an idol that someone had made.

---

*32.5 The landfill on the east side: The Hebrew text has "the Millo", which probably refers to a landfill to strengthen and extend the hill where the city was built.

*32.12 worship: Hezekiah actually had torn down the places where idols were worshipped, and he had told the people to worship the LORD at the one place of worship in Jerusalem. But the Assyrian leader was confused and thought these were also places where the LORD was supposed to be worshipped.

438

The death of King Sennacherib

This is also told in 2 Kings 19.14–19,35–37; Isaiah 37.14–20; 37.36–38

20 Hezekiah and the prophet Isaiah son of Amoz asked the LORD for help, 21 and he sent an angel who killed every soldier and commander in the Assyrian camp.

Sennacherib returned to Assyria, completely disgraced. Then one day he went into the temple of his god where some of his sons killed him.

22 The LORD rescued Hezekiah and the people of Jerusalem from Sennacherib and also protected them from other enemies. 23 People brought offerings to the LORD and expensive gifts for Hezekiah, and from that day on, every nation on earth respected Hezekiah.

Hezekiah gets sick and almost dies

This is also told in 2 Kings 20.1–11; Isaiah 38.1–8

24 About this same time, Hezekiah got sick and was almost dead. He prayed, and the LORD gave him a sign that he would recover. 25 But Hezekiah was so proud that he refused to thank the LORD for everything he had done for him. This made the LORD angry, and he punished Hezekiah and the people of Judah and Jerusalem. 26 Hezekiah and the people later felt sorry and asked the LORD to forgive them. So the LORD did not punish them as long as Hezekiah was king.

Hezekiah's wealth

This is also told in 2 Kings 20.12–19; Isaiah 39.1–8

27 Hezekiah was very rich, and everyone respected him. He built special rooms to store the silver, the gold, the precious stones and spices, the shields, and the other valuable possessions. 28 Storehouses were also built for his supply of grain, wine, and olive oil; barns were built for his cattle, and pens were put up for his sheep. 29 God made Hezekiah extremely rich, so he bought even more sheep, goats, and cattle. And he built towns where he could keep all these animals.

30 It was Hezekiah who built a tunnel that carried the water from Gihon Spring into the city of Jerusalem. In fact, everything he did was successful! 31 Even when the leaders of Babylonia sent messengers to ask Hezekiah about the sign God had given him, God let Hezekiah give his own answer to test him and to see if he would remain faithful.

Hezekiah dies

This is also told in 2 Kings 20.20,21

32 Everything else Hezekiah did while he was king, including how faithful he was to the LORD, is included in the records kept by Isaiah the prophet. These are written in *The History of the Kings of Judah and Israel*. 33 When Hezekiah died, he was buried in the section of the royal tombs that was reserved for the most respected kings,* and everyone in Judah and Jerusalem honoured him. His son Manasseh then became king.

King Manasseh and King Amon

CHAPTER 33

King Manasseh of Judah

This is also told in 2 Kings 21.1–9,17,18

1 Manasseh was twelve years old when he became king of Judah, and he ruled fifty-five years from Jerusalem. 2 Manasseh disobeyed the LORD by following the disgusting customs of the nations that the LORD had forced out of Judah. 3 He rebuilt the local shrines* that his father Hezekiah had torn down. He built altars for the god Baal and set up sacred poles * for worshipping the goddess Asherah. And he faithfully worshipped the stars in the sky.

4 In the temple, where only the LORD was supposed to be worshipped, Manasseh built altars for pagan gods 5 and for the stars. He placed these altars in both courtyards of the temple 6–7 and even set up a stone image of a foreign god. Manasseh practised magic and witchcraft; he asked fortune-tellers for advice and sacrificed his own sons in Hinnom Valley. He did many other sinful things and made the LORD very angry.

Years ago, God had told David and Solomon:

Jerusalem is the place I prefer above all others in Israel. It belongs to me, and there in the temple I will be worshipped for ever. 8 If my people will faithfully obey all the laws and teaching I gave to my servant Moses, I will never again force them to leave the land I gave to their ancestors.

---

*33.3 sacred poles: See the note at 14.3.

See also: 33.2: Jer 15.4.   33.4: 2 Chron 6.6.
33.7,8: 1 King 9.3–5; 2 Chron 7.12–18.

⁹ But the people of Judah and Jerusalem listened to Manasseh and did even more sinful things than the nations the LORD had wiped out.

¹⁰ The LORD tried to warn Manasseh and the people about their sins, but they ignored the warning. ¹¹ So he let Assyrian army commanders invade Judah and capture Manasseh. They put a hook in his nose and tied him up in chains, and they took him to Babylon. ¹² While Manasseh was held captive there, he asked the LORD God to forgive him and to help him. ¹³ The LORD listened to Manasseh's prayer and saw how sorry he was, and so he let him go back to Jerusalem and rule as king. Manasseh knew from then on that the LORD was God.

¹⁴ Later, Manasseh rebuilt the eastern section of Jerusalem's outer wall and made it taller. This section went from Gihon Valley north to Fish Gate and around the part of the city called Mount Ophel. He also assigned army officers to each of the fortified cities in Judah.*

¹⁵ Manasseh also removed the idols and the stone image of the foreign god from the temple, and he gathered the altars he had built near the temple and in other parts of Jerusalem. He threw all these things outside the city. ¹⁶ Then he repaired the LORD's altar and offered sacrifices to thank him and sacrifices to ask his blessing.* He gave orders that everyone in Judah must worship the LORD God of Israel. ¹⁷ The people obeyed Manasseh, but they worshipped the LORD at their own shrines.

¹⁸ Everything else Manasseh did while he was king, including his prayer to the LORD God and the warnings from his prophets, is written in *The History of the Kings of Israel*. ¹⁹ Hozai* wrote a lot about Manasseh, including his prayer and God's answer. But Hozai also recorded the evil things Manasseh did before turning back to God, as well as a list of places where Manasseh set up idols, and where he built local shrines and places to worship Asherah. ²⁰ Manasseh died and was buried near the palace, and his son Amon became king.

King Amon of Judah

This is also told in 2 Kings 21.19–26

²¹ Amon was twenty-two years old when he became king of Judah, and he ruled from Jerusalem for two years. ²² Amon disobeyed the LORD, just as his father Manasseh had done, and he worshipped and offered sacrifices to the idols his father had made. ²³ Manasseh had turned back to the LORD, but Amon refused to do that. Instead, he sinned even more than his father.

²⁴ Some of Amon's officials plotted against him and killed him in his palace. ²⁵ But the people of Judah killed the murderers of Amon and made his son Josiah king.

King Josiah and "The Book of God's Law"

CHAPTER 34

King Josiah of Judah

This is also told in 2 Kings 22.1,2

¹ Josiah was eight years old when he became king of Judah, and he ruled thirty-one years from Jerusalem. ² He followed the example of his ancestor David and always obeyed the LORD.

Josiah stops the worship of foreign gods

This is also told in 2 Kings 23.4–20

³ When Josiah was only sixteen years old he began worshipping God, just as his ancestor David had done. Then, four years later, he decided to destroy the local shrines* in Judah and Jerusalem, as well as the sacred poles* for worshipping the goddess Asherah and the idols of foreign gods. ⁴ He watched as the altars for the worship of the god Baal were torn down, and as the nearby incense altars were smashed. The Asherah poles, the idols, and the stone images were also smashed, and the pieces were scattered over the graves of their worshippers. ⁵ Josiah then had the bones of the pagan priests burnt on the altars.*

---

*33.14 fortified cities in Judah: At this time, Judah was under the control of Assyria. The fortifications mentioned in this verse may have been done under orders from Assyrian officials, hoping to strengthen their southern border against the rising power of Egypt.
*33.16 sacrifices to ask his blessing: See the note at 29.33.

*34.3 sacred poles: See the note at 14.3.
*34.5 the bones of the pagan priests burnt on the altars: This made the altars unclean, so that they could not be used in worshipping any god.
See also: 34.1: Jer 3.6. 34.4: 2 King 21.3; 2 Chron 33.3. 34.5: 1 King 13.2.

And so Josiah got rid of the worship of foreign gods in Judah and Jerusalem. 6 He did the same things in the towns and ruined villages* in the territories of West Manasseh, Ephraim, and Simeon, as far as the border of Naphtali. 7 Everywhere in the northern kingdom of Israel, Josiah tore down pagan altars and Asherah poles; he crushed idols to dust and smashed incense altars.

Then Josiah went back to Jerusalem.

Hilkiah finds *The Book of God's Law*

This is also told in 2 Kings 22.3–20

8 In the eighteenth year of Josiah's rule in Judah, after he had got rid of all the sinful things from the land and from the LORD's temple, he sent three of his officials to repair the temple. They were Shaphan son of Azaliah, Governor Maaseiah of Jerusalem, and Joah son of Joahaz, who kept the government records.

9 These three men went to Hilkiah the high priest. They gave him the money that the Levite guards had collected from the people of West Manasseh, Ephraim, and the rest of Israel, as well as those living in Judah, Benjamin, and Jerusalem. 10 Then the money was turned over to the men who supervised the repairs to the temple. They used some of it to pay the workers, 11 and they gave the rest of it to the carpenters and builders, who used it to buy the stone and wood they needed to repair the other buildings that Judah's kings had not taken care of.

12 The workers were honest, and their supervisors were Jahath and Obadiah from the Levite clan of Merari, and Zechariah and Meshullam from the Levite clan of Kohath. Other Levites, who were all skilled musicians, 13 were in charge of carrying supplies and supervising the workers. Other Levites were appointed to stand guard around the temple.

14 While the money was being given to these supervisors, Hilkiah found the book that contained the laws that the LORD had given to Moses. 15 Hilkiah handed the book to Shaphan the official and said, "Look what I found here in the temple – *The Book of God's Law.*"

16 Shaphan took the book to Josiah and reported, "Your officials are doing everything you wanted. 17 They have collected the money from the temple and have given it to the men supervising the repairs. 18 But there's something else, Your Majesty. The priest Hilkiah gave me this book." Then Shaphan read it aloud.

19 When Josiah heard what was in *The Book of God's Law,* he tore his clothes in sorrow. 20 At once he called together Hilkiah, Shaphan, Ahikam son of Shaphan, Abdon son of Micah,* and his own servant Asaiah. He said, 21 "The LORD must be furious with me and everyone else in Israel and Judah, because our ancestors did not obey the laws written in this book. Go and find out what the LORD wants us to do."

22 Hilkiah and the four other men left straight away and went to talk with Huldah the prophet. Her husband was Shallum,* who was in charge of the king's clothes. Huldah lived in the northern part of Jerusalem, and when they met in her home, 23 she said:

You were sent here by King Josiah, and this is what the LORD God of Israel says to him: 24 "Josiah, I am the LORD! And I intend to punish this country and everyone in it, just as this book says. 25 The people of Judah and Israel have rejected me. They have offered sacrifices to foreign gods and have worshipped their own idols. I can't stand it any longer. I am furious.

26-27 "Josiah, listen to what I am going to do. I noticed how sad you were when you heard that this country and its people would be completely wiped out. You even tore your clothes in sorrow, and I heard you cry. 28 So before I destroy this place, I will let you die in peace."

The men left and reported to Josiah what Huldah had said.

Josiah reads *The Book of God's Law*

This is also told in 2 Kings 23.1–3

29 King Josiah called together the leaders of Judah and Jerusalem. 30 Then he went to the LORD's temple, together with all the people of Judah and Jerusalem, the priests, and the Levites.

Finally, when everybody was there, he read aloud *The Book of God's Law** that had been found in the temple. 31 After Josiah had finished reading, he stood in the place reserved for the king. He promised in the LORD's name to obey the LORD faithfully and to follow his laws and teachings that were written in the book.

*34.30 *The Book of God's Law:* The Hebrew text has "The Book of God's Agreement", which is the same as *The Book of God's Law* in verses 15 and 19. In traditional translations this is called "The Book of the Covenant".

441

³² Then he asked the people of Jerusalem and Benjamin to make that same promise and to obey the God their ancestors had worshipped.

³³ Josiah destroyed all the idols in the territories of Israel, and he commanded everyone in Israel to worship only the LORD God. The people did not turn away from the LORD God of their ancestors for the rest of Josiah's rule as king.

CHAPTER 35

Passover is celebrated

This is also told in 2 Kings 23.21–23

¹ Josiah commanded that Passover be celebrated in Jerusalem to honour the LORD. So, on the fourteenth day of the first month,* the lambs were killed for the Passover celebration.

² On that day, Josiah made sure the priests knew what duties they were to do in the temple. ³ He called together the Levites who served the LORD and who taught the people his laws, and he said:

No longer will you have to carry the sacred chest from place to place. It will stay in the temple built by King Solomon son of David, where you will serve the LORD and his people Israel. ⁴ Get ready to do the work that David and Solomon assigned to you, according to your clans. ⁵ Divide yourselves into groups, then arrange yourselves throughout the temple so that each family of worshippers will be able to get help from one of you.* ⁶ When the people bring you their Passover lamb, you must kill it and prepare it to be sacrificed to the LORD. Make sure the people celebrate according to the instructions that the LORD gave Moses, and don't do anything to make yourselves unclean and unacceptable.

⁷ Josiah donated thirty thousand sheep and goats, and three thousand bulls from his own flocks and herds for the people to offer as sacrifices. ⁸ Josiah's officials also voluntarily gave some of their animals to the people, the priests, and the Levites as sacrifices. Hilkiah, Zechariah, and Jehiel, who were the officials in charge of the temple, gave the priests twenty-six hundred sheep and lambs and three hundred bulls to sacrifice during the Passover celebration. ⁹ Conaniah, his two

brothers Shemaiah and Nethanel, as well as Hashabiah, Jeiel, and Jozabad were leaders of the Levites, and they gave the other Levites five thousand sheep and goats, and five hundred bulls to offer as sacrifices.

¹⁰ When everything was ready to celebrate Passover, the priests and the Levites stood where Josiah had told them. ¹¹ Then the Levites killed and skinned the Passover lambs, and they handed some of the blood to the priests, who splattered it on the altar. ¹² The Levites set aside the parts of the animal that the worshippers needed for their sacrifices to please the LORD,* just as the Law of Moses required. They also did the same thing with the bulls. ¹³ They sacrificed the Passover animals on the altar and boiled the meat for the other offerings in pots, kettles, and pans. Then they quickly handed the meat to the people so they could eat it.

¹⁴ All day long, the priests were busy offering sacrifices and burning the animals' fat on the altar. And when everyone had finished, the Levites prepared Passover animals for themselves and for the priests.

¹⁵ During the celebration some of the Levites prepared Passover animals for the musicians and the guards, so that the Levite musicians would not have to leave their places, which had been assigned to them according to the instructions of David, Asaph, Heman, and Jeduthun the king's prophet. Even the guards at the temple gates did not have to leave their posts.

¹⁶ So on that day, Passover was celebrated to honour the LORD, and sacrifices were offered on the altar to him, just as Josiah had commanded. ¹⁷ The worshippers then celebrated the Festival of Thin Bread for the next seven days.

¹⁸ People from Jerusalem and from towns all over Judah and Israel were there. Passover had not been observed like this since the days of Samuel the prophet. In fact, this was the greatest Passover celebration in Israel's history! ¹⁹ All these things happened in the eighteenth year of Josiah's rule in Judah.

Josiah dies in battle

This is also told in 2 Kings 23.28–30

²⁰ Some time later, King Neco of Egypt led his army to the city of Carchemish on the River

---

*35.1 first month: See the note at 29.3.

See also: 35.4: 2 Chron 8.14.

*35.12 sacrifices to please the LORD: See the note at 1.6.

See also: 35.13: Exod 12.8,9.   35.15: 1 Chron 25.1.
35.17: Exod 12.1–20.

Euphrates. And Josiah led his troops north to meet the Egyptians in battle.*

21 Neco sent the following message to Josiah:

I'm not attacking you, king of Judah! We're not even at war. But God has told me to attack my enemy quickly. God is on my side, so if you try to stop me, he will punish me.

22 But Josiah ignored Neco's warning, even though it came from God! Instead, he disguised himself and marched into battle against Neco in the valley near Megiddo.

23 During the battle an Egyptian soldier shot Josiah with an arrow. Josiah told his servants, "Get me out of here! I've been hit." 24 They carried Josiah out of his chariot, then put him in the other chariot he had there and took him back to Jerusalem, where he soon died. He was buried beside his ancestors, and everyone in Judah and Jerusalem mourned his death.

25 Jeremiah the prophet wrote a funeral song in honour of Josiah. And since then, anyone in Judah who mourns the death of Josiah sings that song. It is included in the collection of funeral songs.

26 Everything else Josiah did while he was king, including how he faithfully obeyed the LORD, 27 is written in *The History of the Kings of Israel and Judah*.

The last kings of Judah

CHAPTER 36

King Jehoahaz of Judah

This is also told in 2 Kings 23.30–35

1 After the death of Josiah, the people of Judah crowned his son Jehoahaz their new king. 2 He was twenty-three years old at the time, and he ruled only three months from Jerusalem. 3 King Neco of Egypt captured Jehoahaz and forced Judah to pay three thousand four hundred kilogrammes of silver and thirty-four kilogrammes of gold as taxes. 4 Then Neco appointed Jehoahaz's brother Eliakim king of Judah and changed his name to Jehoiakim. He led Jehoahaz away to Egypt as his prisoner.

*35.20 battle: At this time, King Neco of Egypt (609–595 BC) was fighting on the side of the Assyrians. He marched north to fight the Babylonian army and help Assyria keep control of its land. Since Josiah considered Assyria an enemy, he set out to stop Neco and the Egyptian troops.
See also: 36.4: Jer 22.11,12.

King Jehoiakim of Judah

This is also told in 2 Kings 23.36—24.7

5 Jehoiakim was twenty-five years old when he was appointed king, and he ruled eleven years from Jerusalem. Jehoiakim disobeyed the LORD his God by doing evil.

6 During Jehoiakim's rule, King Nebuchadnezzar of Babylonia invaded Judah. He arrested Jehoiakim and put him in chains, and he sent him to the capital city of Babylon. 7 Nebuchadnezzar also carried off many of the valuable things in the LORD's temple, and he put them in his palace in Babylon.

8 Everything else Jehoiakim did while he was king, including all the disgusting and evil things, is written in *The History of the Kings of Israel and Judah*. His son Jehoiachin then became king.

King Jehoiachin of Judah

This is also told in 2 Kings 24.8–17

9 Jehoiachin was eighteen' years old when he became king of Judah, and he ruled only three months and ten days from Jerusalem. Jehoiachin also disobeyed the LORD by doing evil. 10 In the spring of the year, King Nebuchadnezzar of Babylonia had Jehoiachin arrested and taken to Babylon, along with more of the valuable items in the temple. Then Nebuchadnezzar appointed Zedekiah king of Judah.

King Zedekiah of Judah

This is also told in 2 Kings 24.18–20; Jeremiah 52.1-3

11 Zedekiah was twenty-one years old when he was appointed king of Judah, and he ruled from Jerusalem for eleven years. 12 He disobeyed the LORD his God and refused to change his ways, even after a warning from Jeremiah, the LORD's prophet. 13 King Nebuchadnezzar of Babylonia had forced Zedekiah to promise in God's name that he would be loyal. Zedekiah was stubborn and refused to turn back to the LORD God of Israel, so he rebelled against Nebuchadnezzar. 14 The people of Judah and even the priests who were their leaders became more unfaithful. They followed the disgusting example of the nations around them and made the LORD's holy temple unfit for worship. 15 But the LORD God felt sorry for his

See also: 36.5: Jer 22.18,19; 26.1–6; 35.1–19.
36.6: Jer 25.1-38; 36.1–12; 45.1–5; Dan 1.1,2.
36.10: a Jer 22.24–30; 24.1–10; 29.1,2; Ezek 17.12; b Jer 37.1;
Ezek 17.13.   36.11: Jer 27.1–22; 28.1–17. 36.13: Ezek 17.15.

people, and instead of destroying the temple, he sent prophets who warned the people over and over again about their sins. ¹⁶ But the people only laughed and insulted these prophets. They ignored what the LORD God was trying to tell them, until he finally became so angry that nothing could stop him from punishing Judah and Jerusalem.

Jerusalem is destroyed and the people are taken to Babylonia

This is also told in 2 Kings 25.1–21; Jeremiah 52.3–30

¹⁷ The LORD sent King Nebuchadnezzar of Babylonia to attack Jerusalem. Nebuchadnezzar killed the young men who were in the temple, and he showed no mercy to anyone, whether man or woman, young or old. God let him kill everyone in the city. ¹⁸ Nebuchadnezzar carried off everything that was left in the temple; he robbed the treasury and the personal storerooms of the king and his officials. He took everything back to Babylon.

¹⁹ Nebuchadnezzar's troops burnt down the temple and destroyed every important building in the city. Then they broke down the city wall. ²⁰ The survivors were taken to Babylonia as prisoners, where they were slaves of the king and his sons, until Persia became a powerful nation.

²¹ Judah was an empty desert, and it stayed that way for seventy years, to make up for all the years it was not allowed to rest. These things happened just as Jeremiah the LORD's prophet had said.*

King Cyrus of Persia lets the Jews return to Judah

Cyrus lets the Jews return home

This is also told in Ezra 1.1–4

²² In the first year that Cyrus was king of Persia,* the LORD told Cyrus to send a message

to all parts of his kingdom. This happened just as Jeremiah the LORD's prophet had promised. ²³ The message said:

I am King Cyrus of Persia.
The LORD God of heaven has made me the ruler of every nation on earth. He has also chosen me to build a temple for him in Jerusalem, which is in Judah. The LORD God will watch over any of his people who want to go back to Judah.

See also: 36.23: Isa 44.28.

Additional notes

•**1.2–5 Bezalel:** Hebrew "Bezalel son of Uri son of Hur".

•**3.1,2 Araunah:** The Hebrew text has "Ornan", another spelling of the name (see 2 Samuel 24.18–25; 1 Chronicles 21.18—22.1).

•**3.4 nine metres:** Some manuscripts of two ancient translations; Hebrew "fifty-four metres".

•**3.9 The walls . . . gold:** One possible meaning for the difficult Hebrew text.

•**3.16 designs that looked like chains:** One possible meaning for the difficult Hebrew text.

•**5.10 Sinai:** Hebrew "Horeb".

•**6.42 the love you had for your servant David:** Or "how loyal your servant David was to you".

•**9.3,4 his palace:** Or "the temple".

•**9.10–12 steps:** Or "stools" or "railings".

•**9.21 peacocks:** Or "baboons".

•**10.10 Compared . . . weak:** Hebrew "My little finger is bigger than my father's waist".

•**10.15–19 Adoniram:** The Hebrew text has "Hadoram", another spelling of the name.

•**11.15 local shrines:** The Hebrew text has "high places", which were local places to worship foreign gods.

•**13.1 Abijah:** In 1 Kings 15.1–8 his name is spelt "Abijam".

•**14.3 local shrines:** See the note at 11.15.

•**14.13 the Ethiopians could not even fight back:** Or "not one of the Ethiopians survived!"

•**15.17 local shrines:** See the note at 11.15.

•**16.4 Abel-Maim:** Also called "Abel-Bethmaacah" (see 1 Kings 15.20).

•**16.10 Asa was also cruel . . . people:** Or "Asa also started being cruel to some of his people."

•**17.6 local shrines:** See the note at 11.15.

•**19.11 Zebadiah, the leader:** Hebrew "Zebadiah son of Ishmael, who is the leader".

•**20.1 Meunites:** One ancient translation (see 26.7); Hebrew "Ammonites".

•**20.2 Edom:** The Hebrew text has "Syria"; in Hebrew there is only one letter difference between "Edom" and "Aram", which is the usual Hebrew name for Syria in the Bible.

---

*36.21 not allowed to rest . . . Jeremiah . . . said: Jeremiah 25.11,12; 29.10. According to the Law, the people had to allow the land to rest one out of every seven years (see Leviticus 25.1–7).
*36.22 the first year that Cyrus was king of Persia: Probably 539 BC, when Cyrus captured Babylonia. He had actually ruled Persia since 549 BC.

See also: 36.17: Jer 21.1–10; 34.1–5.   36.19: 1 King 9.8. 36.21: Jer 25.11; 29.10.

›20.14 Jahaziel, a Levite from the Asaph clan:
Hebrew "Jahaziel son of Zechariah son of Benaiah son
of Jeiel son of Mattaniah, who was a Levite from the
Asaph clan."

›20.21 to march in front . . . singing: Or "to put on
their sacred robes, lead the army into battle, and
praise the LORD by singing".

›20.25 a large herd of livestock: One ancient
translation; Hebrew "among the bodies a large herd
of".

›20.25 clothes: One ancient translation; Hebrew
"dead bodies".

›20.33 local shrines: See the note at 11.15.

›20.37 Eliezer: Hebrew "Eliezer son of Dodavahu
from Mareshah".

›21.11 local shrines: See the note at 11.15.

›21.17 Ahaziah: The Hebrew text has "Jehoahaz",
another spelling of the name.

›22.2 twenty-two: One ancient translation (see also
2 Kings 8.26); Hebrew "forty-two".

›22.11 Jehosheba: The Hebrew text has
"Jehoshabeath", another spelling of the name.

›24.25,26 Zabad and Jehozabad: Hebrew "Zabad
son of Shimeath from Ammon and Jehozabad son of
Shimrith from Moab".

›25.1 Jehoaddin: The Hebrew text has "Jehoaddan",
another spelling of the name.

›25.17 King Jehoash: The Hebrew text has "King
Joash son of Jehoahaz son of Jehu"; Jehoash is
another spelling for the name Joash.

›26.1–3 Uzziah: In the parallel passages in 2 Kings,
he is called "Azariah" (see also 1 Chronicles 3.10–15).
He is also called "Uzziah" in 2 Kings 15.13; Isaiah 1.1;
Hosea 1.1; and Amos 1.1. One of these names was
probably his birth name, while the other was his
name after he became king.

›26.9 the place where the city wall turned inward:
One possible meaning for the difficult Hebrew text.

›28.4 local shrines: See the note at 11.15.

›28.5,6 Pekah: Hebrew "Pekah son of Remaliah".

›28.25 local shrines: See the note at 11.15.

›29.21 goats: Hebrew "male goats".

›31.1 local shrines: See the note at 11.15.

›31.15,16 thirty: The Hebrew text has "three" instead
of "thirty"; in Hebrew, these two words look almost
exactly the same (see also Numbers 4.3;
1 Chronicles 23.3).

›32.33 in the section . . . reserved for the most
respected kings: One possible meaning for the
difficult Hebrew text.

›33.3 local shrines: See the note at 11.15.

›33.19 Hozai: Or "The prophets".

›34.3 local shrines: See the note at 11.15.

›34.6 ruined villages: One possible meaning for the
difficult Hebrew text.

›34.20 Abdon son of Micah: Also called "Achbor son
of Micaiah" (see 2 Kings 22.12).

›34.22 Shallum: Hebrew "Shallum son of Tokhath
son of Hasrah".

›35.5 each family of worshippers . . . you: One
possible meaning for the difficult Hebrew text.

›36.9 eighteen: Some manuscripts of one ancient
translation (see also 2 Kings 24.8); Hebrew "eight".

445

Ezra

A quick look at this book

The Jews return home from exile *page 446*

The altar is rebuilt, and work on the temple
begins *page 448*

Later trouble rebuilding Jerusalem *page 449*

The temple is rebuilt *page 450*

Ezra leads many Jews back to Jerusalem
page 452

Ezra forces men to divorce their Gentile wives
page 454

Additional notes *page 456*

This book is named after the main character of
its second part.

The book of 2 Chronicles ended with an official
message that King Cyrus of Persia sent in 538 BC,
which allowed the Jews to return to their land
and to rebuild the Lord's temple. The first part of
the book of Ezra (1—6) begins with that same
message and then tells how many of the Jews
returned to Jerusalem and began work on the
temple. But the people in nearby areas caused a
lot of trouble for them, and so the work went
slowly and even stopped for several years. But
the temple was finally finished in 515 BC.

The first part of the book also tells about
problems at a later time, when the Jews had to
stop rebuilding the city walls during the rule of
Artaxerxes (4.6–23).

The second part of the book (7—10) begins
with Ezra arriving in Jerusalem to teach God's
laws to the people of Judah. Ezra was horrified
to learn that the people of Israel were
committing the same sins as other nations.

446

Israel was in serious danger of being punished
or even destroyed by the Lord. So Ezra prayed
and confessed Israel's sins, and the people
agreed to begin obeying God's laws. The book
of Nehemiah reports other things that Ezra did.

God's people were no longer an independent
nation, but Ezra realized that God was in
control, no matter what empire ruled over
them. And so Ezra said:

> Praise the LORD God of our ancestors! He made
> sure that the king honoured the LORD's temple
> in Jerusalem. God has told the king, and his
> advisers, and his powerful officials to treat me
> with kindness. The LORD God has helped me,
> and I have been able to bring many Jewish
> leaders back to Jerusalem.

(7.27b,28)

The Jews return home
from exile

CHAPTER 1

¹ Years ago the LORD sent Jeremiah with a
message about a promise* for the people of
Israel. Then in the first year that Cyrus was
king of Persia,* the LORD kept his promise by
telling Cyrus to send this official message to
all parts of his kingdom:

---

*1.1 a promise: That the people of Israel would be
set free from Babylonia after seventy years (see
Jeremiah 25.11; 29.10).
*1.1 the first year that Cyrus was king of Persia:
Probably 539 BC, when Cyrus captured Babylonia. He
had actually ruled Persia since 549 BC.
See also: 1.1: Jer 25.11; 29.10.

2-3 I am King Cyrus of Persia.

The LORD God of heaven, who is also the God of Israel, has made me the ruler of all nations on earth. And he has chosen me to build a temple for him in Jerusalem, which is in Judah. The LORD God will watch over and encourage any of his people who want to go back to Jerusalem and help build the temple.

4 Everyone else must provide what is needed. They must give money, supplies, and animals, as well as gifts for rebuilding God's temple.

5 Many people felt that the LORD God wanted them to help rebuild his temple, and they made plans to go to Jerusalem. Among them were priests, Levites, and leaders of the tribes of Judah and Benjamin. 6 The others helped by giving silver articles, gold, personal possessions, cattle, and other valuable gifts, as well as offerings for the temple.

7 King Cyrus gave back the things that Nebuchadnezzar* had taken from the LORD's temple in Jerusalem and had put in the temple of his own gods. 8 Cyrus placed Mithredath, his chief treasurer, in charge of these things. Mithredath counted them and gave a list to Sheshbazzar, the governor of Judah. 9-10 Included among them were: 30 large gold dishes; 1,000 large silver dishes; 29 other dishes;* 30 gold bowls; 410 silver bowls; and 1,000 other articles.

11 Altogether, there were 5,400 gold and silver dishes, bowls, and other articles. Sheshbazzar took them with him when he and the others returned to Jerusalem from Babylonia.

CHAPTER 2

A list of people who returned from exile

This is also told in Nehemiah 7.4–73

1 King Nebuchadnezzar* of Babylonia had captured many of the people of Judah and had taken them as prisoners to Babylonia. Now they were on their way back to Jerusalem and to their own towns everywhere in Judah.

2-20 Zerubbabel, Joshua,* Nehemiah, Seraiah, Reelaiah, Mordecai, Bilshan, Mispar,

Bigvai, Rehum, and Baanah were in charge of the ones who were coming back. And here is a list of how many returned from each family group: 2,172 from the family of Parosh; 372 from the family of Shephatiah; 775 from the family of Arah; 2,812 descendants of Jeshua and Joab* from the family of Pahath Moab; 1,254 from the family of Elam; 945 from the family of Zattu; 760 from the family of Zaccai; 642 from the family of Bani; 623 from the family of Bebai; 1,222 from the family of Azgad; 666 from the family of Adonikam; 2,056 from the family of Bigvai; 454 from the family of Adin; 98 from the family of Ater, also known as Hezekiah; 323 from the family of Bezai; 112 from the family of Jorah; 223 from the family of Hashum; and 95 from the family of Gibbar.

21-35 Here is how many people returned whose ancestors had come from the following towns: 123 from Bethlehem; 56 from Netophah; 128 from Anathoth; 42 from Azmaveth; 743 from Kiriatharim, Chephirah, and Beeroth; 122 from Michmas; 223 from Bethel and Ai; 52 from Nebo; 156 from Magbish; 1,254 from Elam;* 320 from Harim; 725 from Lod, Hadid, and Ono; 345 from Jericho; and 3,630 from Senaah.

36-39 Here is a list of how many returned from each family of priests: 973 descendants of Jeshua from the family of Jedaiah; 1,052 from the family of Immer; 1,247 from the family of Pashhur; and 1,017 from the family of Harim.

40-42 And here is a list of how many returned from the families of Levites: 74 descendants of Hodaviah from the families of Jeshua and Kadmiel; 128 descendants of Asaph from the temple musicians; and 139 descendants of Shallum, Ater, Talmon, Akkub, Hatita, and Shobai from the temple guards.

43-54 Here is a list of the families of temple workers whose descendants returned: Ziha, Hasupha, Tabbaoth, Keros, Siaha, Padon, Lebanah, Hagabah, Akkub, Hagab, Shamlai, Hanan, Giddel, Gahar, Reaiah, Rezin, Nekoda, Gazzam, Uzza, Paseah, Besai, Asnah, Meunim, Nephisim, Bakbuk, Hakupha, Harhur, Bazluth, Mehida, Harsha, Barkos, Sisera, Temah, Neziah, and Hatipha.

55-57 Here is a list of Solomon's servants whose descendants returned: Sotai, Hassophereth, Peruda, Jaalah, Darkon, Giddel, Shephatiah, Hattil, Pochereth Hazzebaim, and Ami.

*1.7 Nebuchadnezzar: Known as Nebuchadnezzar II, who ruled Babylonia from 605 to 562 BC. In 586 BC he destroyed Jerusalem and took many of its people to Babylonia.

*2.1 Nebuchadnezzar: See the note at 1.7.

See also: 1.2: Isa 44.28.

⁵⁸ A total of 392 descendants of temple workers and of Solomon's servants returned.

⁵⁹⁻⁶⁰ There were 652 who returned from the families of Delaiah, Tobiah, and Nekoda, though they could not prove that they were Israelites. They had lived in the Babylonian towns of Tel-Melah, Tel-Harsha, Cherub, Addan, and Immer.

⁶¹⁻⁶² The families of Habaiah, Hakkoz, and Barzillai could not prove that they were priests. The ancestor of the family of Barzillai had married the daughter of Barzillai from Gilead and had taken his wife's family name. But the records of these three families could not be found, and none of them were allowed to serve as priests. ⁶³ In fact, the governor* told them, "You cannot eat the food offered to God until we find out if you really are priests."*

⁶⁴⁻⁶⁷ There were 42,360 who returned, in addition to 7,337 servants and 200 musicians, both women and men. They brought with them 736 horses, 245 mules, 435 camels, and 6,720 donkeys.

⁶⁸ When the people came to where the LORD's temple had been in Jerusalem, some of the family leaders gave gifts so it could be rebuilt in the same place. ⁶⁹ They gave all they could, and it came to a total of 500 kilogrammes of gold, 2,800 kilogrammes of silver, and 100 robes for the priests.

⁷⁰ Everyone returned to the towns from which their families had come, including the priests, the Levites, the musicians, the temple guards, and the workers.*

The altar is rebuilt, and work on the temple begins

CHAPTER 3

The first offering on the new altar

¹ During the seventh month* of the year, the Israelites who had settled in their towns went to Jerusalem. ² The priest Joshua son of

Jozadak, together with the other priests, and Zerubbabel son of Shealtiel and his relatives rebuilt the altar of Israel's God. Then they were able to offer sacrifices there by following the instructions God had given to Moses. ³ And they built the altar where it had stood before,* even though they were afraid of the people who were already living around there. Then every morning and evening they burnt sacrifices and offerings to the LORD.

⁴ The people followed the rules for celebrating the Festival of Shelters and offered the proper sacrifices each day. ⁵ They offered sacrifices to please the LORD,* sacrifices at each New Moon Festival, and sacrifices at the rest of the LORD's festivals. Every offering the people had brought was presented to the LORD.

⁶ Although work on the temple itself had not yet begun, the people started offering sacrifices on the LORD's altar on the first day of the seventh month of that year.

The rebuilding of the temple begins

⁷ King Cyrus of Persia had said the Israelites could have cedar trees brought from Lebanon to Joppa by sea. So they sent grain, wine, and olive oil to the cities of Tyre and Sidon as payment for these trees, and they gave money to the stoneworkers and carpenters.

⁸ During the second month* of the second year after the people had returned from Babylonia, they started rebuilding the LORD's temple. Zerubbabel son of Shealtiel, Joshua son of Jozadak, the priests, the Levites, and everyone else who had returned started working. Every Levite over twenty years of age was put in charge of some part of the work. ⁹ The Levites in charge of the whole project were Joshua and his sons and relatives and Kadmiel and his sons from the family of Hodaviah.* The family of Henadad worked along with them.

¹⁰ When the builders had finished laying the foundation of the temple, the priests put on their robes and blew trumpets in honour of the LORD, while the Levites from the family of Asaph praised God with cymbals. All of them followed the instructions

---

*2.63 governor: In Nehemiah 8.9; 10.1, this same title is used of Nehemiah, though it is doubtful if he is the one referred to here.
*2.63 until . . . priests: The Hebrew text has "until a priest comes with the urim and thummim", sacred objects which were used in some way to receive answers from God.
*3.1 seventh month: Tishri (also called Ethanim), the seventh month of the Hebrew calendar, from about mid-September to mid-October.

See also: 2.63: Num 27.21. 2.70: 1 Chron 9.2; Neh 11.3. 3.2: Exod 27.1.

*3.5 sacrifices to please the LORD: In traditional translations these sacrifices are usually called "whole burnt offerings" (see Leviticus 1.1-16).
*3.8 second month: Ziv, the second month of the Hebrew calendar, from about mid-April to mid-May.

See also: 3.3: Num 28.1-8. 3.4: Num 29.12-38. 3.5: Num 28.11-29.39. 3.10: 1 Chron 25.1.

given years before by King David.* [11] They praised the LORD and gave thanks as they took turns singing:

> "The LORD is good!
> His faithful love for Israel
>   will last for ever."

Everyone started shouting and praising the LORD because work on the foundation of the temple had begun. [12] Many of the older priests and Levites and the heads of families cried aloud because they remembered seeing the first temple years before. But others were so happy that they celebrated with joyful shouts. [13] Their shouting and crying were so noisy that it all sounded alike and could be heard a long way off.

CHAPTER 4

Foreigners* want to help rebuild the temple

[1] The enemies of the tribes of Judah and Benjamin heard that the people had come back to rebuild the temple of the LORD God of Israel. [2] So they went to Zerubbabel and to the family leaders and said, "Let us help! Ever since King Esarhaddon of Assyria* brought us here, we have worshipped your God and offered sacrifices to him."

[3] But Zerubbabel, Joshua, and the family leaders answered, "You cannot take part in building a temple for the LORD our God! We will build it ourselves, just as King Cyrus of Persia commanded us."

[4] Then the neighbouring people began to do everything possible to frighten the Jews* and to make them stop building. [5] During the time when Cyrus was king and even until Darius* became king, they kept bribing government officials to slow down the work.

Later trouble rebuilding Jerusalem

Trouble rebuilding Jerusalem*

[6] In the first year that Xerxes was king,* the neighbouring people brought written charges against the people of Judah and Jerusalem.

[7] Later, Bishlam, Mithredath, Tabeel, and their advisers got together and wrote a letter to Artaxerxes when he was king of Persia.* It was written in Aramaic and had to be translated.*

[8-10] A letter was also written to Artaxerxes about Jerusalem by Governor Rehum, Secretary Shimshai, and their advisers, including the judges, the governors, the officials, and the local leaders. They were joined in writing this letter by people from Erech and Babylonia, the Elamites from Susa,* and people from other foreign nations that the great and famous Ashurbanipal* had forced to settle in Samaria and other parts of Western Province.* [11] This letter said:

Your Majesty King Artaxerxes, we are your servants from everywhere in Western Province, and we send you our greetings.

[12] You should know that the Jews who left your country have moved back to Jerusalem and are now rebuilding that terrible city. In fact, they have almost finished rebuilding the walls and repairing the foundations. [13] You should also know that if the walls are completed and the city is rebuilt, the Jews won't pay any kind of taxes, and there will be less money in your treasury.

---

*3.10 King David: Ruled from about 1010 to 970 BC.
*4.1 Foreigners: People from foreign countries who had been captured by Assyrian and Babylonian kings and forced to settle in Palestine.
*4.2 King Esarhaddon of Assyria: Ruled from 681 to 669 BC. These people may have been brought to Palestine in 677 or 676 BC, when Esarhaddon invaded Syria.
*4.4 Jews: This was the name given to those Israelites who settled in Judah after returning from Babylonia.
*4.5 Cyrus . . . Darius: Cyrus ruled 539–530 BC (see the note at 1.1); Darius I, known as Darius the Great, ruled 522–486 BC.

See also: 3.11: 1 Chron 16.34; 2 Chron 5.13; 7.3; Psa 100.5; 106.1; 107.1; 118.1; 136.1; Jer 33.11. 4.2: 2 King 17.24–41.

*4.6 Jerusalem: Verses 6–23, which tell about the events of a later period, are placed here because they are also concerned with the problem of stopping or slowing down work on the temple.
*4.6 first year that Xerxes was king: Either the end of 486 or the beginning of 485 BC. The Hebrew has the king's Persian name "Ahasuerus", but he is better known as "Xerxes", the Greek form of the name.
*4.7 Artaxerxes: Persia: Artaxerxes I (465–425 BC).
*4.7 It was . . . translated: One possible meaning for the difficult Hebrew text. Ezra 4.8–6.18 is written in Aramaic, instead of in Hebrew like most of the Old Testament.
*4.8-10 Ashurbanipal: King of Assyria 669–633 (or possibly 627) BC. In Aramaic the king's name is "Osnapper", but he is better known as Ashurbanipal.
*4.8-10 Western Province: The land from the River Euphrates west to the Mediterranean Sea.

See also: 4.6: Esth 1.1.

¹⁴ We are telling you this, because you have done so much for us, and we want everyone to respect you. ¹⁵ If you look up the official records of your ancestors, you will find that Jerusalem has constantly rebelled and has led others to rebel against kings and provinces. That's why the city was destroyed in the first place. ¹⁶ If Jerusalem is rebuilt and its walls completed, you will no longer have control over Western Province.

¹⁷ King Artaxerxes answered:

Greetings to Governor Rehum, Secretary Shimshai, and to your advisers in Samaria and other parts of Western Province.

¹⁸ After your letter was translated and read to me, ¹⁹ I had the old records checked. It is true that for years Jerusalem has rebelled and caused trouble for other kings and nations. ²⁰ And powerful kings have ruled Western Province from Jerusalem and have collected all kinds of taxes.

²¹ I want you to command the people to stop rebuilding the city until I give further notice. ²² Do this straight away, so that no harm will come to the kingdom.

²³ As soon as this letter was read, Governor Rehum, Secretary Shimshai, and their advisers went to Jerusalem and forced everyone to stop rebuilding the city.

The temple is rebuilt

Work on the temple starts again

²⁴ The Jews were forced to stop work on the temple and were not able to do any more building until the year after Darius became king of Persia.*

CHAPTER 5

¹ Then the LORD God of Israel told the prophets Haggai and Zechariah* to speak in his name to the people of Judah and Jerusalem. And they did. ² So Zerubbabel the governor and Joshua the priest urged the people to start working on the temple again, and God's prophets encouraged them.

³ Governor Tattenai of Western Province and his assistant Shethar Bozenai got together with some of their officials. Then they went to Jerusalem and said to the people, "Who told

you to rebuild this temple? ⁴ Give us the names of the workers!"

⁵ But God was looking after the Jewish leaders. So the governor and his group decided not to make the people stop working on the temple until they could report to Darius and get his advice.

⁶ Governor Tattenai, Shethar Bozenai, and their advisers sent a report to Darius, ⁷ which said:

King Darius, we wish you the best! ⁸ We went to Judah, where the temple of the great God is being built with huge stones and wooden beams set in the walls. Everyone is working hard, and the building is going up fast.

⁹ We asked those in charge to tell us who gave them permission to rebuild the temple. ¹⁰ We also asked for the names of their leaders, so that we could write them down for you.

¹¹ They claimed to be servants of the God who rules heaven and earth. And they said they were rebuilding the temple that was built many years ago by one of Israel's greatest kings.*

¹² We were told that their people had made God angry, and he let them be captured by Nebuchadnezzar,* the Babylonian king* who took them away as captives to Babylonia. Nebuchadnezzar tore down their temple, ¹³⁻¹⁵ took its gold and silver articles, and put them in the temple of his own god in Babylon.

They also said that during the first year Cyrus was king of Babylonia,* he gave orders for God's temple to be rebuilt in Jerusalem where it had stood before. So Cyrus appointed Sheshbazzar governor of Judah and sent these gold and silver articles for him to put in the temple. Sheshbazzar then went to Jerusalem and laid the foundation for the temple, and the work is still going on.

¹⁷ Your Majesty, please order someone to look up the old records in Babylonia and find out if King Cyrus really did give orders to rebuild God's temple in Jerusalem. We will do whatever you think we should.

---

*5.11 one of Israel's greatest kings: Solomon (ruled from about 970 to 931 BC).
*5.12 Nebuchadnezzar: See the note at 1.7.
*5.13–15 Cyrus was king of Babylonia: King Cyrus of Persia became king of Babylonia when the Persians conquered the city of Babylon in 539 BC.

See also: 5.12: 2 King 25.8–12; 2 Chron 36.17–20; Jer 52.12–15. 5.13: Ezra 1.2–11.

---

*4.24 year after . . . king of Persia: 520 BC.

See also: 4.24: Hag 1.1; Zech 1.1. 5.1: Hag 1.1; Zech 1.1.
5.2: Hag 1.12; Zech 4.6–9.

CHAPTER 6

King Cyrus' order is rediscovered

¹ King Darius ordered someone to go through the old records kept in Babylonia. ² Finally, a scroll* was found in Ecbatana, the capital of Media Province, and it said:

This official record will show ³ that in the first year Cyrus was king, he gave orders to rebuild God's temple in Jerusalem, so that sacrifices and offerings could be presented there.' It is to be built twenty-seven metres high and twenty-seven metres wide, ⁴ with one' row of wooden beams for each three rows of large stones. The royal treasury will pay for everything. ⁵ Then return to their proper places the gold and silver things that Nebuchadnezzar took from the temple and brought to Babylonia.

King Darius orders the work to continue

⁶ King Darius sent this message:

Governor Tattenai of Western Province and Shethar Bozenai, you and your advisers must stay away from the temple. ⁷ Let the Jewish governor and leaders rebuild it where it stood before. And stop slowing them down!

⁸ Starting at once, I am ordering you to help the leaders by paying their expenses from the tax money collected in Western Province. ⁹ And don't fail to let the priests in Jerusalem have whatever they need each day so they can offer sacrifices to the God of heaven. Give them young bulls, rams, sheep, as well as wheat, salt, wine, and olive oil. ¹⁰ I want them to be able to offer pleasing sacrifices to God and to pray for me and my family.

¹¹ If any of you don't obey this order, a wooden beam will be taken from your house and sharpened on one end. Then it will be driven through your body,* and your house will be torn down and turned into a rubbish dump. ¹² I ask the God who is worshipped in Jerusalem to destroy any king or nation who tries either to change what I have said or to tear down his temple. I, Darius, give these orders, and I expect them to be followed carefully.

The temple is dedicated

¹³ Governor Tattenai, Shethar Bozenai, and their advisers carefully obeyed King Darius. ¹⁴ With great success the Jewish leaders continued working on the temple, while Haggai and Zechariah encouraged them by their preaching. And so, the temple was completed at the command of the God of Israel and by the orders of kings Cyrus, Darius, and Artaxerxes of Persia.* ¹⁵ On the third day of the month of Adar* in the sixth year of the rule of Darius,* the temple was finished.

¹⁶ The people of Israel, the priests, the Levites, and everyone else who had returned from exile were happy and celebrated as they dedicated God's temple. ¹⁷ One hundred bulls, two hundred rams, and four hundred lambs were offered as sacrifices at the dedication. Also twelve goats were sacrificed as sin offerings for the twelve tribes of Israel. ¹⁸ Then the priests and Levites were assigned their duties in God's temple in Jerusalem, according to the instructions Moses had written.

The Passover

¹⁹ Everyone who had returned from exile celebrated Passover on the fourteenth day of the first month.* ²⁰ The priests and Levites had gone through a ceremony to make themselves acceptable to lead in worship. Then some of them killed Passover lambs for those who had returned, including the other priests and themselves.

²¹ The sacrifices were eaten by the Israelites who had returned and by the neighbouring people who had given up the sinful customs of other nations in order to worship the LORD God of Israel. ²² For seven days they celebrated the Festival of Thin Bread. Everyone was happy because the LORD God of Israel had made sure that the king of Assyria* would be kind to them and help them build the temple.

---

*6.2 scroll: A roll of paper or special leather used for writing on.

*6.11 driven through your body: A well-known punishment in the ancient Near East.

*6.14 Artaxerxes of Persia: See the note at 4.7.

*6.15 Adar: The twelfth month of the Hebrew calendar, from about mid-February to about mid-March.

*6.15 sixth year . . . Darius: 515 BC.

*6.19 the first month: Nisan or Abib, the first month of the Hebrew calendar, from about mid-March to mid-April.

*6.22 king of Assyria: Meaning the king of Persia, because Assyria was now part of the Persian Empire.

See also: 6.14: a Hag 1.1; b Zech 1.1. 6.19: Exod 12.1-20.

Ezra leads many Jews back to Jerusalem

CHAPTER 7

Ezra comes to Jerusalem

1–6 Much later, when Artaxerxes* was king of Persia, Ezra came to Jerusalem from Babylonia. Ezra was the son of Seraiah and the grandson of Azariah. His other ancestors were Hilkiah, Shallum, Zadok, Ahitub, Amariah, Azariah, Meraioth, Zerahiah, Uzzi, Bukki, Abishua, Phinehas, Eleazar, and Aaron, the high priest.

Ezra was an expert in the Law that the LORD God of Israel had given to Moses, and the LORD made sure that the king gave Ezra everything he asked for.

7 Other Jews, including priests, Levites, musicians, the temple guards, and servants, came to Jerusalem with Ezra. This happened during the seventh year that Artaxerxes* was king.

8–9 God helped Ezra, and he arrived in Jerusalem on the first day of the fifth month* of that seventh year, after leaving Babylonia on the first day of the first month.* 10 Ezra had spent his entire life studying and obeying the Law of the LORD and teaching it to others.

Artaxerxes gives a letter to Ezra

11 Ezra was a priest and an expert in the laws and commands that the LORD had given to Israel. One day King Artaxerxes gave Ezra a letter which said:

12 Greetings from the great King Artaxerxes to Ezra the priest and expert in the teachings of the God of heaven.

13–14 Any of the people of Israel or their priests or Levites in my kingdom may go with you to Jerusalem if they want to. My seven advisers and I agree that you may go to Jerusalem and Judah to find out if the laws of your God are being obeyed.

15 When you go, take the silver and gold that I and my advisers are freely giving to the God of Israel, whose temple is in Jerusalem. 16 Take the silver and gold that you collect from everywhere in Babylonia. Also take the gifts that your own people and priests have so willingly contributed for the temple of your God in Jerusalem.

17 Use the money carefully to buy the best bulls, rams, lambs, grain, and wine. Then sacrifice them on the altar at God's temple in Jerusalem. 18 If any silver or gold is left, you and your people may use it for whatever pleases your God. 19 Give your God the other articles that have been contributed for use in his temple. 20 If you need to get anything else for the temple, you may have the money you need from the royal treasury.

21 Ezra, you are a priest and an expert in the laws of the God of heaven, and I order all treasurers in Western Province to do their very best to help you. 22 They will be allowed to give as much as 3,400 kilogrammes of silver, 10,000 kilogrammes of wheat, 2,000 litres of wine, 2,000 litres of olive oil, and all the salt you need.

23 They must provide whatever the God of heaven demands for his temple, so that he won't be angry with me and with the kings who rule after me. 24 We want you to know that no priests, Levites, musicians, guards, temple servants, or any other temple workers will have to pay any kind of taxes.

25 Ezra, use the wisdom God has given you and choose officials and leaders to govern the people of Western Province. These leaders should know God's laws and have them taught to anyone who doesn't know them. 26 Everyone who fails to obey God's Law or the king's law will be punished without pity. They will be executed or put in prison or forced to leave their country, or have all their own taken away.

Ezra praises God

27 Because King Artaxerxes was so kind, Ezra said:

Praise the LORD God of our ancestors! He made sure that the king honoured the LORD's temple in Jerusalem. 28 God has told the king, his advisers, and his powerful officials to treat me with kindness. The LORD God has helped me, and I have been able to bring many Jewish leaders back to Jerusalem.

---

*7.1–6 Artaxerxes: Either Artaxerxes I (ruled from 465 to 425 BC) or Artaxerxes II (ruled from 405–358 BC).

*7.7 seventh year . . . Artaxerxes: 458 BC if this is Artaxerxes I; 398 BC, if this is Artaxerxes II (see the note at 7.1–6).

*7.8,9 fifth month: Ab, the fifth month of the Hebrew calendar, from about mid-July to mid-August.

*7.8,9 first month: See the note at 6.19.

CHAPTER 8

The families who came back with Ezra

¹ Artaxerxes was king of Persia when I* led the following chiefs of the family groups from Babylonia to Jerusalem:

²⁻¹⁴ Gershom of the Phinehas family;
  Daniel of the Ithamar family;
  Hattush son of Shecaniah of the
    David family;
  Zechariah and 150 other men of the
    Parosh family, who had family records;
  Eliehoenai son of Zerahiah with 200 men
    of the Pahath Moab family;
  Shecaniah son of Jahaziel with 300 men
    of the Zattu family;*
  Ebed son of Jonathan with 50 men of the
    Adin family;
  Jeshaiah son of Athaliah with 70 men of
    the Elam family;
  Zebadiah son of Michael with 80 men of
    the Shephatiah family;
  Obadiah son of Jehiel with 218 men of
    the Joab family;
  Shelomith son of Josiphiah with
    160 men of the Bani family;*
  Zechariah son of Bebai with 28 men of
    the Bebai family;
  Johanan son of Hakkatan with 110 men
    of the Azgad family;
  Eliphelet, Jeuel, and Shemaiah who
    returned some time later with 60 men
    of the Adonikam family;
  Uthai and Zaccur with 70 men of the
    Bigvai family.

Ezra finds Levites for the temple

¹⁵ I* brought everyone together by the river* that flows to the town of Ahava* where we camped for three days. Not one Levite could be found among the people and priests. ¹⁶ So I sent for the leaders Eliezer, Ariel, Shemaiah, Elnathan, Jarib, Elnathan, Nathan, Zechariah, and Meshullam. I also sent for Joiarib and Elnathan, who were very wise. ¹⁷ Then I sent them to Iddo, the leader at Casiphia,* and I told them to ask him and his temple workers to send people to serve in God's temple. ¹⁸ God was kind to us and made them send a skilful man named Sherebiah, who was a Levite from the family of Mahli. Eighteen of

his relatives came with him. ¹⁹ We were also sent Hashabiah and Jeshaiah from the family of Merari along with twenty of their relatives. ²⁰ In addition, 220 others came to help the Levites in the temple. The ancestors of these workers had been chosen years ago by King David* and his officials, and they were all listed by name.

Ezra asks the people to go without eating and to pray

²¹ Beside the River* Ahava, I* asked the people to go without eating* and to pray. We humbled ourselves and asked God to bring us and our children safely to Jerusalem with all our possessions. ²² I was ashamed to ask the king to send soldiers and cavalry to protect us against enemies along the way. After all, we had told the king that our God takes care of everyone who truly worships him, but that he gets very angry and punishes anyone who refuses to obey. ²³ So we went without food and asked God himself to protect us, and he answered our prayers.

The gifts for the temple

²⁴ I* chose twelve of the leading priests — Sherebiah, Hashabiah and ten of their relatives. ²⁵⁻²⁷ Then I weighed the gifts that had been given for God's temple, and I divided them among the twelve priests I had chosen. There were gifts of silver and gold, as well as the articles that the king, his advisers and officials, and the people of Israel had contributed. In all there were 22 tonnes of silver; 100 silver articles weighing 70 kilogrammes; 3,400 kilogrammes of gold; 20 gold bowls weighing over 8 kilogrammes; and 2 polished bronze articles as valuable as gold. ²⁸ I said to the priests:

You belong to the LORD, the God of your ancestors, and these things also belong to him. The silver and gold were willingly given as gifts to the LORD. ²⁹ Be sure to guard them and keep them safe until you reach Jerusalem. Then weigh them inside God's temple in the presence of the chief priests, the Levites, and the heads of the Israelite families.

---

*8.1 I: Ezra.
*8.15 I: See the note at 8.1.
*8.15 town of Ahava: A town (or place) in Babylonia, but the exact location is unknown.
*8.17 Casiphia: The location is not known.

*8.20 King David: See the note at 3.10.
*8.21,24 I: See the note at 8.1.
*8.21 to go without eating: The Jews often went without eating as a way of worshipping God. This is sometimes called "fasting".

³⁰ The priests and Levites then took charge of the gifts that had been weighed, so they could take them to the temple of our God in Jerusalem.

The return to Jerusalem

³¹ On the twelfth day of the first month,* we left the River' Ahava and started for Jerusalem. Our God watched over us, and as we travelled along, he kept our enemies from ambushing us.

³² After arriving in Jerusalem, we rested for three days. ³³ Then on the fourth day we went to God's temple, where the silver, the gold, and the other things were weighed and given to the priest Meremoth son of Uriah. With him were Eleazar son of Phinehas and the two Levites, Jozabad son of Jeshua and Noadiah son of Binnui. ³⁴ Everything was counted, weighed, and recorded.

³⁵ Those who had returned from exile offered sacrifices on the altar to the God of Israel. Twelve bulls were offered for all Israel. Ninety-six rams and seventy-seven* lambs were offered on the altar. And twelve goats were sacrificed for the sins of the people. ³⁶ Some of those who had returned took the king's orders to the governors and officials in Western Province. Then the officials did what they could for the people and for the temple of God.

Ezra forces men to divorce their Gentile wives

CHAPTER 9

Ezra condemns mixed marriages

¹ Later the Jewish leaders came to me* and said:

Many Israelites, including priests and Levites, are living just like the people around them. They are even guilty of some of the horrible sins of the Canaanites, the Hittites, the Perizzites, the Jebusites, the Ammonites, the Moabites, the Egyptians, and the Amorites. ² Some Israelite men have married foreign women and have let their sons do the same thing. Our own officials and leaders were the first to commit this disgusting sin, and now God's holy people are mixed with foreigners.

³ This news made me so angry that I ripped my clothes and tore hair from my head and beard. Then I just sat in shock * until time for the evening sacrifice. Many of our people were greatly concerned and gathered around me, because the God of Israel had warned us to stay away from foreigners.

Ezra's prayer

⁵ At the time of the evening sacrifice, I was still sitting there in sorrow with my clothes all torn. So I got down on my knees, then lifted my arms, ⁶ and prayed:

I am much too ashamed to face you, LORD God. Our sins and our guilt have swept over us like a flood that reaches up to the heavens. ⁷ Since the time of our ancestors, all of us have sinned. That's why we, our kings, and our priests have often been defeated by other kings. They have killed some of us and made slaves of others; they have taken our possessions and made us ashamed, just as we are today.

⁸ But for now, LORD God, you have shown great kindness to us. You made us truly happy by letting some of us settle in this sacred place and by helping us in our time of slavery.* ⁹ We are slaves, but you have never turned your back on us. You love us, and because of you, the kings of Persia have helped us. It's as though you have given us new life! You let us rebuild your temple and live safely in Judah and Jerusalem.

¹⁰ Our God, what can we say now? Even after all this, we have disobeyed the commands ¹¹ that were given to us by your servants the prophets. They said the land you are giving us is full of sinful and wicked people, who never stop doing disgusting things.* ¹² And we were warned not to let our daughters and sons marry their sons and daughters.

Your prophets also told us never to help those foreigners or even let them live in peace. You wanted us to become strong and to enjoy the good things in the land, then some day to leave it to our children for ever. ¹³ You punished us because of our terrible sins. But you did not punish us nearly as much as we deserve, and you have brought some of us back home. ¹⁴ Why should we disobey your commands again by letting our sons and daughters marry these

---

*8.31 first month: See the note at 6.19.
*8.35 seventy-seven: Or "seventy-two".
*9.1 me: Ezra.

*9.11 doing disgusting things: Probably worshipping idols.
See also: 9.12: Exod 34.11–16; Deut 7.1–5.

foreigners who do such disgusting things? That would make you angry enough to destroy us all! ¹⁵ LORD God of Israel, you have been more than fair by letting a few of us survive. But once again, our sins have made us ashamed to face you.

CHAPTER 10

The plan for ending mixed marriages

¹ While Ezra was down on his knees in front of God's temple, praying with tears in his eyes, and confessing the sins of the people of Israel, a large number of men, women, and children gathered around him and cried bitterly.

² Shecaniah son of Jehiel from the family of Elam said:

Ezra, we have disobeyed God by marrying these foreign women. But there is still hope for the people of Israel, ³ if we follow your advice and the advice of others who truly respect the laws of God. We must promise God that we will divorce our foreign wives and send them away, together with their children.

⁴ Ezra, it's up to you to do something! We will support whatever you do. So be brave!

⁵ Ezra stood up and made the chief priests, the Levites, and everyone else in Israel swear that they would follow the advice of Shecaniah. ⁶ Then Ezra left God's temple and went to spend the night in the living quarters of Jehohanan son of Eliashib. He felt sorry for what the people had done, and he did not eat or drink a thing.

⁷⁻⁸ The officials and leaders sent a message to all who had returned from Babylonia and were now living in Jerusalem and Judah. It told them to meet in Jerusalem within three days, or else they would lose everything they owned and would no longer be considered part of the people that had returned from Babylonia.

⁹ Three days later, on the twentieth day of the ninth month,* everyone from Judah and Benjamin came to Jerusalem and sat in the temple courtyard. It was a serious meeting, and they sat there, trembling in the rain.

¹⁰ Ezra the priest stood up and said:

You have broken God's Law by marrying foreign women, and you have made the whole nation guilty! ¹¹ Now you must confess your sins to the LORD God of your ancestors and obey him. Divorce your foreign wives and don't have anything to do with the rest of the foreigners who live around here.

¹² Everyone in the crowd shouted:

You're right! We will do what you say. ¹³ But there are so many of us, and we can't just stay out here in this downpour. A lot of us have sinned by marrying foreign women, and the matter can't be settled in only a day or two.

¹⁴ Why can't our officials stay on in Jerusalem and take care of this for us? Let everyone who has sinned in this way meet here at a certain time with leaders and judges from their own towns. If we take care of this problem, God will surely stop being so terribly angry with us.

¹⁵ Jonathan son of Asahel and Jahzeiah son of Tikvah were the only ones who objected, except for the two Levites, Meshullam and Shabbethai.

¹⁶ Everyone else who had returned from exile agreed with the plan. So Ezra the priest chose men* who were heads of the families, and he listed their names. They started looking into the matter on the first day of the tenth month,* ¹⁷ and they did not finish until the first day of the first month* of the next year.

The men who had foreign wives

¹⁸⁻¹⁹ Here is a list of the priests who had agreed to divorce their foreign wives and to sacrifice a ram as a sin offering:
Maaseiah, Eliezer, Jarib, and Gedaliah from the family of Joshua son of Jozadak and his brothers; ²⁰ Hanani and Zebadiah from the family of Immer; ²¹ Maaseiah, Elijah, Shemaiah, Jehiel, and Uzziah from the family of Harim; ²² Elioenai, Maaseiah, Ishmael, Nethanel, Jozabad, and Elasah from the family of Pashhur.

²³ Those Levites who had foreign wives were: Jozabad, Shimei, Kelaiah (also known as Kelita), Pethahiah, Judah, and Eliezer.

---

*10.9 ninth month: Chislev, the ninth month of the Hebrew calendar, from about mid-November to mid-December.

*10.16 tenth month: Tebeth, the tenth month of the Hebrew calendar, from about mid-December to mid-January.

*10.17 first month: See the note at 6.19.

²⁴ Eliashib, the musician, had a foreign wife.

These temple guards had foreign wives: Shallum, Telem, and Uri.

²⁵ Here is a list of the others from Israel who had foreign wives:

Ramiah, Izziah, Malchijah, Mijamin, Eleazar, Hashabiah,ᵝ and Benaiah from the family of Parosh;

²⁶ Mattaniah, Zechariah, Jehiel, Abdi, Jeremoth, and Elijah from the family of Elam;

²⁷ Elioenai, Eliashib, Mattaniah, Jeremoth, Zabad, and Aziza from the family of Zattu;

²⁸ Jehohanan, Hananiah, Zabbai, and Athlai from the family of Bebai;

²⁹ Meshullam, Malluch, Adaiah, Jashub, Sheal, and Jeremoth from the family of Bani;

³⁰ Adna, Chelal, Benaiah, Maaseiah, Mattaniah, Bezalel, Binnui, and Manasseh from the family of Pahath Moab;

³¹⁻³² Eliezer, Isshijah, Malchijah, Shemaiah, Shimeon, Benjamin, Malluch, and Shemariah from the family of Harim;

³³ Mattenai, Mattattah, Zabad, Eliphelet, Jeremai, Manasseh, and Shimei from the family of Hashum;

³⁴⁻³⁷ Maadai, Amram, Uel, Benaiah, Bedeiah, Cheluhi, Vaniah, Meremoth, Eliashib, Mattaniah, Mattenai, and Jaasu from the family of Bani;

³⁸⁻⁴² Shimei, Shelemiah, Nathan, Adaiah, Machnadebai, Shashai, Sharai, Azarel, Shelemiah, Shemariah, Shallum, Amariah, and Joseph from the family of Binnui;ᵝ

⁴³ Jeiel, Mattithiah, Zabad, Zebina, Jaddai, Joel, and Benaiah from the family of Nebo.

⁴⁴ These men divorced their foreign wives, then sent them and their children away.ᵝ

Additional notes

ᵝ**1.9,10 other dishes:** One possible meaning for the difficult Hebrew text.
ᵝ**2.2–20 Joshua:** Hebrew "Jeshua". In this translation the name "Joshua" is used of the descendant of Jozadak, the last chief priest before the exile; this same Joshua is often mentioned together with Zerubbabel (2.2–20; 3.2,8,9; 4.3; 5.2; 10.18,19). In other places the name "Jeshua" is used (2.2–20,36–39,40–42; 8.33).
ᵝ**2.2–20 Jeshua and Joab:** Hebrew "Jeshua Joab".
ᵝ**2.21–35 Elam:** Hebrew "the other Elam".
ᵝ**2.70 workers:** One possible meaning for the difficult Hebrew text of verse 70.

ᵝ**3.3 where it had stood before:** One possible meaning for the difficult Hebrew text.
ᵝ**3.9 Hodaviah:** Or "Yehudah" or "Hodiah".
ᵝ**4.8–10 the judges . . . Susa:** One possible translation for the names and titles.
ᵝ**5.1 Zechariah:** Aramaic "Zechariah son of Iddo".
ᵝ**5.12 the Babylonian king:** Aramaic "the Babylonian king from Chaldea", but Chaldea is another name for Babylonia.
ᵝ**6.3 so that . . . there:** One possible meaning for the difficult Aramaic text.
ᵝ**6.4 one:** One possible meaning for the difficult Aramaic text.
ᵝ**7.13,14 find out if:** Or "make sure that".
ᵝ**8.2–14 of the Zattu family:** One ancient translation; these words are not in the Hebrew text, but see 2.2–20, where Zattu is mentioned.
ᵝ**8.2–14 of the Bani family:** One ancient translation; these words are not in the Hebrew text, but see 2.2–20.
ᵝ**8.15 river:** Or "canal".
ᵝ**8.21 River:** See the note at 8.15.
ᵝ**8.31 River:** See the note at 8.15.
ᵝ**10.16 So . . . men:** One possible meaning for the difficult Hebrew text.
ᵝ**10.25 Hashabiah:** One ancient translation; Hebrew "Malchijah".
ᵝ**10.38–42 from the family of Binnui:** One possible meaning for the difficult Hebrew text.
ᵝ**10.44 away:** One possible meaning for the difficult Hebrew text of verse 44.

Nehemiah

A quick look at this book

Twelve years after the last events of the book of Ezra, a Jew named Nehemiah received bad news about Jerusalem: the walls of the city were still broken down, and the burnt gates had never been replaced.

Nehemiah lived in the Persian city of Susa and was a personal servant to King Artaxerxes. So Nehemiah prayed and asked God to make Artaxerxes send him to Jerusalem to rebuild the city. Artaxerxes did send Nehemiah, and he even provided the materials for the repairs.

After Nehemiah had arrived in Jerusalem and the repair work had begun, the officials from neighbouring areas insulted the Jews and accused them of wanting to rebel against Persia. These enemies even planned attacks against Jerusalem and tried to have Nehemiah killed. Finally, the walls and gates were finished and dedicated to God, and they became a sign that God had blessed his people.

But Nehemiah realized that God would continue to bless his people only if they obeyed him. As Nehemiah said in one of his prayers:

> LORD God of heaven, you are great and fearsome. And you faithfully keep your promises to everyone who loves you and obeys your commands.

(1.5)

King Artaxerxes sends Nehemiah to Jerusalem

CHAPTER 1

Nehemiah's prayer

¹ I am Nehemiah son of Hacaliah, and in this book I tell what I have done.

During the month of Chislev* in the twentieth year that Artaxerxes* ruled Persia, I was in his fortress city of Susa,* ² when my

---

*1.1 Chislev: The ninth month of the Hebrew calendar, from about mid-November to mid-December.

*1.1 Artaxerxes: Probably Artaxerxes I, who ruled Persia 465-425 BC.

*1.1 Susa: Capital of Elam Province, the winter home of Persian kings.

brother Hanani came with some men from Judah. So I asked them about the Jews who had escaped* from being captives in Babylonia. I also asked them about the city of Jerusalem.

³ They told me, "Those captives who have come back are having all kinds of troubles. They are terribly disgraced. Jerusalem's walls are broken down, and its gates have been burnt."

⁴ When I heard this, I sat down and cried. Then for several days, I mourned; I went without eating to show my sorrow, and I prayed:

⁵ LORD God of heaven, you are great and fearsome. And you faithfully keep your promises to everyone who loves you and obeys your commands. ⁶ I am your servant, so please have mercy on me and answer the prayer that I make day and night for these people of Israel who serve you. I, my family, and the rest of your people have sinned ⁷ by choosing to disobey you and the laws and teachings you gave to your servant Moses.

⁸ Please remember the promise you made to Moses. You told him that if we were unfaithful, you would scatter us among foreign nations. ⁹ But you also said that no matter how far away we were, we could turn to you and start obeying your laws. Then you would bring us back to the place where you have chosen to be worshipped.

¹⁰ Our LORD, I am praying for your servants — those you rescued by your great strength and mighty power. ¹¹ Please answer my prayer and the prayer of your other servants who gladly honour your name. When I serve the king his wine today, make him pleased with me and let him do what I ask.

CHAPTER 2

Nehemiah goes to Jerusalem

¹ During the month of Nisan* in the twentieth year that Artaxerxes was king, I served him his wine, as I had done before. But this was the first time I had ever looked depressed. ² So the king said, "Why do you look so sad? You're not sick. Something must be bothering you."

Even though I was frightened, ³ I answered, "Your Majesty, I hope you live for ever! I feel sad because the city where my ancestors are buried is in ruins, and its gates have been burnt down."

⁴ The king asked, "What do you want me to do?"

I prayed to the God who rules from heaven. ⁵ Then I told the king, "Sir, if it's all right with you, please send me back to Judah, so that I can rebuild the city where my ancestors are buried."

⁶ The queen was sitting beside the king when he asked me, "How long will it take, and when will you be back?" The king agreed to let me go, and I told him when I would return.

⁷ Then I asked, "Your Majesty, would you be willing to give me letters to the governors of the provinces west of the River Euphrates, so that I can travel safely to Judah? ⁸ I will need timber to rebuild the gates of the fortress near the temple and more timber to construct the city wall and to build a place for me to live. And so, I would appreciate a letter to Asaph, who is in charge of the royal forest." God was good to me, and the king did everything I asked.

⁹ The king sent some army officers and cavalry troops along with me, and as I travelled through the Western Provinces, I gave the letters to the governors. ¹⁰ But when Sanballat from Horon* and Tobiah the Ammonite official heard about what had happened, they became very angry, because they didn't want anyone to help the people of Israel.

Rebuilding the walls of Jerusalem

Nehemiah inspects the wall of Jerusalem

¹¹ Three days after arriving in Jerusalem, ¹² I got up during the night and left my house. I took some men with me, without telling anyone what I thought God wanted me to do for the city. The only animal I took was the donkey I rode on. ¹³ I went through Valley Gate on the west, then south past Dragon Spring, before coming to Rubbish Gate. As I rode along, I took a good look at the crumbled walls of the city and the gates that

---

*2.1 Nisan: Or Abib, the first month of the Hebrew calendar, from about mid-March to mid-April.

See also: 1.8: Lev 26.33. 1.9: Deut 30.1-5.

*2.10 Horon: Possibly meaning that Sanballat was the official in charge of Beth-Horon, an important town on the road from Jerusalem to Lydda and the Mediterranean Sea.

See also: 2.3: 2 King 25.8-10; 2 Chron 36.19; Jer 52.12-14.

had been torn down and burnt. [14] On the east side of the city, I headed north to Fountain Gate and King's Pool, but then the path became too narrow for my donkey. [15] So I went down to Kidron Valley and looked at the wall from there. Then before daylight I returned to the city through Valley Gate.

[16] None of the city officials knew what I had in mind. And I had not even told any of the Jews — not the priests, the leaders, the officials, or any other Jews who would be helping in the work. [17] But when I got back, I said to them, "Jerusalem is truly in a mess! The gates have been torn down and burnt, and everything is in ruins. We must rebuild the city wall so that we can again take pride in our city."

[18] Then I told them how kind God had been and what the king had said.

Immediately, they replied, "Let's start building now!" So they got everything ready.

[19] When Sanballat, Tobiah, and Geshem the Arab heard about our plans, they started insulting us and saying, "Just look at you! Do you plan to rebuild the walls of the city and rebel against the king?"

[20] I answered, "We are servants of the God who rules from heaven, and he will make our work succeed. So we will start rebuilding Jerusalem, but you have no right to any of its property, because you have had no part in its history."

CHAPTER 3

Rebuilding the wall of Jerusalem

[1] These are the people who helped rebuild the wall and gates of Jerusalem:

The high priest Eliashib and the other priests rebuilt Sheep Gate and hung its doors. Then they dedicated Sheep Gate and the section of the wall as far as Hundred Tower and Hananel Tower.

[2] The people of Jericho rebuilt the next section of the wall, and Zaccur son of Imri rebuilt the section after that.

[3] The family of Hassenaah built Fish Gate. They put the beams in place and hung the doors, then they added metal bolts and wooden beams as locks.

[4] Meremoth, son of Uriah and grandson of Hakkoz, completed the next section of the wall.

Meshullam, son of Berechiah and grandson of Meshezabel, rebuilt the next section, and Zadok son of Baana rebuilt the section beside that.

[5] The next section was to be repaired by the men of Tekoa, but their town leaders refused to do the hard work they were assigned.*

[6] Joiada son of Paseah and Meshullam son of Besodeiah restored Ancient Gate. They put the beams in place, hung the doors, and added metal bolts and wooden beams as locks. [7] Melatiah from Gibeon, Jadon from Meronoth, and the men from Gibeon and Mizpah rebuilt the next section of the wall. This section reached as far as the house of the governor of West Euphrates Province.*

[8] Uzziel son of Harhaiah the goldsmith rebuilt the next section.

Hananiah the perfume maker rebuilt the section next after that, and it went as far as Broad Wall.

[9] Rephaiah son of Hur ruled half of the Jerusalem District, and he rebuilt the next section of the wall.

[10] The section after that was close to the home of Jedaiah son of Harumaph, and he rebuilt it.

Hattush son of Hashabneiah constructed the next section of the wall.

[11] Malchijah son of Harim and Hasshub son of Pahath Moab rebuilt the section after that, and they also built Oven Tower.

[12] Shallum son of Hallohesh ruled the other half of the Jerusalem District, and he rebuilt the next section of the wall. Shallum's daughters also worked with him.

[13] Hanun and the people who lived in the town of Zanoah rebuilt Valley Gate. They hung the doors and added metal bolts and wooden beams as locks. They also rebuilt the wall for four hundred and forty metres, all the way to Rubbish Gate.

[14] Malchijah son of Rechab ruled the district of Beth-Haccherem, and he rebuilt Rubbish Gate. He hung the doors and added metal bolts and wooden beams as locks.

[15] Shallum* son of Colhozeh ruled the district of Mizpah, and he rebuilt Fountain Gate. He put a cover over the gateway, then hung the doors and added metal bolts and wooden beams as locks. He also rebuilt the wall at Shelah Pool. This section was next to the king's garden and went as far as the stairs leading down from David's City.

[16] Nehemiah son of Azbuk ruled half of the district of Beth-Zur, and he rebuilt the next section of the wall. It went as far as the royal cemetery,* the artificial pool, and the army barracks.

Levites who worked on the wall

17 The Levites who worked on the next sections of the wall were Rehum son of Bani; Hashabiah, who ruled half of the district of Keilah and did this work for his district; 18 Binnui* son of Henadad, who ruled the other half of the district of Keilah; 19 Ezer son of Jeshua, who ruled Mizpah, rebuilt the section of the wall that was in front of the armoury and reached to the corner of the wall; 20 Baruch son of Zabbai eagerly rebuilt the section of the wall that went all the way to the door of the house of Eliashib the high priest; 21 Meremoth, son of Uriah and grandson of Hakkoz, built up to the far end of Eliashib's house.

Priests who worked on the wall

22 Here is a list of the priests who worked on the wall:

Priests from the region around Jerusalem rebuilt the next section of the wall.

23 Benjamin and Hasshub rebuilt the wall in front of their own houses.

Azariah, who was the son of Maaseiah and the grandson of Ananiah, rebuilt the section in front of his house.

24 Binnui son of Henadad rebuilt the section of the wall from Azariah's house to the corner of the wall.

25 Palal son of Uzai rebuilt the next section, which began at the corner of the wall and the tower of the upper palace near the court of the guard.

Pedaiah son of Parosh rebuilt the next section of the wall. 26 He stopped at a place near the Water Gate on the east and the tower guarding the temple. This was close to a section in the city called Ophel, where the temple workers lived.*

Other builders who worked on the wall

27 The men from Tekoa rebuilt the next section of the wall, and it was their second section.* It started at a place opposite the large tower that guarded the temple, and it went all the way to the wall near Ophel.

28 Some priests rebuilt the next section of the wall. They began working north of Horse Gate, and each one worked on a section in front of his own home.

29 Zadok son of Immer rebuilt the wall in front of his house.

Shemaiah son of Shecaniah, who looked after the East Gate, rebuilt the section after that.

30 Hananiah and Hanun* rebuilt the next section, which was the second section* for them.

Meshullam son of Berechiah rebuilt the next section, which happened to be in front of his house.

31 Malchijah, a goldsmith, rebuilt the next section, as far as the house used by the temple workers and merchants. This area was opposite Gathering Gate, near the room on top of the wall at the north-east corner.

32 The goldsmiths and merchants rebuilt the last section of the wall, which went from the corner room all the way to Sheep Gate.

CHAPTER 4

Nehemiah's enemies

1 When Sanballat, the governor of Samaria, heard that we were rebuilding the walls of Jerusalem, he became angry and started insulting our people. 2 In front of his friends and the Samaritan army he said, "What is this feeble bunch of Jews trying to do? Are they going to rebuild the wall and offer sacrifices all in one day? Do they think they can make something out of this pile of scorched stones?"

3 Tobiah from Ammon was standing beside Sanballat and said, "Look at the wall they are building! Why, even a fox could knock over this pile of stones."

4 But I prayed, "Our God, these people hate us and have wished horrible things for us. Please answer our prayers and make their insults fall on them! Let them be the ones to be dragged away as prisoners of war. 5 Don't forgive the mean and evil way they have insulted the builders."

6 The people worked hard, and we built the walls of Jerusalem halfway up again. 7 But Sanballat, Tobiah, the Arabs, the Ammonites, and the people from the city of Ashdod saw the walls going up and the holes being repaired. So they became angry 8 and decided to stir up trouble, and to fight against the people of Jerusalem. 9 But we kept on praying to our God, and we also stationed guards day and night.

10 Meanwhile, the people of Judah were singing a sorrowful song:

---

*3.27 second section: See verse 5.

*3.30 second section: See verses 8,13.

"So much rubble for us to haul!
 Worn out and weary,
 will we ever finish this wall?"

[11] Our enemies were saying, "Before those Jews know what has happened, we will sneak up and kill them and put an end to their work."

[12] On at least ten different occasions, the Jews living near our enemies warned us against attacks from every side,' [13] and so I sent people to guard the wall at its lowest places and where there were still holes in it. I placed them according to families, and they stood guard with swords and spears and with bows and arrows. [14] Then I looked things over and told the leaders, the officials, and the rest of the people, "Don't be afraid of your enemies! The Lord is great and fearsome. So think of him and fight for your relatives and children, your wives and homes!"

[15] Our enemies found out that we knew about their plot against us, but God kept them from doing what they had planned. So we went back to work on the wall.

[16] From then on, I let half of the young men work while the other half stood guard. They wore armour and had spears and shields, as well as bows and arrows. The leaders helped the workers [17] who were rebuilding the wall. Everyone who hauled building materials kept one hand free to carry a weapon. [18] Even the workers who were rebuilding the wall strapped on a sword. The worker who was to blow the signal trumpet stayed with me.

[19] I told the people and their officials and leaders, "Our work is so spread out, that we are a long way from one another. [20] If you hear the sound of the trumpet, come quickly and gather around me. Our God will help us fight."

[21] Every day from dawn to dark, half of the workers rebuilt the walls, while the rest stood guard with their spears.

[22] I asked the men in charge and their workers to stay inside Jerusalem and stand guard at night. So they guarded the city at night and worked during the day. [23] I even slept in my work clothes at night; my children, the workers, and the guards slept in theirs as well. And we always kept our weapons close by.'

Nehemiah's concern for the poor

CHAPTER 5

[1] Some of the men and their wives complained about the Jews in power [2] and said, "We have large families, and it takes a lot of grain merely to keep them alive."

[3] Others said, "During the famine we even had to mortgage our fields, vineyards, and homes to them in order to buy grain."

[4] Then others said, "We had to borrow money from those in power to pay the government tax on our fields and vineyards. [5] We are Jews just as they are, and our children are as good as theirs. But we still have to sell our children as slaves, and some of our daughters have already been raped. We are completely helpless; our fields and vineyards have even been taken from us."

[6] When I heard their complaints and their charges, I became very angry. [7] So I thought it over and said to the leaders and officials, "How can you charge your own people interest?"

Then I called a public meeting and accused the leaders [8] by saying, "We have tried to buy back all of our people who were sold into exile. But here you are, selling more of them for us to buy back!" The officials and leaders did not say a word, because they knew this was true.

[9] I continued, "What you have done is wrong! We must honour our God by the way we live, so the Gentiles can't find fault with us. [10] My relatives, my friends, and I are also lending money and grain, but we must no longer demand payment in return. [11] Now give back the fields, vineyards, olive orchards, and houses you have taken and also the interest you have been paid."

[12] The leaders answered, "We will do whatever you say and return their property, without asking to be repaid."

So I made the leaders promise in front of the priests to give back the property. [13] Then I emptied my pockets and said, "If you don't keep your promise, that's what God will do to you. He will empty out everything you own, even taking away your houses."

The people answered, "We will keep our promise." Then they praised the LORD and did as they had promised.

See also: **5.7:** Exod 22.25; Lev 25.35–37; Deut 23.19,20.

Nehemiah is generous

¹⁴ I was governor of Judah from the twentieth year that Artaxerxes* was king until the thirty-second year. And during these entire twelve years, my relatives and I refused to accept the food that I was allowed. ¹⁵ Each governor before me had been a burden to the people by making them pay for his food and wine and by demanding forty silver coins a day. Even their officials had been a burden to the people. But I respected God, and I didn't think it was right to be so hard on them. ¹⁶ I spent all my time getting the wall rebuilt and did not buy any property. Everyone working for me did the same thing. ¹⁷ I usually fed a hundred and fifty of our own Jewish people and their leaders, as well as foreign visitors from surrounding lands. ¹⁸ Each day one ox, six of the best sheep, and lots of chickens were prepared. Then every ten days, a large supply of wine was brought in. I knew what a heavy burden this would have been for the people, and so I did not ask for my food allowance as governor.

¹⁹ I pray that God will bless me for everything I have done for my people.

The wall is finished, in spite of enemy plots

CHAPTER 6

Plots against Nehemiah

¹ Sanballat, Tobiah, Geshem, and our other enemies learnt that I had completely rebuilt the wall. All I lacked was hanging the doors in the gates. ² Then Sanballat and Geshem sent a message, asking me to meet with them in one of the villages in Ono Valley. I knew they were planning to harm me in some way. ³ So I sent messengers to tell them, "My work is too important to stop now and go there. I can't afford to slow down the work just to visit you." ⁴ They invited me four times, but each time I refused to go.

⁵ Finally, Sanballat sent an official to me with an unsealed letter, ⁶ which said:

A rumour is going around among the nations that you and the other Jews are rebuilding the wall and planning to rebel, because you want to be their king. And Geshem* says it's true! ⁷ You even have prophets in Jerusalem, claiming you are now the king of Judah. You know the Persian king will hear about this, so let's get together and talk it over.

⁸ I sent a message back to Sanballat, saying, "None of this is true! You are making it all up."

⁹ Our enemies were trying to frighten us and to keep us from our work. But I asked God to give me strength.

¹⁰ One day I went to visit Shemaiah.* He was looking very worried, and* he said, "Let's hurry to the holy place of the temple and hide there.* We will lock the temple doors, because your enemies are planning to kill you tonight."

¹¹ I answered, "Why should someone like me have to run and hide in the temple to save my life? I won't go!"

¹² Suddenly I realized that God had not given Shemaiah this message. But Tobiah and Sanballat had paid him to trick me ¹³ and to frighten me into doing something wrong, because they wanted to ruin my good name.

¹⁴ Then I asked God to punish Tobiah and Sanballat for what they had done. I prayed that God would punish the prophet Noadiah and the other prophets who, together with her, had tried to frighten me.

The work is finished

¹⁵ On the twenty-fifth day of the month Elul,* the wall was completely rebuilt. It had taken fifty-two days. ¹⁶ When our enemies in the surrounding nations learnt that the work was finished, they felt helpless, because they knew that our God had helped us rebuild the wall.

¹⁷ All this time the Jewish leaders and Tobiah had been writing letters back and forth. ¹⁸ Many people in Judah were loyal to Tobiah for two reasons: Shecaniah son of Arah was his father-in-law, and Tobiah's son Jehohanan had married the daughter of Meshullam son of Berechiah.* ¹⁹ The people would always tell me about the good things Tobiah had done, and then they would tell Tobiah everything I had said. So Tobiah kept sending letters, trying to frighten me.

---

*6.10 holy place . . . hide there: Only priests were allowed to enter the holy place; anyone else could be put to death.
*6.15 Elul: The sixth month of the Hebrew calendar, from about mid-August to mid-September.
*6.18 Shecaniah . . . Berechiah: Jews who had helped rebuild the Jerusalem wall (see 3.4,29,30).

---

*5.14 Artaxerxes: See the note at 1.1.

CHAPTER 7

¹ After the wall had been rebuilt and the gates hung, then the temple guards, the singers, and the other Levites were assigned their work. ² I put my brother Hanani in charge of Jerusalem, along with Hananiah, the commander of the fortress, because Hananiah could be trusted, and he respected God more than most people did. ³ I said to them, "Don't let the gates to the city be opened until the sun has been up for a while. And make sure that they are closed and barred before the guards go off duty at sunset. Choose people from Jerusalem to stand guard at different places around the wall and others to stand guard near their own houses."

Exiles who returned

A list of exiles who returned

This is also told in Ezra 2.1–70

⁴ Although Jerusalem covered a large area, not many people lived there, and no new houses had been built. ⁵⁻⁶ So God gave me the idea to bring together the people, their leaders, and officials and to check the family records of those who had returned from captivity in Babylonia, after having been taken there by King Nebuchadnezzar.* About this same time, I found records of those who had been the first to return to Jerusalem from Babylon Province.* By reading these records, I learnt that they settled in their own home towns, ⁷ and that they had come with Zerubbabel, Joshua, Nehemiah, Azariah, Raamiah, Nahamani, Mordecai, Bilshan, Mispereth, Bigvai, Nehum, and Baanah.

⁸⁻²⁵ Here is how many had returned from each family group: 2,172 from Parosh; 372 from Shephatiah; 652 from Arah; 2,818 from Pahath Moab, who were all descendants of Jeshua and Joab; 1,254 from Elam; 845 from Zattu; 760 from Zaccai; 648 from Binnui; 628 from Bebai; 2,322 from Azgad; 667 from Adonikam; 2,067 from Bigvai; 655 from Adin; 98 from Ater, also known as Hezekiah; 328 from Hashum; 324 from Bezai; 112 from Hariph; and 95 from Gibeon.

²⁶⁻³⁸ Here is how many people returned whose ancestors had come from the following towns: 188 from Bethlehem and Netophah; 128 from Anathoth; 42 from Beth-Azmaveth; 743 from Kiriath-Jearim, Chephirah, and Beeroth; 621 from Ramah and Geba; 122 from Michmas; 123 from Bethel and Ai; 52 from Nebo;* 1,254 from Elam;* 320 from Harim; 345 from Jericho; 721 from Lod, Hadid, and Ono; and 3,930 from Senaah.

³⁹⁻⁴² Here is how many returned from each family of priests: 973 descendants of Jeshua from Jedaiah; 1,052 from Immer; 1,247 from Pashhur; and 1,017 from Harim.

⁴³⁻⁴⁵ Here is how many returned from the families of Levites: 74 descendants of Hodevah from the families of Jeshua and Kadmiel; 148 descendants of Asaph from the temple musicians; and 138 descendants of Shallum, Ater, Talmon, Akkub, Hatita, and Shobai the temple guards.

⁴⁶⁻⁵⁶ Here are the names of the families of temple workers whose descendants returned: Ziha, Hasupha, Tabbaoth, Keros, Sia, Padon, Lebana, Hagaba, Shalmai, Hanan, Giddel, Gahar, Reaiah, Rezin, Nekoda, Gazzam, Uzza, Paseah, Besai, Meunim, Nephushesim, Bakbuk, Hakupha, Harhur, Bazlith, Mehida, Harsha, Barkos, Sisera, Temah, Neziah, and Hatipha.

⁵⁷⁻⁵⁹ Here are the names of Solomon's servants whose descendants returned: Sotai, Sophereth, Perida, Jaala, Darkon, Giddel, Shephatiah, Hattil, Pochereth Hazzebaim, and Amon.

⁶⁰ A total of 392 descendants of temple workers and of Solomon's servants returned.

⁶¹⁻⁶² There were 642 who returned from the families of Delaiah, Tobiah, and Nekoda, though they could not prove they were Israelites. They had lived in the Babylonian towns of Tel-Melah, Tel-Harsha, Cherub, Addon, and Immer.

⁶³⁻⁶⁴ The families of Hobaiah, Hakkoz, and Barzillai could not prove they were priests. The ancestor of the family of Barzillai had married the daughter of Barzillai from Gilead and had taken his wife's family name. But the records of these three families could not be found, and none of them were allowed to serve as priests. ⁶⁵ In fact, the governor told them, "You cannot eat the food offered to God until he lets you know if you really are priests."

---

*7.5,6 Nebuchadnezzar: Known as Nebuchadnezzar II, who ruled Babylonia from 605 to 562 BC. In 586 BC he destroyed Jerusalem and took many of its people to Babylonia.

*7.5,6 first to return . . . Province: Probably 539 BC, when Cyrus, the ruler of Persia, captured the city of Babylon.

*7.65 until . . . priests: The Hebrew text has "until a priest comes with the urim and thummim", sacred objects which were used in some way to receive answers from God.

See also: 7.65: Exod 28.30; Deut 33.8.

66-69 There were 42,360 who returned, in addition to 7,337 servants, and 245 musicians. Altogether, they brought with them 736 horses, 245 mules,' 435 camels, and 6,720 donkeys.

70-72 Many people gave gifts to help pay for the materials to rebuild the temple. The governor himself gave 8 kilogrammes of gold, 50 bowls to be used in the temple, and 530 robes for the priests. Family leaders gave 153 kilogrammes of gold and 1,458 kilogrammes of silver. The rest of the people gave 153 kilogrammes of gold, 1,325 kilogrammes of silver, and 67 robes for the priests.

73 And so, by the seventh month,* priests, Levites, temple guards, musicians, workers, and many of the ordinary people had settled in the towns of Judah.

Ezra reads God's Law to the people, and they celebrate the Festival of Shelters

CHAPTER 8

Ezra reads God's Law to the people

1-2 On the first day of the seventh month,* the people came together in the open area in front of the Water Gate. Then they asked Ezra, who was a teacher of the Law of Moses, to read to them from this Law that the LORD had given his people. Ezra the priest came with the Law and stood before the crowd of men, women, and the children who were old enough to understand. 3 From early morning till midday, he read the Law of Moses to them, and they listened carefully. 4 Ezra stood on a high wooden platform that had been built for this occasion. Mattithiah, Shema, Anaiah, Uriah, Hilkiah, and Maaseiah were standing to his right, while Pedaiah, Mishael, Malchijah, Hashum, Hash Baddanah, Zechariah, and Meshullam were standing to his left.

5 Ezra was up on the high platform, where he could be seen by everyone, and when he opened the book, they all stood up. 6 Ezra praised the great LORD God, and the people shouted, "Amen! Amen!" Then they bowed

with their faces to the ground and worshipped the LORD.

7-8 After this, the Levites Jeshua, Bani, Sherebiah, Jamin, Akkub, Shabbethai, Hodiah, Maaseiah, Kelita, Azariah, Jozabad, Hanan, and Pelaiah went among the people, explaining the meaning of what Ezra had read.

9 The people started crying when God's Law was read to them. Then Nehemiah the governor, Ezra the priest and teacher, and the Levites who had been teaching the people all said, "This is a special day for the LORD your God. So don't be sad and don't cry!"

10 Nehemiah told the people, "Enjoy your good food and wine and share some with those who didn't have anything to bring. Don't be sad! This is a special day for the LORD, and he will make you happy and strong."

11 The Levites encouraged the people by saying, "This is a sacred day, so don't worry or mourn!" 12 When the people returned to their homes, they celebrated by eating and drinking and sharing their food with those in need, because they had understood what had been read to them.

Celebrating the Festival of Shelters

13 On the second day of the seventh month,' the leaders of all the family groups came together with the priests and the Levites, so Ezra could teach them the Law 14 that the LORD had given to Moses. They learnt from the Law that the people of Israel were to live in shelters when they celebrated the festival in the seventh month of the year. 15 They also learnt that they were to go into the woods and gather branches of leafy trees such as olives, myrtles, and palms for making these shelters.

16 So the people gathered branches and made shelters on the flat roofs of their houses, in their yards, in the courtyard of the temple, and in the open areas around the Water Gate and Ephraim Gate. 17 Everyone who had returned from Babylonia built shelters. They lived in them and joyfully celebrated the Festival of Shelters for the first time since the days of Joshua son of Nun. 18 On each of the first seven days of the festival, Ezra read to the people from God's Law. Then on the eighth day, everyone gathered for worship, just as the Law had said they must.

---

*7.73 seventh month: Tishri (also called Ethanim), the seventh month of the Hebrew calendar, from about mid-September to mid-October.
*8.1,2 seventh month: See the note at 7.73.
See also: 7.73: 1 Chron 9.2; Neh 11.3.

See also: 8.14,15: Lev 23.33–36,39–43; Deut 16.13–15.

The people confess their sins

CHAPTER 9

¹ On the twenty-fourth day of the seventh month,ᵃ the people of Israel went without eating, and they dressed in sackcloth and threw dust on their heads to show their sorrow. ² They refused to let foreigners join them, as they met to confess their sins and the sins of their ancestors. ³ For three hours they stood and listened to the Law of the LORD their God, and then for the next three hours they confessed their sins and worshipped the LORD.

⁴ Jeshua, Bani, Kadmiel, Shebaniah, Bunni, Sherebiah, Bani, and Chenani stood on the special platform for the Levites and prayed aloud to the LORD their God. ⁵ Then the Levites Jeshua, Kadmiel, Bani, Hashabneiah, Sherebiah, Hodiah, Shebaniah, and Pethahiah said:

"Stand and shout praises
   to your LORD,
      the eternal God!ᵇ
Praise his wonderful name,
though he is greater
   than words can express."

The people pray

⁶ You alone are the LORD,
   Creator of the heavens
      and all the stars,
   Creator of the earth
      and those who live on it,
   Creator of the ocean
      and all its creatures.
You are the source of life,
   praised by the stars
      that fill the heavens.
⁷ You are the LORD our God,
   the one who chose Abram —
you brought him from Ur
   in Babylonia
and named him Abraham.
⁸ Because he was faithful,
   you made an agreement
to give his descendants
   the land of the Canaanites
      and Hittites,
   of the Amorites and Perizzites,
   and of the Jebusites and Girgashites.

Now you have kept your promise,
   just as you always do.

⁹ When our ancestors were in Egypt,
   you saw their suffering;
when they were at the Red Sea,*
   you heard their cry for help.
¹⁰ You knew that the King of Egypt
   and his officials and his nation
      had ill-treated your people.
So you worked fearsome miracles
   against the Egyptians
and earned a reputation
   that still remains.
¹¹ You divided the deep sea,
   and your people walked through
      on dry land.
But you tossed their enemies in,
   and they sank down
      like a heavy stone.
¹² Each day you led your people
   with a thick cloud,
and at night you showed the way
   with a flaming fire.
¹³ At Sinai you came down from heaven,
   and you gave your people
good laws and teachings
   that are fair and honest.
¹⁴ You commanded them to respect
   your holy Sabbath,
and you instructed
   your servant Moses
to teach them your laws.
¹⁵ When they were hungry,
   you sent bread from heaven,
and when they were thirsty,
   you let water flow from a rock.
Then you commanded them
   to capture the land
that you had solemnly promised.

¹⁶⁻¹⁷ Our stubborn ancestors
   refused to obey —
they forgot about the miracles
   you had worked for them,
and they were determined

*9.9 Red Sea: Hebrew *yam suph* "Sea of Reeds", one of the marshes or fresh water lakes near the eastern part of the Nile Delta. This identification is based on Exodus 13.17—14.9, which lists the towns on the route of the Israelites before crossing the sea. In the Greek translation of the Scriptures made about 200 BC, the "Sea of Reeds" was named "Red Sea".

See also: 9.1: a Exod 3.7; b Exod 14.10-12. 9.10: a Exod 14.21-29; b Exod 15.4,5. 9.12: Exod 13.21,22. 9.13,14: Exod 19.18—23.33. 9.15: a Exod 16.4-15; b Exod 17.1-7; c Deut 1.21. 9.16,17: Num 14.1-4; Deut 1.26-33. 9.17: Exod 34.6; Num 14.18.

to return to Egypt
and become slaves again.
But, our God, you are merciful
and quick to forgive;
you are loving, kind,
and very patient.
So you never turned away from them —
18 not even when they made
an idol shaped like a calf
and insulted you by claiming,
"This is the god who rescued us
from Egypt."

19 Because of your great mercy,
you never abandoned them
in the desert.
And you always guided them
with a cloud by day and a fire at night.
20 Your gentle Spirit instructed them,'
and you gave them manna* to eat
and water to drink.
21 You took good care of them,
and for forty years
they never lacked a thing.
Their shoes didn't wear out,
and their feet were never swollen.

22 You let them conquer kings
and take their land,
including King Sihon of Heshbon
and King Og of Bashan.'
23 You brought them into the land
that you had promised their ancestors,
and you blessed their nation
with people who outnumbered
the stars in the sky.

24 Then their descendants
conquered the land.
You helped them defeat
the kings and nations
and treat their enemies
however they wished.
25 They captured strong cities
and rich farmland;
they took furnished houses,
as well as cisterns,*
vineyards, olive orchards,
and numerous fruit trees.
They ate till they were satisfied,
and they celebrated
your abundant blessings.

26 In spite of this, they rebelled
and disobeyed your laws.
They killed your prophets,
who warned them
to turn back to you,
and they cursed your name.
27 So you handed them over
to their enemies,
who treated them terribly.
But in their sufferings,
they begged you to help.
From heaven you listened
to their prayers
and because of your great mercy,
you sent leaders to rescue them.

28 But when they were at peace,
they would turn against you,
and you would hand them over
to their enemies.
Then they would beg for help,
and because you are merciful,
you rescued them
over and over again.
29 You warned them to turn back
and discover true life
by obeying your laws.
But they stubbornly refused
and continued to sin.
30 For years, you were patient,
and your Spirit' warned them
with messages spoken
by your prophets.
Still they refused to listen,
and you handed them over
to their enemies.
31 But you are merciful and kind,
and so you never forgot them
or let them be destroyed.

32 Our God, you are powerful,
fearsome, and faithful,
always true to your word.
So please keep in mind
the terrible sufferings
of our people, kings, leaders,
priests, and prophets,
from the time Assyria ruled
until this very day.
33 You have always been fair
when you punished us for our sins.

34 Our kings, leaders, and priests
have never obeyed your commands
or heeded your warnings.

---

*9.20 manna: This was something like a thin wafer
(see Exodus 16.1–36).
*9.25 cisterns: Pits dug into the ground to hold water.

See also: 9.18: Exod 32.1–4. 9.19–21: Deut 8.2–4.
9.22: Num 21.21–35. 9.23: a Gen 15.5; 22.17;
b Josh 3.14–17. 9.24: Josh 11.23. 9.25: Deut 6.10,11.

See also: 9.26–28: Judg 2.11–16. 9.29: Lev 18.5.
9.30: 2 King 17.13–18; 2 Chron 36.15,16.
9.32: 2 King 15.19,29; 17.3–6; Ezra 4.2,10.

³⁵ You blessed them with a kingdom
and with an abundance
of rich, fertile land,
but they refused to worship you
or turn from their evil.
³⁶ Now we are slaves
in this fruitful land
you gave to our ancestors.
³⁷ Its plentiful harvest is taken
by kings you placed over us
because of our sins.
Our suffering is unbearable,
because they do as they wish
to us and our livestock.

The people sign an agreement to obey the Lord

³⁸ And so, a firm agreement was made that
had the official approval of the leaders, the
Levites, and priests.

CHAPTER 10

¹ As governor, I* signed the agreement
together with Zedekiah and the following
priests: ²⁻⁸ Seraiah, Azariah, Jeremiah,
Pashhur, Amariah, Malchijah, Hattush,
Shebaniah, Malluch, Harim, Meremoth,
Obadiah, Daniel, Ginnethon, Baruch,
Meshullam, Abijah, Mijamin, Maaziah,
Bilgai, and Shemaiah.

⁹ The Levites who signed were: Jeshua son
of Azaniah, Binnui from the clan of Henadad,
Kadmiel, ¹⁰ Shebaniah, Hodiah, Kelita,
Pelaiah, Hanan, ¹¹ Mica, Rehob, Hashabiah,
¹² Zaccur, Sherebiah, Shebaniah, ¹³ Hodiah,
Bani, and Beninu.

¹⁴ The leaders who signed were: Parosh,
Pahath Moab, Elam, Zattu, Bani, ¹⁵ Bunni,
Azgad, Bebai, ¹⁶ Adonijah, Bigvai, Adin,
¹⁷ Ater, Hezekiah, Azzur, ¹⁸ Hodiah, Hashum,
Bezai, ¹⁹ Hariph, Anathoth, Nebai,
²⁰ Magpiash, Meshullam, Hezir,
²¹ Meshezabel, Zadok, Jaddua, ²² Pelatiah,
Hanan, Anaiah, ²³ Hoshea, Hananiah,
Hasshub, ²⁴ Hallohesh, Pilha, Shobek,
²⁵ Rehum, Hashabnah, Maaseiah, ²⁶ Ahiah,
Hanan, Anan, ²⁷ Malluch, Harim, and
Baanah.

The agreement

²⁸⁻²⁹ All of us, including priests, Levites,
temple guards, singers, temple workers and
leaders, together with our wives and

children, have separated ourselves from
the foreigners in this land and now enter
into an agreement with a complete
understanding of what we are doing. And
so, we now place ourselves under the curse
of the LORD our God, if we fail to obey his
laws and teachings that were given to us by
his servant Moses.

³⁰ We won't let our sons and daughters
marry foreigners.

³¹ We won't buy goods or grain on the
Sabbath or on any other sacred day, not
even from foreigners.

Every seven years we will let our fields
rest, and we will cancel all debts.

³² Once a year we will each donate a
small amount of silver to the temple of our
God. ³³ This is to pay for the sacred bread,
as well as for the daily sacrifices and special
sacrifices such as those offered on the
Sabbath and during the New Moon Festival
and the other festivals. It will also pay for
the sacrifices to forgive our sins and for all
expenses connected with the worship of
God in the temple.

³⁴ We have decided that the families* of
priests, Levites, and ordinary people will
supply firewood for the temple each year,
so that sacrifices can be offered on the altar,
just as the LORD our God has commanded.

³⁵ Each year we will bring to the temple
the first part of our harvest of grain and
fruit.

³⁶ We will bring our firstborn sons and
the firstborn males of our herds and flocks
and offer them to the priests who serve in
the temple, because this is what is written
in God's Law.*

³⁷ To the priests in the temple of our God,
we will bring the bread dough from the first
harvest, together with our best fruit, and an
offering of new wine and olive oil.

We will bring ten per cent of our grain
harvest to those Levites who are
responsible for collecting it in our towns.
³⁸ A priest from the family of Aaron must
be there when we give this to the Levites.
Then the Levites will put one tenth of this
part in the temple storeroom, ³⁹ which is
also the place for the sacred objects used by

---

*10.36 firstborn sons . . . God's Law: See
Exodus 13.2,12–15; 34.19,20.

See also: 10.30: Exod 34.16; Deut 7.3.
10.31: a Exod 23.10,11; Lev 25.1–7; b Deut 15.1,2.
10.32: Exod 30.11–16. 10.35: Exod 23.19; 34.26; Deut 26.2.
10.36: Exod 13.2. 10.37: Num 18.21. 10.38: Num 18.26.

*10.1 I: Hebrew "Nehemiah son of Hacaliah".

the priests, the temple guards, and the singers.

Levites and everyone else must bring their gifts of grain, wine, and olive oil to this room.

We will not neglect the temple of our God.

The people who settled in Jerusalem and Judah

CHAPTER 11

People who settled in Jerusalem

[1] The nation's leaders and their families settled in Jerusalem. But there was room for only one out of every ten of the remaining families, and so they asked God to show them* who would live there. [2] Then everyone else asked God to bless those who were willing to live in Jerusalem.

[3] Some of the people of Israel, the priests, the Levites, the temple workers, and the descendants of Solomon's servants lived on their own property in the towns of Judah. But the leaders of the province lived in Jerusalem with their families.

The Judah tribe

[4-6] From the Judah tribe, two leaders settled in Jerusalem with their relatives. One of them was Athaiah son of Uzziah. His ancestors were Zechariah, Amariah, Shephatiah, Mahalalel, and Perez, the son of Judah. From the descendants of Perez, four hundred and sixty-eight of the best men lived in Jerusalem.

The other leader from Judah was Maaseiah the son of Baruch. His ancestors were Colhozeh, Hazaiah, Adaiah, Joiarib, Zechariah, and Shelah, the son of Judah.

The Benjamin tribe

[7-8] From the Benjamin tribe, three leaders settled in Jerusalem. The first was Sallu son of Meshullam, and the others were Gabbai and Sallai. Sallu's ancestors were Joed, Pedaiah, Kolaiah, Maaseiah, Ithiel, and Jeshaiah. Altogether, there were nine hundred and twenty-eight men of the Benjamin tribe living in Jerusalem. [9] Joel son of Zichri was

their leader, and Judah son of Hassenuah was second in command.

Priests

[10] Four priests settled in Jerusalem. The first was Jedaiah; he was the son of Joiarib and the uncle of Jachin.*

[11] The second priest to settle there was Seraiah son of Hilkiah. His ancestors were Meshullam, Zadok, Meraioth, and Ahitub, who had been a high priest. [12] Altogether, there were eight hundred and twenty-two from his clan who served in the temple.

The third priest to settle there was Adaiah son of Jeroham. His ancestors were Pelaliah, Amzi, Zechariah, Pashhur, and Malchijah. [13] Altogether, there were two hundred and forty-two clan leaders among his relatives.

The fourth priest to settle there was Amashsai son of Azarel. His ancestors were Ahzai, Meshillemoth, and Immer. [14] Altogether, there were one hundred and twenty-eight brave warriors from their clans, and their leader was Zabdiel son of Haggedolim.

Levites

[15] Several Levites settled in Jerusalem. First, there was Shemaiah son of Hasshub. His ancestors were Azrikam, Hashabiah, and Bunni.

[16] Next, there were Shabbethai and Jozabad, who were in charge of the work outside the temple.

[17] Then there was Mattaniah son of Mica. His ancestors were Zabdi and Asaph. Mattaniah led the temple choir in the prayer of praise. Bakbukiah, who also settled in Jerusalem, was his assistant.

Finally, there were Abda son of Shammua; his grandfather was Galal, and his great-grandfather was Jeduthun.

[18] Altogether, two hundred and eighty-four Levites settled in the holy city.

Temple guards and others

[19] One hundred and seventy-two temple guards settled in Jerusalem; their leaders were Akkub and Talmon.

[20] The rest of the Israelites, including priests and Levites, lived on their own property in the other towns of Judah. [21] But

---

*11.1 asked God to show them: The Hebrew text has "cast lots". These were made of wood or stone and were thrown on the ground by a priest or official to find out how and when to do something.

See also: 11.3,4; Neh 7.73.

*11.10 son of Joiarib and the uncle of Jachin: See 1 Chronicles 9.10; the Hebrew text has "son of Joiarib, Jachin".

the temple workers lived in the section of Jerusalem known as Ophel, and the two men in charge of them were Ziha and Gishpa.

²² Uzzi son of Bani was the leader of the Levites in Jerusalem. His grandfather was Hashabiah, his great-grandfather was Mattaniah, and his great-great-grandfather was Mica. He belonged to the Asaph clan that was in charge of the music for the temple services, ²³ though the daily choice of singers and musicians was decided by royal decree of the Persian king.

²⁴ The people of Israel were represented at the Persian court by Pethahiah son of Meshezabel from the Zerah clan of the Judah tribe.

The people in the other towns and villages

²⁵ Some of the people of Judah lived in the following towns near their farms: Kiriath-Arba, Dibon, Jekabzeel, ²⁶ Jeshua, Moladah, Beth-Pelet, ²⁷ Hazar-Shual, Beersheba, ²⁸ Ziklag, Meconah, ²⁹ Enrimmon, Zorah, Jarmuth, ³⁰ Zanoah, Adullam, Lachish, and Azekah. In fact, they settled the towns from Beersheba in the south to Hinnom Valley in the north.

³¹ The people of Benjamin lived in the towns of Geba, Michmash, Aija, Bethel with its nearby villages, ³² Anathoth, Nob, Ananiah, ³³ Hazor, Ramah, Gittaim, ³⁴ Hadid, Zeboim, Neballat, ³⁵ Lod, and Ono, as well as in Craft Valley. ³⁶ Several groups of Levites from the territory of Judah were sent to live among the people of Benjamin.

Priests and Levites who returned from exile

CHAPTER 12

A list of priests and Levites

¹ Many priests and Levites had returned from Babylonia with Zerubbabel* and Joshua as their leaders. Those priests were Seraiah, Jeremiah, Ezra, ² Amariah, Malluch, Hattush, ³ Shecaniah, Rehum, Meremoth, ⁴ Iddo, Ginnethoi, Abijah, ⁵ Mijamin, Maadiah, Bilgah, ⁶ Shemaiah, Joiarib, Jedaiah, ⁷ Sallu, Amok, Hilkiah, and another Jedaiah. These were the leading priests and their assistants during the time of Joshua.*

⁸ The Levites who returned were Jeshua, Binnui, Kadmiel, Sherebiah, Judah, and Mattaniah. They and their assistants were responsible for the songs of praise, ⁹ while Bakbukiah and Unno, together with their assistants, were responsible for the choral responses.

Descendants of Joshua the high priest

¹⁰ Joshua was the father of Joiakim, the grandfather of Eliashib, and the great-grandfather of Joiada. ¹¹ Joiada was the father of Jonathan and the grandfather of Jaddua.

Leaders of the priestly clans

¹² When Joiakim was high priest, the following priests were leaders of their clans: Meraiah of the Seraiah clan, Hananiah of Jeremiah, ¹³ Meshullam of Ezra, Jehohanan of Amariah, ¹⁴ Jonathan of Malluchi, Joseph of Shebaniah, ¹⁵ Adna of Harim, Helkai of Meraioth, ¹⁶ Zechariah of Iddo, Meshullam of Ginnethon, ¹⁷ Zichri of Abijah,* Piltai of Moadiah, ¹⁸ Shammua of Bilgah, Jehonathan of Shemaiah, ¹⁹ Mattenai of Joiarib, Uzzi of Jedaiah, ²⁰ Kallai of Sallai, Eber of Amok, ²¹ Hashabiah of Hilkiah, and Nethanel of Jedaiah.

The priestly and Levite families

²² During the time of the high priests Eliashib, Joiada, Johanan, and Jaddua, and including the time that Darius was king of Persia, a record was kept of the heads of the Levite and priestly families. ²³ However, no official record was kept of the heads of the Levite clans after the death of Johanan,* the grandson of Eliashib.

²⁴ Hashabiah, Sherebiah, Jeshua son of Kadmiel,* and their assistants organized two choirs of Levites to offer praises to God, just as King David, the man of God, had commanded.

²⁵ Mattaniah, Bakbukiah, Obadiah, Meshullam, Talmon, and Akkub were responsible for guarding the storerooms near the temple gates.

²⁶ All these men lived during the time of Joiakim* and during the time that I was governor and Ezra, a teacher of the Law of Moses, was priest.

---

*12.7 Joshua: Joshua the high priest and friend of Zerubbabel (see verse 1 and Haggai 1.1; 2.2).

*12.23 death of Johanan: Probably between 408 and 405 BC, when Darius II died.

Nehemiah dedicates the city wall

27 When the city wall was dedicated, Levites from everywhere in Judah were invited to join in the celebration with songs of praise and with the music of cymbals, small harps, and other stringed instruments. 28-29 The Levite singers lived in villages around Jerusalem, and so they came from there, as well as from the villages around Netophah, Beth-Gilgal, Geba, and Azmaveth. 30 The priests and Levites held special ceremonies to make themselves holy, and then they did the same for the rest of the people and for the gates and walls of the city.

31 I brought the leaders of Judah to the top of the city wall and put them in charge of the two groups that were to march around on top of the wall, singing praises to God. One group marched to the right in the direction of Rubbish Gate. 32 Hoshaiah and half of the leaders followed them. 33 Then came the priests Azariah, Ezra, Meshullam, 34 Judah, Benjamin, Shemaiah, and Jeremiah, 35 all of them blowing trumpets. Next, there was Zechariah the Asaph clan* 36 and his relatives, Shemaiah, Azarel, Milalai, Gilalai, Maai, Nethanel, Judah, and Hanani. They played musical instruments like those that had been played by David, the man of God. And they marched behind Ezra, the teacher of the Law. 37 When they reached Fountain Gate, they climbed the steps to David's City and went past his palace, before stopping at the Water Gate near the eastern wall of the city.

38 The second group of singers marched along the wall in the opposite direction, and I followed them, together with the other half of the leaders of Judah. We went past Oven Tower, Broad Wall, 39 Ephraim Gate, Old Gate, Fish Gate, Hananel Tower, Hundred Tower, and on to Sheep Gate. Finally, we stopped at Gate of the Guard, 40 where we stood in front of the temple with the other group, praising God. In the group with me were half of the leaders, 41 as well as the priests Eliakim, Maaseiah, Miniamin, Micaiah, Elioenai, Zechariah, and Hananiah, who were blowing trumpets. 42 Maaseiah, Shemaiah, Eleazar, Uzzi, Jehohanan, Malchijah, Elam, and Ezer also stood there, as Jezrahiah led the singers. 43 God had made the people very happy, and so on that day they celebrated and offered many sacrifices. The women and children joined in the festivities, and joyful shouts could be heard far from the city of Jerusalem.

Preparation for worship

44 On that same day, some leaders were appointed to be responsible for the safekeeping of gifts for the temple and to be in charge of receiving the first part of the harvest and the ten per cent of the crops and livestock that was offered to God. These same leaders also collected the part of crops that the Law of Moses taught was to be given to the Levites.

Everyone was pleased with the work of the priests and Levites, 45 when they performed the ceremonies to make people acceptable to worship God. And the singers and the temple guards did their jobs according to the instructions given by David and his son Solomon. 46 In fact, ever since the days of David and Asaph, there had been song leaders and songs of praise and worship. 47 During the time when Zerubbabel and I were in charge, everyone in Israel gave what they were supposed to give for the daily needs of the singers and temple guards from the Levi tribe. Then the Levites would give the priests their share from what they had received.

Changes Nehemiah made

CHAPTER 13

Foreigners are sent away

1 On that day when the Law of Moses was read aloud to everyone, it was discovered that Ammonites and Moabites were forbidden to belong to the people of God. 2 This was because they had refused to give food and water to Israel and had hired Balaam* to call down a curse on them. However, our God turned the curse into a blessing. 3 Following the reading of the Law of Moses, the people of Israel started sending away anyone who had any foreign ancestors.

Nehemiah makes other changes

4 The priest Eliashib was a relative of Tobiah and had earlier been put in charge of the temple storerooms. 5 So he let Tobiah live in one of these rooms, where all kinds of things had been stored — the grain offerings, incense, utensils for the temple, as well as the tenth of

---

*13.2 Balaam: See Numbers 22.1–6.

See also: 12.45: a 1 Chron 25.1–8; b 1 Chron 26.12.
13.1,2: Deut 23.3–5. 13.2: Num 22.1–6.

the grain, wine, and olive oil that had been given for the use of the Levites, singers, and temple guards, and the gifts for the priests.

[6] This happened in the thirty-second year that Artaxerxes* ruled Babylonia. I was away from Jerusalem at the time, because I was visiting him. Later I received permission from the king [7] to return to Jerusalem. Only then did I find out that Eliashib had done this terrible thing of letting Tobiah have a room in the temple. [8] It upset me so much that I threw out every bit of Tobiah's furniture. [9] Then I ordered the room to be cleaned and the temple utensils, the grain offerings, and the incense to be brought back into the room.

[10] I also found out that the temple singers and several other Levites had returned to work on their farms, because they had not been given their share of the harvest. [11] I called the leaders together and angrily asked them, "Why is the temple neglected?" Then I told them to start doing their jobs. [12] After this, everyone in Judah brought a tenth of their grain, wine, and olive oil to the temple storeroom. [13] Finally, I appointed three men with good reputations to be in charge of what was brought there and to distribute it to the others. They were Shelemiah the priest, Zadok the teacher of the Law, and Pedaiah the Levite. Their assistant was Hanan, the son of Zaccur and the grandson of Mattaniah.

[14] I pray that my God will remember these good things that I have done for his temple and for those who worship there.

The Sabbath

[15] I also noticed what the people of Judah were doing on the Sabbath. Not only were they trampling grapes to make wine, but they were harvesting their grain, grapes, figs, and other crops, and then loading these on donkeys to sell in Jerusalem. So I warned them not to sell food on the Sabbath. [16] People who had moved to Jerusalem from the city of Tyre were bringing in fish and other things to sell there on the Sabbath. [17] I got angry and said to the leaders of Judah, "This evil you are doing is an insult to the Sabbath! [18] Didn't God punish us and this city because our ancestors did these very same things? And here you are, about to make God furious again by disgracing the Sabbath!"

[19] I ordered the gates of Jerusalem to be closed on the eve of the Sabbath* and not to be opened until after the Sabbath had ended. Then I put some of my own men in charge of the gates to make certain that nothing was brought in on the Sabbath. [20] Once or twice some merchants spent the night outside Jerusalem with their goods. [21] But I warned them, "If you do this again, I'll have you arrested." From then on, they did not come on the Sabbath. [22] I ordered the Levites to make themselves holy and to guard the gates on the Sabbath, so that it would be kept holy.

God is truly merciful, and I pray that he will treat me with kindness and bless me for doing this.

Mixed marriages

[23] I discovered that some Jewish men had married women from Ashdod, Ammon, and Moab. [24] About half of their children could not speak Hebrew — they spoke only the language of Ashdod or some other foreign language. [25] So in my anger, I called down curses on those men. I had them beaten and even pulled out the hair of some of them. Then I made them promise:

In the name of God we solemnly promise not to let our sons and daughters marry foreigners. [26] God dearly loved King Solomon of Israel and made him the greatest king on earth, but Solomon's foreign wives led him into sin. [27] So we will obey you and not rebel against our God by marrying foreign women.

[28] Jehoiada, the son of the high priest Eliashib, had a son who had married a daughter of Sanballat from Horon,* and I forced his son to leave.

[29] I pray that God will punish them for breaking their priestly vows and disgracing the Levi tribe.

[30] Then I made sure that the people were free from every foreign influence, and I assigned duties for the priests and Levites. [31] I also arranged for the people to bring firewood to the altar each day and for them to bring the first part of their harvest to the temple.

I pray that God will bless me for the good I have done.

---

*13.19 eve of the Sabbath: The Jewish day began at sunset.
*13.28 Horon: See the note at 2.10.
See also: 13.23–25: Exod 34.11–16; Deut 7.1–5.
13.26: a 2 Sam 12.24,25; b 1 King 11.1–8. 13.28: Neh 4.1.

---

*13.6 Artaxerxes: See the note at 1.1.
See also: 13.10: Deut 12.19. 13.12: Mal 3.10.
13.15: Exod 20.8-10; Deut 5.12–14; Jer 17.21,22.

Additional notes

'1.2 escaped: Or "returned".

'3.5 refused . . . assigned: One possible meaning for the difficult Hebrew text.

'3.7 as far as . . . Province: One possible meaning for the difficult Hebrew text.

'3.15 Shallum: A few Hebrew manuscripts and one ancient translation; most Hebrew manuscripts "Shallun"; one ancient translation "Solomon".

'3.16 royal cemetery: Hebrew "David's tombs".

'3.18 Binnui: Two ancient translations; Hebrew "Bavvai".

'3.26 This . . . lived: One possible meaning for the difficult Hebrew text.

'3.30 Hananiah and Hanun: Hebrew "Hananiah son of Shelemiah and Hanun, Zalaph's sixth son".

'4.12 against . . . side: One possible meaning for the difficult Hebrew text.

'4.23 And . . . by: One possible meaning for the difficult Hebrew text.

'6.6 Geshem: Hebrew "Gashmu" (see verse 1 and 2.19).

'6.10 Shemaiah: Hebrew "Shemaiah son of Delaiah son of Mehetabel."

'6.10 was . . . worried, and: Or "wasn't supposed to leave his house, but".

'7.26–38 Nebo: Hebrew "the other Nebo".

'7.26–38 Elam: Hebrew "the other Elam".

'7.66–69 736 horses, 245 mules: A few Hebrew manuscripts; this is not found in most Hebrew manuscripts of verse 68.

'8.13 seventh month: Hebrew "same month".

'9.1 seventh month: See the note at 8.13.

'9.5 shout . . . God: Or "shout eternal praises to the LORD your God."

'9.20 Your gentle Spirit instructed them: Or "You gently instructed them".

'9.22 Bashan: One possible meaning for the difficult Hebrew text of verse 22.

'9.30 your Spirit: Or "you".

'10.34 that the families: Or "which families".

'12.1 Zerubbabel: Hebrew "Zerubbabel son of Shealtiel".

'12.17 of Abijah: The Hebrew text adds " . . . of Miniamin".

'12.24 son of Kadmiel: Or possibly "Binnui, Kadmiel" (see 10.9; 12.8).

'12.26 Joiakim: Hebrew "Joiakim son of Joshua son of Jozadak".

'12.35 Zechariah of the Asaph clan: Hebrew "Zechariah son of Jonathan son of Shemaiah son of Mattaniah son of Micaiah son of Zaccur son of Asaph".

Esther

A quick look at this book

The story of Esther takes place in the city of Susa, in the winter palace of the Persian king. After King Xerxes divorced his queen, he chose a young Jewish woman named Esther as his new queen. She was an orphan but had been adopted and cared for by her cousin, Mordecai, who was given a job as a palace official. Mordecai warned her not to tell anyone that she was a Jew, and she obeyed.

The king's highest official was a man named Haman. He hated the Jews, and he tricked the king into giving permission to have them all killed. The rest of the book tells how Esther risked her own life to save the lives of her people.

Afterwards, Mordecai and Esther wrote a letter telling all Jews to celebrate the Festival of Purim every year to remember how the nation was saved.

The Hebrew text of the book of Esther doesn't mention God, but the whole plot shows that God was protecting his people by making Esther queen, and as Mordecai put it:

> It could be that you were made queen for a time like this!

(4.14b)

Esther becomes queen

CHAPTER 1

Queen Vashti disobeys King Xerxes

¹⁻² King Xerxes* of Persia lived in his capital city of Susa* and ruled one hundred and twenty-seven provinces from India to Ethiopia.* ³ During the third year of his rule, Xerxes gave a big dinner for all his officials and officers. The governors and leaders of the provinces were also invited, and even the commanders of the Persian and Median armies came. ⁴ For one hundred and eighty days he showed off his wealth and spent a lot of money to impress his guests with the greatness of his kingdom.

---

*1.1,2 Xerxes: The Hebrew text has "Ahasuerus", who was better known as King Xerxes I (485–465 BC).
*1.1,2 in his capital city of Susa: Or "in his royal fortress in the city of Susa". Susa was a city east of Babylon and a winter home for Persian kings.
*1.1,2 Ethiopia: The Hebrew text has "Cush", which was a region south of Egypt that included parts of the present countries of Ethiopia and Sudan.
See also: 1.1: Ezra 4.6.

⁵ King Xerxes soon gave another dinner and invited everyone in the city of Susa, no matter who they were. The eating and drinking lasted seven days in the beautiful palace gardens.
⁶ The area was decorated with blue and white cotton curtains tied back with purple linen cords that ran through silver rings fastened to marble columns. Couches of gold and silver rested on pavement that had all kinds of designs made from costly bright-coloured stones and marble and mother-of-pearl.
⁷ The guests drank from gold cups, and each cup had a different design. The king was generous ⁸ and said to them, "Drink all you want!" Then he told his servants, "Keep their cups full."

⁹ While the men were enjoying themselves, Queen Vashti gave the women a big dinner inside the royal palace.

¹⁰ By the seventh day, King Xerxes was feeling happy because of so much wine. And he asked his seven personal servants, Mehuman, Biztha, Harbona, Bigtha, Abagtha, Zethar, and Carkas, ¹¹ to bring Queen Vashti to him. The king wanted her to wear her crown and let his people and his officials see how beautiful she was. ¹² The king's servants told Queen Vashti what he had said, but she refused to go to him, and this made him terribly angry.

¹³⁻¹⁴ The king called in the seven highest officials of Persia and Media. They were Carshena, Shethar, Admatha, Tarshish, Meres, Marsena, and Memucan. These men were very wise and understood all the laws and customs of the country, and the king always asked them what they thought about such matters.

¹⁵ The king said to them, "Queen Vashti refused to come to me when I sent my servants for her. What does the law say I should do about that?"

¹⁶ Then Memucan told the king and the officials:

Your Majesty, Queen Vashti has not only embarrassed you, but she has insulted your officials and everyone else in all the provinces.
¹⁷ The women in the kingdom will hear about this, and they will refuse to respect their husbands. They will say, "If Queen Vashti doesn't obey her husband, why should we?" ¹⁸ Before this day is over, the wives of the officials of Persia and Media will find out what Queen Vashti has done, and they will refuse to obey their husbands. They won't respect their husbands, and their husbands will be angry with them.

¹⁹ Your Majesty, if you agree, you should write for the Medes and Persians a law that can never be changed. This law would keep Queen Vashti from ever seeing you again. Then you could let someone who respects you be queen in her place.
²⁰ When the women in your great kingdom hear about this new law, they will respect their husbands, no matter if they are rich or poor.

²¹ King Xerxes and his officials liked what Memucan had said, ²² and he sent letters to all his provinces. Each letter was written in the language of the province to which it was sent, and it said that husbands should have complete control over their wives and children.

CHAPTER 2

Esther becomes queen

¹ After a while, King Xerxes got over being angry. But he kept thinking about what Vashti had done and the law that he had written because of her. ² Then the king's personal servants said:

Your Majesty, a search must be made to find you some beautiful young women.
³ You can select officers in every province to bring them to the place where you keep your wives in the capital city of Susa. Put your servant Hegai in charge of them since that is his job. He can see to it that they are given the proper beauty treatments. ⁴ Then let the young woman who pleases you most take Vashti's place as queen.

King Xerxes liked these suggestions, and he followed them.

⁵ At this time a Jew named Mordecai was living in Susa. His father was Jair, and his grandfather Shimei was the son of Kish from the tribe of Benjamin. ⁶ Kish* was one of the people whom Nebuchadnezzar had taken from Jerusalem, when he took King Jeconiah of Judah to Babylonia.
⁷ Mordecai had a very beautiful cousin named Esther, whose Hebrew name was Hadassah. He had raised her as his own daughter, after her father and mother died.
⁸ When the king ordered that beautiful women, many were taken to the king's palace in Susa, and Esther was one of them.

See also: **2.6:** 2 King 24.10–16; 2 Chron 36.10.

Hegai was put in charge of all the women, 9 and from the first day, Esther was his favourite. He began her beauty treatments at once. He also gave her plenty of food and seven special maids from the king's palace, and they had the best rooms.

10 Mordecai had warned Esther not to tell anyone that she was a Jew, and she obeyed him. 11 He was anxious to see how Esther was getting on and to learn what had happened to her. So each day he would walk back and forth in front of the court where the women lived.

12 The young women were given beauty treatments for one whole year. The first six months their skin was rubbed with olive oil and myrrh, and the last six months it was treated with perfumes and cosmetics. Then each of them spent the night alone with King Xerxes. 13 When a young woman went to the king, she could wear whatever clothes or jewellery she chose from the women's living quarters. 14 In the evening she would go to the king, and the following morning she would go to the place where his wives stayed after being with him. There a man named Shaashgaz was in charge of the king's wives.* Only the ones the king wanted and asked for by name could go back to the king.

15-16 Xerxes had been king for seven years when Esther's turn came to go to him during Tebeth,* the tenth month of the year. Everyone liked Esther. The king's personal servant Hegai was in charge of the women, and Esther trusted Hegai and asked him what she ought to take with her.*

17 Xerxes liked Esther more than he did any of the other young women. None of them pleased him as much as she did, and straight away he fell in love with her and crowned her queen in place of Vashti. 18 In honour of Esther he gave a big dinner for his leaders and officials. Then he declared a holiday everywhere in his kingdom and gave expensive gifts.

Mordecai saves the king's life

19 When the young women were brought together again, Esther's cousin Mordecai had become a palace official. 20 He had told

Esther never to tell anyone that she was a Jew, and she obeyed him, just as she had always done.

21 Bigthana and Teresh were the two men who guarded King Xerxes' rooms, but they got angry with the king and decided to kill him. 22 Mordecai found out about their plans and asked Queen Esther to tell the king what he had found out. 23 King Xerxes learnt that Mordecai's report was true, and he had the two men hanged. Then the king had all of this written down in his record book as he watched.

Haman plans to destroy the Jews

CHAPTER 3

1 Later, King Xerxes promoted Haman the son of Hammedatha to the highest position in his kingdom. Haman was a descendant of Agag,* 2 and the king had given orders for his officials at the royal gate to honour Haman by kneeling down to him. All of them obeyed except Mordecai. 3 When the other officials asked Mordecai why he disobeyed the king's command, 4 he said, "Because I am a Jew." They spoke to him for several days about kneeling down, but he still refused to obey. Finally, they reported this to Haman, to find out if he would let Mordecai get away with it.

5 Haman was furious to learn that Mordecai refused to kneel down and honour him. 6 And when he found out that killing only Mordecai was not enough. Every Jew in the whole kingdom had to be killed.

7 It was now the twelfth year of the rule of King Xerxes. During Nisan,* the first month of the year, Haman said, "Find out the best time for me to do this."* The time chosen was Adar,* the twelfth month.

8 Then Haman went to the king and said:

---

*2.14 wives: This translates a Hebrew word for women who were legally bound to a man, but without the full privileges of a wife.
*2.15,16 Tebeth: The tenth month of the Hebrew calendar, from about mid-December to mid-January.

---

*3.1 Agag: Agag was a king who had fought against the Jews long before the time of Esther (see 1 Samuel 15.1–33).
*3.7 Nisan: Or Abib, the first month of the Hebrew calendar, from about mid-March to mid-April.
*3.7 Find out . . . do this: The Hebrew text has "cast lots", which were pieces of wood or stone used to find out how and when to do something. For "lots" the Hebrew text uses the Babylonian word "purim".
*3.7 Adar: The twelfth month of the Hebrew calendar, from about mid-February to mid-March.

Your Majesty, there are some people who live all over your kingdom and won't have a thing to do with anyone else. They have customs that are different from everyone else's, and they refuse to obey your laws. We would be better off to get rid of them! 9 Why not give orders for all of them to be killed? I can promise that you will get a great deal of silver for your treasury.

10 The king handed his official ring to Haman, who hated the Jews, and the king told him, 11 "Do what you want with those people! You can keep their money."

12 On the thirteenth day of Nisan, Haman called in the king's secretaries and ordered them to write letters in every language used in the kingdom. The letters were written in the name of the king and sealed by using the king's own ring.* At once they were sent to the king's highest officials, the governors of each province, and the leaders of the different nations in the kingdom of Xerxes.

13 The letters were taken by messengers to every part of the kingdom, and this is what was said in the letters:

> On the thirteenth day of Adar, the twelfth month, all Jewish men, women, and children are to be killed. And their property is to be taken.

14-15 King Xerxes gave orders for these letters to be posted where they could be seen by everyone all over the kingdom. The king's command was obeyed, and one of the letters was read aloud to the people in the walled city of Susa. Then the king and Haman sat down to drink together, but no one in the city* could work out what was going on.

Mordecai asks for Esther's help

CHAPTER 4

1 When Mordecai heard about the letter, he tore his clothes in sorrow and put on sackcloth. Then he covered his head with ashes and went through the city, crying and weeping. 2 But he could go only as far as the palace gate, because no one wearing sackcloth was allowed inside the palace. 3 In every province where the king's orders were

read, the Jews cried and mourned, and they went without eating.* Many of them even put on sackcloth and sat in ashes.

4 When Esther's servant girls and her other servants told her what Mordecai was doing, she became very upset and sent Mordecai some clothes to wear in place of the sackcloth. But he refused to take them.

5 Esther had a servant named Hathach, who had been given to her by the king. So she called him in and said, "Find out what's wrong with Mordecai and why he's acting this way."

6 Hathach went to Mordecai in the city square in front of the palace gate, 7 and Mordecai told him everything that had happened. He also told him how much money Haman had promised to add to the king's treasury, if all the Jews were killed.

8 Mordecai gave Hathach a copy of the orders for the murder of the Jews and told him that these had been read in Susa. He said, "Show this to Esther and explain what it means. Ask her to go to the king and beg him to have pity on her people, the Jews!"

9 Hathach went back to Esther and told her what Mordecai had said. 10 She answered, "Tell Mordecai 11 there is a law about going in to see the king, and all his officials and his people know about this law. Anyone who goes in to see the king without being invited by him will be put to death. The only way that anyone can be saved is for the king to hold out the gold sceptre to that person. And it's been thirty days since he has asked for me."

12 When Mordecai was told what Esther had said, 13 he sent back this reply, "Don't think that you will escape being killed with the rest of the Jews, just because you live in the king's palace. 14 If you don't speak up now, we will somehow get help, but you and your family will be killed. It could be that you were made queen for a time like this!"

15 Esther sent a message to Mordecai, saying, 16 "Bring together all the Jews in Susa and tell them to go without eating for my sake! Don't eat or drink for three days and nights. My servant girls and I will do the same. Then I will go in to see the king, even if it means I must die."

17 Mordecai did everything Esther told him to do.

---

*3.12 king's own ring: Melted wax was used to seal a letter, and while the wax was still soft, the king's ring was pressed in the wax to show that the letter was official.

*4.3 went without eating: The Israelites would sometimes go without eating (also called "fasting") in times of great sorrow or danger.

Mordecai is honoured, not killed

CHAPTER 5

Esther invites the king and Haman to a dinner

¹ Three days later, Esther dressed in her royal robes and went to the inner court of the palace in front of the throne. The king was sitting there, facing the open doorway. ² He was happy to see Esther, and he held out the gold sceptre to her.

When Esther came up and touched the tip of the sceptre, ³ the king said, "Esther, what brings you here? Just ask, and I will give you as much as half of my kingdom."

⁴ Esther answered, "Your Majesty, please come with Haman to a dinner I will prepare for you later today."

⁵ The king said to his servants, "Hurry and get Haman, so we can accept Esther's invitation."

The king and Haman went to Esther's dinner, ⁶ and while they were drinking wine, the king asked her, "What can I do for you? Just ask, and I will give you as much as half of my kingdom."

⁷⁻⁸ Esther replied, "Your Majesty, if you really care for me and are willing to do what I want, please come again tomorrow with Haman to the dinner I will prepare for you. At that time I will answer Your Majesty's question."

Haman plans to kill Mordecai

⁹ Haman was feeling great as he left. But when he saw Mordecai at the palace gate, he noticed that Mordecai did not stand up or show him any respect. This made Haman really angry, ¹⁰ but he did not say a thing.

When Haman got home, he called together his friends and his wife Zeresh ¹¹ and started boasting about his great wealth and all his sons. He told them the many ways that the king had honoured him and how all the other officials and leaders had to respect him. ¹² Haman added, "That's not all! Besides the king himself, I'm the only person Queen Esther invited for dinner. She has also invited the king and me to dinner tomorrow. ¹³ But none of this makes me happy, as long as I see that Jew Mordecai sitting at the palace gate."

¹⁴ Haman's wife and friends said to him, "Have a tower built about twenty-two metres high, and tomorrow morning ask the king to

hang Mordecai there. Then later, you can have dinner with the king and enjoy yourself."

This seemed like a good idea to Haman, and he had the tower built.

CHAPTER 6

The king honours Mordecai

¹ That night the king could not sleep, and he got a servant to read him the records of what had happened since he had been king. ² When the servant read how Mordecai had kept Bigthana and Teresh from killing the king, ³ the king asked, "What has been done to reward Mordecai for this?"

"Nothing, Your Majesty!" the king's servants replied.

⁴ About this time, Haman came in to ask the king to have Mordecai hanged on the tower he had built. The king saw him and asked, "Who is that man waiting in front of the throne room?"

⁵ The king's servants answered, "Your Majesty, it is Haman."

"Tell him to come in," the king commanded.

⁶ When Haman entered the room, the king asked him, "What should I do for a man I want to honour?"

Haman was sure that he was the one the king wanted to honour. ⁷ So he replied, "Your Majesty, if you wish to honour a man, ⁸ get someone to bring him one of your own robes and one of your own horses with a fancy head-dress. ⁹ Tell one of your highest officials to place your robe on this man and lead him through the streets on your horse, while someone shouts, 'This is how the king honours a man!'"

¹⁰ The king replied, "Hurry and do just what you have said! Don't forget a thing. Get the robe and the horse for Mordecai the Jew, who is on duty at the palace gate!"

¹¹ Haman got the king's robe and put it on Mordecai. He led him through the city on the horse and shouted as he went, "This is how the king honours a man!"

¹² Afterwards, Mordecai returned to his duties at the palace gate, and Haman hurried home, hiding his face in shame. ¹³ Haman told his wife and friends what had happened. Then his wife and his advisers said, "If Mordecai is a Jew, this is just the beginning of your troubles! You will end up a ruined man." ¹⁴ They were still talking, when the king's servants came and quickly took Haman to the dinner that Esther had prepared.

See also: 6.2: Esth 2.21,22.

Haman is put to death

CHAPTER 7

[1] The king and Haman were dining with Esther [2] and drinking wine during the second dinner, when the king again said, "Esther, what can I do for you? Just ask, and I will give you as much as half of my kingdom!"

[3] Esther answered, "Your Majesty, if you really care for me and are willing to help, you can save me and my people. That's what I really want, [4] because a reward has been promised to anyone who kills my people. Your Majesty, if we were merely going to be sold as slaves, I would not have bothered you."*

[5] "Who would dare to do such a thing?" the king asked.

[6] Esther replied, "That evil Haman is the one to blame for all this!"

Haman was terrified, as he looked at the king and the queen.

[7] The king was so angry that he got up, left his wine, and went out into the palace garden.

Haman realized that the king had already decided what to do with him, and he stayed and begged Esther to save his life.

[8] Just as the king came back into the room, Haman got down on his knees beside Esther, who was lying on the couch. The king shouted, "Now you're even trying to rape my queen here in my own palace!"

As soon as the king said this, his servants covered Haman's head. [9] Then Harbona, one of the king's personal servants, said, "Your Majesty, Haman built a tower twenty-two metres high beside his house, so he could hang Mordecai on it. And Mordecai is the very one who spoke up and saved your life."

"Hang Haman from his own tower!" the king commanded. [10] Straight away, Haman was hanged on the tower he had built to hang Mordecai, and the king calmed down.

The Jews defend themselves and kill their enemies

CHAPTER 8

A happy ending for the Jews

[1] Before the end of the day, King Xerxes gave Esther everything that had belonged to Haman, the enemy of the Jews. Esther told the king that Mordecai was her cousin. So the king made Mordecai one of his highest

officials [2] and gave him the royal ring that Haman had worn. Then Esther put Mordecai in charge of Haman's property.

[3] Once again Esther went to speak to the king. This time she fell down at his feet, crying and begging, "Please stop Haman's evil plan to have the Jews killed!" [4] King Xerxes held out the golden sceptre to Esther, [5] and she got up and said, "Your Majesty, I know that you will do the right thing and that you really love me. Please stop what Haman has planned. He has already sent letters demanding that the Jews in all your provinces be killed, [6] and I can't bear to see my people and my own relatives destroyed."

[7] King Xerxes then said to Esther and Mordecai, "I have already ordered Haman to be hanged and his house given to Esther, because of his evil plans to kill the Jews. [8] I now give you permission to make a law that will save the lives of your people. You may use my ring to seal the law, so that it can never be changed."

[9] On the twenty-third day of Sivan,* the third month, the king's secretaries wrote the law. They obeyed Mordecai and wrote to the Jews, the rulers, the governors, and the officials of all one hundred and twenty-seven provinces from India to Ethiopia.* The letters were written in every language used in the kingdom, including the Jewish language. [10] They were written in the name of King Xerxes and sealed with his ring. Then they were taken by messengers who rode the king's finest and fastest horses.

[11-13] In these letters the king said:

On the thirteenth day of Adar,* the twelfth month, the Jews in every city and province will be allowed to get together and defend themselves. They may destroy any army that attacks them, and they may kill all their enemies, including women and children. They may also take everything that belongs to their enemies.

A copy of this law was to be posted in every province and read by everyone.

[14-15] Then the king ordered his messengers to take their fastest horses and deliver the law as quickly as possible to every province. When Mordecai left, he was wearing clothes fit for a king. He wore blue and white robes, a large gold crown, and a cape made of fine linen and purple cloth.

---

*8.9 Sivan: The third month of the Hebrew calendar, from about mid-May to mid-June.
*8.9 Ethiopia: See the note at 1.1,2.
*8.11–13 Adar: See the note at 3.7.

After the law was announced in Susa, everyone shouted and cheered, [16] and the Jews were no longer afraid. In fact, they were very happy and felt that they had won a victory.

[17] In every province and city where the law was sent, the Jews had parties and celebrated. Many of the people in the provinces accepted the Jewish religion, because they were now afraid of the Jews.

CHAPTER 9

The Jews destroy their enemies

[1] The first law that the king had made was to be followed on the thirteenth day of Adar,* the twelfth month. This was the very day that the enemies of the Jews had hoped to do away with them. But the Jews turned things around, [2] and in the cities of every province they came together to attack their enemies. Everyone was afraid of the Jews, and no one could do anything to oppose them.

[3] The leaders of the provinces, the rulers, the governors, and the court officials were afraid of Mordecai and took sides with the Jews. [4] Everyone in the provinces knew that the king had promoted him and had given him a lot of power.

[5] The Jews took their swords and did away with their enemies, without showing any mercy. [6-10] They killed five hundred people in Susa,* but they did not take anything that belonged to the ones they killed. Haman had been one of the worst enemies of the Jews, and ten of his sons were among those who were killed. Their names were Parshandatha, Dalphon, Aspatha, Poratha, Adalia, Aridatha, Parmashta, Arisai, Aridai, and Vaizatha.

[11] Later that day, someone told the king how many people had been killed in Susa.* [12] Then he told Esther, "Five hundred people, including Haman's ten sons, have been killed in Susa alone. If that many were killed here, what must have happened in the provinces? Is there anything else you want done? Just tell me, and it will be done."

[13] Esther answered, "Your Majesty, please let the Jews in Susa fight to defend themselves tomorrow, just as they did today. And order the bodies of Haman's ten sons to be hanged in public."

[14] King Xerxes did what Esther had requested, and the bodies of Haman's sons were hung in Susa. [15] Then on the fourteenth day of Adar the Jews of the city got together and killed three hundred more people. But they still did not take anything that belonged to their enemies.

[16-17] On the thirteenth day of Adar, the Jews in the provinces had come together to defend themselves. They killed seventy-five thousand of their enemies, but the Jews did not take anything that belonged to the ones they killed. Then on the fourteenth day of the month the Jews celebrated with a feast.

[18] On the fifteenth day of the month the Jews in Susa held a holiday and celebrated, after killing their enemies on the thirteenth and the fourteenth. [19] This is why the Jews in the villages now celebrate on the fourteenth day of the month. It is a joyful holiday that they celebrate by feasting and sending gifts of food to each other.

The Festival of Purim

[20] Mordecai wrote down everything that had happened. Then he sent letters to the Jews everywhere in the provinces [21] and told them:

Each year you must celebrate on both the fourteenth and the fifteenth [22] the days when we Jews defeated our enemies. Remember this month as a time when our sorrow was turned to joy, and celebration took the place of crying. Celebrate by having parties and by giving to the poor and by sharing gifts of food with each other.

[23] They followed Mordecai's instructions and set aside these two days every year as a time of celebration.

The reason for the Festival of Purim

[24] Haman was the son of Hammedatha and a descendant of Agag. He hated the Jews so much that he planned to destroy them, but he wanted to find out the best time to do it. So he cast lots.*

[25] Esther went to King Xerxes and asked him to save her people. Then the king gave written orders for Haman and his sons to be punished in the same terrible way that Haman had in mind for the Jews. So they were hanged. [26] Mordecai's letter had said that the Jews must celebrate for two days because of what happened to them. This

---

*9.1 Adar: See the note at 3.7.

*9.24 cast lots: See the note at 3.7.
See also: 9.24: Esth 3.7.

time of celebration is called Purim,* which is the Hebrew word for the lots that were cast. [27] Now every year the Jews set aside these two days for having parties and celebrating, just as they were told to do. [28] From now on, all Jewish families must remember to celebrate Purim on these two days each year.

[29] Queen Esther, daughter of Abihail, wanted to give full authority to Mordecai's letter about the Festival of Purim, and with his help she wrote a letter about the feast. [30] Copies of this letter were sent to Jews in the one hundred and twenty-seven provinces of King Xerxes. In the letter they said:

> We pray that all of you will live in peace and safety.
>
> [31] You and your descendants must always remember to celebrate Purim at the time and in the way that we have said. You must also follow the instructions that we have given you about mourning and going without eating.*
>
> [32] These laws about Purim are written by the authority of Queen Esther.

The greatness of Xerxes and Mordecai

CHAPTER 10

[1] King Xerxes made everyone in his kingdom pay taxes, even those in lands across the sea. [2] All the great and famous things that King Xerxes did are written in the record books of the kings of Media and Persia. These records also tell about the honours that the king gave to Mordecai. [3] Next to the king himself, Mordecai was the highest official in the kingdom. He was a popular leader of the Jews, because he helped them in many ways and would even speak to the king for them.

*9.26 Purim: The Jewish Festival of Purim got its name from "purim", which is the Babylonian name for the lots that Haman used. Purim is celebrated each year on the 14th and 15th of Adar, which is about the first of March.
*9.31 going without eating: See the note at 4.3.

Additional notes

*2.6 Kish: Or "Mordecai". The Hebrew text has "He".
*2.15,16 her: The Hebrew text adds, "Esther was the daughter of Abihail and was the cousin of Mordecai, who had adopted her after her parents died" (see verse 7).

*3.14,15 walled city . . . city: Or "royal fortress . . . rest of the city".
*7.4 I would . . . bothered you: One possible meaning for the difficult Hebrew text.
*9.6–10 in Susa: Or "in the royal fortress in Susa".
*9.11 in Susa: See the note at 9.6–10.

Job

A quick look at this book

Job was a very rich man, and although he did not belong to the people of Israel, he worshipped the Lord and was a truly good person. But Satan talked to God and accused Job of serving God only because God was blessing him. God agreed to let Satan take away Job's wealth, his children, and, finally, his health, to see whether Job would stay faithful to God. Job did remain faithful.

Then three of Job's friends came to comfort him. They believed that health and prosperity were signs of God's blessing. And because Job had lost both his health and his prosperity, the three friends insisted that God must be punishing Job for some sin. Job answered that he was innocent, and this meant that they

were wrong. Job and the friends argued back and forth, with neither side really proving the other wrong, although at the end of the argument, the friends gave up.

Job was suffering deeply, and several times during the argument he asked God to appear and explain the reason for his suffering. Then, after the friends stopped speaking, Job decided that human beings cannot find the kind of wisdom that gives answers to the deep questions of life. Only God has that wisdom. Job ended his speeches by swearing that he was innocent of doing wrong.

At this point, a young bystander named Elihu began talking. He repeated some of what had already been said, but he also criticized both sides of the argument. Elihu finished with a poem praising God's care for nature.

God finally did appear to Job, but he did not explain Job's suffering. Instead, God showed that the many things he does cannot be understood by humans; humans cannot do what God does. God criticized Job for talking so much when he knew so little, but he also said that Job had remained his faithful servant. And so, at the very end, the book tells how God blessed Job and made him twice as wealthy as he had been before.

Job never did understand why he had suffered; he felt bitter, but he never rejected God or turned away from him. Job was convinced that some day, God would rescue him:

I know that my Saviour lives,
    and at the end he will stand on this earth.
My flesh may be destroyed,
    yet from this body I will see God.
Yes, I will see him for myself,
    and I long for that moment.

(19.25-27)

Job loses his wealth, family, and health

CHAPTER 1

Job and his family

¹ Many years ago, a man named Job lived in the land of Uz.* He was a truly good person, who respected God and refused to do evil.

² Job had seven sons and three daughters. ³ He owned seven thousand sheep, three thousand camels, five hundred pair of oxen, five hundred donkeys, and a large number of servants. He was the richest person in the East.

⁴ Job's sons took turns having feasts in their homes, and they always invited their three sisters to join in the eating and drinking. ⁵ After each feast, Job would send for his children and perform a ceremony, as a way of asking God to forgive them for any wrongs they might have done. He would get up early the next morning and offer a sacrifice for each of them, just in case they had sinned or silently cursed God.

Angels, the LORD, and Satan

⁶ One day, when the angels* had gathered around the LORD, and Satan* was there with them, ⁷ the LORD asked, "Satan, where have you been?"

Satan replied, "I have been going all over the earth."

⁸ Then the LORD asked, "What do you think of my servant Job? No one on earth is like him — he is a truly good person, who respects me and refuses to do evil."

⁹ "Why shouldn't he respect you?" Satan remarked. ¹⁰ "You are like a wall protecting not only him, but his entire family and all

his property. You make him successful in whatever he does, and his flocks and herds are everywhere. ¹¹ Try taking away everything he owns, and he will curse you to your face."

¹² The LORD replied, "All right, Satan, do what you want with anything that belongs to him, but don't harm Job."

Then Satan left.

Job loses everything

¹³ Job's sons and daughters were having a feast in the home of his eldest son, ¹⁴ when someone rushed up to Job and said, "While your servants were ploughing with your oxen, and your donkeys were nearby eating grass, ¹⁵ a gang of Sabeans* attacked and stole the oxen and donkeys! Your other servants were killed, and I was the only one who escaped to tell you."

¹⁶ That servant was still speaking, when a second one came running up and saying, "God sent down a fire that killed your sheep and your servants. I am the only one who escaped to tell you."

¹⁷ Before that servant finished speaking, a third one raced up and said, "Three gangs of Chaldeans* attacked and stole your camels! All your other servants were killed, and I am the only one who escaped to tell you."

¹⁸ That servant was still speaking, when a fourth one dashed up and said, "Your children were having a feast and drinking wine at the home of your eldest son, ¹⁹ when suddenly a storm from the desert blew the house down, crushing all your children. I am the only one who escaped to tell you."

²⁰ When Job heard this, he tore his clothes and shaved his head because of his great sorrow. He knelt on the ground, then worshipped God ²¹ and said:

"We bring nothing at birth;
    we take nothing with us at death.
The LORD alone gives and takes.
    Praise the name of the LORD!"

²² In spite of everything, Job did not sin or accuse God of doing wrong.

---

*1.1 Uz: The exact location of this place is unknown, though it was possibly somewhere in north-west Arabia.
*1.6 angels: See the note at 15.8.
See also: 1.6: Gen 6.2.   1.9-11: Rev 12.10.

*1.15 Sabeans: Perhaps the people of Sheba in what is now south-west Arabia (see Isaiah 60.6).
*1.17 Chaldeans: People from the region of Babylonia, north-east of Palestine.

CHAPTER 2

Job loses his health

[1] When the angels* gathered around the LORD again, Satan* was there with them,
[2] and the LORD asked, "Satan, where have you been?"

Satan replied, "I have been going all over the earth."

[3] Then the LORD asked, "What do you think of my servant Job? No one on earth is like him — he is a truly good person, who respects me and refuses to do evil. And he hasn't changed, even though you persuaded me to destroy him for no reason."

[4] Satan answered, "There's no pain like your own.* People will do anything to stay alive. [5] Try striking Job's own body with pain, and he will curse you to your face."

[6] "All right!" the LORD replied. "Make Job suffer as much as you want, but just don't kill him." [7] Satan left and caused painful sores to break out all over Job's body — from head to toe.

[8] Then Job sat on the ash-heap to show his sorrow. And while he was scraping his sores with a broken piece of pottery, [9] his wife asked, "Why do you still trust God? Why don't you curse him and die?"

[10] Job replied, "Don't talk like a fool! If we accept blessings from God, we must accept trouble as well." In all that happened, Job never once said anything against God.

Job's three friends

[11] Eliphaz from Teman, Bildad from Shuah, and Zophar from Naamah* were three of Job's friends, and they heard about his troubles. So they agreed to visit Job and comfort him. [12] When they came near enough to see Job, they could hardly recognize him. And in their great sorrow, they tore their clothes, then sprinkled dust on their heads and cried bitterly. [13] For seven days and nights, they sat silently on the ground beside him, because they realized what terrible pain he was in.

Job curses the day of his birth

CHAPTER 3

Job's first speech

Blot out the day of my birth

[1] Finally, Job cursed the day of his birth [2] by saying to God:

[3] Blot out the day of my birth
    and the night when my parents
    created a son.
[4] Forget about that day,
    cover it with darkness,
[5] and send thick, gloomy shadows
    to fill it with dread.
[6] Erase that night from the calendar
    and conceal it with darkness.
[7] Don't let children be created
    or joyful shouts be heard ever again
    in that night.
[8] Let those with magic powers*
    place a curse on that day.
[9] Darken its morning stars
    and remove all hope of light,
[10] because it let me be born
    into a world of trouble.

Why didn't I die at birth?

[11] Why didn't I die at birth?
[12] Why was I accepted*
    and allowed to nurse
    at my mother's breast?
[13] Now I would be at peace
    in the silent world below
[14] with kings and their advisers
    whose palaces lie in ruins,
[15] and with rulers once rich
    with silver and gold.
[16] I wish I had been born dead
    and then buried,
    never to see the light of day.
[17] In the world of the dead,
    the wicked and the weary rest
    without a worry.

18-19 Everyone is there —
    where captives and slaves
    are free at last.

Why does God let me live?

20 Why does God let me live
    when life is miserable and so bitter?
21 I keep longing for death
    more than I would seek
    a valuable treasure.
22 Nothing could make me happier
    than to be in the grave.
23 Why do I go on living
    when God has me surrounded,
    and I can't see the road?
24 Moaning and groaning
    are my food and drink,
25   and my worst fears
    have all come true.
26 I have no peace or rest —
    only troubles and worries.

The first round of the debate

CHAPTER 4

Eliphaz's first speech

Please be patient and listen

1 Eliphaz from Teman* said:

2 Please be patient and listen
    to what I have to say.
3-4 Remember how your words
    have guided and encouraged
    many in need.
5 But now you feel discouraged
    when struck by trouble.
6 You respect God and live right,
    so don't lose hope!
7 No truly innocent person
    has ever died young.
8 In my experience, only those
    who plant seeds of evil
    harvest trouble,
9 and then they are swept away
    by the angry breath of God.
10 They may roar and growl
    like powerful lions.
    But when God breaks their teeth,
11   they starve,
    and their children are scattered.

A secret was told to me

12 A secret was told to me
    in a faint whisper —
13 I was overcome by sleep,
    but disturbed by dreams;
14 I trembled with fear,
15   and my hair stood on end,
    as a wind blew past my face.
16 It stopped and stood still.
    Then a form appeared —
    a shapeless form.
    And from the silence,
    I heard a voice say,
17 "No humans are innocent
    in the eyes of God their Creator.
18 He finds fault with his servants
    and even with his angels.
19 Humans are formed from clay
    and are fragile as moths,
    so what chance do you have?
20 Born after daybreak,
    you die before nightfall
    and disappear for ever.
21 Your tent pegs are pulled up,
    and you leave this life,
    having gained no wisdom."

CHAPTER 5

Eliphaz continues

Call out for help

1 Job, call out for help
    and see if an angel comes!

2 Envy and jealousy
    will kill a stupid fool.
3 I have seen fools take root.
    But God sends a curse,
    suddenly uprooting them
4   and leaving their children
    helpless in court.
5 Then hungry and greedy people
    gobble up their crops
    and grab their wealth.*
6 Our suffering isn't caused
    by the failure of crops;
7   it's all part of life,
    like sparks shooting skyward.

8 Job, if I were you,
    I would ask God for help.
9 His miracles are marvellous,
    more than we can count.
10 God sends showers on earth
    and waters the fields.
11 He protects the sorrowful

---

*4.1 Teman: See the note at 2.11.
See also: 3.21: Rev 9.6.

See also: 4.13: Job 33.15.

and lifts up those
who have been disgraced.
12-13 God swiftly traps the wicked
in their own evil schemes,
and their wisdom fails.
14 Darkness is their only companion,
hiding their path at midday.
15 God rescues the needy
from the words of the wicked
and the fist of the mighty.
16 The poor are filled with hope,
and injustice is silenced.

Consider yourself fortunate

17 Consider yourself fortunate
if God All-Powerful
chooses to correct you.
18 He may cause injury and pain,
but he will bandage and heal
your cuts and bruises.
19 God will protect you from harm,
no matter how often trouble may strike.

20 In times of war and famine,
God will keep you safe.
21 You will be sheltered,
without fear of hurtful words
or any other weapon.
22 You will laugh at the threat
of destruction and famine.
And you won't be afraid
of wild animals —
23 they will no longer be fierce,
and your rocky fields
will become friendly.
24 Your home will be secure,
and your sheep will be safe.
25 You will have more descendants
than there are blades of grass
on the face of the earth.
26 You will live a long life,
and your body will be strong
until the day you die.
27 Our experience has proved
these things to be true,
so listen and learn.

CHAPTER 6

Job's reply to Eliphaz

It's impossible

1 Job said:

2 It's impossible to weigh
my misery and grief!

See also: **5.13:** 1 Cor 3.19. **5.17:** Prov 3.11,12; Heb 12.5,6.
5.18: Hos 6.1.

3 They outweigh the sand
along the beach,
and that's why I have spoken
without thinking first.
4 The fearsome arrows of God All-Powerful
have filled my soul with their poison.
5 Do oxen and wild donkeys
cry out in distress
unless they are hungry?
6 What is food without salt?
What is more tasteless
than the white of an egg?*
7 That's how my food tastes,
and my appetite is gone.

8-9 How I wish that God
would answer my prayer
and do away with me.
10 Then I would be comforted,
knowing that in all my pain
I have never disobeyed God.
11 Why should I patiently hope
when my strength is gone?
12 I am not strong as stone or bronze,
13 and I have finally reached
the end of my rope.

My friends, I am desperate

14 My friends, I am desperate,
and you should help me,
even if I no longer respect
God All-Powerful.*
15-16 But you are treacherous
as streams that swell with
melting snow,
17 then suddenly disappear
in the summer heat.
18 I am like a caravan,
lost in the desert
while searching for water.
19 Caravans from Tema and Sheba*
20 thought they would find water.
But they were disappointed,
21 just as I am with you.*
Only one look at my suffering,
and you run away scared.

What have I done wrong?

22 Have I ever asked any of you
to give me a gift
23 or to purchase my freedom
from brutal enemies?
24 What have I done wrong?

*6.19 Tema and Sheba: Tema was a region in
north-west Arabia, and Sheba was probably a region
in south-west Arabia.

Show me, and I will keep quiet.
25 The truth is always painful,
but your arguments prove nothing.
26 Here I am desperate,
and you consider my words
as worthless as wind.
27 Why, you would sell an orphan
or your own neighbour!
28 Look me straight in the eye;
I won't lie to you.
29 Stop accusing me falsely;
my reputation is at stake.
30 I know right from wrong,
and I am not telling lies.

CHAPTER 7

Job continues

Why is life so hard?

1 Why is life so hard? Why do we suffer?
2 We are slaves in search of shade;
we are labourers longing for our wages.
3 God has made my days drag on
and my nights miserable.
4 I pray for night to end,
but it stretches out
while I toss and turn.
5 My parched skin is covered
with worms, dirt, and sores,
6 and my days are running out
quicker than the thread
of a fast-moving needle.

Don't forget!

7 I beg you, God, don't forget!
My life is just a breath,
and trouble lies ahead.
8 I will vanish from sight,
and no one, including you,
will ever see me again.
9 I will disappear in the grave
or vanish from sight like a passing cloud.
10 Never will I return home;
soon I will be forgotten.

11 And so, I cry out to you
in agony and distress.
12 Am I the sea or a sea monster?
Is that why you imprison me?*
13 I go to bed, hoping for rest,

14 but you torture me with terrible dreams.
15-16 I'd rather choke to death
than live in this body.
Leave me alone and let me die;
my life has no meaning.
17 What makes you so concerned
about us humans?
18 Why do you test us
from sunrise to sunset?
19 Won't you look away
just long enough
for me to swallow?
20 Why do you watch us so closely?
What's it to you, if I sin?
Why am I your target
and such a heavy burden?
21 Why do you refuse to forgive?
Soon you won't find me,
because I'll be dead.

CHAPTER 8

Bildad's first speech

How long will you talk?

1 Bildad from Shuah* said:

2 How long will you talk
and keep saying nothing?
3 Does God All-Powerful
stand in the way of justice?
4 He made your children pay
for their sins.
5 So why don't you turn to him
6 and start living right?
Then he will decide
to rescue and restore you
to your place of honour.
7 Your future will be brighter
by far than your past.

Our ancestors were wise

8 Our ancestors were wise,
so learn from them.
9 Our own time has been short,
like a fading shadow,
and we know very little.
10 But they will instruct you
with great understanding.

11 Papyrus reeds grow healthy
only in a swamp,
12 and if the water dries up,
they die sooner than grass.

---

*7.12 sea monster . . . imprison me: "Sea monster" translates the Hebrew word "Tannin," which was possibly a sea monster similar to Leviathan (3.8), Rahab (9.13), and Behemoth (40.15). According to 38.8-11, God makes the sea his prisoner by setting its boundaries.

---

*8.1 Shuah: See the note at 2.11.
See also: 7.17: Psa 8.4; 144.3.

13 Such is the hopeless future
  of all who turn from God
14 and trust in something as frail
  as a spider's web —
15   they take hold and fall
  because it's so flimsy.
16 Sinful people are like plants
  with spreading roots
  and plenty of sun and water.
17 They wrap their roots tightly
  around rocks.'
18 But once they are pulled up,
  they have no more place;
19   their life slips away,'
  and other plants grow there.

20 We know God doesn't reject
  an innocent person
  or help a sinner.
21 And so, he will make you happy
  and give you something to smile about.
22 But your evil enemies
  will be put to shame
  and disappear for ever.

CHAPTER 9

Job's reply to Bildad

What you say is true

1 Job said:

2 What you say is true.
  No human is innocent
  in the sight of God.
3 Not once in a thousand times
  could we win our case
  if we took him to court.
4 God is wise and powerful —
  who could possibly
  oppose him and win?
5 When God becomes angry,
  he can move mountains
  before they even know it.
6 God can shake the earth loose
  from its foundations
7   or command the sun and stars
  to hold back their light.
8 God alone stretched out the sky,
  stepped on the sea,*
9 and set the stars in place —
  the Great Bear and Orion,
  the Pleiades and the stars
  in the southern sky.

10 Of all the miracles God works,
  we cannot understand a single one.
11 God walks right past me,
  without making a sound.
12 And if he grabs something,
  who can stop him
  or raise a question?
13 When God showed his anger,
  the servants of the sea monster*
  fell at his feet.
14 How, then, could I possibly
  argue my case with God?

Though I am innocent

15 Even though I am innocent,
  I can only beg for mercy.
16 And if God came into court
  when I called him,
  he would not hear my case.
17 He would strike me with a storm'
  and increase my injuries
  for no reason at all.
18 Before I could get my breath,
  my miseries would multiply.
19 God is much stronger than I am,
  and who would call me into court
  to give me justice?
20 Even if I were innocent,
  God would prove me wrong.'
21 I am not guilty, but I no longer care
  what happens to me.
22 What difference does it make?
  God destroys the innocent
  along with the guilty.
23 When a good person dies a sudden death,
  God sits back and laughs.
24 And who else but God
  blindfolds the judges,
  then lets the wicked
  take over the earth?

My life is speeding by

25 My life is speeding by,
  without a hope of happiness.
26 Each day passes swifter
  than a sailing ship
  or an eagle swooping down.
27 Sometimes I try to be cheerful
  and to stop complaining,
28 but my sufferings frighten me,
  because I know that God
  still considers me guilty.

---

*9.8 sea: Or "sea monster" (see verse 13 and the note there).
See also: 9.2: Job 4.17. 9.9: Job 38.31; Amos 5.8.

*9.13 the sea monster: The Hebrew text has "Rahab", which was some kind of sea monster with supernatural powers (see the notes at 3.8 and 26.12).

29 So what's the use of trying
  to prove my innocence?
30 Even if I washed myself
  with the strongest soap,
31 God would throw me into a pit
  of stinking slime,
  leaving me disgusting to my clothes.

32 God isn't a mere human like me.
  I can't put him on trial.
33 Who could possibly judge
  between the two of us?
34 Can someone snatch away the stick
  God carries to frighten me?
35 Then I could speak up
  without fear of him,
  but for now, I cannot speak.'

CHAPTER 10

Job complains to God

I am sick of life!

1 I am sick of life!
  And from my deep despair,
  I complain to you, my God.
2 Don't just condemn me!
  Point out my sin.
3 Why do you take such delight
  in destroying those you created
  and in smiling on sinners?
4 Do you look at things
  the way we humans do?
5 Is your life as short as ours?
6 Is that why you are so quick
  to find fault with me?
7 You know I am innocent,
  but who can defend me against you?
8 Will you now destroy
  someone you created?
9 Remember that you moulded me
  like a piece of clay.
  So don't turn me back
  into dust once again.
10 As cheese is made from milk,
  you created my body
  from a tiny drop.
11 Then you tied my bones together
  with muscles
  and covered them with flesh
  and skin.
12 You, the source of my life,
  showered me with kindness
  and watched over me.

You have not explained

13 You have not explained
  all your mysteries,

14 but you catch and punish me
  each time I sin.
15 Guilty or innocent,
  I am condemned and ashamed
  because of my troubles.
16 No matter how hard I try,
  you keep hunting me down
  like a powerful lion.'
17 You never stop accusing me;
  you become furious and attack
  over and over again.

18 Why did you let me be born?
  I would rather have died before birth
19 and been carried to the grave
  without ever breathing.
20 I have only a few days left.
  Why don't you leave me alone?'
  Let me find some relief,
21-22 before I travel to the land
  of darkness and despair,
  the place of no return.

CHAPTER 11

Zophar's first speech

So much foolish talk

1 Zophar from Naamah* said:

2 So much foolish talk
  cannot go unanswered.
3 Your words have silenced others
  and made them ashamed;
  now it is only right for you
  to be put to shame.
4 You claim to be innocent
  and argue that your beliefs
  are acceptable to God.
5 But I wish he would speak
6 and let you know
  that wisdom has many different sides.
  You would then discover
  that God has punished you less
  than you deserve.

7 Can you understand the mysteries
  surrounding God All-Powerful?
8 They are higher than the heavens
  and deeper than the grave.
  So what can you do
  when you know so little,
9 and these mysteries outreach
  the earth and the sea?

10 If God puts you in prison
  or drags you to court,
  what can you do?

*11.1 Naamah: See the note at 2.11.

11 God has the wisdom to know
    when someone is worthless and sinful,
12 but it's easier to tame
    a wild donkey
    than to make a fool wise.*

Surrender your heart to God

13 Surrender your heart to God,
    turn to him in prayer,
14 and give up your sins —
    even those you do in secret.
15 Then you won't be ashamed;
    you will be confident and fearless.
16 Your troubles will go away
    like water beneath a bridge,
17 and your darkest night
    will be brighter than midday.
18 You will rest safe and secure,
    filled with hope and emptied of worry.
19 You will sleep without fear
    and be greatly respected.
20 But those who are evil
    will go blind and lose their way.
    Their only escape is death!

CHAPTER 12

Job's reply to Zophar

You think you are so great

1-2 Job said to his friends:

    You think you are so great,
    with all the answers.
3 But I know as much as you do,
    and so does everyone else.
4 I have always lived right,
    and God answered my prayers;
    now friends make fun of me.
5 It's easy to condemn
    those who are suffering,
    when you have no troubles.
6 Robbers and other godless people
    live safely at home
    and say, "God is in our hands!"*

If you want to learn

7 If you want to learn,
    then go and ask
    the wild animals and the birds,
8 the flowers and the fish.
9 Any of them can tell you
    what the LORD has done.*
10 Every living creature
    is in the hands of God.
11 We hear with our ears,
    taste with our tongues,

12 and gain some wisdom from those
    who have lived a long time.
13 But God is the real source
    of wisdom and strength.
14 No one can rebuild
    what he destroys,
    or release those he has imprisoned.
15 God can hold back the rain
    or send a flood,
16 just as he rules over liars
    and those they lie to.
17 God destroys counsellors,
    turns judges into fools,
18 and makes slaves of kings.
19 God removes priests and others
    who have great power —
20 he confuses wise,
    experienced advisers,
21 puts mighty kings to shame,
    and takes away their power.
22 God turns darkness to light;
23 he makes nations strong,
    then shatters their strength.
24 God strikes their rulers senseless,
    then leaves them to roam
    through barren deserts,
25 lost in the dark, staggering
    like someone drunk.

CHAPTER 13

Job continues

I know and understand

1 I know and understand
    every bit of this.
2 None of you are cleverer than I am;
    there's nothing you know that I don't.
3 But I prefer to argue my case
    with God All-Powerful —
4 you are merely useless doctors,
    who treat me with lies.
5 The wisest thing you can do
    is to keep quiet
6 and listen to my argument.
7 Are you telling lies for God
8 and not telling the whole truth
    when you argue his case?
9 If he took you to court,
    could you fool him,
    just as you fool others?
10 If you were secretly unfair,
    he would correct you,
11 and his glorious splendour
    would make you terrified.
12 Your wisdom and arguments
    are as delicate as dust.

Be quiet while I speak

¹³ Be quiet while I speak,
   then say what you will.
¹⁴ I will be responsible
   for what happens to me.
¹⁵ God may kill me, but still
   I will trust him*
   and offer my defence.
¹⁶ This may be what saves me,
   because no guilty person
   would come to his court.
¹⁷ Listen carefully to my words!
¹⁸ I have prepared my case well,
   and I am certain to win.
¹⁹ If you can prove me guilty,
   I will give up and die.

Job prays

I ask only two things

²⁰ I ask only two things
   of you, my God,
   and I will no longer hide from you —
²¹ stop punishing and terrifying me!

²² Then speak, and I will reply;
   or else let me speak,
   and you reply.
²³ Please point out my sins,
   so I will know them.
²⁴ Why have you turned your back
   and count me your enemy?
²⁵ Do you really enjoy
   frightening a fallen leaf?
²⁶ Why do you accuse me
   of horrible crimes
   and make me pay for sins
   I did in my youth?
²⁷ You have tied my feet down
   and keep me surrounded;
²⁸ I am rotting away like cloth
   eaten by worms.

CHAPTER 14

Job continues his prayer

Life is short and sorrowful

¹ Life is short and sorrowful
   for every living soul.
² We are flowers that fade
   and shadows that vanish.
³ And so, I ask you, God,
   why pick on me?
⁴ There's no way a human
   can be completely pure.

⁵ Our time on earth is brief;
   the number of our days
   is already decided by you.
⁶ Why don't you leave us alone
   and let us find some happiness
   while we toil and labour?

When a tree is chopped down

⁷ When a tree is chopped down,
   there is always the hope
   that it will sprout again.
⁸ Its roots and stump may rot,
⁹ but at the touch of water,
   fresh twigs shoot up.
¹⁰ Humans are different —
   we die, and that's the end.
¹¹ We are like streams and lakes
   after the water has gone;
¹² we fall into the sleep of death,
   never to rise again,
   until the sky disappears.
¹³ Please hide me, God,
   deep in the ground —
   and when you are angry no more,
   remember to rescue me.

Will we humans live again?

¹⁴ Will we humans live again?
   I would gladly suffer
   and wait for my time.
¹⁵ My Creator, you would want me;
   you would call out,
   and I would answer.
¹⁶ You would take care of me,
   but not count my sins —
¹⁷ you would put them in a bag,
   tie it tight,
   and toss them away.
¹⁸ But in the real world,
   mountains tumble,
   and rocks crumble;
¹⁹ streams wear away stones
   and wash away soil.
   And you destroy our hopes!
²⁰ You change the way we look,
   then send us away,
   wiped out for ever.
²¹ We never live to know
   if our children are praised
   or disgraced.
²² We feel no pain but our own,
   and when we mourn,
   it's only for ourselves.

See also: 13.27: Job 33.11.

The second round of the debate

CHAPTER 15

Eliphaz's second speech

If you had any sense

¹ Eliphaz from Teman* said:

²⁻³ Job, if you had any sense,
  you would stop spreading
  all this hot air.
⁴ Your words are enough
  to make others turn from God
  and lead them to doubt.
⁵ And your sinful, scheming mind
  is the source of all you say.
⁶ I am not here as your judge;
  your own words are witnesses
  against you.

⁷ Were you the first human?
  Are you older than the hills?
⁸ Have you ever been present
  when God's council* meets?
  Do you alone have wisdom?
⁹ Do you know and understand
  something we don't?
¹⁰ We have the benefit of wisdom
  older than your father.
¹¹ And you have been offered
  comforting words from God.
  Isn't this enough?

¹² Your emotions are out of control,
  making you look fierce;
¹³ that's why you attack God
  with everything you say.
¹⁴ No human is pure and innocent,
¹⁵ and neither are angels —
  not in the sight of God.
  If God doesn't trust his angels,
¹⁶ what chance do humans have?
  We are so terribly evil
  that we thirst for sin.

Just listen to what I know

¹⁷ Just listen to what I know,
  and you will learn
¹⁸ wisdom known by others
  since ancient times.

¹⁹ Those who gained such insights
  also gained the land,
  and they were not influenced
  by foreign teachings.
²⁰ But suffering is in store
  each day for those who sin.
²¹ Even in times of success,
  they constantly hear
  the threat of doom.
²² Darkness, despair, and death
  are their destiny.
²³ They scrounge around for food,
  all the while dreading
  the approaching darkness.
²⁴ They are overcome with despair,
  like a terrified king
  about to go into battle.
²⁵ This is because they rebelled
  against God All-Powerful
²⁶ and have attacked him
  with their weapons.

²⁷ They may be rich and fat,
²⁸ but they will live in the ruins
  of deserted towns.
²⁹ Their property and wealth
  will shrink and disappear.
³⁰ They won't escape the darkness,
  and the blazing breath of God
  will set their future aflame.
³¹⁻³² They have put their trust
  in something worthless;
  now they will become worthless
  like a date palm tree without a leaf.ᵉ
³³ Or like vineyards or orchards
  whose blossoms and unripe fruit
  drop to the ground.
³⁴ Yes, the godless and the greedy
  will have nothing but flames
  feasting on their homes,
³⁵ because they are the parents
  of trouble and vicious lies.

CHAPTER 16

Job's reply to Eliphaz

I have often heard this

¹ Job said:

² I have often heard this,
  and it offers no comfort.
³ So why don't you keep quiet?
  What's bothering you?
⁴ If I were in your place,
  it would be easy to criticize
  or to give advice.
⁵ But I would offer hope
  and comfort instead.

---

*15.1 **Teman:** See the note at 2.11.
*15.8 **God's council:** The angels and others who
gather to discuss matters with God (see 1.6; 2.1).
See also: 15.14-16: Job 25.4-6.

491

⁶ If I speak, or if I don't,
  I suffer all the same.
  My torment continues.
⁷ God has worn me down
  and destroyed my family;
⁸ my shrivelled up skin proves
  that I am his prisoner.
⁹ God is my hateful enemy,
  glaring at me
  and attacking with his sharp teeth.
¹⁰ Everyone is against me;
  they sneer and slap my face.
¹¹ And God is the one
  who handed me over
  to this merciless mob.

Everything was going well

¹² Everything was going well,
  until God grabbed my neck
  and shook me to pieces.
  God set me up as the target
¹³ for his arrows,
  and without showing mercy,
  he slashed my stomach open,
  spilling out my insides.
¹⁴ God never stops attacking,
¹⁵ and so, in my sorrow
  I dress in sackcloth* and sit in the dust.
¹⁶ My face is red with tears,
  and dark shadows circle my eyes,
¹⁷ though I am not violent,
  and my prayers are sincere.

¹⁸ If I should die, I beg the earth
  not to cover my cry for justice.
¹⁹ Even now, God in heaven
  is both my witness
  and my protector.
²⁰ My friends have rejected me,
  but God is the one*
²¹ to show that I am right,
  just as a friend should.
²² Because in only a few years,
  I will be dead and gone.

CHAPTER 17

Job complains to God

My hopes have died

¹ My hopes have died,
  my time is up,
  and the grave is ready.

---

² All I can see are angry crowds,
  making fun of me.
³ If you, LORD, don't help,
  who will pay the price for my release?
⁴ My friends won't really listen,
  all because of you,
  and so you must be the one
  to prove them wrong.
⁵ They have condemned me,
  just to benefit themselves;
  now blind their children.

⁶ You, God, are the reason
  I am insulted and spat on.
⁷ I am almost blind with grief;
  my body is a mere shadow.

⁸ People who are truly good
  would feel so alarmed,
  that they would become angry
  with my worthless friends.
⁹ They would do the right thing
  and because they did,
  they would grow stronger.*
¹⁰ But none of my friends show any sense.

¹¹ My life is drawing to an end;
  hope has disappeared.
¹² But all my friends can do
  is offer empty hopes.*
¹³ I could tell the world below
  to prepare me a bed.
¹⁴ Then I could greet the grave as my father
  and say to the worms,
  "Hello, mother and sisters!"

¹⁵ But what kind of hope is that?
¹⁶ Will it keep me company
  in the world of the dead?

CHAPTER 18

Bildad's second speech

How long will you talk?

¹ Bildad from Shuah* said:

² How long will you talk?
  Be sensible! Let us speak.
³ Or do you think that we
  are dumb animals?
⁴ You cut yourself in anger.
  Will that shake the earth
  or even move the rocks?

⁵⁻⁶ The lamps of sinful people
  soon are snuffed out,
  leaving their tents dark.

---

*16.15 sackcloth: A rough, dark-coloured cloth made
from goat or camel hair and used to make grain
sacks. It was worn in times of trouble or sorrow.
See also: 16.19: Job 19.25.
492

*18.1 Shuah: See the note at 2.11.
See also: 18.5,6: Job 21.17.

7 Their powerful legs become weak,
   and they stumble on schemes
   of their own doing.
8-10 Before they know it,
   they are trapped
   in a net, hidden along the path.
11 Terror strikes and pursues from every side.
12 Starving, they run, only to meet disaster,
13   then afterwards to be eaten alive
   by death itself.

14 Those sinners are dragged
   from the safety of their tents
   to die a gruesome death.
15 Then their tents and possessions
   are burnt to ashes,
16   and they are left like trees,
   dried up from the roots.
17 They are gone and forgotten,
18 thrown far from the light
   into a world of darkness,
19   without any children
   to carry on their name.
20 Everyone, from east to west,
   is overwhelmed with horror.
21 Such is the fate of sinners
   and their families
   who don't know God.

CHAPTER 19

Job's reply to Bildad

How long will you torture me?

1 Job said:

2 How long will you torture me
   with your words?
3   Isn't ten times enough
   for you to accuse me?
   Aren't you ashamed?
4   Even if I have sinned,
   you haven't been harmed.
5 You boast of your goodness,
   claiming I am suffering
   because I am guilty.
6   But God is the one at fault
   for finding fault with me.

7 Though I pray to be rescued
   from this torment,
   no whisper of justice answers me.
8 God has me trapped with a wall of darkness
9   and stripped of respect.
10 God rips me apart, uproots my hopes,
11   and attacks with fierce anger,
   as though I were his enemy.
12 His entire army advances,
   then surrounds my tent.

I am forgotten

13-14 God has turned relatives
   and friends against me,
   and I am forgotten.
15 My guests and my servants
   consider me a stranger,
16   and when I call my servants,
   they pay no attention.
17 My breath disgusts my wife;
   everyone in my family turns away.
18 Young children can't stand me,
   and when I come near, they make fun.
19 My best friends and loved ones
   have turned from me.
20 I am skin and bones — just barely alive.
21   My friends, I beg you for pity!
   God has made me his target.
22 Hasn't he already done enough?
   Why do you join the attack?

23 I wish that my words
   could be written down
24   or chiselled into rock.
25 I know that my Saviour° lives,
   and at the end
   he will stand on this earth.
26 My flesh may be destroyed,
   yet from this body I will see God.°
27 Yes, I will see him for myself,
   and I long for that moment.

28 My friends, you think up ways
   to blame and torment me,
   saying I brought it on myself.
29 But watch out for the judgment,
   when God will punish you!

CHAPTER 20

Zophar's second speech

Your words are disturbing

1 Zophar from Naamah* said:

2 Your words are disturbing;
   now I must speak.
3 You have accused and insulted me,
   and reason requires a reply.
4 Since the time of creation,
   everyone has known
5   that sinful people are happy
   for only a while.
6 Though their pride and power
   may reach to the sky,
7   they will disappear like dust,
   and those who knew them
   will wonder what happened.

---

*20.1 *Naamah:* See the note at 2.11.

493

⁸ They will be forgotten like a dream
⁹   and vanish from the sight
      of family and friends.
¹⁰ Their children will have to repay
    what the parents took from the poor.
¹¹ Indeed, the wicked will die
    and go to their graves
    in the prime of life.

Sinners love the taste of sin

¹² Sinners love the taste of sin;
    they relish every bite
¹³   and swallow it slowly.
¹⁴ But their food will turn sour
    and poison their stomachs.
¹⁵ Then God will make them lose
    the wealth they gobbled up.
¹⁶ They will die from the fangs
    of poisonous snakes
¹⁷   and never enjoy rivers flowing
    with milk and honey.
¹⁸ Their hard work will result
    in nothing gained,
¹⁹   because they cheated the poor
    and took their homes.

²⁰ Greedy people want everything
    and are never satisfied.
²¹ But when nothing remains
    for them to grab,
    they will be nothing.
²² Once they have everything,
    distress and despair
    will strike them down,
²³   and God will make them swallow
    his blazing anger.

²⁴ While running from iron spears,
    they will be killed
    by arrows of bronze,
²⁵   whose shining tips go straight
    through their bodies.
    They will be trapped by terror,
²⁶   and what they treasure most
    will be lost in the dark.
    God will send flames
    to destroy them in their tents
    with all their property.
²⁷ The heavens and the earth
    will testify against them,
²⁸ and all their possessions
    will be dragged off
    when God becomes angry.
²⁹ This is what God has decided
    for those who are evil.

CHAPTER 21

Job's reply to Zophar

If you want to offer comfort

¹ Job said:

² If you want to offer comfort,
    then listen to me.
³ And when I have finished,
    you can start your insults
    all over again.
⁴ My complaint is against God;
    that's why I am impatient.
⁵ Just looking at me is enough
    to make you sick,
⁶   and the very thought of myself
    fills me with disgust.

⁷ Why do evil people live so long
    and gain such power?
⁸ Why are they allowed to see
    their children grow up?
⁹ They have no worries at home,
    and God never punishes them.
¹⁰ Their cattle have lots of calves
    without ever losing one;
¹¹   their children play and dance
    safely by themselves.
¹² These people sing and celebrate
    to the sound of tambourines,
    small harps, and flutes,
¹³ and they are successful,
    without a worry,
    until the day they die.

Leave us alone!

¹⁴ Those who are evil say
    to God All-Powerful,
    "Leave us alone! Don't bother us
    with your teachings.
¹⁵ What do we gain from praying
    and worshipping you?
¹⁶ We succeeded all on our own."
    And so, I keep away from them
    and their evil schemes.

¹⁷ How often does God become angry
    and send disaster and darkness
    to punish sinners?
¹⁸ How often does he strike them
    like a storm that scatters straw?
¹⁹ You say, "God will punish
    those sinners' children
    in place of those sinners."
    But I say, "Let him punish
    those sinners themselves
    until they really feel it.

20 Let God All-Powerful force them to drink
their own destruction
from the cup of his anger.
21 Because after they are dead,
they won't care what happens
to their children."

Who can tell God what to do?

22 Who can tell God what to do?
He judges powerful rulers.
23-24 Some of us die prosperous,
enjoying good health,
25 while others die in poverty,
having known only pain.
26 But we all end up dead,
beneath a blanket of worms.

27 My friends, I know that you
are plotting against me.
28 You ask, "Where is the home
of that important person
who does so much evil?"

29 Everyone, near and far, agrees
30 that those who do wrong
never suffer disaster,
when God becomes angry.
31 No one points out their sin
or punishes them.
32 Then at their funerals,
they are highly praised;
33 the earth welcomes them home,
while crowds mourn.

34 But empty, meaningless words
are the comfort you offer me.

The third round
of the debate

CHAPTER 22

Eliphaz's third speech

What use are we humans to God?

1 Eliphaz from Teman* said:

2 What use are we humans to God,
even the wisest of us?
3 If you were completely sinless,
that would still mean nothing
to God All-Powerful.
4 Is he correcting you for worshipping him?
5 No! It's because
of your terrible sins.

22.1 Teman: See the note at 2.11.
See also: 22.2,3: Job 35.6–8.

6 To guarantee payment of a debt,
you have taken clothes
from the poor.
7 And you refused bread and water
to the hungry and thirsty,
8 although you were rich,
respected, and powerful.
9 You have turned away widows
and have broken the arms of orphans.
10 That's why you were suddenly
trapped by terror,
11 blinded by darkness,
and drowned in a flood.

God lives in the heavens

12 God lives in the heavens
above the highest stars,
where he sees everything.
13 Do you think the deep darkness
hides you from God?
14 Do thick clouds cover his eyes,
as he walks around heaven's dome
high above the earth?
15 Give up those ancient ideas
believed by sinners,
16 who were swept away
without warning.
17 They rejected God All-Powerful,
feeling he was helpless,
18 although he had been kind
to their families.
The beliefs of these sinners
are truly disgusting.
19 When God's people see
the godless swept away,
they celebrate,
20 saying, "Our enemies are gone,
and fire has destroyed
their possessions."

Surrender to God All-Powerful

21 Surrender to God All-Powerful!
You will find peace and prosperity.
22 Listen to his teachings
and take them to heart.
23 If you return to God
and turn from sin,
all will go well for you.
24 So get rid of your finest gold,
as though it were sand.
25 Let God All-Powerful
be your silver and gold,
26 and you will find happiness
by worshipping him.
27 God will answer your prayers,
and you will keep the promises
you made to him.

28 He will do whatever you ask,
   and life will be bright.
29 When others are disgraced,
   God will clear their names
   in answer to your prayers.
30 Even those who are guilty will be forgiven,
   because you obey God.'

CHAPTER 23

Job's reply to Eliphaz

Today I complain bitterly

1 Job said:

2 Today I complain bitterly,
   because God has been cruel
   and made me suffer.
3 If I knew where to find God,
   I would go there
4 and argue my case.
5 Then I would discover
   what he wanted to say.
6 Would he overwhelm me
   with his greatness?
   No! He would listen
7 because I am innocent,
   and he would say, "I now set you free!"

8 I cannot find God anywhere —
   in front of or behind me,
9 to my left or my right.
   God is always at work,
   though I never see him.
10 But he knows what I am doing,
   and when he tests me,
   I will be pure as gold.
11-12 I have never refused to follow
   any of his commands,
   and I have always treasured
   his teachings.'
13 But he alone is God,
   and who can oppose him?
   God does as he pleases,
14 and he will do exactly
   what he intends with me.
15-16 Merely the thought of God All-Powerful
   makes me tremble with fear.
17 God has covered me with darkness,
   but I refuse to be silent.'

CHAPTER 24

Job continues

Why doesn't God set a time?

1 Why doesn't God set a time for court?
   Why don't his people know
   where he can be found?

2 Sinners remove boundary markers
   and take care of sheep they have stolen.
3 They cheat orphans and widows
   by taking their donkeys and oxen.
4 The poor are trampled
   and forced to hide
5 in the desert,
   where they and their children
   must live like wild donkeys
   and search for food.
6 If they want grain or grapes,*
   they must go to the property
   of these sinners.
7 They sleep naked in the cold,
   because they have no cover,
8 and during a storm
   their only shelters are caves
   among the rocky cliffs.

9 Children whose fathers have died
   are taken from their mothers
   as payment for a debt.
10 Then they are forced to work
   naked in the grain fields
   because they have no clothes,
   and they go hungry.
11 They crush olives to make oil
   and grapes to make wine —
   but still they go thirsty.
12 And along the city streets,
   the wounded and dying cry out,
   yet God does nothing.

Some reject the light

13 Some rebel and refuse
   to follow the light.
14 Soon after learn they murder
   the poor and the needy,
   and at night they steal.

15 Others wait for the dark,
   thinking they won't be seen
   if they sleep with the wife
   or husband of someone else.
16 Robbers hide during the day,
   then break in after dark
   because they reject the light.
17 They prefer night to day,
   since the terrors of the night
   are their friends.

Sinners are filthy foam

18 Those sinners are filthy foam
   on the surface of the water.

---

*24.6 If they want grain or grapes: Poor people
were allowed to gather what was left in the fields and
vineyards after the harvest.

And so, their fields and vineyards
will fall under a curse
and won't produce.
19 Just as the heat of summer
swallows the snow,
the world of the dead
swallows those who sin.
20 Forgotten here on earth,
and with their power broken,
they taste sweet to worms.

21 Sinners take advantage of widows
and other helpless women.◆
22 But God's mighty strength
destroys those in power.
Even if they seem successful,
they are doomed to fail.
23 God may let them feel secure,
but they are never
out of his sight.
24 Great for a while; gone for ever!
Sinners are mowed down like weeds,
then they wither and die.
25 If I haven't spoken the truth,
then prove me wrong.

CHAPTER 25

Bildad's third speech

God is the one to fear

1 Bildad from Shuah* said:

2 God is the one to fear,
because God is in control
and rules the heavens.
3 Who can count his army of stars?
Isn't God the source of light?
4 How can anyone be innocent
in the sight of God?
5 To him, not even the light
of the moon and stars
can ever be pure.
6 So how can we humans,
when we are merely worms?

CHAPTER 26

Job's reply to Bildad

You have really been helpful

1 Job said:

2 You have really been helpful
to someone weak and weary.
3 You have given great advice
and wonderful wisdom
to someone truly in need.

4 How can anyone possibly speak
with such understanding?
5 Remember the terrible trembling
of those in the world of the dead
below the mighty ocean.
6 Nothing in that land
of death and destruction
is hidden from God,
7 who hung the northern sky
and suspended the earth
on empty space.
8 God stores water in clouds,
but they don't burst,
9 and he wraps them around
the face of the moon.
10 On the surface of the sea,
God has drawn a boundary line
between light and darkness.
11 And columns supporting the sky
tremble at his command.

12 By his power and wisdom,
God conquered the force
of the mighty ocean.◆
13 The heavens became bright
when he breathed,
and the escaping sea monster*
died at the hands of God.
14 These things are merely a whisper
of God's power at work.
How little we would understand
if this whisper
ever turned into thunder!

Job's closing statements

CHAPTER 27

Job continues

I am desperate

1 Job said:

2 I am desperate because
God All-Powerful
refuses to do what is right.
As surely as God lives,
3 and while he gives me breath,
4 I will tell only the truth.
5 Until the day I die,
I will refuse to do wrong
by saying you are right,
6 because each day my conscience
agrees that I am innocent.

---

*25.1 Shuah: See the note at 2.11.

*26.13 sea monster: The Hebrew text has "snake",
which probably stands for some kind of fearsome sea
monster, such as Leviathan (see Isaiah 27.1).

7 I pray that my enemies
will suffer no less than the wicked.

8 Such people are hopeless,
and God All-Powerful
will cut them down,

9 without listening
when they beg for mercy.

10 And that is what God should do,
because they don't like him or ever pray.

11 Now I will explain in detail
what God All-Powerful does.

12 All of you have seen these things
for yourselves.
So you have no excuse.

How God treats the wicked

13 Here is how God All-Powerful
treats those who are wicked
and brutal.

14 They may have many children,
but most of them
will go hungry
or suffer a violent death.

15 Others will die of disease,
and their widows won't be able to weep.

16 The wicked may collect riches
and clothes in abundance
as easily as clay.

17 But God's people will wear
clothes taken from them
and divide up their riches.

18 No homes built by the wicked
will outlast a cocoon
or a shack.

19 Those sinners may go to bed rich,
but they will wake up poor.*

20 Terror will strike at night
like a flood or a storm.

21 Then a scorching wind
will sweep them away

22 without showing mercy,
as they try to escape.

23 At last, the wind will celebrate
because they are gone.

CHAPTER 28

Job continues

Gold and silver are mined

1 Gold and silver are mined,
then purified;

2 the same is done with iron and copper.

3 Miners carry lanterns
deep into the darkness
to search for these metals.

4 They dig tunnels
in distant, unknown places,
where they dangle by ropes.

5 Far beneath the grain fields,
fires are built to break loose those rocks

6 that have jewels or gold.*

7 Miners go to places unseen
by the eyes of hawks;

8 they walk on soil unknown
to the proudest lions.

9 With their own hands
they remove sharp rocks
and uproot mountains.

10 They dig through the rocks
in search of jewels
and precious metals.

11 They also uncover the sources of* rivers
and discover secret places.

Where is wisdom found?

12 But where is wisdom found?

13 No human knows the way.*

14 Nor can it be discovered
in the deepest sea.

15-16 It is worth much more
than silver or pure gold
or precious stones.

17 Nothing is its equal —
not gold or costly glass.*

18 Wisdom is worth much more than
coral, jasper,* or rubies.

19 All the topaz* of Ethiopia*
and the finest gold
cannot compare with it.

20 Where then is wisdom?

21 It is hidden from human eyes
and even from birds.

22 Death and destruction
have merely heard rumours
about where it is found.

23 God is the only one who knows
the way to wisdom,

24 because he sees everything
beneath the heavens.

25 When God divided out
the wind and the water,

26 and when he decided the path
for rain and lightning,

---

*28.17 costly glass: In the ancient world, objects
made of glass were costly.

*28.18 jasper: A valuable stone, usually green or clear.

*28.19 topaz: A valuable, yellow stone.

*28.19 Ethiopia: The Hebrew text has "Cush", which
was a region south of Egypt that included parts of the
present countries of Ethiopia and Sudan.

²⁷ he also determined the truth
and defined wisdom.
²⁸ God told us, "Wisdom means
that you respect me, the Lord,
and turn from sin."

CHAPTER 29

Job continues

I long for the past

¹ Job said:

² I long for the past,
when God took care of me,
³ and the light from his lamp
showed me the way through the dark.
⁴ I was in the prime of life,
God All-Powerful was my closest friend,
⁵ and all my children were nearby.
⁶ My herds gave enough milk
to bathe my feet,
and from my olive harvest
flowed rivers of oil.
⁷⁻⁸ When I sat down at the meeting
of the city council,
the young leaders stepped aside,
while the older ones stood
⁹⁻¹⁰ and remained silent.

Everyone was pleased

¹¹ Everyone was pleased
with what I said and did.
¹² When poor people or orphans
cried out for help,
I came to their rescue.
¹³ And I was highly praised
for my generosity to widows
and others in poverty.
¹⁴ Kindness and justice
were my coat and hat;
¹⁵ I was good to the blind and to the lame.
¹⁶ I was a father to the needy,
and I defended them in court,
even if they were strangers.
¹⁷ When criminals attacked,
I broke their teeth
and set their victims free.

¹⁸ I felt certain that I would live
a long and happy life,
then die in my own bed.
¹⁹ In those days I was strong
like a tree with deep roots
and with plenty of water,
²⁰ or like an archer's new bow.

²¹ Everyone listened in silence
to my welcome advice,
²² and when I finished speaking,
nothing needed to be said.
²³ My words were eagerly accepted
like the showers of spring,
²⁴ and the smile on my face
renewed everyone's hopes.
²⁵ My advice was followed
as though I were a king leading my troops,
or someone comforting those in sorrow.

CHAPTER 30

Job continues

Young people now insult me

¹ Young people now insult me,
although their fathers
would have been a disgrace
to my sheep dogs.
² And those who insult me
are helpless themselves.
³ They must claw the desert sand
in the dark for something
to satisfy their hunger.◗
⁴ They gather tasteless shrubs
for food and firewood,
⁵ and they are driven out of towns,
as though they were thieves.
⁶ Their only homes are ditches
or holes between rocks,
⁷ where they bray like donkeys
gathering around shrubs.
⁸ And like senseless donkeys
they are chased away.

Those worthless nobodies

⁹ Those worthless nobodies
make up jokes and songs
to disgrace me.
¹⁰ They are hateful
and keep their distance,
even while spitting in my direction.
¹¹ God has destroyed me,
and so they don't care what they do.◗
¹² Their attacks never stop,
though I am defenceless,
and my feet are trapped.◗
¹³ Without any help,
they prevent my escape,
destroying me completely◗
¹⁴ and leaving me crushed.
¹⁵ Terror has me surrounded;
my reputation and my riches
have vanished like a cloud.

I am sick at heart

16 I am sick at heart!
   Pain has taken its toll.
17 Night chews on my bones,
   causing endless torment,
18 and God has shrunk my skin,
   choking me to death.
19 I have been thrown in the dirt
   and now am dirt myself.
20 I beg God for help,
   but there is no answer;
   and when I stand up,
   he simply stares.
21 God has turned brutal,
22 stirring up a storm to toss me about.
23 Soon he will send me home
   to the world of the dead,
   where we all must go.

24 No one refuses help to others,
   when disaster strikes.◆
25 I mourned for the poor
   and those who suffered.
26 But when I beg for relief and light,
   all I receive are disaster
   and darkness.
27 My stomach is tied in knots;
   pain is my daily companion.
28 Suffering has scorched my skin,
   and in the city council
   I stand and cry out,
29 making mournful sounds
   like jackals* and owls.
30 My skin is so parched,
   that it peels right off,
   and my bones are burning.
31 My only songs are sorrow
   and sadness.

Job swears that he is innocent

CHAPTER 31

Job continues

I promised myself

1 I promised myself
   never to stare with desire
   at a young woman.
2 God All-Powerful punishes
   men who do that.

3 In fact, God sends disaster
   on all who sin,
4 and he keeps a close watch
   on everything I do.

5 I am not dishonest or deceitful,
6 and I beg God to prove my innocence.
7 If I have disobeyed him
   or even wanted to,
8 then others can eat my harvest
   and uproot my crops.
9 If I have desired someone's wife
   and chased after her,
10 then let some stranger
   steal my wife from me.
11 If I took someone's wife,
   it would be a horrible crime,
12 sending me to destruction
   and my crops to the flames.◆

13 When my servants
   complained against me,
   I was fair to them.
14 Otherwise, what answer
   would I give to God
   when he judges me?
15 After all, God is the one
   who gave life to each of us
   before we were born.

I have never cheated anyone

16 I have never cheated widows
   or others in need,
17 and I have always shared
   my food with orphans.
18 Since the time I was young,
   I have cared for orphans
   and helped widows.◆
19 I provided clothes for the poor,
20 and I was praised
   for supplying woollen garments
   to keep them warm.
21 If I have ever raised my arm
   to threaten an orphan
   when the power was mine,
22 I hope that arm will fall
   from its socket.
23 I could not have been abusive;
   I was terrified at the thought
   that God might punish me.
24 I have never trusted the power of wealth,
25 or taken pride in owning
   many possessions.
26-27 I have never openly or secretly
   worshipped the sun or moon.
28 Such horrible sins
   would have deserved
   punishment from God.

---

*30.29 jackals: Desert animals related to wolves, but smaller.

29 I have never laughed
    when my enemies
    were struck by disaster.
30 Neither have I sinned by asking God
    to send down on them
    the curse of death.
31 No one ever went hungry*
    at my house,
32 and travellers were always welcome.
33 Many have attempted to hide
    their sins from others —
    but I refused.
34 And the fear of public disgrace
    never forced me
    to keep silent
    about what I had done.

Why doesn't God listen?

35 Why doesn't God All-Powerful
    listen and answer?
    If God has something against me,
    let him speak up
    or put it in writing!
36 Then I would wear his charges
    on my clothes and forehead.
37 And with my head held high,
    I would tell him everything
    I have ever done.

38 I have never ill-treated
    the land I farmed
    and made it mourn.*
39 Nor have I cheated my workers
    and caused them pain.'
40 If I had, I would pray
    for weeds instead of wheat
    to grow in my fields.

After saying these things, Job was silent.

Elihu's speeches

CHAPTER 32

Elihu is upset with Job's friends

1 Finally, these three men stopped arguing with Job, because he refused to admit that he was guilty.

2 Elihu from Buz* was there, and he had become upset with Job for blaming God instead of himself. 3 He was also angry with Job's three friends for not being able to prove that Job was wrong. 4 Elihu was younger than these three, and he let them speak first. 5 But he became irritated when they could not answer Job, 6 and he said to them:

    I am much younger than you,
        so I have shown respect
        by keeping silent.
7 I once believed age
        was the source of wisdom;
8 now I truly realize
        wisdom comes from God.
9 Age is no guarantee of wisdom
        and understanding.
10 That's why I ask you
        to listen to me.

I eagerly listened

11-12 I eagerly listened
        to each of your arguments,
        but not one of you proved
        Job to be wrong.
13 You shouldn't say,
        "We know what's right!
        Let God punish him."
14 Job hasn't spoken against me,
        and so I won't answer him
        with your arguments.

15 All of you are shocked;
        you don't know what to say.
16 But am I to remain silent,
        just because you
        have stopped speaking?
17 No! I will give my opinion,
18 because I have so much to say,
        that I can't keep quiet.
19 I am like a swollen wineskin,
        and I will burst*
20   if I don't speak.
21-22 I don't know how to be unfair
        or to flatter anyone —
        if I did, my Creator
        would quickly destroy me!

---

*31.31 ever went hungry: Or "was ever sexually abused" (see Genesis 19.1–11; Judges 17.22–30). In ancient Israel, the lives of one's guests were sacred and had to be protected at any cost.
*31.38 mourn: In biblical times there were strict regulations for proper use of the land, and land that was abused was said to "mourn" and become no longer productive.

*32.2 Elihu from Buz: The Hebrew text has "Elihu son of Barachel from Buz of the family of Ram". Buz may have been somewhere in the territory of Edom; in Jeremiah 25.23 it is mentioned along with Dedan and Tema (see 6.19).
*32.19 swollen wineskin . . . burst: While the juice from grapes was becoming wine, it would swell and stretch the skins in which it had been stored; sometimes the swelling would burst the wineskins.

CHAPTER 33

Elihu speaks

Job, listen to me!

¹ Job, listen to me!
  Pay close attention.
²⁻³ Everything I will say
  is true and sincere,
⁴ just as surely as the Spirit
  of God All-Powerful•
  gave me the breath of life.
⁵ Now line up your arguments
  and prepare to face me.
⁶ We were each made from clay,
  and God has no favourites,
⁷ so don't be afraid of me
  or what I might do.

I have heard you argue

⁸ I have heard you argue
⁹ that you are innocent,
  guilty of nothing.
¹⁰ You claim that God
  has made you his enemy,
¹¹ that he has bound your feet
  and blocked your path.
¹² But, Job, you're wrong —
  God is greater than any human.
¹³ So why do you challenge God
  to answer you?•
¹⁴ God speaks in different ways,
  and we don't always
  recognize his voice.
¹⁵⁻¹⁶Sometimes in the night,
  he uses terrifying dreams
  to give us warnings.
¹⁷ God does this to make us turn
  from sin and pride
¹⁸ and to protect us
  from being swept away
  to the world of the dead.
¹⁹ Sometimes we are punished
  with a serious illness
  and aching joints.
²⁰ Merely the thought
  of our favourite food
  makes our stomachs sick,
²¹ and we become so skinny
  that our bones stick out.
²² We feel death and the grave
  taking us in their grip.

²³ One of a thousand angels
  then comes to our rescue
  by saying we are innocent.
²⁴ The angel shows kindness,
  commanding death to release us,
  because the price was paid.
²⁵ Our health is restored,
  we feel young again,
²⁶ and we ask God to accept us.
  Then we joyfully worship God,
  and we are rewarded
  because we are innocent.
²⁷ When that happens,
  we tell everyone,
  "I sinned and did wrong,
  but God forgave me
²⁸ and rescued me from death!
  Now I will see the light."

²⁹ God gives each of us
  chance after chance
³⁰ to be saved from death
  and brought into the light
  that gives life.
³¹ So, Job, pay attention
  and don't interrupt,
³² though I would gladly listen
  to anything you say
  that proves you are right.
³³ Otherwise, listen in silence
  to my wisdom.

CHAPTER 34

Elihu continues

You men think you are wise

¹ Elihu said:

² You men think you are wise,
  but just listen to me!
³ Think about my words,
  as you would taste food.
⁴ Then we can decide the case
  and give a just verdict.
⁵ Job claims he is innocent
  and God is guilty
  of ill-treating him.
⁶ Job also argues that God
  considers him a liar
  and that he is suffering severely
  in spite of his innocence.
⁷ But to tell the truth,
  Job is shameless!
⁸ He spends his time with sinners,
⁹ because he has said,
  "It doesn't pay to please God."

See also: **33.11:** Job 13.27. **33.15:** Job 4.13.

If any of you are clever

¹⁰ If any of you are clever,
  you will listen and learn
  that God All-Powerful
  does what is right.

¹¹ God always treats everyone
  the way they deserve,
¹² and he is never unfair.

¹³ From the very beginning,
  God has been in control
  of all the world.

¹⁴ If God took back the breath
  that he breathed into us,
¹⁵ we humans would die
  and return to the soil.

¹⁶ So be wise and listen!

¹⁷ The mighty God is the one
  who brings about justice,
  and you are condemning him.

¹⁸ Indeed, God is the one
  who condemns unfair rulers.

¹⁹ And God created us all;
  he has no favourites,
  whether rich or poor.

²⁰ Even powerful rulers die
  in the darkness of night
  when they least expect it,
  just like the rest of us.

God watches everything we do

²¹ God watches everything we do.

²² No evil person can hide
  in the deepest darkness.

²³ And so, God doesn't need
  to set a time for judgment.

²⁴ Without asking for advice,
  God removes mighty leaders
  and puts others in their place.

²⁵ He knows what they are like,
  and he wipes them out
  in the middle of the night.

²⁶ And while others look on,
  he punishes them
  because they were evil
²⁷ and refused to obey him.

²⁸ The persons they ill-treated
  had prayed for help,
  until God answered their prayers.

²⁹ When God does nothing,
  can any person or nation
  find fault with him?

³⁰ But still, he punishes rulers
  who abuse their people.◆

³¹ Job, you should tell God
  that you are guilty
  and promise to do better.

³² Then ask him to point out
  what you did wrong,
  so you won't do it again.

³³ Do you make the rules,
  or does God?
  You have to decide —
  I can't do it for you;
  now make up your mind.

³⁴ Job, anyone with good sense
  can easily see
³⁵ that you are speaking nonsense
  and lack good judgment.

³⁶ So I pray for you to suffer
  as much as possible
  for talking like a sinner.

³⁷ You have rebelled against God,
  time after time,
  and have even insulted us.

CHAPTER 35

Elihu continues

Are you really innocent?

¹ Elihu said:

² Job, are you really innocent
  in the sight of God?◆

³ Don't you honestly believe
  it pays to obey him?

⁴ I will give the answers
  to you and your friends.

⁵⁻⁶ Look up to the heavens and think!
  Do your sins hurt God?

⁷ Is any good you may have done
  at all helpful to him?

⁸ The evil or good you do
  only affects other humans.

⁹ In times of trouble,
  everyone begs the mighty God
  to have mercy.

¹⁰ But after their Creator
  helps them through hard times,
  they forget about him,
¹¹ though he makes us wiser
  than animals or birds.

¹² God won't listen to the prayers
  of proud and evil people.

¹³ If God All-Powerful refuses
  to answer their empty prayers,
¹⁴ he will surely deny your impatient request
  to face him in court.

See also: 34.11: Psa 62.12.

See also: 35.6–8: Job 22.2,3.

15 Job, you were wrong to say
God doesn't punish sin.
16 Everything you have said
adds up to nonsense.

CHAPTER 36

Elihu continues

Be patient a while longer

1 Elihu said:

2 Be patient a while longer;
I have something else to say
in God's defence.
3 God always does right —
and this knowledge
comes straight from God.*
4 You can rest assured
that what I say is true.
5 Although he is mighty,
he cares about everyone
and makes fair decisions.
6 The wicked are cut down,
and those who are wronged
receive justice.
7 God watches over good people
and places them
in positions of power and honour
for ever.
8 But when people are prisoners
of suffering and pain,
9-10 God points out their sin and their pride,
then he warns them to turn back to him.
11 And if they obey, they will be successful
and happy from then on.
12 But if they foolishly refuse,
they will be rewarded
with a violent death.

Godless people are too angry

13 Godless people are too angry
to ask God for help
when he punishes them.
14 So they die young
in shameful disgrace.
15 Hard times and trouble
are God's way of getting our attention!
16 And at this very moment,
God deeply desires
to lead you from trouble
and to spread your table
with your favourite food.

17 Now that the judgment for your sins
has fallen upon you,
18 don't let your anger
and the pain you endured
make you sneer at God.
19 Your reputation and riches
cannot protect you from distress,
20 nor can you find safety
in the dark world below.◆
21 Be on guard! Don't turn to evil
as a way of escape.
22 God's power is unlimited.
He needs no teachers
23 to guide or correct him.

Others have praised God

24 Others have praised God
for what he has done,
so join with them.
25 From down here on earth,
everyone has looked up and seen
26 how great God is —
God is more than we imagine;
no one can count the years
he has lived.
27-28 God gathers moisture into the clouds
and supplies us with rain.
29 Who can understand
how God scatters the clouds
and speaks from his home
in the thunderstorm?
30 And when God sends lightning,
it can be seen
at the bottom of the sea.
31 By producing such rainstorms,
God rules the world
and provides us with food.
32 Each flash of lightning
is one of his arrows
striking its target,
33 and the thunder tells
of his anger against sin.◆

CHAPTER 37

Elihu continues

I am frightened

1 I am frightened and tremble all over,
2 when I hear the roaring voice
of God in the thunder,
3 and when I see his lightning
flash across the sky.
4 God's majestic voice
thunders his commands,◆
5 creating miracles too marvellous
for us to understand.

---

*36.3 comes straight from God: The Hebrew text
has "comes from a distant place", which refers to the
place where God lives; Elihu is claiming that he learnt
this from God.

6 Snow and heavy rainstorms
7 make us stop and think about
    God's power,
8   and they force animals to seek shelter.
9 The storms of winter strike,
10 and the breath of God
    freezes streams and rivers.
11 Rain clouds filled with lightning
    appear at God's command,
12 travelling across the sky
13 to release their cargo —
    sometimes as punishment for sin,
    sometimes as kindness.

Consider carefully

14 Job, consider carefully
    the many wonders of God.
15 Can you explain why lightning flashes
    at the orders
16 of God who knows all things?
    Or how he hangs the clouds
    in empty space?
17 You almost melt in the heat
    of fierce desert winds
    when the sky is like brass.
18 God can spread out the clouds
    to get relief from the heat,
    but can you?

19 Tell us what to say to God!
    Our minds are in the dark,
    and we don't know how
    to argue our case.
20 Should I risk my life by telling God
    that I want to speak?
21 No one can stare at the sun
    after a breeze has blown
    the clouds from the sky.
22 Yet the glorious splendour
    of God All-Powerful
    is brighter by far.
23 God cannot be seen —
    but his power is great,
    and he is always fair.
24 And so we humans fear God,
    because he shows no respect
    for those who are proud
    and think they know so much.

God's first speech

CHAPTER 38

The LORD speaks

From out of a storm

1 From out of a storm, the LORD said to Job:

2 Why do you talk so much
    when you know so little?
3 Now get ready to face me!
    Can you answer the questions I ask?
4 How did I lay the foundation
    for the earth?
    Were you there?
5 Doubtless you know who decided
    its length and width.
6 What supports the foundation?
    Who placed the cornerstone,
7   while morning stars sang,
    and angels rejoiced?

8 When the ocean was born,
    I set its boundaries
9   and wrapped it in blankets of thickest fog.
10 Then I built a wall around it,
    locked the gates,
11 and said,
    "Your powerful waves stop here!
    They can go no further."

Did you ever tell the sun to rise?

12 Did you ever tell the sun to rise?
    And did it obey?
13 Did it take hold of the earth
    and shake out the wicked
    like dust from a rug?
14 Early dawn outlines the hills
    like stitches on clothing
    or sketches on clay.
15 But its light is too much
    for those who are evil,
    and their power is broken.

16 Job, have you ever walked
    on the ocean floor?
17 Have you seen the gate
    to the world of the dead?
18 And how large is the earth?
    Tell me, if you know?

19 Where is the home of light,
    and where does darkness live?
20 Can you lead them home?
21 I'm certain you must be able to,
    since you were already born
    when I created everything.

22 Have you been to the places
    where I keep snow and hail,
23 until I use them to punish
    and conquer nations?
24 From where does lightning leap,
    or the east wind blow?

See also: **38.8-11:** Jer 5.22.

²⁵ Who carves out a path
   for thunderstorms?
   Who sends torrents of rain
²⁶ on empty deserts where no one lives?
²⁷ Rain that changes barren land
   to meadows green with grass.
²⁸ Who is the father of the dew
   and of the rain?
²⁹ Who gives birth to the sleet
   and the frost
³⁰ that fall in winter,
   when streams and lakes
   freeze solid as a rock?

Can you arrange stars?

³¹ Can you arrange stars in groups
   such as Orion and the Pleiades?
³² Do you control the stars
   or set in place the Great Bear
   and the Little Bear?
³³ Do you know the laws
   that govern the heavens,
   and can you make them rule the earth?
³⁴ Can you order the clouds
   to send a downpour,
³⁵ or will lightning flash at your command?
³⁶ Did you teach birds to know
   that rain or floods
   are on their way?'
³⁷ Can you count the clouds
   or pour out their water
³⁸ on the dry, lumpy soil?

³⁹ When lions are hungry,
   do you help them hunt?
⁴⁰ Do you send an animal into their den?
⁴¹ And when starving young ravens
   cry out to me for food,
   do you satisfy their hunger?

CHAPTER 39

The LORD continues

When do mountain goats give birth?

¹ When do mountain goats
   and deer give birth?
   Have you been there
   when their young are born?
²⁻³ How long are they pregnant
   before they deliver?
⁴ Soon their young grow strong
   and then leave to be on their own.

⁵ Who set wild donkeys free?
⁶ I alone help them survive
   in salty desert sand.

⁷ They stay far from crowded cities
   and refuse to be tamed.
⁸ Instead, they roam the hills,
   searching for pasture land.

⁹ Would a wild ox agree to live in your barn
   and labour for you?
¹⁰ Could you force him to plough
   or to drag a heavy log
   to smooth out the soil?
¹¹ Can you depend on him
   to use his great strength
   and do your heavy work?
¹² Can you trust him to harvest your grain
   or take it to your barn
   from the threshing place?

An ostrich proudly flaps her wings

¹³ An ostrich proudly flaps her wings,
   but not because she loves her young.
¹⁴ She abandons her eggs
   and lets the dusty ground
   keep them warm.
¹⁵ And she doesn't seem to worry
   that the feet of an animal
   could crush them all.
¹⁶ She treats her eggs as though
   they were not her own,
   unconcerned that her work
   might be for nothing.
¹⁷ I myself made her foolish
   and without common sense.
¹⁸ But once she starts running,'
   she laughs at a rider on the fastest horse.

Did you give horses their strength?

¹⁹ Did you give horses their strength
   and the flowing hair along their necks?
²⁰ Did you make them able
   to jump like grasshoppers
   or to frighten people with their snorting?

²¹ Before horses are ridden into battle,
   they paw at the ground,
   proud of their strength.
²² Laughing at fear, they rush
   towards the fighting,
²³ while the weapons of their riders
   rattle and flash in the sun.
²⁴ Unable to stand still,
   they gallop eagerly into battle
   when trumpets blast.
²⁵ Stirred by the distant smells
   and sounds of war,
   they snort in reply to the trumpet.

²⁶ Did you teach hawks to fly south
   for the winter?

See also: 38.31: Job 9.9; Amos 5.8.

27-28Did you train eagles' to build
their nests on rocky cliffs,
29 where they can look down
to spot their next meal?
30 Then their young gather to feast
wherever the victim lies.

God's second speech and Job's responses

CHAPTER 40

The LORD continues

I am the LORD All-Powerful

1-2 I am the LORD All-Powerful,
but you have argued that I am wrong.
Now you must answer me.

3 Job said to the LORD:

4 Who am I to answer you?
5 I did speak once or twice,
but never again.

6 Then out of the storm the LORD said to Job:

7 Face me and answer the questions I ask!
8 Are you trying to prove
that you are innocent
by accusing me of injustice?
9 Do you have a powerful arm
and a thundering voice
that compare with mine?
10 If so, then surround yourself
with glory and majesty.
11-12Show your furious anger!
Throw down and crush
all who are proud and evil.
13 Wrap them in grave clothes
and bury them together
in the dusty soil.
14 Do this, and I will agree
that you have won this argument.

I created you

15 I created both you
and the hippopotamus.*
It eats only grass like an ox,
16 but look at the mighty muscles
in its body
17 and legs.

Its tail is like a cedar tree,
and its thighs are thick.
18 The bones in its legs
are like bronze or iron.

19 I made it more powerful
than any other creature,
yet I am stronger still.
20 Undisturbed, it eats grass
while the other animals play nearby.'
21-22It rests in the shade of trees
along the river bank
or hides among reeds in the swamp.
23 It remains calm and unafraid
with the River Jordan rushing
and splashing in its face.
24 There is no way to capture
a hippopotamus —
not even by hooking its nose
or blinding its eyes.

CHAPTER 41

The LORD continues

Can you catch a sea monster?

1 Can you catch a sea monster*
by using a fish-hook?
Can you tie its mouth shut with a rope?
2 Can it be led around by a ring in its nose
or a hook in its jaw?
3 Will it beg for mercy?
4 Will it surrender as a slave for life?
5 Can it be tied by the leg
like a pet bird for little girls?
6 Is it ever chopped up
and its pieces bargained for
in the fish-market?
7 Can it be killed with harpoons or spears?
8 Wrestle with it just once —
that will be the end.
9 Merely a glimpse of this monster
makes all courage melt.
10 And if it is too fierce for anyone to attack,
who would dare oppose me?
11 I am in command of the world
and in debt to no one.
12 What powerful legs, what a stout body
this monster possesses!
13 Who could strip off its armour
or bring it under control with a harness?
14 Who would try to open its jaws,
full of fearsome teeth?

*40.15 the hippopotamus: The Hebrew text has "Behemoth", which was sometimes understood to be a sea monster like Rahab (9.13; 26.12), Leviathan (3.8; 41.1), and Tannin (7.12).
See also: 39.30: Matt 24.28; Luke 17.37.

*41.1 sea monster: The Hebrew text has "Leviathan", which may refer to a sea monster or possibly to a crocodile in this verse (see the note at 3.8).
See also: 41.1: Psa 74.14; 104.26; Isa 27.1.

15-17Its back' is covered
with shield after shield,
firmly bound and closer together
than breath to breath.

When this monster sneezes

18 When this monster sneezes,
lightning flashes,
and its eyes glow like the dawn.
19 Sparks and fiery flames
explode from its mouth.
20 And smoke spews from its nose
like steam from a boiling pot,
21 while its blazing breath
scorches everything in sight.

22 Its neck is so tremendous
that everyone trembles,
23 the weakest parts of its body
are harder than iron,
24 and its heart is stone.
25 When this noisy monster appears,
even the most powerful'
turn and run in fear.

26 No sword or spear can harm it,
27 and weapons of bronze
or iron are as useless
as straw or rotten wood.
28 Stones thrown from a sling
cause it no more harm
than husks of grain.
This monster fears no arrows,
29 it simply smiles at spears,
and striking it with a stick
is like slapping it with straw.

30 As it crawls through the mud,
its sharp and spiny hide
tears the ground apart.
31 And when it swims down deep,
the sea starts churning like boiling oil,
32 and it leaves behind a trail
of shining white foam.
33 No other creature on earth
is so fearless.
34 It is king of all proud creatures,
and it looks upon the others
as nothing.

CHAPTER 42

Job's reply to the LORD

No one can oppose you

1 Job said:

2 No one can oppose you,
because you have the power
to do what you want.

3 You asked why I talk so much
when I know so little.
I have talked about things
that are far beyond my understanding.
4 You told me to listen
and answer your questions.'
5 I heard about you from others;
now I have seen you
with my own eyes.
6 That's why I hate myself
and sit here in dust and ashes
to show my sorrow.

The Lord again blesses Job with health, wealth, and family

The LORD corrects Job's friends

7 The LORD said to Eliphaz:

What my servant Job has said about me
is true, but I am angry with you and your two
friends for not telling the truth. 8 So I want
you to go over to Job and offer seven bulls
and seven goats on an altar as a sacrifice to
please me.* After this, Job will pray, and I
will agree not to punish you for your
foolishness.

9 Eliphaz, Bildad, and Zophar obeyed the
LORD, and he answered Job's prayer.

A happy ending

10 After Job had prayed for his three friends,
the LORD made Job twice as rich as he had
been before. 11 Then Job gave a feast for his
brothers and sisters and for his old friends.
They expressed their sorrow for the
suffering the LORD had brought on him, and
they each gave Job some silver and a gold
ring.

12 The LORD now blessed Job more than
ever; he gave him fourteen thousand sheep,
six thousand camels, a thousand pair of
oxen, and a thousand donkeys.

13 In addition to seven sons, Job had three
daughters, 14 whose names were Jemimah,
Keziah, and Keren Happuch. 15 They were the

---

*42.8 sacrifice to please me: These sacrifices have
traditionally been called "whole burnt offerings"
because the whole animal was burnt on the altar.
A main purpose of such sacrifices was to please the
LORD with the smell of the sacrifice, and so in the CEV
they are often called "sacrifices to please the LORD."
See also: 42.3: Job 38.2. 42.4: Job 38.3. 42.10: Job 1.1-3.

most beautiful women in that part of the world, and Job gave them shares of his property, along with their brothers.

¹⁶ Job lived for another one hundred and forty years — long enough to see his great-grandchildren have children of their own — ¹⁷ and when he finally died, he was very old.

Additional notes

¹1.6 Satan: Hebrew "the accuser".

¹2.1 Satan: See the note at 1.6.

¹2.4 There's no pain like your own: The Hebrew text has "Skin for skin", which was probably a popular saying.

¹3.12 Why was I accepted: The Hebrew text has "Why were there knees to receive me", which may refer either to Job's mother or to his father, who would have placed Job on his knees to show that he had accepted him as his child.

¹5.5 wealth: One possible meaning for the difficult Hebrew text of verse 5.

¹6.6 What is more tasteless . . . egg: One possible meaning for the difficult Hebrew text.

¹6.14 and you should help me . . . God All-Powerful: Or "and if you don't help me, you no longer respect God All-Powerful."

¹6.21 just . . . you: One possible meaning for the difficult Hebrew text.

¹8.17 rocks: One possible meaning for the difficult Hebrew text of verse 17.

¹8.19 their . . . away: One possible meaning for the difficult Hebrew text.

¹9.17 strike . . . storm: One possible meaning for the difficult Hebrew text.

¹9.20 God . . . wrong: Or "my own words would prove me wrong."

¹9.35 but . . . speak: One possible meaning for the difficult Hebrew text.

¹10.16 lion: One possible meaning for the difficult Hebrew text of verse 16.

¹10.20 I have only . . . alone: One possible meaning for the difficult Hebrew text.

¹11.12 it's . . . wise: One possible meaning for the difficult Hebrew text.

¹12.6 God is in our hands: One possible meaning for the difficult Hebrew text.

¹12.9 Any . . . done: One possible meaning for the difficult Hebrew text.

¹13.15 God . . . trust him: Or "God will surely kill me; I have lost all hope."

¹15.31,32 leaf: One possible meaning for the difficult Hebrew text of verses 31,32.

¹16.20 My friends . . . beg: Or "God is my friend, and he is the one I beg".

¹17.9 stronger: One possible meaning for the difficult Hebrew text of verse 12.

¹17.12 hopes: One possible meaning for the difficult Hebrew text of verse 12.

¹19.25 Saviour: Or "Defender".

¹19.26 God: One possible meaning for the difficult Hebrew text of verses 25,26.

¹20.20 are never satisfied: One possible meaning for the difficult Hebrew text.

¹20.23 anger: One possible meaning for the difficult Hebrew text of verse 23.

¹21.8 up: One possible meaning for the difficult Hebrew text of verse 8.

¹22.30 God: One possible meaning for the difficult Hebrew text of verses 29,30.

¹23.11,12 treasured his teachings: One possible meaning for the difficult Hebrew text.

¹23.17 silent: One possible meaning for the difficult Hebrew text of verse 17.

¹24.21 women: One possible meaning for the difficult Hebrew text of verse 21.

¹26.12 the force of the mighty ocean: The Hebrew text has "the ocean . . . Rahab". In this passage the sea monster Rahab stands for the fearsome power of the ocean (see the notes at 3.8 and 9.13).

¹27.19 poor: Or "dead".

¹28.6 gold: One possible meaning for the difficult Hebrew text of verses 5,6.

¹28.11 uncover the sources of: Two ancient translations; Hebrew "dam up".

¹28.13 the way: Or "its worth".

¹30.3 hunger: One possible meaning for the difficult Hebrew text of verse 3.

¹30.11 God . . . do: Or "They have destroyed me, and so they don't care what else they do."

¹30.12 trapped: One possible meaning for the difficult Hebrew text of verse 12.

¹30.13 destroying . . . completely: One possible meaning for the difficult Hebrew text.

¹30.24 strikes: One possible meaning for the difficult Hebrew text of verse 24.

¹31.12 flames: One possible meaning for the difficult Hebrew text of verse 12.

¹31.18 widows: One possible meaning for the difficult Hebrew text of verse 18.

¹31.39 pain: One possible meaning for the difficult Hebrew text of verse 39.

¹33.4 the Spirit of God All-Powerful: Or "God All-Powerful".

¹33.13 answer you: One possible meaning for the difficult Hebrew text of verse 13.

¹34.30 people: One possible meaning for the difficult Hebrew text of verses 29,30.

¹35.2 are . . . God: Or "is it right for you to accuse God?"

¹36.20 below: One possible meaning for the difficult Hebrew text of verses 18–20.

¹36.33 sin: One possible meaning for the difficult Hebrew text of verse 33.

¹37.4 commands: One possible meaning for the difficult Hebrew text of verse 4.

'38.36 way: One possible meaning for the difficult
Hebrew text of verse 36.
'39.18 starts running: One possible meaning for the
difficult Hebrew text.
'39.27,28 eagles: Or "vultures".
'40.20 nearby: One possible meaning for the difficult
Hebrew text of verse 20.
'41.15-17 back: Two ancient translations; Hebrew
"pride".
'41.25 most powerful: Or "gods".
'42.4 questions: One possible meaning for the
difficult Hebrew text of verse 4.

Psalms

A quick look at this book

The book of Psalms is divided into five sections or "books". Most of the psalms in Books 1 and 2 were written by David, while many in Book 3 were written by either Asaph or the people of Korah. Psalms 120—134 are all "celebration psalms". The five sections of the book of Psalms are:

The book of Psalms is the longest book in the Bible. Psalms are poems that can either be sung as songs or spoken as prayers by individuals or groups. There are 150 psalms in this book, and many of them list King David as their author. They were collected over a long period of time and became a very important part of the worship of the people of Israel.

Some of the psalms tell the music leader what instruments should be used and what tunes should be followed. For example, look at Psalm 4 and Psalm 45.

Many of the Bible's main ideas are echoed in the Psalms: praise, thankfulness, faith, hope, sorrow for sin, God's loyalty and help. And at the heart of all the psalms there is a deep trust in God. The writers of the psalms always express their true feelings, whether they are praising God for his blessings or complaining in times of trouble.

In ancient Israel the psalms were used in several different ways: (1) to praise God, as in Psalm 105; (2) to express sorrow, as in Psalm 13; (3) to teach, as in Psalm 1; (4) to honour Israel's king and pray for fairness in his rule, as in Psalm 72; (5) to tell of God's power over all creation, as in Psalm 47; (6) to show love for Jerusalem, as in Psalm 122; and (7) to celebrate festivals, as in Psalm 126. Of course, many of the psalms could be used for more than one purpose.

Jesus used the psalms when he preached and taught, and they were often quoted by the writers of the New Testament. The earliest Christians also used the psalms in worship, teaching, and telling others the good news about what God has done through Jesus Christ. A verse from Psalm 118, for example, is directly referred to six times in the New Testament:

> The stone that the builders
>   tossed aside
>   has now become
>   the most important stone.

(118.22)

BOOK 1

(Psalms 1–41)

Psalm 1

The way to happiness

¹ God blesses those people
who refuse evil advice
and won't follow sinners
or join in sneering at God.
² Instead, the Law of the LORD
makes them happy,
and they think about it day and night.

³ They are like trees
growing beside a stream,
trees that produce fruit in season
and always have leaves.
Those people succeed
in everything they do.

⁴ That isn't true of those who are evil,
because they are like straw
blown by the wind.
⁵ Sinners won't have an excuse
on the day of judgment,
and they won't have a place
with the people of God.
⁶ The LORD protects everyone
who follows him,
but the wicked follow a road
that leads to ruin.

Psalm 2

The LORD's chosen king

¹ Why do the nations plot,*
and why do their people
make useless plans?*
² The kings of this earth
have all joined together
to turn against the LORD
and his chosen one.
³ They say, "Let's cut the ropes
and set ourselves free!"

⁴ In heaven the LORD laughs
as he sits on his throne,
making fun of the nations.
⁵ The LORD becomes furious
and threatens them.
His anger terrifies them as he says,
⁶ "I've put my king on Zion,
my sacred hill."

⁷ I will tell the promise
that the LORD made to me:
"You are my son, because today
I have become your father.
⁸ Ask me for the nations,
and every nation on earth
will belong to you.
⁹ You will smash them with an iron rod
and shatter them like dishes of clay."

¹⁰ Be wise, all you rulers,
and pay close attention.
¹¹ Serve and honour the LORD;
be glad and tremble.
¹² Show respect to his son
because if you don't,
the LORD might become furious
and suddenly destroy you.*
But he blesses and protects
everyone who runs to him.

Psalm 3

*(Written by David when he was running
from his son Absalom.)*

An early morning prayer

¹ I have a lot of enemies, LORD.
Many fight against
² me and say,
"God won't rescue you!"

³ But you are my shield,
and you give me victory
and great honour.
⁴ I pray to you, and you answer
from your sacred hill.
⁵ I sleep and wake up refreshed
because you, LORD, protect me.
⁶ Ten thousand enemies attack
from every side,
but I am not afraid.

⁷ Come and save me, LORD God!
Break my enemies' jaws
and shatter their teeth,
⁸ because you protect
and bless your people.

See also: 1.3: Jer 17.8. 2.1,2: Acts 4.25,26.

See also: 2.7: Acts 13.33; Heb 1.5; 5.5. 2.9: Rev 2.26,27;
12.5; 19.15. 3 Title: 2 Sam 15.13—17.22.

You alone keep me safe.
Don't reject or desert me.
¹⁰ Even if my father and mother
should desert me,
you will take care of me.

¹¹ Teach me to follow, LORD,
and lead me on the right path
because of my enemies.
¹² Don't let them do to me
what they want.
People tell lies about me
and make terrible threats,
¹³ but I know I will live
to see how kind you are.

¹⁴ Trust the LORD!
Be brave and strong
and trust the LORD.

Psalm 28

(By David.)

A prayer for help

¹ Only you, LORD,
are a mighty rock!*
Don't refuse to help me when I pray.
If you don't answer me,
I will soon be dead.
² Please listen to my prayer
and my cry for help,
as I lift my hands
towards your holy temple.

³ Don't drag me away, LORD,
with those cruel people,
who speak kind words,
while planning trouble.
⁴ Treat them as they deserve!
Punish them for their sins.
⁵ They don't pay any attention
to your wonderful deeds.
Now you will destroy them
and leave them in ruin.

⁶ I praise you, LORD,
for answering my prayers.
⁷ You are my strong shield,
and I trust you completely.
You have helped me,
and I will celebrate
and thank you in song.

⁸ You give strength to your people, LORD,
and you save and protect
your chosen ones.

⁹ Come, save us and bless us.
Be our shepherd and always
carry us in your arms.

Psalm 29

(A psalm by David.)

The voice of the LORD in a storm

¹ All you angels* in heaven,
honour the glory and power
of the LORD!
² Honour the wonderful name
of the LORD,
and worship the LORD
most holy and glorious.*

³ The voice of the LORD
echoes over the oceans.
The glorious LORD God thunders
above the roar of the raging sea,
⁴ and his voice is mighty
and marvellous.
⁵ The voice of the LORD
destroys the cedar trees;
the LORD shatters cedars
on Mount Lebanon.
⁶ God makes Mount Lebanon
skip like a calf
and Mount Hermon
jump like a wild ox.

⁷ The voice of the LORD
makes lightning flash
⁸ and the desert tremble.
And because of the LORD,
the desert near Kadesh
shivers and shakes.

⁹ The voice of the LORD
makes deer give birth
before their time.*
Forests are stripped of leaves,
and the temple is filled
with shouts of praise.

¹⁰ The LORD rules on his throne,
king of the flood* for ever.
¹¹ Pray that our LORD
will make us strong
and give us peace.

---

*28.1 mighty rock: See the note at 18.2.
See also: 28.4: Rev 22.12.

*29.10 king of the flood: In ancient times the people of Israel believed that a mighty ocean surrounded all of creation, and that God could release the water to flood the earth.
See also: 29.1,2: Psa 96.7–9.

525

Psalm 30

(A psalm by David for the dedication of the temple.)

A prayer of thanks

1 I will praise you, LORD!
  You saved me from the grave
  and kept my enemies
  from celebrating my death.
2 I prayed to you, LORD God,
  and you healed me,
3 saving me from death and the grave.

4 Your faithful people, LORD,
  will praise you with songs
  and honour your holy name.
5 Your anger lasts a little while,
  but your kindness lasts for a lifetime.
  At night we may cry,
  but when morning comes
  we will celebrate.

6 I was carefree and thought,
  "I'll never be shaken!"
7 You, LORD, were my friend,
  and you made me strong
  as a mighty mountain.
  But when you hid your face,
  I was crushed.

8 I prayed to you, LORD,
  and in my prayer I said,
9 "What good will it do you
  if I am in the grave?
  Once I have turned to dust,
  how can I praise you
  or tell how loyal you are?
10 Have pity, LORD! Help!"

11 You have turned my sorrow
  into joyful dancing.
  No longer am I sad
  and wearing sackcloth.*
12 I thank you from my heart,
  and I will never stop
  singing your praises,
  my LORD and my God.

Psalm 31

(A psalm by David for the music leader.)

A prayer for protection

1 I come to you, LORD, for protection.
  Don't let me be ashamed.
  Do as you have promised
  and rescue me.
2 Listen to my prayer
  and hurry to save me.
  Be my mighty rock*
  and the fortress where I am safe.

3 You, LORD God,
  are my mighty rock and my fortress.
  Lead me and guide me,
  so that your name will be honoured.
4 Protect me from hidden traps
  and keep me safe.
5 You are faithful,
  and I trust you
  because you rescued me.

6 I hate the worshippers
  of worthless idols,
  but I trust you, LORD.
7 I celebrate and shout
  because you are kind.
  You saw all my suffering,
  and you cared for me.
8 You kept me from the hands
  of my enemies,
  and you set me free.

9 Have pity, LORD!
  I am suffering and almost blind.
  My whole body aches.
10 I have known only sorrow
  all my life long,
  and I suffer year after year.
  I am weak from sin,
  and my bones are limp.

11 My enemies insult me.
  Neighbours are even worse,
  and I disgust my friends.
  People meet me in the street,
  and they turn and run.
12 I am completely forgotten
  like someone dead.
  I am merely a broken dish.
13 I hear the crowds whisper,
  "Everyone is afraid!"
  They are plotting and scheming
  to murder me.

14 But I trust you, LORD,
  and I claim you as my God.
15 My life is in your hands.
  Save me from enemies
  who hunt me down.
16 Smile on me, your servant.
  Have pity and rescue me.

---

*30.11 sackcloth: A rough, dark-coloured cloth made from goat or camel hair and used to make grain sacks. It was worn in times of trouble or sorrow.

*31.2 mighty rock: See the note at 18.2.
See also: 31.5: Luke 23.46.

[17] I pray only to you.
   Don't disappoint me.
Disappoint my cruel enemies
   until they lie silent in their graves.
[18] Silence those proud liars!
   Make them stop boasting
   and insulting your people.

[19] You are wonderful,
   and while everyone watches,
you store up blessings for all
   who honour and trust you.
[20] You are their shelter
   from harmful plots,
   and you are their protection
   from vicious gossip.

[21] I will praise you, LORD,
   for showing great kindness
   when I was like a city under attack.
[22] I was terrified and thought,
   "They've chased me
   far away from you!"
But you answered my prayer
   when I shouted for help.

[23] All who belong to the LORD,
   show how you love him.
The LORD protects the faithful,
   but he severely punishes
   everyone who is proud.
[24] All who trust the LORD,
   be cheerful and strong.

Psalm 32

(A special psalm by David.)

The joy of forgiveness

[1] Our God, you bless everyone
   whose sins you forgive and wipe away.
[2] You bless them by saying,
   "You told me your sins,
   without trying to hide them,
   and now I forgive you."

[3] Before I confessed my sins,
   my bones felt limp,
   and I groaned all day long.
[4] Night and day your hand
   weighed heavily on me,
   and my strength was gone
   as in the summer heat.

[5] So I confessed my sins
   and told them all to you.
I said, "I'll tell the LORD
   each one of my sins."

See also: 32.1,2: Rom 4.7,8.

Then you forgave me
   and took away my guilt.

[6] We worship you, Lord,
   and we should always pray
whenever we find out
   that we have sinned.[?]
Then we won't be swept away
   by a raging flood.
[7] You are my hiding place!
   You protect me from trouble,
   and you put songs in my heart
   because you have saved me.

[8] You said to me,
   "I will point out the road
   that you should follow.
I will be your teacher
   and watch over you.
[9] Don't be stupid like horses and mules
   that must be led with ropes
   to make them obey."

[10] All kinds of troubles
   will strike the wicked,
   but your kindness shields those
   who trust you, LORD.
[11] And so your good people
   should celebrate and shout.

Psalm 33

Sing praises to the LORD

[1] You are the LORD's people.
   Obey him and celebrate!
   He deserves your praise.
[2] Praise the LORD with harps!
   Use harps with ten strings
   to make music for him.
[3] Sing a new song. Shout!
   Play beautiful music.

[4] The LORD is truthful; he can be trusted.
[5] He loves justice and fairness,
   and he is kind to everyone
   everywhere on earth.

[6] The LORD made the heavens
   and everything in them by his word.
[7] He scooped up the ocean
   and stored the water.
[8] Everyone in this world
   should worship
   and honour the LORD!
[9] As soon as he spoke
   the world was created;
   at his command, the earth was formed.

[10] The LORD destroys the plans
   and spoils the schemes of the nations.

11 But what the LORD has planned
   will stand for ever.
   His thoughts never change.
12 The LORD blesses each nation
   that worships only him.
   He blesses his chosen ones.
13 The LORD looks at the world
14 from his throne in heaven,
   and he watches us all.
15 The LORD gave us each a mind,
   and nothing we do
   can be hidden from him.

16 Mighty armies alone
   cannot win wars for a king;
   great strength by itself
   cannot keep a soldier safe.
17 In war the strength of a horse
   cannot be trusted
   to take you to safety.
18 But the LORD watches over all
   who honour him
   and trust his kindness.
19 He protects them from death
   and starvation.

20 We depend on you, LORD,
   to help and protect us.
21 You make our hearts glad
   because we trust you,
   the only God.
22 Be kind and bless us!
   We depend on you.

Psalm 34

*(Written by David when he pretended to be mad
in front of Abimelech, so that Abimelech would
send him away, and David could leave.)*

Honour the LORD

1 I will always praise the LORD.
2 With all my heart,
   I will praise the LORD.
   Let all who are helpless,
   listen and be glad.
3 Honour the LORD with me!
   Celebrate his great name.

4 I asked the LORD for help,
   and he saved me from all my fears.
5 Keep your eyes on the LORD!
   You will shine like the sun
   and never blush with shame.
6 I was a nobody, but I prayed,
   and the LORD saved me
   from all my troubles.

7 If you honour the LORD,
   his angel will protect you.
8 Discover for yourself
   that the LORD is kind.
   Come to him for protection,
   and you will be glad.

9 Honour the LORD!
   You are his special people.
   No one who honours the LORD
   will ever be in need.
10 Young lions* may go hungry
   or even starve,
   but if you trust the LORD,
   you will never miss out
   on anything good.

11 Come, my children, listen
   as I teach you to respect the LORD.
12 Do you want to live
   and enjoy a long life?
13 Then don't say cruel things
   and don't tell lies.
14 Do good instead of evil
   and try to live at peace.

15 If you obey the LORD,
   he will watch over you
   and answer your prayers.
16 But God despises evil people,
   and he will wipe them all
   from the earth,
   till they are forgotten.
17 When his people pray for help,
   he listens and rescues them
   from their troubles.
18 The LORD is there to rescue all
   who are discouraged
   and have given up hope.
19 The LORD's people may suffer a lot,
   but he will always
   bring them safely through.
20 Not one of their bones
   will ever be broken.
21 Wicked people are killed
   by their own evil deeds,
   and if you hate God's people
   you will be punished.
22 The LORD saves the lives
   of his servants.
   Run to him for protection,
   and you won't be punished.

---

*34.10 **Young lions:** In the Psalms wild animals often
stand for God's enemies.

See also: 34.8: 1 Pet 2.3. 34.12-16: 1 Pet 3.10-12.
34.20: John 19.36.

See also: 34 Title: 1 Sam 21.13–15.

Psalm 35

(A psalm by David.)

A prayer for protection from enemies

1 Fight my enemies, LORD!
   Attack my attackers!
2 Shield me and help me.
3 Aim your spear at everyone
   who hunts me down,
   but promise to save me.

4 Let all who want to kill me
   be disappointed and disgraced.
   Chase away and confuse
   all who plan to harm me.
5 Send your angel after them
   and let them be like straw in the wind.
6 Make them run in the dark
   on a slippery road,
   as your angel chases them.
7 I did them no harm,
   but they hid a net to trap me,
   and they dug a deep pit
   to catch and kill me.
8 Surprise them with disaster!
   Trap them in their own nets
   and let them fall and rot
   in the pits they have dug.

9 I will celebrate and be joyful
   because you, LORD, have saved me.
10 Every bone in my body will shout:
   "No one is like the LORD!"
   You protect the helpless
   from those in power;
   you save the poor and needy
   from those who hurt them.

11 Liars accuse me of crimes
   I know nothing about.
12 They repay evil for good,
   and I feel all alone.
13 When they were sick,
   I wore sackcloth*
   and went without food.*
   I truly prayed for them,*
14 as I would for a friend
   or a relative.
   I was in sorrow and mourned,
   as I would for my mother.

15 I have stumbled,
   and worthless liars
   I don't even know
   surround me and sneer.

16 Worthless people make fun*
   and never stop laughing.
17 But all you do is watch!
   When will you do something?
   Save me from the attack
   of those vicious lions.
18 And when your people meet,
   I will praise you
   and thank you, Lord,
   in front of them all.

19 Don't let my brutal enemies
   be glad because of me.
   They hate me for no reason.
   Don't let them wink behind my back.
20 They say hurtful things,
   and they lie to people
   who want to live in peace.
21 They are quick to accuse me.
   They say, "You did it!
   We saw you ourselves."

22 You see everything, LORD!
   Please don't keep silent
   or stay so far away.
23 Fight to defend me, Lord God,
24   and prove that I am right
   by your standards.
   Don't let them laugh at me
25   or say to each other,
   "Now we've got what we want!
   We'll gobble him up!"

26 Disappoint and confuse
   all who are glad to see me in trouble,
   but disgrace and embarrass
   my proud enemies who say to me,
   "You are nothing!"

27 Let all who want me to win
   be happy and joyful.
   From now on let them say,
   "The LORD is wonderful!
   God is glad when all goes well
   for his servant."
28 Then I will shout all day,
   "Praise the LORD God!
   He did what was right."

Psalm 36

*(For the music leader by David,
the LORD's servant.)*

Human sin and God's goodness

1 Sinners don't respect God;
   sin is all they think about.

*35.13 sackcloth: See the note at 30.11.
*35.13 without food: People sometimes went without food (called "fasting") to show sorrow.

See also: 35.19: Psa 69.4; John 15.25. 36.1: Rom 3.18.

529

2 They like themselves too much
   to hate their own sins
   or even to see them.
3 They tell deceitful lies,
   and they don't have the sense
   to live right.
4 Those people stay awake,
   thinking up mischief,
   and they follow the wrong road,
   refusing to turn from sin.

5 Your love is faithful, LORD,
   and even the clouds in the sky
   can depend on you.
6 Your decisions are always fair.
   They are firm like mountains,
   deep like the sea,
   and all people and animals
   are under your care.

7 Your love is a treasure,
   and everyone finds shelter
   in the shadow of your wings.
8 You give your guests a feast
   in your house,
   and you serve a tasty drink
   that flows like a river.
9 The life-giving fountain
   belongs to you,
   and your light gives light
   to each of us.

10 Our LORD, keep showing love
   to everyone who knows you,
and use your power to save
   all whose thoughts please you.
11 Don't let those proud
   and merciless people
   kick me around or chase me away.

12 Look at those wicked people!
   They are knocked down,
   never to get up again.

Psalm 37

(By David.)

Trust the LORD

1 Don't be annoyed by anyone
   who does wrong,
   and don't envy them.
2 They will soon disappear
   like grass without rain.

3 Trust the LORD and live right!
   The land will be yours,
   and you will be safe.

4 Do what the LORD wants,
   and he will give you
   your heart's desire.

5 Let the LORD lead you
   and trust him to help.
6 Then it will be as clear
   as the noonday sun
   that you were right.

7 Be patient and trust the LORD.
   Don't let it bother you
   when all goes well for those
   who do sinful things.
8 Don't be angry or furious.
   Anger can lead to sin.
9 All sinners will disappear,
   but if you trust the LORD,
   the land will be yours.

10 Sinners will soon disappear,
   never to be found,
11 but the poor will take the land
   and enjoy a big harvest.

12 Merciless people make plots
   against good people
   and snarl like animals,
13 but the Lord laughs and knows
   their time is coming soon.
14 The wicked kill with swords
   and shoot arrows
   to murder the poor and the needy
   and all who do right.
15 But they will be killed
   by their own swords,
   and their arrows will be broken.

16 It is better to live right and be poor
   than to be sinful and rich.
17 The wicked will lose
   all of their power,
   but the LORD gives strength
   to everyone who is good.

18 Those who obey the LORD
   are daily in his care,
   and what he has given them
   will be theirs for ever.
19 They won't be in trouble
   when times are bad,
   and they will have plenty
   when food is scarce.

20 Wicked people are enemies
   of the LORD
   and will vanish like smoke
   from a field on fire.

See also: 37.11: Matt 5.5.

21 An evil person borrows
    and never pays back;
    a good person is generous
    and never stops giving.
22 Everyone the LORD blesses
    will receive the land;
    everyone the LORD curses
    will be destroyed.

23 If you do what the LORD wants,
    he will make certain
    each step you take is sure.
24 The LORD will hold your hand,
    and if you stumble,
    you still won't fall.

25 As long as I can remember,
    good people have never
    been left helpless,
    and their children have never
    gone begging for food.
26 They gladly give and lend,
    and their children turn out good.

27 If you stop sinning
    and start doing right,
    you will keep living
    and be secure for ever.
28 The LORD loves justice,
    and he won't ever desert
    his faithful people.
    He always protects them,
    but destroys the children of the wicked.
29 God's people will own the land
    and live here for ever.

30 Words of wisdom come
    when good people speak for justice.
31 They remember God's teachings,
    and they never take a wrong step.
32 The wicked try to trap
    and kill good people,
33 but the LORD is on their side,
    and he will defend them
    when they are on trial.

34 Trust the LORD and follow him.
    He will give you the land,
    and you will see the wicked destroyed.

35 I have seen brutal people abuse others
    and grow strong like trees in rich soil.
36 Suddenly they disappeared!
    I looked, but they were gone
    and no longer there.

37 Think of the bright future waiting
    for all the families of honest
    and innocent and peace-loving people.

38 But not a trace will be left
    of the wicked or their families.

39 The LORD protects his people,
    and they can come to him
    in times of trouble.
40 The LORD helps them
    and saves them from the wicked
    because they run to him.

Psalm 38

(A psalm by David to be used when an offering is made.)

A prayer in times of trouble

1 When you are angry, LORD,
    please don't punish me
    or even correct me.
2 You shot me with your arrows,
    and you struck me with your hand.

3 My body hurts all over
    because of your anger.
    Even my bones are in pain,
    and my sins
4 are so heavy that I am crushed.

5 Because of my foolishness,
    I am covered with sores
    that stink and spread.
6 My body is twisted and bent,
    and I groan all day long.
7 Fever has my back in flames,
    and I hurt all over.
8 I am worn out and weak,
    moaning and in distress.

9 You, Lord, know every one
    of my deepest desires,
    and my noisy groans
    are no secret to you.
10 My heart is beating fast.
    I feel weak all over,
    and my eyes are red.
11 Because of my sickness,
    no friends or neighbours
    will come near me.
12 All who want me dead
    set traps to catch me,
    and those who want
    to harm and destroy me
    plan and plot all day.

13 I am not able to hear or speak a word;
14 I am completely deaf
    and can't make a sound.

15 I trust you, LORD God,
    and you will do something.

16 I said, "Don't let them laugh
    or boast because I slip."

17 I am about to collapse
    from constant pain.
18 I told you my sins,
    and I am sorry for them.
19 Many deadly and powerful
    enemies hate me,
20 and they repay evil for good
    because I try to do right.

21 You are the LORD God!
    Stay nearby and don't desert me.
22 You are the one who saves me.
    Please hurry and help.

Psalm 39

*(A psalm by David for Jeduthun,
the music leader.)*

A prayer for forgiveness

1 I told myself, "I'll be careful
   not to sin by what I say,
   and I'll muzzle my mouth
   when evil people are near."
2 I kept completely silent,
   but it did no good,'
   and I suffered even more.

3 I felt a fire burning inside,
   and the more I thought,
   the more it burnt,
   until at last I said:
4 "Please, LORD, show me my future.
   Will I soon be gone?
5 You made my life short,
   so brief that the time
   means nothing to you.

   "Human life is but a breath,
6 and it disappears like a shadow.
   Our struggles are senseless;
   we store up more and more,
   without ever knowing
   who will get it all.

7 "What am I waiting for?
   I depend on you, Lord!
8 Save me from my sins.
   Don't let fools sneer at me.
9 You treated me like this,
   and I kept silent, not saying a word.

10 "Won't you stop punishing me?
   You have worn me down.
11 You punish us severely
   because of our sins.

Like a moth, you destroy
what we treasure most.
We are as frail as a breath.

12 "Listen, LORD, to my prayer!
   My eyes are flooded with tears,
   as I pray to you.
   I am merely a stranger
   visiting your home
   as my ancestors did.
13 Stop being angry with me
   and let me smile again
   before I am dead and gone."

Psalm 40

(A psalm by David for the music leader.)

A prayer for help

1 I patiently waited, LORD,
   for you to hear my prayer.
   You listened
2 and pulled me from a lonely pit
   full of mud and mire.
   You let me stand on a rock
   with my feet firm,
3 and you gave me a new song,
   a song of praise to you.
   Many will see this,
   and they will honour
   and trust you, the LORD God.

4 You bless all of those
   who trust you, LORD,
   and refuse to worship idols
   or follow false gods.
5 You, LORD God, have done
   many wonderful things,
   and you have planned
   marvellous things for us.
   No one is like you!
   I would never be able to tell
   all you have done.

6 Sacrifices and offerings
   are not what please you;
   gifts and payment for sin
   are not what you demand.
   But you made me willing
   to listen and obey.
7 And so, I said, "I am here
   to do what is written
   about me in the book,
   where it says,
8 'I enjoy pleasing you.
   Your Law is in my heart.' "

See also: **40.6–8:** Heb 10.5–7.

⁹ When your people worshipped,
    you know I told them,
    "Our LORD always helps!"
¹⁰ When all your people met,
    I did not keep silent.
    I said, "Our LORD is kind.
    He is faithful and caring,
    and he saves us."
¹¹ You, LORD, never fail
    to have pity on me;
    your love and faithfulness
    always keep me secure.

¹² I have more troubles
    than I can count.
    My sins are all around me,
    and I can't find my way.
    My sins outnumber
    the hairs on my head,
    and I feel weak.
¹³ Please show that you care
    and come to my rescue.
    Hurry and help me!

¹⁴ Disappoint and confuse
    all who want me dead;
    turn away and disgrace
    all who want to hurt me.
¹⁵ Embarrass and shame
    all those who say,
    "Just look at you now!"

¹⁶ Our LORD, let your worshippers
    rejoice and be glad.
    They love you for saving them,
    so let them always say,
    "The LORD is wonderful!"

¹⁷ I am poor and needy,
    but, LORD God,
    you care about me,
    and you come to my rescue.
    Please hurry and help.

Psalm 41

(A psalm by David for the music leader.)

A prayer in time of sickness

¹ You, LORD God, bless everyone
    who cares for the poor,
    and you rescue those people
    in times of trouble.
² You protect them
    and keep them alive.
    You make them happy
    here in this land,
    and you don't hand them over
    to their enemies.

³ You always heal them
    and restore their strength
    when they are sick.
⁴ I prayed, "Have pity, LORD!
    Heal me,
    though I have sinned
    against you."

⁵ My vicious enemies ask me,
    "When will you die and be forgotten?"
⁶ When visitors come,
    all they ever bring are worthless words,
    and when they leave,
    they spread gossip.

⁷ My enemies whisper about me.
    They think the worst,
⁸   and they say,
    "You have some fatal disease!
    You'll never get well."
⁹ My most trusted friend
    has turned against me,
    though he ate at my table.

¹⁰ Have pity, LORD! Heal me,
    so I can pay them back.
¹¹ Then my enemies won't defeat me,
    and I will know that you really care.
¹² You have helped me
    because I am innocent,
    and you will always be close to my side.

¹³ You, the LORD God of Israel,
    will be praised for ever!
    Amen and amen.

BOOK 2

(Psalms 42–72)

Psalm 42

*(A special psalm for the people of Korah
and for the music leader.)*

Longing for God

¹ As a deer gets thirsty
    for streams of water,
    I truly am thirsty for you, my God.
² In my heart, I am thirsty
    for you, the living God.
    When will I see your face?
³ Day and night my tears
    are my only food,
    as everyone keeps asking,
    "Where is your God?"

See also: 41.9: Matt 26.23; Mark 14.18; Luke 22.21;
John 13.18.   41.13: Psa 106.48.

⁴ Sorrow floods my heart,
    when I remember
    leading the worshippers
    to your house.
I can still hear them shout
    their joyful praises.
⁵ Why am I discouraged?
    Why am I restless?
I trust you!
    And I will praise you again
    because you help me,
⁶   and you are my God.

I am deeply discouraged
    as I think about you
    from where the Jordan begins
    at Mount Hermon
    and from Mount Mizar.*
⁷ Your vicious waves have swept over me
    like an angry ocean
    or a roaring waterfall.

⁸ Every day, you are kind,
    and at night you give me a song
    as my prayer to you,
    the living LORD God.
⁹ You are my mighty rock.*
    Why have you forgotten me?
Why must enemies ill-treat me
    and make me sad?
¹⁰ Even my bones are in pain,
    while all day long
    my enemies sneer and ask,
    "Where is your God?"

¹¹ Why am I discouraged?
    Why am I restless?
I trust you!
    And I will praise you again
    because you help me,
    and you are my God.

Psalm 43

A prayer in times of trouble

¹ Show that I am right, God!
    Defend me against everyone
    who doesn't know you;
    rescue me from each
    of those deceitful liars.
² I run to you for protection.
    Why have you turned me away?
Why must enemies ill-treat me
    and make me sad?

³ Send your light and your truth
    to guide me.
Let them lead me to your house
    on your sacred mountain.
⁴ Then I will worship at your altar
    because you make me joyful.
You are my God,
    and I will praise you.
Yes, I will praise you as I play my harp.

⁵ Why am I discouraged?
    Why am I restless?
I trust you!
    And I will praise you again
    because you help me,
    and you are my God.

Psalm 44

(A special psalm for the people of Korah and for the music leader.)

A prayer for help

¹ Our God, our ancestors told us
    what wonders you worked
    and we listened carefully.
² You chased off the nations
    by causing them trouble
    with your powerful arm.
Then you let our ancestors
    take over their land.
³ Their strength and weapons were not
    what won the land
    and gave them victory!
You loved them and fought
    with your powerful arm
    and your shining glory.

⁴ You are my God and King,
    and you give victory
    to the people of Jacob.
⁵ By your great power,
    we knocked our enemies down
    and trampled on them.
⁶ I don't depend on my arrows
    or my sword to save me.
⁷ But you saved us
    from our hateful enemies,
    and you put them to shame.
⁸ We boast about you, our God,
    and we are always grateful.

⁹ But now you have rejected us;
    you don't lead us into battle,
    and we look foolish.
¹⁰ You made us retreat,
    and our enemies have taken
    everything we own.

---

*42.6 Mount Mizar: The location is not known.
*42.9 mighty rock: See the note at 18.2.
534

11 You let us be slaughtered like sheep,
    and you scattered us
      among the nations.
12 You sold your people
    for little or nothing,
      and you earned no profit.

13 You made us look foolish
    to our neighbours,
      and people who live nearby
      insult us and sneer.
14 Foreigners joke about us
    and shake their heads.
15 I am embarrassed every day,
    and I blush with shame.
16 But others mock and sneer,
    as they watch my enemies
      take revenge on me.

17 All of this has happened to us,
    though we didn't forget you
      or break our agreement.
18 We always kept you in mind
    and followed your teaching.
19 But you crushed us,
    and you covered us
      with deepest darkness
      where wild animals live.

20 We did not forget you
    or lift our hands in prayer
      to foreign gods.
21 You would have known it
    because you discover
      every secret thought.
22 We face death all day for you.
    We are like sheep on their way
      to be slaughtered.

23 Wake up! Do something, Lord!
    Why are you sleeping?
      Don't desert us for ever.
24 Why do you keep looking away?
    Don't forget our sufferings
      and all our troubles.
25 We are flat on the ground,
    holding on to the dust.
26 Do something! Help us!
    Show how kind you are
      and come to our rescue.

Psalm 45

(A special psalm for the people of Korah and for the music leader. To the tune "Lilies". A love song.)

For a royal wedding

1 My thoughts are filled
    with beautiful words
      for the king,
    and I will use my voice
      as a writer would use pen and ink.

2 No one is as handsome as you!
    Your words are always kind.
      That is why God will always bless you.
3 Mighty king, glorious ruler,
    strap on your sword
4   and ride out in splendour!
    Win victories for truth
      and mercy and justice.
    Do fearsome things
      with your powerful arm.
5 Send your sharp arrows
    through enemy hearts
      and make all nations fall at your feet.

6 You are God, and you will rule
    for ever as king.'
      Your royal power brings about justice.
7 You love justice and hate evil.
    And so, your God chose you
      and made you happier
      than any of your friends.
8 The sweet aroma of the spices
    myrrh, aloes, and cassia,
      covers your royal robes.
    You enjoy the music of harps
      in palaces decorated with ivory.
9 Daughters of kings are here,
    and your bride stands at your right side,
      wearing a wedding gown
      trimmed with pure gold.*

10 Bride of the king,
    listen carefully to me.
      Forget your own people
      and your father's family.
11 The king is your husband,
    so do what he desires.
12 All the richest people
    from the city of Tyre
      will try to influence you
13   with precious treasures.

*45.9 trimmed with pure gold: Hebrew has "with gold from Ophir", which may have been in Africa or India. Gold from there was considered the very best.

See also: 44.22: Rom 8.36.

See also: 45.6,7: Heb 1.8,9.

Your bride, my king,
has inward beauty,*
and her wedding gown is woven
with threads of gold.

¹⁴ Wearing the finest garments,
she is brought to you,
followed by her young friends,
the bridesmaids.

¹⁵ Everyone is excited,
as they follow you to the royal palace.

¹⁶ Your sons and your grandsons
will also be kings
as your ancestors were.
You will make them the rulers
everywhere on earth.

¹⁷ I will make your name famous
from now on,
and you will be praised
for ever and ever.

Psalm 46

*(A special song for the people of Korah
and for the music leader.)*

God is our mighty fortress

¹ God is our mighty fortress,
always ready to help
in times of trouble.

² And so, we won't be afraid!
Let the earth tremble
and the mountains tumble
into the deepest sea.

³ Let the ocean roar and foam,
and its raging waves
shake the mountains.

⁴ A river and its streams
bring joy to the city,
which is the sacred home
of God Most High.

⁵ God is in that city,
and it won't be shaken.
He will help it at dawn.

⁶ Nations rage! Kingdoms fall!
But at the voice of God
the earth itself melts.

⁷ The LORD All-Powerful is with us.
The God of Jacob is our fortress.

⁸ Come! See the fearsome things
the LORD has done on earth.

⁹ God brings wars to an end
all over the world.
He breaks the arrows,
shatters the spears,
and burns the shields.*

¹⁰ Our God says, "Calm down,
and learn that I am God!
All nations on earth will honour me."

¹¹ The LORD All-Powerful is with us.
The God of Jacob is our fortress.

Psalm 47

*(A psalm for the people of Korah
and for the music leader.)*

God rules the nations

¹ All you nations, clap your hands
and shout joyful praises to God.

² The LORD Most High is fearsome,
the ruler of all the earth.

³ God has put every nation
under our power,

⁴ and he chose for us the land
that was the pride of Jacob,
his favourite.

⁵ God goes up to his throne,
as people shout and trumpets blast.

⁶ Sing praises to God our King,
⁷   the ruler of all the earth!
Praise God with songs.

⁸ God rules the nations
from his sacred throne.

⁹ Their leaders come together
and are now the people
of Abraham's God.
All rulers on earth
surrender their weapons,
and God is greatly praised!

Psalm 48

(A song and a psalm for the people of Korah.)

The city of God

¹ The LORD God is wonderful!
He deserves all praise
in the city where he lives.
His holy mountain,

²   beautiful and majestic,
brings joy to all on earth.
Mount Zion, truly sacred,
is home for the Great King.

³ God is there to defend it
and has proved to be its protector.

⁴ Kings joined forces to attack the city,
⁵ but when they saw it,
they were terrified and ran away.

See also: 48.2: Matt 5.35.

536

6 They trembled all over
   like women giving birth
7 or like seagoing ships*
   wrecked by eastern winds.
8 We had heard about it,
   and now we have seen it
   in the city of our God,
   the LORD All-Powerful.
   This is the city that God
   will let stand for ever.

9 Our God, here in your temple
   we think about your love.
10 You are famous and praised
    everywhere on earth,
    as you win victories
    with your powerful arm.
11 Mount Zion will celebrate,
    and all Judah will be glad,
    because you bring justice.

12 Let's walk around Zion
    and count its towers.
13 We will see its strong walls
    and visit each fortress.
    Then you can say
    to future generations,
14 "Our God is like this for ever
    and will always* guide us."

Psalm 49

*(A psalm for the people of Korah
and for the music leader.)*

Don't depend on wealth

1 Everyone on this earth,
   now listen to what I say!
2 Listen, no matter who you are,
   rich or poor.
3 I speak words of wisdom,
   and my thoughts make sense.
4 I have in mind a mystery
   that I will explain
   while playing my harp.

5 Why should I be afraid
   in times of trouble,
   when I am surrounded
   by vicious enemies?
6 They trust in their riches
   and boast about all their wealth.
7 You cannot buy back your life
   or pay off God!

8 It costs far too much
   to buy back your life.
   You can never pay God enough
9 to stay alive for ever
   and safe from death.

10 We see that wise people die,
    and so do stupid fools.
    Then their money is left
    for someone else.
11 The grave* will be their home
    for ever and ever,
    although they once had land
    of their own.
12 Our human glory disappears,
    and, like animals, we die.

13 Here is what happens to fools
    and to those who trust
    the words of fools:
14 They are like sheep
    with death as their shepherd,
    leading them to the grave.*
    In the morning God's people
    will walk all over them,
    as their bodies lie rotting
    in their home, the grave.
15 But God will rescue me
    from the power of death.

16 Don't let it bother you
    when others get rich and live in luxury.
17 Soon they will die
    and all their wealth will be left behind.

18 We humans are praised
    when we do well,
    and all of us are glad to be alive.
19 But we will each go down
    to our ancestors,
    never again to see the light of day.
20 Our human glory disappears,
    and, like animals, we die.

Psalm 50

(A psalm by Asaph.)

What pleases God

1 From east to west,
   the powerful LORD God
   has been calling together
   everyone on earth.
2 God shines brightly from Zion,
   the most beautiful city.

3 Our God approaches, but not silently;
   a flaming fire comes first,
   and a storm surrounds him.

---

*48.7 seagoing ships: The Hebrew text has "ships of
Tarshish," which probably means large, seagoing
ships.

⁴ God comes to judge his people.
  He shouts to the heavens
  and to the earth,
⁵ "Call my followers together!
  They offered me a sacrifice,
  and we made an agreement."

⁶ The heavens announce,
  "God is the judge,
  and he is always honest."

⁷ My people, I am God!
  Israel, I am your God.
  Listen to my charges against you.
⁸ Although you offer sacrifices
  and always bring gifts,
⁹ I won't accept your offerings
  of bulls and goats.

¹⁰ Every animal in the forest belongs to me,
  and so do the cattle on a thousand hills.
¹¹ I know all the birds
  in the mountains,
  and every wild creature is in my care.

¹² If I were hungry, I wouldn't tell you,
  because I own the world
  and everything in it.
¹³ I don't eat the meat of bulls
  or drink the blood of goats.
¹⁴ I am God Most High!
  The only sacrifice I want
  is for you to be thankful
  and to keep your word.

¹⁵ Pray to me in time of trouble.
  I will rescue you,
  and you will honour me.

¹⁶ But to the wicked I say:
  "You don't have the right
  to mention my laws
  or claim to keep our agreement!
¹⁷ You refused correction
  and rejected my commands.
¹⁸ You made friends
  with every criminal you met,
  and you liked people who break
  their wedding vows.
¹⁹ You talked only about violence
  and told nothing but lies;
²⁰ you sat around gossiping,
  ruining the reputation
  of your own relatives."

²¹ When you did all this,
  I didn't say a word,
  and you thought, "God is just like us!"
  But now I will accuse you.
²² You have ignored me!
  So pay close attention

or I will tear you apart,
  and no one can help you.

²³ The sacrifice that honours me
  is a thankful heart.
  Obey me,* and I, your God,
  will show my power to save.

Psalm 51

*(For the music leader. A psalm by David when
the prophet Nathan came to him after David
had been with Bathsheba.)*

A prayer for forgiveness

¹ You are kind, God!
  Please have pity on me.
  You are always merciful!
  Please wipe away my sins.
² Wash me clean from all
  of my sin and guilt.
³ I know about my sins,
  and I cannot forget my terrible guilt.
⁴ You are really the one
  I have sinned against;
  I have disobeyed you
  and have done wrong.
  So it is right and fair for you
  to correct and punish me.

⁵ I have sinned and done wrong
  since the day I was born.
⁶ But you want complete honesty,
  so teach me true wisdom.
⁷ Wash me with hyssop*
  until I am clean and whiter than snow.
⁸ Let me be happy and joyful!
  You crushed my bones,
  now let them celebrate.
⁹ Turn your eyes from my sin
  and cover my guilt.
¹⁰ Create pure thoughts in me
  and make me faithful again.
¹¹ Don't chase me away from you
  or take your Holy Spirit away from me.

¹² Make me as happy as you did
  when you saved me;
  make me want to obey!
¹³ I will teach sinners your Law,
  and they will return to you.
¹⁴ Keep me from any deadly sin.
  Only you can save me!

---

*51.7 hyssop: A small bush with bunches of small,
white flowers. It was sometimes used as a symbol for
making a person clean from sin.
See also: 51 Title: 2 Sam 12.1–15. 51.4: Rom 3.4.

Then I will shout and sing
about your power to save.

15 Help me to speak,
and I will praise you, Lord.
16 Offerings and sacrifices
are not what you want.
17 The way to please you
is to feel sorrow deep in our hearts.
This is the kind of sacrifice
you won't refuse.

18 Please be willing, Lord,
to help the city of Zion
and to rebuild its walls.
19 Then you will be pleased
with the proper sacrifices,
and we will offer bulls
on your altar once again.

Psalm 52

(A special psalm by David for the music leader. He wrote this when Doeg from Edom went to Saul and said, "David has gone to Ahimelech's house.")

God is in control

1 You people may be strong
and boast about your sins,
but God can be trusted day after day.
2 You plan brutal crimes,
and your lying words cut
like a sharp razor.
3 You would rather do evil than good,
and tell lies than speak the truth.
4 You love to say cruel things,
and your words are a trap.

5 God will destroy you for ever!
He will grab you and drag you
from your homes.
You will be uprooted
and left to die.
6 When good people see
this fearsome sight,
they will laugh and say,
7 "Just look at them now!
Instead of trusting God,
they trusted their wealth
and their cruelty."

8 But I am like an olive tree
growing in God's house,
and I can count on his love
for ever and ever.

9 I will always thank God
for what he has done;
I will praise his good name
when his people meet.

Psalm 53

(A special psalm by David for the music leader. To the tune "Mahalath".)

No one can ignore God

1 Only a fool would say,
"There is no God!"
People like that are worthless!
They are heartless and cruel
and never do right.

2 From heaven God looks down to see
if anyone is wise enough
to search for him.
3 But all of them are crooked and corrupt.
Not one of them does right.

4 Won't you lawbreakers learn?
You refuse to pray,
and you gobble up the people of God.
5 But you will be more terrified
than ever before.
God will scatter the bones
of his enemies,
and you will be ashamed
when God rejects you.

6 I long for someone from Zion
to come and save Israel!
Our God, when you bless
your people again,
Jacob's family will be glad,
and Israel will celebrate.

Psalm 54

(For the music leader. Use with stringed instruments. A special psalm that David wrote when the people of Ziph went to Saul and said, "David is hiding here with us.")

Trusting God in times of trouble

1 Save me, God, by your power
and prove that I am right.
2 Listen to my prayer
and hear what I say.
3 Cruel strangers have attacked
and want me dead.
Not one of them cares about you.

See also: 52 Title: 1 Sam 22.9,10.

See also: 53.1–3: Rom 3.10–12.   54 Title: 1 Sam 23.19; 26.1.

⁴ You will help me, Lord God,
and keep me from falling;
⁵ you will punish my enemies
for their evil deeds.
Be my faithful friend and destroy them.

⁶ I will bring a gift
and offer a sacrifice to you, LORD.
I will praise your name
because you are good.
⁷ You have rescued me
from all my troubles,
and my own eyes have seen
my enemies fall.

Psalm 55

*(A special psalm by David for the music
leader. Use with stringed instruments.)*

Betrayed by a friend

¹ Listen, God, to my prayer!
Don't reject my request.
² Please listen and help me.
My thoughts are troubled,
and I keep groaning
³ because my loud enemies
shout and attack.
They treat me terribly
and hold angry grudges.
⁴ My heart is racing fast,
and I am afraid of dying.
⁵ I am trembling with fear,
completely terrified.

⁶ I wish I had wings like a dove,
so I could fly far away
and be at peace.
⁷ I would go and live
in some distant desert.
⁸ I would quickly find shelter
from howling winds
and raging storms.

⁹ Confuse my enemies, Lord!
Upset their plans.
Cruelty and violence
are all I see in the city,
¹⁰ and they are like guards
on patrol day and night.
The city is full of trouble, evil,
¹¹ and corruption.
Troublemakers and liars
freely roam the streets.

¹² My enemies are not the ones
who sneer and make fun.
I could put up with that
or even hide from them.

¹³ But it was my closest friend,
the one I trusted most.
¹⁴ We enjoyed being together,
and we went with others
to your house, our God.

¹⁵ All who hate me are controlled
by the power of evil.
Sentence them to death
and send them down alive
to the world of the dead.
¹⁶ I ask for your help, LORD God,
and you will keep me safe.
¹⁷ Morning, noon, and night
you hear my concerns
and my complaints.
¹⁸ I am attacked from all sides,
but you will rescue me
unharmed by the battle.
¹⁹ You have always ruled,
and you will hear me.
You will defeat my enemies
because they won't turn
and worship you.

²⁰ My friend turned against me
and broke his promise.
²¹ His words were smoother than butter,
and softer than olive oil.
But hatred filled his heart,
and he was ready to attack
with a sword.

²² Our LORD, we belong to you.
We tell you what worries us,
and you won't let us fall.
²³ But what about those people
who are cruel and brutal?
You will throw them down
into the deepest pit
long before their time.
I trust you, LORD!

Psalm 56

*(For the music leader. To the tune "A Silent Dove
in the Distance".* A special psalm by David
when the Philistines captured him in Gath.)*

A prayer of trust in God

¹ Have pity, God Most High!
My enemies chase me all day.
² Many of them are pursuing
and attacking me,
³ but even when I am afraid,
I keep on trusting you.

See also: **56** Title: 1 Sam 21.13–15.

⁴ I praise your promises!
I trust you and am not afraid.
No one can harm me.

⁵ Enemies spend the whole day
finding fault with me;
all they think about
is how to do me harm.

⁶ They attack from ambush,
watching my every step
and hoping to kill me.

⁷ They won't get away'
with these crimes, God,
because when you get angry,
you destroy people.

⁸ You have kept record
of my days of wandering.
You have stored my tears in your bottle
and counted each of them.

⁹ When I pray, LORD God,
my enemies will retreat,
because I know for certain
that you are with me.

¹⁰ I praise your promises!
¹¹ I trust you and am not afraid.
No one can harm me.

¹² I will keep my promises
to you, my God,
and bring you gifts.

¹³ You protected me from death
and kept me from stumbling,
so that I would please you
and follow the light that leads to life.

⁴ I live among lions,
who gobble up people!
They have spears and arrows
instead of teeth,
and they have sharp swords
instead of tongues.

⁵ May you, my God, be honoured
above the heavens;
may your glory be seen
everywhere on earth.

⁶ Enemies set traps for my feet
and struck me down.
They dug a pit in my path,
but fell in it themselves.

⁷ I am faithful to you,
and you can trust me.
I will sing and play music
for you, my God.

⁸ I feel wide awake!
I will wake up my harp
and wake up the sun.

⁹ I will praise you, Lord,
for everyone to hear,
and I will sing hymns to you
in every nation.

¹⁰ Your love reaches higher
than the heavens;
your loyalty extends
beyond the clouds.

¹¹ May you, my God, be honoured
above the heavens;
may your glory be seen
everywhere on earth.

Psalm 57

*(For the music leader. To the tune "Don't
Destroy".' A special psalm by David when he
was in the cave while running from Saul.)*

Praise and trust in times of trouble

¹ God Most High, have pity on me!
Have mercy.
I run to you for safety.
In the shadow of your wings,
I seek protection till danger dies down.

² I pray to you, my protector.
³ You will send help from heaven
and save me,
but you will bring trouble
on my attackers.
You are faithful,
and you can be trusted.

Psalm 58

*(A special psalm by David for the music leader.
To the tune "Don't Destroy".')*

A prayer when all goes wrong

¹ Do you mighty people' talk
only to oppose justice?'
Don't you ever judge fairly?

² You are always planning evil,
and you are brutal.

³ You have done wrong and lied
from the day you were born.

⁴ Your words spread poison
like the bite of a cobra

⁵ that refuses to listen
to the snake charmer.

⁶ My enemies are fierce
as lions, LORD God!
Shatter their teeth.
Snatch out their fangs.

See also: **57 Title:** 1 Sam 22.1; 24.3.

7 Make them disappear like leaking water,
   and make their arrows miss.
8 Let them dry up like snails
   or be like a child that dies
   before seeing the sun.
9 Wipe them out quicker
   than a pot can be heated
   by setting thorns on fire.*
10 Good people will be glad
   when they see the wicked
   getting what they deserve,
   and they will wash their feet
   in their enemies' blood.
11 Everyone will say, "It's true!
   Good people are rewarded.
   God does rule the earth with justice."

Psalm 59

(For the music leader. To the tune "Don't Destroy". A special psalm by David when Saul had David's house watched so that he could kill him.)*

A prayer for protection

1 Save me, God! Protect me
   from enemy attacks!
2 Keep me safe from brutal people
   who want to kill me.

3 Merciless enemies, LORD,
   are hiding and plotting,
   hoping to kill me.
   I have not hurt them in any way at all.
4 But they are ready to attack.
   Do something! Help me!
   Look at what's happening.
5 LORD God All-Powerful,
   you are the God of Israel.
   Punish the other nations
   and don't pity those terrible
   and rebellious people.

6 My enemies return at evening,
   growling like dogs roaming the city.
7 They curse and their words
   cut like swords,
   as they say to themselves,
   "No one can hear us!"

8 You, LORD, laugh at them
   and sneer at the nations.
9 You are my mighty fortress,
   and I depend on you.
10 You love me and will let me
   see my enemies defeated.

11 Don't kill them,
   or everyone may forget!
   Just use your mighty power
   to make them tremble and fall.

You are a shield for your people.
12 My enemies are liars!
   So let them be trapped
   by their boastful lies.
13 Get angry and destroy them.
   Leave them in ruin.
   Then all the nations will know
   that you rule in Israel.

14 Those liars return at evening,
   growling like dogs roaming the city.
15 They search for scraps of food,
   and they snarl until they are full.

16 But I will sing about
   your strength, my God,
   and I will celebrate
   because of your love.
   You are my fortress,
   my place of protection
   in times of trouble.
17 I will sing your praises!
   You are my mighty fortress,
   and you love me.

Psalm 60

(For the music leader. To the tune "Lily of the Promise". A special psalm by David for teaching. He wrote it during his wars with the Arameans of northern Syria, when Joab came back and killed twelve thousand Edomites* in Salt Valley.)*

You can depend on God

1 You, God, are angry with us!
   We are rejected and crushed.
   Make us strong again!
2 You made the earth shake
   and split wide open;
   now heal its wounds
   and stop its trembling.
3 You brought hard times
   on your people,
   and you gave us wine
   that made us stagger.

4 You gave a signal to those
   who worship you,

---

*Psalm 60 wars . . . Syria: See 2 Samuel 8.3–8;
10.16–18; 1 Chronicles 18.3–11; 19.6–19.
*Psalm 60 killed . . . Edomites: See 2 Samuel 8.13;
1 Chronicles 18.12.

See also: 60 Title: 2 Sam 8.13; 1 Chron 18.12.

See also: 59 Title: 1 Sam 19.11.

so they could escape
from enemy arrows.'

5 Answer our prayers!
Use your powerful arm
and give us victory.
Then the people you love will be safe.

6 Our God, you solemnly promised,
"I would gladly divide up
the city of Shechem
and give away Succoth Valley
piece by piece.
7 The lands of Gilead
and Manasseh are mine.
Ephraim is my war helmet,
and Judah is the symbol
of my royal power.
8 Moab is merely my washbasin.
Edom belongs to me,
and I shout in triumph
over the Philistines."

9 Our God, who will bring me
to the fortress,
or lead me to Edom?
10 Have you rejected us
and deserted our armies?
11 Help us defeat our enemies!
No one else can rescue us.
12 You will give us victory
and crush our enemies.

Psalm 61

(A psalm by David for the music leader.
Use with stringed instruments.)

Under the protection of God

1 Please listen, God,
and answer my prayer!
2 I feel hopeless,
and I cry out to you
from a faraway land.

Lead me to the mighty rock*
high above me.
3 You are a strong tower,
where I am safe
from my enemies.

4 Let me live with you for ever
and find protection
under your wings, my God.
5 You heard my promises,
and you have blessed me,
just as you bless everyone
who worships you.

6 Let the king have a long and healthy life.
7 May he always rule
with you, God, at his side;
may your love and loyalty
watch over him.

8 I will sing your praises for ever
and will always keep my promises.

Psalm 62

(A psalm by David for Jeduthun, the music leader.)

God is powerful and kind

1 Only God can save me,
and I calmly wait for* him.
2 God alone is the mighty rock*
that keeps me safe
and the fortress where I am secure.

3 I feel like a shaky fence or a sagging wall.
How long will all of you
attack and assault me?
4 You want to bring me down
from my place of honour.
You love to tell lies,
and when your words are kind,
hatred hides in your heart.

5 Only God gives inward peace,
and I depend on him.
6 God alone is the mighty rock
that keeps me safe,
and he is the fortress where I feel secure.
7 God saves me and honours me.
He is that mighty rock
where I find safety.
8 Trust God, my friends,
and always tell him
each one of your concerns.
God is our place of safety.

9 We humans are only a breath;
none of us are truly great.
All of us together weigh less
than a puff of air.
10 Don't trust in violence
or depend on dishonesty
or rely on great wealth.

11 I heard God say two things:
"I am powerful,
12   and I am very kind."
The Lord rewards each of us
according to what we do.

---

*61.2 mighty rock: See the note at 18.2.

*62.2 mighty rock: See the note at 18.2.

See also: 62.12: Job 34.11; Jer 17.10; Matt 16.27; Rom 2.6;
Rev 2.23.

Psalm 63

(A psalm by David when he was in the desert of Judah.)

God's love means more than life

1 You are my God. I worship you.
  In my heart, I long for you,
    as I would long for a stream
    in a scorching desert.

2 I have seen your power
    and your glory
    in the place of worship.

3 Your love means more than life to me,
    and I praise you.

4 As long as I live,
    I will pray to you.

5 I will sing joyful praises
    and be filled with excitement
    like a guest at a banquet.

6 I think about you before I go to sleep,
    and my thoughts turn to you
    during the night.

7 You have helped me,
    and I sing happy songs
    in the shadow of your wings.

8 I stay close to you,
    and your powerful arm supports me.

9 All who want to kill me
    will end up in the ground.

10 Swords will run them through,
    and wild dogs will eat them.

11 Because of you, our God,
    the king will celebrate
    with your faithful followers,
    but liars will be silent.

Psalm 64

(A psalm by David for the music leader.)

Celebrate because of the LORD

1 Listen to my concerns, God,
    and protect me
    from my terrible enemies.

2 Keep me safe from secret plots
    of corrupt and evil gangs.

3 Their words cut like swords,
    and their cruel remarks
    sting like sharp arrows.

4 They fearlessly ambush
    and shoot innocent people.

5 They are determined to do evil,
    and they tell themselves,
    "Let's set traps! No one can see us."*

6 They make evil plans and say,
    "We'll commit a perfect crime.
    No one knows our thoughts."*

7 But God will shoot his arrows
    and quickly wound them.

8 They will be destroyed
    by their own words,
    and everyone who sees them
    will tremble with fear.*

9 They will be afraid and say,
    "Look at what God has done
    and keep it all in mind."

10 May the LORD bless his people
    with peace and happiness
    and let them celebrate.

Psalm 65

(A psalm by David and a song for the music leader.)

God answers prayer

1 Our God, you deserve* praise in Zion,
    where we keep our promises to you.

2 Everyone will come to you
    because you answer prayer.

3 Our terrible sins get us down,
    but you forgive us.

4 You bless your chosen ones,
    and you invite them
    to live near you in your temple.
  We will enjoy your house,
    the sacred temple.

5 Our God, you save us,
    and your fearsome deeds
    answer our prayers for justice!
  You give hope to people
    everywhere on earth,
    even those across the sea.

6 You are strong,
    and your mighty power
    put the mountains in place.

7 You silence the roaring waves
    and the noisy shouts of the nations.

8 People far away marvel
    at your fearsome deeds,
  and all who live under the sun
    celebrate and sing because of you.

9 You take care of the earth
    and send rain
    to help the soil
    grow all kinds of crops.

Your rivers never run dry,
   and you prepare the earth
   to produce much grain.
10 You water all its fields
   and level the lumpy ground.
   You send showers of rain
   to soften the soil
   and help the plants sprout.
11 Wherever your footsteps
   touch the earth,
   a rich harvest is gathered.
12 Desert pastures blossom,
   and mountains celebrate.
13 Meadows are filled
   with sheep and goats;
   valleys overflow with grain
   and echo with joyful songs.

Psalm 66

(A song and a psalm for the music leader.)

Shout praises to God

1 Tell everyone on this earth
   to shout praises to God!
2 Sing about his glorious name.
   Honour him with praises.
3 Say to God, "Everything you do
   is fearsome,
   and your mighty power makes
   your enemies come crawling.
4 You are worshipped by everyone!
   We all sing praises to you."

5 Come and see the fearsome things
   our God has done!
6 When God made the sea dry up,
   our people walked across,
   and because of him,
   we celebrated there.
7 His mighty power rules for ever,
   and nothing the nations do
   can be hidden from him.
   So don't turn against God.

8 All you people, come, praise our God!
   Let his praises be heard.
9 God protects us from death
   and keeps us steady.
10 Our God, you tested us,
   just as silver is tested.
11 You trapped us in a net
   and gave us heavy burdens.
12 You sent war chariots
   to crush our skulls.

We travelled through fire
   and through floods,
   but you brought us
   to a land of plenty.

13 I will bring sacrifices
   into your house, my God,
   and I will do what I promised
14   when I was in trouble.
15 I will sacrifice my best sheep
   and offer bulls and goats on your altar.

16 All who worship God,
   come here and listen;
   I will tell you everything
   God has done for me.
17 I prayed to the Lord,
   and I praised him.
18 If my thoughts had been sinful,
   he would have refused to hear me.
19 But God did listen
   and answered my prayer.
20 Let's praise God!
   He listened when I prayed,
   and he is always kind.

Psalm 67

*(A psalm and a song for the music leader.
Use with stringed instruments.)*

Tell the nations to praise God

1 Our God, be kind and bless us!
   Be pleased and smile.
2 Then everyone on earth
   will learn to follow you,
   and all nations will see
   your power to save us.

3 Make everyone praise you
   and shout your praises.
4 Let the nations celebrate
   with joyful songs,
   because you judge fairly
   and guide all nations.
5 Make everyone praise you
   and shout your praises.

6 Our God has blessed the earth
   with a wonderful harvest!
7 Pray for his blessings to continue
   and for everyone on earth
   to worship our God.

See also: 66.6: a Exod 14.21; b Josh 3.14–17.

Psalm 68

*(A psalm and a song by David
for the music leader.)*

God will win the battle

¹ Do something, God!
  Scatter your hateful enemies.
  Make them turn and run.
² Scatter them like smoke!
  When you come near,
  make them melt like wax in a fire.
³ But let your people be happy
  and celebrate because of you.

⁴ Our God, you are the one
  who rides on the clouds,
  and we praise you.
  Your name is the LORD,
  and we celebrate as we worship you.

⁵ Our God, from your sacred home
  you take care of orphans
  and protect widows.
⁶ You find families
  for those who are lonely.
  You set prisoners free
  and let them prosper,•
  but all who rebel will live
  in a scorching desert.

⁷ You set your people free,
  and you led them
  through the desert.
⁸ God of Israel,
  the earth trembled,
  and rain poured down.
  You alone are the God
  who rules from Mount Sinai.
⁹ When your land was thirsty,
  you sent showers to refresh it.
¹⁰ Your people settled there,
  and you were generous
  to everyone in need.

¹¹ You gave the command,
  and a chorus of women told
  what had happened:
¹² "Kings and their armies
  retreated and ran,
  and everything they left
  is now being divided.
¹³ And for those who stayed back
  to guard the sheep,
  there are metal doves
  with silver-coated wings
  and shiny gold feathers."

¹⁴ God All-Powerful, you scattered the kings
  like snow falling
  on Mount Zalmon.*

¹⁵ Our LORD and our God,
  Bashan is a mighty mountain
  covered with peaks.
¹⁶ Why is it jealous of Zion,
  the mountain you chose
  as your home for ever?

¹⁷ When you, LORD God, appeared
  to your people• at Sinai,
  you came with thousands
  of mighty chariots.
¹⁸ When you climbed
  the high mountain,
  you took prisoners with you
  and were given gifts.
  Your enemies didn't want you
  to live there,
  but they gave you gifts.

¹⁹ We praise you, Lord God!
  You treat us with kindness
  day after day,
  and you rescue us.
²⁰ You always protect us
  and save us from death.

²¹ Our Lord and our God,
  your terrible enemies
  are ready for war,•
  but you will crush their skulls.
²² You promised to bring them
  from Bashan
  and from the deepest sea.
²³ Then we could stamp
  on their blood,
  and our dogs could chew
  on their bones.

²⁴ We have seen crowds marching
  to your place of worship,
  our God and King.
²⁵ The singers come first,
  and then the musicians,
  surrounded by young women
  playing tambourines.
²⁶ They come shouting,
  "People of Israel,
  praise the LORD God!"
²⁷ The small tribe of Benjamin
  leads the way,
  followed by the leaders from Judah.

*68.14 Mount Zalmon: The location of this mountain
is not known.

See also: 68.18: Eph 4.8.

Then come the leaders
  from Zebulun and Naphtali.
28 Our God, show your strength!
  Show us once again.
29 Then kings will bring gifts
  to your temple in Jerusalem.'

30 Punish that animal
  that lives in the swamp!*
  Punish that nation
  whose leaders and people
  are like wild bulls.
  Make them come crawling
  with gifts of silver.
  Scatter those nations
  that enjoy making war.'
31 Force the Egyptians to bring
  gifts of bronze;
  make the Ethiopians* hurry
  to offer presents.'

32 Now sing praises to God!
  Every kingdom on earth,
  sing to the Lord!
33 Praise the one who rides
  across the ancient skies;
  listen as he speaks
  with a mighty voice.

34 Tell about God's power!
  He is honoured in Israel,
  and he rules the skies.
35 The God of Israel is fearsome
  in his temple,
  and he makes us strong.
  Let's praise our God!

Psalm 69

*(By David for the music leader.
To the tune "Lilies".)*

God can be trusted

1 Save me, God!
  I am about to drown.
2 I am sinking deep in the mud,
  and my feet are slipping.
  I am about to be swept under
  by a mighty flood.
3 I am worn out from crying,
  and my throat is dry.

I have waited for you
  till my eyes are blurred.
4 There are more people
  who hate me for no reason
  than there are hairs on my head.
  Many terrible enemies
  want to destroy me, God.
  Am I supposed to give back
  something I didn't steal?
5 You know my foolish sins.
  Not one is hidden from you.

6 Lord God All-Powerful, ruler of Israel,
  don't let me embarrass anyone
  who trusts and worships you.
7 It is for your sake alone
  that I am insulted
  and blush with shame.
8 I am like a stranger to my relatives
  and like a foreigner to my own family.

9 My love for your house
  burns in me like a fire,
  and when others insulted you,
  they insulted me as well.
10 I cried and went without food,*
  but they still insulted me.
11 They sneered at me
  for wearing sackcloth*
  to show my sorrow.
12 Rulers and judges gossip about me,
  and drunkards make up songs
  to mock me.

13 But I pray to you, LORD.
  So when the time is right, answer me
  and help me
  with your wonderful love.
14 Don't let me sink in the mud,
  but save me from my enemies
  and from the deep water.
15 Don't let me be swept away by a flood
  or drowned in the ocean
  or swallowed by death.

16 Answer me, LORD!
  You are kind and good.
  Pay attention to me!
  You are truly merciful.
17 Don't turn away from me.
  I am your servant,
  and I am in trouble.
  Please hurry and help!
18 Come and save me from my enemies.

---

*68.30 animal . . . swamp: Probably Egypt.
*68.31 the Ethiopians: The Hebrew text has "the people of Cush", which was a region south of Egypt that included parts of the present countries of Ethiopia and Sudan.

*69.10 went without food: See the note at 35.13.
*69.11 sackcloth: See the note at 30.11.
See also: 69.4: Psa 35.19; John 15.25. 69.9: John 2.17; Rom 15.3.

19 You know how I am insulted,
    mocked, and disgraced;
    you know every one of my enemies.
20 I am crushed by insults, and I feel sick.
    I had hoped for mercy and pity,
    but there was none.
21 Enemies poisoned my food,
    and when I was thirsty,
    they gave me vinegar.

22 Make their table a trap
    for them and their friends.
23 Blind them with darkness
    and make them tremble.
24 Show them how angry you are!
    Be furious and catch them.
25 Destroy their camp
    and don't let anyone live in their tents.

26 They cause trouble for people
    you have already punished;
    their gossip hurts those
    you have wounded.
27 Make them guiltier than ever
    and don't forgive them.
28 Wipe their names from the book
    of the living;
    remove them from the list
    of the innocent.
29 I am ill-treated and in pain.
    Protect me, God,
    and keep me safe!

30 I will praise the LORD God
    with a song and a thankful heart.
31 This will please the LORD
    better than offering an ox
    or a full-grown bull.
32 When those in need see this,
    they will be happy,
    and the LORD's worshippers
    will be encouraged.
33 The LORD will listen
    when the homeless cry out,
    and he will never forget
    his people in prison.

34 Heaven and earth will praise our God,
    and so will the oceans
    and everything in them.
35 God will rescue Jerusalem,
    and he will rebuild the towns of Judah.
    His people will live there
    on their own land,
36 and when the time comes,
    their children will inherit the land.

Then everyone who loves God
    will also settle there.

Psalm 70

(By David for the music leader.
To be used when an offering is made.)

God is wonderful

1 Save me, LORD God!
    Hurry and help.
2 Disappoint and confuse
    all who want to kill me.
Turn away and disgrace
    all who want to hurt me.
3 Embarrass and shame those
    who say, "We told you so!"

4 Let your worshippers celebrate
    and be glad because of you.
They love your saving power,
    so let them always say,
    "God is wonderful!"
5 I am poor and needy,
    but you, the LORD God,
    care about me.
You are the one who saves me.
    Please hurry and help!

Psalm 71

A prayer for God's protection

1 I run to you, LORD, for protection.
    Don't disappoint me.
2 You do what is right,
    so come to my rescue.
    Listen to my prayer and keep me safe.
3 Be my mighty rock,*
    the place where I can always run
    for protection.
Save me by your command!
    You are my mighty rock and my fortress.

4 Come and save me, LORD God,
    from vicious and cruel
    and brutal enemies!
5 I depend on you,
    and I have trusted you
    since I was young.
6 I have relied on you
    from the day I was born.
You brought me safely through birth,
    and I always praise you.

7 Many people think of me
    as something evil.

See also: 69.21: Matt 27.48; Mark 15.36; Luke 23.26;
John 19.28,29.   **69.22,23:** Rom 11.9,10.   **69.25:** Acts 1.20.
69.28: Exod 32.32; Rev 3.5; 13.8; 17.8.

*71.3 mighty rock: See the note at 18.2.

¹⁵ With your own arm you rescued
your people,
the descendants of Jacob and Joseph.

¹⁶ The ocean looked at you, God,
and it trembled deep down with fear.

¹⁷ Water flowed from the clouds.
Thunder was heard above
as your arrows of lightning flashed about.

¹⁸ Your thunder roared like chariot wheels.
The world was made bright by lightning,
and all the earth trembled.

¹⁹ You walked through the water
of the mighty sea,
but your footprints were never seen.

²⁰ You guided your people
like a flock of sheep,
and you chose Moses and Aaron
to be their leaders.

Psalm 78

(A special psalm by Asaph.)

What God has done for his people

¹ My friends, I beg you
to listen as I teach.

² I will give instruction
and explain the mystery
of what happened long ago.

³ These are things we learnt
from our ancestors,

⁴ and we will tell them
to the next generation.
We won't keep secret the glorious deeds
and the mighty miracles of the LORD.

⁵ God gave his Law
to Jacob's descendants,
the people of Israel.
And he told our ancestors
to teach their children,

⁶ so that each new generation
would know his Law
and tell it to the next.

⁷ Then they would trust God
and obey his teachings,
without forgetting anything
God had done.

⁸ They would be different
from their ancestors,
who were stubborn, rebellious,
and unfaithful to God.

⁹ The warriors from Ephraim
were armed with arrows,

but they ran away when the battle began.

¹⁰ They broke their agreement with God,
and they turned their backs
on his teaching.

¹¹ They forgot all he had done,
even the mighty miracles

¹² he did for their ancestors
near Zoan* in Egypt.

¹³ God made a path in the sea
and piled up the water
as he led them across.

¹⁴ He guided them during the day
with a cloud,
and each night he led them
with a flaming fire.

¹⁵ God made water flow from rocks
he split open in the desert,
and his people drank freely,
as though from a lake.

¹⁶ He made streams gush out
like rivers from rocks.

¹⁷ But in the desert,
the people of God Most High
kept sinning and rebelling.

¹⁸ They stubbornly tested God
and demanded from him
what they wanted to eat.

¹⁹ They challenged God by saying,
"Can God provide food
out here in the desert?

²⁰ It's true God struck the rock
and water gushed out like a river,
but can he give his people
bread and meat?"

²¹ When the LORD heard this,
he was angry and furious
with Jacob's descendants,
the people of Israel.

²² They had refused to trust him,
and they had doubted his saving power.

²³ But God gave a command to the clouds,
and he opened the doors in the skies.

²⁴ From heaven he sent grain
that they called manna.*

---

*78.12 Zoan: A city in the eastern part of the Nile
Delta.
*78.24 manna: When the people of Israel were
wandering through the desert, the Lord gave them a
special kind of food to eat. It tasted like a wafer and
was called "manna", which in Hebrew means, "What
is this?"

See also: 78.12: Exod 7.8—12.32. 78.13: Exod 14.21,22.
78.14: Exod 13.21,22. 78.15,16: Exod 17.1–7;
Num 20.2–13. 78.18-31: Exod 16.2–15;
Num 11.4–23,31–35. 78.24: John 6.31.

See also: 78.2: Matt 13.35.

²⁵ He gave them more than enough,
  and each one of them ate
    this special food.

²⁶ God's mighty power
  brought a strong wind
    from the south-east,
²⁷ and it brought birds
  that covered the ground,
    like sand on the beach.
²⁸ Then God made the birds fall
  in the camp of his people
    near their tents.

²⁹ God gave his people all they wanted,
  and each of them ate
    until they were full.
³⁰ But before they had swallowed the last bite,
³¹ God became angry and killed the strongest
  and best from the families of Israel.

³² But the rest kept on sinning
  and would not trust God's miracles.
³³ So he cut their lives short
  and made them terrified.
³⁴ After he killed some of them,
  the others turned to him
    with all their hearts.
³⁵ They remembered God Most High,
  the mighty rock* that kept them safe.
³⁶ But they tried to flatter God,
  and they told him lies;
³⁷   they were unfaithful
  and broke their promises.

³⁸ Yet God was kind.
  He kept forgiving their sins
    and didn't destroy them.
  He often became angry,
    but never lost his temper.
³⁹ God remembered that they
  were made of flesh
    and were like a wind that blows once
      and then dies down.

⁴⁰ While they were in the desert,
  they often rebelled and made God sad.
⁴¹ They kept testing him
  and caused terrible pain
    for the Holy One of Israel.
⁴² They forgot about his power
  and how he had rescued them
    from their enemies.

⁴³ God showed them all kinds
  of wonderful miracles
    near Zoan* in Egypt.

⁴⁴ He turned the rivers
  of Egypt into blood,
    and no one could drink
      from the streams.
⁴⁵ He sent swarms of flies
  to pester the Egyptians,
    and he sent frogs
      to cause them trouble.

⁴⁶ God let worms and grasshoppers
  eat their crops.
⁴⁷ He destroyed their grapevines
  and their fig trees
    with hail and floods.ᵇ
⁴⁸ Then he killed their cattle with hail
  and their other animals
    with lightning.

⁴⁹ God was so angry and furious
  that he went into a rage
    and caused them great trouble
      by sending swarms
        of destroying angels.
⁵⁰ God gave in to his anger
  and slaughtered them
    in a terrible way.
⁵¹ He killed the firstborn son
  of each Egyptian family.

⁵² Then God led his people out of Egypt
  and guided them in the desert
    like a flock of sheep.
⁵³ He led them safely along,
  and they were not afraid,
    but their enemies drowned in the sea.

⁵⁴ God brought his people
  to the sacred mountain
    that he had taken by his own power.
⁵⁵ He made nations run
  from the tribes of Israel,
    and he let the tribes
      take over their land.

⁵⁶ But the people tested God Most High,
  and they refused to obey his laws.
⁵⁷ They were as unfaithful
  as their ancestors,
    and they were as crooked
      as a twisted arrow.
⁵⁸ God demanded all their love,
  but they made him angry
    by worshipping idols.

---

*78.35 mighty rock: See the note at 18.2.
*78.43 Zoan: See the note at 78.12.

See also: 78.37: Acts 8.21.

See also: 78.44: Exod 7.17-21. 78.45: a Exod 8.20-24;
b Exod 8.1-6. 78.46: Exod 10.12-15.
78.47,48: Exod 9.22-25. 78.51: Exod 12.29.
78.52: Exod 13.17-22. 78.53: Exod 14.26-28.
78.54: Exod 15.17; Josh 3.14-17. 78.55: Josh 11.16-23.
78.56: Judg 2.11-15.

59 So God became furious
   and completely rejected
   the people of Israel.
60 Then he deserted his home at Shiloh,
   where he lived here on earth.
61 He let enemies capture
   the sacred chest*
   and let them dishonour him.

62 God took out his anger
   on his chosen ones
   and let them be killed by enemy swords.
63 Fire destroyed the young men,
   and the young women were left
   with no one to marry.
64 Priests died violent deaths,
   but their widows
   were not allowed to mourn.

65 Finally the Lord woke up,
   and he shouted like a drunken soldier.
66 God scattered his enemies
   and made them ashamed for ever.

67 Then the Lord decided
   not to make his home
   with Joseph's descendants in Ephraim.*
68 Instead he chose the tribe of Judah,
   and he chose Mount Zion,
   the place he loves.
69 There he built his temple
   as lofty as the mountains
   and as solid as the earth
   that he had made to last for ever.

70 The Lord God chose David
   to be his servant
   and took him from tending sheep
71   and from caring for lambs.
   Then God made him the leader
   of Israel, his own nation.
72 David treated the people fairly
   and guided them with wisdom.

Psalm 79

(A psalm by Asaph.)

Have pity on Jerusalem

1 Our God, foreign nations
   have taken your land,
   disgraced your temple,
   and left Jerusalem in ruins.
2 They have fed the bodies
   of your servants
   to flesh-eating birds;
   your loyal people are food
   for savage animals.
3 All Jerusalem is covered
   with their blood,
   and there is no one left to bury them.
4 Every nation around us
   sneers and makes fun.

5 Our LORD,
   will you keep on being angry?
   Will your angry feelings
   keep flaming up like fire?
6 Get angry with those nations
   that don't know you
   and won't worship you!
7 They have gobbled up
   Jacob's descendants
   and left the land in ruins.

8 Don't make us pay for the sins
   of our ancestors.
   Have pity and come quickly!
   We are completely helpless.
9 Our God, you keep us safe.
   Now help us! Rescue us.
   Forgive our sins
   and bring honour to yourself.

10 Why should nations ask us,
   "Where is your God?"
   Let us and the other nations
   see you take revenge
   for your servants who died
   a violent death.

11 Listen to the prisoners groan!
   Let your mighty power save all
   who are sentenced to die.
12 Each of those nations sneered
   at you, our Lord.
   Now let others sneer at them,
   seven times as much.
13 Then we, your people,
   will always thank you.

---

*78.61 sacred chest: The Hebrew text has "his power", which refers to the sacred chest. In Psalm 132.8 it is called "powerful".
*78.67 with . . . Ephraim: Ephraim was Joseph's youngest son. One of the twelve tribes was named after him, and sometimes the northern kingdom of Israel was also known as Ephraim. The town of Shiloh was in the territory of Ephraim, but the place where God was worshipped was moved from there to Zion (Jerusalem) in the territory of Judah.

See also: 78.60: Josh 18.1; Jer 7.12–14; 26.6.
78.61: 1 Sam 4.4–22.   78.70,71: 1 Sam 16.11,12; 2 Sam 7.8; 1 Chron 17.7.

See also: 79.1: 2 King 25.8–10; 2 Chron 36.17–19; Jer 52.12–14.

We are like sheep
with you as our shepherd,
and all generations
will hear us praise you.

Psalm 80

*(A psalm by Asaph for the music leader.
To the tune "Lilies of the Agreement".)*

Help our nation

¹ Shepherd of Israel, you lead
the descendants of Joseph,
and you sit on your throne
above the winged creatures.*
Listen to our prayer
and let your light shine
² for the tribes of Ephraim,
Benjamin, and Manasseh.
Save us by your power.

³ Our God, make us strong again!
Smile on us and save us.

⁴ LORD God All-Powerful,
how much longer
will the prayers of your people
make you angry?
⁵ You gave us tears for food,
and you made us drink them
by the bowlful.
⁶ Because of you,
our enemies who live nearby
laugh and joke about us.
⁷ But if you smile on us, we will be saved.

⁸ We were like a grapevine
you brought out of Egypt.
You chased other nations away
and planted us here.
⁹ Then you cleared the ground,
and we put our roots deep,
spreading over the land.
¹⁰ Shade from this vine
covered the mountains.
Its branches climbed the mighty cedars
¹¹ and stretched to the sea;
its new growth reached to the river.*

¹² Our Lord, why have you
torn down the wall
from around the vineyard?
You let everyone who walks by
pick the grapes.
¹³ Now the vine is gobbled up
by pigs from the forest
and other wild animals.

¹⁴ God All-Powerful,
please do something!
Look down from heaven
and see what's happening
to this vine.
¹⁵ With your own hands
you planted its roots,
and you raised it as your very own.

¹⁶ Enemies chopped the vine down
and set it on fire.
Now show your anger and destroy them.
¹⁷ But help the one who sits
at your right side,*
the one you raised to be your own.
¹⁸ Then we will never turn away.
Put new life into us,
and we will worship you.

¹⁹ LORD God All-Powerful,
make us strong again!
Smile on us and save us.

Psalm 81

(By Asaph for the music leader.)*

God makes us strong

¹ Be happy and shout to God
who makes us strong!
Shout praises to the God of Jacob.
² Sing as you play tambourines
and the lovely sounding
stringed instruments.
³ Sound the trumpets and start
the New Moon Festival.*
We must also celebrate
when the moon is full.
⁴ This is the law in Israel,
and it was given to us
by the God of Jacob.

---

*80.1 winged creatures: Two winged creatures
made of gold were on the top of the sacred chest
and were symbols of the LORD's throne on earth
(see Exodus 25.18).
*80.11 the sea . . . the river: The Mediterranean Sea
and the River Euphrates were part of the ideal
boundaries for Israel.
See also: 80.1: Exod 25.22.

*80.17 right side: See the note at 16.11.
*Psalm 81 leader: See the note at Psalm 8.
*81.3 New Moon Festival: Celebrated on the first
day of each new moon, which was the beginning of
the month. But this may refer to either the New Year
celebration or the Harvest Festival. "The moon is full"
suggests a festival in the middle of the month.
See also: 81.3: Num 10.10.

5 The descendants of Joseph
were told to obey it,
when God led them out
from the land of Egypt.

In a language unknown to me,
I heard someone say:
6 "I lifted the burden from your shoulder
and took the heavy basket
from your hands.
7 When you were in trouble,
I rescued you,
and from the thunderclouds,
I answered your prayers.
Later I tested you at Meribah Spring.*

8 "Listen, my people,
while I, the Lord, correct you!
Israel, if you would only
pay attention to me!
9 Don't worship foreign gods
or bow down to gods
you know nothing about.
10 I am the LORD your God.
I rescued you from Egypt.
Just ask, and I will give you
whatever you need.

11 "But, my people, Israel,
you refused to listen,
and you would have nothing
to do with me!
12 So I let you be stubborn
and keep on following
your own advice.

13 "My people, Israel,
if only you would listen
and do as I say!
14 I, the LORD, would quickly
defeat your enemies
with my mighty power.
15 Everyone who hates me
would come crawling,
and that would be the end of them.
16 But I would feed you
with the finest bread
and with the best honey
until you were full."

Psalm 82

(A psalm by Asaph.)

Please do something, God!

1 When all the other gods*
have come together,
the Lord God judges them and says:
2 "How long will you keep judging unfairly
and favouring evil people?
3 Be fair to the poor and to orphans.
Defend the helpless
and everyone in need.
4 Rescue the weak and homeless
from the powerful hands
of heartless people.

5 "None of you know
or understand a thing.
You live in darkness,
while the foundations
of the earth tremble.*

6 "I, the Most High God, say
that all of you are gods*
and also my own children.
7 But you will die,
just like everyone else,
including powerful rulers."

8 Do something, God!
Judge the nations of the earth;
they belong to you.

Psalm 83

(A song and a psalm by Asaph.)

God rules all the earth

1 Our God, don't just sit there,
silently doing nothing!
2 Your hateful enemies
are turning against you and rebelling.
3 They are sly, and they plot
against those you treasure.
4 They say, "Let's wipe out
the nation of Israel
and make sure that no one
remembers its name!"

*81.7 Meribah Spring: When the people of Israel complained to Moses about the need for water, God commanded Moses to strike a rock with his walking stick, and water came out. The place was then named Massah ("test") and Meribah ("complaining").
See also: 81.7: Exod 17.7; Num 20.13. 81.9: Exod 20.2,3; Deut 5.6,7.

*82.1 the other gods: This probably refers to the gods of the nations that God defeated, but it could refer to God's servants (angels) in heaven or even to human rulers.
*82.5 foundations . . . tremble: In ancient times it was believed that the earth was flat and supported by columns.
*82.6 all of you are gods: See the note at 82.1.
See also: 82.6: John 10.34.

⁵ All of them fully agree
in their plans against you,
and among them are
⁶ Edom and the Ishmaelites;
Moab and the Hagrites;
⁷ Gebal, Ammon, and Amalek;
Philistia and Phoenicia.ᵃ
⁸ Even Assyria has joined forces
with Moab and Ammon.ᵇ

⁹ Our Lord, punish all of them
as you punished Midian.
Destroy them, as you destroyed
Sisera and Jabin
at Kishon Creek
¹⁰ near Endor,
and let their bodies rot.
¹¹ Treat their leaders as you did
Oreb and Zeeb,
Zebah and Zalmunna.
¹² All of them said, "We'll take
God's valuable land!"

¹³ Our God, scatter them around
like dust in a whirlwind.
¹⁴ Just as flames destroy forests
on the mountains,
¹⁵ pursue and terrify them
with storms of your own.
¹⁶ Make them blush with shame,
until they turn and worship
you, our Lord.
¹⁷ Let them be for ever ashamed
and confused.
Let them die in disgrace.
¹⁸ Make them realize that you
are the Lord Most High,
the only ruler of earth!

Psalm 84

(For the music leader. A psalm for
the people of Korah.)*

The joy of worship

¹ Lord God All-Powerful,
your temple is so lovely!
² Deep in my heart I long for your temple,
and with all that I am
I sing joyful songs to you.

³ Lord God All-Powerful,
my King and my God,
sparrows find a home near your altars;
swallows build nests there
to raise their young.

⁴ You bless everyone
who lives in your house,
and they sing your praises.
⁵ You bless all who depend
on you for their strength
and all who deeply desire
to visit your temple.
⁶ When they reach Dry Valley,ᵃ
springs start flowing,
and the autumn rain fills it
with pools of water.ᵇ

⁷ Your people grow stronger,
and you, the God of gods,
will be seen in Zion.

⁸ Lord God All-Powerful,
the God of Jacob,
please answer my prayer!
⁹ You are the shield
that protects your people,
and I am your chosen one.
Won't you smile on me?

¹⁰ One day in your temple is better
than a thousand anywhere else.
I would rather serve in your house,
than live in the homes of the wicked.

¹¹ Our Lord and our God,
you are like the sun
and also like a shield.
You treat us with kindness
and with honour,
never denying any good thing
to those who live right.

¹² Lord God All-Powerful,
you bless everyone who trusts in you.

Psalm 85

*(A psalm by the people of Korah
for the music leader.)*

A prayer for peace

¹ Our Lord, you have blessed your land
and made all go well
for Jacob's descendants.
² You have forgiven the sin
and taken away the guilt
of your people.
³ Your fierce anger is no longer
aimed at us.

---

*83.8 Moab and Ammon: The Hebrew text has "the
descendants of Lot", whose elder daughter was the
mother of the Moabites and whose younger
daughter was the mother of the Ammonites (see
Genesis 19.30–38).
*Psalm 84 leader: See the note at Psalm 8.
See also: 83.9: a Judg 7.1–23; b Judg 4.6–22.
83.11: a Judg 7.25; b Judg 8.12.

⁴ Our LORD and our God, you save us!
  Please bring us back home
  and don't be angry.
⁵ Will you always be angry
  with us and our families?
⁶ Won't you give us fresh life
  and let your people be glad
  because of you?
⁷ Show us your love and save us!

⁸ I will listen to you, LORD God,
  because you promise peace to those
  who are faithful and no longer foolish.
⁹ You are ready to rescue
  everyone who worships you,
  so that you will live with us
  in all your glory.

¹⁰ Love and loyalty will come together;
  goodness and peace will unite.
¹¹ Loyalty will sprout from the ground;
  justice will look down
  from the sky above.

¹² Our LORD, you will bless us;
  our land will produce wonderful crops.
¹³ Justice will march in front,
  making a path for you to follow.

Psalm 86

(A prayer by David.)

A prayer for help

¹ Please listen, LORD,
  and answer my prayer!
  I am poor and helpless.
² Protect me and save me
  because you are my God.
  I am your faithful servant,
  and I trust you.
³ Be kind to me! I pray to you all day.
⁴ Make my heart glad!
  I serve you, and my prayer is sincere.
⁵ You willingly forgive,
  and your love is always there
  for those who pray to you.
⁶ Please listen, LORD!
  Answer my prayer for help.
⁷ When I am in trouble, I pray,
  knowing you will listen.

⁸ No other gods are like you;
  only you work miracles.
⁹ You created each nation,
  and they will all bow down
  to worship and honour you.

¹⁰ You perform great wonders
  because you alone are God.
¹¹ Teach me to follow you,
  and I will obey your truth.
  Always keep me faithful.
¹² With all my heart I thank you.
  I praise you, LORD God.
¹³ Your love for me is so great
  that you protected me
  from death and the grave.

¹⁴ Proud and violent enemies,
  who don't care about you,
  have ganged up to attack and kill me.
¹⁵ But you, the Lord God,
  are kind and merciful.
  You don't easily get angry,
  and your love can always be trusted.
¹⁶ I serve you, LORD,
  and I am the child of one of your servants.
  Look on me with kindness.
  Make me strong and save me.
¹⁷ Show that you approve of me!
  Then my hateful enemies
  will feel like fools,
  because you have helped
  and comforted me.

Psalm 87

(A psalm and a song by the people of Korah.)

The glory of Mount Zion

¹ Zion was built by the LORD
  on the holy mountain,
² and he loves that city
  more than any other place in all of Israel.
³ Zion, you are the city of God,
  and wonderful things are told about you.

⁴ Egypt,* Babylonia, Philistia,
  Phoenicia,* and Ethiopia*
  are some of those nations that know you,
  and their people all say,
  "I was born in Zion."

⁵ God Most High will strengthen
  the city of Zion.
  Then everyone will say,
  "We were born here too."
⁶ The LORD will make a list of his people,
  and all who were born here
  will be included.

⁷ All who sing or dance will say,
  "I too am from Zion."

---

*87.4 Phoenicia: See the note at 83.7.
*87.4 Ethiopia: See the note at 68.31.

See also: 86.9: Rev 15.4.

Psalm 88

(A song and a psalm by the people of Korah for the music leader. To the tune "Mahalath Leannoth"." A special psalm by Heman the Ezrahite.)

A prayer when you can't find the way

¹ You keep me safe, LORD God.
  So when I pray at night,
² please listen carefully
  to each of my concerns.

³ I am deeply troubled
  and close to death;
⁴ I am as good as dead
  and completely helpless.
⁵ I am no better off
  than those in the grave,
  those you have forgotten
  and no longer help.

⁶ You have put me in the deepest
  and darkest grave;
⁷ your anger rolls over me
  like ocean waves.
⁸ You have made my friends turn
  in horror from me.
  I am a prisoner who cannot escape,
⁹ and I am almost blind
  because of my sorrow.

Each day I lift my hands
  in prayer to you, LORD.
¹⁰ Do you work miracles for the dead?
  Do they stand up and praise you?
¹¹ Are your love and loyalty announced
  in the world of the dead?
¹² Do they know of your miracles
  or your saving power
  in the dark world below
  where all is forgotten?

¹³ Each morning I pray to you, LORD.
¹⁴ Why do you reject me?
  Why do you turn from me?
¹⁵ Ever since I was a child,
  I have been sick and close to death.
  You have terrified me
  and made me helpless.'

¹⁶ Your anger is like a flood!
  And I am shattered by your furious attacks
¹⁷ that strike each day
  and from every side.
¹⁸ My friends and neighbours
  have turned against me because of you,
  and now darkness
  is my only companion.

Psalm 89

(A special psalm by Ethan the Ezrahite.)

The LORD's agreement with David

¹ Our LORD, I will sing
  of your love for ever.
  Everyone yet to be born
  will hear me praise your faithfulness.
² I will tell them,
  "God's love can always be trusted,
  and his faithfulness lasts
  as long as the heavens."

³ You said, "David, my servant,
  is my chosen one,
  and this is the agreement
  I made with him:
⁴ David, one of your descendants
  will always be king."

⁵ Our LORD, let the heavens
  now praise your miracles,
  and let all your angels
  praise your faithfulness.

⁶ None who live in the heavens
  can compare with you.
⁷ You are the most fearsome
  of all who live in heaven;
  all the others fear
  and greatly honour you.
⁸ You are LORD God All-Powerful!
  No one is as loving
  and faithful as you are.
⁹ You rule the roaring sea
  and calm its waves.
¹⁰ You crushed the monster Rahab,*
  and with your powerful arm
  you scattered your enemies.
¹¹ The heavens and the earth belong to you.
  And so does the world
  with all its people,
  because you created them
¹² and everything else.'

Mount Tabor and Mount Hermon
  gladly praise you.
¹³ You are strong and mighty!
¹⁴ Your kingdom is ruled
  by justice and fairness,
  with love and faithfulness
  leading the way.

---

*89.10 Rahab: Many people in the ancient world thought that the world was controlled by this sea monster that the Lord destroyed at the time of creation (see Isaiah 51.9).

See also: 89 Title: 1 King 4.31. 89.4: 2 Sam 7.12–16; 1 Chron 17.11–14; Psa 132.11; Acts 2.30.

15 Our LORD, you bless those
who join in the festival
and walk in the brightness
of your presence.
16 We are happy all day because of you,
and your saving power
brings honour to us.
17 Your own glorious power
makes us strong,
and because of your kindness,
our strength increases.
18 Our LORD and our King,
the Holy One of Israel,
you are truly our shield.

19 In a vision, you once said
to your faithful followers:
"I have helped a mighty hero.
I chose him from my people
and made him famous.
20 David, my servant, is the one
I chose to be king,
21 and I will always be there
to help and strengthen him.

22 "No enemy will outsmart David,
and he won't be defeated
by any hateful people.
23 I will strike down and crush
his troublesome enemies.
24 He will always be able
to depend on my love,
and I will make him strong
with my own power.
25 I will let him rule the lands
across the rivers and seas.
26 He will say to me,
'You are my Father and my God,
as well as the mighty rock*
where I am safe.'

27 "I have chosen David
as my firstborn son,
and he will be the ruler
of all kings on earth.
28 My love for him will last,
and my agreement with him
will never be broken.

29 "One of David's descendants
will always be king,
and his family will rule
until the sky disappears.
30 Suppose some of his children
should reject my Law
and refuse my instructions.

31 Or suppose they should disobey
all of my teachings.
32 Then I will correct
and punish them
because of their sins.
33 But I will always love David
and faithfully keep all
of my promises to him.

34 "I won't break my agreement
or go back on my word.
35 I have sworn once and for all
by my own holy name,
and I won't lie to David.
36 His family will always rule.
I will let his kingdom last
as long as the sun
37 and moon appear in the sky."

38 You are now angry, God,
and you have turned your back
on your chosen king.
39 You broke off your agreement
with your servant, the king,
and you completely destroyed
his kingdom.
40 The walls of his city
have been broken through,
and every fortress now lies in ruin.
41 All who pass by take what they want,
and nations everywhere
joke about the king.

42 You made his enemies powerful
and let them celebrate.
43 But you forced him to retreat
because you did not
fight on his side.
44 You took his crown†
and threw his throne to the ground.
45 You made an old man of him
and put him to shame.

46 How much longer, LORD?
Will you hide for ever?
How long will your anger
keep burning like fire?
47 Remember, life is short!†
Why did you empty our lives
of all meaning?
48 No one can escape the power
of death and the grave.

49 Our Lord, where is the love
you have always shown
and that you promised
so faithfully to David?
50 Remember your servant, Lord!
People make jokes about me,
and I suffer many insults.

*89.26 mighty rock: See the note at 18.2.
See also: 89.20: a 1 Sam 13.14; Acts 13.22; b 1 Sam 16.12.
89.27: Rev 1.5.

561

⁵¹ I am your chosen one,
   but your enemies chase
   and make fun of me.

⁵² Our LORD, we praise you
   for ever. Amen and amen.

BOOK 4

(Psalms 90–106)

Psalm 90

(A prayer by Moses, the man of God.)

God is eternal

¹ Our Lord, in all generations
   you have been our home.
² You have always been God —
   long before the birth
   of the mountains,
   even before you created
   the earth and the world.

³ At your command we die
   and turn back to dust,
⁴ but a thousand years
   mean nothing to you!
   They are merely a day gone by
   or a few hours in the night.

⁵ You bring our lives to an end
   just like a dream.
   We are merely tender grass
⁶ that sprouts and grows
   in the morning,
   but dries up by evening.

⁷ Your furious anger frightens
   and destroys us,
⁸ and you know all our sins,
   even those we do in secret.

⁹ Your anger is a burden
   each day we live,
   then life ends like a sigh.
¹⁰ We can expect seventy years,
   or perhaps eighty,
   if we are healthy,
   but even our best years
   bring trouble and sorrow.
   Suddenly our time is up,
   and we disappear.
¹¹ No one knows the full power
   of your furious anger,
   but it is as great as the fear
   that we owe to you.

¹² Teach us to use wisely
   all the time we have.

¹³ Help us, LORD! Don't wait!
   Pity your servants.

¹⁴ When morning comes,
   let your love satisfy all our needs.
   Then we can celebrate
   and be glad for what time we have left.

¹⁵ Make us happy for as long
   as you caused us trouble and sorrow.

¹⁶ Do wonderful things for us,
   your servants,
   and show your mighty power
   to our children.

¹⁷ Our Lord and our God,
   treat us with kindness
   and let all go well for us.
   Please let all go well!

Psalm 91

The LORD is my fortress

¹ Live under the protection
   of God Most High
   and stay in the shadow
   of God All-Powerful.
² Then you will say to the LORD,
   "You are my fortress,
   my place of safety;
   you are my God,
   and I trust you."

³ The Lord will keep you safe
   from secret traps and deadly diseases.
⁴ He will spread his wings over you
   and keep you secure.
   His faithfulness is like
   a shield or a city wall.ᵇ

⁵ You won't need to worry
   about dangers at night
   or arrows during the day.
⁶ And you won't fear diseases
   that strike in the dark
   or sudden disaster at midday.

⁷ You will not be harmed,
   though thousands fall all around you.
⁸ And with your own eyes you will see
   the punishment of the wicked.
⁹ The LORD Most High is your fortress.
   Run to him for safety,
¹⁰ and no terrible disasters
   will strike you or your home.

¹¹ God will command his angels
   to protect you wherever you go.

See also: 90.4: 2 Pet 3.8.

See also: 91.11: Matt 4.6; Luke 4.10.

¹² They will carry you in their arms,
    and you won't hurt your feet
      on the stones.
¹³ You will overpower the strongest lions
    and the most deadly snakes.

¹⁴ The Lord says,
    "If you love me
    and truly know who I am,
      I will rescue you and keep you safe.
¹⁵ When you are in trouble,
      call out to me.
    I will answer and be there
      to protect and honour you.
¹⁶ You will live a long life
    and see my saving power."

Psalm 92

(A psalm and a song for the Sabbath.)

Sing praises to the LORD

¹ It is wonderful to be grateful
    and to sing your praises,
    LORD Most High!
² It is wonderful each morning
    to tell about your love
    and at night to announce
      how faithful you are.
³ I enjoy praising your name
    to the music of harps,
⁴ because everything you do
    makes me happy,
    and I sing joyful songs.

⁵ You do great things, LORD.
    Your thoughts are too deep
⁶ for an ignorant fool
    to know or understand.
⁷ Though the wicked sprout
    and spread like grass,
      they will be pulled up by their roots.
⁸ But you will rule over all of us for ever,
⁹ and your hateful enemies
    will be scattered
      and then destroyed.

¹⁰ You have given me
    the strength of a wild ox,
    and you have chosen me
      to be your very own.
¹¹ My eyes have seen,
    and my ears have heard
      the doom and destruction
    of my terrible enemies.

¹² Good people will prosper
    like palm trees,
    and they will grow strong
      like the cedars of Lebanon.
¹³ They will take root
    in your house, LORD God,
    and they will do well.
¹⁴ They will be like trees
    that stay healthy and fruitful,
      even when they are old.
¹⁵ And they will say about you,
    "The LORD always does right!
    God is our mighty rock."*

Psalm 93

The LORD is king

¹ Our LORD, you are King!
    Majesty and power are your royal robes.
    You put the world in place,
      and it will never be moved.
² You have always ruled,
    and you are eternal.

³ The ocean is roaring, LORD!
    The sea is pounding hard.
⁴ Its mighty waves are majestic,
    but you are more majestic,
      and you rule over all.
⁵ Your decisions are firm,
    and your temple will always
      be beautiful and holy.

Psalm 94

The LORD punishes the guilty

¹ LORD God, you punish the guilty.
    Show what you are like
      and punish them now.
² You judge the earth.
    Come and help us!
    Pay back those proud people
      for what they have done.
³ How long will the wicked
    celebrate and be glad?

⁴ All those cruel people strut and boast,
⁵ and they crush and wound
    your chosen nation, LORD.
⁶ They murder widows,
    foreigners, and orphans.
⁷ Then they say,
    "The LORD God of Jacob
    doesn't see or know."

See also: 91.12: Matt 4.6; Luke 4.11. **91.13:** Luke 10.19.   ***92.15 mighty rock:** See the note at 18.2.

8 Can't you fools see?
  Won't you ever learn?
9 God gave us ears and eyes!
  Can't he hear and see?
10 God instructs the nations
  and gives knowledge to us all.
  Won't he also correct us?
11 The LORD knows how useless
  our plans really are.
12 Our LORD, you bless everyone
  whom you instruct and teach
  by using your Law.
13 You give them rest from their troubles,
  until a pit can be dug for the wicked.
14 You won't turn your back
  on your chosen nation.
15 Justice and fairness will go hand in hand,
  and all who do right will follow along.

16 Who will stand up for me
  against those cruel people?
17 If you had not helped me, LORD,
  I would soon have gone
  to the land of silence.*
18 When I felt my feet slipping,
  you came with your love
  and kept me steady.
19 And when I was burdened with worries,
  you comforted me
  and made me feel secure.
20 But you are opposed
  to dishonest lawmakers
21 who gang up to murder
  innocent victims.
22 You, LORD God, are my fortress,
  that mighty rock* where I am safe.
23 You will pay back my enemies,
  and you will wipe them out
  for the evil they did.

Psalm 95

Worship and obey the LORD

1 Sing joyful songs to the LORD!
  Praise the mighty rock*
  where we are safe.
2 Come to worship him
  with thankful hearts
  and songs of praise.

3 The LORD is the greatest God,
  king over all other gods.

4 He holds the deepest part
  of the earth in his hands,
  and the mountain peaks
  belong to him.
5 The ocean is the Lord's
  because he made it,
  and with his own hands
  he formed the dry land.

6 Bow down and worship
  the LORD our Creator!
7 The LORD is our God,
  and we are his people,
  the sheep he takes care of
  in his own pasture.

Listen to God's voice today!
8 Don't be stubborn and rebel
  as your ancestors did
  at Meribah and Massah*
  out in the desert.
9 For forty years they tested God
  and saw the things he did.
10 Then God got tired of them and said,
  "You never show good sense,
  and you don't understand
  what I want you to do."
11 In his anger, God told them,
  "You people will never enter
  my place of rest."

Psalm 96

Sing a new song to the LORD

1 Sing a new song to the LORD!
  Everyone on this earth,
  sing praises to the LORD,
2 sing and praise his name.

Day after day announce,
  "The LORD has saved us!"
3 Tell every nation on earth,
  "The LORD is wonderful
  and does marvellous things!
4 The LORD is great and deserves
  our greatest praise!
  He is the only God
  worthy of our worship.
5 Other nations worship idols,
  but the LORD created the heavens.
6 Give honour and praise to the LORD,
  whose power and beauty
  fill his holy temple."

---

*94.17 land of silence: The grave or the world of the dead.
*94.22; 95.1 mighty rock: See the note at 18.2.
See also: 94.11: 1 Cor 3.20.

*95.8 Meribah and Massah: See the note at 81.7.
See also: 95.7-11: Heb 3.7-11. 95.7,8: Heb 3.15; 4.7.
95.8,9: Exod 17.1-7; Num 20.2-13. 95.11: a Num 14.20-23;
Deut 1.34-36; Heb 4.3,5; b Deut 12.9,10.

7 Tell everyone of every nation,
    "Praise the glorious power of the LORD.
8 He is wonderful! Praise him
    and bring an offering into his temple.
9 Everyone on earth, now tremble
    and worship the LORD,
    majestic and holy."

10 Announce to the nations,
    "The LORD is King!
    The world stands firm,
    never to be shaken,
    and he will judge its people with fairness."

11 Tell the heavens and the earth
    to be glad and celebrate!
    Command the ocean to roar
    with all its creatures,
12 and the fields to rejoice
    with all their crops.
    Then every tree in the forest
    will sing joyful songs
13 to the LORD.
    He is coming to judge
    all people on earth
    with fairness and truth.

Psalm 97

The LORD brings justice

1 The LORD is King!
    Tell the earth to celebrate
    and all islands to shout.
2 Dark clouds surround him,
    and his throne is supported
    by justice and fairness.
3 Fire leaps from his throne,
    destroying his enemies,
4 and his lightning is so bright
    that the earth sees it and trembles.
5 Mountains melt away like wax
    in the presence of the LORD
    of all the earth.

6 The heavens announce,
    "The LORD brings justice!"
    Everyone sees God's glory.
7 Those who boast about
    the useless idols they worship
    are terribly ashamed,
    and all the false gods
    bow down to the LORD.

8 When the people of Zion
    and of the towns of Judah
    hear that God brings justice,
    they will celebrate.

9 The LORD rules the whole earth,
    and he is more glorious
    than all the false gods.

10 Love the LORD and hate evil!
    God protects his loyal people
    and rescues them from violence.
11 If you obey and do right,
    a light will show you the way
    and fill you with happiness.
12 You are the LORD's people!
    So celebrate and praise the only God.

Psalm 98

The LORD works miracles

1 Sing a new song to the LORD!
    He has worked miracles,
    and with his own powerful arm,
    he has won the victory.
2 The LORD has shown the nations
    that he has the power to save
    and to bring justice.
3 God has been faithful
    in his love for Israel,
    and his saving power is seen
    everywhere on earth.

4 Tell everyone on this earth
    to sing happy songs
    in praise of the LORD.
5 Make music for him on harps.
    Play beautiful melodies!
6 Sound the trumpets and horns
    and celebrate with joyful songs
    for our LORD and King!

7 Command the ocean to roar
    with all its creatures,
    and the earth to shout with all its people.
8 Order the rivers to clap their hands,
    and all the hills to sing together.
9 Let them worship the LORD!
    He is coming to judge
    everyone on the earth,
    and he will be honest and fair.

Psalm 99

Our LORD is King

1 Our LORD, you are King!
    You rule from your throne
    above the winged creatures,*
    as people tremble
    and the earth shakes.

See also: 96.7–9: Psa 29.1,2.

*99.1 winged creatures: See the note at 80.1.
See also: 99.1: Exod 25.22.

² You are praised in Zion,
    and you control all nations.
³ Only you are God!
    And your power alone,
    so great and fearsome,
    is worthy of praise.
⁴ You are our mighty King,’
    a lover of fairness,
    who sees that justice is done
    everywhere in Israel.
⁵ Our LORD and our God,
    we praise you
    and kneel down to worship you,
    the God of holiness!

⁶ Moses and Aaron were two
    of your priests.
    Samuel was also one of those
    who prayed in your name,
    and you, our LORD,
    answered their prayers.
⁷ You spoke to them from a thick cloud,
    and they obeyed your laws.

⁸ Our LORD and our God,
    you answered their prayers
    and forgave their sins,
    but when they did wrong,
    you punished them.
⁹ We praise you, LORD God,
    and we worship you
    at your sacred mountain.
    Only you are God!

Psalm 100

(A psalm of praise.)

The LORD is God

¹ Shout praises to the LORD,
    everyone on this earth.
² Be joyful and sing
    as you come in to worship the LORD!

³ You know the LORD is God!
    He created us,
    and we belong to him;
    we are his people,
    the sheep in his pasture.

⁴ Be thankful and praise the LORD
    as you enter his temple.
⁵ The LORD is good!
    His love and faithfulness
    will last for ever.

See also: 99.7: Exod 33.9. 100.5: 1 Chron 16.34;
2 Chron 5.13; 7.3; Ezra 3.11; Psa 106.1; 107.1; 118.1; 136.1;
Jer 33.11.
566

Psalm 101

(A psalm by David.)

A king and his promises

¹ I will sing to you, LORD!
    I will celebrate your kindness
    and your justice.
² Please help me learn
    to do the right thing,
    and I will be honest and fair
    in my own kingdom.

³ I refuse to be corrupt
    or to take part in anything crooked,
⁴   and I won’t be dishonest or deceitful.

⁵ Anyone who spreads gossip
    will be silenced,
    and no one who is conceited
    will be my friend.

⁶ I will find trustworthy people
    to serve as my advisers,
    and only an honest person
    will serve as an official.

⁷ No one who cheats or lies
    will have a position in my royal court.
⁸ Each morning I will silence
    any lawbreakers I find
    in the countryside
    or in the city of the LORD.

Psalm 102

*(A prayer for someone who suffers
and needs to ask the LORD for help.)*

A prayer in time of trouble

¹ I pray to you, LORD! Please listen.
²   Don’t hide from me
    in my time of trouble.
    Pay attention to my prayer
    and quickly give an answer.

³ My days disappear like smoke,
    and my bones are burning
    as though in a furnace.
⁴ I am wasting away like grass,
    and my appetite is gone.
⁵ My groaning never stops,
    and my bones can be seen
    through my skin.
⁶ I am like a lonely owl in the desert
⁷   or a restless sparrow
    alone on a roof.

⁸ My enemies insult me all day,
    and they use my name
    for a curse word.

9 Instead of food,
I have ashes to eat and tears to drink,
10 because you are furious
and have thrown me aside.
11 My life fades like a shadow
at the end of day
and withers like grass.

12 Our LORD, you are King for ever
and will always be famous.
13 You will show pity to Zion
because the time has come.
14 We, your servants,
love each stone in the city,
and we are sad to see them
lying in the dust.

15 Our LORD, the nations
will honour you,
and all kings on earth
will praise your glory.
16 You will rebuild the city of Zion.
Your glory will be seen,
17 and the prayers of the homeless
will be answered.

18 Future generations must also
praise the LORD,
so write this for them:
19 "From his holy temple,
the LORD looked down at the earth.
20 He listened to the groans of prisoners,
and he rescued everyone
who was doomed to die."

21 All Jerusalem should praise you, our LORD,
22 when people from every nation
meet to worship you.

23 I should still be strong,
but you, LORD, have made
an old person of me.
24 You will live for ever!
Years mean nothing to you.
Don't cut my life in half!

25 In the beginning, LORD,
you laid the earth's foundation
and created the heavens.
26 They will all disappear
and wear out like clothes.
You change them,
as you would a coat,
but you last for ever.
27 You are always the same.
Years cannot change you.
28 Every generation of those
who serve you will
live in your presence.

Psalm 103

(By David.)

The LORD's wonderful love

1 With all my heart I praise the LORD,
and with all that I am
I praise his holy name!
2 With all my heart I praise the LORD!
I will never forget how kind he has been.

3 The LORD forgives our sins,
heals us when we are sick,
4 and protects us from death.
His kindness and love
are a crown on our heads.
5 Each day that we live,'
he provides for our needs
and gives us the strength
of a young eagle.

6 For all who are ill-treated,
the LORD brings justice.
7 He taught his Law to Moses
and showed all Israel
what he could do.

8 The LORD is merciful!
He is kind and patient,
and his love never fails.
9 The LORD won't always be angry
and point out our sins;
10 he doesn't punish us
as our sins deserve.

11 How great is God's love for all
who worship him?
Greater than the distance
between heaven and earth!
12 How far has the LORD taken
our sins from us?
Further than the distance
from east to west!

13 Just as parents are kind to their children,
the LORD is kind to all who worship him,
14 because he knows
we are made of dust.
15 We humans are like grass
or wild flowers that quickly bloom.
16 But a scorching wind blows,
and they quickly wither
to be for ever forgotten.

17 The LORD is always kind
to those who worship him,
and he keeps his promises
to their descendants
18 who faithfully obey him.

See also: 102.25-27: Heb 1.10-12.

See also: 103.8: Jam 5.11.

¹⁹ God has set up his kingdom in heaven,
  and he rules the whole creation.
²⁰ All you mighty angels,
  who obey God's commands,
  come and praise your LORD!
²¹ All you thousands
  who serve and obey God,
  come and praise your LORD!
²² All God's creation
  and all that he rules,
  come and praise your LORD!
  With all my heart I praise the LORD!

Psalm 104

The LORD takes care of his creation

¹ I praise you, LORD God,
  with all my heart.
  You are glorious and majestic,
  dressed in royal robes
² and surrounded by light.
  You spread out the sky like a tent,
³ and you built your home
  over the mighty ocean.
  The clouds are your chariot
  with the wind as its wings.
⁴ The winds are your messengers,
  and flames of fire are your servants.

⁵ You built foundations for the earth,
  and it will never be shaken.
⁶ You covered the earth with the ocean
  that rose above the mountains.
⁷ Then your voice thundered!
  And the water flowed
⁸   down the mountains
  and through the valleys
  to the place you prepared.
⁹ Now you have set boundaries,
  so that the water will never
  flood the earth again.

¹⁰ You provide streams of water
  in the hills and valleys,
¹¹ so that the donkeys
  and other wild animals
  can satisfy their thirst.
¹² Birds build their nests nearby
  and sing in the trees.
¹³ From your home above
  you send rain on the hills
  and water the earth.
¹⁴ You let the earth produce
  grass for cattle,
  plants for our food,
¹⁵   wine to cheer us up,

olive oil for our skin,
  and grain for our health.

¹⁶ Our LORD, your trees always have water,
  and so do the cedars
  you planted in Lebanon.
¹⁷ Birds nest in those trees,
  and storks make their home
  in the fir trees.
¹⁸ Wild goats find a home
  in the tall mountains,
  and small animals can hide
  between the rocks.

¹⁹ You created the moon
  to tell us the seasons.
  The sun knows when to set,
²⁰   and you made the darkness,
  so the animals in the forest
  could come out at night.
²¹ Lions roar as they hunt
  for the food you provide.
²² But when morning comes,
  they return to their dens,
²³   then we go out to work
  until the end of day.

²⁴ Our LORD, by your wisdom
  you made so many things;
  the whole earth is covered
  with your living creatures.
²⁵ But what about the ocean
  so big and wide?
  It is alive with creatures,
  large and small.
²⁶ And there are the ships,
  as well as Leviathan,*
  the monster you created
  to splash in the sea.

²⁷ All of these depend on you
  to provide them with food,
²⁸ and you feed each one
  with your own hand,
  until they are full.
²⁹ But when you turn away,
  they are terrified;
  when you end their life,
  they die and rot.
³⁰ You created all of them by your Spirit,
  and you give new life to the earth.
³¹ Our LORD, we pray that your glory
  will last for ever
  and that you will be pleased
  with what you have done.

---

*104.26 Leviathan: See the note at 74.14.

See also: 104.4: Heb 1.7.

See also: 104.26: Job 41.1; Psa 74.14; Isa 27.1.

32 You look at the earth, and it trembles.
   You touch the mountains,
   and smoke goes up.
33 As long as I live,
   I will sing and praise you,
   the LORD God.
34 I hope my thoughts will please you,
   because you are the one
   who makes me glad.

35 Destroy all wicked sinners
   from the earth once and for all.
   With all my heart I praise you, LORD!
   I praise you!

Psalm 105

The LORD can be trusted

1 Praise the LORD and pray in his name!
   Tell everyone what he has done.
2 Sing praises to the LORD!
   Tell about his miracles.
3 Celebrate and worship
   his holy name with all your heart.

4 Trust the LORD and his mighty power.
5 Remember his miracles
   and all his wonders
   and his fair decisions.
6 You belong to the family
   of Abraham, his servant;
   you are his chosen ones,
   the descendants of Jacob.

7 The LORD is our God,
   bringing justice everywhere on earth.
8 He will never forget
   his agreement or his promises,
   not in thousands of years.
9-10 God made an eternal promise
   to Abraham, Isaac, and Jacob,
11   when he said, "I'll give you
   the land of Canaan."

12 At the time there were only a few of us,
   and we were homeless.
13 We wandered from nation to nation,
   from one country to another.
14 God did not let anyone
   ill-treat our people.
   Instead he protected us
   by punishing rulers
15   and telling them,
   "Don't touch my chosen leaders
   or harm my prophets!"

16 God kept crops from growing
   until food was scarce
   everywhere in the land.
17 But he had already sent Joseph,
   sold as a slave into Egypt,
18   with chains of iron
   around his legs and neck.

19 Joseph remained a slave
   until his own words had come true,
   and the LORD had finished testing him.
20 Then the king of Egypt set Joseph free
21   and put him in charge
   of everything he owned.
22 Joseph was in command of the officials,
   and he taught the leaders
   how to use wisdom.

23 Jacob and his family came
   and settled in Egypt as foreigners.
24 They were the LORD's people,
   so he let them grow stronger
   than their enemies.
25 They served the LORD,
   and he made the Egyptians plan
   hateful things against them.
26 God sent his servant Moses.
   He also chose and sent Aaron
27   to his people in Egypt,
   and they worked miracles
   and wonders there.
28 Moses and Aaron obeyed God,
   and he sent darkness to cover Egypt.
29 God turned their rivers
   into streams of blood,
   and the fish all died.
30 Frogs were everywhere,
   even in the royal palace.
31 When God gave the command,
   flies and gnats swarmed all around.

32 In place of rain,
   God sent hailstones
   and flashes of lightning.
33 He destroyed their grapevines
   and their fig trees,
   and he made splinters
   of all the other trees.
34 God gave the command,
   and more grasshoppers came
   than could be counted.

See also: 105.16: Gen 41.53–57. 105.17: Gen 37.28; 45.5.
105.18,19: Gen 39.20—40.23. 105.20: Gen 41.14.
105.21: Gen 41.39–41. 105.23: a Gen 46.6; b Gen 47.11.
105.24,25: Exod 1.7–14. 105.26: Exod 3.1—4.17.
105.28: Exod 10.21-23. 105.29: Exod 7.17–21.
105.30: Exod 8.1–6. 105.31: a Exod 8.20–24;
b Exod 8.16,17. 105.32,33: Exod 9.22–25.
105.34,35: Exod 10.12–15.

See also: 105.9: a Gen 12.7; 17.8; b Gen 26.3.
105.10,11: Gen 28.13. 105.14,15: Gen 20.3–7.

³⁵ They ate every green plant
  and all the crops that grew
  in the land of Egypt.
³⁶ Then God took the life
  of every firstborn son.

³⁷ When God led Israel from Egypt,
  they took silver and gold,
  and no one was left behind.
³⁸ The Egyptians were afraid
  and gladly let them go.
³⁹ God hid them under a cloud
  and guided them by fire
  during the night.

⁴⁰ When they asked for food,
  he sent more birds than they could eat.
⁴¹ God even split open a rock,
  and streams of water
  gushed into the desert.
⁴² God never forgot his sacred promise
  to his servant Abraham.

⁴³ When the Lord rescued
  his chosen people from Egypt,
  they celebrated with songs.
⁴⁴ The Lord gave them the land
  and everything else
  the nations had worked for.
⁴⁵ He did this so that his people
  would obey all his laws.
  Shout praises to the LORD!

Psalm 106

A nation asks for forgiveness

¹ We will celebrate
  and praise you, LORD!
  You are good to us,
  and your love never fails.
² No one can praise you enough
  for all the mighty things you have done.
³ You bless those people
  who are honest and fair
  in everything they do.

⁴ Remember me, LORD,
  when you show kindness
  by saving your people.
⁵ Let me prosper with the rest
  of your chosen ones,
  as they celebrate with pride
  because they belong to you.

⁶ We and our ancestors
  have sinned terribly.
⁷ When they were in Egypt,
  they paid no attention
  to your marvellous deeds
  or your wonderful love.
  And they turned against you
  at the Red Sea.*

⁸ But you were true to your name,
  and you rescued them to prove
  how mighty you are.
⁹ You said to the Red Sea,*
  "Dry up!"
  Then you led your people across
  on land as dry as a desert.
¹⁰ You saved all of them
¹¹ and drowned every one
  of their enemies.
¹² Then your people trusted you
  and sang your praises.

¹³ But they soon forgot
  what you had done
  and rejected your advice.
¹⁴ They became greedy for food
  and tested you there in the desert.
¹⁵ So you gave them what they wanted,
  but later you destroyed them
  with a horrible disease.

¹⁶ Everyone in camp was jealous
  of Moses and of Aaron,
  your chosen priest.
¹⁷ Dathan and Abiram rebelled,
  and the earth opened up
  and swallowed them.
¹⁸ Then fire broke out
  and destroyed all of their followers.

¹⁹ At Horeb your people
  made and worshipped the statue
²⁰ of a bull, instead of you,
  their glorious God.
²¹ You worked powerful miracles
  to save them from Egypt,
  but they forgot about you
²² and the fearsome things
  you did at the Red Sea.*

---

*106.7,9,22 Red Sea:** Hebrew *yam suph* "Sea of
Reeds", one of the marshes or fresh water lakes near
the eastern part of the Nile Delta. This identification is
based on Exodus 13.17—14.9, which lists the towns
on the route of the Israelites before crossing the sea.
In the Greek translation of the Scriptures made about
200 BC, the "Sea of Reeds" was named "Red Sea".

See also: 105.36: Exod 12.29. 105.37,38: Exod 12.33–36.
105.39: Exod 13.21,22. 105.40: Exod 16.2–15.
105.41: Exod 17.1–7; Num 20.2–13. 105.44: Josh 11.16–23.
106.1: 1 Chron 16.34; 2 Chron 5.13; 7.3; Ezra 3.11; Psa 100.5;
107.1; 118.1; 136.1; Jer 33.11.

See also: 106.7: Exod 14.10-12. 106.9–12: Exod 14.21–31.
106.12: Exod 15.1–21. 106.14,15: Num 11.4–34.
106.16-18: Num 16.1–35. 106.19-23: Exod 32.1–14.

23 You were angry and started
  to destroy them,
  but Moses, your chosen leader,
  begged you not to do it.

24 They would not trust you, LORD,
  and they did not like
  the promised land.

25 They would not obey you,
  and they grumbled in their tents.

26 So you threatened them by saying,
  "I'll kill you out here in the desert!

27 I'll scatter your children
  everywhere in the world."

28 Your people became followers
  of a god named Baal Peor,
  and they ate sacrifices
  offered to the dead.*

29 They did such terrible things
  that you punished them
  with a deadly disease.

30 But Phinehas* helped them,
  and the sickness stopped.

31 Now he will always be highly honoured.

32 At Meribah Spring*
  they turned against you
  and made you furious.

33 Then Moses got into trouble
  for speaking in anger.

34 Our LORD, they disobeyed you
  by refusing to destroy the nations.

35 Instead they were friendly
  with those foreigners
  and followed their customs.

36 Then they fell into the trap
  of worshipping idols.

37 They sacrificed their sons
  and their daughters to demons

38 and to the gods of Canaan.
  Then they poured out the blood
  of these innocent children
  and made the land filthy.

39 By doing such gruesome things,
  they also became filthy.

40 Finally, LORD, you were angry
  and terribly disgusted with your people.

41 So you put them in the power

of nations that hated them.

42 They were ill-treated and abused
  by their enemies,

43 but you saved them time after time.
  They were determined to rebel,
  and their sins caused their downfall.

44 You answered their prayers
  when they were in trouble.

45 You kept your agreement
  and were so merciful

46 that their enemies had pity on them.

47 Save us, LORD God!
  Bring us back from among the nations.
  Let us celebrate and shout
  in praise of your holy name.

48 LORD God of Israel,
  you deserve to be praised
  for ever and ever.
  Let everyone say, "Amen!
  Shout praises to the LORD!"

BOOK 5

(Psalms 107–150)

Psalm 107

The LORD is good to his people

1 Shout praises to the LORD!
  He is good to us,
  and his love never fails.

2 Everyone the LORD has rescued
  from trouble should praise him,

3 everyone he has brought
  from the east and the west,
  the north and the south.*

4 Some of you were lost
  in the scorching desert,
  far from a town.

5 You were hungry and thirsty
  and about to give up.

6 You were in serious trouble,
  but you prayed to the LORD,
  and he rescued you.

7 Straight away he brought you
  to a town.

8 You should praise the LORD for his love
  and for the wonderful things
  he does for all of us.

9 To everyone who is thirsty,
  he gives something to drink;

---

*106.30 Phinehas: The grandson of Aaron, who put two people to death and kept the Lord from being angry with the rest of his people (see Numbers 25.1–13).
*106.32 Meribah Spring: See the note at 81.7.

See also: 106.24–26: Num 14.1–35. 106.27: Lev 26.33.
106.28–31: Num 25.1–13. 106.32,33: Num 20.2–13.
106.34–36: Judg 2.1–3; 3.5,6. 106.37: 2 King 17.17.
106.38: Num 35.33. 106.40–46: Judg 2.14–18.

See also: 106.47,48: 1 Chron 16.35,36.
107.1: 1 Chron 16.34; 2 Chron 5.13; 7.3; Ezra 3.11; Psa 100.5;
106.1; 118.1; 136.1; Jer 33.11.

to everyone who is hungry,
he gives good things to eat.

10 Some of you were prisoners
suffering in deepest darkness
and bound by chains,
11 because you had rebelled
against God Most High
and refused his advice.
12 You were worn out
from working like slaves,
and no one came to help.
13 You were in serious trouble,
but you prayed to the LORD,
and he rescued you.
14 He brought you out
of the deepest darkness
and broke your chains.

15 You should praise the LORD
for his love
and for the wonderful things
he does for all of us.
16 He breaks down bronze gates
and shatters iron locks.

17 Some of you had foolishly
committed a lot of sins
and were in terrible pain.
18 The very thought of food
was disgusting to you,
and you were almost dead.
19 You were in serious trouble,
but you prayed to the LORD,
and he rescued you.
20 By the power of his own word,
he healed you and saved you
from destruction.

21 You should praise the LORD
for his love
and for the wonderful things
he does for all of us.
22 You should celebrate
by offering sacrifices
and singing joyful songs
to tell what he has done.

23 Some of you made a living
by sailing the mighty sea,
24 and you saw the miracles
the LORD performed there.
25 At his command a storm arose,
and waves covered the sea.
26 You were tossed to the sky
and to the ocean depths,
until things looked so bad
that you lost your courage.
27 You staggered like drunkards
and gave up all hope.

28 You were in serious trouble,
but you prayed to the LORD,
and he rescued you.
29 He made the storm stop
and the sea be quiet.
30 You were happy because of this,
and he brought you to the port
where you wanted to go.

31 You should praise the LORD
for his love
and for the wonderful things
he does for all of us.
32 Honour the LORD
when you and your leaders
meet to worship.

33 If you start doing wrong,
the LORD will turn rivers into deserts,
34 flowing streams into scorched land,
and fruitful fields into beds of salt.

35 But the LORD can also turn
deserts into lakes
and scorched land
into flowing streams.
36 If you are hungry,
you can settle there
and build a town.
37 You can plant fields
and vineyards that produce
a good harvest.
38 The LORD will bless you
with many children
and with herds of cattle.

39 Sometimes you may be crushed
by troubles and sorrows,
until only a few of you
are left to survive.
40 But the LORD will take revenge
on those who conquer you,
and he will make them wander
across desert sands.
41 When you are suffering and in need,
he will come to your rescue,
and your families will grow
as fast as a herd of sheep.
42 You will see this because
you obey the LORD,
but everyone who is wicked
will be silenced.

43 Be wise! Remember this
and think about the kindness
of the LORD.

Psalm 108

(A song and a psalm by David.)

With God on our side

1 Our God, I am faithful to you
    with all my heart,
    and you can trust me.
  I will sing and play music for you
    with all that I am.
2 I will start playing my harps
    before the sun rises.
3 I will praise you, LORD,
    for everyone to hear;
  I will sing hymns to you
    in every nation.
4 Your love reaches higher
    than the heavens,
  and your loyalty extends
    beyond the clouds.

5 Our God, may you be honoured
    above the heavens;
  may your glory be seen
    everywhere on earth.
6 Answer my prayers
    and use your powerful arm
    to give us victory.
  Then the people you love
    will be safe.

7 Our God, from your holy place
    you made this promise:
  "I will gladly divide up
    the city of Shechem
  and give away Succoth Valley
    piece by piece.
8 The lands of Gilead
    and Manasseh are mine.
  Ephraim is my war helmet,
    and Judah is my symbol
    of royal power.
9 Moab is merely my washbasin,
    and Edom belongs to me.
  I shout with victory
    over the Philistines."

10 Our God, who will bring me
    to the fortress
    or lead me to Edom?
11 Have you rejected us?
    You don't lead our armies.
12 Help us defeat our enemies!
    No one else can rescue us.
13 You are the one
    who gives us victory
    and crushes our enemies.

Psalm 109

(A psalm by David for the music leader.)

A prayer for the LORD's help

1 I praise you, God! Don't keep silent.
2 Destructive and deceitful lies
    are told about me,
3   and hateful things are said
    for no reason.
4 I had pity and prayed*
    for my enemies,
  but their words to me
    were harsh and cruel.
5 For being friendly and kind,
    they paid me back
    with meanness and hatred.

6 My enemies said,
  "Find some worthless fools
    to accuse him of a crime.
7   Try him and find him guilty!
    Consider his prayers a lie.
8 Cut his life short
    and let someone else have his job.
9 Make orphans of his children
    and a widow of his wife;
10   make his children beg for food
    and live in the slums.

11 "Let the people he owes
    take everything he owns.
  Give it all to strangers.
12 Don't let anyone be kind to him
    or have pity on the children
    he leaves behind.
13 Bring an end to his family,
    and from now on let him be
    a forgotten man.

14 "Don't let the LORD forgive
    the sins of his parents
    and his ancestors.
15 Don't let the LORD forget
    the sins of his family,
  or let anyone remember
    his family ever lived.
16 He was so cruel to the poor,
    homeless, and discouraged
    that they died young.

17 "He cursed others.
    Now place a curse on him!
  He never wished others well.
    Wish only trouble for him!
18 He cursed others more often
    than he dressed himself.
  Let his curses strike him deep,

See also: 109.8: Acts 1.20.

573

just as water and olive oil
   soak through to our bones.
19 Let his curses surround him,
   just like the clothes he wears each day."

20 Those are the cruel things
   my enemies wish for me.
   Let it all happen to them!
21 Be true to your name, LORD God!
   Show your great kindness and rescue me.

22 I am poor and helpless,
   and I have lost all hope.
23 I am fading away
   like an evening shadow;
   I am tossed aside like a crawling insect.
24 I have gone without eating,*
   until my knees are weak,
   and my body is bony.
25 When my enemies see me,
   they say cruel things
   and shake their heads.

26 Please help me, LORD God!
   Come and save me
   because of your love.
27 Let others know that you alone
   have saved me.
28 I don't care if they curse me,
   as long as you bless me.
   You will make my enemies fail
   when they attack,
   and you will make me glad
   to be your servant.
29 You will cover them with shame,
   just as their bodies
   are covered with clothes.

30 I will sing your praises
   and thank you, LORD,
   when your people meet.
31 You help everyone in need,
   and you defend them
   when they are on trial.

Psalm 110

(A psalm by David.)

The LORD gives victory

1 The LORD said to my Lord,
   "Sit at my right side,*
   until I make your enemies
   into a footstool for you."

2 The LORD will let your power
   reach out from Zion,
   and you will rule over your enemies.
3 Your glorious power will be seen
   on the day you begin to rule.
   You will wear the sacred robes
   and shine like the morning sun
   in all your strength.
4 The LORD has made a promise
   that will never be broken:
   "You will be a priest for ever,
   just like Melchizedek."

5 My Lord is at your right side,
   and when he gets angry he will crush
   the other kings.
6 He will judge the nations
   and crack their skulls,
   leaving piles of dead bodies
   all over the earth.
7 He will drink from any stream
   that he chooses,
   while winning victory after victory.

Psalm 111

Praise the LORD for all he has done

1 Shout praises to the LORD!
   With all my heart
   I will thank the LORD
   when his people meet.
2 The LORD has done
   many wonderful things!
   Everyone who is pleased
   with God's marvellous deeds
   will keep them in mind.
3 Everything the LORD does
   is glorious and majestic,
   and his power to bring justice
   will never end.

4 The LORD God is famous
   for his wonderful deeds,
   and he is kind and merciful.
5 He gives food to his worshippers
   and always keeps his agreement
   with them.
6 He has shown his mighty power
   to his people
   and has given them the lands
   of other nations.

7 God is always honest and fair,
   and his laws can be trusted.
8   They are true and right
   and will stand for ever.

---

*109.24 without eating: See the note at 35.13.
*110.1 right side: See the note at 16.11.

See also: 109.25: Matt 27.39; Mark 15.29.
110.1: Matt 22.44; Mark 12.36; Luke 20.42,43; Acts 2.34,35;
1 Cor 15.25; Eph 1.20–22; Col 3.1; Heb 1.13; 8.1; 10.12,13.

See also: 110.4: Heb 5.6; 6.20; 7.17,21.

9 God rescued his people,
and he will never break
his agreement with them.
He is fearsome and holy.

10 Respect and obey the LORD!
This is the first step
to wisdom and good sense.*
God will always be respected.

Psalm 112

God blesses his worshippers

1 Shout praises to the LORD!
The LORD blesses everyone
who worships him and gladly
obeys his teachings.

2 Their descendants will have
great power in the land,
because the LORD blesses
all who do right.

3 They will get rich and prosper
and will always be remembered
for their fairness.

4 They will be so kind and merciful and good,
that they will be a light
in the dark for others
who do the right thing.

5 Life will go well for those who freely lend
and are honest in business.

6 They won't ever be troubled,
and the kind things they do
will never be forgotten.

7 Bad news won't bother them;
they have decided to trust the LORD.

8 They are dependable and not afraid,
and they will live to see
their enemies defeated.

9 They will always be remembered
and greatly praised,
because they were kind
and freely gave to the poor.

10 When evil people see this,
they angrily bite their tongues
and disappear.
They will never get what they really want.

Psalm 113

The LORD helps people in need

1 Shout praises to the LORD!
Everyone who serves him,
come and praise his name.

2 Let the name of the LORD
be praised now and for ever.

3 From dawn until sunset
the name of the LORD
deserves to be praised.

4 The LORD is far above all the nations;
he is more glorious than the heavens.

5 No one can compare
with the LORD our God.
His throne is high above,

6 and he looks down to see
the heavens and the earth.

7 God lifts the poor and needy
from dust and ashes,

8 and he lets them take part
in ruling his people.

9 When a wife has no children,
he blesses her with some,
and she is happy.
Shout praises to the LORD!

Psalm 114

The LORD works wonders

1 God brought his people out of Egypt,
that land with a strange language.

2 He made Judah his holy place
and ruled over Israel.

3 When the sea looked at God,
it ran away,
and the River Jordan flowed upstream.

4 The mountains and the hills
skipped around like goats.

5 Ask the sea why it ran away
or ask the Jordan
why it flowed upstream.

6 Ask the mountains and the hills
why they skipped like goats!

7 Earth, you will tremble,
when the Lord God of Jacob
comes near,

8 because he turns solid rock
into flowing streams
and pools of water.

Psalm 115

The LORD deserves to be praised

1 We don't deserve praise!
The LORD alone deserves all the praise,
because of his love and faithfulness.

See also: 111.10: Job 28.28; Prov 1.7; 9.10.
112.9: 2 Cor 9.9.

See also: 114.1: Exod 12.51. 114.3: a Exod 14.21;
b Josh 3.16. 114.8: Exod 17.1–7; Num 20.2–13.

² Why should the nations ask,
   "Where is your God?"

³ Our God is in the heavens,
   doing as he chooses.
⁴ The idols of the nations
   are made of silver and gold.
⁵ They have a mouth and eyes,
   but they can't speak or see.
⁶ Their ears can't hear,
   and their noses can't smell.
⁷ Their hands have no feeling,
   their legs don't move,
   and they can't make a sound.
⁸ Everyone who made the idols
   and all who trust them
   are just as helpless as those useless gods.

⁹ People of Israel, you must trust the LORD
   to help and protect you.
¹⁰ Family of Aaron the priest,
   you must trust the LORD
   to help and protect you.
¹¹ All of you who worship the LORD,
   so you must trust him
   to help and protect you.

¹² The LORD will not forget
   to give us his blessing;
   he will bless all Israel
   and the family of Aaron.
¹³ All who worship the LORD,
   no matter who they are,
   will receive his blessing.

¹⁴ I pray that the LORD
   will let your family
   and your descendants
   always grow strong.
¹⁵ May the LORD who created
   the heavens and the earth
   give you his blessing.

¹⁶ The LORD has kept the heavens
   for himself, but he has given the earth
   to us humans.
¹⁷ The dead are silent
   and cannot praise the LORD,
¹⁸ but we will praise him
   now and for evermore.
   Shout praises to the LORD!

Psalm 116

When the LORD saves you from death

¹ I love you, LORD!
   You answered my prayers.

² You paid attention to me,
   and so I will pray to you
   as long as I live.
³ Death attacked from all sides,
   and I was captured
   by its painful chains.
   But when I was really suffering,
⁴ I prayed and said,
   "LORD, please don't let me die!"

⁵ You are kind, LORD,
   so good and merciful.
⁶ You protect ordinary people,
   and when I was helpless,
   you saved me
⁷ and treated me so kindly
   that I don't need
   to worry any more.

⁸ You, LORD, have saved
   my life from death,
   my eyes from tears,
   my feet from stumbling.
⁹ Now I will walk at your side
   in this land of the living.
¹⁰ I was faithful to you
   when I was suffering,
¹¹ though in my confusion I said,
   "I can't trust anyone!"

¹² What must I give you, LORD,
   for being so good to me?
¹³ I will pour out an offering
   of wine to you,
   and I will pray in your name
   because you have saved me.
¹⁴ I will keep my promise to you
   when your people meet.
¹⁵ You are deeply concerned
   when one of your loyal people
   faces death.

¹⁶ I worship you, LORD,
   just as my mother did,
   and you have rescued me
   from the chains of death.
¹⁷ I will offer you a sacrifice
   to show how grateful I am,
   and I will pray.
¹⁸ I will keep my promise to you
   when your people
¹⁹ gather at your temple in Jerusalem.
   Shout praises to the LORD!

See also: 115.4–8: Psa 135.15–18; Rev 9.20.
115.13: Rev 11.18; 19.5.

See also: 116.10: 2 Cor 4.13.

Psalm 117

Come, praise the LORD

[1] All you nations,
come, praise the LORD!
Let everyone praise him.
[2] His love for us is wonderful;
his faithfulness never ends.
Shout praises to the LORD!

Psalm 118

The LORD is always merciful

[1] Tell the LORD how thankful you are,
because he is kind and always merciful.

[2] Let Israel shout,
"God is always merciful!"
[3] Let the family of Aaron
the priest shout,
"God is always merciful!"
[4] Let every true worshipper
of the LORD shout,
"God is always merciful!"

[5] When I was really suffering,
I prayed to the LORD.
He answered my prayer,
and took my worries away.
[6] The LORD is on my side,
and I am not afraid
of what others can do to me.
[7] With the LORD on my side,
I will defeat all of my hateful enemies.
[8] It is better to trust the LORD
for protection
than to trust anyone else,
[9] including strong leaders.

[10] Nations surrounded me,
but I got rid of them
by the power of the LORD.
[11] They attacked from all sides,
but I got rid of them
by the power of the LORD.
[12] They swarmed around like bees,
but by the power of the LORD,
I got rid of them and their fiery sting.
[13] Their attacks were so fierce
that I nearly fell,
but the LORD helped me.
[14] My power and my strength
come from the LORD,
and he has saved me.

[15] From the tents of God's people
come shouts of victory:
"The LORD is powerful!
[16] With his mighty arm
the LORD wins victories!
The LORD is powerful!"

[17] And so my life is safe,
and I will live to tell
what the LORD has done.
[18] He punished me terribly,
but he did not let death
lay its hands on me.

[19] Open the gates of justice!
I will enter and tell the LORD
how thankful I am.

[20] Here is the gate of the LORD!
Everyone who does right
may enter this gate.

[21] I praise the LORD
for answering my prayers
and saving me.
[22] The stone that the builders
tossed aside has now become
the most important stone.

[23] The LORD has done this,
and it is amazing to us.
[24] This day belongs to the LORD!
Let's celebrate and be glad today.
[25] We'll ask the LORD to save us!
We'll sincerely ask the LORD
to let us win.

[26] God bless the one who comes
in the name of the LORD!
We praise you from here
in the house of the LORD.

[27] The LORD is our God,
and he has given us light!
Start the celebration!
March with palm branches
all the way to the altar.◆

[28] The LORD is my God!
I will praise him and tell him
how thankful I am.

[29] Tell the LORD
how thankful you are,
because he is kind
and always merciful.

See also: 117.1: Rom 15.11.   **118.1:** 1 Chron 16.34;
2 Chron 5.13; 7.3; Ezra 3.11; Psa 100.5; 106.1; 107.1; 136.1;
Jer 33.11.   **118.6:** Heb 13.6.   **118.14:** Exod 15.2; Isa 12.2.

See also: 118.22: Luke 20.17; Acts 4.11; 1 Pet 2.7.
118.22,23: Matt 21.42; Mark 12.10,11.   **118.25:** Matt 21.9;
Mark 11.9; John 12.13.   **118.26:** Matt 21.9; 23.39; Mark 11.9;
Luke 13.35; 19.38; John 12.13.

Psalm 119

In praise of the Law of the LORD

¹ Our LORD, you bless everyone
   who lives right
   and obeys your Law.
² You bless all those
   who follow your commands
   from deep in their hearts
³ and who never do wrong
   or turn from you.
⁴ You have ordered us always
   to obey your teachings;
⁵ I don't ever want to stray
   from your laws.
⁶ Thinking about your commands
   will keep me from doing
   some foolish thing.
⁷ I will do right and praise you
   by learning to respect
   your perfect laws.
⁸ I will obey all of them!
   Don't turn your back on me.

⁹ Young people can live a clean life
   by obeying your word.
¹⁰ I worship you with all my heart.
   Don't let me walk away
   from your commands.
¹¹ I treasure your word above all else;
   it keeps me from sinning against you.
¹² I praise you, LORD!
   Teach me your laws.
¹³ With my own mouth,
   I tell others the laws
   that you have spoken.
¹⁴ Obeying your instructions
   brings as much happiness
   as being rich.
¹⁵ I will study your teachings
   and follow your footsteps.
¹⁶ I will take pleasure in your laws
   and remember your words.

¹⁷ Treat me with kindness, LORD,
   so that I may live
   and do what you say.
¹⁸ Open my mind and let me discover
   the wonders of your Law.
¹⁹ I live here as a stranger.
   Don't keep me from knowing
   your commands.
²⁰ What I want most of all
   and at all times
   is to honour your laws.
²¹ You punish those boastful,
   worthless nobodies who turn
   from your commands.

²² Don't let them sneer and insult me
   for following you.
²³ I keep thinking about
   your teachings, LORD,
   even if rulers plot against me.
²⁴ Your laws are my greatest joy!
   I follow their advice.

²⁵ I am at the point of death.
   Let your teachings
   breathe new life into me.
²⁶ When I told you my troubles,
   you answered my prayers.
   Now teach me your laws.
²⁷ Help me to understand your teachings,
   and I will think about
   your marvellous deeds.
²⁸ I am overcome with sorrow.
   Encourage me,
   as you have promised to do.
²⁹ Keep me from being deceitful,
   and be kind enough
   to teach me your Law.
³⁰ I am determined to be faithful
   and to respect your laws.
³¹ I follow your rules, LORD.
   Don't let me be ashamed.
³² I am eager to learn all
   that you want me to do;
   help me to understand
   more and more.

³³ Point out your rules to me,
   and I won't disobey even one of them.
³⁴ Help me to understand your Law;
   I promise to obey it with all my heart.
³⁵ Direct me by your commands!
   I love to do what you say.
³⁶ Make me want to obey you,
   rather than to be rich.
³⁷ Take away my foolish desires,
   and let me find life
   by walking with you.
³⁸ I am your servant!
   Do for me what you promised
   to those who worship you.
³⁹ Your wonderful teachings
   protect me from the insults
   that I hate so much.
⁴⁰ I long for your teachings.
   Be true to yourself and let me live.

⁴¹ Show me your love
   and save me, LORD,
   as you have promised.
⁴² Then I will have an answer
   for everyone who insults me
   for trusting your word.

43 I rely on your laws!
  Don't take away my chance
    to speak your truth.
44 I will keep obeying your Law
    for ever and ever.
45 I have gained perfect freedom
    by following your teachings,
46 and I trust them so much
    that I tell them to kings.
47 I love your commands!
    They bring me happiness.
48 I love and respect them
    and will keep them in mind.

49 Don't forget your promise
    to me, your servant.
    I depend on it.
50 When I am suffering,
    I find comfort in your promise
    that leads to life.
51 Conceited people sneer at me,
    but I obey your Law.
52 I find true comfort, LORD,
    because your laws have stood
    the test of time.
53 I get furious when evil people
    turn against your Law.
54 No matter where I am,
    your teachings fill me with songs.
55 Even in the night
    I think about you, LORD,
    and I obey your Law.
56 You have blessed me
    because I have always followed
    your teachings.

57 You, LORD, are my choice,
    and I will obey you.
58 With all my heart
    I beg you to be kind to me,
    just as you have promised.
59 I pay careful attention as you lead me,
    and I follow closely.
60 As soon as you command,
    I do what you say.
61 Evil people may set a trap,
    but I obey your Law.
62 Your laws are so fair that I wake up
    and praise you
    in the middle of the night.
63 I choose as my friends
    everyone who worships you
    and follows your teachings.
64 Our LORD, your love is seen
    all over the world.
    Teach me your laws.

65 I am your servant, LORD,
    and you have kept your promise
    to treat me with kindness.
66 Give me wisdom and good sense.
    I trust your commands.
67 Once you corrected me
    for not obeying you,
    but now I obey.
68 You are kindhearted,
    and you do good things,
    so teach me your laws.
69 My reputation is being ruined
    by conceited liars,
    but with all my heart
    I follow your teachings.
70 Those liars have no sense,
    but I find happiness in your Law.
71 When you corrected me,
    it did me good because it taught me
    to study your laws.
72 I would rather obey you
    than have a thousand pieces
    of silver and gold.

73 You created me and put me together.
    Make me wise enough to learn
    what you have commanded.
74 Your worshippers will see me,
    and they will be glad
    that I trust your word.
75 Your decisions are correct,
    and you were right to punish me.
76 I serve you, LORD.
    Comfort me with your love,
    just as you have promised.
77 I love to obey your Law!
    Have mercy and let me live.
78 Put down those proud people
    who hurt me with their lies,
    because I have chosen
    to study your teachings.
79 Let your worshippers come to me,
    so they will learn to obey your rules.
80 Let me truly respect your laws,
    so I won't be ashamed.

81 I long for you to rescue me!
    Your word is my only hope.
82 I am worn out from waiting
    for you to keep your word.
    When will you have mercy?
83 My life is wasting away
    like a dried-up wineskin,*
    but I have not forgotten your teachings.

*119.83 a dried-up wineskin: The Hebrew text has "a
wineskin in the smoke." In ancient times bags were
made from animal skins to hold wine, but when the
bags dried up they cracked and could no longer be used.

84 I am your servant!
How long must I suffer?
When will you punish
those troublemakers?
85 Those proud people reject
your teachings,
and they dig pits for me to fall in.
86 Your laws can be trusted!
Protect me from cruel liars.
87 They have almost killed me,
but I have been faithful
to your teachings.
88 Show that you love me
and let me live,
so that I may obey
all of your commands.

89 Our LORD, you are eternal!
Your word will last as long
as the heavens.*
90 You remain faithful
in every generation,
and the earth you created
will keep standing firm.
91 All things are your servants,
and the laws you made
are still in effect today.
92 If I had not found happiness
in obeying your Law,
I would have died in misery.
93 I won't ever forget your teachings,
because you give me new life
by following them.
94 I belong to you,
and I have respected your laws,
so keep me safe.
95 Brutal enemies are waiting
to ambush and destroy me,
but I obey your rules.
96 Nothing is completely perfect,
except your teachings.

97 I deeply love your Law!
I think about it all day.
98 Your laws never leave my mind,
and they make me much wiser
than my enemies.
99 Thinking about your teachings
gives me better understanding
than my teachers.
100 and obeying your laws
makes me wiser than those
who have lived a long time.
101 I obey your word
instead of following a way
that leads to trouble.
102 You have been my teacher,
and I won't reject your instructions.

103 Your teachings are sweeter
than honey.
104 They give me understanding
and make me hate all lies.

105 Your word is a lamp
that gives light wherever I walk.
106 Your laws are fair,
and I have given my word
to respect them all.
107 I am in terrible pain!
Save me, LORD,
as you said you would.
108 Accept my offerings of praise
and teach me your laws.
109 I never forget your teachings,
although my life is always in danger.
110 Some merciless people
are trying to trap me,
but I never turn my back
on your teachings.
111 They will always be
my most prized possession
and my source of joy.
112 I have made up my mind
to obey your laws for ever,
no matter what.

113 I hate anyone
whose loyalty is divided,
but I love your Law.
114 You are my place of safety
and my shield;
Your word is my only hope.
115 All you worthless people,
get away from me!
I am determined to obey
the commands of my God.
116 Be true to your word, LORD.
Keep me alive and strong;
don't let me be ashamed
because of my hope.
117 Keep me safe and secure,
so that I will always respect your laws.
118 You reject all deceitful liars
because they refuse your teachings.
119 As far as you are concerned,
all evil people are* rubbish,
and so I follow yours.
120 I tremble all over when I think of you
and the way you judge.

121 I did what was fair and right!
Don't hand me over to those
who want to ill-treat me.
122 Take good care of me, your servant,
and don't let me be harmed
by those conceited people.

123 My eyes are weary from waiting
   to see you keep your promise
   to come and save me.
124 Show your love for me, your servant,
   and teach me your laws.
125 I serve you,
   so let me understand your teachings.
126 Do something, LORD!
   They have broken your Law.
127 Your laws mean more to me
   than the finest gold.
128 I follow all your commands,'
   but I hate anyone who leads me astray.

129 Your teachings are wonderful,
   and I respect them all.
130 Understanding your word
   brings light to the minds
   of ordinary people.
131 I honestly want to know
   everything you teach.
132 Think about me and be kind,
   just as you are to everyone
   who loves your name.
133 Keep your promise
   and don't let me stumble
   or let sin control my life.
134 Protect me from abuse,
   so I can obey your laws.
135 Smile on me, your servant,
   and teach me your laws.
136 When anyone disobeys you,
   my eyes overflow with tears.

137 Our LORD, you always do right,
   and your decisions are fair.
138 All your teachings are true
   and trustworthy.
139 It upsets me greatly
   when my enemies neglect
   your teachings.
140 Your word to me, your servant,
   is like pure gold;
   I treasure what you say.
141 Everyone calls me a nobody,
   but I remember your laws.
142 You will always do right,
   and your teachings are true.
143 I am in deep distress,
   but I love your teachings.
144 Your rules are always fair.
   Help me to understand them
   and live.

145 I pray to you, LORD!
   Please answer me.
   I promise to obey your laws.
146 I beg you to save me,
   so I can follow your rules.

147 Even before sunrise,
   I pray for your help,
   and I put my hope
   in what you have said.
148 I lie awake at night,
   thinking of your promises.
149 Show that you love me, LORD,
   and answer my prayer.
   Please do the right thing
   and save my life.
150 People who disobey your Law
   have made evil plans
   and want to hurt me,
151 but you are with me,
   and all your commands can be trusted.
152 From studying your laws,
   I found out long ago
   that you made them to last for ever.

153 I have not forgotten your Law!
   Look at the trouble I am in,
   and rescue me.
154 Be my defender and protector!
   Keep your promise and save my life.
155 Evil people won't obey you,
   and so they have no hope of being saved.
156 You are merciful, LORD!
   Please do the right thing
   and save my life.
157 I have a lot of brutal enemies,
   but still I never turn from your laws.
158 All those unfaithful people
   who refuse to obey you
   are disgusting to me.
159 Remember how I love your laws,
   and show your love for me
   by keeping me safe.
160 All you say can be trusted;
   your teachings are true
   and will last for ever.

161 Rulers are cruel to me for no reason.
   But with all my heart
   I respect your words,
162 because they bring happiness
   like treasures taken in war.
163 I can't stand liars,
   but I love your Law.
164 I praise you seven times a day
   because your laws are fair.
165 You give peace of mind
   to all who love your Law.
   Nothing can make them fall.
166 You are my only hope
   for being saved, LORD,
   and I do all you command.
167 I love and obey your laws
   with all my heart.

168 You know everything I do.
  You know I respect every law
  you have given.

169 Please, LORD, hear my prayer
  and give me the understanding
  that comes from your word.

170 Listen to my concerns
  and keep me safe,
  just as you have promised.

171 If you will teach me your laws,
  I will praise you

172 and sing about your promise,
  because all your teachings
  are what they ought to be.

173 Be ready to protect me
  because I have chosen.
  to obey your laws.

174 I am waiting for you
  to save me, LORD.
  Your Law makes me happy.

175 Keep me alive, so I can praise you,
  and let me find help in your teachings.

176 I am your servant,
  but I have wandered away
  like a lost sheep.
  Please come after me,
  because I have not forgotten
  your teachings.

Psalm 120

(A song for worship.)

A prayer for the LORD's help

1 When I am in trouble, I pray,
2   "Come and save me, LORD,
  from deceitful liars!"

3 What punishment is fitting
  for you deceitful liars?
4   Your reward should be
  sharp and flaming arrows!

5 But I must live as a foreigner
  among the people of Meshech
  and in the tents of Kedar.*

6 I have spent too much time
  living among people who hate peace.

7 I am in favour of peace,
  but when I speak of it,
  all they want is war.

Psalm 121

(A song for worship.)

The LORD will protect his people

1 I look to the hills!
  Where will I find help?

2 It will come from the LORD,
  who created the heavens
  and the earth.

3 The LORD is your protector,
  and he won't go to sleep
  or let you stumble.

4 The protector of Israel doesn't doze
  or ever get drowsy.

5 The LORD is your protector,
  there at your right side
  to shade you from the sun.

6 You won't be harmed
  by the sun during the day
  or by the moon* at night.

7 The LORD will protect you
  and keep you safe from all dangers.

8 The LORD will protect you
  now and always wherever you go.

Psalm 122

(A song by David for worship.)

A song of praise

1 It made me glad to hear them say,
  "Let's go to the house of the LORD!"

2 Jerusalem, we are standing
  inside your gates.

3 Jerusalem, what a strong
  and beautiful city you are!

4 Every tribe of the LORD obeys him
  and comes to you to praise his name.

5 David's royal throne is here
  where justice rules.

6 Jerusalem, we pray
  that you will have peace,
  and that all will go well
  for those who love you.

7 May there be peace
  inside your city walls
  and in your palaces.

---

*120.5 Meshech . . . Kedar: Meshech was a country near the Black Sea, and Kedar was a tribe of the Syrian desert.

*121.6 harmed . . . sun . . . moon: In ancient times people saw the harmful effects of the rays of the sun, and they thought that certain illnesses (especially mental disorders) were also caused by the rays of the moon.

⁸ Because of my friends
and my relatives,
I will pray for peace.
⁹ And because of the house
of the LORD our God,
I will work for your good.

Psalm 123

(A song for worship.)

A prayer for mercy

¹ Our LORD and our God,
I turn my eyes to you,
on your throne in heaven.
² Servants look to their master,
but we will look to you,
until you have mercy on us.

³ Please have mercy, LORD!
We have been insulted
more than we can stand,
⁴ and we can't take more abuse
from those proud, conceited people.

Psalm 124

(A song by David for worship.)

Thanking the LORD for victory

¹ The LORD was on our side!
Let everyone in Israel say:
² "The LORD was on our side!
Otherwise, the enemy attack
³ would have killed us all,
because it was furious.
⁴ We would have been swept away
in a violent flood
⁵ of high and roaring waves."

⁶ Let's praise the LORD!
He protected us from enemies
who were like wild animals,
⁷ and we escaped like birds
from a hunter's torn net.

⁸ The LORD made heaven and earth,
and he is the one who sends us help.

Psalm 125

(A song for worship.)

The LORD's people are safe

¹ Everyone who trusts the LORD
is like Mount Zion
that cannot be shaken
and will stand for ever.

² Just as Jerusalem is protected
by mountains on every side,
the LORD protects his people
by holding them in his arms
now and for ever.

³ He won't let the wicked rule his people
or lead them to do wrong.
⁴ Let's ask the LORD to be kind
to everyone who is good
and completely obeys him.

⁵ When the LORD punishes the wicked,
he will punish everyone else
who lives a crooked life.
Pray for peace in Israel!

Psalm 126

(A song for worship.)

Celebrating the harvest

¹ It seemed like a dream
when the LORD brought us back
to the city of Zion.•
² We celebrated with laughter
and joyful songs.
In foreign nations it was said,
"The LORD has worked miracles
for his people."
³ And so we celebrated
because the LORD had indeed
worked miracles for us.

⁴ Our LORD, we ask you to bless
our people again,
and let us be like streams
in the Southern Desert.
⁵ We cried as we went out
to plant our seeds.
Now let us celebrate
as we bring in the crops.
⁶ We cried on the way to plant our seeds,
but we will celebrate and shout
as we bring in the crops.

Psalm 127

(A song by Solomon for worship.)

Only the LORD can bless a home

¹ Without the help of the LORD
it is useless to build a home
or to guard a city.
² It is useless to get up early
and stay up late
in order to earn a living.
God takes care of his own,
even while they sleep.•

³ Children are a blessing
    and a gift from the LORD.
⁴ Having a lot of children
    to take care of you in your old age
    is like a warrior with a lot of arrows.
⁵ The more you have,
    the better off you will be,
    because they will protect you
    when your enemies attack
    with arguments.

Psalm 128

(A song for worship.)

The LORD rewards his faithful people

¹ The LORD will bless you
    if you respect him
    and obey his laws.
² Your fields will produce,
    and you will be happy
    and all will go well.
³ Your wife will be as fruitful
    as a grapevine,
    and just as an olive tree
    is rich with olives,
    your home will be rich
    with healthy children.
⁴ That is how the LORD will bless
    everyone who respects him.

⁵ I pray that the LORD
    will bless you from Zion
    and let Jerusalem prosper
    as long as you live.
⁶ May you live long enough
    to see your grandchildren.
    Let's pray for peace in Israel!

Psalm 129

(A song for worship.)

A prayer for protection

¹ Since the time I was young,
    enemies have often attacked!
    Let everyone in Israel say:
² "Since the time I was young,
    enemies have often attacked!
    But they have not defeated me,
³ though my back is like a field
    that has just been ploughed."

⁴ The LORD always does right,
    and he has set me free
    from the ropes
    of those cruel people.

⁵ I pray that all who hate the city of Zion
    will be made ashamed
    and forced to turn and run.
⁶ May they be like grass
    on the flat roof of a house,
    grass that dries up as soon as it sprouts.
⁷ Don't let them be like wheat
    gathered in bundles.
⁸ And don't let anyone
    who passes by say to them,
    "The LORD bless you!
    I give you my blessing
    in the name of the LORD."

Psalm 130

(A song for worship.)

Trusting the LORD in times of trouble

¹ From a sea of troubles
    I call out to you, LORD,
² Won't you please listen
    as I beg for mercy?

³ If you kept record of our sins,
    no one could last long.
⁴ But you forgive us,
    and so we will worship you.

⁵ With all my heart,
    I am waiting, LORD, for you!
    I trust your promises.
⁶ I wait for you more eagerly
    than a soldier on guard duty
    waits for the dawn.
    Yes, I wait more eagerly
    than a soldier on guard duty
    waits for the dawn.

⁷ Israel, trust the LORD!
    He is always merciful,
    and he has the power to save you.
⁸ Israel, the LORD will save you
    from all your sins.

Psalm 131

(A song by David for worship.)

Trust the LORD!

¹ I am not conceited, LORD,
    and I don't waste my time
    on impossible schemes.
² But I have learnt to feel safe
    and satisfied,

See also: **130.8:** Matt 1.21; Titus 2.14.

just like a young child
on its mother's lap.

³ People of Israel,
you must trust the LORD
now and for ever.

Psalm 132

(A song for worship.)

The LORD is always with his people

¹ Our LORD, don't forget David
and how he suffered.
² Mighty God of Jacob,
remember how he promised:
³ "I won't go home or crawl into bed
⁴ or close my eyelids,
⁵ until I find a home for you,
the mighty LORD God of Jacob."

⁶ When we were in Ephrath,
we heard that the sacred chest
was somewhere near Jaar.
⁷ Then we said, "Let's go
to the throne of the LORD
and worship at his feet."

⁸ Come to your new home, LORD,
you and the sacred chest
with all its power.
⁹ Let victory be like robes for the priests;
let your faithful people
celebrate and shout.
¹⁰ David is your chosen one,
so don't reject him.
¹¹ You made a solemn promise
to David, when you said,
"I, the LORD, promise
that someone in your family
will always be king.
¹² If they keep our agreement
and follow my teachings,
then someone in your family
will rule for ever."

¹³ You have gladly chosen Zion
as your home, our LORD.
¹⁴ You said, "This is my home!
I will live here for ever.
¹⁵ I will bless Zion with food,
and even the poor will eat
until they are full.
¹⁶ Victory will be like robes for the priests,
and its faithful people
will celebrate and shout.

¹⁷ I will give mighty power
to the kingdom of David.
Each one of my chosen kings
will shine like a lamp
¹⁸ and wear a sparkling crown.
But I will disgrace their enemies."

Psalm 133

(A song for worship.)

Living together in peace

¹ It is truly wonderful
when relatives live together in peace.
² It is as beautiful as olive oil
poured on Aaron's head*
and running down his beard
and the collar of his robe.
³ It is like the dew from Mount Hermon,
falling on Zion's mountains,
where the LORD has promised
to bless his people
with life for evermore.

Psalm 134

(A song for worship.)

Praising the LORD at night

¹ Everyone who serves the LORD,
come and offer praises.
Everyone who has gathered
in his temple tonight,
² lift your hands in prayer
towards his holy place
and praise the LORD.

³ The LORD is the Creator
of heaven and earth,
and I pray that the LORD
will bless you from Zion.

Psalm 135

In praise of the LORD's kindness

¹ Shout praises to the LORD!
You are his servants,
so praise his name.
² All who serve in the temple
of the LORD our God,
³ come and shout praises.
Praise the name of the LORD!
He is kind and good.

See also: **132.6–10:** 2 Chron 6.41,42.
132.11: 2 Sam 7.12–16; 1 Chron 17.11–14; Psa 89.3,4;
Acts 2.30.

*133.2 head: Olive oil was poured on Aaron's head to
show that God had chosen him to be the high priest.
See also: **132.17:** 1 King 11.36.

⁴ He chose the family of Jacob
  and the people of Israel
  for his very own.

⁵ The LORD is much greater
  than any other god.
⁶ He does as he chooses
  in heaven and on earth
  and deep in the sea.
⁷ The LORD makes the clouds rise
  from far across the earth,
  and he makes lightning
  to go with the rain.
  Then from his secret place
  he sends out the wind.
⁸ The LORD killed the firstborn
  of people and animals
  in the land of Egypt.
⁹ God used miracles and wonders
  to fight the king of Egypt
  and all his officials.
¹⁰ He destroyed many nations
  and killed powerful kings,
¹¹ including King Sihon of the Amorites
  and King Og of Bashan.
  He conquered every kingdom
  in the land of Canaan
¹² and gave their property
  to his people Israel.

¹³ The name of the LORD
  will be remembered for ever,
  and he will be famous
  for all time to come.
¹⁴ The LORD will bring justice
  and show mercy
  to all who serve him.

¹⁵ Idols of silver and gold are made
  and worshipped in other nations.
¹⁶ They have a mouth and eyes,
  but they can't speak or see.
¹⁷ They are completely deaf,
  and they can't breathe.
¹⁸ Everyone who makes idols
  and all who trust them
  will end up as helpless as their idols.

¹⁹ Everyone in Israel,
  come, praise the LORD!
  All the family of Aaron
²⁰ and all the tribe of Levi,*
  come, praise the LORD!

All of his worshippers,
  come, praise the LORD.
²¹ Praise the LORD from Zion!
  He lives here in Jerusalem.
  Shout praises to the LORD!

Psalm 136

God's love never fails

¹ Praise the LORD! He is good.
  God's love never fails.
² Praise the God of all gods.
  God's love never fails.
³ Praise the Lord of lords.
  God's love never fails.

⁴ Only God works great miracles.*
  God's love never fails.
⁵ With wisdom he made the sky.
  God's love never fails.
⁶ The Lord stretched the earth over the ocean.
  God's love never fails.
⁷ He made the bright lights in the sky.
  God's love never fails.
⁸ He lets the sun rule each day.
  God's love never fails.
⁹ He lets the moon and the stars
  rule each night.
  God's love never fails.

¹⁰ God struck down the firstborn
  in every Egyptian family.
  God's love never fails.
¹¹ He rescued Israel from Egypt.
  God's love never fails.
¹² God used his great strength
  and his powerful arm.
  God's love never fails.
¹³ He split the Red Sea* apart.
  God's love never fails.

¹⁴ The Lord brought Israel safely
  through the sea.
  God's love never fails.
¹⁵ He destroyed the Egyptian king
  and his army there.
  God's love never fails.
¹⁶ The Lord led his people
  through the desert.
  God's love never fails.

¹⁷ Our God defeated mighty kings.
  God's love never fails.

---

*135.19,20 Aaron . . . Levi: Aaron was from the tribe of Levi, and all priests were from his family. The temple helpers, singers, and musicians were also from the tribe of Levi.
See also: 135.15–18: Psa 115.4–8; Rev 9.20.

*136.13 Red Sea: See the note at 106.7.
See also: 136.1: 1 Chron 16.34; 2 Chron 5.13; 7.3; Ezra 3.11; Psa 100.5; 106.1; 107.1; 118.1; Jer 33.11. 136.5: Gen 1.1. 136.6: Gen 1.2. 136.7–9: Gen 1.16. 136.10: Exod 12.29. 136.11: Exod 12.51. 136.13–15: Exod 14.21–29.

¹⁸ And he killed famous kings.
    God's love never fails.
¹⁹ One of them was Sihon,
    king of the Amorites.
    God's love never fails.
²⁰ Another was King Og of Bashan.
    God's love never fails.
²¹ God took away their land.
    God's love never fails.
²² He gave their land to Israel,
    the people who serve him.
    God's love never fails.

²³ God saw the trouble we were in.
    God's love never fails.
²⁴ He rescued us from our enemies.
    God's love never fails.
²⁵ He gives food to all who live.
    God's love never fails.

²⁶ Praise God in heaven!
    God's love never fails.

Psalm 137

A prayer for revenge

¹ Beside the rivers of Babylon
    we thought about Jerusalem,
    and we sat down and cried.
² We hung our small harps
    on the willow⋅ trees.
³ Our enemies had brought us here
    as their prisoners,
    and now they wanted us to sing
    and entertain them.
    They insulted us and shouted,
    "Sing about Zion!"

⁴ Here in a foreign land,
    how can we sing about the LORD?
⁵ Jerusalem, if I forget you,
    let my right hand go limp.
⁶ Let my tongue stick
    to the roof of my mouth,
    if I don't think about you
    above all else.

⁷ Our LORD, punish the Edomites!
    Because the day Jerusalem fell,
    they shouted,
    "Completely destroy the city!
    Tear down every building!"

⁸ Babylon, you are doomed!
    I pray the Lord's blessings
    on anyone who punishes you
    for what you did to us.

⁹ May the Lord bless everyone
    who beats your children
    against the rocks!

Psalm 138

(By David.)

Praise the LORD with all your heart

¹ With all my heart I praise you, LORD.
    In the presence of angels⋅
    I sing your praises.
² I worship at your holy temple
    and praise you for your love
    and your faithfulness.
    You were true to your word
    and made yourself more famous
    than ever before.⋅
³ When I asked for your help,
    you answered my prayer
    and gave me courage.⋅

⁴ All kings on this earth
    have heard your promises, LORD,
    and they will praise you.
⁵ You are so famous
    that they will sing
    about the things you have done.
⁶ Though you are above us all,
    you care for humble people,
    and you keep a close watch
    on everyone who is proud.

⁷ I am surrounded by trouble,
    but you protect me
    against my angry enemies.
    With your own powerful arm
    you keep me safe.

⁸ You, LORD, will always
    treat me with kindness.
    Your love never fails.
    You have made us what we are.
    Don't give up on us now!⋅

Psalm 139

(A psalm by David for the music leader.)

The LORD is always near

¹ You have looked deep
    into my heart, LORD,
    and you know all about me.
² You know when I am resting
    or when I am working,
    and from heaven
    you discover my thoughts.

See also: 136.19: Num 21.21-30.   **136.20:** Num 21.31-35.
137.8: Rev 18.6.

³ You notice everything I do
  and everywhere I go.
⁴ Before I even speak a word,
  you know what I will say,
⁵ and with your powerful arm
  you protect me from every side.
⁶ I can't understand all this!
  Such wonderful knowledge
  is far above me.

⁷ Where could I go to escape
  from your Spirit
  or from your sight?
⁸ If I were to climb up
  to the highest heavens,
  you would be there.
  If I were to dig down
  to the world of the dead
  you would also be there.

⁹ Suppose I had wings
  like the dawning day
  and flew across the ocean.
¹⁰ Even then your powerful arm
  would guide and protect me.
¹¹ Or suppose I said, "I'll hide
  in the dark until night comes
  to cover me over."
¹² But you see in the dark
  because daylight and dark
  are all the same to you.

¹³ You are the one who put me together
  inside my mother's body,
¹⁴ and I praise you
  because of the wonderful way
  you created me.
  Everything you do is marvellous!
  Of this I have no doubt.

¹⁵ Nothing about me
  is hidden from you!
  I was secretly woven together
  deep in the earth below,
¹⁶ but with your own eyes
  you saw my body being formed.
  Even before I was born,
  you had written in your book
  everything I would do.

¹⁷ Your thoughts are far beyond
  my understanding,
  much more than
  I could ever imagine.
¹⁸ I try to count your thoughts,
  but they outnumber the grains
  of sand on the beach.
  And when I awake,
  I will find you nearby.

¹⁹ How I wish that you would kill
  all cruel and heartless people
  and protect me from them!
²⁰ They are always rebelling
  and speaking evil of you.⁕
²¹ You know I hate anyone
  who hates you, LORD,
  and refuses to obey.
²² They are my enemies too,
  and I truly hate them.

²³ Look deep into my heart, God,
  and find out everything
  I am thinking.
²⁴ Don't let me follow evil ways,
  but lead me in the way
  that time has proved true.

Psalm 140

(A psalm by David for the music leader.)

A prayer for the LORD's help

¹ Rescue me from cruel
  and violent enemies, LORD!
² They think up evil plans
  and always cause trouble.
³ Their words bite deep
  like the poisonous fangs of a snake.

⁴ Protect me, LORD, from cruel
  and brutal enemies,
  who want to destroy me.
⁵ Those proud people have hidden
  traps and nets to catch me as I walk.

⁶ You, LORD, are my God!
  Please listen to my prayer.
⁷ You have the power to save me,
  and you keep me safe in every battle.

⁸ Don't let the wicked succeed
  in doing what they want,
  or else they might never
  stop planning evil.
⁹ They have me surrounded,
  but make them the victims
  of their own vicious lies.⁕
¹⁰ Tip flaming coals on them
  and throw them into pits
  where they can't climb out.
¹¹ Chase those cruel liars away!
  Let trouble hunt them down.

¹² Our LORD, I know that you
  defend the homeless
  and see that the poor
  are given justice.

See also: 140.3: Rom 3.13.

588

¹³ Your people will praise you
     and will live with you
     because they do right.

Psalm 141

(A psalm by David.)

A prayer for the LORD's protection

¹ I pray to you, LORD!
   Please listen when I pray
   and hurry to help me.
² Think of my prayer
   as sweet-smelling incense,
   and think of my lifted hands
   as an evening sacrifice.

³ Help me to guard my words
   whenever I say something.
⁴ Don't let me want to do evil
   or waste my time doing wrong
   with wicked people.
   Don't let me even taste
   the good things they offer.

⁵ Let your faithful people
   correct and punish me.
   My prayers condemn the deeds
   of those who do wrong,
   so don't let me be friends
   with any of them.
⁶ Everyone will admit that I was right
   when their rulers are thrown
   down a rocky cliff,
⁷ and their bones lie scattered
   like broken rocks on top of a grave.ʼ

⁸ You are my LORD and God,
   and I look to you for safety.
   Don't let me be harmed.
⁹ Protect me from the traps
   of those violent people,
¹⁰ and make them fall
   into their own traps
   while you help me escape.

Psalm 142

*(A special psalm and a prayer by David
when he was in the cave.)*

A prayer for help

¹ I pray to you, LORD. I beg for mercy.
² I tell you all my worries and my troubles,
³   and whenever I feel low,
     you are there to guide me.

A trap has been hidden
   along my pathway.
⁴ Even if you look,
   you won't see anyone
   who cares enough to walk beside me.
There is no place to hide,
   and no one who really cares.

⁵ I pray to you, LORD!
   You are my place of safety,
   and you are my choice
   in the land of the living.
   Please answer my prayer.
   I am completely helpless.

⁶ Help! They are chasing me,
   and they are too strong.
⁷   Rescue me from this prison,
     so I can praise your name.
And when your people notice
   your wonderful kindness to me,
   they will rush to my side.

Psalm 143

(A psalm by David.)

A prayer in time of danger

¹ Listen, LORD, as I pray!
   You are faithful and honest
   and will answer my prayer.
² I am your servant.
   Don't try me in your court,
   because no one is innocent
   by your standards.
³ My enemies are chasing me,
   crushing me in the ground.
   I am in total darkness,
   like someone long dead.
⁴ I have given up all hope,
   and I feel numb all over.

⁵ I remember to think about
   the many things you did
   in years gone by.
⁶ Then I lift my hands in prayer,
   because my soul is a desert,
   thirsty for water from you.

⁷ Please hurry, LORD,
   and answer my prayer.
I feel hopeless.
   Don't turn away
   and leave me here to die.
⁸ Each morning let me learn
   more about your love
   because I trust you.

See also: 141.2: Rev 5.8. **142 Title:** 1 Sam 22.1; 24.3.   **See also:** 143.2: Rom 3.20; Gal 2.16.

I come to you in prayer,
asking for your guidance.
⁹ Please rescue me from my enemies, LORD!
I come to you for safety.'
¹⁰ You are my God. Show me
what you want me to do,
and let your gentle Spirit
lead me in the right path.
¹¹ Be true to your name, LORD,
and keep my life safe.
Use your saving power
to protect me from trouble.
¹² I am your servant.
Show how much you love me
by destroying my enemies.

Psalm 144

(By David.)

A prayer for the nation

¹ I praise you, LORD!
You are my mighty rock,*
and you teach me
how to fight my battles.
² You are my friend,
and you are my fortress where I am safe.
You are my shield,
and you made me the ruler
of our people.'
³ Why do we humans mean anything
to you, our LORD?
Why do you care about us?
⁴ We disappear like a breath;
we last no longer than a faint shadow.
⁵ Open the heavens like a curtain
and come down, LORD.
Touch the mountains
and make them send up smoke.
⁶ Use your lightning as arrows
to scatter my enemies
and make them run away.
⁷ Reach down from heaven and set me free.
Save me from the mighty flood
⁸ of those lying foreigners
who can't tell the truth.
⁹ In praise of you, our God,
I will sing a new song,
while playing my harp.
¹⁰ By your power, kings win wars,
and your servant David is saved
from deadly swords.

¹¹ Won't you keep me safe
from those lying foreigners
who can't tell the truth?
¹² Let's pray that our young sons
will grow like strong plants
and that our daughters
will be as lovely as columns
in the corner of a palace.
¹³ May our barns be filled
with all kinds of crops.
May our fields be covered
with sheep by the thousands,
¹⁴   and every cow have calves.'
Don't let our city be captured
or any of us be taken away,
and don't let cries of sorrow
be heard in our streets.
¹⁵ Our LORD and our God,
you give these blessings
to all who worship you.

Psalm 145

(By David for praise.)

The LORD is kind and merciful

¹ I will praise you, my God and King,
and always honour your name.
² I will praise you each day
and always honour your name.
³ You are wonderful, LORD,
and you deserve all praise,
because you are much greater
than anyone can understand.
⁴ Each generation will announce
to the next your wonderful
and powerful deeds.
⁵ I will keep thinking about
your marvellous glory
and your mighty miracles.'
⁶ Everyone will talk about
your fearsome deeds,
and I will tell all nations
how great you are.
⁷ They will celebrate and sing
about your matchless mercy
and your power to save.
⁸ You are merciful, LORD!
You are kind and patient
and always loving.
⁹ You are good to everyone,
and you take care of all your creation.
¹⁰ All creation will thank you,
and your loyal people
will praise you.

---

*144.1 mighty rock: See the note at 18.2.
See also: 144.3: Job 7.17,18; Psa 8.4.

11 They will tell about
your marvellous kingdom
and your power.
12 Then everyone will know about
the mighty things you do
and your glorious kingdom.
13 Your kingdom will never end,
and you will rule for ever.

Our Lord, you keep your word
and do everything you say.[*]
14 When someone stumbles or falls,
you give a helping hand.
15 Everyone depends on you,
and when the time is right,
you provide them with food.
16 By your own hand you satisfy
the desires of all who live.

17 Our Lord, everything you do
is kind and thoughtful,
18 and you are near to everyone
whose prayers are sincere.
19 You satisfy the desires
of all your worshippers,
and you come to save them
when they ask for help.
20 You take care of everyone
who loves you,
but you destroy the wicked.

21 I will praise you, Lord,
and everyone will respect
your holy name for ever.

Psalm 146

Shout praises to the Lord

1 Shout praises to the Lord!
With all that I am,
I will shout his praises.
2 I will sing and praise
the Lord God for as long as I live.

3 You can't depend on anyone,
not even a great leader.
4 Once they die and are buried,
that will be the end of all their plans.

5 The Lord God of Jacob blesses
everyone who trusts him
and depends on him.
6 God made heaven and earth;
he created the sea and everything else.
God always keeps his word.
7 He gives justice to the poor
and food to the hungry.

The Lord sets prisoners free
8 and heals blind eyes.
He gives a helping hand
to everyone who falls.
The Lord loves good people
9 and looks after strangers.
He defends the rights
of orphans and widows,
but destroys the wicked.

10 The Lord God of Zion
will rule for ever!
Shout praises to the Lord!

Psalm 147

Sing and praise the Lord

1 Shout praises to the Lord!
Our God is kind,
and it is right and good
to sing praises to him.
2 The Lord rebuilds Jerusalem
and brings the people of Israel
back home again.
3 He renews our hopes
and heals our bodies.
4 He decided how many stars
there would be in the sky
and gave each one a name.
5 Our Lord is great and powerful!
He understands everything.
6 The Lord helps the poor,
but he pulls the wicked to the ground.

7 Celebrate and sing!
Play your harps to the Lord our God.
8 He fills the sky with clouds
and sends rain to the earth,
so that the hills will be green with grass.
9 He provides food for cattle
and for the young ravens,
when they cry out.
10 The Lord doesn't care about
the strength of horses
or powerful armies.
11 The Lord is pleased only
with those who worship him
and trust his love.

12 Everyone in Jerusalem,
come and praise the Lord your God!
13 He makes your city gates strong
and blesses your people
by giving them children.
14 God lets you live in peace,
and he gives you the very best wheat.

15 As soon as God speaks,
the earth obeys.

See also: 146.6: Acts 4.24; 14.15.

591

¹⁶ He covers the ground with snow
  like a blanket of wool,
  and he scatters frost
  like ashes on the ground.
¹⁷ God sends down hailstones
  like chips of rocks.
  Who can stand the cold?
¹⁸ At his command the ice melts,
  the wind blows,
  and streams begin to flow.

¹⁹ God gave his laws and teachings
  to the descendants of Jacob,
  the nation of Israel.
²⁰ But he has not given his laws
  to any other nation.
  Shout praises to the LORD!

Psalm 148

Come, praise the LORD

¹ Shout praises to the LORD!
  Shout the LORD's praises
  in the highest heavens.
² All you angels,
  and all who serve him above,
  come and offer praise.

³ Sun and moon,
  and all you bright stars,
  come and offer praise.
⁴ Highest heavens, and the water
  above the highest heavens,*
  come and offer praise.

⁵ Let all things praise the name of the LORD,
  because they were created
  at his command.
⁶ He made them to last for ever,
  and nothing can change
  what he has done.*

⁷ All creatures on earth,
  you obey his commands,
  so come, praise the LORD!

⁸ Sea monsters and the deep sea,
  fire and hail,
  snow and frost,
  and every stormy wind,
  come, praise the LORD!

⁹ All mountains and hills,
  fruit trees and cedars,
¹⁰ every wild and tame animal,
  all reptiles and birds,
  come, praise the LORD!

¹¹ Every king and every ruler,
  all nations on earth,
¹² every man and every woman,
  young people and old,
  come, praise the LORD!

¹³ All creation, come and praise
  the name of the LORD.
  Praise his name alone.
  The glory of God is greater
  than heaven and earth.

¹⁴ Like a bull with mighty horns,
  the LORD protects his faithful nation Israel,
  because they belong to him.
  Shout praises to the LORD!

Psalm 149

A new song of praise

¹ Shout praises to the LORD!
  Sing him a new song of praise
  when his loyal people meet.
² People of Israel, rejoice
  because of your Creator.
  People of Zion, celebrate
  because of your King.
³ Praise his name by dancing
  and playing music on harps
  and tambourines.
⁴ The LORD is pleased
  with his people,
  and he gives victory
  to those who are humble.
⁵ All you faithful people,
  praise our glorious LORD!
  Celebrate and worship.
⁶ Praise God with songs on your lips
  and a sword in your hand.
⁷ Take revenge and punish the nations.
⁸ Put chains of iron
  on their kings and rulers.
⁹ Punish them as they deserve;
  this is the privilege
  of God's faithful people.
  Shout praises to the LORD!

Psalm 150

The LORD is good to his people

¹ Shout praises to the LORD!
  Praise God in his temple.
  Praise him in heaven,
  his mighty fortress.
² Praise our God!
  His deeds are wonderful,
  too marvellous to describe.

---

*148.4 the water . . . heavens: It was believed that
the earth and the heavens were surrounded by water.

3 Praise God with trumpets
    and all kinds of harps.
4 Praise him with tambourines
    and dancing,
    with stringed instruments
    and woodwinds.
5 Praise God with cymbals,
    with clashing cymbals.
6 Let every living creature
    praise the LORD.
    Shout praises to the LORD!

Additional notes

›2.1 **Why . . . plot?:** Or "Why are the nations restless?"

›2.1 **make useless plans:** Or "grumble uselessly".

›2.11,12 **Serve . . . you:** One possible meaning for the difficult Hebrew text of verses 11,12.

›4.2 **me:** Or "my God".

›4.3 **has chosen . . . very own:** Some Hebrew manuscripts have "work miracles for his faithful people".

›5.1 **when I groan:** Or "to my thoughts" or "to my words".

›5.3 **requests:** Or "sacrifices".

›7.4 **had pity on an enemy:** Or "failed to have pity on an enemy".

›7.7 **sit . . . throne:** Or "return to your place".

›8.1 **You . . . seen:** Or "I will worship your glory".

›8.5 **you yourself:** Or "the angels" or "the beings in heaven".

›11.6 **fiery coals:** Or "trouble, fire".

›12.8 **while . . . deeds:** One possible meaning for the difficult Hebrew text.

›16.3 **Your people . . . happy:** Or "I was happy worshipping gods I thought were powerful."

›16.4 **but . . . sorrow:** One possible meaning for the difficult Hebrew text.

›17.14 **last:** One possible meaning for the difficult Hebrew text of verse 14.

›20.9 **victory . . . prayers:** Or "victory. He (God or the king) answers us."

›22.16 **tearing at:** One possible meaning for the difficult Hebrew text.

›24.6 **worship . . . Jacob:** Two ancient translations; Hebrew "worship God and serve the descendants of Jacob".

›26.3 **I am . . . to you:** Or "I trust your faithfulness."

›29.1 **angels:** Or "supernatural beings" or "gods".

›29.2 **most . . . glorious:** Or "in his holy place" or "and wear your glorious clothes".

›29.9 **makes . . . time:** Or "twists the oak trees around".

›32.6 **whenever . . . sinned:** Hebrew "at a time of finding only".

›35.13 **I . . . them:** Or "My prayer wasn't answered, but I prayed".

›35.16 **Worthless . . . fun:** One possible meaning for the difficult Hebrew text.

›37.35 **like . . . soil:** One possible meaning for the difficult Hebrew text.

›39.2 **but . . . good:** One possible meaning for the difficult Hebrew text.

›42.4 **leading . . . house:** One possible meaning for the difficult Hebrew text.

›44.4 **and . . . victory:** One ancient translation; Hebrew "please give victory".

›45.6 **You . . . king:** Or "God has made you king, and you will rule for ever."

›45.13 **has inward beauty:** Or "is dressed in her room".

›46.9 **shields:** Or "chariots".

›48.14 **always:** One possible meaning for the difficult Hebrew text.

›49.11 **The grave:** Some ancient translations; Hebrew "Their inward thoughts".

›49.14 **as their . . . grave:** One possible meaning for the difficult Hebrew text.

›50.23 **Obey me:** One possible meaning for the difficult Hebrew text.

›**Psalm 53 Mahalath:** Or "For flutes", one possible meaning for the difficult Hebrew text.

›**Psalm 56 A Silent . . . Distance:** One possible meaning for the difficult Hebrew text.

›56.7 **They . . . away:** One possible meaning for the difficult Hebrew text.

›**Psalm 57 Don't Destroy:** One possible meaning for the difficult Hebrew text.

›**Psalm 58 Don't Destroy:** See the note at Psalm 57.

›58.1 **mighty people:** Or "mighty rulers" or "mighty gods".

›58.1 **Do . . . justice:** One possible meaning for the difficult Hebrew text.

›58.9 **Wipe . . . fire:** One possible meaning for the difficult Hebrew text..

›**Psalm 59 Don't Destroy:** See the note at Psalm 57.

›60.4 **so . . . arrows:** Some ancient translations and one possible meaning for the difficult Hebrew text.

›62.1 **calmly wait for:** Or "am at peace with".

›64.5 **us:** One ancient translation; Hebrew "them".

›64.6 **thoughts:** One possible meaning for the difficult Hebrew text of verse 6.

›64.8 **tremble with fear:** Or "turn and run".

›65.1 **deserve:** One possible meaning for the difficult Hebrew text.

›68.6 **and let them prosper:** Or "and give them a song".

›68.17 **to your people:** Or "in all your holiness" or "in your holy place".

›68.21 **are ready for war:** The Hebrew text has "have long hair", which probably refers to the ancient custom of wearing long hair on special occasions, such as a "holy war".

›68.28,29 **Our God . . . Jerusalem:** One possible meaning for the difficult Hebrew text of verses 28,29.

›68.30 **war:** One possible meaning for the difficult Hebrew text of verse 30.

ᵗ**68.31 presents:** One possible meaning for the difficult Hebrew text of verse 31.

ᵘ**71.6 I . . . you:** One possible meaning for the difficult Hebrew text.

ᵛ**72.5 Let the king live:** One ancient translation; Hebrew "Let them worship you".

ᵂ**73.1 to Israel:** Or "to those who do right".

ˣ**73.4 . . . suffer:** Or "They die a painless death".

ʸ**73.10 gives:** One possible meaning for the difficult Hebrew text of verse 10.

ᶻ**73.24 in glory:** Or "with honour".

ᵃ**74.5 pieces:** One meaning for the difficult Hebrew text of verse 5.

ᵇ**74.17 gave . . . earth:** Or "made boundaries for the earth".

ᶜ**Psalm 75 Don't Destroy:** See the note at Psalm 57.

ᵈ**76.4 the eternal mountains:** One ancient translation; Hebrew "the mountains of victims (of wild animals)".

ᵉ**76.10 furious:** One possible meaning for the difficult Hebrew text of verse 10.

ᶠ**77.6 my mind . . . questions:** One ancient translation; Hebrew "I remember my music".

ᵍ**78.47 floods:** Or "frost".

ʰ**81.16 the best honey:** The Hebrew text has "honey from rocks", referring to honey taken from beehives in holes or cracks in large rocks.

ⁱ**83.7 Phoenicia:** The Hebrew text has "Tyre", the main city in Phoenicia.

ʲ**84.6 Dry Valley:** Or "Balsam Tree Valley". The exact location is not known.

ᵏ**84.6 and . . . water:** One possible meaning for the difficult Hebrew text.

ˡ**87.4 Egypt:** The Hebrew text has "Rahab", the name of a monster that stands for Egypt (see Isaiah 30.7).

ᵐ**Psalm 88 To . . . Leannoth:** Or "For the flutes", one possible meaning for the difficult Hebrew text.

ⁿ**88.15 and made me helpless:** One possible meaning for the difficult Hebrew text.

ᵒ**89.12 and everything else:** The Hebrew text has "Zaphon and Yamin", which may either be the names of mountains or refer to the directions "north and south", with the meaning "everything from north to south".

ᵖ**89.44 You took . . . crown:** One possible meaning for the difficult Hebrew text.

ᵠ**89.47 Remember . . . short:** One possible meaning for the difficult Hebrew text.

ʳ**91.4 city wall:** One possible meaning for a difficult Hebrew word; it may possibly mean some kind of shield or weapon.

ˢ**99.4 You . . . King:** One possible meaning for the difficult Hebrew text.

ᵗ**103.5 Each . . . live:** One possible meaning for the difficult Hebrew text.

ᵘ**106.28 the dead:** Or "lifeless idols".

ᵛ**107.3 south:** The Hebrew text has "sea", probably referring to the Mediterranean Sea.

ᵂ**109.4 and prayed:** One possible meaning for the difficult Hebrew text.

ˣ**110.3 You will . . . strength:** One possible meaning for the difficult Hebrew text.

ʸ**110.7 while . . . victory:** Or "God will give him victory after victory."

ᶻ**111.10 This . . . sense:** Or "This is what wisdom and good sense are all about."

ᵃ**118.27 Start . . . altar:** One possible meaning for the difficult Hebrew text.

ᵇ**119.89 Our . . . heavens:** Or "Our LORD, your word is eternal. It will last as long as the heavens."

ᶜ**119.119 As far as . . . are:** A few Hebrew manuscripts and ancient translations. Most Hebrew manuscripts have "You get rid of evil people as if they were".

ᵈ**119.128 I . . . commands:** One possible meaning for the difficult Hebrew text.

ᵉ**126.1 brought . . . Zion:** Or "made the city of Zion prosperous again."

ᶠ**127.2 God . . . sleep:** One possible meaning for the difficult Hebrew text.

ᵍ**136.4 great miracles:** One Hebrew manuscript and one ancient translation have "miracles".

ʰ**137.2 willow:** Or "poplar".

ⁱ**138.1 angels:** Or "gods" or "supernatural beings" who worship and serve God in heaven or "rulers" or "leaders".

ʲ**138.2 You were . . . before:** One possible meaning for the difficult Hebrew text.

ᵏ**138.3 and gave me courage:** One possible meaning for the difficult Hebrew text.

ˡ**138.8 You have . . . now:** Or "Please don't desert your people."

ᵐ**139.20 you:** One possible meaning for the difficult Hebrew text of verse 20.

ⁿ**140.8,9 or else . . . lies:** One possible meaning for the difficult Hebrew text.

ᵒ**141.5–7 Let . . . grave:** One possible meaning for the difficult Hebrew text of verses 5–7.

ᵖ**143.9 I . . . safety:** Or "You are my hiding place."

ᵠ**144.2 of our people:** Some Hebrew manuscripts and ancient translations have "of the nations".

ʳ**144.14 have calves:** Or "grow fat".

ˢ**145.5 and . . . miracles:** One Hebrew manuscript and two ancient translations have "as others tell about your mighty miracles".

ᵗ**145.13 Our . . . say:** These words are found in one Hebrew manuscript and two ancient translations.

ᵘ**148.6 nothing . . . done:** Or "his laws will never change".

6 All wisdom comes from the LORD,
   and so do common sense
   and understanding.
7 God gives helpful advice'
   to everyone who obeys him
   and protects all those
   who live as they should.
8 God sees that justice is done,
   and he watches over everyone
   who is faithful to him.
9 With wisdom you will learn
   what is right
   and honest and fair.

10 Wisdom will control your mind,
   and you will be pleased
   with knowledge.
11 Sound judgment and good sense
   will watch over you.
12 Wisdom will protect you
   from evil schemes
   and from those liars
13 who turned from doing good
   to live in the darkness.
14 Most of all they enjoy
   being mean and deceitful.
15 They are dishonest themselves,
   and all they do is crooked.

Wisdom and sexual purity

16 Wisdom will protect you
   from the smooth talk
   of a sinful woman,
17 who breaks her wedding vows
   and leaves the man she married
   when she was young.
18 The road to her house leads down
   to the dark world of the dead.
19 Visit her, and you will never
   find the road to life again.

20 Follow the example of good people
   and live an honest life.
21 If you are honest and innocent,
   you will keep your land;
22 if you do wrong
   and can never be trusted,
   you will be rooted out.

CHAPTER 3

Trust God

1 My child, remember
   my teachings and instructions
   and obey them completely.
2 They will help you live
   a long and prosperous life.

3 Let love and loyalty
   always show like a necklace,
   and write them in your mind.
4 God and people will like you
   and consider you a success.

5 With all your heart
   you must trust the LORD
   and not your own judgment.
6 Always let him lead you,
   and he will clear the road
   for you to follow.
7 Don't ever think that you
   are wise enough,
   but respect the LORD
   and stay away from evil.
8 This will make you healthy,
   and you will feel strong.
9 Honour the LORD
   by giving him your money
   and the first part of all your crops.
10 Then you will have
   more grain and grapes
   than you will ever need.

11 My child, don't turn away
   or become bitter
   when the LORD corrects you.
12 The LORD corrects everyone he loves,
   just as parents correct
   their favourite child.

The value of wisdom

13 God blesses everyone who has wisdom
   and common sense.
14 Wisdom is worth more than silver;
   it makes you much richer than gold.
15 Wisdom is more valuable
   than precious jewels;
   nothing you want compares with her.

16 In her right hand
   Wisdom holds a long life,
   and in her left hand
   are wealth and honour.
17 Wisdom makes life pleasant
   and leads us safely along.
18 Wisdom is a life-giving tree,
   the source of happiness
   for all who hold on to her.

19 By his wisdom and knowledge
   the LORD created heaven and earth.
20 By his understanding
   he let the ocean break loose
   and clouds release the rain.

See also: 3.4: Luke 2.52. 3.7: Rom 12.16. 3.11: Job 5.17.
3.11,12: Heb 12.5,6. 3.12: Rev 3.19.

21 My child, use common sense
and sound judgment!
Always keep them in mind.
22 They will help you to live
a long and beautiful life.
23 You will walk safely and never stumble;
24   you will rest without a worry
and sleep soundly.
25 So don't be afraid of sudden disasters
or storms that strike those who are evil.
26 You can be sure that the LORD
will protect you from harm.

27 Do all you can for everyone
who deserves your help.
28 Don't tell your neighbour
to come back tomorrow,
if you can help today.
29 Don't try to be mean
to neighbours who trust you.
30 Don't argue just to be arguing,
when you haven't been hurt.
31 Don't be jealous of cruel people
or follow their example.

32 The LORD doesn't like
anyone who is dishonest,
but he lets good people be his friends.
33 He places a curse on the home
of everyone who is evil,
but he blesses the home
of every good person.
34 The LORD sneers at those
who sneer at him,
but he is kind to everyone
who is humble.
35 You will be praised if you are wise,
but you will be disgraced
if you are a stubborn fool.

CHAPTER 4

Advice to young people

1 My child, listen closely
to my teachings
and learn common sense.
2 My advice is useful,
so don't turn away.
3 When I was still very young
and my mother's favourite child,
my father
4   said to me:
"If you follow my teachings
and keep them in mind,
you will live.
5 Be wise and learn good sense;
remember my teachings

and do what I say.
6 If you love Wisdom and don't reject her,
she will watch over you.
7 The best thing about Wisdom
is Wisdom herself;
good sense is more important
than anything else.
8 If you value Wisdom
and hold tightly to her,
great honours will be yours.
9 It will be like wearing
a glorious crown
of beautiful flowers.

The right way and the wrong way

10 My child, if you listen
and obey my teachings,
you will live a long time.
11 I have shown you the way
that makes sense;
I have guided you along the right path.
12 Your road won't be blocked,
and you won't stumble when you run.
13 Hold firmly to my teaching
and never let go.
It will mean life for you.
14 Don't follow the bad example
of cruel and evil people.
15   Turn aside and keep going.
Stay away from them.
16 They can't sleep or rest
until they do wrong
or harm some innocent victim.
17 Their food and drink
are violence and cruelty.

18 The lifestyle of good people
is like sunlight at dawn
that keeps getting brighter
until broad daylight.
19 The lifestyle of the wicked
is like total darkness,
and they will never know
what makes them stumble.

20 My child, listen carefully
to everything I say.
21   Don't forget a single word,
but think about it all.
22 Knowing these teachings
will mean true life
and good health for you.
23 Carefully guard your thoughts
because they are the source of true life.
24 Never tell lies or be deceitful
in what you say.
25   Keep looking straight ahead,
without turning aside.

See also: **3.34:** Jam 4.6; 1 Pet 5.5.

²⁶ Know where you are headed,
  and you will stay on solid ground.
²⁷ Don't make a mistake by turning
  to the right or the left.

CHAPTER 5

Be faithful to your wife

¹ My son, if you listen closely
  to my wisdom and good sense,
² you will have sound judgment,
  and you will always know
  the right thing to say.
³ The words of an immoral woman
  may be as sweet as honey
  and as smooth as olive oil.
⁴ But all that you really get
  from being with her
  is bitter poison and pain.
⁵ If you follow her,
  she will lead you down
  to the world of the dead.
⁶ She has missed the path that leads to life
  and doesn't even know it.

⁷ My son, listen to me
  and do everything I say.
⁸ Stay away from a bad woman!
  Don't even go near the door
  of her house.
⁹ You will lose your self-respect
  and end up in debt
  to some cruel person
  for the rest of your life.
¹⁰ Strangers will get your money
  and everything else you have worked for.
¹¹ When it's all over,
  your body will waste away,
  as you groan
¹² and shout,
  "I hated advice and correction!
¹³ I paid no attention to my teachers,
¹⁴ and now I am disgraced
  in front of everyone."

¹⁵ You should be faithful to your wife,
  just as you take water
  from your own well.*
¹⁶ And don't be like a stream
  from which just any woman
  may take a drink.
¹⁷ Save yourself for your wife
  and don't have sex with other women.
¹⁸ Be happy with the wife you married
  when you were young.

¹⁹ She is beautiful and graceful,
  just like a deer;
  you should be attracted to her
  and stay deeply in love.
²⁰ Don't go mad over a woman
  who is unfaithful to her own husband!
²¹ The LORD sees everything,
  and he watches us closely.
²² Sinners are trapped and caught
  by their own evil deeds.
²³ They get lost and die
  because of their foolishness
  and lack of self-control.

CHAPTER 6

Don't be foolish

¹ My child, suppose you agree
  to pay the debt of someone,
  who cannot repay a loan.
² Then you are trapped
  by your own words,
³ and you are now in the power
  of someone else.
  Here is what you should do:
  go and beg for permission
  to call off the agreement.
⁴ Do this before you fall asleep
  or even get sleepy.
⁵ Save yourself, just as a deer or a bird
  tries to escape from a hunter.

⁶ You lazy people can learn
  by watching an anthill.
⁷ Ants don't have leaders,
⁸ but they store up food
  during harvest season.
⁹ How long will you lie there
  doing nothing at all?
  When are you going to get up
  and stop sleeping?
¹⁰ Sleep a little. Doze a little.
  Fold your hands
  and twiddle your thumbs.
¹¹ Suddenly, everything is gone,
  as though it had been taken
  by an armed robber.

¹² Worthless liars go around
¹³ winking and giving signals
  to deceive others.
¹⁴ They are always thinking up
  something cruel and evil,
  and they stir up trouble.
¹⁵ But they will be struck by sudden disaster
  and left without a hope.

---

*5.15 own well: In biblical times water was scarce
and wells were carefully guarded.

See also: 4.26: Heb 12.13.

See also: 6.10,11: Prov 24.33,34.

16 There are six or seven kinds of people
   the LORD doesn't like:
17 Those who are too proud
   or tell lies or murder,
18 those who make evil plans
   or are quick to do wrong,
19 those who tell lies in court
   or stir up trouble in a family.

20 Obey the teaching of your parents —
21 always keep it in mind
   and never forget it.
22 Their teaching will guide you
   when you walk,
   protect you when you sleep,
   and talk to you when you are awake.

23 The Law of the Lord is a lamp,
   and its teachings shine brightly.
   Correction and self-control
   will lead you through life.
24 They will protect you
   from the flattering words
   of someone else's wife.*
25 Don't let yourself be attracted
   by the charm
   and lovely eyes of someone like that.
26 A woman who sells her love
   can be bought for as little
   as the price of a meal.
   But making love
   to another man's wife
   will cost you everything.
27 If you carry burning coals,
   you burn your clothes;
28 if you step on hot coals,
   you burn your feet.
29 And if you go to bed
   with another man's wife,
   you pay the price.

30 We don't put up with thieves,
   not even* with one who steals
   for something to eat.
31 And thieves who get caught must pay back
   seven times what was stolen
   and lose everything.
32 But if you go to bed
   with another man's wife,
   you will destroy yourself
   by your own stupidity.
33 You will be beaten
   and for ever disgraced,
34 because a jealous husband
   can be furious and merciless
   when he takes revenge.
35 He won't let you pay him off,
   no matter what you offer.

CHAPTER 7

The foolishness of unfaithfulness

1 My son, pay close attention
   and don't forget what I tell you to do.
2 Obey me, and you will live!
   Let my instructions be
   your greatest treasure.
3 Keep them at your fingertips
   and write them in your mind.
4 Let wisdom be your sister
   and make common sense
   your closest friend.
5 They will protect you
   from the flattering words
   of someone else's wife.

6 From the window of my house,
   I once happened to see
7 some foolish young men.
8 It was late in the evening,
   some time after dark.
9 One of these young men
   turned the corner
   and was walking by the house
   of an unfaithful wife.
10 She was dressed up
   like a woman of the street
   with only one thing in mind.
11 She was one of those women
   who are loud and restless
   and never stay at home,
12 who walk street after street,
   waiting to trap a man.

13 She grabbed him and kissed him,
   and with no sense of shame, she said:
14 "I had to offer a sacrifice,
   and there is enough meat
   left over for a feast.
15 So I came looking for you,
   and here you are!
16 The sheets on my bed
   are bright-coloured cloth from Egypt.
17 And I have covered it with perfume
   made of myrrh, aloes, and cinnamon.

18 "Let's go there and make love all night.
19 My husband is travelling,
   and he's far away.
20 He took a lot of money along,
   and he won't be back home
   before the middle of the month."

21 And so, she tricked him
   with all her sweet talk and her flattery.
22 Straight away he followed her
   like an ox on the way to be slaughtered,
   or like a fool on the way to be punished*

²³ and killed with arrows.
  He was no more than a bird
    rushing into a trap,
  without knowing
    it would cost him his life.

²⁴ My son, pay close attention
  to what I have said.
²⁵ Don't even think about
    that kind of woman
  or let yourself be misled
    by someone like her.
²⁶ Such a woman has caused the downfall
    and destruction of a lot of men.
²⁷ Her house is a one-way street
    leading straight down
  to the world of the dead.

In praise of wisdom

CHAPTER 8

¹ With great understanding,
    Wisdom* is calling out
² as she stands at the crossroads
    and on every hill.
³ She stands by the city gate
    where everyone enters the city,
  and she shouts:
⁴ "I am calling out to each one of you!
⁵ Good sense and sound judgment
    can be yours.
⁶ Listen, because what I say
    is worthwhile and right.
⁷ I always speak the truth
    and refuse to tell a lie.
⁸ Every word I speak is honest,
    not one is misleading or deceptive.

⁹ "If you have understanding,
    you will see that my words
  are just what you need.
¹⁰ Let instruction and knowledge
    mean more to you
  than silver or the finest gold.
¹¹ Wisdom is worth much more
    than precious jewels
  or anything else you desire."

Wisdom speaks

¹² I am Wisdom* — Common Sense
    is my closest friend;
  I possess knowledge
    and sound judgment.

¹³ If you respect the LORD,
    you will hate evil.
  I hate pride and conceit
    and deceitful lies.
¹⁴ I am strong,
    and I offer sensible advice
    and sound judgment.
¹⁵ By my power kings govern,
    and rulers make laws that are fair.
¹⁶ Every honest leader rules
    with help from me.

¹⁷ I love everyone who loves me,
    and I will be found by all
  who honestly search.
¹⁸ I can make you rich and famous,
    important and successful.
¹⁹ What you receive from me
    is more valuable
  than even the finest gold
    or the purest silver.
²⁰ I always do what is right,
²¹ and I give great riches
    to everyone who loves me.

²² From the beginning,
    I was with the LORD.'
  I was there before he began
²³ to create the earth.
  At the very first,
    the LORD gave life to' me.
²⁴ When I was born,
    there were no oceans
  or springs of water.
²⁵ My birth was before
    mountains were formed
  or hills were put in place.
²⁶ It happened long before God
    had made the earth
  or any of its fields or even the dust.

²⁷ I was there when the LORD
    put the heavens in place
  and stretched the sky
    over the surface of the sea.
²⁸ I was with him when he placed
    the clouds in the sky
  and created the springs
    that fill the ocean.
²⁹ I was there when he set
    boundaries for the sea
  to make it obey him,
    and when he laid foundations
  to support the earth.

³⁰ I was right beside the LORD,
    helping him plan and build.'

---

*8.1,12 Wisdom: See the note at 1.20.
See also: 8.1-3: Prov 1.20,21.

See also: 8.22: Rev 3.14.

I made him happy each day,
and I was happy at his side.
31 I was pleased with his world
and pleased with its people.
32 Pay attention, my children!
Follow my advice,
and you will be happy.
33 Listen carefully to my instructions,
and you will be wise.

34 Come to my home each day
and listen to me.
You will find happiness.
35 By finding me, you find life,
and the LORD will be pleased with you.
36 But if you don't find me,
you hurt only yourself,
and if you hate me,
you are in love with death.

Wisdom's feast

CHAPTER 9

1 Wisdom has built her house
with its seven columns.
2 She has prepared the meat
and set out the wine.
Her feast is ready.

3 She has sent her servant women
to announce her invitation
from the highest hills:
4 "Everyone who is ignorant
or foolish is invited!
5 All of you are welcome
to my meat and wine.
6 If you want to live,
give up your foolishness
and let understanding
guide your steps."

True wisdom

7 Correct a worthless boaster,
and all you will get
are insults and injuries.
8 Any boaster you correct
will only hate you.
But if you correct someone
who has common sense,
you will be loved.
9 If you have good sense,
instruction will help you
to have even better sense.
And if you live right,
education will help you
to know even more.

10 Respect and obey the LORD!
This is the beginning of wisdom.*
To have understanding,
you must know the Holy God.
11 I am Wisdom.
If you follow me,
you will live a long time.
12 Good sense is good for you,
but if you boast,*
you hurt yourself.

A foolish invitation

13 Stupidity* is reckless,
senseless, and foolish.
14 She sits in front of her house
and on the highest hills in the town.
15 She shouts to everyone who passes by,
16 "If you are stupid, come on inside!"
And to every fool she says,
17 "Stolen water tastes best,
and the food you eat in secret
tastes best of all."
18 None who listen to Stupidity understand
that her guests are as good as dead.

Solomon's wise sayings

CHAPTER 10

1 Here are some proverbs of Solomon:
Children with good sense
make their parents happy,
but foolish children make them sad.
2 What you gain by doing evil
won't help you at all,
but being good*
can save you from death.

3 If you obey the LORD,
you won't go hungry;
if you are wicked,
God won't let you have what you want.
4 Laziness leads to poverty;
hard work makes you rich.
5 At harvest season
it's clever to work hard,
but stupid to sleep.

6 Everyone praises good people,
but evil hides behind
the words of the wicked.
7 Good people are remembered
long after they are gone,
but the wicked are soon forgotten.

See also: 9.10: Job 28.28; Psa 111.10; Prov 1.7.

8 If you have good sense,
   you will listen and obey;
   if all you do is talk,
   you will destroy yourself.
9 You will be safe,
   if you always do right,
   but you will get caught,
   if you are dishonest.
10 Deceit causes trouble,
   and foolish talk will bring you to ruin.†
11 The words of good people
   are a source of life,
   but evil hides behind
   the words of the wicked.

12 Hatred stirs up trouble;
   love overlooks the wrongs
   that others do.
13 If you have good sense,
   it will show when you speak.
   But if you are stupid,
   you will be beaten with a stick.
14 If you have good sense,
   you will learn all you can,
   but foolish talk will soon destroy you.

15 Great wealth can be a fortress,
   but poverty is no protection at all.
16 If you live right,
   the reward is a good life;
   if you are evil, all you have is sin.

17 Accept correction,
   and you will find life;
   reject correction,
   and you will miss the road.
18 You can hide your hatred by telling lies,
   but you are a fool to spread lies.
19 You will say the wrong thing
   if you talk too much —
   so be sensible and watch what you say.
20 The words of a good person
   are like pure silver,
   but the thoughts of an evil person
   are almost worthless.
21 Many are helped by useful instruction,
   but fools are killed
   by their own stupidity.

22 When the LORD blesses you with riches,
   you have nothing to regret.†
23 Fools enjoy doing wrong,
   but anyone with good sense
   enjoys acting wisely.
24 What evil people dread most
   will happen to them,
   but good people will get
   what they want most.

25 Those crooks will disappear
   when a storm strikes,
   but God will keep safe
   all who obey him.
26 Having a lazy person on the job
   is like a mouth full of vinegar
   or smoke in your eyes.

27 If you respect the LORD,
   you will live longer;
   if you keep doing wrong,
   your life will be cut short.
28 If you obey the Lord,
   you will be happy,
   but there is no future for the wicked.
29 The LORD protects everyone
   who lives right,
   but he destroys anyone who does wrong.
30 Good people will stand firm,
   but the wicked will lose their land.
31 Honest people speak sensibly,
   but deceitful liars will be silenced.
32 If you obey the Lord,
   you will always know
   the right thing to say.
   But no one will trust you if you tell lies.

CHAPTER 11

Watch what you say and do

1 The LORD hates anyone who cheats,
   but he likes everyone who is honest.
2 Too much pride can put you to shame.
   It's wiser to be humble.
3 If you do the right thing,
   honesty will be your guide.
   But if you are crooked,
   you will be trapped
   by your own dishonesty.

4 When God is angry,
   money won't help you.
   Obeying God is the only way
   to be saved from death.
5 If you are truly good, you will do right;
   if you are wicked,
   you will be destroyed by your own sin.
6 Honesty can keep you safe,
   but if you can't be trusted,
   you trap yourself.
7 When the wicked die,
   their hopes die with them.
8 Trouble goes right past the LORD's people
   and strikes the wicked.

9 Dishonest people use gossip
   to destroy their neighbours;
   good people are protected
   by their own good sense.

See also: 10.12: Jam 5.20; 1 Pet 4.8.

10 When honest people prosper
and the wicked disappear,
the whole city celebrates.
11 When God blesses his people,
their city prospers,
but deceitful liars can destroy a city.

12 It's stupid to say bad things
about your neighbours.
If you are sensible,
you will keep quiet.
13 A gossip tells everything,
but a true friend will keep a secret.
14 A city without wise leaders
will end up in ruin;
a city with many wise leaders
will be kept safe.

15 It's a dangerous thing
to guarantee payment
for someone's debts.
Don't do it!
16 A gracious woman will be respected,
but a man must work hard to get rich.'
17 Kindness is rewarded —
but if you are cruel,
you hurt yourself.
18 Meanness gets you nowhere,
but goodness is rewarded.
19 Always do the right thing,
and you will live;
keep on doing wrong, and you will die.

20 The LORD hates cunning people,
but he likes everyone who lives right.
21 You can be sure of this:
all crooks will be punished,
but God's people won't.
22 A beautiful woman who acts foolishly
is like a gold ring on the snout of a pig.
23 Good people want what is best,
but troublemakers
hope to stir up trouble.'

24 Sometimes you can become rich
by being generous
or poor by being greedy.
25 Generosity will be rewarded:
give a cup of water,
and you will receive
a cup of water in return.
26 Charge too much for grain,
and you will be cursed;
sell it at a fair price,
and you will be praised.
27 Try hard to do right,
and you will win friends;
go looking for trouble,
and you will find it.

28 Trust in your wealth,
and you will be a failure,
but God's people will prosper
like healthy plants.
29 Fools who cause trouble
in the family won't inherit a thing.
They will end up as slaves
of someone with good sense.
30 Live right, and you will eat
from the life-giving tree.
And if you act wisely,
others will follow.'
31 If good people are rewarded'
here on this earth,
all who are cruel and mean
will surely be punished.

CHAPTER 12

You can't hide behind evil

1 To accept correction is wise,
to reject it is stupid.
2 The LORD likes everyone who lives right,
but he punishes everyone
who makes evil plans.
3 Sin cannot offer security!
But if you live right,
you will be as secure
as a tree with deep roots.
4 A helpful wife is a jewel
for her husband,
but a shameless wife
will make his bones rot.

5 Good people have kind thoughts,
but you should never trust
the advice of someone evil.
6 Bad advice is a deadly trap,
but good advice is like a shield.
7 Once the wicked are defeated,
they are gone for ever,
but no one who obeys God
will ever be thrown down.
8 Good sense is worthy of praise,
but stupidity is a curse.
9 It's better to be ordinary
and have only one servant'
than to think you are somebody
and starve to death.
10 Good people are kind to their animals,
but a mean person is cruel.
11 Hard working farmers have more
than enough food;
daydreamers are nothing more
than stupid fools.

See also: 11.31: 1 Pet 4.18.

12 An evil person tries to hide behind evil;'
good people are like trees
with deep roots.

13 We trap ourselves by telling lies,
but we stay out of trouble
by living right.

14 We are rewarded or punished
for what we say and do.

15 Fools think they know what is best,
but a sensible person listens to advice.

16 Losing your temper is foolish;
ignoring an insult is sensible.

17 An honest person
tells the truth in court,
but a dishonest person
tells nothing but lies.

18 Sharp words cut like a sword,
but words of wisdom heal.

19 Truth will last for ever;
lies are soon found out.

20 An evil mind is deceitful,
but gentle thoughts bring happiness.

21 Good people never have trouble,
but troublemakers
have more than enough.

22 The LORD hates every liar,
but he is the friend of all
who can be trusted.

23 Be sensible and don't tell
everything you know —
only fools spread
foolishness everywhere.

24 Work hard, and you will be a leader;
be lazy, and you will end up a slave.

25 Worry is a heavy burden,
but a kind word always brings cheer.

26 You are better off doing right,
than losing your way
by doing wrong.'

27 Anyone too lazy to cook will starve,
but a hard worker
is a valuable treasure.'

28 Follow the road to life,
and you won't be bothered by death.

CHAPTER 13

Wise friends make you wise

1 Children with good sense
accept correction from their parents,
but stubborn children
ignore it completely.

2 You will be well rewarded
for saying something kind,
but all some people think about
is how to be cruel and mean.

3 Keep what you know to yourself,
and you will be safe;
talk too much, and you are done for.

4 No matter how much you want,
laziness won't help a bit,
but hard work will reward you
with more than enough.

5 A good person hates deceit,
but those who are evil
cause shame and disgrace.

6 Live right, and you are safe!
But sin will destroy you.

7 Some who have nothing
may pretend to be rich,
and some who have everything
may pretend to be poor.

8 The rich may have to pay a ransom,
but the poor don't have that problem.

9 The lamp of a good person
keeps on shining;
the lamp of an evil person
soon goes out.

10 Too much pride causes trouble.
Be sensible and take advice.

11 Money wrongly got
will disappear bit by bit;
money earned little by little
will grow and grow.

12 Not getting what you want
can make you feel sick,
but a wish that comes true
is a life-giving tree.

13 If you reject God's teaching,
you will pay the price;
if you obey his commands,
you will be rewarded.

14 Sensible instruction
is a life-giving fountain
that helps you escape all deadly traps.

15 Sound judgment is praised,
but people without good sense
are on the way to disaster.'

16 If you have good sense,
you will act sensibly,
but fools act like fools.

17 Whoever delivers your message
can make things better
or worse for you.

18 All who refuse correction
will be poor and disgraced,
but all who accept correction will be praised.

19 It's a good feeling
to get what you want,
but only a stupid fool
hates to turn from evil.

²⁰ Wise friends make you wise,
but you hurt yourself
by going around with fools.
²¹ You are in for trouble if you sin,
but you will be rewarded if you live right.
²² If you obey God,
you will have something
to leave your grandchildren.
If you don't obey God,
those who live right
will get what you leave.
²³ Even when the land of the poor
produces good crops,
they get cheated out of what they grow.¹
²⁴ If you love your children,
you will correct them;
if you don't love them,
you won't correct them.
²⁵ If you live right,
you will have plenty to eat;
if you don't live right,
you will go away empty.

CHAPTER 14

Wisdom makes good sense

¹ A woman's family is held together
by her wisdom,
but it can be destroyed
by her foolishness.
² By living right, you show
that you respect the LORD;
by being deceitful, you show
that you despise him.
³ Proud fools are punished
for their stupid talk,
but sensible talk can save your life.
⁴ Without the help of an ox
there can be no crop,
but with a strong ox
a big crop is possible.
⁵ An honest witness tells the truth;
a dishonest witness
tells nothing but lies.
⁶ Make fun of wisdom,
and you will never find it.
But if you have understanding,
knowledge comes easily.
⁷ Stay away from fools,
or you won't learn a thing.
⁸ Wise people have enough sense
to find their way,
but stupid fools get lost.
⁹ Fools don't care if they are wrong,²
but God is pleased
when people do right.

¹⁰ No one else can really know
how sad or happy you are.
¹¹ The tent of a good person stands longer
than the house of someone evil.
¹² You may think you are
on the right road
and still end up dead.
¹³ Sorrow may hide behind laughter,
and happiness may end in sorrow.
¹⁴ You harvest what you plant,
whether good or bad.
¹⁵ Don't be stupid and believe all you hear;
be clever and know
where you are headed.
¹⁶ Only a stupid fool is never cautious —
so be extra careful
and stay out of trouble.
¹⁷ Fools have quick tempers,
and no one likes you
if you can't be trusted.
¹⁸ Stupidity leads to foolishness;
be clever and learn.
¹⁹ The wicked will come crawling
to those who obey God.
²⁰ You have no friends if you are poor,
but you have lots of friends
if you are rich.
²¹ It's wrong to hate others,
but God blesses everyone
who is kind to the poor.
²² It's a mistake to make evil plans,
but you will have loyal friends
if you want to do right.
²³ Hard work is worthwhile,
but empty talk will make you poor.
²⁴ Wisdom can make you rich,
but foolishness leads
to more foolishness.
²⁵ An honest witness can save your life,
but liars can't be trusted.
²⁶ If you respect the LORD,
you and your children have
a strong fortress
²⁷ and a life-giving fountain
that keeps you safe from deadly traps.
²⁸ Rulers of powerful nations
are held in honour;
rulers of weak nations are nothing at all.
²⁹ It's clever to be patient,
but it's stupid to lose your temper.
³⁰ It's healthy to be content,
but envy can eat you up.
³¹ If you ill-treat the poor,
you insult your Creator;

See also: 14.12: Prov 16.25.

if you are kind to them,
    you show him respect.
32 In times of trouble
    the wicked are destroyed,
    but even at death
    the innocent have faith.*

33 Wisdom is found in the minds
    of people with good sense,
    but fools don't know it.*

34 Doing right brings honour to a nation,
    but sin brings disgrace.

35 Kings reward servants who act wisely,
    but they punish those
    who act foolishly.

CHAPTER 15

The LORD sees everything

1 A kind answer soothes angry feelings,
    but harsh words stir them up.

2 Words of wisdom come from the wise,
    but fools speak foolishness.

3 The LORD sees everything,
    whether good or bad.

4 Kind words are good medicine,
    but deceitful words can really hurt.

5 Don't be a fool
    and disobey your parents.
    Be clever! Accept correction.

6 Good people become wealthy,
    but those who are evil
    will lose what they have.

7 Words of wisdom make good sense;
    the thoughts of a fool
    make no sense at all.

8 The LORD is disgusted
    by gifts from the wicked,
    but it makes him happy
    when his people pray.

9 The LORD is disgusted
    with all who do wrong,
    but he loves everyone who does right.

10 If you turn from the right way,
    you will be punished;
    if you refuse correction,
    you will die.

11 If the LORD can see everything
    in the world of the dead,
    he can see in our hearts.

12 Those who sneer at others
    don't like to be corrected,
    and they won't ask help
    from someone with sense.

13 Happiness makes you smile;
    sorrow can crush you.

14 Anyone with good sense
    is eager to learn more,
    but fools are hungry for foolishness.

15 The poor have a hard life,
    but being content is as good
    as an endless feast.

16 It's better to obey the LORD
    and have only a little,
    than to be very rich
    and terribly confused.

17 A simple meal with love
    is better than a feast
    where there is hatred.

18 Losing your temper
    causes a lot of trouble,
    but staying calm settles arguments.

19 Being lazy is like walking
    in a thorn patch,
    but everyone who does right
    walks on a smooth road.

20 Children with good sense
    make their parents happy,
    but foolish children
    are hateful to them.

21 Stupidity brings happiness
    to senseless fools,
    but everyone with good sense
    follows the straight path.

22 Without good advice
    everything goes wrong —
    it takes careful planning
    for things to go right.

23 Giving the right answer at the right time
    makes everyone happy.

24 All who are wise follow a road
    that leads upward to life
    and away from death.

25 The LORD destroys the homes
    of those who are proud,
    but he protects the property of widows.

26 The LORD hates evil thoughts,
    but kind words please him.

27 Being greedy causes trouble
    for your family,
    but you protect yourself
    by refusing bribes.

28 Good people think before they answer,
    but the wicked speak evil
    without ever thinking.

29 The LORD never even hears
    the prayers of the wicked,
    but he answers the prayers
    of all who obey him.

30 A friendly smile makes you happy,
    and good news makes you feel strong.

³¹ Healthy correction is good,
   and if you accept it,
   you will be wise.
³² You hurt only yourself
   by rejecting instruction,
   but it makes good sense to accept it.
³³ Showing respect to the LORD
   will make you wise,
   and being humble
   will bring honour to you.

CHAPTER 16

The LORD has the final word

¹ We humans make plans,
   but the LORD has the final word.
² We may think we know what is right,
   but the LORD is the judge of our motives.
³ Share your plans with the LORD,
   and you will succeed.

⁴ The LORD has a reason
   for everything he does,
   and he lets evil people live
   only to be punished.
⁵ The LORD doesn't like
   anyone who is conceited —
   you can be sure they will be punished.
⁶ If we truly love God,
   our sins will be forgiven;
   if we show him respect,
   we will keep away from sin.
⁷ When we please the LORD,
   even our enemies make friends with us.
⁸ It's better to be honest and poor
   than to be dishonest and rich.

⁹ We make our own plans,
   but the LORD decides where we will go.
¹⁰ Rulers speak with authority
   and are never wrong.
¹¹ The LORD doesn't like it
   when we cheat in business.
¹² Justice makes rulers powerful.
   They should hate evil
¹³ and like honesty and truth.
¹⁴ An angry ruler can put you to death.
   So be wise!
   Don't make one angry.
¹⁵ When a ruler is happy
   and pleased with you,
   it's like refreshing rain,
   and you will live.

¹⁶ It's much better to be wise
   and sensible than to be rich.
¹⁷ God's people avoid evil ways,
   and they protect themselves
   by watching where they go.

¹⁸ Too much pride will destroy you.
¹⁹ You are better off being humble and poor
   than getting rich
   from what you take by force.
²⁰ If you know what you're doing,
   you will prosper.
   God blesses everyone who trusts him.
²¹ Good judgment proves
   that you are wise,
   and if you speak kindly,
   you can teach others.
²² Good sense is a fountain that gives life,
   but fools are punished
   by their foolishness.
²³ You can persuade others
   if you are wise
   and speak sensibly.

²⁴ Kind words are like honey —
   they cheer you up
   and make you feel strong.
²⁵ Sometimes what seems right
   is really a road to death.
²⁶ The hungrier you are,
   the harder you work.
²⁷ Worthless people plan trouble.
   Even their words burn
   like a flaming fire.
²⁸ Gossip is no good!
   It causes hard feelings
   and comes between friends.

²⁹ Don't trust violent people.
   They will mislead you
   to do the wrong thing.
³⁰ When someone winks
   or grins behind your back,
   trouble is on the way.
³¹ Grey hair is a glorious crown
   worn by those who have lived right.
³² Controlling your temper
   is better than being a hero
   who captures a city.
³³ We make our own decisions,
   but the LORD alone
   determines what happens.

CHAPTER 17

Our thoughts are tested by the LORD

¹ A dry crust of bread eaten
   in peace and quiet
   is better than a feast eaten
   where everyone argues.
² A hard-working slave
   will be placed in charge
   of a no-good child,

See also: **16.25:** Prov 14.12.

and that slave will be given
the same inheritance
that each child receives.
³ Silver and gold are tested by flames of fire;
our thoughts are tested by the LORD.
⁴ Troublemakers listen to troublemakers,
and liars listen to liars.
⁵ By insulting the poor,
you insult your Creator.
You will be punished
if you make fun
of someone in trouble.
⁶ Grandparents are proud
of their grandchildren,
and children should be proud
of their parents.

⁷ It sounds strange for a fool
to talk sensibly,
but it's even worse for a ruler to tell lies.
⁸ A bribe works miracles like a magic charm
that brings good luck.
⁹ You will keep your friends
if you forgive them,
but you will lose your friends
if you keep talking about
what they did wrong.
¹⁰ A sensible person accepts correction,
but you can't beat sense into a fool.

¹¹ Cruel people want to rebel,
and so vicious attackers
will be sent against them.
¹² A bear robbed of her cubs
is far less dangerous
than a stubborn fool.
¹³ You will always have trouble
if you are mean to those
who are good to you.
¹⁴ The start of an argument
is like a water leak —
so stop it before real trouble breaks out.
¹⁵ The LORD doesn't like those
who defend the guilty
or condemn the innocent.
¹⁶ Why should fools have money
for an education
when they refuse to learn?

¹⁷ A friend is always a friend,
and relatives are born
to share our troubles.
¹⁸ It's stupid to guarantee
someone else's loan.
¹⁹ The wicked and the proud love trouble
and keep begging to be hurt.
²⁰ Dishonesty does you no good,
and telling lies will get you in trouble.
²¹ It's never pleasant

to be the parent of a fool
and have nothing but pain.
²² If you are cheerful, you feel good;
if you are sad, you hurt all over.

²³ Crooks accept secret bribes
to keep justice from being done.
²⁴ Anyone with wisdom knows
what makes good sense,
but fools can never
make up their minds.
²⁵ Foolish children bring sorrow
to their father
and pain to their mother.
²⁶ It isn't fair to punish the innocent
and those who do right.
²⁷ It makes a lot of sense
to be a person of few words
and to stay calm.
²⁸ Even fools seem clever
when they are quiet.

CHAPTER 18

It's wrong to favour the guilty

¹ It's selfish and stupid
to think only of yourself
and to sneer at people
who have sense.'
² Fools have no desire to learn;
they would much rather
give their own opinion.
³ Wrongdoing leads to shame and disgrace.
⁴ Words of wisdom are a stream
that flows from a deep fountain.
⁵ It's wrong to favour the guilty
and keep the innocent
from getting justice.

⁶ Foolish talk will get you
into a lot of trouble.
⁷ Saying foolish things
is like setting a trap
to destroy yourself.
⁸ There's nothing so delicious
as the taste of gossip!
It melts in your mouth.
⁹ Being lazy is no different
from being a troublemaker.

¹⁰ The LORD is a mighty tower
where his people can run for safety —
¹¹ the rich think their money
is a wall of protection.

¹² Pride leads to destruction;
humility leads to honour.
¹³ It's stupid and embarrassing
to give an answer before you listen.

14 Being cheerful helps when we are sick,
   but nothing helps when we give up.
15 Everyone with good sense wants to learn.
16   A gift will get you in to see anyone.
17 You may think you have won
     your case in court,
   until your opponent speaks.
18 Drawing straws is one way
     to settle a difficult case.
19 Making up with a friend
     you have offended'
   is harder than breaking
     through a city wall.
20 Make your words good —
     you will be glad you did.
21 Words can bring death or life!
   Talk too much, and you will eat
     everything you say.
22 A man's greatest treasure is his wife —
     she is a gift from the LORD.
23 The poor must beg for help,
     but the rich can give a harsh reply.
24 Some friends don't help,'
     but a true friend is closer
     than your own family.

CHAPTER 19

It's wise to be patient

1 It's better to be poor
     and live right
   than to be a stupid liar.
2 Willingness and stupidity
     don't go well together.
   If you are too eager,
     you will miss the road.
3 We are ruined by our own stupidity,
     though we blame the LORD.

4 The rich have many friends;
     the poor have none.
5   Dishonest witnesses and liars
     won't escape punishment.
6 Everyone tries to be friends
     of those who can help them.
7 If you are poor,
     your own relatives reject you,
     and your friends are worse.
   When you really need them,
     they are not there.'
8 Do yourself a favour
     by having good sense —
     you will be glad you did.
9 Dishonest witnesses and liars
     will be destroyed.

10 It isn't right for a fool
     to live in luxury
   or for a slave to rule in place of a king.
11 It's wise to be patient
     and show what you are like
     by forgiving others.
12 An angry king roars like a lion,
     but when a king is pleased,
     it's like dew on the crops.
13 A foolish son brings disgrace
     to his father.
   A nagging wife goes on and on
     like the drip, drip, drip of the rain.
14 You may inherit all you own
     from your parents,
   but a sensible wife
     is a gift from the LORD.
15 If you are lazy and sleep your time away,
     you will starve.
16 Obey the Lord's teachings
     and you will live —
   disobey and you will die.
17 Caring for the poor
     is lending to the LORD,
     and you will be well repaid.
18 Correct your children
     before it's too late;
   if you don't punish them,
     you are destroying them.
19 People with bad tempers
     are always in trouble,
   and they need help over and over again.'
20 Pay attention to advice
     and accept correction,
     so you can live sensibly.
21 We may make a lot of plans,
     but the LORD will do
     what he has decided.
22 What matters most is loyalty.
   It's better to be poor than to be a liar.
23 Showing respect to the LORD
     brings true life —
   if you do it, you can relax
     without fear of danger.

24 Some people are too lazy
     to lift a hand to feed themselves.
25 Stupid fools learn good sense
     by seeing others punished;
   a sensible person learns
     by being corrected.
26 Children who bring disgrace
     rob their father
     and chase their mother away.
27 If you stop learning, you will forget
     what you already know.

28 A lying witness makes fun
   of the court system,
   and criminals think crime
   is really delicious.
29 Every stupid fool is just waiting
   to be punished.

CHAPTER 20

Words of wisdom are better than gold

1 It isn't clever to get drunk!
   Drinking makes a fool of you
   and leads to fights.
2 An angry ruler is like a roaring lion —
   make either one angry,
   and you are dead.
3 It makes you look good
   when you avoid a fight —
   only fools love to quarrel.
4 If you are too lazy to plough,
   don't expect a harvest.
5 Someone's thoughts may be
   as deep as the ocean,
   but if you are clever,
   you will discover them.
6 There are many who say,
   "You can trust me!"
   But can they be trusted?
7 Good people live right,
   and God blesses the children
   who follow their example.
8 When rulers decide cases,
   they weigh the evidence.
9 Can any of us really say,
   "My thoughts are pure,
   and my sins are gone"?
10 Two things the LORD hates
    are dishonest scales
    and dishonest measures.
11 The good or bad that children do
    shows what they are like.
12 Hearing and seeing
    are gifts from the LORD.
13 If you sleep all the time,
    you will starve;
    if you get up and work,
    you will have enough food.
14 Everyone likes to boast
    about getting a bargain.
15 Sensible words are better
    than gold or jewels.
16 You deserve to lose your coat
    if you loan it to someone
    to guarantee payment
    for the debt of a stranger.

17 The food you get by cheating
    may taste delicious,
    but it turns to gravel.
18 Be sure you have sound advice
    before making plans
    or starting a war.
19 Stay away from gossips —
    they tell everything.
20 Children who curse their parents
    will go to the land of darkness
    long before their time.
21 Getting rich quick'
    may turn out to be a curse.
22 Don't try to get even.
    Trust the LORD,
    and he will help you.
23 The LORD hates dishonest scales
    and dishonest weights.
    So don't cheat!
24 How can we know
    what will happen to us
    when the LORD alone decides?
25 Don't fall into the trap
    of making promises to God
    before you think!
26 A wise ruler severely punishes
    every criminal.
27 Our inner thoughts are a lamp
    from the LORD,
    and they search our hearts.
28 Rulers are protected
    by God's mercy and loyalty,
    but' they must be merciful
    for their kingdoms to last.
29 Young people take pride
    in their strength,
    but the grey hairs of wisdom
    are even more beautiful.
30 A severe beating can knock all
    of the evil out of you!

CHAPTER 21

The LORD is in charge

1 The LORD controls rulers,
   just as he determines
   the course of rivers.
2 We may think we are doing
   the right thing,
   but the LORD always knows
   what is in our hearts.
3 Doing what is right and fair
   pleases the LORD
   more than an offering.
4 Evil people are proud and arrogant,
   but sin is the only crop they produce.'

5 If you plan and work hard,
   you will have plenty;
   if you get in a hurry,
   you will end up poor.

6 Cheating to get rich is a foolish dream
   and no less than suicide.•

7 You destroy yourself
   by being cruel and violent
   and refusing to live right.

8 All crooks are liars,
   but anyone who is innocent
   will do right.

9 It's better to stay outside
   on the roof of your house
   than to live inside with a nagging wife.

10 Evil people want to do wrong,
   even to their friends.

11 An ignorant fool learns
   by seeing others punished;
   a sensible person learns
   by being instructed.

12 God is always fair!
   He knows what the wicked do
   and will punish them.

13 If you won't help the poor,
   don't expect to be heard
   when you cry out for help.

14 A secret bribe will save you
   from someone's fierce anger.

15 When justice is done,
   good citizens are glad
   and crooks are terrified.

16 If you stop using good sense,
   you will find yourself in the grave.

17 Heavy drinkers and others
   who live only for pleasure
   will lose all they have.

18 God's people will escape,
   but all who are wicked
   will pay the price.

19 It's better out in the desert
   than at home with a nagging,
   complaining wife.

20 Be sensible and store up
   precious treasures —
   don't waste them like a fool.

21 If you try to be kind and good,
   you will be blessed with life
   and goodness and honour.

22 One wise person can defeat
   a city full of soldiers
   and capture their fortress.

23 Watching what you say
   can save you a lot of trouble.

24 If you are proud and conceited,
   everyone will say, "You're a snob!"

25 If you want too much
   and are too lazy to work,
   it could be fatal.

26 But people who obey God
   are always generous.

27 The Lord despises the offerings
   of wicked people
   with evil motives.

28 If you tell lies in court, you are done for;
   only a reliable witness can do the job.

29 Wicked people bluff their way,
   but God's people think
   before they take a step.

30 No matter how much you know
   or what plans you make,
   you can't defeat the Lord.

31 Even if your army has horses
   ready for battle,
   the Lord will always win.

CHAPTER 22

The value of a good reputation

1 A good reputation and respect
   are worth much more
   than silver and gold.

2 The rich and the poor
   are all created by the Lord.

3 When you see trouble coming,
   don't be stupid
   and walk right into it —
   be clever and hide.

4 Respect and serve the Lord!
   Your reward will be wealth,
   a long life, and honour.

5 Crooks walk down a road
   full of thorny traps.
   Stay away from there!

6 Teach your children right from wrong,
   and when they are grown
   they will still do right.

7 The poor are ruled by the rich,
   and those who borrow
   are slaves of moneylenders.

8 Troublemakers get in trouble,
   and their terrible anger
   will get them nowhere.

9 The Lord blesses everyone
   who freely gives food to the poor.

10 Arguments and fights will come to an end,
   if you chase away those
   who insult others.

11 The king is the friend of all
   who are sincere
   and speak with kindness.

¹² The LORD watches over everyone
who shows good sense,
but he frustrates the plans
of deceitful liars.
¹³ Don't be so lazy that you say,
"If I go to work, a lion will eat me!"
¹⁴ The words of a bad woman
are like a deep pit;
if you make the LORD angry,
you will fall right in.
¹⁵ All children are foolish,
but firm correction
will make them change.
¹⁶ Cheat the poor to make profit
or give gifts to the rich —
either way you lose.

Thirty wise sayings

¹⁷ Here are some sayings
of people with wisdom,
so listen carefully as I teach.
¹⁸ You will be glad
that you know these sayings
and can recite them.
¹⁹ I am teaching them today,
so that you may trust the LORD.
²⁰ I have written thirty sayings
filled with sound advice.
²¹ You can trust them completely
to give you the right words
for those in charge of you.

First saying

²² Don't take advantage of the poor
or cheat them in court.
²³ The LORD is their defender,
and what you do to them,
he will do to you.

Second saying

²⁴ Don't make friends with anyone
who has a bad temper.
²⁵ You might turn out like them
and get caught in a trap.

Third saying

²⁶ Don't guarantee to pay
someone else's debt.
²⁷ If you don't have the money,
you might lose your bed.

Fourth saying

²⁸ Don't move a boundary marker*
set up by your ancestors.

Fifth saying

²⁹ If you do your job well,
you will work for a ruler
and never be a slave.

CHAPTER 23

Sixth saying

¹ When you are invited to eat with a king,
use your best manners.
² Don't go and stuff yourself!
That would be just the same
as cutting your throat.
³ Don't be greedy for all that fancy food!
It may not be so tasty.

Seventh saying

⁴ Give up trying so hard to get rich.
⁵ Your money flies away before you know it,
just like an eagle suddenly taking off.

Eighth saying

⁶ Don't accept an invitation
to eat a selfish person's food,
no matter how good it is.
⁷ People like that take note
of how much you eat.
They say, "Take all you want!"
But they don't mean it.
⁸ Each bite will come back up,
and all your kind words will be wasted.

Ninth saying

⁹ Don't talk to fools —
they will just make fun of you.

Tenth saying

¹⁰ Don't move a boundary marker*
or take the land that belongs to orphans.
¹¹ God All-Powerful is there
to defend them against you.

Eleventh saying

¹² Listen to instruction
and do your best to learn.

Twelfth saying

¹³ Don't fail to correct your children.
You won't kill them by being firm,
¹⁴ and it may even save their lives.

Thirteenth saying

¹⁵ My children, if you show good sense,
I will be happy,
¹⁶ and if you are truthful, I will really be glad.

*22.28 marker: In ancient Israel boundary lines were sacred because all property was a gift from the Lord (see Deuteronomy 19.14).

*23.10 marker: See the note at 22.28.

Fourteenth saying

17 Don't be jealous of sinners,
   but always honour the LORD.
18 Then you will truly have hope
   for the future.

Fifteenth saying

19 Listen to me, my children!
   Be wise and have enough sense
   to follow the right path.
20 Don't be a heavy drinker
   or stuff yourself with food.
21 It will make you feel drowsy,
   and you will end up poor
   with only rags to wear.

Sixteenth saying

22 Pay attention to your father,
   and don't neglect your mother
   when she grows old.
23 Invest in truth and wisdom,
   discipline and good sense,
   and don't part with them.
24 Make your father truly happy
   by living right
   and showing sound judgment.
25 Make your parents proud,
   especially your mother.

Seventeenth saying

26 My son, pay close attention,
   and gladly follow my example.
27 Bad women and unfaithful wives
   are like a deep pit —
28 they are waiting to attack you
   like a gang of robbers
   with victim after victim.

Eighteenth saying

29 Who is always in trouble?
   Who argues and fights?
   Who has cuts and bruises?
   Whose eyes are red?
30 Everyone who stays up late,
   having just one more drink.
31 Don't even look
   at that colourful stuff
   bubbling up in the glass!
   It goes down so easily,
32 but later it bites
   like a poisonous snake.
33 You will see weird things,
   and your mind will play tricks on you.
34 You will feel tossed about
   like someone trying to sleep
   on a ship in a storm.

35 You will be bruised all over,
   without even remembering
   how it all happened.
   And you will lie awake asking,
   "When will morning come,
   so I can drink some more?"

CHAPTER 24

Nineteenth saying

1 Don't be jealous of crooks
   or want to be their friends.
2 All they think about
   and talk about is violence and cruelty.

Twentieth saying

3 Use wisdom and understanding
   to establish your home;
4 let good sense fill the rooms
   with priceless treasures.

Twenty-first saying

5 Wisdom brings strength,
   and knowledge gives power.
6 Battles are won by listening to advice
   and making a lot of plans.

Twenty-second saying

7 Wisdom is too much for fools!
   Their advice is no good.

Twenty-third saying

8 No one but troublemakers
   think up trouble.
9 Everyone hates senseless fools
   who think up ways to sin.

Twenty-fourth saying

10 Don't give up and be helpless
   in times of trouble.

Twenty-fifth saying

11 Don't fail to rescue those
   who are doomed to die.
12 Don't say, "I didn't know it!"
   God can read your mind.
   He watches each of us
   and knows our thoughts.
   And God will pay us back
   for what we do.

Twenty-sixth saying

13 Honey is good for you, my children,
   and it tastes sweet.
14 Wisdom is like honey for your life —
   if you find it, your future is bright.

Twenty-seventh saying

15 Don't be a cruel person
who attacks good people
and hurts their families.
16 Even if good people fall seven times,
they will get back up.
But when trouble strikes the wicked,
that's the end of them.

Twenty-eighth saying

17 Don't be happy to see your enemies trip
and fall down.
18 The LORD will find out and be unhappy.
Then he will stop
being angry with them.

Twenty-ninth saying

19 Don't let evil people worry you
or make you jealous.
20 They will soon be gone
like the flame of a lamp that burns out.

Thirtieth saying

21 My children, you must respect
the LORD and the king,
and you must not make friends
with anyone
who rebels against either of them.
22 Who knows what sudden disaster
the LORD or a ruler might bring?

More sayings that make good sense

23 Here are some more sayings
that make good sense:
When you judge,
you must be fair.
24 If you let the guilty go free,
people of all nations
will hate and curse you.
25 But if you punish the guilty,
things will go well for you,
and you will prosper.
26 Giving an honest answer
is a sign of true friendship.
27 Get your fields ready
and plant your crops
before setting up home.
28 Don't accuse anyone who isn't guilty.
Don't ever tell a lie
29 or say to someone,
"I'll get even with you!"

30 I once walked by the field
and the vineyard of a lazy fool.
31 Thorns and weeds were everywhere,
and the stone wall had fallen down.
32 When I saw this,

it taught me a lesson:
33 Sleep a little. Doze a little.
Fold your hands
and twiddle your thumbs.
34 Suddenly poverty hits you
and everything is gone!

More of Solomon's wise sayings

CHAPTER 25

1 Here are more of Solomon's proverbs.
They were copied by the officials
of King Hezekiah of Judah.
2 God is praised for being mysterious;
rulers are praised for explaining mysteries.
3 Who can fully understand
the thoughts of a ruler?
They reach beyond the sky
and go deep in the earth.

4 Silver must be purified
before it can be used
to make something of value.
5 Evil people must be removed
before anyone can rule with justice.

6 Don't try to seem important
in the court of a ruler.
7 It's better for the ruler
to give you a high position
than for you to be embarrassed
in front of royal officials.
Be sure you are right
8 before you sue someone,
or you might lose your case
and be embarrassed.

9 When you and someone else
can't get along,
don't gossip about it.•
10 Others will find out,
and your reputation will then be ruined.

11 The right word at the right time
is like precious gold set in silver.
12 Listening to good advice
is worth much more
than jewellery made of gold.
13 A messenger you can trust
is just as refreshing
as cool water in summer.
14 Broken promises
are worse than rain clouds
that don't bring rain.

See also: 24.33,34: Prov 6.10,11. 25.6,7: Luke 14.8-10.

¹⁵ Patience and gentle talk
     can convince a ruler
     and overcome any problem.

¹⁶ Eating too much honey
     can make you sick.
¹⁷ Don't visit friends too often,
     or they will get tired of it
     and start hating you.
¹⁸ Telling lies about friends
     is like attacking them
     with clubs and swords
     and sharp arrows.
¹⁹ A friend you can't trust in times of trouble
     is like having a toothache
     or a sore foot.
²⁰ Singing to someone in deep sorrow
     is like pouring vinegar in an open cut.*

²¹ If your enemies are hungry,
     give them something to eat.
     And if they are thirsty,
     give them something to drink.
²² This will be the same
     as piling burning coals on their heads.
     And the LORD will reward you.
²³ As surely as rain blows in from the north,
     anger is caused by cruel words.
²⁴ It's better to stay outside
     on the roof of your house
     than to live inside with a nagging wife.

²⁵ Good news from far away
     refreshes like cold water
     when you are thirsty.
²⁶ When a good person gives in
     to the wicked,
     it's like dumping rubbish
     in a stream of clear water.
²⁷ Don't eat too much honey
     or always want praise.*
²⁸ Losing self-control
     leaves you as helpless
     as a city without a wall.

CHAPTER 26

Don't be a fool

¹ Expecting snow in summer
   and rain in the dry season
   makes more sense
   than honouring a fool.
² A curse you don't deserve will take wings
   and fly away like a sparrow or a swallow.
³ Horses and donkeys
   must be beaten and bridled —
   and so must fools.

⁴ Don't make a fool of yourself
   by answering a fool.
⁵ But if you answer any fools,
   show how foolish they are,
   so they won't feel clever.

⁶ Sending a message by a fool
   is like chopping off your foot
   and drinking poison.
⁷ A fool with words of wisdom
   is like an athlete
   with legs that can't move.*
⁸ Are you going to honour a fool?
   Why not shoot a slingshot
   with the stone tied tight?
⁹ A thorn bush waved around
   in the hand of a drunkard
   is no worse than a proverb
   in the mouth of a fool.

¹⁰ It's no cleverer to shoot arrows
   at every passer-by
   than it is to hire a bunch
   of worthless nobodies.*
¹¹ Dogs return to eat their vomit,
   just as fools repeat their foolishness.
¹² There is more hope for a fool
   than for someone who says,
   "I'm really clever!"

¹³ Don't be lazy and keep saying,
   "There's a lion outside!"
¹⁴ A door turns on its hinges,
   but a lazy person just turns over in bed.
¹⁵ Some of us are so lazy
   that we won't lift a hand
   to feed ourselves.
¹⁶ A lazy person says,
   "I am cleverer than everyone else."

¹⁷ It's better to take hold
   of a mad dog by the ears
   than to take part
   in someone else's argument.
¹⁸ It's no crazier to shoot
   sharp and flaming arrows
¹⁹ than to cheat someone and say,
   "I was only fooling!"

²⁰ Where there is no fuel a fire goes out;
   where there is no gossip
   arguments come to an end.
²¹ Troublemakers start trouble,
   just as sparks and fuel start a fire.
²² There is nothing so delicious
   as the taste of gossip!
   It melts in your mouth.

See also: **25.21,22:** Rom 12.20.   See also: **26.11:** 2 Pet 2.22.

616

²³ Hiding hateful thoughts
    behind smooth' talk
is like coating a clay pot
    with a cheap glaze.
²⁴ The pleasant talk of an enemy
    hides more evil plans
²⁵ than can be counted —
    so don't believe a word!
²⁶ Everyone will see through
    those evil plans.
²⁷ If you dig a pit, you will fall in;
    if you start a stone rolling,
    it will roll back on you.
²⁸ Watch out for anyone
    who tells lies and flatters —
    they are out to get you.

CHAPTER 27

Don't boast about tomorrow

¹ Don't boast about tomorrow!
    Each day brings its own surprises.
² Don't boast about yourself —
    let others praise you.
³ Stones and sand are heavy,
    but trouble caused by a fool
    is a much heavier load.
⁴ An angry person is dangerous,
    but a jealous person is even worse.
⁵ A truly good friend
    will openly correct you.
⁶ You can trust a friend who corrects you,
    but kisses from an enemy
    are nothing but lies.
⁷ If you have had enough to eat,
    honey doesn't taste good,
    but if you are really hungry,
    you will eat anything.
⁸ When you are far from home,
    you feel like a bird without a nest.
⁹ The sweet smell of incense
    can make you feel good,
    but true friendship is better still.'
¹⁰ Don't desert an old friend of your family
    or visit your relatives
    when you are in trouble.
    A friend nearby is better
    than relatives far away.
¹¹ My child, show good sense!
    Then I will be happy
    and able to answer anyone
    who criticizes me.

¹² Be cautious and hide
    when you see danger —
    don't be stupid and walk
    right into trouble.
¹³ Don't loan money to a stranger
    unless you are given something
    to guarantee payment.
¹⁴ A loud greeting
    early in the morning
    is the same as a curse.
¹⁵ The steady dripping of rain
    and the nagging of a wife
    are one and the same.
¹⁶ It's easier to catch the wind
    or hold olive oil in your hand
    than to stop a nagging wife.
¹⁷ Just as iron sharpens iron,
    friends sharpen the minds of each other.
¹⁸ Take care of a tree,
    and you will eat its fruit;
    look after your master,
    and you will be praised.
¹⁹ You see your face in a mirror
    and your thoughts
    in the minds of others.
²⁰ Death and the grave are never satisfied,
    and neither are we.
²¹ Gold and silver are tested
    in a red-hot furnace,
    but we are tested by praise.
²² No matter how hard you beat a fool,
    you can't pound out the foolishness.
²³ You should take good care
    of your sheep and goats,
²⁴ because wealth and honour
    don't last for ever.
²⁵ After the hay is cut
    and the new growth appears
    and the harvest is over,
²⁶ you can sell lambs and goats
    to buy clothes and land.
²⁷ From the milk of the goats,
    you can make enough cheese
    to feed your family and all your servants.

CHAPTER 28

The Law of God makes sense

¹ Wicked people run away
    when no one chases them,
    but those who live right
    are as brave as lions.
² In time of civil war
    there are many leaders,
    but a sensible leader
    restores law and order.'

See also: 27.1: Jam 4.13-16.

3 When someone poor takes over
  and ill-treats the poor,
  it's like a heavy rain
  destroying the crops.

4 Lawbreakers praise criminals,
  but law-abiding citizens
  always oppose them.

5 Criminals don't know what justice means,
  but all who respect the LORD
  understand it completely.

6 It's better to be poor and live right,
  than to be rich and dishonest.

7 It makes good sense
  to obey the Law of God,
  but you disgrace your parents
  if you make friends
  with worthless nobodies.

8 If you make money by charging
  high interest rates,
  you will lose it all to someone
  who cares for the poor.

9 God cannot stand the prayers
  of anyone who disobeys his Law.

10 By leading good people to sin,
  you dig a pit for yourself,
  but all who live right
  will have a bright future.

11 The rich think highly of themselves,
  but anyone poor and sensible
  sees right through them.

12 When an honest person wins,
  it's time to celebrate;
  when crooks are in control,
  it's best to hide.

13 If you don't confess your sins,
  you will be a failure.
  But God will be merciful
  if you confess your sins and give them up.

14 The LORD blesses everyone
  who is afraid to do evil,
  but if you are cruel,
  you will end up in trouble.

15 A ruler who ill-treats the poor
  is like a roaring lion
  or a bear hunting for food.

16 A heartless leader is a fool,
  but anyone who refuses
  to get rich by cheating others
  will live a long time.

17 Don't give help to murderers!
  Make them stay on the run
  for as long as they live.'

18 Honesty will keep you safe,
  but everyone who is crooked
  will suddenly fall.

19 Work hard, and you will have
  a lot of food;
  waste time, and you will have
  a lot of trouble.

20 God blesses his loyal people,
  but punishes all who want
  to get rich quick.

21 It isn't right to be unfair,
  but some people can be bribed
  with only a piece of bread.

22 Don't be selfish and eager to get rich —
  you will end up worse off
  than you can imagine.

23 Honest correction is appreciated
  more than flattery.

24 If you cheat your parents
  and don't think it's wrong,
  you are a common thief.

25 Selfish people cause trouble,
  but you will live a full life
  if you trust the LORD.

26 Only fools would trust
  what they alone think,
  but if you live by wisdom,
  you will do all right.

27 Giving to the poor
  will keep you from poverty,
  but if you close your eyes to their needs,
  everyone will curse you.

28 When crooks are in control,
  everyone tries to hide,
  but when they lose power,
  good people are everywhere.

CHAPTER 29

Use good sense

1 If you keep being stubborn
  after many warnings,
  you will suddenly discover
  you have gone too far.

2 When justice rules a nation,
  everyone is glad;
  when injustice rules,
  everyone groans.

3 If you love wisdom,
  your parents will be glad,
  but chasing after bad women
  will cost you everything.

4 An honest ruler
  makes the nation strong;
  a ruler who takes bribes
  will bring it to ruin.

5 Flattery is nothing less
  than setting a trap.

⁶ Your sins will catch you,
   but everyone who lives right
      will sing and celebrate.
⁷ The wicked don't care
   about the rights of the poor,
      but good people do.
⁸ Sneering at others is a spark
   that sets a city on fire;
      using good sense can put out
         the flames of anger.

⁹ Be wise and don't sue a fool.
   You won't get satisfaction,
      because all the fool will do
         is sneer and shout.
¹⁰ A murderer hates everyone
   who is honest and lives right.
¹¹ Don't be a fool
   and quickly lose your temper —
      be sensible and patient.

¹² A ruler who listens to lies
   will have corrupt officials.
¹³ The poor and all who abuse them
   must each depend on God for light.
¹⁴ Kings who are fair to the poor
   will rule for ever.

¹⁵ Correct your children,
   and they will be wise;
      children out of control
         disgrace their mothers.
¹⁶ Crime increases
   when crooks are in power,
      but law-abiding citizens
         will see them fall.
¹⁷ If you correct your children,
   they will bring you peace and happiness.

¹⁸ Without guidance from God,
   law and order disappear,
      but God blesses everyone
         who obeys his Law.
¹⁹ Even when servants are clever,
   it takes more than words
      to make them obey.
²⁰ There is more hope for a fool
   than for someone who speaks
      without thinking.
²¹ Slaves you treat kindly
   from their childhood
      will cause you sorrow.
²² A person with a quick temper
   stirs up arguments
      and commits a lot of sins.

²³ Too much pride brings disgrace;
   humility leads to honour.
²⁴ If you take part in a crime,
   you are your worst enemy,
      because even under oath
         you can't tell the truth.
²⁵ Don't fall into the trap
   of being a coward —
      trust the LORD, and you will be safe.
²⁶ Many try to make friends with a ruler,
   but justice comes from the LORD.
²⁷ Good people and criminals
   can't stand each other.

The sayings of Agur

CHAPTER 30

¹ These are the sayings
   and the message of Agur son of Jakeh.
      Someone cries out to God,
         "I am completely worn out!
            How can I last?"
² I am far too stupid
   to be considered human.
³ I never was wise,
   and I don't understand what God is like."

⁴ Has anyone gone up to heaven
   and come back down?
      Has anyone grabbed hold of the wind?
      Has anyone wrapped up the sea
         or marked out boundaries
            for the earth?
   If you know of any
      who have done such things,
         then tell me their names
            and their children's names.

⁵ Everything God says is true —
   and it's a shield for all
      who come to him for safety.
⁶ Don't change what God has said!
   He will correct you and show
      that you are a liar.

⁷ There are two things, Lord,
   I want you to do for me before I die:
⁸ make me absolutely honest,
   and don't let me be too poor or too rich.
      Give me just what I need.
⁹ If I have too much to eat,
   I might forget about you;
      if I don't have enough,
         I might steal and disgrace your name.

¹⁰ Don't tell a slave owner something bad
   about one of the slaves.
      That slave will curse you,
         and you will be in trouble.

¹¹ Some people curse their father
   and even their mother;

12 others think they are perfect,
  but they are stained by sin.
13 Some people are stuck-up
  and act like snobs;
14 others are so greedy
  that they gobble up
  the poor and homeless.

15 Greed' has twins,
  each named "Give me!"
There are three or four things
  that are never satisfied:
16 the world of the dead
  and a childless wife,
  the thirsty earth and a flaming fire.

17 Don't make fun of your father
  or disobey your mother —
crows will peck out your eyes,
  and vultures will eat the rest of you.

18 There are three or four things
  I cannot understand:
19 how eagles fly so high
  or snakes crawl on rocks,
  how ships sail the ocean
  or people fall in love.

20 An unfaithful wife says,
  "Sleeping with another man
  is as natural as eating."

21 There are three or four things
  that make the earth tremble
  and are unbearable:
22 a slave who becomes king,
  a fool who eats too much,
23 a hateful woman
  who finds a husband, and a slave
  who takes the place
  of the woman who owns her.

24 On this earth four things
  are small but very wise:
25 ants, who seem to be feeble,
  but store up food all summer long;
26 badgers, who seem to be weak,
  but live among the rocks;
27 locusts, who have no king,
  but march like an army;
28 lizards,' which can be caught
  in your hand,
  but sneak into palaces.

29 Three or four creatures
  really strut around:
30 those fearless lions
  who rule the jungle,
31 those proud cocks,
  those mountain goats,
  and those rulers who have no enemies.'

32 If you are foolishly boasting
  or planning something evil,
  then stop it now!
33 If you churn milk you get butter;
  if you hit your nose,
  you get blood —
  and if you stay angry,
  you get in trouble.

What King Lemuel's mother taught him

CHAPTER 31

1 These are the sayings
  that King Lemuel of Massa
  was taught by his mother.
2 My son Lemuel, you were born
  in answer to my prayers,
  so listen carefully.
3 Don't waste your life
  chasing after women!
  This has ruined many kings.

4 Kings and leaders should not get drunk
  or even want to drink.
5 Drinking makes you forget
  your responsibilities,
  and you ill-treat the poor.
6 Beer and wine are only for the dying
  or for those who have lost all hope.
7 Let them drink and forget
  how poor and miserable they feel.
8 But you must defend
  those who are helpless
  and have no hope.
9 Be fair and give justice
  to the poor and homeless.

In praise of a good wife

10 A truly good wife
  is the most precious treasure
  a man can find!
11 Her husband depends on her,
  and she never lets him down.
12 She is good to him every day of her life,
13 and with her own hands
  she gladly makes clothes.

14 She is like a sailing ship
  that brings food from across the sea.
15 She gets up before daylight
  to prepare food for her family
  and for her servants.'
16 She knows how to buy land
  and how to plant a vineyard,
17 and she always works hard.

¹⁸ She knows when to buy or sell,
      and she stays busy until late at night.
¹⁹ She spins her own cloth,
²⁰   and she helps the poor and the needy.
²¹ Her family has warm clothing,
      and so she doesn't worry when it snows.
²² She does her own sewing,
      and everything she wears is beautiful.

²³ Her husband is a well-known
      and respected leader
         in the city.
²⁴ She makes clothes to sell
      to the shop owners.
²⁵ She is strong and graceful,ʲ
      as well as cheerful about the future.
²⁶ Her words are sensible,
      and her advice is thoughtful.
²⁷ She takes good care
      of her family and is never lazy.
²⁸ Her children praise her,
      and with great pride her husband says,
²⁹ "There are many good women,
      but you are the best!"

³⁰ Charm can be deceiving,
      and beauty fades away,
   but a woman who honours the LORD
      deserves to be praised.
³¹ Show her respect —
      praise her in public
         for what she has done.

Additional notes

ʲ1.7 the beginning of knowledge: Or "what knowledge is all about".
ʲ1.17 They are . . . trap: Or "Be like a bird that won't go for the bait, if it sees the trap."
ʲ2.7 helpful advice: Or "wisdom".
ʲ6.24 someone else's wife: Or "an evil woman".
ʲ6.30 not even: Or "except".
ʲ7.22 is . . . punished: One possible meaning for the difficult Hebrew text.
ʲ8.22 From the beginning . . . with the LORD: Or "In the very beginning, the LORD created me."
ʲ8.23 gave life to: Or "formed".
ʲ8.30 helping . . . build: Or "like his own child".
ʲ9.10 the beginning of wisdom: Or "what wisdom is all about".
ʲ9.13 Stupidity: Or "A foolish woman".
ʲ10.2 good: Or "generous".
ʲ10.10 and foolish . . . ruin: One ancient translation "but you can help people by correcting them."
ʲ10.22 When . . . regret: Or "No matter how hard you work, your riches really come from the Lord."

ʲ11.16 but . . . rich: Or "a ruthless man will only get rich".
ʲ11.23 Good people . . . trouble: Or "Good people do what is best, but troublemakers just stir up trouble."
ʲ11.30 act . . . follow: Hebrew; one ancient translation "but violence leads to death."
ʲ11.31 rewarded: Or "punished".
ʲ12.9 It's . . . servant: Or "It is better just to have an ordinary job."
ʲ12.12 An evil . . . evil: Or "Evil people love what they get from being evil".
ʲ12.26 wrong: One possible meaning for the difficult Hebrew text of verse 26.
ʲ12.27 but . . . treasure: One possible meaning for the difficult Hebrew text.
ʲ13.15 people . . . disaster: One possible meaning for the difficult Hebrew text.
ʲ13.23 grow: One possible meaning for the difficult Hebrew text of verse 23.
ʲ14.9 Fools . . . wrong: One possible meaning for the difficult Hebrew text.
ʲ14.32 but even . . . faith: One possible meaning for the difficult Hebrew text. Some ancient translations "but good people trust their innocence."
ʲ14.33 but . . . it: One possible meaning for the difficult Hebrew text. Some ancient translations "but not in the mind of a fool."
ʲ16.20 know what . . . doing: Or "do what you're taught".
ʲ18.1 sense: One possible meaning for the difficult Hebrew text of verse 1.
ʲ18.19 Making . . . offended: One possible meaning for the difficult Hebrew text.
ʲ18.24 Some . . . help: One possible meaning for the difficult Hebrew text.
ʲ19.7 When . . . there: One possible meaning for the difficult Hebrew text.
ʲ19.19 and they . . . again: One possible meaning for the difficult Hebrew text.
ʲ20.21 quick: Or "the wrong way".
ʲ20.28 by God's mercy . . . but: Or "by their mercy . . . and".
ʲ21.4 but sin . . . produce: Or "but sin is the only light they ever follow."
ʲ21.6 and . . . suicide: One possible meaning for the difficult Hebrew text.
ʲ23.7 People . . . eat: One possible meaning for the difficult Hebrew text.
ʲ25.9 When . . . it: Or "Settle a problem privately between you and your neighbour and don't involve others."
ʲ25.20 cut: One possible meaning for the difficult Hebrew text of verse 20.
ʲ25.27 or . . . praise: One possible meaning for the difficult Hebrew text.
ʲ26.7 with . . . move: One possible meaning for the difficult Hebrew text.
ʲ26.10 nobodies: One possible meaning for the difficult Hebrew text of verse 10.
ʲ26.23 smooth: One ancient translation; Hebrew "hateful".

'27.9 still: One possible meaning for the difficult Hebrew text of verse 9.

'28.2 but . . . order: One possible meaning for the difficult Hebrew text.

'28.17 live: One possible meaning for the difficult Hebrew text of verse 17.

'29.10 and lives right: Or "and those who live right are friends of honest people."

'29.21 will . . . sorrow: One possible meaning for the difficult Hebrew text.

'30.1 last: One possible meaning for the difficult Hebrew text of verse 1.

'30.15 Greed: Or "A leech".

'30.28 lizards: Or "spiders".

'30.31 enemies: One possible meaning for the difficult Hebrew text of verse 31.

'31.15 and . . . servants: Or "and to tell her servants what to do."

'31.25 She . . . graceful: Or "The clothes she makes are attractive and of good quality."

Ecclesiastes

A quick look at this book

This book is a search for meaning in life. What can humans do to find satisfaction and happiness? What is worthwhile in life? The search begins with a gloomy outlook — life is boring and as senseless as chasing the wind.

Ecclesiastes looks at one area of life after another, to see whether meaning and purpose for living can be found. The book decides that humans cannot understand the meaning of life, and that life is too short and unfair. This may seem depressing, but Ecclesiastes also shows that some things in life are better than others. For example, it is better to be wise than to be foolish. And God does intend people to enjoy his gifts of work, food, drink, friendship, and marriage. And most important of all:

> Respect and obey God!
>   This is what life is all about.
> God will judge everything we do,
>   even what is done in secret,
>   whether good or bad.

(12.13,14)

The search for meaning in life

CHAPTER 1

Nothing makes sense

¹ When the son of David was king in Jerusalem, he was known to be very wise,* and he said:

² Nothing makes sense!
    Everything is nonsense.
    I have seen it all —
    nothing makes sense!
³ What is there to show
    for all our hard work
    here on this earth?
⁴ People come, and people go,
    but still the world never changes.

⁵ The sun comes up, the sun goes down;
    it hurries right back
    to where it started from.
⁶ The wind blows south,
    the wind blows north;
    round and round it blows
    over and over again.
⁷ All rivers empty into the sea,
    but it never spills over;
    one by one the rivers return
    to their source.'

⁸ All of life is far more boring
    than words could ever say.

---

*1.1 known to be very wise: This stands for the Hebrew word often translated "preacher" or "teacher". The word may refer to someone who was a very wise leader or to someone who had become wise from collecting sayings about wisdom.

Our eyes and our ears are never satisfied
with what we see and hear.
9 Everything that happens
has happened before;
nothing is new, nothing under the sun.
10 Someone might say,
"Here is something new!"
But it happened before,
long before we were born.
11 No one who lived in the past
is remembered any more,
and everyone yet to be born
will be forgotten too.

It is senseless to be wise

12 I said these things when I lived in
Jerusalem as king of Israel. 13 With all my
wisdom I tried to understand everything that
happens here on earth. And God has made
this so hard for us humans to do. 14 I have
seen it all, and everything is just as senseless
as chasing the wind.*

15 If something is crooked,
it can't be made straight;
if something isn't there,
it can't be counted.

16 I said to myself, "You are by far the wisest
person who has ever lived in Jerusalem. You
are eager to learn, and you have learnt a lot."
17 Then I decided to find out all I could about
wisdom and foolishness. Soon I realized that
this too was as senseless as chasing the wind.*

18 The more you know,
the more it hurts;
the more you understand,
the more you suffer.

CHAPTER 2

It is senseless to be selfish

1 I said to myself, "Have fun and enjoy
yourself!" But this didn't make sense.
2 Laughing and having fun is mad. What good
does it do? 3 I wanted to find out what was
best for us during the short time we have on
this earth. So I decided to make myself happy
with wine and find out what it means to be
foolish, without really being foolish myself.

4 I did some great things. I built houses and
planted vineyards. 5 I had flower gardens and
orchards full of fruit trees. 6 And I had pools
where I could get water for the trees.

7 I owned slaves, and their sons and
daughters became my slaves. I had more
sheep and goats than anyone who had ever
lived in Jerusalem. 8 Foreign rulers brought
me silver, gold, and precious treasures. Men
and women sang for me, and I had many
wives* who gave me great pleasure.

9 I was the most famous person who had
ever lived in Jerusalem, and I was very wise.
10 I got whatever I wanted and did whatever
made me happy. But most of all, I enjoyed
my work. 11 Then I thought about everything
I had done, including the hard work, and it
was just chasing the wind.* Nothing on
earth is worth the trouble.

Wisdom makes sense

12 I asked myself, "What can the next king do
that I haven't done?" Then I decided to
compare wisdom with foolishness and
stupidity. 13 And I discovered that wisdom is
better than foolishness, just as light is better
than darkness. 14 Wisdom is like having two
good eyes; foolishness leaves you in the dark.
But wise or foolish, we all end up the same.

15 Finally, I said to myself, "Being wise got
me nowhere! The same thing will happen to
me that happens to fools. Nothing makes
sense. 16 Wise or foolish, we all die and are
soon forgotten." 17 This made me hate life.
Everything we do is painful; it's just as
senseless as chasing the wind.*

18 Suddenly I realized that others would
some day get everything I had worked so
hard for, then I started hating it all. 19 Who
knows if those people will be sensible or
stupid? Either way, they will own everything
I have earned by hard work and wisdom. It
doesn't make sense.

20 I thought about all my hard work, and
I felt depressed. 21 When we use our wisdom,
knowledge, and skill to get what we own, why
do we have to leave it to someone who didn't
work for it? This is senseless and wrong.
22 What do we really gain from all our hard
work? 23 Our bodies ache during the day, and
work is torture. Then at night our thoughts
are troubled. It just doesn't make sense.

24 The best thing we can do is to enjoy
eating, drinking, and working.* I believe
these are God's gifts to us, 25 and no one
enjoys eating and living more than I do.
26 If we please God, he will make us wise,

See also: 1.16: 1 King 4.29–31.   2.4–8: 1 King 10.23–27;
2 Chron 9.22–27.

See also: 2.7: 1 King 4.23.   2.8: 1 King 10.10,14–22.
2.9: 1 Chron 29.25.   2.23: Job 5.7; 14.1.   2.24: Ecc 3.13; 5.18;
9.7; Isa 56.12; Luke 12.19; 1 Cor 15.32.   2.26: Job 32.8;
Prov 2.6.

understanding, and happy. But if we sin, God will make us struggle for a living, then he will give all we own to someone who pleases him. This makes no more sense than chasing the wind.◆

Everything has its time

CHAPTER 3

¹ Everything on earth has its own time
and its own season.
² There is a time for birth and death,
planting and reaping,
³ for killing and healing,
destroying and building,
⁴ for crying and laughing,
weeping and dancing,
⁵ for throwing stones
and gathering stones,
embracing and parting.
⁶ There is a time for finding and losing,
keeping and giving,
⁷ for tearing and sewing,
listening and speaking.
⁸ There is also a time for love and hate,
for war and peace.

Life isn't always fair, so live wisely

What God has given us to do

⁹ What do we gain by all our hard work? ¹⁰ I have seen what difficult things God demands of us. ¹¹ God makes everything happen at the right time. Yet none of us can ever fully understand all he has done, and he puts questions in our minds about the past and the future. ¹² I know the best thing we can do is always to enjoy life, ¹³ because God's gift to us is the happiness we get from our food and drink and from the work we do. ¹⁴ Everything God has done will last for ever; nothing he does can ever be changed. God has done all this, so that we will worship him.

¹⁵ Everything that happens
has happened before,
and all that will be has already been —
God does everything
over and over again.◆

The future is known only to God

¹⁶ Everywhere on earth I saw violence and injustice instead of fairness and justice. ¹⁷ So I told myself that God has set a time and

a place for everything. He will judge everyone, both the wicked and the good. ¹⁸ I know that God is testing us to show us that we are merely animals. ¹⁹ Like animals we breathe and die, and we are no better off than they are. It just doesn't make sense. ²⁰ All living creatures go to the same place. We are made from earth, and we return to the earth. ²¹ Who really knows if our spirits go up and the spirits of animals go down into the earth? ²² We were meant to enjoy our work, and that's the best thing we can do. We can never know the future.

CHAPTER 4

¹ I looked again and saw people being ill-treated everywhere on earth. They were crying, but no one was there to offer comfort, and those who ill-treated them were powerful. ² I said to myself, "The dead are better off than the living. ³ But those who have never been born are better off than anyone else, because they have never seen the terrible things that happen on this earth."

⁴ Then I realized that we work and do wonderful things just because we are jealous of others. This makes no more sense than chasing the wind.◆

⁵ Fools will fold their hands
and starve to death.
⁶ Yet a very little food eaten in peace
is better than twice as much
earned from overwork
and chasing the wind.◆

⁷ Once again I saw that nothing on earth makes sense. ⁸ For example, some people don't have friends or family. But they are never satisfied with what they own, and they never stop working to get more. They should ask themselves, "Why am I always working to have more? Who will get what I leave behind?" What a senseless and miserable life!

It is better to have a friend

⁹ You are better off having a friend than being all alone, because then you will get more enjoyment out of what you earn. ¹⁰ If you fall, your friend can help you up. But if you fall without having a friend nearby, you are really in trouble. ¹¹ If you sleep alone, you won't have anyone to keep you warm on a cold night. ¹² Someone might be able to beat up one of you, but not both of you. As the saying goes, "A rope made from three strands of cord is hard to break."

13 You may be poor and young. But if you are wise, you are better off than a foolish old king who won't listen to advice. 14 Even if you were not born into the royal family and have been a prisoner and poor, you can still be king. 15 I once saw everyone in the world follow a young leader who came to power after the king was gone. His followers could not even be counted. But years from now, no one will praise him — this makes no more sense than chasing the wind.*

CHAPTER 5

Be careful how you worship

1 Be careful what you do when you enter the house of God. Some fools go there to offer sacrifices, even though they haven't sinned.* But it's just to listen when you go to worship. 2 Don't talk before you think or make promises to God without thinking them through. God is in heaven, and you are on earth, so don't talk too much. 3 If you keep thinking about something, you will dream about it. If you talk too much, you will say the wrong thing.

4 God doesn't like fools. So don't be slow to keep your promises to God. 5 It's better not to make a promise at all than to make one and not keep it. 6 Don't let your mouth get you in trouble! And don't say to the worship leader,* "I didn't mean what I said." God can destroy everything you have worked for, so don't say something that makes God angry.

7 Respect and obey God! Daydreaming leads to a lot of senseless talk.*

8 Don't be surprised if the poor of your country are abused, and injustice takes the place of justice. After all, the lower officials must do what the higher ones order them to do. 9 And since the king is the highest official, he benefits most from the taxes paid on the land.*

10 If you love money and wealth, you will never be satisfied with what you have. This doesn't make sense either. 11 The more you have, the more everyone expects from you. Your money won't do you any good — others will just spend it for you. 12 If you have to work hard for a living, you can rest well at night, even if you don't have much to eat. But if you are rich, you can't even sleep.

13 I have seen something terribly unfair. People get rich, but it does them no good. 14 Suddenly they lose everything in a bad business deal, then have nothing to leave for

their children. 15 They came into this world naked, and when they die, they will be just as naked. They can't take anything with them, and they won't have anything to show for all their work. 16 That's terribly unfair. They leave the world just as they came into it. They gained nothing from running after the wind. 17 Besides all this, they are always gloomy at mealtimes, and they are troubled, sick, and bitter.*

18 What is the best thing to do in the short life that God has given us? I think we should enjoy eating, drinking, and working hard. This is what God intends us to do. 19 Suppose you are very rich and able to enjoy everything you own. Then go ahead and enjoy it — this is God's gift to you. 20 God will keep you so happy that you won't have time to worry about each day.

CHAPTER 6

Don't depend on wealth

1 There is something else terribly unfair, and it troubles everyone on earth. 2 God may give you everything you want — money, property, and wealth. Then God doesn't let you enjoy it, and someone you don't even know gets it all. That's senseless and terribly unfair!

3 You may live a long time and have a hundred children. But a child born dead is better off than you, unless you enjoy life and have a decent burial. 4-5 That child will never live to see the sun or to have a name, and it will go straight to the world of darkness. But it will still find more rest than you, 6 even if you live two thousand years and don't enjoy life. As you know, we all end up in the same place.

7 We struggle just to have enough to eat, but we are never satisfied. 8 We may be sensible, yet we are no better off than a fool. And if we are poor, it still doesn't do us any good to try to live right. 9 It's better to enjoy what we have than always to want something else, because that makes no more sense than chasing the wind.*

10 Everything that happens was decided long ago. We humans know what we are like, and we can't argue with God, because he is* too strong for us. 11 The more we talk, the less sense we make, so what good does it do to talk? 12 Life is short and meaningless, and it fades away like a shadow. Who knows what is best for us? Who knows what will happen after we are gone?

No one knows what the future will bring

CHAPTER 7

The best in life

¹ A good reputation
   at the time of death
is better than loving care
   at the time of birth.'

² It's better to go to a funeral
   than to attend a feast;
funerals remind us
   that we all must die.

³ Choose sorrow over laughter
   because a sad face
may hide a happy heart.

⁴ A sensible person mourns,
   but fools always laugh.

⁵ Harsh correction is better
   than the songs of a fool.

⁶ Foolish laughter is stupid.
   It sounds like thorns crackling in a fire.

⁷ Corruption' makes fools
   of sensible people,
and bribes can ruin you.

⁸ Something completed is better
   than something just begun;
patience is better than too much pride.

⁹ Only fools get angry quickly
   and hold a grudge.

¹⁰ It isn't wise to ask,
   "Why is everything worse
      than it used to be?"

¹¹ Having wisdom is better
   than an inheritance.

¹² Wisdom will protect you just like money;
   knowledge with good sense
      will lead you to life.

¹³ Think of what God has done!
   If God makes something crooked,
      can you make it straight?

¹⁴ When times are good,
   you should be cheerful;
when times are bad,
   think what it means.
God makes them both
   to keep us from knowing
      what will happen next.

Some of life's questions

¹⁵ I have seen everything during this senseless life of mine. I have seen good citizens die for doing the right thing, and I have seen

criminals live to a ripe old age. ¹⁶ So don't destroy yourself by being too good or acting too clever! ¹⁷ Don't die before your time by being too evil or acting like a fool. ¹⁸ Keep to the middle of the road. You can do this if you truly respect God.

¹⁹ Wisdom will make you stronger than the ten most powerful leaders in your city.

²⁰ No one in this world always does right.

²¹ Don't listen to everything that everyone says, or you might hear your servant cursing you. ²² Haven't you cursed many others?

²³ I told myself that I would be clever and try to understand all of this, but it was too much for me. ²⁴ The truth is beyond us. It's far too deep. ²⁵ So I decided to learn everything I could and become wise enough to discover what life is all about. At the same time, I wanted to understand why it's stupid and senseless to be an evil fool.

²⁶ Here is what I discovered: a bad woman is worse than death. She is a trap, reaching out with body and soul to catch you. But if you obey God, you can escape. If you don't obey, you are done for. ²⁷ With all my wisdom I have tried to find out how everything fits together, ²⁸ but so far I have not been able to. I do know there is one good man in a thousand, but never have I found a good woman. ²⁹ I did learn one thing: we were completely honest when God created us, but now we have twisted minds.

CHAPTER 8

¹ Who is clever enough
   to explain everything?
Wisdom makes you cheerful
   and gives you a smile.

Obey the king

² If you promised God that you would be loyal to the king, I advise you to keep that promise. ³ Don't quickly oppose the king or argue when he has already made up his mind. ⁴ The king's word is law. No one can ask him, "Why are you doing this?" ⁵ If you obey the king, you will stay out of trouble. So be clever and learn what to do and when to do it. ⁶ Life is hard, but there is a time and a place for everything, ⁷ though no one can tell the future. ⁸ We cannot control the wind' or determine the day of our death. There is no escape in time of war, and no one can hide behind evil.

⁹ I noticed all this and thought seriously about what goes on in the world. Why does one person have the power to hurt another?

See also: 7.1: Prov 22.1. 7.9: Jam 1.19.

Who can understand the ways of God?

¹⁰ I saw the wicked buried with honour, but God's people had to leave the holy city and were forgotten.* None of this makes sense. ¹¹ When we see criminals commit crime after crime without being punished, it makes us want to start a life of crime. ¹² They commit hundreds of crimes and live to a ripe old age, in spite of the saying:

> Everyone who lives right
> and respects God will prosper,
> ¹³ but no one who sins
> and rejects God
> will prosper or live very long.

¹⁴ There is something else that doesn't make sense to me. Good citizens are treated as criminals, while criminals are honoured as though they were good citizens. ¹⁵ So I think we should get as much out of life as we possibly can. There is nothing better than to enjoy our food and drink and to have a good time. Then we can make it through this troublesome life that God has given us here on earth.

¹⁶ Day and night I went without sleep, trying to understand what goes on in this world. ¹⁷ I saw everything God does, and I realized that no one can really understand what happens. We may be very wise, but no matter how much we try or how much we claim to know, we cannot understand it all.

CHAPTER 9

One day at a time

¹ I thought about these things. Then I understood that God has power over everyone, even those of us who are wise and live right. Anything can happen to any of us, and so we never know if life will be good or bad.* ² But exactly* the same thing will finally happen to all of us, whether we live right and respect God or sin and don't respect God. Yes, the same thing will happen if we offer sacrifices to God or if we don't, if we keep our promises or break them.

³ It's terribly unfair for the same thing to happen to each of us. We are mean and foolish while we live, and then we die. ⁴ As long as we are alive, we still have hope, just as a live dog is better off than a dead lion. ⁵ We know that we will die, but the dead don't know a thing. Nothing good will happen to them — they are gone and forgotten. ⁶ Their loves, their hates, and their jealous feelings have all disappeared with them. They will never again take part in anything that happens on this earth.

⁷ Be happy and enjoy eating and drinking! God decided long ago that this is what you should do. ⁸ Dress up, comb your hair, and look your best. ⁹ Life is short, and you love your wife, so enjoy being with her. This is what you are supposed to do as you struggle through life on this earth. ¹⁰ Work hard at whatever you do. You will soon go to the world of the dead, where no one works or thinks or reasons or knows anything.

¹¹ Here is something else I have learnt:

> The fastest runners
> and the greatest heroes
> don't always win races and battles.
> Wisdom, intelligence, and skill
> don't always make you healthy,
> rich, or popular.
> We each have our share of bad luck.

¹² None of us know when we might fall victim to a sudden disaster and find ourselves like fish in a net or birds in a trap.

Better to be wise than foolish

¹³ Once I saw what people really think of wisdom. ¹⁴ It happened when a powerful ruler surrounded and attacked a small city where only a few people lived. The enemy army was getting ready to break through the city walls. ¹⁵ But the city was saved by the wisdom of a poor person who was soon forgotten. ¹⁶ So I decided that wisdom is better than strength. Yet if you are poor, no one pays any attention to you, no matter how clever you are.

> ¹⁷ Words of wisdom spoken softly
> make much more sense
> than the shouts of a ruler
> to a crowd of fools.
> ¹⁸ Wisdom is more powerful than weapons,
> yet one mistake can destroy
> all the good you have done.

CHAPTER 10

> ¹ A few dead flies in perfume
> make all of it stink,
> and a little foolishness
> outweighs a lot of wisdom.
> ² Sensible thoughts lead you to do right;
> foolish thoughts lead you to do wrong.
> ³ Fools show their stupidity
> by the way they live;
> it's easy to see they have no sense.

4 Don't give up your job
when your boss gets angry.
If you stay calm, you'll be forgiven.

5 Some things rulers do are terribly unfair:
6 they honour fools, but dishonour the rich;
7 they let slaves ride on horses, but force slave
owners to walk.

8 If you dig a pit,
you might fall in;
if you break down a wall,
a snake might bite you.*

9 You could even get hurt
by chiselling a stone
or chopping a log.

10 If you don't sharpen your axe,
it will be harder to use;
if you are clever,
you'll know what to do.'

11 The power to charm a snake does you
no good if it bites you anyway.

12 If you talk sensibly,
you will have friends;
if you talk foolishly,
you will destroy yourself.

13 Fools begin with nonsense,
and their stupid chatter
ends with disaster.

14 They never tire of talking,
but none of us really know
what the future will bring.

15 Fools wear themselves out —
they don't know enough
to find their way home.'

16 A country is in for trouble
when its ruler is childish,
and its leaders feast all day long.

17 But a nation will prosper
when its ruler is mature,
and its leaders don't feast too much.

18 Some people are too lazy
to fix a leaky roof —
then the house falls in.

19 Eating and drinking
make you feel happy,
and bribes can buy
everything you need.

20 Don't even think about cursing the king;
don't curse the rich,
not even in secret.
A little bird might hear
and tell everything.

CHAPTER 11

It pays to work hard

1 Be generous, and some day
you will be rewarded.'

2 Share what you have
with seven or eight others,
because you never know
when disaster may strike.

3 Rain clouds always bring rain;
trees always stay wherever they fall.

4 If you worry about the weather
and don't plant seeds,
you won't harvest a crop.

5 No one can explain how a baby breathes
before it is born.' So how can anyone explain
what God does? After all, he created
everything.

6 Plant your seeds early in the morning and
keep working in the field until dark. Who
knows? Your work might pay off, and your
seeds might produce.

Respect and obey God

Youth and old age

7 Nothing on earth is more beautiful than the
morning sun. 8 Even if you live to a ripe old
age, you should try to enjoy each day,
because darkness will come and will last a
long time. Nothing makes sense.'

9 Be cheerful and enjoy life while you are
young! Do what you want and find pleasure
in what you see. But don't forget that God
will judge you for everything you do.

10 Rid yourself of all worry and pain,
because the wonderful moments of youth
quickly disappear.

CHAPTER 12

1 Keep your Creator in mind while you are
young! In years to come, you will be
burdened down with troubles and say,
"I don't enjoy life any more."

2 Some day the light of the sun
and the moon and the stars
will all seem dim to you.
Rain clouds will remain over your head.

---

*10.8 a snake might bite you: Walls of houses were
often made of stones with mud to fill in the cracks
between them. If some of the mud washed out, a
snake could be living inside the wall.
See also: 10.8: Psa 7.15; Prov 26.27.

³ Your body will grow feeble,
  your teeth will decay,
  and your eyesight fail.
⁴ The noisy grinding of grain
  will be shut out by your deaf ears,
  but even the song of a bird
  will keep you awake.

⁵ You will be afraid to climb up a hill
  or walk down a road.
  Your hair will turn as white
  as almond blossoms.
  You will feel lifeless and drag along
  like an old grasshopper.

  We each go to our eternal home,
  and the streets are filled
  with those who mourn.

⁶ The silver cord snaps,
  the golden bowl breaks;
  the water pitcher is smashed,
  and the pulley at the well is shattered.
⁷ So our bodies return to the earth,
  and the life-giving breath¹
  returns to God.

⁸ Nothing makes sense.
  I have seen it all —
  nothing makes sense.

Respect and obey God

⁹ I was a wise teacher with much
understanding, and I collected a number of
proverbs that I had carefully studied. ¹⁰ Then
I tried to explain these things in the best and
most accurate way.

¹¹ Words of wisdom are like the stick a
farmer uses to make animals move. These
sayings come from God, our only shepherd,
and they are like nails that fasten things
together.¹ ¹² My child, I warn you to stay
away from any teachings except these.

  There is no end to books,
  and too much study will wear you out.

¹³ Everything you were taught can be put into
a few words:

  Respect and obey God!
  This is what life is all about.

¹⁴ God will judge everything we do,
  even what is done in secret,
  whether good or bad.

Additional notes

'**1.7 return to their source:** Or "flow into the sea".
'**1.14 chasing the wind:** Or "eating the wind."
'**1.17 chasing the wind:** See the note at 1.14.
'**2.8 many wives:** One possible meaning for the difficult Hebrew text.
'**2.11 chasing the wind:** See the note at 1.14.
'**2.17 chasing the wind:** See the note at 1.14.
'**2.24 The best . . . working:** One possible meaning for the difficult Hebrew text.
'**2.26 chasing the wind:** See the note at 1.14.
'**3.15 God does . . . again:** One possible meaning for the difficult Hebrew text.
'**4.4 chasing the wind:** See the note at 1.14.
'**4.6 chasing the wind:** See the note at 1.14.
'**4.16 chasing the wind:** See the note at 1.14.
'**5.1 even . . . sinned:** One possible meaning for the difficult Hebrew text.
'**5.6 worship leader:** Or "messenger".
'**5.7 Daydreaming . . . talk:** One possible meaning for the difficult Hebrew text.
'**5.9 land:** One possible meaning for the difficult Hebrew text of verse 9.
'**5.17 bitter:** One possible meaning for the difficult Hebrew text of verse 17.
'**6.9 chasing the wind:** See the note at 1.14.
'**6.10 with God, because he is:** Or "with anyone who is".
'**7.1 birth:** One possible meaning for the difficult Hebrew text of verse 1.
'**7.7 Corruption:** Or "Oppression".
'**8.8 control the wind:** Or "escape from death".
'**8.10 but . . . forgotten:** One possible meaning for the difficult Hebrew text.
'**9.1 or bad:** Three ancient translations; the Hebrew text does not have these words.
'**9.2 exactly:** One possible meaning for the difficult Hebrew text.
'**10.10 do:** One possible meaning for the difficult Hebrew text of verse 10.
'**10.15 home:** One possible meaning for the difficult Hebrew text of verse 15.
'**11.1 Be generous . . . rewarded:** Or "Don't be afraid to invest. Some day it will pay off."
'**11.5 how . . . born:** Or "what makes the wind blow or how a baby grows inside its mother".
'**11.8 Nothing makes sense:** Or "There's nothing to look forward to!"
'**12.7 life-giving breath:** Or "spirit".
'**12.11 These sayings . . . together:** One possible meaning for the difficult Hebrew text.

Song of Songs

A quick look at this book

The title of this book means "the most beautiful of songs"; in some translations, it is called "The Song of Solomon" (see 1.1).

This book is a collection of songs, or poems, in which a woman and a man tell about their love for each other. Sometimes they speak to themselves, sometimes to each other or to friends, and in some of the poems they seem to be remembering earlier times in their relationship.

The poems have been interpreted in different ways. Some have thought that the man was King Solomon himself. Others read the book as a drama: the woman was taken to the court of Solomon, but she was still in love with a man back in her home town, and finally the two are reunited. Some interpreters believe that the man and woman stand for God and his people or Christ and the Church.

But it is also possible to take the book as a collection of poems expressing the deep and powerful love that a woman and a man can have for each other. In fact, they may have been part of marriage celebrations in ancient Israel. As one of the poems says:

> *The passion of love bursting into flame*
> *is more powerful than death,*
> *stronger than the grave.*
> *Love cannot be drowned*
> *by oceans or floods;*
> *it cannot be bought,*
> *no matter what is offered.*
>
> (8.6b,7)

Love is better than wine

CHAPTER 1

¹ This is Solomon's
most beautiful song.

She speaks:

² Kiss me tenderly!
Your love is better than wine,
³ and you smell so sweet.
All the young women adore you;
the very mention of your name
is like spreading perfume.
⁴⁻⁵ Hurry, my king! Let's hurry.
Take me to your home.

The young women speak:

We are happy for you!
And we praise your love
even more than wine.

She speaks:

> Young women of Jerusalem,
>   it is only right
>   that you should adore him.
> My skin is dark and beautiful,
>   like a tent in the desert
>   or like Solomon's curtains.
> ⁶ Don't stare at me just because the sun
>   has darkened my skin.
> My brothers were angry with me;
>   they made me work in the vineyard,
>   and so I neglected my complexion.
>
> Don't let the other shepherds
>   think badly of me.⸰
> ⁷ I'm not one of those women
>   who shamelessly follow
>   after shepherds.⸰
> My darling, I love you!
>   Where do you feed your sheep
>   and let them rest at midday?

He speaks:

> ⁸ My dearest, if you don't know,
>   just follow the path of the sheep.
> Then feed your young goats
>   near the shepherds' tents.
> ⁹ You move as gracefully as the pony
>   that leads the chariot of the king.
> ¹⁰ Earrings add to your beauty,
>   and you wear a necklace
>   of precious stones.
> ¹¹ Let's make you some jewellery
>   of gold, woven with silver.

She speaks:

> ¹² My king, while you
>   were on your couch,
>   my love was a magic charm.⸰
> ¹³ My darling, you are perfume
>   between my breasts;
> ¹⁴ you are flower blossoms
>   from the gardens of En-Gedi.＊

He speaks:

> ¹⁵ My darling, you are lovely,
>   so very lovely —
>   your eyes are those of a dove.

She speaks:

> ¹⁶ My love, you are handsome,
>   truly handsome —
>   the fresh green grass
>   will be our wedding bed
> ¹⁷ in the shade of cedar
>   and cypress trees.

Love makes everything beautiful

CHAPTER 2

She speaks:

> ¹ I am merely a rose＊
>   from the land of Sharon,
>   a lily from the valley.

He speaks:

> ² My darling, when compared
>   with other young women,
>   you are a lily among thorns.

She speaks:

> ³ And you, my love,
>   are an apple tree
>   among trees of the forest.
> Your shade brought me pleasure;
>   your fruit was sweet.
> ⁴ You led me to your banquet room
>   and showered me with love.
> ⁵ Refresh and strengthen me
>   with raisins and apples.
> I am hungry for love!
> ⁶ Put your left hand under my head
>   and embrace me with your right arm.
>
> ⁷ Young women of Jerusalem,
>   promise me by the power
>   of deer and gazelles＊
>   never to awaken love before it is ready.

Winter is past

She speaks:

> ⁸ I hear the voice of the one I love,
>   as he comes leaping
>   over mountains and hills
> ⁹ like a deer or a gazelle.
> Now he stands outside our wall,
>   looking through the window
> ¹⁰ and speaking to me.

He speaks:

> My darling, I love you!
>   Let's go away together.
> ¹¹ Winter is past,
>   the rain has stopped;

＊1.14 En-Gedi: An oasis west of the Dead Sea.

＊2.1 rose: The traditional translation. The exact variety of the flower is not known, though it may have been a crocus.

＊2.7 deer and gazelles: Deer and gazelles were sacred animals in some religions of Old Testament times, and they were thought to have special powers.

12 flowers cover the earth,
it's time to sing.'
The cooing of doves
is heard in our land.
13 Fig trees are bearing fruit,
while blossoms on grapevines
fill the air with perfume.
My darling, I love you!
Let's go away together.
14 You are my dove
hiding among the rocks
on the side of a cliff.
Let me see how lovely you are!
Let me hear the sound
of your melodious voice.
15 Our vineyards are in blossom;
we must catch the little foxes
that destroy the vineyards.'

She speaks:

16 My darling, I am yours,
and you are mine,
as you feed your sheep
among the lilies.
17 Pretend to be a young deer
dancing on mountain slopes'
until daylight comes
and shadows fade away.

CHAPTER 3

Beautiful dreams

She speaks:

1 While in bed at night,
I reached for the one I love
with heart and soul.
I looked for him,
but he wasn't there.
2 So I searched through the town
for the one I love.
I looked in every street,
but he wasn't there.
3 I even asked the guards
patrolling the town,
"Have you seen the one
I love so much?"
4 Straight after that, I found him.
I held him and would not let go
until I had taken him
to the home of my mother.
5 Young women of Jerusalem,
promise me by the power
of deer and gazelles,*
never to awaken love
before it is ready.

*3.5 deer and gazelles: See the note at 2.7.

The wedding

The groom and the wedding party

Their friends speak:

6 What do we see approaching
from the desert
like a cloud of smoke?
With it comes the sweet smell of spices,
including myrrh and frankincense.
7 It is King Solomon carried on a throne,
surrounded by sixty
of Israel's best soldiers.
8 Each of them wears a sword.
They are experts at fighting,
even in the dark.
9 The throne is made of trees
from Lebanon.
10 Its posts are silver, the back is gold,
and the seat is covered
with purple cloth.
You women of Jerusalem
have taken great care
to furnish the inside.'
11 Now come and see the crown
given to Solomon by his mother
on his happy wedding day.

CHAPTER 4

What a beautiful bride

He speaks:

1 My darling, you are lovely,
so very lovely —
as you look through your veil,
your eyes are those of a dove.
Your hair tosses about
as gracefully as goats
coming down from Gilead.
2 Your teeth are whiter
than sheep freshly washed;
they match perfectly,
not one is missing.
3 Your lips are crimson cords,
your mouth is shapely;
behind your veil are hidden
beautiful rosy cheeks.'
4 Your neck is more graceful
than the tower of David,
decorated with thousands
of warriors' shields.
5 Your breasts are perfect;
they are twin deer
feeding among lilies.
6 I will hasten to those hills
sprinkled with sweet perfume
and stay there till sunrise.

⁷ My darling, you are lovely in every way.
⁸ My bride, together
    we will leave Lebanon!
We will say goodbye to the peaks
    of Mount Amana, Senir, and Hermon,
    where lions and leopards
    live in the caves.

⁹ My bride, my very own,
    you have stolen my heart!
With one glance from your eyes
    and the glow of your necklace,
    you have stolen my heart.

¹⁰ Your love is sweeter than wine;
    the smell of your perfume
    is more fragrant than spices.

¹¹ Your lips are a honeycomb;
    milk and honey flow from your tongue.
Your dress has the aroma
    of cedar trees from Lebanon.

¹² My bride, my very own,
    you are a garden,
    a fountain closed off to all others.

¹³ Your arms' are vines,
    covered with delicious fruits
    and all sorts of spices —
    henna, nard,

¹⁴ saffron, calamus, cinnamon,
    frankincense, myrrh, and aloes —
    all the finest spices.

¹⁵ You are a spring in the garden,
    a fountain of pure water,
    and a refreshing stream
    from Mount Lebanon.

She speaks:

¹⁶ Let the north wind blow,
    the south wind too!
Let them spread the aroma of my garden,
    so the one I love may enter
    and taste its delicious fruits.

CHAPTER 5

He speaks:

¹ My bride, my very own,
    I come to my garden
    and enjoy its spices.
I eat my honeycomb and honey;
    I drink my wine and milk.

Their friends speak:

Eat and drink
    until you are drunk with love.

Why is the one you love more special than others?

Another dream

She speaks:

² I was asleep, but dreaming:
    the one I love was at the door,
    knocking and saying,
    "My darling, my very own,
    my flawless dove,
    open the door for me!
My head is drenched with evening dew."

³ But I had already undressed
    and bathed my feet.
Should I dress again
    and get my feet dirty?

⁴ Then my darling's hand
    reached to open the latch,
    and my heart stood still.

⁵ When I rose to open the door,
    my hands and my fingers
    dripped with perfume.

⁶ My heart stood still
    while he spoke to me,
but when I opened the door,
    my darling had disappeared.
I searched and shouted,
    but I could not find him —
    there was no answer.

⁷ Then I was found by the guards
    patrolling the town
    and guarding the wall.
They beat me up
    and stripped off my robe.

⁸ Young women of Jerusalem,
    if you find the one I love,
    please say to him,
    "She is weak with desire."

Their friends speak:

⁹ Most beautiful of women,
    why is the one you love
    more special than others?
Why do you ask us
    to tell him how you feel?

She speaks:

¹⁰ He is handsome and healthy,
    the most outstanding
    among ten thousand.

¹¹ His head is purest gold;
    his hair is wavy,
    black as a raven.

¹² His eyes are a pair of doves
 bathing in a stream
 flowing with milk.ᵇ
¹³ His face is a garden
 of sweet-smelling spices;
 his lips are lilies
 dripping with perfume.
¹⁴ His arms are branches of gold
 covered with jewels;
 his body is ivoryᶜ
 decorated with sapphires.
¹⁵ His legs are columns of marble
 on feet of gold.
 He stands there majestic
 like Mount Lebanon
 and its choice cedar trees.
¹⁶ His kisses are sweet.
 I desire him so much!
 Young women of Jerusalem,
 he is my lover and friend.

CHAPTER 6

Their friends speak:

¹ Most beautiful of women,
 tell us where he has gone.
 Let us help you find him.

She speaks:

² My darling has gone down
 to his garden of spices,
 where he will feed his sheep
 and gather lilies.
³ I am his, and he is mine,
 as he feeds his sheep among the lilies.

He speaks:

⁴ My dearest, the cities of Tirzah
 and Jerusalem
 are not as lovely as you.
 Your charms are more powerful
 than all the stars in the heavens.ᵃ
⁵ Turn away your eyes —
 they make me melt.
 Your hair tosses about
 as gracefully as goats
 coming down from Gilead.
⁶ Your teeth are whiter
 than sheep freshly washed;
 they match perfectly,
 not one is missing.
⁷ Behind your veil are hidden
 beautiful rosy cheeks.ᵇ
⁸ What if I could have
 sixty queens, eighty wives,
 and thousands of others!

⁹ You would be my only choice,
 my flawless dove,
 the favourite child of your mother.
 The young women, the queens,
 and all the others
 tell how excited you are
 as they sing your praises:
¹⁰ "You are as majestic
 as the morning sky —
 glorious as the moon —
 blinding as the sun!
 Your charms are more powerful
 than all the stars above."ᶜ

She speaks:

¹¹ I went down to see if blossoms
 were on the walnut trees,
 grapevines, and fruit trees.
¹² But in my imagination
 I was suddenly riding
 on a glorious chariot.ᵈ

Their friends speak:

¹³ Dance! Dance!
 Beautiful woman from Shulam,
 let us see you dance!

She speaks:

 Why do you want to see
 this woman from Shulam
 dancing with the others?ᵉ

CHAPTER 7

The wedding dance

He speaks:

¹ You are a princess,
 and your feet are graceful
 in their sandals.
 Your thighs are works of art,
 each one a jewel;
² your navel is a wine glass
 filled to overflowing.
 Your body is full and slender
 like a bundle of wheat
 bound together by lilies.
³ Your breasts are like twins of a deer.
⁴ Your neck is like ivory,
 and your eyes sparkle
 like the pools of Heshbon
 by the gate of Bath-Rabbim.
 Your nose is beautiful
 like Mount Lebanon
 above the city of Damascus.

635

⁵ Your head is held high
   like Mount Carmel;
   your hair is so lovely
   it holds a king prisoner.*

⁶ You are beautiful, so very desirable!
⁷ You are tall and slender
   like a palm tree,
   and your breasts are full.
⁸ I will climb that tree
   and cling to its branches.
   I will discover that your breasts
   are clusters of grapes,
   and that your breath
   is the aroma of apples.
⁹ Kissing you is more delicious
   than drinking the finest wine.
   How wonderful and tasty!*

She speaks:

¹⁰ My darling, I am yours,
   and you desire me.
¹¹ Let's stroll through the fields
   and sleep in the villages.
¹² At dawn let's slip out and see
   if grapevines and fruit trees
   are covered with blossoms.
   When we are there,
   I will give you my love.
¹³ Perfume from the magic flower*
   fills the air, my darling.
   Right at our doorstep
   I have stored up for you
   all kinds of tasty fruits.

If only you and I . . .

CHAPTER 8

She speaks:

¹ If you were my brother,
   I could kiss you
   whenever we happen to meet,
   and no one would say I did wrong.
² I could take you to the home
   of my mother,
   who taught me all I know.*
   I would give you delicious wine
   and fruit juice as well.
³ Put your left hand under my head
   and embrace me with your right arm.

⁴ Young women of Jerusalem,
   promise me by the power

of deer and gazelles*
   never to awaken love before it is ready.

Their friends speak:

⁵ Who is this young woman
   coming in from the desert
   and leaning on the shoulder
   of the one she loves?

She speaks:

   I stirred up your passions
   under the apple tree
   where you were born.
⁶ Always keep me in your heart
   and wear this bracelet
   to remember me by.
   The passion of love bursting into flame
   is more powerful than death,
   stronger than the grave.
⁷ Love cannot be drowned
   by oceans or floods;
   it cannot be bought,
   no matter what is offered.

Their friends speak:

⁸ We have a little sister whose breasts
   are not yet formed.
   If someone asks to marry her,
   what should we do?
⁹ She isn't a wall that we can defend
   behind a silver shield.
   Neither is she a room that we can protect
   behind a wooden door.

She speaks:

¹⁰ I am a wall around a city,
   my breasts are towers,
   and just looking at me
   brings him great pleasure.
¹¹ Solomon has a vineyard
   at Baal-Hamon,
   which he rents to others
   for a thousand pieces of silver each.
¹² My vineyard is mine alone!
   Solomon can keep his silver
   and the others can keep
   their share of the profits.

He speaks:

¹³ You are in the garden
   with friends all around.
   Let me hear your voice!

---

*7.13 magic flower: The Hebrew text has
"mandrake", a plant that was thought to give sexual
powers.

*8.4 deer and gazelles: See the note at 2.7.

She speaks:

¹⁴ Hurry to me, my darling!
Run faster than a deer
to mountains of spices.

Additional notes

ꞌ1.6 Don't . . . me: One possible meaning for the difficult Hebrew text.

ꞌ1.7 I'm . . . shepherds: One possible meaning for the difficult Hebrew text.

ꞌ1.12 magic charm: The Hebrew text has "spikenard" (or "nard"), a sweet-smelling ointment made from a plant that comes from India. The ointment was sometimes used as a love charm.

ꞌ2.12 sing: Or "trim the vines".

ꞌ2.15 vineyards: One possible meaning for the difficult Hebrew text of verse 15.

ꞌ2.17 mountain slopes: One possible meaning for the difficult Hebrew text.

ꞌ3.10 inside: One possible meaning for the difficult Hebrew text.

ꞌ4.3 beautiful rosy cheeks: One possible meaning for the difficult Hebrew text.

ꞌ4.13 Your arms: One possible meaning for the difficult Hebrew text.

ꞌ5.12 milk: One possible meaning for the difficult Hebrew text of verse 12.

ꞌ5.14 his . . . ivory: One possible meaning for the difficult Hebrew text.

ꞌ6.4 all . . . heavens: Or "a mighty army ready for war."

ꞌ6.7 cheeks: One possible meaning for the difficult Hebrew text of verse 7.

ꞌ6.10 all . . . above: Or "a mighty army ready for war."

ꞌ6.12 chariot: One possible meaning for the difficult Hebrew text of verse 12.

ꞌ6.13 dancing . . . others: One possible meaning for the difficult Hebrew text.

ꞌ7.5 it . . . prisoner: One possible meaning for the difficult Hebrew text.

ꞌ7.9 How . . . tasty: One possible meaning for the difficult Hebrew text.

ꞌ8.2 who . . . know: One possible meaning for the difficult Hebrew text.

Isaiah

A quick look at this book

Isaiah spoke for the Lord to the people of Judah during the reigns of four kings of Judah. Over this period of about forty years, the Assyrian empire was expanding. Nations joined together to fight Assyria, but Assyria finally conquered Israel and most other nearby countries. Thousands of people were led away as prisoners. And although the kingdom of Judah wasn't completely conquered, it had to pay heavy taxes.

The messages in this book can be divided into three parts. The first part (1—39) is especially concerned about the Lord's holiness and his power as king of the whole earth. As a holy king, the Lord was angry about evil in Judah. Government officials were corrupt; violence and injustice were everywhere. The Lord said he was going to make Assyria and Babylonia punish the people of Judah and other nations. But the Lord offered his people hope for the future, if they turned back to him and trusted him to protect their nation.

In the second part (40—55) the Lord spoke to people who had been punished (40.1,2). They were discouraged, and he offered them hope. But the Lord wanted them to understand that idols have no power, and that he alone is the true God. If the people of Israel turned back to him, then he would rescue them from Babylonia and the other nations where they had been scattered. They would return to their own land, and he would bless them and make them prosperous. The Lord was able to make this tremendous promise to his people because he created and rules the entire earth.

In the third part (56—66) the Lord promises an especially bright future for those who are faithful to him. And in this section, people from all nations are included, not just the people of Judah. These promises are like windows that allow a glimpse into a future

time when the Lord will create a new world
full of joy and free from suffering:

I am creating new heavens
and a new earth;
everything of the past
will be forgotten.
Celebrate and be glad for ever!
I am creating a Jerusalem,
full of happy people.
I will celebrate with Jerusalem
and all its people;
there will be no more crying
or sorrow in that city.

(65.17-19)

Introduction

CHAPTER 1

¹ I am Isaiah, the son of Amoz.
And this is the message⁺ that I was given
about Judah and Jerusalem when Uzziah,
Jotham, Ahaz, and Hezekiah were the kings
of Judah:⁺

A guilty nation

² The LORD has said,
"Listen, heaven and earth!
The children I raised
have turned against me.
³ Oxen and donkeys know
who owns and feeds them,
but my people won't ever learn."

⁴ Israel, you are a sinful nation
loaded down with guilt.
You are wicked and corrupt
and have turned from the LORD,
the holy God of Israel.
⁵ Why be punished more?
Why not give up your sin?
Your head is badly bruised,
and you are weak all over.
⁶ From your head to your toes
there isn't a healthy spot.
Bruises, cuts, and open sores
go without care
or oil to ease the pain.

A country in ruins

⁷ Your country lies in ruins;
your towns are in ashes.
Foreigners and strangers
take and destroy your land
while you watch.
⁸ Enemies surround Jerusalem,
alone like a hut in a vineyard⁺
or in a cucumber field.
⁹ Zion would have disappeared
like Sodom and Gomorrah,⁺
if the LORD All-Powerful
had not let a few of its people survive.

Justice, not sacrifices

¹⁰ You are no better
than the leaders and people
of Sodom and Gomorrah!
So listen to the LORD God:
¹¹ "Your sacrifices
mean nothing to me.
I am sick of your offerings
of rams and choice cattle;
I don't like the blood
of bulls or lambs or goats.

¹² "Who asked you to bring all this
when you come to worship me?
Stay out of my temple!
¹³ Your sacrifices are worthless,
and incense is disgusting.
I can't stand the evil you do
on your New Moon Festivals
or on your Sabbaths
and other times of worship.
¹⁴ I hate your New Moon Festivals
and all others as well.
They are a heavy burden
I am tired of carrying.

¹⁵ "No matter how much you pray,
I won't listen.
You are too violent.
¹⁶ Wash yourselves clean!
I am disgusted
with your filthy deeds.
Stop doing wrong
¹⁷ and learn to live right.

⁺1.1 kings of Judah: Uzziah (783-742 BC);
Jotham (742-735 BC); Ahaz (735-715 BC);
Hezekiah (715-687 BC).
See also: 1.1: a 2 King 15.1-7; 2 Chron 26.1-23;
b 2 King 15.32-38; 2 Chron 27.1-9; c 2 King 16.1-20;
2 Chron 28.1-27; d 2 King 18.1-20.21; 2 Chron 29.1-32.33.

⁺1.8 a hut in a vineyard: When it was almost time for
grapes to ripen, farmers would put up a temporary
shelter or hut in the field or vineyard and stay there to
keep thieves and wild animals away.
⁺1.9 Sodom and Gomorrah: Two ancient cities of
Palestine that God destroyed because the people
were so wicked (see Genesis 19.1-29).
See also: 1.9: Gen 19.24; Rom 9.29.
1.11-14: Amos 5.21,22.

See that justice is done.
Defend widows and orphans
and help those in need."'

An invitation from the LORD

18 I, the LORD, invite you
to come and talk it over.
Your sins are scarlet red,
but they will be whiter
than snow or wool.
19 If you willingly obey me,
the best crops in the land
will be yours.
20 But if you turn against me,
your enemies will kill you.
I, the LORD, have spoken.

The LORD condemns Jerusalem

21 Jerusalem, you are like
an unfaithful wife.
Once your judges were honest
and your people lived right;
now you are a city
full of murderers.
22 Your silver is fake,
and your wine is watered down.
23 Your leaders have rejected me
to become friends of crooks;
your rulers are looking
for gifts and bribes.
Widows and orphans
never get a fair trial.

24 I am the LORD All-Powerful,
the mighty ruler of Israel,
and I make you a promise:
you are now my enemy,
and I will show my anger
by taking revenge on you.
25 I will punish you terribly
and burn away everything
that makes you unfit
to worship me.
26 Jerusalem, I will choose
judges and advisers
like those you had before.
Your new name will be
"Justice and Faithfulness".

The LORD will save Jerusalem

27 Jerusalem, you will be saved
by showing justice;
Zion's people who turn to me
will be saved by doing right.
28 But those rebellious sinners
who turn against me, the LORD,
will all disappear.

29 You will be made ashamed
of those groves of trees
where you worshipped idols.
30 You will be like a grove of trees
dying in a drought.
31 Your strongest leaders
will be like dry wood
set on fire by their idols.'
No one will be able to help,
as they all go up in flames.

Messages about Judah and Israel

CHAPTER 2

Peace that lasts for ever

1 This is the message' that I was given about
Judah and Jerusalem:

2 In the future, the mountain
with the LORD's temple
will be the highest of all.
It will reach above the hills;
every nation will rush to it.
3 Many people will come and say,
"Let's go to the mountain
of the LORD God of Jacob
and worship in his temple."

The LORD will teach us his Law
from Jerusalem,
and we will obey him.
4 He will settle arguments
between nations.
They will beat their swords
and their spears
into rakes and shovels;
they will never make war
or attack one another.
5 People of Israel, let's live
by the light of the LORD.

Following sinful customs

6 Our LORD, you have deserted
your people, Israel,
because they follow customs
of nations from the east.
They worship Philistine gods
and are close friends
of foreigners.'
7 They have endless treasures
of silver and gold;
they have countless horses
and war chariots.

See also: 2.4: Joel 3.10; Mic 4.3.

8 Everywhere in the country
they worship the idols
they have made.
9 And so, all of them
will be ashamed and disgraced.
Don't help them!

A day of judgment

10 Every one of you,
hide among the rocks
and in the ground,
because the LORD is fearsome,
marvellous, and glorious.
11 When the LORD comes,
everyone who is proud
will be made humble,
and the LORD alone
will be honoured.
12 The LORD All-Powerful
has chosen a day
when those who are proud and conceited
will be put down.

13 The tall and towering
cedars of Lebanon will be destroyed.
So will the oak trees of Bashan,
14 all high mountains and hills,
15 every strong fortress,
16 all the seagoing ships,*
and every beautiful boat.
17 When that day comes,
everyone who is proud
will be put down.
Only the LORD will be honoured.
18 Idols will be gone for good.

19 You had better hide
in caves and holes —
the LORD will be fearsome,
marvellous, and glorious
when he comes to terrify
people on earth.
20 On that day everyone will throw
to the rats and bats
their idols of silver and gold
they made to worship.
21 The LORD will be fearsome,
marvellous, and glorious
when he comes to terrify
people on earth —
they will hide in caves
and in the hills.

22 Stop trusting the power
of humans.
They are all going to die,
so how can they help?

CHAPTER 3

Judgment on Jerusalem and Judah

1 The mighty LORD All-Powerful
is going to take away
from Jerusalem and Judah
everything you need —
your bread and water,
2-3 soldiers and heroes,
judges and prophets,
leaders and army officers,
officials and advisers,
fortune-tellers and others
who tell the future.
4 He will let children and babies'
become your rulers.
5 You will each be cruel
to friends and neighbours.
Young people will insult
their elders;
no one will show respect
to those who deserve it.

6 Some of you will grab hold
of a relative and say,
"You still have a coat.
Be our leader and rule
this pile of ruins."
7 But the answer will be,
"I can't do you any good.
Don't make me your leader.
There's no food or clothing
left in my house."

8 Jerusalem and Judah,
you rebelled against
your glorious LORD —
your words and your actions,
made you stumble and fall.
9 The look on your faces shows
that you are sinful as Sodom,
and you don't try to hide it.
You are in for trouble,
and you have brought it all
on yourselves.

The wrong kind of leaders

10 Tell those who obey God,
"You're very fortunate —
you will be rewarded
for what you have done."

---

*2.16 seagoing ships: The Hebrew text has "ships of
Tarshish", which may have been a Phoenician city in
Spain. "Ships of Tarshish" probably means large,
seagoing ships.

See also: 2.10: Rev 6.15; 2 Thes 1.9.

11 Tell those who disobey,
"You're in big trouble —
what you did to others
will come back to you."
12 Though you are God's people,
you are ruled and abused
by women and children.
You are confused by leaders
who guide you
down the wrong path.

13 The LORD is ready to accuse
and judge all nations.
14 He will even judge
you rulers and leaders
of his own nation.
You destroyed his vineyard*
and filled your houses
by robbing the poor.
15 The LORD All-Powerful says,
"You have crushed my people
and rubbed in the dust
the faces of the poor."

The women of Jerusalem

16 The LORD says:

The women of Jerusalem
are proud and strut around,
winking shamelessly.
They wear anklets that jingle
and call attention
to the way they walk.
17 But I, the LORD, will cover
their heads with sores,
and I will uncover
their private parts.

18-23 When that day comes, I will take away
from those women all the fine jewellery they
wear on their ankles, heads, necks, ears,
arms, noses, fingers, and on their clothes.
I will remove their veils, their belts, their
perfume, their magic charms, their royal
robes, and all their fine dresses, hats, and
purses.

24 In place of perfume,
there will be a stink;
in place of belts,
there will be ropes;
in place of fancy hair styles,
they will have bald heads.
Instead of expensive clothes,
they will wear sackcloth;
instead of beauty,
they will have ugly scars.

25 The fighting men of Jerusalem
will be killed in battle.
26 The city will mourn
and sit in the dust,
emptied of its people.

CHAPTER 4

1 When this happens, seven women will grab
the same man, and each of them will say,
"I'll buy my own food and clothes! Just
marry me and take away my disgrace."*

The LORD will bless
his people who survive

2 The time is coming when the LORD will
make his land fruitful and glorious again,
and the people of Israel who survive will take
great pride in what the land produces.
3 Everyone who is left alive in Jerusalem will
be called special, 4 after the LORD sends a
fiery judgment to clean the city and its
people of their violent deeds.

5 Then the LORD will cover the whole city
and its meeting places with a thick cloud
each day and with a flaming fire* each night.
God's glory will be like a huge tent that
covers everything. 6 It will provide shade
from the heat of the sun and a place of
shelter and protection from storms and rain.

CHAPTER 5

A song about a vineyard

The LORD said:

1 I will sing a song
about my friend's vineyard
that was on the side
of a fertile hill.
2 My friend dug the ground,
removed the stones,
and planted the best vines.
He built a watchtower
and dug a pit in rocky ground
for pressing the grapes.
He hoped they would be sweet,
but bitter grapes
were all it produced.

---

*3.14 his vineyard: The nation Israel (see 5.1-7).

*4.1 take away my disgrace: If a woman did not
have a husband or children, it was thought that God
was punishing her.
*4.5 fire . . . fire: This is how the LORD led the
people of Israel during the forty years they were in
the desert (see Exodus 13.20-22; 40.36-38).
See also: 4.5: Exod 13.21; 24.16. 5.1,2: Matt 21.33;
Mark 12.1; Luke 20.9.

3 Listen, people of Jerusalem
   and of Judah!
You be the judge of me
   and my vineyard.
4 What more could I have done
   for my vineyard?
I hoped for sweet grapes,
   but bitter grapes
   were all that grew.

5 Now I will let you know
   what I am going to do.
I will cut down the hedge
   and tear down the wall.
My vineyard will be trampled
   and left in ruins.
6 It will turn into a desert,
   neither pruned nor hoed;
it will be covered
   with thorns and briars.
I will command the clouds
   not to send rain.

7 I am the LORD All-Powerful!
Israel is the vineyard,
   and Judah is the garden
   I tended with care.
I had hoped for honesty
   and for justice,
but dishonesty
   and cries for mercy
   were all I found.

Isaiah condemns social injustice

8 You are in for trouble! You take over house
after house and field after field, until there is
no room left for anyone else in all the land.
9 But the LORD All-Powerful has made this
promise to me:

Those large and beautiful homes will be
left empty, with no one to take care of
them. 10 Four hectares of grapevines will
produce only twenty-seven litres of juice,
and a hundred and eighty litres of seed will
produce merely eighteen litres of grain.

11 You are in for trouble! You get up early to
start drinking, and you keep it up late into
the night. 12 At your drinking parties you
have the music of stringed instruments,
tambourines, and flutes. But you never even
think about all the LORD has done, 13 and so
his people know nothing about him. That's
why many of you will be dragged off to
foreign lands. Your leaders will starve to
death, and everyone else will suffer from
thirst.

14 The world of the dead has opened its
mouth wide and is eagerly waiting for the
leaders of Jerusalem and for its noisy crowds,
especially for those who take pride in that
city. 15 Its citizens have been put down, and
its proud people have been brought to
shame. 16 But the holy LORD God All-Powerful
is praised, because he has shown who he is by
bringing justice. 17 His people will be like
sheep grazing in their own pasture, and they
will take off what was left by others.*

18 You are in for trouble! The lies you tell
are like ropes by which you drag along sin
and evil. 19 And you say, "Let the holy God of
Israel hurry up and do what he has promised,
so we can see it for ourselves." 20 You are
headed for trouble! You say wrong is right,
darkness is light, and bitter is sweet.

21 You think you are clever and wise. 22 And
you are great at drinking and mixing drinks.
But you are in for trouble. 23 You accept
bribes to let the guilty go free, and you cheat
the innocent out of a fair trial.

24 You will go up in flames like straw and
hay! You have rejected the teaching of the
holy LORD God All-Powerful of Israel. Now
your roots will rot, and your blossoms will
turn to dust.

25 You are the LORD's people, but you made
him terribly angry, and he struck you with
his mighty arm. Mountains shook, and dead
bodies covered the streets like rubbish. The
LORD is still angry, and he is ready to strike
you again.*

Foreign nations will attack

26 The LORD has signalled for the foreign
nations to come and attack you. He has
already whistled, and they are coming as fast
as they can. 27 None of them are tired. They
don't sleep or get drowsy, and they run
without stumbling. Their belts don't come
loose; their sandal straps don't break. 28 Their
arrows are sharp, and their bows are ready.
The hoofs of their horses are hard as flint; the
wheels of their war chariots turn as fast as a
whirlwind.

29 They roar and growl like fierce young
lions as they grab their victims and drag
them off where no one can rescue them.
30 On the day they attack, they will roar like
the sea. And across the land you will see
nothing but darkness and trouble, because
the light of day will be covered by thick
clouds.

Events from Isaiah's ministry

CHAPTER 6

A vision of the LORD in the temple

[1] In the year that King Uzziah died,* I had a vision of the LORD. He was on his throne high above, and his robe filled the temple. [2] Flaming creatures with six wings each were flying over him. They covered their faces with two of their wings and their bodies with two more. They used the other two wings for flying, [3] as they shouted,

> "Holy, holy, holy,
> LORD All-Powerful!
> The earth is filled
>   with your glory."

[4] As they shouted, the doorposts of the temple shook, and the temple was filled with smoke. [5] Then I cried out, "I'm doomed! Everything I say is sinful, and so are the words of everyone around me. Yet I have seen the King, the LORD All-Powerful."

[6] One of the flaming creatures flew over to me with a burning coal that it had taken from the altar with a pair of metal tongs. [7] It touched my lips with the hot coal and said, "This has touched your lips. Your sins are forgiven, and you are no longer guilty."

[8] After this, I heard the LORD ask, "Is there anyone I can send? Will someone go for us?"

"I'll go," I answered. "Send me!"

[9] Then the LORD told me to go and speak this message to the people:

> "You will listen and listen,
>   but never understand.
> You will look and look,
>   but never see."

The LORD also said,

[10] "Make these people stubborn!
> Make them stop up their ears,
>   cover their eyes,
> and fail to understand.
>   Don't let them turn to me
>   and be healed."

[11] Then I asked the LORD, "How long will this last?"

The LORD answered:

Until their towns are destroyed and their houses are deserted, until their fields are empty, [12] and I have sent them far away, leaving their land in ruins. [13] If only a tenth of the people are left, even they will be destroyed. But just as stumps remain after trees have been cut down,* some of my chosen ones will be left.

CHAPTER 7

Isaiah offers hope to King Ahaz

[1] Ahaz, the son of Jotham and the grandson of Uzziah, was king of Judah when King Rezin of Syria and King Pekah son of Remaliah of Israel went to attack Jerusalem. But they were not able to do what they had planned.* [2] When news reached the royal palace that Syria had joined forces with Israel, King Ahaz and everyone in Judah were so terrified that they shook like trees in a storm.

[3] Then the LORD said to me:

Take your son Shearjashub* and go and see King Ahaz. You will find him on the road near the cloth makers' shops at the end of the canal that brings water from the upper pool. [4] Tell Ahaz to stop worrying. There's no need for him to be afraid of King Rezin and King Pekah. They are very angry, but they are nothing more than a dying fire. Ahaz doesn't need to fear [5] their evil threats [6] to invade and defeat Judah and Jerusalem and to let the son of Tabeel be king in his place.

[7] I, the LORD, promise that this will never happen. [8-9] Damascus is just the capital of Syria, and King Rezin rules only in Damascus. Samaria is just the capital of Israel, and King Pekah rules only in Samaria. But in less than sixty-five years, Israel will be destroyed. And if Ahaz and his officials don't trust me, they will be defeated.

A son named Immanuel

[10] Once again the LORD God spoke to King Ahaz. This time he said, [11] "Ask me for proof that my promise will come true. Ask for something to happen deep in the world of the dead or high in the heavens above."

---

*6.1 the year that King Uzziah died: Probably 742 BC.

See also: 6.1: 2 King 15.7; 2 Chron 26.23. 6.3: Rev 4.8.
6.4: Rev 15.8. 6.9,10: Matt 13.14,15; Mark 4.12; Luke 8.10;
John 12.40; Acts 28.26,27.

*7.3 Shearjashub: In Hebrew "Shearjashub" means "a few will return".

See also: 7.1: 2 King 16.5; 2 Chron 28.5,6.

¹² "No, Lᴏʀᴅ," Ahaz answered. "I won't test you!"

¹³ Then I said:

Listen, every one of you in the royal family of David. You have already tried my patience. Now you are trying God's patience by refusing to ask for proof. ¹⁴ But the Lᴏʀᴅ will still give you proof. A virgin* is pregnant; she will have a son and will name him Immanuel.* ¹⁵⁻¹⁶ Even before the boy is old enough to know how to choose between right and wrong, he will eat yoghurt and honey,* and the countries of the two kings you fear will be destroyed. ¹⁷ But the Lᴏʀᴅ will make more trouble for your people and your kingdom than any of you have known since Israel broke away from Judah. He will even bring the king of Assyria to attack you.

The threat of an invasion

¹⁸ When that time comes, the Lᴏʀᴅ will whistle, and armies will come from Egypt like flies and from Assyria like bees. ¹⁹ They will settle everywhere — in the deep valleys and between the rocks, on every bush and all over the pasture land.

²⁰ The Lᴏʀᴅ will pay the king of Assyria to bring a razor from across the River Euphrates and shave your head and every hair on your body, including your beard.*

²¹ No one will have more than one young cow and two sheep, ²² but those who do will have enough milk to make yoghurt. In fact, everyone left in the land will eat yoghurt and honey.*

²³ Vineyards that had a thousand vines and were worth a thousand pieces of silver will turn into thorn patches. ²⁴ You will go there to hunt with your bow and arrows, because the whole country will be covered with thorn bushes. ²⁵ The hills where you once planted crops will be overgrown with thorns and thistles. You will be afraid to go there, and your cattle, sheep, and goats will be turned loose on those hills.

CHAPTER 8

A warning and a hope

¹ The Lᴏʀᴅ said, "Isaiah, get something to write on. Then write in big clear letters* the name, MAHER-SHALAL-HASH-BAZ.* ² I will tell Uriah the priest and Zechariah son of Jeberechiah to serve as witnesses for me."

³ Some time later, my wife and I had a son, and the Lᴏʀᴅ said, "Name him Maher-Shalal-Hash-Baz. ⁴ Because before he can say 'Mummy' or 'Daddy', the king of Assyria will attack and take everything of value from Damascus and Samaria."

⁵ The Lᴏʀᴅ spoke to me again and said:

⁶ These people have refused the gentle waters of Shiloah* and have gladly gone over to the side of King Rezin and King Pekah. ⁷ Now I will send the king of Assyria against them with his powerful army, which will attack like the mighty River Euphrates overflowing its banks. ⁸ Enemy soldiers will cover Judah like a flood reaching up to your neck.

But God is with us.*
He will spread his wings
and protect our land.*
⁹ All you foreign nations,
go ahead and prepare for war,
but you will be crushed.
¹⁰ Get together and make plans,
but you will fail
because God is with us.

¹¹ The Lᴏʀᴅ took hold of me with his powerful hand and said:

I'm warning you! Don't act like these people. ¹² Don't call something a rebellious plot, just because they do, and don't be

*7.14 virgin: Or "young woman". In this context the difficult Hebrew word did not imply a virgin birth. However, in the Greek translation made about 200 bc and used by the early Christians, the word parthenos had a double meaning. While the translator took it to mean "young woman", Matthew understood it to mean "virgin" and quoted the passage (Matthew 1.23) because it was the appropriate description of Mary, the mother of Jesus.
*7.14 Immanuel: In Hebrew "Immanuel" means "God is with us".
*7.15,16,22 yoghurt and honey: This may refer either to expensive foods eaten in a time of plenty or to a limited diet eaten in times of a food shortage.
*7.20 shave . . . head . . . body . . . beard: This would have been a terrible insult.
See also: 7.14: Matt 1.23.

*8.1 MAHER-SHALAL-HASH-BAZ: In Hebrew "Maher-Shalal-Hash-Baz" means "suddenly attacked, quickly taken".
*8.6 Shiloah: The canal that brought water from Gihon Spring to Jerusalem.
*8.8 God is with us: Here and in verse 10 this translates the Hebrew word "Immanuel" (see 7.14).
See also: 8.12,13: 1 Pet 3.14,15.

afraid of something, just because they are. [13] I am the one you should fear and respect. I am the holy God, the LORD All-Powerful! [14-15] Run to me for protection. I am a rock that will make both Judah and Israel stumble and break their bones. I am a trap that will catch the people of Jerusalem — they will be captured and dragged away.

Isaiah and his followers

[16] My message and my teachings are to be sealed and given to my followers. [17] Meanwhile, I patiently trust the LORD, even though he is no longer pleased with Israel. [18] My children and I are warning signs to Israel from the LORD All-Powerful, who lives on Mount Zion.

[19] Someone may say to you, "Go to the fortune-tellers who make soft chirping sounds or ask the spirits of the dead. After all, a nation ought to be able to ask its own gods [20] what it should do."

None of those who talk like that will live to see the light of day! [21] They will go around in great pain and will become so hungry that they will angrily curse their king and their gods. And when they try to find help in heaven [22] and on earth, they will find only trouble and darkness, terrible trouble and deepest darkness.

CHAPTER 9

[1] But those who have suffered will no longer be in pain.* The territories of Zebulun and Naphtali in Galilee were once hated. But this land of the Gentiles across the River Jordan and along the Mediterranean Sea will be greatly respected.

War is over

[2] Those who walked in the dark
    have seen a bright light.
And it shines upon everyone
    who lives in the land
    of darkest shadows.
[3] Our LORD, you have made
    your nation stronger.*
Because of you, its people
    are glad and celebrate
like workers at harvest time
    or like soldiers dividing up
    what they have taken.

[4] You have broken the power
    of those who abused
    and enslaved your people.
You have rescued them
    just as you saved your people
    from Midian.*
[5] The boots of marching warriors
    and the blood-stained uniforms
    have been fed to flames
    and eaten by fire.

A child has been born

[6] A child has been born for us.
We have been given a son
    who will be our ruler.
His names will be
Wonderful Adviser and Mighty God,
Eternal Father and Prince of Peace.
[7] His power will never end;
    peace will last for ever.
He will rule David's kingdom
    and make it grow strong.
He will always rule
    with honesty and justice.
The LORD All-Powerful
will make certain that all of this is done.

More messages about Judah and Israel

God will punish Israel

[8] The Lord had warned the people of Israel, [9] and all of them knew it, including everyone in the capital city of Samaria. But they were proud and stubborn and said,

[10] "Houses of brick and sycamore
    have fallen to the ground,
but we will build houses
    with stones and cedar."

[11] The LORD made their enemies' attack them. [12] He sent the Arameans from the east and the Philistines from the west, and they swallowed up Israel. But even this did not stop him from being angry, so he kept on punishing them.* [13] The people of Israel still did not turn back to the LORD All-Powerful and worship him.

[14] In one day he cut off their head and tail, their leaves and branches. [15] Their rulers and leaders were the head, and the lying prophets

---

*9.4 rescued . . . from Midian: The time when Gideon defeated the people of Midian in Jezreel Valley (see Judges 6—8).

See also: 9.7: Luke 1.32,33.

See also: 8.14,15: 1 Pet 2.8. 8.17: Heb 2.13.
8.18: Heb 2.13. 9.1: Matt 4.15. 9.2: Matt 4.16; Luke 1.79.

were the tail. ¹⁶ They had led the nation down the wrong path, and the people were confused. ¹⁷ The Lord was angry with his people and kept punishing them, because they had turned against him.' They were evil and spoke foolishly. That's why he did not have pity on their young people or on their widows and orphans.

¹⁸ Evil had spread like a raging forest fire sending thorn bushes up in smoke. ¹⁹ The LORD All-Powerful was angry and used the people as fuel for a fire that scorched the land. They turned against each other ²⁰ like wild animals attacking and eating everyone around them, even their own relatives.' But still they were not satisfied. ²¹ The tribes of Ephraim and Manasseh turned against each other, then joined forces to attack Judah. But the LORD was still angry and ready to punish the nation even more.

CHAPTER 10

¹ You people are in for trouble! You have made cruel and unfair laws ² that let you cheat the poor and needy and rob widows and orphans. ³ But what will you do when you are fiercely attacked and punished by foreigners? Where will you run for help? Where will you hide your valuables? ⁴ How will you escape being captured' or killed? The Lord is still angry, and he isn't through with you yet!'

The Lord's purpose and the king of Assyria

⁵ The Lord says:

I am furious! And I will use the king of Assyria* as a club ⁶ to beat down you godless people. I am angry with you, and I will send him to attack you. He will take what he wants and walk on you like mud in the streets. ⁷ He has even bigger plans in mind, because he wants to destroy many nations.

⁸ The king of Assyria says:

My army commanders are kings! ⁹ They have already captured* the cities of Calno, Carchemish, Hamath, Arpad, Samaria, and

Damascus. ¹⁰⁻¹¹ The gods of Jerusalem and Samaria are weaker than the gods of those powerful nations. I will destroy Jerusalem, together with its gods and idols, just as I did Samaria.

¹² The Lord will do what he has planned against Jerusalem and Mount Zion. Then he will punish the proud and boastful king of Assyria, ¹³ who says:

I did these things by my own power because I am clever and wise. I attacked kings like a wild bull, and I took the land and the treasures of their nations. ¹⁴ I have conquered the whole world! And it was easier than taking eggs from an unguarded nest. No one even flapped a wing or made a cheep.

¹⁵ King of Assyria, can an axe or a saw overpower the one who uses it? Can a wooden pole lift whoever holds it? ¹⁶ The mighty LORD All-Powerful will send a terrible disease to strike down your army, and you will burn with fever under your royal robes. ¹⁷ The holy God, who is the light of Israel, will turn into a fire, and in one day you will go up in flames, just like a thorn bush. ¹⁸ The Lord will make your beautiful forests and fertile fields slowly rot. ¹⁹ There will be so few trees that even a young child can count them.

Only a few will come back

²⁰ A time is coming when the survivors from Israel and Judah will completely depend on the holy LORD of Israel, instead of the nation* that defeated them. ²¹⁻²² There were as many people as there are grains of sand along the seashore, but only a few will survive to come back to Israel's mighty God. This is because he has threatened to destroy their nation, just as they deserve. ²³ The LORD All-Powerful has promised that everyone on this earth' will be punished.

²⁴ Now the LORD God All-Powerful says to his people in Jerusalem:

The Assyrians will beat you with sticks and abuse you, just as the Egyptians did. But don't be afraid of them. ²⁵ Soon I will stop being angry with you, and I will punish them for their crimes. ²⁶ I will beat the Assyrians with a whip, as I did the people of Midian near the rock at Oreb. And I will show the same mighty power that I used

---

*10.5 king of Assyria: Probably King Sennacherib who invaded Israel in 701 BC.
*10.9 already captured: Calno (in northern Syria), Carchemish (on the River Euphrates), Hamath (on the River Orontes), Arpad (near Aleppo in northern Syria), Samaria, and Damascus had already been captured by Assyrian kings (738–717 BC).
See also: 10.5–34: Isa 14.24–27; Nah 1.1–3.19; Zeph 2.13–15.

*10.20 nation: That is, Assyria.
See also: 10.22,23: Rom 9.27.

when I made a path through the sea in Egypt. ²⁷ Then they will no longer rule your nation. All will go well for you,' and your burden will be lifted.

²⁸ Enemy troops have reached the town of Aiath.* They have gone through Migron, and they stored their supplies at Michmash, ²⁹ before crossing the valley and spending the night at Geba.* The people of Ramah are terrified; everyone in Gibeah, the home town of Saul, has run away. ³⁰ Loud crying can be heard in the towns of Gallim, Laishah, and sorrowful Anathoth. ³¹ No one is left in Madmenah or Gebim. ³² Today the enemy will camp at Nob* and shake a threatening fist at Mount Zion in Jerusalem.

³³ But the LORD All-Powerful
    will use his fearsome might
to bring down the tallest trees
    and chop off every branch.
³⁴ With an axe, the glorious Lord
    will destroy every tree
in the forests of Lebanon.'

CHAPTER 11

Peace at last

¹ Like a branch that sprouts
    from a stump,
someone from David's family*
    will some day be king.
² The Spirit of the LORD
    will be with him
to give him understanding,
    wisdom, and insight.
He will be powerful,
    and he will know
    and honour the LORD.
³ His greatest joy will be
    to obey the LORD.

This king won't judge
    by appearances
    or listen to rumours.
⁴ The poor and the needy
    will be treated with fairness
    and with justice.

His word will be law
    everywhere in the land,
and criminals
    will be put to death.
⁵ Honesty and fairness
    will be his royal robes.

⁶ Leopards will lie down
    with young goats,
and wolves will rest
    with lambs.
Calves and lions
    will eat together
and be cared for
    by little children.
⁷ Cows and bears will share
    the same pasture;
their young will rest
    side by side.
Lions and oxen
    will both eat straw.
⁸ Little children will play
    near snake holes.
They will stick their hands
    into dens of poisonous snakes
    and never be hurt.

⁹ Nothing harmful will take place
    on the LORD's holy mountain.
Just as water fills the sea,
    the land will be filled
with people who know
    and honour the LORD.

God's people will come back home

¹⁰ The time is coming when one of David's descendants* will be the signal for the people of all nations to come together. They will follow his advice, and his own nation will become famous.

¹¹ When that day comes, the Lord will again reach out his mighty arm and bring home his people who have survived in Assyria, Egypt, Pathros, Ethiopia,* Elam, Shinar, Hamath, and the land along the coast.* ¹² He will give a signal to the nations, and he will bring together the refugees from Judah and Israel, who have been scattered all over the earth. ¹³ Israel will stop being jealous of Judah, and Judah will no longer be the enemy of Israel. ¹⁴ Instead, they

---

*10.28 Aiath: Probably Ai (Joshua 7.2).
*10.29 Geba: Only nine kilometres from Jerusalem.
*10.32 Nob: Perhaps within three kilometres of Jerusalem.
*11.1 David's family: Hebrew "Jesse's family". Jesse was the father of King David.
See also: 11.1: Rev 5.5; 22.16. 11.4: 2 Thes 2.8.

*11.10 David's descendants: Hebrew "Jesse's descendants" (see the note at 11.1).
*11.11 Ethiopia: The Hebrew text has "Cush", which was a region south of Egypt that included parts of the present countries of Ethiopia and Sudan.
See also: 11.5: Eph 6.14. 11.6-9: Isa 65.25.
11.9: Hab 2.14. 11.10: Rom 15.12.

will get together and attack the Philistines in the west. Then they will defeat the Edomites, the Moabites, and the Ammonites in the east. They will rule those people and take from them whatever they want.

15 The Lord will dry up the arm of the Red Sea near Egypt,* and he will send a scorching wind to divide the River Euphrates into seven streams that anyone can step across. 16 Then for his people who survive, there will be a good road from Assyria, just as there was a good road for their ancestors when they left Egypt.

CHAPTER 12

A song of praise

1 At that time you will say,
   "I thank you, LORD!
    You were angry with me,
    but you stopped being angry
      and gave me comfort.

2 I trust you to save me, LORD God,
    and I won't be afraid.
  My power and my strength'
    come from you,
    and you have saved me."

3 With great joy, you people
    will get water
    from the well of victory.

4 At that time you will say,
   "Our LORD, we are thankful,
    and we worship only you.
  We will tell the nations
    how glorious you are
    and what you have done.

5 Because of your wonderful deeds
  we will sing your praises
    everywhere on earth."

6 Sing, people of Zion!
  Celebrate the greatness
    of the holy LORD of Israel.
  God is here to help you.

God will punish other nations

CHAPTER 13

Babylon will be punished

1 This is the message' that I was given about Babylon:

2 From high on a barren hill
    give a signal, shout the orders,
      and point the way
    to enter the gates
      of Babylon's proud rulers.

3 The LORD has commanded
    his very best warriors
  and his proud heroes
    to show how angry he is.

4 Listen to the noisy crowds
    on the mountains!
  Kingdoms and nations
    are joining forces.
  The LORD All-Powerful
    is bringing together
    an army for battle.

5 From a distant land
    the LORD is coming
    fierce and furious —
  he brings his weapons
    to destroy the earth.

6 Cry and weep!
    The day is coming
  when the mighty LORD
    will bring destruction.

7-8 All people will be terrified.
  Hands will grow limp;
    courage will melt away.
  Everyone will tremble with pain
    like a woman giving birth;
  they will stare at each other
    with horror on their faces.

There will be no mercy

9 I, the LORD,
    will show no mercy or pity
    when that time comes.
  In my anger I will destroy
    the earth and every sinner
    who lives on it.

10 Light will disappear
    from the stars in the sky;
  the dawning sun will turn dark,
    and the moon
    will lose its glow.

11 I will punish this evil world
    and its people
    because of their sins.
  I will crush the horrible pride
    of those who are cruel.

12 Survivors will be harder to find
    than the purest gold.

---

*11.15 arm of the Red Sea near Egypt: Gulf of Suez.
See also: 11.15: Rev 16.12. 12.2: Exod 15.2; Psa 118.14.
13.1–14.23: Isa 47.1–15; Jer 50.1–51.64.

See also: 13.6: Joel 1.15. 13.10: Ezek 32.7; Matt 24.29;
Mark 13.24,25; Luke 21.25; Rev 6.12,13; 8.12.

¹³ I, the LORD All-Powerful,
    am terribly angry —
I will make the sky tremble
    and the earth shake loose.

¹⁴ Everyone will run
    to their homelands,
just as hunted deer run,
    and sheep scatter
when they have no shepherd.

¹⁵ Those who are captured
    will be killed by a sword.

¹⁶ They will see their children
    beaten against rocks,
their homes robbed,
    and their wives abused.

¹⁷ The Medes* can't be bought off
    with silver or gold,
and I'm sending them
    to attack Babylonia.

¹⁸ Their arrows will slaughter
    the young men;
no pity will be shown
    to babies and children.

The LORD will destroy Babylon

¹⁹ The city of Babylon
    is glorious and powerful,
    the pride of the nation.
But it will be like the cities
    of Sodom and Gomorrah
after I, the Lord,
    destroyed them.

²⁰ No one will live in Babylon.
Even nomads won't camp nearby,
    and shepherds won't let
    their sheep rest there.

²¹ Only desert creatures,
    owls, and ostriches
will live in its ruins,
    and goats* will leap about.

²² Hyenas and wolves will howl
    from Babylon's fortresses
    and beautiful palaces.
Its time is almost up!

CHAPTER 14

The LORD's people will come home

¹ The LORD will have mercy on Israel and will
let them be his chosen people once again. He
will bring them back to their own land, and

foreigners will join them as part of Israel.
² Other nations will lead them home, and
Israel will make slaves of them in the land that
belongs to the Lord. Israel will rule over those
who once governed and ill-treated them.

Death to the king of Babylonia!

³ The LORD will set you free from your
sorrow, suffering, and slavery. ⁴ Then you
will make fun of the king of Babylonia by
singing this song:

That cruel monster is done for!
    He won't attack us again.•

⁵ The LORD has crushed the power
    of those evil kings,

⁶ who were furious
    and never stopped abusing
    the people of other nations.

⁷ Now all the world is at peace;
    its people are celebrating
    with joyful songs.

⁸ King of Babylonia,
    even the cypress trees
and the cedars of Lebanon
    celebrate and say,
"Since you were put down,
    no one comes along
    to chop us down."

⁹ The world of the dead
    eagerly waits for you.
With great excitement,
    the spirits of ancient rulers
    hear about your coming.

¹⁰ Each one of them will say,
"Now you are just as weak as any of us!

¹¹ Your pride and your music
    have ended here
in the world of the dead.
    Worms are your blanket,
    maggots are your bed."

¹² You, the bright morning star,
    have fallen from the sky!
You brought down other nations;
    now you are brought down.

¹³ You said to yourself,
    "I'll climb to heaven
and place my throne
    above the highest stars.
I'll sit there with the gods
    far away in the north.

¹⁴ I'll be above the clouds,
    just like God Most High."

---

*13.17 Medes: People of a nation north-east of
Babylonia, which became part of the Persian Empire.
See also: 13.19: Gen 19.24. 13.21: Isa 34.14; Zeph 2.14;
Rev 18.2.

See also: 14.12: Rev 8.10; 9.1. 14.13–15: Matt 11.23;
Luke 10.15.

¹⁵ But now you are deep
in the world of the dead.
¹⁶ Those who see you will stare
and wonder, "Is this the man
who made the world tremble
and shook up kingdoms?
¹⁷ Did he capture every city
and make earth a desert?
Is he the one who refused
to let prisoners go home?"

¹⁸ When kings die, they are buried
in glorious tombs.
¹⁹ But you will be left unburied,
just another dead body
lying underfoot like a broken branch.
You will be one of many
killed in battle and gone down
to the deep rocky pit.*
²⁰ You won't be buried with kings;
you ruined your country
and murdered your people.

You evil monster!
We hope that your family
will be forgotten for ever.
²¹ We will slaughter your sons
to make them pay for the crimes
of their ancestors.
They won't take over the world
or build cities
anywhere on this earth.

²² The LORD All-Powerful has promised to attack Babylonia and destroy everyone there, so that none of them will ever be remembered again. ²³ The LORD will sweep out the people, and the land will become a swamp for wild animals.

Assyria will be punished

²⁴ The LORD All-Powerful has made this promise:

Everything I have planned
will happen just as I said.
²⁵ I will wipe out every Assyrian
in my country,
and I will crush those
on my mountains.
I will free my people from slavery
to the Assyrians.
²⁶ I have planned this for the whole world,
and my mighty arm
controls every nation.

²⁷ I, the LORD All-Powerful,
have made these plans.
No one can stop me now!

The Philistines will be punished

²⁸ This message came from the LORD in the year King Ahaz died:*

²⁹ Philistines, don't be happy
just because the rod
that punished you is broken.
That rod will become
a poisonous snake, and then
a flying fiery dragon.

³⁰ The poor and needy will find
pastures for their sheep
and will live in safety.
But I will starve some of you,
and others will be killed.

³¹ Cry and weep in the gates of your towns,
you Philistines!
Smoke blows in from the north,*
and every soldier is ready.
³² If a messenger comes
from a distant nation,
you must say:
"The LORD built Zion.
Even the poorest of his people
will find safety there."

CHAPTER 15

Moab will be punished

¹This is a message about Moab:

The towns of Ar and Kir
were destroyed in a night.
Moab is left in ruins!
² Everyone in Dibon has gone up
to the temple* and the shrines
to cry and weep.
All of Moab is crying.
Heads and beards are shaved*
because of what happened
at Nebo and Medeba.
³ In the towns and at home,
everyone wears sackcloth
and cries loud and long.

---

*14.19 deep rocky pit: The world of the dead.
*14.28 King Ahaz died: 715 BC.
*14.31 north: The Assyrian and Babylonian attacks came from the north.
*15.2 Heads . . . shaved: As a sign of sorrow and mourning.

See also: 14.28: 2 King 16.20; 2 Chron 28.27.
14.29–31: Jer 47.1–7; Ezek 25.15–17; Joel 3.4–8; Amos 1.6–8; Zeph 2.4–7; Zech 9.5–7. 15.1–16.14: Isa 25.10–12; Jer 48.1–47; Ezek 25.8–11; Amos 2.1–3; Zeph 2.8–11.

⁴ From Heshbon and Elealeh,
    weeping is heard in Jahaz;
Moab's warriors scream
    while trembling with fear.

Pity Moab

⁵ I pity Moab!
Its people are running to Zoar
    and to Eglath-Shelishiyah.
They cry on their way up
    to the town of Luhith;
on the road to Horonaim
    they tell of disasters.
⁶ The streams of Nimrim
    and the grasslands
    have dried up.
Every plant is parched.

⁷ The people of Moab are leaving,
    crossing over Willow Brook,
taking everything they own
    and have worked for.
⁸ In the towns of Eglaim
    and of Beerelim
and everywhere else in Moab
    mournful cries are heard.
⁹ The streams near Dimon
    are flowing with blood.
But the Lord will bring
    even worse trouble to Dimon,ᵇ
because all in Moab who escape
    will be attacked by lions.

CHAPTER 16

More troubles for Moab

¹ Send lambs* as gifts
    to the ruler of the land.
Send them across the desert
    from Sela* to Mount Zion.
² The women of Moab
    crossing the River Arnon
are like a flock of birds
    scattered from their nests.
³ Moab's messengers say
    to the people of Judah,
"Be kind and help us!
Shade us from the heat
    of the noonday sun.
Hide our refugees!
    Don't turn them away.
⁴ Let our people live
    in your country
    and find safety here."

Moab, your cruel enemies will disappear;
    they will no longer attack
    and destroy your land.
⁵ Then a kingdom of love
    will be set up,
and someone from David's family
    will rule with fairness.
He will do what is right
    and quickly bring justice.

Moab's pride is destroyed

⁶ We have heard of Moab's pride.
Its people strut and boast,
    but without reason.
⁷ Tell everyone in Moab
    to mourn for their nation.
Tell them to cry and weep
    for those fine raisins*
    of Kir-Hareseth.

⁸ Vineyards near Heshbon and Sibmah
    have turned brown.
The rulers of nations used to get drunk
    on wine from those vineyards,
    that spread to Jazer,
then across the desert
    and beyond the sea.

⁹ Now I mourn like Jazer
    for the vineyards of Sibmah.
I shed tears for Heshbon
    and for Elealeh.
There will be no more
    harvest celebrations
¹⁰ or joyful and happy times,
    while bringing in the crops.
Singing and shouting are gone
    from the vineyards.
There are no joyful shouts
    where grapes were pressed.
    God has silenced them all.

¹¹ Deep in my heart I suffer
    for Moab and Kir-Heres.
¹² It's useless for Moab's people
    to wear themselves out
by going to their altars
    to worship and pray.

¹³ The Lord has already said all this about
Moab. ¹⁴ Now he says, "The contract of a
hired worker is good for three years, but
Moab's glory and greatness won't last any
longer than that. Only a few of its people will
survive, and they will be left helpless."

---

*16.1 lambs: The main product of Moab.
*16.1 Sela: A town in Edom.

*16.7 fine raisins: The Hebrew text has
"raisin-cakes," which could mean either the rich
produce or the prosperous farmers.

CHAPTER 17

Damascus will be punished

¹ This is a message about Damascus:

Damascus is doomed!
It will end up in ruins.
² The villages around Aroer*
will be deserted,
with only sheep living there
and no one to bother them.
³ Israel* will lose its fortresses.
The kingdom of Damascus
will be destroyed;
its survivors will suffer
the same fate as Israel.
The LORD All-Powerful
has promised this.

Sin and suffering

⁴ When that time comes,
the glorious nation of Israel
will be brought down;
its prosperous people
will be skin and bones.
⁵ Israel will be like wheat fields
in Rephaim Valley
picked clean of grain.
⁶ It will be like an olive tree
beaten with a stick,
leaving two or three olives
or perhaps four or five
on the highest
or most fruitful branches.
The LORD God of Israel
has promised this.

⁷ At that time the people will turn and trust their Creator, the holy God of Israel. ⁸ They have built altars and places for burning incense to their goddess Asherah, and they have set up sacred poles* for her. But they will stop worshipping at these places.

⁹ Israel captured powerful cities and chased out the people who lived there. But these cities will lie in ruins, covered over with weeds and undergrowth.»

¹⁰ Israel, you have forgotten
the God who saves you,
the one who is the mighty rock*
where you find protection.
You plant the finest flowers
to honour a foreign god.
¹¹ The plants may sprout and blossom
that very same morning,
but it will do you no good,
because you will suffer
endless agony.

God defends his people

¹² The nations are a noisy,
thunderous sea.
¹³ But even if they roar
like a fearsome flood,
God will give the command
to turn them back.
They will be like dust,
or like straw
blowing across the hills
in a storm.
¹⁴ In the evening
their attack is fierce,
but by morning
they are destroyed.
This is what happens to those
who raid and rob us.

CHAPTER 18

Ethiopia will be punished

¹ Downstream from Ethiopia*
lies the country of Egypt,
swarming with insects.»
² Egypt sends messengers
up the River Nile
on ships made of reeds.*
Send them fast to Ethiopia,
whose people are tall
and have smooth skin.
Their land is divided by rivers;
they are strong and brutal,
feared all over the world.»
³ Everyone on this earth,
listen with care!

---

*17.2 Aroer: Either a city near Damascus with the same name as the Moabite city or the Moabite city itself, here used as an example of what will happen to Damascus.
*17.8 sacred poles: Or "trees", used as symbols of Asherah, the goddess of fertility.
See also: 17.1–3; Jer 49.23–27; Amos 1.3–5; Zech 9.1.

*17.10 mighty rock: The Hebrew text has "rock", which is sometimes used in poetry to compare the Lord to a mountain where his people can run for protection from their enemies.
*18.1 Ethiopia: See the note at 11.11.
*18.2 reeds: Ancient Egypt was famous for the papyrus reeds that grew in the Nile Delta.
See also: 18.1–7: Zeph 2.12.

A signal will be given
on the mountains,
and you will hear a trumpet.
4 The LORD said to me,
"I will calmly look down
from my home above —
as calmly as the sun at midday
or clouds in the heat
of harvest season."

5 Before the blossoms
can turn into grapes,
God will cut off the shoots
and hack off the branches.
6 Ethiopians will be food
for mountain eagles
during the summer
and for wild animals
during the winter.

7 Those Ethiopians are tall and their skin is smooth. They are feared all over the world, because they are strong and brutal. But at that time they will come from their land divided by rivers, and they will bring gifts to the LORD All-Powerful, who is worshipped on Mount Zion.

CHAPTER 19

Egypt will be punished

1 This is a message about Egypt:

The LORD comes to Egypt,
riding swiftly on a cloud.
The people are weak from fear.
Their idols tremble
as he approaches and says,
2 "I will punish Egypt with civil war —
neighbours, cities, and kingdoms
will fight each other.

3 "Egypt will be discouraged
when I confuse their plans.
They will try to get advice
from their idols,
from the spirits of the dead,
and from fortune-tellers.
4 I will put the Egyptians
under the power of a cruel,
heartless king.
I, the LORD All-Powerful,
have promised this."

Trouble along the Nile

5 The River Nile will dry up
and become parched land.

6 Its streams will stink,
Egypt will have no water,
and the reeds and tall grass
will dry up.
7 Fields along the Nile
will be completely barren;
every plant will disappear.

8 Those who fish in the Nile
will be discouraged
and mourn.
9 None of the cloth makers*
will know what to do,
and they will turn pale.◆
10 Weavers will be confused;
paid workers will cry and mourn.

Egypt's helpless leaders

11 The king's officials in Zoan*
are foolish themselves
and give stupid advice.
How can they say to him,
"We are very wise,
and our families go back
to kings of long ago"?
12 Where are those wise men now?
If they can, let them say
what the LORD All-Powerful
intends for Egypt.

13 The royal officials in Zoan
and in Memphis
are foolish and deceived.
The leaders in every state
have given bad advice
to the nation.
14 The LORD has confused Egypt;
its leaders have made it stagger
and vomit like a drunkard.
15 No one in Egypt can do a thing,
no matter who they are.

16 When the LORD All-Powerful punishes Egypt with his mighty arm, the Egyptians will become terribly weak and will tremble with fear. 17 They will be so terrified of Judah that they will be frightened by the very mention of its name. This will happen because of what the LORD All-Powerful is planning against Egypt.

The LORD will bless Egypt, Assyria, and Israel

18 The time is coming when Hebrew will be spoken in five Egyptian cities, and their

---

*19.9 **cloth makers:** Cloth was made from several kinds of plants that grew in the fields along the Nile.
*19.11 **Zoan:** The city of Tanis in the Nile delta.

See also: 19.1-25: Jer 46.2-26; Ezek 29.1—32.32.

people will become followers of the LORD. One of these cities will be called City of the Sun.*

19 In the heart of Egypt an altar will be set up for the LORD; at its border a shrine will be built to honour him. 20 These will remind the Egyptians that the LORD All-Powerful is with them. And when they are in trouble and ask for help, he will send someone to rescue them from their enemies. 21 The LORD will show the Egyptians who he is, and they will know and worship the LORD. They will bring him sacrifices and offerings, and they will keep their promises to him. 22 After the LORD has punished Egypt, the people will turn to him. Then he will answer their prayers, and the Egyptians will be healed.

23 At that time a good road will run from Egypt to Assyria. The Egyptians and the Assyrians will travel back and forth from Egypt to Assyria, and they will worship together. 24 Israel will join with these two countries. They will be a blessing to everyone on earth, 25 then the LORD All-Powerful will bless them by saying,

"The Egyptians are my people.
I created the Assyrians
and chose the Israelites."

CHAPTER 20

Isaiah acts out the defeat of Egypt and Ethiopia

1 King Sargon of Assyria gave orders for his army commander to capture the city of Ashdod.* 2 About this same time the LORD had told me, "Isaiah, take off everything, including your sandals!" I did this and went around naked and barefoot 3 for three years.

Then the LORD said:

What Isaiah has done is a warning to Egypt and Ethiopia.* 4 Everyone in these two countries will be led away naked and barefoot by the king of Assyria. Young or old, they will be taken prisoner, and Egypt will be disgraced. 5 They will be confused and frustrated, because they depended on Ethiopia and boasted about Egypt. 6 When this happens, the people who live along the coast* will say, "Look what happened

to them! We ran to them for safety, hoping they would protect us from the king of Assyria. But now, there is no escape for us."

CHAPTER 21

The fall of Babylonia*

1 This is a message about a desert beside the sea:*

Enemies from a hostile nation
attack like a whirlwind
from the Southern Desert.
2 What a horrible vision
was shown to me —
a vision of betrayal and destruction.
Tell Elam and Media*
to surround and attack
the Babylonians.
The LORD has sworn to end
the suffering they caused.

3 I'm in terrible pain
like a woman giving birth.
I'm shocked and hurt so much
that I can't hear or see.
4 My head spins; I'm horrified!
Early evening, my favourite time,
has become a nightmare.

5 In Babylon the high officials
were having a feast.
They were eating and drinking,
when someone shouted,
"Officers, take your places!
Grab your shields."

6 The LORD said to me,
"Send guards to find out
what's going on.
7 When they see cavalry troops
and columns of soldiers
on donkeys and camels,
tell them to be ready!"

8 Then a guard* said,
"I have stood day and night
on this watchtower, Lord.

*20.1 Ashdod: King Sargon II of Assyria captured this Philistine city in 711 BC.
*20.3 Ethiopia: See the note at 11.11.
*20.6 people . . . coast: Probably the Philistines.

*21.1 Babylonia: King Cyrus and his army of Medes and Persians captured the city of Babylon in 539 BC.
*21.1 This . . . sea: One possible meaning for the difficult Hebrew text. The prophet may be speaking of Babylonia as a desert, because of the terrible punishment God will bring on it. The southern part of Babylonia on the Persian Gulf was sometimes called "the land beside the sea".
*21.2 Elam and Media: People from the Iranian highlands; the capital of Elam was Susa, in the hill country east of Babylon.

⁹ Now I see column after column
  of cavalry troops."
Straight away someone shouted,
  "Babylon has fallen!
Every idol in the city
  lies broken on the ground."

¹⁰ Then I said, "My people,
  you have suffered terribly,
but I have a message for you
  from the LORD All-Powerful,
  the God of Israel."

How much longer?

¹¹ This is a message about Dumah:

From the country of Seir,*
  someone shouts to me,
"Guard, how much longer
  before daylight?"

¹² From my guard post, I answered,
  "Morning will soon be here,
  but night will return.
If you want to know more,
  come back later."

¹³ This is a message for Arabs who live in the
barren desert in the region of Dedan:*

You must order your caravans
¹⁴ to bring water for those
  who are thirsty.
You people of Tema*
  must bring food
  for the hungry refugees.
¹⁵ They are worn out and weary
  from being chased by enemies
  with swords and arrows.

¹⁶ The Lord said to me:

A year from now the glory of the people of
Kedar* will all come to an end, just as a
worker's contract ends after a year. ¹⁷ Only
a few of their warriors will be left with
bows and arrows. This is a promise that I,
the LORD God of Israel, have made.

CHAPTER 22

Trouble in Vision Valley

¹ This is a message about Vision Valley:*

Why are you celebrating
  on the flat roofs*
  of your houses?
² Your city is filled
  with noisy shouts.
Those who lie drunk
  in your streets
  were not killed in battle.
³ Your leaders ran away,
  but they were captured
  without a fight.
No matter how far they ran,
  they were found and caught.*

⁴ Then I said, "Leave me alone!
  Let me cry bitter tears.
My people have been destroyed,
  so don't try to comfort me."

⁵ The LORD All-Powerful
  had chosen a time
for noisy shouts and confusion
  to fill Vision Valley,
and for everyone to beg
  the mountains for help.*
⁶ The people of Elam and Kir*
  attacked with chariots*
  and carried shields.
⁷ Your most beautiful valleys
  were covered with chariots;
  your cities were surrounded
  by cavalry troops.
⁸ Judah was left defenceless.

At that time you trusted in the weapons you
had stored in Forest Palace.* ⁹ You saw the
holes in the outer wall of Jerusalem, and you
brought water from the lower pool.* ¹⁰ You
counted the houses in Jerusalem and tore

---

*21.11 Dumah . . . Seir: Dumah was an oasis in the
Arabian desert. One ancient translation has "Edom",
which may be what is meant. Seir is a mountainous
region of Edom south-west of the Dead Sea.
*21.13 Dedan: A region in north-west Arabia.
*21.14 Tema: A region in north Arabia.
*21.16 Kedar: A region in the Arabian desert.
See also: 21.9; Rev 14.8; 18.2.

*22.1 Vision Valley: The exact location is not known.
In Hebrew the name sounds something like
"Hinnom Valley", where the people of Jerusalem
sometimes offered human sacrifices to the gods of
Canaan.
*22.1 flat roofs: In Palestine the houses usually had a
flat roof. Stairs on the outside led up to the roof,
which was made of beams and boards covered with
packed earth.
*22.6 Elam and Kir: Regions in the Iranian highlands.
*22.8 Forest Palace: Built by Solomon (1 Kings 7.2)
and used as a place for storing weapons.
*22.9 the lower pool: Mentioned only here;
probably in the southern part of the Central Valley
(Tyropoean Valley) of Jerusalem.

down some of them, so you could get stones to repair the city wall. ¹¹ Then you built a large tank between the walls* to store the water. But you refused to trust the God who planned this long ago and made it happen.

A time to weep

¹² When all this happened,
the LORD All-Powerful told you
        to weep and mourn,
        to shave your heads,
        and wear sackcloth.
¹³ But instead, you celebrated
by feasting on beef and lamb
        and by drinking wine,
because you said,
        "Let's eat and drink!
        Tomorrow we may die."

¹⁴ The LORD All-Powerful
has spoken to me
        this solemn promise:
"I won't forgive them for this,
        not as long as they live."

Selfish officials are doomed

¹⁵ The LORD All-Powerful is sending you with this message for Shebna, the prime minister:

¹⁶ Shebna, what gives you the right to have a tomb carved out of rock in this burial place of royalty? None of your relatives are buried here. ¹⁷ You may be powerful, but the LORD is about to snatch you up and throw you away. ¹⁸ He will roll you into a ball and throw you into a wide open country, where you will die and your chariots will be destroyed. You're a disgrace to those you serve.

¹⁹ The LORD is going to take away your job! ²⁰⁻²¹ He will give your official robes and your authority to his servant Eliakim son of Hilkiah.

Eliakim will be like a father to the people of Jerusalem and to the royal family of Judah. ²² The LORD will put him in charge of the key that belongs to King David's family. No one will be able to unlock what he locks, and no one will be able to lock what he unlocks. ²³ The LORD will make

him as firm in his position as a tent peg hammered in the ground, and Eliakim will bring honour to his family.

²⁴ His children and relatives will be supported by him, like pans hanging from a peg on the wall. ²⁵ That peg is fastened firmly now, but some day it will be shaken loose and fall down. Then everything that was hanging on it will be destroyed. This is what the LORD All-Powerful has promised.

CHAPTER 23

The city of Tyre will be punished

¹ This is a message from distant islands about the city of Tyre:*

        Cry, you seagoing ships!*
        Tyre and its houses lie in ruins.•
² Mourn in silence,
        you shop owners of Sidon,*
        you people on the coast.
        Your sailors crossed oceans,
        making your city rich.
³ Your merchants sailed the seas,
        making you wealthy by trading
        with nation after nation.
        They brought back grain
        that grew along the Nile.•
⁴ Sidon, you are a mighty fortress
        built along the sea.
        But you will be disgraced
        like a married woman
        who never had children.•

⁵ When Egypt hears about Tyre,
        it will tremble.
⁶ All of you along the coast
        had better cry and sail
        far across the ocean.•
⁷ Can this be the happy city
        that has stood for centuries?
        Its people have spread to distant lands;
⁸ its merchants were kings
        honoured all over the world.
        Who planned to destroy Tyre?
⁹ The LORD All-Powerful planned it
        to bring shame and disgrace
        to those who are honoured
        by everyone on earth.

---

*22.11 between the walls: Some cities had two walls with a space between them. If the enemy broke through the outer wall, the city was still protected by the inner wall. The houses that were torn down to repair the outer wall were probably squatters' huts that had been built between the two walls.
See also: 22.13: 1 Cor 15.32. **22.22:** Rev 3.7.

*23.1 Tyre: A fortress city built on an island in the Mediterranean Sea off the coast of what is now Lebanon.
*23.1 seagoing ships: See the note at 2.16.
*23.2 Sidon: A coastal city just north of Tyre.
See also: 23.1–18: Ezek 26.1—28.19; Joel 3.4–8; Amos 1.9,10; Zech 9.1–4; Matt 11.21,22; Luke 10.13,14.

¹⁰ People of Tyre,•
   your harbour is destroyed!
   You will have to become farmers
      just like the Egyptians.•

Tyre will be forgotten

¹¹ The LORD's hand has reached
      across the sea,
      upsetting the nations.
   He has given a command
      to destroy fortresses
      in the land of Canaan.
¹² The LORD has said
      to the people of Sidon,
   "Your celebrating is over —
      you are crushed.
   Even if you escape to Cyprus,
      you won't find peace."

¹³ Look what the Assyrians have done to
Babylonia! They have attacked, destroying
every palace in the land. Now wild animals
live among the ruins.• ¹⁴ Not a fortress will
be left standing, so tell all the seagoing ships*
to mourn.

¹⁵ The city of Tyre will be forgotten for
seventy years, which is the lifetime of a king.
Then Tyre will be like that evil woman in the
song:

¹⁶ You're gone and forgotten,
      you evil woman!
   So strut through the town,
      singing and playing
   your favourite tune
      to be remembered again.

¹⁷ At the end of those seventy years, the LORD
will let Tyre get back into business. The city
will be like a woman who sells her body to
everyone of every nation on earth, ¹⁸ but none
of what is earned will be kept in the city. That
money will belong to the LORD, and it will be
used to buy more than enough food and good
clothes for those who worship the LORD.

Messages of hope for the Lord's people who are suffering

CHAPTER 24

The earth will be punished

¹ The LORD is going to twist the earth out of
shape and turn it into a desert. Everyone will
be scattered, ² including ordinary people and
priests, slaves and slave owners, buyers and
sellers, lenders and borrowers, the rich and
the poor. ³ The earth will be stripped bare and
left that way. This is what the LORD has
promised.

⁴ The earth wilts away;
   its mighty leaders melt
      to nothing.•
⁵ The earth is polluted
      because its people
   disobeyed the laws of God,
      breaking their agreement
      that was to last for ever.

⁶ The earth is under a curse;
      its people are dying out
      because of their sins.
⁷ Grapevines have dried up;
      wine is almost gone —
   mournful sounds are heard
      instead of joyful shouts.

⁸ No one plays tambourines
      or stringed instruments;
   all noisy celebrating
      has come to an end.
⁹ They no longer sing
      as they drink their wine,
      and it tastes sour.

¹⁰ Towns are crushed and in chaos;
      houses are locked tight.
¹¹ Happy times have disappeared
      from the earth,
   and people shout in the streets,
      "We're out of wine!"
¹² Cities are destroyed;
      their gates are torn down.
¹³ Nations will be stripped bare,
      like olive trees or vineyards
      after the harvest season.

Praise the God of justice

¹⁴ People in the west shout;
      they joyfully praise
      the majesty of the LORD.
¹⁵ And so, everyone in the east
      and those on the islands
   should praise the LORD,
      the God of Israel.
¹⁶ From all over the world
      songs of praise are heard
      for the God of justice.•
   But I feel awful,
      terribly miserable.
   Can anyone be trusted?
      So many are treacherous!

---

*23.14 seagoing ships: See the note at 2.16.

There's no escape

17 Terror, traps, and pits
   are waiting for everyone.
18 If you are terrified and run,
   you will fall into a pit;
   if you crawl out of the pit,
   you will get caught in a trap.

The sky has split apart
   like a window thrown open.
The foundations of the earth
   have been shaken;
19 the earth is shattered,
   ripped to pieces.
20 It staggers and shakes like a drunkard
   or a hut in a storm.
It is burdened down with sin;
   the earth will fall,
   never again to get up.

21 On that day the LORD
   will punish the powers
   in the heavens*
   and the kings of the earth.
22 He will put them in a pit
   and keep them prisoner.
Then later on,
   he will punish them.
23 The moon and sun will both
   be embarrassed and ashamed.
The LORD All-Powerful will rule
   on Mount Zion in Jerusalem,
   where he will show its rulers
   his wonderful glory.

CHAPTER 25

A prayer of thanks to God

1 You, LORD, are my God!
   I will praise you
   for doing the wonderful things
   you had planned and promised
   since ancient times.
2 You have destroyed the fortress
   of our enemies,
   leaving their city in ruins.
Nothing in that foreign city
   will ever be rebuilt.
3 Now strong and cruel nations
   will fear and honour you.

4 You have been a place of safety
   for the poor and needy
   in times of trouble.
Brutal enemies pounded us

like a heavy rain
   or the heat of the sun at midday,
   but you were our shelter.
5 Those wild foreigners struck
   like scorching desert heat.
But you were like a cloud,
   protecting us from the sun.
You kept our enemies from singing
   songs of victory.

The LORD has saved us

6 On this mountain
   the LORD All-Powerful
   will prepare for all nations
   a feast of the finest foods.
Choice wines and the best meats
   will be served.
7 Here the LORD will strip away
   the burial clothes
   that cover the nations.
8 The LORD All-Powerful
   will destroy the power of death
   and wipe away all tears.
No longer will his people
   be insulted everywhere.
   The LORD has spoken!

9 At that time, people will say,
   "The LORD has saved us!
   Let's celebrate.
We waited and hoped —
   now our God is here."
10 The powerful arm of the LORD
   will protect this mountain.

The Moabites will be put down
   and trampled on like straw
   in a pit of manure.
11 They will struggle to get out,
   but God will humiliate them
   no matter how hard they try.
12 The walls of their fortresses
   will be knocked down
   and scattered in the dust.

CHAPTER 26

A song of victory

1 The time is coming
   when the people of Judah
   will sing this song:
   "Our city* is protected.

---

*24.21 the powers in the heavens: In ancient times
the stars were thought of as powerful spiritual beings,
and sometimes they stood for pagan gods.

*26.1 city: Probably Jerusalem.

See also: 25.8: a 1 Cor 15.54; b Rev 7.17; 21.4.
25.10–12: Isa 15.1–16.14; Jer 48.1–47; Ezek 25.8–11;
Amos 2.1–3; Zeph 2.8–11.

The LORD is our fortress,
and he gives us victory.
2 Open the city gates
for a law-abiding nation
that is faithful to God.
3 The LORD gives perfect peace
to those whose faith is firm.
4 So always trust the LORD
because he is for ever
our mighty rock.*
5 God has put down our enemies
in their mountain city*
and rubbed it in the dust.
6 Now the poor and abused
trample all over that city."

The LORD can be trusted

7 Our LORD, you always do right,
and you make the path smooth
for those who obey you.
8 You are the one we trust
to bring about justice;
above all else we want
your name to be honoured.
9 Throughout the night,
my heart searches for you,
because your decisions
show everyone on this earth
how to live right.

10 Even when the wicked
are treated with mercy
in this land of justice,
they do wrong and are blind
to your glory, our LORD.
11 Your hand is raised and ready
to punish them,
but they don't see it.
Put them to shame!
Show how much you care for us
and throw them into the fire
intended for your enemies.

12 You will give us peace, LORD,
because everything we have done
was by your power.
13 Others have ruled over us
besides you, our LORD God,
but we obey only you.
14 Those enemies are now dead
and can never live again.
You have punished them —
they are destroyed,
completely forgotten.

15 Our nation has grown
because of you, our LORD.
We have more land than before,
and you are honoured.

The LORD gives life to the dead

16 When you punished our people,
they turned and prayed
to you, our LORD.'
17 Because of what you did to us,
we suffered like a woman
about to give birth.
18 But instead of having a child,
our terrible pain
produced only wind.
We have won no victories,
and we have no descendants
to take over the earth.

19 Your people will rise to life!
Tell them to leave their graves
and celebrate with shouts.
You refresh the earth
like morning dew;
you give life to the dead.

20 Go inside and lock the doors,
my people.
Hide there for a little while,
until the LORD is no longer angry.

The earth and the sea will be punished

21 The LORD will come out
to punish everyone on earth
for their sins.
And when he does,
those who did violent crimes
will be known and punished.

CHAPTER 27

1 On that day, Leviathan,*
the sea monster,
will squirm and try to escape,
but the LORD will kill him
with a cruel, sharp sword.

Protection and forgiveness

The LORD said:

2 At that time you must sing
about a fruitful* vineyard.

---

*26.4 mighty rock: See the note at 17.10.

See also: 26.11: Heb 10.27.

*27.1 Leviathan: God's victory over this monster
sometimes stands for God's power over all creation
and sometimes for his defeat of his enemies,
especially Egypt.

See also: 27.1: Job 41.1; Psa 74.14; 104.26.

³ I, the LORD, will protect it
  and always keep it watered.
I will guard it day and night
  to keep it from harm.
⁴ I am no longer angry.
  But if it produces thorns,
I will go to war against it
  and burn it to the ground.
⁵ Yet if the vineyard depends
  on me for protection,
it will become my friend
  and be at peace with me.

⁶ Some day Israel will take root
  like a vine.
It will blossom and bear fruit
  that covers the earth.

⁷ I, the LORD, didn't punish and kill
  the people of Israel
as fiercely as I punished
  and killed their enemies.
⁸ I carefully measured out
  Israel's punishment'
and sent the scorching heat
  to chase them far away.

⁹ There's only one way
  that Israel's sin and guilt
  can be completely forgiven:
they must crush the stones
  of every pagan altar
  and place of worship.

The LORD will bring
his people together

¹⁰ Fortress cities are left
  like a desert
  where no one lives.
Cattle walk through the ruins,
  stripping the trees bare.
¹¹ When broken branches
  fall to the ground,
women pick them up
  to feed the fire.
But these people are so stupid
  that the God who created them
  will show them no mercy.

¹² The time is coming when the LORD will
shake the land between the River Euphrates
and the border of Egypt, and one by one he
will bring all his people together. ¹³ A loud
trumpet will be heard. Then the people of
Israel who were dragged away to Assyria and
Egypt will return to worship the LORD on his
holy mountain in Jerusalem.

The Lord will punish
his rebellious people

CHAPTER 28

Samaria will be punished

¹ The city of Samaria
  above a fertile valley
  is in for trouble!
Its leaders are drunkards,
  who stuff themselves
  with food and wine.
But they will be like flowers
  that dry up and wilt.
² Only the Lord is strong and powerful!
  His mighty hand
  will strike them down
with the force of a hailstorm
  or a mighty whirlwind
  or an overwhelming flood.

³ Every drunkard in Ephraim*
  takes pride in Samaria,
  but it will be crushed.
⁴ Samaria above a fertile valley
  will quickly lose its glory.
It will be gobbled up
  like the first ripe fig
  at harvest season.
⁵ When this time comes,
  the LORD All-Powerful
  will be a glorious crown
  for his people who survive.
⁶ He will see that justice rules
  and that his people are able
  to defend their cities.

Corrupt leaders will be punished

⁷ Priests and prophets stumble
  because they are drunk.
Their minds are too confused
  to receive God's messages
  or give honest decisions.
⁸ Their tables are covered,
  completely covered,
  with their stinking vomit.

⁹ You drunken leaders are like babies!
How can you possibly understand
  or teach the LORD's message?
¹⁰ You don't even listen —
  all you hear is senseless sound
  after senseless sound.'

*28.3 Ephraim: The northern kingdom of Israel;
Samaria was its capital.

661

¹¹ So, the Lord will speak
to his people in strange sounds
and foreign languages.*
¹² He promised you
perfect peace and rest,
but you refused to listen.
¹³ Now his message to you
will be senseless sound
after senseless sound.'
Then you will fall backwards,
injured and trapped.

False security is fatal

¹⁴ You rulers of Jerusalem
do nothing but sneer;
now you must listen
to what the LORD says.
¹⁵ Do you think you have
an agreement with death
and the world of the dead?
Why do you trust in your lies
to keep you safe from danger
and the mighty flood?

¹⁶ And so the LORD says,
"I'm laying a firm foundation
for the city of Zion.
It's a valuable cornerstone
proved to be trustworthy;
no one who trusts it
will ever be disappointed.
¹⁷ Justice and fairness
will be the measuring lines
that help me build."

Hailstones and floods
will destroy and wash away
your shelter of lies.
¹⁸ Your agreement with death
and the world of the dead
will be broken.
Then angry, roaring waves
will sweep over you.
¹⁹ Morning, noon, and night
an overwhelming flood
will wash you away.
The terrible things that happen
will teach you this lesson:
²⁰ your bed is too short,
your blanket too skimpy.*

²¹ The LORD will fiercely attack
as he did at Mount Perazim*
and in Gibeon Valley.*
But this time the LORD
will do something surprising,
not what you expect.
²² So you had better stop sneering
or you will be in worse shape
than ever before.
I heard the LORD All-Powerful
threaten the whole country
with destruction.

All wisdom comes from the LORD

²³ Pay close attention
to what I am saying.
²⁴ Farmers don't just plough
and break up the ground.
²⁵ When a field is ready,
they scatter the seeds
of dill and cumin;
they plant the seeds
of wheat and barley
in the proper places.
²⁶ They learn this from their God.

²⁷ After dill and cumin
have been harvested,
the stalks are beaten,
not run over with a wagon.
²⁸ Wheat and barley are pounded,
but not beaten to pulp;
they are run over with a wagon,
but not ground to dust.
²⁹ This wonderful knowledge comes
from the LORD All-Powerful,
who has such great wisdom.

CHAPTER 29

Jerusalem will suffer

The LORD said:

¹ Jerusalem, city of David,
the place of my altar,'
you are in trouble!
Celebrate your festivals year after year.
² I will still make you suffer,
and your people will cry
when I make an altar of you.'

28.11 in . . . foreign languages: This probably refers
to the language of the Assyrians.
28.20 your bed . . . skimpy: Isaiah quotes a popular
saying to teach that the treaty made with Egypt
(verse 18) cannot give the nation security from its
enemies.

See also: 28.11,12: 1 Cor 14.21. **28.16:** Psa 118.22,23;
Rom 9.33; 10.11; 1 Pet 2.6.

662

28.21 Mount Perazim: This may refer to
David's defeat of the Philistines at Baal Perazim
(2 Samuel 5.17–21).
28.21 Gibeon Valley: This refers to Joshua's
victory at Gibeon (Joshua 10.1–11).
See also: 28.21: a 2 Sam 5.20; 1 Chron 14.11;
b Josh 10.10–12.

3 I will surround you and prepare
   to attack from all sides.⁍
4 From deep in the earth,
   you will call out for help
   with only a faint whisper.

5 Then your cruel enemies
   will suddenly be swept away
   like dust in a storm.
6 I, the LORD All-Powerful,
   will come to your rescue
   with a thundering earthquake
   and a fiery whirlwind.

7 Every brutal nation
   that attacks Jerusalem
   and makes it suffer
   will disappear like a dream
   when night is over.
8 Those nations that attack
   Mount Zion
   will suffer from hunger and thirst.
   They will dream of food and drink
   but wake up weary and hungry
   and thirsty as ever.

Prophets who fool themselves

9 Be shocked and stunned,
   you prophets!
   Refuse to see.
   Get drunk and stagger,
   but not from wine.
10 The LORD has made you drowsy;
   he put you into a deep sleep
   and covered your head.

11 Now his message is like a sealed letter to
you. Some of you say, "We can't read it,
because it's sealed." 12 Others say, "We can't
read it, because we don't know how to read."
   13 The Lord has said:

   "These people praise me
      with their words,
   but they never really
      think about me.
   They worship me by repeating
      rules made up by humans.
14 So once again I will do things
   that shock and amaze them,
   and I will destroy the wisdom
   of those who claim to know
      and understand."

15 You are in for trouble,
   if you try to hide your plans
   from the LORD!

Or if you think what you do
   in the dark can't be seen.
16 You have it all backwards.
   A clay dish doesn't say to the potter,
   "You didn't make me.
   You don't even know how."

Hope for the future

17 Soon the forest of Lebanon
   will become a field with crops,
   thick as a forest.⁍
18 The deaf will be able to hear
   whatever is read to them;
   the blind will be freed
   from a life of darkness.
19 The poor and the needy
   will celebrate and shout
   because of the LORD,
   the holy God of Israel.

20 All who are cruel and arrogant
   will be gone for ever.
   Those who live by crime will disappear,
21 together with everyone
   who tells lies in court
   and keeps innocent people
   from getting a fair trial.

22 The LORD who rescued Abraham
   has this to say
   about Jacob's descendants:
   "They will no longer
   be ashamed and disgraced.
23 When they see how great
   I have made their nation,
   they will praise and honour me,
   the holy God of Israel.
24 Everyone who is confused
   will understand,
   and all who have complained
   will obey my teaching."

CHAPTER 30

Don't expect help from Egypt

1 This is the LORD's message for his rebellious
people:

   "You follow your own plans
      instead of mine;
   you make treaties
      without asking me,
   and you keep on sinning.
2 You trust Egypt for protection.
   So you refuse my advice
   and send messengers to Egypt
   to beg their king for help.

See also: 29.10: Rom 11.8. 29.13: Matt 15.8,9; Mark 7.6,7.
29.14: 1 Cor 1.19.

See also: 29.16: Isa 45.9; Rom 9.20.

³ You will be disappointed,
completely disgraced
for trusting Egypt.
⁴ The king's power reaches
from the city of Zoan
as far south as Hanes.*
⁵ But Egypt can't protect you,
and to trust that nation
is useless and foolish.

⁶ This is a message about the animals of the Southern Desert:

You people carry treasures
on donkeys and camels.
You travel to a feeble nation
through a troublesome desert
filled with lions
and flying fiery dragons.
⁷ Egypt can't help you!
That's why I call that nation
a helpless monster.ª

Israel refuses to listen

⁸ The LORD told me to write down his message to his people, so that it would be there for ever. ⁹ They have turned against the LORD and can't be trusted. They have refused his teaching ¹⁰ and have said to his messengers and prophets:

Don't tell us what God has shown you and don't preach the truth. Just say what we want to hear, even if it's false. ¹¹ Stop telling us what God has said! We don't want to hear any more about the holy God of Israel.

¹² Now this is the answer
of the holy God of Israel:
"You rejected my message,
and you trust in violence and lies.
¹³ This sin is like a crack
that makes a high wall
quickly crumble
¹⁴ and shatter like a crushed bowl.
There's not a piece left
big enough to carry hot coals
or to scoop up water."

Trust the LORD

¹⁵ The holy LORD God of Israel
had told all of you,
"I will keep you safe
if you turn back to me
and calm down.

I will make you strong
if you quietly trust me."

Then you stubbornly
¹⁶ said, "No! We will safely escape
on speedy horses."

But those who chase you
will be even faster.
¹⁷ As few as five of them,
or even one, will be enough
to chase a thousand of you.
Finally, all that will be left
will be a few survivors
as lonely as a flag pole
on a barren hill.

The LORD will show mercy

¹⁸ The LORD God is waiting
to show how kind he is
and to have pity on you.
The LORD always does right;
he blesses those who trust him.

¹⁹ People of Jerusalem, you don't need to cry any more. The Lord is kind, and as soon as he hears your cries for help, he will come. ²⁰ The Lord has given you trouble and sorrow as your food and drink. But now you will again see the Lord, your teacher, and he will guide you. ²¹ Whether you turn to the right or to the left, you will hear a voice saying, "This is the road! Now follow it." ²² Then you will treat your idols of silver and gold like rubbish; you will throw them away like filthy rags.

²³ The Lord will send rain to water the seeds you have planted — your fields will produce more crops than you need, and your cattle will graze in open pastures. ²⁴ Even the oxen and donkeys that plough your fields will be fed the finest grain.*

²⁵ On that day people will be slaughtered and towers destroyed, but streams of water will flow from high hills and towering mountains. ²⁶ Then the LORD will bandage his people's injuries and heal the wounds he has caused. The moon will shine as bright as the sun, and the sun will shine seven times brighter than usual. It will be like the light of seven days all at once.

Assyria will be punished

²⁷ The LORD is coming from far away
with his fiery anger

---

*30.4 Zoan . . . Hanes: Or "Your messengers have reached the city of Zoan and gone as far as Hanes." Zoan was in north-east Egypt; Hanes was to the south.

*30.24 the finest grain: The Hebrew text refers to grain with the husks removed.

and thick clouds of smoke.*
His angry words flame up
   like a destructive fire;
²⁸ he breathes out a flood
   that comes up to the neck.
He sifts the nations
   and destroys them.
Then he puts a bridle
   in every foreigner's mouth
   and leads them to doom.

²⁹ The LORD's people will sing as they do
when they celebrate a religious festival* at
night. The LORD is Israel's mighty rock,* and
his people will be as happy as they are when
they follow the sound of flutes to the
mountain where he is worshipped.

³⁰ The LORD will get furious. His fearsome
voice will be heard, his arm will be seen
ready to strike, and his anger will be like a
destructive fire, followed by thunderstorms
and hailstones. ³¹ When the Assyrians hear
the LORD's voice and see him striking with
his iron rod, they will be terrified. ³² He will
attack them in battle, and each time he
strikes them, it will be to the music of
tambourines and harps.

³³ Long ago the LORD got a place ready for
burning the body of the dead king.* The
place for the fire is deep and wide, the wood
is piled high, and the LORD will start the fire
by breathing out flaming sulphur.

CHAPTER 31

Don't trust the power of Egypt

¹ You are in for trouble
   if you go to Egypt for help,
or if you depend on
   an army of chariots
   or a powerful cavalry.
Instead you should depend on
   and trust the holy LORD God
   of Israel.
² The LORD isn't stupid!
   He does what he promises,
   and he can bring doom.
If you are cruel yourself,
   or help those who are evil,
   you will be destroyed.

---

*30.29 a religious festival: Probably Passover.
*30.29 mighty rock: See the note at 17.10.
*30.33 burning . . . king: Or "sacrificing the king" or
"sacrificing to Molech". Human sacrifices were
sometimes offered to Molech, a god whose name
sounds like the Hebrew word for "king" (see
2 Kings 23.10; Jeremiah 32.35).

³ The Egyptians are mere humans.
   They aren't God.
Their horses are made of flesh;
   they can't live for ever.
When the LORD shows his power,
   he will destroy the Egyptians
   and all who depend on them.
Together they will fall.

⁴ The LORD All-Powerful
   said to me,
"I will roar and attack
   like a fearless lion
not frightened by the shouts
   of shepherds trying to protect
   their sheep.
That's how I will come down
   and fight on Mount Zion.
⁵ I, the LORD All-Powerful,
   will protect Jerusalem
like a mother bird circling
   over her nest."

Come back to the LORD

⁶ People of Israel, come back!
   You have completely turned
   from the LORD.
⁷ The time is coming
   when you will throw away
your idols of silver and gold,
   made by your sinful hands.

⁸ The Assyrians will be killed,
   but not by the swords
   of humans.
Their young men will try
   to escape,
but they will be captured
   and forced into slavery.
⁹ Their fortress* will fall
   when terror strikes;
their army officers
   will be frightened
   and run from the battle.
This is what the LORD has said,
   the LORD whose fiery furnace
   is built on Mount Zion.

The Lord will punish Edom and bless Jerusalem

CHAPTER 32

Justice will rule

¹ A king and his leaders
   will rule with justice.

2 They will be a place of safety
  from stormy winds,
  a stream in the desert,
  and a rock that gives shade
  from the heat of the sun.
3 Then everyone who has eyes
  will open them and see,
  and those who have ears
  will pay attention.
4 All who are impatient
  will take time to think;
  everyone who stutters
  will talk clearly.
5 Fools will no longer
  be highly respected,
  and crooks won't be given
  positions of honour.
6 Fools talk foolishness.
  They always make plans
  to do sinful things,
  to lie about the LORD,
  to let the hungry starve,
  and to keep water from those
  who are thirsty.
7 Cruel people tell lies —
  they do evil things,
  and make cruel plans
  to destroy the poor and needy,
  even when they beg
  for justice.
8 But helpful people
  can always be trusted
  to make helpful plans.

Punishment for the women of Jerusalem

9 Listen to what I say,
  you women who are carefree
  and careless!
10 You may not have worries now,
  but in about a year,
  the grape harvest will fail,
  and you will tremble.

11 Shake and shudder,
  you women without a care!
  Strip off your clothes —
  put on sackcloth.
12 Slap your breasts in sorrow
  because of what happened
  to the fruitful fields
  and vineyards,
13 and to the happy homes
  in Jerusalem.
  The land of my people
  is covered with thorns.

14 The palace will be deserted,
  the crowded city empty.
  Fortresses and towers
  will for ever become
  playgrounds for wild donkeys
  and pastures for sheep.

God's Spirit makes the difference

15 When the Spirit is given to us
  from heaven,
  deserts will become orchards
  thick as fertile forests.
16 Honesty and justice will prosper there,
17 and justice will produce
  lasting peace and security.
18 You, the LORD's people,
  will live in peace,
  calm and secure,
19 even if hailstones flatten
  forests and cities.
20 You will have God's blessing,
  as you plant your crops
  beside streams,
  while your donkeys and cattle
  roam freely about.

CHAPTER 33

Jerusalem will be safe

1 You defeated my people.
  Now you're in for trouble!
  You've never been destroyed,
  but you will be destroyed;
  you've never been betrayed,
  but you will be betrayed.
  When you have finished
  destroying and betraying,
  you will be destroyed
  and betrayed in return.

2 Please, LORD, be kind to us!
  We depend on you.
  Make us strong each morning,
  and come to save us
  when we are in trouble.
3 Nations scatter when you roar
  and show your greatness.'
4 We attack our enemies
  like swarms of locusts;*
  we take everything
  that belongs to them.'

5 You, LORD, are above all others,
  and you live in the heavens.

---

*33.4 locusts: Insects like grasshoppers that travel in swarms and cause great damage to crops.

You have brought justice
and fairness to Jerusalem;
6 you are the foundation
on which we stand today.
You always save us and give
true wisdom and knowledge.
Nothing means more to us'
than obeying you.

The LORD will do something

7 Listen! Our bravest soldiers
are running through the streets,
screaming for help.'
Our messengers hoped for peace,
but came home crying.
8 No one travels any more;
every road is empty.
Treaties are broken,
and no respect is shown
to any who keep promises.'
9 Fields are dry and barren;
Mount Lebanon wilts with shame.
Sharon Valley is a desert;
the forests of Bashan and Carmel
have lost their leaves.

10 But the LORD says,
"Now I will do something
and be greatly praised.
11 Your deeds are straw
that will be set on fire
by your very own breath.
12 You will be burnt to ashes
like thorns in a fire.
13 Everyone, both far and near,
come, look at what I have done.
See my mighty power!"

Punishment and rewards

14 Those terrible sinners
on Mount Zion tremble
as they ask in fear,
"How can we possibly live
where a raging fire
never stops burning?"

15 But there will be rewards
for those who live right
and tell the truth,
for those who refuse
to take money by force
or accept bribes,
for all who hate murder
and violent crimes.
16 They will live in a fortress
high on a rocky cliff,
where they will have food
and plenty of water.

The LORD is our King

17 With your own eyes
you will see the glorious King;
you will see his kingdom
reaching far and wide.
18 Then you will ask yourself,
"Where are those officials
who terrified us and forced us
to pay such heavy taxes?"
19 You will never again have to see
the proud people who spoke
a strange and foreign language
you could not understand.

20 Look to Mount Zion
where we celebrate
our religious festivals.
You will see Jerusalem,
secure as a tent with pegs
that cannot be pulled up
and fastened with ropes
that can never be broken.
21 Our wonderful LORD
will be with us!
There will be deep rivers
and wide streams
safe from enemy ships.*

The LORD is our judge

22 The LORD is our judge
and our ruler;
the LORD is our king
and will keep us safe.
23 But your nation* is a ship
with its rigging loose,
its mast shaky,
and its sail not spread.

Some day even you who are lame
will take everything you want
from your enemies.
24 The LORD will forgive your sins,
and none of you will say, "I feel ill."

CHAPTER 34

The nations will be judged

1 Everyone of every nation,
the entire earth,
and all its creatures,
come here and listen!
2 The LORD is terribly angry
with the nations;

---

*33.21 safe . . . ships: This probably means that
Jerusalem will have a lot of water, without the danger
of attacks from enemy ships.
*33.23 your nation: Possibly Judah or Assyria.

he has condemned them
to be slaughtered.
³ Their dead bodies will be left
to rot and stink;
their blood will flow
down the mountains.
⁴ Each star* will disappear —
the sky will roll up
like a scroll.*
Everything in the sky
will dry up and wilt
like leaves on a vine
or fruit on a tree.

Trouble for Edom

⁵ After the sword of the LORD
has done what it wants
to the skies above,•
it will come down on Edom,
the nation that the LORD
has doomed for destruction.

⁶ The sword of the LORD
is covered with blood
from lambs and goats,
together with fat
from kidneys of rams.
This is because the LORD
will slaughter many people
and make a sacrifice of them
in the city of Bozrah
and everywhere else
in Edom.

⁷ Edom's leaders are wild oxen.
They are powerful bulls,
but they will die
with the others.
Their country will be soaked
with their blood,
and its soil made fertile
with their fat.

⁸ The LORD has chosen
the year and the day,
when he will take revenge
and come to Zion's defence.
⁹ Edom's streams will turn into tar
and its soil into sulphur —
then the whole country
will go up in flames.

¹⁰ It will burn night and day
and never stop smoking.
Edom will be a desert,
generation after generation;
no one will ever travel
through that land.
¹¹ Owls, hawks, and wild animals•
will make it their home.
God will leave it in ruins,
merely a pile of rocks.

The end of Edom

¹² Edom will be called
"Kingdom of Nothing".
Its rulers will also be nothing.
¹³ Its palaces and fortresses
will be covered with thorns;
only wolves and ostriches
will make their home there.
¹⁴ Wildcats and hyenas
will hunt together,
demons will scream to demons,
and creatures of the night
will live among the ruins.
¹⁵ Owls will nest there
to raise their young
among its shadows,•
while families of vultures
circle around.

¹⁶ In *The Book of the LORD*•
you can search and find
where it is written,
"The LORD brought together
all his creatures
by the power of his Spirit.
Not one is missing."
¹⁷ The LORD has decided
where they each should live;
they will be there for ever,
generation after generation.

CHAPTER 35

God's splendour will be seen

¹ Thirsty deserts will be glad;
barren lands will celebrate
and blossom with flowers.
² Deserts will bloom everywhere
and sing joyful songs.
They will be as majestic
as Mount Lebanon,
as glorious as Mount Carmel
or Sharon Valley.

•34.4 star: Stars were worshipped as gods.
•34.4 scroll: A roll of paper or specially prepared
leather used for writing on.

See also: 34.4: Matt 24.29; Mark 13.25; Luke 21.26;
Rev 6.13,14.   **34.5–17:** Isa 63.1–6; Jer 49.7–22;
Ezek 25.12–14; 35.1–15; Amos 1.11,12; Obad 1–14;
Mal 1.2–5.

•34.16 *The Book of the LORD*: The book that Isaiah
refers to is unknown.
See also: 34.10: Rev 14.11; 19.3.

Everyone will see
the wonderful splendour
of the LORD our God.

God changes everything

3-4 Here is a message for all who are weak,
trembling, and worried:

"Cheer up! Don't be afraid.
Your God is coming
to punish your enemies.
God will take revenge on them
and rescue you."

5 The blind will see,
and the ears of the deaf
will be healed.
6 Those who were lame
will leap around like deer;
tongues once silent
will begin to shout.
Water will rush
through the desert.
7 Scorching sand
will turn into a lake,
and thirsty ground
will flow with fountains.
Grass will grow in wetlands,
where packs of wild dogs
once made their home.'

God's sacred highway

8 A good road will be there,
and it will be named
"God's Sacred Highway".
It will be for God's people;
no one unfit to worship God
will walk on that road.
And no fools can travel
on that highway.'
9 No lions or other wild animals
will come near that road;
only those the LORD has saved
will travel there.

10 The people the LORD has rescued
will come back singing
as they enter Zion.
Happiness will be a crown
they will always wear.
They will celebrate and shout
because all sorrows and worries
will be gone far away.

Assyria, Babylonia, King Hezekiah, and Isaiah

CHAPTER 36

The Assyrians surround Jerusalem

This is also told in 2 Kings 18.13–27;
2 Chronicles 32.1–19

1 Hezekiah had been king of Judah for
fourteen years when King Sennacherib of
Assyria invaded the country and captured
every walled city 2 except Jerusalem. The
Assyrian king ordered his army commander
to leave the city of Lachish and to take a large
army to Jerusalem.

The commander went there and stood on
the road near the cloth makers' shops along
the canal from the upper pool. 3 Three of the
king's highest officials came out of Jerusalem
to meet him. One of them was Hilkiah's son
Eliakim, who was the prime minister. The
other two were Shebna, assistant to the prime
minister, and Joah son of Asaph, keeper of
the government records.
4 The Assyrian commander told them:

I have a message for Hezekiah from the
great king of Assyria. Ask Hezekiah why he
feels so sure of himself. 5 Does he think he
can plan and win a war with nothing but
words? Who is going to help him, now
that he has turned against the king of
Assyria? 6 Is he depending on Egypt and its
king? That's the same as leaning on a
broken stick, and it will go right through
his hand.
7 Is Hezekiah now depending on the
LORD, your God? Didn't Hezekiah tear
down all except one of the LORD's altars
and places of worship?* Didn't he tell the
people of Jerusalem and Judah to worship
at that one place?
8 The king of Assyria wants to make a bet
with you people! He will give you two
thousand horses, if you have enough
troops to ride them. 9 How could you
defeat even our lowest ranking officer,
when you have to depend on Egypt for
chariots and cavalry? 10 Don't forget that it

---

*36.7 worship: Hezekiah actually had torn down the
places where idols were worshipped, and he had told
the people to worship the LORD at the one place of
worship in Jerusalem. But the Assyrian leader was
confused and thought these were also places where
the LORD was supposed to be worshipped.

See also: 35.3: Heb 12.12. 35.5,6: Matt 11.5; Luke 7.22.

See also: 36.6: Ezek 29.6,7.

was the LORD who sent me here with orders to destroy your nation!

[11] Eliakim, Shebna, and Joah said, "Sir, we don't want the people listening from the city wall to understand what you are saying. So please speak to us in Aramaic instead of Hebrew."

[12] The Assyrian army commander answered, "My king sent me to speak to everyone, not just to you leaders. These people will soon have to eat their own body waste and drink their own urine! And so will the three of you!"

[13] Then, in a voice loud enough for everyone to hear, he shouted out in Hebrew:

Listen to what the great king of Assyria says! [14] Don't be fooled by Hezekiah. He can't save you. [15] Don't trust him when he tells you that the LORD will protect you from the king of Assyria. [16] Stop listening to Hezekiah. Pay attention to my king. Surrender to him. He will let you keep your own vineyards, fig trees, and cisterns [17] for a while. Then he will come and take you away to a country just like yours, where you can plant vineyards and raise your own grain.

[18] Hezekiah claims the LORD will save you. But don't be fooled by him. Were any other gods able to defend their land against the king of Assyria? [19] What happened to the gods of Hamath, Arpad, and Sepharvaim? Were the gods of Samaria able to protect their land against the Assyrian forces? [20] None of these gods kept their people safe from the king of Assyria. Do you think the LORD, your God, can do any better?

[21-22] Eliakim, Shebna, and Joah had been warned by King Hezekiah not to answer the Assyrian commander. So they tore their clothes in sorrow and reported to Hezekiah everything the commander said.

CHAPTER 37

Hezekiah asks Isaiah for advice

This is also told in 2 Kings 19.1–13

[1] As soon as Hezekiah heard the news, he tore off his clothes in sorrow and put on sackcloth. Then he went into the temple of the LORD. [2] He told Prime Minister Eliakim, Assistant Prime Minister Shebna, and the senior priests to dress in sackcloth and tell me:

[3] Isaiah, these are difficult and disgraceful times. Our nation is like a woman too weak to give birth, when it's time for her baby to be born. [4] Please pray for those of us who are left alive. The king of Assyria sent his army commander to insult the living God. Perhaps the LORD heard what he said and will do something, if you will pray.

[5] When these leaders came to me, [6] I told them that the LORD had this message for Hezekiah:

I am the LORD. Don't worry about the insulting things that have been said about me by these messengers from the king of Assyria. [7] I will upset him with rumours about what's happening in his own country. He will go back, and there I will make him die a violent death.

[8] Meanwhile the commander of the Assyrian forces heard that his king had left the town of Lachish and was now attacking Libnah. So he went there.

[9] About this same time, the king of Assyria learnt that King Tirhakah of Ethiopia* was on his way to attack him. Then the king of Assyria sent some messengers with this note for Hezekiah:

[10] Don't trust your God or be fooled by his promise to defend Jerusalem against me. [11] You have heard how we Assyrian kings have completely wiped out other nations. What makes you feel so safe? [12] The Assyrian kings before me destroyed the towns of Gozan, Haran, Rezeph, and everyone from Eden who lived in Telassar. What good did their gods do them? [13] The kings of Hamath, Arpad, Sepharvaim, Hena, and Ivvah have all disappeared.

Hezekiah prays

This is also told in 2 Kings 19.14–19

[14] After Hezekiah had read the note from the king of Assyria, he took it to the temple and spread it out for the LORD to see. [15] Then he prayed:

[16] LORD God All-Powerful of Israel, your throne is above the winged creatures.* You

---

*37.9 Ethiopia: See the note at 11.11.
*37.16 winged creatures: Two winged creatures made of gold were on the top of the sacred chest and were symbols of the LORD's throne on earth (see Exodus 25.18; 2 Samuel 6.2).
See also: 37.16: Exod 25.22.

created the heavens and the earth, and you alone rule the kingdoms of this world. ¹⁷ Just look and see how Sennacherib has insulted you, the living God.

¹⁸ It is true, our LORD, that Assyrian kings have turned nations into deserts. ¹⁹ They destroyed the idols of wood and stone that the people of those nations had made and worshipped. ²⁰ But you are our LORD and our God! We ask you to keep us safe from the Assyrian king. Then everyone in every kingdom on earth will know that you are the only LORD.

Isaiah gives the LORD's answer to Hezekiah

This is also told in 2 Kings 19.20-34

²¹⁻²² I went to Hezekiah and told him that the LORD God of Israel had said:

Hezekiah, you prayed to me about King Sennacherib of Assyria.* Now this is what I say to that king:

The people of Jerusalem
hate and make fun of you;
    they laugh behind your back.

²³ Sennacherib, you cursed,
    shouted, and sneered at me,
    the holy God of Israel.
²⁴ You let your officials
    insult me, the Lord.
And here is what you
    have said about yourself,
"I led my chariots
to the highest heights
    of Lebanon's mountains.
I went deep into its forest,
cutting down the best cedar
    and cypress trees.
²⁵ I dried up every stream
    in the land of Egypt,
and I drank water
    from wells I had dug."

²⁶ Sennacherib, now listen
    to me, the LORD.
I planned all this long ago.
And you don't even know
    that I alone am the one
who decided that you
    would do these things.
I let you make ruins
    of fortified cities.
²⁷ Their people became weak,
    terribly confused,

They were like wild flowers
or like tender young grass
    growing on a flat roof
or like a field of grain
    before it matures.*

²⁸ I know all about you,
    even how fiercely angry
    you are with me.
²⁹ I have seen your pride
    and the tremendous hatred
    you have for me.
Now I will put a hook in your nose,
    a bit in your mouth,*
    then I will send you back
    to where you came from.

³⁰ Hezekiah, I will tell you what's going to happen. This year you will eat crops that grow on their own, and the next year you will eat whatever springs up where those crops grew. But the third year, you will plant grain and vineyards, and you will eat what you harvest. ³¹ Those who survive in Judah will be like a vine that puts down deep roots and bears fruit. ³² I, the LORD All-Powerful, will see to it that some who live in Jerusalem will survive.

³³ I promise that the king of Assyria won't get into Jerusalem, or shoot an arrow into the city, or even surround it and prepare to attack. ³⁴ As surely as I am the LORD, he will return by the way he came and will never enter Jerusalem. ³⁵ I will protect it for the sake of my own honour and because of the promise I made to my servant David.

The death of King Sennacherib

This is also told in 2 Kings 19.35-37

³⁶ The LORD sent an angel to the camp of the Assyrians, and he killed one hundred and eighty-five thousand of them all in one night. The next morning, the camp was full of dead bodies. ³⁷ After this, King Sennacherib went back to Assyria and lived in the city of Nineveh. ³⁸ One day he was

---

*37.27 tender young grass . . . matures: The Standard Hebrew Text; the Dead Sea Scrolls and some Hebrew manuscripts "tender young grass, growing on a flat roof and scorched by the heat". Many of the houses had roofs made of packed earth. Grass would sometimes grow on the roof, but would die quickly because of the sun and hot winds.
*37.29 I will put . . . your mouth: This is how the Assyrians treated their prisoners, and now the LORD will treat Sennacherib the same way.

worshipping in the temple of his god Nisroch, when his sons, Adrammelech and Sharezer, killed him with their swords. They escaped to the land of Ararat, and his son Esarhaddon became king.*

CHAPTER 38

Hezekiah gets sick and almost dies

This is also told in 2 Kings 20.1–11; 2 Chronicles 32.24–26

¹ About this time, Hezekiah got sick and was almost dead. So I went in and told him, "The LORD says you won't ever get well. You are going to die, and so you had better start doing what needs to be done."

² Hezekiah turned towards the wall and prayed, ³ "Don't forget that I have been faithful to you, LORD. I have obeyed you with all my heart, and I do whatever you say is right." After this, he cried hard.

⁴ Then the LORD sent me ⁵ with this message for Hezekiah:

I am the LORD God, who was worshipped by your ancestor David. I heard you pray, and I saw you cry. I will let you live fifteen years more, ⁶ while I protect you and your city from the king of Assyria. ⁷ Now I will prove to you that I will keep my promise. ⁸ Do you see the shadow made by the setting sun on the stairway built for King Ahaz? I will make the shadow go back ten steps.

Then the shadow went back ten steps.*

King Hezekiah's song of praise

⁹ This is what Hezekiah wrote after he got well:

¹⁰ I thought I would die
   during my best years
   and stay as a prisoner for ever
   in the world of the dead.
¹¹ I thought I would never again
   see you, my LORD,
   or any of the people
   who live on this earth.
¹² My life was taken from me
   like the tent that a shepherd
   pulls up and moves.
   You cut me off like thread
   from a weaver's loom;

   you make a wreck of me
   day and night.
¹³ Until morning came, I thought
   you would crush my bones
   just like a hungry lion;
   both night and day
   you make a wreck of me.*
¹⁴ I cry like a swallow;
   I mourn like a dove.
   My eyes are red
   from looking to you, LORD.
   I am terribly abused.
   Please come and help me.*
¹⁵ There's nothing I can say
   in answer to you,
   since you are the one
   who has done this to me.*
   My life has turned sour;
   I will limp until I die.

¹⁶ Your words and your deeds
   bring life to everyone,
   including me.*
   Please make me healthy
   and strong again.
¹⁷ It was for my own good
   that I had such hard times.
   But your love protected me
   from doom in the deep pit,*
   and you turned your eyes
   away from my sins.

¹⁸ No one in the world of the dead
   can thank you or praise you;
   none of those in the deep pit
   can hope for you to show them
   how faithful you are.
¹⁹ Only the living can thank you,
   as I am doing today.
   Each generation tells the next
   about your faithfulness.*

²⁰ You, LORD, will save me,
   and every day that we live
   we will sing in your temple
   to the music
   of stringed instruments.

Isaiah's advice to Hezekiah

²¹ I had told King Hezekiah's servants to put some mashed figs on the king's open sore, and he would get well. ²² Then Hezekiah asked for proof that he would again worship in the LORD's temple.

---

*37.38 Esarhaddon became king: He ruled Assyria 681–669 BC.

*38.17 deep pit: The world of the dead, as in verse 18.

CHAPTER 39

Isaiah speaks the LORD's message to Hezekiah

This is also told in 2 Kings 20.12–19

¹ Merodach Baladan, the son of Baladan, was now king of Babylonia. And when he learnt that Hezekiah was well, he sent messengers with letters and a gift for him. ² Hezekiah welcomed the messengers and showed them all the silver, the gold, the spices, and the fine oils that were in his storehouse. He even showed them where he kept his weapons. Nothing in his palace or in his entire kingdom was kept hidden from them.

³ I asked Hezekiah, "Where did these men come from? What did they want?"

"They came all the way from Babylonia," Hezekiah answered.

⁴ "What did you show them?" I asked.

Hezekiah answered, "I showed them everything in my kingdom."

⁵ Then I told Hezekiah:

I have a message for you from the LORD All-Powerful. ⁶ One day everything you and your ancestors have stored up will be taken to Babylonia. The LORD has promised that nothing will be left. ⁷ Some of your own sons will be taken to Babylonia, where they will be disgraced and made to serve in the king's palace.

⁸ Hezekiah thought, "At least our nation will be at peace for a while." So he told me, "The message you brought from the LORD is good."

The Lord will rescue his people

CHAPTER 40

Encourage God's people

¹ Our God has said:

"Encourage my people!
Give them comfort.
² Speak kindly to Jerusalem
and announce:
Your slavery is past;
your punishment is over.
I, the LORD, made you pay
double for your sins."

³ Someone is shouting:
"Clear a path in the desert!
Make a straight road
for the LORD our God.
⁴ Fill in the valleys;
flatten every hill
and mountain.
Level the rough
and rugged ground.
⁵ Then the glory of the LORD
will appear for all to see.
The LORD has promised this!"

⁶ Someone told me to shout,
and I asked,
"What should I shout?"
We humans are merely grass,
and we last no longer
than wild flowers.
⁷ At the LORD's command,
flowers and grass disappear,
and so do we.
⁸ Flowers and grass fade away,
but what our God has said
will never change.

Your God is here!

⁹ There is good news
for the city of Zion.
Shout it as loud as you can
from the highest mountain.
Don't be afraid to shout
to the towns of Judah,
"Your God is here!"
¹⁰ Look! The powerful LORD God
is coming to rule
with his mighty arm.
He brings with him
what he has taken in war,
and he rewards his people.
¹¹ The LORD cares for his nation,
just as shepherds care
for their flocks.
He carries the lambs
in his arms,
while gently leading
the mother sheep.

Who compares with God?

¹² Did any of you measure
the ocean by yourself
or stretch out the sky
with your own hands?

See also: **39.7:** Dan 1.1–7; 2 King 24.10–16; 2 Chron 36.10.

See also: **40.3:** Matt 3.3; Mark 1.3; John 1.23.
40.3–5: Luke 3.4–6. **40.6–8:** Jam 1.10,11; 1 Pet 1.24,25.
40.10: Isa 62.11; Rev 22.12. **40.11:** Ezek 34.15; John 10.11.

Did you put the soil
   of the earth in a bucket
or weigh the hills and mountains
   on balance scales?

¹³ Has anyone told the LORD'
   what he must do
   or given him advice?
¹⁴ Did the LORD ask anyone
   to teach him wisdom
   and justice?
Who gave him knowledge
   and understanding?
¹⁵ To the LORD, all nations
   are merely a drop in a bucket
   or dust on balance scales;
all the islands
   are but a handful of sand.
¹⁶ The cattle on Lebanon's mountains
   would not be enough to offer
   as a sacrifice to God,
and the trees would not
   be enough for the fire.
¹⁷ God thinks of the nations
   as far less than nothing.

¹⁸ Who compares with God?
   Is anything like him?
¹⁹ Is an idol at all like God?
   It is made of bronze
with a thin layer of gold,
   and decorated with silver.
²⁰ Or special wood may be chosen*
   because it doesn't rot —
then skilled hands
   take care to make an idol
   that won't fall on its face.

God rules the whole earth

²¹ Don't you know?
   Haven't you heard?
Isn't it clear that God
   created the world?'
²² God is the one who rules
   the whole earth,
and we who live here
   are merely insects.
He spread out the heavens
   like a curtain or an open tent.
²³ God brings down rulers
   and turns them into nothing.

²⁴ They are like flowers
   freshly sprung up
   and starting to grow.
But when God blows on them,
   they wilt and are carried off
   like straw in a storm.

²⁵ The holy God asks,
   "Who compares with me?
   Is anyone my equal?"

²⁶ Look at the evening sky!
   Who created the stars?
Who gave them each a name?
   Who leads them like an army?
The LORD is so powerful
   that none of the stars
   are ever missing.

The LORD gives strength

²⁷ You people of Israel, say,
   "God pays no attention to us!
He doesn't care if we
   are treated unjustly."

But how can you say that?
²⁸ Don't you know?
   Haven't you heard?
The LORD is the eternal God,
   Creator of the earth.
He never gets weary or tired;
   his wisdom cannot be measured.

²⁹ The LORD gives strength
   to those who are weary.
³⁰ Even young people get tired,
   then stumble and fall.
³¹ But those who trust the LORD
   will find new strength.
They will be strong like eagles
   soaring upward on wings;
they will walk and run
   without getting tired.

CHAPTER 41

The LORD controls human events

¹ Be silent and listen,
   every island in the sea.
Have courage and come near,
   every one of you nations.
Let's settle this matter!
² Who appointed this ruler
   from the east?*

---

*40.20 Or . . . chosen: One possible meaning for the difficult Hebrew text. Two kinds of idols seem to be described: bronze idols covered with gold (verse 19) and wooden idols (verse 20).

See also: 40.13: Rom 11.34; 1 Cor 2.16.
40.18,19: Acts 17.29.

---

*41.2 ruler from the east: Probably Cyrus (see 44.28; 45.1; 48.14).

Who puts nations and kings
in his power?*
His sword and his arrows
turn them to dust
blown by the wind.
³ He goes after them so quickly
that his feet barely touch the ground —
he doesn't even get hurt.

⁴ Who makes these things happen?
Who controls human events?
I do! I am the LORD.
I was there at the beginning;
I will be there at the end.
⁵ Islands and foreign nations
saw what I did and trembled
as they came near.

What can idols do?

⁶ Worshippers of idols comfort each other,
saying, "Don't worry!"
⁷ Woodcarvers, goldsmiths,
and other workers*
encourage one another and say,
"We've done a great job!"
Then they nail the idol down,
so it won't fall over.

The LORD's chosen servant

⁸ Israel, you are my servant.
I chose you, the family
of my friend Abraham.
⁹ From far across the earth
I brought you here and said,
"You are my chosen servant.
I haven't forgotten you."

¹⁰ Don't be afraid. I am with you.
Don't tremble with fear.
I am your God.
I will make you strong,
as I protect you with my arm
and give you victories.
¹¹ Everyone who hates you
will be terribly disgraced;
those who attack
will vanish into thin air.
¹² You will look around
for those brutal enemies,
but you won't find them
because they will be gone.

¹³ I am the LORD your God.
I am holding your hand,
so don't be afraid.
I am here to help you.

¹⁴ People of Israel, don't worry,
though others may say,
"Israel is only a worm!"
I am the holy God of Israel,
who saves and protects you.
¹⁵ I will let you be like a log
covered with sharp spikes.*
You will grind and crush
every mountain and hill*
until they turn to dust.
¹⁶ A strong wind will scatter them
in all directions.
Then you will celebrate
and praise me, your LORD,
the holy God of Israel.

The LORD helps the poor

¹⁷ When the poor and needy
are dying of thirst
and cannot find water,
I, the LORD God of Israel,
will come to their rescue.
I won't forget them.
¹⁸ I will make rivers flow
on mountain peaks.
I will send streams
to fill the valleys.
Dry and barren land
will flow with springs
and become a lake.
¹⁹ I will fill the desert
with all kinds of trees —
cedars, acacias, and myrtles;
olive and cypress trees;
fir trees and pines.
²⁰ Everyone will see this
and know that I,
the holy LORD God of Israel,
created it all.

Idols are useless

²¹ I am the LORD,
the King of Israel!
Come, argue your case with me.
Present your evidence.
²² Come near me, you idols.*
Tell us about the past,
and we will think about it.

*41.15 I will let . . . sharp spikes: In ancient times a heavy object was sometimes dragged over wheat or barley to separate the grain from the husk. This was called threshing.
*41.15 mountain and hill: These stand for the power and pride of Israel's enemies.

Tell us about the future,
so we will know
what is going to happen.
²³ Prove that you are gods
by making your predictions come true.
Do something good or evil,
so we can be amazed
and terrified.'
²⁴ You idols are nothing,
and you are powerless.'
To worship you
would be disgusting.

²⁵ I, the LORD, appointed a ruler
in the north;
now he comes from the east
to honour my name.
He tramples' kings like mud,
as potters trample clay.*
²⁶ Did any of you idols predict
what would happen?
Did any of you get it right?
None of you told about this
or even spoke a word.
²⁷ I was the first to tell
the people of Jerusalem,
"Look, it's happening!"'
I was the one who announced
this good news to Zion.

²⁸ None of these idols
are able to give advice
or answer questions.
²⁹ They are nothing,'
and they can do nothing —
they are less than a passing breeze.

CHAPTER 42

The LORD's servant

¹ Here is my servant!
I have made him strong.
He is my chosen one;
I am pleased with him.
I have given him my Spirit,
and he will bring justice
to the nations.
² He won't shout or yell
or call out in the streets.
³ He won't break off a bent reed
or put out a dying flame,
but he will make sure
that justice is done.

⁴ He won't stop or give up
until he brings justice
everywhere on earth,
and people in foreign nations
long for his teaching.

⁵ I am the LORD God.
I created the heavens
like an open tent above.
I made the earth and everything
that grows on it.
I am the source of life
for all who live on this earth,
so listen to what I say.
⁶ I chose you to bring justice,
and I am here at your side.
I selected and sent you'
to bring light
and my promise of hope
to the nations.
⁷ You will give sight
to the blind;
you will set prisoners free
from dark dungeons.

⁸ My name is the LORD!
I won't let idols or humans
share my glory and praise.
⁹ Everything has happened
just as I said it would;
now I will announce
what will happen next.

Sing praises to the LORD

¹⁰ Tell the whole world to sing
a new song to the LORD!
Tell those who sail the ocean
and those who live far away
to join in the praise.
¹¹ Tell the tribes of the desert
and everyone in the mountains'
to celebrate and sing.
¹² Let them announce
his praises everywhere.
¹³ The LORD is marching out
like an angry soldier,
shouting with all his might
while attacking his enemies.

The LORD will help his people

¹⁴ For a long time, I, the LORD,
have held my temper;
now I will scream and groan
like a woman giving birth.

---

*41.25 trample clay: This was done to soften the clay
and make it easier to shape.
See also: 41.1: Matt 3.17; 17.5; Mark 1.11; Luke 3.22; 9.35.
42.1-4: Matt 12.18-21.

See also: 42.5: Acts 17.24,25. 42.6: Isa 49.6; Luke 2.32;
Acts 13.47; 26.23.

¹⁵ I will destroy the mountains
and what grows on them;
I will dry up rivers and ponds.

¹⁶ I will lead the blind on roads
they have never known;
I will guide them on paths
they have never travelled.
Their road is dark and rough,
but I will give light
to keep them from stumbling.
This is my solemn promise.

¹⁷ Everyone who worships idols
as though they were gods
will be terribly ashamed.

God's people won't obey

¹⁸ You people are deaf and blind,
but the LORD commands you
to listen and to see.

¹⁹ No one is as blind or deaf
as his messenger,
his chosen servant,

²⁰ who sees and hears so much,
but pays no attention.

²¹ The LORD always does right,
and so he wanted his Law
to be greatly praised.'

²² But his people were trapped
and imprisoned in holes
with no one to rescue them.
All they owned had been taken,
and no one was willing
to give it back.

²³ Why won't his people
ever learn to listen?

²⁴ Israel sinned and refused
to obey the LORD
or follow his instructions.
So the LORD let them be robbed
of everything they owned.

²⁵ He was furious with them
and punished their nation
with the fires of war.
Still they paid no attention.
They didn't even care
when they were surrounded
and scorched by flames.

CHAPTER 43

The LORD has rescued his people

¹ Descendants of Jacob,
I, the LORD, created you
and formed your nation.

Israel, don't be afraid.
I have rescued you.
I have called you by name;
now you belong to me.

² When you cross deep rivers,
I will be with you,
and you won't drown.
When you walk through fire,
you won't be burnt
or scorched by the flames.

³ I am the LORD, your God,
the Holy One of Israel,
the God who saves you.
I gave up Egypt, Ethiopia,*
and the region of Seba*
in exchange for you.

⁴ To me, you are very dear,
and I love you.
That's why I gave up nations
and people to rescue you.

⁵ Don't be afraid! I am with you.
From both east and west
I will bring you together.

⁶ I will say to the north
and to the south,
"Free my sons and daughters!
Let them return
from distant lands.

⁷ They are my people —
I created each of them
to bring honour to me."

The LORD alone is God

The LORD said:

⁸ Bring my people together.
They have eyes and ears,
but they can't see or hear.

⁹ Tell everyone of every nation
to gather around.
None of them can honestly say,
"We told you so!"
If someone heard them say this,
then tell us about it now.

¹⁰ My people, you are my witnesses
and my chosen servant.
I want you to know me,
to trust me, and understand
that I alone am God.
I have always been God;
there can be no others.

---

*43.3 Ethiopia: See the note at 11.11.
*43.3 Seba: A region in south-west Arabia. Egypt,
Ethiopia, and Seba probably stood for all that was
known of Africa in biblical times.

11 I alone am the LORD;
    only I can rescue you.
12 I promised to save you,
    and I kept my promise.
    You are my witnesses
    that no other god did this.
    I, the LORD, have spoken.
13 I am God now and for ever.
    No one can snatch you from me
    or stand in my way.

The LORD will prepare the way

14 I, the LORD, will rescue you!
    I am Israel's holy God,
    and this is my promise:
    For your sake, I will send
    an army against Babylon
    to drag its people away,
    crying as they go.*

15 I am the LORD, your holy God,
    Israel's Creator and King.
16 I am the one who cut a path
    through the mighty ocean.
17 I sent an army to chase you
    with chariots and horses;
    now they lie dead,
    unable to move.
    They are like an oil lamp
    with the flame snuffed out.

Forget the past

The LORD said:

18 Forget what happened long ago!
    Don't think about the past.
19 I am creating something new.
    There it is! Do you see it?
    I have put roads in deserts,
    streams* in thirsty lands.
20 Every wild animal honours me,
    even jackals* and owls.
    I provide water in deserts —
    streams in thirsty lands
    for my chosen people.
21 I made them my own nation,
    so they would praise me.

22 I, the LORD, said to Israel:
    You have become weary,
    but not from worshipping me.
23 You have not honoured me
    by sacrificing sheep
    or other animals.

And I have not burdened you
    with demands for sacrifices
    or sweet-smelling incense.
24 You have not brought
    delicious spices for me
    or given me the best part
    of your sacrificed animals.
    Instead, you burden me down
    with your terrible sins.
25 But I wipe away your sins
    because of who I am.
    And so, I will forget
    the wrongs you have done.

26 Meet me in court!
    State your case and prove
    that you are right.
27 Your earliest ancestor*
    and all your leaders*
    rebelled against me.
28 That's why I don't allow
    your priests to serve me;
    I let Israel be destroyed
    and your people disgraced.

CHAPTER 44

The LORD's promise to Israel

1 People of Israel,
    I have chosen you as my servant.
2 I am your Creator.
    You were in my care
    even before you were born.
    Israel, don't be terrified!
    You are my chosen servant,
    my very favourite.*

3 I will bless the thirsty land
    by sending streams of water;
    I will bless your descendants
    by giving them my Spirit.
4 They will spring up like grass*
    or like willow trees
    near flowing streams.
5 They will worship me
    and become my people.
    They will write my name
    on the back of their hands.*

6 I am the LORD All-Powerful,
    the first and the last,
    the one and only God.

---

*43.20 jackals: Desert animals related to wolves, but smaller.

*43.27 earliest ancestor: Jacob, also known as Israel.
*43.27 leaders: Probably prophets, but perhaps also priests and kings.
*44.5 write . . . hands: To show that they belong to the LORD and to Israel.
See also: 44.6: Isa 48.12; Rev 1.17; 2.8; 22.13.

Israel, I have rescued you!
  I am your King.
7 Can anyone compare with me?
    If so, let them speak up
      and tell me now.
  Let them say what has happened
    since I made my nation long ago,
    and let them tell
      what is going to happen.'
8 Don't tremble with fear!
    Didn't I tell you long ago?
    Didn't you hear me?
  I alone am God —
    no one else is a mighty rock.*

Idols can't do a thing

The LORD said:

9 Those people who make idols
    are nothing themselves,
  and the idols they treasure
    are just as worthless.
  Worshippers of idols are blind,
    stupid, and foolish.
10 Why make an idol or an image
    that can't do a thing?
11 Everyone who makes idols
    and all who worship them
    are mere humans,
  who will end up
    sadly disappointed.
  Let them face me in court
    and be terrified.

Idols and firewood

12 A metalworker shapes an idol
    by using a hammer'
    and heat from the fire.
  In his powerful hand
    he holds a hammer,
  as he pounds the metal
    into the proper shape.
  But he gets hungry and thirsty
    and loses his strength.

13 Some woodcarver measures
    a piece of wood,
    then draws an outline.
  The idol is carefully carved
    with each detail exact.
  At last it looks like a person
    and is placed in a temple.
14 Cedar, cypress, oak,
    or any tree from the forest
    may be chosen.

Or even a pine tree planted
    by the woodcarver
    and watered by the rain.

15 Some of the wood is used
    to make a fire for heating
    or for cooking.
  One piece is made into an idol,
    then the woodcarver bows down
    and worships it.
16 He enjoys the warm fire
    and the meat that was roasted
    over the burning coals.
17 Afterwards, he bows down
    to worship the wooden idol.
  "Protect me!" he says.
    "You are my god."

18 Those who worship idols are stupid and
blind! 19 They don't have enough sense to
say to themselves, "I made a fire with half of
the wood and cooked my bread and meat
on it. Then I made something worthless
with the other half. Why worship a block of
wood?"

20 How can anyone be stupid enough to
trust something that can be burnt to ashes?'
No one can save themselves like that. Don't
they realize that the idols they hold in their
hands are not really gods?

The LORD won't forget his people

21 People of Israel,
    you are my servant,
    so remember all of this.
  Israel, I created you,
    and you are my servant.
    I won't forget you.'
22 Turn back to me!
    I have rescued you
    and swept away your sins
    as though they were clouds.

Sing praises to the LORD

23 Tell the heavens and the earth
    to start singing!
  Tell the mountains
    and every tree in the forest
    to join in the song!

  The LORD has rescued his people;
    now they will worship him.

The LORD created everything

24 Israel, I am your LORD.
  I am your source of life,
    and I have rescued you.

---

*44.8 mighty rock: See the note at 17.10.

I created everything
from the sky above
    to the earth below.

25 I make liars of false prophets
    and fools of fortune-tellers.
I take human wisdom
    and turn it into nonsense.
26 I will make the message
    of my prophets come true.
They are saying, "Jerusalem
    will be filled with people,
and the LORD will rebuild
    the towns of Judah."

27 I am the one who commands
    the sea and its streams to run dry.
28 I am also the one who says,
    "Cyrus will lead my people
    and obey my orders.
Jerusalem and the temple
    will be rebuilt."

CHAPTER 45

Cyrus obeys the LORD's commands

1 The LORD said to Cyrus, his chosen one:

I have taken hold
    of your right hand
to help you capture nations
    and remove kings from power.
City gates will open for you;
    not one will stay closed.
2 As I lead you,
    I will level mountains*
and break the iron bars
    on bronze gates of cities.
3 I will give you treasures
    hidden in dark
    and secret places.
Then you will know that I,
    the LORD God of Israel,
    have called you by name.
4 Cyrus, you don't even know me!
But I have called you by name
    and highly honoured you*
because of Israel,
    my chosen servant.
5 Only I am the LORD!
    There are no other gods.
I have made you strong,
    though you don't know me.
6 Now everyone from east to west
    will learn that I am the LORD.

No other gods are real.
7 I create light and darkness,
    happiness and sorrow.
    I, the LORD, do all of this.

8 Tell the heavens
    to send down justice
    like showers of rain.
Prepare the earth
    for my saving power
to sprout and produce justice
    that I, the LORD, create.'

The LORD's mighty power

The LORD said:

9 Israel, you have no right
    to argue with your Creator.
You are merely a clay pot
    shaped by a potter.
The clay doesn't ask,
    "Why did you make me this way?
    Where are the handles?"
10 Children don't have the right
    to demand of their parents,
    "What have you done
    to make us what we are?"

11 I am the LORD, the Creator,
    the holy God of Israel.
Do you dare question me
    about my own nation
    or about what I have done?
12 I created the world
    and covered it with people;
I stretched out the sky
    and filled it with stars.
13 I have done the right thing
    by placing Cyrus in power,
and I will make the roads easy
    for him to follow.
I am the LORD All-Powerful!
    Cyrus will rebuild my city
and set my people free
    without being paid a thing.
I, the LORD, have spoken.

The LORD alone can save

14 My people, I, the LORD, promise
    that the riches of Egypt
    and the treasures of Ethiopia*
    will belong to you.
You will force into slavery
    those tall people of Seba.*

---

*45.14 Ethiopia: See the note at 11.11.
*45.14 Seba: See the note at 43.3.
See also: 45.9: Isa 29.16; Rom 9.20.

They will bow down and say,
"The only true God is with you;
    there are no other gods."

15 People of Israel,
    your God is a mystery,
    though he alone can save.

16 Anyone who makes idols
    will be confused
    and terribly disgraced.

17 But Israel, I, the LORD,
    will always keep you safe
    and free from shame.

Everyone is invited

18 The LORD alone is God!
He created the heavens
    and made a world
where people can live,
    instead of creating an empty desert.
The LORD alone is God;
    there are no others.

19 The LORD did not speak
    in a dark secret place
or command Jacob's descendants
    to search for him in vain.

The LORD speaks the truth,
    and this is what he says

20 to every survivor
    from every nation:
"Gather around me!
Learn how senseless it is
    to worship wooden idols
    or pray to helpless gods.

21 "Why don't you get together
    and meet me in court?
Didn't I tell you long ago
    what would happen?
I am the only God!
    There are no others.
I bring about justice,
    and have the power to save.

22 "I invite the whole world
    to turn to me and be saved.
I alone am God!
    No others are real.

23 I have made a solemn promise,
    one that won't be broken:
everyone will bow down
    and worship me.

24 They will admit that I alone
    can bring about justice.
Everyone who is angry with me
    will be terribly ashamed
    and will turn to me.

25 I, the LORD, will give
    victory and great honour
    to the people of Israel."

CHAPTER 46

Babylonia's gods are helpless

The LORD said:

1 The gods Bel and Nebo*
    are down on their knees,
as wooden images of them
    are carried away
    on weary animals.*

2 They are down on their knees
    to rescue the heavy load,
but the images are still taken
    to a foreign country.

3 You survivors in Israel,
    listen to me, the LORD.
Since the day you were born,
    I have carried you along.

4 I will still be the same
    when you are old and grey,
    and I will take care of you.
I created you. I will carry you
    and always keep you safe.

5 Can anyone compare with me?
    Is anyone my equal?

6 Some people hire a goldsmith
    and give silver and gold
to be formed into an idol
    for them to worship.

7 They carry the idol
    on their shoulders,
then put it on a stand,
    but it cannot move.

They call out to the idol
    when they are in trouble,
but it doesn't answer,
    and it cannot help.

8 Now keep this in mind,*
    you sinful people.
And don't ever forget it.

The LORD alone is God

9 I alone am God!
There are no other gods;
    no one is like me.
Think about what happened
    many years ago.

---

*46.1 Bel and Nebo: Bel was another name for Marduk, the chief god of the Babylonians. Nebo was the son of Marduk and also an important god.

¹⁰ From the very beginning,
    I told what would happen
    long before it took place.

I kept my word
¹¹ and brought someone from a distant land
    to do what I wanted.
He attacked from the east,
    like a hawk swooping down.
Now I will keep my promise
    and do what I planned.

¹² You people are stubborn
    and far from being safe,
    so listen to me.
¹³ I will soon come to save you.
    I am not far away
    and will waste no time;
I take pride in Israel
    and will save Jerusalem.

CHAPTER 47

Babylon will fall

The LORD said:

¹ City of Babylon,
    you are delicate and untouched,
    but that will change.
Surrender your royal power
    and sit in the dust.
² Start grinding grain!
    Take off your veil.
Strip off your fine clothes
    and cross over rivers.*
³ You will suffer the shame
    of going naked,
because I will take revenge,
    and no one can escape.'
⁴ I am the LORD All-Powerful,
    the holy God of Israel.
    I am their Saviour.

⁵ Babylon, be silent!
    Sit in the dark.
No longer will nations
    accept you as their queen.
⁶ I was angry with my people.
    So I let you take their land
    and bring disgrace on them.
You showed them no mercy,
    but were especially cruel
    to those who were old.

⁷ You thought that you
    would be queen for ever.
You didn't care what you did;
    it never entered your mind
    that you might get caught.

⁸ You think that you alone
    are all-powerful,
that you won't be a widow
    or lose your children.
All you care about is pleasure,
    but listen to what I say.
⁹ Your magic powers and charms
    will suddenly fail,
then you will be a widow
    and lose your children.

¹⁰ You hid behind evil
    like a shield and said,
    "No one can see me!"
You were fooled by your wisdom
    and your knowledge;
you felt sure that you alone
    were in full control.
¹¹ But without warning,
    disaster will strike —
and your magic charms
    won't help at all.

¹² Keep using your magic powers
    and your charms
    as you have always done.
Perhaps — just perhaps —
    you will frighten somebody!
¹³ You have worn yourself out,
    asking for advice
from those who study the stars
    and tell the future
    month after month.
Go and ask them how to be saved
    from what will happen.

¹⁴ People who trust the stars
    are as helpless as straw
    in a flaming fire.
No one can even keep warm,'
    sitting by a fire
    that feeds only on straw.
¹⁵ These are the fortune-tellers
    you have done business with
    all your life.
But they don't know
    where they are going,
    and they can't save you.

---

*47.2 Strip . . . rivers: This may be a command to get
ready for work that requires wading in the river, or it
may be a warning that they are going to be taken
away as slaves.

See also: 47.1-15: Isa 13.1–14.23; Jer 50.1–51.64.

See also: 47.8,9: Rev 18.7,8.

and stretched out the sky.
They obey my every command.

CHAPTER 48

The LORD corrects his people

[1] People of Israel,
you come from Jacob's family
and the tribe* of Judah.
You claim to worship me,
the LORD God of Israel,
but you are lying.
[2] You call Jerusalem your home
and say you depend on me,
the LORD All-Powerful,
the God of Israel.

[3] Long ago I announced
what was going to be,
then without warning,
I made it happen.
[4] I knew you were stubborn
and hard-headed.
[5] And I told you these things,
so that when they happened
you would not say,
"The idols we worship did this."

[6] You heard what I said,
and you have seen it happen.
Now admit that it's true!
I will show you secrets
you have never known.
[7] Today I am doing something new,
something you cannot say
you have heard before.
[8] You have never been willing
to listen to what I say;
from the moment of your birth,
I knew you would rebel.

The LORD warns Israel

[9] I, the LORD, am true to myself;
I will be praised for not punishing
and destroying you.
[10] I tested you in hard times
just as silver is refined
in a heated furnace.*
[11] I did this because of who I am.
I refuse to be dishonoured*
or share my praise
with any other god.

[12] Israel, my chosen people,
listen to me.
I alone am the LORD,
the first and the last.
[13] With my own hand
I created the earth

The LORD speaks to the nations

[14] Gather around me, all of you!
Listen to what I say.
Did any of your idols
predict this would happen?
Did they say that my friend*
would do what I want done
to Babylonia?*
[15] I was the one who chose him.
I have brought him this far,
and he will be successful.
[16] Come closer and listen!
I have never kept secret
the things I have said,
and I was here before time began.

It is best to obey the LORD

By the power of his Spirit the LORD God has
sent me [17] with this message:

People of Israel,
I am the holy LORD God,
the one who rescues you.
For your own good,
I teach you, and I lead you
along the right path.
[18] How I wish that you
had obeyed my commands!
Your success and good fortune
would then have overflowed
like a flooding river.
[19] Your nation would be blessed
with more people
than there are grains of sand
along the seashore.
And I would never have let
your country be destroyed.

[20] Now leave Babylon!
Celebrate as you go.
Be happy and shout
for everyone to hear,
"The LORD has rescued
his servant Israel!"
[21] He led us through the desert
and made water flow from a rock
to satisfy our thirst.
[22] But the LORD has promised
that none who are evil
will live in peace."

---

*48.14 my friend: Probably Cyrus (see 44.28; 45.1).

See also: 48.12: Isa 44.6; Rev 1.17; 22.13.   See also: 48.20: Rev 18.4. 48.22: Isa 57.21.

The Lord's servant

CHAPTER 49

The work of the LORD's servant

¹ Everyone, listen,
    even you foreign nations across the sea.
The LORD chose me
    and gave me a name
    before I was born.
² He made my words pierce
    like a sharp sword
    or a pointed arrow;
he kept me safely hidden
    in the palm of his hand.
³ The LORD said to me,
    "Israel, you are my servant;
    and because of you
    I will be highly honoured."

⁴ I said to myself,
    "I'm completely worn out;
    my time has been wasted.
But I did it for the LORD God,
    and he will reward me."

⁵ Even before I was born,
    the LORD God chose me
to serve him and to lead back
    the people of Israel.
So the LORD has honoured me
    and made me strong.

⁶ Now the LORD says to me,
    "It isn't enough for you
    to be merely my servant.
You must do more than lead back
    survivors from the tribes of Israel.
I have placed you here as a light
    for other nations;
you must take my saving power
    to everyone on earth."

The LORD will rescue his people

⁷ Israel, I am the holy LORD God,
    the one who rescues you.
You are slaves of rulers
    and of a nation
    who despises you.*
Now this is what I promise:
    kings and rulers will honour you
    by kneeling at your feet.
You can trust me! I am your LORD,
    the holy God of Israel,
    and you are my chosen ones.

The LORD will lead his people home

⁸ This is what the LORD says:

I will answer your prayers
    because I have set a time
    when I will help
    by coming to save you.
I have chosen you
    to take my promise of hope
    to other nations.*
You will rebuild the country
    from its ruins,
then people will come
    and settle there.
⁹ You will set prisoners free
    from dark dungeons
    to see the light of day.

On their way home,
    they will find plenty to eat,
    even on barren hills.
¹⁰ They won't go hungry
    or get thirsty;
they won't be bothered
    by the scorching sun
    or hot desert winds.
I will be merciful
    while leading them along
    to streams of water.
¹¹ I will level the mountains
    and make roads.
¹² Then my people will return
    from distant lands
in the north and the west
    and from the city of Syene.*

The LORD's mercy

¹³ Tell the heavens and the earth
    to celebrate and sing;
command every mountain
    to join in the song.
The LORD's people have suffered,
    but he has shown mercy
    and given them comfort.

¹⁴ The people of Zion said,
    "The LORD has turned away
    and forgotten us."
¹⁵ The LORD answered,
    "Could a mother forget a child
    who nurses at her breast?
Could she fail to love an infant
    who came from her own body?

---

*49.12 Syene: The Dead Sea Scrolls; the Standard Hebrew Text "Sinim". The reference may be to modern Aswan, a city in southern Egypt.
See also: 49.8: 2 Cor 6.2. 49.10: Rev 7.16,17.

See also: 49.1: Jer 1.5. 49.2: Heb 4.12; Rev 1.16.
49.6: a Isa 42.6; Luke 2.32; Acts 26.23; b Acts 13.47.

Even if a mother could forget,
I will never forget you.
16 A picture of your city
is drawn on my hand.
You are always in my thoughts!

17 "Your city will be built faster
than it was destroyed* —
those who attacked it
will retreat and leave.
18 Look around! You will see
your people coming home.
As surely as I live,
I, the LORD, promise
that your city with its people
will be as lovely as a bride
wearing her jewellery."

Jerusalem's bright future

19 Jerusalem is now in ruins!
Nothing is left of the city.
But it will be rebuilt
and soon overcrowded;
its cruel enemies
will be gone far away.

20 Jerusalem is a woman
whose children were born
while she was in deep sorrow*
over the loss of her husband.
Now those children
will come and seek room
in the crowded city,
21 and Jerusalem will ask,
"Am I really their mother?
How could I have given birth
when I was still mourning
in a foreign land?
Who raised these children?
Where have they come from?"

22 The LORD God says:
"I will soon give a signal
for the nations
to return your sons
and your daughters
to the arms of Jerusalem.
23 The kings and queens
of those nations
where they were raised
will come and bow down.
They will take care of you
just like a slave

taking care of a child.
Then you will know
that I am the LORD.
You won't be disappointed
if you trust me."

The LORD is on our side

24 Is it possible to rescue victims
from someone strong
and cruel?*
25 But the LORD has promised
to fight on our side
and to rescue our children
from those strong
and violent enemies.
26 He will make those cruel people
dine on their own flesh
and get drunk from drinking
their own blood.
Then everyone will know
that the LORD is our Saviour;
the powerful God of Israel
has rescued his people.

CHAPTER 50

The LORD's power to punish

1 The LORD says, "Children,
I didn't divorce your mother
or sell you to pay debts;
I divorced her and sold you
because of your sins.
2 I came and called out,
but you didn't answer.
Have I lost my power
to rescue and save?
At my command oceans and rivers
turn into deserts;
fish rot and stink
for lack of water.
3 I make the sky turn dark
like the sackcloth
you wear at funerals."

God's servant must suffer

4 The LORD God gives me
the right words
to encourage the weary.
Each morning he awakens me
eager to learn his teaching;
5 he made me willing to listen
and not rebel or run away.

6 I let them beat my back
and pull out my beard.

*49.20 whose children . . . sorrow: These "children" are Jews who were born in foreign countries during the time that Jerusalem was in ruins. Jerusalem probably stands for all the cities in Judah that were destroyed by the Babylonians.

See also: 50.6: Matt 26.67; Mark 14.65.

685

I didn't turn aside
when they insulted me
and spat in my face.
⁷ But the LORD God keeps me
from being disgraced.
So I refuse to give up,
because I know
God will never let me down.

⁸ My protector is nearby;
no one can stand here
to accuse me of wrong.
⁹ The LORD God will help me
and prove I am innocent.
My accusers will wear out
like moth-eaten clothes.

¹⁰ None of you respect the LORD
or obey his servant.
You walk in the dark
instead of the light;
you don't trust the name
of the LORD your God.'
¹¹ Go ahead and walk in the light
of the fires you have lit.'
But with his own hand,
the LORD will punish you
and make you suffer.

CHAPTER 51

The LORD will bring comfort

¹ If you want to do right
and obey the LORD,
follow Abraham's example.
He was the rock from which
you were chipped.
² God chose Abraham and Sarah
to be your ancestors.
The LORD blessed Abraham,
and from that one man
came many descendants.

³ Though Zion is in ruins,
the LORD will bring comfort,
and the city will be as lovely
as the garden of Eden
that he provided.
Then Zion will celebrate;
it will be thankful
and sing joyful songs.

The LORD's victory will last

⁴ The LORD says:

You are my people and nation!
So pay attention to me.

My teaching will cause justice
to shine like a light
for every nation.
⁵ Those who live across the sea
are eagerly waiting
for me to rescue them.
I am strong and ready;
soon I will come to save
and to rule all nations.

⁶ Look closely at the sky!
Stare at the earth.
The sky will vanish like smoke;
the earth will wear out like clothes.
Everyone on this earth
will die like flies.
But my victory will last;
my saving power never ends.

⁷ If you want to do right
and to obey my teaching
with all your heart,
then pay close attention.
Don't be discouraged
when others insult you
and say hurtful things.
⁸ They will be eaten away
like a moth-eaten coat.
But my victory will last;
my saving power will never end.

A prayer for the LORD's help

⁹ Wake up! Do something, LORD.
Be strong and ready.
Wake up! Do what you did
for our people long ago.
Didn't you chop up
Rahab* the monster?
¹⁰ Didn't you dry up the deep sea
and make a road for your people
to follow safely across?
¹¹ Now those you have rescued
will return to Jerusalem,
singing on their way.
They will be crowned
with great happiness,
never again to be burdened
with sadness and sorrow.

The LORD gives hope

¹² I am the LORD, the one
who encourages you.
Why are you afraid
of mere humans?
They dry up and die like grass.

---

*51.9 Rahab: This may refer to Egypt at the time of
the exodus.

[13] I spread out the heavens
and laid foundations
for the earth.
But you have forgotten me,
your LORD and Creator.
All day long you were afraid
of those who were angry
and hoped to abuse you.
Where are they now?

[14] Everyone crying out in pain
will be quickly set free;
they will be rescued
from the power of death
and never go hungry.

[15] I will help them
because I am your God,
the LORD All-Powerful,
who makes the ocean roar.

[16] I have told you what to say,
and I will keep you safe
in the palm of my hand.
I spread out the heavens
and laid foundations
for the earth.
Now I say, "Jerusalem,
your people are mine."

A warning to Jerusalem

[17] Jerusalem, wake up! Stand up!
You've drunk too much
from the cup filled
with the LORD's anger.
You have swallowed every drop,
and you can't walk straight.

[18] Not one of your many children
is there to guide you
or to offer a helping hand.

[19] You have been destroyed
by war and by famine;
I cannot comfort you.'

[20] The LORD your God is angry,
and on every street corner
your children lie helpless,
like deer trapped in nets.

[21] You are in trouble and drunk,
but not from wine.
So pay close attention

[22] to the LORD your God,
who defends you and says,
"I have taken from your hands
the cup filled with my anger
that made you drunk.
You will never be forced
to drink it again.

[23] Instead I will give it
to your brutal enemies,
who treated you like dirt
and walked all over you."

CHAPTER 52

Jerusalem can celebrate

[1] Jerusalem, wake up!
Stand up and be strong.
Holy city of Zion,
dress in your best clothes.
Those foreigners who ruined
your sacred city
won't bother you again.

[2] Zion, rise from the dust!
Free yourself from the rope
around your neck.

Suffering will end

[3] The LORD says:

My people, you were sold,
but not for money;
now you will be set free,
but not for a payment.

[4] Long ago you went to Egypt
where you lived as foreigners.
Then Assyria was cruel to you,

[5] and now another nation*
has taken you prisoner
for no reason at all.
Your leaders groan with pain,'
and day after day
my own name is cursed.

[6] My people, you will learn
who I am and who is speaking
because I am here.

A message of hope for Jerusalem

[7] What a beautiful sight!
On the mountains a messenger
announces to Jerusalem,
"Good news! You're saved.
There will be peace.
Your God is now King."

[8] Everyone on guard duty,
sing and celebrate!
Look! You can see the LORD
returning to Zion.

[9] Jerusalem, rise from the ruins!
Join in the singing.

---

*52.5 another nation: Babylonia.
See also: 52.1: Rev 21.2,27. 52.5: Rom 2.24.
52.7: Nah 1.15; Rom 10.15; Eph 6.15.

See also: 51.17: Rev 14.10; 16.19.

The LORD has given comfort
to his people;
  he comes to your rescue.
[10] The LORD has shown all nations
his mighty strength;
  now everyone will see
  the saving power of our God.

A command to leave Babylon

[11] Leave the city of Babylon!
Don't touch anything filthy.
Wash yourselves. Be ready
to carry back everything sacred
  that belongs to the LORD.
[12] You won't need to run.
No one is chasing you.
The LORD God of Israel
will lead and protect you
  from enemy attacks.

The suffering servant

[13] The LORD says:

My servant will succeed!
He will be given great praise
  and the highest honours.
[14] Many were horrified
at what happened to him.*
But everyone who saw him
was even more horrified
because he suffered until
  he no longer looked human.*
[15] My servant will make
nations worthy to worship me;*
  kings will be silent
as they bow in wonder.*
They will see and think about
things they have never seen
  or thought of before.

CHAPTER 53

What God's servant did for us

[1] Has anyone believed us
or seen the mighty power
  of the LORD in action?
[2] Like a young plant or a root
that sprouts in dry ground,
the servant grew up
  obeying the LORD.
He wasn't some handsome king.
Nothing about the way he looked
  made him attractive to us.

[3] He was hated and rejected;
his life was filled with sorrow
  and terrible suffering.
No one wanted to look at him.
We despised him and said,
  "He is a nobody!"
[4] He suffered and endured
  great pain for us,
but we thought his suffering
  was punishment from God.
[5] He was wounded and crushed
because of our sins;
by taking our punishment,
  he made us completely well.
[6] All of us were like sheep
that had wandered off.
We had each gone our own way,
but the LORD gave him
  the punishment we deserved.

[7] He was painfully abused,
but he did not complain.
He was silent like a lamb
being led to the butcher,
as quiet as a sheep
  having its wool cut off.
[8] He was condemned to death
without a fair trial.
Who could have imagined
what would happen to him?
His life was taken away
because of the sinful things
  my people* had done.
[9] He wasn't dishonest or violent,
but he was buried in a tomb
  of cruel and rich people.*

[10] The LORD decided his servant
would suffer as a sacrifice
to take away the sin
  and guilt of others.
Now the servant will live
to see his own descendants.*
He did everything
  the LORD had planned.

[11] By suffering, the servant
will learn the true meaning
  of obeying the LORD.
Although he is innocent,
he will take the punishment
for the sins of others,
so that many of them
  will no longer be guilty.

See also: 52.11: 2 Cor 6.17. 52.15: Rom 15.21.
53.1: Rom 10.16; John 12.38.

See also: 53.4: Matt 8.17. 53.5: 1 Pet 2.24.
53.6: 1 Pet 2.25. 53.7: Rev 5.6. 53.7,8: Acts 8.32,33.
53.9: 1 Pet 2.22.

¹² The LORD will reward him
    with honour and power
    for sacrificing his life.
Others thought he was a sinner,
    but he suffered for our sins
    and asked God to forgive us.

The Lord will keep all his promises

CHAPTER 54

A promise of the LORD's protection

¹ Sing and shout,
    even though you have never
        had children!
The LORD has promised that you
    will have more children
    than someone married
        for a long time.
² Make your tents larger!
    Spread out the tent pegs;
    fasten them firmly.
³ You and your descendants
    will take over the land
        of other nations.
You will settle in towns
    that are now in ruins.

⁴ Don't be afraid or ashamed
    and don't be discouraged.
    You won't be disappointed.
Forget how sinful you were
    when you were young;
stop feeling ashamed
    for being left a widow.
⁵ The LORD All-Powerful,
    the Holy God of Israel,
    rules all the earth.
He is your Creator and husband,
    and he will rescue you.
⁶ You were like a young wife,
    brokenhearted and crying
    because her husband
        had divorced her.

But the LORD your God says,
    "I am taking you back!
⁷ I rejected you for a while,
    but with love and tenderness
    I will embrace you again.
⁸ For a while, I turned away
    in furious anger.

Now I will have mercy
    and love you for ever!
I, your protector and LORD,
    make this promise."

The LORD promises lasting peace

⁹ I once promised Noah that I
    would never again destroy
        the earth by a flood.
Now I have promised that I
    will never again get angry
        and punish you.
¹⁰ Every mountain and hill
        may disappear.
But I will always be kind
    and merciful to you;
I won't break my agreement
    to give your nation peace.

The new Jerusalem

¹¹ Jerusalem, you are sad
        and discouraged,
    tossed around in a storm.
But I, the LORD,
    will rebuild your city
    with precious stones;*
for your foundation
    I will use blue sapphires.
¹² Your fortresses* will be built of rubies,
    your gates of jewels,
    and your walls of gems.
¹³ I will teach your children
    and make them successful.

¹⁴ You will be built on fairness
    with no fears of injustice;
every one of your worries
    will be taken far from you.
¹⁵ I will never send anyone
    to attack your city,
and you will make prisoners
    of those who do attack.
¹⁶ Don't forget that I created
    metalworkers who make weapons
        over burning coals.
I also created armies
    that can bring destruction.
¹⁷ Weapons made to attack you
    won't be successful;
words spoken against you
    won't hurt at all.

My servants, Jerusalem is yours!
I, the LORD, promise
    to bless you with victory.

See also: 53.12: Mark 15.28; Luke 22.37. 54.1: Gal 4.27.

See also: 54.9: Gen 9.8–17. 54.11,12: Rev 21.18–21. 54.13: John 6.45.

CHAPTER 55

The LORD's invitation

¹ If you are thirsty,
  come and drink water!
If you don't have any money,
  come, eat what you want!
Drink wine and milk
  without paying a penny.
² Why waste your money
  on what isn't really food?
Why work hard for something
  that doesn't satisfy?
Listen carefully to me,
  and you will enjoy the very best foods.

³ Pay close attention!
  Come to me and live.
I will promise you
  the eternal love and loyalty
  that I promised David.
⁴ I made him the leader and ruler
  of the nations;
  he was my witness to them.
⁵ You will call out to nations
  you have never known.
And they have never known you,
  but they will come running
  because I am the LORD,
  the holy God of Israel,
  and I have honoured you.

God's words are powerful

⁶ Turn to the LORD!
  He can still be found.
  Call out to God! He is near.
⁷ Give up your crooked ways
  and your evil thoughts.
Return to the LORD our God.
  He will be merciful
  and forgive your sins.

⁸ The LORD says:
  "My thoughts and my ways
  are not like yours.
⁹ Just as the heavens
  are higher than the earth,
my thoughts and my ways
  are higher than yours.

¹⁰ "Rain and snow fall from the sky.
  But they don't return
  without watering the earth
  that produces seeds to plant
  and grain to eat.

¹¹ That's how it is with my words.
  They don't return to me
  without doing everything
  I send them to do."

God's people will celebrate

¹² When you are set free,
  you will celebrate
  and travel home in peace.
Mountains and hills will sing
  as you pass by,
  and trees will clap.
¹³ Cypress and myrtle trees
  will grow in fields
  once covered by thorns.
And then those trees will stand
  as a lasting witness
  to the glory of the LORD.

All nations will be part of God's people

CHAPTER 56

¹ The LORD said:

  Be honest and fair!
  Soon I will come to save you;
  my saving power will be seen
  everywhere on earth.

² I will bless everyone
  who respects the Sabbath
  and refuses to do wrong.

³ Foreigners who worship me
  must not say,
  "The LORD won't let us
  be part of his people."
Men who are unable
  to become fathers
  must no longer say,
  "We are dried-up trees."

⁴ To them, I, the LORD, say:
  Respect the Sabbath,
  obey me completely,
  and keep our agreement.
⁵ Then I will set up monuments
  in my temple with your names
  written on them.
This will be much better
  than having children,
because these monuments
  will stand there for ever.

⁶ Foreigners will follow me.
  They will love me and worship
  in my name;

they will respect the Sabbath
and keep our agreement.
7 I will bring them
to my holy mountain,
where they will celebrate
in my house of worship.
Their sacrifices and offerings
will always be welcome
on my altar.
Then my house will be known
as a house of worship
for all nations.
8 I, the LORD, promise
to bring together my people
who were taken away,
and let them join the others.

Leaders unfaithful to God will be punished

God promises to punish Israel's leaders

9 Come from the forest,
you wild animals!
Attack and gobble up
your victims.
10 You leaders of Israel
should be watchdogs,
protecting my people.
But you can't see a thing,
and you never warn them.
Dozing and daydreaming
are all you ever do.
11 You stupid leaders are a pack
of hungry and greedy dogs
that never get enough.
You are shepherds
who ill-treat your own sheep
for selfish gain.
12 You say to each other,
"Let's drink till we're drunk!
Tomorrow we'll do it again.
We'll really enjoy ourselves."

CHAPTER 57

God's faithful people suffer

1 God's faithful people
are dragged off and killed,
and no one even cares.
Evil sweeps them away,
2 but in death they find peace
for obeying God.◆

The LORD condemns idolatry

3 You people are unfaithful!
You go to fortune-tellers,
and you worship idols.
Now pay close attention!
4 Who are you making fun of?
Who are you sneering at?
Look how your sins
have made fools of you.

5 All you think about is sex
under those green trees
where idols are worshipped.
You sacrifice your children
on altars built in valleys
under rocky slopes.
6 You have chosen to worship
idols made of stone;◆
you have given them offerings
of wine and grain.
Should I be pleased?

7 You have spread out your beds
on the tops of high mountains,
where you sacrifice to idols.
8 Even in your homes
you have placed pagan symbols
all around your huge beds.
Yes, you have rejected me,
sold yourselves to your lovers,
and gone to bed with them.◆

9 You smear on olive oil
and all kinds of perfume
to worship the god Molech.◆
You even seek advice
from spirits of the dead.
10 Though you tired yourself out
by running after idols,
you refused to stop.
Your desires were so strong
that they kept you going.

11 Did you forget about me
and become unfaithful
because you were more afraid
of someone else?
Have I been silent so long◆
that you no longer fear me?
12 You think you're so good,
but I'll point out the truth.
13 Ask your idols to save you
when you are in trouble.
Be careful though —
it takes only a faint breath
to blow them over.
But if you come to me for protection,
this land and my holy mountain
will always belong to you.

The LORD helps the helpless

¹⁴ The LORD says,
"Clear the road!
    Get it ready for my people."

¹⁵ Our holy God lives for ever in the highest
heavens, and this is what he says:

Though I live high above
    in the holy place,
I am here to help those
    who are humble
    and depend only on me.

¹⁶ My people, I won't stay angry
    and keep on accusing you.
After all, I am your Creator.
I don't want you to give up
    in complete despair.

¹⁷ Your greed made me furious.
That's why I punished you
    and refused to be found,
while you kept returning
    to your old sinful ways.

¹⁸ I know what you are like!
But I will heal you, lead you,
    and give you comfort,
until those who are mourning
¹⁹ start singing my praises.*
No matter where you are,
I, the LORD, will heal you*
    and give you peace.

²⁰ The wicked are a restless sea
    tossing up mud.
²¹ But I, the LORD, have promised
    that none who are evil
    will live in peace.

CHAPTER 58

True religion

¹ Shout the message!
    Don't hold back.
Say to my people Israel:
You've sinned! You've turned
    against the LORD.
² Day after day, you worship him
    and seem eager to learn
    his teachings.
You act like a nation
    that wants to do right
    by obeying his laws.
You ask him about justice,
    and say you enjoy
    worshipping the LORD.

³ You wonder why the LORD
    pays no attention
when you go without eating
    and act humble.
But on those same days
    that you give up eating,
you think only of yourselves*
    and abuse your workers.
⁴ You even get angry
    and ready to fight.
No wonder God won't listen
    to your prayers!

⁵ Do you think the LORD
    wants you to give up eating
and to act as humble
    as a bent-over bush?
Or to dress in sackcloth
    and sit in ashes?
Is this really what he wants
    on a day of worship?

⁶ I'll tell you
    what it really means
    to worship the LORD.
Remove the chains of prisoners
    who are chained unjustly.
Free those who are abused!
⁷ Share your food with everyone
    who is hungry;
share your home
    with the poor and homeless.
Give clothes to those in need;
    don't turn away your relatives.

⁸ Then your light will shine
    like the dawning sun, and you
    will quickly be healed.
Your honesty* will protect you
    as you advance,
and the glory of the LORD
    will defend you from behind.
⁹ When you beg the LORD for help,
    he will answer, "Here I am!"

Don't ill-treat others
    or falsely accuse them
    or say something cruel.
¹⁰ Give your food to the hungry
    and care for the homeless.
Then your light will shine
    in the dark;
your darkest hour will be
    like the noonday sun.

¹¹ The LORD will always guide you
    and provide good things to eat
    when you are in the desert.

See also: 57.19: Eph 2.17. 57.21: Isa 48.22.
See also: 58.7: Matt 25.34.

He will make you healthy.
You will be like a garden
   that has plenty of water
or like a stream that never runs dry.
¹² You will rebuild those houses
   left in ruins for years;
you will be known
   as a builder and repairer
   of city walls and streets.

¹³ But first, you must start
respecting the Sabbath
   as a joyful day of worship.
You must stop doing and saying
   whatever you please
   on this special day.
¹⁴ Then you will truly enjoy
   knowing the LORD.
He will let you rule
   from the highest mountains
and bless you with the land
   of your ancestor Jacob.
   The LORD has spoken!

CHAPTER 59

Social injustice is condemned

¹ The LORD hasn't lost
   his powerful strength;
he can still hear
   and answer prayers.
² Your sins are the roadblock
   between you and your God.
That's why he doesn't answer
   your prayers or let you see his face.

³ Your talk is filled with lies
   and plans for violence;
every finger on your hands
   is covered with blood.
⁴ You falsely accuse others
   and tell lies in court;
sin and trouble are the names
   of your children.
⁵ You eat the deadly eggs
   of poisonous snakes,
and more snakes crawl out
   from the eggs left to hatch.
You weave spider's webs,
⁶ but you can't make clothes
   with those webs
   or hide behind them.

You're sinful and brutal.
⁷ You hurry off to do wrong
   or murder innocent victims.

All you think about is sin;
you leave ruin and destruction
   wherever you go.
⁸ You don't know how to live in peace
   or to be fair with others.
The roads you make are crooked;
   your followers cannot find peace.

The people confess their sins

⁹ No one has come to defend us
   or to bring about justice.
We hoped for a day of sunshine,
   but all we found
   was a dark, gloomy night.
¹⁰ We feel our way along,
   as if we were blind;
we stumble at midday,
   as if it were night.
We can see no better
   than someone dead.ᵛ

¹¹ We growl like bears
   and mourn like doves.
We hope for justice and victory,
   but they escape us.
¹² How often have we sinned
   and turned against you,
   the LORD God?
Our sins condemn us!
   We have done wrong.
¹³ We have rebelled and refused
   to follow you.
Our hearts were deceitful,
   and so we lied;
we planned to abuse others
   and turn our backs on you.
¹⁴ Injustice is everywhere;
   justice seems far away.
Truth is chased out of court;
   honesty is shoved aside.
¹⁵ Everyone tells lies;
   those who turn from crime
   end up ruined.

The LORD will rescue his people

When the LORD noticed
   that justice had disappeared,
   he became very displeased.
¹⁶ It disgusted him even more
   to learn that no one
   would do a thing about it.
So with his own powerful arm,
   he won victories for truth.
¹⁷ Justice was the LORD's armour;
   saving power was his helmet;

See also: 59.7,8: Rom 3.15–17.   See also: 59.16: Isa 63.5.   59.17: Eph 6.14,17; 1 Thes 5.8.

anger and revenge
were his clothes.
18 Now the LORD will get furious
and do to his enemies,
both near and far,
what they did to his people.
19 He will attack like a flood
in a mighty storm.
Nations in the west and the east
will then honour and praise
his wonderful name.
20 The LORD has promised to rescue
the city of Zion
and Jacob's descendants
who turn from sin.

21 The LORD says: "My people,
I promise to give you my Spirit
and my message.
These will be my gifts to you
and your families for ever.
I, the LORD, have spoken."

The future glory of Jerusalem

CHAPTER 60

A new day for Jerusalem

1 Jerusalem, stand up! Shine!
Your new day is dawning.
The glory of the LORD
shines brightly on you.
2 The earth and its people
are covered with darkness,
but the glory of the LORD
is shining upon you.
3 Nations and kings
will come to the light
of your dawning day.

Crowds are coming to Jerusalem

The LORD said:

4 Open your eyes! Look around!
Crowds are coming.
Your sons are on their way
from distant lands;
your daughters are being carried
like little children.
5 When you see this,
your faces will glow;
your hearts will pound
and swell with pride.*

Treasures from across the sea
and the wealth of nations
will be brought to you.
6 Your country will be covered
with caravans of young camels
from Midian and Ephah.*
The people of Sheba*
will bring gold and spices
in praise of me, the LORD.
7 Every sheep of Kedar
will come to you;
rams from Nebaioth*
will be yours as well.
I will accept them as offerings
and bring honour to my temple.

8 What is that sailing by
like clouds
or like doves flying home?
9 On those distant islands
your people are waiting
for me, the LORD.*
Seagoing ships* lead the way
to bring them home
with their silver and gold.
I, the holy LORD God of Israel,
do this to honour your people,
so they will honour me.

Jerusalem will be rebuilt

The LORD said:

10 Jerusalem, your city walls
will be rebuilt by foreigners;
their rulers will become
your slaves.
I punished you in my anger;
now I will be kind
and treat you with mercy.
11 Your gates will be open day and night
to let the rulers of nations
lead their people to you
with all their treasures.
12 Any nation or kingdom
that refuses to serve you
will be wiped out.

---

*60.6 Midian . . . Ephah: Midian was the ancestor of a nomadic tribe of the Arabian desert, east of the Gulf of Aqaba. Ephah was a clan within the tribe of Midian.
*60.6 Sheba: Perhaps a place in what is now south-west Arabia. The Queen of Sheba brought gifts to Solomon (1 Kings 10.1–13).
*60.7 Kedar . . . Nebaioth: Regions in northern Arabia.
*60.9 Seagoing ships: See the note at 2.16.

See also: 60.11: Rev 21.25,26.

See also: 59.20: Rom 11.26.

13 Wood from Lebanon's best trees
will be brought to you —
  the pines, the firs,
  and the cypress trees.
It will be used in my temple
to make beautiful the place
  where I rest my feet.

14 The descendants of enemies
  who hated and ill-treated you
  will kneel at your feet.
They will say, "You are Zion,
  the city of the LORD,
  the holy God of Israel."

15 You were hated and deserted,
  rejected by everyone.
But I will make you beautiful,
  a city to be proud of for all time to come.

16 You will drain the wealth
  of kings and foreign nations.
You will know that I,
  the mighty LORD God of Israel,
  have saved and rescued you.

17 I will bring bronze and iron
  in place of wood and stone;
  in place of bronze and iron,
  I will bring gold and silver.
I will appoint peace and justice
  as your rulers and leaders.

18 Violence, destruction, and ruin
  will never again be heard of
  within your borders.
"Victory" will be the name
  you give to your walls;
"Praise" will be the name
  you give to your gates.

19 You won't need the light
  of the sun or the moon.
I, the LORD your God,
  will be your eternal light
  and bring you honour.

20 Your sun will never set
  or your moon go down.
I, the LORD, will be your everlasting light,
  and your days of sorrow
  will come to an end.

21 Your people will live right
  and always own the land;
they are the trees I planted
  to bring praise to me.

22 Even the smallest family
  will be a powerful nation.
I am the LORD,
  and when the time comes,
  I will quickly do all this.

CHAPTER 61

The good news of victory

1 The Spirit of the LORD God
  has taken control of me!
The LORD has chosen and sent me
  to tell the oppressed
  the good news,
to heal the brokenhearted,
  and to announce freedom
  for prisoners and captives.

2 This is the year
  when the LORD God
  will show kindness to us
  and punish our enemies.

The LORD has sent me
  to comfort those who mourn,
3 especially in Jerusalem.
He sent me to give them flowers
  in place of their sorrow,
olive oil in place of tears,
  and joyous praise
  in place of broken hearts.
They will be called
  "Trees of Justice",
  planted by the LORD
  to honour his name.

4 Then they will rebuild cities
  that have been in ruins
  for many generations.

5 They will hire foreigners
  to take care of their sheep
  and their vineyards.

6 But they themselves will be
  priests and servants
  of the LORD our God.
The treasures of the nations
  will belong to them,
  and they will be famous.'

7 They were terribly insulted
  and horribly ill-treated;
now they will be greatly blessed
  and joyful for ever.

The LORD loves justice

8 I, the LORD, love justice!
But I hate robbery
  and injustice.'
My people, I solemnly promise
  to reward you
  with an eternal agreement.

9 Your descendants will be known
  in every nation.

See also: 60.14: Rev 3.9. 60.19: Rev 21.23; 22.5.

See also: 61.1: Matt 11.5; Luke 7.22. 61.1,2: Luke 4.18,19.
61.2: Matt 5.4.

All who see them will realize
that they have been blessed,
by me, the LORD.

Celebrate and shout

¹⁰ I celebrate and shout
because of my LORD God.
His saving power and justice
are the very clothes I wear.
They are more beautiful
than the jewellery worn
by a bride or a groom.
¹¹ The LORD will bring about
justice and praise
in every nation on earth,
like flowers blooming in a garden.

CHAPTER 62

Jerusalem will be saved

¹ Jerusalem, I will speak up
for your good.
I will never be silent
till you are safe and secure,
sparkling like a flame.
² Your great victory will be seen
by every nation and king;
the LORD will even give you
a new name.
³ You will be a glorious crown,
a royal headband,
for the LORD your God.

⁴ Your name will no longer be
"Deserted and Childless",
but "Happily Married".
You will please the LORD;
your country
will be his bride.
⁵ Your people will take the land,
just as a young man
takes a bride.
The LORD will be pleased
because of you,
just as a husband is pleased
with his bride.

⁶ Jerusalem, on your walls
I have stationed guards,
whose duty it is
to speak out day and night,
without resting.
They must remind the LORD
⁷ and not let him rest
till he makes Jerusalem strong
and famous everywhere.

⁸ The LORD has given his word
and made this promise:
"Never again will I give
to your enemies
the grain and grapes
for which you struggled.
⁹ As surely as you harvest
your grain and grapes,
you will eat your bread
with thankful hearts,
and you will drink your wine
in my temple."

¹⁰ People of Jerusalem,
open your gates!
Repair the road to the city
and clear it of stones;
raise a banner to help
the nations find their way.
¹¹ Here is what the LORD has said
for all the earth to hear:
"Soon I will come to save
the city of Zion,
and to reward you.
¹² Then you will be called,
The LORD's Own People,
The Ones He Rescued!
Your city will be known
as a good place to live
and a city full of people."

God's wonderful new creation

CHAPTER 63

The LORD's victory over the nations

¹ Who is this coming
from Bozrah* in Edom
with clothes stained red?
Who is this hero marching
in his glorious uniform?

"It's me, the LORD!
I have won the battle,
and I can save you!"

² What are those red spots?
Your clothes look stained
from trampling on grapes.*

---

*63.1 Bozrah: The main city of Edom.
*63.2 trampling on grapes: This is one way that grapes were crushed to make them into juice.

See also: 62.11: Isa 40.10; Rev 22.12. 63.1–6: Isa 34.5–17; Jer 49.7–22; Ezek 25.12–14; 35.1–15; Amos 1.11,12; Obad 1–14; Mal 1.2–5.

See also: 61.10: Rev 21.2.

3 "I alone trampled the grapes!
      None of the nations helped.
  I trampled nations in my anger
      and stained my clothes
      with their blood.
4 I did this because I wanted
      to take revenge —
  the time had come to rescue my people.
5 No one was there to help me
      or to give support;
  my mighty arm won the battle,
      strengthened by my anger.
6 In my fury I trampled on nations
      and made them drunk;
  their blood poured out
      everywhere on earth."

The LORD's goodness to his people

7 I will tell about the kind deeds
      the LORD has done.
      They deserve praise!
  The LORD has shown mercy
      to the people of Israel;
      he has been kind and good.

8 The LORD rescued his people,
      and said, "They are mine.
      They won't betray me."
9 It troubled the LORD
      to see them in trouble,
      and his angel saved them.*
  The LORD was truly merciful,
      so he rescued his people.
  He took them in his arms
      and carried them all those years.

10 Then the LORD's people
      turned against him and made
      his Holy Spirit sad.
  So he became their enemy
      and attacked them.
11 But his people remembered
      what had happened
      during the time of Moses.*
  Didn't the LORD* bring them
      and their leaders
      safely through the sea?
  Didn't he* give them his Holy Spirit?
12 The glorious power of the LORD
      marched beside Moses.
  The LORD will be praised for ever
      for dividing the sea.
13 He led his people across
      like horses running wild
      without stumbling.

14 His Spirit gave them rest,
      just as cattle find rest
      when led into a valley.*
  The name of the LORD was praised
      for doing these things.

A prayer for mercy and help

15 Please, LORD, look down
      from your holy and glorious
      home in the heavens
  and see what's going on.
  Have you lost interest?
      Where is your power?
  Show that you care about us*
      and have mercy!
16 Our ancestors Abraham and Jacob
      have both rejected us.
  But you are still our Father;
      you have been our protector
      since ancient times.

17 Why did you make us turn away
      from you, our LORD?
  Why did you make us want
      to disobey you?
  Please change your mind!
  We are your servants,
      your very own people.
18 For a little while,
      your temple belonged to us;*
  and now our enemies
      have torn it down.
19 We act as though you
      had never ruled us
      or called us your people.

CHAPTER 64

1 Rip the heavens apart!
  Come down, LORD;
      make the mountains tremble.
2 Be a spark that starts a fire
      causing water to boil.*
  Then your enemies will know
      who you are;
  all nations will tremble
      because you are nearby.

3 Your fearsome deeds
      have completely amazed us;
  even the mountains shake
      when you come down.
4 You are the only God
      ever seen or heard of
  who works miracles
      for his followers.

See also: 63.3: a Rev 14.20; 19.15; b Rev 19.13.
63.5: Isa 59.16. 63.12: Exod 14.21.

See also: 64.4: 1 Cor 2.9.

⁵ You help all who gladly obey
and do what you want,
  but sin makes you angry.
Only by your help
  can we ever be saved.ᵇ
⁶ We are unfit to worship you;
each of our good deeds
  is merely a filthy rag.
We dry up like leaves;
our sins are storm winds
  sweeping us away.
⁷ No one worships in your name
  or remains faithful.
You have turned your back on us
and let our sins melt us away.ᵇ

⁸ You, LORD, are our Father.
  We are nothing but clay,
but you are the potter
  who moulded us.
⁹ Don't be so furious
or keep our sins
  in your thoughts for ever!
Remember that all of us are your people.
¹⁰ Every one of your towns
has turned into a desert,
  especially Jerusalem.
¹¹ Zion's glorious and holy temple
where our ancestors praised you
  has been destroyed by fire.
Our beautiful buildings
  are now a pile of ruins.
¹² When you see these things,
how can you just sit there
and make us suffer more?

CHAPTER 65

The LORD will punish the guilty

¹ I, the LORD, was ready
to answer even those
  who were not asking
and to be found by those
  who were not searching.
To a nation that refused to worship me,ᵇ
  I said, "Here I am!"

² All day long I have reached out
to stubborn and sinful people
  going their own way.
³ They keep making me angry
  by sneering at me,
while offering sacrifices
  to idols in gardens
and burning incense
  to them on bricks.

⁴ They spend their nights
  hiding in burial caves;
they eat the meat of pigs,•
  cooked in sauces
made of stuff unfit to eat.
⁵ And then they say to others,
"Don't come near us!
  We're dedicated to God."
Such people are like smoke,
irritating my nose all day.
⁶ I have written this down;
  I won't keep silent.
I'll pay them back
  just as their sins deserve.
⁷ I, the LORD, will make them pay
for their sins and for those
  of their ancestors —
they have disgraced me
  by burning incense
on mountains.

⁸ Here is what the LORD says:
  A cluster of grapes
that produces wine
  is worth keeping!
So, because of my servants,
  I won't destroy everyone.
⁹ I have chosen the people
  of Israel and Judah,
and I will bless them
  with many descendants.
They will settle here
in this land of mountains,
  and it will be theirs.
¹⁰ My people will worship me.
Then the coastlands of Sharon
  and the land as far
as Achor Valley•
will turn into pasture land
where cattle and sheep
  will feed and rest.

¹¹ What will I, the LORD, do
if any of you reject me
  and my holy mountain?
What will happen to you
for offering food and wine
to the gods you call
  "Good Luck" and "Fate"?

•65.4 burial . . . pigs: Coming in contact with the
dead or eating the meat of pigs made a person
unacceptable to God.
•65.10 coastlands of Sharon . . . Achor Valley:
Sharon is the coastal plain on the west, and Achor
Valley is in the east near Jericho. These two places
stand for the whole country.

See also: 65.1: Rom 10.20.   65.2: Rom 10.21.

See also: 65.10: Josh 7.24-26.

¹² Your luck will end!
I will see to it that you
are slaughtered with swords.
You refused to answer
when I called out;
you paid no attention
to my instructions.
Instead, you did what I hated,
knowing it was wrong.

¹³ I, the LORD God, will give
food and drink to my servants,
and they will celebrate.
But all of you sinners
will go hungry and thirsty,
overcome with disgrace.
¹⁴ My servants will laugh and sing,
but you will be sad
and cry out in pain.
¹⁵ I, the LORD God, promise
to see that you are killed
and that my chosen servants use
your names as curse words.
But I will give new names*
to my servants.’
¹⁶ I am God! I can be trusted.
Your past troubles are gone;
I no longer think of them.
When you pray for someone
to receive a blessing,
or when you make a promise,
you must do it in my name.
I alone am the God
who can be trusted.

The LORD's new creation

¹⁷ I am creating new heavens
and a new earth;
everything of the past
will be forgotten.
¹⁸ Celebrate and be glad for ever!
I am creating a Jerusalem,
full of happy people.
¹⁹ I will celebrate with Jerusalem
and all its people;
there will be no more crying
or sorrow in that city.

²⁰ No child will die in infancy;
everyone will live
to a ripe old age.
Anyone a hundred years old
will be considered young,

and to die younger than that
will be considered a curse.

²¹ My people will live
in the houses they build;
they will enjoy grapes
from their own vineyards.
²² No one will take away
their homes or vineyards.
My chosen people will live
to be as old as trees,
and they will enjoy
what they have earned.
²³ Their work won't be wasted,
and their children won't die
of dreadful diseases.’
I will bless their children
and their grandchildren.
²⁴ I will answer their prayers
before they finish praying.

²⁵ Wolves and lambs
will graze together;
lions and oxen
will feed on straw.
Snakes will eat only dust!
They won't bite or harm anyone
on my holy mountain.
I, the LORD, have spoken!

CHAPTER 66

True worship

¹ The LORD said:

Heaven is my throne;
the earth is my footstool.
What kind of house
could you build for me?
In what place will I rest?
² I have made everything;
that's how it all came to be.’
I, the LORD, have spoken.

The people I treasure most
are the humble —
they depend only on me
and tremble when I speak.

³ You sacrifice oxen to me,
and you commit murder;
you sacrifice lambs to me
and dogs to other gods;
you offer grain to me
and pigs' blood to idols;
you burn incense to me
and praise your idols.’

---

*65.15 **new names:** The giving of a new name
suggests the beginning of a new life.
See also: 65.17: Isa 66.22; 2 Pet 3.13; Rev 21.1.
65.19: Rev 21.4.

See also: 65.25: Isa 11.6–9. 66.1: a Matt 5.34; 23.22;
b Matt 5.35. 66.1,2a: Acts 7.49,50.

You have made your own choice
to do these disgusting things
that you enjoy so much.
⁴ You refused to answer
when I called out;
you paid no attention
to my instructions.
Instead, you did what I hated,
knowing it was wrong.
Now I will punish⁴ you
in a way you dread the most.

The Lord will help Jerusalem

⁵ If you tremble
when the Lord speaks,
listen to what he says:
"Some of your own people hate
and reject you because of me.
They make fun and say,
'Let the Lord show his power!
Let us see him
make you truly happy.'
But those who say these things
will be terribly ashamed."

⁶ Do you hear that noise
in the city and those shouts
coming from the temple?
It is the Lord shouting
as he punishes his enemies.

⁷ Have you ever heard of a woman
who gave birth to a child
before having labour pains?
⁸ Who ever heard of such a thing
or imagined it could happen?
Can a nation be born in a day
or come to life in a second?
Jerusalem is like a mother
who gave birth to her children
as soon as she was in labour.
⁹ The Lord is the one
who makes birth possible.
And he will see that Zion
has many more children.
The Lord has spoken.

¹⁰ If you love Jerusalem,
celebrate and shout!
If you were in sorrow
because of the city,
you can now be glad.
¹¹ She will nurse and comfort you,
just like your own mother,
until you are satisfied.
You will fully enjoy
her wonderful glory.

¹² The Lord has promised:
"I will flood Jerusalem
with the wealth of nations
and make the city prosper.
Zion will nurse you at her breast,
carry you in her arms,
and hold you in her lap.
¹³ I will comfort you there
like a mother
comforting her child."

¹⁴ When you see this happen,
you will celebrate;
your strength will return
faster than grass can sprout.
Then everyone will know
that the Lord is present
with his servants,
but he is angry
with his enemies.
¹⁵ The Lord will come down
like a whirlwind
with his flaming chariots.
He will be terribly furious
and punish his enemies
with fire.
¹⁶ The Lord's fiery sword
will bring justice
everywhere on this earth
and execute many people.

A threat and a promise

¹⁷ Some of you get yourselves ready and go to
a garden to worship a foreign goddess.⁴ You
eat the meat of pigs, lizards, and mice. But I,
the Lord, will destroy you for this.

¹⁸ I know everything you do and think!
The time has now come⁴ to bring together
the people of every language and nation and
to show them my glory ¹⁹ by proving what I
can do.⁴ I will send the survivors to Tarshish,
Pul,⁴ Lud, Meshech,⁴ Tubal, Javan,⁴ and to
the distant islands. I will send them to
announce my wonderful glory to nations
that have never heard about me.

²⁰ They will bring your relatives from the
nations as an offering to me, the Lord. They
will come on horses, chariots, wagons,
mules, and camels⁴ to Jerusalem, my holy

*66.19 Pul: Hebrew; one ancient translation "Put", a
country in Africa, but the location of neither Pul nor
Put is known for certain.
*66.19 Tarshish . . . Javan: Tarshish may have been a
Phoenician city in Spain; Put (see note on Pul) and
Lud were African people; Meshech and Tubal were
regions south or south-east of the Black Sea; the Javan
were people of Asia Minor and the Greek islands.

See also: 66.7: Rev 12.5.

mountain. It will be like the people of Israel bringing the right offering to my temple. ²¹ I promise that some of them will be priests and others will be helpers in my temple. I, the LORD, have spoken.

²² I also promise that you will always have descendants and will never be forgotten, just as the new heavens and the new earth that I create will last for ever. ²³ On the first day of each month and on each Sabbath, everyone will worship me. I, the LORD, have spoken.

²⁴ My people will go out and look at the dead bodies of those who turned against me. The worms there never die, the fire never stops burning, and the sight of those bodies will be disgusting to everyone.

See also: 66.22: Isa 65.17; 2 Pet 3.13; Rev 21.1.
66.24: Mark 9.48.

Additional notes

⸰1.1 **message:** Or "vision".
⸰1.17 **and help those in need:** Or "and punish cruel people".
⸰1.27 **by showing justice:** Or "by my saving power".
⸰1.31 **Your . . . idols:** Or "Your wealth will be like dry wood, set on fire by its owners."
⸰2.1 **message:** See the note at 1.1.
⸰2.6 **because . . . foreigners:** One possible meaning for the difficult Hebrew text.
⸰3.4 **babies:** Or "worthless nobodies".
⸰5.17 **and they . . . others:** One possible meaning for the difficult Hebrew text.
⸰5.25 **is ready . . . again:** Or "hasn't given up on you yet".
⸰6.13 **But just . . . down:** One possible meaning for the difficult Hebrew text.
⸰7.1 **went . . . had planned:** Or "attacked Jerusalem, but could not capture it".
⸰8.1 **in big clear letters:** One possible meaning for the difficult Hebrew text.
⸰8.8 **But . . . land:** One possible meaning for the difficult Hebrew text.
⸰9.1 **will . . . pain:** One possible meaning for the difficult Hebrew text.
⸰9.3 **stronger:** Or "happy" or "larger".
⸰9.11 **their enemies:** Hebrew "the enemies of Rezin".
⸰9.12 **so . . . them:** Or "but he hasn't given up on them yet".
⸰9.17 **and kept . . . against him:** Or "but even though they had turned against him, he still had not given up on them."
⸰9.20 **their own relatives:** One possible meaning for the difficult Hebrew text.
⸰10.4 **escape being captured:** One possible meaning for the difficult Hebrew text.
⸰10.4 **and he . . . yet:** Or "but he hasn't given up on you yet!"

⸰10.23 **on this earth:** Or "in this land".
⸰10.25 **punish . . . crimes:** Or "completely destroy them".
⸰10.27 **All . . . you:** One possible meaning for the difficult Hebrew text.
⸰10.34 **Lebanon:** One possible meaning for the difficult Hebrew text of verse 34.
⸰11.11 **land along the coast:** Or "islands".
⸰12.2 **strength:** Or "song".
⸰13.1 **message:** See the note at 1.1.
⸰13.21 **goats:** Or "demons".
⸰14.4 **He . . . again:** One possible meaning for the difficult Hebrew text.
⸰15.2 **Everyone . . . temple:** One possible meaning for the difficult Hebrew text.
⸰15.9 **Dimon . . . Dimon:** The Standard Hebrew Text; the Dead Sea Scrolls and one ancient translation have *Dibon . . . Dibon.*
⸰16.8 **The rulers . . . vineyards:** Or "The rulers of nations have destroyed those vineyards."
⸰17.3 **Israel:** The Hebrew text has "Ephraim," another name for the northern kingdom.
⸰17.9 **covered . . . undergrowth:** Hebrew; one ancient translation "like the cities of the Hivites and the Amorites".
⸰18.1 **insects:** Or "sailing ships".
⸰18.2 **world:** One possible meaning for the difficult Hebrew text of verse 2.
⸰19.9 **turn pale:** One possible meaning for the difficult Hebrew text.
⸰19.18 **City of the Sun:** Some manuscripts of the Standard Hebrew Text, the Dead Sea Scrolls, and one ancient translation; most manuscripts of the Standard Hebrew Text have "City of Destruction". This probably refers to Heliopolis which means "City of the Sun" (see Jeremiah 43.13).
⸰21.8 **guard:** The Dead Sea Scrolls and one ancient translation; the Standard Hebrew text has "lion".
⸰22.3 **No matter . . . caught:** One possible meaning for the difficult Hebrew text.
⸰22.5 **and for . . . help:** One possible meaning for the difficult Hebrew text.
⸰22.6 **chariots:** One possible meaning for the difficult Hebrew text.
⸰23.1 **Tyre . . . ruins:** One possible meaning for the difficult Hebrew text.
⸰23.3 **along the Nile:** The Hebrew text has "grain of Shihor, the harvest of the Nile", but Shihor is probably a name for a region near the lower part of the Nile.
⸰23.4 **children:** One possible meaning for the difficult Hebrew text.
⸰23.6 **far across the ocean:** The Hebrew text has "to Tarshish", probably meaning a long distance.
⸰23.10 **People of Tyre:** The Hebrew text has "the people of Tarshish", which stands for the colonies of Tyre.
⸰23.10 **Egyptians:** One possible meaning for the difficult Hebrew text of verse 10.
⸰23.13 **ruins:** One possible meaning for the difficult Hebrew text of verse 13.

'24.4 its . . . to nothing: One possible meaning for the difficult Hebrew text.

'24.16 God of justice: Or "people who do right".

'25.11 no matter . . . try: One possible meaning for the difficult Hebrew text.

'26.5 our enemies . . . city: One possible meaning for the difficult Hebrew text.

'26.16 LORD: One possible meaning for the difficult Hebrew text of verse 16.

'27.2 fruitful: Some Hebrew manuscripts have "lovely".

'27.8 I . . . punishment: One possible meaning for the difficult Hebrew text.

'28.10 sound: One possible meaning for the difficult Hebrew text of verses 9,10.

'28.13 Now . . . sound: One possible meaning for the difficult Hebrew text.

'29.1 the place of my altar: One possible meaning for "ariel, ariel" of the Hebrew text. In Hebrew "ariel" can mean "God's hero" or "God's lion" or "God's altar".

'29.2 when . . . you: One possible meaning for the difficult Hebrew text.

'29.3 from all sides: One possible meaning for the difficult Hebrew text. One ancient translation has "like David".

'29.17 with . . . forest: Or "and Mount Carmel will be covered with forests".

'30.7 a helpless monster: One possible meaning for the difficult Hebrew text.

'30.27 with . . . smoke: One possible meaning for the difficult Hebrew text.

'31.9 fortress: The Hebrew text has "rock", which may refer to the Assyrian god or king, or to their army.

'33.3 greatness: One possible meaning for the difficult Hebrew text of verse 3.

'33.4 them: One possible meaning for the difficult Hebrew text of verse 4.

'33.6 Nothing . . . us: One possible meaning for the difficult Hebrew text.

'33.7 Listen . . . help: Or "The LORD heard our shouts and will come to help us."

'33.8 to any . . . promises: The Dead Sea Scrolls; the Standard Hebrew Text "to those in the cities".

'34.5 has done . . . above: The Standard Hebrew Text; the Dead Sea Scrolls "appears in the skies above".

'34.11 Owls . . . animals: One possible meaning for the difficult Hebrew text.

'34.15 Owls . . . shadows: One possible meaning for the difficult Hebrew text.

'35.7 where . . . home: One possible meaning for the difficult Hebrew text.

'35.8 And . . . highway: Or "And not even a fool can miss that highway."

'37.21,22 Hezekiah, you prayed . . . Assyria: One possible meaning for the difficult Hebrew text.

'38.8 steps: One possible meaning for the difficult Hebrew text of verse 8.

'38.13 of me: One possible meaning for the difficult Hebrew text of verse 13.

'38.14 help me: One possible meaning for the difficult Hebrew text of verse 14.

'38.15 There's . . . me: One possible meaning for the difficult Hebrew text.

'38.16 Your . . . me: One possible meaning for the difficult Hebrew text.

'38.19 about your faithfulness: One possible meaning for the difficult Hebrew text.

'40.9 There . . . can: Or "City of Jerusalem, you have good news. Shout it as loud as you can."

'40.13 the LORD: Or "the LORD's Spirit".

'40.21 Isn't . . . world: Or "Hasn't it been clear since the time of creation?"

'41.2 Who puts . . . power: One possible meaning for the difficult Hebrew text.

'41.7 and other workers: One possible meaning for the difficult Hebrew text.

'41.22 Come near . . . idols: One possible meaning for the difficult Hebrew text.

'41.23 and terrified: Or "when we see it".

'41.24 powerless: One possible meaning for the difficult Hebrew text.

'41.25 tramples: One possible meaning for the difficult Hebrew text.

'41.27 Look . . . happening: One possible meaning for the difficult Hebrew text.

'41.29 nothing: One possible meaning for the difficult Hebrew text.

'42.6 I selected . . . you: One possible meaning for the difficult Hebrew text.

'42.11 desert . . . mountains: The Hebrew text includes the place names of Kedar in the desert and Sela in the mountains.

'42.21 greatly praised: One possible meaning for the difficult Hebrew text of verse 21.

'43.14 crying as they go: Or "in their glorious ships".

'43.19 streams: The Standard Hebrew Text; the Dead Sea Scrolls "paths".

'44.2 my very favourite: Or "Jeshurun".

'44.4 like grass: One possible meaning for the difficult Hebrew text.

'44.7 Let them say . . . happen: One possible meaning for the difficult Hebrew text.

'44.12 by using a hammer: One possible meaning for the difficult Hebrew text.

'44.20 How . . . ashes: One possible meaning for the difficult Hebrew text.

'44.21 I won't forget you: One possible meaning for the difficult Hebrew text.

'45.2 mountains: The Dead Sea Scrolls and one ancient translation; the Standard Hebrew Text "rising waves".

'45.4 But . . . you: One possible meaning for the difficult Hebrew text.

'45.8 Prepare . . . create: One possible meaning for the difficult Hebrew text.

'46.1 as . . . animals: One possible meaning for the difficult Hebrew text.

'46.8 Now . . . mind: One possible meaning for the difficult Hebrew text.

'47.3 escape: Or "oppose me".

'47.14 keep warm: Or "cook food".

'48.1 tribe: Hebrew "waters".

'48.10 furnace: One possible meaning for the difficult Hebrew text of verse 10.

'48.11 I refuse to be dishonoured: One possible meaning for the difficult Hebrew text.

'48.14 Babylonia: One possible meaning for the difficult Hebrew text of verse 14.

'49.7 You . . . you: One possible meaning for the difficult Hebrew text.

'49.8 my . . . nations: One possible meaning for the difficult Hebrew text.

'49.17 Your city . . . destroyed: One possible meaning for the difficult Hebrew text.

'49.24 cruel: The Dead Sea Scrolls and two ancient translations; the Standard Hebrew Text "good".

'50.10 God: One possible meaning for the difficult Hebrew text of verse 10.

'50.11 Go . . . lit: One possible meaning for the difficult Hebrew text.

'51.19 I . . . you: One possible meaning for the difficult Hebrew text.

'52.5 groan with pain: One possible meaning for the difficult Hebrew text.

'52.14 him: One ancient translation; Hebrew "you".

'52.14 human: One possible meaning for the difficult Hebrew text of verse 14.

'52.15 My . . . me: Hebrew; one ancient translation "The nations will be amazed at him."

'52.15 kings . . . wonder: One possible meaning for the difficult Hebrew text.

'53.8 my people: Or "his people".

'53.9 but he . . . people: One possible meaning for the difficult Hebrew text.

'53.10 The LORD . . . descendants: One possible meaning for the difficult Hebrew text.

'54.11 with precious stones: One possible meaning for the difficult Hebrew text.

'54.12 fortresses: One possible meaning for the difficult Hebrew text.

'57.1,2 Evil . . . God: One possible meaning for the difficult Hebrew text.

'57.6 You have . . . stone: One possible meaning for the difficult Hebrew text.

'57.8 them: One possible meaning for the difficult Hebrew text of verse 8.

'57.9 the god Molech: Or "the king". In Hebrew "Molech" and "king" sound alike.

'57.11 so long: One possible meaning for the difficult Hebrew text.

'57.18,19 until . . . praises: One possible meaning for the difficult Hebrew text.

'57.19 heal you: One possible meaning for the difficult Hebrew text.

'58.3 you think . . . yourselves: One possible meaning for the difficult Hebrew text.

'58.8 honesty: Or "honest leader".

'59.10 We can . . . dead: One possible meaning for the difficult Hebrew text.

'60.5 swell with pride: One possible meaning for the difficult Hebrew text.

'60.9 On . . . LORD: One possible meaning for the difficult Hebrew text.

'61.6 and . . . famous: One possible meaning for the difficult Hebrew text.

'61.8 But . . . injustice: One possible meaning for the difficult Hebrew text.

'62.5 Your . . . land: One possible meaning for the difficult Hebrew text.

'63.9 It . . . them: One possible meaning for the difficult Hebrew text.

'63.11 But . . . Moses: One possible meaning for the difficult Hebrew text.

'63.11 the LORD: Or "Moses".

'63.11 he: Or "Moses".

'63.14 His . . . valley: One possible meaning for the difficult Hebrew text.

'63.15 us: Hebrew "me".

'63.18 For . . . us: One possible meaning for the difficult Hebrew text.

'64.2 Be . . . boil: One possible meaning for the difficult Hebrew text.

'64.5 saved: One possible meaning for the difficult Hebrew text of verse 5.

'64.7 and let . . . away: One possible meaning for the difficult Hebrew text.

'65.1 refused . . . me: One possible meaning for the difficult Hebrew text.

'65.15 But I . . . servants: One possible meaning for the difficult Hebrew text.

'65.23 their children . . . diseases: One possible meaning for the difficult Hebrew text.

'66.2 that's . . . be: One possible meaning for the difficult Hebrew text.

'66.3 You sacrifice oxen . . . idols: Or "Sacrificing oxen to me is the same as murder; sacrificing lambs to me is the same as sacrificing dogs to other gods; offering grain to me is the same as offering pigs' blood to idols; and burning incense to me is the same as praising idols."

'66.4 punish: One possible meaning for the difficult Hebrew text.

'66.5 Some . . . happy: One possible meaning for the difficult Hebrew text.

'66.17 Some . . . goddess: One possible meaning for the difficult Hebrew text.

'66.18 I . . . come: One possible meaning for the difficult Hebrew text.

'66.19 by . . . do: One possible meaning for the difficult Hebrew text.

'66.19 Meshech: One ancient translation; Hebrew "those who use bows and arrows".

'66.20 camels: One possible meaning for the difficult Hebrew text.

Jeremiah

A quick look at this book

The world of Jeremiah's time was full of wars
as new empires conquered the old ones. The
tiny kingdom of Judah was caught in the
middle, and during Jeremiah's lifetime,
Babylonia conquered Judah and ended its
freedom as a nation.

Jeremiah began bringing the Lord's message
to the people of Judah when he was young,
possibly less than 20 years old. He continued
until 586 BC, when the Babylonians captured
Jerusalem. Some of the people of Judah soon
forced him to go with them to Egypt, where he
continued to speak to them for the Lord.

Many of Jeremiah's messages include the date
when they were originally spoken. But when
his friend Baruch helped him put the messages
into writing, they did not arrange the
messages by these dates. Usually the messages
are grouped together because they are about
similar subjects.

Jeremiah acted out many of his messages, so
that the people would know exactly what the
Lord was saying (see 13.1–11; 19.1–11;
27.1–28.17; 32.1–44; 43.7–13).

Time after time, Jeremiah said God was going
to punish Judah. But because he also said the
people of Judah should surrender to the
Babylonians, his enemies accused him of being
a traitor. They had him thrown in prison and
even tried to have him killed. Jeremiah
complained to God about his problems, and
these complaints are now known as his
"Confessions" (see 11.18–23; 12.1–6;
15.10,11,15–21; 17.14–18; 18.19–23;
20.7–18).

Jeremiah often reminded the people of Judah
that they had broken their agreement to
worship only the Lord. And so the Lord was
going to punish them by letting the
Babylonians take them away to Babylonia. But
the Lord had also promised to bring his people
back to their land some day, and at that time
the Lord would make a new agreement with
them:

*I will write my laws
    on their hearts and minds.
I will be their God,
    and they will be my people.*

*No longer will they have to teach one another
to obey me. I, the LORD, promise that all of
them will obey me, ordinary people and rulers
alike. I will forgive their sins and forget the evil
things they have done.*

(31.33b,34)

God chooses Jeremiah to speak for him

CHAPTER 1

¹ My name is Jeremiah. I am a priest, and my father Hilkiah and everyone else in my family are from Anathoth in the territory of the Benjamin tribe. This book contains the things that the LORD told me to say. ² The LORD first spoke to me in the thirteenth year that Josiah* was king of Judah, ³ and he continued to speak to me during the rule of Josiah's son Jehoiakim.* The last time the LORD spoke to me was in the fifth month* of the eleventh year that Josiah's son Zedekiah* was king. That was also when the people of Jerusalem were taken away as prisoners.

The LORD chooses Jeremiah

⁴ The LORD said:

⁵ "Jeremiah, I am your Creator,
    and before you were born,
    I chose you to speak for me
        to the nations."

⁶ I replied, "I'm not a good speaker, LORD, and I'm too young."

⁷ "Don't say you're too young," the LORD answered. "If I tell you to go and speak to someone, then go! And when I tell you what to say, don't leave out a word! ⁸ I promise to be with you and keep you safe, so don't be afraid."

⁹ The LORD reached out his hand, then he touched my mouth and said, "I am giving you the words to say, ¹⁰ and I am sending you with authority to speak to the nations for me. You will tell them of doom and destruction, and of rising and rebuilding again."

¹¹ The LORD showed me something in a vision. Then he asked, "What do you see, Jeremiah?"

I answered, "A branch of almonds that ripen early."

¹² "That's right," the LORD replied, "and I always rise early* to keep a promise."

¹³ Then the LORD showed me something else and asked, "What do you see now?"

I answered, "I see a pot of boiling water in the north, and it's about to spill out towards us."

¹⁴ The LORD said:

I will pour out destruction
    all over the land.
¹⁵ Just watch while I send
    for the kings of the north.
They will attack and capture
    Jerusalem and other towns,
    then set up their thrones
        at the gates of Jerusalem.

¹⁶ I will punish my people,
    because they are guilty
    of turning from me
        to worship idols.

¹⁷ Jeremiah, get ready!
Go and tell the people
    what I command you to say.
Don't be frightened by them,
    or I will make you terrified
        while they watch.

¹⁸ My power will make you strong
    like a fortress
    or a column of iron
        or a wall of bronze.
You will oppose all of Judah,
    including its kings and leaders,
        its priests and people.

¹⁹ They will fight back,
    but they won't win.
I, the LORD, give my word —
    I won't let them harm you.

---

*1.2 Josiah: Ruled 640–609 BC.

*1.3 Jehoiakim: Ruled 609–598 BC.

*1.3 fifth month: Ab, the fifth month of the Hebrew calendar, from about mid-July to mid-August.

*1.3 Zedekiah: Ruled 598–586 BC.

See also: 1.2: 2 King 22.3–23.27; 2 Chron 34.8–35.19.
1.3: a 2 King 23.36–24.7; 2 Chron 36.5–8;
b 2 King 24.18–25.21; 2 Chron 36.11–21.

*1.11,12 almonds . . . rise early: In Hebrew "almonds that ripen early" sounds like "always rise early".

God will punish the people of Judah and Jerusalem

CHAPTER 2

Israel's unfaithfulness

¹ The LORD told me ² to go to Jerusalem and tell everyone that he had said:

> When you were my young bride,
> you loved me
> and followed me
> through the barren desert.
> ³ You belonged to me alone,
> like the first part of the harvest,
> and I severely punished
> those who ill-treated you.

⁴ Listen, people of Israel,*
⁵ and I, the LORD, will speak.
I was never unfair
to your ancestors,
but they left me
and became worthless
by following worthless idols.
⁶ Your ancestors refused
to ask for my help,
though I had rescued them from Egypt
and led them through
a treacherous, barren desert,
where no one lives
or dares to travel.

⁷ I brought you here to my land,
where food is abundant,
but you made my land filthy
with your sins.
⁸ The priests who teach my laws
don't care to know me.
Your leaders rebel against me;
your prophets
give messages from Baal
and worship false gods.

The LORD accuses his people

The LORD said:

⁹ I will take you to court and accuse you
and your descendants
¹⁰⁻¹¹ of a crime that no nation
has ever committed before.

Just ask anyone, anywhere,
from the eastern deserts
to the islands in the west.
You will find that no nation
has ever abandoned its gods
even though they were false.
I am the true and glorious God,
but you have rejected me
to worship idols.
¹² Tell the heavens
to tremble with fear!
¹³ You, my people, have sinned
in two ways —
you have rejected me, the source
of life-giving water,
and you've tried to collect water
in cracked and leaking pits
dug in the ground.

¹⁴ People of Israel,
you weren't born slaves;
you were captured in war.
¹⁵ Enemies roared like lions
and destroyed your land;
towns lie burnt and empty.
¹⁶ Soldiers from the Egyptian towns
of Memphis and Tahpanhes
have cracked your skulls.
¹⁷ It's all your own fault!
You stopped following me,
the LORD your God,
¹⁸ and you trusted the power
of Egypt and Assyria.*
¹⁹ Your own sins will punish you,
because it was a bitter mistake
for you to reject me
without fear of punishment.
I, the LORD All-Powerful,
have spoken.

²⁰ Long ago you left me
and broke all ties between us,
refusing to be my servant.
Now you worship other gods
by having sex
on hilltops or in the shade
of large trees.*
²¹ You were a choice grapevine,
but now you produce nothing
but small, rotten grapes.

---

*2.4 Israel: After the nation was divided, the northern kingdom was called "Israel", and the southern kingdom was called "Judah" (see 1 Kings 12.1–20). In 722 BC the Assyrians conquered the northern kingdom, and Judah was all that was left. So in the book of Jeremiah the name "Israel" is most often used of the southern kingdom.

*2.20 having sex . . . trees: In some Canaanite religions, worshippers had sex with temple prostitutes, who represented their gods; many of the Canaanite places of worship were on hilltops or under large trees.

Israel is stained with guilt

22 The LORD said:

People of Israel,
    you are stained with guilt,
and no soap or bleach
    can wash it away.
23 You deny your sins
and say, "We aren't unclean.
    We haven't worshipped Baal."*
But think about what you do
    in Hinnom Valley.*
And you run back and forth
    like young camels,
as you rush to worship one idol
    after another.
24 You are a female donkey
    sniffing the desert air,
wanting to mate with just anyone.
    You are an easy catch!
25 Your shoes are worn out,
    and your throat is parched
from running here and there
    to worship foreign gods.
"Stop!" I shouted, but you replied, "No!
    I love those gods too much."

26 You and your leaders
    are more disgraceful
    than thieves —
you and your kings,
    your priests and prophets
27 worship stone idols
    and sacred poles
as if they had created you
    and had given you life.
You have rejected me,
    but when you're in trouble,
    you cry to me for help.
28 Go and cry to the gods you made!
There should be enough of them
    to save you,
because Judah has as many gods
    as it has towns.

Israel rebels against the LORD

29 The LORD said to Israel:

You accuse me of not saving you,
    but I say you have rebelled.
30 I tried punishing you,
    but you refused
    to come back to me,
and like fierce lions
    you killed my prophets.

31 Now listen to what I say!
Did I abandon you in the desert
    or surround you with darkness?
You are my people,
    yet you have told me,
"We'll do what we want,
    and we refuse
    to worship you!"
32 A bride could not forget
    to wear her jewellery
    to her wedding,
but you have forgotten me
    day after day.
33 You are so clever
    at finding lovers
that you could give lessons
    to a prostitute.
34 You killed innocent people
    for no reason at all.
And even though their blood
    can be seen on your clothes,
35 you claim to be innocent,
    and you want me to stop
    being angry with you.
So I'll take you to court,
    and we'll see who is right.

36 When Assyria let you down,
    you ran to Egypt,
but you'll find no help there,
37 and you will leave
    in great sadness.*
I won't let you find help
    from those you trust.

CHAPTER 3

Sin and shame

1 The LORD said to the people of Israel:

If a divorced woman marries,
    can her first husband
    ever marry her again?
No, because this
    would pollute the land.
But you have more gods
    than a prostitute has lovers.
    Why should I take you back?
2 Just try to find one hilltop
    where you haven't gone
    to worship other gods
    by having sex.*
You sat beside the road
    like a robber in ambush,
except you offered yourself
    to every passer-by.

---

*2.23 Hinnom Valley: Hebrew "the valley" (see 7.31-32; 19.1-6).

*3.2 hilltop . . . sex: See the note at 2.20.

Your sins of unfaithfulness
have polluted the land.
3 So I, the LORD, refused
to let the spring rains fall.
But just like a prostitute,
you still have no shame
for what you have done.
4 You call me your father
or your long-lost friend;
5 you beg me to stop being angry,
but you won't stop sinning.

The LORD asks Israel to come back to him

6 When Josiah* was king, the LORD said:

Jeremiah, the kingdom of Israel* was like an unfaithful wife who became a prostitute on the hilltops and in the shade of large trees.* 7-8 I knew that the kingdom of Israel had been unfaithful and committed many sins, yet I still hoped she might come back to me. But she didn't, so I divorced her and sent her away.

Her sister, the kingdom of Judah, saw what happened, but she wasn't worried in the least, and I watched her become unfaithful like her sister. 9 The kingdom of Judah wasn't sorry for being a prostitute, and she didn't care that she had made both herself and the land unclean by worshipping idols of stone and wood. 10 And worst of all, the people of Judah pretended to come back to me. 11 Even the people of Israel were honest enough not to pretend.

12 Jeremiah, shout towards the north:

Israel, I am your LORD —
come back to me!
You were unfaithful
and made me furious,
but I am merciful,
and so I will forgive you.
13 Just admit that you rebelled
and worshipped foreign gods
under large trees everywhere.
14 You are unfaithful children,
but you belong to me.
Come home!
I'll take one or two of you
from each town and clan
and bring you to Zion.

15 Then I'll appoint wise rulers
who will obey me,
and they will care for you
like shepherds.
16 You will increase in numbers,
and there will be no need
to remember the sacred chest
or to make a new one.*
17 The whole city of Jerusalem
will be my throne.*
All nations will come here
to worship me,
and they will no longer follow
their stubborn, evil hearts.
18 Then, in countries to the north,
you people of Judah and Israel
will be reunited,
and you will return to the land
I gave your ancestors.
19 I have always wanted
to treat you as my children
and give you the best land,
the most beautiful on earth.
I wanted you to call me "Father"
and not turn from me.
20 But instead, you are like a wife
who broke her wedding vows.
You have been unfaithful to me.
I, the LORD, have spoken.

The people confess their sins

The LORD said:

21 Listen to the noise
on the hilltops!
It's the people of Israel,
weeping and begging me
to answer their prayers.
They forgot about me
and chose the wrong path.
22 I will tell them, "Come back,
and I will cure you
of your unfaithfulness."

They will answer,
"We will come back, because you
are the LORD our God.
23 On hilltops, we worshipped idols
and made loud noises,
but it was all for nothing —
only you can save us.

---

*3.6 Josiah: See the note at 1.2.
*3.6 Israel: The northern kingdom (see the note at 2.4).
*3.6 prostitute . . . trees: See the note at 2.20.
See also: 3.6: 2 King 22.1—23.30; 2 Chron 34.1—35.27.

*3.16 make a new one: The sacred chest was probably destroyed or taken away by the Babylonians when they captured Jerusalem in 586 BC.
*3.16,17 sacred chest . . . throne: The sacred chest was thought to be God's throne on earth.

²⁴ Since the days of our ancestors
    when our nation was young,
that shameful god Baal* has taken
    our crops and livestock,
    our sons and daughters.
²⁵ We have rebelled against you
    just like our ancestors,
and we are ashamed of our sins."

CHAPTER 4

How Israel can return to the LORD

¹ The LORD said:

Israel, if you really want
    to come back to me, get rid
    of those disgusting idols.
² Make promises only in my name,
    and do what you promise!
Then all nations will praise me,
    and I will bless them.
³ People of Jerusalem and Judah,
    don't be so stubborn!
Your hearts have become hard,
    like unploughed ground
    where thorn bushes grow.
⁴ With all your hearts,
    keep the agreement
    I made with you.
But if you are stubborn
    and keep on sinning,
my anger will burn like a fire
    that cannot be put out.

Disaster is coming

The LORD said:

⁵⁻⁶ "Sound the trumpets, my people.
Warn the people of Judah,'
    'Run for your lives!
Head for Jerusalem
    or another walled town!'

"Jeremiah, tell them I'm sending
    disaster from the north.
⁷ An army will come out,
    like a lion from its den.
It will destroy nations
    and leave your towns empty
    and in ruins."

⁸ Then I said
    to the people of Israel,
"Put on sackcloth!*

Mourn and cry out,
    'The LORD is still angry
    with us'."

⁹ The LORD said,

"When all this happens,
    the king and his officials,
    the prophets and the priests
    will be shocked and terrified."

¹⁰ I said, "You are the LORD God. So why have
you fooled everyone, especially the people of
Jerusalem? Why did you promise peace,
when a knife is at our throats?"

The coming disaster

¹¹⁻¹² When disaster comes, the LORD will tell
you people of Jerusalem,

"I am sending a storm
    from the desert —
    not a welcome breeze.*
And it will sweep you away
    as punishment for your sins.
¹³ Look! The enemy army
    swoops down like an eagle;
their cavalry and chariots
    race faster than storm clouds
    blown by the wind."

Then you will answer,
    "We are doomed!"

¹⁴ But Jerusalem, there is still time
    for you to be saved.
Wash the evil from your hearts
    and stop making sinful plans,
¹⁵ before a message of disaster
    arrives from the hills of Ephraim
    and the town of Dan.*

¹⁶⁻¹⁷ The LORD said,

"Tell the nations that my people
    have rebelled against me.
And so an army will come
    from far away
to surround Jerusalem
    and the towns of Judah.
I, the LORD, have spoken.

---

*4.8 sackcloth:** A rough, dark-coloured cloth made
from goat or camel hair and used to make grain
sacks. It was worn in times of trouble or sorrow.
See also: 4.3: Hos 10.12.

*4.11,12 a welcome breeze:** Hebrew "a wind to
blow away the husks". Farmers used a special shovel
to pitch grain and husks into the air. Wind would
blow away the light husks, and the grain would fall
back to the ground, where it could be gathered up.
*4.15 Ephraim . . . Dan:** The hills of Ephraim were to
the north of Jerusalem, and Dan was even further
north. They would be reached by the invading army
first.

18 "People of Judah,
      your hearts will be in pain,
   but it's your own fault
      that you will be punished."

Jeremiah's vision
of the coming punishment

19 I can't stand the pain!
   My heart pounds,
      as I twist and turn in agony.
   I hear the signal trumpet
      and the battle cry of the enemy,
      and I cannot be silent.
20 I see the enemy defeating us
      time after time,
   leaving everything in ruins.
   Even my own home
      is destroyed in a moment.
21 How long will I see enemy flags
      and hear their trumpets?

22 I heard the LORD say,
      "My people ignore me.
   They are foolish children
      who do not understand
      that they will be punished.
   All they know is how to sin."

23 After this, I looked around.
   The earth was barren,
      with no form of life.
   The sun, moon, and stars
      had disappeared.
24 The mountains were shaking;
25 no people could be seen,
      and all the birds
      had flown away.
26 Farmland had become a desert,
      and towns were in ruins.
   The LORD's fierce anger
      had done all of this.

The death of Jerusalem

27-28 The LORD said:

   I have made my decision,
      and I won't change my mind.
   This land will be destroyed,
      although not completely.
   The sky will turn dark,
      and the earth will mourn.

29 Enemy cavalry and archers
      shout their battle cry.
   People run for their lives
      and try to find safety
      among trees and rocks.
   Every town is empty.

30 Jerusalem, your land
      has been wiped out.
   But you act like a prostitute
      and try to win back your lovers,
      who now hate you.
   You can put on a red dress,
      gold jewellery, and eye shadow,
      but it's no use —
   your lovers are out to kill you!

31 I heard groaning and crying.
   Was it a woman giving birth
      to her first child?
   No, it was Jerusalem.
   She was gasping for breath
      and begging for help.
   "I'm dying!" she said.
   "They have murdered me."

CHAPTER 5

Is anyone honest and faithful?

The LORD said to me:

1 "Search Jerusalem
      for honest people
      who try to be faithful.
   If you can find even one,
      I'll forgive the whole city.
2 Everyone breaks promises
      made in my name."

3 I answered, "I know
      that you look for truth.
   You punished your people
      for their lies,
   but in spite of the pain,
      they became more stubborn
      and refused to turn back
      to you."

4 Then I thought to myself,
   "These common people
      act like fools,
   and they have never learnt
      what the LORD their God
      demands of them.
5 I'll go and talk to the leaders.
   They know what God demands."
   But even they had decided
      not to obey the LORD.

6 The people have rebelled
      and rejected the LORD
      too many times.
   So enemies will attack
      like lions from the forest
      or wolves from the desert.
   Those enemies will watch
      the towns of Judah,

and like leopards
they will tear to pieces
whoever goes outside.

Enemies will punish Judah

The LORD said:

7 People of Judah,
how can I forgive you?
I gave you everything,
but you abandoned me
and worshipped idols.
You men go to prostitutes
and are unfaithful
to your wives.
8 You are no better than animals,
and you always want sex
with someone else's wife.

9 Why shouldn't I punish
the people of Judah?
10 I will tell their enemies,
"Go through my vineyard.
Don't destroy the vines,
but cut off the branches,
because they are the people
who don't belong to me."

11 In every way, Judah and Israel
have been unfaithful to me.
12-13 Their prophets lie and say,
"The LORD won't punish us.
We will have peace
and plenty of food."
They tell these lies in my name,
so now they will be killed in war
or starve to death.

14 I am the LORD God All-Powerful.
Jeremiah, I will tell you
exactly what to say.
Your words will be a fire;
Israel and Judah
will be the fuel.

15 People of Israel,
I have made my decision.
An army from a distant country
will attack you.
I've chosen an ancient nation,
and you won't understand
their language.
16 All of them are warriors,
and their arrows bring death.
17 This nation will eat your crops
and livestock;
they will leave no fruit
on your vines or trees.
And although you feel safe
behind thick walls,

your towns will be destroyed
and your children killed.

Israel refused to worship the LORD

18 The LORD said:

Jeremiah, the enemy army won't kill
everyone in Judah. 19 And the people who
survive will ask, "Why did the LORD our
God do such terrible things to us?" Then
tell them:

I am the LORD,
but you abandoned me
and worshipped other gods
in your own land.
Now you will be slaves
in a foreign country.
20 Tell these things to each other,
you people of Judah,
you descendants of Jacob.

21 You fools! Why don't you listen
when I speak?
Why can't you understand
22 that you should worship me
with fear and trembling?
I'm the one who made the shore
to hold back the ocean.
Waves may crash on the beach,
but they can come no further.
23 You stubborn people have rebelled
and turned your backs on me.
24 You refuse to say,
"Let's worship the LORD!
He's the one who sends rain
in spring and autumn
and gives us a good harvest."
25 That's why I cannot bless you!

26-27 A hunter traps birds
and puts them in a cage,
but some of you trap humans
and make them your slaves.
You are evil, and you lie and cheat
to make yourselves rich.
You are powerful
28 and prosperous,
but you refuse to help* the poor
get the justice they deserve.
29 You need to be punished,
and so I will take revenge.
30 Look at the terrible things
going on in this country.
I am shocked!

See also: **5.21:** Isa 6.9,10; Ezek 12.2; Mark 8.18.
5.22: Job 38.8–11.

711

³¹ Prophets give their messages
  in the name of a false god,'
  my priests don't want to serve me,'
  and you — my own people —
  like it this way!
  But on the day of disaster,
  where will you turn for help?

CHAPTER 6

A warning for the people of Jerusalem

The LORD said:

¹ Run for your lives,
  people of Benjamin.
  Get out of Jerusalem.
  Sound a trumpet in Tekoa
  and light a signal fire
  in Beth-Haccherem.
  Soon you will be struck
  by disaster from the north.
²⁻³ Jerusalem is a lovely pasture,
  but shepherds will surround it
    and divide it up,
  then let their flocks
    eat all the grass.'
⁴ Kings will tell their troops,
    "If we reach Jerusalem
    in the morning,
  we'll attack at midday.
  But if we arrive later,
⁵ we'll attack after dark
    and destroy its fortresses."

⁶ I am the LORD All-Powerful,
  and I will command these armies
    to chop down trees
  and build a ramp up to the walls
    of Jerusalem.

People of Jerusalem,
  I must punish you
    for your injustice.
⁷ Evil pours from your city
  like water from a spring.
  Sounds of violent crimes
  echo within your walls;
  victims are everywhere,
    wounded and dying.

⁸ Listen to me,
  you people of Jerusalem and Judah.
  I will abandon you,
  and your land will become
    an empty desert.
⁹ I will tell your enemies
  to leave your nation bare
  like a vine stripped of grapes.
  I, the LORD All-Powerful,
    have spoken.

Jeremiah's anger

¹⁰ I have told the people
  that you, LORD,
    will punish them,
  but they just laugh
    and refuse to listen.
¹¹ Your anger against Judah
  flames up inside me,
  and I can't hold it in
    much longer.

The LORD's anger will sweep everyone away

The LORD answered:

Don't hold back my anger!
  Let it sweep away everyone —
  the children at play and all adults,
    young and old alike,
¹² I'll punish the people of Judah
    and give to others
  their houses and fields,
    as well as their wives.
  I, the LORD, have spoken.

¹³ Everyone is greedy and dishonest,
    whether poor or rich.
  Even the prophets and priests
    cannot be trusted.
¹⁴ All they ever offer
  to my deeply wounded people
    are empty hopes for peace.
¹⁵ They should be ashamed
  of their disgusting sins,
  but they don't even blush.
  And so, when I punish Judah,
  they will end up on the ground,
    dead like everyone else.
  I, the LORD, have spoken.

The people of Judah rejected God's way of life

¹⁶ The LORD said:

My people, when you stood
    at the crossroads,
  I told you, "Follow the road
    your ancestors took,
  and you will find peace."
  But you refused.
¹⁷ I also sent prophets
  to warn you of danger,
  but when they sounded the alarm,
    you paid no attention.
¹⁸⁻¹⁹ So I tell all nations on earth,
    "Watch what I will do!

See also: 6.12–15: Jer 8.10–12. 6.14: Ezek 13.10.

My people ignored me
and rejected my laws.
They planned to do evil,
and now the evil they planned
will happen to them."

²⁰ People of Judah,
you bring me incense from Sheba
and spices from distant lands.
You offer sacrifices of all kinds.
But why bother?
I hate these gifts of yours!
²¹ So I will put stumbling blocks
in your path,
and everyone will die,
including parents and children,
neighbours and friends.

An army from the north

²² The LORD said,

"Look towards the north,
where a powerful nation
has prepared for war.
²³ Its well-armed troops are cruel
and never show mercy.
Their galloping horses sound
like ocean waves
pounding on the shore.
This army will attack you,
lovely Jerusalem."

²⁴ Then the people said,

"Just hearing about them
makes us tremble with fear,
and we twist and turn in pain
like a woman giving birth."

²⁵ The LORD said,

"Don't work in your fields
or walk along the roads.
It's too dangerous.
The enemy is well armed
²⁶ and attacks without warning.
So mourn, my people, as though
your only child had died.
Wear clothes made of sackcloth*
and roll in the ash heap."

The LORD's people must be tested

The LORD said:

²⁷ Jeremiah, test my people
as though they were metal.
²⁸ And you'll find they are hard
like bronze and iron.

They are stubborn rebels,
always spreading lies.
²⁹⁻³⁰ Silver can be purified
in a fiery furnace,
but my people are too wicked
to be made pure,
and so I have rejected them.

CHAPTER 7

Jeremiah speaks in the temple

This is also told in Jeremiah 26.1–6

¹⁻³ The LORD told me to stand by the gate of
the temple* and to tell the people who were
going in that the LORD All-Powerful, the God
of Israel, had said:

Pay attention, people of Judah! Change
your ways and start living right, then I will
let you keep on living in your own country.*
⁴ Don't fool yourselves! My temple is here
in Jerusalem, but that doesn't mean I will
protect you. ⁵ I will keep you safe only if you
change your ways. Be fair and honest with
each other. ⁶ Stop taking advantage of
foreigners, orphans, and widows. Don't kill
innocent people. And stop worshipping
other gods. ⁷ Then I will let you enjoy a long
life in this land I gave your ancestors.

⁸ But just look at what is happening! You
put your trust in worthless lies. ⁹ You steal
and murder; you lie in court and are
unfaithful in marriage. You worship idols
and offer incense to Baal, when these gods
have never done anything for you. ¹⁰ And
then you come into my temple and worship
me! Do you think I will protect you so that
you can go on sinning? ¹¹ You are thieves,
and you have made my temple your hide-
out. But I've seen everything you have done.

¹² Go to Shiloh, where my sacred tent
once stood. Take a look at what I did there.
My people Israel sinned, and so I destroyed
Shiloh!

¹³ While you have been sinning, I have
been trying to talk to you, but you refuse to
listen. ¹⁴ Don't think this temple will protect
you. Long ago I told your ancestors to build
it and worship me here, but now I have
decided to tear it down, just as I destroyed
Shiloh. ¹⁵ And as for you, people of Judah,
I'm going to send you away from my land,
just as I sent away the people of Ephraim
and the other northern tribes.

See also: 7.11: Matt 21.13; Mark 11.17; Luke 19.46.
7.12–14: Josh 18.1; Psa 78.60; Jer 26.6.

---

*6.26 sackcloth: See the note at 4.8.

Punishment for worshipping other gods

The LORD said:

¹⁶ Jeremiah, don't pray for these people! I, the LORD, would refuse to listen. ¹⁷ Do you see what the people of Judah are doing in their towns and in the streets of Jerusalem? ¹⁸ Children gather firewood, their fathers build fires, and their mothers mix dough to bake bread for the goddess they call the Queen of Heaven.* They even offer wine sacrifices to other gods, just to insult me. ¹⁹ But they are not only insulting me; they are also insulting themselves by doing these shameful things.

²⁰ And now, I, the LORD All-Powerful, will flood Judah with my fiery anger until nothing is left — no people or animals, no trees or crops.

It is useless to offer sacrifices

²¹ The LORD told me to say to the people of Judah:

I am the LORD All-Powerful, the God of Israel, but I won't accept sacrifices from you. So don't even bother bringing them to me. You might as well just cook the meat for yourselves.

²² At the time I brought your ancestors out of Egypt, I didn't command them to offer sacrifices to me. ²³ Instead, I told them, "If you listen to me and do what I tell you, I will be your God, you will be my people, and all will go well for you." ²⁴ But your ancestors refused to listen. They were stubborn, and whenever I wanted them to go one way, they always went the other. ²⁵ Ever since your ancestors left Egypt, I have been sending my servants the prophets to speak for me. ²⁶ But you have ignored me and become even more stubborn and sinful than your ancestors ever were!

Slaughter Valley

The LORD said:

²⁷ Jeremiah, no matter what you do, the people won't listen. ²⁸ So you must say to them:

People of Judah, I am the LORD your God, but you have refused to obey me, and you didn't change when I punished you. And

now, you no longer even pretend to be faithful to me.

²⁹ Shave your head bald
   and throw away the hair.
Sing a funeral song
   on top of a barren hill.
You people have made me angry,
   and I have abandoned you.

³⁰ You have disobeyed me by putting your disgusting idols in my temple, and now the temple itself is disgusting to me. ³¹ At Topheth in Hinnom Valley you have built altars where you kill your children and burn them as sacrifices to other gods. I would never think of telling you to do this. ³² So watch out! Some day that place will no longer be called Topheth or Hinnom Valley. It will be called Slaughter Valley, because you will bury your dead there until you run out of room, ³³ and then bodies will lie scattered on the ground. Birds and wild animals will come and eat, and no one will be around to scare them off. ³⁴ When I have finished with your land, there will be deathly silence in the empty ruins of Jerusalem and the towns of Judah — no happy voices, no sounds of parties or wedding celebrations.

CHAPTER 8

The LORD said:

¹ Then the bones of the dead kings of Judah and their officials will be dug up, along with the bones of the priests, the prophets, and everyone else in Jerusalem ² who loved and worshipped the sun, moon, and stars. These bones will be scattered and left lying on the ground like rubbish, where the sun and moon and stars can shine on them.

³ Some of you people of Judah will be left alive, but I will force you to go to foreign countries, and you will wish you were dead. I, the LORD God All-Powerful, have spoken.

The people took the wrong road

⁴ The LORD said:

People of Jerusalem,
when you stumble and fall,
   you get back up,
and if you take a wrong road,
   you turn round and go back.'

---

*7.18 Queen of Heaven: Probably another name for the goddess Astarte.

See also: 7.18: Jer 44.17-19.

See also: 7.31: a 2 King 23.10; Jer 32.35; b Lev 18.21. 7.34: Jer 16.9; 25.10; Rev 18.23.

⁵ So why do you refuse
  to come back to me?
Why do you hold so tightly
  to your false gods?

⁶ I listen carefully,
  but none of you admit
  that you've done wrong.
Without a second thought,
  you run down the wrong road•
  like cavalry troops
  charging into battle.

⁷ Storks, doves, swallows,
  and thrushes
all know when it's time
  to fly away for the winter
  and when to come back.
But you, my people,
  don't know what I demand.

⁸ You say, "We are wise
because we have the teachings
  and laws of the LORD."
But I say that your teachers
  have turned my words into lies!

⁹ Your wise men have rejected what I say,
  and so they have no wisdom.
Now they will be trapped
  and put to shame;
  they won't know what to do.

¹⁰ I'll give their wives and fields
  to strangers.

Everyone is greedy and dishonest,
  whether poor or rich.
Even the prophets and priests
  cannot be trusted.

¹¹ All they ever offer
to my deeply wounded people
  are empty hopes for peace.

¹² They should be ashamed
of their disgusting sins,
  but they don't even blush.
And so, when I punish Judah,
  they will end up on the ground,
  dead like everyone else.

¹³ I will wipe them out.•
They are vines without grapes;
fig trees without figs or leaves.
They have not done a thing
  that I told them!•
I, the LORD, have spoken.

The people and their punishment

¹⁴ The people of Judah
  say to each other,
"What are we waiting for?

Let's run to a town with walls
  and die there.
We rebelled against the LORD,
  and we were sentenced to die
  by drinking poison.

¹⁵ We had hoped for peace
  and a time of healing,
  but all we got was terror.

¹⁶ Our enemies have reached
  the town of Dan in the north,
  and the snorting of their horses
  makes us tremble with fear.
The enemy will destroy Jerusalem
  and our entire nation.
  No one will survive."

¹⁷ "Watch out!" the LORD says.
"I'm sending poisonous snakes
  to attack you,
  and no one can stop them."

Jeremiah mourns for his people

¹⁸ I'm burdened with sorrow
  and feel like giving up.

¹⁹ In a foreign land
  my people are crying.
Listen! You'll hear them say,
"Has the LORD deserted Zion?
  Is he no longer its king?"

I hear the LORD reply,
"Why did you make me angry
  by worshipping useless idols?"

²⁰ The people complain,
"Spring and summer
  have come and gone,
  but still the LORD
  hasn't rescued us."

²¹ My people are crushed,
  and so is my heart.
  I am horrified and mourn.

²² If medicine and doctors
  may be found in Gilead,
  why aren't my people healed?

CHAPTER 9

¹ I wish that my eyes
  were fountains of tears,
so I could cry day and night
  for my people who were killed.

² I wish I could go into the desert
  and find a hiding place
from all who are treacherous
  and unfaithful to God.

See also: 8.10–12: Jer 6.12–15. **8.11:** Ezek 13.10.

The LORD answers Jeremiah

3 The LORD replied:

Lies come from the mouths
of my people,
    like arrows from a bow.
With each dishonest deed
    their power increases,
and not one of them will admit
    that I am God.

4 Jeremiah, all your friends
    and relatives
tell lies about you,
    so don't trust them.
5 They wear themselves out,
    always looking for a new way
    to cheat their friends.
6 Everyone takes advantage
    of everyone else,
and no one will admit
    that I am God.

7 And so I will purify
    the hearts of my people
just as gold is purified in a furnace.
    I have no other choice.
8 They say they want peace,
    but this lie is deadly,
like an arrow that strikes
    when you least expect it.
9 Give me one good reason
    not to punish them
    as they deserve.
I, the LORD All-Powerful, have spoken.

Jeremiah weeps for his people

10 I weep for the pasture land
    in the hill country.
It's so barren and scorched
    that no one travels there.
No cattle can be found there,
    and birds and wild animals
    have all disappeared.
11 I heard the LORD reply,
    "When I have finished,
Jerusalem and the towns of Judah
    will be piles of ruins
    where only jackals* live."

Why the land was destroyed

12 I said to the LORD, "None of us can
understand why the land has become like an
uncrossable desert. Won't you explain why?"

13 The LORD said:

I destroyed the land because the people
disobeyed me and rejected my laws and
teachings. 14 They were stubborn and
worshipped Baal,* just as their ancestors
did. 15 So I, the LORD All-Powerful, the God
of Israel, promise them poison to eat and
drink.* 16 I'll scatter them in foreign
countries that they and their ancestors
have never even heard of. Finally, I will
send enemy soldiers to kill every last one
of them.

The women who are paid to weep

17 The LORD All-Powerful said,
    "Send for the women
    who are paid to weep
    at funerals,*
    especially the women
    who can cry the loudest."

18 The people answered,
    "Let them come quickly
    and cry for us,
until our own eyes
    are flooded with tears.
19 Now those of us on Zion cry,
    'We are ruined!
    We can't stand the shame.
Our homes have been destroyed,
    and we must leave our land.'

20 "We ask you women
    to pay attention
    to what the LORD says.
We will teach you a funeral song
    that you can teach
    your daughters and friends:
21 'We were in our fortress,
    but death sneaked in
    through our windows.
It even struck down
    children at play
    and our strongest young men.'

22 "The LORD has told us
    the ground will be covered
    with dead bodies,
like stalks of ungathered grain
    or like manure."

9.11 jackals: Desert animals related to wolves, but
smaller.

9.17 women . . . weep at funerals: Or "the women
who weep for Baal"; the god Baal was believed to
have died and come back to life, and some women
would go to places of worship and weep over the
death of Baal.

What the LORD likes best

23 The LORD says:

Don't boast about your wisdom
or strength or wealth.
24 If you feel you must boast,
then have enough sense
to boast about worshipping me,
the LORD.
What I like best
is showing kindness,
justice, and mercy
to everyone on earth.

25-26 Some day I will punish the nations of
Egypt, Edom, Ammon, and Moab, and the
tribes of the desert.• The men of these
nations are circumcised, but they don't
worship me. And it's the same with you
people of Judah. Your bodies are
circumcised, but your hearts are unchanged.

CHAPTER 10

The LORD talks about idols

1-2 The LORD said:

Listen to me,
you people of Israel.
Don't follow the customs
of those nations
who become frightened
when they see something strange
happen in the sky.
3 Their religion is worthless!
They chop down a tree,
carve the wood into an idol,
4 cover it with silver and gold,
and then nail it down
so it won't fall over.

5 An idol is no better
than a scarecrow.
It can't speak,
and it has to be carried,
because it can't walk.
Why worship an idol
that can't help or harm you?

Jeremiah praises the LORD

6 Our LORD, great and powerful,
you alone are God.
7 You are King of the nations.
Everyone should worship you.
No human anywhere on earth
is wiser than you.

8 Idols are worthless,
and anyone who worships them
is a fool!
9 Idols are made by humans.
A carver shapes the wood.
A metalworker hammers out
a covering of gold from Uphaz
or of silver from Tarshish.
Then the idol is dressed
in blue and purple clothes.

10 You, LORD, are the only true
and living God.
You will rule for all time.
When you are angry
the earth shakes,
and nations are destroyed.

11 You told me to say
that idols did not create
the heavens and the earth,
and that you, the LORD,
will destroy every idol.

12 With your wisdom and power
you created the earth
and spread out the heavens.
13 The waters in the heavens roar
at your command.
You make clouds appear —
you send the winds
from your storehouse
and make lightning flash
in the rain.

14 People who make idols
are so stupid!
They will be disappointed,
because their false gods
are not alive.
15 Idols are merely a joke,
and when the time is right,
they will be destroyed.

16 But you, Israel's God,
created all things,
and you chose Israel
to be your very own.
Your name is the LORD
All-Powerful.

Judah will be thrown from its land

17 I said to the people of Judah,
"Gather your things;
you are surrounded.
18 The LORD said these troubles
will lead to your capture,
and he will throw you from this land
like a stone from a sling."•

See also: 9.24: 1 Cor 1.31; 2 Cor 10.17. **10.7:** Rev 15.4.

¹⁹ The people answered,
"We are wounded
and doomed to die.
Why did we say
we could stand the pain?
²⁰ Our homes are destroyed;
our children are dead.
No one is left
to help us find shelter."

²¹ But I told them,
"Our leaders were stupid failures,
because they refused
to listen to the LORD.
And so we've been scattered
like sheep.

²² "Sounds of destruction
rumble from the north
like distant thunder.
Soon our towns will be ruins
where jackals* live."

Jeremiah prays

²³ I know, LORD, that we humans
are not in control
of our own lives.
²⁴ Correct me, as I deserve,
but not in your anger,
or I will be dead.
²⁵ Our enemies refuse
to admit that you are God
or to worship you.
They have wiped out our people
and left our nation
lying in ruins.
So get angry
and sweep them away!

CHAPTER 11

Judah has broken the LORD's agreement

¹⁻³ The LORD God told me to say to the people of Judah and Jerusalem:

I, the LORD, am warning you that I will put a curse on anyone who doesn't keep the agreement I made with Israel. So pay attention to what it says. ⁴ My commands haven't changed since I brought your ancestors out of Egypt, a nation that seemed like a blazing furnace where iron ore is melted. I told your ancestors that if they obeyed my commands, I would be their God, and they would be my people.

⁵ Then I did what I had promised and gave them this wonderful land, where you now live.

"Yes, LORD," I replied, "that's true."
⁶ Then the LORD told me to say to everyone in the streets of Jerusalem and in the towns of Judah:

Pay attention to the commands in my agreement with you. ⁷ Ever since I brought your ancestors out of Egypt, I have been telling your people to obey me. But you and your ancestors ⁸ have always been stubborn. You have refused to listen, and instead you have done whatever your sinful hearts have desired.

You have not kept the agreement we made, so I will make you suffer every curse that goes with it.

⁹ The LORD said to me:

Jeremiah, the people of Judah and Jerusalem are plotting against me. ¹⁰ They have sinned in the same way their ancestors did, by turning from me and worshipping other gods. The northern kingdom of Israel broke the agreement I made with your ancestors, and now the southern kingdom of Judah* has done the same.

¹¹ Here is what I've decided to do. I will bring suffering on the people of Judah and Jerusalem, and no one will escape. They will beg me to help, but I won't listen to their prayers. ¹²⁻¹³ Then they will offer sacrifices to their other gods and ask them for help. After all, the people of Judah have more gods than towns, and more altars for Baal than there are streets in Jerusalem. But those gods won't be able to rescue the people of Judah from disaster.

¹⁴ Jeremiah, don't pray for these people or beg me to rescue them. If you do, I won't listen, and I certainly won't listen if they pray!

¹⁵ Then the LORD told me to say to the people of Judah:

You are my chosen people,
but you have no right
to be here in my temple,
doing such terrible things.
The sacrifices you offer me
won't protect you from disaster,
so stop celebrating.

---

*10.22 jackals: See the note at 9.11.
718

*11.10 Israel . . . Judah: See the note at 2.4.

16 Once you were like an olive tree
    covered with fruit.
  But soon I will send a noisy mob
    to break off your branches
    and set you on fire.

17 I am the LORD All-Powerful. You people of
Judah were like a tree that I had planted, but
you have made me angry by offering
sacrifices to Baal, just as the northern
kingdom did. And now I'm going to pull
you up by the roots.

The plot to kill Jeremiah

18-19Some people plotted to kill me.
    And like a lamb
      being led to the butcher,
    I knew nothing about their plans.
  But then the LORD told me
    that they had planned
  to chop me down like a tree —
    fruit and all —
  so that no one would ever
    remember me again.

20 I prayed, "LORD All-Powerful,
    you always do what is right,
    and you know every thought.
  So I trust you to help me
    and to take revenge."

21 Then the LORD said:

  Jeremiah, some men from Anathoth* say
  they will kill you, if you keep on speaking
  for me. 22 But I will punish them. Their
  young men will die in battle, and their
  children will starve to death. 23 And when I
  have finished, no one from their families
  will be left alive.

CHAPTER 12

Jeremiah complains to the LORD

1 Whenever I complain to you, LORD,
    you are always fair.
  But now I have questions
    about your justice.
  Why is life easy for sinners?
    Why are they successful?

2 You plant like trees;
    you let them prosper and produce fruit.
  Yet even when they praise you,
    they don't mean it.

3 But you know, LORD,
    how faithful I've always been,
    even in my thoughts.

  So drag my enemies away
    and butcher them like sheep!

4 How long will the ground be dry
    and the pasture lands parched?
  The birds and animals
    are dead and gone.
  And all this happened because
    the people are so sinful.
  They even boast, "God can't see
    the sins we commit."

The LORD answers Jeremiah

The LORD said:

5 Jeremiah, if you get tired
    in a race against people,
  how can you possibly run
    against horses?
  If you fall in open fields,
    what will happen in the forest
    along the River Jordan?

6 Even your own family
    has turned against you.
  They act friendly,
    but don't trust them.
  They're out to get you,
    and so is everyone else.

The LORD is furious with his people

The LORD said:

7 I loved my people and chose them
    as my very own.
  But now I will reject them
    and hand them over
    to their enemies.

8 My people have turned against me
    and roar at me like lions.
  That's why I hate them.

9 My people are like a hawk
    surrounded and attacked
    by other hawks.
  Tell the wild animals
    to come and eat their fill.

10 My beautiful land is ruined
    like a field or a vineyard
  trampled by shepherds
    and stripped bare
    by their flocks.

11 Every field I see lies barren,
    and no one cares.

12 A destroying army
    marches along desert roads
    and attacks everywhere.
  They are my deadly sword;
    no one is safe from them.

---

*11.21 Anathoth: Jeremiah's home town (see 1.1).

13 My people, you planted wheat,
    but because I was furious,
    I let only weeds grow.
You wore yourselves out for nothing!

The LORD will have pity
on other nations

14 The LORD said:

I gave this land to my people Israel, but
enemies around it have attacked and robbed
it. So I will uproot them from their own
countries just as I will uproot Judah from its
land. 15 But later, I will have pity on these
nations and bring them back to their own
lands. 16 They once taught my people to
worship Baal. But if they admit I am the only
true God, and if they let my people teach
them how to worship me, these nations will
also become my people. 17 However, if they
don't listen to me, I will uproot them from
their lands and completely destroy them.
I, the LORD, have spoken.

CHAPTER 13

Jeremiah's linen shorts

1 The LORD told me, "Go and buy a pair of
linen shorts. Wear them for a while, but don't
wash them." 2 So I bought a pair of shorts and
put them on.

3 Then the LORD said, 4 "Take off the shorts.
Go to Parah* and hide the shorts in a crack
between some large rocks." 5 And that's what
I did.

6 Some time later the LORD said, "Go back
and get the shorts." 7 I went back and dug the
shorts out of their hiding place, but the cloth
had rotted, and the shorts were ruined.

8 Then the LORD said:

9 Jeremiah, I will use Babylonia to* destroy
the pride of the people of Judah and
Jerusalem. 10 The people of Judah are evil
and stubborn. So instead of listening to me,
they do whatever they want and even
worship other gods. When I have finished
with these people, they will be good for
nothing, just like this pair of shorts. 11 These
shorts were tight around your waist, and
that's how tightly I held on to the kingdoms
of Israel and Judah. I wanted them to be my
people. I wanted to make them famous, so
that other nations would praise and honour
me, but they refused to obey me.

Wine jars

The LORD said:

12 Jeremiah, tell the people of Judah, "The
LORD God of Israel orders you to fill your
wine jars with wine."

They will answer, "Of course we fill our
wine jars with wine! Why are you telling us
something we already know?"

13 Then say to them:

I am the LORD, and what I'm going to do
will make everyone in Judah and Jerusalem
appear to be full of wine. And the worst
ones will be the kings of David's family
and the priests and the prophets. 14 Then
I will smash them against each other like
jars. I will have no pity on the young or the
old, and they will all be destroyed. I, the
LORD, have spoken.

The people of Judah
will be taken away

15 People of Judah,
    don't be too proud to listen
    to what the LORD has said.
16 You hope for light,
    but God is sending darkness.
Evening shadows already deepen
    in the hills.
So return to God
    and confess your sins to him
    before you trip and fall.
17 If you are too proud to listen,
    I will weep alone.
Tears will stream from my eyes
    when the LORD's people
    are taken away as prisoners.

18 The LORD told me to tell you
    that your king and his mother*
    must surrender their thrones
    and remove their crowns.'
19 The cities in the Southern Desert
    are surrounded;
    no one can get in or out.
Everyone in Judah will be taken away.
20 Jerusalem, you were so proud
    of ruling the people of Judah.
    But where are they now?

Look north, and you will see
    your enemies approaching.
21 You once trusted them to help,
    but now I'll let them rule you.'

---

*13.4 Parah: Or "the River Euphrates". Parah was a
village about nine kilometres north-east of Jerusalem.
720

*13.18 mother: The king's mother usually had an
important position in the royal court.

What do you say about that?
You will be in pain
    like a woman giving birth.

22 Do you know why
    your clothes were torn off
    and you were abused?
It was because of your terrible sins.

23 Can you ever change
    and do what's right?
Can people change the colour
    of their skin,
or can a leopard remove its spots?
If so, then perhaps you can change
    and learn to do right.

24 I will scatter you,
    just as the desert wind
blows husks from grain
    tossed in the air.

25 I won't change my mind.
I, the LORD, have spoken.

You rejected me
    and worshipped false gods.

26-27 You were married to me,
    but you were unfaithful.
You even became a prostitute*
by worshipping disgusting gods
    on hilltops and in fields.
So I'll rip off your clothes
and leave you naked and ashamed
    for everyone to see.
You are doomed!
Will you ever be worthy
    to worship me again?

CHAPTER 14

The land dries up

1 When there had been no rain for a long
time, the LORD told me to say to the people:

2 Judah and Jerusalem weep
    as the land dries up.

3 Rulers send their servants
    to the storage pits for water.*
But there's none to be found;
    they return in despair
    with their jars still empty.

4 There has been no rain,
    and farmers feel sick
as they watch cracks appear
    in their dry ground.'

---

*13.26,27 prostitute: See the note at 2.20.
*14.3 storage pits for water: Since water was scarce,
pits were dug into solid rock for collecting and
storing rainwater. These pits were called "cisterns".

---

5 A deer gives birth in a field,
    then abandons her newborn fawn
    and leaves in search of grass.

6 Wild donkeys go blind from starvation.
So they stand on barren hilltops
    and sniff the air,'
    hoping to smell green grass.

The LORD's people pray

7 Our terrible sins may demand
    that we be punished.
But if you rescue us, LORD,
    everyone will see
    how great you are.

8 You're our only hope;
    you alone can save us now.
You help us one day,
    but you're gone the next.

9 Did this disaster take you by surprise?
Are you a warrior
    with your hands tied?
You have chosen us,
    and your temple is here.
    Don't abandon us!

The LORD's answer

The LORD said:

10 My people,
    you love to wander away;
you don't even try
    to stay close to me.
So now I will reject you
    and punish you for your sins.
I, the LORD, have spoken.

Lying prophets

11 The LORD said, "Jeremiah, don't ask me to
help these people. 12 They may even go
without eating* and offer sacrifices to please
me* and to give thanks.* But when they cry
out for my help, I won't listen, and I won't

---

*14.12 go without eating: The people of Israel
sometimes went without eating to show sorrow for
their sins.
*14.12 sacrifices to please me: These sacrifices have
traditionally been called "whole burnt offerings"
because the whole animal was burnt on the altar.
A main purpose of such sacrifices was to please the LORD
with the smell of the sacrifice, and so in the CEV they are
sometimes called "sacrifices to please the LORD".
*14.12 sacrifices . . . to give thanks: These sacrifices
have traditionally been called "grain offerings". A main
purpose of such sacrifices was to thank the LORD with a
gift of grain, and so in the CEV they are sometimes
called "sacrifices to give thanks to the LORD".

13 I replied, "The other prophets keep telling everyone that you won't send starvation or war, and that you're going to give us peace."

14 The LORD answered:

They claim to speak for me, but they're lying! I didn't even speak to them, much less choose them to be my prophets. Their messages come from worthless dreams, useless fortune-telling, and their own imaginations.

15 Those lying prophets say that there will be peace and plenty of food. But I say that those same prophets will die from war and hunger.
16 And everyone who listens to them will be killed, just as they deserve. Their dead bodies will be thrown out into the streets of Jerusalem, because their families will also be dead, and no one will be left to bury them.*
17 Jeremiah, go and tell the people how you feel about all this.

So I told them:

"Tears will flood my eyes
    both day and night,
because my nation suffers
    from a deadly wound.
18 In the fields I see the bodies
    of those killed in battle.
And in the towns I see crowds
    dying of hunger.
But the prophets and priests
    go about their business,
without understanding
    what has happened."*

Jeremiah prays to the LORD

19 Have you rejected Judah, LORD?
    Do you hate Jerusalem?
Why did you strike down Judah
    with a fatal wound?
We had hoped for peace
    and a time of healing,
but all we got was terror.
20 We and our ancestors are guilty
    of rebelling against you.
21 If you save us, it will show
    how great you are.
Don't let our enemies
    disgrace your temple,
    your beautiful throne.
Don't forget that you promised
    to rescue us.

22 Idols can't send rain,
    and showers don't fall
    by themselves.
Only you control the rain,
    so we put our trust in you,
    the LORD our God.

CHAPTER 15

The people of Judah will die

1 The LORD said to me:

Even if Moses and Samuel were here,
praying with you, I wouldn't change my
mind. So send the people of Judah away.
2 And when they ask where they are going,
tell them that I, the LORD, have said:

Some of you are going to die
    of horrible diseases.
Others are going to die in war
    or from starvation.
The rest will be led away
    to a foreign country.
3 I will punish you
    in four different ways:
You will be killed in war
    and your bodies dragged off by dogs,
your flesh will be eaten by birds,
    and your bones will be chewed on
    by wild animals.
4 This punishment will happen
    because of the horrible things*
    your King Manasseh* did.
And you will be disgusting
    to all nations on earth.
5 People of Jerusalem,
    who will feel sorry for you?
Will anyone bother
    to ask if you are well?

6 My people, you abandoned me
    and walked away.
I am tired of showing mercy;
    that's why I'll destroy you
7 by scattering you like straw
    blown by the wind.
I will punish you with sorrow and death,
    because you refuse
    to change your ways.
8 There will be more widows in Judah
    than grains of sand on a beach.

---

*14.16 dead bodies . . . bury them: A proper burial was considered very important.

722

*15.4 the horrible things: See 2 Kings 21.1–16.
*15.4 Manasseh: Hebrew "Manasseh son of Hezekiah"; he ruled 687–642 BC.

See also: 15.1: a Exod 32.11–14; Num 14.13–19;
b 1 Sam 7.5–9. 15.2: Rev 13.10. 15.4: 2 King 21.1–16;
2 Chron 33.1–9.

A surprise attack at midday!
And the mothers in Jerusalem
mourn for their children.
⁹ A mother is in deep despair
and struggles for breath.
Her daylight has turned
to darkness —
she has suffered the loss
of her seven sons.

I will kill anyone who survives.
I, the LORD, have spoken.

Jeremiah complains

¹⁰ I wish I had never been born!
I'm always in trouble
with everyone in Judah.
I never lend or borrow money,
but everyone curses me
just the same.

¹¹ Then the LORD replied,
"I promise to protect you,
and when disaster comes,
even your enemies
will beg you for help."'

The enemy cannot be defeated

The LORD told me to say:

¹² People of Judah,
just as you can't break iron
mixed with bronze,
you can't defeat the enemies
who will attack from the north.
¹³ I will give them
everything you own,
because you have sinned
everywhere in your country.
¹⁴ My anger is a fire
that cannot be put out,'
so I will make you slaves
of your enemies
in a foreign land.'

Jeremiah complains again

¹⁵ You can see how I suffer
insult after insult,
all because of you, LORD.
Don't be so patient
with my enemies;
take revenge on them
before they kill me.

¹⁶ When you spoke to me,
I was glad to obey,
because I belong to you,
the LORD All-Powerful.

¹⁷ I don't go to parties
and have a good time.
Instead, I keep to myself,
because you have filled me
with your anger.

¹⁸ I am badly injured
and in constant pain.
Are you going to disappoint me,
like a stream that goes dry
in the heat of summer?

The LORD replies

¹⁹ Then the LORD told me:

Stop talking like a fool!
If you turn back to me
and speak my message,
I will let you be my prophet
once again.
I hope the people of Judah
will accept what you say.
But you can ignore their threats,
²⁰⁻²¹because I am making you strong,
like a bronze wall.
They are evil and violent,
but when they attack,
I will be there to rescue you.
I, the LORD, have spoken.

CHAPTER 16

Jeremiah must live his message

¹ The LORD said to me:

² Jeremiah, don't get married and have
children — Judah is no place to raise a
family. ³ I'll tell you what's going to happen
to children and their parents here. ⁴ They
will die of horrible diseases and of war and
starvation. No one will give them a funeral
or bury them,* and their bodies will be
food for the birds and wild animals. And
what's left will lie on the ground like
manure.

⁵ When someone dies, don't visit the
family or show any sorrow. I will no
longer love or bless or have any pity on
the people of Judah. ⁶ Rich and poor
alike will die and be left unburied. No
one will mourn and show their sorrow by
cutting themselves or shaving their heads.*
⁷ No one will bring food and wine to help

---

*16.4 bury them: See the note at 14.16.
*16.6 mourn and show their sorrow by cutting
themselves or shaving their heads: A custom in
some Canaanite religions.

comfort those who are mourning the death of their father or mother.

8 Don't even set foot in a house where there is eating and drinking and celebrating. 9 Warn the people of Judah that I, the LORD All-Powerful, will put an end to all their parties and wedding celebrations. 10 They will ask, "Why has the LORD our God threatened us with so many disasters? Have we done something wrong or sinned against him?"

11 Then tell them I have said:

People of Judah, your ancestors turned away from me; they rejected my laws and teachings and started worshipping other gods. 12 And you have done even worse! You are stubborn, and instead of obeying me, you do whatever evil comes to your mind. 13 So I will throw you into a land that you and your ancestors know nothing about, a place where you will have to worship other gods both day and night. And I won't feel the least bit sorry for you.

14 A time will come when you will again worship me. But you will no longer call me the Living God who rescued Israel from Egypt. 15 Instead, you will call me the Living God who rescued you from that country in the north and from the other countries where I had forced you to go.

Some day I will bring you back to this land that I gave your ancestors. 16 But for now, I am sending enemies who will catch you like fish and hunt you down like wild animals in the hills and the caves.

17 I can see everything you are doing, even if you try to hide your sins from me. 18 I will punish you double for your sins, because you have made my own land disgusting. You have filled it with lifeless idols that remind me of dead bodies.

The LORD gives strength

I prayed to the LORD:

19 Our LORD, you are the one
    who gives me strength
    and protects me like a fortress
    when I am in trouble.
People will come to you
    from distant nations and say,
"Our ancestors worshipped
    false and useless gods,
20 worthless idols
    made by human hands."

21 Then the LORD replied,
    "That's why I will teach them
        about my power,
    and they will know
        that I am the true God."

CHAPTER 17

The LORD will punish Judah

The LORD said:

1 People of Judah,
    your sins cannot be erased.
They are written on your hearts
    like words chiselled in stone
    or carved on the corners
    of your altars.*
2-3 One generation after another
    has set up pagan altars
and worshipped the goddess Asherah
    everywhere in your country —
    on hills and mountains,
    and under large trees.
So I'll take everything you own,
    including your altars,
    and give it all to your enemies.▸
4 You will lose▸ the land
    that I gave you,
and I will make you slaves
    in a foreign country,
because you have made my anger
    blaze up like a fire
    that won't stop burning.

Trust the LORD

The LORD said:

5 I, the LORD, have put a curse
    on those who turn from me
    and trust in human strength.
6 They will dry up like a bush
    in salty desert soil,
    where nothing can grow.

7 But I will bless those who trust me.
8 They will be like trees
    growing beside a stream —
    trees with roots that reach
        down to the water,
    and with leaves
        that are always green.

---

*17.1 carved on the corners of your altars: When sacrifices were offered to the LORD to ask him to forgive sins, some of the blood was smeared on the corners of the altar (see Leviticus 4.7,18–20,25,26,30,31,34,35; 16.18). But now the LORD refuses to accept these sacrifices.

See also: 16.9: Jer 7.34; 25.10; Rev 18.23.

See also: 17.8: Psa 1.3.

They bear fruit every year
and are never worried
by a lack of rain.

⁹ You people of Judah
are so deceitful
that you even fool yourselves,
and you can't change.
¹⁰ But I know your deeds
and your thoughts,
and I will make sure
you get what you deserve.
¹¹ You cheated others,
but everything you gained
will fly away, like birds
hatched from stolen eggs.
Then you will discover
what fools you are.

Jeremiah prays to the LORD

¹² Our LORD, your temple
is a glorious throne
that has stood on a mountain
from the beginning.
¹³ You are a spring of water
giving Israel life and hope.
But if the people reject
what you have told me,
they will be swept away
like words written in dust.ᵇ

¹⁴ You, LORD, are the one I praise.
So heal me and rescue me!
Then I will be completely well
and perfectly safe.

¹⁵ The people of Judah say to me,
"Jeremiah, you claimed to tell us
what the LORD has said.
So why hasn't it come true?"

¹⁶ Our LORD, you chose me
to care for your people,
and that's what I have done.
You know everything I have said,
and I have never once
asked you to punish them.ᵇ
¹⁷ I trust you for protection
in times of trouble,
so don't frighten me.
¹⁸ Keep me from failure
and disgrace,
but make my enemies fail
and be disgraced.
Send destruction to make
their worst fears come true.

Resting on the Sabbath

¹⁹⁻²⁰ The LORD said:

Jeremiah, stand at each city gate in
Jerusalem, including the one the king uses,
and speak to him and everyone else. Tell
them I have said:

I am the LORD, so pay attention. ²¹⁻²⁴ If you
value your lives, don't do any work on the
Sabbath. Don't carry anything through the
city gates or through the door of your
house, or anywhere else. Keep the Sabbath
day sacred!

I gave this command to your ancestors,
but they were stubborn and refused to
obey or to be corrected. But if you obey,
²⁵ then Judah and Jerusalem will always be
ruled by kings from David's family. The
king and his officials will ride through
these gates on horses or in chariots, and
the people of Judah and Jerusalem will be
with them. There will always be people
living in Jerusalem, ²⁶ and others will come
here from the nearby villages, from the
towns of Judah and Benjamin,* from the
hill country and the foothills to the west,
and from the Southern Desert. They will
bring sacrifices to please me and to give me
thanks,* as well as offerings of grain and
incense.

²⁷ But if you keep on carrying things
through the city gates on the Sabbath and
keep treating it as any other day, I will set
fire to these gates and burn down the
whole city, including the fortresses.

CHAPTER 18

Jeremiah goes to the pottery shop

¹ The LORD told me, ² "Go to the pottery
shop, and when you get there, I will tell you
what to say to the people."

³ I went there and saw the potter making
clay pots on his pottery wheel. ⁴ And
whenever the clay would not take the shape
he wanted, he would change his mind and
form it into some other shape.

⁵ Then the LORD told me to say:

⁶ People of Israel, I, the LORD, have power
over you, just as a potter has power over

*17.26 Judah and Benjamin: These two tribes made
up the southern kingdom of Judah.
*17.26 sacrifices to please me and to give me
thanks: See the notes at 14.12.
See also: 17.21: Neh 13.15–22. 17.22: Exod 20.8–10;
Deut 5.12–14.

clay. ⁷ If I threaten to uproot and shatter an evil nation ⁸ and that nation turns from its evil, I will change my mind.

⁹ If I promise to make a nation strong, ¹⁰ but its people start disobeying me and doing evil, then I will change my mind and not help them at all.

¹¹ So listen to me, people of Judah and Jerusalem! I have decided to strike you with disaster, and I won't change my mind unless you stop sinning and start living right. ¹² But I know you won't listen. You might as well answer, "We don't care what you say. We have made plans to sin, and we are going to be stubborn and do what we want!"

¹³ So I, the LORD, command you to ask the nations, and find out if they have ever heard of such a horrible sin as what you have done.

¹⁴ The snow on Lebanon's mountains
    never melts away,
    and the streams there
    never run dry.*

¹⁵ But you, my people,
    have turned from me
to burn incense to worthless idols.
You have left the ancient road
    to follow an unknown path
    where you stumble over idols.

¹⁶ Your land will be ruined,
    and every passer-by
will look at it with horror
    and make insulting remarks.

¹⁷ When your enemies attack,
    I will scatter you like dust
    blown by an eastern wind.
Then, on that day of disaster,
    I will turn my back on you.

The plot against Jeremiah

¹⁸ Some of the people said, "Let's get rid of Jeremiah! We will always have priests to teach us God's laws, as well as wise people to give us advice, and prophets to speak the LORD's messages. So, instead of listening to Jeremiah any longer, let's accuse him of a crime."

Jeremiah prays about his enemies

¹⁹ Please, LORD, answer my prayer.
    Make my enemies stop
    accusing me of evil.

²⁰ I tried to help them,
    but they are paying me back
    by digging a pit to trap me.
I even begged you
    not to punish them.

²¹ But now I am asking you
    to let their children starve
    or be killed in war.
Let women lose
    their husbands and sons
    to disease and violence.

²² These people have dug pits
    and set traps for me, LORD.
Make them scream in fear
    when you send enemy troops
    to attack their homes.

²³ You know they plan to kill me.
    So get angry and punish them!
Don't ever forgive
    their terrible crimes.

CHAPTER 19

Jeremiah and the clay jar

¹ The LORD said:

Jeremiah, go to the pottery shop and buy a clay jar. Then take along some of the city officials and leading priests ² and go to Hinnom Valley, just outside Potsherd* Gate. Tell the people that I have said:

³ I am the LORD All-Powerful, the God of Israel, and you kings of Judah and you people of Jerusalem had better pay attention. I am going to bring so much trouble on this valley that everyone who hears about it will be shocked. ⁴⁻⁵ The people of Judah stopped worshipping me and made this valley into a place of worship for Baal and other gods that have never helped them or their ancestors or their kings. And they have committed murder here, burning their young, innocent children as sacrifices to Baal. I have never even thought of telling you to do that. ⁶ So watch out! Some day this place will no longer be called Topheth or Hinnom Valley. It will be called Slaughter Valley!

⁷ You people of Judah and Jerusalem may have big plans, but here in this valley I'll ruin* those plans. I'll let your enemies kill you, and I'll tell the birds and wild animals to eat your dead bodies. ⁸ I will turn Jerusalem into a pile of rubble, and every passer-by will be shocked and horrified and will make insulting remarks. ⁹ And while your enemies are trying to break through

---

*19.2 Potsherd: A piece of broken pottery.
*19.7 ruin: In Hebrew "ruin" sounds like "jar" (see verse 1).
See also: 19.2: 2 King 23.10; Jer 7.30–32; 32.34,35.
19.5: Lev 18.21.

your city walls to kill you, the food supply will run out. You will become so hungry that you will eat the flesh of your friends and even of your own children.

¹⁰ Jeremiah, as soon as you have said this, smash the jar while the people are watching. ¹¹ Then tell them that I have also said:

I am the LORD All-Powerful, and I warn you that I will shatter Judah and Jerusalem just like this jar that is broken beyond repair. You will bury your dead here in Topheth, but so many of you will die that there won't be enough room.

¹²⁻¹³ I will make Jerusalem as unclean as Topheth, by filling the city with your dead bodies. I will do this because you and your kings have gone up to the roofs of your houses and burnt incense to the stars in the sky, as though they were gods. And you have given sacrifices of wine to foreign gods.

Jeremiah speaks in the temple courtyard

¹⁴ I went to Topheth, where I told the people what the LORD had said. Then I went to the temple courtyard and shouted to the people, ¹⁵ "Listen, everyone! Some time ago, the LORD All-Powerful, the God of Israel, warned us that he would bring disaster on Jerusalem and all nearby villages. But you were stubborn and refused to listen. Now the LORD is going to bring the disaster he promised."

CHAPTER 20

Pashhur arrests Jeremiah

¹ Pashhur son of Immer was a priest and the chief of temple security. He heard what I had said, ² and so he hit me.ᵃ Then he had me arrested and put in chains* at the Benjamin Gate in the LORD's temple.* ³ The next day, when Pashhur let me go free, I told him that the LORD had said:

No longer will I call you Pashhur. Instead, I will call you Afraid-of-Everything.ᵇ ⁴ You will be afraid, and you will bring fear to your friends as well. You will see enemies kill them in battle. Then I will make the king of Babylonia take everyone in Judah prisoner, killing some and dragging the rest away to Babylonia. ⁵ He will clean out

the royal treasury and take everything else of value from Jerusalem.

⁶ Pashhur, you are guilty of telling lies and claiming they were messages from me. That's why I will make the Babylonians take you, your family, and your friends as prisoners to Babylonia, where you will all die and be buried.

Jeremiah complains to the LORD

⁷ You tricked me, LORD,
    and I was really fooled.
You are stronger than I am,
    and you have defeated me.
People never stop sneering
    and insulting me.
⁸ You have let me announce
    only destruction and death.
Your message has brought me
    nothing but insults
    and trouble.
⁹ Sometimes I tell myself
    not to think about you, LORD,
    or even mention your name.
But your message burns
    in my heart and bones,
    and I cannot keep silent.

¹⁰ I heard the crowds whisper,
    "Everyone is afraid.
Now's our chance
    to accuse Jeremiah!"
All of my so-called friends
    are just waiting
    for me to make a mistake.
They say, "Perhaps Jeremiah
    can be tricked.
Then we can overpower him
    and get even at last."

¹¹ But you, LORD,
    are a mighty soldier,
    standing at my side.
Those troublemakers
    will fall down and fail —
    terribly embarrassed,
    for ever ashamed.

¹² LORD All-Powerful,
    you test those who do right,
    and you know every heart
    and mind.
I have told you my complaints,
    so let me watch you
    take revenge on my enemies.
¹³ I sing praises to you, LORD.
    You rescue the oppressed
    from the wicked.

---

*20.2 the Benjamin Gate in the LORD's temple: The Hebrew text has "the upper Benjamin Gate in the temple"; the lower Benjamin Gate may have been the city gate of that name.

¹⁴ Put a curse on the day I was born!
   Don't bless my mother.
¹⁵ Put a curse on the man
   who told my father, "Good news!
   You have a son."
¹⁶ May that man be like the towns
   you destroyed without pity.
   Let him hear shouts of alarm
   in the morning
   and battle cries at midday.
¹⁷ He deserves to die
   for not killing me
   before I was born.
   Then my mother's body
   would have been my grave."
¹⁸ Why did I have to be born?
   Was it just to suffer
   and die in shame?

CHAPTER 21

The LORD will fight against Jerusalem

¹ King Zedekiah* of Judah sent for Pashhur son of Malchiah and for a priest named Zephaniah son of Maaseiah. Then he told them, "Talk with Jeremiah for me."

So they came to me and said, ² "King Nebuchadnezzar* of Babylonia has attacked Judah. Please ask the LORD to work miracles for our people, as he has done in the past, so that Nebuchadnezzar will leave us alone."

³⁻⁷ I told them that the LORD God of Israel had told me to say to King Zedekiah:

The Babylonians have surrounded Jerusalem and want to kill you and your people. You are asking me to save you, but you have made me furious. So I will stretch out my mighty arm and fight against you myself. Your army is using spears and swords to fight the Babylonians, but I will make your own weapons turn and attack you. I will send a horrible disease to kill many of the people and animals in Jerusalem, and there will be nothing left to eat. Finally, I will let King Nebuchadnezzar and his army fight their way to the centre of Jerusalem and capture everyone who is left alive, including you and your officials. But Nebuchadnezzar won't be kind or show any mercy — he will have you killed! I, the LORD, have spoken.

⁸ Then I told them that the LORD had said:

People of Jerusalem, I, the LORD, give you the choice of life or death. ⁹ The Babylonian army has surrounded Jerusalem, so if you want to live, you must go out and surrender to them. But if you want to die because of hunger, disease, or war, then stay here in the city. ¹⁰ I have decided not to rescue Jerusalem. Instead, I am going to let the king of Babylonia burn it to the ground. I, the LORD, have spoken.

The LORD warns the king of Judah

The LORD said:

¹¹⁻¹² Pay attention, you who belong
   to the royal family.
   Each new day, make sure
   that justice is done,
   and rescue those
   who are being robbed.
   Or else my anger will flame up
   like a fire that never goes out.

¹³ Jerusalem,
   from your mountaintop
   you look out over the valleys*
   and think you are safe.
   But I, the LORD, am angry,
¹⁴ and I will punish you
   as you deserve.
   I'll set your palace* on fire,
   and everything around you
   will go up in smoke.

CHAPTER 22

The LORD will punish
the king of Judah

¹⁻³ The LORD sent me to the palace of the king of Judah to speak to the king, his officials, and everyone else who was there. The LORD told me to say:

I am the LORD, so pay attention! You have been allowing people to cheat, rob, and take advantage of widows, orphans, and foreigners who live here. Innocent people have become victims of violence, and some of them have even been killed. But now I command you to do what is right and see that justice is done. Rescue everyone who has suffered from injustice.

---

*21.1 Zedekiah: See the note at 1.3.
*21.2 Nebuchadnezzar: Ruled 605–562 BC.
See also: 20.14-18: Job 3.1-19. 21.2: 2 King 25.1-11;
2 Chron 36.17-21.

*21.14 your palace: The Hebrew text has "the forest"; the largest room in the king's palace was known as Forest Hall (see 1 Kings 7.2,3).

⁴ If you obey me, the kings from David's family will continue to rule Judah from this palace. They and their officials will ride in and out on their horses or in their chariots. ⁵ But if you ignore me, I promise in my own name that this palace will lie in ruins. ⁶ Listen to what I think about it:

> The palace of Judah's king
> is as glorious as Gilead
>   or Lebanon's highest peaks.
> But it will be as empty
>   as a ghost town
> when I'm through with it.
> ⁷ I'll send troops to tear it apart,
>   and its beautiful cedar beams
>   will be used for firewood.

⁸ People from different nations will pass by and ask, "Why did the LORD do this to such a great city as Jerusalem?" ⁹ Others will answer, "It's because the people worshipped foreign gods and broke the agreement that the LORD their God had made with them."

King Jehoahaz

The LORD said:

> ¹⁰ King Josiah is dead,
>   so don't cry for him.*
> Instead, cry for his son
>   King Jehoahaz,*
> dragged off to another country,
>   never to return.

¹¹⁻¹² Jehoahaz* became king of Judah after his father King Josiah died. But Jehoahaz was taken as a prisoner to a foreign country. Now I, the LORD, promise that he will die there without ever seeing his own land again.

King Jehoiakim

The LORD told me to say:

> ¹³⁻¹⁴ King Jehoiakim,* you are doomed!
> You built a palace
>   with large rooms upstairs.

> You put in big windows
> and used cedar panelling
>   and red paint.
> But you were unfair
> and forced the builders to work
>   without pay.

> ¹⁵⁻¹⁶ More cedar in your palace
>   doesn't make you a better king
>   than your father Josiah.
> He always did right —
>   he gave justice to the poor
>   and was honest.
> That's what it means
>   to truly know me.
> So he lived a comfortable life
>   and always had enough
>   to eat and drink.

> ¹⁷ But all you think about
>   is how to cheat
> or abuse or murder
>   some innocent victim.
> ¹⁸ Jehoiakim, no one will cry
>   at your funeral.
> They won't turn to each other
>   and ask,
> "Why did our great king have to die?"
> ¹⁹ You will be given a burial
>   fit for a donkey;
> your body will be dragged
>   outside the city gates
>   and tossed in the dust.
> I, the LORD, have spoken.

King Jehoiachin and the people of Jerusalem

The LORD told me to say:

> ²⁰ People of Jerusalem,
>   the nations* you trusted
>   have been crushed.
> Go to Lebanon and weep;
>   cry in the land of Bashan
>   and in Moab.
> ²¹ When times were good,
>   I warned you.
> But you ignored me,
>   just as you have done
>   since Israel was young.
> ²² Now you will be disgraced
>   because of your sins.
> Your leaders will be swept away
>   by the wind,
> and the nations you trusted
>   will be captured and dragged
>   to a foreign country.

---

*22.10 **King Josiah . . . him:** The Hebrew text has "don't cry for the dead one", meaning King Josiah, who ruled 640–609 BC.
*22.10 **his son, King Jehoahaz . . . country:** The Hebrew text has "the one who was dragged off to another country", meaning King Jehoahaz, who ruled for three months in 609 BC.
*22.13,14 **Jehoiakim:** See the note at 1.3.

See also: 22.5: Matt 23.28; Luke 13.35.
22.11: 2 King 23.31–34; 2 Chron 36.1–4.

See also: 22.18: 2 King 23.36–24.6; 2 Chron 36.5–7.

²³ Those who live in the palace
panelled with cedar*
will groan with pain
like women giving birth.

²⁴ King Jehoiachin,* son of Jehoiakim,*
even if you were the ring I wear as the sign
of my royal power, I would still pull you
from my finger. ²⁵ I would hand you over
to the enemy you fear, to King
Nebuchadnezzar* and his army, who want
to kill you. ²⁶ You and your mother* were
born in Judah, but I will throw both of you
into a foreign country, where you will die,
²⁷ longing to return home.

²⁸ Jehoiachin, you are unwanted
like a broken clay pot.
So you and your children
will be thrown into a country
you know nothing about.

²⁹ Land of Judah, I am the LORD.
Now listen to what I say!
³⁰ Erase the names
of Jehoiachin's children
from the royal records.
He is a complete failure,
and so none of them
will ever be king.
I, the LORD, have spoken.

CHAPTER 23

A message of hope

The LORD said:

¹ You leaders of my people are like
shepherds that kill and scatter the sheep.
² You were supposed to take care of my
people, but instead you chased them away.
So now I'll really take care of you, and
believe me, you will pay for your crimes!

³ I will bring the rest of my people home
from the lands where I have scattered them,
and they will grow into a mighty nation.

⁴ I promise to choose leaders who will care
for them like real shepherds. All my people
will be there, and they will never again be
frightened.

⁵ Some day I will appoint
an honest king
from the family of David,
a king who will be wise
and rule with justice.
⁶ As long as he is king,
Israel will have peace,
and Judah will be safe.
The name of this king will be
"The LORD Gives Justice".

⁷ A time will come when you will again
worship me. But you will no longer call me
the Living God who rescued Israel from
Egypt. ⁸ Instead, you will call me the Living
God who rescued you from the land in the
north and from all the other countries
where I had forced you to go. And you will
once again live in your own land.

Jeremiah thinks about unfaithful prophets

⁹ When I think of the prophets,
I am shocked, and I tremble*
like someone drunk,
because of the LORD
and his sacred words.
¹⁰ Those unfaithful prophets
misuse their power
all over the country.
So God turned the pasture lands
into scorching deserts.*

The LORD will punish unfaithful prophets

¹¹ The LORD told me to say:

You prophets and priests
think so little of me, the LORD,
that you even sin
in my own temple!
¹² Now I will punish you with disaster,
and you will slip and fall
in the darkness.
I, the LORD, have spoken.

¹³ The prophets in Samaria
were disgusting to me,
because they preached
in the name of Baal
and led my people astray.

---

*22.23 who live in the palace panelled with cedar:
The Hebrew text has "who live in Lebanon and who
nest among the cedars", which probably means
Forest Hall in the royal palace at Jerusalem, which
was panelled with cedar and had cedar columns and
a cedar ceiling, all from Lebanon (see 1 Kings 7.2,3).
*22.24 Jehoiachin: The Hebrew text has "Coniah",
another form of Jehoiachin's name; he ruled for three
months in 598 BC.
*22.24 Jehoiakim: See the note at 1.3.
*22.25 Nebuchadnezzar: See the note at 21.2.
*22.26 mother: See the note at 13.18.

See also: 22.24: 2 King 24.8–15; 2 Chron 36.9,10.

See also: 23.5,6: Jer 33.14–16.

14 And you prophets in Jerusalem
are even worse.
You're unfaithful in marriage[*]
and never tell the truth.[*]
You even lead others to sin
instead of helping them
turn back to me.
You and the people of Jerusalem
are evil like Sodom
and Gomorrah.[*]
15 You prophets in Jerusalem
have spread evil everywhere.
That's why I, the LORD, promise
to give you bitter poison
to eat and drink.

The LORD gives a warning

The LORD said:

16 Don't listen to the lies
of these false prophets,
you people of Judah!
The message they preach
is something they imagined;
it did not come from me,
the LORD All-Powerful.

17 These prophets go to people
who refuse to respect me
and who do whatever they want.
The prophets tell them,
"The LORD has promised
everything will be fine."

18 But I, the LORD, tell you
that these prophets
have never attended a meeting
of my council in heaven[*]
or heard him speak.

19 They are evil! So in my anger
I will strike them
like a violent storm.

20 I won't calm down,
until I have finished
what I have decided to do.
Some day you will understand
exactly what I mean.

21 I did not send these prophets
or speak to them,
but they ran to find you
and to preach their message.

22 If they had been in a meeting
of my council in heaven,
they would have told
you people of Judah
to give up your sins
and come back to me.

23 I am everywhere —
both near and far,
24 in heaven and on earth.
There are no secret places
where you can hide from me.

25 These unfaithful prophets claim that I
have given them a dream or a vision, and
then they tell lies in my name. 26 But
everything they say comes from their own
twisted minds. How long can this go on?
27 They tell each other their dreams and try
to get my people to reject me, just as their
ancestors left me and worshipped Baal.
28 Their dreams and my truth are as different
as straw and wheat. But when prophets
speak for me, they must say only what I
have told them. 29 My words are a powerful
fire; they are a hammer that shatters rocks.
30-32 These unfaithful prophets claim I
give them their dreams, but it isn't true. I
didn't choose them to be my prophets, and
yet they babble on and on, speaking in my
name, while stealing words from each
other. And when my people hear these liars,
they are led astray instead of being helped.
So I warn you that I am now the enemy of
these prophets. I, the LORD, have spoken.

News and nuisance

The LORD said to me:

33 Jeremiah, when a prophet or a priest or
anyone else comes to you and asks, "Does
the LORD have news for us?" tell them,
"You people are a nuisance[*] to the LORD,
and he[*] will get rid of you."

34 If any of you say, "Here is news from
the LORD," I will punish you and your
families, even if you are a prophet or a
priest. 35 Instead, you must ask your friends
and relatives, "What answer did the LORD
give?" or "What has the LORD said?" 36 It
seems that you each have your own news!
So if you say, "Here is news from the
LORD," you are twisting my words into a lie.
Remember that I am your God, the LORD
All-Powerful.

23.14 Sodom and Gomorrah: Two cities that the
LORD destroyed because their people were so evil
(see Genesis 18.16—19.29).
23.18 a meeting of my council in heaven:
Sometimes, prophets had visions of the LORD meeting
with his angels (see 1 Kings 22.19–23).
See also: 23.14: Gen 18.20; Ezek 16.49.

23.33 news . . . nuisance: The Hebrew word for
"news" in verses 33–38 is the same as "nuisance" and
is related to "pick up" in verse 39.

731

37 If you go to a prophet, it's all right to ask, "What answer did the LORD give to my question?" or "What has the LORD said?" 38 But if you disobey me and say, "Here is news from the LORD," 39 I will pick you up* and throw you far away. And I will abandon this city of Jerusalem that I gave to your ancestors. 40 You will never be free from your shame and disgrace.

CHAPTER 24

Jeremiah has a vision of two baskets of figs

1 The LORD spoke to me in a vision after King Nebuchadnezzar* of Babylonia had come to Judah and taken King Jehoiachin,* his officials, and all the skilled workers back to Babylonia. In this vision I saw two baskets of figs in front of the LORD's temple. 2 One basket was full of very good figs that ripened early, and the other was full of rotten figs that were not fit to eat.

3 "Jeremiah," the LORD asked, "what do you see?"

"Figs," I said. "Some are very good, but the others are too rotten to eat."

4 Then the LORD told me to say:

5 People of Judah, the good figs stand for those of you I sent away as exiles to Babylonia, 6 where I am watching over them. Then some day I will bring them back to this land. I will plant them, instead of uprooting them, and I will build them up, rather than tearing them down. 7 I will give them a desire to know me and to be my people. They will want me to be their God, and they will turn back to me with all their heart.

8 The rotten figs stand for King Zedekiah* of Judah, his officials, and all the others who were not taken away to Babylonia, whether they stayed here in Judah or went to live in Egypt. 9 I will punish them with a terrible disaster, and everyone on earth will tremble when they hear about it. I will force the people of Judah to go to foreign countries, where they will be cursed and insulted. 10 War and hunger and disease will strike them,

until they finally disappear from the land that I gave them and their ancestors.

CHAPTER 25

Seventy years of exile

1-2 In the fourth year that Jehoiakim was king of Judah,* which was the first year that Nebuchadnezzar* was king of Babylonia, the LORD told me to speak to the people of Judah and Jerusalem. So I told them:

3 For twenty-three years now, ever since the thirteenth year that Josiah* was king, I have been telling you what the LORD has told me. But you have not listened. 4 The LORD has sent prophets to you time after time, but you refused to listen. 5 They told you that the LORD had said:

Change your ways! If you stop doing evil, I will let you stay for ever in this land that I gave your ancestors. 6 I don't want to harm you. So don't make me angry by worshipping idols and other gods.

7 But you refused to listen to my prophets. So I, the LORD, say that you have made me angry by worshipping idols, and you are the ones who were hurt by what you did. 8 You refused to listen to me, 9 and now I will let you be attacked by nations from the north, and especially by my servant, King Nebuchadnezzar of Babylonia. You and other nearby nations will be destroyed and left in ruins for ever. Everyone who sees what has happened will be shocked, but they will still make fun of you. 10 I will put an end to your parties and wedding celebrations; no one will grind grain or be here to light the lamps at night. 11 This country will be as empty as a desert, because I will make all of you the slaves of the king of Babylonia for seventy years.

12 When that time is up, I will punish the king of Babylonia and his people for everything they have done wrong, and I will turn that country into a wasteland for ever. 13 My servant Jeremiah has told you what I said I will do to Babylonia and to the other nations, and he wrote it all down in this book. I will do everything I

---

*24.1 Nebuchadnezzar: See the note at 21.2.
*24.1 Jehoiachin: The Hebrew text has "Jeconiah", another form of Jehoiachin's name; he ruled for three months in 598 BC.
*24.8 Zedekiah: See the note at 1.3.
See also: 24.1: 2 King 24.12–16; 2 Chron 36.10.

*25.1,2 Jehoiakim . . . Judah: See the note at 1.3.
*25.1,2 Nebuchadnezzar: See the note at 21.2.
*25.3 Josiah: Hebrew "Josiah son of Amon"; see also the note at 1.2.
See also: 25.1: 2 King 24.1; 2 Chron 36.5–7; Dan 1.1,2. 25.10: a Jer 7.34; 16.9; b Rev 18.22,23. 25.11: 2 Chron 36.21; Jer 29.10; Dan 9.2.

threatened. [14] I will pay back the Babylonians for every wrong they have done. Great kings from many other nations will conquer the Babylonians and force them to be slaves.

The cup full of God's anger

[15] The LORD God of Israel showed me a vision in which he said, "Jeremiah, here is a cup filled with the wine of my anger. Take it and make every nation drink some. [16] They will vomit and act mad, because of the war this cup of anger will bring to them."

[17] I took the cup from the LORD's hand, and I went to the kings of the nations and made each of them drink some. [18] I started with Jerusalem and the towns of Judah, and the king and his officials were removed from power in disgrace. Everyone still makes insulting jokes about them and uses their names as curse words. [19] The second place I went was Egypt, where everyone had to drink from the cup, including the king and his officials, the other government workers, the rest of the Egyptians, [20] and all the foreigners who lived in the country.

Next I went to the king of Uz, and then to the four kings of Philistia, who ruled from Ashkelon, Gaza, Ekron, and what was left of Ashdod.* [21] Then I went to the kings of Edom, Moab, Ammon, [22] and to the kings of Tyre, Sidon, and their colonies across the sea. [23-24] After this, I went to the kings of Dedan, Tema, Buz, the tribes of the Arabian Desert,' [25] Zimri, Elam, Media, [26] and the countries in the north, both near and far.

I went to all the countries on earth, one after another, and finally to Babylonia.'

[27] The LORD had said I must tell each king, "The LORD All-Powerful, the God of Israel, commands you to drink from this cup that is full of the wine of his anger. It will make you so drunk that you will vomit. And when the LORD sends war against the nations, you will be completely defeated."

[28] The LORD told me that if any of them refused to drink from the cup, I must tell them that he had said, "I, the LORD All-Powerful, command you to drink." [29] Starting with my own city of Jerusalem, everyone on earth will suffer from war. So there is no way I will let you escape unharmed."

[30] The LORD told me to say:

From my sacred temple
  I will roar like thunder,
while I trample my people
  and everyone else
  as though they were grapes.
[31] My voice will be heard
  everywhere on earth,
accusing nations of their crimes
  and sentencing the guilty
  to death.

Disaster is coming

[32] The LORD All-Powerful says:

You can see disaster spreading
  from far across the earth,
from nation to nation
  like a horrible storm.

[33] When it strikes, I will kill so many people that their bodies will cover the ground like manure. No one will be left to bury them* or to mourn.

The leaders of Judah will be punished

[34] The LORD's people are his flock,
  and you leaders
  were the shepherds.
But now it's your turn
  to be butchered like sheep.
You'll shatter like fine pottery
  dropped on the floor.'
So roll on the ground,
  crying and mourning.
[35] You have nowhere to run,
  nowhere to hide.
[36-38] Listen to the cries
  of the shepherds,
as the LORD's burning anger
  turns' peaceful meadows
  into barren deserts.
The LORD has abandoned
  his people'
  like a lion leaving its den.

CHAPTER 26

Jeremiah's message in the temple

This is also told in Jeremiah 7.1-15

[1] Soon after Jehoiakim* became king of Judah, the LORD said:

---

*25.20 what was left of Ashdod: It was defeated by the king of Egypt after being surrounded for twenty-nine years.

*25.33 bury them: See the note at 14.16.
*26.1 Jehoiakim: See the note at 1.3.
See also: 26.1: 2 King 23.36–24.6; 2 Chron 36.5-7.

² Jeremiah, I have a message for everyone who comes from the towns of Judah to worship in my temple. Go to the temple courtyard and speak every word that I tell you. ³ Perhaps the people will listen this time. And if they stop doing wrong, I will change my mind and not punish them for their sins. ⁴ Tell them that I have said:

You have refused to listen to me and to obey my laws and teachings. ⁵ Again and again I have sent my servants the prophets to preach to you, but you ignored them as well. Now I am warning you that if you don't start obeying me straight away, ⁶ I will destroy this temple, just as I destroyed the town of Shiloh.* Then everyone on earth will use the name "Jerusalem" as a curse word.

Jeremiah on trial

⁷ The prophets, the priests, and everyone else in the temple heard what I said, ⁸⁻⁹ and as soon as I finished, they all crowded around me and started shouting, "Why did you preach that the LORD will destroy this temple, just as he destroyed Shiloh*? Why did you say that Jerusalem will be empty and lie in ruins? You ought to be put to death for saying such things in the LORD's name!" Then they had me arrested.

¹⁰ The royal officers heard what had happened, and they came from the palace to the new gate of the temple to be the judges at my trial.* ¹¹ While they listened, the priests and the prophets said to the crowd, "All of you have heard Jeremiah prophesy that Jerusalem will be destroyed. He deserves the death penalty."

¹²⁻¹³ Then I told the judges and everyone else:

The LORD himself sent me to tell you about the terrible things he will do to you, to Jerusalem, and to the temple. But if you change your ways and start obeying the LORD, he will change his mind.

¹⁴ You must decide what to do with me. Just do whatever you think is right. ¹⁵ But if you put me to death, you and everyone else in Jerusalem will be guilty of

murdering an innocent man, because everything I preached came from the LORD.

¹⁶ The judges and the other people told the priests and prophets, "Since Jeremiah only told us what the LORD our God said, we don't think he deserves to die."

¹⁷ Then some of the leaders from other towns stepped forward. They told the crowd that ¹⁸ years ago when Hezekiah* was king of Judah, a prophet named Micah from the town of Moresheth had said:

"I, the LORD All-Powerful, say Jerusalem will be ploughed under and left in ruins.
Thorns will cover the mountain where the temple now stands."*

¹⁹ Then the leaders continued:

No one put Micah to death for saying that. Instead, King Hezekiah prayed to the LORD with fear and trembling and asked him to have mercy. Then the LORD decided not to destroy Jerusalem, even though he had already said he would.

People of Judah, if Jeremiah is killed, we will bring a terrible disaster on ourselves.

²⁰⁻²⁴ After these leaders finished speaking, an important man named Ahikam son of Shaphan spoke up for me as well. And so, I wasn't handed over to the crowd to be killed.

Uriah the prophet

While Jehoiakim* was still king of Judah, a man named Uriah son of Shemaiah left his home town of Kiriath-Jearim and came to Jerusalem. Uriah was one of the LORD's prophets, and he was saying the same things about Judah and Jerusalem that I had been saying. And when Jehoiakim and his officials and military officers heard what Uriah said, they tried to arrest him, but he escaped to Egypt. So Jehoiakim sent Elnathan son of Achbor and some other men after Uriah, and they brought him back. Then Jehoiakim had Uriah killed and his body dumped in a common burial pit.

---

*26.6,8-9 Shiloh: The sacred tent had once stood at Shiloh.

*26.10 new gate . . . trial: Public trials were often held in an open area at a gate of a city, palace, or temple.

See also: 26.6: Josh 18.1; Psa 78.60; Jer 7.12-14.

*26.18 Hezekiah: Ruled 716–687 BC.

*26.18 Jerusalem . . . stands: See Micah 3.12.

*26.20-24 Jehoiakim: See the note at 1.3.

See also: 26.18: Mic 3.12.

Jeremiah against the lying prophets

CHAPTER 27

Slaves of Nebuchadnezzar

1-2 Not long after Zedekiah became king of Judah,* the LORD told me:

Jeremiah, make a wooden yoke* with leather straps, and place it on your neck. ³ Then send a message to the kings of Edom, Moab, Ammon, Tyre, and Sidon. Some officials from these countries are in Jerusalem, meeting with Zedekiah. ⁴ So order them to tell their kings that I have said:

I am the All-Powerful LORD God of Israel, ⁵ and with my power I created the earth, its people, and all animals. I decide who will rule the earth, ⁶⁻⁷ and I have chosen my servant Nebuchadnezzar* of Babylonia to rule all nations, including yours. I will even let him rule the wild animals. All nations will be slaves of Nebuchadnezzar, his son, and his grandson. Then many nations will join together, and their kings will be powerful enough to make slaves of the Babylonians.

⁸ This yoke stands for the power of King Nebuchadnezzar, and I will destroy any nation that refuses to obey him. Nebuchadnezzar will attack, and many will die in battle or from hunger and disease. ⁹ You might have people in your kingdom who claim they can tell the future by magic or by talking with the dead or by dreams or messages from a god. But don't pay attention if any of them tell you not to obey Nebuchadnezzar. ¹⁰ If you listen to such lies, I will have you dragged far from your country and killed. ¹¹ But if you and your nation are willing to stay in your country, and your people will continue to live and work on their farms.

¹² After I had spoken to the officials from the nearby kingdoms, I went to King Zedekiah and told him the same thing. Then I said:

Zedekiah, if you and the people of Judah want to stay alive, you must obey

Nebuchadnezzar and the Babylonians. ¹³ But if you refuse, then you and your people will die from war, hunger, and disease, just as the LORD has warned. ¹⁴ Your prophets have told you that you don't need to obey Nebuchadnezzar, but don't listen to their lies. ¹⁵ Those prophets claim to be speaking for the LORD, but he didn't send them. They are lying! If you do what they say, he will have both you and them dragged off to another country and killed. The LORD has spoken.

¹⁶ When I finished talking to the king, I went to the priests and told them that the LORD had said:

Don't listen to the prophets when they say that very soon the Babylonians will return the things they took from my temple. Those prophets are lying! ¹⁷ If you choose to obey the king of Babylonia, you will live. But if you listen to those prophets, this whole city will be nothing but a pile of rubble.

¹⁸ If I really had spoken to those prophets, they would know what I am going to do. Then they would be begging me not to let everything else be taken from the temple and the king's palace and the rest of Jerusalem. ¹⁹⁻²¹ After all, when Nebuchadnezzar took King Jehoiachin* to Babylonia as a prisoner, he didn't take everything of value from Jerusalem. He left the bronze pillars, the huge bronze bowl called the Sea, and the moveable bronze stands in the temple, and he left a lot of other valuable things in the palace and in the rest of Jerusalem.

But now I, the LORD All-Powerful, the God of Israel, say that all these things ²² will be taken to Babylonia, where they will remain until I decide to bring them back to Jerusalem. I, the LORD, have spoken.

CHAPTER 28

Jeremiah accuses Hananiah of being a false prophet

¹ Later that same year, in the fifth month of the fourth year that Zedekiah* was king,* the prophet Hananiah son of Azzur from Gibeon came up to me in the temple. And while the

---

27.1,2 yoke: A wooden collar that fits around the neck of an ox, so the ox can be made to pull a plough or a cart.
27.6,7 Nebuchadnezzar: See the note at 21.2.
See also: 27.1: 2 King 24.18–20; 2 Chron 36.11–13.

27.19–21 Jehoiachin: Hebrew "Jeconiah" (see the note at 24.1).
28.1 Zedekiah: See the note at 1.3.
See also: 28.1: 2 King 24.18–20; 2 Chron 36.11–13.

priests and others in the temple were listening, [2] he told me that the LORD had said:

I am the LORD All-Powerful, the God of Israel, and I will smash the yoke* that Nebuchadnezzar* put on the necks of the nations to make them his slaves. [3] And within two years, I will bring back to Jerusalem everything that he took from my temple and carried off to Babylonia. [4] King Jehoiachin* and the other people who were taken from Judah to Babylonia were allowed to come back here as well. All this will happen because I will smash the power of the king of Babylonia!

[5] The priests and the others were still standing there, so I said:

[6] Hananiah, I hope the LORD will do exactly what you said. I hope he does bring back everything the Babylonians took from the temple, and that our people who were taken to Babylonia will be allowed to return home. [7] But let me remind you and everyone else [8] that long before we were born, prophets were saying powerful kingdoms would be struck by war, disaster, and disease. [9] Now you are saying we will have peace. We will just have to wait and see if that is really what the LORD has said.*

[10] Hananiah grabbed the wooden yoke from my neck and smashed it. [11] Then he said, "The LORD says this is the way he will smash the power Nebuchadnezzar has over the nations, and it will happen in less than two years."

I left the temple, [12] and a little while later, the LORD told me [13-14] to go back and say to Hananiah:

I am the LORD All-Powerful, the God of Israel. You smashed a wooden yoke, but I will replace it with one made of iron. I will put iron yokes on all the nations, and they will have to do what King Nebuchadnezzar commands. I will even let him rule the wild animals.

[15-16] Hananiah, I have never sent you to speak for me. And yet you have talked my people into believing your lies and rebelling against me. So now I will send

you — I'll send you right off the face of the earth! You will die before this year is over.

[17] Two months later, Hananiah died.

CHAPTER 29

Jeremiah's letter to the people of Judah in Babylonia

[1-2] I had been left in Jerusalem when King Nebuchadnezzar* took many of the people of Jerusalem and Judah to Babylonia as prisoners, including King Jehoiachin,* his mother, his officials, and the metal workers and others in Jerusalem who were skilled in making things. So I wrote a letter to the prophets, the priests, the leaders, and the rest of our people in Babylonia. [3] I gave the letter to Elasah and Gemariah,* two men that King Zedekiah* of Judah was sending to Babylon to talk with Nebuchadnezzar. In the letter, I wrote [4] that the LORD All-Powerful, the God of Israel, had said:

I had you taken from Jerusalem to Babylonia. Now I tell you [5] to settle there and build houses. Plant gardens and eat what you grow in them. [6] Get married and have children, then help your sons find wives and help your daughters find husbands, so they can have children as well. I want your numbers to grow, not to get smaller.

[7] Pray for peace in Babylonia and work hard to make it prosperous. The more successful that nation is, the better off you will be.

[8-9] Some of your people there in Babylonia are fortune-tellers, and you have asked them to tell you what will happen in the future. But they will only lead you astray. And don't let the prophets fool you, either. They speak in my name, but they are liars. I have not spoken to them.

[10] After Babylonia has been the strongest nation for seventy years, I will be kind and bring you back to Jerusalem, just as I have promised. [11] I will bless you with a future filled with hope — a future of success, not of suffering. [12] You will turn back to me and ask for help, and I will answer your prayers. [13] You will worship me with all your heart,

---

*28.2 yoke: See the note at 27.1,2.
*28.2 Nebuchadnezzar: See the note at 21.2.
*28.4 Jehoiachin: Hebrew "Jeconiah" (see the note at 24.1).
*28.9 We will . . . said: See Deuteronomy 18.21,22.

*29.1,2 Nebuchadnezzar: See the note at 21.2.
*29.1,2 Jehoiachin: Hebrew "Jeconiah" (see the note at 24.1).
*29.3 Zedekiah: See the note at 1.3.
See also: 29.1,2: 2 King 24.12-16; 2 Chron 36.10.
29.10: 2 Chron 36.21; Jer 25.11; Dan 9.2. 29.13: Deut 4.29.

and I will be with you [14] and accept your worship. Then I will gather you from all the nations where I scattered you, and you will return to Jerusalem.

[15] You feel secure, because you think I have sent prophets to speak for me in Babylonia.

[16-19] But I have been sending prophets to the people of Judah for a long time, and the king from David's family and the people who are left in Jerusalem and Judah still don't obey me. So I, the LORD All-Powerful, will keep attacking them with war and hunger and disease, until they are as useless as rotten figs. I will force them to leave the land, and all nations will be disgusted and shocked at what happens to them. The nations will sneer and make fun of them and use the names "Judah" and "Jerusalem" as curse words.

And you have not obeyed me, even though [20] I had you taken from Jerusalem to Babylonia. But you had better listen to me now. [21-23] You think Ahab son of Kolaiah and Zedekiah son of Maaseiah are prophets because they claim to speak for me. But they are lying! I haven't told them anything. They are also committing other horrible sins in your community, such as sleeping with the wives of their friends. So I will hand them over to King Nebuchadnezzar, who will put them to death while the rest of you watch. And in the future, when you want to put a curse on someone, you will say, "I pray that the LORD will kill you in the same way the king of Babylonia burnt Zedekiah and Ahab to death!"

A message for Shemaiah

[24-25] The LORD All-Powerful, the God of Israel, told me what would happen to Shemaiah,* who was one of our people in Babylonia. After my letter reached Babylonia, Shemaiah wrote letters to the people of Jerusalem, including the priest Zephaniah son of Maaseiah, and the other priests. The letter to Zephaniah said:

[26] After the death of Jehoiada the priest, the LORD chose you to be the priest in charge of the temple security force. You know that anyone who acts mad and pretends to be a prophet should be arrested and put in chains' and iron collars. [27] Jeremiah from the town of Anathoth is pretending to be a prophet there in Jerusalem, so why haven't you punished him? [28] He even wrote a letter to the people here in Babylonia, saying we

would be here a long time. He told us to build homes and to plant gardens and grow our own food.

[29] When Zephaniah received Shemaiah's letter, he read it to me. [30] Then the LORD told me what to write in a second letter [31] to the people of Judah who had been taken to Babylonia. In this letter, I wrote that the LORD had said:

I, the LORD, have not chosen Shemaiah to be one of my prophets, and he has misled you by telling lies in my name. [32] He has even talked you into disobeying me. So I will punish Shemaiah. And his descendants won't live to see the good things I will do for my people. I, the LORD, have spoken.

God will some day bring his people back to their land

CHAPTER 30

The LORD will rescue Israel and Judah

[1-2] The LORD God of Israel said, "Jeremiah, get a scroll* and write down everything I have told you. [3] Some day I will let my people from both Israel* and Judah return to the land I gave their ancestors."

[4-5] Then the LORD told me to say to Israel and Judah:

I, the LORD, hear screams
of terror,
    and there is no peace.
[6] Can men give birth?
Then why do I see them
    looking so pale
and clutching their stomachs
    like women in labour?
[7] My people, soon you will suffer
worse than ever before,
    but I will save you.

[8] Now you are slaves of other nations,
but I will break the chains
    and smash the yokes*
    that keep you in slavery.
[9] Then you will be my servants,
and I will choose a king for you
    from the family of David.

---

*30.1,2 scroll: A roll of paper or special leather used for writing on.
*30.3 Israel: The northern kingdom.
*30.8 yokes: See the note at 27.1,2.

10-11 Israel,* you belong to me,
so don't be afraid.
You deserved to be punished;
that's why I scattered you
in distant nations.
But I am with you,
and some day I will destroy
those nations.
Then I will bring you
and your descendants
back to your land,
where I will protect you
and give you peace.
Then your fears will be gone.
I, the LORD, have spoken.

The LORD will heal Israel and Judah

12 The LORD said:

My people, you are wounded
and near death.
13 You are accused of a crime
with no one to defend you,
and you are covered with sores
that no medicine can cure.
14-15 Your friends have forgotten you;
they don't care any more.
Even I have acted like an enemy.
And because your sins
are horrible and countless,
I will be cruel
as I punish you.
So don't bother to cry out
for relief from your pain.

16 But if your enemies try to rob
or destroy you,
I will rob and destroy them,
and they will be led as captives
to foreign lands.
17 No one wants you as a friend
or cares what happens to you.
But I will heal your injuries,
and you will get well.

The LORD will rescue Israel and Judah

18 The LORD said:

Israel, I will be kind to you
and let you come home.
Jerusalem now lies in ruins,
but you will rebuild it,
complete with a new palace.♦

19 Other nations will respect
and honour you.
Your homes will be filled
with children,
and you will celebrate,
singing praises to me.
20 It will be just like old times.
Your nation will worship me,
and I will punish anyone
who abuses you.
21 One of your own people
will become your ruler.
And when I invite him
to come near me
at the place of worship,
he will do so.
No one would dare to come near
without being invited.
22 You will be my people,
and I will be your God.
I, the LORD, have spoken.

23 I am furious!
And like a violent storm
I will strike those
who do wrong.
24 I won't calm down
until I have finished
what I have decided to do.
Some day, you will understand
what I mean.

CHAPTER 31

Israel will return to God

1 The LORD said:

Israel, I promise
that some day all your tribes
will again be my people,
and I will be your God.
2 In the desert I was kind
to those who escaped death.
I gave them peace,
and when the time is right,
I'll do the same for you.♦
I, the LORD, have spoken.

The LORD will rebuild Israel

3 Some time ago, the LORD appeared to me♦
and told me to say:

Israel, I will always love you;
that's why I've been so patient and kind.
4 You are precious to me,
and so I will rebuild your nation.
Once again you will dance for joy
and play your tambourines.

*30.10,11 Israel: The people of the northern and
southern kingdoms.
See also: 30.10,11: Jer 46.27,28.
738

⁵ You will plant vineyards
on the hills of Samaria
and enjoy the grapes.
⁶ Some day those who guard
the hill country of Ephraim
will shout, "Let's go to Zion
and worship the LORD our God."

Israel will return to its own land

⁷ The LORD says:

Celebrate and sing for Israel,
the greatest of nations.
Offer praises and shout,
"Come and rescue
your people, LORD!
Save what's left of Israel."

⁸ I, the LORD, will bring
my people back from Babylonia⁹
and everywhere else on earth.
The blind and the lame
will be there.
Expectant mothers
and women about to give birth
will come and be part
of that great crowd.
⁹ They will weep and pray
as I bring them home.
I will lead them
to streams of water.
They will walk on a level⁹ road
and not stumble.
I am a father to Israel,⁹
my favourite children.

¹⁰ Listen to me, you nations
nearby or across the sea.
I scattered the people of Israel,
but I will gather them again.
I will protect them like a shepherd
guarding a flock;
¹¹ I will rescue them from enemies
who could overpower them.
¹² My people will come
to Mount Zion and celebrate;
their faces will glow
because of my blessings.
I'll give them grain, grapes,
and olive oil,
as well as sheep and cattle.
Israel will be prosperous
and grow like a garden
with plenty of water.
¹³ Young women and young men,
together with the elderly,
will celebrate and dance,
because I will comfort them

and turn their sorrow
into happiness.
¹⁴ I will bless my people
with more food
than they need,
and the priests will enjoy
the choice cuts of meat.
I, the LORD, have spoken.

The LORD offers hope

The LORD said:

¹⁵ In Ramah⁹ a voice is heard,
crying and weeping loudly.
Rachel mourns for her children*
and refuses to be comforted,
because they are dead.
¹⁶⁻¹⁷ But I, the LORD, tell you
to dry your tears.
Some day your children
will come home
from the enemy's land.
Then all you have done for them
will be greatly rewarded.
So don't lose hope.
I, the LORD, have spoken.

¹⁸ The people of Israel⁹ moan
and say to me,
"We were like wild bulls,
but you, LORD, broke us,
and we learnt to obey.
You are our God —
please let us come home.
¹⁹ When we were young,
we strayed and sinned,
but then we realized
what we had done.
We are ashamed and disgraced
and want to return to you."

²⁰ People of Israel,
you are my own dear children.
Don't I love you best of all?
Though I often make threats,
I want you to be near me,
so I will have mercy on you.
I, the LORD, have spoken.

²¹ With rock piles and signposts,
mark the way home,
my dear people.

---

*31.15 Rachel . . . children: Rachel was one of the
wives of Jacob, the ancestor of the nation of Israel. She
was the mother of Joseph and Benjamin. Joseph's two
sons Ephraim and Manasseh were the ancestors of the
leading tribes of the northern kingdom of Israel.
See also: 31.15: a Gen 35.16–19; **b** Matt 2.18.

It is the same road
by which you left.
²² Will you ever decide
to be faithful?
I will make sure that some day
things will be different,
as different as a woman
protecting a man.•

The LORD will bring Judah home

²³ The LORD All-Powerful, the God of Israel,
said:

I promise to set the people of Judah free
and to lead them back to their home
towns. And when I do, they will once again
say,

"We pray that the LORD
will bless his home,
the sacred hill in Jerusalem
where his temple stands."

²⁴ The people will live in Jerusalem and in
the towns of Judah. Some will be farmers,
and others will be shepherds. ²⁵ Those who
feel tired and worn out will find new life
and energy, ²⁶ and when they sleep, they
will wake up refreshed.•
²⁷ Some day, Israel and Judah will be my
field where my people and their livestock
will grow. ²⁸ In the past, I took care to
uproot them, to tear them down, and to
destroy them. But when that day comes,
I will take care to plant them and help
them grow. ²⁹ No longer will anyone go
around saying,

"Sour grapes eaten by parents
leave a sour taste in the mouths
of their children."

³⁰ When that day comes, only those who
eat sour grapes will get the sour taste, and
only those who sin will be put to death.

The new agreement with Israel and Judah

³¹ The LORD said:

The time will surely come when I will make
a new agreement with the people of Israel
and Judah. ³² It will be different from the
agreement I made with their ancestors
when I led them out of Egypt. Although I
was their God, they broke that agreement.

³³ Here is the new agreement that I, the
LORD, will make with the people of Israel:

"I will write my laws
on their hearts and minds.
I will be their God,
and they will be my people.

³⁴ "No longer will they have to teach one
another to obey me. I, the LORD, promise
that all of them will obey me, ordinary
people and rulers alike. I will forgive their
sins and forget the evil things they have
done."

³⁵ I am the LORD All-Powerful.
I command the sun
to give light each day,
the moon and stars
to shine at night,
and ocean waves to roar.
³⁶ I will never forget
to give those commands,
and I will never let Israel
stop being a nation.
I, the LORD, have spoken.

³⁷ Can you measure the heavens?
Can you explore
the depths of the earth?
That's how hard it would be
for me to reject Israel for ever,
even though they have sinned.
I, the LORD, have spoken.

Jerusalem will be rebuilt

³⁸ The LORD said:

Some day, Jerusalem will truly belong to
me. It will be rebuilt with a boundary line
running from Hananel Tower to Corner
Gate. ³⁹ From there, the boundary will go
in a straight line to Gareb Hill, then turn
towards Goah. ⁴⁰ Even that disgusting
Hinnom Valley* will be sacred to me,
and so will the eastern slopes that go
down from Horse Gate into Kidron
Valley. Jerusalem will never again be
destroyed.

---

*31.40 that disgusting Hinnom Valley: The Hebrew
text has "the whole valley of the dead bodies and of
the fatty ashes", which probably refers to Hinnom
Valley, just south-west of Jerusalem, where human
sacrifices had been offered to foreign gods.
See also: 31.33: Heb 10.16. 31.34: Heb 10.17.

CHAPTER 32

Jeremiah buys a field

[1] The LORD spoke to me in the tenth year that Zedekiah* was king of Judah, which was the eighteenth year that Nebuchadnezzar* was king of Babylonia. [2] At that time, the Babylonian army had surrounded Jerusalem, and I was in the prison at the courtyard of the palace guards. [3] Zedekiah had ordered me to be held there because I told everyone that the LORD had said:

I am the LORD, and I am about to let the king of Babylonia conquer Jerusalem. [4] King Zedekiah will be captured and taken to King Nebuchadnezzar, who will speak with him face to face. [5] Then Zedekiah will be led away to Babylonia, where he will stay until I have finished with him. So, if you people of Judah fight against the Babylonians, you will lose. I, the LORD, have spoken.

[6] Later, when I was in prison, the LORD said:

[7] Jeremiah, your cousin Hanamel, the son of your uncle Shallum, will visit you. He must sell his field near the town of Anathoth, and because you are his nearest relative, you have the right and the responsibility to buy it and keep it in the family.*

[8] Hanamel came, just as the LORD had promised. And he said, "Please buy my field near Anathoth in the territory of the Benjamin tribe. You have the right to buy it, and if you do, it will stay in our family."

The LORD had told me to buy it, [9] so I bought it from Hanamel, and so I did. The price was seventeen pieces of silver, and I weighed out the full amount on a scale. [10-11] I had two copies of the bill of sale written out, each containing all the details of our agreement. Some witnesses and I signed the official copy, which was folded and tied, before being sealed shut with hot wax.* Then I gave Hanamel the silver. [12] And while he, the witnesses, and all the other Jews sitting in the

courtyard were still watching, I gave both copies to Baruch son of Neriah.'

[13-14] I told Baruch that the LORD had said:

Take both copies of this bill of sale, one sealed shut and the other open, and put them in a clay jar so they will last a long time. [15] I am the LORD All-Powerful, the God of Israel, and I promise you that people will once again buy and sell houses, farms, and vineyards in this country.

Jeremiah questions the LORD

[16] Then I prayed:

[17] LORD God, you stretched out your mighty arm and made the sky and the earth. You can do anything. [18] You show kindness for a thousand generations,' but you also punish people for the sins of their parents. You are the LORD All-Powerful. [19] With great wisdom you make plans, and with your great power you do all the mighty things you planned. Nothing was too hidden from your eyes, and you reward or punish us as we deserve.

[20] You are famous because you worked miracles in Egypt, and you are still working them in Israel and in the rest of the world as well. [21] You terrified the Egyptians with your miracles, and you reached out your mighty arm and rescued your people Israel from Egypt. [22] Then you gave Israel this land rich with milk and honey, just as you had promised our ancestors.

[23] But when our ancestors took over the land, they did not obey you. And now you have punished Israel with disaster.

[24] Jerusalem is under attack, and we suffer from hunger and disease. The Babylonians have already built earth ramps up to the city walls, and you can see that Jerusalem will be captured just as you said.

[25] So why did you tell me to get some witnesses and buy a field with my silver, when Jerusalem is about to be captured by the Babylonians?

The LORD explains about the field

[26] The LORD explained:

[27] Jeremiah, I am the LORD God. I rule the world, and I can do anything! [28] It is true that I am going to let King Nebuchadnezzar* of Babylonia capture

---

*32.1 Zedekiah: See the note at 1.3.
*32.1 Nebuchadnezzar: See the note at 21.2.
*32.7 you have the right . . . in the family: See Leviticus 25.25–32.
*32.10,11 signed the official copy, which was folded and tied, before being sealed shut with hot wax: The signing was actually done by pressing a carved clay stamp (called a "seal") into the hot wax, leaving the design in the wax.
See also: 32.1: 2 King 25.1–7.

*32.28 Nebuchadnezzar: See the note at 21.2.
See also: 32.28: 2 King 25.1–11; 2 Chron 36.17–21.

Jerusalem. ²⁹ The Babylonian army is already attacking, and they will capture the city and set it on fire. The people of Jerusalem have made me angry by going up to the flat roofs of their houses and burning incense to Baal and offering wine sacrifices to other gods. Now these houses will be burnt to the ground!

³⁰⁻³³ The kings and the officials, the priests and the prophets, and everyone else in Israel and Judah have turned from me and made me angry by worshipping idols. Again and again I have tried to teach my people to obey me, but they refuse to be corrected.

I am going to get rid of Jerusalem, because its people have done nothing but evil. ³⁴ They have set up disgusting idols in my temple, and now it isn't a fit place to worship me. ³⁵ And they led Judah into sin by building places to worship Baal in Hinnom Valley, where they also sacrificed their sons and daughters to the god Molech. I have never even thought of telling them to commit such disgusting sins.

³⁶ Jeremiah, what you said is true. The people of Jerusalem are suffering from hunger and disease, and so the king of Babylonia will be able to capture Jerusalem.

³⁷ I am angry with the people of Jerusalem, and I will scatter them in foreign countries. But some day I will bring them back here and let them live in safety. ³⁸ They will be my people, and I will be their God. ³⁹⁻⁴¹ I will make their thoughts and desires pure. Then they will realize that, for their own good and the good of their children, they must worship only me. They will even be afraid to turn away from me. I will make an agreement with them that will never end, and I won't ever stop doing good things for them. With all my heart I promise that they will be planted in this land once again. ⁴² Even though I have brought disaster on the people, I will some day do all these good things for them.

⁴³ Jeremiah, when you bought the field, you showed that fields will some day be bought and sold again. You say that this land will be conquered by the Babylonians and has become a desert, emptied of people and animals. ⁴⁴ But some day, people will again spend their silver to buy fields everywhere — in the territory of Benjamin, the region around Jerusalem and the towns

of Judah, and in the hill country, the foothills to the west, and the Southern Desert. Buyers and sellers and witnesses will sign and seal the bills of sale for the fields. It will happen, because I will give this land back to my people. I, the LORD, have spoken.

CHAPTER 33

The LORD promises to give the land back to his people

¹⁻² I was still being held prisoner in the courtyard of the palace guards when the LORD told me:

I am the LORD, and I created the whole world. ³ Ask me, and I will tell you things that you don't know and can't find out.

⁴⁻⁵ Many of the houses in Jerusalem and some of the buildings at the royal palace have been torn down to be used in repairing the walls to keep out the Babylonian attackers.ᵇ Now there are empty spaces where the buildings once stood. But I am furious, and these spaces will be filled with the bodies of the people I kill. The people of Jerusalem will cry out to me for help, but they are evil, and I will ignore their prayers.

⁶ Then some day, I will heal this place and my people as well, and let them enjoy unending peace.ᶜ ⁷ I will give this land to Israel and Judah once again, and I will make them as strong as they were before. ⁸ They sinned and rebelled against me, but I will forgive them and take away their guilt. ⁹ When that happens, all nations on earth will see the good things I have done for Jerusalem, and how I have given it complete peace. The nations will celebrate and praise and honour me, but they will also tremble with fear.

¹⁰ Jeremiah, you say that this land is a desert without people or animals, and for now, you are right. The towns of Judah and the streets of Jerusalem are deserted, and people and animals are nowhere to be seen. But some day you will hear ¹¹ happy voices and the sounds of parties and wedding celebrations. And when people come to my temple to offer sacrifices to thank me, you will hear them say:

> "We praise you,
> LORD All-Powerful!
> You are good to us,
> and your love never fails."

See also: 32.34: 2 King 23.10; Jer 7.30,31; 19.1–6.
32.35: a 2 King 23.10; Jer 7.31; b Lev 18.21.

See also: 33.11: 1 Chron 16.34; 2 Chron 5.13; 7.3; Ezra 3.11;
Psa 100.5; 106.1; 107.1; 118.1; 136.1.

The land will once again be productive.
12-13 Now it is empty, without people or
animals. But when that time comes,
shepherds will take care of their flocks in
pastures near every town in the hill
country, in the foothills to the west, in the
Southern Desert, in the land of the
Benjamin tribe, and around Jerusalem and
the towns of Judah.

I, the LORD, have spoken.

The LORD's wonderful promise

14 The LORD said:

I made a wonderful promise to Israel and
Judah,* and the days are coming when I
will keep it.

15 I promise that the time will come
when I will appoint a king
from the family of David,
a king who will be honest
and rule with justice.
16 In those days, Judah will be safe;
Jerusalem will have peace
and will be named,
"The LORD Gives Justice".

17 The king of Israel will be one of David's
descendants, 18 and there will always be
priests from the Levi tribe serving at my
altar and offering sacrifices to please me
and to give thanks.*

19 Then the LORD told me:

20 I, the LORD, have an agreement with day
and night, so they always come at the right
time. You can't break the agreement I made
with them, 21 and you can't break the
agreements I have made with David's family
and with the priests from the Levi tribe who
serve at my altar. A descendant of David will
always rule as king of Israel, 22 and there
will be more descendants of David and of
the priests from the Levi tribe than stars in
the sky or grains of sand on the beach.

23 The LORD also said:

24 You've heard foreigners insult my people
by saying, "The LORD chose Israel and
Judah, but now he has rejected them, and
they are no longer a nation."

25 Jeremiah, I will never break my
agreement with the day and the night or let

the sky and the earth stop obeying my
commands. 26 In the same way, I will never
reject the descendants of Abraham, Isaac,
and Jacob or break my promise that they
will always have a descendant of David as
their king. I will be kind to my people
Israel, and they will be successful again.

Scenes from Jeremiah's ministry

CHAPTER 34

Jeremiah warns Zedekiah

1 King Nebuchadnezzar* had a large army
made up of people from every kingdom in
his empire. He and his army were attacking
Jerusalem and all the nearby towns, when the
LORD told me 2 to say to King Zedekiah:*

I am the LORD, and I am going to let
Nebuchadnezzar capture this city and burn
it down. 3 You will be taken prisoner and
brought to Nebuchadnezzar, and he will
speak with you face to face. Then you will
be led away to Babylonia.

4 Zedekiah, I promise that you won't die
in battle. 5 You will die a peaceful death.
People will mourn when you die, and they
will light bonfires in your honour, just as
they did for your ancestors, the kings who
ruled before you.

6 I went to Zedekiah and told him what the
LORD had said. 7 Meanwhile, the king of
Babylonia was trying to break through the
walls of Lachish, Azekah, and Jerusalem, the
only three towns of Judah that had not been
captured.

The people break a promise

8-10 King Zedekiah,* his officials, and
everyone else in Jerusalem made an
agreement to free all Hebrew* men and
women who were slaves. No Jew would ever
another as a slave. And so, all the Jewish
slaves were given their freedom.

11 But those slave owners changed their
minds and forced their former slaves back
into slavery. 12 That's when the LORD told me
to say to the people:

---

*33.14 Israel and Judah: See the note at 2.4.
*33.18 sacrifices to please me and to give thanks:
See the notes at 14.12.
See also: 33.14-16: Jer 23.5,6. 33.17: 2 Sam 7.12-16;
1 King 2.4; 1 Chron 17.11-14. 33.18: Num 3.5-10.

*34.1 Nebuchadnezzar: See the note at 21.2.
*34.2,8-10 Zedekiah: See the note at 1.3.
*34.8-10 Hebrew: An earlier term for "Israelite" and
"Jewish".
See also: 34.1: 2 King 25.1-11; 2 Chron 36.17-21.

[13] I am the LORD God of Israel, and I made an agreement with your ancestors when I brought them out of Egypt, where they had been slaves. [14] As part of this agreement, you must let a Hebrew slave go free after six years of service.

Your ancestors did not obey me, [15-16] but you decided to obey me and do the right thing by setting your Hebrew slaves completely free. You even went to the temple, and in my name you made an agreement to set them free. But you have abused my name, because you broke your agreement and forced your former slaves back into slavery.

[17] You have disobeyed me by not giving your slaves their freedom. So I will give you freedom — the freedom to die in battle or from disease or hunger. I will make you disgusting to all other nations on earth.

[18] You asked me to be a witness when you made the agreement to set your slaves free. And as part of the ceremony you cut a calf into two parts, then walked between the parts. But you people of Jerusalem have broken that agreement as well as my agreement with Israel. So I will do to you what you did to that calf. [19-20] I will let your enemies take all of you prisoner, including the leaders of Judah and Jerusalem, the royal officials, the priests, and everyone else who walked between the two parts of the calf. These enemies will kill you and leave your bodies lying on the ground as food for birds and wild animals.

[21-22] These enemies are King Nebuchadnezzar* of Babylonia and his army. They have stopped attacking Jerusalem, but they want to kill King Zedekiah and his high officials. So I will command them to return and attack again. This time they will conquer the city and burn it down, and they will capture Zedekiah and his officials. I will also let them destroy the towns of Judah, so that no one can live there any longer.

CHAPTER 35

Learn a lesson from the Rechabites

[1] When Jehoiakim* was king of Judah, the LORD told me, [2] "Go to the Rechabite clan and invite them to meet you in one of the side rooms* of the temple. When they arrive, offer them a drink of wine."

[3] So I went to Jaazaniah,* the leader of the clan, and I invited him and all the men of his clan. [4] I brought them into the temple courtyard and took them upstairs to a room belonging to the prophets who were followers of Hanan son of Igdaliah. It was next to a room belonging to some of the officials, and that room was the one belonging to Maaseiah, a priest who was one of the high officials in the temple.

[5] I set out some large bowls full of wine together with some cups, and then I said to the Rechabites, "Have some wine!"

[6] But they answered:

No! The ancestor of our clan, Jonadab son of Rechab,* made a rule that we must obey. He said, "Don't ever drink wine [7] or build houses or plant crops and vineyards. Instead, you must always live in tents and move from place to place. If you obey this command, you will live a long time."

[8-10] Our clan has always obeyed Jonadab's command. To this very day, we and our wives and sons and daughters don't drink wine or build houses or plant vineyards or crops. And we have lived in tents, [11] except now we have to live inside Jerusalem because Nebuchadnezzar* has taken over the countryside with his army from Babylonia and Syria.

[12-13] Then the LORD told me to say to the people of Judah and Jerusalem:

I, the LORD All-Powerful, the God of Israel, want you to learn a lesson [14] from the Rechabite clan. Their ancestor Jonadab told his descendants never to drink wine, and to this very day they have obeyed him. But I have spoken to you over and over, and you haven't obeyed me! [15] You refused to listen to my prophets, who kept telling you, "Stop doing evil and worshipping other gods! Start obeying the LORD, and he will let you live in this land he gave your ancestors."

[16] The Rechabites have obeyed the command of their ancestor Jonadab, but

---

*34.21,22 Nebuchadnezzar: See the note at 21.2.
*35.1 Jehoiakim: See the note at 1.3.
See also: 34.14: Exod 21.2; Deut 15.12.
35.1: 2 King 23.36—24.6; 2 Chron 36.5—7.

*35.2 side rooms: Probably a room with walls on three sides, and open to the courtyard on the fourth side.
*35.6 Jonadab son of Rechab: See 2 Kings 10.15—23. In the Hebrew of this chapter, "Jonadab" is sometimes spelt "Jehonadab".
*35.11 Nebuchadnezzar: See the note at 21.2.

you have not obeyed me, 17 your God. I am the LORD All-Powerful, and I warned you about the terrible things that would happen to you if you did not listen to me. You have ignored me, so now disaster will strike you. I, the LORD, have spoken.

The LORD makes a promise to the Rechabites

18 Then the LORD told me to say to the Rechabite clan:

I am the LORD All-Powerful, the God of Israel. You have obeyed your ancestor Jonadab, 19 so I promise that your clan will be my servants and will never die out.

CHAPTER 36

King Jehoiakim burns Jeremiah's first scroll

1 During the fourth year that Jehoiakim* son of Josiah* was king of Judah, the LORD said to me, "Jeremiah, 2 since the time Josiah was king, I have been speaking to you about Israel, Judah, and the other nations. Now, get a scroll* and write down everything I have told you, 3 then read it to the people of Judah. Perhaps they will stop sinning when they hear what terrible things I plan for them. And if they turn to me, I will forgive them."

4 I sent for Baruch son of Neriah and asked him to help me. I repeated everything the LORD had told me, and Baruch wrote it all down on a scroll. 5 Then I said,

Baruch, the officials refuse to let me go into the LORD's temple, 6 so you must go instead. Wait for the next holy day when the people of Judah come to the temple to pray and to go without eating.* Then take this scroll to the temple and read it aloud. 7 The LORD is furious, and if the people hear how he is going to punish them, perhaps they will ask to be forgiven.

8-10 In the ninth month* of the fifth year that Jehoiakim was king, the leaders set a day

when everyone who lived in Jerusalem or who was visiting here had to pray and go without eating. So Baruch took the scroll to the upper courtyard of the temple. He went over to the side of the courtyard and stood in a covered area near New Gate, where he read the scroll aloud.

This covered area belonged to Gemariah,* one of the king's highest officials.
11 Gemariah's son Micaiah was there and heard Baruch read what the LORD had said. 12 When Baruch finished reading, Micaiah went down to the palace. His father Gemariah was in the officials' room, meeting with the rest of the king's officials, including Elishama, Delaiah, Elnathan, and Zedekiah.* 13 Micaiah told them what he had heard Baruch reading to the people. 14 Then the officials sent Jehudi and Shelemiah* to tell Baruch, "Bring us that scroll."

When Baruch arrived with the scroll, 15 the officials said, "Please sit down and read it to us," which he did. 16 After they heard what was written on the scroll, they were worried and said to each other, "The king needs to hear this!" Turning to Baruch, they asked, 17 "Did someone tell you what to write on this scroll?"

18 "Yes, Jeremiah did," Baruch replied. "I wrote down just what he told me."

19 The officials said, "You and Jeremiah must go into hiding, and don't tell anyone where you are."

20-22 The officials put the scroll in Elishama's room and went to see the king, who was in one of the rooms where he lived and worked during the winter. It was the ninth month* of the year, so there was a fire burning in the fireplace,* and the king was sitting nearby. After the officials told the king about the scroll, he sent Jehudi to get it. Then Jehudi started reading the scroll to the king and his officials. 23-25 But every time Jehudi finished reading three or four columns, the king would tell him to cut them off with his penknife and throw them in the fire. Elnathan, Delaiah, and Gemariah begged the king not to burn the scroll, but he ignored them, and soon there was nothing left of it.

---

*36.1 Jehoiakim: See the note at 1.3.
*36.1 Josiah: See the note at 1.2.
*36.2 scroll: See the note at 30.1,2.
*36.6 to go without eating: As a way of asking for God's help.
*36.8-10 ninth month: Chislev, the ninth month of the Hebrew calendar, from about mid-November to mid-December.
See also: 36.1: 2 King 24.1; 2 Chron 36.5-7; Dan 1.1,2.

*36.8-10 Gemariah: Hebrew "Gemariah son of Shaphan"; Gemariah's brother Ahikam had earlier protected Jeremiah (see 26.20-24).
*36.20-22 ninth month: See the note at 36.8-10.
*36.20-22 fireplace: Probably a large metal or clay pot on a moveable stand, with the fire burning inside.

The king and his servants listened to what was written on the scroll, but they were not afraid, and they did not tear their clothes in sorrow.*

26 The king told his son Jerahmeel to take Seraiah and Shelemiah† and to go and arrest Baruch and me.* But the LORD kept them from finding us.

Jeremiah's second scroll

27 I had told Baruch what to write on that first scroll,* but King Jehoiakim* had burnt it. So the LORD told me 28 to get another scroll and write down everything that had been on the first one. 29 Then he told me to say to King Jehoiakim:

Not only did you burn Jeremiah's scroll, you had the nerve to ask why he had written that the king of Babylonia would attack and ruin the land, killing all the people and even the animals. 30 So I, the LORD, promise that you will be killed and your body thrown out on the ground. The sun will beat down on it during the day, and the frost will settle on it at night. And none of your descendants will ever be king of Judah. 31 You, your children, and your servants are evil, and I will punish all of you. I warned you and the people of Judah and Jerusalem that I would bring disaster, but none of you have listened. So now you are doomed!

32 After the LORD finished speaking to me, I got another scroll and gave it to Baruch. Then I told him what to write, so this second scroll would contain even more than was on the scroll Jehoiakim had burnt.

CHAPTER 37

King Zedekiah asks Jeremiah to pray

1 King Nebuchadnezzar* of Babylonia had removed Jehoiachin* son of Jehoiakim* from being the king of Judah and had made Josiah's* son Zedekiah* king instead.* 2 But Zedekiah, his officials, and everyone else in Judah ignored everything the LORD had told me.

3-5 Later, the Babylonian army attacked Jerusalem, but they left after learning that the Egyptian army† was headed in this direction.

One day, Zedekiah sent Jehucal and the priest Zephaniah† to talk with me. At that time, I was free to go wherever I wanted, because I had not yet been put in prison. Jehucal and Zephaniah said, "Jeremiah, please pray to the LORD our God for us."

6-7 Then the LORD told me to send them back to Zedekiah with this message:

Zedekiah, you wanted Jeremiah to ask me, the LORD God of Israel, what is going to happen. So I will tell you. The king of Egypt and his army came to your rescue, but soon they will go back to Egypt. 8 Then the Babylonians will return and attack Jerusalem, and this time they will capture the city and set it on fire. 9 Don't fool yourselves into thinking that the Babylonians will leave as they did before. 10 Even if you could defeat their entire army, their wounded survivors would still be able to leave their tents and set Jerusalem on fire.

Jeremiah is put in prison

11 The Babylonian army had left because the Egyptian army was on its way to help us. 12 So I decided to leave Jerusalem and go to the territory of the Benjamin tribe to claim my share of my family's land. 13 I was leaving Jerusalem through Benjamin Gate, when I was stopped by Irijah,* the officer in charge of the soldiers at the gate. He said, "Jeremiah, you're under arrest for trying to join the Babylonians."

14 "I'm not trying to join them!" I answered. But Irijah wouldn't listen, and he took me to the king's officials. 15-16 They were angry and ordered the soldiers to beat me. Then I was taken to the house that belonged to Jonathan, one of the king's officials. It had been turned into a prison, and I was kept in a basement room.

*36.23–25 they did not tear their clothes in sorrow: Such actions would have shown that they were sorry for disobeying the LORD and were turning back to him.
*36.26 me: Jeremiah.
*36.27 scroll: See the note at 30.1,2.
*36.27; 37.1 Jehoiakim: See the note at 1.3.
*37.1 Nebuchadnezzar: See the note at 21.2.
*37.1 Jehoiachin: Hebrew "Coniah" (see the note at 1.2).
See also: 37.1: 2 King 24.17; 2 Chron 36.10.

*37.1 Josiah's: Josiah was the father of both Jehoiakim and Zedekiah. Josiah ruled 640–609 BC.
*37.1 Zedekiah: See the note at 1.3.
*37.1 King Nebuchadnezzar . . . instead: See 2 Kings 24.10–17.

After I had spent a long time there, [17] King Zedekiah secretly had me brought to his palace, where he asked, "Is there any message for us from the LORD?"

"Yes, there is, Your Majesty," I replied. "The LORD is going to let the king of Babylonia capture you."

[18] Then I continued, "Your Majesty, why have you put me in prison? Have I committed a crime against you or your officials or the nation? [19] Have you locked up the prophets who lied to you and said that the king of Babylonia would never attack Jerusalem? [20] Please, don't send me back to that prison at Jonathan's house. If you do, I will die."

[21] King Zedekiah had me taken to the prison cells in the courtyard of the palace guards. He told the soldiers to give me a loaf of bread* from one of the bakeries every day until the city ran out of grain.

CHAPTER 38

Jeremiah is held prisoner in a dry well

[1] One day, Shephatiah, Gedaliah, Jehucal,* and Pashhur* heard me tell the people of Judah [2-3] that the LORD had said, "If you stay here in Jerusalem, you will die in battle or from disease or hunger, and the Babylonian army will capture the city anyway. But if you surrender to the Babylonians, they will let you live."

[4] So the four of them went to the king and said, "You should put Jeremiah to death, because he is making the soldiers and everyone else lose hope. He isn't trying to help our people; he's trying to harm them."

[5] Zedekiah replied, "Do what you want with him. I can't stop you."

[6] Then they took me back to the courtyard of the palace guards and let me down with ropes into the well that belonged to Malchiah, the king's son. There was no water in the well, and I sank down in the mud.

[7-8] Ebedmelech from Ethiopia* was an official at the palace, and he heard what they had done to me. So he went to speak with King Zedekiah, who was holding court at Benjamin Gate. [9] Ebedmelech said, "Your

Majesty, Jeremiah is a prophet, and those men were wrong to throw him into a well. And when Jerusalem runs out of food, Jeremiah will starve to death down there."

[10] Zedekiah answered, "Take thirty* of my soldiers and pull Jeremiah out before he dies."

[11] Ebedmelech and the soldiers went to the palace and got some rags from the room under the treasury. He used ropes to lower them into the well. [12] Then he said, "Put these rags under your arms so the ropes won't hurt you." After I had done that, [13] the men pulled me out. And from then on, I was kept in the courtyard of the palace guards.

King Zedekiah questions Jeremiah

[14] King Zedekiah* had me brought to his private entrance* to the temple, and he said, "I'm going to ask you something, and I want to know the truth."

[15] "Why?" I replied. "You won't listen, and you might even have me killed!"

[16] He said, "I swear in the name of the living LORD our Creator that I won't have you killed. No one else can hear what we say, and I won't let anyone kill you."

[17] Then I told him that the LORD had said: "Zedekiah, I am the LORD God All-Powerful, the God of Israel. I promise that if you surrender to King Nebuchadnezzar's* officers, you and your family won't be killed, and Jerusalem won't be burnt down. [18] But if you don't surrender, I will let the Babylonian army capture Jerusalem and burn it down, and you will be taken prisoner."

[19] Zedekiah answered, "I can't surrender to the Babylonians. I'm too afraid of the Jews who have already joined them. The Babylonians might hand me over to those Jews, and they would torture me."

[20] I said, "If you will just obey the LORD, the Babylonians won't hand you over to those Jews. You will be allowed to live, and all will go well for you. [21] But the LORD has shown me that if you refuse to obey, [22] then the women of your palace will be taken prisoner by Nebuchadnezzar's officials. And those women will say to you:

> Friends you trusted led you astray.
> Now you're trapped in mud,
> and those friends you trusted
> have all turned away.

*37.21 a loaf of bread: Bread was the main food of the Israelites. During this time of emergency in Jerusalem, everyone probably received the same amount each day.
*38.7,8 Ethiopia: The Hebrew text has "Cush," a region south of Egypt that included parts of the present countries of Ethiopia and Sudan.

*38.14 Zedekiah: See the note at 1.3.
*38.17 Nebuchadnezzar's: See the note at 21.2.

23 The Babylonian army will take your wives and children captive, you will be taken as a prisoner to the King of Babylonia, and Jerusalem will be burnt down."

24 Zedekiah said, "Jeremiah, if you tell anyone what we have talked about, you might lose your life. 25 And I'm sure that if my officials hear about our meeting, they will ask you what we said to each other. They might even threaten to kill you if you don't tell them. 26 So if they question you, tell them you were begging me not to send you back to the prison at Jonathan's house, because going back there would kill you."

27 The officials did come and question me about my meeting with the king, and I told them exactly what he had ordered me to say. They never spoke to me about the meeting again, since no one had heard us talking.

28 I was held in the courtyard of the palace guards until the day Jerusalem was captured.

The fall of Jerusalem and later events in Judah

CHAPTER 39

Jerusalem is captured by the Babylonians

This is also told in Jeremiah 52.4-16; 2 Kings 25.1-12

1-3 In the tenth month* of the ninth year that Zedekiah* was king of Judah, King Nebuchadnezzar* and the Babylonian army began their attack on Jerusalem. They kept the city surrounded for a year and a half. Then, on the ninth day of the fourth month* of the eleventh year that Zedekiah was king, they broke through the city walls.

After Jerusalem was captured,* Nebuchadnezzar's highest officials,' including Nebo Sarsechim' and Nergal Sharezer from Simmagir,' took their places at Middle Gate to show they were in control of the city.*

39.1-3 the tenth month: Tebeth, the tenth month of the Hebrew calendar, from about mid-December to mid-January.
39.1-3 Zedekiah: See the note at 1.3.
39.1-3 Nebuchadnezzar: See the note at 21.2.
39.1-3 fourth month: Tammuz, the fourth month of the Hebrew calendar, from about mid-June to mid-July.
39.1-3 After Jerusalem was captured: This phrase is from 38.28.
39.1-3 took their places . . . control of the city: The rulers and leaders often sat in the broad open area at the gate of a city to take care of official business and hold trials.
See also: 38.28: Ezek 33.21.

4 When King Zedekiah and his troops saw that Jerusalem had been captured, they tried to escape from the city that same night. They went to the king's garden, where they slipped through the gate between the two city walls* and headed towards the valley of the River Jordan. 5 But the Babylonian troops caught up with them near Jericho. They arrested Zedekiah and took him to the town of Riblah in the land of Hamath, where Nebuchadnezzar put him on trial, then found him guilty 6 and gave orders for him to be punished. Zedekiah's sons were killed there in front of him, and so were the leaders of Judah's ruling families. 7 His eyes were put out, and he was put in chains, so he could be dragged off to Babylonia.

8 Meanwhile, the Babylonian army had burnt the houses in Jerusalem, including* the royal palace, and they had broken down the city walls. 9 Nebuzaradan, the Babylonian officer in charge of the guards, led away everyone from the city as prisoners, even those who had deserted to Nebuchadnezzar. 10 Only the poorest people who owned no land were left behind in Judah, and Nebuzaradan gave them fields and vineyards.

11 Nebuchadnezzar had given the following orders to Nebuzaradan: 12 "Find Jeremiah and keep him safe. Take good care of him and do whatever he asks."

13 Nebuzaradan, Nebushazban, Nergal Sharezer, and the other officers of King Nebuchadnezzar 14 sent some of their troops to bring me from the courtyard of the royal palace guards. They put me in the care of Gedaliah son of Ahikam* and told me to take me to my home. And so I was allowed to stay with the people who remained in Judah.

The LORD promises to protect Ebedmelech

15 While I was a prisoner in the courtyard of the palace guard, the LORD told me to say 16 to Ebedmelech from Ethiopia:*

I am the LORD All-Powerful, the God of Israel. I warned everyone that I would bring disaster, not prosperity, to this city. Now very soon I will do what I said, and you will see it happen. 17-18 But because you trusted me,* I will protect you from

---

39.4 the gate between the two city walls: The construction of the city walls at this point is not known.
39.16 Ethiopia: See the note at 38.7,8.
39.17,18 you trusted me: See 38.7-13, where Ebedmelech helped Jeremiah.

the officials of Judah, and when Judah is struck by disaster, I will rescue you and keep you alive. I, the LORD, have spoken.

CHAPTER 40

Jeremiah is set free

[1] I was led away in chains along with the people of Judah and Jerusalem who were being taken to Babylonia. Nebuzaradan was the officer in charge of the guard, and when we stopped at Ramah, the LORD made him set me free. [2] Nebuzaradan said:

Jeremiah, the LORD your God warned your people that he would bring disaster on this land. [3] But they continued to rebel against him, and now he has punished them just as he threatened.

[4] Today I am taking the chains off your wrists and setting you free! If you want to, you can come with me to Babylonia, and I will see that you are taken care of. Or if you decide to stay here, you can go wherever you wish. [5] King Nebuchadnezzar* has chosen Gedaliah to rule Judah. You can live near Gedaliah, and he will provide for you, or you can live anywhere else you want.

Nebuzaradan gave me a supply of food, then let me leave. [6] I decided to stay with the people of Judah, and I went to live near Gedaliah in Mizpah.

The harvest is brought in

[7-8] Ishmael the son of Nethaniah, together with Johanan and Jonathan, the two sons of Kareah, had been officers in Judah's army. And so had Seraiah the son of Tanhumeth, the sons of Ephai the Netophathite, and Jezaniah from Maacah. They and their troops had been stationed outside Jerusalem and had not been captured. They heard that Gedaliah had been chosen to rule Judah, and that the poorest men, women, and children had not been taken away to Babylonia. So they went to Mizpah and met with their new ruler.

[9] Gedaliah told them, "There's no need to be afraid of the Babylonians. Everything will be fine, if we live peacefully and obey King Nebuchadnezzar.* [10] I will stay here at Mizpah and meet with the Babylonian officials on each of their visits. But you must

go back to your towns and bring in the harvest, then store the wine, olive oil, and dried fruit."

[11-12] Earlier, when the Babylonians had invaded Judah, many of the Jews escaped to Moab, Ammon, Edom, and several other countries. But these Jews heard that the king of Babylonia had appointed Gedaliah as ruler of Judah, and that only a few people were left there. So the Jews in these other countries came back to Judah and helped with the grape and fruit harvest, which was especially large that year.

Gedaliah is murdered

[13] One day, Johanan got together with some of the other men who had been army officers, and they came to Mizpah and met with Gedaliah. [14] They said, "Gedaliah, we came to warn you that King Baalis of Ammon hired Ishmael to murder you!"

Gedaliah refused to believe them, [15] so Johanan went to Gedaliah privately and said, "Let me kill Ishmael. No one will find out who did it. There are only a few people left in Judah, but they are depending on you. And if you are murdered, they will be scattered or killed."

[16] Gedaliah answered, "Don't kill Ishmael! What you've said about him can't be true."

CHAPTER 41

[1] But in the seventh month,* Ishmael¹ came to Mizpah with ten of his soldiers. He had been one of the king's officials and was a member of the royal family. Ishmael and his men were invited to eat with Gedaliah. [2] During the meal, Ishmael and his soldiers killed Gedaliah, the man chosen as ruler of Judah by the king of Babylonia. [3] Then they killed the Jews who were with Gedaliah, and they also killed the Babylonian soldiers who were there.

[4] The next day, the murders had still not been discovered, [5] when eighty men came down the road towards Mizpah from the towns of Shechem, Shiloh, and Samaria. They were on their way to the temple to offer gifts of grain and incense to the LORD. They had shaved off their beards, torn their clothes, and cut themselves, because they were mourning.

---

*40.5,9 Nebuchadnezzar: See the note at 21.2.
See also: 40.7–9: 2 King 25.22–24.

*41.1 seventh month: Tishri, also called Ethanim, the seventh month of the Hebrew calendar, from about mid-September to mid-October.
See also: 41.1–3: 2 King 25.25.

749

6 Ishmael went out of the town gate to meet them. He pretended to be weeping, and he asked them to come into Mizpah to meet with Gedaliah, the ruler of Judah. 7 But after they were inside the town, Ishmael ordered his soldiers to kill them and throw their bodies into a well. 8 He let ten of the men live, because they offered to give him supplies of wheat, barley, olive oil, and honey they had hidden in a field. 9 The well that he filled with bodies had been dug by King Asa* of Judah to store rainwater, because he was afraid that King Baasha* of Israel might surround Mizpah and keep the people from getting to their water supply.

10 Nebuzaradan, King Nebuchadnezzar's* officer in charge of the guard, had left King Zedekiah's* daughters and many other people at Mizpah, and he had put Gedaliah in charge of them. But now Ishmael took them all prisoner and led them towards Ammon, on the other side of the River Jordan.

11 Johanan and the other army officers heard what Ishmael had done. 12 So they and their troops chased Ishmael and caught up with him at the large pit at Gibeon. 13 When Ishmael's prisoners saw Johanan and the officers, they were happy 14 and turned round and ran towards Johanan. 15 But Ishmael and eight of his men escaped and went to Ammon.

Johanan decides to take the people to Egypt

16 Johanan and the officers had rescued the women, children, and royal officials whom Ishmael had taken prisoner after killing Gedaliah. Johanan led the people from Gibeon 17-18 towards Egypt. They wanted to go there, because they were afraid of what the Babylonians would do when they found out that Ishmael had killed Gedaliah, the ruler appointed by King Nebuchadnezzar.*

The people ask Jeremiah to pray for them

On the way to Egypt, we* stopped at the town of Geruth Chimham near Bethlehem.

---

*41.9 Asa: Ruled 911–870 BC.
*41.9 Baasha: Ruled 909–886 BC.
*41.10,17,18 Nebuchadnezzar's: See the note at 21.2.
*41.10 Zedekiah's: See the note at 1.3.
*41.17,18 we: The group of people included Jeremiah, since he had been staying with Gedaliah near Mizpah (see 40.6).

CHAPTER 42

1 Johanan, Jezaniah,* the other army officers, and everyone else in the group, came to me 2 and said, "Please pray to the LORD your God for us. Judah used to have many people, but as you can see, only a few of us are left. 3 Ask the LORD to tell us where he wants us to go and what he wants us to do."

4 "All right," I answered, "I will pray to the LORD your God, and I will tell you everything he says."

5 They answered, "The LORD himself will be our witness that we promise to do whatever he says, 6 even if it isn't what we want to do. We will obey the LORD so that all will go well for us."

7 Ten days later, the LORD gave me an answer for 8 Johanan, the officers, and the other people. So I called them together 9 and told them that the LORD God of Israel had said:

You asked Jeremiah to pray and find out what you should do. 10 I am sorry that I had to punish you, and so I now tell you to stay here in Judah, where I will plant you and build you up, instead of tearing you down and uprooting you. 11 Don't be afraid of the King of Babylonia. I will protect you from him, 12 and I will even force him to have mercy on you and give back your farms.

13 But you might keep on saying, "We won't stay here in Judah, and we won't obey the LORD our God. 14 We are going to Egypt, where there is plenty of food and no danger of war."

15 People of Judah, you survived when the Babylonian army attacked. Now you are planning to move to Egypt, and if you do go, this is what will happen. 16-17 You are afraid of war, starvation, and disease here in Judah, but they will follow you to Egypt and kill you there. None of you will survive the disasters I will send.

18 I, the LORD, was angry with the people of Jerusalem and punished them. And if you go to Egypt, I will be angry and punish you the same way. You will never again see your homeland. People will be horrified at what I do to you, and they will use the name of your city as a curse word.

Jeremiah gives a warning

19 I told the people:

You escaped the disaster that struck Judah, but now the LORD warns you to stay away from Egypt. ²⁰ You asked me to pray and find out what the LORD our God wants you to do, and you promised to obey him. But that was a terrible mistake, ²¹ because now that I have given you the LORD's answer, you refuse to obey him. ²² And so, you will die in Egypt from war, hunger, and disease.

Jeremiah in Egypt

CHAPTER 43

The people go to Egypt

¹ I told the people everything the LORD had told me. ² But Azariah, Johanan' and some other arrogant men said to me, "You're lying! The LORD didn't tell you to say that we shouldn't go to Egypt. ³ Baruch son of Neriah must have told you to say that. He wants the Babylonians to capture us, so they can take us away to Babylonia or even kill us."

⁴ Johanan, the other army officers, and everyone else refused to stay in Judah in spite of the LORD's command. ⁵ So Johanan and the officers led us away towards Egypt. The group that left Judah included those who had been scattered in other countries and who had then come back to live in Judah. ⁶ Baruch and I and others in the group had been staying with Gedaliah, because Nebuzaradan, the Babylonian officer in charge of the guard, had ordered him to take care of the king's daughters and quite a few men, women, and children.

⁷ The people disobeyed the LORD and went to Egypt. The group had settled in Tahpanhes, ⁸ when the LORD told me:

⁹ Jeremiah, carry some large stones to the entrance of the government building in Tahpanhes. Bury the stones underneath the brick pavement' and be sure the Jews are watching.

¹⁰ Then tell them that I, the LORD All-Powerful, the God of Israel, have sent for my servant, Nebuchadnezzar* of Babylonia. I will bring him here and make him set up his throne and his royal tent over these stones that I told you to bury. ¹¹ He will attack Egypt and kill many of its people; others will die of disease or be dragged away as prisoners. ¹²⁻¹³ I will let him set Egypt's temples on fire, and he will either burn or carry off their idols. He will

destroy the sacred monuments at the temple of the sun-god.' Then Nebuchadnezzar will pick the land clean, just like a shepherd picking the lice off his clothes. And he will return safely home.

CHAPTER 44

The LORD will destroy the people of Judah

¹ The LORD told me to speak with the Jews who were living in the towns of Migdol, Tahpanhes, and Memphis in northern Egypt, and also to those living in southern Egypt. He told me to tell them:

² I am the LORD All-Powerful, the God of Israel. You saw how I destroyed Jerusalem and the towns of Judah. They lie empty and in ruins today, ³ because the people of Judah made me angry by worshipping gods that had never helped them or their ancestors.

⁴ Time after time I sent my servants the prophets to tell the people of Judah how much I hated their disgusting sins. The prophets warned them to stop sinning, ⁵ but they refused to listen and would not stop worshipping other gods. ⁶ Finally, my anger struck like a raging flood, and today Jerusalem and the towns of Judah are nothing but empty ruins.

⁷ Why do you now insist on heading for another disaster? A disaster that will destroy not only you, but also your children and babies. ⁸ You have made me angry by worshipping idols and burning incense to other gods after you came here to Egypt. You will die such a disgusting death, that other nations will use the name of Judah as a curse word. ⁹ When you were living in Jerusalem and Judah, you followed the example of your ancestors in doing evil things, just like your kings and queens. ¹⁰ Even now, your pride keeps you from respecting me and obeying the laws and teachings I gave you and your ancestors.

¹¹ I, the LORD All-Powerful, have decided to wipe you out with disasters. ¹² There were only a few of you left in Judah, and you decided to go to Egypt. But you will die such horrible deaths in war or from starvation, that people of other countries will use the name of Judah as a curse word. ¹³ I punished Jerusalem with war, hunger, and disease, and that's how I will punish you. ¹⁴ None of you will survive. You may

---

*43.10 Nebuchadnezzar: See the note at 21.2.
See also: 43.5–7: 2 King 25.26.

hope to return to Judah some day, but only a very few of you will escape death and be able to go back.

The people refuse to worship the LORD

15 A large number of Jews from both northern and southern Egypt listened to me as I told them what the LORD had said. Most of the men in the crowd knew that their wives often burnt incense to other gods. So they and their wives shouted:

16 Jeremiah, what do we care if you speak in the LORD's name? We refuse to listen! 17 We have promised to worship the goddess Astarte, the Queen of Heaven,' and that is exactly what we are going to do. We will burn incense and offer sacrifices of wine to her, just as we, our ancestors, our kings, and our leaders did when we lived in Jerusalem and the other towns of Judah. We had plenty of food back then. We were well off, and nothing bad ever happened to us. 18 But since the time we stopped burning incense and offering wine sacrifices to her, we have been dying from war and hunger.

19 Then the women said, "When we lived in Judah, we worshipped the Queen of Heaven and offered sacrifices of wine and special loaves of bread shaped like her. Our husbands knew what we were doing, and they approved of it."

20 Then I told the crowd:

21 Don't you think the LORD knew that you and your ancestors, your leaders and kings, and the rest of the people were burning incense to other gods in Jerusalem and everywhere else in Judah? 22 And when he could no longer put up with your disgusting sins, he placed a curse on your land and turned it into a desert, as it is today. 23 This disaster happened because you worshipped other gods and rebelled against the LORD by refusing to obey him or follow his laws and teachings.

24-25 Then I told the men and their wives, that the LORD All-Powerful, the God of Israel, had said:

Here in Egypt you still keep your promises to burn incense and offer sacrifices of wine to the so-called Queen of Heaven. 26 Keep these promises! But let me tell you what will happen. As surely as I am the LORD God, I swear that I will never again accept any promises you make in my name.

27 Instead of watching over you, I will watch for chances to harm you. Some of you will die in war, and others will starve to death. 28 Only a few will escape and return to Judah. Then everyone who went to live in Egypt will know that when I say something will happen, it will — no matter what you say.

29 And here is how you will know that I will keep my threats to punish you in Egypt. 30 I will hand over King Hophra of Egypt to those who want to kill him,* just as I handed Zedekiah* over to Nebuchadnezzar,* who wanted to kill him.

A message for Baruch

CHAPTER 45

The LORD will not let Baruch be killed

1 In the fourth year that Jehoiakim* was king of Judah, Baruch wrote down everything I had told him.* 2 Then later, the LORD God of Israel told me to say to Baruch:

3 You are moaning and blaming me, the LORD, for your troubles and sorrow, and for being so tired that you can't even rest. 4 But all over the earth I am tearing down what I built and pulling up what I planted. 5 I am bringing disaster everywhere, so don't even think about making any big plans for yourself. However, I promise that wherever you go, I will at least protect you from death. I, the LORD, have spoken.

The Lord speaks about the nations

CHAPTER 46

1 The LORD often told me what to say about the different nations of the world.

---

*44.30 King Hophra . . . kill him: Hophra, also known as Apries, ruled Egypt from 589 to 570 BC, when he was killed by Ahmosis II, who then became king of Egypt and ruled until 526 BC.
*44.30 Zedekiah: See the note at 1.3.
*44.30 Nebuchadnezzar: See the note at 21.2.
*45.1 Jehoiakim: See the note at 1.3.
*45.1 Baruch wrote down everything I had told him: See 36.1–32.

See also: 44.30: 2 King 25.1–7. 45.1: 2 King 24.1; 2 Chron 36.5–7; Dan 1.1,2.

What the LORD says about Egypt

² In the fourth year that Jehoiakim* was king of Judah, King Nebuchadnezzar* of Babylonia defeated King Neco of Egypt* in a battle at the city of Carchemish near the River Euphrates. And here is what the LORD told me to say about the Egyptian army:

³ It's time to go into battle!
So grab your shields,
⁴ saddle your horses,
and polish your spears.
Put on your helmets and armour,
then take your positions.

⁵ I can see the battle now —
you are defeated
and running away,
never once looking back.
Terror is all around.
⁶ You are strong and run fast,
but you can't escape.
You fall in battle
near the River Euphrates.

⁷ What nation is this,
that rises like the River Nile
overflowing its banks?
⁸ It is Egypt, rising with a roar
like a raging river
and saying,
"I'll flood the earth,
destroying cities, and killing
everyone in them."

⁹ Go ahead, Egypt.
Tell your chariots and cavalry
to attack and fight hard.
Order your troops to march out,
with Ethiopians* and Libyans
carrying shields,
and the Lydians* armed with bows
and arrows.

¹⁰ But the LORD All-Powerful
will win this battle
and take revenge
on his enemies.

His sword will eat them
and drink their blood
until it is full.
They will be killed in the north
near the River Euphrates,
as a sacrifice to the LORD.

¹¹ Egypt, no medicine can heal you,
not even the soothing lotion
from Gilead.
¹² All nations have heard you weep;
you are disgraced,
and they know it.
Your troops fall to the ground,
stumbling over each other.

A warning for Egypt

¹³⁻¹⁴ When King Nebuchadnezzar* of Babylonia was on his way to attack Egypt, the LORD sent me with a warning for every Egyptian town, but especially for Migdol, Memphis, and Tahpanhes. He said I must tell them:

Prepare to defend yourselves!
Everywhere in your nation,
people are dying in war.
¹⁵ I have struck down
your mighty god Apis*
and chased him away.◊
¹⁶ Your soldiers stumble
over each other
and say, "Get up!
The enemy will kill us,
unless we can escape
to our own land."

¹⁷ Give the king of Egypt
this new name,
"Talks-Big-Does-Nothing".

¹⁸ Egypt, I am the true king,
the LORD All-Powerful,
and as surely as I live,
those enemies who attack
will tower over you
like Mount Tabor among the hills
or Mount Carmel by the sea.
¹⁹ You will be led away captive,
so pack a few things
to bring with you.
Your capital, Memphis,
will lie empty and in ruins.

---

*46.2 Jehoiakim: See the note at 1.3.
*46.2 King Nebuchadnezzar: Ruled 605–562 BC. At the time of the battle in 605 BC, he was crown prince, but his father died a few months later, and he became king.
*46.2 King Neco of Egypt: Neco II, ruled 609–594 BC.
*46.9 Ethiopians: See the note at 38.7,8.
*46.9 Lydians: Probably hired soldiers from Lydia, an area in west-central Asia minor.
See also: 46.2-26: Isa 19.1-25; Ezek 29.1–32.32.

*46.13,14 Nebuchadnezzar: See the note at 21.2.
*46.15 Apis: A sacred bull, kept in a temple at Memphis, Egypt, and worshipped as a god.
See also: 46.13: Jer 43.10–13.

20 An enemy from the north
    will attack you, beautiful Egypt,
    like a fly biting a cow.
21 The foreign soldiers you hired
    will turn and run.
    But they are doomed,
    like well-fed calves
    being led to the butcher.
22-23 The enemy army will go forward
    like a swarm of locusts.*
    Your troops will feel helpless,
    like a snake in a forest
    when men with axes
    start chopping down trees.
    It can only hiss
    and try to escape.
24 Your people will be disgraced
    and captured by the enemy
    from the north.

25 I am the LORD All-Powerful, the God of
Israel. Soon I will punish the god Amon of
Thebes* and the other Egyptian gods, the
Egyptian kings, the people of Egypt, and
everyone who trusts in the Egyptian power.
26 I will hand them over to King
Nebuchadnezzar and his army. But I also
promise that Egypt will some day have
people living here again, just as it had
before. I, the LORD, have spoken.

The LORD will bring Israel home

The LORD said:

27 Israel,* don't be afraid.
    Some day I will bring you home
    from foreign lands.
    You and your descendants
    will live in peace and safety,
    with nothing to fear.
28 So don't be afraid,
    even though now
    you deserve to be punished
    and have been scattered
    among other nations.
    But when I destroy them,
    I will protect you.
    I, the LORD, have spoken.

CHAPTER 47

What the LORD says about
the Philistines

1 Before the king of Egypt attacked the town
of Gaza,* the LORD told me to say to the
Philistines:

2 I, the LORD, tell you
    that your land will be flooded
    with an army from the north.
    It will destroy your towns
    and sweep you away,
    moaning and screaming.
3 When you hear the thunder
    of horses and chariots,
    your courage will vanish,
    and parents will abandon
    their own children.

4 You refugees from Crete,'
    your time has now come,
    and I will destroy you.
    None of you will be left
    to help the cities
    of Tyre and Sidon.
5-6 The Anakim who survive*
    in Gaza and Ashkelon
    will mourn for you
    by shaving their heads
    and sitting in silence.
    You ask how long I will continue
    to attack you with my sword,
    then you tell me to put it away
    and leave you alone.
7 But how can my sword rest,
    when I have commanded it
    to attack Ashkelon
    and the coast?

CHAPTER 48

What the LORD says about Moab

1 The LORD All-Powerful, the God of Israel,
told me to say to the nation of Moab:

46.22,23 locusts: A type of grasshopper that comes
in swarms and causes great damage to plant life.
46.25 the god Amon of Thebes: Amon was the king
of the Egyptian gods and was the special god of the
Egyptian kings.
46.27 Israel: See the note at 30.10,11.

See also: 46.27,28: Jer 30.10,11.

754

47.1 attacked the town of Gaza: One of the major
Philistine towns; nothing is known about this attack.
47.5,6 Anakim who survive: One ancient
translation; Hebrew "people in the valley who
survive". The Anakim may have been a group of
people of great stature that lived in Palestine before
the Israelites (see Numbers 13.33; Deuteronomy
2.10,11,20,21; and Joshua 11.21,22).

See also: 47.1–7: Isa 14.29–31; Ezek 25.15–17; Joel 3.4–8;
Amos 1.6–8; Zeph 2.4–7; Zech 9.5–7.   48.1–47: Isa 15.1–16.14;
25.10–12; Ezek 25.8–11; Amos 2.1–3; Zeph 2.8–11.

The town of Nebo is doomed;
Kiriathaim will be captured
and disgraced,
and even its fortress
will be left in ruins.

2 No one honours you, Moab.
In Heshbon, enemies make plans
to end your life.
My sword will leave only silence
in your town named "Quiet".*

3 The people of Horonaim
will cry for help,
as their town is attacked
and destroyed.

4 Moab will be shattered!
Your children will sob

5 and cry on their way up
to the town of Luhith;
on the road to Horonaim
they will tell of disasters.

6 Run for your lives!
Head into the desert
like a wild donkey.*

7 You thought you could be saved
by your power and wealth,
but you will be captured
along with your god Chemosh,
his priests, and officials.

8 Not one of your towns
will escape destruction.

I have told your enemies,
"Wipe out the valley
and the flat lands of Moab.

9 Spread salt on the ground
to kill the crops.*
Leave its towns in ruins,
with no one living there.

10 I want you to kill the Moabites,
and if you let them escape,
I will put a curse on you."

11 Moab, you are like wine
left to settle undisturbed,
never poured from jar to jar.
And so, your nation continues
to prosper and improve.*

12 But now, I will send enemies
to pour out the wine
and smash the jars!

13 Then you will be ashamed,
because your god Chemosh
cannot save you,

just as Bethel* could not help
the Israelites.

14 You claim that your soldiers
are strong and brave.

15 But I am the LORD,
the all-powerful King,
and I promise that enemies
will overpower your towns.
Even your best warriors
will die in the battle.

16 It won't be long now —
disaster will hit Moab!

17 I will order the nearby nations
to mourn for you and say,
"Isn't it sad? Moab ruled others,
but now its glorious power
has been shattered."

18 People in the town of Dibon,*
you will be honoured no more,
so have a seat in the dust.
Your walls will be torn down
when the enemies attack.

19 You people of Aroer,*
wait beside the road,
and when refugees run by,
ask them, "What happened?"

20 They will answer,
"Moab has been defeated!
Weep with us in shame.
Tell everyone at the River Arnon
that Moab is destroyed."

21-24 I will punish every town
that belongs to Moab,
but especially Holon,
Jahzah, Mephaath,
Dibon, Nebo,
Beth-Diblathaim, Kiriathaim,
Beth-Gamul, Beth-Meon,
Kerioth, and Bozrah.*

25 My decision is final —
your army will be crushed,
and your power broken.

26 People of Moab, you claim
to be stronger than I am.
Now I will tell other nations
to make you drunk

---

*48.2 silence . . . Quiet: In Hebrew the name of the town was "Madmen", which sounds like the word for "silence".

*48.13 Bethel: It may refer to the Phoenician or Canaanite god of that name; or it may refer to the town where people of the northern kingdom worshipped at a local shrine (see 1 Kings 12.26–30).
*48.18 Dibon: The capital city of Moab.
*48.19 Aroer: A Moabite town just north of the River Arnon.

and to laugh while you collapse
in your own vomit.
27 You made fun of my people
and treated them like criminals
caught in the act.
28 Now you must leave your towns
and live like doves
in the shelter of cliffs
and canyons.

29 I know about your pride,
and how you strut and boast.
30 But I also know boasting
will never save you.
31 So I will cry and mourn
for Moab
and its town of Kir-Heres.

32 People of Sibmah,
you were like a vineyard
heavy with grapes,
and with branches reaching
north to the town of Jazer
and west to the Dead Sea.ᵉ
But you have been destroyed,
and so I will weep for you,
as the people of Jazer weep
for the vineyards.

33 Harvest celebrations are gone
from the orchards and farms
of Moab.
There are no happy shouts
from people making wine.

34 Weeping from Heshbon
can be heard as far
as Elealeh and Jahaz;
cries from Zoar are heard
in Horonaim
and Eglath-Shelishiyah.
And Nimrim Brook has run dry.

35 I will get rid of anyone
who burns incense
to the gods of Moab
or offers sacrifices
at their shrines.
I, the LORD, have spoken.

36 In my heart I moan for Moab,
like a funeral song
played on a flute.
I mourn for the people
of the town of Kir-Heres,
because their wealth is gone.

37-38 The people of Moab
mourn on the rooftops
and in the streets.

Men cut off their beards,
people shave their heads;
they make cuts on their hands
and wear sackcloth.*
And it's all because I, the LORD,
have shattered Moab like a jar
that no one wants.
39 Moab lies broken!
Listen to its people cry
as they turn away in shame.
Other nations are horrified
at what happened,
but still they laugh.

40 Moab, an enemy swoops down
like an eagle spreading its wings
over your land.
41 Your cities* and fortresses
will be captured,
and your warriors gripped by fear.ᵉ
42 You are finished as a nation,
because you dared oppose me,
the LORD.
43 Terror, pits, and traps
are waiting for you.
44 If you are terrified and run,
you will fall into a pit;
and if you crawl out of the pit,
you'll get caught in a trap.
The time has come
for you to be punished.

45 Near the city of Heshbon,
where Sihon once ruled,
tired refugees stand in shadows
cast by the flames
of their burning city.
Soon, the towns on other hilltops,
where those warlike people live,
will also go up in smoke.

46 People of Moab, you worshipped
Chemosh, your god,
but now you are done for,
and your children are prisoners
in a foreign country.
47 Yet some day, I will bring
your people back home.
I, the LORD, have spoken.

CHAPTER 49

What the LORD says about Ammon

1 The LORD has this to say about the nation of
Ammon:

---

*48.37,38 sackcloth: See the note at 4.8.

See also: 49.1–6: Ezek 21.28–32; 25.1–7; Amos 1.13–15;
Zeph 2.8–11.

The people of Israel
have plenty of children
to inherit their lands.
So why have you worshippers
of the god Milcom*
taken over towns and land
belonging to the Gad tribe?
2 Some day I will send an army
to attack you in Rabbah,
your capital city.
It will be left in ruins,
and the surrounding villages
will lie in ashes.
You took some of Israel's land,
but on that day
Israel will take yours!

3 Cry, people of Heshbon;*
your town will become
a pile of rubble.↑
You will turn here and there,
but your path will be blocked.↑

Put on sackcloth* and mourn,
you citizens of Rabbah,
because the idol you worship*
will be taken
to a foreign country,
along with its priests
and temple officials.
4 You rebellious Ammonites
trust your wealth and ask,
"Who could attack us?"
But I warn you not to boast
when your strength is fading.↑
5 I, the LORD All-Powerful,
will send neighbouring nations
to strike you with terror.
You will be scattered,
with no one to care
for your refugees.
6 Yet some day, I will bring
your people back home.
I, the LORD, have spoken.

What the LORD says about Edom

7-8 The LORD All-Powerful says about Edom:

Wisdom and common sense
have vanished from Teman.*
I will send disaster to punish
you descendants of Esau,*
so anyone from Dedan*
had better turn round
and run back home.
9 People who harvest grapes
leave some for the poor.
Thieves who break in at night
take only what they want.
10 But I will take everything
that belongs to you,
people of Edom,
and I will uncover every place
where you try to hide.
Then you will die,
and so will your children,
relatives, and neighbours.
11 But I can be trusted
to care for your orphans
and widows.

12 Even those nations that don't deserve to
be punished will have to drink from the
cup of my anger. So how can you possibly
hope to escape? 13 I, the LORD, swear in my
own name that your city of Bozrah* and all
your towns will suffer a horrible fate. They
will lie in ruins for ever, and people will use
the name "Bozrah" as a curse word.

14 I have sent a messenger
to command the nations
to prepare for war
against you people of Edom.
15 Your nation will be small,
yet hated by other nations.
16 Pride tricks you into thinking
that other nations
look at you with fear.↑
You live along the cliffs
and high in the mountains
like the eagles,
but I am the LORD,
and I will bring you down.
17 People passing by your country
will be shocked and horrified
to see a disaster

---

*49.1 Milcom: The national god of Ammon, probably
the same as the god Molech in 32.35.
*49.3 Heshbon: See also 48.45; since Heshbon was
near the border of Moab and Ammon, it was probably
ruled by the country that was stronger at the time.
*49.3 sackcloth: See the note at 4.8.
*49.3 the idol you worship: Hebrew "Milcom" (see
verse 1 and the note there).

See also: 49.7–22: Isa 34.5–17; 63.1–6; Ezek 25.12–14;
35.1–15; Amos 1.11,12; Obad 1–14; Mal 1.2–5.

*49.7,8 Teman: The name of a town in Edom,
sometimes used as the name of the northern half of
the nation of Edom; here it probably stands for the
whole nation.
*49.7,8 Esau: The ancestor of the nation of Edom.
*49.7,8 Dedan: The name of a town in north-west
Arabia, also used of the north-west region of Arabia
along the Red Sea.
*49.13 Bozrah: The main city and capital of Edom.

18 as bad as the destruction
    of Sodom and Gomorrah
    and towns nearby.
  The towns of Edom will be empty.

19 I will attack you
    like a lion from the forest,
  attacking sheep in a meadow
    along the Jordan.
  In a moment the flock runs,
    and the land is empty.
  Who will I choose to attack you?
    I will do it myself!
  No one can force me to fight
    or chase me away.
20 Listen to my plans for you,
    people of Edom.*
  Your children will be dragged off
    and your country destroyed.
21 The sounds of your destruction
    will reach the Red Sea*
    and cause the earth to shake.
22 An enemy will swoop down
    to attack you,
  like an eagle spreading its wings
    and circling over Bozrah.
  Your warriors will be gripped
    by fear.*

What the LORD says about Damascus

23 The LORD says about Damascus:

  The towns of Hamath and Arpad*
    have heard your bad news.
  They have lost hope,
    and worries roll over them
    like ocean waves.*
24 You people of Damascus
    have lost your courage,
  and in panic you turn to run,
    gripped by fear and pain.*

25 I once was pleased
    with your famous city.
  But now I warn you, "Escape
    while you still can!"*
26 Soon, even your best soldiers
    will lie dead in your streets.

---

*49.21 Red Sea: Hebrew *yam suph*, here referring to
the Gulf of Aqaba, since the term is extended to
include the north-eastern arm of the Red Sea (see also
the note at Exodus 13.18).
*49.23 Hamath and Arpad: Two towns in Syria that
had been the capitals of small kingdoms allied with
the more powerful kingdom whose capital was
Damascus.
See also: 49.18: Gen 19.24,25. 49.23–27: Isa 17.1–3;
Amos 1.3–5; Zech 9.1.
758

  I, the LORD All-Powerful,
    have spoken.
27 I will set fire to your city walls
    and burn down the fortresses
    King Benhadad built.

**Nebuchadnezzar and the
people of the desert**

28 Here is what the LORD says about the Kedar
tribe and the desert villages* that were
conquered by King Nebuchadnezzar* of
Babylonia:

  Listen, you people of Kedar
    and the other tribes
    of the eastern desert.
  I have told Nebuchadnezzar
    to attack and destroy you.
29 His fearsome army
    will surround you,
  taking your tents and possessions,
    your sheep and camels.

30 Run and hide,
    you people of the desert
    who live in villages!*
  Nebuchadnezzar has big plans
    for you.
31 You have no city walls
    and no neighbours to help,
  yet you think you're safe —
    so I told him to attack.
32 Then your camels and large herds
    will be yours no longer.

  People of the Arabian Desert,*
    disaster will strike you
    from every side,
  and you will be scattered
    everywhere on earth.
33 Only jackals* will live
    where your villages* once stood.
  I, the LORD, have spoken.

What the LORD says about Elam

34-35 Not long after Zedekiah* became king of
Judah, the LORD told me to say:

  People of Elam,*
  I, the LORD All-Powerful,
    will kill the archers
    who make your army strong.

---

*49.28 Nebuchadnezzar: See the note at 21.2.
*49.33 jackals: See the note at 9.11.
*49.34,35 Zedekiah: See the note at 1.3.
*49.34,35 Elam: A nation east of Babylonia, attacked
by Nebuchadnezzar about 596 BC.

36 Enemies will attack
    from all directions,
and you will be led captive
    to every nation on earth.
37 Their armies will crush
    and kill you,
and you will face the disaster
    that my anger brings.
38 Your king and his officials
    will die, and I will rule
    in their place.
I, the LORD, have spoken.
39 But I promise that some day
    I will bring your people
    back to their land.

CHAPTER 50

Babylon will be captured

1-2 The LORD told me to say:

Announce what will happen
    and don't leave anything out.
Raise the signal flags;
shout so all nations can hear —
    Babylon will be captured!

Marduk,* Babylon's god,
    will be ashamed and terrified,
    and his idols broken.
3 The attack on the Babylonians
    will come from the north;
they and their animals will run,
    leaving the land empty.

Israel and Judah will return to their land

4 The LORD said:

People of Israel and Judah,
    when these things happen
you will weep, and together
    you will return to your land
    and worship me,
    the LORD your God.
5 You will ask the way to Zion
    and then come and join with me
    in making an agreement
    you won't break or forget.

6 My people, you are lost sheep
    abandoned by their shepherds
    in the mountains.
You don't even remember
    your resting place.

7 I am your true pasture land,
    the one who gave hope
    to your ancestors.
But you abandoned me,
    so when your enemies found you,
they felt no guilt
    as they gobbled you up.

8 Escape from Babylonia,
    my people.
Get out of that country!
    Don't wait for anyone else.
9 In the north I am bringing
    great nations together.
They will attack Babylon
    and capture it.
The arrows they shoot
    are like the best soldiers,*
    always finding their target.
10 Babylonia will be conquered,
    and its enemies will carry off
    everything they want.

Babylon will be disgraced

The LORD said:

11 People of Babylonia,
    you were glad
    to rob my people.
You had a good time,
    making more noise
    than horses
    and jumping around
    like calves threshing grain.*
12 The city of Babylon
    was like a mother to you.
But it will be disgraced
    and become nothing
    but a barren desert.
13 My anger will destroy Babylon,
    and no one will live there.
Everyone who passes by
    will be shocked to see
    what has happened.

14 Babylon has rebelled against me.
    Archers, take your places.
Shoot all your arrows at Babylon.
15 Attack from every side!

Babylon surrenders!
The enemy tears down
    its walls and towers.
I am taking my revenge
    by doing to Babylon what it did
    to other cities.

16 There is no one in Babylonia
to plant or harvest crops.
Even foreigners who lived there
have left for their homelands,
afraid of the enemy armies.

17 Israel is a flock of sheep
scattered by hungry lions.
The king of Assyria*
first gobbled Israel up.
Then Nebuchadnezzar,*
king of Babylonia,
crunched on Israel's bones.

18 I, the LORD All-Powerful,
the God of Israel,
punished the king of Assyria,
and I will also punish
the king of Babylonia.

19 But I will bring Israel
back to its own land.
The people will be like sheep
eating their fill
on Mount Carmel
and in Bashan,
in the hill country of Ephraim
and in Gilead.

20 I will rescue a few people
from Israel and Judah.
I will forgive them so completely
that their sin and guilt
will disappear,
never to be found.

The LORD's commands to the enemies of Babylonia

21 The LORD said:

I have told
the enemies of Babylonia,
"Attack the people of Meratharim
and Pekod.*
Kill them all!
Destroy their possessions!"

22 Sounds of war
and the noise of destruction
can be heard.

23 Babylonia was a hammer
pounding every country,
but now it lies broken.
What a shock to the nations
of the world!

24 Babylonia challenged me,
the LORD God All-Powerful,
but that nation doesn't know
it is caught in a trap that I set.

25 I've brought out my weapons,
and with them
I will put a curse on Babylonia.

26 Come from far away,
you enemies of Babylon!
Pile up the grain
from its storehouses,
and destroy it completely,
along with everything else.

27 Kill the soldiers of Babylonia,
because the time has come
for them to be punished.

28 The Babylonian army
destroyed my temple,
but soon I will take revenge.
Then refugees from Babylon
will tell about it in Zion.

29 Attack Babylon, enemy archers;
set up camp around the city,
and don't let anyone escape.
It challenged me, the holy God,
so do to it
what it did to other cities.

Proud Babylon will fall

The LORD said:

30 People of Babylon,
I, the LORD, promise
that even your best soldiers
will lie dead in the streets.

31 Babylon, you should be named,
"The Proud One".
But the time has come when I,
the LORD All-Powerful,
will punish you.

32 You are proud,
but you will stumble and fall,
and no one will help you up.
I will set your villages on fire,
and everything around you
will go up in flames.

33 You Babylonians were cruel
to Israel and Judah.
You took them captive, and now
you refuse to let them go.

34 But I, the LORD All-Powerful,
will rescue and protect them.
I will bring peace to their land
and trouble to yours.

---

*50.17 king of Assyria: Either Shalmaneser V, who
ruled 726–722 BC, conquered most of the northern
kingdom, and surrounded its capital city Samaria; or
Sargon II, who ruled 721–705 BC and took thousands
of prisoners back to Assyria.
*50.17 Nebuchadnezzar: See the note at 21.2.

See also: 50.29: Rev 18.6.

⁵ I have declared war on you,
    your officials, and advisers.
³⁶ This war will prove
    that your prophets
    are liars and fools.
And it will frighten
    your warriors.
³⁷ Then your chariot horses
    and the foreigners in your army
    will refuse to go into battle,
    and the enemy will carry away
    everything you treasure.
³⁸ Your rivers and canals
    will dry up.

All this will happen,
because your land
    is full of idols,
and they have made fools
    of you.
³⁹ Never again will people live
    in your land —
    only desert animals, jackals,*
    and unclean birds.
⁴⁰ I destroyed Sodom and Gomorrah
    and the nearby towns,
    and I will destroy Babylon
    just as completely.
No one will live there again.

Babylonia is invaded

The LORD said:

⁴¹ Far to the north,
    a nation and its allies
    have been awakened.
They are powerful
    and ready for war.
⁴² Bows and arrows and swords
    are in their hands.
The soldiers are cruel
    and show no pity.
The hoofbeats of their horses
    echo like ocean waves
    crashing against the shore.
The army has lined up for battle
    and is coming to attack you,
    people of Babylonia!
⁴³ Ever since your king heard
    about this army,
    he has been weak with fear;
    he twists and turns in pain
    like a woman giving birth.
⁴⁴ Babylonia, I will attack you
    like a lion from the forest,

attacking sheep in a meadow
    along the Jordan.
In a moment the flock runs,
    and the land is empty.
Who will I choose to attack you?
    I will do it myself!
No one can force me to fight
    or chase me away.
⁴⁵ Listen to my plans for you,
    people of Babylonia.
Your children will be dragged off,
    and your country destroyed.
⁴⁶ The sounds of your destruction
    will be heard among the nations,
    and the earth will shake.

CHAPTER 51

Babylon will be destroyed

The LORD said:

¹ I, the LORD, am sending
    a wind* to destroy
    the people of Babylonia*
    and Babylon, its capital.
² Foreign soldiers will come
    from every direction,
    and when the disaster is over,
    Babylonia will be empty
    and worthless.
³ I will tell these soldiers,
    "Attack quickly,
    before the Babylonians
    can string their bows
    or put on their armour.*
Kill their best soldiers
    and destroy their army!"
⁴ Their troops will fall wounded
    in the streets of Babylon.

⁵ Everyone in Israel and Judah
    is guilty.
But I, the LORD All-Powerful,
    their holy God,
    have not abandoned them.

⁶ Get out of Babylon!
    Run for your lives!
If you stay, you will be killed
    when I take revenge on the city
    and punish it for its sins.
⁷ Babylon was my golden cup,
    filled with the wine
    of my anger.
The nations of the world
    got drunk on this wine
    and went insane.

*50.39 jackals: See the note at 9.11.
See also: 50.39: Rev 18.2. 50.40: Gen 19.24,25.

See also: 51.7: Rev 17.2–4; 18.3.

761

8 But suddenly, Babylon will fall
   and be destroyed.

I, the LORD, told the foreigners*
   who lived there,
"Weep for the city!
Get medicine for its wounds;
   perhaps they will heal."

9 The foreigners answered,
   "We have already tried
to treat Babylon's wounds,
   but they would not heal.
Come on, let's all go home
   to our own countries.
Nothing is left in Babylonia;
   everything is destroyed."

10 The people of Israel said,
   "Tell everyone in Zion!
The LORD has taken revenge
   for what Babylon did to us."

The LORD wants Babylon destroyed

The LORD said:

11 I, the LORD,
   want Babylon destroyed,
because its army
   destroyed my temple.
So, you kings of Media,*
   sharpen your arrows
and pick up your shields.

12 Raise the signal flag
   and attack the city walls.
Post more guards.
Command soldiers to watch the city
   and set up ambushes.
I have made plans to destroy Babylon,
   and nothing will stop me.

13 People of Babylon, you live
   along the River Euphrates
and are surrounded by canals.
You are rich,
   but now the time has come
   for you to die.*

14 I, the LORD All-Powerful,
   swear by my own life
that enemy soldiers
   will fill your streets
   like a swarm of locusts.*
They will shout
   and celebrate their victory.

A hymn of praise

This is also told in Jeremiah 10.12–16

15 God used his wisdom and power
   to create the earth
   and spread out the heavens.

16 The waters in the heavens roar
   at his command.
He makes clouds appear;
   he sends the wind
   from his storehouse
and makes lightning flash
   in the rain.

17 People who make idols
   are stupid!
They will be disappointed,
   because their false gods
   cannot breathe.

18 Idols are merely a joke,
   and when the time is right,
   they will be destroyed.

19 But the LORD, Israel's God,
   is all-powerful.
He created everything,
   and he chose Israel
   to be his very own.

God's hammer

The LORD said:

20 Babylonia, you were my hammer;
   I used you to pound nations
   and break kingdoms,

21 to shatter cavalry and chariots,

22 as well as men and women,
   young and old,

23 shepherds and their flocks,
   farmers and their oxen,
   and governors and leaders.

24 But now, my people will watch,
   while I repay you
   for what you did to Zion.

25 You destroyed the nations
   and seem strong as a mountain,
   but I am your enemy.
I might even grab you
   and roll you off a cliff.
When I have finished,
   you'll only be a pile
   of scorched bricks.

26 Your stone blocks won't be reused
   for cornerstones
   or foundations,
and I promise that for ever
   you will be a desert.
I, the LORD, have spoken.

---

*51.11 kings of Media: Probably kings of smaller
kingdoms that were part of the Median empire (see
also verse 27 and the note there).
*51.14 locusts: See the note at 46.22,23.
See also: 51.9: Rev 18.5. 51.13: Rev 17.1.

The nations will attack Babylon

The LORD said:

27 Signal the nations
to get ready to attack.
Raise a flag and blow a trumpet.
Send for the armies of Ararat,
Minni, and Ashkenaz.*
Choose a commander;
let the cavalry attack
like a swarm of locusts.

28 Tell the kings and governors,
the leaders and the people
of the kingdoms of the Medes
to prepare for war!

29 The earth twists and turns
in torment,
because I have decided
to make Babylonia a desert
where no one can live,
and I won't change my mind.

30 The Babylonian soldiers
have lost their strength
and courage.*
They stay in their fortresses,
unable to fight,
while the enemy breaks through
the city gates,
then sets their homes on fire.

31 One messenger after another
announces to the king,
"Babylon has been captured!

32 The enemy now controls
the river crossings.
The marshes* are on fire!
Your army has panicked!"

33 I am the LORD All-Powerful,
the God of Israel,
and I make this promise —
"Soon Babylon will be levelled
and packed down
like a threshing place
at harvest time."*

Babylonia will pay!

34 The people of Jerusalem say,
"King Nebuchadnezzar*
made us panic.
That monster stuffed himself
with us and our treasures,
leaving us empty —
he gobbled up
what he wanted
and spat out the rest.

35 The people of Babylonia
harmed some of us*
and killed others.
Now, LORD, make them pay!"

The LORD will take revenge on Babylon

The LORD said:

36 My people, I am on your side,
and I will take revenge on Babylon.
I will cut off its water supply,
and its stream* will dry up.

37 Babylon will be a pile of rubble
where only jackals* live.
People will laugh,
but they will be afraid
to walk among the ruins.

38 The Babylonians roar and growl
like young lions.

39 And since they are hungry,
I will give them a banquet.
They will celebrate, get drunk,
then fall asleep,
never to wake up!

40 I will lead them away to die,
like sheep, lambs, and goats
being led to the butcher.

41 All nations now praise Babylon,*
but when it is captured,
those same nations
will be horrified.

42 Babylon's enemies will rise
like ocean waves
and flood the city.

43 Horrible destruction will strike
the nearby towns.
The land will become
a barren desert,
where no one can live
or even travel.

44 I will punish Marduk,*
the god of Babylon,
and make him vomit
everything he gobbled up.

---

*51.27 Ararat, Minni, and Ashkenaz: Kingdoms
to the north of Babylonia that were part of the
Median empire (see also verse 28).
*51.32 marshes: The tall grass in the marshes
could have provided hiding places for people trying
to escape from Babylon.
*51.33 levelled . . . harvest time: A threshing
place with an earth surface had to be levelled and
packed down before it could be used.

*51.34 Nebuchadnezzar: See the note at 21.2.
*51.36 stream: Probably the River Euphrates.
*51.37 jackals: See the note at 9.11.

Then nations will no longer
bring him gifts,
and Babylon's walls will crumble.

The LORD offers hope to his people

The LORD said:

45 Get out of Babylon, my people,
and run for your lives,
before I strike the city
in my anger!
46 Don't be afraid or lose hope,
though year after year
there are rumours
of leaders fighting for control
in the city of Babylon.
47 The time will come
when I will punish
Babylon's false gods.
Everyone there will die,
and the whole nation
will be disgraced,
48 when an army attacks
from the north
and brings destruction.
Then the earth and the heavens
and everything in them will celebrate.
49 Babylon must be overthrown,
because it slaughtered
the people of Israel
and of many other nations.

50 My people, you escaped death
when Jerusalem fell.
Now you live far from home,
but you should trust me
and think about Jerusalem.
Leave Babylon! Don't stay!
51 You feel ashamed and disgraced,
because foreigners have entered
my sacred temple.
52 Soon I will send a war
to punish Babylon's idols
and leave its wounded people
moaning everywhere.
53 Although Babylon's walls
reach to the sky,
the army I send
will destroy that city.
I, the LORD, have spoken.

Babylon will be destroyed

The LORD said:

54 Listen to the cries for help
coming from Babylon.

Everywhere in the country
the sounds of destruction
can be heard.
55 The shouts of the enemy,
like crashing ocean waves,
will drown out Babylon's cries
as I level the city.

56 An enemy will attack
and destroy Babylon.
Its soldiers will be captured
and their weapons broken,
because I am a God
who takes revenge against nations
for what they do.
57 I, the LORD All-Powerful,
the true King, promise
that the officials and advisers,
the governors and leaders
and the soldiers of Babylon
will get drunk, fall asleep,
and never wake up.
58 The thick walls of that city
will be torn down,
and its huge gates burnt.
Everything that nation
worked so hard to gain
will go up in smoke.

Jeremiah gives Seraiah a scroll

59 During Zedekiah's* fourth year as king of
Judah, he went to Babylon. And Baruch's
brother Seraiah* went along as the officer in
charge of arranging for places to stay
overnight.*

60 Before they left, I wrote on a scroll* all the
terrible things that would happen to Babylon.
61 I gave the scroll to Seraiah and said:

When you get to Babylon, read this scroll
aloud, 62 then pray, "Our LORD, you
promised to destroy this place and make it
into a desert where no people or animals
will ever live."

63 When you finish praying, tie the scroll
to a rock and throw it in the River
Euphrates. Then say, 64 "This is how
Babylon will sink when the LORD destroys
it. Everyone in the city will die, and it
won't have the strength to rise again."

---

*51.59 Zedekiah's: See the note at 1.3.
*51.59 Baruch's brother Seraiah: Hebrew "Seraiah
son of Neriah and grandson of Mahseiah"; Baruch
helped Jeremiah write down his messages (see 32.12;
36.4–10).
*51.60 scroll: See the note at 30.1,2.

See also: 51.63,64: Rev 18.21.

The end of Jeremiah's writing

Jeremiah's writing ends here.

Another account of the fall of Jerusalem

CHAPTER 52

Jerusalem is captured

This is also told in 2 Kings 24.18—25.30; 2 Chronicles 36.11–21

¹ Zedekiah was twenty-one years old when he was appointed king of Judah,* and he ruled from Jerusalem for eleven years.* His mother Hamutal was the daughter of Jeremiah from the town of Libnah.* ² Zedekiah disobeyed the LORD, just as Jehoiakim had done, ³ and it was Zedekiah who finally rebelled against Nebuchadnezzar.*

The people of Judah and Jerusalem had made the LORD so angry that he finally turned his back on them. That's why horrible things were happening.

⁴ In Zedekiah's ninth year as king, on the tenth day of the tenth month,* King Nebuchadnezzar of Babylonia led his entire army to attack Jerusalem. The troops set up camp outside the city and built ramps up to the city walls.

⁵⁻⁶ After a year and a half,* all the food in Jerusalem was gone. Then on the ninth day of the fourth month,* ⁷ the Babylonian troops broke through the city wall. That same night, Zedekiah and his soldiers tried to escape through the gate near the royal garden, even though they knew the enemy had the city surrounded. They headed towards the Jordan Valley, ⁸ but the Babylonian troops caught up with them near Jericho. The Babylonians arrested Zedekiah, but his soldiers scattered in every direction. ⁹ Zedekiah was taken to Riblah in the land of Hamath, where Nebuchadnezzar put him on trial and found him guilty. ¹⁰ Zedekiah's sons and the officials

of Judah were killed while he watched, ¹¹ then his eyes were put out. He was put in chains, then dragged off to Babylon and kept in prison until he died.

¹² Jerusalem was captured during Nebuchadnezzar's nineteenth year as king of Babylonia.

About a month later,* Nebuchadnezzar's officer in charge of the guards arrived in Jerusalem. His name was Nebuzaradan, ¹³ and he burnt down the LORD's temple, the king's palace, and every important building in the city, as well as all the houses. ¹⁴ Then he ordered the Babylonian soldiers to break down the walls around Jerusalem. ¹⁵ He led away the people left in the city, including everyone who had become loyal to Nebuchadnezzar, the rest of the skilled workers,* and even some of the poor people of Judah. ¹⁶ Only the very poorest were left behind to work the vineyards and the fields.

¹⁷⁻²⁰ Nebuzaradan ordered his soldiers to go to the temple and take everything made of gold or silver, including bowls, fire pans, sprinkling bowls, pans, lampstands, dishes for incense, and the cups for wine offerings. The Babylonian soldiers took all the bronze things used for worship at the temple, including the pans for hot ashes, and the shovels, lamp snuffers, sprinkling bowls, and dishes for incense. The soldiers also took everything else made of bronze, including the two columns that stood in front of the temple, the large bowl called the Sea, the twelve bulls that held it up, and the moveable stands.* The soldiers broke these things into pieces so they could take them to Babylon. There was so much bronze that it could not be weighed. ²¹ For example, the columns were about eight metres high and five metres around. They were hollow, but the bronze was about seventy-five millimetres thick. ²² Each column had a bronze cap over two metres high that was decorated with bronze designs. Some of these designs were like chains and others were like pomegranates.* ²³ There were ninety-six pomegranates evenly spaced* around each column, and a total of one hundred pomegranates were above the chains.

---

*52.1 appointed king of Judah: By Nebuchadnezzar (see 37.1).
*52.1 he ruled . . . years: Ruled 598–586 BC.
*52.1 Jeremiah from the town of Libnah: Not the same Jeremiah as the author of this book (see 1.1).
*52.3 Nebuchadnezzar: See the note at 21.2.
*52.4 tenth month: See the note at 39.1–3.
*52.5,6 After a year and a half: Jerusalem was captured in 586 BC.
*52.5,6 fourth month: See the note at 39.1–3.
See also: 52.4: Ezek 24.2. 52.7: Ezek 33.21.

*52.15 the rest of the skilled workers: Nebuchadnezzar had taken away some of the skilled workers eleven years before (see 2 Kings 24.14–16).
*52.22 pomegranates: A small red fruit that looks like an apple.
See also: 52.11: Ezek 12.13. 52.13: 1 King 9.8.
52.17–23: 1 King 7.15–47.

24 Next, Nebuzaradan arrested Seraiah the chief priest, Zephaniah his assistant, and three temple officials. 25 Then he arrested one of the army commanders, seven of King Zedekiah's personal advisers, and the officer in charge of gathering the troops for battle. He also found sixty more soldiers who were still in Jerusalem. 26-27 Nebuzaradan led them to Riblah in the land of Hamath, where Nebuchadnezzar had them killed.

The people of Judah no longer lived in their own country.

People of Judah taken prisoner

28-30 Here is a list of the number of the people of Judah that Nebuchadnezzar* took to Babylonia as prisoners:

In his seventh year as king, he took 3,023 people.
In his eighteenth year as king, he took 832 from Jerusalem.
In his twenty-third year as king, his officer Nebuzaradan took 745 people.

So, Nebuchadnezzar took a total of 4,600 people from Judah to Babylonia.

Jehoiachin is set free

This is also told in 2 Kings 25.27-30

31 Jehoiachin* was a prisoner in Babylon for thirty-seven years. Then Evil-Merodach* became king of Babylonia, and in the first year of his rule, on the twenty-fifth day of the twelfth month,* he let Jehoiachin out of prison. 32 Evil-Merodach was kind to Jehoiachin and honoured him more than any of the other kings held prisoner there. 33 Jehoiachin was allowed to wear ordinary clothes instead of a prison uniform, and he even ate at the king's table every day. 34 As long as Jehoiachin lived, he was paid a daily allowance to buy whatever he needed.

*52.28-30 Nebuchadnezzar: See the note at 21.2.
*51.31 Jehoiachin: See the note at 24.1.
*52.31 Evil-Merodach: The son of Nebuchadnezzar who ruled Babylonia from 562-560 BC.
*52.31 twelfth month: Adar, the twelfth month of the Hebrew calendar, from about mid-February to mid-March.

Additional notes

'2.18 trusted . . . Assyria: Hebrew "went to Egypt and drank from the River Shihor, and you went to Assyria and drank from the River Euphrates."

'2.23 Baal: The Hebrew text has "the Baals", probably because the god Baal was believed to be present in different forms at different places of worship.
'2.37 in great sadness: Or "as prisoners".
'3.24 that shameful god Baal: The Hebrew text has "The Shame", which was sometimes used as a way of making fun of the Canaanite god Baal.
'4.5,6 Judah: Hebrew "Judah and Jerusalem".
'5.28 refuse to help: One possible meaning for the difficult Hebrew text.
'5.31 give . . . god: Or "tell lies".
'5.31 don't . . . me: Or "don't care what I want".
'6.2,3 Jerusalem . . . grass: One possible meaning for the difficult Hebrew text.
'7.1-3 temple: The Hebrew text has "house of the LORD", another name for the temple.
'7.1-3 let you . . . own country: Or "live here with you".
'8.4 if you take . . . go back: One possible meaning for the difficult Hebrew text.
'8.6 you run down the wrong road: One possible meaning for the difficult Hebrew text.
'8.13 I will wipe them out: One possible meaning for the difficult Hebrew text.
'8.13 They have not . . . them: One possible meaning for the difficult Hebrew text.
'9.14 Baal: See the note at 2.23.
'9.15 poison to eat and drink: Or "bitter disappointment to eat, and tears to drink".
'9.25,26 the tribes of the desert: One possible meaning for the difficult Hebrew text.
'10.18 like a stone from a sling: One possible meaning for the difficult Hebrew text.
'11.15 celebrating: One possible meaning for the difficult Hebrew text of verse 15.
'12.4 God can't see the sins we commit: Or "Jeremiah won't live to see what happens to us."
'12.9 My people . . . other hawks: Or "My land has become a hyena's den with vultures circling above."
'13.9 I will use Babylonia to: Or "that's how I'm going to".
'13.18 and remove their crowns: One possible meaning for the difficult Hebrew text.
'13.21 You once . . . rule you: One possible meaning for the difficult Hebrew text.
'14.4 cracks . . . ground: One possible meaning for the difficult Hebrew text.
'14.6 sniff the air: The Hebrew text has "sniff the air, like jackals" (see the footnote at 9.11).
'14.18 go about . . . has happened: One possible meaning for the difficult Hebrew text.
'15.11 Hebrew: One possible meaning for the difficult Hebrew text of verse 11.
'15.14 that cannot be put out: Some Hebrew manuscripts; most Hebrew manuscripts "against you".
'15.14 I will make . . . land: Many Hebrew manuscripts; most Hebrew manuscripts "I will make your enemies go through to a land you don't know about."

'17.2,3 enemies: One possible meaning for the difficult Hebrew text of verses 2,3.

'17.4 You will lose: One possible meaning for the difficult Hebrew text.

'17.13 reject . . . dust: One possible meaning for the difficult Hebrew text.

'17.16 you chose . . . punish them: One possible meaning for the difficult Hebrew text.

'18.14 dry: One possible meaning for the difficult Hebrew text of verse 14.

'20.2 hit me: Or "beat me up" or "had me beaten up".

'20.2 in chains: Or "in the stocks" (a wooden frame with holes for the hands, neck, or feet of a prisoner) or "in a prison cell".

'20.3 Afraid-of-Everything: Hebrew "Magor-Missabib".

'21.13 Jerusalem . . . valleys: One possible meaning for the difficult Hebrew text.

'22.11,12 Jehoahaz: The Hebrew text has "Shallum", another name for Jehoahaz.

'22.20 nations: Or "gods".

'23.9 tremble: Or "become weak".

'23.10 deserts: One possible meaning for the difficult Hebrew text of verse 10.

'23.14 in marriage: Or "to me".

'23.14 never tell the truth: Or "worship other gods".

'23.33 You people are a nuisance to the LORD, and he: Two ancient translations; Hebrew "Does the LORD have news for us? He".

'23.39 pick you up: A few Hebrew manuscripts and three ancient translations; most Hebrew manuscripts "forget you completely".

'25.23,24 the tribes of the Arabian Desert: One possible meaning for the difficult Hebrew text.

'25.26 Babylonia: The Hebrew text has "Sheshach", a secret way of writing "Babylonia".

'25.34 You'll shatter . . . floor: One possible meaning for the difficult Hebrew text.

'25.36-38 anger turns: Or "anger and enemy armies turn".

'25.36-38 The LORD has . . . people: Or "And his people leave their homes".

'27.1,2 Not long after Zedekiah became king of Judah: A few manuscripts and one ancient translation; most Hebrew manuscripts "Not long after Jehoiakim became king of Judah"; most manuscripts of another ancient translation do not have these words. Jehoiakim ruled 609–598 BC, and Zedekiah ruled 598–586 BC.

'28.1 Later . . . king: One possible meaning for the difficult Hebrew text.

'29.3 Elasah and Gemariah: Hebrew "Elasah son of Shaphan and Gemariah son of Hilkiah".

'29.24,25 Shemaiah: Hebrew "Shemaiah, who came from the town of Nehelam".

'29.26 in chains: See the note at 20.2.

'30.18 Jerusalem . . . palace: Or "Your towns lie in ruins, but you will rebuild them, and your homes will be where they were there".

'31.2 In the desert . . . same for you: One possible meaning for the difficult Hebrew text.

'31.3 Some time . . . me: Or "The LORD appeared to me from far away".

'31.8 Babylonia: The Hebrew text has "that country in the north", referring to Babylonia.

'31.9 level: Or "straight".

'31.9 Israel: The Hebrew text also has "Ephraim", the leading tribe of the northern kingdom of Israel, which sometimes stands for the whole northern kingdom.

'31.15 In Ramah: Or "In the hills".

'31.18 Israel: Hebrew "Ephraim" (see the note at 31.9).

'31.22 I will make sure . . . a woman protecting a man: One possible meaning for the difficult Hebrew text.

'31.26 and when they sleep . . . refreshed: One possible meaning for the difficult Hebrew text.

'32.12 Baruch son of Neriah: Hebrew "Baruch son of Neriah and grandson of Mahseiah".

'32.18 for a thousand generations: Or "to thousands of people".

'33.1,2 the whole world: One ancient translation; Hebrew "it".

'33.4,5 have been torn down . . . Babylonian attackers: One possible meaning for the difficult Hebrew text.

'33.6 let them enjoy unending peace: One possible meaning for the difficult Hebrew text.

'35.3 Jaazaniah: The Hebrew text has "Jaazaniah son of Jeremiah son of Habazziniah"; this is a different Jeremiah from the author of the book.

'35.4 Maaseiah . . . temple: Hebrew "Maaseiah son of Shallum, the keeper of the temple door".

'36.12 Delaiah, Elnathan, and Gemariah: Hebrew "Delaiah son of Shemaiah, Elnathan son of Achbor, and Zedekiah son of Hananiah".

'36.14 Jehudi and Shelemiah: Hebrew "Jehudi son of Nethaniah and Shelemiah son of Cushi".

'36.26 Seraiah and Shelemiah: Hebrew "Seraiah son of Azriel and Shelemiah son of Abdeel".

'37.3-5 Egyptian army: Led by King Apries, also known as Hophra.

'37.3-5 Jehucal and the priest Zephaniah: Hebrew "Jehucal son of Shelemiah, and the priest Zephaniah son of Maaseiah".

'37.13 Irijah: Hebrew "Irijah son of Shelemiah and grandson of Hananiah".

'38.1 Jehucal: The Hebrew text has "Jucal", another form of the name.

'38.1 Shephatiah, Gedaliah, Jehucal, and Pashhur: Hebrew "Shephatiah son of Mattan, Gedaliah son of Pashhur, Jucal son of Shelemiah, and Pashhur son of Malchiah".

'38.10 thirty: Most Hebrew manuscripts; one Hebrew manuscript "three".

'38.14 his private entrance: One possible meaning for the difficult Hebrew text.

'38.23 Jerusalem will be burnt down: A few Hebrew manuscripts and three ancient translations; most Hebrew manuscripts "you will burn Jerusalem down"; one ancient translation "he will burn Jerusalem down".

'39.1–3 highest officials: The Hebrew text gives Nergal Sharezer's title as "the Rabmag", and Nebo Sarsechim's title as "the Rabsaris", but the exact meaning of the titles and the duties of these offices are not known.

'39.1–3 Nebo Sarsechim: Probably another form of the name Nebushazban (see verse 13).

'39.1–3 Nergal Sharezer from Simmagir: One possible meaning for the difficult Hebrew text. Probably Nebuchadnezzar's son-in-law, who was king of Babylonia 560–556 BC. It is also possible that the Hebrew text mentions a second official named Nergal Sharezer.

'39.8 the houses in Jerusalem, including: Or "the temple and".

'39.14 son of Ahikam: Hebrew "son of Ahikam and grandson of Shaphan".

'41.1 Ishmael: Hebrew "Ishmael son of Nethaniah and grandson of Elishama".

'42.1 Jezaniah: Hebrew "Jezaniah son of Hoshaiah"; one ancient translation "Azariah son of Hoshaiah" (see also 43.2 and the note there).

'43.2 Azariah, Johanan: Hebrew "Azariah son of Hoshaiah, Johanan son of Kareah".

'43.9 underneath the brick pavement: One possible meaning for the difficult Hebrew text.

'43.12,13 at the temple of the sun-god: Or "in the city of Heliopolis".

'44.17 the goddess Astarte, the Queen of Heaven: The Hebrew text has "the queen of heaven", which probably refers to the goddess Astarte.

'46.15 I have . . . him away: One possible meaning for the difficult Hebrew text.

'47.4 Crete: Hebrew "Caphtor", another name for Crete, the original homeland of the ancestor of the Philistines.

'48.6 like a wild donkey: One ancient translation; Hebrew "like (the town of) Aroer" (see verse 19).

'48.9 Spread salt . . . crops: One possible meaning for the difficult Hebrew text.

'48.11 continues . . . improve: Or "remains as evil as ever".

'48.21–24 Bozrah: Not the same Bozrah as in 49.13.

'48.32 reaching north . . . Dead Sea: One possible meaning for the difficult Hebrew text.

'48.41 Your cities: Or "Kerioth".

'48.41 gripped by fear: One possible meaning for the difficult Hebrew text.

'49.3 your town will become a pile of rubble: Or "because the town of Ai has been destroyed"; referring to an Ammonite town named Ai, not the town of that name near Bethel in the land of Israel.

'49.3 You will turn . . . blocked: One possible meaning for the difficult Hebrew text.

'49.4 when . . . fading: One possible meaning for the difficult Hebrew text.

'49.7,8 anyone . . . home: One possible meaning for the difficult Hebrew text.

'49.16 Pride . . . fear: One possible meaning for the difficult Hebrew text.

'49.20 Edom: The Hebrew text also uses the name "Teman" (see the note at verses 7–8).

'49.22 will be gripped by fear: One possible meaning for the difficult Hebrew text.

'49.23 worries . . . waves: One possible meaning for the difficult Hebrew text.

'49.24 gripped by fear and pain: One possible meaning for the difficult Hebrew text.

'49.25 can: One possible meaning for the difficult Hebrew text of verse 25.

'49.28 desert villages: The Hebrew text has "kingdoms of Hazor", which probably refers to several kingdoms of desert peoples who were not nomads, but who lived in small villages.

'49.30 villages: See the note at 49.28.

'49.32 People of the Arabian Desert: One possible meaning for the difficult Hebrew text.

'49.33 villages: See the note at 49.28.

'50.1,2 Marduk: The Hebrew text has "Bel" and "Marduk", two names for the same god.

'50.9 the best soldiers: Some Hebrew manuscripts and two ancient translations; most Hebrew manuscripts "soldiers who kill children".

'50.11 threshing grain: Hebrew; two ancient translations "in a pasture".

'50.21 Merathaim . . . Pekod: Hebrew forms of two Babylonian names that refer to the land of Babylonia. Merathaim probably referred to lagoons near the mouth of the Rivers Tigris and Euphrates or to the Persian Gulf, but in Hebrew it means "Twice as Rebellious". Pekod referred to a tribe of south-eastern Babylonia, but in Hebrew it means "Punishment".

'51.1 wind: Or "spirit".

'51.1 Babylonia: The Hebrew text has "Leb-Qamai", a secret way of writing "Babylonia".

'51.3 I will tell . . . armour: Or "Attack quickly! String your bows and put on your armour."

'51.8 the foreigners: Or "my people".

'51.13 for you to die: One possible meaning for the difficult Hebrew text.

'51.30 have lost their strength and courage: Hebrew "have lost their strength and have become like women".

'51.35 harmed some of us: One possible meaning for the difficult Hebrew text.

'51.41 Babylon: The Hebrew text has "Sheshach", a secret way of writing the name "Babylon".

'51.44 Marduk: Hebrew "Bel" (see the note at 50.2).

'51.59 arranging for places to stay overnight: Hebrew and one ancient translation; two ancient translations, "the tax money".

'52.12 About a month later: Hebrew "On the seventh day of the fifth month".

'52.17–20 the large bowl called the Sea, the twelve bulls that held it up, and the moveable stands: One ancient translation; Hebrew "the large bowl called the Sea, and the twelve bulls under the moveable stands".

'52.23 evenly spaced: One possible meaning for the difficult Hebrew text.

Lamentations

A quick look at this book

This book is a collection of five poems expressing deep sorrow about the destruction of Jerusalem. The poems, sometimes called laments, are presented as being spoken by the city of Jerusalem and by the writer, who is called "the prophet" in the CEV.

The prophet realized that Jerusalem was being punished because its people had sinned, but the suffering seemed greater than what their sins deserved. Still, there was hope. Some day, God would be merciful again if the people would give up their sins and turn back to him.

> Then I remember something
> that fills me with hope.
> The LORD's kindness never fails!
> If he had not been merciful,
> we would have been destroyed.
> The LORD can always be trusted
> to show mercy each morning.
> Deep in my heart I say,
> "The LORD is all I need;
> I can depend on him!"

(3.21–24)

First lament

CHAPTER 1

Lonely Jerusalem

The prophet speaks:

1 Jerusalem, once so crowded,
   lies deserted and lonely.
  This city that was known
   all over the world
  is now like a widow.
  This queen of the nations
   has been made a slave.

2 Each night, bitter tears
   flood her cheeks.
  None of her former lovers
   are there to offer comfort;
  her friends* have betrayed her
   and are now her enemies.

3 The people of Judah are slaves,
   suffering in a foreign land,
   with no rest from sorrow.
  Their enemies captured them
   and were terribly cruel.•

4 The roads to Zion mourn
   because no one travels there
   to celebrate the festivals.
  The city gates are deserted;
   priests are weeping.
  Young women are raped;•
  Zion is in sorrow!

5 Enemies now rule the city
   and live as they please.
  The LORD has punished Jerusalem
   because of her awful sins;
  he has let her people
   be dragged away.

---

*1.2 lovers . . . friends: Israel's former allies.

⁶ Zion's glory has disappeared.
   Her leaders are like deer
      that cannot find pasture;
   they are hunted down
      till their strength is gone.
⁷ Her people recall the good life
      that once was theirs;
   now they suffer and are scattered.
   No one was there to protect them
      from their enemies
   who sneered when their city was taken.

⁸ Jerusalem's horrible sins
      have made the city a joke.
   Those who once admired her
      now hate her instead —
   she has been disgraced;
      she groans and turns away.

⁹ Her sins had made her filthy,
      but she wasn't worried
      about what could happen.
   And when Jerusalem fell,
      it was so tragic.
   No one gave her comfort
      when she cried out,
   "Help! I'm in trouble, LORD!
      The enemy has won."

¹⁰ Zion's treasures were stolen.
   Jerusalem saw foreigners
      enter her place of worship,
   though the LORD
      had forbidden them
      to belong to his people.'
¹¹ Everyone in the city groans
      while searching for food;
   they trade their valuables
      for barely enough scraps to stay alive.

Jerusalem speaks:

   Jerusalem shouts to the LORD,
      "Please look and see
      how miserable I am!"
¹² No passer-by even cares.'
   Why doesn't someone notice
      my terrible sufferings?
   You were fiercely angry, LORD,
      and you punished me worst of all.
¹³ From heaven you sent a fire
      that burnt in my bones;
   you set a trap for my feet
      and made me turn back.
   All day long you leave me
      in shock from constant pain.
¹⁴ You have tied my sins
      around my neck,'
   and they weigh so heavily
      that my strength is gone.

   You have put me in the power of enemies
      too strong for me.
¹⁵ You, LORD, have turned back my warriors
      and crushed my young heroes.
   Judah was a woman untouched,
      but you let her be trampled
      like grapes in a wine-pit.
¹⁶ Because of this, I mourn,
      and tears flood my eyes.
   No one is here to comfort
      or to encourage me;
   we have lost the war —
      my people are suffering.

The prophet speaks:

¹⁷ Zion reaches out her hands,
      but no one offers comfort.
   The LORD has turned
      the neighbouring nations
      against Jacob's descendants.
   Jerusalem is merely a filthy rag
      to her neighbours.

Jerusalem speaks:

¹⁸ The LORD was right,
      but I refused to obey him.
   Now I ask all of you to look
      at my sufferings —
   even my young people
      have been dragged away.
¹⁹ I called out to my lovers,
      but they betrayed me.
   My priests and my leaders died
      while searching the city
      for scraps of food.
²⁰ Won't you look and see
      how upset I am, our LORD?
   My stomach is in knots,
      and my heart is broken
      because I betrayed you.
   In the streets and at home,
      my people are slaughtered.
²¹ Everyone heard my groaning,
      but no one offered comfort.
   My enemies know of the trouble
      that you have brought on me,
      and it makes them glad.
   Hurry and punish them,
      as you have promised.
²² Don't let their evil deeds
      escape your sight.
   Punish them as much
      as you have punished me
      because of my sins.
   I never stop groaning —
      I've lost all hope!

Second lament

CHAPTER 2

The LORD was like an enemy

The prophet speaks:

¹ The Lord was angry!
    So he disgraced* Zion
    though it was Israel's pride
    and his own place of rest.
In his anger he threw Zion down
    from heaven to earth.
² The LORD had no mercy!
    He destroyed the homes
    of Jacob's descendants.
In his anger he tore down
    every walled city in Judah;
he toppled the nation
    together with its leaders,
    leaving them in shame.

³ The Lord was so furiously angry
    that he wiped out
    the whole army* of Israel
by not supporting them
    when the enemy attacked.
He was like a raging fire
    that swallowed up
    the descendants of Jacob.
⁴ He attacked like an enemy
    with a bow and arrows,
    killing our loved ones.
He has burnt to the ground
    the homes on Mount Zion.*

⁵ The Lord was like an enemy!
    He left Israel in ruins
    with its palaces
    and fortresses destroyed,
    and with everyone in Judah
    moaning and weeping.
⁶ He shattered his temple
    like a hut in a garden;*
    he completely wiped out
    his meeting place,
and did away with festivals and Sabbaths
    in the city of Zion.
In his fierce anger he rejected
    our king and priests.

⁷ The Lord abandoned his altar
    and his temple;
    he let Zion's enemies
    capture her fortresses.
Noisy shouts were heard
    from the temple,
    as if it were a time of celebration.

⁸ The LORD had decided
    to tear down the walls of Zion
    stone by stone.
So he started destroying
    and did not stop
until walls and fortresses
    mourned and trembled.
⁹ Zion's gates have fallen
    face down on the ground;
    the bars that locked the gates
    are smashed to pieces.
Her king and royal family
    are prisoners in foreign lands.
Her priests don't teach,
    and her prophets don't have
    a message from the LORD.

¹⁰ Zion's leaders are silent.
    They just sit on the ground,
    tossing dust on their heads
    and wearing sackcloth.
Her young women can do nothing
    but stare at the ground.

¹¹ My eyes are red from crying,
    my stomach is in knots,
    and I feel sick all over.
My people are being wiped out,
    and children lie helpless
    in the streets of the city.
¹² A child begs its mother
    for food and drink,
    then blacks out like a wounded soldier
    lying in the street.
The child slowly dies
    in its mother's arms.

¹³ Zion, how can I comfort you?
    How great is your pain?*
Lovely city of Jerusalem,
    how can I heal your wounds,
    gaping as wide as the sea?
¹⁴ Your prophets deceived you
    with false visions and lying messages —
    they should have warned you
    to leave your sins
    and be saved from disaster.
¹⁵ Those who pass by
    shake their heads and sneer
    as they make fun and shout,
    "What a lovely city you were,
    the happiest on earth,
    but look at you now!"

¹⁶ Zion, your enemies curse you
    and snarl like wild animals,
    while shouting,
    "This is the day we've waited for!
    At last, we've got you!"

17 The LORD has done everything
    that he had planned
    and threatened long ago.
He destroyed you without mercy
    and let your enemies boast
    about their powerful forces.*

18 Zion, deep in your heart
    you cried out to the Lord.
Now let your tears overflow
    your walls day and night.
Don't ever lose hope
    or let your tears stop.

19 Get up and pray for help
    all through the night.
Pour out your feelings
    to the Lord,
    as you would pour water
    out of a jug.
Beg him to save your people,
    who are starving to death
    at every street crossing.

Jerusalem speaks:

20 Think about it, LORD!
    Have you ever been this cruel
    to anyone before?
Is it right for mothers
    to eat their children,
    or for priests and prophets
    to be killed in your temple?

21 My people, both young and old,
    lie dead in the streets.
Because you were angry,
    my young men and women
    were brutally slaughtered.

22 When you were angry, LORD,
    you invited my enemies
    like guests for a party.
No one survived that day;
    enemies killed my children,
    my own little ones.

Third lament

CHAPTER 3

There is still hope

The prophet speaks:

1 I have suffered much
    because God was angry.

2 He chased me into a dark place,
    where no light could enter.

3 I am the only one he punishes
    over and over again,
    without ever stopping.

4 God caused my skin and flesh
    to waste away,
    and he crushed my bones.

5 He attacked and surrounded me
    with hardships and trouble;

6 he forced me to sit in the dark
    like someone long dead.

7 God built a fence around me
    that I cannot climb over,
    and he chained me down.

8 Even when I shouted
    and prayed for help,
    he refused to listen.

9 God put big rocks in my way
    and made me follow a crooked path.

10 God was like a bear or a lion
    waiting in ambush for me;

11 he dragged me from the road,
    then tore me to shreds.*

12 God took careful aim and shot his arrows
13 straight through my heart.

14 I am a joke to everyone —
    no one ever stops
    making fun of me.

15 God has turned my life sour.

16 He made me eat gravel
    and rubbed me in the earth.

17 I cannot find peace
    or remember happiness.

18 I tell myself, "I am finished!
    I can't count on the LORD
    to do anything for me."

19 Just thinking of my troubles
    and my lonely wandering
    makes me miserable.

20 That's all I ever think about,
    and I am depressed.*

21 Then I remember something
    that fills me with hope.

22 The LORD's kindness never fails!
    If he had not been merciful,
    we would have been destroyed.*

23 The LORD can always be trusted
    to show mercy each morning.

24 Deep in my heart I say,
    "The LORD is all I need;
    I can depend on him!"

25 The LORD is kind to everyone
    who trusts and obeys him.

26 It is good to wait patiently
    for the LORD to save us.

27 When we are young,
    it is good to struggle hard

28 and to sit silently alone,
    if this is what the LORD intends.

29 Being rubbed in the earth
   can teach us a lesson;*
30 we can also learn from insults
   and hard knocks.

31 The Lord won't always reject us!
32 He causes a lot of suffering,
   but he also has pity
   because of his great love.
33 The Lord doesn't enjoy
   sending grief or pain.

34 Don't trample prisoners
   under your feet
35 or cheat anyone out of
   what is rightfully theirs.
   God Most High sees everything,
36 and he knows
   when you refuse
   to give someone a fair trial.

37 No one can do anything
   without the Lord's approval.
38 Good and bad each happen
   at the command
   of God Most High.
39 We're still alive!
   We shouldn't complain
   when we are being punished
   for our sins.
40 Instead, we should think
   about the way we are living,
   and turn back to the LORD.

41 When we lift our hands
   in prayer to God in heaven,
   we should offer him our hearts and say,
42 "We've sinned!
   We've rebelled against you,
   and you haven't forgiven us!
43 Anger is written all over you,
   as you pursue and slaughter us
   without showing pity.
44 You are behind a wall of clouds
   that blocks out our prayers.
45 You allowed nations
   to treat us like rubbish;
46 our enemies curse us.
47 We are terrified and trapped,
   caught and crushed."

48 My people are destroyed!
   Tears flood my eyes,
49 and they won't stop
50 until the LORD looks down
   from heaven and helps.
51 I am horrified when I see
   what enemies have done
   to the young women of our city.

52 No one had reason to hate me,
   but I was hunted down like a bird.
53 Then they tried to kill me
   by tossing me into a pit
   and throwing stones at me.
54 Water covered my head —
   I thought I was gone.

55 From the bottom of the pit,
   I prayed to you, LORD.
56 I begged you to listen.
   "Help!" I shouted. "Save me!"
   You answered my prayer
57 and came when I was in need.
   You told me, "Don't worry!"
58 You rescued me and saved my life.

59 You saw them abuse me, LORD,
   so make things right.
60 You know every plot
   they have made against me.
61 Yes, you know their insults
   and their evil plans.
62 All day long they attack
   with words and whispers.
63 No matter what they are doing,
   they keep on mocking me.

64 Pay them back for everything
   they have done, LORD!
65 Put your curse on them
   and make them suffer.*
66 Get angry and go after them
   until not a trace is left
   under the heavens.

Fourth lament

CHAPTER 4

The punishment of Jerusalem

The prophet speaks:

1 The purest gold is ruined
   and has lost its shine;
   jewels from the temple
   lie scattered in the streets.
2 These are Zion's people,
   worth more than purest gold;
   yet they are counted worthless
   like dishes of clay.

3 Even jackals* nurse their young,
   but my people are like ostriches
   that abandon their own.
4 Babies are so thirsty that their tongues
   are stuck to the roof of the mouth.

---

*4.3 jackals: Desert animals related to wolves, but smaller.

Children go begging for food,
but no one gives them any.
⁵ All who ate expensive foods
lie starving in the streets;
those who grew up in luxury
now sit on rubbish heaps.

⁶ My nation was punished worse
than the people of Sodom,
whose city was destroyed in a flash
without the help of human hands.▸

⁷ The leaders of Jerusalem
were purer than snow
and whiter than milk;
their bodies were healthy
and glowed like jewels.▸

⁸ Now they are blacker than tar,
and no one recognizes them;
their skin clings to their bones
and is drier than firewood.

⁹ Being killed with a sword is better
than slowly starving to death.

¹⁰ Life in the city is so bad
that loving mothers
have boiled and eaten
their own children.

¹¹ The LORD was so fiercely angry
that he burnt the city of Zion
to the ground.

¹² Not a king on this earth
or the people of any nation
believed enemies could break
through her gates.

¹³ Jerusalem was punished because
her prophets and her priests
had sinned and caused the death
of innocent victims.

¹⁴ Yes, her prophets and priests
were covered with blood;
no one would come near them,
as they wandered
from street to street.

¹⁵ Instead, everyone shouted,
"Go away! Don't touch us!
You're filthy and unfit
to belong to God's people!"

So they had to leave
and become refugees.
But foreign nations told them,
"You can't stay here!"▸

¹⁶ The LORD is the one
who sent them scattering,
and he has forgotten them.
No respect or kindness will be shown
to the priests or leaders.

¹⁷ Our eyes became weary,
hopelessly looking for help
from a nation* that could not save us.

¹⁸ Enemies hunted us down
on every public street.
Our time was up;
our doom was near.

¹⁹ They swooped down faster
than eagles from the sky.
They hunted for us in the hills
and set traps to catch us
out in the desert.

²⁰ The LORD's chosen leader*
was our hope for survival!
We thought he would keep us safe
somewhere among the nations,
but even he was caught
in one of their traps.

²¹ You people of Edom
can celebrate now!
But your time will come to suffer
and stagger around naked.

²² The people of Zion
have paid for their sins,
and the Lord will soon
let them return home.
But, people of Edom,
you will be punished,
and your sins exposed.

Fifth lament

CHAPTER 5

A prayer for mercy

The people of Jerusalem pray:▸

¹ Our LORD, don't forget
how we have suffered
and been disgraced.
² Foreigners and strangers
have taken our land
and our homes.
³ We are like children
whose mothers are widows.
⁴ The water we drink
and the wood we burn
cost far too much.
⁵ We are terribly ill-treated;▸
we are worn out and can find no rest.
⁶ We had to surrender
to† Egypt and Assyria
because we were hungry.

*4.17 nation: Egypt, a former ally of Judah.
*4.20 chosen leader: Probably Zedekiah, the last
king of Judah, taken away to Babylonia in 586 BC.

See also: 4.6: Gen 19.24.   4.10: Deut 28.57; Ezek 5.10.
774

7 Our ancestors sinned,
   but they are dead,
   and we are left to pay
   for their sins.
8 Slaves are now our rulers,
   and there is no one
   to set us free.
9 We are in danger
   from brutal desert tribes;
   we must risk our lives
   just to bring in our crops.ᵇ
10 Our skin is scorched
   from fever and hunger.

11 On Zion and everywhere in Judah
   our wives and daughters
   are being raped.
12 Our rulers are strung up
   by their arms,
   and our nation's advisers
   are treated shamefully.
13 Young men are forced
   to do the work of slaves;
   boys must carry
   heavy loads of wood.
14 Our leaders are not allowed
   to decide cases in court,
   and young people
   no longer play music.

15 Our hearts are sad;
   instead of dancing,
   we mourn.
16 Zion's glory has disappeared!
   And we are doomed
   because of our sins.
17 We feel sick all over
   and can't even see straight;
18 our city is in ruins,
   overrun by wild dogs.

19 You will rule for ever, LORD!
   You are King for all time.
20 Why have you forgotten us
   for so long?
21 Bring us back to you!
   Give us a fresh start.
22 Or do you despise us so much
   that you don't want us?

ᵇ**1.12 No . . . cares:** One possible meaning for the difficult Hebrew text.
ᵇ**1.14 You . . . neck:** One possible meaning for the difficult Hebrew text.
ᶜ**2.1 disgraced:** One possible meaning for the difficult Hebrew text.
ᵈ**2.3 army:** The Hebrew text has "horn", which refers to the horn of a bull, one of the most powerful animals in ancient Palestine.
ᵉ**2.4 the homes on Mount Zion:** Or "the temple on Mount Zion."
ᶠ**2.6 He . . . garden:** Or "He shattered the temple walls, as if they were the walls of a garden".
ᵍ**2.13 How great . . . pain:** Or "What are you really like?" or "What can I say about you?"
ʰ**2.17 powerful forces:** See the note at 2.3.
ⁱ**3.11 shreds:** One possible meaning for the difficult Hebrew text of verse 11.
ʲ**3.20 I am depressed:** One possible meaning for the difficult Hebrew text.
ᵏ**3.22 destroyed:** One possible meaning for the difficult Hebrew text of verse 22.
ˡ**3.29 lesson:** One possible meaning for the difficult Hebrew text of verse 29.
ᵐ**3.65 make them suffer:** One possible meaning for the difficult Hebrew text.
ⁿ**4.6 hands:** One possible meaning for the difficult Hebrew text of verse 6.
ᵒ**4.7 jewels:** One possible meaning for the difficult Hebrew text of verse 7.
ᵖ**4.15 here:** One possible meaning for the difficult Hebrew text of verse 15.
ᵠ**5.1 The people of Jerusalem pray:** Or "The prophet prays".
ʳ**5.5 We . . . ill-treated:** One possible meaning for the difficult Hebrew text.
ˢ**5.6 surrender to:** Or "make treaties with".
ᵗ**5.9 crops:** One possible meaning for the difficult Hebrew text of verse 9.

Additional notes

ᵃ**1.3 Their . . . cruel:** One possible meaning for the difficult Hebrew text.
ᵃ**1.4 raped:** One possible meaning for the difficult Hebrew text.
ᵃ**1.10 to . . . people:** Or "to enter his temple."

Ezekiel

A quick look at this book

Ezekiel was a priest and a prophet. He had been taken away as a prisoner to Babylonia, where he lived among the other exiles from Judah. The Lord chose Ezekiel to be his prophet and to preach his message, not only to the exiles in Babylonia, but also to the people still living in Jerusalem. Ezekiel's

ministry probably began around 593 BC, during the last years of the kingdom of Judah, and it ended some time around 570 BC, several years after the fall of Jerusalem (586 BC). Ezekiel preached before and after this horrible disaster, and so some of his messages threatened judgment and others offered hope.

The book of Ezekiel can be divided into five main parts. The first part (1—3) describes Ezekiel's vision of the Lord's glory and tells how the Lord appointed Ezekiel to be his prophet. The second part (4—24) includes several messages warning the people of Judah that they will soon be punished for turning away from the Lord. Ezekiel acted out many of these warnings. And the third part of the book (25—32) includes the Lord's judgments on nearby nations.

The fourth part of the book (33—39) is made up of Ezekiel's messages after he heard that Jerusalem had been captured. These are messages of hope. The Lord promises he will forgive his people and bring them back to Judah and Jerusalem. Finally, the fifth part of the book (40—48) is Ezekiel's vision of the new temple in Jerusalem, its regulations for proper worship, and how the restored land of Israel will be divided among the tribes.

When the Lord speaks to Ezekiel, he calls him "son of man". Although this expression shows that Ezekiel is a mere human, it also shows that he has been appointed to preach the Lord's message to the people of Judah and Jerusalem.

One of the most familiar passages in the book is Ezekiel's vision of the valley full of dried-out bones. Ezekiel watches the Lord's Spirit blow life into the dead bodies, and he sees them come back to life. The Lord then tells Ezekiel:

> The people of Israel are like dead bones. They complain that they are dried up and that they have no hope for the future. So tell them, "I, the LORD God, promise to open your graves and set you free. I will bring you back to Israel . . . My Spirit will give you breath, and you will live again."

(37.11,12,14a)

Ezekiel sees the Lord's glory and is chosen to be his prophet

CHAPTER 1

1-3 I am Ezekiel — a priest and the son of Buzi.•

Five years after King Jehoiachin of Judah had been led away as a prisoner to Babylonia, I was living near the River Chebar among those who had been taken there with him. Then on the fifth day of the fourth month• of the thirtieth year,• the heavens suddenly opened. The LORD placed his hand upon me• and showed me some visions.

4 I saw a storm blowing in from the north. Lightning flashed from a huge cloud and lit up the whole sky with a dazzling brightness. The fiery centre of the cloud was as shiny as polished metal, 5 and in that centre I saw what looked like four living creatures. They were somewhat like humans, 6 except that each one had four faces and four wings. 7 Their legs were straight, but their feet looked like the hoofs of calves and sparkled like bronze. 8 Under each of their wings, these creatures had a human hand. 9 The four creatures were standing back-to-back with the tips of their wings touching. They moved together in every direction, without turning their bodies.

10 Each creature had the face of a human in front, the face of a lion on the right side, the face of a bull on the left, and the face of an eagle at the back. 11 Two wings• of each creature were spread out and touched the wings of the creatures on either side. The other two wings of each creature were folded against its body.

12 Wherever the four living creatures went, they moved together without turning their bodies, because each creature faced straight ahead. 13 The creatures were glowing like hot coals, and I saw something like a flaming torch moving back and forth among them. Lightning flashed from the torch every time its flame blazed up.• 14 The creatures themselves moved as quickly as sparks jumping from a fire.•

15 I then noticed that on the ground beside each of the four living creatures was a wheel,• 16 shining like chrysolite.• Each wheel was exactly the same and had a second wheel that cut through the middle of it,• 17 so that they could move in any direction without turning. 18 The rims of the wheels were large and had eyes all the way around them.• 19-21 The creatures controlled when and where the wheels moved — the wheels went wherever the four creatures went and stopped whenever they stopped. Even when the creatures flew in the air, the wheels were beside them.

22-23 Above the living creatures, I saw something that was sparkling like ice, and it reminded me of a dome. Each creature had two of its wings stretched out towards the creatures on either side, while the other two wings folded against its body. 24 Whenever the creatures flew, their wings roared like an ocean or a large army or even the voice of God All-Powerful. And whenever the creatures stopped, they folded their wings against their bodies.

25 When the creatures stopped flapping their wings, I heard a sound coming from above the dome. 26 I then saw what looked like a throne made of sapphire,• and sitting on the throne was a figure in the shape of a human. 27 From the waist up, it was glowing

---

1.1–3 Five years . . . prisoner . . . fourth month: Jehoiachin ruled for three months in 598 BC. The fourth month was probably July of 593 BC.
1.1–3 thirtieth year: The event from which this date is worked out is unknown.
1.1–3 The LORD placed his hand upon me: This was a sign that the LORD had chosen Ezekiel to be his prophet.
See also: 1.1: Rev 19.11. 1.2: 2 King 24.10–16; 2 Chron 36.9,10. 1.5: Rev 4.6.

1.16 chrysolite: A precious stone that has an olive green colour.
1.26 sapphire: A precious stone that has a blue colour.
See also: 1.10: Ezek 10.14; Rev 4.7. 1.13: Rev 4.5. 1.15–21: Ezek 10.9–13. 1.18: Rev 4.8. 1.22: Rev 4.6. 1.24: Rev 1.4–15; 19.6. 1.26: Rev 10.1; Rev 4.2,3. 1.27: Ezek 8.2.

like metal in a hot furnace, and from the waist down it looked like the flames of a fire. The figure was surrounded by a bright light, [28] as colourful as a rainbow that appears after a storm.

I realized I was seeing the brightness of the LORD's glory! So I bowed with my face to the ground, and just then I heard a voice speaking to me.

CHAPTER 2

The LORD chooses Ezekiel

[1] The LORD* said, "Ezekiel, son of man,* I want you to stand up and listen." [2] After he said this, his Spirit took control of me and lifted me to my feet. Then the LORD said:

[3] Ezekiel, I am sending you to the people of Israel. They are just like their ancestors who rebelled against me and refused to stop. [4] They are stubborn and hard-headed. But I, the LORD God, have chosen you to tell them what I say. [5] Those rebels may not even listen, but at least they will know that a prophet has come to them.

[6] Don't be afraid of them or of anything they say. You may think you're in the middle of thorn bushes or scorpions. But be brave [7] and preach my message to them, whether they choose to listen or not. [8] Ezekiel, don't rebel against me, as they have done. Instead, listen to everything I tell you.

And now, Ezekiel, open your mouth and eat what I am going to give you.

[9] Just then, I saw a hand stretched out towards me. And in it was a scroll.* [10] The hand opened the scroll, and both sides of it were filled with words of sadness, mourning, and grief.

CHAPTER 3

[1] The LORD said, "Ezekiel, son of man, after you eat this scroll, go and speak to the people of Israel."

[2-3] He handed me the scroll and said, "Eat this and fill your stomach with it." So I ate the scroll, and it tasted sweet as honey.

[4] The LORD said:

Ezekiel, I am sending you to your own people. [5-6] They are Israelites, not strangers who speak a foreign language you can't understand. If I were to send you to foreign nations, they would listen to you. [7] But the people of Israel will refuse to listen, because they have refused to listen to me. All of them are stubborn and hard-headed, [8] so I will make you as stubborn as they are. [9] You will be so determined to speak my message that nothing will stop you. I will make you hard like a diamond, and you'll have no reason to be afraid of those arrogant rebels.

[10] Listen carefully to everything I say and then think about it. [11] Then go to the people who were brought here to Babylonia with you and tell them you have a message from me, the LORD God. Do this, whether they listen to you or not.

[12] The Spirit* lifted me up, and as the glory of the LORD started to leave,* I heard a loud, thundering noise behind me. [13] It was the sound made by the creatures' wings as they brushed against each other, and by the rumble of the wheels beside them. [14] Then the Spirit carried me away.

The LORD's power had taken complete control of me, and I was both annoyed and angry.

[15] When I was back with the others living at Abib Hill near the River Chebar, I sat among them for seven days, shocked at what had happened to me.

The LORD appoints Ezekiel to stand watch

This is also told in Ezekiel 33.1–9

[16] Seven days after I had seen the brightness of the LORD's glory, the LORD said:

[17] Ezekiel, son of man, I have appointed you to stand watch for the people of Israel. So listen to what I say, then warn them for me. [18] When I tell wicked people they will die because of their sins, you must warn them to turn from their sinful ways so they won't be punished. If you refuse, you are responsible for their death. [19] However, if you do warn them, and they keep on sinning, they will die because of their sins, and you will be innocent.

---

*2.1 Ezekiel, son of man: The Hebrew text has "Son of man", which is often used in this book when the LORD speaks directly to Ezekiel. It means that Ezekiel is a mere human, yet he is the one the LORD has chosen to be his prophet who speaks for him to the people of Israel.
*2.9 scroll: A roll of paper or special leather used for writing on.
See also: 2.9,10: Rev 5.1. 3.1–3: Rev 10.9,10.

²⁰ Now suppose faithful people start sinning, and I decide to put stumbling blocks in their paths to make them fall. They deserve to die because of their sins. So if you refuse to warn them, I will forget about the times they were faithful, and I will hold you responsible for their death. ²¹ But if you do warn them, and they listen to you and stop sinning, I will let them live. And you will be innocent.

Ezekiel cannot talk

²² The LORD took control of me and said, "Stand up! Go into the valley, and I will talk with you there."

²³ I immediately went to the valley, where I saw the brightness of the LORD's glory, just as I had seen near the River Chebar, and I bowed with my face to the ground. ²⁴ His Spirit took control of me and lifted me to my feet. Then the LORD said:

Go back and lock yourself in your house! ²⁵ You will be tied up to keep you inside, ²⁶ and I will make you unable to talk or to warn those who have rebelled against me. ²⁷ But the time will come, when I will tell you what to say, and you will again be able to speak my message.* Some of them will listen; others will be stubborn and refuse to listen.

Ezekiel acts out the coming destruction of Judah and Jerusalem

CHAPTER 4

The LORD said:

¹ Ezekiel, son of man, find a brick and sketch a picture of Jerusalem on it. ² Then prepare to attack the brick as if it were a real city. Build an earth mound and a ramp up to the top and surround the brick with enemy camps. On every side put large wooden poles as though you were going to break down the gate to the city. ³ Set up an iron pan like a wall between you and the brick. All this will be a warning for the people of Israel.

⁴⁻⁵ After that, lie down on your left side and stay there for three hundred and ninety days as a sign of Israel's punishment* —

one day for each year of its suffering. ⁶ Then turn over and lie on your right side forty more days. That will be a sign of Judah's punishment — one day for each year of its suffering.

⁷ The brick stands for Jerusalem, so attack it! Stare at it and shout angry warnings. ⁸ I will tie you up, so you can't leave until your attack has ended.

⁹ Get a large bowl. Then mix together wheat, barley, beans, lentils, and millet, and make some bread. This is what you will eat for the three hundred and ninety days you are lying down. ¹⁰ Eat only a small loaf of bread each day ¹¹ and drink only two large cups of water. ¹² Use dried human waste to start a fire, then bake the bread on the coals where everyone can watch you. ¹³ When I scatter the people of Israel among the nations, they will also have to eat food that is unclean, just as you must do.*

¹⁴ I said, "LORD God, please don't make me do that! Never in my life have I eaten food that would make me unacceptable to you. I've never eaten anything that died a natural death or was killed by a wild animal or that you said was unclean."

¹⁵ The LORD replied, "Instead of human waste, I will let you bake your bread on a fire made from cow manure. ¹⁶ Ezekiel, the people of Jerusalem will starve. They will have so little food and water that they will be afraid and hopeless. ¹⁷ Everyone will be shocked at what is happening, and, because of their sins, they will die a slow death."

CHAPTER 5

Jerusalem's coming destruction

The LORD said:

¹ Ezekiel, son of man, get a sharp sword and use it to cut off your hair and beard. Weigh the hair and divide it into three equal piles. ² After you attack the brick that stands for Jerusalem, burn one pile of your hair on the brick. Chop up the second pile and let the small pieces of hair fall around the brick. Throw the third pile into the wind, and I will strike it with my own sword.

---

*3.27 again . . . speak my message: See 33.21,22.
*4.4,5 Israel's punishment: Israel here refers to the northern kingdom that was destroyed in 722 BC.

*4.13 have to eat food that is unclean, just as you must do: The LORD had forbidden the people of Israel to mix certain things (see Deuteronomy 22.9–11), and so the people would not have been allowed to eat this bread under normal conditions. It is used here to show that when a city is under attack, people eat whatever food is left, even if the LORD had said it was unclean.

³ Keep a few of the hairs and wrap them in the hem of your clothes. ⁴ Then pull out a few of those hairs and throw them in the fire, so they will also burn. This fire will spread, destroying everyone in Israel.

⁵ I am the LORD God, and I have made Jerusalem the most important place in the world, and all other nations admire it. ⁶ But the people of Jerusalem rebelled and refuse to obey me. They ignored my laws and have become even more sinful than the nations around them.

⁷ So tell the people of Jerusalem:

I am the LORD God! You have refused to obey my laws and teachings, and instead you have obeyed the laws of the surrounding nations. You have become more rebellious than any of them! ⁸ Now all those nations will watch as I turn against you and punish you ⁹ for your sins. Your punishment will be more horrible than anything I've ever done or will ever do again. ¹⁰ Parents will be so desperate for food that they will eat their own children, and children will eat their parents. Those who survive this horror will be scattered in every direction.

¹¹ Your disgusting sins have made my temple unfit as a place to worship me. So I swear by my own life that I will turn my back on you and show you no pity. ¹² A third of you will die here in Jerusalem from disease or starvation. Another third will be killed in war. And I will scatter the last third of you in every direction, then track you down and kill you.

¹³ You will feel my fierce anger until I have finished taking revenge. Then you will know that I, the LORD, was furious because of your disobedience. ¹⁴ Every passer-by will laugh at your destruction. Foreign nations ¹⁵ will insult you and make fun of you, but they will also be shocked and terrified at what I did in my anger. ¹⁶ I will destroy your crops until you starve to death, and disasters will strike you like arrows. ¹⁷ Starvation and wild animals will kill your children. I'll punish you with horrible diseases, and your enemies will strike you down with their swords. I, the LORD, have spoken.

Disaster is near

CHAPTER 6

Israel is doomed

¹ The LORD God said:

² Ezekiel, son of man, face the hills of Israel and tell them:

³ Listen, you mountains and hills, and every valley and gorge! I, the LORD, am about to turn against you and crush all the places where foreign gods are worshipped. ⁴ Every altar will be smashed, and in front of the idols I will put to death the people who worship them. ⁵ Dead bodies and bones will be lying around the idols and the altars. ⁶ Every town in Israel will be destroyed to make sure that each shrine, idol, and altar is smashed — everything the Israelites made will be a pile of ruins. ⁷ All over the country, your people will die. And those who survive will know that I, the LORD, did these things. ⁸ I will let some of the people live through this punishment, but I will scatter them among the nations, ⁹ where they will be prisoners. And when they think of me, they will realize that they disgraced me by rebelling and by worshipping idols. They will hate themselves for the evil things they did, ¹⁰ and they will know that I am the LORD and that my warnings must be taken seriously.

¹¹ The LORD God then said:

Ezekiel, beat your fists together and stamp your feet in despair! Moan in sorrow, because the people of Israel have done disgusting things and now will be killed by enemy troops, or they will die from starvation and disease. ¹² Those who live far away will be struck with deadly diseases. Those who live nearby will be killed in war. And the ones who are left will starve to death. I will let loose my anger on them! ¹³ These people used to offer incense to idols at altars built on hills and mountaintops and in the shade of large oak trees. But when they see dead bodies lying around those altars, they will know that I am the LORD. ¹⁴ I will make their country a barren wasteland, from the Southern Desert to the town of Diblah in the north. Then they will know that I, the LORD, have done these things.

See also: 5.10: Lam 4.10. 5.17: Rev 6.8.

CHAPTER 7

Disaster is near

[1] The LORD God said:

[2] Ezekiel, son of man, tell the people of Israel that I am saying:

Israel will soon come to an end! Your whole country is about to be destroyed [3] as punishment for your disgusting sins. I, the LORD, am so angry [4] that I will show no pity. I will punish you for the evil you've done, and you will know that I am the LORD.

[5] There's never been anything like the coming disaster.* [6] And when it comes, your life will be over. [7] You people of Israel are doomed! Soon there will be panic on the mountaintops instead of celebration.*
[8] I will let loose my anger and punish you for the evil things you've done. You'll get what you deserve. [9] Your sins are so terrible, that you'll get no mercy from me. Then you will know that I, the LORD, have punished you.

[10] Disaster is near! Injustice and arrogance are everywhere, [11] and violent criminals run free. None of you will survive the disaster, and everything you own and value will be shattered.* [12] The time is coming when everyone will be ruined. Buying and selling will stop, [13] and people who sell property will never get it back, because all of you must be punished for your sins. And I won't change my mind!*

[14] A signal has been blown on the trumpet, and weapons are prepared for battle. But no one goes to war, because in my anger I will strike down everyone in Israel.

Israel is surrounded

The LORD said to the people of Israel:

[15] War, disease, and starvation are everywhere! People who live in the countryside will be killed in battle, and those who live in towns will die from starvation or deadly diseases. [16] Anyone who survives will escape into the hills, like doves who leave the valleys to find safety. All of you will moan* because of your sins. [17] Your hands will tremble, and your knees will go limp. [18] You will put on sackcloth* to show your sorrow, but terror

will overpower you. Shame will be written all over your faces, and you will shave your heads in despair. [19] Your silver and gold will be thrown into the streets like rubbish, because those are the two things that led you into sin, and now they cannot save you from my anger. They are not even worth enough to buy food. [20] You took great pride in using your beautiful jewellery to make disgusting idols of foreign gods. So I will make your jewellery worthless.

[21] Wicked foreigners will rob and disgrace you. [22] They will break into my temple* and leave it unfit as a place to worship me, but I will look away and let it happen.

[23] Your whole country is in confusion!* Murder and violence are everywhere in Israel, [24] so I will tell the most wicked nations to come and take over your homes. They will put an end to the pride you have in your strong army, and they will make your places of worship unfit to use. [25] You will be terrified and will desperately look for peace — but there will be no peace.
[26] One tragedy will follow another, and you'll hear only bad news. People will beg prophets to give them a message from me. Priests will stop teaching my Law, and wise leaders won't be able to give advice. [27] Even your king and his officials will lose hope and cry in despair. Your hands will tremble with fear.

I will punish you for your sins and treat you the same way you have treated others. Then you will know that I am the LORD.

The Lord's glory leaves sinful Jerusalem

CHAPTER 8

Ezekiel sees the terrible sins of Jerusalem

[1] Six years after King Jehoiachin and the rest of us had been led away as prisoners to Babylonia, the leaders of Judah were meeting with me in my house. On the fifth day of the sixth month,* the LORD God suddenly took control of me, [2] and I saw something in the shape of a human.* This figure was like fire from the waist down, and it was bright as polished metal from the waist up. [3] It reached

---

*7.18 sackcloth: A rough, dark-coloured cloth made from goat or camel hair and used to make grain sacks. It was worn in times of trouble or sorrow.

*8.1 Six years . . . sixth month: Probably September of 592 BC.
See also: 8.2: Ezek 1.27.

out what seemed to be a hand and grabbed my hair. Then in my vision the LORD's Spirit lifted me into the sky and carried me to Jerusalem.

The Spirit took me to the north gate of the temple's inner courtyard, where there was an idol that disgusted the LORD and made him furious. 4 Then I saw the brightness of the glory of the God of Israel, just as I had seen it near the River Chebar.

5 God said to me, "Ezekiel, son of man, look north." And when I did, I saw that disgusting idol by the altar near the gate.

6 God then said, "Do you see the terrible sins of the people of Israel? Their sins are making my holy temple unfit as a place to worship me. Yet you will see even worse things than this."

7 Next, I was taken to the entrance of the courtyard, where I saw a hole in the wall.

8 God said, "Make this hole bigger." And when I did, I realized it was a doorway. 9 "Go in," God said, "and see what horrible and evil things the people are doing."

10 Inside, I saw that the walls were covered with pictures of reptiles and disgusting, unclean animals,* as well as with idols that the Israelites were worshipping. 11 Seventy Israelite leaders were standing there, including Jaazaniah son of Shaphan. Each of these leaders was holding an incense burner, and the smell of incense filled the room.

12 God said, "Ezekiel, do you see what horrible things Israel's leaders are doing in secret? They have filled their rooms with idols. And they say I can't see them, because they think I have already deserted Israel. 13 But I will show you something even worse than this."

14 He took me to the north gate of the temple, where I saw women mourning for the god Tammuz.* 15 God asked me, "Can you believe what these women are doing? But now I want to show you something worse."

16 I was then led into the temple's inner courtyard, where I saw about twenty-five men standing near the entrance, between the porch and the altar. Their backs were to the LORD's temple, and they were bowing down to the rising sun.

17 God said, "Ezekiel, it's bad enough that the people of Judah are doing these disgusting things. But they have also spread violence and injustice everywhere in Israel and have made me very angry. They have disgraced and insulted me in the worst possible way.* 18 So in my fierce anger, I will punish them without mercy and refuse to help them when they cry out to me."

CHAPTER 9

The LORD gives the command to punish Jerusalem

1 After that, I heard the LORD shout, "Come to Jerusalem, you men chosen to destroy the city. And bring your weapons!"

2 I saw six men come through the north gate of the temple, each one holding a deadly weapon. A seventh man dressed in a linen robe was with them, and he was carrying things to write with. The men went into the temple and stood by the bronze altar.

3 The brightness of God's glory then left its place above the statues of the winged creatures* inside the temple and moved to the entrance. The LORD said to the man in the linen robe, 4 "Walk through the city of Jerusalem and mark the forehead of anyone who is truly upset and sad about the disgusting things that are being done here."

5-6 He turned to the other six men and said, "Follow him and put to death everyone who doesn't have a mark on their forehead. Show no mercy or pity! Kill men and women, parents and children. Begin here at my temple and be sure not to harm those who are marked."

The men immediately killed the leaders who were standing there.

7 Then the LORD said, "Pollute the temple by piling the dead bodies in the courtyards. Now get busy!" They left and started killing the people of Jerusalem.

8 I was then alone, so I bowed down and cried out to the LORD, "Why are you doing this? Are you so angry at the people of Jerusalem that everyone must die?"

9 The LORD answered, "The people of Israel and Judah have done horrible things. Their country is filled with murderers, and Jerusalem itself is filled with violence. They

---

*8.10 disgusting, unclean animals: See, for example, Leviticus 11.9–19.
*8.14 the god Tammuz: A god of vegetation who was thought to die in the dry season. During the Hebrew month of Tammuz (from about mid-June to mid-July), women mourned the death of this god, hoping to bring him back to life.
See also: 8.4: Ezek 1.28.

*9.3 the statues of the winged creatures: These were symbols of the LORD's throne on earth (see Exodus 25.18–22; 1 Kings 6.23–28).
See also: 9.4: Rev 7.3; 9.4; 14.1.

think that I have deserted them, and that I can't see what they are doing. [10] And so I will not have pity on them or forgive them. They will be punished for what they have done."

[11] Just then, the man in the linen robe returned and said, "I have done what you commanded."

CHAPTER 10

The Lord's glory leaves the temple

[1] I saw the dome that was above the four winged creatures,* and on it was the sapphire* throne.* [2] The LORD said to the man in the linen robe, "Walk among the four wheels beside the creatures and pick up as many hot coals as you can carry. Then scatter them over the city of Jerusalem." I watched him as he followed the LORD's instructions.

[3] The winged creatures were standing south of the temple when the man walked among them. A cloud filled the inner courtyard, [4] and the brightness of the LORD's glory moved from above the creatures and stopped at the entrance of the temple. The entire temple was filled with his glory, and the courtyard was dazzling bright. [5] The sound of the creatures' wings was as loud as the voice of God All-Powerful and could even be heard in the outer courtyard.

[6] The man in the robe was now standing beside a wheel. [7] One of the four creatures reached its hand into the fire among them and gave the man some of the hot coals. The man took the coals and left.

[8] I noticed again that each of the four winged creatures had what looked like human hands under their wings, [9] and I saw the four wheels near the creatures. These wheels were shining like chrysolite.* [10] Each wheel was exactly the same and had a second wheel that cut through the middle of it,' [11] so that they could move in any direction without turning. The wheels moved together whenever the creatures moved. [12] I also noticed that the wheels and the creatures' bodies, including their backs, their hands, and their wings, were covered with eyes. [13] And I heard a voice calling these "the wheels that spin."

[14] Each of the winged creatures had four faces: the face of a bull,* the face of a human, the face of a lion, and the face of an eagle. [15-17] These were the same creatures I had seen near the River Chebar. They controlled when and where the wheels moved — the wheels went wherever the creatures went and stopped whenever they stopped. Even when the creatures flew in the air, the wheels stayed beside them.

[18] Then I watched the brightness of the LORD's glory move from the entrance of the temple and stop above the winged creatures. [19] They spread their wings and flew into the air with the wheels at their side. They stopped at the east gate of the temple, and the LORD's glory was above them.

[20] I knew for certain that these were the same creatures I had seen beneath the LORD's glory near the River Chebar. [21-22] They had four wings with hands beneath them, and they had the same four faces as those near the River. Each creature moved straight ahead without turning.

CHAPTER 11

Ezekiel condemns Jerusalem's wicked leaders

[1] The LORD's Spirit' lifted me up and took me to the east gate of the temple, where I saw twenty-five men, including the two leaders, Jaazaniah son of Azzur and Pelatiah son of Benaiah. [2] The LORD said, "Ezekiel, son of man, these men are making evil plans and giving dangerous advice to the people of Jerusalem. [3] They say things like, 'Let's build more houses.' This city is like a cooking pot over a fire, and we are the meat, but at least the pot keeps us from being burnt in the fire.'* [4] So, Ezekiel, condemn them!"

[5] The LORD's Spirit took control of me and told me to tell these leaders:

I, the LORD God, know what you leaders are saying. [6] You have murdered so many people that the city is filled with dead bodies! [7] This city is indeed a cooking pot, but the bodies of those you killed are the meat. And so I will force you to leave Jerusalem, [8] and I'll

---

*10.1 winged creatures: See the note at 9.3.
*10.1 sapphire: See the note at 1.26.
*10.1 dome . . . creatures . . . throne: See 1.22-26.
*10.9 chrysolite: See the note at 1.16.
See also: 10.1: Ezek 1.26; Rev 4.2. 10.2: Rev 8.5.
10.9-13: Ezek 1.15-21. 10.12: Rev 4.8.

*10.14 a bull: The Hebrew text has "a winged creature", but see 1.10.
*11.3 the pot keeps us from being burnt in the fire: These leaders were trying to convince the people of Jerusalem that they were secure, and that their future was bright.
See also: 10.14: Ezek 1.10; Rev 4.7.

send armies to attack you, just as you fear. ⁹ Then you will be captured and punished by foreign enemies.* ¹⁰ You will be killed in your own country, but not before you realize that I, the LORD, have done these things.

¹¹ You leaders claim to be meat in a cooking pot, but you won't be protected by this city. No, you will die at the border of Israel. ¹² You will realize that while you were following the laws of nearby nations, you were disobeying my laws and teachings. And I am the LORD!

¹³ Before I finished speaking, Pelatiah dropped dead. I bowed down and cried out, "Please, LORD God, don't kill everyone left in Israel."

A promise of hope

¹⁴ The LORD replied:

¹⁵ Ezekiel, son of man, the people living in Jerusalem claim that you and the other Israelites who were taken to Babylonia are too far away to worship me. They also claim that the land of Israel now belongs only to them. ¹⁶ But here is what I want you to tell the Israelites in Babylonia:

It's true that I, the LORD God, have forced you out of your own country and made you live among foreign nations. But for now, I will be with you wherever you are, so that you can worship me. ¹⁷ And some day, I will gather you from the nations where you are scattered and let you live in Israel again. ¹⁸ When that happens, I want you to clear the land of all disgusting idols. ¹⁹ Then I will take away your stubbornness and make you eager to be completely faithful to me. You will want to obey me ²⁰ and all my laws and teachings. You will be my people, and I will be your God. ²¹ But those who worship idols will be punished and get what they deserve. I, the LORD God, have spoken.

The LORD's glory leaves Jerusalem

²² After the LORD had finished speaking, the winged creatures spread their wings and flew into the air, and the wheels were beside them. The brightness of the LORD's glory above them ²³ left Jerusalem and stopped at a hill east of the city.

²⁴ Then in my vision, the LORD's Spirit* lifted me up and carried me back to the other exiles in Babylonia. The vision faded away, ²⁵ and I told them everything the LORD had shown me.

Messages of doom for Judah and Jerusalem

CHAPTER 12

Ezekiel acts out Israel's captivity

¹ The LORD said:

² Ezekiel, son of man, you are living among rebellious people. They have eyes, but refuse to see; they have ears, but refuse to listen. ³ So before it gets dark, here is what I want you to do. Pack a few things as though you were going to be taken away as a prisoner. Then go outside where everyone can see you and walk around from place to place. Perhaps as they watch, they will realize what rebels they are. ⁴ After you have done this, return to your house.

Later that evening leave your house as if you were going into exile. ⁵ Dig through the wall of your house* and crawl out, carrying the bag with you. Make sure everyone is watching. ⁶ Lift the bag to your shoulders, and with your face covered, take it into the darkness, so that you cannot see the land you are leaving. All this will be a warning for the people of Israel.

⁷ I did everything the LORD had said. I packed a few things. Then as the sun was going down, and while everyone was watching, I dug a hole through one of the walls of my house. I pulled out my bag, then lifted it to my shoulders and left in the darkness.

⁸ The next morning, the LORD ⁹ reminded me that these rebellious people didn't even ask what I was doing. ¹⁰ So he sent me back to tell them:

The LORD God has a message for the leader of Jerusalem and everyone living there! ¹¹ I have done these things to show them what will happen when they are taken away as prisoners.

¹² The leader of Jerusalem will lift his own bag to his shoulders at sunset and leave through a hole that the others have dug in

---

*11.9 foreign enemies: That is, the Babylonians.
See also: 11.19,20: Ezek 36.26–28. 11.22,23: Ezek 43.2–5.

*12.5 Dig through the wall of your house: The walls of most houses in Babylonia were made of mud bricks that had been dried in the sun. A hole could easily have been dug through these bricks.
See also: 12.2: Isa 6.9,10; Jer 5.21; Mark 8.18.

the wall of his house. He will cover his face, so he can't see the land he is leaving. ¹³ The LORD will spread out a net and trap him as he leaves Jerusalem. He will then be led away to the city of Babylon, but will never see that place,* even though he will die there. ¹⁴ His own officials and troops will scatter in every direction, and the LORD will track them down and put them to death.

¹⁵ The LORD will force the rest of the people in Jerusalem to live in foreign nations, where they will realize that he has done all these things. ¹⁶ Some of them will survive the war, the starvation, and the deadly diseases. That way, they will be able to tell foreigners how disgusting their sins were, and that it was the LORD who punished them in this way.

A sign of fear

¹⁷ The LORD said:

¹⁸ Ezekiel, son of man, shake with fear when you eat, and tremble when you drink. ¹⁹ Tell the people of Israel that I, the LORD, say that some day everyone in Jerusalem will shake when they eat and tremble when they drink. Their country will be destroyed and left empty, because they have been cruel and violent. ²⁰ Every town will lie in ruins, and the land will be a barren desert. Then they will know that I am the LORD.

The words of the LORD will come true

²¹ The LORD said:

²² Ezekiel, son of man, you've heard people in Israel use the saying, "Time passes, and prophets are proved wrong." ²³ Now tell the people that I, the LORD, am going to prove that saying wrong. No one will ever be able to use it again in Israel, because very soon everything I have said will come true! ²⁴ The people will hear no more useless warnings and false messages. ²⁵ I will give them my message, and what I say will certainly happen. Warn those rebels that the time has come for them to be punished. I, the LORD, make this promise.

²⁶⁻²⁷ Ezekiel, the people of Israel are also saying that your visions and messages are only about things in the future. ²⁸ So tell

them that my words will soon come true, just as I have warned. I, the LORD, have spoken.

CHAPTER 13

Lying prophets

¹ The LORD said:

² Ezekiel, son of man, condemn the prophets of Israel who say they speak in my name, but who preach messages that come from their own imagination. Tell them it's time to hear my message. ³ I, the LORD God, say those lying prophets are doomed! They don't see visions — they make up their own messages! ⁴ Israel's prophets are no better than jackals* that hunt for food among the ruins of a city. ⁵ They don't warn the people about coming trouble or tell them how dangerous it is to sin against me. ⁶ Those prophets lie by claiming they speak for me, but I have not even chosen them to be my prophets. And they still think their words will come true. ⁷ They say they're preaching my messages, but they are full of lies — I did not speak to them!

⁸ So I am going to punish those lying prophets for deceiving the people of Israel with false messages. ⁹ I will turn against them and no longer let them belong to my people. They will not be allowed to call themselves Israelites or even to set foot in Israel. Then they will realize that I am the LORD God.

¹⁰ Those prophets refuse to be honest. They tell my people there will be peace, even though there's no peace to be found. They are like workers who think they can fix a shaky wall by covering it with paint. ¹¹ But when I send rainstorms, hailstones, and strong winds, the wall will surely collapse. ¹² People will then ask the workers why the paint didn't hold it up.

¹³ That wall is the city of Jerusalem. And I, the LORD God, am so angry that I will send strong winds, rainstorms, and hailstones to destroy it. ¹⁴ The lying prophets have tried to cover up the evil in Jerusalem, but I will tear down the city, all the way to its foundations. And when it collapses, those prophets will be killed, and everyone will know that I have done these things.

¹⁵ The city of Jerusalem and its lying prophets will feel my fierce anger. Then I

---

*12.13 He will then be led away . . . that place: According to 2 Kings 25.6,7, King Zedekiah of Judah was blinded before he was taken to Babylon.
See also: 12.13: 2 King 25.7; Jer 52.11.

*13.4 jackals: Desert animals related to wolves, but smaller.
See also: 13.10: Jer 6.14; 8.11.

will announce that the city has fallen and that the lying prophets are dead, [16] because they promised my people peace, when there was no peace. I, the LORD God, have spoken.

Women who wear magic charms

The LORD said:

[17] Ezekiel, son of man, now condemn the women of Israel who preach messages that come from their own imagination. [18] Tell them they're doomed! They wear magic charms on their wrists and scarves on their heads, then trick others into believing they can predict the future.' They won't get away with telling those lies. [19] They charge my people a few handfuls of barley and a couple of pieces of bread, and then give messages that are insulting to me. They use lies to sentence the innocent to death and to help the guilty go free. And my people believe them!

[20] I hate the magic charms they use to trick people into believing their lies. I will rip those charms from their wrists and set free the people they have trapped like birds.' [21] I will tear the scarves from their heads and rescue my people from their power once and for all. Then they will know that I am the LORD God.

[22] They do things I would never do. They lie to good people and encourage them to do wrong, and they convince the wicked to keep sinning and ruin their lives. [23] I will no longer let these women give false messages and use magic, and I will free my people from their control. Then they will know that I, the LORD, have done these things.

CHAPTER 14

Ezekiel encourages the people to turn back to the LORD

[1] One day, some of Israel's leaders came to me and asked for a message from the LORD. [2] While they were there, the LORD said:

[3] Ezekiel, son of man, these men have started worshipping idols, though they know it will cause them to sin even more. So I refuse to give them a message!

[4] Tell the people of Israel that if they sin by worshipping idols and then go to a prophet to find out what I say, I will give them the answer their sins deserve. [5] When they hear my message, perhaps they will see that they need to turn back to me and stop worshipping those idols.

[6] Now, Ezekiel, tell everyone in Israel:

I am the LORD God. Stop worshipping your disgusting idols and come back to me.

[7] Suppose one of you Israelites or a foreigner living in Israel rejects me and starts worshipping idols. If you then go to a prophet to find out what I say, I will answer [8] by turning against you. I will make you a warning to anyone who might think of doing the same thing, and you will no longer belong to my people. Then you will know that I am the LORD and that you have sinned against me.

[9] If a prophet gives a false message, I am the one who caused that prophet to lie. But I will still reject him and cut him off from my people, [10] and anyone who goes to that prophet for a message will be punished in the same way. [11] I will do this, so that you will come back to me and stop destroying yourselves with these disgusting sins. So turn back to me! Then I will be your God, and you will be my people. I, the LORD God, make this promise.

Judgment on a sinful nation

[12] The LORD God said:

[13] Ezekiel, son of man, suppose an entire nation sins against me, and I punish it by destroying the crops and letting its people and livestock starve to death. [14] Even if Noah, Daniel,* and Job were living in that nation, their faithfulness would not save anyone but themselves.

[15] Or suppose I punish a nation by sending wild animals to eat people and scare away every passer-by, so that the land becomes a barren desert. [16] As surely as I live, I promise that even if these three men lived in that nation, their own children would not be spared. The three men would live, but the land would be an empty desert.

[17] Or suppose I send an enemy to attack a sinful nation and kill its people and livestock. [18] If these three men were in that nation when I punished it, not even their children would be spared. Only the three men would live.

[19] And suppose I am so angry that I send a deadly disease to wipe out the people and livestock of a sinful nation. [20] Again, even if Noah, Daniel, and Job were living

---

*14.14 Daniel: Or "Danel", possibly a well-known hero or wise man.

there, I, the LORD, promise that the children of these faithful men would also die. Only the three of them would be spared.

²¹ I am the LORD God, and I promise to punish Jerusalem severely. I will send war, starvation, wild animals, and deadly disease to slaughter its people and livestock. ²² And those who survive will be taken from their country and led here to Babylonia. Ezekiel, when you see how sinful they are, you will know why I did all these things to Jerusalem. ²³ You will be convinced that I, the LORD God, was right in doing what I did.

CHAPTER 15

Jerusalem is a useless vine

¹ Some time later, the LORD said:

² Ezekiel, son of man, what happens to the wood of a grapevine after the grapes have been picked? It isn't like other trees in the forest, ³ because the wood of a grapevine can't be used to make anything, not even a small peg to hang things on. ⁴ It can only be used as firewood. But after its ends are burnt and its middle is charred, it can't be used for anything. ⁵ The wood is useless before it is burnt, and afterwards, it is completely worthless.

⁶ I, the LORD God, promise that just as the wood of a grapevine is burnt as firewood, ⁷ I will punish the people of Jerusalem with fire. Some of them have escaped one destruction, but soon they will be completely burnt. And when that happens, you, Ezekiel, will know that I am the LORD. ⁸ I will make their country an empty wasteland, because they have not been loyal to me. I, the LORD God, have spoken.

CHAPTER 16

Jerusalem is unfaithful

¹ The LORD said:

² Ezekiel, son of man, remind the people of Jerusalem of their disgusting sins ³ and tell them that I, the LORD God, am saying:

Jerusalem, you were born in the country where Canaanites lived. Your father was an Amorite, and your mother was a Hittite.*

⁴ When you were born, no one cut you loose from your mother or washed your body. No one rubbed your skin with salt and olive oil,* and wrapped you in warm blankets. ⁵ Not one person loved you enough to do any of these things, and no one even felt sorry for you. You were despised, thrown into a field, and forgotten.

⁶ I saw you lying there, rolling around in your own blood, and I couldn't let you die. ⁷ I took care of you, like someone caring for a tender, young plant. You grew up to be a beautiful young woman with perfect breasts and long hair, but you were still naked.

⁸ When I saw you again, you were old enough to have sex. So I covered your naked body with my own robe.* Then I solemnly promised that you would belong to me and that I, the LORD God, would take care of you.

⁹ I washed the blood off you and rubbed your skin with olive oil. ¹⁰ I gave you the finest clothes and the most expensive robes,* as well as sandals made from the best leather. ¹¹ I gave you bracelets, a necklace, ¹² a ring for your nose, some earrings, and a beautiful crown. ¹³ Your jewellery was gold and silver, and your clothes were made of only the finest material and embroidered linen. Your bread was baked from fine flour, and you ate honey and olive oil. You were as beautiful as a queen, ¹⁴ and everyone on earth knew it. I, the LORD God, had helped you become a lovely young woman.

¹⁵ You learnt that you were attractive enough to have any man you wanted, so you offered yourself to every passer-by.* ¹⁶ You made shrines for yourself and decorated them with some of your clothes. That's where you took your visitors to have sex with them. These things should never have happened!* ¹⁷ You made idols out of the gold and silver jewellery I gave you, then you sinned by worshipping those idols. ¹⁸ You dressed them in the clothes you got from me, and you offered them the olive oil and incense I gave you. ¹⁹ I supplied you with fine flour, olive oil, and honey, but you sacrificed it all as offerings to please those idols. I, the LORD God, watched this happen.

---

*16.3 Amorite . . . Hittite: People who lived in Canaan before the Israelites and who worshipped idols.
See also: 14.21; Rev 6.8.

*16.4 rubbed your skin with salt and olive oil: People believed this toughened the skin of the babies.
*16.8 I covered your naked body with my own robe: To show that he would protect and take care of her.

²⁰ But you did something even worse than that — you sacrificed your own children to those idols! ²¹ You slaughtered my children, so you could offer them as sacrifices. ²² You were so busy sinning and being a prostitute that you refused to think about the days when you were young and were rolling around naked in your own blood.

²³ Now I, the LORD God, say you are doomed! Not only did you do these evil things, ²⁴ but you also built places on every street corner ²⁵ where you disgraced yourself by having sex with anyone who walked by. And you did that more and more every day! ²⁶ To make me angry, you even offered yourself to Egyptians, who were always ready to sleep with you.

²⁷ So I punished you by letting those greedy Philistine enemies take over some of your territory. But even they were offended by your disgusting behaviour.

²⁸ You couldn't get enough sex, so you chased after Assyrians and slept with them. You still weren't satisfied, ²⁹ so you went after Babylonians. But those merchants could not satisfy you either.

³⁰ I, the LORD God, say that you were so disgusting that you would have done anything to get what you wanted.* ³¹ You had sex on every street corner, and when you finished, you refused to accept money. That's worse than being a prostitute! ³² You are nothing but an unfaithful wife who would rather have sex with strangers than with your own husband. ³³ Prostitutes accept money for having sex, but you bribe men from everywhere to have sex with you. ³⁴ You're not like other prostitutes. Men don't ask you for sex — you offer to pay them!

Jerusalem must be punished

The LORD said:

³⁵ Jerusalem, you prostitute, listen to me. ³⁶ You chased after lovers, then took off your clothes and had sex. You even worshipped disgusting idols and sacrificed your own children as offerings to them. ³⁷ So I, the LORD God, will gather every one of your lovers, those you liked and those you hated. They will stand around you, and I will rip off your clothes and let all those lovers stare at your nakedness. ³⁸ I will find you guilty of being an unfaithful wife and a murderer, and in my fierce anger I will sentence you to death! ³⁹ Then I will hand you over to your lovers, who will tear down the places where you had sex. They will take

your clothes and jewellery, leaving you naked and empty-handed.

⁴⁰ Your lovers and an angry mob will stone you to death; they will cut your dead body into pieces ⁴¹ and burn down your houses. Other women will watch these terrible things happen to you. I promise to stop you from being a prostitute and paying your lovers for sex.

⁴² Only then will I calm down and stop being angry and jealous. ⁴³ You made me furious by doing all these disgusting things and by forgetting how I took care of you when you were young. Then you made things worse by acting like a prostitute. You must be punished! I, the LORD God, have spoken.

Jerusalem's two sisters

The LORD said:

⁴⁴ People will use this saying about you, Jerusalem: "If the mother is bad, so is her daughter." ⁴⁵ You are just like your mother, who hated her husband and her own children. You are also like your sisters, who hated their husbands and children. Your father was an Amorite, and your mother was a Hittite.* ⁴⁶ Your elder sister was Samaria, that city to your north with her nearby villages. Your younger sister was Sodom, that city to your south with her nearby villages. ⁴⁷ You followed their way of life and their wicked customs, and soon you were more disgusting than they were.

⁴⁸ As surely as I am the living LORD God, the people of Sodom and its nearby villages were never as sinful as you. ⁴⁹ They were arrogant and spoilt; they had everything they needed and still refused to help the poor and needy. ⁵⁰ They thought they were better than everyone else, and they did things I hate. And so I destroyed them.

⁵¹ You people of Jerusalem have sinned twice as much as the people of Samaria. In fact, your evil ways have made both Sodom and Samaria look innocent. ⁵² So their punishment will seem light compared to yours. You will be disgraced and put to shame because of your disgusting sins.

Jerusalem will be ashamed

The LORD said to Jerusalem:

⁵³ Some day I will bless Sodom and Samaria and their nearby villages. I will also bless

---

*16.45 Amorite . . . Hittite: See the note at 16.3.

you, Jerusalem. ⁵⁴ Then you will be ashamed of how you've acted, and Sodom and Samaria will be relieved that they weren't as sinful as you. ⁵⁵ When that day comes, you and Sodom and Samaria will once again be well off, and all nearby villages will be restored.

⁵⁶ Jerusalem, you were so arrogant that you sneered at Sodom. ⁵⁷ But now everyone has learnt how wicked you really are. The countries of Syria and Philistia, as well as your other neighbours, hate you and make insulting remarks. ⁵⁸ You must pay for all the vulgar and disgusting things you have done. I, the LORD, have spoken.

The LORD makes a promise to Jerusalem

The LORD said:

⁵⁹ Jerusalem, you deserve to be punished, because you broke your promises and ignored our agreement. ⁶⁰ But I remember the agreement I made with you when you were young,* and so I will make you a promise that will last for ever. ⁶¹ When you think about how you acted, you will be ashamed, especially when I return your sisters* to you as daughters, even though this was not part of our agreement.* ⁶² I will keep this solemn promise, and you will know that I am the LORD. ⁶³ I will forgive you, but you will think about your sins and be too ashamed to say a word. I, the LORD God, have spoken.

CHAPTER 17

A story about two eagles and a vine

¹ The LORD said:

² Ezekiel, son of man, tell the people of Israel the following story, ³ so they will understand what I am saying to them:

A large eagle with strong wings and beautiful feathers once flew to Lebanon. It broke the top branch off a cedar tree, ⁴ then carried it to a nation of merchants and left it in one of their cities. ⁵ The eagle also took seed from Israel and planted it in a fertile field with plenty of water, like a willow tree beside a stream.* ⁶ The seed sprouted and grew into a grapevine that spread over the ground. It had lots of

leaves and strong, deep roots, and its branches grew upward towards the eagle.

⁷ There was another eagle with strong wings and thick feathers. The roots and branches of the grapevine soon turned towards this eagle, hoping it would bring water for the soil. ⁸ But the vine was already growing in fertile soil, where there was plenty of water to produce healthy leaves and large grapes.

⁹ Now tell me, Ezekiel, do you think this grapevine will live? Or will the first eagle pull it up by its roots and pluck off the grapes and let its new leaves die? The eagle could easily kill it without the help of a large and powerful army. ¹⁰ The grapevine is strong and healthy, but as soon as the scorching desert wind blows, it will quickly wither.

The LORD explains the story

¹¹ The LORD said:

¹² Ezekiel, ask the rebellious people of Israel if they know what this story means.

Tell them that the king of Babylonia came to Jerusalem, then captured the king of Judah* and his officials, and took them back to Babylon as prisoners. ¹³ He chose someone from the family of Judah's king* and signed a treaty with him, then made him swear to be loyal. He also led away other important citizens, ¹⁴ so that the rest of the people of Judah would obey only him and never gain control of their own country again.

¹⁵ But this new king of Judah later rebelled against Babylonia and sent officials to Egypt to get horses and troops. Will this king be successful in breaking the treaty with Babylonia? Or will he be punished for what he's done?

¹⁶ As surely as I am the living LORD God, I swear that the king of Judah will die in Babylon, because he broke the treaty with the king of Babylonia, who appointed him king. ¹⁷ Even the king of Egypt and his powerful army will be useless to Judah when the Babylonians attack and build earth ramps to invade the cities of Judah and kill its people. ¹⁸ The king of Judah broke his own promises and ignored the treaty with Babylonia. And so he will be punished!

---

*16.60 the agreement . . . when you were young: See verse 8.
*16.61 sisters: Sodom and Samaria (see verses 44–52).

*17.12 king of Judah: Probably King Jehoiachin (see 2 Kings 24.10–12,15,16).
*17.13 someone from the family of Judah's king: Probably King Zedekiah (see 2 Kings 24.17).
See also: 17.12–15: 2 King 24.15–20; 2 Chron 36.10–13.

¹⁹ He made a promise in my name and swore to honour the treaty. And now that he has broken that promise, my name is disgraced. He must pay for what he's done. ²⁰ I will spread out a net to trap him. Then I will drag him to Babylon and see that he is punished for his unfaithfulness to me. ²¹ His best troops* will be killed in battle, and the survivors will be scattered in every direction. I, the LORD, have spoken.

²²⁻²³ Some day, I, the LORD,
will cut a tender twig
    from the top of a cedar tree,
then plant it on the peak
    of Israel's tallest mountain,
where it will grow
    strong branches
    and produce large fruit.
All kinds of birds will find
    shelter under the tree,
and they will rest in the shade
    of its branches.

²⁴ Every tree in the forest
    will know that I, the LORD,
can bring down tall trees
    and help short ones grow.
I dry up green trees
    and make dry ones green.
I, the LORD, have spoken,
    and I will keep my word.

CHAPTER 18

Those who sin will die

¹ The LORD said:

² Ezekiel, I hear the people of Israel using the old saying,

> "Sour grapes eaten by parents
> leave a sour taste in the mouths
> of their children."

³ Now tell them that I am the LORD God, and as surely as I live, that saying will no longer be used in Israel. ⁴ The lives of all people belong to me — parents as well as children. Only those who sin will be put to death.

⁵ Suppose there is a truly good man who always does what is fair and right. ⁶ He refuses to eat meat sacrificed to foreign gods at local shrines or to worship Israel's idols. He doesn't have sex with someone else's wife or with a woman having her monthly period. ⁷ He never cheats or robs anyone and always returns anything taken as security for a loan; he gives food and clothes to the poor ⁸ and doesn't charge interest when lending money. He refuses to do anything evil; he is fair to everyone ⁹ and faithfully obeys my laws and teachings. This man is good, and I promise he will live.

¹⁰ But suppose this good man has an evil son who is violent and commits sins ¹¹ his father never did. He eats meat at local shrines, has sex with someone else's wife, ¹² cheats the poor, and robs people. He keeps what is given to him as security for a loan. He worships idols, does disgusting things, ¹³ and charges high interest when lending money. An evil man like that will certainly not live. He is the one who has done these horrible sins, so it's his own fault that he will be put to death.

¹⁴ But suppose this evil man has a son who sees his father do these things and refuses to act like him. ¹⁵ He doesn't eat meat at local shrines or worship Israel's idols, and he doesn't have sex with someone else's wife. ¹⁶ He never cheats or robs anyone and doesn't even demand security for a loan. He gives food and clothes to the poor ¹⁷ and refuses to do anything evil* or to charge interest. And he obeys all my laws and teachings. Such a man will live. His own father sinned, but this good man will not be put to death for the sins of his father. ¹⁸ It is his father who will die for cheating and robbing and doing evil.

¹⁹ You may wonder why a son isn't punished for the sins of his father. It is because the son does what is right and obeys my laws. ²⁰ Only those who sin will be put to death. Children won't suffer for the sins of their parents, and parents won't suffer for the sins of their children. Good people will be rewarded for what they do, and evil people will be punished for what they do.

²¹ Suppose wicked people stop sinning and start obeying my laws and doing right. They won't be put to death. ²² All their sins will be forgiven, and they will live because they did right. ²³ I, the LORD God, don't like to see wicked people die. I enjoy seeing them turn from their sins and live.

²⁴ But when good people start sinning and doing disgusting things, will they live? No! All their good deeds will be forgotten, and they will be put to death because of their sins.

²⁵ You people of Israel accuse me of being unfair! But listen — I'm not unfair; you are!

See also: 18.2: Jer 31.29.

See also: 18.9: Lev 18.5. 18.20: Deut 24.16.

26 If good people start doing evil, they must be put to death, because they have sinned. 27 And if wicked people start doing right, they will save themselves from punishment. 28 They will think about what they've done and stop sinning, and so they won't be put to death. 29 But you still say that I am unfair. You are the ones who have done wrong and are unfair!

30 I will judge each of you for what you've done. So stop sinning, or else you will certainly be punished. 31 Give up your evil ways and start thinking pure thoughts. And be faithful to me! Do you really want to be put to death for your sins? 32 I, the LORD God, don't want to see that happen to anyone. So stop sinning and live!

CHAPTER 19

A funeral song for Israel's leaders

The LORD said:

1 Ezekiel, sing a funeral song for two of Israel's leaders:*

2 Your mother was a brave lioness
   who raised her cubs
      among lions.
3 She taught one of them to hunt,
   and he learnt to eat people.
4 When the nations heard of him,
   they trapped him in a pit,
then they used hooks
   to drag him to Egypt.

5 His mother waited
   for him to return.
But soon she lost all hope
   and raised another cub,
who also became fierce.
6 He hunted with other lions
   and learnt to eat people.
7 He destroyed fortresses'
   and ruined towns;
his mighty roar
   terrified everyone.
8 Nations plotted to kill him,
   and people came from everywhere
      to spread out a net
      and catch him in a trap.
9 They put him in a cage
   and took him to Babylonia.
The lion was locked away,
   so that his mighty roar

would never again be heard
   on Israel's hills.

10 Your mother was a vine'
   growing near a stream.
There was plenty of water,
so she was filled with branches
   and with lots of fruit.
11 Her strong branches
   became symbols of authority,
and she was taller
   than all other trees —
everyone could see how strong
   and healthy she was.
12 But in anger, I pulled her up
   by the roots
and threw her to the ground,
   where the scorching desert wind
   dried out her fruit.
Her strong branches wilted
   and burnt up.
13 Then she was planted
   in a hot, dry desert,
14 where her stem caught fire,
   and flames burnt
      her branches and fruit.
Not one strong branch is left;
   she is stripped bare.

This funeral song must be sung with sorrow.

CHAPTER 20

Israel keeps on rebelling

1 Seven years after King Jehoiachin and the rest of us had been led away as prisoners to Babylonia, some of Israel's leaders came to me on the tenth day of the fifth month.* They sat down and asked for a message from the LORD. 2 Just then, the LORD God said:

3 Ezekiel, son of man, these leaders have come to find out what I want them to do. As surely as I live, I will not give them an answer of any kind.

4 Are you willing to warn them, Ezekiel? Then remind them of the disgusting sins of their ancestors. 5 Tell them that long ago I, the LORD God, chose Israel to be my own. I appeared to their ancestors in Egypt and made a solemn promise that I would be their God and the God of their descendants. 6 I swore that I would rescue them from Egypt and lead them to a land I had already chosen. This

---

*19.1 two of Israel's leaders: Probably Jehoahaz (ruled three months in 609 BC) and Jehoiachin (ruled three months in 598 BC) or Zedekiah (598–586 BC).

*20.1 Seven years . . . fifth month: Probably August of 591 BC.

See also: 20.5,6: Exod 6.2–8.

land was rich with milk and honey and was the most splendid land of all. 7 I told them to get rid of their disgusting idols and not to sin by worshipping the gods of Egypt. I reminded them that I was the LORD their God, 8 but they still rebelled against me. They refused to listen and kept on worshipping their idols and foreign gods.

In my anger, I decided to punish the Israelites in Egypt. 9 But that would have made me look like a liar, because I had already promised in front of everyone that I would lead them out of Egypt. 10 So I brought them out and led them into the desert. 11 I gave them my laws and teachings, so they would know how to live right. 12 And I commanded them to respect the Sabbath as a way of showing that they were holy and belonged to me. 13 But the Israelites rebelled against me in the desert. They refused to obey my laws and teachings, and they treated the Sabbath like any other day.

Then in my anger, I decided to destroy the Israelites in the desert once and for all. 14 But that would have disgraced me, because many other nations had seen me bring the Israelites out of Egypt. 15 Instead, I told them in the desert that I would not lead them into the beautiful, fertile land I had promised. 16 I said this because they had not only ignored my laws and teachings, but had disgraced my Sabbath and worshipped idols.

17 Yet, I felt sorry for them and could not let them die in the desert. 18 So I warned the children not to act like their parents or follow their evil ways or worship their idols. 19 I reminded them that I was the LORD their God and that they should obey my laws and teachings. 20 I told them to respect my Sabbath to show that they were my people and that I was the LORD their God. 21 But the children also rebelled against me. They refused to obey my laws and teachings, and they treated the Sabbath as any other day.

I became angry and decided to punish them in the desert. 22 But I did not. That would have disgraced me in front of the nations that had seen me bring the Israelites out of Egypt. 23 So I solemnly swore that I would scatter the people of Israel across the nations, 24 because they had disobeyed my laws and ignored my teachings; they had disgraced my Sabbath and worshipped the idols their ancestors had made. 25 I gave them laws that bring punishment instead of life,

26 and I let them offer me unacceptable sacrifices, including their firstborn sons. I did this to horrify them and to let them know that I, the LORD, was punishing them.

27 Ezekiel, tell the people of Israel that their ancestors also rejected and insulted me 28 by offering sacrifices, incense, and wine to gods on every hill and under every large tree. I was very angry, because they did these things in the land I had given them! 29 I asked them where they went to worship those gods, and they answered, "At the local shrines."* And those places of worship are still called shrines.

30 Then ask the Israelites why they are following the example of their wicked ancestors 31 by worshipping idols and by sacrificing their own children as offerings. They commit these sins and still think they can ask me for a message. As surely as I am the living LORD God, I will give them no answer. 32 They may think they can be like other nations and get away with worshipping idols made of wood and stone. But that will never happen!

The LORD promises to restore Israel

The LORD said to the people of Israel:

33 As surely as I am the living LORD God, I will rule over you with my powerful arm. You will feel my fierce anger 34 and my power, when I gather you from the places where you are scattered 35 and lead you into a desert surrounded by nations. I will meet you there face to face. Then I will pass judgment on you 36 and punish you, just as I punished your ancestors in the desert near Egypt.* 37 I will force each of you to obey the regulations of our solemn agreement. 38 I will separate the sinful rebels from the rest of you, and even though I will bring them from the nations where they live in exile, they won't be allowed to return to Israel. Then you will know that I am the LORD.

39 Go ahead and worship your idols for now, you Israelites, because soon I will no longer let you dishonour me by offering gifts to them. You will have no choice but to obey me!* 40 When that day comes, everyone in Israel will worship me on Mount Zion, my holy mountain in Jerusalem. I will once

---

*20.29 where they went to worship those gods . . . local shrines: In Hebrew "where they went" sounds like "local shrines". These were places to worship foreign gods.
*20.36 the desert near Egypt: The Sinai Desert.

See also: 20.11,13: Lev 18.5. 20.12: Exod 31.13–17. 20.15: Num 14.26–35. 20.23: Lev 26.33.

792

again call you my own, and I will accept your sacred offerings and sacrifices. ⁴¹ When I bring you home from the places where you are now scattered, I will be pleased with you, just as I am pleased with the smell of the smoke from your sacrifices. Every nation on earth will see that I am holy, ⁴² and you will know that I, the LORD, am the one who brought you back to Israel, the land I promised your ancestors. ⁴³ Then you will remember your wicked sins, and you will hate yourselves for doing such horrible things. They have made you unacceptable to me, ⁴⁴ so you deserve to be punished. But I will treat you in a way that will bring honour to my name, and you will know that I am the LORD God.

Fire from the south

⁴⁵ The LORD said, ⁴⁶ "Ezekiel, son of man, turn towards the south and warn the forests ⁴⁷ that I, the LORD God, will start a fire that will burn up every tree, whether green or dry. Nothing will be able to put out the blaze of that fire as it spreads to the north and burns everything in its path. ⁴⁸ Everyone will know that I started it, and that it cannot be stopped."

⁴⁹ But I complained, "LORD God, I don't want to do that! People already say I confuse them with my messages."

CHAPTER 21

The LORD will punish Jerusalem

¹ The LORD said:

² Ezekiel, son of man, condemn the places in Jerusalem where people worship. Warn everyone in Israel ³ that I am about to punish them. I will pull out my sword and have it ready to kill everyone, whether good or evil. ⁴ From south to north, people will die, ⁵ knowing that my sword will never be put away.

⁶ Ezekiel, groan in sorrow and despair so that everyone can hear you. ⁷ When they ask why you are groaning, tell them you have terrifying news that will make them faint and tremble in fear and lose all courage. These things will happen soon. I, the LORD God, make this promise!

A sword is ready to attack Israel

⁸ The LORD said:

⁹⁻¹⁰ Ezekiel, son of man, tell the people of Jerusalem:

I have sharpened my sword
to slaughter you;
it is shiny and will flash
like lightning!
Don't celebrate —
punishment is coming,
because everyone has ignored
my warnings.'
¹¹ My sword has been polished;
it's sharp and ready to kill.

¹² Groan in sorrow, Ezekiel;
the sword is drawn against
my people
and their leaders.
They will die!
So give up all hope.
¹³ I am testing my people,
and they can do nothing
to stop me.'
I, the LORD, have spoken.

¹⁴ Ezekiel, warn my people,
then celebrate my victory
by clapping your hands.
My vicious sword will attack
again and again,
killing my people
with every stroke.
¹⁵ They will lose all courage
and stumble with fear.
My slaughtering sword
is waiting at every gate,
flashing and ready to kill.'
¹⁶ It will slash right and left,
wherever the blade is pointed.
¹⁷ Then I will stop being angry,
and I will clap my hands
in victory.
I, the LORD, have spoken.

The king of Babylonia and his sword

¹⁸ The LORD said:

¹⁹ Ezekiel, son of man, mark two roads for the king of Babylonia to follow when he comes with his sword. The roads will begin at the same place, but be sure to put up a signpost where the two roads separate and go in different directions. ²⁰ Clearly mark where the two roads lead. One goes to Rabbah, the capital of Ammon, and the other goes to Jerusalem, the fortified capital of Judah. ²¹ When the Babylonian king stands at that signpost, he will decide which way to go by shaking his arrows, by asking his idols, and by carefully looking at the liver of a sacrificed

animal.* [22] His right hand will pull out the arrow marked "Jerusalem". Then he will immediately give the signal to shout the battle cry, to build earth ramps to the top of the city walls, to break down its walls and gates with large wooden poles, and to kill the people. [23] Everyone in Jerusalem had promised to be loyal to Babylonia, and so none of them will believe that this could happen to them. But Babylonia's king will remind them of their sinful ways and warn them of their coming captivity.

[24] Ezekiel, tell the people of Jerusalem and their ruler that I, the LORD God, am saying:

Everything you do is wicked and shows how sinful you are. You are guilty and will be taken away as prisoners.

[25] And you, you evil and wicked ruler of Israel, your day of final punishment is almost here. [26] I, the LORD God, command you to take off your royal turban and your crown, because everything will be different. Those who had no power will be put in charge, and those who now rule will become nobodies. [27] I will leave Jerusalem in ruins when my chosen one comes to punish this city.

Judgment against Ammon

[28] The LORD God said:

Ezekiel, son of man, the Ammonites have insulted Israel, so condemn them and tell them I am saying:

A sword is drawn,
    ready to slaughter;
it is polished and prepared
    to kill as fast as lightning.

[29] You wicked Ammonites see false visions and believe untrue messages. But your day of punishment is coming soon, and my sword will slaughter you! [30] Your days of punishing others are over, so put your swords away.* You will be punished in the land of your birth. [31] My furious anger will scorch you like fire, and I will hand you over to cruel men who are experts in killing. [32] You will be burnt and will die in your own land. Then you will be forgotten for ever. I, the LORD, have spoken.

*21.21 shaking . . . animal: These were ways the Babylonians found out what their gods wanted them to do.
See also: 21.28–32: Jer 49.1–6; Ezek 25.1–7; Amos 1.3–15; Zeph 2.8–11.

CHAPTER 22

Jerusalem is condemned

[1] Some time later, the LORD said:

[2] Ezekiel, son of man, are you ready to condemn Jerusalem? That city is filled with murderers, so remind the people of their sins [3] and tell them I am saying:

Jerusalem, you have murdered many of your own people and have worshipped idols. You will soon be punished! [4] Those crimes have made you guilty, and the idols have made you unacceptable to me. So your final punishment is near. Other nations will laugh at you and make insulting remarks, [5] and people far and near will make fun of your misery.

[6] Your own leaders use their power to murder. [7] None of you honour your parents, and you cheat foreigners, orphans, and widows. [8] You show no respect for my sacred places and treat the Sabbath just like any other day. [9] Some of your own people tell lies, so that others will be put to death. Some of you eat meat sacrificed to idols at local shrines, and others never stop doing vulgar things. [10] Men have sex with their father's wife or with women who are having their monthly period [11] or with someone else's wife. Some men even sleep with their own daughter-in-law or half-sister. [12] Others of you accept money to murder someone. Your own people charge high interest when making a loan to other Israelites, and they get rich by cheating. Worst of all, you have forgotten me, the LORD God.

[13] I will shake my fist in anger at your violent crimes. [14] When I've finished with you, your courage will disappear, and you will be so weak that you won't be able to lift your hands. I, the LORD, have spoken and will not change my mind. [15] I will scatter you throughout every nation on earth and put a stop to your sinful ways. [16] You* will be humiliated in the eyes of other nations. Then you will know that I, the LORD God, have done these things.

Jerusalem must be purified

[17] The LORD said:

See also: 22.7: a Exod 20.12; Deut 5.16; b Exod 22.21,22; Deut 24.17. 22.8: Lev 19.30; 26.2. 22.10,11: Lev 18.7–20. 22.12: Exod 23.8; Deut 16.19; Exod 22.25; Lev 25.36,37; Deut 23.19.

¹⁸ Ezekiel, son of man, I consider the people of Israel as worthless as the leftover metal in a furnace after silver has been purified. ¹⁹ So I am going to bring them together in Jerusalem. ²⁰⁻²¹ I will be like a metalworker who collects that metal from the furnace and melts it down. I will collect the Israelites and blow on them with my fiery anger. They will melt inside the city of Jerusalem ²² like silver in a furnace. Then they will know that I, the LORD, have punished them in my anger.

Everyone in Jerusalem is guilty

²³ The LORD said:

²⁴ Ezekiel, son of man, tell the people of Israel that their country is full of sin, and that I, the LORD, am furious! ²⁵ Their leaders are like* roaring lions, tearing apart their victims. They put people to death, then steal everything of value. Husbands are killed, and many women are left as widows.

²⁶ The priests of Israel ignore my Law! Not only do they refuse to respect any of my sacred things, but they don't even teach the difference between what is sacred and what is ordinary, or between what is clean and what is unclean. They treat my Sabbath like any other day, and so my own people no longer honour me.

²⁷ Israel's officials are like ferocious wolves, ripping their victims apart. They make a dishonest living by injuring and killing people.

²⁸ And then the prophets in Israel cover up these sins by giving false visions. I have never spoken to them, but they lie and say they have a message from me. ²⁹ The people themselves cheat and rob; they abuse the poor and take advantage of foreigners.

³⁰ I looked for someone to defend the city and to protect it from my anger, as well as to stop me from destroying it. But I found no one. ³¹ So in my fierce anger, I will punish the Israelites for what they have done, and they will know that I am furious. I, the LORD, have spoken.

CHAPTER 23

Two sinful sisters

¹ The LORD said:

² Ezekiel, son of man, listen to this story about two sisters. ³ While they were young

and living in Egypt, they became prostitutes. ⁴ The elder one was named Oholah, which stands for Samaria; the younger one was Oholibah, which stands for Jerusalem.* They became my wives and gave birth to my children.

⁵ Even though Oholah was my wife, she continued to be a prostitute and chased after Assyrian lovers. ⁶ She offered herself to soldiers in purple uniforms, to every handsome, high-ranking officer, and to cavalry troops. ⁷ She had sex with all the important Assyrian officials and even worshipped their disgusting idols. ⁸ Once she started doing these things in Egypt, she never stopped. Men slept with her, and she was always ready for sex.

⁹ So I gave Oholah to the Assyrian lovers she wanted so badly. ¹⁰ They ripped off her clothes, then captured her children and killed her. Women everywhere talked about what had happened to Oholah.

¹¹ Oholibah saw all this, but she was more sinful and wanted sex more than her sister Oholah ever did. ¹² Oholibah also chased after good-looking Assyrian officers, uniformed soldiers, and cavalry troops. ¹³ Just like her sister, she did vulgar things.

¹⁴ But Oholibah behaved worse than her sister. Oholibah saw images of Babylonian men carved into walls and painted red. ¹⁵ They had belts around their waists and large turbans on their heads, and they reminded her of Babylonian cavalry officers. ¹⁶ As soon as she looked at them, she wanted to have sex with them. And so, she sent messengers to bring them to her. ¹⁷ Men from Babylonia came and had sex with her so many times that she got disgusted with them. ¹⁸ She let everyone see her naked body and didn't care if they knew she was a prostitute. That's why I turned my back on her, just as I had done with her elder sister.

¹⁹ Oholibah didn't stop there, but became even more immoral and acted as she had back in Egypt. ²⁰ She eagerly wanted to go to bed with Egyptian men, who were famous for their sexual powers. ²¹ And she longed for the days when she was a young prostitute, when men enjoyed having sex with her.

*23.4 Samaria . . . Jerusalem: After the nation of Israel was divided, the northern kingdom was called "Israel", and the southern kingdom was called "Judah". Samaria was the capital of the northern kingdom, and Jerusalem was the capital of the southern kingdom.

See also: 22.26: Lev 10.10.

The LORD will punish Oholibah

22 The LORD God said:

Oholibah,* though you no longer want to be with your lovers, they will surround you like enemies, when I turn them against you. 23 I will gather all the handsome young officials and the high-ranking cavalry officers from Babylonia and Assyria, as well as from the Chaldean tribes of Pekod, Shoa, and Koa. 24 Their large armies will come from the north* with chariots and wagons carrying weapons. They will wear shields and helmets and will surround you, and I will let them judge and sentence you according to their own laws. 25 I am angry with you, so I will let them be very cruel. They will cut off your nose and ears; they will kill your children and put to death anyone in your family who is still alive. 26 Your clothes and jewellery will be torn off. 27 I will stop your wickedness and the prostitution you started back in Egypt. You will never want to think about those days again.

28 I, the LORD God, am ready to hand you over to those hateful enemies that you find so disgusting. 29 They will cruelly take away everything you have worked for and strip you naked. Then everyone will see you for the prostitute you really are. Your own vulgar sins 30 have led to this. You were the one determined to have sex with men from other nations and to worship their idols. 31 You have turned out no better than your elder sister, and now you must drink from the cup filled with my anger.

32 I, the LORD God, gave your sister a large, deep cup filled with my anger. And when you drink from that cup, you will be mocked and insulted. 33 You will end up drunk and devastated, because that cup is filled with horror and ruin. 34 But you must drink every drop! Then smash the cup to pieces and use them to cut your breasts in sorrow. I, the LORD God, have spoken.

35 You have completely rejected me, and so I promise that you will be punished for the disgusting things you did as a prostitute.

The two sisters are condemned

36 The LORD said:

Ezekiel, son of man, it's time for you to tell Oholah and Oholibah* that they are guilty.

Remind them of their evil ways! 37 They have been unfaithful by worshipping idols, and they have committed murder by sacrificing my own children as offerings to idols. 38-39 They came into my temple that same day, and that made it unfit as a place to worship me. They have even stopped respecting the Sabbath.

40 They sent messengers to attract men from far away. When those men arrived, the two sisters took baths and put on eye shadow and jewellery. 41 They sat on a fine couch, and in front of them was a table for the olive oil and incense that had belonged to me. 42 Their room was always filled with a noisy crowd of drunkards brought in from the desert. These men gave the women bracelets and beautiful crowns, 43 and I noticed that the men were eager to have sex with these women, though they were exhausted from being prostitutes. 44 In fact, the men had sex over and over with Oholah and Oholibah, the two sinful sisters. 45 But good men will some day accuse those two of murder and of being unfaithful, because they are certainly guilty.

46 So I, the LORD God, now say to these sisters:

I will call together an angry mob that will abuse and rob you. 47 They will stone you to death and cut you to pieces; they will kill your children and burn down your houses. 48 I will get rid of sinful prostitution in this country, so that women everywhere will be warned not to act as you have. 49 You will be punished for becoming prostitutes and for worshipping idols, and you will know that I am the LORD God.

CHAPTER 24

A cooking pot

1 Nine years after King Jehoiachin and the rest of us had been led away as prisoners to Babylonia, the LORD spoke to me on the tenth day of the tenth month.* He said:

2 Ezekiel, son of man, write down today's date, because the king of Babylonia has just begun attacking the city of Jerusalem. 3 Then tell my rebellious people:

"Pour water in a cooking pot
and set it over a fire.

---

*23.22 Oholibah: That is, Jerusalem (see verse 4).
*23.36 Oholah and Oholibah: That is, Samaria and Jerusalem (see verse 4).

*24.1 Nine years . . . tenth month: Probably January of 588 BC.

See also: 24.2: 2 King 25.1; Jer 52.4.

4-5 Throw in the legs and shoulders
    of your finest sheep
        and put in the juicy bones.
    Pile wood* underneath the pot,
    and let the meat and bones
        boil until they are done."

6 These words mean that Jerusalem is
doomed! The city is filled with murderers
and is like an old, rusty pot. The meat is
taken out piece by piece, and no one cares
what happens to it.* 7 The people of
Jerusalem murdered innocent people in the
city and didn't even try to cover up the
blood that flowed out on the hard ground.
8 But I have seen that blood, and it cries out
for me to take revenge.

9 I, the LORD God, will punish that city of
violence! I will make a huge pile of
firewood, 10 so bring more wood and light
it. Cook the meat and boil away the broth*
to let the bones scorch. 11 Then set the
empty pot over the hot coals until it is
red-hot. That will clean the pot and burn off
the rust. 12 I've tried everything else. Now
the rust must be burnt away.*

13 Jerusalem is so full of sin and evil that I
can't get it clean, even though I have tried.
It will stay filthy until I let loose my fierce
anger against it. 14 That time will certainly
come! And when it does, I won't show the
people of Jerusalem any pity or change my
mind. They must be punished for the evil
they have done. I, the LORD God, have
spoken.

Ezekiel's wife dies

15 The LORD said, 16 "Ezekiel, son of man,
I will suddenly take the life of the person you
love most. But I don't want you to complain
or cry. 17 Mourn in silence and don't show
that you are grieving. Don't remove your
turban or take off your sandals; don't cover
your face to show your sorrow, or eat the
food that mourners eat."*

18 One morning, I was talking with the
people as usual, and by sunset my wife was
dead. The next day I did what the LORD told
me, 19 when people saw me, they asked,
"Why aren't you mourning for your wife?"

20 I answered:

The LORD God says 21 he is ready to destroy
the temple in which you take such pride
and which makes you feel so safe. Your
children who now live in Jerusalem will be
killed. 22 Then you will do the same things
I have done. You will leave your face
uncovered and refuse to eat the food that
mourners usually eat. 23 You won't take off
your turbans and your sandals.* You won't
cry or mourn, but all day long you will go
around groaning because of your sins.

24 I am a warning sign — everything I
have done, you will also do. And then you
will know the LORD God has made these
things happen.

25 The LORD said, "Ezekiel, I will soon destroy
the temple that makes everyone feel proud
and safe, and I will take away their children
as well. 26 On that same day, someone will
escape from the city and come to tell you
what has happened. 27 Then you will be able
to speak again,* and the two of you will talk.
You will be a warning sign to the people, and
they will know that I am the LORD."

Judgment on foreign nations

CHAPTER 25

Judgment on Ammon

1 The LORD God said:

2 Ezekiel, son of man, condemn the people
of Ammon 3 and tell them:

You celebrated when my temple was
destroyed, when Israel was defeated, and
when my people were taken away as
prisoners. 4 Now I am going to let you be
conquered by tribes from the eastern
desert. They will set up their camps in your
land and eat your fruit and drink your milk.
5 Your capital city of Rabbah will be
nothing but pasture land for camels, and
the rest of the country will be pastures for
sheep. Then you will know that I am the
LORD God.

---

*24.17 Don't remove your turban . . . take off your
sandals . . . cover your face . . . eat the food that
mourners eat: The usual way people mourned was to
remove anything worn on the head, to go barefoot,
to cover their faces, and to eat special food to show
they were grieving.
*24.22,23 You will leave your face uncovered . . .
refuse to eat the food . . . won't take off your
turbans and your sandals: See the note at 24.17.
*24.27 you will be able to speak again: See 3.25-27;
33.21,22.
See also: 25.1-7: Jer 49.1-6; Ezek 21.28-32; Amos 1.13-15;
Zeph 2.8-11.

⁶ You hated Israel so much that you clapped and shouted and celebrated. ⁷ And so I will hand you over to enemies who will rob you. I will completely destroy you. There won't be enough of your people left to be a nation ever again, and you will know that I, the LORD, have done these things.

Judgment on Moab

⁸ The LORD God said, "The people of Moab* thought Judah was no different from any other nation. ⁹ So I will let Moab's fortress towns along its border be attacked, including Beth-Jeshimoth, Baal-Meon, and Kiriathaim. ¹⁰ The same eastern desert tribes that invade Ammon will invade Moab, and just as Ammon will be forgotten for ever, ¹¹ Moab will be punished. Then the people there will know that I am the LORD."

Judgment on Edom

¹² The LORD God then said, "The people of Edom are guilty of taking revenge on Judah. ¹³ So I will punish Edom by killing all its people and livestock. It will be an empty wasteland all the way from Teman to Dedan. ¹⁴ I will send my own people to take revenge on the Edomites by making them feel my fierce anger. And when I punish them, they will know that I am the LORD God."

Judgment on Philistia

¹⁵ The LORD God said, "The cruel Philistines have taken revenge on their enemies over and over and have tried to destroy them. ¹⁶ Now it's my turn to treat the Philistines as my enemies and to kill everyone* living in their towns along the coast. ¹⁷ In my fierce anger, I will take revenge on them. And when I punish them, they will know that I am the LORD."

CHAPTER 26

Judgment on the city of Tyre

¹ Eleven years* after King Jehoiachin and the rest of us had been led away as prisoners to Babylonia, the LORD spoke to me on the first day of the month. He said:

---

*26.1 Eleven years: Probably late in 587 BC.

See also: 25.8-11: Isa 15.1–16.14; 25.10-12; Jer 48.1-47; Amos 2.1–3; Zeph 2.8-11. 25.12-14: Isa 34.5-17; 63.1-6; Jer 49.7-22; Ezek 35.1-15; Amos 1.11,12; Obad 1-14; Mal 1.2-5. 25.15–17: Isa 14.29-31; Jer 47.1-7; Joel 3.4-8; Amos 1.6-8; Zeph 2.4-7; Zech 9.5-7.
26.1–28.19: Isa 23.1-18; Joel 3.4-8; Amos 1.9,10; Zech 9.1-4; Matt 11.21,22; Luke 10.13,14.
798

² Ezekiel, son of man, the people of the city of Tyre* have celebrated Jerusalem's defeat by singing,

"Jerusalem has fallen!
It used to be powerful,
a centre of trade.
Now the city is shattered,
and we will take its place."

³ Because the people of Tyre have sung that song, I have the following warning for them: I am the LORD God, and I am now your enemy! I will send nations to attack you, like waves crashing against the shore. ⁴ They will tear down your city walls and defence towers. I will sweep away the ruins until all that's left of you is a bare rock, ⁵ where fishermen can dry their nets along the coast. I promise that you will be robbed ⁶ and that the people who live in your towns along the coast will be killed. Then you will know that I am the LORD.

⁷ King Nebuchadnezzar of Babylonia is the world's most powerful king, and I will send him to attack you. He will march from the north with a powerful army, including horses and chariots and cavalry troops. ⁸ First, he will attack your towns along the coast and kill the people who live there. Then he will build earth ramps up to the top of your city walls and set up rows of shields around you. ⁹ He will command some of his troops to use large wooden poles to beat down your walls, while others use iron rods to knock down your watchtowers. ¹⁰ He will have so many horses that the dust they stir up will seem like a thick fog. And as his chariots and cavalry approach, even the walls will shake, especially when he proudly enters your ruined city. ¹¹ His troops will ride through your streets, killing people left and right, and your strong columns will crumble to the ground. ¹² The troops will steal your valuable possessions; they will break down your walls, and crush your expensive houses. Then the stones and wood and all the remains will be dumped into the sea. ¹³ You will have no reason to sing or play music on harps, ¹⁴ because I will turn you into a bare rock where fishermen can dry their nets. And you will never rebuild your city. I, the LORD God, make this promise.

---

*26.2 Tyre: One of the two major cities of Phoenicia; Sidon was the other.

See also: 26.13: Rev 18.22.

¹⁵ The people of the nations up and down the coast will shudder when they hear your screams and moans of death. ¹⁶ The kings will step down from their thrones, then take off their royal robes and fine clothes, and sit on the ground, trembling. They will be so shocked at the news of your defeat that they will shake in fear ¹⁷ and sing this funeral song:

"The great city beside the sea
is destroyed!'
Its people once ruled the coast
and terrified everyone there.
¹⁸ But now Tyre is in ruins,
and the people on the coast
stare at it in horror
and tremble in fear."

¹⁹ I, the LORD God, will turn you into a ghost town. The ocean depths will rise over you ²⁰ and carry you down to the world of the dead, where you will join people of ancient times and towns ruined long ago. You will stay there and never again be a city filled with people.' ²¹ You will die a horrible death! People will come looking for your city, but it will never be found. I, the LORD, have spoken.

CHAPTER 27

A funeral song for Tyre

¹ The LORD said:

² Ezekiel, son of man, sing a funeral song for Tyre,* ³ the city that is built along the sea and that trades with nations along the coast. Tell the people of Tyre that the following message is from me:

Tyre, you boast about
your perfect beauty,
⁴ and your control of the sea.'

You are a ship
built to perfection.
⁵ Builders used cypress trees
from Mount Hermon
to make your planks
and a cedar tree from Lebanon
for your tall mast.
⁶ Oak trees from Bashan
were shaped into oars;
pine trees from Cyprus'
were cut for your deck,
which was then decorated

with strips of ivory.
⁷ The builders used fine linen
from Egypt for your sails,
so everyone could see you.
Blue and purple cloth
from Cyprus was used
to shade your deck.
⁸ Men from Sidon and Arvad
did the rowing,
and your own skilled workers
were the captains.
⁹ Experienced men from Byblos
repaired any damages.
Sailors from all over
shopped at the stores
in your port.

¹⁰ Brave soldiers from Persia,
Lydia, and Libya
served in your navy,
protecting you with shields
and helmets,
and making you famous.
¹¹ Your guards came from
Arvad and Cilicia,
and men from Gamad
stood watch in your towers.
With their weapons
hung on your walls,
your beauty was complete.

¹² Merchants from southern Spain' traded silver, iron, tin, and lead for your products. ¹³ The people of Greece, Tubal, and Meshech traded slaves and things made of bronze, ¹⁴ and those from Beth-Togarmah traded work horses, war horses, and mules. ¹⁵ You also did business with people from Rhodes,' and people from nations along the coast gave you ivory and ebony* in exchange for your goods. ¹⁶ Edom' traded emeralds, purple cloth, embroidery, fine linen, coral, and rubies. ¹⁷ Judah and Israel gave you their finest wheat, best figs,' honey, olive oil, and spices in exchange for your merchandise. ¹⁸ The people of Damascus saw what you had to offer and brought you wine from Helbon and wool from Zahar. ¹⁹ Vedan and Javan near Uzal' traded you iron and spices. ²⁰ The people of Dedan supplied you with saddle blankets, ²¹ while people from Arabia and the rulers of Kedar traded lambs, sheep, and goats. ²² Merchants from Sheba and Raamah gave you excellent spices, precious stones, and gold in exchange for your products. ²³ You

---

*27.2 Tyre: See the note at 26.2.
See also: 26.16–18: Rev 18.9,10. 26.21: Rev 18.21.

*27.15 ebony: A valuable black wood.

also did business with merchants from the cities of Haran, Canneh, Eden, Sheba, Asshur, and Chilmad, ²⁴ and they gave you expensive clothing, purple and embroidered cloth, brightly-coloured rugs, and strong rope. ²⁵ Large, seagoing ships* carried your goods wherever they needed to go.

> You were like a ship
> loaded with heavy cargo
> ²⁶ and sailing across the sea,
> but you were wrecked
> by strong eastern winds.
> ²⁷ Everything on board was lost —
> your valuable cargo,
> your sailors and carpenters,
> merchants and soldiers.
> ²⁸ The shouts of your drowning crew
> were heard on the shore.

> ²⁹ Every ship is deserted;
> rowers and sailors and captains
> all stand on shore,
> ³⁰ mourning for you.
> They show their sorrow
> by putting dust on their heads
> and rolling in ashes;
> ³¹ they shave their heads
> and dress in sackcloth*
> as they cry in despair.
> ³² In their grief they sing
> a funeral song for you:
> "Tyre, you were greater
> than all other cities.
> But now you lie in silence
> at the bottom of the sea.'

> ³³ "Nations that received
> your merchandise
> were always pleased;
> kings everywhere got rich
> from your costly goods.
> ³⁴ But now you are wrecked
> in the deep sea,
> with your cargo and crew
> scattered everywhere.
> ³⁵ People living along the coast
> are shocked at the news.
> Their rulers are horrified,
> and terror is written
> across their faces.
> ³⁶ The merchants of the world

can't believe what happened.
Your death was gruesome,
and you are gone for ever."

CHAPTER 28

Judgment on the king of Tyre

¹ The LORD God said:

²Ezekiel, son of man, tell the king of Tyre* that I am saying:

You are so arrogant that you think you're a god and that the city of Tyre is your throne. You may claim to be a god, though you're nothing but a mere human. ³ You think you're wiser than Daniel*and know everything.'

⁴ Your wisdom has certainly made you rich, because you have storehouses filled with gold and silver. ⁵ You're a clever businessman and are extremely wealthy, but your wealth has led to arrogance!

⁶ You compared yourself to a god, so now I, the LORD God, ⁷ will make you the victim of cruel enemies. They will destroy all the possessions you've worked so hard to get. ⁸ Your enemies will brutally kill you, and the sea will be your only grave. ⁹ When you face your enemies, will you still claim to be a god? They will attack, and you will suffer like any other human. ¹⁰ Foreigners will kill you, and you will die the death of those who don't worship me. I, the LORD, have spoken.

A funeral song for the king of Tyre

¹¹ The LORD said:

¹² Ezekiel, son of man, sing a funeral song for the king of Tyre* and tell him I am saying:

At one time, you were perfect,' intelligent, and good-looking. ¹³ You lived in the garden of Eden and wore jewellery made of brightly-coloured gems and precious stones. They were all set in gold* and were ready for you on the day you were born.' ¹⁴ I appointed a winged creature to guard your home* on my holy mountain, where you walked among gems that dazzled like fire.

¹⁵ You were truly good from the time of your birth, but later you started doing wicked things. ¹⁶ You traded with other nations and became more and more cruel

---

*27.25 **Large, seagoing ships:** The Hebrew text has "Ships of Tarshish," which may have been a Phoenician city in Spain. "Ships of Tarshish" probably means large, seagoing ships.

*27.31 **sackcloth:** See the note at 7.18.

See also: 27.25–36: Rev 18.11–19.

*28.2,12 **Tyre:** See the note at 26.2.

*28.3 **Daniel:** See the note at 14.14.

and evil. So I forced you to leave my mountain, and the creature that had been your protector now chased you away from the gems.

¹⁷ It was your good looks that made you arrogant, and you were so famous that you started acting like a fool. That's why I threw you to the ground and let other kings sneer at you. ¹⁸ You have cheated so many merchants that your places of worship are corrupt. So I set your city on fire and burnt it down. Now everyone sees only ashes where your city once stood, ¹⁹ and the people of other nations are shocked. Your punishment was horrible, and you are gone for ever.

Judgment on Sidon and peace for Israel

²⁰ The LORD said:

²¹ Ezekiel, son of man, condemn the city of Sidon*²² and tell its people:

I, the LORD God, am your enemy! People will praise me when I punish you, and they will see that I am holy. ²³ I will send deadly diseases to wipe you out, and I will send enemies to invade and surround you. Your people will be killed, and you will know that I am the LORD.

²⁴ When that happens, the people of Israel will no longer have cruel neighbours that abuse them and make them feel as though they are in a field of thorns and briers. And the Israelites will know that I, the LORD God, have done these things.

A blessing for Israel

²⁵ The LORD God said:

Some day I will gather the people of Israel from the nations where they are now scattered, and every nation will see that I am holy. The Israelites will once again live in the land I gave to my servant Jacob. ²⁶ They will be safe and will build houses and plant vineyards. They will no longer be in danger, because I will punish their hateful neighbours. Israel will know that I am the LORD their God.

CHAPTER 29

Judgment on the king of Egypt

¹ Ten years after King Jehoiachin and the rest of us had been led away as prisoners to Babylonia, the LORD spoke to me on the twelfth day of the tenth month.* He said:

² Ezekiel, son of man, condemn the king of Egypt. Tell him and his people ³ that I am saying:

King of Egypt, you were like a giant crocodile lying in a river. You acted as though you owned the Nile and made it for yourself. But now I, the LORD God, am your enemy! ⁴ I will put a hook in your jaw and pull you out of the water, and all the fish in your river will stick to your scaly body.* ⁵ I'll throw you and these fish into the desert, and your body will fall on the hard ground. You will be left unburied,* and wild animals and birds will eat your flesh. ⁶ Then everyone in Egypt will know that I am the LORD.

You and your nation refused to help the people of Israel and were nothing more than a broken stick. ⁷ When they reached out to you for support, you broke in half, cutting their arms and making them fall.*

⁸ So I, the LORD God, will send troops to attack you, king of Egypt. They will kill your people and livestock, ⁹ until your land is a barren desert. Then you will know that I have done these things.

You claimed that you made the River Nile and control it. ¹⁰ Now I am turning against you and your river. Your nation will be nothing but an empty wasteland all the way from the town of Migdol in the north to Aswan in the south, and as far as the border of Ethiopia.* ¹¹ No human or animal will even dare travel through Egypt, because no sign of life will be found there for forty years.

---

*28.21 Sidon: See the note at 26.2.
See also: 28.20–26: Joel 3.4–8; Zech 9.1,2; Matt 11.21,22;
Luke 10.13,14.

*29.1 Ten years . . . tenth month: Probably January
of 587 BC.
*29.4 all the fish in your river will stick to your scaly
body: All the king's officials will be removed from
power and destroyed along with the king himself.
*29.5 You will be left unburied: A proper burial in a
royal tomb was extremely important to Egyptian kings,
because they often thought of themselves as gods.
*29.10 Ethiopia: The Hebrew text has "Cush," which
was a region south of Egypt that included parts of the
present countries of Ethiopia and Sudan.
See also: 29.1–32.32: Isa 19.1–25; Jer 46.2–26.
29.6: Isa 36.6.

12 It will be the most barren place on earth. Every city in Egypt will lie in ruins during those forty years, and I will scatter your people throughout the nations of the world.

13 Then after those forty years have passed, I will bring your people back from the places where I scattered them. 14 They will once again live in their homeland in southern Egypt. But they will be a weak kingdom 15 and won't ever be strong enough to rule nations, as they did in the past. 16 My own people Israel will never again depend on your nation. In fact, when the Israelites remember what happened to you Egyptians, they will realize how wrong they were to turn to you for help. Then the Israelites will know that I, the LORD God, did these things.

King Nebuchadnezzar of Babylonia will conquer Egypt

17 Twenty-seven years after King Jehoiachin and the rest of us had been led away as prisoners to Babylonia, the LORD spoke to me on the first day of the first month.* He said:

18 King Nebuchadnezzar of Babylonia has attacked the city of Tyre. He forced his soldiers to carry so many heavy loads that their heads were rubbed bald, and their shoulders were red and sore. Nebuchadnezzar and his army still could not capture the city. 19 So now I will hand over the nation of Egypt to him. He will take Egypt's valuable treasures and give them to his own troops. 20 Egypt will be his reward, because he and his army have been following my orders. I, the LORD God, have spoken.

21 Ezekiel, when Egypt is defeated, I will make the people of Israel strong, and I will give you the power to speak to them. Then they will know that I, the LORD, have done these things.

CHAPTER 30

Egypt will be a barren desert

1 The LORD said:

2 Ezekiel, son of man, tell the people of Egypt that I am saying:

Cry out in despair,
  3 because you will soon
    be punished!

That will be a time
of darkness and doom
  for all nations.
4 Your own nation of Egypt
  will be attacked,
    and Ethiopia* will suffer.
  You will be killed in battle,
    and your land will be robbed
    and left in ruins.

5 Soldiers hired from Ethiopia, Libya, Lydia, Arabia, Kub, as well as from Israel,* will die in that battle. 6 All your allies will be killed, and your proud strength will crumble. People will die from Migdol in the north to Aswan in the south. I, the LORD, have spoken.

7 Your nation of Egypt will be the most deserted place on earth, and its cities will lie in complete ruin. 8 I will set fire to your land, and anyone who defended your nation will die. Then you will know that I am the LORD.

9 On the same day I destroy Egypt, I will send messengers to the Ethiopians to announce their coming destruction. They think they are safe, but they will be terrified.

10 Your Egyptian army is very strong, but I will send King Nebuchadnezzar of Babylonia to completely defeat that army. 11 He and his cruel troops will invade and destroy your land and leave your dead bodies piled everywhere. 12 I will dry up the River Nile, then sell the land to evil buyers. I will send foreigners to turn your entire nation into a barren desert. I, the LORD, have spoken.

Egypt's proud cities will lie in ruins

The LORD said to the people of Egypt:

13 All the idols and images you Egyptians worship in the city of Memphis* will be smashed. No one will be left to rule your nation, and terror will fill the land. 14 The city of Pathros will be left in ruins, and Zoan will be burnt to the ground. Thebes,* your capital city, will also be destroyed! 15 The fortress city of Pelusium will feel my fierce anger, and all the troops stationed at Thebes will be slaughtered.

16 I will set fire to your entire nation of Egypt! The city of Pelusium will be in anguish. Thebes will fall, and the people of Memphis will live in constant fear.* 17 The young soldiers in the cities of Heliopolis and Bubastis* will die in battle, and the rest of

---

*29.17 Twenty-seven . . . first month: Probably March of 571 BC.

*30.4 Ethiopia: See the note at 29.10.

the people will be taken prisoner. [18] You were so proud of your nation's power, but when I crush that power and kill that pride, darkness will fall over the city of Tahpanhes. A dark, gloomy cloud will cover the land as you are being led away into captivity. [19] When I've finished punishing Egypt, you will know that I am the LORD.

Egypt's king is powerless

[20] Eleven years after King Jehoiachin and the rest of us had been led away as prisoners to Babylonia, the LORD spoke to me on the seventh day of the first month.* He said:

[21] Ezekiel, son of man, I, the LORD, have defeated the king of Egypt! I broke his arm, and no one has wrapped it or put it in a sling, so that it could heal and get strong enough to hold a sword. [22] So tell him that I am now his worst enemy. I will break both his arms — the good one and the broken one! His sword will drop from his hand for ever, [23] and I will scatter the Egyptians all over the world.

[24-25] I will strengthen the power of Babylonia's king and give him my sword to use against Egypt. I will also make the wounded king of Egypt powerless, and he will moan in pain and die in front of the Babylonian king. Then everyone on earth will know that I am the LORD. [26] I will force the Egyptians to live as prisoners in foreign nations, and they will know that I, the LORD, have punished them.

CHAPTER 31

Egypt's king will be chopped down like a cedar tree

[1] Eleven years after King Jehoiachin and the rest of us had been led away as prisoners to Babylonia, the LORD spoke to me on the first day of the third month.* He said:

[2] Ezekiel, son of man, tell the king of Egypt and his people that I am saying:

You are more powerful
  than anyone on earth.
  Now listen to this.
[3] There was once a cedar tree
  in Lebanon

with large, strong branches
  reaching to the sky.•
[4] This tree had plenty of water
  to help it grow tall,
and nearby streams watered
  the other trees
  in the forest.
[5] But this tree towered over
  those other trees,
and its branches
  grew long and thick.
[6] Birds built nests
  in its branches,
and animals were born
  beneath it.
People from all nations
  lived in the shade
  of this strong tree.

[7] It had beautiful,
  long branches,
and its roots found water
  deep in the soil.
[8] None of the cedar trees
  in my garden of Eden
were as beautiful
  as this tree;
no tree of any kind
  had such long branches.
[9] I, the LORD, gave this tree
  its beauty,
and I helped the branches
  grow strong.
All other trees in Eden
  wanted to be just like it.

[10] King of Egypt, now listen to what I, the LORD God, am saying about that tree:

The tree grew so tall that it reached the sky• and became very proud and arrogant. [11] So I, the LORD God, will reject the tree and hand it over to a foreign ruler, who will punish it for its wickedness. [12] Cruel foreigners will chop it down and leave it wherever it falls. Branches and broken limbs will be scattered over the mountains and in the valleys. The people living in the shade of those branches will go somewhere else. [13] Birds will then nest on the stump of the fallen tree, and wild animals will trample its branches.

[14] Never again will any tree dare to grow as tall as this tree, no matter how much water it has. Every tree must die, just as humans die and go down to the world of the dead.

[15] On the day this tree dies and goes to the world below, I, the LORD God, will

*30.20 **Eleven years . . . first month:** Probably March of 587 BC.
*31.1 **Eleven years . . . third month:** Probably May of 587 BC.

See also: 31.8: Gen 2.9.

command rivers and streams to mourn its death. Every underground spring of water and every river will stop flowing.* The mountains in Lebanon will be covered with darkness as a sign of their sorrow, and all the trees in the forest will wither. ¹⁶ This tree will crash to the ground, and I will send it to the world below. Then the nations of the earth will tremble.

The trees from Eden and the choice trees from Lebanon are now in the world of the dead, and they will be comforted when this tree falls. ¹⁷ Those people who found protection in its shade will also be sent to the world below, where they will join the dead.*

¹⁸ King of Egypt, all these things will happen to you and your people! You were like this tree at one time — taller and stronger than anyone on earth. But now you will be chopped down, just as every tree in the garden of Eden must die. You will be sent down to the world of the dead, where you will join the godless and the other victims of violent death. I, the LORD God, have spoken.

CHAPTER 32

A funeral song for the king of Egypt

¹ Twelve years after King Jehoiachin and the rest of us had been led away as prisoners to Babylonia, the LORD spoke to me on the first day of the twelfth month.* He said:

² Ezekiel, son of man, condemn the king of Egypt and tell him I am saying:

You act like a lion
    roaming the earth;
but you are nothing more than
    a crocodile in a river,
churning up muddy water
    with your feet.

³ King of Egypt, listen to me. I, the LORD God, will catch you in my net and let a crowd of foreigners drag you to shore. ⁴ I will throw you into an open field, where birds and animals will come to feed on your body. ⁵ I will spread your rotting flesh* over the mountains and in the valleys, ⁶ and your blood will flow throughout the land and fill up the streams. ⁷ I will cover the whole sky and every star with thick clouds, so that the sun and moon will stop shining. ⁸ The

heavens will become black, leaving your country in total darkness. I, the LORD, have spoken.

⁹ Foreign nations you have never heard of will be shocked when I tell them how I destroyed you.* ¹⁰ They will be horrified, and when I flash my sword in victory on the day of your death, their kings will tremble in the fear of what could happen to them.

¹¹ The king of Babylonia is coming to attack you, king of Egypt! ¹² Your soldiers will be killed by the cruellest army in the world, and everything you take pride in will be crushed. ¹³ I will slaughter your cattle that graze by the river,* and no people or livestock will be left to muddy its water. ¹⁴ The water will be clear, and streams will be calm. I, the LORD God, have spoken.

¹⁵ Egypt will become a barren wasteland, and no living thing will ever survive there. Then you and your people will know that I am the LORD.

¹⁶ This is your warning, and it will be used as a funeral song by foreign women to mourn the death of your people. I, the LORD God, have spoken.

A sad ending for Egypt

¹⁷ On the fifteenth day of that same month,* the LORD said:

¹⁸ Ezekiel, son of man, mourn for the Egyptians and condemn them to the world of the dead, where they will be buried beside the people of other powerful nations.* ¹⁹ Say to them:

You may be more beautiful
    than the people
    of other nations,
but you will also die
    and join the godless
    in the world below.

²⁰ You cannot escape! The enemy's sword is ready to slaughter every one of you.* ²¹ Brave military leaders killed in battle will gladly welcome you and your allies into the world of the dead. ²²⁻²³ The graves of soldiers from Assyria are there. They once terrified people, but they were killed in battle and now lie deep in the world of the dead.*

---

*32.1 Twelve years . . . twelfth month: Probably February of 585 BC.
See also: 32.7: Isa 13.10; Matt 24.29; Mark 13.24,25; Luke 21.25; Rev 6.12,13; 8.12.

*32.13 the river: This possibly refers to the River Nile.
*32.17 that same month: See verse 1.
*32.22,23 deep in the world of the dead: The place of greatest dishonour.

24-25 The graves of soldiers from Elam are there. The very sight of those godless soldiers once terrified their enemies and made them panic. But now they are disgraced and ashamed as they lie in the world of the dead, beside others who were killed in battle.

26 The graves of soldiers from Meshech and Tubal are there. These godless soldiers who terrified people were all killed in battle. 27 They were not given a proper burial like the heroes of long ago,* who were buried with their swords under their heads and with their shields* over their bodies. These were the heroes who made their enemies panic.

28 You Egyptians will be cruelly defeated, and you will be buried beside these other godless soldiers who died in battle.

29 The graves of kings and leaders from Edom are there. They were powerful at one time. Now they are buried in the world of the dead with other godless soldiers killed in battle.

30 The graves of the rulers of the north* are there, as well as those of the Sidonians. Their powerful armies once terrified enemies. Now they lie buried in the world of the dead, where they are disgraced like other soldiers killed in battle.

31 The LORD God says:

When your king of Egypt sees all these graves, he and his soldiers will be glad they are not the only ones suffering. 32 I sent him to terrify people all over the earth. But he and his army will be killed and buried beside other godless soldiers in the world of the dead. I, the LORD God, have spoken.

Ezekiel must warn the people to turn from their sinful ways

CHAPTER 33

The LORD appoints Ezekiel to stand watch
This is also told in Ezekiel 3.16–21

1 The LORD said:

2 Ezekiel, son of man, warn your people by saying:

Some day, I, the LORD, may send an enemy to invade a country. And suppose its people

choose someone to stand watch 3 and to sound a warning signal when the enemy is seen coming. 4-5 If any of these people hear the signal and ignore it, they will be killed in battle. But it will be their own fault, because they could have escaped if they had paid attention.

6 But suppose the person watching fails to sound the warning signal. The enemy will attack and kill some of the sinful people in that country, and I, the LORD, will hold that person responsible for their death.

7 Ezekiel, I have appointed you to stand watch for the people of Israel. So listen to what I say, then warn them for me. 8 When I tell wicked people they will die because of their sins, you must warn them to turn from their sinful ways. But if you refuse to warn them, you are responsible for their death. 9 If you do warn them, and they keep sinning, they will die because of their sins, and you will be innocent.

The LORD is always fair
This is also told in Ezekiel 18.21–30

10 The LORD said:

Ezekiel, son of man, the people of Israel are complaining that the punishment for their sins is more than they can stand. They have lost all hope for survival, and they blame me. 11 Tell them that as surely as I am the living LORD God, I don't like to see wicked people die. I enjoy seeing them turn from their sins and live. So if the Israelites want to live, they must stop sinning and turn back to me.

12 Tell them that when good people start sinning, all the good they did in the past cannot save them from being punished. And remind them that when wicked people stop sinning, their past sins will be completely forgiven, and they won't be punished.

13 Suppose I promise good people that they will live, then later they start sinning and believe they will be saved by the good they did in the past. These people will certainly be put to death because of their sins. Their good deeds will be forgotten.

14 Suppose I warn wicked people that they will die because of their sins, and they stop sinning and start doing right. 15 For example, they need to return anything they have taken as security for a loan and anything they have stolen. Then if they stop doing evil and start obeying my Law, they will live.

---

*32.30 the rulers of the north: Probably the Phoenicians.

16 Their past sins will be forgiven, and they will live because they have done right.

17 Ezekiel, your people accuse me of being unfair. But they are the ones who are unfair. 18 If good people start doing evil, they will be put to death, because they have sinned. 19 And if wicked people stop sinning and start doing right, they will save themselves from punishment. 20 But the Israelites still think I am unfair. So warn them that they will be punished for what they have done.

The news of Jerusalem's fall

21 Twelve years after King Jehoiachin and the rest of us had been led away as prisoners to Babylonia, a refugee who had escaped from Jerusalem came to me on the fifth day of the tenth month.* He told me that the city had fallen.

22 The evening before this man arrived at my house, the LORD had taken control of me. So when the man came to me the next morning, I could once again speak.*

What will happen to those left in Israel?

23 Then the LORD said:

24 Ezekiel, son of man, the people living in the ruined cities of Israel are saying, "Abraham was just one man, and the LORD gave him this whole land of Israel. There are many of us, and so this land must be ours."

25 So, Ezekiel, tell them I am saying:

How can you think the land is still yours? You eat meat with blood in it and worship idols. You commit murder 26 and spread violence throughout the land. Everything you do is wicked; you are even unfaithful in marriage. And you claim the land is yours!

27 As surely as I am the living LORD God, you people in the ruined cities will be killed in battle. Those of you living in the countryside will be eaten by wild animals, and those hiding in caves and on rocky cliffs will die from deadly diseases. 28 I will make the whole country an empty wasteland and crush the power in which you take such pride. Even the mountains will be bare, and no one will try to cross them. 29 I will punish you because of your

sins, and I will turn your nation into a barren desert. Then you will know that I am the LORD.

The people listen, but don't change

The LORD said:

30 Ezekiel, son of man, the people with you in Babylonia talk about you when they meet by the city walls or in the doorways of their houses. They say, "Let's ask Ezekiel what the LORD has said today." 31 So they all come and listen to you, but they refuse to do what you tell them. They claim to be faithful, but they are for ever trying to cheat others out of their money. 32 They treat you as though you were merely singing love songs or playing music. They listen, but don't do anything you say.

33 Soon they will be punished, just as you warned, and they will know that a prophet has been among them.

The Lord promises to bring the people home and to restore Judah

CHAPTER 34

Israel's leaders are worthless shepherds

1 The LORD God said:

2 Ezekiel, son of man, Israel's leaders are like shepherds taking care of my sheep, the people of Israel. But I want you to condemn these leaders and tell them:

I, the LORD God, say you shepherds of Israel are doomed! You take care of yourselves while ignoring my sheep. 3 You drink their milk and use their wool to make your clothes. Then you butcher the best ones for food. But you don't take care of the flock! 4 You have never protected the weak ones or healed the sick ones or bandaged those that get hurt. You let them wander off and never look for those that get lost. You are cruel and mean to my sheep. 5 They strayed in every direction, and because there was no shepherd to watch them, they were attacked and eaten by wild animals. 6 So my sheep were scattered across the earth. They roamed on hills and mountains, without anyone even bothering to look for them.

---

*33.21 Twelve years . . . tenth month: Probably December of 586 BC.

*33.22 I could once again speak: See 3.27.

See also: 33.21: 2 King 25.3–10; Jer 39.2–8; 52.4–14.

See also: 34.5: Num 27.17; 1 King 22.17; Matt 9.36; Mark 6.34.

⁷⁻⁸ Now listen to what I, the living LORD God, am saying to you shepherds. My sheep have been attacked and eaten by wild animals, because you refused to watch them. You never went looking for the lost ones, and you fed yourselves without feeding my sheep. ⁹⁻¹⁰ So I, the LORD, will punish you! I will rescue my sheep from you and never let you be their shepherd again or butcher them for food. I, the LORD, have spoken.

The LORD is the good shepherd

¹¹ The LORD God then said:

I will look for my sheep and take care of them myself, ¹² just as a shepherd looks for lost sheep. My sheep have been lost since that dark and miserable day when they were scattered throughout the nations.* But I will rescue them ¹³ and bring them back from the foreign nations where they now live. I will be their shepherd and will let them graze on Israel's mountains and in the valleys and fertile fields. ¹⁴ They will be safe as they feed on grassy meadows and green hills. ¹⁵ I promise to take care of them and keep them safe, ¹⁶ to look for those that are lost and bring back the ones that wander off, to bandage those that are hurt and protect the ones that are weak. I will also slaughter⁹ those that are fat and strong, because I always do right.

Judgment on the strong sheep

¹⁷ The LORD God said to his sheep, the people of Israel:

I will carefully watch each one of you to decide which ones are the strong sheep and which ones are weak. ¹⁸ Some of you eat the greenest grass, then trample down what's left when you finish. Others drink clean water, then step in the water to make the rest of it muddy. ¹⁹ That means my other sheep have nothing fit to eat or drink.

²⁰ So I, the LORD God, will separate you strong sheep from the weak. ²¹ You strong ones have used your powerful horns to chase off those that are weak, ²² but I will rescue them and no longer let them be ill-treated. I will separate the good from the bad.

²³ After that, I will give you a shepherd from the family of my servant King David. All of you, both strong and weak, will have the same shepherd, and he will take good care of you. ²⁴ He will be your leader, and I will be your God. I, the LORD, have spoken.

A bright future for the LORD's sheep

The LORD God said:

²⁵ The people of Israel are my sheep, and I solemnly promise that they will live in peace. I will chase away every wild animal from the desert and the forest, so my sheep will not be afraid. ²⁶ They will live around my holy mountain,* and I will bless them by sending more than enough rain ²⁷ to make their trees produce fruit and their crops grow. I will set them free from slavery and let them live safely in their own land. Then they will know that I am the LORD. ²⁸ Foreign nations will never again rob them, and wild animals will no longer kill and eat them. They will have nothing to fear. ²⁹ I will make their fields produce large amounts of crops, so they will never again go hungry or be laughed at by foreigners. ³⁰ Then everyone will know that I protect my people Israel. I, the LORD, make this promise. ³¹ They are my sheep; I am their God, and I take care of them.

CHAPTER 35

Edom will be a wasteland

¹ The LORD said:

² Ezekiel, son of man, condemn the people of Edom⁹ ³ and say to them:

I, the LORD God,
am now your enemy!
And I will turn your nation
into an empty wasteland,
⁴ leaving your towns in ruins.
Your land will be a desert,
and then you will know
that I am the LORD.

⁵ People of Edom, not only have you been Israel's longtime enemy, you simply watched when disaster wiped out its people as punishment for their sins. ⁶ And so, as

---

*34.12 dark and miserable day . . . nations: That is, the day the Babylonians defeated Jerusalem and led its people away as prisoners.

*34.26 my holy mountain: That is, Mount Zion in Jerusalem.

See also: 34.23: Rev 7.17. 34.24: Ezek 37.24. 35.1–15: Isa 34.5–17; 63.1–6; Jer 49.7–22; Ezek 25.12–14; Amos 1.11,12; Obad 1–14; Mal 1.2–5.

surely as I am the living LORD God, you are guilty of murder and must be put to death. [7] I will destroy your nation and kill anyone who travels through it. [8] Dead bodies will cover your mountains and fill up your valleys, [9] and your land will lie in ruins for ever. No one will live in your towns ever again. You will know that I am the LORD.

[10] You thought the nations of Judah and Israel belonged to you, and that you could take over their territory. But I am their God, [11] and as surely as I live, I will punish you for treating my people with anger and hatred. Then they will know that I, the LORD, am punishing you! [12] And you will finally realize that I heard you laugh at their destruction and say their land was yours to take. [13] You even insulted me, but I heard it all.

[14] Everyone on earth will celebrate when I destroy you, [15] just as you celebrated when Israel was destroyed. Your nation of Edom will be nothing but a wasteland. Then everyone will know that I am the LORD.

CHAPTER 36

A message for Israel's mountains

[1] The LORD said:

Ezekiel, son of man, tell the mountains of Israel [2] that I, the LORD God, am saying:

Your enemies sneered and said that you mountains belonged to them. [3] They ruined and crushed you from every side, and foreign nations captured and made fun of you. [4] So all you mountains and hills, streams and valleys, listen to what I will do. Your towns may now lie in ruins, and nations may laugh and insult you. [5] But in my fierce anger, I will turn against those nations, and especially the Edomites, because they laughed at you the loudest and took over your pasture lands. [6] You have suffered long enough, and, I, the LORD God, am very angry! Nations have insulted you, [7] so I will now insult and disgrace them. That is my solemn promise.

[8] Trees will grow on you mountains of Israel and produce fruit for my people, because they will soon come home. [9] I will take care of you by ploughing your soil and planting crops on your fertile slopes. [10] The people of Israel will return and rebuild your ruined towns and live in them. [11] Children will be born, and animals will give birth to their young. You will no longer be deserted as you are now, but you will be covered

with people and treated better than ever. Then you will know that I am the LORD.

[12] I will bring my people Israel home, and they will live on you mountains, because you belong to them, and your fertile slopes will never again let them starve. [13] It's true that you have been accused of not producing enough food and of letting your people starve. [14-15] But I, the LORD, promise that you won't kill any more people and sneer at you ever again. From now on, you will always produce plenty of food for your people. I, the LORD God, have spoken.

The LORD will be honoured

[16] The LORD said:

[17] Ezekiel, son of man, when the people of Israel were living in their own country, they made the land unclean by the way they behaved, just as a woman's monthly period makes her unclean. [18] They committed murders and worshipped idols, which made the land even worse. So in my anger, I punished my people [19] and scattered them throughout the nations, just as they deserved. [20] Wherever they went, my name was disgraced, because foreigners insulted my people by saying I had forced them out of their own land.

[21] I care what those foreigners think of me, [22] so tell the Israelites that I am saying:

You have disgraced my holy name among the nations where you now live. But you don't deserve what I'm going to do for you. I will lead you home to bring honour to my name [23] and to show foreign nations that I am holy. Then they will know that I am the LORD God. I have spoken.

[24] I will gather you from the foreign nations and bring you home. [25] I will sprinkle you with clean water, and you will be clean and acceptable to me. I will wash away everything that makes you unclean, and I will remove your disgusting idols. [26] I will take away your stubborn heart and give you a new heart and a desire to be faithful. You will have only pure thoughts, [27] because I will put my Spirit in you and make you eager to obey my laws and teachings. [28] You will once again live in the land I gave your ancestors; you will be my people, and I will be your God. [29] I will protect you from anything that makes you unclean. Your fields will

---

See also: **36.26–28:** Ezek 11.19,20.

overflow with grain, and no one will starve. [30] Your trees will be filled with fruit, and crops will grow in your fields, so that you will never again feel ashamed for not having enough food. [31] You will remember your evil ways and hate yourselves for what you've done. [32] People of Israel, I'm not doing these things for your sake. You sinned against me, and you must suffer shame and disgrace for what you have done. I, the LORD God, have spoken.

[33] After I have made you clean, I will let you rebuild your ruined towns and let you live in them. [34] Your land will be ploughed again, and everywhere I looked I saw bones that it was once barren. [35] Instead, they will say that it looks as beautiful as the garden of Eden. They won't see towns lying in ruins, but they will see your strong cities filled with people. [36] Then the nearby nations that survive will know that I am the one who rebuilt the ruined places and replanted the barren fields. I, the LORD, make this promise.

[37] I will once again answer your prayers, and I will let your nation grow until you are like a large flock of sheep. [38] The towns that now lie in ruins will be filled with people, just as Jerusalem was once filled with sheep to be offered as sacrifices during a festival. Then you will know that I am the LORD.

CHAPTER 37

Dry bones live again

[1] Some time later, I felt the LORD's power take control of me, and his Spirit carried me to a valley full of bones. [2] The LORD showed me all around, and everywhere I looked I saw bones that were dried out. [3] He said, "Ezekiel, son of man, can these bones come back to life?"

I replied, "LORD God, only you can answer that."

[4] He then told me to say:

Dry bones, listen to what the LORD is saying to you, [5] "I, the LORD God, will put breath in you, and once again you will live. [6] I will wrap you with muscles and skin and breathe life into you. Then you will know that I am the LORD."

[7] I did what the LORD said, but before I finished speaking, I heard a rattling noise. The bones were coming together! [8] I saw muscles and skin cover the bones, but they had no life in them.

[9] The LORD said:

Ezekiel, now say to the wind,* "The LORD God commands you to blow from every

direction and to breathe life into these dead bodies, so they can live again."

[10] As soon as I said this, the wind blew among the bodies, and they came back to life! They all stood up, and there were enough to make a large army.

[11] The LORD said:

Ezekiel, the people of Israel are like dead bones. They complain that they are dried up and that they have no hope for the future. [12] So tell them, "I, the LORD God, promise to open your graves and set you free. I will bring you back to Israel, [13] and when that happens, you will realize that I am the LORD. [14] My Spirit will give you breath, and you will live again. I will bring you home, and you will know that I have kept my promise. I, the LORD, have spoken."

Judah and Israel together again

[15] The LORD said:

[16] Ezekiel, son of man, get a stick and write on it, "The kingdom of Judah". Then get another stick and write on it, "The kingdom of Israel". [17] Hold these two sticks end to end, so they look like one stick. [18] And when your people ask you what this means, [19] tell them that I, the LORD, will join together the stick of Israel and the stick of Judah. I will hold them in my hand, and they will become one.

[20] Hold these two sticks where they can be seen by everyone [21] and then say:

I, the LORD God, will gather the people of Israel and bring them home from the foreign nations where they now live. [22] I will make them into one nation and let them once again live in the land of Israel. Only one king will rule them, and they will never again be divided into two nations. [23] They will no longer worship idols and do things that make them unacceptable to me. I will wash away their sin and make them clean, and I will protect them from everything that makes them unclean. They will be my people, and I will be their God.

[24-25] Their king will always come from the family of my servant King David and will care for them like a shepherd. The people of Israel will faithfully obey my laws. They and their descendants will live in the land I gave my servant Jacob, just as their ancestors did. [26] I solemnly promise to bless the people of

See also: **37.10:** Rev 11.11. **37.24:** Ezek 34.24.

Israel with unending peace. I will protect them and let them become a powerful nation. My temple will stand in Israel for all time, [27] and I will live among my people and be their God. [28] Every nation on earth will know that my temple is in Israel and that I have chosen the Israelites to be my people.

Gog will be defeated and Israel will be restored

CHAPTER 38

Gog invades Israel

[1] The LORD said:

[2] Ezekiel, son of man, condemn Gog, that wicked ruler of the kingdoms of Meshech and Tubal in the land of Magog. Tell him:

[3] I, the LORD God, am your enemy, [4] and I will make you powerless! I will put a hook in your jaw and drag away both you and your large army. You command cavalry troops that wear heavy armour and carry shields and swords. [5] Your army includes soldiers from Persia, Ethiopia,* and Libya, [6] as well as from Gomer and Beth-Togarmah in the north. Your army is enormous!

[7] So keep your troops prepared to fight, [8] because in a few years, I will command you to invade Israel, a country that was ruined by war. It was deserted for a long time, but its people have returned from the foreign nations where they once lived. The Israelites now live in peace in the mountains of their own land. [9] But you and your army will attack them like a fierce thunderstorm and surround them like a cloud.

[10] When that day comes, I know that you will have an evil plan [11] to take advantage of Israel, that weak and peaceful country where people live safely inside towns that have no walls or gates or locks. [12] You will rob the people in towns that were once a pile of rubble. These people lived as prisoners in foreign nations, but they have returned to Israel, the most important place in the world, and they own livestock and property. [13] The people of Sheba and Dedan, along with merchants from villages in* southern Spain,* will be your allies. They will want some of the silver and gold, as

well as the livestock and property that your army takes from Israel.

[14] I, the LORD God, know that when you see* my people living in peace, [15] you will lead your powerful cavalry from your kingdom in the north. [16] You will attack my people like a storm-cloud that covers their land. I will let you invade my country Israel, so that every nation on earth will know that I, the LORD, am holy.

Judgment on Gog

[17] The LORD said to Gog:

Long ago, I made my prophets warn the people of Israel that some day I would send an enemy to attack them. You, Gog, are that enemy, and that day is coming. [18] When you invade Israel, I will become furious, [19] and in my anger I will send a terrible earthquake to shake Israel. [20] Every living thing on earth will tremble in fear of me — every fish and bird, every wild animal and reptile, and every human. Mountains will crumble, cliffs will fall, and cities will collapse. [21] I, the LORD, will make the mountains of Israel turn against you.* Your troops will be so terrified that they will attack each other. [22] I will strike you with diseases and punish you with death. You and your army will be pounded with rainstorms, hailstones, and burning sulphur. [23] I will do these things to show the world that I, the LORD, am holy.

CHAPTER 39

Gog is defeated

The LORD said:

[1] Ezekiel, son of man, condemn Gog and tell him:

You are the ruler of Meshech and Tubal, but I, the LORD, am your enemy! [2] I will turn you around and drag you from the north until you reach the mountains of Israel. [3] I will knock the bow out of your left hand and the arrows out of your right hand, [4] and you and your army will die on those mountains. Then birds and wild animals will eat the flesh [5] of your dead bodies left lying in open fields. I, the LORD, have spoken.

[6] I will set fire to the land of Magog and to those nations along the coast that think they are so secure, and they will know that I am the LORD.

[7] My people Israel will know me, and they will no longer disgrace my holy name.

---

*38.5 Ethiopia: See the note at 29.10.
See also: 37.27: 2 Cor 6.16; Rev 21.3. 38.2: Rev 20.8.

Everyone on earth will know that I am the holy LORD God of Israel. ⁸ The day is coming when these things will happen, just as I have promised.

⁹ When that day comes, the people in the towns of Israel will collect the weapons of their dead enemies. They will use these shields, bows and arrows, spears, and clubs as firewood, and there will be enough to last for seven years. ¹⁰ They will burn these weapons instead of gathering sticks or chopping down trees. That's how the Israelites will take revenge on those who robbed and abused them. I, the LORD, have spoken.

The burial of Gog

The LORD said:

¹¹ After Gog has been destroyed, I will bury him and his army in Israel, in Travellers'ᵇ Valley, east of the Dead Sea. That graveyard will be so large that it will block the way of anyone who tries to walk through the valley,ᶜ which will then be known as "The Valley of Gog's Army".ᵈ ¹² The Israelites will spend seven months burying dead bodies and cleaning up their land. ¹³ Everyone will help with the burial, and they will be honoured for this on the day the brightness of my glory is seen. ¹⁴ After those seven months, the people will appoint a group of men to look for any dead bodies left unburied. This must be done for seven months to make sure that the land is no longer unclean. ¹⁵ Whenever they find a human bone, they will set up a marker next to it. Then the gravediggers will bury it in "The Valley of Gog's Army". ¹⁶ near the town of "Gog's Army". After that, the land will be pure again.

¹⁷ Ezekiel, son of man, I am going to hold a feast on Israel's mountains and offer sacrifices there. So invite all the birds and wild animals to come from every direction and eat the meat of sacrifices and drink the blood. ¹⁸ The birds and animals will feast on the bodies of warriors and foreign rulers that I will sacrifice like sheep, goats, and bulls. ¹⁹ I want the birds and animals to eat until they are full and drink until they are drunk. ²⁰ They will come to my table and stuff themselves with the flesh of horses and warriors of every kind. I, the LORD God, have spoken.

Israel will be restored

The LORD said:

²¹ When I punish the nations of the earth, they will see the brightness of my glory.
²² The people of Israel will know from then on that I am the LORD their God. ²³ Foreign nations will realize that the Israelites were forced to leave their own land because they sinned against me. I turned my back on my people and let enemies attack and kill them.
²⁴ Their lives were wicked and corrupt, and they deserved to be punished.

²⁵ Now I will show mercy to the people of Israel and bring them back from the nations where they are living. They are Jacob's descendants, so I will bless them and show that I am holy. ²⁶ They will live safely in their own land, but will be ashamed when they remember their evil ways and how they disgraced me.ᵉ ²⁷ Foreign nations will watch as I take the Israelites from enemy lands and bring them back home, and those nations will see that I am holy.

²⁸ My people will realize that I, the LORD their God, sent them away as prisoners and now will bring them back to their own land. ²⁹ Never again will I turn my back on the people of Israel, and my Spirit will live in them. I, the LORD, have spoken.

Ezekiel sees the future temple in Jerusalem

CHAPTER 40

¹⁻² Twenty-five years after King Jehoiachin and the rest of us had been led away as prisoners to Babylonia, and fourteen years after the Babylonians had captured Jerusalem, the LORD's power took control of me on the tenth day of the first month.* The LORD showed me some visions in which I was carried to the top of a high mountain in Jerusalem. I looked to the south and saw what looked like a city full of buildings. ³ In my vision the LORD took me closer, and I saw a man who was sparkling like polished bronze. He was standing near one of the gates and was holding a tape measure in one hand and a measuring stick in the other. ⁴ The man said, "Ezekiel, son of man, pay close attention to everything I'm going to show you — that's why you've been brought here.

---

*40.1,2 **Twenty-five years . . . first month:** Probably March of 573 BC.

See also: 40.2: Rev 21.10. 40.3: Rev 11.1; 21.15.

See also: 39.17-20: Rev 19.17,18.

Listen carefully, because you must tell the people of Israel what you see."

The east gate

5 The first thing I saw was an outer wall that completely surrounded the temple area. The man took his measuring stick, which was three metres long, and measured the wall; it was three metres high and three metres thick. 6-7 Then he went to the east gate, where he walked up steps that led to a long passageway. On each side of this passageway were three guardrooms, which were three metres square, and they were separated by walls two and a half metres thick. The man measured the distance between the opening of the gate and the first guardroom, and it was three metres, the thickness of the outer wall.

At the far end of this passageway, I saw an entrance room that faced the courtyard of the temple itself. There was also a distance of three metres between the last guardroom and the entrance room 8-9 at the end of the passageway. The man measured this room: it was four metres from the doorway to the opposite wall, and the distance from the doorway to the wall on either side was one metre. 10 The three guardrooms on each side of the passageway were the same size, and the walls that separated them were the same thickness.

11 Next, the man measured the width of the passageway, and it was six and a half metres, but the two doors of the gate were only five metres wide.* 12 In front of the guardrooms, which were three metres square, was a railing about fifty centimetres high and fifty centimetres thick. 13 The man measured the distance from the back wall* of one of these rooms to the same spot in the room directly across the passageway, and it was twelve and a half metres. 14 He measured the entrance room at the far end of the passageway, and it was ten metres wide.* 15 Finally, he measured the total length of the passageway, from the outer wall to the entrance room, and it was twenty-five metres. 16 The three walls in the guardrooms had small windows in them, just like the ones in the entrance room.* The walls along the passageway were decorated with carvings of palm trees.

The outer courtyard

17 The man then led me through the passageway and into the outer courtyard of the temple, where I saw thirty rooms built around the outside of the courtyard.* These side rooms were built against the outer wall, and in front of them was a pavement that circled the courtyard. 18 This was known as the lower pavement, and it was twenty-five metres wide.

19 I saw the gates that led to the inner courtyard of the temple and noticed that they were higher than those leading to the outer courtyard. The man measured the distance between the outer and inner gates, and it was fifty metres.*

The north gate

20 Next, the man measured the north gate that led to the outer courtyard. 21 This gate also had three guardrooms on each side of a passageway. The measurements of these rooms, the walls between them, and the entrance room at the far end of the passageway were exactly the same as those of the east gate. The north gate was also twenty-five metres long and twelve and a half metres wide, 22 and the windows, the entrance room, and the carvings of palm trees were just like those in the east gate. The entrance room also faced the courtyard of the temple and had seven steps leading up to it. 23 Directly across the outer courtyard was a gate that led to the inner courtyard, just as there was for the east gate. The man measured the distance between the outer and inner gate, and it was fifty metres.

The south gate

24 The man then took me to the south gate. He measured the walls and the entrance room of this gate, and the measurements were exactly the same as those of the other two gates. 25 There were windows in the guardrooms of this gate and in the entrance room, just like the others, and this gate was also twenty-five metres long and twelve and a half metres wide. 26 Seven steps led up to the gate; the entrance room was at the far end of the passageway and faced the

---

*40.11 the width of the passageway . . . six and a half metres . . . the two doors of the gate . . . five metres wide: The doors themselves were probably were hung on stone sockets, which could explain the one-and-a-half-metre difference in width between the passageway and the doors.

See also: 40.5–42.20: 1 King 6.1–38; 2 Chron 3.1–9.

---

*40.17 thirty rooms built around the outside of the courtyard: These were probably used by worshippers as places to meet and share sacrificial meals (see, for example, Jeremiah 35.2).

courtyard of the temple. Carvings of palm trees decorated the walls along the passageway. [27] And directly across the outer courtyard was a gate on the south side of the inner courtyard. The man measured the distance between the outer and inner gate, and it was also fifty metres.

The gates leading to the inner courtyard

[28] We then went into the inner courtyard, through the gate on the south side of the temple. The man measured the gate, and it was the same size as the gates in the outer wall. [29-30] In fact, everything along the passageway was also the same size, including the guardrooms, the walls separating them, the entrance room at the far end, and the windows. This gate, like the others, was twenty-five metres long and twelve and a half metres wide. [31] The entrance room of this gate faced the outer courtyard, and carvings of palm trees decorated the walls of the passageway. Eight steps led up to this gate.

[32] Next, we went through the east gate to the inner courtyard. The man measured this gate, and it was the same size as the others. [33] The guardrooms, the walls separating them, and its entrance room had the same measurements as the other gates. The guardrooms and the entrance room had windows, and the gate was twenty-five metres long and twelve and a half metres wide. [34] The entrance room faced the outer courtyard, and the walls in the passageway were decorated with carvings of palm trees. Eight steps also led up to this gate.

[35] Then the man took me to the north gate. He measured it, and it was the same size as the others, [36] including the guardrooms, the walls separating them, and the entrance room. There were also windows in this gate. It was twenty-five metres long and twelve and a half metres wide, [37] and like the other inner gates, its entrance room faced the outer courtyard, and its walls were decorated with carvings of palm trees. Eight steps also led up to this gate.

The rooms for sacrificing animals

[38-39] Inside the entrance room of the north gate, I saw four tables, two on each side of the room, where the animals to be sacrificed were killed. Just outside* this room was a small building used for washing the animals

before they were offered as sacrifices to please the LORD* or sacrifices for sin* or sacrifices to make things right.* [40] Four more tables were in the outer courtyard, two on each side of the steps leading into the entrance room. [41] So there was a total of eight tables, four inside and four outside, where the animals were killed, [42-43] and where the meat was placed until it was sacrificed on the altar.*

Next to the tables in the entrance room were four stone tables fifty centimetres high and seventy-five centimetres square; the equipment used for killing the animals was kept on each of these tables. All around the walls of this room was a seventy-five-millimetre shelf.*

The rooms belonging to the priests

[44] The man then took me to the inner courtyard, where I saw two buildings, one beside the inner gate on the north and the other beside the inner gate on the south.* [45] He said, "The building beside the north gate belongs to the priests who serve in the temple, [46] and the building beside the south gate belongs to those who serve at the altar. All of them are descendants of Zadok and are the only Levites allowed to serve as the LORD's priests."

The inner courtyard and the temple

[47] Now the man measured the inner courtyard; it was fifty metres square. I also saw an altar in front of the temple.

[48] We walked to the porch of the temple, and the man measured the doorway of the porch: it was seven metres long,* two and a half metres wide, and the distance from the doorway to the wall on either side was one and a half metres. [49] The porch itself was ten metres by six* metres, with steps* leading up to it. There was a column on each side of these steps.

---

*40.38,39 sacrifices to please the LORD: These sacrifices have traditionally been called "whole burnt offerings" because the whole animal was burnt on the altar. A main purpose of such sacrifices was to please the LORD with the smell of the sacrifice, and so in the CEV they are often called "sacrifices to please the LORD."
*40.38,39 sacrifices for sin: See Leviticus 4.1,2; 6.24-30.
*40.38,39 sacrifices to make things right: See Leviticus 5.14-19; 7.1-10.

CHAPTER 41

¹ Next we went into the main room of the temple. The man measured the doorway of this room: it was three metres wide,' ² five metres long, and the distance from the doorway to the wall on either side was two and a half metres. The main room itself was twenty metres by ten metres.

³⁻⁴ Then the man walked to the far end of the temple's main room and said, "Beyond this doorway is the most holy place." He first measured the doorway: it was one metre wide, three metres long, and the distance from the doorway to the wall on either side was three and a half metres. Then he measured the most holy place, and it was ten metres square.

The storage rooms of the temple

⁵ The man measured the wall of the temple, and it was three metres thick. Storage rooms two metres wide were built against the outside of the wall. ⁶ There were three levels of rooms, with thirty rooms on each level, and they rested on ledges that were attached to the temple walls, so that nothing was built into the walls. ⁷ The walls of the temple were thicker at the bottom than at the top, which meant that the storage rooms on the top level were wider than those on the bottom level.' Steps led from the bottom level, through the middle level, and into the top level.

⁸ The temple rested on a stone base three metres high, which also served as the foundation for the storage rooms. ⁹ The outside walls of the storage rooms were two and a half metres thick; there was nothing between these walls ¹⁰ and the nearest buildings ten metres away. ¹¹ One door led into the storage rooms on the north side of the temple, and another door led to those on the south side. The stone base extended two and a half metres beyond the outside wall of the storage rooms.

The west building and the measurements of the temple

¹² I noticed another building: it faced the west end of the temple and was thirty-five metres wide, forty-five metres long, and had walls over two and a half metres thick.

¹³ The man measured the length of the temple, and it was fifty metres. He then measured from the back wall of the temple, across the open space behind the temple, to the back wall of the west building; it was fifty metres. ¹⁴ The distance across the front of the temple, including the open space on either side, was also fifty metres.

¹⁵ Finally, the man measured the length of the west building, including the side rooms on each end, and it was also fifty metres.

The inside of the temple

The inside walls of the temple's porch and main room' ¹⁶ were panelled with wood all the way from the floor to the windows, while the doorways, the small windows, and the three side rooms were trimmed in wood.' ¹⁷ The panelling stopped just above the doorway. These walls were decorated' ¹⁸⁻²⁰ with carvings of winged creatures and had a carving of a palm tree between the creatures. Each winged creature had two faces: a human face looking at the palm tree on one side, and a lion's face looking at the palm tree on the other side. These designs were carved into the panelling all the way around the two rooms.

²¹ The doorframe to the temple's main room was in the shape of a rectangle.

The wooden altar

In front of the doorway to the most holy place was something that looked like ²² a wooden altar. It was one and a half metres high and one metre square,' and its corners, its base,' and its sides were made of wood. The man said, "This is a reminder that the LORD is constantly watching over his temple."

The doors in the temple

²³ Both the doorway to the main room of the temple and the doorway to the most holy place had two doors, ²⁴ and each door had two sections that could fold open. ²⁵ The doors to the main room were decorated with carvings of winged creatures and palm trees just like those on the walls, and there was a wooden covering over the porch just outside these doors. ²⁶ The walls on each side of this porch had small windows and were also decorated with carvings of palm trees.

CHAPTER 42

The sacred rooms for the priests

¹⁻² After the man and I left the temple and walked back to the outer courtyard, he showed me a set of rooms on the north side of the west building.' This set of rooms was fifty metres long and twenty-five metres wide. ³ On one side of them was the ten metres of open space

that ran beside the temple,* and on the other side was the pavement that circled the outer courtyard.* The rooms were arranged in three levels [4] with doors that opened towards the north, and in front of them was a passage five metres wide and fifty metres long.* [5] The rooms on the top level were narrower than those on the middle level, and the rooms on the middle level were narrower than those on the bottom level. [6] The rooms on the bottom level supported those on the two upper levels, and so these rooms did not have columns like other buildings in the courtyard. [7-8] To the north was a screening wall twenty-five metres long,* [9-10] and at the east end of this wall was the door leading from the courtyard to these rooms.

There was also a set of rooms on the south* side of the west building. [11] These rooms were exactly like those on the north side, and they also had a passage in front of them. [12] The door to these rooms was at the east end of the wall that stood in front of them.

[13] The man then said to me:

These rooms on the north and south sides of the temple are the sacred rooms where the LORD's priests will eat the most holy offerings. These offerings include the grain sacrifices,* the sacrifices for sin,* and the sacrifices to make things right.* [14] When the priests are ready to leave the temple, they must go through these rooms before they return to the outer courtyard. They must leave their sacred clothes in these rooms and put on ordinary clothes before going anywhere near other people.

The size of the temple area

[15] After the man had finished measuring the buildings inside the temple area, he took me back through the east gate and measured the wall around this area. [16] He used his measuring stick to measure the east side of this wall; it was two hundred and fifty metres long. [17-19] Then he measured the north side, the south side, and the west side of the wall, and they were each two hundred and fifty-five metres long, [20] and so the temple area was a perfect square. The wall

around this area separated what was sacred from what was ordinary.

CHAPTER 43

The LORD's glory returns to the temple

[1] The man took me back to the east gate of the temple, [2] where I saw the brightness of the glory of Israel's God coming from the east. The sound I heard was as loud as ocean waves, and everything around was shining with the dazzling brightness of his glory. [3] This vision was like the one I had seen when God came to destroy Jerusalem and like the one I had seen near the River Chebar.

I immediately bowed with my face to the ground, [4] and the LORD's glory came through the east gate and into the temple.* [5] The LORD's Spirit lifted me to my feet and carried me to the inner courtyard, where I saw that the LORD's glory had filled the temple.

[6] The man was standing beside me, and I heard the LORD say from inside the temple:

[7] Ezekiel, son of man, this temple is my throne on earth. I will live here among the people of Israel for ever. They and their kings will never again disgrace me by worshipping idols at local shrines or by setting up memorials to their dead kings.' [8] Israel's kings built their palaces so close to my holy temple that only a wall separated them from me. Then these kings disgraced me with their evil ways, and in my fierce anger I destroyed them. [9] But if the people and their kings stop worshipping other gods and tear down those memorials, I will live among them for ever.

[10] The people of Israel must suffer shame for sinning against me, so tell them about my holy temple. Let them think about it, [11] then if they are truly sorry, describe for them the design and shape of the temple, the gates, the measurements, and how the buildings are arranged. Explain the regulations about worshipping them, then write down these things, so they can study and obey them.

[12] The temple area on my holy mountain must be kept sacred! This is the most important law about the temple.

---

*42.3 the ten metres of open space . . . the temple: See 41.10.

*42.3 the pavement that circled the outer courtyard: See 40.17.

*42.13 grain sacrifices: See Leviticus 2.1.

*42.13 sacrifices for sin: See the note at 40.38,39.

*42.13 sacrifices to make things right: See the note at 40.38,39.

*43.4 the LORD's glory . . . temple: This was the same gate the LORD's glory went through when it left Jerusalem (see 10.19 and 11.22,23).

See also: 43.2: Ezek 10.3,4,18,19; 11.22,23; Rev 1.15.

The altar

13 According to the official standards, the altar in the temple had the following measurements: around the bottom of the altar was a gutter fifty centimetres wide and fifty centimetres deep, with a twenty-five-centimetre ledge on the outer rim. 14-17 The altar rested on a base and had three sections, each one of them square. The bottom section was eight metres on each side and one metre high. The middle section was seven metres on each side and two metres high, and it had a twenty-five-centimetre rim around its outer edge. The top section, which was six metres on each side and two metres high, was the place where sacrifices were burnt, and the four corners of the top section looked like the horns of a bull. The steps leading up to the altar were on the east side.

The dedication of the altar

18 The LORD God said:

Ezekiel, son of man, after the altar is built, it must be dedicated by offering sacrifices on it and by splattering it with blood. Here is what you must do: 19 the priests of the Levi tribe from the family of Zadok the priest are the only ones who may serve in my temple — this is my law. So give them a young bull to slaughter as a sacrifice for sin. 20 Take some of the animal's blood and smear it on the four corners of the altar, some on the corners of the middle section, and some more on the rim around its edge. That will purify the altar and make it fit for offering sacrifices to me. 21 Then take the body of the bull outside the temple area and burn it at the special place.

22 The next day, a goat* that has nothing wrong with them it must be offered as a sacrifice for sin. Purify the altar with its blood, just as you did with the blood of the bull. 23 Then choose a young bull and a young ram that have nothing wrong with them, 24 and bring them to my temple. The priests will sprinkle salt on them* and offer them as sacrifices to please me.*

25 Each day for the next seven days, you must offer a goat and a bull and a ram as sacrifices for sin. These animals must have

nothing wrong with them. 26 The priests will purify the altar during those days, so that it will be acceptable to me and ready to use. 27 From then on, the priests will use this altar to offer sacrifices to please me and sacrifices to ask my blessing.* Then I will be pleased with the people of Israel. I, the LORD God, have spoken.

CHAPTER 44

The east gate must remain closed

1 The man took me back to the outer courtyard, near the east gate of the temple area. I saw that the doors to this gate were closed. 2 The LORD said:

I, the LORD God of Israel, came through this gate, so it must remain closed for ever! No one must ever use it. 3 The ruler of Israel may come here to eat a sacrificial meal that has been offered to me, but he must use only the entrance room of this gate.

People who are not allowed in the temple

4 Then the man took me through the north gate to the front of the temple. I saw that the brightness of the LORD's glory had filled the temple, and I immediately bowed with my face to the ground. 5 The LORD said:

Ezekiel, son of man, I am going to give you the laws for my temple. So pay attention and listen carefully to what kind of people are allowed to come in the temple, and what kind are not. 6 Tell those rebellious people of Israel:

I, the LORD God, command you to stop your evil ways! 7 My temple has been disgraced, because you have let godless, stubborn foreigners come here when sacrifices are being offered to me. You have sinned and have broken our solemn agreement. 8 Instead of following the proper ways to worship me, you have put foreigners in charge of worship at my temple.

9 And so I, the LORD God, say that no godless foreigner who disobeys me will be allowed in my temple. This includes any foreigner living in Israel.

---

*43.24 The priests will sprinkle salt on them: See Leviticus 2.13.
*43.24 sacrifices to please me: See the note at 40.38,39.
See also: 43.13–17: Exod 27.1,2; 2 Chron 4.1. 43.18–27: Exod 29.35–37.

*43.27 sacrifices to ask my blessing: These sacrifices have traditionally been called "peace offerings" or "offerings of well-being". A main purpose was to ask for the LORD's blessing, and so in the CEV they are sometimes called "sacrifices to ask the LORD's blessing".

816

The Levites are punished

The LORD said:

¹⁰ Some of the Levites turned their backs on me and joined the other people of Israel in worshipping idols. So these Levites must be punished! ¹¹ They will still be allowed to serve me as temple workers by guarding the gates and by killing the animals to be sacrificed and by helping the worshippers. ¹² But because these Levites served the people of Israel when they worshipped idols, I, the LORD God, promise that the Levites will be punished. They did not stop the Israelites from sinning, ¹³ and now I will no longer let the Levites serve as my priests or come near anything sacred to me. They must suffer shame and disgrace for their disgusting sins. ¹⁴ They will be responsible for all the hard work that must be done in the temple.

Rules for priests

The LORD said:

¹⁵ The priests of the Levi tribe who are descendants of Zadok the priest were faithful to me, even when the rest of the Israelites turned away. And so, these priests will continue to serve as my priests and to offer the fat and the blood of sacrifices. ¹⁶ They will come into my temple, where they will offer sacrifices at my altar and lead others in worship.

¹⁷ When they come to the inner courtyard, they must wear their linen priestly clothes. My priests must never wear anything made of wool when they are on duty in this courtyard or in the temple. ¹⁸ Even their turbans and underwear must be made of linen to keep my priests from sweating when they work. ¹⁹ And before they leave to join the other people in the outer courtyard, they must take off their priestly clothes, then place them in the sacred rooms and put on their ordinary clothes.* That way, no one will touch their sacred clothes and be harmed.*

²⁰ Priests must never shave their heads when they are mourning. But they must keep their hair properly trimmed and not let it grow too long. ²¹ They must not drink wine before going to the inner courtyard.

²² A priest must not marry a divorced woman; he can marry only a virgin from Israel or the widow of another priest.

²³ Priests must teach my people the difference between what is sacred and what is ordinary, and between what is clean and what is unclean. ²⁴ They will make decisions in difficult legal cases, according to my own laws. They must also observe the religious festivals my Law requires and must always respect the Sabbath.

²⁵ Touching a dead body will make a person unclean. So a priest must not go near a dead body, unless it is one of his parents or children, or his brother or unmarried sister.* ²⁶ If a priest touches a dead body, he is unclean and must go through a ceremony to make himself clean. Then seven days later, ²⁷ he must go to the inner courtyard of the temple and offer a sacrifice for sin.* After that, he may once again serve as my priest. I, the LORD God, have spoken.

²⁸ I myself will provide for my priests, and so they won't receive any land of their own. ²⁹ Instead, they will receive part of the grain sacrifices,* as well as part of the sacrifices for sin* and sacrifices to make things right.* They will also be given everything in Israel that has been completely dedicated to me.* ³⁰ The first part of every harvest will belong to the priests. They will also receive part of all special gifts and offerings the Israelites bring to me. And whenever any of my people bake bread, they will give their first loaf as an offering to the priests, and I will bless the homes of the people when they do this.

³¹ Priests must not eat any bird or animal that died a natural death or that has been killed by a wild animal.

---

*44.19 take off their priestly clothes . . . put on their ordinary clothes: See 42.14.
*44.19 no one will touch . . . and be harmed: Ordinary people were forbidden to touch anything that was sacred. If they did, it was believed they would somehow be harmed.

See also: 44.17,18: Exod 28.39–43; Lev 16.4. 44.19: Lev 16.23. 44.20: Lev 21.5.

*44.27,29 sacrifice(s) for sin: See the note at 40.38,39.
*44.29 grain sacrifices: See the note at 42.13.
*44.29 sacrifices to make things right: See the note at 40.38,39.
*44.29 that has been completely dedicated to me: This translates a Hebrew word that describes property and things that were taken away from humans and given to God. In the early history of Israel, such things often had to be destroyed (see Joshua 6.15–19).

See also: 44.21: Lev 10.9. 44.22: Lev 21.7,13,14. 44.23: Lev 10.10. 44.25: Lev 21.1–4. 44.28: Num 18.20. 44.29,30: Num 18.8–19. 44.31: Lev 22.8.

CHAPTER 45

The LORD's sacred land

The LORD said:

¹ When the land of Israel is divided among the twelve tribes, you must set aside an area that will belong to me. This sacred area will be twelve and a half kilometres long and ten* kilometres wide. ² The temple will be on a piece of land two hundred and fifty-five metres square, and the temple will be completely surrounded by an open space twenty-five metres wide.

³⁻⁴ I will give half of my sacred land, a section twelve and a half kilometres long and five kilometres wide, to the priests who serve in the temple. Their houses will be in this half, as will my temple, which is the most sacred place of all.

⁵ I will give the other half of my land to the Levites who work in my temple, and the towns* where they will live will be there.

⁶ Next to my sacred land will be an area twelve and a half kilometres long and three kilometres wide. This will belong to the people of Israel and will include the city of Jerusalem.

Land for Israel's ruler

The LORD said:

⁷⁻⁸ The regions west and east of my sacred land and the city of Jerusalem will belong to the ruler of Israel. He will be given the region between the western edge of my land and the Mediterranean Sea, and between the eastern edge of my land and the River Jordan. This will mean that the length of his property will be the same as the sections of land given to the tribes.

This property will belong to every ruler of Israel, so they will always be fair to my people and will let them live peacefully in the land given to their tribes.

Israel's rulers must be honest

⁹ The LORD God said:

You leaders of Israel have robbed and cheated my people long enough! I want you to stop sinning and start doing what is right and fair. You must never again force my people off their own land. I, the LORD, have spoken.

¹⁰ So from now on, you must use honest weights and measures. ¹¹ The *ephah* will be the standard dry measure, and the *bath* will be the standard liquid measure. Their size will be based on the *homer*, which will equal ten *ephahs* or ten *baths.**

¹² The standard unit of weight will be the *shekel.** One *shekel* will equal twenty *gerahs*, and sixty *shekels* will equal one *mina.*

¹³ Leaders of Israel, the people must bring you one sixtieth of their grain harvests as offerings to me. ¹⁴ They must also bring one per cent of their olive oil. These things will be measured according to the *bath*, and ten *baths* is the same as one *homer* or one *cor.*

¹⁵ Finally, they must bring one sheep out of every two hundred from their flocks.

These offerings will be used as grain sacrifices, as well as sacrifices to please me* and those to ask my blessing.* I, the LORD, will be pleased with these sacrifices and will forgive the sins of my people.

¹⁶ The people of Israel will bring you these offerings. ¹⁷ But during New Moon Festivals, Sabbath celebrations, and other religious feasts, you leaders will be responsible for providing animals for the sacrifices, as well as the grain and wine. All these will be used for the sacrifices for sin,* the grain sacrifices,* the sacrifices to please me,* and those to ask my blessing.* I will be pleased and will forgive the sins of my people.

The festivals

This is also told in Exodus 12.1–20; Leviticus 23.33–43

¹⁸ The LORD God said:

On the first day of the first month,* a young bull that has nothing wrong with it must be offered as a sacrifice to purify the temple. ¹⁹ The priest will take some blood from this sacrifice and smear it on the doorposts of

---

*45.11 the *homer* . . . ten *ephahs* . . . ten *baths*: A *homer* was either a dry or a liquid measure and equalled about one hundred and seventy-five litres; an *ephah* would be about nine kilogrammes, and a *bath* would be about seventeen and a half litres.
*45.12 the *shekel*: The *shekel* was about eleven grammes.
*45.15,17 sacrifices to please me: See the note at 40.38,39.
*45.15,17 sacrifices . . . to ask my blessing: See the note at 43.27.
*45.17 sacrifices for sin: See the note at 40.38,39.
*45.17 grain sacrifices: See the note at 42.13.
*45.18 the first month: Abib (also called Nisan), the first month of the Hebrew calendar, from about mid-March to mid-April.

the temple, as well as on the four corners of the altar and on the doorposts of the gates that lead into the inner courtyard.

20 The same ceremony must also be done on the seventh day of the month, so that anyone who sins accidentally or without knowing it will be forgiven, and so that my temple will remain holy.

21 Beginning on the fourteenth day of the first month, and continuing for seven days, everyone will celebrate Passover and eat bread made without yeast. 22 On the first day, the ruler will bring a bull to offer as a sacrifice for his sins and for the sins of the people. 23 Each day of the festival he is to bring seven bulls and seven rams as sacrifices to please me,* and he must bring a goat* as a sacrifice for sin. These animals must have nothing wrong with them. 24 He will also provide nine kilogrammes of grain and three litres of olive oil to be offered with each bull and each ram.

25 The Festival of Shelters will begin on the fifteenth day of the seventh month* and will continue for seven days. On each day of this festival, the ruler will provide the same number of animals that he did each day during Passover, as well as the same amount of grain and olive oil for the sacrifices.

CHAPTER 46

Various laws for the ruler and the people

1 The LORD said:

The east gate of the inner courtyard must remain closed during the six working days of each week. But on the Sabbath and on the first day of the month, this gate will be opened. 2 Israel's ruler will go from the outer courtyard into the entrance room of this gate and stand in the doorway while the priest offers sacrifices to ask my blessing* and sacrifices to please me.* The ruler will bow with his face to the ground to show that he has worshipped me. Then he will leave, and the gate will remain open until evening.

3 Each Sabbath and on the first day of each month, the people of Israel must also come to the east gate and worship me. 4 On the Sabbath, the ruler will bring six lambs and one ram to be offered as sacrifices to please me. There must be nothing wrong with any of these animals. 5 With the ram, he is to offer nine kilogrammes of grain, and with each of the lambs, he can offer as much as he wants. He must also offer three litres of olive oil with every nine kilogrammes of grain.

6 The ruler is to bring six lambs, a bull, and a ram to be offered as sacrifices at the New Moon Festival. There must be nothing wrong with any of these animals. 7 With the bull and the ram, he is to offer nine kilogrammes of grain, and with each of the lambs, he can offer as much as he wants. He must also offer three litres of olive oil with every nine kilogrammes of grain. 8 The ruler must come through the entrance room of the east gate and leave the same way.

9 When my people come to worship me during any festival, they must always leave by the opposite gate from which they came: those who come in the north gate must leave by the south gate, and those who come in the south gate must leave by the north gate. 10 Their ruler will come in at the same time they do and leave at the same time they leave.

11 At all other festivals and celebrations, nine kilogrammes of grain will be offered with a bull, and nine kilogrammes will be offered with a ram. The worshippers can offer as much grain as they want with each lamb. Three litres of olive oil must be offered with every nine kilogrammes of grain.

12 If the ruler voluntarily offers a sacrifice to please me or to ask my blessing, the east gate of the inner courtyard will be opened for him. He will offer his sacrifices just as he does on each Sabbath; then he will leave, and the gate will be closed.

13 Each morning a year-old lamb that has nothing wrong with it must be offered as a sacrifice to please me. 14 Along with it, two kilogrammes of fine flour mixed with a litre of olive oil must be offered as a grain sacrifice. This law will never change — 15 the lamb, the flour, and the olive oil will be offered to me every morning for all time.

---

*45.23; 46.2 sacrifices to please me:** See the note at 40.38,39.
*45.25 seventh month:** Tishri (also called Ethanim), the seventh month of the Hebrew calendar, from about mid-September to mid-October.
*46.2 sacrifices to ask my blessing:** See the note at 43.27.
See also: 45.21: Exod 12.1–20; Num 28.16–25.
45.25: Lev 23.33–36; Num 29.12–38.

Laws about the ruler's land

16 The LORD God said:

If the ruler of Israel gives some of his land to one of his children, it will belong to the ruler's child as part of the family property. 17 But if the ruler gives some of his land to one of his servants, the land will belong to the servant until the Year of Celebration, when it will be returned to the ruler.* Only the ruler's children can keep what is given to them.

18 The ruler must never abuse my people by taking land from them. Any land he gives his children must already belong to him.

The sacred kitchens

19 The man who was showing me the temple* then took me back to the inner courtyard. We walked to the south side of the courtyard and stopped at the door to the sacred rooms that belonged to the priests. He showed me more rooms at the western edge of the courtyard 20 and said, "These are the kitchens where the priests must boil the meat to be offered as sacrifices to make things right* and as sacrifices for sin.* They will also bake the grain for sacrifices in these kitchens. That way, these sacred offerings won't have to be carried through the outer courtyard, where someone could accidentally touch them and be harmed."*

21 We went back to the outer courtyard and walked past the four corners. 22 At each corner I saw a smaller courtyard, twenty metres long and fifteen metres wide. 23 Around the inside of these smaller courtyards was a low wall of stones, and against the wall were places to build fires.* 24 The man said, "These are the kitchens where the temple workers will boil the meat that worshippers offer as sacrifices."

The stream flowing from the temple

CHAPTER 47

1 The man took me back to the temple, where I saw a stream flowing from under the entrance. It began in the south part of the temple, where it ran past the altar and continued east through the courtyard. 2 We walked out of the temple area through the north gate and went around to the east gate. I saw the small stream of water flowing east from the south side of the gate.

3 The man walked east, then took out his measuring stick and measured five hundred metres downstream. He told me to wade through the stream there, and the water came up to my ankles. 4 Then he measured another five hundred metres downstream, and told me to wade through it there. The water came up to my knees. Another five hundred metres downstream the water came up to my waist. 5 Another five hundred metres downstream, the stream had become a river that could be crossed only by swimming. 6 The man said, "Ezekiel, son of man, pay attention to what you've seen."

We walked to the river bank, 7 where I saw dozens of trees on each side. 8 The man said:

This water flows eastwards to the valley of the River Jordan and empties into the Dead Sea, where it turns the salt water into fresh water. 9 Wherever this water flows, there will be all kinds of animals and fish, because it will bring life and fresh water to the Dead Sea. 10 From En-Gedi to Eneglaim, people will fish in the sea and dry their nets along the coast. There will be as many kinds of fish in the Dead Sea as there are in the Mediterranean Sea. 11 But the marshes along the shore will remain salty, so that people can use the salt from them.

12 Fruit trees will grow all along this river and produce fresh fruit every month. The leaves will never dry out, because they will always have water from the stream that flows from the temple, and they will be used for healing people.

---

*46.17 the Year of Celebration . . . to the ruler: This was a sacred year for Israel, traditionally called the "Year of Jubilee". During this year, all property had to go back to its original owner (see Leviticus 25.8–34).
*46.19 The man . . . temple: See 40.3.
*46.20 sacrifices to make things right: See the note at 40.38,39.
*46.20 sacrifices for sin: See the note at 40.38,39.
*46.20 someone . . . touch them and be harmed: See the note at 44.19.
See also: 46.17: Lev 25.10.

See also: 47.1: Zech 14.8; John 7.38; Rev 22.1.
47.12: Rev 22.2.

The borders of the restored land and its division among the tribes

The borders of the land

13-14 The LORD God said to the people of Israel:

When the land is divided among the twelve tribes of Israel, the Joseph tribe* will receive two shares. Divide the land equally, because I promised your ancestors that this land would some day belong to their descendants. These are the borders of the land:

15 The northern border will begin at the Mediterranean Sea, then continue eastward to Hethlon, to Lebo-Hamath, then across to Zedad, 16 Berothah,* and Sibraim, which is on the border between the two kingdoms of Damascus and Hamath. The border will end at Hazer-Hatticon, which is on the border of Hauran. 17 So the northern border will run between the Mediterranean Sea and Hazar-Enon, which is on the border between Damascus and Hamath.*

18 The eastern border will begin on the border between the two kingdoms of Hauran and Damascus. It will run south along the River Jordan, which separates the territories of Gilead and Israel, and it will end at the Dead Sea near the town of Tamar.*

19 The southern border will begin at Tamar, then run south-west to the springs near Meribath-Kadesh. It will continue along the Egyptian Gorge and will end at the Mediterranean Sea.

20 The western border will run north along the Mediterranean Sea to a point just west of Lebo-Hamath.

21 That is the land to be divided among the tribes of Israel. 22 It will belong to the Israelites and to any foreigners living among them whose children were born in Israel. These foreigners must be treated like any other Israelite citizen, and they will receive 23 a share of the land given to the tribe where they live. I, the LORD God, have spoken.

---

*47.13,14 the Joseph tribe: That is, the two tribes of Manasseh and Ephraim, Joseph's sons.

CHAPTER 48

The division of land among tribes in the north

The LORD said:

1-7 Each tribe will receive a section of land that runs from the eastern border of Israel west to the Mediterranean Sea. The northern border of Israel will run along the towns of Hethlon and Lebo-Hamath, and will end at Hazar-Enon, which is on the border between the kingdoms of Damascus and Hamath. The tribes will receive their share of land in the following order, from north to south: Dan, Asher, Naphtali, Manasseh, Ephraim, Reuben, and Judah.

The special section of land

The LORD said:

8 South of Judah's territory will be a special section of land. Its length will be twelve and a half kilometres, and its width will run from the eastern border of Israel west to the Mediterranean Sea. My temple will be in this section of land.

9 An area in the centre of this land will belong to me. It will be twelve and a half kilometres long and ten* kilometres wide.

10 I, the LORD, will give half of my sacred land to the priests. Their share will be twelve and a half kilometres long and five kilometres wide, and my temple will be right in the middle. 11 Only priests who are descendants of Zadok will receive a share of this sacred land, because they remained faithful to me when the Levites and the rest of the Israelites started sinning. 12 The land belonging to the priests will be the most sacred area and will lie south of the area that belongs to the Levites.

13 I will give the other half of my sacred land to the Levites. Their share will also be twelve and a half kilometres long and five kilometres wide, 14 and they must never sell or trade any of this land — it is the best land and belongs to me.

15 South of my sacred land will be a section twelve and a half kilometres long and three kilometres wide. It will not be sacred, but will belong to the people of Israel and will include the city of Jerusalem, together with its houses and pasture land. 16 The city will be a square: each side will be two kilometres long, 17 and an open area one hundred and twenty-five metres wide will surround the city. 18 The land on the

east and west sides of the city boundaries will be farmland for the people of Jerusalem; both sections will be five kilometres long and three kilometres wide. [19] People from the city will farm the land, no matter which tribe they belong to.

[20] And so the centre of this special section of land will be for my sacred land, as well as for the city and its property. The land will be a square, twelve and a half kilometres on each side.

[21] The regions east and west of this square of land will belong to the ruler of Israel. His property will run east to the River Jordan and west to the Mediterranean Sea. In the very centre of his property will be my sacred land, as well as the temple, [22] together with the share belonging to the Levites and the city of Jerusalem. The northern border of the ruler's property will be the land that belongs to Judah, and the southern border will be the land that belongs to Benjamin.

The division of land among tribes in the south

The LORD God said:

[23-27] South of this special section will be the land that belongs to the rest of Israel's tribes. Each tribe will receive a section of land that runs from the eastern border of Israel west to the Mediterranean Sea. The tribes will receive their share of land in the following order, from north to south: Benjamin, Simeon, Issachar, Zebulun, and Gad.

[28] Gad's southern border is also the southern border of Israel. It will begin at the town of Tamar, then run south-west to the springs near Meribath-Kadesh. It will continue along the Egyptian Gorge and end at the Mediterranean Sea.

[29] That's how the land of Israel will be divided among the twelve tribes. I, the LORD God, have spoken.

The gates of Jerusalem

The LORD said:

[30-34] The city of Jerusalem will have twelve gates, three on each of the four sides of the city wall. These gates will be named after the twelve tribes of Israel. The gates of Reuben, Judah, and Levi will be in the north; Joseph, Benjamin, and Dan will be in the east; Simeon, Issachar, and Zebulun will be in the south; Gad, Asher, and Naphtali will be in

the west. Each side of the city wall will be two kilometres long, [35] and so the total length of the wall will be ten kilometres. The new name of the city will be "The-LORD-Is-Here!"

Additional notes

[1.1-3] a priest and the son of Buzi: Or "the son of Buzi the priest".

[1.11] Two wings: One possible meaning for the difficult Hebrew text.

[1.13] up: One possible meaning for the difficult Hebrew text of verse 13.

[1.14] as sparks jumping from a fire: Or "as flashes of lightning".

[1.15] wheel: One possible meaning for the difficult Hebrew text of verse 15.

[1.16] a second wheel that cut through the middle of it: Or "a smaller wheel inside it".

[1.18] them: One possible meaning for the difficult Hebrew text of verse 18.

[2.1] The LORD: Hebrew "The voice".

[3.12] The Spirit: Or "A wind".

[3.12] as the glory of the LORD started to leave: One possible meaning for the difficult Hebrew text.

[7.5] disaster: One possible meaning for the difficult Hebrew text of verse 5.

[7.7] celebration: One possible meaning for the difficult Hebrew text of verse 7.

[7.11] shattered: One possible meaning for the difficult Hebrew text of verses 10,11.

[7.13] mind: One possible meaning for the difficult Hebrew text of verse 13.

[7.16] will moan: Hebrew; two ancient translations "will die".

[7.22] my temple: The Hebrew text has "my treasure", which may refer to the temple, to Jerusalem, or to Israel itself.

[7.23] Your whole country is in confusion: One ancient translation; Hebrew "Get chains ready to drag away the dead bodies of your people."

[8.2] a human: One ancient translation; Hebrew "a fiery figure".

[8.17] disgraced and insulted me . . . way: One possible meaning for the difficult Hebrew text.

[10.10] a second wheel that cut through the middle of it: See the note at 1.16.

[11.1] The LORD's Spirit: See the note at 3.12.

[11.3] Let's . . . houses: One possible meaning for the difficult Hebrew text.

[11.24] The LORD's Spirit: See the note at 3.12.

[13.18] They wear . . . the future: One possible meaning for the difficult Hebrew text.

[13.20] like birds: One possible meaning for the difficult Hebrew text.

[16.10] most expensive robes: One possible meaning for the difficult Hebrew text.

See also: 48.30–34: Rev 21.12,13.

˒16.15 so you offered yourself to every passer-by: One possible meaning for the difficult Hebrew text.
˒16.16 These things should never have happened: One possible meaning for the difficult Hebrew text.
˒16.30 wanted: One possible meaning for the difficult Hebrew text of verse 30.
˒16.61 even though this was not part of our agreement: One possible meaning for the difficult Hebrew text.
˒17.5 like a willow tree beside a stream: One possible meaning for the difficult Hebrew text.
˒17.21 best troops: Two ancient translations; Hebrew "troops that ran away".
˒18.17 evil: One ancient translation; Hebrew "for the poor".
˒19.7 He destroyed fortresses: One possible meaning for the difficult Hebrew text.
˒19.10 Your mother was a vine: One possible meaning for the difficult Hebrew text.
˒20.39 me: One possible meaning for the difficult Hebrew text of verse 39.
˒21.9,10 Don't celebrate . . . my warnings: One possible meaning for the difficult Hebrew text.
˒21.13 I am testing . . . me: One possible meaning for the difficult Hebrew text.
˒21.15 My slaughtering sword . . . ready to kill: One possible meaning for the difficult Hebrew text.
˒21.30 Your days . . . put your swords away: One possible meaning for the difficult Hebrew text.
˒22.16 You: Hebrew; two ancient translations "Because of you, I".
˒22.25 Their leaders are like: One ancient translation; Hebrew "Their prophets are like herds of".
˒23.24 from the north: One ancient translation; Hebrew "with weapons".
˒23.43 prostitutes: One possible meaning for the difficult Hebrew text of verse 43.
˒24.4,5 Pile wood: Or "Stack the bones".
˒24.6 and no one cares what happens to it: One possible meaning for the difficult Hebrew text.
˒24.10 boil away the broth: One ancient translation; Hebrew "mix the spices".
˒24.12 away: One possible meaning for the difficult Hebrew text of verse 12.
˒25.8 Moab: One ancient translation; Hebrew "Moab and Edom".
˒25.16 kill everyone: The Hebrew text also has the name "Cherethites", which was a group of people that lived just south-east of Philistia, and was often identified with the Philistines.
˒26.17 The great city . . . is destroyed: One possible meaning for the difficult Hebrew text.
˒26.20 You will stay there . . . with people: One possible meaning for the difficult Hebrew text.
˒27.4 and your control of the sea: One possible meaning for the difficult Hebrew text.
˒27.6 pine trees from Cyprus: One possible meaning for the difficult Hebrew text.
˒27.12 southern Spain: The Hebrew text has "Tarshish", which may have been a Phoenician city in southern Spain.

˒27.15 Rhodes: One ancient translation; Hebrew "Dedan".
˒27.16 Edom: Some Hebrew manuscripts and one ancient translation; most Hebrew manuscripts "Syria".
˒27.17 their finest wheat, best figs: One possible meaning for the difficult Hebrew text.
˒27.19 Vedan and Javan near Uzal: One possible meaning for the difficult Hebrew text.
˒27.32 Tyre, you were greater . . . the bottom of the sea: One possible meaning for the difficult Hebrew text.
˒28.3 and know everything: One possible meaning for the difficult Hebrew text.
˒28.12 you were perfect: One possible meaning for the difficult Hebrew text.
˒28.13 They were all set in gold: One possible meaning for the difficult Hebrew text.
˒28.14 I appointed a winged creature to guard your home: One possible meaning for the difficult Hebrew text.
˒29.7 making them fall: One possible meaning for the difficult Hebrew text.
˒30.5 as well as from Israel: One possible meaning for the difficult Hebrew text.
˒30.13 Memphis: Hebrew "Noph".
˒30.14 Thebes: Hebrew "No".
˒30.16 the people of Memphis . . . constant fear: One possible meaning for the difficult Hebrew text.
˒30.17 Heliopolis and Bubastis: Hebrew "On and Pi-Beseth".
˒31.3 sky: One possible meaning for the difficult Hebrew text of verse 3.
˒31.10 the sky: One ancient translation; Hebrew "over the thick branches".
˒31.15 rivers and streams . . . stop flowing: One possible meaning for the difficult Hebrew text.
˒31.17 dead: One possible meaning for the difficult Hebrew text of verse 17.
˒32.5 rotting flesh: One possible meaning for the difficult Hebrew text.
˒32.9 when I tell them how I destroyed you: Hebrew; one ancient translation "when I scatter you like prisoners among them."
˒32.18 where they will be buried . . . powerful nations: One possible meaning for the difficult Hebrew text.
˒32.20 The enemy's sword . . . you: One possible meaning for the difficult Hebrew text.
˒32.27 heroes of long ago: One ancient translation; Hebrew "godless heroes".
˒32.27 shields: One possible meaning for the difficult Hebrew text.
˒34.16 slaughter: Hebrew; three ancient translations "take care of".
˒35.2 Edom: The Hebrew text has "Mount Seir", another name for Edom.
˒37.9 wind: Or "breath". The Hebrew word may mean either.
˒37.16 Israel: The Hebrew text has "Joseph, that is, Ephraim", the leading tribe in the northern kingdom.

'38.13 from villages in: One ancient translation; Hebrew "and soldiers from".

'38.13 southern Spain: See the note at 27.12.

'38.14 when you see: One possible meaning for the difficult Hebrew text.

'38.21 I, the LORD . . . against you: One possible meaning for the difficult Hebrew text.

'39.11 Travellers': Hebrew "Abarim".

'39.11 That graveyard . . . the valley: One possible meaning for the difficult Hebrew text.

'39.11 Gog's Army: Hebrew "Hamon-Gog".

'39.26 me: One possible meaning for the difficult Hebrew text of verse 26.

'40.13 back wall: One ancient translation; Hebrew "roof".

'40.14 wide: One possible meaning for the difficult Hebrew text of verse 14.

'40.16 just like the ones in the entrance room: One possible meaning for the difficult Hebrew text.

'40.19 metres: The Hebrew text adds "the east and the north".

'40.38,39 Just outside: Or "Inside".

'40.42,43 where the meat . . . altar: One possible meaning for the difficult Hebrew text.

'40.42,43 was a seventy-five-millimetre shelf: Or "were seventy-five-millimetre pegs".

'40.44 south: One possible meaning for the difficult Hebrew text of verse 44.

'40.48 seven metres long: One ancient translation; these words are not in the Hebrew text of this verse.

'40.49 six: One ancient translation; Hebrew "five and a half".

'40.49 steps: Hebrew; one ancient translation "ten steps".

'41.1 it was three metres wide: One possible meaning for the difficult Hebrew text.

'41.7 which meant that . . . on the bottom level: One possible meaning for the difficult Hebrew text.

'41.15 The inside walls of the temple's porch and main room: One possible meaning for the difficult Hebrew text.

'41.16 were trimmed in wood: One possible meaning for the difficult Hebrew text.

'41.17 decorated: One possible meaning for the difficult Hebrew text of verse 17.

'41.22 one metre square: One ancient translation; Hebrew "one metre wide".

'41.22 base: One ancient translation; Hebrew "length".

'42.1,2 he showed me . . . the west building: One possible meaning for the difficult Hebrew text.

'42.4 fifty metres long: Two ancient translations; Hebrew "fifty centimetres long".

'42.7,8 long: One possible meaning for the difficult Hebrew text of verses 5–8.

'42.9,10 south: One ancient translation; Hebrew "east".

'43.6 the LORD: Hebrew "a voice".

'43.7 by setting up memorials to their dead kings: One possible meaning for the difficult Hebrew text.

'43.22 goat: Hebrew "male goat".

'45.1 ten: One ancient translation; Hebrew "five".

'45.5 the towns: One ancient translation; Hebrew "the twenty rooms".

'45.23 goat: See the note at 43.22.

'46.23 fires: One possible meaning for the difficult Hebrew text of verse 23.

'47.15,16 to Lebo-Hamath, then across to Zedad, ¹⁶ Berothah: One ancient translation; Hebrew "to Lebo-Zedad, ¹⁶ then across to Hamath, Berothah".

'47.17 which is on the border between Damascus and Hamath: One possible meaning for the difficult Hebrew text.

'47.18 near the town of Tamar: One possible meaning for the difficult Hebrew text.

'48.9 ten: The Hebrew text has "five" (but see 45.1 and the note there).

Daniel

A quick look at this book

As a young man, Daniel had been taken prisoner by the Babylonian army when Jerusalem was captured. The first half of this book (1—6) tells how he and three of his friends from Judah became important officials in the government at Babylon. They remained completely faithful to the Lord, even when it meant risking their lives. This half of the book concludes with Daniel serving in the government of the Medo-Persian empire after it had conquered Babylonia.

In the second half of the book (7—12) Daniel reports several visions that he had and how

the meanings of those visions were explained to him by angels.

This book shows that God is in control of human events. He guides empires into power, but later he lets them be conquered by other empires. God also cares for individuals who are faithful to him, and some day he will finally bring justice to the world and provide victory for his people. Here is how Daniel spoke about this future time of victory:

> I saw what looked like
>   a son of man
> coming with the clouds of heaven,
> and he was presented
>   to the Eternal God.
> He was crowned king
>   and given power and glory,
> so that all people
> of every nation and race
>   would serve him.
> He will rule for ever,
> and his kingdom is eternal,
>   never to be destroyed.

(7.13,14)

Daniel and his three friends

CHAPTER 1

[1] In the third year that Jehoiakim was king of Judah,* King Nebuchadnezzar of Babylonia

---

*1.1 Jehoiakim . . . king of Judah: Ruled 609–598 BC.
See also: 1.1: 2 King 24.1; 2 Chron 36.5–7.

attacked Jerusalem. [2] The Lord let Nebuchadnezzar capture Jehoiakim and take away some of the things used in God's temple. And when the king returned to Babylonia,* he put these things in the temple of his own god.

[3] One day the king ordered Ashpenaz, his highest palace official, to choose some young men from the royal family of Judah and from other leading Jewish families. [4] The king said, "They must be healthy, handsome, clever, wise, educated, and fit to serve in the royal palace. Teach them how to speak and write our language [5] and give them the same food and wine that I am served. Train them for three years, and then they can become court officials."

[6] Four of the young Jews chosen were Daniel, Hananiah, Mishael, and Azariah, all from the tribe of Judah. [7] But the king's official gave them Babylonian names: Daniel became Belteshazzar, Hananiah became Shadrach, Mishael became Meshach, and Azariah became Abednego.

[8] Daniel made up his mind to eat and drink only what God approved for his food to eat. And he asked the king's chief official for permission not to eat the food and wine served in the royal palace. [9] God made the official friendly and kind to Daniel. [10] But the man still told him, "The king has decided what you must eat and drink. And I am afraid he will kill me, if you eat something else and end up looking worse than the other young men."

[11] The king's official had put a guard in charge of Daniel and his three friends. So Daniel said to the guard, [12] "For the next ten days, let us have only vegetables and water at mealtimes. [13] When the ten days are up, compare how we look with the other young men, and decide what to do with us." [14] The guard agreed to do what Daniel had asked.

[15] Ten days later, Daniel and his friends looked healthier and better than the young men who had been served food from the royal palace. [16] After this, the guard let them eat vegetables instead of the rich food and wine.

[17] God made the four young men clever and wise. They read a lot of books and became well educated. Daniel could also tell the meaning of dreams and visions.

[18] At the end of the three-year period set by King Nebuchadnezzar, his chief palace official brought all the young men to him. [19] The king interviewed them and discovered that none of the others were as outstanding as Daniel, Hananiah, Mishael, and Azariah. So they were given positions in the royal court. [20] From then on, whenever the king asked for advice, he found their wisdom was ten times better than that of any of his other advisers and magicians. [21] Daniel served there until the first year of King Cyrus.*

King Nebuchadnezzar's dream

CHAPTER 2

[1] During the second year that Nebuchadnezzar was king, he had such horrible nightmares that he could not sleep. [2] So he called in his counsellors, advisers, magicians, and wise men, [3] and said, "I am disturbed by a dream that I don't understand, and I want you to explain it."

[4] They answered in Aramaic,* "Your Majesty, we hope you live for ever! We are your servants. Please tell us your dream, and we will explain what it means."

[5] But the king replied, "No! I have made up my mind. If you don't tell me both the dream and its meaning, you will be chopped to pieces and your houses will be torn down. [6] However, if you do tell me both the dream and its meaning, you will be greatly rewarded and highly honoured. Now tell me the dream and explain what it means."

[7] "Your Majesty," they said, "if you will only tell us your dream, we will interpret it for you."

[8] The king replied, "You're just stalling for time, [9] because you know what's going to happen if you don't come up with the answer. You've decided to make up a pack of lies, hoping I might change my mind. Now tell me the dream, and that will prove that you can interpret it."

[10] His advisers explained, "Your Majesty, you are demanding the impossible! No king, not even the most famous and powerful, has ever ordered his advisers, magicians, or wise men to do such a thing. [11] It can't be done, except by the gods, and they don't live here on earth."

See also: 1.2–4: 2 King 20.17,18; 24.10–16; 2 Chron 36.10; Isa 39.7,8.

*1.21 first year of King Cyrus: 539 BC.
*2.4 Aramaic: Chapters 2.4–7.28 are written in Aramaic, a language closely related to Hebrew.

12-13 This made the king so angry that he gave orders for every wise man in Babylonia to be put to death, including Daniel and his three friends.

God tells Nebuchadnezzar's dream to Daniel

14 Arioch was the king's official in charge of putting the wise men to death. He was on his way to have it done, when Daniel very wisely went to him 15 and asked, "Why did the king give such cruel• orders?" After Arioch explained what had happened, 16 Daniel rushed off and said to the king, "If you will just give me some time, I'll explain your dream."

17 Daniel returned home and told his three friends. 18 Then he said, "Pray that the God who rules from heaven will be merciful and explain this mystery, so that we and the others won't be put to death." 19 In a vision one night, Daniel was shown the dream and its meaning. Then he praised the God who rules from heaven:

20 "Our God, your name
will be praised
for ever and for ever.
You are all-powerful,
and you know everything.
21 You control human events —
you give rulers their power
and take it away,
and you are the source
of wisdom and knowledge.

22 "You explain deep mysteries,
because even the dark
is light to you.
23 You are the God
who was worshipped
by my ancestors.
Now I thank you and praise you
for making me wise
and telling me the king's dream,
together with its meaning."

Daniel interprets the dream

24 Daniel went back to Arioch, the official in charge of executing the wise men. Daniel said, "Don't kill these men! Take me to the king, and I will explain the meaning of his dream."

25 Arioch rushed Daniel to the king and announced, "Your Majesty, I have found out that one of the men brought here from Judah can explain your dream."

26 The king asked Daniel,• "Can you tell me my dream and what it means?"

27 Daniel answered:

Your Majesty, not even the cleverest person in all the world can do what you are demanding. 28-29 But the God who rules from heaven can explain mysteries. And while you were sleeping, he showed you what will happen in the future. 30 However, you must realize that these mysteries weren't explained to me because I am cleverer than everyone else. Instead, it was done so that you would understand what you have seen.

31 Your Majesty, what you saw standing in front of you was a huge and terrifying statue, shining brightly. 32 Its head was made of gold, its chest and arms were silver, and from its waist down to its knees, it was bronze. 33 From there to its ankles it was iron, and its feet were a mixture of iron and clay.

34 As you watched, a stone was cut from a mountain — but not by human hands. The stone struck the feet, completely shattering the iron and clay. 35 Then the iron, the clay, the bronze, the silver, and the gold were crushed and blown away without a trace, like husks of wheat at threshing time. But the stone became a tremendous mountain that covered the entire earth.

36 That was the dream, and now I'll tell you what it means. 37 Your Majesty, you are the greatest of kings, and God has highly honoured you with power 38 over all humans, animals, and birds. You are the head of gold. 39 After you are gone, another kingdom will rule, but it won't be as strong. Then it will be followed by a kingdom of bronze that will rule the whole world. 40 Next, a kingdom of iron will come to power, crushing and shattering everything.•

41-42 This fourth kingdom will be divided — it will be both strong and brittle, just as you saw that the feet and toes were a mixture of iron and clay. 43 This kingdom will be the result of a marriage between kingdoms, but it will crumble, just as iron and clay don't stick together.

44-45 During the time of those kings, the God who rules from heaven will set up an eternal kingdom that will never fall. It will be like the stone that was cut from the mountain, but not by human hands — the stone that crushed the iron, bronze, clay, silver, and gold. Your Majesty, in your dream the great God has told you what is going to happen, and you can trust this interpretation.

Daniel is promoted

46 King Nebuchadnezzar bowed low to the ground and worshipped Daniel. Then he gave orders for incense to be burnt and a sacrifice of grain to be offered in honour of Daniel. 47 The king said, "Now I know that your God is above all other gods and kings, because he gave you the power to explain this mystery." 48 The king then presented Daniel with a lot of gifts; he promoted him to governor of Babylon Province and put him in charge of the other wise men. 49 At Daniel's request, the king appointed Shadrach, Meshach, and Abednego to high positions in Babylon Province, and he let Daniel stay on as a palace official.

God rescues Shadrach, Meshach, and Abednego

CHAPTER 3

King Nebuchadnezzar's gold statue

1 King Nebuchadnezzar ordered a gold statue to be built twenty-seven metres high and nearly three metres wide. He had it set up in Dura Valley near the city of Babylon, 2 and he commanded his governors, advisers, treasurers, judges, and his other officials to come from everywhere in his kingdom to the dedication of the statue. 3 So all of them came and stood in front of it.

4 Then an official stood up and announced:

People of every nation and race, now listen to the king's command! 5 Trumpets, flutes, harps, and all other kinds of musical instruments will soon start playing. When you hear the music, you must bow down and worship the statue that King Nebuchadnezzar has set up. 6 Anyone who refuses will at once be thrown into a flaming furnace.

7 As soon as the people heard the music, they bowed down and worshipped the gold statue that the king had set up.

8 Some Babylonians used this as a chance to accuse the Jews to King Nebuchadnezzar. 9 They said, "Your Majesty, we hope you live for ever! 10 You commanded everyone to bow down and worship the gold statue when the music played. 11 And you said that anyone who did not bow down and worship it would be thrown into a flaming furnace. 12 Sir, you appointed three men to high positions in Babylon Province, but they have disobeyed

you. Those Jews, Shadrach, Meshach, and Abednego, refuse to worship your gods and the statue you have set up."

13 King Nebuchadnezzar was furious. So he sent for the three young men and said, 14 "I hear that you refuse to worship my gods and the gold statue I have set up. 15 Now I am going to give you one more chance. If you bow down and worship the statue when you hear the music, everything will be all right. But if you don't, you will at once be thrown into a flaming furnace. No god can save you from me."

16 The three men replied, "Your Majesty, we don't need to defend ourselves. 17 The God we worship can save us from you and your flaming furnace. 18 But even if he doesn't, we still won't worship your gods and the gold statue you have set up."

19 Nebuchadnezzar's face twisted with anger at the three men. And he ordered the furnace to be heated seven times hotter than usual. 20 Next, he commanded some of his strongest soldiers to tie up the men and throw them into the flaming furnace. 21-23 The king wanted it done at that very moment. So the soldiers tied up Shadrach, Meshach, and Abednego and threw them into the flaming furnace with all their clothes still on, including their turbans. The fire was so hot that flames leaped out and killed the soldiers.

24 Suddenly the king jumped up and shouted, "Weren't only three men tied up and thrown into the fire?"

"Yes, Your Majesty," the people answered.

25 "But I see four men walking around in the fire," the king replied. "None of them is tied up or harmed, and the fourth one looks like a god."

26 Nebuchadnezzar went closer to the flaming furnace and said to the three young men, "You servants of the Most High God, come out at once!"

They came out, 27 and the king's high officials, governors, and advisers all crowded around them. The men were not burnt, and their hair wasn't scorched, and their clothes didn't even smell of smoke. 28 King Nebuchadnezzar said:

Praise their God for sending an angel to rescue his servants! They trusted their God and refused to obey my commands. Yes, they chose to die rather than to worship or serve any god except their own. 29 And I won't allow people of any nation or race to say anything against their God. Anyone who does will be chopped up and their houses will be torn down, because no other god has such great power to save.

³⁰ After this happened, the king appointed Shadrach, Meshach, and Abednego to even higher positions in Babylon Province.

Nebuchadnezzar loses his kingdom for seven years

CHAPTER 4

King Nebuchadnezzar's letter about his second dream

¹ King Nebuchadnezzar sent the following letter to the people of all nations and races on the earth:

Greetings to all of you! ² I am glad to tell about the wonderful miracles God Most High has done for me. ³ His miracles are mighty and marvellous. He will rule for ever, and his kingdom will never end.

⁴ I was enjoying a time of peace and prosperity, ⁵ when suddenly I had some horrifying dreams and visions. ⁶ Then I commanded every wise man in Babylonia to appear in my court, so they could explain the meaning of my dream. ⁷ After they arrived, I told them my dream, but they were not able to say what it meant. ⁸ Finally, a young man named Daniel came in, and I told him the dream. The holy gods had given him special powers, and I had renamed him Belteshazzar after my own god.

⁹ I said, "Belteshazzar, not only are you the wisest of all advisers and counsellors, but the holy gods have given you special powers to solve the most difficult mysteries. So listen to what I dreamed and tell me what it means:

¹⁰ In my sleep I saw a very tall tree in the centre of the world. ¹¹ It grew stronger and higher, until it reached to heaven and could be seen from anywhere on earth.

¹² It was covered with leaves and heavy with fruit — enough for all nations. Wild animals enjoyed its shade, birds nested in its branches, and all creatures on earth lived on its fruit.

¹³ "While I was in bed, having this vision, a holy angel• came down from heaven ¹⁴ and shouted:

'Chop down the tree and cut off its branches; strip off its leaves and scatter its fruit. Make the animals leave its shade and send the birds flying from its branches.

¹⁵ But leave its stump and roots in the ground, surrounded by grass and held by chains of iron and bronze.

'Make sure that this ruler lives like the animals out in the open fields, unprotected from the dew.

¹⁶ Give him the mind of a wild animal for seven long years.•

¹⁷ This punishment is given at the command of the holy angels.•

It will show to all who live that God Most High controls all kingdoms and chooses for their rulers persons of humble birth.'

¹⁸ "Daniel,• that was the dream that none of the wise men in my kingdom were able to understand. But I am sure that you will understand what it means, because the holy gods have given you some special powers."

¹⁹ For a while, Daniel• was terribly confused and worried by what he was thinking. But I said, "Don't be bothered either by the dream or by what it means." Daniel replied:

Your Majesty, I wish the dream had been against your enemies. ²⁰ You saw a tree that grew so big and strong that it reached up to heaven and could be seen from anywhere on earth. ²¹ Its leaves were beautiful, and it produced enough fruit for all living creatures; animals lived in its shade, and birds nested in its branches. ²² Your

Majesty, that tree is you. Your glorious reputation has reached heaven, and your kingdom covers the earth.

²³ Then you saw a holy angel* come down from heaven and say, "Chop down the tree and destroy it! But leave its stump and roots in the ground, fastened there by a chain of iron and bronze. Let it stay for seven years* out in the field with the wild animals, unprotected from the dew."

²⁴ Your Majesty, God Most High has sent you this message, and it means ²⁵ that you will be forced to live with the wild animals, far away from humans. You will eat grass like a wild animal and live outdoors for seven years,* until you learn that God Most High controls all earthly kingdoms and chooses their rulers. ²⁶ But he gave orders not to disturb the stump and roots. This is to show that you will be king once again, after you learn that the God who rules from heaven is in control. ²⁷ Your Majesty, please be willing to do what I say. Turn from your sins and start living right; have mercy on those who are ill-treated. Then all will go well with you for a long time.

The rest of Nebuchadnezzar's letter about his second dream

²⁸⁻³⁰ About twelve months later, I was walking on the flat roof of my royal palace and admiring the beautiful city of Babylon, when these things started happening to me. I was saying to myself, "Just look at this wonderful capital city that I have built by my own power and for my own glory!"

³¹ But before I could finish speaking, a voice from heaven interrupted:

King Nebuchadnezzar, this kingdom is no longer yours. You will be forced to live with the wild animals, away from people. For seven years* you will eat grass, as though you were an ox, until you learn that God Most High is in control of all earthly kingdoms and that he is the one who chooses their rulers.

³³ This was no sooner said than done — I was forced to live like a wild animal; I ate grass and was unprotected from the dew. As time went by, my hair grew longer than eagle feathers, and my fingernails looked like the claws of a bird.

³⁴ Finally, I prayed to God in heaven, and my mind was healed. Then I said:

"I praise and honour
God Most High.
He lives for ever,
and his kingdom
will never end.
³⁵ To him the nations
are far less than nothing;
God controls the stars in the sky
and everyone on this earth.
When God does something,
we cannot change it
or even ask why."

³⁶ At that time my mind was healed, and once again I became the ruler of my glorious kingdom. My advisers and officials returned to me, and I had greater power than ever before. ³⁷ That's why I say:

"Praise and honour the King
who rules from heaven!
Everything he does
is honest and fair,
and he can shatter the power
of those who are proud."

King Belshazzar and the writing on the wall

CHAPTER 5

King Belshazzar's banquet

¹ One evening, King Belshazzar gave a great banquet for a thousand of his highest officials, and he drank wine with them. ² He got drunk and ordered his servants to bring in the gold and silver cups that his father Nebuchadnezzar* had taken from the temple in Jerusalem. Belshazzar wanted the cups, so that he and all his wives and officials could drink from them.

³⁻⁴ When the gold cups were brought in, everyone at the banquet drank from them and praised their idols made of gold, silver, bronze, iron, wood, and stone.

⁵ Suddenly a human hand was seen writing on the plaster wall of the palace. The hand was just behind the lampstand, and the king could see it writing. ⁶ He was so frightened that his face turned pale, his knees started shaking, and his legs became weak.

---

*5.2 his father Nebuchadnezzar: Belshazzar was actually the son of King Nabonidus, who was from another family. But in ancient times, it was possible to refer to a previous king as the "father" of the present king.

⁷ The king called in his advisers, who claimed they could talk with the spirits of the dead and understand the meanings found in the stars. He told them, "The man who can read this writing and tell me what it means will become the third most powerful man in my kingdom. He will wear robes of royal purple and a gold chain around his neck."

⁸ All of King Belshazzar's highest officials came in, but not one of them could read the writing or tell what it meant, ⁹ and they were completely puzzled. Now the king was more afraid than ever before, and his face turned white as a ghost.

¹⁰ When the queen heard the king and his officials talking, she came in and said:

Your Majesty, I hope you live for ever! Don't be afraid or look so pale. ¹¹ In your kingdom there is a man who has been given special powers by the holy gods. When your father Nebuchadnezzar was king, this man was known to be as clever, intelligent, and wise as the gods themselves. Your father put him in charge of all who claimed they could talk with the spirits or understand the meanings in the stars or tell about the future. ¹² He also changed the man's name from Daniel to Belteshazzar. Not only is he wise and intelligent, but he can explain dreams and riddles and solve difficult problems. Send for Daniel, and he will tell you what the writing means.

¹³ When Daniel was brought in, the king said:

So you are Daniel, one of the captives my father brought back from Judah! ¹⁴ I was told that the gods have given you special powers and that you are intelligent and very wise. ¹⁵ Neither my advisers nor the men who talk with the spirits of the dead could read this writing or tell me what it means. ¹⁶ But I have been told that you understand everything and that you can solve difficult problems. Now then, if you can read this writing and tell me what it means, you will become the third most powerful man in my kingdom. You will wear royal purple robes and have a gold chain around your neck.

¹⁷ Daniel answered:

Your Majesty, I will read the writing and tell you what it means. But you may keep your gifts or give them to someone else. ¹⁸ Sir, the Most High God made your father a great and powerful man and brought him

much honour and glory. ¹⁹ God did such great things for him that people of all nations and races shook with fear.

Your father had the power of life or death over everyone, and he could honour or ruin anyone he chose. ²⁰ But when he became proud and stubborn, his glorious kingdom was taken from him. ²¹ His mind became like that of an animal, and he was forced to stay away from people and live with wild donkeys. Your father ate grass like an ox, and he slept outside where his body was soaked with dew. He was forced to do this until he learnt that the Most High God rules all kingdoms on earth and chooses their kings.

²² King Belshazzar, you knew all this, but you still refused to honour the Lord who rules from heaven. ²³ Instead, you turned against him and ordered the cups from his temple to be brought here, so that you and your wives and officials could drink wine from them. You praised idols made of silver, gold, bronze, iron, wood, and stone, even though they cannot see or hear or think. You refused to worship the God who gives you breath and controls everything you do. ²⁴ That's why he sent the hand to write this message on the wall.

²⁵⁻²⁸ The words written there are *mene*, which means "numbered", *tekel*, which means "weighed", and *parsin*,ᵇ which means "divided". God has numbered the days of your kingdom and has brought it to an end. He has weighed you on his balance scales, and you fall short of what it takes to be king. So God has divided your kingdom between the Medes and the Persians.

²⁹ Belshazzar gave a command for Daniel to be made the third most powerful man in his kingdom and to be given a purple robe and a gold chain.

³⁰ That same night, the king was killed. ³¹ Then Darius the Mede, who was sixty-two years old, took over his kingdom.

God rescues Daniel from the pit of lions

CHAPTER 6

¹ Darius divided his kingdom into a hundred and twenty states and placed a governor in charge of each one. ² In order to make sure that his government was run properly, Darius put three other officials in charge of the

governors. One of these officials was Daniel. ³ And he did his work so much better than the other governors and officials that the king decided to let him govern the whole kingdom.

⁴ The other men tried to find something wrong with the way Daniel did his work for the king. But they could not accuse him of anything wrong, because he was honest and faithful and did everything he was supposed to do. ⁵ Finally, they said to one another, "We will never be able to bring any charge against Daniel, unless it has to do with his religion."

⁶ They all went to the king and said:

Your Majesty, we hope you live for ever! ⁷ All of your officials, leaders, advisers, and governors agree that you should make a law forbidding anyone to pray to any god or human except you for the next thirty days. Everyone who disobeys this law must be thrown into a pit of lions. ⁸ Order this to be written and then sign it, so it cannot be changed, just as no written law of the Medes and Persians can be changed."

⁹ So King Darius made the law and had it written down.

¹⁰ Daniel heard about the law, but when he returned home, he went upstairs and prayed in front of the window that faced Jerusalem. In the same way that he had always done, he knelt down in prayer three times a day, giving thanks to God.

¹¹ The men who had spoken to the king watched Daniel and saw him praying to his God for help. ¹² They went back to the king and said, "Didn't you make a law that forbids anyone to pray to any god or human except you for the next thirty days? And doesn't the law say that everyone who disobeys it will be thrown into a pit of lions?"

"Yes, that's the law I made," the king agreed. "And just like all written laws of the Medes and Persians, it cannot be changed."

¹³ The men then told the king, "That Jew named Daniel, who was brought here as a captive, refuses to obey you or the law that you ordered to be written. And he still prays to his god three times a day." ¹⁴ The king was really upset to hear about this, and for the rest of the day he tried to think how he could save Daniel.

¹⁵ At sunset the men returned and said, "Your Majesty, remember that no written law

of the Medes and Persians can be changed, not even by the king."

¹⁶ So Darius ordered Daniel to be brought out and thrown into a pit of lions. But he said to Daniel, "You have been faithful to your God, and I pray that he will rescue you."

¹⁷ A stone was rolled over the pit, and it was sealed. Then Darius and his officials stamped the seal to show that no one should let Daniel out. ¹⁸ All night long the king could not sleep. He did not eat anything, and he would not let anyone come in to entertain him.

¹⁹ At daybreak the king got up and ran to the pit. ²⁰ He was anxious and shouted, "Daniel, you were faithful and served your God. Was he able to save you from the lions?"

²¹ Daniel answered, "Your Majesty, I hope you live for ever! ²² My God knew that I was innocent, and he sent an angel to keep the lions from eating me. Your Majesty, I have never done anything to hurt you."

²³ The king was relieved to hear Daniel's voice, and he gave orders for him to be taken out of the pit. Daniel's faith in his God had kept him from being harmed. ²⁴ And the king ordered the men who had brought charges against Daniel to be thrown into the pit, together with their wives and children. But before they even reached the bottom, the lions ripped them to pieces.

²⁵ King Darius then sent this message to all people of every nation and race in the world:

"Greetings to all of you! ²⁶ I command everyone
      in my kingdom
   to worship and honour
      the God of Daniel.
He is the living God,
   the one who lives for ever.
His power and his kingdom
   will never end.
²⁷ He rescues people
   and sets them free
      by working great miracles.
Daniel's God has rescued him
   from the power of the lions."

²⁸ All went well for Daniel while Darius was king, and even when Cyrus the Persian ruled.*

*6.28 Cyrus the Persian ruled: 539–530 BC.

Daniel's vision of four beasts

CHAPTER 7

1-2 Daniel wrote:

In the first year of King Belshazzar* in Babylonia, I had some dreams and visions while I was asleep one night, and I wrote them down.

The four winds were stirring up the mighty sea, ³ when suddenly four powerful beasts came out of the sea. Each beast was different. ⁴ The first was like a lion with the wings of an eagle. As I watched, its wings were pulled off. Then it was lifted to an upright position and made to stand on two feet, just like a human, and it was given a human mind.

⁵ The second beast looked like a bear standing on its hind legs.♦ It held three ribs in its teeth, and it was told, "Attack! Eat all the flesh you want."

⁶ The third beast was like a leopard — except that it had four wings and four heads. It was given authority to rule.

⁷ The fourth beast was stronger and more terrifying than the others. Its huge teeth were made of iron, and what it didn't grind with its teeth, it smashed with its feet. It was different from the others, and it had horns on its head — ten of them. ⁸ Just as I was thinking about these horns, a smaller horn appeared, and three of the other horns were pulled up by the roots to make room for it. This horn had the eyes of a human and a mouth that spoke with great pride.

Judgment

Daniel wrote:

⁹ Thrones were set up
    while I was watching,
and the Eternal God♦
    took his place.
His clothing and his hair
    were white as snow.
His throne was a blazing fire
    with fiery wheels,
¹⁰ and flames were dashing out
    from all around him.
Countless thousands

were standing there
    to serve him.
The time of judgment began,
    and the books* were opened.

¹¹ I watched closely to see what would happen to this smaller horn because of the arrogant things it was saying. Then before my very eyes, the fourth beast was killed and its body destroyed by fire. ¹² The other three beasts had their authority taken from them, but they were allowed to live a while longer.♦ ¹³ As I continued to watch the vision that night,

I saw what looked like
    a son of man♦
coming with the clouds of heaven,
    and he was presented
        to the Eternal God.♦
¹⁴ He was crowned king
    and given power and glory,
so that all people
    of every nation and race
        would serve him.
He will rule for ever,
    and his kingdom is eternal,
        never to be destroyed.

The meaning of Daniel's vision

¹⁵ Daniel wrote:

I was terrified by these visions, and I didn't know what to think. ¹⁶ So I asked one of those standing there, and he explained, ¹⁷ "The four beasts are four earthly kingdoms. ¹⁸ But God Most High will give his kingdom to his chosen ones, and it will be theirs for ever and ever."

¹⁹ I wanted to know more about the fourth beast,* because it was so different and much more terrifying than the others. What was the meaning of its iron teeth and bronze claws and of its feet that smashed what the teeth and claws had not ground and crushed? ²⁰ I also wanted to know more about all ten of those horns on its head. I especially wanted to know more about the one that took the place of three of the

---

*7.10 books: Containing the record of the good and evil that each person has done.
*7.16 one of those standing there: Possibly an angel sent to interpret the visions or one of those thousands mentioned in verse 10.
*7.19 fourth beast: See verses 7,8.
See also: 7.13: Matt 24.30; 26.64; Mark 13.26; 14.62; Luke 21.27; Rev 1.7,13; 14.14. 7.14: Rev 11.15.
7.18: Rev 22.5.

---

*7.1,2 first year of King Belshazzar: 554 BC.
See also: 7.3: Rev 13.1; 17.8. 7.4–6: Rev 13.2.
7.7: Rev 12.3; 13.1. 7.8: Rev 13.5,6. 7.9: a Rev 20.4;
b Rev 1.14. 7.10: a Rev 5.11; b Rev 20.12.

others — the horn that had eyes and spoke with arrogance and seemed greater than the others. 21 While I was looking, this horn attacked God's chosen ones and was winning the battle. 22 Then God Most High, the Eternal God,* came and judged in favour of his chosen ones, because the time had arrived for them to be given the kingdom.

23 Then I was told
by the one standing there:
"The fourth beast
will be a fourth kingdom
to appear on earth.
It will be different
from all the others —
it will trample the earth
and crush it to pieces.
24 All ten of those horns are kings
who will come from this kingdom,
and one more will follow.
This horn will be different
from the others,
and it will conquer
three other kings.

25 "This king will speak evil
of God Most High,
and he will be cruel
to God's chosen ones.
He will try to change God's Law
and the sacred seasons.
And he will be able to do this
for a time, two times,
and half a time.*

26 But he will finally be judged,
and his kingdom
completely destroyed.

27 "Then the greatest kingdom of all
will be given
to the chosen ones
of God Most High.
His kingdom will be eternal,
and all others will serve
and obey him."

28 That was what I saw and heard. I turned pale with fear and kept it all to myself.

Daniel's vision of a ram and a goat

CHAPTER 8

1 Daniel wrote:

In the third year of King Belshazzar of Babylonia,* I had a second vision 2 in which I was in Susa, the chief city of Babylonia's Elam Province. I was beside the River* Ulai, 3 when I looked up and saw a ram standing there with two horns on its head — both of them were long, but the second one was longer than the first. 4 The ram went charging towards the west, the north, and the south. No other animals were strong enough to oppose him, and nothing could save them from his power. So he did as he pleased and became even more powerful.

5 I kept on watching and saw a goat come from the west and charge across the entire earth, without even touching the ground. Between his eyes was a powerful horn,* 6 and with tremendous anger the goat started towards the ram that I had seen beside the river. 7 The goat was so fierce that its attack broke both horns of the ram, leaving him powerless. Then the goat trampled on the ram, and no one could do anything to help. 8 After this, the goat became even more powerful. But at the peak of his power, his mighty horn was broken, and four other mighty horns took its place — one pointing to the north and one to the east, one to the south and one to the west.

9 A little horn came from one of these, and its power reached to the south, to the east, and even to the holy land.* 10 It became so strong that it attacked the stars in the sky, which were heaven's army.* Then it threw some of them down to the earth and trampled on them. 11–12 It humiliated heaven's army and dishonoured its leader* by keeping him from offering the daily sacrifices. In fact, it was so terrible that it even disgraced the temple and wiped out true worship. It also did everything else it wanted to do.

13 Then one of the holy angels asked another, "When will the daily sacrifices be offered again? What about this horrible

---

*8.1 third year . . . Babylonia: 552 BC, two years after the first vision (see 7.1,2).

*8.10 heaven's army: In verses 10–13 the Hebrew word translated "heaven's army" may also mean "God's people."

See also: 8.10: Rev 12.4.

See also: 7.21: Rev 13.7. 7.22: Rev 20.4. 7.24: Rev 17.12. 7.25: Rev 12.14; 13.5,6. 7.27: a Rev 20.4; b Rev 22.5.

rebellion? When will the temple and heaven's army no longer be trampled in the dust?"

14 The other answered, "It will be two thousand three hundred evenings and mornings before the temple is dedicated and in use again."

Gabriel interprets the vision

15 Daniel wrote:

I was trying to understand the meaning of the vision, when someone suddenly appeared there beside me. 16 And from beside the River* Ulai, a voice like that of a human said, "Gabriel, help him understand the vision."

17 Gabriel came over, and I fell to the ground in fear. Then he said, "You are merely a human, but you need to understand that this vision is about the end of time."

18 While he was speaking, I fell face down in a deep sleep. But he lifted me to my feet 19 and said:

Listen, and I will tell you what will happen at the end of time, when God has chosen to show his anger. 20 The two horns of the ram are the kings of Media and Persia, 21 the goat is the kingdom of Greece, and the powerful horn between his eyes is the first of its kings. 22 After this horn is broken, four other kingdoms will appear, but they won't be as strong.

23 When these rulers have become as evil as possible, their power will end, and then a king who is dangerous and cannot be trusted will appear. 24 He will gain strength, but not on his own, and he will cause terrible destruction. He will wipe out powerful leaders and God's people as well. 25 His deceitful lies will make him so successful, that he will think he is really great. Suddenly he will kill many people, and he will even attack God, the Supreme Ruler. But God will crush him!

26 This vision about the evenings and mornings is true, but these things won't happen for a long time, so don't tell it to others.

27 After this, I was so worn out and weak that it was several days before I could get out of bed and go about my duties for the king. I was disturbed by this vision that made no sense to me.

Daniel prays for his people

CHAPTER 9

1-2 Daniel wrote:

Some years later, Darius the Mede,* who was the son of Xerxes,* had become king of Babylonia. And during his first year as king, I found out from studying the writings of the prophets that the LORD had said to Jeremiah, "Jerusalem will lie in ruins for seventy years."* 3-4 Then, to show my sorrow, I went without eating and dressed in sackcloth* and sat in ashes. I confessed my sins and earnestly prayed to the LORD my God:

Our Lord, you are a great and fearsome God, and you faithfully keep your agreement with those who love and obey you. 5 But we have sinned terribly by rebelling against you and rejecting your laws and teachings. 6 We have ignored the message your servants the prophets spoke to our kings, our leaders, our ancestors, and everyone else.

7 Everything you do is right, our Lord. But still we suffer public disgrace because we have been unfaithful and have sinned against you. This includes all of us, both far and near — the people of Judah, Jerusalem, and Israel, as well as those you dragged away to foreign lands, 8 and even our kings, our officials, and our ancestors. 9 LORD God, you are merciful and forgiving, even though we have rebelled against you 10 and rejected your teachings that came to us from your servants the prophets.

11 Everyone in Israel has stubbornly refused to obey your laws, and so these curses written by your servant Moses have fallen upon us. 12 You warned us and our leaders that Jerusalem would suffer the worst disaster in human history, and you did exactly as you had threatened. 13 We have not escaped any of the terrible curses written by Moses, and yet we have refused to beg you for mercy and to remind ourselves of how faithful you have always been. 14 And when you finally punished us with this horrible disaster, that was also the right thing to do, because we deserved it so much.

*9.1,2 Darius the Mede: See 5.31.
*9.1,2 seventy years: See Jeremiah 25.11–13; 29.10.
*9.3,4 sackcloth: A rough, dark-coloured cloth made from goat or camel hair and used to make grain sacks. It was worn in times of trouble or sorrow.

See also: 8.16: Luke 1.19,26.
See also: 9.2: Jer 25.11; 29.10.

15 Our Lord God, with your own mighty arm you rescued us from Egypt and made yourself famous to this very day, but we have sinned terribly. 16 In the past, you treated us with such kindness, that we now beg you to stop being so terribly angry with Jerusalem. After all, it is your chosen city built on your holy mountain, even though it has suffered public disgrace because of our sins and those of our ancestors.

17 I am your servant, Lord God, and I beg you to answer my prayers and bring honour to yourself by having pity on your temple that lies in ruins. 18 Please show mercy to your chosen city, not because we deserve it, but because of your great kindness.

19 Forgive us! Hurry and do something, not only for your city and your chosen people, but to bring honour to yourself.

The seventy weeks

Daniel wrote:

20 I was still confessing my sins and those of all Israel to the LORD my God, and I was praying for the good of his holy mountain,• 21 when Gabriel suddenly came flying in at the time of the evening sacrifice. This was the same Gabriel I had seen in my vision, 22 and he explained:

Daniel, I am here to help you understand the vision. 23 God thinks highly of you, and at the very moment you started praying, I was sent to give you the answer. 24 God has decided that for seventy weeks,• your people and your holy city must suffer as the price of their sins. Then evil will disappear, and justice will rule for ever; the visions and words of the prophets will come true, and a most holy place will be dedicated.•

25 You need to realize that from the command to rebuild Jerusalem until the coming of the Chosen Leader,• it will be seven weeks and another sixty-two weeks.• Streets will be built in Jerusalem, and a trench will be dug around the city for protection, but these will be difficult times.• 26 At the end of the sixty-two weeks,• the Chosen Leader• will be killed and left with nothing.

A foreign ruler and his army will sweep down like a mighty flood, leaving both the city and the temple in ruins, and war and

destruction will continue until the end, just as God has decided. 27 For one week• this foreigner• will make a firm agreement with many people, and halfway through this week,• he will end all sacrifices and offerings. Then the "Horrible Thing" that causes destruction will be put there. And it will stay there until the time God has decided to destroy this one who destroys.

Daniel has a vision beside the River Tigris

CHAPTER 10

1 In the third year• of Cyrus the king of Persia, a message came to Daniel• from God, and it was explained in a vision. The message was about a horrible war, and it was true. 2 Daniel wrote:

For three weeks I was in sorrow. 3 I ate no fine food or meat, I drank no wine, and I put no olive oil on my face or hair.• 4 Then, on the twenty-fourth day of the first month,• I was standing on the banks of the great River Tigris, 5 when I looked up and saw someone dressed in linen and wearing a solid gold belt.• 6 His body was like a precious stone,• his face like lightning, his eyes like flaming fires, his arms and legs like polished bronze, and his voice like the roar of a crowd. 7 Although the people who were with me did not see the vision, they became so frightened that they scattered and hid. 8 Only I saw this great vision. I became weak and pale, 9 and at the sound of his voice, I fell face down in a deep sleep.

10 He raised me to my hands and knees 11 and then said, "Daniel, your God thinks highly of you, and he has sent me. So stand up and pay close attention." I stood trembling, while the angel said:

12 Daniel, don't be afraid! God has listened to your prayers since the first day you humbly asked for understanding, and he has sent me here. 13 But the guardian angel• of Persia opposed me for twenty-one days.

•9.20 holy mountain: Jerusalem (see verse 16) or the temple.

See also: 9.21: Luke 1.19,26.

•10.1 third year: 536 BC.
•10.3 olive oil . . . hair: On special occasions, it was the custom to put olive oil on one's face and hair.
•10.4 first month: Nisan (also known as Abib), the first month of the Hebrew calendar, from about mid-March to mid-April.

See also: 9.27: Dan 11.31; 12.11; Matt 24.15; Mark 13.14. 10.5,6: Rev 1.13–15; 2.18; 19.12. 10.13: Rev 12.7.

Then Michael, who is one of the strongest guardian angels,' came to rescue me from the kings of Persia.' ¹⁴ Now I have come here to give you another vision about what will happen to your people in the future.

¹⁵ While this angel was speaking to me, I stared at the ground, speechless. ¹⁶ Then he appeared in human form and touched my lips. I said, "Sir, this vision has brought me great pain and has drained my strength. ¹⁷ I am merely your servant. How can I possibly speak with someone so powerful, when I am almost too weak to get my breath?"

¹⁸⁻¹⁹ The angel touched me a second time and said, "Don't be frightened! God thinks highly of you, and he intends this for your good, so be brave and strong."

At this, I regained my strength and replied, "Please speak! You have already made me feel much better." ²⁰ Then the angel said:

Now do you understand why I have come? Soon I must leave to fight against the guardian angel of Persia. Then after I have defeated him, the guardian angel of Greece will attack me. ²¹ I will tell you what is written in *The Book of Truth*. But first, you must realize that no one except Michael, the guardian angel of Israel, is on my side.

CHAPTER 11

¹ You also need to know that I protected and helped Darius the Mede* in his first year as king.

The angel's message to Daniel

Part one: the four kings and their successors

² What I am going to tell you is certain to happen. Four kings will rule Persia, one after the other, but the fourth one will become much richer than the others. In fact, his wealth will make him so powerful that he will turn everyone against the kingdom of Greece. ³ Then a mighty king will come to power and will be able to do whatever he pleases. ⁴ But suddenly his kingdom will be crushed and scattered to the four corners of the earth, where four more kingdoms will rise. But these won't be ruled by his descendants or be as powerful as his kingdom.

⁵ The king of the south will grow powerful. Then one of his generals will rebel and take over most of the kingdom. ⁶ Years later the southern kingdom and the northern kingdom will make a treaty, and the daughter of the king of the south will marry the king of the north. But she will lose her power. Then she, her husband, their child,' and the servants who came with her will all be killed.

After this, ⁷ one of her relatives will become the ruler of the southern kingdom. He will attack the army of the northern kingdom and capture its fortresses. ⁸ Then he will carry their idols to Egypt, together with their precious treasures of silver and gold, but it will be a long time before he attacks the northern kingdom again. Some years later ⁹ the king of the north will invade the southern kingdom, but he will be forced back to his own country.

¹⁰ The sons of the king of the north will gather a huge army that will sweep down like a roaring flood, reaching all the way to the fortress of the southern kingdom. ¹¹ But this will make the king of the south angry, and he will defeat this large army from the north. ¹² The king of the south will feel proud because of the many thousands he has killed. But his victories won't last long, ¹³ because the king of the north will gather a larger and more powerful army than ever before. Then in a few years, he will start invading other countries.

¹⁴ At this time many of your own people will try to make this vision come true by rebelling against the king of the south, but their rebellion will fail. ¹⁵ Then the army from the north will surround and capture a fortress in the south, and not even the most experienced troops of the southern kingdom will be able to make them retreat. ¹⁶ The king who invaded from the north will do as he pleases, and he will even capture and destroy the holy land.' ¹⁷ In fact, he will decide to invade the south with his entire army. Then he will attempt to make peace by giving the king of the south a bride from the northern kingdom, but this won't be successful.

¹⁸ Afterwards, this proud king of the north will invade and conquer many of the nations along the coast, but a military leader will defeat him and make him lose his pride. ¹⁹ He will retreat to his fortresses in his own country, but on the way he will be defeated and never again be seen.

*11.1 Darius the Mede: See 5.31.
See also: 10.21; Rev 12.7.

20 The next king of the north will try to collect taxes for the glory of his kingdom. However, he will come to a sudden end in some mysterious way, instead of in battle or because of someone's anger.

Part two: the evil king from the north

21 The successor of this king of the north will be a worthless nobody, who doesn't come from a royal family. He will suddenly appear and gain control of the kingdom by treachery. 22 Then he will destroy armies and remove God's chosen high priest. 23 He will make a treaty, but he will be deceitful and break it, even though he has only a few followers. 24 Without warning, he will successfully invade a wealthy province, which is something his ancestors never did. Then he will divide among his followers all of its treasures and property. But none of this will last very long.

25 He will gather a large and powerful army, and with great courage he will attack the king of the south. The king of the south will meet him with a much stronger army, but he will lose the battle, because he will be betrayed 26 by members of the royal court. He will be ruined, and most of his army will be slaughtered.

27 The two kings will meet around a table and tell evil lies to each other. But their plans will fail, because God has already decided what will happen. 28 Then the king of the north will return to his own country with great treasures. But on the way, he will attack the religion of God's people and do whatever else he pleases.

29 At the time God has decided, the king of the north will invade the southern kingdom again, but this time, things will be different. 30 Ships from the west will come to attack him, and he will be discouraged. Then he will start back to his own country and take out his anger on the religion of God's faithful people, while showing kindness to those who are unfaithful. 31 He will send troops to pollute the temple and the fortress, and he will stop the daily sacrifices. Then he will set up that "Horrible Thing" that causes destruction. 32 The king will use deceit to win followers from those who are unfaithful to God, but those who remain faithful will do everything possible to oppose him.

33 Wise leaders will instruct many of the people. But for a while, some of these leaders will either be killed with swords or burnt alive, or else robbed of their possessions and thrown into prison. 34 They will receive only a little help in their time of trouble, and many of their followers will be treacherous. 35 Some of those who are wise will suffer, so that God will make them pure and acceptable until the end, which will still come at the time he has decided.

36 This king will do as he pleases. He will proudly claim to be greater than any god and will insult the only true God. Indeed, he will be successful until God is no longer angry with his people. 37 This king will reject the gods his ancestors worshipped and the god preferred by women.* In fact, he will put himself above all gods 38 and worship only the so-called god of fortresses, who was unknown to his ancestors. And he will honour it with gold, silver, precious stones, and other costly gifts. 39 With the help of this foreign god, he will capture the strongest fortresses. Everyone who worships this god will be put in a position of power and rewarded with wealth and land.

Part three: the time of the end

40 At the time of the end, the king of the south will attack the kingdom of the north. But its king will rush out like a storm with war chariots, cavalry, and many ships. Indeed, his forces will flood one country after another, 41 and when they reach the holy land,* tens of thousands will be killed. But the countries of Edom and Moab and the ruler of Ammon* will escape.

42 The king of the north will invade many countries, including Egypt, 43 and he will take its rich treasures of gold and silver. He will also conquer Libya and Ethiopia.* 44 But he will be alarmed by news from the east and the north, and he will become furious and cause great destruction. 45 After this, he will set up camp between the Mediterranean Sea and Mount Zion. Then he will be destroyed, and no one will be able to save him.

*11.37 god preferred by women: Perhaps Tammuz or Adonis, which were popular among the women of that time.

*11.43 Ethiopia: The Hebrew text has "Cush", which was a region south of Egypt that included parts of the present countries of Ethiopia and Sudan.

See also: 11.31: Dan 9.27; 12.11; Matt 24.15; Mark 13.14.

See also: 11.36: a 2 Thes 2.3,4; b Rev 13.5,6.

CHAPTER 12

Part four: the dead will rise to life

¹ Michael, the chief of the angels, is the protector of your people, and he will come at a time of terrible suffering, the worst in all of history. And your people who have their names written in *The Book** will be protected. ² Many of those who lie dead in the ground will rise from death. Some of them will be given eternal life, and others will receive nothing but eternal shame and disgrace. ³ Everyone who has been wise will shine as bright as the sky above, and everyone who has led others to please God will shine like the stars.

⁴ Daniel, I now command you to keep the message of this book secret until the end of time, even though many people will go everywhere, searching for the knowledge to be found in it.*

The end of time

⁵ Daniel wrote:

I looked around and saw two other people — one on this side of the river and one on the other side. ⁶ The angel who had spoken to me was dressed in linen and was standing upstream from them.* So one of the two beside the river asked him, "How long before these amazing things happen?"

⁷ The angel then raised both hands towards heaven and said, "In the name of the God who lives for ever, I solemnly promise that it will be a time, two times, and half a time.* Everything will be over, when the suffering of God's holy people comes to an end."

⁸ I heard what the angel said, but I didn't understand. So I asked, "Sir, how will it all end?"

⁹ The angel in my vision then replied:

Daniel, go about your business, because the meaning of this message will remain secret until the end of time. ¹⁰ Many people will have their hearts and lives made pure

and clean, but those who are evil will keep on being evil and never understand. Only the wise will understand. ¹¹ There will be one thousand two hundred and ninety days from the time that the daily sacrifices are stopped, until someone sets up the "Horrible Thing" that causes destruction. ¹² God will bless everyone who patiently waits until one thousand three hundred and thirty-five days have gone by.

¹³ So, Daniel, be faithful until the end! You will rest, and at the end of time, you will rise from death to receive your reward.

See also: 12.11: Dan 9.27; 11.31; Matt 24.15; Mark 13.14.

Additional notes

•1.2 Babylonia: The Hebrew text has "Shinar", another name for Babylonia.

•2.15 cruel: Or "urgent".

•2.26 Daniel: Aramaic "Daniel whose name was Belteshazzar" (see 1.7).

•2.40 crushing . . . everything: Three ancient translations; Aramaic adds "and like iron crushing".

•3.25 a god: Aramaic, "a son of the gods".

•4.13 angel: The Aramaic text has "watcher", which may be some special class of angel.

•4.16 long years: Aramaic "times".

•4.17 angels: See the note at 4.13.

•4.18 Daniel: See the note at 2.26.

•4.19 Daniel: See the note at 2.26.

•4.23 angel: See the note at 4.13.

•4.25 years: See the note at 4.16.

•4.32 years: See the note at 4.16.

•5.25–28 mene . . . tekel . . . parsin: In the Aramaic text of verse 25, the words "mene, tekel, parsin," are used, and in verses 26–28 the words "mene, tekel, peres" (the singular of "parsin") are used. "Parsin" means "divided", but "peres" can mean either "divided" or "Persia".

•7.5 standing on its hind legs: Or "higher on one side than the other" or "with a paw lifted up".

•7.9 Eternal God: Aramaic "Ancient of Days".

•7.12 a while longer: Aramaic "for a time and a season".

•7.13 son of man: Or "human". In Aramaic "son of man" may mean a human or even "oneself" ("I" or "me"). Jesus often used the phrase "the Son of Man" when referring to himself.

•7.13 Eternal God: See the note at 7.9.

•7.22 Eternal God: See the note at 7.9.

•7.25 for . . . time: Or "for a year, two years, and half a year".

•8.2 River: Or "Gate".

•8.5 powerful horn: Hebrew "horn of vision".

•8.6 river: See the note at 8.2.

---

*12.1 The Book: Either the book with the names of God's people in it or the book with the record of the good and evil that people have done.

*12.6 angel . . . upstream from them: See 10.4–6.

*12.7 a time, two times, and half a time: Or "a year, two years, and half a year", that is, about 1260 days.

See also: 12.1: a Rev 12.7; b Matt 24.21; Mark 13.19; Rev 7.14; 12.7. **12.2:** Isa 26.19; Matt 25.46; John 5.29. **12.4:** Rev 22.10. **12.7:** a Rev 10.5; b Rev 12.14. **12.10:** Rev 22.11.

9.9 holy land: Hebrew "the lovely land".
9.11,12 leader: Hebrew "prince".
8.16 River: See the note at 8.2.
9.1,2 Xerxes: Hebrew "Ahasuerus".
9.24 seventy weeks: Or "seventy times seven years".
9.24 a most holy place will be dedicated: Or "God's Holy One will appear".
9.25 the Chosen Leader: Or "a chosen leader". In Hebrew the word "chosen" means "to pour oil (on someone's head)". In Old Testament times it was the custom to pour oil on a person's head when that person was chosen to be a priest or a king.
9.25 seven weeks and another sixty-two weeks: Or "seven times seven years and another sixty-two times seven years".
9.25 it will be seven . . . difficult times: Or "it will be seven weeks. Then streets will be built in Jerusalem, and a trench will be dug around the city for protection. But Jerusalem will have difficult times for sixty-two weeks."
9.26 sixty-two weeks: Or "sixty-two times seven years".
9.26 the Chosen Leader: See the note at 9.25.
9.26 left with nothing: Or "no one will take his place".
9.27 one week: Or "seven years".
9.27 this foreigner: Or "the Chosen Leader".
9.27 halfway through this week: Or "for half of this week of seven years."
10.1 Daniel: See the note at 2.26.
10.5 solid gold belt: Hebrew "belt of gold from Uphaz".
10.6 a precious stone: The Hebrew text has "beryl", which is green or bluish-green.
10.13 guardian angel: Hebrew "prince".
10.13 one of the strongest guardian angels: Hebrew "chief prince".
10.13 came . . . Persia: One possible meaning for the difficult Hebrew text.
11.6 their child: One Hebrew manuscript and two ancient translations; most Hebrew manuscripts "her father".
11.16 the holy land: See the note at 8.9.
11.41 the holy land: See the note at 8.9.
11.41 the ruler of Ammon: Or "what is left of Ammon".
12.4 even though . . . in it: One possible meaning for the difficult Hebrew text.

Hosea

A quick look at this book

Hosea was a prophet in the northern kingdom during its final years as a nation. In the first three chapters of this book, Hosea's family life became a living picture of the message he preached to his country. The Lord told Hosea to marry a prostitute, as a way of showing how unfaithful Israel had been. Then the Lord told Hosea what to name his children, and these names were reminders that Israel was going to be punished. But Hosea was told to love his unfaithful wife, and his love was to be a picture of the Lord's continuing love for unfaithful Israel.

The rest of the book emphasizes the agreement that the Lord had made with Israel. This agreement demanded that Israel and the Lord be loyal and faithful to each other. The Lord had always lived up to the agreement, but the people had broken it time after time. They had trusted their own military strength and the power of foreign countries, rather than depending on the Lord to protect their nation. And the people had worshipped other gods and trusted them to provide good crops and large herds of livestock.

In this book the Lord put Israel and Judah on trial and charged them with breaking their agreement with him. They were guilty and would be punished.

But the Lord still loved his people in spite of everything they had done. And so he promised to forgive them and bless them again after they learnt to be faithful to him:

> *Israel, you have rejected me,*
>   *but my anger is gone;*
> *I will heal you and love you*
>   *without limit.*

(14.4)

Hosea's family is a picture of the Lord's unfaithful people

CHAPTER 1

[1] I am Hosea son of Beeri. When Uzziah, Jotham, Ahaz, and Hezekiah were the kings

---

See also: **1.1:** a 2 King 15.1–7; 2 Chron 26.1–23; b 2 King 15.32–38; 2 Chron 27.1–8; c 2 King 16.1–20; 2 Chron 28.1–27; d 2 King 18.1–20.21; 2 Chron 29.1–32.33; e 2 King 14.23–29.

of Judah, and when Jeroboam son of Jehoash* was king of Israel,* the LORD spoke this message to me.

Hosea's family

2 The LORD said, "Hosea, Israel has betrayed me like an unfaithful wife.* Marry such a woman and have children by her." 3 So I married Gomer the daughter of Diblaim, and we had a son.

4 Then the LORD said, "Hosea, name your son Jezreel,* because I will soon punish the descendants of King Jehu of Israel for the murders he committed in Jezreel Valley.* I will destroy his kingdom, 5 and in Jezreel Valley I will break the power of Israel."

6 Later, Gomer had a daughter, and the LORD said, "Name her Lo-Ruhamah,* because I will no longer have mercy and forgive Israel. 7 But I am the LORD God of Judah, and I will have mercy and save Judah by my own power — not by wars and arrows or swords or cavalry."

8 After Gomer had stopped nursing Lo-Ruhamah, she had another son. 9 Then the LORD said, "Name him Lo-Ammi,* because these people are not mine, and I am not their God."

Hope for Israel

The LORD said:

10 Some day it will be impossible to count the people of Israel, because there will be as many of them as there are grains of sand along the seashore. They are now called "Not My People", but in the future they will be called "Children of the Living God". 11 Israel and Judah will unite and choose one leader. Then they will take back their land, and this will be a great day for Jezreel.*

CHAPTER 2

1 So let your brothers be called "My People" and your sisters be called "Shown Mercy".*

The LORD promises to punish Israel

2 Accuse! Accuse your mother!
    She is no longer my wife,
    and now I, the LORD,
    am not her husband.
Beg her to give up prostitution
    and stop being unfaithful,*
3 or I will strip her naked
    like the day she was born.
I will make her barren like a desert,
    and she will die of thirst.
4 You children are the result
    of her unfaithfulness,
    and I'll show you no pity.
5 Your mother was unfaithful.
    She was disgraceful and said,
    "I'll run after my lovers.
Everything comes from them —
    my food and drink,
    my linen and wool,
    my olive oil and wine."

6 I, the LORD, will build
    a fence of thorns
    to block her path.
7 She will run after her lovers,
    but not catch them;
    she will search,
    but not find them.
Then she will say, "I'll return
    to my first husband.
    Life was better then."
8 She didn't know that her grain,
    wine, and olive oil
    were gifts from me,
    as were the gold and silver
    she used in worshipping Baal.*

---

*1.1 kings of Judah . . . king of Israel: Uzziah (781–740 BC), Jotham (740–736), Ahaz (736–716), Hezekiah (716–687), and Jeroboam II (783–743).

*1.2 unfaithful wife: In some Canaanite religions of Old Testament times, young women were expected to have sex with the worshippers of their god before marriage. Such women were called "temple prostitutes". Many of the Israelite women did this same thing, and Hosea is told to marry one of them to show that the nation has turned from the LORD to worship idols.

*1.4 Jezreel: In Hebrew "Jezreel" means "God scatters (seed)". Here the name is used as a threat (meaning the LORD will punish Israel by scattering its people), while in verse 11 it is used as a promise (meaning the LORD will bless Israel by giving their nation many people, just as a big harvest comes when many seeds are scattered in a field).

*1.4 murders . . . Valley: Jehu murdered the wife and relatives of King Ahab (see 2 Kings 9.15—10.14).

*1.6 Lo-Ruhamah: In Hebrew "Lo-Ruhamah" means "No Mercy".

*1.9 Lo-Ammi: In Hebrew "Lo-Ammi" means "Not My People".

See also: 1.4: 2 King 10.11. 1.10: Rom 9.26.

*1.11 Jezreel: See the note at verse 4.

*2.1 My People . . . Shown Mercy: In Hebrew "My People" is "Ammi" and "Shown Mercy" is "Ruhamah" (see Lo-Ruhamah in 1.6 and Lo-Ammi in 1.9).

*2.2 prostitution . . . unfaithful: See the note at 1.2.

*2.8 Baal: A Canaanite god of fertility.

⁹ So I'll hold back the harvest
    of grain and grapes.
I'll take back
    my wool and my linen
    that cover her body.
¹⁰ Then I'll strip her naked
    in the sight of her lovers.*
    No one can rescue her.

¹¹ I'll stop Israel's celebrations —
    no more New Moon Festivals,
    Sabbaths, and other feasts.
¹² She said, "My lovers gave me
    vineyards and fig trees
    as payment* for sex."

Now I, the LORD, will ruin
    her vineyards and fig trees;
    they will become clumps of weeds
    eaten by wild animals.

¹³ I'll punish her for the days
    she worshipped Baal
    and burnt incense to him.
I'll punish her for the times
    she forgot about me
    and wore jewellery and rings
    to attract her lovers.
    I, the LORD, have spoken!

The LORD will help Israel

¹⁴ Israel, I, the LORD,
    will lure you into the desert
    and speak gently to you.
¹⁵ I will return your vineyards,
    and then Trouble Valley*
    will become Hopeful Valley.
You will say "Yes" to me
    as you did in your youth,
    when leaving Egypt.

¹⁶ I promise that from that day on, you will
call me your husband instead of your
master.* ¹⁷ I will no longer even let you
mention the names of those pagan gods that
you called "Master". ¹⁸ And I will agree to let
you live in peace — you will no longer be

attacked by wild animals and birds or by
weapons of war. ¹⁹ I will accept you as my
wife for ever, and instead of a bride price* I
will give you justice, fairness, love, kindness,
²⁰ and faithfulness. Then you will truly know
who I am.

²¹ I will command the sky to send rain on
the earth, ²² and it will produce grain, grapes,
and olives in Jezreel Valley. ²³ I will scatter
the seeds and show mercy to Lo-Ruhamah.*
I will say to Lo-Ammi,* "You are my people,"
and they will answer, "You are our God."

CHAPTER 3

God's love offers hope

¹ Once again the LORD spoke to me. And this
time he said, "Hosea, fall in love with an
unfaithful woman* who has a lover. Do this
to show that I love the people of Israel, even
though they worship idols and enjoy the
offering cakes made with fruit."

² So I paid fifteen pieces of silver and about
a hundred and fifty kilograms of grain for
such a woman. ³ Then I said, "Now you are
mine! You will have to remain faithful to me,
though it will be a long time before we sleep
together."

⁴ It will also be a long time before Israel has
a king or before sacrifices are offered at the
temple or before there is any way to get
guidance from God. ⁵ But later, Israel will turn
back to the LORD their God and to David their
king. At that time they will come to the LORD
with fear and trembling, and he will be good
to them.

The Lord accuses Israel, Judah, and their leaders

CHAPTER 4

Israel is unfaithful

¹ Israel, listen
    as the LORD accuses
    everyone in the land!

---

*2.15 **Trouble Valley**: Or "Achor Valley". The exact
location of the valley is unknown, but in Hebrew
"Achor" sounds like "Achan", who brought trouble on
Israel by disobeying the Lord (see Joshua 7.24–26).
*2.16 **husband . . . master**: In Hebrew the word
"master" is the same as the name of the god Baal. But
the LORD promises that his people will have a deep
personal relationship with him (like a devoted wife
and husband) rather than merely a legal tie (like a
wife and "master").
See also: 2.15: Josh 7.24–26.

*2.19 **bride price**: It was the custom for the husband
to pay his wife's parents a bride price. Instead of
money, the LORD will give much better benefits to
Israel.
*2.23 **Lo-Ruhamah**: See the note at 1.6.
*2.23 **Lo-Ammi**: See the note at 1.9.
*3.1 **unfaithful woman**: This may refer to Gomer, the
woman Hosea married (see 1.3), or it may refer to
another woman.
See also: 2.23: Rom 9.25; 1 Pet 2.10.

No one is faithful or loyal
or truly cares about God.
² Cursing, dishonesty, murder,
robbery, unfaithfulness —
these happen all the time.
Violence is everywhere.
³ And so your land is a desert.
Every living creature is dying —
people and wild animals,
birds and fish.

The LORD warns the priests

⁴ Don't accuse just anyone!
Not everyone is at fault.
My case is against you,
the priests.*
⁵ You and the prophets
will stumble day and night;
I'll silence your mothers.
⁶ You priests have rejected me,
and my people are destroyed
by refusing to obey.
Now I'll reject you and forget
your children, because you
have forgotten my Law.

⁷ By adding more of you priests,
you multiply the number
of people who sin.
Now I'll change your pride
into shame.
⁸ You encourage others to sin,
so you can stuff yourselves
on their sin offerings.

⁹ That's why I will punish
the people for their deeds,
just as I will punish
you priests.
¹⁰ Their food won't satisfy,
and having sex at pagan shrines
won't produce children.
My people have rebelled
¹¹ and have been unfaithful
to me, their LORD.

God condemns Israel's idolatry

My people, you are foolish
because of too much pleasure
and too much wine.
¹² You expect wooden idols
and other objects of wood
to give you advice.
Lusting for sex at pagan shrines
has made you unfaithful
to me, your God.
¹³ You offer sacrifices
on mountaintops and hills,

under oak trees, and wherever
good shade is found.

Your own daughters
and daughters-in-law
sell themselves for sex.
¹⁴ But I won't punish them.
You men are to blame,
because you go to prostitutes
and offer sacrifices with them
at pagan shrines.
Your own foolishness
will lead to your ruin.
¹⁵ Israel, you are unfaithful,
but don't lead Judah to sin.
Stop worshipping at Gilgal
or at sinful Bethel.*
And stop making promises
in my name — the name
of the living LORD.
¹⁶ You are nothing more
than a stubborn cow —
so stubborn that I, the LORD,
cannot feed you like lambs
in an open pasture.

¹⁷ You people of Israel*
are charmed by* idols.
Leave them alone!
¹⁸ You get drunk, then sleep
with prostitutes;
you would rather be vulgar
than lead a decent life.*
¹⁹ And so you will be swept away
in a whirlwind
for sacrificing to idols.

CHAPTER 5

Israel and Judah will be judged

The LORD said:

¹ Listen, you priests!
Pay attention, Israel!*
Listen, you members
of the royal family.
Justice was your duty.
But* at Mizpah and Mount Tabor
you trapped the people.
² At the place of worship
you were a treacherous pit,*
and I will punish you.

---

*4.15 sinful Bethel: The Hebrew text has "Beth-Aven",
which means "house of sin" or "house of nothing",
referring to "Bethel", which means "house of God".
*5.1 Israel: Probably meaning the tribal leaders of
Israel.

³ Israel, I know all about you,
   and because of your unfaithfulness,
   I find you unacceptable.
⁴ Your evil deeds are the reason
   you won't return to me,
   your LORD God.
   And your constant craving for sex
   keeps you from knowing me.

⁵ Israel, your pride
   testifies to your guilt;
   it makes you stumble,
   and Judah stumbles too.
⁶ You offer sheep and cattle
   as sacrifices to me,
   but I have turned away
   and refuse to be found.
⁷ You have been unfaithful
   to me, your LORD;
   you have had children
   by prostitutes.*
   So at the New Moon Festival,
   you and your crops
   will be destroyed.▸

The LORD warns Israel and Judah

⁸ Give a warning on the trumpet!
   Let it be heard in Gibeah,
   Ramah, and sinful Bethel.*
   Benjamin, watch out!▸
⁹ I, the LORD, will punish
   and wipe out Israel.
   This is my solemn promise
   to every tribe of Israel.
¹⁰ Judah's leaders are like crooks
   who move boundary markers;
   that's why I will flood them
   with my anger.

¹¹ Israel was brutally crushed.
   They got what they deserved
   for worshipping useless idols.▸
¹² Now I, the LORD,
   will fill Israel with maggots
   and make Judah rot.
¹³ When Israel and Judah saw
   their sickness and wounds,
   Israel asked help from Assyria
   and its mighty king.▸

   But the king cannot cure them
   or heal their wounds.
¹⁴ So I'll become a fierce lion
   attacking Israel and Judah.
   I'll snatch and carry off
   what I want,
   and no one can stop me.
¹⁵ Then I'll return to my temple
   until they confess their guilt
   and worship me,
   until they are desperate
   and beg for my help.

The people pretend to turn to the Lord

CHAPTER 6

The LORD's people speak

¹ Let's return to the LORD.
   He has torn us to shreds,
   but he will bandage our wounds
   and make us well.
² In two or three days
   he will heal us
   and restore our strength
   that we may live with him.
³ Let's do our best
   to know the LORD.
   His coming is as certain
   as the morning sun;
   he will refresh us like rain
   renewing the earth
   in the springtime.

The LORD speaks to Israel and Judah

⁴ People of Israel and Judah,
   what can I do with you?
   Your love for me disappears
   more quickly than mist
   or dew at sunrise.
⁵ That's why I slaughtered you
   with the words
   of my prophets.
   That's why my judgments blazed
   like the dawning sun.▸
⁶ I'd rather you were faithful
   and knew me
   than offered sacrifices.

⁷ At a place named Adam,
   you▸ betrayed me
   by breaking our agreement.

---

*5.7 prostitutes: See at 4.14, and the note at 1.2.
*5.8 sinful Bethel: See the note at 4.15. Gibeah is about five kilometres north of Jerusalem, Ramah is eight kilometres north, and Bethel is seventeen and a half kilometres north. The attack comes from the south, and all the land of Benjamin (belonging to Israel) is in danger.

See also: 6.6: Matt 9.13; 12.7.

8 Everyone in Gilead is evil;
   your hands are stained
      with the blood of victims.*
9 You priests are like a gang
      of robbers in ambush.
   On the road to Shechem*
      you murder and commit
      other horrible crimes.
10 I have seen a terrible thing
      in Israel —
   you are unfaithful
      and unfit to worship me.
11 People of Judah,
      your time is coming too.

The LORD wants to help Israel

I, the LORD, would like to make
   my nation prosper again

CHAPTER 7

1 and to heal its wounds.
   But then I see the crimes
      in Israel* and Samaria.
   Everyone is deceitful;
      robbers roam the streets.
2 No one realizes
      that I have seen their sins
   surround them like a flood.

3 The king and his officials
      take great pleasure
      in their sin and deceit.
4 Everyone burns with desire —
      they are like coals in an oven,
      ready to burst into flames.
5 On the day their king
      was crowned,
   his officials got him drunk,
      and he joined
      in their foolishness.*

6 Their anger is a fire
      that smoulders all night,
      then flares up at dawn.
7 They are flames
      destroying their leaders.
   And their kings are powerless;
      none of them trust me.

8 The people of Israel*
      have mixed with foreigners;

they are a thin piece of bread
   scorched on one side.
9 They don't seem to realize
   how weak and feeble they are;
      their hair has turned grey,
      while foreigners rule.
10 I am the LORD, their God,
      but in all their troubles
      their pride keeps them
      from returning to me.

Israel refused to trust the Lord

No help from foreign nations

The LORD said:

11 Israel* is a senseless bird,
      fluttering back and forth
      between Egypt and Assyria.
12 But I will catch them in a net
      as hunters trap birds;
   I threatened to punish them,
      and indeed I will.*
13 Trouble and destruction
      will be their reward
      for rejecting me.
   I would have rescued them,
      but they told me lies.

14 They don't really pray to me;
      they just howl in their beds.
   They have rejected me for Baal
      and slashed themselves,*
   in the hope that Baal
      will bless their crops.
15 I taught them what they know,
      and I made them strong.
   Now they plot against me
16   and refuse to obey.*
   They are more useless
      than a crooked arrow.
   Their leaders will die in war
      for saying foolish things.
   Egyptians will laugh at them.

CHAPTER 8

Israel rejects the LORD

The LORD said:

1 Sound a warning!
   Israel, you broke our agreement
      and ignored my teaching.
   Now an eagle is swooping down
      to attack my land.
2 Israel, you say, "We claim you,
      the LORD, as our God."

6.8 your hands . . . victims: This may refer to child
sacrifice.
6.9 Shechem: This was one of the towns where
people could run for safety, if they had accidentally
killed someone (see Joshua 20.1–9).

³ But your enemies
  will chase you for rejecting
  our good agreement.ᐟ

⁴ You chose kings and leaders
  without consulting me;
  you made silver and gold idols
  that led to your downfall.

⁵ City of Samaria, I'm angry
  because of your idol
  in the shape of a calf.
  When will you ever
  be innocent again?

⁶ Someone from Israel built
  that idol for you,
  but only I am God.
  And so it will be smashed
  to pieces.ᐟ

⁷ If you scatter wind
  instead of wheat,
  you will harvest a whirlwind
  and have no wheat.
  Even if you harvest grain,
  enemies will steal it all.

⁸ Israel, you are ruined,
  and now the nations
  consider you worthless.

⁹ You are like a wild donkey
  that goes its own way.
  You've run off to Assyria
  and hired them as allies.

¹⁰ You can bargain with nations,
  but I'll catch you anyway.
  Soon you will suffer abuse
  by kings and rulers.

¹¹ Israel, you have built
  many altars where you offer
  sacrifices for sin.
  But these altars have become
  places for sin.

¹² My instructions for sacrifices
  were written in detail,
  but you ignored them.

¹³ You sacrifice your best animals
  and eat the sacrificial meals,ᐟ
  but I, the LORD,
  refuse your offerings.

I will remember your sins
  and punish you.
  Then you will return to Egypt.ᐟ

¹⁴ Israel, I created you,
  but you forgot me.
  You and Judah built palaces
  and many strong cities.ᐟ
  Now I will send fire to destroy
  your towns and fortresses.

Israel will get the punishment it deserves

CHAPTER 9

¹ Israel, don't celebrateᐟ
  or make noisy shoutsᐟ
  like other nations.
  You have been unfaithful
  to your God.
  Wherever grain is threshed,
  you behave like prostitutes
  because you enjoy
  the money you receive.ᐟ

² But you will run short
  of grain and wine,

³ and you will have to leave
  the land of the LORD.
  Some of you will go to Egypt;
  others will go to Assyria
  and eat unclean food.

⁴ You won't be able to offer
  sacrifices of wine
  to the LORD.
  None of your sacrifices
  will please him —
  they will be unclean
  like food offered to the dead.
  Your food will only be used
  to satisfy your hunger;
  none of it will be brought
  to the LORD's temple.

---

*8.13 sacrifice . . . sacrificial meals:** One possible
meaning for the difficult Hebrew text. Two kinds of
sacrifices are referred to: those in which the whole
animal is burnt on the altar ("whole burnt offerings"
in traditional translations) and those in which part is
eaten by the worshippers ("fellowship offerings" in
traditional translations).

*8.13 return to Egypt:** Either as slaves or to find help
against Assyria.
*8.14 built palaces . . . cities:** They did this because
they no longer trusted the LORD to protect them.
"Palaces" may also mean "temples".
*9.1 Wherever . . . receive:** Grain was threshed on
hills or other places where the wind could blow away
the husks. People also met at these places to worship
Baal, the god they thought had given them the grain
harvest.

5 You will no longer be able
  to celebrate the festival
  of the LORD.*
6 Even if you escape alive,
  you will end up in Egypt
  and be buried in Memphis.*
  Your silver treasures
  will be lost among weeds;'
  thorns will sprout in your tents.

7 Israel, the time has come.
  You will get what you deserve,
  and you will know it.
  "Prophets are fools," you say.
  "And God's messengers are mad."
  Your terrible guilt
  has filled you with hatred.

8 Israel, the LORD sent me
  to look after you.'
  But you trap his prophets
  and flood his temple
  with your hatred.
9 You are brutal and corrupt,
  as were the men of Gibeah.*
  But God remembers your sin,
  and you will be punished.

Sin's terrible results

The LORD said:

10 Israel, when I, the LORD,
   found you long ago
   it was like finding
   grapes in a barren desert
   or tender young figs.
   Then you worshipped Baal Peor,
   that disgusting idol,
   and you became as disgusting
   as the idol you loved.

11 And so, Israel, your glory —
   will fly away like birds —
   your women will no longer
   be able to give birth.
12 Even if you do have children,
   I will take them all
   and leave you to mourn.
   I will turn away,
   and you will sink down
   in deep trouble.

13 Israel, when I first met you,
   I thought of you as palm trees
   growing in fertile ground.'
   Now you lead your people out,
   only to be slaughtered.

Hosea's advice

14 Our LORD, do just one thing
   for your people —
   make their women unable
   to have children
   or to nurse their babies.

The LORD's judgment on Israel

15 Israel, I first began
   to hate you because
   you did evil at Gilgal.*
   Now I will chase you
   out of my house.
   No longer will I love you;
   your leaders betrayed me.
16 Israel, you are a vine
   with dried-up roots
   and fruitless branches.
   Even if you had more children
   and loved them dearly,
   I would slaughter them all.

Warnings for Israel

17 Israel, you disobeyed my God.
   Now he will force you to roam
   from nation to nation.

CHAPTER 10

1 You were a healthy vine
  covered with grapes.
  But the more grapes you grew,
  the more altars you built;
  the better off you became,
  the better shrines you set up
  for pagan gods.
2 You are deceitful and disloyal.
  So you will pay
  for your sins,
  because the LORD will destroy
  your altars and images.

3 "We don't have a king,"
  you will say.
  "We don't fear the LORD.
  And what good are kings?"
4 Israel, you break treaties
  and don't keep promises;

---

*9.5 festival of the LORD: Probably the Festival of
Shelters.
*9.6 Memphis: An Egyptian city with a famous
cemetery.
*9.9 the men of Gibeah: They raped and murdered a
woman (see Judges 19).
See also: 9.7: Luke 21.22. 9.9: Judg 19.1-30.
9.10: Num 25.1-5.

*9.15 Gilgal: See 4.15.

you turn justice
into poisonous weeds
where healthy plants should grow.'

⁵ All who live in Samaria tremble
with concern for the idols'
at sinful Bethel.*
The idol there was the pride
of the priests,
but it has been put to shame;
now everyone will cry.
⁶ It will be taken to Assyria
and given to the great king.
Then Israel will be disgraced
for worshipping that idol.

⁷ Like a twig in a stream,
the king of Samaria
will be swept away.
⁸ The altars at sinful Bethel
will be destroyed
for causing Israel to sin;
they will be overgrown
with thorns and thistles.
Then everyone will beg
the mountains and hills
to cover and protect them.

The LORD promises to punish Israel

⁹ Israel, you have never
stopped sinning'
since that time at Gibeah.*
That's why you
will be attacked at Gibeah.'
¹⁰ Your sins have doubled,
and you are rebellious.
Now I have decided
to send nations to attack
and put you in chains.
¹¹ Once you were obedient
like a calf
that loved to thresh grain.
But I will put a harness
on your powerful neck;
you and Judah must plough
and cultivate the ground.
¹² Plough your fields,
scatter seeds of justice,
and harvest faithfulness.
Worship me, the LORD,
and I will send my saving power
down like rain.

¹³ You have planted evil,
harvested injustice, and eaten
the fruit of your lies.
You trusted your own strength
and your powerful forces.
¹⁴ So war will break out,
and your fortresses
will be destroyed.
Your enemies will do to you
what Shalman* did to the people
of Beth-Arbel —
mothers and their children
will be beaten to death
against rocks.
¹⁵ Bethel, this will be your fate
because of your evil.
Israel, at dawn your king
will be killed.

God's love for his people

CHAPTER 11

¹ When Israel was a child,
I loved him, and I called
my son out of Egypt.
² But as the saying goes,
"The more they were called,
the more they rebelled."'
They never stopped offering
incense and sacrifices
to the idols of Baal.

³ I took Israel by the arm
and taught them to walk.
But they would not admit
that I was the one
who had healed them.
⁴ I led them with kindness
and with love,
not with ropes.
I held them close to me;'
I bent down to feed them.

⁵ But they trusted Egypt
instead of returning to me;
now Assyria will rule them.
⁶ War will visit their cities,
and their plans will fail.'
⁷ My people are determined
to reject me for a god
they think is stronger,
but he can't help.'

---

*10.5 sinful Bethel: See the note at 4.15.
*10.9 Gibeah: See the note at 9.9.
See also: 10.8: Luke 23.30; Rev 6.16.   10.9: Judg 19.1–30.
10.12: Jer 4.3.

*10.14 Shalman: Perhaps a Moabite king, also
known as Salamanu.
See also: 11.1: Exod 4.22; Matt 2.15.

8 Israel, I can't let you go.
   I can't give you up.
   How could I possibly destroy you
   as I did the towns of Admah
   and Zeboiim?*
   I just can't do it.
   My feelings for you
   are much too strong.
9 Israel, I won't lose my temper
   and destroy you again.
   I am the Holy God —
   not merely a human being,
   and I won't stay angry.
10 I, the LORD, will roar like a lion,
   and my children will return,
   trembling from the west.
11 They will come back,
   fluttering like birds from Egypt
   or like doves from Assyria.
   Then I will bring them
   back to their homes.
   I, the LORD, have spoken!

Israel and Judah are doomed

Israel and Judah compared

12 Israel is deceitful to me,
   their loyal and holy God;
   they surround me with lies,
   and Judah worships
   other gods.*

CHAPTER 12

1 All day long Israel chases
   wind from the desert;
   deceit and violence
   are found everywhere.
   Treaties are made with Assyria;
   olive oil is taken to Egypt.

Israel and Judah condemned

2 The LORD also brings charges
   against the people of Judah,
   the descendants of Jacob.
   He will punish them
   for what they have done.

3 Even before Jacob was born,
   he cheated his brother,*
   and when he grew up,
   he fought against God.*

4 At Bethel, Jacob wrestled
   with an angel and won;
   then with tears in his eyes,
   he asked for a blessing,
   and God spoke to us* there.
5 God's name is the LORD,
   the LORD God All-Powerful.
6 So return to your God.
   Patiently trust him,
   and show love and justice.

7 Israel, you enjoy cheating
   and taking advantage
   of others.
8 You say to yourself, "I'm rich!
   I earned it all on my own,
   without committing a sin."*

The LORD is still the God of Israel

9 Israel, I, the LORD,
   am still your God,
   just as I have been
   since the time
   you were in Egypt.
   Now I will force you
   to live in tents once again,
   as you did in the desert.*
10 I spoke to the prophets —
   often I spoke in visions.
   And so, I will send my prophets
   with messages of doom.
11 Gilead is terribly sinful
   and will end up ruined.
   Bulls are sacrificed in Gilgal
   on altars made of stones,
   but those stones will be scattered
   in every field.

---

*11.8 Admah and Zeboiim: When the LORD destroyed Sodom and Gomorrah, he also destroyed these two towns (see Deuteronomy 29.23).
See also: 11.8: Deut 29.23.

850

---

*12.3 Jacob . . . cheated . . . brother: In Hebrew "Jacob" sounds like "cheat" and also like "heel". Jacob grabbed his twin brother Esau by the heel at the time of their birth (see Genesis 25.26). Later he cheated him out of his rights and blessings as the firstborn son (see Genesis 25.29–34; 27.1–40).
*12.3 fought against God: See Genesis 32.22–32.
*12.9 as . . . desert: One possible meaning for the difficult Hebrew text. This probably refers to the forty years of wandering through the desert after leaving Egypt, though it could refer to the "tents" (or "shelters") in which the Israelites lived during the Festival of Shelters (see 9.5,6).
See also: 12.3: Gen 25.26. 12.3,4: Gen 32.24–26. 12.4: Gen 28.10–22. 12.9: Lev 23.42,43.

12 Jacob* escaped to Syria'
where he tended sheep
to earn himself a wife.
13 I sent the prophet Moses
to lead Israel from Egypt
and to keep them safe.
14 Israel, I will make you pay
for your terrible sins
and for insulting me.

CHAPTER 13

Israel is doomed

The LORD said:

1 When your leaders' spoke,
everyone in Israel trembled
and showed great respect.
But you sinned by worshipping Baal,
and you were destroyed.
2 Now you continue to sin
by designing and making
idols of silver
in the shape of calves.
You are told to sacrifice
to these idols' —
yes, even to kiss them.
3 And so, all of you will vanish
like the mist or the dew
of early morning,
or husks of grain in the wind
or smoke from a chimney.

4 I, the LORD, have been your God
since the time
you were in Egypt.
I am the only God you know,
the only one who can save.
5 I took care of you
in a thirsty desert.*
6 I fed you till you were satisfied,
then you became proud
and forgot about me.
7 Now I will attack like a lion,
ambush you like a leopard,
8 and rip you apart like a bear
robbed of her cubs.
I will gnaw on your bones,
as though I were a lion
or some other wild animal.
9 Israel, you are done for.

Don't expect help from me.'
10 You wanted a king and rulers.
Where is your king now?
What cities have rulers?
11 In my anger, I gave you a king;
in my fury, I took him away.

Israel's terrible fate

The LORD said:

12 Israel, your terrible sins
are written down
and stored away.
13 You are like a senseless child
who refuses to be born
at the proper time.
14 Should I, the LORD, rescue you
from death and the grave?
No! I call death and the grave
to strike you like a plague.
I refuse to show mercy.

15 No matter how much you prosper
more than the other tribes,'
I, the LORD, will wipe you out,
just as a scorching desert wind
dries up streams of water.
I will take away
your precious treasures.
16 Samaria* will be punished
for turning against me.
It will be destroyed in war —
children will be beaten
against rocks,
and pregnant women
will be ripped open.

Future forgiveness and blessings

CHAPTER 14

Turn back to the LORD

1 Israel, return! Come back
to the LORD, your God.
Sin has made you fall.
2 Return to the LORD and say,
"Please forgive our sins.
Accept our good sacrifices
of praise instead of bulls.'

---

*12.12 Jacob: His name was later changed to Israel
(see Genesis 32.28), and he became the ancestor of
the nation by that name.
*13.5 thirsty desert: The forty years that Israel
wandered through the desert, after leaving Egypt.
See also: 12.12: Gen 29.1–20. 12.13: Exod 12.50,51.
13.5,6: Deut 8.11–17.

*13.16 Samaria: The capital of the northern kingdom
of Israel.
See also: 13.10: 1 Sam 8.5,6. 13.11: a 1 Sam 10.17–24;
b 1 Sam 15.26. 13.14: 1 Cor 15.55.

³ Assyria can't save us,
and chariots can't help.
So we will no longer worship
the idols we have made.
Our LORD, you show mercy
to orphans."

The LORD promises to forgive

⁴ Israel, you have rejected me,
but my anger is gone;
I will heal you and love you
without limit.
⁵ I will be like the dew —
then you will blossom like lilies
and have roots like a tree.ᵇ
⁶ Your branches will spread
with the beauty
of an olive tree
and with the aroma
of Lebanon Forest.
⁷ You will rest in my shade,
and your grain will grow.
You will blossom
like a vineyard
and be famous as the wine
from Lebanon.

⁸ Israel, give up your idols!
I will answer your prayers
and take care of you.ᶜ
I am that glorious tree,
the source of your fruit.ᵈ

⁹ If you are wise, you will know
and understand what I mean.
I am the LORD, and I lead you
along the right path.
If you obey me,
we will walk together,
but if you are wicked,
you will stumble.

ᵈ**14.8 I am . . . fruit:** This is the only place in the Old Testament where the LORD is compared to a tree. Hosea reminds the people that it is the LORD who is the source of life, rather than the Canaanite gods and goddesses that are worshipped under trees at the local shrines.

Additional notes

ᵃ**1.1 Jehoash:** The Hebrew text has "Joash", another spelling of the name.

ᵃ**2.10 I'll strip . . . lovers:** Or "I'll show her lovers how disgusting she is."

ᵇ**2.12 fig trees . . . payment:** Hosea uses an unusual word for "fig tree", which is spelt something like the word for "payment".

ᵃ**4.4 priests:** One possible meaning for the difficult Hebrew text of verse 4. Hosea may have had in mind only one priest, possibly the chief priest.

ᵃ**4.17 Israel:** The Hebrew text has "Ephraim", the leading tribe of the northern kingdom of Israel, which sometimes stands for the whole kingdom.

ᵇ**4.17 charmed by:** Or "joined to".

ᶜ**4.18 life:** One possible meaning for the difficult Hebrew text of verse 18.

ᵃ**5.1 Justice . . . duty. But:** Or "You are doomed, because".

ᵇ**5.2 At . . . pit:** One possible meaning for the difficult Hebrew text.

ᶜ**5.7 So . . . destroyed:** One possible meaning for the difficult Hebrew text.

ᵈ**5.8 watch out:** Or "lead the way".

ᵉ**5.11 for . . . idols:** One possible meaning for the difficult Hebrew text.

ᶠ**5.13 and . . . king:** One possible meaning for the difficult Hebrew text.

ᵃ**6.5 That's why my . . . sun:** One possible meaning for the difficult Hebrew text.

ᵇ**6.7 At . . . you:** Or "Like Adam, you" or "Each one of you".

ᶜ**6.9 You . . . ambush:** One possible meaning for the difficult Hebrew text.

ᵃ**7.1 Israel:** See the note at 4.17. Samaria was the capital city of Israel.

ᵇ**7.5 foolishness:** One possible meaning for the difficult Hebrew text of verse 5.

ᶜ**7.8 Israel:** See the note at 4.17.

ᵈ**7.11 Israel:** See the note at 4.17.

ᵉ**7.12 I threatened . . . will:** One possible meaning for the difficult Hebrew text.

ᶠ**7.14 slashed themselves:** One ancient translation and some Hebrew manuscripts; other Hebrew manuscripts "gather together". Slashing themselves was one way of worshipping Baal (see 1 Kings 18.28).

ᵃ**7.16 and . . . obey:** One possible meaning for the difficult Hebrew text.

ᵃ**8.3 our good agreement:** Or "me, the Good One" (referring to God).

ᵇ**8.6 smashed to pieces:** Or "destroyed by fire".

ᵃ**9.1 or . . . shouts:** One possible meaning for the difficult Hebrew text.

ᵇ**9.6 Your silver . . . weeds:** One possible meaning for the difficult Hebrew text.

ᶜ**9.8 Israel . . . you:** One possible meaning for the difficult Hebrew text.

ᵈ**9.13 Israel, when . . . ground:** One possible meaning for the difficult Hebrew text.

ᵃ**10.4 you turn . . . grow:** One possible meaning for the difficult Hebrew text.

ᵇ**10.5 idols:** The Hebrew text has "calves", referring to the idols made in the shape of calves.

ᶜ**10.9 never stopped sinning:** One possible meaning for the difficult Hebrew text.

ᵈ**10.9 That's why . . . Gibeah:** One possible meaning for the difficult Hebrew text.

›11.2 But . . . rebelled: One possible meaning for the difficult Hebrew text.
›11.4 I held . . . to me: One possible meaning for the difficult Hebrew text.
›11.6 fail: One possible meaning for the difficult Hebrew text of verse 6.
›11.7 help: One possible meaning for the difficult Hebrew text of verse 7.
›11.12 and Judah worships other gods: Or "but Judah remains faithful".
›12.4 us: Hebrew; two ancient translations "him".
›12.8 without . . . sin: One possible meaning for the difficult Hebrew text.
›12.12 Syria: The Hebrew text has "Aram", probably referring to northern Syria in the region of Haran.
›13.1 your leaders: The Hebrew text has "Ephraim", here meaning Mount Ephraim, where the royal palace of Samaria (capital of the northern kingdom of Israel) was situated.
›13.2 You are told . . . idols: One possible meaning for the difficult Hebrew text.
›13.9 Don't . . . me: Or "You are against me, the one who helps you."
›13.15 more . . . tribes: One possible meaning for the difficult Hebrew text.
›14.2 Accept . . . bulls: One possible meaning for the difficult Hebrew text.
›14.5 like a tree: The Hebrew text has "like Lebanon", probably referring to the famous cedar trees on Mount Lebanon.
›14.8 Israel . . . you: One possible meaning for the difficult Hebrew text.

Joel

A quick look at this book

Joel was a prophet who had watched swarm after swarm of locusts cover the land of Israel and wipe out the crops. He described these locusts as though they were an enemy army destroying everything in sight, and he said that the Lord had sent the locusts as punishment for the sins of Israel. Joel also used the locusts as a way of talking about a real army that was going to attack Israel. But the Lord promised that if the people would turn back to him, he would forgive them and bless them once again.

The locusts caused horrible destruction, but it was only a small taste of what will happen on the judgment day of the Lord. At that time the Lord will put all nations on trial for what they have done to his people, and those who are guilty will be punished.

> Crowds fill Decision Valley.
> The judgment day of the LORD
>   will soon be here —
> no light from the sun or moon,
>   and stars no longer shine.
> From the heart of Jerusalem
> the LORD roars like a lion,
>   shaking the earth and sky.
> But the LORD is a fortress,
> a place of safety
>   for his people Israel.

(3.14–16)

Locusts and an enemy army

CHAPTER 1

> [1] I am Joel the son of Pethuel.
>   And this is the message
>   the LORD gave to me.

Locusts cover the land

> [2] Listen, you leaders
>   and everyone else
>   in the land.
>   Has anything like this
>   ever happened before?
> [3] Tell our children!
>   Let it be told
>   to our grandchildren
>   and their children too.
>
> [4] Swarm after swarm of locusts*
>   has attacked our crops,
>   eating everything in sight.
> [5] Sober up, you drunkards!
>   Cry long and loud;
>   your wine supply is gone.
> [6] A powerful nation*
>   with countless troops
>   has invaded our land.
>   They have the teeth and jaws
>   of powerful lions.
> [7] Our grapevines and fig trees
>   are stripped bare;
>   only naked branches remain.

---

*1.4 Swarm . . . locusts: The Hebrew text lists either four kinds of locusts or locusts in four stages of their development. Locusts are a type of grasshopper that comes in swarms and causes great damage to plant life.

*1.6 A powerful nation: The swarms of locusts.

See also: 1.6: Rev 9.8.

8 Grieve like a young woman
    mourning for the man
        she was to marry.
9 Offerings of grain and wine
    are no longer brought
        to the LORD's temple.
His servants, the priests,
    are deep in sorrow.
10 Barren fields mourn;
    grain, grapes, and olives
        are scorched and shrivelled.

11 Mourn for our farms
    and our vineyards!
There's no wheat or barley
    growing in our fields.
12 Grapevines have dried up
    and so has every tree —
        figs and pomegranates,*
    date palms and apples.
All happiness has faded away.

Return to God

13 Mourn, you priests who serve
    at the altar of my God.
Spend your days and nights
    wearing sackcloth.*
Offerings of grain and wine
    are no longer brought
        to the LORD's temple.

14 Tell the leaders and people
    to come together
        at the temple.
Order them to go without eating*
    and to pray sincerely.
15 We are in for trouble!
Soon the LORD All-Powerful
    will bring disaster.
16 Our food is already gone;
    there's no more celebrating
        at the temple of our God.

17 Seeds dry up in the ground;'
    no harvest is possible.
Our barns are in bad shape,
    with no grain
        to store in them.

18 Our cattle wander aimlessly,
    moaning for lack of pasture,
        and sheep are suffering.'
19 I cry out to you, LORD.
Grasslands and forests are eaten
    by the scorching heat.
20 Wild animals have no water
    because of you;
rivers and streams are dry,
    and pastures are parched.

CHAPTER 2

Locusts and an enemy army

1 Sound the trumpet on Zion,
    the LORD's sacred hill.
Warn everyone to tremble!
The judgment day of the LORD
    is coming soon.
2 It will be dark and gloomy
    with storm clouds overhead.
Troops will cover the mountains
    like thunderclouds.
No army this powerful
    has ever been gathered before
        or will ever be again.
3 Fiery flames surround them;
    no one escapes.
Before they invaded,
    the land was like Eden;
now only a desert remains.

4 They look like horses
    and charge like cavalry.
5 They roar over mountains
    like noisy chariots,
or a mighty army
    ready for battle.
They are a forest fire
    that feasts on straw.
6 The very sight of them
    is frightening.'
7 They climb over walls
    like warriors;
they march in columns
    and never turn aside.
8 They charge straight ahead,
    without pushing each other;
even arrows and spears
    cannot make them retreat.
9 They swarm over city walls
    and enter our homes;
they crawl in through windows,
    just like thieves.

---

*1.12 pomegranates: A bright red fruit that looks like
an apple.
*1.13 sackcloth: A rough, dark-coloured cloth made
from goat or camel hair and used to make grain
sacks. It was worn in times of trouble or sorrow.
*1.14 go without eating: As a way of showing
sorrow for their sins.
See also: 1.15: Isa 13.6.

See also: 2.4,5: Rev 9.7–9.

¹⁰ They make the earth tremble
      and the heavens shake;
   the sun and moon turn dark,
      and stars stop shining.
¹¹ The LORD God leads this army
      of countless troops,
      and they obey his commands.
   The day of his judgment is so terrible
      that no one can stand it.

The LORD's invitation

¹² The LORD said:

   It isn't too late.
   You can still return to me
      with all your heart.
   Start crying and mourning!
      Go without eating.
¹³ Don't rip your clothes
      to show your sorrow.
   Instead, turn back to me
      with broken hearts.
   I am merciful, kind, and caring.
   I don't easily lose my temper,
      and I don't like to punish.

¹⁴ I am the LORD your God.
   Perhaps I will change my mind
      and treat you with mercy.
   Then you will be blessed
      with enough grain and wine
      for offering sacrifices to me.

¹⁵ Sound the trumpet on Zion!
   Call the people together.
   Show your sorrow
      by going without food.
¹⁶ Make sure that everyone
      is fit to worship me.*
   Bring adults, children, babies,
      and even bring newlyweds
      from their festivities.

¹⁷ Tell my servants, the priests,
      to cry inside the temple
   and to offer this prayer
      near the altar:*
   "Save your people, LORD God!
   Don't let foreign nations
      make jokes about us.
   Don't let them laugh and ask,
      'Where is your God?' "

The Lord will bless his people

The LORD will bless the land

¹⁸ The LORD was deeply concerned
      about his land
   and had pity on his people.
¹⁹ In answer to their prayers
      he said,
   "I will give you enough grain,
      wine, and olive oil
      to satisfy your needs.
   No longer will I let you
      be insulted by the nations.
²⁰ An army attacked from the north,
   but I will chase it
      into a scorching desert.
   There it will rot and stink
      from the Dead Sea
      to the Mediterranean."

   The LORD works wonders
²¹   and does great things.
   So tell the soil to celebrate
²²   and wild animals
      to stop being afraid.
   Grasslands are green again;
   fruit trees and fig trees
      are loaded with fruit.
   Grapevines are covered
      with grapes.

²³ People of Zion,*
   celebrate in honour
      of the LORD your God!
   He is generous and has sent
      the autumn and spring rains
      in the proper seasons.*
²⁴ Grain will cover
      your threshing places;
   jars will overflow
      with wine and olive oil.

The LORD will rescue his people

²⁵ I, the LORD your God,
   will make up for the losses
      caused by those swarms
      and swarms of locusts*
   I sent to attack you.
²⁶ My people, you will eat
      until you are satisfied.
   Then you will praise me
      for the wonderful things
      I have done.

---

*2.16 fit to worship me: This required going through
certain kinds of ceremonies.

See also: 2.10: Rev 8.12. 2.11: Rev 6.17.

856

*2.23 Zion: Jerusalem.

*2.25 swarms . . . locusts: See the note at 1.4.

Never again will you
be put to shame.

²⁷ Israel, you will know
that I stand at your side.
I am the LORD your God —
there are no other gods.
Never again will you
be put to shame.

The LORD will work wonders

The LORD said:

²⁸ Later, I will give my Spirit to everyone.
Your sons and daughters will prophesy.
Your old men will have dreams,
and your young men
will see visions.

²⁹ In those days I will even give
my Spirit to my servants,
both men and women.

³⁰ I will work wonders
in the sky above
and on the earth below.
There will be blood and fire
and clouds of smoke.

³¹ The sun will turn dark,
and the moon
will be as red as blood
before that great
and terrible day
when I appear.

³² Then the LORD will save everyone who
faithfully worships him. He has promised
there will be survivors on Mount Zion and in
Jerusalem, and among them will be his
chosen ones.

The Lord will punish
the nations

CHAPTER 3

The LORD said:

¹ At that time I, the LORD, will make Judah
and Jerusalem prosperous again. ² Then in
Judgment Valley⸲ I will bring together the
nations that scattered my people Israel
everywhere in the world, and I will bring
charges against those nations. They divided
up my land ³ and gambled to see who would
get my people; they sold boys and girls to
pay for prostitutes and wine.

⁴ You people of Tyre and Sidon* and you
Philistines, why are you doing this? Are you
trying to get even with me? I'll strike back
before you know what's happened. ⁵ You've
taken my prized possessions, including my
silver and gold, and carried them off to your
temples.⸲ ⁶ You have dragged the people of
Judah and Jerusalem from their land and
sold them to the Greeks.

⁷ But I'll make the people of Judah
determined to come home, and what
happened to them will happen to you. ⁸ I'll
hand over your sons and daughters to the
people of Judah, and they will sell them to
the Sabeans,* who live far away. I, the
LORD, have spoken!

Judgment in Judgment Valley

The LORD said:

⁹ Say to the nations:

"Get ready for war!
Be eager to fight.
Line up for battle
and prepare to attack.

¹⁰ Make swords out of ploughs
and spears out of garden tools.
Strengthen every weakling."

¹¹ Hurry, all you nations!
Come quickly.
Ask the LORD to bring
his warriors along.⸲

¹² You must come now
to Judgment Valley,⸲
where the LORD will judge
the surrounding nations.

¹³ They are a field of ripe crops.
Bring in the harvest!
They are grapes piled high.
Start trampling them now!*
If our enemy's sins were wine,
every jar would overflow.

¹⁴ Crowds fill Decision Valley.
The judgment day of the LORD
will soon be here —

---

*3.4 Tyre and Sidon: Two Phoenician coastal cities.
*3.8 Sabeans: The people of Seba, a region in
south-west Arabia.
*3.13 grapes . . . now: People trampled grapes with
their bare feet to squeeze out the juice.

See also: 3.4–8: Isa 23.1–18; Ezek 26.1—28.26; Amos 1.9,10;
Zech 9.1–4; Matt 11.21,22; Luke 10.13,14.
3.4–8: Isa 14.29–31; Jer 47.1–7; Ezek 25.15–17; Amos 1.6–8;
Zeph 2.4–7; Zech 9.5–7. 3.10: Isa 2.4; Mic 4.3.
3.13: a Rev 14.14–16; b Rev 14.19,20; 19.15.

See also: 2.28–32: Acts 2.17–21. 2.31: Matt 24.29;
Mark 13.24,25; Luke 21.25; Rev 6.12,13. 2.32: Rom 10.13.

¹⁵ no light from the sun or moon,
    and stars no longer shine.
¹⁶ From the heart of Jerusalem
    the LORD roars like a lion,
       shaking the earth and sky.
But the LORD is a fortress,
    a place of safety
       for his people Israel.

God will bless his people

¹⁷ I am the LORD your God.
    And you will know I live on Zion,
       my sacred hill,
because Jerusalem will be sacred,
    untouched by foreign troops.
¹⁸ On that day, fruitful vineyards
    will cover the mountains.
And your cattle and goats
    that graze on the hills
       will produce a lot of milk.
Streams in Judah
    will never run dry;
a stream from my house
    will flow in Acacia Valley.*

¹⁹ Egypt and Edom were cruel
    and brutal to Judah,
       without a reason.
Now their countries will become
    a barren desert,
²⁰ but Judah and Jerusalem
    will always have people.
²¹ I, the LORD, live on Mount Zion.
    I will punish the guilty
       and defend the innocent.'

---

*3.18 Acacia Valley: In the plains of Moab,
north-east of the Dead Sea.
See also: 3.16: Amos 1.2.

Additional notes

'1.17 Seeds . . . ground: One possible meaning for
the difficult Hebrew text.
'1.18 sheep are suffering: One possible meaning for
the difficult Hebrew text.
'2.6 The very . . . frightening: One possible meaning
for the difficult Hebrew text.
'2.17 inside . . . altar: The Hebrew text has "between
the porch and the altar", which is the place where the
priests usually prayed for the people.
'2.23 in . . . seasons: Or "as he used to do".
'3.2 Judgment Valley: The Hebrew text has
"Jehoshaphat Valley", which means "Valley of the
LORD's Judgment". This valley is mentioned here and
in verse 12, but nowhere else in the Bible.
'3.5 temples: Or "palaces".

'3.11 Ask . . . along: One possible meaning for the
difficult Hebrew text.
'3.12 Judgment Valley: See the note at 3.2.
'3.21 I will . . . innocent: One possible meaning for
the difficult Hebrew text.

Amos

A quick look at this book

Amos wasn't a professional prophet and had never been trained to be a prophet (7.14). But when the Lord gave him messages for the people in the northern kingdom, Amos left his home town of Tekoa in Judah and went to preach in the town of Bethel in Israel, probably at the famous place of worship.

In this book, Amos first condemns many of the nearby nations, and then he condemns the people of Israel, especially the rich who lived in luxury. They had great power and used it to rob the poor and to make slaves of them. And even though most of the people were worshipping other gods besides the Lord, they still expected the Lord to protect them. But Amos warned the people that they would be punished, and he said:

> Choose good instead of evil!
>   See that justice is done.
> Perhaps I, the LORD All-Powerful,
> will be kind to what's left
>   of your people.

(5.15)

Crimes of the nations will be punished

CHAPTER 1

1 I am Amos. And I raised sheep near the town of Tekoa* when Uzziah was king of Judah and Jeroboam* son of Jehoash' was king of Israel.

Two years before the earthquake,* the LORD gave me several messages' about Israel, 2 and I said:

> When the LORD roars
>   from Jerusalem,
> pasture lands and Mount Carmel
>   dry up and turn brown.

Judgment on Syria

3 The LORD said:

> I will punish Syria'
>   for countless crimes,
>   and I won't change my mind.
> They dragged logs with spikes*
>   over the people of Gilead.

---

*1.1 Tekoa: In the hill country of Judah about eight kilometres south of Bethlehem.
*1.1 Uzziah . . . Jeroboam: Uzziah was king of Judah 781–740 BC, and Jeroboam II was king of Israel 783–743 BC.
*1.1 Two years . . . earthquake: Possibly the earthquake of 760 BC, which seems to have been especially violent.
*1.3 logs with spikes: These were dragged over grain to thresh it.
See also: 1.1: a 2 King 15.1–7; 2 Chron 26.1–23; b 2 King 14.23–29. 1.2: Joel 3.16. 1.3–5: Isa 17.1–3; Jer 49.23–27; Zech 9.1.

⁴ Now I will burn down the palaces
  and fortresses
    of King Hazael
    and of King Benhadad.*
⁵ I will break through
    the gates of Damascus.
  I will destroy the people›
    of Wicked Valley›
    and the ruler of Beth-Eden.›
  Then the Syrians will be dragged
    as prisoners to Kir.
  I, the LORD, have spoken!

Judgment on Philistia

⁶ The LORD said:

  I will punish Philistia›
    for countless crimes,
    and I won't change my mind.
  They dragged off my people*
    from town after town
  to sell them as slaves
    to the Edomites.

⁷ That's why I will burn down
    the walls and fortresses
    of the city of Gaza.
⁸ I will destroy the king› of Ashdod
    and the ruler of Ashkelon.
  I will strike down Ekron,*
  and that will be the end
    of the Philistines.
  I, the LORD, have spoken!

Judgment on Phoenicia

⁹ The LORD said:

  I will punish Phoenicia›
    for countless crimes,
    and I won't change my mind.
  They broke their treaty
  and dragged off my people*
    from town after town
  to sell them as slaves
    to the Edomites.

¹⁰ That's why I will send flames
    to burn down the city of Tyre
    along with its fortresses.

Judgment on Edom

¹¹ The LORD said:

  I will punish Edom
    for countless crimes,
    and I won't change my mind.
  They killed their own relatives*
    and were so terribly furious
    that they showed no mercy.
¹² Now I will send fire to wipe out
    the fortresses of Teman
    and Bozrah.*

Judgment on Ammon

¹³ The LORD said:

  I will punish Ammon
    for countless crimes,
    and I won't change my mind.
  In Gilead they ripped open
    pregnant women,
    just to take the land.

¹⁴ Now I will send fire to destroy
    the walls and fortresses
    of Rabbah.*
  Enemies will shout and attack
    like a whirlwind.
¹⁵ Ammon's king and leaders
    will be dragged away.
  I, the LORD, have spoken!

CHAPTER 2

Judgment on Moab

¹ The LORD said:

  I will punish Moab
    for countless crimes,
    and I won't change my mind.

---

*1.4 Hazael . . . Benhadad: Two Syrian kings.
*1.5 Kir: The exact location of this country is not
known; in 9.7 Amos refers to Kir as the original home
of the Syrians, and so the verse probably means that
the Syrians will lose everything they have gained as a
people.
*1.6 my people: The people of Israel.
*1.8 Ashdod . . . Ashkelon . . . Ekron: Philistine cities.
*1.9 my people: See the note at 1.6.
See also: **1.6–8:** Isa 14.29–31; Jer 47.1–7; Ezek 25.15–17;
Joel 3.4–8; Zeph 2.4–7; Zech 9.5–7.   **1.9,10:** Isa 23.1–18;
Ezek 26.1—28.19; Joel 3.4–8; Zech 9.1–4; Matt 11.21,22;
Luke 10.13,14.

*1.11 their own relatives: The Edomites were
descendants of Esau, the brother of Jacob, the
ancestor of the Israelites.
*1.12 Teman and Bozrah: These stand for all of
Edom; Teman may have been a city or a district.
Bozrah, the chief city of northern Edom, was
forty-eight kilometres south-east of the Dead Sea.
*1.14 Rabbah: The capital city of Ammon.
See also: **1.11,12:** Isa 34.5–17; 63.1–6; Jer 49.7–22;
Ezek 25.12–14; 35.1–15; Obad 1–14; Mal 1.2–5.
1.13–15: Jer 49.1–6; Ezek 21.28–32; 25.1–7; Zeph 2.8–11.
2.1–3: Isa 15.1—16.14; 25.10–12; Jer 48.1–47; Ezek 25.8–11;
Zeph 2.8–11.

They made lime from the bones*
  of the king of Edom.
² Now I will send fire to destroy
  the fortresses of Kerioth.*
Battle shouts and trumpet blasts
  will be heard
  as I destroy Moab
³ with its king and leaders.
I, the LORD, have spoken!

Judgment on Judah

⁴ The LORD said:

I will punish Judah for countless crimes,
  and I won't change my mind.
They have rejected their teachings
  and refused to obey me.
They were led astray
  by the same false gods
  their ancestors worshipped.
⁵ Now I will send fire on Judah
  and destroy the fortresses
  of Jerusalem.

Judgment on Israel

⁶ The LORD said:

I will punish Israel
  for countless crimes,
  and I won't change my mind.
They sell honest people for money,
  and the needy are sold
  for the price of sandals.
⁷ They throw the poor to the ground
  and push aside
  those who are helpless.

My holy name is dishonoured,
  because fathers and sons sleep
  with the same young women.
⁸ They lie down beside altars
  on clothes taken
  as security for loans.
And they drink wine in my temple,
  wine bought with the money
  they received from fines.

⁹ Israel, the Amorites* were there
  when you entered Canaan.

They were tall as cedars
  and strong as oaks.
But I wiped them out —
  I destroyed their branches
  and their roots.
¹⁰ I had rescued you from Egypt,
  and for forty years I had led you
  through the desert.
Then I gave you the land
  of the Amorites.

¹¹ I chose some of you
  to be prophets
  and others to be Nazirites.*
People of Israel,
you know this is true.
I, the LORD, have spoken!
¹² But you commanded the prophets
  not to speak their message,
and you pressured the Nazirites
  into drinking wine.

¹³ And so I will crush you,
  just as a wagon full of grain
  crushes the ground.»
¹⁴ No matter how fast you run,
  you won't escape.
No matter how strong you are,
  you will lose your strength
  and your life.
¹⁵ Even if you are an expert
  with a bow and arrow,
  you will retreat.
And you won't get away alive,
  not even if you run fast
  or ride a horse.
¹⁶ You may be brave and strong,
  but you will run away,
  stripped naked.
I, the LORD, have spoken!

CHAPTER 3

¹ People of Israel,
  I rescued you from Egypt.
Now listen to my judgment
  against you.
² Of all nations on earth,
  you are the only one
  I have chosen.
That's why I will punish you
  because of your sins.

---

*2.1 They . . . bones: They dug up the bodies of
kings and made lime out of them to use as whitewash
on their houses and walls.
*2.2 Kerioth: A leading city of Moab and a centre for
the worship of Chemosh, the chief god of Moab.
*2.9 Amorites: This word is used for all the people
who lived in Canaan at the time Israel took over the
land.
See also: 2.9: Deut 3.8-11.

*2.11 Nazirites: People who promised the LORD that
they would never drink wine or cut their hair or come
in contact with a dead body.
See also: 2.11: Num 6.1-8.

Israel and Samaria will be destroyed

The work of a prophet

³ Can two people walk together
without agreeing to meet?
⁴ Does a lion roar in the forest
unless it has caught
a victim?
Does it growl in its den
unless it is eating?
⁵ How can anyone catch a bird
without using a net?
Does a trap spring shut
unless something is caught?
⁶ Isn't the whole city frightened
when the trumpet
signals an attack?
Isn't it the LORD who brings
disaster on a city?
⁷ Whatever the LORD God
plans to do,
he tells his servants,
the prophets.
⁸ Everyone is terrified
when a lion roars —
and ordinary people
become prophets
when the LORD God speaks.

Samaria is doomed

⁹ Here is a message
for the leaders
of Philistia* and Egypt*
tell everyone to come together
on the hills of Samaria.
Let them see the injustice
and the lawlessness
in that city.
¹⁰ The LORD has said
that they don't even know how
to do right.
They have become rich
from violence and robbery.
¹¹ And so the LORD God has sworn
that they will be surrounded.
Enemies will break through
their defences
and steal their treasures.

¹² The LORD has promised
that only a few from Samaria
will escape with their lives
and with some broken pieces
of their beds and couches.*

It will be like when a shepherd
rescues two leg bones
and part of a sheep's ear
from the jaws of a lion.*

The altars at Bethel

¹³ The LORD God All-Powerful
told me to speak this message
against Jacob's descendants:

¹⁴ When I, the LORD, punish Israel
for their sins,
I will destroy the altars
at Bethel.
Even the corners of the altar*
will be left in the dust.
¹⁵ I will tear down winter homes
and summer homes.
Houses decorated with ivory
and all other mansions
will be gone for ever.
I, the LORD, have spoken!

CHAPTER 4

The women of Samaria

The LORD said:

¹ You women of Samaria
are fat cows!*
You ill-treat and abuse
the poor and needy,
then you say to your husbands,
"Bring us more drinks!"
² I, the LORD God, have sworn
by my own name
that your time is coming.
Not one of you will be left —
you will be taken away
by sharp hooks.*
³ You will be dragged through holes
in your city walls,
and you will be thrown
towards Harmon.*
I, the LORD, have spoken!

---

*3.12 lion: When a wild animal attacked and killed a
sheep, the shepherd had to rescue part of the sheep
and take it to the owner as proof that it had been
killed by an animal. Otherwise, the shepherd had to
pay the owner the cost of the sheep.
*3.14 altar: Altars were places of worship but also
places of protection. People whose lives were in
danger could grab hold of the corners of an altar, and
no one was allowed to kill them.
See also: 3.14: 2 King 23.15.

Israel refuses to obey

The LORD said:

4 Come to Bethel and Gilgal.*
  Sin all you want!
  Offer sacrifices the next morning
  and bring a tenth of your crops
    on the third day.*
5 Bring offerings to show me
    how thankful you are.
  Gladly bring more offerings
    than I have demanded.
  You really love to do this.
  I, the LORD God, have spoken!

How the LORD warned Israel

6 I, the LORD, took away the food
  from every town and village,
    but still you rejected me.
7 Three months before harvest,
    I kept back the rain.
  Sometimes I would let it fall
    on one town or field
  but not on another,
    and pastures dried up.
8 People from two or three towns
    would go to a town
  that still had water,
    but it wasn't enough.
  Even then you rejected me.
  I, the LORD, have spoken!

9 I dried up your grain fields;
  your gardens and vineyards
    turned brown.
  Locusts* ate your fig trees
    and olive orchards,
  but even then you rejected me.
  I, the LORD, have spoken!

10 I did terrible things to you,
    just as I did to Egypt —
  I killed your young men in war;
  I let your horses be stolen,
  and I made your camp stink
    with dead bodies.
  Even then you rejected me.
  I, the LORD, have spoken!

11 I destroyed many of you,
  just as I did the cities
    of Sodom and Gomorrah.
  You were a burning stick
    I rescued from the fire.
  Even then you rejected me.
  I, the LORD, have spoken!

12 Now, Israel, I myself
  will deal with you.
  Get ready to face your God!

13 I created the mountains
    and the wind.
  I let humans know
    what I am thinking.'
  I bring darkness at dawn
    and step over hills.
  I am the LORD God All-Powerful!

CHAPTER 5

Turn back to the LORD

1 Listen, nation of Israel,
    to my mournful message:
2 you, dearest Israel, have fallen,
    never to rise again —
  you lie deserted in your own land,
    with no one to help you up.

3 The LORD God has warned,
  "From every ten soldiers
    only one will be left;
  from a thousand troops,
    only a hundred will survive."

4 The LORD keeps saying,
  "Israel, turn back to me
    and you will live!
5 Don't go to Gilgal or Bethel
    or even to Beersheba.*
  Gilgal will be dragged away,
  and Bethel will end up
    as nothing."'

6 Turn back to the LORD,
  you descendants of Joseph,*
    and you will live.
  If you don't, the LORD
  will attack like fire.
  Bethel will burn to the ground,
    and no one can save it.

*4.4 Bethel and Gilgal: These were two of the most important centres of worship in northern Israel. Amos mentions these together again in 5.5.
*4.4 Offer . . . day: Or "Offer sacrifices each morning and bring a tenth of your crops every three days." In verses 4,5 God is condemning the people for meaningless acts of worship.
*4.9 Locusts: A type of grasshopper that comes in swarms and causes great damage to plant life.

*5.5 Gilgal, . . . Bethel . . . Beersheba: These were ancient places of worship, but the LORD had warned his people to stay away from them.
*5.6 descendants of Joseph: Another name for the people of the northern kingdom of Israel.
See also: 4.11: Gen 19.24.

7 You people are doomed!
  You twist the truth
    and trample on justice.

8 But the LORD created the stars
    and put them in place.*
  He turns darkness to dawn
    and daylight to darkness;
  he scoops up the ocean
    and empties it on the earth.

9 God destroys mighty soldiers
    and strong fortresses.

Choose good instead of evil!

The LORD said:

10 You people hate judges
    and honest witnesses;

11 you abuse the poor and demand
    heavy taxes from them.
  You have built expensive homes,
    but you won't enjoy them;
  you have planted vineyards,
    but you will get no wine.

12 I am the LORD, and I know
    your terrible sins.
  You cheat honest people and take bribes;
    you rob the poor of justice.

13 Times are so evil
    that anyone with good sense
    will keep quiet.

14 If you really want to live,
    you must stop doing wrong
    and start doing right.
  I, the LORD God All-Powerful,
    will then be on your side,
    just as you claim I am.

15 Choose good instead of evil!
    See that justice is done.
  Perhaps I, the LORD All-Powerful,
    will be kind to what's left
    of your people.*

Judgment is coming

16 This is what the LORD has sworn:

  Noisy crying will be heard
    in every town and street.

Even farmers will be told
  to mourn for the dead,
  together with those
  who are paid to mourn.*

17 Your vineyards will be filled
    with crying and weeping,*
  because I will punish you.
  I, the LORD, have spoken!

When the LORD judges

18 You look forward to the day
    when the LORD comes to judge.
  But you are in for trouble!
  It won't be a time of sunshine;
    all will be darkness.

19 You will run from a lion,
    only to meet a bear.
  You will escape to your house,
    rest your hand on the wall,
    and be bitten by a snake.

20 The day when the LORD judges
    will be dark, very dark,
    without a ray of light.

What the LORD demands

The LORD said:

21 I, the LORD, hate and despise
    your religious celebrations
    and your times of worship.

22 I won't accept your offerings
    or animal sacrifices —
    not even your very best.

23 No more of your noisy songs!
  I won't listen when you play your harps.

24 But let justice and fairness
    flow like a river
    that never runs dry.

25 Israel, for forty years
    you wandered in the desert,
  without bringing offerings
    or sacrifices to me.

26 Now you will have to carry
    the two idols you made —
  Sakkuth, the one you call king,
    and Kaiwan,
    the one you built
    in the shape of a star.*

27 I will force you to march
    as captives beyond Damascus.

---

*5.8 the stars . . . place: The Hebrew text mentions two groups of stars, Pleiades and Orion. Since the LORD is the Creator of the stars, he controls the seasons that are signalled by the different positions of the stars. Moreover, the stars are created objects and should not be worshipped.
*5.15 your people: Hebrew "Joseph's descendants" (see the note at verse 6).
See also: 5.8: Job 9.9; 38.31.

*5.16 paid to mourn: In ancient times some people were paid to mourn and make loud cries at funerals.
*5.17 Your vineyards . . . weeping: Instead of happy celebrations that were often held in vineyards after the harvest.
See also: 5.21,22: Isa 1.11-14. 5.25-27: Acts 7.42,43.

I, the LORD God All-Powerful,
have spoken!*

CHAPTER 6

Israel will be punished

1 Do you rulers in Jerusalem
and in the city of Samaria
feel safe and at ease?
Everyone bows down to you,
and you think you are better
than any other nation.
But you are in for trouble!

2 Look what happened
to the cities of Calneh,
powerful Hamath,
and Gath* in Philistia.
Are you greater than any
of those kingdoms?

3 You are cruel, and you forget
the coming day of judgment.

4 You rich people lounge around
on beds with ivory posts,
while dining on the meat
of your lambs and calves.

5 You sing foolish songs
to the music of harps,
and you make up new tunes,
just as David used to do.

6 You drink all the wine you want
and wear expensive perfume,
but you don't care about
the ruin of your nation.*

7 So you will be the first
to be dragged off as captives;
your good times will end.

8 The LORD God All-Powerful
has sworn by his own name:
"You descendants of Jacob
make me angry by your pride,
and I hate your fortresses.
And so I will surrender your city
and possessions
to your enemies."

9 If only ten of you survive

by hiding in a house
you will still die.

10 As you carry out a corpse
to prepare it for burial,'
your relative in the house
will ask, "Are there others?"
You will answer, "No!"
Then your relative will reply,
"Be quiet!
Don't dare mention
the name of the LORD."*

11 At the LORD's command,
houses great and small
will be smashed to pieces.

12 Horses can't gallop on rocks;
oceans' can't be ploughed.
But you have turned justice and fairness
into bitter poison.

13 You celebrate the defeat
of Lo-Debar and Karnaim,*
and you boast by saying,
"We did it on our own."

14 But the LORD God All-Powerful
will send a nation to attack
you people of Israel.
They will capture Lebo-Hamath
in the north,
Arabah Brook* in the south,
and everything in between.

Five visions of Israel's punishment

CHAPTER 7

A vision of locusts

1 The LORD God showed me that he is going
to send locusts* to attack your crops. It will
happen after the king has already been given

---

*5.27 I, the LORD . . . spoken: Israel did not offer
sacrifices and gifts to the LORD during the time they
wandered through the desert. But now they have
made idols to carry during their ceremonies. So the
LORD warns that he will make them "march" away as
captives beyond Damascus, where Israel had
extended its borders by victories in war (see 2 Kings
14.28). *6.6 your nation: Hebrew "Joseph's descendants"
(see the note at 5.6).

*6.10 the name of the LORD: Two relatives seem to
be carrying out corpses for burial. One of them warns
the other to be careful not even to say "Thank the
LORD!" for fear that the mention of his name may
cause something worse to happen. *6.13 Lo-Debar and Karnaim: Two cities east of the
River Jordan that were captured by Jeroboam II (see
2 Kings 14.25). In Hebrew "Lo-Debar" can mean
"nothing," and "Karnaim" means "two horns (of a
bull)". Horns were symbols of strength, and so the
people are boasting about their military power
(defeat of "two horns"), which Amos says is
"nothing" (Lo-Debar). *6.14 Lebo-Hamath . . . Arabah Brook: The northern
and southern boundaries of the northern kingdom.
*7.1 locusts: See the note at 4.9.

his share of the grain and before the rest of the grain has been harvested.* ² In my vision the locusts ate every crop in the land, and I said to the LORD, "Forgive me for asking, but how can the nation survive? It's so weak."

³ Then the LORD felt sorry and answered, "I won't let it be destroyed."

A vision of fire

⁴ The LORD showed me that he is going to send a ball of fire to burn up everything on earth, including the sea. ⁵ Then I said, "Won't you please stop? How can our weak nation survive?"

⁶ Again the LORD felt sorry and answered, "I won't let it be destroyed."

A vision of a measuring line

⁷ The LORD showed me a vision of himself standing beside a wall and holding a string with a weight tied to the end of it. The string and weight had been used to measure the straightness of the wall. ⁸ Then he asked, "Amos, what do you see?"

"A measuring line," I answered.

The LORD said, "I'm using this measuring line to show that my people Israel don't measure up, and I won't forgive them any more. ⁹ Their sacred places will be destroyed, and I will send war against the nation of King Jeroboam."*

Amos and Amaziah

¹⁰ Amaziah the priest at Bethel sent this message to King Jeroboam of Israel, "Amos is plotting against you in the very heart of Israel. Our nation cannot put up with his message for very long. ¹¹ Here is what he is saying:

'Jeroboam will be put to death,
and the people will be taken
   to a foreign country.' "

¹² Then Amaziah told me, "Amos, take your visions and get out! Go back to Judah and earn your living there as a prophet. ¹³ Don't do any more preaching at Bethel. The king worships here at our national temple."

¹⁴ I answered:

I'm not a prophet! And I wasn't trained to be a prophet. I am a shepherd, and I take care of fig trees. ¹⁵ But the LORD told me to leave my herds and preach to the people of Israel. ¹⁶ And here you are, telling me not to preach! ¹⁷ Now, listen to what the LORD says about you:

Your wife will become
   a prostitute in the city,
your sons and daughters
   will be killed in war,
and your land will be divided
   among others.
You will die in a country
   of foreigners,
and the people of Israel
will be dragged
   from their homeland.

CHAPTER 8

A basket of fruit

¹ The LORD God showed me a basket of ripe fruit ² and asked, "Amos, what do you see?"

"A basket of ripe fruit," I replied.

Then he said,

"This is the end*
for my people Israel.
   I won't forgive them again.
³ Instead of singing
in the temple,
   they will cry and weep.
Dead bodies will be everywhere.
   So keep silent!
I, the LORD, have spoken!"

Israel is doomed

The LORD said:

⁴ You people crush those in need
   and wipe out the poor.
⁵ You say to yourselves,
"How much longer before the end
   of the New Moon Festival?
When will the Sabbath* be over?
Our wheat is ready,
   and we want to sell it now.
We can't wait to cheat
   and charge high prices
      for the grain we sell.

---

*7.1 harvested: This would have been an especially bad time for a locust attack. The non-grain crops such as vegetables and onions were just beginning to sprout, and the grain crops were almost ready to be harvested.

*7.9 Jeroboam: Jeroboam II, who ruled Israel 783–743 BC.

*8.2 end: In Hebrew "ripe fruit" and "end" sound alike.

*8.5 New Moon Festival . . . Sabbath: Selling grain at these times was forbidden by the Law of Moses.

'8.14 You made . . . Beersheba: Or "You made promises to the goddess Ashimah at Samaria, and you made vows in the names of other gods at the shrines of Dan and Beersheba."
'9.6 He built . . . earth: One possible meaning for the difficult Hebrew text.
'9.7 Crete: Hebrew "Caphtor".

Obadiah

A quick look at this book

Obadiah was a prophet, but nothing else is known about him. His name, meaning "worshipper of the Lord", was fairly common in ancient Israel.

Obadiah wrote about the nation of Edom, which was south of the Dead Sea. The Edomites had been cruel to the Lord's people Israel, and so the Lord was going to punish them and give their land to Israel.

The book of Obadiah is so short that it wasn't divided into chapters.

Edom's pride and punishment

1 The LORD God gave Obadiah
    a message' about Edom,
    and this is what we heard:
"I, the LORD, have sent a messenger
    with orders for the nations
    to attack Edom."

2 The LORD said to Edom:
I will make you the weakest
    and most despised nation.
3 You live in a mountain fortress,'

because your pride
    makes you feel safe from attack,
    but you are mistaken.
4 I will still bring you down,
    even if you fly higher
        than an eagle
    or nest among the stars.
    I, the LORD, have spoken!

5 If thieves break in at night, they steal
    only what they want.
And people who harvest grapes
    always leave some unpicked.
But, Edom, you are doomed!
6 Everything you treasure most
    will be taken from you.
7 Your allies can't be trusted.
    They will force you out
    of your own country.
Your best friends
    will trick and trap you,
    even before you know it.

8 Edom, when this happens,
    I, the LORD, will destroy
    all your marvellous wisdom.
9 Warriors from the city of Teman*
    will be terrified,
    and you descendants of Esau*
    will be wiped out.

Edom's cruelty

The LORD condemns Edom's cruelty

10 You were cruel to your relatives,
    the descendants of Jacob.*

---

*v9 Teman: A famous city in Edom.
*v9 descendants of Esau: The people of Edom were descendants of Esau, the brother of Jacob (Israel).
*v10 descendants of Jacob: Jacob and Esau were brothers (see the note on Esau at verse 9).

See also: v1–14: Isa 34.5–17; 63.1–6; Jer 49.7–22;
Ezek 25.12–14; 35.1–15; Amos 1.11,12; Mal 1.2–5.

Now you will be destroyed,
    disgraced for ever.
¹¹ You stood there and watched
    as foreigners entered Jerusalem
    and took what they wanted.
    In fact, you were no better
    than those foreigners.

¹² Why did you celebrate
    when such a dreadful disaster
    struck your relatives?
    Why were you so pleased
    when everyone in Judah
    was suffering?
¹³ They are my people,
    and you were cruel to them.
    You went through their towns,
    sneering and stealing
    whatever was left.
¹⁴ In their time of torment,
    you ambushed refugees
    and handed them over
    to their attackers.

Victory for Israel

The LORD will judge the nations

¹⁵ The day is coming
    when I, the LORD,
    will judge the nations.
    And, Edom, you will pay in full
    for what you have done.

¹⁶ I forced the people of Judah▸
    to drink the wine of my anger
    on my sacred mountain.
    Soon the neighbouring nations
    must drink their fill —
    then vanish without a trace.

Victory for Israel

¹⁷ The LORD's people who escape
    will go to Mount Zion,
    and it will be holy.
    Then Jacob's descendants
    will capture the land of those
    who took their land.
¹⁸ Israel▸ will be a fire,
    and Edom will be straw
    going up in flames.
    The LORD has spoken!

¹⁹ The people of Israel
    who live in the Southern Desert
    will take the land of Edom.
    Those who live in the hills
    will capture Philistia,
    Ephraim, and Samaria.

And the tribe of Benjamin
    will conquer Gilead.

²⁰ Those who return from captivity
    will control Phoenicia
    as far as Zarephath.▸
    Captives from Jerusalem
    who were taken to Sepharad*
    will capture the towns
    of the Southern Desert.
²¹ Those the LORD has saved
    will live on Mount Zion
    and rule over Edom.▸
    Then the kingdom will belong
    to the LORD.

---

*v20 Sepharad: Possibly the city of Sardis, the capital of Lydia, a country north and west of Media. This would refer to those captives from Judah who had been taken beyond the kingdom of Babylonia.

Additional notes

▸v1 message: Or "vision".
▸v3 mountain fortress: The Hebrew text has "rocky cliff", which sounds like "Sela", the capital of Edom, a fortress city built on a mountain.
▸v16 I forced . . . Judah: Or "I will force the people of Edom".
▸v18 Israel: Hebrew "The descendants of Jacob and of Joseph".
▸v20 Those who return . . . Zarephath: One possible meaning for the difficult Hebrew text.
▸v21 Those the LORD . . . Edom: Or "Leaders on (from) Mount Zion will save the people and rule over Edom."

Jonah

The book of Jonah is different from the other prophetic books, because it gives only one sentence of what the prophet Jonah preached. Instead, this book tells how Jonah disobeyed the Lord and refused to warn Nineveh that it was going to be destroyed. Jonah even wanted the city to be destroyed, because it was the capital city of Assyria, a hated enemy of Israel. But the Lord corrected Jonah; then Jonah went to Nineveh and preached the Lord's message.

When many people think about the book of Jonah, they think only of Jonah being swallowed by a huge fish. However, the message of this book is that the Lord wants to have mercy on everyone; as Jonah says to him:

> You are a kind and merciful God, and you are
> very patient. You always show love, and you
> don't like to punish anyone, not even
> foreigners.

(4.2b)

Jonah runs from the Lord

CHAPTER 1

¹ One day the LORD told Jonah, the son of Amittai, ² to go to the great city of Nineveh* and say to the people, "The LORD has seen your terrible sins. You are doomed!"

³ Instead, Jonah ran from the LORD. He went to the seaport of Joppa and bought a ticket on a ship that was going to Spain. Then he got on the ship and sailed away to escape.

⁴ But the LORD made a strong wind blow, and such a bad storm came up that the ship was about to be broken to pieces. ⁵ The sailors were frightened, and they all started praying to their gods. They even threw the ship's cargo overboard to make the ship lighter.

All this time, Jonah was down below deck, sound asleep. ⁶ The ship's captain went to him and said, "How can you sleep at a time like this? Get up and pray to your God! Perhaps he will have pity on us and keep us from drowning."

⁷ Finally, the sailors got together and said, "Let's ask our gods to show us* who caused all this trouble." It turned out to be Jonah.

⁸ They started asking him, "Are you the one who brought all this trouble on us? What business are you in? Where do you come from? What is your country? Who are your people?"

---

*1.2 Nineveh: Capital city of Assyria, a hated enemy of Israel.

*1.7 ask . . . show us: The Hebrew text has "cast lots", which were pieces of wood or stone used to find out how and when to do something. In this case, the lots would show who was the guilty person.

See also: 1.1: 2 King 14.25.

⁹ Jonah answered, "I'm a Hebrew, and I worship the LORD God of heaven, who made the sea and the dry land."

¹⁰ When the sailors heard this, they were frightened, because Jonah had already told them he was running from the LORD. Then they said, "Do you know what you have done?"

¹¹ The storm kept getting worse, until finally the sailors asked him, "What should we do with you to make the sea calm down?"

¹² Jonah told them, "Throw me into the sea, and it will calm down. I'm the cause of this terrible storm."

¹³ The sailors tried their best to row to the shore. But they could not do it, and the storm kept getting worse every minute. ¹⁴ So they prayed to the LORD, "Please don't let us drown for taking this man's life. Don't hold us guilty for killing an innocent man. All this happened because you wanted it to." ¹⁵ Then they threw Jonah overboard, and the sea calmed down. ¹⁶ The sailors were so terrified that they offered a sacrifice to the LORD and made all kinds of promises.

¹⁷ The LORD sent a big fish to swallow Jonah, and Jonah was inside the fish for three days and three nights.

Jonah prays to the Lord

CHAPTER 2

¹ From inside the fish, Jonah prayed to the LORD his God:

² When I was in trouble, LORD,
I prayed to you,
  and you listened to me.
From deep in the world
  of the dead,
I begged for your help,
  and you answered my prayer.

³ You threw me down
  to the bottom of the sea.
The water was churning all around;
I was completely covered
  by your mighty waves.

⁴ I thought I was swept away
  from your sight,
never again to see
  your holy temple.

⁵ I was almost drowned
  by the swirling waters
    that surrounded me.

Seaweed had wrapped
  around my head.
⁶ I had sunk down below
  the underwater mountains;
I knew that for ever,
  I would be a prisoner there.

But, you, LORD God,
  rescued me from that pit.
⁷ When my life was slipping away,
  I remembered you —
and in your holy temple
  you heard my prayer.

⁸ All who worship worthless idols
turn from the God
  who offers them mercy.
⁹ But with shouts of praise,
  I will offer a sacrifice
    to you, my LORD.
I will keep my promise,
because you are the one
  with power to save.

¹⁰ The LORD commanded the fish to vomit up Jonah on the shore. And it did.

Jonah goes to Nineveh, and its people believe God's message

CHAPTER 3

¹ Once again the LORD told Jonah ² to go to that great city of Nineveh and preach his message of doom.

³ Jonah obeyed the LORD and went to Nineveh. The city was so big that it took three days just to walk through it. ⁴ After walking for a day, Jonah warned the people, "Forty days from now, Nineveh will be destroyed!"

⁵ They believed God's message and set a time when they would go without eating to show their sorrow. Then everyone in the city, no matter who they were, dressed in sackcloth.

⁶ When the king of Nineveh heard what was happening, he also dressed in sackcloth; he left the royal palace and sat in dust.*

*3.5,6 dressed in sackcloth . . . sat in dust: Sackcloth was a rough, dark-coloured cloth made from goat or camel hair and used to make grain sacks. Sometimes people wore sackcloth and sat in dust to show how sorry they were for their sins.

See also: 3.4,5: Matt 12.41; Luke 11.32.

See also: 1.17: Matt 12.40.

[7-9] Then he and his officials sent out an order for everyone in the city to obey. It said:

> None of you or your animals may eat or drink a thing. Each of you must wear sackcloth, and you must even put sackcloth on your animals.
>
> You must also pray to the LORD God with all your heart and stop being sinful and cruel. Perhaps God will change his mind and have mercy on us, so we won't be destroyed.

[10] When God saw that the people had stopped doing evil things, he had pity and did not destroy them as he had planned.

Jonah is angry because the Lord showed mercy

CHAPTER 4

[1] Jonah was really upset and angry. [2] So he prayed:

> Our LORD, I knew from the very beginning that you wouldn't destroy Nineveh. That's why I left my own country and headed for Spain. You are a kind and merciful God, and you are very patient. You always show love, and you don't like to punish anyone, not even foreigners.
>
> [3] Now let me die! I'd be better off dead.

[4] The LORD replied, "What right do you have to be angry?"

[5] Jonah then left through the east gate of the city and made a shelter to protect himself from the sun. He sat under the shelter, waiting to see what would happen to Nineveh.

[6] The LORD made a vine grow up to shade Jonah's head and protect him from the sun. Jonah was very happy to have the vine, [7] but early the next morning the LORD sent a worm to chew on the vine, and the vine dried up. [8] During the day the LORD sent a scorching wind, and the sun beat down on Jonah's head, making him feel faint. Jonah was ready to die, and he shouted, "I wish I were dead!"

[9] But the LORD asked, "Jonah, do you have the right to be angry about the vine?"

"Yes, I do," he answered, "and I'm angry enough to die."

[10] But the LORD said:

You are concerned about a vine that you did not plant or take care of, a vine that grew up in one night and died the next. [11] In that city of Nineveh there are more than a hundred and twenty thousand people who cannot tell right from wrong, and many cattle are also there. Don't you think I should be concerned about that big city?

Micah

A quick look at this book

The messages in this book were especially for Samaria, the capital of Israel, and for Jerusalem, the capital of Judah. Instead of leading their nations to worship and obey the Lord, the officials and people of these capital cities had led their nations to worship other gods and to cheat and rob the poor. And so the Lord was going to punish Israel and Judah.

But the Lord had also promised that in the future the people of Israel and Judah would return to him. Then he and his chosen king would take care of the people, just as shepherds take care of sheep, and there would be peace everywhere:

He will settle arguments
between distant
* and powerful nations.*
They will beat their swords
and their spears
* into rakes and shovels;*
they will never again make war
* or attack one another.*
Everyone will find rest
beneath their own fig trees
* or grape vines,*
and they will live in peace.

(4.3,4a)

The Lord will punish his people

CHAPTER 1

¹ I am Micah from Moresheth.* And this is the message about Samaria and Jerusalem* that the LORD gave to me when Jotham, Ahaz, and Hezekiah* were the kings of Judah.

---

*1.1 Moresheth: A town in southern Judah not far from Gath. In verse 14 it is called Moresheth-Gath.
*1.1 Samaria and Jerusalem: Samaria was the capital of the northern kingdom (Israel), and Jerusalem was the capital of the southern kingdom (Judah).
*1.1 Jotham, Ahaz, and Hezekiah: Jotham, the son of Uzziah, ruled Judah 740–736 BC; Ahaz, the son of Jotham, ruled 736–716 BC; Hezekiah, the son of Ahaz, ruled 716–687 BC.

See also: 1.1: a 2 King 15.32–38; 2 Chron 27.1–7; b 2 King 16.1–20; 2 Chron 28.1–27; c 2 King 16.1—20.21; 2 Chron 29.1—32.33.

Judgment on Samaria

2 Listen, all of you!
Earth and everything on it,
pay close attention.
The LORD God accuses you
from his holy temple.*

3 And he will come down
to crush underfoot
every pagan altar.

4 Mountains will melt
beneath his feet
like wax beside a fire.
Valleys will vanish like water
rushing down a ravine.

5 This will happen because of
the terrible sins of Israel,
the descendants of Jacob.
Samaria has led Israel to sin,
and pagan altars at Jerusalem
have made Judah sin.

6 So the LORD will leave Samaria
in ruins —
merely an empty field
where vineyards are planted.
He will scatter its stones
and destroy its foundations.

7 Samaria's idols will be smashed,
and the wages
of temple prostitutes*
will be destroyed by fire.
Silver and gold from those idols
will then be used
by foreigners
as payment for prostitutes.

Judah is doomed

8 Because of this tragedy,*
I go barefoot and naked.
My crying and weeping
sound like howling wolves
or ostriches.

9 The nation is fatally wounded.
Judah is doomed.
Jerusalem will fall.

10 Don't tell it in Gath!
Don't even cry.

Instead, roll in the dust
at Beth-Leaphrah.*

11 Depart naked and ashamed,
you people of Shaphir.'
The town of Bethezel' mourns
because no one from Zaanan'
went out to help.'

12 Everyone in Maroth'
hoped for the best,
but the LORD sent disaster
down on Jerusalem.

13 Get the war chariots ready,
you people of Lachish.*
You led Jerusalem into sin,
just as Israel did.*

14 Now you will have to give
a going-away gift*
to Moresheth.*
Israel's kings will discover
that they cannot trust
the town of Achzib.*

15 People of Mareshah,*
the LORD will send someone
to capture your town.
Then Israel's glorious king
will be forced to hide
in Adullam Cave.*

---

*1.2 holy temple: Possibly the one in heaven, though it may be the Jerusalem temple.

*1.7 wages of temple prostitutes: At pagan temples, people had sex with prostitutes as a way of worshipping the idols, and the money earned in this way was used to support the pagan religion.

*1.8 this tragedy: Either the destruction of Samaria (verses 6,7) or the coming destruction of Judah and Jerusalem.

*1.10 Gath . . . Beth-Leaphrah: Gath was a Philistine city; Beth-Leaphrah is unknown, but in Hebrew it sounds like "House of Dust".

*1.13 Lachish: The chief city of south-west Judah, about forty-eight kilometres from Jerusalem.

*1.13 led . . . sin . . . did: Or "You led Jerusalem and Israel into sin." In Hebrew "Lachish" sounds like "a team of horses (that pulls a war chariot)". And the sin may be that Lachish led the nation to trust the power of war chariots instead of the LORD. But the sin could be idolatry or some false teachings that were brought in from Egypt by way of Lachish.

*1.14 going-away gift: The gift (dowry) that a bride's father gave her when she left the home of her parents to live with the family of her husband. In Hebrew the word for "bride" or "fiancee" sounds like "Moresheth".

*1.14 Moresheth: Hebrew "Moresheth-Gath"; the home of Micah (see verse 1).

*1.14 Achzib: Meaning "lie" or "deception" was near Adullam Cave (verse 15), where David hid from King Saul (see 1 Samuel 22.1,2). Micah probably means that the people of Israel (including their king) will have to run for their lives, but will find that all hope for escape is merely a "lie" (see verse 15).

*1.15 Mareshah: Sounds something like the Hebrew word for "conqueror" and was only a few kilometres north-east of Lachish.

*1.15 Adullam Cave: See the note at 1.14.

16 Judah, shave your head
as bald as a vulture
and start mourning.
Your precious children*
will be dragged off
to a foreign country.

CHAPTER 2

Punishment for those
who abuse their power

1 Doomed! You're doomed!
At night you lie in bed,
making evil plans.
And when morning comes,
you do what you've planned
because you have the power.
2 You grab any field or house
that you want;
you cheat families
out of homes and land.

3 But here is what the LORD says:
"I am planning trouble for you.
Your necks will be caught
in a noose,
and you will be disgraced
in this time of disaster."

4 When that happens,
this sorrowful song
will be sung about you:
"Ruined! Completely ruined!
The LORD has taken our land
and given it to traitors."

5 And so you will never again
own property
among the LORD's people.

6 "Enough of your preaching!"
That's what you tell me.
"We won't be disgraced,
so stop preaching!"

7 Descendants of Jacob,
is it right for you to claim
that the LORD did what he did
because he was angry?
Doesn't he always bless
those who do right?
8 My people, you have even stolen
clothes right off the backs
of your unsuspecting soldiers
returning home from battle.

9 You take over lovely homes
that belong to the women
of my nation.
Then you cheat their children
out of the inheritance
that comes from the LORD.

10 Get out of here, you crooks!
You'll find no rest here.
You're not fit to belong
to the LORD's people,
and you will be destroyed.

11 The only prophet you want
is a liar who will say,
"Drink and get drunk!"

A promise of hope

The LORD said:

12 I, the LORD, promise
to bring together
the people of Israel
who have survived.
I will gather them,
just as a shepherd
brings sheep together,
and there will be many.
13 I will break down the gate
and lead them out —
then I will be their king.

The Lord will punish evil
rulers and lying prophets

CHAPTER 3

1 Listen to me,
you rulers of Israel!
You know right from wrong,
2 but you prefer to do evil
instead of what is right.
You skin my people alive.
You strip off their flesh,
3 break their bones,
cook it all in a pot,
and gulp it down.

4 Some day you will beg the LORD
to help you,
but he will turn away
because of your sins.

5 You lying prophets promise
security for anyone
who gives you food,
but disaster for anyone
who refuses to feed you.

---

*1.16 precious children: The towns mentioned in
verses 10–15.

Here is what the LORD says to you prophets:

6 "You will live in the dark,
  far from the sight of the sun,
  with no message from me.
7 You prophets and fortune-tellers
  will all be disgraced,
  with no message from me."

8 But the LORD has filled me
  with power and his Spirit.
I have been given the courage
  to speak about justice
and to tell you people of Israel
  that you have sinned.
9 So listen to my message,
  you rulers of Israel!
You hate justice
  and twist the truth.
10 You make cruelty and murder
  a way of life in Jerusalem.
11 You leaders accept bribes
  for dishonest decisions.
You priests and prophets
  teach and preach,
  but only for money.

Then you say,
  "The LORD is on our side.
  No harm will come to us."
12 And so, because of you,
Jerusalem will be ploughed under
  and left in ruins.
Thorns will cover the mountain
  where the temple now stands.

A new temple in a new Israel

CHAPTER 4

Peace and prosperity

1 In the future, the mountain
  with the LORD's temple
  will be the highest of all.
It will reach above the hills,
  and every nation will rush to it.
2 People of many nations
  will come and say,
  "Let's go up to the mountain
  of the LORD God of Jacob
  and worship in his temple."

The LORD will teach us his Law
  from Jerusalem,
  and we will obey him.

3 He will settle arguments
  between distant
  and powerful nations.
They will beat their swords
  and their spears
  into rakes and shovels;
they will never again make war
  or attack one another.
4 Everyone will find rest
  beneath their own fig trees
  or grape vines,
and they will live in peace.
This is a solemn promise
  of the LORD All-Powerful.

5 Others may follow their gods,
  but we will always follow
  the LORD our God.

The LORD will lead his people home

6 The LORD said:

At that time
  I will gather my people —
  the lame and the outcasts,
  and all into whose lives
  I have brought sorrow.
7 Then the lame and the outcasts
  will belong to my people
  and become a strong nation.
I, the LORD, will rule them
  from Mount Zion for ever.
8 Mount Zion in Jerusalem,
  guardian of my people,
  you will rule again.

9 Jerusalem, why are you crying?
  Don't you have a king?
  Have your advisers gone?
Are you suffering
  like a woman in childbirth?
10 Keep on groaning with pain,
  you people of Jerusalem!
If you escape from your city
  to the countryside,
  you will still be taken
  as prisoners to Babylonia.
But later I will rescue you
  from your enemies.

11 Zion, because of your sins
  you are surrounded
  by many nations who say,
  "We can hardly wait
  to see you disgraced."
12 But they don't know
  that I, the LORD,

have gathered them here
    to grind them like grain.
¹³ Smash them to pieces, Zion!
I'll let you be like a bull
    with iron horns and bronze hoofs.
Crush those nations
and bring their wealth to me,
    the LORD of the earth.

CHAPTER 5

A promised ruler

¹ Jerusalem, enemy troops
    have surrounded you;*
they have struck Israel's ruler
    in the face with a stick.

² Bethlehem Ephrath,
you are one of the smallest towns
    in the nation of Judah.
But the LORD will choose
one of your people
    to rule the nation —
someone whose family
    goes back to ancient times.*
³ The LORD will abandon Israel
    only until this ruler is born,
and the rest of his family
    returns to Israel.
⁴ Like a shepherd
    taking care of his sheep,
this ruler will lead
    and care for his people
by the power and glorious name
    of the LORD his God.
His people will live securely,
    and the whole earth will know
    his true greatness,
⁵ because he will bring peace.

Assyria will be defeated

Let Assyria attack our country
    and our palaces.
We will counter-attack,
    led by a number of rulers
⁶ whose strong army will defeat
    the nation of Assyria.
Yes, our leaders will rescue us,
    if those Assyrians
    dare to invade our land.

The survivors will be safe

⁷ A few of Jacob's descendants
survived and are scattered
    among the nations.

But the LORD will let them
cover the earth
    like dew and rain
    that refreshes the soil.
⁸ At present they are scattered,
    but later they will attack,
as though they were fierce lions
    pouncing on sheep.
Their enemies will be torn to shreds,
    with no one to save them;
⁹ they will be helpless,
    completely destroyed.

Idols will be destroyed in Israel

¹⁰ The LORD said:

At that time I will wipe out
    your cavalry and chariots,
¹¹ as well as your cities
    and your fortresses.
¹² I will stop you
    from telling fortunes
    and practising witchcraft.
¹³ You will no longer worship
    the idols or stone images
    you have made —
I will destroy them,
¹⁴ together with the sacred poles*
    and even your towns.
¹⁵ I will become furious
    and take revenge
    on the nations
    that refuse to obey me.

Israel is declared guilty

CHAPTER 6

The LORD's challenge to his people

¹ The LORD said to his people:

Come and present your case
    to the hills and mountains.
² Israel, I am bringing charges
    against you —
I call upon the mountains
    and the earth's firm foundation
    to be my witnesses.

³ My people, have I wronged you
    in any way at all?
    Please tell me.
⁴ I rescued you from Egypt,
    where you were slaves.

*5.14 sacred poles: Used in the worship of Asherah,
the fertility goddess.

See also: 5.2: Matt 2.6; John 7.42. 5.6: Gen 10.8–11.

See also: 6.4: a Exod 12.50,51; b Exod 4.10–16; c Exod 15.20.

I sent Moses, Aaron, and Miriam
  to be your leaders.
5 Don't forget the evil plans
  of King Balak of Moab
or what Balaam son of Beor*
  said to him.
Remember how I, the LORD,
  saved you many times
on your way from Acacia
  to Gilgal.*

True obedience

6 What offering should I bring
  when I bow down to worship
  the LORD God Most High?
Should I try to please him*
  by sacrificing
  calves a year old?
7 Will thousands of sheep
  or rivers of olive oil
  make God satisfied with me?
Should I sacrifice to the LORD
  my firstborn child as payment
  for my terrible sins?
8 The LORD God has told us
  what is right
  and what he demands:
"See that justice is done,
  let mercy be your first concern,
  and humbly obey your God."

Cheating and violence

The LORD said:

9 I am the LORD,
  and it makes sense to respect
  my power to punish.
So listen to my message
  for the city of Jerusalem:⸽
10 You store up stolen treasures
  and use dishonest scales.⸽
11 But I, the LORD, will punish you
  for cheating with weights
  and with measures.
12 You rich people are violent,
  and everyone tells lies.

13 Because of your sins,
  I will wound you and leave you
  ruined and defenceless.
14 You will eat,
  but still be hungry;
you will store up goods,
  but lose everything —
I, the LORD, will let it all
  be captured in war.
15 You won't harvest what you plant
  or use the oil
  from your olive trees
or drink the wine
  from grapes you grow.

16 Jerusalem, this will happen
  because you followed
the sinful example
  of kings Omri and Ahab.*
Now I will destroy you
  and your property.
Then the people of every nation
  will make fun and insult you.

CHAPTER 7

Israel is corrupt

1 I feel so empty inside —
  like someone starving
  for grapes or figs,
after the vines and trees
  have all been picked clean.
2 No one is loyal to God;
  no one does right.
Everyone is brutal
  and eager to deceive
  everyone else.
3 People co-operate to commit crime.
Judges and leaders demand bribes,
  and rulers cheat in court.⸽
4 The most honest of them
  is worse than a thorn patch.

Your doom has come!
Lookouts sound the warning,
  and everyone panics.
5 Don't trust anyone,
  not even your best friend,
and be careful what you say
  to the one you love.

---

*6.5 Balak . . . Beor: See Numbers 22—24.
*6.5 Acacia to Gilgal: Acacia was where the Israelites
camped after the experience with Balaam (see
Numbers 25.1; Joshua 2.1; 3.1); Gilgal was where
they camped while waiting to attack Jericho (see
Joshua 4.19—5.12).
*6.6 try to please him: This refers to what are
traditionally called "burnt sacrifices", which were
offered as a way of pleasing the LORD.
See also: 6.5: a Num 22.2—24.25; b Josh 3.1—4.19.

*6.16 Omri and Ahab: King Ahab was the son of
Omri and the husband of the evil Jezebel. Almost two
centuries before Micah, the prophet Elijah had
spoken against the idolatry and the other sinful
practices that Ahab had encouraged in Israel (see
1 Kings 16.21—34; 18.1—18; 21.1—26).
See also: 6.16: a 1 King 16.23—28; b 1 King 16.29—34;
21.25,26.

6 Sons refuse to respect
   their own fathers,
   daughters rebel against
   their own mothers,
   and daughters-in-law despise
   their mothers-in-law.
   Your family is now your enemy.
7 But I trust the LORD God
   to save me,
   and I will wait for him
   to answer my prayer.

The nation turns to God

8 My enemies, don't be glad
   because of my troubles!
   I may have fallen,
   but I will get up;
   I may be sitting in the dark,
   but the LORD is my light.
9 I have sinned against the LORD.
   And so I must endure his anger,
   until he comes to my defence.
   But I know that I will see him
   making things right for me
   and leading me to the light.

10 You, my enemies, said,
   "The LORD God is helpless."
   Now each of you
   will be disgraced
   and put to shame.
   I will see you trampled
   like mud in the street.

A bright future

11 Towns of Judah, the day is coming
   when your walls will be rebuilt,
   and your boundaries enlarged.
12 People will flock to you
   from Assyria and Egypt,
   from Babylonia*
   and everywhere else.
13 Those nations will suffer disaster
   because of what they did.

Micah's prayer and the LORD's answer

14 Lead your people, LORD!
   Come and be our shepherd.
   Grasslands surround us,
   but we live in a forest.
   So lead us to Bashan and Gilead,*

and let us find pasture
   as we did long ago.
The LORD said:
15 I, the LORD, will work miracles
   just as I did when I led you
   out of Egypt.
16 Nations will see this
   and be ashamed because
   of their helpless armies.
   They will be in shock,
   unable to speak or hear,
17 because of their fear of me,
   your LORD and God.
   Then they will come trembling,
   crawling out of their fortresses
   like insects or snakes,
   lapping up the dust.

No one is like God

The people said:
18 Our God, no one is like you.
   We are all that is left
   of your chosen people,
   and you freely forgive
   our sin and guilt.
   You don't stay angry for ever;
   you're glad to have pity
19   and pleased to be merciful.
   You will trample on our sins
   and throw them in the sea.
20 You will keep your word
   and be faithful to Jacob
   and to Abraham,
   as you promised our ancestors
   many years ago.

Additional notes

•1.11 **Shaphir:** Mentioned only here in the Old Testament; in Hebrew "Shaphir" means "beautiful".
•1.11 **Bethezel:** Mentioned only here in the Old Testament; in Hebrew "Bethezel" means "house next door".
•1.11 **Zaanan:** Mentioned only here in the Old Testament; in Hebrew "Zaanan" means "one who goes out".
•1.11 **The town . . . help:** Or "No one from Zaanan refused to desert their town, and Bethezel mourns because it is left undefended."
•1.12 **Maroth:** Mentioned only here in the Old Testament; in Hebrew "Maroth" means "bitter".
•2.4 **The LORD . . . traitors:** One possible meaning for the difficult Hebrew text.

*7.14 **Bashan and Gilead:** Two regions east of the River Jordan, known for their fertile pasture lands.
See also: 7.6: Matt 10.35,36; Luke 12.53.

²2.9 inheritance . . . Lord: The Hebrew text has "my glory", which refers to the inheritance of land that the Lord had promised his people.
²2.10 destroyed: One possible meaning for the difficult Hebrew text.
²4.11 We . . . disgraced: Or "We'll pull up your skirt and expose your nakedness!"
⁵5.1 Jerusalem . . . you: Or "Jerusalem, you are slashing yourself in sorrow, because of the enemy troops".
⁵5.2 family . . . times: Or "kingdom is eternal".
⁵5.6 the nation of Assyria: The Hebrew text uses both "land of Assyria" and "land of Nimrod", which was a poetic name for Assyria.
⁶6.9 Jerusalem: One possible meaning for the difficult Hebrew text of verse 9.
⁶6.10 scales: One possible meaning for the difficult Hebrew text of verse 10.
⁷7.3 court: One possible meaning for the difficult Hebrew text of verse 3.
⁷7.12 Babylonia: The Hebrew text has "the river", meaning the River Euphrates, which stood for Babylonia.

Nahum

A quick look at this book

In this book, the prophet Nahum said the Lord was going to bring justice and punish Assyria, because it had been so cruel to other nations. Many Old Testament books also talk about the Lord's mercy when they discuss the Lord's justice. But in this book the Lord is merciful and good only to those who turn to him (1.7). Nahum also hinted that one way God has mercy on his people is to punish enemies like Assyria and give his people freedom from their power (1.13–15). And the Lord can do this because he rules the earth:

> The LORD God demands loyalty.
> In his anger, he takes revenge
>   on his enemies.
> The LORD is powerful,
>   yet patient;
> he makes sure that the guilty
>   are always punished.
> He can be seen in storms
>   and in whirlwinds;
> clouds are the dust from his feet.

(1.2,3)

The fierce anger of the Lord

CHAPTER 1

¹ I am Nahum from Elkosh.* And this is the message* that I wrote down about Nineveh.*

The fierce anger of the LORD

² The LORD God demands loyalty.
  In his anger, he takes revenge
    on his enemies.
³ The LORD is powerful,
    yet patient;
  he makes sure that the guilty
    are always punished.
  He can be seen in storms
    and in whirlwinds;
  clouds are the dust from his feet.

⁴ At the LORD's command,
    oceans and rivers dry up.
  Bashan, Mount Carmel,
    and Lebanon* wither,
  and their flowers fade.
⁵ At the sight of the LORD,
    mountains and hills
    tremble and melt;
  the earth and its people
    shudder and shake.
⁶ Who can stand the heat
    of his furious anger?
  It flashes out like fire
    and shatters stones.

---

*1.1 Elkosh: The location of Elkosh is not known.
*1.1 Nineveh: The capital of Assyria, the hated enemy of Israel.
*1.4 Bashan, Mount Carmel, and Lebanon: Three regions noted for their trees and flowers.
See also: 1.1–3.19: Isa 10.5–34; 14.24–27; Zeph 2.13–15.

Assyria's doom brings hope for the Lord's people

The power of Assyria will be broken

⁷ The LORD is good.
He protects those who trust him
in times of trouble.

⁸ But like a roaring flood,
the LORD chases his enemies
into dark places and destroys them.

⁹ So don't plot against the LORD!
He wipes out his enemies,
and they never revive.

¹⁰ They are like drunkards
overcome by wine,
or like dry thorn bushes
burning in a fire.*

¹¹ Assyria, one of your rulers
has made evil plans
against the LORD.

¹² But the LORD says, "Assyria,
no matter how strong you are,
you are doomed!
My people Judah,
I have troubled you before,
but I won't do it again.

¹³ I'll snap your chains and set you free
from the Assyrians."

¹⁴ Assyria, this is what else
the LORD says to you:
"Your name will be forgotten.
I will destroy every idol
in your temple,
and I will send you to the grave,
because you are worthless."

¹⁵ Look towards the mountains,
people of Judah!
Here comes a messenger
with good news of peace.
Celebrate your festivals.
Keep your promises to God.
Your evil enemies are destroyed
and will never again
invade your country.

Nineveh, the capital of Assyria, will be destroyed

CHAPTER 2

¹ Nineveh, someone is coming
to attack and scatter you.

Guard your fortresses!
Watch the road!
Be brave!
Prepare for battle!

² Judah and Israel are like trees
with branches broken
by their enemies.
But the LORD is going to restore
their power and glory.

³⁻⁴ Nineveh, on this day of attack,
your enemies' shields are red;
their uniforms are crimson.
Their horses* prance,
and their armoured* chariots
dart around like lightning
or flaming torches.

⁵ An officer gives a command.
But his soldiers stumble,
as they hasten to build
a shelter to protect themselves
against rocks thrown down
from the city wall.

⁶ The river gates* fly open,
and panic floods the palace.

⁷ Nineveh is disgraced.
The queen is dragged off.
Her servant women mourn;
they sound like doves,
and they beat their breasts
in sorrow.*

⁸ Nineveh is like a pond
with leaking water.
Shouts of "Stop! Don't go!"
can be heard everywhere.
But everyone is leaving.

⁹ Enemy soldiers shout,
"The city is full of treasure
and all kinds of wealth.
Steal her silver! Grab her gold!"

¹⁰ Nineveh is doomed! Destroyed!
Her people tremble with fear;
their faces turn pale.*

¹¹ What happened to this city?
They were safer there
than powerful lions in a den,
with no one to disturb them.

¹² These are the same lions
that ferociously attacked
their victims,
then dragged away the flesh
to feed their young.

See also: 1.15: Isa 52.7.

*2.6 river gates: Nineveh was protected by a moat
filled with water from the nearby River Tigris.

¹³ The LORD All-Powerful,
   is against you, Nineveh.
   God will burn your chariots
   and send an army to kill
   those young lions of yours.
   You will never again
   make victims of others
   or send messengers to threaten
   everyone on this earth.

CHAPTER 3

Punishment for Nineveh

The LORD said:

¹ Doom to the crime capital!
   Nineveh, city of murder
   and treachery,
² here is your fate —
   cracking whips,
   churning wheels;
   galloping horses,
   roaring chariots;
³ cavalry attacking,
   swords and spears flashing;
   soldiers stumbling
   over piles of dead bodies.
⁴ You were nothing more
   than a prostitute
   using your magical charms
   and witchcraft
   to attract and trap nations.

⁵ But I, the LORD All-Powerful,
   am now your enemy.
   I will pull up your skirt
   and let nations and kingdoms
   stare at your nakedness.
⁶ I will cover you with rubbish!
   treat you like trash,
   and rub you in the dirt.
⁷ Everyone who sees you
   will turn away and shout,
   "Nineveh is done for!
   Is anyone willing to mourn
   or to give her comfort?"

Nineveh's fate is sealed

⁸ Nineveh, do you feel safer
   than the city of Thebes?*
   The River Nile
   was its wall of defence.◆

⁹ Thebes trusted the mighty power
   of Ethiopia* and Egypt;
   the nations of Put* and Libya
   were her allies.
¹⁰ But she was captured and taken
   to a foreign country.
   Her children were murdered
   at every street corner.
   The members of her royal family
   were auctioned off,
   and her high officials
   were bound in chains.

¹¹ Nineveh, now it's your turn!
   You will get drunk and try to hide
   from your enemy.
¹² Your fortresses are fig trees
   with ripe figs.
   Merely shake the trees,
   and fruit will fall
   into every open mouth.
¹³ Your army is weak.
   Fire has destroyed the crossbars
   on your city gates;
   now they stand wide open
   to your enemy.

¹⁴ Your city is under attack.
   Haul in extra water!
   Strengthen your defences!
   Start making bricks!
   Stir the mortar!
¹⁵ You will still go up in flames
   and be cut down by swords
   that will wipe you out like wheat
   attacked by grasshoppers.
   So, go ahead and increase
   like a swarm of locusts!*

¹⁶ More merchants are in your city
   than there are stars
   in the sky —
   but they are like locusts
   that eat everything,
   then fly away.
¹⁷ Your guards and your officials
   are swarms of locusts.
   On a chilly day
   they settle on a fence,

---

*3.8 Thebes: In 663 BC, the Assyrian King
Ashurbanipal captured this Egyptian city, which
seems to have been built with protection similar to
that of Nineveh.

*3.9 Ethiopia: The Hebrew text has "Cush", which
was a region south of Egypt that included parts of the
present countries of Ethiopia and Sudan.
*3.9 Put: A region in Africa, possibly part of the
present country of Libya.
*3.15 locusts: A type of grasshopper that comes in
swarms and causes great damage to plant life.

but when the sun comes out,
they take off
   to who-knows-where.

¹⁸ King of Assyria,
   your officials and leaders
      sleep the eternal sleep,
while your people are scattered
   in the mountains.
Yes, your people are sheep
   without a shepherd.
¹⁹ You're fatally wounded.
   There's no hope for you.
But everyone claps
   when they hear this news,
because your constant cruelty
   has caused them pain.

Additional notes

›**1.1 message:** Or "vision".
›**1.10 fire:** One possible meaning for the difficult Hebrew text of verse 10.
›**2,3,4 horses:** Two ancient translations; Hebrew "spears".
›**2,3,4 armoured:** One possible meaning for the difficult Hebrew text.
›**2.7 sorrow:** One possible meaning for the difficult Hebrew text of verse 7.
›**2.10 faces turn pale:** Or "ashes cover their faces".
›**3.8 was its . . . defence:** One possible meaning for the difficult Hebrew text.

Habakkuk

A quick look at this book

The first two chapters of this book report a conversation between Habakkuk and the Lord. Habakkuk complained that Judah was full of injustice and crime. The Lord answered that he was going to send the Babylonians to punish the people of Judah. But then Habakkuk complained that this would be unfair, because the Babylonians were even worse sinners than the people of Judah! The Lord answered that Babylonia would be punished later.

The last chapter of the book is a prayer in which Habakkuk praises the Lord's power and glory.

Habakkuk complains, and the Lord answers

CHAPTER 1

¹ I am Habakkuk the prophet. And this is the message' that the LORD gave me.

Habakkuk complains to the LORD

² Our LORD, how long must I beg
for your help
before you listen?

How long before you save us
from all this violence?
³ Why do you make me watch
such terrible injustice?
Why do you allow violence,
lawlessness, crime, and cruelty
to spread everywhere?
⁴ Laws cannot be enforced;
justice is always the loser;
criminals crowd out honest people
and twist the laws around.

The LORD answers Habakkuk

⁵ Look and be amazed
at what's happening
among the nations!
Even if you were told,
you would never believe
what's taking place now.
⁶ I am sending the Babylonians.
They are fierce and cruel —
marching across the land,
conquering cities and towns.

⁷ How fearsome and frightening.
Their only laws and rules
are the ones they make up.
⁸ Their cavalry troops are faster
than leopards,
more ferocious than wolves
hunting at sunset,
and swifter than hungry eagles
suddenly swooping down.

⁹ They are eager to destroy,'
and they gather captives
like handfuls of sand.
¹⁰ They make fun of rulers
and laugh at fortresses,

while building earth mounds
so they can capture cities.*
¹¹ Then suddenly they disappear
like a gust of wind —
those sinful people who worship
their own strength.

Habakkuk complains again

¹² Holy LORD God, mighty rock,*
you are eternal,
and we' are safe from death.
You are using those Babylonians
to judge and punish others.'
¹³ But you can't stand sin or wrong.
So don't sit by in silence
while they gobble up people
who are better than they are.

¹⁴ The people you put on this earth
are like fish or reptiles
without a leader.
¹⁵ Then an enemy comes along
and takes them captive
with hooks and nets.
It makes him so happy
¹⁶ that he offers sacrifices
to his fishing nets,
because they make him rich
and provide choice foods.

¹⁷ Will he keep hauling in his nets
and destroying nations
without showing mercy?

CHAPTER 2

The LORD answers Habakkuk again

¹ While standing guard
on the watchtower,
I waited for the LORD's answer,
before explaining the reason
for my complaint.'

² Then the LORD told me:
"I will give you my message
in the form of a vision.
Write it clearly enough
to be read at a glance.
³ At the time I have decided,
my words will come true.

You can trust what I say
about the future.
It may take a long time,
but keep on waiting —
it will happen!

⁴ "I, the LORD, refuse to accept
anyone who is proud.
Only those who live by faith
are acceptable to me."'

Trouble for evil people

⁵ Wine' is treacherous,
and arrogant people
are never satisfied.
They are no less greedy
than death itself —
they open their mouths as wide
as the world of the dead
and swallow everyone.

⁶ But they will be mocked
with these words:
You're doomed!
You stored up stolen goods
and cheated others
of what belonged to them.
⁷ But without warning,
those you owe
will demand payment.
Then you will become
a frightened victim.
⁸ You robbed cities and nations
everywhere on earth
and murdered their people.
Now those who survived
will be as cruel to you.

⁹ You're doomed!
You made your family rich
at the expense of others.
You even said to yourself,
"I'm above the law."
¹⁰ But you will bring shame
on your family
and ruin to yourself
for what you did to others.
¹¹ The very stones and wood
in your home
will testify against you.

¹² You're doomed! You built a city
on crime and violence.
¹³ But the LORD All-Powerful
sends up in flames
what nations and people
work so hard to gain.

---

*1.10 earth mounds . . . cities: Attacking armies
often built earth mounds against city walls to make it
easier for them to climb the wall and capture the city.
*1.12 mighty rock: The Hebrew text has "rock,"
which is sometimes used in poetry to compare the
LORD to a mountain where his people can run for
protection from their enemies.
See also: 2.3: Heb 10.37.

See also: 2.4: Rom 1.17; Gal 3.11; Heb 10.38.

¹⁴ Just as water fills the sea,
the land will be filled
with people who know
and honour the LORD.

¹⁵ You're doomed!
You get your friends drunk,
just to see them naked.

¹⁶ Now you will be disgraced
instead of praised.
The LORD will make you drunk,
and when others see you naked,
you will lose their respect.

¹⁷ You destroyed trees and animals
on Mount Lebanon;
you were ruthless to towns
and people everywhere.
Now you will be terrorized.

Idolatry is foolish

¹⁸ What is an idol worth?
It's merely a false god.
Why trust a speechless image
made from wood or metal
by human hands?

¹⁹ What can you learn from idols
covered with silver or gold?
They can't even breathe.
Pity anyone who says to an idol
of wood or stone,
"Get up and do something!"

²⁰ Let all the world be silent —
the LORD is present
in his holy temple.

Habakkuk gives praise to the Lord

CHAPTER 3

Habakkuk's prayer

¹ This is my prayer:*

² I know your reputation, LORD,
and I am amazed
at what you have done.
Please turn from your anger
and be merciful;
do for us what you did
for our ancestors.

³ You are the same Holy God
who came from Teman
and Paran* to help us.
The brightness of your glory
covered the heavens,
and your praises were heard
everywhere on earth.

⁴ Your glory shone like the sun,
and light flashed from your hands,
hiding your mighty power.

⁵ Dreadful diseases and plagues
marched in front
and followed behind.

⁶ When you stopped,
the earth shook;
when you stared,
nations trembled;
when you walked
along your ancient paths,
eternal mountains and hills
crumbled and collapsed.

⁷ The tents of desert tribes
in Cushan and Midian*
were ripped apart.

⁸ Our LORD, were you angry
with the monsters
of the deep?*
You attacked in your chariot
and wiped them out.

⁹ Your arrows were ready
and obeyed your commands.*

You split the earth apart
with rivers and streams;

¹⁰ mountains trembled
at the sight of you;
rain poured from the clouds;
ocean waves roared and rose.

¹¹ The sun and moon stood still,
while your arrows and spears
flashed like lightning.

¹² In your furious anger,
you trampled on nations

¹³ to rescue your people
and save your chosen one.*
You crushed a nation's ruler
and stripped his evil kingdom
of its power.*

---

*3.3 Teman . . . Paran: Teman is a district in Edom,
but the name is sometimes used of the whole country
of Edom; Paran is the hill country along the western
border of the Gulf of Aqaba. In Judges 5.4, the LORD
is said to have marched from Edom to help his
people; in Deuteronomy 33.2, Paran is mentioned in
connection with the LORD's appearance at Sinai.
*3.7 Cushan and Midian: Tribes of the Arabian
desert who were enemies of Israel.

See also: 2.14: Isa 11.9.

¹⁴ His troops had come like a storm,
    hoping to scatter us
      and glad to gobble us up.
To them we were refugees
    in hiding —
but you smashed their heads
    with their own weapons.'
¹⁵ Then your chariots churned
    the waters of the sea.

Habakkuk's response to God's message

¹⁶ When I heard this message,'
    I felt weak from fear,
    and my lips quivered.
My bones seemed to melt,
    and I stumbled around.
But I will patiently wait.
Some day those vicious enemies
    will be struck by disaster.'

Trust in a time of trouble

¹⁷ Fig trees may no longer bloom,
    or vineyards produce grapes;
olive trees may be fruitless,
    and harvest time a failure;
sheep pens may be empty,
    and cattle stalls vacant —
¹⁸ but I will still celebrate
    because the LORD God
      saves me.
¹⁹ The LORD gives me strength.
He makes my feet as sure
    as those of a deer,
and he helps me stand
    on the mountains.'

To the music director:
Use stringed instruments.

See also: 3.19: 2 Sam 22.34; Psa 18.33.

Additional notes

'1.1 message: Or "vision".
'1.9 eager to destroy: One possible meaning for the difficult Hebrew text.
'1.12 we: Hebrew; one ancient Jewish tradition "you".
'1.12 You . . . others: Or "You will judge and punish those Babylonians."
'2.1 I . . . complaint: One possible meaning for the difficult Hebrew text.
'2.4 Only . . . me: Or "But those who are acceptable to me will live because of their faithfulness."
'2.5 Wine: The Standard Hebrew Text; the Dead Sea Scrolls "Wealth".

'3.1 prayer: The Hebrew text adds "according to the shigionoth", which may mean a prayer of request or a prayer to be accompanied by a special musical instrument.
'3.8 monsters of the deep: The Hebrew text has "rivers and oceans", which may stand for the powerful monsters that were thought to have lived there before the LORD defeated them.
'3.9 obeyed your commands: One possible meaning for the difficult Hebrew text.
'3.13 chosen one: Or "chosen ones".
'3.13 You crushed . . . power: One possible meaning for the difficult Hebrew text.
'3.14 but you . . . weapons: One possible meaning for the difficult Hebrew text.
'3.16 heard this message: Or "saw this vision".
'3.16 I will . . . disaster: One possible meaning for the difficult Hebrew text.
'3.19 stand on the mountains: One possible meaning for the difficult Hebrew text.

Zephaniah

A quick look at this book

Judah and Jerusalem will be punished on the day of the Lord *page 891*

Turn to the Lord *page 892*

The nations will be punished *page 892*

Judah and other nations will turn to the Lord *page 893*

Additional notes *page 894*

The people of Judah had thought that at a certain time in the future, the Lord was going to make them powerful and would wipe out their enemies. This future time of justice, victory, and celebration was called "the day of the Lord". But Zephaniah told the people that when the day of the Lord did come, the Lord would punish everyone who had not obeyed him. And this included Judah, as well as other nations. The only way that Judah could avoid being swept away by the Lord's anger was to obey the Lord and worship only him:

> If you humbly obey the LORD,
>   then come and worship him.
> If you do right and are humble,
>   perhaps you will be safe
> on that day when the LORD
>   turns loose his anger.

(2.3)

Judah and Jerusalem will be punished on the day of the Lord

CHAPTER 1

¹ I am Zephaniah, the son of Cushi, the grandson of Gedaliah, the great-grandson of Amariah, and the great-great-grandson of Hezekiah.*

When Josiah son of Amon was king of Judah,* the LORD gave me this message.

Judgment on Judah

² I, the LORD, now promise
    to destroy everything
        on this earth —
³ people and animals,
    birds and fish.
Everyone who is evil
    will crash to the ground,'
and I will wipe out
    the entire human race.
⁴ I will reach out to punish
    Judah and Jerusalem —
nothing will remain of the god Baal;*
    nothing will be remembered
        of his pagan priests.
⁵ Not a trace will be found
    of those who worship stars
        from their rooftops,
or bow down to the god Milcom,*
    while claiming loyalty
        to me, the LORD.

---

*1.1 **Hezekiah:** Ruled 716–687 BC.
*1.1 **Josiah . . . king of Judah:** Ruled 640–609 BC.
*1.4 **Baal:** A Canaanite fertility god.
*1.5 **Milcom:** An Ammonite fertility god.
See also: 1.1: 2 King 22.1—23.30; 2 Chron 34.1—35.27.

⁶ Nothing will remain of anyone
  who has turned away
  and rejected me.

⁷ Be silent! I am the LORD God,
  and the time is near.
  I am preparing
  to sacrifice my people
  and to invite my guests.
⁸ On that day I will punish
  national leaders
  and sons of the king,
  along with all who follow
  foreign customs.⋆
⁹ I will punish worshippers
  of pagan gods⋆
  and cruel palace officials
  who abuse their power.

¹⁰ I, the LORD, promise
  that on that day
  noisy crying will be heard
  from Fish Gate, New Town,
  and Upper Hills.
¹¹ Everyone in Lower Hollow⋆
  will mourn loudly,
  because merchants
  and money changers
  will be wiped out.
¹² I'll search Jerusalem with lamps
  and punish those people
  who sit there unworried
  while thinking,
  "The LORD won't do anything,
  good or bad."
¹³ Their possessions will be taken,
  their homes left in ruins.
  They won't get to live
  in the houses they build,
  or drink wine from the grapes
  in their own vineyards.

A terrible day

¹⁴ The great day of the LORD
  is coming soon, very soon.
  On that terrible day,
  fearsome shouts of warriors
  will be heard everywhere.
¹⁵ It will be a time of anger —
  of trouble and torment,

of disaster and destruction,
  of darkness and despair,
  of storm clouds and shadows,
¹⁶ of trumpet calls
  and battle cries
  against fortified cities
  and mighty fortresses.

¹⁷ The LORD warns everyone
  who has sinned against him,
  "I'll strike you blind!
  Then your blood and your insides
  will gush out like vomit.
¹⁸ Not even your silver or gold
  can save you on that day
  when I, the LORD, am angry.
  My anger will flare up
  like a furious fire
  scorching the earth
  and everyone on it."

Turn to the Lord

CHAPTER 2

¹ You disgraceful nation,
  gather around,
²   before it's too late.
  The LORD has set a time
  when his fierce anger
  will strike like a storm
  and sweep you away.
³ If you humbly obey the LORD,
  then come and worship him.
  If you do right and are humble,
  perhaps you will be safe
  on that day when the LORD
  turns loose his anger.

The nations will be punished

Judgment on Philistia

⁴ Gaza and Ashkelon
  will be deserted
  and left in ruins.
  Ashdod will be emptied
  in broad daylight,
  and Ekron⋆ uprooted.

⋆1.10,11 **Fish Gate, New Town, and Upper Hills . . .
Lower Hollow:** Names for different sections of
Jerusalem: Fish Gate was probably the main gate on
the north side of the city; New Town was a newer
section; Upper Hills may have been a suburb north of
the city; Lower Hollow was probably on the southern
edge of town.

⋆2.4 **Gaza . . . Ekron:** Gaza, Ashkelon, Ashdod, Ekron,
and Gath (not mentioned because it was already
destroyed) were the five major Philistine towns.
See also: 2.4–7: Isa 14.29–31; Jer 47.1–7; Ezek 25.15–17;
Joel 3.4–8; Amos 1.6–8; Zech 9.5–7.

⁵ To you people of Philistia♦
who live along the coast,
    the Lord has this to say:
"I am now your enemy,
    and I'll wipe you out!"

⁶ Your coast will be changed
into pasture land
    and sheep pens.♦
⁷ The Lord God hasn't forgotten
those survivors in Judah,
    and he will help them —
his people will take your land
    to use for pasture.
And when evening comes,
they will rest
    in houses at Ashkelon.*

Judgment on Moab and Ammon

⁸⁻⁹ The Lord All-Powerful,
    the God of Israel, said:
I've heard Moab and Ammon
insult my people
    and threaten their nation.♦
And so, I swear by my very life
that Moab and Ammon will end up
    like Sodom and Gomorrah —
covered with thorn bushes
    and salt pits for ever.
Then my people who survive
    will take their land.
¹⁰ This is how Moab and Ammon
will at last be repaid
    for their pride —
and for sneering at the nation
    that belongs to me,
the Lord All-Powerful.
¹¹ I will fiercely attack.
Then every god on this earth
    will shrink to nothing,
and everyone of every nation
    will bow down to me,
right where they are.

Judgment on Ethiopia

¹² People of Ethiopia,*
    the sword of the Lord
    will slaughter you!

Judgment on Assyria

¹³ The Lord will reach to the north
    to crush Assyria
    and overthrow Nineveh.*
¹⁴ Herds of wild animals
    will live in its rubble;
all kinds of desert owls
    will perch on its stones
    and hoot in the windows.
Noisy ravens will be heard
    inside its buildings,
    stripped bare of cedar.♦
¹⁵ This is the glorious city
that felt secure and said,
    "I am the only one!"
Now it's merely ruins,
    a home for wild animals.
Every passer-by simply sneers
    and makes vulgar signs.

Judah and other nations will turn to the Lord

CHAPTER 3

Sinful Jerusalem

¹ Too bad for that disgusting,
    corrupt, and lawless city!
² For ever rebellious
    and rejecting correction,
Jerusalem refuses to trust
    or obey the Lord God.
³ Its officials are roaring lions,
    its judges are wolves;
in the evening they attack,
    by morning nothing is left.
⁴ Jerusalem's prophets are proud
    and not to be trusted.
The priests have disgraced
    the place of worship
    and abused God's Law.
⁵ All who do evil are shameless,
    but the Lord does right
    and is always fair.
With the dawn of each day,
    God brings about justice.

⁶ The Lord wiped out nations
    and left fortresses
    crumbling in the dust.

---

*2.7 Ashkelon: A Philistine town; see the note at 2.4.
*2.12 Ethiopia: The Hebrew text has "Cush", which
was a region south of Egypt that included parts of the
present countries of Ethiopia and Sudan.
See also: 2.8–11: a Isa 15.1–16.14; 25.10–12; Jer 48.1–47;
Ezek 25.8–11; Amos 1.13–15; b Jer 49.1–6; Ezek 21.28–32;
25.1–7; Amos 1.13–15. 2.9: Gen 19.24. 2.12: Isa 18.1–7.

*2.13 Nineveh: The capital of Assyria; Nineveh was
protected by a moat filled with water from the nearby
River Tigris.
See also: 2.13–15: Isa 10.5–34; 14.24–27; Nah 1.1–3.19.

Their streets and towns
were reduced to ruins
and emptied of people.
⁷ God felt certain that Jerusalem
would learn to respect
and obey him.
Then he would hold back
from punishing the city
and not wipe it out.
But everyone there was eager
to start sinning again.

Nations will turn to the LORD

⁸ The LORD said:
Just wait for the day
when I accuse you nations.
I have decided on a day,
when I will bring together
every nation and kingdom
and punish them all
in my fiery anger.
I will become furious
and destroy the earth.

⁹ I will purify each language
and make those languages
acceptable for praising me.ᵇ
Then, with hearts united,
everyone will serve
only me, the LORD.
¹⁰ From across the rivers of Ethiopia,*
my scattered people,
my true worshippers,
will bring offerings to me.

¹¹ When that time comes,
you won't rebel against me
and be put to shame.
I'll do away with those
who are proud and arrogant.
Never will any of them strut around
on my holy mountain.
¹² But I, the LORD, won't destroy
any of your people
who are truly humble
and turn to me for safety.
¹³ The people of Israel who survive
will live right and refuse to tell lies.
They will eat and rest
with nothing to fear.

A song of celebration

¹⁴ Everyone in Jerusalem and Judah,
celebrate and shout
with all your heart!

¹⁵ Zion, your punishment is over.
The LORD has forced your enemies
to turn and retreat.
Your LORD is King of Israel
and stands at your side;
you don't have to worry
about any more troubles.

¹⁶ Jerusalem, the time is coming,
when it will be said to you:
"Don't be discouraged
or grow weak from fear!
¹⁷ The LORD your God
wins victory after victory
and is always with you.
He celebrates and sings
because of you,
and he will refresh your life
with his love."ᵇ

The LORD's promise to his people

¹⁸ The LORD has promised:
Your sorrow has ended,
and you can celebrate.ᵇ
¹⁹ I will punish those who ill-treat you.
I will bring together the lame
and the outcasts,
then they will be praised,
instead of despised,
in every country on earth.
²⁰ I will lead you home,
and with your own eyes
you will see me bless you
with all you once owned.
Then you will be famous
everywhere on this earth.
I, the LORD, have spoken!

Additional notes

ᵇ1.3 Everyone . . . ground: One possible meaning for
the difficult Hebrew text.
ᵇ1.8 follow foreign customs: Hebrew "wear foreign
clothes".
ᵇ1.9 worshippers . . . gods: The Hebrew text has "all
who jump over the threshold", which was a Philistine
religious practice (see 1 Samuel 5.5).
ᵇ2.5 people of Philistia: The Hebrew text also
mentions "Canaan" and "Cherethites", which are
other ways of referring to the Philistines.
ᵇ2.6 pens: One possible meaning for the difficult
Hebrew text of verse 6.
ᵇ2.8,9 threaten their nation: Or "boast about their
own nation".
ᵇ2.14 stripped . . . cedar: One possible meaning for
the difficult Hebrew text.

*3.10 Ethiopia: See the note at 2.12.
See also: 3.13: Rev 14.5.

'3.9 I will . . . praising me: Or "I will change the
hearts of all people and make them fit for praising
me."
'3.17 refresh . . . love: Two ancient translations;
Hebrew "silently show you his love".
'3.18 celebrate: One possible meaning for the
difficult Hebrew text of verse 18.

Haggai

A quick look at this book

By 520 BC, many of the Jews had returned to
Judah from the exile in Babylonia. The leaders
were fairly well off, but most of the people
were struggling just to survive. The Lord told
Haggai that the reason the people had to
struggle was because the temple still had not
been rebuilt. Their lack of respect for the Lord's
temple showed that they did not respect the
Lord himself, and so he refused to bless them.

The people began work on the temple, and
then the Lord promised to bless them and
make them prosperous.

The Lord says the temple must be rebuilt

CHAPTER 1

¹ On the first day of the sixth month of the
second year that Darius was king of Persia,*
the LORD told Haggai the prophet to speak

his message to the governor of Judah and to
the high priest.

So Haggai told Governor Zerubbabel and
High Priest Joshua⁴ ²⁻⁵ that the LORD
All-Powerful had said to them and to the
people:

> You say this isn't the right time to build a
> temple for me. But is it right for you to live
> in expensive houses,* while my temple is a
> pile of ruins? Just look at what's
> happening. ⁶ You harvest less than you
> plant, you never have enough to eat or
> drink, your clothes don't keep you warm,
> and your wages are stored in bags full of
> holes.
>
> ⁷ Think about what I have said! ⁸ But
> first, go to the hills and get wood for my
> temple, so I can take pride in it and be
> worshipped there. ⁹ You expected much,
> but received only a little. And when you
> brought it home, I made that little
> disappear. Why have I done this? It's
> because you hurry off to build your own
> houses, while my temple is still in ruins.
> ¹⁰ That's also why the dew doesn't fall and
> your harvest fails. ¹¹ And so, at my
> command everything will become
> barren — your farmland and pastures, your
> vineyards and olive trees, your animals and
> you yourselves. All your hard work will be
> for nothing.

¹² Zerubbabel and Joshua, together with the
others who had returned from exile in
Babylonia, obeyed the LORD's message
spoken by his prophet Haggai, and they
started showing proper respect for the LORD.
¹³ Haggai then told them that the LORD had

---

*1.1 sixth month . . . king of Persia: Elul, the sixth
month of the Hebrew calendar, from about
mid-August to mid-September; the second year of the
rule of Darius was 520 BC.

See also: 1.1: Ezra 4.24—5.2; 6.14.

896

*1.2–5 expensive houses: Either houses with
panelled interiors or with roofs; the temple was not
yet completely rebuilt at this time.

promised to be with them. [14] So the LORD God All-Powerful made everyone eager to work on his temple, especially Zerubbabel and Joshua. [15] And the work began on the twenty-fourth day of that same month.

The Lord promises to bless his people

CHAPTER 2

The glorious new temple

[1-2] On the twenty-first day of the next month,* the LORD told Haggai the prophet to speak this message to Governor Zerubbabel, High Priest Joshua, and everyone else:

[3] Does anyone remember how glorious this temple used to be? Now it looks like nothing. [4] But cheer up! Because I, the LORD All-Powerful, will be here to help you with the work, [5] just as I promised your ancestors when I brought them out of Egypt. Don't worry. My Spirit is* here with you.

[6] Soon I will again shake the heavens and the earth, the sea and the dry land. [7] I will shake the nations, and their treasures* will be brought here. Then the brightness of my glory will fill this temple. [8] All silver and gold belong to me, [9] and I promise that this new temple will be more glorious than the first one. I will also bless this city* with peace.

The past and the future

[10] On the twenty-fourth day of the ninth month,* the LORD God All-Powerful told the prophet Haggai [11] to ask the priests for their opinion on the following matter:

[12] Suppose meat ready to be sacrificed to God is being carried in the folds of someone's clothing, and the clothing rubs against some bread or stew or wine or olive oil or any other food. Would those foods that were touched then become acceptable for sacrifice?

"Of course not," the priests answered.

[13] Then Haggai said, "Suppose someone has touched a dead body and is considered unacceptable to worship God. If that person touches these foods, would they become unclean?"

"Of course they would," the priests answered.

[14] So the LORD told Haggai to say:

That's how it is with this entire nation. Everything you do and every sacrifice you offer is unacceptable to me. [15] But from now on, things will get better. Before you started building the foundation for the temple, [16] you recalled what life was like in the past.* When you wanted two hundred kilogrammes of wheat, there were only a hundred, and when you wanted fifty jars of wine, there were only twenty. [17] I made all your hard work useless by sending mildew, mould, and hail — but you still did not return to me, your LORD.

[18] Today you have completed the foundation for my temple, so listen to what your future will be like. [19] Although you have not yet harvested any grain, grapes, figs, pomegranates,* or olives, I will richly bless you in the days ahead.

The Lord promises to be with Zerubbabel

[20] That same day the LORD spoke to Haggai again and said:

[21] Tell Governor Zerubbabel of Judah that I am going to shake the heavens and the earth [22] and wipe out kings and their kingdoms. I will overturn war chariots, and then cavalry troops will start slaughtering each other. [23] But tell my servant Zerubbabel that I, the LORD All-Powerful, have chosen him, and he will rule in my name.*

---

*2.19 pomegranates: A bright red fruit that looks like an apple.
See also: 2.13: Num 19.11–22.

---

*2.1,2 the next month: Tishri (also called Ethanim), the seventh month of the Hebrew calendar, from about mid-September to mid-October (see the note at 1.1).
*2.10 ninth month: Chislev, the ninth month of the Hebrew calendar, from about mid-November to mid-December.
See also: 2.3: Ezra 3.12. 2.5: Exod 29.45,46. 2.6: Heb 12.26.

Additional notes

*1.1 Governor . . . Joshua: Hebrew "Governor Zerubbabel son of Shealtiel and High Priest Joshua son of Jehozadak".
*2.5 My Spirit is: Or "I am".
*2.7 their treasures: Hebrew "what they most desire".

'2.9 **city:** Or "temple".
'2.16 **you recalled . . . past:** One possible meaning for the difficult Hebrew text.
'2.23 **rule in my name:** The Hebrew text has "be my signet ring", which signified authority.

Zechariah

A quick look at this book

The people of Jerusalem had problems. They had begun to rebuild the temple, but the new temple could never be as great as the original one. There was no king from David's family, and Judah was only a small part of the Medo-Persian empire.

In the first part of this book (1—8) Zechariah tells how the Lord gave him eight meaningful visions to help the people overcome these problems. Some day, the Lord's chosen king would again rule in Jerusalem, and all the nations would turn to the Lord and become his people. But for now, the Lord had chosen Zerubbabel to be the governor and Joshua to be the high priest, and they were to be in charge of the Lord's people.

In the second part of this book (9—11) the Lord promised to punish some of the nearby nations and also the leaders of Judah who had been unfaithful.

In the third part (12—14) the Lord gave Zechariah messages about a time even further in the future, when Jerusalem and Judah will be attacked by all nations. Many of the people of Judah will be killed, but the Lord himself will appear and rescue his people. They will turn back to him, and he will forgive them. Then mountains around Jerusalem will be flattened, but Jerusalem will remain on the mountain towering high above the land around it. Life-giving streams will flow from Jerusalem, and all people on earth will worship the Lord.

The Lord promised that some day he would again choose a king for his people. In the New Testament both Matthew and John quote part of this verse from the book of Zechariah, to show that God had chosen Jesus to be that king:

> Everyone in Jerusalem,
>   celebrate and shout!
> Your king has won a victory,
>   and he is coming to you.
> He is humble
>   and rides on a donkey;
> he comes on the colt
>   of a donkey.

(9.9)

CHAPTER 1

Turn to the LORD

¹ I am the prophet Zechariah, the son of Berechiah and the grandson of Iddo.

In the eighth month of the second year that Darius was king of Persia,* the LORD told me to say:

²⁻³ Israel, I, the LORD All-Powerful, was very angry with your ancestors. But if you people will return to me, I will turn and help you. ⁴ Don't be stubborn like your ancestors. They were warned by the earlier prophets* to give up their evil and turn back to me, but they paid no attention.

⁵ Where are your ancestors now? Not even prophets live for ever. ⁶ But my warnings and my words spoken by the prophets caught up with your ancestors. So they turned back to me and said, "LORD All-Powerful, you have punished us for our sins, just as you had planned."

First vision: horses and riders

⁷⁻⁸ On the twenty-fourth day of Shebat,* which was the eleventh month of that same year,* the LORD spoke to me in a vision during the night: in a valley among myrtle trees,* I saw someone on a red horse, with riders on red, brown, and white horses behind him. ⁹ An angel was there to explain things to me, and I asked, "Sir, who are these riders?"

"I'll tell you," the angel answered.

¹⁰ Straight away, the man standing among the myrtle trees said, "These are the ones the LORD has sent to find out what's happening on earth."

¹¹ Then the riders spoke to the LORD's angel, who was standing among the myrtle trees, and they said, "We have gone everywhere and have discovered that the whole world is at peace."

¹² At this, the angel said, "LORD All-Powerful, for seventy years you have been angry with Jerusalem and the towns of Judah. When are you ever going to have mercy on them?"

¹³ The LORD's answer was kind and comforting. ¹⁴ So the angel told me to announce:

I, the LORD All-Powerful, am very protective of Jerusalem. ¹⁵ For a while I was angry with the nations, but now I am furious, because they have made things worse for Jerusalem and are not the least bit concerned. ¹⁶ And so, I will have pity on Jerusalem. The city will be completely rebuilt, and my temple will stand again. ¹⁷ I also promise that my towns will prosper — Jerusalem will once again be my chosen city, and I will comfort the people of Zion.

Second vision: animal horns

¹⁸ Next, I saw four animal horns.* ¹⁹⁻²¹ The angel was there to explain what was there, and so I asked, "What do these mean?"

His answer was, "These horns are the nations that scattered the people of Judah, Israel, and Jerusalem, and took away their freedom."

Then the LORD showed me four blacksmiths, and I asked, "What are they going to do?"

He replied, "They are going to terrify and crush those horns."

Third vision: a measuring line

CHAPTER 2

¹ This time I saw someone holding a measuring line, ² and I asked, "Where are you going?"

"To measure Jerusalem," was the answer. "To find out how wide and long it is."

³ The angel who had spoken to me was leaving, when another angel came up to him ⁴ and said, "Hurry! Tell that man with the measuring line that Jerusalem won't have any boundaries. It will be too full of people and animals even to have a wall. ⁵ The LORD

1.1 eighth month . . . second year . . . king of Persia: Bul, the eighth month of the Hebrew calendar, from about mid-October to mid-November; the second year of the rule of Darius was 520 BC.
1.4 the earlier prophets: Those who preached before the fall of Jerusalem in either 587 or 586 BC.
1.7,8 Shebat: The eleventh month of the Hebrew calendar, from about mid-January to mid-February.
1.7,8 that same year: See verse 1 and the note there.
1.7,8 myrtle trees: Evergreen shrubs, which in ancient times were symbols of fertility and renewal.
See also: 1.1: Ezra 4.24–5.1; 6.14. 1.8: a Rev 6.4; b Rev 6.2.

1.18 animal horns: Horns, especially those of a bull, were symbols of power in ancient times. The number "four" would signal completeness, one representing each of the four directions.

himself has promised to be a protective wall of fire surrounding Jerusalem, and he will be its shining glory in the heart of the city."

A call to action

⁶ The LORD says to his people, "Run! Escape from the land in the north, where I scattered you to the four winds. ⁷ Leave Babylonia and hurry back to Zion."

⁸ Then the glorious LORD All-Powerful ordered me to say to the nations that had raided and robbed Zion:

Zion is as precious to the LORD as are his eyes. Whatever you do to Zion, you do to him. ⁹ And so, he will put you in the power of your slaves, and they will raid and rob you. Then you will know that I am a prophet of the LORD All-Powerful.

¹⁰ City of Zion, sing and celebrate! The LORD has promised to come and live with you. ¹¹ When he does, many nations will turn to him and become his people. At that time you will know that I am a prophet of the LORD All-Powerful. ¹² Then Judah will be his part of the holy land, and Jerusalem will again be his chosen city.

¹³ Everyone, be silent!
   The LORD is present
   and moving about
   in his holy place.

Fourth vision: Joshua and Satan

CHAPTER 3

¹ I was shown another vision. This time Joshua the high priest was standing in front of the LORD's angel. And there was Satan, standing at Joshua's right side, ready to accuse him. ² But the LORD said, "Satan, you are wrong. Jerusalem is my chosen city, and this man was rescued like a stick from a flaming fire."

³ Joshua's clothes were filthy. ⁴ So the angel told some of the people to remove Joshua's filthy clothes. Then he said to Joshua, "This means you are forgiven. Now I will dress you in priestly clothes."

⁵ I spoke up and said, "Also put a clean priestly turban on his head." Then they dressed him in priestly clothes and put the turban on him, while the LORD's angel stood there watching.

⁶ After this, the angel encouraged Joshua by telling him that the LORD All-Powerful had promised:

⁷ If you truly obey me, I will put you in charge of my temple, including the courtyard around it, and you will be allowed to speak at any time with the angels standing beside me.* ⁸ Listen carefully, High Priest Joshua and all you other priests. You are a sign of things to come, because I am going to bring back my servant, the Chosen King.†

⁹ Joshua, I have placed in front of you a stone with seven sides. I will engrave something on that stone, and in a single day I will forgive this guilty country. ¹⁰ Then each of you will live at peace and entertain your friends in your own vineyard and under your own fig trees.

Fifth vision: a lampstand and olive trees

CHAPTER 4

¹ The angel who explained the visions woke me from what seemed like sleep. ² Then he asked, "What do you see?"

"A solid gold lampstand with an oil container above it," I answered. "On the stand are seven lamps, each with seven flames. ³ One olive tree is on the right side and another on the left of the oil container." ⁴ But, sir, what do these mean?"

⁵ Then he asked, "Don't you know?"

"No sir," I replied.

⁶ So the angel explained that it was the following message of the LORD to Zerubbabel:*

I am the LORD All-Powerful. So don't depend on your own power or strength, but on my Spirit. ⁷ Zerubbabel, that mountain in front of you will be levelled to the ground. Then you will bring out the temple's most important stone and shout, "God has been very kind."†

⁸ The LORD spoke to me again and said:

---

*3.7 with the angels . . . me: Or "with me". The angels are members of God's Council, who stand beside the throne of God in heaven and are allowed to speak with him and for him.
*4.6 Zerubbabel: Governor of Judah (see Haggai 1.1).

See also: 3.8: Jer 23.5; 33.15; Zech 6.12. 3.10: Mic 4.4.
4.3: Rev 11.4. 4.6: Ezra 5.2.

See also: 3.1: a Ezra 5.2; b Rev 12.10. 3.2: Jude 9.

9 Zerubbabel laid the foundation for the temple, and he will complete it. Then everyone will know that you were sent by me, the LORD All-Powerful. 10 Those who have made fun of this day of small beginnings will celebrate when they see Zerubbabel holding this important stone.•

Those seven lamps represent my eyes — the eyes of the LORD — and they see everything on this earth.

11 Then I asked the angel, "What about the olive trees on each side of the lampstand? What do they represent? 12 And what is the meaning of the two branches from which golden olive oil• flows through the two gold pipes?"

13 "Don't you know?" he asked.

"No sir, I don't," was my answer.

14 Then he told me, "These branches are the two chosen leaders• who stand beside the Lord of all the earth."

Sixth vision: a flying scroll

CHAPTER 5

1 When I looked the next time, I saw a flying scroll,• 2 and the angel asked, "What do you see?"

"A flying scroll," I answered. "About nine metres long and four and a half metres wide."

3 Then he told me:

This scroll puts a curse on everyone in the land who steals or tells lies. The writing on one side tells about the destruction of those who steal, while the writing on the other side tells about the destruction of those who lie.

4 The LORD All-Powerful has said, "I am sending this scroll into the house of everyone who is a robber or tells lies in my name, and it will remain there until every piece of wood and stone in that house crumbles."

Seventh vision: a woman in a basket

5 Now the angel who was there to explain the visions came over and said, "Look up and tell me what you see coming."

6 "I don't know what it is," was my reply.

"It's a big basket," he said. "And it shows what everyone in the land has in mind."•

7 The lead cover of the basket was opened, and in the basket was a woman. 8 "This woman represents evil," the angel explained. Then he threw her back into the basket and slammed the heavy cover down tight.

9 Straight after this I saw two women coming through the sky like storks with wings outstretched in the wind. Suddenly they lifted the basket into the air, 10 and I asked the angel, "Where are they taking the basket?"

11 "To Babylonia,"• he answered, "where they will build a house for the basket and set it down inside."

Eighth vision: four chariots

CHAPTER 6

1 Finally, I looked up and saw four chariots coming from between two bronze mountains. 2 The first chariot was pulled by red horses, and the second by black horses; 3 the third chariot was pulled by white horses, and the fourth by spotted grey horses.

4 "Sir," I asked the angel. "What do these stand for?"

5 Then he explained, "These are the four winds• of heaven, and now they are going out, after presenting themselves to the Lord of all the earth. 6 The chariot with black horses goes towards the north, the chariot with white horses goes towards the west,• and the one with spotted horses goes towards the south."

7 The horses came out eager to patrol the earth, and the angel told them, "Start patrolling the earth."

When they had gone on their way, 8 he shouted to me, "Those that have gone to the country in the north will do what the LORD's Spirit• wants them to do there."

Mourning and celebrating

The chosen leader

9 The LORD said to me:

10-11 Heldai, Tobijah, and Jedaiah have returned from Babylonia. Collect enough silver and gold from them to make a crown.• Then go with them to the house of Josiah son of Zephaniah and put the crown on the head of the high priest Joshua son of Jehozadak.• 12-13 Tell him that I, the

---

*5.1 scroll: A roll of paper or special leather used for writing on.

See also: 4.10: Rev 5.6. 4.11: Rev 11.4.

See also: 6.2: a Rev 6.4; b Rev 6.5. 6.3: Rev 6.2.
6.5: Rev 7.1. 6.12: Jer 23.5; 33.15; Zech 3.8.

LORD All-Powerful, say, "Someone will reach out from here like a branch and build a temple for me. I will name him 'Branch', and he will rule with royal honours. A priest will stand beside his throne,* and the two of them will be good friends. ¹⁴ This crown will be kept in my temple as a reminder and will be taken care of by Heldai,* Tobijah, Jedaiah, and Josiah.'"

¹⁵ When people from distant lands come and help build the temple of the LORD All-Powerful, you will know that the LORD is the one who sent me. And this will happen, if you truly obey the LORD your God.

CHAPTER 7

A question about going without eating

¹ On the fourth day of Chislev, the ninth month of the fourth year that Darius was king of Persia,* the LORD again spoke to me. ²⁻³ It happened after the people of Bethel had sent Sharezer with Regem-Melech and his men to ask the priests in the LORD's temple and the prophets to pray for them. So they prayed, "Should we mourn and go without eating during the fifth month,* as we have done for many years?"

⁴⁻⁵ It was then that the LORD All-Powerful told me to say to everyone in the country, including the priests:

For seventy years you have gone without eating during the fifth and seventh months of the year. But did you do it for me? ⁶ And when you eat and drink, isn't it for your own enjoyment? ⁷ My message today is the same one I commanded the earlier prophets* to speak to Jerusalem and its villages when they were prosperous, and when all of Judah, including the Southern Desert and the hill country, was filled with people.

⁸⁻⁹ So once again, I, the LORD All-Powerful, tell you, "See that justice is done and be kind and merciful to one another! ¹⁰ Don't ill-treat widows or orphans or foreigners or anyone who is poor, and stop making plans to hurt each other."

¹¹⁻¹² But everyone who heard those prophets, stubbornly refused to obey. Instead, they turned their backs on everything my Spirit* had commanded the earlier prophets to preach. So I, the LORD, became angry ¹³ and said, "You people paid no attention when I called out to you, and now I'll pay no attention when you call out to me."

¹⁴ That's why I came with a whirlwind and scattered them among foreign nations, leaving their lovely country empty of people and in ruins.

CHAPTER 8

The LORD's promises to Zion

¹ The LORD All-Powerful said to me:

² I love Zion so much that her enemies make me angry. ³ I will return to Jerusalem and live there on Mount Zion. Then Jerusalem will be known as my faithful city, and Zion will be known as my holy mountain.

⁴ Very old people with walking sticks will once again sit around in Jerusalem, ⁵ while boys and girls play in the streets. ⁶ This may seem impossible for my people who are left, but it isn't impossible for me, the LORD All-Powerful. ⁷ I will save those who were taken to lands in the east and west, ⁸ and I will bring them to live in Jerusalem. They will be my people, and I will be their God, faithful to bring about justice.

⁹ I am the LORD All-Powerful! So don't give up. Think about the message my prophets spoke when the foundation of my temple was laid. ¹⁰ Before that time, neither people nor animals were rewarded for their work, and no one was safe anywhere, because I had turned them against each other.

¹¹ My people, only a few of you are left, and I promise not to punish you as I did before. ¹² Instead, I will make sure that your crops are planted in peace and your vineyards are fruitful, that your fields are fertile and the dew falls from the sky. ¹³ People of Judah and Israel, you have been a curse to the nations, but I will save you and make you a blessing to them. So don't be afraid or lose courage.

¹⁴ When your ancestors made me angry, I decided to punish you with disasters, and

---

*7.1 Chislev . . . fourth year . . . king of Persia: Chislev, the ninth month of the Hebrew calendar, from about mid-November to mid-December; the fourth year of the rule of Darius was 518 BC.
*7.2,3 fifth month: Ab, the fifth month of the Hebrew calendar, from about mid-July to mid-August. The temple was destroyed by the Babylonians in the year 587 or 586 BC.
*7.7 the earlier prophets: See the note at 1.4.

I didn't hold back. 15 Now you no longer
need to be afraid. I have decided to treat
Jerusalem and Judah with kindness. 16 But
you must be truthful with each other, and
in court you must give fair decisions that
lead to peace. 17 Don't ever plan evil things
against others or tell lies under oath. I, the
LORD, hate such things.

A time of celebration

18 The LORD All-Powerful told me to say:

19 People of Judah, I, the LORD, demand
that whenever you go without food as a
way of worshipping me, it should become
a time of celebration. No matter if it's the
fourth month, the fifth month, the
seventh month, or the tenth month, you
should have a joyful festival. So love truth
and live at peace.

20 I tell you that people will come here
from cities everywhere. 21 Those of one
town will go to another and say, "We're
going to ask the LORD All-Powerful to treat
us with kindness. Come and join us."

22 Many people from strong nations will
come to Jerusalem to worship me and to
ask me to treat them with kindness.
23 When this happens, ten people from
nations with different languages will grab a
Jew by his clothes and say, "Let us go with
you. We've heard that God is on your
side." I, the LORD All-Powerful, have
spoken!

The Lord will rescue his people and punish their enemies

CHAPTER 9

Israel's enemies will be punished

1 This is a message
    from the LORD:
His eyes are on everyone,
    especially the tribes of Israel.*
So he pronounces judgment
    against the cities
    of Hadrach and Damascus.*

2 Judgment will also fall
    on the nearby city of Hamath,
as well as on Tyre and Sidon,*
    whose people are clever.
3 Tyre has built a fortress
    and piled up silver and gold,
as though they were dust
    or mud from the streets.
4 Now the Lord will punish Tyre
    with poverty;
he will sink its ships
    and send it up in flames.

5 Both Ashkelon and Gaza
    will tremble with fear;
    Ekron will lose all hope.
Gaza's king will be killed,
    and Ashkelon emptied
    of its people.
6 A mob of half-breeds
    will settle in Ashdod,*
    and the Lord himself
    will rob Philistia of pride.

7 No longer will the Philistines
    eat meat with blood in it
    or any unclean food.*
They will become part
    of the people of our God
    from the tribe of Judah.
And God will accept
    the people of Ekron,
    as he did the Jebusites.*

8 God says, "I will stand guard
    to protect my temple from those
    who come to attack.
I know what's happening,
    and no one will ill-treat
    my people ever again."

The LORD tells about the coming king

9 Everyone in Jerusalem,
    celebrate and shout!

---

*9.1 Hadrach and Damascus: Hadrach was north of
both Damascus (the main city of Syria) and Hamath
(verse 2).

See also: 8.16: Eph 4.25. 9.1: Isa 17.1-3; Jer 49.23-27;
Amos 1.3-5. 9.1-4: Isa 23.1-18; Ezek 26.1—28.26; Joel 3.4-8;
Amos 1.9,10; Matt 11.21,22; Luke 10.13,14.

*9.2 Tyre and Sidon: Phoenician cities.
*9.5,6 Ashkelon and Gaza . . . Ekron . . . Ashdod:
Philistine cities.
*9.7 eat . . . food: The Philistines will become part
of Judah and no longer eat meat with blood in it (see
Genesis 9.4) or any other forbidden foods (see
Leviticus 11.1-23; Deuteronomy 14.3-21).
*9.7 Jebusites: The original people of Canaan, who
lived in Jerusalem before it was captured by David
(see 2 Samuel 5.6-10) and were later accepted as
part of Israel.

See also: 9.5-7: Isa 14.29-31; Jer 47.1-7; Ezek 25.15-17;
Joel 3.4-8; Amos 1.6-8; Zeph 2.4-7. 9.9: Matt 21.5;
John 12.15.

Your king has won a victory,
and he is coming to you.
He is humble
and rides on a donkey;
he comes on the colt
of a donkey.
¹⁰ I, the LORD, will take away
war chariots and horses
from Israel* and Jerusalem.
Bows that were made for battle
will be broken.
I will bring peace to nations,
and your king will rule
from sea to sea.
His kingdom will reach
from the River Euphrates
across the earth.

The LORD promises to rescue captives

¹¹ When I made a sacred agreement
with you, my people,
we sealed it with blood.*
Now some of you are captives
in waterless pits,
but I will come to your rescue
¹² and offer you hope.
Return to your fortress,
because today I will reward you
with twice what you had.
¹³ I will use Judah as my bow
and Israel* as my arrow.
I will take the people of Zion
as my sword
and attack the Greeks.

The LORD will protect his people

¹⁴ Like a cloud, the LORD God
will appear over his people,
and his arrows will flash
like lightning.
God will sound his trumpet
and attack in a whirlwind
from the south.
¹⁵ The LORD All-Powerful
will protect his people,
and they will trample down
the sharpshooters
and their slingshots.
They will drink and get rowdy;
they will be as full as a bowl
at the time of sacrifice.

¹⁶ The LORD God will save them
on that day,
because they are his people,
and they will shine on his land
like jewels in a crown.
¹⁷ How lovely they will be.
Young people will grow there
like grain in a field
or grapes in a vineyard.

CHAPTER 10

A bright future for Judah and Israel

¹ I, the LORD, am the one
who sends storm clouds
and showers of rain
to make fields produce.
So when the crops need rain,
you should pray to me.

² You can't believe idols
and fortune-tellers,
or depend on the hope
you receive from witchcraft
and interpreters of dreams.
But you have tried all of these,
and now you are like sheep
without a shepherd.

³ I, the LORD All-Powerful,
am fiercely angry
with you leaders,
and I will punish you.
I care for my people,
the nation of Judah,
and I will change
this flock of sheep
into charging war horses.

⁴ From this flock will come leaders
who will be strong
like cornerstones and tent pegs
and weapons of war.
⁵ They will join in the fighting,
and together they will trample
their enemies like mud.
They will fight,
because I, the LORD,
will be on their side.
And they will crush
the enemy cavalry.

⁶ I will strengthen
the kingdoms of Judah and Israel.*
And I will show mercy
because I am the LORD, their God.
I will answer their prayers
and bring them home.

---

*9.11 agreement . . . blood: The agreement at
Mount Sinai (see Exodus 24.7,8).
See also: 9.10: Psa 72.8. 9.11: Exod 24.8.

See also: 10.2: Matt 9.36; Mark 6.34.

Then it will seem as though
I had never rejected them.
7 Israel* will be like a tribe of warriors
celebrating with wine.
When their children see this,
they will also be happy
because of me, the LORD.

8 I will give a signal
for them to come together
because I have rescued them.
And there will be as many
as ever before.
9 Although I scattered my people
in distant countries,
they won't forget me.
Once their children are raised,*
they will return —
10 I will bring them home
from Egypt and Assyria,
then let them settle
as far as Gilead and Lebanon,
until the land overflows with them.
11 My people will go through
an ocean of troubles,
but I will overcome the waves
and dry up the deepest part
of the Nile.
Assyria's great pride
will be put down,
and the power of Egypt will disappear.
12 I'll strengthen my people
because of who I am,
and they will follow me.
I, the LORD, have spoken!

CHAPTER 11

Trouble for Israel's enemies

1 Lebanon, open your gates!
Let the fire come in
to destroy your cedar trees.
2 Cry, you cypress trees!
The glorious cedars have fallen
and are rotting.
Cry, you oak trees of Bashan!
The dense forest
has been chopped down.
3 Listen! Shepherds are crying.
Their glorious pastures
have been ruined.
Listen! Lions are roaring.
The forests of the Jordan Valley
are no more to be found.

Israel's leaders are worthless shepherds

4 The LORD my God said to me:

Tend those sheep doomed for slaughter!
5 The people who buy and butcher them go
unpunished, while everyone who sells
them says, "Praise the LORD! I'm rich." Not
even their shepherds have pity on them.

6 Tend those sheep because I, the LORD,
will no longer have pity on the people of
this earth. I'll turn neighbour against
neighbour and make them slaves of a king.
They will bring disaster on the earth, and
I'll do nothing to rescue any of them.

7 So I became a shepherd of those sheep
doomed to be slaughtered by the sheep
dealers.* And I gave names to the two sticks I
used for tending the sheep: one of them was
named "Mercy" and the other "Unity". 8 In
less than a month, I became impatient with
three shepherds who didn't like me, and I got
rid of them. 9 Then I said, "I refuse to be your
shepherd. Let the sheep that are going to die,
go on and die, and those that are going to be
destroyed, go on and be destroyed. Then let
the others eat one another alive."

10 On that same day, I broke the stick
named "Mercy" to show that the LORD had
cancelled his agreement with all people.
11 The sheep dealers who saw me knew
straight away that this was a message from
the LORD. 12-13 I told them, "Pay me my
wages, if you think you should; otherwise,
forget it." So they handed me my wages, a
measly thirty pieces of silver.

Then the LORD said, "Throw the money
into the treasury."* So I threw the money into
the treasury at the LORD's temple. 14 Then I
broke the stick named "Unity" and cancelled
the ties between Judah and Israel.

15 Next, the LORD said to me, "Act like a
shepherd again — this time a worthless
shepherd. 16 Once more I am going to let a
worthless nobody rule the land — one who
won't care for the strays or search for the
young or heal the sick or feed the healthy. He
will just dine on the fattest sheep, leaving
nothing but a few bones."

17 You worthless shepherd,
deserting the sheep!
I hope a sword
will cripple your arm
and blind your right eye.

See also: 11.12,13: Matt 27.9,10. 11.12: Matt 26.15.

Victory for Jerusalem

CHAPTER 12

[1] This is a message from the LORD about Israel:

I am the LORD! I stretched out the heavens; I put the earth on its foundations and gave breath to humans. [2] I have decided that Jerusalem will become a bowl of wine that makes the neighbouring nations drunk. And when Jerusalem is attacked, Judah will also be attacked.* [3] But I will turn Jerusalem into a heavy stone that crushes anyone who tries to lift it.

When all nations on earth surround Jerusalem, [4] I will make every horse panic and every rider confused. But at the same time, I will watch over Judah. [5] Then every clan in Judah will realize that I, the LORD All-Powerful, am their God, and that I am the source of their strength.

[6] At that time I will let the clans of Judah be like a ball of fire in a wood pile or a fiery torch in a hay stack. Then Judah will send the surrounding nations up in smoke. And once again the city of Jerusalem will be filled with people.

[7] But I will first give victory to Judah, so the kingdom of David and the city of Jerusalem in all their glory won't be thought of more highly than Judah itself. [8] I, the LORD God, will protect Jerusalem. Even the weakest person there will be as strong as David, and David's kingdom will rule as though my very own angel were its leader. [9] I am determined to wipe out every nation that attacks Jerusalem.

The people will mourn and return to the Lord

Mourning for the one pierced with a spear

[10] I, the LORD, will make the descendants of David and the people of Jerusalem feel deep sorrow and pray when they see the one they pierced with a spear. They will mourn and weep for him, as parents weep over the death of their only child or their firstborn. [11] On that day the people of Jerusalem will mourn as much as everyone did for Hadad Rimmon* on the flat lands near Megiddo. [12] Everyone of each family in the land will mourn, and the

men will mourn separately from the women. This includes those from the family of David, and the families of Nathan, [13] Levi, Shimei,* [14] and all other families as well.

CHAPTER 13

Getting rid of idols and false prophets

[1] In the future there will be a fountain, where David's descendants and the people of Jerusalem can wash away their sin and guilt.

[2] The LORD All-Powerful says:

When that time comes, I will get rid of every idol in the country, and they will be forgotten for ever. I will also do away with their prophets and those evil spirits that control them. [3] If any such prophets ever appear again, their own parents must warn them that they will die for telling lies in my name — the name of the LORD. If those prophets don't stop speaking, their parents must then kill them with a sword.

[4] Those prophets will be ashamed of their so-called visions, and they won't deceive anyone by dressing like a true prophet. [5] Instead, they will say, "I'm no prophet. I've been a farmer all my life."* [6] And if any of them are asked why they are wounded,* they will answer, "It happened at the house of some friends."

A wounded shepherd and scattered sheep

[7] The LORD All-Powerful said:

My sword, wake up! Attack
   my shepherd and friend.
Strike down the shepherd!
Scatter the little sheep,
   and I will destroy them.
[8] Nowhere in the land
   will more than a third of them be left alive.
[9] Then I will purify them
   and put them to the test,
just as gold and silver
   are purified and tested.
They will pray in my name,
   and I will answer them.
I will say, "You are my people,"
   and they will reply,
   "You, LORD, are our God!"

*12.13 Shimei: A descendant of Gershon son of Levi (see Numbers 3.18).
*13.6 wounded: Probably from slashing themselves in the worship of a false god (see 1 Kings 18.28).
See also: 13.7: Matt 26.31; Mark 14.27.

See also: 12.10: John 19.37; Rev 1.7. 12.10–14: Matt 24.20; Rev 1.7.

The final war and the Lord's victory

CHAPTER 14

[1] The LORD will have his day. And when it comes, everything that was ever taken from Jerusalem will be returned and divided among its people. [2] But first, he will bring many nations to attack Jerusalem — homes will be robbed, women raped, and half of the population dragged off, though the others will be allowed to remain.

[3] The LORD will attack those nations like a warrior fighting in battle. [4] He will take his stand on the Mount of Olives east of Jerusalem, and the mountain will split in half, forming a wide valley that runs from east to west. [5] Then you people will escape from the LORD's mountain, through this valley, which reaches to Azal.* You will run in all directions, just as everyone did when the earthquake struck* in the time of King Uzziah of Judah. Afterwards, the LORD my God will appear with his holy angels.

[6] It will be a bright day that won't turn cloudy.* [7] And the LORD has decided when it will happen — this time of unending day.

[8] In both summer and winter, life-giving streams will flow from Jerusalem, half of them to the Dead Sea in the east and half to the Mediterranean Sea in the west. [9] Then there will be only one LORD who rules as King and whose name is worshipped everywhere on earth.

[10-11] From Geba down to Rimmon* south of Jerusalem, the entire country will be turned into flat lands, with Jerusalem still towering above. Then the city will be full of people, from Benjamin Gate, Old Gate Place, and Hananel Tower in the north-east part of the city over to Corner Gate in the north-west and down to King's Wine Press in the south. Jerusalem will always be secure and will never again be destroyed.

[12] Here is what the LORD will do to those who attack Jerusalem: while they are standing there, he will make their flesh rot and their eyes fall from their sockets and their tongues drop out. [13] The LORD will make them go into a frenzy and start attacking each other, [14-15] until even the people of Judah turn against those in Jerusalem.* This same terrible disaster will also strike every animal nearby, including horses, mules, camels, and donkeys. Finally, everything of value in the surrounding nations will be collected and brought to Jerusalem — gold, silver, and piles of clothing.

[16] Afterwards, the survivors from those nations that attacked Jerusalem will go there each year to worship the King, the LORD All-Powerful, and to celebrate the Festival of Shelters. [17] No rain will fall on the land of anyone in any country who refuses to go to Jerusalem to worship the King, the LORD All-Powerful. [18-19] This horrible disaster will strike the Egyptians and everyone else who refuses to go there for the celebration.

[20-21] At that time the words "Dedicated to the LORD" will be engraved on the bells worn by horses. In fact, every ordinary cooking pot in Jerusalem will be just as sacred to the LORD All-Powerful as the bowls used at the altar. Any one of them will be acceptable for boiling the meat of sacrificed animals, and there will no longer be a need to sell special pots and bowls.*

---

*14.20,21 special pots and bowls: Since all pots and bowls will be considered acceptable for use in the temple, there will be no more need for merchants to sell special ones to those people who come to offer sacrifices.

See also: 14.16: Lev 23.39–43.

Additional notes

*3.8 Chosen King: The Hebrew text has "Sprout" or "Branch", a term used of royalty (see Isaiah 11.1).

*4.7 God . . . kind: Or "What a beautiful stone."

*4.10 important stone: Or "measuring line (with a stone attached to the end)".

*4.12 golden olive oil: The Hebrew text has "gold", which possibly refers to the colour of the olive oil as it flows through the gold pipe.

*4.14 clean leaders: The Hebrew text has "people of oil". In ancient times prophets, priests, and kings had olive oil poured over their heads to show that they had been chosen (see 1 Samuel 10.1; 16.13).

*5.6 What . . . mind: Hebrew; one ancient translation "the sin of everyone in the land".

*5.11 Babylonia: The Hebrew text has "Shinar", an ancient name for Babylonia.

---

*14.5 earthquake struck: See Amos 1.1.

*14.10,11 From Geba down to Rimmon: Approximately the northern and southern borders of Judah before the exile (see 2 Kings 23.8); Geba is about sixteen kilometres north of Jerusalem, and Rimmon is about sixteen kilometres north of Beersheba.

See also: 14.8: Ezek 47.1; John 7.38; Rev 22.1.
14.11: Rev 22.3.

6.5 winds: Or "spirits". The Hebrew word may mean either.

6.6 goes towards the west: Or "follows behind".

6.8 LORD's Spirit: Or "LORD".

6.10,11 a crown: Two ancient translations; Hebrew "some crowns".

6.10,11 Heldai . . . Jehozadak: Or "Go to the house of Josiah son of Zephaniah, where you will find Heldai, Tobijah, and Jedaiah, who have returned from Babylonia. Collect enough silver and gold from them to make a crown. Then put it on the head of the high priest Joshua son of Jehozadak."

6.12,13 stand beside his throne: Or "sit on a throne".

6.14 Heldai: One ancient translation; Hebrew "Helem".

6.14 Josiah: One ancient translation; Hebrew "Hen".

7.11,12 my Spirit: Or "I".

9.1 His . . . Israel: One possible meaning for the difficult Hebrew text.

9.10 Israel: The Hebrew text has "Ephraim", the leading tribe of the northern kingdom of Israel, which sometimes stands for the whole kingdom.

9.13 Israel: See the note at 9.10.

10.6 Israel: The Hebrew text has "family of Joseph", the ancestor of Ephraim and Manasseh, the leading tribes of the northern kingdom (Israel).

10.7 Israel: See the note at 9.10.

10.9 Once . . . raised: One possible meaning for the difficult Hebrew text.

11.7 by the sheep dealers: One ancient translation; Hebrew "especially the weak ones".

11.12,13 Throw . . . treasury: Hebrew "Throw the money to the potter."

12.2 Judah . . . attacked: One possible meaning for the difficult Hebrew text.

12.11 Hadad Rimmon: Not mentioned elsewhere in the Old Testament.

13.5 I've . . . my life: One possible meaning for the difficult Hebrew text.

14.5 to Azal: One possible meaning for the difficult Hebrew text. The location of Azal is unknown.

14.6 a bright . . . cloudy: One possible meaning for the difficult Hebrew text.

14.13–15 each other . . . Jerusalem: Or "each other. 14-15 But the people of Judah will fight on the side of Jerusalem."

Malachi

The book of Malachi comes from a time after
many people of Judah had returned from
Babylonia, but just before Ezra and Nehemiah
returned. The temple had been rebuilt, and
the priests were again offering the people's
sacrifices to the Lord. But times were hard, and
the people had lost most of their hope for a
bright new future in Judah. The people and
the priests were no longer showing the proper
respect for the Lord or for his temple. They
were also making wrong sacrifices and
disobeying the laws of God. They were
ill-treating the poor and powerless, and men
were divorcing their wives.

Malachi challenged the people and especially
the priests to be faithful to the agreement the
Lord had made with Israel. They were to
honour the Lord by offering the right kind of
sacrifices and by giving ten per cent of their
harvest to him. Then the Lord would bless
them.

The Lord's love for Israel

CHAPTER 1

¹ I am Malachi. And this is the message that
the LORD gave me for Israel.

The LORD's love for Israel

The LORD said:

² Israel, I, the LORD, have loved you. And yet
you ask in what way have I loved you. Don't
forget that Esau was the brother of your
ancestor Jacob, but I chose Jacob ³ instead of
Esau. And I turned Esau's hill country into a
barren desert where jackals* roam. ⁴ Esau's
descendants may say, "Although our nation
Edom is in ruins, we will rebuild."
  But I, the LORD All-Powerful, promise to
tear down whatever they build. Then everyone will know that I will never stop being
angry with them as long as they are so sinful.
  ⁵ Israel, when you see this, you will shout,
"The LORD's great reputation reaches
beyond our borders."

Against the priests

The LORD said:

⁶ I, the LORD All-Powerful, have something
to say to you priests. Children respect their
fathers, and servants respect their masters.
I am your father and your master, so why
don't you respect me? You priests have
insulted me, and now you ask, "How did we
insult you?"

---

*1.3 **jackals:** Desert animals related to wolves, but
smaller.
See also: 1.2,3: Rom 9.13. 1.2–5: Isa 34.5–17; 63.1–6;
Jer 49.7–22; Ezek 25.12–14; 35.1–15; Amos 1.11–12; Obad 1–14.

⁷ You embarrass me by offering worthless food on my altar. Then you ask, "How have we embarrassed you?" You have done it by saying, "What's so great about the LORD's altar?"

⁸ But isn't it wrong to offer animals that are blind, crippled, or sick? Just try giving those animals to your governor. That certainly wouldn't please him or make him want to help you. ⁹ I am the LORD God All-Powerful, and you had better try to please me. You have sinned. Now see if I will have mercy on any of you.

¹⁰ I wish someone would lock the doors of my temple, so you would stop wasting time building fires on my altar. I am not pleased with you priests, and I refuse to accept any more of your offerings. ¹¹ From dawn until dusk my name is praised by every nation on this earth, as they burn incense and offer the proper sacrifices to me. ¹² But you priests insult me by saying, "There's nothing special about the LORD's altar, and these sacrifices are worthless."

¹³ You get so disgusted that you even make vulgar signs at me.* And for an offering, you bring stolen* animals or those that are crippled or sick. Should I accept these? ¹⁴ Instead of offering the acceptable animals you have promised, you bring me those that are unhealthy. I will punish you for this, because I am the great King, the LORD All-Powerful, and I am worshipped by nations everywhere.

CHAPTER 2

True and false priests

The LORD said:

¹ I, the LORD All-Powerful, have something else to say to you priests. ² You had better take seriously the need to honour my name. Otherwise, when you give a blessing, I will turn it into a curse. In fact, I have already done this, because you haven't taken to heart your duties as priests. ³ I will punish your descendants and rub your faces in the manure from your animal sacrifices, and then be done with you.*

⁴ I am telling you this, so I can continue to keep my agreement with your ancestor Levi. ⁵ I blessed him with a full life, as I had promised, and he kept his part of the agreement by honouring me and respecting my name. ⁶ He taught the truth and never told lies, and he led a lot of people to turn from sin, because he obeyed me and lived right.

⁷ You priests should be eager to spread knowledge, and everyone should come to you for instruction, because you speak for me, the LORD All-Powerful. ⁸ But you have turned your backs on me. Your teachings have led others to do sinful things, and you have broken the agreement I made with your ancestor Levi. ⁹ So I caused everyone to hate and despise you, because you disobeyed me and failed to treat all people alike.

Broken agreements

¹⁰ Don't you know that we all have God as our Father? Didn't the one God create each of us? Then why do you cheat each other by breaking the agreement God made with your ancestors? ¹¹ You people in Judah and Jerusalem have been unfaithful to the LORD. You have disgraced the temple that he loves, and you have committed the disgusting sin of worshipping other gods.* ¹² I pray that the LORD will no longer let those who are guilty belong to his people, even if they eagerly decide to offer the LORD a gift.

¹³ And what else are you doing? You cry noisily and flood the LORD's altar with your tears, because he isn't pleased with your offerings and refuses to accept them. ¹⁴ And why isn't God pleased? It's because he knows that each of you men has been unfaithful to the wife you married when you were young. You promised that she would be your partner, but now you have broken that promise. ¹⁵ Didn't God create you to become like one person with your wife?* And why did he do this? It was so you would have children, and then lead them to become God's people. Don't ever be unfaithful to your wife. ¹⁶ The LORD God All-Powerful of Israel hates anyone who is cruel enough to divorce his wife. So take care never to be unfaithful!

¹⁷ You have worn out the LORD with your words. And yet, you ask, "How did we do that?"

You did it by saying, "The LORD is pleased with evil and doesn't care about justice."

See also: 1.8: Deut 15.21. 2.4: Num 3.11–13.
2.5: Num 25.12.

The Lord will come

CHAPTER 3

The promised messenger

¹ I, the LORD All-Powerful,
 will send my messenger
 to prepare the way for me.
Then suddenly the Lord
 you are looking for
 will appear in his temple.
The messenger you desire
 is coming with my promise,
 and he is on his way.

A day of change

² On the day the Lord comes, he will be like a furnace that purifies silver or like strong soap in a washbasin. No one will be able to stand up to him. ³ The LORD will purify the descendants of Levi,* as though they were gold or silver. Then they will bring the proper offerings to the LORD, ⁴ and the offerings of the people of Judah and Jerusalem will please him, just as they did in the past.

Don't cheat God

⁵ The LORD All-Powerful said:

I'm now on my way to judge you. And I will quickly condemn all who practise witchcraft or cheat in marriage or tell lies in court or rob workers of their pay or ill-treat widows and orphans or steal the property of foreigners or refuse to respect me.

⁶ Descendants of Jacob, I am the LORD All-Powerful, and I never change. That's why you haven't been wiped out, ⁷ even though you have ignored and disobeyed my laws ever since the time of your ancestors. But if you return to me, I will return to you.

And yet you ask, "How can we return?"

⁸ You people are robbing me, your God. And, here you are, asking, "How are we robbing you?"

You are robbing me of the offerings and of the ten per cent that belongs to me.*

⁹ That's why your whole nation is under a curse. ¹⁰ I am the LORD All-Powerful, and I challenge you to put me to the test. Bring the entire ten per cent into the storehouse, so there will be food in my house. Then I will open the windows of heaven and flood you with blessing after blessing.* ¹¹ I will also stop locusts* from destroying your crops and keeping your vineyards from producing. ¹² Everyone of every nation will talk about how I have blessed you and about your wonderful land. I, the LORD All-Powerful, have spoken!

¹³ You have said horrible things about me, and yet you ask, "What have we said?"

¹⁴ Here is what you have said: "It's foolish to serve the LORD God All-Powerful. What do we get for obeying him and from going around looking sad? ¹⁵ See how happy those arrogant people are. Everyone who does wrong is successful, and when they put God to the test, they always get away with it."

The Lord will reward faithful people and punish those who are evil

Faithfulness is rewarded

¹⁶ All those who truly respected the LORD and honoured his name started discussing these things, and when God saw what was happening, he had their names* written as a reminder at this time.

¹⁷ Then the LORD All-Powerful said:

You people are precious to me, and when I come to bring justice, I will protect you, just as parents protect an obedient child. ¹⁸ Then everyone will once again see the difference between those who obey me by doing right and those who reject me by doing wrong.

---

*3.3 descendants of Levi: The priests.
*3.8 the ten per cent . . . to me: The people of Israel were supposed to give a tenth of their harvests and of their flocks and herds to the LORD (see Leviticus 27.30–33; Deuteronomy 14.22–29).

See also: 3.1: Matt 11.10; Mark 1.2; Luke 1.76; 7.27.
3.2: Joel 2.11; Rev 6.17.

*3.10 open the windows . . . blessing: This may refer to rain, since there seems to have been a terrible drought at this time.
*3.11 locusts: A kind of grasshopper that comes in swarms and causes great damage to plant life.

See also: 3.10: Lev 27.30; Num 18.21–24; Deut 12.6; 14.22–29; Neh 13.12.

CHAPTER 4

The day of judgment

The LORD said:

¹ The day of judgment is certain to come. And it will be like a red-hot furnace with flames that burn up proud and sinful people, as though they were straw. Not a branch or a root will be left. I, the LORD All-Powerful, have spoken! ² But for you who honour my name, victory will shine like the sun with healing in its rays, and you will jump around like calves at play. ³ When I come to bring justice, you will trample those who are evil, as though they were ashes under your feet. I, the LORD All-Powerful, have spoken!

⁴ Don't ever forget the laws and teachings I gave my servant Moses on Mount Sinai.*

⁵ I, the LORD, promise to send the prophet Elijah before that great and terrible day comes. ⁶ He will lead children and parents to love each other more, so that when I come, I won't bring doom to the land.

See also: 4.5: Matt 11.14; 17.10–13; Mark 9.11–13; Luke 1.17; John 1.21.

Additional notes

'1.13 me: Or "the altar".
'1.13 stolen: Or "injured".
'2.3 and then be done with you: One possible meaning for the difficult Hebrew text.
'2.11 worshipping other gods: Or "marrying the worshippers of other gods".
'2.12 even if . . . gift: One possible meaning for the difficult Hebrew text.
'2.15 Didn't . . . wife: One possible meaning for the difficult Hebrew text.
'3.16 names: Or "deeds".
'4.4 Sinai: Hebrew "Horeb".

The New Testament

Matthew

tells the good news

A quick look at this book

The ancestors and birth of Jesus *page 2*

The message of John the Baptist *page 3*

The baptism and temptation of Jesus *page 4*

Jesus in Galilee *page 4*

Jesus goes from Galilee to Jerusalem *page 25*

Jesus' last week: his trial and death *page 27*

Jesus is alive *page 40*

Additional notes *page 41*

The Sermon on the Mount (5.1—7.28), the Lord's Prayer (6.9–13), and the Golden Rule (7.12: "Treat others as you want them to treat you") are all in this book. It is perhaps the best known and the most quoted of all the books that have ever been written about Jesus. That is one reason why Matthew was placed first among the four books about Jesus called Gospels.

One of the most important ideas found here is that God expects his people to obey him, and this is what is meant by the Greek word that appears in many translations as *righteousness*. It is used seven times by Matthew, but only once by Luke, and not at all by Mark. So it is an important clue to much of what Matthew wants his readers to understand about the teaching of Jesus.

Jesus first uses this word at his own baptism, when he tells John the Baptist, "We must do all that God wants us to do" (3.15). Then, during

his Sermon on the Mount, he speaks five more times of what God's people must do to obey him (5.6,10,20; 6.1,33). And finally, he reminds the chief priests and leaders of the people, "John the Baptist showed you how to do right" (21.32).

Matthew wanted to provide for the people of his time a record of Jesus' message and ministry. It is clear that the Old Testament Scriptures were very important to these people. And Matthew never fails to show when these texts point to the coming of Jesus as the Messiah sent from God. Matthew wrote this book to make sure Christians knew that their faith in Jesus as the Messiah was well anchored in the Old Testament Scriptures, and to help them grow in faith.

Matthew ends his story with the words of Jesus to his followers, which tell what they are to do after he leaves them:

I have been given all authority in heaven and on earth! Go to the people of all nations and make them my disciples. Baptize them in the name of the Father, the Son, and the Holy Spirit, and teach them to do everything I have told you. I will be with you always, even until the end of the world.

(28.18b–20)

1

The ancestors and birth of Jesus

CHAPTER 1

The ancestors of Jesus

This is also told in Luke 3.23–38

[1] Jesus Christ came from the family of King David and also from the family of Abraham. And this is a list of his ancestors. [2–6a] From Abraham to King David, his ancestors were:

Abraham, Isaac, Jacob, Judah and his brothers (Judah's sons were Perez and Zerah, and their mother was Tamar), Hezron;

Ram, Amminadab, Nahshon, Salmon, Boaz (his mother was Rahab), Obed (his mother was Ruth), Jesse, and King David.

[6b–11] From David to the time of the exile in Babylonia, the ancestors of Jesus were:

David, Solomon (his mother had been Uriah's wife), Rehoboam, Abijah, Asa, Jehoshaphat, Jehoram;

Uzziah, Jotham, Ahaz, Hezekiah, Manasseh, Amon, Josiah, and Jehoiachin and his brothers.

[12–16] From the exile to the birth of Jesus, his ancestors were:

Jehoiachin, Shealtiel, Zerubbabel, Abiud, Eliakim, Azor, Zadok, Achim;

Eliud, Eleazar, Matthan, Jacob, and Joseph, the husband of Mary, the mother of Jesus, who is called the Messiah.

[17] There were fourteen generations from Abraham to David. There were also fourteen from David to the exile in Babylonia and fourteen more to the birth of the Messiah.

The birth of Jesus

This is also told in Luke 2.1–7

[18] This is how Jesus Christ was born. A young woman named Mary was engaged to Joseph from King David's family. But before they were married, she learnt that she was going to have a baby by God's Holy Spirit. [19] Joseph was a good man* and did not want to embarrass Mary in front of everyone. So he decided to call off the wedding quietly.

[20] While Joseph was thinking about this, an angel from the Lord came to him in a dream. The angel said, "Joseph, the baby that Mary will have is from the Holy Spirit.

Go ahead and marry her. [21] Then after her baby is born, name him Jesus,* because he will save his people from their sins."

[22] So the Lord's promise came true, just as the prophet had said, [23] "A virgin will have a baby boy, and he will be called Immanuel," which means "God is with us."

[24] After Joseph woke up, he and Mary were soon married, just as the Lord's angel had told him to do. [25] But they did not sleep together before her baby was born. Then Joseph named him Jesus.

CHAPTER 2

The wise men

[1] When Jesus was born in the village of Bethlehem in Judea, Herod was king. During this time some wise men* from the east came to Jerusalem [2] and said, "Where is the child born to be king of the Jews? We saw his star in the east* and have come to worship him."

[3] When King Herod heard about this, he was worried, and so was everyone else in Jerusalem. [4] Herod brought together the chief priests and the teachers of the Law of Moses and asked them, "Where will the Messiah be born?"

[5] They told him, "He will be born in Bethlehem, just as the prophet wrote,

[6] 'Bethlehem in the land
of Judea,
you are very important
among the towns of Judea.
From your town
will come a leader,
who will be like a shepherd
for my people Israel.' "

[7] Herod secretly called in the wise men and asked them when they had first seen the star. [8] He told them, "Go to Bethlehem and search carefully for the child. As soon as you find him, let me know. I want to go and worship him too."

[9] The wise men listened to what the king said and then left. And the star they had seen in the east went on ahead of them until it stopped over the place where the child was. [10] They were thrilled and excited to see the star.

*1.21 name him Jesus: In Hebrew the name "Jesus" means "the Lord saves".
*2.1 wise men: People famous for studying the stars.

See also: 1.21: Luke 1.31.   1.23: Isa 7.14 (LXX).
1.25: Luke 2.21.   2.6: Mic 5.2.

See also: 1.11: 2 King 24.14,15; 2 Chron 36.10; Jer 27.20.
1.18: Luke 1.27.
2

11 When the men went into the house and saw the child with Mary, his mother, they knelt down and worshipped him. They took out their gifts of gold, frankincense, and myrrh* and gave them to him. 12 Later they were warned in a dream not to return to Herod, and they went back home by another road.

The escape to Egypt

13 After the wise men had gone, an angel from the Lord appeared to Joseph in a dream and said, "Get up! Hurry and take the child and his mother to Egypt! Stay there until I tell you to return, because Herod is looking for the child and wants to kill him."

14 That night, Joseph got up and took his wife and the child to Egypt, 15 where they stayed until Herod died. So the Lord's promise came true, just as the prophet had said, "I called my son out of Egypt."

The killing of the children

16 When Herod found out that the wise men from the east had tricked him, he was very angry. He gave orders for his men to kill all the boys who lived in or near Bethlehem and were two years old and younger. This was based on what he had learnt from the wise men.

17 So the Lord's promise came true, just as the prophet Jeremiah had said,

18 "In Ramah a voice was heard
crying and weeping loudly.
Rachel was mourning
for her children,
and she refused
to be comforted,
because they were dead."

The return from Egypt

19 After King Herod died, an angel from the Lord appeared in a dream to Joseph while he was still in Egypt. 20 The angel said, "Get up and take the child and his mother back to Israel. The people who wanted to kill him are now dead."

21 Joseph got up and left with them for Israel. 22 But when he heard that Herod's son Archelaus was now ruler of Judea, he was afraid to go there. Then in a dream he was told to go to Galilee, 23 and they went to live there in the town of Nazareth. So the Lord's promise came true, just as the prophet said, "He will be called a Nazarene."*

The message of John the Baptist

CHAPTER 3

The preaching of John the Baptist

This is also told in Mark 1.1–8; Luke 3.1–18; John 1.19–28

1 Years later, John the Baptist started preaching in the desert of Judea. 2 He said, "Turn back to God! The kingdom of heaven▸ will soon be here."▸

3 John was the one the prophet Isaiah was talking about, when he said,

"In the desert someone
is shouting,
'Get the road ready
for the Lord!
Make a straight path
for him.' "

4 John wore clothes made of camel's hair. He had a leather strap around his waist and ate grasshoppers and wild honey. 5 From Jerusalem and all Judea and from the River Jordan Valley crowds of people went to John. 6 They told how sorry they were for their sins, and he baptized them in the river.

7 Many Pharisees and Sadducees also came to be baptized. But John said to them:

You snakes! Who warned you to run from the coming judgment? 8 Do something to show that you have really given up your sins. 9 And don't start telling yourselves that you belong to Abraham's family. I tell you that God can turn these stones into children for Abraham. 10 An axe is ready to cut the trees down at their roots. Any tree that doesn't produce good fruit will be chopped down and thrown into a fire.

11 I baptize you with water so that you will give up your sins. But someone more powerful is going to come, and I am not good enough even to carry his

---

*2.11 frankincense and myrrh: Frankincense was a valuable powder that was burnt to make a sweet smell. Myrrh was a valuable sweet-smelling powder often used in perfume.

See also: 2.15: Hos 11.1. 2.18: Jer 31.15.

*2.23 He will be called a Nazarene: The prophet who said this is not known.

See also: 2.23: Mark 1.24; Luke 2.39; John 1.45.
3.2: Matt 4.17; Mark 1.15. 3.3: Isa 40.3 (LXX). 3.4: 2 King 1.8.
3.7: Matt 12.34; 23.33. 3.9: John 8.33. 3.10: Matt 7.19.

sandals.* He will baptize you with the Holy Spirit and with fire. [12] His threshing fork is in his hand, and he is ready to separate the wheat from the husks.* He will store the wheat in a barn and burn the husks in a fire that never goes out.

The baptism and temptation of Jesus

The baptism of Jesus

This is also told in Mark 1.9–11; Luke 3.21,22

[13] Jesus left Galilee and went to the River Jordan to be baptized by John. [14] But John kept objecting and said, "I ought to be baptized by you. Why have you come to me?" [15] Jesus answered, "For now this is how it should be, because we must do all that God wants us to do." Then John agreed.

[16] So Jesus was baptized. And as soon as he came out of the water, the sky opened, and he saw the Spirit of God coming down on him like a dove. [17] Then a voice from heaven said, "This is my own dear Son, and I am pleased with him."

CHAPTER 4

Jesus and the devil

This is also told in Mark 1.12,13; Luke 4.1–13

[1] The Holy Spirit led Jesus into the desert, so that the devil could test him. [2] After Jesus had gone without eating* for forty days and nights, he was very hungry. [3] Then the devil came to him and said, "If you are God's Son, tell these stones to turn into bread."

[4] Jesus answered, "The Scriptures say:

'No one can live only on food.
    People need every word
        that God has spoken.' "

[5] Next, the devil took Jesus to the holy city and made him stand on the highest part of the temple. [6] The devil said, "If you are God's Son, jump off. The Scriptures say:

'God will give his angels
    orders about you.
They will catch you
    in their arms,
and you won't hurt
    your feet on the stones.' "

[7] Jesus answered, "The Scriptures also say, 'Don't try to test the Lord your God!' "

[8] Finally, the devil took Jesus up on a very high mountain and showed him all the kingdoms on earth and their power. [9] The devil said to him, "I will give all this to you, if you will bow down and worship me."

[10] Jesus answered, "Go away Satan! The Scriptures say:

'Worship the Lord your God
    and serve only him.' "

[11] Then the devil left Jesus, and angels came to help him.

Jesus in Galilee

Jesus begins his work

This is also told in Mark 1.14,15; Luke 4.14,15

[12] When Jesus heard that John had been put in prison, he went to Galilee. [13] But instead of staying in Nazareth, Jesus moved to Capernaum. This town was beside Lake Galilee in the territory of Zebulun and Naphtali.* [14] So God's promise came true, just as the prophet Isaiah had said,

[15] "Listen, lands of Zebulun
        and Naphtali,
    lands along the road
    to the sea and east
        of the Jordan!
    Listen Galilee,
        land of the Gentiles!
[16] Although your people
    live in darkness,
        they will see a bright light.

---

*3.11 carry his sandals: This was one of the duties of a slave.
*3.12 His threshing fork is in his hand, and he is ready to separate the wheat from the husks: After Jewish farmers had trampled out the grain, they used a large fork to pitch the grain and the husks into the air. Wind would blow away the light husks, and the grain would fall back to the ground, where it could be gathered up.
*4.2 had gone without eating: The Jewish people sometimes went without eating (also called "fasting") to show their love for God or to show sorrow for their sins.
See also: 3.17: Gen 22.2; Psa 2.7; Isa 42.1; Matt 12.18; 17.5; Mark 1.11; Luke 9.35. 4.1: Heb 2.18; 4.15. 4.4: Deut 8.3.

*4.13 Zebulun and Naphtali: In Old Testament times these tribes were in northern Palestine, and in New Testament times many Gentiles lived where these tribes had once been.
See also: 4.6: Psa 91.11,12. 4.7: Deut 6.16.
4.10: Deut 6.13. 4.12: Matt 14.3; Mark 6.17; Luke 3.19,20.
4.13: John 2.12. 4.15,16: Isa 9.1,2.

Although they live
in the shadow of death,
a light will shine on them."

[17] Then Jesus started preaching, "Turn back to God! The kingdom of heaven will soon be here."*

Jesus chooses four fishermen

This is also told in Mark 1.16-20; Luke 5.1-11

[18] While Jesus was walking along the shore of Lake Galilee, he saw two brothers. One was Simon, also known as Peter, and the other was Andrew. They were fishermen, and they were casting their net into the lake. [19] Jesus said to them, "Come with me! I will teach you how to bring in people instead of fish." [20] At once the two brothers dropped their nets and went with him.

[21] Jesus walked on until he saw James and John, the sons of Zebedee. They were in a boat with their father, mending their nets. Jesus asked them to come with him too. [22] Straight away they left the boat and their father and went with Jesus.

Jesus teaches, preaches, and heals

This is also told in Luke 6.17-19

[23] Jesus went all over Galilee, teaching in the Jewish meeting places and preaching the good news about God's kingdom. He also healed every kind of disease and sickness. [24] News about him spread all over Syria, and people with every kind of sickness or disease were brought to him. Some of them had a lot of demons in them, others were thought to be mad,* and still others could not walk. But Jesus healed them all.

[25] Large crowds followed Jesus from Galilee and the region around the ten cities known as Decapolis.* They also came from Jerusalem, Judea, and from across the River Jordan.

CHAPTER 5

The sermon on the mount

[1] When Jesus saw the crowds, he went up on the side of a mountain and sat down.*

Blessings

This is also told in Luke 6.20-23

Jesus' disciples gathered around him, [2] and he taught them.

[3] God blesses those people
who depend only on him.
They belong to the kingdom
of heaven!'

[4] God blesses those people
who grieve.
They will find comfort!

[5] God blesses those people
who are humble.
The earth will belong
to them!

[6] God blesses those people
who want to obey him*
more than to eat or drink.
They will be given
what they want!

[7] God blesses those people
who are merciful.
They will be treated
with mercy!

[8] God blesses those people
whose hearts are pure.
They will see him!

[9] God blesses those people
who make peace.
They will be called
his children!

[10] God blesses those people
who are treated badly
for doing right.
They belong to the kingdom
of heaven.'

[11] God will bless you when people insult you, ill-treat you, and tell all kinds of evil lies about you because of me. [12] Be happy and excited! You will have a great reward in heaven. People did these same things to the prophets who lived long ago.

---

*4.24 thought to be mad: In ancient times people with epilepsy were thought to be mad.

*4.25 the ten cities known as Decapolis: A group of ten cities east of Samaria and Galilee, where the people followed the Greek way of life.

See also: 4.17: Matt 3.2. 4.23: Matt 9.35; Mark 1.39.

*5.1 sat down: Teachers in the ancient world, including Jewish teachers, usually sat down when they taught.

See also: 5.4: Isa 61.2. 5.5: Psa 37.11. 5.6: Isa 55.1,2. 5.8: Psa 24.3,4. 5.10: 1 Pet 3.14. 5.11: 1 Pet 4.14. 5.12: 2 Chron 36.16; Acts 7.52.

Salt and light

This is also told in Mark 9.50; Luke 14.34,35

Jesus continued:

¹³ You are like salt for everyone on earth. But if salt no longer tastes like salt, how can it make food salty? It is good for is to be thrown out and walked on.

¹⁴ You are like light for the whole world. A city built on top of a hill cannot be hidden, ¹⁵ and no one would light a lamp and put it under a clay pot. A lamp is placed on a lampstand, where it can give light to everyone in the house. ¹⁶ Make your light shine, so that others will see the good that you do and will praise your Father in heaven.

The Law of Moses

Jesus continued:

¹⁷ Don't suppose that I came to do away with the Law and the Prophets.* I did not come to do away with them, but to give them their full meaning. ¹⁸ Heaven and earth may disappear. But I promise you that not even a full stop or comma will ever disappear from the Law. Everything written in it must happen.

¹⁹ If you reject even the least important command in the Law and teach others to do the same, you will be the least important person in the kingdom of heaven. But if you obey and teach others its commands, you will have an important place in the kingdom. ²⁰ You must obey God's commands better than the Pharisees and the teachers of the Law obey them. If you don't, I promise you that you will never get into the kingdom of heaven.

Anger

Jesus continued:

²¹ You know that our ancestors were told, "Do not murder" and "A murderer must be brought to trial." ²² But I promise you that if you are angry with someone,* you will have to stand trial. If you call someone a fool, you will be taken to court. And if you say that someone is worthless, you will be in danger of the fires of hell.

²³ So if you are about to place your gift on the altar and remember that someone is angry with you, ²⁴ leave your gift there in front of the altar. Make peace with that person, then come back and offer your gift to God.

²⁵ Before you are dragged into court, make friends with the person who has accused you of doing wrong. If you don't, you will be handed over to the judge and then to the officer who will put you in jail. ²⁶ I promise you that you will not get out until you have paid the last penny you owe.

Marriage

Jesus continued:

²⁷ You know the commandment which says, "Be faithful in marriage." ²⁸ But I tell you that if you look at another woman and want her, you are already unfaithful in your thoughts. ²⁹ If your right eye causes you to sin, poke it out and throw it away. It is better to lose one part of your body, than for your whole body to end up in hell. ³⁰ If your right hand causes you to sin, chop it off and throw it away! It is better to lose one part of your body, than for your whole body to be thrown into hell.

Divorce

This is also told in Matthew 19.9; Mark 10.11,12; Luke 16.18

Jesus continued:

³¹ You have been taught that a man who divorces his wife must write out divorce papers for her.* ³² But I tell you not to divorce your wife unless she has committed some terrible sexual sin.* If you divorce her, you will cause her to be unfaithful, just as any man who marries her is guilty of taking another man's wife.

---

*5.17 the Law and the Prophets: The Jewish Scriptures, that is, the Old Testament.

See also: 5.13: Mark 9.50; Luke 14.34,35. 5.14: John 8.12; 9.5. 5.15: Mark 4.21; Luke 8.16; 11.33. 5.16: 1 Pet 2.12. 5.18: Luke 16.17. 5.21: Exod 20.13; Deut 5.17.

*5.31 write out divorce papers for her: Jewish men could divorce their wives, but the women could not divorce their husbands. The purpose of writing these papers was to make it harder for a man to divorce his wife. Before this law was made, all a man had to do was to send his wife away and say that he was no longer his wife.

*5.32 some terrible sexual sin: This probably refers to the laws about the wrong kinds of marriages that are forbidden in Leviticus or to some serious sexual sin.

See also: 5.27: Exod 20.14; Deut 5.18. 5.29: Matt 18.9; Mark 9.47. 5.30: Matt 18.8; Mark 9.43. 5.31: Deut 24.1-4; Matt 19.7; Mark 10.4. 5.32: Matt 19.9; Mark 10.11,12; Luke 16.18; 1 Cor 7.10,11.

Promises

Jesus continued:

33 You know that our ancestors were told, "Don't use the Lord's name to make a promise unless you are going to keep it." 34 But I tell you not to swear by anything when you make a promise! Heaven is God's throne, so don't swear by heaven. 35 The earth is God's footstool, so don't swear by the earth. Jerusalem is the city of the great king, so don't swear by it. 36 Don't swear by your own head. You cannot make one hair white or black. 37 When you make a promise, say only "Yes" or "No". Anything else comes from the devil.

Revenge

This is also told in Luke 6.29,30

Jesus continued:

38 You know that you have been taught, "An eye for an eye and a tooth for a tooth." 39 But I tell you not to try to get even with a person who has done something to you. When someone slaps your right cheek,* turn and let that person slap your other cheek. 40 If someone sues you for your shirt, give up your coat as well. 41 If a soldier forces you to carry his pack one kilometre, carry it two kilometres.* 42 When people ask you for something, give it to them. When they want to borrow money, lend it to them.

Love

This is also told in Luke 6.27,28,32–36

Jesus continued:

43 You have heard people say, "Love your neighbours and hate your enemies." 44 But I tell you to love your enemies and pray for anyone who ill-treats you. 45 Then you will be acting like your Father in heaven. He makes the sun rise on both good and bad people. And he sends rain for the ones who do right and for the ones who

do wrong. 46 If you love only those people who love you, will God reward you for that? Even tax collectors* love their friends. 47 If you greet only your friends, what's so great about that? Don't even unbelievers act like that? 48 But you must always act like your Father in heaven.

CHAPTER 6

Giving

Jesus said:

1 When you do good deeds, don't try to show off. If you do, you won't get a reward from your Father in heaven.

2 When you give to the poor, don't blow a loud horn. That's what show-offs do in the meeting places and on the street corners, because they are always looking for praise. I can assure you that they already have their reward.

3 When you give to the poor, don't let anyone know about it.* 4 Then your gift will be given in secret. Your Father knows what is done in secret, and he will reward you.

Prayer

This is also told in Luke 11.2–4

Jesus continued:

5 When you pray, don't be like those show-offs who love to stand up and pray in the meeting places and on the street corners. They do this just to look good. I can assure you that they already have their reward.

6 When you pray, go into a room alone and close the door. Pray to your Father in private. He knows what is done in private, and he will reward you.

7 When you pray, don't talk on and on as people do who don't know God. They think God likes to hear long prayers. 8 Don't be like them. Your Father knows what you need before you ask. 9 You should pray like this:

Our Father in heaven,
    help us to honour
        your name.

---

*5.39 right cheek: A slap on the right cheek was a bad insult.
*5.41 two kilometres: A Roman soldier had the right to force a person to carry his pack as far as approximately one and a half kilometres.
See also: 5.33: a Lev 19.12; b Num 30.2; Deut 23.21. 5.34: a Jam 5.12; b Isa 66.1; Matt 23.22. 5.35: a Isa 66.1; b Psa 48.2. 5.38: Exod 21.24; Lev 24.20; Deut 19.21.

*5.46 tax collectors: These were usually Jewish people who paid the Romans for the right to collect taxes. They were hated by other Jews who thought of them as traitors to their country and to their religion.
See also: 5.48: Lev 19.2; Deut 18.13. 6.1: Matt 23.5. 6.5: Luke 18.10–14.

¹⁰ Come and set up
    your kingdom,
so that everyone on earth
    will obey you,
    as you are obeyed
    in heaven.
¹¹ Give us our food for today.•
¹² Forgive us for doing wrong,
    as we forgive others.
¹³ Keep us from being tempted
    and protect us from evil.•

¹⁴ If you forgive others for the wrongs they do to you, your Father in heaven will forgive you. ¹⁵ But if you don't forgive others, your Father will not forgive your sins.

Worshipping God by going without eating

Jesus continued:

¹⁶ When you go without eating,• don't try to look gloomy as those show-offs do when they go without eating. I can assure you that they already have their reward. ¹⁷ Instead, comb your hair and wash your face. ¹⁸ Then others won't know that you are going without eating. But your Father sees what is done in private, and he will reward you.

Treasures in heaven

This is also told in Luke 12.33,34

Jesus continued:

¹⁹ Don't store up treasures on earth! Moths and rust can destroy them, and thieves can break in and steal them. ²⁰ Instead, store up your treasures in heaven, where moths and rust cannot destroy them, and thieves cannot break in and steal them. ²¹ Your heart will always be where your treasure is.

Light

This is also told in Luke 11.34–36

Jesus continued:

²² Your eyes are like a window for your body. When they are good, you have all the light you need. ²³ But when your eyes are bad, everything is dark. If the light inside you is dark, you are in the dark.

Money

This is also told in Luke 16.13

Jesus continued:

²⁴ You cannot be the slave of two masters! You will like one more than the other or be more loyal to one than the other. You cannot serve both God and money.

Worry

This is also told in Luke 12.22–31

Jesus continued:

²⁵ I tell you not to worry about your life. Don't worry about having something to eat, drink, or wear. Isn't life more than food or clothing? ²⁶ Look at the birds in the sky! They don't plant or harvest. They don't even store grain in barns. Yet your Father in heaven takes care of them. Aren't you worth more than birds?

²⁷ Can worry make you live longer?• ²⁸ Why worry about clothes? Look how the wild flowers grow. They don't work hard to make their clothes. ²⁹ But I tell you that Solomon with all his wealth• wasn't as well clothed as one of them. ³⁰ God gives such beauty to everything that grows in the fields, even though it is here today and thrown into a fire tomorrow. He will surely do even more for you! Why do you have such little faith?

³¹ Don't worry and ask yourselves, "Will we have anything to eat? Will we have anything to drink? Will we have any clothes to wear?" ³² Only people who don't know God are always worrying about such things. Your Father in heaven knows that you need all these. ³³ But more than anything else, put God's work first and do what he wants. Then the other things will be yours as well.

³⁴ Don't worry about tomorrow. It will take care of itself. You have enough to worry about today.

---

*6.16 without eating: See the note at 4.2.
See also: 6.14,15: Mark 11.25,26. 6.19: Jam 5.2,3.

*6.29 Solomon with all his wealth: The Jewish people thought that Solomon was the richest person who had ever lived.
See also: 6.29: 1 King 10.4–7; 2 Chron 9.3–6.

CHAPTER 7

Judging others

This is also told in Luke 6.37,38,41,42

Jesus said:

¹ Don't condemn others, and God won't condemn you. ² God will be as hard on you as you are on others! He will treat you exactly as you treat them.

³ You can see the speck in your friend's eye, but you don't notice the log in your own eye. ⁴ How can you say, "My friend, let me take the speck out of your eye," when you don't see the log in your own eye? ⁵ You're nothing but show-offs! First, take the log out of your own eye. Then you can see how to take the speck out of your friend's eye.

⁶ Don't give to dogs what belongs to God. They will only turn and attack you. Don't throw pearls down in front of pigs. They will trample all over them.

Ask, search, knock

This is also told in Luke 11.9–13

Jesus continued:

⁷ Ask, and you will receive. Search, and you will find. Knock, and the door will be opened for you. ⁸ Everyone who asks will receive. Everyone who searches will find. And the door will be opened for everyone who knocks. ⁹ Would any of you give your hungry child a stone, if the child asked for some bread? ¹⁰ Would you give your child a snake if the child asked for a fish? ¹¹ As bad as you are, you still know how to give good gifts to your children. But your heavenly Father is even more ready to give good things to people who ask.

¹² Treat others as you want them to treat you. This is what the Law and the Prophets* are all about.

The narrow gate

This is also told in Luke 13.24

Jesus continued:

¹³ Go in through the narrow gate. The gate to destruction is wide, and the road that leads there is easy to follow. A lot of people go through that gate. ¹⁴ But the gate to life is very narrow. The road that leads there is so hard to follow that only a few people find it.

A tree and its fruit

This is also told in Luke 6.43–45

Jesus continued:

¹⁵ Watch out for false prophets! They dress up like sheep, but inside they are wolves who have come to attack you. ¹⁶ You can tell what they are by what they do. No one picks grapes or figs from thorn bushes. ¹⁷ A good tree produces good fruit, and a bad tree produces bad fruit. ¹⁸ A good tree cannot produce bad fruit, and a bad tree cannot produce good fruit. ¹⁹ Every tree that produces bad fruit will be chopped down and burnt. ²⁰ You can tell who the false prophets are by their deeds.

A warning

This is also told in Luke 13.26,27

Jesus continued:

²¹ Not everyone who calls me their Lord will get into the kingdom of heaven. Only the ones who obey my Father in heaven will get in. ²² On the day of judgment many will call me their Lord. They will say, "We preached in your name, and in your name we forced out demons and performed many miracles." ²³ But I will tell them, "I will have nothing to do with you! Get out of my sight, you evil people!"

Two builders

This is also told in Luke 6.47–49

Jesus continued:

²⁴ Anyone who hears and obeys these teachings of mine is like a wise person who built a house on solid rock. ²⁵ Rain poured down, rivers flooded, and winds beat against that house. But it did not fall, because it was built on solid rock.

²⁶ Anyone who hears my teachings and doesn't obey them is like a foolish person who built a house on sand. ²⁷ The rain poured down, the rivers flooded, and the winds blew and beat against that house. Finally, it fell with a crash.

---

*7.12 the Law and the Prophets: See the note at 5.17.
See also: 7.2: Mark 4.24. 7.12: Luke 6.31.

See also: 7.19: Matt 3.10; Luke 3.9. 7.20: Matt 12.33. 7.23: Psa 6.8.

28 When Jesus finished speaking, the crowds were surprised at his teaching. 29 He taught them like someone with authority, and not like their teachers of the Law of Moses.

CHAPTER 8

Jesus heals a man

This is also told in Mark 1.40–45; Luke 5.12–16

1 As Jesus came down the mountain, he was followed by large crowds. 2 Suddenly a man with leprosy* came and knelt in front of Jesus. He said, "Lord, you have the power to make me well, if only you wanted to."

3 Jesus put his hand on the man and said, "I want to! Now you are well." At once the man's leprosy disappeared. 4 Jesus told him, "Don't tell anyone about this, but go and show the priest that you are well. Then take a gift to the temple just as Moses commanded, and everyone will know that you have been healed."*

Jesus heals an army officer's servant

This is also told in Luke 7.1–10; John 4.43–54

5 When Jesus was going into the town of Capernaum, an army officer came up to him and said, 6 "Lord, my servant is at home in such terrible pain that he can't even move."

7 "I will go and heal him," Jesus replied.

8 But the officer said, "Lord, I'm not good enough for you to come into my house. Just give the order, and my servant will get well. 9 I have officers who give orders to me, and I have soldiers who take orders from me. I can say to one of them, 'Go!' and he goes. I can say to another, 'Come!' and he comes. I can say to my servant, 'Do this!' and he will do it."

10 When Jesus heard this, he was so surprised that he turned and said to the crowd following him, "I tell you that in all of Israel I've never found anyone with this much faith! 11 Many people will come from everywhere to enjoy the feast in the

kingdom of heaven with Abraham, Isaac, and Jacob. 12 But the ones who should have been in the kingdom will be thrown out into the dark. They will cry and grit their teeth in pain."

13 Then Jesus said to the officer, "You may go home now. Your faith has made it happen."

At once his servant was healed.

Jesus heals many people

This is also told in Mark 1.29–34; Luke 4.38–41

14 Jesus went to the home of Peter, where he found that Peter's mother-in-law was sick in bed with fever. 15 He took her by the hand, and the fever left her. Then she got up and served Jesus a meal.

16 That evening many people with demons in them were brought to Jesus. And with only a word he forced out the evil spirits and healed everyone who was sick. 17 So God's promise came true, just as the prophet Isaiah had said,

"He healed our diseases
    and made us well."

Some who wanted to go with Jesus

This is also told in Luke 9.57–62

18 When Jesus saw the crowd,* he went across Lake Galilee. 19 A teacher of the Law of Moses came up to him and said, "Teacher, I'll go anywhere with you!"

20 Jesus replied, "Foxes have dens, and birds have nests. But the Son of Man doesn't have a place to call his own."

21 Another disciple said to Jesus, "Lord, let me wait till I bury my father."

22 Jesus answered, "Come with me, and let the dead bury their dead."*

A storm

This is also told in Mark 4.35–41; Luke 8.22–25

23 After Jesus left in a boat with his disciples, 24 a terrible storm suddenly struck the lake, and waves started splashing into their boat.

Jesus was sound asleep, 25 so the disciples went over to him and woke him up. They said, "Lord, save us! We're going to drown!"

---

*8.2 leprosy: In biblical times the word "leprosy" was used for many different kinds of skin diseases.
*8.4 everyone will know that you have been healed: People with leprosy had to be examined by a priest and told that they were well (that is "clean") before they could once again live a normal life in the Jewish community. The gift that Moses commanded was the sacrifice of some lambs together with flour mixed with olive oil.
See also: 7.28,29; Mark 1.22; Luke 4.32. 8.4: Lev 14.1–32. 8.11: Luke 13.29.

*8.22 let the dead bury their dead: For the Jewish people a proper burial of their dead was a very important duty. But Jesus teaches that following him is even more important.
See also: 8.12: Matt 22.13; 25.30; Luke 13.28. 8.17: Isa 53.4.

26 But Jesus replied, "Why are you so afraid? You don't have much faith." Then he got up and ordered the wind and the waves to calm down. And everything was calm.

27 The men in the boat were amazed and said, "Who is this? Even the wind and the waves obey him."

Two men with demons in them

This is also told in Mark 5.1–20; Luke 8.26–39

28 After Jesus had crossed the lake, he came to shore near the town of Gadara.* Two men with demons in them came to him from the tombs.* They were so fierce that no one could travel that way. 29 Suddenly they shouted, "Jesus, Son of God, what do you want with us? Have you come to punish us before our time?"

30 Not far from there a large herd of pigs was feeding. 31 So the demons begged Jesus, "If you force us out, please send us into those pigs!" 32 Jesus told them to go, and they went out of the men and into the pigs. All at once the pigs rushed down the steep bank into the lake and drowned.

33 The people taking care of the pigs ran to the town and told everything, especially what had happened to the two men. 34 Everyone in town came out to meet Jesus. When they saw him, they begged him to leave their part of the country.

CHAPTER 9

Jesus heals a crippled man

This is also told in Mark 2.1–12; Luke 5.17–26

1 Jesus got into a boat and crossed back over to the town where he lived.* 2 Some people soon brought to him a crippled man lying on a mat. When Jesus saw how much faith they had, he said to the crippled man, "My friend, don't worry! Your sins are forgiven."

3 Some teachers of the Law of Moses said to themselves, "Jesus must think he is God!"

4 But Jesus knew what was in their minds, and he said, "Why are you thinking such evil things? 5 Is it easier for me to tell this crippled man that his sins are forgiven or to tell him to get up and walk? 6 But I will show you that the Son of Man has the right to forgive sins here on earth." So Jesus said to

the man, "Get up! Pick up your mat and go on home." 7 The man got up and went home. 8 When the crowds saw this, they were afraid' and praised God for giving such authority to people.

Jesus chooses Matthew

This is also told in Mark 2.13–17; Luke 5.27–32

9 As Jesus was leaving, he saw a tax collector* named Matthew sitting at the place for paying taxes. Jesus said to him, "Come with me." Matthew got up and went with him.

10 Later, Jesus and his disciples were having dinner at Matthew's house.* Many tax collectors and other sinners were also there. 11 Some Pharisees asked Jesus' disciples, "Why does your teacher eat with tax collectors and other sinners?"

12 Jesus heard them and answered, "Healthy people don't need a doctor, but sick people do. 13 Go and learn what the Scriptures mean when they say, 'Instead of offering sacrifices to me, I want you to be merciful to others.' I didn't come to invite good people to be my followers. I came to invite sinners."

People ask about going without eating

This is also told in Mark 2.18–22; Luke 5.33–39

14 One day some followers of John the Baptist came and asked Jesus, "Why do we and the Pharisees often go without eating,* while your disciples never do?"

15 Jesus answered:

The friends of a bridegroom don't go without eating while he is still with them. But the time will come when he will be taken from them. Then they will go without eating.

16 No one uses a new piece of cloth to patch old clothes. The patch would shrink and tear a bigger hole.

17 No one pours new wine into old wineskins. The wine would swell and burst the old skins.* Then the wine would be lost, and the skins would be

---

8.28 tombs: It was thought that demons and evil spirits lived in tombs and in caves that were used for burying the dead.
9.1 where he lived: Capernaum. See 4.13.

9.9 tax collector: See the note at 5.46.
9.14 without eating: See the note at 4.2.
9.17 swell and burst the old skins: While the juice from grapes was becoming wine, it would swell and stretch the skins in which it had been stored. If the skins were old and stiff, they would burst.
See also: 9.10,11: Luke 15.1,2. 9.13: a Matt 12.7; b Hos 6.6.

ruined. New wine must be put into new wineskins. Both the skins and the wine will then be safe.

A dying girl and a sick woman

This is also told in Mark 5.21–43; Luke 8.40–56

18 While Jesus was still speaking, an official came and knelt in front of him. The man said, "My daughter has just died! Please come and place your hand on her. Then she will live again."

19 Jesus and his disciples got up and went with the man.

20 A woman who had been bleeding for twelve years came up behind Jesus and barely touched his clothes. 21 She had said to herself, "If I can just touch his clothes, I will get well."

22 Jesus turned. He saw the woman and said, "Don't worry! You are now well because of your faith." At that moment she was healed.

23 When Jesus went into the home of the official and saw the musicians and the crowd of mourners,* 24 he said, "Get out of here! The little girl isn't dead. She is just asleep." Everyone started laughing at Jesus. 25 But after the crowd had been sent out of the house, Jesus went to the girl's bedside. He took her by the hand and helped her up.

26 News about this spread all over that part of the country.

Jesus heals two blind men

27 As Jesus was walking along, two blind men began following him and shouting, "Son of David,* have pity on us!"

28 After Jesus had gone indoors, the two blind men came up to him. He asked them, "Do you believe I can make you well?"

"Yes, Lord," they answered.

29 Jesus touched their eyes and said, "Because of your faith, you will be healed." 30 They were able to see, and Jesus strictly warned them not to tell anyone about him. 31 But they left and talked about him to everyone in that part of the country.

---

*9.23 the crowd of mourners: The Jewish people often hired mourners for funerals.
*9.27 Son of David: The Jewish people expected the Messiah to be from the family of King David, and for this reason the Messiah was often called the "Son of David".

12

Jesus heals a man who could not talk

32 As Jesus and his disciples were on their way, some people brought to him a man who could not talk because a demon was in him. 33 After Jesus had forced the demon out, the man started talking. The crowds were so amazed that they began saying, "Nothing like this has ever happened in Israel!"

34 But the Pharisees said, "The leader of the demons gives him the power to force out demons."

Jesus has pity on people

35 Jesus went to every town and village. He taught in their meeting places and preached the good news about God's kingdom. Jesus also healed every kind of disease and sickness. 36 When he saw the crowds, he felt sorry for them. They were confused and helpless, like sheep without a shepherd. 37 He said to his disciples, "A large crop is in the fields, but there are only a few workers. 38 Ask the Lord in charge of the harvest to send out workers to bring it in."

CHAPTER 10

Jesus chooses his twelve apostles

This is also told in Mark 3.13–19; Luke 6.12–16

1 Jesus called together his twelve disciples. He gave them the power to force out evil spirits and to heal every kind of disease and sickness. 2 The first of the twelve apostles was Simon, better known as Peter. His brother Andrew was an apostle, and so were James and John, the two sons of Zebedee. 3 Philip, Bartholomew, Thomas, Matthew the tax collector,* James the son of Alphaeus, and Thaddaeus were also apostles. 4 The others were Simon, known as the Eager One,* and Judas Iscariot,* who later betrayed Jesus.

---

*10.3 tax collector: See the note at 5.46.
*10.4 known as the Eager One: The Greek text has "Cananaean", which probably comes from a Hebrew word meaning "zealous" (see Luke 6.15). "Zealot" was the name later given to the members of a Jewish group which resisted and fought against the Romans.
*10.4 Iscariot: This may mean "a man from Kerioth" (a place in Judea). But more probably it means "a man who was a liar" or "a man who was a betrayer".
See also: 9.34: Matt 10.25; 12.24; Mark 3.22; Luke 11.15. 9.35: Matt 4.23; Mark 1.39; Luke 4.44. 9.36: Num 27.17; 1 Kings 22.17; 2 Chron 18.16; Ezek 34.5; Mark 6.34. 9.37,38: Luke 10.2.

Instructions for the twelve apostles

This is also told in Mark 6.7–13; Luke 9.1–6

[5] Jesus sent out the twelve apostles with these instructions:

Stay away from the Gentiles and don't go to any Samaritan town. [6] Go only to the people of Israel, because they are like a flock of lost sheep. [7] As you go, announce that the kingdom of heaven will soon be here. [8] Heal the sick, raise the dead to life, heal people who have leprosy,* and force out demons. You received without paying, now give without being paid. [9] Don't take along any gold, silver, or copper coins. [10] And don't carry* a travelling bag or an extra shirt or sandals or a walking stick.

Workers deserve their food. [11] So when you go to a town or a village, find someone worthy enough to have you as their guest and stay with them until you leave. [12] When you go to a home, give it your blessing of peace. [13] If the home is deserving, let your blessing remain with them. But if the home isn't deserving, take back your blessing of peace. [14] If someone won't welcome you or listen to your message, leave their home or town. And shake the dust from your feet at them.* [15] I promise you that the day of judgment will be easier for the towns of Sodom and Gomorrah* than for that town.

Warning about trouble

This is also told in Mark 13.9–13; Luke 21.12–17

Jesus continued:

[16] I am sending you like lambs into a pack of wolves. So be as wise as snakes and as innocent as doves. [17] Watch out for people who will take you to court and have you beaten in their meeting places. [18] Because of me, you will be dragged before rulers and kings to tell them and the Gentiles about your faith. [19] But when someone arrests you, don't worry about what you will say or how you will say it. At that time you will be given the words to say. [20] But you will not really be the one speaking. The Spirit from your Father will tell you what to say.

[21] Brothers and sisters will betray one another and have each other put to death. Parents will betray their own children, and children will turn against their parents and have them killed. [22] Everyone will hate you because of me. But if you remain faithful until the end, you will be saved. [23] When people ill-treat you in one town, hurry to another one. I promise you that before you have gone to all the towns of Israel, the Son of Man will come.

[24] Disciples are not better than their teacher, and slaves are not better than their master. [25] It is enough for disciples to be like their teacher and for slaves to be like their master. If people call the head of the family Satan, what will they say about the rest of the family?

The one to fear

This is also told in Luke 12.2–7

Jesus continued:

[26] Don't be afraid of anyone! Everything that is hidden will be found out, and every secret will be known. [27] Whatever I say to you in the dark, you must tell in the light. And you must announce from the housetops whatever I have whispered to you. [28] Don't be afraid of people. They can kill you, but they cannot harm your soul. Instead, you should fear God who can destroy both your body and your soul in hell. [29] Aren't two sparrows sold for only a penny? But your Father knows when any one of them falls to the ground. [30] Even the hairs on your head are counted. [31] So don't be afraid! You are worth much more than many sparrows.

Telling others about Christ

This is also told in Luke 12.8,9

Jesus continued:

[32] If you tell others that you belong to me, I will tell my Father in heaven that you are my followers. [33] But if you reject me, I will tell my Father in heaven that you don't belong to me.

---

*10.8 leprosy: See the note at 8.2.

*10.14 shake the dust from your feet at them: This was a way of showing rejection. See Acts 13.51.

*10.15 Sodom and Gomorrah: During the time of Abraham the Lord destroyed these towns because the people there were so evil.

See also: 10.7–15: Luke 10.4–12. **10.10:** 1 Cor 9.14; 1 Tim 5.18. **10.14:** Acts 13.51. **10.15:** a Matt 11.24; b Gen 19.24–28. **10.16:** Luke 10.3. **10.17–20:** Mark 13.9–11; Luke 12.11,12; 21.12–15.

See also: 10.21: Mark 13.12; Luke 21.16. **10.22:** a Matt 24.9; Mark 13.13; Luke 21.17; b Matt 24.13; Mark 13.13. **10.24:** a Luke 6.40; b John 13.16; 15.20. **10.25:** Matt 9.34; 12.24; Mark 3.22; Luke 11.15. **10.26:** Mark 4.22; Luke 8.17. **10.33:** 2 Tim 2.12.

Not peace, but trouble

This is also told in Luke 12.51–53; 14.26,27

Jesus continued:

³⁴ Don't think that I came to bring peace to the earth! I came to bring trouble, not peace. ³⁵ I came to turn sons against their fathers, daughters against their mothers, and daughters-in-law against their mothers-in-law. ³⁶ Your worst enemies will be in your own family.

³⁷ If you love your father or mother or even your sons and daughters more than me, you are not fit to be my disciples. ³⁸ And unless you are willing to take up your cross and come with me, you are not fit to be my disciples. ³⁹ If you try to save your life, you will lose it. But if you give it up for me, you will find it.

Rewards

This is also told in Mark 9.41

Jesus continued:

⁴⁰ Anyone who welcomes you welcomes me. And anyone who welcomes me also welcomes the one who sent me. ⁴¹ Anyone who welcomes a prophet, just because that person is a prophet, will be given the same reward as a prophet. Anyone who welcomes a good person, just because that person is good, will be given the same reward as a good person. ⁴² And anyone who gives one of my most humble followers a cup of cool water, just because that person is my follower, will be rewarded.

CHAPTER 11

John the Baptist

This is also told in Luke 7.18–35

¹ After Jesus had finished instructing his twelve disciples, he left and began teaching and preaching in the towns.

² John was in prison when he heard what Christ was doing. So John sent some of his followers ³ to ask Jesus, "Are you the one we should be looking for? Or must we wait for someone else?"

⁴ Jesus answered, "Go and tell John what you have heard and seen. ⁵ The blind are now able to see, and the lame can walk. People with leprosy* are being healed, and the deaf can hear. The dead are raised to life, and the poor are hearing the good news. ⁶ God will bless everyone who doesn't reject me because of what I do."

⁷ As John's followers were going away, Jesus spoke to the crowds about John:

What sort of person did you go out into the desert to see? Was he like tall grass blown about by the wind? ⁸ What kind of man did you go out to see? Was he someone dressed in fine clothes? People who dress like that live in the king's palace. ⁹ What did you really go out to see? Was he a prophet? He certainly was. I tell you that he was more than a prophet. ¹⁰ In the Scriptures God says about him, "I am sending my messenger ahead of you to get things ready for you." ¹¹ I tell you that no one ever born on this earth is greater than John the Baptist. But whoever is least in the kingdom of heaven is greater than John.

¹² From the time of John the Baptist until now, violent people have been trying to take over the kingdom of heaven by force. ¹³ All the Books of the Prophets and the Law of Moses* told what was going to happen up to the time of John. ¹⁴ And if you believe them, John is Elijah,* the prophet you are waiting for. ¹⁵ If you have ears, pay attention!

¹⁶ You people are like children sitting in the market and shouting to each other,

¹⁷ "We played the flute,
    but you would not dance!
We sang a funeral song,
    but you would not mourn!"

¹⁸ John the Baptist did not go around eating and drinking, and you said, "That man has a demon in him!" ¹⁹ But the Son of Man goes around eating and drinking, and you say, "That man eats and drinks too much! He is even a friend of tax collectors* and sinners." Yet Wisdom is shown to be right by what it does.

---

*11.5 leprosy: See the note at 8.2.
*11.13 the Books of the Prophets and the Law of Moses: See the note at 5.17.
*11.14 Elijah: Many of the Jewish people expected the prophet Elijah to prepare the way for the Messiah.
*11.19 tax collectors: See the note at 5.46.

See also: 11.10: Mal 3.1. 11.12,13: Luke 16.16.
11.14: Mal 4.5; Matt 17.10–13; Mark 9.11–13.

See also: 10.35,36: Mic 7.6. 10.38: Matt 16.24; Mark 8.34; Luke 9.23. 10.39: Matt 16.25; Mark 8.35; Luke 9.24; 17.33; John 12.25. 10.40: a Luke 10.16; John 13.20; b Mark 9.37; Luke 9.48. 11.5: a Isa 35.5,6; b Isa 61.1.

The unbelieving towns

This is also told in Luke 10.13–15

20 In the towns where Jesus had performed most of his miracles, the people refused to turn to God. So Jesus was upset with them and said:

21 You people of Chorazin are in for trouble! You people of Bethsaida are in for trouble too! If the miracles that took place in your towns had happened in Tyre and Sidon, the people there would have turned to God long ago. They would have dressed in sackcloth and put ashes on their heads.*
22 I tell you that on the day of judgment the people of Tyre and Sidon will get off easier than you will.
23 People of Capernaum, do you think you will be honoured in heaven? You will go down to hell! If the miracles that took place in your town had happened in Sodom, that town would still be standing. 24 So I tell you that on the day of judgment the people of Sodom will get off easier than you.

Come to me and rest

This is also told in Luke 10.21,22

25 At that moment Jesus said:

My Father, Lord of heaven and earth, I am grateful that you hid all this from wise and educated people and showed it to ordinary people. 26 Yes, Father, that is what pleased you.
27 My Father has given me everything, and he is the only one who knows the Son. The only one who truly knows the Father is the Son. But the Son wants to tell others about the Father, so that they can know him too.
28 If you are tired from carrying heavy burdens, come to me and I will give you rest. 29 Take the yoke* I give you. Put it on your shoulders and learn from me. I am gentle and humble, and you will find rest. 30 This yoke is easy to bear, and this burden is light.

*11.21 sackcloth . . . ashes on their heads: This was one way that people showed how sorry they were for their sins.
*11.29 yoke: Yokes were put on the necks of animals, so that they could pull a plough or wagon. A yoke was a symbol of obedience and hard work.
See also: 11.21: Isa 23.1–18; Ezek 26.1–28.26; Joel 3.4–8; Amos 1.9,10; Zech 9.2–4.   11.23: a Isa 14.13–15; b Gen 19.24–28.   11.24: Matt 10.15; Luke 10.12.
11.27: a John 3.35; b John 1.18; 10.15.   11.29: Jer 6.16.

CHAPTER 12

A question about the Sabbath

This is also told in Mark 2.23–28; Luke 6.1–5

1 One Sabbath, Jesus and his disciples were walking through some wheat fields. His disciples were hungry and began picking and eating grains of wheat.* 2 Some Pharisees noticed this and said to Jesus, "Why are your disciples picking grain on the Sabbath? They are not supposed to do that!"
3 Jesus answered:

You must have read what David did when he and his followers were hungry. 4 He went into the house of God, and then they ate the sacred loaves of bread that only priests were supposed to eat. 5 Haven't you read in the Law of Moses that the priests are allowed to work in the temple on the Sabbath? But no one says that they are guilty of breaking the law of the Sabbath. 6 I tell you that there is something here greater than the temple. 7 Don't you know what the Scriptures mean when they say, "Instead of offering sacrifices to me, I want you to be merciful to others"? If you knew what this means, you would not condemn these innocent disciples of mine. 8 So the Son of Man is Lord over the Sabbath.

A man with a crippled hand

This is also told in Mark 3.1–6; Luke 6.6–11

9 Jesus left and went into one of the Jewish meeting places, 10 where there was a man whose hand was crippled. Some Pharisees wanted to accuse Jesus of doing something wrong, and they asked him, "Is it right to heal someone on the Sabbath?"
11 Jesus answered, "If you had a sheep that fell into a ditch on the Sabbath, wouldn't you lift it out? 12 People are worth much more than sheep, and so it is right to do good on the Sabbath." 13 Then Jesus told the man, "Hold out your hand." The man did, and it became as healthy as the other one.
14 The Pharisees left and started making plans to kill Jesus.

*12.1 picking . . . grains of wheat: It was the custom to let hungry travellers pick grains of wheat.
See also: 12.1: Deut 23.25. 12.3,4: 1 Sam 21.1–6.
12.4: Lev 24.9. 12.5: Num 28.9,10. 12.7: a Matt 9.13; b Hos 6.6. 12.11: Luke 14.5.

God's chosen servant

[15] When Jesus found out what was happening, he left there and large crowds followed him. He healed all their sick, [16] but warned them not to tell anyone about him. [17] So God's promise came true, just as Isaiah the prophet had said,

[18] "Here is my chosen servant!
   I love him,
      and he pleases me.
   I will give him my Spirit,
   and he will bring justice
      to the nations.
[19] He won't shout or yell
   or call out in the streets.
[20] He won't break off a bent reed
   or put out a dying flame,
   but he will make sure
      that justice is done.
[21] All nations will place
   their hope in him."

Jesus and the ruler of the demons

This is also told in Mark 3.20–30;
Luke 11.14–23; 12.10

[22] Some people brought to Jesus a man who was blind and could not talk because he had a demon in him. Jesus healed the man, and then he was able to talk and see. [23] The crowds were so amazed that they asked, "Could Jesus be the Son of David?"*

[24] When the Pharisees heard this, they said, "He forces out demons by the power of Beelzebul, the ruler of the demons!"

[25] Jesus knew what they were thinking, and he said to them:

Any kingdom where people fight each other will end up ruined. And a town or family that fights will soon destroy itself. [26] So if Satan fights against himself, how can his kingdom last? [27] If I use the power of Beelzebul to force out demons, whose power do your own followers use to force them out? Your followers are the ones who will judge you. [28] But when I force out demons by the power of God's Spirit, it proves that God's kingdom has already come to you. [29] How can anyone break into a strong man's house and steal his things,

unless he first ties up the strong man? Then he can take everything.

[30] If you are not on my side, you are against me. If you don't gather in the harvest with me, you scatter it. [31–32] I tell you that any sinful thing you do or say can be forgiven. Even if you speak against the Son of Man, you can be forgiven. But if you speak against the Holy Spirit, you can never be forgiven, either in this life or in the life to come.

A tree and its fruit

This is also told in Luke 6.43–45

Jesus continued:

[33] A good tree produces only good fruit, and a bad tree produces bad fruit. You can tell what a tree is like by the fruit it produces. [34] You are evil snakes, so how can you say anything good? Your words show what is in your hearts. [35] Good people bring good things out of their hearts, but evil people bring evil things out of their hearts. [36] I promise you that on the day of judgment, everyone will have to account for every careless word they have spoken. [37] On that day they will be told that they are either innocent or guilty because of the things they have said.

A sign from heaven

This is also told in Mark 8.11,12; Luke 11.29–32

[38] Some Pharisees and teachers of the Law of Moses said, "Teacher, we want you to show us a sign from heaven."

[39] But Jesus replied:

You want a sign because you are evil and won't believe! But the only sign you will get is the sign of the prophet Jonah. [40] He was in the stomach of a big fish for three days and nights, just as the Son of Man will be deep in the earth for three days and nights. [41] On the day of judgment the people of Nineveh* will stand there with you and condemn you. They turned to God

---

*12.23 Could Jesus be the Son of David: Or "Does Jesus think he is the Son of David?" See the note at 9.27.

See also: 12.18–21: Isa 42.1–4 (LXX).
12.24: Matt 9.34; 10.25.

*12.41 Nineveh: During the time of Jonah this city was the capital of the Assyrian Empire, which was Israel's worst enemy. But Jonah was sent there to preach, so that the people would turn to the Lord and be saved.

See also: 12.30: Matt 9.40. 12.32: Luke 12.10.
12.33: Matt 7.20; Luke 6.44. 12.34: a Matt 3.7; 23.33;
Luke 3.7; b Matt 15.18; Luke 6.45. 12.38: Matt 16.1;
Mark 8.11; Luke 11.16. 12.39: Matt 16.4; Mark 8.12.
12.40: Jon 1.17. 12.41: Jon 3.5.

when Jonah preached, and yet here is something far greater than Jonah. 42 The Queen of the South* will also stand there with you and condemn you. She travelled a long way to hear Solomon's wisdom, and yet here is something much greater than Solomon.

Return of an evil spirit

This is also told in Luke 11.24-26

Jesus continued:

43 When an evil spirit leaves a person, it travels through the desert, looking for a place to rest. But when the demon doesn't find a place, 44 it says, "I will go back to the home I left." When it gets there and finds the place empty, clean, and tidy, 45 it goes off and finds seven other evil spirits even worse than itself. They all come and make their home there, and the person ends up in a worse state than before. That's how it will be with you evil people of today.

Jesus' mother and brothers

This is also told in Mark 3.31-35; Luke 8.19-21

46 While Jesus was still speaking to the crowds, his mother and brothers came and stood outside because they wanted to talk with him. 47 Someone told Jesus, "Your mother and brothers are standing outside and want to talk with you."

48 Jesus answered, "Who is my mother and who are my brothers?" 49 Then he pointed to his disciples and said, "These are my mother and my brothers! 50 Anyone who obeys my Father in heaven is my brother or sister or mother."

CHAPTER 13

A story about a farmer

This is also told in Mark 4.1-9; Luke 8.4-8

1 That same day Jesus left the house and went out beside Lake Galilee, where he sat down to teach. 2 Such large crowds gathered around him that he had to sit in a boat, while the people stood on the shore. 3 Then he taught them many things by using stories. He said:

A farmer went out to scatter seed in a field. 4 While the farmer was scattering the seed, some of it fell along the road and was eaten by birds. 5 Other seeds fell on thin, rocky ground and quickly started growing because the soil wasn't very deep. 6 But when the sun came up, the plants were scorched and dried up, because they did not have enough roots. 7 Some other seeds fell where thorn bushes grew up and choked the plants. 8 But a few seeds did fall on good ground where the plants produced a hundred or sixty or thirty times as much as was scattered. 9 If you have ears, pay attention!

Why Jesus used stories

This is also told in Mark 4.10-12; Luke 8.9,10

10 Jesus' disciples came to him and asked, "Why do you use nothing but stories when you speak to the people?"

11 Jesus answered:

I have explained the secrets about the kingdom of heaven to you, but not to others. 12 Everyone who has something will be given more. But people who don't have anything will lose even what little they have. 13 I use stories when I speak to them because when they look, they cannot see, and when they listen, they cannot hear or understand. 14 So God's promise came true, just as the prophet Isaiah had said,

"These people will listen
and listen,
   but never understand.
They will look and look,
   but never see.
15 All of them have
stubborn minds!
Their ears are stopped up,
   and their eyes are covered.
They cannot see or hear
or understand.
If they could,
they would turn to me,
   and I would heal them."

16 But God has blessed you, because your eyes can see and your ears can hear! 17 Many prophets and good people were eager to see what you see and to hear what you hear. But I tell you that they did not see or hear.

---

*12.42 Queen of the South: Sheba, probably a country in southern Arabia.

*13.1 sat down to teach: See the note at 5.1.

See also: 12.42: 1 King 10.1-10; 2 Chron 9.1-12.
13.2: Luke 5.1-3.

See also: 13.12: Matt 25.29; Mark 4.25; Luke 8.18; 19.26.
13.14,15: Isa 6.9,10 (LXX).   13.16,17: Luke 10.23,24.

Jesus explains the story about the farmer

This is also told in Mark 4.13–20; Luke 8.11–15

Jesus continued:

18 Now listen to the meaning of the story about the farmer: 19 The seeds that fell along the road are the people who hear the message about the kingdom, but don't understand it. Then the evil one comes and snatches the message from their hearts. 20 The seeds that fell on rocky ground are the people who gladly hear the message and accept it straight away. 21 But they don't have deep roots, and they don't last very long. As soon as life gets hard or the message gets them in trouble, they give up. 22 The seeds that fell among the thorn bushes are also people who hear the message. But they start worrying about the needs of this life and are fooled by the desire to get rich. So the message gets choked out, and they never produce anything. 23 The seeds that fell on good ground are the people who hear and understand the message. They produce as much as a hundred or sixty or thirty times what was planted.

Weeds among the wheat

24 Jesus then told them this story:

The kingdom of heaven is like what happened when a farmer scattered good seed in a field. 25 But while everyone was sleeping, an enemy came and scattered weeds in the field and then left.

26 When the plants came up and began to ripen, the farmer's servants could see the weeds. 27 The servants came and asked, "Sir, didn't you scatter good seed in your field? Where did these weeds come from?"

28 "An enemy did this," he replied.

His servants then asked, "Do you want us to go out and pull up the weeds?"

29 "No!" he answered. "You might also pull up the wheat. 30 Leave the weeds alone until harvest time. Then I'll tell my workers to gather the weeds and tie them up and burn them. But I'll order them to store the wheat in my barn."

Stories about a mustard seed and yeast

This is also told in Mark 4.30–32; Luke 13.18–21

31 Jesus told them another story:

The kingdom of heaven is like what happens when a farmer plants a mustard seed in a field. 32 Although it is the smallest of all seeds, it grows larger than any garden plant and becomes a tree. Birds even come and nest on its branches.

33 Jesus also said:

The kingdom of heaven is like what happens when a woman mixes a little yeast into three big batches of flour. Finally, all the dough rises.

The reason for teaching with stories

This is also told in Mark 4.33,34

34 Jesus used stories when he spoke to the people. In fact, he did not tell them anything without using stories. 35 So God's promise came true, just as the prophet* had said,

"I will use stories
    to speak my message
and to explain things
    that have been hidden
since the creation
    of the world."

Jesus explains the story about the weeds

36 After Jesus left the crowd and went inside,* his disciples came to him and said, "Explain to us the story about the weeds in the wheat field."

37 Jesus answered:

The one who scattered the good seed is the Son of Man. 38 The field is the world, and the good seeds are the people who belong to the kingdom. The weeds are those who belong to the evil one, 39 and the one who scattered them is the devil. The harvest is the end of time, and angels are the ones who bring in the harvest.

40 Weeds are gathered and burnt. That's how it will be at the end of time. 41 The Son of Man will send out his angels, and they will gather from his kingdom everyone who does wrong or causes others to sin. 42 Then he will throw them into a flaming furnace, where people will cry and grit

See also: 13.35: Psa 78.2.

their teeth in pain. ⁴³ But everyone who has done right will shine like the sun in their Father's kingdom. If you have ears, pay attention!

A hidden treasure

Jesus continued:

⁴⁴ The kingdom of heaven is like what happens when someone finds treasure hidden in a field and buries it again. A person like that is happy and goes and sells everything in order to buy that field.

A valuable pearl

Jesus continued:

⁴⁵ The kingdom of heaven is like what happens when a shop owner is looking for fine pearls. ⁴⁶ After finding a very valuable one, the owner goes and sells everything in order to buy that pearl.

A fish net

Jesus continued:

⁴⁷ The kingdom of heaven is like what happens when a net is thrown into a lake and catches all kinds of fish. ⁴⁸ When the net is full, it is dragged to the shore, and the fishermen sit down to separate the fish. They keep the good ones, but throw the bad ones away. ⁴⁹ That's how it will be at the end of time. Angels will come and separate the evil people from the ones who have done right. ⁵⁰ Then those evil people will be thrown into a flaming furnace, where they will cry and grit their teeth in pain.

New and old treasures

⁵¹ Jesus asked his disciples if they understood all these things. They said, "Yes, we do."

⁵² So he told them, "Every student of the Scriptures who becomes a disciple in the kingdom of heaven is like someone who brings out new and old treasures from the storeroom."

The people of Nazareth turn against Jesus

This is also told in Mark 6.1–6; Luke 4.16–30

⁵³ When Jesus had finished telling these stories, he left ⁵⁴ and went to his home town. He taught in their meeting place, and the people were so amazed that they asked, "Where does he get all this wisdom and the power to perform these miracles! ⁵⁵ Isn't he the son of the carpenter? Isn't Mary his mother, and aren't James, Joseph, Simon, and Judas his brothers? ⁵⁶ Don't his sisters still live here in our town? How can he do all this?" ⁵⁷ So the people were very unhappy because of what he was doing.

But Jesus said, "Prophets are honoured by everyone, except the people of their home town and their own family." ⁵⁸ And because the people did not have any faith, Jesus did not perform many miracles there.

CHAPTER 14

The death of John the Baptist

This is also told in Mark 6.14–29; Luke 9.7–9

¹ About this time Herod the ruler* heard the news about Jesus ² and told his officials, "This is John the Baptist! He has come back from death, and that's why he has the power to perform these miracles."

³⁻⁴ Herod had earlier arrested John and had him chained and put in prison. He did this because John had told him, "It isn't right for you to take Herodias, the wife of your brother Philip." ⁵ Herod wanted to kill John. But the people thought John was a prophet, and Herod was afraid of what they might do.

⁶ When Herod's birthday came, the daughter of Herodias danced for the guests. She pleased Herod ⁷ so much that he swore to give her whatever she wanted. ⁸ But the girl's mother told her to say, "Here on a dish I want the head of John the Baptist!"

⁹ The king was sorry for what he had said. But he did not want to break the promise he had made in front of his guests. So he ordered a guard ¹⁰ to go to the prison and cut off John's head. ¹¹ It was taken on a dish to the girl, and she gave it to her mother. ¹² John's followers took his body and buried it. Then they told Jesus what had happened.

Jesus feeds five thousand

This is also told in Mark 6.30–44; Luke 9.10–17; John 6.1–14

¹³ After Jesus heard about John, he crossed Lake Galilee* to go to some place where he could be alone. But the crowds found out and followed him on foot from the towns.

*14.1 Herod the ruler: Herod Antipas, the son of Herod the Great (see 2.1).
*14.13 crossed Lake Galilee: To the east side.
See also: 13.57; John 4.44. 14.3,4; Luke 3.19,20.
14.4: Lev 18.16; 20.21.

19

14 When Jesus got out of the boat, he saw the large crowd. He felt sorry for them and healed everyone who was sick.

15 That evening the disciples came to Jesus and said, "This place is like a desert, and it is already late. Let the crowds leave, so they can go to the villages and buy some food."

16 Jesus replied, "They don't have to leave. Why don't you give them something to eat?"

17 But they said, "We have only five small loaves of bread* and two fish." 18 Jesus asked his disciples to bring the food to him, 19 and he told the crowd to sit down on the grass. Jesus took the five loaves and the two fish. He looked up towards heaven and blessed the food. Then he broke the bread and handed it to his disciples, and they gave it to the people.

20 After everyone had eaten all they wanted, Jesus' disciples picked up twelve large baskets of leftovers.

21 There were about five thousand men who ate, not counting the women and children.

Jesus walks on the water

This is also told in Mark 6.45–52; John 6.15–21

22 Straight away, Jesus made his disciples get into a boat and start back across the lake.* But he stayed until he had sent the crowds away. 23 Then he went up on a mountain where he could be alone and pray. Later that evening, he was still there.

24 By this time the boat was a long way from the shore. It was going against the wind and was being tossed around by the waves. 25 A little while before morning, Jesus came walking on the water towards his disciples. 26 When they saw him, they thought he was a ghost. They were terrified and started screaming.

27 At once, Jesus said to them, "Don't worry! I am Jesus. Don't be afraid."

28 Peter replied, "Lord, if it is really you, tell me to come to you on the water."

29 "Come on!" Jesus said. Peter then got out of the boat and started walking on the water towards him.

30 But when Peter saw how strong the wind was, he was afraid and started sinking. "Save me, Lord!" he shouted.

31 Straight away, Jesus reached out his hand. He helped Peter up and said, "You don't have much faith. Why do you doubt?"

32 When Jesus and Peter got into the boat, the wind died down. 33 The men in the boat worshipped Jesus and said, "You really are the Son of God!"

Jesus heals sick people in Gennesaret

This is also told in Mark 6.53–56

34 Jesus and his disciples crossed the lake and came to shore near the town of Gennesaret. 35 The people found out that he was there, and they sent word to everyone who lived in that part of the country. So they brought all the sick people to him. 36 They begged him just to let them touch his clothes, and everyone who did was healed.

CHAPTER 15

The teaching of the ancestors

This is also told in Mark 7.1–13

1 About this time some Pharisees and teachers of the Law of Moses came from Jerusalem. They asked Jesus, 2 "Why don't your disciples obey what our ancestors taught us to do? They don't even wash their hands* before they eat."

3 Jesus answered:

Why do you disobey God and follow your own teaching? 4 Didn't God command you to respect your father and mother? Didn't he tell you to put to death all who curse their parents? 5 But you let people get by without helping their parents when they should. You let them say that what they have been offered to God.* 6 Is this any way to show respect to your parents? You ignore God's commands in order to follow your own teaching. 7 And you are nothing but show-offs! Isaiah the prophet was right when he wrote that God had said,

8 "All of you praise me
    with your words,
but you never really
    think about me.

---

*14.17 small loaves of bread: These would have been flat and round or in the shape of a bun.
*14.22 back across the lake: To the west side.

*15.2 wash their hands: The Jewish people had strict laws about washing their hands before eating, especially if they had been out in public.
*15.5 has been offered to God: According to Jewish custom, when people said something was offered to God, it belonged to him and could not be used for anyone else, not even for their own parents.
See also: 15.4: a Exod 20.12; Deut 5.16; b Exod 21.17; Lev 20.9. 15.8,9: Isa 29.13 (LXX).

⁹ It is useless for you
   to worship me,
   when you teach rules
   made up by humans."

What really makes people unclean

This is also told in Mark 7.14–23

¹⁰ Jesus called the crowd together and said, "Pay attention and try to understand what I mean. ¹¹ The food that you put into your mouth doesn't make you unclean and unfit to worship God. The bad words that come out of your mouth are what make you unclean."

¹² Then his disciples came over to him and asked, "Do you know that you insulted the Pharisees by what you said?"

¹³ Jesus answered, "Every plant that my Father in heaven did not plant will be pulled up by the roots. ¹⁴ Stay away from those Pharisees! They are like blind people leading other blind people, and all of them will fall into a ditch."

¹⁵ Peter replied, "What did you mean when you talked about the things that make people unclean?"

¹⁶ Jesus then said:

Don't any of you know what I am talking about by now? ¹⁷ Don't you know that the food you put into your mouth goes into your stomach and then out of your body? ¹⁸ But the words that come out of your mouth come from your heart. And they are what make you unfit to worship God. ¹⁹ Out of your heart come evil thoughts, murder, unfaithfulness in marriage, vulgar deeds, stealing, telling lies, and insulting others. ²⁰ These are what make you unclean. Eating without washing your hands will not make you unfit to worship God.

A woman's faith

This is also told in Mark 7.24–30

²¹ Jesus left and went to the territory near the cities of Tyre and Sidon. ²² Suddenly a Canaanite woman* from there came out shouting, "Lord and Son of David,* have pity on me! My daughter is full of demons."

²³ Jesus did not say a word. But the woman kept following along and shouting, so his disciples came up and asked him to send her away.

²⁴ Jesus said, "I was sent only to the people of Israel! They are like a flock of lost sheep."

²⁵ The woman came closer. Then she knelt down and begged, "Please help me, Lord!"

²⁶ Jesus replied, "It isn't right to take food away from children and feed it to dogs."*

²⁷ "Lord, that's true," the woman said, "but even dogs get the crumbs that fall from their owner's table."

²⁸ Jesus answered, "Dear woman, you really do have a lot of faith, and you will be given what you want." At that moment her daughter was healed.

Jesus heals many people

²⁹ From there, Jesus went along Lake Galilee. Then he climbed a hill and sat down. ³⁰ Large crowds came and brought many people who were crippled or blind or lame or unable to talk. They placed them, and many others, in front of Jesus, and he healed them all. ³¹ Everyone was amazed at what they saw and heard. People who had never spoken could now speak. The lame were healed, the crippled could walk, and the blind were able to see. Everyone was praising the God of Israel.

Jesus feeds four thousand

This is also told in Mark 8.1–10

³² Jesus called his disciples together and told them, "I feel sorry for these people. They have been with me for three days, and they don't have anything to eat. I don't want to send them away hungry. They might faint on their way home."

³³ His disciples said, "This place is like a desert. Where can we find enough food to feed such a crowd?"

³⁴ Jesus asked them how much food they had. They replied, "Seven small loaves of bread* and a few little fish."

³⁵ After Jesus had told the people to sit down, ³⁶ he took the seven loaves of bread and the fish and gave thanks. He then broke them and handed them to his disciples, who passed them around to his crowds.

³⁷ Everyone ate all they wanted, and the leftovers filled seven large baskets.

---

*15.22 Canaanite woman: This woman was not Jewish.
*15.22 Son of David: See the note at 9.27.
See also: 15.14: Luke 6.39. 15.18: Matt 12.34.

*15.26 feed it to dogs: The Jewish people sometimes referred to Gentiles as dogs.
*15.34 small loaves of bread: See the note at 14.17.

[38] There were four thousand men who ate, not counting the women and children.

[39] After Jesus had sent the crowds away, he got into a boat and sailed across the lake. He came to shore near the town of Magadan.*

CHAPTER 16

A demand for a sign from heaven

This is also told in Mark 8.11–13; Luke 12.54–56

[1] The Pharisees and Sadducees came to Jesus and tried to test him by asking for a sign from heaven. [2] He told them:

> If the sky is red in the evening, you say the weather will be good. [3] But if the sky is red and gloomy in the morning, you say it is going to rain. You can tell what the weather will be like by looking at the sky. But you don't understand what is happening now.* [4] You want a sign because you are evil and won't believe! But the only sign you will be given is what happened to Jonah.*

Then Jesus left.

The yeast of the Pharisees and Sadducees

This is also told in Mark 8.14–21

[5] The disciples had forgotten to bring any bread when they crossed the lake.* [6] Jesus then warned them, "Watch out! Guard against the yeast of the Pharisees and Sadducees."

[7] The disciples talked this over and said to each other, "He must be saying this because we didn't bring along any bread."

[8] Jesus knew what they were thinking and said:

> You don't have much faith! Why are you talking about not having any bread? [9] Don't you understand? Have you forgotten about the five thousand people and all those baskets of leftovers from just five loaves of bread? [10] And what about the four thousand people and all those baskets of leftovers from only seven loaves of bread? [11] Don't

you know by now that I am not talking to you about bread? Watch out for the yeast of the Pharisees and Sadducees!

[12] Finally, the disciples understood that Jesus wasn't talking about the yeast used to make bread, but about the teaching of the Pharisees and Sadducees.

Who is Jesus?

This is also told in Mark 8.27–30; Luke 9.18–21

[13] When Jesus and his disciples were near the town of Caesarea Philippi, he asked them, "What do people say about the Son of Man?"

[14] The disciples answered, "Some people say you are John the Baptist or perhaps Elijah* or Jeremiah or some other prophet."

[15] Then Jesus asked them, "But who do you say I am?"

[16] Simon Peter spoke up, "You are the Messiah, the Son of the living God."

[17] Jesus told him:

> Simon, son of Jonah, you are blessed! You didn't discover this on your own. It was shown to you by my Father in heaven. [18] So I will call you Peter, which means "a rock". On this rock I will build my church, and death itself will not have any power over it. [19] I will give you the keys to the kingdom of heaven, and God in heaven will allow whatever you allow on earth. But he will not allow anything that you don't allow.

[20] Jesus told his disciples not to tell anyone that he was the Messiah.

Jesus speaks about his suffering and death

This is also told in Mark 8.31–9.1; Luke 9.22–27

[21] From then on, Jesus began telling his disciples what would happen to him. He said, "I must go to Jerusalem. There the nation's leaders, the chief priests, and the teachers of the Law of Moses will make me suffer terribly. I will be killed, but three days later I will rise to life."

[22] Peter took Jesus aside and told him to stop talking like that. He said, "God would never let this happen to you, Lord!"

---

*15.39 Magadan:** The location is unknown.
*16.4 what happened to Jonah:** Jonah was in the stomach of a big fish for three days and nights. See 12.40.
*16.5 crossed the lake:** To the east side.

See also: **16.1:** Matt 12.38; Luke 11.16. **16.4:** Matt 12.39; Luke 11.29. **16.6:** Luke 12.1. **16.9:** Matt 14.17–21. **16.10:** Matt 15.34–38.

*16.14 Elijah:** See the note at 11.14.
See also: **16.14:** Matt 14.1,2; Mark 6.14,15; Luke 9.7,8. **16.16:** John 6.68,69. **16.19:** Matt 18.18; John 20.23.

23 Jesus turned to Peter and said, "Satan, get away from me! You're in my way because you think like everyone else and not like God." 24 Then Jesus said to his disciples:

If any of you want to be my followers, you must forget about yourself. You must take up your cross and follow me. 25 If you want to save your life,' you will destroy it. But if you give up your life for me, you will find it. 26 What will you gain, if you own the whole world but destroy yourself? What would you give to get back your soul?

27 The Son of Man will soon come in the glory of his Father and with his angels to reward all people for what they have done. 28 I promise you that some of those standing here will not die before they see the Son of Man coming with his kingdom.

CHAPTER 17

The true glory of Jesus
This is also told in Mark 9.2–13; Luke 9.28–36

1 Six days later Jesus took Peter and the brothers James and John with him. They went up on a very high mountain where they could be alone. 2 There in front of the disciples, Jesus was completely changed. His face was shining like the sun, and his clothes became white as light.

3 All at once Moses and Elijah were there talking with Jesus. 4 So Peter said to him, "Lord, it is good for us to be here! Let us make three shelters, one for you, one for Moses, and one for Elijah."

5 While Peter was still speaking, the shadow of a bright cloud passed over them. From the cloud a voice said, "This is my own dear Son, and I am pleased with him. Listen to what he says!" 6 When the disciples heard the voice, they were so afraid that they fell flat on the ground. 7 But Jesus came over and touched them. He said, "Get up and don't be afraid!" 8 When they opened their eyes, they saw only Jesus.

9 On their way down from the mountain, Jesus warned his disciples not to tell anyone what they had seen until after the Son of Man had been raised from death.

10 The disciples asked Jesus, "Don't the teachers of the Law of Moses say that Elijah must come before the Messiah does?"

11 Jesus told them, "Elijah certainly will come and get everything ready. 12 In fact, he has already come. But the people did not recognize him and treated him just as they wanted to. They will soon make the Son of Man suffer in the same way." 13 Then the disciples understood that Jesus was talking to them about John the Baptist.

Jesus heals a boy
This is also told in Mark 9.14–29; Luke 9.37–43a

14 Jesus and his disciples returned to the crowd. A man knelt in front of him 15 and said, "Lord, have pity on my son! He has a bad case of epilepsy and often falls into a fire or into water. 16 I brought him to your disciples, but none of them could heal him."

17 Jesus said, "You people are too stubborn to have any faith! How much longer must I be with you? Why do I have to put up with you? Bring the boy here." 18 Then Jesus spoke sternly to the demon. It went out of the boy, and at once the boy was healed.

19 Later the disciples went to Jesus in private and asked him, "Why couldn't we force out the demon?"

20-21 Jesus replied:

It is because you don't have enough faith! But I can promise you this. If you had faith no larger than a mustard seed, you could tell this mountain to move from here to there. And it would. Everything would be possible for you.'

Jesus again speaks about his death
This is also told in Mark 9.30–32; Luke 9.43b–45

22 While Jesus and his disciples were going from place to place in Galilee, he told them, "The Son of Man will be handed over to people 23 who will kill him. But three days later he will rise to life." All this made the disciples very sad.

Paying the temple tax

24 When Jesus and the others arrived in Capernaum, the collectors for the temple tax came to Peter and asked, "Does your teacher pay the temple tax?"

See also: 16.24: Matt 10.38; Luke 14.27.   16.25: Matt 10.39; Luke 17.33; John 12.25.   16.27: a Matt 25.31; b Psa 62.12; Rom 2.6.   17.1–5: 2 Pet 1.17,18.   17.5: a Gen 22.2; Psa 2.7; Isa 42.1; Matt 3.17; 12.18; Mark 1.11; Luke 3.22; b Deut 18.15.

See also: 17.10: Mal 4.5.   17.12: Matt 11.14. 17.20: Matt 21.21; Mark 11.23; 1 Cor 13.2. 17.24: Exod 30.13–15; 38.26.

²⁵ "Yes, he does," Peter answered.

After they had returned home, Jesus went up to Peter and asked him, "Simon, what do you think? Do the kings of this earth collect taxes and fees from their own people or from foreigners?"

²⁶ Peter answered, "From foreigners."

Jesus replied, "Then their own people' don't have to pay. ²⁷ But we don't want to cause trouble. So go and cast a line into the lake and pull out the first fish you hook. Open its mouth, and you will find a coin. Use it to pay your taxes and mine."

CHAPTER 18

Who is the greatest?

This is also told in Mark 9.33–37; Luke 9.46–48

¹ About this time the disciples came to Jesus and asked him who would be the greatest in the kingdom of heaven. ² Jesus called a child over and made the child stand near him. ³ Then he said:

I promise you this. If you don't change and become like a child, you will never get into the kingdom of heaven. ⁴ But if you are as humble as this child, you are the greatest in the kingdom of heaven. ⁵ And when you welcome one of these children because of me, you welcome me.

Temptations to sin

This is also told in Mark 9.42–48; Luke 17.1,2

Jesus continued:

⁶ It will be terrible for people who cause even one of my little followers to sin. Those people would be better off thrown into the deepest part of the sea with a heavy stone tied around their necks! ⁷ The world is in for trouble because of the way it causes people to sin. There will always be something to cause people to sin, but anyone who does this will be in for trouble.

⁸ If your hand or foot causes you to sin, chop it off and throw it away! You would be better off to go into life crippled or lame than to have two hands or two feet and be thrown into the fire that never goes out. ⁹ If your eye causes you to sin, poke it out and get rid of it. You would be better off to go into life with only one eye than to have two eyes and be thrown into the fires of hell.

The lost sheep

This is also told in Luke 15.3–7

Jesus continued:

¹⁰–¹¹ Don't be cruel to any of these little ones! I promise you that their angels are always with my Father in heaven.' ¹² Let me ask you this. What would you do if you had a hundred sheep and one of them wandered off? Wouldn't you leave the ninety-nine on the hillside and go and look for the one that had wandered away? ¹³ I am sure that finding it would make you happier than having the ninety-nine that never wandered off. ¹⁴ That's how it is with your Father in heaven. He doesn't want any of these little ones to be lost.

When someone sins

This is also told in Luke 17.3

Jesus continued:

¹⁵ If one of my followers* sins against you, go and point out what was wrong. But do it in private, just between the two of you. If that person listens, you have won back a follower. ¹⁶ But if that one refuses to listen, take along one or two others. The Scriptures teach that every complaint must be proved true by two or more witnesses. ¹⁷ If the follower refuses to listen to them, report the matter to the church. Anyone who refuses to listen to the church must be treated like an unbeliever or a tax collector.*

Allowing and not allowing

Jesus continued:

¹⁸ I promise you that God in heaven will allow whatever you allow on earth, but he will not allow anything you don't allow. ¹⁹ I promise that when any two of you on earth agree about something you are praying for, my Father in heaven will do it for you. ²⁰ Whenever two or three of you come together in my name,' I am there with you.

---

*18.15 followers: The Greek text has "brother", which is used here and elsewhere in this chapter to refer to a follower of Christ.
*18.17 tax collector: See the note at 5.46.

See also: 18.1: Luke 22.24. 18.3: Mark 10.15; Luke 18.17.
18.8: Matt 5.30. 18.9: Matt 5.29.

See also: 18.11: Luke 19.10. 18.15: Luke 17.3.
18.16: Deut 19.15. 18.18: Matt 16.19; John 20.23.

An official who refused to forgive

21 Peter came up to the Lord and asked, "How many times should I forgive someone* who does something wrong to me? Is seven times enough?"

22 Jesus answered:

Not just seven times, but seventy-seven times!* 23 This story will show you what the kingdom of heaven is like:

One day a king decided to call in his officials and ask them to give an account of what they owed him. 24 As he was doing this, one official was brought in who owed him fifty million silver coins. 25 But he didn't have any money to pay what he owed. The king ordered him to be sold, along with his wife and children and all he owned, in order to pay the debt.

26 The official got down on his knees and began begging, "Have pity on me, and I will pay you every penny I owe!" 27 The king felt sorry for him and let him go free. He even told the official that he did not have to pay back the money.

28 As the official was leaving, he happened to meet another official, who owed him a hundred silver coins. So he grabbed the man by the throat. He started choking him and said, "Pay me what you owe!"

29 The man got down on his knees and began begging, "Have pity on me, and I will pay you back." 30 But the first official refused to have pity. Instead, he went and had the other official put in jail until he could pay what he owed.

31 When some other officials found out what had happened, they felt sorry for the man who had been put in jail. Then they told the king what had happened. 32 The king called the first official back in and said, "You're an evil man! When you begged for mercy, I said you did not have to pay back a penny. 33 Don't you think you should show pity to someone else, as I did to you?" 34 The king was so angry that he ordered the official to be tortured until he could pay back everything he owed. 35 That is how

my Father in heaven will treat you, if you don't forgive each of my followers with all your heart.

Jesus goes from Galilee to Jerusalem

CHAPTER 19

Teaching about divorce

This is also told in Mark 10.1–12

1 When Jesus finished teaching, he left Galilee and went to the part of Judea that is east of the River Jordan. 2 Large crowds followed him, and he healed their sick people.

3 Some Pharisees wanted to test Jesus. They came up to him and asked, "Is it right for a man to divorce his wife for just any reason?"

4 Jesus answered, "Don't you know that in the beginning the Creator made a man and a woman? 5 That's why a man leaves his father and mother and gets married. He becomes like one person with his wife. 6 Then they are no longer two people, but one. And no one should separate a couple that God has joined together."

7 The Pharisees asked Jesus, "Why did Moses say that a man could write out divorce papers and send his wife away?"

8 Jesus replied, "You are so heartless! That's why Moses allowed you to divorce your wife. But from the beginning God did not intend it to be that way. 9 I say that if your wife has not committed some terrible sexual sin,* you must not divorce her to marry someone else. If you do, you are unfaithful."

10 The disciples said, "If that's how it is between a man and a woman, it's better not to get married."

11 Jesus told them, "Only those people who have been given the gift of staying single can accept this teaching. 12 Some people are unable to marry because of birth defects or because of what someone has done to their bodies. Others stay single for the sake of the kingdom of heaven. Anyone who can accept this teaching should do so."

---

*18.21 someone: Or "a follower". See the note at 18.15.

*18.22 seventy-seven times: Or "seventy times seven". The large number means that one follower should never stop forgiving another.

See also: 18.21,22: Luke 17.3,4. 18.22: Gen 4.24.

*19.9 some terrible sexual sin: See the note at 5.32.

See also: 19.4: Gen 1.27; 5.2. 19.5: Gen 2.24.
19.7: Deut 24.1–4; Matt 5.31. 19.9: Matt 5.32;
1 Cor 7.10,11.

Jesus blesses little children

This is also told in Mark 10.13–16; Luke 18.15–17

13 Some people brought their children to Jesus, so that he could place his hands on them and pray for them. His disciples told the people to stop bothering him. 14 But Jesus said, "Let the children come to me, and don't try to stop them! People who are like these children belong to God's kingdom." 15 After Jesus had placed his hands on the children, he left.

A rich young man

This is also told in Mark 10.17–31; Luke 18.18–30

16 A man came to Jesus and asked, "Teacher, what good thing must I do to have eternal life?"

17 Jesus said to him, "Why do you ask me about what is good? Only God is good. If you want to have eternal life, you must obey his commandments."

18 "Which ones?" the man asked.

Jesus answered, "Do not murder. Be faithful in marriage. Do not steal. Do not tell lies about others. 19 Respect your father and mother. And love others as much as you love yourself." 20 The young man said, "I have obeyed all these. What else must I do?"

21 Jesus replied, "If you want to be perfect, go and sell everything you own! Give the money to the poor, and you will have riches in heaven. Then come and be my follower." 22 When the young man heard this, he was sad, because he was very rich.

23 Jesus said to his disciples, "It's terribly hard for rich people to get into the kingdom of heaven! 24 In fact, it's easier for a camel to go through the eye of a needle than for a rich person to get into God's kingdom."

25 When the disciples heard this, they were greatly surprised and asked, "How can anyone ever be saved?"

26 Jesus looked straight at them and said, "There are some things that people cannot do, but God can do anything."

27 Peter replied, "Remember, we have left everything to be your followers! What will we get?"

28 Jesus answered:

Yes, all of you have become my followers. And so in the future world, where the Son of Man sits on his glorious throne, I promise that you will sit on twelve thrones to judge the twelve tribes of Israel. 29 All who have given up home or brothers and sisters or father and mother or children or land for me will be given a hundred times as much. They will also have eternal life. 30 But many who are now first will be last, and many who are last will be first.

CHAPTER 20

Workers in a vineyard

1 As Jesus was telling what the kingdom of heaven would be like, he said:

Early one morning a man went out to hire some workers for his vineyard. 2 After he had agreed to pay them the usual amount for a day's work, he sent them off to his vineyard.

3 About nine that morning, the man saw some other people standing in the market with nothing to do. 4 He said he would pay them what was fair, if they would work in his vineyard. 5 So they went.

At midday and again about three in the afternoon he returned to the market. And each time he made the same agreement with others who were lazing around with nothing to do.

6 Finally, about five in the afternoon the man went back and found some others standing there. He asked them, "Why have you been standing here all day long doing nothing?"

7 "Because no one has hired us," they answered. Then he told them to go and work in his vineyard.

8 That evening the owner of the vineyard told the man in charge of the workers to call them in and give them their money. He also told the man to begin with the ones who were hired last. 9 When the workers arrived, the ones who had been hired at five in the afternoon were given a full day's pay.

10 The workers who had been hired first thought they would be given more than the others. But when they were given the same, 11 they began complaining to the owner of the vineyard. 12 They said, "The ones who were hired last worked for only one hour. But you paid them the same that you did us. And we worked in the hot sun all day long!"

13 The owner answered one of them, "Friend, I didn't cheat you. I paid you

See also: **19.18:** a Exod 20.13; Deut 5.17; b Exod 20.14; Deut 5.18; c Exod 20.15; Deut 5.19. d Exod 20.16; Deut 5.20. **19.19:** a Exod 20.12; Deut 5.16; b Lev 19.18. **19.28:** a Matt 25.31; b Luke 22.30.

See also: **19.30:** Matt 20.16; Luke 13.30. **20.8:** Lev 19.13; Deut 24.15.

exactly what we agreed on. ¹⁴ Take your money now and go! What business is it of yours if I want to pay them the same that I paid you? ¹⁵ Don't I have the right to do what I want with my own money? Why should you be jealous, if I want to be generous?"

¹⁶ Jesus then said, "So it is. Everyone who is now first will be last, and everyone who is last will be first."

Jesus again tells about his death

This is also told in Mark 10.32–34; Luke 18.31–34

¹⁷ As Jesus was on his way to Jerusalem, he took his twelve disciples aside and told them in private:

¹⁸ We are now on our way to Jerusalem, where the Son of Man will be handed over to the chief priests and the teachers of the Law of Moses. They will sentence him to death, ¹⁹ and then they will hand him over to foreigners* who will make fun of him. They will beat him and nail him to a cross. But on the third day he will rise from death.

A mother's request

This is also told in Mark 10.35–45

²⁰ The mother of James and John* came to Jesus with her two sons. She knelt down and started begging him to do something for her. ²¹ Jesus asked her what she wanted, and she said, "When you come into your kingdom, please let one of my sons sit at your right side and the other at your left."*

²² Jesus answered, "Not one of you knows what you are asking. Are you able to drink from the cup* that I must soon drink from?"

James and John said, "Yes, we are!"

²³ Jesus replied, "You certainly will drink from my cup! But it isn't for me to say who will sit at my right side and at my left. That is for my Father to say."

²⁴ When the ten other disciples heard this, they were angry with the two brothers. ²⁵ But Jesus called the disciples together and said:

You know that foreign rulers like to order their people around. And their great leaders have full power over everyone they rule. ²⁶ But don't act like them. If you want to be great, you must be the servant of all the others. ²⁷ And if you want to be first, you must be the slave of the rest. ²⁸ The Son of Man did not come to be a slave master, but a slave who will give his life to rescue* many people.

Jesus heals two blind men

This is also told in Mark 10.46–52; Luke 18.35–43

²⁹ Jesus was followed by a large crowd as he and his disciples were leaving Jericho. ³⁰ Two blind men were sitting beside the road. And when they heard that Jesus was coming their way, they shouted, "Lord and Son of David,* have pity on us!"

³¹ The crowd told them to be quiet, but they shouted even louder, "Lord and Son of David, have pity on us!"

³² When Jesus heard them, he stopped and asked, "What do you want me to do for you?"

³³ They answered, "Lord, we want to see!"

³⁴ Jesus felt sorry for them and touched their eyes. Straight away they could see, and they became his followers.

Jesus' last week: his trial and death

CHAPTER 21

Jesus enters Jerusalem

This is also told in Mark 11.1–11; Luke 19.28–38; John 12.12–19

¹ When Jesus and his disciples came near Jerusalem, he went to Bethphage on the Mount of Olives and sent two of them on ahead. ² He told them, "Go into the next village, where you will at once find a donkey and her colt. Untie the two donkeys and bring them to me. ³ If anyone asks why you are doing that, just say, 'The Lord' needs them.' Straight away he will let you have the donkeys."

---

*20.19 foreigners: The Romans, who ruled Judea at this time.
*20.21 right side . . . left: The most powerful people in a kingdom sat at the right and left side of the king.
*20.22 drink from the cup: In the Scriptures a cup is sometimes used as a symbol of suffering. To "drink from the cup" is to suffer.

See also: 20.16: Matt 19.30; Mark 10.31; Luke 13.30.
20.25,26: Luke 22.25,26.

*20.28 rescue: The Greek word often, though not always, means the payment of a price to free a slave or a prisoner.
*20.30 Son of David: See the note at 9.27.

See also: 20.26,27: Matt 23.11; Mark 9.35; Luke 22.26.

[4] So God's promise came true, just as the prophet had said,

[5] "Announce to the people
    of Jerusalem:
'Your king is coming to you!
He is humble
    and rides on a donkey.
He comes on the colt
    of a donkey.' "

[6] The disciples left and did what Jesus had told them to do. [7] They brought the donkey and its colt and laid some clothes on their backs. Then Jesus got on.

[8] Many people spread clothes in the road, while others put down branches* which they had cut from trees. [9] Some people walked ahead of Jesus and others followed behind. They were all shouting,

"Hooray* for the Son of David!*
God bless the one who comes
    in the name of the Lord.
Hooray for God
    in heaven above!"

[10] The crowd went to Jerusalem, everyone in the city was excited and asked, "Who can this be?"

[11] The crowd answered, "This is Jesus, the prophet from Nazareth in Galilee."

Jesus in the temple

This is also told in Mark 11.15–19; Luke 19.45–48; John 2.13–22

[12] Jesus went into the temple and chased out everyone who was selling or buying. He turned over the tables of the moneychangers and the benches of the ones who were selling doves. [13] He told them, "The Scriptures say, 'My house should be called a place of worship.' But you have turned it into a place where robbers hide."

[14] Blind and lame people came to Jesus in the temple, and he healed them. [15] But the chief priests and the teachers of the Law of Moses were angry when they saw his miracles and heard the children

shouting praises to the Son of David.* [16] The men said to Jesus, "Don't you hear what those children are saying?"

"Yes, I do!" Jesus answered. "Don't you know that the Scriptures say, 'Children and infants will sing praises'?" [17] Then Jesus left the city and went out to the village of Bethany, where he spent the night.

Jesus puts a curse on a fig tree

This is also told in Mark 11.12–14,20–24

[18] When Jesus got up the next morning, he was hungry. He started out for the city, [19] and along the way he saw a fig tree. But when he came to it, he found only leaves and no figs. So he told the tree, "You will never again grow any fruit!" At once the fig tree dried up.

[20] The disciples were shocked when they saw how quickly the tree had dried up. [21] But Jesus said to them, "If you have faith and don't doubt, I promise that you can do what I did to this tree. And you will be able to do even more. You can tell this mountain to get up and jump into the sea, and it will. [22] If you have faith when you pray, you will be given whatever you ask for.

A question about Jesus' authority

This is also told in Mark 11.27–33; Luke 20.1–8

[23] Jesus had gone into the temple and was teaching when the chief priests and the leaders of the people came up to him. They asked, "What right do you have to do these things? Who gave you this authority?"

[24] Jesus answered, "I have just one question to ask you. If you answer it, I will tell you where I got the right to do these things. [25] Who gave John the right to baptize? Was it God in heaven or merely some human being?"

They thought it over and said to each other, "We can't say that God gave John this right. Jesus will ask us why we didn't believe John. [26] On the other hand, these people think that John was a prophet, and we are afraid of what they might do to us. That's why we can't say that it was merely some human who gave John the right to baptize." [27] So they told Jesus, "We don't know."

Jesus said, "Then I won't tell you who gave me the right to do what I do."

---

*21.8 spread clothes . . . put down branches: This was one way that the Jewish people welcomed a famous person.
*21.9 Hooray: This translates a word that can mean "please save us". But it is most often used as a shout of praise to God.
*21.9 Son of David: See the note at 9.27.
See also: 21.5: Zech 9.9. 21.9: Psa 118.25,26.
21.13: Isa 56.7; Jer 7.11.

*21.15 Son of David: See the note at 9.27.
See also: 21.16: Psa 8.2 (LXX). 21.21: Matt 17.20;
1 Cor 13.2.

A story about two sons

28 Jesus said:

I will tell you a story about a man who had two sons. Then you can tell me what you think. The father went to the elder son and said, "Go and work in the vineyard today!" 29 His son told him that he would not do it, but later he changed his mind and went. 30 The man then told his younger son to go and work in the vineyard. The boy said he would, but he didn't go. 31 Which one of the sons obeyed his father?

"The elder one," the chief priests and leaders answered.

Then Jesus told them:

You can be sure that tax collectors* and prostitutes will get into the kingdom of God before you ever will! 32 When John the Baptist showed you how to do right, you would not believe him. But these evil people did believe. And even when you saw what they did, you still would not change your minds and believe.

Tenants of a vineyard

This is also told in Mark 12.1–12; Luke 20.9–19

33 Jesus told the chief priests and leaders to listen to this story:

A land owner once planted a vineyard. He built a wall around it and dug a pit to crush the grapes in. He also built a lookout tower. Then he let his vineyard and left the country.

34 When it was harvest time, the owner sent some servants to get his share of the grapes. 35 But the tenants grabbed those servants. They beat up one, killed one, and stoned one of them to death. 36 He then sent more servants than he did the first time. But the tenants treated them in the same way.

37 Finally, the owner sent his own son to the tenants, because he thought they would respect him. 38 But when they saw the man's son, they said, "Some day he will own the vineyard. Let's kill him! Then we can have it all for ourselves." 39 So they grabbed him, threw him out of the vineyard, and killed him.

40 Jesus asked, "When the owner of that vineyard comes, what do you suppose he will do to those tenants?"

41 The chief priests and leaders answered, "He will kill them in some horrible way. Then he will let his vineyard to people who will give him his share of grapes at harvest time."

42 Jesus replied, "Surely you know that the Scriptures say,

'The stone that the builders
   tossed aside
is now the most important
   stone of all.
This is something
   the Lord has done,
   and it is amazing to us.'

43 I tell you that God's kingdom will be taken from you and given to people who will do what he demands. 44 Anyone who stumbles over this stone will be crushed, and anyone it falls on will be smashed to pieces."

45 When the chief priests and the Pharisees heard these stories, they knew that Jesus was talking about them. 46 So they looked for a way to arrest Jesus. But they were afraid to, because the people thought he was a prophet.

CHAPTER 22

The great banquet

This is also told in Luke 14.15–24

1 Once again Jesus used stories to teach people:

2 The kingdom of heaven is like what happened when a king gave a wedding banquet for his son. 3 The king sent some servants to tell the invited guests to come to the banquet, but the guests refused.

4 He sent other servants to say to the guests, "The banquet is ready! My cattle and prize calves have all been prepared. Everything is ready. Come to the banquet!"

5 But the guests did not pay any attention. Some of them left for their farms, and some went to their places of business. 6 Others grabbed the servants, then beat them up and killed them.

7 This made the king so furious that he sent an army to kill those murderers and burn down their city. 8 Then he said to the servants, "It is time for the wedding banquet, and the invited guests don't deserve to come. 9 Go out to the street corners and tell everyone you meet to come to the banquet." 10 They went out into the streets and brought in everyone they could find, good and bad

---

*21.31 tax collectors: See the note at 5.46.
See also: 21.32: Luke 3.12; 7.29,30. 21.33: Isa 5.1,2.

See also: 21.42: Psa 118.22,23.

alike. And the banquet room was filled with guests.

[11] When the king went in to meet the guests, he found that one of them wasn't wearing the right kind of clothes for the wedding. [12] The king asked, "Friend, why didn't you wear proper clothes for the wedding?" But the guest had no excuse. [13] So the king gave orders for that person to be tied hand and foot and to be thrown outside into the dark. That's where people will cry and grit their teeth in pain. [14] Many are invited, but only a few are chosen.

Paying taxes

This is also told in Mark 12.13–17; Luke 20.20–26

[15] The Pharisees got together and planned how they could trick Jesus into saying something wrong. [16] They sent some of their followers and some of Herod's followers* to say to him, "Teacher, we know that you are honest. You teach the truth about what God wants people to do. And you treat everyone with the same respect, no matter who they are. [17] Tell us what you think! Should we pay taxes to the Emperor or not?"

[18] Jesus knew their evil thoughts and said, "Why are you trying to test me? You show-offs! [19] Let me see one of the coins used for paying taxes." They brought him a silver coin, [20] and he asked, "Whose picture and name are on it?"

[21] "The Emperor's," they answered.

Then Jesus told them, "Give the Emperor what belongs to him and give God what belongs to God." [22] His answer surprised them so much that they walked away.

Life in the future world

This is also told in Mark 12.18–27; Luke 20.27–40

[23] The Sadducees did not believe that people would rise to life after death. So that same day some of the Sadducees came to Jesus and said:

[24] Teacher, Moses wrote that if a married man dies and has no children, his brother should marry the widow. Their first son would then be thought of as the son of the dead brother.

[25] Once there were seven brothers who lived here. The first one married, but

died without having any children. So his wife was left to his brother. [26] The same thing happened to the second and third brothers and finally to all seven of them. [27] At last the woman died. [28] When God raises people from death, whose wife will this woman be? She had been married to all seven brothers.

[29] Jesus answered:

You are completely wrong! You don't know what the Scriptures teach. And you don't know anything about the power of God. [30] When God raises people to life, they won't marry. They will be like the angels in heaven. [31] And as for people being raised to life, God was speaking to you when he said, [32] "I am the God worshipped by Abraham, Isaac, and Jacob."* He isn't the God of the dead, but of the living.

[33] The crowds were surprised to hear what Jesus was teaching.

The most important commandment

This is also told in Mark 12.28–34; Luke 10.25–28

[34] After Jesus had made the Sadducees look foolish, the Pharisees heard about it and got together. [35] One of them was an expert in the Jewish Law. So he tried to test Jesus by asking, [36] "Teacher, what is the most important commandment in the Law?"

[37] Jesus answered:

Love the Lord your God with all your heart, soul, and mind. [38] This is the first and most important commandment. [39] The second most important commandment is like this one. And it is, "Love others as much as you love yourself." [40] All the Law of Moses and the Books of the Prophets* are based on these two commandments.

About David's son

This is also told in Mark 12.35–37; Luke 20.41–44

[41] While the Pharisees were still there, Jesus asked them, [42] "What do you think about the Messiah? Whose family will he come from?"

---

*22.16 Herod's followers: People who were political followers of the family of Herod the Great (see 2.1) and his son Herod Antipas (see 14.1), and who wanted Herod to be king in Jerusalem.
See also: 22.13; Matt 8.12; 25.30; Luke 13.28.
22.23: Acts 23.8. **22.24:** Deut 25.5.

*22.32 I am the God worshipped by Abraham, Isaac, and Jacob: Jesus argues that if God is worshipped by these three, they must still be alive, because he is the God of the living.
*22.40 the Law of Moses and the Books of the Prophets: See the note at 5.17.
See also: 22.32: Exod 3.6. 22.35–40: Luke 10.25–28. 22.37: Deut 6.5. 22.39: Lev 19.18.

They answered, "He will be a son of King David."*

[43] Jesus replied, "How then could the Spirit lead David to call the Messiah his Lord? David said,

[44] 'The Lord said to my Lord:
Sit at my right side*
until I make your enemies
into a footstool for you.'

[45] If David called the Messiah his Lord, how can the Messiah be a son of King David?" [46] No one was able to give Jesus an answer, and from that day on, no one dared ask him any more questions.

CHAPTER 23

Jesus condemns the Pharisees and the teachers of the Law of Moses

This is also told in Mark 12.38–40; Luke 11.37–52; 20.45–47

[1] Jesus said to the crowds and to his disciples:

[2] The Pharisees and the teachers of the Law are experts in the Law of Moses. [3] So obey everything they teach you, but don't do as they do. After all, they say one thing and do something else. [4] They pile heavy burdens on people's shoulders and won't lift a finger to help. [5] Everything they do is just to show off in front of others. They even make a big show of wearing Scripture verses on their foreheads and arms, and they wear big tassels* for everyone to see. [6] They love the best seats at banquets and the front seats in the meeting places. [7] And when they are in the market, they like to have people greet them as their teachers.

[8] But none of you should be called a teacher. You have only one teacher, and all of you are like brothers and sisters. [9] Don't call anyone on earth your father. All of you have the same Father in heaven. [10] None of

you should be called the leader. The Messiah is your only leader. [11] Whoever is the greatest should be the servant of the others. [12] If you put yourself above others, you will be put down. But if you humble yourself, you will be honoured.

[13–14] You Pharisees and teachers of the Law of Moses are in for trouble! You're nothing but show-offs. You lock people out of the kingdom of heaven. You won't go in yourselves, and you keep others from going in.◆

[15] You Pharisees and teachers of the Law of Moses are in for trouble! You're nothing but show-offs. You travel over land and sea to win one follower. And when you have done so, you make that person twice as fit for hell as you are.

[16] You are in for trouble! You are supposed to lead others, but you are blind. You teach that it doesn't matter if a person swears by the temple. But you say that it does matter if someone swears by the gold in the temple. [17] You blind fools! Which is greater, the gold or the temple that makes the gold sacred? [18] You also teach that it doesn't matter if a person swears by the altar. But you say that it does matter if someone swears by the gift on the altar. [19] Are you blind? Which is more important, the gift or the altar that makes the gift sacred? [20] Anyone who swears by the altar also swears by everything on it. [21] And anyone who swears by the temple also swears by God, who lives there. [22] To swear by heaven is the same as swearing by God's throne and by the one who sits on that throne.

Jesus continued:

[23] You Pharisees and teachers are show-offs, and you're in for trouble! You give God a tenth of the spices from your garden, such as mint, dill, and cumin. Yet you neglect the more important matters of the Law, such as justice, mercy, and faithfulness. These are the important things you should have done, though you should not have left the others undone either. [24] You blind leaders! You strain out a small fly but swallow a camel.

[25] You Pharisees and teachers are show-offs, and you're in for trouble! You wash the outside of your cups and dishes,

---

*22.42 son of King David: See the note at 9.27.
*22.44 right side: The place of power and honour.
*23.5 wearing Scripture verses on their foreheads and arms . . . tassels: As a sign of their love for the Lord and his teachings, the Jewish people had started wearing Scripture verses in small leather boxes. But the Pharisees tried to show off by making the boxes bigger than necessary. The Jewish people were also taught to wear tassels on the four corners of their robes to show their love for God.

See also: 22.44: Psa 110.1. 23.5: a Matt 6.1; b Deut 6.8;
c Num 15.38.

See also: 23.11: Matt 20.26,27; Mark 9.35; 10.43,44;
Luke 22.26. 23.12: Luke 14.11; 18.14. 23.22: Isa 66.1;
Matt 5.34. 23.23: Lev 27.30.

while inside there is nothing but greed and selfishness. 26 You blind Pharisee! First clean the inside of a cup, and then the outside will also be clean.

27 You Pharisees and teachers are in for trouble! You're nothing but show-offs. You're like tombs that have been whitewashed.* On the outside they are beautiful, but inside they are full of bones and filth. 28 That's what you are like. Outside you look good, but inside you are evil and only pretend to be good.

29 You Pharisees and teachers are nothing but show-offs, and you're in for trouble! You build monuments for the prophets and decorate the tombs of good people. 30 And you claim that you would not have taken part with your ancestors in killing the prophets. 31 But you prove that you really are the relatives of the ones who killed the prophets. 32 So keep on doing everything they did. 33 You are nothing but snakes and the children of snakes! How can you escape going to hell?

34 I will send prophets and wise people and experts in the Law of Moses to you. But you will kill them or nail them to a cross or beat them in your meeting places or chase them from town to town. 35 That's why you will be held guilty for the murder of every good person, beginning with the good man Abel. This also includes Barachiah's son Zechariah,* the man you murdered between the temple and the altar. 36 I can promise that you people living today will be punished for all these things!

Jesus loves Jerusalem

This is also told in Luke 13.34,35

Jesus continued:

37 Jerusalem, Jerusalem! Your people have killed the prophets and have stoned the messengers who were sent to you. I have often wanted to gather your people, as a

hen gathers her chicks under her wings. But you wouldn't let me. 38 And now your temple will be deserted. 39 You won't see me again until you say,

"Blessed is the one who comes
in the name of the Lord."

CHAPTER 24

The temple will be destroyed

This is also told in Mark 13.1,2; Luke 21.5,6

1 After Jesus left the temple, his disciples came over and said, "Look at all these buildings!"

2 Jesus replied, "Do you see these buildings? They will certainly be torn down! Not one stone will be left in place."

Warning about trouble

This is also told in Mark 13.3–13; Luke 21.7–19

3 Later, as Jesus was sitting on the Mount of Olives, his disciples came to him in private and asked, "When will this happen? What will be the sign of your coming and of the end of the world?"

4 Jesus answered:

Don't let anyone fool you. 5 Many will come and claim to be me. They will say that they are the Messiah, and they will fool many people.

6 You will soon hear about wars and threats of wars, but don't be afraid. These things will have to happen first, but that isn't the end. 7 Nations and kingdoms will go to war against each other. People will starve to death, and in some places there will be earthquakes. 8 But this is just the beginning of troubles.

9 You will be arrested, punished, and even killed. Because of me, you will be hated by people of all nations. 10 Many will give up and will betray and hate each other. 11 Many false prophets will come and fool a lot of people. 12 Evil will spread and cause many people to stop loving others. 13 But if you keep on being faithful to the end, you will be saved. 14 When the good news about the kingdom has been preached all over the world and told to all nations, the end will come.

---

*23.27 whitewashed: Tombs were whitewashed to keep anyone from accidentally touching them. A person who touched a dead body or a tomb was considered unclean and could not worship with the rest of the Jewish people.
*23.35 Zechariah: Genesis is the first book in the Jewish Scriptures, and it tells that Abel was the first person to be murdered. The Second Book of Chronicles is the last book in the Jewish Scriptures, and the last murder that it tells about is that of Zechariah.

See also: 23.27: Acts 23.3. 23.33: Matt 3.7; 12.34; Luke 3.7. 23.35: a Gen 4.8; b 2 Chron 24.20,21.

See also: 23.38: Jer 22.5. 23.39: Psa 118.26. 24.9: Matt 10.22. 24.13: Matt 10.22.

The Horrible Thing

This is also told in Mark 13.14–23; Luke 21.20–24

Jesus continued:

15 Some day you will see that "Horrible Thing" in the holy place, just as the prophet Daniel said. Everyone who reads this must try to understand! 16 If you are living in Judea at that time, run to the mountains. 17 If you are on the roof* of your house, don't go inside to get anything. 18 If you are out in the field, don't go back for your coat. 19 It will be a terrible time for women who are expecting babies or nursing young children. 20 And pray that you won't have to escape in winter or on a Sabbath.* 21 This will be the worst time of suffering since the beginning of the world, and nothing this terrible will ever happen again. 22 If God doesn't make the time shorter, no one will be left alive. But because of God's chosen ones, he will make the time shorter.

23 Someone may say, "Here is the Messiah!" or "There he is!" But don't believe it. 24 False messiahs and false prophets will come and perform great miracles and signs. They will even try to fool God's chosen ones. 25 But I have warned you beforehand. 26 If you are told that the Messiah is out in the desert, don't go there! And if you are told that he is in some secret place, don't believe it! 27 The coming of the Son of Man will be like lightning that can be seen from east to west. 28 Where there is a corpse, there will always be vultures.*

When the Son of Man appears

This is also told in Mark 13.24–27; Luke 21.25–28

Jesus continued:

29 Straight after those days of suffering,

"The sun will become dark,
   and the moon
      will no longer shine.
The stars will fall,
   and the powers in the sky*
      will be shaken."

30 Then a sign will appear in the sky. And there will be the Son of Man.* All nations on earth will weep when they see the Son of Man coming on the clouds of heaven with power and great glory. 31 At the sound of a loud trumpet, he will send his angels to bring his chosen ones together from all over the earth.

A lesson from a fig tree

This is also told in Mark 13.28–31; Luke 21.29–33

Jesus continued:

32 Learn a lesson from a fig tree. When its branches sprout and start putting out leaves, you know that summer is near. 33 So when you see all these things happening, you will know that the time has almost come.* 34 I can promise you that some of the people of this generation will still be alive when all this happens. 35 The sky and the earth won't last for ever, but my words will.

No one knows the day or time

This is also told in Mark 13.32–37;
Luke 17.26–30,34–36

Jesus continued:

36 No one knows the day or hour. The angels in heaven don't know, and the Son himself doesn't know.* Only the Father knows. 37 When the Son of Man appears, things will be just as they were when Noah lived. 38 People were eating, drinking, and getting married right up to the day that the flood came and Noah went into the big boat. 39 They didn't know anything was happening until the flood came and swept

---

*24.17 roof: In Palestine the houses usually had a flat roof. Stairs on the outside led up to the roof, which was made of beams and boards covered with packed earth.
*24.20 in winter or on a Sabbath: In Palestine the winters are cold and rainy and make travel difficult. The Jewish people were not allowed to travel much more than a kilometre on the Sabbath. For these reasons it was hard for them to escape from their enemies in the winter or on a Sabbath.
*24.28 Where there is a corpse, there will always be vultures: This saying may mean that when anything important happens, people soon know about it. Or the saying may mean that whenever something bad happens, curious people gather around and stare. But the word translated "vulture" also means "eagle" and may refer to the Roman army, which had an eagle as its symbol.
See also: 24.15: Dan 9.27; 11.31; 12.11.
24.17,18: Luke 17.31. 24.21: Dan 12.1; Rev 7.14.
24.26,27: Luke 17.23,24. 24.28: Luke 17.37.

*24.29 the powers in the sky: In ancient times people thought that the stars were spiritual powers.
See also: 24.29: a Isa 13.10; Joel 2.10,31; 3.15; Rev 6.12; b Isa 13.10; Ezek 32.7; Joel 2.10; 3.15; c Isa 34.4; Rev 6.13. 24.30: Dan 7.13; Zech 12.10–14; Rev 1.7. 24.37: Gen 6.5–8. 24.39: Gen 7.6–24.

them all away. That is how it will be when the Son of Man appears.

⁴⁰ Two men will be in the same field, but only one will be taken. The other will be left. ⁴¹ Two women will be together grinding grain, but only one will be taken. The other will be left. ⁴² So be on your guard! You don't know when your Lord will come.

⁴³ Homeowners never know when a thief is coming, and they are always on guard to keep one from breaking in. ⁴⁴ Always be ready! You don't know when the Son of Man will come.

Faithful and unfaithful servants

This is also told in Luke 12.35–48

Jesus continued:

⁴⁵ Who are faithful and wise servants? Who are the ones the master will put in charge of giving the other servants their food supplies at the proper time? ⁴⁶ Servants are fortunate if their master comes and finds them doing their job. ⁴⁷ You may be sure that a servant who is always faithful will be put in charge of everything the master owns. ⁴⁸ But suppose one of the servants thinks that the master won't return until late. ⁴⁹ Suppose that evil servant starts beating the other servants and eats and drinks with people who are drunk. ⁵⁰ If that happens, the master will come on a day and at a time when the servant least expects him. ⁵¹ That servant will then be punished and thrown out with the ones who only pretended to serve their master. There they will cry and grit their teeth in pain.

CHAPTER 25

A story about ten girls

Jesus said:

¹ The kingdom of heaven is like what happened one night when ten girls took their oil lamps and went to a wedding to meet the groom.* ² Five of the girls were foolish and five were wise. ³ The foolish ones took their lamps, but no extra oil.

*25.1 to meet the groom: Some manuscripts add "and the bride". It was the custom for the groom to go to the home of the bride's parents to get his bride. Young girls and other guests would then go with them to the home of the groom's parents, where the wedding feast would take place.

See also: 24.43,44: Luke 12.39,40.   25.1: Luke 12.35.

⁴ The ones who were wise took along extra oil for their lamps.

⁵ The groom was late arriving, and the girls became drowsy and fell asleep. ⁶ Then in the middle of the night someone shouted, "Here's the groom! Come to meet him!"

⁷ When the girls got up and started getting their lamps ready, ⁸ the foolish ones said to the others, "Let us have some of your oil! Our lamps are going out."

⁹ The girls who were wise answered, "There's not enough oil for all of us! Go and buy some for yourselves."

¹⁰ While the foolish girls were on their way to get some oil, the groom arrived. The girls who were ready went into the wedding, and the doors were closed.

¹¹ Later the other girls returned and shouted, "Sir, sir! Open the door for us!"

¹² But the groom replied, "I don't even know you!"

¹³ So, my disciples, always be ready! You don't know the day or the time when all this will happen.

A story about three servants

This is also told in Luke 19.11–27

Jesus continued:

¹⁴ The kingdom is also like what happened when a man went away and put his three servants in charge of all he owned. ¹⁵ The man knew what each servant could do. So he handed five thousand coins to the first servant, two thousand to the second, and one thousand to the third. Then he left the country.

¹⁶ As soon as the man had gone, the servant with the five thousand coins used them to earn five thousand more. ¹⁷ The servant who had two thousand coins did the same with his money and earned two thousand more. ¹⁸ But the servant with one thousand coins dug a hole and hid his master's money in the ground.

¹⁹ Some time later the master of those servants returned. He called them in and asked what they had done with his money. ²⁰ The servant who had been given five thousand coins brought them in with the five thousand that he had earned. He said, "Sir, you gave me five thousand coins, and I have earned five thousand more."

²¹ "Wonderful!" his master replied. "You are a good and faithful servant. I left you in

See also: 25.11,12: Luke 13.25.   25.14–30: Luke 19.11–27.

charge of only a little, but now I will put you in charge of much more. Come and share in my happiness!"

²² Next, the servant who had been given two thousand coins came in and said, "Sir, you gave me two thousand coins, and I have earned two thousand more."

²³ "Wonderful!" his master replied. "You are a good and faithful servant. I left you in charge of only a little, but now I will put you in charge of much more. Come and share in my happiness!"

²⁴ The servant who had been given one thousand coins then came in and said, "Sir, I know that you are hard to get along with. You harvest what you don't plant and gather crops where you haven't scattered seed. ²⁵ I was frightened and went out and hid your money in the ground. Here is every single coin!"

²⁶ The master of the servant told him, "You are lazy and good-for-nothing! You know that I harvest what I don't plant and gather crops where I haven't scattered seed. ²⁷ You could have at least put my money in the bank, so that I could have earned interest on it."

²⁸ Then the master said, "Now your money will be taken away and given to the servant with ten thousand coins! ²⁹ Everyone who has something will be given more, and they will have more than enough. But everything will be taken from those who don't have anything. ³⁰ You are a worthless servant, and you will be thrown out into the dark where people will cry and grit their teeth in pain."

The final judgment

Jesus continued:

³¹ When the Son of Man comes in his glory with all his angels, he will sit on his royal throne. ³² The people of all nations will be brought before him, and he will separate them, as shepherds separate their sheep from their goats.

³³ He will place the sheep on his right and the goats on his left. ³⁴ Then the king will say to those on his right, "My father has blessed you! Come and receive the kingdom that was prepared for you before the world was created. ³⁵ When I was hungry, you gave me something to eat,

and when I was thirsty, you gave me something to drink. When I was a stranger, you welcomed me, ³⁶ and when I was naked, you gave me clothes to wear. When I was sick, you took care of me, and when I was in jail, you visited me."

³⁷ Then the ones who pleased the Lord will ask, "When did we give you something to eat or drink? ³⁸ When did we welcome you as a stranger or give you clothes to wear ³⁹ or visit you while you were sick or in jail?"

⁴⁰ The king will answer, "Whenever you did it for any of my people, no matter how unimportant they seemed, you did it for me."

⁴¹ Then the king will say to those on his left, "Get away from me! You are under God's curse. Go into the everlasting fire prepared for the devil and his angels! ⁴² I was hungry, but you did not give me anything to eat, and I was thirsty, but you did not give me anything to drink. ⁴³ I was a stranger, but you did not welcome me, and I was naked, but you did not give me any clothes to wear. I was sick and in jail, but you did not take care of me."

⁴⁴ Then the people will ask, "Lord, when did we fail to help you when you were hungry or thirsty or a stranger or naked or sick or in jail?"

⁴⁵ The king will say to them, "Whenever you failed to help any of my people, no matter how unimportant they seemed, you failed to do it for me."

⁴⁶ Then Jesus said, "Those people will be punished for ever. But the ones who pleased God will have eternal life."

CHAPTER 26

The plot to kill Jesus

This is also told in Mark 14.1,2; Luke 22.1,2; John 11.45–53

¹ When Jesus had finished teaching, he told his disciples, ² "You know that two days from now will be Passover. That is when the Son of Man will be handed over to his enemies and nailed to a cross."

³ At that time the chief priests and the nation's leaders were meeting at the home of Caiaphas the high priest. ⁴ They secretly planned to have Jesus arrested and put to death. ⁵ But they said, "We must not do it during Passover, because the people will riot."

See also: **25.29:** Matt 13.12; Mark 4.25; Luke 8.18. **25.30:** Matt 8.12; 22.13; Luke 13.28. **25.31:** a Matt 16.27; b Matt 19.28.

See also: **25.46:** Dan 12.2. **26.2:** Exod 12.1–27.

At Bethany

This is also told in Mark 14.3–9; John 12.1–8

⁶ Jesus was in the town of Bethany, eating at the home of Simon, who had leprosy.*
⁷ A woman came in with a bottle of expensive perfume and poured it on Jesus' head. ⁸ But when his disciples saw this, they became angry and complained, "Why such a waste? ⁹ We could have sold this perfume for a lot of money and given it to the poor."

¹⁰ Jesus knew what they were thinking, and he said:

Why are you bothering this woman? She has done a beautiful thing for me. ¹¹ You will always have the poor with you, but you won't always have me. ¹² She has poured perfume on my body to prepare it for burial.* ¹³ You may be sure that wherever the good news is told all over the world, people will remember what she has done. And they will tell others.

Judas and the chief priests

This is also told in Mark 14.10,11; Luke 22.3–6

¹⁴ Judas Iscariot* was one of the twelve disciples. He went to the chief priests ¹⁵ and asked, "How much will you give me if I help you arrest Jesus?" They paid Judas thirty silver coins, ¹⁶ and from then on he started looking for a good chance to betray Jesus.

Jesus eats the Passover meal with his disciples

This is also told in Mark 14.12–21; Luke 22.7–13; John 13.21–30

¹⁷ On the first day of the Festival of Thin Bread, Jesus' disciples came to him and asked, "Where do you want us to prepare the Passover meal?"

¹⁸ Jesus told them to go to a certain man in the city and tell him, "Our teacher says, 'My time has come! I want to eat the Passover meal with my disciples in your home.'" ¹⁹ They did as Jesus told them and prepared the meal.

²⁰⁻²¹ When Jesus was eating with his twelve disciples that evening, he said, "One of you will hand me over to my enemies."

²² The disciples were very sad, and each one said to Jesus, "Lord, you can't mean me!"

²³ He answered, "One of you men who has eaten with me from this dish will betray me.
²⁴ The Son of Man will die, as the Scriptures say. But it's going to be terrible for the one who betrays me! That man would be better off if he had never been born."

²⁵ Judas said, "Teacher, surely you don't mean me!"

"That's what you say!" Jesus replied. But later, Judas did betray him.

The Lord's Supper

This is also told in Mark 14.22–26; Luke 22.14–23; 1 Corinthians 11.23–25

²⁶ During the meal Jesus took some bread in his hands. He blessed the bread and broke it. Then he gave it to his disciples and said, "Take this and eat it. This is my body."

²⁷ Jesus picked up a cup of wine and gave thanks to God. He then gave it to his disciples and said, "Take this and drink it. ²⁸ This is my blood, and with it God makes his agreement with you. It will be poured out, so that many people will have their sins forgiven. ²⁹ From now on I am not going to drink any wine, until I drink new wine with you in my Father's kingdom." ³⁰ Then they sang a hymn and went out to the Mount of Olives.

Peter's promise

This is also told in Mark 14.27–31; Luke 22.31–34; John 13.36–38

³¹ Jesus said to his disciples, "During this very night, all of you will reject me, as the Scriptures say,

'I will strike down
    the shepherd,
and the sheep
    will be scattered.'

³² But after I am raised to life, I will go to Galilee ahead of you."

³³ Peter spoke up, "Even if all the others reject you, I never will!"

³⁴ Jesus replied, "I promise you that before a cock crows tonight, you will say three times that you don't know me." ³⁵ But Peter said, "Even if I have to die with you, I will never say I don't know you."

All the others said the same thing.

---

*26.6 leprosy: See the note at 8.2.
*26.12 poured perfume on my body to prepare it for burial: The Jewish people taught that giving someone a proper burial was even more important than helping the poor.
*26.14 Iscariot: See the note at 10.4.

See also: 26.7: Luke 7.37,38. 26.11: Deut 15.11. 26.15: Zech 11.12.

See also: 26.23: Psa 41.9. 26.28: a Exod 24.8; b Jer 31.31–34. 26.31: Zech 13.7. 26.32: Matt 28.16.

Jesus prays

This is also told in Mark 14.32–42; Luke 22.39–46

36 Jesus went with his disciples to a place called Gethsemane. When they got there, he told them, "Sit here while I go over there and pray."

37 Jesus took along Peter and the two brothers, James and John.* He was very sad and troubled, 38 and he said to them, "I am so sad that I feel as if I am dying. Stay here and keep awake with me."

39 Jesus walked on a little way. Then he knel. with his face to the ground and prayed, "My Father, if it is possible, don't make me suffer by making me drink from this cup.* But do what you want, and not what I want."

40 He came back and found his disciples sleeping. So he said to Peter, "Can't any of you stay awake with me for just one hour? 41 Stay awake and pray that you won't be tested. You want to do what is right, but you are weak."

42 Again Jesus went to pray and said, "My Father, if there is no other way, and I must suffer, I will still do what you want."

43 Jesus came back and found them sleeping again. They simply could not keep their eyes open. 44 He left them and prayed the same prayer once more.

45 Finally, Jesus returned to his disciples and said, "Are you still sleeping and resting? The time has come for the Son of Man to be handed over to sinners. 46 Get up! Let's go. The one who will betray me is already here."

Jesus is arrested

This is also told in Mark 14.43–50; Luke 22.47–53; John 18.3–12

47 Jesus was still speaking, when Judas the betrayer came up. He was one of the twelve disciples, and a large mob armed with swords and clubs was with him. They had been sent by the chief priests and the nation's leaders. 48 Judas had told them beforehand, "Arrest the man I greet with a kiss."*

49 Judas walked right up to Jesus and said, "Hello, teacher." Then Judas kissed him.

50 Jesus replied, "My friend, why are you here?"▸

The men grabbed Jesus and arrested him. 51 One of Jesus' followers pulled out a sword. He struck the servant of the high priest and cut off his ear.

52 But Jesus told him, "Put your sword away. Anyone who lives by fighting will die by fighting. 53 Don't you know that I could ask my Father, and straight away he would send me more than twelve armies of angels? 54 But then, how could the words of the Scriptures come true, which say that this must happen?"

55 Jesus said to the mob, "Why do you come with swords and clubs to arrest me like a criminal? Day after day I sat and taught in the temple, and you didn't arrest me. 56 But all this happened, so that what the prophets wrote would come true."

All Jesus' disciples left him and ran away.

Jesus is questioned by the council

This is also told in Mark 14.53–65; Luke 22.54,55,63–71; John 18.13,14,19–24

57 After Jesus had been arrested, he was led off to the house of Caiaphas the high priest. The nation's leaders and the teachers of the Law of Moses were meeting there. 58 But Peter followed along at a distance and came to the courtyard of the high priest's palace. He went in and sat down with the guards to see what was going to happen.

59 The chief priests and the whole council wanted to put Jesus to death. So they tried to find some people who would tell lies about him in court.* 60 But they could not find any, even though many did come and tell lies. At last, two men came forward 61 and said, "This man claimed that he would tear down God's temple and build it again in three days."

62 The high priest stood up and asked Jesus, "Why don't you say something in your own defence? Don't you hear the charges they are making against you?" 63 But Jesus did not answer. So the high priest said, "With the living God looking on, you must tell the truth. Tell us, are you the Messiah, the Son of God?"*

*26.59 some people who would tell lies about him in court: The Law of Moses taught that two witnesses were necessary before a person could be put to death. See verse 60.

*26.63 Son of God: One of the titles used for the kings of Israel.

See also: 26.55: Luke 19.47; 21.37. 26.61: John 2.19.

*26.39 making me drink from this cup: See the note at 20.22.

*26.48 the man I greet with a kiss: It was the custom for people to greet each other with a kiss on the cheek.

[64] "That is what you say!" Jesus answered. "But I tell all of you,

> 'Soon you will see
> the Son of Man
> sitting at the right side*
> of God All-Powerful
> and coming on the clouds
> of heaven.' "

[65] The high priest then tore his robe and said, "This man claims to be God! We don't need any more witnesses! You have heard what he said. [66] What do you think?"

They answered, "He is guilty and deserves to die!" [67] Then they spat in his face and hit him with their fists. Others slapped him [68] and said, "You think you are the Messiah! So tell us who hit you!"

Peter says he doesn't know Jesus

This is also told in Mark 14.66-72; Luke 22.56-62; John 18.15-18,25-27

[69] While Peter was sitting out in the courtyard, a servant girl came up to him and said, "You were with Jesus from Galilee."

[70] But in front of everyone Peter said, "That isn't so! I don't know what you are talking about!"

[71] When Peter had gone out to the gate, another servant girl saw him and said to some people there, "This man was with Jesus from Nazareth."

[72] Again Peter denied it, and this time he swore, "I don't even know that man!"

[73] A little while later some people standing there walked over to Peter and said, "We know that you are one of them. We can tell it because you talk like someone from Galilee."

[74] Peter began to curse and swear, "I don't know that man!"

At once a cock crowed, [75] and Peter remembered that Jesus had said, "Before a cock crows, you will say three times that you don't know me." Then Peter went out and cried hard.

CHAPTER 27

Jesus is taken to Pilate

This is also told in Mark 15.1; Luke 23.1,2; John 18.28-32

[1] Early the next morning all the chief priests and the nation's leaders met and decided

that Jesus should be put to death. [2] They tied him up and led him away to Pilate the governor.

The death of Judas

This is also told in Acts 1.18,19

[3] Judas had betrayed Jesus, but when he learnt that Jesus had been sentenced to death, he was sorry for what he had done. He returned the thirty silver coins to the chief priests and leaders [4] and said, "I have sinned by betraying a man who has never done anything wrong."

"So what? That's your problem," they replied. [5] Judas threw the money into the temple and then went out and hanged himself.

[6] The chief priests picked up the money and said, "This money was paid to have a man killed. We can't put it in the temple treasury." [7] Then they had a meeting and decided to buy a field that belonged to someone who made clay pots. They wanted to use it as a graveyard for foreigners. [8] That's why people still call that place "Field of Blood." [9] So the words of the prophet Jeremiah came true,

> "They took
> the thirty silver coins,
> the price of a person
> among the people of Israel.
> [10] They paid it
> for a potter's field,*
> as the Lord
> had commanded me."

Pilate questions Jesus

This is also told in Mark 15.2-5; Luke 23.3-5; John 18.33-38

[11] Jesus was brought before Pilate the governor, who asked him, "Are you the king of the Jews?"

"Those are your words!" Jesus answered. [12] And when the chief priests and leaders brought their charges against him, he did not say a thing.

[13] Pilate asked him, "Don't you hear what crimes they say you have done?" [14] But Jesus did not say anything, and the governor was greatly amazed.

---

*26.64 right side: See the note at 22.44.
See also: 26.64: Dan 7.13. 26.65,66: Lev 24.16. 26.67: Isa 50.6.

---

*27.10 a potter's field: Perhaps a field owned by someone who made clay pots. But it may have been a field where potters came to get clay or to make pots or to throw away their broken pieces of pottery.
See also: 27.3-8: Acts 1.18,19. 27.9,10: Zech 11.12,13.

The death sentence

This is also told in Mark 15.6–15; Luke 23.13–26; John 18.39–19.16

15 During Passover the governor always freed a prisoner chosen by the people. 16 At that time a well-known terrorist named Jesus Barabbas* was in jail. 17 So when the crowd came together, Pilate asked them, "Which prisoner do you want me to set free? Do you want Jesus Barabbas or Jesus who is called the Messiah?" 18 Pilate knew that the leaders had brought Jesus to him because they were jealous.

19 While Pilate was judging the case, his wife sent him a message. It said, "Don't have anything to do with that innocent man. I have had nightmares because of him."

20 But the chief priests and the leaders convinced the crowds to ask for Barabbas to be set free and for Jesus to be killed. 21 Pilate asked the crowd again, "Which of these two men do you want me to set free?"

"Barabbas!" they replied.

22 Pilate asked them, "What am I to do with Jesus, who is called the Messiah?"

They all yelled, "Nail him to a cross!"

23 Pilate answered, "But what crime has he done?"

"Nail him to a cross!" they yelled even louder.

24 Pilate saw that there was nothing he could do and that the people were starting to riot. So he took some water and washed his hands* in front of them and said, "I won't have anything to do with killing this man. You are the ones doing it!"

25 Everyone answered, "We and our own families will take the blame for his death!"

26 Pilate set Barabbas free. Then he ordered his soldiers to beat Jesus with a whip and nail him to a cross.

Soldiers make fun of Jesus

This is also told in Mark 15.16–21; John 19.2,3

27 The governor's soldiers led Jesus into the fortress* and brought together the rest of the troops. 28 They stripped off Jesus' clothes and put a scarlet robe* on him. 29 They made a crown out of thorn branches and placed it on his head, and they put a stick in his right hand. The soldiers knelt down and pretended to worship him. They made fun of him and shouted, "Hey, you king of the Jews!" 30 Then they spat on him. They took the stick from him and beat him on the head with it.

Jesus is nailed to a cross

This is also told in Mark 15.22–32; Luke 23.27–43; John 19.17–27

31 When the soldiers had finished making fun of Jesus, they took off the robe. They put his own clothes back on him and led him off to be nailed to a cross. 32 On the way they met a man from Cyrene named Simon, and they forced him to carry Jesus' cross.

33 They came to a place named Golgotha, which means "Place of a Skull." * 34 There they gave Jesus some wine mixed with a drug to ease the pain. But when Jesus tasted what it was, he refused to drink it.

35 The soldiers nailed Jesus to a cross and gambled to see who would get his clothes. 36 Then they sat down to guard him. 37 Above his head they put a sign that told why he was nailed there. It said, "This is Jesus, the King of the Jews." 38 The soldiers also nailed two criminals on crosses, one to the right of Jesus and the other to his left.

39 People who passed by said terrible things about Jesus. They shook their heads and 40 shouted, "So you're the one who claimed you could tear down the temple and build it again in three days! If you are God's Son, save yourself and come down from the cross!"

41 The chief priests, the leaders, and the teachers of the Law of Moses also made fun of Jesus. They said, 42 "He saved others, but he can't save himself. If he is the king of Israel, he should come down from the cross! Then we will believe him. 43 He trusted God, so let God save him, if he wants to. He even said he was God's Son." 44 The two criminals also said cruel things to Jesus.

*27.24 washed his hands: To show that he was innocent.
*27.27 fortress: The place where the Roman governor stayed. It was probably at Herod's palace west of Jerusalem, though it may have been Fortress Antonia north of the temple, where the Roman troops were stationed.
See also: 27.24: Deut 21.6–9.

*27.28 scarlet robe: This was probably a Roman soldier's robe.
*27.33 Place of a Skull: The place given this name because it was near a large rock in the shape of a human skull.
See also: 27.34: Psa 69.21. 27.35: Psa 22.18.
27.39: Psa 22.7; 109.25. 27.40: Matt 26.61; John 2.19.
27.43: Psa 22.8.

The death of Jesus

This is also told in Mark 15.33–41; Luke 23.44–49; John 19.28–30

45 At midday the sky turned dark and stayed that way until three o'clock. 46 Then about that time Jesus shouted, "Eli, Eli, lema sabachthani?"* which means, "My God, my God, why have you deserted me?"

47 Some of the people standing there heard Jesus and said, "He's calling for Elijah."* 48 One of them at once ran and grabbed a sponge. He soaked it in wine, then put it on a stick and held it up to Jesus.

49 Others said, "Wait! Let's see if Elijah will come* and save him." 50 Once again Jesus shouted, and then he died.

51 At once the curtain in the temple* was torn in two from top to bottom. The earth shook, and rocks split apart. 52 Graves opened, and many of God's people were raised to life. 53 Then after Jesus had risen to life, they came out of their graves and went into the holy city, where they were seen by many people.

54 The officer and the soldiers guarding Jesus felt the earthquake and saw everything else that happened. They were frightened and said, "This man really was God's Son!"

55 Many women had come with Jesus from Galilee to be of help to him, and they were there, looking on at a distance. 56 Mary Magdalene, Mary the mother of James and Joseph, and the mother of James and John* were some of these women.

Jesus is buried

This is also told in Mark 15.42–47; Luke 23.50–56; John 19.38–42

57 That evening a rich disciple named Joseph from the town of Arimathea 58 went and asked for Jesus' body. Pilate gave orders for it to be given to Joseph, 59 who took the body and wrapped it in a clean linen cloth. 60 Then

Joseph put the body in his own tomb that had been cut into solid rock* and had never been used. He rolled a big stone against the entrance to the tomb and went away.

61 All this time Mary Magdalene and the other Mary were sitting across from the tomb.

62 On the next day, which was a Sabbath, the chief priests and the Pharisees went together to Pilate. 63 They said, "Sir, we remember what that liar said while he was still alive. He claimed that in three days he would come back from death. 64 So please order the tomb to be carefully guarded for three days. If you don't, his disciples may come and steal his body. They will tell the people that he has been raised to life, and this last lie will be worse than the first one."*

65 Pilate said to them, "All right, take some of your soldiers and guard the tomb as well as you know how." 66 So they sealed it tight and placed soldiers there to guard it.

Jesus is alive

CHAPTER 28

Jesus is alive

This is also told in Mark 16.1–8; Luke 24.1–12; John 20.1–10

1 The Sabbath was over, and it was almost daybreak on Sunday when Mary Magdalene and the other Mary went to see the tomb. 2 Suddenly a strong earthquake struck, and the Lord's angel came down from heaven. He rolled away the stone and sat on it. 3 The angel looked as bright as lightning, and his clothes were white as snow. 4 The guards shook from fear and fell down, as though they were dead.

5 The angel said to the women, "Don't be afraid! I know you are looking for Jesus, who was nailed to a cross. 6 He isn't here! God has raised him to life, just as Jesus said he would. Come, see the place where his body was lying. 7 Now hurry! Tell his disciples that he has been raised to life and is on his way to Galilee. Go there, and you will see him. That is what I came to tell you."

---

*27.46 Eli . . . sabachthani: These words are in Hebrew.
*27.47 Elijah: In Aramaic the name "Elijah" sounds like "Eli," which means "my God".
*27.49 Elijah will come: See the note at 16.14.
*27.51 curtain in the temple: There were two curtains in the temple. One was at the entrance, and the other separated the holy place from the most holy place that the Jewish people thought of as God's home on earth. The second curtain is probably the one that is meant.

See also: 27.46: Psa 22.1. 27.48: Psa 69.21. 27.51: Exod 26.31–33. 27.55,56: Luke 8.2,3.

*27.60 tomb . . . solid rock: Some of the Jewish people buried their dead in rooms carved into solid rock. A heavy stone was rolled against the entrance.
*27.64 the first one: Probably the belief that Jesus is the Messiah.

See also: 27.63: Matt 16.21; 17.23; 20.19; Mark 8.31; 9.31; 10.33,34; Luke 9.22; 18.31–33.

⁸ The women were frightened and yet very happy, as they hurried from the tomb and ran to tell his disciples. ⁹ Suddenly Jesus met them and greeted them. They went near him, held on to his feet, and worshipped him. ¹⁰ Then Jesus said, "Don't be afraid! Tell my followers to go to Galilee. They will see me there."

Report of the guard

¹¹ While the women were on their way, some soldiers who had been guarding the tomb went into the city. They told the chief priests everything that had happened. ¹² So the chief priests met with the leaders and decided to bribe the soldiers with a lot of money. ¹³ They said to the soldiers, "Tell everyone that Jesus' disciples came during the night and stole his body while you were asleep. ¹⁴ If the governor* hears about this, we will talk to him. You won't have anything to worry about." ¹⁵ The soldiers took the money and did what they were told. Some of the Jewish people still tell each other this story.

What Jesus' followers must do

This is also told in Mark 16.14–18; Luke 24.36–49; John 20.19–23; Acts 1.6-8

¹⁶ Jesus' eleven disciples went to a mountain in Galilee, where Jesus had told them to meet him. ¹⁷ They saw him and worshipped him, but some of them doubted.

¹⁸ Jesus came to them and said:

I have been given all authority in heaven and on earth! ¹⁹ Go to the people of all nations and make them my disciples. Baptize them in the name of the Father, the Son, and the Holy Spirit, ²⁰ and teach them to do everything I have told you. I will be with you always, even until the end of the world.

*28.14 governor: Pontius Pilate.
See also: 28.16: Matt 26.32; Mark 14.28. 28.19: Acts 1.8.

Additional notes

›1.19 good man: Or "kind man", or "man who always did the right thing".
›2.2 his star in the east: Or "his star rise".
›3.2 kingdom of heaven: In the Gospel of Matthew "kingdom of heaven" is used with the same meaning as "God's kingdom" in Mark and Luke.
›3.2 will soon be here: Or "is already here."

›3.11 so that you will give up your sins: Or "because you have given up your sins."
›4.17 The kingdom of heaven will soon be here: See the two notes at 3.2.
›5.3 They belong to the kingdom of heaven: Or "The kingdom of heaven belongs to them."
›5.6 who want to obey him: Or "who want to do right" or "who want everyone to be treated right".
›5.10 They belong to the kingdom of heaven: See the note at 5.3.
›5.22 someone: In verses 22–24 the Greek text has "brother", which may refer to people in general or to other followers.
›6.3 don't let anyone know about it: The Greek text has, "Don't let your left hand know what your right hand is doing."
›6.11 our food for today: Or "the food that we need" or "our food for the coming day."
›6.13 evil: Or "the evil one", that is, the devil. Some manuscripts add, "The kingdom, the power, and the glory are yours for ever. Amen."
›6.27 live longer: Or "grow taller".
›8.18 saw the crowd: Some manuscripts have "large crowd". Others have "large crowds".
›8.28 Gadara: Some manuscripts have "Gergesa". Others have "Gerasa".
›9.8 afraid: Some manuscripts have "amazed".
›9.10 Matthew's house: Or "Jesus' house".
›10.7 will soon be here: See the note at 3.2.
›10.9,10 Don't take along . . . don't carry: Or "Don't accept . . . don't accept".
›11.1 the towns: The Greek text has "their towns", which may refer to the towns of Galilee or to the towns where Jesus' disciples had lived.
›12.47 with you: Some manuscripts do not have verse 47.
›13.35 the prophet: Some manuscripts have "the prophet Isaiah".
›13.36 went inside: Or "went home".
›16.2,3 If the sky is red . . . what is happening now: The words of Jesus in verses 2 and 3 are not in some manuscripts.
›16.25 life: In verses 25 and 26 the same Greek word is translated "life", "yourself", and "soul".
›17.20,21 for you: Some manuscripts add, "But the only way to force out that kind of demon is by praying and going without eating."
›17.25 from their own people or from foreigners: Or "from their children or from others."
›17.26 From foreigners . . . their own people: Or "From others . . . their children".
›18.10,11 in heaven: Some manuscripts add, "The Son of Man came to save people who are lost."
›18.20 in my name: Or "as my followers".
›19.14 People who are like these children belong to God's kingdom: Or "God's kingdom belongs to people who are like these children".
›20.20 mother of James and John: The Greek text has "mother of the sons of Zebedee". See 26.37.
›21.3 The Lord: Or "the master of the donkeys".
›21.44 pieces: Verse 44 is not in some manuscripts.

'23.13,14 from going in: Some manuscripts add,
"You Pharisees and teachers are in for trouble! And
you're nothing but show-offs! You cheat widows out
of their homes and then pray long prayers just to
show off. So you will be punished most of all."
'24.30 And there will be the Son of Man: Or "And it
will be the Son of Man."
'24.33 the time has almost come: Or "he (that is, the
Son of Man) will soon be here."
'24.36 and the Son himself doesn't know: These
words are not in some manuscripts.
'26.37 the two brothers, James and John: The Greek
text has "the two sons of Zebedee". See 27.56.
'26.45 Are you still sleeping and resting?: Or "You
may as well keep on sleeping and resting."
'26.50 why are you here?: Or "do what you came
for."
'27.16 Jesus Barabbas: Here and in verse 17 many
manuscripts have "Barabbas".
'27.56 of James and John: The Greek text has "of
Zebedee's sons". See 26.37.

Mark

tells the good news

A quick look at this book

This is the shortest of the four New Testament books that tell about the life and teachings of Jesus, but it is also the most action-packed. From the very beginning of his ministry, Jesus worked mighty wonders. After choosing four followers (1.16–20), he immediately performed many miracles of healing. Among those healed were a man with an evil spirit in him (1.21–28), Simon's mother-in-law (1.30,31), crowds of sick people (1.32–34), and a man with leprosy (1.40–45). Over and over Mark tells how Jesus healed people, but always in such a way as to show that he did these miracles by the power of God.

The religious leaders refused to accept Jesus. This led to conflicts (2.2–3.6) that finally made them start looking for a way to kill him (11.18). But the demons saw the power of Jesus, and they knew that he was the Son of God, although Jesus would not let them tell anyone.

This book is full of miracles that amazed the crowds and Jesus' followers. But, according to Mark, the most powerful miracle of Jesus is his suffering and death. The first person to understand this miracle was the Roman soldier who saw Jesus die on the cross and said, "This man really was the Son of God!" (15.39).

This Gospel is widely thought to be the first one written. The many explanations of Aramaic words and Jewish customs in Mark suggest that Mark wrote to Gentile or non-Jewish Christians. He wants to tell about Jesus and to encourage readers to believe in the power of Jesus to rescue them from sickness, demons, and death. He also wants to remind them that the new life of faith is not an easy life, and that they must follow Jesus by serving others and being ready to suffer as he did.

The first followers of Jesus to discover the empty tomb were three women, and the angel told them:

> *Don't be alarmed! You are looking for Jesus from Nazareth, who was nailed to a cross. God has raised him to life, and he isn't here.*
>
> (16.6)

The message of John the Baptist

CHAPTER 1

The preaching of John the Baptist

This is also told in Matthew 3.1–12; Luke 3.1–18; John 1.19–28

¹ This is the good news about Jesus Christ, the Son of God.' ² It began just as God had said in the book written by Isaiah the prophet,

"I am sending my messenger
to get the way ready
for you.
³ In the desert
someone is shouting,
'Get the road ready
for the Lord!
Make a straight path
for him.' "

⁴ So John the Baptist appeared in the desert and told everyone, "Turn back to God and be baptized! Then your sins will be forgiven." ⁵ From all Judea and Jerusalem crowds of people went to John. They told how sorry they were for their sins, and he baptized them in the River Jordan.

⁶ John wore clothes made of camel's hair. He had a leather strap around his waist and ate grasshoppers and wild honey. ⁷ John also told the people, "Someone more powerful is going to come. And I am not good enough even to stoop down and untie his sandals." ⁸ I baptize you with water, but he will baptize you with the Holy Spirit!"

The baptism and temptation of Jesus

The baptism of Jesus

This is also told in Matthew 3.13–17; Luke 3.21,22

⁹ About that time Jesus came from Nazareth in Galilee, and John baptized him in the River Jordan. ¹⁰ As soon as Jesus came out of the water, he saw the sky open and the Holy Spirit coming down to him like a dove. ¹¹ A voice from heaven said, "You are my own dear Son, and I am pleased with you."

Jesus and Satan

This is also told in Matthew 4.1–11; Luke 4.1–13

¹² Straight away God's Spirit made Jesus go into the desert. ¹³ He stayed there for forty days while Satan tested him. Jesus was with the wild animals, but angels took care of him.

Jesus in Galilee

Jesus begins his work

This is also told in Matthew 4.12–17; Luke 4.14,15

¹⁴ After John was arrested, Jesus went to Galilee and told the good news that comes from God.' ¹⁵ He said, "The time has come! God's kingdom will soon be here.' Turn back to God and believe the good news!"

Jesus chooses four fishermen

This is also told in Matthew 4.18–22; Luke 5.1–11

¹⁶ As Jesus was walking along the shore of Lake Galilee, he saw Simon and his brother Andrew. They were fishermen and were casting their nets into the lake. ¹⁷ Jesus said to them, "Come with me! I will teach you how to bring in people instead of fish." ¹⁸ At once the two brothers dropped their nets and went with him.

¹⁹ Jesus walked on and soon saw James and John, the sons of Zebedee. They were in a boat, mending their nets. ²⁰ At once Jesus asked them to come with him. They left their father in the boat with the hired workers and went with him.

A man with an evil spirit

This is also told in Luke 4.31–37

²¹ Jesus and his disciples went to the town of Capernaum. Then on the next Sabbath he went into the Jewish meeting place and started teaching. ²² Everyone was amazed at his teaching. He taught with authority, and not like the teachers of the Law of Moses. ²³ Suddenly a man with an evil spirit* in him entered the meeting place and yelled, ²⁴ "Jesus from Nazareth, what do you want with us? Have you come to destroy us? I know who you are! You are God's Holy One."

---

*1.7 untie his sandals: This was the duty of a slave.

See also: 1.2: Mal 3.1. 1.3: Isa 40.3 (LXX). 1.6: 2 King 1.8.
1.11: Gen 22.2; Psa 2.7; Isa 42.1; Matt 3.17; 12.18; Mark 9.7;
Luke 3.22.

*1.23 evil spirit: A Jewish person who had an evil spirit was considered "unclean" and was not allowed to eat or worship with other Jewish people.
See also: 1.15: Matt 3.2. 1.22: Matt 7.28,29.

²⁵ Jesus told the evil spirit, "Be quiet and come out of the man!" ²⁶ The spirit shook him. Then it gave a loud shout and left.

²⁷ Everyone was completely surprised and kept saying to each other, "What is this? It must be some new kind of powerful teaching! Even the evil spirits obey him." ²⁸ News about Jesus quickly spread all over Galilee.

Jesus heals many people

This is also told in Matthew 8.14–17; Luke 4.38–41

²⁹ As soon as Jesus left the meeting place with James and John, they went home with Simon and Andrew. ³⁰ When they got there, Jesus was told that Simon's mother-in-law was sick in bed with fever. ³¹ Jesus went to her. He took hold of her hand and helped her up. The fever left her, and she served them a meal.

³² That evening after sunset,* all who were sick or had demons in them were brought to Jesus. ³³ In fact, the whole town gathered around the door of the house. ³⁴ Jesus healed all kinds of terrible diseases and forced out a lot of demons. But the demons knew who he was, and he did not let them speak.

³⁵ Very early the next morning, Jesus got up and went to a place where he could be alone and pray. ³⁶ Simon and the others started looking for him. ³⁷ And when they found him, they said, "Everyone is looking for you!"

³⁸ Jesus replied, "We must go to the nearby towns, so that I can tell the good news to those people. This is why I have come." ³⁹ Then Jesus went to Jewish meeting places everywhere in Galilee, where he preached and forced out demons.

Jesus heals a man

This is also told in Matthew 8.1–4; Luke 5.12–16

⁴⁰ A man with leprosy* came to Jesus and knelt down. He begged, "You have the power to make me well, if only you wanted to."

⁴¹ Jesus felt sorry for* the man. So he put his hand on him and said, "I want to! Now you are well." ⁴² At once the man's leprosy disappeared, and he was well.

⁴³ After Jesus strictly warned the man, he sent him on his way. ⁴⁴ He said, "Don't tell anyone about this. Just go and show the priest that you are well. Then take a gift to the temple as Moses commanded, and everyone will know that you have been healed."*

⁴⁵ The man talked about it so much and told so many people, that Jesus could no longer go openly into a town. He had to stay away from the towns, but people still came to him from everywhere.

CHAPTER 2

Jesus heals a crippled man

This is also told in Matthew 9.1–8; Luke 5.17–26

¹ Jesus went back to Capernaum, and a few days later people heard that he was at home.* ² Then so many of them came to the house that there wasn't even standing room left in front of the door.

Jesus was still teaching ³ when four people came up, carrying a crippled man on a mat. ⁴ But because of the crowd, they could not get him to Jesus. So they made a hole in the roof* above him and let the man down in front of everyone.

⁵ When Jesus saw how much faith they had, he said to the crippled man, "My friend, your sins are forgiven."

⁶ Some of the teachers of the Law of Moses were sitting there. They started wondering, ⁷ "Why would he say such a thing? He must think he is God! Only God can forgive sins."

⁸ Straight away, Jesus knew what they were thinking, and he said, "Why are you thinking such things? ⁹ Is it easier for me to tell this crippled man that his sins are forgiven or to tell him to get up and pick up his mat and go on home? ¹⁰ I will show you that the Son of Man has the right to forgive sins here on earth." So Jesus said to the man, ¹¹ "Get up! Pick up your mat and go on home."

---

*1.32 after sunset: The Sabbath was over, and a new day began at sunset.
*1.40 leprosy: In biblical times the word "leprosy" was used for many different kinds of skin diseases.
See also: 1.39; Matt 4.23; 9.35.

*1.44 everyone will know that you have been healed: People with leprosy had to be examined by a priest and told that they were well (that is, "clean") before they could once again live a normal life in the Jewish community. The gift that Moses commanded was the sacrifice of some lambs together with flour mixed with olive oil.
*2.4 roof: In Palestine the houses usually had a flat roof. Stairs on the outside led up to the roof that was made of beams and boards covered with packed earth.
See also: 1.44: Lev 14.1–32.

45

¹² The man got straight up. He picked up his mat and went out while everyone watched in amazement. They praised God and said, "We have never seen anything like this!"

Jesus chooses Levi

This is also told in Matthew 9.9–13; Luke 5.27–32

¹³ Once again, Jesus went to the shore of Lake Galilee. A large crowd gathered around him, and he taught them. ¹⁴ As he walked along, he saw Levi, the son of Alphaeus. Levi was sitting at the place for paying taxes, and Jesus said to him, "Come with me!" So he got up and went with Jesus.

¹⁵ Later, Jesus and his disciples were having dinner at Levi's house.* Many tax collectors* and other sinners had become followers of Jesus, and they were also guests at the dinner.

¹⁶ Some of the teachers of the Law of Moses were Pharisees, and they saw that Jesus was eating with sinners and tax collectors. So they asked his disciples, "Why does he eat with tax collectors and sinners?"

¹⁷ Jesus heard them and answered, "Healthy people don't need a doctor, but sick people do. I didn't come to invite good people to be my followers. I came to invite sinners."

People ask about going without eating

This is also told in Matthew 9.14–17; Luke 5.33–39

¹⁸ The followers of John the Baptist and the Pharisees often went without eating. Some people came and asked Jesus, "Why do the followers of John and those of the Pharisees often go without eating, while your disciples never do?"

¹⁹ Jesus answered:

The friends of a bridegroom don't go without eating while he is still with them. ²⁰ But the time will come when he will be taken from them. Then they will go without eating.

²¹ No one patches old clothes by sewing on a piece of new cloth. The new piece would shrink and tear a bigger hole.

²² No one pours new wine into old wineskins. The wine would swell and burst the old skins.* Then the wine would be lost, and the skins would be ruined. New wine must be put into new wineskins.

A question about the Sabbath

This is also told in Matthew 12.1–8; Luke 6.1–5

²³ One Sabbath Jesus and his disciples were walking through some wheat fields. His disciples were picking grains of wheat* as they went along. ²⁴ Some Pharisees asked Jesus, "Why are your disciples picking grain on the Sabbath? They are not supposed to do that!"

²⁵ Jesus answered, "Haven't you read what David did when he and his followers were hungry and in need? ²⁶ It was during the time of Abiathar the high priest. David went into the house of God and ate the sacred loaves of bread that only priests are allowed to eat. He also gave some to his followers."

²⁷ Jesus finished by saying, "People were not made for the good of the Sabbath. The Sabbath was made for the good of people. ²⁸ So the Son of Man is Lord over the Sabbath."

CHAPTER 3

A man with a crippled hand

This is also told in Matthew 12.9–14; Luke 6.6–11

¹ The next time that Jesus went into the meeting place, a man with a crippled hand was there. ² The Pharisees* wanted to accuse Jesus of doing something wrong, and they kept watching to see if Jesus would heal him on the Sabbath.

³ Jesus told the man to stand up where everyone could see him. ⁴ Then he asked, "On the Sabbath should we do good deeds or evil deeds? Should we save someone's life or destroy it?" But no one said a word.

⁵ Jesus was angry as he looked around at the people. Yet he felt sorry for them because they were so stubborn. Then he

---

*2.15 tax collectors: These were usually Jewish people who paid the Romans for the right to collect taxes. They were hated by other Jews who thought of them as traitors to their country and to their religion.
*2.18 without eating: The Jewish people sometimes went without eating (also called "fasting") to show their love for God or to show sorrow for their sins.

*2.22 swell and burst the old skins: While the juice from grapes was becoming wine, it would swell and stretch the skins in which it had been stored. If the skins were old and stiff, they would burst.
*2.23 picking grains of wheat: It was the custom to let hungry travellers pick grains of wheat.
*3.2 Pharisees: The Greek text has "they," but see verse 6.
See also: 2.23: Deut 23.25. 2.25–26: 1 Sam 21.1–6. 2.26: Lev 24.9.

told the man, "Stretch out your hand." He did, and his bad hand was healed.

⁶ The Pharisees left. And straight away they started making plans with Herod's followers* to kill Jesus.

Large crowds come to Jesus

⁷ Jesus led his disciples down to the shore of the lake. Large crowds followed him from Galilee, Judea, ⁸ and Jerusalem. People came from Idumea, as well as other places east of the River Jordan. They also came from the region around the cities of Tyre and Sidon. All these crowds came because they had heard what Jesus was doing. ⁹ He even had to tell his disciples to get a boat ready to keep him from being crushed by the crowds.

¹⁰ After Jesus had healed many people, the other sick people begged him to let them touch him. ¹¹ And whenever any evil spirits saw Jesus, they would fall to the ground and shout, "You are the Son of God!" ¹² But Jesus warned the spirits not to tell who he was.

Jesus chooses his twelve apostles

This is also told in Matthew 10.1–4; Luke 6.12–16

¹³ Jesus decided to ask some of his disciples to go up on a mountain with him, and they went. ¹⁴ Then he chose twelve of them to be his apostles,* so that they could be with him. He also wanted to send them out to preach ¹⁵ and to force out demons. ¹⁶ Simon was one of the twelve, and Jesus named him Peter. ¹⁷ There were also James and John, the two sons of Zebedee. Jesus called them Boanerges, which means "Thunderbolts". ¹⁸ Andrew, Philip, Bartholomew, Matthew, Thomas, James son of Alphaeus, and Thaddaeus were also apostles. The others were Simon, known as the Eager One,* ¹⁹ and Judas Iscariot,* who later betrayed Jesus.

---

*3.6 Herod's followers: People who were political followers of the family of Herod the Great and his son Herod Antipas.
*3.18 known as the Eager One: The Greek text has "Cananaean", which probably comes from a Hebrew word meaning "zealous" (see Luke 6.15). "Zealot" was the name later given to the members of a Jewish group which resisted and fought against the Romans.
*3.19 Iscariot: This may mean "a man from Kerioth" (a place in Judea). But more probably it means "a man who was a liar" or "a man who was a betrayer".

See also: 3.9,10: Mark 4.1; Luke 5.1–3.

Jesus and the ruler of demons

This is also told in Matthew 12.22–32; Luke 11.14–23; 12.10

²⁰ Jesus went back home,' and once again such a large crowd gathered that there was no chance even to eat. ²¹ When Jesus' family heard what he was doing, they thought he was mad and went to get him under control.

²² Some teachers of the Law of Moses came from Jerusalem and said, "This man is under the power of Beelzebul, the ruler of demons! He is even forcing out demons with the help of Beelzebul."

²³ Jesus told the people to gather around him. Then he spoke to them in riddles and said:

How can Satan force himself out?
²⁴ A nation whose people fight each other won't last very long. ²⁵ And a family that fights won't last long either. ²⁶ So if Satan fights against himself, that will be the end of him.

²⁷ How can anyone break into the house of a strong man and steal his things, unless he first ties up the strong man? Then he can take everything.

²⁸ I promise you that any of the sinful things you say or do can be forgiven, no matter how terrible those things are. ²⁹ But if you speak against the Holy Spirit, you can never be forgiven. That sin will be held against you for ever.

³⁰ Jesus said this because the people were saying that he had an evil spirit in him.

Jesus' mother and brothers

This is also told in Matthew 12.46–50; Luke 8.19–21

³¹ Jesus' mother and brothers came and stood outside. Then they sent someone with a message for him to come out to them. ³² The crowd that was sitting around Jesus told him, "Your mother and your brothers and sisters' are outside and want to see you."

³³ Jesus asked, "Who is my mother and who are my brothers?" ³⁴ Then he looked at the people sitting around him and said, "Here are my mother and my brothers. ³⁵ Anyone who obeys God is my brother or sister or mother."

See also: 3.22: Matt 9.34; 10.25. 3.29: Luke 12.10.

CHAPTER 4

A story about a farmer

This is also told in Matthew 13.1–9; Luke 8.4–8

¹ The next time Jesus taught beside Lake Galilee, a big crowd gathered. It was so large that he had to sit in a boat out on the lake, while the people stood on the shore. ² He used stories to teach them many things, and this is part of what he taught:

³ Now listen! A farmer went out to scatter seed in a field. ⁴ While the farmer was scattering the seed, some of it fell along the road and was eaten by birds. ⁵ Other seeds fell on thin, rocky ground and quickly started growing because the soil wasn't very deep. ⁶ But when the sun came up, the plants were scorched and dried up, because they did not have enough roots. ⁷ Some other seeds fell where thorn bushes grew up and choked out the plants. So they did not produce any grain. ⁸ But a few seeds did fall on good ground where the plants grew and produced thirty or sixty or even a hundred times as much as was scattered.

⁹ Then Jesus said, "If you have ears, pay attention."

Why Jesus used stories

This is also told in Matthew 13.10–17; Luke 8.9,10

¹⁰ When Jesus was alone with the twelve apostles and some others, they asked him about these stories. ¹¹ He answered:

I have explained the secret about God's kingdom to you, but for others I can use only stories. ¹² The reason is,

"These people will look
   and look, but never see.
They will listen and listen,
   but never understand.
If they did,
   they would turn to God,
   and he would forgive them."

Jesus explains the story about the farmer

This is also told in Matthew 13.18–23; Luke 8.11–15

¹³ Jesus told them:

If you don't understand this story, you won't understand any others. ¹⁴ What the farmer is spreading is really the message

about the kingdom. ¹⁵ The seeds that fell along the road are the people who hear the message. But Satan soon comes and snatches it away from them. ¹⁶ The seeds that fell on rocky ground are the people who gladly hear the message and accept it straight away. ¹⁷ But they don't have any roots, and they don't last very long. As soon as life gets hard or the message gets them in trouble, they give up.

¹⁸ The seeds that fell among the thorn bushes are also people who hear the message. ¹⁹ But they start worrying about the needs of this life. They are fooled by the desire to get rich and to have all kinds of other things. So the message gets choked out, and they never produce anything. ²⁰ The seeds that fell on good ground are the people who hear and welcome the message. They produce thirty or sixty or even a hundred times as much as was planted.

Light

This is also told in Luke 8.16–18

²¹ Jesus also said:

You don't light a lamp and put it under a clay pot or under a bed. Don't you put a lamp on a lampstand? ²² There is nothing hidden that will not be made public. There is no secret that will not be well known. ²³ If you have ears, pay attention!

²⁴ Listen carefully to what you hear! The way you treat others will be the way you will be treated—and even worse. ²⁵ Everyone who has something will be given more. But people who don't have anything will lose what little they have.

Another story about seeds

²⁶ Again Jesus said:

God's kingdom is like what happens when a farmer scatters seed in a field. ²⁷ The farmer sleeps at night and is up and around during the day. Yet the seeds keep sprouting and growing, and he doesn't understand how. ²⁸ It is the ground that makes the seeds sprout and grow into plants that produce grain. ²⁹ Then when harvest season comes and the grain is ripe, the farmer cuts it with a sickle.*

---

*4.29 sickle: A knife with a long curved blade, used to cut grain and other crops.

See also: 4.21: Matt 5.15; Luke 11.33. 4.22: Matt 10.26; Luke 12.2. 4.24: Matt 7.2; Luke 6.38. 4.25: Matt 13.12; 25.29; Luke 19.26. 4.29: Joel 3.13.

See also: 4.1: Luke 5.1–3. 4.12: Isa 6.9,10 (LXX).

A mustard seed

This is also told in Matthew 13.31,32; Luke 13.18,19

30 Finally, Jesus said:

What is God's kingdom like? What story can I use to explain it? 31 It is like what happens when a mustard seed is planted in the ground. It is the smallest seed in all the world. 32 But once it is planted, it grows larger than any garden plant. It even puts out branches that are big enough for birds to nest in its shade.

The reason for teaching with stories

This is also told in Matthew 13.34,35

33 Jesus used many other stories when he spoke to the people, and he taught them as much as they could understand. 34 He did not tell them anything without using stories. But when he was alone with his disciples, he explained everything to them.

A storm

This is also told in Matthew 8.23–27; Luke 8.22–25

35 That evening, Jesus said to his disciples, "Let's cross to the east side." 36 So they left the crowd, and his disciples started across the lake, with him in the boat. Some other boats followed along. 37 Suddenly a storm struck the lake. Waves started splashing into the boat, and it was about to sink.

38 Jesus was in the back of the boat with his head on a pillow, and he was asleep. His disciples woke him and said, "Teacher, don't you care that we're about to drown?"

39 Jesus got up and ordered the wind and the waves to be quiet. The wind stopped, and everything was calm.

40 Jesus asked them, "Why were you afraid? Don't you have any faith?"

41 Now they were more afraid than ever and said to each other, "Who is this? Even the wind and the waves obey him!"

CHAPTER 5

A man with evil spirits

This is also told in Matthew 8.28–34; Luke 8.26–39

1 Jesus and his disciples crossed Lake Galilee and came to shore near the town of Gerasa.ᐟ 2 When he was getting out of the boat, a man with an evil spirit quickly ran to him 3 from the graveyard* where he had been living. No one was able to tie the man up any more, not even with a chain. 4 He had often been put in chains and leg irons, but he broke the chains and smashed the leg irons. No one could control him. 5 Night and day he was in the graveyard or on the hills, yelling and cutting himself with stones.

6 When the man saw Jesus in the distance, he ran up to him and knelt down. 7 He shouted, "Jesus, Son of God in heaven, what do you want with me? Promise me in God's name that you won't torture me!" 8 The man said this because Jesus had already told the evil spirit to come out of him.

9 Jesus asked, "What is your name?"

The man answered, "My name is Lots, because I have 'lots' of evil spirits." 10 He then begged Jesus not to send them away.

11 Over on the hillside a large herd of pigs was feeding. 12 So the evil spirits begged Jesus, "Send us into those pigs! Let us go into them." 13 Jesus let them go, and they went out of the man and into the pigs. The whole herd of about two thousand pigs rushed down the steep bank into the lake and drowned.

14 The men taking care of the pigs ran to the town and the farms to spread the news. Then the people came out to see what had happened. 15 When they came to Jesus, they saw the man who had once been full of demons. He was sitting there with his clothes on and in his right mind, and they were terrified.

16 Everyone who had seen what had happened told about the man and the pigs. 17 Then the people started begging Jesus to leave their part of the country.

18 When Jesus was getting into the boat, the man begged to go with him. 19 But Jesus would not let him. Instead, he said, "Go home to your family and tell them how much the Lord has done for you and how good he has been to you."

20 The man went away into the region near the ten cities known as Decapolis* and began telling everyone how much Jesus had done for him. Everyone who heard what had happened was amazed.

---

*5.3 graveyard: It was thought that demons and evil spirits lived in graveyards.

*5.20 the ten cities known as Decapolis: A group of ten cities east of Samaria and Galilee, where the people followed the Greek way of life.

A dying girl and a sick woman

This is also told in Matthew 9.18–26; Luke 8.40–56

21 Once again Jesus got into the boat and crossed Lake Galilee.* Then as he stood on the shore, a large crowd gathered around him. 22 The person in charge of the Jewish meeting place was also there. His name was Jairus, and when he saw Jesus, he went over to him. He knelt at Jesus' feet 23 and started begging him for help. He said, "My daughter is about to die! Please come and touch her, so she will get well and live." 24 Jesus went with Jairus. Many people followed along and kept crowding around.

25 In the crowd was a woman who had been bleeding for twelve years. 26 She had gone to many doctors, and they had not done anything except cause her a lot of pain. She had paid them all the money she had. But instead of getting better, she only got worse.

27 The woman had heard about Jesus, so she came up behind him in the crowd and barely touched his clothes. 28 She had said to herself, "If I can just touch his clothes, I will get well." 29 As soon as she touched them, her bleeding stopped, and she knew she was well.

30 At that moment Jesus felt power go out from him. He turned to the crowd and asked, "Who touched my clothes?"

31 His disciples said to him, "Look at all these people crowding around you! How can you ask who touched you?" 32 But Jesus turned to see who had touched him.

33 The woman knew what had happened to her. She came shaking with fear and knelt down in front of Jesus. Then she told him the whole story.

34 Jesus said to the woman, "You are now well because of your faith. May God give you peace! You are healed, and you will no longer be in pain."

35 While Jesus was still speaking, some men came from Jairus' home and said, "Your daughter has died! Why bother the teacher any more?"

36 Jesus heard* what they said, and he said to Jairus, "Don't worry. Just have faith!"

37 Jesus did not let anyone go with him except Peter and the two disciples, James and John. 38 They went home with Jairus and saw the people crying and making a lot of noise.*

39 Then Jesus went inside and said to them, "Why are you crying and carrying on like this? The child isn't dead. She is just asleep." 40 But the people laughed at him.

After Jesus had sent them all out of the house, he took the girl's father and mother and his three disciples and went to where she was. 41–42 He took the twelve-year-old girl by the hand and said, "Talitha, koum!"* which means, "Little girl, get up!" The girl got straight up and started walking around.

Everyone was greatly surprised. 43 But Jesus ordered them not to tell anyone what had happened. Then he said, "Give them something to eat."

CHAPTER 6

The people of Nazareth turn against Jesus

This is also told in Matthew 13.53–58; Luke 4.16–30

1 Jesus left and returned to his home town* with his disciples. 2 The next Sabbath he taught in the Jewish meeting place. Many of the people who heard him were amazed and asked, "How can he do all this? Where did he get such wisdom and the power to perform these miracles? 3 Isn't he the carpenter,* the son of Mary? Aren't James, Joseph, Judas, and Simon his brothers? Don't his sisters still live here in our town?" The people were very unhappy because of what he was doing.

4 But Jesus said, "Prophets are honoured by everyone, except the people of their home town and their relatives and their own family." 5 Jesus could not perform any miracles there, except to heal a few sick people by placing his hands on them. 6 He was surprised that the people did not have any faith.

Instructions for the twelve apostles

This is also told in Matthew 10.5–15; Luke 9.1–6

Jesus taught in all the neighbouring villages. 7 Then he called together his twelve apostles and sent them out two by two with power over evil spirits. 8 He told them, "You may take along a walking stick. But don't carry food or a travelling bag or any money. 9 It's all right to wear sandals, but don't take along

---

*5.21 crossed Lake Galilee: To the west side.
*5.38 crying and making a lot of noise: The Jewish people often hired mourners for funerals.

*5.41,42 Talitha, koum: These words are in Aramaic, a language spoken in Palestine during the time of Jesus.
*6.1 home town: Nazareth.
See also: 6.4: John 4.44. 6.8–11: Luke 10.4–11.

a change of clothes. ¹⁰ When you are welcomed into a home, stay there until you leave that town. ¹¹ If any place won't welcome you or listen to your message, leave and shake the dust from your feet* as a warning to them."

¹² The apostles left and started telling everyone to turn to God. ¹³ They forced out many demons and healed a lot of sick people by putting olive oil* on them.

The death of John the Baptist
This is also told in Matthew 14.1–12; Luke 9.7–9

¹⁴ Jesus became so well-known that Herod the ruler* heard about him. Some people thought he was John the Baptist, who had come back to life with the power to perform miracles. ¹⁵ Others thought he was Elijah* or some other prophet who had lived long ago. ¹⁶ But when Herod heard about Jesus, he said, "This must be John! I had his head cut off, and now he has come back to life."

¹⁷⁻¹⁸ Herod had earlier married Herodias, the wife of his brother Philip. But John had told him, "It isn't right for you to take your brother's wife!" So, in order to please Herodias, Herod arrested John and put him in prison.

¹⁹ Herodias had a grudge against John and wanted to kill him. But she could not do it ²⁰ because Herod was afraid of John and protected him. He knew that John was a good and holy man. Even though Herod was confused by what John said,* he was glad to listen to him. And he often did.

²¹ Finally, Herodias got her chance when Herod gave a great birthday celebration for himself and invited his officials, his army officers, and the leaders of Galilee. ²² The daughter of Herodias* came in and danced for Herod and his guests. She pleased them so much that Herod said, "Ask for anything, and it's yours! ²³ I swear that I will give you as much as half of my kingdom, if you want it."

²⁴ The girl left and asked her mother, "What do you think I should ask for?"

Her mother answered, "The head of John the Baptist!"

²⁵ The girl hurried back and told Herod, "Straight away on a dish I want the head of John the Baptist!"

²⁶ The king was very sorry for what he had said. But he did not want to break the promise he had made in front of his guests. ²⁷ At once he ordered a guard to cut off John's head there in prison. ²⁸ The guard put the head on a dish and took it to the girl. Then she gave it to her mother.

²⁹ When John's followers learnt that he had been killed, they took his body and put it in a tomb.

Jesus feeds five thousand
This is also told in Matthew 14.13–21; Luke 9.10–17; John 6.1–14

³⁰ After the apostles returned to Jesus,* they told him everything they had done and taught. ³¹ But so many people were coming and going that Jesus and the apostles did not even have a chance to eat. Then Jesus said, "Let's go to a place* where we can be alone and get some rest." ³² They left in a boat for a place where they could be alone. ³³ But many people saw them leave and worked out where they were going. So people from every town ran on ahead and got there first.

³⁴ When Jesus got out of the boat, he saw the large crowd that was like sheep without a shepherd. He felt sorry for the people and started teaching them many things.

³⁵ That evening the disciples came to Jesus and said, "This place is like a desert, and it is already late. ³⁶ Let the crowds leave, so they can go to the farms and villages near here and buy something to eat."

³⁷ Jesus replied, "You give them something to eat."

But they asked him, "Don't you know that it would take almost a year's wages* to buy all these people something to eat?"

---

*6.11 shake the dust from your feet: This was a way of showing rejection.
*6.13 olive oil: The Jewish people used olive oil as a way of healing people. Sometimes olive oil is a symbol for healing by means of a miracle (see James 5.14).
*6.14 Herod the ruler: Herod Antipas, the son of Herod the Great.
*6.15 Elijah: Many of the Jewish people expected the prophet Elijah to come and prepare the way for the Messiah.

See also: 6.11: Acts 13.51. 6.13: Jam 5.14.
6.14,15: Matt 16.14; Mark 8.28; Luke 9.19.
17,18: Luke 3.19,20.

*6.30 the apostles returned to Jesus: From the mission on which he had sent them (see 6.7,12,13).
*6.31 a place: This was probably north-east of Lake Galilee (see verse 45).
*6.37 almost a year's wages: The Greek text has "two hundred silver coins". Each coin was the average day's wage for a worker.

See also: 6.34: Num 27.17; 1 King 22.17; 2 Chron 18.16; Ezek 34.5; Matt 9.36.

[38] Then Jesus said, "How much bread do you have? Go and see!"

They found out and answered, "We have five small loaves of bread* and two fish."
[39] Jesus told his disciples to make the people sit down on the green grass. [40] They sat down in groups of a hundred and groups of fifty.

[41] Jesus took the five loaves and the two fish. He looked up towards heaven and blessed the food. Then he broke the bread and handed it to his disciples to give to the people. He also divided the two fish, so that everyone could have some.

[42] After everyone had eaten all they wanted, [43] Jesus' disciples picked up twelve large baskets of leftover bread and fish.

[44] There were five thousand men who ate the food.

Jesus walks on the water

This is also told in Matthew 14.22–33; John 6.15–21

[45] Straight away, Jesus made his disciples get into the boat and start back across to Bethsaida. But he stayed until he had sent the crowds away. [46] Then he said goodbye to them and went up on the side of a mountain to pray.

[47] Later that evening he was still there by himself, and the boat was somewhere in the middle of the lake. [48] He could see that the disciples were struggling hard, because they were rowing against the wind. Not long before morning, Jesus came towards them. He was walking on the water and was about to pass the boat.

[49] When the disciples saw Jesus walking on the water, they thought he was a ghost, and they started screaming. [50] All of them saw him and were terrified. But at that same time he said, "Don't worry! I am Jesus. Don't be afraid." [51] He then got into the boat with them, and the wind died down. The disciples were completely confused. [52] Their minds were closed, and they could not understand the true meaning of the loaves of bread.

Jesus heals sick people in Gennesaret

This is also told in Matthew 14.34–36

[53] Jesus and his disciples crossed the lake and brought the boat to shore near the town of Gennesaret. [54] As soon as they got out of the boat, the people recognized Jesus. [55] So they

ran all over that part of the country to bring their sick people to him on mats. They brought them each time they heard where he was. [56] In every village or farm or market place where Jesus went, the people brought their sick to him. They begged him to let them just touch his clothes, and everyone who did was healed.

CHAPTER 7

The teaching of the ancestors

This is also told in Matthew 15.1–9

[1] Some Pharisees and several teachers of the Law of Moses from Jerusalem came and gathered around Jesus. [2] They noticed that some of his disciples ate without first washing their hands.*

[3] The Pharisees and many other Jewish people obey the teachings of their ancestors. They always wash their hands in the proper way* before eating. [4] None of them will eat anything they buy in the market until it is washed. They also follow a lot of other teachings, such as washing cups, jugs, and bowls.*

[5] The Pharisees and teachers asked Jesus, "Why don't your disciples obey what our ancestors taught us to do? Why do they eat without washing their hands?"

[6] Jesus replied:

You are nothing but show-offs! The prophet Isaiah was right when he wrote that God had said,

"All of you praise me
   with your words,
but you never really
   think about me.
[7] It is useless for you
   to worship me,
when you teach rules
   made up by humans."

[8] You disobey God's commands in order to obey what humans have taught. [9] You are good at rejecting God's commands so that you can follow your own teachings! [10] Didn't Moses command you to respect your father and mother? Didn't he tell you to put to death all who curse their parents? [11] But you let people get by without

---

*6.38 small loaves of bread: These would have been flat and round or in the shape of a bun.

*7.2 without first washing their hands: The Jewish people had strict laws about washing their hands before eating, especially if they had been out in public.

See also: 7.6,7: Isa 29.13 (LXX). 7.10: a Exod 20.12; Deut 5.16; b Exod 21.17; Lev 20.9.

helping their parents when they should. You let them say that what they own has been offered to God.* ¹² You won't let those people help their parents. ¹³ And you ignore God's commands in order to follow your own teaching. You do a lot of other things that are just as bad.

What really makes people unclean

This is also told in Matthew 15.10–20

¹⁴ Jesus called the crowd together again and said, "Pay attention and try to understand what I mean. ¹⁵⁻¹⁶ The food that you put into your mouth doesn't make you unclean and unfit to worship God. The bad words that come out of your mouth are what make you unclean."*

¹⁷ After Jesus and his disciples had left the crowd and had gone into the house, they asked him what these sayings meant. ¹⁸ He answered, "Don't you know what I am talking about by now? Surely you know that the food you put into your mouth cannot make you unclean. ¹⁹ It doesn't go into your heart, but into your stomach, and then out of your body." By saying this, Jesus meant that all foods were fit to eat.

²⁰ Then Jesus said:

What comes from your heart is what makes you unclean. ²¹ Out of your heart come evil thoughts, vulgar deeds, stealing, murder, ²² unfaithfulness in marriage, greed, meanness, deceit, indecency, envy, insults, pride, and foolishness. ²³ All these come from your heart, and they are what make you unfit to worship God.

A woman's faith

This is also told in Matthew 15.21–28

²⁴ Jesus left and went to the region near the city of Tyre, where he stayed in someone's home. He did not want people to know he was there, but they found out anyway. ²⁵ A woman whose daughter had an evil spirit in her heard where Jesus was. And straight away she came and knelt down at his feet. ²⁶ The woman was Greek and had been born in the part of Syria known as Phoenicia. She begged Jesus to force the demon out of

her daughter. ²⁷ But Jesus said, "The children must first be fed! It isn't right to take away their food and feed it to dogs."*

²⁸ The woman replied, "Lord, even dogs eat the crumbs that children drop from the table."

²⁹ Jesus answered, "That's true! You may go now. The demon has left your daughter."

³⁰ When the woman got back home, she found her child lying on the bed. The demon had gone.

Jesus heals a man who was deaf and could hardly talk

³¹ Jesus left the region around Tyre and went by way of Sidon towards Lake Galilee. He went through the land near the ten cities known as Decapolis.* ³² Some people brought to him a man who was deaf and could hardly talk. They begged Jesus just to touch him.

³³ After Jesus had taken him aside from the crowd, he stuck his fingers in the man's ears. Then he spat and put the spit on the man's tongue. ³⁴ Jesus looked up towards heaven, and with a groan he said, "Effatha!"* which means "Open up!" ³⁵ At once the man could hear, and he had no more trouble talking clearly.

³⁶ Jesus told the people not to say anything about what he had done. But the more he told them, the more they talked about it. ³⁷ They were completely amazed and said, "Everything he does is good! He even heals people who cannot hear or talk."

CHAPTER 8

Jesus feeds four thousand

This is also told in Matthew 15.32–39

¹ One day another large crowd gathered around Jesus. They had not brought along anything to eat. So Jesus called his disciples together and said, ² "I feel sorry for these people. They have been with me for three days, and they don't have anything to eat. ³ Some of them live a long way from here. If I send them away hungry, they might faint on their way home."

---

*7.11 has been offered to God: According to Jewish custom, when anything was offered to God, it could not be used for anyone else, not even for a person's parents.

*7.27 feed it to dogs: The Jewish people often referred to Gentiles as dogs.

*7.31 the ten cities known as Decapolis: See the note at 5.20.

*7.34 Effatha: This word is in Aramaic, a language spoken in Palestine during the time of Jesus.

⁴ The disciples said, "This place is like a desert. Where can we find enough food to feed such a crowd?"

⁵ Jesus asked them how much food they had. They replied, "Seven small loaves of bread."*

⁶ After Jesus told the crowd to sit down, he took the seven loaves and blessed them. He then broke the loaves and handed them to his disciples, who passed them out to the crowd. ⁷ They also had a few little fish, and after Jesus had blessed these, he told the disciples to pass them around.

⁸⁻⁹ The crowd of about four thousand people ate all they wanted, and the leftovers filled seven large baskets.

As soon as Jesus had sent the people away, ¹⁰ he got into the boat with the disciples and crossed to the territory near Dalmanutha.*

A sign from heaven

This is also told in Matthew 16.1–4

¹¹ The Pharisees came out and started an argument with Jesus. They wanted to test him by asking for a sign from heaven. ¹² Jesus groaned and said, "Why are you always looking for a sign? I can promise you that you will not be given one!" ¹³ Then he left them. He again got into a boat and crossed over to the other side of the lake.

The yeast of the Pharisees and of Herod

This is also told in Matthew 16.5–12

¹⁴ The disciples had forgotten to bring any bread, and they had only one loaf with them in the boat. ¹⁵ Jesus warned them, "Watch out! Guard against the yeast of the Pharisees and of Herod."*

¹⁶ The disciples talked this over and said to each other, "He must be saying this because we don't have any bread."

¹⁷ Jesus knew what they were thinking and asked, "Why are you talking about not having any bread? Don't you understand? Are your minds still closed? ¹⁸ Are your eyes blind and your ears deaf? Don't you remember ¹⁹ how many baskets of leftovers

you picked up when I fed those five thousand people with only five small loaves of bread?"

"Yes," the disciples answered. "There were twelve baskets."

²⁰ Jesus then asked, "And how many baskets of leftovers did you pick up when I broke seven small loaves of bread for those four thousand people?"

"Seven," they answered.

²¹ "Don't you know what I am talking about by now?" Jesus asked.

Jesus heals a blind man at Bethsaida

²² As Jesus and his disciples were going into Bethsaida, some people brought a blind man to him and begged him to touch the man. ²³ Jesus took him by the hand and led him out of the village, where he spat into the man's eyes. He placed his hands on the blind man and asked him if he could see anything. ²⁴ The man looked up and said, "I see people, but they look like trees walking around." ²⁵ Once again Jesus placed his hands on the man's eyes, and this time the man stared. His eyes were healed, and he saw everything clearly. ²⁶ Jesus said to him, "You may return home now, but don't go into the village."

Who is Jesus?

This is also told in Matthew 16.13–20; Luke 9.18–21

²⁷ Jesus and his disciples went to the villages near the town of Caesarea Philippi. As they were walking along, he asked them, "What do people say about me?"

²⁸ The disciples answered, "Some say you are John the Baptist or perhaps Elijah.* Others say you are one of the prophets."

²⁹ Then Jesus asked them, "But who do you say I am?"

"You are the Messiah!" Peter replied.

³⁰ Jesus warned the disciples not to tell anyone about him.

Jesus speaks about his suffering and death

This is also told in Matthew 16.21–28; Luke 9.22–27

³¹ Jesus began telling his disciples what would happen to him. He said, "The nation's leaders, the chief priests, and the teachers of the Law of Moses will make the Son of Man suffer

---

*8.5 small loaves of bread: See the note at 6.38.
*8.10 Dalmanutha: The place is unknown.
*8.15 Herod: See the note at 6.14.

See also: 8.11: Matt 12.38; Luke 11.16. 8.12: Matt 12.39; Luke 11.29. 8.15: Luke 12.1. 8.18: Jer 5.21; Ezek 12.2; Mark 4.12.

---

*8.28 Elijah: See the note at 6.15.
See also: 8.28: Mark 6.14,15; Luke 9.7,8.
8.29: John 6.68,69.

terribly. He will be rejected and killed, but three days later he will rise to life." 32 Then Jesus explained clearly what he meant.

Peter took Jesus aside and told him to stop talking like that. 33 But when Jesus turned and saw the disciples, he corrected Peter. He said to him, "Satan, get away from me! You are thinking like everyone else and not like God."

34 Jesus then told the crowd and the disciples to come closer, and he said:

If any of you want to be my followers, you must forget about yourself. You must take up your cross and follow me. 35 If you want to save your life,* you will destroy it. But if you give up your life for me and for the good news, you will save it. 36 What will you gain, if you own the whole world but destroy yourself? 37 What could you give to get back your soul?

38 Don't be ashamed of me and my message among these unfaithful and sinful people! If you are, the Son of Man will be ashamed of you when he comes in the glory of his Father with the holy angels.

CHAPTER 9

Jesus continued:

1 I can assure you that some of the people standing here will not die before they see God's kingdom come with power.

The true glory of Jesus

This is also told in Matthew 17.1–13; Luke 9.28–36

2 Six days later Jesus took Peter, James, and John with him. They went up on a high mountain, where they could be alone. There in front of the disciples, Jesus was completely changed. 3 And his clothes became much whiter than any bleach on earth could make them. 4 Then Moses and Elijah were there talking with Jesus.

5 Peter said to Jesus, "Teacher, it is good for us to be here! Let us make three shelters, one for you, one for Moses, and one for Elijah." 6 But Peter and the others were terribly frightened, and he did not know what he was talking about.

7 The shadow of a cloud passed over and covered them. From the cloud a voice said, "This is my Son, and I love him. Listen to

what he says!" 8 At once the disciples looked around, but they saw only Jesus.

9 As Jesus and his disciples were coming down the mountain, he told them not to say a word about what they had seen, until the Son of Man had been raised from death. 10 So they kept it to themselves. But they wondered what he meant by the words "raised from death."

11 The disciples asked Jesus, "Don't the teachers of the Law of Moses say that Elijah must come before the Messiah does?"

12 Jesus answered:

Elijah certainly will come* to get everything ready. But don't the Scriptures also say that the Son of Man must suffer terribly and be rejected? 13 I can assure you that Elijah has already come. And people treated him just as they wanted to, as the Scriptures say they would.

Jesus heals a boy

This is also told in Matthew 17.14–20; Luke 9.37–43a

14 When Jesus and his three disciples came back down, they saw a large crowd around the other disciples. The teachers of the Law of Moses were arguing with them.

15 The crowd was really surprised to see Jesus, and everyone hurried over to greet him. 16 Jesus asked, "What are you arguing about?"

17 Someone from the crowd answered, "Teacher, I brought my son to you. A demon keeps him from talking. 18 Whenever the demon attacks my son, it throws him to the ground and makes him foam at the mouth and grit his teeth in pain. Then he becomes stiff. I asked your disciples to force out the demon, but they couldn't do it."

19 Jesus said, "You people don't have any faith! How much longer must I be with you? Why do I have to put up with you? Bring the boy to me."

20 They brought the boy, and as soon as the demon saw Jesus, it made the boy shake all over. He fell down and began rolling on the ground and foaming at the mouth. 21 Jesus asked the boy's father, "How long has he been like this?"

The man answered, "Ever since he was a child. 22 The demon has often tried to kill him by throwing him into a fire or into water. Please have pity and help us if you can!"

See also: **8.34:** Matt 10.38; Luke 14.27. **8.35:** Matt 10.39; Luke 17.33; John 12.25. **9.2–7:** 2 Pet 1.17,18. **9.7:** Matt 3.17; Mark 1.11; Luke 3.22.

*9.12 Elijah certainly will come: See the note at 6.15.
See also: **9.11:** Mal 4.5; Matt 11.14. **9.12:** Luke 22.24.

²³ Jesus replied, "Why do you say 'if you can'? Anything is possible for someone who has faith!"

²⁴ Straight away the boy's father shouted, "I do have faith! Please help me to have even more."

²⁵ When Jesus saw that a crowd was gathering fast, he spoke sternly to the evil spirit that had kept the boy from speaking or hearing. He said, "I order you to come out of the boy! Don't ever bother him again."

²⁶ The spirit screamed and made the boy shake all over. Then it went out of him. The boy looked dead, and almost everyone said he was. ²⁷ But Jesus took hold of his hand and helped him stand up.

²⁸ After Jesus and the disciples had gone back home and were alone, they asked him, "Why couldn't we force out that demon?"

²⁹ Jesus answered, "Only prayer can force out that kind of demon."

Jesus again speaks about his death

This is also told in Matthew 17.22,23; Luke 9.43b–45

³⁰ Jesus left with his disciples and started through Galilee. He did not want anyone to know about it, ³¹ because he was teaching the disciples that the Son of Man would be handed over to people who would kill him. But three days later he would rise to life. ³² The disciples did not understand what Jesus meant, and they were afraid to ask.

Who is the greatest?

This is also told in Matthew 18.1–5; Luke 9.46–48

³³ Jesus and his disciples went to his home in Capernaum. After they were inside the house, Jesus asked them, "What were you arguing about along the way?" ³⁴ They had been arguing about which one of them was the greatest, and so they did not answer.

³⁵ After Jesus sat down and told the twelve disciples to gather around him, he said, "If you want the place of honour, you must become a slave and serve others!"

³⁶ Then Jesus made a child stand near him. He put his arm around the child and said, ³⁷ "When you welcome even a child because of me, you welcome me. And when you welcome me, you welcome the one who sent me."

For or against Jesus

This is also told in Luke 9.49,50

³⁸ John said, "Teacher, we saw a man using your name to force demons out of people. But he wasn't one of us, and we told him to stop."

³⁹ Jesus said to his disciples:

Don't stop him! No one who performs miracles in my name is going to say something bad about me the next minute. ⁴⁰ Anyone who isn't against us is for us. ⁴¹ And anyone who gives you a cup of water in my name, just because you belong to me, will surely be rewarded.

Temptations to sin

This is also told in Matthew 18.6–9; Luke 17.1,2

Jesus continued:

⁴² It will be terrible for people who cause even one of my little followers to sin. Those people would be better off thrown into the sea with a heavy stone tied around their necks. ⁴³⁻⁴⁴ So if your hand causes you to sin, cut it off! You would be better off to go into life crippled than to have two hands and be thrown into the fires of hell that never go out.* ⁴⁵⁻⁴⁶ If your foot causes you to sin, chop it off. You would be better off to go into life lame than to have two feet and be thrown into hell.* ⁴⁷ If your eye causes you to sin, get rid of it. You would be better off to go into God's kingdom with only one eye than to have two eyes and be thrown into hell. ⁴⁸ The worms there never die, and the fire never stops burning.

⁴⁹ Everyone must be salted with fire.*

⁵⁰ Salt is good. But if it no longer tastes like salt, how can it be made salty again? Have salt among you and live at peace with each other.*

***9.49 salted with fire:** Some manuscripts add "and every sacrifice will be seasoned with salt." The verse may mean that Christ's followers must suffer because of their faith.

***9.50 Have salt among you and live at peace with each other:** This may mean that when Christ's followers have to suffer because of their faith, they must still try to live at peace with each other.

See also: 9.34: Matt 18.1; Luke 22.24.   9.35: Matt 20.26,27; 23.11; Mark 10.43,44; Luke 22.26.   9.37: Matt 10.40; Luke 10.16; John 13.20.

See also: 9.40: Matt 12.30; Luke 11.23.   9.41: Matt 10.42.
9.43: Matt 5.30.   9.47: Matt 5.29.   9.48: Isa 66.24.
9.50: Matt 5.13; Luke 14.34,35.

Jesus goes from Galilee to Jerusalem

CHAPTER 10

Teaching about divorce

This is also told in Matthew 19.1–12; Luke 16.18

¹ After Jesus left, he went to Judea and then on to the other side of the River Jordan. Once again large crowds came to him, and as usual, he taught them.

² Some Pharisees wanted to test Jesus. So they came up to him and asked if it was right for a man to divorce his wife. ³ Jesus asked them, "What does the Law of Moses say about that?"

⁴ They answered, "Moses allows a man to write out divorce papers and send his wife away."

⁵ Jesus replied, "Moses gave you this law because you are so heartless. ⁶ But in the beginning God made a man and a woman. ⁷ That's why a man leaves his father and mother and gets married. ⁸ He becomes like one person with his wife. Then they are no longer two people, but one. ⁹ And no one should separate a couple that God has joined together."

¹⁰ When Jesus and his disciples were back in the house, they asked him about what he had said. ¹¹ He told them, "A man who divorces his wife and marries someone else is unfaithful to his wife. ¹² A woman who divorces her husband* and marries again is also unfaithful."

Jesus blesses little children

This is also told in Matthew 19.13–15; Luke 18.15–17

¹³ Some people brought their children to Jesus so that he could bless them by placing his hands on them. But his disciples told the people to stop bothering them.

¹⁴ When Jesus saw this, he became angry and said, "Let the children come to me! Don't try to stop them. People who are like these little children belong to the kingdom of God.▸ ¹⁵ I promise you that you cannot get into God's kingdom, unless you accept it the way a child does." ¹⁶ Then Jesus took the children

in his arms and blessed them by placing his hands on them.

A rich man

This is also told in Matthew 19.16–30; Luke 18.18–30

¹⁷ As Jesus was walking down a road, a man ran up to him. He knelt down, and asked, "Good teacher, what can I do to have eternal life?"

¹⁸ Jesus replied, "Why do you call me good? Only God is good. ¹⁹ You know the commandments. 'Do not murder. Be faithful in marriage. Do not steal. Do not tell lies about others. Do not cheat. Respect your father and mother.' "

²⁰ The man answered, "Teacher, I have obeyed all these commandments since I was a young man."

²¹ Jesus looked closely at the man. He liked him and said, "There's one thing you still need to do. Go and sell everything you own. Give the money to the poor, and you will have riches in heaven. Then come with me."

²² When the man heard Jesus say this, he went away gloomy and sad because he was very rich.

²³ Jesus looked around and said to his disciples, "It's hard for rich people to get into God's kingdom!" ²⁴ The disciples were shocked to hear this. So Jesus told them again, "It's terribly hard▸ to get into God's kingdom! ²⁵ In fact, it's easier for a camel to go through the eye of a needle than for a rich person to get into God's kingdom."

²⁶ Jesus' disciples were even more amazed. They asked each other, "How can anyone ever be saved?"

²⁷ Jesus looked at them and said, "There are some things that people cannot do, but God can do anything."

²⁸ Peter replied, "Remember, we left everything to be your followers!"

²⁹ Jesus told him:

You can be sure that anyone who gives up home or brothers or sisters or mother or father or children or land for me and for the good news ³⁰ will be rewarded. In this world they will be given a hundred times as many houses and brothers and sisters and mothers and children and pieces of land, though they will also be ill-treated. And in the world to come, they will have eternal life. ³¹ But many who are now first will be last, and many who are now last will be first.

---

*10.12 A woman who divorces her husband: Roman law let a woman divorce her husband, but Jewish law did not let a woman do this.

See also: 10.4: Deut 24.1–4; Mark 5.31. 10.6: Gen 1.27; 5.2. 10.7,8: Gen 2.24. 10.11,12: Matt 5.32; 1 Cor 7.10,11. 10.15: Matt 18.3.

See also: 10.19: a Exod 20.13; Deut 5.17; b Exod 20.14; Deut 5.18; c Exod 20.15; Deut 5.19; d Exod 20.16; Deut 5.20; e Exod 20.12; Deut 5.16. 10.31: Matt 20.16; Luke 13.30.

Jesus again tells about his death

This is also told in Matthew 20.17–19; Luke 18.31–34

³² The disciples were confused as Jesus led them towards Jerusalem, and his other followers were afraid. Once again, Jesus took the twelve disciples aside and told them what was going to happen to him. He said:

³³ We are now on our way to Jerusalem where the Son of Man will be handed over to the chief priests and the teachers of the Law of Moses. They will sentence him to death and hand him over to foreigners,* ³⁴ who will make fun of him and spit on him. They will beat him and kill him. But three days later he will rise to life.

The request of James and John

This is also told in Matthew 20.20–28

³⁵ James and John, the sons of Zebedee, came up to Jesus and asked, "Teacher, will you do us a favour?"

³⁶ Jesus asked them what they wanted, ³⁷ and they answered, "When you come into your glory, please let one of us sit at your right side and the other at your left."*

³⁸ Jesus told them, "You don't really know what you're asking! Are you able to drink from the cup* that I must soon drink from or be baptized as I must be baptized?"*

³⁹ "Yes, we are!" James and John answered.

Then Jesus replied, "You certainly will drink from the cup from which I must drink. And you will be baptized just as I must! ⁴⁰ But it isn't for me to say who will sit at my right side and at my left. That is for God to decide."

⁴¹ When the ten other disciples heard this, they were angry with James and John. ⁴² But Jesus called the disciples together and said:

You know that those foreigners who call themselves kings like to order their people around. And their great leaders have full power over the people they rule. ⁴³ But don't act like them. If you want to be great, you

must be the servant of all the others. ⁴⁴ And if you want to be first, you must be everyone's slave. ⁴⁵ The Son of Man did not come to be a slave master, but a slave who will give his life to rescue* many people.

Jesus heals blind Bartimaeus

This is also told in Matthew 20.29–34; Luke 18.35–43

⁴⁶ Jesus and his disciples went to Jericho. And as they were leaving, they were followed by a large crowd. A blind beggar called Bartimaeus son of Timaeus was sitting beside the road. ⁴⁷ When he heard that it was Jesus from Nazareth, he shouted, "Jesus, Son of David,* have pity on me!" ⁴⁸ Many people told the man to stop, but he shouted even louder, "Son of David, have pity on me!"

⁴⁹ Jesus stopped and said, "Call him over!"

They called out to the blind man and said, "Don't be afraid! Come on! He is calling for you." ⁵⁰ The man threw off his coat as he jumped up and ran to Jesus.

⁵¹ Jesus asked, "What do you want me to do for you?"

The blind man answered, "Master,* I want to see!"

⁵² Jesus told him, "You may go. Your eyes are healed because of your faith."

Straight away the man could see, and he went down the road with Jesus.

Jesus' last week: his trial and death

CHAPTER 11

Jesus enters Jerusalem

This is also told in Matthew 21.1–11; Luke 19.28–40; John 12.12–19

¹ Jesus and his disciples reached Bethphage and Bethany near the Mount of Olives. When they were getting close to Jerusalem, Jesus sent two of them on ahead. ² He told them, "Go into the next village. As soon as you enter it, you will find a young donkey that has never been ridden. Untie the donkey and bring it here. ³ If anyone asks why you are doing that, say, 'The Lord* needs it and will soon bring it back.' "

---

*10.33 foreigners: The Romans who ruled Judea at this time.

*10.37 right side . . . left: The most powerful people in a kingdom sat at the right and left side of the king.

*10.38 drink from the cup: In the Scriptures a "cup" is sometimes used as a symbol of suffering. To "drink from the cup" would be to suffer.

*10.38 as I must be baptized: Baptism is used with the same meaning that "cup" has in this verse.

See also: 10.38: Luke 12.50. 10.42,43: Luke 22.25,26. 10.43,44: Matt 23.11; Mark 9.35; Luke 22.26.

*10.45 rescue: The Greek word often, though not always, means the payment of a price to free a slave or a prisoner.

*10.47 Son of David: The Jewish people expected the Messiah to be from the family of King David, and for this reason the Messiah was often called the "Son of David".

⁴ The disciples left and found the donkey tied near a door that faced the street. While they were untying it, ⁵ some of the people standing there asked, "Why are you untying the donkey?" ⁶ They told them what Jesus had said, and the people let them take it.

⁷ The disciples led the donkey to Jesus. They put some of their clothes on its back, and Jesus got on. ⁸ Many people spread clothes on the road, while others went to cut branches from the fields.*

⁹ In front of Jesus and behind him, people went along shouting,

"Hooray!*
God bless the one who comes
    in the rame of the Lord!
¹⁰ God bless the coming kingdom
    of our ancestor David.
Hooray for God
    in heaven above!"

¹¹ After Jesus had gone to Jerusalem, he went into the temple and looked around at everything. But since it was already late in the day, he went back to Bethany with the twelve disciples.

Jesus puts a curse on a fig tree

This is also told in Matthew 21.18,19

¹² When Jesus and his disciples left Bethany the next morning, he was hungry. ¹³ From a distance Jesus saw a fig tree covered with leaves, and he went to see if there were any figs on the tree. But there were not any, because it wasn't the season for figs. ¹⁴ So Jesus said to the tree, "Never again will anyone eat fruit from this tree!" The disciples heard him say this.

Jesus in the temple

This is also told in Matthew 21.12–17; Luke 19.45–48; John 2.13–22

¹⁵ After Jesus and his disciples reached Jerusalem, he went into the temple and began chasing out everyone who was selling and buying. He turned over the tables of the moneychangers and the benches of those who were selling doves. ¹⁶ Jesus would not let anyone carry things through the temple.

¹⁷ Then he taught the people and said, "The Scriptures say, 'My house should be called a place of worship for all nations.' But you have made it a place where robbers hide!"

¹⁸ The chief priests and the teachers of the Law of Moses heard what Jesus said, and they started looking for a way to kill him. They were afraid of him, because the crowds were completely amazed at his teaching.

¹⁹ That evening, Jesus and the disciples went outside the city.

A lesson from the fig tree

This is also told in Matthew 21.20–22

²⁰ As the disciples walked past the fig tree the next morning, they noticed that it was completely dried up, roots and all. ²¹ Peter remembered what Jesus had said to the tree. Then Peter said, "Teacher, look! The tree you put a curse on has dried up."

²² Jesus told his disciples:

Have faith in God! ²³ If you have faith in God and don't doubt, you can tell this mountain to get up and jump into the sea, and it will. ²⁴ Everything you ask for in prayer will be yours, if you only have faith.

²⁵⁻²⁶ Whenever you stand up to pray, you must forgive what others have done to you. Then your Father in heaven will forgive your sins.'

A question about Jesus' authority

This is also told in Matthew 21.23–27; Luke 20.1–8

²⁷ Jesus and his disciples returned to Jerusalem. And as he was walking through the temple, the chief priests, the nation's leaders, and the teachers of the Law of Moses came over to him. ²⁸ They asked, "What right do you have to do these things? Who gave you this authority?"

²⁹ Jesus answered, "I have just one question to ask you. If you answer it, I will tell you where I got the right to do these things. ³⁰ Who gave John the right to baptize? Was it God in heaven or merely some human being?"

³¹ They thought it over and said to each other, "We can't say that God gave John this right. Jesus will ask us why we didn't believe John. ³² On the other hand, these people think that John was a prophet. So we can't say that it was merely some human who gave John the right to baptize."

---

*11.8 spread . . . branches from the fields: This was one way that the Jewish people welcomed a famous person.
*11.9 Hooray: This translates a word that can mean "please save us". But it is most often used as a shout of praise to God.
See also: 11.9: Psa 118.25,26.

See also: 11.17: a Isa 56.7; b Jer 7.11. 11.23: Matt 17.20; 1 Cor 13.2. 11.25,26: Matt 6.14,15.

They were afraid of the crowd ³³ and told Jesus, "We don't know."

Jesus replied, "Then I won't tell you who gave me the right to do what I do."

CHAPTER 12

Tenants of a vineyard

This is also told in Matthew 21.33–46; Luke 20.9–19

¹ Jesus then told them this story:

A farmer once planted a vineyard. He built a wall around it and dug a pit to crush the grapes. He also built a lookout tower. Then he let his vineyard and left the country.

² When it was harvest time, he sent a servant to get his share of the grapes. ³ The tenants grabbed the servant. They beat him up and sent him away without a thing.

⁴ The owner sent another servant, but the tenants beat him on the head and insulted him terribly. ⁵ Then the man sent another servant, and they killed him. He kept sending servant after servant. They beat some of them and killed others.

⁶ The owner had a son he loved very much. Finally, he sent his son to the tenants because he thought they would respect him. ⁷ But they said to themselves, "Some day he will own this vineyard. Let's kill him! That way we can have it all for ourselves." ⁸ So they grabbed the owner's son and killed him. Then they threw his body out of the vineyard.

⁹ Jesus asked, "What do you think the owner of the vineyard will do? He will come and kill those tenants and let someone else have his vineyard. ¹⁰ Surely you know that the Scriptures say,

'The stone that the builders
    tossed aside
is now the most important
    stone of all.
¹¹ This is something
    the Lord has done,
    and it is amazing to us.'"

¹² The leaders knew that Jesus was really talking about them, and they wanted to arrest him. But because they were afraid of the crowd, they let him alone and left.

Paying taxes

This is also told in Matthew 22.15–22; Luke 20.20–26

¹³ The Pharisees got together with Herod's followers.* Then they sent some men to trick Jesus into saying something wrong. ¹⁴ They went to him and said, "Teacher, we know that you are honest. You treat everyone with the same respect, no matter who they are. And you teach the truth about what God wants people to do. Tell us, should we pay taxes to the Emperor or not?"

¹⁵ Jesus knew what they were up to, and he said, "Why are you trying to test me? Show me a coin!"

¹⁶ They brought him a silver coin, and he asked, "Whose picture and name are on it?"

"The Emperor's," they answered.

¹⁷ Then Jesus told them, "Give the Emperor what belongs to him and give God what belongs to God." The men were amazed at Jesus.

Life in the future world

This is also told in Matthew 22.23–33; Luke 20.27–40

¹⁸ The Sadducees did not believe that people would rise to life after death. So some of them came to Jesus and said:

¹⁹ Teacher, Moses wrote that if a married man dies and has no children, his brother should marry the widow. Their first son would then be thought of as the son of the dead brother. ²⁰ There were once seven brothers. The first one married, but died without having any children. ²¹ The second brother married his brother's widow, and he also died without having children. The same thing happened to the third brother, ²² and finally to all seven brothers. At last the woman died. ²³ When God raises people from death, whose wife will this woman be? After all, she had been married to all seven brothers.

²⁴ Jesus answered:

You are completely wrong! You don't know what the Scriptures teach. And you don't know anything about the power of God. ²⁵ When God raises people to life, they won't marry. They will be like the angels in heaven. ²⁶ You know

*12.13 Herod's followers: See the note at 3.6.

See also: 12.18: Acts 23.8. 12.19: Deut 25.5.
12.26: Exod 3.6.

See also: 12.1: Isa 5.1,2. 12.10,11: Psa 118.22,23.

about people being raised to life. You know that in the story about Moses and the burning bush, God said, "I am the God worshipped by Abraham, Isaac, and Jacob."* ²⁷ He isn't the God of the dead, but of the living. You Sadducees are all wrong.

The most important commandment

This is also told in Matthew 22.34–40; Luke 10.25–28

²⁸ One of the teachers of the Law of Moses came up while Jesus and the Sadducees were arguing. When he heard Jesus give a good answer, he asked him, "What is the most important commandment?"

²⁹ Jesus answered, "The most important one says: 'People of Israel, you have only one Lord and God. ³⁰ You must love him with all your heart, soul, mind, and strength.' ³¹ The second most important commandment says: 'Love others as much as you love yourself.' No other commandment is more important than these."

³² The man replied, "Teacher, you are certainly right to say there is only one God. ³³ It is also true that we must love God with all our heart, mind, and strength, and that we must love others as much as we love ourselves. These commandments are more important than all the sacrifices and offerings that we could possibly make."

³⁴ When Jesus saw that the man had given a sensible answer, he told him, "You are not far from God's kingdom." After this, no one dared ask Jesus any more questions.

About David's son

This is also told in Matthew 22.41–46; Luke 20.41–44

³⁵ As Jesus was teaching in the temple, he said, "How can the teachers of the Law of Moses say that the Messiah will come from the family of King David? ³⁶ The Holy Spirit led David to say,

'The Lord said to my Lord:
    Sit at my right side*
until I make your enemies
    into a footstool for you.'

³⁷ If David called the Messiah his Lord, how can the Messiah be his son?"*

The large crowd enjoyed listening to Jesus teach.

Jesus condemns the Pharisees and the teachers of the Law of Moses

This is also told in Matthew 23.1–36; Luke 20.45–47

³⁸ As Jesus was teaching, he said:

Guard against the teachers of the Law of Moses! They love to walk around in long robes and be greeted in the market. ³⁹ They like the front seats in the meeting places and the best seats at banquets. ⁴⁰ But they cheat widows out of their homes and pray long prayers just to show off. They will be punished most of all.

A widow's offering

This is also told in Luke 21.1–4

⁴¹ Jesus was sitting in the temple near the offering box and watching people put in their gifts. He noticed that many rich people were giving a lot of money. ⁴² Finally, a poor widow came up and put in two coins that were worth only a few pennies. ⁴³ Jesus told his disciples to gather around him. Then he said:

I tell you that this poor widow has put in more than all the others. ⁴⁴ Everyone else gave what they didn't need. But she is very poor and gave everything she had. Now she doesn't have a penny to live on.

CHAPTER 13

The temple will be destroyed

This is also told in Matthew 24.1,2; Luke 21.5,6

¹ As Jesus was leaving the temple, one of his disciples said to him, "Teacher, look at these beautiful stones and wonderful buildings!"

² Jesus replied, "Do you see these huge buildings? They will certainly be torn down! Not one stone will be left in place."

Warning about trouble

This is also told in Matthew 24.3–14; Luke 21.7–19

³ Later, as Jesus was sitting on the Mount of Olives across from the temple, Peter, James, John, and Andrew came to him in private. ⁴ They asked, "When will these things happen? What will be the sign that they are about to take place?"

---

*12.26 "I am the God worshipped by Abraham, Isaac, and Jacob": Jesus argues that if God is worshipped by these three, they must still be alive, because he is the God of the living.
*12.36 right side: The place of power and honour.
See also: 12.28–34: Luke 10.25–28. 12.29,30: Deut 6.4,5. 12.31: Lev 19.18. 12.32: Deut 4.35. 12.33: Hos 6.6. 12.36: Psa 110.1.

*12.37 David . . . his son: See the note at 10.47.

⁵ Jesus answered:

Watch out and don't let anyone fool you!
⁶ Many will come and claim to be me.
They will use my name and fool many
people.

⁷ When you hear about wars and threats
of wars, don't be afraid. These things will
have to happen first, but that isn't the end.
⁸ Nations and kingdoms will go to war
against each other. There will be
earthquakes in many places, and people
will starve to death. But this is just the
beginning of troubles.

⁹ Be on your guard! You will be taken to
courts and beaten with whips in their
meeting places. And because of me, you
will have to stand before rulers and kings
to tell about your faith. ¹⁰ But before the
end comes, the good news must be
preached to all nations.

¹¹ When you are arrested, don't worry
about what you will say. You will be given
the right words when the time comes. But
you will not really be the ones speaking.
Your words will come from the Holy
Spirit.

¹² Brothers and sisters will betray each
other and have each other put to death.
Parents will betray their own children,
and children will turn against their parents
and have them killed. ¹³ Everyone will
hate you because of me. But if you keep
on being faithful right to the end, you will
be saved.

The Horrible Thing

This is also told in Matthew 24.15–21; Luke 21.20–24

Jesus continued:

¹⁴ Some day you will see that "Horrible
Thing" where it should not be.*
Everyone who reads this must try to
understand! If you are living in Judea
at that time, run to the mountains. ¹⁵ If
you are on the roof* of your house, don't
go inside to get anything. ¹⁶ If you are out
in the field, don't go back for your coat.
¹⁷ It will be an awful time for women who
are expecting babies or nursing young
children. ¹⁸ Pray that it won't happen in

winter.* ¹⁹ This will be the worst time of
suffering since God created the world, and
nothing this terrible will ever happen
again. ²⁰ If the Lord doesn't make the time
shorter, no one will be left alive. But
because of his chosen and special ones, he
will make the time shorter.

²¹ If someone should say, "Here is the
Messiah!" or "There he is!" don't believe
it. ²² False messiahs and false prophets will
come and perform miracles and signs.
They will even try to fool God's chosen
ones. ²³ But be on your guard! That's why I
am telling you these things now.

When the Son of Man appears

This is also told in Matthew 24.29–31; Luke 21.25–28

Jesus continued:

²⁴ In those days, straight after that time of
suffering,

"The sun will become dark,
    and the moon
    will no longer shine.
²⁵ The stars will fall,
    and the powers in the sky*
    will be shaken."

²⁶ Then the Son of Man will be seen
coming in the clouds with great power
and glory. ²⁷ He will send his angels to
gather his chosen ones from all over the
earth.

A lesson from a fig tree

This is also told in Matthew 24.32–35; Luke 21.29–33

Jesus continued:

²⁸ Learn a lesson from a fig tree. When
its branches sprout and start putting out
leaves, you know summer is near. ²⁹ So
when you see all these things happening,
you will know that the time has almost
come. ³⁰ You can be sure that some of the
people of this generation will still be alive
when all this happens. ³¹ The sky and the
earth will not last for ever, but my words
will.

---

*13.18 in winter: In Palestine the winters are cold
and rainy and make travel difficult.
*13.25 the powers in the sky: In ancient times
people thought that the stars were spiritual powers.

See also: 13.19: Dan 12.1; Rev 7.14. 13.24: a Isa 13.10;
Joel 2.10,31; 3.15; Rev 6.12; b Isa 13.10; Ezek 32.7.
13.25: a Isa 34.4; Rev 6.13; b Joel 2.10. 13.26: Dan 7.13;
Rev 1.7.

*13.14 where it should not be: Probably the holy
place in the temple.
*13.15 roof: See the note at 2.4.

See also: 13.9–11: Matt 10.17–20; Luke 12.11,12.
13.13: Matt 10.22. 13.14: Dan 9.27; 11.31; 12.11.
13.15,16: Luke 17.31.

No one knows the day or time

This is also told in Matthew 24.36–44

Jesus continued:

³² No one knows the day or the time. The angels in heaven don't know, and the Son himself doesn't know. Only the Father knows. ³³ So watch out and be ready! You don't know when the time will come. ³⁴ It is like what happens when a man goes away for a while and places his servants in charge of everything. He tells each of them what to do, and he orders the guard to keep alert. ³⁵ So be alert! You don't know when the master of the house will come back. It could be in the evening or at midnight or before dawn or in the morning. ³⁶ But if he comes suddenly, don't let him find you asleep. ³⁷ I tell everyone just what I have told you. Be alert!

CHAPTER 14

A plot to kill Jesus

This is also told in Matthew 26.1–5; Luke 22.1,2; John 11.45–53

¹ It was now two days before Passover and the Festival of Thin Bread. The chief priests and the teachers of the Law of Moses were secretly planning to have Jesus arrested and put to death. ² They were saying, "We must not do it during the festival, because the people will riot."

At Bethany

This is also told in Matthew 26.6–13; John 12.1–8

³ Jesus was eating in Bethany at the home of Simon, who once had leprosy,* when a woman came in with a very expensive bottle of sweet-smelling perfume.* After breaking it open, she poured the perfume on Jesus' head. ⁴ This made some of the guests angry, and they complained, "Why such a waste? ⁵ We could have sold this perfume for more than three hundred silver coins and given the money to the poor!" So they started saying cruel things to the woman.

⁶ But Jesus said:

Leave her alone! Why are you bothering her? She has done a beautiful thing for me. ⁷ You will always have the poor with you. And whenever you want to, you can give to them. But you won't always have me here with you. ⁸ She has done all she could by pouring perfume on my body to prepare it for burial. ⁹ You may be sure that wherever the good news is told all over the world, people will remember what she has done. And they will tell others.

Judas and the chief priests

This is also told in Matthew 26.14–16; Luke 22.3–6

¹⁰ Judas Iscariot* was one of the twelve disciples. He went to the chief priests and offered to help them arrest Jesus. ¹¹ They were glad to hear this, and they promised to pay him. So Judas started looking for a good chance to betray Jesus.

Jesus eats with his disciples

This is also told in Matthew 26.17–25; Luke 22.7–14,21–23; John 13.21–30

¹² It was the first day of the Festival of Thin Bread, and the Passover lambs were being killed. Jesus' disciples asked him, "Where do you want us to prepare the Passover meal?"

¹³ Jesus said to two of the disciples, "Go into the city, where you will meet a man carrying a jar of water.* Follow him, ¹⁴ and when he goes into a house, say to the owner, 'Our teacher wants to know if you have a room where he can eat the Passover meal with his disciples.' ¹⁵ The owner will take you upstairs and show you a large room furnished and ready for you to use. Prepare the meal there."

¹⁶ The two disciples went into the city and found everything just as Jesus had told them. So they prepared the Passover meal.

¹⁷⁻¹⁸ While Jesus and the twelve disciples were eating together that evening, he said, "The one who will betray me is now eating with me."

¹⁹ This made the disciples sad, and one after another they said to Jesus, "Surely you don't mean me!"

²⁰ He answered, "It is one of you twelve men who is eating from this dish with me. ²¹ The Son of Man will die, just as the Scriptures say. But it is going to be terrible for the one who betrays me. That man would be better off if he had never been born."

*14.3 leprosy: See the note at 1.40.
See also: 13.32: Matt 24.36.   13.34: Luke 12.36–38.
14.1: Exod 12.1–27.   14.3: Luke 7.37,38.   14.7: Deut 15.11.

*14.10 Iscariot: See the note at 3.19.
*14.13 a man carrying a jar of water: A male slave carrying water could mean that the family was rich.
See also: 14.18: Psa 41.9.

The Lord's Supper

This is also told in Matthew 26.26–30; Luke 22.14–23;
1 Corinthians 11.23–25

22 During the meal Jesus took some bread in
his hands. He blessed the bread and broke it.
Then he gave it to his disciples and said,
"Take this. It is my body."

23 Jesus picked up a cup of wine and gave
thanks to God. He gave it to his disciples,
and said, "Drink it!" So they all drank some.
24 Then he said, "This is my blood, which is
poured out for many people, and with it
God makes his agreement. 25 From now on
I will not drink any wine, until I drink new
wine in God's kingdom." 26 Then they sang
a hymn and went out to the Mount of
Olives.

Peter's promise

This is also told in Matthew 26.31–35; Luke 22.31–34;
John 13.36–38

27 Jesus said to his disciples, "All of you will
reject me, as the Scriptures say,

'I will strike down
    the shepherd,
and the sheep
    will be scattered.'

28 But after I am raised to life, I will go ahead
of you to Galilee."

29 Peter spoke up, "Even if all the others
reject me, I never will!"

30 Jesus replied, "This very night before a
cock crows twice, you will say three times
that you don't know me."

31 But Peter was so sure of himself that he
said, "Even if I have to die with you, I will
never say that I don't know you!"

All the others said the same thing.

Jesus prays

This is also told in Matthew 26.36–46; Luke 22.39–46

32 Jesus went with his disciples to a place
called Gethsemane, and he told them, "Sit
here while I pray."

33 Jesus took along Peter, James, and John.
He was sad and troubled and 34 told them,
"I am so sad that I feel as if I am dying. Stay
here and keep awake with me."

35–36 Jesus walked on a little way. Then he
knelt down on the ground and prayed,
"Father,* if it is possible, don't let this

happen to me! Father, you can do anything.
Don't make me suffer by making me drink
from this cup.* But do what you want, and
not what I want."

37 When Jesus came back and found the
disciples sleeping, he said to Simon Peter,
"Are you asleep? Can't you stay awake for just
one hour? 38 Stay awake and pray that you
won't be tested. You want to do what is right,
but you are weak."

39 Jesus went back and prayed the same
prayer. 40 But when he returned to the
disciples, he found them sleeping again.
They simply could not keep their eyes open,
and they did not know what to say.

41 When Jesus returned to the disciples the
third time, he said, "Are you still sleeping
and resting? Enough of that! The time has
come for the Son of Man to be handed over
to sinners. 42 Get up! Let's go. The one who
will betray me is already here."

Jesus is arrested

This is also told in Matthew 26.47–56; Luke 22.47–53;
John 18.3–12

43 Jesus was still speaking, when Judas the
betrayer came up. He was one of the twelve
disciples, and a mob of men armed with
swords and clubs were with him. They had
been sent by the chief priests, the nation's
leaders, and the teachers of the Law of Moses.
44 Judas had told them beforehand, "Arrest
the man I greet with a kiss.* Tie him up tight
and lead him away."

45 Judas walked right up to Jesus and said,
"Teacher!" Then Judas kissed him, 46 and the
men grabbed Jesus and arrested him.

47 Someone standing there pulled out a
sword. He struck the servant of the high
priest and cut off his ear.

48 Jesus said to the mob, "Why do you
come with swords and clubs to arrest me like
a criminal? 49 Day after day I was with you
and taught in the temple, but you didn't
arrest me. But what the Scriptures say must
come true."

50 All Jesus' disciples ran off and left him.
51 One of them was a young man who was
wearing only a linen cloth. And when the
men grabbed him, 52 he left the cloth behind
and ran away naked.

*14.35,36 making me drink from this cup: See
the note at 10.38.

*14.44 greet with a kiss: It was the custom for
people to greet each other with a kiss on the cheek.
See also: 14.49: Luke 19.47; 21.37.

See also: 14.24: a Exod 24.8; b Jer 31.31–34.
14.27: Zech 13.7. 14.28: Matt 28.16.

Jesus is questioned by the council

This is also told in Matthew 26.57–68;
Luke 22.54,55,63–71; John 18.13,14,19–24

53 Jesus was led off to the high priest. Then
the chief priests, the nation's leaders, and the
teachers of the Law of Moses all met together.
54 Peter had followed at a distance. And when
he reached the courtyard of the high priest's
house, he sat down with the guards to warm
himself beside a fire.

55 The chief priests and the whole council
tried to find someone to accuse Jesus of a
crime, so they could put him to death. But
they could not find anyone to accuse him.
56 Many people did tell lies against Jesus,
but they did not agree on what they said.
57 Finally, some men stood up and lied about
him. They said, 58 "We heard him say he
would tear down this temple that we built.
He also claimed that in three days he would
build another one without any help." 59 But
even then they did not agree on what they
said.

60 The high priest stood up in the council
and asked Jesus, "Why don't you say
something in your own defence? Don't you
hear the charges they are making against
you?" 61 But Jesus kept quiet and did not say a
word. The high priest asked him another
question, "Are you the Messiah, the Son of
the glorious God?"*

62 "Yes, I am!" Jesus answered.

> "Soon you will see
> the Son of Man
> sitting at the right side*
> of God All-Powerful,
> and coming with the clouds
> of heaven."

63 At once the high priest ripped his robe
apart and shouted, "Why do we need more
witnesses? 64 You heard him claim to be God!
What is your decision?" They all agreed that
he should be put to death.

65 Some of the people started spitting on
Jesus. They blindfolded him, hit him with
their fists, and said, "Tell us who hit you!"
Then the guards took charge of Jesus and
beat him.

Peter says he doesn't know Jesus

This is also told in Matthew 26.69–75; Luke 22.56–62;
John 18.15–18,25–27

66 While Peter was still in the courtyard,
a servant girl of the high priest came up
67 and saw Peter warming himself by the fire.
She stared at him and said, "You were with
Jesus from Nazareth!"

68 Peter replied, "That isn't true! I don't
know what you're talking about. I don't have
any idea what you mean." He went out to the
gate, and a cock crowed.◆

69 The servant girl saw Peter again and said
to the people standing there, "This man is
one of them!"

70 "No, I'm not!" Peter replied.

A little while later some of the people said
to Peter, "You certainly are one of them.
You're a Galilean!"

71 This time Peter began to curse and swear,
"I don't even know the man you're talking
about!"

72 Straight away the cock crowed a second
time. Then Peter remembered that Jesus had
told him, "Before a cock crows twice, you
will say three times that you don't know
me." So Peter started crying.

CHAPTER 15

Pilate questions Jesus

This is also told in Matthew 27.1,2,11–14;
Luke 23.1–5; John 18.28–38

1 Early the next morning the chief priests, the
nation's leaders, and the teachers of the Law
of Moses met together with the whole Jewish
council. They tied up Jesus and led him off to
Pilate.

2 He asked Jesus, "Are you the king of the
Jews?"

"Those are your words," Jesus answered.

3 The chief priests brought many charges
against Jesus. 4 Then Pilate questioned him
again, "Don't you have anything to say?
Don't you hear what crimes they say you
have done?" 5 But Jesus did not answer, and
Pilate was amazed.

The death sentence

This is also told in Matthew 27.15–26; Luke 23.13–25;
John 18.39—19.16

6 During Passover, Pilate always freed one
prisoner chosen by the people. 7 And at
that time there was a prisoner named
Barabbas. He and some others had been
arrested for murder during a riot. 8 The

---

*14.61 Son of the glorious God: "Son of God" was
one of the titles used for the kings of Israel.
*14.62 right side: See the note at 12.36.
See also: 14.58: John 2.19. 14.62: Dan 7.13.
14.64: Lev 24.16.

crowd now came and asked Pilate to set a prisoner free, as he usually did.

⁹ Pilate asked them, "Do you want me to free the king of the Jews?" ¹⁰ Pilate knew that the chief priests had brought Jesus to him because they were jealous.

¹¹ But the chief priests had stirred up the crowd to ask Pilate to free Barabbas.

¹² Then Pilate asked the crowd, "What do you want me to do with this man you say is' king of the Jews?"

¹³ They yelled, "Nail him to a cross!"

¹⁴ Pilate asked, "But what crime has he done?"

"Nail him to a cross!" they yelled even louder.

¹⁵ Pilate wanted to please the crowd. So he set Barabbas free. Then he ordered his soldiers to beat Jesus with a whip and nail him to a cross.

Soldiers make fun of Jesus

This is also told in Matthew 27.27–30; John 19.2,3

¹⁶ The soldiers led Jesus inside the courtyard of the fortress* and called together the rest of the troops. ¹⁷ They put a purple robe* on him, and on his head they placed a crown that they had made out of thorn branches. ¹⁸ They made fun of Jesus and shouted, "Hey, you king of the Jews!" ¹⁹ Then they beat him on the head with a stick. They spat on him and knelt down and pretended to worship him.

²⁰ When the soldiers had finished making fun of Jesus, they took off the purple robe. They put his own clothes back on him and led him off to be nailed to a cross. ²¹ Simon from Cyrene happened to be coming in from a farm, and they forced him to carry Jesus' cross. Simon was the father of Alexander and Rufus.

Jesus is nailed to a cross

This is also told in Matthew 27.31–44; Luke 23.27–43; John 19.17–27

²² The soldiers took Jesus to Golgotha, which means "Place of a Skull."* ²³ There

they gave him some wine mixed with a drug to ease the pain, but he refused to drink it.

²⁴ They nailed Jesus to a cross and gambled to see who would get his clothes. ²⁵ It was about nine o'clock in the morning when they nailed him to the cross. ²⁶ On it was a sign that told why he was nailed there. It read, "This is the King of the Jews." ²⁷⁻²⁸ The soldiers also nailed two criminals on crosses, one to the right of Jesus and the other to his left.'

²⁹ People who passed by said terrible things about Jesus. They shook their heads and shouted, "Ha! So you're the one who claimed you could tear down the temple and build it again in three days. ³⁰ Save yourself and come down from the cross!"

³¹ The chief priests and the teachers of the Law of Moses also made fun of Jesus. They said to each other, "He saved others, but he can't save himself. ³² If he is the Messiah, the king of Israel, let him come down from the cross! Then we will see and believe." The two criminals also said cruel things to Jesus.

The death of Jesus

This is also told in Matthew 27.45–56; Luke 23.44–49; John 19.28–30

³³ About midday the sky turned dark and stayed that way until around three o'clock. ³⁴ Then about that time Jesus shouted, "Eloi, Eloi, lema sabachthani?" * which means, "My God, my God, why have you deserted me?"

³⁵ Some of the people standing there heard Jesus and said, "He is calling for Elijah."*

³⁶ One of them ran and grabbed a sponge. After he had soaked it in wine, he put it on a stick and held it up to Jesus. He said, "Let's wait and see if Elijah will come* and take him down!" ³⁷ Jesus shouted and then died.

³⁸ At once the curtain in the temple* tore in two from top to bottom.

*15.16 fortress: The place where the Roman governor stayed. It was probably at Herod's palace west of Jerusalem, though it may have been Fortress Antonia, north of the temple, where the Roman troops were stationed.
*15.17 purple robe: This was probably a Roman soldier's robe.
*15.22 Place of a Skull: The place was probably given this name because it was near a large rock in the shape of a human skull.
See also: 15.21: Rom 16.13.

*15.34 Eloi . . . sabachthani: These words are in Aramaic, a language spoken in Palestine during the time of Jesus.
*15.35 Elijah: The name "Elijah" sounds something like "Eloi," which means "my God."
*15.36 see if Elijah will come: See the note at 6.15.
*15.38 curtain in the temple: There were two curtains in the temple. One was at the entrance, and the other separated the holy place from the most holy place that the Jewish people thought of as God's home on earth. The second curtain is probably the one which is meant.

See also: 15.24: Psa 22.18. 15.28: Isa 53.12. 15.29: a Psa 22.7; 109.25; b Mark 14.58; John 2.19. 15.34: Psa 22.1. 15.36: Psa 69.21. 15.38: Exod 26.31–33.

[39] A Roman army officer was standing in front of Jesus. When the officer saw how Jesus died, he said, "This man really was the Son of God!"

[40-41] Some women were looking on from a distance. They had come with Jesus to Jerusalem. But even before this they had been his followers and had helped him while he was in Galilee. Mary Magdalene and Mary the mother of the younger James and of Joseph were two of these women. Salome was also one of them.

Jesus is buried

This is also told in Matthew 27.57–61; Luke 23.50–56; John 19.38–42

[42] It was now the evening before the Sabbath, and the Jewish people were getting ready for that sacred day. [43] A man named Joseph from Arimathea was brave enough to ask Pilate for the body of Jesus. Joseph was a highly respected member of the Jewish council, and he was also waiting for God's kingdom to come.

[44] Pilate was surprised to hear that Jesus was already dead, and he called in the army officer to find out if Jesus had been dead very long. [45] After the officer told him, Pilate let Joseph have Jesus' body.

[46] Joseph bought a linen cloth and took the body down from the cross. He had it wrapped in the cloth, and he put it in a tomb that had been cut into solid rock. Then he rolled a big stone against the entrance to the tomb. [47] Mary Magdalene and Mary the mother of Joseph were watching and saw where the body was placed.

Jesus is alive

CHAPTER 16

This is also told in Matthew 28.1–8; Luke 24.1–12; John 20.1–10

[1] After the Sabbath, Mary Magdalene, Salome, and Mary the mother of James bought some spices to put on Jesus' body. [2] Very early on Sunday morning, just as the sun was coming up, they went to the tomb. [3] On their way, they were asking one another, "Who will roll the stone away from the entrance for us?" [4] But when they looked, they saw that the stone had already been rolled away. And it was a huge stone!

[5] The women went into the tomb, and on the right side they saw a young man in a white robe sitting there. They were alarmed. [6] The man said, "Don't be alarmed! You are looking for Jesus from Nazareth, who was nailed to a cross. God has raised him to life, and he isn't here. You can see the place where they put his body. [7] Now go and tell his disciples, and especially Peter, that he will go ahead of you to Galilee. You will see him there, just as he told you."

[8] When the women ran from the tomb, they were confused and shaking all over. They were too afraid to tell anyone what had happened.

Jesus appears to his followers

ONE OLD ENDING TO MARK'S GOSPEL[1]

Jesus appears to Mary Magdalene

This is also told in Matthew 28.9,10; John 20.11–18

[9] Very early on the first day of the week, after Jesus had risen to life, he appeared to Mary Magdalene. Earlier he had forced seven demons out of her. [10] She left and told his friends, who were crying and mourning. [11] Even though they heard that Jesus was alive and that Mary had seen him, they would not believe it.

Jesus appears to two disciples

This is also told in Luke 24.13–35

[12] Later, Jesus appeared in another form to two disciples, as they were on their way out of the city. [13] But when these disciples told what had happened, the others would not believe.

What Jesus' followers must do

This is also told in Matthew 28.16–20; Luke 24.36–49; John 20.19–23; Acts 1.6-8

[14] Afterwards, Jesus appeared to his eleven disciples as they were eating. He scolded them because they were too stubborn to believe the ones who had seen him after he had been raised to life. [15] Then he told them:

> Go and preach the good news to everyone in the world. [16] Anyone who believes me and is baptized will be saved. But anyone who refuses to believe me will be condemned. [17] Everyone who believes me will be able to do wonderful things. By using my name they will force out demons,

See also: 15.40,41: Luke 8.2,3.   See also: 16.7: Matt 26.32; Mark 14.28.   16.15: Acts 1.8.

67

and they will speak new languages. ¹⁸ They will handle snakes and will drink poison and not be hurt. They will also heal sick people by placing their hands on them.

Jesus returns to heaven

This is also told in Luke 24.50–53; Acts 1.9–11

¹⁹ After the Lord Jesus had said these things to the disciples, he was taken back up to heaven where he sat down at the right side* of God. ²⁰ Then the disciples left and preached everywhere. The Lord was with them, and the miracles they performed proved that their message was true.

ANOTHER OLD ENDING TO MARK'S GOSPEL⁹

⁹⁻¹⁰ The women quickly told Peter and his friends what had happened. Later, Jesus sent the disciples to the east and to the west with his sacred and everlasting message of how people can be saved for ever.

*16.19 right side: See the note at 12.36.
See also: 16.19: Acts 1.9–11.

Additional notes

'1.1 the Son of God: These words are not in some manuscripts.
'1.14 that comes from God: Or "that is about God".
'1.15 will soon be here: Or "is already here".
'1.40 and knelt down: These words are not in some manuscripts.
'1.41 felt sorry for: Some manuscripts have "was angry with".
'2.1 at home: Or "in the house" (perhaps Simon Peter's home).
'2.15 Levi's house: Or "Jesus' house".
'3.14 to be his apostles: These words are not in some manuscripts.
'3.20 went back home: Or "entered a house" (perhaps the home of Simon Peter).
'3.32 and sisters: These words are not in some manuscripts.
'5.1 Gerasa: Some manuscripts have "Gadara", and others have "Gergesa".
'5.36 heard: Or "ignored".
'6.3 carpenter: The Greek word may also mean someone who builds or works with stone or brick.
'6.20 was confused by what John said: Some manuscripts have "did many things because of what John said".
'6.22 Herodias: Some manuscripts have "Herod".

'7.3 in the proper way: The Greek text has "with the fist", but the exact meaning is not clear. It could mean "to the wrist" or "to the elbow".
'7.4 bowls: Some manuscripts add "and sleeping mats".
'7.15,16 unclean: Some manuscripts add, "If you have ears, pay attention."
'8.35 life: In verses 35–37 the same Greek word is translated "life", "yourself", and "soul".
'9.43,44 never go out: Some manuscripts add, "The worms there never die, and the fire never stops burning."
'9.45,46 thrown into hell: See the note at 9.43,44.
'10.14 People who are like these little children belong to the kingdom of God: Or "The kingdom of God belongs to people who are like these little children."
'10.24 hard: Some manuscripts add "for people who trust in their wealth". Others add "for the rich".
'10.51 Master: A Hebrew word that may also mean "Teacher".
'11.3 The Lord: Or "The master of the donkey".
'11.25,26 your sins: Some manuscripts add, "But if you do not forgive others, God will not forgive you."
'13.29 the time has almost come: Or "he (that is, the Son of Man) will soon be here."
'14.3 sweet-smelling perfume: The Greek text has "perfume made of pure spikenard", a plant used to make perfume.
'14.35,36 Father: The Greek text has "Abba", which is an Aramaic word meaning "father".
'14.41 Are you still sleeping and resting?: Or "You may as well keep on sleeping and resting."
'14.68 a cock crowed: These words are not in some manuscripts.
'15.12 this man you say is: These words are not in some manuscripts.
'15.27–28 left: Some manuscripts add, "So the Scriptures came true which say, 'He was accused of being a criminal.' "
'16.9 One old ending to Mark's Gospel: Verses 9–20 are not in some manuscripts.
'16.9,10 Another old ending to Mark's Gospel: Some manuscripts and early translations have both this shorter ending and the longer one (verses 9–20).

Luke

tells the good news

A quick look at this book

God's love is for everyone! Jesus came into the world to be the Saviour of all people! These are two of the main thoughts in this book. Two of the best known stories that Jesus used for teaching about God's love are found only in Luke's Gospel: The Good Samaritan (10.25–37) and A Lost Son (15.11–32). Only Luke tells how Jesus stayed in the home of a hated tax collector (19.1–10) and promised life in paradise to a dying criminal (23.39–43).

Luke mentions God's Spirit more than any of the other New Testament writers. For example, the power of the Spirit was with John the Baptist from the time he was born (1.15). And the angel promised Mary, "The Holy Spirit will come down to you . . . So your child will be called the holy Son of God" (1.35). Jesus followed the Spirit (4.1,14,18; 10.21) and taught that the Spirit is God's greatest gift (11.13).

Luke shows how important prayer was to Jesus. Jesus prayed often: after being baptized (3.21), before choosing the disciples (6.12), before asking his disciples who they thought he was (9.18), and before giving up his life on the cross (23.34,46). From Luke we learn of three stories that Jesus told to teach about prayer (11.5–9; 18.1–8,9–14).

An important part of Luke's story is the way in which he shows the concern of Jesus for the poor: the good news is preached to them (4.18; 7.22), they receive God's blessings (6.20), they are invited to the great feast (14.13,21), the poor man Lazarus is taken to heaven by angels (16.20,22), and Jesus commands his disciples to sell what they have and give the money to the poor (12.33).

To make sure that readers would understand that Jesus was raised physically from death, Luke reports that the risen Jesus ate a piece of fish (24.42,43). There could be no mistake about the risen Jesus: he was not a ghost. His being raised from death was real and not someone's imagination. Luke also wrote another book — the Acts of the Apostles — to show what happened to Jesus' followers after he was raised from death and taken up to heaven. No other Gospel has a second volume that continues the story.

Luke closes this first book that he wrote by telling that Jesus returned to heaven. But just before Jesus leaves, he tells his disciples:

The Scriptures say that the Messiah must suffer, then three days later he will rise from death. They also say that all people of every nation must be told in my name to turn to God, in order to be forgiven. So beginning in Jerusalem, you must tell everything that has happened.

(24.46–48)

Why Luke wrote this book

CHAPTER 1

¹ Many people have tried to tell the story of what God has done among us. ² They wrote what we had been told by the ones who were there in the beginning and saw what happened. ³ So I made a careful study* of everything and then decided to write and tell you exactly what took place. Honourable Theophilus,* ⁴ I have done this to let you know the truth about what you have heard.

The births of John the Baptist and Jesus

An angel tells about the birth of John

⁵ When Herod was king of Judea, there was a priest called Zechariah from the priestly group of Abijah. His wife Elizabeth was from the family of Aaron.* ⁶ Both of them were good people and pleased the Lord God by obeying all that he had commanded. ⁷ But they did not have children. Elizabeth could not have any, and both Zechariah and Elizabeth were already old.

⁸ One day Zechariah's group of priests were on duty, and he was serving God as a priest. ⁹ According to the custom of the priests, he had been chosen to go into the Lord's temple that day and to burn incense,* ¹⁰ while the people stood outside praying.

¹¹ All at once an angel from the Lord appeared to Zechariah at the right side of the altar. ¹² Zechariah was confused and afraid when he saw the angel. ¹³ But the angel told him:

Don't be afraid, Zechariah! God has heard your prayers. Your wife Elizabeth will have a son, and you must name him John. ¹⁴ His birth will make you very happy, and many people will be glad. ¹⁵ Your son will be a great servant of the Lord. He must never drink wine or beer, and the power of the Holy Spirit will be with him from the time he is born.

¹⁶ John will lead many people in Israel to turn back to the Lord their God. ¹⁷ He will go ahead of the Lord with the same power and spirit that Elijah* had. And because of John, parents will be more thoughtful of their children. And people who now disobey God will begin to think as they ought to. That is how John will get people ready for the Lord.

¹⁸ Zechariah said to the angel, "How will I know this is going to happen? My wife and I are both very old."

¹⁹ The angel answered, "I am Gabriel, God's servant, and I was sent to tell you this good news. ²⁰ You have not believed what I have said. So you will not be able to say a thing until all this happens. But everything will take place when it is supposed to."

²¹ The crowd was waiting for Zechariah and kept wondering why he was staying so long in the temple. ²² When he did come out, he could not speak, and they knew he had seen a vision. He motioned to them with his hands, but did not say a thing.

²³ When Zechariah's time of service in the temple was over, he went home. ²⁴ Soon after that, his wife was expecting a baby, and for five months she did not leave the house. She said to herself, ²⁵ "What the Lord has done for me will keep people from looking down on me."*

An angel tells about the birth of Jesus

²⁶ One month later God sent the angel Gabriel to the town of Nazareth in Galilee ²⁷ with a message for a virgin named Mary. She was engaged to Joseph from the family of King David. ²⁸ The angel greeted Mary and said, "You are truly blessed! The Lord is with you."

---

*1.3 Honourable Theophilus: Luke dedicated his Gospel and the Acts of the Apostles to this man, probably a high Roman official.
*1.5 Aaron: The brother of Moses and the first priest.
*1.9 burn incense: This was done twice a day, once in the morning and again in the late afternoon.
See also: 1.5: 1 Chron 24.10.

*1.17 Elijah: The prophet Elijah was known for his power to perform miracles.
*1.25 keep people from looking down on me: When a married woman could not have children, it was thought that the Lord was punishing her.
See also: 1.15: Num 6.3. 1.17: Mal 4.5,6. 1.19: Dan 8.16; 9.21. 1.27: Matt 1.18.

29 Mary was confused by the angel's words and wondered what they meant. 30 Then the angel told Mary, "Don't be afraid! God is pleased with you, 31 and you will have a son. His name will be Jesus. 32 He will be great and will be called the Son of God Most High. The Lord God will make him king, as his ancestor David was. 33 He will rule the people of Israel for ever, and his kingdom will never end."

34 Mary asked the angel, "How can this happen? I am not married!"

35 The angel answered, "The Holy Spirit will come down to you, and God's power will come over you. So your child will be called the holy Son of God. 36 Your relative Elizabeth is also going to have a son, even though she is old. No one thought she could ever have a baby, but in three months she will have a son. 37 Nothing is impossible for God!"

38 Mary said, "I am the Lord's servant! Let it happen as you have said." And the angel left her.

Mary visits Elizabeth

39 A short time later Mary hurried to a town in the hill country of Judea. 40 She went into Zechariah's home, where she greeted Elizabeth. 41 When Elizabeth heard Mary's greeting, her baby moved within her.

The Holy Spirit came upon Elizabeth. 42 Then in a loud voice she said to Mary:

God has blessed you more than any other woman! He has also blessed the child you will have. 43 Why should the mother of my Lord come to me? 44 As soon as I heard your greeting, my baby became happy and moved within me. 45 The Lord has blessed you because you believed that he will keep his promise.

Mary's song of praise

46 Mary said:

With all my heart
    I praise the Lord,
47 and I am glad
    because of God my Saviour.
48 He cares for me,
    his humble servant.
From now on,
all people will say
    God has blessed me.

49 God All-Powerful has done
    great things for me,
    and his name is holy.
50 He always shows mercy
    to everyone
    who worships him.
51 The Lord has used
    his powerful arm
    to scatter those
    who are proud.
52 He drags strong rulers
    from their thrones
    and puts humble people
    in places of power.
53 God gives the hungry
    good things to eat,
    and sends the rich away
    with nothing.
54 He helps his servant Israel
    and is always merciful
    to his people.
55 The Lord made this promise
    to our ancestors,
    to Abraham and his family
    for ever!

56 Mary stayed with Elizabeth about three months. Then she went back home.

The birth of John the Baptist

57 When Elizabeth's son was born, 58 her neighbours and relatives heard how kind the Lord had been to her, and they too were glad.

59 Eight days later they did for the child what the Law of Moses commands.* They were going to name him Zechariah, after his father. 60 But Elizabeth said, "No! His name is John."

61 The people argued, "No one in your family has ever been named John." 62 So they motioned to Zechariah to find out what he wanted to name his son.

63 Zechariah asked for a writing tablet. Then he wrote, "His name is John." Everyone was amazed. 64 Straight away Zechariah started speaking and praising God.

65 All the neighbours were frightened because of what had happened, and everywhere in the hill country people kept talking about these things. 66 Everyone who heard about this wondered what this

---

*1.59 what the Law of Moses commands: This refers to circumcision. It is the custom of cutting off skin from the private part of Jewish boys eight days after birth to show that they belong to the Lord.

See also: 1.52: Job 5.11; 12.19. **1.55:** Gen 17.7.
1.59: Lev 12.3.

See also: 1.31: Matt 1.21. **1.32,33:** 2 Sam 7.12,13,16;
Isa 9.7. **1.37:** Gen 18.14. **1.46–55:** 1 Sam 2.1–10.
1.48: 1 Sam 1.11.

71

child would grow up to be. They knew
that the Lord was with him.

Zechariah praises the Lord

⁶⁷ The Holy Spirit came upon Zechariah, and
he began to speak:

⁶⁸ Praise the Lord,
  the God of Israel!
He has come
  to save his people.
⁶⁹ Our God has given us
  a mighty Saviour*
from the family
  of David his servant.
⁷⁰ Long ago the Lord promised
  by the words
  of his holy prophets
⁷¹ to save us from our enemies
  and from everyone
  who hates us.
⁷² God said he would be kind
  to our people and keep
  his sacred promise.
⁷³ He told our ancestor Abraham
⁷⁴ that he would rescue us
  from our enemies.
Then we could serve him
  without fear,
⁷⁵ by being holy and good
  as long as we live.

⁷⁶ You, my son, will be called
  a prophet of God
  in heaven above.
You will go ahead of the Lord
  to get everything ready
  for him.
⁷⁷ You will tell his people
  that they can be saved
  when their sins
  are forgiven.
⁷⁸ God's love and kindness
  will shine upon us
like the sun that rises
  in the sky.*
⁷⁹ On us who live
  in the dark shadow
  of death
this light will shine
  to guide us
  into a life of peace.

⁸⁰ As John grew up, God's Spirit gave him
great power. John lived in the desert until
the time he was sent to the people of Israel.

CHAPTER 2

The birth of Jesus

This is also told in Matthew 1.18-25

¹ About that time Emperor Augustus gave
orders for the names of all the people to be
listed in record books.* ² These first records
were made when Quirinius was governor of
Syria.*

³ Everyone had to go to their own home
town to be listed. ⁴ So Joseph had to leave
Nazareth in Galilee and go to Bethlehem in
Judea. Long ago Bethlehem had been King
David's home town, and Joseph went there
because he was from David's family.

⁵ Mary was engaged to Joseph and travelled
with him to Bethlehem. She was soon going
to have a baby, ⁶ and while they were there,
⁷ she gave birth to her firstborn* son. She
dressed him in baby clothes* and laid him on
a bed of hay, because there was no room for
them in the inn.

The shepherds

⁸ That night in the fields near Bethlehem
some shepherds were guarding their sheep.
⁹ All at once an angel came down to them
from the Lord, and the brightness of the
Lord's glory flashed around them. The
shepherds were frightened. ¹⁰ But the angel
said, "Don't be afraid! I have good news for
you, which will make everyone happy. ¹¹ This
very day in King David's home town a
Saviour was born for you. He is Christ the
Lord. ¹² You will know who he is, because
you will find him dressed in baby clothes*
and lying on a bed of hay."

---

*1.69 a mighty Saviour: The Greek text has "a horn
of salvation". In the Scriptures animal horns are often
a symbol of great strength.
See also: 1.76: Mal 3.1. 1.79: Isa 9.2.

*2.1 names . . . listed in record books: This was
done so that everyone could be made to pay taxes to
the Emperor.
*2.2 Quirinius was governor of Syria: It is known
that Quirinius made a record of the people in AD 6 or
7. But the exact date of the record taking that Luke
mentions is not known.
*2.7 firstborn: The Jewish people said that the
firstborn son in each of their families belonged to the
Lord.
*2.7,12 dressed him in baby clothes: The Greek text
has "wrapped him in wide strips of cloth", which was
how young babies were dressed.

¹³ Suddenly many other angels came down from heaven and joined in praising God. They said:

¹⁴ "Praise God in heaven!
   Peace on earth to everyone
      who pleases God."

¹⁵ After the angels had left and gone back to heaven, the shepherds said to each other, "Let's go to Bethlehem and see what the Lord has told us about." ¹⁶ They hurried off and found Mary and Joseph, and they saw the baby lying on a bed of hay.

¹⁷ When the shepherds saw Jesus, they told his parents what the angel had said about him. ¹⁸ Everyone listened and was surprised. ¹⁹ But Mary kept thinking about all this and wondering what it meant.

²⁰ As the shepherds returned to their sheep, they were praising God and saying wonderful things about him. Everything they had seen and heard was just as the angel had said.

²¹ Eight days later Jesus' parents did for him what the Law of Moses commands.* And they named him Jesus, just as the angel had told Mary when he promised she would have a baby.

Simeon praises the Lord

²² The time came for Mary and Joseph to do what the Law of Moses says a mother is supposed to do after her baby is born.*

They took Jesus to the temple in Jerusalem and presented him to the Lord, ²³ just as the Law of the Lord says, "Each firstborn* baby boy belongs to the Lord." ²⁴ The Law of the Lord also says that parents have to offer a sacrifice, giving at least a pair of doves or two young pigeons. So that is what Mary and Joseph did.

²⁵ At this time a man named Simeon was living in Jerusalem. Simeon was a good man. He loved God and was waiting for God to save the people of Israel. God's Spirit came to him ²⁶ and told him that he would not die until he had seen Christ the Lord.

²⁷ When Mary and Joseph brought Jesus to the temple to do what the Law of Moses says should be done for a new baby, the Spirit told Simeon to go into the temple. ²⁸ Simeon took the baby Jesus in his arms and praised God,

²⁹ "Lord, I am your servant,
   and now I can die in peace,
   because you have kept
      your promise to me.
³⁰ With my own eyes I have seen
   what you have done
      to save your people,
³¹ and foreign nations
   will also see this.
³² Your mighty power is a light
   for all nations,
   and it will bring honour
      to your people Israel."

³³ Jesus' parents were surprised at what Simeon had said. ³⁴ Then he blessed them and told Mary, "This child of yours will cause many people in Israel to fall and others to stand. The child will be like a warning sign. Many people will reject him, ³⁵ and you, Mary, will suffer as though you had been stabbed by a dagger. But all this will show what people are really thinking."

Anna speaks about the child Jesus

³⁶ The prophet Anna was also there in the temple. She was the daughter of Phanuel from the tribe of Asher, and she was very old. In her youth she had been married for seven years, but her husband had died. ³⁷ And now she was eighty-four years old.* Night and day she served God in the temple by praying and often going without eating.*

³⁸ At that time Anna came in and praised God. She spoke about the child Jesus to everyone who hoped for Jerusalem to be set free.

The return to Nazareth

³⁹ After Joseph and Mary had done everything that the Law of God commands, they returned home to Nazareth in Galilee. ⁴⁰ The child Jesus grew. He became strong and wise, and God blessed him.

*2.21 what the Law of Moses commands: See the note at 1.59.
*2.22 after her baby is born: After a Jewish mother gave birth to a son, she was considered "unclean" and had to stay at home until he was circumcised (see the note at 1.59). Then she had to stay at home for another 33 days, before offering a sacrifice to the Lord.
*2.23 firstborn: See the note at 2.7.
See also: 2.21: a Lev 12.3; b Luke 1.31. 2.22–24: Lev 12.6–8. 2.23: Exod 13.2,12.

*2.37 without eating: The Jewish people sometimes went without eating (also called "fasting") to show their love for God or to show sorrow for their sins.
See also: 2.32: Isa 42.6; 49.6; 52.10. 2.39: Matt 2.23.

The boy Jesus in the temple

⁴¹ Every year Jesus' parents went to Jerusalem for Passover. ⁴² And when Jesus was twelve years old, they all went there as usual for the celebration. ⁴³ After Passover his parents left, but they did not know that Jesus had stayed on in the city. ⁴⁴ They thought he was travelling with some other people, and they went a whole day before they started looking for him. ⁴⁵ When they could not find him with their relatives and friends, they went back to Jerusalem and started looking for him there.

⁴⁶ Three days later they found him sitting in the temple, listening to the teachers and asking them questions. ⁴⁷ Everyone who heard him was surprised at how much he knew and at the answers he gave.

⁴⁸ When his parents found him, they were amazed. His mother said, "Son, why have you done this to us? Your father and I have been very worried, and we have been searching for you!"

⁴⁹ Jesus answered, "Why did you have to look for me? Didn't you know that I would be in my Father's house?" ⁵⁰ But they did not understand what he meant.

⁵¹ Jesus went back to Nazareth with his parents and obeyed them. His mother kept on thinking about all that had happened.

⁵² Jesus became wise, and he grew strong. God was pleased with him and so were the people.

The message of John the Baptist

CHAPTER 3

The preaching of John the Baptist

This is also told in Matthew 3.1-12; Mark 1.1-8; John 1.19-28

¹ For fifteen years* Emperor Tiberius had ruled that part of the world. Pontius Pilate was governor of Judea, and Herod* was the ruler of Galilee. Herod's brother, Philip, was the ruler in the countries of Iturea and Trachonitis, and Lysanias was the ruler of

Abilene. ² Annas and Caiaphas were the Jewish high priests.*

At that time God spoke to Zechariah's son John, who was living in the desert. ³ So John went along the Jordan Valley, telling the people, "Turn back to God and be baptized! Then your sins will be forgiven." ⁴ Isaiah the prophet wrote about John when he said,

"In the desert
    someone is shouting,
'Get the road ready
    for the Lord!
Make a straight path
    for him.
⁵ Fill up every valley
    and level every mountain
        and hill.
Straighten the crooked paths
    and smooth out
        the rough roads.
⁶ Then everyone will see
    the saving power of God.' "

⁷ Crowds of people came out to be baptized, but John said to them, "You snakes! Who warned you to run from the coming judgment? ⁸ Do something to show that you really have given up your sins. Don't start saying that you belong to Abraham's family. God can turn these stones into children for Abraham.* ⁹ An axe is ready to cut the trees down at their roots. Any tree that doesn't produce good fruit will be cut down and thrown into a fire."

¹⁰ The crowds asked John, "What should we do?"

¹¹ John told them, "If you have two coats, give one to someone who doesn't have any. If you have food, share it with someone else."

¹² When tax collectors* came to be baptized, they asked John, "Teacher, what should we do?"

¹³ John told them, "Don't make people pay more than they owe."

---

*3.1 For fifteen years: This was either AD 28 or 29, and Jesus was about thirty years old (see 3.23).
*3.1 Herod: Herod Antipas, the son of Herod the Great.

See also: 2.41: Exod 12.1–27; Deut 16.1–8. 2.52: 1 Sam 2.26; Prov 3.4.

*3.2 Annas and Caiaphas . . . high priests: Annas was high priest from AD 6 until 15. His son-in-law Caiaphas was high priest from AD 18 until 37.
*3.8 children for Abraham: The Jewish people thought they were God's chosen people because of God's promises to their ancestor Abraham.
*3.12 tax collectors: These were usually Jewish people who paid the Romans for the right to collect taxes. They were hated by other Jews who thought of them as traitors to their country and to their religion.

See also: 3.4–6: Isa 40.3–5 (LXX). 3.7: Matt 12.34; 23.33. 3.8: John 8.33. 3.9: Matt 7.19. 3.12: Luke 7.29.

14 Some soldiers asked him, "And what about us? What do we have to do?"

John told them, "Don't force people to pay money to make you leave them alone. Be satisfied with your pay."

15 Everyone became excited and wondered, "Could John be the Messiah?"

16 John said, "I am just baptizing with water. But someone more powerful is going to come, and I am not good enough even to untie his sandals.* He will baptize you with the Holy Spirit and with fire. 17 His threshing fork* is in his hand, and he is ready to separate the wheat from the husks. He will store the wheat in his barn and burn the husks with a fire that never goes out."

18 In many different ways John preached the good news to the people. 19 But to Herod the ruler, he said, "It was wrong for you to take Herodias, your brother's wife." John also said that Herod had done many other bad things. 20 Finally, Herod put John in jail, and this was the worst thing he had done.

The baptism and temptation of Jesus

The baptism of Jesus

This is also told in Matthew 3.13–17; Mark 1.9–11

21 While everyone else was being baptized, Jesus himself was baptized. Then as he prayed, the sky opened up, 22 and the Holy Spirit came down upon him in the form of a dove. A voice from heaven said, "You are my own dear Son, and I am pleased with you."

The ancestors of Jesus

This is also told in Matthew 1.1–17

23 When Jesus began to preach, he was about thirty years old. Everyone thought he was the son of Joseph. But his family went back through Heli, 24 Matthat, Levi, Melchi, Jannai, Joseph, 25 Mattathias, Amos, Nahum, Esli, Naggai, 26 Maath, Mattathias, Semein, Josech, Joda;

27 Joanan, Rhesa, Zerubbabel, Shealtiel, Neri, 28 Melchi, Addi, Cosam, Elmadam, Er, 29 Joshua, Eliezer, Jorim, Matthat, Levi;

30 Simeon, Judah, Joseph, Jonam, Eliakim, 31 Melea, Menna, Mattatha, Nathan, David, 32 Jesse, Obed, Boaz, Salmon, Nahshon;

33 Amminadab, Admin, Arni, Hezron, Perez, Judah, 34 Jacob, Isaac, Abraham, Terah, Nahor, 35 Serug, Reu, Peleg, Eber, Shelah;

36 Cainan, Arphaxad, Shem, Noah, Lamech, 37 Methuselah, Enoch, Jared, Mahalaleel, Kenan, 38 Enosh, and Seth.

The family of Jesus went all the way back to Adam and then to God.

CHAPTER 4

Jesus and the devil

This is also told in Matthew 4.1–11; Mark 1.12,13

1 When Jesus returned from the River Jordan, the power of the Holy Spirit was with him, and the Spirit led him into the desert. 2 For forty days Jesus was tested by the devil, and during that time he went without eating.* When it was all over, he was hungry.

3 The devil said to Jesus, "If you are God's Son, tell this stone to turn into bread."

4 Jesus answered, "The Scriptures say, 'No one can live only on bread.' "

5 Then the devil led Jesus up to a high place and quickly showed him all the nations on earth. 6 The devil said, "I will give all this power and glory to you. It has been given to me, and I can give it to anyone I want to. 7 Just worship me, and you can have it all."

8 Jesus answered, "The Scriptures say:

'Worship the Lord your God
    and serve only him!' "

9 Finally, the devil took Jesus to Jerusalem and had him stand on top of the temple. The devil said, "If you are God's Son, jump off. 10-11 The Scriptures say:

'God will tell his angels
    to take care of you.
They will catch you
    in their arms,
and you will not hurt
    your feet on the stones.' "

12 Jesus answered, "The Scriptures also say, 'Don't try to test the Lord your God!' "

---

*3.16 untie his sandals:** This was the duty of a slave.
*3.17 threshing fork:** After Jewish farmers had trampled out the grain, they used a large fork to pitch the grain and the husks into the air. Wind would blow away the light husks, and the grain would fall back to the ground, where it could be gathered up.
See also: 3.19,20: Matt 14.3,4; Mark 6.17,18. 3.22: Gen 22.2; Psa 2.7; Isa 42.1; Matt 3.17; Mark 1.11; Luke 9.35.

*4.2 went without eating:** See the note at 2.37.
See also: 4.4: Deut 8.3. 4.8: Deut 6.13. 4.10,11: Psa 91.11,12. 4.12: Deut 6.16.

¹³ After the devil had finished testing Jesus in every way possible, he left him for a while.

Jesus' ministry in Galilee

Jesus begins his work

This is also told in Matthew 4.12–17; Mark 1.14,15

¹⁴ Jesus returned to Galilee with the power of the Spirit. News about him spread everywhere. ¹⁵ He taught in the Jewish meeting places, and everyone praised him.

The people of Nazareth turn against Jesus

This is also told in Matthew 13.53–58; Mark 6.1–6

¹⁶ Jesus went back to Nazareth, where he had been brought up, and as usual he went to the meeting place on the Sabbath. When he stood up to read from the Scriptures, ¹⁷ he was given the book of Isaiah the prophet. He opened it and read,

> ¹⁸ "The Lord's Spirit
> has come to me,
> because he has chosen me
> to tell the good news
> to the poor.
> The Lord has sent me
> to announce freedom
> for prisoners,
> to give sight to the blind,
> to free everyone
> who suffers,
> ¹⁹ and to say, 'This is the year
> the Lord has chosen.' "

²⁰ Jesus closed the book, then handed it back to the man in charge and sat down. Everyone in the meeting place looked straight at Jesus. ²¹ Then Jesus said to them, "What you have just heard me read has come true today."

²² All the people started talking about Jesus and were amazed at the wonderful things he said. They kept on asking, "Isn't he Joseph's son?"

²³ Jesus answered:

You will certainly want to tell me this saying, "Doctor, first make yourself well." You will tell me to do the same things here in my own home town that you heard I did in Capernaum. ²⁴ But you can be sure that no prophets are liked by the people of their own home town.

²⁵ Once during the time of Elijah there was no rain for three and a half years, and people everywhere were starving. There were many widows in Israel, ²⁶ but Elijah was sent only to a widow in the town of Zarephath near the city of Sidon. ²⁷ During the time of the prophet Elisha, many men in Israel had leprosy.* But no one was healed, except Naaman who lived in Syria.

²⁸ When the people in the meeting place heard Jesus say this, they became so angry ²⁹ that they got up and threw him out of town. They dragged him to the edge of the cliff on which the town was built, because they wanted to throw him down from there. ³⁰ But Jesus slipped through the crowd and got away.

A man with an evil spirit

This is also told in Mark 1.21–28

³¹ Jesus went to the town of Capernaum in Galilee and taught the people on the Sabbath. ³² His teaching amazed them because he spoke with power. ³³ There in the Jewish meeting place was a man with an evil spirit. He yelled out, ³⁴ "Hey, Jesus of Nazareth, what do you want with us? Are you here to get rid of us? I know who you are! You are God's Holy One."

³⁵ Jesus ordered the evil spirit to be quiet and come out. The demon threw the man to the ground in front of everyone and left without harming him.

³⁶ They all were amazed and kept saying to each other, "What kind of teaching is this? He has power to order evil spirits out of people!" ³⁷ News about Jesus spread all over that part of the country.

Jesus heals many people

This is also told in Matthew 8.14–17; Mark 1.29–34

³⁸ Jesus left the meeting place and went to Simon's home. When Jesus got there, he was told that Simon's mother-in-law was sick with a high fever. ³⁹ So Jesus went over to her and ordered the fever to go away. At once she was able to get up and serve them a meal.

⁴⁰ After the sun had set, people with all kinds of diseases were brought to Jesus. He put his hands on each one of them and

---

4.27 leprosy: In biblical times the word "leprosy" was used for many different kinds of skin diseases.

See also: 4.25: 1 King 17.1. 4.26: 1 King 17.8–16. 4.27: 2 King 5.1–14. 4.32: Matt 7.28,29.

See also: 4.18,19: Isa 61.1,2 (LXX). 4.24: John 4.44.

healed them. ⁴¹ Demons went out of many people and shouted, "You are the Son of God!" But Jesus ordered the demons not to speak because they knew he was the Messiah.

⁴² The next morning Jesus went out to a place where he could be alone, and crowds came looking for him. When they found him, they tried to stop him from leaving. ⁴³ But Jesus said, "People in other towns must hear the good news about God's kingdom. That's why I was sent." ⁴⁴ So he kept on preaching in the Jewish meeting places in Judea.ᵇ

CHAPTER 5

Jesus chooses his first disciples

This is also told in Matthew 4.18–22; Mark 1.16–20

¹ Jesus was standing on the shore of Lake Gennesaret,* teaching the people as they crowded around him to hear God's message. ² Near the shore he saw two boats left there by some fishermen who had gone to wash their nets. ³ Jesus got into the boat that belonged to Simon and asked him to row it out a little way from the shore. Then Jesus sat down* in the boat to teach the crowd.

⁴ When Jesus had finished speaking, he told Simon, "Row the boat out into the deep water and let your nets down to catch some fish."

⁵ "Master," Simon answered, "we have worked hard all night long and have not caught a thing. But if you tell me to, I will let the nets down." ⁶ They did it and caught so many fish that their nets began ripping apart. ⁷ Then they signalled for their partners in the other boat to come and help them. The men came, and together they filled the two boats so full that they both began to sink.

⁸ When Simon Peter saw this happen, he knelt down in front of Jesus and said, "Lord, don't come near me! I am a sinner." ⁹ Peter and everyone with him were completely surprised at all the fish they had caught. ¹⁰ His partners James and John, the sons of Zebedee, were surprised too.

Jesus told Simon, "Don't be afraid! From now on you will bring in people instead of

fish." ¹¹ The men pulled their boats up on the shore. Then they left everything and went with Jesus.

Jesus heals a man

This is also told in Matthew 8.1–4; Mark 1.40–45

¹² Jesus came to a town where there was a man who had leprosy.* When the man saw Jesus, he knelt down on the ground in front of Jesus and begged, "Lord, you have the power to make me well, if only you wanted to."

¹³ Jesus put his hand on him and said, "I want to! Now you are well." At once the man's leprosy disappeared. ¹⁴ Jesus told him, "Don't tell anyone about this, but go and show yourself to the priest. Offer a gift to the priest, just as Moses commanded, and everyone will know that you have been healed."*

¹⁵ News about Jesus kept spreading. Large crowds came to listen to him teach and to be healed of their diseases. ¹⁶ But Jesus would often go to some place where he could be alone and pray.

Jesus heals a crippled man

This is also told in Matthew 9.1–8; Mark 2.1–12

¹⁷ One day some Pharisees and experts in the Law of Moses sat listening to Jesus teach. They had come from every village in Galilee and Judea and from Jerusalem.

God had given Jesus the power to heal the sick, ¹⁸ and some people came carrying a crippled man on a mat. They tried to take him inside the house and put him in front of Jesus. ¹⁹ But because of the crowd, they could not get him to Jesus. So they went up on the roof,* where they removed some tiles and let the mat down in the middle of the room.

---

*5.12 leprosy: See the note at 4.27.
*5.14 everyone will know that you have been healed: People with leprosy had to be examined by a priest and told that they were well (that is, "clean") before they could once again live a normal life in the Jewish community. The gift that Moses commanded was the sacrifice of some lambs together with flour mixed with olive oil.
*5.19 roof: In Palestine the houses usually had a flat roof. Stairs on the outside led up to the roof, which was made of beams and boards covered with packed earth. Luke says that the roof was made of (clay) tiles, which were also used for making roofs in New Testament times.

See also: 5.14: Lev 14.1–32.

---

*5.1 Lake Gennesaret: Another name for Lake Galilee.
*5.3 sat down: Teachers in the ancient world, including Jewish teachers, usually sat down when they taught.

See also: 5.1–3: Matt 13.1,2; Mark 3.9,10; 4.1.
5.5: John 21.3. 5.6: John 21.6.

20 When Jesus saw how much faith they had, he said to the crippled man, "My friend, your sins are forgiven."

21 The Pharisees and the experts began arguing, "Jesus must think he is God! Only God can forgive sins."

22 Jesus knew what they were thinking, and he said, "Why are you thinking that? 23 Is it easier for me to tell this crippled man that his sins are forgiven or to tell him to get up and walk? 24 But now you will see that the Son of Man has the right to forgive sins here on earth." Jesus then said to the man, "Get up! Pick up your mat and walk home."

25 At once the man stood up in front of everyone. He picked up his mat and went home, giving thanks to God. 26 Everyone was amazed and praised God. What they saw surprised them, and they said, "We have seen a great miracle today!"

Jesus chooses Levi

This is also told in Matthew 9.9–13; Mark 2.13–17

27 Later, Jesus went out and saw a tax collector* named Levi sitting at the place for paying taxes. Jesus said to him, "Come with me." 28 Levi left everything and went with Jesus.

29 In his home Levi gave a big dinner for Jesus. Many tax collectors and other guests were also there.

30 The Pharisees and some of their teachers of the Law of Moses grumbled to Jesus' disciples, "Why do you eat and drink with those tax collectors and other sinners?"

31 Jesus answered, "Healthy people don't need a doctor, but sick people do. 32 I didn't come to invite good people to turn to God. I came to invite sinners."

People ask about going without eating

This is also told in Matthew 9.14–17; Mark 2.18–22

33 Some people said to Jesus, "John's followers often pray and go without eating,* and so do the followers of the Pharisees. But your disciples never go without eating or drinking."

34 Jesus told them, "The friends of a bridegroom don't go without eating while he is still with them. 35 But the time will come when he will be taken from them. Then they will go without eating."

36 Jesus then told them these sayings:

No one uses a new piece of cloth to patch old clothes. The patch would shrink and make the hole even bigger.

37 No one pours new wine into old wineskins. The new wine would swell and burst the old skins.* Then the wine would be lost, and the skins would be ruined.

38 New wine must be put only into new wineskins.

39 No one wants new wine after drinking old wine. They say, "The old wine is better."

CHAPTER 6

A question about the Sabbath

This is also told in Matthew 12.1–8; Mark 2.23–28

1 One Sabbath when Jesus and his disciples were walking through some wheat fields, the disciples picked some wheat.* They rubbed the husks off with their hands and started eating the grain.

2 Some Pharisees said, "Why are you picking grain on the Sabbath? You're not supposed to do that!"

3 Jesus answered, "Surely you have read what David did when he and his followers were hungry. 4 He went into the house of God and took the sacred loaves of bread that only priests were supposed to eat. He not only ate some himself, but even gave some to his followers."

5 Jesus finished by saying, "The Son of Man is Lord over the Sabbath."

A man with a crippled hand

This is also told in Matthew 12.9–14; Mark 3.1–6

6 On another Sabbath' Jesus was teaching in a Jewish meeting place, and a man with a crippled right hand was there. 7 Some Pharisees and teachers of the Law of Moses kept watching Jesus to see if he would heal the man. They did this because they wanted to accuse Jesus of doing something wrong.

---

*5.27 tax collector: See the note at 3.12.
*5.33 without eating: See the note at 2.37.
See also: 5.30: Luke 15.1,2.

*5.37 swell and burst the old skins: While the juice from grapes was becoming wine, it would swell and stretch the skins in which it had been stored. If the skins were old and stiff, they would burst.
*6.1 picked some wheat: It was the custom to let hungry travellers pick grains of wheat.
See also: 6.1: Deut 23.25. 6.3,4: 1 Sam 21.1–6. 6.4: Lev 24.9.

8 Jesus knew what they were thinking. So he told the man to stand up where everyone could see him. And the man stood up. 9 Then Jesus asked, "On the Sabbath should we do good deeds or evil deeds? Should we save someone's life or destroy it?"

10 After he had looked around at everyone, he told the man, "Stretch out your hand." He did, and his bad hand became completely well.

11 The teachers and the Pharisees were furious and started saying to each other, "What can we do about Jesus?"

Jesus chooses his twelve apostles

This is also told in Matthew 10.1–4; Mark 3.13–19

12 About that time Jesus went off to a mountain to pray, and he spent the whole night there. 13 The next morning he called his disciples together and chose twelve of them to be his apostles. 14 One was Simon, and Jesus named him Peter. Another was Andrew, Peter's brother. There were also James, John, Philip, Bartholomew, 15 Matthew, Thomas, and James the son of Alphaeus. The rest of the apostles were Simon, known as the Eager One,* 16 Jude, who was the son of James, and Judas Iscariot,* who later betrayed Jesus.

Jesus teaches, preaches, and heals

This is also told in Matthew 4.23–25

17 Jesus and his apostles went down from the mountain and came to some flat, level ground. Many other disciples were there to meet him. Large crowds of people from all over Judea, Jerusalem, and the coastal cities of Tyre and Sidon were there too. 18 These people had come to listen to Jesus and to be healed of their diseases. All who were troubled by evil spirits were also healed. 19 Everyone was trying to touch Jesus, because power was going out from him and healing them all.

*6.15 known as the Eager One:** The word "eager" translates the Greek word "zealot", which was a name later given to the members of a Jewish group that resisted and fought against the Romans.
*6.16 Iscariot:** This may mean "a man from Kerioth" (a place in Judea). But more probably it means "a man who was a liar" or "a man who was a betrayer".

Blessings and troubles

This is also told in Matthew 5.1–12

20 Jesus looked at his disciples and said:

God will bless you people
who are poor.
His kingdom belongs to you!
21 God will bless
you hungry people.
You will have plenty
to eat!
God will bless you people
who are crying.
You will laugh!

22 God will bless you when others hate you and won't have anything to do with you. God will bless you when people insult you and say cruel things about you, all because you are a follower of the Son of Man. 23 Long ago your own people did these same things to the prophets. So when this happens to you, be happy and jump for joy! You will have a great reward in heaven.

24 But you rich people
are in for trouble.
You have already had
an easy life!
25 You well-fed people
are in for trouble.
You will go hungry!
You people
who are laughing now
are in for trouble.
You are going to cry
and weep!

26 You are in for trouble when everyone says good things about you. That is what your own people said about those prophets who told lies.

Love for enemies

This is also told in Matthew 5.38–48; 7.12a

Jesus continued:

27 This is what I say to all who will listen to me:
Love your enemies, and be good to everyone who hates you. 28 Ask God to bless anyone who curses you, and pray for everyone who is cruel to you. 29 If someone slaps you on one cheek, don't stop that person from slapping you on the other

See also: 6.22: 1 Pet 4.14. **6.23:** 2 Chron 36.16; Acts 7.52.

cheek. If someone wants to take your coat, don't try to keep back your shirt. ³⁰ Give to everyone who asks and don't ask people to return what they have taken from you. ³¹ Treat others just as you want to be treated.

³² If you love only someone who loves you, will God praise you for that? Even sinners love people who love them. ³³ If you are kind only to someone who is kind to you, will God be pleased with you for that? Even sinners are kind to people who are kind to them. ³⁴ If you lend money only to someone you think will pay you back, will God be pleased with you for that? Even sinners lend to sinners because they think they will get it all back.

³⁵ But love your enemies and be good to them. Lend without expecting to be paid back.' Then you will get a great reward, and you will be the true children of God in heaven. He is good even to people who are unthankful and cruel. ³⁶ Have pity on others, just as your Father has pity on you.

Judging others

This is also told in Matthew 7.1–5

Jesus said:

Don't judge others, and God won't judge you. Don't be hard on others, and God won't be hard on you. Forgive others, and God will forgive you. ³⁸ If you give to others, you will be given a full amount in return. It will be packed down, shaken together, and spilling over into your lap. The way you treat others is the way you will be treated.

³⁹ Jesus also used some sayings as he spoke to the people. He said:

Can one blind person lead another blind person? Won't they both fall into a ditch? ⁴⁰ Are students better than their teacher? But when they are fully trained, they will be like their teacher.

⁴¹ You can see the speck in your friend's eye. But you don't notice the log in your own eye. ⁴² How can you say, "My friend, let me take the speck out of your eye," when you don't see the log in your own eye? You show-offs! First, get the log out of your own eye. Then you can see how to take the speck out of your friend's eye.

A tree and its fruit

This is also told in Matthew 7.17–20; 12.34b,35

Jesus continued:

⁴³ A good tree cannot produce bad fruit, and a bad tree cannot produce good fruit. ⁴⁴ You can tell what a tree is like by the fruit it produces. You cannot pick figs or grapes from thorn bushes. ⁴⁵ Good people do good things because of the good in their hearts. Bad people do bad things because of the evil in their hearts. Your words show what is in your heart.

Two builders

This is also told in Matthew 7.24–27

Jesus continued:

⁴⁶ Why do you keep on saying that I am your Lord, when you refuse to do what I say? ⁴⁷ Anyone who comes and listens to me and obeys me ⁴⁸ is like someone who dug down deep and built a house on solid rock. When the flood came and the river rushed against the house, it was built so well that it didn't even shake. ⁴⁹ But anyone who hears what I say and doesn't obey me is like someone whose house wasn't built on solid rock. As soon as the river rushed against that house, it was smashed to pieces!

CHAPTER 7

Jesus heals an army officer's servant

This is also told in Matthew 8.5–13; John 4.43–54

¹ After Jesus had finished teaching the people, he went to Capernaum. ² In that town an army officer's servant was sick and about to die. The officer liked this servant very much. ³ And when he heard about Jesus, he sent some Jewish leaders to ask him to come and heal the servant.

⁴ The leaders went to Jesus and begged him to do something. They said, "This man deserves your help! ⁵ He loves our nation and even built us a meeting place." ⁶ So Jesus went with them.

When Jesus wasn't far from the house, the officer sent some friends to tell him, "Lord, don't go to any trouble for me! I am not good enough for you to come into my house. ⁷ And I am certainly not worthy to come to you. Just say the word, and my servant will get well. ⁸ I have officers who give orders to

See also: **6.31:** Matt 7.12. **6.39:** Matt 15.14.
6.40: Matt 10.24,25; John 13.16; 15.20.

6.44: Matt 12.33. **6.45:** Matt 12.34.

80

me, and I have soldiers who take orders from me. I can say to one of them, 'Go!' and he goes. I can say to another, 'Come!' and he comes. I can say to my servant, 'Do this!' and he will do it."

⁹ When Jesus heard this, he was so surprised that he turned and said to the crowd following him, "In all of Israel I've never found anyone with this much faith!"

¹⁰ The officer's friends returned and found the servant well.

A widow's son

¹¹ Soon Jesus and his disciples were on their way to the town of Nain, and a big crowd was going along with them. ¹² As they came near the gate of the town, they saw people carrying out the body of a widow's only son. Many people from the town were walking along with her.

¹³ When the Lord saw the woman, he felt sorry for her and said, "Don't cry!"

¹⁴ Jesus went over and touched the stretcher on which the people were carrying the dead boy. They stopped, and Jesus said, "Young man, get up!" ¹⁵ The boy sat up and began to speak. Jesus then gave him back to his mother.

¹⁶ Everyone was frightened and praised God. They said, "A great prophet is here with us! God has come to his people."

¹⁷ News about Jesus spread all over Judea and everywhere else in that part of the country.

John the Baptist
This is also told in Matthew 11.1–19

¹⁸⁻¹⁹ John's followers told John everything that was being said about Jesus. So he sent two of them to ask the Lord, "Are you the one we should be looking for? Or must we wait for someone else?"

²⁰ When these messengers came to Jesus, they said, "John the Baptist sent us to ask, 'Are you the one we should be looking for? Or are we supposed to wait for someone else?'"

²¹ At that time Jesus was healing many people who were sick or in pain or were troubled by evil spirits, and he was giving sight to a lot of blind people. ²² Jesus said to the messengers sent by John, "Go and tell John what you have seen and heard. Blind people are now able to see, and the lame can

walk. People who have leprosy* are being healed, and the deaf can now hear. The dead are raised to life, and the poor are hearing the good news. ²³ God will bless everyone who doesn't reject me because of what I do."

²⁴ After John's messengers had gone, Jesus began speaking to the crowds about John:

What kind of person did you go out to the desert to see? Was he like tall grass blown about by the wind? ²⁵ What kind of man did you really go out to see? Was he someone dressed in fine clothes? People who wear expensive clothes and live in luxury are in the king's palace. ²⁶ What then did you go out to see? Was he a prophet? He certainly was! I tell you that he was more than a prophet. ²⁷ In the Scriptures, God calls John his messenger and says, "I am sending my messenger ahead of you to get things ready for you." ²⁸ No one ever born on this earth is greater than John. But whoever is least important in God's kingdom is greater than John.

²⁹ Everyone had been listening to John. Even the tax collectors* had obeyed God and had done what was right by letting John baptize them. ³⁰ But the Pharisees and the experts in the Law of Moses refused to obey God and be baptized by John.

³¹ Jesus went on to say:

What are you people like? What kind of people are you? ³² You are like children sitting in the market and shouting to each other,

"We played the flute,
 but you would not dance!
We sang a funeral song,
 but you would not cry!"

³³ John the Baptist did not go around eating and drinking, and you said, "John has a demon in him!" ³⁴ But because the Son of Man goes around eating and drinking, you say, "Jesus eats and drinks too much! He is even a friend of tax collectors and sinners." ³⁵ Yet Wisdom is shown to be right by what its followers do.

*7.22 leprosy: See the note at 4.27.
*7.29 tax collectors: See the note at 3.12.

See also: 7.22: a Isa 35.5,6; b Isa 61.1.   See also: 7.27: Mal 3.1. 7.29,30: Matt 21.32; Luke 3.12.

81

Simon the Pharisee

36 A Pharisee invited Jesus to have dinner with him. So Jesus went to the Pharisee's home and got ready to eat.*

37 When a sinful woman in that town found out that Jesus was there, she bought an expensive bottle of perfume. 38 Then she came and stood behind Jesus. She cried and started washing his feet with her tears and drying them with her hair. The woman kissed his feet and poured the perfume on them.

39 The Pharisee who had invited Jesus saw this and said to himself, "If this man really were a prophet, he would know what kind of woman is touching him! He would know that she is a sinner."

40 Jesus said to the Pharisee, "Simon, I have something to say to you."

"Teacher, what is it?" Simon replied.

41 Jesus told him, "Two people were in debt to a moneylender. One of them owed him five hundred silver coins, and the other owed him fifty. 42 Since neither of them could pay him back, the moneylender said that they didn't have to pay him anything. Which one of them will like him more?"

43 Simon answered, "I suppose it would be the one who had owed more and didn't have to pay it back."

"You are right," Jesus said.

44 He turned towards the woman and said to Simon, "Have you noticed this woman? When I came into your home, you didn't give me any water so I could wash my feet. But she has washed my feet with her tears and dried them with her hair. 45 You didn't greet me with a kiss, but from the time I came in, she has not stopped kissing my feet. 46 You didn't even pour olive oil on my head,* but she has poured expensive perfume on my feet. 47 So I tell you that all her sins are forgiven, and that is why she has shown great love. But anyone who has been forgiven for only a little will show only a little love."

48 Then Jesus said to the woman, "Your sins are forgiven."

49 Some other guests started saying to one another, "Who is this who dares to forgive sins?"

50 But Jesus told the woman, "Because of your faith, you are now saved.• May God give you peace!"

CHAPTER 8

Women who helped Jesus

1 Soon after this, Jesus was going through towns and villages, telling the good news about God's kingdom. His twelve apostles were with him, 2 and so were some women who had been healed of evil spirits and all sorts of diseases. One of the women was Mary Magdalene,* who once had seven demons in her. 3 Joanna, Susanna, and many others had also used what they owned to help Jesus* and his disciples. Joanna's husband Chuza was one of Herod's officials.*

A story about a farmer

This is also told in Matthew 13.1–9; Mark 4.1–9

4 When a large crowd from several towns had gathered around Jesus, he told them this story:

5 A farmer went out to scatter seed in a field. While the farmer was doing it, some of the seeds fell along the road and were stepped on or eaten by birds. 6 Other seeds fell on rocky ground and started growing. But the plants did not have enough water and soon dried up. 7 Some other seeds fell where thorn bushes grew up and choked the plants. 8 The rest of the seeds fell on good ground where they grew and produced a hundred times as many seeds.

When Jesus had finished speaking, he said, "If you have ears, pay attention!"

---

*7.36 got ready to eat: On special occasions the Jewish people often followed the Greek and Roman custom of lying down on their left side and leaning on their left elbow, while eating with their right hand. This is how the woman could come up behind Jesus and wash his feet (see verse 38).
*7.44–46 washed my feet . . . greet me with a kiss . . . pour olive oil on my head: Guests in a home were usually offered water they could wash their feet, because most people either went barefoot or wore sandals and would come into the house with very dusty feet. Guests were also greeted with a kiss on the cheek, and special ones often had sweet-smelling olive oil poured on their head.
See also: 7.37,38; Matt 26.7; Mark 14.3; John 12.3.

*8.2 Magdalene: Meaning "from Magdala", a small town on the western shore of Lake Galilee. There is no hint that she is the sinful woman in 7.36–50.
*8.3 used what they owned to help Jesus: Women often helped Jewish teachers by giving them money.
*8.3 Herod's officials: Herod Antipas, the son of Herod the Great.
See also: 8.2,3; Matt 27.55,56; Mark 15.40,41; Luke 23.49.

Why Jesus used stories

This is also told in Matthew 13.10–17; Mark 4.10–12

[9] Jesus' disciples asked him what the story meant. [10] So he answered:

I have explained the secrets about God's kingdom to you, but for others I can only use stories. These people look, but they don't see, and they hear, but they don't understand.

Jesus explains the story about a farmer

This is also told in Matthew 13.18–23; Mark 4.13–20

[11] This is what the story means: The seed is God's message, [12] and the seeds that fell along the road are the people who hear the message. But the devil comes and snatches the message out of their hearts, so that they will not believe and be saved. [13] The seeds that fell on rocky ground are the people who gladly hear the message and accept it. But they don't have deep roots, and they believe only for a little while. As soon as life gets hard, they give up.

[14] The seeds that fell among the thorn bushes are also people who hear the message. But they are so eager for riches and pleasures that they never produce anything. [15] Those seeds that fell on good ground are the people who listen to the message and keep it in good and honest hearts. They last and produce a harvest.

Light

This is also told in Mark 4.21–25

Jesus continued:

[16] No one lights a lamp and puts it under a bowl or under a bed. A lamp is always put on a lampstand, so that people who come into a house will see the light. [17] There is nothing hidden that will not be found. There is no secret that will not be well known. [18] Pay attention to how you listen! Everyone who has something will be given more, but people who have nothing will lose what little they think they have.

Jesus' mother and brothers

This is also told in Matthew 12.46–50; Mark 3.31–35

[19] Jesus' mother and brothers went to see him, but because of the crowd they could not

get near him. [20] Someone told Jesus, "Your mother and brothers are standing outside and want to see you."

[21] Jesus answered, "My mother and my brothers are those people who hear and obey God's message."

A storm

This is also told in Matthew 8.23–27; Mark 4.35–41

[22] One day, Jesus and his disciples got into a boat, and he said, "Let's cross the lake."* They started out, [23] and while they were sailing across, he went to sleep.

Suddenly a storm struck the lake, and the boat started sinking. They were in danger. [24] So they went to Jesus and woke him up, "Master, Master! We are about to drown!"

Jesus got up and ordered the wind and waves to stop. They obeyed, and everything was calm. [25] Then Jesus asked the disciples, "Don't you have any faith?"

But they were frightened and amazed. They said to each other, "Who is this? He can give orders to the wind and the waves, and they obey him!"

A man with demons in him

This is also told in Matthew 8.28–34; Mark 5.1–20

[26] Jesus and his disciples sailed across Lake Galilee and came to shore near the town of Gerasa.* [27] As Jesus was getting out of the boat, he was met by a man from that town. The man had demons in him. He had gone naked for a long time and no longer lived in a house, but in the graveyard.*

[28] The man saw Jesus and screamed. He knelt down in front of him and shouted, "Jesus, Son of God in heaven, what do you want with me? I beg you not to torture me!" [29] He said this because Jesus had already told the evil spirit to go out of him.

The man had often been attacked by the demon. And even though he had been bound with chains and leg irons and kept under guard, he smashed whatever bound him. Then the demon would force him out into lonely places.

[30] Jesus asked the man, "What is your name?"

He answered, "My name is Lots." He said this because there were 'lots' of demons in

---

*8.22 cross the lake: To the eastern shore of Lake Galilee, where most of the people were not Jewish.
*8.27 graveyard: It was thought that demons and evil spirits lived in graveyards.

him. [31] They begged Jesus not to send them to the deep pit,* where they would be punished.

[32] A large herd of pigs was feeding there on the hillside. So the demons begged Jesus to let them go into the pigs, and Jesus let them go. [33] Then the demons left the man and went into the pigs. The whole herd rushed down the steep bank into the lake and drowned.

[34] When the men taking care of the pigs saw this, they ran to spread the news in the town and on the farms. [35] The people went out to see what had happened, and when they came to Jesus, they also found the man. The demons had gone out of him, and he was sitting there at the feet of Jesus. He had clothes on and was in his right mind. But the people were terrified.

[36] Then all who had seen the man healed told about it. [37] Everyone from around Gerasa* begged Jesus to leave, because they were so frightened.

When Jesus got into the boat to start back, [38] the man who had been healed begged to go with him. But Jesus sent him off and said, [39] "Go back home and tell everyone how much God has done for you." The man then went all over town, telling everything that Jesus had done for him.

A dying girl and a sick woman

This is also told in Matthew 9.18–26; Mark 5.21–43

[40] Everyone had been waiting for Jesus, and when he came back, a crowd was there to welcome him. [41] Just then the man in charge of the Jewish meeting place came and knelt down in front of Jesus. His name was Jairus, and he begged Jesus to come to his home [42] because his twelve-year-old child was dying. She was his only daughter.

While Jesus was on his way, people were crowding all around him. [43] In the crowd was a woman who had been bleeding for twelve years. She had spent everything she had on doctors,* but none of them could make her well.

[44] As soon as she came up behind Jesus and barely touched his clothes, her bleeding stopped.

[45] "Who touched me?" Jesus asked.

While everyone was denying it, Peter said, "Master, people are crowding all around and pushing you from every side."*

[46] But Jesus answered, "Someone touched me, because I felt power going out from me."
[47] The woman knew that she could not hide, so she came trembling and knelt down in front of Jesus. She told everyone why she had touched him and that she had been healed straight away.

[48] Jesus said to the woman, "You are now well because of your faith. May God give you peace!"

[49] While Jesus was speaking, someone came from Jairus' home and said, "Your daughter has died! Why bother the teacher any more?"

[50] When Jesus heard this, he told Jairus, "Don't worry! Have faith, and your daughter will get well."

[51] Jesus went into the house, but he did not let anyone else go with him, except Peter, John, James, and the girl's father and mother. [52] Everyone was crying and weeping for the girl. But Jesus said, "The child isn't dead. She is just asleep." [53] The people laughed at him because they knew she was dead.

[54] Jesus took hold of the girl's hand and said, "Child, get up!" [55] She came back to life and got straight up. Jesus told them to give her something to eat. [56] Her parents were surprised, but Jesus ordered them not to tell anyone what had happened.

CHAPTER 9

Instructions for the twelve apostles

This is also told in Matthew 10.5–15; Mark 6.7–13

[1] Jesus called together his twelve apostles and gave them complete power over all demons and diseases. [2] Then he sent them to tell about God's kingdom and to heal the sick. [3] He told them, "Don't take anything with you! Don't take a walking stick or a travelling bag or food or money or even a change of clothes. [4] When you are welcomed into a home, stay there until you leave that town. [5] If people won't welcome you, leave the town and shake the dust from your feet* as a warning to them."

[6] The apostles left and went from village to village, telling the good news and healing people everywhere.

---

*8.31 deep pit: The place where evil spirits are kept and punished.

*9.5 shake the dust from your feet: This was a way of showing rejection.

See also: 9.3–5: Luke 10.4–11. 9.5: Acts 13.51.

Herod is worried

This is also told in Matthew 14.1–12; Mark 6.14–29

⁷ Herod* the ruler heard about all that was happening, and he was worried. Some people were saying that John the Baptist had come back to life. ⁸ Others were saying that Elijah had come* or that one of the prophets from long ago had come back to life. ⁹ But Herod said, "I had John's head cut off! Who is this I hear so much about?" Herod was eager to meet Jesus.

Jesus feeds five thousand

This is also told in Matthew 14.13–21; Mark 6.30–44; John 6.1–14

¹⁰ The apostles came back and told Jesus everything they had done. He then took them with him to the village of Bethsaida, where they could be alone. ¹¹ But a lot of people found out about this and followed him. Jesus welcomed them. He spoke to them about God's kingdom and healed everyone who was sick.

¹² Late in the afternoon the twelve apostles came to Jesus and said, "Send the crowd to the villages and farms around here. They need to find a place to stay and something to eat. There is nothing in this place. It is like a desert!"

¹³ Jesus answered, "You give them something to eat."

But they replied, "We have only five small loaves of bread* and two fish. If we are going to feed all these people, we will have to go and buy food." ¹⁴ There were about five thousand men in the crowd.

Jesus said to his disciples, "Tell the people to sit in groups of fifty." ¹⁵ They did this, and all the people sat down. ¹⁶ Jesus took the five loaves and the two fish. He looked up towards heaven and blessed the food. Then he broke the bread and fish and handed them to his disciples to give to the people.

¹⁷ Everyone ate all they wanted. What was left over filled twelve baskets.

Who is Jesus?

This is also told in Matthew 16.13–19; Mark 8.27–29

¹⁸ When Jesus was alone praying, his disciples came to him, and he asked them, "What do people say about me?"

¹⁹ They answered, "Some say that you are John the Baptist or Elijah* or a prophet from long ago who has come back to life."

²⁰ Jesus then asked them, "But who do you say I am?"

Peter answered, "You are the Messiah sent from God."

²¹ Jesus strictly warned his disciples not to tell anyone about this.

Jesus speaks about his suffering and death

This is also told in Matthew 16.20–28; Mark 8.30–9.1

²² Jesus told his disciples, "The nation's leaders, the chief priests, and the teachers of the Law of Moses will make the Son of Man suffer terribly. They will reject him and kill him, but three days later he will rise to life."

²³ Then Jesus said to all the people:

If any of you want to be my followers, you must forget about yourself. You must take up your cross each day and follow me. ²⁴ If you want to save your life, you will destroy it. But if you give up your life for me, you will save it. ²⁵ What will you gain, if you own the whole world but destroy yourself or waste your life? ²⁶ If you are ashamed of me and my message, the Son of Man will be ashamed of you when he comes in his glory and in the glory of his Father and the holy angels. ²⁷ You can be sure that some of the people standing here will not die before they see God's kingdom.

The true glory of Jesus

This is also told in Matthew 17.1–8; Mark 9.2–8

²⁸ About eight days later Jesus took Peter, John, and James with him and went up on a mountain to pray. ²⁹ While he was praying, his face changed, and his clothes became white. ³⁰ Suddenly Moses and Elijah were there speaking with him. ³¹ They appeared in heavenly glory and talked about all that Jesus' death* in Jerusalem would mean.

---

*9.7 Herod: See the note at 3.1.
*9.8 Elijah had come: Many of the Jewish people expected the prophet Elijah to come and prepare the way for the Messiah.
*9.13 small loaves of bread: These would have been flat and round or in the shape of a bun.
See also: 9.7,8; Matt 16.14; Mark 8.28; Luke 9.19.

*9.19 Elijah: See the note at 9.8.
See also: 9.19: Matt 14.1,2; Mark 6.14,15; Luke 9.7,8.
9.20: John 6.68,69. 9.23: Matt 10.38; Luke 14.27.
9.24: Matt 10.39; Luke 17.33; John 12.25.
9.28–35: 2 Pet 1.17,18.

32 Peter and the other two disciples had been sound asleep. All at once they woke up and saw how glorious Jesus was. They also saw the two men who were with him.

33 Moses and Elijah were about to leave, when Peter said to Jesus, "Master, it is good for us to be here! Let us make three shelters, one for you, one for Moses, and one for Elijah." But Peter did not know what he was talking about.

34 While Peter was still speaking, a shadow from a cloud passed over them, and they were frightened as the cloud covered them. 35 From the cloud a voice said, "This is my chosen Son. Listen to what he says!"

36 After the voice had spoken, Peter, John, and James saw only Jesus. For some time they kept quiet and did not say anything about what they had seen.

Jesus heals a boy

This is also told in Matthew 17.14–18; Mark 9.14–27

37 The next day Jesus and his three disciples came down from the mountain and were met by a large crowd. 38 Just then someone in the crowd shouted, "Teacher, please do something for my son! He is my only child! 39 A demon often attacks him and makes him scream. It shakes him until he foams at the mouth, and it won't leave him until it has completely worn the boy out. 40 I begged your disciples to force out the demon, but they couldn't do it."

41 Jesus said to them, "You people are stubborn and don't have any faith! How much longer must I be with you? Why do I have to put up with you?"

Then Jesus said to the man, "Bring your son to me." 42 While the boy was being brought, the demon attacked him and made him shake all over. Jesus ordered the demon to stop. Then he healed the boy and gave him back to his father. 43 Everyone was amazed at God's great power.

Jesus again speaks about his death

This is also told in Matthew 17.22,23; Mark 9.30–32

While everyone was still amazed at what Jesus was doing, he said to his disciples, 44 "Pay close attention to what I am telling you! The Son of Man will be handed over to his enemies." 45 But the disciples did not know what he meant. The meaning

was hidden from them. They could not understand it, and they were afraid to ask.

Who is the greatest?

This is also told in Matthew 18.1–5; Mark 9.33–37

46 Jesus' disciples were arguing about which one of them was the greatest. 47 Jesus knew what they were thinking, and he had a child stand there beside him. 48 Then he said to his disciples, "When you welcome even a child because of me, you welcome me. And when you welcome me, you welcome the one who sent me. Whichever one of you is the most humble is the greatest."

For or against Jesus

This is also told in Mark 9.38–40

49 John said, "Master, we saw a man using your name to force demons out of people. But we told him to stop, because he isn't one of us."

50 "Don't stop him!" Jesus said. "Anyone who isn't against you is for you."

Jesus goes from Galilee to Jerusalem

A Samaritan village refuses to receive Jesus

51 Not long before it was time for Jesus to be taken up to heaven, he made up his mind to go to Jerusalem. 52 He sent some messengers on ahead to a Samaritan village to get things ready for him. 53 But he was on his way to Jerusalem, so the people there refused to welcome him. 54 When the disciples James and John saw what was happening, they asked, "Lord, do you want us to call down fire from heaven to destroy these people?"

55 But Jesus turned and corrected them for what they had said. 56 Then they all went on to another village.

Three people who wanted to be followers

This is also told in Matthew 8.19–22

57 Along the way someone said to Jesus, "I'll go anywhere with you!"

See also: 9.35: Isa 42.1; Matt 3.17; 12.18; Mark 1.11; Luke 3.22.

See also: 9.46: Luke 22.24. 9.48: Matt 10.40; Luke 10.16; John 13.20. 9.54: 2 Kings 1.9–16.

⁵⁸ Jesus said, "Foxes have dens, and birds have nests, but the Son of Man doesn't have a place to call his own."

⁵⁹ Jesus told someone else to come with him. But the man said, "Lord, let me wait until I bury my father."*

⁶⁰ Jesus said, "Let the dead take care of the dead, while you go and tell about God's kingdom."

⁶¹ Then someone said to Jesus, "I want to go with you, Lord, but first let me go back and take care of things at home."

⁶² Jesus answered, "Anyone who starts ploughing and keeps looking back isn't worth a thing to God's kingdom!"

CHAPTER 10

The work of the seventy-two followers

¹ Later the Lord chose seventy-two* other followers and sent them out two by two to every town and village where he was about to go. ² He said to them:

A large crop is in the fields, but there are only a few workers. Ask the Lord in charge of the harvest to send out workers to bring it in. ³ Now go, but remember, I am sending you like lambs into a pack of wolves. ⁴ Don't take along a money bag or a travelling bag or sandals. And don't waste time greeting people on the road.* ⁵ As soon as you enter a home, say, "God bless this home with peace." ⁶ If the people living there are peace-loving, your prayer for peace will bless them. But if they are not peace-loving, your prayer will return to you. ⁷ Stay with the same family, eating and drinking whatever they give you, because workers are worth what they earn. Don't move around from house to house.

⁸ If the people of a town welcome you, eat whatever they offer. ⁹ Heal their sick and say, "God's kingdom will soon be here!"*

¹⁰ But if the people of a town refuse to welcome you, go out into the street and say, ¹¹ "We are shaking the dust from our feet* as a warning to you. And you can be sure that God's kingdom will soon be here!"* ¹² I tell you that on the day of judgment the people of Sodom will get off easier than the people of that town!

The unbelieving towns

This is also told in Matthew 11.20–24

Jesus continued:

¹³ You people of Chorazin are in for trouble! You people of Bethsaida are also in for trouble! If the miracles that took place in your towns had happened in Tyre and Sidon, the people there would have turned to God long ago. They would have dressed in sackcloth and put ashes on their heads.* ¹⁴ On the day of judgment the people of Tyre and Sidon will get off easier than you will. ¹⁵ People of Capernaum, do you think you will be honoured in heaven? Well, you will go down to hell!

¹⁶ My followers, whoever listens to you is listening to me. Anyone who says "No" to you is saying "No" to me. And anyone who says "No" to me is really saying "No" to the one who sent me.

The return of the seventy-two

¹⁷ When the seventy-two* returned, they were excited and said, "Lord, even the demons obeyed when we spoke in your name!"

¹⁸ Jesus told them:

I saw Satan fall from heaven like a flash of lightning. ¹⁹ I have given you the power to trample on snakes and scorpions and to defeat the power of your enemy Satan.

---

*9.59 bury my father: The Jewish people taught that giving someone a proper burial was even more important than helping the poor.
*10.1 seventy-two: Some manuscripts have "seventy." According to Jewish tradition there were seventy nations on earth. But the ancient Greek translation of the Old Testament has "seventy-two" in place of "seventy." Jesus probably chose this number of followers to show that his message was for everyone in the world.
*10.4 waste time greeting people on the road: In those days a polite greeting could take a long time.
See also: 9.61: 1 King 19.20. 10.2: Matt 9.37,38. 10.3: Matt 10.16. 10.4–11: Matt 10.7–14; Mark 6.8–11; Luke 9.3–5. 10.7: 1 Cor 9.14; 1 Tim 5.18.

*10.11 shaking the dust from our feet: See the note at 9.5.
*10.13 dressed in sackcloth . . . ashes on their heads: This was one way that people showed how sorry they were for their sins.
*10.17 seventy-two: See the note at 10.1.
See also: 10.10,11: Acts 13.51. 10.12: a Gen 19.24–28; Matt 11.24; b Matt 10.15. 10.13: Isa 23.1–18; Ezek 26.1—28.26; Joel 3.4–8; Amos 1.9,10; Zech 9.2–4. 10.15: Isa 14.13–15. 10.16: Matt 10.40; Mark 9.37; Luke 9.48; John 13.20. 10.19: Psa 91.13.

Nothing can harm you. 20 But don't be happy because evil spirits obey you. Be happy that your names are written in heaven!

Jesus thanks his Father

This is also told in Matthew 11.25–27; 13.16,17

21 At that same time, Jesus felt the joy that comes from the Holy Spirit,' and he said:

My Father, Lord of heaven and earth, I am grateful that you hid all this from wise and educated people and showed it to ordinary people. Yes, Father, that is what pleased you.

22 My Father has given me everything, and he is the only one who knows the Son. The only one who really knows the Father is the Son. But the Son wants to tell others about the Father, so that they can know him too.

23 Jesus then turned to his disciples and said to them in private, "You are really blessed to see what you see! 24 Many prophets and kings were eager to see what you see and to hear what you hear. But I tell you that they did not see or hear."

The good Samaritan

25 An expert in the Law of Moses stood up and asked Jesus a question to see what he would say. "Teacher," he asked, "what must I do to have eternal life?"

26 Jesus answered, "What is written in the Scriptures? How do you understand them?"

27 The man replied, "The Scriptures say, 'Love the Lord your God with all your heart, soul, strength, and mind.' They also say, 'Love your neighbours as much as you love yourself.' "

28 Jesus said, "You have given the right answer. If you do this, you will have eternal life."

29 But the man wanted to show that he knew what he was talking about. So he asked Jesus, "Who are my neighbours?"

30 Jesus replied:

As a man was going down from Jerusalem to Jericho, robbers attacked him and grabbed everything he had. They beat him up and ran off, leaving him half dead.

31 A priest happened to be going down the same road. But when he saw the man,

he walked by on the other side. 32 Later a temple helper* came to the same place. But when he saw the man who had been beaten up, he also went by on the other side.

33 A man from Samaria then came travelling along that road. When he saw the man, he felt sorry for him 34 and went over to him. He treated his wounds with olive oil and wine* and bandaged them. Then he put him on his own donkey and took him to an inn, where he took care of him. 35 The next morning he gave the innkeeper two silver coins and said, "Please take care of the man. If you spend more than this on him, I will pay you when I return."

36 Then Jesus asked, "Which one of these three people was a real neighbour to the man who was beaten up by robbers?"

37 The teacher answered, "The one who showed pity."

Jesus said, "Go and do the same!"

Martha and Mary

38 The Lord and his disciples were travelling along and came to a village. When they got there, a woman named Martha welcomed him into her home. 39 She had a sister named Mary, who sat down in front of the Lord and was listening to what he said. 40 Martha was worried about all that had to be done. Finally, she went to Jesus and said, "Lord, doesn't it bother you that my sister has left me to do all the work by myself? Tell her to come and help me!"

41 The Lord answered, "Martha, Martha! You are worried and upset about so many things, 42 but only one thing is necessary. Mary has chosen what is best, and it will not be taken away from her."

CHAPTER 11

Prayer

This is also told in Matthew 6.9–13; 7.7–11

1 When Jesus had finished praying, one of his disciples said to him, "Lord, teach us to pray, just as John taught his followers to pray."

---

*10.32 temple helper: A man from the tribe of Levi, whose job it was to work around the temple.

*10.34 olive oil and wine: In New Testament times these were used as medicine. Sometimes olive oil is a symbol for healing by means of a miracle (see James 5.14).

See also: 10.33,34: 2 Chron 28.15. 10.38,39: John 11.1.

See also: 10.22: a John 3.35; b John 10.15.
10.25–28: Matt 22.35–40; Mark 12.28–34. 10.27: a Deut 6.5;
b Lev 19.18. 10.28: Lev 18.5.

2 So Jesus told them, "Pray in this way:

'Father, help us
   to honour your name.
Come and set up
   your kingdom.
3 Give us each day
   the food we need.'
4 Forgive our sins,
   as we forgive everyone
   who has done wrong to us.
And keep us
   from being tempted.' "

5 Then Jesus went on to say:

Suppose one of you goes to a friend in the middle of the night and says, "Let me borrow three loaves of bread. 6 A friend of mine has dropped in, and I don't have a thing for him to eat." 7 And suppose your friend answers, "Don't bother me! The door is bolted, and my children and I are in bed. I cannot get up to give you something."

8 He may not get up and give you the bread, just because you are his friend. But he will get up and give you as much as you need, simply because you are not ashamed to keep on asking.

9 So I tell you to ask and you will receive, search and you will find, knock and the door will be opened for you. 10 Everyone who asks will receive, everyone who searches will find, and the door will be opened for everyone who knocks. 11 Which one of you fathers would give your hungry child a snake if the child asked for a fish? 12 Which one of you would give your child a scorpion if the child asked for an egg? 13 As bad as you are, you still know how to give good gifts to your children. But your heavenly Father is even more ready to give the Holy Spirit to anyone who asks.

Jesus and the ruler of demons

This is also told in Matthew 12.22–30; Mark 3.20–27

14 Jesus forced a demon out of a man who could not talk. And after the demon had gone out, the man started speaking, and the crowds were amazed. 15 But some people said, "He forces out demons by the power of Beelzebul, the ruler of the demons!"

16 Others wanted to put Jesus to the test. So they asked him to show them a sign from God. 17 Jesus knew what they were thinking, and he said:

A kingdom where people fight each other will end up in ruin. And a family that fights will break up. 18 If Satan fights against himself, how can his kingdom last? Yet you say that I force out demons by the power of Beelzebul. 19 If I use his power to force out demons, whose power do your own followers use to force them out? They are the ones who will judge you. 20 But if I use God's power to force out demons, it proves that God's kingdom has already come to you.

21 When a strong man arms himself and guards his home, everything he owns is safe. 22 But if a stronger man comes and defeats him, he will carry off the weapons in which the strong man trusted. Then he will divide with others what he has taken. 23 If you are not on my side, you are against me. If you don't gather in the crop with me, you scatter it.

Return of an evil spirit

This is also told in Matthew 12.43–45

Jesus continued:

24 When an evil spirit leaves a person, it travels through the desert, looking for a place to rest. But when it doesn't find a place, it says, "I will go back to the home I left." 25 When it gets there and finds the place clean and tidy, 26 it goes off and finds seven other evil spirits even worse than itself. They all come and make their home there, and that person ends up in a worse state than before.

Being really blessed

27 While Jesus was still talking, a woman in the crowd spoke up, "The woman who gave birth to you and nursed you is blessed!"

28 Jesus replied, "That's true, but the people who are really blessed are the ones who hear and obey God's message!"

A sign from God

This is also told in Matthew 12.38–42; Mark 8.12

29 As crowds were gathering around Jesus, he said:

You people of today are evil! You keep looking for a sign from God. But what happened to Jonah* is the only sign you will be given. 30 Just as Jonah was a sign to the people of Nineveh, the Son of Man will be a sign to the people of today. 31 When the judgment comes, the Queen of the South* will stand there with you and condemn you. She travelled a long way to hear Solomon's wisdom, and yet here is something far greater than Solomon. 32 The people of Nineveh will also stand there with you and condemn you. They turned to God when Jonah preached, and yet here is something far greater than Jonah.

Light

This is also told in Matthew 5.15; 6.22,23

Jesus continued:

33 No one lights a lamp and then hides it or puts it under a clay pot. A lamp is put on a lampstand, so that everyone who comes into the house can see the light. 34 Your eyes are the lamp for your body. When your eyes are good, you have all the light you need. But when your eyes are bad, everything is dark. 35 So be sure that your light isn't darkness. 36 If you have light, and nothing is dark, then light will be everywhere, as when a lamp shines brightly on you.

Jesus condemns the Pharisees and teachers of the Law of Moses

This is also told in Matthew 23.1–36; Mark 12.38–40; Luke 20.45–47

37 When Jesus finished speaking, a Pharisee invited him home for a meal. Jesus went and sat down to eat.* 38 The Pharisee was surprised that he did not wash his hands* before eating. 39 So the Lord said to him:

You Pharisees clean the outside of cups and dishes, but on the inside you are greedy and evil. 40 You fools! Didn't God make both the outside and the inside?' 41 If you would only give what you have to the poor, everything you do would please God.

42 You Pharisees are in for trouble! You give God a tenth of the spices from your gardens, such as mint and rue. But you cheat people, and you don't love God. You should be fair and kind to others and still give a tenth to God.

43 You Pharisees are in for trouble! You love the front seats in the meeting places, and you like to be greeted with honour in the market. 44 But you are in for trouble! You are like unmarked graves* that people walk on without even knowing it.

45 A teacher of the Law of Moses spoke up, "Teacher, you said cruel things about us."

46 Jesus replied:

You teachers are also in for trouble! You load people down with heavy burdens, but you won't lift a finger to help them carry the loads. 47 Yes, you are really in for trouble. You build monuments to honour the prophets your own people murdered long ago. 48 You must think that was the right thing for your people to do, or else you would not have built monuments for the prophets they murdered.

49 Because of your evil deeds, the Wisdom of God said, "I will send prophets and apostles to you. But you will murder some and ill-treat others." 50 You people living today will be punished for all the prophets who have been murdered since the beginning of the world. 51 This includes every prophet from the time of Abel to the time of Zechariah,* who was murdered between the altar and the temple. You people will certainly be punished for all this.

---

*11.29 what happened to Jonah: Jonah was in the stomach of a big fish for three days and nights. See Matthew 12.40.
*11.31 Queen of the South: Sheba, probably a country in southern Arabia.
*11.37 sat down to eat: See the note at 7.36.
*11.38 did not wash his hands: The Jewish people had strict laws about washing their hands before eating, especially if they had been out in public.

See also: 11.30: Jon 3.4. 11.31: 1 King 10.1–10; 2 Chron 9.1–12. 11.32: Jon 3.5. 11.33: Matt 5.15; Mark 4.21; Luke 8.16.

11.44 unmarked graves: Tombs were whitewashed to keep anyone from accidentally touching them. A person who touched a dead body or a tomb was considered unclean and could not worship with other Jewish people.
*11.51 from the time of Abel . . . Zechariah: Genesis is the first book in the Jewish Scriptures, and it tells that Abel was the first person to be murdered. The Second Book of Chronicles is the last book in the Jewish Scriptures, and the last murder that it tells about is that of Zechariah.

See also: 11.42: Lev 27.30. 11.51: a Gen 4.8; b 2 Chron 24.20,21.

52 You teachers of the Law of Moses are really in for trouble! You carry the keys to the door of knowledge about God. But you never go in, and you keep others from going in.

53 Jesus was about to leave, but the teachers and the Pharisees wanted to get even with him. They tried to make him say what he thought about other things, 54 so that they could catch him saying something wrong.

CHAPTER 12

Warnings

1 As thousands of people crowded around Jesus and were stepping on each other, he told his disciples:

Be sure to guard against the dishonest teaching* of the Pharisees! It is their way of fooling people. 2 Everything that is hidden will be found out, and every secret will be known. 3 Whatever you say in the dark will be heard when it is day. Whatever you whisper in a closed room will be shouted from the housetops.

The one to fear

This is also told in Matthew 10.28-31

Jesus continued:

4 My friends, don't be afraid of people. They can kill you, but after that, there is nothing else they can do. 5 God is the one you must fear. Not only can he take your life, but he can throw you into hell. God is certainly the one you should fear!

6 Five sparrows are sold for just two pennies, but God doesn't forget a single one of them. 7 Even the hairs on your head are counted. So don't be afraid! You are worth much more than many sparrows.

Telling others about Christ

This is also told in Matthew 10.32,33; 12.32; 10.19,20

Jesus continued:

8 If you tell others that you belong to me, the Son of Man will tell God's angels that you are my followers. 9 But if you reject me, you will be rejected in front of them.

10 If you speak against the Son of Man, you can be forgiven, but if you speak against the Holy Spirit, you cannot be forgiven.

11 When you are brought to trial in the Jewish meeting places or before rulers or officials, don't worry about how you will defend yourselves or what you will say. 12 At that time the Holy Spirit will tell you what to say.

A rich fool

13 A man in a crowd said to Jesus, "Teacher, tell my brother to give me my share of what our father left us when he died."

14 Jesus answered, "Who gave me the right to settle arguments between you and your brother?"

15 Then he said to the crowd, "Don't be greedy! Owning a lot of things won't make your life safe."

16 So Jesus told them this story:

A rich man's farm produced a big crop, 17 and he said to himself, "What can I do? I don't have a place large enough to store everything."

18 Later, he said, "Now I know what I'll do. I'll tear down my barns and build bigger ones, where I can store all my grain and other goods. 19 Then I'll say to myself, 'You have stored up enough good things to last for years to come. Live it up! Eat, drink, and enjoy yourself.' "

20 But God said to him, "You fool! Tonight you will die. Then who will get what you have stored up?"

21 "This is what happens to people who store up everything for themselves, but are poor in the sight of God."

Worry

This is also told in Matthew 6.25-34

22 Jesus said to his disciples:

I tell you not to worry about your life! Don't worry about having something to eat or wear. 23 Life is more than food or clothing. 24 Look at the crows! They don't plant or harvest, and they don't have storehouses or barns. But God takes care of them. You are much more important than any birds. 25 Can worry make you live longer?* 26 If you don't have power over small things, why worry about everything else?

---

*12.1 dishonest teaching: The Greek text has "yeast", which is used here of a teaching that is not true. See Matthew 16.6,12.

See also: 12.1: Matt 16.6; Mark 8.15. 12.2: Mark 4.22; Luke 8.17.

See also: 12.10: Matt 12.32; Mark 3.29.
12.11,12: Matt 10.19,20; Mark 13.11; Luke 21.14,15.

27 Look how the wild flowers grow! They don't work hard to make their clothes. But I tell you that Solomon with all his wealth* wasn't as well clothed as one of these flowers. 28 God gives such beauty to everything that grows in the fields, even though it is here today and thrown into a fire tomorrow. Won't he do even more for you? You have such little faith!

29 Don't keep worrying about having something to eat or drink. 30 Only people who don't know God are always worrying about such things. Your Father knows what you need. 31 But put God's work first, and these things will be yours as well.

Treasures in heaven

This is also told in Matthew 6.19–21

Jesus continued:

32 My little group of disciples, don't be afraid! Your Father wants to give you the kingdom. 33 Sell what you have and give the money to the poor. Make yourselves money bags that never wear out. Make sure your treasure is safe in heaven, where thieves cannot steal it and moths cannot destroy it. 34 Your heart will always be where your treasure is.

Faithful and unfaithful servants

This is also told in Matthew 24.45–51

Jesus continued:

35 Be ready and keep your lamps burning 36 just like those servants who wait up for their master to return from a wedding feast. As soon as he comes and knocks, they open the door for him. 37 Servants are fortunate if their master finds them awake and ready when he comes! I promise you that he will get ready and make his servants sit down so that he can serve them. 38 Those servants are really fortunate if their master finds them ready, even though he comes late at night or early in the morning. 39 You would not let a thief break into your home, if you knew when the thief was coming. 40 So always be

ready! You don't know when the Son of Man will come.

41 Peter asked Jesus, "Did you say this just for us or for everyone?"

42 The Lord answered:

Who are faithful and wise servants? Who are the ones the master will put in charge of giving the other servants their food supplies at the proper time? 43 Servants are fortunate if their master comes and finds them doing their job. 44 A servant who is always faithful will be put in charge of everything the master owns.

45 But suppose one of the servants thinks that the master won't return until late. Suppose that servant starts beating all the other servants and eats and drinks and gets drunk. 46 If that happens, the master will come on a day and at a time when the servant least expects him. That servant will then be punished and thrown out with the servants who cannot be trusted.

47 If servants are not ready or willing to do what their master wants them to do, they will be beaten hard. 48 But servants who don't know what their master wants them to do will not be beaten so hard for doing wrong. If God has been generous with you, he will expect you to serve him well. But if he has been more than generous, he will expect you to serve him even better.

Not peace, but trouble

This is also told in Matthew 10.34–36

Jesus continued:

49 I came to set fire to the earth, and I wish it were already on fire! 50 I am going to be put to a hard test. And I will have to suffer a lot of pain until it is over. 51 Do you think that I came to bring peace to earth? No indeed! I came to make people choose sides. 52 A family of five will be divided, with two of them against the other three. 53 Fathers and sons will turn against one another, and mothers and daughters will do the same. Mothers-in-law and daughters-in-law will also turn against each other.

---

*12.27 Solomon with all his wealth: The Jewish people thought that Solomon was the richest person who had ever lived.

See also: 12.27: 1 King 10.4–7; 2 Chron 9.3–6.
12.35: Matt 25.1–13.   **12.36:** Mark 13.34–36.
12.39,40: Matt 24.43,44.

See also: 12.50: Mark 10.38.   12.53: Mic 7.6.

Knowing what to do

This is also told in Matthew 16.2,3; 5.25,26

[54] Jesus said to all the people:

As soon as you see a cloud coming up in the west, you say, "It's going to rain," and it does. [55] When the south wind blows, you say, "It's going to get hot," and it does. [56] Are you trying to fool someone? You can predict the weather by looking at the earth and sky, but you don't really know what's going on right now. [57] Why don't you understand the right thing to do? [58] When someone accuses you of something, try to settle things before you are taken to court. If you don't, you will be dragged before the judge. Then the judge will hand you over to the jailer, and you will be locked up. [59] You won't get out until you have paid the last penny you owe.

CHAPTER 13

Turn back to God

[1] About this same time Jesus was told that Pilate had given orders for some people from Galilee to be killed while they were offering sacrifices. [2] Jesus replied:

Do you think that these people were worse sinners than everyone else in Galilee just because of what happened to them? [3] Not at all! But you can be sure that if you don't turn back to God, every one of you will also be killed. [4] What about those eighteen people who died when the tower in Siloam fell on them? Do you think they were worse than everyone else in Jerusalem? [5] Not at all! But you can be sure that if you don't turn back to God, every one of you will also die.

A story about a fig tree

[6] Jesus then told them this story:

A man had a fig tree growing in his vineyard. One day he went out to pick some figs, but he didn't find any. [7] So he said to the gardener, "For three years I have come looking for figs on this tree, and I haven't found any yet. Chop it down! Why should it take up space?"

[8] The gardener answered, "Master, leave it for another year. I'll dig around it and put some manure on it to make it grow. [9] Perhaps it will have figs on it next year. If it doesn't, you can have it cut down."

Healing a woman on the Sabbath

[10] One Sabbath, Jesus was teaching in a Jewish meeting place, [11] and a woman was there who had been crippled for eighteen years. She was completely bent over and could not straighten up. [12] When Jesus saw the woman, he called her over and said, "You are now well." [13] He placed his hands on her, and at once she stood up straight and praised God.

[14] The man in charge of the meeting place was angry because Jesus had healed someone on the Sabbath. So he said to the people, "Each week has six days when we can work. Come and be healed on one of those days, but not on the Sabbath."

[15] The Lord replied, "Are you trying to fool someone? Won't any one of you untie your ox or donkey and lead it out to drink on a Sabbath? [16] This woman belongs to the family of Abraham, but Satan has kept her bound for eighteen years. Isn't it right to set her free on the Sabbath?" [17] Jesus' words made his enemies ashamed. But everyone else in the crowd was happy about the wonderful things he was doing.

A mustard seed and yeast

This is also told in Matthew 13.31–33; Mark 4.30–32

[18] Jesus said, "What is God's kingdom like? What can I compare it with? [19] It is like what happens when someone plants a mustard seed in a garden. The seed grows as big as a tree, and birds nest in its branches."

[20] Then Jesus said, "What can I compare God's kingdom with? [21] It is like what happens when a woman mixes yeast into three batches of flour. Finally, all the dough rises."

The narrow door

This is also told in Matthew 7.13,14,21–23

[22] As Jesus was on his way to Jerusalem, he taught the people in the towns and villages. [23] Someone asked him, "Lord, are only a few people going to be saved?"

Jesus answered:

[24] Do all you can to go in by the narrow door! A lot of people will try to get in, but will not be able to. [25] Once the owner of the house gets up and locks the door, you will be left standing outside. You will knock on the door and say, "Sir, open the door for us!"

See also: 13.14: Exod 20.9,10; Deut 5.13,14.

But the owner will answer, "I don't know a thing about you!"

26 Then you will start saying, "We dined with you, and you taught in our streets."

27 But he will say, "I really don't know who you are! Get away from me, you evil people!"

28 Then when you have been thrown outside, you will weep and grit your teeth because you will see Abraham, Isaac, Jacob, and all the prophets in God's kingdom. 29 People will come from all directions and sit down to feast in God's kingdom. 30 There the ones who are now least important will be the most important, and those who are now most important will be least important.

Jesus and Herod

31 At that time some Pharisees came to Jesus and said, "You had better get away from here! Herod* wants to kill you."

32 Jesus said to them:

Go and tell that fox, "I am going to force out demons and heal people today and tomorrow, and three days later I'll have finished." 33 But I am going on my way today and tomorrow and the next day. After all, Jerusalem is the place where prophets are killed.

Jesus loves Jerusalem

This is also told in Matthew 23.37–39

Jesus continued:

34 Jerusalem, Jerusalem! Your people have killed the prophets and have stoned the messengers who were sent to you. I have often wanted to gather your people, as a hen gathers her chicks under her wings. But you wouldn't let me. 35 Now your temple will be deserted. You won't see me again until the time when you say,

"Blessed is the one who comes in the name of the Lord."

CHAPTER 14

Jesus heals a sick man

1 One Sabbath, Jesus was having dinner in the home of an important Pharisee, and everyone was carefully watching Jesus. 2 All of a sudden a man with swollen legs stood up in front of him. 3 Jesus turned and asked the Pharisees and the teachers of the Law of Moses, "Is it right to heal on the Sabbath?" 4 But they did not say a word.

Jesus took hold of the man. Then he healed him and sent him away. 5 Afterwards, Jesus asked the people, "If your son or ox falls into a well, wouldn't you pull him out straight away, even on the Sabbath?" 6 There was nothing they could say.

How to be a guest

7 Jesus saw how the guests had tried to take the best seats. So he told them:

8 When you are invited to a wedding feast, don't sit in the best place. Someone more important may have been invited. 9 Then the one who invited you will come and say, "Give your place to this other guest!" You will be embarrassed and will have to sit in the worst place.

10 When you are invited to be a guest, go and sit in the worst place. Then the one who invited you may come and say, "My friend, take a better seat!" You will then be honoured in front of all the other guests. 11 If you put yourself above others, you will be put down. But if you humble yourself, you will be honoured.

12 Then Jesus said to the man who had invited him:

When you give a dinner or a banquet, don't invite your friends and family and relatives and rich neighbours. If you do, they will invite you in return, and you will be paid back. 13 When you give a feast, invite the poor, the crippled, the lame, and the blind. 14 They cannot pay you back. But God will bless you and reward you when his people rise from death.

The great banquet

This is also told in Matthew 22.1–10

15 After Jesus had finished speaking, one of the guests said, "The greatest blessing of all is to be at the banquet in God's kingdom!"

16 Jesus told him:

A man once gave a great banquet and invited a lot of guests. 17 When the banquet was ready, he sent a servant to tell the guests, "Everything is ready! Please come."

---

*13.31 Herod: See the note at 3.1.

See also: 13.27: Psa 6.8. 13.28: Matt 22.13; 25.30.
13.28,29: Matt 8.11,12. 13.30: Matt 19.30; 20.16;
Mark 10.31. 13.35: Psa 118.26.

See also: 14.5: Matt 12.11. 14.8-10: Prov 25.6,7.
14.11: Matt 23.12; Luke 18.14.

[18] One guest after another started making excuses. The first one said, "I bought some land, and I've got to look it over. Please excuse me."

[19] Another guest said, "I bought five teams of oxen, and I need to try them out. Please excuse me."

[20] Still another guest said, "I have just got married, and I can't be there."

[21] The servant told his master what happened, and the master became so angry that he said, "Go as fast as you can to every street and alley in town! Bring in everyone who is poor or crippled or blind or lame."

[22] When the servant returned, he said, "Master, I've done what you told me, and there is still plenty of room for more people."

[23] His master then told him, "Go out along the back roads and lanes and make people come in, so that my house will be full. [24] Not one of the guests I first invited will get even a bite of my food!"

Being a disciple

This is also told in Matthew 10.37,38

[25] Large crowds were walking along with Jesus, when he turned and said:

[26] You cannot be my disciple, unless you love me more than you love your father and mother, your wife and children, and your brothers and sisters. You cannot come with me unless you love me more than you love your own life.

[27] You cannot be my disciple unless you carry your own cross and come with me.

[28] Suppose one of you wants to build a tower. What is the first thing you will do? Won't you sit down and figure out how much it will cost and if you have enough money to pay for it? [29] Otherwise, you will start building the tower, but not be able to finish. Then everyone who sees what is happening will laugh at you. [30] They will say, "You started building, but could not finish the job." [31] What will a king do if he has only ten thousand soldiers to defend himself against a king who is about to attack him with twenty thousand soldiers? Before he goes out to battle, won't he first sit down and decide if he can win? [32] If he thinks he won't be able to defend himself, he will

send messengers and ask for peace while the other king is still a long way off. [33] So then, you cannot be my disciple unless you give away everything you own.

Salt

This is also told in Matthew 5.13; Mark 9.50

Jesus continued:

[34] Salt is good, but if it no longer tastes like salt, how can it be made to taste salty again? [35] It is no longer good for the soil or even for the manure pile. People simply throw it out. If you have ears, pay attention!

CHAPTER 15

One sheep

This is also told in Matthew 18.12–14

[1] Tax collectors* and sinners were all crowding around to listen to Jesus. [2] So the Pharisees and the teachers of the Law of Moses started grumbling, "This man is friendly with sinners. He even eats with them."

[3] Then Jesus told them this story:

[4] If any of you has a hundred sheep, and one of them gets lost, what will you do? Won't you leave the ninety-nine in the field and go and look for the lost sheep until you find it? [5] And when you find it, you will be so glad that you will put it on your shoulder [6] and carry it home. Then you will call in your friends and neighbours and say, "Let's celebrate! I've found my lost sheep."

[7] Jesus said, "In the same way there is more happiness in heaven because of one sinner who turns to God than over ninety-nine good people who don't need to."

One coin

[8] Jesus told the people another story:

What will a woman do if she has ten silver coins and loses one of them? Won't she light a lamp, sweep the floor, and look carefully until she finds it? [9] Then she will call in her friends and neighbours and say, "Let's celebrate! I've found the coin I lost."

[10] Jesus said, "In the same way God's angels are happy when even one person turns to him."

See also: 14.26: Matt 10.37.   14.27: Matt 10.38; 16.24; Mark 8.34; Luke 9.23.

*15.1 Tax collectors: See the note at 3.12.
See also: 15.1,2: Luke 5.29,30.

Two sons

[11] Jesus also told them another story:

Once a man had two sons. [12] The younger son said to his father, "Give me my share of the property." So the father divided his property between his two sons.

[13] Not long after that, the younger son packed up everything he owned and left for a foreign country, where he wasted all his money in wild living. [14] He had spent everything, when a bad famine spread through that whole land. Soon he had nothing to eat.

[15] He went to work for a man in that country, and the man sent him out to take care of his pigs.* [16] He would have been glad to eat what the pigs were eating,* but no one gave him a thing.

[17] Finally, he came to his senses and said, "My father's workers have plenty to eat, and here I am, starving to death! [18] I will go to my father and say to him, 'Father, I have sinned against God in heaven and against you. [19] I am no longer good enough to be called your son. Treat me like one of your workers.'"

[20] The younger son got up and started back to his father. But when he was still a long way off, his father saw him and felt sorry for him. He ran to his son and hugged him and kissed him.

[21] The son said, "Father, I have sinned against God in heaven and against you. I am no longer good enough to be called your son."

[22] But his father said to the servants, "Hurry and bring the best clothes and put them on him. Give him a ring for his finger and sandals* for his feet. [23] Get the best calf and prepare it, so we can eat and celebrate. [24] This son of mine was dead, but has now come back to life."

He was lost and has now been found." And they began to celebrate.

[25] The elder son had been out in the field. But when he came near the house, he heard the music and dancing. [26] So he called one of the servants over and asked, "What's going on here?"

[27] The servant answered, "Your brother has come home safe and sound, and your father ordered us to kill the best calf." [28] The elder brother got so angry that he would not even go into the house.

His father came out and begged him to go in. [29] But he said to his father, "For years I have worked for you like a slave and have always obeyed you. But you have never even given me a little goat, so that I could give a dinner for my friends. [30] This other son of yours wasted your money on prostitutes. And now that he has come home, you ordered the best calf to be killed for a feast."

[31] His father replied, "My son, you are always with me, and everything I have is yours. [32] But we should be glad and celebrate! Your brother was dead, but he is now alive. He was lost and has now been found."

CHAPTER 16

A dishonest manager

[1] Jesus said to his disciples:

A rich man once had a manager to take care of his business. But he was told that his manager was wasting money. [2] So the rich man called him in and said, "What is this I hear about you? Tell me what you have done! You are no longer going to work for me."

[3] The manager said to himself, "What shall I do now that my master is going to fire me? I can't dig ditches, and I'm ashamed to beg. [4] I know what I'll do, so that people will welcome me into their homes after I've lost my job. [5] Then one by one he called in the people who were in debt to his master. He asked the first one, "How much do you owe my master?"

[6] "A hundred barrels of olive oil," the man answered.

So the manager said, "Take your bill and sit down and quickly write 'fifty'."

---

*15.15 pigs: The Jewish religion taught that pigs were not fit to eat or even to touch. A Jewish man would have felt terribly insulted if he had to feed pigs, much less eat with them.

*15.16 the pigs were eating: The Greek text has "(bean) pods", which came from a tree in Palestine. These were used to feed animals. Poor people sometimes ate them too.

*15.22 ring . . . sandals: These show that the young man's father fully accepted him as his son. A ring was a sign of high position in the family. Sandals showed that he was a son instead of a slave, since slaves did not usually wear sandals.

⁷ The manager asked someone else who was in debt to his master, "How much do you owe?"

"A thousand sacks* of wheat," the man replied.

The manager said, "Take your bill and write 'eight hundred'."

⁸ The master praised his dishonest manager for looking out for himself so well. That's how it is! The people of this world look out for themselves better than the people who belong to the light.

⁹ My disciples, I tell you to use wicked wealth to make friends for yourselves. Then when it is gone, you will be welcomed into an eternal home. ¹⁰ Anyone who can be trusted in little matters can also be trusted in important matters. But anyone who is dishonest in little matters will be dishonest in important matters. ¹¹ If you cannot be trusted with this wicked wealth, who will trust you with true wealth? ¹² And if you cannot be trusted with what belongs to someone else, who will give you something that will be your own? ¹³ You cannot be the slave of two masters. You will like one more than the other or be more loyal to one than to the other. You cannot serve God and money.

Some sayings of Jesus

This is also told in Matthew 11.12,13; 5.31,32; Mark 10.11,12

¹⁴ The Pharisees really loved money. So when they heard what Jesus said, they made fun of him. ¹⁵ But Jesus told them:

You are always making yourselves look good, but God sees what is in your heart. The things that most people think are important are worthless as far as God is concerned.

¹⁶ Until the time of John the Baptist, people had to obey the Law of Moses and the Books of the Prophets.* But since God's kingdom has been preached, everyone is trying hard to get in. ¹⁷ Heaven and earth will disappear before the smallest letter of the Law does.

¹⁸ It is a terrible sin* for a man to divorce his wife and marry another woman. It is also a terrible sin for a man to marry a divorced woman.

Lazarus and the rich man

Jesus continued:

¹⁹ There was once a rich man who wore expensive clothes and every day ate the best food. ²⁰ But a poor beggar named Lazarus was brought to the gate of the rich man's house. ²¹ He was happy just to eat the scraps that fell from the rich man's table. His body was covered with sores, and dogs kept coming up to lick them. ²² The poor man died, and angels took him to the place of honour next to Abraham.*

The rich man also died and was buried. ²³ He went to hell* and was suffering terribly. When he looked up and saw Abraham far off and Lazarus at his side, ²⁴ he said to Abraham, "Have pity on me! Send Lazarus to dip his finger in water and touch my tongue. I'm suffering terribly in this fire."

²⁵ Abraham answered, "My friend, remember that while you lived, you had everything good, and Lazarus had everything bad. Now he is happy, and you are in pain. ²⁶ And besides, there is a deep ditch between us, and no one from either side can cross over."

²⁷ But the rich man said, "Abraham, then please send Lazarus to my father's home. ²⁸ Let him warn my five brothers, so they won't come to this horrible place."

²⁹ Abraham answered, "Your brothers can read what Moses and the prophets* wrote. They should pay attention to that."

³⁰ Then the rich man said, "No, that's not enough! If only someone from the dead would go to them, they would listen and turn to God."

---

*16.7 a thousand sacks: The Greek text has "a hundred measures", and each measure is about 300 kilograms.
*16.16 the Law of Moses and the Books of the Prophets: The Jewish Scriptures, that is, the Old Testament.
See also: 16.13: Matt 6.24. 16.16: Matt 11.12,13. 16.17: Matt 5.18.

*16.18 a terrible sin: The Greek text uses a word that means the sin of being unfaithful in marriage.
*16.22 the place of honour next to Abraham: The Jewish people thought that heaven would be a banquet that God would give for them. Abraham would be the most important person there, and the guest of honour would sit next to him.
*16.23 hell: The Greek text has "hades", which the Jewish people often thought of as the place where the dead wait for the final judgment.
*16.29 Moses and the prophets: See the note at 16.16.
See also: 16.18: Matt 5.32; 1 Cor 7.10,11.

³¹ So Abraham said, "If they won't pay attention to Moses and the prophets, they won't listen even to someone who comes back from the dead."

CHAPTER 17

Faith and service

This is also told in Matthew 18.6,7,21,22; Mark 9.42

¹ Jesus said to his disciples:

There will always be something that causes people to sin. But anyone who causes them to sin is in for trouble. A person who causes even one of my little followers to sin ² would be better off thrown into the ocean with a heavy stone tied around their neck. ³ So be careful what you do.

Correct any followers* of mine who sin, and forgive the ones who say they are sorry. ⁴ Even if one of them ill-treats you seven times in one day and says, "I am sorry," you should just forgive that person.

⁵ The apostles said to the Lord, "Make our faith stronger!"

⁶ Jesus replied:

If you had faith no bigger than a tiny mustard seed, you could tell this mulberry tree to pull itself up, roots and all, and to plant itself in the ocean. And it would!

⁷ If your servant comes in from ploughing or from taking care of the sheep, would you say, "Welcome! Come on in and have something to eat"? ⁸ No, you wouldn't say that. You would say, "Prepare me something to eat. Get ready to serve me, so I can have my meal. Then later on you can eat and drink." ⁹ Servants don't deserve special thanks for doing what they are supposed to. ¹⁰ And that's how it should be with you. When you've done all you should, then say, "We are merely servants, and we have simply done our duty."

Ten men with leprosy

¹¹ On his way to Jerusalem, Jesus went along the border between Samaria and Galilee. ¹² As he was going into a village, ten men with leprosy* came towards him. They stood at a distance ¹³ and shouted, "Jesus, Master, have pity on us!"

¹⁴ Jesus looked at them and said, "Go and show yourselves to the priests."*

On their way they were healed. ¹⁵ When one of them discovered that he was healed, he came back, shouting praises to God. ¹⁶ He bowed down at the feet of Jesus and thanked him. The man was from the country of Samaria.

¹⁷ Jesus asked, "Weren't ten men healed? Where are the other nine? ¹⁸ Why was this foreigner the only one who came back to thank God?" ¹⁹ Then Jesus told the man, "You may get up and go. Your faith has made you well."

God's kingdom

This is also told in Matthew 24.23–28,37–41

²⁰ Some Pharisees asked Jesus when God's kingdom would come. He answered, "God's kingdom isn't something you can see. ²¹ There is no use saying, 'Look! Here it is' or 'Look! There it is.' God's kingdom is here with you."*

²² Jesus said to his disciples:

The time will come when you will long to see one of the days of the Son of Man, but you will not. ²³ When people say to you, "Look there," or "Look here," don't go looking for him. ²⁴ The day of the Son of Man will be like lightning flashing across the sky. ²⁵ But first he must suffer terribly and be rejected by the people of today. ²⁶ When the Son of Man comes, things will be just as they were when Noah lived. ²⁷ People were eating, drinking, and getting married right up to the day when Noah went into the big boat. Then the flood came and drowned everyone on earth. ²⁸ When Lot* lived, people were also eating and drinking. They were buying, selling, planting, and building. ²⁹ But on the very day Lot left Sodom, fiery flames poured down from the sky and killed everyone. ³⁰ The same will happen on the day when the Son of Man appears.

---

*17.14 show yourselves to the priests: See the note at 5.14.

*17.27,28 Noah . . . Lot: When God destroyed the earth by a flood, he saved Noah and his family. And when God destroyed the cities of Sodom and Gomorrah and the evil people who lived there, he rescued Lot and his family (see Genesis 9.1–29).

See also: 17.14: Lev 14.1–32. 17.26: Gen 6.5–8.
17.27: Gen 7.6–24. 17.28,29: Gen 18.20–19.25.

---

*17.3 followers: The Greek text has "brothers", which is often used in the New Testament for followers of Jesus.

*17.12 leprosy: See the note at 4.27.

See also: 17.3: Matt 18.15.

³¹ At that time no one on a rooftop* should go down into the house to get anything. No one in a field should go back to the house for anything. ³² Remember what happened to Lot's wife.*

³³ People who try to save their lives will lose them, and those who lose their lives will save them. ³⁴ On that night two people will be sleeping in the same bed, but only one will be taken. The other will be left. ³⁵-³⁶ Two women will be together grinding wheat, but only one will be taken. The other will be left.*

³⁷ Then Jesus' disciples spoke up, "But where will this happen, Lord?"

Jesus said, "Where there is a corpse, there will always be vultures."*

CHAPTER 18

A widow and a judge

¹ Jesus told his disciples a story about how they should keep on praying and never give up:

² In a town there was once a judge who didn't fear God or care about people. ³ In that same town there was a widow who kept going to the judge and saying, "Make sure that I get fair treatment in court."

⁴ For a while the judge refused to do anything. Finally, he said to himself, "Even though I don't fear God or care about people, ⁵ I will help this widow because she keeps on bothering me. If I don't help her, she will wear me out."

⁶ The Lord said:

Think about what that crooked judge said. ⁷ Won't God protect his chosen ones who pray to him day and night? Won't he be concerned for them? ⁸ He will hurry and help them. But when the Son of Man comes, will he find on this earth anyone with faith?

A Pharisee and a tax collector

⁹ Jesus told a story to some people who thought they were better than others and who looked down on everyone else:

¹⁰ Two men went into the temple to pray.* One was a Pharisee and the other a tax collector.* ¹¹ The Pharisee stood over by himself and prayed,* "God, I thank you that I am not greedy, dishonest, and unfaithful in marriage like other people. And I am really glad that I am not like that tax collector over there. ¹² I go without eating* for two days a week, and I give you one tenth of all I earn."

¹³ The tax collector stood off at a distance and did not think he was good enough even to look up towards heaven. He was so sorry for what he had done that he pounded his chest and prayed, "God, have pity on me! I am such a sinner."

¹⁴ Then Jesus said, "When the two men went home, it was the tax collector and not the Pharisee who was pleasing to God. If you put yourself above others, you will be put down. But if you humble yourself, you will be honoured."

Jesus blesses little children

This is also told in Matthew 19.13–15; Mark 10.13–16

¹⁵ Some people brought their little children for Jesus to bless. But when his disciples saw them doing this, they told the people to stop bothering him. ¹⁶ So Jesus called the children over to him and said, "Let the children come to me! Don't try to stop them. People who are like these children belong to God's kingdom.* ¹⁷ You will never get into God's kingdom unless you enter it like a child!"

---

*17.31 rooftop: See the note at 5.19.
*17.32 what happened to Lot's wife: She turned into a block of salt when she disobeyed God (see Genesis 19.26).
*17.37 Where there is a corpse, there will always be vultures: This saying may mean that when anything important happens, people soon know about it. Or the saying may mean that whenever something bad happens, curious people gather around and stare. But the word translated "vulture" also means "eagle" and may refer to the Roman army, which had an eagle as its symbol.
See also: 17.31: Matt 24.17,18; Mark 13.15,16. 17.32: Gen 19.26. 17.33: Matt 10.39; 16.25; Mark 8.35; Luke 9.24; John 12.25.

*18.10 into the temple to pray: Jewish people usually prayed there early in the morning and late in the afternoon.
*18.10 tax collector: See the note at 3.12.
*18.12 without eating: See the note at 2.37.
See also: 18.14: Matt 23.12; Luke 14.11.

A rich and important man

This is also told in Matthew 19.16–30; Mark 10.17–31

¹⁸ An important man asked Jesus, "Good Teacher, what must I do to have eternal life?"

¹⁹ Jesus said, "Why do you call me good? Only God is good. ²⁰ You know the commandments: 'Be faithful in marriage. Do not murder. Do not steal. Do not tell lies about others. Respect your father and mother.' "

²¹ He told Jesus, "I have obeyed all these commandments since I was a young man."

²² When Jesus heard this, he said, "There is one thing you still need to do. Go and sell everything you own! Give the money to the poor, and you will have riches in heaven. Then come and be my follower." ²³ When the man heard this, he was sad, because he was very rich.

²⁴ Jesus saw how sad the man was. So he said, "It's terribly hard for rich people to get into God's kingdom! ²⁵ In fact, it's easier for a camel to go through the eye of a needle than for a rich person to get into God's kingdom."

²⁶ When the crowd heard this, they asked, "How can anyone ever be saved?"

²⁷ Jesus replied, "There are some things that people cannot do, but God can do anything."

²⁸ Peter said, "Remember, we left everything to be your followers!"

²⁹ Jesus answered, "You can be sure that anyone who gives up home or wife or brothers or family or children because of God's kingdom ³⁰ will be given much more in this life. And in the future world they will have eternal life."

Jesus again tells about his death

This is also told in Matthew 20.17–19; Mark 10.32–34

³¹ Jesus took the twelve apostles aside and said:

We are now on our way to Jerusalem. Everything that the prophets wrote about the Son of Man will happen there. ³² He will be handed over to foreigners,* who will make fun of him, ill-treat him, and spit on him. ³³ They will beat him and kill him, but three days later he will rise to life.

³⁴ The apostles did not understand what Jesus was talking about. They did not understand, because the meaning of what he said was hidden from them.

Jesus heals a blind beggar

This is also told in Matthew 20.29–34; Mark 10.46–52

³⁵ When Jesus was coming close to Jericho, a blind man sat begging beside the road. ³⁶ The man heard the crowd walking by and asked what was happening. ³⁷ Some people told him that Jesus from Nazareth was passing by. ³⁸ So the blind man shouted, "Jesus, Son of David,* have pity on me!" ³⁹ The people who were going along with Jesus told the man to be quiet. But he shouted even louder, "Son of David, have pity on me!"

⁴⁰ Jesus stopped and told some people to bring the blind man over to him. When the blind man was getting near, Jesus asked, ⁴¹ "What do you want me to do for you?"

"Lord, I want to see!" he answered.

⁴² Jesus replied, "Look and you will see! Your eyes are healed because of your faith." ⁴³ Straight away the man could see, and he went with Jesus and started thanking God. When the crowds saw what happened, they praised God.

CHAPTER 19

Zacchaeus

¹ Jesus was going through Jericho, ² where a man named Zacchaeus lived. He was in charge of collecting taxes* and was very rich. ³⁻⁴ Jesus was heading his way, and Zacchaeus wanted to see what he was like. But Zacchaeus was a short man and could not see over the crowd. So he ran ahead and climbed up into a sycamore tree.

⁵ When Jesus got there, he looked up and said, "Zacchaeus, hurry down! I want to stay with you today." ⁶ Zacchaeus hurried down and gladly welcomed Jesus.

⁷ Everyone who saw this started grumbling, "This man Zacchaeus is a sinner! And Jesus is going home to eat with him."

⁸ Later that day Zacchaeus stood up and said to the Lord, "I will give half of my property to the poor. And I will now pay back four times as much* to everyone I have ever cheated."

---

*18.32 foreigners: The Romans, who ruled Judea at this time.

See also: 18.20: a Exod 20.14; Deut 5.18; b Exod 20.13; Deut 5.17; c Exod 20.15; Deut 5.19; d Exod 20.16; Deut 5.20; e Exod 20.12; Deut 5.16.

*18.38 Son of David: The Jewish people expected the Messiah to be from the family of King David, and for this reason the Messiah was often called the "Son of David".

*19.2 in charge of collecting taxes: See the note at 3.12.

*19.8 pay back four times as much: Both Jewish and Roman law said that a person must pay back four times the amount that was taken.

9 Jesus said to Zacchaeus, "Today you and your family have been saved,* because you are a true son of Abraham.* 10 The Son of Man came to look for and to save people who are lost."

A story about ten servants

This is also told in Matthew 25.14-30

11 The crowd was still listening to Jesus as he was getting close to Jerusalem. Many of them thought that God's kingdom would soon appear, 12 and Jesus told them this story:

A prince once went to a foreign country to be crowned king and then to return. 13 But before leaving, he called in ten servants and gave each of them some money. He told them, "Use this to earn more money until I get back."

14 But the people of his country hated him, and they sent messengers to the foreign country to say, "We don't want this man to be our king."

15 After the prince had been made king, he returned and called in his servants. He asked them how much they had earned with the money they had been given.

16 The first servant came and said, "Sir, with the money you gave me I have earned ten times as much."

17 "That's fine, my good servant!" the king said. "Since you have shown that you can be trusted with a small amount, you will be given ten cities to rule."

18 The second one came and said, "Sir, with the money you gave me, I have earned five times as much."

19 The king said, "You will be given five cities."

20 Another servant came and said, "Sir, here is your money. I kept it safe in a handkerchief. 21 You are a hard man, and I was afraid of you. You take what isn't yours, and you harvest crops you didn't plant."

22 "You worthless servant!" the king told him. "You have condemned yourself by what you have just said. You knew that I am a hard man, taking what isn't mine and harvesting what I haven't planted.

23 Why didn't you put my money in the bank? On my return, I could have had the money together with interest."

24 Then he said to some other servants standing there, "Take the money away from him and give it to the servant who earned ten times as much."

25 But they said, "Sir, he already has ten times as much!"

26 The king replied, "Those who have something will be given more. But everything will be taken away from those who don't have anything. 27 Now bring me the enemies who didn't want me to be their king. Kill them while I watch!"

Jesus' last week: his trial and death

Jesus enters Jerusalem

This is also told in Matthew 21.1-11; Mark 11.1-11; John 12.12-19

28 When Jesus had finished saying all this, he went on towards Jerusalem. 29 As he was getting near Bethphage and Bethany on the Mount of Olives, he sent two of his disciples on ahead. 30 He told them, "Go into the next village, where you will find a young donkey that has never been ridden. Untie the donkey and bring it here. 31 If anyone asks why you are doing that, just say, 'The Lord needs it.'"

32 They went off and found everything just as Jesus had said. 33 While they were untying the donkey, its owners asked, "Why are you doing that?"

34 They answered, "The Lord needs it."

35 Then they led the donkey to Jesus. They put some of their clothes on its back and helped Jesus get on. 36 And as he rode along, the people spread clothes on the road* in front of him. 37 When Jesus was setting off down the Mount of Olives, his large crowd of disciples were happy and praised God because of all the miracles they had seen. 38 They shouted,

"Blessed is the king who comes
in the name of the Lord!
Peace in heaven
and glory to God."

*19.9 saved: Zacchaeus was Jewish, but it is only now that he is rescued from sin and placed under God's care.
*19.9 son of Abraham: As used in this verse, the words mean that Zacchaeus is truly one of God's special people.
See also: 19.10: Matt 18.11. 19.11-27: Matt 25.14-30.

*19.36 spread clothes on the road: This was one way that the Jewish people welcomed a famous person.
See also: 19.26: Matt 13.12; Mark 4.25; Luke 8.18. 19.38: Psa 118.26.

³⁹ Some Pharisees in the crowd said to Jesus, "Teacher, make your disciples stop shouting!"

⁴⁰ But Jesus answered, "If they keep quiet, these stones will start shouting."

⁴¹ As Jesus came closer and could see Jerusalem, he cried ⁴² and said:

Today your people don't know what will bring them peace! Now it is hidden from them. ⁴³ Jerusalem, the time will come when your enemies will build walls around you to attack you. Armies will surround you and close in on you from every side. ⁴⁴ They will level you to the ground and kill your people. Not one stone in your buildings will be left on top of another. This will happen because you did not see that God had come to save you.*

Jesus in the temple

This is also told in Matthew 21.12–17; Mark 11.15–19; John 2.13–22

⁴⁵ When Jesus entered the temple, he started chasing out the people who were selling things. ⁴⁶ He told them, "The Scriptures say, 'My house should be a place of worship.' But you have made it a place where robbers hide!"

⁴⁷ Each day, Jesus kept on teaching in the temple. So the chief priests, the teachers of the Law of Moses, and some other important people tried to have him killed. ⁴⁸ But they could not find any way to do it, because everyone else was eager to listen to him.

CHAPTER 20

A question about Jesus' authority

This is also told in Matthew 21.23–27; Mark 11.27–33

¹ One day, Jesus was teaching in the temple and telling the good news. So the chief priests, the teachers, and the nation's leaders ² asked him, "What right do you have to do these things? Who gave you this authority?"

³ Jesus replied, "I want to ask you a question. ⁴ Who gave John the right to baptize? Was it God in heaven or merely some human being?"

⁵ They talked this over and said to each other, "We can't say that God gave John this

right. Jesus will ask us why we didn't believe John. ⁶ And we can't say that it was merely some human who gave John the right to baptize. The crowd will stone us to death, because they think John was a prophet."

⁷ So they told Jesus, "We don't know who gave John the right to baptize."

⁸ Jesus replied, "Then I won't tell you who gave me the right to do what I do."

Tenants of a vineyard

This is also told in Matthew 21.33–46; Mark 12.1–12

⁹ Jesus told the people this story:

A man once planted a vineyard and let it. Then he left the country for a long time. ¹⁰ When it was time to harvest the crop, he sent a servant to ask the tenants for his share of the grapes. But they beat up the servant and sent him away without anything. ¹¹ So the owner sent another servant. The tenants also beat him up. They insulted him terribly and sent him away without a thing. ¹² The owner sent a third servant. He was also beaten terribly and thrown out of the vineyard.

¹³ The owner then said to himself, "What am I going to do? I know what. I'll send my son, the one I love so much. They will surely respect him!"

¹⁴ When the tenants saw the owner's son, they said to one another, "Some day he will own the vineyard. Let's kill him! Then we can have it all for ourselves." ¹⁵ So they threw him out of the vineyard and killed him.

Jesus asked, "What do you think the owner of the vineyard will do? ¹⁶ I'll tell you what. He will come and kill those tenants and let someone else have his vineyard."

When the people heard this, they said, "This must never happen!"

¹⁷ But Jesus looked straight at them and said, "Then what do the Scriptures mean when they say, 'The stone that the builders tossed aside is now the most important stone of all'? ¹⁸ Anyone who stumbles over this stone will get hurt, and anyone it falls on will be smashed to pieces."

¹⁹ The chief priests and the teachers of the Law of Moses knew that Jesus was talking about them when he was telling this story. They wanted to arrest him at once, but they were afraid of the people.

*19.44 that God had come to save you: The Jewish people looked for the time when God would come and rescue them from their enemies. But when Jesus came, many of them refused to obey him.

See also: 19.46: Isa 56.7; Jer 7.11. 19.47: Luke 21.37.

See also: 20.9: Isa 5.1. 20.17: Psa 118.22.

Paying taxes

This is also told in Matthew 22.15–22; Mark 12.13-17

²⁰ Jesus' enemies kept watching him closely, because they wanted to hand him over to the Roman governor. So they sent some men who pretended to be good. But they were really spies trying to catch Jesus saying something wrong. ²¹ The spies said to him, "Teacher, we know that you teach the truth about what God wants people to do. And you treat everyone with the same respect, no matter who they are. ²² Tell us, should we pay taxes to the Emperor or not?"

²³ Jesus knew that they were trying to trick him. So he told them, ²⁴ "Show me a coin." Then he asked, "Whose picture and name are on it?"

"The Emperor's," they answered.

²⁵ Then he told them, "Give the Emperor what belongs to him and give God what belongs to God." ²⁶ Jesus' enemies could not catch him saying anything wrong there in front of the people. They were amazed at his answer and kept quiet.

Life in the future world

This is also told in Matthew 22.23–33; Mark 12.18-27

²⁷ The Sadducees did not believe that people would rise to life after death. So some of them came to Jesus ²⁸ and said:

Teacher, Moses wrote that if a married man dies and has no children, his brother should marry the widow. Their first son would then be thought of as the son of the dead brother. ²⁹ There were once seven brothers. The first one married, but died without having any children. ³⁰ The second one married his brother's widow, and he also died without having any children. ³¹ The same thing happened to the third one. Finally, all seven brothers married that woman and died without having any children. ³² At last the woman died. ³³ When God raises people from death, whose wife will this woman be? All seven brothers had married her.

³⁴ Jesus answered:

The people in this world get married. ³⁵ But in the future world no one who is worthy to rise from death will either marry ³⁶ or die. They will be like the angels and will be God's children, because they have been raised to life.

³⁷ In the story about the burning bush, Moses clearly shows that people will live again. He said, "The Lord is the God worshipped by Abraham, Isaac, and Jacob."* ³⁸ So the Lord isn't the God of the dead, but of the living. This means that everyone is alive as far as God is concerned.

³⁹ Some of the teachers of the Law of Moses said, "Teacher, you have given a good answer!" ⁴⁰ From then on, no one dared to ask Jesus any questions.

About David's son

This is also told in Matthew 22.41–46; Mark 12.35-37

⁴¹ Jesus asked, "Why do people say that the Messiah will be the son of King David?* ⁴² In the book of Psalms, David himself says,

'The Lord said to my Lord,
    Sit at my right side*
⁴³ until I make your enemies
    into a footstool for you.'

⁴⁴ David spoke of the Messiah as his Lord, so how can the Messiah be his son?"

Jesus and the teachers of the Law of Moses

This is also told in Matthew 23.1-36; Mark 12.38-40; Luke 11.37-54

⁴⁵ While everyone was listening to Jesus, he said to his disciples:

⁴⁶ Guard against the teachers of the Law of Moses! They love to walk around in long robes, and they like to be greeted in the market. They want the front seats in the meeting places and the best seats at banquets. ⁴⁷ But they cheat widows out of their homes and then pray long prayers just to show off. These teachers will be punished most of all.

*20.37 "The Lord is the God worshipped by Abraham, Isaac, and Jacob": Jesus argues that if God is worshipped by these three, they must be alive, because he is the God of the living.
*20.41 the son of King David: See the note at 18.38.
*20.42 right side: The place of power and honour.
See also: 20.37: Exod 3.6. 20.42,43: Psa 110.1.

See also: 20.27: Acts 23.8. 20.28: Deut 25.5.

103

CHAPTER 21

A widow's offering

This is also told in Mark 12.41-44

[1] Jesus looked up and saw some rich people tossing their gifts into the offering box. [2] He also saw a poor widow putting in two pennies. [3] And he said, "I tell you that this poor woman has put in more than all the others. [4] Everyone else gave what they didn't need. But she is very poor and gave everything she had."

The temple will be destroyed

This is also told in Matthew 24.1,2; Mark 13.1,2

[5] Some people were talking about the beautiful stones used to build the temple and about the gifts that had been placed in it. Jesus said, [6] "Do you see these stones? The time is coming when not one of them will be left in place. They will all be knocked down."

Warning about trouble

This is also told in Matthew 24.3-14; Mark 13.3-13

[7] Some people asked, "Teacher, when will all this happen? How can we know when these things are about to take place?"

[8] Jesus replied:

Don't be fooled by those who will come and claim to be me. They will say, "I am Christ!" and "Now is the time!" But don't follow them. [9] When you hear about wars and riots, don't be afraid. These things will have to happen first, but that isn't the end.

[10] Nations will go to war against one another, and kingdoms will attack each other. [11] There will be great earthquakes, and in many places people will starve to death and suffer terrible diseases. All sorts of frightening things will be seen in the sky.

[12] Before all this happens, you will be arrested and punished. You will be tried in your meeting places and put in jail. Because of me you will be placed on trial before kings and governors. [13] But this will be your chance to tell about your faith. [14] Don't worry about what you will say to defend yourselves. [15] I will give you the wisdom to know what to say. None of your enemies will be able to oppose you or to say that you are wrong. [16] You will be betrayed

by your own parents, brothers, family, and friends. Some of you will even be killed. [17] Because of me, you will be hated by everyone. [18] But don't worry! [19] You will be saved by being faithful to me.

Jerusalem will be destroyed

This is also told in Matthew 24.15-21; Mark 13.14-19

Jesus continued:

[20] When you see Jerusalem surrounded by soldiers, you will know that it will soon be destroyed. [21] If you are living in Judea at that time, run to the mountains. If you are in the city, leave it. And if you are out in the country, don't go back into the city. [22] This time of punishment is what is written about in the Scriptures. [23] It will be an awful time for women who are expecting babies or nursing young children! Everywhere in the land people will suffer horribly and be punished. [24] Some of them will be killed by swords. Others will be carried off to foreign countries. Jerusalem will be overrun by foreign nations until their time comes to an end.

When the Son of Man appears

This is also told in Matthew 24.29-31; Mark 13.24-27

Jesus continued:

[25] Strange things will happen to the sun, moon, and stars. The nations on earth will be afraid of the roaring sea and tides, and they won't know what to do. [26] People will be so frightened that they will faint because of what is happening to the world. Every power in the sky will be shaken.* [27] Then the Son of Man will be seen, coming in a cloud with great power and glory. [28] When all this starts happening, stand up straight and be brave. You will soon be set free.

A lesson from a fig tree

This is also told in Matthew 24.32-35; Mark 13.28-31

[29] Then Jesus told them a story:

When you see a fig tree or any other tree [30] putting out leaves, you know that summer will soon come. [31] So, when you

---

*21.26 Every power in the sky will be shaken: In ancient times people thought that the stars were spiritual powers.
See also: 21.22: Hos 9.7. 21.25: Isa 13.10; Ezek 32.7; Joel 2.31; Rev 6.12,13. 21.27: Dan 7.13; Rev 1.7.

See also: 21.14,15: Luke 12.11,12.

New Testament: the Gospels Luke 22

see these things happening, you know that God's kingdom will soon be here. ³² You can be sure that some of the people of this generation will still be alive when all this takes place. ³³ The sky and the earth won't last for ever, but my words will.

A warning

Jesus continued:

³⁴ Don't spend all your time thinking about eating or drinking or worrying about life. If you do, the final day will suddenly catch you ³⁵ like a trap. That day will surprise everyone on earth. ³⁶ Watch out and keep praying that you can escape all that is going to happen and that the Son of Man will be pleased with you.

³⁷ Jesus taught in the temple each day, and he spent each night on the Mount of Olives. ³⁸ Everyone got up early and came to the temple to hear him teach.

CHAPTER 22

A plot to kill Jesus

This is also told in Matthew 26.1–5,14,16; Mark 14.1,2,10,11; John 11.45–53

¹ The Festival of Thin Bread, also called Passover, was near. ² The chief priests and the teachers of the Law of Moses were looking for a way to get rid of Jesus, because they were afraid of what the people might do. ³ Then Satan entered the heart of Judas Iscariot,* who was one of the twelve apostles.

⁴ Judas went to talk with the chief priests and the officers of the temple police about how he could help them arrest Jesus. ⁵ They were very pleased and offered to pay Judas some money. ⁶ He agreed and started looking for a good chance to betray Jesus when the crowds were not around.

Jesus eats with his disciples

This is also told in Matthew 26.17–25; Mark 14.12–21; John 13.21–30

⁷ The day had come for the Festival of Thin Bread, and it was time to kill the Passover lambs. ⁸ So Jesus said to Peter and John, "Go and prepare the Passover meal for us to eat." ⁹ But they asked, "Where do you want us to prepare it?"

¹⁰ Jesus told them, "As you go into the city, you will meet a man carrying a jar of water.* Follow him into the house ¹¹ and say to the owner, 'Our teacher wants to know where he can eat the Passover meal with his disciples.' ¹² The owner will take you upstairs and show you a large room ready for you to use. Prepare the meal there."

¹³ Peter and John left. They found everything just as Jesus had told them, and they prepared the Passover meal.

The Lord's Supper

This is also told in Matthew 26.26–30; Mark 14.22–26; 1 Corinthians 11.23–25

¹⁴ When the time came for Jesus and the apostles to eat, ¹⁵ he said to them, "I have very much wanted to eat this Passover meal with you before I suffer. ¹⁶ I tell you that I will not eat another Passover meal until it is finally eaten in God's kingdom."

¹⁷ Jesus took a cup of wine in his hands and gave thanks to God. Then he told the apostles, "Take this wine and share it with each other. ¹⁸ I tell you that I will not drink any more wine until God's kingdom comes."

¹⁹ Jesus took some bread in his hands and gave thanks for it. He broke the bread and handed it to his apostles. Then he said, "This is my body, which is given for you. Eat this as a way of remembering me!"

²⁰ After the meal he took another cup of wine in his hands. Then he said, "This is my blood. It is poured out for you, and with it God makes his new agreement. ²¹ The one who will betray me is here at the table with me! ²² The Son of Man will die in the way that has been decided for him, but it will be terrible for the one who betrays him!"

²³ Then the apostles started arguing about who would ever do such a thing.

An argument about greatness

²⁴ The apostles got into an argument about which one of them was the greatest. ²⁵ So Jesus told them:

Foreign kings order their people around, and powerful rulers call themselves

---

*22.3 Iscariot: See the note at 6.16.
See also: 21.37: Luke 19.47. 22.1: Exod 12.1–27.

*22.10 a man carrying a jar of water: A male slave carrying water would probably mean that the family was rich.

See also: 22.20: Jer 31.31–34. 22.21: Psa 41.9.
22.24: Matt 18.1; Mark 9.34; Luke 9.46.
22.25,26: Matt 20.25–27; Mark 10.42–44.

everyone's friends.* ²⁶ But don't be like them. The most important one of you should be like the least important, and your leader should be like a servant. ²⁷ Who do people think is the greatest, a person who is served or one who serves? Isn't it the one who is served? But I have been with you as a servant.

²⁸ You have stayed with me in all my troubles. ²⁹ So I will give you the right to rule as kings, just as my Father has given me the right to rule as a king. ³⁰ You will eat and drink with me in my kingdom, and you will each sit on a throne to judge the twelve tribes of Israel.

Jesus' disciples will be tested

This is also told in Matthew 26.31–35; Mark 14.27–31; John 13.36–38

³¹ Jesus said, "Simon, listen to me! Satan has demanded the right to test each one of you, as a farmer does when he separates wheat from the husks.* ³² But Simon, I have prayed that your faith will be strong. And when you have come back to me, help the others."

³³ Peter said, "Lord, I am ready to go with you to jail and even to die with you."

³⁴ Jesus replied, "Peter, I tell you that before a cock crows tomorrow morning, you will say three times that you don't know me."

Money bags, travelling bags, and swords

³⁵ Jesus asked his disciples, "When I sent you out without a money bag or a travelling bag or sandals, did you need anything?"

"No!" they answered.

³⁶ Jesus told them, "But now, if you have a money bag, take it with you. Also take a travelling bag, and if you don't have a sword,* sell some of your clothes and buy

one. ³⁷ Do this because the Scriptures say, 'He was considered a criminal.' This was written about me, and it will soon come true."

³⁸ The disciples said, "Lord, here are two swords!"

"Enough of that!" Jesus replied.

Jesus prays

This is also told in Matthew 26.36–46; Mark 14.32–42

³⁹ Jesus went out to the Mount of Olives, as he often did, and his disciples went with him. ⁴⁰ When they got there, he told them, "Pray that you won't be tested."

⁴¹ Jesus walked on a little way before he knelt down and prayed, ⁴² "Father, if you will, please don't make me suffer by making me drink from this cup.* But do what you want, and not what I want."

⁴³ Then an angel from heaven came to help him. ⁴⁴ Jesus was in great pain and prayed so sincerely that his sweat fell to the ground like drops of blood.⁰

⁴⁵ Jesus got up from praying and went over to his disciples. They were asleep and worn out from being so sad. ⁴⁶ He said to them, "Why are you asleep? Wake up and pray that you won't be tested."

Jesus is arrested

This is also told in Matthew 26.47–56; Mark 14.43–50; John 18.3–11

⁴⁷ While Jesus was still speaking, a crowd came up. It was led by Judas, one of the twelve apostles. He went over to Jesus and greeted him with a kiss.*

⁴⁸ Jesus asked Judas, "Are you betraying the Son of Man with a kiss?"

⁴⁹ When Jesus' disciples saw what was about to happen, they asked, "Lord, should we attack them with a sword?" ⁵⁰ One of the disciples even struck at the high priest's servant with his sword and cut off the servant's right ear.

⁵¹ "Enough of that!" Jesus said. Then he touched the servant's ear and healed it.

⁵² Jesus spoke to the chief priests, the temple police, and the leaders who had come to arrest him. He said, "Why do you come

---

*22.25 everyone's friends: This translates a Greek word that rulers sometimes used as a title for themselves or for special friends.

*22.31 separates wheat from the husks: See the note at 3.17.

*22.36 money bag . . . travelling bag . . . sword: These were things that someone would take on a dangerous journey. Jesus was telling his disciples to be ready for anything that might happen. They seem to have understood what he meant (see 22.49–51).

See also: 22.26: Matt 23.11; Mark 9.35.
22.27: John 13.12–15.   22.30: Matt 19.28.
22.35: Mark 10.9,10; Mark 6.8,9; Luke 9.3; 10.4.

---

*22.42 making me drink from this cup: In the Scriptures "to drink from a cup" sometimes means to suffer.

*22.47 greeted him with a kiss: It was the custom for people to greet each other with a kiss on the cheek.

See also: 22.37: Isa 53.12.

out with swords and clubs and treat me like a criminal? [53] I was with you every day in the temple, and you didn't arrest me. But this is your time, and darkness* is in control."

Peter says he doesn't know Jesus

This is also told in Matthew 26.57,58,67–75; Mark 14.53,54,66–72; John 18.12–18,25–27

[54] Jesus was arrested and led away to the house of the high priest, while Peter followed at a distance. [55] Some people built a fire in the middle of the courtyard and were sitting around it. Peter sat there with them, [56] and a servant girl saw him. Then after she had looked at him carefully, she said, "This man was with Jesus!"

[57] Peter said, "Woman, I don't even know that man!"

[58] A little later someone else saw Peter and said, "You are one of them!"

"No, I'm not!" Peter replied.

[59] About an hour later another man insisted, "This man must have been with Jesus. They both come from Galilee."

[60] Peter replied, "I don't know what you are talking about!" At once, while Peter was still speaking, a cock crowed.

[61] The Lord turned and looked at Peter. And Peter remembered that the Lord had said, "Before a cock crows tomorrow morning, you will say three times that you don't know me." [62] Then Peter went out and cried hard.

[63] The men who were guarding Jesus made fun of him and beat him. [64] They put a blindfold on him and said, "Tell us who struck you!" [65] They kept on insulting Jesus in many other ways.

Jesus is questioned by the council

This is also told in Matthew 26.59–66; Mark 14.55–64; John 18.19–24

[66] At daybreak the nation's leaders, the chief priests, and the teachers of the Law of Moses got together and brought Jesus before their council. [67] They said, "Tell us! Are you the Messiah?"

Jesus replied, "If I said so, you wouldn't believe me. [68] And if I asked you a question, you wouldn't answer. [69] But from now on, the Son of Man will be seated at the right side of God All-Powerful."

[70] Then they asked, "Are you the Son of God?"*

Jesus answered, "You say I am!"

[71] They replied, "Why do we need more witnesses? He said it himself!"

CHAPTER 23

Pilate questions Jesus

This is also told in Matthew 27.1,2,11–14; Mark 15.1–5; John 18.28–38

[1] Everyone in the council got up and led Jesus off to Pilate. [2] They started accusing him and said, "We caught this man trying to get our people to riot and to stop paying taxes to the Emperor. He also claims that he is the Messiah, our king."

[3] Pilate asked Jesus, "Are you the king of the Jews?"

"Those are your words," Jesus answered.

[4] Pilate told the chief priests and the crowd, "I don't find him guilty of anything."

[5] But they all kept on saying, "He has been teaching and causing trouble all over Judea. He started in Galilee and has now come all the way here."

Jesus is brought before Herod

[6] When Pilate heard this, he asked, "Is this man from Galilee?" [7] After Pilate learnt that Jesus came from the region ruled by Herod,* he sent him to Herod, who was in Jerusalem at that time.

[8] For a long time Herod had wanted to see Jesus and was very happy because he finally had this chance. He had heard many things about Jesus and hoped to see him perform a miracle.

[9] Herod asked him a lot of questions, but Jesus did not answer. [10] Then the chief priests and the teachers of the Law of Moses stood up and accused him of all kinds of bad things.

[11] Herod and his soldiers made fun of Jesus and insulted him. They put a fine robe on him and sent him back to Pilate. [12] That same day Herod and Pilate became friends, even though they had been enemies before this.

---

*22.53 darkness: Darkness stands for the power of the devil.
See also: 22.53: Luke 19.47; 21.37.

*22.70 Son of God: This was one of the titles used for the kings of Israel.
*23.7 Herod: See the note at 3.1.

The death sentence

This is also told in Matthew 27.15–26; Mark 15.6–15; John 18.39–19.16

13 Pilate called together the chief priests, the leaders, and the people. 14 He told them, "You brought Jesus to me and said he was a troublemaker. But I have questioned him here in front of you, and I have not found him guilty of anything that you say he has done. 15 Herod didn't find him guilty either and sent him back. This man doesn't deserve to be put to death! 16–17 I will just have him beaten with a whip and set free."*

18 But the whole crowd shouted, "Kill Jesus! Give us Barabbas!" 19 Now Barabbas was in jail because he had started a riot in the city and had murdered someone.

20 Pilate wanted to set Jesus free, so he spoke again to the crowds. 21 But they kept shouting, "Nail him to a cross! Nail him to a cross!"

22 Pilate spoke to them a third time, "But what crime has he done? I have not found him guilty of anything for which he should be put to death. I will have him beaten with a whip and set free."

23 The people kept on shouting as loud as they could for Jesus to be put to death. 24 Finally, Pilate gave in. 25 He freed the man who was in jail for rioting and murder, because he was the one the crowd wanted to be set free. Then Pilate handed Jesus over for them to do what they wanted with him.

Jesus is nailed to a cross

This is also told in Matthew 27.31–44; Mark 15.21–32; John 19.17–27

26 As Jesus was being led away, some soldiers grabbed hold of a man from Cyrene named Simon. He was coming in from the fields, but they put the cross on him and made him carry it behind Jesus.

27 A large crowd was following Jesus, and in the crowd a lot of women were crying and weeping for him. 28 Jesus turned to the women and said:

Women of Jerusalem, don't cry for me! Cry for yourselves and for your children. 29 Some day people will say, "Women who never had children are really fortunate!" 30 At that time everyone will say to the mountains, "Fall on us!" They will say to the hills, "Hide us!" 31 If this can

happen when the wood is green, what do you think will happen when it is dry?*

32 Two criminals were led out to be put to death with Jesus. 33 When the soldiers came to the place called "The Skull",* they nailed Jesus to a cross. They also nailed the two criminals to crosses, one on each side of Jesus.

34–35 Jesus said, "Father, forgive these people! They don't know what they're doing."*

While the crowd stood there watching Jesus, the soldiers gambled for his clothes. The leaders insulted him by saying, "He saved others. Now he should save himself, if he really is God's chosen Messiah!"

36 The soldiers made fun of Jesus and brought him some wine. 37 They said, "If you are the king of the Jews, save yourself!"

38 Above him was a sign that said, "This is the King of the Jews."

39 One of the criminals hanging there also insulted Jesus by saying, "Aren't you the Messiah? Save yourself and save us!"

40 But the other criminal told the first one off, "Don't you fear God? Aren't you getting the same punishment as this man? 41 We got what was coming to us, but he didn't do anything wrong." 42 Then he said to Jesus, "Remember me when you come into power!"

43 Jesus replied, "I promise that today you will be with me in paradise."*

The death of Jesus

This is also told in Matthew 27.45–56; Mark 15.33–41; John 19.28–30

44 Around midday the sky turned dark and stayed that way until the middle of the afternoon. 45 The sun stopped shining, and

---

*23.31 If this can happen when the wood is green, what do you think will happen when it is dry?: This saying probably means, "If this can happen to an innocent person, what do you think will happen to one who is guilty?"

*23.33 "The Skull": The place was probably given this name because it was near a large rock in the shape of a human skull.

*23.43 paradise: In the Greek translation of the Old Testament, this word is used for the Garden of Eden. In New Testament times it was sometimes used for the place where God's people are happy and at rest, as they wait for the final judgment.

See also: 23.34: Psa 22.18. 23.35: Psa 22.7. 23.36: Psa 69.21. 23.45: Exod 26.31–33.

See also: 23.30: Hos 10.8; Rev 6.16.

the curtain in the temple* split down the middle. 46 Jesus shouted, "Father, I put myself in your hands!" Then he died.

47 When the Roman officer saw what had happened, he praised God and said, "Jesus must really have been a good man!"

48 A crowd had gathered to see the terrible sight. Then after they had seen it, they felt brokenhearted and went home. 49 All Jesus' close friends and the women who had come with him from Galilee stood at a distance and watched.

Jesus is buried

This is also told in Matthew 27.57–61; Mark 15.42–47; John 19.38–42

50-51 There was a man named Joseph, who was from Arimathea in Judea. Joseph was a good and honest man, and he was eager for God's kingdom to come. He was also a member of the Jewish council, but he did not agree with what they had decided.

52 Joseph went to Pilate and asked for Jesus' body. 53 He took the body down from the cross and wrapped it in fine cloth. Then he put it in a tomb that had been cut out of solid rock and had never been used. 54 It was Friday, and the Sabbath was about to begin.*

55 The women who had come with Jesus from Galilee followed Joseph and watched how Jesus' body was placed in the tomb. 56 Then they went to prepare some sweet-smelling spices for his burial. But on the Sabbath they rested, as the Law of Moses commands.

Jesus is alive

CHAPTER 24

This is also told in Matthew 28.1–10; Mark 16.1–8; John 20.1–10

1 Very early on Sunday morning the women went to the tomb, carrying the spices that they had prepared. 2 When they found the stone rolled away from the entrance, 3 they went in.

But they did not find the body of the Lord* Jesus, 4 and they did not know what to think.

Suddenly two men in shining white clothes stood beside her. 5 The women were afraid and bowed to the ground. But the men said, "Why are you looking in the place of the dead for someone who is alive? 6 Jesus isn't here! He has been raised from death. Remember that while he was still in Galilee, he told you, 7 'The Son of Man will be handed over to sinners who will nail him to a cross. But three days later he will rise to life.' " 8 Then they remembered what Jesus had said.

9-10 Mary Magdalene, Joanna, Mary the mother of James, and some other women were the ones who had gone to the tomb. When they returned, they told the eleven apostles and the others what had happened. 11 The apostles thought it was all nonsense, and they would not believe.

12 But Peter ran to the tomb. And when he stooped down and looked in, he saw only the burial clothes. Then he returned, wondering what had happened.*

Jesus appears. He is taken to heaven

Jesus appears to two disciples

This is also told in Mark 16.12,13

13 That same day two of Jesus' disciples were going to the village of Emmaus, which was about eleven kilometres from Jerusalem. 14 As they were talking and thinking about what had happened, 15 Jesus came near and started walking along beside them. 16 But they did not know who he was.

17 Jesus asked them, "What were you talking about as you walked along?"

The two of them stood there looking sad and gloomy. 18 Then the one named Cleopas asked Jesus, "Are you the only person from Jerusalem who didn't know what was happening there these last few days?"

19 "What do you mean?" Jesus asked. They answered:

Those things that happened to Jesus from Nazareth. By what he did and said he showed that he was a powerful prophet, who pleased God and all the people. 20 Then the chief priests and our leaders had him arrested and sentenced to die on a cross.

---

*23.45 curtain in the temple: There were two curtains in the temple. One was at the entrance, and the other separated the holy place from the most holy place that the Jewish people thought of as God's home on earth. The second curtain is probably the one which is meant.
*23.54 the Sabbath was about to begin: The Sabbath begins at sunset on Friday.

See also: 23.46: Psa 31.5. 23.49: Luke 8.2,3. 23.56: Exod 20.10; Deut 5.14.

See also: 24.6,7: Matt 16.21; 17.22,23; 20.18,19; Mark 8.31; 9.31; 10.33,34; Luke 9.22; 18.31–33.

21 We had hoped that he would be the one to set Israel free! But it has already been three days since all this happened.

22 Some women in our group surprised us. They had gone to the tomb early in the morning, 23 but did not find the body of Jesus. They came back, saying that they had seen a vision of angels who told them that he is alive. 24 Some men from our group went to the tomb and found it just as the women had said. But they didn't see Jesus either.

25 Then Jesus asked the two disciples, "Why can't you understand? How can you be so slow to believe all that the prophets said? 26 Didn't you know that the Messiah would have to suffer before he was given his glory?" 27 Jesus then explained everything written about himself in the Scriptures, beginning with the Law of Moses and the Books of the Prophets.*

28 When the two of them came near the village where they were going, Jesus seemed to be going further. 29 They begged him, "Stay with us! It's already late, and the sun is going down." So Jesus went into the house to stay with them.

30 After Jesus sat down to eat, he took some bread. He blessed it and broke it. He gave it to them. 31 At once they knew who he was, but he disappeared. 32 They said to each other, "When he talked with us along the road and explained the Scriptures to us, didn't it warm our hearts?" 33 So they got up at once and returned to Jerusalem.

The two disciples found the eleven apostles and the others gathered together. 34 And they learnt from the group that the Lord was really alive and had appeared to Peter. 35 Then the disciples from Emmaus told what happened on the road and how they knew he was the Lord when he broke the bread.

What Jesus' followers must do

This is also told in Matthew 28.16–20; Mark 16.14–18; John 20.19–23; Acts 1.6–8

36 While Jesus' disciples were talking about what had happened, Jesus appeared and greeted them. 37 They were frightened and terrified because they thought they were seeing a ghost.

38 But Jesus said, "Why are you so frightened? Why do you doubt? 39 Look at my

*24.27 the Law of Moses and the Books of the Prophets: See the note at 16.16.

hands and my feet and see who I am! Touch me and find out for yourselves. Ghosts don't have flesh and bones as you see I have."

40 After Jesus said this, he showed them his hands and his feet. 41 The disciples were so glad and amazed that they could not believe it. Jesus then asked them, "Do you have something to eat?" 42 They gave him a piece of baked fish. 43 He took it and ate it as they watched.

44 Jesus said to them, "While I was still with you, I told you that everything written about me in the Law of Moses, the Books of the Prophets, and in the Psalms* had to happen." 45 Then he helped them understand the Scriptures. 46 He told them:

The Scriptures say that the Messiah must suffer, then three days later he will rise from death. 47 They also say that all people of every nation must be told in my name to turn to God, in order to be forgiven. So beginning in Jerusalem, 48 you must tell everything that has happened. 49 I will send you the one my Father has promised,* but you must stay in the city until you are given power from heaven.

Jesus returns to heaven

This is also told in Mark 16.19,20; Acts 1.9–11

50 Jesus led his disciples out to Bethany, where he raised his hands and blessed them. 51 As he was doing this, he left and was taken up to heaven.* 52 After his disciples had worshipped him,* they returned to Jerusalem and were very happy. 53 They spent their time in the temple, praising God.

*24.44 Psalms: The Jewish Scriptures were made up of three parts: (1) the Law of Moses, (2) the Books of the Prophets, and (3) the Writings, which included the Psalms. Sometimes the Scriptures were just called the Law or the Law (of Moses) and the Books of the Prophets.
*24.49 the one my Father has promised: Jesus means the Holy Spirit.
See also: 24.49: Acts 1.4. 24.50,51: Acts 1.9–11.

Additional notes

•1.3 a careful study: Or "a study from the beginning".
•1.78 like the sun that rises in the sky: Or "like the Messiah coming from heaven."
•2.37 And now she was eighty-four years old: Or "And now she had been a widow for eighty-four years."
•2.49 in my Father's house: Or "doing my Father's work".

4.44 Judea: Some manuscripts have "Galilee".

6.6 On another Sabbath: Some manuscripts have a reading which may mean "the Sabbath after the next".

6.35 without expecting to be paid back: Some manuscripts have "without giving up on anyone".

7.50 saved: Or "healed". The Greek word may have either meaning.

8.26 Gerasa: Some manuscripts have "Gergesa".

8.37 Gerasa: See the note at 8.26.

8.43 She had spent everything she had on doctors: Some manuscripts do not have these words.

8.45 from every side: Some manuscripts add "and you ask, 'Who touched me?' "

9.24 life: In verses 24,25 a Greek word which often means "soul" is translated "life" and "yourself".

9.31 Jesus' death: In Greek this is "his departure", which probably includes his rising to life and his return to heaven.

9.54 to destroy these people: Some manuscripts add "as Elijah did".

9.55 what they had said: Some manuscripts add, "and said, 'Don't you know what spirit you belong to? The Son of Man did not come to destroy people's lives, but to save them.' "

10.9 will soon be here: Or "is already here".

10.11 will soon be here: See the note at 10.9.

10.21 the Holy Spirit: Some manuscripts have "his spirit".

11.3 the food we need: Or "food for today" or "food for the coming day".

11.28 "That's true, but the people who are really blessed . . . message": Or " 'That's not true, the people who are blessed . . . message.' "

11.40 Didn't God make both the outside and the inside?: Or "Doesn't the person who washes the outside always wash the inside too?"

12.25 live longer: Or "grow taller".

17.21 here with you: Or "in your hearts".

17.35,36 will be left: Some manuscripts add, "Two men will be in the same field, but only one will be taken. The other will be left."

18.11 stood over by himself and prayed: Some manuscripts have "stood up and prayed to himself".

18.16 People who are like these children belong to God's kingdom: Or "God's kingdom belongs to people who are like these children."

19.31 The Lord: Or "The master of the donkey".

19.34 The Lord: See the note at 19.31.

21.18 But don't worry: The Greek text has "Not a hair of your head will be lost", which means, "There's no need to worry".

22.43,44 Then an angel . . . like drops of blood: Verses 43,44 are not in some manuscripts.

22.70 You say I am: Or "That's what you say."

23.16,17 set free: Some manuscripts add, "Pilate said this, because at every Passover he was supposed to set one prisoner free for the Jewish people."

23.34,35 Jesus said, "Father, forgive these people! They don't know what they're doing.": These words are not in some manuscripts.

24.3 the Lord: These words are not in some manuscripts.

24.12 what had happened: Verse 12 is not in some manuscripts.

24.51 and was taken up to heaven: These words are not in some manuscripts.

24.52 After his disciples had worshipped him: These words are not in some manuscripts.

John
tells the good news

A quick look at this book

Who is Jesus Christ? John answers this question in the first chapter of his Gospel. Using the words of an early Christian hymn, he calls Jesus the "Word" by which God created everything and by which he gave life to everyone (1.3,4). He shows how John the Baptist announced Jesus' coming, "Here is the Lamb of God who takes away the sin of the world" (1.29). When Philip met Jesus he knew Jesus was "the one that Moses and the Prophets wrote about" (1.45). And, in the words of Nathanael, Jesus is "the Son of God and the King of Israel" (1.49).

In John's Gospel we learn a lot about who Jesus is by observing what he said and did when he was with other people. These include a Samaritan woman who received Jesus' offer of life-giving water, a woman who had been caught in sin, his friend Lazarus who was brought back to life by Jesus, and his follower Thomas who doubted that Jesus was raised from death. Jesus also refers to himself as

"I am", a phrase which translates the most holy name for God in the Hebrew Scriptures. He uses this name for himself when he makes his claim to be the life-giving bread, the light of the world, the good shepherd, and the true vine.

Jesus performs seven miracles that are more than miracles. Each of them is a "sign" that tells us something about Jesus as the Son of God. For example, by healing a lame man (5.1–8), Jesus shows that he is just like his Father, who never stops working (5.17). This sign also teaches that the Son does only what he sees his Father doing (5.19), and that like the Father "the Son gives life to anyone he wants to" (5.21).

The way John tells the story of Jesus is quite different from the other three Gospels. Here, Jesus has long conversations with people about who he is and what God sent him to do. In these conversations he teaches many important things — for example, that he is the way, the truth, and the life.

Why did John write? John himself tells us, "So that you will put your faith in Jesus as the Messiah and the Son of God" (20.31). How is this possible? Jesus answers that question in his words to Nicodemus:

> God loved the people of this world so much that he gave his only Son, so that everyone who has faith in him will have eternal life and never really die.
>
> (3.16)

In praise of the Word

CHAPTER 1

The Word of life

¹ In the beginning was the one
   who is called the Word.
   The Word was with God
   and was God.
² From the very beginning
   the Word was with God.

³ And with this Word,
   God created all things.
   Nothing was made
   without the Word.
   Everything that was created
⁴ received its life from him,
   and his life gave light
   to everyone.
⁵ The light keeps shining
   in the dark,
   and darkness has never
   put it out.◆
⁶ God sent a man named John,
⁷ who came to tell
   about the light
   and to lead all people
   to have faith.
⁸ John wasn't that light.
   He came only to tell
   about the light.

⁹ The true light that shines
   on everyone
   was coming into the world.
¹⁰ The Word was in the world,
    but no one knew him,
    though God had made the world
    with his Word.
¹¹ He came into his own world,
    but his own nation
    did not welcome him.
¹² Yet some people accepted him
    and put their faith in him.
    So he gave them the right
    to be the children of God.
¹³ They were not God's children
    by nature or because
    of any human desires.
    God himself was the one
    who made them his children.

¹⁴ The Word became
    a human being
    and lived here with us.

We saw his true glory,
   the glory of the only Son
   of the Father.
From him all the kindness
   and all the truth of God
   have come down to us.

¹⁵ John spoke about him and shouted, "This
is the one I told you would come! He is
greater than I am, because he was alive before
I was born."

¹⁶ Because of all that the Son is, we have
been given one blessing after another.◆ ¹⁷ The
Law was given by Moses, but Jesus Christ
brought us undeserved kindness and truth.
¹⁸ No one has ever seen God. The only Son,
who is truly God and is closest to the Father,
has shown us what God is like.

The message of John the Baptist

John the Baptist tells about Jesus

This is also told in Matthew 3.1–12; Mark 1.1–8;
Luke 3.15–17

¹⁹⁻²⁰ The Jewish leaders in Jerusalem sent
priests and temple helpers to ask John who
he was. He told them plainly, "I am not the
Messiah." ²¹ Then when they asked him if he
were Elijah, he said, "No, I am not!" And
when they asked if he were the Prophet,* he
also said "No!"

²² Finally, they said, "Who are you then?
We have to give an answer to the ones who
sent us. Tell us who you are!"

²³ John answered in the words of the prophet
Isaiah, "I am only someone shouting in the
desert, 'Get the road ready for the Lord!' "

²⁴ Some Pharisees had also been sent to
John. ²⁵ They asked him, "Why are you
baptizing people, if you are not the Messiah
or Elijah or the Prophet?"

²⁶ John told them, "I use water to baptize
people. But here with you is someone you
don't know. ²⁷ Even though I come first, I am
not good enough to untie his sandals."

²⁸ John said this as he was baptizing east of
the River Jordan in Bethany.*

---

*1.21 the Prophet: Many of the Jewish people
expected God to send them a prophet who would be
like Moses, but with even greater power. See
Deuteronomy 18.15,18.
*1.28 Bethany: An unknown village east of the Jordan
with the same name as the village near Jerusalem.

See also: 1.21: a Mal 4.5; b Deut 18.15,18.
1.23: Isa 40.3 (LXX).

The Lamb of God

29 The next day, John saw Jesus coming towards him and said:

Here is the Lamb of God who takes away the sin of the world! 30 He is the one I told you about when I said, "Someone else will come. He is greater than I am, because he was alive before I was born." 31 I didn't know who he was. But I came to baptize you with water, so that everyone in Israel would see him.

32 I was there and saw the Spirit come down on him like a dove from heaven. And the Spirit stayed on him. 33 Before this I didn't know who he was. But the one who sent me to baptize with water had told me, "You will see the Spirit come down and stay on someone. Then you will know that he is the one who will baptize with the Holy Spirit." 34 I saw this happen, and I tell you that he is the Son of God.

Jesus chooses his first disciples

35 The next day, John was there again, and two of his followers were with him. 36 When he saw Jesus walking by, he said, "Here is the Lamb of God!" 37 John's two followers heard him, and they went with Jesus.

38 When Jesus turned and saw them, he asked, "What do you want?"

They answered, "Rabbi, where do you live?" The Hebrew word "Rabbi" means "Teacher".

39 Jesus replied, "Come and see!" It was already about four o'clock in the afternoon when they went with him and saw where he lived. So they stayed on for the rest of the day.

40 One of the two men who had heard John and had gone with Jesus was Andrew, the brother of Simon Peter. 41 The first thing Andrew did was to find his brother and tell him, "We have found the Messiah!" The Hebrew word "Messiah" means the same as the Greek word "Christ".

42 Andrew brought his brother to Jesus. And when Jesus saw him, he said, "Simon son of John, you will be called Cephas." This name can be translated as "Peter".*

*1.42 Peter: The Aramaic name "Cephas" and the Greek name "Peter" each mean "rock".

114

Jesus chooses Philip and Nathanael

43-44 The next day Jesus decided to go to Galilee. There he met Philip, who was from Bethsaida, the home town of Andrew and Peter. Jesus said to Philip, "Come with me."

45 Philip then found Nathanael and said, "We have found the one that Moses and the Prophets* wrote about. He is Jesus, the son of Joseph from Nazareth."

46 Nathanael asked, "Can anything good come from Nazareth?"

Philip answered, "Come and see."

47 When Jesus saw Nathanael coming towards him, he said, "Here is a true descendant of our ancestor Israel. And he isn't deceitful."*

48 "How do you know me?" Nathanael asked.

Jesus answered, "Before Philip called you, I saw you under the fig tree."

49 Nathanael said, "Rabbi, you are the Son of God and the King of Israel!"

50 Jesus answered, "Did you believe me just because I said that I saw you under the fig tree? You will see something even greater. 51 I tell you for certain that you will see heaven open and God's angels going up and coming down on the Son of Man."*

Jesus' seven special miracles

CHAPTER 2

Jesus at a wedding in Cana

1 Three days later Mary, the mother of Jesus, was at a wedding feast in the village of Cana in Galilee. 2 Jesus and his disciples had also been invited and were there.

3 When the wine was all gone, Mary said to Jesus, "They don't have any more wine."

*1.45 Moses and the Prophets: The Jewish Scriptures, that is, the Old Testament.
*1.47 Israel . . . isn't deceitful: Israel (meaning "a man who wrestled with God" or "a prince of God") was the name that the Lord gave to Jacob (meaning "cheater" or "deceiver"), the famous ancestor of the Jewish people.
*1.51 going up and coming down on the Son of Man: When Jacob (see the note at verse 47) was running from his brother Esau, he had a dream in which he saw angels going up and down on a ladder from earth to heaven. See Genesis 32.22–32.
See also: 1.51: Gen 28.12.

⁴ Jesus replied, "Mother, my time hasn't yet come!* You must not tell me what to do."

⁵ Mary then said to the servants, "Do whatever Jesus tells you to do."

⁶ At the feast there were six stone water jars that were used by the people for washing themselves in the way that their religion said they must. Each jar held about a hundred litres. ⁷ Jesus told the servants to fill them to the top with water. Then after the jars had been filled, ⁸ he said, "Now take some water and give it to the man in charge of the feast."

The servants did as Jesus told them, ⁹ and the man in charge drank some of the water that had now turned into wine. He did not know where the wine had come from, but the servants did. He called the bridegroom over ¹⁰ and said, "The best wine is always served first. Then after the guests have had plenty, the other wine is served. But you have kept the best until last!"

¹¹ This was Jesus' first miracle,* and he did it in the village of Cana in Galilee. There Jesus showed his glory, and his disciples put their faith in him. ¹² After this, he went with his mother, his brothers, and his disciples to the town of Capernaum, where they stayed for a few days.

Jesus in the temple

This is also told in Matthew 21.12,13; Mark 11.15–17; Luke 19.45,46

¹³ Not long before the Jewish festival of Passover, Jesus went to Jerusalem. ¹⁴ There he found people selling cattle, sheep, and doves in the temple. He also saw moneychangers sitting at their tables. ¹⁵ So he took some rope and made a whip. Then he chased everyone out of the temple, together with their sheep and cattle. He turned over the tables of the moneychangers and scattered their coins.

¹⁶ Jesus said to the people who had been selling doves, "Get those doves out of here! Don't make my Father's house a market place."

¹⁷ The disciples then remembered that the Scriptures say, "My love for your house burns in me like a fire."

¹⁸ The Jewish leaders asked Jesus, "What miracle* will you perform to show us why you have done this?"

¹⁹ "Destroy this temple," Jesus answered, "and in three days I will build it again!"

²⁰ The leaders replied, "It took forty-six years to build this temple. What makes you think you can rebuild it in three days?"

²¹ But Jesus was talking about his body as a temple. ²² And when he was raised from death, his disciples remembered what he had told them. Then they believed the Scriptures and the words of Jesus.

Jesus knows what people are like

²³ In Jerusalem during Passover many people put their faith in Jesus, because they saw him perform miracles.* ²⁴ But Jesus knew what was in their hearts, and he would not let them have power over him. ²⁵ No one had to tell him what people were like. He already knew.

CHAPTER 3

Jesus and Nicodemus

¹ There was a man named Nicodemus who was a Pharisee and a Jewish leader. ² One night he went to Jesus and said, "Sir, we know that God has sent you to teach us. You could not perform these miracles, unless God were with you."

³ Jesus replied, "I tell you for certain that you must be born from above* before you can see God's kingdom!"

⁴ Nicodemus asked, "How can a grown man ever be born a second time?"

⁵ Jesus answered:

I tell you for certain that before you can get into God's kingdom, you must be born not only by water, but by the Spirit. ⁶ Humans give life to their children. Yet only God's Spirit can change you into a child of God. ⁷ Don't be surprised when I say that you must be born from above. ⁸ Only God's Spirit gives new life. The Spirit is like the wind that blows wherever it wants to. You can hear the wind, but you don't know where it comes from or where it is going.

---

*2.4 my time hasn't yet come!: The time when the true glory of Jesus would be seen, and he would be recognized as God's Son. See 12.23.
*2.11 miracle: The Greek text has "sign". In the Gospel of John the word "sign" is used for the miracle itself and as a way of pointing to Jesus as the Son of God.
See also: 2.12: Matt 4.13. 2.13: Exod 12.1–27.
2.17: Psa 69.9.

*2.18,23 miracle(s): See the note at 2.11.
*3.3 from above: Or "in a new way". The same Greek word is used in verses 7,31.
See also: 2.19: Matt 26.61; 27.40; Mark 14.58; 15.29.

9 "How can this be?" Nicodemus asked.

10 Jesus replied:

How can you be a teacher of Israel and not know these things? 11 I tell you for certain that we know what we are talking about because we have seen it ourselves. But none of you will accept what we say. 12 If you don't believe when I talk to you about things on earth, how can you possibly believe if I talk to you about things in heaven?

13 No one has gone up to heaven except the Son of Man, who came down from there. 14 And the Son of Man must be lifted up, just as that metal snake was lifted up by Moses in the desert.* 15 Then everyone who has faith in the Son of Man will have eternal life.

16 God loved the people of this world so much that he gave his only Son, so that everyone who has faith in him will have eternal life and never really die. 17 God did not send his Son into the world to condemn its people. He sent him to save them! 18 No one who has faith in God's Son will be condemned. But everyone who doesn't have faith in him has already been condemned for not having faith in God's only Son.

19 The light has come into the world, and people who do evil things are judged guilty because they love the dark more than the light. 20 People who do evil hate the light and won't come to the light, because it clearly shows what they have done. 21 But everyone who lives by the truth will come to the light, because they want others to know that God is really the one doing what they do.

Jesus and John the Baptist

22 Later, Jesus and his disciples went to Judea, where he stayed with them for a while and was baptizing people.

23–24 John had not yet been put in jail. He was at Aenon near Salim, where there was a lot of water, and people were coming there for John to baptize them.

25 John's followers got into an argument with a Jewish man* about a ceremony of washing.* 26 They went to John and said, "Rabbi, you spoke about a man when you were with him east of the Jordan. He is now baptizing people, and everyone is going to him."

27 John replied:

No one can do anything unless God in heaven allows it. 28 Surely you remember how I told you that I am not the Messiah. I am only the one sent ahead of him.

29 At a wedding the groom is the one who gets married. The best man is glad just to be there and to hear the groom's voice. That's why I am so glad. 30 Jesus must become more important, while I become less important.

The one who comes from heaven

John continued:

31 God's Son comes from heaven and is above all others. Everyone who comes from the earth belongs to the earth and speaks about earthly things. The one who comes from heaven is above all others. 32 He speaks about what he has seen and heard, and yet no one believes him. 33 But everyone who does believe him has shown that God is truthful. 34 The Son was sent to speak God's message, and he has been given the full power of God's Spirit.

35 The Father loves the Son and has given him everything. 36 Everyone who has faith in the Son has eternal life. But no one who rejects him will ever share in that life, and God will be angry with them for ever.

CHAPTER 4

1 Jesus knew that the Pharisees had heard that he was winning and baptizing more followers than John was. 2 But Jesus' disciples were really the ones doing the baptizing, and not Jesus himself.

Jesus and the Samaritan woman

3 Jesus left Judea and started for Galilee again. 4 This time he had to go through Samaria,

---

*3.14 just as that metal snake was lifted up by Moses in the desert: When the Lord punished the people of Israel by sending snakes to bite them, he told Moses to hold a metal snake up on a pole. Everyone who looked at the snake was cured of the snake bites. See Numbers 21.4–9.

See also: 3.14: Num 21.9. **3.24:** Matt 14.3; Mark 6.17; Luke 3.19,20.

---

*3.25 about a ceremony of washing: The Jewish people had some rules about washing themselves and their dishes, in order to make themselves fit to worship God.

See also: 3.28: John 1.20. **3.35:** Matt 11.27; Luke 10.22.

5 and on his way he came to the town of Sychar. It was near the field that Jacob had long ago given to his son Joseph. 6-8 The well that Jacob had dug was still there, and Jesus sat down beside it because he was tired from travelling. It was midday, and after Jesus' disciples had gone into town to buy some food, a Samaritan woman came to draw water from the well.

Jesus asked her, "Would you please give me a drink of water?"

9 "You are a Jew," she replied, "and I am a Samaritan woman. How can you ask me for a drink of water when Jews and Samaritans won't have anything to do with each other?"*

10 Jesus answered, "You don't know what God wants to give you, and you don't know who is asking you for a drink. If you did, you would ask me for the water that gives life."

11 "Sir," the woman said, "you don't even have a bucket, and the well is deep. Where are you going to get this life-giving water? 12 Our ancestor Jacob dug this well for us, and his family and animals got water from it. Are you greater than Jacob?"

13 Jesus answered, "Everyone who drinks this water will get thirsty again. 14 But no one who drinks the water I give will ever be thirsty again. The water I give is like a flowing fountain that gives eternal life."

15 The woman replied, "Sir, please give me a drink of that water! Then I won't get thirsty and have to come to this well again."

16 Jesus told her, "Go and bring your husband."

17-18 The woman answered, "I don't have a husband."

"That's right," Jesus replied, "you're telling the truth. You don't have a husband. You have already been married five times, and the man you are now living with isn't your husband."

19 The woman said, "Sir, I can see that you are a prophet. 20 My ancestors worshipped on this mountain,* but you Jews say Jerusalem is the only place to worship."

21 Jesus said to her:

Believe me, the time is coming when you won't worship the Father either

on this mountain or in Jerusalem. 22 You Samaritans don't really know the one you worship. But we Jews do know the God we worship, and by using us, God will save the world. 23 But a time is coming, and it is already here! Even now the true worshippers are being led by the Spirit to worship the Father according to the truth. These are the ones the Father is seeking to worship him. 24 God is Spirit, and those who worship God must be led by the Spirit to worship him according to the truth.

25 The woman said, "I know that the Messiah will come. He is the one we call Christ. When he comes, he will explain everything to us."

26 "I am that one," Jesus told her, "and I am speaking to you now."

27 The disciples returned about this time and were surprised to find Jesus talking with a woman. But none of them asked him what he wanted or why he was talking with her.

28 The woman left her water jar and ran back into town. She said to the people, 29 "Come and see a man who told me everything I have ever done! Could he be the Messiah?" 30 Everyone in town went out to see Jesus.

31 While this was happening, Jesus' disciples were saying to him, "Teacher, please eat something."

32 But Jesus told them, "I have food that you don't know anything about."

33 His disciples started asking each other, "Has someone brought him something to eat?"

34 Jesus said:

My food is to do what God wants! He is the one who sent me, and I must finish the work that he gave me to do. 35 You may say that there are still four months until harvest time. But I tell you to look, and you will see that the fields are ripe and ready to harvest.

36 Even now the harvest workers are receiving their reward by gathering a harvest that brings eternal life. Then everyone who planted the seed and everyone who harvests the crop will celebrate together. 37 So the saying proves true, "Some plant the seed, and others harvest the crop." 38 I am sending you to harvest crops in fields where others have done all the hard work.

39 A lot of Samaritans in that town put their faith in Jesus because the woman had said, "This man told me everything I have ever

---

*4.9 won't have anything to do with each other: Or "won't use the same cups." The Samaritans lived in the land between Judea and Galilee. They worshipped God differently from the Jews and did not get along with them.

*4.20 this mountain: Mount Gerizim, near the city of Shechem.

See also: 4.5: Gen 33.19; Josh 24.32. 4.9: Ezra 4.1–5; Neh 4.1,2.

done." ⁴⁰ They came and asked him to stay in their town, and he stayed on for two days.

⁴¹ Many more Samaritans put their faith in Jesus because of what they heard him say. ⁴² They told the woman, "We no longer have faith in Jesus just because of what you told us. We have heard him ourselves, and we are certain that he is the Saviour of the world!"

Jesus heals an official's son

This is also told in Matthew 8.5–13; Luke 7.1–10

⁴³⁻⁴⁴ Jesus had said, "Prophets are honoured everywhere, except in their own country." Then two days later he left ⁴⁵ and went to Galilee. The people there welcomed him, because they had gone to the festival in Jerusalem and had seen everything he had done.

⁴⁶ While Jesus was in Galilee, he returned to the village of Cana, where he had turned the water into wine. There was an official in Capernaum whose son was sick. ⁴⁷ And when the man heard that Jesus had come from Judea, he went and begged him to keep his son from dying.

⁴⁸ Jesus told the official, "You won't have faith unless you see miracles and wonders!"

⁴⁹ The man replied, "Lord, please come before my son dies!"

⁵⁰ Jesus then said, "Your son will live. Go on home to him." The man believed Jesus and set off to return home.

⁵¹ Some of the official's servants met him along the road and told him, "Your son is better!" ⁵² He asked them when the boy got better, and they answered, "The fever left him yesterday at one o'clock."

⁵³ The boy's father realized that at one o'clock the day before, Jesus had told him, "Your son will live." So the man and everyone in his family put their faith in Jesus.

⁵⁴ This was the second miracle* that Jesus performed after he left Judea and went to Galilee.

CHAPTER 5

Jesus heals a sick man

¹ Later, Jesus went to Jerusalem for another Jewish festival.* ² In the city near the Sheep Gate was a pool with five porches, and its name in Hebrew was Bethzatha.◊

³⁻⁴ Many sick, blind, lame, and crippled people were lying close to the pool.◊

⁵ Beside the pool was a man who had been sick for thirty-eight years. ⁶ When Jesus saw the man and realized that he had been crippled for a long time, he asked him, "Do you want to be healed?"

⁷ The man answered, "Lord, I don't have anyone to put me in the pool when the water is stirred up. I try to get in, but someone else always gets there first."

⁸ Jesus told him, "Pick up your mat and walk!" ⁹ At once the man was healed. He picked up his mat and started walking around. The day on which this happened was a Sabbath.

¹⁰ When the Jewish leaders saw the man carrying his mat, they said to him, "This is the Sabbath! No one is allowed to carry a mat on the Sabbath."

¹¹ But he replied, "The man who healed me told me to pick up my mat and walk."

¹² They asked him, "Who is this man that told you to pick up your mat and walk?" ¹³ But he did not know who Jesus was, and Jesus had left because of the crowd.

¹⁴ Later, Jesus met the man in the temple and told him, "You are now well. But don't sin any more or something worse might happen to you." ¹⁵ The man left and told the leaders that Jesus was the one who had healed him. ¹⁶ They started making a lot of trouble for Jesus because he did things like this on the Sabbath.

¹⁷ But Jesus said, "My Father has never stopped working, and that is why I keep on working." ¹⁸ Now the leaders wanted to kill Jesus for two reasons. First, he had broken the law of the Sabbath. But even worse, he had said that God was his Father, which made him equal with God.

The Son's authority

¹⁹ Jesus told the people:

I tell you for certain that the Son cannot do anything on his own. He can do only what he sees the Father doing, and he does exactly what he sees the Father do. ²⁰ The Father loves the Son and has shown him everything he does. The Father will show him even greater things, and you will be amazed. ²¹ Just as the Father raises the dead

---

*4.54 miracle: See the note at 2.11.
*5.1 another Jewish festival: Either the Festival of Shelters or Passover.

See also: 4.44: Matt 13.57; Mark 6.4; Luke 4.24.
4.45: John 2.23. 4.46: John 2.1–11.

See also: 5.10: Neh 13.19; Jer 17.21.

and gives life, so the Son gives life to anyone he wants to.

²² The Father doesn't judge anyone, but he has made his Son the judge of everyone. ²³ The Father wants all people to honour the Son as much as they honour him. When anyone refuses to honour the Son, that is the same as refusing to honour the Father who sent him. ²⁴ I tell you for certain that everyone who hears my message and has faith in the one who sent me has eternal life and will never be condemned. They have already gone from death to life.

²⁵ I tell you for certain that the time will come, and it is already here, when all the dead will hear the voice of the Son of God. And those who listen to it will live! ²⁶ The Father has the power to give life, and he has given that same power to the Son. ²⁷ And he has given his Son the right to judge everyone, because he is the Son of Man.

²⁸ Don't be surprised! The time will come when all the dead will hear the voice of the Son of Man, ²⁹ and they will come out of their graves. Everyone who has done good things will rise to life, but everyone who has done evil things will rise and be condemned.

³⁰ I cannot do anything on my own. The Father sent me, and he is the one who told me how to judge. I judge with fairness, because I obey him, and I don't just try to please myself.

Witnesses to Jesus

Jesus continued:

³¹ If I speak for myself, there is no way to prove I am telling the truth. ³² But there is someone else who speaks for me, and I know what he says is true. ³³ You sent messengers to John, and he told them the truth. ³⁴ I don't depend on what people say about me, but I tell you these things so that you may be saved. ³⁵ John was a lamp that gave a lot of light, and you were glad to enjoy his light for a while.

³⁶ But something more important than John speaks for me. I mean the things that the Father has given me to do! All of these speak for me and prove that the Father sent me.

³⁷ The Father who sent me also speaks for me, but you have never heard his voice or seen his face to face. ³⁸ You have not

believed his message, because you refused to have faith in the one he sent.

³⁹ You search the Scriptures, because you think you will find eternal life in them. The Scriptures tell about me, ⁴⁰ but you refuse to come to me for eternal life.

⁴¹ I don't care about human praise, ⁴² but I do know that none of you love God. ⁴³ I have come with my Father's authority, and you have not welcomed me. But you will welcome people who come on their own. ⁴⁴ How could you possibly believe? You like to have your friends praise you, and you don't care about praise that the only God can give!

⁴⁵ Don't think that I will be the one to accuse you to the Father. You have put your hope in Moses, yet he is the very one who will accuse you. ⁴⁶ Moses wrote about me, and if you had believed Moses, you would have believed me. ⁴⁷ But if you don't believe what Moses wrote, how can you believe what I say?

CHAPTER 6

Feeding five thousand

This is also told in Matthew 14.13–21; Mark 6.30–44; Luke 9.10–17

¹ Jesus crossed Lake Galilee, which was also known as Lake Tiberias. ² A large crowd had seen him perform miracles to heal the sick, and those people went with him. ³⁻⁴ It was almost time for the Jewish festival of Passover, and Jesus went up on a mountain with his disciples and sat down.*

⁵ When Jesus saw the large crowd coming towards him, he asked Philip, "Where will we get enough food to feed all these people?" ⁶ He said this to test Philip, since he already knew what he was going to do.

⁷ Philip answered, "Don't you know that it would take almost a year's wages* just to buy only a little bread for each of these people?"

⁸ Andrew, the brother of Simon Peter, was one of the disciples. He spoke up and said, ⁹ "There is a boy here who has five small loaves* of barley bread and two fish. But what good is that with all these people?"

*6.3,4 sat down: Possibly to teach. Teachers in the ancient world, including Jewish teachers, usually sat down to teach.
*6.7 almost a year's wages: The Greek text has "two hundred silver coins". Each coin was worth the average day's wages for a worker.
*6.9 small loaves: These would have been flat and round or in the shape of a bun.

See also: 5.29: Dan 12.2. 5.33: John 1.19–27; 3.27–30. 5.37: Matt 3.17; Mark 1.11; Luke 3.22.

¹⁰ The ground was covered with grass, and Jesus told his disciples to make everyone sit down. About five thousand men were in the crowd. ¹¹ Jesus took the bread in his hands and gave thanks to God. Then he passed the bread to the people, and he did the same with the fish, until everyone had plenty to eat.

¹² The people ate all they wanted, and Jesus told his disciples to gather up the leftovers, so that nothing would be wasted. ¹³ The disciples gathered them up and filled twelve large baskets with what was left over from the five barley loaves.

¹⁴ After the people had seen Jesus perform this miracle,* they began saying, "This must be the Prophet* who is to come into the world!" ¹⁵ Jesus realized that they would try to force him to be their king. So he went up on a mountain, where he could be alone.

Jesus walks on the water

This is also told in Matthew 14.22–27; Mark 6.45–52

¹⁶ That evening, Jesus' disciples went down to the lake. ¹⁷ They got into a boat and set off for Capernaum. Later that evening Jesus had still not come to them, ¹⁸ and a strong wind was making the water rough.

¹⁹ When the disciples had rowed for five or six kilometres, they saw Jesus walking on the water. He kept coming closer to the boat, and they were terrified. ²⁰ But he said, "I am Jesus!* Don't be afraid!" ²¹ The disciples wanted to take him into the boat, but suddenly the boat reached the shore where they were headed.

The bread that gives life

²² The people who had stayed on the east side of the lake knew that only one boat had been there. They also knew that Jesus had not left in it with his disciples. But the next day ²³ some boats from Tiberias sailed near the place where the crowd had eaten the bread for which the Lord had given thanks. ²⁴ They saw that Jesus and his disciples had left. Then they got into the boats and went to Capernaum to look for Jesus. ²⁵ They found him on the west side of the lake and asked, "Rabbi, when did you get here?"

²⁶ Jesus answered, "I tell you for certain that you are not looking for me because you saw the miracles,* but because you ate all the food you wanted. ²⁷ Don't work for food that spoils. Work for food that gives eternal life. The Son of Man will give you this food, because God the Father has given him the right to do so."

²⁸ "What exactly does God want us to do?" the people asked.

²⁹ Jesus answered, "God wants you to have faith in the one he sent."

³⁰ They replied, "What miracle will you perform, so that we can have faith in you? What will you do? ³¹ For example, when our ancestors were in the desert, they were given manna* to eat. It happened just as the Scriptures say, 'God gave them bread from heaven to eat.'"

³² Jesus then told them, "I tell you for certain that Moses wasn't the one who gave you bread from heaven. My Father is the one who gives you the true bread from heaven. ³³ And the bread that God gives is the one who came down from heaven to give life to the world."

³⁴ The people said, "Lord, give us this bread and don't ever stop!"

³⁵ Jesus replied:

I am the bread that gives life! No one who comes to me will ever be hungry. No one who has faith in me will ever be thirsty. ³⁶ I have told you already that you have seen me and still do not have faith in me. ³⁷ Everything and everyone that the Father has given me will come to me, and I won't turn any of them away.

³⁸ I didn't come from heaven to do what I want! I came to do what the Father wants me to do. He sent me, ³⁹ and he wants to make certain that none of the ones he has given me will be lost. Instead, he wants me to raise them to life on the last day.* ⁴⁰ My Father wants everyone who sees the Son to have faith in him and to have eternal life. Then I will raise them to life on the last day.

*6.26 miracles: The Greek text has "signs" here and "sign" in verse 30. See the note at 2.11.
*6.31 manna: When the people of Israel were wandering through the desert, the Lord gave them a special kind of food to eat. It tasted like a wafer and was called "manna", which in Hebrew means, "What is this?"
*6.39 the last day: When God will judge all people.
See also: 6.31: Exod 16.4,15; Psa 78.24.

*6.14 miracle: See the note at 2.11.
*6.14 the Prophet: See the note at 1.21.
*6.20 I am Jesus: The Greek text has "I am". See the note at 8.24.

[41] The people started grumbling because Jesus had said he was the bread that had come down from heaven. [42] They were asking each other, "Isn't he Jesus, the son of Joseph? Don't we know his father and mother? How can he say that he has come down from heaven?"

[43] Jesus told them:

Stop grumbling! [44] No one can come to me, unless the Father who sent me makes them want to come. But if they do come, I will raise them to life on the last day. [45] One of the prophets wrote, "God will teach all of them." And so everyone who listens to the Father and learns from him will come to me.

[46] The only one who has seen the Father is the one who has come from him. No one else has ever seen the Father. [47] I tell you for certain that everyone who has faith in me has eternal life.

[48] I am the bread that gives life! [49] Your ancestors ate manna* in the desert, and later they died. [50] But the bread from heaven has come down, so that no one who eats it will ever die. [51] I am that bread from heaven! Everyone who eats it will live for ever. My flesh is the life-giving bread that I give to the people of this world.

[52] They started arguing with each other and asked, "How can he give us his flesh to eat?"

[53] Jesus answered:

I tell you for certain that you won't live unless you eat the flesh and drink the blood of the Son of Man. [54] But if you do eat my flesh and drink my blood, you will have eternal life, and I will raise you to life on the last day. [55] My flesh is the true food, and my blood is the true drink. [56] If you eat my flesh and drink my blood, you are one with me, and I am one with you.

[57] The living Father sent me, and I have life because of him. Now everyone who eats my flesh will live because of me. [58] The bread that comes down from heaven isn't like what your ancestors ate. They died, but whoever eats this bread will live for ever.

[59] Jesus was teaching in a Jewish place of worship in Capernaum when he said these things.

The words of eternal life

[60] Many of Jesus' disciples heard him and said, "This is too hard for anyone to understand."

[61] Jesus knew that his disciples were grumbling. So he asked, "Does this bother you? [62] What if you should see the Son of Man go up to heaven where he came from? [63] The Spirit is the one who gives life! Human strength can do nothing. The words that I have spoken to you are from that life-giving Spirit. [64] But some of you refuse to have faith in me." Jesus said this, because from the beginning he knew who would have faith in him. He also knew which one would betray him.

[65] Then Jesus said, "You cannot come to me, unless the Father makes you want to come. That is why I have told these things to all of you."

[66] Because of what Jesus said, many of his disciples turned their backs on him and stopped following him. [67] Jesus then asked his twelve disciples if they were going to leave him. [68] Simon Peter answered, "Lord, there is no one else that we can go to! Your words give eternal life. [69] We have faith in you, and we are sure that you are God's Holy One."

[70] Jesus told his disciples, "I chose all twelve of you, but one of you is a demon!" [71] Jesus was talking about Judas, the son of Simon Iscariot.* He would later betray Jesus, even though he was one of the twelve disciples.

CHAPTER 7

Jesus' brothers don't have faith in him

[1] Jesus decided to leave Judea and to start going through Galilee because the Jewish leaders wanted to kill him. [2] It was almost time for the Festival of Shelters, [3] and Jesus' brothers said to him, "Why don't you go to Judea? Then your disciples can see what you are doing. [4] No one does anything in secret, if they want others to know about them. So let the world know what you are doing!" [5] Even Jesus' own brothers had not yet become his followers.

[6] Jesus answered, "My time hasn't yet come,* but your time is always now. [7] The people of this world cannot hate you. They hate me, because I tell them that they do evil things. [8] Go on to the festival. My time hasn't yet come, and I am not going." [9] Jesus said this and stayed on in Galilee.

---

*6.49 manna: See the note at 6.31.

See also: 6.45: Isa 54.13.

*6.71 Iscariot: This may mean "a man from Kerioth" (a place in Judea). But more probably it means "a man who was a liar" or "a man who was a betrayer".

*7.6 My time hasn't yet come: See the note at 2.4.

See also: 6.68,69: Matt 16.16; Mark 8.29; Luke 9.20. 7.2: Lev 23.34; Deut 16.13.

Jesus at the Festival of Shelters

10 After Jesus' brothers had gone to the festival, he went secretly, without telling anyone.

11 During the festival the Jewish leaders looked for Jesus and asked, "Where is he?" 12 The crowds even got into an argument about him. Some were saying, "Jesus is a good man," while others were saying, "He is lying to everyone." 13 But the people were afraid of their leaders, and none of them talked in public about him.

14 When the festival was about half over, Jesus went into the temple and started teaching. 15 The leaders were surprised and said, "How does this man know so much? He has never been taught!"

16 Jesus replied:

I am not teaching something that I thought up. What I teach comes from the one who sent me. 17 If you really want to obey God, you will know if what I teach comes from God or from me. 18 If I wanted to bring honour to myself, I would speak for myself. But I want to honour the one who sent me. That is why I tell the truth and not a lie. 19 Didn't Moses give you the Law? Yet none of you obey it! So why do you want to kill me?

20 The crowd replied, "You're mad! What makes you think someone wants to kill you?"

21 Jesus answered:

I performed one miracle,* and it amazed you. 22 Moses commanded you to circumcise your sons. But it wasn't really Moses who gave you this command. It was your ancestors, and even on the Sabbath you circumcise your sons 23 in order to obey the Law of Moses. Why are you angry with me for making someone completely well on the Sabbath? 24 Don't judge by appearances. Judge by what is right.

25 Some of the people from Jerusalem were saying, "Isn't this the man they want to kill? 26 Yet here he is, speaking for everyone to hear. And no one is arguing with him. Do you suppose the authorities know that he is the Messiah? 27 But how could that be? No one knows where the Messiah will come from, but we know where this man comes from."

28 As Jesus was teaching in the temple, he shouted, "Do you really think you know me

and where I came from? I didn't come on my own! The one who sent me is truthful, and you don't know him. 29 But I know the one who sent me, because I came from him."

30 Some of the people wanted to arrest Jesus there and then. But no one even laid a hand on him, because his time had not yet come.* 31 A lot of people in the crowd put their faith in him and said, "When the Messiah comes, he won't perform more miracles* than this man has done!"

Officers sent to arrest Jesus

32 When the Pharisees heard the crowd arguing about Jesus, they got together with the chief priests and sent some temple police to arrest him. 33 But Jesus told them, "I will be with you a little while longer, and then I will return to the one who sent me. 34 You will look for me, but you won't find me. You cannot go where I am going."

35 The Jewish leaders asked each other, "Where can he go to keep us from finding him? Is he going to some foreign country where our people live? Is he going there to teach the Greeks?* 36 What did he mean by saying that we will look for him, but won't find him? Why can't we go where he is going?"

Streams of life-giving water

37 On the last and most important day of the festival, Jesus stood up and shouted, "If you are thirsty, come to me and drink! 38 Have faith in me, and you will have life-giving water flowing from deep inside you, just as the Scriptures say." 39 Jesus was talking about the Holy Spirit, who would be given to everyone that had faith in him. The Spirit had not yet been given to anyone, since Jesus had not yet been given his full glory.*

The people take sides

40 When the crowd heard Jesus say this, some of them said, "He must be the Prophet!"* 41 Others said, "He is the Messiah!" Others

---

*7.21 one miracle: The healing of the lame man (5.1–18; see also the note at 2.11).
See also: 7.22: a Lev 12.3; b Gen 17.10.   7.23: John 5.9.

*7.30 his time had not yet come: See the note at 2.4.
*7.31 miracles: See the note at 2.11.
*7.35 Greeks: Perhaps Gentiles or Jews who followed Greek customs.
*7.39 had not yet been given his full glory: In the Gospel of John, Jesus is given his full glory both when he is nailed to the cross and when he is raised from death to sit beside his Father in heaven.
*7.40 the Prophet: See the note at 1.21.
See also: 7.37: Lev 23.36.   7.38: Ezek 47.1; Zech 14.8.

even said, "Can the Messiah come from Galilee? [42] The Scriptures say that the Messiah will come from the family of King David. Doesn't this mean that he will be born in David's home town of Bethlehem?" [43] The people started taking sides against each other because of Jesus. [44] Some of them wanted to arrest him, but no one laid a hand on him.

The leaders refuse to have faith in Jesus

[45] When the temple police returned to the chief priests and Pharisees, they were asked, "Why didn't you bring Jesus here?"

[46] They answered, "No one has ever spoken like that man!"

[47] The Pharisees said to them, "Have you also been fooled? [48] Not one of the chief priests or the Pharisees has faith in him. [49] And these people who don't know the Law are under God's curse anyway."

[50] Nicodemus was there at the time. He was a member of the council, and was the same one who had earlier come to see Jesus.* He said, [51] "Our Law doesn't let us condemn people before we hear what they have to say. We cannot judge them before we know what they have done."

[52] Then they said, "Nicodemus, you must be from Galilee! Read the Scriptures, and you will find that no prophet is to come from Galilee."

CHAPTER 8

A woman caught in sin

[53] Everyone else went home, [1] but Jesus walked out to the Mount of Olives. [2] Then early the next morning he went to the temple. The people came to him, and he sat down* and started teaching them.

[3] The Pharisees and the teachers of the Law of Moses brought in a woman who had been caught in bed with a man who wasn't her husband. They made her stand in the middle of the crowd. [4] Then they said, "Teacher, this woman was caught sleeping with a man who isn't her husband. [5] The Law of Moses teaches that a woman like this should be stoned to death! What do you say?"

[6] They asked Jesus this question, because they wanted to test him and bring some

charge against him. But Jesus simply bent over and started writing on the ground with his finger.

[7] They kept on asking Jesus about the woman. Finally, he stood up and said, "If any of you have never sinned, then go ahead and throw the first stone at her!" [8] Once again he bent over and began writing on the ground. [9] The people left one by one, beginning with the oldest. Finally, Jesus and the woman were there alone.

[10] Jesus stood up and asked her, "Where is everyone? Isn't there anyone left to accuse you?"

[11] "No sir," the woman answered.

Then Jesus told her, "I am not going to accuse you either. You may go now, but don't sin any more."

Jesus is the light for the world

[12] Once again Jesus spoke to the people. This time he said, "I am the light for the world! Follow me, and you won't be walking in the dark. You will have the light that gives life."

[13] The Pharisees objected, "You are the only one speaking for yourself, and what you say isn't true!"

[14] Jesus replied:

Even if I do speak for myself, what I say is true! I know where I came from and where I am going. But you don't know where I am from or where I am going. [15] You judge in the same way that everyone else does, but I don't judge anyone. [16] If I did judge, I would judge fairly, because I would not be doing it alone. The Father who sent me is here with me. [17] Your Law requires two witnesses to prove that something is true. [18] I am one of my witnesses, and the Father who sent me is the other one.

[19] "Where is your Father?" they asked.

"You don't know me or my Father!" Jesus answered. "If you knew me, you would know my Father."

[20] Jesus said this while he was still teaching in the place where the temple treasures were stored. But no one arrested him, because his time had not yet come.*

You cannot go where I am going

[21] Jesus also told them, "I am going away, and you will look for me. But you cannot go

---

*7.50 who had earlier come to see Jesus: See 3.1–21.
*8.2 sat down: See the note at 6.3,4.
See also: 7.42: 2 Sam 7.12; Mic 5.2. 7.50: John 3.1,2.
8.5: Lev 20.10; Deut 22.22–24.

*8.20 his time had not yet come: See the note at 2.4.
See also: 8.12: Matt 5.14; John 9.5. 8.13: John 5.31.
8.17: Deut 19.15.

where I am going, and you will die with your sins unforgiven."

²² The Jewish leaders asked, "Does he intend to kill himself? Is that what he means by saying we cannot go where he is going?"

²³ Jesus answered, "You are from below, but I am from above. You belong to this world, but I don't. ²⁴ That is why I said you will die with your sins unforgiven. If you don't have faith in me for who I am,* you will die, and your sins will not be forgiven."

²⁵ "Who are you?" they asked Jesus.

Jesus answered, "I am exactly who I told you at the beginning. ²⁶ There is a lot more I could say to condemn you. But the one who sent me is truthful, and I tell the people of this world only what I have heard from him."

²⁷ No one understood that Jesus was talking to them about the Father.

²⁸ Jesus went on to say, "When you have lifted up the Son of Man,* you will know who I am. You will also know that I don't do anything on my own. I say only what my Father taught me. ²⁹ The one who sent me is with me. I always do what pleases him, and he will never leave me."

³⁰ After Jesus said this, many of the people put their faith in him.

The truth will set you free

³¹ Jesus told the people who had faith in him, "If you keep on obeying what I have said, you truly are my disciples. ³² You will know the truth, and the truth will set you free."

³³ They answered, "We are Abraham's children! We have never been anyone's slaves. How can you say we will be set free?"

³⁴ Jesus replied:

I tell you for certain that anyone who sins is a slave of sin! ³⁵ And slaves don't stay in the family for ever, though the Son will always remain in the family. ³⁶ If the Son gives you freedom, you are free! ³⁷ I know that you are from Abraham's family. Yet you want to kill me, because my message isn't really in your hearts. ³⁸ I am telling you what my Father has shown me, just as you are doing what your father has taught you.

Your father is the devil

³⁹ The people said to Jesus, "Abraham is our father!"

Jesus replied, "If you were Abraham's children, you would do what Abraham did. ⁴⁰ Instead, you want to kill me for telling you the truth that God gave me. Abraham never did anything like that. ⁴¹ But you are doing exactly what your father does."

"Don't accuse us of having someone else as our father!" they said. "We just have one father, and he is God."

⁴² Jesus answered:

If God were your Father, you would love me, because I came from God and only from him. He sent me. I did not come on my own. ⁴³ Why can't you understand what I am talking about? Can't you stand to hear what I am saying? ⁴⁴ Your father is the devil, and you do exactly what he wants. He has always been a murderer and a liar. There is nothing truthful about him. He speaks on his own, and everything he says is a lie. Not only is he a liar himself, but he is also the father of all lies.

⁴⁵ Everything I have told you is true, and you still refuse to have faith in me. ⁴⁶ Can any of you accuse me of sin? If you cannot, why won't you have faith in me? After all, I am telling you the truth. ⁴⁷ Anyone who belongs to God will listen to his message. But you refuse to listen, because you don't belong to God.

Jesus and Abraham

⁴⁸ The people told Jesus, "We were right to say that you are a Samaritan* and that you have a demon in you!"

⁴⁹ Jesus answered, "I don't have a demon in me. I honour my Father, and you refuse to honour me. ⁵⁰ I don't want honour for myself. But there is one who wants me to be honoured, and he is also the one who judges. ⁵¹ I tell you for certain that if you obey my words, you will never die."

⁵² Then the people said, "Now we are sure that you have a demon. Abraham is dead, and so are the prophets. How can you say that no one who obeys your words will ever die? ⁵³ Are you greater than our father Abraham? He died, and so did the prophets. Who do you think you are?"

⁵⁴ Jesus replied, "If I honoured myself, it would mean nothing. My Father is the one

---

*8.24 I am: For the Jewish people the most holy name of God is "Yahweh", which may be translated "I am". In the Gospel of John "I am" is sometimes used by Jesus to show that he is that one.
*8.28 lifted up the Son of Man: See the note at 7.39.
See also: 8.33: Matt 3.9; Luke 3.8.

*8.48 Samaritan: See 4.9 and the note there.

who honours me. You claim that he is your God, 55 even though you don't really know him. If I said I didn't know him, I would be a liar, just like all of you. But I know him, and I do what he says. 56 Your father Abraham was really glad to see me."

57 "You are not even fifty years old!" they said. "How could you have seen Abraham?"

58 Jesus answered, "I tell you for certain that even before Abraham was, I was, and I am."* 59 The people picked up stones to kill Jesus, but he hid and left the temple.

CHAPTER 9

Jesus heals a man born blind

1 As Jesus walked along, he saw a man who had been blind since birth. 2 Jesus' disciples asked, "Teacher, why was this man born blind? Was it because he or his parents sinned?"

3 "No, it wasn't!" Jesus answered. "But because of his blindness, you will see God perform a miracle for him. 4 As long as it is day, we must do what the one who sent me wants me to do. When night comes, no one can work. 5 While I am in the world, I am the light for the world."

6 After Jesus said this, he spat on the ground. He made some mud and smeared it on the man's eyes. 7 Then he said, "Go and wash off the mud in Siloam Pool." The man went and washed in Siloam, which means "One who is sent". When he had washed off the mud, he could see.

8 The man's neighbours and the people who had seen him begging wondered if he really could be the same man. 9 Some of them said he was the same beggar, while others said he only looked like him. But he told them, "I am that man."

10 "Then how can you see?" they asked.

11 He answered, "Someone named Jesus made some mud and smeared it on my eyes. He told me to go and wash it off in Siloam Pool. When I did, I could see."

12 "Where is he now?" they asked.

"I don't know," he answered.

The Pharisees try to find out what happened

13-14 The day when Jesus made the mud and healed the man was a Sabbath. So the people took the man to the Pharisees. 15 They asked

him how he was able to see, and he answered, "Jesus made some mud and smeared it on my eyes. Then after I washed it off, I could see."

16 Some of the Pharisees said, "This man Jesus doesn't come from God. If he did, he would not break the law of the Sabbath."

Others asked, "How could someone who is a sinner perform such a miracle?"*

Since the Pharisees could not agree among themselves, 17 they asked the man, "What do you say about this one who healed your eyes?"

"He is a prophet!" the man told them.

18 But the Jewish leaders would not believe that the man had once been blind. They sent for his parents 19 and asked them, "Is this the son that you said was born blind? How can he now see?"

20 The man's parents answered, "We are certain that he is our son, and we know that he was born blind. 21 But we don't know how he got his sight or who gave it to him. Ask him! He is old enough to speak for himself."

22-23 The man's parents said this because they were afraid of the Jewish leaders. The leaders had already agreed that no one was to have anything to do with anyone who said Jesus was the Messiah.

24 The leaders called the man back and said, "Swear by God to tell the truth! We know that Jesus is a sinner."

25 The man replied, "I don't know if he is a sinner or not. All I know is that I used to be blind, but now I can see!"

26 "What did he do to you?" the Jewish leaders asked. "How did he heal your eyes?"

27 The man answered, "I have already told you once, and you refused to listen. Why do you want me to tell you again? Do you also want to become his disciples?"

28 The leaders insulted the man and said, "You are his follower! We are followers of Moses. 29 We are sure that God spoke to Moses, but we don't even know where Jesus comes from."

30 "How strange!" the man replied. "He healed my eyes, and yet you don't know where he comes from. 31 We know that God listens only to people who love and obey him. God doesn't listen to sinners. 32 And this is the first time in history that anyone has ever given sight to someone born blind. 33 Jesus could not do anything unless he came from God."

34 The leaders told the man, "You have been a sinner since the day you were born!

---

*8.58 I am: See the note at 8.24.

See also: 9.5: Matt 5.14; John 8.12.

*9.16 miracle: See the note at 2.11.

Do you think you can teach us anything?" Then they said, "You can never come back into any of our meeting places!"

³⁵ When Jesus heard what had happened, he went and found the man. Then Jesus asked, "Do you have faith in the Son of Man?"

³⁶ He replied, "Sir, if you will tell me who he is, I will put my faith in him."

³⁷ "You have already seen him," Jesus answered, "and right now he is talking with you."

³⁸ The man said, "Lord, I put my faith in you!" Then he worshipped Jesus.

³⁹ Jesus told him, "I came to judge the people of this world. I am here to give sight to the blind and to make blind everyone who can see."

⁴⁰ When the Pharisees heard Jesus say this, they asked, "Are we blind?"

⁴¹ Jesus answered, "If you were blind, you would not be guilty. But now that you claim to see, you will keep on being guilty."

CHAPTER 10

A story about sheep

¹ Jesus said:

I tell you for certain that only thieves and robbers climb over the fence instead of going in through the gate to the sheep pen. ²⁻³ But the gatekeeper opens the gate for the shepherd, and he goes in through it. The sheep know their shepherd's voice. He calls each of them by name and leads them out.

⁴ When he has led out all his sheep, he walks in front of them, and they follow, because they know his voice. ⁵ The sheep will not follow strangers. They don't recognize a stranger's voice, and they run away.

⁶ Jesus told the people this story. But they did not understand what he was talking about.

Jesus is the good shepherd

⁷ Jesus said:

I tell you for certain that I am the gate for the sheep. ⁸ Everyone who came before me was a thief or a robber, and the sheep did not listen to any of them. ⁹ I am the gate. All who come in through me will be saved. Through me they will come and go and find pasture.

¹⁰ A thief comes only to rob, kill, and destroy. I came so that everyone would

have life, and have it fully. ¹¹ I am the good shepherd, and the good shepherd gives up his life for his sheep. ¹² Hired workers are not like the shepherd. They don't own the sheep, and when they see a wolf coming, they run off and leave the sheep. Then the wolf attacks and scatters the flock. ¹³ Hired workers run away because they don't care about the sheep.

¹⁴ I am the good shepherd. I know my sheep, and they know me. ¹⁵ Just as the Father knows me, I know the Father, and I give up my life for my sheep. ¹⁶ I have other sheep that are not in this sheep pen. I must bring them together too, when they hear my voice. Then there will be one flock of sheep and one shepherd.

¹⁷ The Father loves me, because I give up my life, so that I may receive it back again. ¹⁸ No one takes my life from me. I give it up willingly! I have the power to give it up and the power to receive it back again, just as my Father commanded me to do.

¹⁹ The people took sides because of what Jesus had told them. ²⁰ Many of them said, "He has a demon in him! He is mad! Why listen to him?"

²¹ But others said, "How could anyone with a demon in him say these things? No one like that could give sight to a blind person!"

Jesus is rejected

²² That winter, Jesus was in Jerusalem for the Temple Festival. ²³ One day he was walking in that part of the temple known as Solomon's Porch,* ²⁴ and the people gathered all around him. They said, "How long are you going to keep us guessing? If you are the Messiah, tell us plainly!"

²⁵ Jesus answered:

I have told you, and you refused to believe me. The things I do by my Father's authority show who I am. ²⁶ But since you are not my sheep, you don't believe me. ²⁷ My sheep know my voice, and I know them. They follow me, ²⁸ and I give them eternal life, so that they will never be lost. No one can snatch them out of my hand. ²⁹ My Father gave them to me, and he is greater than all others.• No one can snatch them from his hands, ³⁰ and I am one with the Father.

---

*10.23 Solomon's Porch: A public place with tall columns along the east side of the temple.
See also: 10.15: Matt 11.27; Luke 10.22.

³¹ Once again the Jewish leaders picked up stones in order to kill Jesus. ³² But he said, "I have shown you many good things that my Father sent me to do. Which one are you going to stone me for?"

³³ They answered, "We are not stoning you because of any good thing you did. We are stoning you because you did a terrible thing. You are just a man, and here you are claiming to be God!"

³⁴ Jesus replied:

In your Scriptures doesn't God say, "You are gods"? ³⁵ You can't argue with the Scriptures, and God spoke to those people and called them gods. ³⁶ So why do you accuse me of a terrible sin for saying that I am the Son of God? After all, it is the Father who prepared me for this work. He is also the one who sent me into the world. ³⁷ If I don't do as my Father does, you should not believe me. ³⁸ But if I do what my Father does, you should believe because of that, even if you don't have faith in me. Then you will know for certain that the Father is one with me, and I am one with the Father.

³⁹ Again they wanted to arrest Jesus. But he escaped ⁴⁰ and crossed the Jordan to the place where John had earlier been baptizing. While Jesus was there, ⁴¹ many people came to him. They were saying, "John didn't perform any miracles, but everything he said about Jesus is true." ⁴² A lot of those people also put their faith in Jesus.

CHAPTER 11

The death of Lazarus

¹⁻² A man called Lazarus was sick in the village of Bethany. He had two sisters, Mary and Martha. This was the same Mary who later poured perfume on the Lord's head and wiped his feet with her hair. ³ The sisters sent a message to the Lord and told him that his good friend Lazarus was sick.

⁴ When Jesus heard this, he said, "His sickness won't end in death. It will bring glory to God and his Son."

⁵ Jesus loved Martha and her sister and brother. ⁶ But he stayed where he was for two more days. ⁷ Then he said to his disciples, "Now we will go back to Judea."

⁸ "Teacher," they said, "the people there want to stone you to death! Why do you want to go back?"

⁹ Jesus answered, "Aren't there twelve hours in each day? If you walk during the day, you will have light from the sun, and you won't stumble. ¹⁰ But if you walk during the night, you will stumble, because you don't have any light." ¹¹ Then he told them, "Our friend Lazarus is asleep, and I am going there to wake him up."

¹² They replied, "Lord, if he is asleep, he will get better." ¹³ Jesus really meant that Lazarus was dead, but they thought he was talking only about sleep.

¹⁴ Then Jesus told them plainly, "Lazarus is dead! ¹⁵ I am glad that I wasn't there, because now you will have a chance to put your faith in me. Let's go to him."

¹⁶ Thomas, whose nickname was "Twin", said to the other disciples, "Come on. Let's go, so we can die with him."

Jesus brings Lazarus to life

¹⁷ When Jesus got to Bethany, he found that Lazarus had already been in the tomb four days. ¹⁸ Bethany was less than three kilometres from Jerusalem, ¹⁹ and many people had come from the city to comfort Martha and Mary because their brother had died.

²⁰ When Martha heard that Jesus had arrived, she went out to meet him, but Mary stayed in the house. ²¹ Martha said to Jesus, "Lord, if you had been here, my brother would not have died. ²² Yet even now I know that God will do anything you ask.

²³ Jesus told her, "Your brother will live again!"

²⁴ Martha answered, "I know that he will be raised to life on the last day,* when all the dead are raised."

²⁵ Jesus then said, "I am the one who raises the dead to life! Everyone who has faith in me will live, even if they die. ²⁶ And everyone who lives because of faith in me will never really die. Do you believe this?"

²⁷ "Yes, Lord!" she replied. "I believe that you are Christ, the Son of God. You are the one we hoped would come into the world."

²⁸ After Martha said this, she went and privately said to her sister Mary, "The Teacher is here, and he wants to see you." ²⁹ As soon as Mary heard this, she got up and went out to Jesus. ³⁰ He was still outside the village where Martha had gone to meet him. ³¹ Many people had come to comfort Mary, and when they saw her quickly leave the

---

See also: 10.33: Lev 24.16. 10.34: Psa 82.6. 10.40: John 1.28. 11.1: Luke 10.38,39. 11.2: John 12.3.

*11.24 the last day: See the note at 6.39.

house, they thought she was going out to the tomb to cry. So they followed her.

32 Mary went to where Jesus was. Then as soon as she saw him, she knelt at his feet and said, "Lord, if you had been here, my brother would not have died."

33 When Jesus saw that Mary and the people with her were crying, he was terribly upset 34 and asked, "Where have you put his body?"

They replied, "Lord, come and you will see."

35 Jesus started crying, 36 and the people said, "See how much he loved Lazarus."

37 Some of them said, "He gives sight to the blind. Why couldn't he have kept Lazarus from dying?"

38 Jesus was still terribly upset. So he went to the tomb, which was a cave with a stone rolled against the entrance. 39 Then he told the people to roll the stone away. But Martha said, "Lord, you know that Lazarus has been dead four days, and there will be a bad smell."

40 Jesus replied, "Didn't I tell you that if you had faith, you would see the glory of God?"

41 After the stone had been rolled aside, Jesus looked up towards heaven and prayed, "Father, I thank you for answering my prayer. 42 I know that you always answer my prayers. But I said this, so that the people here would believe that you sent me."

43 When Jesus finished praying, he shouted, "Lazarus, come out!" 44 The man who had been dead came out. His hands and feet were wrapped with strips of burial cloth, and a cloth covered his face.

Jesus then told the people, "Untie him and let him go."

The plot to kill Jesus

This is also told in Matthew 26.1–5; Mark 14.1,2; Luke 22.1,2

45 Many of the people who had come to visit Mary saw the things that Jesus did, and they put their faith in him. 46 Others went to the Pharisees and told what Jesus had done. 47 Then the chief priests and the Pharisees called the council together and said, "What should we do? This man is performing a lot of miracles.* 48 If we don't stop him now, everyone will put their faith in him. Then the Romans will come and destroy our temple and our nation."*

49 One of the council members was Caiaphas, who was also high priest that year. He spoke up and said, "You people don't have any sense at all! 50 Don't you know it is better for one person to die for the people than for the whole nation to be destroyed?"

51 Caiaphas did not say this on his own. As high priest that year, he was prophesying that Jesus would die for the nation. 52 Yet Jesus would not die just for the Jewish nation. He would die to bring together all God's scattered people. 53 From that day on, the council started making plans to put Jesus to death.

54 Because of this plot against him, Jesus stopped going around in public. He went to the town of Ephraim, which was near the desert, and he stayed there with his disciples.

55 It was almost time for Passover. Many of the Jewish people who lived out in the country had come to Jerusalem to get themselves ready* for the festival. 56 They looked around for Jesus. Then when they were in the temple, they asked each other, "You don't think he will come here for Passover, do you?"

57 The chief priests and the Pharisees told the people to let them know if any of them saw Jesus. That is how they hoped to arrest him.

CHAPTER 12

At Bethany

This is also told in Matthew 26.6-13; Mark 14.3-9

1 Six days before Passover Jesus went back to Bethany, where he had raised Lazarus from death. 2 A meal had been prepared for Jesus. Martha was doing the serving, and Lazarus himself was there.

3 Mary took a very expensive bottle of perfume* and poured it on Jesus' feet. She wiped them with her hair, and the sweet smell of the perfume filled the house.

4 A disciple named Judas Iscariot* was there. He was the one who was going to betray Jesus, and he asked, 5 "Why wasn't this perfume sold for three hundred silver coins and the money given to the poor?" 6 Judas did not really care about the poor. He asked this because he carried the money bag and sometimes would steal from it.

---

*11.47 miracles: See the note at 2.11.
*11.48 destroy our temple and our nation: The Jewish leaders were afraid that Jesus would lead his followers to rebel against Rome and that the Roman army would then destroy their nation.

*11.55 get themselves ready: The Jewish people had to do certain things to prepare themselves to worship God.
*12.4 Iscariot: See the note at 6.71.
See also: 12.3: Luke 7.37,38.

[7] Jesus replied, "Leave her alone! She has kept this perfume for the day of my burial. [8] You will always have the poor with you, but you won't always have me."

A plot to kill Lazarus

[9] A lot of people came when they heard that Jesus was there. They also wanted to see Lazarus, because Jesus had raised him from death. [10] So the chief priests made plans to kill Lazarus. [11] He was the reason that many of the Jewish people were turning from them and putting their faith in Jesus.

Jesus enters Jerusalem

This is also told in Matthew 21.1–11; Mark 11.1–11; Luke 19.28–40

[12] The next day a large crowd was in Jerusalem for Passover. When they heard that Jesus was coming for the festival, [13] they took palm branches and went out to greet him.* They shouted,

"Hooray!*
God bless the one who comes
    in the name of the Lord!
God bless the King
    of Israel!"

[14] Jesus found a donkey and rode on it, just as the Scriptures say,

[15] "People of Jerusalem,
    don't be afraid!
Your King is now coming,
    and he is riding
    on a donkey."

[16] At first, Jesus' disciples did not understand. But after he had been given his glory,* they remembered all this. Everything had happened exactly as the Scriptures said it would.

[17-18] A crowd had come to meet Jesus because they had seen him call Lazarus out of the tomb. They kept talking about him and this miracle.* [19] But the Pharisees said to each other, "There is nothing that can be done! Everyone in the world is following Jesus."

Some Greeks want to meet Jesus

[20] Some Greeks* had gone to Jerusalem to worship during Passover. [21] Philip from Bethsaida in Galilee was there too. So they went to him and said, "Sir, we would like to meet Jesus." [22] Philip told Andrew. Then the two of them went to Jesus and told him.

The Son of Man must be lifted up

[23] Jesus said:

The time has come for the Son of Man to be given his glory.* [24] I tell you for certain that a grain of wheat that falls on the ground will never be more than one grain unless it dies. But if it dies, it will produce lots of wheat. [25] If you love your life, you will lose it. If you give it up in this world, you will be given eternal life. [26] If you serve me, you must go with me. My servants will be with me wherever I am. If you serve me, my Father will honour you.

[27] Now I am deeply troubled, and I don't know what to say. But I must not ask my Father to keep me from this time of suffering. In fact, I came into the world to suffer. [28] So Father, bring glory to yourself.

A voice from heaven then said, "I have already brought glory to myself, and I will do it again!" [29] When the crowd heard the voice, some of them thought it was thunder. Others thought an angel had spoken to Jesus.

[30] Then Jesus told the crowd, "That voice spoke to help you, not me. [31] This world's people are now being judged, and the ruler of this world* is already being thrown out! [32] If I am lifted up above the earth, I will make everyone want to come to me." [33] Jesus was talking about the way he would be put to death.

[34] The crowd said to Jesus, "The Scriptures teach that the Messiah will live for ever. How can you say that the Son of Man must be lifted up? Who is this Son of Man?"

---

*12.13 took palm branches and went out to greet him: This was one way that the Jewish people welcomed a famous person.
*12.13 Hooray: This translates a word that can mean "please save us". But it is most often used as a shout of praise to God.
*12.16 had been given his glory: See the note at 7.39.
*12.17,18 miracle: See the note at 2.11.
See also: 12.8: Deut 15.11. 12.13: Psa 118.25,26. 12.15: Zech 9.9.

*12.20 Greeks: Perhaps Gentiles who worshipped with the Jews. See the note at 7.35.
*12.23 be given his glory: See the note at 7.39.
*12.31 world: In the Gospel of John "world" sometimes refers to the people who live in this world and to the evil forces that control their lives.
See also: 12.25: Matt 10.39; 16.25; Mark 8.35; Luke 9.24; 17.33. 12.34: Psa 110.4; Isa 9.7; Ezek 37.25; Dan 7.14.

35 Jesus answered, "The light will be with you for only a little longer. Walk in the light while you can. Then you won't be caught walking blindly in the dark. 36 Have faith in the light while it is with you, and you will be children of the light."

The people refuse to have faith in Jesus

After Jesus had said these things, he left and went into hiding. 37 He had performed a lot of miracles* among the people, but they were still not willing to have faith in him. 38 This happened so that what the prophet Isaiah had said would come true,

"Lord, who has believed
    our message?
And who has seen
    your mighty strength?"

39 The people could not have faith in Jesus, because Isaiah had also said,

40 "The Lord has blinded
    the eyes of the people,
and he has made
    the people stubborn.
He did this so that they
    could not see
    or understand,
and so that they
    would not turn to the Lord
    and be healed."

41 Isaiah said this, because he saw the glory of Jesus and spoke about him. 42 Even then, many of the leaders put their faith in Jesus, but they did not tell anyone about it. The Pharisees had already given orders for the people not to have anything to do with anyone who had faith in Jesus. 43 And besides, the leaders liked praise from others more than they liked praise from God.

Jesus came to save the world

44 In a loud voice Jesus said:

Everyone who has faith in me also has faith in the one who sent me. 45 And everyone who has seen me has seen the one who sent me. 46 I am the light that has come into the world. No one who has faith in me will stay in the dark.

47 I am not the one who will judge those who refuse to obey my teachings. I came to save the people of this world, not to be their judge. 48 But everyone who rejects me and my teachings will be judged on the last day* by what I have said. 49 I don't speak on my own. I say only what the Father who sent me has told me to say. 50 I know that his commands will bring eternal life. That is why I tell you exactly what the Father has told me.

Jesus' last week: his trial and death

CHAPTER 13

Jesus washes the feet of his disciples

1 It was before Passover, and Jesus knew that the time had come for him to leave this world and to return to the Father. He had always loved his followers in this world, and he loved them to the very end.

2 Even before the evening meal started, the devil had made Judas, the son of Simon Iscariot,* decide to betray Jesus. 3 Jesus knew that he had come from God and would go back to God. He also knew that the Father had given him complete power. 4 So during the meal Jesus got up, removed his outer garment, and wrapped a towel around his waist. 5 He put some water into a large bowl. Then he began washing his disciples' feet and drying them with the towel he was wearing.

6 But when he came to Simon Peter, that disciple asked, "Lord, are you going to wash my feet?"

7 Jesus answered, "You don't really know what I am doing, but later you will understand."

8 "You will never wash my feet!" Peter replied.

"If I don't wash you," Jesus told him, "you don't really belong to me."

9 Peter said, "Lord, don't wash just my feet. Wash my hands and my head."

10 Jesus answered, "People who have bathed and are clean all over need to wash just their feet. And you, my disciples, are clean, except for one of you." 11 Jesus knew who would betray him. That is why he said, "except for one of you."

---

*12.37 miracles: See the note at 2.11.
See also: 12.38: Isa 53.1 (LXX). 12.40: Isa 6.10 (LXX).

*12.48 the last day: See the note at 6.39.
*13.2 Iscariot: See the note at 6.71.

[12] After Jesus had washed his disciples' feet and had put his outer garment back on, he sat down again.* Then he said:

Do you understand what I have done? [13] You call me your teacher and Lord, and you should, because that is who I am. [14] And if your Lord and teacher has washed your feet, you should do the same for each other. [15] I have set the example, and you should do for each other exactly what I have done for you. [16] I tell you for certain that servants are not greater than their master, and messengers are not greater than the one who sent them. [17] You know these things, and God will bless you, if you do them.

[18] I am not talking about all of you. I know the ones I have chosen. But what the Scriptures say must come true. And they say, "The man who ate with me has turned against me!" [19] I am telling you this before it all happens. Then when it does happen, you will believe who I am.* [20] I tell you for certain that anyone who welcomes my messengers also welcomes me, and anyone who welcomes me welcomes the one who sent me.

Jesus tells what will happen to him

This is also told in Matthew 26.20–25; Mark 14.17–21; Luke 22.21–23

[21] After Jesus had said these things, he was deeply troubled and told his disciples, "I tell you for certain that one of you will betray me." [22] They were confused about what he meant. And they just stared at each other.

[23] Jesus' favourite disciple was sitting next to him at the meal, [24] and Simon motioned for that disciple to find out which one Jesus meant. [25] So the disciple leaned towards Jesus and asked, "Lord, which one of us are you talking about?"

[26] Jesus answered, "I will dip this piece of bread in the sauce and give it to the one I was talking about."

Then Jesus dipped the bread and gave it to Judas, the son of Simon Iscariot.* [27] At once Satan took control of Judas.

Jesus said, "Judas, go quickly and do what you have to do." [28] No one at the meal understood what Jesus meant. [29] But because Judas was in charge of the money, some of them thought that Jesus had told him to buy something they needed for the festival. Others thought that Jesus had told him to give some money to the poor. [30] Judas took the piece of bread and went out.

It was already night.

The new command

[31] After Judas had gone, Jesus said:

Now the Son of Man will be given glory, and he will bring glory to God. [32] Then, after God is given glory because of him, God will bring glory to him, and God will do it very soon.

[33] My children, I will be with you for a little while longer. Then you will look for me, but you won't find me. I tell you just as I told the people, "You cannot go where I am going." [34] But I am giving you a new command. You must love each other, just as I have loved you. [35] If you love each other, everyone will know that you are my disciples.

Peter's promise

This is also told in Matthew 26.31–35; Mark 14.27–31; Luke 22.31–34

[36] Simon Peter asked, "Lord, where are you going?"

Jesus answered, "You can't go with me now, but later on you will."

[37] Peter asked, "Lord, why can't I go with you now? I would die for you!"

[38] "Would you really die for me?" Jesus asked. "I tell you for certain that before a cock crows, you will say three times that you don't even know me."

CHAPTER 14

Jesus is the way to the Father

[1] Jesus said to his disciples, "Don't be worried! Have faith in God and have faith in me.♦ [2] There are many rooms in my Father's house. I wouldn't tell you this, unless it was true. I am going there to prepare a place for each of you. [3] After I have done this, I will come back and take you with me. Then we will be together. [4] You know the way to where I am going."

---

*13.12 sat down again: On special occasions the Jewish people followed the Greek and Roman custom of lying down on their left side and leaning on their left elbow, while eating with their right hand.
*13.19 I am: See the note at 8.24.
*13.26 Iscariot: See the note at 6.71.

See also: 13.12–15: Luke 22.27. 13.16: Matt 10.24; Luke 6.40; John 15.20. 13.18: Psa 41.9. 13.20: Matt 10.40; Mark 9.37; Luke 9.48; 10.16.

See also: 13.33: John 7.34. 13.34: John 15.12,17; 1 John 3.23; 2 John 5.

5 Thomas said, "Lord, we don't even know where you are going! How can we know the way?"

6 "I am the way, the truth, and the life!" Jesus answered. "Without me, no one can go to the Father. 7 If you had known me, you would have known the Father. But from now on, you do know him, and you have seen him."

8 Philip said, "Lord, show us the Father. That is all we need."

9 Jesus replied:

Philip, I have been with you for a long time. Don't you know who I am? If you have seen me, you have seen the Father. How can you ask me to show you the Father? 10 Don't you believe that I am one with the Father and that the Father is one with me? What I say isn't said on my own. The Father who lives in me does these things.

11 Have faith in me when I say that the Father is one with me and that I am one with the Father. Or else have faith in me simply because of the things I do. 12 I tell you for certain that if you have faith in me, you will do the same things that I am doing. You will even do greater things, now that I am going back to the Father. 13 Ask me, and I will do whatever you ask. This way the Son will bring honour to the Father. 14 I will do whatever you ask me to do.

The Holy Spirit is promised

15 Jesus said to his disciples:

If you love me, you will do as I command. 16 Then I will ask the Father to send you the Holy Spirit who will help* you and always be with you. 17 The Spirit will show you what is true. The people of this world cannot accept the Spirit, because they don't see or know him. But you know the Spirit, who is with you and will keep on living in you.

18 I won't leave you like orphans. I will come back to you. 19 In a little while the people of this world won't be able to see me, but you will see me. And because I live, you will live. 20 Then you will know that I am one with the Father. You will know that you are one with me, and I am one with you. 21 If you love me, you will do what I have said, and my Father will love you. I will also love you and show you what I am like.

22 The other Judas, not Judas Iscariot,* then spoke up and asked, "Lord, what do you mean by saying that you will show us what you are like, but you will not show the people of this world?"

23 Jesus replied:

If anyone loves me, they will obey me. Then my Father will love them, and we will come to them and live in them. 24 But anyone who doesn't love me, won't obey me. What they have heard me say doesn't really come from me, but from the Father who sent me.

25 I have told you these things while I am still with you. 26 But the Holy Spirit will come and help* you, because the Father will send the Spirit to take my place. The Spirit will teach you everything and will remind you of what I said while I was with you.

27 I give you peace, the kind of peace that only I can give. It isn't like the peace that this world can give. So don't be worried or afraid.

28 You have already heard me say that I am going and that I will also come back to you. If you really love me, you should be glad that I am going back to the Father, because he is greater than I am.

29 I am telling you this before I leave, so that when it does happen, you will have faith in me. 30 I cannot speak with you much longer, because the ruler of this world is coming. But he has no power over me. 31 I obey my Father, so that everyone in the world might know that I love him.

It is time for us to go now.

CHAPTER 15

Jesus is the true vine

1 Jesus said to his disciples:

I am the true vine, and my Father is the gardener. 2 He cuts away every branch of mine that doesn't produce fruit. But he trims clean every branch that does produce fruit, so that it will produce even more fruit. 3 You are already clean because of what I have said to you.

4 Stay joined to me, and I will stay joined to you. Just as a branch cannot produce fruit unless it stays joined to the vine, you cannot produce fruit unless you stay joined to me. 5 I am the vine, and you are the

---

*14.22 Iscariot: See the note at 6.71.

branches. If you stay joined to me, and I stay joined to you, then you will produce lots of fruit. But you cannot do anything without me. ⁶ If you don't stay joined to me, you will be thrown away. You will be like dry branches that are gathered up and burnt in a fire.

⁷ Stay joined to me and let my teachings become part of you. Then you can pray for whatever you want, and your prayer will be answered. ⁸ When you become fruitful disciples of mine, my Father will be honoured. ⁹ I have loved you, just as my Father has loved me. So remain faithful to my love for you. ¹⁰ If you obey me, I will keep loving you, just as my Father keeps loving me, because I have obeyed him.

¹¹ I have told you this to make you as completely happy as I am. ¹² Now I tell you to love each other, as I have loved you. ¹³ The greatest way to show love for friends is to die for them. ¹⁴ And you are my friends, if you obey me. ¹⁵ Servants don't know what their master is doing, and so I don't speak to you as my servants. I speak to you as my friends, and I have told you everything that my Father has told me.

¹⁶ You did not choose me. I chose you and sent you out to produce fruit, the kind of fruit that will last. Then my Father will give you whatever you ask for in my name.' ¹⁷ So I command you to love each other.

The world's hatred

Jesus continued:

¹⁸ If the people of this world* hate you, just remember that they hated me first. ¹⁹ If you belonged to the world, its people would love you. But you don't belong to the world. I have chosen you to leave the world behind, and that is why its people hate you. ²⁰ Remember how I told you that servants are not greater than their master. So if people ill-treat me, they will ill-treat you. If they do what I say, they will do what you say.

²¹ People will do to you exactly what they did to me. They will do it because you belong to me, and they don't know the one who sent me. ²² If I had not come and spoken to them, they would not be guilty of sin. But now they have no excuse for their sin.

²³ Everyone who hates me also hates my Father. ²⁴ I have done things that no one else has ever done. If they had not seen me do these things, they would not be guilty. But they did see me do these things, and they still hate me and my Father too. ²⁵ That is why the Scriptures are true when they say, "People hated me for no reason."

²⁶ I will send you the Spirit who comes from the Father and shows what is true. The Spirit will help' you and will tell you about me. ²⁷ Then you will also tell others about me, because you have been with me from the beginning.

CHAPTER 16

Jesus continued:

¹ I am telling you this to keep you from being afraid. ² You will be chased out of the Jewish meeting places. And the time will come when people will kill you and think they are doing God a favour. ³ They will do these things because they don't know either the Father or me. ⁴ I am saying this to you now, so that when the time comes, you will remember what I have said.

The work of the Holy Spirit

Jesus continued:

I was with you at the first, and so I didn't tell you these things. ⁵ But now I am going back to the Father who sent me, and none of you asks me where I am going. ⁶ You are very sad from hearing all this. ⁷ But I tell you that I am going to do what is best for you. That is why I am going away. The Holy Spirit cannot come to help' you until I leave. But after I am gone, I will send the Spirit to you.

⁸ The Spirit will come and show the people of this world the truth about sin and God's justice and the judgment. ⁹ The Spirit will show them that they are wrong about sin, because they didn't have faith in me. ¹⁰ They are wrong about God's justice, because I am going to the Father, and you won't see me again. ¹¹ And they are wrong about the judgment, because God has already judged the ruler of this world.

¹² I have much more to say to you, but right now it would be more than you could understand. ¹³ The Spirit shows what is true and will come and guide you into the full truth. The Spirit doesn't speak on his own.

---

*15.18 world: See the note at 12.31.

See also: 15.12: John 13.34; 15.17; 1 John 3.23; 2 John 5.
15.20: Matt 10.24; Luke 6.40; John 13.16.

See also: 15.25: Psa 35.19; 69.4.

He will tell you only what he has heard from me, and he will let you know what is going to happen. ¹⁴ The Spirit will bring glory to me by taking my message and telling it to you. ¹⁵ Everything that the Father has is mine. That is why I have said that the Spirit takes my message and tells it to you.

Sorrow will turn into joy

¹⁶ Jesus told his disciples, "For a little while you won't see me, but after a while you will see me."

¹⁷ They said to each other, "What does Jesus mean by saying that for a little while we won't see me, but after a while we will see him? What does he mean by saying that he is going to the Father? ¹⁸ What is this 'little while' that he is talking about? We don't know what he means."

¹⁹ Jesus knew that they had some questions, so he said:

You are wondering what I meant when I said that for a little while you won't see me, but after a while you will see me. ²⁰ I tell you for certain that you will cry and be sad, but the world will be happy. You will be sad, but later you will be happy.

²¹ When a woman is about to give birth, she is in great pain. But after it is all over, she forgets the pain and is happy, because she has brought a child into the world. ²² You are now very sad. But later I will see you, and you will be so happy that no one will be able to change the way you feel. ²³ When that time comes, you won't have to ask me about anything. I tell you for certain that the Father will give you whatever you ask for in my name. ²⁴ You have not asked for anything in this way before, but now you must ask in my name.* Then it will be given to you, so that you will be completely happy.

²⁵ I have used examples to explain to you what I have been talking about. But the time will come when I will speak to you plainly about the Father and will no longer use examples like these. ²⁶ You will ask the Father in my name,* and I won't have to ask him for you. ²⁷ God the Father loves you because you love me, and you believe that I have come from him. ²⁸ I came from the Father into the world, but I am leaving the world and returning to the Father.

²⁹ The disciples said, "Now you are speaking plainly to us! You are not using examples. ³⁰ At last we know that you understand everything, and we don't have any more questions. Now we believe that you truly have come from God."

³¹ Jesus replied:

Do you really believe me? ³² The time will come and is already here when all of you will be scattered. Each of you will go back home and leave me by myself. But the Father will be with me, and I won't be alone. ³³ I have told you this, so that you might have peace in your hearts because of me. While you are in the world, you will have to suffer. But cheer up! I have defeated the world.*

CHAPTER 17

Jesus prays

¹ After Jesus had finished speaking to his disciples, he looked up towards heaven and prayed:

Father, the time has come for you to bring glory to your Son, in order that he may bring glory to you. ² And you gave him power over all people, so that he would give eternal life to everyone you give him. ³ Eternal life is to know you, the only true God, and to know Jesus Christ, the one you sent. ⁴ I have brought glory to you here on earth by doing everything that you gave me to do. ⁵ Now, Father, give me back the glory that I had with you before the world was created.

⁶ You have given me some followers from this world, and I have shown them what you are like. They were yours, but you gave them to me, and they have obeyed you. ⁷ They know that you gave me everything I have. ⁸ I told my followers what you told me, and they accepted it. They know that I came from you, and they believe that you are the one who sent me. ⁹ I am praying for them, but not for those who belong to this world.* My followers belong to you, and I am praying for them. ¹⁰ All that I have is yours, and all that you have is mine, and they will bring glory to me.

¹¹ Holy Father, I am no longer in the world. I am coming to you, but my followers are still in the world. So keep

*16.33; 17.9 world: See the note at 12.31.

them safe by the power of the name that you have given me. Then they will be one with each other, just as you and I are one. [12] While I was with them, I kept them safe by the power you have given me. I guarded them, and not one of them was lost, except the one who had to be lost. This happened so that what the Scriptures say would come true.

[13] I am on my way to you. But I say these things while I am still in the world, so that my followers will have the same complete joy that I do. [14] I have told them your message. But the people of this world hate them, because they don't belong to this world, just as I don't.

[15] Father, I don't ask you to take my followers out of the world, but keep them safe from the evil one. [16] They don't belong to this world, and neither do I. [17] Your word is the truth. So let this truth make them completely yours. [18] I am sending them into the world, just as you sent me. [19] I have given myself completely for their sake, so that they may belong completely to the truth.

[20] I am not praying just for these followers. I am also praying for everyone else who will have faith because of what my followers will say about me. [21] I want all of them to be one with each other, just as I am one with you and you are one with me. I also want them to be one with us. Then the people of this world will believe that you sent me.

[22] I have honoured my followers in the same way that you honoured me, in order that they may be one with each other, just as we are one. [23] I am one with them, and you are one with me, so that they may become completely one. Then the people of this world will know that you sent me. They will know that you love my followers as much as you love me.

[24] Father, I want everyone you have given me to be with me, wherever I am. Then they will see the glory that you have given me, because you loved me before the world was created. [25] Good Father, the people of this world don't know you. But I know you, and my followers know that you sent me. [26] I told them what you are like, and I will tell them even more. Then the love that you have for me will become part of them, and I will be one with them.

See also: 17.12: Psa 41.9; John 13.18.

CHAPTER 18

Jesus is betrayed and arrested

This is also told in Matthew 26.47–56; Mark 14.43–50; Luke 22.47–53

[1] When Jesus had finished praying, he and his disciples crossed the Kidron Valley and went into a garden.* [2] Jesus had often met there with his disciples, and Judas knew where the place was.

[3-5] Judas had promised to betray Jesus. So he went to the garden with some Roman soldiers and temple police, who had been sent by the chief priests and the Pharisees. They carried torches, lanterns, and weapons. Jesus already knew everything that was going to happen, but he asked, "Who are you looking for?"

They answered, "We are looking for Jesus from Nazareth."

Jesus told them, "I am Jesus!"* [6] At once they all backed away and fell to the ground.

[7] Jesus again asked, "Who are you looking for?"

"We are looking for Jesus from Nazareth," they answered.

[8] This time Jesus replied, "I have already told you that I am Jesus. If I am the one you are looking for, let these others go. [9] Then everything will happen, just as I said, 'I did not lose anyone you gave me.' "

[10] Simon Peter had brought along a sword. He now pulled it out and struck at the servant of the high priest. The servant's name was Malchus, and Peter cut off his right ear. [11] Jesus told Peter, "Put your sword away. I must drink from the cup* that the Father has given me."

Jesus is brought to Annas

This is also told in Matthew 26.57,58; Mark 14.53,54; Luke 22.54

[12] The Roman officer and his men, together with the temple police, arrested Jesus and tied him up. [13] They took him first to Annas, who was the father-in-law of Caiaphas, the high priest that year. [14] He was the same Caiaphas

*18.1 garden: The Greek word is usually translated "garden", but probably referred to an olive orchard.
*18.3-5 I am Jesus: The Greek text has "I am". See the note at 8.24.
*18.11 drink from the cup: In the Scriptures a cup is sometimes used as a symbol of suffering. To "drink from the cup" is to suffer.

See also: 18.11: Matt 26.39; Mark 14.36; Luke 22.42. **18.14:** John 11.49,50.

who had told the Jewish leaders, "It is better if one person dies for the people."

Peter says he doesn't know Jesus

This is also told in Matthew 26.69,70; Mark 14.66–68; Luke 22.55–57

15 Simon Peter and another disciple followed Jesus. That disciple knew the high priest, and he followed Jesus into the courtyard of the high priest's house. 16 Peter stayed outside near the gate. But the other disciple came back out and spoke to the girl at the gate. She let Peter go in, 17 but asked him, "Aren't you one of that man's followers?"

"No, I am not!" Peter answered.

18 It was cold, and the servants and temple police had made a charcoal fire. They were warming themselves around it, when Peter went over and stood near the fire to warm himself.

Jesus is questioned by the high priest

This is also told in Matthew 26.59–66; Mark 14.55–64; Luke 22.66–71

19 The high priest questioned Jesus about his followers and his teaching. 20 But Jesus told him, "I have spoken freely in front of everyone. And I have always taught in our meeting places and in the temple, where all our people come together. I have not said anything in secret. 21 Why are you questioning me? Why don't you ask the people who heard me? They surely know what I have said."

22 As soon as Jesus said this, one of the temple police hit him and said, "That's no way to talk to the high priest!"

23 Jesus answered, "If I have done something wrong, say so. But if not, why did you hit me?" 24 Jesus was still tied up, and Annas sent him to Caiaphas the high priest.

Peter again denies that he knows Jesus

This is also told in Matthew 26.71–75; Mark 14.69–72; Luke 22.58–62

25 While Simon Peter was standing there warming himself, someone asked him, "Aren't you one of Jesus' followers?"

Again Peter denied it and said, "No, I am not!"

26 One of the high priest's servants was there. He was a relative of the servant whose ear Peter had cut off, and he asked, "Didn't I see you in the garden with that man?"

27 Once more Peter denied it, and at once a cock crowed.

Jesus is tried by Pilate

This is also told in Matthew 27.1,2,11–14; Mark 15.1–5; Luke 23.1–5

28 It was early in the morning when Jesus was taken from Caiaphas to the building where the Roman governor stayed. But the crowd waited outside. Any of them who had gone inside would have become unclean and would not be allowed to eat the Passover meal.*

29 Pilate came out and asked, "What charges are you bringing against this man?"

30 They answered, "He is a criminal! That's why we brought him to you."

31 Pilate told them, "Take him and judge him by your own laws."

The crowd replied, "We are not allowed to put anyone to death." 32 And so what Jesus said about his death* would soon come true.

33 Pilate then went back inside. He called Jesus over and asked, "Are you the king of the Jews?"

34 Jesus answered, "Are you asking this on your own or did someone tell you about me?"

35 "You know I'm not a Jew!" Pilate said. "Your own people and the chief priests brought you to me. What have you done?"

36 Jesus answered, "My kingdom doesn't belong to this world. If it did, my followers would have fought to keep me from being handed over to the Jewish leaders. No, my kingdom doesn't belong to this world."

37 "So you are a king," Pilate replied.

"You are saying that I am a king," Jesus told him. "I was born into this world to tell about the truth. And everyone who belongs to the truth knows my voice."

38 Pilate asked Jesus, "What is truth?"

Jesus is sentenced to death

This is also told in Matthew 27.15–31; Mark 15.6–20; Luke 23.13–25

Pilate went back out and said, "I don't find this man guilty of anything! 39 And since I usually set a prisoner free for you at Passover, would you like me to set free the king of the Jews?"

*18.28 would have become unclean and would not be allowed to eat the Passover meal: Jewish people who came in close contact with foreigners just before Passover were not allowed to eat the Passover meal.
*18.32 about his death: Jesus had said that he would die by being "lifted up," which meant that he would die on a cross. The Romans killed criminals by nailing them on a cross, but they did not let the Jews kill anyone in this way.

See also: 18.28: John 3.14; 12.32.

40 They shouted, "No, not him! We want Barabbas." Now Barabbas was a terrorist.*

CHAPTER 19

1 Pilate gave orders for Jesus to be beaten with a whip. 2 The soldiers made a crown out of thorn branches and put it on Jesus. Then they put a purple robe on him. 3 They came up to him and said, "Hey, you king of the Jews!" They also hit him with their fists.

4 Once again Pilate went out. This time he said, "I will have Jesus brought out to you again. Then you can see for yourselves that I have not found him guilty."

5 Jesus came out, wearing the crown of thorns and the purple robe. Pilate said, "Here is the man!"*

6 When the chief priests and the temple police saw him, they yelled, "Nail him to a cross! Nail him to a cross!"

Pilate told them, "You take him and nail him to a cross! I don't find him guilty of anything."

7 The crowd replied, "He claimed to be the Son of God! Our Jewish Law says that he must be put to death."

8 When Pilate heard this, he was terrified. 9 He went back inside and asked Jesus, "Where are you from?" But Jesus did not answer.

10 "Why won't you answer my question?" Pilate asked. "Don't you know that I have the power to let you go free or to nail you to a cross?"

11 Jesus replied, "If God had not given you the power, you couldn't do anything at all to me. But the one who handed me over to you did something even worse."

12 Then Pilate wanted to set Jesus free. But the crowd again yelled, "If you set this man free, you are no friend of the Emperor! Anyone who claims to be a king is an enemy of the Emperor."

13 When Pilate heard this, he brought Jesus out. Then he sat down on the judge's bench at the place known as "The Stone Pavement". In Aramaic this pavement is called "Gabbatha". 14 It was about midday on the day before Passover, and Pilate said to the crowd, "Look at your king!"

15 "Kill him! Kill him!" they yelled. "Nail him to a cross!"

"So you want me to nail your king to a cross?" Pilate asked.

The chief priests replied, "The Emperor is our king!" 16 Then Pilate handed Jesus over to be nailed to a cross.

Jesus is nailed to a cross

This is also told in Matthew 27.32–44; Mark 15.21–32; Luke 23.26–43

Jesus was taken away, 17 and he carried his cross to a place known as "The Skull".* In Aramaic this place is called "Golgotha". 18 There Jesus was nailed to the cross, and on each side of him a man was also nailed to a cross.

19 Pilate ordered the charge against Jesus to be written on a board and put above the cross. It read, "Jesus of Nazareth, King of the Jews." 20 The words were written in Hebrew, Latin, and Greek.

The place where Jesus was taken wasn't far from the city, and many of the Jewish people read the charge against him. 21 So the chief priests went to Pilate and said, "Why did you write that he is King of the Jews? You should have written, 'He claimed to be King of the Jews.' "

22 But Pilate told them, "What is written will not be changed!"

23 After the soldiers had nailed Jesus to the cross, they divided up his clothes into four parts, one for each of them. But his outer garment was made from a single piece of cloth, and it did not have any seams. 24 The soldiers said to each other, "Let's not rip it apart. We will gamble to see who gets it." This happened so that the Scriptures would come true, which say,

> "They divided up my clothes
> and gambled
> for my garments."

The soldiers then did what they had decided.

25 Jesus' mother stood beside his cross with her sister and Mary the wife of Clopas. Mary Magdalene was standing there too.* 26 When Jesus saw his mother and his favourite disciple with her, he said to his mother, "This man is now your son." 27 Then he said to the disciple, "She is now your mother." From then on, that disciple took her into his own home.

---

*18.40 terrorist: Someone who stirred up trouble against the Romans in the hope of gaining freedom for the Jewish people.

*19.17 The Skull: The place was probably given this name because it was near a large rock in the shape of a human skull.
See also: 19.24: Psa 22.18.

The death of Jesus

This is also told in Matthew 27.45–56;
Mark 15.33–41; Luke 23.44–49

28 Jesus knew that he had now finished his
work. And in order to make the Scriptures
come true, he said, "I am thirsty!" 29 A jar of
cheap wine was there. Someone then soaked a
sponge with the wine and held it up to Jesus'
mouth on the stem of a hyssop plant. 30 After
Jesus drank the wine, he said, "Everything is
done!" He bowed his head and died.

A spear is stuck in Jesus' side

31 This would be both a Sabbath and
the Passover. It was a special day for the Jewish
people,* and they did not want the bodies to
stay on the crosses during that day. So they
asked Pilate to break the men's legs* and take
their bodies down. 32 The soldiers first broke
the legs of the other two men who were nailed
there. 33 But when they came to Jesus, they
saw that he was already dead, and they did not
break his legs.
34 One of the soldiers stuck his spear into
Jesus' side, and blood and water came out.
35 We know this is true, because it was told by
someone who saw it happen. Now you can
have faith too. 36 All this happened so that the
Scriptures would come true, which say, "No
bone of his body will be broken" 37 and, "They
will see the one in whose side they stuck a
spear."

Jesus is buried

This is also told in Matthew 27.57–61;
Mark 15.42–47; Luke 23.50–56

38 Joseph from Arimathea was one of Jesus'
disciples. He had kept it secret though,
because he was afraid of the Jewish leaders.
But now he asked Pilate to let him have Jesus'
body. Pilate gave him permission, and Joseph
took it down from the cross.
39 Nicodemus also came with about thirty
kilogrammes of spices made from myrrh and
aloes. This was the same Nicodemus who had

*19.31 a special day for the Jewish people: Passover
could be any day of the week. But according to the
Gospel of John, Passover was on a Sabbath in the year
that Jesus was nailed to a cross.
*19.31 break the men's legs: This was the way that
the Romans sometimes speeded up the death of a
person who had been nailed to a cross.

See also: 19.28: Psa 69.21; 22.15. 19.36: Exod 12.46;
Num 9.12; Psa 34.20. 19.37: Zech 12.10; Rev 1.7.
19.39: John 3.1,2.

138

visited Jesus one night.* 40 The two men
wrapped the body in a linen cloth, together
with the spices, which was how the Jewish
people buried their dead. 41 In the place
where Jesus had been nailed to a cross, there
was a garden with a tomb that had never
been used. 42 The tomb was nearby, and since
it was the time to prepare for the Sabbath,
they were in a hurry to put Jesus' body there.

Jesus is alive

CHAPTER 20

This is also told in Matthew 28.1–10; Mark 16.1–8;
Luke 24.1–12

1 On Sunday morning while it was still dark,
Mary Magdalene went to the tomb and saw
that the stone had been rolled away from the
entrance. 2 She ran to Simon Peter and to
Jesus' favourite disciple and said, "They have
taken the Lord from the tomb! We don't
know where they have put him."
3 Peter and the other disciple set off for the
tomb. 4 They ran side by side, until the other
disciple ran faster than Peter and got there
first. 5 He bent over and saw the strips of
linen cloth lying inside the tomb, but he did
not go in.
6 When Simon Peter got there, he went
into the tomb and saw the strips of cloth.
7 He also saw the piece of cloth that had been
used to cover Jesus' face. It was rolled up and
in a place by itself. 8 The disciple who got
there first then went into the tomb, and
when he saw it, he believed. 9 At that time
Peter and the other disciple did not know
that the Scriptures said Jesus would rise to
life. 10 So the two of them went back to the
other disciples.

Jesus appears to his disciples

Jesus appears to Mary Magdalene

This is also told in Mark 16.9–11

11 Mary Magdalene stood crying outside the
tomb. She was still weeping, when she
stooped down 12 and saw two angels inside.
They were dressed in white and were sitting
where Jesus' body had been. One was at the
head and the other was at the foot. 13 The
angels asked Mary, "Why are you crying?"

*19.39 Nicodemus who had visited Jesus one night:
See 3.1–21.

She answered, "They have taken away my Lord's body! I don't know where they have put him."

[14] As soon as Mary said this, she turned around and saw Jesus standing there. But she did not know who he was. [15] Jesus asked her, "Why are you crying? Who are you looking for?"

She thought he was the gardener and said, "Sir, if you have taken his body away, please tell me, so I can go and get him."

[16] Then Jesus said to her, "Mary!"

She turned and said to him, "Rabboni." The Aramaic word "Rabboni" means "Teacher".

[17] Jesus told her, "Don't hold on to me! I have not yet gone to the Father. But tell my disciples that I am going to the one who is my Father and my God, as well as your Father and your God." [18] Mary Magdalene then went and told the disciples that she had seen the Lord. She also told them what he had said to her.

Jesus appears to his disciples

This is also told in Matthew 28.16–20; Mark 16.14–18; Luke 24.36–49

[19] The disciples were afraid of the Jewish leaders, and on the evening of that same Sunday they locked themselves in a room. Suddenly, Jesus appeared in the middle of the group. He greeted them [20] and showed them his hands and his side. When the disciples saw the Lord, they became very happy.

[21] After Jesus had greeted them again, he said, "I am sending you, just as the Father has sent me." [22] Then he breathed on them and said, "Receive the Holy Spirit. [23] If you forgive anyone's sins, they will be forgiven. But if you don't forgive their sins, they will not be forgiven."

Jesus and Thomas

[24] Although Thomas the Twin was one of the twelve disciples, he wasn't with the others when Jesus appeared to them. [25] So they told him, "We have seen the Lord!"

But Thomas said, "First, I must see the nail scars in his hands and touch them with my finger. I must put my hand where the spear went into his side. I won't believe unless I do this!"

[26] A week later the disciples were together again. This time, Thomas was with them. Jesus came in while the doors were still locked and stood in the middle of the group.

He greeted his disciples [27] and said to Thomas, "Put your finger here and look at my hands! Put your hand into my side. Stop doubting and have faith!"

[28] Thomas replied, "You are my Lord and my God!"

[29] Jesus said, "Thomas, do you have faith because you have seen me? The people who have faith in me without seeing me are the ones who are really blessed!"

Why John wrote his book

[30] Jesus performed many other miracles* for his disciples, and not all of them are written in this book. [31] But these are written so that you will put your faith in Jesus as the Messiah and the Son of God. If you have faith in* him, you will have true life.

CHAPTER 21

Jesus appears to seven disciples

[1] Jesus later appeared to his disciples along the shore of Lake Tiberias. [2] Simon Peter, Thomas the Twin, Nathanael from Cana in Galilee, and the brothers James and John, were there, together with two other disciples. [3] Simon Peter said, "I'm going fishing!"

The others said, "We will go with you." They went out in their boat. But they didn't catch a thing that night.

[4] Early the next morning Jesus stood on the shore, but the disciples did not realize who he was. [5] Jesus shouted, "Friends, have you caught anything?"

"No!" they answered.

[6] So he told them, "Let your net down on the right side of your boat, and you will catch some fish."

They did, and the net was so full of fish that they could not drag it up into the boat.

[7] Jesus' favourite disciple told Peter, "It's the Lord!" When Simon heard that it was the Lord, he put on the clothes that he had taken off while he was working. Then he jumped into the water. [8] The boat was only about a hundred metres from shore. So the other disciples stayed in the boat and dragged in the net full of fish.

[9] When the disciples got out of the boat, they saw some bread and a charcoal fire with fish on it. [10] Jesus told his disciples, "Bring some of the fish you have just caught."

[11] Simon Peter got back into the boat and

---

*20.30 miracles: See the note at 2.11.

See also: 20.23: Matt 16.19; 18.18.   See also: 21.3: Luke 5.5. 21.6: Luke 5.6.

dragged the net to shore. In it were one hundred and fifty-three large fish, but still the net did not rip.

¹² Jesus said, "Come and eat!" But none of the disciples dared ask who he was. They knew he was the Lord. ¹³ Jesus took the bread in his hands and gave some of it to his disciples. He did the same with the fish. ¹⁴ This was the third time that Jesus appeared to his disciples after he was raised from death.

Jesus and Peter

¹⁵ When Jesus and his disciples had finished eating, he asked, "Simon son of John, do you love me more than the others do?"

Simon Peter answered, "Yes, Lord, you know I do!"

"Then feed my lambs," Jesus said.

¹⁶ Jesus asked a second time, "Simon son of John, do you love me?"

Peter answered, "Yes, Lord, you know I love you!"

"Then take care of my sheep," Jesus told him.

¹⁷ Jesus asked a third time, "Simon son of John, do you love me?"

Peter was hurt because Jesus had asked him three times if he loved him. So he told Jesus, "Lord, you know everything. You know I love you."

Jesus replied, "Feed my sheep. ¹⁸ I tell you for certain that when you were a young man, you dressed yourself and went wherever you wanted to go. But when you are old, you will hold out your hands. Then others will tie your belt around you and lead you where you don't want to go."

¹⁹ Jesus said this to tell how Peter would die and bring honour to God. Then he said to Peter, "Follow me!"

Jesus and his favourite disciple

²⁰ Peter turned and saw Jesus' favourite disciple following them. He was the same one who had sat next to Jesus at the meal and had asked, "Lord, who is going to betray you?" ²¹ When Peter saw that disciple, he asked Jesus, "Lord, what about him?"

²² Jesus answered, "What is it to you, if I want him to live until I return? You must follow me." ²³ So the rumour spread among the other disciples that this disciple would not die. But Jesus did not say he would not die. He simply said, "What is it to you, if I want him to live until I return?"

²⁴ This disciple is the one who told all this. He wrote it, and we know he is telling the truth.

²⁵ Jesus did many other things. If they were all written in books, I don't suppose there would be room enough in the whole world for all the books.

Additional notes

'1.5 put it out: Or "understood it."

'1.16 one blessing after another: Or "one blessing in place of another."

'3.25 a Jewish man: Some manuscripts have "some Jewish men."

'5.2 Bethzatha: Some manuscripts have "Bethesda" and others have "Bethsaida."

'5.3,4 pool: Some manuscripts add, "They were waiting for the water to be stirred, because an angel from the Lord would sometimes come down and stir it. The first person to get into the pool after that would be healed."

'8.11 don't sin any more: Verses 1–11 are not in some manuscripts. In other manuscripts these verses are placed after 7.36 or after 21.25 or after Luke 21.38, with some differences in the text.

'10.29 he is greater than all others: Some manuscripts have "they are greater than all others."

'12.3 very expensive bottle of perfume: The Greek text has "expensive perfume made of pure spikenard", a plant used to make perfume.

'12.41 he saw the glory of Jesus and spoke about him: Or "he saw the glory of God and spoke about Jesus."

'14.1 Have faith in God and have faith in me: Or "You have faith in God, so have faith in me."

'14.16 help: The Greek word may mean "comfort," "encourage," or "defend."

'14.26 help: See the note at 14.16.

'15.16 in my name: Or "because you are my followers."

'15.26 help: See the note at 14.16.

'16.7 help: See the note at 14.16.

'16.23,24 in my name . . . in my name: Or "as my disciples . . . as my disciples."

'16.26 in my name: Or "because you are my followers."

'19.5 "Here is the man!" Or "Look at the man!"

'19.25 Jesus' mother stood beside his cross with her sister and Mary the wife of Clopas. Mary Magdalene was standing there too: The Greek text may also be understood to include only three women ("Jesus' mother stood beside the cross with her sister, Mary the mother of Clopas. Mary Magdalene was standing there too.") or merely two women ("Jesus' mother was standing there with her sister Mary of Clopas, that is, Mary Magdalene.") "Of Clopas" may mean "daughter of" or "mother of".

See also: 21.20: John 13.25.

›**20.31 put your faith in . . . have faith in:** Some
manuscripts have "keep on having faith in . . . keep
on having faith in".
›**21.2 the brothers James and John:** Greek "the two
sons of Zebedee".
›**21.15 more than the others do?:** Or "more than you
love these things?"

The Acts

of the apostles

A quick look at this book

This is the second book written by Luke. His
first one is commonly known as the Gospel of
Luke. In it he told "all that Jesus did and
taught from the very first until he was taken up
to heaven" (1.1,2). In this book Luke continues
the story by describing some of the struggles
the disciples faced as they tried to obey the
command of Jesus: "You will tell everyone
about me in Jerusalem, in all Judea, in Samaria,
and everywhere in the world" (1.8).

So many different countries are mentioned in
Acts that the book may seem to have been
written only to tell about the spread of the
Christian message. But that is only part of the
story. After Jesus was taken up to heaven, one
of the big problems for his followers was

deciding who could belong to God's people.
And since Jesus and his first followers were
Jews, it was only natural for many of them to
think that his message was only for Jews. But
in Acts, the Spirit is always present to show
that Jesus came to save both Jews and
Gentiles, and that God wants followers from
every nation and race to be part of his people.

The first conflict between Christians and Jews
took place when some of the Jewish religious
leaders rejected the message about Jesus
(4.1–31; 7.1–59). But the most serious problems
for the early church happened because the
disciples at first failed to understand that
anyone could become a follower of Jesus
without first becoming a Jew. This began to
change when Philip dared to take the message
to the Samaritans (8.7–25), and when Peter
went to the home of Cornelius, a captain in the
Roman army (10.1–48).

Finally, Peter reported to the church in
Jerusalem (11.1–18) and a meeting was held
there (15.3–35) to discuss the question of
who could become followers of Christ. Before
the meeting was over, everyone agreed that
the Spirit of God was leading them to reach
out to Gentiles as well as Jews with the good
news of Jesus.

The one who did the most for the spread of
the faith was a man named Paul, and much
of the book tells about his preaching among
the Gentiles. Finally, he took the message to
Rome, the world's most important city at
that time (28.16–31). One of Luke's main

reasons for writing was to show that nothing could keep the Christian message from spreading everywhere.

For two years Paul stayed in a rented house and welcomed everyone who came to see him. He bravely preached about God's kingdom and taught about the Lord Jesus Christ, and no one tried to stop him.

(28.30,31)

Telling the good news in Jerusalem

CHAPTER 1

¹ Theophilus, I first wrote to you* about all that Jesus did and taught from the very first ² until he was taken up to heaven. But before he was taken up, he gave orders to the apostles he had chosen with the help of the Holy Spirit.

³ For forty days after Jesus had suffered and died, he proved in many ways that he had been raised from death. He appeared to his apostles and spoke to them about God's kingdom. ⁴ While he was still with them, he said:

Don't leave Jerusalem yet. Wait here for the Father to give you the Holy Spirit, just as I told you he has promised to do. ⁵ John baptized with water, but in a few days you will be baptized with the Holy Spirit.

Jesus is taken to heaven

⁶ While the apostles were still with Jesus, they asked him, "Lord, are you now going to give Israel its own king again?"*

⁷ Jesus said to them, "You don't need to know the time of those events that only the Father controls. ⁸ But the Holy Spirit will come upon you and give you power. Then you will tell everyone about me in Jerusalem, in all Judea, in Samaria, and everywhere in the world." ⁹ After Jesus had said this and while they were watching, he was taken up into a cloud. They could not see him, ¹⁰ but as he went up, they kept looking up into the sky.

Suddenly two men dressed in white clothes were standing there beside them. ¹¹ They said,

"Why are you men from Galilee standing here and looking up into the sky? Jesus has been taken to heaven. But he will come back in the same way that you have seen him go."

Someone to take the place of Judas

¹²⁻¹³ The Mount of Olives was about a kilometre from Jerusalem. The apostles who had gone there were Peter, John, James, Andrew, Philip, Thomas, Bartholomew, Matthew, James the son of Alphaeus, Simon, known as the Eager One,* and Judas the son of James.

After the apostles returned to the city, they went upstairs to the room where they had been staying.

¹⁴ The apostles often met together and prayed with a single purpose in mind.* The women and Mary the mother of Jesus would meet with them, and so would his brothers. ¹⁵ One day there were about a hundred and twenty of the Lord's followers meeting together, and Peter stood up to speak to them. ¹⁶⁻¹⁷ He said:

My friends, long ago by the power of the Holy Spirit, David said something about Judas, and what he said has now happened. Judas was one of us and had worked with us, but he brought the mob to arrest Jesus. ¹⁸ Then Judas bought some land with the money he was given for doing that evil thing. He fell head-first into the field. His body burst open, and all his insides came out. ¹⁹ When the people of Jerusalem found out about this, they called the place Akeldama, which in the local language means "Field of Blood."

²⁰ In the book of Psalms it says,

"Leave his house empty,
and don't let anyone
live there."

It also says,

"Let someone else
have his job."

²¹⁻²² So we need someone else to help us tell others that Jesus has been raised from

---

*1.1 I first wrote to you: The Gospel of Luke.

See also: 1.1: Luke 1.1–4. 1.4: Luke 24.49. 1.5: Matt 3.11; Mark 1.8; Luke 3.16; John 1.33. 1.8: Matt 28.19; Mark 16.15; Luke 24.47,48. 1.9: Mark 16.19; Luke 24.50,51.

*1.12,13 known as the Eager One: The Greek text has "Zealot", a name later given to the members of a Jewish group which resisted and fought against the Romans.

See also: 1.13: Matt 10.2–4; Mark 3.16–19; Luke 6.14–16. 1.18,19: Matt 27.3–8. 1.20: a Psa 69.25; b Psa 109.8. 1.22: a Matt 3.16; Mark 1.9; Luke 3.21; b Mark 16.19; Luke 24.51.

death. He must also be one of the men who was with us from the very beginning. He must have been with us from the time the Lord Jesus was baptized by John until the day he was taken to heaven.

23 Two men were suggested: one of them was Joseph Barsabbas, known as Justus, and the other was Matthias. 24 Then they all prayed, "Lord, you know what everyone is like! Show us the one you have chosen 25 to be like an apostle and to serve in place of Judas, who got what he deserved." 26 They drew names, and Matthias was chosen to join the group of the eleven apostles.

CHAPTER 2

The coming of the Holy Spirit

1 On the day of Pentecost* all the Lord's followers were together in one place. 2 Suddenly there was a noise from heaven like the sound of a mighty wind! It filled the house where they were meeting. 3 Then they saw what looked like fiery tongues moving in all directions, and a tongue came and settled on each person there. 4 The Holy Spirit took control of everyone, and they began speaking whatever languages the Spirit let them speak.

5 Many religious Jews from every country in the world were living in Jerusalem. 6 And when they heard this noise, a crowd gathered. But they were surprised, because they were hearing everything in their own languages. 7 They were excited and amazed, and said:

Don't all these who are speaking come from Galilee? 8 Then why do we hear them speaking our very own languages? 9 Some of us are from Parthia, Media, and Elam. Others are from Mesopotamia, Judea, Cappadocia, Pontus, Asia, 10 Phrygia, Pamphylia, Egypt, parts of Libya near Cyrene, Rome, 11 Crete, and Arabia. Some of us were born Jews, and others of us have chosen to be Jews. Yet we all hear them using our own languages to tell the wonderful things God has done.

12 Everyone was excited and confused. Some of them even kept asking each other, "What does all this mean?"

13 Others made fun of the Lord's followers and said, "They are drunk."

Peter speaks to the crowd

14 Peter stood with the eleven apostles and spoke in a loud and clear voice to the crowd:

Friends and everyone else living in Jerusalem, listen carefully to what I have to say! 15 You are wrong to think that these people are drunk. After all, it is only nine o'clock in the morning. 16 But this is what God led the prophet Joel to say,

17 "When the last days come,
   I will give my Spirit
      to everyone.
   Your sons and daughters
      will prophesy.
   Your young men
      will see visions,
   and your old men
      will have dreams.
18 In those days I will give
      my Spirit to my servants,
   both men and women,
      and they will prophesy.
19 I will perform miracles
      in the sky above
   and wonders
      on the earth below.
   There will be blood and fire
      and clouds of smoke.
20 The sun will turn dark,
   and the moon
      will be as red as blood
   before the great
      and wonderful day
   of the Lord appears.
21 Then the Lord
   will save everyone
      who asks for his help."

22 Now, listen to what I have to say about Jesus from Nazareth. God proved that he sent Jesus to you by having him perform miracles, wonders, and signs. All of you know this. 23 God had already planned and decided that Jesus would be handed over to you. So you took him and had evil men put him to death on a cross. 24 But God set him free from death and raised him to life. Death could not hold him in its power.

---

*2.1 Pentecost: A Jewish festival that came fifty days after Passover and celebrated the wheat harvest. Jews later celebrated Pentecost as the time when they were given the Law of Moses.
See also: 2.1: Lev 23.15–21; Deut 16.9–11.

See also: 2.17–21: Joel 2.28–32 (LXX). 2.23: Matt 27.35; Mark 15.24; Luke 23.33; John 19.18. 2.24: Matt 28.5,6; Mark 16.6; Luke 24.5.

25 What David said are really the words of Jesus,

"I always see the Lord
near me,
and I will not be afraid
with him at my right side.
26 Because of this,
my heart will be glad,
my words will be joyful,
and I will live in hope.
27 The Lord won't leave me
in the grave.
I am his holy one,
and he won't let
my body decay.
28 He has shown me
the path to life,
and he makes me glad
by being near me."

29 My friends, it is right for me to speak to you about our ancestor David. He died and was buried, and his tomb is still here. 30 But David was a prophet, and he knew that God had made a promise he would not break. He had told David that someone from his own family would some day be king.

31 David knew this would happen, and so he told us that Christ would be raised to life. He said that God would not leave him in the grave or let his body decay. 32 All of us can tell you that God has raised Jesus to life!

33 Jesus was taken up to sit at the right side* of God, and he was given the Holy Spirit, just as the Father had promised. Jesus is also the one who has given the Spirit to us, and that is what you are now seeing and hearing.

34 David didn't go up to heaven. So he wasn't talking about himself when he said,
"The Lord told my Lord to sit at his right side,
35 until he made my Lord's enemies into a footstool for him." 36 Everyone in Israel should then know for certain that God has made Jesus both Lord and Christ, even though you put him to death on a cross.

37 When the people heard this, they were very upset. They asked Peter and the other apostles, "Friends, what shall we do?"

38 Peter said, "Turn back to God! Be baptized in the name of Jesus Christ, so that your sins will be forgiven. Then you will be given the Holy Spirit. 39 This promise is for you and your children. It is for everyone our Lord God will choose, no matter where they live."

40 Peter told them many other things as well. Then he said, "I beg you to save yourselves from what will happen to all these evil people." 41 On that day about three thousand believed his message and were baptized. 42 They spent their time learning from the apostles, and they were like family to each other. They also broke bread* and prayed together.

Life among the Lord's followers

43 Everyone was amazed by the many miracles and wonders that the apostles performed. 44 All the Lord's followers often met together, and they shared everything they had. 45 They would sell their property and possessions and give the money to whoever needed it. 46 Day after day they met together in the temple. They broke bread* together in different homes and shared their food happily and freely, 47 while praising God. Everyone liked them, and each day the Lord added to their group others who were being saved.

CHAPTER 3

Peter and John heal a lame man

1 The time of prayer* was about three o'clock in the afternoon, and Peter and John were going into the temple. 2 A man who had been born lame was being carried to the temple door. Each day he was placed beside this door, known as the Beautiful Gate. He sat there and begged from the people who were going in.

3 The man saw Peter and John entering the temple, and he asked them for money. 4 But they looked straight at him and said, "Look up at us!"

5 The man stared at them and thought he was going to get something. 6 But Peter said, "I don't have any silver or gold! But I will give you what I do have. In the name of Jesus Christ from Nazareth, get up and start walking." 7 Peter then took him by the right hand and helped him up.

---

*2.42,46 broke bread: They ate together and celebrated the Lord's Supper.
*3.1 The time of prayer: Many of the Jewish people prayed in their homes at regular times each day (see Daniel 6.11), and on special occasions they prayed in the temple.
See also: 2.44: Acts 4.32–35.

*2.33 right side: The place of honour and power.
See also: 2.25–28: Psa 16.8–11 (LXX). 2.30: Psa 132.11; 2 Sam 7.12,13. 2.34,35: Psa 110.1.

At once the man's feet and ankles became strong, [8] and he jumped up and started walking. He went with Peter and John into the temple, walking and jumping and praising God. [9] Everyone saw him walking around and praising God. [10] They knew that he was the beggar who had been lying beside the Beautiful Gate, and they were completely surprised. They could not imagine what had happened to the man.

Peter speaks in the temple

[11] While the man kept holding on to Peter and John, the whole crowd ran to them in amazement at the place known as Solomon's Porch.* [12] Peter saw that a crowd had gathered, and he said:

Friends, why are you surprised at what has happened? Why are you staring at us? Do you think we have some power of our own? Do you think we were able to make this man walk because we are so religious? [13] The God that Abraham, Isaac, Jacob, and our other ancestors worshipped has brought honour to his Servant* Jesus. He is the one you betrayed. You turned against him when he was being tried by Pilate, even though Pilate wanted to set him free.

[14] You rejected Jesus, who was holy and good. You asked for a murderer to be set free, [15] and you killed the one who leads people to life. But God raised him from death, and all of us can tell you what he has done. [16] You see this man, and you know him. He put his faith in the name of Jesus and was made strong. Faith in Jesus made this man completely well while everyone was watching.

[17] My friends, I am sure that you and your leaders didn't know what you were doing. [18] But God had his prophets tell that his Messiah would suffer, and now he has kept that promise. [19] So turn to God! Give up your sins, and you will be forgiven. [20] Then that time will come when the Lord will give you fresh strength. He will send you Jesus, his chosen Messiah. [21] But Jesus must stay in heaven until God makes all things new, just as his holy prophets promised long ago.

[22] Moses said, "The Lord your God will choose one of your own people to be a prophet, just as he chose me. Listen to everything he tells you. [23] No one who disobeys that prophet will be one of God's people any longer."

[24] Samuel and all the other prophets who came later also spoke about what is now happening. [25] You are really the ones God told his prophets to speak to. And you were given the promise that God made to your ancestors. He said to Abraham, "All nations on earth will be blessed because of someone from your family." [26] God sent his chosen Son* to you first, because God wanted to bless you and make each one of you turn away from your sins.

CHAPTER 4

Peter and John are brought in front of the council

[1] The apostles were still talking to the people, when some priests, the captain of the temple guard, and some Sadducees arrived. [2] These men were angry because the apostles were teaching the people that the dead would be raised from death, just as Jesus had been raised from death. [3] It was already late in the afternoon, and they arrested Peter and John and put them in jail for the night. [4] But a lot of people who had heard the message believed it. So by now there were about five thousand followers of the Lord.

[5] The next morning the leaders, the elders, and the teachers of the Law of Moses met in Jerusalem. [6] The high priest Annas was there, as well as Caiaphas, John, Alexander, and other members of the high priest's family. [7] They brought in Peter and John and made them stand in the middle while they questioned them. They asked, "By what power and in whose name have you done this?"

[8] Peter was filled with the Holy Spirit and told the nation's leaders and the elders:

[9] You are questioning us today about a kind deed in which a crippled man was healed. [10] But there is something we must tell you and everyone else in Israel. This man is standing here completely well because of the power of Jesus Christ from Nazareth. You put Jesus to death on a cross, but God raised him to life. [11] He is the stone that you builders thought was worthless, and now he is the most important stone of all.

---

*3.11 Solomon's Porch: A public place with tall columns along the east side of the temple.

See also: 3.13: Exod 3.15. 3.14: Matt 27.15–23; Mark 15.6–14; Luke 23.13–23; John 19.12–15. 3.22: Deut 18.15,18 (LXX).

See also: 3.23: Deut 18.19. 3.25: Gen 22.18. 4.11: Psa 118.22.

¹² Only Jesus has the power to save! His name is the only one in all the world that can save anyone.

¹³ The officials were amazed to see how brave Peter and John were, and they knew that these two apostles were only ordinary men and not well educated. The officials were certain that these men had been with Jesus. ¹⁴ But they could not deny what had happened. The man who had been healed was standing there with the apostles.

¹⁵ The officials commanded them to leave the council room. Then the officials said to each other, ¹⁶ "What can we do with these men? Everyone in Jerusalem knows about this miracle, and we cannot say it didn't happen. ¹⁷ But to keep this thing from spreading, we will warn them never again to speak to anyone about the name of Jesus." ¹⁸ So they called the two apostles back in and told them that they must never, for any reason, teach anything about the name of Jesus.

¹⁹ Peter and John answered, "Do you think God wants us to obey you or to obey him? ²⁰ We cannot keep quiet about what we have seen and heard."

²¹⁻²² The officials could not find any reason to punish Peter and John. So they threatened them and let them go. The man who was healed by this miracle was more than forty years old, and everyone was praising God for what had happened.

Peter and others pray for courage

²³ As soon as Peter and John had been set free, they went back and told the others everything that the chief priests and the leaders had said to them. ²⁴ When the rest of the Lord's followers heard this, they prayed together and said:

Master, you created heaven and earth, the sea, and everything in them. ²⁵ And by the Holy Spirit you spoke to our ancestor David. He was your servant, and you told him to say:

"Why are all the Gentiles
    so furious?
Why do people
    make foolish plans?
²⁶ The kings of earth
    prepare for war,
and the rulers
    join together

against the Lord
    and his Messiah."

²⁷ Here in Jerusalem, Herod* and Pontius Pilate got together with the Gentiles and the people of Israel. Then they turned against your holy Servant* Jesus, your chosen Messiah. ²⁸ They did what you in your power and wisdom had already decided would happen.

²⁹ Lord, listen to their threats! We are your servants. So make us brave enough to speak your message. ³⁰ Show your mighty power, as we heal people and perform miracles and wonders in the name of your holy Servant* Jesus.

³¹ After they had prayed, the meeting place shook. They were all filled with the Holy Spirit and bravely spoke God's message.

Sharing possessions

³² The group of followers all felt the same way about everything. None of them claimed that their possessions were their own, and they shared everything they had with each other. ³³ In a powerful way the apostles told everyone that the Lord Jesus was now alive. God greatly blessed his followers, ³⁴ and no one went in need of anything. Everyone who owned land or houses would sell them and bring the money ³⁵ to the apostles. Then they would give the money to anyone who needed it.

³⁶⁻³⁷ Joseph was one of the followers who had sold a piece of property and brought the money to the apostles. He was a Levite from Cyprus, and the apostles called him Barnabas, which means "one who encourages others".

CHAPTER 5

Peter condemns Ananias and Sapphira

¹ Ananias and his wife Sapphira also sold a piece of property. ² But they agreed to cheat and keep some of the money for themselves. So when Ananias took the rest of the money to the apostles, ³ Peter said, "Why has Satan made you keep back some of the money from the sale of the property? Why have you lied to the Holy Spirit? ⁴ The property was yours before you sold it, and even after you sold it, the money was still

---

*4.27 **Herod:** Herod Antipas, the son of Herod the Great.

See also: 4.27: a Luke 23.7–11; b Matt 27.1,2; Mark 15.1; Luke 23.1; John 18.28,29 **4.32:** Acts 2.44,45.

See also: 4.24: Exod 20.11; Neh 9.6; Psa 146.6.
4.25,26: Psa 2.1,2 (LXX).

147

yours. What made you do such a thing? You didn't lie to people. You lied to God!"

[5] As soon as Ananias heard this, he dropped dead, and everyone who heard about it was frightened. [6] Some young men came in and wrapped up his body. Then they took it out and buried it.

[7] Three hours later Sapphira came in, but she did not know what had happened to her husband. [8] Peter asked her, "Tell me, did you sell the property for this amount?"

"Yes," she answered, "that's the amount."

[9] Then Peter said, "Why did the two of you agree to test the Lord's Spirit? The men who buried Ananias are by the door, and they will carry you out!" [10] At once they fell at Peter's feet and died.

When the young men came back in, they found Sapphira lying there dead. So they carried her out and buried her beside her husband. [11] The church members were afraid, and so was everyone else who heard what had happened.

Peter's unusual power

[12] The apostles performed many miracles and wonders among the people. All the Lord's followers often met in the part of the temple known as Solomon's Porch.* No one outside their group dared join them, even though everyone liked them very much.

[14] Many men and women started having faith in the Lord. [15] Then sick people were brought out to the road and placed on stretchers and mats. It was hoped that Peter would walk by, and his shadow would fall on them and heal them. [16] A lot of people living in the towns near Jerusalem brought those who were sick or troubled by evil spirits, and they were all healed.

Trouble for the apostles

[17] The high priest and all the other Sadducees who were with him became jealous. [18] They arrested the apostles and put them in the city jail. [19] But that night an angel from the Lord opened the doors of the jail and led the apostles out. The angel said, [20] "Go to the temple and tell the people everything about this new life." [21] So they went into the temple before sunrise and started teaching.

The high priest and his men called together their council, which included all Israel's leaders. Then they ordered the apostles to be brought to them from the jail.

[22] The temple police who were sent to the jail did not find the apostles. They returned and said, [23] "We found the jail locked tight and the guards standing at the doors. But when we opened the doors and went in, we didn't find anyone there." [24] The captain of the temple police and the chief priests listened to their report, but they did not know what to think about it.

[25] Just then someone came in and said, "Now those men you put in jail are in the temple, teaching the people!" [26] The captain went with some of the temple police and brought the apostles back. But they did not use force. They were afraid that the people might start throwing stones at them.

[27] When the apostles were brought before the council, the high priest said to them, [28] "We told you plainly not to teach in the name of Jesus. But look what you have done! You have been teaching all over Jerusalem, and you are trying to blame us for his death."

[29] Peter and the apostles replied:

We don't obey people. We obey God. [30] You killed Jesus by nailing him to a cross. But the God our ancestors worshipped raised him to life [31] and made him our Leader and Saviour. Then God gave him a place at his right side,* so that the people of Israel would turn back to him and be forgiven. [32] We are here to tell you about all this, and so is the Holy Spirit, who is God's gift to everyone who obeys God.

[33] When the council members heard this, they became so angry that they wanted to kill the apostles. [34] But one of the members was the Pharisee Gamaliel, a highly respected teacher. He ordered the apostles to be taken out of the room for a little while. [35] Then he said to the council:

People of Israel, be careful what you do with these men. [36] Not long ago Theudas claimed to be someone important, and about four hundred men joined him. But he was killed. All his followers were scattered, and that was the end of that. [37] Later, when the people of our nation were being counted, Judas from Galilee appeared. A lot of people followed him, but he was killed, and all his followers were scattered.

---

*5.12 Solomon's Porch: See the note at 3.11.

*5.31 right side: See the note at 2.33.

See also: 5.28: Matt 27.25.

[38] So I advise you to stay away from these men. Leave them alone. If what they are planning is something of their own doing, it will fail. [39] But if God is behind it, you cannot stop it anyway, unless you want to fight against God.

The council members agreed with what he said, [40] and they called the apostles back in. They had them beaten with a whip and warned them not to speak in the name of Jesus. Then they let them go.

[41] The apostles left the council and were happy, because God had considered them worthy to suffer for the sake of Jesus. [42] Every day they spent time in the temple and in one home after another. They never stopped teaching and telling the good news that Jesus is the Messiah.

CHAPTER 6

Seven leaders for the church

[1] A lot of people were now becoming followers of the Lord. But some of the ones who spoke Greek started complaining about the ones who spoke Aramaic. They complained that the Greek-speaking widows were not given their share when the food supplies were handed out each day.

[2] The twelve apostles called the whole group of followers together and said, "We should not give up preaching God's message in order to serve at tables.* [3] My friends, choose seven men who are respected and wise and filled with God's Spirit. We will put them in charge of these things. [4] We can spend our time praying and serving God by preaching."

[5] This suggestion pleased everyone, and they began by choosing Stephen. He had great faith and was filled with the Holy Spirit. Then they chose Philip, Prochorus, Nicanor, Timon, Parmenas, and also Nicolaus, who worshipped with the Jewish people* in Antioch. [6] These men were brought to the apostles. Then the apostles prayed and placed their hands on the men to show that they had been chosen to do this work. [7] God's message spread, and many

more people in Jerusalem became followers. Even a large number of priests put their faith in the Lord.

Stephen is arrested

[8] God gave Stephen the power to perform great miracles and wonders among the people. [9] But some Jews from Cyrene and Alexandria were members of a group who called themselves "Free Men".* They started arguing with Stephen. Some others from Cilicia and Asia also argued with him. [10] But they were no match for Stephen, who spoke with the great wisdom that the Spirit gave him. [11] So they talked some men into saying, "We heard Stephen say terrible things against Moses and God!"

[12] They turned the people and their leaders and the teachers of the Law of Moses against Stephen. Then they all grabbed Stephen and dragged him in front of the council.

[13] Some men agreed to tell lies about Stephen, and they said, "This man keeps on saying terrible things about this holy temple and the Law of Moses. [14] We have heard him claim that Jesus from Nazareth will destroy this place and change the customs that Moses gave us." [15] Then all the council members stared at Stephen. They saw that his face looked like the face of an angel.

CHAPTER 7

Stephen's speech

[1] The high priest asked Stephen, "Are they telling the truth about you?"

[2] Stephen answered:

Friends, listen to me. Our glorious God appeared to our ancestor Abraham while he was still in Mesopotamia, before he had moved to Haran. [3] God told him, "Leave your country and your relatives and go to a land that I will show you." [4] Then Abraham left the land of the Chaldeans and settled in Haran.

After his father died, Abraham came and settled in this land where you now live. [5] God didn't give him any part of it, not even a square metre. But God did promise to give it to him and his family for ever, even though Abraham didn't have any children. [6] God said that Abraham's descendants

---

*6.2 to serve at tables: This may mean either that they were in charge of handing out food to the widows or that they were in charge of the money, since the Greek word "table" may also mean "bank".
*6.5 worshipped with the Jewish people: This translates the Greek word "proselyte" that means a Gentile who had accepted the Jewish religion.

*6.9 Free Men: A group of Jewish men who had once been slaves, but had been freed.
See also: 7.2,3: Gen 12.1. 7.4: a Gen 11.31; b Gen 12.4.
7.5: Gen 12.7; 13.15; 15.18; 17.8. 7.6,7: Gen 15.13,14.

would live for a while in a foreign land. There they would be slaves and would be ill-treated four hundred years. [7] But he also said, "I will punish the nation that makes them slaves. Then later they will come and worship me in this place."

[8] God said to Abraham, "Every son in each family must be circumcised to show that you have kept your agreement with me." So when Isaac was eight days old, Abraham circumcised him. Later, Isaac circumcised his son Jacob, and Jacob circumcised his twelve sons. [9] These men were our ancestors.

Joseph was also one of our famous ancestors. His brothers were jealous of him and sold him as a slave to be taken to Egypt. But God was with him [10] and rescued him from all his troubles. God made him so wise that the Egyptian king Pharaoh* thought highly of him. Pharaoh even made Joseph governor over Egypt and put him in charge of everything he owned.

[11] Everywhere in Egypt and Canaan the grain crops failed. There was terrible suffering, and our ancestors could not find enough to eat. [12] But when Jacob heard that there was grain in Egypt, he sent our ancestors there for the first time. [13] It was on their second trip that Joseph told his brothers who he was, and Pharaoh learnt about Joseph's family.

[14] Joseph sent for his father and his relatives. In all, there were seventy-five of them. [15] His father went to Egypt and died there, just as our ancestors did. [16] Later their bodies were taken back to Shechem and placed in the tomb that Abraham had bought from the sons of Hamor.

Stephen continued:

[17] Finally, the time came for God to do what he had promised Abraham. By then the number of our people in Egypt had greatly increased. [18] Another king was ruling Egypt, and he didn't know anything about Joseph. [19] He tricked our ancestors

and was cruel to them. He even made them leave their babies outside, so they would die.

[20] During this time Moses was born. He was a very beautiful child, and for three months his parents took care of him in their home. [21] Then when they were forced to leave him outside, the king's daughter found him and raised him as her own son. [22] Moses was given the best education in Egypt. He was a strong man and a powerful speaker.

[23] When Moses was forty years old, he wanted to help the Israelites because they were his own people. [24] One day he saw an Egyptian ill-treating one of them. So he rescued the man and killed the Egyptian. [25] Moses thought the rest of his people would realize that God was going to use him to set them free. But they didn't understand.

[26] The next day Moses saw two of his own people fighting, and he tried to make them stop. He said, "Men, you are both Israelites. Why are you so cruel to each other?"

[27] But the man who had started the fight pushed Moses aside and asked, "Who made you our ruler and judge? [28] Are you going to kill me, just as you killed that Egyptian yesterday?" [29] When Moses heard this, he ran away to live in the country of Midian. His two sons were born there.

Stephen continued:

[30] Forty years later, an angel appeared to Moses from a burning bush in the desert near Mount Sinai. [31] Moses was surprised by what he saw. He went closer to get a better look, and the Lord said, [32] "I am the God who was worshipped by your ancestors, Abraham, Isaac, and Jacob." Moses started shaking all over and didn't dare to look at the bush.

[33] The Lord said to him, "Take off your sandals. The place where you are standing is holy. [34] With my own eyes I have seen the suffering of my people in Egypt. I have heard their groans and have come down to rescue them. Now I am sending you back to Egypt."

[35] This was the same Moses that the people rejected by saying, "Who made you our leader and judge?" God's angel had

*7.10 Pharaoh: A Hebrew word sometimes used for the title of the king of Egypt.

See also: 7.7: Exod 3.12. 7.8: a Gen 17.10–14; b Gen 21.2–4; c Gen 25.26; d Gen 29.31–35.18. 7.9: a Gen 37.11; b Gen 37.28; c Gen 39.2,21. 7.10: Gen 41.39–41. 7.11: Gen 42.1,2. 7.13: a Gen 45.1; b Gen 45.16. 7.14: a Gen 45.9,10,17,18; b Gen 46.27 (LXX). 7.15: a Gen 46.1–7; b Gen 49.33. 7.16: a Gen 23.3–16; 33.19; 50.7–13; Josh 24.32. 7.17,18: Exod 1.7,8. 7.19: a Exod 1.10,11; b Exod 1.22.

See also: 7.20: Exod 2.2. 7.21: Exod 2.3–10. 7.23–29: Exod 2.11–15. 7.29: Exod 18.3,4. 7.30–34: Exod 3.1–10. 7.35: Exod 2.14.

spoken to Moses from the bush. And God had even sent the angel to help Moses rescue the people and be their leader.

36 In Egypt and at the Red Sea* and in the desert, Moses rescued the people by performing miracles and wonders for forty years. 37 Moses is the one who told the people of Israel, "God will choose one of your people to be a prophet, just as he chose me." 38 Moses brought our people together in the desert, and the angel spoke to him on Mount Sinai. There he was given these life-giving words to pass on to us. 39 But our ancestors refused to obey Moses. They rejected him and wanted to go back to Egypt.

40 The people said to Aaron, "Make some gods to lead us! Moses led us out of Egypt, but we don't know what's happened to him now." 41 Then they made an idol in the shape of a calf. They offered sacrifices to the idol and were pleased with what they had done.

42 God turned his back on his people and left them. Then they worshipped the stars in the sky, just as it says in the Book of the Prophets, "People of Israel, you didn't offer sacrifices and offerings to me during those forty years in the desert. 43 Instead, you carried the tent where the star Molech is worshipped, and you took along the star of your god Rephan. You made those idols and worshipped them. So now I will have you carried off beyond Babylonia."

Stephen continued:

44 The tent where our ancestors worshipped God was with them in the desert. This was the same tent that God had commanded Moses to make. And it was made like the model that Moses had seen. 45 Later it was given to our ancestors, and they took it with them when they went with Joshua. They carried the tent along as they took over the land from those people that God had chased out for them. Our ancestors

used this tent until the time of King David. 46 He pleased God and asked him if he could build a house of worship for the people♦ of Israel. 47 And it was finally King Solomon who built a house for God.♦

48 But the Most High God doesn't live in houses made by humans. It is just as the prophet said, when he spoke for the Lord,

49 "Heaven is my throne,
    and the earth
    is my footstool.
What kind of house
    will you build for me?
In what place will I rest?
50 I have made everything."

51 You stubborn and hardheaded people! You are always fighting against the Holy Spirit, just as your ancestors did. 52 Is there one prophet that your ancestors didn't ill-treat? They killed the prophets who told about the coming of the One Who Obeys God.* And now you have turned against him and killed him. 53 Angels gave you God's Law, but you still don't obey it.

Stephen is stoned to death

54 When the council members heard Stephen's speech, they were angry and furious. 55 But Stephen was filled with the Holy Spirit. He looked towards heaven, where he saw our glorious God and Jesus standing at his right side.* 56 Then Stephen said, "I see heaven open and the Son of Man standing at the right side of God!"

57 The council members shouted and covered their ears. At once they all attacked Stephen 58 and dragged him out of the city. Then they started throwing stones at him. The men who had brought charges against him put their coats at the feet of a young man named Saul.*

59 As Stephen was being stoned to death, he called out, "Lord Jesus, please welcome me!" 60 He knelt down and shouted, "Lord, don't blame them for what they have done." Then he died.

*7.36 Red Sea: This name comes from the Bible of the early Christians, a translation made into Greek about 200 BC. It refers to the body of water that the Israelites crossed and was one of the marshes or fresh water lakes near the eastern part of the Nile Delta, where they lived and where the towns of Exodus 13.17—14.9 were located.

See also: 7.36: a Exod 7.3; b Exod 14.21; c Num 14.33. 7.37: Deut 18.15,18. 7.38: Exod 19.1—20.17; Deut 5.1–33. 7.40: Exod 32.1. 7.41: Exod 32.2–6. 7.42,43: Amos 5.25–27 (LXX). 7.44: Exod 25.9,40. 7.45: Josh 3.14–17.

*7.52 One Who Obeys God: That is, Jesus.
*7.55 standing at his right side: The "right side" is the place of honour and power. "Standing" may mean that Jesus is welcoming Stephen (see verse 59).
*7.58 Saul: Better known as Paul, who became a famous follower of Jesus.

See also: 7.46: 2 Sam 7.1–16; 1 Chron 17.1–14. 7.47: 1 King 6.1–38; 2 Chron 3.1–17. 7.49,50: Isa 66.1,2. 7.51: Isa 63.10.

CHAPTER 8

1-2 Saul approved the stoning of Stephen. Some faithful followers of the Lord buried Stephen and mourned very much for him.

Saul makes trouble for the church

At that time the church in Jerusalem suffered terribly. All the Lord's followers, except the apostles, were scattered everywhere in Judea and Samaria. 3 Saul started making a lot of trouble for the church. He went from house to house, arresting men and women and putting them in jail.

The good news in Judea and Samaria

The good news is preached in Samaria

4 The Lord's followers who had been scattered went from place to place, telling the good news. 5 Philip went to the city of Samaria and told the people about Christ. 6 They crowded around Philip because they were eager to hear what he was saying and to see him perform miracles. 7 Many people with evil spirits were healed, and the spirits went out of them with a shout. A lot of crippled and lame people were also healed. 8 Everyone in that city was very glad because of what was happening.

9 For some time a man named Simon had lived in the city of Samaria and had amazed the people. He practised witchcraft and claimed to be somebody great. 10 Everyone, rich and poor, crowded around him. They said, "This man is the power of God called 'The Great Power'."

11 For a long time, Simon had used witchcraft to amaze the people, and they kept crowding around him. 12 But when they believed what Philip was saying about God's kingdom and about the name of Jesus Christ, they were all baptized. 13 Even Simon believed and was baptized. He stayed close to Philip, because he marvelled at all the miracles and wonders.

14 The apostles in Jerusalem heard that some people in Samaria had accepted God's message, and they sent Peter and John. 15 When the two apostles arrived, they prayed that the people would be given the Holy Spirit. 16 Before this, the Holy Spirit had not been given to anyone in Samaria, though some of them had been baptized in

the name of the Lord Jesus. 17 Peter and John then placed their hands on everyone who had faith in the Lord, and they were given the Holy Spirit.

18 Simon noticed that the Spirit was given only when the apostles placed their hands on the people. So he brought money 19 and said to Peter and John, "Let me have this power too! Then anyone I place my hands on will also be given the Holy Spirit."

20 Peter said to him, "You and your money will both end up in hell if you think you can buy God's gift! 21 You don't have any part in this, and God sees that your heart isn't right. 22 Get rid of these evil thoughts and ask God to forgive you. 23 I can see that you are jealous and bound by your evil ways."

24 Simon said, "Please pray to the Lord, so that what you said won't happen to me."

25 After Peter and John had preached about the Lord, they returned to Jerusalem. On their way they told the good news in many villages of Samaria.

Philip and an Ethiopian official

26 The Lord's angel said to Philip, "Go south along the desert road that leads from Jerusalem to Gaza." 27 So Philip left.

An important Ethiopian official happened to be going along that road in his chariot. He was the chief treasurer for Candace, the Queen of Ethiopia. The official had gone to Jerusalem to worship 28 and was now on his way home. He was sitting in his chariot, reading the book of the prophet Isaiah.

29 The Spirit told Philip to catch up with the chariot. 30 Philip ran up close and heard the man reading aloud from the book of Isaiah. Philip asked him, "Do you understand what you are reading?"

31 The official answered, "How can I understand unless someone helps me?" He then invited Philip to come up and sit beside him.

32 The man was reading the passage that said,

"He was led like a sheep
on its way to be killed.
He was silent as a lamb
whose wool
is being cut off,
and he did not say
a word.

³³ He was treated like a nobody
   and did not receive
   a fair trial.
How can he have children,
   if his life
   is snatched away?"

³⁴ The official said to Philip, "Tell me, was the prophet talking about himself or about someone else?" ³⁵ So Philip began at this place in the Scriptures and explained the good news about Jesus.

³⁶⁻³⁷ As they were going along the road, they came to a place where there was some water. The official said, "Look! Here is some water. Why can't I be baptized?"• ³⁸ He ordered the chariot to stop. Then they both went down into the water, and Philip baptized him.

³⁹ After they had come out of the water, the Lord's Spirit took Philip away. The official never saw him again, but he was very happy as he went on his way.

⁴⁰ Philip later appeared in Azotus. He went from town to town, all the way to Caesarea, telling people about Jesus.

CHAPTER 9

Saul becomes a follower of the Lord

This is also told in Acts 22.6–16; 26.12–18

¹ Saul kept on threatening to kill the Lord's followers. He even went to the high priest ² and asked for letters to the Jewish leaders in Damascus. He did this because he wanted to arrest and take to Jerusalem any man or woman who had accepted the Lord's Way.• ³ When Saul had almost reached Damascus, a bright light from heaven suddenly flashed around him. ⁴ He fell to the ground and heard a voice that said, "Saul! Saul! Why are you so cruel to me?"

⁵ "Who are you?" Saul asked.

"I am Jesus," the Lord answered. "I am the one you are so cruel to. ⁶ Now get up and go into the city, where you will be told what to do."

⁷ The men who were with Saul stood there speechless. They had heard the voice, but they had not seen anyone. ⁸ Saul got up from the ground, and when he opened his eyes, he could not see a thing. Someone then led him by the hand to Damascus, ⁹ and for three days he was blind and did not eat or drink.

¹⁰ A follower named Ananias lived in Damascus, and the Lord spoke to him in a vision. Ananias answered, "Lord, here I am."

¹¹ The Lord said to him, "Get up and go to the house of Judas in Straight Street. When you get there, you will find a man named Saul from the city of Tarsus. Saul is praying, ¹² and he has seen a vision. He saw a man named Ananias coming to him and putting his hands on him, so that he could see again."

¹³ Ananias replied, "Lord, a lot of people have told me about the terrible things this man has done to your followers in Jerusalem. ¹⁴ Now the chief priests have given him the power to come here and arrest anyone who worships in your name."

¹⁵ The Lord said to Ananias, "Go! I have chosen him to tell foreigners, kings, and the people of Israel about me. ¹⁶ I will show him how much he must suffer for worshipping in my name."

¹⁷ Ananias left and went into the house where Saul was staying. Ananias placed his hands on him and said, "Saul, the Lord Jesus has sent me. He is the same one who appeared to you along the road. He wants you to be able to see and to be filled with the Holy Spirit."

¹⁸ Suddenly something like fish scales fell from Saul's eyes, and he could see. He got up and was baptized. ¹⁹ Then he ate and felt much better.

Saul preaches in Damascus

For several days Saul stayed with the Lord's followers in Damascus. ²⁰ Soon he went to the Jewish meeting places and started telling people that Jesus is the Son of God. ²¹ Everyone who heard Saul was amazed and said, "Isn't this the man who caused so much trouble for those people in Jerusalem who worship in the name of Jesus? Didn't he come here to arrest them and take them to the chief priests?"

²² Saul preached with such power that he completely confused the Jewish people in Damascus, as he tried to show them that Jesus is the Messiah.

²³ Later some of them made plans to kill Saul, ²⁴ but he found out about it. He learnt that they were guarding the gates of the city day and night in order to kill him. ²⁵ Then one night his followers let him down over the city wall in a large basket.

•**9.2 accepted the Lord's Way:** In the book of Acts, this means to become a follower of the Lord Jesus.

See also: 9.23–25: 2 Cor 11.32,33.

Saul in Jerusalem

²⁶ When Saul arrived in Jerusalem, he tried to join the followers. But they were all afraid of him, because they did not believe he was a true follower. ²⁷ Then Barnabas helped him by taking him to the apostles. He explained how Saul had seen the Lord and how the Lord had spoken to him. Barnabas also said that when Saul was in Damascus, he had spoken bravely in the name of Jesus.

²⁸ Saul moved about freely with the followers in Jerusalem and told everyone about the Lord. ²⁹ He was always arguing with the Jews who spoke Greek, and so they tried to kill him. ³⁰ But the followers found out about this and took Saul to Caesarea. From there they sent him to the city of Tarsus.

³¹ The church in Judea, Galilee, and Samaria now had a time of peace and kept on worshipping the Lord. The church became stronger, as the Holy Spirit encouraged it and helped it grow.

Peter heals Aeneas

³² While Peter was travelling from place to place, he visited the Lord's followers who lived in the town of Lydda. ³³ There he met a man named Aeneas, who for eight years had been sick in bed and could not move. ³⁴ Peter said to Aeneas, "Jesus Christ has healed you! Get up and make up your bed."* Straight away he stood up.

³⁵ Many people in the towns of Lydda and Sharon saw Aeneas and became followers of the Lord.

Peter brings Dorcas back to life

³⁶ In Joppa there was a follower named Tabitha. Her Greek name was Dorcas, which means "deer". She was always doing good things for people and had given much to the poor. ³⁷ But she became ill and died, and her body was washed and placed in an upstairs room. ³⁸ Joppa wasn't far from Lydda, and the followers heard that Peter was there. They sent two men to say to him, "Please come with us as quickly as you can!" ³⁹ Straight away, Peter went with them.

The men took Peter upstairs into the room. Many widows were there crying. They showed him the coats and clothes that Dorcas had made while she was still alive.

⁴⁰ After Peter had sent everyone out of the room, he knelt down and prayed. Then he turned to the body of Dorcas and said, "Tabitha, get up!" The woman opened her eyes, and when she saw Peter, she sat up. ⁴¹ He took her by the hand and helped her to her feet.

Peter called in the widows and the other followers and showed them that Dorcas had been raised from death. ⁴² Everyone in Joppa heard what had happened, and many of them put their faith in the Lord. ⁴³ Peter stayed on for a while in the house of a man named Simon, who made leather.

CHAPTER 10

Peter and Cornelius

¹ In Caesarea there was a man named Cornelius, who was the captain of a group of soldiers called "The Italian Unit". ² Cornelius was a very religious man. He worshipped God, and so did everyone else who lived in his house. He had given a lot of money to the poor and was always praying to God.

³ One afternoon at about three o'clock,* Cornelius had a vision. He saw an angel from God coming to him and calling him by name. ⁴ Cornelius was surprised and stared at the angel. Then he asked, "What is this all about?"

The angel answered, "God has heard your prayers and knows about your gifts to the poor. ⁵ Now send some men to Joppa for a man named Simon Peter. ⁶ He is staying with Simon the leather maker, who lives in a house near the sea." ⁷ After saying this, the angel left.

Cornelius called in two of his servants and one of his soldiers who worshipped God. ⁸ He explained everything to them and sent them off to Joppa.

⁹ The next day about midday these men were coming near Joppa. Peter went up on the roof* of the house to pray ¹⁰ and became very hungry. While the food was being prepared, he fell sound asleep and had a vision. ¹¹ He saw heaven open, and something came down like a huge sheet held up by its four corners. ¹² In it were all kinds of animals, snakes, and birds. ¹³ A voice said to him, "Peter, get up! Kill these and eat them."

¹⁴ But Peter said, "Lord, I can't do that! I've never eaten anything that is unclean and not fit to eat."*

---

*10.3 at about three o'clock: Probably while he was praying. See 3.1 and the note there.
*10.9 roof: In Palestine the houses usually had a flat roof. Stairs on the outside led up to the roof, which was made of beams and boards covered with packed earth.
*10.14 unclean and not fit to eat: The Law of Moses taught that some foods were not fit to eat.

¹⁵ The voice spoke to him again, "When God says that something can be used for food, don't say it isn't fit to eat."

¹⁶ This happened three times before the sheet was suddenly taken back to heaven.

¹⁷ Peter was still wondering what all this meant, when the men sent by Cornelius came and stood at the gate. They had found their way to Simon's house ¹⁸ and were asking if Simon Peter was staying there.

¹⁹ While Peter was still thinking about the vision, the Holy Spirit said to him, "Three• men are here looking for you. ²⁰ Hurry down and go with them. Don't worry, I sent them."

²¹ Peter went down and said to the men, "I am the one you are looking for. Why have you come?"

²² They answered, "Captain Cornelius sent us. He is a good man who worships God and is liked by the Jewish people. One of God's holy angels told Cornelius to send for you, so he could hear what you have to say." ²³ Peter invited them to spend the night.

The next morning, Peter and some of the Lord's followers in Joppa left with the men who had come from Cornelius. ²⁴ The next day they arrived in Caesarea where Cornelius was waiting for them. He had also invited his relatives and close friends.

²⁵ When Peter arrived, Cornelius greeted him. Then he knelt at Peter's feet and started worshipping him. ²⁶ But Peter took hold of him and said, "Stand up! I am nothing more than a human."

²⁷ As Peter entered the house, he was still talking with Cornelius. Many people were there, ²⁸ and Peter said to them, "You know that we Jews are not allowed to have anything to do with other people. But God has shown me that he doesn't think anyone is unclean or unfit. ²⁹ I agreed to come here, but I want to know why you sent for me."

³⁰ Cornelius answered:

Four days ago at about three o'clock in the afternoon I was praying at home. Suddenly a man in bright clothes stood in front of me. ³¹ He said, "Cornelius, God has heard your prayers, and he knows about your gifts to the poor. ³² Now send to Joppa for Simon Peter. He is staying in the home of Simon the leather maker, who lives near the sea."

³³ I sent for you straight away, and you have been good enough to come. All of us are here in the presence of the Lord God, so that we can hear what he has to say.

³⁴ Peter then said:

Now I am certain that God treats all people alike. ³⁵ God is pleased with everyone who worships him and does right, no matter what nation they come from. ³⁶ This is the same message that God gave to the people of Israel, when he sent Jesus Christ, the Lord of all, to offer peace to them.

³⁷ You know what happened• everywhere in Judea. It all began in Galilee after John had told everyone to be baptized. ³⁸ God gave the Holy Spirit and power to Jesus from Nazareth. He was with Jesus, as he went around doing good and healing everyone who was under the power of the devil. ³⁹ We all saw what Jesus did both in Israel and in the city of Jerusalem.

Jesus was put to death on a cross. ⁴⁰ But three days later, God raised him to life and let him be seen. ⁴¹ Not everyone saw him. He was seen only by us, who ate and drank with him after he was raised from death. We were the ones God chose to tell others about him.

⁴² God told us to announce clearly to the people that Jesus is the one he has chosen to judge the living and the dead. ⁴³ Every one of the prophets has said that all who have faith in Jesus will have their sins forgiven in his name.

⁴⁴ While Peter was still speaking, the Holy Spirit took control of everyone who was listening. ⁴⁵ Some Jewish followers of the Lord had come with Peter, and they were surprised that the Holy Spirit had been given to Gentiles. ⁴⁶ Now they were hearing Gentiles speaking unknown languages and praising God.

Peter said, ⁴⁷ "These Gentiles have been given the Holy Spirit, just as we have! I am certain that no one would dare stop us from baptizing them." ⁴⁸ Peter ordered them to be baptized in the name of Jesus Christ, and they asked him to stay on for a few days.

CHAPTER 11

Peter reports to the church in Jerusalem

¹ The apostles and the followers in Judea heard that Gentiles had accepted God's message. ² So when Peter came to Jerusalem, some of the Jewish followers started arguing with him. They wanted Gentile followers to be circumcised, and ³ they said, "You stayed in the homes of Gentiles, and you even ate with them!"

See also: 10.34: Deut 10.17.

⁴ Then Peter told them exactly what had happened:

⁵ I was in the town of Joppa and was praying when I fell sound asleep and had a vision. I saw heaven open, and something like a huge sheet held by its four corners came down to me. ⁶ When I looked in it, I saw animals, wild beasts, snakes, and birds. ⁷ I heard a voice saying to me, "Peter, get up! Kill these and eat them."

⁸ But I said, "Lord, I can't do that! I've never taken a bite of anything that is unclean and not fit to eat."*

⁹ The voice from heaven spoke to me again, "When God says that something can be used for food, don't say it isn't fit to eat." ¹⁰ This happened three times before it was all taken back into heaven.

¹¹ Suddenly three men from Caesarea stood in front of the house where I was staying. ¹² The Holy Spirit told me to go with them and not to worry. Then six of the Lord's followers went with me to the home of a man ¹³ who told us that an angel had appeared to him. The angel had ordered him to send to Joppa for someone named Simon Peter. ¹⁴ Then Peter would tell him how he and everyone in his house could be saved.

¹⁵ After I started speaking, the Holy Spirit was given to them, just as the Spirit had been given to us at the beginning. ¹⁶ I remembered that the Lord had said, "John baptized with water, but you will be baptized with the Holy Spirit." ¹⁷ God gave those Gentiles the same gift that he gave us when we put our faith in the Lord Jesus Christ. So how could I have gone against God?

¹⁸ When they heard Peter say this, they stopped arguing and started praising God. They said, "God has now let Gentiles turn to him, and he has given life to them!"

The church in Antioch

¹⁹ Some of the Lord's followers had been scattered because of the terrible trouble that started when Stephen was killed. They went as far as Phoenicia, Cyprus, and Antioch, but they told the message only to the Jews.

²⁰ Some of the followers from Cyprus and Cyrene went to Antioch and started telling Gentiles* the good news about the Lord Jesus. ²¹ The Lord's power was with them, and many people turned to the Lord and put their faith in him. ²² News of what was happening reached the church in Jerusalem. Then they sent Barnabas to Antioch.

²³ When Barnabas got there and saw what God had been kind enough to do for them, he was very glad. So he begged them to remain faithful to the Lord with all their hearts. ²⁴ Barnabas was a good man of great faith, and he was filled with the Holy Spirit. Many more people turned to the Lord.

²⁵ Barnabas went to Tarsus to look for Saul. ²⁶ He found Saul and brought him to Antioch, where they met with the church for a whole year and taught many of its people. There in Antioch the Lord's followers were first called Christians.

²⁷ During this time some prophets from Jerusalem came to Antioch. ²⁸ One of them was Agabus. Then with the help of the Spirit, he told that there would be a terrible famine everywhere in the world. And it happened when Claudius was Emperor.* ²⁹ The followers in Antioch decided to send whatever help they could to the followers in Judea. ³⁰ So they asked Barnabas and Saul to take their gifts to the church leaders in Jerusalem.

CHAPTER 12

Herod causes trouble for the church

¹ At that time King Herod* caused terrible suffering for some members of the church. ² He ordered soldiers to cut off the head of James, the brother of John. ³ When Herod saw that this pleased the Jewish people, he had Peter arrested during the Festival of Thin Bread. ⁴ He put Peter in jail and ordered four squads of soldiers to guard him. Herod planned to put him on trial in public after the festival.

⁵ While Peter was being kept in jail, the church never stopped praying to God for him.

Peter is rescued

⁶ The night before Peter was to be put on trial, he was asleep and bound by two chains.

---

*11.8 unclean and not fit to eat: See the note at 10.14.

See also: 11.16: Acts 1.5. 11.19: Acts 8.1-4.

*11.28 when Claudius was Emperor: AD 41-54.
*12.1 Herod: Herod Agrippa I, the grandson of Herod the Great.

See also: 11.28: Acts 21.10. 12.4: Exod 12.1-27.

A soldier was guarding him on each side, and two other soldiers were guarding the entrance to the jail. 7 Suddenly an angel from the Lord appeared, and light flashed around in the cell. The angel poked Peter in the side and woke him up. Then he said, "Quick! Get up!"

8 The chains fell off his hands, 8 and the angel said, "Get dressed and put on your sandals." Peter did what he was told. Then the angel said, "Now put on your coat and follow me." 9 Peter left with the angel, but he thought everything was only a dream. 10 They went past the two groups of soldiers, and when they came to the iron gate to the city, it opened by itself. They went out and were going along the street, when all at once the angel disappeared.

11 Peter now realized what had happened, and he said, "I am certain that the Lord sent his angel to rescue me from Herod and from everything the Jewish leaders planned to do to me." 12 Then Peter went to the house of Mary the mother of John whose other name was Mark. Many of the Lord's followers had come together there and were praying.

13 Peter knocked on the gate, and a servant named Rhoda came to answer. 14 When she heard Peter's voice, she was too excited to open the gate. She ran back into the house and said that Peter was standing there.

15 "You are mad!" everyone told her. But she kept saying that it was Peter. Then they said, "It must be his angel."* 16 But Peter kept on knocking, until finally they opened the gate. They saw him and were completely amazed.

17 Peter motioned for them to keep quiet. Then he told how the Lord had led him out of jail. He also said, "Tell James* and the others what has happened." After that, he left and went somewhere else.

18 The next morning the soldiers who had been on guard were terribly worried and wondered what had happened to Peter. 19 Herod ordered his own soldiers to search for him, but they could not find him. Then he questioned the guards and had them put to death. After this, Herod left Judea to stay in Caesarea for a while.

Herod dies

20 Herod and the people of Tyre and Sidon were very angry with each other. But their country got its food supply from the region that he ruled. So a group of them went to see Blastus, who was one of Herod's high officials. They convinced Blastus that they wanted to make peace between their cities and Herod, 21 and a day was set for them to meet with him.

Herod came dressed in his royal robes. He sat down on his throne and made a speech. 22 The people shouted, "You speak more like a god than a man!" 23 At once an angel from the Lord struck him down because he took the honour that belonged to God. Later, Herod was eaten by worms and died.

24 God's message kept spreading. 25 And after Barnabas and Saul had done the work they were sent to do, they went back to Jerusalem* with John, whose other name was Mark.

Paul's first journey to tell the good news

CHAPTER 13

Barnabas and Saul are chosen and sent

1 The church at Antioch had several prophets and teachers. They were Barnabas, Simeon, also called Niger, Lucius from Cyrene, Manaen, who was Herod's* close friend, and Saul. 2 While they were worshipping the Lord and going without eating,* the Holy Spirit told them, "Appoint Barnabas and Saul to do the work for which I have chosen them." 3 Everyone prayed and went without eating for a while longer. Next, they placed their hands on Barnabas and Saul to show that they had been appointed to do this work. Then everyone sent them on their way.

Barnabas and Saul in Cyprus

4 After Barnabas and Saul had been sent by the Holy Spirit, they went to Seleucia. From there they sailed to the island of Cyprus. 5 They arrived at Salamis and began to preach God's message in the Jewish meeting places. They also had John* as a helper.

6 Barnabas and Saul went all the way to the city of Paphos on the other end of the island, where they met a Jewish man named

---

*13.1 Herod's: See the note at 4.27.
*13.2 going without eating: The Jews often went without eating as a way of showing how much they loved God. This is also called "fasting".
*13.5 John: Whose other name was Mark (see 12.12,25).

*12.17 James: The brother of the Lord.

Bar-Jesus. He practised witchcraft and was a false prophet. [7] He also worked for Sergius Paulus, who was very clever and was the governor of the island. Sergius Paulus wanted to hear God's message, and he sent for Barnabas and Saul. [8] But Bar-Jesus, whose other name was Elymas, was against them. He even tried to keep the governor from having faith in the Lord.

[9] Then Saul, better known as Paul, was filled with the Holy Spirit. He looked straight at Elymas [10] and said, "You son of the devil! You are a liar, a criminal, and an enemy of everything that is right. When will you stop speaking against the true ways of the Lord? [11] The Lord is going to punish you by making you completely blind for a while."

Suddenly the man's eyes were covered by a dark mist, and he went around trying to get someone to lead him by the hand. [12] When the governor saw what had happened, he was amazed at this teaching about the Lord. So he put his faith in the Lord.

Paul and Barnabas in Antioch of Pisidia

[13] Paul and the others left Paphos and sailed to Perga in Pamphylia. But John* left them and went back to Jerusalem. [14] The rest of them went on from Perga to Antioch in Pisidia. Then on the Sabbath they went to the Jewish meeting place and sat down.

[15] After the reading of the Law and the Prophets,* the leaders sent someone over to tell Paul and Barnabas, "Friends, if you have anything to say that will help the people, please say it."

[16] Paul got up. He motioned with his hand and said:

People of Israel, and everyone else who worships God, listen! [17] The God of Israel chose our ancestors, and he let our people prosper while they were living in Egypt. Then with his mighty power he led them out, [18] and for about forty years he took care of them in the desert. [19] He destroyed seven nations in the land of Canaan and gave their land to our people. [20] All this happened in about 450 years.

Then God gave our people judges until the time of the prophet Samuel, [21] but the people demanded a king. For forty years God gave them King Saul, the son of Kish from the tribe of Benjamin. [22] Later, God removed Saul and let David rule in his place. God said about him, "David the son of Jesse is the kind of person who pleases me most! He does everything I want him to do."

[23] God promised that someone from David's family would come to save the people of Israel, and that one is Jesus. [24] But before Jesus came, John was telling everyone in Israel to turn back to God and be baptized. [25] Then, when John's work was almost done, he said, "Who do you people think I am? Do you think I am the Promised One? He will come later, and I am not good enough to untie his sandals."

[26] Now listen, you descendants of Abraham! Pay attention, all you Gentiles who are here to worship God! Listen to this message about how to be saved, because it is for everyone. [27] The people of Jerusalem and their leaders didn't realize who Jesus was. And they didn't understand the words of the prophets that they read each Sabbath. So they condemned Jesus just as the prophets had said.

[28-29] They did exactly what the Scriptures said they would. Even though they couldn't find any reason to put Jesus to death, they still asked Pilate to have him killed.

After Jesus had been put to death, he was taken down from the cross* and placed in a tomb. [30] But God raised him from death! [31] Then for many days Jesus appeared to his followers who had gone with him from Galilee to Jerusalem. Now they are telling our people about him.

[32] God made a promise to our ancestors. And we are here to tell you the good news [33] that he has kept this promise to us. It is just as the second Psalm says about Jesus,

"You are my son because today
    I have become your Father."

[34] God raised Jesus from death and will never let his body decay. It is just as God said,

---

*13.13 John: See the note at 13.5.
*13.15 the Law and the Prophets: The Jewish Scriptures, that is, the Old Testament.

See also: 13.17: a Exod 1.7; b Exod 12.51.
13.18: Num 14.34; Deut 1.31. 13.19: a Deut 7.1;
b Josh 14.1. 13.20: a Judg 2.16; b 1 Sam 3.20.

13.21: a 1 Sam 8.5; b 1 Sam 10.21.
13.22: a 1 Sam 13.14; b 1 Sam 16.12; Psa 89.20.
13.24: Mark 1.4; Luke 3.3. 13.25: a John 1.20; b Matt 3.11;
Mark 1.7; Luke 3.16; John 1.27. 13.28: Matt 27.22,23;
Mark 15.13,14; Luke 23.21-23; John 19.15.
13.29: Matt 27.57-61; Mark 15.42-47; Luke 23.50-56;
John 19.38-42. 13.31: Acts 1.3. 13.33: Psa 2.7.
13.34: Isa 55.3 (LXX).

"I will make to you
  the same holy promise
  that I made to David."

35 And in another psalm it says, "God will never let the body of his Holy One decay." 36 When David was alive, he obeyed God. Then after he died, he was buried in the family grave, and his body decayed. 37 But God raised Jesus from death, and his body did not decay.

38 My friends, the message is that Jesus can forgive your sins! The Law of Moses could not set you free from all your sins. 39 But everyone who has faith in Jesus is set free. 40 Make sure that what the prophets have said doesn't happen to you. They said,

41 "Look, you people
  who make fun of God!
  Be amazed
    and disappear.
  I will do something today
    that you won't believe,
  even if someone
    tells you about it!"

42 As Paul and Barnabas were leaving the meeting, the people begged them to say more about these same things on the next Sabbath. 43 After the service, many Jews and a lot of Gentiles who worshipped God went with them. Paul and Barnabas begged them all to remain faithful to God, who had been so kind to them.

44 The next Sabbath almost everyone in town came to hear the message about the Lord.* 45 When the Jewish people saw the crowds, they were very jealous. They insulted Paul and spoke against everything he said.

46 But Paul and Barnabas bravely said:

We had to tell God's message to you before we told it to anyone else. But you rejected the message! This proves that you don't deserve eternal life. Now we are going to the Gentiles. 47 The Lord has given us this command,

"I have placed you here
  as a light
  for the Gentiles.
You are to take
  the saving power of God
to people everywhere on earth."

48 This message made the Gentiles glad, and they praised what they had heard about the Lord. Everyone who had been chosen for eternal life then put their faith in the Lord.

49 The message about the Lord spread all over that region. 50 But the Jewish leaders went to some of the important men in the town and to some respected women who were religious. They turned them against Paul and Barnabas and started making trouble for them. They even chased them out of that part of the country. 51 Paul and Barnabas shook the dust from that place off their feet* and went on to the city of Iconium. 52 But the Lord's followers in Antioch were very happy and were filled with the Holy Spirit.

CHAPTER 14

Paul and Barnabas in Iconium

1 Paul and Barnabas spoke in the Jewish meeting place in Iconium, just as they had done at Antioch, and many Jews and Gentiles* put their faith in the Lord. 2 But the Jews who did not have faith in him made the other Gentiles angry and turned them against the Lord's followers.

3 Paul and Barnabas stayed there for a while, having faith in the Lord and bravely speaking his message. The Lord gave them the power to perform miracles and wonders, and he showed that their message about his great kindness was true.

4 The people of Iconium did not know what to think. Some of them believed the Jewish group, and others believed the apostles. 5 Finally, some Gentiles and Jews, together with their leaders, decided to make trouble for Paul and Barnabas and to stone them to death. 6-7 But when the two apostles found out what was happening, they escaped to the region of Lycaonia. They preached the good news there in the towns of Lystra and Derbe and in the nearby countryside.

---

*13.51 shook the dust from that place off their feet: This was a way of showing rejection.
*14.1 Gentiles: The Greek text has "Greeks," which probably means people who were not Jews. But it may mean Gentiles who worshipped with the Jews.

See also: 13.51: Matt 10.14; Mark 6.11; Luke 9.5; 10.11.

See also: 13.35: Psa 16.10. 13.41: Hab 1.5 (LXX).
13.47: Isa 42.6; 49.6.

Paul and Barnabas in Lystra

8 In Lystra there was a man who had been born with crippled feet and had never been able to walk. 9 The man was listening to Paul speak, when Paul saw that he had faith in Jesus and could be healed. So he looked straight at the man 10 and shouted, "Stand up!" The man jumped up and started walking around.

11 When the crowd saw what Paul had done, they yelled out in the language of Lycaonia, "The gods have turned into humans and have come down to us!" 12 The people then gave Barnabas the name Zeus, and they gave Paul the name Hermes,* because he did the talking.

13 The temple of Zeus was near the entrance to the city. Its priest and the crowds wanted to offer a sacrifice to Barnabas and Paul. So the priest brought some bulls and flowers to the city gates. 14 When the two apostles found out about this, they tore their clothes in horror and ran to the crowd, shouting:

15 Why are you doing this? We are humans just like you. Please give up all this foolishness. Turn to the living God, who made the sky, the earth, the sea, and everything in them. 16 In times past, God let each nation go its own way. 17 But he showed that he was there by the good things he did. God sends rain from heaven and makes your crops grow. He gives food to you and makes your hearts glad.

18 Even after Paul and Barnabas had said all this, they could hardly keep the people from offering a sacrifice to them.

19 Some Jewish leaders from Antioch and Iconium came and turned the crowds against Paul. They hit him with stones and dragged him out of the city, thinking he was dead. 20 But when the Lord's followers gathered around Paul, he stood up and went back into the city. The next day he and Barnabas went to Derbe.

Paul and Barnabas return to Antioch in Syria

21 Paul and Barnabas preached the good news in Derbe and won some people to the Lord. Then they went back to Lystra, Iconium, and Antioch in Pisidia. 22 They encouraged the followers and begged them to remain faithful. They told them, "We have to suffer a lot before we can get into God's kingdom." 23 Paul and Barnabas chose some leaders for each of the churches. Then they went without eating* and prayed that the Lord would take good care of these leaders.

24 Paul and Barnabas went on through Pisidia to Pamphylia, 25 where they preached in the town of Perga. Then they went down to Attalia 26 and sailed to Antioch in Syria. It was there that they had been placed in God's care for the work they had now completed.*

27 After arriving in Antioch, they called the church together. They told the people what God had helped them do and how he had made it possible for the Gentiles to believe. 28 Then they stayed there with the followers for a long time.

An important decision in Jerusalem

CHAPTER 15

1 Some people came from Judea and started teaching the Lord's followers that they could not be saved, unless they were circumcised as Moses had taught. 2 This caused trouble, and Paul and Barnabas argued with them about this teaching. So it was decided to send Paul and Barnabas and a few others to Jerusalem to discuss this problem with the apostles and the church leaders.

The church leaders meet in Jerusalem

3 The men who were sent by the church went through Phoenicia and Samaria, telling how the Gentiles had turned to God. This news made the Lord's followers very happy. 4 When the men arrived in Jerusalem, they were welcomed by the church, including the apostles and the leaders. They told them everything God had helped them do. 5 But some Pharisees had become followers of the Lord. They stood up and said, "Gentiles who have faith in the Lord must be circumcised and told to obey the Law of Moses."

6 The apostles and church leaders met to discuss this problem about Gentiles.

---

*14.12 Hermes: The Greeks thought of Hermes as the messenger of the other gods, especially of Zeus, their chief god.

See also: 14.15: Exod 20.11; Psa 146.6.

*14.23 went without eating: See the note at 13.2.
*14.26 the work they had now completed: See 13.1-3.

See also: 15.1: Lev 12.3.

[7] They had talked it over for a long time, when Peter got up and said:

My friends, you know that God decided long ago to let me be the one from your group to preach the good news to the Gentiles. God did this so that they would hear and obey him. [8] He knows what is in everyone's heart. And he showed that he had chosen the Gentiles, when he gave them the Holy Spirit, just as he had given his Spirit to us. [9] God treated them in the same way that he treated us. They put their faith in him, and he made their hearts pure.

[10] Now why are you trying to make God angry by placing a heavy burden on these followers? This burden was too heavy for us or our ancestors. [11] But our Lord Jesus was kind to us, and we are saved by faith in him, just as the Gentiles are.

[12] Everyone kept quiet and listened as Barnabas and Paul told how God had given them the power to perform a lot of miracles and wonders for the Gentiles.

[13] After they had finished speaking, James* said:

My friends, listen to me! [14] Simon Peter* has told how God first came to the Gentiles and made some of them his own people. [15] This agrees with what the prophets wrote,

[16] "I, the Lord, will return
 and rebuild
 David's fallen house.
 I will build it from its ruins
 and set it up again.
[17] Then other nations
 will turn to me
 and be my chosen ones.
 I, the Lord, say this.
[18] I promised it long ago."

[19] And so, my friends, I don't think we should place burdens on the Gentiles who are turning to God. [20] We should simply write and tell them not to eat anything that has been offered to idols. They should be told not to eat the meat of any animal that has been strangled or that still has blood in it. They must also not commit any terrible sexual sins.*

[21] We must remember that the Law of Moses has been preached in city after city for many years, and every Sabbath it is read when we Jews meet.

A letter to Gentiles who had faith in the Lord

[22] The apostles, the leaders, and all the church members decided to send some men to Antioch along with Paul and Barnabas. They chose Silas and Judas Barsabbas,* who were two leaders of the Lord's followers. [23] They wrote a letter that said:

We apostles and leaders send friendly greetings to all you Gentiles who are followers of the Lord in Antioch, Syria, and Cilicia.

[24] We have heard that some people from here have terribly upset you by what they said. But we did not send them! [25] So we met together and decided to choose some men and to send them to you along with our good friends Barnabas and Paul. [26] These men have risked their lives for our Lord Jesus Christ. [27] We are also sending Judas and Silas, who will tell you in person the same things that we are writing.

[28] The Holy Spirit has shown us that we should not place any extra burden on you. [29] But you should not eat anything offered to idols. You should not eat any meat that still has the blood in it or any meat of any animal that has been strangled. You must also not commit any terrible sexual sins. If you follow these instructions, you will do well.

We send our best wishes.

[30] The four men left Jerusalem and went to Antioch. Then they called the church members together and gave them the letter. [31] When the letter was read, everyone was pleased and greatly encouraged. [32] Judas and Silas were prophets, and they spoke a long time, encouraging and helping the Lord's followers.

[33] The men from Jerusalem stayed on in Antioch for a while. And when they left to

---

*15.13 James: See the note at 12.17.
*15.14 Simon Peter: The Greek text has "Simeon", which is another form of the name "Simon". The apostle Peter is meant.
See also: 15.7: Acts 10.1–43. 15.8: Acts 10.44; Acts 2.4.
15.16–18: Amos 9.11,12 (LXX). 15.20: a Exod 34.15–17;
b Lev 18.6–23; c Lev 17.10–16.

*15.20 not commit any terrible sexual sins: This probably refers to the laws about the wrong kind of marriages that are forbidden in Leviticus 18.6–18 or to some serious sexual sin.
*15.22 Judas Barsabbas: He may have been a brother of Joseph Barsabbas (see 1.23), but the name "Barsabbas" was often used by the Jewish people.

return to the ones who had sent them, the followers wished them well. 34-35 But Paul and Barnabas stayed on in Antioch, where they and many others taught and preached about the Lord.•

Paul's second journey to tell the good news

Paul and Barnabas go their separate ways

36 Some time later Paul said to Barnabas, "Let's go back and visit the Lord's followers in the cities where we preached his message. Then we will know how they are doing." 37 Barnabas wanted to take along John, whose other name was Mark. 38 But Paul did not want to, because Mark had left them in Pamphylia and had stopped working with them.

39 Paul and Barnabas argued, then each of them went his own way. Barnabas took Mark and sailed for Cyprus, 40 but Paul took Silas and left after the followers had placed them in God's care. 41 They travelled through Syria and Cilicia, encouraging the churches.

CHAPTER 16

Timothy works with Paul and Silas

1 Paul and Silas went back to Derbe and Lystra, where there was a follower named Timothy. His mother was also a Jewish, and his father was Greek. 2 The Lord's followers in Lystra and Iconium said good things about Timothy, 3 and Paul wanted him to go with them. But Paul first had him circumcised, because all the Jewish people around there knew that Timothy's father was Greek.•

4 As Paul and the others went from city to city, they told the followers what the apostles and leaders in Jerusalem had decided, and they urged them to follow these instructions. 5 The churches became stronger in their faith, and each day more people put their faith in the Lord.

Paul's vision in Troas

6 Paul and his friends went through Phrygia and Galatia, but the Holy Spirit would not let

them preach in Asia. 7 After they arrived in Mysia, they tried to go into Bithynia, but the Spirit of Jesus would not let them. 8 So they went on through• Mysia until they came to Troas.

9 During the night, Paul had a vision of someone from Macedonia who was standing there and begging him, "Come over to Macedonia and help us!" 10 After Paul had seen the vision, we began looking for a way to go to Macedonia. We were sure that God had called us to preach the good news there.

Lydia becomes a follower of the Lord

11 We sailed straight from Troas to Samothrace, and the next day we arrived in Neapolis. 12 From there we went to Philippi, which is a Roman colony in the first district of Macedonia.•

We stayed several days in Philippi. 13 Then on the Sabbath we went outside the city gate to a place by the river, where we thought there would be a Jewish meeting place for prayer. We sat down and talked with the women who came. 14 One of them was Lydia, who was from the city of Thyatira and sold expensive purple cloth. She was a worshipper of the Lord God, and he made her willing to accept what Paul was saying. 15 Then after she and her family were baptized, she kept on begging us, "If you think I really do have faith in the Lord, come and stay in my home." Finally, we accepted her invitation.

Paul and Silas are put in jail

16 One day on our way to the place of prayer, we were met by a slave girl. She had a spirit in her that gave her the power to tell the future. By doing this she made a lot of money for her owners. 17 The girl followed Paul and the rest of us and kept yelling, "These men are servants of the Most High God! They are telling you how to be saved."

18 This went on for several days. Finally, Paul got so upset that he turned and said to the spirit, "In the name of Jesus Christ, I order you to leave this girl alone!" At once the evil spirit left her.

19 When the girl's owners realized that they had lost all chances for making more money, they grabbed Paul and Silas and dragged them into court. 20 They told the officials, "These Jews are upsetting our city! 21 They are telling us to do things we Romans are not allowed to do."

---

*16.3 had him circumcised . . . Timothy's father was Greek: Timothy would not have been acceptable to the Jews unless he had been circumcised, and Greeks did not circumcise their sons.

See also: 15.38: Acts 13.13.

²² The crowd joined in the attack on Paul and Silas. Then the officials tore the clothes off the two men and ordered them to be beaten with a whip. ²³ After they had been badly beaten, they were put in jail, and the jailer was told to guard them carefully. ²⁴ The jailer did as he was told. He put them deep inside the jail and chained their feet to heavy blocks of wood.

²⁵ About midnight Paul and Silas were praying and singing praises to God, while the other prisoners listened. ²⁶ Suddenly a strong earthquake shook the jail to its foundations. The doors opened, and the chains fell from all the prisoners.

²⁷ When the jailer woke up and saw that the doors were open, he thought that the prisoners had escaped. He pulled out his sword and was about to kill himself. ²⁸ But Paul shouted, "Don't harm yourself! No one has escaped."

²⁹ The jailer asked for a torch and went into the jail. He was shaking all over as he knelt down in front of Paul and Silas. ³⁰ After he had led them out of the jail, he asked, "What must I do to be saved?"

³¹ They replied, "Have faith in the Lord Jesus and you will be saved! This is also true for everyone who lives in your home."

³² Then Paul and Silas told him and everyone else in his house about the Lord. ³³ While it was still night, the jailer took them to a place where he could wash their cuts and bruises. Then he and everyone in his home were baptized. ³⁴ They were very glad that they had put their faith in God. After this, the jailer took Paul and Silas to his home and gave them something to eat.

³⁵ The next morning the officials sent some police with orders for the jailer to let Paul and Silas go. ³⁶ The jailer told Paul, "The officials have ordered me to set you free. Now you can leave in peace."

³⁷ But Paul told the police, "We are Roman citizens,* and the Roman officials had us beaten in public without giving us a trial. They threw us into jail. Now do they think they can secretly send us away? No, they cannot! They will have to come here themselves and let us out."

³⁸ When the police told the officials that Paul and Silas were Roman citizens, the officials were afraid. ³⁹ So they came and apologized. They led them out of the jail and

asked them to leave town. ⁴⁰ But Paul and Silas went straight to the home of Lydia, where they saw the Lord's followers, and encouraged them. Then they left.

CHAPTER 17

Trouble in Thessalonica

¹ After Paul and his friends had travelled through Amphipolis and Apollonia, they went on to Thessalonica. A Jewish meeting place was in that city. ² So as usual, Paul went there to worship, and on three Sabbaths he spoke to the people. He used the Scriptures ³ to show them that the Messiah had to suffer, but that he would rise from death. Paul also told them that Jesus is the Messiah he was preaching about. ⁴ Some of them believed what Paul had said, and they became followers with Paul and Silas. Some Gentiles* and many important women also believed the message.

⁵ The Jewish leaders were jealous and got some worthless louts who hung around the market place to start a riot in the city. They wanted to drag Paul and Silas out to the mob, and so they went straight to Jason's home. ⁶ But when they did not find them there, they dragged out Jason and some of the Lord's followers. They took them to the city authorities and shouted, "Paul and Silas have been upsetting things everywhere. Now they have come here, ⁷ and Jason has welcomed them into his home. All of them break the laws of the Roman Emperor by claiming that someone named Jesus is king."

⁸ The officials and the people were upset when they heard this. ⁹ So they made Jason and the other followers pay bail before letting them go.

People in Berea welcome the message

¹⁰ That same night the Lord's followers sent Paul and Silas on to Berea, and after they arrived, they went to the Jewish meeting place. ¹¹ The people in Berea were much nicer than those in Thessalonica, and they gladly accepted the message. Day after day they studied the Scriptures to see if these things were true. ¹² Many of them put their faith in the Lord, including some important Greek women and several men.

¹³ When the Jewish leaders in Thessalonica heard that Paul had been preaching God's message in Berea, they went there and caused trouble by turning the crowds against Paul.

---

*16.37 Roman citizens: Only a small number of the people living in the Roman Empire were citizens, and they had special rights and privileges.

*17.4 Gentiles: See the note at 14.1.

¹⁴ Straight away the followers sent Paul down to the coast, but Silas and Timothy stayed in Berea. ¹⁵ Some men went with Paul as far as Athens, and then returned with instructions for Silas and Timothy to join him as soon as possible.

Paul in Athens

¹⁶ While Paul was waiting in Athens, he was upset to see all the idols in the city. ¹⁷ He went to the Jewish meeting place to speak to the Jews and to anyone who worshipped with them. Day after day he also spoke to everyone he met in the market. ¹⁸ Some of them were Epicureans* and some were Stoics,* and they started arguing with him.

People were asking, "What is this know-all trying to say?"

Some even said, "Paul must be preaching about foreign gods! That's what he means when he talks about Jesus and about people rising from death."*

¹⁹ They brought Paul before a council called the Areopagus and said, "Tell us what your new teaching is all about. ²⁰ We have heard you say some strange things, and we want to know what you mean."

²¹ More than anything else the people of Athens and the foreigners living there loved to hear and to talk about anything new. ²² So Paul stood up in front of the council and said:

People of Athens, I see that you are very religious. ²³ As I was going through your city and looking at the things you worship, I found an altar with the words, "To an Unknown God." You worship this God, but you don't really know him. So I want to tell you about him. ²⁴ This God made the world and everything in it. He is Lord of heaven and earth, and he doesn't live in temples built by human hands. ²⁵ He doesn't need help from anyone. He gives life, breath, and everything else to all people. ²⁶ From one person God made all nations who live on earth, and he decided when and where every nation would be. ²⁷ God has done all this, so that we will look for him and reach out and find him. He isn't far from any of us, ²⁸ and he gives

us the power to live, to move, and to be who we are. "We are his children," just as some of your poets have said.

²⁹ Since we are God's children, we must not think that he is like an idol made out of gold or silver or stone. He isn't like anything that humans have thought up and made. ³⁰ In the past, God forgave all this because people did not know what they were doing. But now he says that everyone everywhere must turn to him. ³¹ He has set a day when he will judge the world's people with fairness. And he has chosen the man Jesus to do the judging for him. God has given proof of this to all of us by raising Jesus from death.

³² As soon as the people heard Paul say that a man had been raised from death, some of them started laughing. Others said, "We will hear you talk about this some other time." ³³ When Paul left the council meeting, ³⁴ some of the men put their faith in the Lord and went with Paul. One of them was a council member named Dionysius. A woman named Damaris and several others also put their faith in the Lord.

CHAPTER 18

Paul in Corinth

¹ Paul left Athens and went to Corinth, ² where he met Aquila, a Jewish man from Pontus. Not long before this, Aquila had come from Italy with his wife Priscilla, because Emperor Claudius had ordered the Jewish people to leave Rome.* Paul went to see Aquila and Priscilla ³ and found out that they were tent makers. Paul was a tent maker too. So he stayed with them, and they worked together.

⁴ Every Sabbath, Paul went to the Jewish meeting place. He spoke to Jews and Gentiles* and tried to win them over. ⁵ But after Silas and Timothy came from Macedonia, he spent all his time preaching to the Jews about Jesus the Messiah. ⁶ Finally, they turned against him and insulted him. So he shook the dust from his clothes* and told them, "Whatever happens to you will be your own fault! I am

---

*17.18 Epicureans: People who followed the teaching of a man named Epicurus, who taught that happiness should be the main goal in life.
*17.18 Stoics: Followers of a man named Zeno, who taught that people should use self-control and be guided by their consciences.
See also: 17.24,25: 1 King 8.27; Isa 42.5; Acts 7.48.

*18.2 Emperor Claudius had ordered the Jewish people to leave Rome: Probably AD 49, though it may have been AD 41.
*18.4 Gentiles: Here the word is "Greeks". But see the note at 14.1.
*18.6 shook the dust from his clothes: This means the same as shaking dust from the feet. See the note at 13.51.

not to blame. From now on I am going to preach to the Gentiles."

⁷ Paul then moved into the house of a man named Titius Justus, who worshipped God and lived next door to the Jewish meeting place. ⁸ Crispus was the leader of the meeting place. He and everyone in his family put their faith in the Lord. Many others in Corinth also heard the message, and all the people who had faith in the Lord were baptized.

⁹ One night, Paul had a vision, and in it the Lord said, "Don't be afraid to keep on preaching. Don't stop! ¹⁰ I am with you, and you won't be harmed. Many people in this city belong to me." ¹¹ Paul stayed on in Corinth for a year and a half, teaching God's message to the people.

¹² While Gallio was governor of Achaia, some of the Jewish leaders got together and grabbed Paul. They brought him into court ¹³ and said, "This man is trying to make our people worship God in a way that is against our Law!"

¹⁴ Even before Paul could speak, Gallio said, "If you were charging this man with a crime or some other wrong, I would have to listen to you. ¹⁵ But since this concerns only words, names, and your own law, you will have to take care of it. I refuse to judge such matters." ¹⁶ Then he sent them out of the court. ¹⁷ The crowd grabbed Sosthenes, the Jewish leader, and beat him up in front of the court. But none of this mattered to Gallio.

Paul returns to Antioch in Syria

¹⁸ After Paul had stayed for a while with the Lord's followers in Corinth, he said goodbye to them and sailed on to Syria with Aquila and Priscilla. But before he left, he had his head shaved* at Cenchreae because he had made a promise to God.

¹⁹ The three of them arrived in Ephesus, where Paul left Priscilla and Aquila. He then went into the Jewish meeting place to talk with the people there. ²⁰ They asked him to stay longer, but he refused. ²¹ He said goodbye to them and told them, "If God lets me, I will come back."

Paul's third journey to tell the good news

²² Paul sailed to Caesarea, where he greeted the church. Then he went on to Antioch. ²³ After staying there for a while, he left and visited several places in Galatia and Phrygia. He helped the followers there to become stronger in their faith.

Apollos in Ephesus

²⁴ A Jewish man named Apollos came to Ephesus. Apollos had been born in the city of Alexandria. He was a very good speaker and knew a lot about the Scriptures. ²⁵ He also knew much about the Lord's Way,* and he spoke about it with great excitement. What he taught about Jesus was right, but all he knew was John's message about baptism.

²⁶ Apollos started speaking bravely in the Jewish meeting place. But when Priscilla and Aquila heard him, they took him to their home and helped him understand God's Way even better.

²⁷ Apollos decided to travel through Achaia. So the Lord's followers wrote letters, encouraging the followers there to welcome him. After Apollos arrived in Achaia, he was a great help to everyone who had put their faith in the Lord Jesus because of God's kindness. ²⁸ He got into fierce arguments with the Jewish people, and in public he used the Scriptures to prove that Jesus is the Messiah.

CHAPTER 19

Paul in Ephesus

¹ While Apollos was in Corinth, Paul travelled across the hill country to Ephesus, where he met some of the Lord's followers. ² He asked them, "When you put your faith in Jesus, were you given the Holy Spirit?"

"No!" they answered. "We have never even heard of the Holy Spirit."

³ "Then why were you baptized?" Paul asked.

They answered, "Because of what John taught."*

⁴ Paul replied, "John baptized people so that they would turn to God. But he also told them that someone else was coming,

---

*18.18 he had his head shaved: Paul had promised to be a "Nazirite" for a while. This meant that for the time of the promise, he could not cut his hair or drink wine. When the time was over, he would have to cut his hair and offer a sacrifice to God.

See also: 18.18: Num 6.18.

*18.25 the Lord's Way: See the note at 9.2.

See also: 19.4: Matt 3.11; Mark 1.4,7,8; Luke 3.4,16; John 1.26,27.

and that they should put their faith in him. Jesus is the one that John was talking about." ⁵ After the people heard Paul say this, they were baptized in the name of the Lord Jesus. ⁶ Then Paul placed his hands on them. The Holy Spirit was given to them, and they spoke unknown languages and prophesied. ⁷ There were about twelve men in this group.

⁸ For three months Paul went to the Jewish meeting place and talked bravely with the people about God's kingdom. He tried to win them over, ⁹ but some of them were stubborn and refused to believe. In front of everyone they said terrible things about God's Way. Paul left and took the followers with him to the lecture hall of Tyrannus. He spoke there every day ¹⁰ for two years, until every Jew and Gentile* in Asia had heard the Lord's message.

The sons of Sceva

¹¹ God gave Paul the power to perform great miracles. ¹² People even took handkerchiefs and aprons that had touched Paul's body, and they carried them to everyone who was sick. All the sick people were healed, and the evil spirits went out.

¹³ Some Jewish men started going around trying to force out evil spirits by using the name of the Lord Jesus. They said to the spirits, "Come out in the name of that same Jesus that Paul preaches about!"

¹⁴ Seven sons of a Jewish high priest named Sceva were doing this, ¹⁵ when an evil spirit said to them, "I know Jesus! And I have heard about Paul. But who are you?" ¹⁶ Then the man with the evil spirit jumped on them and beat them up. They ran out of the house, naked and bruised.

¹⁷ When the Jews and Gentiles* in Ephesus heard about this, they were so frightened that they praised the name of the Lord Jesus. ¹⁸ Many who were followers now started telling everyone about the evil things they had been doing. ¹⁹ Some who had been practising witchcraft even brought their books and burnt them in public. These books were worth about fifty thousand silver coins. ²⁰ So the Lord's message spread and became even more powerful.

The riot in Ephesus

²¹ After all this had happened, Paul decided to visit Macedonia and Achaia on his way to Jerusalem. Paul had said, "From there I will go on to Rome." ²² So he sent his two helpers, Timothy and Erastus, to Macedonia. But he stayed on in Asia for a while.

²³ At that time there was serious trouble because of the Lord's Way.* ²⁴ A silversmith named Demetrius had a business that made silver models of the temple of the goddess Artemis. Those who worked for him earned a lot of money. ²⁵ Demetrius brought together everyone who was in the same business and said:

> Friends, you know that we make a good living at this. ²⁶ But you have seen and heard how this man Paul is upsetting a lot of people, not only in Ephesus, but almost everywhere in Asia. He claims that the gods we humans make are not really gods at all. ²⁷ Everyone will start saying terrible things about our business. They will stop respecting the temple of the goddess Artemis, who is worshipped in Asia and all over the world. Our great goddess will be forgotten!

²⁸ When the workers heard this, they got angry and started shouting, "Great is Artemis, the goddess of the Ephesians!" ²⁹ Soon the whole city was in a riot, and some men grabbed Gaius and Aristarchus, who had come from Macedonia with Paul. Then everyone in the crowd rushed to the place where the town meetings were held.

³⁰ Paul wanted to go out and speak to the people, but the Lord's followers would not let him. ³¹ A few of the local officials were friendly to Paul, and they sent someone to warn him not to go.

³² Some of the people in the meeting were shouting one thing, and others were shouting something else. Everyone was completely confused, and most of them did not even know why they were there.

³³ Several of the Jewish leaders pushed a man named Alexander to the front of the crowd and started telling him what to say. He motioned with his hand and tried to explain what was going on. ³⁴ But when the crowd saw that he was Jewish, they all shouted for two hours, "Great is Artemis, the goddess of the Ephesians!"

---

*19.10,17 Gentile(s): The text has "Greek(s)" (see the note at 14.1).

*19.23 the Lord's Way: See the note at 9.2.

35 Finally, a town official made the crowd be quiet. Then he said:

People of Ephesus, who in the world doesn't know that our city is the centre for worshipping the great goddess Artemis? Who doesn't know that her image which fell from heaven is here? 36 No one can deny this, and so you should calm down and not do anything foolish. 37 You have brought men in here who have not robbed temples or spoken against our goddess.

38 If Demetrius and his workers have a case against these men, we have courts and judges. Let them take their complaints there. 39 But if you want to do more than that, the matter will have to be brought before the city council. 40 We could easily be accused of starting a riot today. There is no excuse for it! We cannot even give a reason for this uproar.

41 After saying this, he told the people to leave.

CHAPTER 20

Paul goes through Macedonia and Greece

1 When the riot was over, Paul sent for the followers and encouraged them. He then said goodbye to them and left for Macedonia. 2 As he travelled from place to place, he encouraged the followers with many messages. Finally, he went to Greece* and stayed there for three months.

Paul was about to sail to Syria. But some of the Jewish leaders plotted against him, so he decided to return by way of Macedonia. 4 With him were Sopater, son of Pyrrhus from Berea, and Aristarchus and Secundus from Thessalonica. Gaius from Derbe was also with him, and so were Timothy and the two Asians, Tychicus and Trophimus. 5 They went on ahead to Troas and waited for us there. 6 After the Festival of Thin Bread, we sailed from Philippi. Five days later we met them in Troas and stayed there for a week.

Paul's last visit to Troas

7 On the first day of the week* we met to break bread together.* Paul spoke to the people until midnight because he was leaving

the next morning. 8 In the upstairs room where we were meeting, there were a lot of lamps. 9 A young man called Eutychus was sitting on a window sill. While Paul was speaking, the young man got very sleepy. Finally, he went to sleep and fell three floors all the way down to the ground. When they picked him up, he was dead.

10 Paul went down and bent over Eutychus. He took him in his arms and said, "Don't worry! He's alive." 11 After Paul had gone back upstairs, he broke bread, and ate with us. He then spoke until dawn and left.

12 Then the followers took the young man home alive and were very happy.

The voyage from Troas to Miletus

13 Paul decided to travel by land to Assos. The rest of us went on ahead by ship, and we were to take him aboard there. 14 When he met us in Assos, he came aboard, and we sailed on to Mitylene. 15 The next day we came to a place near Chios, and the following day we reached Samos. The day after that we sailed to Miletus. 16 Paul had decided to sail on past Ephesus, because he did not want to spend too much time in Asia. He was in a hurry and wanted to be in Jerusalem in time for Pentecost.*

Paul says goodbye to the church leaders of Ephesus

17 From Miletus, Paul sent a message for the church leaders at Ephesus to come and meet with him. 18 When they got there, he said:

You know everything I did during the time I was with you when I first came to Asia. 19 Some of the Jews plotted against me and caused me a lot of sorrow and trouble. But I served the Lord and was humble. 20 When I preached in public or taught in your homes, I didn't hold back from telling anything that would help you. 21 I told Jews and Gentiles to turn to God and have faith in our Lord Jesus.

22 I don't know what will happen to me in Jerusalem, but I must obey God's Spirit and go there. 23 In every city I visit, I am told by the Holy Spirit that I will be put in jail and will be in trouble in Jerusalem. 24 But I don't care what happens to me, as

*20.2 Greece: Probably Corinth.
*20.7 On the first day of the week: Since the Jewish day began at sunset, the meeting would have begun in the evening.
*20.7 break bread together: See the note at 2.46.

*20.16 in time for Pentecost: The Jewish people liked to be in Jerusalem for this festival. See the note at 2.1.
See also: 20.24: 2 Tim 4.7.

long as I finish the work that the Lord Jesus gave me to do. And that work is to tell the good news about God's great kindness.

25 I have gone from place to place, preaching to you about God's kingdom, but now I know that none of you will ever see me again. 26 I tell you today that I am no longer responsible for any of you! 27 I have told you everything God wants you to know. 28 Look after yourselves and everyone the Holy Spirit has placed in your care. Be like shepherds to God's church. It is the flock that he bought with the blood of his own Son.•

29 I know that after I am gone, others will come like fierce wolves to attack you. 30 Some of your own people will tell lies to win over the Lord's followers. 31 Be on your guard! Remember how day and night for three years I kept warning you with tears in my eyes.

32 I now place you in God's care. Remember the message about his great kindness! This message can help you and give you what belongs to you as God's people. 33 I have never wanted anyone's money or clothes. 34 You know how I have worked with my own hands to make a living for myself and my friends. 35 By everything I did, I showed you how you should work to help everyone who is weak. Remember that our Lord Jesus said, "More blessings come from giving than from receiving."

36 After Paul had finished speaking, he knelt down with all of them and prayed. 37 Everyone cried and hugged and kissed him. 38 They were especially sad because Paul had told them, "You will never see me again."

Then they went with him to the ship.

CHAPTER 21

Paul goes to Jerusalem

1 After saying goodbye, we sailed straight to Cos. The next day we reached Rhodes and from there sailed on to Patara. 2 We found a ship going to Phoenicia, so we got on board and sailed off.

3 We came within sight of Cyprus and then sailed south of it on to the port of Tyre in Syria, where the ship was going to unload its cargo. 4 We found the Lord's followers and stayed with them for a week. The Holy Spirit had told them to warn Paul not to go to Jerusalem. 5 But when the week was over, we started on our way again. All the men,

together with their wives and children, walked with us from the town to the seashore. We knelt on the beach and prayed. 6 Then after saying goodbye to each other, we got into the ship, and they went back home.

7 We sailed from Tyre to Ptolemais, where we greeted the followers and stayed with them for a day. 8 The next day we went to Caesarea and stayed with Philip, the preacher. He was one of the seven men who helped the apostles, 9 and he had four unmarried• daughters who prophesied.

10 We had been in Caesarea for several days, when the prophet Agabus came to us from Judea. 11 He took Paul's belt, and with it he tied up his own hands and feet. Then he told us, "The Holy Spirit says that some of the Jewish leaders in Jerusalem will tie up the man who owns this belt. They will also hand him over to the Gentiles." 12 After Agabus said this, we and the followers living there begged Paul not to go to Jerusalem.

13 But Paul answered, "Why are you crying and breaking my heart? I am not only willing to be put in jail for the Lord Jesus. I am even willing to die for him in Jerusalem!"

14 Since we could not get Paul to change his mind, we gave up and prayed, "Lord, please make us willing to do what you want."

15 Then we got ready to go to Jerusalem. 16 Some of the followers from Caesarea went with us and took us to stay in the home of Mnason. He was from Cyprus and had been a follower from the beginning.

Paul's arrest in Jerusalem

Paul visits James

17 When we arrived in Jerusalem, the Lord's followers gladly welcomed us. 18 Paul went with us to see James• the next day, and all the church leaders were present. 19 Paul greeted them and told how God had used him to help the Gentiles. 20 Everyone who heard this praised God and said to Paul:

My friend, you can see how many tens of thousands of the Jewish people have become followers! And all of them are eager to obey the Law of Moses. 21 But they have been told that you are teaching those who live among the Gentiles to disobey this Law. They claim that you are telling them not to circumcise their sons or to follow Jewish customs.

*21.18 James: See the note at 12.17.

See also: 21.8: Acts 6.5; 8.5. 21.10: Acts 11.28.

22 What should we do now that our people have heard that you are here? 23 Please do what we ask, because four of our men have made special promises to God. 24 Join with them and prepare yourself for the ceremony that goes with the promises. Pay the cost for their heads to be shaved. Then everyone will learn that the reports about you are not true. They will know that you do obey the Law of Moses.

25 Some while ago we told the Gentile followers what we think they should do. We instructed them not to eat anything offered to idols. They were told not to eat any meat with blood still in it or the meat of an animal that has been strangled. They were also told not to commit any terrible sexual sins.*

26 The next day Paul took the four men with him and got himself ready at the same time they did. Then he went into the temple and told when the final ceremony would take place and when an offering would be made for each of them.

Paul is arrested

27 When the period of seven days for the ceremony was almost over, some of the Jewish people from Asia saw Paul in the temple. They got a large crowd together and started attacking him. 28 They were shouting, "Friends, help us! This man goes around everywhere, saying bad things about our nation and about the Law of Moses and about this temple. He has even brought shame to this holy temple by bringing in Gentiles." 29 Some of them thought that Paul had brought Trophimus from Ephesus into the temple, because they had seen them together in the city.

30 The whole city was in an uproar, and the people turned into a mob. They grabbed Paul and dragged him out of the temple. Then suddenly the doors were shut. 31 The people were about to kill Paul when the Roman army commander heard that all Jerusalem was starting to riot. 32 So he quickly took some soldiers and officers and ran to where the crowd had gathered.

As soon as the mob saw the commander and soldiers, they stopped beating Paul.

33 The army commander went over and arrested him and had him bound with two chains. Then he tried to find out who Paul was and what he had done. 34 Part of the crowd shouted one thing, and part of them shouted something else. But they were making so much noise that the commander could not find out a thing. Then he ordered Paul to be taken into the fortress. 35 As they reached the steps, the crowd became so wild that the soldiers had to lift Paul up and carry him. 36 The crowd followed and kept shouting, "Kill him! Kill him!"

Paul speaks to the crowd

37 When Paul was about to be taken into the fortress, he asked the commander, "Can I say something to you?"

"How do you know Greek?" the commander asked. 38 "Aren't you that Egyptian who started a riot not long ago and led four thousand terrorists into the desert?"

39 "No!" Paul replied. "I am a Jew from Tarsus, an important city in Cilicia. Please let me speak to the crowd."

40 The commander told him he could speak, so Paul stood on the steps and motioned to the people. When they were quiet, he spoke to them in Aramaic:

CHAPTER 22

1 "My friends and leaders of our nation, listen as I explain what happened!" 2 When the crowd heard Paul speak to them in Aramaic, they became even quieter. Then Paul said:

3 I am a Jew, born and raised in the city of Tarsus in Cilicia. I was a student of Gamaliel and was taught to follow every single law of our ancestors. In fact, I was just as eager to obey God as any of you are today.

4 I made trouble for everyone who followed the Lord's Way,* and I even had some of them killed. I had others arrested and put in jail. I didn't care if they were men or women. 5 The high priest and all the council members can tell you that this is true. They even gave me letters to the Jewish leaders in Damascus, so that I could arrest people there and bring them to Jerusalem to be punished.

6 One day about midday I was getting close to Damascus, when a bright light

---

*21.25 not to commit any terrible sexual sins: See the note at 15.20.
See also: 21.23,24: Num 6.13–21. 21.25: Acts 15.29. 21.29: Acts 20.4.

*22.4 followed the Lord's Way: See the note at 9.2.
See also: 22.3: Acts 5.34–39. 22.4,5: Acts 8.3; 26.9–11.

from heaven suddenly flashed around me. ⁷ I fell to the ground and heard a voice asking me, "Saul, Saul, why are you so cruel to me?"

⁸ "Who are you?" I answered.

The Lord replied, "I am Jesus from Nazareth! I am the one you are so cruel to." ⁹ The men who were travelling with me saw the light, but did not hear the voice.

¹⁰ I asked, "Lord, what do you want me to do?"

Then he told me, "Get up and go to Damascus. When you get there, you will be told what to do." ¹¹ The light had been so bright that I couldn't see. And the other men had to lead me by the hand to Damascus.

¹² In that city there was a man named Ananias, who faithfully obeyed the Law of Moses and was well liked by all the Jewish people living there. ¹³ He came to me and said, "Saul, my friend, you can now see again!"

At once I could see. ¹⁴ Then Ananias told me, "The God that our ancestors worshipped has chosen you to know what he wants done. He has chosen you to see the One Who Obeys God* and to hear his voice. ¹⁵ You must tell everyone what you have seen and heard. ¹⁶ What are you waiting for? Get up! Be baptized, and wash away your sins by praying to the Lord."

¹⁷ After this I returned to Jerusalem and went to the temple to pray. There I had a vision ¹⁸ of the Lord who said to me, "Hurry and leave Jerusalem! The people won't listen to what you say about me."

¹⁹ I replied, "Lord, they know that in many of our meeting places I arrested and beat people who had faith in you. ²⁰ Stephen was killed because he spoke for you, and I stood there and cheered them on. I even guarded the clothes of the men who murdered him."

²¹ But the Lord told me to go, and he promised to send me far away to the Gentiles.

²² The crowd listened until Paul said this. Then they started shouting, "Get rid of this man! He doesn't deserve to live." ²³ They kept shouting. They waved their clothes around and threw dust into the air.

Paul and the Roman army commander

²⁴ The Roman commander ordered Paul to be taken into the fortress and beaten with a whip. He did this to find out why the people were screaming at Paul.

²⁵ While the soldiers were tying Paul up to be beaten, he asked the officer standing there, "Is it legal to beat a Roman citizen before he has been tried in court?"

²⁶ When the officer heard this, he went to the commander and said, "What are you doing? This man is a Roman citizen!"

²⁷ The commander went to Paul and asked, "Tell me, are you a Roman citizen?"

"Yes," Paul answered.

²⁸ The commander then said, "I paid a lot of money to become a Roman citizen."*

But Paul replied, "I was born a Roman citizen."

²⁹ The men who were about to beat and question Paul quickly backed off. And the commander himself was frightened when he realized that he had put a Roman citizen in chains.

Paul is tried by the council

³⁰ The next day the commander wanted to know the real reason why the Jewish leaders had brought charges against Paul. So he had Paul's chains removed, and he ordered the chief priests and the whole council to meet. Then he had Paul led in and made him stand in front of them.

CHAPTER 23

¹ Paul looked straight at the council members and said, "My friends, to this day I have served God with a clear conscience!"

² Then Ananias the high priest ordered the men standing beside Paul to hit him on the mouth. ³ Paul turned to the high priest and said, "You whitewashed wall!* God will hit you. You sit there to judge me by the Law of Moses. But at the same time you order men to break the Law by hitting me."

⁴ The men standing beside Paul asked, "Don't you know you are insulting God's high priest?"

⁵ Paul replied, "Oh! I didn't know he was the high priest. The Scriptures do tell us not to speak evil about a leader of our people."

---

*22.14 One Who Obeys God: See the note at 7.52.

See also: 22.20: Acts 7.58.

*22.28 Roman citizen: See the note at 16.37.

*23.3 whitewashed wall: Someone who pretends to be good, but really isn't.

See also: 23.3: Matt 23.27,28.   23.5: Exod 22.28.

⁶ When Paul saw that some of the council members were Sadducees and others were Pharisees, he shouted, "My friends, I am a Pharisee and the son of a Pharisee. I am on trial simply because I believe that the dead will be raised to life."

⁷ As soon as Paul said this, the Pharisees and the Sadducees got into a big argument, and the council members started taking sides. ⁸ The Sadducees do not believe in angels or spirits or that the dead will rise to life. But the Pharisees believe in all these, ⁹ and so there was a lot of shouting. Some of the teachers of the Law of Moses were Pharisees. Finally, they became angry and said, "We don't find anything wrong with this man. Perhaps a spirit or an angel really did speak to him."

¹⁰ The argument became fierce, and the commander was afraid that Paul would be pulled apart. So he ordered the soldiers to go in and rescue Paul. Then they took him back into the fortress.

¹¹ That night the Lord stood beside Paul and said, "Don't worry! Just as you have told others about me in Jerusalem, you must also tell about me in Rome."

A plot to kill Paul

¹²⁻¹³ The next morning more than forty Jewish men got together and vowed that they would not eat or drink anything until they had killed Paul. ¹⁴ Then some of them went to the chief priests and the nation's leaders and said, "We have promised God that we would not eat or drink a thing until we have killed Paul. ¹⁵ You and everyone in the council must go to the commander and pretend that you want to find out more about the charges against Paul. Ask for him to be brought before your court. Meanwhile, we will be waiting to kill him before he gets there."

¹⁶ When Paul's nephew heard about the plot, he went to the fortress and told Paul about it. ¹⁷ So Paul said to one of the army officers, "Take this young man to the commander. He has something to tell him."

¹⁸ The officer took him to the commander and said, "The prisoner named Paul asked me to bring this young man to you, because he has something to tell you."

¹⁹ The commander took the young man aside and asked him in private, "What do you want to tell me?"

²⁰ He answered, "Some men are planning to ask you to bring Paul down to the Jewish council tomorrow. They will claim that they want to find out more about him. ²¹ But please don't do what they say. More than forty men are going to attack Paul. They have made a vow not to eat or drink anything until they have killed him. Even now they are waiting to hear what you decide."

²² The commander sent the young man away after saying to him, "Don't let anyone know that you told me this."

Paul is taken to Caesarea

Paul is sent to Felix the governor

²³ The commander called in two of his officers and told them, "By nine o'clock tonight have two hundred soldiers ready to go to Caesarea. Take along seventy men on horseback and two hundred foot soldiers with spears. ²⁴ Get a horse ready for Paul and make sure that he gets safely through to Felix the governor."

²⁵ The commander wrote a letter that said:

²⁶ Greetings from Claudius Lysias to the Honourable Governor Felix:

²⁷ Some Jews grabbed this man and were about to kill him. But when I found out that he was a Roman citizen, I took some soldiers and rescued him. ²⁸ I wanted to find out what they had against him. So I brought him before their council ²⁹ and learnt that the charges concern only their religious laws. This man isn't guilty of anything for which he should die or even be put in jail.

³⁰ As soon as I learnt that there was a plot against him, I sent him to you and told their leaders to bring charges against him in your court.

³¹ The soldiers obeyed the commander's orders, and that same night they took Paul to the city of Antipatris. ³² The next day the foot soldiers returned to the fortress and let the soldiers on horseback take him the rest of the way. ³³ When they came to Caesarea, they gave the letter to the governor and handed Paul over to him.

³⁴ The governor read the letter. Then he asked Paul and found out that he was from

See also: 23.6: Acts 26.5; Phil 3.5. 23.8: Matt 22.23; Mark 12.18; Luke 20.27.

171

Cilicia. ³⁵ The governor said, "I will listen to your case as soon as the people come to bring their charges against you." After saying this, he gave orders for Paul to be kept as a prisoner in Herod's palace.*

CHAPTER 24

Paul is accused in the court of Felix

¹ Five days later Ananias the high priest, together with some of their leaders and a lawyer named Tertullus, went to the governor to present their case against Paul. ² So Paul was called in, and Tertullus stated the case against him:*

Honourable Felix, you have brought our people a long period of peace, and because of your concern our nation is much better off. ³ All of us are always grateful for what you have done. ⁴ I don't want to bother you, but please be patient with us and listen for just a few minutes.

⁵ This man has been found to be a real pest and troublemaker for Jews all over the world. He is also a leader of a group called Nazarenes. ⁶⁻⁸ When he tried to disgrace the temple, we arrested him.* If you question him, you will find out for yourself that our charges are true.

⁹ The Jewish crowd spoke up and agreed with what Tertullus had said.

Paul defends himself

¹⁰ The governor motioned for Paul to speak, and he began:

I know that you have judged the people of our nation for many years, and I am glad to defend myself in your court.

¹¹ It was no more than twelve days ago that I went to worship in Jerusalem. You can find this out easily enough. ¹² Never once did the Jews find me arguing with anyone in the temple. I didn't cause trouble in the Jewish meeting places or in the city itself. ¹³ There is no way that they can prove these charges that they are now bringing against me.

¹⁴ I admit that their leaders think that the Lord's Way* which I follow is based on wrong beliefs. But I still worship the same God that my ancestors worshipped. And I believe everything written in the Law of Moses and in the Prophets.* ¹⁵ I am just as sure as these people are that God will raise from death everyone who is good or evil. ¹⁶ And because I am sure, I try my best to have a clear conscience in whatever I do for God or for people.

¹⁷ After being away for several years, I returned here to bring gifts for the poor people of my nation and to offer sacrifices. ¹⁸ This is what I was doing when I was found going through a ceremony in the temple. I wasn't with a crowd, and there was no uproar.

¹⁹ Some Jews from Asia were there at that time, and if they have anything to say against me, they should be here now. ²⁰ Or ask the ones who are here. They can tell you that they didn't find me guilty of anything when I was tried by their own council. ²¹ The only charge they can bring against me is what I shouted out in court, when I said, "I am on trial today because I believe that the dead will be raised to life!"

²² Felix knew a lot about the Lord's Way.* But he brought the trial to an end and said, "I will make my decision after Lysias the commander arrives." ²³ He then ordered the army officer to keep Paul under guard, but not to lock him up or to stop his friends from helping him.

Paul is kept under guard

²⁴ Several days later Felix and his wife Drusilla, who was Jewish, went to the place where Paul was kept under guard. They sent for Paul and listened while he spoke to them about having faith in Christ Jesus. ²⁵ But Felix was frightened when Paul started talking to them about doing right, about self-control, and about the coming judgment. So he said to Paul, "That's enough for now. You may go. But when I have time I will send for you." ²⁶ After this, Felix often sent for Paul and talked with him, because he hoped that Paul would offer him a bribe.

²⁷ Two years later Porcius Festus became governor in place of Felix. But since Felix wanted to do the Jewish leaders a favour, he kept Paul in jail.

---

*23.35 Herod's palace: The palace built by Herod the Great and used by the Roman governors of Palestine.
*24.14 the Lord's Way: See the note at 9.2.

*24.14 Law of Moses . . . the Prophets: See the note at 13.15.
*24.22 the Lord's Way: See the note at 9.2.
See also: 24.17,18: Acts 21.17–28. 24.21: Acts 23.6.

CHAPTER 25

Paul asks to be tried by the Roman Emperor

¹ Three days after Festus had become governor, he went from Caesarea to Jerusalem. ² There the chief priests and some Jewish leaders told him about their charges against Paul. They also asked Festus ³ if he would be willing to bring Paul to Jerusalem. They begged him to do this because they were planning to attack and kill Paul on the way. ⁴ But Festus told them, "Paul will be kept in Caesarea, and I am soon going there myself. ⁵ If he has done anything wrong, let your leaders go with me and bring charges against him there."

⁶ Festus stayed in Jerusalem for eight or ten more days before going to Caesarea. Then the next day he took his place as judge and had Paul brought into court. ⁷ As soon as Paul came in, the Jewish leaders from Jerusalem crowded around him and said he was guilty of many serious crimes. But they could not prove anything. ⁸ Then Paul spoke in his own defence, "I have not broken the Law of my people. And I have not done anything against either the temple or the Emperor."

⁹ Festus wanted to please the leaders. So he asked Paul, "Are you willing to go to Jerusalem and be tried by me on these charges?"

¹⁰ Paul replied, "I am on trial in the Emperor's court, and that's where I should be tried. You know very well that I have not done anything to harm the Jewish nation. ¹¹ If I had done something deserving death, I would not ask to escape the death penalty. But I am not guilty of any of these crimes, and no one has the right to hand me over to these people. I now ask to be tried by the Emperor himself."

¹² After Festus had talked this over with members of his council, he told Paul, "You have asked to be tried by the Emperor, and to the Emperor you will go!"

Paul speaks to Agrippa and Bernice

¹³ A few days later King Agrippa and Bernice came to Caesarea to visit Festus. ¹⁴ Festus had been there for several days, when Festus told the king about the charges against Paul. He said:

Felix left a man here in jail, ¹⁵ and when I went to Jerusalem, the chief priests and the Jewish leaders came and asked me to find him guilty. ¹⁶ I told them that it isn't the Roman custom to hand a man over to people who are bringing charges against him. He must first have the chance to meet them face to face and to defend himself against their charges.

¹⁷ So when they came here with me, I wasted no time. On the very next day I took my place on the judge's bench and ordered him to be brought in. ¹⁸ But when the men stood up to make their charges against him, they did not accuse him of any of the crimes that I thought they would. ¹⁹ Instead, they argued with him about some of their beliefs and about a dead man named Jesus, who Paul said was alive.

²⁰ Since I did not know how to find out the truth about all this, I asked Paul if he would be willing to go to Jerusalem and be put on trial there. ²¹ But Paul asked to be kept in jail until the Emperor could decide his case. So I ordered him to be kept here until I could send him to the Emperor.

²² Then Agrippa said to Festus, "I would also like to hear what this man has to say."

Festus answered, "You can hear him tomorrow."

²³ The next day Agrippa and Bernice made a big show as they came into the meeting room. High ranking army officers and leading citizens of the town were also there. Festus then ordered Paul to be brought in ²⁴ and said:

King Agrippa and other guests, look at this man! Every Jew from Jerusalem and Caesarea has come to me, demanding for him to be put to death. ²⁵ I have not found him guilty of any crime deserving death. But because he has asked to be judged by the Emperor, I have decided to send him to Rome.

²⁶ I have to write some facts about this man to the Emperor. So I have brought him before all of you, but especially before you, King Agrippa. After we have talked about his case, I will then have something to write. ²⁷ It makes no sense to send a prisoner to the Emperor without stating the charges against him.

CHAPTER 26

Paul's defence before Agrippa

[1] Agrippa told Paul, "You may now speak for yourself."

Paul stretched out his hand and said:

[2] King Agrippa, I am glad for this chance to defend myself before you today on all these charges that my own people have brought against me. [3] You know a lot about our religious customs and the beliefs that divide us. So I ask you to listen patiently to me.

[4-5] All the Jews have known me since I was a child. They know what kind of life I have lived in my own country and in Jerusalem. And if they were willing, they could tell you that I was a Pharisee, a member of a group that is stricter than any other. [6] Now I am on trial because I believe the promise God made to our people long ago.

[7] Day and night our twelve tribes have earnestly served God, waiting for his promised blessings. King Agrippa, because of this hope, the Jewish leaders have brought charges against me. [8] Why should any of you doubt that God raises the dead to life?

[9] I once thought that I should do everything I could to oppose Jesus from Nazareth. [10] I did this first in Jerusalem, and with the authority of the chief priests I put many of God's people in jail. I even voted for them to be killed. [11] I often had them punished in our meeting places, and I tried to make them give up their faith. In fact, I was so angry with them, that I went looking for them in foreign cities.

[12] King Agrippa, one day I was on my way to Damascus with the authority and permission of the chief priests. [13] About midday I saw a light brighter than the sun. It flashed from heaven on me and on everyone travelling with me. [14] We all fell to the ground. Then I heard a voice say to me in Aramaic, "Saul, Saul, why are you so cruel to me? It's foolish to fight against me!"

[15] "Who are you?" I asked.

Then the Lord answered, "I am Jesus! I am the one you are so cruel to. [16] Now stand up. I have appeared to you, because I have chosen you to be my servant. You are to tell others what you have learnt about me and what I will show you later."

[17] The Lord also said, "I will protect you from the Jews and from the Gentiles that I am sending you to. [18] I want you to open their eyes, so that they will turn from darkness to light and from the power of Satan to God. Then their sins will be forgiven, and by faith in me they will become part of God's holy people."

[19] King Agrippa, I obeyed this vision from heaven. [20] First I preached to the people in Damascus, and then I went to Jerusalem and all over Judea. Finally, I went to the Gentiles and said, "Stop sinning and turn to God! Then prove what you have done by the way you live."

[21] That is why some men grabbed me in the temple and tried to kill me. [22] But all this time God has helped me, and I have preached both to the rich and to the poor. I have told them only what the prophets and Moses said would happen. [23] I told them how the Messiah would suffer and be the first to be raised from death, so that he could bring light to his own people and to the Gentiles.

[24] Before Paul finished defending himself, Festus shouted, "Paul, you're mad! Too much learning has driven you out of your mind."

[25] But Paul replied, "Honourable Festus, I am not mad. What I am saying is true, and it makes sense. [26] None of these things happened off in a corner somewhere. I am sure that King Agrippa knows what I am talking about. That's why I can speak so plainly to him."

[27] Then Paul said to Agrippa, "Do you believe what the prophets said? I know you do."

[28] Agrippa asked Paul, "In such a short time do you think you can talk me into being a Christian?"

[29] Paul answered, "Whether it takes a short time or a long time, I wish you and everyone else who hears me today would become just like me! Except, of course, for these chains."

[30] Then King Agrippa, Governor Festus, Bernice, and everyone who was with them got up. [31] But before they left, they said, "This man isn't guilty of anything. He doesn't deserve to die or to be put in jail."

[32] Agrippa told Festus, "Paul could have been set free, if he had not asked to be tried by the Roman Emperor."

See also: 26.5: Acts 23.6; Phil 3.5. 26.9–11: Acts 8.3; 22.4,5.

See also: 26.20: Acts 9.20,28,29. 26.23: a 1 Cor 15.20; b Isa 42.6; 49.6.

Paul is taken to Rome

CHAPTER 27

¹ When it was time for us to sail to Rome, Captain Julius from the Emperor's special troops was put in charge of Paul and the other prisoners. ² We went aboard a ship from Adramyttium that was about to sail to some ports along the coast of Asia. Aristarchus from Thessalonica in Macedonia sailed on the ship with us.

³ The next day we came to shore at Sidon. Captain Julius was very kind to Paul. He even let him visit his friends, so they could give him whatever he needed. ⁴ When we left Sidon, the winds were blowing against us, and we sailed close to the island of Cyprus to be safe from the wind. ⁵ Then we sailed south of Cilicia and Pamphylia until we came to the port of Myra in Lycia. ⁶ There the army captain found a ship from Alexandria that was going to Italy. So he ordered us to board that ship.

⁷ We sailed along slowly for several days and had a hard time reaching Cnidus. The wind would not let us go any further in that direction, so we sailed past Cape Salmone, where the island of Crete would protect us from the wind. ⁸ We went slowly along the coast and finally reached a place called Fair Havens, not far from the town of Lasea.

⁹ By now we had already lost a lot of time, and sailing was no longer safe. In fact, even the Great Day of Forgiveness* was past. ¹⁰ Then Paul spoke to the crew of the ship, "Men, listen to me! If we sail now, our ship and its cargo will be badly damaged, and many lives will be lost." ¹¹ But Julius listened to the captain of the ship and its owner, rather than to Paul.

¹² The harbour at Fair Havens wasn't a good place to spend the winter. Because of this, almost everyone agreed that we should at least try to sail along the coast of Crete as far as Phoenix. It had a harbour that opened towards the south-west and north-west,* and we could spend the winter there.

---

*27.9 Great Day of Forgiveness: This Jewish festival took place near the end of September. The sailing season was dangerous after the middle of September, and it was stopped completely between the middle of November and the middle of March.

The storm at sea

¹³ When a gentle wind from the south started blowing, the men thought it was a good time to do what they had planned. So they pulled up the anchor, and we sailed along the coast of Crete. ¹⁴ But soon a strong wind called "The North-easter" blew against us from the island. ¹⁵ The wind struck the ship, and we could not sail against it. So we let the wind carry the ship.

¹⁶ We went around the island of Cauda on the side that was protected from the wind. We had a hard time holding the lifeboat in place, ¹⁷ but finally we got it where it belonged. Then the sailors tied ropes around the ship to hold it together. They lowered the sail and let the ship drift along, because they were afraid it might hit the sandbanks in the gulf of Syrtis.

¹⁸ The storm was so fierce that the next day they threw some of the ship's cargo overboard. ¹⁹ Then on the third day, with their bare hands they threw overboard some of the ship's gear. ²⁰ For several days we could not see either the sun or the stars. A strong wind kept blowing, and we finally gave up all hope of being saved.

²¹ Since none of us had eaten anything for a long time, Paul stood up and told the men:

> You should have listened to me! If you had stayed on in Crete, you would not have had this damage and loss. ²² But now I beg you to cheer up, because you will be safe. Only the ship will be lost.
> ²³ I belong to God, and I worship him. Last night he sent an angel ²⁴ to tell me, "Paul, don't be afraid! You will stand trial before the Emperor. And because of you, God will save the lives of everyone on the ship." ²⁵ Cheer up! I am sure that God will do exactly what he promised. ²⁶ But we will first be shipwrecked on some island.

²⁷ For fourteen days and nights we had been blown around over the Mediterranean Sea. But about midnight the sailors realized that we were getting near land. ²⁸ They measured and found that the water was about forty metres deep. A little later they measured again and found it was only about thirty metres. ²⁹ The sailors were afraid that we might hit some rocks, and they let down four anchors from the back of the ship. Then they prayed for daylight.

30 The sailors wanted to escape from the ship. So they lowered the lifeboat into the water, pretending that they were letting down an anchor from the front of the ship. 31 But Paul said to Captain Julius and the soldiers, "If the sailors don't stay on the ship, you won't have any chance to save your lives." 32 The soldiers then cut the ropes that held the lifeboat and let it fall into the sea.

33 Just before daylight Paul begged the people to eat something. He told them, "For fourteen days you have been so worried that you haven't eaten a thing. 34 I beg you to eat something. Your lives depend on it. Do this and not one of you will be hurt."

35 After Paul had said this, he took a piece of bread and gave thanks to God. Then in front of everyone, he broke the bread and ate some. 36 They all felt encouraged, and each of them ate something. 37 There were 276 people on the ship, 38 and after everyone had eaten, they threw the cargo of wheat into the sea to make the ship lighter.

The shipwreck

39 Morning came, and the ship's crew saw a coast that they did not recognize. But they did see a cove with a beach. So they decided to try to run the ship aground on the beach. 40 They cut the anchors loose and let them sink into the sea. At the same time they untied the ropes that were holding the rudders. Next, they raised the sail at the front of the ship and let the wind carry the ship towards the beach. 41 But it ran aground on a sandbank. The front of the ship stuck firmly in the sand, and the rear was being smashed by the force of the waves.

42 The soldiers decided to kill the prisoners to keep them from swimming away and escaping. 43 But Captain Julius wanted to save Paul's life, and he did not let the soldiers do what they had planned. Instead, he ordered everyone who could swim to dive into the water and head for shore. 44 Then he told the others to hold on to planks of wood or parts of the ship. At last, everyone safely reached shore.

CHAPTER 28

On the island of Malta

1 When we came ashore, we learnt that the island was called Malta. 2 The local people were very friendly, and they welcomed us by building a fire, because it was rainy and cold.

3 After Paul had gathered some wood and had put it on the fire, the heat caused a snake to crawl out, and it bit him on the hand. 4 When the local people saw the snake hanging from Paul's hand, they said to each other, "This man must be a murderer! He didn't drown in the sea, but the goddess of justice will kill him anyway."

5 Paul shook the snake off into the fire and wasn't harmed. 6 The people kept thinking that Paul would either swell up or suddenly drop dead. They watched him for a long time, and when nothing happened to him, they changed their minds and said, "This man is a god."

7 The governor of the island was named Publius, and he owned some of the land around there. Publius was very friendly and welcomed us into his home for three days. 8 His father was in bed, sick with fever and stomach trouble, and Paul went to visit him. Paul healed the man by praying and placing his hands on him.

9 After this happened, everyone on the island brought their sick people to Paul, and they were all healed. 10 The people were very respectful to us, and when we sailed, they gave us everything we needed.

From Malta to Rome

11 Three months later we sailed in a ship that had been docked at Malta for the winter. The ship was from Alexandria in Egypt and was known as "The Twin Gods".* 12 We arrived in Syracuse and stayed for three days. 13 From there we sailed to Rhegium. The next day a south wind began to blow, and two days later we arrived in Puteoli. 14 There we found some of the Lord's followers, who begged us to stay with them. A week later we left for the city of Rome.

15 Some of the followers in Rome heard about us and came to meet us at the Market of Appius and at the Three Inns. When Paul saw them, he thanked God and was encouraged.

Paul in Rome

16 We arrived in Rome, and Paul was allowed to live in a house by himself with a soldier to guard him.

---

*28.11 known as "The Twin Gods": Or "carried on its bow a wooden carving of the Twin Gods." These gods were Castor and Pollux, two of the favourite gods among sailors.

17 Three days after we got there, Paul called together some of the Jewish leaders and said:

My friends, I have never done anything to hurt our people, and I have never gone against the customs of our ancestors. But in Jerusalem I was handed over as a prisoner to the Romans. 18 They looked into the charges against me and wanted to release me. They found that I had not done anything deserving death. 19 The Jewish leaders disagreed, so I asked to be tried by the Emperor.

But I don't have anything to say against my own nation. 20 I am bound by these chains because of what we people of Israel hope for. That's why I have called you here to talk about this hope of ours.

21 The leaders replied, "No one from Judea has written us a letter about you. And not one of them has come here to report on you or to say anything against you. 22 But we would like to hear what you have to say. We understand that people everywhere are against this new group."

23 They agreed on a time to meet with Paul, and many of them came to his house. From early morning until late in the afternoon, Paul talked to them about God's kingdom. He used the Law of Moses and the Books of the Prophets* to try to win them over to Jesus.

24 Some of the leaders agreed with what Paul said, but others did not. 25 Since they could not agree among themselves, they started leaving. But Paul said, "The Holy Spirit said the right thing when he sent Isaiah the prophet 26 to tell our ancestors,

'Go to these people
    and tell them:
You will listen and listen,
    but never understand.
You will look and look,
    but never see.
27 All of you
    have stubborn hearts.
Your ears are stopped up,
    and your eyes are covered.
You cannot see or hear
    or understand.
If you could,
    you would turn to me,
    and I would heal you.' "

28-29 Paul said, "You may be sure that God wants to save the Gentiles! And they will listen."

30 For two years Paul stayed in a rented house and welcomed everyone who came to see him. 31 He bravely preached about God's kingdom and taught about the Lord Jesus Christ, and no one tried to stop him.

Additional notes

1.6 are you now going to give Israel its own king again?: Or "Are you now going to rule Israel as its king?"
1.14 met together and prayed with a single purpose in mind: Or "met together in a special place for prayer".
3.13 Servant: Or "Son".
3.26 Son: Or "Servant".
4.27 Servant: See the note at 3.13.
4.30 Servant: See the note at 3.13.
4.33 God greatly blessed his followers: Or "Everyone highly respected his followers".
7.46 the people: Some manuscripts have "God".
7.47 God: Or "the people".
8.26 Go south: Or "About midday go".
8.26 the desert road that leads from Jerusalem to Gaza: Or "the road that leads from Jerusalem to Gaza in the desert".
8.36,37 Why can't I be baptized: Some manuscripts add, "Philip replied, 'You can, if you believe with all your heart.' The official answered, 'I believe that Jesus Christ is the Son of God.' "
9.34 and make up your bed: Or "and prepare something to eat."
10.19 Three: One manuscript has "two"; some manuscripts have "some".
10.37 what happened: Or "the message that went".
11.20 Gentiles: This translates a Greek word that may mean "people who speak Greek" or "people who live as Greeks do". Here the word seems to mean "people who are not Jews". Some manuscripts have "Greeks", which also seems to mean "people who are not Jews".
12.15 his angel: Probably meaning "his guardian angel".
12.25 went back to Jerusalem: Some manuscripts have "left Jerusalem", and others have "went to Antioch".
13.18 took care of: Some manuscripts have "put up with".
13.28,29 cross: This translates a Greek word that means "wood", "pole", or "tree".
13.44 the Lord: Some manuscripts have "God".
13.48 the Lord: See the note at 13.44.
15.34,35 Verse 34, which says that Silas decided to stay on in Antioch, is not in some manuscripts.

*28.23 Law of Moses and the Books of the Prophets: See the note at 13.15.
See also: 28.19: Acts 25.11. 28.26,27: Isa 6.9,10 (LXX).

*16.8 went on through: Or "passed by".

*16.12 in the first district of Macedonia: Some manuscripts have "and the leading city of Macedonia."

*17.18 people rising from death: Or "a goddess named 'Rising from Death'."

*19.3 Then why were you baptized? . . . Because of what John taught: Or "In whose name were you baptized? . . . We were baptized in John's name."

*19.21 Paul decided: Or "Paul was led by the Holy Spirit".

*20.28 the blood of his own Son: Or "his own blood."

*21.9 unmarried: Or "virgin".

*24.2 Paul was called in, and Tertullus stated the case against him: Or "Tertullus was called in and stated the case against Paul.

*24.6–8 we arrested him: Some manuscripts add, "We wanted to judge him by our own laws. But Lysias the commander took him away from us by force. Then Lysias ordered us to bring our charges against this man in your court."

*27.12 south-west and north-west: Or "north-east and south-east".

*28.28,29 And they will listen: Some manuscripts add, "After Paul said this, the people left, but they got into a fierce argument among themselves."

Romans

Paul's letter to the church
in Rome

A quick look at this letter

Paul wrote this letter to introduce himself
and his message to the church at Rome. He
had never been to this important city,
although he knew the names of many
Christians there and hoped to visit them soon
(15.22—16.21). Paul tells them that he is an
apostle, chosen to preach the good news
(1.1). And the message he proclaims "is
God's powerful way of saving all people who
have faith, whether they are Jews or Gentiles"
(1.16).

Paul reminds his readers, "All of us have
sinned and fallen short of God's glory" (3.23).
But how can we be made acceptable to God?
This is the main question that Paul answers in
this letter. He begins by showing how
everyone has failed to do what God requires.
The Jews have not obeyed the Law of Moses,
and the Gentiles have refused even to think
about God, although God has spoken to them
in many different ways (1.18—3.20).

*Now we see how God does make us acceptable
to him.*

*He accepts people only because they have faith
in Jesus Christ . . . God treats us much better
than we deserve, and because of Christ Jesus,
he freely accepts us and sets us free from our
sins.*

(3.21a,22b–24)

*God gave Jesus to die for our sins, and he
raised him to life, so that we would be made
acceptable to God.*

(4.25)

Paul and his message of good news

CHAPTER 1

[1] *From Paul, a servant of Christ Jesus.*

God chose me to be an apostle, and he
appointed me to preach the good news [2] that
he promised long ago by what his prophets
said in the Holy Scriptures. [3-4] This good
news is about his Son, our Lord Jesus Christ!
As a human, he was from the family of David.
But the Holy Spirit* proved that Jesus is the
powerful Son of God,* because he was raised
from death.

[5] Jesus was kind to me and chose me to be
an apostle,* so that people of all nations
would obey and have faith. [6] You are some of
those people chosen by Jesus Christ.

⁷ This letter is to all of you in Rome. God loves you and has chosen you to be his very own people.

I pray that God our Father and our Lord Jesus Christ will be kind to you and will bless you with peace!

A prayer of thanks

⁸ First, I thank God in the name of Jesus Christ for all of you. I do this because people everywhere in the world are talking about your faith. ⁹ God has seen how I never stop praying for you, while I serve him with all my heart and tell the good news about his Son.

¹⁰ In all my prayers, I ask God to make it possible for me to visit you. ¹¹ I want to see you and share with you the same blessings that God's Spirit has given me. Then you will grow stronger in your faith. ¹² What I am saying is that we can encourage each other by the faith that is ours.

¹³ My friends, I want you to know that I have often planned to come for a visit. But something has always kept me from doing it. I want to win followers to Christ in Rome, as I have done in many other places. ¹⁴⁻¹⁵ It doesn't matter if people are civilized and educated, or if they are uncivilized and uneducated. I must tell the good news to everyone. That's why I am eager to visit all of you in Rome.

The power of the good news

¹⁶ I am proud of the good news! It is God's powerful way of saving all people who have faith, whether they are Jews or Gentiles. ¹⁷ The good news tells how God accepts everyone who has faith, but only those who have faith.' It is just as the Scriptures say, "The people God accepts because of their faith will live."'

Everyone is guilty

¹⁸ From heaven God shows how angry he is with all the wicked and evil things that sinful people do to crush the truth. ¹⁹ They know everything that can be known about God, because God has shown it all to them. ²⁰ God's eternal power and character cannot be seen. But from the beginning of creation, God has shown what these are like by all he has made. That's why those people don't have any excuse. ²¹ They know about God,

but they don't honour him or even thank him. Their thoughts are useless, and their stupid minds are in the dark. ²² They claim to be wise, but they are fools. ²³ They don't worship the glorious and eternal God. Instead, they worship idols that are made to look like humans who cannot live for ever, and like birds, animals, and reptiles.

²⁴ So God let these people go their own way. They did what they wanted to do, and their filthy thoughts made them do shameful things with their bodies. ²⁵ They gave up the truth about God for a lie, and they worshipped God's creation instead of God, who will be praised for ever. Amen.

²⁶ God let them follow their own evil desires. Women no longer wanted to have sex in a natural way, and they did things with each other that were not natural. ²⁷ Men behaved in the same way. They stopped wanting to have sex with women and had strong desires for sex with other men. They did shameful things with each other, and what has happened to them is punishment for their foolish deeds.

²⁸ Since these people refused even to think about God, he let their useless minds rule over them. That's why they do all sorts of indecent things. ²⁹ They are evil, wicked, and greedy, as well as mean in every possible way. They want what others have, and they murder, argue, cheat, and are hard to get along with. They gossip, ³⁰ say cruel things about others, and hate God. They are proud, conceited, and boastful, always thinking up new ways to do evil.

These people don't respect their parents. ³¹ They are stupid, unreliable, and don't have any love or pity for others. ³² They know that God has said that anyone who acts this way deserves to die. But they keep on doing evil things, and they even encourage others to do them.

CHAPTER 2

God's judgment is fair

¹ Some of you accuse others of doing wrong. But there is no excuse for what you do. When you judge others, you condemn yourselves, because you are guilty of doing the very same things. ² We know that God is right to judge everyone who behaves in this way. ³ Do you really think God won't punish you, when you behave exactly like the people you accuse? ⁴ You don't think much of God's

---

See also: 1.13: Acts 19.21. 1.16: Mark 8.38. 1.17: Hab 2.4. 1.21: Eph 4.17,18.

See also: 1.23: Deut 4.16–18. 2.1: Matt 7.1; Luke 6.37.

wonderful goodness or of his patience and willingness to put up with you. Don't you know that the reason God is good to you is because he wants you to turn to him?

5 But you are stubborn and refuse to turn to God. So you are making things even worse for yourselves on that day when he will show how angry he is and will judge the world with fairness. 6 God will reward each of us for what we have done. 7 He will give eternal life to everyone who has patiently done what is good in the hope of receiving glory, honour, and life that lasts for ever. 8 But he will show how angry and furious he can be with every selfish person who rejects the truth and wants to do evil. 9 All who are wicked will be punished with trouble and suffering. It doesn't matter if they are Jews or Gentiles. 10 But all who do right will be rewarded with glory, honour, and peace, whether they are Jews or Gentiles. 11 God doesn't have any favourites!

12 Those people who don't know about God's Law will still be punished for what they do wrong. And the Law will be used to judge everyone who knows what it says. 13 God accepts those who obey his Law, but not those who simply hear it.

14 Some people naturally obey the Law's commands, even though they don't have the Law. 15 This proves that the conscience is like a law written in the human heart. And it will show whether we are forgiven or condemned, 16 when God appoints Jesus Christ to judge everyone's secret thoughts, just as my message says.

The Jews and the Law

17 Some of you call yourselves Jews. You trust in the Law and take pride in God. 18 By reading the Scriptures you learn how God wants you to behave, and you discover what is right. 19 You are sure that you are a guide for the blind and a light for all who are in the dark. 20 And since there is knowledge and truth in God's Law, you think you can instruct fools and teach young people.

21 But how can you teach others when you refuse to learn? You preach that it is wrong to steal. But do you steal? 22 You say people should be faithful in marriage. But are you faithful? You hate idols, yet you rob their temples. 23 You take pride in the Law, but you disobey the Law and bring shame to God. 24 It is just as the Scriptures tell us, "You have made foreigners say insulting things about God."

25 Being circumcised is worthwhile, if you obey the Law. But if you don't obey the Law, you are no better off than people who are not circumcised. 26 In fact, if they obey the Law, they are as good as anyone who is circumcised. 27 So everyone who obeys the Law, but has never been circumcised, will condemn you. Even though you are circumcised and have the Law, you still don't obey its teachings.

28 Just because you live like a Jew and are circumcised doesn't make you a real Jew. 29 To be a real Jew you must obey the Law. True circumcision is something that happens deep in your heart, not something done to your body. And besides, you should want praise from God and not from humans.

CHAPTER 3

1 What good is it to be a Jew? What good is it to be circumcised? 2 It is good in a lot of ways! First of all, God's messages were spoken to the Jews. 3 It is true that some of them did not believe the message. But does this mean that God cannot be trusted, just because they did not have faith? 4 No, indeed! God tells the truth, even if everyone else is a liar. The Scriptures say about God,

"Your words
    will be proved true,
and in court
    you will win your case."

5 If our evil deeds show how right God is, then what can we say? Is it wrong for God to become angry and punish us? What a foolish thing to ask. 6 But the answer is, "No." Otherwise, how could God judge the world? 7 Since your lies bring great honour to God by showing how truthful he is, you may ask why God still says you are a sinner. 8 You might as well say, "Let's do something evil, so that something good will come of it!" Some people even claim that we are saying this. But God is fair and will judge them as well.

No one is good

9 What does all this mean? Does it mean that we Jews are better off* than the Gentiles? No, it doesn't! Jews, as well as Gentiles, are ruled by sin, just as I have said. 10 The Scriptures tell us,

See also: 2.6: Psa 62.12; Prov 24.12. 2.11: Deut 10.17.
2.24: Isa 52.5 (LXX).

See also: 2.29: Deut 30.6. 3.4: Psa 51.4 (LXX).
3.10–12: Psa 14.1-3 (LXX); Psa 53.1-3 (LXX).

181

"No one is acceptable to God!
[11] Not one of them understands
  or even searches for God.
[12] They have all turned away
  and are worthless.
There isn't one person
  who does right.
[13] Their words are like
  an open pit,
  and their tongues are good
  only for telling lies.
Each word is as deadly
  as the fangs of a snake,
[14] and they say nothing
  but bitter curses.
[15] These people quickly
  become violent.
[16] Wherever they go,
  they leave ruin
  and destruction.
[17] They don't know how
  to live in peace.
[18] They don't even fear God."

[19] We know that everything in the Law was written for those who are under its power. The Law says these things to stop anyone from making excuses and to let God show that the whole world is guilty. [20] God doesn't accept people simply because they obey the Law. No, indeed! All the Law does is to point out our sin.

God's way of accepting people

[21] Now we see how God does make us acceptable to him. The Law and the Prophets* tell how we become acceptable, and it isn't by obeying the Law of Moses. [22] God treats everyone alike. He accepts people only because they have faith in Jesus Christ. [23] All of us have sinned and fallen short of God's glory. [24] But God treats us much better than we deserve,* and because of Christ Jesus, he freely accepts us and sets us free from our sins. [25-26] God sent Christ to be our sacrifice. Christ offered his life's blood, so that by faith

in him we could come to God. And God did this to show that in the past he was right to be patient and forgive sinners. This also shows that God is right when he accepts people who have faith in Jesus.

[27] What is left for us to boast about? Not a thing! Is it because we obeyed some law? No! It is because of faith. [28] We see that people are acceptable to God because they have faith, and not because they obey the Law. [29] Does God belong only to the Jews? Isn't he also the God of the Gentiles? Yes, he is! [30] There is only one God, and he accepts Gentiles as well as Jews, simply because of their faith. [31] Do we destroy the Law by our faith? Not at all! We make it even more powerful.

CHAPTER 4

The example of Abraham

[1] Well then, what can we say about our ancestor Abraham? [2] If he became acceptable to God because of what he did, then he would have something to boast about. But he would never be able to boast about it to God. [3] The Scriptures say, "God accepted Abraham because Abraham had faith in him."

[4] Money paid to workers isn't a gift. It is something they earn by working. [5] But you cannot make God accept you because of something you do. God accepts sinners only because they have faith in him. [6] In the Scriptures David talks about the blessings that come to people who are acceptable to God, even though they don't do anything to deserve these blessings. David says,

[7] "God blesses people
  whose sins are forgiven
  and whose evil deeds
  are forgotten.
[8] The Lord blesses people
  whose sins are erased
  from his book."

[9] Are these blessings meant for circumcised people or for those who are not circumcised? Well, the Scriptures say that God accepted Abraham because Abraham had faith in him. [10] But when did this happen? Was it before or after Abraham was circumcised? Of course, it was before.

[11] Abraham let himself be circumcised to show that he had been accepted because of his faith even before he was circumcised. This makes Abraham the father of all who are

---

*3.21 The Law and the Prophets: The Jewish Scriptures, that is, the Old Testament.
*3.24 treats us much better than we deserve: The Greek word *charis*, traditionally rendered "grace", is translated here and in other places in the CEV to express the overwhelming kindness of God.

See also: 3.13: a Psa 5.9 (LXX); b Psa 140.3.
3.14: Psa 10.7 (LXX). 3.15–17: Isa 59.7,8. 3.18: Psa 36.1.
3.20: Psa 143.2; Gal 2.16. 3.22: a 2.16.

See also: 3.30: Deut 6.4; Gal 3.20. 4.3: Gen 15.6; Gal 3.6.
4.7,8: Psa 32.1,2. 4.11: Gen 17.10.

acceptable to God because of their faith, even though they are not circumcised. ¹² This also makes Abraham the father of everyone who is circumcised and has faith in God, as Abraham did before he was circumcised.

The promise is for all who have faith

¹³ God promised Abraham and his descendants that he would give them the world. This promise wasn't made because Abraham had obeyed a law, but because his faith in God made him acceptable. ¹⁴ If Abraham and his descendants were given this promise because they had obeyed a law, then faith would mean nothing, and the promise would be worthless.

¹⁵ God becomes angry when his Law is broken. But where there isn't a law, it cannot be broken. ¹⁶ Everything depends on having faith in God, so that God's promise is assured by his great kindness. This promise isn't only for Abraham's descendants who have the Law. It is for all who are Abraham's descendants because they have faith, just as he did. Abraham is the ancestor of us all. ¹⁷ The Scriptures say that Abraham would become the ancestor of many nations. This promise was made to Abraham because he had faith in God, who raises the dead to life and creates new things.

¹⁸ God promised Abraham a lot of descendants. And when it all seemed hopeless, Abraham still had faith in God and became the ancestor of many nations. ¹⁹ Abraham's faith never became weak, not even when he was nearly a hundred years old. He knew that he was almost dead and that his wife Sarah could not have children. ²⁰ But Abraham never doubted or questioned God's promise. His faith made him strong, and he gave all the credit to God.

²¹ Abraham was certain that God could do what he had promised. ²² So God accepted him, ²³ just as we read in the Scriptures. But these words were not written only for Abraham. ²⁴ They were written for us, since we will also be accepted because of our faith in God, who raised our Lord Jesus to life. ²⁵ God gave Jesus to die for our sins, and he raised him to life, so that we would be made acceptable to God.

See also: 4.13: Gen 17.4–6; 22.17,18; Gal 3.29.
4.14: Gal 3.18. **4.16:** Gal 3.7. **4.17:** Gen 17.5.
4.18: Gen 15.5. **4.19:** Gen 17.17. **4.25:** Isa 53.4,5.

A new life for God's people

CHAPTER 5

What it means to be acceptable to God

¹ By faith we have been made acceptable to God. And now, because of our Lord Jesus Christ, we live at peace* with God. ² Christ has also introduced us* to God's undeserved kindness on which we take our stand. So we are happy, as we look forward to sharing in the glory of God. ³ But that's not all! We gladly suffer,* because we know that suffering helps us to endure. ⁴ And endurance builds character, which gives us a hope ⁵ that will never disappoint us. All this happens because God has given us the Holy Spirit, who fills our hearts with his love.

⁶ Christ died for us at a time when we were helpless and weak. ⁷ No one is really willing to die for an honest person, though someone might be willing to die for a truly good person. ⁸ But God showed how much he loved us by having Christ die for us, even though we were sinful.

⁹ But there is more! Now that God has accepted us because Christ sacrificed his life's blood, we will also be kept safe from God's anger. ¹⁰ Even when we were God's enemies, he made peace with us, because his Son died for us. Yet something even greater than friendship is ours. Now that we are at peace with God, we will be saved by his Son's life. ¹¹ And in addition to everything else, we are happy because God sent our Lord Jesus Christ to make peace with us.

Adam and Christ

¹² Adam sinned, and that sin brought death into the world. Now everyone has sinned, and so everyone must die. ¹³ Sin was in the world before the Law came. But no record of sin was kept, because there was no Law. ¹⁴ Yet death still had power over all who lived from the time of Adam to the time of Moses. This happened, though not everyone disobeyed a direct command from God, as Adam did.

In some ways Adam is like Christ who came later. ¹⁵ But the gift that God was kind enough to give was very different from Adam's sin. That one sin brought death to many others. Yet in an even greater way, Jesus Christ alone brought God's gift of kindness to many people.

See also: 5.12: Gen 3.6.

16 There is a lot of difference between Adam's sin and God's gift. That one sin led to punishment. But God's gift made it possible for us to be acceptable to him, even though we have sinned many times. 17 Death ruled like a king because Adam had sinned. But that cannot compare with what Jesus Christ has done. God has been so kind to us, and he has accepted us because of Jesus. And so we will live and rule like kings.

18 Everyone was going to be punished because Adam sinned. But because of the good thing that Christ has done, God accepts us and gives us the gift of life. 19 Adam disobeyed God and caused many others to be sinners. But Jesus obeyed him and will make many people acceptable to God.

20 The Law came, so that the full power of sin could be seen. Yet where sin was powerful, God's kindness was even more powerful. 21 Sin ruled by means of death. But God's kindness now rules, and God has accepted us because of Jesus Christ our Lord. This means that we will have eternal life.

CHAPTER 6

Dead to sin but alive because of Christ

1 What should we say? Should we keep on sinning, so that God's wonderful kindness will show up even better? 2 No, we should not! If we are dead to sin, how can we go on sinning? 3 Don't you know that all who share in Christ Jesus by being baptized also share in his death? 4 When we were baptized, we died and were buried with Christ. We were baptized, so that we would live a new life, as Christ was raised to life by the glory of God the Father.

5 If we shared in Jesus' death by being baptized, we will be raised to life with him. 6 We know that the persons we used to be were nailed to the cross with Jesus. This was done, so that our sinful bodies would no longer be the slaves of sin. 7 We know that sin doesn't have power over dead people.

8 As we died with Christ, we believe we will also live with him. 9 We know that death no longer has any power over Christ. He died and was raised to life, never again to die. 10 When Christ died, he died for sin once and for all. But now he is alive, and he lives only for God. 11 In the same way, you must think of yourselves as dead to the power of sin. But Christ Jesus has given life to you, and you live for God.

12 Don't let sin rule your body. After all, your body is bound to die, so don't obey its desires 13 or let any part of it become a slave of evil. Give yourselves to God, as people who have been raised from death to life. Make every part of your body a slave that pleases God. 14 Don't let sin keep ruling your lives. You are ruled by God's kindness and not by the Law.

Slaves who do what pleases God

15 What does all this mean? Does it mean we are free to sin, because we are ruled by God's wonderful kindness and not by the Law? Certainly not! 16 Don't you know that you are slaves of anyone you obey? You can be slaves of sin and die, or you can be obedient slaves of God and be acceptable to him. 17 You used to be slaves of sin. But I thank God that with all your heart you obeyed the teaching you received from me. 18 Now you are set free from sin and are slaves who please God.

19 I am using these everyday examples, because in some ways you are still weak. You used to let the different parts of your body be slaves of your evil thoughts. But now you must make every part of your body serve God, so that you will belong completely to him.

20 When you were slaves of sin, you didn't have to please God. 21 But what good did you receive from the things you did? All you have to show for them is your shame, and they lead to death. 22 Now you have been set free from sin, and you are God's slaves. This will make you holy and will lead you to eternal life. 23 The reward for sin is death. But God's gift is eternal life given by Jesus Christ our Lord.

CHAPTER 7

An example from marriage

1 My friends, you understand enough about law to know that laws only have power over people who are alive. 2 For example, the Law says that a man's wife must remain his wife as long as he lives. But once her husband is dead, she is free 3 to marry someone else. However, if she goes off with another man while her husband is still alive, she is said to be unfaithful.

4 That is how it is with you, my friends. You are now part of the body of Christ and are dead to the power of the Law. You are free to belong to Christ, who was raised to life so that we could serve God. 5 When we thought

See also: 6.4: Col 2.12.

New Testament: letters   **Romans 8**

only of ourselves, the Law made us have sinful desires. It made every part of our bodies into slaves who are doomed to die. 6 But the Law no longer rules over us. We are like dead people, and it cannot have any power over us. Now we can serve God in a new way by obeying his Spirit, and not in the old way by obeying the written Law.

The battle with sin

7 Does this mean that the Law is sinful? Certainly not! But if it had not been for the Law, I would not have known what sin is really like. For example, I would not have known what it means to want something that belongs to someone else, unless the Law had told me not to do that. 8 It was sin that used this command as a way of making me have all kinds of desires. But without the Law, sin is dead.

9 Before I knew about the Law, I was alive. But as soon as I heard that command, sin came to life, 10 and I died. The very command that was supposed to bring life to me, instead brought death. 11 Sin used this command to trick me, and because of it I died. 12 Still, the Law and its commands are holy and correct and good.

13 Am I saying that something good caused my death? Certainly not! It was sin that killed me by using something good. Now we can see how terrible and evil sin really is. 14 We know that the Law is spiritual. But I am merely a human, and I have been sold as a slave to sin. 15 In fact, I don't understand why I act the way I do. I don't do what I know is right. I do the things I hate. 16 Although I don't do what I know is right, I agree that the Law is good. 17 So I am not the one doing these evil things. The sin that lives in me is what does them.

18 I know that my selfish desires won't let me do anything that is good. Even when I want to do right, I cannot. 19 Instead of doing what I know is right, I do wrong. 20 And so, if I don't do what I know is right, I am no longer the one doing these evil things. The sin that lives in me is what does them.

21 The Law has shown me that something in me keeps me from doing what I know is right. 22 With my whole heart I agree with the Law of God. 23 But in every part of me I discover something fighting against my mind, and it makes me a prisoner of sin that

controls everything I do. 24 What a miserable person I am. Who will rescue me from this body that is doomed to die? 25 Thank God! Jesus Christ will rescue me.

So with my mind I serve the Law of God, although my selfish desires make me serve the law of sin.

CHAPTER 8

Living by the power of God's Spirit

1 If you belong to Christ Jesus, you won't be punished. 2 The Holy Spirit will give you life that comes from Christ Jesus and will set you free from sin and death. 3 The Law of Moses cannot do this, because our selfish desires make the Law weak. But God set you free when he sent his own Son to be like us sinners and to be a sacrifice for our sin. God used Christ's body to condemn sin. 4 He did this, so that we would do what the Law commands by obeying the Spirit instead of our own desires.

5 People who are ruled by their desires think only of themselves. Everyone who is ruled by the Holy Spirit thinks about spiritual things. 6 If our minds are ruled by our desires, we will die. But if our minds are ruled by the Spirit, we will have life and peace. 7 Our desires fight against God, because they do not and cannot obey God's laws. 8 If we follow our desires, we cannot please God.

9 You are no longer ruled by your desires, but by God's Spirit, who lives in you. People who don't have the Spirit of Christ in them don't belong to him. 10 But Christ lives in you. So you are alive because God has accepted you, even though your bodies must die because of your sins. 11 Yet God raised Jesus to life! God's Spirit now lives in you, and he will raise you to life by his Spirit.

12 My dear friends, we must not live to satisfy our desires. 13 If you do, you will die. But you will live, if by the help of God's Spirit you say "No" to your desires. 14 Only those people who are led by God's Spirit are his children. 15 God's Spirit doesn't make us slaves who are afraid of him. Instead, we become his children and call him our Father.* 16 God's Spirit makes us sure that we are his children. 17 His Spirit lets us know that together with Christ we will be given what

---

*8.15 our Father: The Greek text uses the Aramaic word "Abba" (meaning "father"), which shows the close relation between the children and their father.

See also: 7.7: Exod 20.17; Deut 5.21.   7.11: Gen 3.13.
7.15: Gal 5.17.

See also: 8.11: 1 Cor 3.16.   8.15-17: Gal 4.5-7.
8.15: Mark 14.36; Gal 4.6.

God has promised. We will also share in the glory of Christ, because we have suffered with him.

A wonderful future for God's people

18 I am sure that what we are suffering now cannot compare with the glory that will be shown to us. 19 In fact, all creation is eagerly waiting for God to show who his children are. 20 Meanwhile, creation is confused, but not because it wants to be confused. God made it this way in the hope 21 that creation would be set free from decay and would share in the glorious freedom of his children. 22 We know that all creation is still groaning and is in pain, like a woman about to give birth.

23 The Spirit makes us sure about what we will be in the future. But now we groan silently, while we wait for God to show that we are his children.* This means that our bodies will also be set free. 24 And this hope is what saves us. But if we already have what we hope for, there is no need to keep on hoping. 25 However, we hope for something we have not yet seen, and we patiently wait for it.

26 In certain ways we are weak, but the Spirit is here to help us. For example, when we don't know what to pray for, the Spirit prays for us in ways that cannot be put into words. 27 All our thoughts are known to God. He can understand what is in the mind of the Spirit, as the Spirit prays for God's people. 28 We know that God is always at work for the good of everyone who loves him.* They are the ones God has chosen for his purpose, 29 and he has always known who his chosen ones would be. He had decided to let them become like his own Son, so that his Son would be the first of many children. 30 God then accepted the people he had already decided to choose, and he has shared his glory with them.

God's love

31 What can we say about all this? If God is on our side, can anyone be against us? 32 God did not keep back his own Son, but he gave him for us. If God did this, won't he freely give us everything else? 33 If God says his chosen ones are acceptable to him, can anyone bring charges against them? 34 Or can anyone condemn them? No indeed! Christ died and was raised to life, and now he is at God's right side,* speaking to him for us.

35 Can anything separate us from the love of Christ? Can trouble, suffering, and hard times, or hunger and nakedness, or danger and death? 36 It is exactly as the Scriptures say,

> "For you we face death
>   all day long.
> We are like sheep
>   on their way
>   to be butchered."

37 In everything we have won more than a victory because of Christ who loves us. 38 I am sure that nothing can separate us from God's love — not life or death, not angels or spirits, not the present or the future, 39 and not powers above or powers below. Nothing in all creation can separate us from God's love for us in Christ Jesus our Lord!

What about the people of Israel?

CHAPTER 9

God's choice of Israel

1 I am a follower of Christ, and the Holy Spirit is a witness to my conscience. So I tell the truth and I am not lying when I say 2 my heart is broken and I am in great sorrow. 3 I would gladly be placed under God's curse and be separated from Christ for the good of my own people. 4 They are the descendants of Israel, and they are also God's chosen people. God showed them his glory. He made agreements with them and gave them his Law. The temple is theirs and so are the promises that God made to them. 5 They have those famous ancestors, who were also the ancestors of Jesus Christ. I pray that God, who rules over all, will be praised for ever! Amen.

6 It cannot be said that God broke his promise. After all, not all the people of Israel are the true people of God. 7-8 In fact, when God made the promise to Abraham, he meant only Abraham's descendants by his son Isaac. God was talking only about Isaac when he promised 9 Sarah, "At this time next year I will return, and you will already have a son."

---

*8.34 right side: The place of power and honour.

See also: 8.20: Gen 3.17–19. 8.23: 2 Cor 5.2–4.

See also: 8.36: Psa 44.22. 9.4: Exod 4.22. 9.7: Gen 21.12. 9.9: Gen 18.10.

¹⁰ Don't forget what happened to the twin sons of Isaac and Rebekah. ¹¹⁻¹² Even before they were born or had done anything good or bad, the Lord told Rebekah that her elder son would serve the younger one. The Lord said this to show that he makes his own choices and that it wasn't because of anything either of them had done. ¹³ That's why the Scriptures say that the Lord liked Jacob more than Esau.

¹⁴ Are we saying that God is unfair? Certainly not! ¹⁵ The Lord told Moses that he has pity and mercy on anyone he wants to. ¹⁶ Everything then depends on God's mercy and not on what people want or do. ¹⁷ In the Scriptures the Lord says to Pharaoh* of Egypt, "I let you become king, so that I could show you my power and be praised by all people on earth." ¹⁸ Everything depends on what God decides to do, and he can either have pity on people or make them stubborn.

God's anger and mercy

¹⁹ Someone may ask, "How can God blame us, if he makes us behave in the way he wants us to?" ²⁰ But, my friend, I ask, "Who do you think you are to question God? Does the clay have the right to ask the potter why he shaped it the way he did? ²¹ Doesn't a potter have the right to make a fancy bowl and a plain bowl out of the same lump of clay?"

²² God wanted to show his anger and reveal his power against everyone who deserved to be destroyed. But instead, he patiently put up with them. ²³ He did this by showing how glorious he is when he has pity on the people he has chosen to share in his glory. ²⁴ Whether Jews or Gentiles, we are those chosen ones, ²⁵ just as the Lord says in the book of Hosea,

> "Although they are not
> my people,
>   I will make them my people.
> I will treat with love
>   those nations
>   that have never been loved.

²⁶ "Once they were told,
>   'You are not my people.'
> But in that very place
>   they will be called
>   children of the living God."

²⁷ And this is what the prophet Isaiah said about the people of Israel,

> "The people of Israel
>   are as many
> as the grains of sand
>   along the beach.
> But only a few who are left
>   will be saved.
> ²⁸ The Lord will be quick
>   and sure to do on earth
> what he has warned
>   he will do."

²⁹ Isaiah also said,

> "If the Lord All-Powerful
>   had not spared some
>   of our descendants,
> we would have been destroyed
> like the cities of Sodom
>   and Gomorrah."*

Israel and the good news

³⁰ What does all this mean? It means that the Gentiles were not trying to be acceptable to God, but they found that he would accept them if they had faith. ³¹⁻³² It also means that the people of Israel were not acceptable to God. And why not? It was because they were trying' to be acceptable by obeying the Law instead of by having faith in God. The people of Israel fell over the stone that makes people stumble, ³³ just as God says in the Scriptures,

> "Look! I am placing in Zion
>   a stone to make people
>   stumble and fall.
> But those who have faith
>   in that one will never
>   be disappointed."

CHAPTER 10

¹ Dear friends, my greatest wish and my prayer to God is for the people of Israel to be saved. ² I know they love God, but they don't understand ³ what makes people acceptable to him. So they refuse to trust God, and they try to be acceptable by obeying the Law. ⁴ But Christ makes the Law no longer necessary' for those who become acceptable to God by faith.

---

*9.17 Pharaoh: A Hebrew word sometimes used for the title of the king of Egypt.
See also: 9.12: Gen 25.23. 9.13: Mal 1.2,3.
9.15: Exod 33.19. 9.17: Exod 9.16 (LXX). 9.20: Isa 29.16;
45.9. 9.25: Hos 2.23. 9.26: Hos 1.10.

*9.29 Sodom and Gomorrah: During the time of Abraham the Lord destroyed these two cities because their people were so sinful.
See also: 9.27,28: Isa 10.22,23 (LXX). 9.29: Isa 1.9 (LXX).
9.33: Isa 28.16 (LXX).

Anyone can be saved

⁵ Moses said that a person could become acceptable to God by obeying the Law. He did this when he wrote, "If you want to live, you must do all that the Law commands."

⁶ But people whose faith makes them acceptable to God will never ask, "Who will go up to heaven to bring Christ down?" ⁷ Neither will they ask, "Who will go down into the world of the dead to raise him to life?"

⁸ All who are acceptable because of their faith simply say, "The message is as near as your mouth or your heart." And this is the same message we preach about faith. ⁹ So you will be saved, if you honestly say, "Jesus is Lord," and if you believe with all your heart that God raised him from death. ¹⁰ God will accept you and save you, if you truly believe this and tell it to others.

¹¹ The Scriptures say that no one who has faith will be disappointed, ¹² no matter if that person is a Jew or a Gentile. There is only one Lord, and he is generous to everyone who asks for his help. ¹³ All who call out to the Lord will be saved.

¹⁴ How can people have faith in the Lord and ask him to save them, if they have never heard about him? And how can they hear, unless someone tells them? ¹⁵ And how can anyone tell them without being sent by the Lord? The Scriptures say it is a beautiful sight to see even the feet of someone coming to preach the good news. ¹⁶ Yet not everyone has believed the message. For example, the prophet Isaiah asked, "Lord, has anyone believed what we said?"

¹⁷ No one can have faith in the Lord without hearing the message about Christ. ¹⁸ But am I saying that the people of Israel did not hear? No, I am not! The Scriptures say,

"The message was told
    everywhere on earth.
It was announced
    all over the world."

¹⁹ Did the people of Israel understand or not? Moses answered this question when he told that the Lord had said,

"I will make Israel jealous
    of people

who are a nation
    of nobodies.
I will make them angry
    with people
who don't understand
    a thing."

²⁰ Isaiah was fearless enough to tell that the Lord had said,

"I was found by people
    who were not looking
    for me.
I appeared to the ones
    who were not asking
    about me."

²¹ And Isaiah said about the people of Israel,

"All day long the Lord
    has reached out
to people who are stubborn
    and refuse to obey."

CHAPTER 11

God has not rejected his people

¹ Am I saying that God has turned his back on his people? Certainly not! I am one of the people of Israel, and I myself am a descendant of Abraham from the tribe of Benjamin. ² God did not turn his back on his chosen people. Don't you remember reading in the Scriptures how Elijah complained to God about the people of Israel? ³ He said, "Lord, they killed your prophets and destroyed your altars. I am the only one left, and now they want to kill me."

⁴ But the Lord told Elijah, "I still have seven thousand followers who have not worshipped Baal." ⁵ It is the same way now. God was kind to the people of Israel, and so a few of them are still his followers. ⁶ This happened because of God's undeserved kindness and not because of anything they have done. It could not have happened except for God's kindness.

⁷ This means that only a chosen few of the people of Israel found what all of them were searching for. And the rest of them were stubborn, ⁸ just as the Scriptures say,

"God made them so stupid
    that their eyes are blind,
and their ears
    are still deaf."

See also: 10.5: Lev 18.5.   10.6-8: Deut 30.12-14.
10.11: Isa 28.16 (LXX).   10.13: Joel 2.32.   10.15: Isa 52.7.
10.16: Isa 53.1 (LXX).   10.18: Psa 19.4 (LXX).
10.19: Deut 32.21.

See also: 10.20: Isa 65.1 (LXX).   10.21: Isa 65.2 (LXX).
11.1: Phil 3.5.   11.3: 1 King 19.10,14.   11.4: 1 King 19.18.
11.8: Deut 29.4; Isa 29.10.

[9] Then David said,

> "Turn their meals
>   into bait for a trap,
> so that they will stumble
> and be given
>   what they deserve.
> [10] Blindfold their eyes!
>   Don't let them see.
> Bend their backs
>   beneath a burden
>   that will never be lifted."

Gentiles will be saved

[11] Do I mean that the people of Israel fell, never to get up again? Certainly not! Their failure made it possible for the Gentiles to be saved, and this will make the people of Israel jealous. [12] But if the rest of the world's people were helped so much by Israel's sin and loss, they will be helped even more by their full return.

[13] I am now speaking to you Gentiles, and as long as I am an apostle to you, I will take pride in my work. [14] I hope in this way to make some of my own people jealous enough to be saved. [15] When Israel rejected God,* the rest of the people in the world were able to turn to him. So when God makes friends with Israel, it will be like bringing the dead back to life. [16] If part of a batch of dough is made holy by being offered to God, then all the dough is holy. If the roots of a tree are holy, the rest of the tree is holy too.

[17] You Gentiles are like branches of a wild olive tree that were made to be part of a cultivated olive tree. You have taken the place of some branches that were cut away from it. And because of this, you enjoy the blessings that come from being part of that cultivated tree. [18] But don't think you are better than the branches that were cut away. Just remember that you are not supporting the roots of that tree. Its roots are supporting you.

[19] Perhaps you think those branches were cut away, so that you could be put in their place. [20] That's true enough. But they were cut away because they did not have faith, and you are where you are because you do have faith. So don't be proud, but be afraid. [21] If God cut away those natural branches, couldn't he do the same to you?

[22] Now you see both how kind and how hard God can be. He was hard on those who fell, but he was kind to you. And he will keep on being kind to you, if you keep on trusting in his kindness. Otherwise, you will be cut away too.

[23] If those other branches will start having faith, they will be made a part of that tree again. God has the power to put them back. [24] After all, it wasn't natural for branches to be cut from a wild olive tree and to be made part of a cultivated olive tree. So it is much more likely that God will join the natural branches back to the cultivated olive tree.

The people of Israel will be brought back

[25] My friends, I don't want you Gentiles to be too proud of yourselves. So I will explain the mystery of what has happened to the people of Israel. Some of them have become stubborn, and they will stay like that until the complete number of you Gentiles has come in. [26] In this way all Israel will be saved, as the Scriptures say,

> "From Zion someone will come
>   to rescue us.
> Then Jacob's descendants
>   will stop being evil.
> [27] This is what the Lord
>   has promised to do
>   when he forgives their sins."

[28] The people of Israel are treated as God's enemies, so that the good news can come to you Gentiles. But they are still the chosen ones, and God loves them because of their famous ancestors. [29] God doesn't take back the gifts he has given or forget about the people he has chosen.

[30] At one time you Gentiles rejected God. But now Israel has rejected God, and you have been shown mercy. [31] And because of the mercy shown to you, they will also be shown mercy. [32] All people have disobeyed God, and that's why he treats them as prisoners. But he does this, so that he can have mercy on all of them.

[33] Who can measure the wealth and wisdom and knowledge of God? Who can understand his decisions or explain what he does?

> [34] "Has anyone known
>   the thoughts of the Lord
>   or given him advice?
> [35] Has anyone loaned
>   something to the Lord
>   that must be repaid?"

See also: 11.9,10: Psa 69.22,23 (LXX).

See also: 11.26: Isa 59.20,21 (LXX). 11.27: Isa 27.9 (LXX). 11.33: Isa 55.8. 11.34: Isa 40.13 (LXX). 11.35: Job 41.11.

36 Everything comes from the Lord. All things were made because of him and will return to him. Praise the Lord for ever! Amen.

How to live the new life of love

CHAPTER 12

Christ brings new life

1 Dear friends, God is good. So I beg you to offer your bodies to him as a living sacrifice, pure and pleasing. That's the most sensible way to serve God. 2 Don't be like the people of this world, but let God change the way you think. Then you will know how to do everything that is good and pleasing to him.

3 I realize how kind God has been to me, and so I tell each of you not to think you are better than you really are. Use good sense and measure yourself by the amount of faith that God has given you. 4 A body is made up of many parts, and each of them has its own use. 5 That's how it is with us. There are many of us, but we are each part of the body of Christ, as well as part of one another.

6 God has also given each of us different gifts to use. If we can prophesy, we should do it according to the amount of faith we have. 7 If we can serve others, we should serve. If we can teach, we should teach. 8 If we can encourage others, we should encourage them. If we can give, we should be generous. If we are leaders, we should do our best. If we are good to others, we should do it cheerfully.

Rules for Christian living

9 Be sincere in your love for others. Hate everything that is evil and hold tight to everything that is good. 10 Love each other as brothers and sisters and honour others more than you do yourself. 11 Never give up. Eagerly follow the Holy Spirit and serve the Lord. 12 Let your hope make you glad. Be patient in time of trouble and never stop praying. 13 Take care of God's needy people and welcome strangers into your home.

14 Ask God to bless everyone who ill-treats you. Ask him to bless them and not to curse them. 15 When others are happy, be happy with them, and when they are sad, be sad.

16 Be friendly with everyone. Don't be proud and feel that you are cleverer than others. Make friends with ordinary people.* 17 Don't ill-treat someone who has ill-treated you. But try to earn the respect of others, 18 and do your best to live at peace with everyone.

19 Dear friends, don't try to get even. Let God take revenge. In the Scriptures the Lord says,

"I am the one to take revenge
and pay them back."

20 The Scriptures also say,

"If your enemies are hungry,
give them something to eat.
And if they are thirsty,
give them something
to drink.
This will be the same
as piling burning coals
on their heads."

21 Don't let evil defeat you, but defeat evil with good.

CHAPTER 13

Obey rulers

1 Obey the rulers who have authority over you. Only God can give authority to anyone, and he puts these rulers in their places of power. 2 People who oppose the authorities are opposing what God has done, and they will be punished. 3 Rulers are a threat to evil people, not to good people. There is no need to be afraid of the authorities. Just do right, and they will praise you for it. 4 After all, they are God's servants, and it is their duty to help you.

If you do something wrong, you ought to be afraid, because these rulers have the right to punish you. They are God's servants who punish criminals to show how angry God is. 5 But you should obey the rulers because you know it is the right thing to do, and not just because of God's anger.

6 You must also pay your taxes. The authorities are God's servants, and it is their duty to take care of these matters. 7 Pay all that you owe, whether it is taxes and fees or respect and honour.

See also: 11.36: 1 Cor 8.6. 12.4,5: 1 Cor 12.12.
12.6–8: 1 Cor 12.4–11. 12.14: Matt 5.44; Luke 6.28.
See also: 12.16: Prov 3.7. 12.19: Deut 32.35.
12.20: Prov 25.21,22 (LXX). 13.6,7: Matt 22.21; Mark 12.17;
Luke 20.25.

Love

[8] Let love be your only debt! If you love others, you have done all that the Law demands. [9] In the Law there are many commands, such as, "Be faithful in marriage. Do not murder. Do not steal. Do not want what belongs to others." But all these are summed up in the command that says, "Love others as much as you love yourself." [10] No one who loves others will harm them. So love is all that the Law demands.

The day when Christ returns

[11] You know what sort of times we live in, and so you should live properly. It is time to wake up. You know that the day when we will be saved is nearer now than when we first put our faith in the Lord. [12] Night is almost over, and day will soon appear. We must stop behaving as people do in the dark and be ready to live in the light. [13] So behave properly, as people do in the day. Don't go to wild parties or get drunk or be vulgar or indecent. Don't quarrel or be jealous. [14] Let the Lord Jesus Christ be as near to you as the clothes you wear. Then you won't try to satisfy your selfish desires.

CHAPTER 14

Don't criticize others

[1] Welcome all the Lord's followers, even those whose faith is weak. Don't criticize them for having beliefs that are different from yours. [2] Some think it is all right to eat anything, while those whose faith is weak will eat only vegetables. [3] But you should not criticize others for eating or for not eating. After all, God welcomes everyone. [4] What right do you have to criticize someone else's servants? Only their Lord can decide if they are doing right, and the Lord will make sure that they do right.

[5] Some of the Lord's followers think one day is more important than another. Others think all days are the same. But each of you should make up your own mind. [6] Any followers who count one day more important than another day do it to honour their Lord. And any followers who eat meat give thanks to God, just like the ones who don't eat meat.

[7] Whether we live or die, it must be for God, rather than for ourselves. [8] Whether we live or die, it must be for the Lord. Alive or dead, we still belong to the Lord. [9] This is because Christ died and rose to life, so that he would be the Lord of the dead and of the living. [10] Why do you criticize other followers of the Lord? Why do you look down on them? The day is coming when God will judge all of us. [11] In the Scriptures God says,

> "I swear by my very life
> that everyone will kneel down
> and praise my name!"

[12] And so, each of us must give an account to God for what we do.

Don't cause problems for others

[13] We must stop judging others. We must also make up our minds not to upset anyone's faith. [14] The Lord Jesus has made it clear to me that God considers all foods fit to eat. But if you think some foods are unfit to eat, then for you they are not fit.

[15] If you are hurting others by the foods you eat, you are not guided by love. Don't let your appetite destroy someone Christ died for. [16] Don't let your eating to eat bring shame to Christ. [17] God's kingdom isn't about eating and drinking. It is about pleasing God, about living in peace, and about true happiness. All this comes from the Holy Spirit. [18] If you serve Christ in this way, you will please God and be respected by people. [19] We should try* to live at peace and help each other have a strong faith.

[20] Don't let your appetite destroy what God has done. All foods are fit to eat, but it is wrong to cause problems for others by what you eat. [21] It is best not to eat meat or drink wine or do anything else that causes problems for other followers of the Lord. [22] What you believe about these things should be kept between you and God. You are fortunate, if your actions don't make you have doubts. [23] But if you do have doubts about what you eat, you are going against your beliefs. And you know that is wrong, because anything you do against your beliefs is sin.

See also: **13.9:** a Exod 20.14; Deut 5.18; b Exod 20.13; Deut 5.17; c Exod 20.15; Deut 5.19; d Exod 20.17; Deut 5.21; e Lev 19.18. **14.1–6:** Col 2.16.

See also: **14.10:** 2 Cor 5.10. **14.11:** Isa 45.23 (LXX).

CHAPTER 15

Please others and not yourself

¹ If our faith is strong, we should be patient with the Lord's followers whose faith is weak. We should try to please them instead of ourselves. ² We should think of their good and try to help them by doing what pleases them. ³ Even Christ did not try to please himself. But as the Scriptures say, "The people who insulted you also insulted me." ⁴ And the Scriptures were written to teach and encourage us by giving us hope. ⁵ God is the one who makes us patient and cheerful. I pray that he will help you live at peace with each other, as you follow Christ. ⁶ Then all of you together will praise God, the Father of our Lord Jesus Christ.

The good news is for Jews and Gentiles

⁷ Honour God by accepting each other, as Christ has accepted you. ⁸ I tell you that Christ came as a servant of the Jews to show that God has kept the promises he made to their famous ancestors. Christ also came, ⁹ so that the Gentiles would praise God for being kind to them. It is just as the Scriptures say,

> "I will tell the nations
>   about you,
> and I will sing praises
>   to your name."

¹⁰ The Scriptures also say to the Gentiles, "Come and celebrate with God's people." ¹¹ Again the Scriptures say,

> "Praise the Lord,
>   all you Gentiles.
> All you nations, come
>   and worship him."

¹² Isaiah says,

> "Someone from David's family
>   will come to power.
> He will rule the nations,
>   and they will put their hope
>   in him."

¹³ I pray that God, who gives hope, will bless you with complete happiness and peace because of your faith. And may the power of the Holy Spirit fill you with hope.

Paul's plans and personal greetings

Paul's work as a missionary

¹⁴ My friends, I am sure that you are very good and that you have all the knowledge you need to teach each other. ¹⁵ But I have spoken to you plainly and have tried to remind you of some things. God was so kind to me! ¹⁶ He chose me to be a servant of Christ Jesus for the Gentiles and to do the work of a priest in the service of his good news. God did this so that the Holy Spirit could make the Gentiles into a holy offering, pleasing to him.

¹⁷ Because of Christ Jesus, I can take pride in my service for God. ¹⁸ In fact, all I will talk about is how Christ let me speak and work, so that the Gentiles would obey him. ¹⁹ Indeed, I will tell how Christ performed miracles and wonders by the power of the Holy Spirit. I have preached the good news about him all the way from Jerusalem to Illyricum. ²⁰ But I have always tried to preach where people have never heard about Christ. I am like a builder who doesn't build on anyone else's foundation. ²¹ It is just as the Scriptures say,

> "All who haven't been told
>   about him
>   will see him,
> and those who haven't heard
>   about him
>   will understand."

Paul's plan to visit Rome

²² My work has always kept me from coming to see you. ²³ Now there is nothing left for me to do in this part of the world, and for years I have wanted to visit you. ²⁴ So I plan to stop off on my way to Spain. Then after a short, but refreshing, stay with you, I hope you will quickly send me on.

²⁵⁻²⁶ I am now on my way to Jerusalem to deliver the money that the Lord's followers in Macedonia and Achaia collected for God's needy people. ²⁷ This is something they really wanted to do. But sharing their money with the Jews was also like paying back a debt, because the Jews had already shared their spiritual blessings with the Gentiles. ²⁸ After I have safely delivered this money, I will visit

See also: 15.3: Psa 69.9. 15.9: 2 Sam 22.50; Psa 18.49.
15.10: Deut 32.43. 15.11: Psa 117.1.
15.12: Isa 11.10 (LXX).

See also: 15.21: Isa 52.15 (LXX). 15.22: Rom 1.13.
15.25,26: 1 Cor 16.1–4. 15.27: 1 Cor 9.11.

you and then go on to Spain. ²⁹ And when I do arrive in Rome, I know it will be with the full blessings of Christ.

³⁰ My friends, by the power of the Lord Jesus Christ and by the love that comes from the Holy Spirit, I beg you to pray sincerely with me and for me. ³¹ Pray that God will protect me from the unbelievers in Judea, and that his people in Jerusalem will be pleased with what I am doing. ³² Ask God to let me come to you and have a pleasant and refreshing visit. ³³ I pray that God, who gives peace, will be with all of you. Amen.

CHAPTER 16

Personal greetings

¹ I have good things to say about Phoebe, who is a leader in the church at Cenchreae. ² Welcome her in a way that is proper for someone who has faith in the Lord and is one of God's own people. Help her in any way you can. After all, she has proved to be a respected leader for many others, including me.

³ Give my greetings to Priscilla and Aquila. They have not only served Christ Jesus together with me, ⁴ but they have even risked their lives for me. I am grateful for them and so are all the Gentile churches. ⁵ Greet the church that meets in their home.

Greet my dear friend Epaenetus, who was the first person in Asia to have faith in Christ.

⁶ Greet Mary, who has worked so hard for you.

⁷ Greet my relatives⁹ Andronicus and Junias⁹, who were in jail with me. They are highly respected by the apostles and were followers of Christ before I was.

⁸ Greet Ampliatus, my dear friend whose faith is in the Lord.

⁹ Greet Urbanus, who serves Christ along with us.

Greet my dear friend Stachys.

¹⁰ Greet Apelles, a faithful servant of Christ. Greet Aristobulus and his family.

¹¹ Greet Herodion, who is a relative⁹ of mine. Greet Narcissus and the others in his family, who have faith in the Lord.

¹² Greet Tryphaena and Tryphosa, who work hard for the Lord.

Greet my dear friend Persis. She also works hard for the Lord.

¹³ Greet Rufus, that special servant of the Lord, and greet his mother, who has been like a mother to me.

¹⁴ Greet Asyncritus, Phlegon, Hermes, Patrobas, and Hermas, as well as our friends who are with them.

¹⁵ Greet Philologus, Julia, Nereus and his sister, and Olympas, and all God's people who are with them.

¹⁶ Be sure to give each other a warm greeting.

All Christ's churches greet you.

¹⁷ My friends, I beg you to watch out for anyone who causes trouble and divides the church by refusing to do what all of you were taught. Stay away from them! ¹⁸ They want to serve themselves and not Christ the Lord. Their flattery and fancy talk fool people who don't know any better. ¹⁹ I am glad that everyone knows how well you obey the Lord. But still, I want you to understand what is good and not have anything to do with evil. ²⁰ Then God, who gives peace, will soon crush Satan under your feet. I pray that our Lord Jesus will be kind to you.

²¹ Timothy, who works with me, sends his greetings, and so do my relatives,⁹ Lucius, Jason, and Sosipater.

²² I, Tertius, also send my greetings. I am a follower of the Lord, and I wrote this letter.*

²³⁻²⁴ Gaius welcomes me and the whole church into his home, and he sends his greetings.

Erastus, the city treasurer, and our dear friend Quartus send their greetings too.⁹

Paul's closing prayer

²⁵ Praise God! He can make you strong by means of my good news, which is the message about⁹ Jesus Christ. For many ages this message was kept secret, ²⁶ but now at last it has been told. The eternal God commanded his prophets to write about the good news, so that all nations would obey and have faith. ²⁷ And now, because of Jesus Christ, we can praise the only wise God for ever! Amen.⁹

*16.22 I wrote this letter: Paul probably dictated this letter to Tertius.

See also: 16.21; Acts 16.1.

Additional notes

⁹1.4 the Holy Spirit: Or "his own spirit of holiness".
⁹1.4 proved that Jesus is the powerful Son of God: Or "proved in a powerful way that Jesus is the Son of God".

See also: 16.3: Acts 18.2. 16.13: Mark 15.21.

'1.5 Jesus was kind to me and chose me to be an apostle: Or "Jesus was kind to us and chose us to be his apostles".

'1.17 but only those who have faith: Or "and faith is all that matters."

'1.17 The people God accepts because of their faith will live: Or "The people God accepts will live because of their faith."

'3.9 better off: Or "worse off".

'5.1 we live at peace: Some manuscripts have "let us live at peace".

'5.2 introduced us: Some manuscripts add "by faith".

'5.3 We gladly suffer: Or "Let us gladly suffer".

'8.2 you: Some manuscripts have "me".

'8.23 to show that we are his children: These words are not in some manuscripts. The translation of the remainder of the verse would then read, "while we wait for God to set our bodies free."

'8.28 God is always at work for the good of everyone who loves him: Or "All things work for the good of everyone who loves God" or "God's Spirit always works for the good of everyone who loves God."

'9.5 Christ. I pray that God, who rules over all, will be praised for ever: Or "Christ, who rules over all. I pray that God will be praised for ever" or "Christ. And I pray that Christ, who is God and rules over all, will be praised for ever."

'9.31 because they were trying: Or "while they were trying" or "even though they were trying".

'10.4 But Christ makes the Law no longer necessary: Or "But Christ gives the full meaning to the Law".

'11.15 When Israel rejected God: Or "When Israel was rejected".

'12.16 Make friends with ordinary people: Or "Do ordinary jobs."

'14.19 We should try: Some manuscripts have "We try".

'16.7 relatives: Or "Jewish friends".

'16.7 Junias: Or "Junia". Some manuscripts have "Julia".

'16.11 relative(s): See the note at 16.7.

'16.21 relative(s): See the note at 16.7.

'16.23,24 send their greetings too: Some manuscripts add, "I pray that our Lord Jesus Christ will always be kind to you. Amen."

'16.25 about: Or "from".

'16.27 Amen: Some manuscripts have verses 25–27 after 14.23. Others have the verses here and after 14.23, and one manuscript has them after 15.33.

1 Corinthians

Paul's first letter to the church
in Corinth

A quick look at this letter

Although this letter is called the First Letter to the Corinthians, it is not really the first one that Paul wrote to this church. We know this because he mentions in this letter that he had written one before (5.9). The Christians in Corinth had also written to him (7.1), and part of 1 Corinthians contains Paul's answers to questions they had asked.

Corinth is a large city port in southern Greece. Paul began his work there in a Jewish meeting place, but he had to move next door to the home of a Gentile who had become a follower of Jesus (Acts 18.1–17). Most of the followers in Corinth were poor people (1 Corinthians 1.26–29), though some of them were wealthy (1 Corinthians 11.18–21), and one was even the city treasurer (Romans 16.23). While he was in Corinth, Paul worked

as a tent maker to earn a living (Acts 18.3; 1 Corinthians 4.12; 9.1–18).

Paul was especially concerned about the way the Corinthian Christians were always arguing and dividing themselves into groups (1.10–4.21) and about the way they treated one another (5.1–6.20). These are two of Paul's main concerns as he writes this letter. But he also wants to answer the questions they asked him about marriage (7.1–40) and food offered to idols (8.1–13). Paul encourages them to worship God the right way (10.1–14.40) and to be firm in their belief that God has given them victory over death (15.1–58).

Love, Paul tells them, is even more important than faith or hope. All the problems in the church could be solved, if all the members would love one another, as Christians should:

> Love is kind and patient,
>   never jealous, boastful,
>   proud, or rude.
> Love rejoices in the truth,
>   but not in evil.
> Love is always supportive,
>   loyal, hopeful,
>   and trusting.
> Love never fails!

(13.4,5a,6–8a)

Paul's greeting and prayer

CHAPTER 1

¹ *From Paul, chosen by God to be an apostle of Christ Jesus, and from Sosthenes, who is also a follower.*

² *To God's church in Corinth.* Christ Jesus chose you to be his very own people, and you worship in his name, as we and all others do who call him Lord.

³ My prayer is that God our Father and the Lord Jesus Christ will be kind to you and will bless you with peace!

⁴ I never stop thanking my God for being kind enough to give you Christ Jesus, ⁵ who helps you speak and understand so well. ⁶ Now you are certain that everything we told you about our Lord Christ Jesus is true. ⁷ You are not missing out on any blessings, as you wait for him to return. ⁸ And until the day Christ does return, he will keep you completely innocent. ⁹ God can be trusted, and he chose you to be partners with his Son, our Lord Jesus Christ.

A call for unity

Taking sides

¹⁰ My dear friends, as a follower of our Lord Jesus Christ, I beg you to get along with each other. Don't take sides. Always try to agree in what you think. ¹¹ Several people from Chloe's family* have already reported to me that you keep arguing with each other. ¹² They have said that some of you claim to follow me, while others claim to follow Apollos or Peter* or Christ.

¹³ Has Christ been divided up? Was I nailed to a cross for you? Were you baptized in my name? ¹⁴ I thank God* that I didn't baptize any of you except Crispus and Gaius. ¹⁵ Not one of you can say that you were baptized in my name. ¹⁶ I did baptize the family* of Stephanas, but I don't remember if I baptized anyone else. ¹⁷ Christ did not send me to baptize. He sent me to tell the good news

without using big words that would make the cross of Christ lose its power.

Christ is God's power and wisdom

¹⁸ The message about the cross doesn't make any sense to lost people. But for those of us who are being saved, it is God's power at work. ¹⁹ As God says in the Scriptures,

"I will destroy the wisdom
   of all who claim
      to be wise.
I will confuse those
   who think they know
      so much."

²⁰ What happened to those wise people? What happened to those experts in the Scriptures? What happened to the ones who think they have all the answers? Didn't God show that the wisdom of this world is foolish? ²¹ God was wise and decided not to let the people of this world use their wisdom to learn about him.

Instead, God chose to save only those who believe the foolish message we preach. ²² Jews ask for miracles, and Greeks want something that sounds wise. ²³ But we preach that Christ was nailed to a cross. Most Jews have problems with this, and most Gentiles think it is foolish. ²⁴ Our message is God's power and wisdom for the Jews and the Greeks that he has chosen. ²⁵ Even when God is foolish, he is wiser than everyone else, and even when God is weak, he is stronger than everyone else.

²⁶ My dear friends, remember what you were when God chose you. The people of this world didn't think that many of you were wise. Only a few of you were in places of power, and not many of you came from important families. ²⁷ But God chose the foolish things of this world to put the wise to shame. He chose the weak things of this world to put the powerful to shame. ²⁸ What the world thinks is worthless, useless, and nothing at all is what God has used to destroy what the world considers important. ²⁹ God did all this to keep anyone from boasting to him. ³⁰ You are God's children. He sent Christ Jesus to save us and to make us wise, acceptable, and holy. ³¹ So if you want to boast, do what the Scriptures say and boast about the Lord.

1.11 family: Family members and possibly slaves and others who may have lived in the house.
1.12 Peter: The Greek text has "Cephas," which is an Aramaic name meaning "rock." Peter is the Greek name with the same meaning.
1.16 family: See the note at 1.11.

See also: 1.2: Acts 18.1. 1.12: Acts 18.24. 1.14: a Acts 18.8; b Acts 19.29; Rom 16.23. 1.16: 1 Cor 16.15.

See also: 1.19: Isa 29.14 (LXX). 1.20: a Job 12.17; Isa 19.12; 33.18; b Isa 44.25. 1.31: Jer 9.24.

CHAPTER 2

Telling about Christ and the cross

¹ Friends, when I came and told you the mystery* that God had shared with us, I didn't use big words or try to sound wise. ² In fact, while I was with you, I made up my mind to speak only about Jesus Christ, who had been nailed to a cross.

³ At first, I was weak and trembling with fear. ⁴ When I talked with you or preached, I didn't try to prove anything by sounding wise. I simply let God's Spirit show his power. ⁵ That way you would have faith because of God's power and not because of human wisdom.

⁶ We do use wisdom when speaking to people who are mature in their faith. But it isn't the wisdom of this world or of its rulers, who will soon disappear. ⁷ We speak of God's hidden and mysterious wisdom that God decided to use for our glory long before the world began. ⁸ The rulers of this world didn't know anything about this wisdom. If they had known about it, they would not have nailed the glorious Lord to a cross. ⁹ But it is just as the Scriptures say,

"What God has planned
for people who love him
is more than eyes have seen
or ears have heard.
It has never even
entered our minds!"

¹⁰ God's Spirit has shown you everything. His Spirit finds out everything, even what is deep in the mind of God. ¹¹ You are the only one who knows what is in your own mind, and God's Spirit is the only one who knows what is in God's mind. ¹² But God has given us his Spirit. That's why we don't think the same way that the people of this world think. That's also why we can recognize the blessings that God has given us.

¹³ Every word we speak was taught to us by God's Spirit, not by human wisdom. And this same Spirit helps us teach spiritual things to spiritual people.* ¹⁴ That's why only someone who has God's Spirit can understand spiritual blessings. Anyone who doesn't have God's Spirit thinks these blessings are foolish. ¹⁵ People who are guided by the Spirit can make all kinds of judgments, but they cannot be judged by others. ¹⁶ The Scriptures ask,

"Has anyone ever known
the thoughts of the Lord
or given him advice?"

But we understand what Christ is thinking.*

CHAPTER 3

Working together for God

¹ My friends, you are acting like the people of this world. That's why I could not speak to you as spiritual people. You are like babies as far as your faith in Christ is concerned. ² So I had to treat you like babies and feed you milk. You could not take solid food, and you still cannot, ³ because you are not yet spiritual. You are jealous and argue with each other. This proves that you are not spiritual and that you are acting like the people of this world.

⁴ Some of you say that you follow me, and others claim to follow Apollos. Isn't that how ordinary people behave? ⁵ Apollos and I are merely servants who helped you to have faith. It was the Lord who made it all happen. ⁶ I planted the seeds, Apollos watered them, but God made them sprout and grow. ⁷ What matters isn't those who planted or watered, but God who made the plants grow. ⁸ The one who plants is just as important as the one who waters. And each one will be paid for what they do. ⁹ Apollos and I work together for God, and you are God's garden and God's building.

Only one foundation

¹⁰ God was kind and let me become an expert builder. I laid a foundation on which others have built. But we must each be careful how we build, ¹¹ because Christ is the only foundation. ¹²⁻¹³ Whatever we build on that foundation will be tested by fire on the day of judgment. Then everyone will find out if we have used gold, silver, and precious stones, or wood, hay, and straw. ¹⁴ We will be rewarded if our building is left standing. ¹⁵ But if it is destroyed by the fire, we will lose everything. Yet we ourselves will be saved, like someone escaping from flames.

¹⁶ All of you know that you are God's temple and that his Spirit lives in you. ¹⁷ Together you are God's holy temple, and God will destroy anyone who destroys his temple.

See also: 2.3: Acts 18.9. 2.9: Isa 64.4.
2.16: Isa 40.13 (LXX).

See also: 3.2: Heb 5.12,13. 3.4: 1 Cor 1.12.
3.6: a Acts 18.4–11; b Acts 18.24–28. 3.16: 1 Cor 6.19;
2 Cor 6.16.

18 Don't fool yourselves! If any of you think you are wise in the things of this world, you will have to become foolish before you can be truly wise. 19 This is because God considers the wisdom of this world to be foolish. It is just as the Scriptures say, "God catches the wise when they try to outsmart him." 20 The Scriptures also say, "The Lord knows that the plans made by wise people are useless." 21-22 So stop boasting about what anyone has done. Paul and Apollos and Peter* all belong to you. In fact, everything is yours, including the world, life, death, the present, and the future. Everything belongs to you, 23 and you belong to Christ, and Christ belongs to God.

CHAPTER 4

The work of the apostles

1 Think of us as servants of Christ who have been given the work of explaining God's mysterious ways. 2 And since our first duty is to be faithful to the one we work for, 3 it doesn't matter to me if I am judged by you or even by a court of law. In fact, I don't judge myself. 4 I don't know of anything against me, but that doesn't prove that I am right. The Lord is my judge. 5 So don't judge anyone until the Lord returns. He will show what is hidden in the dark and what is in everyone's heart. Then God will be the one who praises each of us.

6 Friends, I have used Apollos and myself as examples to teach you the meaning of the saying, "Follow the rules." I want you to stop saying that one of us is better than the other. 7 What is so special about you? What do you have that you were not given? And if it was given to you, how can you boast? 8 Are you already satisfied? Are you now rich? Have you become kings while you are still nobodies? I wish you were kings. Then we could have a share in your kingdom.

9 It seems to me that God has put us apostles in the worst possible place. We are like prisoners on their way to death. Angels and the people of this world just laugh at us. 10 Because of Christ we are thought of as fools, but Christ has made you wise. We are weak and hated, but you are powerful and respected. 11 Even today we go hungry and thirsty and don't have anything to wear except rags. We are ill-treated and don't have

a place to live. 12 We work hard with our own hands, and when people abuse us, we wish them well. When we suffer, we are patient. 13 When someone curses us, we answer with kind words. Until now we are thought of as nothing more than the trash and rubbish of this world.

14 I am not writing to embarrass you. I want to help you, just as parents help their own dear children. 15 Ten thousand people may teach you about Christ, but I am your only father. You became my children when I told you about Christ Jesus, 16 and I want you to be like me. 17 That's why I sent Timothy to you. I love him like a son, and he is a faithful servant of the Lord. Timothy will tell you what I do to follow Christ and how it agrees with what I always teach about Christ in every church.

18 Some of you think I am not coming for a visit, and so you are boasting. 19 But if the Lord lets me come, I will soon see these. Then I will find out if the ones who are doing all this boasting really have any power. 20 God's kingdom isn't just a lot of words. It is power. 21 What do you want me to do when I arrive? Do you want me to be hard on you or to be kind and gentle?

Problems in relationships

CHAPTER 5

Immoral followers

1 I have heard terrible things about some of you. In fact, you are behaving worse than the Gentiles. A man is even sleeping with his own stepmother.* 2 You are proud, when you ought to feel bad enough to chase away anyone who acts like that.

3-4 I am with you only in my thoughts. But in the name of our Lord Jesus I have already judged this man, as though I were with you in person. So when you meet together and the power of the Lord Jesus is with you, I will be there too. 5 You must then hand that man over to Satan. His body will be destroyed, but his spirit will be saved when the Lord Jesus returns.

6 Stop being proud! Don't you know how a little yeast can spread through the whole batch of dough? 7 Get rid of the old yeast! Then you will be like fresh bread made without yeast, and that is what you are. Our

---

*3.21,22 Peter: See the note at 1.12.

See also: 3.19: Job 5.13. 3.20: Psa 94.11.

See also: 4.12: Acts 18.3. 4.16: 1 Cor 11.1; Phil 3.17. 5.1: Deut 22.30. 5.6: Gal 5.9. 5.7: Exod 12.5.

Passover lamb is Christ, who has already been sacrificed. [8] So don't celebrate the festival by being evil and sinful, which is like serving bread made with yeast. Be pure and truthful and celebrate by using bread made without yeast.

[9] In my other letter* I told you not to have anything to do with immoral people. [10] But I wasn't talking about the people of this world. You would have to leave this world to get away from everyone who is immoral or greedy or who cheats or worships idols. [11] I was talking about your own people who are immoral or greedy or worship idols or curse others or get drunk or cheat. Don't even eat with them! [12] Why should I judge outsiders? Aren't we supposed to judge only church members? [13] God judges everyone else. The Scriptures say, "Chase away any of your own people who are evil."

CHAPTER 6

Taking each other to court

[1] When one of you has a complaint against another, do you take your complaint to a court of sinners? Or do you take it to God's people? [2] Don't you know that God's people will judge the world? And if you are going to judge the world, can't you settle small problems? [3] Don't you know that we will judge angels? And if that is so, we can surely judge everyday matters. [4] Why do you take everyday complaints to judges who are not respected by the church? [5] I say this to your shame. Aren't any of you wise enough to act as a judge between one follower and another? [6] Why should one of you take another to be tried by unbelievers?

[7] When one of you takes another to court, all of you lose. It would be better to let yourselves be cheated and robbed. [8] But instead, you cheat and rob other followers.

[9] Don't you know that evil people won't have a share in the blessings of God's kingdom? Don't fool yourselves! No one who is immoral or worships idols or is unfaithful in marriage or is a pervert or behaves like a homosexual [10] will share in God's kingdom. Neither will any thief or greedy person or drunkard or anyone who curses and cheats others. [11] Some of you used to be like that. But now the name of our Lord Jesus Christ and the power of God's Spirit have washed you and made you holy and acceptable to God.

Honour God with your body

[12] Some of you say, "We can do anything we want to." But I tell you that not everything is good for us. So I refuse to let anything have power over me. [13] You also say, "Food is meant for our bodies, and our bodies are meant for food." But I tell you that God will destroy them both. We are not supposed to do indecent things with our bodies. We are to use them for the Lord who is in charge of our bodies. [14] God will raise us from death by the same power that he used when he raised our Lord to life.

[15] Don't you know that your bodies are part of the body of Christ? Is it right for me to join part of the body of Christ to a prostitute? No, it isn't! [16] Don't you know that a man who does that becomes part of her body? The Scriptures say, "The two of them will be like one person." [17] But anyone who is joined to the Lord is one in spirit with him.

[18] Don't be immoral in matters of sex. That is a sin against your own body in a way that no other sin is. [19] You know that your body is a temple where the Holy Spirit lives. The Spirit is in you and is a gift from God. You are no longer your own. [20] God paid a great price for you. So use your body to honour God.

CHAPTER 7

Questions about marriage

[1] Now I will answer the questions that you asked in your letter. You asked, "Is it best for people not to marry?"* [2] Well, having your own husband or wife should keep you from doing something immoral. [3] Husbands and wives should be fair with each other about having sex. [4] A wife belongs to her husband instead of to herself, and a husband belongs to his wife instead of to himself. [5] So don't refuse sex to each other, unless you agree not to have sex for a little while, in order to spend time in prayer. Then Satan won't be able to tempt you because of your lack of self-control. [6] In my opinion that is what should be done, though I don't know of anything the Lord said about this matter. [7] I wish that all of you were like me, but God has given different gifts to each of us.

---

*5.9 other letter: An unknown letter that Paul wrote to the Christians at Corinth before he wrote this one.
See also: 5.8: Exod 13.7; Deut 16.3.   5.13: Deut 13.5; 17.7 (LXX).

See also: 6.12: 1 Cor 10.23.   6.16: Gen 2.24.
6.19: 1 Cor 3.16; 2 Cor 6.16.

[8] Here is my advice for people who have never been married and for widows. You should stay single, just as I am. [9] But if you don't have enough self-control, then go ahead and get married. After all, it is better to marry than to burn with desire.'

[10] I instruct married couples to stay together, and this is exactly what the Lord himself taught. A wife who leaves her husband [11] should either stay single or go back to her husband. And a husband should not leave his wife.

[12] I don't know of anything else the Lord said about marriage. All I can do is to give you my own advice. If your wife isn't a follower of the Lord, but is willing to stay with you, don't divorce her. [13] If your husband isn't a follower, but is willing to stay with you, don't divorce him. [14] Your husband or wife who isn't a follower is made holy by having you as a partner. This also makes your children holy and keeps them from being unclean in God's sight.

[15] If your husband or wife isn't a follower of the Lord and decides to divorce you, then you should agree to it. You are no longer bound to that person. After all, God chose you and wants you to live at peace. [16] And besides, how do you know if you will be able to save your husband or wife who isn't a follower?

Obeying the Lord at all times

[17] In every church I tell the people to stay as they were when the Lord Jesus chose them and God called them to be his own. Now I say the same thing to you. [18] If you are already circumcised, don't try to change it. If you are not circumcised, don't get circumcised. [19] Being circumcised or uncircumcised isn't really what matters. The important thing is to obey God's commands. [20] So don't try to change what you were when God chose you. [21] Are you a slave? Don't let that bother you. But if you can win your freedom, you should. [22] When the Lord chooses slaves, they become his free people. And when he chooses free people, they become slaves of Christ. [23] God paid a great price for you. So don't become slaves of anyone else. [24] Stay what you were when God chose you.

Unmarried people

[25] I don't know of anything that the Lord said about people who have never been married.' But I will tell you what I think. And you can trust me, because the Lord has treated me with kindness. [26] We are now going through hard times, and I think it is best for you to stay as you are. [27] If you are married, stay married. If you are not married, don't try to get married. [28] It isn't wrong to marry, even if you have never been married before. But those who marry will have a lot of trouble, and I want to protect you from that.

[29] My friends, what I mean is that the Lord will soon come,' and it won't matter if you are married or not. [30] It will be all the same if you are crying or laughing, or if you are buying or are completely broke. [31] It won't make any difference how much good you are getting from this world or how much you like it. This world as we know it is now passing away.

[32] I want all of you to be free from worry. An unmarried man worries about how to please the Lord. [33] But a married man has more worries. He must worry about the things of this world, because he wants to please his wife. [34] So he is pulled in two directions. Unmarried women and women who have never been married' worry only about pleasing the Lord, and they keep their bodies and minds pure. But a married woman worries about the things of this world, because she wants to please her husband. [35] What I am saying is for your own good — it isn't to limit your freedom. I want to help you to live right and to love the Lord above all else.

[36] But suppose you are engaged to someone old enough to be married, and you want her so much that all you can think about is getting married. Then go ahead and marry.' There is nothing wrong with that. [37] But it is better to have self-control and to make up your mind not to marry. [38] It is perfectly all right to marry, but it is better not to get married at all.

[39] A wife should stay married to her husband until he dies. Then she is free to marry again, but only to a man who is a follower of the Lord. [40] However, I think I am obeying God's Spirit when I say she would be happier to stay single.

See also: 7.10,11: Matt 5.32; 19.9; Mark 10.11,12; Luke 16.18.

Honouring God instead of idols

CHAPTER 8

Food offered to idols

[1] In your letter you asked me about food offered to idols. All of us know something about this subject. But knowledge makes us proud of ourselves, while love makes us helpful to others. [2] In fact, people who think they know so much don't know anything at all. [3] But God has no doubts about who loves him.

[4] Even though food is offered to idols, we know that none of the idols in this world are alive. After all, there is only one God. [5] Many things in heaven and on earth are called gods and lords, but none of them really are gods or lords. [6] We have only one God, and he is the Father. He created everything, and we live for him. Jesus Christ is our only Lord. Everything was made by him, and by him life was given to us.

[7] Not everyone knows these things. In fact, many people have grown up with the belief that idols have life in them. So when they eat meat offered to idols, they are bothered by a weak conscience. [8] But food doesn't bring us any closer to God. We are no worse off if we don't eat, and we are no better off if we do.

[9] Don't cause problems for someone with a weak conscience, just because you have the right to eat anything. [10] You know all this, and so it doesn't bother you to eat in the temple of an idol. But suppose a person with a weak conscience sees you and decides to eat food that has been offered to idols. [11] Then what you know has destroyed someone Christ died for. [12] When you sin by hurting a follower with a weak conscience, you sin against Christ. [13] So if I hurt one of the Lord's followers by what I eat, I will never eat meat as long as I live.

CHAPTER 9

The rights of an apostle

[1] I am free. I am an apostle. I have seen the Lord Jesus and have led you to have faith in him. [2] Others may think that I am not an apostle, but you are proof that I am an apostle to you.

[3] When people question me, I tell them [4] that Barnabas and I have the right to our food and drink. [5] We each have the right to marry one of the Lord's followers and to take her along with us, just as the other apostles and the Lord's brothers and Peter* do. [6] Are we the only ones who have to support ourselves by working at another job? [7] Do soldiers pay their own salaries? Don't people who raise grapes eat some of what they grow? Don't shepherds get milk from their own goats?

[8-9] I am not saying this on my own authority. The Law of Moses tells us not to muzzle an ox when it is grinding grain. But was God concerned only about an ox? [10] No, he wasn't! He was talking about us. This was written in the Scriptures so that all who plough and all who grind the grain will look forward to sharing in the harvest.

[11] When we told the message to you, it was like planting spiritual seed. So we have the right to accept material things as our harvest from you. [12] If others have the right to do this, we have an even greater right. But we haven't used this right of ours. We are willing to put up with anything to keep from causing trouble for the message about Christ.

[13] Don't you know that people who work in the temple make their living from what is brought to the temple? Don't you know that a person who serves at the altar is given part of what is offered? [14] In the same way, the Lord wants everyone who preaches the good news to make a living from preaching this message.

[15] But I have never used these privileges of mine, and I am not writing this because I want to start now. I would rather die than let someone rob me of the right to take pride in this. [16] I don't have any reason to boast about preaching the good news. Preaching is something God told me to do, and if I don't do it, I am doomed. [17] If I preach because I want to, I will be paid. But even if I don't want to, it is still something God has sent me to do. [18] What pay am I given? It is the chance to preach the good news free of charge and not to use the privileges that are mine because I am a preacher.

[19] I am not anyone's slave. But I have become a slave to everyone, so that I can win as many people as possible. [20] When I am with the Jews, I live like a Jew to win them. They are ruled by the Law of Moses, and I am not. But I live by the Law to win them. [21] And when I am with people who are not ruled by

---

*9.5 Peter: See the note at 1.12.

See also: 9.9: Deut 25.4; 1 Tim 5.18. 9.11: Rom 15.27.
9.13: Deut 18.1. 9.14: Matt 10.10; Luke 10.7.

the Law, I forget about the Law to win them. Of course, I never really forget about the law of God. In fact, I am ruled by the law of Christ. 22 When I am with people whose faith is weak, I live as they do to win them. I do everything I can to win everyone I possibly can. 23 I do all this for the good news, because I want to share in its blessings.

A race and a fight

24 You know that many runners enter a race, and only one of them wins the prize. So run to win! 25 Athletes work hard to win a crown that cannot last, but we do it for a crown that will last for ever. 26 I don't run without a goal. And I don't box by waving my fists in the air. 27 I keep my body under control and make it my slave, so I won't lose out after telling the good news to others.

CHAPTER 10

Don't worship idols

1 Friends, I want to remind you that all our ancestors walked under the cloud and went through the sea. 2 This was like being baptized and becoming followers of Moses. 3 All of them also ate the same spiritual food 4 and drank the same spiritual drink, which flowed from the spiritual rock that followed them. That rock was Christ. 5 But most of them did not please God. So they died, and their bodies were scattered all over the desert.

6 What happened to them is a warning to keep us from wanting to do the same evil things. 7 They worshipped idols, just as the Scriptures say, "The people sat down to eat and drink. Then they got up to dance around." So don't worship idols. 8 Some of those people did shameful things, and in a single day about twenty-three thousand of them died. Don't do shameful things as they did. 9 And don't try to test Christ,* as some of them did and were later bitten by poisonous snakes. 10 Don't even grumble, as some of them did and were killed by the destroying angel. 11 These things happened to them as a warning to us. All this was written in the Scriptures to teach us who live in these last days.

12 Even if you think you can stand up to temptation, be careful not to fall. 13 You are tempted in the same way that everyone else is tempted. But God can be trusted not to let you be tempted too much, and he will show you how to escape from your temptations.

14 My friends, you must keep away from idols. 15 I am speaking to you as people who have enough sense to know what I am talking about. 16 When we drink from the cup that we ask God to bless, isn't that sharing in the blood of Christ? When we eat the bread that we break, isn't that sharing in the body of Christ? 17 By sharing in the same loaf of bread, we become one body, even though there are many of us.

18 Aren't the people of Israel sharing in the worship when they gather around the altar and eat the sacrifices offered there? 19 Am I saying that either the idols or the food sacrificed to them is anything at all? 20 No, I am not! That food is really sacrificed to demons and not to God. I don't want you to have anything to do with demons. 21 You cannot drink from the cup of demons and still drink from the Lord's cup. You cannot eat at the table of demons and still eat at the Lord's table. 22 We would make the Lord jealous if we did that. And we are not stronger than the Lord.

Always honour God

23 Some of you say, "We can do whatever we want to!" But I tell you that not everything may be good or helpful. 24 We should think about others and not about ourselves. 25 However, when you buy meat in the market, go ahead and eat it. Keep your conscience clear by not asking where the meat came from. 26 The Scriptures say, "The earth and everything in it belong to the Lord."

27 If an unbeliever invites you to dinner, and you want to go, then go. Eat whatever you are served. Don't cause a problem for someone's conscience by asking where the food came from. 28-29 But if you are told that it has been sacrificed to idols, don't cause a problem by eating it. I don't mean a problem for yourself, but for the one who told you. Why should my freedom be limited by someone else's conscience? 30 If I give thanks for what I eat, why should anyone accuse me of doing wrong?

See also: 10.1: a Exod 13.21,22; b Exod 14.22–29.
10.3: Exod 16.35.   10.4: Exod 17.6; Num 20.11.
10.5: Num 14.29,30.   10.6: Num 11.4.   10.7: Exod 32.6.
10.8: Num 25.1–18.   10.9: Num 21.5,6.
10.10: Num 16.41–49.

See also: 10.16: Matt 26.26–28; Mark 14.22–24;
Luke 22.19,20.   10.18: Lev 7.6.   10.20: Deut 32.17 (LXX).
10.22: Deut 32.21.   10.23: 1 Cor 6.12.   10.26: Psa 24.1.

31 When you eat or drink or do anything else, always do it to honour God. 32 Don't cause problems for Jews or Greeks or anyone else who belongs to God's church. 33 I always try to please others instead of myself, in the hope that many of them will be saved.

CHAPTER 11

1 You must follow my example, as I follow the example of Christ.

Guidance for worship and church life

Rules for worship

2 I am proud of you, because you always remember me and obey the teachings I gave you. 3 Now I want you to know that Christ is the head over all men, and a man is the head over a woman. But God is the head over Christ. 4 This means that any man who prays or prophesies with something on his head brings shame to his head.

5 But any woman who prays or prophesies without something on her head brings shame to her head. In fact, she may as well shave her head.* 6 A woman should wear something on her head. It is a disgrace for a woman to shave her head or cut her hair. But if she refuses to wear something on her head, let her cut off her hair.

7 Men were created to be like God and to bring honour to God. This means that a man should not wear anything on his head. Women were created to bring honour to men. 8 It was the woman who was made from a man, and not the man who was made from a woman. 9 He wasn't created for her. She was created for him. 10 And so, because of this, and also because of the angels, a woman ought to wear something on her head, as a sign of her authority.*

11 As far as the Lord is concerned, men and women need each other. 12 It is true that the first woman came from a man, but all other men have been given birth by women. Yet God is the one who created everything.

13 Ask yourselves if it is proper for a woman to pray without something on her head. 14 Isn't it unnatural and disgraceful for men to have long hair? 15 But long hair is a beautiful way for a woman to cover her head. 16 This is how things are done in all God's churches,' and that's why none of you should argue about what I have said.

Rules for the Lord's Supper

17 Your worship services do you more harm than good. I am certainly not going to praise you for this. 18 I am told that you can't get along with each other when you worship, and I am sure that some of what I have heard is true. 19 You are bound to argue with each other, but it is easy to see which of you have God's approval.

20 When you meet together, you don't really celebrate the Lord's Supper. 21 You even start eating before everyone gets to the meeting, and some of you go hungry, while others get drunk. 22 Don't you have homes where you can eat and drink? Do you hate God's church? Do you want to embarrass people who don't have anything? What can I say to you? I certainly cannot praise you.

The Lord's Supper

This is also told in Matthew 26.26–29; Mark 14.22–25; Luke 22.14–20

23 I have already told you what the Lord Jesus did on the night he was betrayed. And it came from the Lord himself.

He took some bread in his hands. 24 Then after he had given thanks, he broke it and said, "This is my body, which is given for you. Eat this and remember me."

25 After the meal, Jesus took a cup of wine in his hands and said, "This is my blood, and with it God makes his new agreement with you. Drink this and remember me."

26 The Lord meant that when you eat this bread and drink from this cup, you tell about his death until he comes.

27 But if you eat the bread and drink the wine in a way that isn't worthy of the Lord, you sin against his body and blood. 28 That's why you must examine the way you eat and drink. 29 If you fail to understand that you are the body of the Lord, you will condemn yourselves by the way you eat and drink. 30 That's why many of you are sick and weak

---

*11.5 she may as well shave her head: A woman's hair was a mark of beauty, and it was shameful for a woman to cut hair short or to shave her head, so that she looked like a man.

*11.10 as a sign of her authority: Or "as a sign that she is under someone's authority."

See also: 11.1: 1 Cor 4.16; Phil 3.17.   11.7: Gen 1.26,27. 11.8,9: Gen 2.18–23.

See also: 11.25: a Exod 24.8; Jer 31.31–34; b Exod 24.6–8.

and why a lot of others have died. ³¹ If we carefully judge ourselves, we won't be punished. ³² But when the Lord judges and punishes us, he does it to keep us from being condemned with the rest of the world.

³³ My dear friends, you should wait until everyone gets there before you start eating. ³⁴ If you really are hungry, you can eat at home. Then you won't condemn yourselves when you meet together.

After I arrive, I will instruct you about the other matters.

CHAPTER 12

Spiritual gifts

¹ My friends, you asked me about spiritual gifts. ² I want you to remember that before you became followers of the Lord, you were led in all the wrong ways by idols that cannot even talk. ³ Now I want you to know that if you are led by God's Spirit, you will say that Jesus is Lord, and you will never curse Jesus.

⁴ There are different kinds of spiritual gifts, but they all come from the same Spirit. ⁵ There are different ways to serve the same Lord, ⁶ and we can each do different things. Yet the same God works in all of us and helps us in everything we do.

⁷ The Spirit has given each of us a special way of serving others. ⁸ Some of us can speak with wisdom, while others can speak with knowledge, but these gifts come from the same Spirit. ⁹ To others the Spirit has given great faith or the power to heal the sick ¹⁰ or the power to perform mighty miracles. Some of us are prophets, and some of us recognize when God's Spirit is present.* Others can speak different kinds of languages, and still others can tell what these languages mean. ¹¹ But it is the Spirit who does all this and decides which gifts to give to each of us.

One body with many parts

¹² The body of Christ has many different parts, just as any other body does. ¹³ Some of us are Jews, and others are Gentiles. Some of us are slaves, and others are free. But God's Spirit baptized each of us and made us part of the body of Christ. Now we each drink from that same Spirit.*

¹⁴ Our bodies don't have just one part. They have many parts. ¹⁵ Suppose a foot says, "I'm not a hand, and so I'm not part of the body." Wouldn't the foot still belong to the body? ¹⁶ Or suppose an ear says, "I'm not an eye, and so I'm not part of the body." Wouldn't the ear still belong to the body? ¹⁷ If our bodies were only an eye, we couldn't hear a thing. And if they were only an ear, we couldn't smell a thing. ¹⁸ But God has put all parts of our body together in the way that he decided was best.

¹⁹ A body isn't really a body, unless there is more than one part. ²⁰ It takes many parts to make a single body. ²¹ That's why the eyes cannot say they don't need the hands. That's also why the head cannot say it doesn't need the feet. ²² In fact, we cannot get along without the parts of the body that seem to be the weakest. ²³ We take special care to dress up some parts of our bodies. We are modest about our personal parts, ²⁴ but we don't have to be modest about other parts.

God put our bodies together in such a way that even the parts that seem the least important are valuable. ²⁵ He did this to make all parts of the body work together smoothly, with each part caring about the others. ²⁶ If one part of our body hurts, we hurt all over. If one part of our body is honoured, the whole body will be happy.

²⁷ Together you are the body of Christ. Each one of you is part of his body. ²⁸ First, God chose some people to be apostles and prophets and teachers for the church. But he also chose some to perform miracles or heal the sick or help others or be leaders or speak different kinds of languages. ²⁹ Not everyone is an apostle. Not everyone is a prophet. Not everyone is a teacher. Not everyone can perform miracles. ³⁰ Not everyone can heal the sick. Not everyone can speak different kinds of languages. Not everyone can tell what these languages mean. ³¹ I want you to desire the best gifts. So I will show you a much better way.

CHAPTER 13

Love

¹ What if I could speak
all languages of humans
and of angels?
If I did not love others,
I would be nothing more

---

*12.10 and some of us . . . present: Or "and some of us recognize the difference between God's Spirit and other spirits."

See also: 12.4-11: Rom 12.6-8. 12.12: Rom 12.4,5.

See also: 12.28: Eph 4.11.

than a noisy gong
or a clanging cymbal.
² What if I could prophesy
and understand all secrets
and all knowledge?
And what if I had faith
that moved mountains?
I would be nothing,
unless I loved others.
³ What if I gave away all
that I owned
and let myself
be burnt alive?*
I would gain nothing,
unless I loved others.
⁴ Love is kind and patient,
never jealous, boastful,
proud, or ⁵ rude.
Love isn't selfish
or quick-tempered.
It doesn't keep a record
of wrongs that others do.
⁶ Love rejoices in the truth,
but not in evil.
⁷ Love is always supportive,
loyal, hopeful,
and trusting.
⁸ Love never fails!

Everyone who prophesies
will stop,
and unknown languages
will no longer
be spoken.
All that we know
will be forgotten.
⁹ We don't know everything,
and our prophecies
are not complete.
¹⁰ But what is perfect
will some day appear,
and what isn't perfect
will then disappear.

¹¹ When we were children,
we thought and reasoned
as children do.
But when we grew up,
we stopped our childish ways.
¹² Now all we can see of God
is like a cloudy picture
in a mirror.
Later we will see him
face to face.
We don't know everything,
but then we will,

just as God completely
understands us.
¹³ For now there are faith,
hope, and love.
But of these three,
the greatest is love.

CHAPTER 14

Speaking unknown languages and prophesying

¹ Love should be your guide. Be eager to have the gifts that come from the Holy Spirit, especially the gift of prophecy. ² If you speak languages that others don't know, God will understand what you are saying, though no one else will know what you mean. You will be talking about mysteries that only the Spirit understands. ³ But when you prophesy, you will be understood, and others will be helped. They will be encouraged and made to feel better.

⁴ By speaking languages that others don't know, you help only yourself. But by prophesying you help everyone in the church. ⁵ I am glad for you to speak unknown languages, although I would rather you prophesied. In fact, prophesying does much more good than speaking unknown languages, unless someone can help the church by explaining what you mean.

⁶ My friends, what good would it do, if I came and spoke unknown languages to you and didn't explain what I meant? How would I help you, unless I told you what God had shown me or gave you some knowledge or prophecy or teaching? ⁷ If all musical instruments sounded alike, how would you know the difference between a flute and a harp? ⁸ If a bugle call isn't clear, how would you know to get ready for battle?

⁹ That's how it is when you speak unknown languages. If no one can understand what you are talking about, you will only be talking to the wind. ¹⁰ There are many different languages in this world, and all of them make sense. ¹¹ But if I don't understand the language that someone is using, we will be like foreigners to each other. ¹² If you really want spiritual gifts, choose the ones that will be most helpful to the church.

¹³ When we speak languages that others don't know, we should pray for the power to explain what we mean. ¹⁴ For example, if I use an unknown language in my prayers, my spirit prays but my mind is useless. ¹⁵ Then what should I do? There are times

See also: 13.2: Matt 17.20; 21.21; Mark 11.23.

when I should pray with my spirit, and times when I should pray with my mind. Sometimes I should sing with my spirit, and at other times I should sing with my mind.

¹⁶ Suppose some strangers are in your worship service, when you are praising God with your spirit. If they don't understand you, how will they know to say, "Amen"? ¹⁷ You may be worshipping God in a wonderful way, but no one else will be helped. ¹⁸ I thank God that I speak unknown languages more than any of you. ¹⁹ But words that make sense can help the church. That's why in church I had rather speak five words that make sense than speak ten thousand words in a language that others don't know.

²⁰ My friends, stop thinking like children. Think like mature people and be as innocent as tiny babies. ²¹ In the Scriptures the Lord says,

"I will use strangers
    who speak unknown languages
    to talk to my people.
They will speak to them
    in foreign languages,
but still my people
    won't listen to me."

²² Languages that others don't know may mean something to unbelievers, but not to the Lord's followers. Prophecy, on the other hand, is for followers, not for unbelievers. ²³ Suppose everyone in your worship service started speaking unknown languages, and some outsiders or some unbelievers come in. Won't they think you are mad? ²⁴ But suppose all of you are prophesying when those unbelievers and outsiders come in. They will realize that they are sinners, and they will want to change their ways because of what you are saying. ²⁵ They will tell what is hidden in their hearts. Then they will kneel down and say to God, "We are certain that you are with these people."

Worship must be orderly

²⁶ My friends, when you meet to worship, you must do everything for the good of everyone there. That's how it should be when someone sings or teaches or tells what God has said or speaks an unknown language or explains what the language means. ²⁷ No more than two or three of you should speak unknown languages during the meeting. You must take turns, and someone should always be there to

explain what you mean. ²⁸ If no one can explain, you must keep silent in church and speak only to yourself and to God.

²⁹ Two or three persons may prophesy, and everyone else must listen carefully. ³⁰ If someone sitting there receives a message from God, the speaker must stop and let the other person speak. ³¹ Let only one person speak at a time, then all of you will learn something and be encouraged. ³² A prophet should be willing to stop and let someone else speak. ³³ God wants everything to be done peacefully and in order.

When God's people meet in church, ³⁴ the women must not be allowed to speak. They must keep quiet and listen, as the Law of Moses says. ³⁵ If there is something they want to know, they can ask their husbands when they get home. It is disgraceful for women to speak in church. ³⁶ God's message did not start with you people, and you are not the only ones it has reached.

³⁷ If you think of yourself as a prophet or a spiritual person, you will know that I am writing only what the Lord has commanded. ³⁸ So don't pay attention to anyone who ignores what I am writing. ³⁹ My friends, be eager to prophesy and don't stop anyone from speaking languages that others don't know. ⁴⁰ But do everything properly and in order.

Christ's victory over death

CHAPTER 15

Christ was raised to life

¹ My friends, I want you to remember the message that I preached and that you believed and trusted. ² You will be saved by this message, if you hold firmly to it. But if you don't, your faith was all for nothing.

³ I told you the most important part of the message exactly as it was told to me. That part is:

Christ died for our sins,
    as the Scriptures say.
⁴ He was buried,
    and three days later
    he was raised to life,
    as the Scriptures say.
⁵ Christ appeared to Peter,*
    then to the twelve.

---

*15.5 Peter: See the note at 1.12.

See also: 15.3: Isa 53.5–12. 15.4: Psa 16.8–10; Matt 12.40; Acts 2.24–32. 15.5: a Luke 24.34; b Matt 28.16,17; Mark 16.14; Luke 24.36; John 20.19.

⁶ After this, he appeared
to more than five hundred
other followers.
Most of them are still alive,
but some have died.
⁷ He also appeared to James,
and then to all
the apostles.

⁸ Finally, he appeared to me, even though I am like someone who was born at the wrong time.ᵉ

⁹ I am the least important of all the apostles. In fact, I caused so much trouble for God's church that I don't even deserve to be called an apostle. ¹⁰ But God was kind! He made me what I am, and his wonderful kindness wasn't wasted. I worked much harder than any of the other apostles, although it was really God's kindness at work and not me. ¹¹ But it doesn't matter if I preached or if they preached. All of you believed the message just the same.

God's people will be raised to life

¹² If we preach that Christ was raised from death, how can some of you say that the dead will not be raised to life? ¹³ If they won't be raised to life, Christ himself wasn't raised to life. ¹⁴ And if Christ wasn't raised to life, our message is worthless, and so is your faith. ¹⁵ If the dead won't be raised to life, we have told lies about God by saying that he raised Christ to life, when he really did not.

¹⁶ So if the dead won't be raised to life, Christ wasn't raised to life. ¹⁷ Unless Christ was raised to life, your faith is useless, and you are still living in your sins. ¹⁸ And those people who died after putting their faith in him are completely lost. ¹⁹ If our hope in Christ is good only for this life, we are worse off than anyone else.

²⁰ But Christ has been raised to life! And he makes us certain that others will also be raised to life. ²¹ Just as we will die because of Adam, we will be raised to life because of Christ. ²² Adam brought death to all of us, and Christ will bring life to all of us. ²³ But we must each wait our turn. Christ was the first to be raised to life, and his people will be raised to life when he returns. ²⁴ Then after Christ has destroyed all powers and forces, the end will come, and he will give the kingdom to God the Father.

²⁵ Christ will rule until he puts all his enemies under his power, ²⁶ and the last enemy he destroys will be death. ²⁷ When the Scriptures say that he will put everything under his power, they don't include God. It was God who put everything under the power of Christ. ²⁸ After everything is under the power of God's Son, he will put himself under the power of God, who put everything under his Son's power. Then God will mean everything to everyone.

²⁹ If the dead are not going to be raised to life, what will people do who are being baptized for them? Why are they being baptized for those dead people? ³⁰ And why do we always risk our lives ³¹ and face death every day? The pride that I have in you because of Christ Jesus our Lord is what makes me say this. ³² What do you think I gained by fighting wild animals in Ephesus? If the dead are not raised to life,

"Let's eat and drink.
Tomorrow we die."

³³ Don't fool yourselves. Bad friends will destroy you. ³⁴ Be sensible and stop sinning. You should be embarrassed that some people still don't know about God.

What our bodies will be like

³⁵ Some of you have asked, "How will the dead be raised to life? What kind of bodies will they have?" ³⁶ Don't be foolish. A seed must die before it can sprout from the ground. ³⁷ Wheat seeds and all other seeds look different from the sprouts that come up. ³⁸ This is because God gives everything the kind of body he wants it to have. ³⁹ People, animals, birds, and fish are each made of flesh, but none of them are alike.

⁴⁰ Everything in the heavens has a body, and so does everything on earth. But each one is very different from all the others. ⁴¹ The sun isn't like the moon, the moon isn't like the stars, and each star is different.

⁴² That's how it will be when our bodies are raised to life. These bodies will die, but the bodies that are raised will live for ever. ⁴³ These ugly and weak bodies will become beautiful and strong. ⁴⁴ As there are physical bodies, there are spiritual bodies. And our physical bodies will be changed into spiritual bodies.

See also: 15.8: Acts 9.3–6. 15.9: Acts 8.3.

See also: 15.25: Psa 110.1. 15.27: Psa 8.6.
15.32: Isa 22.13.

⁴⁵ The first man was named Adam, and the Scriptures tell us that he was a living person. But Jesus, who may be called the last Adam, is a life-giving spirit. ⁴⁶ We see that the one with a spiritual body did not come first. He came after the one who had a physical body. ⁴⁷ The first man was made from the dust of the earth, but the second man came from heaven. ⁴⁸ Everyone on earth has a body like the body of the one who was made from the dust of the earth. And everyone in heaven has a body like the body of the one who came from heaven. ⁴⁹ Just as we are like the one who was made out of earth, we will be like the one who came from heaven.

⁵⁰ My friends, I want you to know that our bodies of flesh and blood will decay. This means that they cannot share in God's kingdom, which lasts for ever. ⁵¹ I will explain a mystery to you. Not every one of us will die, but we will all be changed. ⁵² It will happen instantly, quicker than the blink of an eye. At the sound of the last trumpet the dead will be raised. We will all be changed, so that we will never die again. ⁵³ Our dead and decaying bodies will be changed into bodies that won't be changed. The bodies we now have are weak and can die. But they will be changed into bodies that are eternal. Then the Scriptures will come true,

"Death has lost the battle!
⁵⁵ Where is its victory?
      Where is its sting?"

⁵⁶ Sin is what gives death its sting, and the Law is the power behind sin. ⁵⁷ But thank God for letting our Lord Jesus Christ give us the victory!

⁵⁸ My dear friends, stand firm and don't be shaken. Always keep busy working for the Lord. You know that everything you do for him is worthwhile.

An offering for the poor

CHAPTER 16

A collection for God's people

¹ When you collect money for God's people, I want you to do exactly what I told the churches in Galatia to do. ² That is, each Sunday each of you must put aside part of what you have earned. If you do this, you won't have to take up a collection when I come. ³ Choose some followers to take the money to Jerusalem. I will send them on with the money and with letters which show that you approve of them. ⁴ If you think I should go along, they can go with me.

Paul's travel plans

⁵ After I have gone through Macedonia, I hope to see you ⁶ and stay with you for a while. I may even stay all winter, so that you can help me on my way to wherever I will be going next. ⁷ If the Lord lets me, I would rather come later for a longer visit than to stop off now for only a short visit. ⁸ I will stay in Ephesus until Pentecost, ⁹ because there is a wonderful welcome. He is doing the Lord's work, just as I am. ¹¹ Don't let anyone ill-treat him. I am looking for him to return to me together with the other followers. So when he leaves, send him off with your blessings.

¹² I have tried hard to get our friend Apollos to visit you with the other followers. He doesn't want to come just now, but he will come when he can.

Personal concerns and greetings

¹³ Keep alert. Be firm in your faith. Stay brave and strong. ¹⁴ Show love in everything you do.

¹⁵ You know that Stephanas and his family were the first in Achaia to have faith in the Lord. They have done all they can for God's people. My friends, I ask you ¹⁶ to obey leaders like them and to do the same for all others who work hard with you.

¹⁷ I was glad to see Stephanas and Fortunatus and Achaicus. Having them here was like having you. ¹⁸ They made me feel much better, just as they made you feel better. You should appreciate people like them.

¹⁹ Greetings from the churches in Asia. Aquila and Priscilla, together with the church that meets in their house, send greetings in the name of the Lord.

²⁰ All the Lord's followers send their greetings.

See also: 15.45: Gen 2.7. 15.51,52: 1 Thes 4.15–17.
15.54: Isa 25.8. 15.55: Hos 13.14 (LXX).
16.1: Rom 15.25,26.

See also: 16.5: Acts 19.21. 16.8: Lev 23.15–21;
Deut 16.9–11. 16.8,9: Acts 19.8–10. 16.10: 1 Cor 4.17.
16.15: 1 Cor 1.16. 16.19: Acts 18.2.

Give each other a warm greeting.

²¹ I am signing this letter myself: PAUL.

²² I pray that God will put a curse on everyone who doesn't love the Lord. And may the Lord come soon.

²³ I pray that the Lord Jesus will be kind to you.

²⁴ I love everyone who belongs to Christ Jesus.

Additional notes

'1.14 I thank God: Some manuscripts have "I thank my God".

'2.1 mystery: Some manuscripts have "testimony".

'2.13 teach spiritual things to spiritual people: Or "compare spiritual things with spiritual things."

'2.16 we understand what Christ is thinking: Or "we think as Christ does."

'5.1 is even sleeping with his own stepmother: Or "has even married his own stepmother."

'7.1 people not to marry: Or "married couples not to have sex".

'7.9 with desire: Or "in the flames of hell".

'7.25 people who have never been married: Or "virgins".

'7.29 the Lord will soon come: Or "there's not much time left" or "the time for decision comes quickly".

'7.34 women who have never been married: Or "virgins".

'7.36 But suppose you are engaged . . . go ahead and marry: Verses 36–38 may also be translated: ³⁶"If you feel that you are not treating your grown-up daughter right by keeping her from getting married, then let her marry. You won't be doing anything wrong. ³⁷But it is better to have self-control and make up your mind not to let your daughter get married. ³⁸It is all right for you to let her marry. But it is better if you don't let her marry at all."

'10.9 Christ: Some manuscripts have "the Lord".

'11.16 This is how things are done in all God's churches: Or "There is no set rule for this in any of God's churches."

'12.13 Some of us are Jews . . . that same Spirit: Verse 13 may also be translated, "God's Spirit is inside each of us, and all around us as well. So it doesn't matter that some of us are Jews and others are Gentiles and that some of us are slaves and others are free. Together we are one body."

'12.31 I want you to desire the best gifts: Or "You desire the best gifts."

'13.3 and let myself be burnt alive: Some manuscripts have "so that I could boast."

'15.8 who was born at the wrong time: The meaning of these words in Greek is not clear.

2 Corinthians

Paul's second letter to the church
in Corinth

A quick look at this letter

In the beginning of this letter Paul answers the concerns of the Christians in Corinth who accused him of not living up to his promise to visit them. Paul had changed his mind for a good reason. He had stayed away from Corinth so that he would not seem to be too hard and demanding (1.23). He also wanted to see if they would follow his instructions about forgiving and comforting people who had sinned (2.5-11).

Paul reminds the Corinthians that God is generous and wants them to be just as generous in their giving to help God's people in Jerusalem and Judea (8.1—9.15).

Paul is a servant of God's new agreement (3.1-17). He is faithful in trying to bring people to God, even if it means terrible suffering for himself (4.1—6.13; 10.1—12.10). And what has God done to make it possible for us to come to him?

God has done it all! He sent Christ to make peace between himself and us, and he has given us the work of making peace between himself and others.

What we mean is that God was in Christ, offering peace and forgiveness to the people of this world. And he has given us the work of sharing his message about peace.

(5.18,19)

Paul gives thanks to God

CHAPTER 1

¹ From Paul, chosen by God to be an apostle of Jesus Christ, and from Timothy, who is also a follower.

To God's church in Corinth and to all God's people in Achaia.
² I pray that God our Father and the Lord Jesus Christ will be kind to you and will bless you with peace!

Paul gives thanks

³ Praise God, the Father of our Lord Jesus Christ! The Father is a merciful God, who always gives us comfort. ⁴ He comforts us when we are in trouble, so that we can share that same comfort with others in trouble. ⁵ We share in the terrible sufferings of Christ, but also in the wonderful comfort he gives. ⁶ We suffer in the hope that you will be comforted and saved. And because we are

See also: 1.1: Acts 18.1.

comforted, you will also be comforted, as you patiently endure suffering like ours. [7] You never disappoint us. You suffered as much as we did, and we know that you will be comforted as we were.

[8] My friends, I want you to know what a hard time we had in Asia. Our sufferings were so horrible and so unbearable that death seemed certain. [9] In fact, we felt sure that we were going to die. But this made us stop trusting in ourselves and start trusting God, who raises the dead to life. [10] God saved us from the threat of death,[*] and we are sure that he will do it again and again. [11] Please help us by praying for us. Then many people will give thanks for the blessings we receive in answer to all these prayers.

The work of an apostle for God's people

Paul's change of plans

[12] We can be proud of our clear conscience. We have always lived honestly and sincerely, especially when we were with you. And we were guided by God's wonderful kindness instead of by the wisdom of this world. [13] I am not writing anything you cannot read and understand. I hope you will understand it completely, [14] just as you already partly understand us. Then when our Lord Jesus returns, you can be as proud of us as we are of you.

[15] I was so sure of your pride in us that I had planned to visit you first of all. In this way you would have the blessing of two visits from me. [16] Once on my way to Macedonia and again on my return from there. Then you could send me on to Judea. [17] Do you think I couldn't make up my mind about what to do? Or do I seem like someone who says "Yes" or "No" simply to please others? [18] God can be trusted, and so can I, when I say that our answer to you has always been "Yes" and never "No". [19] This is because Jesus Christ the Son of God is always "Yes" and never "No". And he is the one that Silas,[*] Timothy, and I told you about. [20] Christ says "Yes" to all of God's promises. That's why we have Christ to say "Amen"[*] for us to the glory of God. [21] And so

God makes it possible for you and us to stand firmly together with Christ. God is also the one who chose us [22] and put his Spirit in our hearts to show that we belong only to him.

[23] God is my witness that I stayed away from Corinth, just to keep from being hard on you. [24] We are not bosses who tell you what to believe. We are working with you to make you glad, because your faith is strong.

CHAPTER 2

[1] I have decided not to make my next visit to you so painful. [2] If I make you feel bad, who would be left to cheer me up, except the people I had made to feel bad? [3] The reason I want to be happy is to make you happy. I wrote as I did because I didn't want to visit you and be made to feel bad, when you should make me feel happy. [4] At the time I wrote, I was suffering terribly. My eyes were full of tears, and my heart was broken. But I didn't want to make you feel bad. I only wanted to let you know how much I cared for you.

Forgiveness

[5] I don't want to be hard on you. But if one of you has made someone feel bad, I am not really the one who has been made to feel bad. Some of you are the ones. [6] Most of you have already pointed out the wrong that person did, and that is punishment enough for what was done.

[7] When people sin, you should forgive and comfort them, so they won't give up in despair. [8] You should make them sure of your love for them.

[9] I also wrote because I wanted to test you and find out if you would follow my instructions. [10] I will forgive anyone you forgive. Yes, for your sake and with Christ as my witness, I have forgiven whatever needed to be forgiven. [11] I have done this to keep Satan from getting the better of us. We all know what goes on in his mind.

[12] When I went to Troas to preach the good news about Christ, I found that the Lord had already prepared the way. [13] But I was worried when I didn't find my friend Titus there. So I left the other followers and went on to Macedonia.

[14] I am grateful that God always makes it possible for Christ to lead us to victory. God also helps us spread the knowledge about Christ everywhere, and this knowledge is like

*1.20 Amen: The word "amen" is used here with the meaning of "yes".

See also: 1.8: 1 Cor 15.32. 1.16: Acts 19.21.
1.19: Acts 18.5.

See also: 2.12,13: Acts 20.1.

the smell of perfume. [15-16] In fact, God thinks of us as a perfume that brings Christ to everyone. For people who are being saved, this perfume has a sweet smell and leads them to a better life. But for people who are lost, it has a bad smell and leads them to a horrible death.

No one really has what it takes to do this work. [17] A lot of people try to get rich from preaching God's message. But we are God's sincere messengers, and by the power of Christ we speak our message with God as our witness.

Guided by the love of Christ

CHAPTER 3

God's new agreement

[1] Are we once again boasting about ourselves? Do we need letters to you or from you to tell others about us? Some people do need letters that tell about them. [2] But you are our letter, and you are in our* hearts for everyone to read and understand. [3] You are like a letter written by Christ and delivered by us. But you are not written with pen and ink or on tablets made of stone. You are written in our hearts by the Spirit of the living God.

[4] We are sure about all this. Christ makes us sure in the very presence of God. [5] We don't have the right to claim that we have done anything on our own. God gives us what it takes to do all that we do. [6] He makes us worthy to be the servants of his new agreement that comes from the Holy Spirit and not from a written Law. After all, the Law brings death, but the Spirit brings life.

[7] The Law of Moses brought only the promise of death, even though it was carved on stones and given in a wonderful way. Still the Law made Moses' face shine so brightly that the people of Israel could not look at it, even though it was a fading glory. [8] So won't the agreement that the Spirit brings to us be even more wonderful? [9] If something that brings the death sentence is glorious, won't something that makes us acceptable to God be even more glorious? [10] In fact, the new agreement is so wonderful that the Law is no longer glorious at all. [11] The Law was given with a glory that faded away. But the glory of the new agreement is much greater, because it will never fade away.

[12] This wonderful hope makes us feel like speaking freely. [13] We are not like Moses. His face was shining, but he covered it to keep the people of Israel from seeing the brightness fade away. [14] The people were stubborn, and something still keeps them from seeing the truth when the Law is read. Only Christ can take away the covering that keeps them from seeing.

[15] When the Law of Moses is read, they have their minds covered over [16] with a covering that is removed only for those who turn to the Lord. [17] The Lord and the Spirit are one and the same, and the Lord's Spirit sets us free. [18] So our faces are not covered. They show the bright glory of the Lord, as the Lord's Spirit makes us more and more like our glorious Lord.

CHAPTER 4

Treasure in clay jars

[1] God has been kind enough to trust us with this work. That's why we never give up. [2] We don't do shameful things that must be kept secret. And we don't try to fool anyone or twist God's message around. God is our witness that we speak only the truth, so others will be sure that we can be trusted. [3] If there is anything hidden about our message, it is hidden only to someone who is lost.

[4] The god who rules this world has blinded the minds of unbelievers. They cannot see the light, which is the good news about our glorious Christ, who shows what God is like. [5] We are not preaching about ourselves. Our message is that Jesus Christ is Lord. He also sent us to be your servants. [6] The Scriptures say, "God commanded light to shine in the dark." Now God is shining in our hearts to let you know that his glory is seen in Jesus Christ.

[7] We are like clay jars in which this treasure is stored. The real power comes from God and not from us. [8] We often suffer, but we are never crushed. Even when we don't know what to do, we never give up. [9] In times of trouble, God is with us, and when we are knocked down, we get up again. [10-11] We face death every day because of Jesus. Our bodies show what his death was like, so that his life can also be seen in us. [12] This means that death is working in us, but life is working in you.

See also: 3.3: a Exod 24.12; b Jer 31.33; Ezek 11.19; 36.26.
3.6: Jer 31.31. 3.7: Exod 34.29.

See also: 3.13: Exod 34.33. 3.16: Exod 34.34.
4.6: Gen 1.3.

13 In the Scriptures it says, "I spoke because I had faith." We have that same kind of faith. So we speak 14 because we know that God raised the Lord Jesus to life. And just as God raised Jesus, he will also raise us to life. Then he will bring us into his presence together with you. 15 All this has been done for you, so that more and more people will know how kind God is and will praise and honour him.

Faith in the Lord

16 We never give up. Our bodies are gradually dying, but we ourselves are being made stronger each day. 17 These little troubles are getting us ready for an eternal glory that will make all our troubles seem like nothing. 18 Things that are seen don't last for ever, but things that are not seen are eternal. That's why we keep our minds on the things that cannot be seen.

CHAPTER 5

1 Our bodies are like tents that we live in here on earth. But when these tents are destroyed, we know that God will give each of us a place to live. These homes will not be buildings that someone has made, but they are in heaven and will last for ever. 2 While we are here on earth, we sigh because we want to live in that heavenly home. 3 We want to put it on like clothes and not be naked.

4 These tents we now live in are like a heavy burden, and we groan. But we don't do this just because we want to leave these bodies that will die. It is because we want to change them for bodies that will never die. 5 God is the one who makes all this possible. He has given us his Spirit to make us certain that he will do it. 6 So always be cheerful!

As long as we are in these bodies, we are away from the Lord. 7 But we live by faith, not by what we see. 8 We should be cheerful, because we would rather leave these bodies and be at home with the Lord. 9 But whether we are at home with the Lord or away from him, we still try our best to please him. 10 After all, Christ will judge each of us for the good or the bad that we do while living in these bodies.

Bringing people to God

11 We know what it means to respect the Lord, and we encourage everyone to turn to him. God himself knows what we are like, and I hope you also know what kind of

people we are. 12 We are not trying once more to boast about ourselves. But we want you to be proud of us, when you are with those who are not sincere and boast about what others think of them.

13 If we seem out of our minds, it is between God and us. But if we are in our right minds, it is for your good. 14 We are ruled by Christ's love for us. We are certain that if one person died for everyone else, then all of us have died. 15 And Christ did die for all of us. He died so we would no longer live for ourselves, but for the one who died and was raised to life for us.

16 We are careful not to judge people by what they seem to be, though we once judged Christ in that way. 17 Anyone who belongs to Christ is a new person. The past is forgotten, and everything is new. 18 God has done it all! He sent Christ to make peace between himself and us, and he has given us the work of making peace between himself and others.

19 What we mean is that God was in Christ, offering peace and forgiveness to the people of this world. And he has given us the work of sharing his message about peace. 20 We were sent to speak for Christ, and God is begging you to listen to our message. We speak for Christ and sincerely ask you to make peace with God. 21 Christ never sinned! But God treated him as a sinner, so that Christ could make us acceptable to God.

CHAPTER 6

1 We work together with God, and we beg you to make good use of God's kindness to you. 2 In the Scriptures God says,

"When the time came,
    I listened to you,
and when you needed help,
    I came to save you."

That time has come. This is the day for you to be saved.

3 We don't want anyone to find fault with our work, and so we try hard not to cause problems. 4 But in everything and in every way we show that we truly are God's servants. We have always been patient, though we have had a lot of trouble, suffering, and hard times. 5 We have been beaten, put in jail, and hurt in riots. We have worked hard and have gone without sleep or food. 6 But we have kept ourselves pure and have been understanding, patient, and kind. The Holy Spirit has been

---

See also: 4.13: Psa 116.10 (LXX).   5.10: Rom 14.10.

See also: 6.2: Isa 49.8.   6.5: Acts 16.23.

with us, and our love has been real. 7 We have spoken the truth, and God's power has worked in us. In all our struggles we have said and done only what is right.

8 Whether we were honoured or dishonoured or praised or cursed, we always told the truth about ourselves. But some people said we did not. 9 We are unknown to others, but well known to you. We seem to be dying, and yet we are still alive. We have been punished, but never killed, 10 and we are always happy, even in times of suffering. Although we are poor, we have made many people rich. And though we own nothing, everything is ours.

11 Friends in Corinth, we are telling the truth when we say that there is room in our hearts for you. 12 We are not holding back on our love for you, but you are holding back on your love for us. 13 I speak to you as I would speak to my own children. Please make room in your hearts for you.

The temple of the living God

14 Stay away from people who are not followers of the Lord! Can someone who is good get along with someone who is evil? Are light and darkness the same? 15 Is Christ a friend of Satan?* Can people who follow the Lord have anything in common with those who don't? 16 Do idols belong in the temple of God? We are the temple of the living God, as God himself says,

> "I will live with these people
>   and walk among them.
> I will be their God,
> and they will be
>   my people."

17 The Lord also says,

> "Leave them and stay away!
>   Don't touch anything
>   that isn't clean.
> Then I will welcome you
> 18   and be your Father.
> You will be my sons
>   and my daughters,
> as surely as I am God,
>   the All-Powerful."

---

*6.15 Satan: The Greek text has "Beliar", which is another form of the Hebrew word "Belial", meaning "wicked" or "useless". The Jewish people sometimes used this as a name for Satan.

See also: 6.16: a 1 Cor 3.16; 6.19; b Lev 26.12; Ezek 37.27. 6.17: Isa 52.11. 6.18: 2 Sam 7.14; 1 Chron 17.13; Isa 43.6; Jer 31.9

CHAPTER 7

1 My friends, God has made us these promises. So we should stay away from everything that keeps our bodies and spirits from being clean. We should honour God and try to be completely like him.

The church makes Paul happy

2 Make a place for us in your hearts! We haven't ill-treated or hurt anyone. We haven't cheated anyone. 3 I am not saying this to be hard on you. But, as I have said before, you will always be in our thoughts, whether we live or die. 4 I trust you completely.* I am always proud of you, and I am greatly encouraged. In all my trouble I am still very happy.

5 After we came to Macedonia, we didn't have any chance to rest. We were faced with all kinds of problems. We were troubled by enemies and troubled by fears. 6 But God cheers up people in need, and that is what he did when he sent Titus to us. 7 Of course, we were glad to see Titus, but what really made us glad was the way you cheered him up. He told how sorry you were and how concerned you were about me. And this made me even happier.

8 I don't feel bad any more, even though my letter* hurt your feelings. I did feel bad at first, but I don't now. I know that the letter hurt you for a while. 9 Now I am happy, but not because I hurt your feelings. It is because God used your hurt feelings to make you turn back to him, and none of you were harmed by us. 10 When God makes you feel sorry enough to turn to him and be saved, you don't have anything to feel bad about. But when this world makes you feel sorry, it can cause your death.

11 Just look what God has done by making you feel sorry! You sincerely want to prove that you are innocent. You are angry. You are shocked. You are eager to see that justice is done. You have proved that you were completely right in this matter. 12 When I wrote to you, it wasn't to accuse the one who was wrong or to stand up for the one who was hurt. I wrote, so that God would show you how much you do care for us. 13 And we were greatly encouraged.

Although we were encouraged, we felt even better when we saw how happy Titus was, because you had shown that he had shown nothing

---

*7.8 my letter: There is no copy of this letter that Paul wrote to the church at Corinth.

See also: 7.5: 2 Cor 2.13.

to worry about. [14] We had told him how much we thought of you, and you did not disappoint us. Just as we have always told you the truth, so everything we told him about you has also proved to be true. [15] Titus loves all of you very much, especially when he remembers how you obeyed him and how you trembled with fear when you welcomed him. [16] It makes me really glad to know that I can depend on you.

Gifts for the poor

CHAPTER 8

Generous giving

[1] My friends, we want you to know that the churches in Macedonia* have shown others how kind God is. [2] Although they were going through hard times and were very poor, they were glad to give generously. [3] They gave as much as they could afford and even more, simply because they wanted to. [4] They even asked and begged us to let them have the joy of giving their money for God's people. [5] And they did more than we had hoped. They gave themselves first to the Lord and then to us, just as God wanted them to do.

[6] Titus was the one who got you started doing this good thing, so we begged him to help you finish what you had begun. [7] You do everything better than anyone else. You have stronger faith. You speak better and know more. You are eager to give, and you love us better.* Now you must give more generously than anyone else.

[8] I am not ordering you to do this. I am simply testing how real your love is by comparing it with the concern that others have shown. [9] You know that our Lord Jesus Christ was kind enough to give up all his riches and become poor, so that you could become rich.

[10] A year ago you were the first ones to give, and you gave because you wanted to. So listen to my advice. [11] I think you should finish what you started. If you give according to what you have, you will prove that you are as eager to give as you were to think about giving. [12] It doesn't matter how much you have. What matters is how much you are willing to give from what you have.

[13] I am not trying to make life easier for others by making life harder for you. But it is only fair [14] for you to share with them when you have so much, and they have so little. Later, when they have more than enough, and you are in need, they can share with you. Then everyone will have a fair share, [15] just as the Scriptures say,

"Those who gathered
 too much
  had nothing left.
Those who gathered
 only a little
  had all they needed."

Titus and his friends

[16] I am grateful that God made Titus care as much about you as we do. [17] When we begged Titus to visit you, he said he would. He wanted to because he cared so much for you. [18] With Titus we are also sending one of the Lord's followers who is well known in every church for spreading the good news. [19] The churches chose this follower to travel with us while we carry this gift that will bring praise to the Lord and show how much we hope to help. [20] We don't want anyone to find fault with the way we handle your generous gift. [21] But we want to do what pleases the Lord and what people think is right.

[22] We are also sending someone else with Titus and the other follower. We approve of this man. In fact, he has already shown us many times that he wants to help. And now he wants to help even more than ever, because he trusts you so much. [23] Titus is my partner, who works with me to serve you. The other two followers are sent by the churches, and they bring honour to Christ. [24] Treat them in such a way that the churches will see your love and will know why we boasted about you.

CHAPTER 9

The money for God's people

[1] I don't need to write to you about the money you plan to give for God's people. [2] I know how eager you are to give. And I have proudly told the Lord's followers in Macedonia that you people in Achaia have been ready for a whole year. Now your desire to give has made them want to give. [3] That's why I am sending Titus and the two others to you. I want you to be ready, just as I promised. This will prove that we were not wrong to boast about you.

*8.1 churches in Macedonia: The churches that Paul had started in Philippi and Thessalonica. The church in Berea is probably also meant.

See also: 8.1–4: Rom 15.26.

See also: 8.15: Exod 16.18.   8.21: Prov 3.4 (LXX).

⁴ Some followers from Macedonia may come with me, and I want them to find that you have the money ready. If you don't, I would be embarrassed for trusting you to do this. But you would be embarrassed even more. ⁵ So I have decided to ask Titus and the others to spend some time with you before I arrive. This way they can arrange to collect the money you have promised. Then you will have the chance to give because you want to, and not because you feel forced to.

⁶ Remember this saying,

"A few seeds make
   a small harvest,
but a lot of seeds make
   a big harvest."

⁷ Each of you must make up your own mind about how much to give. But don't feel sorry that you must give and don't feel that you are forced to give. God loves people who love to give. ⁸ God can bless you with everything you need, and you will always have more than enough to do all kinds of good things for others. ⁹ The Scriptures say,

"God freely gives his gifts
   to the poor,
and always does right."

¹⁰ God gives seed to farmers and provides everyone with food. He will increase what you have, so that you can give even more to those in need. ¹¹ You will be blessed in every way, and you will be able to keep on being generous. Then many people will thank God when we deliver your gift.

¹² What you are doing is much more than a service that supplies God's people with what they need. It is something that will make many others thank God. ¹³ The way in which you have proved yourselves by this service will bring honour and praise to God. You believed the message about Christ, and you obeyed it by sharing generously with God's people and with everyone else. ¹⁴ Now they are praying for you and want to see you, because God used you to bless them so very much. ¹⁵ Thank God for his gift that is too wonderful for words!

Paul is a true apostle

CHAPTER 10

Paul defends his work for Christ

¹ Do you think I am a coward when I am with you and brave when I am far away? Well, I ask you to listen, because Christ himself was humble and gentle. ² Some people have said that we act like the people of this world. So when I arrive, I expect I will have to be firm and forceful in what I say to them. Please don't make me treat you that way. ³ We live in this world, but we don't act like its people ⁴ or fight our battles with the weapons of this world. Instead, we use God's power that can destroy fortresses. We destroy arguments ⁵ and every bit of pride that keeps anyone from knowing God. We capture people's thoughts and make them obey Christ. ⁶ And when you completely obey him, we will punish anyone who refuses to obey.

⁷ You judge by appearances.ᵉ If any of you think you are the only ones who belong to Christ, then think again. We belong to Christ as much as you do. ⁸ Perhaps I boast a little too much about the authority that the Lord gave me to help you and not to hurt you. Yet I am not embarrassed to boast. ⁹ And I am not trying to scare you with my letters. ¹⁰ Some of you are saying, "Paul's letters are harsh and powerful. But in person, he is a weakling and has nothing worth saying." ¹¹ Those people had better understand that when I am with you, I will do exactly what I say in my letters.

¹² We won't dare compare ourselves with those who think so much of themselves. But they are foolish to compare themselves with themselves. ¹³ We won't boast about something we don't have a right to boast about. We will only boast about the work that God has sent us to do, and you are part of that work. ¹⁴ We are not boasting more than we should. After all, we did bring the message about Christ to you.

¹⁵ We don't boast about what others have done, as if we had done those things ourselves. But I hope that as you become stronger in your faith, we will be able to reach many more of the people around you.ᵉ That has always been our goal. ¹⁶ Then we will be able to preach the good news in other lands where we cannot take credit for work someone else has already done. ¹⁷ The

Scriptures say, "If you want to boast, then boast about the Lord." [18] You may boast about yourself, but the only approval that counts is the Lord's approval.

CHAPTER 11

Paul and the false apostles

[1] Please put up with a little of my foolishness. [2] I am as concerned about you as God is. You were like a virgin bride I had chosen only for Christ. [3] But now I fear that you will be tricked, just as Eve was tricked by that lying snake. I am afraid that you might stop thinking about Christ in an honest and sincere way. [4] We told you about Jesus, and you received the Holy Spirit and accepted our message. But you let some people tell you about another Jesus. Now you are ready to receive another spirit and accept a different message. [5] I think I am as good as any of those super apostles. [6] I may not speak as well as they do, but I know as much. And this has already been made perfectly clear to you.

[7] Was it wrong for me to lower myself and honour you by preaching God's message free of charge? [8] I robbed other churches by taking money from them to serve you. [9] Even when I was in need, I still didn't bother you. In fact, some of the Lord's followers from Macedonia brought me what I needed. I have not been a burden to you in the past, and I will never be a burden. [10] As surely as I speak the truth about Christ, no one in Achaia can stop me from boasting about this. [11] And it isn't because I don't love you. God himself knows how much I do love you.

[12] I plan to go on doing just what I have always done. Then those people won't be able to boast about doing the same things we are doing. [13] Anyway, they are no more than false apostles and dishonest workers. They only pretend to be apostles of Christ. [14] And it is no wonder. Even Satan tries to make himself look like an angel of light. [15] So why does it seem strange for Satan's servants to pretend to do what is right? Some day they will get exactly what they deserve.

Paul's sufferings for Christ

[16] I don't want any of you to think that I am a fool. But if you do, then let me be a fool and boast a little. [17] When I do all this boasting, I do it as a fool and not for the Lord. [18] Yet if others want to boast about what they have

done, so will I. [19] And since you are so clever, you will gladly put up with a fool. [20] In fact, you let people make slaves of you and cheat you and steal from you. Why, you even let them strut around and slap you in the face. [21] I am ashamed to say that we are too weak to behave in such a way.

If they can boast, so can I, but it is a foolish thing to do. [22] Are they Hebrews? So am I. Are they Jews? So am I. Are they from the family of Abraham? Well, so am I. [23] Are they servants of Christ? I am a fool to talk this way, but I serve him better than they do. I have worked harder and have been put in jail more times. I have been beaten with whips more and have been in danger of death more often.

[24] Five times the Jews gave me thirty-nine lashes with a whip. [25] Three times the Romans beat me with a big stick, and once my enemies stoned me. I have been shipwrecked three times, and I even had to spend a night and a day in the sea. [26] During my many travels, I have been in danger from rivers, robbers, my own people, and foreigners. My life has been in danger in cities, in deserts, at sea, and with people who only pretended to be the Lord's followers. [27] I have worked and struggled and spent many sleepless nights. I have gone hungry and thirsty and often had nothing to eat. I have been cold from not having enough clothes to keep me warm. [28] Besides everything else, each day I am burdened down, worrying about all the churches. [29] When others are weak, I am weak too. When others are tricked into sin, I am angry.'

[30] If I have to boast, I will boast about how weak I am. [31] God, the Father of our Lord Jesus, knows I am not lying. And God is to be praised for ever! [32] The governor of Damascus at the time of King Aretas had the city gates guarded, so that he could capture me. [33] But I escaped by being let down in a basket through a window in the city wall.

CHAPTER 12

Visions from the Lord

[1] I have to boast. There is nothing to be gained by it, but I must boast about the visions and other things that the Lord has shown me. [2] I know about one of Christ's followers who was taken up into the third

See also: 11.23: Acts 16.23.   11.24: Deut 25.3.
11.25: a Acts 16.22; b Acts 14.19.   11.26: a Acts 9.23;
b Acts 14.5.   11.32,33: Acts 9.23–25.

See also: 11.3: Gen 3.1–5,13.   11.9: Phil 4.15–18.

heaven fourteen years ago. I don't know if the man was still in his body when it happened, but God certainly knows.

³ As I said, only God really knows if this man was in his body at the time. ⁴ But he was taken up into paradise,* where he heard things that are too wonderful to tell. ⁵ I will boast about that man, but not about myself, except to say how weak I am.

⁶ Yet even if I did boast, I would not be foolish. I would simply be speaking the truth. But I will try not to say too much. That way, none of you will think more highly of me than you should because of what you have seen me do and say. ⁷ Of course, I am now referring to the wonderful things I saw. One of Satan's angels was sent to make me suffer terribly, so that I would not feel too proud.'

⁸ Three times I begged the Lord to make this suffering go away. ⁹ But he replied, "My kindness is all you need. My power is strongest when you are weak." So if Christ keeps giving me his power, I will gladly boast about how weak I am. ¹⁰ Yes, I am glad to be weak or insulted or ill-treated or to have troubles and sufferings, if it is for Christ. Because when I am weak, I am strong.

Paul's concern for the Lord's followers at Corinth

¹¹ I have been making a fool of myself. But you forced me to do it, when you should have been speaking up for me. I may be nothing at all, but I am as good as those super apostles. ¹² When I was with you, I was patient and worked all the powerful miracles and signs and wonders of a true apostle. ¹³ You missed out on only one blessing that the other churches received. That is, you didn't have to support me. Forgive me for doing you wrong.

¹⁴ I am planning to visit you for the third time. But I still won't make a burden of myself. What I really want is you, and not what you have. Children are not supposed to save up for their parents, but parents are supposed to take care of their children. ¹⁵ So I will gladly give all that I have and all that I am. Will you love me less for loving you too much? ¹⁶ You agree that I wasn't a burden to you. Perhaps that's because I was trying to

catch you off guard and trick you. ¹⁷ Were you cheated by any of those I sent to you? ¹⁸ I urged Titus to visit you, and I sent another follower with him. But Titus didn't cheat you, and we felt and behaved the same way he did.

¹⁹ Have you been thinking all along that we have been defending ourselves to you? Actually, we have been speaking to God as followers of Christ. But, my friends, we did it all for your good.

²⁰ I am afraid that when I come, we won't be pleased with each other. I fear that some of you may be arguing or jealous or angry or selfish or gossiping or insulting each other. I even fear that you may be proud and acting like a mob. ²¹ I am afraid God will make me ashamed when I visit you again. I will feel like crying because many of you have never given up your old sins. You are still doing things that are immoral, indecent, and shameful.

CHAPTER 13

Final warnings and greetings

¹ I am on my way to visit you for the third time. And as the Scriptures say, "Any charges must be proved true by at least two or three witnesses." ² During my second visit I warned you that I would punish you and anyone else who doesn't stop sinning. I am far away from you now, but I give you the same warning. ³ This should prove to you that I am speaking for Christ. When he corrects you, he won't be weak. He will be powerful! ⁴ Although he was weak when he was nailed to the cross, he now lives by the power of God. We are weak, just as Christ was. But you will see that we will live by the power of God, just as Christ does.

⁵ Test yourselves and find out if you really are true to your faith. If you pass the test, you will discover that Christ is living in you. But if Christ isn't living in you, you have failed. ⁶ I hope you will discover that we have not failed. ⁷ We pray that you will stop doing evil things. We don't pray like this to make ourselves look good, but to get you to do right, even if we are failures.

⁸ All we can do is to follow the truth and not fight against it. ⁹ Even though we are weak, we are glad that you are strong, and we pray that you will do even better. ¹⁰ I am writing these things to you before I arrive. This way I won't have to be hard on you when I use the authority that the Lord has given me. I was given this authority, so that I could help you and not destroy you.

---

*12.4 paradise: In the Greek translation of the Old Testament, this word is used for the Garden of Eden. In New Testament times it was sometimes used for the place where God's people are happy and at rest, as they wait for the final judgment.

See also: 13.1: Deut 17.6; 19.15.

Final greetings

¹¹ Goodbye, my friends. Do better and pay attention to what I have said. Try to get along and live peacefully with each other.

Now I pray that God, who gives love and peace, will be with you. ¹² Give each other a warm greeting. All God's people send their greetings.

¹³ I pray that the Lord Jesus Christ will bless you and be kind to you! May God bless you with his love, and may the Holy Spirit join all your hearts together.

Additional notes

'1.10 the threat of death: Some manuscripts have "many threats of death".

'1.19 Silas: The Greek text has "Silvanus", which is another form of the name Silas.

'3.2 our: Some manuscripts have "your".

'7.4 I trust you completely: Or "I have always spoken the truth to you" or "I can speak freely to you."

'8.7 you love us better: Some manuscripts have "we love you better."

'10.7 You judge by appearances: Or "Take a close look at yourselves."

'10.15 we will be able to reach many more of the people around you: Or "you will praise us even more because of our work among you."

'11.29 When others are tricked into sin, I get angry: Or "When others stumble into sin, I hurt for them."

'12.7 Of course . . . too proud: Or "Because of the wonderful things that I saw, one of Satan's angels was sent to make me suffer terribly, so that I would not feel too proud."

Galatians

Paul's letter to the churches
in Galatia

A quick look at this letter

From the very beginning of this letter to the churches in the region of Galatia (in central Asia Minor), Paul makes two things clear to his readers: he is a true apostle, and his message is the only true message (1.1–10). These statements were very important, because some people claimed that Paul was a false apostle with a false message.

Paul was indeed a true apostle, and his mission to the Gentiles was given to him by the Lord and approved by the apostles in Jerusalem (1.18–2.10). Paul had even corrected the apostle Peter, when he had stopped eating with Gentile followers who were not obeying the Law of Moses (2.1–18).

Faith is the only way to be saved. Paul insists that this was true already for Abraham, who had received God's promise by faith. And Paul leaves no doubt about what his own faith means to him:

> *I have been nailed to the cross with Christ.*
> *I have died, but Christ lives in me. And I now*
> *live by faith in the Son of God, who loved me*
> *and gave his life for me.*
>
> (2.19b,20)

A true apostle and the true message

CHAPTER 1

1-2 *From the apostle Paul and from all the Lord's followers with me.*

I was chosen to be an apostle by Jesus Christ and by God the Father, who raised him from death. No mere human chose or appointed me to this work.

To the churches in Galatia.

3 I pray that God the Father and our Lord Jesus Christ will be kind to you and will bless you with peace! 4 Christ obeyed God our Father and gave himself as a sacrifice for our sins to rescue us from this evil world. 5 God will be given glory for ever and ever. Amen.

The only true message

6 I am shocked that you have so quickly turned from God, who chose you because of his wonderful kindness.* You have believed another message, 7 when there is really only one true message. But some people are causing you trouble and want to make you turn away from the good news about Christ. 8 I pray that God will punish anyone who

preaches anything different from our message to you! It doesn't matter if that person is one of us or an angel from heaven. ⁹ I have said it before, and I will say it again. I hope God will punish anyone who preaches anything different from what you have already believed.

¹⁰ I am not trying to please people. I want to please God. Do you think I am trying to please people? If I were doing that, I would not be a servant of Christ.

God chose Paul to be an apostle

How Paul became an apostle

¹¹ My friends, I want you to know that no one made up the message I preach. It wasn't given or taught to me by some mere human. My message came directly from Jesus Christ when he appeared to me.

¹³ You know how I used to live as a Jew. I was cruel to God's church and even tried to destroy it. ¹⁴ I was a much better Jew than anyone else my own age, and I obeyed every law that our ancestors had given us. ¹⁵ But even before I was born, God had chosen me. He was kind and had decided ¹⁶ to show me his Son, so that I would announce his message to the Gentiles. I didn't talk this over with anyone. ¹⁷ I didn't say a word, not even to the men in Jerusalem who were apostles before I was. Instead, I went at once to Arabia, and afterwards I returned to Damascus.

¹⁸ Three years later I went to visit Peter* in Jerusalem and stayed with him for fifteen days. ¹⁹ The only other apostle I saw was James, the Lord's brother. ²⁰ And in the presence of God I swear I am telling the truth.

²¹ Later, I went to the regions of Syria and Cilicia. ²² But no one who belonged to Christ's churches in Judea had ever seen me in person. ²³ They had only heard that the one who had been cruel to them was now preaching the message that he had once tried to destroy. ²⁴ And because of me, they praised God.

Paul defends his message

CHAPTER 2

¹ Fourteen years later I went to Jerusalem with Barnabas. I also took along Titus. ² But I went there because God had told me to go, and I explained the good news that I had been preaching to the Gentiles. Then I met privately with the ones who seemed to be the most important leaders. I wanted to make sure that my work in the past and my future work would not be for nothing.

³ Titus went to Jerusalem with me. He was a Greek, but still he wasn't forced to be circumcised. ⁴ We went there because of those who pretended to be followers and had sneaked in among us as spies. They had come to take away the freedom that Christ Jesus had given us, and they were trying to make us their slaves. ⁵ But we wanted you to have the true message. That's why we didn't give in to them, not even for a second.

⁶ Some of them were supposed to be important leaders, but I didn't care who they were. God doesn't have any favourites! None of these so-called special leaders added anything to my message. ⁷ They realized that God had sent me with the good news for Gentiles, and that he had sent Peter with the same message for Jews. ⁸ God, who had sent Peter on a mission to the Jews, was now using me to preach to the Gentiles.

⁹ James, Peter,* and John realized that God had given me the message about his undeserved kindness. And these men are supposed to be the backbone of the church. They even gave Barnabas and me a friendly handshake. This was to show that we would work with Gentiles and that they would work with Jews. ¹⁰ They only asked us to remember the poor, and that was something I had always been eager to do.

Paul corrects Peter at Antioch

¹¹ When Peter came to Antioch, I told him face to face that he was wrong. ¹² He used to eat with Gentile followers of the Lord, until James sent some Jewish followers. Peter was afraid of the Jews and soon stopped eating with Gentiles. ¹³ He and the other Jews hid their true feelings so well that even Barnabas

---

*1.18 Peter: The Greek text has "Cephas," which is an Aramaic name meaning "rock". Peter is the Greek name with the same meaning.

See also: 1.13: Acts 8.3; 22.4,5; 26.9–11. 1.14: Acts 22.3.
1.15,16: Acts 9.3–6; 22.6–10; 26.13–18. 1.18: Acts 9.26–30.

*2.9 Peter: See note at 1.18.
See also: 2.1: Acts 11.30; 15.2. 2.6: Deut 10.17.

was fooled. ¹⁴ But when I saw that they were not really obeying the truth that is in the good news, I corrected Peter in front of everyone and said:

Peter, you are a Jew, but you live like a Gentile. So how can you force Gentiles to live like Jews?

¹⁵ We are Jews by birth and are not sinners like Gentiles. ¹⁶ But we know that God accepts only those who have faith in Jesus Christ. No one can please God by simply obeying the Law. So we put our faith in Christ Jesus, and God accepted us because of our faith.

¹⁷ When we Jews started looking for a way to please God, we discovered that we are sinners too. Does this mean that Christ is the one who makes us sinners? No, it doesn't! ¹⁸ But if I tear down something and then build it again, I prove that I was wrong at first. ¹⁹ It was the Law itself that killed me and freed me from its power, so that I could live for God.

I have been nailed to the cross with Christ. ²⁰ I have died, but Christ lives in me. And I now live by faith in the Son of God, who loved me and gave his life for me. ²¹ I don't turn my back on God's undeserved kindness. If we can be acceptable to God by obeying the Law, it was useless for Christ to die.

Faith is the only way to be saved

CHAPTER 3

¹ You stupid Galatians! I told you exactly how Jesus Christ was nailed to a cross. Has someone now put an evil spell on you? ² I want to know only one thing. How were you given God's Spirit? Was it by obeying the Law of Moses or by hearing about Christ and having faith in him? ³ How can you be so stupid? Do you think that by yourself you can complete what God's Spirit started in you? ⁴ Have you gone through all this for nothing? Is it all really for nothing? ⁵ God gives you his Spirit and works miracles in you. But does he do this because you obey the Law of Moses or because you have heard about Christ and have faith in him?

⁶ The Scriptures say that God accepted Abraham because Abraham had faith. ⁷ And so, you should understand that everyone who has faith is a child of Abraham.* ⁸ Long ago the Scriptures said that God would accept the Gentiles because of their faith. That's why God told Abraham the good news that all nations would be blessed because of him. ⁹ This means that everyone who has faith will share in the blessings that were given to Abraham because of his faith.

¹⁰ Anyone who tries to please God by obeying the Law is under a curse. The Scriptures say, "Everyone who doesn't obey everything in the Law is under a curse." ¹¹ No one can please God by obeying the Law. The Scriptures also say, "The people God accepts because of their faith will live."* ¹² The Law isn't based on faith. It promises life only to people who obey its commands. ¹³ But Christ rescued us from the Law's curse, when he became a curse in our place. This is because the Scriptures say that anyone who is nailed to a tree is under a curse. ¹⁴ And because of what Jesus Christ has done, the blessing that was promised to Abraham was taken to the Gentiles. This happened so that by faith we would be given the promised Holy Spirit.

The Law and the promise

¹⁵ My friends, I will use an everyday example to explain what I mean. Once someone agrees to something, no one else can change or cancel the agreement.* ¹⁶ That is how it is with the promises God made to Abraham and his descendant.* The promises were not made to many descendants, but only to one, and that one is Christ. ¹⁷ What I am saying is that the Law cannot change or cancel God's promise that was made 430 years before the Law was given. ¹⁸ If we have to obey the Law in order to receive God's blessings, those blessings don't really come to us because of God's promise. But God was kind to Abraham and made him a promise.

*3.7 a child of Abraham: God chose Abraham, and so it was believed that anyone who was a child of Abraham was also a child of God. See the note at 3.29.
*3.16 descendant: The Greek text has "seed," which may mean one or many descendants. In this verse Paul says it means Christ.

See also: **3.6:** Gen 15.6; Rom 4.3. **3.7:** Rom 4.16.
3.8: Gen 12.3. **3.10:** Deut 27.26 (LXX). **3.11:** Hab 2.4.
3.12: Lev 18.5. **3.13:** Deut 21.23. **3.17:** Exod 12.40.
3.18: Rom 4.14.

¹⁹ What is the use of the Law? It was given later to show that we sin. But it was only supposed to last until the coming of that descendant* who was given the promise. In fact, angels gave the Law to Moses, and he gave it to the people. ²⁰ There is only one God, and the Law did not come directly from him.

Slaves and children

²¹ Does the Law disagree with God's promises? No, it doesn't! If any law could give life to us, we could become acceptable to God by obeying that law. ²² But the Scriptures say that sin controls everyone, so that God's promises will be for anyone who has faith in Jesus Christ.

²³ The Law controlled us and kept us under its power until the time came when we would have faith. ²⁴ In fact, the Law was our teacher. It was supposed to teach us until we had faith and were acceptable to God. ²⁵ But once a person has learnt to have faith, there is no more need to have the Law as a teacher.

²⁶ All of you are God's children because of your faith in Christ Jesus. ²⁷ And when you were baptized, it was as though you had put on Christ in the same way you put on new clothes. ²⁸ Faith in Christ Jesus is what makes each of you equal with each other, whether you are a Jew or a Greek, a slave or a free person, a man or a woman. ²⁹ So if you belong to Christ, you are now part of Abraham's family,* and you will be given what God has promised.

CHAPTER 4

¹ Children who are under age are no better off than slaves, even though everything their parents own will some day be theirs. ² This is because children are placed in the care of guardians and teachers until the time their parents have set. ³ That is how it was with us. We were like children ruled by the powers of this world.

⁴ But when the time was right, God sent his Son, and a woman gave birth to him. His Son obeyed the Law, ⁵ so he could set us free from the Law, and we could become God's children. ⁶ Now that we are his children, God has sent the Spirit of his Son into our hearts.

And his Spirit tells us that God is our Father. ⁷ You are no longer slaves. You are God's children, and you will be given what he has promised.

Paul's concern for the Galatians

⁸ Before you knew God, you were slaves of gods that are not real. ⁹ But now you know God, or better still, God knows you. How can you turn back and become the slaves of those weak and pitiful powers?* ¹⁰ You even celebrate certain days, months, seasons, and years. ¹¹ I am afraid I have wasted my time working with you.

¹² My friends, I beg you to be like me, just as I once tried to be like you. Did you ill-treat me ¹³ when I first preached to you? No you didn't, even though you knew I had come there because I was sick. ¹⁴ My illness must have caused you some trouble, but you didn't hate me or turn me away because of it. You welcomed me as though I were one of God's angels or even Christ Jesus himself. ¹⁵ Where is that good feeling now? I am sure that if it had been possible, you would have taken out your own eyes and given them to me. ¹⁶ Am I now your enemy, just because I told you the truth?

¹⁷ Those people may be paying you a lot of attention, but it isn't for your good. They only want to keep you away from me, so you will pay them a lot of attention. ¹⁸ It is always good to give your attention to something worthwhile, even when I am not with you. ¹⁹ My children, I am in terrible pain until Christ may be seen living in you. ²⁰ I wish I were with you now. Then I would not have to talk this way. You really have me puzzled.

Hagar and Sarah

²¹ Some of you would like to be under the rule of the Law of Moses. But do you know what the Law says? ²² In the Scriptures we learn that Abraham had two sons. The mother of one of them was a slave, while the mother of the other one had always been free. ²³ The son of the slave woman was born in the usual way. But the son of the free woman was born because of God's promise.

²⁴ All this has another meaning as well. Each of the two women stands for one of the agreements God made with his people.

---

*3.19 that descendant: Jesus.
*3.29 you are now part of Abraham's family: Paul tells the Galatians that faith in Jesus Christ is what makes someone a true child of Abraham and of God. See the note at 3.7.

See also: 3.29: Rom 4.13. 4.5–7: Rom 8.15–17.

*4.9 powers: Spirits were thought to control human lives and were believed to be connected with the movements of the stars.

See also: 4.22: a Gen 16.15; b Gen 21.2.

Hagar, the slave woman, stands for the agreement that was made at Mount Sinai. Everyone born into her family is a slave. 25 Hagar also stands for Mount Sinai in Arabia[a] and for the present city of Jerusalem. She[a] and her children are slaves.

26 But our mother is the city of Jerusalem in heaven above, and she isn't a slave. 27 The Scriptures say about her,

"You have never had children,
    but now you can be glad.
You have never given birth,
    but now you can shout.
Once you had no children,
    but now you will have
more children than a woman
    who has been married
    for a long time."

28 My friends, you were born because of this promise, just as Isaac was. 29 But the child who was born in the natural way made trouble for the child who was born because of the Spirit. The same thing is happening today. 30 The Scriptures say, "Get rid of the slave woman and her son! He won't be given anything. The son of the free woman will receive everything." 31 My friends, we are children of the free woman and not of the slave.

Guided by the Spirit and love

CHAPTER 5

Christ gives freedom

1 Christ has set us free! This means we are really free. Now hold on to your freedom and don't ever become slaves of the Law again.

2 I, Paul, promise you that Christ won't do you any good if you get circumcised. 3 If you do, you must obey the whole Law. 4 And if you try to please God by obeying the Law, you have cut yourself off from Christ and his wonderful kindness. 5 But the Spirit makes us sure that God will accept us because of our faith in Christ. 6 If you are a follower of Christ Jesus, it makes no difference whether you are circumcised or not. All that matters is your faith that makes you love others.

7 You were doing so well until someone made you turn from the truth. 8 And that person was certainly not sent by the one who chose you. 9 A little yeast can change a whole batch of dough, 10 but you belong to the Lord. That makes me certain that you will do what I say, instead of what someone else tells you to do. Whoever is causing trouble for you will be punished.

11 My friends, if I still preach that people need to be circumcised, why am I in so much trouble? The message about the cross would no longer be a problem, if I told people to be circumcised. 12 I wish that everyone who is upsetting you would not only get circumcised, but would cut off much more!

13 My friends, you were chosen to be free. So don't use your freedom as an excuse to do anything you want. Use it as an opportunity to serve each other with love. 14 All that the Law says can be summed up in the command to love others as much as you love yourself. 15 But if you keep attacking each other like wild animals, you had better watch out or you will destroy yourselves.

God's Spirit and our own desires

16 If you are guided by the Spirit, you won't obey your selfish desires. 17 The Spirit and your desires are enemies of each other. They are always fighting each other and keeping you from doing what you feel you should. 18 But if you obey the Spirit, the Law of Moses has no control over you.

19 People's desires make them give in to immoral ways, filthy thoughts, and shameful deeds. 20 They worship idols, practise witchcraft, hate others, and are hard to get along with. People become jealous, angry, and selfish. They not only argue and cause trouble, but they are 21 envious. They get drunk, carry on at wild parties, and do other evil things as well. I told you before, and I am telling you again: no one who does these things will share in the blessings of God's kingdom.

22 God's Spirit makes us loving, happy, peaceful, patient, kind, good, faithful, 23 gentle, and self-controlled. There is no law against behaving in any of these ways. 24 And because we belong to Christ Jesus, we have killed our selfish feelings and desires.

See also: 4.27: Isa 54.1. 4.29: Gen 21.9. 4.30: Gen 21.10.

See also: 5.9: 1 Cor 5.6. 5.14: Lev 19.18.
5.17: Rom 7.15–23.

25 God's Spirit has given us life, and so we should follow the Spirit. 26 But don't be conceited or make others jealous by claiming to be better than they are.

CHAPTER 6

Help each other

1 My friends, you are spiritual. So if someone is trapped in sin, you should gently lead that person back to the right path. But watch out, and don't be tempted yourself. 2 You obey the law of Christ when you offer each other a helping hand.

3 If you think you are better than others, when you really aren't, you are wrong. 4 Do your own work well, and then you will have something to be proud of. But don't compare yourself with others. 5 We each must carry our own load.

6 Share every good thing you have with anyone who teaches you what God has said. 7 You cannot fool God, so don't make a fool of yourself! You will harvest what you plant. 8 If you follow your selfish desires, you will harvest destruction, but if you follow the Spirit, you will harvest eternal life. 9 Don't get tired of helping others. You will be rewarded when the time is right, if you don't give up. 10 We should help people whenever we can, especially if they are followers of the Lord.

Final warnings

11 You can see what big letters I make when I write with my own hand.

12 Those people who are telling you to get circumcised are only trying to show how important they are. And they don't want to get into trouble for preaching about the cross of Christ. 13 They are circumcised, but they don't obey the Law of Moses. All they want is to boast about having you circumcised. 14 But I will never boast about anything except the cross of our Lord Jesus Christ. Because of his cross, the world is dead as far as I am concerned, and I am dead as far as the world is concerned.

15 It doesn't matter if you are circumcised or not. All that matters is that you are a new person.

16 If you follow this rule, you will belong to God's true people. God will treat you with undeserved kindness and will bless you with peace.

17 On my own body are scars that prove I belong to Christ Jesus. So I don't want anyone to bother me any more.

18 My friends, I pray that the Lord Jesus Christ will be kind to you! Amen.

Additional notes

▸**1.6 his wonderful kindness:** Some manuscripts have "the wonderful kindness of Christ".

▸**3.11 The people God accepts because of their faith will live:** Or "The people God accepts will live because of their faith."

▸**3.15 Once someone . . . cancel the agreement:** Or "Once a person makes out a will, no one can change or cancel it."

▸**4.25 Hagar also stands for Mount Sinai in Arabia:** Some manuscripts have "Sinai is a mountain in Arabia". This sentence would then be translated: "Sinai is a mountain in Arabia, and Hagar stands for the present city of Jerusalem."

▸**4.25 She:** "Hagar" or "Jerusalem".

Ephesians

Paul's letter to the church in Ephesus

A quick look at this letter

"Praise the God and Father of our Lord Jesus Christ for the spiritual blessings that Christ has brought us from heaven!" (1.3). Paul begins his letter to the Christians in Ephesus with a powerful reminder of the main theme of his message. Christ died on the cross to set us free (1.7,8). But God raised Christ from death, and he now sits at God's right side in heaven, where he rules over this world. And he will rule over the future world as well (1.20,21).

Christ brought Jews and Gentiles together by "breaking down the wall of hatred" that separated them (2.14) and he united them all as part of that holy temple where God's Spirit lives (2.22). This was according to God's eternal plan (3.11).

There is only one Lord, one Spirit of God, and one God, who is the Father of all people (4.4,5). This means that Christians must let the Spirit keep their hearts united, so they can live at peace with each other (4.3). The idea of all Christians being one with Christ is so central to this letter that it occurs twenty times. There is one faith and one baptism by which believers become one body.

Ephesus was a city port on the western shore of Asia Minor (modern-day Turkey). In Paul's time this was the fourth largest city in the Roman Empire. It was also an ancient centre of nature religion where the goddess Artemis was widely worshipped (Acts 19).

Paul lets the Ephesians know that much is expected of people who are called to a new life (4.17—5.20). Followers of the Lord are God's dear children, and they must do as God does (5.1). They used to live in the dark, but they must now live in the light and make their light shine (5.8,9).

Paul then teaches husbands and wives, children and parents, and slaves and masters how to live as Christians (5.21—6.9).

Paul never forgets how kind God is:

> God was merciful! We were dead because of our sins, but God loved us so much that he made us alive with Christ, and God's wonderful kindness is what saves you . . . You were saved by faith in God, who treats us much better than we deserve. This is God's gift to you, and not anything you have done on your own.
>
> (2.4,5,8)

Greetings

CHAPTER 1

¹ *From Paul, chosen by God to be an apostle of Christ Jesus.*

To God's people who live in Ephesus and are faithful followers of Christ Jesus.

² I pray that God our Father and our Lord Jesus Christ will be kind to you and will bless you with peace!

Christ brings spiritual blessings

³ Praise the God and Father of our Lord Jesus Christ for the spiritual blessings that Christ has brought us from heaven! ⁴ Before the world was created, God had Christ choose us to live with him and to be his holy and innocent and loving people. ⁵ God was kind' and decided that Christ would choose us to be God's own adopted children. ⁶ God was very kind to us because of the Son he dearly loves, and so we should praise God.

⁷⁻⁸ Christ sacrificed his life's blood to set us free, which means that our sins are now forgiven. Christ did this because God was so kind to us. God has great wisdom and understanding, ⁹ and by what Christ has done, God has shown us his own mysterious ways. ¹⁰ Then when the time is right, God will do all that he has planned, and Christ will bring together everything in heaven and on earth.

¹¹ God always does what he plans, and that's why he appointed Christ to choose us. ¹² He did this so that we Jews would bring honour to him and be the first ones to have hope because of him. ¹³ Christ also brought you the truth, which is the good news about how you can be saved. You put your faith in Christ and were given the promised Holy Spirit to show that you belong to God. ¹⁴ The Spirit also makes us sure that we will be given what God has stored up for his people. Then we will be set free, and God will be honoured and praised.

Paul's prayer

¹⁵ I have heard about your faith in the Lord Jesus and your love for all God's people. ¹⁶ So I never stop being grateful for you, as I mention you in my prayers. ¹⁷ I ask the

glorious Father and God of our Lord Jesus Christ to give you his Spirit. The Spirit will make you wise and let you understand what it means to know God. ¹⁸ My prayer is that light will flood your hearts and that you will understand the hope that was given to you when God chose you. Then you will discover the glorious blessings that will be yours together with all God's people.

¹⁹ I want you to know about the great and mighty power that God has for us followers. It is the same wonderful power he used ²⁰ when he raised Christ from death and let him sit at his right side* in heaven. ²¹ There Christ rules over all forces, authorities, powers, and rulers. He rules over all beings in this world and will rule in the future world as well. ²² God has put all things under the power of Christ, and for the good of the church he has made him the head of everything. ²³ The church is Christ's body and is filled with Christ who completely fills everything.'

CHAPTER 2

From death to life

¹ In the past you were dead because you sinned and fought against God. ² You followed the ways of this world and obeyed the devil. He rules the world, and his spirit has power over everyone who doesn't obey God. ³ Once we were also ruled by the selfish desires of our bodies and minds. We had made God angry, and we were going to be punished like everyone else.

⁴⁻⁵ But God was merciful! We were dead because of our sins, but God loved us so much that he made us alive with Christ, and God's wonderful kindness is what saves you. ⁶ God raised us from death to life with Christ Jesus, and he has given us a place beside Christ in heaven. ⁷ God did this so that in the future world he could show how truly good and kind he is to us because of what Christ Jesus has done. ⁸ You were saved by faith in God, who treats us much better than we deserve.* This is God's gift to you, and not anything you have done on your own. ⁹ It isn't something you have earned,

---

*1.20 right side: The place of power and honour.
*2.8 treats us much better than we deserve: The Greek word *charis*, traditionally rendered "grace", is translated here and in other places in the CEV to express the overwhelming kindness of God.

See also: 1.20: Psa 110.1. 1.22: Psa 8.6.
1.22,23: Col 1.18. 2.1–5: Col 2.13.

so there is nothing you can boast about. [10] God planned for us to do good things and to live as he has always wanted us to live. That's why he sent Christ to make us what we are.

United by Christ

[11] Don't forget that you are Gentiles. In fact, you used to be called "uncircumcised" by those who take pride in being circumcised. [12] At that time you did not know about Christ. You were foreigners to the people of Israel, and you had no part in the promises that God had made to them. You were living in this world without hope and without God, [13] and you were far from God. But Christ offered his life's blood as a sacrifice and brought you near God.

[14] Christ has made peace between Jews and Gentiles, and he has united us by breaking down the wall of hatred that separated us. Christ gave his own body [15] to destroy the Law of Moses with all its rules and commands. He even brought Jews and Gentiles together as though we were only one person, when he united us in peace. [16] On the cross Christ did away with our hatred for each other. He also made peace* between us and God by uniting Jews and Gentiles in one body. [17] Christ came and preached peace to you Gentiles, who were far from God, and peace to us Jews, who were near God. [18] And because of Christ, all of us can come to the Father by the same Spirit.

[19] You Gentiles are no longer strangers and foreigners. You are citizens with everyone else who belongs to the family of God. [20] You are like a building with the apostles and prophets as the foundation and with Christ as the most important stone. [21] Christ is the one who holds the building together and makes it grow into a holy temple for the Lord. [22] And you are part of that building Christ has built as a place for God's own Spirit to live.

CHAPTER 3

Paul's mission to the Gentiles

[1] Christ Jesus made me his prisoner, so that I could help you Gentiles. [2] You have heard about God's kindness in choosing me to help you. [3] In fact, this letter tells you a little about how God has shown me his mysterious ways.

[4] As you read the letter, you will also find out how well I really do understand the mystery about Christ. [5] No one knew about this mystery until God's Spirit told it to his holy apostles and prophets. [6] And the mystery is this: Because of Christ Jesus, the good news has given the Gentiles a share in the promises that God gave to the Jews. God has also let the Gentiles be part of the same body.

[7] God treated me with kindness. His power worked in me, and it became my job to spread the good news. [8] I am the least important of all God's people. But God was kind and chose me to tell the Gentiles that because of Christ there are blessings that cannot be measured. [9] God, who created everything, wanted me to help everyone understand the mysterious plan that had always been hidden in his mind. [10] Then God would use the church to show the powers and authorities in the spiritual world that he has many different kinds of wisdom.

[11] God did this according to his eternal plan. And he was able to do what he had planned because of all that Christ Jesus our Lord had done. [12] Christ now gives us courage and confidence, so that we can come to God by faith. [13] That's why you should not be discouraged when I suffer for you. After all, it will bring honour to you.

Christ's love for us

[14] I kneel in prayer to the Father. [15] All beings in heaven and on earth receive their life from him.* [16] God is wonderful and glorious. I pray that his Spirit will make you become strong followers [17] and that Christ will live in your hearts because of your faith. Stand firm and be deeply rooted in his love. [18] I pray that you and all God's people will understand what is called wide or long or high or deep.* [19] I want you to know all about Christ's love, although it is too wonderful to be measured. Then your lives will be filled with all that God is.

[20-21] I pray that Christ Jesus and the church will for ever bring praise to God. His power at work in us can do far more than we dare ask or imagine. Amen.

---

*3.18 what is called wide or long or high or deep: This may refer to the heavenly Jerusalem or to God's love or wisdom or to the meaning of the cross.

See also: 2.15: Col 2.14. 2.16: Col 1.20. 2.17: Isa 57.19.

See also: 3.4–6: Col 1.26,27.

A new life in unity with Christ

CHAPTER 4

Unity with Christ

¹ As a prisoner of the Lord, I beg you to live in a way that is worthy of the people God has chosen to be his own. ² Always be humble and gentle. Patiently put up with each other and love each other. ³ Try your best to let God's Spirit keep your hearts united. Do this by living at peace. ⁴ All of you are part of the same body. There is only one Spirit of God, just as you were given one hope when you were chosen to be God's people. ⁵ We have only one Lord, one faith, and one baptism. ⁶ There is one God who is the Father of all people. Not only is God above all others, but he works by using all of us, and he lives in all of us.

⁷ Christ has generously divided out his gifts to us. ⁸ As the Scriptures say,

"When he went up
to the highest place,
he led away many prisoners
and gave gifts to people."

⁹ When it says, "he went up," it means that Christ had been deep in the earth. ¹⁰ This also means that the one who went deep into the earth is the same one who went into the highest heaven, so that he would fill the whole universe.

¹¹ Christ chose some of us to be apostles, prophets, missionaries, pastors, and teachers, ¹² so that his people would learn to serve and his body would grow strong. ¹³ This will continue until we are united by our faith and by our understanding of the Son of God. Then we will be mature, just as Christ is, and we will be completely like him.

¹⁴ We must stop acting like children. We must not let deceitful people trick us by their false teachings, which are like winds that toss us around from place to place. ¹⁵ Love should always make us tell the truth. Then we will grow in every way and be more like Christ, the head ¹⁶ of the body. Christ holds it together and makes all its parts work perfectly, as it grows and becomes strong because of love.

The old life and the new life

¹⁷ As a follower of the Lord, I order you to stop living like stupid, godless people. ¹⁸ Their minds are in the dark, and they are stubborn and ignorant and have missed out on the life that comes from God. They no longer have any feelings about what is right, ¹⁹ and they are so greedy that they do all kinds of indecent things.

²⁰⁻²¹ But that isn't what you were taught about Jesus Christ. He is the truth, and you heard about him and learnt about him. ²² You were told that your foolish desires will destroy you and that you must give up your old way of life with all its bad habits. ²³ Let the Spirit change your way of thinking ²⁴ and make you into a new person. You were created to be like God, and so you must please him and be truly holy.

Rules for the new life

²⁵ We are part of the same body. Stop lying and start telling each other the truth. ²⁶ Don't get so angry that you sin. Don't go to bed angry ²⁷ and don't give the devil a chance. ²⁸ If you are a thief, stop stealing. Be honest and work hard, so you will have something to give to people in need. ²⁹ Stop all your dirty talk. Say the right thing at the right time and help others by what you say. ³⁰ Don't make God's Spirit sad. The Spirit makes you sure that some day you will be free from your sins. ³¹ Stop being bitter and angry with others. Don't yell at one another or curse each other or ever be rude. ³² Instead, be kind and merciful, and forgive others, just as God forgave you because of Christ.

CHAPTER 5

¹ Do as God does. After all, you are his dear children. ² Let love be your guide. Christ loved us* and offered his life for us as a sacrifice that pleases God.

³ You are God's people, so don't let it be said that any of you are immoral or indecent or greedy. ⁴ Don't use dirty or foolish or filthy words. Instead, say how thankful you are. ⁵ Being greedy, indecent, or immoral is just another way of worshipping idols.

See also: **4.2:** Col 3.12,13. **4.8:** Psa 68.18. **4.16:** Col 2.19.
4.22: Col 3.9. **4.24:** a Col 3.10; b Gen 1.26.
4.25: Zech 8.16. **4.26:** Psa 4.4 (LXX). **4.32:** Col 3.13.
5.2: Exod 29.18; Psa 40.6.

You can be sure that people who behave in this way will never be part of the kingdom that belongs to Christ and to God.

Living as people of the light

6 Don't let anyone trick you with foolish talk. God punishes everyone who disobeys him and says' foolish things. 7 So don't have anything to do with anyone like that.

8 You used to be like people living in the dark, but now you are people of the light because you belong to the Lord. So act like people of the light 9 and make your light shine. Be good and honest and truthful, 10 as you try to please the Lord. 11 Don't take part in doing those worthless things that are done in the dark. Instead, show how wrong they are. 12 It is disgusting even to talk about what is done in the dark. 13 But the light will show what these things are really like. 14 Light shows up everything,' just as the Scriptures say,

> "Wake up from your sleep
>   and rise from death.
>   Then Christ will shine on you."

15 Act like people with good sense and not like fools. 16 These are evil times, so make every minute count. 17 Don't be stupid. Instead, find out what the Lord wants you to do. 18 Don't destroy yourself by getting drunk, but let the Spirit fill your life. 19 When you meet together, sing psalms, hymns, and spiritual songs, as you praise the Lord with all your heart. 20 Always use the name of our Lord Jesus Christ to thank God the Father for everything.

Wives and husbands

21 Honour Christ and put others first. 22 A wife should put her husband first, as she does the Lord. 23 A husband is the head of his wife, as Christ is the head and the Saviour of the church, which is his own body. 24 Wives should always put their husbands first, as the church puts Christ first.

25 A husband should love his wife as much as Christ loved the church and gave his life for it. 26 He made the church holy by the power of his word, and he made it pure by washing it with water. 27 Christ did this, so that he would have a glorious and holy church, without faults or spots or wrinkles or any other flaws.

28 In the same way, a husband should love his wife as much as he loves himself. A husband who loves his wife shows that he loves himself. 29 None of us hate our own bodies. We provide for them and take good care of them, just as Christ does for the church, 30 because we are each part of his body. 31 As the Scriptures say, "A man leaves his father and mother to get married, and he becomes like one person with his wife."
32 This is a great mystery, but I understand it to mean Christ and his church. 33 So each husband should love his wife as much as he loves himself, and each wife should respect her husband.

CHAPTER 6

Children and parents

1 Children, you belong to the Lord, and you do the right thing when you obey your parents. The first commandment with a promise says, 2 "Obey your father and your mother, 3 and you will have a long and happy life."

4 Parents, don't be hard on your children. Raise them properly. Teach them and instruct them about the Lord.

Slaves and masters

5 Slaves, you must obey your earthly masters. Show them great respect and be as loyal to them as you are to Christ. 6 Try to please them at all times, and not just when you think they are watching. You are slaves of Christ, so with your whole heart you must do what God wants you to do. 7 Gladly serve your masters, as though they were the Lord himself, and not simply people. 8 You know that you will be rewarded for any good things you do, whether you are slaves or free.

9 Slave owners, you must treat your slaves with this same respect. Don't threaten them. They have the same Master in heaven that you do, and he doesn't have any favourites.

The fight against evil

10 Finally, let the mighty strength of the Lord make you strong. 11 Put on all the armour that God gives, so you can defend yourself against the devil's tricks. 12 We are not fighting against humans. We are fighting against forces and authorities and against

See also: 5.16: Col 4.5. 5.19,20: Col 3.16,17. 5.22: Col 3.18; 1 Pet 3.1. 5.25: Col 3.19; 1 Pet 3.7.

See also: 5.31: Gen 2.24. 6.1: Col 3.20. 6.2,3: Exod 20.12; Deut 5.16. 6.4: Col 3.21. 6.5–8: Col 3.22–25. 6.9: a Col 4.1; b Deut 10.17; Col 3.25.

rulers of darkness and powers in the spiritual world. ¹³ So put on all the armour that God gives. Then when that evil day* comes, you will be able to defend yourself. And when the battle is over, you will still be standing firm.

¹⁴ Be ready! Let the truth be like a belt around your waist, and let God's justice protect you like armour. ¹⁵ Your desire to tell the good news about peace should be like shoes on your feet. ¹⁶ Let your faith be like a shield, and you will be able to stop all the flaming arrows of the evil one. ¹⁷ Let God's saving power be like a helmet, and for a sword use God's message that comes from the Spirit.

¹⁸ Never stop praying, especially for others. Always pray by the power of the Spirit. Stay alert and keep praying for God's people. ¹⁹ Pray that I will be given the message to speak and that I may fearlessly explain the mystery about the good news. ²⁰ I was sent to do this work, and that's the reason I am in jail. So pray that I will be brave and will speak as I should.

Final greetings

²¹⁻²² I want you to know how I am getting along and what I am doing. That's why I am sending Tychicus to you. He is a dear friend, as well as a faithful servant of the Lord. He will tell you how I am doing, and he will cheer you up.

²³ I pray that God the Father and the Lord Jesus Christ will give peace, love, and faith to every follower! ²⁴ May God be kind to everyone who keeps on loving our Lord Jesus Christ.

See also: **6.14:** a Isa 11.5; b Isa 59.17. **6.15:** Isa 52.7.
6.17: Isa 59.17. **6.21:** Acts 20.4; 2 Tim 4.12.
6.21,22: Col 4.7,8.

Additional notes

*1.1 live in Ephesus and: Some manuscripts do not have these words.
*1.4,5 holy and innocent and loving people. ⁵ God was kind: Or "holy and innocent people. God was loving ⁵ and kind."
*1.23 and is filled with Christ who completely fills everything: Or "which completely fills Christ and fully completes his work."
*2.16 He also made peace: Or "The cross also made peace".
*3.15 receive their life from him: Or "know who they really are because of him."

*4.13 and we will be completely like him: Or "and he is completely perfect."
*5.2 us: Some manuscripts have "you".
*5.6 says: Or "does".
*5.14 Light shows up everything: Or "Everything that is seen in the light becomes light itself."
*6.13 that evil day: Either the present (see 5.16) or "the day of death" or "the day of judgment".

Philippians

Paul's letter to the church in Philippi

A quick look at this letter

Paul wrote this letter from jail (1.7) to thank the Lord's followers at Philippi for helping him with their gifts and prayers (1.5; 4.10-19). He hopes to be set free, so that he can continue preaching the good news (3.17-19). But he knows that he might be put to death (1.21; 2.17; 3.10).

The city of Philippi is in the part of northern Greece known as Macedonia. It was at Philippi that Paul had entered Europe for the first time, and there he preached the good news and began a church (Acts 16). He now warns the Christians at Philippi that they may have to suffer, just as Christ suffered and Paul is now suffering. If this happens, the Philippians should count it a blessing that comes from having faith in Christ (1.28-30).

There were problems in the church at Philippi, because some of the members claimed that people must obey the Law of Moses, or they could not be saved. But Paul has no patience

with such members and warns the church, "Watch out for those people who behave like dogs!" (3.2-11). This letter is also filled with joy. Even in jail, Paul is happy because he has discovered how to make the best of a bad situation and because he remembers all the kindness shown to him by the people in the church at Philippi.

Paul reminds them that God's people are to live in harmony (2.2; 4.2,3) and to think the same way that Christ Jesus did:

> Christ was truly God.
> But he did not try to remain
>   equal with God.
> He gave up everything
>   and became a slave,
> when he became
>   like one of us.
>
> (2.6,7)

Greetings and a prayer

CHAPTER 1

[1] *From Paul and Timothy, servants of Christ Jesus.*
  To all God's people who belong to Christ Jesus at Philippi and to all your church officials and officers.[*]
  [2] I pray that God our Father and the Lord Jesus Christ will be kind to you and will bless you with peace!

See also: 1.1: Acts 16.12.

232

Paul's prayer for the church in Philippi

3 Every time I think of you, I thank my God. 4 And whenever I mention you in my prayers, it makes me happy. 5 This is because you have taken part with me in spreading the good news from the first day you heard about it. 6 God is the one who began this good work in you, and I am certain that he won't stop before it is complete on the day that Christ Jesus returns.

7 You have a special place in my heart. So it is only natural for me to feel the way I do. All of you have helped in the work that God has given me, as I defend the good news and tell about it here in jail. 8 God himself knows how much I want to see you. He knows that I care for you in the same way that Christ Jesus does.

9 I pray that your love will keep on growing and that you will fully know and understand 10 how to make the right choices. Then you will still be pure and innocent when Christ returns. And until that day, 11 Jesus Christ will keep you busy doing good deeds that bring glory and praise to God.

What life means to Paul

12 My dear friends, I want you to know that what has happened to me has helped to spread the good news. 13 The Roman guards and all the others know that I am here in jail because I serve Christ. 14 Now most of the Lord's followers have become brave and are fearlessly telling the message.'

15 Some are preaching about Christ because they are jealous and envious of us. Others are preaching because they want to help. 16 They love Christ and know that I am here to defend the good news about him. 17 But the ones who are jealous of us are not sincere. They just want to cause trouble for me while I am in jail. 18 But that doesn't matter. All that matters is that people are telling about Christ, whether they are sincere or not. That is what makes me glad.

I will keep on being glad, 19 because I know that your prayers and the help that comes from the Spirit of Christ Jesus will keep me safe. 20 I honestly expect and hope that I will never do anything to be ashamed of. Whether I live or die, I always want to be as brave as I am now and bring honour to Christ.

21 If I live, it will be for Christ, and if I die, I will gain even more. 22 I don't know what to choose. I could keep on living and doing something useful. 23 It is a hard choice to make. I want to die and be with Christ, because that would be much better. 24-25 But I know that all of you still need me. That's why I am sure I will stay on to help you grow and be happy in your faith. 26 Then, when I visit you again, you will have good reason to take great pride in Christ Jesus because of me.'

27 Above all else, you must live in a way that brings honour to the good news about Christ. Then, whether I visit you or not, I will hear that all of you think alike. I will know that you are working together and that you are struggling side by side to get others to believe the good news.

28 Be brave when you face your enemies. Your courage will show them that they are going to be destroyed, and it will show you that you will be saved. God will make all this happen, 29 and he has blessed you. Not only do you have faith in Christ, but you suffer for him. 30 You saw me suffer, and you still hear about my troubles. Now you must suffer in the same way.

Christ's example of true humility

CHAPTER 2

1 Christ encourages you, and his love comforts you. God's Spirit unites you, and you are concerned for others. 2 Now make me completely happy! Live in harmony by showing love for each other. Be united in what you think, as if you were only one person. 3 Don't be jealous or proud, but be humble and consider others more important than yourselves. 4 Care about them as much as you care about yourselves 5 and think the same way that Christ Jesus thought:'

6 Christ was truly God.
  But he did not try to remain'
    equal with God.
7 Instead he gave up everything'
    and became a slave,
  when he became
    like one of us.
8 Christ was humble.
  He obeyed God and even died
    on a cross.

9 Then God gave Christ
  the highest place
  and honoured his name
  above all others.

10 So at the name of Jesus
  everyone will bow down,
  those in heaven, on earth,
  and under the earth.

11 And to the glory
  of God the Father
  everyone will openly agree,
  "Jesus Christ is Lord!"

Lights in the world

12 My dear friends, you always obeyed when
I was with you. Now that I am away, you
should obey even more. So work with fear
and trembling so that it really
means to be saved. 13 God is working in you
to make you willing and able to obey him.

14 Do everything without grumbling or
arguing. 15 Then you will be the pure and
innocent children of God. You live among
people who are crooked and evil, but you
must not do anything that they can say is
wrong. Try to shine as lights among the
people of this world, 16 as you hold firmly to*
the message that gives life. Then on the day
when Christ returns, I can take pride in you.
I can also know that my work and efforts
were not useless.

17 Your faith in the Lord and your service
are like a sacrifice offered to him. And my
own blood may have to be poured out with
the sacrifice.* If this happens, I will be glad
and rejoice with you. 18 In the same way, you
should be glad and rejoice with me.

News about Paul's friends

Timothy and Epaphroditus

19 I want to be encouraged by news about
you. So I hope the Lord Jesus will soon let me
send Timothy to you. 20 I don't have anyone
else who cares about you as much as he does.
21 The others think only about what interests
them and not about what concerns Christ
Jesus. 22 But you know what kind of person
Timothy is. He has worked with me like a son
in spreading the good news. 23 I hope to send

him to you, as soon as I find out what is
going to happen to me. 24 And I feel sure that
the Lord will also let me come soon.

25 I think I ought to send my dear friend
Epaphroditus back to you. He is a follower
and a worker and a soldier of the Lord, just as
I am. You sent him to look after me, 26 but
now he is eager to see you. He is worried,
because you heard he was sick. 27 In fact, he
was very sick and almost died. But God was
kind to him, and also to me, and he kept me
from being burdened down with sorrow.

28 Now I am more eager than ever to send
Epaphroditus back again. You will be glad to
see him, and I won't have to worry any
longer. 29 Be sure to give him a cheerful
welcome, just as people who serve the Lord
deserve. 30 He almost died working for Christ,
and he risked his own life to do for me what
you could not.

Being acceptable to God

CHAPTER 3

1 Finally, my dear friends, be glad that you
belong to the Lord. It doesn't bother me to
write the same things to you that I have
written before. In fact, it is for your own
good.

2 Watch out for those people who behave
like dogs! They are evil and want to do more
than just circumcise you. 3 But we are the
ones who are truly circumcised, because we
worship by the power of God's Spirit* and
take pride in Christ Jesus. We don't boast
about what we have done, 4 although I could.
Others may boast about themselves, but I
have more reason to boast than anyone else.
5 I was circumcised when I was eight days
old,* and I am from the nation of Israel and
the tribe of Benjamin. I am a true Hebrew. As
a Pharisee, I strictly obeyed the Law of Moses.
6 And I was so eager that I even made trouble
for the church. I did everything the Law
demands in order to please God.

7 But Christ has shown me that I once
thought was valuable is worthless. 8 Nothing
is as wonderful as knowing Christ Jesus my
Lord. I have given up everything else and
count it all as rubbish. All I want is Christ
9 and to know that I belong to him. I could
not make myself acceptable to God by

---

*2.17 my own blood may have to be poured out
with the sacrifice: Offerings of water or wine were
sometimes poured out when animals were sacrificed
on the altar.

See also: 2.10,11: Isa 45.23 (LXX). 2.15: Deut 32.5.

---

*3.5 when I was eight days old: Jewish boys are
circumcised eight days after birth.

See also: 3.5: a Rom 11.1; b Acts 23.6; 26.5. 3.6: Acts 8.3;
22.4; 26.9–11.

obeying the Law of Moses. God accepted me simply because of my faith in Christ. ¹⁰ All I want is to know Christ and the power that raised him to life. I want to suffer and die as he did, ¹¹ so that somehow I also may be raised to life.

Running towards the goal

¹² I have not yet reached my goal, and I am not perfect. But Christ has taken hold of me. So I keep on running and struggling to take hold of the prize. ¹³ My friends, I don't feel that I have already arrived. But I forget what is behind, and I struggle for what is ahead. ¹⁴ I run towards the goal, so that I can win the prize of being called to heaven. This is the prize that God offers because of what Christ Jesus has done. ¹⁵ All of us who are mature should think in this same way. And if any of you think differently, God will make it clear to you. ¹⁶ But we must keep going in the direction that we are now headed.

¹⁷ My friends, I want you to follow my example and learn from others who closely follow the example we set for you. ¹⁸ I often warned you that many people are living as enemies of the cross of Christ. And now with tears in my eyes, I warn you again ¹⁹ that they are headed for hell! They worship their stomachs and boast about the disgusting things they do. All they can think about are the things of this world.

²⁰ But we are citizens of heaven and are eagerly waiting for our Saviour to come from there. Our Lord Jesus Christ ²¹ has power over everything, and he will make these poor bodies of ours like his own glorious body.

CHAPTER 4

¹ Dear friends, I love you and long to see you. Please keep on being faithful to the Lord. You are my pride and joy.

Paul encourages the Lord's followers

² Euodia and Syntyche, you belong to the Lord, so I beg you to stop arguing with each other. ³ And, my true partner,* I ask you to help them. These women have worked together with me and with Clement and with the others in spreading the good news. Their names are now written in the book of life.*

⁴ Always be glad because of the Lord! I will say it again: be glad. ⁵ Always be gentle with others. The Lord will soon be here. ⁶ Don't worry about anything, but pray about everything. With thankful hearts offer up your prayers and requests to God. ⁷ Then, because you belong to Christ Jesus, God will bless you with peace that no one can completely understand. And this peace will control the way you think and feel.

⁸ Finally, my friends, keep your minds on whatever is true, pure, right, holy, friendly, and proper. Don't ever stop thinking about what is truly worthwhile and worthy of praise. ⁹ You know the teachings I gave you, and you know what you heard me say and saw me do. So follow my example. And God, who gives peace, will be with you.

Paul thanks the Philippians

¹⁰ The Lord has made me very grateful that at last you have thought about me once again. Actually, you were thinking about me all along, but you didn't have any chance to show it. ¹¹ I am not complaining about having too little. I have learnt to be satisfied with* whatever I have. ¹² I know what it is to be poor or to have plenty, and I have lived under all kinds of conditions. I know what it means to be full or to be hungry, to have too much or too little. ¹³ Christ gives me the strength to face anything.

¹⁴ It was good of you to help me when I was having such a hard time. ¹⁵ My friends at Philippi, you remember what it was like when I started preaching the good news in Macedonia.* After I left there, you were the only church that became my partner by giving blessings and by receiving them in return. ¹⁶ Even when I was in Thessalonica, you helped me more than once. ¹⁷ I am not trying to get something from you, but I want you to receive the blessings that come from giving.

¹⁸ I have been paid back everything, and with interest. I am completely satisfied with the gifts that you asked Epaphroditus to bring me. They are like a sweet-smelling offering or like the right kind of sacrifice that pleases

---

*4.3 **the book of life:** A book in which the names of God's people are written.

See also: 3.17: 1 Cor 4.16; 11.1.

*4.15 **when I started preaching the good news in Macedonia:** Paul is talking about his first visit to Philippi. See Acts 16.12–40.

See also: 4.15,16: 2 Cor 11.9. 4.16: Acts 17.1. 4.18: Exod 29.18.

God. ¹⁹ I pray that God will take care of all your needs with the wonderful blessings that come from Christ Jesus! ²⁰ May God our Father be praised for ever and ever. Amen.

Final greetings

²¹ Give my greetings to all who are God's people because of Christ Jesus.

The Lord's followers here with me send you their greetings.

²² All God's people send their greetings, especially those in the service of the Emperor.

²³ I pray that our Lord Jesus Christ will be kind to you and will bless your life!

Additional notes

ª**1.1 church officials and officers:** Or "bishops and deacons".

ª**1.14 the message:** Some manuscripts have "the Lord's message", and others have "God's message".

ª**1.26 take great pride in Christ Jesus because of me:** Or "take great pride in me because of Christ Jesus."

ª**2.5 think the same way that Christ Jesus thought:** Or "think the way you should because you belong to Christ Jesus".

ª**2.6 remain:** Or "become".

ª**2.7 he gave up everything:** Greek, "He emptied himself".

ª**2.16 hold firmly to:** Or "offer them".

ª**3.3 by the power of God's Spirit:** Some manuscripts have "sincerely".

ª**4.3 partner:** Or "Syzygus", a person's name.

ª**4.11 be satisfied with:** Or "get by on".

Colossians

Paul's letter to the church
in Colossae

Colossae was an important city in western Asia Minor, about 160 kilometres east of the city port of Ephesus. Paul had never been to Colossae, but he was pleased to learn that the Christians there were strong in their faith (1.3–7; 2.6,7). They had heard the good news from a man named Epaphras who had lived there (1.7; 4.12,13), but was in jail with Paul (Philemon 23) at the time that Paul wrote this letter (1.14; 4.3,10,18).

Many of the church members in Colossae were Gentiles (1.27), and some of them were influenced by strange religious ideas and practices (2.16–23). They thought that to obey God fully they must give up certain physical desires and worship angels and other spiritual powers. But Paul wanted them to know that Christ was with God in heaven, ruling over all powers in the universe (3.1). And so, their worship should be directed to Christ.

Paul quotes a beautiful hymn that explains who Christ is:

Christ is exactly like God,
who cannot be seen.
He is the firstborn Son,
superior to all creation.

God himself was pleased
to live fully in his Son.
And God was pleased
for him to make peace
by sacrificing his blood
on the cross.

(1.15,19,20a)

Greetings

CHAPTER 1

¹ From Paul, chosen by God to be an apostle of Christ Jesus, and from Timothy, who is also a follower.

² To God's people who live in Colossae and are faithful followers of Christ.

I pray that God our Father will be kind to you and will bless you with peace!

A prayer of thanks

³ Each time we pray for you, we thank God, the Father of our Lord Jesus Christ. ⁴ We have heard of your faith in Christ and of your love for all God's people, ⁵ because what you hope for is kept safe for you in heaven. You first heard about this hope when you believed the true message, which is the good news. ⁶ The good news is spreading all over the world with great success. It has spread in that same way among you, ever since the first day

237

you learnt the truth about God's wonderful kindness[7] from our good friend Epaphras. He works together with us for Christ and is a faithful worker for you.' [8] He is also the one who told us about the love that God's Spirit has given you.

The person and work of Christ

[9] We have not stopped praying for you since the first day we heard about you. In fact, we always pray that God will show you everything he wants you to do and that you may have all the wisdom and understanding that his Spirit gives. [10] Then you will live a life that honours the Lord, and you will always please him by doing good deeds. You will come to know God even better. [11] His glorious power will make you patient and strong enough to endure anything, and you will be truly happy.

[12] I pray that you will be grateful to God for letting you* have part in what he has promised his people in the kingdom of light. [13] God rescued us from the dark power of Satan and brought us into the kingdom of his dear Son, [14] who forgives our sins and sets us free.

[15] Christ is exactly like God,
    who cannot be seen.
He is the firstborn Son,
    superior to all creation.
[16] Everything was created by him,
    everything in heaven
        and on earth,
    everything seen and unseen,
    including all forces
        and powers,
    and all rulers
        and authorities.
All things were created
    by God's Son,
    and everything was made
        for him.

[17] God's Son was before all else,
    and by him everything
        is held together.
[18] He is the head of his body,
    which is the church.
He is the very beginning,
    the first to be raised
        from death,
    so that he would be
        above all others.

[19] God himself was pleased
    to live fully in his Son.
[20] And God was pleased
    for him to make peace
    by sacrificing his blood
        on the cross,
    so that all beings in heaven
        and on earth
    would be brought back to God.

[21] You used to be far from God. Your thoughts made you his enemies, and you did evil things. [22] But his Son became a human and died. So God made peace with you, and now he lets you stand in his presence as people who are holy and faultless and innocent. [23] But you must stay deeply rooted and firm in your faith. You must not give up the hope you received when you heard the good news. It was preached to everyone on earth, and I myself have become a servant of this message.

Paul's service to the church

[24] I am glad that I can suffer for you. I am pleased also that in my own body I can continue* the suffering of Christ for his body, the church. [25] God's plan was to make me a servant of his church and to send me to preach his complete message to you. [26] For many ages this message was kept secret from everyone, but now it has been explained to God's people. [27] God did this because he wanted you Gentiles to understand his wonderful and glorious mystery. And the mystery is that Christ lives in you, and he is your hope of sharing in God's glory.

[28] We announce the message about Christ, and we use all our wisdom to warn and teach everyone, so that all Christ's followers will grow and become mature. [29] That's why I work so hard and use the mighty power he gives me.

CHAPTER 2

[1] I want you to know what a struggle I am going through for you, for God's people at Laodicea, and for all those followers who have never met me. [2] I do it to encourage them. Then as their hearts are joined together in love, they will be wonderfully blessed with complete understanding. And they will truly know Christ. Not only is he the key to God's mystery, [3] but all wisdom and knowledge are hidden away in him.

[4] I tell you these things to keep you from being fooled by fancy talk. [5] Even though I am not with you, I keep thinking about you. I am glad to know that you are living as you should and that your faith in Christ is strong.

Christ brings real life

[6] You have accepted Christ Jesus as your Lord. Now keep on following him. [7] Plant your roots in Christ and let him be the foundation for your life. Be strong in your faith, just as you were taught. And be grateful.

[8] Don't let anyone fool you by using senseless arguments. These arguments may sound wise, but they are only human teachings. They come from the powers of this world* and not from Christ.

[9] God lives fully in Christ. [10] And you are fully grown because you belong to Christ, who is over every power and authority. [11] Christ has also taken away your selfish desires, just as circumcision removes flesh from the body. [12] And when you were baptized, it was the same as being buried with Christ. Then you were raised to life because you had faith in the power of God, who raised Christ from death. [13] You were dead, because you were sinful and were not God's people. But God let Christ make you* alive, when he forgave all our sins.

[14] God wiped out the charges that were against us for disobeying the Law of Moses. He took them away and nailed them to the cross. [15] There Christ defeated all powers and forces. He let the whole world see them being led away as prisoners when he celebrated his victory.

[16] Don't let anyone tell you what you must eat or drink. Don't let them say that you must celebrate the New Moon festival, the Sabbath, or any other festival. [17] These things are only a shadow of what is to come. But Christ is real! [18] Don't be cheated by people who make a show of acting humble and who worship angels.* They boast about seeing visions. But it is all nonsense, because their minds are filled with selfish ideas. [19] They are no longer part of Christ, who is the head of the whole body. Christ gives the body its strength, and he uses its joints and muscles to hold it together, as it grows by the power of God.

New life with Christ

[20] You died with Christ. Now the forces of the universe* don't have any power over you. Why do you live as if you had to obey such rules as, [21] "Don't handle this. Don't taste that. Don't touch this."? [22] After these things are used, they are no longer good for anything. So why be bothered with the rules that humans have made up? [23] Obeying these rules may seem to be the clever thing to do. They appear to make you love God more and to be very humble and to have control over your body. But they don't really have any power over our desires.

CHAPTER 3

[1] You have been raised to life with Christ. Now set your heart on what is in heaven, where Christ rules at God's right side.* [2] Think about what is up there, not about what is here on earth. [3] You died, which means that your life is hidden with Christ, who sits beside God. [4] Christ gives meaning to your* life, and when he appears, you will also appear with him in glory.

[5] Don't be controlled by your body. Kill every desire for the wrong kind of love. Don't be immoral or indecent or have evil thoughts. Don't be greedy, which is the same as worshipping idols. [6] God is angry with people who disobey him by doing* these things. [7] And that is exactly what you did, when you lived among people who behaved in this way. [8] But now you must stop doing such things. You must stop being angry, hateful, and evil. You must no longer say insulting or cruel things about others. [9] And stop lying to each other. You have given up your old way of life with its habits.

[10] Each of you is now a new person. You are becoming more and more like your Creator, and you will understand him better. [11] It doesn't matter if you are a Greek or a Jew, or if you are circumcised or not. You may even be a barbarian or a Scythian;* and you may be a slave or a free person. Yet Christ is all that matters, and he lives in all of us.

---

*2.8 powers of this world: Spirits and unseen forces were thought to control human lives and were believed to be connected with the movements of the stars.

See also: 2.12: Rom 6.4. 2.13: Eph 2.1–5. 2.14: Eph 2.15. 2.16: Rom 14.1–6. 2.19: Eph 4.16.

*2.20 forces of the universe: See the note at 2.8.
*3.1 right side: The place of power and honour.
*3.11 a barbarian or a Scythian: Barbarians were people who could not speak Greek and would be in the lower class of society. Scythians were people who were known for their cruelty.

See also: 3.1: Psa 110.1. 3.9: Eph 4.22. 3.10: a Eph 4.24; b Gen 1.26.

¹² God loves you and has chosen you as his own special people. So be gentle, kind, humble, meek, and patient. ¹³ Put up with each other, and forgive anyone who does you wrong, just as Christ has forgiven you. ¹⁴ Love is more important than anything else. It is what ties everything completely together.

¹⁵ Each one of you is part of the body of Christ, and you were chosen to live together in peace. So let the peace that comes from Christ control your thoughts. And be grateful. ¹⁶ Let the message about Christ completely fill your lives, while you use all your wisdom to teach and instruct each other. With thankful hearts, sing psalms, hymns, and spiritual songs to God. ¹⁷ Whatever you say or do should be done in the name of the Lord Jesus, as you give thanks to God the Father because of him.

Some rules for Christian living

¹⁸ A wife must put her husband first. This is her duty as a follower of the Lord.

¹⁹ A husband must love his wife and not abuse her.

²⁰ Children must always obey their parents. This pleases the Lord.

²¹ Parents, don't be hard on your children. If you are, they might give up.

²² Slaves, you must always obey your earthly masters. Try to please them at all times, and not just when they are watching. Honour the Lord and serve your masters with your whole heart. ²³ Do your work willingly, as though you were serving the Lord himself, and not just your earthly master. ²⁴ In fact, the Lord Christ is the one you are really serving, and you know that he will reward you. ²⁵ But Christ has no favourites! He will punish evil people, just as they deserve.

CHAPTER 4

¹ Slave owners, be fair and honest with your slaves. Don't forget that you have a Master in heaven.

² Never give up praying. And when you pray, keep alert and be thankful. ³ Be sure to pray that God will make a way for us to spread his message and explain the mystery about Christ, even though I am in jail for doing this. ⁴ Please pray that I will make the message as clear as possible.

⁵ When you are with unbelievers, always make good use of the time. ⁶ Be pleasant and hold their interest when you speak the message. Choose your words carefully and be ready to give answers to anyone who asks questions.

Final greetings

⁷ Tychicus is the dear friend, who faithfully works and serves the Lord with us, and he will give you the news about me. ⁸ I am sending him to cheer you up by telling you how we are getting along. ⁹ Onesimus, that dear and faithful follower from your own group, is coming with him. The two of them will tell you everything that has happened here.

¹⁰ Aristarchus is in jail with me. He sends greetings to you, and so does Mark, the cousin of Barnabas. You have already been told to welcome Mark, if he visits you.

¹¹ Jesus, who is known as Justus, sends his greetings. These three men are the only Jewish followers who have worked with me for the kingdom of God. They have given me much comfort.

¹² Your own Epaphras, who serves Christ Jesus, sends his greetings. He always prays hard that you may fully know what the Lord wants you to do and that you may do it completely. ¹³ I have seen how much trouble he has gone through for you and for the followers in Laodicea and Hierapolis.

¹⁴ Our dear doctor Luke sends you his greetings, and so does Demas.

¹⁵ Give my greetings to the followers at Laodicea, especially to Nympha and the church that meets in her home.

¹⁶ After this letter has been read to your people, be sure to have it read in the church at Laodicea. And you should read the letter that I have sent to them.*

¹⁷ Remind Archippus to do the work that the Lord has given him to do.

¹⁸ I am signing this letter myself: PAUL. Don't forget that I am in jail.
I pray that God will be kind to you.

---

*4.16 the letter that I have sent to them: This is the only mention of the letter to the church at Laodicea.

See also: 3.12,13: Eph 4.2. 3.13: Eph 4.32.
3.16,17: Eph 5.19,20. 3.18: Eph 5.22; 1 Pet 3.1.
3.19: Eph 5.25; 1 Pet 3.7. 3.20: Eph 6.1. 3.21: Eph 6.4.
3.22–25: Eph 6.5–8. 3.25: Deut 10.17; Eph 6.9.
4.1: Eph 6.9.

See also: 4.5: Eph 5.16. 4.7: Acts 20.4; 2 Tim 4.12.
4.7,8: Eph 6.21,22. 4.9: Phlm 10–12. 4.10: a Acts 19.29;
27.2; Phlm 24; b Acts 12.12,25; 13.13; 15.37–39.
4.12: Col 1.7; Phlm 23. 4.14: a 2 Tim 4.11; Phlm 24;
b 2 Tim 4.10; Phlm 24. 4.17: Phlm 2.

Additional notes

ʼ1.7 you: Some manuscripts have "us".
ʼ1.12 you: See the note at 1.7.
ʼ1.24 continue: Or "complete".
ʼ2.13 you: See the note at 1.7.
ʼ2.18 worship angels: Or "worship with angels (in visions of heaven)."
ʼ3.4 your: Some manuscripts have "our".
ʼ3.6 people who disobey him by doing: Some manuscripts do not have these words.

1 Thessalonians

Paul's first letter to the church
in Thessalonica

A quick look at this letter

Paul started the church in Thessalonica
(2.13,14), while working hard to support
himself (2.9). In this important city of northern
Greece, many of the followers had worshipped
idols before becoming Christians (1.9). But they
were faithful to the Lord, and because of them
the Lord's message had spread everywhere in
that region (1.8). This letter may have been the
first one that Paul wrote, and perhaps even the
first of all the New Testament writings.

Some people in Thessalonica began to
oppose Paul, and he had to escape to Athens.
But he sent his young friend Timothy to find
out how the Christians were doing (3.1–5).
When Timothy returned, he gave Paul good
reports of their faith and love (3.6–10).

The church itself had problems. Some of its
members had stopped working, since they
thought that the Lord would soon return
(4.11,12). Others were worried because relatives
and friends had already died before Christ's
return. So Paul tried to explain to them more
clearly what would happen when the Lord

returns (4.13–15), and then told them how they
should live meanwhile (5.1–11).

Paul's final instructions are well worth
remembering:

> *Always be joyful and never stop praying.*
> *Whatever happens, keep thanking God*
> *because of Jesus Christ. This is what God wants*
> *you to do.*

(5.16–18)

Greetings

CHAPTER 1

¹ From Paul, Silas,* and Timothy.
   To the church in Thessalonica, the people of
God the Father and of the Lord Jesus Christ.
   I pray that God will be kind to you and will
bless you with peace!
   ² We thank God for you and always
mention you in our prayers. Each time we
pray, ³ we tell God our Father about your
faith and loving work and about your firm
hope in our Lord Jesus Christ.

The Thessalonians' faith
and example

⁴ My dear friends, God loves you, and we
know he has chosen you to be his people.
⁵ When we told you the good news, it was
with the power and assurance that come

See also: 1.1: Acts 17.1.

from the Holy Spirit, and not simply with words. You knew what kind of people we were and how we helped you. 6 So, when you accepted the message, you followed our example and the example of the Lord. You suffered, but the Holy Spirit made you glad.

7 You became an example for all the Lord's followers in Macedonia and Achaia. 8 And because of you, the Lord's message has spread everywhere in those regions. Now the news of your faith in God is known all over the world, and we don't have to say a thing about it. 9 Everyone is talking about how you welcomed us and how you turned away from idols to serve the true and living God. 10 They also tell how you are waiting for his Son Jesus to come from heaven. God raised him from death, and on the day of judgment Jesus will save us from God's anger.

CHAPTER 2

Paul's work in Thessalonica

1 My friends, you know that our time with you wasn't wasted. 2 As you remember, we had been ill-treated and insulted at Philippi. But God gave us the courage to tell you the good news about him, even though many people caused us trouble. 3 We didn't have any hidden motives when we won you over, and we didn't try to fool or trick anyone. 4 God was pleased to trust us with his message. We didn't speak to please people, but to please God who knows our motives.

5 You also know that we didn't try to flatter anyone. God himself knows that what we did wasn't a cover-up for greed. 6 We were not trying to get you or anyone else to praise us. 7 But as apostles, we could have demanded help from you. After all, Christ is the one who sent us. We chose to be like children or like a mother nursing her baby. 8 We cared so much for you, and you became so dear to us, that we were willing to give our lives for you when we gave you God's message.

9 My dear friends, you haven't forgotten our hard work and hardships. You remember how night and day we struggled to make a living, so that we could tell you God's message without being a burden to anyone. 10 Both you and God are witnesses that we were pure and honest and innocent in our dealings with you followers of the Lord. 11 You also know we did everything for you that parents would do for their own children.

12 We begged, encouraged, and urged each of you to live in a way that would honour God. He is the one who chose you to share in his own kingdom and glory.

13 We always thank God that you believed the message we preached. It came from him, and it isn't something made up by humans. You accepted it as God's message, and now he is working in you. 14 My friends, you did just like God's churches in Judea and like the other followers of Christ Jesus there. And so, you were ill-treated by your own people, in the same way they were ill-treated by their people.

15 Those Jews killed the Lord Jesus and the prophets, and they even chased us away. God doesn't like what they do and neither does anyone else. 16 They keep us from speaking his message to the Gentiles and from leading them to be saved. The Jews have always gone too far with their sins. Now God has finally become angry and will punish them.

Paul wants to visit the church again

17 My friends, we were kept from coming to you for a while, but we never stopped thinking about you. We were eager to see you and tried our best to visit you in person. 18 We really wanted to come. I myself tried several times, but Satan stopped us. 19 After all, when the Lord Jesus appears, who else but you will give us hope and joy and be like a glorious crown for us? 20 You alone are our glory and joy!

CHAPTER 3

1 Finally, we couldn't stand it any longer. We decided to stay in Athens by ourselves 2 and send our friend Timothy to you. He works with us as God's servant and preaches the good news about Christ. We wanted him to make you strong in your faith and to encourage you. 3 We didn't want any of you to be discouraged by all these troubles. You knew we would have to suffer, 4 because when we were with you, we told you this would happen. And we did suffer, as you well know. 5 At last, when I could not wait any longer, I sent Timothy to find out about your faith. I hoped that Satan had not tempted you and made all our work useless.

6 Timothy has come back from his visit to you and has told us about your faith and

See also: 1.6: Acts 17.5–9.   2.2: a Acts 16.19–24; b Acts 17.1–9.

See also: 2.14: Acts 17.5.   2.15: Acts 9.23,29; 13.45,50; 14.2,5,19; 17.5,13; 18.12.   3.1: Acts 17.15.   3.6: Acts 18.5.

love. He also said that you always have happy memories of us and that you want to see us as much as we want to see you.

⁷ My friends, even though we have a lot of trouble and suffering, your faith makes us feel better about you. ⁸ Your strong faith in the Lord is like a breath of new life. ⁹ How can we possibly thank God enough for all the happiness you have brought us? ¹⁰ Day and night we sincerely pray that we will see you again and help you to have an even stronger faith.

¹¹ We pray that God our Father and our Lord Jesus will let us visit you. ¹² May the Lord make your love for each other and for everyone else grow by leaps and bounds. That's how our love for you has grown. ¹³ And when our Lord comes with all his people, I pray that he will make your hearts pure and innocent in the sight of God the Father.

A life that pleases God

CHAPTER 4

¹ Finally, my dear friends, since you belong to the Lord Jesus, we beg and urge you to live as we taught you. Then you will please God. You are already living that way, but try even harder. ² Remember the instructions we gave you as followers of the Lord Jesus. ³ God wants you to be holy, so don't be immoral in matters of sex. ⁴ Respect and honour your wife.⁵ ⁵ Don't be a slave of your desires or live like people who don't know God. ⁶ You must not cheat any of the Lord's followers in matters of sex.⁶ Remember, we warned you that he punishes everyone who does such things. ⁷ God didn't choose you to be filthy, but to be pure. ⁸ So if you don't obey these rules, you are not really disobeying us. You are disobeying God, who gives you his Holy Spirit.

⁹ We don't have to write to you about the need to love each other. God has taught you to do this, ¹⁰ and you already have shown your love for all his people in Macedonia. But, my dear friends, we ask you to do even more. ¹¹ Try your best to live quietly, to mind your own business, and to work hard, just as we taught you to do. ¹² Then you will be respected by people who are not followers of the Lord, and you won't have to depend on anyone.

What to expect when the Lord returns

¹³ My friends, we want you to understand how it will be for those followers who have already died. Then you won't grieve over them and be like people who don't have any hope. ¹⁴ We believe that Jesus died and was raised to life. We also believe that when God brings Jesus back again, he will bring with him all who had faith in Jesus before they died. ¹⁵ Our Lord Jesus told us that when he comes, we won't go up to meet him ahead of his followers who have already died.

¹⁶ With a loud command and with the shout of the chief angel and a blast of God's trumpet, the Lord will return from heaven. Then those who had faith in Christ before they died will be raised to life. ¹⁷ Next, all of us who are still alive will be taken up into the clouds together with them to meet the Lord in the sky. From that time on we will all be with the Lord for ever. ¹⁸ Encourage each other with these words.

CHAPTER 5

¹ I don't need to write to you about the time or date when all this will happen. ² You know that the Lord's return⁵ is like a thief coming at night. ³ People will think they are safe and secure. But destruction will suddenly strike them like the pains of a woman about to give birth. And they won't escape.

⁴ My dear friends, you don't live in darkness, and so that day won't surprise you like a thief. ⁵ You belong to the light and live in the day. We don't live in the night or belong to the dark. ⁶ Others may sleep, but we should stay awake and be alert. ⁷ People sleep during the night, and some even get drunk. ⁸ But we belong to the day. So we must stay sober and let our faith and love be like a suit of armour. Our firm hope that we will be saved is our helmet.

⁹ God doesn't intend to punish us, but wants us to be saved by our Lord Jesus Christ. ¹⁰ Christ died for us, so that we could live with him, whether we are alive or dead when he comes. ¹¹ That's why you must encourage and help each other, just as you are already doing.

See also: **4.15-17:** 1 Cor 15.51,52. **5.2:** Matt 24.43; Luke 12.39; 2 Pet 3.10. **5.8:** Isa 59.17; Eph 6.13-17.

Final instructions and greetings

¹² My friends, we ask you to be thoughtful of your leaders who work hard and tell you how to live for the Lord. ¹³ Show them great respect and love because of their work. Try to get along with each other. ¹⁴ My friends, we beg you to warn anyone who isn't living right. Encourage anyone who feels left out, help all who are weak, and be patient with everyone. ¹⁵ Don't be hateful to people, just because they are hateful to you. Rather, be good to each other and to everyone else.

¹⁶ Always be joyful ¹⁷ and never stop praying. ¹⁸ Whatever happens, keep thanking God because of Jesus Christ. This is what God wants you to do.

¹⁹ Don't turn away God's Spirit ²⁰ or ignore prophecies. ²¹ Put everything to the test. Accept what is good ²² and don't have anything to do with evil.

²³ I pray that God, who gives peace, will make you completely holy. And may your spirit, soul, and body be kept healthy and faultless until our Lord Jesus Christ returns. ²⁴ The one who chose you can be trusted, and he will do this.

²⁵ Friends, please pray for us.

²⁶ Give the Lord's followers a warm greeting.

²⁷ In the name of the Lord I beg you to read this letter to all his followers.

²⁸ I pray that our Lord Jesus Christ will be kind to you!

Additional notes

¹1.1 Silas: The Greek text has "Silvanus", which is another form of the name Silas.
¹2.7 like children or like a mother: Some manuscripts have "as gentle as a mother".
¹4.4 your wife: Or "your body".
¹4.6 in matters of sex: Or "in business".
¹5.2 the Lord's return: The Greek text has "the day of the Lord".

2 Thessalonians

Paul's second letter to the church
in Thessalonica

A quick look at this letter

In this letter to the believers in Thessalonica, Paul begins by thanking God that their faith and love keep growing all the time (1.3). They were going through a lot of troubles, but Paul insists that this is God's way of testing their faith, not a way of punishing them (1.4,5).

Someone in Thessalonica claimed to have a letter from Paul, saying that the Lord had already returned (2.2). But Paul warns the church not to be fooled! The Lord will not return until after the "wicked one" has appeared (2.3).

Paul also warns against laziness (3.6–10), and he tells the church to guard against any followers who refuse to obey what he has written in this letter.

The letter closes with a prayer:

I pray that the Lord, who gives peace, will always bless you with peace. May the Lord be with all of you.

(3.16)

Greetings

CHAPTER 1

¹ From Paul, Silas,* and Timothy.
    To the church in Thessalonica, the people of God our Father and of the Lord Jesus Christ.
    ² I pray that God our Father and the Lord Jesus Christ will be kind to you and will bless you with peace!

The Lord's return will bring justice

³ My dear friends, we always have good reason to thank God for you, because your faith in God and your love for each other keep growing all the time. ⁴ That's why we boast about you to all God's churches. We tell them how patient you are and how you keep on having faith, even though you are going through a lot of trouble and suffering.

⁵ All this shows that God judges fairly and that he is making you fit to share in his kingdom for which you are suffering. ⁶ It is only right for God to punish everyone who is causing you trouble, ⁷ but he will give you relief from your troubles. He will do the same for us, when the Lord Jesus comes from heaven with his powerful angels ⁸ and with a flaming fire.

Our Lord Jesus will punish anyone who doesn't know God and won't obey his message. ⁹ Their punishment will be eternal destruction, and they will be kept far from the presence of our Lord and his glorious strength.

See also: 1.1: Acts 17.1. 1.9: Isa 2.10.

246

[10] This will happen on that day when the Lord returns to be praised and honoured by all who have faith in him and belong to him. This includes you, because you believed what we said.

[11] God chose you, and we keep praying that God will make you worthy of being his people. We pray for God's power to help you do all the good things that you hope to do and that your faith makes you want to do. [12] Then, because God and our Lord Jesus Christ are so kind, you will bring honour to the name of our Lord Jesus, and he will bring honour to you.

The Lord has not returned yet

CHAPTER 2

The Lord's return

[1] When our Lord Jesus returns, we will be gathered up to meet him. So I ask you, my friends, [2] not to be easily upset or disturbed by people who claim that the Lord* has already come. They may say that they heard this directly from the Holy Spirit, or from someone else, or even that they read it in one of our letters. [3] But don't be fooled! People will rebel against God. Then before the Lord returns, the wicked* one who is doomed to be destroyed will appear. [4] He will boast and oppose everything that is holy or sacred. He will even sit in God's temple and claim to be God. [5] Don't you remember that I told you this while I was still with you?

[6] You already know what is holding this wicked one back until it is time for him to come. [7] His mysterious power is already at work, but someone is holding him back. And the wicked one won't appear until that someone is out of the way. [8] Then he will appear, but the Lord Jesus will kill him simply by breathing on him. He will be completely destroyed by the Lord's glorious return.

[9] When the wicked one appears, Satan will pretend to perform all kinds of miracles, wonders, and signs. [10] Lost people will be fooled by his evil deeds. They could be saved, but they will refuse to love the truth and accept it. [11] So God will make sure that they are fooled into believing a lie. [12] All of them will be punished, because they would rather do evil than believe the truth.

Be faithful

[13] My friends, the Lord loves you, and it is only natural for us to thank God for you. God chose you to be the first ones to be saved.* His Spirit made you holy, and you put your faith in the truth. [14] God used our preaching as his way of inviting you to share in the glory of our Lord Jesus Christ. [15] My friends, that's why you must remain faithful and follow closely what we taught you in person and by our letters.

[16] God our Father loves us. He is kind and has given us eternal comfort and a wonderful hope. We pray that our Lord Jesus Christ and God our Father [17] will encourage you and help you always to do and say the right thing.

Pray and work

CHAPTER 3

Pray for us

[1] Finally, our friends, please pray for us. This will help the message about the Lord to spread quickly, and others will respect it, just as you do. [2] Pray that we may be kept safe from worthless and evil people. After all, not everyone has faith. [3] But the Lord can be trusted to make you strong and protect you from harm. [4] He has made us sure that you are obeying what we taught you and that you will keep on obeying. [5] I pray that the Lord will guide you to be as loving as God and as patient as Christ.

Warnings against laziness

[6] My dear friends, in the name of* the Lord Jesus, I beg you not to have anything to do with any of your people who waste their time and refuse to obey the instructions we gave you. [7] You know that you should follow our example. We didn't waste our time being lazy, [8] and we didn't accept food from anyone without paying for it. We didn't want to be a burden to any of you, so night and day we worked as hard as we could.

[9] We had the right not to work, but we wanted to set an example for you. [10] We also gave you the rule that if you don't work, you don't eat. [11] Now we learn that some of you waste your time and won't do any work, except the work of a busybody. [12] So, for the sake of our Lord Jesus Christ, we ask and beg

See also: 2.1: 1 Thes 4.15–17. 2.4: Dan 11.36; Ezek 28.2.
2.8: Isa 11.4. 2.9: Matt 24.24.

these people to settle down and start working for a living. ¹³ Dear friends, you must never become tired of doing right.

¹⁴ Be on your guard against any followers who refuse to obey what we have written in this letter. Put them to shame by not having anything to do with them. ¹⁵ Don't consider them your enemies, but speak kindly to them as you would to any other follower.

A final prayer

¹⁶ I pray that the Lord, who gives peace, will always bless you with peace. May the Lord be with all of you.

¹⁷ I always sign my letters as I am now doing: PAUL.

¹⁸ I pray that our Lord Jesus Christ will be kind to all of you.

Additional notes

'1.1 Silas: The Greek text has "Silvanus", which is another form of the name Silas.
'2.2 Lord: The Greek text has "day of the Lord".
'2.3 wicked: Some manuscripts have "sinful".
'2.13 God chose you to be the first ones to be saved: Some manuscripts have "From the beginning God chose you to be saved."
'3.6 in the name of: Or "as a follower of".

1 Timothy

Paul's first letter to Timothy

A quick look at this letter

Timothy travelled and worked with Paul (Romans 16.21; 1 Corinthians 16.10; Philippians 2.19), and because of their shared faith, Timothy was like a son to Paul (1.2). Timothy became one of Paul's most faithful co-workers, and Paul mentions Timothy in five of his letters.

Although this letter is addressed to Timothy personally, it actually addresses many of the concerns Paul had with the life of the entire church. Guidelines are given for choosing church officials (3.1–7), officers (3.8–13), and leaders (5.17–20).

Christians are to pray for everyone and to remember:

> There is only one God,
> and Christ Jesus
>   is the only one
> who can bring us
>   to God.
>   (2.5)

Greetings

CHAPTER 1

[1] *From Paul.*

God our Saviour and Christ Jesus commanded me to be an apostle of Christ Jesus, who gives us hope.

[2] Timothy, because of our faith, you are like a son to me. I pray that God our Father and our Lord Jesus Christ will be kind and merciful to you. May they bless you with peace!

Instructions for church life

Warning against false teaching

[3] When I was leaving for Macedonia, I asked you to stay on in Ephesus and warn certain people there to stop spreading their false teachings. [4] You needed to warn them to stop wasting their time on senseless stories and endless lists of ancestors. Such things only cause arguments. They don't help anyone to do God's work that can only be done by faith.

[5] You must teach people to have genuine love, as well as a good conscience and true faith. [6] There are some who have given up these for nothing but empty talk. [7] They want to be teachers of the Law of Moses. But they don't know what they are talking about, even though they think they do.

[8] We know that the Law is good, if it is used in the right way. [9] We also understand that it wasn't given to control people who please God, but to control lawbreakers, criminals,

---

See also: 1.2: Acts 16.1.

godless people, and sinners. It is for wicked and evil people, and for murderers, who would even kill their own parents. [10] The Law was written for people who are sexual perverts or who live as homosexuals or are kidnappers or liars or won't tell the truth in court. It is for anything else that opposes the correct teaching [11] of the good news that the glorious and wonderful God has given me.

Being thankful for God's kindness

[12] I thank Christ Jesus our Lord. He has given me the strength for my work because he knew that he could trust me. [13] I used to say terrible and insulting things about him, and I was cruel. But he had mercy on me because I didn't know what I was doing, and I had not yet put my faith in him. [14] Christ Jesus our Lord was very kind to me. He has greatly blessed my life with faith and love just like his own.

[15] "Christ Jesus came into the world to save sinners." This saying is true, and it can be trusted. I was the worst sinner of all! [16] But since I was worse than anyone else, God had mercy on me and let me be an example of the endless patience of Christ Jesus. He did this so that others would put their faith in Christ and have eternal life. [17] I pray that honour and glory will always be given to the only God, who lives for ever and is the invisible and eternal King! Amen.

[18] Timothy, my son, the instructions I am giving you are based on what some prophets* once said about you. If you follow these instructions, you will fight like a good soldier. [19] You will be faithful and have a clear conscience. Some people have made a mess of their faith because they didn't listen to their consciences. [20] Two of them are Hymenaeus and Alexander. I have given these men over to the power of Satan, so they will learn not to oppose God.

CHAPTER 2

How to pray

[1] First of all, I ask you to pray for everyone. Ask God to help and bless them all, and tell God how thankful you are for each of them. [2] Pray for kings and others in power, so that we may live quiet and peaceful lives as we worship and honour God. [3] This kind of prayer is good, and it pleases God our Saviour. [4] God wants everyone to be saved and to know the whole truth, which is,

> [5] There is only one God,
>   and Christ Jesus
>   is the only one
>   who can bring us
>   to God.
>   Jesus was truly human,
>   and he gave himself
>   to rescue all of us.
> [6] God showed us this
>   at the right time.

[7] This is why God chose me to be a preacher and an apostle of the good news. I am telling the truth. I am not lying. God sent me to teach the Gentiles about faith and truth.

[8] I want everyone everywhere to lift innocent hands towards heaven and pray, without being angry or arguing with each other.

[9] I would like women to wear modest and sensible clothes. They should not have fancy hair styles, or wear expensive clothes, or put on jewellery made of gold or pearls. [10] Women who claim to love God should do helpful things for others, [11] and they should learn by being quiet and paying attention. [12] They should be silent and not be allowed to teach or to tell men what to do. [13] After all, Adam was created before Eve, [14] and the man Adam wasn't the one who was fooled. It was the woman Eve who was completely fooled and sinned. [15] But women will be saved by having children,* if they stay faithful, loving, holy, and modest.

CHAPTER 3

Church officials

[1] It is true that* anyone who desires to be a church official* wants to be something worthwhile. [2] That's why officials must have a good reputation and be faithful in marriage.* They must be self-controlled, sensible, well-behaved, friendly to strangers, and able to teach. [3] They must not be heavy drinkers or troublemakers. Instead, they must be kind and gentle and not love money.

---

*1.18 prophets: Probably the Christian prophets referred to in 4.14.
See also: 1.13: Acts 8.3; 9.4,5.

*2.15 saved by having children: Or "brought safely through childbirth" or "saved by the birth of a child" (that is, by the birth of Jesus) or "saved by being good mothers".

See also: 2.7: 2 Tim 1.11. 2.9: 1 Pet 3.3. 2.13: a Gen 2.7;
b Gen 2.21,22. 2.14: Gen 3.1–6. 3.2–7: Titus 1.6–9.

⁴ Church officials must be in control of their own families, and they must see that their children are obedient and always respectful. ⁵ If they don't know how to control their own families, how can they look after God's people?

⁶ They must not be new followers of the Lord. If they are, they might become proud and be doomed along with the devil. ⁷ Finally, they must be well respected by people who are not followers. Then they won't be trapped and disgraced by the devil.

Church officers

⁸ Church officers* should be serious. They must not be liars, heavy drinkers, or greedy for money. ⁹ And they must have a clear conscience and hold firmly to what God has shown us about our faith. ¹⁰ They must first prove themselves. Then if no one has anything against them, they can serve as officers.

¹¹ Women* must also be serious. They must not gossip or be heavy drinkers, and they must be faithful in everything they do. ¹² Church officers must be faithful in marriage.* They must be in full control of their children and everyone else in their home. ¹³ Those who serve well as officers will earn a good reputation and will be highly respected for their faith in Christ Jesus.

The mystery of our religion

¹⁴ I hope to visit you soon. But I am writing these instructions, ¹⁵ so that if I am delayed, you will know how everyone who belongs to God's family ought to behave. After all, the church of the living God is the strong foundation of truth.

¹⁶ Here is the great mystery of our religion:

> Christ* came as a human.
> The Spirit proved
>   that he pleased God,
> and he was seen by angels.
>
> Christ was preached
>   to the nations.
> People in this world
>   put their faith in him,
> and he was taken up to glory.

---

*3.11 Women: Either church officers or the wives of church officers.

CHAPTER 4

People will turn from their faith

¹ God's Spirit clearly says that in the last days many people will turn from their faith. They will be fooled by evil spirits and by teachings that come from demons. ² They will also be fooled by the false claims of liars whose consciences have lost all feeling. These liars ³ will forbid people to marry or to eat certain foods. But God created these foods to be eaten with thankful hearts by his followers who know the truth. ⁴ Everything God created is good. And if you give thanks, you may eat anything. ⁵ What God has said and your prayer will make it fit to eat.

Paul's advice to Timothy

⁶ If you teach these things to other followers, you will be a good servant of Christ Jesus. You will show that you have grown up on the teachings about our faith and on the good instructions you have obeyed. ⁷ Don't have anything to do with worthless, senseless stories. Work hard to be truly religious. ⁸⁻⁹ As the saying goes,

> "Exercise is good
>   for your body,
> but religion helps you
>   in every way.
> It promises life
>   now and for ever."

These words are worthwhile and should not be forgotten. ¹⁰ We have put our hope in the living God, who is the Saviour of everyone, but especially of those who have obeyed. That's why we work and struggle so hard.*

¹¹ Teach these things and tell everyone to do what you say. ¹² Don't let anyone make fun of you, just because you are young. Set an example for other followers by what you say and do, as well as by your love, faith, and purity.

¹³ Until I arrive, be sure to keep on reading the Scriptures in worship, and don't stop preaching and teaching. ¹⁴ Use the gift you were given when the prophets spoke and the group of church leaders* blessed you by placing their hands on you. ¹⁵ Remember these things and think about them, so everyone can see how well you are doing. ¹⁶ Be careful about the way you live and about what you teach. Keep on doing this, and you will save not only yourself, but the people who hear you.

CHAPTER 5

How to act towards others

[1] Don't correct an older man. Encourage him, as you would your own father. Treat younger men as you would your own brother, [2] and treat older women as you would your own mother. Show the same respect to younger women that you would to your sister.

[3] Take care of any widow who is really in need. [4] But if a widow has children or grandchildren, they should learn to serve God by taking care of her, as she once took care of them. This is what God wants them to do. [5] A widow who is really in need is one who doesn't have any relatives. She has faith in God, and she keeps praying to him night and day, asking for his help.

[6] A widow who thinks only about having a good time is already dead, even though she is still alive.

[7] Tell all this to everyone, so they will do the right thing. [8] People who don't take care of their relatives, and especially their own families, have given up their faith. They are worse than someone who doesn't have faith in the Lord.

[9] For a widow to be put on the list of widows, she must be at least sixty years old, and she must have been faithful in marriage.[a]

[10] She must also be well known for doing all sorts of good things, such as raising children, giving food to strangers, welcoming God's people into her home,[*] helping people in need, and always making herself useful.

[11] Don't put young widows on the list. They may later have a strong desire to get married. Then they will turn away from Christ [12] and become guilty of breaking their promise to him. [13] Besides, they will become lazy and get into the habit of going from house to house. Next, they will start gossiping and become busybodies, talking about things that are none of their business.

[14] I would prefer that young widows get married, have children, and look after their families. Then the enemy won't have any reason to say insulting things about us. [15] Look what's already happened to some of the young widows! They have turned away to follow Satan.

[16] If a woman who is a follower has any widows in her family, she[*] should help them. This will keep the church from having that burden, and then the church can help widows who are really in need.

Church leaders

[17] Church leaders[*] who do their job well deserve to be paid[*] twice as much, especially if they work hard at preaching and teaching. [18] It is just as the Scriptures say, "Don't muzzle an ox when you are using it to grind grain."[b] You also know the saying, "Workers are worth their pay."

[19] Don't listen to any charge against a church leader, unless at least two or three people bring the charges.[c] [20] But if any of the leaders should keep on sinning, they must be corrected in front of the whole group, as a warning to everyone.

[21] In the presence of God and Christ Jesus and their chosen angels, I order you to follow my instructions! Be fair with everyone, and don't have any favourites.

[22] Don't be too quick to accept people into the service of the Lord[*] by placing your hands on them.

Don't sin because others do, but stay close to God.

[23] Stop drinking only water. Take a little wine to help your stomach trouble and the other illnesses you always have.

[24] Some people get caught in their sins straight away, even before the time of judgment. But other people's sins don't show up until later. [25] It is the same with good deeds. Some are easily seen, but none of them can be hidden.

CHAPTER 6

[1] If you are a slave, you should respect and honour your owner. This will keep people from saying bad things about God and about our teaching. [2] If any of you slaves have owners who are followers, you should show them respect. After all, they are also followers of Christ, and he loves them. So you should serve and help them the best you can.

False teaching and true wealth

These are the things you must teach and tell the people to do. [3] Anyone who teaches something different disagrees with the correct

---

*5.10 welcoming God's people into her home: The Greek text has "washing the feet of God's people". In New Testament times most people either went barefoot or wore sandals, and a host would often wash the feet of special guests.

See also: 5.18: a Deut 25.4; b Matt 10.10; Luke 10.7.
5.19: Deut 17.6; 19.15.

and godly teaching of our Lord Jesus Christ.
⁴ Those people who disagree are proud of themselves, but they don't really know a thing. Their minds are sick, and they like to argue over words. They cause jealousy, disagreements, unkind words, evil suspicions, ⁵ and nasty quarrels. They have wicked minds and have missed out on the truth.

These people think religion is supposed to make you rich. ⁶ And religion does make your life rich, by making you content with what you have. ⁷ We didn't bring anything into this world, and we won't take anything with us when we leave. ⁸ So we should be satisfied just to have food and clothes. ⁹ People who want to be rich fall into all sorts of temptations and traps. They are caught by foolish and harmful desires that drag them down and destroy them. ¹⁰ The love of money causes all kinds of trouble. Some people want money so much that they have given up their faith and caused themselves a lot of pain.

Fighting a good fight for the faith

¹¹ Timothy, you belong to God, so keep away from all these evil things. Try your best to please God and to be like him. Fight a good fight for the faith and claim eternal life. God offered it to you when you clearly told about your faith, while so many people listened. ¹³ Now I ask you to make a promise. Make it in the presence of God, who gives life to all, and in the presence of Jesus Christ, who openly told Pontius Pilate about his faith. ¹⁴ Promise to obey completely and fully all that you have been told until our Lord Jesus Christ returns.

¹⁵ The glorious God
is the only Ruler,
the King of kings
and Lord of lords.
At the time that God
has already decided,
he will send Jesus Christ
back again.

¹⁶ Only God lives for ever!
And he lives in light
that no one can come near.
No human has ever seen God
or ever can see him.
God will be honoured,
and his power
will last for ever. Amen.

¹⁷ Warn the rich people of this world not to be proud or to trust in wealth that is easily lost. Tell them to have faith in God, who is rich and blesses us with everything we need to enjoy life. ¹⁸ Instruct them to do as many good deeds as they can and to help everyone. Remind the rich to be generous and share what they have. ¹⁹ This will lay a solid foundation for the future, so that they will know what true life is like.

²⁰ Timothy, guard what God has placed in your care! Don't pay any attention to that godless and stupid talk that sounds clever but really isn't. ²¹ Some people have even lost their faith by believing this talk.

I pray that the Lord will be kind to all of you!

Additional notes

3.1 It is true that: These words may be taken with 2.15. If so, that verse would be translated: "It is true that women will be saved . . . holy, and modest." And 3.1 would be translated: "Anyone who desires . . . something worthwhile."
3.1 church official: Or "bishop".
3.2 be faithful in marriage: Or "be the husband of only one wife" or "have never been divorced".
3.8 Church officers: Or "Deacons".
3.12 be faithful in marriage: See the note at 3.2.
3.16 Christ: The Greek text has "he", probably meaning "Christ". Some manuscripts have "God".
4.10 struggle so hard: Some manuscripts have "are treated so badly".
4.14 group of church leaders: Or "group of elders" or "group of presbyters" or "group of priests". This translates one Greek word, and it is related to the one used in 5.17,19.
5.9 been faithful in marriage: Or "been the wife of only one husband" or "never been divorced".
5.16 woman . . . she: Some manuscripts have "man or woman . . . that person".
5.17 leaders: Or "elders" or "presbyters" or "priests".
5.17 paid: Or "honoured" or "respected".
5.22 to accept people into the service of the Lord: Or "to forgive people".
6.7 we won't: Some manuscripts have "we certainly won't".

2 Timothy

Paul's second letter to Timothy

A quick look at this letter

Greetings and prayer for Timothy *page 254*

Do not be ashamed of the Lord *page 254*

How to be a good soldier of Christ *page 255*

What people will be like in the last days
page 256

Keep being faithful *page 256*

Personal instructions and final greetings
page 257

Additional notes *page 257*

In his second letter to Timothy, Paul is more
personal than in his first one. Timothy is like a
"dear child" to Paul, and Paul always mentions
him in his prayers (1.2,3) because he wants
Timothy to be a "good soldier" of Christ Jesus
and to learn to endure suffering (2.1,3). Paul
mentions Timothy's mother and grandmother
by name in this letter and reminds Timothy how
he had placed his hands on him as a special
sign that the Spirit was guiding his work.

Some who claimed to be followers of the Lord
had already been trapped by the devil, and Paul
warns Timothy to run from those temptations
that often catch young people (2.20–26; 3.1–9).
He tells Timothy to keep preaching God's
message, even if it is not the popular thing to do
(4.2). He should also beware of false teachers.

Paul knows that he will soon die for his faith, but
he will be rewarded for his faithfulness (4.6–8),
and he reminds Timothy of the true message:

If we died with Christ,
  we will live with him.
If we don't give up,
  we will rule with him.

(2.11,12a)

Greetings and prayer for Timothy

CHAPTER 1

¹ *From Paul, an apostle of Christ Jesus.*
  God himself chose me to be an apostle,
and he gave me the promised life that Jesus
Christ makes possible.
  ² Timothy, you are like a dear child to me.
I pray that God our Father and our Lord
Christ Jesus will be kind and merciful to you
and will bless you with peace!

Do not be ashamed of the Lord

³ Night and day I mention you in my
prayers. I am always grateful for you, as
I pray to the God my ancestors and I have
served with a clear conscience. ⁴ I remember
how you cried, and I want to see you,
because that will make me truly happy.
⁵ I also remember the genuine faith of
your mother Eunice. Your grandmother
Lois had the same sort of faith, and I am
sure that you have it as well. ⁶ So I ask you to

See also: 1.2: Acts 16.1. 1.5: Acts 16.1.

make full use of the gift that God gave you when I placed my hands on you.* Use it well. [7] God's Spirit† doesn't make cowards out of us. The Spirit gives us power, love, and self-control.

[8] Don't be ashamed to speak for our Lord. And don't be ashamed of me, just because I am in jail for serving him. Use the power that comes from God and join with me in suffering for telling the good news.

[9] God saved us and chose us
   to be his holy people.
We did nothing
   to deserve this,
but God planned it
   because he is so kind.
Even before time began
God planned for Christ Jesus
   to show kindness to us.

[10] Now Christ Jesus has come
   to show us the kindness
   of God.
Christ our Saviour defeated death
and brought us
   the good news.
It shines like a light
and offers life
   that never ends.

[11] My work is to be a preacher, an apostle, and a teacher.† [12] That's why I am suffering now. But I am not ashamed! I know the one I have faith in, and I am sure that he can guard until the last day what he has trusted me with.† [13] Now follow the example of the correct teaching I gave you, and let the faith and love of Christ Jesus be your model. [14] You have been trusted with a wonderful treasure. Guard it with the help of the Holy Spirit, who lives within you.

[15] You know that everyone in Asia has turned against me, especially Phygelus and Hermogenes.

[16] I pray that the Lord will be kind to the family of Onesiphorus. He often cheered me up and wasn't ashamed of me when I was put in jail. [17] Then after he arrived in Rome, he searched everywhere until he found me. [18] I pray that the Lord Jesus will ask God to show mercy to Onesiphorus on the day of judgment. You know how much he helped me in Ephesus.

*1.6 when I placed my hands on you: Church leaders placed their hands on people who were being appointed to preach or teach. See 1 Timothy 4.14.
See also: 1.11: 1 Tim 2.7.

How to be a good soldier of Christ

CHAPTER 2

[1] Timothy, my child, Christ Jesus is kind, and you must let him make you strong. [2] You have often heard me teach. Now I want you to tell these same things to followers who can be trusted to tell others.

[3] As a good soldier of Christ Jesus you must endure your share of suffering. [4] Soldiers on duty don't work at outside jobs. They try only to please their commanding officer. [5] No one wins an athletic contest without obeying the rules. [6] And farmers who work hard are the first to eat what grows in their field. [7] If you keep in mind what I have told you, the Lord will help you understand completely.

[8] Keep your mind on Jesus Christ! He was from the family of David and was raised from death, just as my good news says. [9] And because of this message, I am locked up in jail and treated like a criminal. But God's good news isn't locked in jail, [10] and so I am willing to put up with anything. Then God's special people will be saved. They will be given eternal glory because they belong to Christ Jesus. [11] Here is a true message:

   "If we died with Christ,
      we will live with him.
[12] If we don't give up,
      we will rule with him.
   If we deny
      that we know him,
   he will deny
      that he knows us.
[13] If we are not faithful,
      he will still be faithful.
   Christ cannot deny
      who he is."

An approved worker

[14] Don't let anyone forget these things. And with God† as your witness, you must warn them not to argue about words. These arguments don't help anyone. In fact, they ruin everyone who listens to them. [15] Do your best to win God's approval as a worker who doesn't need to be ashamed and who teaches only the true message.

[16] Keep away from worthless and useless talk. It only leads people further away from God. [17] That sort of talk is like a sore that

See also: 2.12: Matt 10.33; Luke 12.9.

255

won't heal. And Hymenaeus and Philetus have been talking this way [18] by teaching that the dead have already been raised to life. This is far from the truth, and it is destroying the faith of some people.

[19] But the foundation that God has laid is solid. On it is written, "The Lord knows who his people are. So everyone who worships the Lord must turn away from evil."

[20] In a large house some dishes are made of gold or silver, while others are made of wood or clay. Some of these are special, and others are not. [21] That's also how it is with people. The ones who stop doing evil and make themselves pure will become special. Their lives will be holy and pleasing to their Master, and they will be able to do all kinds of good deeds.

[22] Run from temptations that capture young people. Always do the right thing. Be faithful, loving, and easy to get along with. Worship with people whose hearts are pure. [23] Stay away from stupid and senseless arguments. These only lead to trouble, [24] and God's servants must not be troublemakers. They must be kind to everyone, and they must be good teachers and very patient.

[25] Be humble when you correct people who oppose you. Perhaps God will lead them to turn to him and learn the truth. [26] They have been trapped by the devil, and he makes them obey him, but God may help them escape.

What people will be like in the last days

CHAPTER 3

[1] You can be certain that in the last days there will be some very hard times. [2] People will love only themselves and money. They will be proud, stuck-up, rude, and disobedient to their parents. They will also be ungrateful, godless, [3] heartless, and hateful. Their words will be cruel, and they will have no self-control or pity. These people will hate everything that is good. [4] They will be sneaky, reckless, and puffed up with pride. Instead of loving God, they will love pleasure. [5] Even though they will make a show of being religious, their religion won't be real. Don't have anything to do with such people.

[6] Some men fool whole families, just to get power over those women who are slaves of sin and are controlled by all sorts of desires.

[7] These women always want to learn something new, but they never can discover the truth. [8] Just as Jannes and Jambres* opposed Moses, these people are enemies of the truth. Their minds are sick, and their faith isn't real. [9] But they won't get very far with their foolishness. Soon everyone will know the truth about them, just as Jannes and Jambres were found out.

Keep being faithful

Paul's last instructions to Timothy

[10] Timothy, you know what I teach and how I live. You know what I want to do and what I believe. You have seen how patient and loving I am, and how in the past I put up with [11] trouble and suffering in the cities of Antioch, Iconium, and Lystra. Yet the Lord rescued me from all those terrible troubles. [12] Anyone who belongs to Christ Jesus and wants to live right will have trouble from others. [13] But evil people who pretend to be what they are not will become worse than ever, as they fool others and are fooled themselves.

[14] Keep on being faithful to what you were taught and to what you believed. After all, you know who taught you these things. [15] Since childhood, you have known the Holy Scriptures that are able to make you wise enough to have faith in Christ Jesus and be saved. [16] Everything in the Scriptures is God's Word. All of it is useful for teaching and helping people and for correcting them and showing them how to live. [17] The Scriptures train God's servants to do all kinds of good deeds.

CHAPTER 4

[1] When Christ Jesus comes as king, he will be the judge of everyone, whether they are living or dead. So with God and Christ as witnesses, I command you [2] to preach God's message. Do it willingly, even if it isn't the popular thing to do. You must correct people and point out their sins. But also cheer them up, and when you instruct them, always be patient. [3] The time is coming when people

---

*3.8 Jannes and Jambres: These names are not found in the Old Testament. But many believe these were the names of the two Egyptian magicians who opposed Moses when he wanted to lead the people of Israel out of Egypt. See Exodus 7.11,22.

See also: 3.8: Exod 7.11. 3.11: a Acts 13.14–52; b Acts 14.1–7; c Acts 14.8–20.

won't listen to good teaching. Instead, they will look for teachers who will please them by telling them only what they are itching to hear. [4] They will turn from the truth and eagerly listen to senseless stories. [5] But you must stay calm and be willing to suffer. You must work hard to tell the good news and to do your job well.

[6] Now the time has come for me to die. My life is like a drink offering* being poured out on the altar. [7] I have fought well. I have finished the race, and I have been faithful. [8] So a crown will be given to me for pleasing the Lord. He judges fairly, and on the day of judgment he will give a crown to me and to everyone else who wants him to appear with power.

Personal instructions and final greetings

Personal instructions

[9] Come to see me as soon as you can. [10] Demas loves the things of this world so much that he left me and went to Thessalonica. Crescens has gone to Galatia, and Titus has gone to Dalmatia. [11] Only Luke has stayed with me.

Mark can be very helpful to me, so please find him and bring him with you. [12] I sent Tychicus to Ephesus.

[13] When you come, bring the coat I left at Troas with Carpus. Don't forget to bring the scrolls, especially the ones made of leather.*

[14] Alexander, the metalworker, has hurt me in many ways. But the Lord will pay him back for what he has done. [15] Alexander opposes what we preach. You had better watch out for him.

[16] When I was first put on trial, no one helped me. In fact, everyone deserted me. I hope it won't be held against them. [17] But the Lord stood beside me. He gave me the strength to tell his full message, so that all

Gentiles would hear it. And I was kept safe from hungry lions. [18] The Lord will always keep me from being harmed by evil, and he will bring me safely into his heavenly kingdom. Praise him for ever and ever! Amen.

Final greetings

[19] Give my greetings to Priscilla and Aquila and to the family of Onesiphorus.

[20] Erastus stayed at Corinth.

Trophimus was sick when I left him at Miletus.

[21] Do your best to come before winter.

Eubulus, Pudens, Linus, and Claudia send you their greetings, and so do the rest of the Lord's followers.

[22] I pray that the Lord will bless your life and will be kind to you.

See also: **4.19:** a Acts 18.2; b 2 Tim 1.16,17. **4.20:** a Acts 19.22; Rom 16.23; b Acts 20.4; 21.29.

Additional notes

*1.7 God's Spirit: Or "God".

*1.11 teacher: Some manuscripts add "of the Gentiles".

*1.12 what he has trusted me with: Or "what I have trusted him with."

*2.14 God: Some manuscripts have "the Lord", and others have "Christ".

4.6 drink offering: Water or wine was sometimes poured out as an offering when an animal sacrifice was made.

*4.13 the ones made of leather: A scroll was a kind of rolled up book, and it could be made out of paper (called "papyrus") or leather (that is, animal skin) or even copper.

See also: **4.10:** a Col 4.14; Phlm 24; b 2 Cor 8.23; Gal 2.3; Titus 1.4. **4.11:** a Col 4.14; Phlm 24; b Acts 12.12,25; 13.13; 15.37–39; Col 4.10; Phlm 24. **4.12:** Acts 20.4; Eph 6.21,22; Col 4.7,8. **4.13:** Acts 20.6. **4.14:** a 1 Tim 1.20; b Psa 62.12; Rom 2.6.

Titus

Paul's letter to Titus

A quick look at this letter

Greetings and a prayer for Titus *page 258*

Instructions for church officials *page 258*

Instructions for church people *page 259*

Personal advice and final greetings *page 260*

Additional notes *page 260*

Paul mentions Titus several times in his letters as someone who worked with him in Asia Minor and Greece (2 Corinthians 2.13; 7.6,13; 8.6,16,23; 12.18; Galatians 2.3). He is told by Paul to appoint church leaders and officials in Crete.

Paul instructs Titus to make sure that church leaders and officials have good reputations (1.5–9) and that all the Lord's followers keep themselves pure and avoid arguments (1.10–2.9).

Paul includes special instructions for the different groups within the church in Crete. He reminds Titus that a new way of life is possible because of what God has done by sending Jesus Christ: God has saved them, washed them by the power of the Holy Spirit, and given them a fresh start and the hope of eternal life.

Paul also tells how we are saved:

*God our Saviour showed us
   how good and kind he is.
He saved us because of his mercy,
   and not because of any good things
   that we have done.*

(3.4,5)

Greetings and a prayer for Titus

CHAPTER 1

¹ *From Paul, a servant of God and an apostle of Jesus Christ.*

I encourage God's own people to have more faith and to understand the truth about religion. ² Then they will have the hope of eternal life that God promised long ago. And God never tells a lie! ³ So, at the proper time, God our Saviour gave this message and told me to announce what he had said.

⁴ Titus, because of our faith, you are like a son to me. I pray that God our Father and Christ Jesus our Saviour will be kind to you and will bless you with peace!

Instructions for church officials

What Titus was to do in Crete

⁵ I left you in Crete to do what had been left undone and to appoint leaders' for the churches in each town. As I told you, ⁶ they must have a good reputation and be faithful in marriage.' Their children must

See also: 1.4: 2 Cor 8.23; Gal 2.3; 2 Tim 4.10.
1.6–9: 1 Tim 3.2–7.

be followers of the Lord and not have a reputation for being wild and disobedient. [7] Church officials' are in charge of God's work, and so they must also have a good reputation. They must not be bossy, quick-tempered, heavy drinkers, bullies, or dishonest in business. [8] Instead, they must be friendly to strangers and enjoy doing good things. They must also be sensible, fair, pure, and self-controlled. [9] They must stick to the true message they were taught, so that their good teaching can help others and correct everyone who opposes it.

[10] There are many who don't respect authority, and they fool others by talking nonsense. This is especially true of some Jewish followers. [11] But you must make them be quiet. They are after money, and they upset whole families by teaching what they should not. [12] It is like one of their own prophets once said,

"The people of Crete
always tell lies.
They are greedy and lazy
like wild animals."

[13] That is a true saying. And you should be hard on such people, so you can help them grow stronger in their faith. [14] Don't pay any attention to any of those senseless Jewish stories and human commands. These are made up by people who won't obey the truth.

[15] Everything is pure for someone whose heart is pure. But nothing is pure for an unbeliever with a dirty mind. That person's mind and conscience are destroyed. [16] Such people claim to know God, but their actions prove that they really don't. They are disgusting. They won't obey God, and they are too worthless to do anything good.

Instructions for church people

CHAPTER 2

Instructions for different groups of people

[1] Titus, you must teach only what is correct. [2] Tell the older men to have self-control and to be serious and sensible. Their faith, love, and patience must never fail.

[3] Tell the older women to behave as those who love the Lord should. They must not gossip about others or be slaves of wine. They must teach what is proper, [4] so the younger women will be loving wives and mothers. [5] Each of the younger women must be sensible and kind, as well as a good homemaker, who puts her own husband first. Then no one can say insulting things about God's message.

[6] Tell the young men to have self-control in everything.

[7] Always set a good example for others. Be sincere and serious when you teach. [8] Use clean language that no one can criticize. Do this, and your enemies will be too ashamed to say anything against you.

[9] Tell slaves always to please their owners by obeying them in everything. Slaves must not talk back to their owners [10] or steal from them. They must be completely honest and trustworthy. Then everyone will show great respect for what is taught about God our Saviour.

God's kindness and the new life

[11] God has shown us how kind he is by coming to save all people. [12] He taught us to give up our wicked ways and our worldly desires and to live decent and honest lives in this world. [13] We are filled with hope, as we wait for the glorious return of our great God and Saviour Jesus Christ.' [14] He gave himself to rescue us from everything that is evil and to make our hearts pure. He wanted us to be his own people and to be eager to do right.

[15] Teach these things, as you use your full authority to encourage and correct people. Make sure you earn everyone's respect.

CHAPTER 3

Doing helpful things

[1] Remind your people to obey the rulers and authorities and not to be rebellious. They must always be ready to do something helpful [2] and not say cruel things or argue. They should be gentle and kind to everyone. [3] We used to be stupid, disobedient, and foolish, as well as slaves of all sorts of desires and pleasures. We were evil and jealous. Everyone hated us, and we hated everyone.

See also: **2.14:** a Psa 130.8; b Exod 19.5; Deut 4.20; 7.6; 14.2; 1 Pet 2.9.

⁴ God our Saviour showed us
how good and kind he is.
⁵ He saved us because
of his mercy,
and not because
of any good things
that we have done.

God washed us by the power
of the Holy Spirit.
He gave us new birth
and a fresh beginning.
⁶ God sent Jesus Christ
our Saviour
to give us his Spirit.
⁷ Jesus treated us much better
than we deserve.
He made us acceptable to God
and gave us the hope
of eternal life.

⁸ This message is certainly true.
These teachings are useful and helpful for everyone. I want you to insist that the people follow them, so that all who have faith in God will be sure to do good deeds. ⁹ But don't have anything to do with stupid arguments about ancestors. And stay away from disagreements and quarrels about the Law of Moses. Such arguments are useless and senseless.

¹⁰ Warn troublemakers once or twice. Then don't have anything else to do with them.
¹¹ You know that their minds are twisted, and their own sins show how guilty they are.

Personal advice and final greetings

¹² I plan to send Artemas or Tychicus to you. After he arrives, please try your best to meet me at Nicopolis. I have decided to spend the winter there.

¹³ When Zenas the lawyer and Apollos get ready to leave, help them as much as you can, so they won't have need of anything.

¹⁴ Our people should learn to spend their time doing something useful and worthwhile.

¹⁵ Greetings to you from everyone here. Greet all our friends who share in our faith.

I pray that the Lord will be kind to all of you!

Additional notes

˙1.5 leaders: Or "elders" or "presbyters" or "priests".
˙1.6 be faithful in marriage: Or "be the husband of only one wife" or "have never been divorced".
˙1.7 Church officials: Or "Bishops".
˙2.13 the glorious return of our great God and Saviour Jesus Christ: Or "the glorious return of our great God and our Saviour Jesus Christ" or "the return of Jesus Christ, who is the glory of our great God and Saviour."

See also: 3.12: Acts 20.4; Eph 6.21,22; Col 4.7,8; 2 Tim 4.12.
3.13: Acts 18.24; 1 Cor 16.12.

Philemon

Paul's letter to Philemon

A quick look at this letter

Philemon was a wealthy man who owned slaves and who used his large house for church meetings (2). He probably lived in Colossae, since Paul's letter to the Colossians mentions Onesimus, a slave of Philemon, and Archippus (Colossians 4.9,17).

Paul is writing from jail on behalf of Onesimus, a runaway slave owned by Philemon. Onesimus had become a follower of the Lord and a valuable friend to Paul, and Paul is writing to encourage Philemon to accept Onesimus also as a friend and follower of the Lord.

This letter is an excellent example of the art of letter-writing in the Roman world, and it is the most personal of all Paul's letters. The way the letter is written suggests that Paul and Philemon were close friends.

Greetings to Philemon

¹ From Paul, who is in jail for serving Christ Jesus, and from Timothy, who is like a brother because of our faith.

Philemon, you work with us and are very dear to us. This letter is to you ² *and to the church that meets in your home. It is also to our dear friend Apphia and to Archippus, who serves the Lord as we do.*
³ I pray that God our Father and our Lord Jesus Christ will be kind to you and will bless you with peace!

Philemon's love and faith

⁴ Philemon, each time I mention you in my prayers, I thank God. ⁵ I hear about your faith in our Lord Jesus and about your love for all God's people. ⁶ As you share your faith with others, I pray that they may come to know all the blessings Christ has given us. ⁷ My friend, your love has made me happy and has greatly encouraged me. It has also cheered the hearts of God's people.

Paul speaks to Philemon about Onesimus

⁸ Christ gives me the courage to tell you what to do. ⁹ But I would rather ask you to do it simply because of love. Yes, as someone* in jail for Christ, ¹⁰ I beg you to help Onesimus!* He is like a son to me because I led him to Christ here in jail. ¹¹ Before this, he was useless to you, but now he is useful both to you and to me.
¹² Sending Onesimus back to you makes me very sad. ¹³ I would like to keep him here with me, where he could take your place in

---

*v10 Onesimus: In Greek this name means "useful".
See also v2: Col 4.17. v10: Col 4.9.

helping me while I am here in prison for preaching the good news. [14] But I won't do anything unless you agree to it first. I want your act of kindness to come from your heart, and not be something you feel forced to do.

[15] Perhaps Onesimus was taken from you for a little while so that you could have him back for good, [16] but not as a slave. Onesimus is much more than a slave. To me he is a dear friend, but to you he is even more, both as a person and as a follower of the Lord.

[17] If you consider me a friend because of Christ, then welcome Onesimus as you would welcome me. [18] If he has cheated you or owes you anything, charge it to my account. [19] With my own hand I write: I, PAUL, WILL PAY YOU BACK. But don't forget that you owe me your life. [20] My dear friend and follower of Christ our Lord, please cheer me up by doing this for me.

[21] I am sure you will do all I have asked, and even more. [22] Please get a room ready for me. I hope your prayers will be answered, and I can visit you.

Final greetings and a prayer

[23] Epaphras is also here in jail for being a follower of Christ Jesus. He sends his greetings, [24] and so do Mark, Aristarchus, Demas, and Luke, who work together with me.

[25] I pray that the Lord Jesus Christ will be kind to you!

See also v23: Col 1.7; 4.12. v24: a Acts 12.12,25; 13.13; 15.37–39; Col 4.10; b Acts 19.29; 27.2; Col 4.10; c Col 4.14; 2 Tim 4.10; d Col 4.14; 2 Tim 4.11.

Additional notes

'v9 someone: Greek "a messenger" or "an old man".

Hebrews

The letter to the Hebrews

A quick look at this letter

Many religious people in the first century after
Jesus' birth, both Jews and Gentiles, had
questions about the religion of the early
Christians. They were looking for evidence that
this new faith was genuine. Jews had the
miracle of crossing the Red Sea and the
agreement made with God at Mount Sinai to
support their faith. But what miracles did
Christians have? Jews had beautiful worship
ceremonies and a high priest who offered
sacrifices in the temple so that the people
would be forgiven. But what did Christians
have? How could this new Christian faith,
centred in Jesus, offer forgiveness of sins and
friendship with God?

The letter to the Hebrews was written to
answer exactly these kinds of questions. In it
the author tells the readers how important
Jesus really is. He is greater than any of God's
angels (1.5–14), greater than any prophet,
and greater even than Moses and Joshua
(2.1—4.14). Jesus is the perfect high priest
because he never sinned, and by offering his
own life he has made the perfect sacrifice for
sin once for all time (9.23—10.18). By his death
and return from death he has opened the way
for all people to come to God (4.14—5.10;
7.1—8.13).

This letter has much to say about the
importance of faith. The writer points out that
what Jesus offers comes only by faith. And this
faith makes his followers sure of what they
hope for and gives them proof of things that
cannot be seen. The writer praises God's
faithful people of the past (11.1–40) and
encourages those who follow Jesus now to
keep their eyes on him as they run the race
(12.1–3).

What does it mean to have a high priest like
Jesus?

Jesus understands every weakness of ours,
because he was tempted in every way that we
are. But he did not sin! So whenever we are in
need, we should come bravely before the
throne of our merciful God. There we will be
treated with undeserved kindness, and we will
find help.

(4.15,16)

The greatness of God's Son

CHAPTER 1

[1] Long ago in many ways and at many times God's prophets spoke his message to our ancestors. [2] But now at last, God sent his Son to bring his message to us. God created the universe by his Son, and everything will some day belong to the Son. [3] God's Son has all the brightness of God's own glory and is like him in every way. By his own mighty word, he holds the universe together.

After the Son had washed away our sins, he sat down at the right side* of the glorious God in heaven. [4] He had become much greater than the angels, and the name he was given is far greater than any of theirs.

Jesus is greater than angels

[5] God has never said
  to any of the angels,
"You are my Son, because today
  I have become your Father!"
Neither has God said
  to any of them,
"I will be his Father,
  and he will be my Son!"

[6] When God brings his firstborn Son* into the world, he commands all his angels to worship him.

[7] And when God speaks about the angels, he says,

"I change my angels into wind
  and my servants
  into flaming fire."

[8] But God says about his Son,

"You are God,
  and you will rule
  as King for ever!
Your royal power
  brings about justice.
[9] You loved justice
  and hated evil,
and so I, your God,
  have chosen you.

I appointed you
and made you happier
  than any of your friends."

[10] The Scriptures also say,

"In the beginning, Lord,
  you were the one
  who laid the foundation
    of the earth
  and created the heavens.
[11] They will all disappear
  and wear out like clothes,
  but you will last for ever.
[12] You will roll them up
  like a robe
  and change them
  like a garment.
But you are always the same,
  and you will live for ever."

[13] God never said to any
  of the angels,
"Sit at my right side
  until I make your enemies
  into a footstool for you!"

[14] Angels are merely spirits sent to serve people who are going to be saved.

CHAPTER 2

This great way of being saved

[1] We must give our full attention to what we were told, so that we won't drift away. [2] The message spoken by angels proved to be true, and all who disobeyed or rejected it were punished as they deserved. [3] So if we refuse this great way of being saved, how can we hope to escape? The Lord himself was the first to tell about it, and people who heard the message proved to us that it was true. [4] God himself showed that his message was true by performing all kinds of powerful miracles and wonders. He also gave his Holy Spirit to anyone he chose to.

The one who leads us to be saved

[5] We know that God did not put the future world under the power of angels. [6] Somewhere in the Scriptures someone says to God,

"What makes you care
  about us humans?
Why are you concerned
  for weaklings such as we?

---

*1.3 right side: The place of honour and power.
*1.6 firstborn Son: The first son born into a family had certain privileges that the other children did not have. In 12.23 "firstborn" refers to God's special people.

See also: 1.5: a Psa 2.7; b 2 Sam 7.14; 1 Chron 17.13.
1.6: Deut 32.43 (LXX). 1.7: Psa 104.4 (LXX).
1.8,9: Psa 45.6,7.

See also: 1.10–12: Psa 102.25–27 (LXX). 1.13: Psa 110.1.
2.6–8: Psa 8.4–6.

earth, he would not be a priest at all, because here the Law appoints other priests to offer sacrifices. ⁵ But the tent where they serve is just a copy and a shadow of the real one in heaven. Before Moses made the tent, he was told, "Be sure to make it exactly like the pattern you were shown on the mountain!" ⁶ Now Christ has been appointed to serve as a priest in a much better way, and he has given us much assurance of a better agreement.

⁷ If the first agreement with God had been all right, there would not have been any need for another one. ⁸ But the Lord found fault with it and said,

> "I tell you the time will come,
>   when I will make
>   a new agreement
> with the people of Israel
>   and the people of Judah.
> ⁹ It won't be like the agreement
>   that I made
>   with their ancestors,
> when I took them by the hand
>   and led them out of Egypt.
> They broke their agreement
>   with me,
> and I stopped caring
>   about them!

¹⁰ "But now I tell the people
    of Israel —
    this is my new agreement:
'The time will come
    when I, the Lord,
will write my laws
    on their minds and hearts.
I will be their God,
    and they will be
    my people.
¹¹ Not one of them
will have to teach another
    to know me, their Lord.'

"All of them will know me,
    no matter who they are.
¹² I will treat them with kindness,
    even though they are wicked.
    I will forget their sins."

¹³ When the Lord talks about a new agreement, he means that the first one is out of date. And anything that is old and useless will soon disappear.

See also: 8.5: Exod 25.40. 8.8–12: Jer 31.31–34 (LXX).

CHAPTER 9

The tent in heaven

¹ The first promise that was made included rules for worship and a tent for worship here on earth. ² The first part of the tent was called the holy place, and a lampstand, a table, and the sacred loaves of bread were kept there.

³ Behind the curtain was the most holy place. ⁴ The gold altar that was used for burning incense was in this holy place. The gold-covered sacred chest was also there, and inside it were three things. First, there was a gold jar filled with manna.* Then there was Aaron's walking stick that sprouted.* Finally, there were the flat stones with the Ten Commandments written on them. ⁵ On top of the chest were the glorious creatures with wings* opened out above the place of mercy.*

Now isn't the time to go into detail about these things. ⁶ But this is how everything was when the priests went each day into the first part of the tent to do their duties. ⁷ However, only the high priest could go into the second part of the tent, and he went in only once a year. Each time he carried blood to offer for his sins and for any sins that the people had committed without meaning to.

⁸ All this is the Holy Spirit's way of saying that no one could enter the most holy place while the tent was still the place of worship. ⁹ This also has a meaning for today. It shows that we cannot make our consciences clear by offering gifts and sacrifices. ¹⁰ These rules are merely about such things as eating and drinking and ceremonies for washing

---

*9.4 manna: When the people of Israel were wandering through the desert, the Lord provided them with food that could be made into thin wafers. This food was called manna, which in Hebrew means "What is it?"

*9.4 Aaron's walking stick that sprouted: According to Numbers 17.1–11, Aaron's walking stick sprouted and produced almonds to show that the Lord was pleased with him and Moses.

*9.5 glorious creatures with wings: Two of these creatures (called "cherubim" in Hebrew and Greek) with outspread wings were on top of the sacred chest and were symbols of God's throne.

*9.5 place of mercy: The lid of the sacred chest, which was thought to be God's throne on earth.

See also: 9.2: a Exod 26.1–30; b Exod 25.31–40; c Exod 25.23–30. 9.3: Exod 26.31–33. 9.4: a Exod 30.1–6; b Exod 25.10–16; c Exod 16.33; d Num 17.8–10; e Exod 25.16; Deut 10.3–5. 9.5: Exod 25.18–22. 9.6: Num 18.2–6. 9.7: Lev 16.2–34.

ourselves. And rules about physical things will last only until the time comes to change them for something better.

¹¹ Christ came as the high priest of the good things that are now here.ᵇ He also went into a much better tent that wasn't made by humans and that doesn't belong to this world. ¹² Then Christ went once for all into the most holy place and freed us from sin for ever. He did this by offering his own blood instead of the blood of goats and bulls.

¹³ According to the Law of Moses, those people who become unclean are not fit to worship God. Yet they will be considered clean, if they are sprinkled with the blood of goats and bulls and with the ashes of a sacrificed calf. ¹⁴ But Christ was sinless, and he offered himself as an eternal and spiritual sacrifice to God. That's why his blood is much more powerful and makes ourᵇ consciences clear. Now we can serve the living God and no longer do things that lead to death.

¹⁵ Christ died to rescue those who had sinned and broken the old agreement. Now he brings his chosen ones a new agreement with its guarantee of God's eternal blessings! ¹⁶ In fact, making an agreement of this kind is like writing a will. This is because the one who makes the will must die before it is of any use. ¹⁷ In other words, a will doesn't go into effect as long as the one who made it is still alive.

¹⁸ Blood was also usedᵇ to put the first agreement into effect. ¹⁹ Moses told the people all that the Law said they must do. Then he used red wool and a hyssop plant to sprinkle the people and the book of the Law with the blood of bulls and goatsᵇ and with water. ²⁰ He told the people, "With this blood God makes his agreement with you."

²¹ Moses also sprinkled the tent and on everything else that was used in worship. ²² The Law says that almost everything must be sprinkled with blood, and no sins can be forgiven unless blood is offered.

Jesus' sacrifice is once and for all

²³ These things are only copies of what is in heaven, and so they had to be made holy by these ceremonies. But the real things in heaven must be made holy by something

better. ²⁴ This is why Christ did not go into a tent that had been made by humans and was only a copy of the real one. Instead, he went into heaven and is now there with God to help us.

²⁵ Christ did not have to offer himself many times. He wasn't like a high priest who goes into the most holy place each year to offer the blood of an animal. ²⁶ If he had offered himself every year, he would have suffered many times since the creation of the world. But instead, near the end of time he offered himself once and for all, so that he could be a sacrifice that does away with sin. ²⁷ We die only once, and then we are judged. ²⁸ So Christ died only once to take away the sins of many people. But when he comes again, it will not be to take away sin. He will come to save everyone who is waiting for him.

CHAPTER 10

¹ The Law of Moses is like a shadow of the good things to come. This shadow isn't the good things themselves, because it cannot free people from sin by the sacrifices that are offered year after year. ² If there were worshippers who already have their sins washed away and their consciences made clear, there would not be any need to go on offering sacrifices. ³⁻⁴ But the blood of bulls and goats cannot take away sins. It only reminds people of their sins from one year to the next.

⁵ When Christ came into the world, he said to God,

> "Sacrifices and offerings
>   are not what you want,
> but you have given me
>   my body.
> ⁶ No, you are not pleased
>   with animal sacrifices
>   and offerings for sin."

⁷ Then Christ said,

> "And so, my God,
>   I have come to do
> what you want,
>   as the Scriptures say."

⁸ The Law teaches that offerings and sacrifices must be made because of sin. But why did Christ mention these things and say that God did not want them? ⁹ Well, it was to do away with offerings and sacrifices and to replace

See also: 9.13: a Lev 16.15,16; b Num 19.9,17–19.
9.19,20: Exod 24.6–8.   **9.21:** Lev 8.15.   **9.22:** Lev 17.11.

See also: 9.28: Isa 53.12. 10.5–7: Psa 40.6–8 (LXX).

them. That is what he meant by saying to God, "I have come to do what you want." [10] So we are made holy because Christ obeyed God and offered himself once for all.

[11] The priests do their work each day, and they keep on offering sacrifices that can never take away sins. [12] But Christ offered himself as a sacrifice that is good for ever. Now he is sitting at God's right side,* [13] and he will stay there until his enemies are put under his power. [14] By his one sacrifice he has for ever set free from sin the people he brings to God.

[15] The Holy Spirit also speaks of this by telling us that the Lord said,

[16] "When the time comes,
  I will make an agreement
    with them.
  I will write my laws
    on their minds and hearts.
[17] Then I will forget
    about their sins
  and no longer remember
    their evil deeds."

[18] When sins are forgiven, there is no more need to offer sacrifices.

Encouragement and warning

[19] My friends, the blood of Jesus gives us courage to enter the most holy place [20] by a new way that leads to life! And this way takes us through the curtain that is Christ himself.

[21] We have a great high priest who is in charge of God's house. [22] So let's come near God with pure hearts and a confidence that comes from having faith. Let's keep our hearts pure, our consciences free from evil, and our bodies washed with clean water. [23] We must hold tightly to the hope that we say is ours. After all, we can trust the one who made the agreement with us. [24] We should keep on encouraging each other to be thoughtful and to do helpful things. [25] Some people have got out of the habit of meeting for worship, but we must not do that. We should keep on encouraging each other, especially since you know that the day of the Lord's coming is getting closer.

[26] No sacrifices can be made for people who decide to sin after they find out about the truth. [27] They are God's enemies, and all they can look forward to is a terrible judgment and a furious fire. [28] If two or more witnesses accuse someone of breaking the Law of Moses, that person could be put to death. [29] But it is much worse to dishonour God's Son and to disgrace the blood of the promise that made us holy. And it is just as bad to insult the Holy Spirit, who shows us mercy. [30] We know that God has said he will punish and take revenge. We also know that the Scriptures say the Lord will judge his people. [31] It is a terrible thing to fall into the hands of the living God!

[32] Don't forget all the hard times you went through when you first received the light. [33] Sometimes you were abused and ill-treated in public, and at other times you shared in the sufferings of others. [34] You were kind to people in jail. And you gladly let your possessions be taken away, because you knew you had something better, something that would last for ever.

[35] Keep on being brave! It will bring you great rewards. [36] Learn to be patient, so that you will please God and be given what he has promised. [37] As the Scriptures say,

"God is coming soon!
  It won't be very long.
[38] The people God accepts
  will live because
    of their faith.▸
But he isn't pleased
  with anyone
    who turns back."

[39] We are not like those people who turn back and get destroyed. We will keep on having faith until we are saved.

Some of God's people who had great faith

CHAPTER 11

[1] Faith makes us sure of what we hope for and gives us proof of what we cannot see. [2] It was their faith that made our ancestors pleasing to God.

[3] Because of our faith, we know that the world was made at God's command. We also know that what can be seen was made out of what cannot be seen.

---

*10.12 right side: See the note at 1.3.

See also: 10.11: Exod 29.38. 10.12,13: Psa 110.1. 10.16: Jer 31.33. 10.17: Jer 31.34. 10.22: Lev 8.30; Ezek 36.25. 10.27: Isa 26.11 (LXX).

See also: 10.28: Deut 17.6; 19.15. 10.29: Exod 24.8. 10.30: a Deut 32.35; b Deut 32.36. 10.37,38: Hab 2.3,4 (LXX). 11.3: Gen 1.1; Psa 33.6,9; John 1.3.

⁴ Because Abel had faith, he offered God a better sacrifice than Cain did. God was pleased with him and his gift, and even though Abel is now dead, his faith still speaks for him.

⁵ Enoch had faith and did not die. He pleased God, and God took him up to heaven. That's why his body was never found. ⁶ But without faith no one can please God. We must believe that God is real and that he rewards everyone who searches for him.

⁷ Because Noah had faith, he was warned about something that had not yet happened. He obeyed and built a boat that saved him and his family. In this way the people of the world were judged, and Noah was given the blessings that come to everyone who pleases God.

⁸ Abraham had faith and obeyed God. He was told to go to the land that God had said would be his, and he left for a country he had never seen. ⁹ Because Abraham had faith, he lived as a stranger in the promised land. He lived there in a tent, and so did Isaac and Jacob, who were later given the same promise. ¹⁰ Abraham did this, because he was waiting for the eternal city that God had planned and built.

¹¹ Even when Sarah was too old to have children, she had faith that God would do what he had promised, and she had a son. ¹² Her husband Abraham was almost dead, but he became the ancestor of many people. In fact, there are as many of them as there are stars in the sky or grains of sand along the beach.

¹³ Every one of those people died. But they still had faith, even though they had not received what they had been promised. They were glad just to see these things from far away, and they agreed that they were only strangers and foreigners on this earth. ¹⁴ When people talk this way, it is clear that they are looking for a place to call their own. ¹⁵ If they had been talking about the land where they had once lived, they could have gone back at any time. ¹⁶ But they were looking forward to a better home in heaven. That's why God wasn't ashamed for them to call him their God. He even built a city for them.

¹⁷⁻¹⁸ Abraham had been promised that Isaac, his only son,* would continue his family. But when Abraham was tested, he had faith and was willing to sacrifice Isaac, ¹⁹ because he was sure that God could raise people to life. This was just like getting Isaac back from death.

²⁰ Isaac had faith, and he promised blessings to Jacob and Esau. ²¹ Later, when Jacob was about to die, he leaned on his walking stick and worshipped. Then because of his faith he blessed each of Joseph's sons. ²² And just before Joseph died, he had faith that God would lead the people of Israel out of Egypt. So he told them to take his bones with them.

²³ Because Moses' parents had faith, they kept him hidden until he was three months old. They saw that he was a beautiful child, and they were not afraid to disobey the king's orders.* ²⁴ Then after Moses grew up, his faith made him refuse to be called Pharaoh's* grandson. ²⁵ He chose to be ill-treated with God's people instead of having the good time that sin could bring for a little while. ²⁶ Moses knew that the treasures of Egypt were not as wonderful as what he would receive from suffering for the Messiah,' and he looked forward to his reward.

²⁷ Because of his faith, Moses left Egypt. Moses had seen the invisible God and wasn't afraid of the king's anger. ²⁸ His faith also made him celebrate Passover. He sprinkled the blood of animals on the doorposts, so that the firstborn sons of the people of Israel would not be killed by the destroying angel.

²⁹ Because of their faith, the people walked through the Red Sea* on dry land. But when the Egyptians tried to do it, they were drowned.

---

*11.23 the king's orders:** The king of Egypt ordered all Israelite baby boys to be left outside their homes, so they would die or be killed.

*11.24 Pharaoh:** A Hebrew word sometimes used for the title of the king of Egypt.

*11.29 Red Sea:** This name comes from the Bible of the early Christians, a translation made into Greek about 200 BC. It refers to the body of water that the Israelites crossed and was one of the marshes or fresh water lakes near the eastern part of the Nile Delta, where they lived and where the towns of Exodus 13.17—14.9 were located.

See also: 11.20: Gen 27.27–29,39,40. 11.21: a Gen 48.1–20; b Gen 47.31 (LXX). 11.22: Gen 50.24,25; Exod 13.19. 11.23: a Exod 2.2; b Exod 1.22. 11.24: Exod 2.10–12. 11.28: Exod 12.21–30. 11.29: Exod 14.21–31.

---

*11.17,18 his only son:** Although Abraham had a son by a slave woman, his son Isaac was considered his only son, because he was born as a result of God's promise to Abraham.

See also: 11.4: Gen 4.3–10. 11.5: Gen 5.21–24 (LXX). 11.7: Gen 6.13–22. 11.8: Gen 12.1–5. 11.9: Gen 35.27. 11.11: Gen 18.11–14; 21.2. 11.12: Gen 15.5; 22.17; 32.12. 11.13: Gen 23.4; 1 Chron 29.15; Psa 39.12. 11.17,18: Gen 21.12; 22.1–14.

30 God's people had faith, and when they had walked around the city of Jericho for seven days, its walls fell down.

31 Rahab had been a prostitute, but she had faith and welcomed the spies. So she wasn't killed with the people who disobeyed.

32 What else can I say? There isn't enough time to tell about Gideon, Barak, Samson, Jephthah, David, Samuel, and the prophets. 33 Their faith helped them conquer kingdoms, and because they did right, God made promises to them. They closed the jaws of lions 34 and put out raging fires and escaped from the swords of their enemies. Although they were weak, they were given the strength and power to chase foreign armies away.

35 Some women received their loved ones back from death. Many of these people were tortured, but they refused to be released. They were sure that they would get a better reward when the dead are raised to life. 36 Others were made fun of and beaten with whips, and some were chained in jail. 37 Still others were stoned to death or sawn in two' or killed with swords. Some had nothing but sheep skins or goat skins to wear. They were poor, ill-treated, and tortured. 38 The world did not deserve these good people, who had to wander in deserts and on mountains and had to live in caves and holes in the ground.

39 All of them pleased God because of their faith! But still they died without being given what had been promised. 40 This was because God had something better in store for us. And he did not want them to reach the goal of their faith without us.

Follow the example of Jesus

CHAPTER 12

A large crowd of witnesses

1 Such a large crowd of witnesses is all around us! So we must get rid of everything that slows us down, especially the sin that just won't let go. And we must be determined to run the race that is ahead of us. 2 We must keep our eyes on Jesus, who leads us and makes our faith complete. He endured the

shame of being nailed to a cross, because he knew that later on he would be glad he did. Now he is seated at the right side* of God's throne! 3 So keep your mind on Jesus, who put up with many insults from sinners. Then you won't get discouraged and give up.

4 None of you have yet been hurt' in your battle against sin. 5 But you have forgotten that the Scriptures say to God's children,

"When the Lord punishes you,
  don't make light of it,
and when he corrects you,
  don't be discouraged.
6 The Lord corrects the people
  he loves
and disciplines those
  he calls his own."

7 Be patient when you are being corrected! This is how God treats his children. Don't all parents correct their children? 8 God corrects all his children, and if he doesn't correct you, then you don't really belong to him. 9 Our earthly fathers correct us, and we still respect them. Isn't it even better to be given true life by letting our spiritual Father correct us?

10 Our human fathers correct us for a short time, and they do it as they think best. But God corrects us for our own good, because he wants us to be holy, as he is. 11 It is never fun to be corrected. In fact, at the time it is always painful. But if we learn to obey by being corrected, we will do right and live at peace.

12 Now stand up straight! Stop your knees from shaking 13 and walk a straight path. Then lame people will be healed, instead of getting worse.

Warning against turning from God

14 Try to live at peace with everyone! Live a clean life. If you don't, you will never see the Lord. 15 Make sure that no one misses out on God's wonderful kindness. Don't let anyone become bitter and cause trouble for the rest of you. 16 Watch out for immoral and ungodly people like Esau, who sold his future blessing* for only one meal. 17 You know how he later wanted it back. But there was

See also: 11.30: Josh 6.12–21. 11.31: a Josh 6.22–25; b Josh 2.1–21. 11.32: a Judg 6.11–8.32; b Judg 4.6–5.31; c Judg 13.2–16.31; d Judg 11.1–12.7; e 1 Sam 16.1–1 King 2.11; f 1 Sam 1.1–25.1. 11.33: Dan 6.1–27. 11.34: Dan 3.1–30. 11.35: 1 King 17.17–24; 2 King 4.25–37. 11.36: 1 King 22.26,27; 2 Chron 18.25,26; Jer 20.2; 37.15; 38.6. 11.37: 2 Chron 24.21.

*12.2 right side: See the note at 1.3.
*12.16 sold his future blessing: As the firstborn son, Esau had certain privileges that were known as a "birthright".
See also: 12.5,6: Job 5.17; Prov 3.11,12 (LXX).
12.12: Isa 35.3 (LXX). 12.13: Prov 4.26 (LXX).
12.15: Deut 29.18 (LXX). 12.16: Gen 25.29–34.
12.17: Gen 27.30–40.

nothing he could do to change things, even though he begged his father and cried.

¹⁸ You have not come to a place like Mount Sinai* that can be seen and touched. There is no flaming fire or dark cloud or storm ¹⁹ or trumpet sound. The people of Israel heard a voice speak. But they begged it to stop, ²⁰ because they could not obey its commands. They were even told to kill any animal that touched the mountain. ²¹ The sight was so frightening that Moses said he shook with fear.

²² You have now come to Mount Zion and to the heavenly Jerusalem. This is the city of the living God, where thousands and thousands of angels have come to celebrate. ²³ Here you will find all God's dearest children,* whose names are written in heaven. And you will find God himself, who judges everyone. Here also are the spirits of those good people who have been made perfect. ²⁴ And Jesus is here! He is the one who makes God's new agreement with us, and his sprinkled blood says much better things than the blood of Abel.*

²⁵ Make sure that you obey the one who speaks to you. The people did not escape, when they refused to obey the one who spoke to them at Mount Sinai. Do you think you can possibly escape, if you refuse to obey the one who speaks to you from heaven? ²⁶ When God spoke the first time, his voice shook only the earth. This time he has promised to shake the earth once again, and heaven too. ²⁷ The words "once again" mean that these created things will some day be shaken and removed. Then what cannot be shaken will last. ²⁸ We should be grateful that we were given a kingdom that cannot be shaken. And in this kingdom we please God by worshipping him and by showing him great honour and respect. ²⁹ Our God is like a destructive fire!

*12.18 a place like Mount Sinai: The Greek text has "a place", but the writer is referring to the time that the Lord spoke to the people of Israel from Mount Sinai (see Exodus 19.16–25).

*12.23 all God's dearest children: The Greek text has "the gathering of the firstborn children". See the note at 1.6.

*12.24 blood of Abel: Cain and Abel were the two sons of Adam and Eve. Cain murdered Abel (see Genesis 4.1–16).

See also: 12.18,19: Exod 19.16–22; 20.18–21; Deut 4.11,12; 5.22–27. 12.20: Exod 19.12,13. 12.21: Deut 9.19. 12.24: Gen 4.10. 12.25: Exod 20.22. 12.26: Hag 2.6 (LXX). 12.29: Deut 4.24.

CHAPTER 13

Service that pleases God

¹ Keep being concerned about each other as the Lord's followers should.

² Be sure to welcome strangers into your home. By doing this, some people have welcomed angels as guests, without even knowing it.

³ Remember the Lord's people who are in jail and be concerned for them. Don't forget those who are suffering, but imagine that you are there with them.

⁴ Have respect for marriage. Always be faithful to your partner, because God will punish anyone who is immoral or unfaithful in marriage.

⁵ Don't fall in love with money. Be satisfied with what you have. The Lord has promised that he will not leave us or desert us. ⁶ That should make you feel like saying,

> "The Lord helps me!
> Why should I be afraid
>   of what people
>   can do to me?"

⁷ Don't forget about your leaders who taught you God's message. Remember what kind of lives they lived and try to have faith like theirs.

⁸ Jesus Christ never changes! He is the same yesterday, today, and for ever. ⁹ Don't be fooled by any kind of strange teachings. It is better to receive strength from God's undeserved kindness than to depend on certain foods. After all, these foods don't really help the people who eat them. ¹⁰ But we have an altar where even the priests who serve in the place of worship have no right to eat.

¹¹ After the high priest offers the blood of animals as a sin offering, the bodies of those animals are burnt outside the camp. ¹² Jesus himself suffered outside the city gate, so that his blood would make people holy. ¹³ That's why we should go outside the camp to Jesus and share in his disgrace. ¹⁴ On this earth we don't have a city that lasts for ever, but we are waiting for such a city.

¹⁵ Our sacrifice is to keep offering praise to God in the name of Jesus. ¹⁶ But don't forget to help others and to share your possessions with them. This too is like offering a sacrifice that pleases God.

See also: 13.2: Gen 18.1–8; 19.1–3. 13.5: Deut 31.6,8; Josh 1.5. 13.6: Psa 118.6 (LXX). 13.11: Lev 16.27.

¹⁷ Obey your leaders and do what they say. They are watching over you, and they must answer to God. So don't make them sad as they do their work. Make them happy. Otherwise, they won't be able to help you at all.

¹⁸ Pray for us. Our consciences are clear, and we always try to live right. ¹⁹ I especially want you to pray that I can visit you again soon.

Final prayers and greetings

²⁰ God gives peace, and he raised our Lord Jesus Christ from death. Now Jesus is like a Great Shepherd whose blood was used to make God's eternal agreement with his flock.* ²¹ I pray that God will make you ready to obey him and that you will always be eager to do right. May Jesus help you do what pleases God. To Jesus Christ be glory for ever and ever! Amen.

²² My friends, I have written only a short letter to encourage you, and I beg you to pay close attention to what I have said.

²³ By now you must know that our friend Timothy is out of jail. If he gets here in time, I will bring him with me when I come to visit you.

²⁴ Please give my greetings to your leaders and to the rest of the Lord's people.

His followers from Italy send you their greetings.

²⁵ I pray that God will be kind to all of you!ʼ

13.20 whose blood was used to make God's eternal agreement with his flock: See 9.18-22.

Additional notes

ʼ1.8 Your: Some manuscripts have "His".

ʼ2.7 and honour: Some manuscripts add "and you have placed us in charge of all you created."

ʼ3.2 all: Some manuscripts do not have this word.

ʼ6.2 baptisms: Or "ceremonies of washing".

ʼ7.25 for ever able to save: Or "able to save for ever".

ʼ9.11 that are now here: Some manuscripts have "that were coming".

ʼ9.14 our: Some manuscripts have "your", and others have "their".

ʼ9.18 Blood was also used: Or "There also had to be a death".

ʼ9.19 blood of bulls and goats: Some manuscripts do not have "and goats".

ʼ10.38 The people God accepts will live because of their faith: Or "The people God accepts because of their faith will live."

ʼ11.26 the Messiah: Or "Christ".

ʼ11.37 sawn in two: Some manuscripts have "tested" or "tempted".

ʼ12.4 hurt: Or "killed".

ʼ13.25 to all of you!: Some manuscripts add "Amen."

James

A letter from James

A quick look at this letter

This is a good example of a general letter, because it is addressed to Christians scattered throughout the Roman Empire. Though written as a letter, it is more like a short book of instructions for daily living.

For James faith means action! In fact, the entire book is a series of examples that show faith in action in wise and practical ways.

His advice was clear and to the point: If you are poor, don't despair! Don't give up when your faith is being tested. Don't get angry quickly. Don't favour the rich over the poor. Do good things for others. Control your tongue and desires. Surrender to God and rely on his wisdom. Resist the devil. Don't boast about what you are going to do. If you are rich, use your money to help the poor. Be patient and kind, and pray for those who need God's help.

Greetings

CHAPTER 1

¹ *From James, a servant of God and of our Lord Jesus Christ.*

Greetings to the twelve tribes scattered all over the world.*

A life of faith and wisdom

² My friends, be glad, even if you have a lot of trouble. ³ You know that you learn to endure by having your faith tested. ⁴ But you must learn to endure everything, so that you will be completely mature and not lacking in anything.

⁵ If any of you need wisdom, you should ask God, and it will be given to you. God is generous and won't correct you for asking. ⁶ But when you ask for something, you must have faith and not doubt. Anyone who doubts is like an ocean wave tossed around in a storm. ⁷⁻⁸ If you are that kind of person, you can't make up your mind, and you can't be trusted. So don't expect the Lord to give you anything at all.

Poor people and rich people

⁹ Any of God's people who are poor should be glad that he thinks so highly of them. ¹⁰ But any who are rich should be glad when God

---

*1.1 twelve tribes scattered all over the world:
James is saying that the Lord's followers are like the tribes of Israel that were scattered everywhere by their enemies.
See also: 1.1: Matt 13.55; Mark 6.3; Acts 15.13; Gal 1.19.
1.10,11: Isa 40.6,7 (LXX).

makes them humble. Rich people will disappear like wild flowers [11] scorched by the burning heat of the sun. The flowers lose their blossoms, and their beauty is destroyed. That is how the rich will disappear, as they go about their business.

Trials and temptations

[12] God will bless you, if you don't give up when your faith is being tested. He will reward you with a glorious life,* just as he rewards everyone who loves him.

[13] Don't blame God when you are tempted! God cannot be tempted by evil, and he doesn't use evil to tempt others. [14] We are tempted by our own desires that drag us off and trap us. [15] Our desires make us sin, and when sin is finished with us, it leaves us dead.

[16] Don't be fooled, my dear friends. [17] Every good and perfect gift comes down from the Father who created all the lights in the heavens. He is always the same and never makes dark shadows by changing. [18] He wanted us to be his own special people,* and so he sent his true message to give us new birth.

Hearing and obeying God's message

[19] My dear friends, you should be quick to listen and slow to speak or to get angry. [20] If you are angry, you cannot do any of the good things that God wants done. [21] You must stop doing anything immoral or evil. Instead be humble and accept the message that is planted in you to save you.

[22] Obey God's message! Don't fool yourselves by just listening to it. [23] If you hear the message and don't obey it, you are like people who stare at themselves in a mirror [24] and forget what they look like as soon as they leave. [25] But you must never stop looking at the perfect law that sets you free. God will bless you in everything you do, if you listen and obey, and don't just hear and forget.

[26] If you think you are being religious, but can't control your tongue, you are fooling yourself, and everything you do is useless. [27] Religion that pleases God the Father must be pure and spotless. You must help needy orphans and widows and not let this world make you evil.

Don't favour the rich and powerful

CHAPTER 2

Warning against having favourites

[1] My friends, if you have faith in our glorious Lord Jesus Christ, you won't treat some people better than others. [2] Suppose a rich person wearing fine clothes and a gold ring comes to one of your meetings. And suppose a poor person dressed in worn-out clothes also comes. [3] You must not give the best seat to the one in fine clothes and tell the one who is poor to stand at the side or sit on the floor. [4] That is the same as saying that some people are better than others, and you would be acting like a crooked judge.

[5] My dear friends, pay attention. God has given a lot of faith to the poor people in this world. He has also promised them a share in his kingdom that he will give to everyone who loves him. [6] You ill-treat the poor. But isn't it the rich who boss you around and drag you off to court? [7] Aren't they the ones who make fun of your Lord?

[8] You will do well, if you obey the most important law* in the Scriptures. It is the law that commands us to love others as much as we love ourselves. [9] But if you treat some people better than others, you have done wrong, and the Scriptures teach that you have sinned.

[10] If you obey every law except one, you are still guilty of breaking them all. [11] The same God who told us to be faithful in marriage also told us not to murder. So even if you are faithful in marriage, but murder someone, you have still broken God's Law.

[12] Speak and act like people who will be judged by the law that sets us free. [13] Do this, because on the day of judgment there will be no pity for those who serve others as much as others. But even in judgment, God is merciful!

---

*1.12 a glorious life: The Greek text has "the crown of life". In ancient times an athlete who had won a contest was rewarded with a crown of flowers as a sign of victory.
*1.18 his own special people: The Greek text has "the first of his creatures". The Law of Moses taught that the firstborn of all animals and first part of the harvest were special and belonged to the Lord.

*2.8 most important law: The Greek text has "royal law", meaning the one given by the king (that is, God).
See also: 2.8: Lev 19.18. 2.11: a Exod 20.14; Deut 5.18; b Exod 20.13; Deut 5.17.

Faith and works

14 My friends, what good is it to say you have faith, when you don't do anything to show that you really do have faith? Can that kind of faith save you? 15 If you know someone who doesn't have any clothes or food, 16 you shouldn't just say, "I hope all goes well for you. I hope you will be warm and have plenty to eat." What good is it to say this, unless you do something to help? 17 Faith that doesn't lead us to do good deeds is all alone and dead!

18 Suppose someone disagrees and says, "It is possible to have faith without doing kind deeds."

I would answer, "Prove that you have faith without doing kind deeds, and I will prove that I have faith by doing them." 19 You believe there is only one God. That's fine. Even demons believe this, and it makes them shake with fear.

20 Does some stupid person want proof that faith without deeds is useless? 21 Well, our ancestor Abraham pleased God by putting his son Isaac on the altar to sacrifice him. 22 Now you see how Abraham's faith and deeds worked together. He proved that his faith was real by what he did. 23 This is what the Scriptures mean by saying, "Abraham had faith in God, and God was pleased with him." That's how Abraham became God's friend.

24 You can now see that we please God by what we do and not only by what we believe. 25 For example, Rahab had been a prostitute. But she pleased God when she welcomed the spies and sent them home by another way.

26 Anyone who doesn't breathe is dead, and faith that doesn't do anything is just as dead!

Wisdom and words

CHAPTER 3

The tongue

1 My friends, we should not all try to become teachers. In fact, teachers will be judged more strictly than others. 2 All of us do many wrong things. But if you can control your tongue, you are mature and able to control your whole body.

3 By putting a bit into the mouth of a horse, we can turn the horse in different directions. 4 It takes strong winds to move a large sailing ship, but the captain uses only a small rudder to make it go in any direction. 5 Our tongues are small too, and yet they boast about big things.

It takes only a spark to start a forest fire! 6 The tongue is like a spark. It is an evil power that dirties the rest of the body and sets a person's entire life on fire with flames that come from hell itself. 7 All kinds of animals, birds, reptiles, and sea creatures can be tamed and have been tamed. 8 But our tongues get out of control. They are restless and evil, and always spreading deadly poison.

9-10 My dear friends, with our tongues we speak both praises and curses. We praise our Lord and Father, and we curse people who were created to be like God, and this isn't right. 11 Can clean water and dirty water both flow from the same spring? 12 Can a fig tree produce olives or a grapevine produce figs? Does fresh water come from a well full of salt water?

Wisdom from above

13 Are any of you wise or sensible? Then show it by living right and by being humble and wise in everything you do. 14 But if your heart is full of bitter jealousy and selfishness, don't boast or lie to cover up the truth. 15 That kind of wisdom doesn't come from above. It is earthly and selfish and comes from the devil himself. 16 Whenever people are jealous or selfish, they cause trouble and do all sorts of cruel things. 17 But the wisdom that comes from above leads us to be pure, friendly, gentle, sensible, kind, helpful, genuine, and sincere. 18 When peacemakers plant seeds of peace, they will harvest justice.

Warning against friendship with the world

CHAPTER 4

1 Why do you fight and argue with each other? Isn't it because you are full of selfish desires that fight to control your body? 2 You want something you don't have, and you will do anything to get it. You will even kill! But you still cannot get what you want, and you won't get it by fighting and arguing. You should pray for it. 3 Yet even when you do pray, your prayers are not answered, because you pray just for selfish reasons.

4 You people aren't faithful to God! Don't you know that if you love the world, you are

See also: 2.21: Gen 22.1–14. 2.23: a Gen 15.6;
b 2 Chron 20.7; Isa 41.8. 2.25: Josh 2.1–21.

See also: 3.9: Gen 1.26.

God's enemies? And if you decide to be a friend of the world, you make yourself an enemy of God. [5] Do you doubt the Scriptures that say, "God truly cares about the Spirit he has put in us"?* [6] In fact, God treats us with even greater kindness, just as the Scriptures say,

"God opposes everyone
   who is proud,
but he is kind to everyone
   who is humble."

[7] Surrender to God! Resist the devil, and he will run from you. [8] Come near to God, and he will come near to you. Clean up your lives, you sinners. Purify your hearts, you people who can't make up your mind. [9] Be sad and sorry and weep. Stop laughing and start crying. Be gloomy instead of glad. [10] Be humble in the Lord's presence, and he will honour you.

Saying cruel things about others

[11] My friends, don't say cruel things about others! If you do, or if you condemn others, you are condemning God's Law. And if you condemn the Law, you put yourself above the Law and refuse to obey either it [12] or God who gave it. God is our judge, and he can save or destroy us. What right do you have to condemn anyone?

Warning against boasting

[13] You should know better than to say, "Today or tomorrow we will go to the city. We will do business there for a year and make a lot of money!" [14] What do you know about tomorrow? How can you be so sure about your life? It is nothing more than mist that appears for only a little while before it disappears. [15] You should say, "If the Lord lets us live, we will do these things." [16] Yet you are stupid enough to boast, and it is wrong to be so proud. [17] If you don't do what you know is right, you have sinned.

CHAPTER 5

Warning to the rich

[1] You rich people should cry and weep! Terrible things are going to happen to you. [2] Your treasures have already rotted, and moths have eaten your clothes. [3] Your money has rusted, and the rust will be evidence against you, as it burns your body like fire. Yet you keep on storing up wealth in these last days. [4] You refused to pay the people who worked in your fields, and now their unpaid wages are shouting out against you. The Lord All-Powerful has heard the cries of the workers who harvested your crops.

[5] While here on earth, you have thought only of filling your own stomachs and having a good time. But now you are like fat cattle on their way to be butchered. [6] You have condemned and murdered innocent people, who couldn't even fight back.

Patience, kindness, and prayer

[7] My friends, be patient until the Lord returns. Think of farmers who wait patiently for the spring and summer rains to make their valuable crops grow. [8] Be patient like those farmers and don't give up. The Lord will soon be here! [9] Don't grumble about each other or you will be judged, and the judge is just outside the door.

[10] My friends, follow the example of the prophets who spoke for the Lord. They were patient, even when they had to suffer. [11] In fact, we praise the ones who endured the most. You remember how patient Job was and how the Lord finally helped him. The Lord did this because he is so merciful and kind.

[12] My friends, above all else, don't take an oath. You must not swear by heaven or by earth or by anything else. "Yes" or "No" is all you need to say. If you say anything more, you will be condemned.

[13] If you are having trouble, you should pray. And if you are feeling good, you should sing praises. [14] If you are sick, ask the church leaders* to come and pray for you. Ask them to put olive oil* on you in the name of the Lord. [15] If you have faith when you pray for sick people, they will get well. The Lord will heal them, and if they have sinned, he will forgive them.

[16] If you have sinned, you should tell each other what you have done. Then you can pray for one another and be healed. The prayer of an innocent person is powerful, and it can help a lot. [17] Elijah was just as human

---

*5.14 olive oil: The Jewish people used olive oil for healing.

See also: **5.4:** Deut 24.14,15. **5.11:** a Job 1.21,22; 2.10; b Psa 103.8. **5.12:** Matt 5.34–37. **5.14:** Mark 6.13. **5.17:** 1 King 17.1; 18.1.

See also: **4.6:** Prov 3.34 (LXX). **4.13,14:** Prov 27.1. **5.2,3:** Matt 6.19.

as we are, and for three and a half years his prayers kept the rain from falling. [18] But when he did pray for rain, it fell from the skies and made the crops grow.

[19] My friends, if any followers have wandered away from the truth, you should try to lead them back. [20] If you turn sinners from the wrong way, you will save them from death, and many of their sins will be forgiven.

See also: 5.18: 1 King 18.42–45. 5.20: Prov 10.12; 1 Pet 4.8.

Additional notes

'2.13 But even in judgment, God is merciful!: Or "So be merciful, and you will be shown mercy on the day of judgment."

'4.5 God truly cares about the Spirit he has put in us: One possible meaning for the difficult Greek text; other translations are possible, such as, "the Spirit that God put in us truly cares."

'5.14 church leaders: Or "elders" or "presbyters" or "priests".

1 Peter

Peter's first letter

A quick look at this letter

In this letter Peter has much to say about suffering. He shows how it can be a way of serving the Lord, of sharing the faith, and of being tested. The letter was written to Christians scattered all over the northern part of Asia Minor. In this part of the Roman Empire many Christians had already suffered unfair treatment from people who did not believe in Jesus. And they could expect to suffer even more.

Peter was quick to offer encouragement. His letter reminds the readers that some of the Lord's followers may have to go through times of hard testing. But this should make them glad, Peter declares, because it will strengthen their faith and bring them honour on the day when Jesus Christ returns (1.6,7).

Peter reminds them that Christ suffered here on earth, and when his followers suffer for doing right they are sharing his sufferings

(2.18-25; 4.12-17). In fact, Christians should expect to suffer for their faith (3.8—4.19).

But because of who God is and because of what God has done by raising Jesus Christ from death, Christians can have hope in the future. Just as Christ suffered before he received honour from God, so will Christians be tested by suffering before they receive honour when the Lord returns. Peter uses poetic language to remind his readers of what Christ has done:

> Christ died once for our sins.
> An innocent person died
>   for those who are guilty.
> Christ did this
>   to bring you to God,
> when his body
>   was put to death
> and his spirit
>   was made alive.

(3.18)

Greetings and prayer

CHAPTER 1

[1] *From Peter, an apostle of Jesus Christ.*
To God's people who are scattered like foreigners in Pontus, Galatia, Cappadocia, Asia, and Bithynia.
    [2] God the Father decided to choose you as his people, and his Spirit has made you holy.

You have obeyed Jesus Christ and are sprinkled with his blood.*

I pray that God will be kind to you and will keep on giving you peace!

A real reason for hope

3 Praise God, the Father of our Lord Jesus Christ. God is so good, and by raising Jesus from death, he has given us new life and a hope that lives on. 4 God has something stored up for you in heaven, where it will never decay or be ruined or disappear.

5 You have faith in God, whose power will protect you until the end.* Then he will save you, just as he has always planned to do. 6 On that day you will be glad, even if you have to go through many hard trials for a while. 7 Your faith will be like gold that has been tested in a fire. And these trials will prove that your faith is worth much more than gold that can be destroyed. They will show that you are to be given praise and honour and glory when Jesus Christ returns.

8 You have never seen Jesus, and you don't see him now. But still you love him and have faith in him, and no words can tell how glad and happy 9 you are to be saved. That's why you have faith.

10 Some prophets told how kind God would be to you, and they searched hard to find out more about the way you would be saved. 11 The Spirit of Christ was in them and was telling them how Christ would suffer and would then be given great honour. So they searched to find out exactly who Christ would be and when this would happen. 12 But they were told that they were serving you and not themselves. They preached to you by the power of the Holy Spirit, who was sent from heaven. And their message was only for you, even though angels would like to know more about it.

Living as God's holy people

13 Be alert and think straight. Put all your hope in how kind God will be to you when Jesus Christ appears. 14 Behave like obedient children. Don't let your lives be controlled by your desires, as they used to be. 15 Always live as God's holy people should, because God is the one who chose you, and he is holy. 16 That's why the Scriptures say, "I am the holy God, and you must be holy too."

17 You say that God is your Father, but God doesn't have favourites! He judges all people by what they do. So you must honour God while you live as strangers here on earth. 18 You were rescued* from the useless way of life that you learnt from your ancestors. But you know that you were not rescued by such things as silver or gold that don't last for ever. 19 You were rescued by the precious blood of Christ, that spotless and innocent lamb. 20 Christ was chosen even before the world was created, but because of you, he did not come until these last days. 21 And when he did come, it was to lead you to have faith in God, who raised him from death and honoured him in a glorious way. That's why you have put your faith and hope in God.

22 You obeyed the truth,* and your souls were made pure. Now you sincerely love each other. But you must keep on loving with all your heart. 23 Do this because God has given you new birth by his message that lives on for ever. 24 The Scriptures say,

"Humans wither like grass,
    and their glory fades
        like wild flowers.
Grass dries up,
    and flowers fall
        to the ground.
25 But what the Lord has said
    will stand for ever."

Our good news to you is what the Lord has said.

CHAPTER 2

A living stone and a holy nation

1 Stop being hateful! Stop trying to fool people, and start being sincere. Don't be jealous or say cruel things about others. 2 Be like newborn babies who are thirsty for the pure spiritual milk that will help you grow and be saved. 3 You have already found out how good the Lord really is.

---

*1.2 sprinkled with his blood: According to Exodus 24.3–8 the people of Israel were sprinkled with the blood of cows to show they kept their agreement with God. Peter says that it is the blood of Jesus that seals the agreement between God and his people. See Hebrews 9.18–21.
*1.5 the last day: When God will judge all people.

*1.18 rescued: The Greek word often, though not always, means payment of a price to free a slave or prisoner.
See also: 1.16: Lev 11.44,45; 19.2.
1.24,25: Isa 40.6–8 (LXX). 2.3: Psa 34.8.

4 Come to Jesus Christ. He is the living stone that people have rejected, but which God has chosen and highly honoured. 5 And now you are living stones that are being used to build a spiritual house. You are also a group of holy priests, and with the help of Jesus Christ you will offer sacrifices that please God. 6 It is just as God says in the Scriptures,

"Look! I am placing in Zion
a choice and precious
cornerstone.
No one who has faith
in that one
will be disappointed."

7 You are followers of the Lord, and that stone is precious to you. But it isn't precious to those who refuse to follow him. They are the builders who tossed aside the stone that turned out to be the most important one of all. 8 They disobeyed the message and stumbled and fell over that stone, because they were doomed.

9 But you are God's chosen and special people. You are a group of royal priests and a holy nation. God has brought you out of darkness into his marvellous light. Now you must tell all the wonderful things that he has done. The Scriptures say,

10 "Once you were nobody.
Now you are God's people.
At one time no one
had pity on you.
Now God has treated you
with kindness."

Live as God's servants should

11 Dear friends, you are foreigners and strangers on this earth. So I beg you not to surrender to those desires that fight against you. 12 Always let others see you behaving properly, even though they may still accuse you of doing wrong. Then on the day of judgment, they will honour God by telling the good things they saw you do.

13 The Lord wants you to obey all human authorities, especially the Emperor, who rules over everyone. 14 You must also obey governors, because they are sent by the Emperor to punish criminals and to praise good citizens. 15 God wants you to silence stupid and ignorant people by doing right.

16 You are free, but still you are God's servants, and you must not use your freedom as an excuse for doing wrong. 17 Respect everyone and show special love for God's people. Honour God and respect the Emperor.

The example of Christ's suffering

18 Servants, you must obey your masters and always show respect to them. Do this, not only to those who are kind and thoughtful, but also to those who are cruel. 19 God will bless you, even if others treat you unfairly for being loyal to him. 20 You don't gain anything by being punished for some wrong you have done. But God will bless you, if you have to suffer for doing something good. 21 After all, God chose you to suffer as you follow in the footsteps of Christ, who set an example by suffering for you.

22 Christ did not sin
or ever tell a lie.
23 Although he was abused,
he never tried to get even.
And when he suffered,
he made no threats.
Instead, he had faith in God,
who judges fairly.
24 Christ carried the burden
of our sins.
He was nailed to the cross,
so that we would stop sinning
and start living right.
By his cuts and bruises
you are healed.
25 You had wandered away
like sheep.
Now you have returned
to the one
who is your shepherd
and protector.

Being a Christian and suffering

CHAPTER 3

Wives and husbands

1 If you are a wife, you must put your husband first. Even if he opposes our message, you will win him over by what you do. No one else

See also: 2.6: Isa 28.16 (LXX). 2.7: Psa 118.22.
2.8: Isa 8.14,15. 2.9: a Exod 19.5,6; Isa 43.20 (LXX);
b Exod 19.5; Deut 4.20; 7.6; 14.2; Titus 2.14; c Isa 43.21;
d Isa 9.2. 2.10: Hos 2.23.

See also: 2.22: Isa 53.9. 2.23: Isa 53.7.
2.24,25: Isa 53.5,6 (LXX). 3.1: Eph 5.22; Col 3.18.

will have to say anything to him, ² because he will see how you honour God and live a pure life. ³ Don't depend on things like fancy hair styles or gold jewellery or expensive clothes to make you look beautiful. ⁴ Be beautiful in your heart by being gentle and quiet. This kind of beauty will last, and God considers it very special.

⁵ Long ago those women who worshipped God and put their hope in him made themselves beautiful by putting their husbands first. ⁶ For example, Sarah obeyed Abraham and called him her master. You are her true children, if you do right and don't let anything frighten you.

⁷ If you are a husband, you should be thoughtful of your wife. Treat her with honour, because she isn't as strong as you are, and she shares with you in the gift of life. Then nothing will stand in the way of your prayers.

Suffering for doing right

⁸ Finally, all of you should agree and have concern and love for each other. You should also be kind and humble. ⁹ Don't be hateful and insult people just because they are hateful and insult you. Instead, treat everyone with kindness. You are God's chosen ones, and he will bless you. The Scriptures say,

¹⁰ "Do you really love life?
    Do you want to be happy?
  Then stop saying cruel things
    and stop telling lies.
¹¹ Give up your evil ways
    and do right,
  as you find and follow
    the road that leads
      to peace.
¹² The Lord watches over
    everyone who obeys him,
  and he listens
    to their prayers.
  But he opposes everyone
    who does evil."

¹³ Can anyone really harm you for being eager to do good deeds? ¹⁴ Even if you have to suffer for doing good things, God will bless you. So stop being afraid and don't worry about what people might do. ¹⁵ Honour Christ and let him be the Lord of your life.

Always be ready to give an answer when someone asks you about your hope. ¹⁶ Give a kind and respectful answer and keep your conscience clear. This way you will make people ashamed for saying bad things about your good conduct as a follower of Christ. ¹⁷ You are better off to obey God and suffer for doing right than to suffer for doing wrong.

¹⁸ Christ died once for our sins.
    An innocent person died
      for those who are guilty.
  Christ did this
    to bring you to God,
  when his body
    was put to death
  and his spirit
    was made alive.

¹⁹ Christ then preached to the spirits that were being kept in prison. ²⁰ They had disobeyed God while Noah was building the boat, but God had been patient with them. Eight people went into that boat and were brought safely through the flood.

²¹ Those flood waters were like baptism that now saves you. But baptism is more than just washing your body. It means turning to God with a clear conscience, because Jesus Christ was raised from death. ²² Christ is now in heaven, where he sits at the right side* of God. All angels, authorities, and powers are under his control.

CHAPTER 4

Being faithful to God

¹ Christ suffered here on earth. Now you must be ready to suffer as he did, because suffering shows that you have stopped sinning. ² It means you have turned from your own desires and want to obey God for the rest of your life. ³ You have already lived long enough like people who don't know God. You were immoral and followed your evil desires. You went around drinking and feasting and carrying on. In fact, you even worshipped disgusting idols. ⁴ Now your former friends wonder why you have stopped running around with them, and they curse you for it. ⁵ But they will have to answer to God, who judges the living and the dead. ⁶ The good news has even been

---

See also: **3.3:** 1 Tim 2.9. **3.6:** Gen 18.12. **3.7:** Eph 5.25; Col 3.19. **3.10–12:** Psa 34.12–16 (LXX). **3.14:** Matt 5.10. **3.14,15:** Isa 8.12,13.

*3.22 right side: The place of honour and power.
See also: **3.20:** Gen 6.1—7.24.

preached to the dead,* so that after they have been judged for what they have done in this life, their spirits will live with God.

⁷ Everything will soon come to an end. So be serious and be sensible enough to pray.

⁸ Most important of all, you must sincerely love each other, because love wipes away many sins.

⁹ Welcome people into your home and don't grumble about it.

¹⁰ Each of you has been blessed with one of God's many wonderful gifts to be used in the service of others. So use your gift well.
¹¹ If you have the gift of speaking, preach God's message. If you have the gift of helping others, do it with the strength that God supplies. Everything should be done in a way that will bring honour to God because of Jesus Christ, who is glorious and powerful for ever. Amen.

Suffering for being a Christian

¹² Dear friends, don't be surprised or shocked that you are going through testing that is like walking through fire. ¹³ Be glad for the chance to suffer as Christ suffered. It will prepare you for even greater happiness when he makes his glorious return.

¹⁴ Count it a blessing when you suffer for being a Christian. This shows that God's glorious Spirit is with you. ¹⁵ But you deserve to suffer if you are a murderer, a thief, a criminal, or a busybody. ¹⁶ Don't be ashamed to suffer for being a Christian. Praise God that you belong to him. ¹⁷ God has already begun judging his own people. And if his judgment begins with us, imagine how terrible it will be for those who refuse to obey his message. The Scriptures say,

¹⁸ "If good people barely escape,
    what will happen to sinners
    and to others
    who don't respect God?"

¹⁹ If you suffer for obeying God, you must have complete faith in your faithful Creator and keep on doing right.

Advice for church leaders

CHAPTER 5

Helping Christian leaders

¹ Church leaders,† I am writing to encourage you. I too am a leader, as well as a witness to Christ's suffering, and I will share in his glory when it is shown to us.

² Just as shepherds watch over their sheep, you must watch over everyone God has placed in your care. Do it willingly in order to please God, and not simply because you think you must. Let it be something you want to do, instead of something you do merely to make money.
³ Don't be bossy to those people who are in your care, but set an example for them.
⁴ Then when Christ the Chief Shepherd returns, you will be given a crown that will never lose its glory.

⁵ All you young people should obey your elders. In fact, everyone should be humble towards everyone else. The Scriptures say,

"God opposes proud people,
    but he helps everyone
        who is humble."

⁶ Be humble in the presence of God's mighty power, and he will honour you when the time comes. ⁷ God cares for you, so turn all your worries over to him.

⁸ Be on your guard and stay awake. Your enemy, the devil, is like a roaring lion, prowling around to find someone to attack.
⁹ But you must resist the devil and stay strong in your faith. You know that all over the world the Lord's followers are suffering just as you are. ¹⁰ But God shows undeserved kindness to everyone. That's why he appointed Christ Jesus to choose you to share in his eternal glory. You will suffer for a while, but God will make you complete, steady, strong, and firm. ¹¹ God will be in control for ever! Amen.

Final greetings

¹² Silvanus helped me write this short letter, and I consider him a faithful follower of the Lord. I wanted to encourage you and tell you how kind God really is, so that you will keep on having faith in him.

---

*4.6 the dead: Either people who died after becoming followers of Christ or the people of Noah's day (see 3.19).
See also: 4.8: Prov 10.12. 4.18: Prov 11.31 (LXX).

See also: 5.2: John 21.15–17. 5.5: Prov 3.34 (LXX).
5.6: Matt 23.12; Luke 14.11; 18.14. 5.12: Acts 15.22,40.

¹³ Greetings from the Lord's followers in Babylon.* They are God's chosen ones.

Mark, who is like a son to me, sends his greetings too.

¹⁴ Give each other a warm greeting. I pray that God will give peace to everyone who belongs to Christ.ᵇ

---

*5.13 Babylon: This may be a secret name for the city of Rome.

See also: 5.13: Acts 12.12,25; 13.13; 15.37–39; Col 4.10; Phlm 24.

Additional notes

ᵃ1.22 You obeyed the truth: Some manuscripts add "by the power of the Spirit".
ᵇ5.1 Church leaders: Or "Elders" or "Presbyters" or "Priests".
ᵇ5.14 Christ: Some manuscripts add "Amen."

2 Peter

Peter's second letter

A quick look at this letter

The writer of this letter wants the readers to know that Christians must live in a way that pleases God (1.3) and hold firmly to the truth they were given (1.12).

He warns them that false prophets and teachers had entered the Christian community and were trying to lead the Lord's followers away from the truth. But they will be punished for their evil deeds (2.1–22). When false teachers are at work, Christians must stick to their faith and be examples for others of right living. They must have understanding, self-control, and patience, and they should show love for God and all people.

The readers must never forget that the Lord's return is certain, no matter what others may say (3.1–18).

Don't forget that for the Lord one day is the same as a thousand years, and a thousand years is the same as one day. The Lord isn't slow about keeping his promises, as some people think he is. In fact, God is patient, because he wants everyone to turn from sin and no one to be lost.

(3.8,9)

Greetings and prayer

CHAPTER 1

¹ *From Simon Peter, a servant and an apostle of Jesus Christ.*
  To everyone who shares with us in the privilege of believing that our God and Saviour Jesus Christ will do what is just and fair.
  ² I pray that God will be kind to you and will let you live in perfect peace! May you keep learning more and more about God and our Lord Jesus.

How the Lord's followers should live

³ We have everything we need to live a life that pleases God. It was all given to us by God's own power, when we learnt that he had invited us to share in his wonderful goodness. ⁴ God made great and marvellous promises, so that his nature would become part of us. Then we could escape our evil desires and the corrupt influences of this world.

⁵ Do your best to improve your faith. You can do this by adding goodness, understanding, ⁶ self-control, patience, devotion to God, ⁷ concern for others, and love. ⁸ If you keep growing in this way, it will show that what you know about our Lord Jesus Christ has made your lives useful and meaningful. ⁹ But if you don't grow, you are like someone who is nearsighted or blind, and you have forgotten that your past sins are forgiven.

¹⁰ My friends, you must do all you can to show that God has really chosen and selected

you. If you keep on doing this, you won't stumble and fall. ¹¹ Then our Lord and Saviour Jesus Christ will give you a glorious welcome into his kingdom that will last for ever.

¹² You are holding firmly to the truth that you were given. But I am still going to remind you of these things. ¹³ In fact, I think I should keep on reminding you until I leave this body. ¹⁴ And our Lord Jesus Christ has already told me that I will soon leave it behind. ¹⁵ That is why I am doing my best to make sure that each of you remembers all this after I am gone.

The glory of Christ

¹⁶ When we told you about the power and the return of our Lord Jesus Christ, we were not telling clever stories that someone had made up. But with our own eyes we saw his true greatness. ¹⁷ God, our great and wonderful Father, truly honoured him by saying, "This is my own dear Son, and I am pleased with him." ¹⁸ We were there with Jesus on the holy mountain and heard this voice speak from heaven.

¹⁹ All this makes us even more certain that what the prophets said is true. So you should pay close attention to their message, as you would to a lamp shining in some dark place. You must keep on paying attention until daylight comes and the morning star rises in your hearts. ²⁰ But you need to realize that no one alone can understand any of the prophecies in the Scriptures. ²¹ The prophets did not think these things up on their own, but they were guided by the Spirit of God.

False prophets and teachers

CHAPTER 2

¹ Sometimes false prophets spoke to the people of Israel. False teachers will also sneak in and speak harmful lies to you. But these teachers don't really belong to the Master who paid a great price for them, and they will quickly destroy themselves. ² Many people will follow their evil ways and cause others to tell lies about the true way. ³ They will be greedy and cheat you with smooth talk. But long ago God decided to punish them, and God doesn't sleep.

⁴ God did not have pity on the angels that sinned. He had them tied up and thrown into the dark pits of hell until the time of judgment. ⁵ And during Noah's time, God did not have pity on the ungodly people of the world. He destroyed them with a flood, though he did save eight people, including Noah, who preached the truth.

⁶ God punished the cities of Sodom and Gomorrah* by burning them to ashes, and this is a warning to anyone else who wants to sin.

⁷⁻⁸ Lot lived right and was greatly troubled by the terrible way those wicked people were living. He was a good man, and day after day he suffered because of the evil things he saw and heard. So the Lord rescued him. ⁹ This shows that the Lord knows how to rescue godly people from their sufferings and to punish evil people while they wait for the day of judgment.

¹⁰ The Lord is especially hard on people who disobey him and don't think of anything except their own filthy desires. They are reckless and proud and are not afraid of cursing the glorious beings in heaven. ¹¹ Although angels are more powerful than these evil beings,ᵇ even the angels don't dare to accuse them to the Lord.

¹² These people are no better than senseless animals that live by their feelings and are born to be caught and killed. They speak evil of things they don't know anything about. But their own corrupt deeds will destroy them. ¹³ They have done evil, and they will be rewarded with evil.

They think it is fun to have wild parties during the day. They are immoral, and the meals they eat with you are spoilt by the shameful and selfish way they carry on.ᶜ ¹⁴ All they think about is having sex with someone else's husband or wife. There is no end to their wicked deeds. They trick people who are easily fooled, and their minds are filled with greedy thoughts. But they are headed for trouble!

¹⁵ They have left the true road and have gone down the wrong path by following the example of the prophet Balaam. He was the son of Beor and loved what he got from being a criminal. ¹⁶ But a donkey corrected him for this evil deed. It spoke to him with a human voice and made him stop his foolishness.

---

*2.6 Sodom and Gomorrah: During the time of Abraham the Lord destroyed these cities because the people there were so evil. See Genesis 19.24.

See also: 1.17,18: Matt 17.1–5; Mark 9.2–7; Luke 9.28–35.

See also: 2.5: Gen 6.1–7.24. 2.6: Gen 19.24.
2.7: Gen 19.1–16. 2.15,16: Num 22.4–35.

¹⁷ These people are like dried-up water holes and clouds blown by a storm. The darkest part of hell is waiting for them.
¹⁸ They boast out loud about their stupid nonsense. And by being vulgar and crude, they trap people who have barely escaped from living the wrong kind of life. ¹⁹ They promise freedom to everyone. But they are merely slaves of filthy living, because people are slaves of whatever controls them.

²⁰ When they learnt about our Lord and Saviour Jesus Christ, they escaped from the filthy things of this world. But they are again caught up and controlled by these filthy things, and now they are in a worse state than they were at first. ²¹ They would have been better off if they had never known about the right way. Even after they knew what was right, they turned their backs on the holy commandments that they were given. ²² What happened to them is just like the true saying,

> "A dog will come back
>   to lick up its own vomit.
> A pig that has been washed
>   will roll in the mud."

The Lord's return is certain

CHAPTER 3

¹ My dear friends, this is the second letter I have written to encourage you to do some honest thinking. I don't want you to forget ² what God's prophets said would happen. You must never forget what the holy prophets taught in the past. And you must remember what the apostles told you our Lord and Saviour has commanded us to do.

³ But first you must realize that in the last days some people won't think about anything except their own selfish desires. They will make fun of you ⁴ and say, "Didn't your Lord promise to come back? Yet the first leaders have already died, and the world hasn't changed a bit."

⁵ They will say this because they want to forget that long ago the heavens and the earth were made at God's command. The earth came out of water and was made from water. ⁶ Later it was destroyed by the waters of a mighty flood. ⁷ But God has commanded the present heavens and earth to remain until the day of judgment. Then they will be set on fire, and ungodly people will be destroyed.

⁸ Dear friends, don't forget that for the Lord one day is the same as a thousand years, and a thousand years is the same as one day. ⁹ The Lord isn't slow about keeping his promises, as some people think he is. In fact, God is patient, because he wants everyone to turn from sin and no one to be lost.

¹⁰ The day of the Lord's return will surprise us like a thief. The heavens will disappear with a loud noise, and the heat will melt the whole universe.* Then the earth and everything on it will be seen for what they are.*

¹¹ Everything will be destroyed. So you should serve and honour God by the way you live. ¹² You should look forward to the day when God judges everyone, and you should try to make it come soon.* On that day the heavens will be destroyed by fire, and everything else will melt in the heat. ¹³ But God has promised us a new heaven and a new earth, where justice will rule. We are really looking forward to that!

¹⁴ My friends, while you are waiting, you should make certain that the Lord finds you pure, spotless, and living at peace.
¹⁵ Don't forget that the Lord is patient because he wants people to be saved. This is also what our dear friend Paul said when he wrote to you with the wisdom that God had given him. ¹⁶ Paul talks about these same things in all his letters, but part of what he says is hard to understand. Some ignorant and unsteady people even destroy themselves by twisting what he said. They do the same thing with other Scriptures too.

¹⁷ My dear friends, you have been warned beforehand! So don't let the errors of evil people lead you down the wrong path and make you lose your balance. ¹⁸ Let the wonderful kindness and the understanding that come from our Lord and Saviour Jesus Christ help you to keep on growing. Praise Jesus now and for ever! Amen.*

---

*3.10 the whole universe: Probably the sun, moon, and stars, or the elements that everything in the universe is made of.

See also: 2.22: Prov 26.11. 3.3: Jude 18. 3.5: Gen 1.6–9. 3.6: Gen 7.11.

See also: 3.8: Psa 90.4. 3.10: Matt 24.43; Luke 12.39; 1 Thes 5.2; Rev 16.15. 3.13: Isa 65.17; 66.22; Rev 21.1.

289

Additional notes

¹1.1 To everyone who . . . just and fair: Or "To everyone whose faith in the justice and fairness of our God and Saviour Jesus Christ is as precious as our own faith."

²2.11 evil beings: Or "evil teachers".

²2.13 and the meals they eat with you are spoilt by the shameful and selfish way they carry on: Some manuscripts have "and the meals they eat with you are spoilt by the shameful way they carry on during your feasts of Christian love."

³3.10 will be seen for what they are: Some manuscripts have "will go up in flames."

³3.12 and you should try to make it come soon: Or "and you should eagerly desire for that day to come."

³3.18 Amen: Some manuscripts do not have "Amen."

1 John

John's first letter

A quick look at this letter

John wants Christian believers to know that when we tell God about our sins, God will forgive us and take them away (1.9).

The true test of faith is love for each other (3.11–24). Because God is love, his people must be like him (4.1–21). For a complete victory over sin, we must not only love others, but we must believe that Jesus, the Son of God, is truly Christ, and that his death for us was real (5.1–12).

Remember:

> The Word that gives life
>   was from the beginning,
> and this is the one
>   our message is about.

(1.1a)

The Word that gives life

CHAPTER 1

¹ The Word that gives life
  was from the beginning,
and this is the one
  our message is about.

Our ears have heard,
  our own eyes have seen,
and our hands touched
  this Word.

² The one who gives life appeared! We saw it happen, and we are witnesses to what we have seen. Now we are telling you about this eternal life that was with the Father and appeared to us. ³ We are telling you what we have seen and heard, so that you may share in this life with us. And we share in it with the Father and with his Son Jesus Christ. ⁴ We are writing to tell you these things, because this makes us' truly happy.

God is light and Christ is our example

⁵ Jesus told us that God is light and doesn't have any darkness in him. Now we are telling you.
⁶ If we say that we share in life with God and keep on living in the dark, we are lying and are not living by the truth. ⁷ But if we live in the light, as God does, we share in life with each other. And the blood of his Son Jesus

See also: 1.1: John 1.1. 1.2: John 1.14.

washes all our sins away. ⁸ If we say that we have not sinned, we are fooling ourselves, and the truth isn't in our hearts. ⁹ But if we confess our sins to God, he can always be trusted to forgive us and take our sins away.

¹⁰ If we say that we have not sinned, we make God a liar, and his message isn't in our hearts.'

CHAPTER 2

Christ helps us

¹ My children, I am writing this so that you won't sin. But if you do sin, Jesus Christ always does the right thing, and he will speak to the Father for us. ² Christ is the sacrifice that takes away our sins and the sins of all the world's people.

³ When we obey God, we are sure that we know him. ⁴ But if we claim to know him and don't obey him, we are lying and the truth isn't in our hearts. ⁵ We truly love God only when we obey him as we should, and then we know that we belong to him. ⁶ If we say we are his, we must follow the example of Christ.

The new commandment

⁷ My dear friends, I am not writing to give you a new commandment. It is the same one that you were first given, and it is the message you heard. ⁸ But it really is a new commandment, and you know its true meaning, just as Christ does. You can see the darkness fading away and the true light already shining.

⁹ If we claim to be in the light and hate someone, we are still in the dark. ¹⁰ But if we love others, we are in the light, and we don't cause problems for them.' ¹¹ If we hate others, we are living and walking in the dark. We don't know where we are going, because we can't see in the dark.

¹² Children, I am writing to you,
   because your sins
   have been forgiven
   in the name of Christ.
¹³ Parents, I am writing to you,
   because you have known
   the one who was there
   from the beginning.
   Young people, I am writing to you,
   because you have defeated
   the evil one.

¹⁴ Children, I am writing to you,
   because you have known
   the Father.
   Parents, I am writing to you,
   because you have known
   the one who was there
   from the beginning.
   Young people, I am writing to you,
   because you are strong.
   God's message is firm
   in your hearts,
   and you have defeated
   the evil one.

¹⁵ Don't love the world or anything that belongs to the world. If you love the world, you cannot love the Father. ¹⁶ Our foolish pride comes from this world, and so do our selfish desires and our desire to have everything we see. None of this comes from the Father. ¹⁷ The world and the desires it causes are disappearing. But if we obey God, we will live for ever.

The enemies of Christ and God's children

The enemy of Christ

¹⁸ Children, this is the last hour. You heard that the enemy of Christ would appear at this time, and many of Christ's enemies have already appeared. So we know that the last hour is here. ¹⁹ These people came from our own group, yet they were not part of us. If they had been part of us, they would have stayed with us. But they left, which proves that they did not belong to our group.

²⁰ Christ, the Holy One,' has blessed* you, and now all of you understand.' ²¹ I did not need to write to you about the truth, since you already know it. You also know that liars do not belong to the truth. ²² And a liar is anyone who says that Jesus isn't truly Christ. Anyone who says this is an enemy of Christ and rejects both the Father and the Son. ²³ If we reject the Son, we reject the Father. But if we say that we accept the Son, we have the

---

2.20 blessed: This translates a word which means "to pour olive oil on (someone's head)". In Old Testament times it was the custom to pour olive oil on a person's head when that person was chosen to be a priest or a king. Here the meaning is not clear. It may refer to the ceremony of pouring olive oil on the followers of the Lord just before they were baptized or it may refer to the gift of the Holy Spirit which were given at baptism (see verse 27).

Father. ²⁴ Keep thinking about the message you first heard, and you will always be one in your heart with the Son and with the Father. ²⁵ The Son* has promised us* eternal life.

²⁶ I am writing to warn you about those people who are misleading you. ²⁷ But Christ has blessed you with the Holy Spirit.* Now the Spirit stays in you, and you don't need any teachers. The Spirit is truthful and teaches you everything. So stay united in your heart with Christ, just as the Spirit has taught you to do.

Children of God

²⁸ Children, stay united in your hearts with Christ. Then when he returns, we will have confidence and won't have to hide in shame. ²⁹ You know that Christ always does right and that everyone who does right is a child of God.

CHAPTER 3

¹ Think how much the Father loves us. He loves us so much that he lets us be called his children, as we truly are. But since the people of this world did not know who Christ* is, they don't know who we are. ² My dear friends, we are already God's children, though what we will be hasn't yet been seen. But we do know that when Christ returns, we will be like him, because we will see him as he truly is. ³ This hope makes us keep ourselves holy, just as Christ* is holy.

⁴ Everyone who sins breaks God's law, because sin is the same as breaking God's law. ⁵ You know that Christ came to take away sins. He isn't sinful, ⁶ and people who stay united in their hearts with him won't keep on sinning. If they do keep on sinning, they don't know Christ, and they have never seen him.

⁷ Children, don't be fooled. Anyone who does right is good, just like Christ himself. ⁸ Anyone who keeps on sinning belongs to the devil. He has sinned from the beginning, but the Son of God came to destroy all that he has done. ⁹ God's children cannot keep on being sinful. His life-giving power* lives in them and makes them his children, so that they cannot keep on sinning. ¹⁰ You can tell God's children from the devil's children, because those who belong to the devil refuse to do right or to love each other.

God's love and our love

Love each other

¹¹ From the beginning you were told that we must love each other. ¹² Don't be like Cain, who belonged to the devil and murdered his own brother. Why did he murder him? He did it because his brother was good, and he was evil. ¹³ My friends, don't be surprised if the people of this world hate you. ¹⁴ Our love for each other proves that we have gone from death to life. But if you don't love each other, you are still under the power of death.

¹⁵ If you hate each other, you are murderers, and we know that murderers do not have eternal life. ¹⁶ We know what love is because Jesus gave his life for us. That's why we must give our lives for each other. ¹⁷ If we have all we need and see one of our own people in need, we must have pity on that person, or else we cannot say we love God. ¹⁸ Children, you show love for others by truly helping them, and not merely by talking about it.

¹⁹ When we love others, we know that we belong to the truth, and we feel at ease in the presence of God. ²⁰ But even if we don't feel at ease, God is greater than our feelings, and he knows everything. ²¹ Dear friends, if we feel at ease in the presence of God, we will have the courage to come near him. ²² He will give us whatever we ask, because we obey him and do what pleases him. ²³ God wants us to have faith in his Son Jesus Christ and to love each other. This is also what Jesus taught us to do. ²⁴ If we obey God's commandments, we will stay united in our hearts with him, and he will stay united with us. The Spirit that he has given us is proof that we are one with him.

CHAPTER 4

God is love

¹ Dear friends, don't believe everyone who claims to have the Spirit of God. Test them all to find out if they really do come from God. Many false prophets have already gone out into the world, ² and you can know which ones come from God. His Spirit says that Jesus Christ had a truly human body. ³ But when someone doesn't say this about Jesus, you know that person has a spirit that

See also: 3.1: John 1.12. 3.5: John 1.29.

See also: 3.11: John 13.34. 3.12: Gen 4.8. 3.14: John 5.24. 3.23: John 13.34; 15.12,17.

doesn't come from God and is the enemy of Christ. You knew that this enemy was coming into the world and now is already here.

[4] Children, you belong to God, and you have defeated these enemies. God's Spirit* is in you and is more powerful than the one that is in the world. [5] These enemies belong to this world, and the world listens to them, because they speak its language. [6] We belong to God, and everyone who knows God will listen to us. But the people who don't know God won't listen to us. That is how we can tell the Spirit that speaks the truth from the one that tells lies.

[7] My dear friends, we must love each other. Love comes from God, and when we love each other, it shows that we have been given new life. We are now God's children, and we know him. [8] God is love, and anyone who doesn't love others has never known him. [9] God showed his love for us when he sent his only Son into the world to give us life. [10] Real love isn't our love for God, but his love for us. God sent his Son to be the sacrifice by which our sins are forgiven. [11] Dear friends, since God loved us this much, we must love each other.

[12] No one has ever seen God. But if we love each other, God lives in us, and his love is truly in our hearts.

[13] God has given us his Spirit. That is how we know that we are one with him, just as he is one with us. [14] God sent his Son to be the Saviour of the world. We saw his Son and are now telling others about him. [15] God stays united with everyone who openly says that Jesus is the Son of God. That's how we stay united with God [16] and are sure that God loves us.

God is love. If we keep on loving others, we will stay united in our hearts with God, and he will stay united with us. [17] If we truly love others and live as Christ did in this world, we won't be worried about the day of judgment. [18] A real love for others will chase those worries away. The thought of being punished is what makes us afraid. It shows that we have not really learnt to love.

[19] We love because God loved us first. [20] But if we say we love God and don't love each other, we are liars. We cannot see God. So how can we love God, if we don't love the people we can see? [21] The commandment that God has given us is: "Love God and love each other!"

See also: 4.12: John 1.18.
294

Victory over the world

CHAPTER 5

[1] If we believe that Jesus is truly Christ, we are God's children. Everyone who loves the Father will also love his children. [2] If we love and obey God, we know that we will love his children. [3] We show our love for God by obeying his commandments, and they are not hard to follow.

[4] Every child of God can defeat the world, and our faith is what gives us this victory. [5] No one can defeat the world without having faith in Jesus as the Son of God.

Who Jesus is

[6] Water and blood came out from the side of Jesus Christ. It wasn't just water, but water and blood.* The Spirit tells about this, because the Spirit is truthful. [7] In fact, there are three who tell about it. [8] They are the Spirit, the water, and the blood, and they all agree.

[9] We believe what people tell us. But we can trust what God says even more, and God is the one who has spoken about his Son. [10] If we have faith in God's Son, we have believed what God has said. But if we don't believe what God has said about his Son, it is the same as calling God a liar. [11] God has also said that he gave us eternal life and that this life comes to us from his Son. [12] And so, if we have God's Son, we have this life. But if we don't have the Son, we don't have this life.

Knowing about eternal life

[13] All of you have faith in the Son of God, and I have written to let you know that you have eternal life. [14] We are certain that God will hear our prayers when we ask for what pleases him. [15] And if we know that God listens when we pray, we are sure that our prayers have already been answered.

[16] Suppose you see one of our people commit a sin that isn't a sin. You can pray, and that person will be given eternal

*5.6 Water and blood came out from the side of Jesus Christ. It wasn't just water, but water and blood: See John 19.34. It is also possible to translate, "Jesus Christ came by the water of baptism and by the blood of his death! He was not only baptized, but he bled and died." The purpose of the verse is to tell that Jesus was truly human and that he really died.
See also: 5.3: John 14.15. 5.11: John 3.36.

life. But the sin must not be one that is deadly. ¹⁷ Everything that is wrong is sin, but not all sins are deadly.

¹⁸ We are sure that God's children do not keep on sinning. God's own Son protects them, and the devil cannot harm them.

¹⁹ We are certain that we come from God and that the rest of the world is under the power of the devil.

²⁰ We know that Jesus Christ the Son of God has come and has shown us the true God. And because of Jesus, we now belong to the true God who gives eternal life.

²¹ Children, you must stay away from idols.

Additional notes

›**1.4 us:** Some manuscripts have "you".

›**1.10 and his message isn't in our hearts:** Or "because we have not accepted his message."

›**2.10 and we don't cause problems for them:** Or "and we can see anything that might make us fall."

›**2.20 Christ, the Holy One:** The Greek text has "the Holy One" which may refer either to Christ or to God the Father.

›**2.20 now all of you understand:** Some manuscripts have "you understand all things."

›**2.25 The Son:** The Greek text has "he" and may refer to God the Father.

›**2.25 us:** Some manuscripts have "you".

›**2.27 Christ has blessed you with the Holy Spirit:** The Greek text has "You received a pouring on of olive oil from him" (see verse 20). The "pouring on of olive oil" is here taken to refer to the gift of the Holy Spirit, and "he" may refer either to Christ or to the Father.

›**3.1 Christ:** The Greek text has "he" and may refer to God.

›**3.3 Christ:** The Greek text has "that one" and may refer to God.

›**3.9 His life-giving power:** The Greek text has "His seed".

›**4.4 God's Spirit:** The Greek text has "he" and may refer to the Spirit or to God or to Jesus.

2 John

John's second letter

A quick look at this letter

John writes again about the importance of love in a Christian's life. He points out that truth and love must go together. We must also believe that Christ was truly human, and we must love each other.

Greetings and prayer

[1] *From the church leader.**
*To a very special woman and her children.**
I truly love all of you, and so does everyone else who knows the truth. [2] We love you because the truth is now in our hearts, and it will be there for ever.

[3] I pray that God the Father and Jesus Christ his Son will be kind and merciful to us! May they give us peace and truth and love.

Truth and love

[4] I was very glad to learn that some of your children are obeying the truth, as the Father told us to do. [5] Dear friend, I am not writing to tell you and your children to do something you have not done before. I am writing to tell you to love each other, which is the first thing you were told to do. [6] Love means that we do what God tells us. And from the beginning, he told you to love him.

[7] Many liars have gone out into the world. These deceitful liars are saying that Jesus Christ did not have a truly human body. But they are liars and the enemies of Christ. [8] So be sure not to lose what we* have worked for. If you do, you won't be given your full reward. [9] Don't keep changing what you were taught about Christ, or else God will no longer be with you. But if you hold firmly to what you were taught, both the Father and the Son will be with you. [10] If people won't agree to this teaching, don't welcome them into your home or even greet them. [11] Greeting them is the same as taking part in their evil deeds.

Final greetings

[12] I have much more to tell you, but I don't want to write it with pen and ink. I want to come and talk to you in person, because that will make us* really happy.

[13] Greetings from the children of your very special sister.**

---

v13 sister: See the note at verse 1.

---

v1 very special woman and her children: A group of the Lord's followers who met together for worship. "The children of your . . . sister" (see verse 13) is another group of followers. "Very special" (here and verse 13) probably means "chosen (by the Lord)".
See also: v5: John 13.34; 15.12,17.

Additional notes

v1 church leader: Or "elder" or "presbyter" or "priest".
v8 we: Some manuscripts have "you".
v12 us: Some manuscripts have "you".

3 John

John's third letter

A quick look at this letter

In this letter the writer reminds Christian readers that they should help support those who go to know parts of the world to tell others about the Lord. The letter is written to an important church member named Gaius, who had been very helpful to Christians who travelled around and preached the good news.

Greetings to Gaius

¹ *From the church leader.*
  To my dear friend Gaius.
  I love you because we follow the truth, ² dear friend, and I pray that all goes well for you. I hope that you are as strong in body, as I know you are in spirit. ³ It makes me very happy when the Lord's followers come by and speak openly of how you obey the truth. ⁴ Nothing brings me greater happiness than to hear that my children* are obeying the truth.

The importance of working together

⁵ Dear friend, you have always been faithful in helping other followers of the Lord, even the ones you didn't know before. ⁶ They have told the church about your love. They say you were good enough to welcome them and to send them on their mission in a way that God's servants deserve. ⁷ When they left to tell others about the Lord, they decided not to accept help from anyone who wasn't a follower. ⁸ We must support people like them, so that we can take part in what they are doing to spread the truth.

⁹ I wrote to the church. But Diotrephes likes to be the number-one leader, and he won't pay any attention to us. ¹⁰ So if I come, I will remind him of how he has been attacking us with gossip. Not only has he been doing this, but he refuses to welcome any of the Lord's followers who come by. And when other church members want to welcome them, he puts them out of the church.

¹¹ Dear friend, don't copy the evil deeds of others! Follow the example of people who do kind deeds. They are God's children, but those who are always doing evil have never seen God.

¹² Everyone speaks well of Demetrius, and so does the true message that he teaches. I also speak well of him, and you know what I say is true.

---

*v4 children: Probably persons that the leader had led to be followers of the Lord.
See also: v1: Acts 19.29; Rom 16.23; 1 Cor 1.14.

297

Final greetings

[13] I have much more to say to you, but I don't want to write it with pen and ink. [14] I hope to see you soon, and then we can talk in person. [15] I pray that God will bless you with peace!

Your friends send their greetings. Please give a personal greeting to each of our friends.

Additional notes

*v1 church leader: Or "elder" or "presbyter" or "priest".

Jude

A letter from Jude

A quick look at this letter

Jude has much to say about false teachers. They are evil! God will punish them, and Christians should not follow their teaching or imitate the way they live.

Jude ends with a beautiful prayer-like blessing:

> *Offer praise to God our Saviour because of our Lord Jesus Christ! Only God can keep you from falling and make you pure and joyful in his glorious presence. Before time began and now and for evermore, God is worthy of glory, honour, power, and authority. Amen.*

(24,25)

Greetings

¹ *From Jude, a servant of Jesus Christ and the brother of James.*
 To all who are chosen and loved by God the Father and are kept safe by Jesus Christ.
 ² I pray that God will greatly bless you with kindness, peace, and love!

See also: **v1:** Matt 13.55; Mark 6.3.

Defending the faith against false teachers

³ My dear friends, I really wanted to write to you about God's saving power at work in our lives. But instead, I must write and ask you to defend the faith that God has once for all given to his people. ⁴ Some godless people have sneaked in among us and are saying, "God treats us much better than we deserve, and so it is all right to be immoral." They even deny that we must obey Jesus Christ as our only Master and Lord. But long ago the Scriptures warned that these godless people were doomed.

⁵ Don't forget what happened to those people that the Lord rescued from Egypt. Some of them did not have faith, and he later destroyed them. ⁶ You also know about the angels* who didn't do their work and left their proper places. God chained them with everlasting chains and is now keeping them in dark pits until the great day of judgment. ⁷ We should also be warned by what happened to the cities of Sodom and Gomorrah* and the nearby towns. Their people became immoral and did all sorts of sexual sins. Then God made an example of them and punished them with eternal fire.

*v6 angels: This may refer to the angels who liked the women on earth so much that they came down and married them (see Genesis 6.2).
*v7 Sodom and Gomorrah: During the time of Abraham the Lord destroyed these cities because the people there were so evil.
See also: **v5:** a Exod 12.51; b Num 14.29,30.
v7: Gen 19.1–24.

⁸ The people I am talking about are behaving just like those dreamers who destroyed their own bodies. They reject all authority and insult angels. ⁹ Even Michael, the chief angel, didn't dare to insult the devil, when the two of them were arguing about the body of Moses.* All Michael said was, "The Lord will punish you!"

¹⁰ But these people insult powers they don't know anything about. They are like senseless animals that end up getting destroyed, because they live only by their feelings. ¹¹ Now they are in for real trouble. They have followed Cain's example* and have made the same mistake that Balaam* did by caring only for money. They have also rebelled against God, just as Korah did.* Because of all this, they will be destroyed.

¹² These people are filthy minded, and by their shameful and selfish actions they spoil the meals you eat together. They are like clouds blown along by the wind, but never bringing any rain. They are like leafless trees, uprooted and dead, and unable to produce fruit. ¹³ Their shameful deeds show up like foam on wild ocean waves. They are like wandering stars for ever doomed to the darkest pits of hell.

¹⁴ Enoch was the seventh person after Adam, and he was talking about these people when he said:

Look! The Lord is coming with thousands and thousands of holy angels ¹⁵ to judge everyone. He will punish all those ungodly people for all the evil things they have done. The Lord will punish those ungodly sinners for every evil thing they have ever said about him.

¹⁶ These people grumble and complain and live by their own selfish desires. They boast about themselves and flatter others to get what they want.

More warnings

¹⁷ My dear friends, remember the warning you were given by the apostles of our Lord Jesus Christ. ¹⁸ They told you that near the end of time, selfish and godless people would start making fun of God. ¹⁹ And now these people are already making you turn against each other. They think only about this life, and they don't have God's Spirit.

²⁰ Dear friends, keep building on the foundation of your most holy faith, as the Holy Spirit helps you to pray. ²¹ And keep in step with God's love, as you wait for our Lord Jesus Christ to show how kind he is by giving you eternal life. ²² Be helpful to* all who may have doubts. ²³ Rescue any who need to be saved, as you would rescue someone from a fire. Then with fear in your own hearts, have mercy on everyone who needs it. But hate even the clothes of those who have been made dirty by their filthy deeds.

Final prayer

²⁴⁻²⁵ Offer praise to God our Saviour because of our Lord Jesus Christ! Only God can keep you from falling and make you pure and joyful in his glorious presence. Before time began and now and for evermore, God is worthy of glory, honour, power, and authority. Amen.

See also: v18: 2 Pet 3.3.

---

*v9 Michael . . . the body of Moses: This refers to what was said in an ancient Jewish book about Moses.
*v11 Cain's example: Cain murdered his brother Abel.
*v11 Balaam: According to the biblical account, Balaam refused to curse the people of Israel for profit (see Numbers 22.18; 24.13), though he led them to be unfaithful to the Lord (see Numbers 25.1–3; 31.16). But by New Testament times, some Jewish teachers taught that Balaam was greedy and did accept money to curse them.
*v11 just as Korah did: Together with Dathan and Abiram, Korah led a rebellion against Moses and Aaron (see Numbers 16.1–35; 26.9,10).
See also: v9: a Dan 10.13,21; 12.1; Rev 12.7; b Deut 34.6; c Zech 3.2. v11: a Gen 4.3–8; b Num 22.1–35; c Num 16.1–35. v14: Gen 5.18,21–24.

Additional notes

*v22 Be helpful to: Some manuscripts have "Correct".

Revelation

A quick look at this book

This book tells what John had seen in a vision about God's message and about what Jesus Christ had said and done (1.2). The message has three main parts: (1) There are evil forces at work in the world, and Christians may have to suffer and die; (2) Jesus is Lord, and he will conquer all people and powers who oppose God; and (3) God has wonderful rewards in store for his faithful people, who remain faithful to him, especially for those who lose their lives in his service.

This was a powerful message of hope for those early Christians who had to suffer or die for their faith. In this book they learnt that, in spite of the cruel power of the Roman Empire, the Lamb of God would win the final victory. And this gave them the courage to be faithful.

Because this book is so full of visions that use ideas and word pictures from the Old Testament, it was like a book with secret messages for the early Christians. The book could be passed around and be understood by Christians, but an official of the Roman Empire would not be able to understand it. For example, when the fall of Babylon is described (chapter 18), the early Christians knew that this pointed to the fall of the Roman Empire. This knowledge gave them hope.

At the beginning of this book there are seven letters to seven churches. These letters show what different groups of the Lord's followers will do in times of persecution (2.1—3.22).

The author uses many powerful images to describe God's power and judgment. The vision of God's throne (4.1-11) and of the scroll and the Lamb (5.1-14) show that God and Christ are in control of all human and supernatural events. Opening seven seals (6.1—8.5), blowing the seven trumpets (8.6—11.19), and emptying the seven bowls (16.1-21) are among the visions that show God's fierce judgment on the world.

After the suffering has ended, God's faithful people will receive the greatest blessing of all:

> God's home is now with his people. He will live with them, and they will be his own. Yes, God will make his home among his people. He will wipe all tears from their eyes, and there will be no more death, suffering, crying, or pain. These things of the past are gone for ever.

(21.3b,4)

A prophecy from John

CHAPTER 1

[1] This is what God showed to Jesus Christ, so that he could tell his servants what must happen soon. Christ then sent his angel with the message to his servant John. [2] And John told everything that he had seen about God's message and about what Jesus Christ had said and done.

[3] God will bless everyone who reads this prophecy to others,* and he will bless everyone who hears and obeys it. The time is almost here.

[4] From John to the seven churches in Asia.*

> I pray that you
>   will be blessed
> with kindness and peace
> from God, who is and was
>   and is coming.
> May you receive
>   kindness and peace
> from the seven spirits
>   before the throne of God.
> [5] May kindness and peace
>   be yours
> from Jesus Christ,
>   the faithful witness.

> Jesus was the first
>   to conquer death,
> and he is the ruler
>   of all earthly kings.
> Christ loves us,
>   and by his blood

he set us free
    from our sins.
[6] He lets us rule as kings
    and serve God his Father
    as priests.
To him be glory and power
    for ever and ever! Amen.
[7] Look! He is coming
    with the clouds.
Everyone will see him,
    even the ones who stuck
    a sword through him.
All people on earth
    will weep because of him.
    Yes, it will happen! Amen.

[8] The Lord God says, "I am Alpha and Omega,* the one who is and was and is coming. I am God All-Powerful!"

A vision of the living Lord

[9] I am John, a follower together with all of you. We suffer because Jesus is our king, but he gives us the strength to endure. I was sent to Patmos Island,* because I had preached God's message and had told about Jesus. [10] On the Lord's day the Spirit took control of me, and behind me I heard a loud voice that sounded like a trumpet. [11] The voice said, "Write in a book what you see. Then send it to the seven churches in Ephesus, Smyrna, Pergamum, Thyatira, Sardis, Philadelphia, and Laodicea."*

[12] When I turned to see who was speaking to me, I saw seven gold lampstands. [13] There with the lampstands was someone who seemed to be the Son of Man.* He was wearing a robe that reached down to his feet, and a gold cloth was wrapped around his chest. [14] His head and his hair were white as wool or snow, and his eyes looked like flames of fire. [15] His feet were glowing like bronze

---

*1.3 who reads this prophecy to others: A public reading, in a worship service.
*1.4 Asia: The section 1.4–3.22 is in the form of a letter. Asia was in the eastern part of the Roman Empire and is present-day Turkey.

See also: 1.4: a Exod 3.14; b Rev 4.5. 1.5: a Isa 55.4; b Psa 89.27.

302

*1.8 Alpha and Omega: The first and last letters of the Greek alphabet, which sometimes mean "first" and "last".
*1.9 Patmos Island: A small island where prisoners were sometimes kept by the Romans.
*1.11 Ephesus . . . Laodicea: Ephesus was in the centre with the six other cities forming a half-circle around it.
*1.13 Son of Man: That is, Jesus.

See also: 1.6: Exod 19.6; Rev 5.10. 1.7: a Dan 7.13; Matt 24.30; Mark 13.26; Luke 21.27; 1 Thes 4.17; b Zech 12.10; John 19.34,37; c Zech 12.10; Matt 24.30. 1.8: a Rev 22.13; b Exod 3.14. 1.13: a Dan 7.13; b Dan 10.5. 1.14: Dan 7.9. 1.14,15: Dan 10.6. 1.15: Ezek 1.24; 43.2.

being heated in a furnace, and his voice sounded like the roar of a waterfall. ¹⁶ He held seven stars in his right hand, and a sharp double-edged sword was coming from his mouth. His face was shining as bright as the sun at midday.

¹⁷ When I saw him, I fell at his feet like a dead person. But he put his right hand on me and said:

Don't be afraid! I am the first, the last, ¹⁸ and the living one. I died, but now I am alive for evermore, and I have the keys to death and the world of the dead.*

¹⁹ Write what you have seen and what is and what will happen after these things. ²⁰ I will explain the mystery of the seven stars that you saw at my right side and the seven gold lampstands. The seven stars are the angels* of the seven churches, and the lampstands are the seven churches.

Letters to the seven churches

CHAPTER 2

The letter to Ephesus

The risen Lord said:

¹ This is what you must write to the angel of the church in Ephesus:

I am the one who holds the seven stars in my right hand, and I walk among the seven gold lampstands. Listen to what I say.

² I know everything you have done, including your hard work and how you have endured. I know you won't put up with anyone who is evil. When some people pretended to be apostles, you tested them and found out that they were liars. ³ You have endured and gone through hard times because of me, and you have not given up.

⁴ But I do have something against you! And it is this: you don't have as much love as you used to. ⁵ Think about where you have fallen from, and then turn back and do as you did at first. If you don't turn

back, I will come and take away your lampstand. ⁶ But there is one thing you are doing right. You hate what the Nicolaitans* are doing, and so do I.

⁷ If you have ears, listen to what the Spirit says to the churches. I will let everyone who wins the victory eat from the life-giving tree in God's wonderful garden.

The letter to Smyrna

The risen Lord continued:

⁸ This is what you must write to the angel of the church in Smyrna:

I am the first and the last. I died, but now I am alive! Listen to what I say.

⁹ I know how much you suffer and how poor you are, but you are rich. I also know the cruel things being said about you by people who claim to be Jews. But they are not really Jews. They are a group that belongs to Satan.

¹⁰ Don't worry about what you will suffer. The devil will throw some of you into jail, and you will be tested and made to suffer for ten days. But if you are faithful until you die, I will reward you with a glorious life.*

¹¹ If you have ears, listen to what the Spirit says to the churches. Whoever wins the victory will not be hurt by the second death.*

The letter to Pergamum

The risen Lord continued:

¹² This is what you must write to the angel of the church in Pergamum:

I am the one who has the sharp double-edged sword! Listen to what I say.

¹³ I know that you live where Satan has his throne. But you have kept true to my name. There where Satan lives, my faithful

---

*1.18 keys to death and the world of the dead: That is, power over death and the world of the dead.
*1.20 angels: Perhaps guardian angels that represent the churches, or they may be church leaders or messengers sent to the churches.

See also: 1.17: Isa 44.6; 48.12; Rev 2.8; 22.13.

*2.6 Nicolaitans: Nothing else is known about these people, though it is possible that they claimed to be followers of Nicolaus from Antioch (see Acts 6.5).
*2.10 a glorious life: The Greek text has "a crown of life." In ancient times an athlete who had won a contest was rewarded with a crown of flowers as a sign of victory.
*2.11 second death: The first death is physical death, and the "second death" is eternal death.
*2.13 where Satan has his throne: The meaning is uncertain, but it may refer to the city as a centre of pagan worship or of Emperor worship.

See also: 2.7: a Gen 2.9; Rev 22.2; b Ezek 28.13; 31.8 (LXX). 2.8: Isa 44.6; 48.12; Rev 1.17; 22.13. 2.11: Rev 20.14; 21.8.

witness Antipas* was taken from you and put to death. Even then you did not give up your faith in me.

14 I do have a few things against you. Some of you are following the teaching of Balaam.* Long ago he told Balak to teach the people of Israel to eat food that had been offered to idols and to be immoral. 15 Now some of you are following the teaching of the Nicolaitans.* 16 Turn back! If you don't, I will come quickly and fight against these people. And my words will cut like a sword.

17 If you have ears, listen to what the Spirit says to the churches. To everyone who wins the victory, I will give some of the hidden food.* I will also give each one a white stone* with a new name* written on it. No one will know that name except the one who is given the stone.

The letter to Thyatira

The risen Lord continued:

18 This is what you must write to the angel of the church in Thyatira:

I am the Son of God! My eyes are like flames of fire, and my feet are like bronze. Listen to what I say.

19 I know everything about you, including your love, your faith, your service, and how you have endured. I know that you are doing more now than you have ever done before. 20 But I still have something against you because of that woman Jezebel.* She calls herself a prophet, and you let her teach and mislead my servants to do immoral things and to eat food offered to idols. 21 I gave her a chance to turn from her sins, but she did not want to stop doing these immoral things.

22 I am going to strike down Jezebel. Everyone who does these immoral things with her will also be punished, if they don't stop. 23 I will even kill her followers.* Then all the churches will see that I know everyone's thoughts and feelings. I will treat each of you as you deserve.

24 Some of you in Thyatira don't follow Jezebel's teaching. You don't know anything about what her followers call the "deep secrets of Satan." So I won't burden you down with any other commands. 25 But until I come, you must hold firmly to the teaching you have.

26 I will give power over the nations to everyone who wins the victory and keeps on obeying me until the end. 27-28 I will give each of them the same power that my Father has given me. They will rule the nations with an iron rod and smash those nations to pieces like clay pots. I will also give them the morning star.*

29 If you have ears, listen to what the Spirit says to the churches.

CHAPTER 3

The letter to Sardis

The risen Lord said:

1 This is what you must write to the angel of the church in Sardis:

I have the seven spirits of God and the seven stars. Listen to what I say.

I know what you are doing. Everyone may think you are alive, but you are dead. 2 Wake up! You have only a little strength left, and it is almost gone. So try to become stronger. I have found that you are not completely obeying God. 3 Remember the

---

2.13 Antipas: Nothing else is known about this man, who is mentioned only here in the New Testament.
2.14 Balaam: According to Numbers 22–24, Balaam refused to disobey the Lord. But in other books of the Old Testament, he is spoken of as evil (see Deuteronomy 23.4,5; Joshua 13.22; 24.9,10; Nehemiah 13.2).
2.15 Nicolaitans: See the note at 2.6.
2.17 hidden food: When the people of Israel were going through the desert, the Lord provided a special food for them. Some of this was placed in a jar and stored in the sacred chest (see Exodus 16). According to later Jewish teaching, the prophet Jeremiah rescued the sacred chest when the temple was destroyed by the Babylonians. He hid the chest in a cave, where it would stay until God came to save his people.
2.17 white stone: The meaning of this is uncertain, though it may be the same as a ticket that lets a person into God's banquet where the "hidden food" is eaten. Or it may be a symbol of victory.
2.17 a new name: Either the name of Christ or God or the name of the follower who is given the stone.

See also: 2.14: a Num 22.5,7; 31.16; Deut 23.4; b Num 25.1–3. 2.17: a Exod 16.14,15; 16.33,34; John 6.48–50; b Isa 62.2; 65.15.

2.20 Jezebel: Nothing else is known about her. This may have been her real name or a name that was given to her because she was like Queen Jezebel, who opposed the Lord (see 1 Kings 19.1,2; 21.1–26).
2.27,28 the morning star: Probably thought of as the star that signals the end of night and the beginning of day. In 22.16 Christ is called the "morning star."

See also: 2.20: 1 King 16.31; 2 King 9.22,30. 2.23: a Psa 7.9; Jer 17.10; b Psa 62.12. 2.26,27: Psa 2.8,9 (LXX). 3.3: Matt 24.43,44; Luke 12.39,40; Rev 16.15.

teaching that you were given and that you heard. Hold firmly to it and turn from your sins. If you don't wake up, I will come when you least expect it, just as a thief does.

⁴ A few of you in Sardis have not dirtied your clothes with sin. You will walk with me in white clothes, because you are worthy. ⁵ Everyone who wins the victory will wear white clothes. Their names will not be erased from the book of life,* and I will tell my Father and his angels that they are my followers.

⁶ If you have ears, listen to what the Spirit says to the churches.

The letter to Philadelphia

The risen Lord continued:

⁷ This is what you must write to the angel of the church in Philadelphia:

I am the one who is holy and true, and I have the keys that belonged to David.* When I open a door, no one can close it. And when I close a door, no one can open it. Listen to what I say.

⁸ I know everything you have done. And I have placed before you an open door that no one can close. You were not very strong, but you obeyed my message and did not deny that you are my followers. ⁹ Now you will see what I will do with those people who belong to Satan's group. They claim to be Jews, but they are liars. I will make them come and kneel down at your feet. Then they will know that I love you.

¹⁰ You obeyed my message and endured. So I will protect you from the time of testing that everyone in all the world must go through. ¹¹ I am coming soon. So hold firmly to what you have, and no one will take away the crown that you will be given as your reward.

¹² Everyone who wins the victory will be made into a pillar in the temple of my God, and they will stay there for ever. I will write on each of them the name of my God and the name of his city. It is the new Jerusalem that my God will send down from heaven. I will also write on them my own new name.

¹³ If you have ears, listen to what the Spirit says to the churches.

The letter to Laodicea

The risen Lord continued:

¹⁴ This is what you must write to the angel of the church in Laodicea:

I am the one called Amen!* I am the faithful and true witness and the source* of God's creation. Listen to what I say.

¹⁵ I know everything you have done, and you are not cold or hot. I wish you were either one or the other. ¹⁶ But since you are lukewarm and neither cold nor hot, I will spit you out of my mouth. ¹⁷ You claim to be rich and successful and to have everything you need. But you don't know how badly off you are. You are pitiful, poor, blind, and naked.

¹⁸ Buy your gold from me. It has been refined in a fire, and it will make you rich. Buy white clothes from me. Wear them and you can cover up your shameful nakedness. Buy medicine for your eyes, so that you will be able to see.

¹⁹ I correct and punish everyone I love. So make up your minds to turn away from your sins. ²⁰ Listen! I am standing and knocking at your door. If you hear my voice and open the door, I will come in and we will eat together. ²¹ Everyone who wins the victory will sit with me on my throne, just as I won the victory and sat with my Father on his throne.

²² If you have ears, listen to what the Spirit says to the churches.

A vision of worship in heaven

CHAPTER 4

¹ After this, I looked and saw a door that opened into heaven. Then the voice that had spoken to me at first and that sounded like a trumpet said, "Come up here! I will show you what must happen next." ² At once the Spirit took control of me, and there in heaven I saw a throne and someone sitting on it. ³ The one who was sitting there sparkled like precious stones of

---

3.5 book of life: The book in which the names of God's people are written.
3.7 the keys that belonged to David: The keys stand for authority over David's kingdom.

See also: **3.5:** a Exod 32.32,33; Psa 69.28; Rev 20.12; b Matt 10.32; Luke 12.8. **3.7:** Isa 22.22; Job 12.14. **3.9:** a Isa 49.23; 60.14; b Isa 43.4. **3.12:** a Rev 21.2; b Isa 62.2; 65.15.

3.14 Amen: Meaning "Trustworthy".
3.14 source: Or "beginning".
See also: **3.14:** Prov 8.22. **3.19:** Prov 3.12; Heb 12.6. **4.2,3:** Ezek 1.26–28; 10.1.

jasper* and carnelian.* A rainbow that looked like an emerald* surrounded the throne.

⁴ Twenty-four other thrones were in a circle around that throne. And on each of these thrones there was an elder dressed in white clothes and wearing a gold crown. ⁵ Flashes of lightning and roars of thunder came out from the throne in the centre of the circle. Seven torches, which are the seven spirits of God, were burning in front of the throne. ⁶ Also in front of the throne was something that looked like a glass sea, clear as crystal.

Around the throne in the centre were four living creatures covered front and back with eyes. The first creature was like a lion, the second one was like a bull, the third one had the face of a human, and the fourth was like a flying eagle. ⁸ Each of the four living creatures had six wings, and their bodies were covered with eyes. Day and night they never stopped singing,

> "Holy, holy, holy is the Lord,
>   Lord God All-Powerful,
> who was and is
>   and is coming!"

⁹ The living creatures kept praising, honouring, and thanking the one who sits on the throne and who lives for ever and ever. ¹⁰ At the same time the twenty-four elders knelt down before the one sitting on the throne. And as they worshipped the one who lives for ever, they placed their crowns in front of the throne and said,

> ¹¹ "Our Lord and God,
>   you are worthy
> to receive glory,
>   honour, and power.
> You created all things,
>   and by your decision they are
>   and were created."

A scroll with seven seals

CHAPTER 5

The scroll and the Lamb

¹ In the right hand of the one sitting on the throne I saw a scroll* that had writing on the inside and on the outside. And it was sealed in seven places. ² I saw a mighty angel ask with a loud voice, "Who is worthy to open the scroll and break its seals?" ³ No one in heaven or on earth or under the earth was able to open the scroll or see inside it.

⁴ I cried hard because no one was found worthy to open the scroll or see inside it. ⁵ Then one of the elders said to me, "Stop crying and look! The one who is called both the 'Lion from the Tribe of Judah'* and 'King David's Great Descendant'* has won the victory. He will open the book and its seven seals."

⁶ Then I looked and saw a Lamb standing in the centre of the throne that was surrounded by the four living creatures and the elders. The Lamb looked as if it had once been killed. It had seven horns and seven eyes, which are the seven spirits* of God, sent out to all the earth. ⁷ The Lamb went over and took the scroll from the right hand of the one who sat on the throne. ⁸ After he had taken it, the four living creatures and the twenty-four elders knelt down before him. Each of them had a harp and a gold bowl full of incense,* which are the prayers of God's people. ⁹ Then they sang a new song,

> "You are worthy
>   to receive the scroll
> and open its seals,
>   because you were killed.
> And with your own blood
>   you bought for God

4.3 jasper: Usually green or clear.
4.3 carnelian: Usually deep-red or reddish-white.
4.3 emerald: A precious stone, usually green.
See also: 4.5: a Exod 19.16; Rev 8.5; 11.19; 16.18; b Ezek 1.13; c Rev 1.4; Zech 4.2. 4.6: Ezek 1.22. 4.6,7: Ezek 1.5–10; 10.14. 4.8: a Ezek 1.18; 10.12; b Isa 6.2,3.

5.1 scroll: A roll of paper or special leather used for writing on. Sometimes a scroll would be sealed on the outside with one or more pieces of wax.
5.5 'Lion from the Tribe of Judah': In Genesis 49.9 the tribe of Judah is called a young lion, and King David was from Judah.
5.5 'King David's Great Descendant': The Greek text has "the root of David" which is a title for the Messiah based on Isaiah 11.1,10.
5.8 incense: A material that produces a sweet smell when burnt. Sometimes it is a symbol for the prayers of God's people.
See also: 5.1: Ezek 2.9,10; Isa 29.11. 5.5: a Gen 49.9; b Isa 11.1,10. 5.6: a Isa 53.7; b Zech 4.10. 5.8: Psa 141.2. 5.9: Psa 33.3; 98.1; Isa 42.10.

people from every tribe,
language, nation, and race.
¹⁰ You let them become kings
and serve God as priests,
and they will rule on earth."

¹¹ As I looked, I heard the voices of a lot of angels around the throne and the voices of the living creatures and of the elders. There were millions and millions of them, ¹² and they were saying in a loud voice,

"The Lamb who was killed
is worthy to receive power,
riches, wisdom, strength,
honour, glory, and praise."

¹³ Then I heard all beings in heaven and on the earth and under the earth and in the sea offer praise. Together, all of them were saying,

"Praise, honour, glory,
and strength
for ever and ever
to the one who sits
on the throne
and to the Lamb!"

¹⁴ The four living creatures said "Amen," while the elders knelt down and worshipped.

CHAPTER 6

Opening the seven seals

¹ At the same time that I saw the Lamb open the first of the seven seals, I heard one of the four living creatures shout with a voice like thunder. It said, "Come out!" ² Then I saw a white horse. Its rider carried a bow and was given a crown. He had already won some victories, and he went out to win more.

³ When the Lamb opened the second seal, I heard the second living creature say, "Come out!" ⁴ Then another horse came out. It was fiery red. And its rider was given the power to take away all peace from the earth, so that people would slaughter one another. He was also given a big sword.

⁵ When the Lamb opened the third seal, I heard the third living creature say, "Come out!" Then I saw a black horse, and its rider had a balance scale in one hand. ⁶ I heard what sounded like a voice from somewhere among the four living creatures. It said, "A litre of wheat will cost you a whole day's wages! Three litres of barley will cost you a day's wages too. But don't ruin the olive oil or the wine."

⁷ When the Lamb opened the fourth seal, I heard the voice of the fourth living creature say, "Come out!" ⁸ Then I saw a pale green horse. Its rider was named Death, and Death's Kingdom followed behind. They were given power over one fourth of the earth, and they could kill its people with swords, famines, diseases, and wild animals.

⁹ When the Lamb opened the fifth seal, I saw under the altar the souls of everyone who had been killed for speaking God's message and telling about their faith. ¹⁰ They shouted, "Master, you are holy and faithful! How long will it be before you judge and punish the people of this earth who killed us?"

¹¹ Then each of those who had been killed was given a white robe and told to rest for a little while. They had to wait until the complete number of the Lord's other servants and followers would be killed.

¹² When I saw the Lamb open the sixth seal, I looked and saw a great earthquake. The sun turned as dark as sackcloth,* and the moon became as red as blood. ¹³ The stars in the sky fell to earth, just like figs shaken loose by a storm. ¹⁴ Then the sky was rolled up like a scroll,* and all mountains and islands were moved from their places.

¹⁵ The kings of the earth, its famous people, and its military leaders hid in caves or behind rocks on the mountains. They hid there together with the rich and the powerful and with all the slaves and free people. ¹⁶ Then they shouted to the mountains and the rocks, "Fall on us! Hide us from the one who sits on the throne and from the anger of the Lamb. ¹⁷ That terrible day has come! God and the Lamb will show their anger, and who can face it?"

Worship in front of God's throne

CHAPTER 7

The 144,000 are marked for God

¹⁻² After this I saw four angels. Each one was standing on one of the earth's four corners.

---

*6.12 sackcloth: A rough, dark-coloured cloth made from goat or camel hair and used to make grain sacks. It was worn in times of trouble or sorrow.
*6.14 scroll: See the note at 5.1.

See also: 6.8: Ezek 14.21. 6.12: a Rev 11.13; 16.18; b Isa 13.10; Joel 2.10,31; 3.15; Matt 24.29; Mark 13.24,25; Luke 21.25. 6.13,14: Isa 34.4. 6.14: Rev 16.20.
6.15: Isa 2.19,21. 6.16: Hos 10.8; Luke 23.30.
6.17: Joel 2.11; Mal 3.2. 7.1: Jer 49.36; Dan 7.2; Ezek 6.5.

See also: **5.10:** Exod 19.6; Rev 1.6. **5.11:** Dan 7.10.
6.2: Zech 1.8; 6.3,6. **6.4:** Zech 1.8; 6.2. **6.5:** Zech 6.2,6.

The angels held back the four winds, so that no wind would blow on the earth or on the sea or on any tree. These angels had also been given the power to harm the earth and the sea. Then I saw another angel come up from where the sun rises in the east, and he was ready to put the mark of the living God on people. He shouted to the four angels, ³ "Don't harm the earth or the sea or any tree! Wait until I have marked the foreheads of the servants of our God."

⁴ Then I heard how many people had been marked on the forehead. There were one hundred and forty-four thousand, and they came from every tribe of Israel:

⁵ 12,000 from Judah,
   12,000 from Reuben,
   12,000 from Gad,
⁶ 12,000 from Asher,
   12,000 from Naphtali,
   12,000 from Manasseh,
⁷ 12,000 from Simeon,
   12,000 from Levi,
   12,000 from Issachar,
⁸ 12,000 from Zebulun,
   12,000 from Joseph,
   12,000 from Benjamin.

People from every nation

⁹ After this, I saw a large crowd with more people than could be counted. They came from every race, tribe, nation, and language, and they stood before the throne and before the Lamb. They wore white robes and held palm branches in their hands, ¹⁰ as they shouted,

"Our God, who sits
   upon the throne,
has the power
   to save his people,
   and so does the Lamb."

¹¹ The angels who stood around the throne knelt in front of it with their faces to the ground. The elders and the four living creatures knelt there with them. Then they all worshipped God ¹² and said,

"Amen! Praise, glory, wisdom,
   thanks, honour, power,
and strength belong to our God
   for ever and ever! Amen!"

¹³ One of the elders asked me, "Do you know who these people are that are dressed in white robes? Do you know where they come from?"

¹⁴ "Sir," I answered, "you must know." Then he told me:

"These are the ones
   who have gone through
      the great suffering.
They have washed their robes
   in the blood of the Lamb
      and have made them white.
¹⁵ And so they stand
   before the throne of God
and worship him in his temple
      day and night.
The one who sits on the throne
   will spread his tent
      over them.
¹⁶ They will never hunger
      or thirst again,
and they won't be troubled
      by the sun
   or any scorching heat.

¹⁷ The Lamb in the centre
   of the throne
   will be their shepherd.
He will lead them to streams
      of life-giving water,
and God will wipe all tears
      from their eyes."

Seven trumpets

CHAPTER 8

The seventh seal is opened

¹ When the Lamb opened the seventh seal, there was silence in heaven for about half an hour. ² I noticed that the seven angels who stood before God were each given a trumpet.

³ Another angel, who had a gold container for incense,* came and stood at the altar. This one was given a lot of incense to offer with the prayers of God's people on the gold altar in front of the throne. ⁴ Then the smoke of the incense, together with the prayers of God's people, went up to God from the hand of the angel.

⁵ After this, the angel filled the incense container with fire from the altar and threw it on the earth. Thunder roared, lightning flashed, and the earth shook.

---

*8.3 incense: See the note at 5.8.

See also: 7.14: Dan 12.1; Matt 24.21; Mark 13.19.
7.16: Isa 49.10. 7.17: a Psa 23.1; Ezek 34.23; b Psa 23.2;
Isa 49.10; c Isa 25.8. 8.3: a Amos 9.1; b Exod 30.1,3.
8.5: a Lev 16.12; Ezek 10.2; b Exod 19.16; Rev 11.19; 16.18.

The trumpets

⁶ The seven angels now got ready to blow their trumpets.

⁷ When the first angel blew his trumpet, hail and fire mixed with blood were thrown down on the earth. A third of the earth, a third of the trees, and a third of all green plants were burnt.

⁸ When the second angel blew his trumpet, something like a great fiery mountain was thrown into the sea. A third of the sea turned to blood, ⁹ a third of the living creatures in the sea died, and a third of the ships were destroyed.

¹⁰ When the third angel blew his trumpet, a great star fell from heaven. It was burning like a torch, and it fell on a third of the rivers and on a third of the springs of water. ¹¹ The name of the star was Bitter, and a third of the water turned bitter. Many people died because the water was so bitter.

¹² When the fourth angel blew his trumpet, a third of the sun, a third of the moon, and a third of the stars were struck. They each lost a third of their light. So during a third of the day there was no light, and a third of the night was also without light.

¹³ Then I looked and saw a lone eagle flying across the sky. It was shouting, "Trouble, trouble, trouble to everyone who lives on earth! The other three angels are now going to blow their trumpets."

CHAPTER 9

¹ When the fifth angel blew his trumpet, I saw a star* fall from the sky to earth. It was given the key to the tunnel that leads down to the deep pit. ² As it opened the tunnel, smoke poured out like the smoke of a great furnace. The sun and the air turned dark because of the smoke. ³ Locusts* came out of the smoke and covered the earth. They were given the same power that scorpions have.

⁴ The locusts were told not to harm the grass on the earth or any plant or any tree. They were to punish only those people who did not have God's mark on their foreheads. ⁵ The locusts were allowed to make their suffer for five months, but not to kill them.

The suffering they caused was like the sting of a scorpion. ⁶ In those days people will want to die, but they will not be able to. They will hope for death, but it will escape from them.

⁷ These locusts looked like horses ready for battle. On their heads they wore something like gold crowns, and they had human faces. ⁸ Their hair was like a woman's long hair, and their teeth were like those of a lion. ⁹ On their chests they wore armour made of iron. Their wings roared like an army of horse-drawn chariots rushing into battle. ¹⁰ Their tails were like a scorpion's tail with a sting that had the power to hurt someone for five months. ¹¹ Their king was the angel in charge of the deep pit. In Hebrew his name was Abaddon, and in Greek it was Apollyon.*

¹² The first horrible thing had happened! But wait. Two more horrible things will happen soon.

¹³ Then the sixth angel blew his trumpet. I heard a voice speak from the four corners of the gold altar that stands in the presence of God. ¹⁴ The voice spoke to this angel and said, "Release the four angels who are tied up beside the great River Euphrates." ¹⁵ The four angels had been prepared for this very hour and day and month and year. Now they were set free to kill a third of all people.

¹⁶ By listening, I could tell there were more than two hundred million of these war horses. ¹⁷ In my vision their riders wore fiery red, dark blue, and yellow armour on their chests. The heads of the horses looked like lions, with fire and smoke and sulphur coming out of their mouths. ¹⁸ One-third of all people were killed by the three terrible troubles caused by the fire, the smoke, and the sulphur. ¹⁹ The horses had powerful mouths, and their tails were like poisonous snakes that bite and hurt.

²⁰ The people who lived through these terrible troubles did not turn away from the idols they had made, and they did not stop worshipping demons. They kept on worshipping idols that were made of gold, silver, bronze, stone, and wood. Not one of these idols could see, hear, or walk. ²¹ No one stopped murdering or practising witchcraft or being immoral or stealing.

---

*9.1 star: In the ancient world, stars were often thought of as living beings, such as angels.
*9.3 Locusts: A type of grasshopper that comes in swarms and causes great damage to crops.

See also: 8.7: Exod 9.23–25; Ezek 38.22.   8.10: Isa 14.12.
8.11: Jer 9.15.   8.12: Isa 13.10; Joel 3.27; Joel 2.10,31; 3.15.
9.2: Gen 19.28.   9.3: Exod 10.12–15.   9.4: Ezek 9.4.

*9.11 Abaddon . . . Apollyon: The Hebrew word "Abaddon" and the Greek word "Apollyon" each mean "destruction".

See also: 9.6: Job 3.21; Jer 8.3.   9.7: Joel 2.4.   9.8: Joel 1.6.
9.9: Joel 2.5.   9.13: Exod 30.1–3.   9.20: Psa 115.4–7;
135.15–17; Dan 5.23.

CHAPTER 10

The angel and the little scroll

[1] I saw another powerful angel come down from heaven. This one was covered with a cloud, and a rainbow was over his head. His face was like the sun, his legs were like columns of fire, [2] and with his hand he held a little scroll* that had been unrolled. He stood there with his right foot on the sea and his left foot on the land. [3] Then he shouted with a voice that sounded like a growling lion. Thunder roared seven times.

[4] After the thunder stopped, I was about to write what it had said. But a voice from heaven shouted, "Keep it secret! Don't write these things."

[5] The angel I had seen standing on the sea and the land then held his right hand up towards heaven. [6] He made a promise in the name of God who lives for ever and who created heaven, earth, the sea, and every living creature. The angel said, "You won't have to wait any longer. [7] God told his secret plans to his servants the prophets, and it will all happen by the time the seventh angel sounds his trumpet."

[8] Once again the voice from heaven spoke to me. It said, "Go and take the open scroll from the hand of the angel standing on the sea and the land."

[9] When I went over to ask the angel for the little scroll, the angel said, "Take the scroll and eat it! Your stomach will turn sour, but the taste in your mouth will be as sweet as honey." [10] I took the little scroll from the hand of the angel and ate it. The taste was as sweet as honey, but my stomach turned sour.

[11] Then some voices said, "Keep on telling what will happen to the people of many nations, races, and languages, and also to kings."

CHAPTER 11

The two witnesses

[1] An angel gave me a measuring stick and said:

Measure around God's temple. Be sure to include the altar and everyone worshipping there. [2] But don't measure the courtyard outside the temple building. Leave it out. It has been given to those people who don't know God, and they will trample all over the holy city for forty-two months. [3] My two witnesses will wear sackcloth,* while I let them preach for one thousand two hundred and sixty days.

[4] These two witnesses are the two olive trees and the two lampstands that stand in the presence of the Lord who rules the earth. [5] Any enemy who tries to harm them will be destroyed by the fire that comes out of their mouths. [6] They have the power to lock up the sky and to keep rain from falling while they are prophesying. And whenever they want to, they can turn water to blood and cause all kinds of terrible troubles on earth.

[7] After the two witnesses have finished preaching God's message, the beast that lives in the deep pit will come up and fight against them. It will win the battle and kill them. [8] Their bodies will be left lying in the streets of the same great city where their Lord was nailed to a cross. And that city is spiritually like the city of Sodom or the country of Egypt.

[9] For three and a half days the people of every nation, tribe, language, and race will stare at the bodies of these two witnesses and refuse to let them be buried. [10] Everyone on earth will celebrate and be happy. They will give gifts to each other, because of what happened to the two prophets who caused them so much trouble. [11] But three and a half days later, God will breathe life into their bodies. They will stand up, and everyone who sees them will be terrified.

[12] The witnesses then heard a loud voice from heaven, saying, "Come up here." And while their enemies were watching, they were taken up to heaven in a cloud. [13] At that same moment there was a terrible earthquake that destroyed a tenth of the city. Seven thousand people were killed, and the rest were frightened and praised the God who rules in heaven.

[14] The second horrible thing has now happened! But the third one will be here soon.

The seventh trumpet

[15] At the sound of the seventh trumpet, loud voices were heard in heaven. They said,

---

*10.2 scroll: See the note at 5.1.

See also: 10.5-7: Exod 20.11; Deut 32.40; Dan 12.7; Amos 3.7. 10.8-10: Ezek 2.8–3.3. 11.1: Ezek 40.3; Zech 2.1,2. 11.2: Luke 21.24.

*11.3 sackcloth: See the note at 6.12.

See also: 11.4: Zech 4.3,11–14. 11.6: a 1 King 17.1; b Exod 7.17–19; c 1 Sam 4.1. 11.7: Rev 13.5–7; 17.8. b Dan 7.21. 11.8: Isa 1.9,10. 11.11: Ezek 37.10. 11.12: 2 King 2.11. 11.13: Rev 6.12; 16.18. 11.15: Exod 15.18; Dan 2.44; 7.14,27.

"Now the kingdom
of this world
belongs to our Lord
and to his Chosen One!
And he will rule
for ever and ever!"

[16] Then the twenty-four elders, who were
seated on thrones in God's presence, knelt
down and worshipped him. [17] They said,

"Lord God All-Powerful,
you are and you were,
and we thank you.
You used your great power
and started ruling.
[18] When the nations got angry,
you became angry too!
Now the time has come
for the dead
to be judged.
It is time for you to reward
your servants the prophets
and all your people
who honour your name,
no matter who they are.
It is time to destroy everyone
who has destroyed
the earth."

[19] The door to God's temple in heaven was
then opened, and the sacred chest* could be
seen inside the temple. I saw lightning and
heard roars of thunder. The earth trembled
and huge hailstones fell to the ground.

A dragon and two beasts

CHAPTER 12

The woman and the dragon

[1] Something important appeared in the sky. It
was a woman whose clothes were the sun.
The moon was under her feet, and a crown
made of twelve stars was on her head. [2] She
was about to give birth, and she was crying
because of the great pain.

[3] Something else appeared in the sky. It was
a huge red dragon with seven heads and ten
horns, and a crown on each of its seven
heads. [4] With its tail, it dragged a third of the

stars from the sky and threw them down to
the earth. Then the dragon turned towards
the woman, because it wanted to eat her
child as soon as it was born.

[5] The woman gave birth to a son, who
would rule all nations with an iron rod. The
boy was snatched away. He was taken to God
and placed on his throne. [6] The woman ran
into the desert to a place that God had
prepared for her. There she would be taken
care of for one thousand two hundred and
sixty days.

Michael fights the dragon

[7] A war broke out in heaven. Michael and his
angels were fighting the dragon and
its angels. [8] But the dragon lost the battle. It
and its angels were forced out of their places
in heaven [9] and were thrown down to the
earth. Yes, that old snake and his angels were
thrown out of heaven! That snake, who fools
everyone on earth, is known as the devil and
Satan. [10] Then I heard a voice from heaven
shout,

"Our God has shown
his saving power,
and his kingdom has come!
God's own Chosen One
has shown his authority.
Satan accused our people
in the presence of God
day and night.
Now he has been thrown out!
[11] Our people defeated Satan
because of the blood*
of the Lamb
and the message of God.
They were willing
to give up their lives.
[12] The heavens should rejoice,
together with everyone
who lives there.
But pity the earth
and the sea,
because the devil
was thrown down
to the earth.
He knows his time is short,
and he is very angry."

[13] When the dragon realized that it had been
thrown down to the earth, it tried to make
trouble for the woman who had given birth

---

*11.19 sacred chest: In Old Testament times the
sacred chest was kept in the tent used for worship. It
was the symbol of God's presence with his people
and also of his agreement with them.

See also: 11.18: a Psa 2.5; 110.5; b Psa 115.13.
11.19: a Rev 8.5; 16.18; b Rev 16.21. 12.3: Dan 7.7.
12.4: Dan 8.10.

See also: 12.5: a Isa 66.7; b Psa 2.9. 12.7: Dan 10.13,21;
12.1; Jude 9. 12.9: a Gen 3.1; b Luke 10.18.
12.10: Job 1.9–11; Zech 3.1.

to a son. ¹⁴ But the woman was given two wings like those of a huge eagle, so that she could fly into the desert. There she would escape from the snake and be taken care of for a time, two times, and half a time.

¹⁵ The snake then spewed out water like a river to sweep the woman away. ¹⁶ But the earth helped her and swallowed the water that had come from the dragon's mouth. ¹⁷ This made the dragon terribly angry with the woman. So it started a war against the rest of her children. They are the people who obey God and are faithful to what Jesus did and taught. ¹⁸ The dragon· stood·on the beach beside the sea.

CHAPTER 13

The two beasts

¹ I looked and saw a beast coming up from the sea. This one had ten horns and seven heads, and a crown was on each of its ten horns. On each of its heads were names that were an insult to God. ² The beast that I saw had the body of a leopard, the feet of a bear, and the mouth of a lion. The dragon handed over its own power and throne and great authority to this beast. ³ One of its heads seemed to have been fatally wounded, but now it was well. Everyone on earth marvelled at this beast, ⁴ and they worshipped the dragon who had given its authority to the beast. They also worshipped the beast and said, "No one is like this beast! No one can fight against it."

⁵ The beast was allowed to boast and claim to be God, and for forty-two months it was allowed to rule. ⁶ The beast cursed God, and it cursed the name of God. It even cursed the place where God lives, as well as everyone who lives in heaven with God. ⁷ It was allowed to fight against God's people and defeat them. It was also given authority over the people of every tribe, nation, language, and race. ⁸ The beast was worshipped by everyone whose name wasn't written before the time of creation in the book of the Lamb who was killed.·

⁹ If you have ears,
then listen!
¹⁰ If you are doomed
to be captured,
you will be captured.

If you are doomed
to be killed by a sword,
you will be killed
by a sword.

This means that God's people must learn to endure and be faithful!

¹¹ I now saw another beast. This one came out of the ground. It had two horns like a lamb, but spoke like a dragon. ¹² It worked for the beast whose fatal wound had been healed. And it used all its authority to force the earth and its people to worship that beast. ¹³ It performed mighty miracles, and while people watched, it even made fire come down from the sky.

¹⁴ This second beast fooled people on earth by performing miracles for the first one. Then it talked them into making an idol in the form of the beast that did not die after being wounded by a sword. ¹⁵ It was allowed to put breath into the idol, so that it could speak. Everyone who refused to worship the idol of the beast was put to death. ¹⁶ All people were forced to put a mark on their right hand or forehead. Whether they were powerful or weak, rich or poor, free people or slaves, ¹⁷ they all had to have this mark, or else they could not buy or sell anything. This mark stood for the name of the beast and for the number of its name.

¹⁸ You need wisdom to understand the number of the beast! But if you are clever enough, you can work this out. Its number is six hundred and sixty-six, and it stands for a person.

Visions of God's judgment and protection

CHAPTER 14

The Lamb and his 144,000 followers

¹ I looked and saw the Lamb standing on Mount Zion!* With him were a hundred and forty-four thousand, who had his name and his Father's name written on their foreheads. ² Then I heard a sound from heaven that was like a roaring flood or loud thunder or even like the music of harps. ³ And a new song was being sung in front of God's throne and in front of the four living creatures and the elders. No one could learn that song, except the one hundred and forty-four thousand

---

See also: 12.14: Dan 7.25; 12.7. 13.1: a Dan 7.3;
b Rev 17.3,7–12. 13.2: Dan 7.4–6. 13.5,6: Dan 7.8,25; 11.36.
13.7: Dan 7.21. 13.8: Psa 69.28. 13.10: Jer 15.2; 43.11.

*14.1 Mount Zion: Another name for Jerusalem.
See also: 14.1: Ezek 9.4; Rev 7.3.

who had been rescued from the earth. ⁴ All these are pure virgins, and they follow the Lamb wherever he leads. They have been rescued to be presented to God and the Lamb as the most precious people* on earth. ⁵ They never tell lies, and they are innocent.

The messages of the three angels

⁶ I saw another angel. This one was flying across the sky and had the eternal good news to announce to the people of every race, tribe, language, and nation on earth. ⁷ The angel shouted, "Worship and honour God! The time has come for him to judge everyone. Kneel down before the one who created heaven and earth, the oceans, and every stream."

⁸ A second angel followed and said, "The great city of Babylon has fallen! This is the city that made all nations drunk and immoral. Now God is angry, and Babylon has fallen."

⁹ Finally, a third angel came and shouted:

Here is what will happen if you worship the beast and the idol and have the mark of the beast on your hand or forehead. ¹⁰ You will have to drink the wine that God gives to everyone who makes him angry. You will feel his mighty anger, and you will be tortured with fire and burning sulphur, while the holy angels and the Lamb look on. ¹¹ If you worship the beast and the idol and accept the mark of its name, you will be tortured day and night. The smoke from your torture will go up for ever and ever, and you will never be able to rest.

¹² God's people must learn to endure. They must also obey his commands and have faith in Jesus. ¹³ Then I heard a voice from heaven say, "Put this in writing. From now on, the Lord will bless everyone who has faith in him when they die."

The Spirit answered, "Yes, they will rest from their hard work, and they will be rewarded for what they have done."

The earth is harvested

¹⁴ I looked and saw a bright cloud, and someone who seemed to be the Son of Man* was sitting on the cloud. He wore a gold crown on his head and held a sharp sickle* in his hand. ¹⁵ An angel came out of the temple and shouted, "Start cutting with your sickle! Harvest season is here, and all crops on earth are ripe." ¹⁶ The one on the cloud swung his sickle and harvested the crops.

¹⁷ Another angel with a sharp sickle then came out of the temple in heaven. ¹⁸ After this, an angel with power over fire came from the altar and shouted to the angel who had the sickle. He said, "All grapes on earth are ripe! Harvest them with your sharp sickle." ¹⁹ The angel swung his sickle on earth and cut off its grapes. He threw them into a pit* where they were trampled on as a sign of God's anger. ²⁰ The pit was outside the city, and when the grapes were squashed, blood flowed out. The blood turned into a river that was about three hundred kilometres long and almost deep enough to cover a horse.

CHAPTER 15

The last of the terrible troubles

¹ After this, I looked at the sky and saw something else that was strange and important. Seven angels were bringing the last seven terrible troubles. When these are ended, God will no longer be angry.

² Then I saw something that looked like a glass sea mixed with fire, and people were standing on it. They were the ones who had defeated the beast and the idol and the number that tells the name of the beast. God had given them harps, ³ and they were singing the song that his servant Moses and the Lamb had sung. They were singing,

"Lord God All-Powerful,
    you have done great
        and marvellous things.
You are the ruler
    of all nations,
and you do what is
    right and fair.

---

*14.4 the most precious people: The Greek text has "the first people". The Law of Moses taught that the firstborn of all animals and the first part of the harvest were special and belonged to the Lord.

See also: 14.5: Zeph 3.13. 14.8: Isa 21.9; Jer 51.8; Rev 18.2. 14.10: a Isa 51.17; b Gen 19.24; Ezek 38.22. 14.11: Isa 34.10.

*14.14 Son of Man: See the note at 1.13.
*14.14 sickle: A knife with a long curved blade, used to cut grain and other crops.
*14.19 pit: It was the custom to put grapes in a pit (called a wine press) and trample on them to make juice that would later turn to wine.

See also: 14.14: Dan 7.13. 14.15: Joel 3.13. 14.20: Isa 63.3; Lam 1.15; Rev 19.15. 15.3: Exod 15.1.

⁴ Lord, who doesn't honour
    and praise your name?
You alone are holy,
    and all nations will come
    and worship you,
because you have shown
    that you judge
    with fairness."

⁵ After this, I noticed something else in heaven. The sacred tent used for a temple was open. ⁶ And the seven angels who were bringing the terrible troubles were coming out of it. They were dressed in robes of pure white linen and wore belts made of pure gold. ⁷ One of the four living creatures gave each of the seven angels a bowl made of gold. These bowls were filled with the anger of God who lives for ever and ever. ⁸ The temple quickly filled with smoke from the glory and power of God. No one could enter it until the seven angels had finished pouring out the seven last troubles.

Seven bowls of God's anger

CHAPTER 16

¹ From the temple I heard a voice shout to the seven angels, "Go and empty the seven bowls of God's anger on the earth."

² The first angel emptied his bowl on the earth. At once ugly and painful sores broke out on everyone who had the mark of the beast and worshipped the idol.

³ The second angel emptied his bowl on the sea. Straight away the sea turned into blood like that of a dead person, and every living thing in the sea died.

⁴ The third angel emptied his bowl into the rivers and streams. At once they turned to blood. ⁵ Then I heard the angel, who has power over water, say,

"You have always been,
    and you always will be
    the holy God.
You had the right
    to judge in this way.
⁶ They poured out the blood*
    of your people
    and your prophets.
So you gave them blood
    to drink, as they deserve!"

*16.6 They poured out the blood: A way of saying, "They murdered."

See also: 15.4: a Jer 10.7; b Psa 86.9. 15.5: Exod 38.21.
15.8: Exod 40.34; 1 King 8.10,11; 2 Chron 5.13,14; Isa 6.4.
16.2: Exod 9.10. 16.4: Exod 7.17–21; Psa 78.44.

314

⁷ After this, I heard
    the altar shout,
"Yes, Lord God All-Powerful,
    your judgments are honest
    and fair."

⁸ The fourth angel emptied his bowl on the sun, and it began to scorch people like fire. ⁹ Everyone was scorched by its great heat, and all of them cursed the name of God who had power over these terrible troubles. But no one turned to God and praised him.

¹⁰ The fifth angel emptied his bowl on the throne of the beast. At once darkness covered its kingdom, and its people began biting their tongues in pain. ¹¹ And because of their painful sores, they cursed the God who rules in heaven. But still they did not stop doing evil things.

¹² The sixth angel emptied his bowl on the great River Euphrates, and it completely dried up to make a road for the kings from the east. ¹³ An evil spirit that looked like a frog came out of the mouth of the dragon. One also came out of the mouth of the beast, and another out of the mouth of the false prophet. ¹⁴ These evil spirits had the power to perform miracles. They went to every king on earth, to bring them together for a war against God All-Powerful. But that will be the day of God's great victory.

¹⁵ Remember that Christ says, "When I come, it will surprise you like a thief! But God will bless you, if you are awake and ready. Then you won't have to walk around naked and be ashamed."

¹⁶ Those armies came together in a place that in Hebrew is called Armageddon.*

¹⁷ As soon as the seventh angel emptied his bowl in the air, a loud voice from the throne in the temple shouted, "It's done!" ¹⁸ There were flashes of lightning, roars of thunder, and the worst earthquake in all history. ¹⁹ The great city of Babylon split into three parts, and the cities of other nations fell. So God made Babylon drink from the wine cup that was filled with his anger. ²⁰ Every island ran away, and the mountains disappeared. ²¹ Hailstones, weighing about fifty kilograms each, fell

*16.16 Armageddon: The Hebrew form of the name would be "Har Megiddo", meaning "Hill of Megiddo", where many battles were fought in ancient times (see Judges 5.19; 2 Kings 23.29,30).

See also: 16.10: Exod 10.21. 16.12: Isa 11.15.
16.15: Matt 24.43,44; Luke 12.39,40; Rev 3.3.
16.16: 2 King 23.29; Zech 12.11. 16.18: Rev 8.5; 11.13,19.
16.19: Isa 51.17. 16.20: Rev 6.14. 16.21: Exod 9.23;
Rev 11.19.

from the sky on people. Finally, the people cursed God, because the hail was so terrible.

God's enemies are defeated

CHAPTER 17

The prostitute and the beast

¹ One of the seven angels who had emptied the bowls came over and said to me, "Come on! I will show you how God will punish that shameless prostitute who sits on many oceans. ² Every king on earth has slept with her, and her shameless ways are like wine that has made everyone on earth drunk."

³ With the help of the Spirit, the angel took me into the desert, where I saw a woman sitting on a red beast. The beast was covered with names that were an insult to God, and it had seven heads and ten horns. ⁴ The woman was dressed in purple and scarlet robes, and she wore jewellery made of gold, precious stones, and pearls. In her hand she held a gold cup filled with the filthy and nasty things she had done. ⁵ On her forehead a mysterious name was written:

I AM THE GREAT CITY OF BABYLON,
THE MOTHER OF EVERY IMMORAL
AND FILTHY THING ON EARTH.

⁶ I could tell that the woman was drunk on the blood of God's people who had given their lives for Jesus. This surprising sight amazed me, ⁷ and the angel said:

Why are you so amazed? I will explain the mystery about this woman and about the beast she is sitting on, with its seven heads and ten horns. ⁸ The beast you saw is one that used to be and no longer is. It will come back from the deep pit, but only to be destroyed. Everyone on earth whose names were not written in the book of life* before the time of creation will be amazed. They will see this beast that used to be and no longer is, but will be once more.

⁹ Anyone with wisdom can work this out. The seven heads that the woman is sitting on stand for seven hills. These heads are also seven kings. ¹⁰ Five of the kings are dead. One is ruling now, and the other one has not yet come. But when he does, he will rule for only a little while.

¹¹ You also saw a beast that used to be and no longer is. That beast is one of the seven kings who will return as the eighth king, but only to be destroyed.

¹² The ten horns that you saw are ten more kings, who have not yet come into power, and they will rule with the beast for only a short time. ¹³ They will all think alike and will give their power and authority to the beast. ¹⁴ These kings will go to war against the Lamb. But he will defeat them, because he is Lord over all lords and King over all kings. His followers are chosen and special and faithful.

¹⁵ The oceans that you saw the prostitute sitting on are crowds of people from all races and languages. ¹⁶ The ten horns and the beast will start hating the shameless woman. They will strip off her clothes and leave her naked. Then they will eat her flesh and throw the rest of her body into a fire. ¹⁷ God is the one who made these kings all think alike and decide to give their power to the beast. And they will do this until what God has said comes true.

¹⁸ The woman you saw is the great city that rules over all kings on earth.

CHAPTER 18

The fall of Babylon

¹ I saw another angel come from heaven. This one had great power, and the earth was bright because of his glory. ² The angel shouted,

"Fallen! Powerful Babylon
  has fallen
and is now the home
  of demons.
It is the den
  of every filthy spirit
and of all unclean birds,
and every dirty
  and hated animal.
³ Babylon's evil and immoral wine
  has made all nations drunk.
Every king on earth
  has slept with her,
and every merchant on earth
is rich because of
  her evil desires."

⁴ Then I heard another voice
  from heaven shout,

---

*17.8 book of life: See the note at 3.5.

See also: 17.1: Jer 51.13. 17.2: Isa 23.17; Jer 51.7.
17.3: Rev 13.1. 17.4: Jer 51.7. 17.8: a Dan 7.7; Rev 11.7;
b Psa 69.28.

See also: 17.12: Dan 7.24. 18.2: a Isa 21.9; Jer 51.8;
Rev 14.8; b Isa 13.21; Jer 50.39. 18.3: Isa 23.17; Jer 51.7.
18.4: Isa 48.20; Jer 50.8; 51.6,45.

"My people, you must escape
   from Babylon.
Don't take part in her sins
   and share her punishment.
⁵ Her sins are piled
   as high as heaven.
God has remembered the evil
   she has done.
⁶ Treat her as she
   has treated others.
Make her pay double
   for what she has done.
Make her drink twice as much
   of what she mixed
   for others.
⁷ That woman honoured herself
   with a life of luxury.
Reward her now
   with suffering and pain.

"Deep in her heart
Babylon said,
   'I am the queen!
Never will I be a widow
   or know what it means
   to be sad.'
⁸ And so, in a single day
   she will suffer the pain
   of sorrow, hunger, and death.
Fire will destroy
   her dead body,
because her judge
   is the powerful Lord God."

⁹ Every king on earth who slept with her
and shared in her luxury will mourn. They
will weep, when they see the smoke from
that fire. ¹⁰ Her sufferings will frighten
them, and they will stand at a distance and
say,

"Pity that great
   and powerful city!
Pity Babylon!
In a single hour
   her judgment has come."

¹¹ Every merchant on earth will mourn,
because there is no one to buy their goods.
¹² There won't be anyone to buy their gold,
silver, jewels, pearls, fine linen, purple
cloth, silk, scarlet cloth, sweet-smelling
wood, fancy carvings of ivory and wood,
as well as things made of bronze, iron,
or marble. ¹³ No one will buy their
cinnamon, spices, incense, myrrh,

frankincense,* wine, olive oil, fine flour,
wheat, cattle, sheep, horses, chariots, slaves,
and other humans.

¹⁴ Babylon, the things
   your heart desired
have all escaped
   from you.
Every luxury
and all your glory
   will be lost for ever.
You will never
   get them back.

¹⁵ The merchants had become rich because of
her. But when they saw her sufferings, they
were terrified. They stood at a distance,
crying and mourning. ¹⁶ Then they shouted,

"Pity the great city
   of Babylon!
She dressed in fine linen
   wore purple
   and scarlet cloth.
She had jewellery
   made of gold
and precious stones
   and pearls.
¹⁷ Yet in a single hour
   her riches disappeared."

Every ship's captain and passenger and sailor
stood at a distance, together with everyone
who does business by travelling on the sea.
¹⁸ When they saw the smoke from her fire,
they shouted, "This was the greatest city
ever!"

¹⁹ They cried loudly, and in their sorrow
they threw dust on their heads, as they said,

"Pity the great city
   of Babylon!
Everyone who sailed the seas
   became rich
   from her treasures.
But in a single hour
   the city was destroyed.
²⁰ The heavens should be happy
   with God's people
   and apostles and prophets.
God has punished her
   for them."

*18.13 myrrh, frankincense: Myrrh was a valuable
sweet-smelling powder often used in perfume.
Frankincense was a valuable powder that was burnt
to make a sweet smell.

See also: 18.5: Gen 18.20,21; Jer 51.9. 18.6: Psa 137.8;
Jer 50.29. 18.7,8: Isa 47.7–9. 18.9,10: Ezek 26.16,17.
18.11: Ezek 27.31,36. 18.12,13: Ezek 27.12,13,22.

See also: 18.15: Ezek 27.31,36. 18.17: Isa 23.14;
Ezek 27.26–30. 18.18: Ezek 27.32. 18.19: Ezek 27.30–34.
18.20: Deut 32.43; Jer 51.48.

²¹ A powerful angel then picked up a huge stone and threw it into the sea. The angel said,

"This is how the great city
of Babylon
will be thrown down,
never to rise again.
²² The music of harps and singers
and of flutes and trumpets
will no longer be heard.
No workers will ever
set up shop in that city,
and the sound
of grinding grain
will be silenced for ever.
²³ Lamps will no longer shine
anywhere in Babylon,
and couples will never again
say wedding vows there.
Her merchants ruled
the earth,
and by her witchcraft
she fooled all nations.
²⁴ On the streets of Babylon
is found the blood
of God's people
and of his prophets,
and everyone else."

CHAPTER 19

¹ After this, I heard what sounded like a lot of voices in heaven, and they were shouting,

"Praise the Lord!
To our God belongs
the glorious power to save,
² because his judgments
are honest and fair.
That filthy prostitute
ruined the earth
with shameful deeds.
But God has judged her
and made her pay
the price for murdering
his servants."

³ Then the crowd shouted,

"Praise the Lord!
Smoke will never stop rising
from her burning body."

⁴ After this, the twenty-four elders and the four living creatures all knelt before the throne of God and worshipped him. They said, "Amen! Praise the Lord!"

The marriage supper of the Lamb

⁵ From the throne a voice said,

"If you worship
and fear our God,
give praise to him,
no matter who you are."

⁶ Then I heard what seemed to be a large crowd that sounded like a roaring flood and loud thunder all mixed together. They were saying,

"Praise the Lord!
Our Lord God All-Powerful
now rules as king.
⁷ So we will be glad and happy
and give him praise.
The wedding day of the Lamb
is here,
and his bride is ready.
⁸ She will be given
a wedding dress
made of pure
and shining linen.
This linen stands for
the good things
God's people have done."

⁹ Then the angel told me, "Put this in writing. God will bless everyone who is invited to the wedding feast of the Lamb." The angel also said, "These things that God has said are true."

¹⁰ I knelt at the feet of the angel and began to worship him. But the angel said, "Don't do that! I am a servant, just like you and everyone else who tells about Jesus. Don't worship anyone but God. Everyone who tells about Jesus does it by the power of the Spirit."

The rider on the white horse

¹¹ I looked and saw that heaven was open, and a white horse was there. Its rider was called Faithful and True, and he is always fair when he judges or goes to war. ¹² He had eyes like flames of fire, and he was wearing a lot of crowns. His name was written on him, but he was the only one who knew what the name meant.

¹³ The rider wore a robe that was covered with' blood, and he was known as "The Word of God." ¹⁴ He was followed by armies from heaven that rode on horses and were

See also: **18.21:** a Jer 51.63,64; b Ezek 26.21.
18.22: Ezek 26.13; Isa 24.8. **18.22,23:** Jer 7.34; 25.10.
18.24: Jer 51.49. **19.2:** Deut 32.43; 2 King 9.7.
19.3: Isa 34.10.

See also: **19.5:** Psa 115.13. **19.6:** a Ezek 1.24; b Psa 93.1;
97.1; 99.1. **19.9:** Matt 22.2,3. **19.11:** a Ezek 1.1; b Psa 96.13;
Isa 11.4. **19.12:** Dan 10.6.

dressed in pure white linen. ¹⁵ From his mouth a sharp sword went out to attack the nations. He will rule them with an iron rod and will show the fierce anger of God All-Powerful by trampling on the grapes in the pit where wine is made. ¹⁶ On the part of the robe that covered his thigh was written, "KING OF KINGS AND LORD OF LORDS".

¹⁷ I then saw an angel standing on the sun, and he shouted to all the birds flying in the sky, "Come and join in God's great feast! ¹⁸ You can eat the flesh of kings, rulers, leaders, horses, riders, free people, slaves, important people, and everyone else."

¹⁹ I also saw the beast and all kings of the earth come together. They fought against the rider on the white horse and against his army. ²⁰ But the beast was captured and so was the false prophet. This is the same prophet who had performed miracles for the beast, so that he could fool everyone who had the mark of the beast and worshipped the idol. The beast and the false prophet were thrown alive into a lake of burning sulphur. ²¹ But the rest of their army was killed by the sword that came from the mouth of the rider on the horse. Then birds stuffed themselves on the dead bodies.

CHAPTER 20

The thousand years

¹ I saw an angel come down from heaven, carrying the key to the deep pit and a big chain. ² He chained the dragon for a thousand years. It is that old snake, who is also known as the devil and Satan. ³ Then the angel threw the dragon into the pit. He locked and sealed it, so that a thousand years would go by before the dragon could fool the nations again. But after that, it would have to be set free for a little while.

⁴ I saw thrones, and sitting on those thrones were the ones who had been given the right to judge. I also saw the souls of the people who had their heads cut off because they had told about Jesus and preached God's message. They were the same ones who had not worshipped the beast or the idol, and they had refused to let its mark be put on their hands or foreheads. They will come to life and rule with Christ for a thousand years.

⁵⁻⁶ These people are the first to be raised to life, and they are especially blessed and

holy. The second death* has no power over them. They will be priests for God and Christ and will rule with them for a thousand years.

No other dead people were raised to life until a thousand years later.

Satan is defeated

⁷ At the end of the thousand years, Satan will be set free. ⁸ He will fool the countries of Gog and Magog, which are at the far ends of the earth, and their people will follow him into battle. They will have as many followers as there are grains of sand along the beach, ⁹ and they will march all the way across the earth. They will surround the camp of God's people and the city that his people love. But fire will come down from heaven and destroy the whole army. ¹⁰ Then the devil who fooled them will be thrown into the lake of fire and burning sulphur. He will be there with the beast and the false prophet, and they will be in pain day and night for ever and ever.

The final judgment

The judgment at the great white throne

¹¹ I saw a great white throne with someone sitting on it. Earth and heaven tried to run away, but there was nowhere for them to go. ¹² I also saw all the dead people standing in front of that throne. Every one of them was there, no matter who they had ever been. Several books were opened, and then the book of life* was opened. The dead were judged by what those books said they had done.

¹³ The sea gave up the dead people who were in it, and death and its kingdom also gave up their dead. Then everyone was judged by what they had done. ¹⁴ Afterwards, death and its kingdom were thrown into the lake of fire. This is the second death.* ¹⁵ Anyone whose name wasn't written in the book of life was thrown into the lake of fire.

---

*20.5,6,14 second death: See the note at 2.11.
*20.12 book of life: See the note at 3.5.
See also: 20.8: a Ezek 7.2; b Ezek 38.2,9,15.
20.11,12: Dan 7.9,10.

See also: 19.15: a Psa 2.9; b Isa 63.3; Joel 3.13; Rev 14.20.
19.17,18: Ezek 39.17–20. 19.20: Rev 13.1–18.
20.2: Gen 3.1. 20.4: Dan 7.9,22.

A new heaven and a new earth

CHAPTER 21

¹ I saw a new heaven and a new earth. The first heaven and the first earth had disappeared, and so had the sea. ² Then I saw New Jerusalem, that holy city, coming down from God in heaven. It was like a bride dressed in her wedding gown and ready to meet her husband.

³ I heard a loud voice shout from the throne:

God's home is now with his people. He will live with them, and they will be his own. Yes, God will make his home among his people. ⁴ He will wipe all tears from their eyes, and there will be no more death, suffering, crying, or pain. These things of the past are gone for ever.

⁵ Then the one sitting on the throne said:

I am making everything new. Write down what I have said. My words are true and can be trusted. ⁶ Everything is finished! I am Alpha and Omega,* the beginning and the end. I will freely give water from the life-giving fountain to everyone who is thirsty. ⁷ All who win the victory will be given these blessings. I will be their God, and they will be my people.

⁸ But I will tell you what will happen to cowards and to everyone who is unfaithful or dirty-minded or who murders or is sexually immoral or uses witchcraft or worships idols or tells lies. They will be thrown into that lake of fire and burning sulphur. This is the second death.*

New Jerusalem

⁹ I saw one of the seven angels who had the bowls filled with the seven last terrible troubles. The angel came to me and said, "Come on! I will show you the one who will be the bride and wife of the Lamb." ¹⁰ Then with the help of the Spirit, he took me to the top of a very high mountain. There he showed me the holy city of Jerusalem coming down from God in heaven.

¹¹ The glory of God made the city bright. It was dazzling and crystal clear like a precious jasper stone. ¹² The city had a high and thick wall with twelve gates, and each one of them was guarded by an angel. On each of the gates was written the name of one of the twelve tribes of Israel. ¹³ Three of these gates were on the east, three were on the north, three more were on the south, and the other three were on the west. ¹⁴ The city was built on twelve foundation stones. On each of the stones was written the name of one of the Lamb's twelve apostles.

¹⁵ The angel who spoke to me had a gold measuring stick to measure the city and its gates and its walls. ¹⁶ The city was shaped like a cube, because it was just as high as it was wide. When the angel measured the city, it was about two thousand four hundred kilometres high and two thousand four hundred kilometres wide. ¹⁷ Then the angel measured the wall, and by our measurements it was about sixty metres high.

¹⁸ The wall was built of jasper, and the city was made of pure gold, clear as crystal. ¹⁹ Each of the twelve foundations was a precious stone. The first was jasper,* the second was sapphire, the third was agate, the fourth was emerald, ²⁰ the fifth was onyx, the sixth was carnelian, the seventh was chrysolite, the eighth was beryl, the ninth was topaz, the tenth was chrysoprase, the eleventh was jacinth, and the twelfth was amethyst. ²¹ Each of the twelve gates was a solid pearl. The streets of the city were made of pure gold, clear as crystal.

²² I did not see a temple there. The Lord God All-Powerful and the Lamb were its temple. ²³ And the city did not need the sun or the moon. The glory of God was shining on it, and the Lamb was its light. ²⁴ Nations will walk by the light of that city, and kings will bring their riches there. ²⁵ Its gates are always open during the day, and night never comes. ²⁶ The glorious

---

*21.6 Alpha and Omega: See the note at 1.8.
*21.8 second death: See the note at 2.11.

See also: 21.1: Isa 65.17; 66.22; 2 Pet 3.13. 21.2: a Isa 52.1; b Rev 3.12; c Isa 61.10. 21.3: Ezek 37.27; Lev 26.11,12. 21.4: a Isa 25.8; b Isa 35.10; 65.19. 21.6: Isa 55.1. 21.7: Psa 89.26,27. 21.10: Ezek 40.2.

*21.19 jasper: The precious and semi-precious stones mentioned in verses 19,20 are of different colours. *Jasper* is usually green or clear; *sapphire* is blue; *agate* has circles of brown and white; *emerald* is green; *onyx* has different bands of colour; *carnelian* is deep red or reddish-white; *chrysolite* is olive green; *beryl* is green or bluish-green; *topaz* is yellow; *chrysoprase* is apple green; *jacinth* is reddish-orange; and *amethyst* is deep purple.

See also: 21.12,13: Ezek 48.30–35. 21.15: Ezek 40.3. 21.18–21: Isa 54.11,12. 21.23: Isa 60.19,20. 21.24: Isa 60.3. 21.25,26: Isa 60.11.

treasures of nations will be brought into the city. ²⁷ But nothing unworthy will be allowed to enter. No one who is dirty-minded or who tells lies will be there. Only those whose names are written in the Lamb's book of life* will be in the city.

CHAPTER 22

¹ The angel showed me a river that was crystal clear, and its waters gave life. The river came from the throne where God and the Lamb were seated. ² Then it flowed down the middle of the city's main street. On each side of the river are trees* that grow a different kind of fruit each month of the year. The fruit gives life, and the leaves are used as medicine to heal the nations.

³ God's curse will no longer be on the people of that city. He and the Lamb will be seated there on their thrones, and his people will worship God ⁴ and will see him face to face. God's name will be written on the foreheads of the people. ⁵ Never again will night appear, and no one who lives there will ever need a lamp or the sun. The Lord God will be their light, and they will rule for ever.

Christ will soon return

⁶ Then I was told:

These words are true and can be trusted. The Lord God controls the spirits of his prophets, and he is the one who sent his angel to show his servants what must happen straight away. ⁷ Remember, I am coming soon! God will bless everyone who pays attention to the message of this book.

⁸ My name is John, and I am the one who heard and saw these things. Then after I had heard and seen all this, I knelt down and began to worship at the feet of the angel who had shown it to me.

⁹ But the angel said,

Don't do that! I am a servant, just like you. I am the same as a follower or a prophet or anyone else who obeys what is written in this book. God is the one you should worship.

¹⁰ Don't keep the prophecies in this book a secret. These things will happen soon.

¹¹ Evil people will keep on being evil, and everyone who is dirty-minded will still be dirty-minded. But good people will keep on doing right, and God's people will always be holy.

¹² Then I was told:

I am coming soon! And when I come, I will reward everyone for what they have done. ¹³ I am Alpha and Omega,* the first and the last, the beginning and the end.

¹⁴ God will bless all who have washed their robes. They will each have the right to eat fruit from the tree that gives life, and they can enter the gates of the city. ¹⁵ But outside the city will be dogs, witches, immoral people, murderers, idol worshippers, and everyone who loves to tell lies and do wrong.

¹⁶ I am Jesus! And I am the one who sent my angel to tell all of you these things for the churches. I am David's Great Descendant,* and I am also the bright morning star.*

¹⁷ The Spirit and the bride say, "Come!" Everyone who hears this* should say, "Come!"

If you are thirsty, come! If you want life-giving water, come and take it. It's free!

¹⁸ Here is my warning for everyone who hears the prophecies in this book:

If you add anything to them, God will make you suffer all the terrible troubles written in this book. ¹⁹ If you take anything away from these prophecies, God will not let you have part in the life-giving tree and in the holy city described in this book.

²⁰ The one who has spoken these things says, "I am coming soon!"

So, Lord Jesus, please come soon!

²¹ I pray that the Lord Jesus will be kind to all of you.

---

*22.13 Alpha and Omega: See the note at 1.8.
*22.16 David's Great Descendant: See the note at 5.5.
*22.16 the bright morning star: Probably thought of as the brightest star. See 2.27,28.
*22.17 who hears this: The reading of the book of Revelation in a service of worship.

*21.27 book of life: See the note at 3.5.
*22.2 trees: The Greek has "tree", which is used in a collective sense of trees on both sides of the heavenly river.

See also: 21.27: Isa 52.1; Ezek 44.9. 22.2: a Ezek 47.1; Zech 14.8. 22.2: Gen 2.9. 22.5: Zech 14.11 (cp. Gen 3.17). 22.5: a Isa 60.19; b Dan 7.18.

See also: 22.11: Dan 12.10. 22.12: a Isa 40.10; 62.11; b Psa 28.4; Isa 40.10; Jer 17.10. 22.13: a Rev 1.8; b Isa 44.6; 48.12; Rev 1.17; 2.8. 22.14: Gen 2.9; 3.22. 22.16: Isa 11.1,10. 22.17: Isa 55.1. 22.18,19: Deut 4.2; 12.32.

Additional notes

▸**2.23 her followers:** Or "her children".
▸**3.8 did not deny that you are my followers:** Or "did not say evil things about me."
▸**5.6 the seven spirits:** Some manuscripts have "the spirits".
▸**12.11 blood:** Or "death".
▸**12.18 The dragon:** The text has "he", and some manuscripts have "I".
▸**13.8 wasn't written . . . was killed:** Or "wasn't written in the book of the Lamb who was killed before the time of creation."
▸**19.13 covered with:** Some manuscripts have "sprinkled with".

Mini dictionary for the Bible

This dictionary is divided into 21 sections. The indexes below list all of the sections, and all of the entries in alphabetical order, so that you can find what you are looking for more easily.

Section Index

Alphabetical Index

Numbers refer to the sections (listed above) in which the entry is included.

1. A few basics

CEV	The *Contemporary English Version* of the Bible.
Old Testament	This first part of the Bible is made up of the 39 books from Genesis to Malachi. They were written mostly in Hebrew, with a few passages in Aramaic.
New Testament	This second part of the Bible is made up of the 27 books from Matthew to Revelation. They were written in Greek.
Chapter and verse numbers	These numbers were not part of the original books, but were added hundreds of years later as a way to refer to specific parts of the books of Scripture. For example, Genesis 1.3 means "the book of Genesis, chapter 1, verse 3". Genesis 2.4,5 means "the book of Genesis, chapter 2, verses 4 to 5". And Genesis 1—2 means, "the book of Genesis, chapters 1 to 2". A few books are so short that they were not divided up into chapters, and so these books only have verse numbers. In the text of the CEV, sometimes verse numbers have been combined, for example, ³⁻⁴. One reason verse numbers might be combined is that contemporary English says things in a different order from ancient Greek and Hebrew, and so two or more verses are sometimes blended together in the CEV translation. And in lists, the verse numbers are sometimes combined into a single heading to avoid confusion. But all the meaning from the original Greek and Hebrew has been carefully included in the CEV text.

2. Scriptures, manuscripts

Ancient translations	The Old Testament was translated into Greek over the period 250—150 BC. Later, the whole Bible was translated into Latin, Syriac, and some other languages. These ancient translations can sometimes show what the Hebrew or Greek text said at the time they were translated, and so the CEV notes will sometimes refer to them.
Commandments	God's rules for his people to live by. The most famous are the Ten Commandments (see Exodus 20.1-17; Deuteronomy 5.6-21).
Dead Sea Scrolls	Manuscripts found near the Dead Sea from 1947—1954. They date from about 250 BC to AD 68. These manuscripts include at least some parts of nearly all Old Testament books.
God's Law	God's rules for his people to live by. They are found in the Old Testament, especially the first five books.
Law and the Prophets	A term used in New Testament times to refer to the sacred writings of the Jews. The Law and the Prophets were two of the three sections of the Old Testament, but the expression sometimes refers to the entire Old Testament.
Law of Moses and Law of the Lord	Usually refers to the first five books of the Old Testament, but sometimes to the entire Old Testament.

Manuscript	In ancient times, all books were copied by hand. A copy made this way was called "a manuscript".
Proverb	A wise saying that is short and easy to remember.
Psalm	A Hebrew poem. Psalms were often written in such a way that they could be prayed or sung by an individual or a group. Some of the psalms thank and praise God, while others ask God to take away sins or to give protection, comfort, vengeance, or mercy.
Samaritan Hebrew Text	The Hebrew text of Genesis to Deuteronomy used and preserved by the Samaritans (see also "Samaria"). This text uses forms of letters and many spellings that are different from the Standard Hebrew Text. It has traditionally been called the "Samaritan Pentateuch".
Scriptures	Although this term now refers to the whole Bible, in the New Testament it refers to the Old Testament.
Standard Hebrew Text	The Hebrew text that is found in most Hebrew manuscripts of the Old Testament. Almost all of these manuscripts were copied after AD 900 (but see also "Dead Sea Scrolls").
Wisdom	Often refers to the common sense and practical skill needed to solve everyday problems, but sometimes involves trying to find answers to the hard questions about the meaning of life.

3. Languages

Aramaic	A language closely related to Hebrew. In New Testament times Aramaic was spoken by many Jews including Jesus. Ezra 4.8–6.18; 7.12–26; and Daniel 2.4b–7.28 were written in Aramaic.
Greek	The language used throughout the Mediterranean world in New Testament times, and the language in which the New Testament was written.
Hebrew	The language used by most of the people of Israel until the Exile. But after the people returned, more and more people spoke Aramaic instead. Most of the Old Testament was written in Hebrew.

4. People

Aaron	The brother of Moses. Only he and his descendants were to serve as priests and offer sacrifices for the people of Israel (see Exodus 4.14–16; 28.1; Numbers 16.1–18.7).
Abel	The second son of Adam and Eve and the younger brother of Cain. Abel was killed by Cain after God accepted Abel's offering and refused to accept Cain's (see Genesis 4.1–17).
Abraham	The first of the three great ancestors of the people of Israel. Abraham was the husband of Sarah and the father of Isaac. At first Abraham's name was Abram, meaning "Great Father". Then, when Abram was ninety-nine years old, God changed Abram's name to Abraham, which means "Father of a Crowd". Abraham trusted God, and so God promised that Abraham and his wife Sarah would have

a son and more descendants than could be counted. God also promised that Abraham would be a blessing to everyone on earth (see Genesis 12.1–7; 17.1–18.15).

Abram	See "Abraham".
Adam	The first man and the husband of Eve (see Genesis 1.26–3.21).
Agrippa	(1) Herod Agrippa was king of Judea AD 41–44 and ill-treated Christians (see Acts 12.1–5). (2) Agrippa II was the son of Herod Agrippa and ruled parts of Palestine from AD 53 to AD 93 or later. He and his sister Bernice listened to Paul defend himself (see Acts 25.13–26,32).
Antipas	(1) Herod Antipas, son of Herod the Great (see "Herod"). (2) An otherwise unknown Christian at Pergamum, who was killed because he was a follower of Christ (see Revelation 2.13).
Augustus	A title meaning "honoured", which was given to Octavian by the Romans when he began ruling the Roman world in 27 BC. He was the Roman Emperor when Jesus was born.
Cain	The first son of Adam and Eve; Cain killed his brother Abel after God accepted Abel's offering and refused to accept Cain's (see Genesis 4.1–17).
David	King of Israel from about 1010–970 BC. David was the most famous king Israel ever had, and many of the people of Israel hoped that one of his descendants would always be their king (see 1 Samuel 16–30; 2 Samuel; 1 Kings 12).
Esau	The elder son of Isaac and Rebekah, and the brother of Jacob. Esau was also known as Edom and as the ancestor of the Edomites (see Genesis 25.20–34; 26.34–46; 32.1–33.16).
Eve	The first woman and the wife of Adam (see Genesis 1.26–3.21).
Felix	The Roman governor of Palestine AD 52–60, who listened to Paul speak and kept him in jail (see Acts 23.24–24.27).
Festus	The Roman governor after Felix, who sent Paul to stand trial in Rome (see Acts 24.27–26.32).
Hagar	A slave of Sarah, the wife of Abraham. When Sarah could not have any children, she followed the ancient custom of letting her husband have a child by Hagar, her slave. The boy's name was Ishmael (see Genesis 16; 21.8–21).
Herod	(1) Herod the Great was the king of all Palestine 37–4 BC, and so he was king at the time that Jesus was born (see the note at "AD"). (2) Herod Antipas was the son of Herod the Great and was the ruler of Galilee 4 BC–AD 39. (3) Herod Agrippa I, the grandson of Herod the Great, ruled Palestine AD 41–44.
Isaac	The second of the three great ancestors of the people of Israel. He was the son of Abraham and Sarah, and he was the father of Esau and Jacob.

Ishmael	The son of Abraham and Hagar.
Israel	See "Jacob".
Jacob	The third great ancestor of the people of Israel. He was the son of Isaac and Rebekah, and his name was changed to Israel when he struggled with God at Peniel near the River Jabbok (see Genesis 32.22–32).
Joseph	A son of Jacob and Rachel. Joseph was sold as a slave by his brothers, but later became governor of Egypt (see Genesis 37.12–36; 41.1–57).
Lot	A nephew of Abraham and the ancestor of the Moabites and Ammonites (see Genesis 11.27; 13.1–13; 18.16—19.38).
Noah	When God destroyed the world by a flood, Noah and his family were kept safe in a big boat that God had told him to build (see Genesis 6—8).
Rebekah	The wife of Isaac, and the mother of Jacob and Esau (see Genesis 24.1–67; 25.19–28).
Sarah	The wife of Abraham and the mother of Isaac. At first her name was Sarai, but when she was old, God promised her that she would have a son, and he changed her name to Sarah. Both names mean "princess" (see Genesis 11.29,30; 17.15–19; 18.9–15; 21.1–7).
Solomon	A son of King David and Bathsheba. After David's death, Solomon ruled Israel about 970–931 BC. Solomon built the temple in Jerusalem and was widely known for his wisdom. The Hebrew text indicates that he wrote many of the proverbs and two of the psalms.

5. Prophets

Anna	A woman prophet who stayed in the temple night and day. Soon after Jesus was born, Mary and Joseph took him to the temple and presented him to the Lord, and Anna talked about the child Jesus to everyone who hoped for Jerusalem to be set free (see Luke 2.36-38).
Balaam	A foreign prophet. Balaam was hired by the king of Moab to put a curse on Israel, but instead Balaam blessed Israel (see Numbers 22—24).
Deborah	A prophet and judge who helped lead Israel to defeat King Jabin of Hazor (see Judges 4—5).
Elijah	A prophet who spoke for God in the early ninth century BC and who opposed the evil King Ahab and Queen Jezebel of the northern kingdom. Many Jews in later centuries thought Elijah would return to get everything ready for the day of judgment or for the coming of the Messiah (see 1 Kings 17—21; 2 Kings 1—2; Malachi 4.1-6; Matthew 17.10,11; Mark 9.11,12).
Elisha	A prophet who assisted Elijah and later took his place. Elisha spoke for God in the late ninth century BC, and was the prophet who healed Naaman (see 1 Kings 19.19–21; 2 Kings 2—9; 13.14–21).

Huldah	A prophet who spoke for God during the late seventh century BC. After *The Book of God's Law* was found in the temple, King Josiah asked her what the Lord wanted him to do (see 2 Kings 22.14–20).
Micaiah	A prophet who told King Ahab that he would die in battle against the Syrian army (see 1 Kings 22.5–38).
Moses	The prophet who led the people of Israel when God rescued them from slavery in Egypt. Moses also received laws from God and gave them to Israel (see Exodus 2–12; 19–24; Numbers 12.68).
Prophesy	To speak as a prophet (see "Prophet").
Prophet	Someone who spoke God's message, which at times included telling what would happen in the future. Sometimes when the Spirit of God took control of prophets, they lost some or all control of their speech and actions or were not aware of what was happening around them.

6. Twelve tribes of Israel

The Bible speaks of all the people in a tribe as having descended from one of the twelve sons of Jacob. The tribes of Ephraim and Manasseh were a little different, because the people in those tribes descended from the two sons of Joseph, who was one of Jacob's sons. That would make a total of thirteen tribes, but the Bible always counts only twelve. In some passages Ephraim and Manasseh are counted as one tribe, and in other passages the Levi tribe is left out, probably because they were designated for priestly service to all the tribes, and as such, were scattered throughout the land belonging to the other tribes. People from other nations were sometimes allowed to become Israelites (see Exodus 12.38; Deuteronomy 23.1-8; and the book of Ruth), and these people would then belong to one of the tribes.

Asher	Occupied land along the Mediterranean coast from Mount Carmel to the border with the city of Tyre.
Benjamin	Occupied land between Bethel and Jerusalem. When the northern tribes of Israel broke away following the death of Solomon, only the tribes of Benjamin and Judah were left to form the southern kingdom.
Dan	First occupied land west of Judah, Benjamin, and Ephraim. But after the Philistines took control of this area, part of the tribe then moved to the northernmost area of Israel.
Ephraim	One of the largest tribes. Ephraim occupied the land north of Benjamin and south of West Manasseh.
Gad	Occupied land east of the River Jordan from the northern end of the Dead Sea north to the River Jabbok.
Issachar	Occupied land south-west of Lake Galilee.
Judah	Occupied the hill country west of the Dead Sea. When the ten northernmost tribes of Israel broke away following the death of Solomon, only the tribes of Judah and Benjamin were left to form the southern kingdom, and it was also called "Judah".
Levi	The men of this tribe were to be the special servants of the Lord at the sacred tent and later at the temple, and so the people of this

	tribe were not given tribal land. Instead, they were given towns scattered throughout the other twelve tribes (see also "Levites").
Manasseh	Occupied two areas of land: (1) East Manasseh lived east of the River Jordan and north of the River Jabbok in the areas of Bashan and northern Gilead. (2) West Manasseh lived west of the River Jordan and to the north of Ephraim.
Naphtali	Occupied land north and west of Lake Galilee.
Reuben	Occupied land east of the Dead Sea, from the River Arnon in the south to the northern end of the Dead Sea.
Simeon	Occupied land south-west of Judah, and was later practically absorbed into Judah.
Zebulun	Occupied land north of Manasseh from the eastern end of Mount Carmel to Mount Tabor.

7. Christ's twelve apostles

Apostle	A person chosen and sent by Christ to take his message to others. Lists of the names of Christ's twelve apostles can be found in Matthew 10.2–4; Mark 3.16–19; Luke 6.14–16; Acts 1.12,13. Later, others such as Paul and James the brother of Jesus also became known as apostles.
Simon	Also known as Peter or Cephas.
Andrew	Simon Peter's brother.
James	The son of Zebedee.
John	The son of Zebedee (James and John were also known as the "Thunderbolts").
Philip	From Bethsaida, the home town of Simon and Andrew.
Bartholomew	Mentioned in all New Testament lists of the apostles, but nowhere else.
Thomas	Also know as "The Twin".
Matthew	Also known as Levi.
James	The son of Alphaeus.
Thaddeus	Also known as Judas or Jude the son of James.
Simon	Also known as "the Eager One".
Judas Iscariot	He betrayed Jesus.
Matthias	He was chosen to replace Judas Iscariot.

8. Cities, nations, and groups of people

Amalekites	A nomadic nation living mostly in the area south and east of the Dead Sea. They were enemies of Israel.

Ammon	A nation that lived east of Israel. According to Genesis 19.30-38, the people of Ammon descended from Lot, a nephew of Abraham.
Amorites	Usually a name for all the non-Israelite nations who lived in Canaan, but in some passages it may refer to one nation scattered in several areas of Canaan.
Anakim	Perhaps a group of people of great stature who lived in Palestine before the Israelites (see Numbers 13.33 and Deuteronomy 2.10,11,20,21).
Asia	A Roman province in what is today the nation of Turkey.
Assyria	An empire of Old Testament times, whose capital city Nineveh was located in what is today northern Iraq. In 722 BC Assyria conquered the kingdom of Israel and took many Israelites as captives. The Assyrians then forced people from other parts of its empire to settle on Israel's land (see 2 Kings 18.9-12).
Avvites	A nation that lived along the Mediterranean coast before the Philistines came and took their land. The Avvites who survived lived south of the Philistines.
Babylonia	A large empire of Old Testament times, whose capital city Babylon was located in south-central Mesopotamia. The Babylonians defeated the southern kingdom of Judah in 586 BC and forced many of its people to live in Babylonia (see 2 Kings 25.1-12).
Canaanites	The nations who lived in Canaan before the Israelites. Many Canaanites continued to live there even after the Israelites came.
Cush	The Hebrew term for Ethiopia (see "Ethiopia" below).
Disciples	Those who were followers of Jesus and learnt from him. The term often refers to his twelve apostles.
Edomites	A nation living in Edom or Seir, an area south and south-east of the Dead Sea. According to Genesis 36.1-43, the Edomites descended from Esau, Jacob's brother.
Empire	A number of kingdoms ruled by one strong military power.
Epicureans	People who followed the teachings of a man named Epicurus, who taught that happiness should be the main goal in life.
Ethiopia	A region south of Egypt that included parts of the present countries of Ethiopia and Sudan.
Exiles	Israelites who were taken away as prisoners to Babylonia (see also "Exile").
Gentiles	Those people who are not Jews.
Girgashites	One of the nations that lived in Canaan before the Israelites.
Hebrew	An older term for "Israelite" or "Jewish".
Hittites	A nation whose capital was in what is now Turkey. The Hittites had an empire that at times controlled some kingdoms in Canaan before 1200 BC, and many Hittites remained in Canaan even after the Israelites came.

Hivites	A nation that lived in Canaan before the Israelites, probably related to the Horites.
Horites	A nation that lived in Canaan before the Israelites. The Horites were also known as "Hurrians".
Israel	(1) The nation made up of the twelve tribes descended from Jacob (see Section 6, "Twelve tribes of Israel"). (2) The northern kingdom, after the northern tribes broke away following the death of Solomon (see 1 Kings 12.1–20).
Jebusites	A group of Canaanite people who lived at Jebus, also known as Jerusalem (see 2 Samuel 5.6–10).
Jews	A name first used in referring to someone belonging to the tribe of Judah. Later, the term came to be used of any Israelite.
Kadesh	A town in the desert of Paran south-west of the Dead Sea, near the southern border of Israel and the western border of Edom. Israel camped at Kadesh while the twelve tribal leaders explored Canaan (see Numbers 13–14).
Levites	Those Israelites who belonged to the tribe of Levi. God chose the men of one Levite family, the descendants of Aaron, to be Israel's priests. The other men from this tribe helped with the work in the sacred tent and later in the temple (see Numbers 3.5–10).
Medes	A nation that lived in what is today north-west Iran. Their kingdom, called "Media", later became one of the most important provinces of the Persian Empire, and Persian laws were referred to as the laws of the Medes and Persians (see Esther 1.19; Daniel 6.8,12,15).
Midianites	A nomadic nation that lived mainly in the desert along the eastern shore of the Gulf of Aqaba.
Moab	A nation that lived east of the Dead Sea. According to Genesis 19.30–38, the people of Moab descended from Lot, the nephew of Abraham.
Nazarenes	A name that was sometimes used for the followers of Jesus, who came from the small town of Nazareth (see Acts 24.5).
Perizzites	A nation that lived in the central hill country of Canaan, before the Israelites.
Persia	A large empire of Old Testament times, whose capital was located in what is now southern Iran. It is sometimes called "the Medo-Persian Empire", because of the importance of the province of Media.
Pharisees	A group of Jews who thought they could best serve God by strictly obeying the laws of the Old Testament, as well as their own rules, traditions, and teachings.
Philistines	The land along the Mediterranean coast controlled by the Philistine people was called "Philistia". There were five main cities, each with its own ruler: Ashod, Ashkelon, Ekron, Gath, and Gaza. The Philistines were often at war with Israel.

Phoenicia	The territory along the Mediterranean Sea controlled by the cities of Tyre, Sidon, Arvad, and Byblos. The coast of modern Lebanon covers about the same area.
Rapha	Perhaps a group of people of great stature who lived in Palestine before the Israelites (see Deuteronomy 2.11,20).
Roman Empire	Controlled the area around the Mediterranean Sea in New Testament times. Its capital was Rome.
Sadducees	A small and powerful group of Jews in New Testament times. They were closely connected with the high priests and accepted only the first five books of the Old Testament as their Bible. They also did not believe in life after death.
Samaria	(1) The capital city of the northern kingdom of Israel beginning with the rule of King Omri (ruled 885–874 BC). (2) In New Testament times, a district between Judea and Galilee, named after the city of Samaria. The people of this district, called "Samaritans", worshipped God differently from the Jews, and these two groups refused to have anything to do with one another.
Sidon	See "Phoenicia".
Stoics	Followers of a man named Zeno, who taught that people should learn self-control and be guided by their consciences.
Tyre	See "Phoenicia".

9. Places

Bashan	The flat highlands and wooded hills of southern Syria. Bashan was just north of the region of Gilead and was known for its fat cattle and fine grain.
Canaan	The area now covered by Israel plus Gaza, the West Bank of Jordan, Lebanon, and southern Syria (see Numbers 34.1–12). Many passages use the term to refer only to the area south of Lebanon.
Gethsemane	A garden or olive orchard on the Mount of Olives (see "Mount of Olives").
Gilead	A region east of the River Jordan. Moab lay to the south of Gilead, and Bashan was to the north.
Hinnom Valley	A valley west and south of Jerusalem, where human sacrifice was sometimes made in Old Testament times (see "Molech").
Mount of Olives	A mountain just east of Jerusalem, across Kidron Valley from the temple. Gethsemane, a place where Jesus and his disciples often went to pray, was on this mountain, and so were the villages of Bethany, Bethphage, and Bahurim (see Matthew 26.36; Mark 14.32; Luke 22.39; John 18.1,2).
Palestine	The area now covered by Israel, Gaza, and Jordan.
Peniel	A place near the River Jabbok where Jacob wrestled with God. Then God changed Jacob's name to Israel (see Genesis 32.22–32).

Zion	Another name for Jerusalem. Zion can also refer to the hill in Jerusalem where the temple was built.

10. Objects

Chariot	A two-wheeled cart that was open at the back and was pulled by horses.
Cistern	A hole or pit used for storing rainwater. Cisterns were sometimes dug in the ground and lined with stones and plaster, and at other times they were cut into the rock. The CEV sometimes translates "cistern" as "well".
Cross	A device used by the Romans to put people to death. It was made of two pieces of timber crossed in a "T", "†", or "X" shape.
Piece of silver	In the Old Testament, this usually refers to an amount of silver weighing about 11 grammes. Coins were not invented until late Old Testament times, so when silver or gold was used to buy things, it was weighed. In traditional translations this amount is called "a shekel". Silver and gold were worth more in biblical times than they are today.
Sackcloth	A rough, dark-coloured cloth made from goat or camel hair. Sackcloth was usually used to make grain sacks, but clothing made from it was worn in times of trouble or sorrow.
Sceptre	A decorated rod, often made of gold, that a king held in his hand as a symbol of royal power.
Scroll	A roll of paper or special thin leather used for writing on.
Sling	A weapon used to throw stones a little smaller than a tennis ball. A sling was made of a piece of leather that wrapped almost around the stone and had a leather strap at each end. The person would hold the ends of the straps and swing the sling round and round. When the person let go of one strap, the stone would fly out of the sling.
Tomb	A burial place, often made by cutting a small room out of the rock.

11. Festivals and holy days

Many of these festivals are still celebrated by Jewish people.

Festival of Purim	A festival held on the fourteenth and fifteenth of Adar, near the end of winter, when the Jews celebrated how they were saved from Haman, the evil prime minister of Persia who wanted to have them killed (see Esther 9.20–32).
Festival of Shelters	A festival in the early autumn celebrating the period of forty years when the people of Israel walked through the desert and lived in small shelters. This happy celebration began on the fifteenth day of Tishri, and for the next seven days, the people lived in small shelters made of tree branches. The name of this festival in Hebrew is "Succoth".
Festival of Thin Bread	A seven-day festival straight after Passover. During this festival the Israelites ate a thin, flat bread made without yeast to remind themselves how God freed the people of Israel from slavery in Egypt

	and made them into a nation. The name of this festival in Hebrew is "Mazzoth".
Festival of Trumpets	See "New Moon Festival".
Great Day of Forgiveness	The tenth day of Tishri in the early autumn. On this one day of the year, the high priest was allowed to go into the most holy part of the temple and sprinkle some of the blood of a sacrificed bull on the sacred chest. This was done so that the people's sins would be forgiven. In English this holy day has traditionally been called "the Day of Atonement", and its name in Hebrew is "Yom Kippur".
Harvest Festival	See "Pentecost".
New Moon Festival	A religious festival held on the day of the new moon, the day when only a thin edge of the moon can be seen. This day was always the first day of the month for the Hebrew calendar. The New Moon Festival was a time for rest from work, and a time for worship, sacrifices, celebration, and eating. The New Moon Festival in the month of Tishri in the early autumn was also called "the Festival of Trumpets", and it involved even more sacrifices.
Passover	A festival held on the fourteenth day of Abib in the early spring. At Passover the Israelites celebrated the time God rescued them from slavery in Egypt. The name of this festival in Hebrew is "Pesach".
Pentecost	A Jewish festival held in mid-spring, fifty days after Passover. At this festival Israelites celebrated the wheat harvest. Pentecost was also known as "the Harvest Festival" and has traditionally been called "the Feast of Weeks"; in Hebrew, its name is "Shavuoth".
Sabbath	The seventh day of the week, from sunset on Friday to sunset on Saturday. Israelites worshipped on the Sabbath and rested from work.
Temple Festival	In 165 BC the Jewish people recaptured the temple in Jerusalem from their enemies and made it fit for worship again. They celebrated this event each year by an eight-day festival that began on the twenty-fifth day of the month of Chislev in the late autumn. This festival is traditionally called "the Festival of Dedication", or in Hebrew, "Hanukkah".

12. Sacrifice, temple, worship

Altar	A raised structure where sacrifices and offerings were presented to God or to pagan gods. Altars could be made of rock, packed earth, metal, or pottery.
Amen	A Hebrew word used after a prayer or a blessing and meaning that what had been said was right and true.
Fire pan	A metal pan used for burning incense or carrying hot coals from the altar.
God's tent	See "Sacred tent".
High priest	See "Priest".

Holy place	The main room of the sacred tent and of the temple. This room contained the sacred bread, the golden incense altar, and the golden lampstand. A curtain or wall separated the holy place from the most holy place. A priest would go into the holy place once each morning and evening to burn incense on the golden altar (see also "Most holy place").
Incense	A material that makes a sweet smell when burnt. It was used in the worship of God.
Local shrine	See "Place of worship".
Most holy place	The inner room of the sacred tent and of the temple. In the sacred tent this room contained only the sacred chest. In Solomon's temple, the most holy place also held statues of winged creatures. Only the high priest could enter the most holy place, and even he could enter it only once a year on the Great Day of Forgiveness. The most holy place has traditionally been called "the holy of holies".
Offerings	See "Sacrifices".
Place of worship	A place to worship God or pagan gods. These places were often on a hill outside a town and have traditionally been called "high places". In the CEV they are sometimes called "local shrines".
Priest	A man who led the worship in the sacred tent or in the temple and who offered sacrifices. Some of the more important priests were called "chief priests", and the most important priest was called the "high priest".
Sacred chest	The chest or box that contained the two flat stones with the Ten Commandments written on them. The chest was covered with gold, and two golden statues of winged creatures were on the lid of the chest. These winged creatures and the chest represented God's throne on earth. Two wooden poles, one on each side, were put through rings at the corners of the chest, so that the Levites could carry the chest without touching it. The chest was kept in the most holy place (see Exodus 25.10–22).
Sacred tent	The tent where the people of Israel worshipped God before the temple was built. It has traditionally been called "the tabernacle" (see Exodus 26).
Sacrifices	These gifts to God included certain animals, grains, fruits, and sweet-smelling spices. Israelites offered sacrifices to give thanks to God, to ask him for his forgiveness and his blessing, and to make a payment for a wrong. Some sacrifices were completely burnt on the altar. In the case of other sacrifices, a portion was given to the LORD and burnt on the altar, then the rest was eaten by the priests or the worshippers who had offered the sacrifice.
Sacrifices to ask the LORD's blessing	Traditionally called "peace offerings" or "offerings of well-being". A main purpose was to ask for the LORD's blessing, and so in the CEV they are sometimes called "sacrifices to ask the LORD's blessing" (see Leviticus 3).

Sacrifices to give thanks to the LORD	Traditionally called "grain offerings". A main purpose of such sacrifices was to thank the LORD with a gift of grain, and so in the CEV they are sometimes called "sacrifices to give thanks to the LORD" (see Leviticus 2).
Sacrifices to make things right	Traditionally called "guilt offerings". A main purpose was to make things right when a person had cheated someone or the LORD. These sacrifices were also made when a person had broken certain religious rules (see Leviticus 5.14—6.7).
Sacrifices to please the LORD	Traditionally called "whole burnt offerings" because the whole animal was burnt on the altar. While these sacrifices did involve forgiveness for sin, a main purpose was to please the LORD with the smell of the smoke from the sacrifice, and so in the CEV they are often called "sacrifices to please the LORD" (see Leviticus 1).
Snuffer	A small tool used for putting out the flame of an oil lamp, or for trimming off the charred part of the wick.
Temple	A building used as a place of worship. The god who was worshipped in a particular temple was believed to be present there in a special way. The LORD's temple was in Jerusalem.

13. Customs

Ashes	People put ashes, dust, or earth on their heads, or they rolled in ash piles, dust, or earth, as a way of showing sorrow.
Circumcise	To cut off the foreskin from the male organ. This was done for Israelite boys eight days after they were born. God commanded that all newborn Israelite boys be circumcised to show that they belonged to his people (see Genesis 17.9–14).
Clean and unclean	(1) In Old Testament times, a person who was acceptable to worship God was called "clean". A person who had certain kinds of diseases, who had touched a dead body, or who had broken certain laws became "unclean", and was unacceptable to worship God. If a person was unclean because of disease, the disease would have to be cured before the person could be clean again. And becoming clean again involved performing certain ceremonies that sometimes included sacrifices. (2) Animals that were acceptable as food were called "clean". Those that were not acceptable were called "unclean" (see Leviticus 11.1–47; Deuteronomy 14.3–21). (3) Many things including tools, dishes, houses, and land could also become unclean and unusable, especially if they were touched by something unclean. Some unclean objects had to be destroyed, but others could be made clean by being washed or placed in a fire for a short time.
Going without eating	This was a way of showing sorrow, or of asking for God's help. It is also called "fasting".

| Tearing clothes | A way of showing sorrow or anger, or of asking for God's help. |

14. God, Jesus, angels

Angel	A supernatural being who tells God's messages to people or protects those who belong to God.
Christ	A Greek work meaning "the Chosen One" and used to translate the Hebrew word "Messiah". In New Testament times, many of the Jews believed that God was going to send the Messiah to set them free from the power of their enemies. The term "Christ" is used in the New Testament both as a title and as a name for Jesus.
Eternal life	Life that is the gift of God and that never ends.
Glory	Something seen, heard, or felt that shows a person or thing is important, wonderful, or powerful. When God appeared to people, his glory was often seen as a bright light or as fire and smoke. Jesus' glory was seen when he performed miracles, when he was lifted up on the cross, and when he was raised from death.
God's kingdom	God's rule over people, both in this life and in the next.
Holy One	A name for the Saviour that God had promised to send (see "Saviour").
Kingdom of heaven	See "God's kingdom".
LORD	In the Old Testament the word "LORD" in capital letters stands for the Hebrew consonants YHWH, the personal name of God. Ancient Hebrew did not have vowel letters, and so anyone reading Hebrew would have to know what vowels to put with the consonants. It is not known for certain what vowel sounds were originally used with the consonants YHWH. The word "LORD" represents the Hebrew term *Adonai*, the usual word for "LORD". By late Old Testament times, Jews considered God's personal name too holy to be pronounced. So they said *Adonai*, "LORD", whenever they read YHWH. When the Jewish scribes first translated the Hebrew Scriptures into ancient Greek, they translated the personal name of God as *Kurios*, "LORD". Since that time, most translations, including the CEV, have followed their example and have avoided using the personal name of God.
Messiah	See "Christ".
Promised One	A title for the Saviour that God promised to send (see "Saviour").
Save	To rescue people from the power of their enemies or from the power of evil, and to give them new life and place them under God's care (see also "Saviour").
Saviour	The one whom God has chosen to rescue or save his people (see also "Save").
Sin	Turning away from God and disobeying the teachings or commandments of God.

Son of Man	A title often used by Jesus to refer to himself. This title is also found in the Hebrew text of Daniel 7.13 and Psalm 8.4, and God uses it numerous times in the book of Ezekiel to refer to Ezekiel.
Way	In the book of Acts the Christian life is sometimes called "the Way" or "the Way of the LORD" or "God's Way".
Winged creature	These supernatural beings represented the presence of God and supported his throne in Ezekiel 1.4–25; 10.1–22. Statues of winged creatures were on top of the sacred chest, and larger ones were in the most holy place in the temple built by Solomon. Wood carvings of winged creatures decorated the inside walls and doors of the temple, and figures of winged creatures were woven into the curtain separating the holy place from the most holy place in the sacred tent. The traditional term for winged creature is "cherub" (or "cherubim" for more than one).

15. Foreign gods, fortune-tellers, evil spirits

Astarte	A Canaanite goddess. Those who worshipped her believed that she gave them fertile land and many children, and that she helped their animals give birth to lots of young.
Baal	A Canaanite god. The Canaanites believed that Baal was the most powerful of all the gods.
Dagon	The chief god of the Philistines.
Demons and evil spirits	Supernatural beings that do harmful things to people and sometimes cause them to do bad things. In the New Testament they are sometimes called "unclean spirits", because people under their power were thought to be unclean and unfit to worship God.
Devil	The chief of the demons and evil spirits, also known as "Ṣatan".
Evil spirits	See "Demons".
Fortune-teller	Fortune-tellers thought they could learn secrets or learn about the future by doing such things as watching the flight of birds, looking at the livers of animals, and rolling dice.
Hermes	The Greek god of skilful speaking and the messenger of the other Greek gods.
Molech or Milcom	The national god of the Ammonites. Some Israelites offered human sacrifices to Molech in Hinnom Valley near Jerusalem.
Satan	See "Devil".
Zeus	The chief god of the Greeks.

16. Plants, animals, and farming

Acacia	A flowering tree that produces a hard, durable wood. The sacred chest, the altars, and certain other wooden objects in the sacred tent were made of acacia wood.

Aloes	A sweet-smelling spice that was mixed with myrrh and used as a perfume.
Barley	A grain that was used to make bread.
Cedar	A tall tree once common in the Lebanon mountains and used for many of the royal building projects in Jerusalem.
Cumin	A plant with small seeds used for seasoning food.
Flax	The stalks of flax plants were harvested, soaked in water, and dried. Then their fibres were separated and spun into thread, which was woven to make linen cloth.
Hyssop	A bush with clusters of small branches. In religious ceremonies, hyssop was sometimes dipped in a liquid and then used to sprinkle people or objects.
Jackal	A wild desert animal related to wolves, but smaller.
Leviathan	A legendary sea monster representing revolt and evil, also known from Canaanite writings.
Locust	A type of grasshopper that comes in huge swarms and causes great damage to plant life.
Mint	A garden plant used for seasoning and medicine.
Mustard	A large plant with very small seeds, which were ground up and used as a spice.
Myrrh	A valuable sweet-smelling powder used in perfume.
Pomegranate	A reddish fruit with a hard rind. Figures of pomegranates were used as decorations on the high priest's robe and in the temple.
Reed	Several kinds of tall plant related to the grass family can be called "reeds". Some varieties are hollow, and some grow in shallow water. The stems are strong and can be up to 5 metres long and 7 centimetres across at the base.
Rue	A garden plant used for seasoning and medicine.
Threshing	The process of separating grain from its husks. Grain was spread out at a "threshing place", a flat area of stone or packed earth. People or animals walked on the grain or dragged heavy boards across it to remove the husks. Then the grain and husks were tossed into the air with a special shovel called a "threshing fork". The wind would blow the light husks away, but the heavy grain would fall back to the surface of the threshing place.
Wine-pit	A hollow place cut into the rock where the juice was squeezed from grapes to make wine.
Yoke	A strong, heavy, wooden collar that fitted around the neck of an ox, so that the ox could pull a plough or a cart.

17. Society and its leaders

Citizen	A person who is given special rights and privileges by a nation or state. In return, a citizen was expected to be loyal to that nation or state.

Council	(1) A group of leaders who meet and make decisions for their people. (2) The Old Testament refers to God's council as a group of angels who meet and talk with God in heaven.
Elders	Men whose age and wisdom made them respected leaders.
Emperor	The person who ruled an empire.
Generation	One way of describing a group of people who lived during the same period of time. In the Bible the time of one generation is often understood to be about forty years.
Judges	Leaders chosen by the LORD for the people of Israel after the time of Joshua and before the time of the kings.
Tax collectors	See "Taxes".
Taxes	Special fees collected by the government. Taxes are usually part of the value of crops, property, or income. Taxes were collected at markets, city gates, ports, and border crossings. In New Testament times, Jews were hired by the Roman government to collect taxes from other Jews, and these tax collectors were hated by their own people.

18. Families, relatives

Ancestor	Someone born earlier in a family line, especially several generations earlier.
Clan	A group of families who were related to each other and who often lived close to each other. A group of clans made up a tribe.
Descendant	Someone born one or more generations later in a family line.
Tribe	A large group of people descended from a common ancestor (see also "Clan" and Section 6, "Twelve tribes of Israel").

19. Events

Exile	The time in Israel's history (597—539 BC) when the Babylonians took away many of the people of Jerusalem and Judah as prisoners of war and made them live in Babylonia. The northern tribes had been taken away by Assyria in 722 BC.
Exodus	The people of Israel leaving Egypt, led by Moses and Aaron. This event is celebrated each year as Passover.

20. Dates

AD	*Anno Domini*, Latin for "in the year of the LORD". Used to date events that happened after Christ's birth. "AD" is often used before the number of the year. The numbering system now in use was developed about AD 525. The plan was that the year of Christ's birth would be AD 1, and then the years would be numbered before and after. But an error was made in assigning AD 1, and by the time the error was discovered, the numbering system could not be changed. And so, the correct year of Christ's birth according to the numbering system is probably about 6 BC.

BC	Before Christ. Used to date events that happened before Christ's birth. "BC" is used after the number of the year.
931 BC	The nation of Israel split into two parts, Israel, the northern kingdom, and Judah, the southern kingdom.
722 BC	Samaria, the capital of the northern kingdom, was captured by the Assyrian army.
586 BC	Jerusalem, the capital of the southern kingdom, was captured by the Babylonian army.
538 BC	Cyrus of Persia allowed the Jews to return to Judah.
333 BC	Alexander the Great took control of Palestine.
323 BC	Palestine was taken over by Ptolemy, who was one of Alexander's generals and who became the ruler of Egypt after Alexander's death.
198 BC	Palestine was taken over by the Seleucids, the descendants of one of Alexander's generals. They had been the rulers of Syria since Alexander's death.
166 BC	The Jews revolted, led by Judas Maccabeus and his brothers.
63 BC	Rome took control of Palestine.
37 BC	Herod the Great was appointed king of the Jews by the Roman government.
6 BC	Jesus was born (see the note following "AD" above).
AD 30 (or possibly AD 33)	Jesus died and was raised to life.

21. The Hebrew Calendar

Nisan or Abib	First month, about mid-March to mid-April.
Iyyar or Ziv	Second month, about mid-April to mid-May.
Sivan	Third month, about mid-May to mid-June.
Tammuz	Fourth month, about mid-June to mid-July.
Ab	Fifth month, about mid-July to mid-August.
Elul	Sixth month, about mid-August to mid-September.
Tishri or Ethanim	Seventh month, about mid-September to mid-October.
Marchesvan or Bul	Eighth month, about mid-October to mid-November.
Chislev	Ninth month, about mid-November to mid-December.
Tebeth	Tenth month, about mid-December to mid-January.
Shebat	Eleventh month, about mid-January to mid-February.
Adar	Twelfth month, about mid-February to mid-March.

THE ROUTE
OF THE EXODUS

THE DIVISION OF CANAAN

Sidon
Mount Lebanon
Mount Hermon
Damascus

Tyre

Dan (Laish)
DAN
Kedesh

Hazor

ASHER

ZEBULUN
NAPHTALI
Mount Tabor
Lake Galilee
Golan
Ashtaroth

ISSACHAR
EAST MANASSEH

Dor
Megiddo
Jezreel
Valley of Jezreel
Villages of Jair

Ramoth in Gilead

WEST MANASSEH

GILEAD

GAD

Mount Ebal
Shechem
Mount Gerizim

River Jordan

AMMON

River Jabbok

Timnath Serah
Shiloh
EPHRAIM
Bethel • Ai
Gibeon • Jericho • Gilgal
Ekron
BENJAMIN
Libnah
Jerusalem

Ashdod

PHILISTIA

Ashkelon
Gath • Lachish
Gaza
Debir
JUDAH
Hebron
Engedi
DEAD SEA
River Arnon

Beersheba
Hormah
SIMEON

MOAB

MEDITERRANEAN SEA

EDOM

0   20   40   60
Kilometres

JERUSALEM IN OLD TESTAMENT TIMES

Tower of Hananel

East wall of Nehemiah's City

Solomon's Wall

THE TEMPLE

THE ALTAR

THE PALACE

Manasseh's Wall

K I D R O N   V A L L E Y

C E N T R A L   V A L L E Y

UPPER CITY

NEW CITY

Solomon's Wall

Gate

Wall of Zion

CITY OF DAVID

OPHEL

Water Tunnel

Gihon

Upper Pool

Hezekiah's Tunnel

Old Ditch

Manasseh's Wall

Lower Pool

Old Pool

Steps from David's City

Gate

V A L L E Y   O F   H I N N O M

| 0 | 100 | 200 | 300 |

Metres

● Spring of Enrogel

JERUSALEM IN NEW
TESTAMENT TIMES

Garden Tomb

Pool of
Bethesda

Sheep Gate

Antonia
Fortress

Temple
Mount

The Temple

Traditional
Golgotha

THE TYROPOEAN VALLEY

Gethsemane

THE KIDRON VAL

Herod's
Palace

Hasmonean
Palace

THE
UPPER
CITY

THE

LOWER

CITY

? House of
Caiaphas

Siloam Pool

0   300
Metres